PENGUIN

POCKET FR

Raymond Escoffey was born in 1923 in Neuchâtel, Switzerland. He was educated at Haberdashers' Aske's Hampstead School and at Cambridge University, where he gained a First Class Honours degree in Modern and Medieval Languages. He also has a Diploma in Education. He taught modern languages at Dulwich College from 1945 to 1954. Following this he was modern languages programme producer in the Schools Broadcasting Department of the BBC and subsequently executive producer. In 1982 he retired from the BBC to become a freelance writer. He wrote scripts for radio and television schools language programmes in French and English in Great Britain and Germany, where he has also directed programmes. He was for many years an awarder and examiner in French for Oxford and Cambridge Schools Examination Board.

Merlin Thomas was born in 1920 and educated at Taunton School, Somerset, and New College, Oxford. Following a brief period in the army from 1943 to 1945 he returned to New College, first as lecturer and, from 1953, as Fellow and Tutor in French, until his retirement in 1987. His publications include editions of Anouilh's *L'Alouette* and Giraudoux's *Électre* (both in collaboration with Simon Lee) and *Louis-Ferdinand Céline* (1979); and he was co-editor (with Professor W. D. Howarth) of *Molière: Stage and Study*. He also published articles on Rabelais, Molière and Anouilh. He was engaged upon a general book on the French novel from Laclos to Zola, which was to be his *magnum opus*, but unfortunately illness prevented its completion. Dr Thomas was a senior member of the Oxford University Dramatic Society and at the Oxford Playhouse he directed plays by Shakespeare and, in French, works by Corneille, Molière, Racine and Beaumarchais.

Merlin Thomas died in Sicily in July 1996. In its obituary *The Times* praised him 'for his expertise in his subject, his skill as a teacher of both undergraduates and graduates, and his devotion to the success of his students ... He was an exceptionally gifted teacher.'

# POCKET
# FRENCH DICTIONARY

---

### COMPILED BY MERLIN THOMAS
### AND RAYMOND ESCOFFEY

PENGUIN BOOKS

## PENGUIN BOOKS

Published by the Penguin Group
Penguin Books Ltd, 80 Strand, London WC2R 0RL, England
Penguin Putnam Inc., 375 Hudson Street, New York, New York 10014, USA
Penguin Books Australia Ltd, 250 Camberwell Road, Camberwell, Victoria 3124, Australia
Penguin Books Canada Ltd, 10 Alcorn Avenue, Toronto, Ontario, Canada M4V 3B2
Penguin Books India (P) Ltd, 11 Community Centre, Panchsheel Park, New Delhi – 110 017, India
Penguin Books (NZ) Ltd, Cnr Rosedale and Airborne Roads, Albany, Auckland, New Zealand
Penguin Books (South Africa) (Pty) Ltd, 24 Sturdee Avenue, Rosebank 2196, South Africa

Penguin Books Ltd, Registered Offices: 80 Strand, London WC2R 0RL, England

www.penguin.com

First published as *The Penguin French Dictionary* 1985
Reissued under the present title 2001
5

Copyright © Merlin Thomas and Raymond Escoffey, 1985
All rights reserved

Printed in England by Clays Ltd, St Ives plc

# CONTENTS

# INTRODUCTION

All dictionaries, since those early miracles in the sixteenth century, rely greatly on their predecessors. We have taken as ultimate arbiters the various Oxford dictionaries on the English side, the *Grand* and *Petit Robert* dictionaries on the French side, with occasional reference to *Littré*, and only very rarely indeed have we challenged their authority. We have also used, as a guide for the selection of words in a dictionary of this size, G.N. Garmonsway's *Penguin English Dictionary*.

The *Pocket French Dictionary* sets out to provide a useful and manageable guide to the present state of the vocabulary of French and English languages, and also to that of the literary languages from about 1800. This means that many slang and colloquial words are included, as are also a number of so-called 'obscene' words – preceded by the indication *vulg* – which are now to be found in the written as well as in the spoken languages. In a dictionary of this size there clearly have to be limits when it comes to technical vocabularies, but we have sought to provide as large as possible a range of useful terms in domains such as natural history, the sciences, the law, sport, motoring, seafaring, politics etc. Words common in American are also given (though, to save space, words spelt slightly differently in American – e.g. *theater* instead of *theatre* – are not normally separately included), preceded by the indication *US*. However, many American words have passed firmly into at least the *spoken* English language: conservative English readers may be surprised in some cases that these are *not* noted as *US*.

Again in order to save space in what is essentially a reading/translating dictionary, no indications about pronunciation are given. (No one, we feel, except perhaps the occasional trained phonetician, ever acquired a convincing accent in a foreign language from a dictionary.)

## Introduction

A brief summary of certain points of *French* grammar follows this Introduction. There is no parallel summary of *English* grammar, but, apart from this, the dictionary is also designed to help French students of the English language.

### *Layout and conventions*

Words are listed in alphabetical order. Inside each entry, alternative synonymous translations are separated by *commas*, whereas *semi-colons* separate different meanings. Where phrases are given within an entry (and we have tried to give as many as possible), the head-word is represented by a tilde (~). The order in which phrases are given is as follows. First come phrases which begin with the head-word. The alphabetical order of these phrases depends on the letter immediately following the head-word: e.g. in the entry (English–French) **party** the order of such phrases is '~ **line** ligne partagée; ~ **politics** politique *f* de partis; ~ **wall** mur mitoyen'. Then come phrases which do *not* begin with the head-word. They follow obvious alphabetical order (examples again taken from the English–French entry **party**) thus: 'a third ~ un tiers; **be a small** ~ être peu nombreux; **be no** ~ **to sth** ne pas s'associer à qch.' Homonyms with major semantic differences are indicated by separate head-words preceded by a numeral 1, 2, etc:

¹**vice** *n* vice *m*; (trait) défaut *m*
²**vice** *n* (tool) étau *m*
³**vice** *prep* à la place de

Adverbs formed *regularly* (see the grammatical summary below) in either French or English are usually omitted, unless there is some special reason for their inclusion. Genders are shown for nouns in French – *nm*, *nf* – but if *no* gender indication is given it means that the word can be both masculine and feminine – e.g. '**dactylo(graphe)** *n* typist'. If it differs from the masculine form the feminine form of a noun is shown as part of the head-word, thus – '**défendeur -eresse** *n leg* defendant'. Plurals of nouns and compound nouns which do not conform to the 'regular' pattern indicated below in the grammatical summary are shown. Adjectives which in the feminine and the plural do not conform to

the 'regular' pattern indicated below in the grammatical section
are also shown.

As far as possible we have of course sought to give *translations*
of both French and English words and phrases rather than
*descriptions*. From time to time, however, descriptive entries are
unavoidable, e.g. '**barrière de dégel** barrier on road to protect
surface during thaw'. Sometimes an *equivalent* is provided,
preceded by an equals sign, e.g. '**arpent** *nm ar* = (nearly) acre'.

Both languages are of course changing fast, especially in spoken
usage. This is most clearly seen in the use of abbreviations such as
*vulg, sl* and *coll*. Only a few years ago, most of the words we list as
*vulg* would not have been printed in ordinary dictionaries in either
language. A number of these now seem in some usages no more
than *sl*, e.g. '**con** *nm* . . . fool', or '**ball** *n* . . . *sl* ~s! conneries!'.
The distinction between *sl* and *coll* is often very hard to draw: our
decisions on this have been along the following lines: *sl* indicates a
term certainly unacceptable in the formal written languages, and
also in formal speech, whereas *coll* suggests a term not really
acceptable in the formal written languages, but already very
common in the spoken languages.

Two other abbreviations need brief comment – *ar* and *obs*. Our
principle has been to use *ar* for words that have an out-dated
flavour – e.g. '**forsooth** *adv ar+joc* en vérité' – and *obs* for words
likely in time to disappear from current usage – e.g. '**shilling** *n
obs* shilling *m*'. We know this to be a dangerous area: the French
word **sou** is still very alive, and we have not yet heard of anyone
threatening to cut off his heir with 5 p. . . .

Bracketed Roman numerals after certain *verb* head-words in the
French–English section refer to the verb section of the grammatical summary – e.g. '**déjeter** *vt* (5)'.

Where the only necessary translation of a French word is an English
word of identical spelling (except for accents) – e.g. **déformation**
(French), **deformation** (English) – the word is *omitted* from the
French–English section, allowing space for further entries. Accents
and genders, where appropriate, are given in the English–French
section.

# LIST OF ABBREVIATIONS

| | | | | | |
|---|---|---|---|---|---|
| *abbr* | abbreviation | *econ* | economics | *log* | logic |
| *adj* | adjective | *eg* | for example | | |
| *adv* | adverb | *elect* | electricity | *m* | masculine |
| *aer* | aeronautics | *eng* | engineering | *magn* | magnetism |
| *agr* | agriculture | *ent* | entomology | *math* | mathematics |
| *anat* | anatomical | *esp* | especially | *mech* | mechanics |
| *anthrop* | anthropology | *euph* | euphemistic | *med* | medical |
| *antiq* | antiquity | | | *met* | metaphysics |
| *ar* | archaic | *f* | feminine | *metal* | metallurgy |
| *arch* | archaeology | *fig* | figurative(ly) | *meteor* | meteorology |
| *archi* | architecture | *Fr* | French | *mil* | military |
| *art* | article | *fut* | future | *min* | mineralogy |
| *arts* | in the arts | | | *mot* | motoring |
| *astrol* | astrology | *geneal* | genealogy | *mus* | music |
| *astron* | astronomy | *geog* | geography | *myth* | mythology |
| *aux* | auxiliary | *geol* | geology | | |
| | | *geom* | geometry | *n* | noun |
| *bibl* | biblical | *gramm* | grammar | *naut* | nautical |
| *bioch* | biochemistry | | | *neg* | negative |
| *biol* | biology | *her* | heraldry | *neut* | neuter |
| *bot* | botany | *hist* | history, his-torical | *nom* | nominative |
| *bui* | building | | | *num* | numeral |
| | | *hort* | horticulture | | |
| *cap* | capital letter | | | *obs* | obsolete |
| *carp* | carpentry | *ie* | that is | *opp* | opposite |
| *cer* | ceramics | *imper* | imperative | *opt* | optics |
| *chem* | chemistry | *impers* | impersonal | *orig* | originally |
| *cin* | cinema | *incl* | including | *orni* | ornithology |
| *coll* | colloquial | *ind* | indicative | | |
| *collect* | collective | *indef* | indefinite | *path* | pathology |
| *comm* | commerce | *infin* | infinitive | *pej* | pejorative |
| *comp* | comparative | *inter* | interrogative | *pers* | person |
| *conj* | conjunction | *interj* | interjection | *phil* | philology |
| *cont* | contemptuous | *invar* | invariable | *philos* | philosophy |
| *cul* | culinary | *iron* | ironical | *phon* | phonetics |
| | | | | *phot* | photography |
| *def* | definite | *joc* | jocular | *phr* | phrase |
| *dem* | demonstrative | | | *phys* | physics |
| *dial* | dialect | *lang* | language | *physiol* | physiology |
| *dim* | diminutive | *leg* | legal | *pl* | plural |
| | | *lit* | literary | *poet* | poetic(al) |
| *eccles* | ecclesiastical | *liturg* | liturgical | *pol* | politics |

x

# List of Abbreviations

| | | | | | |
|---|---|---|---|---|---|
| *p part* | past participle | *Rom* | Roman | *typ* | typography |
| *pref* | prefix | | | | |
| *prep* | preposition | *sci* | science | *US* | United States |
| *pres* | present | *Scots* | Scots, Scottish | *usu* | usually |
| *pres part* | present | *sing* | singular | | |
| | participle | *sl* | slang | *v aux* | auxiliary verb |
| *print* | printing | *sp* | sport | *vi* | intransitive |
| *pron* | pronoun | *subj* | subjunctive | | verb |
| *pros* | prosody | *superl* | superlative | *v refl* | reflexive verb |
| *psych* | psychology | *surg* | surgery | *vt* | transitive verb |
| | | | | *vet* | veterinary |
| *rad* | radio | *tel* | telegraphy | *vulg* | vulgar |
| *refl* | reflexive | *theat* | of the theatre | | |
| *rel* | relative | *theol* | theology | *zool* | zoology |
| *rhet* | rhetoric(al) | *TV* | television | | |
| *RC* | Roman Catholic | | | | |

# LISTE DES ABRÉVIATIONS

Dans la plupart des cas le lecteur français comprendra tout de suite pourquoi les abréviations – calquées sur l'anglais – sont établies comme elles le sont. Dans les cas où une abréviation est liée uniquement à un mot ou à une phrase anglais, le mot ou la phrase anglais est donné en parenthèse.

| | | | | | |
|---|---|---|---|---|---|
| abbr | abréviation | comm | commerce | her | héraldique |
| adj | adjectif | comp | comparatif | hist | historique, |
| adv | adverbe | conj | conjonction | | histoire |
| aer | aéronautique | cont | méprisant | hort | horticulture |
| agr | agriculture | | [con- | | |
| anat | anatomique | | temptuous] | ie | c'est à dire [id |
| anthrop | anthropologie | cul | culinaire | | est] |
| antiq | antiquité | | | imper | impératif |
| ar | archaïque | def | défini | impers | impersonnel |
| arch | archéologie | dem | démonstratif | ind | indicatif |
| archi | architecture | dial | dialecte | indef | indéfini |
| art | article | dim | diminutif | infin | infinitif |
| arts | langage des | | | inter | interrogatif |
| | arts | eccles | ecclésiastique | interj | interjection |
| astrol | astrologie | econ | économie | invar | invariable |
| astrom | astronomie | eg | par exemple | iron | ironique |
| aux | auxiliaire | | [exempli | | |
| | | | gratia] | joc | facétieux |
| bibl | biblique | elect | électricité | | [jocular] |
| bioch | biochimie | eng | ingénierie [en- | | |
| biol | biologie | | gineering] | lang | langage |
| bot | botanique | ent | entomologie | leg | droit [legal] |
| bui | construction | esp | spécialement | lit | littéraire |
| | (bâtiments) | | [especially] | liturg | liturgique |
| | [building] | euph | euphémique | log | logique |
| cap | majuscule | f | féminin | m | masculin |
| | [capital] | fig | figuré | magn | magnétique |
| carp | menuiserie | Fr | français | math | mathématique |
| | [carpentry] | fut | futur | mech | mécanique |
| cer | céramique | | | med | médical |
| chem | chimie | geneal | généalogie | met | métaphysique |
| cin | cinéma | geog | géographie | metal | métallurgie |
| coll | familier [col- | geol | géologie | meteor | météorologie |
| | loquial] | geom | géométrie | mil | militaire |
| collect | collectif | gramm | grammaire | min | minéralogie |

# Liste des Abréviations

| | | | | | |
|---|---|---|---|---|---|
| *mot* | automobile [motoring] | *physiol* | physiologie | *subj* | subjonctif |
| *mus* | musique | *pl* | pluriel | *superl* | superlatif |
| *myth* | mythologie | *poet* | poétique | *surg* | chirurgie [surgery] |
| | | *pol* | politique | | |
| | | *p part* | participe passé | | |
| *n* | nom | *pref* | préfixe | *tel* | télégraphie |
| *naut* | nautique | *prep* | préposition | *theat* | théâtre |
| *neg* | négatif | *pres* | présent | *theol* | théologie |
| *neut* | neutre | *pres part* | participe | *TV* | télévision |
| *nom* | nominatif | | présent | *typ* | typographie |
| *num* | nombre [numeral] | *print* | imprimerie [printing] | *US* | américain [United States] |
| | | *pron* | pronom | | |
| *obs* | vieux, vieilli [obsolete] | *pros* | prosodie | *usu* | normalement [usually] |
| | | *psych* | psychologie | | |
| *opp* | opposé | | | | |
| *opt* | optique | *rad* | radio | *v aux* | verbe auxiliaire |
| *orig* | originalement | *refl* | réfléchi | | |
| *orni* | ornithologie | *rel* | relatif | *vi* | verbe intransitif |
| | | *rhet* | rhétorique | | |
| *path* | pathologie | *RC* | Catholique [Roman Catholic] | *v refl* | verbe réfléchi |
| *pej* | péjoratif | | | *vt* | verbe transitif |
| *pers* | personne | | | *vet* | vétérinaire |
| *phil* | philologie | *Rom* | romain | *vulg* | indécent [vulgar] |
| *philos* | philosophie | | | | |
| *phon* | phonétique | *sci* | scientifique | | |
| *phot* | photographie | *sing* | singulier | *zool* | zoologie |
| *phr* | phrase | *sl* | argot [slang] | | |
| *phys* | physique | *sp* | sport | | |

# MAIN POINTS OF FRENCH GRAMMAR

## The Article

Definite article (the)

**le** *m*, **la** *f*, **l'** (before vowel and **h** mute), **les** *mfpl*

(of the) **du** *m*, **de la** *f*, **de l'** (before vowel and **h** mute), **des** *mfpl*

(to the) **au** *m*, **à la** *f*, **à l'** (before vowel and **h** mute), **aux** *mfpl*

Note: the definite article, in addition to its meaning of 'the', is used with nouns in a general sense e.g. **l'alcool est mauvais pour la santé, les salades sont vertes.**

Indefinite article (a)

**un** *m*, **une** *f*, **des** *mfpl*, **de** (**d'**) after negative and often before adjective preceding a plural noun.

Partitive article (some, any)

As for definite article (of the): all forms become **de** or **d'** after a negative, and these latter forms are also used after expressions denoting quantity (e.g. **un kilo de pommes, un verre d'eau**).

## Nouns

Gender

Nouns are either masculine or feminine. As a rough guide, it may be said that those ending in **-e** are feminine (with the notable exception of those ending in **-isme** and nearly all in **-age**), and that most others are masculine (with the notable exception of those ending in **-ion** and **-té**).

Masculine nouns which can also have a feminine meaning normally add **-e**, e.g. **ami, amie.** Exceptions to this are masculine nouns in **-iste**, which remain unaltered, in **-er**, which change to **-ère**, **-on, -ien, -eur,** and **-ateur,** which change to **-onne, -ienne, -euse** and **-atrice.** Some conform to none of these patterns, e.g. **acteur, actrice; maître, maîtresse; mari, femme; neveu, nièce; roi, reine;** and **cheval, jument.**

Plural

The plural is normally formed by adding **-s** to the singular form. Nouns ending in **-s, -x** and **-z** do not change.

Nouns ending in **-au** and **-eu** add **-x** (except **bleu** *m*), as do **bijou, chou, caillou, genou, hibou,** and **pou.** Those ending in **-al** change to **-aux.** Those ending in **-ail** take **-s,** sometimes **-aux,** e.g. **détails, détails; travail, travaux.** There are a few totally irregular ones, e.g. **ciel, cieux; œil, yeux; bal, bals.**

Compound nouns

When written as one word, compound nouns normally take **-s.** Note the exceptions **bonhomme, bonshommes; gentilhomme, gentilshommes.**

Hyphened compound nouns vary. The plural of any which take anything other than -s at the end (or already end in -s, -x or -z in the singular), e.g. **avant-poste, avant-postes**, will be indicated in the body of the dictionary, e.g. **choufleur** *nm* (*pl* **choux-fleurs**).

## *Adjectives*

### Position

Adjectives normally follow the noun, although meaning and considerations of style or emphasis can require them to precede. A few common adjectives normally precede the noun, e.g. **bon, meilleur, beau, grand, petit, mauvais, vieux.**

### Agreement

Adjectives agree with the noun they qualify in number and gender. The feminine is normally formed by adding **-e** to the masculine form, e.g. **grand, grande**, unless this already ends in **-e**.

The following are important variations:

| | |
|---|---|
| -if -ive | e.g. **vif, vive** |
| -eux -euse | e.g. **peureux, peureuse** |
| -er -ère | e.g. **amer, amère** |
| -as -asse | e.g. **bas, basse** |
| -el -elle | e.g. **formel, formelle** |
| -eil -eille | e.g. **pareil, pareille** |
| -en -enne | e.g. **ancien, ancienne** |
| -on -onne | e.g. **bon, bonne** |
| -et -ète or -ette | e.g. **complet, complète aigrelet, aigrelette** |
| -ic -ique | e.g. **public, publique** |
| -eur -euse | e.g. **moqueur, moqueuse** |

Some are totally irregular, e.g. **doux, douce; vieux, vieille; grec, grecque; meilleur, meilleure; favori, favorite; blanc, blanche; sec, sèche; fou, folle.**

A few adjectives have two masculine forms, as follows (the second form being used before a vowel or **h** mute): **vieux, vieil; beau, bel; nouveau, nouvel; fou, fol; mou, mol.**

A very few have no feminine form, e.g. **chic**, and nouns used as adjectives, especially of colour.

### Plural

The general rule, as for nouns, is to add **-s** to the singular form.

Adjectives ending in **-s, -x** and **-z** are unchanged.

Those ending in **-al** form their plural in **-aux** (exceptions **banal, fatal, final, glacial, natal, naval**, which all take **-s**), e.g. **loyal, loyaux.**

**Tout** becomes **tous** in the plural.

### Comparative

The comparative is formed by using **plus** (more) before the adjective, e.g. **grand, plus grand**. The following are exceptions: **bon, meilleur; mauvais, pire** (or **plus mauvais); petit, moindre** (only when not denoting size).

The following words are used in comparisons: **plus** (more), **aussi** (as, so), **si** (so), **moins** (less) and the second part of the comparison is introduced by **que** (as, than).

**Aussi . . . que** renders as . . . as,

**pas si . . . que** not so . . . as.

In comparisons of quantity **plus, moins, autant** etc., are followed by **de** or **d'**.

### Superlative

The appropriate form of the article is used with the comparative form, e.g. **la plus belle voiture, le film le plus intéressant.**

# Main Points of French Grammar

Note that after a superlative 'in' is normally rendered by **de**, e.g. **le plus grand du monde**, the biggest in the world.

## Numeral adjectives (cardinal)

**Un, deux, trois, quatre, cinq, six, sept, huit, neuf, dix, onze, douze, treize, quatorze, quinze, seize, dix-sept, dix-huit, dix-neuf, vingt, vingt et un, vingt-deux, trente, quarante, cinquante, soixante, soixante-dix, soixante et onze, quatre-vingts, quatre-vingt-dix, quatre-vingt-onze, cent, cent un, deux cents, mille, deux mille, deux mille un, un million.**

Nearly all numerals are invariable.

The **un** of **vingt et un**, etc., agrees in the feminine, e.g. **vingt et une maisons**.

**Quatre-vingts** drops the **-s** in compounds, e.g. **quatre-vingt-onze**. Similarly **cents**, when followed by another number, drops its plural **-s**.

**Mille** is invariable (the form **mil** is used in dates).

**Un million**, a million, is a noun, not an adjective.

## Numeral adjective (ordinal)

Ordinal numeral adjectives are formed by adding **-ième** to the cardinal number (note the spellings **cinquième** and **neuvième**).

The exception is **premier, première** (first) and **second** (second), which is less used than the form **deuxième**.

## Fractions

$\frac{1}{2}$ **une moitié**, $\frac{1}{3}$ **un tiers**, $\frac{1}{4}$ **un quart**.

For other fractions, the ordinal is used, e.g. $\frac{3}{11}$ **trois onzièmes**, $\frac{1}{50}$ **un cinquantième**.

Note: Cardinal numbers are used instead of ordinals, with the exception of **premier**, in:

(a) Titles of sovereigns, e.g. Élisabeth II (**Deux**).

(b) Dates, e.g. **le 3 (trois) mars**.

## Demonstrative adjectives

The equivalent of 'this' and 'that' is normally **ce** *m* **cet** *m* (before a vowel or **h** mute), **cette** *f*, **ces** *mfpl*. Differentiation between 'this' and 'that' is conveyed by the addition of **-ci** or **-là** after the noun, e.g. **ce crayon-ci, cette lampe-là**.

## Possessive adjectives

| | |
|---|---|
| My | **mon** *m*, **ma** *f*, **mon** *f* (before vowel or **h** mute), **mes** *mfpl* |
| Your | (familiar form) **ton** *m*, **ta** *f*, **ton** *f* (before vowel or **h** mute), **tes** *mfpl* **votre, vos** *pl* |
| His, its | **son** *m*, **sa** *f*, **son** *f* (before vowel or **h** mute), **ses** *pl* |
| Our | **notre, nos** *pl* |
| Their | **leur** *mf*, **leurs** *pl* |

Examples: **mon frère, mon amie, sa jupe, tes livres, son toit, leurs amies**.

## Interrogative adjective

Which: **quel** *m*, **quelle** *f*, **quels** *mpl*, **quelles** *fpl*

Note: **quel** is also used to convey the exclamatory what a . . .!, e.g. **Quel beau paysage!**

# Pronouns

## Personal subject pronouns

**Je, tu, il, elle, nous, vous, ils, elles.**

Note: **tu** and its related words and forms are used when addressing relatives, close friends and children and also normally among young people.

## Personal object pronouns

Direct (accusative): **me, te, le, la, nous, vous, les**

Indirect (dative): **me, te, lui, y** (referring to anything but persons), **nous, vous, leur, y** (referring to anything

xvi

but persons)

**En** (of it or of them) is not used to refer to persons. Meaning some or any, it can refer to both persons and things. The following table indicates the order of object pronouns before the verb.

| me | | | | |
|----|----|-----|---|----|
| te | **le** | | | |
| | **la** | **lui** | | |
| nous | | **leur** | y | en |
| vous | **les** | | | |

e.g. **Elle nous en offre.**
**Je vous y ai vu.**

But note that object pronouns follow the imperative affirmative, e.g. **mangez-les. Moi** is used instead of **me**, e.g. **regardez-moi**, but note **donnez-m'en.**

When two pronouns follow an imperative the order is as in English, e.g. **donnez-le-moi, passe-le-lui.**

Reflexive pronouns (accusative and dative)

**me, te, se, nous, vous, se.**

Stressed pronouns

**moi, toi, lui, elle, nous, vous, eux, elles** and the third person singular reflexive **soi.**

These forms are mainly used:

(a) after prepositions, e.g. **avec moi**

(b) for emphasis, e.g. **toi, tu ne fais rien**

(c) in double subjects, e.g. **eux et leur mère**

(d) to indicate possession, after **être**, e.g. **cette voiture est à lui**

(e) when the pronoun stands alone, e.g. **Qui est-ce? – Moi.**

The form **soi** is used with reference to the indefinite subjects **on** and **il** (impersonal), e.g. **il faut penser à soi, on s'occupe de soi**

(f) with **c'est** and **ce sont**, e.g. **c'est lui, ce sont eux**

Demonstrative pronouns

This one: **celui-ci** *m*, **celle-ci** *f*; that one: **celui-là** *m*, **celle-là** *f*; these: **ceux-ci** *mpl*, **celles-ci** *fpl*; those: **ceux-là** *mpl*, **celles-là** *fpl*.

**Ceci** and **cela (ça)** (this and that) are invariable and refer to things, facts etc.

The unstressed form **ce** is used as subject to the verb **être**, e.g. **c'est possible**. Where **être** has as its complement a pronoun in the third person plural it often becomes plural, e.g. **c'est lui, ce sont eux.**

**Ce** also frequently occurs as antecedent to a relative pronoun, e.g. **Ce que vous me dites n'a aucun sens.**

**Celui** *m* (the one, he, him), **celle** *f* (the one, she, her) and the plural forms **ceux, celles** (those) are followed:

(a) by a relative clause, e.g. **J'ai vu celui que vous m'avez décrit.**

(b) by **de**, e.g. **Donnez-moi celle de votre frère.**

Possessive pronouns

**Le mien, la mienne, les miens, les miennes** – mine
**Le tien, la tienne, les tiens, les tiennes** – yours (thine)
**Le sien, la sienne, les siens, les siennes** – his, hers
**Le nôtre, la nôtre, les nôtres** – ours
**Le vôtre, la vôtre, les vôtres** – yours
**Le leur, la leur, les leurs** – theirs

The predicative mine, his, etc. is normally expressed by **à moi, à lui**, etc., e.g. **ce livre est à moi, cette serviette est à lui.**

Interrogative pronouns

| | |
|---|---|
| Who, whom | **qui**, e.g. **Qui vous l'a dit? Qui avez-vous vu?** The compound forms **qui est-ce qui** (who) and **qui est-ce que** (whom) are also used, generally in conversation. |
| What | **qu'est-ce qui** (subject), e.g. **Qu'est-ce qui se passe?** **que** or **qu'est-ce que** (object), e.g. **Que faites-vous là?** **quoi** (after a preposition, alone and before |

partitive **de**), e.g. **À quoi rêves-tu?, Quoi? Que dis-tu?, Quoi de neuf?**

Relative pronouns

Who, which (subject)  **qui**, e.g. **la table qui se trouve dans le salon**

Whom, which (object)  **que**, e.g. **le monsieur que nous avons vu**

To whom  **à qui**, e.g. **l'enfant à qui j'ai donné cela**

Whose, of whom, of which  **dont**, e.g. **la chose dont je parle, le garçon dont j'ai vu les devoirs**

Note: which, after a preposition, is normally translated by **lequel** (except where **dont** is appropriate), e.g. **la table sur laquelle j'ai posé le livre, les maisons derrière lesquelles passe le train.**

## Adverbs

Adverbs are formed in most cases by adding **-ment** to the feminine singular form of the adjective, e.g. **heureusement.**

Adjectives in **-ant** and **-ent** form their adverbs with the endings **-amment** and **-emment**, e.g. **indépendamment, patiemment.**

In a few cases the **-e** of the feminine becomes **-é**, e.g. **profondément.**

In cases where the masculine ends in a vowel, the feminine **-e** is dropped, e.g. **hardiment.**

Certain irregularities to the above rules do occur, e.g. **bon, bien; meilleur, mieux; mauvais, mal; pire, pis; petit, peu; moindre, moins; assidu, assidûment; gentil, gentiment; gai, gaîment (gaiement); lent, lentement; présent, présentement.**

## Negation

A negation which accompanies a verb has two components, the first, **ne**, coming before the verb, the latter after, e.g. **je ne vois rien, il ne dort jamais.**

In the case of compound tenses the second component comes immediately after the auxiliary, e.g. **nous n'avons** **rien vu.** The exception is **ne . . . personne**, e.g. **ils n'ont rencontré personne.**

Where a negation stands on its own without a verb, the **ne** is not used, e.g. **Vient-il quelquefois chez vous? – Jamais.**

## Verbs

There are four regular conjugations.

Compound tenses are formed with **avoir** or **être** and the past participle. **Avoir** is used in all cases except for reflexive verbs and a number of common verbs, mostly indicating

movement or change of state: **aller, arriver, décéder, devenir, échoir, éclore, entrer, mourir, naître, partir, re-partir, rentrer, rester, retourner, sortir, tomber, venir.**

The past participle appears mostly in

the masculine singular form. In cases of verbs conjugated with **être** in compound tenses it agrees with the subject. In reflexive verbs it agrees with the reflexive pronoun in all cases where the latter is the direct object of the verb. In verbs whose compound tenses are conjugated with **avoir** it agrees with the direct object whenever this precedes it (e.g. **nous les avons vus**). As an adjective or when used to form the passive, it agrees with the noun or pronoun to which it refers (e.g. **elle a été achetée, ils sont cassés**).

Below is set out the conjugation of regular verbs followed by a list of irregular verbs with their particular irregularities. The latter are each given a number. These numbers are given in the body of the dictionary and refer users to the verb in the table to whose type it conforms.

### Regular conjugation in -er

### PORTER, carry

#### INDICATIVE

| Present | Future | Imperfect | Past definite |
|---|---|---|---|
| je porte | je porterai | je portais | je portai |
| tu portes | tu porteras | tu portais | tu portas |
| il porte | il portera | il portait | il porta |
| nous portons | nous porterons | nous portions | nous portâmes |
| vous portez | vous porterez | vous portiez | vous portâtes |
| ils portent | ils porteront | ils portaient | ils portèrent |

| Perfect | Pluperfect | Future perfect | Past anterior |
|---|---|---|---|
| j'ai porté | j'avais porté | j'aurai porté | j'eus porté |
| tu as porté | tu avais porté | tu auras porté | tu eus porté |
| il a porté | il avait porté | il aura porté | il eut porté |
| nous avons porté | nous avions porté | nous aurons porté | nous eûmes porté |
| vous avez porté | vous aviez porté | vous aurez porté | vous eûtes porté |
| ils ont porté | ils avaient porté | ils auront porté | ils eurent porté |

#### CONDITIONAL

| Present | Past |
|---|---|
| je porterais | j'aurais porté |
| tu porterais | tu aurais porté |
| il porterait | il aurait porté |
| nous porterions | nous aurions porté |
| vous porteriez | vous auriez porté |
| ils porteraient | ils auraient porté |

# Main Points of French Grammar

### SUBJUNCTIVE

| Present | Imperfect | Perfect | Pluperfect |
|---------|-----------|---------|------------|
| je porte | je portasse | j'aie porté | j'eusse porté |
| tu portes | tu portasses | tu aies porté | tu eusses porté |
| il porte | il portât | il ait porté | il eût porté |
| nous portions | nous portassions | nous ayons porté | nous eussions porté |
| vous portiez | vous portassiez | vous ayez porté | vous eussiez porté |
| ils portent | ils portassent | ils aient porté | ils eussent porté |

### INFINITIVE

| Present | Past |
|---------|------|
| porter | avoir porté |

### IMPERATIVE

| Present | Past |
|---------|------|
| porte | aie porté |
| portons | ayons porté |
| portez | ayez porté |

### PARTICIPLE

| Present | Past |
|---------|------|
| portant | porté (passive) |
| | ayant porté (active) |

### Regular conjugation in -ir
### PUNIR, punish

### INDICATIVE

| Present | Future | Imperfect | Past definite |
|---------|--------|-----------|---------------|
| je punis | je punirai | je punissais | je punis |
| tu punis | tu puniras | tu punissais | tu punis |
| il punit | il punira | il punissait | il punit |
| nous punissons | nous punirons | nous punissions | nous punîmes |
| vous punissez | vous punirez | vous punissiez | vous punîtes |
| ils punissent | ils puniront | ils punissaient | ils punirent |

# Main Points of French Grammar

| Perfect | Pluperfect | Future perfect | Past anterior |
|---------|-----------|----------------|---------------|
| j'ai puni | j'avais puni | j'aurai puni | j'eus puni |
| tu as puni | tu avais puni | tu auras puni | tu eus puni |
| il a puni | il avait puni | il aura puni | il eut puni |
| nous avons puni | nous avions puni | nous aurons puni | nous eûmes puni |
| vous avez puni | vous aviez puni | vous aurez puni | vous eûtes puni |
| ils ont puni | ils avaient puni | ils auront puni | ils eurent puni |

## CONDITIONAL

| Present | Past |
|---------|------|
| je punirais | j'aurais puni |
| tu punirais | tu aurais puni |
| il punirait | il aurait puni |
| nous punirions | nous aurions puni |
| vous puniriez | vous auriez puni |
| ils puniraient | ils auraient puni |

## SUBJUNCTIVE

| Present | Imperfect | Perfect | Pluperfect |
|---------|-----------|---------|-----------|
| je punisse | je punisse | j'aie puni | j'eusse puni |
| tu punisses | tu punisses | tu aies puni | tu eusses puni |
| il punisse | il punît | il ait puni | il eût puni |
| nous punissions | nous punissions | nous ayons puni | nous eussions puni |
| vous punissiez | vous punissiez | vous ayez puni | vous eussiez puni |
| ils punissent | ils punissent | ils aient puni | ils eussent puni |

## INFINITIVE

| Present | Past |
|---------|------|
| punir | avoir puni |

## IMPERATIVE

| Present | Past |
|---------|------|
| punis | aie puni |
| punissons | ayons puni |
| punissez | ayez puni |

# Main Points of French Grammar

| Present | Past |
|---|---|
| punissant | puni (passive) |
| | ayant puni (active) |

## Regular conjugation in -re
### RENDRE, give back

INDICATIVE

| Present | Future | Imperfect | Past definite |
|---|---|---|---|
| je rends | je rendrai | je rendais | je rendis |
| tu rends | tu rendras | tu rendais | tu rendis |
| il rend | il rendra | il rendait | il rendit |
| nous rendons | nous rendrons | nous rendions | nous rendîmes |
| vous rendez | vous rendrez | vous rendiez | vous rendîtes |
| ils rendent | ils rendront | ils rendaient | ils rendirent |

| Perfect | Pluperfect | Future perfect | Past anterior |
|---|---|---|---|
| j'ai rendu | j'avais rendu | j'aurai rendu | j'eus rendu |
| tu as rendu | tu avais rendu | tu auras rendu | tu eus rendu |
| il a rendu | il avait rendu | il aura rendu | il eut rendu |
| nous avons rendu | nous avions rendu | nous aurons rendu | nous eûmes rendu |
| vous avez rendu | vous aviez rendu | vous aurez rendu | vous eûtes rendu |
| ils ont rendu | ils avaient rendu | ils auront rendu | ils eurent rendu |

CONDITIONAL

| Present | Past |
|---|---|
| je rendrais | j'aurais rendu |
| tu rendrais | tu aurais rendu |
| il rendrait | il aurait rendu |
| nous rendrions | nous aurions rendu |
| vous rendriez | vous auriez rendu |
| ils rendraient | ils auraient rendu |

SUBJUNCTIVE

| Present | Imperfect | Perfect | Pluperfect |
|---|---|---|---|
| je rende | je rendisse | j'aie rendu | j'eusse rendu |
| tu rendes | tu rendisses | tu aies rendu | tu eusses rendu |
| il rende | il rendît | il ait rendu | il eût rendu |

| nous rendions | nous rendissions | nous ayons rendu | nous eussions rendu |
| vous rendiez | vous rendissiez | vous ayez rendu | vous eussiez rendu |
| ils rendent | ils rendissent | ils aient rendu | ils eussent rendu |

### INFINITIVE

| *Present* | *Past* |
|-----------|--------|
| rendre | avoir rendu |

### IMPERATIVE

| *Present* | *Past* |
|-----------|--------|
| rends | aie rendu |
| rendons | ayons rendu |
| rendez | ayez rendu |

### PARTICIPLE

| *Present* | *Past* |
|-----------|--------|
| rendant | rendu (passive) |
| | ayant rendu (active) |

Regular conjugation in **-oir**

RECEVOIR, receive

### INDICATIVE

| *Present* | *Future* | *Imperfect* | *Past definite* |
|-----------|----------|-------------|-----------------|
| je reçois | je recevrai | je recevais | je reçus |
| tu reçois | tu recevras | tu recevais | tu reçus |
| il reçoit | il recevra | il recevait | il reçut |
| nous recevons | nous recevrons | nous recevions | nous reçûmes |
| vous recevez | vous recevrez | vous receviez | vous reçûtes |
| ils reçoivent | ils recevront | ils recevaient | ils reçurent |

| *Perfect* | *Pluperfect* | *Future perfect* | *Past anterior* |
|-----------|--------------|------------------|-----------------|
| j'ai reçu | j'avais reçu | j'aurai reçu | j'eus reçu |
| tu as reçu | tu avais reçu | tu auras reçu | tu eus reçu |
| il a reçu | il avait reçu | il aura reçu | il eut reçu |
| nous avons reçu | nous avions reçu | nous aurons reçu | nous eûmes reçu |
| vous avez reçu | vous aviez reçu | vous aurez reçu | vous eûtes reçu |
| ils ont reçu | ils avaient reçu | ils auront reçu | ils eurent reçu |

# Main Points of French Grammar

| *Present* | *Past* |
|---|---|
| je recevrais | j'aurais reçu |
| tu recevrais | tu aurais reçu |
| il recevrait | il aurait reçu |
| nous recevrions | nous aurions reçu |
| vous recevriez | vous auriez reçu |
| ils recevraient | ils auraient reçu |

SUBJUNCTIVE

| *Present* | *Imperfect* | *Perfect* | *Pluperfect* |
|---|---|---|---|
| je reçoive | je reçusse | j'aie reçu | j'eusse reçu |
| tu reçoives | tu reçusses | tu aies reçu | tu eusses reçu |
| il reçoive | il reçût | il ait reçu | il eût reçu |
| nous recevions | nous reçussions | nous ayons reçu | nous eussions reçu |
| vous receviez | vous reçussiez | vous ayez reçu | vous eussiez reçu |
| ils reçoivent | ils reçussent | ils aient reçu | ils eussent reçu |

INFINITIVE

| *Present* | *Past* |
|---|---|
| recevoir | avoir reçu |

IMPERATIVE

| *Present* | *Past* |
|---|---|
| reçois | aie reçu |
| recevons | ayons reçu |
| recevez | ayez reçu |

PARTICIPLE

| *Present* | *Past* |
|---|---|
| recevant | reçu (passive) |
| | ayant reçu (active) |

# Main Points of French Grammar

Irregular Verbs

1   AVOIR, have

INDICATIVE

| Present | Future | Imperfect | Past definite |
|---|---|---|---|
| j'ai | j'aurai | j'avais | j'eus |
| tu as | tu auras | tu avais | tu eus |
| il a | il aura | il avait | il eut |
| nous avons | nous aurons | nous avions | nous eûmes |
| vous avez | vous aurez | vous aviez | vous eûtes |
| ils ont | ils auront | ils avaient | ils eurent |

| Perfect | Pluperfect | Future perfect | Past anterior |
|---|---|---|---|
| j'ai eu | j'avais eu | j'aurai eu | j'eus eu |
| tu as eu | tu avais eu | tu auras eu | tu eus eu |
| il a eu | il avait eu | il aura eu | il eut eu |
| nous avons eu | nous avions eu | nous aurons eu | nous eûmes eu |
| vous avez eu | vous aviez eu | vous aurez eu | vous eûtes eu |
| ils ont eu | ils avaient eu | ils auront eu | ils eurent eu |

CONDITIONAL

| Present | Past |
|---|---|
| j'aurais | j'aurais eu |
| tu aurais | tu aurais eu |
| il aurait | il aurait eu |
| nous aurions | nous aurions eu |
| vous auriez | vous auriez eu |
| ils auraient | ils auraient eu |

SUBJUNCTIVE

| Present | Imperfect | Perfect | Pluperfect |
|---|---|---|---|
| j'aie | j'eusse | j'aie eu | j'eusse eu |
| tu aies | tu eusses | tu aies eu | tu eusses eu |
| il ait | il eût | il ait eu | il eût eu |
| nous ayons | nous eussions | nous ayons eu | nous eussions eu |
| vous ayez | vous eussiez | vous ayez eu | vous eussiez eu |
| ils aient | ils eussent | ils aient eu | ils eussent eu |

## Main Points of French Grammar

| Present | Past |
|---------|------|
| avoir | avoir eu |

IMPERATIVE

Present
aie
ayons
ayez

PARTICIPLE

| Present | Past |
|---------|------|
| ayant | eu (passive) |
| | ayant eu (active) |

## 2   ÊTRE, be

INDICATIVE

| Present | Future | Imperfect | Past definite |
|---------|--------|-----------|---------------|
| je suis | je serai | j'étais | je fus |
| tu es | tu seras | tu étais | tu fus |
| il est | il sera | il était | il fut |
| nous sommes | nous serons | nous étions | nous fûmes |
| vous êtes | vous serez | vous étiez | vous fûtes |
| ils sont | ils seront | ils étaient | ils furent |

| Perfect | Pluperfect | Future perfect | Past anterior |
|---------|------------|----------------|---------------|
| j'ai été | j'avais été | j'aurai été | j'eus été |
| tu as été | tu avais été | tu auras été | tu eus été |
| il a été | il avait été | il aura été | il eut été |
| nous avons été | nous avions été | nous aurons été | nous eûmes été |
| vous avez été | vous aviez été | vous aurez été | vous eûtes été |
| ils ont été | ils avaient été | ils auront été | ils eurent été |

# Main Points of French Grammar

CONDITIONAL

| *Present* | *Past* |
|-----------|--------|
| je serais | j'aurais été |
| tu serais | tu aurais été |
| il serait | il aurait été |
| nous serions | nous aurions été |
| vous seriez | vous auriez été |
| ils seraient | ils auraient été |

SUBJUNCTIVE

| *Present* | *Imperfect* | *Perfect* | *Pluperfect* |
|-----------|-------------|-----------|--------------|
| je sois | je fusse | j'aie été | j'eusse été |
| tu sois | tu fusses | tu aies été | tu eusses été |
| il soit | il fût | il ait été | il eût été |
| nous soyons | nous fussions | nous ayons été | nous eussions été |
| vous soyez | vous fussiez | vous ayez été | vous eussiez été |
| ils soient | ils fussent | ils aient été | ils eussent été |

INFINITIVE

| *Present* | *Past* |
|-----------|--------|
| être | avoir été |

IMPERATIVE

*Present*

sois
soyons
soyez

PARTICIPLE

| *Present* | *Past* |
|-----------|--------|
| étant | été |
|  | ayant été |

# Main Points of French Grammar

3 Verbs in **-ger** add e before endings in **a** and **o**, e.g. **manger, mangeais, mangeons**

4 Verbs in **-cer** change **c** to **ç** before endings in **a** and **o**, e.g. **menacer, menaçais, menaçons**

5 Verbs in **-eler** and **-eter** double **l** or **t** before **e** mute, e.g. **appeler, appelle, jeter, jette**. The following verbs are exceptions, the **e** before **l** or **t** changing to **è**: **acheter, agneler, becqueter, cacheter, celer, ciseler, congeler, corseter, déceler, dégeler, démanteler, écarteler, fureter, geler, haleter, harceler, marteler, modeler, peler, racheter, receler, regeler**, e.g. **acheter, achète**

6 Verbs having mute **e** or **é** in the penultimate syllable of the infinitive change these to **è** before a mute syllable (except in the future and conditional), e.g. **espérer, espère**

7 Verbs in **-yer**: Those ending in **-oyer** and **-uyer** change the **y** to **i** before **e** mute, e.g. **essuyer, essuie**. Those ending in **-ayer** may either keep the **y** or change to **i** before **e** mute. Those ending in **-eyer** keep the **y** throughout

8 **absoudre** *Pres ind* **absous, absous, absout, absolvons, absolvez, absolvent.** *Imperf* **absolvais.** *Fut* **absoudrai.** *Condit* **absoudrais.** *Imp* **absous, absolvons, absolvez.** *Pres subj* **absolve, absolvions.** *Pres part* **absolvant.** *P part* **absous, absoute.** No *p def*, no *imperf subj*

9 **abstraire** *Pres ind* **abstrais, abstrayons.** *Imperf* **abstrayais.** *Fut* **abstrairai.** *Condit* **abstrairais.** *Imp* **abstrais, abstrayons, abstrayez.** *Pres subj* **abstraie, abstrayions.** *Pres part* **abstrayant.** *P part* **abstrait.** No *p def*, no *imperf subj*

10 **accroire** Used only in *infin*, and always after **faire**

11 **advenir** Used only in third pers. Conjugated like **venir**

12 **aller** *Pres indic* **vais, vas, va, vont.** *Imperf* **allais.** *Fut* **irai.** *Condit* **irais.** *Imp* **va (vas-y), allons, allez.** *Pres subj* **aille, ailles, aille, allions, alliez, aillent.** *Pres part* **allant.** *P part* **allé**

13 **apparoir** *Pres indic third pers* only **appert**

14 **assaillir** *Pres indic* **assaille, assaillons.** *Imperf* **assaillais.** *Imp* **assaille, assaillons, assaillez.** *Pres subj* **assaille, assaillions.** *Pres part* **assaillant**

15 **asseoir** *Pres indic* **assieds, assieds, assied, asseyons, asseyez, asseyent (assois, assoyons, assoient).** *Imperf* **asseyais (assoyais).** *P def* **assis.** *Fut* **assiérai (assoirai).** *Condit* **assiérais (assoirais).** *Imper* **assieds, asseyons, asseyez (assois, assoyons).** *Pres subj* **asseye, asseyions (assoie, assoyions, assoient).** *Pres part* **asseyant (assoyant).** *P part* **assis**

16 **battre** *Pres indic* **bats, battons.** *Imperf* **battais.** *Imper* **bats, battons, battez.** *Pres subj* **batte, battions.** *Pres part* **battant**

17 **boire** *Pres indic* **bois, bois, boit, buvons, buvez, boivent.** *Imperf* **buvais.** *P def* **bus.** *Fut* **boirai.** *Condit* **boirais.** *Imper* **bois, buvons, buvez.** *Pres subj* **boive, buvions.** *Pres part* **buvant.** *P part* **bu**

18 **bouillir** *Pres indic* **bous, bous, bout, bouillons, bouillez, bouillent.** *Imperf* **bouillais.** *P def* **bouillis** . *Fut* **bouillirai.** *Imper* **bous, bouillons, bouillez.** *Pres subj* **bouille, bouillions.** *Pres part* **bouillant.** *P part* **bouilli**

19 **braire** *Third pers* only. *Pres indic* **brait, braient.** *Fut* **braira, brairont**

20 **bruire** *Third pers* only. *Pres indic* **bruit, bruissent.** *Imperf* **bruissait, bruissaient.** *Pres part* **bruissant**

21 **choir** Only in: *Pres indic* **chois, chois, choit.** *P def* **chus, chûmes.** *Fut* **choirai.** *P part* **chu**

22 **circoncire** *Pres indic* **circoncis, circoncisons.** *Imperf* **circoncisais, circoncisions.** *P def* **circoncis.** *Fut* **circoncirai.** *Imper* **circoncis, circoncisons, circoncisez.** *Pres subj* **circoncisse.** *Pres part* **circoncisant.** *P part* **circoncis**

23 **clore** Only in: *Pres indic* **clos, clos, clôt.** *Fut* **clorai, clorons.** *Condit* **clorais, clorions.** *Pres subj* **close, closions.** *P part* **clos**

24 **comparoir** Only in *infin* and *pres part* **comparant**

25 **conclure** *Pres indic* **conclus, conclus, conclut, concluons, concluez, concluent.** *Imperf* **concluais, concluions.** *P def* **conclus.** *Fut* **conclurai.** *Imper* **conclus, concluons, concluez.** *Pres subj* **conclue, concluions.** *Pres part* **concluant.** *P part* **conclu**

26 **confire** *Pres indic* **confis, confisons.** *Imperf* **confisais.** *P def* **confis.** *Fut* **confirai, confirons.** *Imper* **confis, confisons, confisez.** *Pres subj* **confise, confisions.** *Pres part* **confisant.** *P part* **confit**

27 **conquérir** *Pres indic* **conquiers, conquiers, conquiert, conquérons, conquérez, conquièrent.** *Imperf* **conquérais.** *P def* **conquis.** *Fut* **conquerrai.** *Pres subj* **conquière, conquières, conquière, conquérions, conquériez, conquièrent.** *Pres part* **conquérant.** *P part* **conquis**

28 **coudre** *Pres indic* **couds, couds, coud, cousons, cousez, cousent.** *Imperf* **cousais.** *P def* **cousis.** *Fut* **coudrai.** *Imper* **couds, cousons, cousez.** *Pres subj* **couse.** *Pres part* **cousant.** *P part* **cousu**

29 **courir** *Pres indic* **cours, cours, court, courons, courez, courent.** *Imperf* **courais.** *P def* **courus.** *Fut* **courrai.** *Imper* **cours, courons, courez.** *Pres subj* **coure.** *Pres part* **courant.** *P part* **couru**

30 **couvrir** *Pres indic* **couvre, couvres, couvre, couvrons, couvrez, couvrent.** *Imperf* **couvrais.** *P def* **couvris.** *Fut* **couvrirai.** *Imper* **couvre, couvrons, couvrez.** *Pres subj* **couvre.** *Pres part* **couvrant.** *P part* **couvert**

31 **croire** *Pres indic* **crois, crois, croit, croyons, croyez, croient.** *Imperf* **croyais.** *P def* **crus.** *Fut* **croirai.** *Imper* **crois, croyons, croyez.** *Pres subj* **croie, croyions.** *Pres part* **croyant.** *P part* **cru**

32 **croître** *Pres indic* **croîs, croîs, croît, croissons, croissez, croissent.** *Imperf* **croissais.** *P def* **crûs.** *Fut* **croîtrai.** *Imper* **croîs, croissons, croissez.** *Pres subj* **croisse.** *Pres part* **croissant.** *P part* **crû**

# Main Points of French Grammar

33 **cueillir** *Pres indic* **cueille, cueilles, cueille, cueillons, cueillez, cueillent.** *Imperf* **cueillais, cueillions.** *P def* **cueillis.** *Fut* **cueillerai.** *Imper* **cueille, cueillons, cueillez.** *Pres subj* **cueille, cueillions.** *Pres part* **cueillant.** *P part* **cueilli**

34 **déchoir** *Pres indic* **déchois, déchois, déchoit, déchoient.** *P def* **déchus.** *Pres subj* **déchoie, déchoyions.** *P part* **déchu**

35 **déconfire** Only in *infin* and *p part* **déconfit**

36 **défaillir** *Pres indic* **défaille, défailles, défaille (défaut), défaillons, défaillez, défaillent.** *Imperf* **défaillais.** *P def* **défaillis.** *Fut* **défaillerai (défaillirai).** *Pres subj* **défaille.** *Pres part* **défaillant**

37 **devoir** *Pres indic* **dois, dois, doit, devons, devez, doivent.** *Imperf* **devais.** *P def* **dus.** *Fut* **devrai.** *Imper* **dois, devons, devez.** *Pres subj* **doive, devions.** *Pres part* **devant.** *P part* **dû** (*f* **due**)

38 **dire** *Pres indic* **dis, dis, dit, disons, dites, disent.** *Imperf* **disais.** *P def* **dis.** *Fut* **dirai.** *Imper* **dis, disons, dites.** *Pres subj* **dise.** *Pres part* **disant.** *P part* **dit**

39 **dormir** *Pres indic* **dors, dors, dort, dormons, dormez, dorment.** *Imperf* **dormais.** *P def* **dormis.** *Fut* **dormirai.** *Imper* **dors, dormons, dormez.** *Pres subj* **dorme.** *Pres part* **dormant.** *P part* **dormi**

40 **échoir** *Third pers sing* only. *Pres indic* **échoit.** *P def* **échut.** *Fut* **il échoira (écherra).** *Pres part* **échéant.** *P part* **échu**

41 **éclore** *Third pers* only. *Pres indic* **éclôt, éclosent.** *Fut* **éclora, écloront.** *Pres subj* **éclose, éclosent.** *P part* **éclos**

42 **écrire** *Pres indic* **écris, écris, écrit, écrivons, écrivez, écrivent.** *Imperf* **écrivais.** *P def* **écrivis.** *Fut* **écrirai.** *Imper* **écris, écrivons, écrivez.** *Pres subj* **écrive.** *Pres part* **écrivant.** *P part* **écrit**

43 **ensuivre (s')** *Third pers* only. *Pres indic* **s'ensuit, s'ensuivent.** *Imperf* **s'ensuivait, s'ensuivaient.** *P def* **s'ensuivit, s'ensuivirent.** *Fut* **s'ensuivra, s'ensuivront.** *Pres subj* **s'ensuive, s'ensuivent.** *Pres part* **s'ensuivant.** *P part* **ensuivi**

44 **envoyer** *Pres indic* **envoie, envoies, envoie, envoyons, envoyez, envoient.** *Imperf* **envoyais.** *Fut* **enverrai.** *Pres subj* **envoie, envoyions.** *Pres part* **envoyant.** *P part* **envoyé**

45 **faillir** Only in: *P def* **faillis.** *Fut* **faudrai (faillirai).** *Condit* **faudrais (faillirais).** *Pres part* **faillant.** *P part* **failli**

46 **faire** *Pres indic* **fais, fais, fait, faisons, faites, font.** *Imperf* **faisais.** *P def* **fis.** *Fut* **ferai.** *Imper* **fais, faisons, faites.** *Pres subj* **fasse.** *Pres part* **faisant.** *P part* **fait**

47 **falloir** *Third pers* only. *Pres indic* **faut.** *Imperf* **fallait.** *P def* **fallut.** *Fut* **faudra.** *Pres subj* **faille.** *P part* **fallu**

48 **férir** *Infin* only (in expression **sans coup férir**)

49 **fleurir** Following irregularities when in sense of prosper: *Imperf* **florissais**. *Pres part* **florissant**

50 **forfaire** Only used in *infin*, *pres indic* and compound tenses

51 **frire** Only used in *pres indic* **fris, fris, frit**. *Fut* **frirai**

52 **fuir** *Pres indic* **fuis, fuis, fuit, fuyons, fuyez, fuient**. *Imperf* **fuyais, fuyions**. *P def* **fuis**. *Fut* **fuirai**. *Imper* **fuis, fuyons, fuyez**. *Pres subj* **fuie, fuyions**. *Pres part* **fuyant**. *P part* **fui**

53 **gésir** Only in: *Pres indic* **gît, gisons, gisez, gisent**. *Imperf* **gisais, gisions**. *Pres part* **gisant**

54 **haïr** *Pres indic* **hais, hais, hait, haïssons, haïssez, haïssent**. *Imperf* **haïssais**. *P def* **haïs**. *Fut* **haïrai**. *Pres part* **haïssant**. *P part* **haï**

55 **joindre** *Pres indic* **joins, joins, joint, joignons, joignez, joignent**. *Imperf* **joignais**. *P def* **joignis**. *Fut* **joindrai**. *Imper* **joins, joignons, joignez**. *Pres subj* **joigne**. *Pres part* **joignant**. *P part* **joint**

56 **lire** *Pres indic* **lis, lis, lit, lisons, lisez, lisent**. *Imperf* **lisais**. *P def* **lus**. *Fut* **lirai**. *Imper* **lis, lisons, lisez**. *Pres subj* **lise**. *Pres part* **lisant**. *P part* **lu**

57 **luire** *Pres indic* **luis, luis, luit, luisons, luisez, luisent**. *Imperf* **luisais**. *P def* **luis** or **luisis** (but very rare). *Fut* **luirai**. *Imper* **luis, luisons, luisez**. *Pres subj* **luise**. *Pres part* **luisant**. *P part* **lui**

58 **maudire** *Pres indic* **maudis, maudis, maudit, maudissons, maudissez, maudissent**. *Imperf* **maudissais**. *P def* **maudis**. *Fut* **maudirai**. *Imper* **maudis, maudissons, maudissez**. *Pres subj* **maudisse**. *Pres part* **maudissant**. *P part* **maudit**

59 **mentir** *Pres indic* **mens, mens, ment, mentons, mentez, mentent**. *Imperf* **mentais**. *P def* **mentis**. *Fut* **mentirai**. *Imper* **mens, mentons, mentez**. *Pres subj* **mente**. *Pres part* **mentant**. *P part* **menti**

60 **mettre** *Pres indic* **mets, mets, met, mettons, mettez, mettent**. *Imperf* **mettais**. *P def* **mis**. *Fut* **mettrai**. *Imper* **mets, mettons, mettez**. *Pres subj* **mette**. *Pres part* **mettant**. *P part* **mis**

61 **moudre** *Pres indic* **mouds, mouds, moud, moulons, moulez, moulent**. *Imperf* **moulais**. *P def* **moulus**. *Fut* **moudrai**. *Imper* **mouds, moulons, moulez**. *Pres subj* **moule**. *Pres part* **moulant**. *P part* **moulu**

62 **mourir** *Pres indic* **meurs, meurs, meurt, mourons, mourez, meurent**. *Imperf* **mourais**. *P def* **mourus**. *Fut* **mourrai**. *Imper* **meurs, mourons, mourez**. *Pres subj* **meure, mourions, meurent**. *Pres part* **mourant**. *P part* **mort**

63 **mouvoir** *Pres indic* **meus, meus, meut, mouvons, mouvez, meuvent**. *Imperf* **mouvais**. *P def* **mus**. *Fut* **mouvrai**. *Imper* **meus, mouvons, mouvez**. *Pres subj* **meuve, mouvions, meuvent**. *Pres part* **mouvant**. *P part* **mû** (*f* **mue**)

# Main Points of French Grammar

64 **naître** *Pres indic* **nais, nais, naît, naissons, naissez, naissent.** *Imperf* **naissais.** *P def* **naquis.** *Fut* **naîtrai.** *Imper* **nais, naissons, naissez.** *Pres subj* **naisse.** *Pres part* **naissant.** *P part* **né**

65 **nuire** *P def* **nuisis.** Otherwise like **luire**

66 **ouïr** Used only in *infin*, *imper* **oyez**, *p part* **ouï** and compound tenses

67 **paître** *Pres indic* **pais, pais, paît, paissons, paissez, paissent.** *Imperf* **paissais.** *P def* none. *Fut* **paîtrai.** *Imper* **pais, paissons, paissez.** *Pres subj* **paisse.** *Pres part* **paissant.** *P part* none

68 **paraître** *Pres indic* **parais, parais, paraît, paraissons, paraissez, paraissent.** *Imperf* **paraissais.** *P def* **parus.** *Fut* **paraîtrai.** *Imper* **parais, paraissons, paraissez.** *Pres subj* **paraisse.** *Pres part* **paraissant.** *P part* **paru**

69 **plaire** *Pres indic* **plais, plais, plaît, plaisons, plaisez, plaisent.** *Imperf* **plaisais.** *P def* **plus.** *Fut* **plairai.** *Imper* **plais, plaisons, plaisez.** *Pres subj* **plaise.** *Pres part* **plaisant.** *P part* **plu**

70 **pleuvoir** *Third pers sing* only. *Pres indic* **pleut.** *Imperf* **pleuvait.** *P def* **plut.** *Fut* **pleuvra.** *Pres subj* **pleuve.** *Pres part* **pleuvant.** *P part* **plu**

71 **poindre** Only in: *Pres indic* **point.** *Imperf* **poignait.** *P def* **poignit.** *Fut* **poindra.** *Pres subj* **poigne.** *Pres part* **poignant.** *P part* **point**

72 **pourvoir** *Pres indic* **pourvois, pourvois, pourvoit, pourvoyons, pourvoyez, pourvoient.** *Imperf* **pourvoyais.** *P def* **pourvus.** *Fut* **pourvoirai.** *Imper* **pourvois, pourvoyons, pourvoyez.** *Pres subj* **pourvoie, pourvoyions.** *Pres part* **pourvoyant.** *P part* **pourvu**

73 **pouvoir** *Pres indic* **peux (puis), peux, peut, pouvons, pouvez, peuvent.** *Imperf* **pouvais.** *P def* **pus.** *Fut* **pourrai.** *Imper* none. *Pres subj* **puisse.** *Pres part* **pouvant.** *P part* **pu**

74 **prédire** As **dire**, except for *pres indic* and *imper* **prédisez**

75 **prendre** *Pres indic* **prends, prends, prend, prenons, prenez, prennent.** *Imperf* **prenais.** *P def* **pris.** *Fut* **prendrai.** *Imper* **prends, prenons, prenez.** *Pres subj* **prenne, prenions, prennent.** *Pres part* **prenant.** *P part* **pris**

76 **prévaloir** As **valoir**, except for *pres subj* **prévale**

77 **prévoir** As **voir**, except for *fut* **prévoirai** and *condit* **prévoirais**

78 **promouvoir** As **mouvoir**, but used only in *infin*, compound tenses and *passive*

79 **quérir** Used only in *infin* after verbs **aller, envoyer, faire, venir**

80 **réduire** *Pres indic* **réduis, réduis, réduit, réduisons, réduisez, réduisent.** *Imperf* **réduisais.** *P def* **réduisis.** *Fut* **réduirai.** *Imper* **réduis, réduisons, réduisez.** *Pres subj* **réduise.** *Pres part* **réduisant.** *P part* **réduit**

81 **repaître** As **paître**, but also has *p def* **repus**, *imperf subj* **repusse**, *p part* **repu**

82 **résoudre** *Pres indic* **résous, résous, résout, résolvons, résolvez, résolvent.** *Imperf* **résolvais.** *P def* **résolus.** *Fut* **résoudrai.** *Imper* **résous, résolvons, résolvez.** *Pres subj* **résolve.** *Pres part* **résolvant.** *P part* **résolu**

83 **ressortir** As **sortir** in meaning 'go out again'. As **finir** in *leg* sense

84 **rire** *Pres indic* **ris, ris, rit, rions, riez, rient.** *Imperf* **riais, riions.** *P def* **ris.** *Fut* **rirai.** *Imper* **ris, rions, riez.** *Pres subj* **rie, riions.** *Pres part* **riant.** *P part* **ri**

85 **rompre** As **rendre**, but *third pers pres indic* **rompt**

86 **saillir** (in sense of jut out) Only in: *Third pers pres indic* **saille.** *Imperf* **saillait.** *Fut* **saillera (saillira).** *Condit* **saillerait.** *Pres subj* **saille.** *Pres part* **saillant.** *P part* **sailli**

87 **savoir** *Pres indic* **sais, sais, sait, savons, savez, savent.** *Imperf* **savais.** *P def* **sus.** *Fut* **saurai.** *Imper* **sache, sachons, sachez.** *Pres subj* **sache.** *Pres part* **sachant.** *P part* **su**

88 **seoir** Only in: *Pres indic* **sied, siéent.** *Imperf* **seyait, seyaient.** *Fut* **siéra, siéront.** *Condit* **siérait, siéraient.** *Pres subj* **siée, siéent.** *Pres part* **seyant.** *P part* **sis**

89 **servir** *Pres indic* **sers, sers, sert, servons, servez, servent.** *Imperf* **servais.** *P def* **servis.** *Fut* **servirai.** *Imper* **sers, servons, servez.** *Pres subj* **serve.** *Pres part* **servant.** *P part* **servi**

90 **sourdre** Used only in *infin* and *pres indic third pers* **sourd, sourdent**

91 **suffire** *Pres indic* **suffis, suffis, suffit, suffisons, suffisez, suffisent.** *Imperf* **suffisais.** *P def* **suffis.** *Fut* **suffirai.** *Imper* **suffis, suffisons, suffisez.** *Pres subj* **suffise.** *Pres part* **suffisant.** *P part* **suffi**

92 **suivre** *Pres indic* **suis, suis, suit, suivons, suivez, suivent.** *Imperf* **suivais.** *P def* **suivis.** *Fut* **suivrai.** *Imper* **suis, suivons, suivez.** *Pres subj* **suive.** *Pres part* **suivant.** *P part* **suivi**

93 **surseoir** *Pres indic* **sursois, sursois, sursoit, sursoyons, sursoyez, sursoient.** *Imperf* **sursoyais.** *P def* **sursis.** *Fut* **sursoirai.** *Imper* **sursois, sursoyons, sursoyez.** *Pres subj* **sursoie, sursoyions.** *Pres part* **sursoyant.** *P part* **sursis**

94 **vaincre** *Pres indic* **vaincs, vaincs, vainc, vainquons, vainquez, vainquent.** *Imperf* **vainquais.** *P def* **vainquis.** *Fut* **vaincrai.** *Imper* **vaincs, vainquóns, vainquez.** *Pres subj* **vainque.** *Pres part* **vaincant.** *P part* **vaincu**

95 **valoir** *Pres indic* **vaux, vaux, vaut, valons, valez, valent.** *Imperf* **valais.** *P def* **valus.** *Fut* **vaudrai.** *Imper* not used. *Pres subj* **vaille, valions, vaillent.** *Pres part* **valant.** *P part* **valu**

96 **venir** *Pres indic* **viens, viens, vient, venons, venez, viennent.** *Imperf* **venais.** *P def* **vins.** *Fut* **viendrai.** *Imper* **viens, venons, venez.** *Pres subj* **vienne, venions, viennent.** *Pres part* **venant.** *P part* **venu**

97 vêtir *Pres indic* vêts, vêts, vêt, vêtons, vêtez, vêtent. *Imperf* vêtais. *P def* vêtis. *Fut* vêtirai. *Imper* vêts, vêtons, vêtez. *Pres subj* vête. *Pres part* vêtant. *P part* vêtu

98 vivre *Pres indic* vis, vis, vit, vivons, vivez, vivent. *Imperf* vivais. *P def* vécus. *Fut* vivrai. *Imper* vis, vivons, vivez. *Pres subj* vive. *Pres part* vivant. *P part* vécu

99 voir *Pres indic* vois, vois, voit, voyons, voyez, voient. *Imperf* voyais. *P def* vis. *Fut* verrai. *Imper* vois, voyons, voyez. *Pres subj* voie, voyions. *Pres part* voyant. *P part* vu

100 vouloir *Pres indic* veux, veux, veut, voulons, voulez, veulent. *Imperf* voulais. *P def* voulus. *Fut* voudrai. *Imper* veuille, veuillons, veuillez. *Pres part* voulant. *P part* voulu

# FRENCH-ENGLISH

# A

**à** *prep* at, in; to, into; by, for, from, of, on with; ~ **deux (trois)** both (all three) together; ~ **dix kilomètres** ten kilometres away; ~ **l'anglaise** in the English style; **un homme** ~ **lunettes** a man with glasses

**abaissable** *adj* lowerable

**abaissement** *nm* lowering, fall (price, temperature)

**abaisser** *vt* lower; bring down, pull down; humiliate, humble; s' ~ fall away, sink; humble oneself; condescend, stoop

**abandon** *nm* abandonment, surrender; neglect; abandon, freedom from restraint

**abandonner** *vt* forsake, leave, desert, abandon; renounce, surrender; give up; s' ~ neglect oneself; let oneself go; succumb, become addicted

**abasourdir** *vt* stun, daze; amaze, dumbfound

**abasourdissement** *nm* bewilderment, stupefaction

**abâtardir** *vt* bastardize, degrade, debase

**abâtardissement** *nm* degeneracy; debasement

**abat-jour** *nm invar* lamp-shade; skylight

**abats** *nmpl* offal, giblets

**abattage** *nm* felling; slaughtering; *coll* reprimand, blowing up

**abattant** *nm* leaf (of table), flap (of counter); **siège** ~ tilting seat

**abattement** *nm* deduction, reduction (in tax, price); prostration, depression, dejection

**abattis** *nm* heap, pile; *pl* giblets, offal

**abattre** *vt* fell; slaughter, shoot down; lay (dust); enfeeble; get through (a lot of work); s' ~ fall suddenly, come down; swoop

**abattu** *adj* discouraged; enfeebled; brought down

**abat-vent** *nm* louvre-boards; chimney-cowl; wind-screen

**abat-voix** *nm* sounding-board (over pulpit)

**abbatial** *adj* église ~e minster

**abbaye** *nf* abbey, monastery

**abbé** *nm* abbot; priest

**abbesse** *nf* abbess

**abcès** *nm* abscess, gathering

**abdiquer** *vt* + *vi* abdicate, renounce

**abdominal -aux** *adj* abdominal

**abécédaire** *nm* A B C, spelling-book; *adj* elementary

**abeille** *nf* bee

**aberrant** *adj* aberrant, abnormal, irregular; *coll* absurd, crazy

**abêtir** *vt* stupefy, besot, make s/o stupid; s' ~ become stupid

**abêtissant** *adj* besotting, stupefying

**abêtissement** *nm* stupefaction, stupidity

**abhorrer** *vt* abhor, have a horror of; detest

**abîme** *nm* bottomless gulf, abyss, chasm

**abîmer** *vt* damage, spoil; *coll* ~ **le portrait à qn** smash s/o's face in; s' ~ be swallowed up, sink

**abjurer** *vt* abjure, recant, retract

**ablatif** *nm* ablative

**ablation** *nf* ablation, removal; excision

**ablette** *nf* bleak, ablet

**aboiement** *nm* bark, barking

**abois** *nmpl* être aux ~ be at bay, in a desperate situation

**abolir** *vt* abolish, suppress

**abominer** *vt* abominate

**abondamment** *adv* abundantly, copiously

**abondance** *nf* abundance, plenty; **parler avec (d')** ~ improvise

**abondant** *adj* abundant, rich

**abonder** *vi* abound, be plentiful; ~ **dans le sens de qn** support s/o's opinion to an exaggerated degree

**abonné -e** *n* subscriber

**abonnement** *nm* subscription; season-ticket

**abonner** *vt* take out a subscription for (s/o); s' ~ take out a subscription, subscribe

**abord** *nm* approach, landing; bearing; **d'** ~ at first; **dès l'** ~ from the outset; **d'un** ~ **facile** (person) easy to approach; **au premier** ~ at first sight; **aux abords de** on the outskirts of; **de prime** ~ at first sight, offhand

**abordable** *adj* approachable, accessible

**abordage** *nm* boarding, coming alongside, berthing

**aborder** *vt* board, come alongside; run into; approach

**aborigène** *n* + *adj* aboriginal, native

**abortif -ive** *adj* abortive

**aboutir** *vi* come to an end; lead, end; *med* come to a head, burst; **ne pas** ~ fizzle out

**aboutissement** *nm* outcome, end-product; *med* coming to a head

**aboyer** vi (7) bark, bay, yelp
**aboyeur** nm (fairground) barker
**abracadabrant** adj extraordinary and incoherent
**abrasif -ive** adj abrasive
**abrégé** nm précis, summary, abstract
**abrègement** nm abridgement
**abréger** vt (6,3) shorten, abridge, cut short, abbreviate
**abreuver** vt water (animals); give generously; s' ~ drink copiously
**abreuvoir** nm watering-place, drinking-trough; sl bar, pub
**abréviation** nf abbreviation
**abri** nm shelter, refuge, dug-out; les sans-~ the homeless
**abricot** nm apricot, vulg cunt
**abricotier** nm apricot-tree
**abriter** vt shelter, protect; lodge, put up
**abroger** vt (3) abrogate, repeal, rescind, annul
**abruti -e** n dullard, fool, idiot; adj dull-witted, besotted; tired-out
**abrutir** vt make stupid; besot, stupefy; exhaust, stun
**abrutissant** adj dulling, stupefying
**abrutissement** nm stupefaction, besottedness; exhaustion
**absentéisme** nm absenteeism, truancy
**absentéiste** n absentee; supporter of absenteeism
**absenter (s')** v refl absent oneself, quit; be away
**abside** nf archi apse
**absidial** adj archi apsidal
**absinthe** nf bot wormwood; absinth(e)
**absolu** nm + adj absolute
**absolument** adv absolutely, really, utterly
**absorber** vt drink, consume; absorb; swallow up
**absorption** nf absorption; drinking, eating, swallowing
**absoudre** vt (8) absolve, pardon
**absoute** nf absolution
**abstenir (s')** v refl abstain
**abstentionniste** n one who abstains from voting
**abstraction** nf abstraction; faire ~ de set aside; not to take account of
**abstraire** vt (9) abstract, dissociate; s' ~ become absorbed in thought
**abstrait** adj abstract
**abstrus** adj abstruse
**absurde** nm + adj absurd
**absurdité** nf absurdity
**abus** nm abuse, misuse, violation; coll il y a de l' ~ it's a bit thick, that's going too far
**abuser** vt abuse, deceive; vi ~ de misuse, deceive, take advantage of; s' ~ deceive oneself, be mistaken

**abusif -ive** adj excessive, unauthorized; gramm improper
**abusivement** adv in an unauthorized manner; gramm improperly
**abyssal -aux** adj abyssal; unfathomable
**abysse** nm unfathomable (ocean); depths, abyss
**acabit** nm de cet ~, du même ~ pej of the same kind, birds of a feather
**académie** nf learned society; specialized school; (educational) zone centred on a university; arts painting (or drawing) from the nude; sl figure; elle a une belle (une superbe) ~ she's got a fantastic figure
**académique** adj academic; strictly according to convention
**acajou** nm mahogany; noix d'acajou cashew-nut; adj dark auburn (hair)
**acanthe** nf bot + archi acanthus
**acariâtre** adj difficult, disagreeable (character)
**accablant** adj overwhelming
**accablement** nm overwhelming prostration
**accabler** vt oppress, overwhelm
**accalmie** nf calm, repose
**accaparement** nm keeping for oneself, cornering, monopolizing
**accaparer** vt hoard, monopolize, buttonhole
**accapareur -euse** n hoarder, monopolizer; adj possessive
**accéder** vi (6) have access; accede
**accélérateur** nm accelerator
**accéléré** nm cin quick motion
**accélérer** vt + vi (6) accelerate
**accentué** adj accentuated; stressed, marked
**accentuer** vt accentuate; stress; intensify
**acceptation** nf acceptance
**accepter** vt accept, agree to, consent to
**accès** nm access, way-in; med attack, fit, bout
**accessoire** nm accessory; ~ s accessories; theat props; magasin des ~ s property room; adj accessory, secondary
**accessoirement** adv secondarily
**accessoiriste** n theat property master (mistress); mot dealer in accessories
**accident** nm accident; ~ s de terrain unevenness of the ground
[1]**accidenté** nm casualty, victim (of accident)
[2]**accidenté** adj uneven, rough; eventful; injured
**accidentel -elle** adj accidental
**acclamer** vt acclaim
**acclimatation** nf acclimatization; jardin d' ~ zoological garden
**acclimatement** nm adaptation to an alien environment

**acclimater** *vt* acclimatize; s' ~ become acclimatized

**accointance** *nf* acquaintance; relationship

**accolade** *nf* accolade; hug, embrace; *mus+print* brace

**accoler** *vt* juxtapose, couple; *mus+print* bracket

**accommodant** *adj* accommodating, easygoing

**accommodement** *nm* (friendly) agreement; compromise

**accommoder** *vt* accommodate, adapt; focus; prepare, season a dish

**accompagnateur -trice** *n* accompanist; guide

**accompagnement** *nm* accompaniment, consequence; *cul* garnishing

**accompagner** *vt* accompany, go with; s' ~ de result in

**accompli** *adj* accomplished, perfect; completed

**accomplir** *vt* accomplish; carry out, execute; perform; s' ~ happen, occur; be fulfilled

**accomplissement** *nm* accomplishment; fulfilment

**accord** *nm* agreement, consent; concord, harmony; *mus* chord; tuning; d' ~ agreed; in agreement; en ~ harmoniously; **mettre d' ~** reconcile

**accordéon** *nm* accordion; en ~ rumpled, pleated

**accordéoniste** *n* accordionist

**accorder** *vt* reconcile; harmonize; *mus* tune; concede, admit; grant, bestow; *gramm* make agree; s' ~ be in agreement, get on well; *gramm* agree

**accordeur** *nm mus* tuner

**accordoir** *nm mus* tuning-hammer

**accort** *adj* lively, sprightly; attractive

**accostage** *nm naut* coming alongside; accosting

**accoster** *vt* accost, go up to; *naut* come alongside

**accotement** *nm* verge; ~ non stabilisé soft shoulder

**accoter** *vt* lean, prop; s' ~ lean

**accouchée** *nf* woman who has given birth

**accouchement** *nm* childbirth, parturition

**accoucher** *vt* deliver; *vi* give birth; ~ de give birth to; *sl* explain; cough up

**accoucheur -euse** *n* obstetrician, *f* midwife

**accoudement** *nm* leaning on the elbows

**accouder (s')** *vt refl* lean on one's elbows

**accoudoir** *nm* arm-rest

**accoupler** *vt* couple; s' ~ copulate

**accourir** *vi* run up

**accoutrement** *nm* accoutrement; *coll* absurd get-up

**accoutrer** *vt obs* dress; dress absurdly

**accoutumance** *nf* habit, use; *med* tolerance

**accoutumé** *adj* accustomed, normal

**accoutumer** *vt* accustom, acquire the habit; s' ~ à get used to

**accréditer** *vt* accredit; sanction; s' ~ gain acceptance

**accroc** *nm* tear; snag

**accrochage** *nm* hanging up, attaching; squabble; *mot* slight accident; *mil* encounter, brush

**accroche-cœur** *nm* kiss-curl

**accrocher** *vt* hang up; hook up; take hold of, grip; collide with; attract; *mil* engage; s' ~ hang on; s' ~ à hang on to

**accrocheur -euse** *adj* that catches the eye

**accroire** *vt* (10) faire ~ make believe; en faire ~ delude

**accroissement** *nm* growth, increase; accretion

**accroître** *vt* (32) make bigger, augment, increase; add to, heighten; *leg* accrue

**accroupir (s')** *v refl* squat, crouch

**accroupissement** *nm* squatting, crouching

**accu** *nm coll* accumulator; *coll fig* recharger ses ~s regain one's energies

**accueil** *nm* welcome; reception, reaction; **centre d' ~** reception centre; information bureau; **faire bon ~ à** welcome

**accueillant** *adj* welcoming, friendly

**accueillir** *vt* (33) receive; welcome; greet

**acculer** *vt* corner, bring to bay; ~ à force to; bring close to

**accumulateur** *nm* accumulator

**accumuler** *vt* accumulate; s' ~ accumulate

**accusateur -trice** *n* accuser; *adj* accusing

**accusatif** *nm gramm* accusative

**accusé -e** *n* defendant

**accuser** *vt* accuse; blame; indicate; *coll* ~ le coup take the point; ~ réception acknowledge receipt

**acerbe** *adj* sour, bitter

**acéré** *adj* sharp; biting

**acérer** *vt* (6) sharpen

**acétique** *adj* acetic; vinegary

**acétylène** *nm* acetylene

**achalandage** *nm* customers, clientèle

**achalandé** *adj* well patronized; *coll* well stocked

**acharné** *adj* fierce; inveterate

**acharnement** *nm* fury; obstinacy

**acharner (s')** *v refl* persevere, persist

**achat** *nm* purchase, acquisition; **pouvoir d' ~** purchasing power

**acheminement** *nm* progress; transmission

acheminer

**acheminer** *vt* progress; transmit, forward; s' ~ advance
**acheter** *vt* (5) buy, purchase; bribe
**acheteur -euse** *n* purchaser, buyer
**achevé** *adj* perfect; complete; ended
**achèvement** *nm* completion; perfection
**achever** *vt* (6) complete, finish; round off; finish off; s' ~ end
**achoppement** *nm lit* obstacle; difficulty; **pierre d'** ~ obstacle, snag
**acide** *nm* acid; *coll* L.S.D.; *adj* acid
**acidifier** *vt* acidify; s' ~ become acid
**acidité** *nf* acidity
**acidose** *nf med* acidosis
**aciduler** *vt* acidulate; **bonbon acidulé** acid drop
**acier** *nm* steel
**aciérie** *nf* steelworks
**acmé** *nf* acme; culminating point
**acné** *nf* acne
**acompte** *nm* instalment; down-payment; *coll* something to be going on with
**aconit** *nm* aconite
**acoquiner (s')** *v refl* lower oneself, have an undesirable liaison
**à-côté** *nm* side-issue; ~ s perks
**à-coup** *nm* jerk; **par** ~ s jerkily, intermittently
**acoustique** *nf* acoustics; *adj* acoustic
**acquéreur** *nm* purchaser
**acquérir** *vt* (27) acquire, obtain; purchase, buy; s' ~ obtain
**acquiescement** *nm* acquiescence
**acquiescer** *vt* (4) acquiesce
**acquis** *nm* experience gained; *adj* acquired; bought; ~ **à** belonging to; strongly in favour of
**acquit** *nm* receipt; **pour** ~ received with compliments
**acquit-à-caution** *nm* (*pl* **acquits-à-caution**) document accepting liability for payment of tax, excise, etc
**acquittement** *nm* discharge, payment; *leg* acquittal
**acquitter** *vt* discharge, pay; *leg* acquit; s' ~ free oneself; perform; repay
**âcre** *adj* acrid, bitter
**âcreté** *nf* acridness, bitterness
**acrimonie** *nf* acrimony
**acrimonieux -ieuse** *adj* acrimonious
**acrobate** *n* acrobat
**acrobatie** *nf* acrobatics
**acrobatique** *adj* acrobatic
**acrostiche** *nm* acrostic
**¹acte** *nm* action, deed; document, certificate; ~ s records, proceedings; *bibl* Acts; **demander** ~ **de** request official confirmation of; **donner** ~ **de** give official confirmation of; **étant** ~ duly noted; **faire** ~ **de présence** put in an appearance; **prendre** ~ **de** take due note of
**²acte** *nm theat* act
**acteur** *nm* actor
**actif** *nm* assets; credit; *gramm* active voice; **avoir à son** ~ have to one's credit; *adj* (*f* **-ive**) active; lively, dynamic; **armée active** regular army; **population active** working population
**¹action** *nf* action, deed; activity; lawsuit; *theat* plot; **entrer en** ~ become operative
**²action** *nf fin* share; **compagnie par** ~ s joint-stock company
**actionnaire** *n* share-holder
**actionnement** *nm* setting in motion
**actionner** *vt* set in motion, work, start; *leg* prosecute
**activer** *vt* activate; s' ~ be busy; bustle about
**activisme** *nm* activism
**activiste** *n* activist
**activité** *nf* activity; energy, vivacity; active employment, active service
**actrice** *nf* actress
**actuaire** *n* actuary
**actualiser** *vt* actualize
**actualité** *nf* actuality; relevance; current affairs; ~ s news
**actuel -uelle** *adj* actual; present, contemporary
**acuité** *nf* acuteness, intensity
**acutangle** *adj* acute-angled
**adamantin** *adj* adamantine
**adaptateur -trice** *n* adapter
**adapter** *vt* adapt; s' ~ adapt oneself
**additif** *nm* supplement; additive; *adj* (*f* **-ive**) additive; *math* to be added
**addition** *nf* addition; bill in restaurant
**additionnel -elle** *adj* additional
**additionner** *vt* add up; ~ **de** mix into, enrich
**adducteur** *nm physiol* adductor; water-supply channel; *adj physiol* adducent; carrying water supply
**adduction** *nf physiol* adduction; carrying of water supply
**adénoïde** *adj* adenoid, adenoidal
**adepte** *n* adept; initiate
**adéquat** *adj* adequate, sufficient
**adhérence** *nf* adherence; *med* adhesion
**adhérent -e** *n* + *adj* adherent
**adhérer** *vi* (6) adhere, stick; subscribe; join
**adhésif** *nm* adhesive; *adj* (*f* **-ive**) adhesive; **ruban** ~ adhesive tape
**adhésion** *nf* adhesion; agreement
**adieu** *nm* + *interj* farewell, goodbye
**adipeux -euse** *adj* adipose
**adjectif** *nm* adjective; *adj* (*f* **-ive**) adjectival
**adjoindre** *vt* (55) appoint, allocate; associate; s' ~ take on, engage

4

**adjoint -e** *n* deputy, assistant

**adjudant** *nm mil* warrant-officer, sergeant major; ~ **chef** regimental sergeant major; ~ **major** adjutant

**adjudicateur -trice** *n* adjudicator

**adjudication** *nf* auction; knocking down at auction; acceptance of tender

**adjuger** *vt* award; knock down; **une fois, deux fois, trois fois, adjugé!** going! going! gone!

**adjurant** *nm* additive; stimulant; stimulus

**adjurer** *vt* adjure, entreat

**admettre** *vt* (60) admit, accept; authorize, permit; allow in

**administrateur -trice** *n* administrator; (company) director

**administratif -ive** *adj* administrative

**administration** *nf* administration, management; public service, civil service; **conseil d'** ~ board of directors; board of governors

**administré -e** *n* s/o subject to an authority

**administrer** *vt* administer, manage; rule; *leg* adduce; *coll* give, deal out

**admirateur -trice** *n* admirer

**admiratif -ive** *adj* admiring

**admirer** *vt* admire, wonder at

**admissibilité** *nf* admissibility; (in French examination system) qualification to sit second part of an examination

**admissible** *adj* admissible; tolerable; qualified; admitted to second part of an examination

**admonestation** *nf* reprimand

**admonester** *vt* admonish, reprimand

**adolescent -e** *n* + *adj* adolescent

**adonner (s')** *v refl* devote oneself; ~ **à** go in for; indulge in; **adonné à** given to

**adopter** *vt* adopt; choose, follow

**adoptif -ive** *adj* adoptive

**adorable** *adj* adorable; delightful, charming, marvellous

**adorateur -trice** *n* worshipper; devoted admirer; *adj* adoring

**adorer** *vt* adore; worship; *coll* be terribly fond of, dote on

**adosser** *vt* back on, build against; s' ~ lean one's back

**adouber** *vt* dub; try out a move (chess, draughts)

**adoucir** *vt* soften; s' ~ become soft

**adoucissement** *nm* softening; attenuation

**adrénaline** *nf* adrenalin

**¹adresse** *nf* address; **à l'** ~ **de** directed at

**²adresse** *nf* dexterity, skill; finesse

**adresser** *vt* address; send, direct; s' ~ **à** speak to; go and find; have recourse to

**adroit** *adj* adroit; skilful

**adulateur -trice** *n* adulator, sycophant;

**adj** adulatory, sycophantic

**aduler** *vt* adulate, flatter grossly

**adulte** *n* + *adj* adult

**adultère** *n* adulterer, adulteress; *nm* adultery; *adj* adulterous

**adultérer** *vt* (6) adulterate, falsify

**advenir** *vi* (11) occur, happen; **advienne que pourra** come what may

**adventice** *adj* adventitious

**adverbe** *nm* adverb

**adversaire** *n* adversary

**adversité** *nf* adversity

**aérateur** *nm* ventilator

**aération** *nf* airing, ventilation

**aérer** *vt* (6) air, ventilate; thin, lighten

**aérien -ienne** *adj* aerial; air; airy

**aérodrome** *nm* aerodrome

**aérodynamique** *nf* aerodynamics; *adj* aerodynamic, streamlined

**aérogare** *nf* air-terminal

**aéroglisseur** *nm* hovercraft

**aéronaute** *n* aeronaut

**aéronautique** *nf* aeronautics; *adj* aeronautical

**aéroplane** *nm ar* aeroplane

**aéroport** *nm* airport

**aéroporté** *adj* airborne

**aérospatial** *adj* interplanetary

**affabilité** *nf* affability

**affabulation** *nf* organization of the plot of a narrative

**affadir** *vt* make insipid; make dull; s' ~ become insipid; become dull

**affadissement** *nm* insipidity

**affaiblir** *vt* enfeeble, weaken; attenuate; s' ~ become weak; become weakened

**affaiblissement** *nm* weakening, diminution, enfeebling

**affaire** *nf* affair, matter; lawsuit; trial; *mil* engagement; business, business proposition; ~s affairs, public business; *comm* business; possessions, belongings; ~ **de cœur** love-affair; **avoir** ~ **à** deal with; **avoir** ~ **avec** do business with; **ça fait l'** ~ that will do; **ce n'est pas une** ~ there's nothing in it; **ce n'est pas une** ~ **d'État** it's not a matter of great importance; **c'est toute une** ~ ! it's very complicated!; **faire son** ~ **à qn** settle s/o's hash; **homme d'** ~ s business man; **la belle** ~ ! what a damned nuisance!; so what!; **se tirer d'** ~ get oneself out of trouble

**affairé** *adj* busy

**affairement** *nm* fuss; *coll* flap

**affairer (s')** *v refl* bustle about, fuss; be busy

**affairiste** *nm* profiteer, shark

**affaissement** *nm* subsidence, sinking; collapsing; prostration

**affaisser** *vt* cause to sink; weight down; s' ~ subside, sink; collapse; decline, become weak

**affaler** *vt naut* haul down; cause to run aground; **s' ~** *naut* run aground; slide down; *fig* slump, sink

**affamé -e** *n* starving person; *adj* hungry, starving; **~ de** eager for, avid for

**affamer** *vt* starve

**¹affectation** *nf* allotment, designation, allocation

**²affectation** *nf* affectation, show; putting on

**affecté** *adj* affected; false; put on; mannered

**¹affecter** *vt* allot, designate

**²affecter** *vt* affect; simulate; put on; assume

**³affecter** *vt* affect, touch, move; **s' ~** be upset, be concerned

**affectif -ive** *adj* affective; emotional

**affectionné** *adj* affectionate

**affectionner** *vt* be fond of, be attached to

**affectivité** *nf* sensibility

**affectueux -ueuse** *adj* affectionate

**afférent** *adj* pertaining; *leg* accruing; *physiol* afferent

**affermage** *nm* renting of a farm; renting advertisement space (hoardings, newspapers)

**affermer** *vt* let (farm)

**affermir** *vt* strengthen; harden; consolidate, reinforce; **s' ~** become more stable, become firmer

**afféterie** *nf* affectation, preciosity

**affichage** *nm* bill-posting; display; *sp* **tableau d' ~** score-board

**affiche** *nf* poster; **une pièce qui tient (reste à) l' ~** a play that is still running

**afficher** *vt* post up; announce by posters; display, parade, make no secret of; **défense d' ~** stick no bills; **s' ~ avec** display oneself with, be seen everywhere with

**afficheur** *nm* bill-poster

**affichiste** *n* poster-artist, poster-designer

**affilage** *nm* whetting, sharpening

**affilée (d')** *adv phr* uninterruptedly, without stopping

**affiler** *vt* whet, sharpen; bore; **avoir la langue bien affilée** be very talkative

**affilier** *vt* affiliate; **s' ~** join, belong

**affiloir** *nm* hone, whetstone; knife-sharpener

**affinage** *nm* refining, purification; ripening (cheese)

**affinement** *nm* refinement

**affiner** *vt* purify (metal, glass, etc); ripen (cheese); refine; **s' ~** become sophisticated, become refined

**affinité** *nf* affinity; relationship; mutual understanding

**affirmatif -ive** *adj* affirmative; positive, emphatic, assertive

**affirmation** *nf* affirmation, proposition, assertion, statement; manifestation

**affirmative** *nf* **répondre par l' ~** say yes

**affirmer** *vt* affirm, maintain, assert; swear; **s' ~** assert oneself, assert itself

**affleurement** *nm* levelling; *geol* outcropping; emergence

**affleurer** *vt* level off; *vi* emerge, be manifested

**affligeant** *adj* afflicting, distressing

**affliger** *vt* (3) afflict, cause to suffer, sadden

**affluence** *nf* crowd; affluence; **heures d' ~** rush hour

**affluer** *vi* flow; crowd; flood

**afflux** *nm* influx; crowd; rush (of flood)

**affolant** *adj* disturbing, frightening; *coll* awful, terrible

**affolé** *adj* terrified; excited; bewildered; swinging (compass)

**affolement** *nm* panic; anxiety; swinging (compass)

**affoler** *vt* bewilder; terrify; **s' ~** panic

**affranchi -e** *n* freed slave; *adj* open, free, unprejudiced

**affranchir** *vt* free; grant freedom; pay postage on; exempt (from tax); *sl* put in the know; **s' ~** become free

**affranchissement** *nm* freeing; grant of freedom; payment of postage

**affres** *nfpl lit* torment, torture

**affrètement** *nm naut* chartering

**affréter** *vt* (6) *naut* charter

**affréteur** *nm naut* charterer

**affreux** *nm coll* white mercenary; *adj* (*f* **-euse**) horrible, monstrous, hideous; very disagreeable

**affriolant** *adj* exciting, alluring

**affront** *nm* insult, affront

**affrontement** *nm* confrontation; levelling of two edges

**affronter** *vt* confront, face; level two edges

**affubler** *vt pej* rig out, dress absurdly; **s' ~** rig oneself out

**affût** *nm* ambush; hide; gun carriage; **être à l' ~ de** be on the look-out for

**affûter** *vt* sharpen

**affûtiaux** *nmpl coll* trinkets; *sl* tools

**afin de** *prep phr* in order to

**afin que** *conj phr* in order that

**Africain -e** *n* African

**africain** *adj* African

**afro-asiatique** *adj* Afro-asian

**agaçant** *adj* irritating, annoying; provocative

**agacement** *nm* irritation, impatience

**agacer** *vt* (4) irritate, annoy; provoke

**agacerie** *nf* flirtatious words; flirtatious behaviour

**agape** *nf obs* banquet; **~ s** *joc* feast

**âge** *nm* age; epoch; old age; **deuxième ~**

youth; ~ **critique** change of life; ~
**ingrat** awkward age; **d'un certain** ~
getting on, elderly; **premier** ~ childhood; **troisième** ~ old age

**âgé** *adj* old; aged

**agence** *nf* agency; branch-office of bank

**agencement** *nm* arrangement, disposition, ordering

**agencer** *vt* (4) arrange, dispose, order

**agenda** *nm* diary, engagement-book

**agenouillement** *nm* kneeling

**agenouiller (s')** *v refl* kneel; submit,
humble oneself

**agent** *nm* agent, cause, factor; representative; member of staff; policeman; ~
**comptable** accountant; ~ **de change**
stockbroker; ~ **public** civil servant

**agglomération** *nf* agglomeration; built-
up area; urban area

**aggloméré** *nm* briquette; breeze-block

**agglomérer** *vt* (6) agglomerate

**agglutiner** *vt* agglutinate

**aggravant** *adj* aggravating, making
worse

**aggravation** *nf* aggravation, worsening;
*leg* increase (in sentence)

**aggraver** *vt* aggravate, worsen; augment

**agilité** *nf* agility

**agir** *vi* act, do; behave; take effect, operate; influence; act on; *v impers* s' ~ **de**
be a question of; **de quoi s'agit-il?** what
is the matter?, what's up?; **il ne s'agit
pas de ça** that's not the point

**agissant** *adj* effective, active, efficacious

**agissements** *nmpl pej* dealings, machinations

**agitateur -trice** *n* agitator

**agitation** *nf* agitation; restlessness; turbulence, unrest; commotion

**agité** *adj* agitated; restless; turbulent;
rough (sea); *med* disturbed

**agiter** *vt* move; wave, stir, flap; trouble,
agitate, worry; discuss; s' ~ move
about, go to and fro; become excited;
bustle about; fidget

**agneau** *nm* lamb

**agneler** *vi* (5) lamb

**agnelet** *nm* little lamb

**agnosticisme** *nm* agnosticism

**agnostique** *n* + *adj* agnostic

**agonie** *nf* death agony; **entrer en** ~ , **être
à l'** ~ be on the point of death

**agonisant -e** *n* dying person; *adj* dying

**agoniser** *vi* be dying

**agoraphobie** *nf* agoraphobia

**agrafage** *nm* pinning together; buckling
up; clamping

**agrafe** *nf* clasp; buckle; clip; hook;
clamp, staple

**agrafer** *vt* attach; clip together; hook;
buckle; *sl* nab, arrest

**agraire** *adj* agrarian

**agrandir** *vt* enlarge; make more important; s' ~ grow, expand

**agrandissement** *nm* enlargement, expansion; development

**agrandisseur** *nm phot* enlarger

**agrarien-ienne** *n* + *adj* *hist* + *pol* agrarian

**agréable** *adj* agreeable, pleasant, charming, delightful; *obs* **avoir pour** ~
approve

**agréer** *vt* accept; agree to; **veuillez** ~
**l'assurance de mes sentiments distin-
gués** yours faithfully; *vi* please, suit

**agrégat** *nm* agglomerate; aggregate

**agrégatif -ive** *n* student preparing the
**agrégation**

**agrégation** *nf* competitive graduate examination in France, giving entitle-
ment to posts in lycées and (in certain
faculties) in universities; aggregation,
binding

**agrégé -e** *n* successful candidate at the
**agrégation**

**agréger** *vt* (6) aggregate; incorporate;
s' ~ join

**agrément** *nm* approval; pleasantness;
pleasure, delight; *mus* grace-note

**agrémenter** *vt* ornament, embellish

**agrès** *nmpl naut* rigging, tackle; gymnasium equipment

**agresser** *vt* assault

**agresseur** *nm* aggressor

**agressif -ive** *adj* aggressive, violent

**agression** *nf* aggression

**agressivité** *nf* aggressiveness

**agreste** *adj* rustic

**agricole** *adj* agricultural

**agriculteur** *nm* farmer

**agriculture** *nf* agriculture

**agripper** *vt* clutch; s' ~ seize, clutch at

**agronome** *n* agronomist

**agronomie** *nf* agronomy

**agrumes** *nmpl* citrus fruit

**aguerrir** *vt* train for war; inure; s' ~
harden

**aguets** *nmpl* **aux** ~ on the alert

**aguichant** *adj* alluring, enticing

**aguicher** *vt* excite, entice, arouse

**aguicheur -euse** *n* enticer; *adj* seductive

**ah** *interj* ah!, oh!

**ahuri** *adj* bewildered, amazed, flabbergasted

**ahurir** *vt* bewilder, amaze, flabbergast

**ahurissant** *adj* bewildering, amazing;
unbelievable

**ahurissement** *nm* bewilderment, amazement, stupefaction

**aide** *n* aide, assistant, helper; *nf* aid,
help, assistance; support, collabora-
tion; **à l'** ~ ! help!; **à l'** ~ **de** with, by
means of

**aide-mémoire** *nm* handbook; digest

**aider** *vt* aid, help, assist; support, contribute to; *vi* contribute; s' ~ **de** make use of

**aïe** *interj* ow!

**aïeul -e** *n* (*pl* **aïeuls, aïeules**) grandfather, grandmother; (*pl* **aïeux**) ancestors

**aigle** *nm* eagle; lectern; *coll* **ce n'est pas un ~** he's not very bright; *nf* female eagle; eagle as military emblem; **~ impériale** Napoleonic eagle; **~ romaine** Roman eagle

**aiglefin** *nm* haddock

**aiglon -onne** *n* eaglet

**aigre** *nm* sour taste, bitterness; acrimony; **tourner à l'~** (argument) become heated; *adj* sour, tart; shrill, piercing; bitter; sharp, acrimonious

**aigre-doux** (*f* **aigre-douce**) *adj* bittersweet

**aigrefin** *nm* shark, crook

**aigrelet -ette** *adj* slightly sour; slightly sharp

**aigrette** *nf orni* egret; plume, aigrette; spray

**aigreur** *nf* sour taste, bitterness; acrimony, ill-humour; **~s** *med* heartburn

**aigri** *adj* embittered

**aigrir** *vt* sour, embitter; *vi* turn sour; **s'~** become embittered

**aigu -uë** *adj* pointed; sharp; *geom* + *gramm* acute; shrill; intense, violent; penetrating, subtle

**aiguière** *nf* ewer

**aiguillage** *nm* operation of points (railway); points, switches; *fig* direction

**aiguille** *nf* needle; pointer; hand (clock); spire; sharp rock peak; pine cone; **de fil en ~** little by little

**aiguiller** *vt* direct (train) onto one track or another; direct, orientate; *sl* have sex with

**aiguillette** *nf* aglet; shoulder-knot; cut of beef (part of rump); slice of duck

**aiguilleur** *nm* pointsman (railway); *coll* **~ du ciel** air-traffic controller

**aiguillier** *nm* needle-case

**aiguillon** *nm* goad; sting; prickle, thorn; stimulus, spur

**aiguillonner** *vt* goad, prod; stimulate, animate

**aiguiser** *vt* sharpen, point; stimulate, sharpen

**aiguiseur** *nm* knife-grinder

**aiguisoir** *nm* sharpener

**ail** *nm* garlic

**aile** *nf* wing; **avoir du plomb dans l'~** be compromised, be about to fail; *sl* **avoir un coup dans l'~** be drunk; **battre d'une ~** be in a bad way; **voler de ses propres ~s** cope by oneself, be independent

**ailé** *adj* winged

**aileron** *nm* pinion, wing-tip; fin; aileron; *archi* ornamental scroll

**ailette** *nf* vane, fin, blade

**ailier** *nm sp* winger

**aillade** *nf* vinegar and garlic sauce

**ailleurs** *adv* elsewhere, somewhere else; **d'~** moreover, besides; **par ~** in other respects

**ailloli** *nm* garlic mayonnaise

**aimable** *adj* pleasing, agreeable; amiable, pleasant, nice

**aimant** *nm* magnet; magnetic force

**aimantation** *nf* magnetization

**aimanter** *vt* magnetize

**aimer** *vt* love; like, be fond of; be interested in, enjoy; *vi* be in love; **s'~** be in love with oneself; love one another; make love; **~ autant** like just as well; **~ mieux** prefer; **j'aime autant vous dire** I may as well tell you

**aine** *nf* groin

**aîné -e** *n* older brother (sister); older person; first-born; *lit* **~s** ancestors, predecessors; *adj* older; oldest

**ainsi** *adv* so, thus, in this way; in the same way; **~ que** just as; **~ soit-il** so be it

¹**air** *nm* air; atmosphere; **armée de l'~** air force; **au grand ~** in the open air; **courant d'~** draught; **en l'~** *úg* unfounded; not serious; **en plein ~** in the open air; *coll* **fiche(r) en l'~** throw overboard, give up; **prendre l'~** go for a breath of fresh air; **regarder en l'~** look upwards; **vivre de l'~ du temps** live on next to nothing

²**air** *nm* air, appearance; manner; expression; **avoir l'~** seem, look, appear; **il en a tout l'~** it looks very much like it; *lit* **le bel ~** aristocratic manners; **n'avoir l'~ de rien** seem insignificant, look unimportant

³**air** *nm mus* air, aria

**airain** *nm obs* bronze; *fig* **d'~** implacable, unrelenting

**air-air** *adj invar* air-to-air

**aire** *nf* area, site; flat surface; zone; eyrie; *aer* apron, tarmac; *bui* substructure; *geol* shelf; (motorway) service area

**air-sol, air-terre** *adj invar* air-to-ground

**aisance** *nf* ease, effortlessness, grace; comfortable financial state, sufficiency; **~s de voirie** easements, rights of access; **cabinets d'~, lieux d'~** lavatory

**aise** *nf* ease, comfort; *lit* joy; **~s** comforts; **à l'~** at ease, well-off; **à votre ~** as you will; **en prendre à son ~ avec** be cavalier with; *adj* pleased

**aisé** *adj* easy, effortless; comfortably off

**aisselle** *nf* armpit

**ajiste** *n* youth hosteller

**ajonc** *nm* furze, gorse

**ajour** *nm* aperture; open-work

**ajourer** *vt* pierce holes in; hemstitch

**ajournement** *nm leg* summons; adjournment, postponement; referring (examination candidate); *mil* deferment

**ajourner** *vt leg* summons; adjourn, postpone; refer (examination candidate); *mil* defer

**ajouter** *vt* add; say further; ~ **foi à** give credence to; **s'** ~ be added

**ajustement** *nm* adjustment

**ajuster** *vt* adjust; settle; make fit; **s'** ~ be adjusted; fit

**ajusteur** *nm mech* fitter

**alacrité** *nf* alacrity

**alambic** *nm* alembic

**alambiqué** *adj* tortuous, over-complicated

**alanguir** *vt* weaken, enfeeble, make languid; **s'** ~ become languid

**alanguissement** *nm* languor; decline

**alarme** *nf* alarm, alert; state of alarm

**alarmer** *vt* alarm, disquiet, frighten; **s'** ~ be alarmed, be frightened

**alarmiste** *n* alarmist

**Albanais -e** *n* Albanian

**albanais** *nm* Albanian (language); *adj* Albanian

**albâtre** *nm* alabaster

**albinos** *n* albino

**albumine** *nf* albumin

**alcalescent** *adj* alkalescent

**alcali** *nm* alkali

**alcalin** *adj* alkaline

**alcaloïde** *nm* alkaloid

**alchimie** *nf* alchemy

**alchimiste** *nm* alchemist

**alcool** *nm* alcohol; *coll* spirits; ~ **à brûler** methylated spirits; ~ **à 90°** surgical spirit

**alcoolique** *n* + *adj* alcoholic

**alcooliser** *vt* alcoholize; fortify (wine, etc); **s'** ~ *coll* drink too much

**alcoolisme** *nm* alcoholism

**alcooltest, alcool-test, alcootest** *nm* breathalyser

**alcôve** *nf* alcove; *esp* place for making love; **secrets d'** ~ amorous secrets

**aléa** *nm* hazard, chance; unforseeable occurrence

**aléatoire** *adj* aleatory, chancy, risky, problematical

**alémanique** *nm* Swiss-German (language); *adj* Swiss-German, German-Swiss

**alène** *nf* awl

**alentour** *adv* around; *obs* ~ **de** around

**alentours** *nmpl* surroundings

¹**alerte** *nf* alert; alarm; **fin d'** ~ all clear

²**alerte** *adj* alert, lively, brisk

**alerter** *vt* alert, warn

**alésage** *nm mech* boring; cylinder bore

**aleviner** *vt* stock with fish

**alexandrin** *nm pros* alexandrine; *adj* Alexandrine

**alezan** *adj* reddish-brown, chestnut (of horse, mule)

**algarade** *nf* furious verbal attack, tirade; storm of abuse

**algèbre** *nf* algebra; **c'est de l'** ~ **pour moi** it's double-Dutch to me

**algébrique** *adj* algebraic

**Algérien -ienne** *n* Algerian

**algérien -ienne** *adj* Algerian

**Algérois -e** *n* inhabitant of Algiers

**algorithme** *nm* algorithm

**algue** *nf* seaweed

**aliénable** *adj leg* alienable

**aliénation** *nf leg* alienation, conveyance; insanity, madness; aversion; surrender

**aliéné -e** *n* mental patient

**aliéner** *vt* (6) *leg* alienate, convey; give up; alienate, estrange

**aliéniste** *n med* alienist

**alignement** *nm* alignment; building-line; *mil* dressing; *pol* falling into line; row, line; ~ **monétaire** adjustment of currency exchange rate; **frapper d'** ~ instruct to conform to the building-line

**aligner** *vt* align; conform; adjust (currency); *mil* dress; set out; **s'** ~ get into line, toe the line

**aligoté** *nm* type of white Burgundy grape

**aliment** *nm* food, aliment, nourishment; ~ **s** *leg* subsistance

**alimentaire** *adj* alimentary, nutritious; **pâtes** ~ **s** pasta; **pension** ~ alimony; allowance

**alimentation** *nf* alimentation, nourishment; feeding, providing; **carte d'** ~ ration card; **magasin d'** ~ grocer's shop

**alimenter** *vt* nourish; feed, supply; **s'** ~ feed oneself

**alinéa** *nm typ* indented line; paragraph

**aliquante** *adj math* aliquant

**aliquote** *adj math* aliquot

**aliter** *vt* confine to bed; **s'** ~ take to one's bed

**alizé** *nm* trade-wind; *adj* **vent** ~ trade-wind

**allaitement** *nm* suckling; ~ **artificiel** bottle-feeding; ~ **maternel** breast-feeding

**allaiter** *vt* suckle

**allant** *nm* dash, liveliness; ~ **s et venants** people coming and going; *adj* active, lively

**alléchant** *adj* attractive, alluring

**allécher** *vt* (6) attract, allure

**allée** *nf* tree-lined avenue, tree-lined walk; ~ **(s) et venue(s)** coming(s) and going(s)

**allégation** *nf* allegation

**allège** *nf naut* tender, lighter; *bui* window-breast

**allégeance** *nf* allegiance

**allégement** *nm* lightening, alleviation

**alléger** *vt* (6, 3) lighten

**allégorie** *nf* allegory

**allégorique** *adj* allegorical

**allègre** *adj* lively, spry, gay

**allégresse** *nf* joy, cheerfulness

**alléguer** *vt* (6) cite, produce as evidence, adduce, bring forward; allege

**Allemand -e** *n* German

**allemand** *nm* German (language); *adj* German

**aller** *nm* outward journey; single ticket; ~ **simple** single ticket; ~ **et retour** return ticket; *vi* (12) go; suit, fit; ~+*infin* be about to, be going to; **allez!** go!; come on!; come off it!; **allez donc savoir** find out if you can; **allez-y!** go on!;**allons!** let's go!; come come!; **allons bon!** well!; confound it!; **allons donc!** come off it!; **ça ira** that will be all right; it will work; **ça me va** all right by me, that suits me; **ça va comme ça** that'll do; **cela va de soi** that's obvious; **cela va tout seul** it's working nicely; **comment ça va?** how are you?; **comme vous y allez!** you're really getting on with it!; **il n'en va pas de même** that's a different matter; **il y va de la vie** it's a matter of life or death; **je vais bien** I am well; **les prix vont croissant** prices go on rising; *fig* **où allons-nous?** what are things coming to?; **rien ne va plus** no more bets taken; **va pour quatre francs** four francs – agreed; **s'en** ~ go away, leave, disappear; *euph* die; **je m'en vais vous dire qch** I am going to tell you sth

**allergie** *nf* allergy

**allergique** *adj* allergic

**aller-retour** *nm* return ticket; return journey

**alliage** *nm* alloy

**alliance** *nf* alliance; agreement, union; marriage; relationship by marriage; wedding-ring

**allié -e** *n* ally; *leg* relative; *adj* allied; related

**allier** *vt* ally; alloy; **s'** ~ ally oneself; marry; become connected by marriage; combine, blend

**allô** *interj* hullo!

**allocation** *nf* allocation; allotment; allowance

**allocution** *nf* short speech

**allonger** *vt* (3) lengthen, extend; stretch, stretch out; *cul* thin; *sl* fork out (money); knock down; *coll* ~ **une gifle** slap; *vi* become longer; **s'** ~ become

longer; lie down, stretch oneself out; *coll* fall down flat; *sl* **s'** ~ **qch** treat oneself to sth

**allopathie** *nf med* allopathy

**allotropie** *nf chem* allotropy

**allouer** *vt* allocate; allot; grant

**allumage** *nm* lighting; setting alight; *mot* ignition

**allume-cigares** *nm mot* cigar-lighter

**allume-gaz** *nm invar* gas-lighter

**allumer** *vt* light; set light to; switch on; arouse, excite; **s'** ~ light up

**allumette** *nf* match; *cul* straw, stick; ~ **suédoise** safety match

**allumeur -euse** *n ar* lamp-lighter; *nm mot* distributor; *nf coll* vamp; *vulg* prickteaser

**allure** *nf* speed, pace; gait; air, behaviour; distinction in bearing; appearance; **à toute** ~ at full speed; **avoir de l'** ~ have style; **avoir une drôle** ~ look odd, look strange

**allusif -ive** *adj* allusive

**alluvion** *nf geol* alluvion; alluvium; ~ **s** alluvion, alluvium

**alluvionnement** *nm* alluvium

**almanach** *nm* almanac; ~ **de Gotha** = European Debrett

**aloès** *nm* aloe

**aloi** *nm obs* alloy; official status of coinage; hallmark; *fig* **de bon** ~ of high quality; **de mauvais** ~ of base quality

**alors** *adv* then; in that case; so; therefore; ~ **que** when, whereas; **d'** ~ of that time; **et** ~ so what?; *coll* **non, mais** ~? come off it

**alouette** *nf* lark; *cul* ~ **sans tête** veal olive

**alourdir** *vt* make heavy, weigh down; make dull; **s'** ~ become heavy

**alourdissement** *nm* heaviness; growing heaviness

**aloyau** *nm cul* sirloin

**alpaga** *nm* alpaca

**alpe** *nf* high mountain pasture

**Alpes** *nfpl* Alps

**alpestre** *adj* Alpine

**alphabétique** *adj* alphabetical

**alpin** *adj* Alpine

**alpinisme** *nm* mountaineering

**alpiniste** *n* mountaineer, climber

**Alsacien -ienne** *n* Alsatian

**alsacien** *nm* Alsatian dialect; *adj* (*f* -**ienne**) Alsatian

**altérable** *adj* liable to deterioration

**altérant** *adj* thirst-provoking; causing deterioration

**altération** *nf* change, modification; deterioration, change for the worse; falsification; *mus* sign for altering pitch (sharp, flat, natural)

**altérer** *vt* (6) change, modify; deteriorate, change for the worse; falsify; make thirsty; make desirous

**alternance** *nf* alternation

**alternant** *adj* alternating; **cultures ~ es** rotating crops

**alternateur** *nm elect* alternator

**alternatif -ive** *adj* alternative; *elect* alternating

**alternative** *nf obs* alternation; alternative

**alterné** *adj* in alternation, alternate

**alterner** *vt* rotate (crops); *vi* alternate

**altesse** *nf* Highness

**altier -ière** *adj* haughty, noble

**altimètre** *nm* altimeter

**altiport** *nm* airport at mountain resort

**alto** *nm* viola; counter-tenor; *nf* contralto

**altruisme** *nm* altruism

**altruiste** *n + adj* altruist

**alumine** *nf* alumina

**alun** *nm* alum

**alunir** *vi* land on the moon

**alunissage** *nm* moon landing

**alvéolaire** *adj* alveolar

**alvéole** *nf* alveolus; honeycomb

**amabilité** *nf* amiability; kindness, affability; **veuillez avoir l' ~ de** please be so kind as to

**amadou** *nm* tinder

**amadouer** *vt* soften, wheedle, coax

**amaigrir** *vt* emaciate, make thin; **s' ~** lose weight

**amaigrissant** *adj* slimming, reducing

**amaigrissement** *nm* loss of weight

**amalgame** *nm* alloy of mercury; amalgam, mixture

**amalgamer** *vt* amalgamate, mix

**amande** *nf* almond

**amandier** *nm* almond-tree

**amant -e** *n obs* someone in love; *nm* lover; *nf* mistress; **~ s** lovers

**amarante** *nf bot* amaranth; *adj invar* deep purple

**amariner** *vt naut* put a prize crew on board; make a seaman of

**amarrage** *nm* mooring

**amarre** *nf naut* hawser, mooring-rope

**amarrer** *vt naut* moor; lash

**amas** *nm* heap, pile, store; *astron* nebula

**amasser** *vt* amass, pile up, gather together; **s' ~** pile up, gather together

**amateur** *nm* enthusiast, lover; amateur

**amateurisme** *nm* amateurishness; *sp* amateur status

**amazone** *nf* amazon; horse-woman; **monter en ~** ride side-saddle

**ambages** *nfpl* **sans ~** without circumlocutions, plainly

**ambassade** *nf* embassy; delicate mission; embassy staff

**ambassadeur** *nm* ambassador

**ambassadrice** *nf* woman ambassador; wife of an ambassador

**ambiance** *nf* atmosphere, mood; milieu, environment; *coll* **il y a de l' ~ ici** it's very lively here

**ambiant** *adj* ambient

**ambidextre** *adj* ambidextrous

**ambigu -uë** *adj* ambiguous; equivocal; ambivalent

**ambiguïté** *nf* ambiguity; ambivalence

**ambitieux -ieuse** *n* ambitious person; go-getter; *adj* ambitious; *pej* presumptuous, pretentious

**ambitionner** *vt* aspire to, strongly desire

**ambre** *nm* amber; **~ gris** ambergris; *adj* amber-coloured; smelling of ambergris

**ambroisie** *nf* ambrosia

**ambulance** *nf* ambulance; *mil* mobile field-hospital

**âme** *nf* soul; spirit; living person; guiding spirit; core; bore (rifle, gun); *coll* **~ damnée de s/o** totally devoted to; **~ sœur** kindred spirit; **avoir charge d' ~ s** have care of souls; **état d' ~** state of mind; **être comme une ~ en peine** be inconsolable; *coll* **be like a lost soul**; **ma chère ~** dearest, darling; **rendre l' ~** die

**amélioration** *nf* improvement, betterment, amelioration

**améliorer** *vt* improve, ameliorate; revise, correct; **s' ~** improve

**aménagement** *nm* arranging, fitting out; organization; **~ du territoire** regional economic and social development

**aménager** *vt* (3) arrange, fit out, dispose

**amende** *nf* fine, penalty; **faire ~ honorable** admit one's faults; ask forgiveness; **sous peine d' ~** on pain of a fine

**amendement** *nm* amendment; amelioration of soil; fertilizer

**amender** *vt* improve; correct; amend; improve (soil); **s' ~** mend one's ways

**amène** *adj lit* agreeable, amiable

**amener** *vt* (6) bring; lead; convey; bring about; pull in; **s' ~** *sl* come, turn up

**aménité** *nf* pleasantness, amenity; charm, niceness; *iron* **~ s** disagreeable words

**amenuiser** *vt* diminish; make thinner

**amer** *nm* bitters; *adj* (*f* **-ère**) bitter; sharp, painful; biting

**Américain -e** *n* American

**américain** *nm* American (language); *adj* American

**américaniser** *vt* americanize

**américanisme** *nm* americanism; American studies

**amérindien -ienne** *adj* American Indian

**Amerlo(t), Amerloque** *n sl* Yank

**amerrir** *vt* come down on the sea

**amertume** *nf* bitterness, disquiet,

melancholy

**améthyste** *nf* amethyst

**ameublement** *nm* furniture, furnishings; **tissu d'** ~ furnishing fabric

**ameuter** *vt* muster a crowd; rouse up a crowd; form a pack of hounds; **s'** ~ assemble with hostile intent, band together

**ami -e** *n* friend; *euph* lover, mistress; supporter, fan; **en** ~ as a friend, as friends; **mon** ~ my dear fellow; **petit** ~ boy-friend; **petite** ~ **e** girl-friend; *adj* friendly; kindly; favourable

**amiable** *adj* amicable; **à l'** ~ by agreement

**amiante** *nm* amianthus, asbestos

**amibe** *nf* amoeba

**amical** *adj* friendly

**amicale** *nf* club, association

**amidon** *nm* starch

**amidonner** *vt* starch

**amincir** *vt* make thinner; make look thin; **s'** ~ grow thinner

**amino-acide** *nm* amino-acid

**amiral** *nm* admiral; *adj* **vaisseau** ~ flagship

**amirauté** *nf* naval high command

**amitié** *nf* friendship; friendly gesture, understanding; ~ **particulière** homosexual friendship

**ammoniac -iaque** *adj* ammoniac; **gaz** ~ ammonia

**ammoniaque** *nf* solution ammonia

**amnésie** *nf* amnesia

**amnésique** *adj* amnesic

**amnistie** *nf* amnesty

**amnistier** *vt* amnesty

**amocher** *vt sl* damage, spoil; bash; **s'** ~ get damaged

**amoindrir** *vt* diminish, reduce; **s'** ~ decrease, diminish

**amoindrissement** *nm* diminution, reduction

**amollir** *vt* soften; weaken; **s'** ~ soften

**amonceler** *vt* (5) pile up, accumulate; **s'** ~ increase, pile up

**amoncellement** *nm* piling up, accumulation

**amont** *nm* head waters; **en** ~ **de** upstream; **vent d'** ~ off-shore wind

**amoralisme** *nm* amoralism

**amorçage** *nm* priming; setting off

**amorce** *nf* bait, lure; attraction; detonator; commencement, first step

**amorcer** *vt* (4) bait; attract; commence, begin; prime, inveigle

**amorphe** *adj* amorphous; soft; inconsistent

**amortir** *vt* attenuate, deaden; soften; amortize

**amortissement** *nm* amortization; diminution; deadening; writing off; depre-

ciation

**amortisseur** *nm mot* shock-absorber

**amour** *nm* love; liking; sexual attraction; love-making; person loved; darling; passion; love-affair; ~ **s** love-affairs; ~ **s** *poet nf* feelings of love; **Amour** Cupid; **avec** ~ lovingly; **faire l'** ~ make love, have sex; **filer le parfait** ~ be happily in love; **un** ~ **de robe** a sweet little dress; **vous seriez un** ~ **si** it would be sweet of you to

**amouracher (s')** *v refl pej* fall in love

**amourette** *nf* passing infatuation; calf-love

**amoureux -euse** *n* someone in love; *adj* in love, amorous; avid for

**amour-propre** *nm* self-esteem; self-pride

**amovible** *adj* removable, detachable

**ampère-heure** *nm* ampere-hour

**amphi** *nm coll* lecture-hall

**amphibie** *adj* amphibious

**amphigourique** *adj* (style) rambling, involved

**amphore** *nf* amphora

**ampleur** *nf* spaciousness; fullness, amplitude

**ampli** *nm coll* amplifier

**ampliation** *nf leg* true copy; **pour** ~ certified true copy

**amplificateur** *nm* amplifier

**amplifier** *vt* amplify

**ampoule** *nf* ampoule, phial; *elect* bulb; blister

**ampoulé** *adj* bombastic, inflated

**amputé -e** *n* person with amputated limb

**amputer** *vt* amputate

**amulette** *nf* amulet

**amure** *nf naut* tack (of sail)

**amurer** *vt naut* board, tack

**amusant** *adj* amusing

**amuse-gueule** *nm invar* cocktail snack

**amuser** *vt* amuse, please, entertain; distract; **s'** ~ enjoy oneself; waste one's time; *pej* live it up; **s'** ~ **de** toy with

**amusette** *nf* plaything

**amuseur -euse** *n* entertainer

**amygdale** *nf* tonsil

**amygdalite** *nf* tonsilitis

**an** *nm* year; **bon** ~ **mal** ~ year in year out; **il a vingt** ~ **s** he is twenty years old; **l'** ~ **prochain** next year; **le jour de l'** ~ New Year's Day; **par** ~ per year

**anabaptiste** *n* anabaptist

**anachorète** *nm* hermit

**anachronique** *adj* anachronistic

**anachronisme** *nm* anachronism

**anacoluthe** *nf* anacoluthon

**anagramme** *nf* anagram

**analgésie** *nf* analgesia

**analgésique** *adj* analgesic

**analogie** *nf* analogy
**analogique** *adj* analogous
**analogue** *nm* analogue; *adj* analogous
**analphabète** *n + adj* illiterate
**analphabétisme** *nm* illiteracy
**analyse** *nf* analysis; summary, résumé; **esprit d' ~** analytical mind
**analyser** *vt* analyse; give an abstract of
**analyste** *n* analyst; computer programmer
**analytique** *adj* analytic, analytical
**ananas** *nm* pineapple
**anarchie** *nf* anarchy
**anarchique** *adj* anarchical, anarchic
**anarchisme** *nm* anarchism
**anarchiste** *n* anarchist
**anathématiser** *vt* anathematize; denounce
**anathème** *nm* anathema; curse
**anatomie** *nf* anatomy
**anatomique** *adj* anatomical
**anatomiste** *n* anatomist
**ancêtre** *n* ancestor
**anche** *nf mus* reed
**anchois** *nm* anchovy
**ancien** *nm* senior; **~ s** ancients, peoples of antiquity; *adj* (*f* **-ienne**) ancient, old; antique; former; **~ maire** ex-mayor
**ancienneté** *nf* ancientness; seniority (in post, rank)
**ancrage** *nm* anchorage; anchoring
**ancre** *nf* anchor; *bui* brace; **jeter l' ~** anchor; **lever l' ~** weigh anchor
**ancrer** *vt* fix firmly; *naut ar* anchor; **s' ~** *fig* be rooted in; *naut ar* anchor
**andalou -ouse** *n + adj* Andalusian
**andouille** *nf* chitterlings; *fig sl* idiot, fool
**androgyne** *nm* hermaphrodite; *adj* androgynous
**âne** *nm* ass, donkey; *fig* ass, idiot; **à dos d' ~** humpbacked; **bonnet d' ~** dunce's cap
**anéantir** *vt* annihilate, exterminate, destroy completely; stun, depress; **s' ~** disappear completely; come to nothing
**anéantissement** *nm* annihilation, complete destruction; prostration, depression
**anecdotique** *adj* anecdotal
**anémie** *nf* anaemia
**anémier** *vt* make anaemic, debilitate
**anémique** *adj* anaemic
**anémomètre** *nm* anemometer, windgauge
**ânerie** *nf* stupidity, gross ignorance; silly remark; tomfoolery
**anéroïde** *adj* aneroid
**ânesse** *nf* female donkey, she-ass
**anesthésie** *nf* anaesthesia; *fig* insensibility
**anesthésier** *vt* anaesthetize

**anesthésique** *nm + adj* anaesthetic
**anesthésiste** *n* anaesthetist
**anévrisme** *nm* aneurism
**anfractuosité** *nf* hollow, crack
**ange** *nm* angel; angel fish; **~ gardien** guardian angel; *coll* bodyguard; **être aux ~ s** be delighted; *coll* **faiseuse d' ~ s** abortionist; **un ~ passe** that was an embarrassing silence
¹**angélique** *nf* angelica
²**angélique** *adj* angelic
**angine** *nf* severe sore throat; tonsilitis; quinsy; **~ (de poitrine)** angina (pectoris)
**Anglais -e** *n* Englishman, Englishwoman
**anglais** *nm* English (language); *adj* English; *coll* **capote ~ e** French letter; **filer à l' ~** take French leave
**anglaises** *nfpl* ringlets
**angle** *nm* corner; *geom* angle; *fig* angle, point of view
**anglicanisme** *nm* Anglicanism
**angliciser** *vt* anglicize
**anglicisme** *nm* anglicism
**angliciste** *n* specialist in English studies
**anglomanie** *nf* anglomania
**anglo-normand** *nm* Anglo-Norman (dialect); *adj* Anglo-Norman; **les îles ~ es** the Channel Islands
**anglophobie** *nf* anglophobia
**anglophone** *adj* English-speaking
**angoissant** *adj* agonizing, very painful
**angoisse** *nf* anguish
**angoissé** *adj* anguished, distressed
**anguille** *nf* eel; **~ de mer** conger eel; **il y a ~ sous roche** there's more to this than meets the eye, there's something fishy about this
**angulaire** *adj* angular
**anguleux -euse** *adj* angular; long; difficult.
**anicroche** *nf* snag
**animal** *nm* animal; *pej* idiot, fool; *adj* animal
**animalité** *nf* animality
**animateur -trice** *n* animator; organizer, leader; compère
**animé** *adj* animated
**animer** *vt* animate, give life to; enliven, excite; incite; **s' ~** become alive, become animated; warm up (discussion)
**animisme** *nm* animism
**animosité** *nf* animosity
**anis** *nm* aniseed
**anisette** *nf* (alcoholic) drink made with aniseed
**ankylose** *nf med* anchylosis
**ankyloser** *vt med* stiffen, paralyse; **s' ~** *med* become anchylotic, stiffen; *fig* become paralysed

**annales** *nfpl* annals

**annaliste** *nm* chronicler; annalist

**anneau** *nm* ring; link (chain); coil (spoke); ringlet

**année** *nf* year; **bonne ~!** Happy New Year!; **d' ~ en ~** from year to year

**année-lumière** *nf* (*pl* **années-lumières**) light-year

**annelé** *adj* ringed

**annexe** *nf* annex; *anat + biol* process; *adj* annexed, subsidiary

**annexer** *vt* annex, incorporate; **s' ~** *coll* take for oneself

**annexion** *nf* annexation

**annihiler** *vt* annihilate

**anniversaire** *nm* anniversary; birthday; *adj* anniversary

**annonce** *nf* announcement; advertisement; presage; call (cards); **petites ~ s** small ads

**annoncer** *vt* announce; proclaim; indicate, show; predict; usher in; call (cards); **s' ~** seem likely to happen; promise

**annonceur** *nm* advertiser

**annonciateur -trice** *adj* heralding, presaging

**Annonciation** *nf* Annunciation

**annotateur -trice** *n* commentator (text)

**annoter** *vt* annotate

**annuaire** *nm* (annual) directory, yearbook

**annuel -elle** *adj* annual

**annuité** *nf* annuity

**annulaire** *nm* ring finger; *adj* annular

**annulation** *nf* quashing; cancellation; annulment (marriage)

**annuler** *vt* annul; quash; cancel; **s' ~** cancel out

**anoblir** *vt* ennoble

**anoblissement** *nm* ennoblement

**anodin** *adj* anodyne

**anomalie** *nf* anomaly

**ânon** *nm* little donkey

**ânonnement** *nm* hesitant reading, hesitant speech

**ânonner** *vi* read hesitantly; speak hesitantly; stumble (reading, speaking)

**anonymat** *nm* anonymity

**anonyme** *adj* anonymous; *fig* impersonal

**anorexie** *nf med* anorexia

**anormal** *adj* abnormal; exceptional

**anse** *nf* handle; *geog* cove; **faire danser l' ~ du panier** make a bit on the side (servant when shopping)

**antagonique** *adj* antagonistic

**antagonisme** *nm* antagonism

**antagoniste** *n* antagonist

**antan** *nm lit* **d' ~** of time past, of bygone days

**Antarctique** *nf* Antarctica

**antarctique** *adj* antarctic

**antédiluvien -ienne** *adj* antediluvian

**antenne** *nf* antenna; aerial; **avoir des ~ s** be very perceptive; **passer sur les ~ s** be broadcast; **temps d' ~** duration (broadcast)

**antépénultième** *adj* antepenultimate

**antérieur** *adj* anterior; former

**anthologie** *nf* anthology

**anthropoïde** *nm + adj* anthropoid

**anthropologie** *nf* anthropology

**anthropologiste, anthropologue** *n* anthropologist

**anthropométrie** *nf* anthropometry

**anthropomorphique** *adj* anthropomorphic

**anthropomorphisme** *nm* anthropomorphism

**anthropophage** *nm + adj* cannibal

**anthropophagie** *nf* cannibalism

**antiaérien -ienne** *adj* anti-aircraft

**antibiotique** *nm + adj* antibiotic

**antibrouillard** *nm mot* fog-lamp; *adj* **mot phare ~** fog-lamp

**antibuée** *nm + adj* demister

**antichambre** *nf* antechamber; **faire ~** dance attendance

**antichar** *adj* anti-tank

**anticipé** *adj* early, premature

**anticiper** *vt* anticipate; foresee; *vi* anticipate; **~ sur** encroach on

**anticléricalisme** *nm* anticlericalism

**anticommunisme** *nm* anticommunism

**anticommuniste** *adj* anticommunist

**anticonceptionnel -elle** *adj* contraceptive

**anticorps** *nm* antibody

**antidater** *vt* antedate

**antidémocratique** *adj* antidemocratic

**antidérapant** *adj mot* non-skid

**antienne** *nf eccles* antiphon; *fig* same old tune

**antifasciste** *adj* antifascist

**antigel** *nm mot* antifreeze

**antigène** *nm physiol* antigen

**antigivrant** *nm mot* de-icer

**antihistaminique** *nm + adj* antihistamine

**antilope** *nf* antelope

**antimoine** *nm chem* antimony

**antimonarchique** *adj* antimonarchical

**antinomie** *nf* antinomy, contradiction

**antiparasite** *adj rad* **dispositif ~** suppressor

**antipathie** *nf* antipathy

**antipathique** *adj* antipathetic

**antiphrase** *nf* antiphrasis

**antipode** *nm* exact opposite; **~ s** antipodes; **aux ~ s** far away; poles apart

**antiquaille** *nf pej* junk, valueless antique

**antiquaire** *n* antique dealer

**antique** *nm* art of antiquity; *nf obs* antique (object); *adj* antique, of antiquity; old-fashioned

**antiquité** *nf* antiquity; ~s antiquities; antiques

**antisémitisme** *nm* antisemitism

**antisepsie** *nf* antisepsis

**antiseptique** *nm + adj* antiseptic

**antithèse** *nf* antithesis; sharp contrast

**antithétique** *adj* antithetical

**antitoxine** *nf* antitoxin

**antitoxique** *adj* antitoxic

**antivol** *nm mot* anti-theft device

**antonyme** *nm* antonym

**antre** *nm* den, lair; cavern; *physiol* antrum

**anxiété** *nf* anxiety

**anxieux -ieuse** *adj* anxious, worried; eager, impatient

**aorte** *nf anat* aorta

**août** *nm* August

**aoûtat** *nm dial* harvest-bug

**aoûtien -ienne** *n* August holiday-maker; one who remains in a big city in August

**apaisement** *nm* appeasement, pacification; calming down, assuagement; ~s reassurances

**apaiser** *vt* appease, pacify; calm, assuage; (hunger) satisfy; (thirst) quench; s' ~ become calm, be pacified

**aparté** *nm theat* aside; side conversation

**apathie** *nf* apathy, indolence

**apathique** *adj* apathetic, indolent

**apatride** *n* stateless person

**apercevoir** *vt* see, perceive, discern; laisser ~ show; s' ~ de perceive, become aware of, notice

**aperçu** *nm* glimpse; first idea, notion; outline, summary; remark, observation

**apéritif** *nm* aperitif, cocktail; *adj (f -ive)* which stimulates the appetite

**apesanteur** *nf* weightlessness

**à-peu-près, à peu près** *nm* approximation; imperfection

**apeurer** *vt* frighten

**aphasie** *nf med* aphasia

**aphasique** *adj med* aphasic

**aphone** *adj med* aphonic, voiceless

**aphonie** *nf med* aphonia

**aphorisme** *nm* aphorism

**aphrodisiaque** *nm + adj* aphrodisiac

**aphte** *nm med* aphtha

**aphteux -euse** *adj* covered with aphthae; *vet* **fièvre aphteuse** foot-and-mouth disease

**apiculteur -trice** *n* bee-keeper

**apiculture** *nf* bee-keeping ·

**apitoiement** *nm* pity, compassion

**apitoyer** *vt* touch; s' ~ pity

**aplanir** *vt* level, flatten, smooth; *fig* smooth out, resolve

**aplatir** *vt* flatten, level; (hair) plaster down; s' ~ become flattened; *coll* fall

flat on the ground; *fig* grovel

**aplomb** *nm* verticality; balance; equilibrium; *fig* aplomb, self-possession; *pej* nerve; d' ~ vertical, plumb; in balance; *fig* in good form

**apocalyptique** *adj* apocalyptic

**apocryphe** *nm bibl* apocrypha; *adj* apocryphal

**apogée** *nm astron* apogee; *fig* summit, highest point

**apolitique** *adj* apolitical

**apologétique** *nf eccles* apologetics

**apologie** *nf* apology; justification

**apologiste** *n* apologist

**apophtègme** *nm* apophthegm, maxim

**apoplectique** *adj* apoplectic

**apoplexie** *nf* apoplexy

**apostasie** *nf* apostasy

**apostat** *nm* apostate

**apostille** *nf* marginal note; recommendation

**apostolique** *adj* apostolic

**apostropher** *vt* apostrophize; address rudely; s' ~ exchange insults

**apothéose** *nf* apotheosis

**apothicaire** *nm* apothecary

**apôtre** *nm eccles* apostle; advocate; **faire le bon** ~ sham virtue in order to deceive

**apparaître** *vi* (68) appear, become visible; seem, be apparent

**apparat** *nm* pomp, display; ~ **critique** critical apparatus; **costume d'** ~ ceremonial dress; **discours d'** ~ formal speech

**appareil** *nm ar* = **apparat** *qv*; apparatus, machinery, instrument; mechanism; appliance; (telephone) receiver; aircraft; brace (teeth); ~ **digestif** digestive system; ~ **électrique** electrical appliance; ~ **photo(graphique)** camera; **dans le plus simple** ~ naked; **qui est à l'** ~ ? who is speaking? (telephone)

**appareillage** *nm naut* leaving port, getting under way; equipment; installation

¹**appareiller** *vt* prepare; install; *naut* (ship) make ready for sea; (fishing-net) prepare; *bui* (stone) dress; *vi naut* set sail; depart

²**appareiller** *vt* match

**apparence** *nf* appearance, aspect, form; trace; verisimilitude; **en** ~ apparently; **il y a toute** ~ it would seem that; **sauver les** ~s save face

**apparent** *adj* apparent; ostensible; obvious, evident; illusory, false

**apparenté** *adj* related, allied

**apparentement** *nm pol* alliance for electoral purposes

**apparenter (s')** *v refl* s' ~ **à** marry into;

resemble; *pol* enter into an electoral alliance

**apparier** *vt* mate, couple

**appariteur** *nm* beadle, usher

**apparition** *nf* appearance; apparition; vision; ghost

**apparoir** *vi* (13) *leg* be apparent

**appartement** *nm* flat, *US* apartment

**appartenance** *nf* membership, belonging

**appartenir** *vi* (96) ~ à belong to; (sexually) be possessed by; **il m'appartient de** I am responsible for; **s'** ~ be free, be independent

**appât** *nm* bait; *fig* attraction; ~s *obs* or *joc* (sexual) charms

**appâter** *vt* entice; fatten (poultry)

**appauvrir** *vt* impoverish, exhaust; **s'** ~ become impoverished

**appauvrissement** *nm* impoverishment, exhaustion

**appeau** *nm* decoy

**appel** *nm* call, summons; roll-call; *mil* call up; appeal, exhortation; *leg* appeal; **cour d'** ~ court of appeal; **faire** ~ ask, appeal; **faire l'** ~ call the roll; **sans** ~ irrevocably

**appelant -e** *n* + *adj leg* appellant

**appelé** *nm mil* conscript; *adj* called; **être** ~ à be obliged to

**appeler** *vt* (5) call, summon; call for; require; appoint, designate; name; invoke; *mil* call up; ~ **au téléphone** ring up; ~ **le médecin** send for the doctor; *leg* **en** ~ appeal against sentence; **en** ~ à appeal to; **s'** ~ be called, be named; *coll* **voilà ce qui s'appelle chanter** that's what real singing is like

**appellation** *nf* appellation, designation; *comm* ~ **d'origine** designation of a product's place of origin; **vin d'** ~ **contrôlée** wine certified to come from a designated place

**appendice** *nm* appendage, addition; *anat* appendix; appendix (book)

**appendicite** *nf* appendicitis

**appentis** *nm* lean-to roof; lean-to, outhouse

**appesantir** *vt* weigh down; press down; **s'** ~ become heavy; *fig* insist; talk too much; ~ **sur** weigh upon; dwell on

**appesantissement** *nm* heaviness, dullness

**appétissant** *adj* appetizing; pleasing, attractive

**appétit** *nm* appetite; desire, inclination; ~ **de** strong desire for; ~ **de loup** large appetite; *fig* **l'** ~ **vient en mangeant** the more one has the more one wants

**applaudir** *vt* + *vi* applaud, clap; **s'** ~ **de** be glad about

**applaudissement** *nm* applause, clapping; *fig* approval, satisfaction

**application** *nf* application, applying; employment, use; covering; (mind) concentration; (law) enforcement

**applique** *nf* (sewing) appliqué; *elect* wall-light, sconce

**appliquer** *vt* apply, put; employ, use; (mind) concentrate; (law) enforce; (blow) deal; **s'** ~ apply; apply oneself, concentrate

**appoint** *nm* complement, addition; sum in small change; **d'** ~ supplementary; **faire l'** ~ pay the exact amount; top up

**appointements** *nmpl* emoluments

**¹appointer** *vt* pay emoluments to

**²appointer** *vt* sharpen

**appontement** *nm naut* pier

**apponter** *vi* (aircraft) land on deck of aircraft-carrier

**apport** *nm* contribution; bringing; *leg* ~s assets

**apporter** *vt* bring, carry; provide, furnish; display; produce, cause

**apposer** *vt* place on, put on; affix; (poster) stick up; *leg* ~ **les scellés** put under seals; ~ **sa signature** sign, set one's hand

**appréciable** *adj* appreciable; considerable, notable

**appréciatif -ive** *adj* appreciative

**appréciation** *nf* appreciation; evaluation; judgement, opinion

**apprécier** *vt* appreciate, enjoy, like; evaluate; estimate, judge

**appréhender** *vt leg* arrest; apprehend

**appréhensif -ive** *adj* apprehensive

**apprendre** *vt* (75) learn; hear (of), discover; inform, teach – à learn how to; ~ **à qn à** teach s/o how to; ~ **qch à qn** teach s/o sth; **cela lui apprendra à vivre** that will teach him a lesson

**apprenti -e** *n* apprentice; novice

**apprentissage** *nm* apprenticeship; beginning, first experience

**apprêt** *nm* preparation, making ready; *fig* affectation; **sans** ~(s) naturally, unaffectedly

**apprêté** *adj* affected

**apprêter** *vt* prepare, arrange, make ready; prepare (food); **s'** ~ be being prepared; prepare oneself; dress oneself up

**apprivoisement** *nm* taming

**apprivoiser** *vt* tame, train; soften; **s'** ~ (animal) become tame; become sociable; become accustomed

**approbateur -trice** *n* one who agrees; *adj* approving

**approbatif -ive** *adj* approving

**approchable** *adj* approachable

**approchant** *adj* approaching; approxi-

mate; **qch d'** ~ something like
**approche** *nf* approach, drawing near; access, surround; point of view; approach; **lunette d'** ~ magnifying glass; *mil* **travaux d'** ~ defence works; *fig* subtle manoeuvres
**approcher** *vt* bring near, draw near; come close to; frequent; *vi* approach; be near; be close to; **s'** ~ **de** approach; come close to, be near to
**approfondir** *vt* deepen; examine closely; **s'** ~ become deeper
**approfondissement** *nm* deepening; study, examination
**approprié** *adj* appropriate, pertinent
**approprier** *vt* adapt, make appropriate; **s'** ~ appropriate, seize; usurp
**approuvé** *adj* agreed
**approuver** *vt* approve, agree, accept; recognize
**approvisionnement** *nm* provisioning, stocking; provisions
**approvisionner** *vt* stock, provide, furnish; **s'** ~ stock up
**approximatif -ive** *adj* approximate
**appui** *nm* support; prop, protection; **à l'** ~ **de** in support of; **mur d'** ~ supporting wall; **point d'** ~ fulcrum; key point; **prendre** ~ **sur** rely on
**appui-bras, appuie-bras** *nm* (*pl* **appuis-bras, appuie-bras**) arm rest
**appui-tête, appuie-tête** *nm* (*pl* **appuis-tête, appuie-tête**) head rest; antimacassar
**appuyer** *vt* (7) support; place; maintain, confirm; help, push; press; *vi* ~ **sur** be held up by; weigh upon; emphasize; insist upon; ~ **sur la** *d.* **oite (gauche)** go right (left); **s'** ~ **sur** support oneself on; rely on; lean on, rest on
**âpre** *adj* rough, harsh; biting (wind); bitter, rough (taste); hard (struggle); avid, tough (person)
**après** *adv* after; behind; **et** ~ ? and so what?; what then?; *prep* after; **d'** ~ according to
**après-demain** *adv* the day after tomorrow
**après-dîner** *nm* after dinner
**après-guerre** *nm* post-war period
**après-midi** *nm* afternoon
**après-ski** *nm* soft boot (for use after skiing); activities after skiing
**après-vente** *adj* **service** ~ after-sales service
**âpreté** *nf* roughness, hardness; bitterness (taste)
**à-propos** *nm* appropriateness, suitability
**apte** *adj* apt, capable
**aquaplaning** *nm* *mot* skid on wet surface
**aquatique** *adj* aquatic

**aqueduc** *nm* aqueduct
**aquilin** *adj* aquiline
**aquilon** *nm* *lit* north wind
**Arabe** *n* Arab
**arabe** *nm* Arabic; *adj* Arab
**arabisant -e** *n* specialist in Arabic
**arachide** *nf* peanut, ground-nut
**arachnides** *nmpl zool* arachnids
**araignée** *nf* spider; ~ **de mer** kind of crab; *coll* **avoir une** ~ **au plafond** have a screw loose; **toile d'** ~ spider's web
**araser** *vt* level (wall); plane (plank)
**arbalète** *nf ar* cross-bow
**arbitrage** *nm* arbitration; *sp* refereeing; *comm* arbitrage
**arbitraire** *nm* arbitrary nature; arbitrary action; *adj* arbitrary
**arbitre** *nm* arbitrator, conciliator; arbiter; *sp* referee, umpire; *philos* **libre** ~ free will
**arbitrer** *vt* arbitrate; settle; *sp* referee, umpire
**arborer** *vt* hoist (flag, banner); wear (medal); display; ~ **un sourire** wear a set smile
**arbre** *nm* tree; *mech eng* shaft, axle; ~ **de Noël** Christmas tree; ~ **fruitier** fruit-tree
**arbrisseau** *nm* bush, shrub
**arbuste** *nm* small bush
**arc** *nm* bow; *geom* arc; arch
**arcane** *nm* arcanum, mystery; elixir; ~ **s** secrets
**arc-boutant** *nm* (*pl* **arcs-boutants**) *archi* flying buttress
**arc-bouter** *vt archi* support with a flying buttress; prop up; **s'** ~ *fig* brace oneself
**arceau** *nm* small archway; arch (vault); hoop (croquet)
**arc-en-ciel** *nm* (*pl* **arcs-en-ciel**) *nm* rainbow
**archaïque** *adj* archaic
**archaïsme** *nm* archaism
**archange** *nm* archangel
**¹arche** *nf* ark; ~ **d'alliance** ark of the covenant
**²arche** *nf* arch
**archéologie** *nf* archaeology
**archéologique** *adj* archaeological
**archéologue** *n* archaeologist
**archet** *nm* bow (violin, etc)
**archevêché** *nm* archbishopric; archbishop's palace
**archevêque** *nm* archbishop
**archi-** *pref* very, extremely, super
**archidiacre** *nm* archdeacon
**archidiocèse** *nm* archdiocese
**archiduc** *nm* archduke
**archiduchesse** *nf* archduchess
**archipel** *nm* archipelago
**architecte** *nm* architect

architectonique *adj* architectonic

archiviste *n* archivist

arçon *nm* pommel, saddle-bow; **cheval d'** ~ **s** vaulting horse

Arctique *nm* Arctic

arctique *adj* arctic

ardent *adj* ardent, keen, passionate; burning, scorching; **être sur des charbons** ~ **s** be like a cat on hot bricks

ardeur *nf* heat; ardour

ardoise *nf* slate; debt; slate grey; **avoir des** ~ **s** be in debt

ardu *adj* arduous

arène *nf* arena; ~ **s** bull-ring

arête *nf* fish-bone; ridge; ~ **du nez** bridge of nose

argent *nm* silver; silver coin; money; ~ **de poche** pocket money; **en avoir pour son** ~ have one's money's worth; **être cousu d'** ~ be rolling in money

argentan, argenton *nm* nickel-silver, German silver

argenté *adj* silvery; *coll* rich

argenter *vt* silver, plate with silver

argenterie *nf* silverware, silver-plate

Argentin -e *n* Argentinian

¹argentin *adj* Argentinian

²argentin *adj* clear-sounding, silvery

argile *nf* clay

argileux -euse *adj* clayey

argot *nm* slang; thieves' jargon

argotique *adj* slangy

argotisme *nm* slang term

arguer *vt* deduce, infer; ~ **de** put forward as argument, allege

argument *nm* argument; proof, reason; summary

argumenter *vi* argue

argus *nm lit* vigilant observer, vigilant spy; spy; paper giving specialized information; **Argus de l'automobile** second-hand car price guide

argutie *nf* cavil, quibble

aride *adj* arid, sterile; *fig* dry, tedious

aridité *nf* aridity, sterility; *fig* dryness, tediousness

aristocrate *n* aristocrat, noble

aristocratie *nf* aristocracy, nobility; élite

aristocratique *adj* aristocratic

arithmétique *nf* arithmetic; arithmetic book; *adj* arithmetical

arlequin -e *n* harlequin; **habit d'** ~ motley

armateur *nm* ship-owner

armature *nf* structure, framework; basis; *mus* key-signature

arme *nf* arm, weapon; ~ **absolue** ultimate weapon; ~ **à double tranchant** two-edged weapon; ~ **à feu** firearm; **être sous les** ~ **s** be under arms; **faire ses premières** ~ **s** make one's début; **les** ~ **s** fencing; **maître d'** ~ **s** fencing-master; **passer par les** ~ **s** execute, shoot; **porter**

les ~ **s** bear arms; **portez** ~ **s!** slope arms!; **présentez** ~ **s!** present arms!; **rendre les** ~ **s** surrender; **salle d'** ~ **s** fencing school

armé *adj* armed; provided with; **vol à main** ~ **e** armed robbery

armée *nf* army; vast number, host; ~ **active** regular army; ~ **de l'air** air-force; ~ **de mer** navy; ~ **du Salut** Salvation Army

armement *nm* arming; armament; *naut* commissioning, fitting out; shipowning

Arménien -ienne *n* Armenian

arménien *nm* Armenian (language); *adj* (*f* -ienne) Armenian

armer *vt* arm; cock (gun, rifle); fortify; *naut* commission, equip; s' ~ arm oneself; protect oneself; s' ~ **de** provide oneself with

armoire *nf* cupboard

armoiries *nf pl her* arms

armorial *adj* armorial

armure *nf* armour

armurerie *nf* profession of armourer; *elect* armature; gunsmith's trade

armurier *nm* armourer, gunsmith

aromate *nm* aromatic

aromatique *adj* aromatic

aromatiser *vt* aromatize, flavour

arôme, arome *nm* aroma

aronde *nf ar orni* swallow; *carp* **queue d'** ~ dovetail

arpège *nm mus* arpeggio

arpent *nm ar* = (nearly) acre

arpenter *vt* walk up and down

arpenteur *nm* surveyor

arpion *nm sl* foot

arqué *adj* arched

arquebuse *nf hist* (h)arquebus

arquer *vt* arch, bend, curve; *vi* bend; *sl* walk; s' ~ arch, curve

arrachage *nm* uprooting, pulling out; extraction (tooth)

arrache-clou *nm* wrench (nail)

arrachement *nm* removal; extraction; *fig* wrench

arrache-pied (d') *adv phr* steadily, ceaselessly

arracher *vt* uproot; lift (potatoes); pull out, remove; tear off; extract (tooth); seize, take; save from (danger); obtain, extort; s' ~ **à**, s' ~ **de** detach oneself from, tear oneself away from; s' ~ **les cheveux** tear one's hair, be desperate; s' ~ **les yeux** have a violent quarrel with s/o; s' ~ **qn** compete for s/o's company

arracheur -euse *n* **mentir comme un** ~ **de dents** lie like a trooper

arraisonner *vt* inspect (ship)

arrangeable *adj* repairable; arrangeable

arrangeant *adj* conciliatory, accommodating

**arrangement** *nm* arrangement, ordering, disposition; classification; agreement, accommodation; ~s preparations, measures; terms

**arranger** *vt* (3) arrange, order, dispose; classify; repair; suit; please; *coll* ~ qn de la belle manière sort s/o out; s' ~ manage; become ordered, improve; tidy oneself; be mended; take steps; come to an agreement; s' ~ de put up with

**arrérages** *nmpl* arrears

**arrestation** *nf* arrest

**arrêt** *nm* stop; arrest; halt; *leg* decision, judgement; *mil* ~ s arrest; *mil* ~ s de rigueur close arrest; *mil* ~ s simples open arrest; temps d' ~ pause; sans ~ without pause; temps d' ~ pause

**arrêté** *nm* decision; decree; *adj* decided, fixed

**arrêter** *vt* stop, halt; arrest; interrupt; choose, determine; *vi* stop; s' ~ stop, halt; pay attention

**arrhes** *nfpl comm* deposit, down payment

**arriération** *nf* backwardness

**arrière** *nm* rear; *sp* back; *adj* rear; *adv* behind, back; en ~ backwards, behind; en ~ de behind; *mot* marche ~ reverse

**arriéré** *nm* arrears; *adj* owing, overdue; *pej* out of date, old-fashioned; backward, retarded

**arrière-ban** *nm hist* rear-vassals; ban et ~ the whole lot of them

**arrière-boutique** *nf* room behind shop

**arrière-cour** *nf* back-yard

**arrière-garde** *nf mil* rearguard

**arrière-goût** *nm* after-taste

**arrière-grand-mère** *nf* great-grandmother

**arrière-grand-père** *nm* (*pl* arrière-grands-pères) great-grandfather

**arrière-grands-parents** *nmpl* great-grandparents

**arrière-neveu** *nm* grand-nephew; *lit* remote descendant

**arrière-pays** *nm invar* hinterland; places near a large town

**arrière-pensée** *nf* after-thought

**arrière-petite-fille** *nf* (*pl* arrière-petites-filles) great-granddaughter

**arrière-petit-fils** *nm* (*pl* arrière-petits-fils) great-grandson

**arrière-petits-enfants** *nmpl* great grandchildren

**arrière-plan** *nm* background

**arriérer** *vt* (6) postpone, delay

**arrière-saison** *nf* autumn; *fig* near to old age

**arrière-train** *nm* rear; *coll* backside

**arrimage** *nm naut* loading, stowing

**arrimer** *vt naut* load, stow

**arrivage** *nm* arrival (of goods)

**arrivé -e** *n* arrival (person)

**arrivée** *nf* arrival; arrival platforms (railway); *fig* à l' ~ in the end, in the final instance; ligne d' ~ finishing post

**arriver** *vi* arrive; attain, reach; succeed; happen, occur; en ~ à reach a point where; en ~ là end up there; j'arrive! coming!; n' ~ à rien come to nothing; quoi qu'il arrive come what may

**arrivisme** *nm* place-seeking

**arriviste** *n* place-seeker, climber

**arroger (s')** *v refl* (3) arrogate to oneself; claim

**arrondi** *nm* roundness; *adj* rounded

**arrondir** *vt* round, make round; complete, round off; s' ~ become round

**arrondissement** *nm* rounding off; = district (in France), part of large town

**arrosage** *nm* watering; tuyau d' ~ hose

**arroser** *vt* water; irrigate; wash down (meal with wine); celebrate (with a drink); *cul* baste; *coll* give money to; ~ son café add alcohol to one's coffee; se faire ~ *coll* get soaked with rain

**arroseur** *nm* sprinkler

**arroseuse** *nf* watering-cart

**arrosoir** *nm* watering-can

**arsenal** *nm* arsenal; store of weapons and munitions; *fig* storehouse; stock; ~ de la marine naval dockyard

**arsouille** *n* rogue, blackguard

**art** *nm* art; skill, craft, knack; ~ de faire qch way to do sth; ~s ménagers domestic arts; avoir l' ~ de know how to; beaux ~s fine arts; l' ~ pour l' ~ art for art's sake

**artère** *nf anat* artery; *fig* main road; (town) main street

**artériel -ielle** *adj anat* arterial

**artériosclérose** *nf* arteriosclerosis

**artésien -ienne** *adj* artesian

**arthrite** *nf* arthritis

**arthritique** *adj* arthritic

**artichaut** *nm* artichoke; *coll* avoir un cœur d' ~ be fickle-hearted; fond d' ~ artichoke heart

**article** *nm* clause, section (text); point, topic; article; ~s de Paris fancy goods; à l' ~ de la mort on the point of death; faire l' ~ boost a product, plug

**articulaire** *adj* articular

**articulation** *nf anat* articulation, joint; knuckle; *mech* joint; articulation (speech); pronouncing; *leg* enumeration, enunciation

**articulé** *adj anat* articulated, jointed; articulated (speech)

**articuler** *vt* (speech) articulate, pronounce; *leg* enumerate, enounce; s' ~

# artifice

*anat* be articulated, be jointed; *mech* be jointed

**artifice** *nm* clever device; trick, ruse, artifice; **feux d' ~** fireworks

**artificiel -ielle** *adj* artificial; false; arbitrary; synthetic

**artificieux -ieuse** *adj* cunning, wily

**artillerie** *nf* artillery, ordnance; **tir d' ~** artillery fire

**artilleur** *nm* artilleryman

**artimon** *nm naut* mizzen-mast

**artisan -e** *n* artisan, craftsman; *fig* author, architect

**artisanal** *adj* relating to craft

**artisanat** *nm* craftsman's trade; craftsman

**artiste** *n* artist; actor, actress, performer; **~ peintre** painter; **entrée des ~ s** stagedoor

**artistique** *adj* artistic

**arythmie** *nf* irregular heart-beat

**as** *nm* ace; *sp* champion; *coll* **être ficelé comme l' ~ de pique** be badly dressed; *sl* **être plein aux ~** have packets of money

**asbeste** *nm* asbestos

**ascendance** *nf astron* rising; ancestry, lineage

**ascendant** *nm astron* rising; *astrol* ascendant; *fig* influence, ascendancy; charm; *leg* **~ s** parents; *adj* rising, progressing upwards; *astrol* **astre ~** ascendant

**ascenseur** *nm* lift

**ascension** *nf* ascension; ascent (mountain); *fig* rise, progress; *eccles* **l'Ascension** Ascension

**ascèse** *nf* asceticism

**ascète** *n* ascetic

**ascétique** *adj* ascetic

**ascétisme** *nm* asceticism, austerity

**asepsie** *nf* asepsis

**aseptique** *adj* aseptic

**asexué** *adj biol* asexual; without sexual urges

**Asiate** *n see* Asiatique

**Asiatique** *n* Asiatic, Asian

**asiatique** *adj* Asiatic

**asile** *nm* asylum, refuge; sanctuary; *fig* haven; old people's home; mental hospital; *obs* nursery-school; **~ d'aliénés** mental hospital, psychiatric hospital; **~ de nuit** night-shelter, doss house; **~ de vieillards** old people's home; **~ des morts** tomb

**asocial** *adj* antisocial

**asparagus** *nm bot* asparagus fern

**aspect** *nm* aspect; view, angle; sight, view; **à l' ~ de** at the sight of; **au premier ~** at first sight; **sous cet ~** from this point of view

**asperge** *nf* asparagus; *coll* tall thin person

**asperger** *vt* (3) sprinkle, spray; splash

**aspérité** *nf* asperity; roughness; harshness

**aspersion** *nf eccles* aspersion, sprinkling

**aspersoir** *nm eccles* aspergillum; rose (watering-can)

**asphalte** *nm* asphalt

**asphalter** *vt* asphalt

**asphodèle** *nm bot* asphodel

**asphyxiant** *adj* asphyxiating

**asphyxie** *nf* asphyxiation

**asphyxier** *vt* asphyxiate, gas; *fig* suppress

¹**aspic** *nm zool* asp; **avoir une langue d' ~** have a serpent's tongue

²**aspic** *nm cul* aspic

¹**aspirant -e** *n* candidate, aspirant

²**aspirant** *nm mil* officer-cadet; *naut* = midshipman; *adj* sucking; **pompe ~ e** suction-pump

**aspirateur** *nm* vacuum-cleaner; aspirator

**aspiration** *nf* aspiration; ideal, desire; breathing in

**aspirer** *vt* breathe in, inhale; suck in, draw up; *phon* aspirate; *vi* breathe in; aspire, desire

**aspirine** *nf* aspirin

**assagir** *vt* make wiser; make calmer, moderate; smooth down (hair); **s' ~** become wiser; sober down

**assagissement** *nm* calming down, settling down

**assaillant -e** *n* assailant; *adj* attacking

**assaillir** *vt* (14) assail, attack; assault; *fig* harass, set upon

**assainir** *vt* make healthier; disinfect, decontaminate; drain (marsh); *econ* balance, stabilize; *fig* purify

**assainissement** *nm* disinfection, decontamination; draining (marsh); drainage; *econ* stabilization; *fig* purification

**assaisonnement** *nm cul* seasoning, flavouring; condiment, spice, salad dressing

**assaisonner** *vt cul* season, flavour; dress (salad); *fig* give spice to, season; enliven; *coll* reprimand, tear a strip off

**assassin** *nm* assassin, murderer; *adj* murderous; *lit* killing; seductive, provocative (glance)

**assassinat** *nm* assassination, murder

**assassiner** *vt* assassinate, murder; *coll* overcharge

**assaut** *nm* attack, charge, assault; *sp* bout; **faire ~ de** vie in; **prendre d' ~** take by storm

**assèchement** *nm* drying; draining

**assécher** *vt* (6) dry; drain

**assemblage** *nm mech* assembling, assemblage; putting together; collection; assortment, mixture

**assemblée** *nf* assembly; gathering, audience; meeting (company, society); *pol* national legislative body; **l'Assemblée nationale** national assembly ( = House of Commons, U.S. House of Representatives)

**assembler** *vt* assemble, gather, collect; bring together; *mech* assemble, join, couple; *obs* bring together, summon; **s' ~** come together, meet

**assener, asséner** *vt* (6) hit, strike

**assentiment** *nm* agreement, consent, assent

**asseoir** *vt* (15) seat, install; establish, base; **~ un impôt** make an assessment of tax; **s' ~** sit down

**assermenté** *adj leg* sworn-in, on oath

**asservir** *vt* enslave, subjugate; conquer, master; **s' ~** submit oneself, become enslaved

**asservissement** *nm* bondage, enslavement; subjection

**assesseur** *nm* assessor; *leg* deputy

**assez** *adv* enough, sufficiently; quite, rather, fairly; **~ !** that's enough!, that will do!; **~ de** enough; **~ de personnes imaginent** plenty of people suppose; **~ grand** large enough; quite large; **~ longtemps** long enough; for quite a time; **~ pour** enough to; **c'en est ~**, **en voilà ~** that's enough; **en avoir ~** be bored, be fed up; **j'ai ~ de ça** I have had enough of that

**assidu** *adj* assiduous, regular; diligent; constant

**assiduité** *nf* assiduity, assiduousness; frequent presence; **~ s** (unwelcome) attentions to a woman

**assiéger** *vt* (6,3) besiege, lay siege to; surround, encircle; *fig* harass, assail

**assiette** *nf* plate; plateful; balance; basis; *fig* state of mind, condition; situation, position; *naut* trim; *leg* basis of tax; **~ anglaise** dish of assorted cold meats; *coll* **~ au beurre** cushy job; **avoir une bonne ~** have a good seat (horserider); **ne pas être dans son ~** not feel well, not feel up to the mark

**assiettée** *nf* plateful

**assignation** *nf leg* assignment, allotment, dividing out; *leg* sub-poena

**assigner** *leg* assign, allot; designate; determine, fix; *leg* sub-poena

**assimiler** *vt* assimilate; integrate, incorporate; compare; **s' ~** become assimilated; become similar; *fig* absorb

**assis** *adj* seated; assured; firm, stable; **magistrature ~ e** judiciary, bench; **place ~ e** seat

**assise** *nf* basis, foundation; *bui* course; *geol* stratum

**assises** *nfpl leg* assizes; *pol* congress; formal meeting

**assistance** *nf* audience; assistance, help; **~ judiciaire** legal aid; **~ médicale** medical services; **~ sociale** social services

**assistant -e** *n* assistant, helper; lecturer (university); **~ e sociale** social welfare worker; **~ s** audience; persons present

**assisté -e** *n* person receiving aid; *adj* in receipt of aid

**assister** *vt* help, aid; succour, minister to; *vi* **~ à** be present at

**association** *nf* association; society; *comm* company; *sp* club; analogy, similitude

**associé -e** *n* associate; *comm* partner

**associer** *vt* associate; join, unite, bring together, link; **~ qn à qch** make s/o a party to sth; **s' ~** group together; combine; **s' ~ à** adhere to, associate oneself with; **s' ~ à (avec) qn** join with s/o, enter into partnership with s/o

**assoiffé** *adj* thirsty; arid; eager for

**assolement** *nm* rotation of crops

**assombrir** *vt* darken; sadden; make anxious; **~ s** become dark; become sad; become anxious

**assombrissement** *nm* darkening; gloom, gloominess

**assommant** *adj coll* boring, tedious; tiresome, maddening

**assommer** *vt* kill by a blow on the head, fell; knock (s/o) out; *fig* stun, affect deeply; inconvenience; bore, fatigue

**Assomption** *nf eccles* Assumption

**assorti** *adj* matched, suited, going well together; **~ s** varied, assorted; **bien ~** well stocked

**assortiment** *nm* arrangement, disposition, matching; collection; service, set; *comm* stock

**assortir** *vt* arrange, match, harmonize; (people) bring together, unite; **s' ~** match, go together; **s' ~ de** stock up with

**assoupi** *adj* half-asleep, somnolent; assuaged

**assoupir** *vt* make sleepy; calm, attenuate, assuage

**assoupissement** *nm* somnolence, torpor; calming; attenuation

**assouplir** *vt* make supple; soften, attenuate; **s' ~** become supple; become softer, supple

**assouplissement** *nm* making supple; softening

**assourdir** *vt* deafen; muffle, deaden; **s' ~** *phon* become unvoiced

**assourdissant** *adj* deafening

**assourdissement** *nm* making deaf, deafening; deadening, softening

**assouvir** *vt* satisfy, satiate; quench; gratify; **s'** ~ be gratified, be assuaged

**assouvissement** *nm* satisfaction, satiation; satiety

**assujetti -e** *n* tax-payer; *adj* subject, liable; fixed

**assujettir** *vt* subjugate, enslave; fix, fasten; ~ **à** subject to, make liable to; **s'** ~ submit

**assujettissant** *adj* exacting, demanding

**assujettissement** *nm* subjugation, conquest; submission; constraint, subjection

**assumer** *vt* assume, take upon oneself

**assurance** *nf* assurance, certainty; self-confidence; insurance; *coll* insurance company; *mot* ~ **au tiers** third-party insurance; *mot* ~ **tous risques** comprehensive insurance; ~**s sociales** social security; ~-**vie** life insurance

**assuré -e** *n* insured person, policy-holder; *adj* certain, clear, without doubt; confident, sure

**assurer** *vt* assure, affirm; defend, preserve; guarantee; fix, make firm, strengthen, wedge; insure; ~ **qn de qch** certify sth to s/o; ~ **à qn que** assure s/o that; **s'** ~ check, verify; **s'** ~ **contre** insure oneself against; **s'** ~ **de** guarantee, make sure of

**assureur** *nm* insurance agent; ~ **vie** life-insurance agent

**assyrien -ienne** *adj* Assyrian

**astérie** *nf* starfish

**astérisque** *nm* asterisk

**astéroïde** *nm* asteroid

**asthmatique** *n + adj* asthmatic

**asthme** *nm* asthma

**asticot** *nm* maggot; *coll* chap; *sl* **engraisser les** ~ **s** be pushing up the daisies

**asticoter** *vt coll* nag, worry

**astigmate** *adj* astigmatic

**astigmatisme** *nm* astigmatism

**astiquer** *vt* polish, polish up

**astragale** *nm* astragal

**astrakan** *nm* astrakhan

**astre** *nm* star

**astreindre** *vt* (55) compel, oblige; **s'** ~ force oneself

**astreinte** *nf* constraint; *leg* delay in payment of debt

**astrologie** *nf* astrology

**astronaute** *n* astronaut

**astronautique** *nf* astronautics

**astronef** *nm* space ship

**astronome** *n* astronomer

**astronomie** *nf* astronomy

**astronomique** *adj* astronomic, astronomical

**astrophysique** *nf* astrophysics

**astuce** *nf* ingenious idea, device; joke; *obs pej* trick

**astucieux -ieuse** *adj* ingenious; *obs pej* cunning

**asymétrie** *nf* asymmetry

**asymétrique** *adj* asymmetrical

**ataraxie** *nf phil* ataraxy

**atavique** *adj* atavistic

**atavisme** *nm* atavism

**ataxie** *nf* ataxia

**ataxique** *adj* ataxic

**atelier** *nm* workshop; studio (painter, sculptor); *arts* school

**atermoiement** *nm* leg stay; postponement, delay

**atermoyer** *vi* (7) delay, defer

**athée** *n* atheist; *adj* atheistic

**athéisme** *nm* atheism

**athlétique** *adj* athletic

**athlétisme** *nm* athleticism

**Atlantique** *nm* Atlantic

**atlantique** *adj* Atlantic

**atlantisme** *nm pol* approval of N.A.T.O. policy

**atmosphérique** *adj* atmospheric

**atome** *nm* atom

**atomique** *adj* atomic

**atomiser** *vt* vaporize; pulverize; destroy by atomic weapons

**atomiseur** *nm* atomizer, aerosol, spray

**atonalité** *nf mus* atonality

**atone** *adj path* atonic; inert; dull, lacking in energy; *phon* unaccentuated

**atonie** *nf path* lack of muscular tone; inertia, feebleness

**atour** *nm* finery; ~**s** *obs* or *joc* ornaments

**atout** *nm* trump, winning card; **trois sans** ~**s** three no-trumps

**atrabilaire** *adj* atrabilious, surly; misanthropic

**âtre** *nm* hearth

**atroce** *adj* atrocious, appalling

**atrocité** *nf* atrocity, cruelty; crime

**atrophie** *nf* atrophy

**atrophier** *vt* atrophy; **s'** ~ atrophy, waste away

**attabler** (**s'**) *v refl* sit down to table

**attachant** *adj* attractive, fascinating; interesting

**attache** *nf* fastening; tying up; clip, paper-clip, pin, cord, button, lace, knot; *bot* sucker; *anat* joint; *fig* attachment; ~**s** *anat* wrist and ankle; *fig* links, bonds

**attachement** *nm* attachment, affection; fidelity

**attacher** *vt* attach, fasten, do up; tie; chain; pin together; clip; buckle; button; lace; join; *fig* link, unite; take on, engage; (gaze) fix; (idea) associate; (value) attribute, grant; *vi cul* stick (in pan); **s'** ~ be attached, be fixed; **s'** ~ **à** be joined to; *fig* be attached to, be connected with; be devoted to; apply oneself to

**attaquant -e** *n* attacker, assailant; *sp* forward

**attaque** *nf* attack; *coll* **d'** ~ in good form

**attaquer** *vt* attack; destroy, corrode, eat away; begin, get down to; *coll* start eating; **s'** ~ **à** attack, criticize; seek to resolve (problem)

**attardé -e** *n* someone mentally retarded; *adj* delayed; old-fashioned; retarded

**attarder** *vt* delay; **s'** ~ delay; remain, hang about; remain behind; proceed slowly

**atteindre** *vt* (55) reach, attain, arrive at; equal; strike, wound; affect (illness); *fig* upset, trouble; ~ **à** reach

**atteinte** *nf* injury, blow, attack; *med* symptom; *med* attack; **hors d'** ~ out of reach; **porter** ~ **à** cast a slur on; attack

**attelage** *nm* (animals) harnessing; coupling (railway waggons); harness; yoke

**atteler** *vt* (5) harness, yoke; put between shafts; *fig* put to work; **s'** ~ **à** harness oneself to, apply oneself to

**attelle** *nf* splint

**attenant** *adj* adjacent

**attendre** *vt* await, wait for; expect, foresee; ~ **après qch** need sth; ~ **son heure** bide one's time; **attendez!** (**attends!**) wait!, hang on!; **en attendant** in the meantime; **en attendant de** while waiting to; **en attendant que** until; **faire** ~ **qn** keep s/o waiting; **se faire** ~ be late, be slow in coming; **s'** ~ **à** expect; **s'** ~ **que, s'** ~ **à ce que** expect; *vi* wait, pause

**attendrir** *vt* touch, move; *cul* make tender; **s'** ~ have pity, feel sympathy

**attendrissement** *nm* compassion, pity, feeling

**attendu** *adj* awaited, expected; *prep* given, in view of; ~ **que** given that; *leg* whereas

**attendus** *nmpl leg* reasons

**attentat** *nm* murder attempt; outrage; bomb attack; crime, offence; *leg* ~ **à la pudeur** indecent exposure

**attente** *nf* waiting, wait; desire, expectation; **contre toute** ~ contrary to all expectations; **être dans l'** ~ **de** be waiting for; **salle d'** ~ waiting-room

**attenter** *vi* ~ **à** make an attempt against; ~ **à la vie de qn** make an attempt on s/o's life; ~ **à ses jours** attempt to commit suicide

**attentif -ive** *adj* attentive; mindful; thoughtful; considerate; ~ **à** desirous of; scrupulous

**attention** *nf* attention, notice, heed; care, thoughtfulness; ~ **!** be careful!; ~ **s** solicitude, attentions; ~ **à la marche** mind the step; **faire** ~ **à** take notice of; **faire** ~ **que** take notice that; **faire** ~ **que, faire** ~ **à ce que** take care that

**attentionné** *adj* considerate, attentive

**attentisme** *nm pol* temporization; policy of wait and see

**atténuant** *adj* attenuating

**atténuer** *vt* attenuate; moderate

**atterrer** *vt* astound, stun

**atterrir** *vi* land; *fig* end up

**atterrissage** *nm* landing

**attester** *vt* attest, affirm; show, bear witness

**attiédir** *vt* make tepid (by cooking or by warming); *fig* temper, tone down, cool

**attifer** *vt coll* deck out absurdly

**Attique** *nm geog* Attica

**attique** *nm bui* attic; *adj* Attic

**attirail** *nm* equipment; *coll* paraphernalia, gear, apparatus

**attirant** *adj* attractive, seductive

**attirer** *vt* draw, attract; entice; attract, please, charm; **s'** ~ bring upon oneself

**attiser** *vt* stir up, poke (fire); excite, arouse, revive

**attitré** *adj* appointed; **fournisseur** ~ supplier by appointment

**attouchement** *nm* touching with the hand; ~ **s** (**impurs**) self-abuse

**attractif -ive** *adj phys* attractive; enticing, captivating

**attraction** *nf phys* attraction; fascination; ~ **s** cabaret, floor-show

**attrait** *nm* attraction, charm, fascination; taste, desire; *lit* ~ **s** (female) charms

**attrape** *nf* trick, device; joke, hoax; *obs* trap

**attrape-nigaud** *nm coll* device to deceive the simple-minded

**attraper** *vt* catch; snare; dupe, catch out, have on; scold; catch (illness); hit off (style, likeness); **s'** ~ be catching; *sl* **attrape!** take that!

**attrayant** *adj* attractive, pleasant, agreeable

**attribuable** *adj* attributable

**attribuer** *vt* attribute, assign; grant; confer; allot

**attribut** *nm* attribute, characteristic, quality

**attribution** *nf* attribution, allocation; *gramm* attributive; ~ **s** powers, authority

**attristant** *adj* saddening; deplorable

**attrister** *vt* sadden, pain, afflict; depress

**attroupement** *nm* crowd; *esp* riotous assembly, mob

**attrouper** vt gather together; **s' ~** form into a mob

**atypique** adj atypical

**au, aux** see à + le

**aubaine** nf windfall, stroke of luck

¹**aube** nf dawn; beginning; **dès l' ~** very early in the morning

²**aube** nf eccles alb

³**aube** nf mech vane, blade; **navire à ~s** paddle-steamer

**aubépine** nf hawthorn

**auberge** nf ar inn, tavern; country restaurant; **~ de (la) jeunesse** youth hostel

**aubergine** nf aubergine, egg-plant; coll traffic warden

**aubergiste** n innkeeper

**aucun** adj any; **il n'y a ~ espoir** there is no hope; **ne ... ~** not any; **y a-t-il ~ espoir?** is there any hope?; pron any; no one, nobody

**aucunement** adv not at all; US no way; in any way

**audace** nf daring, courage, audacity, innovation; pej arrogance, cheek; insolence; nerve

**audacieux -ieuse** n audacious person; adj audacious, daring

**au-deça** adv obs on this side; prep phr **~ de** on this side of

**au-dedans** adv inside; prep phr **~ de** inside

**au-dehors** adv outside; prep phr **~ de** outside

**au-delà** nm the beyond; adv beyond, further than; prep phr **~ de** beyond

**au-dessous** adv below, underneath; prep phr **~ de** beneath

**au-dessus** adv above, over; prep phr **~ de** above

**au-devant de** prep phr **aller ~** go to meet; anticipate

**audibilité** nf audibility

**audience** nf hearing; conversation; audience

**audiophone** nm deaf-aid

**audio-visuel** nm audio-visual methods; audio-visual equipment; adj (f -uelle) audio-visual

**auditeur -trice** n listener; **~s** audience, public

**auditif -ive** adj auditory

**audition** nf audition; hearing; mus performance

**auditionner** vt audition; vi give an audition

**auditoire** nm audience; readership

**auge** nf drinking trough; feeding trough

**augmentation** nf augmentation, increase; lengthening; rise (cost, salary); US raise

**augmenter** vt augment, increase; enlarge; lengthen; intensify; **~ qn** give s/o a rise; vi grow, increase, become larger; **s' ~** become larger

**augure** nm augur, prophet; augury, omen, prediction

**augurer** vt augur, predict

**auguste** adj august, venerable

**aujourd'hui** nm the present day; adv today; nowadays, at the present time

**aulne, aune** nm bot alder

**aulx** nmpl obs see ail

**aumône** nf alms; favour

**aumônier** nm eccles chaplain

**aune** nf ell

**auparavant** adv before, first

**auprès** adv near, nearly; prep phr **~ de** near to; attached to (diplomat); according to; compared with

**auquel** see lequel

**auréole** nf aureola, aureole, halo; **~ de martyr** martyr's crown

**auréoler** vt halo

**auréomycine** nf med aureomycin

**auriculaire** nm little finger; adj auricular; **témoin ~** witness testifying to words actually heard

**auricule** nf anat auricle

**aurifère** adj auriferous

**aurore** nf day-break, dawn; origin, commencement

**ausculter** vt med examine, sound (esp with stethoscope)

**auspice** nm antiq auspice; **~s** auspices, protection, patronage

**aussi** adv as, so; also, as well, equally, too; however; therefore; **~ belle qu'elle soit** however pretty she is; **~ bien** equally well; **~ bien que** as well as; just as much as; **~ vite que possible** as fast as possible; **est-ce qu'il est ~ stupide?** is he so stupid?; **mais ~** moreover; **tout ~ bien** just as well

**aussitôt** adv at once, immediately; **~ dit ~ fait** no sooner said than done; conj phr **~ que** as soon as

**austérité** nf austerity; severity, rigour; **~s** eccles mortification, penance

**autan** nm south wind

**autant** adv as many, as much; **~ ... ~** as ... as; **~ que** as much as, as many as; in so far as; **~ (vaut)** one may as well; **d' ~** a great deal; in proportion; **d' ~ plus** all the more; conj phr **d' ~ mieux que** even better because; **d' ~ moins que** even less because; **d' ~ plus que** even more because, all the more so as; **d' ~ que** especially since

**autel** nm altar; **aller à l' ~** get married; **maître ~** high altar; **s'approcher de l' ~** take communion

**auteur** nm author; mus composer; founder, inventor; first cause; **droit d' ~**

copyright; **droits d' ~** royalties; **femme ~** female writer

**authenticité** *nf* authenticity, truth, veracity

**authentifier** *vt* authenticate

**authentique** *adj* authentic, genuine; authoritative

**autisme** *nm* autism

**auto** *nf* car; **~ tamponneuse** dodgem

**auto-accusation** *nf* self-accusation

**autobiographie** *nf* autobiography

**autobiographique** *adj* autobiographical

**autobus** *nm* bus

**autocar** *nm* coach

**autocensure** *nf* self-censoring

**autochtone** *n* autochthon; *adj* autochthonic, autochthonous

**autoclave** *nm* autoclave; pressure-cooker; *adj* self-sealing

**autocollant** *adj* self-sealing (envelope)

**autocopie** *nf* duplicating

**auto-couchettes** *adj invar* **train ~** car-sleeper train

**autocrate** *nm* autocrat

**autocratie** *nf* autocracy

**autocratique** *adj* autocratic

**autocritique** *nf* self-criticism

**autocuiseur** *nm* pressure-cooker

**autodéfense** *nf* self-defence

**autodégivrage** *nm* automatic defrosting (refrigerator)

**autodestruction** *nf* self-destruction

**autodétermination** *nf* self-determination

**autodidacte** *n* self-taught person; *adj* self-taught

**autodrome** *nm* motor-racing track

**auto-école** *nf* driving school

**autogestion** *nf* workers' control (factory)

**autographe** *nm* autograph; *adj* written by hand

**autoguidé** *adj* self-directional

**automate** *nm* robot, automaton

¹**automatique** *nm* automatic pistol; *adj* automatic; involuntary, instructive; *coll* inevitable, bound to happen; **distributeur ~** slot-machine

²**automatique** *nf* science of automation

**automatisation** *nf* automation

**automatiser** *vt* automate

**automatisme** *nf* automatism

**automitrailleuse** *nf* machine-gun carrier

**automnal** *adj* autumnal

**automne** *nm* autumn

**automobile** *nf* car, automobile; *adj* concerning cars; **assurances ~s** car insurance; **industrie ~** car industry

**automobiliste** *n* motorist

**automoteur -trice** *adj* self-propelling

**automotrice** *nf* rail-car

**autonome** *adj* autonomous; independent

**autonomie** *nf* autonomy; independence; range (vehicle)

**autonomiste** *n* autonomist, separatist

**autopompe** *nf* fire-engine

**autoportrait** *nm* self-portrait

**autopropulsé** *adj* self-propelled

**autopropulsion** *nf* self-propulsion

**autopsie** *nf* autopsy, post-mortem

**autopsier** *vt* do a post-mortem on

**autoradio** *nm* car radio

**autorail** *nm* (diesel) railcar

**auto-réglable** *adj* self-adjustable

**autorégulation** *nf* automatic regulation

**autorisation** *nf* authorization; permission; permit, pass

**autorisé** *adj* authorized; official; approved

**autoriser** *vt* authorize; entitle, permit; **s' ~ de** rely upon, base upon

**autoritaire** *adj* authoritarian; authoritative, peremptory

**autoritarisme** *nm* authoritarianism

**autorité** *nf* authority; influence, prestige; **d' ~** without argument, without discussion; **faire ~** be an authority; **faire acte d' ~** bring one's authority to bear

**autoroute** *nf* motorway; **~ de dégagement** toll-free motorway for first few miles outside large city; **~ de liaison** long-distance motorway (with toll)

**auto-stop** *nm* hitch-hiking; **faire de l' ~** hitch-hike

**auto-stoppeur -euse** *n* hitch-hiker

**autour** *adv* around, round; *prep phr* **~ de** around, round; near; about

**autre** *adj* other; different; quite another; **c'est ~ chose** that's quite different; **l' ~ Tois** recently; **une ~ fois** on another occasion; *adv phr* **~ part** elsewhere; **d' ~ part** moreover; *pron* another; **à d' ~ s!** tell that to the marines!; **comme dirait l' ~** as they say; **de temps à ~** from time to time; **d'un bout à l' ~** from start to finish; **d'un moment à l' ~** any minute; **en avoir vu d' ~ s** have seen more surprising things; **entre ~ s** among others; **l'un et l' ~** both of them; **l'un l' ~ ( les uns les ~ s)** each other, one another; **l'un ou l' ~** one or other

**autrefois** *adv* formerly, in the past, of old

**autrement** *adv* otherwise, differently; very; **pas ~** not very, not particularly

**Autriche** *nf* Austria

**autrichien -ienne** *adj* Austrian

**autruche** *nf* ostrich; **la politique de l' ~** burying one's head in the sand

**autrui** *pron* another; other people

**auvent** *nm* lean-to roof, projecting roof

**auxiliaire** *n* auxiliary, assistant, helper; *adj* auxiliary, complementary; *mil* **services ~ s** non-combatant troops

**avachi** *adj* (shoes) shapeless; flabby, soft

**avachir** *vt* soften, make flabby; **s' ~** become soft, become flabby; *coll* become fat; be slipping

**avachissement** *nm* flabbiness

¹**aval** *nm* lower reaches of river; **en ~** downstream

²**aval** *nm* ( *pl* **~ s**) *comm* endorsement

**avaler** *vt* swallow; devour; put up with; conceal; **~ la pilule (le morceau)** accept without protest; **~ sa rage** conceal one's anger; **~ sa salive** keep a hold on one's tongue; **~ un livre** devour a book

**avaliser** *vt comm* endorse; support, back

**à-valoir** *nm invar* instalment

**avance** *nf* advance; lead, start; loan; **à l' ~** before, in advance; **d' ~** in advance; **en ~** early, in advance; **la belle ~ !** that's a fat lot of good!; **par ~** in advance; **prendre de l' ~** go into the lead, increase one's lead

**avancé** *adj* advanced; *mil* forward; late, far gone; precocious; nearing completion; **n'être pas plus ~** be no further ahead; *iron* **vous voilà bien ~ !** that's helped a lot!

**avancement** *nm* advance; progress; improvement; promotion; **~ à l'ancienneté** promotion by seniority

**avancer** *vt* (4) push forward, hold out; advance; propose, affirm; put forward, bring forward (time); make progress; (money) lend; put forward (watch, clock); **ça ne m'avance pas** that doesn't help me; *vi* advance, project; progress, get on; be promoted; be fast (watch, clock); **s' ~** come forward, approach; make progress; jut out; pass by (time); **s' ~ trop** expose oneself to risk

**avanie** *nf* affront, humiliation

**avant** *nm* front; *naut* prow; *sp* forward; *adv* before; first; in front; **bien ~** far in; **en ~** in front, forward, forwards; towards the future; **en ~ de** in front of; **trop ~** too far forward, too far in; *prep* before, earlier; **~ de** before; *conj phr* **~ que** before

**avantage** *nm* advantage, profit, benefit; superiority; *sp* (tennis) advantage; **~ pécuniaire** profit; **avoir ~ à** be well-advised to

**avantager** *vt* (3) favour, benefit

**avantageux -euse** *adj* advantageous, favourable; *pej* conceited, self-satisfied

**avant-bras** *nm invar* forearm

**avant-centre** *nm sp* centre-forward

**avant-coureur** *nm* forerunner, precursor; *adj* precursory, announcing, premonitory

**avant-dernier -ière** *adj* penultimate

**avant-garde** *nf* advance-guard; avant-garde

**avant-goût** *nm* foretaste; anticipation

**avant-guerre** *nm or nf invar* pre-war period

**avant-hier** *adv* two days ago, on the day before yesterday

**avant-poste** *nm mil* forward position

**avant-première** *nf* preview; private showing; advance notice (journalism); **en ~** before public presentation

**avant-propos** *nm* preface, foreword

**avant-scène** *nf* stage-box; proscenium

**avant-toit** *nm* projecting roof; **~ s** eaves

**avare** *n* miser; *adj* avaricious, miserly; **~ de** sparing of

**avaricieux -ieuse** *adj* miserly

**avarie** *nf naut* damage; breakdown

**avarié** *adj* damaged; rotten; *coll obs* poxed

**avarier** *vt* deteriorate

**avec** *adv* with; *coll* **tu viens ~ ?** are you coming along?; *prep* with; at the same time as; in the company of; in the same way as; in addition; by means of; thanks to; **et ~ cela, Madame?** will there be anything else, Madam?; **être bien (mal) ~** be on good (bad) terms with; **marié ~** married to

¹**avenant** *nm* new clause in insurance policy, endorsement

²**avenant** *adj* pleasant, agreeable, charming

³**avenant (à l')** *adv phr* in accordance, in keeping; **~ de** in keeping with

**avènement** *nm eccles* advent of Christ; *pol* accession

**avenir** *nm* future; destiny; posterity; **à l' ~** from now on, in the future; **d' ~** with a future

**Avent** *nm eccles* Advent

**aventure** *nf* adventure; occurrence, incident; love-affair; *obs* future, destiny; **à l' ~** at random; **d' ~, par ~** by chance; **dire la bonne ~ à qn** tell s/o's fortune; **diseuse de bonne ~** fortune-teller

**aventurer** *vt* venture, risk, hazard; **s' ~** venture

**aventureux -euse** *adj* adventurous; hazardous, risky

**aventurier** *nm ar* soldier of fortune, mercenary; pirate; *n* ( *f* **-ière**) adventurer, adventuress

**aventurisme** *nm pol* recklessness

**avenu** *adj leg* **nul et non ~** non-existent, null and void

**avenue** *nf* avenue; tree-lined drive
**avéré** *adj* attested, authenticated
**avérer** *vt* (6) *obs* attest; s' ~ be confirmed, be shown to be true
**averse** *nf* shower; *fig* flood, stream
**averti** *adj* informed, experienced; **un homme ~ en vaut deux** forewarned is forearmed
**avertir** *vt* warn, caution; inform, notify
**avertissement** *nm* warning, caution; premonition; advice, recommendation; foreword; notice; demand (tax); reprimand
**avertisseur** *nm* alarm, warning signal; *mot* horn; *adj* ( *f* -euse) warning
**aveu** *nm* confession, avowal; acknowledgement; declaration (love); *lit* consent, agreement; **de l' ~ de** in the opinion of; **sans ~** of no fixed abode
**aveuglant** *adj* blinding, dazzling
**aveugle** *n* blind person; **en ~** without thought, blindly; *adj* blind; *fig* blind, unreasoning; implicit, unquestioning
**aveuglement** *nm fig* blindness, unreason, folly; *obs* blindness
**aveuglément** *adv* blindly
**aveugler** *vt* make blind, blind; dazzle; *fig* confuse; stop (leak); s' ~ blind oneself, refuse to see the truth
**aveuglette (à l')** *adv phr* blindly
**aveulir** *vt* enfeeble, make limp; s' ~ become feeble, become limp
**aveulissement** *nm* enfeeblement, limpness
**aviateur** -trice *n* aviator; pilot; member of aircrew
**aviculteur** -trice *n* bird-farmer, aviculturalist
**avide** *adj* very hungry, voracious; greedy, rapacious; avid, eager; passionate
**avidité** *nf* voracity; avidity
**avili** *adj* degraded
**avilir** *vt* degrade; discredit, dishonour; *comm* depreciate; s' ~ degrade oneself, become debased; *comm* be depreciated, lose value
**avilissant** *adj* degrading, debasing
**avilissement** *nm* degradation, debasement; dishonour; *comm* depreciation
**aviné** *adj* drunk
**avion** *nm* aircraft, plane; ~ **à réaction** jet; ~ **de ligne** air-liner; **défense contre ~s** anti-aircraft defence; **en ~** by air; **l' ~** aviation, flying; **par ~** by air, air-mail
**avionique** *nf* avionics
**aviron** *nm* oar; *sp* rowing; **faire de l' ~** row
**avis** *nm* view, judgement, opinion; vote; advice; announcement, notification; *lit* warning; ~ **au lecteur** foreword; **à**

**mon ~** in my opinion; **de l' ~ de tous** in everyone's opinion; **être de l' ~ de qn** agree with s/o; **jusqu'à nouvel ~** until further notice; *obs* **m'est ~ que** it seems to me that; **sauf ~ contraire** unless I (you, we) hear to the contrary
**avisé** *adj* prudent, sensible
**¹aviser** *vt* notice, spot; *vi* ~ **à** reflect on, think about, consider; s' ~ realize, discover; have the idea; s' ~ **de** dare to
**²aviser** *vt* notify, advise
**aviver** *vt* stir up, revive; freshen (colour); increase, arouse
**¹avocat** -e *n leg* barrister, counsel; defender, champion (cause); ~ **du diable** devil's advocate
**²avocat** *nm* avocado (pear)
**avoine** *nf* oat, oats; **farine d' ~** oatmeal; **flocons d' ~** porridge
**avoir** *nm* possession(s), wealth; *comm* credit side (of accounts); *v aux* (1) have; *vt* have, possess; be, feel; have on, wear; obtain, buy, get; ~ **beau faire qch** do sth in vain; ~ **faim, soif, chaud, froid** be hungry, thirsty, hot, cold; ~ **lieu** take place; ~ **qn** trick s/o, dupe s/o; *coll* have s/o, make love with s/o; ~ **vingt ans** be twenty years old; *sl* **en ~** have guts; *coll* **en ~ à, contre, après** have it in for; **en ~ assez** have enough of; **en ~ pour son argent** get one's money's worth; **j'en ai pour cinq minutes** it will take me five minutes; **qu'est-ce qu'il a?** what's the matter with him?; (telephone) **vous avez Paris** you've got Paris on the line; **y ~** *impers* **il y a** there is, there are; **il n'y a pas de quoi** it doesn't matter; not at all, don't mention it; **il n'y a pas que lui** he's not the only one; **il n'y a qu'à** it is only necessary to; **il y a deux jours que** it is two days since; **qu'est-ce qu'il y a?** what's the matter?
**avoisinant** *adj* neighbouring, adjacent
**avoisiner** *vt* be near to, be close to
**avortement** *nm* abortion, miscarriage; *fig* failure
**avorter** *vi* abort, miscarry; fail, come to nothing
**avorteur** -euse *n* abortionist
**avorton** *nm* stunted tree, stunted plant; child or animal of arrested development; *pej* squirt, abortion
**avouable** *adj* that can be avowed
**avoué** *nm leg* solicitor; *adj* acknowledged
**avouer** *vt* recognize; approve; avow, admit, confess
**avril** *nm* April; **poisson d' ~** April fool
**avunculaire** *adj* avuncular
**axe** *nm* axis; axle; spindle; direction, line; *pol* axis, alliance; *mot* main road

**axer** *vt* orientate, direct; ~ **sur** centre upon

**axillaire** *adj anat* axillary

**axiome** *nm* axiom

**ayant** *pres part* avoir

**ayant-cause** *nm* (*pl* **ayants-cause**) *leg* assignee, assign

**ayant-droit** *nm* (*pl* **ayants-droit**) *leg* rightful owner

**azalée** *nf bot* azalea

**azimut** *nm* azimuth; **dans tous les** ~ s in all directions; **tous** ~ s in all directions, right, left and centre; of every kind, in every domain

**azote** *nm chem* nitrogen

**Aztèque** *n* Aztec

**aztèque** *adj* Aztec

**azur** *nm* azure, blue; *poet* sky; infinite; **Côte d'Azur** French Riviera

**azuré** *adj* azure, sky-blue

**azuréen -éenne** *n* inhabitant of French Riviera

**azyme** *nm* unleavened bread; *adj* unleavened

# B

**¹baba** *nm* sponge cake steeped in rum

**²baba** *adj invar coll* staggered; **en rester** ~ be speechless with surprise

**babeurre** *nm* buttermilk

**babil** *nm* chattering, babbling; twittering (of birds)

**babillage** *nm see* babil

**babillard -e** *n* chatterbox; *adj* garrulous, talkative

**babiller** *vi* prattle, chatter, babble

**babines** *nfpl* lips, chops (of animal); *sl* **se lécher les** ~ lick one's lips

**babiole** *nf* bauble, trifle, knick-knack

**bâbord** *nm naut* port (side)

**babouche** *nf* Turkish slipper

**babouin** *nm* baboon; little monkey (child)

**baby-foot** *nm* table football

**¹bac** *nm* ferry(-boat)

**²bac** *nm* tank, vat

**³bac** *nm coll* ( = baccalauréat)

**baccalauréat** *nm* advanced school-leaving certificate

**baccara** *nm* baccara (card-game)

**baccarat** *nm* Baccarat glass

**bacchanale** *nf* uproarious dance; drunken revel, orgy

**bâche** *nf* canvas covering, tarpaulin; garden-frame; tank, cistern

**bachelier -ière** *n* one who has passed the baccalauréat examination

**¹bachot** *nm* wherry, punt

**²bachot** *nm* ( = baccalauréat); **boîte à** ~ cramming shop

**bachotage** *nm* cramming

**bachoter** *vi* cram, swot

**bacillaire** *adj* bacillary

**bacille** *nm* bacillus

**bâclage** *nm coll* botching, scamping

**bâcle** *nf* bar (of door)

**bâcler** *vt coll* botch, scamp; bar (door); **travail bâclé** slap-dash job

**bactérie** *nf* bacterium

**bactériologique** *adj* bacteriological; **guerre** ~ germ warfare

**badaud -e** *n* lounger, idler, gaper (in street)

**baderne** *nf naut* fender; *coll* **vieille** ~ old fogey

**badigeon** *nm* whitewash, distemper

**badigeonnage** *nm* whitewashing, distempering

**badigeonner** *vt* whitewash, distemper; *med* paint

**badigeonneur** *nm* whitewasher; *coll* poor painter

**badin** *adj* playful, waggish

**badinage** *nm* banter, fun, trifling

**badine** *nf* cane, switch

**badiner** *vi* trifle, jest

**baffe** *nf sl* blow, cuff

**bafouer** *vt* make fun of, flout, make ridiculous

**bafouillage** *nm* unintelligible speech; *coll* nonsense

**bafouiller** *vt* + *vi* splutter, blurt out; *coll* talk nonsense

**bâfrer** *vt* + *vi sl* stuff, guzzle; **se** ~ guzzle, feed one's face

**bagage** *nm* baggage; stock of knowledge; ~ s luggage; **faire enregistrer ses** ~ s register one's luggage; **plier** ~ *coll* clear out

**bagagiste** *nm* luggage porter (at hotel)

**bagarre** *nf* scuffle, brawl, fight
**bagarrer** *vi coll* fight, struggle; **se ~** fight, quarrel
**bagatelle** *nf* trifle, mere nothing
**bagne** *nm* convict prison; penal servitude; *coll* place where one has to work hard
**bagnole** *nf coll* car
**bagou** *nm coll* gift of the gab
**bague** *nf* ring
**baguenauder** *vi* fool around
¹**baguer** *vt* ring (bird)
²**baguer** *vt* tack (in needlework)
**baguette** *nf* wand, stick, rod; long thin loaf of bread; **faire marcher qn à la ~** be very strict with s/o
**bah** *interj* nonsense!; who cares!
**bahut** *nm* round-topped wooden chest; *sl* school
**bai** *nm* bay (horse)
¹**baie** *nf geog* bay
²**baie** *nf archi* bay, opening
³**baie** *nf bot* berry
**baignade** *nf* bathe; bathing-place
**baigner** *vt* give a bath to, soak, dip; *vi* soak; **se ~** have a bathe; take a bath
**baigneur -euse** *n* bather; bathing attendant; *nm* small celluloid or plastic doll
**baignoire** *nf* bath, bath tub; *theat* box at stalls level
**bail** *nm* (*pl* **baux**) lease
**bâillement** *nm* yawn; gaping
**bâiller** *vi* yawn; fit badly (door or window); be ajar
**bailli** *nm* bailiff
**bâillon** *nm* gag
**bâillonner** *vt* gag
**bain** *nm* bath; **~s** baths, spa; *coll* **être dans le ~** be well up in; **prendre un ~ de foule** *US* press the flesh
**bain-marie** *nm* (*pl* **bains-marie**) double saucepan; *chem* water bath
**baïonnette** *nf* bayonet; **~ au canon!** fix bayonets!; *elect* **douille à ~** bayonet socket
**baise-en-ville** *nm invar* small hold-all
**baisemain** *nm* hand-kissing
**baiser** *nm* kiss; *vt obs + lit* kiss; *vulg* have sex with, fuck; **~ la main à qn** kiss s/o's hand
**baisse** *nf* fall, drop (prices); going down (water); failing (eyesight); **être en ~** be falling (temperature, shares)
**baisser** *vt* lower, let down; hang (head); cast down (eyes); *vi* go, come down, sink (sun); fail (sight, strength); ebb (tide); **se ~** bend down, stoop
**bajoue** *nf* chap, cheek (animal); *coll* falling cheek (person)
**bal** *nm* (*pl* **~s**) ball, dance; dance-hall
**balade** *nf coll* stroll, ramble
**balader** *vt* take for a walk; **se ~** stroll

**baladeur -euse** *n* stroller
**baladeuse** *nf* barrow; inspection lamp; trailer (vehicle)
**baladin** *nm* mountebank, showman (circus), buffoon
**balafre** *nf* gash, cut, scar
**balafrer** *vt* gash, slash, scar
**balai** *nm* broom; *aer* joystick; *sl* last bus; *elect* brush; *mot* blade (windscreen wiper); **manche à ~** broomstick
**balance** *nf* balance, scales; equilibrium; *comm* balance; dipping-net; **faire pencher la ~** turn the scale
**balancé** *adj sl* **bien ~** well stacked
**balancement** *nm* swinging; rocking (boat)
**balancer** *vt* swing, rock, balance; *sl* chuck away, get rid of; *vi* hesitate, be uncertain; **se ~** swing, sway, rock; *sl* **je m'en balance** I couldn't care less
**balancier** *nm* pendulum (clock); balancing-pole
**balançoire** *nf* swing; seesaw
**balayage** *nm* sweeping, sweeping up
**balayer** *vt* (7) sweep, sweep out, sweep up; scour
**balayette** *nf* dusting brush, small broom
**balayeur -euse** *n* sweeper
**balayeuse** *nf* sweeping machine
**balayures** *nfpl* sweepings
**balbutiement** *nm* stammering, stuttering
**balbutier** *vt + vi* stammer, mumble
**balcon** *nm* balcony; *theat* dress-circle; *sl* **il y a du monde au ~!** she's got a bosom!
**baldaquin** *nm* canopy
**Bâle** *nf* Basel, Basle
**baleine** *nf* whale; whalebone (corset); rib (umbrella)
**baleinier** *nm* whaling-ship, whaler
**balise** *nf naut* buoy, beacon, sea-mark; *aer* runway-light
**baliser** *vt naut + aer* mark out (channel, runway)
**balistique** *nf* ballistics, gunnery; *adj* ballistic
**baliverne** *nf* piece of nonsense
**balkanique** *adj* Balkan
**ballade** *nf* ballad
**ballant** *adj* swinging, dangling (arms, legs)
¹**balle** *nf* ball; bullet; **~ perdue** stray shot; **~ traçante** tracer bullet
²**balle** *nf* bale (cotton, etc)
³**balle** *nf* chaff, husk
⁴**balle** *nf sl* franc
**ballerine** *nf* ballerina, ballet-dancer
**ballon** *nm* balloon; large ball, football; **~ d'essai** pilot balloon; *fig* feeler

29

**ballonnement** *nm* swelling, distending (stomach), flatulence

**ballonner** *vt* + *vi* swell, distend; balloon out (skirt)

¹**ballottage** *nm* shaking, jolting

²**ballottage** *nm* indecisive election result

**ballottement** *nm* tossing (of ship); shaking

**ballotter** *vt* toss, shake about; *vi* shake, wobble, rattle (door)

**ballottine** *nf cul* chicken galantine

**ball-trap** *nm* clay-pigeon shoot

**balnéaire** *adj* bathing; **station** ~ spa, seaside resort

**balourd -e** *n* awkward person, idiot; *adj* awkward, stupid

**balourdise** *nf* awkwardness; stupid blunder; **raconter des** ~ s talk rot

**balsamine** *nf bot* balsam

**baluchon** *nm coll* bundle (clothes)

**balustrade** *nf* balustrade, hand-rail

**bambin** *nm coll* little child, kid

**bamboche** *nf* puppet, marionette; *sl* spree, lark; **faire** ~ paint the town red

**bambou** *nm* bamboo

**bamboula** *nm* bamboo drum; *sl* negro

**ban** *nm* proclamation; banns (marriage); ban, exile; **mettre au** ~ banish, send to Coventry

**banal** (*pl* ~ s) *adj* commonplace, hackneyed, banal

**banalité** *nf* triteness, banality; commonplace

**banane** *nf* banana; *mot* over-rider; *coll* medal

**bananier** *nm* banana-tree; banana-boat

**banc** *nm* bench, seat, form, pew; ~ **de glace** ice-field; ~ **de poissons** shoal of fish; ~ **de sable** sandbank; ~ **des accusés** dock, bar; ~ **d'essai** testing bench; ~ **du jury** jury box

**bancaire** *adj* relating to banking

**bancal** *adj* (*pl* ~ s) bandy-legged; rickety

**bandage** *nm* bandaging, bandage; *med* truss; solid tyre

¹**bande** *nf* band, strip; wrapper; reel of film; ~ **dessinée** comic strip; ~ **magnétique** recording tape

²**bande** *nf* band, gang, party; flight, flock, pack; **faire** ~ **à part** keep to oneself

³**bande** *nf naut* list; **donner de la** ~ list

**bandeau** *nm* head-band; bandage (over eyes)

**bander** *vt* bandage, bind up; tighten; ~ **les yeux à qn** blindfold someone; *vi vulg* have an erection

**banderole** *nf* streamer

**bandit** *nm* bandit, brigand; *coll* rascal

**bandoulière** *nf* shoulder-strap; **en** ~ slung over one's shoulder

**bang** *nm* sonic boom

**banlieue** *nf* outskirts (of town), outer suburbs

**banlieusard -e** *n coll* inhabitant of suburbia

**banni -e** *n* exile, outlaw

**bannière** *nf* banner, flag, standard; **en** ~ in one's shirt-tails

**bannir** *vt* banish, exile

**bannissement** *nm* exile, banishment

**banque** *nf* bank; banking

**banqueroute** *nf* bankruptcy

**banqueroutier -ière** *n* bankrupt

**banquette** *nf* bench, seat, form; bunker (golf)

**banquier** *nm* banker

**banquise** *nf* ice-floe, ice-pack

**baptême** *nm* baptism, christening; **nom de** ~ Christian name

**baptiser** *vt* baptize, christen; *coll* call, nickname; *coll* ~ **du vin** add water to wine

**baquet** *nm* tub, bucket

**bar** *nm* sea-perch

**baragouin** *nm coll* gibberish

**baragouiner** *vt* + *vi coll* jabber, talk gibberish

**baraque** *nf* hut, shanty; booth (at fair); *sl* house, hovel

**baraquement** *nm* hutting; ~ s huts, hutments

**baratin** *nm* chatting up, patter

**baratte** *nf* churn (for making butter)

**barbacane** *nf* barbican

**barbant** *adj sl* boring

¹**barbare** *nm* barbarian

²**barbare** *adj* barbaric, uncouth, barbarous

**barbarie** *nf* barbarity; barbarousness

**barbe** *nf* beard; *sl* bore; ~ **à papa** candy-floss; **quelle** ~ ! what a nuisance!; **rire dans sa** ~ laugh up one's sleeve

**barbelé** *adj* barbed; **les** ~ s barbed-wire entanglements

**barber** *vt sl* bore; **se** ~ be bored

**barbiche** *nf* goatee, short beard

**barbier** *nm* barber

**barboter** *vt* paddle, splash about; *sl* steal, pinch

**barboteuse** *nf* child's rompers

**barbouiller** *vt* daub, scrawl, smear; **barbouillé de larmes** tear-stained; **se** ~ get one's face dirty

**barbouze** *nm* unofficial secret agent

**barbu** *adj* bearded

**barde** *nm* bard, poet

¹**barder** *vi coll* **ça va** ~ things are hotting up

²**barder** *vt cul* cover with slices of bacon; *mil* encase in armour

**barème** *nm* ready-reckoner; scale

(marks, etc); printed table

**baril** *nm* barrel, cask, keg

**barillet** *nm* small barrel; chamber (revolver)

**bariolé** *adj* motley, many-coloured

**barioler** *vt* paint in many colours, variegate

**baromètre** *nm* barometer

**baronne** *nf* baroness

**baroque** *nm* baroque style; *adj* odd, quaint, baroque

**baroud** *nm mil sl* fight, scrap

**baroudeur** *nm* fighter, scrapper

**barque** *nf* boat; *coll* **bien mener sa ~** manage one's affairs well

**barrage** *nm* barring, closing, blocking; barrier, block, dam, weir; *mil* **(tir de) ~** barrage; **match de ~** replay

**barre** *nf* bar, rod; **~ fixe** horizontal bar; tiller; stroke (writing); stripe; **avoir ~ sur qn** have a hold over s/o

**barrer** *vt* bar, obstruct, dam; cross out, cross (cheque); *naut* steer; *sl* **se ~** clear off

**¹barrette** *nf* hair-slide; ankle strap; brooch

**²barrette** *nf* biretta; cardinal's cap

**barreur -euse** *n* helmsman

**barrière** *nf* barrier, obstacle; fence; gate; **~ de dégel** barrier on road to protect surface during thaw

**barrique** *nf* large barrel, cask

**barrir** *vi* trumpet (elephant)

**baryton** *nm + adj invar* baritone

**¹bas** *nm* lower part, bottom; **les hauts et les ~** the ups and downs; *adj (f* **basse)** low; base, mean; **au ~ mot** at the lowest estimate; **avoir la vue ~se** be short-sighted; **faire main ~ se sur** lay hands on; *adv* low, low down; **~ !** down with; **en ~** down, downwards; **mettre ~** bring forth (young); lay down (arms); **parler ~** speak softly

**²bas** *nm* stocking

**basané** *adj* sunburnt, tanned, swarthy

**bas-bleu** *nm* blue-stocking

**bas-côté** *nm* aisle (church)

**bascule** *nf* rocker; see-saw; weighing-machine; **chaise à ~** rocking-chair

**basculer** *vt + vi* rock, swing, tip up, lose balance; *fig* **~ dans** tend towards, finish up as

**base** *nf* base, foundation, basis; grass roots, rank and file

**baser** *vt* base, ground, found; **se ~ sur** take as a basis

**bas-fond** *nm* low ground, shallows; **les ~ s** slums; lowest classes of society

**basilique** *nf* basilica

**basquais** *adj* Basque

**basque** *nf* skirt, (coat-)tail, flap

**basse** *nf* bass (voice, instrument)

**basse-cour** *nf* farm-yard, poultry-yard

**bassement** *adv* basely, meanly, scurvily

**bassesse** *nf* baseness, lowness; ignoble action

**bassin** *nm* basin, bowl; dock; ornamental pond; pelvis; **~ houiller** coal field; **entrer au ~** dock

**bassinant** *adj sl* boring, tiresome

**bassine** *nf* pan

**bassinoire** *nf* warming pan

**bastingage** *nm naut* bulwark

**bastringue** *nm sl* slow dance-hall; din; paraphernalia

**bas-ventre** *nm* lower part of abdomen

**bât** *nm* pack-saddle; *coll* **c'est là que le ~ le blesse** that's where the shoe pinches

**bataclan** *nm sl* paraphernalia

**bataille** *nf* battle, fight; **cheveux en ~** ruffled hair

**batailler** *vi* battle, struggle, fight

**batailleur -euse** *adj* pugnacious, quarrelsome

**bataillon** *nm* battalion

**bâtard -e** *n + adj* bastard; **chien ~** mongrel

**bâtarde** *nf* slanting writing (intermediate between round hand and running hand)

**batavia** *nf* kind of lettuce

**¹bateau** *nm* boat, ship

**²bateau** *nm* part of pavement in front of entrance

**³bateau** *nm* hoax; **monter un ~ à qn** hoax s/o

**bateau-citerne** *nm* (*pl* bateaux-citernes) tanker

**bateau-mouche** *nm* (*pl* bateaux-mouches) passenger-boat on the Seine in Paris

**bateau-pêcheur** *nm* (*pl* bateaux-pêcheurs) fishing-boat

**batelier -ière** *n* boatman, boatwoman

**batellerie** *nf* inland waterway transport; canal and river craft (in collective sense)

**bath** *adj invar sl* first-rate, fine, bang on

**bâti** *nm* structure, frame(work); tacking (needlework)

**batifoler** *vi coll* romp, frolic, play about

**bâtiment** *nm* building, building-trade; large ship

**¹bâtir** *vt* build, construct; **terrain à ~** building land

**²bâtir** *vt* baste, tack (needlework)

**bâtisse** *nf* bricks and mortar; masonry; ramshackle building

**batiste** *nf* batiste, cambric

**bâton** *nm* stick, rod, staff; stroke (writing); **~ de rouge** lipstick; **à ~ s rompus** by fits and starts, irregularly; *sl* **mener une vie de ~ de chaise** lead a gay

life, sleep around; **mettre les ～s dans les roues** put a spoke in the wheels
**bâtonner** vt beat, cudgel
**bâtonnier** nm leg president of the Bar
**battage** nm threshing (corn); churning (butter)
**¹battant** nm clapper (bell); flap (table); **porte à deux ～s** double doors
**²battant** adj beating; **pluie ～e** driving rain; **porte ～e** swing door; **tambour ～** with drums beating; hastily, roughly; **tout ～ neuf** brand-new
**battement** nm beating, clapping, fluttering, throbbing (heart), banging (door)
**batterie** nf mil+elect battery; wait, pause; percussion instruments of the orchestra; **～ de cuisine** set of kitchen utensils; **dresser ses ～s** lay one's plans
**¹batteur** nm whisk, beater (machine)
**²batteur -euse** n beater (of gold); thresher; drummer
**batteuse** nf threshing-machine; harvester
**battoir** nm beater (instrument); sl large hand
**battre** vt (16) beat, strike, thrash; defeat; whisk (eggs); shuffle (cards); coin (money); churn (butter); scour (countryside); **～ la mesure** beat time; **～ le pavé** loaf around the streets; **'～ son plein** be in full swing; **un pavillon** fly the flag; vi beat; **～ des mains** clap; **en retraite** beat a retreat; **se ～** fight
**battu** adj beaten; **avoir les yeux ～s** have rings round one's eyes; **chemin ～** beaten track
**battue** nf battue; (police) round-up
**baudet** nm ass, donkey; trestle
**baudrier** nm shoulder-belt
**baume** nm balm, balsam
**bavard -e** n chatterbox; indiscreet person; adj talkative
**bavardage** nm chattering, gossip
**bavarder** vi chatter, gossip
**bavarois** adj Bavarian
**bavaroise** nf cul cold flavoured cream (sweet)
**bave** nf spittle, slaver, foam
**baver** vi dribble, slaver, slobber; run (pen); coll **en ～** be staggered; have a rough time
**bavette** nf bib; skirt (beef)
**baveux -euse** adj dribbling, slavering; moist (omelette)
**Bavière** nf Bavaria
**bavoir** nm bib
**bavure** nf eng burr; smudge; coll fig error; **sans ～** perfect
**bayer** vi obs gape; **～ aux corneilles** stand gaping
**bazar** nm bazaar, general store; coll **tout le ～** the whole lot

**béant** adj gaping (wound); yawning (chasm)
**béat** adj blissful, smug
**béatitude** nf beatitude, bliss; complacency
**beau** nm beauty; beau; **faire le ～** show off; beg (dog); **le plus ～ de l'histoire, c'est...** the best of it is ...; **le temps est au ～ fixe** the weather is set fair; adj (bel) (f belle, mpl beaux) beautiful, handsome, fair; fine, noble; **à la belle étoile** in the open air; **avoir ～ faire qch** do sth in vain; **bel et bien** quite, entirely; **ce n'est pas ～ de votre part** that's not nice of you; **de plus belle** more than ever; **il est ～ joueur** he is a good loser; **il fait ～** the weather is fine; **le ～ côté** the bright side; **le ～ monde** high society; **l'échapper belle** have a narrow escape; **une belle fortune** a large fortune; **une belle occasion** a marvellous opportunity; **voir les choses en ～** see things in a good light; **belle** nf beautiful woman, belle; **faire la ～** play the deciding game; **la Belle et la Bête** Beauty and the Beast
**beaucoup** adv much, very much; **～ de** a lot of, many; **c'est déjà ～ qu'il ne dise pas non** it's something to be thankful for that he does not refuse; **de ～** by far
**beau-fils** nm (pl beaux-fils) son-in-law; step-son
**beau-frère** nm (pl beaux-frères) brother-in-law; step-brother
**beau-père** nm (pl beaux-pères) father-in-law; step-father
**beaupré** nm bowsprit
**beauté** nf beauty; beautiful woman; **～ du diable** bloom of youth; **de toute ～** very beautiful; **être en ～** be looking one's best; **perdre en ～** lose in fine style; **se faire une ～** make up
**beaux-arts** nmpl fine arts
**beaux-parents** nmpl parents-in-law
**bébé** nm baby
**bébé-éprouvette** nm (pl bébés-éprouvette) coll test-tube baby
**bébête** adj coll childish, silly
**bec** nm beak; nib; spout (jug); burner (stove, lamp); mouth-piece (musical instrument); coll mouth; **～ de lièvre** hare-lip; **avoir bon ～** have the gift of the gab; **clouer le ～ à qn** shut s/o up; **fin ～** gourmet; **prise de ～** squabble
**bécane** nf coll bicycle, bike
**bécasse** nf woodcock; fig+coll ninny, goose
**bécassine** nf snipe; fig+coll ninny, goose
**bec-de-cane** nm lever-handle (door)
**béchamel** nf **sauce (à la) ～** white cream sauce

**bêche** nf spade

**bêcher** vt dig; fig+coll criticize, run down

**bécoter** vt coll give little kisses to

**becquée** nf beakful; **donner la ~ à** feed (young birds)

**becqueter** vt (5) peck up; sl eat

**bedaine** nf sl paunch, belly

**bedeau** nm beadle; verger

**bedon** nm coll paunch, belly

**bedonnant** adj pot-bellied

**bée** adj f open, gaping; **bouche ~** open-mouthed

**beffroi** nm belfry

**bégaiement** nm stammering, stuttering

**bégayer** vt+vi (7) stammer (out), stutter

**bègue** n stutterer; adj stammering, stuttering

**bégueule** nf prude; adj prudish, strait-laced

**béguin** nm hood (of Beguine nun); baby's bonnet; fig+coll infatuation

**béguinage** nm (Beguine) convent

**beige** adj beige; natural, raw (wood)

**beignet** nm fritter

**bel** adj see beau

**bêler** vi bleat; fig+coll complain, grouse

**belette** nf weasel

**belge** adj Belgian

**bélier** nm ram; battering ram

**belladone** nf belladonna, deadly nightshade

**bellâtre** nm fop; adj vulgarly handsome

**belle-famille** nf (pl **belles-familles**) in-laws

**belle-fille** nf (pl **belles-filles**) daughter-in-law; step-daughter

**belle-mère** nf (pl **belles-mères**) mother-in-law; step-mother

**belles-lettres** nfpl belles-lettres, humanities

**belle-sœur** nf (pl **belles-sœurs**) sister-in-law; step-sister

**belligérant** adj belligerent

**belliqueux -euse** adj warlike, bellicose

**belvédère** nm belvedere, view-point

**bémol** nm mus flat

**bénédicité** nm grace (before meal)

**bénédictin** nm Benedictine monk; **~ e** nf Benedictine nun; Benedictine (liqueur)

**bénédiction** nf benediction, blessing; godsend

**bénéfice** nm profit, gain, benefit; eccles living; **au ~ de** in aid of; **sous ~ d'inventaire** subject to satisfaction

**bénéficiaire** n beneficiary

**bénéficier** vi benefit, derive advantage

**benêt** nm clot; adj silly, stupid

**bénévole** adj gratuitous, without charge; voluntary

**bénin** (f **bénigne**) adj benign, kind; mild; **maladie bénigne** slight illness

**béni-oui-oui** nm coll yes-man

**bénir** vt bless, consecrate; **~ un mariage** solemnize a marriage; **je bénis la voiture** (I say) thank God for the car

**bénit** adj consecrated, blessed; **eau ~ e** holy water; **pain ~** holy bread

**bénitier** nm font, holy water vessel, stoup

**benne** nf dredger-bucket, cable-car, little truck

**benzine** nf benzine; (in Switzerland) petrol

**béquille** nf crutch

**bercail** nm sheepfold; fig fold (Church), bosom (family)

**berceau** nm cradle, cot; arbour; **dès le ~** from earliest childhood

**bercer** vt (4) rock, lull; **~ qn de promesses** delude s/o with promises

**berceuse** nf lullaby; rocking-chair

**berge** nf steep bank

**berger** nm shepherd; **(chien) ~** sheep-dog

**¹bergère** nf shepherdess

**²bergère** nf easy-chair

**bergerie** nf sheepfold

**berlue** nf fig blindness; **avoir la ~** see things wrong

**berne** nf **en ~** at half-mast

**berner** vt make fun of, hoax

**bernique** interj coll nothing doing, no use

**besace** nf beggar's bag, scrip

**besicles** nfpl coll goggles, specs

**besogne** nf task, job, piece of work; **abattre de la ~** get through a lot of work

**besogner** vi work hard

**besogneux -euse** adj hard-up, needy

**besoin** nm need, want, poverty; **au ~** if necessary; **avoir ~ de** need; **faire ses ~ s** relieve oneself

**bestial** adj bestial, brutish

**bestiaux** nmpl cattle, livestock

**bestiole** nf tiny beast (usu insect)

**bêta** (f **bêtasse**) n sl stupid person, silly ass

**bétail** nm cattle, livestock

**bête** nf beast, animal; stupid person; **~ à bon Dieu** ladybird; **~ de somme** beast of burden; **~ noire** bugbear; coll **chercher la petite ~** split hairs

**bêtise** nf stupidity; foolish act, blunder; trifle

**béton** nm concrete; **~ armé** reinforced concrete

**bette** nf beet; Swiss chard

**betterave** nf beet(root); **~ à salade** beetroot

**beugler** vi low, bellow; coll bawl

**beurre** *nm* butter; **œil au ~ noir** black eye

**beurrer** *vt* butter

**beurrier** *nm* butter-dish

**beuverie** *nf* drinking bout

**bévue** *nf* blunder, slip, howler

**biais** *nm* skew, slant; bias (of bowl); expedient; **de ~** aslant, askew

**biaiser** *vi* be on the slant; be evasive

**bibelot** *nm* curio, knick-knack

**¹biberon** *nm* baby's feeding-bottle

**²biberon** *nm* tippler, drunkard

**bibi** *nm sl* number one, myself; woman's hat

**bibliobus** *nm* mobile library, *US* book-mobile

**bibliographie** *nf* bibliography

**bibliothécaire** *n* librarian

**bibliothèque** *nf* library; bookcase

**biblique** *adj* biblical

**bic** *nm* ball-point pen; *adj* **pointe ~** ball-point pen

**biche** *nf* hind, doe

**bicher** *vi sl* **ça biche?** everything going well?

**bichonner** *vt* smarten up; **se ~** titivate

**bicoque** *nf* shanty, hovel; *coll* little house

**bicyclette** *nf* bicycle

**bidet** *nm* nag, small horse; bidet

**bidon** *nm* can, drum

**bidonville** *nm* shanty town

**bidule** *nm coll* thingummy, thing

**bielle** *nf* connecting-rod; *mot* **j'ai coulé une ~** my big end has gone

**bien** *nm* good; benefit, advantage; property; **~s** property, belongings; **mener à ~** bring to a successful conclusion; **prendre la chose en ~** take sth in good part; *adv* well, good; right, proper; much, very; **~ des** plenty of; **~ entendu** of course; **c'est ~ fait** it serves you (him, her, etc) right; **elle est ~** she is nice-looking; **il y en avait ~ mille** there were at least a thousand; **il va (se porte) ~** he is well; **je suis ~ avec lui** I'm on good terms with him; **nous sommes très ~ ici** we're quite comfortable here; **tant ~ que mal** somehow or other; **vous faites ~ de partir** you are wise to leave; *conj* **~ que** although

**bien-aimé** *adj* beloved, favourite

**bien-être** *nm* well-being, welfare

**bienfaisance** *nf* charity, beneficence

**bienfaisant** *adj* beneficent, charitable, salutary

**bienfait** *nm* kindness, favour; blessing, boon

**bienfaiteur -trice** *n* benefactor, benefactress

**bien-fondé** *nm* justice, merits (of a case)

**bienheureux -euse** *adj* blissful, happy; blessed

**biennal** *adj* biennial, two-yearly

**bienséance** *nf* propriety, decorum, decency

**bienséant** *adj* becoming, seemly, proper

**bientôt** *adv* soon, very soon, shortly, before long; quickly; **à ~** see you soon

**bienveillance** *nf* benevolence, kindness, good-will

**bienveillant** *adj* kind, benevolent, kindly

**bienvenu** *adj* welcome; **soyez le ~!** welcome!

**bienvenue** *nf* welcome; **souhaiter la ~ à qn** welcome s/o

**¹bière** *nf* beer; **~ blonde** light ale; **~ brune** brown ale

**²bière** *nf* coffin

**biffer** *vt* cross out, strike out

**bifteck** *nm* steak, beefsteak; **~ pommes frites** steak and chips

**bifurcation** *nf* fork, bifurcation

**bifurquer** *vi* fork

**bigame** *adj* bigamous

**bigamie** *nf* bigamy

**bigarreau** *nm* white-heart cherry

**bigarrer** *vt* variegate, mottle

**bigorneau** *nm coll* winkle

**bigot -e** *n* bigot; *adj* bigoted

**bigoudi** *nm* hair-curler

**bigre** *interj obs + coll* by jove!

**bigrement** *adv* jolly (well)

**bijou** *nm* gem; sweet thing, sweet person

**bijouterie** *nf* jewellery; jeweller's shop; jeweller's trade

**bijoutier -ière** *n* jeweller

**bilan** *nm* balance-sheet; **déposer son ~** file one's petition (in bankruptcy)

**bile** *nf* bile, gall; bad temper; **s'échauffer la ~** get worked up; *sl* **se faire de la ~** worry

**bileux -euse** *adj coll* easily worried

**biliaire** *adj* biliary; **la vésicule ~** gall bladder

**bilieux -ieuse** *adj* bilious; irascible, irritable

**bilingue** *adj* bilingual

**billard** *nm* billiards; billiard table; billiard saloon; *coll* operating table; *coll* bald head; *coll* **c'est du ~** it's easy

**bille** *nf* billiard ball; marble; **roulement à ~s** ball-bearing; **stylo à ~** ball-point pen

**billet** *nm* note, short letter; ticket; **~ d'aller et retour** return ticket; **~ (de banque)** (bank-)note; **~ simple** single ticket

**billion** *nm* one thousand million

**billot** *nm* block (wood); executioner's block

**bimensuel -uelle** *adj* fortnightly, twice monthly

**bimoteur** *nm* twin-engined plane; *adj invar* twin-engined

**binaire** *adj* binary

**biner** *vt* dig, hoe

[1]**binette** *nf sl* face

[2]**binette** *nf* hoe

**biniou** *nm* Breton bagpipes

**binocle** *nm* pince-nez, eye-glasses

**biochimie** *nf* biochemistry

**biographe** *nm* biographer

**biographie** *nf* biography

**biologie** *nf* biology

**bique** *nf* she-goat; *sl* hag

[1]**bis** *adj* brown (bread)

[2]**bis** *adv* twice; encore!

**bisaïeul** *nm* (*pl* **bisaïeux**) great-grand-father

**bisaïeule** *nf* great-grandmother

**bisannuel -elle** *adj* biannual

**bisbille** *nf coll* petty quarrel

**biscornu** *adj* mis-shapen; queer (ideas)

**biscotte** *nf* rusk

**biscuit** *nm* plain cake; biscuit

[1]**bise** *nf* north wind

[2]**bise** *nf coll* kiss

**biseau** *nm* bevel

**biseauter** *vt* bevel, chamfer

**bisque** *nf cul* shell-fish soup, bisque

**bisser** *vt* encore (performance)

**bissextile** *adj* **année** ~ leap year

**bistouri** *nm med* lancet

**bistre** *nm* bistre (colour); *adj* blackish-brown

**bistré** *adj* swarthy

**bistrot** *nm coll* small restaurant; pub

**bitte** *nf naut* bitt; *vulg* prick

**bitume** *nm* bitumen; asphalt

**bivouaquer** *vi* bivouac, camp

**bizarre** *adj* queer, odd, peculiar; eccentric

**blackbouler** *vt* blackball; *coll* reject (candidate)

**blafard** *adj* pale, wan, pallid, dim

**blague** *nf* tobacco-pouch; *coll* tall story, leg-pull; **sans** ~ ? no joking?, really?

**blaguer** *vt* chaff, make fun of; *vi coll* joke

**blagueur -euse** *n* humbug, joker; *adj* mocking, bantering

**blaireau** *nm* badger; shaving-brush

**blâme** *nm* blame, censure; reprimand

**blâmer** *vt* blame; reprimand

**blanc** *nm* white, whiteness; whitening liquid; blank space (on page); white man; (white) linen; *cul* breast (chicken); **chauffer à** ~ make white hot; **chèque en** ~ blank cheque; **saigner qn à** ~ bleed s/o white; **tirer à** ~ fire blanks; *adj* (*f* **blanche**) white; light-coloured; clean, pure; blank; **donner**

**carte blanche** give unlimited powers; **mariage** ~ unconsummated marriage; **nuit blanche** sleepless night; **voix blanche** expressionless voice

**blanc-bec** *nm coll* (*pl* **blancs-becs**) greenhorn, youngster

**blanchaille** *nf* whitebait

**blanchâtre** *adj* whitish

**blanche** *nf* white woman; *mus* minim; **traite des** ~ s white slave traffic

**blancheur** *nf* whiteness; purity

**blanchir** *vt* make white, whiten, bleach; ~ **du linge** wash clothes; ~ (**à la chaux**) whitewash; *vi* turn white

**blanchissage** *nm* washing, laundering; whitewashing

**blanchisserie** *nf* laundry, wash-house

**blanchisseur** *nm* laundryman

**blanchisseuse** *nf* laundress

**blanc-seing** *nm* (*pl* **blancs-seings**) signed document with blank space above

[1]**blanquette** *nf* blanquette (stew of white meat)

[2]**blanquette** *nf* kind of white wine

**blasé** *adj* indifferent

**blaser** *vt* blunt, cloy, make indifferent

**blason** *nm* coat of arms; heraldry; **redorer son** ~ make a rich marriage (poor nobleman)

**blasphémateur -trice** *n* blasphemer; *adj* blasphemous

**blasphématoire** *adj* blasphemous

**blasphème** *nm* blasphemy

**blatte** *nf* cockroach, black beetle

**blé** *nm* corn, wheat; **manger son** ~ **en herbe** spend one's income before one gets it

**bled** *nm* the interior (in N. Africa); *sl* hole, one-horse town

**blême** *adj* livid, deathly pale

**blêmir** *vi* turn deathly pale, blanch

**blennorragie** *nf* gonorrhoea

**blessé** *adj* + *n* wounded, injured (man or woman)

**blesser** *vt* wound, injure; wrong

**blessure** *nf* wound, injury

**blet** (*f* **blette**) *adj* overripe (fruit)

[1]**bleu** *nm* blue; blue dye; bruise; blue dungarees, overalls; ~ **marine** navy blue; *sl* recruit

[2]**bleu** *adj* blue; **peur** ~ **e** blue funk

**bleuâtre** *adj* bluish

**bleuet** *nm* cornflower

**bleuir** *vt* make blue; *vi* turn blue

**bleuter** *vt* make slightly blue

**blindage** *nm* armour-plating; metal casing; timbering

**blindé** *nm* armoured vehicle; *adj* armour-plated; **division** ~ **e** armoured division

**blinder** *vt* armour-plate; case; timber

**bloc** *nm* block, lump; writing pad; *pol*

coalition; *sl* prison; **à ~** fully, right home; **en ~** in a lump

**blocage** *nm* freeze (prices, etc); *bui* hardcore

**bloc-cuisine** *nm* (*pl* **blocs-cuisines**) kitchen equipment

**blockhaus** *nm* blockhouse; *naut* conning-tower

**bloc-moteur** *nm* (*pl* **blocs-moteurs**) *eng* engine unit

**blocus** *nm* blockade, siege; **forcer le ~** run the blockade

**blond** *nm* blond colour; *adj* fair (-haired), blond

**blondeur** *nf* blondness, fairness

**blondin** *nm* fop; fair-haired person; *adj* fair-haired

**blondir** *vt* bleach, dye blond; *vi* turn yellow

**bloquer** *vt* block up, fill up; lock, clamp; blockade, invest; obstruct; freeze (prices); **~ les freins** brake hard; **~ un chèque** stop a cheque

**blottir (se)** *v refl* hide, huddle, nestle

¹**blouse** *nf* overall, smock, pinafore, blouse

²**blouse** *nf* pocket (billiards)

¹**blouser** *vi* puff out (dress)

²**blouser** *vt* pocket (billiard ball); *coll* take in, deceive

**blouson** *nm* jerkin (windcheater); **~ noir** rocker, leather boy

**blue-jean** *nm* jeans

**bluet** *nm* cornflower

**bluffer** *vt* + *vi* bluff; boast

**bobard** *nm coll* tall story

**bobèche** *nf* sconce, socket (candlestick)

**bobine** *nf* spool, reel, bobbin; *sl* face

**bobiner** *vt* wind, spool, reel

**bobo** *nm coll* (talking to children) sore, bump; **faire ~** hurt

**bocage** *nm* copse, grove; wooded area

**bocal** *nm* jar, bowl

**Boche** *n sl* + *pej* German, Hun

**boche** *adj sl* + *pej* German

**bock** *nm* beer-glass; glass of beer

**bof** *interj* oh well (scorn, resignation, etc)

**boggie** *nm* bogie (railway carriage)

**bohème** *n* + *adj* Bohemian; **(vie de) ~** easy, carefree life

**bohémien -ienne** *n* gipsy

**boire** *vt* (17) drink; soak up, absorb; drink in; **~ un affront** swallow an insult; *coll* **~ un coup** have a drink; *sl* **ce n'est pas la mer à ~** it's not as bad as all that

**bois** *nm* wood, timber; *pl* antlers; *mus* wood instruments; **~ blanc** deal, white wood; **~ de lit** bedstead; **le Bois** the Bois de Boulogne

**boisé** *adj* wooded

**boiser** *vt* wainscot; timber; afforest

**boiserie** *nf* woodwork, panelling

**boisson** *nf* drink, beverage; **pris de** drunk

**boîte** *nf* box, tin; *sl* poky little room, school, place of work; **~ crânienne** brain pan; **~ (de nuit)** night-club; *sl* **mettre en ~** make fun of

**boiter** *vi* limp, hobble

**boiteux -euse** *adj* lame; rickety; **projet ~** poor plan

**boîtier** *nm* case, watch-case

**bol** *nm* bowl, basin

**bolide** *nm* meteor, meteorite; fast-moving car

**bombance** *nf sl* feasting; **faire ~** feast

**bombardement** *nm* bombardment, bombing

**bombarder** *vt* bombard, shell, bomb; pelt; *iron* appoint suddenly

**bombardier** *nm* bomber

**bombe** *nf* bomb; atomizer; aerosol; **~ glacée** ice-cream pudding; **faire la ~** go on the binge

**bomber** *vt* make bulge, swell, arch, camber; **~ la poitrine** throw out one's chest; *vi* bulge out

**bon** *nm* good, goodness; voucher, order, ticket; bond; *adj* (*f* **bonne**) good, virtuous; nice, kind, good-natured; capable, clever; right, correct; fit; profitable, advantageous; **~ à savoir** worth knowing; **~ marché** cheap; **à la ~ne heure!** fine!; **à quoi ~?** what's the use?; **de ~ne heure** early; **si ~ vous semble** if you think fit; **souhaiter la ~ne année** wish a happy New Year; **trouver ~ de** think it advisable to; *adv* agreed!, right!; **c'est ~!** that'll do!; **il fait ~ ici** it's nice here; **pour de ~** for good; seriously speaking; **sentir ~** smell nice; **tenir ~** stand firm

**bonasse** *adj* simple-minded

**bonbon** *nm* sweet(meat)

**bonbonne** *nf* demijohn

**bonbonnière** *nf* sweetmeat box

**bond** *nm* jump, leap, bound; **faire faux ~ à** let down

**bondé** *adj* packed, full

**bondir** *vi* leap, spring up; **cela m'a fait ~** that made me furious

**bonheur** *nm* good fortune, luck; happiness, pleasure; **au petit ~** in a haphazard fashion; **par ~** fortunately; **porter ~ à qn** bring s/o luck; **quel ~!** what a blessing!

**bonhomie** *nf* good nature

**bonhomme** *nm* (*pl* **bonshommes**) (*f* **bonne femme**) good-natured simple fellow (woman); *sl* man, fellow (woman); **aller son petit ~ de chemin** jog quietly along; **conte de bonne**

**femme** old wives' tale; **petit ~** little boy

**boni** *nm* bonus; surplus

**bonification** *nf* improvement; bonus

**bonifier** *vt* improve, make good (shortage)

**boniment** *nm* patter; *coll* spiel

**bonjour** *nm* good morning, good day; **simple comme ~** simple as A B C

**bonne** *nf* maid(-servant)

**bonne-maman** *nf* (*pl* **bonnes-mamans**) *coll* grandma

**bonnement** *adv* **tout ~** simply

**bonnet** *nm* cap; *sl* **gros ~** bigwig; **jeter son ~ par-dessus les moulins** throw propriety to the winds; **prendre sous son ~** invent; act on one's own responsibility; **triste comme un ~ de nuit** dull as ditchwater

**bonneterie** *nf* hosiery

**bon(n)iche** *nf sl* young maid(-servant)

**bon-papa** *nm coll* grandpa

**bonsoir** *nm* good evening, good night

**bonté** *nf* goodness, kindness; **~s** kind actions

**bord** *nm* edge, border, rim; side (ship); shore; **à ~ de** on board; **au ~ de la mer** at the seaside; *coll* **sur les ~s** slightly

**bordeaux** *nm* Bordeaux wine, claret

**bordée** *nf* broadside, volley; **~ d'injures** string of insults

**bordel** *nm* brothel; *sl* **quel ~!** what a shambles!

**bordelais** *adj* of Bordeaux

**border** *vt* border, edge, hem; tuck in; ship (oars)

**bordereau** *nm* memorandum, statement (account, etc)

**bordure** *nf* border, edging, fringe

**borgne** *adj* one-eyed, blind in one eye; *coll* low, disreputable

**borne** *nf* boundary-stone or mark; corner-post, bollard; **~ kilométrique** kilometre marker; **~s** boundaries, limits; **cela dépasse les ~s** that's going too far

**borné** *adj* restricted; narrow-minded

**borner** *vt* limit, restrict

**bosquet** *nm* thicket, grove

**bosse** *nf* bump, bruise, dent, hump; *coll* **avoir la ~ du calcul** be good at figures; *sl* **rouler sa ~** knock about the world

**bosseler** *vt* (5) dent; emboss

**bosser** *vi sl* work hard, slave

**bossu -e** *n + adj* hunch-backed (person)

**bot** *adj invar* **pied-~** club-footed, club-footed person

**botanique** *adj* botanical

¹**botte** *nf* bunch, bundle

²**botte** *nf* high boot, wellington

³**botte** *nf* thrust, lunge

**botter** *vt* put boots or shoes on; kick; **le Chat Botté** Puss in Boots

**bottier** *nm* bootmaker, shoemaker

**Bottin** *nm* street directory (in France)

**bottine** *nf* ankle-boot, bootee

**bouc** *nm* male goat; goatee; **~ émissaire** scapegoat

**boucan** *nm sl* din, row, uproar

**boucanier** *nm* buccaneer, pirate

**bouche** *nf* mouth; muzzle; opening, aperture; **~ d'eau** hydrant; **~ de chaleur** hot-air vent; **~ d'incendie** hydrant; **bonne ~** titbit; **le ~ à ~** the kiss of life

**bouché** *adj* corked, bunged up; *sl* stupid, dense

**bouchée** *nf* mouthful; **~ à la reine** small chicken vol-au-vent; **mettre les ~s doubles** gobble up; **ne faire qu'une ~ de** overcome easily

¹**boucher** *nm* butcher

²**boucher** *vt* stop up, plug, cork

**bouchère** *nf* butcher's wife

**boucherie** *nf* butcher's shop; butcher's trade; slaughter

**bouche-trou** *nm* stop-gap, substitute

**bouchon** *nm* cork, plug, stopper; float (fishing); wisp (straw); **~ de circulation** traffic block, traffic jam

**bouclage** *nm mil* encirclement

**boucle** *nf* buckle; loop (river, road); curl; ring; **~ d'oreille** ear-ring

**bouclé** *adj* curly

**boucler** *vt* buckle, fasten; *coll* lock up, imprison; *mil* encircle; **~ le budget** make both ends meet; *sl* **la ~** shut up

**bouclier** *nm* shield, buckler

**bouddhiste** *n + adj* Buddhist

**bouder** *vt* **~ qch** stay away from sth, not patronize sth; **~ qn** be sulky with s/o; *vi* sulk

**bouderie** *nf* sulkiness, sulks

**boudeur -euse** *n + adj* sulky (person)

**boudin** *nm* black pudding

**boudoir** *nm* boudoir

**boue** *nf* mud, mire, dirt; **traîner qn dans la ~** drag s/o's name in the mud

**bouée** *nf naut* buoy; **~ de sauvetage** life-buoy

**boueur** *nm* dustman

**boueux -euse** *adj* muddy

**bouffant** *adj* puffed, baggy

**bouffe** *adj* **opéra ~** comic opera

**bouffée** *nf* puff, whiff; fit (anger, pride); **~ de chaleur** sudden flush

**bouffer** *vt sl* eat; *vi* puff out (dress)

**bouffi** *adj* puffed, swollen, bloated

**bouffir** *vt* blow out, swell; *vi* become swollen

**bouffissure** *nf* puffiness, swelling

**bouffon** *nm* clown, fool, jester

**bouffonnerie** *nf* buffoonery

**bouge** nm hovel, den; low place; bilge (barrel)

**bougeoir** nm candlestick

**bougeotte** nf coll **avoir la** ~ be fidgety

**bouger** vt (3) move, displace; vi move, budge, stir

**bougie** nf (wax) candle, taper; mot sparking plug

**bougnat** nm coll coal-merchant

**bougon -onne** n+adj coll grumpy (person)

**bougonner** vi coll grumble, grouse

**bougran** nm buckram

**bougre** nm sl chap; ~ **d'idiot!** idiot!; **un bon** ~ a good type; **bougresse** nf sl woman

**bougrement** adv sl very

**bouillabaisse** nf Provençal fish soup

**bouillant** adj boiling(-hot); hot-headed

**bouille** nf sl face, dial, mug

**bouilleur** nm distiller; ~ **de cru** home distiller

**bouilli** nm boiled beef

**bouillie** nf pap; gruel, porridge

**bouillir** vi (18) boil; **faire** ~ **de l'eau** boil water

**bouilloire** nf kettle

**bouillon** nm stock, broth; cheap restaurant; bubbling, bubble; comm remainders

**bouillonnement** nm bubbling, seething

**bouillonner** vi bubble, boil, seethe

**bouillotte** nf hot-water bottle

**boulanger** nm baker

**boulangère** nf baker's wife

**boulangerie** nf baker's shop; bakery

**boule** nf ball, globe; **avoir les nerfs en** ~ be all tensed up; **partie de** ~ **s** game of bowls; sl **perdre la** ~ go mad; **se mettre en** ~ curl up

**bouleau** nm birch-tree

**bouledogue** nm bulldog

**bouler** vt coll muff; vi swell (dough); coll **envoyer** ~ **qn** send s/o to blazes

**boulet** nm cannon-ball; coll dead-weight (person); (coal) ovoid

**boulette** nf meat-ball, bread-ball; sl blunder

**boulevard** nm boulevard

**boulevardier** nm man about town

**bouleversant** adj staggering, upsetting

**bouleversement** nm upheaval, confusion

**bouleverser** vt upset; turn topsy-turvy

**Boul' Mich'** nm coll Boulevard Saint-Michel

**boulon** nm bolt, pin

**boulonner** vt bolt, pin; vi sl work hard

¹**boulot** nm sl work

²**boulot -otte** adj dumpy, fat

**boulotter** vt sl eat

**bouquet** nm bunch; cluster of trees; tuft; aroma, bouquet; prawn; finishing-piece (firework-display); **ça, c'est le** ~! that's the end!

**bouquin** nm coll book; old book

**bouquiner** vi browse, pore over books; hunt for old books

**bouquiniste** nm second-hand bookseller

**bourbe** nf mire, mud

**bourbeux -euse** adj muddy

**bourbier** nm mire, slough; fig mess

**bourdaine** nf bot black alder

**bourde** nf coll blunder, bloomer

**bourdon** nm mus drone; great bell; bumble-bee

**bourdonnement** nm buzz, hum

**bourdonner** vi buzz, hum

**bourg** nm small market town

**bourgade** nf large village

**bourgeois -e** n member of middle class; citizen, townsman (townswoman); nm sl boss; nf sl wife, missus; **les petits** ~ the lower middle classes; adj middle-class; ordinary, unrefined; homely, plain; **cuisine** ~**e** plain cooking

**bourgeoisie** nf the middle class; **la haute** ~ the upper middle class

**bourgeon** nm bud; sl pimple

**bourgeonner** vi bud; coll break out in pimples

**bourgmestre** nm burgomaster

**bourgogne** nm Burgundy (wine)

**bourguignon** nm beef cooked with onions and wine; adj (f **-onne**) Burgundian

**bourlinguer** vi toil (ship); coll travel around

**bourrade** nf blow; dig in the ribs

**bourrage** nm stuffing, padding; ~ **de crâne** eye-wash

**bourrasque** nf squall

**bourre** nf padding, flock (wool); wad (gun)

**bourreau** nm executioner, hangman; inhuman person; ~ **d'enfants** cruel parent

**bourrée** nf bundle of fire-wood; bourrée (dance)

**bourreler** vt (5) to torment, rack (mentally)

**bourrelet** nm pad, cushion; rim (tyre); coll roll (fat)

**bourrelier** nm saddler

**bourrer** vt stuff, pad, fill (pipe); ~ **qn de coups** rain blows on s/o

**bourriche** nf hamper

**bourricot** nm coll little donkey

**bourrique** nf female donkey; sl idiot, ignorant person

**bourru** adj surly, boorish

**bourse** nf purse; scholarship (for studies); pouch (animals); **Bourse** Stock Exchange; **Bourse du Travail**

Labour Exchange; **sans ~ délier** without forking out a penny

**boursette** *nf* lamb's lettuce, corn salad

**boursicoter** *vi* buy and sell shares in a small way

**boursier -ière** *n* holder of a bursary; speculator

**boursouflé** *adj* bloated; turgid (style)

**boursoufler** *vt* puff out (flesh), bloat

**boursouflure** *nf* swelling, puffiness; turgidity (style)

**bousculade** *nf* jostling, scuffle

**bousculer** *vt* knock over, turn upside down, jostle

**bouse** *nf* cow-pat

**bousiller** *vt coll* botch, scamp; *sl* damage badly; kill

**boussole** *nf* compass; *sl* head, conk

**boustifaille** *nf sl* food; tuck-in

**bout** *nm* end, extremity, tip; bit, piece, scrap; **à ~ portant** at point blank range; **au ~ du compte** after all; **être à ~ (de forces)** be exhausted; **pousser qn à ~** drive s/o to extremes; *coll* **un ~ d'homme** a little chap; **venir à ~ de** overcome

**boutade** *nf* flash of wit, joke; whim

**boute-en-train** *nm coll* life and soul of the party

**bouteille** *nf* bottle, bottleful; cylinder (gas); **~ isolante** vacuum flask

**boutique** *nf* shop; boutique; craftsman's workshop

**boutiquier -ière** *n* shopkeeper

**bouton** *nm* bud; button; knob; handle (door); switch; pimple; stud; **~ de col** collar stud; **~ d'or** buttercup

**boutonner** *vt* button up; *vi* bud

**boutonnière** *nf* button-hole

**bouton-poussoir** *nm* (*pl* **boutons-poussoirs**) knob, switch-button

**bouton-pression** *nm* (*pl* **boutons-pression**) snap-fastener

**bouture** *nf hort* cutting

**bouvier** *nm* cowman

**bouvreuil** *nm* bullfinch

**bovin** *adj* bovine

**box** *nm* (*pl* **~**, **~ es**) lock-up garage; horse-box; cubicle (dormitory)

**boxe** *nf* boxing

**boxer** *vi + vt* box

**boxeur** *nm* boxer

**boy** *nm* native servant

**boyau** *nm* intestine (animal); gut; hose-pipe; narrow street

**boycotter** *vt* boycott

**bracelet** *nm* bracelet, bangle

**bracelet-montre** *nm* (*pl* **bracelets-montres**) wrist-watch

**braconnage** *nm* poaching

**braconner** *vt + vi* poach

**braconnier** *nm* poacher

**brader** *vt* sell off cheap

**braderie** *nf* sale of old stock

**braguette** *nf* flies (trousers)

**brahmane** *nm* Brahmin

**braillard** *adj* bawling, noisy

**brailler** *vt + vi* bawl out, shout, yell

**braillerie** *nf* shouting, bawling

**brailleur -euse** *adj* bawling, noisy

**braire** *vi* (19) bray

**braise** *nf* embers

**braiser** *vt cul* braise

**bramer** *vi* bell (stag); *sl* bawl

**brancard** *nm* stretcher; shaft (carriage)

**brancardier** *nm* stretcher-bearer

**branchage** *nm* branches

**branche** *nf* branch; side (spectacles); leg (compasses); blade (propeller); **vieille ~** old chap

**branchement** *nm* branching

**brancher** *vt* plug in, connect; *coll* **être branché** know all about it, understand; *vi* perch, roost

**branchies** *nfpl* gills

**brandade** *nf cul* cod cooked with cream, oil and garlic

**brande** *nf* heather; heath

**brandir** *vt* flourish, brandish

**brandon** *nm* fire-brand

**branlant** *adj* shaky, rickety, loose (tooth)

**branle** *nm* swinging motion; impulse; **mettre en ~** start, set in motion

**branle-bas** *nm coll* bustle, upset

**branler** *vt* swing, shake (leg), wag (head); *vi* be loose, move; *vulg* **se ~** masturbate, toss oneself off

**braquage** *nm* turning (steering-wheel); aiming

**braquer** *vt* point (gun), train (telescope); fix (eyes); turn (steering-wheel); irritate

**bras** *nm* arm; hand (manual labourer); lever; **~ dessus ~ dessous** arm in arm; **à ~ le corps** round the waist; **à plein ~** in armfuls; **à tour de ~** with all one's might; **avoir le ~ long** have great influence; **avoir qn sur les ~** be left with the responsibility for s/o; **en ~ de chemise** in one's shirt sleeves

**braser** *vt* braze

**brasero** *nm* brazier

**brasier** *nm* blazing fire, furnace; fire of live coals; fierce fire

**brasiller** *vt* broil; *vi* sizzle

**brassard** *nm* armlet, arm-band

**brasse** *nf* arm-span; breast-stroke; fathom

**brassée** *nf* armful

**brasser** *vt* brew (beer); mix, stir; **~ des affaires** handle a lot of business

**brasserie** *nf* brewery, brewing; brasserie

39

**brasseur -euse** *n* brewer; breast-stroke swimmer; ~ **d'affaires** big-business man

**brassière** *nf* baby's vest; ~ **s** shoulder straps (rucksack)

**bravache** *adj* blustering, swaggering

**bravade** *nf* bravado

**brave** *adj* brave, bold; worthy, honest; **mon** ~ my good man; *coll* **un** ~ **type** a decent chap

**braver** *vt* brave, defy, face up to

**bravoure** *nf* gallantry, bravery

**break** *nm* estate car, shooting-brake

**brebis** *nf* ewe; sheep; ~ **galeuse** black sheep

**brèche** *nf* breach, gap, opening, notch (blade); **battre en** ~ batter in, make a violent attack on

**bredouille** *adj* empty-handed

**bredouiller** *vt* + *vi* stammer out, mumble

**bref** (*f* **brève**) *adj* brief, short; *adv* briefly, in a word

**breloque** *nf* charm, trinket; *sl* **battre la** ~ be barmy, go haywire

**Brésil** *nm* Brazil

**bretelle** *nf* strap, brace, sling; spur (motorway); ~ **s** braces

**breton -onne** *adj* Breton

**breuvage** *nm* beverage, drink

**brevet** *nm* patent, certificate, warrant; ~ **élémentaire** lower certificate of education; **prendre un** ~ take out a patent

**breveté -e** *n* patentee; *adj* patented, qualified, licensed

**breveter** *vt* (5) grant a patent; patent

**bréviaire** *nm* breviary

**bribes** *nfpl* scraps, fragments

**bric-à-brac** *nm* curios, bric-à-brac; odds and ends; curiosity shop

**brick** *nm naut* brig

**bricole** *nf* strap, breast-strap (harness); *coll* odd job; trifle

**bricoler** *vi* do odd jobs; *vt* arrange (piece of business)

**bricoleur** *nm* handy-man

**bride** *nf* bridle, rein; string (bonnet); **à** ~ **abattue** full tilt; **tenir en** ~ keep a tight rein on

**bridé** *adj* constricted; **yeux** ~ **s** slit eyes

**brider** *vt* bridle, curb, tie up; be tight on (clothes); *cul* truss

**bridgeur -euse** *n* bridge-player

**brièvement** *adv* briefly, succinctly

**brièveté** *nf* brevity; conciseness

**brigade** *nf* brigade; detachment; gang (workmen)

**brigadier** *nm* corporal (cavalry); sergeant (police); brigadier; ganger

**brigand** *nm* robber; brigand

**brigue** *nf* intrigue

**briguer** *vt* intrigue for, solicit

**brillamment** *adv* brilliantly

**brillance** *nf* brilliance

**brillant** *nm* brilliancy, lustre, brightness; *adj* brilliant, sparkling, shining

**briller** *vi* shine, sparkle; be conspicuous, be successful

**brimade** *nf* practical joke (on newcomers), rag; annoying petty regulation or measure

**brimbaler** *vt* cart about; *vi* swing to and fro

**brimer** *vt* rag

**brin** *nm* shoot (tree); blade (grass); strand (rope); *coll* bit, piece; *coll* **un beau** ~ **de fille** a good-looking girl

**brindille** *nf* sprig, tiny branch

**bringue** *nf sl* binge, spree; *sl* **grande** ~ large, gawky woman

**brio** *nm* dash, vigour

**brioche** *nf cul* brioche; *coll* blunder

**brique** *nf* brick; cake (soap); *sl* one million (old) francs

**briquet** *nm* lighter; flint and steel

**brisant** *nm* reef, shoal; breaker

**brise** *nf* breeze

**brisées** *nfpl* broken branches; **aller sur les** ~ **de qn** compete with s/o

**brise-glace** *nm invar* ice-breaker

**brise-jet** *nm invar* anti-splash

**brise-lames** *nm* breakwater

**briser** *vt* smash, shatter, break; wear out, exhaust; interrupt; **se** ~ break

**brise-tout** *nm invar* destructive child or person

**brise-vent** *nm invar* wind-break, windscreen (trees)

**britannique** *adj* British

**broc** *nm* pitcher, large jug; pitcherful

**brocanter** *vt coll* buy and sell; *vi* deal in curios or second-hand goods

**brocanteur -euse** *n* second-hand dealer

**brocart** *nm* brocade

**broche** *nf cul* spit; brooch; peg, pin

**brocher** *vt* brocade; **livre broché** paperback

**brochet** *nm* pike

**brochette** *nf* skewer; kebab

**brochure** *nf* booklet, pamphlet, brochure

**brodequin** *nm* laced boot

**broder** *vt* embroider

**broderie** *nf* embroidery, piece of embroidery

**bromure** *nm* bromide

**broncher** *vi* stumble (horse); shy; *coll* falter

**bronches** *nfpl* bronchial tubes

**bronchite** *nf* bronchitis

**broncho-pneumonie** *nf* bronchial pneumonia

**bronzer** *vt* + *vi* bronze; brown; tan; **se** ~ go brown

**broquette** *nf* tack, tin-tack
**brosse** *nf* brush; *sl* moustache; **cheveux (taillés) en ~** crew-cut; **coup de ~** brushing, brush-up
**brosser** *vt* brush, scrub; paint sketchily; *coll* go without, miss; *coll* beat up
**brou** *nm* husk; **~ de noix** walnut stain
**brouet** *nm* gruel
**brouette** *nf* wheelbarrow
**brouettée** *nf* barrowful
**brouhaha** *nm coll* hubbub, din
**brouillage** *nm rad* jamming
**brouillard** *nm* fog, mist, haze
**brouille** *nf* discord, falling out
**brouiller** *vt* mix up, confuse, entangle; *rad* jam; scramble (eggs); set at loggerheads; **se ~** become confused, grow dim; quarrel, fall out
**¹brouillon** *nm* rough copy
**²brouillon -onne** *adj* muddle-headed
**broussaille** *nf* brushwood, undergrowth; **cheveux en ~** tousled hair
**brousse** *nf* the bush (in Australia and other remote areas); *coll* the country
**brouter** *vt* browse, graze
**broyer** *vt* (7) crush, pound, pulverize; destroy; **~ du noir** be depressed
**bru** *nf* daughter-in-law
**brucelles** *nfpl* tweezers
**brugnon** *nm* nectarine
**bruine** *nf* drizzle
**bruiner** *vi* drizzle
**bruire** *vi* (20) rustle, murmur
**bruissement** *nm* rustling, rustle, murmur
**bruit** *nm* noise, sound; rumour, report; fuss
**brûlant** *adj* burning, scorching, boiling-hot
**brûle-gueule** *nm invar* short clay pipe
**brûle-pourpoint (à)** *adv phr* point-blank
**brûler** *vt* burn; scorch; dry up (sun); pass without stopping; *coll* crack (ring, gang); **~ du café** roast coffee; **~ le pavé** tear along; **être brûlé** be ruined, be done for; **odeur de brûlé** smell of burning; **se ~ la cervelle** blow one's brains out; **tête brûlée** dare-devil; *vi* burn, be on fire; get warm (in games); **~ d'envie** long to
**brûleur -euse** *n* burner; brandy distiller; *nm* gas-jet, burner
**brûlure** *nf* burn, scald
**brumaire** *nm hist* second month of the French Republican calendar (October to November)
**brume** *nf* thick fog, (sea-)mist; **~ artificielle** smoke-screen
**brumeux -euse** *adj* foggy, misty
**brun** *nm* brown; *adj* brown; **à la ~e** at dusk
**brunâtre** *adj* brownish

**brune** *nf* brunette
**brunir** *vt* brown, tan; burnish; *vi* turn brown, darken
**brusque** *adj* rough, abrupt; blunt; sudden; sharp (bend)
**brusquer** *vt* be sharp with; rush (business)
**brusquerie** *nf* abruptness, bluntness
**brut** *adj* rough, brute, raw; crude, unrefined, uncut (diamond); gross (weight, profit); **champagne ~** natural (very dry) champagne
**brutal** *adj* brutal, brutish, savage; rough
**brutaliser** *vt* ill-treat, use roughly, bully
**brutalité** *nf* brutality, savagery; roughness; act of cruelty
**brute** *nf* brute, beast; coarse or cruel person
**Bruxelles** *nf* Brussels
**bruyamment** *adv* noisily
**bruyant** *adj* noisy; loud, boisterous
**bruyère** *nf* heather; heathland; briar
**buanderie** *nf* wash-house
**bubonique** *adj* bubonic
**buccal** *adj* buccal; **par voie ~e** by the mouth, orally
**bûche** *nf* fire-log; **~ de Noël** log-shaped Christmas cake; *coll* dolt; **ramasser une ~** come a cropper
**¹bûcher** *nm* wood-shed; wood-pile; pyre
**²bûcher** *vt + vi* work hard (at), swot (up)
**bûcheron** *nm* woodcutter
**bucolique** *adj* bucolic, pastoral
**budgétaire** *adj* budgetary
**buée** *nf* steam, vapour, mist
**buffet** *nm* sideboard; buffet
**buffle** *nm* buffalo
**building** *nm* large building
**buis** *nm* box-tree, boxwood
**buisson** *nm* bush, thicket
**buissonnier -ière** *adj* that lives in the bushes; **faire l'école buissonnière** play truant
**bulbe** *nm bot + anat* bulb
**bulbeux -euse** *adj* bulbous
**bulle** *nf* bubble; blister; (papal) bull
**bulletin** *nm* bulletin, report (school, weather, etc); receipt, certificate; **~ de commande** order form; **~ de vote** voting paper
**buraliste** *n* clerk (in post-office or tax-office); tobacconist
**bure** *nf* homespun
**bureau** *nm* office; board; writing-desk; **~ de placement** employment agency; **~ de tabac** tobacconist's shop; **le deuxième ~** military intelligence
**bureaucrate** *n* bureaucrat
**bureaucratie** *nf* bureaucracy
**burette** *nf* cruet; oil-can
**burin** *nm* graver, graving-tool
**buriner** *vt* engrave (copperplate)

41

**burnous**

**burnous** *nm* Arab cloak, burnous
**buse** *nf* buzzard; *coll* dolt
**busqué** *adj* hooked (nose), aquiline
**buste** *nm* bust
**but** *nm* target, aim, objective; goal; purpose, design; **de ~ en blanc** point-blank, on the spur of the moment; **marquer un ~** score a goal
**buté** *adj* pig-headed, obstinate
**buter** *vt* prop up, support; *vi* strike, knock; stumble; **~ sur une difficulté** come up against a difficulty; **se ~** be

obstinately set on
**butin** *nm* booty, plunder; *coll* junk
**butiner** *vt* + *vi* gather honey (bees)
**butoir** *nm* buffer-stop
**butor** *nm* bittern; *coll* lout, coarse person
**butte** *nf* hillock, knoll; butts (shooting); **être en ~ à** be exposed to
**butter** *vt* earth up (plants)
**buvable** *adj* drinkable; *coll fig* bearable
**buvard** *nm* blotting-paper, blotting-pad
**buvette** *nf* refreshment room
**buveur -euse** *n* drinker, drunkard

# C

**ça** *pron abbr for* **cela**; *coll* **~ alors!** well I'll be damned!; **~ oui!** yes indeed!; *coll* **~ y est!** got it!; **comme ci comme ~** so-so
**çà** *adv* hither; **~ et là** here and there; **ah ~!** look here!
**cabale** *nf* cabal; intrigue; clique
**cabalistique** *adj* cabalistic
**cabane** *nf* hut, cabin, shanty; hutch (rabbits); *sl* prison, jug
**cabanon** *nm* little hut; tiny house in the country (particularly Provence); padded cell
**cabaret** *nm* tavern, little restaurant; night-club
**cabas** *nm* basket, bag
**cabestan** *nm* capstan, windlass
**cabillaud** *nm* fresh cod
**cabine** *nf* cabin; call-box (telephone); cab (locomotive)
**cabinet** *nm* small room, closet; **~ de toilette** dressing-room, lavatory; **~ de travail** study; consulting-room (doctor); cabinet
**câble** *nm* cable, line, rope; cablegram
**câbler** *vt* cable; twist into a cable
**caboche** *nf sl* head; hobnail
**cabosse** *nf coll* dent, bruise, bump
**cabosser** *vt* dent, bruise, bump
**cabot** *nm coll* dog; bull-head (fish); *sl* corporal
**cabotage** *nm* coasting trade
**cabotin -e** *n* strolling player; *coll* ham actor
**caboulot** *nm* low café, cheap bar
**cabrer (se)** *v refl* rear (horse)

**cabri** *nm* kid (goat)
**cabriole** *nf* caper, leap
**cabriolet** *nm* cabriolet; convertible (car)
**caca** *nm coll* excrement
**cacahouète, cacahuète** *nf* peanut
**cacao** *nm* cocoa
**cacatoès** *nm* cockatoo
**cachalot** *nm* sperm whale
**cache** *nf* hiding-place; cache
**cache-cache** *nm* hide-and-seek
**cache-col** *nm* scarf
**cachemire** *nm* cashmere
**cache-nez** *nm invar* muffler
**cache-pot** *nm* flower-pot case, pot-holder
**cacher** *vt* hide, conceal, keep hidden; **se ~** hide, shun; **je ne m'en cache pas** I make no secret of it
**cache-sexe** *nm* G-string, briefs
**cachet** *nm* seal, stamp, signet; mark, sign; fee (artiste); *med* tablet; **avoir du ~** look distinguished, have character; **lettre de ~** sealed royal order
**cacheter** *vt* (5) seal; **vin cacheté** vintage wine
**cachette** *nf* hiding-place; **en ~** in secret
**cachot** *nm* cell, dungeon; *coll* prison
**cachotterie** *nf* secrecy over trifling matters
**cachottier -ière** *adj* close, secretive
**cacophonie** *nf* cacophony
**cadastre** *nm* cadastral survey
**cadavérique** *adj* cadaverous
**cadavre** *nm* corpse, dead body; carcase; *coll* emptied bottle, 'dead man'
**caddy** *nm* trolley (supermarket)

42

**cadeau** *nm* present, gift

**cadenas** *nm* padlock

**cadenasser** *vt* padlock

**cadence** *nf* rhythm, cadence; **en ~** rhythmically

**cadencé** *adj* rhythmical, measured

**cadencer** *vt* impart rhythm to

**cadet -ette** *n+adj* younger (child), junior; cadet; young player; **le ~ de mes soucis** the least of my worries

**cadran** *nm* dial

**cadre** *nm* frame, framework; border; surroundings; senior rank, senior member of staff

**cadrer** *vi* tally, square with, fit

**caduc -uque** *adj* decrepit, decaying; deciduous; null and void, lapsed

¹**cafard** *nm* cockroach; *coll* **avoir le ~** be fed up

²**cafard** *adj* hypocritical, sanctimonious

**cafarder** *vi* sneak, tell tales

**café** *nm* coffee; café; **~ arrosé** laced coffee; **~ complet** coffee and hot milk with rolls and butter; **~ crème** white coffee; **~ nature (noir)** black coffee; *adj invar* coffee-coloured

**cafetier -ière** *n* café-owner; *nf* coffee-pot

**cafouiller** *vi coll* get into a mess; miss (engine)

**cage** *nf* cage, coop; well (staircase); shaft (lift); **~ thoracique** thorax

**cagneux -euse** *adj* knock-kneed

**cagnotte** *nf* kitty, pool

**cagot -e** *n+adj* hypocritical (person)

**cagoule** *nf* cowl

**cahier** *nm* exercise-book

**cahin-caha** *adv* so-so, middling

**cahot** *nm* jolt (vehicle)

**cahoter** *vt+vi* jolt, bump, shake

**cahoteux -euse** *adj* bumpy (road), rough

**cahute** *nf* hut, hovel

**caïd** *nm* Arab leader; *sl* boss, gang-leader; *sl* super chap, ace

**caille** *nf* quail

**caillé** *nm* curdled milk, curds

**cailler** *vt+vi* curdle

**caillot** *nm* clot (blood)

**caillou** *nm* pebble

**caillouter** *vt* pave with pebbles

**caillouteux -euse** *adj* pebbly, stony, shingly

**caïman** *nm* alligator, cayman

**Caire (le)** *nm* Cairo

**caisse** *nf* case, packing-case, chest; cash-box, till, cashier's desk; fund; body (vehicle); drum; **~ d'épargne** savings bank; **grosse ~** bass drum

**caissier -ière** *n* cashier

**caisson** *nm* large box; locker; *eng* coffer-dam

**cajoler** *vt* coax, cajole

**cajolerie** *nf* coaxing, wheedling

**cake** *nm* fruit-cake

**calamine** *nf* calamine; carbon (deposit in cylinders)

**calamité** *nf* calamity

**calamiteux -euse** *adj* calamitous

**calandre** *nf* mangle, roller (paper, materials); (car-)radiator grille

**calcaire** *adj* chalky, calcareous

**calcéolaire** *nf bot* calceolaria

**calciner** *vt* burn to ashes

**calcul** *nm* reckoning, arithmetic; calculation, plan; *med* stone

**calculateur -trice** *n* computer, reckoner, calculator; *adj* wily

**calculé** *adj* premeditated, intentional, deliberate

**calculer** *vt* calculate, reckon up, compute

**cale** *nf* hold (ship); wedge, chock; **~ sèche** dry dock; **être à fond de ~** be down and out

**calé** *adj coll* knowledgeable, well up

**calèche** *nf* light open four-wheeled carriage

**caleçon** *nm* men's pants; **~ de bain** bathing trunks

**calembour** *nm* pun

**calendes** *nfpl* Kalends; **renvoyer aux ~ grecques** put off indefinitely

**calendrier** *nm* calendar

**calepin** *nm* notebook

**caler** *vt* wedge, scotch, clamp, prop up; *vt+vi* stall (engine); *vi sl* give way, funk

**calfeutrer** *vt* plug, stop up, pad (against draughts); **se ~** make oneself nice and warm

**calibre** *nm* calibre, bore, size; gauge; quality (character)

**calibrer** *vt* gauge, calibrate

**calice** *nm* chalice; *bot* calyx; **boire le ~ jusqu'à la lie** put up with every humiliation

**calicot** *nm* calico; *coll* assistant in draper's shop

**calife** *nm* caliph

**califourchon (à)** *adv phr* astride

**câlin** *adj* coaxing, wheedling, caressing

**calleux -euse** *adj* horny (hands), hard

**calligraphie** *nf* calligraphy, penmanship

**callosité** *nf* callosity, hardness (skin)

**calmant** *nm* sedative, tranquillizer; *adj* soothing

**calme** *nm* calm, stillness, calmness; *adj* calm, quiet, still; unruffled (manner)

**calmer** *vt* calm, still, allay, soothe; **se ~** calm down; die down, abate

**calomniateur -trice** *n* calumniator, slanderer; *adj* slanderous

**calomnie** *nf* calumny, slander

**calomnier** *vt* calumniate, slander

43

**calorifère** nm (slow-burning) stove, heating installation; adj heat-conveying

**calorifuge** adj non-conducting, insulating; heat-proof

**calot** nm forage-cap

**calotte** nf skull-cap; crown (hat); priesthood; coll box on the ears; canopy (heavens)

**calque** nm tracing; slavish imitation

**calquer** vt trace; copy closely

**calvados** nm apple-brandy

**calvaire** nm Calvary; stations of the Cross; moral suffering

**calviniste** n + adj calvinist

**calvitie** nf baldness

**camarade** n comrade, companion, friend, chum

**camaraderie** nf comradeship, friendship; clan, set

**camard** adj flat-nosed; **la Camarde** Death

**cambouis** nm dirty grease or oil (from engine)

**cambrer** vt arch, bend, camber; se ~ throw out one's chest, draw oneself up to full height

**cambriolage** nm housebreaking, burgling, burglary

**cambrioler** vt burgle, break into

**cambrioleur -euse** n housebreaker, burglar

**cambrure** nf camber, arching, arch (foot)

**cambuse** nf naut steward's room; sl dump

**came** nf cam; sl dope (esp cocaine); **arbre à** ~ **s** camshaft

**camée** nm cameo

**camélia** nm camellia

**camelot** nm street-hawker; news-vendor

**camelote** nf sl junk, shoddy piece of work

**camembert** nm Camembert cheese

**caméra** nf ciné-camera

**camion** nm lorry, wagon; US truck

**camionnette** nf van

**camionneur** nm haulier, carrier

**camisole** nf camisole; ~ **de force** strait-jacket

**camomille** nf camomile

**camoufler** vt camouflage; disguise

**camouflet** nm coll insult, snub

**camp** nm camp; side, party; sl **ficher (foutre) le** ~ clear off (out)

**campagnard -e** n countryman (woman); adj of the country, rustic

**campagne** nf countryside, open country; campaign; **battre la** ~ scour the countryside; be delirious; **en pleine** ~ right out in the open country; **faire une** ~ take part in a campaign; **partie de** ~ picnic, country outing; coll **se**

**mettre en** ~ get down to work

**campanule** nf bot bellflower

**campé** adj bien ~ well set-up

**camper** vi camp; put up; coll put; coll **se** ~ plant oneself

**camphre** nm camphor

**camus** adj snub-nosed, pug-nosed

**Canadien -ienne** n Canadian

**canadien -ienne** adj Canadian

**canadienne** nf fur-lined (man's) jacket; estate car

**canaille** nf rabble, riff-raff; scoundrel; adj rascally

**canal** nm canal; channel; duct; means

**canalisation** nf canalization; mains, pipes; wiring

**canaliser** vt canalize; lay down mains

**canapé** nm couch, sofa; cul canapé

**canard** nm (male) duck; coll false piece of news; coll newspaper, rag; coll lump of sugar dipped in liqueur or coffee; mus false note; **froid de** ~ biting cold

**canari** nm canary

**canasson** nm sl nag (horse)

**cancan** nm coll tittle-tattle, piece of scandal; cancan

**cancaner** vi coll talk scandal

**cancanier -ière** adj coll fond of spreading scandal

**cancéreux -euse** n cancer patient; adj cancerous

**cancérigène** adj carcinogenic

**cancre** nm crab; coll dunce

**candélabre** nm branched candelabra; lamp-post (with branches)

**candeur** nf artlessness, ingenuousness

**candi** adj m candied; **sucre** ~ sugar candy

**candidat -e** n applicant, candidate

**candidature** nf candidature; **poser sa** ~ apply (for post)

**candide** adj artless, ingenuous

**cane** nf (female) duck

**caner** vi sl funk

**caneton** nm duckling

**can(n)ette** nf (beer) bottle

**canevas** nm canvas; outline, sketch

**caniche** nf poodle

**caniculaire** adj sultry

**canicule** nf dog-days; heatwave

**canif** nm penknife

**canin** adj canine

**canine** nf canine tooth

**caniveau** nm gutter; conduit

**canne** nf cane, reed; walking stick; ~ **à pêche** fishing rod; ~ **à sucre** sugar cane

**canneler** vt (5) flute; corrugate

**cannelle** nf cinnamon

**canner** vt cane (chair)

**cannette** nf see can(n)ette

**cannibale** n cannibal

**canoë** *nm* canoe

**canon** *nm* cannon; barrel (rifle); glass of wine; *eccles* canon; *mus* canon, round

**canonique** *adj* canonical; *coll* respectable (age)

**canoniser** *vt* canonize

**canonnade** *nf* cannonade

**canonnière** *nf* gun-slit; gun-boat ·

**canot** *nm* dinghy, boat; ~ **de sauvetage** lifeboat

**canotage** *nm* boating, rowing

**canotier** *nm* straw-hat; oarsman

**cantate** *nf* cantata

**cantatrice** *nf* (professional) singer

**cantine** *nf* canteen

**cantique** *nm* hymn, canticle; **Cantique des ~ s** Song of Songs

**canton** *nm* district; canton

**cantonade** *nf theat* wings; **parler à la ~** speak to s/o off-stage

**cantonnement** *nm* billeting, cantonment

**cantonner** *vt* billet; confine; **se ~** shut oneself up, isolate oneself

**cantonnier** *nm* roadmender; platelayer

**canule** *nf* nozzle (syringe); *sl* bore

**canuler** *vt sl* bore

**caoutchouc** *nm* rubber; *pl* galoshes

**caoutchouter** *vt* treat or coat with rubber

**cap** *nm* cape, headland; head (ship); **de pied en ~** from head to foot; **doubler un ~** round a cape; **mettre le ~ sur** set course for

**capable** *adj* capable; able

**capacité** *nf* capacity; ability, competence

**caparaçonner** *vt* caparison

**cape** *nf* cape, cloak; **rire sous ~** laugh up one's sleeve

**capillaire** *adj* capillary

**capitaine** *nm* captain, master (ship), leader

**capital** *nm* capital, assets; *adj* capital, principal, chief; deadly (sin)

**capitale** *nf* chief town, capital

**capitaliser** *vt* capitalize

**capitalisme** *nm* capitalism

**capitaliste** *n* capitalist

**capiteux -euse** *adj* heady

**capitonner** *vt* pad, upholster

**capitulation** *nf* surrender, capitulation

**capituler** *vi* surrender, capitulate

**caporal** *nm* corporal; cheap tobacco

**capot** *nm* hood, casing; *mot* bonnet, *US* hood; hatch

**capote** *nf* hooded cloak; great-coat; hood (car); cowl (chimney); *sl* ~ **anglaise** French letter

**capoter** *vi* turn turtle, capsize, overturn

**câpre** *nf bot* caper

**caprice** *nm* caprice, whim

**capricieux -ieuse** *adj* capricious, whim-sical

**capsule** *nf* capsule; bottle-top

**capter** *vt* obtain (cunningly); pick up (radio programme, message); catch (water)

**captieux -ieuse** *adj* specious, fallacious

**captif -ive** *n + adj* captive, prisoner

**captivant** *adj* captivating, fascinating

**captiver** *vt* captivate, charm

**captivité** *nf* captivity

**capture** *nf* capture, seizure, prize

**capturer** *vt* capture (ship), catch (large animal)

**capuchon** *nm* hood, cowl, cap (fountain-pen)

**capucin** *nm* Capuchin friar

**capucine** *nf* nasturtium; Capuchin nun

**caque** *nf* keg, barrel (herrings); **la ~ sent toujours le hareng** what's bred in the bone will out in the flesh

**caquet** *nm* cackling, cackle, chatter; **rabattre le ~ à qn** shut s/o up

**caqueter** *vi* (5) cackle; chatter, gossip

¹**car** *nm* (motor-)coach; ~ **de police** police van

²**car** *conj* for, because

**carabine** *nf* carbine, rifle

**carabiné** *adj coll* violent, strong; **rhume ~** stinking cold

**caraco** *nm* working jacket (woman)

**caractère** *nm* character, nature, disposition; characteristic; handwriting

**caractériser** *vt* characterize; **se ~** be distinguished

**caractéristique** *nf* characteristic, trait; *adj* characteristic, typical

**carafe** *nf* carafe, decanter

**carafon** *nm* small carafe

**carambolage** *nm* cannon (billiards); collision

**caramel** *nm* caramel, burnt sugar; toffee

**carapace** *nf* carapace, shell (crab, etc)

**caravane** *nf* caravan

**caravansérail** *nm* caravanserai

**caravelle** *nf* caravel

**carbone** *nm* carbon

**carbonique** *adj* carbonic

**carboniser** *vt* carbonize, burn to a cinder

**carburant** *nm* motor-fuel

**carbure** *nm* carbide

**carcan** *nm* iron collar, pillory; *sl* jade (horse)

**carcasse** *nf* carcass; framework; *coll* body

**carcinome** *nm* carcinoma

**carde** *nf bot* chard

**carder** *vt* card (wool)

**cardiaque** *nm* heart-case; *adj* cardiac

**cardon** *nm bot* cardoon

**carême** *nm* Lent; **faire (son) ~** fast, observe Lent

**carénage** *nm* streamlining; careening (ship)

**carence** *nf* insolvency; *med* deficiency; shortcoming, default

**carène** *nf* hull (ship)

**caresse** *nf* caress, pat

**caresser** *vt* caress, stroke, fondle; cherish (a hope)

**cargaison** *nf* cargo, load, freight

**cargo** *nm* cargo-boat

**carie** *nf* decay (teeth); blight (trees)

**carier** *vt* decay, rot; **se ~** decay, rot

**carillon** *nm* carillon, chimes

**carillonner** *vt* announce by ringing; **~ de bal** dance *fig* broadcast; *vi* ring the bells, chime; jingle

**carlingue** *nf naut* ke(e)lson; cockpit, cabin

**carmagnole** *nf* carmagnole; short jacket (worn by 1789 Revolutionaries)

**carmélite** *nf* Carmelite nun

**carmin** *nm* carmine

**carnage** *nm* carnage, slaughter

**carnassier -ière** *adj* carnivorous (animals)

**carnassière** *nf* game-bag

**carnet** *nm* notebook; **~ de bal** dance card; **~ de chèques** cheque-book; **~ de tickets** book of tickets (bus, métro)

**carnier** *nm* game-bag

**carnivore** *adj* carnivorous

**carotte** *nf* carrot; plug (tobacco); *coll* trick; **poil de ~** ginger (hair)

**carotter** *vt coll* wangle; **~ qch à qn** diddle s/o out of sth

**carpe** *nf* carp; **muet comme une ~** dumb as an oyster

**carpette** *nf* rug

**carquois** *nm* quiver

**carré** *nm* square; landing (staircase); *naut* mess-room; bed, patch (garden); four similar cards in one hand; *adj* square, frank, plain; **partie ~e** party of two men and two women

**carreau** *nm* small square, check; tile (floor), floor; window-pane; diamond (cards); *sl* monocle; **~ des Halles** fruit and vegetable section of the Halles; *coll* **rester sur le ~** be left dead

**carrefour** *nm* crossroads; intersection

**carrelage** *nm* tile floor; tiling

**carreler** *vt* (5) lay tiles, pave with tiles

**carrelet** *nm* plaice; square fishing net

**carrément** *adv* frankly, bluntly; squarely

**carrer** *vt* square; **se ~** make oneself comfortable

**¹carrière** *nf* career, profession; scope; **donner (libre) ~ à son imagination** give free rein to one's imagination

**²carrière** *nf* quarry

**carriole** *nf* light cart; ramshackle car

**carrossable** *adj* suitable for vehicles (road)

**carrosse** *nm* carriage, coach; **rouler ~** own a carriage, be well off

**carrosser** *vt* fit coach-work to, put the body on (car)

**carrosserie** *nf* coach-work, body (car); car-body manufacture, coach-building

**carrossier** *nm* coach-builder, car-body builder

**carrousel** *nm* roundabout; tournament

**carrure** *nf* breadth (shoulders, chest)

**cartable** *nm* satchel

**carte** *nf* card; map; playing-card; bill of fare; **~ d'entrée** ticket of admission; **~ grise** car licence; **battre les ~s** shuffle the cards; **brouiller les ~s** embroil matters; **connaître le dessous des ~s** be in the know; **donner ~ blanche à qn** give s/o a free hand; **tirer les ~s** tell fortunes

**carte-lettre** *nf* ( *pl* **cartes-lettres**) letter-card

**carter** *nm* crank-case, gear-case; **fond de ~** sump

**cartographe** *n* map-maker

**cartomancien -ienne** *n* fortune-teller (by means of cards)

**carton** *nm* cardboard; cardboard box, carton; target (shooting-range)

**cartonner** *vt* bind in boards, case

**cartonnier** *nm* file, file-case

**carton-pâte** *nm* papier-mâché

**¹cartouche** *nf* cartridge; cartridge-shaped packing, packet

**²cartouche** *nm* scroll (round title, etc)

**cartouchière** *nf* cartridge pouch

**cas** *nm* case, instance, matter; **au (dans le) ~ où** in case; **dans le ~ de** in a position to; **en tout ~** in any case; **le ~ échéant** should the occasion arise; **faire ~ de** value

**casanier -ière** *adj* stay-at-home

**casaque** *nf obs* coat, jacket; **tourner ~** be a turn-coat

**cascade** *nf* waterfall, cascade

**cascadeur** *nm* stunt-man

**case** *nf* hut, cabin; compartment (drawer); space (on form); square (chess-board)

**caser** *vt* put away, put in order; find a job for, settle (one's daughter); **se ~** settle down

**caserne** *nf* barracks

**casier** *nm* set of pigeon-holes; rack; **~ judiciaire** criminal record

**casque** *nm* helmet; head-phones

**casquer** *vi sl* fork out, pay up

**casquette** *nf* peaked cap

**cassant** *adj* brittle, crisp; abrupt (tone)

**cassation** *nf* quashing; reduction to the ranks; **Cour de ~** Supreme Court of Appeal

**casse** *nf* breakage; **il va y avoir de la ~** there's going to be trouble; *coll* **payer la ~** pay for the damage

**cassé** *adj* broken, worn out

**casse-cou** *nm invar* death-trap; *n* daredevil

**casse-croûte** *nm invar* snack, light meal

**casse-noisettes** *nm* nutcracker

**casse-pieds** *nm coll* bore, pain in the neck

**casser** *vt* break, snap; quash; reduce to the ranks; **~ la tête à qn** deafen s/o; importune s/o; **~ les pieds à qn** get on s/o's nerves; **à tout ~** violently; *sl* **ça ne casse rien** it's not up to much; **se ~ la tête** rack one's brains; **se ~ le nez** find the door closed; fail; *vi* break; **se ~ crack up** (person)

**casserole** *nf* saucepan; *sl* informer, squealer

**casse-tête** *nm invar* club, cosh; task fraught with problems; din

**cassette** *nf* casket; cassette

**casseur** *nm* breaker, smasher; vandal (demonstration, etc)

**¹cassis** *nm* blackcurrant; blackcurrant liqueur

**²cassis** *nm* cross-drain

**cassonade** *nf* brown sugar

**cassure** *nf* break, fracture

**castel** *nm* castle (in S. France)

**castor** *nm* beaver

**¹casuel** *nm* fees

**²casuel -uelle** *adj* accidental, fortuitous

**casuiste** *nm* casuist

**casuistique** *nf* casuistry

**cataclysme** *nm* disaster, cataclysm

**catacombes** *nfpl* catacombs

**catalan** *adj* Catalan, Catalonian

**catalogue** *nm* catalogue, list

**catalyse** *nf* catalysis

**cataplasme** *nm* poultice

**cataracte** *nf* cataract, falls; *med* cataract

**catarrhe** *nm* catarrh

**catastrophe** *nf* catastrophe, disaster

**catastropher** *vt coll* astound; depress

**catéchiser** *vt* catechize; lecture, try to persuade

**catéchisme** *nm* catechism

**catégorie** *nf* category

**catégorique** *adj* categorical; explicit

**cathédrale** *nf* cathedral

**Catherine** *nf* **coiffer Sainte ~** reach one's twenty-fifth birthday without marrying

**catherinette** *nf coll* unmarried girl who celebrates her twenty-fifth birthday

**cathode** *nm elect* cathode

**catholicisme** *nm* Roman Catholicism

**catholique** *n* Catholic; *adj* Roman Catholic; *coll* normal, orthodox

**catimini (en)** *adv phr* stealthily

**catin** *nf coll* whore, tart

**cauchemar** *nm* nightmare

**causant** *adj* talkative, chatty

**cause** *nf* cause, reason; action, suit; **à ~ de** because of; **avoir gain de ~** win, get the better of an argument; **en connaissance de ~** with full knowledge; **en tout état de ~** in any case; **et pour ~** and for a very good reason; **hors de ~** irrelevant; **mettre en ~** implicate

**¹causer** *vt* cause

**²causer** *vi* chat, talk; say too much

**causerie** *nf* talk, chat

**causette** *nf* little chat

**causeur -euse** *n* talker; *nf* small settee; *adj* talkative, chatty

**caustique** *adj* caustic; biting, cutting

**cauteleux -euse** *adj pej* cunning, sly

**cautériser** *vt* cauterize

**caution** *nf* security, guarantee, surety; **en liberté sous ~** out on bail; **se porter ~ pour qn** go bail for someone; **sujet à ~** unconfirmed, suspect

**cautionnement** *nm* security, cautionmoney

**cautionner** *vt* go bail for

**cavalcade** *nf* cavalcade, procession

**cavaler** *vt sl* bore; *sl* **se ~** run, hop it

**cavalerie** *nf* cavalry

**¹cavalier** *nm* horseman, rider; cavalier; escort, dancing-partner; knight (chess); **~ seul** lone wolf

**²cavalier -ière** *adj* cavalier, off-hand

**cavalière** *nf* horsewoman; dancingpartner

**¹cave** *nf* cellar

**²cave** *nf* stake (cards); *nm sl* dupe

**³cave** *adj* hollow, sunken

**caveau** *nm* little cellar, vault; burial vault

**caver** *vt* hollow out, excavate

**caverne** *nf* cave, cavern, den

**caverneux -euse** *adj* cavernous, hollow, sepulchral

**caviar** *nm* caviare

**cavité** *nf* cavity, hollow

**¹ce, c'** *dem pron* (used mainly with **être**) it, this, that; **~ faisant** doing which; **~ que** what, that which; **~ que vous voulez** what you like; *coll* **~ qu'il peut être embêtant!** what a nuisance he can be!; **~ sont eux** it is they; **c'est ici** this is; **c'est là** that is; **pour ~ faire** in order to do this; **sur ~** thereupon; **tout ~ qu'il voudra** everything he wants

**²ce, cet** (*f* **cette**, *pl* **ces**) *dem adj* this, that, these, those; **~ garçon-ci** this boy; **~ garçon-là** that boy

**céans** *adv* in here; **le maître de ~** the master of this place

**ceci** *dem pron* this

**cécité** *nf* blindness

**céder** *vt* (6) give up, surrender, make over; **le ~ à qn** be inferior to s/o; *vi* yield, give way

**cédille** *nf* cedilla

**cèdre** *nm* cedar

**cégétiste** *n + adj* (member) of C.G.T. (French trade union)

**ceindre** *vt* (55) gird, encircle, encompass

**ceinture** *nf* belt, girdle, sash; circle (railway or bus); **~ de sauvetage** lifebelt

**ceinturer** *vt* girdle; tackle

**ceinturon** *nm* mil belt

**cela (ça)** *dem pron* that; **c'est ~** that's right; **comment ~?** how so?; **et avec ~, Madame?** anything else, madam?; **sans ~** but for that

**célèbre** *adj* famous, celebrated

**célébrer** *vt* (6) celebrate, solemnize

**célébrité** *nf* fame, celebrity

**celer** *vt* (5) conceal, hide, keep secret

**céleri** *nm* celery

**célérité** *nf* speed, swiftness, dispatch

**céleste** *adj* celestial, heavenly

**célibat** *nm* celibacy

**célibataire** *n* bachelor, bachelor-girl, spinster; *adj* single, unmarried

**celle** *pron* see **celui**

**cellier** *nm* store-room (wine, provisions)

**cellulaire** *adj* cellular; **voiture ~** prison van, Black Maria

**cellule** *nf* cell

**cellulite** *nf* cellulitis

**Celte** *n* Celt

**celte** *adj* Celtic

**celtique** *adj* Celtic

**celui** (*f* **celle**, *pl* **ceux, celles**) *pron* the one(s); he, she, it, they; **~-ci** this one; the latter; **~-là** that one; the former

**cénacle** *nm* coterie, group

**cendre** *nf* ash, ashes, cinders

**cendré** *adj* ash-coloured, ash-grey

**cendrer** *vt* colour ash-grey; cinder

**cendreux -euse** *adj* ashy; full of ashes, gritty

**cendrier** *nm* ash-tray; ash-pan; *eng* ash-pit

**cène** *nf* **la Sainte Cène** the Last Supper; Holy Communion (in Protestant Church)

**cénotaphe** *nm* cenotaph

**censé** *adj* supposed

**censément** *adv* supposedly; practically

**censeur** *nm* censor; critic; vice-principal (in charge of school discipline)

**censure** *nf* censorship; blame

**censurer** *vt* censor; censure, find fault with

**cent** *nm* a hundred; **pour ~** per cent; *adj* a hundred; **être aux ~ coups** be in despair; **faire les ~ pas** walk up and down; **faire les quatre ~s coups** kick

up a shindy

**centaine** *nf* about a hundred

**centenaire** *nm* centenary, centenarian; *adj* a hundred years old

**centennal** *adj* centennial

**centième** *nm + adj* hundredth

**centimètre** *nm* centimetre; tape-measure

**central ~ téléphonique** telephone exchange; *adj* central; **maison ~e** prison

**centrale** *nf* elect power-station

**centralisation** *nf* centralization

**centraliser** *vt* centralize

**centre** *nm* centre, middle; centre party

**centrer** *vt* centre

**centrifuge** *adj* centrifugal

**centripète** *adj* centripetal

**centuple** *nm + adj* centuple, hundredfold

**cep** *nm* vine-plant

**cépage** *nm* vine-plant

**cèpe** *nm* kind of mushroom

**cependant** *adv* meanwhile; *conj* yet, however, nevertheless

**céramique** *nf* ceramics, pottery; *adj* ceramic

**cerceau** *nm* hoop

**cercle** *nm* circle, ring, hoop; club

**cercler** *vt* ring, encircle, hoop

**cercueil** *nm* coffin

**céréale** *nf + adj* cereal

**cérémonie** *nf* ceremony; **faire des ~s** be excessively polite

**cérémonieux -ieuse** *adj* ceremonious

**cerf** *nm* stag

**cerfeuil** *nm* chervil

**cerf-volant** *nm* (*pl* **cerfs-volants**) kite (toy); stag-beetle

**cerisaie** *nf* cherry-orchard

**cerise** *nf* cherry; *adj invar* cherry-coloured

**cerne** *nm* ring, circle (under eyes)

**cerner** *vt* surround (town), encircle (army); shell (nuts); **avoir les yeux cernés** have rings under the eyes

**certain** *adj* certain, sure; fixed; **~s** *adj + pron* some, certain (people)

**certes** *adv* indeed, to be sure

**certificat** *nm* certificate, testimonial; **~ d'aptitude professionnelle (C.A.P.)** trade qualification or certificate

**certification** *nf* certification, authentication

**certifier** *vt* certify, vouch for

**certitude** *nf* certainty

**céruse** *nf* white lead

**cerveau** *nm* brain; mind, intelligence; **rhume de ~** cold in the head

**cervelas** *nm* saveloy

**cervelet** *nm* cerebellum

**cervelle** *nf* brains (brain-matter); **se brûler la ~** blow out one's brains; **se creuser la ~** rack one's brains

ces *dem pron see* ce

cessation *nf* cessation, ceasing, stopping

cesse *nf* ceasing; sans ~ unceasingly

cesser *vt + vi* stop, cease, leave off; faire ~ qch put a stop to sth

cessez-le-feu *nm invar* cease-fire

cessible *adj* transferable, assignable

cession *nf* transfer, assignment

c'est-à-dire *conj phr* that is to say

césure *nf* caesura

cet *dem pron see* ce

cette *dem pron see* ce

ceux *pron see* celui

chabot *nm* chub

chacal *nm* (*pl* ~s) jackal

chacun *pron* each (one), every one; everybody

chafouin -e *n + adj* sly-looking (person)

chagrin *nm* grief, sorrow, affliction; annoyance; shagreen; *adj* sad, distressed; fretful

chagriner *vt* distress, grieve; vex

chah *nm* Shah

chahut *nm coll* din, noise, shindy; rag

chahutage *nm coll* rowdyism, ragging

chahuter *vt coll* rag (teacher); *vi* make a row

chahuteur -euse *n + adj coll* rowdy

chaîne *nf* chain; range (mountains); channel, network (radio and TV); travail à la ~ work on conveyor belt

chaînette *nf* small chain

chaînon *nm* link (chain)

chair *nf* flesh; meat; ~ à canon cannon-fodder; *coll* ~ de poule goose-flesh; bien en ~ nice and plump; en ~ et en os in the flesh

chaire *nf* chair, throne; pulpit; rostrum; professorship

chaise *nf* chair, seat; ~ de chœur choir stall (church); ~ longue deck-chair; settee; ~ percée night-commode; ~ roulante bath chair

chaisier -ière *n* chair-attendant (park, church)

chaland *nm* lighter, barge

châle *nm* shawl

chalet *nm* chalet; ~ de nécessité public convenience

chaleur *nf* heat, warmth; ardour; craint la ~ keep in a cool place

chaleureux -euse *adj* warm; ardent; cordial

chaloupe *nf* launch

chalumeau *nm* straw; *mus* pipe; blow-pipe

chalut *nm* drag-net, trawl

chalutier *nm* trawler

chamailler (se) *v refl coll* squabble, bicker

chamarrer *vt* bedeck, trim (with lace)

chambard *nm sl* row, upheaval, shindy

chambarder *vt* upset, turn upside down

chambellan *nm* chamberlain

chambouler *vt sl* turn topsy-turvy

chambranle *nm* frame (door, window); mantelpiece

chambre *nf* (bed-)room, chamber; house (government); ~ à air inner tube; Chambre des Députés Chamber of Deputies; garder la ~ be confined to one's room (through illness)

chambrée *nf* roomful (of people); barrack-room

chambrer *vt* bring up to room temperature

chambrette *nf* little room

chambrière *nf* long whip; prop (cart); *obs* chambermaid

chameau *nm* camel; *sl* swine (of man), scoundrel

chamelier *nm* camel-driver

chamois *nm* chamois; peau de ~ shammy-leather

champ *nm* field; scope, range, extent; ~ de courses race-course; ~ de foire fair-ground; à tout bout de ~ at every turn; à travers ~s across country; le ~ est libre the coast is clear; prendre la clef des ~s abscond, clear off; sur le ~ immediately

Champagne *nf* Champagne; (vin de) ~ *nm* champagne (wine); fine ~ brandy

champenois *adj* from Champagne, of Champagne

champêtre *adj* rural, country, rustic; garde ~ kind of village policeman

champignon *nm* mushroom; (milliner's) hatstand; *sl* accelerator (pedal)

champion -ionne *n* champion

championnat *nm* championship

chançard *adj coll* lucky

chance *nf* chance; luck, fortune; ~s likelihood, probability; avoir de la ~ be lucky

chanceler *vi* (5) totter, stagger; santé chancelante precarious health

chancelier *nm* chancellor

chancelière *nf* foot-muff

chancellerie *nf* chancellery; secretaryship of a legation

chanceux -euse *adj coll* lucky; risky, chancy

chancir *vi* (4) go mouldy

chancre *nm* canker; ulcer

chandail *nm* sweater, jumper

Chandeleur (la) *nf* Candlemas

chandelier *nm* candlestick

chandelle *nf* (tallow) candle; support (construction); *coll* drop (on the end of s/o's nose); devoir une fière (belle) ~ à qn owe a great deal to s/o; *coll* économies de bouts de ~ cheeseparing economies; le jeu n'en vaut pas la ~

the game is not worth the candle; **voir trente-six ~ s** see stars

**chanfreiner** *vt* chamfer, bevel

**change** *nm* exchange; **bureau de ~** foreign exchange office; **cours du ~** rate of exchange; **donner le ~ à qn** take s/o in; **lettre de ~** bill of exchange

**changeable** *adj* changeable; exchangeable

**changeant** *adj* changing, changeable, fickle

**changement** *nm* change, alteration; **~ de vitesse** gear change

**changer** *vt* (3) change, exchange, alter, modify; *coll* **ça me changera** it will be a change for me; *coll* **change de disque** give it a rest; *vi* change; **~ d'avis** change one's mind; **se ~** change one's clothes; change

**changeur** *nm* money-changer

**chanoine** *nm eccles* canon

**chanson** *nf* song; **~ à boire** drinking-song; **~ s!** nonsense!; **c'est toujours la même ~** it's the same old story

**chansonnette** *nf* ditty, popular song

**chansonnier -ière** *n* writer of satirical songs

**chant** *nm* song, singing; crowing (cock); canto

**chantage** *nm* blackmail

**chantant** *adj* sing-song; tuneful

**chantepleure** *nf* wine-funnel; tap; spout

**chanter** *vt* + *vi* sing; crow (cock); **~ la gloire** sing the praises; **faire ~** blackmail; **qu'est-ce que vous me chantez?** what's this tale you're telling me?; **si ça vous chante** if this appeals to you

**chanterelle** *nf* kind of mushroom

**chanteur -euse** *n* singer; blackmailer

**chantier** *nm* yard (timber, building, shipping); site (building, road-works); stand (barrels); **fin de ~** road clear

**chantonner** *vt* + *vi* sing softly, hum

**chantre** *nm* bard, singer

**chanvre** *nm* hemp

**chaos** *nm* chaos, disorder; mass (rocks)

**chaotique** *adj* chaotic, confused

**chaparder** *vt sl* pinch, pilfer, steal

**chape** *nf eccles* cope; covering; tread (tyre)

**chapeau** *nm* hat; cap; cowl (chimney); short introduction; **~ de roue** hub-cap; **~ haut de forme** top-hat; **~ melon** bowler-hat; **~ mou** felt hat; **donner un coup de ~** raise one's hat; **(je lui tire mon) ~!** I take my hat off to him

**chapelet** *nm* rosary; string (onions, insults); stick (bombs); **dire (égrener) son ~** tell one's beads

**chapelier** *nm* hatter

**chapelle** *nf* chapel

**chapelure** *nf cul* dried bread-crumbs

**chaperon** *nm* hood; chaperon; coping (wall); **le petit ~ rouge** Little Red Riding Hood

**chaperonner** *vt* hood; chaperon

**chapiteau** *nm* capital (column); circus tent, big top

**chapitre** *nm* chapter; matter, subject; **avoir voix au ~** have a say in the matter

**chapon** *nm* capon

**chaque** *adj* each, every

**char** *nm* chariot; wagon; **~ d'assaut** tank

**charabia** *nm* gibberish

**charançon** *nm* weevil

**charbon** *nm* coal; blight; anthrax; **~ (de bois)** charcoal; **être sur des ~ s ardents** be on tenterhooks

**charbonnage** *nm* coalmining; colliery

**charbonner** *vt* carbonize, char; blacken with charcoal

**charbonnier -ière** *n* coal-merchant; **~ est maître chez lui** a man is master in his own house; *nm* coal-ship, collier

**charcuter** *vt* cut (meat) badly; *coll* butcher (patient)

**charcuterie** *nf* pork butcher's shop; pork-butcher's wares

**charcutier -ière** *n* pork-butcher

**chardon** *nm* thistle

**chardonneret** *nm* goldfinch

**charge** *nf* load, burden; responsibility, charge; duty, office; expense; charge (shell, bomb); caricature; **~ s sociales** social insurance expenses; **être à la ~ de qn** be dependent on s/o; be chargeable to s/o; **témoin à ~** witness for the prosecution

**chargement** *nm* loading, lading; shipment, cargo; charging (accumulator); registration (letter)

**chargé -e** *n* **~ d'affaires** chargé d'affaires; **~ de cours** part-time lecturer

**charger** *vt* (3) load; charge, instruct; *coll* take a fare (taxi); exaggerate; overact; **se ~** become overcast; **se ~ de** undertake

**chariot** *nm* wagon, truck, cart; carriage (typewriter); undercarriage (plane)

**charité** *nf* charity, love; act of charity; **faire la ~** give alms

**charivari** *nm* din; discordant music

**charlatan -e** *n* charlatan, quack

**charmant** *adj* charming

**charme** *nm* charm, spell; attractiveness; **faire du ~** lay on the charm; **se porter comme un ~** be as fit as a fiddle

**charmer** *vt* charm, delight

**charmille** *nf* arbour, bower

**charnel -elle** *adj* carnal, sensual, of the flesh

**charnier** *nm* charnel-house; heap of bodies

**charnière** *nf* hinge

**charnu** *adj* plump, fleshy

**charogne** *nf* carrion, carcass; *sl* swine, scoundrel

**charpente** *nf* frame(work)

**charpenter** *vt* shape, hew (wood); frame; **bien charpenté** well-built (man)

**charpenterie** *nf* carpentry

**charpentier** *nm* carpenter

**charpie** *nf* lint; **mettre en** ~ cut to shreds

**charretée** *nf* cartful

**charretier -ière** *n* carter, carrier; **jurer comme un** ~ swear like a trooper

**charrette** *nf* (two-wheeled) cart; ~ **à bras** barrow

**charrier** *vt* cart, transport, carry down; *sl* make fun of; *vi sl* exaggerate, come it strong

**charron** *nm* wheelwright, cartwright

**charrue** *nf* plough; **mettre la** ~ **devant les bœufs** put the cart before the horse

**charte** *nf* charter; deed

**chartreuse** *nf* Carthusian monastery; chartreuse (liqueur)

**chartreux -euse** *n+adj* Carthusian (monk, nun)

**chas** *nm* eye (needle)

**chasse** *nf* hunting; hunt, hunting-ground; ~ **à courre** hunting with hounds; ~ **d'eau** flush (lavatory); ~ **gardée** private hunting-ground; **avion de** ~ fighter-plane

**châsse** *nf* shrine; frame (spectacles), mounting

**chassé-croisé** *nm* (*pl* **chassés-croisés**) chassé-croisé (dance-step); fruitless running around

**chasse-mouches** *nm invar* fly-swatter

**chasse-neige** *nm invar* snow-plough; **descendre en** ~ (ski-ing) come down braking

**chasser** *vt* hunt, chase; drive away; sack, dismiss, expel; drive (wind); knock in (nail); *vi* hunt, shoot; blow (wind); skid; drag (anchor)

**chasseresse** *nf poet* huntress

**chasseur -euse** *n* hunter, huntsman, huntress; *nm* page-boy, commissionaire; bellhop; rifleman; fighter-plane; *naut* chaser; *adj cul* with mushroom and tomato sauce

**chassie** *nf* rheum

**chassieux -ieuse** *adj* rheumy

**châssis** *nm* frame (door, window); chassis; *phot* slide; garden-frame; ~ **d'atterrissage** landing-gear

**chasteté** *nf* chastity

**chasuble** *nf* chasuble

**chat** (*f* **chatte**) *n* cat; **à bon** ~ **bon rat** tit

for tat; **avoir d'autres** ~**s à fouetter** have other fish to fry; **avoir un** ~ **dans la gorge** be hoarse; **donner sa langue au** ~ give up; **le Chat Botté** Puss-in-Boots; **ma petite** ~**te** darling, *US* honey; **pas un** ~! not a soul anywhere!

**châtaigne** *nf* chestnut

**châtaignier** *nm* chestnut-tree

**châtain** *adj invar* chestnut brown; ~ **clair** auburn

**château** *nm* castle; large country house; royal palace; ~ **d'eau** water-tower; ~ **fort** fortress; ~**x en Espagne** castles in the air

**châteaubriant** *nm* grilled fillet steak (with potatoes)

**châtelain -e** *n* lord (lady) of the manor

**châtelaine** *nf* chain (for keys or jewels)

**chat-huant** *nm* (*pl* **chats-huants**) tawny owl

**châtié** *adj* polished (style)

**châtier** *vt* chastise, punish

**châtiment** *nm* punishment, chastisement

**chatoiement** *nm* sheen; glistening

**chaton -onne** *n* kitten; *nm* catkin

**chatouillement** *nm* tickling

**chatouiller** *vt* tickle; ~ **l'amour-propre de qn** flatter s/o's ego

**chatouilleux -euse** *adj* ticklish; touchy; delicate (matter)

**chatoyer** *vi* (7) shimmer; glisten

**châtrer** *vt* castrate

**chattemite** *nf* flattering hypocrite, toady

**chatterie** *nf* coaxing

**chat-tigre** *nm* (*pl* **chats-tigres**) tiger-cat

**chaud** *nm* warmth, heat; **avoir** ~ be warm (person); **être au** ~ be warm; **cela ne me fait ni** ~ **ni froid** it's all the same to me; *adj* warm, hot; lively; ardent; **il fait** ~ it's hot; **pleurer à** ~**es larmes** weep bitterly

**chaudière** *nf* boiler; copper (for washing)

**chaudron** *nm* cauldron

**chaudronnerie** *nf* boiler-making; copper-smith's workshop

**chaudronnier -ière** *n* boiler-maker; copper-smith

**chauffage** *nm* heating, warming; stoking

**chauffard** *nm coll* road-hog

**chauffe** *nf* heating; stoking

**chauffe-assiettes** *nm invar* plate-warmer

**chauffe-bain** *nm* bath-heater

**chauffe-eau** *nm invar* water-heater

**chauffe-pieds** *nm invar* foot-warmer

**chauffe-plats** *nm invar* hot-plate

**chauffer** *vt* warm, heat; *coll* cram (exam-candidate); ~ **une affaire** expedite a matter; *vi* become warm, hot; overheat

51

(bearings); **ça chauffe** things are warming up

**chaufferette** *nf* foot-warmer

**chauffeur -euse** *n* stoker, fireman (steam-engine); driver, chauffeur

**chaume** *nm* straw; thatch

**chaumière** *nf* thatched cottage

**chaussée** *nf* causeway; roadway

**chausse-pied** *nm* shoe-horn

**chausser** *vt* put shoes on; supply shoes to; **~ du 44** take size 44 in shoes; *coll* **~ ses lunettes** put on one's glasses; **se ~** put on one's shoes

**chausses** *nfpl* hose, breeches

**chaussette** *nf* sock

**chausson** *nm* slipper; dancing-shoe; *cul* turnover

**chaussure** *nf* shoe; footwear; shoe-industry

**chauve** *adj* bald; denuded (mountain)

**chauve-souris** *nf* (*pl* **chauves-souris**) *zool* bat

**chauvin** *adj* jingoistic, chauvinistic

**chauvinisme** *nm* jingoism, chauvinism

**chaux** *nf* lime; **blanchir à la ~** white-wash

**chavirer** *vt* turn upside down; *vi* capsize, overturn

**chef** *nm* chief, principal, leader; heading; *ar* head; **~ de cabinet** principal private secretary; **~ de cuisine** chef; **~ de gare** station-master; **~ d'orchestre** conductor of an orchestra; **~ de rayon** shop-walker, *US* floor-walker; **~ de service** head of department; **~ de train** guard, *US* conductor; **de son propre ~** on one's own responsibility

**chef-d'œuvre** *nm* (*pl* **chefs-d'œuvre**) masterpiece

**chef-lieu** *nm* (*pl* **chefs-lieux**) chief town

**cheik** *nm* sheik

**chemin** *nm* way, road, path; **~ battu** beaten track; **~ de croix** stations of the Cross; **~ de fer** railway, *US* railroad; **~ faisant** on the way; **faire son ~** get on; **ne pas y aller par quatre (trente-six) ~s** not beat about the bush

**chemineau** *nm* tramp, *US* hobo

**cheminée** *nf* chimney, funnel; fireplace, mantelpiece

**cheminer** *vi* make one's way, proceed

**cheminot** *nm* railwayman, *US* railroad man

**chemise** *nf* (man's) shirt; chemise; folder; dust-jacket (book); casing; **~ de nuit** nightshirt (-dress); **en bras de ~** in one's shirt-sleeves

**chemiserie** *nf* shirt shop or factory

**chenal** *nm* channel; mill-race

**chenapan** *nm* rogue, scoundrel

**chêne** *nm* oak

**chéneau** *nm* gutter

**chenet** *nm* fire-dog, andiron

**chenil** *nm* kennels

**chenille** *nf* caterpillar; caterpillar-track

**chenillette** *nf* military tracked vehicle

**chenu** *adj* bleached (hair); hoary

**cheptel** *nm* livestock

**chèque** *nm* cheque, *US* check; **~ barré** crossed cheque; **~ de voyage** traveller's cheque; **~ sans provision** dud cheque; **toucher un ~** cash a cheque

**cher** (*f* **chère**) *n* mon **~** my dear fellow; **ma chère** my dear, darling; *adj* dear, beloved; expensive, costly; *adv* **coûter ~** cost a lot; **il l'a payé ~** he paid dearly (or a lot of money) for it

**chercher** *vt* look for, seek; try; **~ la petite bête** be over-critical; **~ midi à quatorze heures** look for difficulties where there aren't any; **aller ~** fetch; *coll* **cela va ~ dans les mille francs** it fetches about a thousand francs; **envoyer ~** send for; *coll* **tu l'as cherché!** you asked for it!

**chercheur -euse** *n* seeker, investigator; research-worker

**chère** *nf* fare, food, cheer; **faire bonne ~** live well

**chéri -e** *n* + *adj* darling, beloved

**chérir** *vt* cherish, hold dear

**cherté** *nf* dearness, high price

**chérubin** *nm* cherub

**chétif -ive** *adj* weak, puny; wretched

**cheval** *nm* horse; **~ de bataille** pet subject; **à ~** on horseback; **à ~ sur** astride, overlapping; a stickler for; **chevaux de bois** merry-go-round; **fièvre de ~** raging fever; **monter à ~** go in for riding; **monter sur ses grands chevaux** ride one's high horse; **une deux chevaux** a two-horse-power car (French rating)

**chevaleresque** *adj* chivalrous

**chevalerie** *nf* knighthood; chivalry

**chevalet** *nm* support, trestle; easel; clothes-horse; bridge (violin)

**chevalier** *nm* knight; *zool* sandpiper; **~ d'industrie** crook, swindler

**chevalière** *nf* signet-ring

**chevalin** *adj* equine; **boucherie ~e** horse-butcher's

**cheval-vapeur** *nm* (*pl* **chevaux-vapeur**) horse-power

**chevauchée** *nf* ride on horseback; cavalcade

**chevaucher** *vt* sit astride; **se ~** overlap; *vi* ride on horseback; overlap

**chevelu** *adj* hairy, long-haired; **cuir ~** scalp

**chevelure** *nf* head of hair; tail (of comet)

**chevet** *nm* bedhead; bolster; **lampe de ~** bedside lamp; **livre de ~** favourite book

**cheveu** *nm* (single) hair; ~x hair; **comme un ~ sur la soupe** very inappropriate; **couper les ~x en quatre** split hairs; **en ~x** (woman) hatless; **s'arracher les ~x** tear one's hair; *coll* **se faire des ~x** worry; **tenir à un ~** be touch and go; **tiré par les ~x** far-fetched

**cheville** *nf* peg, pin, bolt; ankle; plug; padding (verse); **~ ouvrière** king-pin; mainspring; **il ne vous arrive (vient) pas à la ~** he can't hold a candle to you

**cheviller** *vt* pin, peg, bolt; **avoir l'âme chevillée au corps** be very difficult to kill

**chèvre** *nf* (she-)goat; derrick; **ménager la ~ et le chou** run with the hare and hunt with the hounds

**chevreau** *nm* kid

**chèvrefeuille** *nm* honeysuckle

**chevrette** *nf* kid-goat; roe-deer; tripod; *coll* shrimp or prawn

**chevreuil** *nm* roe-buck; roe-deer; venison

**chevrier -ière** *n* goatherd, goatgirl

**chevron** *nm* rafter; *mil* stripe; chevron

**chevroter** *vi* speak or sing in a quavering voice

**chevrotine** *nf* buckshot

**chez** *prep* at the home or house of; among; with; **~ Dupont** care of Dupont; **~ l'épicier** at the grocer's; **~ Racine** in Racine('s works); **faites comme ~ vous** make yourself at home; **un ~ ~-soi** a home

**chiader** *vt* + *vi coll* swot (for)

**chialer** *vi sl* cry, blubber

**chic** *nm* knack, skill; smartness, chic; **avoir du ~** be smart; **avoir le ~ pour** have the knack of; *adj invar* elegant, smart, stylish; pleasant, nice, first-rate; **elle a été très ~** she behaved very generously; *coll* **un ~ type** a smashing fellow

**chicane** *nf* chicanery, quibbling, wrangling

**chicaner** *vt* quibble, wrangle with; *vi* quibble, carp

**chicanerie** *nf* chicanery, quibbling

**chicaneur -euse** *n* + *adj* quibbling, argumentative (person)

¹**chiche** *nm* **pois ~** chick pea

²**chiche** *adj* poor, scanty; stingy

³**chiche** *interj coll* I dare you, bet you I will (can)

**chichi** *nm coll* affectation; **faire du ~ (des ~s)** put on airs

**chicorée** *nf* endive; chicory

**chicot** *nm* stump (tree or tooth)

**chien** (*f* **chienne**) *n* dog, bitch; hammer (gun); *coll* charm, sex-appeal; **~ de**

(**chienne de**) … wretched …; **~ d'arrêt** pointer; **~ de berger** sheep-dog; **~ de garde** watch-dog; **couché en ~ de fusil** lying curled up; **entre ~ et loup** at dusk; **être ~** be mean; **être coiffé à la ~** ne wear a fringe; **se regarder en ~s de faïence** glare at each other; **temps de ~** filthy weather; **un mal de ~** a lot of trouble; **vie de ~** rotten life; **vivre comme ~ et chat** get on badly

**chiendent** *nm* couch-grass; *coll* difficulty, snag

**chienlit** *nf* mess, chaos; *obs* carnival mask

**chier** *vi vulg* shit

**chiffon** *nm* rag; scrap (paper); *coll* **parler ~s** talk about dress (women)

**chiffonner** *vt* rumple, crumple; vex

**chiffonnier -ière** *n* rag-and-bone man, rag-picker; *nm* chiffonier

**chiffre** *nm* figure, numeral; code, cipher; monogram; **~ d'affaires** turnover; **un zéro en ~** a nonentity, a poor fish

**chiffrer** *vt* number; work out; write in code; mark; *vi* calculate, reckon; mount up (cost, expenses)

**chignon** *nm* coil of hair, bun

**chimère** *nf* chimera, idle dream

**chimérique** *adj* chimerical

**chimie** *nf* chemistry

**chimique** *adj* chemical; **produit ~** chemical

**chimiste** *n* chemist

**chimpanzé** *nm* chimpanzee

**Chine** *nf* China; **encre de ~** Indian ink

**chine** *nm* (**papier de**) rice-paper

**chiner** *vt* cloud, mottle (fabrics); run down, mock at; *vi sl* work hard

**Chinois -e** *n* Chinese (man or woman)

**chinois** *nm* Chinese (language); *adj* Chinese

**chinoiserie** *nf* Chinese curio; *coll* nonsense, futile measure; **~s administratives** red tape

**chiot** *nm* pup, puppy

**chiottes** *nfpl vulg* bog, shit-house, *US* can

**chiourme** *nf* gang of convicts or galley-slaves

**chiper** *vt coll* pinch, swipe

**chipie** *nf coll* shrew, old bitch

**chipoter** *vt* + *vi* nibble (at one's food); *vi* quibble; waste time

**chips** *nmpl* potato crisps; *US* potato chips; game chips

**chique** *nf* quid (tobacco)

**chiqué** *nm coll* affectation, sham; **faire du ~** put it on

**chiquement** *adv* smartly, stylishly

**chiquenaude** *nf* flick of the finger

**chiquer** *vt* + *vi* chew tobacco

**chiromancie** *nf* chiromancy, palmistry

**chiropracteur** *nm* bone-setter
**chirurgical** *adj* surgical; *med* **ventre ~** acute abdomen
**chirurgie** *nf* surgery
**chirurgien** *nm* surgeon
**chlore** *nm* chlorine
**chlorer** *vt* chlorinate
**chloroforme** *nm* chloroform
**chlorophylle** *nf* chlorophyll
**chlorure** *nm* chloride
**chnouf** *nm sl* heroin, snow
**choc** *nm* impact, collision; *med* shock; *adj invar or pl* ~s staggering, amazing
**chocolat** *nm* chocolate; *adj* chocolate-coloured
**chocolatier -ière** *n* chocolate-maker
**chœur** *nm* chorus; choir (singers); *archi* choir; **en ~** unanimously; in chorus
**choir** *vi* (21) *obs* fall
**choisir** *vt* choose, select; **~ ses mots** pick one's words; **société choisie** select company
**choix** *nm* choice, selection; **au ~** all at the same price; **avoir l'embarras du ~** have plenty to choose from; **de ~** choice; **de premier ~** best quality; **je n'ai pas le ~** I have no option, alternative
**chômage** *nm* unemployment; ceasing of work; *coll* dole; **en ~** out of work
**chômer** *vi* stop work; be out of work, be unemployed
**chômeur -euse** *n* unemployed worker
**chope** *nf* beer-mug, tankard; mugful of beer
**choper** *vt coll* catch
**chopine** *nf* half-litre mug
**choquant** *adj* offensive, unpleasant
**choquer** *vt* knock, collide with; clink (glasses); offend; scandalize; **se ~** collide; take offence
**chorale** *nf* choral society
**chorégraphie** *nf* choreography
**choriste** *n* chorus-singer
**chorus** *nm* **faire ~** repeat in chorus; join in agreement
¹**chose** *nf* thing, affair, matter; chattel, slave; **le cours des ~s** the course of events; **Monsieur Chose** Mr So-and-so; **pas grand-~** not much; **porté sur la ~** highly sexed; *nm coll* thingumajig
²**chose** *adj invar coll* **être tout ~** feel queer
**chou** *nm* cabbage; **~ à la crème** cream bun; **~ pommé** garden cabbage; **~x de Bruxelles** Brussels sprouts; **aller planter ses ~x** go and retire into the country; **être (finir) dans les ~x** be among the last in the race; **faire ses ~x gras** feather one's nest; **feuille de ~** rag (newspaper); **mon petit ~** darling,

*US* honey; **oreilles en feuilles de ~** saucer-ears
**chouan** *nm* insurgent Breton royalist
**choucas** *nm* jackdaw
**chouchouter** *vt coll* pet, fondle
**choucroute** *nf cul* sauerkraut
¹**chouette** *nf* owl
²**chouette** *adj coll* fine, *US* swell
**chou-fleur** *nm* (*pl* **choux-fleurs**) cauliflower
**chou-rave** *nm* (*pl* **choux-raves**) kohlrabi
**choyer** *vt* (7) pet, coddle; **~ une idée** entertain an idea
**chrétien -ienne** *n + adj* Christian
**chrétienté** *nf* Christendom
**chris-craft** *nm* small motor-boat
**Christ** *nm* Christ; crucifix
**christianiser** *vt* christianize
**christianisme** *nm* Christianity
**chromage** *nm* chromium plating
**chrome** *nm* chromium
**chromé** *adj* chromium-plated; chrome-tanned
**chromer** *vt* chrome
¹**chronique** *nf* chronicle; news, newspaper report; **défrayer la ~** be in the news
²**chronique** *adj* chronic
**chroniqueur** *nm* chronicler; writer of newspaper articles
**chronologie** *nf* chronology
**chronologique** *adj* chronological
**chronomètre** *nm* chronometer
**chronométrer** *vt* (6) time, keep the time
**chrysalide** *nf* chrysalis, pupa
**chrysanthème** *nm* chrysanthemum
**chu** *p part* choir
**chuchotement** *nm* whispering
**chuchoter** *vt + vi* whisper
**chuinter** *vi* hoot (owl); pronounce 's' as 'j' or 'sh'
**chut** *interj* hush!, quiet!
**chute** *nf* fall; **~ d'eau** waterfall; **~ des reins** small of the back; **~ du jour** nightfall; **faire une ~** fall down; **point de ~** place to settle; situation
**chuter** *vi coll* fall, come a cropper
**Chypre** *nf* Cyprus
¹**ci** *adv* here; **de-~, de-là** on every side; **par-~, par-là** here and there; *see* **ce** *and* **celui**
²**ci** *pron* **~ et ça** this and that; **comme ~, comme ça** so-so
**ci-après** *adv* hereafter; further on (in book)
**ci-bas** *adv* here below
**cible** *nf* target
**ciboire** *nm* pyx
**ciboule** *nf* small onion
**ciboulette** *nf* chive(s)
**cicatrice** *nf* scar

**cicatriser** vt heal up; scar; **se ~** (wound) heal up
**cicérone** nm guide, cicerone
**ci-contre** adv on the page opposite
**ci-dessous** adv below, undermentioned
**ci-dessus** adv above, above-mentioned
**ci-devant** n hist aristocrat of the Ancien Régime; adv formerly
**cidre** nm cider
**ciel** nm (pl **cieux**, **~s**) sky, heaven; climate; Heaven; pl **~s** canopy, skies (in painting); **à ~ ouvert** out of doors; **aide-toi, le ~ t'aidera** God helps those who help themselves; **au ~**, **aux cieux** in Heaven; coll **tomber du ~** come as a godsend; arrive unexpectedly
**cierge** nm eccles wax candle, taper
**cigale** nf cicada
**cigare** nm cigar
**ci-gît, ci-gisant** see gésir
**cigogne** nf stork
**ciguë** nf hemlock
**ci-inclus** adj (invar before n) enclosed, herewith
**ci-joint** adj (invar before n) enclosed, herewith
**cil** nm eyelash
**cilice** nm hair-shirt
**ciller** vi blink
**cime** nf summit, peak; top (tree)
**ciment** nm cement; **~ armé** reinforced concrete
**cimenter** vt cement; consolidate
**cimeterre** nm scimitar
**cimetière** nm cemetery; graveyard
**cimier** nm crest (helmet)
**ciné** nm coll cinema
**ciné-actualités** nm news-theatre
**cinéaste** n member of film-making team
**cinéma** nm cinema; cinema industry; coll **c'est du ~** it's all a farce, it's very unlikely; **faire du ~** act in films
**cinématographe** nm cinematograph
**cinématographie** nf cinematography
**cinématographique** adj cinematographic
**cinéraire** adj cinerary (urn)
**cinglant** adj lashing (wind, rain), bitter, biting; scathing
**cinglé** adj sl daft, barmy, nuts
**¹cingler** vi sail before the wind
**²cingler** vt lash, cut (wind, rain)
**cinq** nm + adj five; fifth; **en ~ sec** in a jiffy; **il était moins ~** it was a near thing; **les ~ lettres** the four letter-word (euphemism for **merde**)
**cinquantaine** nf about fifty; the fifties (age)
**cinquante** nm + adj fifty
**cinquantenaire** nm fiftieth anniversary
**cinquantième** nm + adj fiftieth (part)

**cinquième** nm fifth (part); **être en ~** be in the second year class at the lycée; adj fifth
**cintre** nm interior concave surface (arch or vault); arch; coathanger; bend (handle-bar); **voûte en plein ~** semicircular arch
**cintrer** vt curve, arch, bend
**cirage** nm waxing, polishing; waxpolish; shoe-polish
**circoncire** vt (22) circumcize
**circoncision** nf circumcision
**circonférence** nf circumference; perimeter (town)
**circonflexe** adj circumflex (accent)
**circonlocution** nf circumlocution
**circonscription** nf circumscription; district; electoral district, ward
**circonscrire** vt (42) circumscribe; encircle; limit
**circonspect** adj circumspect, cautious
**circonspection** nf circumspection, caution
**circonstance** nf circumstance, event; **agir en raison des ~s** act in keeping with the circumstances; **à la hauteur des ~s** equal to the occasion; **de ~** improvised for the occasion
**circonstancié** adj detailed
**circonstanciel -ielle** adj circumstantial; gramm adverbial
**circonvenir** vt (96) circumvent; thwart
**circuit** nm circuit; circumference (town); course, lap (race); trip; detour; **~ imprimé** printed circuit; **court ~** short circuit; **mettre en ~** switch on
**circulaire** nf circular (letter); adj circular
**circulation** nf circulation; traffic; **~ interdite** no thoroughfare
**circuler** vi circulate, flow; move about, move along
**cire** nf wax
**cirer** vt wax; polish (shoes); **toile cirée** oilcloth
**cireur -euse** n polisher; shoeblack
**cireux -euse** adj wax-like
**cirque** nm circus; amphitheatre (mountains)
**cisaille** nf parings, shavings (metal); **~s** metal-shears
**cisailler** vt shear (metal)
**cisalpin** adj cisalpine
**ciseau** nm chisel; **~x** scissors
**ciseler** vt (5) engrave; chisel; emboss; shear
**ciselure** nf chiselling; embossing
**citadelle** nf citadel
**citadin -e** n townsman, townswoman
**citation** nf quoting; quotation; summons (to court); subpoena; citation
**cité** nf city; large town; housing estate
**citer** vt quote, cite; **~ qn à l'ordre du**

jour mention s/o in despatches
citerne *nf* cistern, tank; **camion- ~**
tanker (lorry)
cithare *nf* zither
citoyen -enne *n* citizen
citrique *adj* citric
citron *nm* lemon; *adj invar* lemon-
coloured
citronnade *nf* lemonade
citronnier *nm* lemon-tree
citrouille *nf* pumpkin
civet *nm* stew (game); **~ de lièvre**
jugged hare
civette *nf* civet-cat; chives
civière *nf* stretcher; handbarrow
civil *nm* civilian; **dans le ~** in private
life; **en ~** in plain clothes; *adj* civil;
civic; secular; civilian; polite
civilisateur -trice *n* civilizer; *adj* civil-
izing
civilisation *nf* civilization
civiliser *vt* civilize
civilité *nf* civility, courtesy
civique *adj* civic; civil (rights)
clabauder *vi* babble (hound); backbite
claie *nf* wattle; hurdle
clair *nm* light, shine; **en ~** not in cipher;
**tirer une affaire au ~** clear up a matter;
*adj* clear; bright; light (colour); obvious; thin (soup); **voilà qui est ~ !**
that's obvious enough; *adv* clearly,
plainly; **voir ~** see clearly; **y voir ~**
see properly
clairement *adv* distinctly, clearly
clairet -ette *adj* light red (wine); thin
(voice)
claire-voie *nf* (*pl* claires-voies) open-
work, lattice-work; clerestory; **porte à
~** gate
clairière *nf* glade, clearing
clair-obscur *nm* (*pl* clairs-obscurs)
chiaroscuro
clairon *nm* bugle; bugler
claironner *vt* trumpet; noise abroad,
broadcast
clairsemé *adj* scattered, sparse; thinly
sown (corn); thin (hair)
clairvoyance *nf* perspicacity; clairvoyance
clairvoyant *adj* clear-sighted, shrewd;
clairvoyant
clamer *vt* cry out
clameur *nf* clamour, outcry
clan *nm* clan; clique
clandestin *adj* clandestine, secret; **passager ~** stowaway
clapier *nm* rabbit-warren; rabbit-hutch
clapotement *nm* lapping, plashing
clapoter *vi* lap, plash
clapotis *nm* plashing, lapping
claque *nf* smack, slap; *theat* hired
clappers; *nm* opera-hat

claquement *nm* smacking; chattering
(teeth); slamming; crack (whip)
claquemurer *vt* shut up, immure
claquer *vt* + *vi* slap, smack; clap; bang
(door); crack (whip); snap (fingers);
click (heels); *sl* die; fail; *sl* exhaust; *sl* se
**~** wear oneself out
clarifier *vt* clarify, purify
clarinette *nf* clarinet; clarinettist
clarté *nf* clearness; brightness, light
classe *nf* class; division; rank; **aller en ~**
go to school; **faire la ~** teach; **la ~
1952** the contingent of conscripts born
in 1952
classement *nm* classification; filing
(papers); *sp* placing
classer *vt* classify; rate; sort out; file
(papers); **~ une affaire** shelve a matter
classeur *nm* filing-cabinet; file; sorter
classification *nf* classification; classi-
fying, sorting out
classifier *vt* classify; rate; sort out
classique *adj* classic(al); for school use;
**les ~s** the classics
claustral *adj* claustral, monastic
claustration *nf* cloistering
clavecin *nm* harpsichord
clavicule *nf* collar-bone, clavicle
clavier *nm* keyboard (piano, typewriter); range (voice, instrument); key-
ring or charm
clé *nf see* clef
clef *nf* key; spanner; *mus* clef; **~ (à
bascule)** switch-key; **~ anglaise** adjustable spanner; **~ de voûte** keystone; **fausse ~** skeleton key; **fermer à
~** lock
clématite *nf* clematis
clémence *nf* clemency, mercy; mildness
(weather)
clément *adj* clement, merciful; mild
cleptomane *n see* kleptomane
cleptomanie *nf see* kleptomanie
clerc *nm* cleric; scholar; clerk (lawyer's
office); **pas de ~** blunder
clergé *nm* clergy
clic-clac *nm* clatter (shoes); crack (whip)
cliché *nm* *typ* slate, block; *phot* negative; cliché
client -e *n* customer; client; patient;
guest (hotel)
clientèle *nf* customers; goodwill; practice (doctor)
clignement *nm* winking, blinking
cligner *vt* + *vi* wink, blink; **~ de l'œil**
wink
clignotant *nm* *mot* winker, direction
indicator; *econ* warning sign
clignotement *nm* winking; flickering
clignoter *vi* wink; flicker
climat *nm* climate; region
climatique *adj* climatic

**climatisation** *nf* air-conditioning
**climatiser** *vt* air-condition; adapt to a climate
**climatiseur** *nm* air-conditioning apparatus
**clin** *nm* ~ **d'œil** wink
**clinfoc** *nm* flying jib
**clinique** *nf* clinic; medical teaching; *adj* clinical
**clinquant** *nm* tinsel; cheap imitation jewellery; *adj* flashy
**clip** *nm* brooch
**clique** *nf coll + pej* gang
**cliqueter** *vi* (5) click; jingle; rattle; clink; *mot* pink
**cliquetis** *nm* clank(ing), rattling; jingle; clink(ing); *mot* pinking
**cliquette** *nf* castanets
**clivage** *nm* cleavage
**cloaque** *nm* cesspool, sink
**clochard -e** *n coll* tramp, *US* hobo
**cloche** *nf* bell; bell-jar; dish-cover; *sl* clot, dope; *sl* être de la ~ be a tramp, hobo; **sonner les ~ s à qn** tell s/o off
**cloche-pied (à)** *adv phr* hopping, on one foot
**¹clocher** *nm* belfry, steeple; **esprit de ~** parochial mentality
**²clocher** *vi* limp; *coll* be wrong, go wrong
**clocheton** *nm* bell-turret
**clochette** *nf* little bell; bell-shaped flower
**cloison** *nf* partition, division; ~ **étanche** watertight bulkhead
**cloisonné** *adj* cloisonné (enamel)
**cloisonner** *vt* divide into compartments
**cloître** *nm* cloister; monastery; convent
**cloîtrer** *vt* cloister
**clopin-clopant** *adv* with a limp
**clopiner** *vi* limp, hobble
**cloporte** *nm* woodlouse
**cloque** *nf* swelling, blister
**cloquer** *vi + v refl* blister
**clore** *vt* (23) close, shut; conclude
**clos** *nm* enclosure (particularly of vineyard); *adj* closed, shut; **à huis ~** in camera, in secret session; **maison ~ e** brothel
**clôture** *nf* fence, enclosure; closing; conclusion (meeting)
**clôturer** *vt* fence in, enclose; shut down; conclude (meeting); wind up
**clou** *nm* nail; boil; *coll* old car or bicycle; *coll* pawn-shop, *US* hock shop; stud; *coll* star turn; ~ **de girofle** clove; **traverser aux ~ s (dans les ~ s)** cross at the pedestrian crossing (*US* crosswalk)
**clouer** *vt* nail; fix, hold fast; ~ **le bec à qn** shut s/o up; **être cloué au lit** be bedridden
**clouter** *vt* stud; **passage clouté** pedestrian crossing, *US* crosswalk

**club** *nm* club; golf-club
**coadjuteur** *nm* coadjutor
**coagulation** *nf* coagulation
**coaguler** *vt* coagulate; **se ~** clot
**coaliser (se)** *v refl* form a coalition, unite
**coassement** *nm* croaking
**coasser** *vi* croak
**cobalt** *nm* cobalt
**cobaye** *nm* guinea-pig
**cobra** *nm* cobra
**cocagne** *nf* **mât de ~** greasy pole; **pays de ~** land of plenty
**cocaïne** *nf* cocaine
**cocarde** *nf* rosette, cockade
**cocasse** *adj* laughable, ludicrous, comical
**coccinelle** *nf* ladybird
**¹coche** *nm* stagecoach; **mouche du ~** busybody
**²coche** *nf* notch, nick, score
**cochère** *adj f* **porte ~** main entrance, carriage entrance
**cochon** *nm* pig, hog; swine; ~ **de lait** sucking pig; *coll* ~ **de payant** mug, *US* sucker; ~ **d'Inde** guinea-pig; **tour de ~** swinish trick; *adj* (*f* -**onne**) swinish, beastly; dirty, smutty
**cochonnaille** *nf sl* pork meats
**cochonnerie** *nf sl* filthiness; rubbish; filthy trick; smut
**cochonnet** *nm* young pig; jack (bowls); twelve-sided dice
**¹coco** *nm* **mon petit ~** my little darling; **noix de ~** coconut; *sl* fellow; **un drôle de ~** a queer character
**²coco** *nf sl* cocaine, snow
**cocon** *nm* cocoon
**cocorico** *nm* cock-a-doodle-doo
**cocotier** *nm* coconut palm
**cocotte** *nf* stew-pan; high-class tart, floozy; hen (child language); sty (eyelid); *coll* darling
**cocu** *nm + adj* cuckold
**code** *nm* code, law; rules; ~ **de la route** highway code; **mot se mettre en ~** dip one's lights
**codicille** *nm* codicil
**codification** *nf* codification; coding
**codifier** *vt* codify; code
**coéquipier -ière** *n* team-mate
**cœur** *nm* heart; mind, feelings; courage; hearts (cards); midst, core; **à ~ joie** to one's heart's content; **à contre ~** against one's will; **avoir le gros ~** be very sad; **avoir mal au ~** feel sick; **avoir sur le ~** resent; **cela lui tient à ~** he's keen on that; **de bon ~** willingly; **de tout ~** whole-heartedly; **en avoir le ~ net** get to the bottom of a matter; **si le ~ vous en dit** if you feel like it
**coexister** *vi* co-exist

57

**coffrage** *nm* lining (mine-shaft); *bui* framework

**coffre** *nm* chest, bin, coffer; *mot* boot, *US* trunk; mooring buoy; *coll* chest

**coffre-fort** *nm* ( *pl* coffres-forts) safe

**coffrer** *vt* line (shaft); *sl* put in prison

**coffret** *nm* small chest; casket

**cogérer** *vt* (6) manage in common

**cognac** *nm* cognac, brandy

**cognassier** *nm* quince-tree

**cognée** *nf* axe, hatchet

**cogner** *vt* + *vi* knock, beat, hammer

**cohorte** *nf* cohort

**cohue** *nf* mob, crowd

**coi** ( *f* coite) *adj obs* quiet, still; **se tenir ~** keep quiet

**coiffe** *nf* headdress; *med* caul

**coiffer** *vt* cover (head); beat, overtake; **~ Sainte Catherine** be twenty-five and unmarried; **être coiffé de qn** be keen on s/o; **se ~** put on one's hat; do one's hair

**coiffeur -euse** *n* hairdresser; *nf* dressing-table

**coiffure** *nf* headdress; hair-style; hair-dressing

**coin** *nm* corner, angle; wedge; place; stamp, die; **au ~ du feu** by the fireside; **jouer aux quatre ~s** play puss in the corner

**coincer** *vt* (4) wedge, jam; trap

**coïncider** *vi* coincide

**coing** *nm* quince

**coït** *nm* coitus, copulation

**col** *nm* neck; collar; pass (mountains); **faux ~** separate collar; *coll* froth on glass of beer

**coléoptère** *nm* beetle, coleopter

**colère** *nf* anger, fit of anger; **être en ~** be in a temper; **se mettre en ~** get angry; *adj* angry; irascible

**coléreux -euse** *adj* irascible, quick-tempered

**colérique** *adj* choleric

**colibri** *nm* humming-bird

**colifichet** *nm* bauble, trinket

**colimaçon** *nm* snail; **escalier en ~** spiral staircase

**colin-maillard** *nm* blind-man's buff

**colique** *nf* colic; belly-ache

**colis** *nm* parcel, package; article of luggage

**colite** *nf* colitis

**collaborateur -trice** *n* collaborator; associate

**collaborer** *vi* collaborate

**collage** *nm* gluing, sticking; *arts* collage; *sl* cohabitation

**collant** *nm* tights; *adj* sticky; close-fitting; clinging (person)

**collation** *nf* conferment; collation; light meal

**collationner** *vt* collate, compare; *vi* have a snack

**colle** *nf* paste, gum; poser; *coll* detention; **~ à empois** size; **~ forte** glue; **poser une ~** ask a sticky question

**collecte** *nf* (church) collection

**collecteur -trice** *n* collector

**collectif** *nm* block (of flats); *adj* ( *f* -ive) collective

**collection** *nf* collecting; collection

**collectionner** *vt* collect

**collectionneur -euse** *n* collector

**collectivité** *nf* collectivity; community

**collège** *nm* college; school

**collégien -ienne** *n* schoolboy, schoolgirl

**collègue** *n* colleague, fellow worker

**coller** *vt* paste, stick, glue; *coll* place; *coll* give; *coll* floor (s/o); *coll* punish (pupil); *coll* fail, plough, *US* flunk; *vi* stick, adhere; *sl* suit, work out (well); **se ~** stick, cling; *coll* **se ~ avec** live with

**collerette** *nf* little collar

**collet** *nm* collar (coat, etc); cape; flange; snare; **~ monté** prim and proper; **prendre au ~** seize by the scruff of the neck; arrest

**colleter** *vt* (5) collar; grapple; **se ~** come to blows

**collier** *nm* necklace; collar; (type of) beard; *coll* **donner un coup de ~** make a big effort

**colline** *nf* hill

**colloque** *nm* colloquy; conference (scholars, specialists)

**colmater** *vt* warp (land); fill in (holes, etc)

**colombe** *nf* dove, pigeon

**colombier** *nm* dovecot

**colon** *nm* farmer; settler

**colonie** *nf* colony, settlement; **~ de vacances** holiday camp (for children)

**colonisateur -trice** *n* colonizer

**colonisation** *nf* colonization

**coloniser** *vt* colonize

**colonne** *nf* column, pillar; **~ vertébrale** spine

**colorant** *nm* colouring (matter)

**coloration** *nf* colouring; colour

**colorer** *vt* colour, stain

**colorier** *vt* apply colour(s)

**coloris** *nm* colouring, hue

**colosse** *nm* colossus, giant

**colportage** *nm* hawking; spreading of news or rumours

**colporter** *vt* hawk, peddle; propagate, spread (news)

**colporteur -euse** *n* pedlar, hawker

**coltiner** *vt* carry, lug

**colza** *nm* colza, rape

**comateux -euse** *adj* comatose

58

**combat** *nm* combat, fight; **engager le ~** go into action; **hors de ~** out of action, disabled

**combatif -ive** *adj* aggressive, pugnacious

**combattant -e** *n* combatant; **ancien ~** ex-serviceman

**combattre** *vt + vi* combat, struggle

**combe** *nf* dale, valley, combe

**combien** *adv exclam* how; *adv inter* how much (many)?; **c'est ~?** how much is it?; **le ~ sommes-nous?** what is the date?; **tous les ~?** at what intervals?

**combinaison** *nf* combination, arrangement; *coll* scheme; overalls

**combinard** *nm sl* trickster

**combine** *nf* scheme, racket

**combiner** *vt* combine; arrange; devise

**comble** *nm* full measure; roofing; summit, height; **c'est le ~!** that beats everything!; **de fond en ~** from top to bottom; **pour ~ de malheur** worst of all; **sous les ~s** in the attic; *adj* very full; crowded out; **faire salle ~** attract a full house

**combler** *vt* fill, fill up; make up, satisfy fully; **~ qn de bienfaits** heap kindnesses on s/o; **~ un déficit** make up a deficit

**combustible** *nm* fuel; *adj* combustible

**comédie** *nf* comedy; play; **faire la ~** sham

**comédien -ienne** *n* actor, actress; shammer

**comestible** *adj* edible; **~s** provisions, victuals

**comète** *nf* comet

**comices** *nmpl* **~ agricoles** agricultural show

**comique** *nm* comedy; comic actor; comedian; **le ~, c'est** the funny part is; *adj* comic; funny

**comité** *nm* committee; **~ de lecture** (literary) selection committee; **~ d'entreprise** workers' or staff council; **petit ~** small informal gathering

**commandant** *nm* commandant; commanding officer; major; squadron-leader; (naval) captain

**commande** *nf comm* order; *mech* control; **~ ferme** firm order; **de ~** forced, artificial; **levier de ~** control lever; **passer une ~** place an order; **sur ~** to order

**commandement** *nm* command, order; authority

**commander** *vt* command; order; be in command; overlook, dominate; compel (respect); control; **~ à ses passions** control one's passions; **se ~** control oneself

**commanditaire** *nm comm* sleeping partner, *US* silent partner; *theat* backer

**commanditer** *vt* finance

**comme** *adv* as, like, how; as though; **~ de juste** of course; *coll* **c'est tout ~** it comes to the same thing; **qu'est-ce que vous avez ~ fruits?** what have you in the way of fruit?; *conj* as, just as

**commémoratif -ive** *adj* commemorative

**commémorer** *vt* commemorate

**commencement** *nm* beginning

**commencer** *vt + vi* (4) begin, start; **pour ~** to begin with

**comment** *adv inter* how?; what did you say?; *interj* what!; why!; **mais ~ donc!** by all means!

**commentaire** *nm* commentary; comment

**commentateur -trice** *n* commentator

**commenter** *vt* comment, annotate; make remarks on

**commérage** *nm* gossip

**commerçant -e** *n* tradesman, shopkeeper; *adj* commercial; **peu ~** not keen on or good at doing business

**commerce** *nm* commerce; trade; business; dealings; **dans le ~** in the business world; **d'un ~ agréable** pleasant to deal with; **faire le ~ de** deal in; **maison de ~** firm

**commercer** *vi* (4) trade; have dealings

**commercialiser** *vt* commercialize

**commère** *nf* gossip, crony

**commérer** *vi* (6) gossip

**commettre** *vt* (60) commit, perpetrate; **~ une erreur** make a mistake; **se ~** commit oneself

**comminatoire** *adj* comminatory, threatening

**commis** *nm* clerk, shop-assistant; **~ voyageur** (commercial) traveller

**commissaire** *nm* member of commission, commissioner; steward; police superintendent

**commissaire-priseur** *nm* auctioneer

**commissariat** *nm* office of commissioner; **~ (de police)** police station

**commission** *nf* commission; brokerage; errand, message; committee

**commissionnaire** *nm* messenger, commission-agent

**commode** *nf* chest-of-drawers; *adj* suitable, convenient, handy; comfortable; accommodating, good-natured

**commodité** *nf* convenience, comfort

**commotion** *nf* commotion, upheaval; concussion; shell-shock

**commotionné** *adj* suffering from concussion

**commuer** *vt leg* commute

**commun** *nm* common run; generality;

~s outbuildings; **hors du** ~ above average; **le** ~ **des mortels** the common herd; *adj* common, general, usual, widespread; vulgar, commonplace; **d'un** ~ **accord** with one accord; **lieu** ~ truism
**communal** *adj* common (land); communal; *de biens* joint ownership (marriage)
**communauté** *nf* community; society; ~ **de biens** joint ownership (marriage)
**commune** *nf* borough, parish; commune; **la Chambre des Communes** the House of Commons
**communément** *adv* commonly, generally
**communiant -e** *n* communicant
**communicant** *adj* communicating (room)
**communicateur -trice** *adj* connecting (wire)
**communicatif -ive** *adj* communicative, talkative; infectious (laughter)
**communication** *nf* communication, (telephone) call; message; **fausse** ~ wrong number; **obtenir la** ~ get through (telephone); **se mettre en** ~ **avec** get in touch with
**communier** *vi* attend communion; be in communion
**communion** *nf* communion; Holy Communion
**communiquer** *vt* communicate, convey; transmit; *vi* lead into (door); **se** ~ be communicative; spread (fire)
**communisme** *nm* communism
**communiste** *n + adj* communist
**commutateur** *nm* elect switch, commutator
**compact** *adj* compact, dense
**compagne** *n see* **compagnon**
**compagnie** *nf* company; party; firm; **fausser** ~ **à qn** give s/o the slip; **tenir** ~ **à qn** keep s/o company
**compagnon** (*f* **compagne**) *n* companion, comrade; *nm* journeyman
**comparaison** *nf* comparison; **en** ~ **de** compared with
**comparaître** *vi* (68) appear before a court
**comparatif -ive** *adj* comparative
**comparer** *vt* compare; **littérature comparée** comparative literature
**comparse** *n* *theat* actor or actress in walk-on part; confederate
**compartiment** *nm* compartment; division
**compas** *nm* pair of compasses; mariner's compass
**compassé** *adj* formal, stiff
**compasser** *vt* measure with compasses; regulate; weigh (words)
**compassion** *nf* compassion, pity

**compatibilité** *nf* compatibility
**compatir** *vi* sympathize
**compatissant** *adj* compassionate
**compatriote** *n* compatriot
**compensateur -trice** *adj* compensating, equalizing
**compensation** *nf* compensation; **chambre de** ~ clearing house
**compenser** *vt* compensate, make up for; make good; *naut* adjust (compass)
**compère** *nm* accomplice, crony; compère, announcer; godfather
**compère-loriot** *nm* (*pl* **compères-loriots**) sty (eyelid)
**compétence** *nf* leg competence, jurisdiction; ability, skill; **ce n'est pas de ma** ~ that's outside my province
**compétent** *adj* competent (authority)
**compétitif -ive** *adj* competitive
**compilateur -trice** *n* compiler
**compilation** *nf* compiling, compilation
**compiler** *vt* compile
**complainte** *nf* lament
**complaire** *vi* (69) please, humour; **se** ~ **à** take a delight in
**complaisance** *nf* complaisance, obligingness; self-satisfaction; **ayez la** ~ **de** please be so kind as to; **par** ~ out of kindness
**complaisant** *adj* obliging, complaisant; self-satisfied
**complément** *nm* complement; *gramm* object
**complémentaire** *adj* complementary
**complet** *nm* suit; *adj* (*f* **-ète**) complete, entire; full (bus, theatre); **au** ~ full up
**compléter** *vt* (6) complete, finish off; make up
**complexe** *nm* complex; *coll* hang-up; *adj* complex; complicated, intricate
**complexion** *nf* constitution, temperament
**complexité** *nf* complexity
**complication** *nf* complication, intricacy
**complice** *n + adj* accessory, accomplice
**complicité** *nf* complicity
**complies** *nfpl* eccles compline
**compliment** *nm* compliment; **mes** ~ **s à** give my kind regards to
**complimenter** *vt* compliment, congratulate
**compliqué** *adj* complicated, involved
**compliquer** *vt* complicate; **se** ~ **la vie** make life (unnecessarily) difficult for oneself
**complot** *nm* plot, conspiracy
**comploter** *vt + vi* plot, scheme
**componction** *nf* compunction
**comporter** *vt* admit, allow of; require; comprise, entail; **se** ~ behave
**composant** *adj* composing, component

**composé** *nm* compound

**composer** *vt* compose, form, make up; set (type); **temps composé** compound tense; *vi* come to terms

**composition** *nf* composition; arrangement; compromise; type-setting; **de bonne ~** easy to get on with; **entrer en ~ avec qn** come to terms with s/o

**composter** *vt* date-stamp, validate (ticket)

**compote** *nf* stewed fruit, compote

**compotier** *nm* fruit-dish

**compréhensif -ive** *adj* comprehensive; understanding, tolerant

**compréhension** *nf* comprehension; indulgence, understanding

**comprendre** *vt* (75) understand; comprise, include; **cela se comprend** naturally; **faire ~ à qn** give s/o to understand; **je n'y comprends rien** I can't make it out; **se faire ~** make oneself understood; **tout compris** inclusive; **y compris** including, inclusive of

**compresse** *nf med* compress

**compresseur** *nm* compressor; *eng* supercharger; **rouleau ~** steam roller

**compression** *nf* compression; reduction; repression

**comprimable** *adj* compressible

**comprimé** *nm med* tablet

**comprimer** *vt* compress; squeeze; restrain (feelings)

**compris** *p part* **comprendre**

**compromettre** *vt* (60) compromise; endanger, jeopardize; *vi* compromise

**compromis** *nm* compromise

**comptabilité** *nf* book-keeping, accounts; accounts department; **~ en partie simple (double)** single-(double-) entry book-keeping; **tenir la ~** keep the books

**comptable** *n* accountant; *adj* accountable; responsible; **machine ~** calculating machine

**comptant** *adj* **argent ~** ready cash; *adv* **payer ~** pay in cash

**compte** *nm* account, reckoning; amount, score; due; **~ à rebours** count-down; **~ rendu** report, review; **à bon ~** cheap; *sl* **avoir son ~** be drunk; **en fin de ~** all things considered; **le ~ y est** that's the right amount; **pour mon ~** for my part; **régler son ~ à qn** settle s/o's hash; **se rendre ~ de qch** realize; **son ~ est bon** I'll settle him; **tenir ~ de qch** take sth into consideration

**compte-gouttes** *nm invar* dropper, pipette

**compter** *vt* count, number; reckon, value; pay out; charge for; **à pas comptés** with measured tread; **sans ~ ...** not to mention ..., without counting ...; *vi* reckon, rely; be of consequence; **j'y compte bien** I'm banking on it

**compte-tours** *nm invar* rev counter

**compteur** *nm* counter, meter; speedometer; mileage indicator; parking meter

**comptine** *nf* children's song

**comptoir** *nm* counter; warehouse

**compulser** *vt* examine; go through (documents)

**computer** *vt* compute

**comte** *nm* count

**comté** *nm* county; cheese (from Franche-Comté district)

**comtesse** *nf* countess

**con** *nm vulg* cunt; *sl* fool, clot, dope; *adj* (*f* **conne**) *sl* stupid, dumb

**concasser** *vt* pound, crush

**concéder** *vt* (6) grant, concede, admit

**concentration** *nf* concentration; application

**concentré** *nm* extract, concentrate

**concentrer** *vt* concentrate; focus; contain (feelings); **lait concentré** condensed milk; **se ~** concentrate

**concentrique** *adj* concentric

**conception** *nf* conception, idea; conceiving

**concernant** *prep* about, concerning, regarding

**concerner** *vt* concern, relate to, affect

**concert** *nm* concert; agreement, harmony; **agir de ~ avec qn** act in concert with s/o

**concerter** *vt* concert, plan; **se ~** act in concert

**concessif -ive** *adj* concessive

**concession** *nf* concession; grant; conceding

**concessionnaire** *n* authorized agent; holder of a concession

**concevable** *adj* conceivable

**concevoir** *vt* conceive; understand, imagine; **ainsi conçu** worded as follows

**concierge** *n* caretaker, (hall-)porter

**concile** *nm eccles* council

**conciliabule** *nm* secret meeting

**conciliant** *adj* conciliatory

**concilier** *vt* conciliate, reconcile; win over

**concis** *adj* concise, terse

**concision** *nf* conciseness, brevity

**concitoyen -enne** *n* fellow-citizen; fellow-countryman (-countrywoman)

**concluant** *adj* conclusive; **peu ~** inconclusive

**conclure** *vt* (25) conclude, end, finish; **~ un marché** strike a bargain; *vi* come to a conclusion, infer

**conclusif -ive** *adj* conclusive
**conclusion** *nf* conclusion; concluding; end; inference
**concombre** *nm* cucumber
**concomitant** *adj* concomitant, attendant
**concordance** *nf* concordance; agreement
**concordat** *nm eccles* concordat; bankrupt's certificate
**concorde** *nf* harmony, concord
**concorder** *vi* tally, agree
**concourant** *adj* concurrent
**concourir** *vi* (29) converge, concur; combine; compete
**concours** *nm* concourse, gathering; help, assistance; competition, competitive examination; **hors-~** not competing; **se présenter à un ~** go in for an examination (competition)
**concret -ète** *adj* concrete
**concrétion** *nf* coagulation; concretion
**conçu** *p part* **concevoir**
**concupiscence** *nf* lust
**concurrence** *nf* concurrence; competition
**concurrencer** *vt* (4) be in competition with
**concurrent -e** *n* competitor
**concussion** *nf* misappropriation; extortion
**condamnable** *adj* blameworthy, reprehensible
**condamnation** *nf* condemnation; conviction, sentence; censure
**condamné -e** *n* condemned man (woman)
**condamner** *vt* condemn; sentence, convict; censure; **~ un malade** give up hope for a sick person; **~ sa porte** refuse to see anyone; **~ une porte** block up a door
**condensateur** *nm* condenser
**condenser** *vt* condense
**condescendance** *nf* condescension
**condescendre** *vi* condescend
**condiment** *nm* seasoning, condiment
**condisciple** *nm* fellow-student, schoolfellow
**condition** *nf* condition; state; rank; **~s** conditions, circumstances; terms; **acheter sous ~** buy on approval; **à ~ de** providing; **dans ces ~s** under these circumstances; **être en ~** be in service; **être en ~ de faire qch** be in a fit state to do sth; **gens de ~** people of fashion, quality
**conditionnel -elle** *adj* conditional
**conditionner** *vt* condition; season
**condoléance** *nf* condolence
**conducteur -trice** *n* leader, guide, driver; conductor (heat, electricity)

**conductibilité** *nf* conductibility
**conductible** *adj* conductive
**conductivité** *nf* conductivity
**conduire** *vt* (80) conduct, lead, escort, accompany; drive (car, etc), steer; induce; manage; **se ~** behave
**conduit** *nm* conduit, duct, pipe
**conduite** *nf* conducting; driving; behaviour; management; piping, conduit; **~ intérieure** saloon car, *US* sedan; **changer de ~** mend one's ways; **faire un bout de ~ à qn** walk a little way with s/o
**confection** *nf* making, manufacture; ready-made clothes; **s'habiller en ~** get one's clothes off the peg
**confédéré** *adj* confederate
**confédérer** *vt* (6) confederate, unite
**conférence** *nf* conference; lecture; **maître de ~s** university lecturer
**conférencier -ière** *n* lecturer
**conférer** *vt* (6) confer, award; *vi* confer, talk
**confesse** *nf eccles* confession; **aller à ~** go to confession
**confesser** *vt* confess, own up; *eccles* hear confession of; **se ~** confess one's sins
**confesseur** *nm* confessor
**confession** *nf* confession; religious denomination
**confessionnel -elle** *adj* confessional; denominational
**confiance** *nf* trust, confidence; assurance; **abus de ~** breach of trust; **avoir ~ en qn** trust s/o; **crise de ~** credibility gap; **de (toute) ~** reliable; confidently
**confiant** *adj* trustful; confident; assured
**confidence** *nf* confidence (secret); **faire une ~ à qn** tell s/o a secret
**confident -e** *n* confidant
**confidentiel -ielle** *adj* confidential; **à titre ~** confidentially
**confier** *vt* trust, entrust, commit; disclose, confide; **~ qch à qn** entrust s/o with sth; tell s/o sth in confidence; **se ~ à qn** put one's trust in s/o; take s/o into one's confidence
**confiner** *vt* confine, shut up; *vi* border on
**confins** *nmpl* borders, confines
**confire** *vt* (26) preserve; pickle
**confirmatif -ive** *adj* confirmative
**confirmer** *vt* confirm, corroborate
**confiscation** *nf* confiscation, seizure
**confiserie** *nf* confectioner's shop; confectionery; preserving (in sugar)
**confiseur -euse** *n* confectioner; sweetmaker
**confisquer** *vt* confiscate
**confit** *adj* preserved, candied; pickled; **~ en dévotion** steeped in piety
**confiture** *nf* jam
**confiturier** *nm* jam-maker; jam-dish

**conflit** *nm* conflict, struggle; clash
**confluent** *nm* junction (rivers)
**confluer** *vi* meet (rivers)
**confondre** *vt* confound; confuse, mistake; mingle; embarrass; **se ~** blend; be identical; **se ~ en excuses** be profusely apologetic
**confondu** *adj* confounded; confused; dumbfounded
**conforme** *adj* conformable; consistent, corresponding
**conformément** *adv* according, in conformity
**conformer** *vi* shape; conform; **se ~** conform, comply
**conformité** *nf* conformity
**confort** *nm* comfort
**confortable** *adj* comfortable, cosy
**confrère** *nm* (professional) colleague; fellow-member
**confrérie** *nf* brotherhood; confraternity
**confrontation** *nf* confrontation; comparison
**confronter** *vt* confront (witnesses); collate
**confus** *adj* confused, mixed; indistinct, blurred; abashed; obscure
**confusément** *adv* confusedly; indistinctly; obscurely
**confusion** *nf* confusion; disorder; embarrassment
**congé** *nm* leave of absence, holiday; dismissal; discharge; permission; **donner ~** give notice; **donner ~ à qn** dismiss s/o, give s/o notice; **en ~** on leave; **prendre ~ de qn** take leave of s/o
**congédier** *vt* dismiss; discharge
**congélateur** *nm* freezer
**congélation** *nf* congelation, freezing
**congeler** *vt* (5) freeze; congeal
**congestion** *nf med* congestion; **~ cérébrale** stroke; **~ pulmonaire** pneumonia
**congestionné** *adj* congested; flushed
**congestionner** *vt* congest
**conglomérer** *vt* (6) conglomerate
**congratuler** *vt* congratulate, compliment
**congre** *nm* conger-eel
**congrès** *nm* congress
**congru** *adj* adequate, suitable; **portion ~e** barely adequate portion
**conifère** *nm* conifer; *adj* coniferous
**conique** *adj* conical
**conjecture** *nf* conjecture, surmise
**conjecturer** *vt* conjecture, surmise
**conjoindre** *vt* (55) join in marriage
**conjoint -e** *n* marriage partner, spouse
**conjoncteur** *nm elect* switch
**conjonctif -ive** *adj* conjunctive; connective (tissue)

**conjonction** *nf* connection; conjunction
**conjonctivite** *nf* conjunctivitis
**conjoncture** *nf* conjuncture, contingency; (economic) prospect
**conjugaison** *nf* conjugation
**conjugal** *adj* conjugal; **vie ~e** married life
**conjuguer** *vt* conjugate
**conjuration** *nf* plot, conspiracy; spell; **~s** entreaties
**conjuré -e** *n* conspirator
**conjurer** *vt* plot; conjure up; avert (danger); beseech; **se ~** plot together
**connaissance** *nf* knowledge; acquaintance; consciousness; **~s** learning; **en ~ de cause** with full knowledge of the facts; **en pays de ~** in familiar surroundings, among friends; **faire ~ avec qn, faire la ~ de qn** make s/o's acquaintance
**connaisseur -euse** *n* connoisseur, expert
**connaître** *vt* (68) know; be aware of; be acquainted with; *coll* **ça me connaît** I know all there is to know about that; **faire ~ qch** make sth known; **ne plus se ~** be beside oneself with rage; **on lui connaissait cette qualité-là** people knew he had that quality; **se (s'y) ~ en (à) qch** be an expert in, know all about sth; **se faire ~** introduce oneself by name; become well-known
**connard** *nm sl see* con
**connecter** *vt elect* connect
**connerie** *nf sl* nonsense, absurdity; stupid behaviour
**connétable** *nm hist* High Constable
**connexion** *nf* connection
**connexité** *nf* kinship (ideas)
**connivence** *nf* connivance, complicity; **de ~ avec** in collusion with
**connu** *adj* (well-)known; certain
**conque** *nf* conch
**conquérant -e** *n* conqueror
**conquérir** *vt* (27) conquer; win over
**conquête** *nf* conquest; conquered territory
**consacrer** *vt* consecrate; ordain; dedicate; devote, assign; sanction; sanctify; **expression consacrée** stock phrase
**consanguin** *adj* consanguineous; **frère ~** half-brother on father's side
**consciemment** *adv* conscientiously
**conscience** *nf* consciousness; conscience; conscientiousness; **~ large** accommodating conscience; **avoir la ~ nette** have a clear conscience; **en ~** conscientiously; **sans ~** unscrupulous
**conscient** *adj* conscious
**conscrit** *nm* conscript
**consécration** *nf* consecration; dedication; ratification
**consécutif -ive** *adj* consecutive

**conseil** *nm* advice, counsel; council, committee; adviser; ~ **d'administration** board of directors; ~ **de guerre** council of war; court-martial; **homme de bon** ~ wise man; **la nuit porte** ~ better sleep on it; **prendre** ~ **de qn** ask s/o's advice; **tenir** ~ hold a council

**conseillable** *adj* advisable

**¹conseiller -ère** *n* adviser; councillor

**²conseiller** *vt* advise

**consentement** *nm* consent, assent

**consentir** *vt* (59) grant; *vi* consent, agree; **qui ne dit mot consent** silence means consent

**conséquence** *nf* consequence, outcome, result; **de** ~ important; **en** ~ accordingly; **sans** ~ unimportant; **tirer à** ~ be of importance

**conséquent** *adj* consistent; following; *coll* important; **par** ~ consequently

**conservateur -trice** *n* conservator, keeper; curator; conservative

**conservation** *nf* conserving, preserving; preservation; care; state of preservation

**conservatoire** *nm* academy (music, etc)

**conserve** *nf* preserved food; **naviguer de** ~ sail in convoy

**conserver** *vt* preserve; take care of; keep, maintain, keep up; **bien conservé** well preserved; **se** ~ keep

**considérable** *adj* considerable, large; eminent, important

**considération** *nf* consideration; thought; esteem, respect; **prendre en** ~ take into account

**considéré** *adj* circumspect

**considérer** *vt* (6) consider; gaze on; regard

**consignataire** *nm* consignee

**consignateur** *nm* consignor

**consignation** *nf* consignation, deposit; consignment

**consigne** *nf mil* order; confinement to barracks; (school) detention; left-luggage office, *US* check-room; deposit

**consigner** *vt* deposit; consign (goods); confine to barracks; detain; record, write down; put out of bounds

**consistance** *nf* consistency; firmness; **sans** ~ unfounded

**consistant** *adj* firm, solid

**consister** *vi* consist

**consistoire** *nm eccles* consistory

**consolateur -trice** *adj* comforting, consoling

**consolation** *nf* consolation, comfort

**consoler** *vt* console, comfort

**consolidation** *nf* consolidation; healing (fracture); funding

**consolider** *vt* consolidate, strengthen; fund; **se** ~ grow firm; heal (fracture)

**consommable** *adj* consumable

**consommateur -trice** *n* consumer; customer (in café)

**consommation** *nf* consumption; drink (in café); consummation

**¹consommé** *nm* clear soup; stock

**²consommé** *adj* consummate

**consommer** *vt* consume; consummate

**consomption** *nf* wasting, decline

**consonne** *nf* consonant

**consort -e** *n* consort; ~ **s** associates

**consortium** *nm* consortium, trust

**conspirateur -trice** *n* conspirator

**conspiration** *nf* plot, conspiracy

**conspirer** *vt* plot; *vi* plot, conspire; tend

**conspuer** *vt* boo; decry

**constance** *nf* constancy; invariability

**constant** *adj* constant; firm

**constat** *nm* (official) report, affidavit

**constatation** *nf* verification, establishment (fact)

**constater** *vt* establish, ascertain, notice; find out; record

**consteller** *vt* constellate

**consterner** *vt* dismay

**constiper** *vt* constipate

**constituer** *vt* constitute, make up; institute, set up, settle (money); **se** ~ become, make oneself

**constitution** *nf* constitution; constituting; composition; settlement

**constitutionnel -elle** *adj* constitutional

**constricteur** *nm* constrictor

**constructeur -trice** *n* constructor, builder

**constructif -ive** *adj* constructive

**construction** *nf* construction, building; erection; edifice

**construire** *vt* (80) construct, build; put together; construe

**consulaire** *adj* consular

**consulat** *nm* consulate; consulship

**consultatif -ive** *adj* consultative; advisory

**consultation** *nf* consultation; (medical) advice; (legal) opinion; **heures de** ~ surgery hours

**consulter** *vt* consult; take advice

**consumer** *vt* consume; wear out

**contact** *nm* contact, touch; *elect* connection; **clef de** ~ ignition key; **couper le** ~ switch off; **perdre le** ~ lose touch

**contagieux -ieuse** *adj* contagious; infectious

**contagionner** *vt* infect

**contamination** *nf* contamination; infection

**contaminer** *vt* contaminate; infect

**conte** *nm* tale, story; fib

**contemplateur -trice** *n* contemplator

**contempler** *vt* contemplate; behold; reflect

**contemporain -e** *n* contemporary; *adj*

contemporary; contemporaneous

**contenance** *nf* capacity; bearing; **faire bonne ~** put on a good face

**conteneur** *nm* container

**contenir** *vt* (96) contain; restrain; control

**content** *nm* fill, sufficiency; *adj* content, satisfied; pleased, joyful

**contentement** *nm* contentment, satisfaction

**contenter** *vt* content, satisfy; **~ un créancier** pay a creditor; **se ~ de peu** be satisfied with little

**contentieux** *nm* disputed matter; **service du ~** legal department; *adj* (*f* -ieuse) contentious

**contenu** *nm* contents

**conter** *vt* tell, relate; **en ~ de belles** say absurd things; **s'en laisser ~** let oneself be fooled

**contestable** *adj* questionable, debatable

**contestataire** *n* protester; *adj* protesting

**contestation** *nf* contestation, dispute, objection

**conteste** *nf* **sans ~** unquestionably

**contester** *vt* contest, dispute; *vi* dispute

**conteur -euse** *n* story-teller; story-writer

**contexte** *nm* context

**contigu -uë** *adj* adjoining, contiguous

**contiguïté** *nf* contiguity

**continent** *nm* continent; mainland

**contingent** *nm* contingent; share; *mil* (conscript) intake

**contingentement** *nm* limiting; allocation, quota

**contingenter** *vt* fix a quota for; ration out

**continu** *adj* continuous; **courant ~** direct current

**continuel -elle** *adj* continual, unceasing

**continuer** *vt* continue, carry on

**continuité** *nf* continuity

**contorsion** *nf* contortion

**contour** *nm* outline, contour; winding, bend

**contournement** *nm* outlining; skirting, by-passing

**contourner** *vt* shape; by-pass, skirt; warp; **la loi** get round the law

**contraceptif** *nm* contraceptive; *adj* (*f* -ive) contraceptive

**contracter** *vt* contract; incur; acquire (habit); catch (illness); **traits contractés** drawn features

**contraction** *nf* contraction, shrinking; narrowing

**contractuel -uelle** *n* contractual; (**agent**) **~** unestablished public servant, *esp* traffic-warden; *adj* contractual

**contradicteur** *nm* contradictor

**contradiction** *nf* contradiction; discrepancy; **esprit de ~** cussedness

**contradictoire** *adj* contradictory; inconsistent; conflicting

**contraindre** *vt* (55) constrain; restrain; compel, force

**contraint** *adj* constrained; forced, awkward, stiff

**contrainte** *nf* constraint; restraint; compulsion; **sans ~** freely

**contraire** *nm* opposite; **au ~** on the contrary; *adj* contrary, opposite; adverse; harmful

**contrarier** *vt* oppose, cross; annoy; contrast (colours)

**contrariété** *nf* annoyance, vexation; contrariety

**contraste** *nm* contrast; **faire ~ avec** contrast with

**contrat** *nm* contract; deed; agreement; **passer un ~ avec** enter into an agreement with

**contravention** *nf* contravention, infringement, breach; summary conviction; **dresser une ~ à qn** give s/o a ticket

**contre** *nm* opposite; **le pour et le ~** the pros and cons; **par ~** on the other hand; *prep* + *adv* against; contrary to; in exchange for; up against

**contre-amiral** *nm* rear-admiral

**contre-attaque** *nf* counter-attack

**contre-attaquer** *vt* counter-attack

**contre-balancer** *vt* (4) counter-balance, offset

**contrebande** *nf* contraband, smuggling

**contrebandier** *nm* smuggler

**contre-bas (en)** *adv phr* down, below; downwards

**contrebasse** *nf mus* double-bass

**contrebasson** *nm* double-bassoon

**contrecarrer** *vt* thwart, cross

**contrecœur (à)** *adv phr* grudgingly, against one's will

**contre-coup** *nm* rebound, recoil; repercussion; consequence

**contre-courant** *nm* counter-current; **à ~** against the stream

**contre-danse** *nf* quadrille; *sl* police ticket

**contredire** *vt* (74) contradict; be inconsistent with

**contredit (sans)** *adv phr* unquestionably

**contrée** *nf* region; country, district

**contre-écrou** *nm* lock-nut

**contre-espionnage** *nm* counter-espionage

**contrefaçon** *nf* counterfeiting; forgery; infringement (copyright)

**contrefaire** *vt* (46) imitate, mimic; counterfeit; forge; pirate

**contrefait** *adj* feigned; forged; pirated; deformed (person)

**contre-fil** *nm* opposite direction

contre-filet *nm* sirloin
contrefort *nm* buttress; ~s foothills
contre-haut (en) *adv phr* higher up
contre-indication *nf med* contra-indication
contre-indiquer *vt* counter-indicate
contre-interrogatoire *nm* cross-examination
contre-jour *nm* light from behind; à ~ against the light
contremaître *nm* foreman
contremander *vt* countermand, cancel, revoke
contre-manifestation *nf* counter-demonstration
contremarche *nf* countermarch
contremarque *nf* counter-mark (gold, etc); pass-out check; voucher
contre-offensive *nf* counter-offensive
contre-ordre *nm* counter-order, countermand
contrepartie *nf* counterpart; duplicate; cross-entry; opposite view; *sp* return match; en ~ in exchange, as against this
contre-passer *vt* endorse back; reverse (entry in book-keeping)
contrepèterie *nf* spoonerism
contre-pied *nm* opposite; prendre le ~ take the opposite view or course
contre-plaqué *nm* plywood; *adj* laminated
contrepoids *nm* counterweight; counterpoise
contre-poil (à) *adv phr* against the way of the hair (fur); prendre qn à ~ rub s/o the wrong way
contrepoint *nm mus* counterpoint
contrepoison *nm* antidote
contre-proposition *nf* counter-proposal, counter-suggestion
contrer *vt* counter (boxing); double (cards); oppose
contre-révolution *nf* counter-revolution
contre-saison *nf* off-season period
contrescarpe *nf* counterscarp
contre-sceau *nm* counterseal
contresens *nm* wrong way; wrong sense; false interpretation; à ~ in the wrong direction or sense
contresigner *vt* countersign
contretemps *nm* mishap, hitch; inconvenience; *mus* note played against the beat; à ~ inopportunely
contre-torpilleur *nm* destroyer
contrevenant -e *n* infringer; delinquent
contrevenir *vi* (96) contravene, infringe
contrevent *nm* shutter (window)
contre-voie (à) *adv phr* (train) on the wrong side, in the wrong direction
contribuable *n* taxpayer, ratepayer

contribuer *vt* contribute; *vi* conduce
contributif -ive *adj* contributive
contribution *nf* contribution; tax, rate; mettre qn à ~ make s/o contribute
contrister *vt* sadden
contrit *adj* contrite, penitent
contrition *nf* contrition, penitence
contrôle *nm* roll, register; checking, testing, control, verification; auditing; hall-mark; check-point; box-office
contrôler *vt* control; check, inspect; stamp; audit; examine (passport); hold in check
contrôleur -euse *n* controller; ticket-inspector, ticket-collector; tax-inspector; auditor; supervisor; *nm* checking apparatus
controuvé *adj* fabricated, made up
controverse *nf* controversy
controverser *vt* question, dispute
contumace *nf* contumacy, non-appearance; par ~ by default, in absentia
contusion *nf* bruise, contusion
contusionner *vt* bruise
convaincre *vt* (94) convince; prove
convenable *adj* appropriate, suitable, fitting; decent
convenance *nf* fitness, suitability, propriety; conformity; convenience; observer (respecter) les ~s act with propriety
convenir *vi* (96) suit, fit; agree; admit; il convient de the right thing to do is
convention *nf* convention; agreement; de ~ conventional
conventionné *adj* bound by agreement; médecin ~ = doctor in national health service
conventionnel -elle *adj* conventional
convenu *adj* agreed, appointed
converger *vi* (3) converge
conversation *nf* conversation, talk; lier ~ enter into conversation
converser *vi* converse, talk
conversion *nf* conversion, change; *mil* wheeling; altering of interest rate
converti -e *n* convert
convertir *vt* convert
convexe *adj* convex
conviction *nf* conviction; *leg* pièce à ~ exhibit
convier *vt* invite; urge
convive *n* guest, table-companion
convocation *nf* summons, convocation; convening; calling up
convoi *nm* convoy; train, group of vehicles; escort; ~ funèbre funeral procession
convoiter *vt* covet, desire; lust after
convoitise *nf* covetousness, greed, cupidity
convoler *vi* marry, quit the single state

**convoquer** vt summon, convoke; convene; invite

**convoyer** vt (7) convoy, escort

**convulser** vt convulse

**convulsif -ive** adj convulsive

**convulsionner** vt convulse

**coopérateur -trice** n co-operator

**coopératif -ive** adj co-operative stores; co-operative (producers, etc)

**coopérer** vi (6) co-operate, work together

**coopter** vt co-opt

**coordonnées** nfpl coll personal details

**coordonner** vt co-ordinate

**copain** nm coll pal, mate, US buddy

**copeau** nm (wood) shaving; chip (metal)

**copie** nf copy, reproduction; paper, script (examination); imitation; **pour ~ conforme** certified true copy

**copier** vt copy, transcribe; reproduce; imitate

**copieux -ieuse** adj copious

**copilote** n co-pilot

**copine** nf girl friend

**copiste** n copier, copyist; imitator

**copropriétaire** n co-proprietor, joint owner

**copropriété** nf co-proprietorship, joint ownership

**copte** n + adj Copt, coptic

**coq** nm cock; weather-cock; **~ de bruyère** grouse; **au chant du ~** at cockcrow; **comme un ~ en pâte** in clover; **le ~ du village** cock of the walk

**coq-à-l'âne** nm invar string of non-sequiturs

**coque** nf shell; husk; hull; bow (ribbon); **œuf à la ~** soft-boiled egg

**coquelicot** nm (field) poppy

**coqueluche** nf whooping-cough; coll popular person

**coquerico** nm cock-a-doodle-doo

**coquerie** nf ship's galley

**coquet -ette** adj coquettish; smart, attractive, trim

**coqueter** vi (5) flirt, act the coquette

**coquetier** nm egg-cup; egg-seller

**coquette** nf flirt, coquette

**coquetterie** nf coquetry, coquettishness; fastidiousness; smartness

**coquillage** nm shell-fish, sea-shell

**coquille** nf shell (snail, etc); misprint; casing (motor); **~ Saint-Jacques** scallop; **escalier en ~** spiral staircase

**coquin -e** n rascal, rogue; adj rascally, roguish

**coquinerie** nf roguery; knavery

**cor** nm horn; horn-player; corn (foot); tine (antler); **~ anglais** tenor oboe; **à ~ et à cri** vociferously; **sonner du ~** sound the horn

**corail** nm (pl **coraux**) coral

**corallin** adj coral-red

**Coran (le)** nm Koran

**corbeau** nm crow; archi corbel

**corbeille** nf basket; (round) flower-bed; archi bell; theat dress-circle; **~ d'argent** shepherd's purse; **~ de mariage, de noces** wedding presents

**corbillard** nm hearse

**cordage** nm rope; roping; **~s** ropes, cordage

**corde** nf rope, cord, line; string; **~ à linge** clothes line; **~ à sauter** skipping rope; **~ de boyau** catgut; **avoir plusieurs ~s à son arc** have more than one string to one's bow; **ce n'est pas dans mes ~s** that's not in my line; **tenir la ~** be on the inside; have the advantage; **usé jusqu'à la ~** threadbare

**cordeau** nm line, tracing line

**cordée** nf party of mountaineers roped together

**cordelette** nf small cord; plait

**cordelier -ière** n Franciscan friar (nun)

**cordelière** nf friar's girdle; pyjama-cord

**cordelle** nf tow-line

**corder** vt twist into rope, cord; string

**corderie** nf rope-making; rope-trade; rope-walk

**cordial** nm cordial, restorative; adj cordial, hearty; stimulating

**cordialité** nf cordiality, heartiness

**cordier** nm rope-maker; tail-piece (violin)

**cordon** nm cord, string, strand, thread; lace; ribbon (decoration); cordon (troops); **~ de sonnette** bell-pull; **~ souple** flex

**cordon-bleu** nm (pl **cordons-bleus**) coll first-rate cook

**cordonner** vt twist, twine

**cordonnerie** nf shoemaking; cobbler's workshop

**cordonnet** nm braid, cord

**cordonnier** nm shoemaker, cobbler

**Corée** nf Korea

**coreligionnaire** n person of the same religion

**coriace** adj tough, hard; coll obstinate

**Corinthe** nf raisin de **~** currant

**cormoran** nm cormorant

**cornac** nm mahout

**corne** nf horn, horny matter; feeler; antenna; motor-horn; **~ d'abondance** cornucopia; **~ d'une page** dog's ear; **chapeau à ~s** cocked hat; coll **faire les ~s à** jeer at; **porter des ~s** be a cuckold

**corné** adj horny; dog-eared

**cornée** nf cornea

**corneille** nf crow, rook

**cornemuse** nf bagpipes

**corner** vt proclaim; turn down (corner

cornet

of a page); *vi* trumpet, blow the horn, hoot

**cornet** *nm* small horn; dice-box; cornet; cream horn; ~ **à pistons** cornet

**cornette** *nf* nun's cornet; *naut* burgee

**corniaud** *nm sl* fool, clot

**corniche** *nf* cornice; ledge (rock); cliff road

**cornichon** *nm* gherkin; *coll* fool, clot

**Cornouailles** *nf* Cornwall

**cornu** *adj* horned

**cornue** *nf* retort

**corollaire** *nm* corollary

**corolle** *nf bot* corolla

**coron** *nm dial* mining village

**corporatif -ive** *adj* corporate

**corporation** *nf* corporation; guild

**corporel -elle** *adj* corporal, bodily; corporeal

**corps** *nm* body; substance, main part; corps; trunk (tree, body); frame (bicycle); ~ à ~ hand to hand; ~ **composé** compound; ~ **de garde** guard-room; ~ **simple** element; **à bras le** ~ round the waist; **à** ~ **perdu** headlong; **avoir le diable au** ~ be bursting with devilment; **faire** ~ **avec** be an integral part of; **garde du** ~ body-guard; **périr** ~ **et biens** go down with all hands; **prendre** ~ take shape; **se donner** ~ **et âme** give oneself heart and soul

**corpulence** *nf* corpulence, stoutness

**corpulent** *adj* stout, fat, corpulent

**corpus** *nm* body (work, vocabulary)

**corpuscule** *nm* corpuscle

**correct** *adj* correct, accurate; proper (behaviour, etc)

**correcteur -trice** *n* corrector; proof-reader

**correctif -ive** *adj* corrective

**correction** *nf* correction, correcting; proof-reading; punishment; correctness; **maison de** ~ reformatory

**correctionnel -elle** *adj* tribunal ~ magistrate's court, police court

**correctionnelle** *nf* magistrate's court, police court

**corrélatif -ive** *adj* correlative

**correspondance** *nf* correspondence; agreement; connection (train, etc); communication (places)

**correspondant** *nm* correspondent; person in loco parentis; *adj* corresponding; connecting (train, etc)

**correspondre** *vi* correspond; agree, tally; communicate (rooms); run in connection (train, etc)

**corrida** *nf* bull-fight; *coll* free-for-all; complicated business

**corridor** *nm* corridor, passage

**corrigé** *nm* fair copy (exercise)

**corriger** *vt* (3) correct, read (proofs);

sub-edit; rectify; amend; punish, chastise; **se** ~ **d'un défaut** cure a fault

**corroborer** *vt* corroborate

**corroder** *vt* corrode, eat away

**corrompre** *vt* (85) corrupt, pervert, deprave; bribe; taint (meat)

**corrosif -ive** *adj* corrosive

**corrupteur -trice** *n* corrupter; briber; *adj* corrupting, depraving

**corruptible** *adj* corruptible; bribable

**corruption** *nf* corruption; bribing; tainting; decay; corruptness, depravity

**corsage** *nm* bodice

**corsaire** *nm* privateer; pirate, corsaire; **pantalon** ~ calf-length trousers, breeches

**Corse** *nf* Corsica

**corse** *adj* Corsican

**corsé** *adj* full-bodied; stout (cloth); spicy (story)

**corser** *vt* give body to; strengthen; **se** ~ become serious, complex (affair)

**corso** *nm* ~ **fleuri** floral procession

**cortège** *nm* procession; train, retinue

**corvée** *nf* forced labour; *mil* fatigue; *coll* chore, piece of drudgery

**cosaque** *nm* Cossack

**cosinus** *nm* cosine

**cosmétique** *nm + adj* cosmetic

**cosmique** *adj* cosmic

**cosmographie** *nf* cosmography

**cosmonaute** *n* cosmonaut, astronaut, spaceman (-woman)

**cosmopolite** *adj* cosmopolitan

**cosse** *nf* husk, shell, pod; *elect* spade terminal; *sl* **avoir la** ~ feel like doing nothing

**cossu** *adj* rich, well-to-do; rich-looking, grand

**costaud** *nm* tough guy, strong man; *adj* tough, hefty

**costume** *nm* costume dress; suit; (~) **tailleur** lady's tailor-made costume

**costumer** *vt* dress; **bal costumé** fancy-dress ball

**costumier -ière** *n* costumier; wardrobe-keeper

**cote** *nf* mark, number (classification); quota, share; quotation (stock-exchange); odds (race); assessment; marks (school exercise); ~ **d'alerte** danger point; ~ **mal taillée** compromise; **avoir une bonne** ~ be highly thought of

**côte** *nf* coast, shore; rib; slope, hill; ~ **à** ~ side by side; **à mi-** ~ half-way up the hill; **être à la** ~ be on one's beam-ends; **la Côte d'Azur** the French riviera

**côté** *nm* side; ~ **faible** weak spot; **à** ~ to one side; near; **à** ~ **de** next to; **de** ~ on one side; sideways; **de** ~ **et**

68

**d'autre** in all directions; **de mon ~** for my part; **du ~ de** towards; **mettre de ~** save, put by

**coteau** *nm* slope, hillside; hill

**côtelé** *adj* ribbed; **velours ~** corduroy

**côtelette** *nf* chop, cutlet

**coter** *vt* number, classify; assess; quote (shares); award (marks)

**coterie** *nf* set, coterie

**côtier -ière** *adj* coasting; coastal; inshore

**cotillon** *nm* cotillon; *ar* petticoat

**cotisation** *nf* clubbing together; quota, share; contribution; assessment

**cotiser (se)** *v refl* club together, subscribe

**coton** *nm* cotton; *coll* **filer un mauvais ~** be in a bad way

**cotonnade** *nf* cotton fabric

**cotonner (se)** *v refl* become fluffy; become sleepy (fruit)

**cotonneux -euse** *adj* cottony, downy; sleepy (fruit)

**cotonnier** *nm* cotton plant

**coton-poudre** *nm* gun cotton

**côtoyer** *vt* (7) hug (shore), keep close to, skirt; border

**cotte** *nf* skirt, petticoat, tunic; **~ de mailles** coat of mail

**cou** *nm* neck; **prendre ses jambes à son ~** take to one's heels

**couac** *nm* goose-note

**couard -e** *n* coward

**couardise** *nf* cowardice

**couchage** *nm* bedding; **sac de ~** sleeping-bag

**couchant** *nm* sunset; west; *adj* **soleil ~** setting sun

**couche** *nf* layer, bed; nappy, *US* diaper; social stratum; *lit* bed; **~s** confinement; **fausse ~** miscarriage; *sl* **il en a (tient) une ~!** he's a prize idiot!

**coucher** *nm* bedtime; sunset; *vt* put to bed; put up, accommodate; lay down; **~ par écrit** put down in writing; **qn sur son testament** mention s/o in one's will; **être couché** be in bed; be lying down; *vi* sleep, spend the night; **se ~** lie down; go to bed; set (sun)

**coucherie** *nf coll* sleeping around

**couchette** *nf* bunk, berth, couchette; cot

**coucheur -euse** *n* bedfellow; *nm sl* womanizer; **mauvais ~** difficult person to get on with

**couci-couça** *adv coll* so-so

**coude** *nm* elbow; bend (road); knee (pipe); **~ à ~** side by side; **jouer des ~s** elbow one's way; *sl* **lever le ~** drink a lot

**coudée** *nf* cubit; **avoir ses ~s franches** have a free hand; have elbow-room

**cou-de-pied** *nm* (*pl* **cous-de-pied**) instep

**couder** *vt* bend (pipe); crank (shaft)

**coudoyer** *vt* (7) jostle; elbow

**coudre** *vt* (28) sew, stitch; **cousu de fil blanc** easily seen through; **machine à ~** sewing-machine

**coudrier** *nm* hazel-tree

**couenne** *nf* skin (pig), rind; membrane (diphtheria)

**couic** *nm* chirp, cheep, squeak

**couille** *nf vulg* ball, testicle

**couillon** *nm sl* fool, clot, dope; *vulg* ball

**coulage** *nm* pouring (metal); casting; leaking; scuttling; waste

**coulant** *adj* flowing, running; easy-going; **nœud ~** slip-knot

**coulée** *nf* running, flow; outflow (lava); casting

**couler** *vt* pour; sink; scuttle; slip; cast; ruin (person); *coll* slip (coin, note); *sl* **se la ~ douce** take things easy; *vi* flow, run; leak; sink; trickle; pass by (time); **~ de source** happen effortlessly; be self-evident

**couleur** *nf* colour, hue, colouring; paint; appearance; complexion; suit (cards); **boîte de ~s** paint-box; **changer de ~** turn pale; **il m'en fait voir de toutes les ~s** he's a real trial to me; **marchand de ~s** ironmonger; **sous ~ de** under the guise of

**couleuvre** *nf* grass-snake; **avaler des ~s** swallow insults

**coulis** *nm* broth; (plaster) filling

**coulissant** *adj* sliding (*esp* door)

**coulisse** *nf* groove, slide; hem; **~s** wings (theatre); **dans les ~s** back-stage; in the background; **trombone à ~** slide trombone

**couloir** *nm* corridor, passage-way; gully; lane (traffic)

**coup** *nm* blow, knock; stroke; shot; attempt; threat, influence; **~ de coude** nudge; **~ de couteau** stab; **~ de crayon** pencil-stroke; **~ de dents** bite; **~ d'essai** first attempt; *coll* **~ de fil** phone call; **~ de foudre** love at first sight; **~ d'œil** glance; **~ de poing** punch; **~ de sang** apoplectic fit; **~ de téléphone** telephone call; **~ de tête** impulsive act; **~ sur ~** repeatedly; **à ~s de** with (by means of) blows from; **à ~ sûr** certainly; **après ~** too late; **boire un ~** have a drink; **donner un ~ de main à qn** give s/o a helping hand; *coll* **du ~** as a result; **du premier ~** from the very first; **entrer en ~ de vent** burst in; **être aux cent ~s** be at one's wits' end; *coll* **être dans le ~** be with it; **faire d'une pierre deux ~s** kill two birds with one stone; **faire les quatre cents ~s** get up to all sorts of tricks; **il m'a fait un sale ~** he played me a dirty trick; **manquer (rater) son ~** fail; **monter le ~** deceive, fool; **porter un**

~ deal a blow; **pour le** ~ for once;
**sous le** ~ **de** under the threat of, as a
result of; **sur le** ~ immediately; **tenir le**
~ **resist; valoir le** ~ be worth it
**coupable** *adj* guilty; sinful
**coupage** *nm* watering (wine)
**coup-de-poing** *nm* (*pl* **coups-de-poing**)
~ **américain** knuckle duster
**coupe** *nf* (wine-)cup; fruit-bowl;. cutting; cut (coat, etc); division (verse);
section; cut (cards); *coll* **être sous la** ~
**de qn** be under s/o's thumb
**coupé** *nm* brougham; coupé
**coupe-cigares** *nm invar* cigar-cutter
**coupe-circuit** *nm invar elect* cut-out
**coupe-file** *nm invar* pass, police permit
**coupe-gorge** *nm invar* cut-throat alley,
death trap
**coupe-jarret** *nm* ruffian, cut-throat
**coupe-ongles** *nm invar* nail-clippers
**coupe-papier** *nm invar* paper-knife
**couper** *vt* cut; intersect, cross; interrupt,
cut off; water (wine); mix, blend; cut
(cards); trump; switch off; geld; ~ **la**
**parole à qn** cut s/o short; ~ **l'appétit à**
**qn** take s/o's appetite away; *vi* cut; be
sharp; **se** ~ cut oneself; crack (skin);
intersect; contradict oneself
**couperet** *nm* cleaver, chopper; knife
**couperosé** *adj* blotchy
**coupeur -euse** *n* cutter
**couple** *nm* couple, pair; coupling; *nf*
brace, couple; leash
**couplet** *nm* verse (song)
**coupoir** *nm* cutter
**coupole** *nf* cupola; *coll* **sous la Coupole**
in the French Academy
**coupon** *nm* cutting, piece (of material),
remnant; coupon; counterfoil
**coupure** *nf* cut, gash; cutting; section or
piece cut out; note of small denomination
**cour** *nf* court; court of law; yard;
courtyard; playground (school); **être**
**bien en** ~ be in favour; **faire la** ~ **à qn**
pay court to s/o; court s/o
**courage** *nm* courage, bravery
**courageux -euse** *adj* brave, courageous;
spirited, hard-working
**couramment** *adv* fluently; readily; generally, usually
**courant** *nm* current, stream; forward
movement; ~ **d'air** draught; **dans le**
~ **du mois** during the course of the
month; **être au** ~ **de** know all about;
**mettre qn au** ~ inform s/o; *adj*
running, flowing; current; **écriture** ~ **e**
cursive handwriting; **fin** ~ at the end
of this month; **le 5** ~ the fifth inst.
**courbatu** *adj* stiff, aching
**courbature** *nf* stiffness
**courbaturer** *vt* tire out, wear out;

founder (horse)
**courbe** *nf* curve, bend; *adj* curved
**courber** *vt* + *vi* bend, curve; **se** ~ stoop,
bend; bow
**courbette** *nf* **faire des** ~ s bow and
scrape
**courbure** *nf* curvature
**courette** *nf* little yard, small courtyard
**coureur -euse** *n* runner; racer; frequenter; *coll* wolf, tart
**courge** *nf* gourd, marrow
**courgette** *nf* young marrow, courgette
**courir** *vt* (29) hunt, pursue; run (risk);
wander over; frequent; **l'argent ne**
**court pas les rues** money doesn't grow
on trees; *vi* run; race; sail (ship); **le**
**bruit court** rumour has it; **par le temps**
**qui court** nowadays
**courlis** *nm* curlew
**couronne** *nf* crown, coronet; wreath;
crown (coin, tooth)
**couronnement** *nm* crowning, coronation; capping, coping (wall); summit,
perfection
**couronner** *vt* crown; honour, award a
prize; cap, cope
**courre** *vt ar* **chasse à** ~ hunting (with
hounds)
**courrier** *nm* courier, messenger; mail,
correspondence, post; column (newspaper); **par retour de** ~ by return (of
post)
**courroie** *nf* strop, thong; *mech* belt
**courroucer** *vt* (4) *lit* anger
**courroux** *nm lit* anger
**cours** *nm* course; flow, current; lesson,
course of study; text book; currency;
circulation; rate; price (commodities);
~ **d'eau** stream; **avoir** ~ be legal
tender; be generally accepted; **donner**
**libre** ~ **à** give free rein to
**course** *nf* running, run; race; excursion,
trip; errand; course; ~ s (horse) races;
**champ de** ~ s race-course; **faire ses** ~ s
do one's shopping; **n'être plus dans la**
~ be left behind, be out of the running
**coursier** *nm lit* warhorse, charger
¹**court** *nm* tennis-court
²**court** *adj* short, brief; **à** ~ **de** short of;
**avoir la vue** ~ e be short-sighted, lack
foresight; **de** ~ e **durée** short-lived;
**pris de** ~ taken unawares; *adv* short;
**rester (demeurer)** ~ stop short
(speech); **tout** ~ simply
**courtage** *nm* brokerage
**courtaud** *adj* thickset, squat, short and
stocky
**court-bouillon** *nm* (*pl* **courts-bouillons**)
stock for cooking fish (with wine,
butter, spices)
**court-circuit** *nm* (*pl* **courts-circuits**)
short circuit

**courtepointe** *nf* counterpane
**courtier** *nm* broker
**courtisan** *nm* courtier
**courtisane** *nf* courtesan
**courtiser** *vt* court, pay court to; fawn on; woo
**courtois** *adj* courteous, polite; courtly
**courtoisie** *nf* courtesy, politeness
**court-vêtue** *adj f* short-skirted
**couru** *adj* popular, in demand; *coll* **c'est ~** it's a cert
**couseuse** *nf* seamstress
¹**cousin -e** *n* cousin; **~ germain** first cousin
²**cousin** *nm* gnat, daddy-long-legs
**cousinage** *nm* cousinship
**cousiner** *vi* live on good terms
**coussin** *nm* cushion
**coussinet** *nm* small cushion; *mech* bearing, bush; chair (rail)
**cousu** *p part* coudre
**coût** *nm* cost
**couteau** *nm* knife; **~ à découper** carving-knife; **à ~x tirés** at daggers drawn
**coutelas** *nm* cutlass
**coutelier** *nm* cutler
**coutellerie** *nf* cutlery; cutler's shop
**coûter** *vi* cost; be hard, difficult; **~ les yeux de la tête** cost a fortune; **coûte que coûte** at all costs; **prix coûtant** cost price
**coûteux -euse** *adj* costly, expensive; **peu ~** inexpensive
**coutil** *nm* twill, drill
**coutume** *nf* custom, habit, practice; **de ~** usually; **une fois n'est pas ~** one swallow doesn't make a summer
**coutumier -ière** *adj* in the habit of; customary; **~ du fait** in the habit of doing it; **droit ~** common law
**couture** *nf* needlework, sewing; seam; scar; *coll* **battre à plate ~** beat hollow, lick; **examiner sous toutes les ~s** inspect thoroughly; **haute ~** high-class fashion-trade
**couturer** *vt* scar; seam
**couturier -ière** *n* dress-designer; dressmaker
**couvage** *nm* incubation
**couvaison** *nf* brooding time
**couvée** *nf* clutch, sitting (eggs); brood
**couvent** *nm* convent
**couver** *vt* sit on (eggs); brood; sicken for; lavish attention on; **~ des yeux** gaze fondly on s/o; *vi* smoulder; be brewing
**couvercle** *nm* lid, cap, top
**couvert** *nm* shelter, cover; knife, fork and spoon; place (at table); cover charge; **à ~** under cover; **mettre le ~** lay the table; **sous le ~ de** under cover of
**couverture** *nf* cover, covering; blanket, rug; roofing; **~ de lit** bedspread; **tirer la ~ à soi** take the lion's share
**couveuse** *nf* sitting-hen; incubator
**couvre-chef** *nm* headdress, hat
**couvre-feu** *nm* curfew
**couvre-lit** *nm* bedspread, counterpane
**couvre-livre** *nm* dust-jacket
**couvre-pied(s)** *nm* coverlet; bedspread
**couvre-plat** *nm* dish-cover
**couvreur** *nm* roofer; tiler, slater, thatcher
**couvrir** *vt* (30) cover; roof; clothe; shield, protect, safeguard; drown (noise); **se ~** put on clothes; put on a hat; become overcast
**crabe** *nm* crab
**crac** *nm* + *interj* crack, snap
**crachat** *nm* spittle, spit; *coll* **se noyer dans un ~** make a mountain out of a molehill
**crachement** *nm* spitting, spit
**cracher** *vt* spit out; *sl* cough up (money); *coll* **tout craché** the spitting image of; *vi* spit
**crachin** *nm* mist, fine drizzle
**crachoir** *nm* spittoon; *sl* **tenir le ~** hold forth
**crack** *nm coll* ace, champion
**crackage , craquage** *nm* cracking (oil)
**craie** *nf* chalk
**craindre** *vt* (55) fear, dread; be unable to stand (something)
**crainte** *nf* fear, dread; **de (dans la) ~ de** for fear of
**craintif -ive** *adj* timid, fearful
**cramoisi** *adj* crimson
**crampe** *nf* cramp
**crampon** *nm* cramp-iron; hook-nail, stud; *coll* bore; **~s crampons**
**cramponner** *vt* clamp together; *coll* pester, button-hole, stick to; **se ~ à** hang on to
**cran** *nm* notch; cog; *coll* nerve; **~ de sûreté** safety-catch; **couteau à ~ d'arrêt** flick knife; **être à ~** be exasperated
¹**crâne** *nm* skull
²**crâne** *adj* plucky, jaunty
**crâner** *vi coll* show off
**crânien -ienne** *adj* cranial; **boîte ~ne** skull
**crapaud** *nm* toad; low easy chair; baby grand piano; *coll* kid
**crapouillot** *nm coll* (trench) mortar; mortar-bomb
**crapule** *nf* debauchery; riff-raff; scoundrel
**crapuleux -euse** *adj* dissolute, crapulous
**craque** *nf coll* tall story
**craqueler** *vt* (5) *cer* crackle

**craquelure** *nf* crack

**craquer** *vi* crack, crackle; crunch; creak

¹**crasse** *nf* dirt, filth; dross; mire; avarice; *sl* **faire une ~ à qn** play a dirty trick on s/o

²**crasse** *adj* **ignorance ~** gross ignorance

**crasser** *vt* clog, foul

**crasseux -euse** *adj* dirty, filthy; *sl* stingy

**crassier** *nm* slag-heap

**cratère** *nm* crater, shell-hole

**cravache** *nf* riding-whip

**cravacher** *vt* flog (horse); horsewhip

**cravate** *nf* tie; cravat, scarf; *coll* **~ de chanvre** hangman's rope

**crayère** *nf* chalk-pit

**crayeux -euse** *adj* chalky

**crayon** *nm* pencil, crayon

**crayonnage** *nm* pencilling

**crayonner** *vt* pencil; jot down; make a pencil sketch of

**créance** *nf* credit; belief; **lettres de ~** credentials

**créancier -ière** *n* creditor

**créateur -trice** *n* creator; *adj* creative

**création** *nf* creation; founding

**crécelle** *nf* rattle; **voix de ~** rasping voice

**crécerelle** *nf* kestrel

**crèche** *nf* manger; crib, day-nursery

**crédence** *nf* sideboard, buffet

**crédibilité** *nf* credibility

**crédit** *nm* credit; repute; influence; **à ~** on credit; **faire ~ à qn** give s/o credit

**créditer** *vt* credit

**créditeur -trice** *n* creditor

**credo** *nm* creed

**crédule** *adj* credulous

**crédulité** *nf* credulity

**créer** *vt* create; found, establish

**crémaillère** *nf* pot-hanger; *mech* toothed rack; **chemin de fer à ~** cog-wheel railway; **pendre la ~** give a house-warming party

**crémation** *nf* cremation

**crématoire** *adj* crematory; **four ~** crematorium

**crème** *nf* cream; **un (café) ~** a white coffee

**crémer** *vt* (6) cream

**crémerie** *nf* dairy (shop), creamery; small restaurant

**crémeux -euse** *adj* creamy

**crémier -ière** *n* dairyman, dairywoman

**créneau** *nm* crenel, battlement; space, interval

**créneler** *vt* (5) crenelate; notch (wheel); mill (coin)

**crénelure** *nf* crenellation

**créosoter** *vt* creosote

¹**crêpe** *nf* pancake

²**crêpe** *nm* crepe; mourning band

**crêpelé** *adj* fuzzy

**crêper** *vt* frizz; crimp; *coll* **se ~ le chignon** fly at one another (women)

**crépir** *vt* rough-cast (wall); grain (leather)

**crépitement** *nm* crackling

**crépiter** *vi* crackle; patter; sputter

**crépu** *adj* fuzzy, frizzy

**crépusculaire** *adj* twilight, crepuscular

**crépuscule** *nm* twilight, dusk

**cresson** *nm* cress; **~ de fontaine** water-cress

**cressonnière** *nf* water-cress bed

**crête** *nf* comb (bird); crest; ridge, top

**crête-de-coq** *nf* (*pl* **crêtes-de-coq**) cockscomb

**crétin -e** *n* cretin, idiot; *coll* fool

**crétinisme** *nm* cretinism

**cretonne** *nf* cretonne

**creuser** *vt* dig, excavate; hollow out; bore; **~ un sujet** go deeply into a subject; **se ~ la tête** rack one's brains

**creuset** *nm* crucible, melting-pot

**creux** *nm* hollow, cavity; hole; trough (wave); **~ de l'estomac** pit of the stomach; *adj* (*f* **-euse**) hollow; **chemin ~** sunken road; **période creuse** slack period; **ventre ~** empty stomach

**crevaison** *nf* puncture (tyre)

**crevant** *adj coll* exhausting; *coll* funny

**crevasse** *nf* crevasse; crevice; crack (skin)

**crevasser** *vt* crack; chap

**crève** *nf sl* death

**crève-cœur** *nm invar* bitter disappointment; heartbreak

**crève-la-faim** *nm invar sl* starving wretch

**crever** *vt* (6) burst; puncture; **~ le cœur** break the heart; *coll* **~ les yeux** be perfectly obvious; **~ un cheval** exhaust a horse; *vi* burst; split; *sl* die; get a puncture; **~ de rire** split one's sides with laughter

**crevette** *nf* shrimp

**cri** *nm* cry, shout; chirp; squeak, squeal; **à grands ~s** loudly; **dernier ~** latest fashion; **pousser les hauts ~s** complain bitterly

**criailler** *vi* bawl, cry out; complain

**criaillerie** *nf coll* crying, shouting; complaining

**criant** *adj* flagrant, gross, crying

**criard** *adj* crying, noisy, shrill; gaudy

**crible** *nm* sieve, riddle; **passer au ~** sift

**cribler** *vt* sift, riddle; **~ de balles** riddle with bullets; **criblé de dettes** up to one's ears in debt

¹**cric** *nm* lifting-jack

²**cric** *interj* snap!, crack!

**cri-cri** *nm invar coll* cricket

**criée** *nf* auction

**crier** *vt + vi* shout, cry out; call, call out;

squeal; creak; proclaim; hawk
**crieur -ieuse** *n* shouter, crier; ~ **public** town-crier
**crime** *nm* crime
**criminel -elle** *n + adj* criminal
**crin** *nm* horsehair
**crinière** *nf* mane
**crique** *nf* creek
**criquet** *nm* locust
**crise** *nf* crisis; slump; attack, fit (illness); shortage
**crispant** *adj coll* aggravating
**crispation** *nf* crispation, shrivelling up; nervous twitching
**crisper** *vt* contract, clench; *coll* irritate
**crissement** *nm* grating, grinding (teeth)
**crisser** *vi* grate; rasp; grind (teeth); crunch (gravel)
**cristal** *nm* crystal; ~ **taillé** cut glass
**cristalline** *adj* crystalline; clear as crystal
**cristallisation** *nf* crystallization
**cristalliser** *vt* crystallize; **sucre cristallisé** granulated sugar
**critère** *nm* criterion, test
**critérium** *nm sp* competition
**critiquable** *adj* open to criticism
**critique** *n* critic, reviewer; *nf* criticism; censure; review; *adj* critical, crucial
**croassement** *nm* cawing
**croasser** *vi* caw
**croc** *nm* hook; fang, tusk
**croc-en-jambe** *nm* (*pl* **crocs-en-jambe**) **faire un** ~ **à qn** trip s/o up
**croche** *nf mus* quaver, *US* eighth note
**crocher** *vt* hook
**crochet** *nm* hook; fang (snake); sudden turn, swerve; square bracket; *coll* **vivre aux** ~**s de qn** live at s/o's expense
**crocheter** *vt* (5) pick (lock); crochet
**crocheteur** *nm* porter; lock-picker, thief
**crochu** *adj* hooked; crooked; **avoir les doigts** ~**s** be light-fingered; be greedy
**croire** *vt + vi* (31) believe, think; have faith, trust; **à l'en** ~ if one is to believe him; **c'est à ne pas y** ~ it's beyond all belief; **je (le) crois bien** I should think so; **je lui croyais du courage** I thought he was brave; **n'en croyez rien** don't believe a word of it; **se** ~ fancy oneself
**croisade** *nf* crusade
**croisé** *nm* crusader
**croisée** *nf* crossing; casement window
**croisement** *nm* crossing, intersection; cross-breeding, cross(-breed)
**croiser** *vt* cross; fold over; pass, meet (traffic or person coming from opposite direction); meet (eyes); **mots croisés** crossword puzzle(s); **rester les bras croisés** remain arms folded; stay idle; **veston croisé** double-breasted jacket
**croiseur** *nm* cruiser

**croisière** *nf* cruise; **vitesse de** ~ cruising speed
**croisillon** *nm* cross-piece, transom
**croissance** *nf* growth
¹**croissant** *nm* crescent; croissant; bill-hook
²**croissant** *pres part* **croître**
**croître** *vi* (32) grow, increase
**croix** *nf* cross; (print) dagger; **en** ~ crosswise
¹**croquant** *nm* rustic, wretch
²**croquant** *adj* crisp, crunchy
**croque-mitaine** *nm* bogy-man
**croque-monsieur** *nm invar* fried cheese and ham sandwich
**croque-mort** *nm* (undertaker's) mute
**croquer** *vt* crunch, munch; sketch; ~ **le marmot** wait a long time; **belle à** ~ perfectly lovely; *vi* crunch
**croquet** *nm* croquet; *cul* almond biscuit
**croquignole** *nf* flick; kind of biscuit
**croquis** *nm* sketch
**cross** *nm* cross-country
**crosse** *nf* bishop's crook; rifle-butt; hockey-stick
**crotale** *nm* rattlesnake
**crotte** *nf* dung; mud, dirt; ~ **de chocolat** chocolate (drop); *interj sl* blast!
**crotter** *vt* dirty, make muddy
**crottin** *nm* dung (*esp* horses)
**croulant** *nm sl* old fogey; *adj* tumble-down, tottering
**croulement** *nm* collapse, falling-in
**crouler** *vi* collapse; totter
**croupe** *nf* rump, croup, crupper; little hill; **monter en** ~ ride behind, ride pillion
**croupetons (à)** *adv phr* crouching
**croupi** *adj* stagnant, foul
**croupier** *nm* croupier
**croupière** *nf* crupper
**croupion** *nm* rump (bird); parson's nose
**croupir** *vi* wallow (in filth); stagnate
**croustillant** *adj* crisp, crusty; *coll* spicy
**croustiller** *vi* crunch
**croûte** *nf* crust, rind; scab; *coll* daub (painting); *coll* **casser la** ~ eat, have a meal
**croûton** *nm* piece of crust; sippet
**croyable** *adj* believable
**croyance** *nf* belief
**croyant -e** *n* believer
¹**cru** *nm* vineyard; place of growth; **de son** ~ of one's own invention; **grand** ~ great wine
²**cru** *adj* raw; crude, harsh; **à** ~ next to the skin; directly
**cruauté** *nf* cruelty; act of cruelty
**cruche** *nf* jug, pitcher; *coll* fool
**cruchon** *nm* small jug
**crucifier** *vt* crucify
**cruciforme** *adj* cruciform

**cruciverbiste** *n* crossword puzzle enthusiast

**crudité** *nf* crudity, crudeness; coarseness; ~ s raw vegetables (*esp* as hors d'œuvres)

**crue** *nf* rising (river), spate, flood

**cruel -elle** *adj* cruel

**crûment** *adv* crudely, roughly

**crustacés** *nmpl* shell-fish, crustacea

**crypte** *nf* crypt

**cryptogame** *nm* mushroom

**cryptogramme** *nm* cipher, cryptogram

**cubage** *nm* cubic content

**cubain** *adj* Cuban

**cube** *nm* cube; **jeu de ~ s** set of building blocks; *adj* cubic

**cuber** *vt* cube; have a cubic content of

**cubique** *adj* cubical

**cubisme** *nm* cubism

**cueillage** *nm* gathering, picking, plucking

**cueillette** *nf* gathering, picking

**cueillir** *vt* (33) gather, pick, pluck; *coll* nab, pinch, arrest

**cuiller, cuillère** *nf* spoon

**cuillerée** *nf* spoonful

**cuir** *nm* hide, leather; error in liaison

**cuirasse** *nf* cuirass, breast-plate; armour-plate

**cuirassé** *nm* battleship

**cuirasser** *vt* armour-plate

**cuire** *vt* + *vi* (80) cook; *vt* fire, bake (pottery, etc); **~ à l'eau** boil; **il vous en cuira** you will regret it

**cuisant** *adj* smarting, burning, acute

**cuisine** *nf* kitchen; art of cookery, cooking; *coll* jiggery-pokery; **faire la ~** do the cooking

**cuisiner** *vt* + *vi* cook; *vt coll* cook (books); *coll* grill (prisoner)

**cuisinier -ière** *n* cook

**cuisinière** *nf* cooker

**cuissard** *adj* **bottes ~ es** waders, thigh-boots

**cuisse** *nf* thigh

**cuisson** *nf* cooking; firing (pottery, etc); smarting

**cuistre** *nm* pedant

**cuite** *nf sl* **prendre une ~** get drunk

**cuivre** *nm* copper; **~ s** brass (instruments); **~ jaune** brass

**cuivrer** *vt* copper; **teint cuivré** bronzed complexion

**cul** *nm sl* bottom, arse, *US* ass; haunches

**culasse** *nf* breech (firearm); cylinder-head

**culbute** *nf* somersault, tumble

**culbuter** *vt* upset, knock over, tip over; *vi* fall head over heels

**culbuteur** *nm eng* tipper; rocker-arm

**cul-de-jatte** *nm* (*pl* **culs-de-jatte**) legless cripple

**cul-de-sac** *nm* (*pl* **culs-de-sac**) blind alley; dead end

**culinaire** *adj* culinary

**culminant** *adj* **point ~** highest point

**culot** *nm* bottom (church lamp); *coll* cheek, nerve

**culotte** *nf* shorts, knickerbockers; rump (beef); **c'est elle qui porte la ~** she's the one who wears the trousers

**culotté** *adj* cocky, cheeky

**culotter** *vt* put breeches on; season (pipe)

**culpabilité** *nf* culpability, guilt

**culte** *nm* worship; religious service

**cul-terreux** *nm* (*pl* **culs-terreux**) *coll* peasant

**cultivable** *adj* arable

**cultivateur** *nm* farmer

**cultivé** *adj* cultivated; cultured

**cultiver** *vt* cultivate, farm, grow (plants)

**cultuel -uelle** *adj* pertaining to worship

**culture** *nf* cultivation; breeding; culture; **~ s** land under cultivation

**cumul** *nm* cumulation (offices)

**cumuler** *vt* cumulate (offices)

**cunéiforme** *adj* wedge-shaped

**cupide** *adj* greedy, covetous

**cupidité** *nf* cupidity, greed

**Cupidon** *nm* Cupid

**curateur -trice** *n* trustee, guardian

**curatif -ive** *adj* curative

**cure** *nf* care; cure (souls); treatment; curé's residence

**curé** *nm* parish priest

**cure-dents** *nm invar* toothpick

**curée** *nf* quarry (hunting); kill; **âpre à la ~** eager for gain

**cure-pipe** *nm* pipe-cleaner

**curer** *vt* pick (teeth); clean (nails); clean out

**curetage** *nm* curetting, curettage

**curieux** *nm* curious part; *n* (*f* **-ieuse**) sightseer; *adj* (*f* **-ieuse**) curious, inquisitive; inquiring (mind); quaint, odd

**curiosité** *nf* curiosity, inquisitiveness; peculiarity

**cursif -ive** *adj* cursive, running (handwriting); cursory

**cutané** *adj* cutaneous

**cuve** *nf* vat

**cuvée** *nf* vatful; wine produced from vineyard

**cuver** *vt* **~ son vin** sleep it off

**cuvette** *nf* wash-basin; shallow dish; depression (land)

**cuvier** *nm* wash-tub

**cyanose** *nf med* cyanosis

**cyanure** *nm* cyanide

**cyclable** *adj* reserved for bicycles; **piste ~** cycle path

**cyclique** *adj* cyclic

**cyclisme** *nm* cycling

**cycliste** *n* cyclist
**cyclomoteur** *nm* autocycle
**cyclope** *nm* Cyclops
**cygne** *nm* swan
**cylindre** *nm* cylinder
**cylindrée** *nf* cylinder-capacity
**cylindrer** *vt* roll (lawn, road); mangle
**cylindrique** *adj* cylindrical
**cymbale** *nf* cymbal

**cymbalier** *nm* cymbalist
**cynique** *adj* cynical; shameless, impudent
**cynisme** *nm* cynicism; effrontery, shame-lessness
**cynodrome** *nm* greyhound-racing track
**cyprès** *nm* cypress-tree
**cypriote** *adj* Cypriot
**cystite** *nf* cystitis
**cytise** *nm* laburnum; cytisus

# D

**D** *nm coll* **le système D** resourcefulness
**d'abord** *adv phr* at first; **tout ~** first of all
**dac, d'acc** *adv phr* + *interj coll* = d'accord
**dactyle** *nm* dactyl
**dactylo(graphe)** *n* typist
**dactylographie** *nf* typing
**dactylographier** *vt* type
**dada** *nm* gee-gee; *coll* hobby, pet subject; *arts* dada
**dadais** *nm* booby
**dague** *nf* dagger
**daigner** *vi* condescend, deign
**daim** *nm* fallow-deer, buck; buckskin; suède
**dais** *nm* canopy
**dallage** *nm* paving; pavement; tiled floor
**dalle** *nf* flagstone; floor-tile; slab; *sl* **se rincer la ~** wet one's whistle
**daller** *vt* pave; tile (floor)
**daltonien -ienne** *adj* colour-blind
**daltonisme** *nm* colour-blindness
**Damas** *nm* Damascus
**damas** *nm* damask; damson (plum)
**damasser** *vt* damask
**¹dame** *nf* lady; *sl* missus, good lady; queen (cards, chess); king (draughts); **jeu de ~s** draughts
**²dame** *interj* (*usu* with **oui**) indeed
**damer** *vt* crown (draughts)
**damier** *nm* draught-board; **en ~** chequered
**damnable** *adj* damnable; detestable
**damner** *vt* damn; **âme damnée** slave of s/o; **se ~** incur damnation
**damoiseau** *nm* young beau
**dandiner (se)** *v refl* waddle
**Danemark** *nm* Denmark

**danger** *nm* danger, peril; **mettre en ~** endanger; **pas de ~!** no fear of that!
**dangereux -euse** *adj* dangerous
**Danois -e** *n* Dane
**danois** *nm* Danish (language); *adj* Danish
**dans** *prep* in; within; during; **~ le temps** formerly; **boire ~ un verre** drink out of a glass; **cela coûte ~ les cent francs** that costs about a hundred francs; **il arrivera ~ les dix jours** he will arrive during the next ten days
**dansant** *adj* dancing; **thé ~** tea-dance
**danse** *nf* dance, dancing; **~ de Saint-Guy** St Vitus's dance; *coll* **entrer en ~** join in; **mener la ~** be the ringleader
**danser** *vi* dance; **ne savoir sur quel pied ~** not know what to do
**danseur -euse** *n* dancer; ballet-dancer; dancing partner; *sp* **pédaler en danseuse** stand up on one's pedals
**dard** *nm* sting (insect); forked tongue (snake); *ar* dart, spear
**darder** *vt* shoot forth, dart; flash (glance)
**dare-dare** *adv* helter-skelter, straight away, hurriedly
**darne** *nf cul* slice, steak (fish)
**dartre** *nf med* scurfy affection
**date** *nf* date; **de longue ~** of long standing, for a long time; **en ~ de** under date of; **faire ~** be a landmark in history; **prendre ~ pour** fix a date for
**dater** *vt* + *vi* date
**datif** *nm gramm* dative case
**datte** *nf* date
**dattier** *nm* date-palm
**daube** *nf cul* stew

**dauber** *vt cul* stew, braise

**dauphin** *nm* dolphin; Dauphin; *fig* successor-designate

**daurade** *nf see* **dorade**

**davantage** *adv* more; **pas ~** no more; no longer

**de** *prep* from; of; out of; by, with; **~ cette façon** in this way; **~ lui-même** off his own bat; **~ sa propre main** with his own hand; **d'un air drôle** with a strange air, strange-looking; **c'est bien ~ lui** that's just like him; **cette pièce est ~ Sartre** that play is by Sartre; **large ~ trois mètres** three metres wide; **pleurer ~ joie** cry for joy; **quelque chose ~ bon** something good

**dé** *nm* thimble; dice; tee (golf)

**déambuler** *vi coll* stroll about

**débâcle** *nf* downfall, collapse, rout; breaking up (ice on river)

**débâcler** *vt* clear of ice; *vi* break up (ice)

**déballage** *nm* unpacking; *coll* confession

**déballer** *vt* unpack; get sth off one's chest, confess

**déballeur** *nm* hawker

**débandade** *nf* rout; stampede; **à la ~** in confusion

**débander** *vt* relax; unbend (bow); unbandage; rout; disband

**débarbouiller** *vt* wash (*usu* face); **se ~** wash one's face

**débarcadère** *nm* landing-stage

**débarder** *vt* unload

**débardeur** *nm* docker, stevedore; tight-fitting sleeveless pullover

**débarquement** *nm* disembarking, landing; unloading

**débarquer** *vt* unload, discharge (cargo); disembark, set off (passengers); *coll* sack, get rid of; *vi* disembark, land; alight; *coll* turn up; **il débarque de sa province** he's fresh from the country, he's still got straw in his hair

**débarras** *nm* riddance; lumber-room

**débarrasser** *vt* clear, disencumber; **se ~ de** get rid of

**débarrer** *vt* unbar

**débat** *nm* debate, discussion; dispute

**débattable** *adj* debatable

**débattre** *vt* debate, discuss; **se ~** struggle

**débauche** *nf* debauchery

**débauché** *adj* debauched

**débaucher** *vt* lead astray, corrupt, debauch; distract, entice from work; discharge

**débile** *adj* feeble, sickly; *coll* silly

**débilitant** *adj* debilitating

**débilité** *nf* debility, weakness

**débine** *nf sl* poverty

**débiner** *vt coll* run down, disparage; *sl* se

**~ hop it, piss off**

**débit** *nm* sale; shop; output, delivery; flow; delivery (speech); capacity

**débitant -e** *n* retailer

**débiter** *vt* sell, retail; cut up; produce, turn out; debit; recite, deliver

**débiteur -trice** *n* debtor

**déblai** *nm* cutting, excavation; **~s** earth cleared by excavation

**déblatérer** *vt* (6) **~ des injures** fling abuse; *vi* vituperate, rail

**déblayer** *vt* (7) clear away; clear (ground)

**débloquer** *vt* raise the blockade; unclamp; release, defreeze (assets); **se ~** become resolved; (traffic) flow more freely

**débobiner** *vt elect* unwind

**déboire(s)** *nm* (*pl*) disappointment; rebuff

**déboisement** *nm* deforestation

**déboiser** *vt* deforest, clear (woodland)

**déboîter** *vt* disconnect; dislocate; **se ~** come out of joint; *mot* filter

**débonnaire** *adj* affable, good-natured

**débordé** *adj* overwhelmed, snowed under

**débordement** *nm* overflowing; outburst; **~s** excesses

**déborder** *vt* project, protrude, overlap; outflank; untuck; remove the edging from; *vi* overflow; extend beyond; **~ de vie** be full of life

**débotter** *vt* unboot

**débouché** *nm* outlet; issue; opening, opportunity

**déboucher** *vt* clear, remove obstruction from; uncork; *vi* emerge; open out; result

**déboucler** *vt* unbuckle; uncurl

**débouler** *vi coll* fall head over heels, tumble down

**déboulonner** *vt* unrivet

**débourber** *vt* remove mud from; cleanse, clean out; pull out of the mud

**débourrer** *vt* strip; remove stuffing from

**débours** *nmpl* disbursement

**déboursement** *nm* disbursement

**débourser** *vt* pay out, disburse

**déboussolé** *adj coll* confused, disconcerted

**debout** *adv* standing, upright; out of bed; **tenir ~** make sense, hold water (argument); **vent ~** head wind

**débouter** *vt leg* reject (suit)

**déboutonner** *vt* unbutton

**débraillé** *adj* untidy, slovenly (dress); loose (morals)

**débrancher** *vt elect* disconnect; unhook (coaches)

**débrayage** *nm* disconnecting; declutching; downing tools

**débrayer** *vt* (7) disconnect; *vi* declutch;

down tools

**débrider** vt unbridle

**débris** nm fragment; nmpl débris, remains

**débrouillard** adj coll resourceful

**débrouiller** vt disentangle, unravel; clear up (matter); se ~ manage; get out of difficulty

**débusquer** vt drive out of cover or refuge

**début** nm beginning, start; first appearance; first turn (game); dès le ~ from the very beginning

**débutant -e** n beginner, novice; nf débutante

**débuter** vi begin, start; make one's first appearance; play first

**deçà** adv on this side; ~ (et) delà on all sides; en ~ de this side of

**décacheter** vt (5) unseal

**décade** nf period of ten days; decade

**décadence** nf decadence, decline

**décagénaire** n coll teenager

**décalage** nm removal of wedge(s); alteration (time); discrepancy, variation

**décalaminer** vt decarbonize

**décaler** vt remove wedge(s) from; displace (in space or time); shift

**décalque** nm transferring; transfer (picture)

**décalquer** vt transfer (picture)

**décamper** vi decamp, run away

**décantation** nf decanting

**décanter** vt decant

**décapant** nm cleansing or scouring solution; paint remover

**décaper** vt scour, clean

**décapitation** nf decapitation, beheading

**décapiter** vt behead, decapitate

**décapsuler** vt remove the top from (bottle)

**décapsuleur** nm bottle-opener

**décarburer** vt decarbonize

**décarcasser (se)** v refl coll go to great trouble, tear one's guts out

**décasyllabe** nm decasyllable; adj decasyllabic

**décati** adj coll the worse for wear

**décatir** vt take the gloss off

**décaver** vt coll clean out (gambling)

**décédé** adj deceased

**décéder** vi (6) die

**déceler** vt (6) discover, unearth; disclose, divulge

**décembre** nm December

**décemment** adv decently

**décence** nf decency; propriety

**décennal** adj decennial

**décennie** nf decade, period of ten years

**décent** adj decent, modest; proper, becoming

**décentralisation** nf decentralization

**décentraliser** vt decentralize

**décentrer** vt put out of centre (lens)

**déception** nf disappointment; deceit

**décerner** vt award, bestow; decree

**décès** nm decease, death; acte de ~ death certificate

**décevant** adj disappointing; deceptive

**décevoir** vt disappoint

**déchaîné** adj furious, wild, mad

**déchaînement** nm letting loose; breaking loose; outburst

**déchaîner** vt unchain, let loose; se ~ break out; lose one's temper

**déchanter** vi coll climb down, lower one's tone

**décharge** nf unloading, discharge; overflow; relief; dumping-ground (refuse); témoin à ~ witness for the defence

**déchargement** nm unloading; discharging

**décharger** vt unload; discharge; tip; relieve of load; se ~ go off (gun); run down (battery); flow, empty (river); se ~ d'une affaire sur qn shift the responsibility for a matter onto s/o else

**déchargeur** nm docker, unloader

**décharné** adj emaciated, skinny, fleshless

**déchausser** vt take off s/o's shoes; lay bare the roots of (tree); se ~ take off one's shoes; become loose (teeth)

**dèche** nf sl poverty

**déchéance** nf decadence; downfall; expiration; forfeiture

**déchet** nm decrease, diminution, falling off; waste; scrap

**déchiffrable** adj decipherable; legible

**déchiffrer** vt decipher; decode; sight-read (music)

**déchiqueté** adj jagged; mangled

**déchiqueter** vt (5) cut, tear to pieces or shreds; mangle

**déchirant** adj harrowing, heart-rending

**déchirement** nm tearing, rending

**déchirer** vt tear, tear up, rend; se ~ tear, get torn

**déchirure** nf tear, rent, rip; laceration

**déchoir** vi (34) fall (from high position); decline

**déchu** adj fallen

**décidé** adj resolute, determined; decided

**de-ci de-là** adv phr here and there

**décidément** adv resolutely; positively, decidedly; obviously; ~, ça ne va pas aujourd'hui it's just not my day

**décider** vt decide, settle; determine; persuade; se ~ decide, resolve, make up one's mind

**décimale** nf decimal

**décimer** vt decimate

**décisif -ive** adj decisive, final; conclusive; peremptory (tone)

**décision** nf decision; resolve; determination

**déclamateur -trice** n declaimer, tub-thumper

**déclamation** nf declamation; ranting

**déclamatoire** adj declamatory; ranting

**déclamer** vt declaim; vi rant

**déclaration** nf declaration, proclamation; notification

**déclaré** adj declared, professed

**déclarer** vt declare, proclaim, announce; notify; se ~ declare; break out (illness); declare one's feelings

**déclassement** nm change of class (in railway, etc)

**déclasser** vt unclass; transfer from one class to another; bring down; se ~ lower one's social position

**déclenchement** nm releasing, disengaging; launching, setting in motion

**déclencher** vt release, disconnect; start, set in motion; launch

**déclic** nm catch, trigger; noise of catch, click

**déclin** nm decline, wane, falling off, decadence

**déclinaison** nf gramm declension; declination (star)

**décliner** vt decline; refuse; vi wane, decline

**déclivité** nf slope, declivity, incline

**décloisonner** vt fig remove the barriers in

**déclouer** vt unnail

**décocher** vt shoot, let fly

**décodage** nm decoding

**décoder** vt decode

**décoiffer** vt remove (s/o's) hat; disarrange (s/o's) hair

**décolérer** vi (6) calm down, become less angry

**décollage** nm unsticking; take-off (aircraft)

**décoller** vt unstick, unglue; loosen; vi take off (aircraft); get off to a start; se ~ become unstuck, work loose

**décolleté** adj with a low neck (dress); with a low-necked dress (woman)

**décolleter** vt (5) cut out the neck of (a dress); cut (screw)

**décolorant** nm bleaching agent

**décoloration** nf discolouring, bleaching; discolouration, fading

**décolorer** vt discolour, bleach; take the colour out of

**décombres** nmpl débris, rubbish, ruins

**décommander** vt cancel (order, meeting), countermand

**décomplexé** adj free of complexes, relaxed

**décomposer** vt decompose; decay; distort (features); se ~ rot, decay; become distorted (features)

**décomposition** nf decomposition, decay; distortion (features)

**décompte** nm discount, deduction; disappointment

**décompter** vt deduct as discount

**déconcerter** vt upset, confuse; disconcert

**déconfit** adj crestfallen, nonplussed

**déconfiture** nf discomfiture; failure

**décongeler** vt (5) thaw

**décongestionner** vt relieve congestion in; clear

**déconseiller** vt advise against, dissuade

**déconsidérer** vt (6) discredit, bring into disrepute

**décontaminer** vt decontaminate

**décontenancer** vt put out of countenance

**décontracté** adj relaxed; at ease, confident

**décontracter (se)** v refl relax

**déconvenue** nf disappointment; setback

**décor** nm decoration; theat set; scene

**décorateur -trice** n decorator; stage-designer

**décoratif -ive** adj decorative, ornamental

**décoration** nf decoration; ornamentation; medal

**décorer** vt decorate, ornament; bestow a medal on

**décortiquer** vt decorticate, peel bark, husk or shell from

**décorum** nm invar decorum, propriety

**décote** nf tax relief

**découcher** vi sleep away from home, sleep out

**découdre** vt (28) unstitch; se ~ become unstitched or unsewn

**découler** vi drip; proceed, result, follow

**découpage** nm cutting up, carving up

**découper** vt cut up, carve; cut out; stamp, punch; scie à ~ fret-saw; se ~ stand out, show up

**découplé** adj strapping; bien ~ well set up

**découpler** vt uncouple

**découpure** nf piece cut out, cutting; cutting out; punching, stamping; indentation

**découragement** nm discouragement

**décourager** vt discourage, dishearten; deter; se ~ lose heart

**découronner** vt uncrown; pollard (tree)

**décousu** p part découdre + adj unsewn; disconnected, incoherent, scrappy, unmethodical

**découvert** nm overdraft; à ~ in the red; uncovered; adj uncovered; unsheltered, open, exposed

**découverte** *nf* discovery; exposure, detection

**découvrir** *vt* (30) uncover; discover, find out; expose, disclose; discern; **se ~** take one's hat off; clear (sky, weather); expose oneself

**décrasser** *vt* clear, scour

**décrépi** *adj* unplastered; peeling

**décrépit** *adj* senile, decrepit

**décret** *nm* decree, order

**décréter** *vt* (6) decree, enact

**décret-loi** *nm* (*pl* **décrets-lois**) government decree with force of law ( = Order in Council)

**décrier** *vt* disparage, discredit, run down

**décrire** *vt* (42) describe

**décrocher** *vt* unhook; bring down, take down from the peg; take off, disconnect; lift (receiver); *coll* obtain, get; **se ~ la mâchoire** disconnect one's jaw; *vi* abandon contact, leave off; *fig* pack up

**décrochez-moi-ça** *nm invar coll* **acheter au ~** buy cheap ready-made clothes

**décroiser** *vt* uncross (legs)

**décroissance** *nf*, **décroissement** *nm* decrease, diminution; decline, wane

**décroît** *nm* last quarter (moon)

**décroître** *vi* (32) decrease, decline

**décrotter** *vt* clean (boots), remove the mud from; *coll* **~ qn** eradicate s/o's unpolished manners or ignorance

**décrottoir** *nm* shoe-scraper

**décrypter** *vt* decipher

**déçu** *p part* **décevoir**

**déculotter** *vt* take off (s/o's) breeches; **se ~** let down (take off) one's trousers

**décupler** *vt* + *vi* multiply tenfold

**dédaigner** *vt* disdain, scorn

**dédaigneux -euse** *adj* disdainful, scornful

**dédain** *nm* scorn, disdain

**dédale** *nm* maze, labyrinth

**dedans** *nm* inside, interior; **au ~** inside; *adv* inside, within; **en ~** inside

**dédicace** *nf* dedication; *eccles* consecration

**dédicacer** *vt* dedicate (book)

**dédicatoire** *adj* dedicatory

**dédier** *vt* consecrate, dedicate

**dédire (se)** *v refl* (74) retract; go back on one's word

**dédit** *nm* retraction; going back on one's word; forfeit (for non-fulfilment of contract)

**dédommagement** *nm* compensation, damages; indemnification

**dédommager** *vt* compensate, indemnify

**dédoré** *adj* tarnished

**dédouaner** *vt* clear (at customs); rehabilitate

**dédoubler** *vt* undouble; divide into two; run (train) in two portions

**déductif -ive** *adj* deductive

**déduction** *nf* inference; abatement, deduction

**déduire** *vt* (80) deduce, conclude; deduct

**déesse** *nf* goddess

**défaillance** *nf* weakening, lapse; absence, extinction

**défaillant** *adj* failing, waning; dying out

**défaillir** *vi* (36) become weak, lose strength, faint

**défaire** *vt* (46) undo; destroy, cancel, break off; defeat; rid; **~ ses cheveux** let one's hair down; **visage défait** distorted features; **se ~** come undone; **se ~ de** get rid of; part with

**défaite** *nf* defeat

**défaitisme** *nm* defeatism

**défaitiste** *n* defeatist

**défalquer** *vt* deduct (sum of money), write off (debt)

**défaut** *nm* fault, defect, flaw; lack, absence; **à ~ de** failing, for lack of; **faire ~** be absent, lacking

**défaveur** *nf* discredit, disfavour

**défavorable** *adj* unfavourable

**défavoriser** *vt* put at a disadvantage

**défectif -ive** *adj* defective (verb)

**défection** *nf* desertion

**défectueux -ueuse** *adj* faulty, defective

**défectuosité** *nf* defect, imperfection, flaw

**défendable** *adj* defensible

**défendeur -eresse** *n leg* defendant

**défendre** *vt* defend, uphold (opinion); protect; forbid, prohibit; **à son corps défendant** reluctantly; *coll* **se ~** acquit oneself quite well; stay young; **se ~ de faire qch** refrain from doing sth

**défenestrer** *vt* throw out of the window

**défense** *nf* defence; **~ contre avions** anti-aircraft defence; **~ de fumer** no smoking; **~ passive** air-raid precautions; **~s** defences; tusks; prohibition; **sans ~** defenceless

**défenseur** *nm* defender, protector; *leg* counsel for the defence

**défensif -ive** *adj* defensive

**déférence** *nf* respect, regard

**déférer** *vt* (6) *leg* refer; *leg* hand over; **~ à confer** (honour) on; *vi* defer

**déferler** *vt* unfurl; *vi* break (waves); swarm (crowd)

**déferrer** *vt* unshoe (horse); remove fetters from

**défeuiller** *vt* defoliate

**défi** *nm* challenge; defiance; **mettre qn au ~** dare s/o; **relever un ~** take up a challenge

**défiance** *nf* mistrust, suspicion

**défiant** *adj* mistrustful, suspicious, wary

**déficeler** *vt* (5) untie (string)

**déficit** *nm* shortage; **être en ~** be in the red

**déficitaire** *adj* adverse (balance, account)

**défier** *vt* challenge; defy, brave; **se ~ de** mistrust

**défiger** *vt* liquefy

**défiguration** *nf* disfigurement; defacing

**défigurer** *vt* disfigure; deface; distort

**défilé** *nm* defile; *mil* march-past, procession; **~ de mannequins** manequin parade

**défiler** *vt* unthread; *sl* **se ~** clear off; *vi* march past; defile; walk in file

**défini** *adj* clearly defined; definite; **passé ~** past historic, preterite

**définir** *vt* define

**définissable** *adj* definable

**définitif** **-ive** *adj* final, permanent, definitive

**définition** *nf* description, definition

**définitivement** *adv* for good, definitively

**déflationniste** *adj* deflationary

**défleurir** *vi* lose blossoms (tree, bush)

**déflorer** *vt* take away the freshness of; deflower

**défolier** *vt* defoliate

**défoncer** *vt* smash in; break up (road)

**déformer** *vt* deform, put out of shape; distort; warp; **chaussée déformée** rough surface (road)

**défoulement** *nm* liberation from complexes, letting oneself go

**défouler (se)** *v refl coll* get rid of one's complexes, let oneself go

**défourner** *vt* remove from the kiln, oven (pottery, bread)

**défraîchi** *adj* soiled (goods); faded (flower)

**défraîchir** *vt* soil, spoil the freshness of

**défrayer** *vt* (7) pay the expenses of; **~ la chronique** be in the news; **~ la conversation** take the major part in a conversation, be the subject of conversation

**défricher** *vt* clear, make ready for cultivation (ground); **~ un sujet** break new ground in a subject

**défriser** *vt* uncurl

**défroisser** *vt* uncrease

**défroncer** *vt* undo the pleats of

**défroquer** *vt* unfrock

**défunt** *adj* defunct, deceased

**dégagé** *adj* free and easy; untrammelled; **vue ~ e** open view

**dégagement** *nm* disengagement; relieving, slackening; clearing; empty space; redemption (pledge); escape (gas, etc); clearance; **~ de sa parole** going back on one's promise; **voie de ~** relief road

**dégager** *vt* (3) disengage; free; clear; bring out (sense); redeem; emit (gas, etc), give out (heat, etc); get out of one's promise; *vi* clear the way, move along; **se ~** emerge, stand out

**dégainer** *vt* unsheathe; *vt + vi* draw (sword)

**déganter (se)** *v refl* take off one's gloves

**dégarni** *adj* empty; stripped; **il a le front ~** his hair is receding

**dégarnir** *vt* dismantle, empty; strip; **se ~** lose its leaves (tree); lose one's hair; empty

**dégâts** *nmpl* damage

**dégel** *nm* thaw; **barrière de ~** restricted or barred road (after thaw)

**dégelée** *nf sl* shower of blows

**dégeler** *vt + vi* (5) thaw (out)

**dégénéré -e** *n + adj* degenerate

**dégénérer** *vi* (6) degenerate; lower oneself

**dégénérescence** *nf* degeneration

**dégingandé** *adj coll* awkward, ungainly

**dégivrer** *vt* defrost

**déglacer** *vt* (4) thaw, de-ice; *cul* de-glaze

**dégommer** *vt* unstick; *sl* sack, kick out

**dégonfler** *vt* deflate; **se ~** *sl* be scared; back out, climb down

**dégorger** *vt* (3) disgorge; unstop; scour (wool); *vi* overflow; empty

**dégot(t)er** *vt sl* find

**dégouliner** *vi coll* drip, run

**dégourdi** *adj* sharp, wide-awake, quick

**dégourdir** *vt* remove numbness from, revive; smarten, waken up; take the chill off; **se ~** stretch, lose one's stiffness; grow more alert

**dégoût** *nm* disgust, distaste; aversion

**dégoûtant** *adj* disgusting, loathsome

**dégoûter** *vt* disgust; put off

**dégoutter** *vi* drip, be dripping

**dégradant** *adj* degrading

**dégradation** *nf* degradation; dilapidation

**dégrader** *vt* degrade; dilapidate, damage; taper (hair); **se ~** degrade oneself; fall into disrepair

**dégrafer** *vt* unfasten, undo (dress); **se ~** come undone; unfasten one's dress

**dégraissage** *nm* dry-cleaning

**dégraisser** *vt* take the fat off; clean; *comm* cut costs in

**degré** *nm* degree, stage; stair, step; degree (heat, circle)

**dégrever** *vt* (6) diminish (tax), reduce; disencumber (estate)

**dégringolade** *nf coll* tumble; downfall, collapse

**dégringoler** *vt* rush down; *vi coll* tumble down

**dégriser** *vt* sober; remove (s/o's) illusions

**dégrossir** *vt* make roughly ready; rough

down; rough-hew; *coll* lick into shape

**déguenillé** *adj* tattered, ragged

**déguerpir** *vi* clear out

**dégueulasse** *adj sl* bloody awful; disgusting, filthy

**déguisé** *adj* disguised; *coll* got up

**déguisement** *nm* disguise; dissimulation

**déguiser** *vt* disguise; conceal (truth); **se ~ en** get oneself up as

**dégustation** *nf* tasting; **verre à ~** balloon glass

**déguster** *vt* taste, sample; savour, relish

**déhancher (se)** *v refl* sway one's hips (walking); dislocate hip

**dehors** *nm* exterior; outside; *pl* outward appearances; **au ~ (de)** outside, beyond; **en ~ (de)** outside; **en ~ de moi** without my knowledge, participation; *adv* outside, out of doors; *coll* **mettre qn ~** give s/o the sack

**déifier** *vt* deify

**déité** *nf* deity

**déjà** *adv* already; previously; as it is; **d'ores et ~** here and now, from now on

**déjeter** *vt* (5) make lop-sided, warp

**déjeuner** *nm* lunch; breakfast cup and saucer; **petit ~** breakfast; *vi* have breakfast; have lunch

**déjouer** *vt* thwart; frustrate

**delà** *prep* beyond; **au ~ de, par ~ de** beyond

**délabré** *adj* dilapidated, broken-down

**délabrement** *nm* disrepair

**délabrer** *vt* dilapidate, ruin; impair (health); **se ~** fall into decay

**délacer** *vt* undo (shoes), unlace

**délai** *nm* time allotted or allowed; **demander un ~** ask for extra time; **sans ~** immediately

**délaissement** *nm* abandonment; neglect; renunciation

**délaisser** *vt* abandon, desert; relinquish

**délassement** *nm* relaxation

**délasser** *vt* refresh, rest; **se ~** relax

**délateur -trice** *n* informer

**délavé** *adj* washed out

**délayer** *vt* (7) add liquid to; thin; mix; *coll* spin out (speech)

**delco** *nm mot* distributor

**délectable** *adj* delightful, pleasant

**délecter** *vt* delight; **se ~** enjoy oneself

**délégation** *nf* delegation; delegating, assignment

**délégué -e** *n* delegate

**déléguer** *vt* (6) delegate; depute

**délester** *vt* unballast; *coll* relieve of a burden, of money

**délétère** *adj* offensive; noxious; pernicious (doctrine)

**délibération** *nf* discussion, debate; decision, vote (assembly)

**délibéré** *adj* deliberate, intentional; determined; **de propos ~** purposely

**délibérer** *vt* (6) discuss, debate; reflect on; *vi* deliberate; reflect

**délicat** *adj* delicate; tasty; refined, discerning; sensitive, fragile; difficult, ticklish (situation); scrupulous

**délicatesse** *nf* delicacy; fineness; refinement; fragility; awkwardness, difficulty; scrupulousness, tact

**délice** *nm* delight; **~s** *fpl* delights; **faire les ~s de** be the delight of

**délicieux -ieuse** *adj* delicious, delightful

**délictueux -ueuse** *adj* punishable; felonious

**délié** *adj* slender; subtle (mind); *coll* **avoir la langue ~e** talk easily

**délier** *vt* untie, loose; release (s/o from a promise)

**délimiter** *vt* delimit; define (powers)

**délinquance** *nf* delinquency

**délinquant -e** *n* delinquent

**délirant** *adj* delirious, raving

**délire** *nm* delirium; transport; **foule en ~** frenzied crowd

**délirer** *vi* be delirious; wander; rave

**délit** *nm* offence

**délivrance** *nf* rescue, deliverance; handing over; relief

**délivrer** *vt* rescue, deliver, hand over; release; relieve

**déloger** *vt* drive out, dislodge; *vi* move out; go away

**déloyal** *adj* disloyal; false; dishonest

**déloyauté** *nf* treachery, disloyalty; treacherous act

**déluge** *nm* deluge; torrent, mass (insults, etc); *coll* downpour; **après moi le ~!** I couldn't care less what happens when I'm gone!

**déluré** *adj* sharp, smart; forward (girl)

**demain** *adv* tomorrow; in the future; **~ en huit (quinze)** tomorrow week (fortnight)

**démancher** *vt* remove the handle from; put out of joint

**demande** *nf* request, application; *comm* demand; **~s d'emploi** situations required; **~ en mariage** proposal of marriage

**demander** *vt* ask (for); inquire; demand; require; **on vous demande** someone is asking for you; **très demandé** in great demand; **se ~** wonder

**demandeur -eresse** *n leg* plaintiff

**démangeaison** *nf* itch; *coll* urge

**démanger** *vi* itch; *coll* **ça me démange de** I badly want to

**démantèlement** *nm* dismantling

**démanteler** *vt* (5) dismantle

**démantibuler** *vt coll* take to bits; dislocate (jaw)

# démarche

**démarche** *nf* walk, gait; step; intervention

**démarrage** *nm* starting (vehicle); unmooring; *fig* beginning, start

**démarrer** *vi* start (up) (vehicle); start; **faire ~** start (car); cast off; drive off

**démarreur** *nm mot* starter

**démasquer** *vt* expose; unmask; **~ ses batteries** reveal one's plans

**démêlé** *nm usu pl* unpleasant dealings

**démêler** *vt* disentangle; clear up; fathom; **se ~** extricate oneself

**démembrement** *nm* dismembering, breaking up

**démembrer** *vt* dismember, divide up

**déménagement** *nm* removal

**déménager** *vt* (3) move; *vi* move house; *sl* be (going) crazy

**démence** *nf* madness, lunacy

**démener (se)** *v refl* (6) struggle, agitate oneself; *coll* make great efforts

**dément** *adj* mad, crazy

**démenti** *nm* denial; disappointment

**démentir** *vt* (59) give the lie to; deny; belie

**démerder (se)** *v refl vulg* get a move on; extricate oneself from a mess

**démériter** *vi* act in an unworthy manner

**démesuré** *adj* huge, inordinate, immoderate

**démettre** *vt* (60) dislocate; dismiss; **se ~** resign

**demeurant (au)** *adv phr* after all, all the same

**demeure** *nf* dwelling, place of residence; stay; **à ~** permanently; **dernière ~** grave; **mise en ~** summons

**demeuré** *adj* backward

**demeurer** *vi* stay, remain; dwell, live; **demeurons-en là** let's leave it at that

**demi** *nm* half; *sp* half-back; glass of beer; **à ~** half, by halves; *adj* half; **trois heures et ~ e** half past three; three and a half hours; **~-** semi-, half-

**demi-botte** *nf* half-boot

**demi-bouteille** *nf* half-bottle

**demi-cercle** *nm* semi-circle

**demi-dieu** *nm* demigod

**demie** *nf* half-hour

**demi-finale** *nf* semi-final

**demi-fond** *nm* **course de ~** middle-distance race

**demi-frère** *nm* half-brother

**demi-gros** *nm comm* retail supply trade (carried out by middleman)

**demi-heure** *nf* half an hour

**demi-jour** *nm* half-light

**démilitariser** *vt* demilitarize

**demi-litre** *nm* half-litre

**demi-lune** *nf* half-moon

**demi-mondaine** *nf* demi-mondaine, woman of easy virtue

**demi-mot (à)** *adv phr* **comprendre ~** take a hint

**demi-pension** *nf* half-board

**demi-pensionnaire** *n* day-boarder

**demi-place** *nf* half-fare; half-price

**demi-saison** *nf* spring; autumn; **manteau de ~** spring (or autumn) coat

**demi-sœur** *nf* half-sister; step-sister

**demi-solde** *nf mil* half-pay; *nm mil* officer on half-pay

**démission** *nf* resignation; abandonment

**démissionnaire** *n* person resigning; *adj* resigning; outgoing

**démissionner** *vi* resign; *coll* give up

**demi-ton** *nm* semitone

**demi-tour** *nm* half-turn; about turn; **faire ~** turn back, turn about

**demi-voix (à)** *adv phr* softly, under one's breath

**démobiliser** *vt* demobilize; discharge

**démocrate** *n* democrat

**démocratie** *nf* democracy

**démocratique** *adj* democratic

**démocratiser** *vt* democratize

**démodé** *adj* old-fashioned

**démoder (se)** *v refl* go out of fashion

**demoiselle** *nf* single woman, spinster; young woman; dragonfly; paving beetle; **nom de ~** maiden name

**démolir** *vt* demolish, pull down; *coll* beat up, knock flat; *coll* ruin the reputation of

**démolisseur -euse** *n* demolition worker; demolisher

**démon** *nm* demon, devil; genius, spirit; **~ de midi** love in middle age

**démoniaque** *adj* demoniac

**démonstrateur -trice** *n* demonstrator

**démonstratif -ive** *adj* demonstrative, expansive; conclusive

**démonstration** *nf* demonstration; proof (by deduction)

**démontable** *adj* that can be taken to pieces; collapsible

**démonté** *adj* stormy (sea); flustered

**démonter** *vt* take to pieces; dismantle, unhinge; unhorse; upset, disconcert

**démontrable** *adj* demonstrable

**démontrer** *vt* demonstrate

**démoraliser** *vt* demoralize; **se ~** become demoralized

**démordre** *vi* let go one's hold; **ne pas ~ de son opinion** stick to one's opinion

**démouler** *vt* withdraw from the mould; turn out (cake, etc)

**démoustiquer** *vt* clear of mosquitoes

**démultiplication** *nf* gearing down; reduction ratio (gears)

**démultiplier** *vt* reduce the gear ratio of

**démuni** *adj* unprovided; short (of money)

**démunir** *vt* deprive; **se ~** deprive oneself, allow oneself to run short

**démystifier** vt undeceive; coll debunk

**dénantir** vt deprive of securities

**dénatalité** nf fall in the birth rate

**dénationaliser** vt denationalize

**dénaturé** adj unnatural; hard-hearted (parent); ungrateful (child)

**dénaturer** vt alter the nature of; misrepresent, distort

**dénégation** nf denial

**déneigement** nm clearing of snow

**déniaiser** vt teach (s/o) the ways of the world, initiate

**dénicher** vt remove from the nest; dislodge; coll discover

**denier** nm denarius; denier; ~ s publics public funds; **de ses propres** ~ s with one's own money; **jusqu'au dernier** ~ to the last farthing

**dénier** vt deny, disclaim; refuse

**dénigrer** vt disparage

**déniveler** vt (5) make uneven (surface); contour

**dénivellation** nf, **dénivellement** nm difference in level; gradient

**dénombrement** nm census; counting

**dénombrer** vt take a census of; count

**dénominateur** nm denominator

**dénomination** nf name, denomination

**dénommer** vt name, denominate

**dénoncer** vt denounce; inform against; proclaim, betray; **se** ~ give oneself up

**dénonciateur -trice** n informer; adj tell-tale

**dénonciation** nf denunciation; cancellation, annulment

**dénoter** vt denote, show

**dénouement** nm untying; outcome, result, ending

**dénouer** vt untie, unknot; undo (hair); ~ **une intrigue** unravel a plot; **se** ~ end (story)

**denrée** nf commodity; ~ s **alimentaires** foodstuffs

**dense** adj dense, compact, crowded

**densité** nf density; denseness

**dent** nf tooth; cog, prong; **à belles** ~ s with appetite, heartily; **avoir une** ~ **contre qn** bear s/o a grudge; **être sur les** ~ s be harassed; **n'avoir rien à se mettre sous la** ~ have nothing to eat; **ne pas desserrer les** ~ s not utter a word

**dentaire** adj dental

**dent-de-lion** nf (pl dents-de-lion) dandelion

**denté** adj cogged

**denteler** vt (5) jag, notch

**dentelle** nf lace

**dentellerie** nf lace manufacture

**dentellière** nf lace-maker; lace-making machine

**dentelure** nf indentation; serration

**dentier** nm set of false teeth, denture

**dentifrice** nm tooth-paste; adj **pâte** ~ tooth-paste

**dentiste** n dentist; **chirurgien** ~ dental surgeon

**dentition** nf dentition; teething; set of teeth

**denture** nf set of teeth; cogs

**dénudation** nf denudation; stripping

**dénuder** vt lay bare, denude

**dénué** adj devoid, deprived

**dénuement, dénûment** nm need, destitution; bareness

**dénuer** vt strip, divest

**déodoriser** vt deodorize

**dépannage** nm emergency repairs (to engine)

**dépanner** vt repair and get going again (engine); coll help out .

**dépanneuse** nf breakdown lorry

**dépareiller** vt spoil (set); **service dépareillé** incomplete, unmatched service

**déparer** vt strip; spoil (beauty)

**déparier** vt break up, separate (a pair)

**départ** nm departure, start; separation, sorting out; **au** ~ at the outset

**départager** vt decide between (opinion, etc)

**département** nm department, section; French administrative region

**départemental** adj departmental; **route** ~ e secondary road

**départir** vt divide; distribute, dispense; **se** ~ **de** renounce, give up

**dépasser** vt go beyond, overtake, outstrip; project; exceed; coll **cela me dépasse** it beats me

**dépaysé** adj out of one's element; ill-at-ease

**dépayser** vt remove (s/o) from (his) natural surroundings; disorientate

**dépecer** vt (6,4) dismember, carve up

**dépêche** nf telegram; dispatch

**dépêcher** vt despatch; **se** ~ hasten, be quick

**dépeigner** vt ruffle hair of

**dépeindre** vt (55) depict, describe

**dépenaillé** adj ragged, tattered

**dépendance** nf dependence; dependency; ~ s outbuildings

**dépendre** vt take down (hanging object); vi depend; belong, be under the dependence; **il dépend de vous de** it's up to you to

**dépens** nmpl costs; **à ses** ~ to his cost; **aux** ~ **de** at the expense of

**dépense** nf expense, outlay; expenditure; consumption; pantry

**dépenser** vt spend; consume; **se** ~ make strenuous efforts; devote oneself

**dépensier**

**dépensier -ière** *adj* extravagant, spendthrift

**déperdition** *nf* waste; loss

**dépérir** *vi* waste away; wither

**dépersonnaliser** *vt* depersonalize

**dépêtrer** *vt* extricate; **se ~** extricate oneself

**dépeupler** *vt* depopulate

**déphasé** *adj* elect out of phase; lagging behind; *coll* disoriented

**dépilatoire** *n + adj* depilatory

**dépiler** *vt* remove the hairs from

**dépiquer** *vt* unstitch; plant out

**dépistage** *nm* detection

**dépister** *vt* track down; detect; throw off the scent

**dépit** *nm* spite, resèntment; **en ~ de** in spite of; **en ~ du bon sens** badly, stupidly

**dépiter** *vt* vex

**déplacé** *adj* displaced; ill-timed, uncalled-for

**déplacement** *nm* displacement, removing; altering; travelling, journey; **en ~** travelling (on business); **frais de ~** travelling expenses

**déplacer** *vt* (4) displace; transfer, move; alter; have a displacement of (ship)

**déplaire** *vi* (69) displease, offend; **ne vous en déplaise** whatever you may think

**déplaisant** *adj* unpleasant, disagreeable

**déplaisir** *nm* displeasure

**déplanter** *vt* take up, transplant

**déplantoir** *nm* garden trowel

**dépliant** *nm* prospectus, pamphlet; folder; folder insert (in book)

**déplier** *vt* unfold, open out

**déplisser** *vt* take out the folds or creases of

**déploiement** *nm* unfolding; deployment; display, show

**déplomber** *vt* remove the lead seals from

**déplorer** *vt* deplore; grieve over

**déployer** *vt* (7) unfold; spread (sails, wings); deploy

**déplumer** *vt* pluck (chicken); **se ~** moult; *coll* lose one's hair, go bald

**dépolariser** *vt* depolarize

**dépolir** *vt* dull (surface); frost (glass)

**dépolitiser** *vt* take out of politics, remove from the political arena

**déporter** *vt* deport; sweep off course; **se ~** swerve

**déposer** *vt* deposit, set down, lay down; lodge; register; depose; **marque déposée** registered trademark; *vi* give evidence

**dépositaire** *n* trustee; *comm* agent

**déposition** *nf* statement (of evidence); deposing

**déposséder** *vt* (6) dispossess, deprive

**dépôt** *nm* depositing; deposit; depository, store, depot; sediment; **~ de marchandises** warehouse; **en ~** on deposit; in trust; **mandat de ~** order for arrest

**dépoter** *vt* decant; unpot, plant out

**dépotoir** *nm* sewage farm; rubbish dump

**dépouille** *nf* (cast off) skin; **~s** spoils; effects; **~ mortelle** mortal remains

**dépouiller** *vt* skin; cast off; strip, deprive; analyse; **~ le courrier** go through the mail; **se ~ de** divest oneself of

**dépourvu** *adj* devoid, destitute; **être pris au ~** be caught unawares

**dépravation** *nf* depravation; depravity

**dépraver** *vt* deprave

**dépréciateur -trice** *adj* disparaging

**dépréciation** *nf* fall in value; wear; disparagement

**déprécier** *vt* depreciate; belittle

**déprédateur -trice** *n* depredator; *adj* depredatory

**dépression** *nf* hollow; fall; depression

**déprimant** *adj* depressing

**déprime** *nf* *coll* depression

**déprimer** *vt* depress

**depuis** *adv* since then; later; *prep* since, for; from; **~ que** *conj* since

**dépuratif** *nm* depurative

**dépurer** *vt* cleanse, clear

**députation** *nf* delegating; deputation; office of deputy

**député** *nm* delegate, deputy; member of French parliament; **~-maire** member of French parliament and mayor

**députer** *vt* depute; appoint as deputy

**déraciner** *vt* uproot; eradicate

**déraillement** *nm* going off the rails; *fig* diverging from the normal

**dérailler** *vi* become derailed; *coll* be crazy, go off the rails; **faire ~** derail

**dérailleur** *nm* type of gear-change (bicycle)

**déraison** *nf* unreasonableness

**déraisonnable** *adj* unreasonable; senseless, foolish

**déraisonner** *vi* talk nonsense; rave

**dérangement** *nm* derangement; disordering; disturbance; upset

**déranger** *vt* disturb; derange; disarrange; upset; **se ~** move; put oneself out; get out of order (machine)

**dérapage** *nm* skid; dragging, tripping (anchor); *fig* turn for the worse

**déraper** *vi* skid; drag, trip (anchor); *fig* fall, take a bad turn, go off the rails

**dératiser** *vt* clear of rats

**derechef** *adv* once more

**dérèglement** *nm* disorder; irregularity; dissoluteness

**dérégler** *vt* (6) upset, disorder; unsettle; put (clock) out of order

**dérider** vt smooth wrinkles of; coll cheer up; **se ~** cheer up

**dérision** nf mockery, derision; **tourner en ~** hold up to ridicule

**dérisoire** adj laughable; insignificant

**dérivation** nf diversion (of waters); derivation; drift

**dérive** nf drift; **à la ~** adrift

**dérivé** nm derivative; by-product

**dériver** vt divert (stream); vi drift, be carried away by the current

**dermatologie** nf dermatology

**derme** nm dermis

**dernier -ière** adj last; final; latest; abject; utmost; latter

**dernièrement** adv lately, recently

**dernier-né** (f **dernière-née**) n last-born child

**derny** nm light motor-cycle used for pace-making in cycle races

**dérobade** nf escape, avoidance

**dérobé** adj secret, hidden; **à la ~ e** furtively, secretly

**dérober** vt steal; hide; **se ~** escape, slip away; refuse; give way

**dérogation** nf impairment; exception

**dérogatoire** adj derogatory

**déroger** vi (3) depart (from custom, etc); derogate

**dérouiller** vt take the rust off; coll freshen up, polish up

**déroulement** nm unrolling, unwinding; development

**dérouler** vt unroll, unwind; **se ~** come unrolled; develop; unfold; occur

**déroute** nf rout; **en ~** in flight

**dérouter** vt change the route of; baffle, confuse

**derrière** nm back, rear; backside, bottom; adv behind, in the rear; **par ~** from the rear; **porte de ~** back door; prep behind

**derviche, dervis** nm dervish

**des = de + les**

**dès** prep since, from; as early as; **~ aujourd'hui** this very day; **~ lors** ever since, from then onwards; **~ maintenant** already; from now on; **~ que** conj as soon as

**désabusé** adj disillusioned

**désabuser** vt disillusion, undeceive

**désaccord** nm disagreement; clash (of interests); mus discord

**désaccorder** vt set at variance; mus put out of tune

**désaccoutumer** vt disaccustom

**désaffectation** nf putting to different use

**désaffecter** vt put to different use

**désaffection** nf discontent, disaffection

**désaffectionner** vt alienate the affections of

**désagréable** adj unpleasant; surly;

offensive

**désagrégation** nf disintegration; breaking up

**désagréger** vt (6) disintegrate, disaggregate

**désagrément** nm source of annoyance

**désaltérant** adj thirst-quenching

**désaltérer** vt (6) quench, slake; **se ~** quench one's thirst

**désamorcer** vt unprime, prevent the functioning of; fig defuse

**désappointer** vt disappoint

**désapprendre** vt (75) forget, unlearn

**désapprobateur -trice** adj disapproving, censorious

**désapprobation** nf disapproval

**désapprouver** vt + vi disapprove (of), object (to)

**désarçonnant** adj coll staggering

**désarçonner** vt unseat; coll dumbfound, stagger

**désargenter** vt de-silver; coll drain of cash

**désarmement** nm disarming; disarmament; laying up (ship)

**désarmer** vt disarm; unload (gun); lay up (ship); vi disarm; weaken, abandon objections

**désarrimer** vt unstow (cargo); put out of trim (ship)

**désarroi** nm confusion, disorder

**désarticuler** vt disjoint; dislocate

**désassocier** vt disassociate, dissociate

**désassortir** vt break up (collection); **être désassorti** have a reduced stock or selection

**désastre** nm disaster, catastrophe

**désastreux -euse** adj disastrous, catastrophic

**désavantage** nm disadvantage; detriment

**désavantager** vt put at a disadvantage, affect adversely

**désavantageux -euse** adj unfavourable, disadvantageous

**désaveu** nm denial, disavowal

**désavouer** vt repudiate, disavow, deny; disclaim; retract; condemn

**désaxer** vt put out of true (wheel); unbalance (mind)

**desceller** vt unseal, break the seal of; loosen

**descendance** nf lineage, descendants

**descendant -e** n descendant; adj descending, downward

**descendre** vt go down (stairs, etc); bring, take down; lower; shoot down; set down; vi come down, descend, fall; be sloping; raid (police); stay (at hotel); be descended (from); alight

**descente** nf descent, going down; lowering; raid (police); stay (at hotel); **~ de**

descriptible

lit bedside rug, mat
**descriptible** *adj* describable
**descriptif -ive** *adj* descriptive
**désembouteiller** *vt mot* clear, free of traffic-jams
**désemparé** *adj* crippled (ship); at a loss, baffled
**désemparer** *vt* disable (ship); *vi sans* ~ without interruption, ceaselessly
**désemplir** *vt* empty partially; *vi usu* **ne pas** ~ always be full
**désenchantement** *nm* disenchantment; disillusion
**désenchanter** *vt* disenchant; disillusion
**désenclaver** *vt* disenclose; improve communications in
**désencombrer** *vt* disencumber; clear
**désenfler** *vi* become less swollen; go down; **se** ~ become less swollen
**désenfumer** *vt* clear of smoke
**désengager** *vt* (3) free from an obligation
**désengorger** *vt* (3) unchoke, clear (pipe)
**désenivrer** *vt* sober
**désenneiger** *vt* (3) clear the snow from
**désennuyer** *vt* (7) relieve from boredom, amuse
**désensibiliser** *vt* reduce the sensitivity of, desensitize
**désenterrer** *vt* disinter, exhume
**déséquilibrer** *vt* unbalance
**désert** *nm* desert, wilderness; *adj* deserted; uninhabited, lonely
**déserter** *vt* desert
**déserteur** *nm* deserter
**désertique** *adj* barren, desert-like
**désescalade** *nf* de-escalation
**désespérant** *adj* heart-breaking; dreadful, hopeless
**désespéré** *adj* desperate; hopeless
**désespérer** *vt* (6) drive to despair; *vi* despair, lose hope, be without hope; **se** ~ be in despair
**désespoir** *nm* despair; **en** ~ **de cause** as a last resort
**déshabillé** *nm* négligée
**déshabiller** *vt* undress; **se** ~ take off one's clothes
**déshabilloir** *nm* changing room (in clothes shop)
**déshabituer** *vt* break of a habit
**désherbant** *nm* weed-killer
**déshérité** *adj* poor (in natural or material gifts), underprivileged
**déshériter** *vt* disinherit
**déshonneur** *nm* dishonour
**déshonorant** *adj* discreditable, dishonourable
**déshonorer** *vt* dishonour
**déshumaniser** *vt* dehumanize
**déshydrater** *vt* dehydrate
**desiderata** *nmpl* needs, requirements

**désignation** *nf* designation; indicating; nomination
**désigner** *vt* designate, show, point out; fix, appoint, detail
**désillusion** *nf* disillusion
**désillusionner** *vt* disillusion
**désinfectant** *nm* disinfectant
**désinfecter** *vt* disinfect
**désinfection** *nf* disinfection
**désintégration** *nf* disintegration
**désintégrer** *vt* (6) disintegrate, destroy; **se** ~ disintegrate
**désintéressé** *adj* disinterested, unselfish
**désintéressement** *nm* disinterestedness; impartiality; paying off (creditor)
**désintéresser** *vt* buy out, pay off; **se** ~ **de** lose interest in; take no part in
**désintoxication** *nf med* cure for intoxication or for addiction (alcohol, drugs); *fig* relief from the strains and pollution of modern life
**désintoxiquer** *vt med* cure of intoxication or of addiction (alcohol, drugs); *fig* **se** ~ gain relief from the strains and pollution of modern life
**désinvolte** *adj* free, easy; detached; cavalier
**désinvolture** *nf* ease, lack of constraint; cheek, off-hand manner
**désir** *nm* desire, wish
**désirer** *vt* desire, want, wish; covet
**désireux -euse** *adj* desirous
**désistement** *nm* desistance, withdrawal
**désister (se)** *v refl* desist, withdraw
**désobéir** *vi* disobey
**désobéissance** *nf* disobedience
**désobéissant** *adj* disobedient
**désobligeance** *nf* disobligingness; unpleasantness
**désobligeant** *adj* disobliging; unpleasant, ungracious
**désobliger** *vt* (3) offend; disoblige
**désodorisant** *nm* deodorant
**désodoriser** *vt* deodorize
**désœuvré** *adj* unoccupied, idle
**désœuvrement** *nm* idleness
**désolant** *adj* distressing, disheartening
**désolation** *nf* desolation; laying waste; grief
**désolé** *adj* desolate; devastated; very sorry
**désoler** *vt* desolate; devastate; distress; **se** ~ be very sad
**désopilant** *adj* hilarious, very funny
**désordonné** *adj* untidy, disorderly; disordered; dissolute
**désordonner** *vt* throw into disorder
**désordre** *nm* disorder, confusion; disorderliness; tumult; ~ **s** disturbances
**désorganisation** *nf* disorganization
**désorganiser** *vt* disorganize
**désorienté** *adj* bewildered, at a loss

86

**désorienter** *vt* make (s/o) lose his way; disconcert

**désormais** *adv* henceforth, from now on

**désosser** *vt* bone

**désoxyder** *vt* deoxidize

**despote** *nm* despot

**despotique** *adj* despotic

**despotisme** *nm* despotism

**desquels** = de + lesquels

**dessaisir** *vt leg* dispossess; se ~ de drop, relinquish; part with; *leg* not proceed with

**dessalé** *adj* with the salt removed; *sl* wide-awake

**dessaler** *vt* remove the salt from; *coll* ~ qn teach s/o a thing or two

**dessécher** *vt* (6) dry up; desiccate; wither, waste; se ~ dry up, wither, waste

**dessein** *nm* plan, project, design; à ~ on purpose

**desserrer** *vt* loosen, slacken; unclench; release; ne pas ~ les dents refuse to say anything; se ~ work loose

**dessert** *nm* dessert; sweet, pudding

**desservir** *vt* (89) *eccles* minister; ~ une ville serve a town (train, etc)

**dessin** *nm* drawing, sketch; pattern, design; profile; ~ animé cartoon film

**dessinateur -trice** *n* designer; draughtsman (-woman)

**dessiner** *vt* draw, sketch; design; outline; se ~ stand out, be outlined

**dessouder** *vt* unsolder

**dessoûler, dessaouler** *vt* sober; se ~ become sober

**dessous** *nm* underneath, lower part; ~-de-plat table-mat; ~ de robe underslip; avoir le ~ get the worst of it; les ~ the shady side, secret side; underwear; *adv* underneath, below; de ~ under(neath); en ~ furtively, in an underhand fashion

**dessus** *nm* upper surface, upper part; ~-de-lit bedspread; avoir le ~ get, have the upper hand; le ~ du panier the pick, the best; reprendre le ~ rally, get better; *adv* over, above; on top; bras ~ bras dessous arm in arm; de ~ upper, outer; en ~ on top

**destin** *nm* destiny, fate

**destinataire** *n* addressee; payee

**destinée** *nf* destiny

**destiner** *vt* destine; intend, assign; se ~ à une profession intend to take up a profession

**destituer** *vt* dismiss, remove

**destitution** *nf* dismissal

**destructeur -trice** *adj* destructive

**destructif -ive** *adj* destructive

**désuet -uète** *adj* obsolete, antiquated

**désuétude** *nf* disuse

**désuni** *adj* disunited; disjoined

**désunion** *nf* disunion; disconnection

**désunir** *vt* disunite, divide; disconnect

**détachant** *nm* stain-remover

**détaché** *adj* loose; detached, unconcerned; seconded

**détachement** *nm* detaching; indifference; detachment; secondment

**¹détacher** *vt* detach; unfasten, untie, unbind; separate; cut off; tear off; second

**²détacher** *vt* remove stains from

**détail** *nm* detail; dividing up; vendre au ~ sell retail

**détaillant -e** *n* retailer

**détailler** *vt* divide up, cut up; retail; enumerate; relate in detail

**détaler** *vi* run off, scamper away

**détaxe** *nf* remission of tax; tax refund

**détaxer** *vt* suppress (reduce) tax on

**détecter** *vt* detect

**détecteur** *nm* detector

**déteindre** *vt* (55) take the colour out of; *vi* lose colour, fade

**dételer** *vt* (5) unharness, unyoke

**détendre** *vt* loosen, relax; calm; se ~ become slack; relax; ease

**détendu** *adj* slack; relaxed

**détenir** *vt* (96) hold; be in possession of; detain; withhold

**détente** *nf* loosening, slackening, relaxing; easing; rest; trigger; *coll* dur à la ~ close-fisted; hard to get anything out of

**détenteur -trice** *n* holder; owner

**détention** *nf* holding; imprisonment

**détenu -e** *n* prisoner

**détérioration** *nf* deterioration; damage

**détériorer** *vt* worsen; damage; se ~ deteriorate

**déterminé** *adj* definite, specific, well-defined; resolute

**déterminer** *vt* determine; fix; cause, give rise to; se ~ make up one's mind

**déterrer** *vt* dig up, unearth; bring to light

**détersif** *nm* detergent

**détestable** *adj* detestable, hateful

**détester** *vt* hate, detest

**détonateur** *nm* detonator

**détoner** *vi* detonate, explode

**détonner** *vi* sing (play) out of tune; clash, jar

**détordre** *vt* untwist

**détortiller** *vt* untwist, disentangle

**détour** *nm* deviation; roundabout way; turn; curve; devious method; sans ~(s) frankly

**détourné** *adj* indirect, roundabout; unfrequented

**détournement** *nm* diversion; misappropriation; abduction; hi-jacking

**détourner** *vt* divert, turn; avert, turn

away; misappropriate; dissuade; hijack

**détracteur -trice** *n* detractor, disparager

**détraqué** *adj* deranged

**détraquement** *nm* putting out of order; breakdown

**détraquer** *vt* put out of order; upset

**détrempe** *nf* distemper

**détremper** *vt* soak, moisten

**détresse** *nf* distress; grief

**détriment** *nm* detriment, loss

**détritus** *nm* residue; refuse; rubbish

**détroit** *nm* straits

**détromper** *vt* undeceive

**détrôner** *vt* dethrone

**détrousser** *vt* untuck; rob; rifle

**détrousseur** *nm* footpad, highwayman

**détruire** *vt* (80) destroy, demolish; **se ~** kill oneself

**dette** *nf* debt; **faire des ~** s run up debts

**deuil** *nm* mourning, sorrow; bereavement; mourning-clothes; period of mourning; funeral procession; **faire son ~ de qch** give sth up as lost, get along without sth; **quitter le ~** go out of mourning

**deux** *nm* two; second (dates); *adj* two; **à ~ pas d'ici** just near here; **à nous ~** it's a matter between you and me; **en moins de ~** in a jiffy; **tous (les)** both; **tous les ~ jours** every other day

**deuxième** *nm* second floor; *adj* second

**deux-mâts** *nm* two-master

**deux-pièces** *nm* two-piece suit

**deux-points** *nm* colon

**deux-roues** *nm* two-wheeled vehicle

**deux-temps** *nm mus* two-four time; **moteur ~** two-stroke engine

**dévaler** *vt* hurry down, race down; *vi* go down

**dévaliser** *vt* rob; rifle

**dévalorisation** *nf* drop in value

**dévaloriser** *vt* devalue

**dévaluer** *vt* devalue

**devancer** *vt* (4) precede, go before; overtake, outstrip, arrive before; forestall; anticipate

**devancier -ière** *n* predecessor; **~s** forefathers

**devant** *nm* front (part); **prendre les ~s** go on ahead; forestall, make the first move; *adv* ahead, in front; **comme ~** as before; **par ~** in front, the front way; **sens ~ derrière** back to front; *prep* in front of, before; in the presence of, in the face of; in view of

**devanture** *nf* front (shop); display (shop)

**dévastateur -trice** *n* ravager

**dévaster** *vt* devastate, lay waste, ravage

**déveine** *nf coll* bad luck

**développement** *nm* development,

growth; spreading out, expansion; spread; developing

**développer** *vt* develop; spread out, open out; unwrap; expound; **se ~** open out; develop

**devenir** *vi* (96) become, grow; grow into; **c'est à ~ fou!** it's enough to drive one mad!; **qu'est-il devenu?** what has become of him?

**dévergondage** *nm* profligate, extravagant behaviour

**dévergondé** *adj* profligate, shameless

**dévergonder (se)** *v refl* fall into dissolute ways

**dévers** *nm* inclination, slope; banking

**déversement** *nm* discharge; tipping

**déverser** *vt* pour, discharge; tip; divert; slope

**déversoir** *nm* overflow

**dévêtir** *vt* (97) undress, strip

**déviation** *nf* deviation; diversion; variation; curvature (spine)

**dévider** *vt* unwind; reel off

**dévié** *adj* diverted; **route ~e** diversion

**dévier** *vt* deflect, turn aside; **se ~** grow crooked; warp; *vi* deviate, diverge

**devin** *nm* soothsayer

**deviner** *vt* guess; predict; **cela se devine** that's obvious

**devinette** *nf* riddle

**devis** *nm* estimate; specification

**dévisager** *vt* stare at

**devise** *nf* device; motto; slogan; *usu pl* currency

**deviser** *vi* chat, gossip

**dévisser** *vt* unscrew

**dévoiler** *vt* unveil; reveal, disclose, unmask

**devoir** *nm* duty; exercise; **~s** homework; respects; **rentrer dans le ~** return to the path of duty; **se faire un ~ de faire qch** make a point of doing sth; **se mettre en ~ de** prepare to; *vt* (37) owe; *vi* should, ought, have to; be supposed to; must (probability); **il doit être là** he must be there

**dévolter** *vt* lower voltage

**dévolu** *nm coll* **jeter son ~ sur** have designs on; *adj* devolving

**dévolution** *nf* transmission (property); *eccles* lapsing

**dévorant** *adj* consuming, devouring

**dévorateur -trice** *adj* devouring, consuming

**dévorer** *vt* devour, consume

**dévot -e** *n* devout person; **faux ~** religious hypocrite; *adj* devout, religious

**dévotion** *nf* piety, devoutness

**dévoué** *adj* devoted, loyal; **votre ~** yours truly

**dévouer** *vt* dedicate; devote, sacrifice; se

~ devote oneself; throw oneself heart and soul

**dévoyé** *adj* led astray, perverted

**dévoyer** *vt* (7) lead astray, pervert; **se ~** go astray

**dextérité** *nf* dexterity

**diabète** *nm med* diabetes

**diabétique** *n+adj* diabetic

**diable** *nm* devil; two-wheeled trolley; **bruit de tous les ~ s** hell of a din; **ce ~ de ...** that wretched ...; **du ~** terrific; *coll* **faire le ~** be noisy, troublesome; **faire qch à la ~** do sth anyhow; **il habite au ~** he lives miles away; **tirer le ~ par la queue** be hard up; *adj* mischievous

**diablement** *adv* awfully, tremendously

**diablerie** *nf* mischievousness; sorcery

**diablotin** *nm* little devil; imp

**diabolique** *adj* fiendish, diabolical

**diacre** *nm eccles* deacon

**diadème** *nm* diadem

**diagnostic** *nm* diagnosis

**diagonale** *nf* diagonal (line)

**diagramme** *nm* diagram

**dialecte** *nm* dialect

**dialoguer** *vi* converse; put into dialogue form; engage in talks

**diamant** *nm* diamond

**diamanté** *adj* set with diamonds

**diamétral** *adj* diametrical

**diamètre** *nm* diameter

**diane** *nf mil* reveille; **sonner la ~** sound the reveille

**diapason** *nm* pitch; tuning-fork; range (voice); **se mettre au ~** adapt

**diaphane** *adj* translucent

**diaphragme** *nm* diaphragm

**diapositive** *nf phot* slide, transparency

**diaprer** *vt* mottle, variegate, speckle

**diarrhée** *nf* diarrhoea

**diatonique** *adj mus* diatonic

**dichotomie** *nf* dichotomy

**dictame** *nm bot* dittany

**dictateur** *nm* dictator

**dictature** *nf* dictatorship

**dictée** *nf* dictation

**dicter** *vt* dictate

**diction** *nf* diction, delivery; elocution

**dictionnaire** *nm* dictionary

**dicton** *nm* maxim, common saying

**didactique** *adj* didactic

**diérèse** *nf* diaeresis

**dièse** *nm mus* sharp

**diète** *nf* diet

**diététicien -ienne** *n* dietician

**Dieu** *nm* God; *coll* **le bon ~** God; **la maison du bon ~** a hospitable house

**dieu** *nm* god, deity; **jurer ses grands ~x** swear by all that's sacred

**diffamant** *adj* slanderous, libellous

**diffamateur -trice** *n* slanderer, libeller

**diffamation** *nf* slander, libel

**diffamatoire** *adj* slanderous, libellous

**diffamer** *vt* slander, libel

**différé** *adj* postponed; **en ~** recorded (broadcast)

**différence** *nf* difference; **à la ~ de** unlike; **faire la ~** distinguish, discriminate

**différencier** *vt* differentiate

**différend** *nm* difference, disagreement; **partager le ~** split the difference, compromise

¹**différentiel** *nm mot* differential

²**différentiel -ielle** *adj* differential

¹**différer** *vt* (6) postpone, defer, hold over

²**différer** *vi* (6) differ

**difficile** *adj* difficult; trying; *coll* difficult to please, particular; **faire le ~** be fussy

**difficilement** *adv* with difficulty

**difficulté** *nf* difficulty; objection

**difforme** *adj* deformed, misshapen

**difformité** *nf* deformity

**diffus** *adj* diffused; wordy (style)

**diffuser** *vt* diffuse; broadcast

**diffusion** *nf* diffusion; broadcasting; wordiness

**digérer** *vt* (6) digest; assimilate; *sl* put up with, bear, accept; stomach

**digeste** *adj* digestible

**digestif** *nm* digestive; liqueur (after meal)

**digital** *adj* digital; **empreinte ~ e** fingerprint

**digitale** *nf bot* digitalis, foxglove

**digne** *adj* worthy, deserving; dignified; *coll* **c'est bien ~ de lui** that's just like him

**dignitaire** *nm* dignitary

**dignité** *nf* dignity; high position

**digue** *nf* dike, embankment; breakwater; jetty; *fig* obstacle

**dilapidation** *nf* wasting, squandering; peculation

**dilapider** *vt* waste, squander; misappropriate

**dilatation** *nf* dilation, expansion; distension

**dilater** *vt* dilate, expand; distend; **se ~** swell; become distended

**dilemme** *nm* dilemma

**dilettante** *n* amateur, dilettante

**diligence** *nf* application, diligence; haste; stage-coach

**diligent** *adj* industrious, diligent; assiduous

**diluer** *vt* dilute, water down; weaken

**dilution** *nf* dilution, watering down

**diluvien -ienne** *adj* diluvian, diluvial; torrential (rain)

**dimanche** *nm* Sunday; **habits du ~** Sunday best; **le ~** on Sundays

89

**dîme** *nf* tithe

**diminuer** *vt* lessen, diminish, reduce; reduce the pay of; *vi* lessen, diminish, abate, fall off; **les jours diminuent** the days are getting shorter

**diminutif -ive** *adj* diminutive

**diminution** *nf* lessening, diminution, reduction, decrease; shortening (dress)

**dinde** *nf* turkey(-hen); *coll* silly woman

**dindon** *nm* turkey(-cock); **le ~ de la farce** the dupe

**dindonneau** *nm* young turkey

**dîner** *nm* dinner, evening meal; dinner-party; *vi* dine, have dinner; **qui dort dîne** sleep is as good as a meal

**dînette** *nf* children's dinner-party; playing at dinner (with dolls); light meal

**dîneur -euse** *n* diner

**dingue** *adj sl* crazy, cracked

**diocésain** *adj eccles* diocesan

**diphasé** *adj elect* two-phase

**diphtérie** *nf* diphtheria

**diphtongue** *nf* diphthong

**diplomate** *n* diplomat

**diplomatie** *nf* diplomacy

**diplôme** *nm* diploma; **~ s** qualifications

**diplômer** *vt* grant a diploma to; **diplômé** certificated, qualified

**dipsomane** *n* dipsomaniac

**dire** *nm* assertion, statement; *vt* (38) say, tell; recite; express; think; **dis donc, ...** I say, ...; *coll* **à qui le dites-vous?** don't I know it?; **ce disant** with these words; **cela ne me dit rien** that doesn't convey anything to me; I'm not keen on that; **cela ne se dit pas** one doesn't say that; **il n'y a pas à ~** one can't deny it; **il n'y a rien à ~ à cela** there's no objection to that; **on dirait un fou** he looks like a madman; **pour tout ~** in a word; **si le cœur vous en dit** if you feel like it; **tenez-vous cela pour dit** don't let me have to tell you that again; **trouver à ~** to object; **vouloir ~** mean

**direct** *nm* fast train; live transmission; **en ~** live; *adj* direct, straight; fast (train)

**directement** *adv* directly, straight

**directeur -trice** *n* director, directress, manager, manageress; head, chief; headmaster, headmistress, principal; leader; *adj* managing, controlling, directing

**direction** *nf* direction; management; control; conduct; leadership; *mot* steering

**directive** *nf usu pl* directive, guide-lines, rule(s); order(s)

**dirigeable** *nm* airship, dirigible

**dirigeant** *adj* guiding, directing, ruling

**diriger** *vt* (3) direct, control, manage; lead; conduct; edit; drive; level, aim; **se**

**~ vers** make one's way towards, head for

**discal** *adj* **hernie ~e** slipped disc

**discernement** *nm* perception; distinguishing; discernment; understanding

**disciplinaire** *adj* disciplinary

**discipline** *nf* discipline; scourge; branch of study

**discipliner** *vt* discipline, bring under control

**discontinu** *adj* discontinuous

**discontinuation** *nf* discontinuance

**discontinuer** *vt* discontinue, cease; *vi* stop for a moment

**discontinuité** *nf* discontinuity

**disconvenance** *nf* disproportion, inequality; unsuitableness

**disconvenir** *vi* (96) not to agree

**discordance** *nf* discordance, dissonance; clashing (colours); disagreement

**discordant** *adj* discordant; grating, jarring; clashing (colours); conflicting

**discorde** *nf* discord, strife, dissension

**discoureur -euse** *n* talker, speechifier

**discourir** *vi* (29) make discourse, air opinions

**discours** *nm* talk; speech, address; discourse; diction; **parties du ~** parts of speech; **prononcer un ~** make a speech

**discourtois** *adj* discourteous, impolite

**discréditer** *vt* discredit, disparage

**discret -ète** *adj* discreet, cautious; quiet, unassuming, unobtrusive; modest (request)

**discrétion** *nf* discretion; prudence; **manger à ~** eat as much as one likes

**discriminer** *vt* discriminate

**disculpation** *nf* exoneration

**disculper** *vt* exculpate, exonerate; **se ~** clear oneself

**discursif -ive** *adj* discursive

**discussion** *nf* discussion, debate; argument

**discutable** *adj* debatable

**discutailler** *vi coll* argue over trivialities, quibble

**discuté** *adj* contested; criticized

**discuter** *vt* discuss, debate, talk over, argue, question; **ça se discute** it's a debatable point; *vi* talk, chat

**disert** *adj* eloquent

**disette** *nf* dearth, scarcity

**diseur -euse** *n* reciter; **diseuse de bonne aventure** fortune-teller

**disgrâce** *nf* disgrace, fall from favour; misfortune; ugliness; plainness

**disgracier** *vt* dismiss from favour

**disgracieux -ieuse** *adj* uncouth, ungraceful; unpleasant; ugly

**disjoindre** *vt* (55) disjoin, sever

**disjoncteur** *nm* cut-out switch

**dislocation** nf dislocation; dismemberment

**disloquer** vt dislocate, put out of joint; dismember

**disparaître** vi (68) disappear, vanish; be hidden; pass away

**disparate** adj dissimilar; ill-assorted

**disparition** nf disappearance; death

**disparu** adj+p part **disparaître** mil missing; dead, departed; extinct; **être porté** ~ be listed as missing

**dispendieux -ieuse** adj costly, expensive

**dispensaire** nm dispensary; outpatients' department

**dispensation** nf dispensation, distribution

**dispense** nf exemption

**dispenser** vt exempt, dispense; distribute, give out; make up (medicine)

**dispersement** nm dispersing

**disperser** vt scatter, disperse, spread

**dispersion** nf dispersal; rout; scattering

**disponibilité** nf availability; readiness; state of not being committed; ~s available assets

**disponible** adj available; uncommitted

**dispos** adj fit, in good form; **esprit** ~ alert mind

**disposé** adj disposed, inclined; subject

**disposer** vt dispose, arrange, lay out; incline, influence; vi dispose, have at one's disposal; **disposez de moi** I am at your service; **se** ~ **à** make ready to; **vous pouvez** ~ you may go

**dispositif** nm device, appliance, gear

**disposition** nf disposition, arrangement, lay-out; frame of mind; propensity, tendency; aptitude, talent; disposal; ~s arrangements; leg provisions; **prendre des** ~s make arrangements

**disproportionné** adj disproportionate

**dispute** nf dispute; quarrel

**disputer** vt dispute, argue; scold, tell off; ~ **un prix** compete for a prize; vi quarrel; **se** ~ quarrel

**disqualifier** vt disqualify

**disque** nm disk, disc; (gramophone) record; discus; ~ **de stationnement** parking disc

**dissemblable** adj different, dissimilar

**dissemblance** nf dissimilarity

**dissémination** nf scattering, spreading

**disséminer** vt scatter, spread, disseminate

**dissentiment** nm disagreement, dissent

**disséquer** vt (6) dissect

**dissertation** nf dissertation; essay

**disserter** vi dissert; hold forth

**dissidence** nf dissidence, dissent

**dissident** nm dissentient; dissenter; adj dissident; disaffected

**dissimilaire** adj dissimilar, unlike

**dissimulateur -trice** n dissembler, dissimulator

**dissimulation** nf deceit, dissimulation; concealment

**dissimulé** adj secretive

**dissimuler** vt dissemble, dissimulate; conceal; **se** ~ hide

**dissipateur -trice** n squanderer, spendthrift

**dissipation** nf dissipation; dispersion; inattention

**dissiper** vt dissipate, scatter, disperse; dispel, clear up; squander; **se** ~ disappear, clear; amuse oneself; become dissipated; be inattentive

**dissocier** vt dissociate

**dissolu** adj dissolute, profligate

**dissolution** nf dissolution, disintegration, dissolving; breaking up; profligacy

**dissolvant** nm solvent; nail-varnish remover

**dissoudre** vt (8) dissolve, melt; disperse; decompose; **se** ~ dissolve, melt

**dissuader** vt dissuade

**dissyllabique** adj dissyllabic

**distance** nf distance; interval; **à** ~ at a distance

**distancer** vt (4) outrun, outstrip; **se** ~ keep one's distance; keep one's freedom of action

**distant** adj distant; stand-offish

**distendre** vt distend; strain

**distension** nf distension; straining

**distillateur** nm distiller

**distiller** vt distil; secrete

**distillerie** nf distillery; distilling

**distinct** adj distinct, separate; clear

**distinctif -ive** adj distinctive, characteristic

**distinction** nf distinction; honour; eminence; distinguished manner

**distinguable** adj distinguishable

**distingué** adj distinguished; eminent

**distinguer** vt distinguish; characterize; single out; perceive, discern; **se** ~ distinguish oneself, stand out

**distique** nm distich

**distorsion** nf distortion

**distraction** nf division; appropriation; inadvertence, absent-mindedness; entertainment, amusement; **par** ~ inadvertently

**distraire** vt (9) separate; misappropriate; entertain, divert; **se** ~ amuse oneself

**distrait** adj absent-minded

**distrayant** adj entertaining

**distribuer** vt distribute, issue; deliver (letters); deal (cards)

**distributeur -trice** n distributor; ~ **automatique** vending-machine

**distribution** *nf* distribution, allotment; delivery (letters); cast, casting; ~ **des prix** prize-giving

**dit** *adj + p part* **dire** agreed, appointed; (so-)called

**diurne** *adj* diurnal

**diva** *nf* prima-donna

**divagation** *nf* wandering; digression

**divaguer** *vi* wander; digress; talk nonsense, ramble

**divergence** *nf* divergence; disagreement

**diverger** *vi* (3) diverge

**divers** *adj pl* diverse, different; various, miscellaneous; *adj sing* **fait ~** minor news item

**diversifier** *vt* diversify, vary

**diversion** *nf* diversion, change; **faire ~** create a diversion

**diversité** *nf* diversity

**divertir** *vt* divert; entertain

**divertissant** *adj* amusing, entertaining

**divertissement** *nm* entertainment, recreation

**dividende** *nm* dividend

**divin** *adj* divine, holy; exquisite

**divinateur -trice** *n* soothsayer, diviner

**divination** *nf* soothsaying

**divinatoire** *adj* divinatory

**divinité** *nf* divinity; Godhead; deity

**diviser** *vt* divide, separate; **se ~** break up

**diviseur** *nm* divisor; divider

**division** *nf* division, dividing; partition; section, part; department; branch; discord

**divisionnaire** *adj* belonging to a division

**divorce** *nm* divorce; disagreement

**divorcer** *vi* (4) divorce

**divulguer** *vt* divulge, reveal

**dix** *nm + adj* ten

**dix-huit** *nm + adj* eighteen

**dix-huitième** *n + adj* eighteenth

**dixième** *n + adj* tenth

**dix-neuf** *nm + adj* nineteen

**dix-neuvième** *n + adj* nineteenth

**dix-sept** *nm + adj* seventeen

**dix-septième** *n + adj* seventeenth

**dizaine** *nf* about ten

**do** *nm invar mus* C, do(h)

**docile** *adj* docile, submissive, tractable

**docilité** *nf* docility

**dock** *nm naut* dock; warehouse; shop (*usu* food)

**docte** *adj* learned

**docteur** *nm* doctor

**doctoral** *adj* doctoral; pompous

**doctorat** *nm* doctorate

**doctoresse** *nf* woman doctor

**documentaire** *nm* documentary film; *adj* documentary

**documentation** *nf* documentation; documents

**documenter** *vt* document; **se ~ sur** gather information about

**dodeliner** *vi* shake head (of elderly person)

**dodo** *nm coll* bye-byes; **aller au ~** go to bye-byes; **faire ~** sleep

**dodu** *adj* plump

**dogmatique** *adj* dogmatic

**dogme** *nm* dogma

**dogue** *nm* big watch-dog; mastiff

**doigt** *nm* finger; finger's breadth; **~ de pied** toe; **~ de vin** drop of wine; **à deux ~s de la mort** within an inch of death; **mettre le ~ dessus** discover the solution; **montrer du ~** point at; **s'en mordre les ~s** regret it

**doigté** *nm* tact; *mus* fingering

**doit** *nm* debit, liability

**doléances** *nfpl* complaints, grouses

**dolent** *adj* whining, plaintive

**domaine** *nm* domain; estate; field, realm; **~ de l'État**, **~ public** public property; **dans le ~ public** out of copyright

**dôme** *nm* dome

**domesticité** *nf* domesticated state, domesticity; domestic staff

**domestique** *n* servant; *adj* domestic

**domestiquer** *vt* domesticate

**domicile** *nm* residence, domicile; **à ~** at one's place of residence

**domicilié** *adj* resident

**dominance** *nf* dominance; predominance, preponderance

**dominant** *adj* dominant, ruling; prevailing

**dominateur -trice** *adj* domineering

**dominer** *vt* rule; dominate, control; overtake, tower above; master

**dominicain -e** *n + adj eccles* Dominican

**dominical** *adj* dominical, relating to Sunday

**dommage** *nm* damage, injury; *leg* **~s et intérêts** damages; **quel ~!** what a pity!; **réparer les ~s** make good the damage

**domptable** *adj* tameable

**domptage** *nm* taming

**dompter** *vt* tame, break in; subdue, master

**dompteur -euse** *n* tamer

**don** *nm* giving, gift, present; talent

**donateur -trice** *n* giver; *leg* donor (donatrix)

**donc** *conj* therefore, hence, so; *adv* (used for emphasis) **allez ~!** go on!; do go!; **pensez ~!** just imagine!

**dondon** *nf coll* fat woman

**donjon** *nm* keep

**donnant** *adj* generous; **~, ~** fifty-fifty

**donne** *nf* deal (cards)

**donnée** *nf* premise, datum; **~s** data

**donner** *vt* give; provide, furnish; yield;

attribute, ascribe; ~ **la main à qn**
shake hands with s/o; ~ **le bonjour à
qn** wish s/o good day; ~ **tort (raison)
à qn** disagree (agree) with s/o; ~ **une
pièce de théâtre** put on a play; **cela
donne à penser** that gives one food for
thought; **c'est donné** it's dirt cheap;
**étant donné que** given that; **je vous le
donne en mille** you'll never guess; **se
~ au plaisir** give oneself up to
pleasure; **se ~ pour** claim to be;
**s'en ~ à cœur joie** enjoy oneself no
end; *vi* ~ **dans le luxe** like expensive
things; ~ **dans un piège** fall into a
trap; ~ **de la tête contre** bump one's
head against; ~ **sur** look out on, lead
into, shine on

**donneur -euse** *n* giver, donor; dealer
(cards); *sl* informer, nark, sneak

**dont** *rel pron* from, by, with whom or
which; of, concerning whom or which;
whose

**donzelle** *nf coll* wench

**dopant** *nm* dope, stimulant

**doper** *vt* dope; reinforce, improve the
quality of

**dorade** *nf* sea-bream; dolphin

**dorénavant** *adv* henceforth

**dorer** *vt* gild; glaze (cake); brown; ~ **la
pilule** sugar the pill; **doré sur tranches**
gilt-edged (book)

**dorique** *adj* Doric

**dorloter** *vt* fondle; pamper

**dormant** *adj* sleeping; dormant; stagnant

**dormeur -euse** *n* sleeper; sleepy-head

**dormir** *vi* (39) sleep, be asleep; be
dormant; ~ **debout** be dead tired; ~
**sur les deux oreilles** be quite easy in
one's mind; **eau qui dort** stagnant
water; **histoire à ~ debout** tall story,
boring tale

**dortoir** *nm* dormitory

**dorure** *nf* gilding

**doryphore** *nm* Colorado beetle

**dos** *nm* back; **avoir bon ~** be blamed
unfairly; *coll* **en avoir plein le ~** be fed
up; **se mettre tout le monde à ~** put
everyone against oneself

**doser** *vt* proportion

**dossard** *nm* number (on back of competitor's clothing)

**dossier** *nm* back (of seat); documents,
record

**dot** *nf* dowry

**dotation** *nf* endowment

**doter** *vt* give dowry to; endow

**douairière** *nf* dowager; *pej* old woman

**douane** *nf* customs; customs house

**douanier -ière** *n* customs official; *adj*
customs

**doublage** *nm cin* dubbing; *theat* under-

studying; doubling; lining (clothes)

**double** *nm* double; duplicate; *adj*
double, twofold; *ar* two-faced; **faire
coup** ~ kill two birds with one stone

**doubler** *vt* double; fold; line (garment);
*mot* overtake; dub; *vi* double

**doublure** *nf* lining; *theat* understudy;
*cin* stand-in

**douce** *adj see* **doux**

**douceâtre** *adj* sweetish, cloying

**doucement** *adv* softly, gently; smoothly

**doucereux -euse** *adj* sickly; smooth-
tongued

**douceur** *nf* sweetness; smoothness;
pleasantness; ~s sweets; gentleness;
**en ~** gently

**douche** *nf* shower; shower-bath; ~
**écossaise** alternate hot and cold
shower; nasty shock

**doucher** *vt* give (s/o) a shower

**doué** *adj* gifted

**douer** *vt* endow

**douille** *nf* socket; *elect* holder; case
(cartridge)

**douillet -ette** *adj* soft; snug; liking
comfort

**douillette** *nf* quilted coat

**douleur** *nf* pain, suffering; grief

**douloureuse** *nf coll* bill

**douloureux -euse** *adj* painful; distressing

**doute** *nm* uncertainty, doubt; **avoir des
~s** have misgivings; **mettre en ~** cast
doubt on; **sans ~** probably; certainly

**douter** *vi* doubt; **à n'en point ~**
undoubtedly; *coll* **il ne doute de rien**
he's cocksure; **se ~ de** suspect

**douteux -euse** *adj* uncertain, doubtful;
suspect; grubby

**douve** *nf* moat

**doux** (*f* **douce**) *adj* sweet; soft, pleasant,
gentle, meek; **eau douce** fresh water;
*adv* **filer** ~ be submissive; **tout ~!**
gently!, easy!

**douzaine** *nf* dozen, about twelve

**douze** *nm*+*adj* twelve

**douzième** *n*+*adj* twelfth

**doyen -enne** *n* oldest, senior; *nm* dean

**draconien -ienne** *adj* draconian, harsh

**dragage** *nm* dredging; mine-sweeping

**dragée** *nf* sugared almond; **tenir la ~
haute à qn** make s/o pay dearly for
something

**dragon** *nm* dragon; *mil* dragoon

**drague** *nf* dredge; drag-net

**draguer** *vt* dredge; drag, sweep; *coll* pick
up; *vi coll* be out for a pick-up

**dragueur** *nm* dredger; ~ **de mines**
mine-sweeper

**drain** *nm* drainage-tube

**drainer** *vt* drain

**dramatique** *adj* dramatic

93

**dramatiser** vt dramatize

**dramaturge** n dramatist

**drame** nm drama; tragic occurrence, disaster

**drap** nm cloth; sheet; *coll* être dans de beaux ~ s be in a fine mess

**drapeau** nm flag; être sous les ~x be in the army

**draper** vt drape, cover

**draperie** nf drapery

**drapier** nm draper

**drastique** adj drastic

**drelin** nm ting-a-ling

**dressage** nm training; dressage; straightening

**dresser** vt set up, erect; lay (table); pitch (tent); draw up; arrange; train, break in (animal); se ~ rise, straighten up, stand

**dresseur -euse** n trainer; erector

**dressoir** nm dresser, sideboard

**drogue** nf drug; *coll* worthless medicine

**drogué -e** n drug addict; drugged person

**droguer** vt drug; vi *coll* be kept waiting

**droguerie** nf shop selling household goods, paint, dyes, etc

**droguiste** n manager, owner of droguerie

**droit** nm right; law; fee, charge; ~ s d'auteur royalties; à bon ~ with good reason; à qui de ~ to whom it may concern; être en ~ de be entitled to; faire son ~ study law; adj straight, direct; right; upright, frank; angle ~ right angle; adv straight

**droite** nf right hand; *pol* right

**droitier -ière** adj right-handed

**droiture** nf straightforwardness, upright character

**drolatique** adj comic

**drôle** nm rascal; adj funny; ~ de odd, strange, curious

**drôlerie** nf oddness; joke

**drôlesse** nf jade, hussy

**dromadaire** nm dromedary

**dru** adj thick, strong, dense; adv thickly, hard

**druide -esse** n druid, druidess

**du** = **de le**

**dû** nm due; adj (f **due**) owing, due, owed; p part devoir

**dubitatif -ive** adj dubitative

**duc** nm duke; horned owl

**duché** nm dukedom

**duchesse** nf duchess

**duègne** nf duenna

**dulcifier** vt sweeten

**dulcinée** nf lady-love

**dûment** adv duly, in due form

**duo** nm duet

**duper** vt trick, fool, dupe

**duperie** nf deception

**duplex** nm two-way communication system, duplex; two-storey flat

**duplicata** nm invar copy, duplicate

**duplicité** nf double-dealing

**duquel** = **du + lequel**

**dur** nm *coll* tough guy; *pol* hawk; *bui* concrete, stone, etc; adj hard, tough; harsh, severe; à la ~ e in a tough way; avoir la vie ~ e be very resistant, be hard to kill; have a hard life; être ~ d'oreille be hard of hearing; œuf ~ hard-boiled egg; adv hard

**durabilité** nf durability

**durant** prep during

**durcir** vt + vi harden

**durcissement** nm hardening

**durée** nf duration; life, lasting quality; de courte ~ short-lived

**durement** adv hard, harshly

**durer** vi last, endure, hold out

**dureté** nf hardness; difficulty; harshness

**durillon** nm callosity, corn

**duvet** nm down; eiderdown; down sleeping-bag, clothing

**duveteux -euse** adj downy

**dynamique** adj dynamic

**dynamiter** vt blow up, dynamite

**dynastie** nf dynasty

**dysenterie** nf dysentery

**dyslexie** nf dyslexia

**dyslexique** adj dyslexic

**dyspepsie** nf dyspepsia

**dyspepsique, dyspeptique** adj dyspeptic

# E

**eau** *nf* water; ~ **courante** running water; ~ **oxygénée** hydrogen peroxide; **château d'** ~ water tower; **cours d'** ~ stream; **faire** ~ spring a leak (ship); **il tombe de l'** ~ it is raining; **jet d'** ~ fountain; **laver à grande** ~ swill down; **mettre de l'** ~ **dans son vin** draw in one's horns; **pièce d'** ~ ornamental pond or lake; **tomber à l'** ~ fall through; **ville d'** ~ spa

**eau-de-vie** *nf* (*pl* **eaux-de-vie**) spirits, brandy

**eau-forte** *nf* (*pl* **eaux-fortes**) etching; nitric acid

**ébahir** *vt* astound, flabbergast

**ébahissement** *nm* astonishment, amazement

**ébarber** *vt* trim, clip

**ébats** *nmpl* frolic, gambols

**ébattre (s')** *v refl* frolic, gambol, frisk about

**ébaubi** *adj* staggered

**ébauche** *nf* outline; rough sketch; rough pressing, rough cast

**ébaucher** *vt* sketch out, outline; rough-hew

**ébène** *nf* ebony

**ébéniste** *nm* cabinet-maker

**ébénisterie** *nf* cabinet work

**éberlué** *adj* amazed, staggered

**éblouir** *vt* dazzle

**éblouissement** *nm* dazzling; dizziness

**éborgner** *vt* blind in one eye

**éboueur** *nm* dustman

**ébouillanter** *vt* scald; dip in boiling water

**éboulement** *nm* landslide; caving in; rock-fall

**ébouler (s')** *v refl* crumble, cave in, slip

**éboulis** *nm* mass of fallen earth and stones, scree

**ébouriffer** *vt* ruffle, dishevel; amaze, take aback

**ébrancher** *vt* lop off the branches of

**ébranlement** *nm* shock, shaking; agitation

**ébranler** *vt* shake, unsettle; loosen; **s'** ~ get under way

**ébrécher** *vt* (6) chip; *coll* damage, reduce

**ébriété** *nf* state of drunkenness

**ébrouer (s')** *v refl* snort (horse); clean oneself (bird)

**ébruiter** *vt* noise abroad, make known; **s'** ~ become known

**ébullition** *nf* boiling, ebullition

**écaille** *nf* scale (fish); shell; tortoise-shell; flake, splinter

**¹écailler** *vt* remove scales from; open (oyster); **s'** ~ scale off

**²écailler -ère** *n* person who sells or opens oysters

**écailleux -euse** *adj* scaly; splintery, flaky

**écale** *nf* husk, shell

**écarlate** *nf*+*adj* scarlet

**écarquiller** *vt* open wide (eyes); spread out (legs)

**écart** *nm* distance apart; divergence, variation; deviation, swerve; discarding, discard (cards); ~ **de jeunesse** youthful aberration; **à l'** ~ aside, on one side; **faire le grand** ~ do the splits; **faire un** ~ shy, step aside suddenly; make a digression; **tenir qn à l'** ~ keep s/o in the background

**écarté** *adj* isolated, remote

**écarteler** *vt* (5) *hist* quarter (criminal, shield); **être écartelé entre** be torn between

**écartement** *nm* spacing, setting aside; gap, separation

**écarter** *vt* separate, open, draw aside, ward off; exclude; ~ **un obstacle** get rid of an obstacle; **s'** ~ move aside; diverge, stray

**ecchymose** *nf* bruise

**ecclésiastique** *nm* member of clergy, cleric; *adj* ecclesiastical

**écervelé** *adj* scatter-brained, thoughtless

**échafaud** *nm* scaffold

**échafaudage** *nm* scaffolding; erection of scaffolding; constructing

**échafauder** *vt* erect scaffolding on; build up; ~ **des projets** make plans

**échalas** *nm* prop (for vine or other plant); long, skinny person

**échalote** *nf* shallot

**échancrer** *vt* cut out; notch

**échancrure** *nf* cut-out section, opening; notch, indentation

**échange** *nm* exchange

**échangeable** *adj* exchangeable

**échanger** *vt* (3) exchange, swap

**échangeur** *nm* motorway intersection

**échanson** *nm* cup-bearer

**échantillon** *nm* sample, specimen

**échantillonner** *vt* prepare patterns of; check or compare samples of

**échappatoire** *nf* way out, subterfuge; loop-hole

**échappée** *nf* escape; escapade; glimpse; brief moment

échappement

**échappement** *nm* escape (gas, water); escapement (clock); **tuyau d'** ~ exhaust-pipe
**échapper** *vi* escape; pass unnoticed; **cela m'a échappé** I said that quite unintentionally; **l'** ~ **belle** have a narrow escape; **s'** ~ escape; flee, run away; leak
**écharde** *nf* splinter
**écharpe** *nf* sash; scarf; **avoir le bras en** ~ have one's arm in a sling; **mot prendre en** ~ crash into the side of
**écharper** *vt* slash; hack to pieces
**échasse** *nf* stilt
**échassier** *nm orni* wader
**échauder** *vt* scald; plunge in boiling water; ~ **un client** fleece a customer; **se faire** ~ burn one's fingers
**échauffant** *adj* binding (food)
**échauffement** *nm* heating, overheating; overexcitement
**échauffer** *vt* overheat; *coll* ~ **la bile de qn** anger s/o; **s'** ~ get overheated; get excited
**échauffourée** *nf* scuffle; clash
**échauguette** *nf* watch-tower; bartizan
**échéance** *nf* date (for payment, etc); expiration; **à courte (longue)** ~ short-(long-)dated
**échéant** *adj* **le cas** ~ should the occasion arise
**échec** *nm* failure; check; ~ **s** chess; ~ **mat** checkmate; **tenir en** ~ hold in check
**échelle** *nf* ladder; scale; ~ **mobile** sliding scale; **faire la courte** ~ **à qn** give s/o a leg-up, a helping hand; **il n'y a plus qu'à tirer l'** ~ you can't do better than that; you might as well give up
**échelon** *nm* rung; *mil* echelon
**échelonner** *vt* space out; spread out; stagger; dispose in echelon (troops)
**écheveau** *nm* hank, skein
**échevelé** *adj* dishevelled; disordered, wild
**échine** *nf* spike, backbone; *coll* **avoir l'** ~ **souple** be obsequious
**échiner** *vt* break the back of; *coll* **s'** ~ wear oneself out
**échiquier** *nm* chess-board; **Chancelier de l'Échiquier** Chancellor of the Exchequer
**écho** *nm* echo; **les** ~ **s** news items; **se faire l'** ~ **de** repeat
**échoir** *vi* (40) happen; fall due
**échoppe** *nf* street stall
**échouer** *vi* run aground; fail, fall through; *coll* stop, land (in a place)
**échu** *p part* échoir
**éclaboussement** *nm* splashing, spattering
**éclabousser** *vt* splash, spatter
**éclaboussure** *nf* splash, spatter

**éclair** *nm* flash of lightning; flash; *cul* éclair
**éclairage** *nm* lighting; illumination; light
**éclairant** *adj* lighting, illuminating
**éclaircie** *nf* opening, break (in clouds); clearing
**éclaircir** *vt* lighten; clear; solve, explain; thin, thin out; clarify; **s'** ~ clear up; become clearer; thin
**éclaircissement** *nm* explanation, enlightenment, clearing up
**éclairé** *adj* well-informed, enlightened
**éclairer** *vt* light, illuminate; enlighten; reconnoitre
**éclaireur** *nm* scout
**éclaireuse** *nf* girl-guide
**éclat** *nm* chip, splinter; burst; flash, brightness, brilliance, glare, show; scandal; **sans** ~ quietly
**éclatant** *adj* brilliant, shining, dazzling, bright; loud
**éclatement** *nm* bursting; dispersion
**éclater** *vi* splinter; burst, explode; break out; burst out; spill out
**éclectique** *adj* eclectic
**éclipser** *vt* eclipse; **s'** ~ disappear, vanish
**éclopé** *adj* lame, crippled
**éclore** *vi* (41) open, blossom; hatch out; appear
**éclosion** *nf* opening, blossoming; hatching
**écluse** *nf* lock (canal)
**éclusier -ière** *n* lock-keeper
**écœurant** *adj* sickening, disgusting
**écœurement** *nm* disgust
**écœurer** *vt* sicken, disgust; discourage
**école** *nf* school; instruction, training; **être à bonne** ~ be in good hands; **faire** ~ found a school (art, thought); **haute** ~ advanced horsemanship
**écolier -ière** *n* schoolboy(girl); **chemin des** ~ **s** long way round
**écologie** *nf* ecology
**écologique** *adj* ecological
**écologiste** *n* ecologist
**éconduire** *vt* (80) show (s/o) the door, get rid of; refuse, reject
**économat** *nm* stewardship, bursarship; bursar's office, steward's office; staff shop
**économe** *n* bursar, treasurer, steward; *adj* economical, thrifty, sparing
**économie** *nf* economy, management; saving, thrift; **faire des** ~ **s** save money
**économique** *adj* economic; economical, thrifty; inexpensive
**économiser** *vt* save, economize
**économiste** *n* economist
**écoper** *vt* bail out; *vi sl* be wounded; cop it
**écorce** *nf* bark; rind, peel, husk
**écorcer** *vt* remove bark (peel, husk) of
**écorcher** *vt* flay, skin; fleece (customer);

96

graze, bark; scrape; ~ **l'oreille** grate on the ear; ~ **une langue** murder a language

**écorchure** *nf* abrasion, scratch, graze

**écorner** *vt* break, remove horns of (animal); break, chip off the corner of; dog-ear; ~ **sa fortune** break into one's fortune

**écornifler** *vt coll* scrounge, sponge

**Écossais -e** *n* Scot

**écossais** *adj* Scottish, Scots

**Écosse** *nf* Scotland

**écosser** *vt* shell (peas, etc)

**écot** *nm* quota, share

**écoulement** *nm* outflow, discharge; waste-pipe; sale, disposal

**écouler** *vt* get rid of, dispose of, sell; **s' ~** flow out; elapse, pass

**écourter** *vt* shorten, curtail, cut short; dock, crop

¹**écoute** *nf* listening; **être aux ~ s** eavesdrop; **mettre sur ~** bug; **se mettre à l' ~** listen in to the radio

²**écoute** *nf naut* sheet

**écouter** *vt + vi* listen (to); pay attention (to); **s' ~ beaucoup** pay excessive attention to one's health; **s' ~ parler** enjoy hearing oneself speak

**écouteur** *nm* receiver, ear-phone

**écoutille** *nf naut* hatchway

**écrabouiller** *vt coll* squash, crush

**écran** *nm* screen; filter (light)· shade; **le petit ~** television, the box

**écrasant** *adj* crushing

**écrasement** *nm* crushing, squashing; defeat; crashing, collapsing

**écraser** *vt* squash, crush; run over; defeat; overburden; **s' ~** collapse, crash; *vi sl* **écrase!** forget it!

**écrémer** *vt* (6) cream; skim (milk); *fig* cream off

**écrémeuse** *nf* creamer, (cream) separator

**écrevisse** *nf* crayfish; **rouge comme une ~** red as a lobster (beetroot)

**écrier (s')** *v refl* cry out, exclaim

**écrin** *nm* casket, jewel-case

**écrire** *vt + vi* (42) write, write down; **il est écrit que** fate has decided that; **machine à ~** typewriter

**écrit** *nm* writing; written exam, written document; **par ~** in writing

**écriteau** *nm* notice, placard

**écritoire** *nf* writing desk

**écriture** *nf* handwriting; **~ s** documents, papers; accounts; **Écriture Sainte** Holy Scripture

**écrivailler** *vi coll* scribble, write badly

**écrivailleur -euse** *n* scribbler, hackwriter

**écrivain** *nm* writer, author

¹**écrou** *nm* nut

²**écrou** *nm* committal to gaol; **lever l' ~** discharge

**écrouelles** *nfpl* scrofula

**écrouer** *vt* put in prison

**écroulement** *nm* collapse, falling in; downfall

**écrouler (s')** *v refl* collapse, fall down, give way

**écru** *adj* unbleached (material)

**écu** *nm* shield, escutcheon; crown; *hist* five-franc piece

**écueil** *nm* reef; obstacle, peril

**écuelle** *nf* basin, bowl

**éculé** *adj* down at heel

**écume** *nf* froth, foam, scum; dregs (of society); ~ **de mer** meerschaum

**écumeux -euse** *adj* frothy, foamy

**écumoire** *nf* skimmer

**écurer** *vt* clean, scour

**écureuil** *nm* squirrel

**écurie** *nf* stable; horses; writers working with a publisher; cars or cyclists racing for a firm

**écusson** *nm* shield, escutcheon, badge

**écuyer** *nm* squire; equerry; (*f* **-ère**) horse-rider; **monter à l'écuyère** ride astride

**édenté** *adj* toothless

**édicter** *vt* decree

**édifiant** *adj* edifying

**édification** *nf* building, setting up; edification; enlightenment

**édifice** *nm* building, edifice

**édifier** *vt* set up, erect; edify; inform, enlighten

**Édimbourg** *nm* Edinburgh

**édit** *nm* edict

**éditer** *vt* publish; edit

**éditeur -trice** *n* publisher; editor

**édition** *nf* edition, issue, impression; publishing; ~ **originale** first edition

**Édouard** *nm* Edward

**édredon** *nm* eiderdown

**éducateur -trice** *n* educator

**éducatif -ive** *adj* educative

**éducation** *nf* education, upbringing; training; rearing; **homme sans ~** ill-bred man

**édulcorant** *nm* sweetener

**édulcorer** *vt* sweeten; attenuate

**éduquer** *vt* educate, bring up; train

**effacé** *adj* unobtrusive, retiring; retired

**effacement** *nm* obliteration; wearing away; self-effacement, unobtrusiveness

**effacer** *vt* obliterate, rub out, delete; eclipse, surpass; **s' ~** wear away; come off; stand aside, give way

**effarant** *adj* incredible, fantastic

**effarer** *vt* scare, frighten

**effaroucher** *vt* startle, scare

**effectif** *nm mil* establishment; manpower; *usu pl mil* strength; *adj* (*f* **-ive**) effective,

97

efficacious; real

**effectivement** *adv* indeed, yes; effectively; actually

**effectuer** *vt* carry out, effect, realize, accomplish

**efféminé** *adj* effeminate

**effervescence** *nf* effervescence; excitement, agitation

**effet** *nm* result; property, virtue; action; impression, effect; bill; ~ s belongings; **à cet** ~ to this end; **en** ~ indeed; **faire bon** ~ look well, give a good impression; **faire de l'** ~ impress, attract attention; **faire l'** ~ **de** give the impression of; **manquer son** ~ fall flat; **mettre à** ~ carry out, put into operation; **prendre** ~ become operative; **sans** ~ ineffective

**effeuiller** *vt* take off, thin out leaves, petals of; **s'** ~ shed leaves or petals

**effeuilleuse** *nf* stripper

**efficace** *adj* effective, efficacious

**efficacité** *nf* effectiveness, efficacy; efficiency

**effigie** *nf* effigy

**effilé** *adj* slim, slender; tapering

**effiler** *vt* taper; fray; **s'** ~ taper; fray

**effilocher** *vt* fray; ravel out

**efflanqué** *adj* skinny, lean

**effleurement** *nm* light touch, graze; skimming

**effleurer** *vt* touch lightly, graze; skim

**effluve** *nm* emanation

**effondré** *adj* prostrate, shattered

**effondrement** *nm* collapse; subsidence; slump

**effondrer** *vt* break down, bash in; **s'** ~ cave in, fall in, collapse

**efforcer (s')** *v refl* (4) try, strive

**effort** *nm* effort, exertion; strain

**effraction** *nf* breaking in, house-breaking

**effraie** *nf* barn owl, screech owl

**effranger** *vt* (3) fray out (material)

**effrayant** *adj* frightening, terrifying; dreadful; *coll* amazing, tremendous

**effrayer** *vt* (7) frighten, scare; put off, discourage; **s'** ~ be frightened

**effréné** *adj* unbridled; frantic; excessive

**effriter** *vt* reduce to powder, make crumble; **s'** ~ crumble away

**effroi** *nm* terror, fright

**effronté** *adj* bold, shameless, brazen

**effronterie** *nf* effrontery, insolence

**effroyable** *adj* dreadful, frightful; tremendous, awful

**effusion** *nf* effusion; outpouring, overflowing; shedding (blood)

**égailler (s')** *v refl* scatter, disperse

**égal** *adj* equal; same; level, smooth, even, constant; **à armes** ~ **es** on equal terms; **à l'** ~ **de** equally with; **cela m'est** ~ I don't mind, it's all the same to me; *coll* **c'est** ~ well, never mind, all the same; **traiter qn d'** ~ **à** ~ treat s/o as an equal

**également** *adv* equally; also

**égaler** *vt* equal, be equal to; rival

**égaliser** *vt* equalize; level, make even

**égalitaire** *adj* egalitarian

**égalité** *nf* equality; evenness, regularity; **à** ~ equal, even (in games); **à** ~ **de** given equality in; **sur un pied d'** ~ on an equal footing

**égard** *nm* regard; consideration, respect; **à l'** ~ **de** with regard to; **avoir** ~ à allow for

**égaré** *adj* stray, lost; distraught

**égarement** *nm* mislaying; straying; bewilderment; deviation, misconduct; frenzy

**égarer** *vt* lead astray; lose, mislay; bewilder; **s'** ~ lose one's way; become deranged

**égayer** *vt* (7) amuse, cheer up; enliven; brighten up

**égide** *nf* aegis, shield; *coll* protection

**églantier** *nm* wild rose bush

**églantine** *nf* wild rose

**église** *nf* church

**églogue** *nf* eclogue

**égoïsme** *nm* selfishness

**égoïste** *n* + *adj* selfish (person)

**égorger** *vt* (3) cut the throat of; butcher, slaughter

**égosiller (s')** *v refl* bawl, shout one's head off; sing loudly (birds)

**égout** *nm* drainage, draining; sewer, drain; *fig* sink; **tout-à-l'** ~ mains drainage

**égoutter** *vt* + *vi* drain; drip dry; **s'** ~ drain, drip

**égouttoir** *nm* drainer, plate-rack

**égratigner** *vt* scratch; graze; *fig* offend slightly

**égratignure** *nf* scratch; slight

**égrener** *vt* (6) shell; ~ **un chapelet** tell beads; **s'** ~ drop, fall; be dotted along

**égrillard** *adj* ribald, lewd; spicy

**Égypte** *nf* Egypt

**égyptien -ienne** *adj* Egyptian

**eh** *interj* hey!; ~ **bien!** well!

**éhonté** *adj* shameless

**éjecter** *vt* eject

**élaborer** *vt* elaborate; digest

**élaguer** *vt* prune, lop off; cut down

**élan** *nm* bound, spring; impetus; burst; **prendre son** ~ take off, take a run

**élancement** *nm* sudden twinge of pain; transport (feeling)

**élancer (s')** *v refl* (4) spring, bound forward, rush forward

**élargir** *vt* widen, let out, stretch, broaden, enlarge; set free

**élargissement** *nm* widening
**élasticité** *nf* elasticity
**élastique** *nm* elastic; *adj* elastic; springy, buoyant
**électeur -trice** *n* elector, voter
**électif -ive** *adj* elective
**élection** *nf* election, polling; choice, preference
**électoral** *adj* electoral
**électorat** *nm* electorate
**électricien -ienne** *n* electrician
**électricité** *nf* electricity
**électrifier** *vt* electrify
**électrique** *adj* electric
**électro-aimant** *nm* electro-magnet
**électrocardiogramme** *nm* electrocardiogram
**électrocuter** *vt* electrocute
**électrogène** *adj* generating; **groupe ~** generating plant
**électrolyse** *nf* electrolysis
**électroménager** *nm* electrical household appliance department, industry; *adj* (*f* -ère) **appareil ~** electrical household appliance
**électronique** *adj* electronic
**électrophone** *nm* record-player
**élégance** *nf* elegance, stylishness
**élégant** *adj* elegant, well-dressed, stylish
**élégiaque** *adj* elegiac
**élégie** *nf* elegy
**élément** *nm* element; ingredient, component; *elect* cell; **~s** rudiments
**élémentaire** *adj* elementary; rudimentary
**élevage** *nm* raising, rearing
**élévateur** *nm* lift, hoist; elevator muscle
**élévation** *nf* elevation, lifting; setting up; rise; height, altitude; promotion
**élévatoire** *adj* elevatory, lifting
**élève** *n* pupil, student; apprentice; disciple; trainee
**élevé** *adj* high; lofty; **bien ~** well-bred; **peu ~** low
**élever** *vt* (6) raise, elevate; set up, build; rear, bring up; **s' ~** rise; raise oneself; **s' ~ à** amount to; **s' ~ contre** object to, protest against
**éleveur -euse** *n* breeder; wine-producer
**éleveuse** *nf* battery (poultry)
**elfe** *nm* elf
**élider** *vt* elide
**éligibilité** *nf* eligibility
**élimer** *vt* wear (cloth); **s' ~** wear out
**éliminateur -trice** *adj* eliminating
**éliminatoire** *adj* eliminatory
**éliminer** *vt* eliminate, get rid of
**élire** *vt* (56) elect, choose; **~ domicile** take up residence
**élite** *nf* élite, pick, flower; **troupes d' ~** crack troops
**élitisme** *nm* élitism

**elle** (*pl* **elles**) *pron* she, they; it, they; her, it, them
**ellipse** *nf* ellipsis; ellipse
**éloge** *nm* praise; panegyric; **faire l' ~ de** praise
**élogieux -ieuse** *adj* eulogistic, laudatory
**éloigné** *adj* distant, faraway, remote; **~ de trois kilomètres** three kilometres away; **peu ~** near
**éloignement** *nm* removal; distance, remoteness
**éloigner** *vt* remove, send away, put away; put out of the way, banish, set aside, dismiss; put back, postpone; **s' ~** move away, off; deviate; differ (opinion); become detached
**éloquence** *nf* eloquence, oratory
¹**élu -e** *n* elected member; elect; chosen
²**élu** *p part* **élire**
**élucider** *vt* elucidate, clear up
**élucubration** *nf* lucubration; **~s** wild utterances
**éluder** *vt* elude, evade
**Élysée** *nm* Elysium; **(le palais de) l' ~** French President's palace
**émacié** *adj* emaciated
**émail** *nm* (*pl* -aux) enamel
**émailler** *vt* enamel; glaze; stud, spangle; dot (of flowers); enrich, embellish
**émailleur -euse** *n* enameller
**émancipateur -trice** *n* emancipator
**émancipé** *adj* free (in manner)
**émanciper** *vt* emancipate; **s' ~** free oneself; *coll* get out of hand, behave too freely
**émaner** *vi* emanate, issue
**émarger** *vt* trim the margins of; sign or initial in margin (as acknowledgement); *vi* be on the payroll
**émasculer** *vt* emasculate, weaken
**emballage** *nm* wrapping, packing
**emballement** *nm* racing (of engine); *coll* sudden enthusiasm
**emballer** *vt* wrap, pack; *coll* delight; *sl* tell off; race (engine); **s' ~** bolt, run; race (of engine); *coll* be keen, enthusiastic; fly into a rage
**emballeur -euse** *n* packer
**embarcadère** *nm* landing-stage; quay, wharf
**embarcation** *nf* (small) craft
**embardée** *nf* lurch; skid, swerve
**embarquement** *nm* embarkation, embarking; shipment; entraining (troops)
**embarquer** *vt* embark; ship; *coll* arrest, run in; involve, drag (into something); **~ de l'eau** ship water; *vi* embark; **s' ~** embark, go on board; launch (into)
**embarras** *nm* obstacle, obstruction; hold-up (traffic); impediment; shortage of money; trouble, difficulty; indecision, perplexity, hesitation,

embarrassment; ~ **du choix** too much to choose from; ~ **gastrique** gastric upset; **faire des** ~ make a fuss; **tirer qn d'** ~ get s/o out of a tricky situation

**embarrassant** *adj* cumbersome; puzzling; awkward

**embarrasser** *vt* hamper; obstruct, encumber; inconvenience; perplex, embarrass, confuse; **s'** ~ **(de)** worry, trouble (about); be perplexed (about)

**embase** *nf* base, shoulder, base-plate

**embastiller** *vt* put into prison

**embaucher** *vt* take on, engage, hire; *coll* entice, hire

**embauchoir** *nm* boot-tree, shoe-tree

**embaumer** *vt* embalm; perfume, scent; *vi* exhale fragrance

**embellie** *nf* bright spell, lull

**embellir** *vt* embellish; *vi* improve in looks

**embellissement** *nm* embellishment; improvement in looks; ornament

**emberlificoter** *vt coll* trick, get round

**embêtant** *adj coll* annoying

**embêtement** *nm* annoyance; **avoir des** ~ s be in a jam, have trouble

**embêter** *vt* annoy, be a nuisance to

**emblée (d')** *adv phr* straight away, directly

**emblème** *nm* emblem, device, badge; symbol

**embobiner** *vt coll* get round, coax; take in; put on a reel or bobbin

**emboîtage** *nm* packing into boxes

**emboîter** *vt* encase; fit together, dovetail; ~ **le pas** fall into step

**embolie** *nf* embolism, blood-clot

**embonpoint** *nm* plumpness; **prendre de l'** ~ put on flesh

**embouché** *adj sl* **mal** ~ coarse

**embouchure** *nf* mouth (river); mouthpiece (instrument)

**embourber** *vt* put into the mud, mire; **s'** ~ get bogged down, caught up

**embourgeoiser (s')** *v refl* acquire bourgeois attitudes, get into bourgeois ways

**embout** *nm* ferrule, tip

**embouteillage** *nm* congestion, trafficjam; bottling; bottling up

**embouteiller** *vt* congest; bottle; bottle up

**emboutir** *vt* stamp (metal); emboss; bash in; **s'** ~ crash

**embranchement** *nm* branching; branch; road junction; railway junction; pipe junction

**embrancher** *vt* join up (roads, etc); **s'** ~ come together; branch off

**embrasement** *nm* burning, conflagration; illumination

**embraser** *vt* set on fire, set ablaze; illuminate; **s'** ~ catch fire

**embrassade** *nf* embrace

**embrasse** *nf* curtain-loop

**embrassement** *nm* embrace

**embrasser** *vt* embrace, hug; kiss; adopt, take up, undertake; contain, include; take on

**embrasure** *nf* (window) recess; embrasure

**embrayage** *nm* engaging, connection; *mot* clutch

**embrayer** *vt* (7) connect, engage; *vi mot* let in the clutch; *fig* start

**embrigader** *vt* rope in; *ar* brigade, enrol

**embrocher** *vt* spit (meat); *coll* run through

**embrouillement** *nm* entanglement; confusion; intricacy

**embrouiller** *vt* entangle; confuse, muddle, mix up; **s'** ~ get confused, muddled; become complicated; cloud over

**embroussaillé** *adj* covered with bushes; disordered (hair)

**embrumer** *vt* cover with mist; **s'** ~ become misty; cloud over

**embrun** *nm usu pl* spray

**embryon** *nm* embryo

**embûche** *nf* ambush; pitfall

**embuer** *vt* steam over, cloud

**embuscade** *nf* ambush; **dresser une** ~ lay an ambush

**embusqué** *nm coll* shirker (in army)

**embusquer** *vt* place in ambush; **s'** ~ lie in ambush; *coll* shirk (active service)

**éméché** *adj coll* tipsy, slightly drunk

**émeraude** *nf* emerald; *adj invar* emerald green

**émerger** *vi* (3) emerge; come into view

**émeri** *nm* emery; **bouchon à l'** ~ ground (glass) stopper

**émérite** *adj* retired; experienced, practised

**émerveillement** *nm* wonder, amazement

**émerveiller** *vt* amaze, fill with wonder

**émétique** *nm* emetic

**émetteur** *nm* issuer; transmitter; *adj* (*f* -**trice**) issuing; transmitting, broadcasting

**émettre** *vt* (60) emit, send out; utter; issue; express; transmit, broadcast

**émeute** *nf* riot

**émeutier -ière** *n* rioter

**émietter** *vt* crumble; fritter away; **s'** ~ crumble

**émigrant -e** *n* emigrant

**émigration** *nf* migration; emigration

**émigré -e** *n* exile, emigrant; émigré

**émigrer** *vi* migrate; emigrate

**émincé** *nm* thin slice; thinly sliced meat in sauce

**émincer** *vt* (4) slice, shred

**éminence** *nf* eminence; high ground; protuberance; prominence

**éminent** *adj* eminent, distinguished

**émissaire** *nm* emissary; *adj* **bouc ~** scapegoat

**émission** *nf* emission; utterance; transmission, broadcasting; issue, issuing; broadcast

**emmagasiner** *vt* store; accumulate; take in (knowledge)

**emmailloter** *vt* swaddle; bind up

**emmancher** *vt* fix a handle to; *coll* start (an affair); **s' ~** fit

**emmanchure** *nf* arm-hole

**emmêler** *vt* mix up, tangle, muddle

**emménagement** *nm* moving in

**emménager** *vt* move in (furniture); settle in; *vi* move into a new place

**emmener** *vt* (6) lead away, take away, take off

**emmitoufler** *vt* muffle up, wrap up

**émoi** *nm* agitation; **en ~** agitated, all of a flutter

**émoluments** *nmpl* emoluments, salary

**émonder** *vt* prune, trim

**émotionnant** *adj* exciting, thrilling

**émotionner** *vt* move, thrill; **s' ~** get excited

**émoudre** *vt* (61) grind, sharpen

**émouleur** *nm* grinder, knife-grinder

**émoulu** *adj* **frais ~ de** just out of (school, etc)

**émousser** *vt* blunt; dull, deaden; attenuate

**émoustillant** *adj* exhilarating

**émoustiller** *vt* rouse, excite

**émouvant** *adj* moving, touching; thrilling

**émouvoir** *vt* (63) move, touch; rouse; **s' ~** be moved; be roused

**empailler** *vt* pack or stuff with straw; make (chair-seat) with straw

**empailleur -euse** *n* person who makes chair-seats with straw; taxidermist

**empaler** *vt* impale

**empanacher** *vt* adorn with a plume or plumes

**empaqueter** *vt* (5) pack up, make into a parcel

**emparer (s')** *v refl* take possession, lay hold

**empâté** *adj* bloated; **voix ~ e** thick voice

**empâtement** *nm* thickness; bloatedness; fattening

**empâter** *vt* fill with paste; clog; fatten, cram, bloat; **s' ~** become bloated, put on flesh

**empattement** *nm* footing (wall); wheelbase; *typ* serif

**empaumer** *vt* catch or strike with palm of the hand; *coll* take (s/o) in

**empêché** *adj* unable to be present

**empêchement** *nm* hindrance, obstacle, impediment

**empêcher** *vt* hinder, prevent, stop; **(il) n'empêche qu'elle vous a vu** nevertheless she saw you; **il ne peut s' ~ de rire** he can't help laughing; **s' ~ de** prevent oneself from

**empeigne** *nf* upper (shoe)

**empennage** *nm* feathers (arrow); vanes; fins

**empereur** *nm* emperor

**empesé** *adj* starchy, stiff, formal

**empeser** *vt* (6) starch

**empester** *vt* stink out; reek of

**empêtrement** *nm* entanglement

**empêtrer** *vt* hobble; entangle; **s' ~** become entangled, get caught up; become confused

**emphase** *nf* bombast, grandiloquence

**emphatique** *adj* bombastic, grandiloquent, turgid

**empierrer** *vt* metal, macadamize; ballast; pave

**empiètement** *nm* encroachment; infringement

**empiéter** *vi* (6) encroach; infringe

**empiffrer** *vt coll* stuff with food; **s' ~** stuff oneself, gorge

**empiler** *vt* pile up, put in a pile, stack; *coll* cheat, swindle

**empire** *nm* supreme authority, sway; control; empire

**empirer** *vt* make worse; *vi* grow worse

**empirique** *adj* empirical, empiric

**emplacement** *nm* site, location; place; emplacement

**emplâtre** *nm* plaster; *sl* incompetent idler

**emplette** *nf* purchase; **faire ses ~s** go shopping

**emplir** *vt* fill; **s' ~** fill up

**emploi** *nm* employment, use; occupation, post, job; **~ du temps** timetable; **être sans ~** be out of work; **faire double ~** be superfluous, useless; **offres d' ~** situations vacant

**employé -e** *n* employee

**employer** *vt* (7) use, employ; **s' ~** be used, be current; occupy oneself; exert oneself

**employeur -euse** *n* employer

**emplumé** *adj* feathered, adorned with feathers

**empocher** *vt* pocket, cash in

**empoigne** *nf* seizing; **foire d' ~** free-for-all

**empoigner** *vt* seize, grasp, grab; grip, thrill; *coll* arrest; **ils se sont empoignés** they quarrelled, they came to blows

**empois** *nm* starch

**empoisonnant** *adj coll* boring; annoying

**empoisonnement** *nm* poisoning

**empoisonner** vt poison; infect; pollute; coll annoy

**empoisonneur -euse** n poisoner

**emporté** adj quick-tempered, passionate, fiery

**emportement** nm transport (anger)

**emporte-pièce** nm invar punch (tool); **style à l' ~** trenchant style

**emporter** vt carry away, take away; sweep away, blow away; carry along, carry off; take; **l' ~** prevail, win; **se laisser ~** let oneself be carried away; **s' ~** get angry, lose one's temper

**empoté** adj coll awkward, clumsy

**empourprer** vt colour crimson, purple; **s' ~** flush scarlet, turn crimson

**empreindre** vt (55) impress, stamp

**empreint** adj marked, stamped

**empreinte** nf mark; imprint, stamp; print; **~s digitales** finger-prints; **prendre l' ~ de** take an impression of

**empressé** adj eager, zealous, assiduous

**empressement** nm eagerness, alacrity, zeal, assiduity; attention

**empresser (s')** v refl hurry, hasten; show eagerness; be assiduous, attentive

**emprise** nf influence, ascendancy; expropriation

**emprisonnement** nm imprisonment

**emprisonner** vt put in prison, imprison

**emprunt** nm loan; borrowing; loan-word; **nom d' ~** assumed name

**emprunté** adj awkward, stiff; assumed, false

**emprunter** vt borrow; take (road)

**emprunteur -euse** n borrower

**empuantir** vt stink out

**ému** adj moved, affected

**émulation** nf emulation, rivalry

**émule** n emulator, rival

**émulsionner** vt emulsify

**en** pron invar of, about it, them; by it, her, him, them; some, any; **j' ~ ai** have some; **je n' ~ ai pas** I haven't any; **prenez-~** take some; adv from there; because of that, for that reason, on that account; prep in, to; by; within; into; while; of; as a; **~ Angleterre** in, to England; **~ attendant** in the meantime; while waiting; **~ essayant** by trying; **~ souriant** (while) smiling; **~ vacances** on holiday; **de jour ~ jour** from day to day, from one day to the next; **il l'a fait ~ huit jours** he did it in a week; **il m'a traité ~ ami** he treated me as a friend; **une bague tout ~** or a solid gold ring

**énamourer (s')** v refl fall in love

**énarque** nm technocrat, top bureaucrat

**en-avant** nm invar forward pass (rugby)

**encablure** nf naut cable-length (approx two hundred metres)

**encadrement** nm framing; framework, frame; mil officering; straddling (target); **~ du crédit** credit squeeze

**encadrer** vt frame; surround; mil officer; straddle, bracket (target)

**encadreur** nm picture-framer

**encaisse** nf cash in hand

**encaissement** nm encashment, collection; encasing; embankment

**encaisser** vt encash, take in; pack into cases; coll receive, take (punishment); embank (river)

**encan** nm auction; **mettre à l' ~** put up for auction

**encanailler (s')** v refl go around with rogues; get into low habits

**encapuchonner** vt put a hood, cowl on

**en-cas** nm invar ar article kept for emergency; light meal kept ready in case of need

**encastrer** vt set in, embed

**encaustique** nf wax-polish

**¹enceinte** nf enclosure; surrounding, perimeter wall; **~ acoustique** speaker system

**²enceinte** adj f pregnant

**encens** nm incense

**encenser** vt burn incense to; flatter

**encensoir** nm censer

**encerclement** nm encirclement

**encercler** vt encircle

**enchaînement** nm chaining up; series, chain; sequence

**enchaîner** vt chain, put in chains; link up; tie; put in sequence; carry on; **s' ~** be linked together, hang together

**enchantement** nm magic, spell; charm; enchantment; delight; **comme par ~** as though by magic

**enchanté** adj enchanted, bewitched; delighted

**enchanter** vt enchant, bewitch; delight, charm

**enchanteur -eresse** n enchanter, enchantress; adj charming, delightful; entrancing

**enchère** nf bid, bidding; **folle ~** crazy, irresponsible bid; **vente aux ~s (à l' ~)** auction sale

**enchérir** vi grow dearer; make a higher bid; **~ sur qn** outbid s/o, go one further than s/o

**enchevêtrement** nm tangle; tangling up; confusion

**enchevêtrer** vt tangle up, mix up; confuse

**enclaver** vt enclave; wedge in

**enclenchement** nm interlocking; putting into gear

**enclencher** vt engage; put into gear; **s' ~** engage

**enclin** adj disposed, inclined

**enclore** *vt* (23) enclose, fence in
**enclos** *nm* enclosure; paddock; fence
**enclume** *nf* anvil; **entre l' ~ et le marteau** between the devil and the deep blue sea
**encoche** *nf* notch, nick
**encocher** *vt* notch, nick
**encoignure** *nf* corner; corner cupboard
**encoller** *vt* coat with glue, gum
**encolure** *nf* neck and withers (horse); neck (dress); neck; size of collar; **de forte ~** thick-set
**encombrant** *adj* cumbersome, bulky; in the way
**encombre** *nm* **sans ~** without incident, with no difficulty
**encombrement** *nm* jam, congestion, block; litter; bulkiness; space occupied
**encombrer** *vt* congest; encumber, obstruct; overload; **s' ~** saddle oneself
**encontre (à l')** *adv phr* to the contrary; **~ de** against, in opposition to
**encorbellement** *nm* overhang; corbelling
**encorder (s')** *v refl* rope one another together (climbers)
**encore** *adv* still; yet; (yet) another, one … more; again, (once) more; moreover; **~ que** although; **~ qu'il soit malade** even if he is ill; **~ si (si ~) il faisait beau** at least if it were fine; **~ une fois** once again; **~ un peu** a little more; **cent francs! ~ faudrait-il les avoir** a hundred francs! I would need to have them first; **hier ~** only yesterday, as recently as yesterday; **il le vendra cinquante francs, et ~!** he'll sell it for fifty francs, if that!; **mais ~?** what else?, tell me more, out with it; **pas ~** not yet; **quoi ~?** what else?; *interj* what again?, Heavens!
**encourageant** *adj* encouraging, cheering
**encourager** *vt* (3) encourage, incite; foster, aid
**encourir** *vt* (29) incur, expose oneself to
**encrasser** *vt* dirty, foul; clog; **s' ~** get dirty; get clogged
**encre** *nf* ink; **~ de Chine** Indian ink; **~ sympathique** invisible ink; **écrire à l' ~** write in ink
**encrier** *nm* inkpot; inkstand
**encroûté** *adj* stuck in a rut; *fig* fossilized
**encroûter** *vt* encrust; **s' ~** become encrusted; get into a rut
**enculer** *vt vulg* sodomize, bugger
**encyclique** *nf eccles* encyclical
**encyclopédie** *nf* encyclopaedia
**encyclopédique** *adj* encyclopaedic
**endémique** *adj* endemic
**endetter** *vt* get (s/o) into debt; **s' ~** get into debt
**endeuiller** *vt* plunge into mourning

**endiablé** *adj* wild, frenzied
**endiguer** *vt* dam up; contain with dikes; slow up, obstruct
**endimancher (s')** *v refl* dress up in one's Sunday best
**endive** *nf* chicory; endive
**endoctriner** *vt* indoctrinate
**endolori** *adj* sore, tender
**endolorir** *vt* make painful, make ache
**endommager** *vt* (3) damage
**endormeur -euse** *n* flatterer, cajoler
**endormi** *adj* asleep; drowsy; indolent; calm, silent; dormant
**endormir** *vt* (39) put to sleep; anaesthetize; deaden; cajole; lull; bore; allay; **s' ~** fall asleep, drop off; become inactive; fail to be watchful
**endos** *nm* endorsement (on back of cheque)
**endosser** *vt* put on (clothes); endorse (cheque); assume responsibility for
**endroit** *nm* place, spot; passage (book, speech); aspect; right side (material); **à l' ~** right side up, out; **à l' ~ de** regarding; **par ~s** here and there
**enduire** *vt* (80) smear, coat
**enduit** *nm* coat, coating (paint, plaster, etc)
**endurance** *nf* endurance; resistance to wear; *mot* **épreuve d' ~** reliability trial
**endurant** *adj* resistant; patient
**endurci** *adj* hardened, inured; hard, hardened; callous, pitiless
**endurcir** *vt* harden; inure; **s' ~** grow accustomed; become tough, hard
**endurcissement** *nm* hardening; inuring; insensitivity
**endurer** *vt* endure, bear
**énergétique** *adj* relative to energy
**énergie** *nf* energy; vigour, determination, force; efficacy
**énergique** *adj* energetic
**énergumène** *n* energumen, fanatic
**énervant** *adj* aggravating; tiresome; enervating
**énervé** *adj* excited; annoyed
**énervement** *nm* nervous excitement, overexcitement
**énerver** *vt* annoy, aggravate; enervate, weaken; **s' ~** get excited; get irritable
**enfance** *nf* childhood; children; beginning, infancy; **c'est l' ~ de l'art** it's child's play; **tomber en ~** sink into dotage
**enfant** *n* child; **~s** descendants, posterity; **~ de chœur** choirboy; *coll* naïve person; **~ de Paris** native of Paris, true Parisian; **~ trouvé** foundling; **agir en ~** behave like a child; **bon ~** good-natured; **faire l' ~** act childishly
**enfantement** *nm* childbirth; creation (work of art)

**enfantillage** *nm* childish act, childish saying, nonsense

**enfantin** *adj* infantile, childish, puerile; absurdly easy

**enfariné** *adj* covered with flour

**enfer** *nm* hell, the underworld; place in library where licentious books are kept; **d'** ~ terrific, infernal, mad, frenzied

**enfermer** *vt* shut up, confine, lock up; enclose, surround; **s'** ~ lock oneself in; stay in one's room, house

**enferrer** *vt* run through; catch (a fish) on a hook; **s'** ~ get oneself run through; get caught in one's own tangle of lies

**enfiévrer** *vt* (6) make feverish; excite, fire

**enfilade** *nf* succession, series; suit, row, enfilade

**enfiler** *vt* thread; string (beads); run through; take (street); *coll* slip on, put on (clothes); *vulg* fuck

**enfin** *adv* lastly, finally; in a word; at last; well

**enflammé** *adj* blazing; fiery; passionate

**enflammer** *vt* inflame; set on fire, ignite; fire, stir up, rouse

**enfler** *vt* + *vi* swell, puff up; exaggerate

**enflure** *nf* swelling; bombast, turgidity

**enfoncé** *adj* staved in; deep, sunken; low-lying

**enfoncement** *nm* breaking open, staving in; hollow; recess

**enfoncer** *vt* drive in, bang in; break in, stave in, break open; *coll* overcome, get the better of; *vi* sink, go down; **s'** ~ collapse, give way; penetrate; go down, be ruined; become immersed, absorbed

**enfouir** *vt* bury; hide, conceal

**enfourcher** *vt* stick a pitchfork into; bestride, mount; *coll* ~ **son dada** ride one's hobby-horse

**enfourner** *vt* put into the oven; *coll* stuff (food into one's mouth)

**enfreindre** *vt* (55) infringe

**enfuir (s')** *v refl* (52) flee, fly, run away; fly by

**enfumer** *vt* fill with smoke; blacken with smoke; smoke out

**engageant** *adj* engaging, charming, winning

**engagement** *nm* pawning, pledging; commitment; promise; obligation; appointment, engaging; engagement, fight, action; *mil* enlistment, throwing (troops) into battle

**engager** *vt* (3) put in pawn, pledge; commit; engage; begin; throw in (troops); incite, exhort; put in, thrust in, insert; **cela ne vous engage à rien** that does not bind you in any way; **s'** ~ bind oneself, undertake, promise; take up employment; penetrate; enlist; begin; take up a precise position

**engainer** *vt* sheathe

**engeance** *nf coll* crew, breed

**engelure** *nf* chilblain

**engendrement** *nm* begetting; generation

**engendrer** *vt* beget; engender, cause, bring about, breed

**engin** *nm* machine; contrivance, device

**englober** *vt* embody, include, comprise

**engloutir** *vt* swallow, gulp down; engulf; ~ **une fortune** get through a fortune

**engluer** *vt* smear, lime (birds); *fig* ensnare

**engoncé** *adj* tightly wrapped (in one's clothes)

**engorgement** *nm* choking, blocking, clogging; obstruction

**engorger** *vt* (3) obstruct, clog, block

**engouement** *nm* infatuation, craze

**engouer (s')** *v refl* become infatuated, go mad

**engouffrer** *vt* swallow up, engulf; absorb, get through; **s'** ~ be engulfed; rush, dash

**engoulevent** *nm orni* nightjar

**engourdir** *vt* numb, benumb; dull; **s'** ~ go numb, become dull

**engourdissement** *nm* numbness; dullness

**engrais** *nm* fertilizer, manure; fattening food

**engraisser** *vt* fatten, make fat; fertilize; make rich; *vi* grow fat, put on weight

**engranger** *vt* garner

**engraver (s')** *v refl* run aground

**engrenage** *nm* gears, gearing, gearwheels; mesh (of circumstances)

**engrener** *vt* (6) engage, connect

**engrosser** *vt sl* make pregnant

**engueulade** *nf sl* slanging, quarrel

**engueuler** *vt sl* slang, blow up; **ils s'engueulent toute la journée** they go on at each other all day long

**enhardir** *vt* embolden; **s'** ~ pluck up courage

**énigmatique** *adj* enigmatic

**énigme** *nf* enigma, riddle, puzzle; difficult subject

**enivrant** *adj* intoxicating, heady

**enivrement** *nm* intoxication, drunken state; transport, ecstasy

**enivrer** *vt* intoxicate, make drunk; elate; **s'** ~ get drunk, become intoxicated

**enjambée** *nf* stride

**enjambement** *nm* enjambment; flyover, overpass

**enjamber** *vt* step over; bestride; *vi* stride; encroach, project

**enjeu** *nm* stake

**enjoindre** *vt* (55) enjoin, charge

**enjôlement** *nm* cajoling; cajolery
**enjôler** *vt* cajole, wheedle, coax; trick
**enjôleur -euse** *n* cajoler, wheedler; *adj* coaxing, wheedling, cajoling
**enjoliver** *vt* embellish, beautify
**enjoliveur -euse** *n* beautifier, embellisher; *nm mot* hub-cap
**enjolivure** *nf* embellishment
**enjoué** *adj* sprightly, playful
**enjouement** *nm* cheerful good-humour
**enlacer** *vt* (4) interlace, entwine; hug
**enlaidir** *vt* disfigure, make ugly; *vi* grow ugly
**enlèvement** *nm* carrying away, removal; abduction, kidnapping; *mil* storming
**enlever** *vt* (6) take away, carry away, remove; take up; carry off, kidnap, abduct; raise, bear up; perform brilliantly; delight, enrapture; *mil* storm
**enlisement** *nm* getting bogged down
**enliser (s')** *v refl* sink, get bogged, stuck
**enluminer** *vt* illuminate (manuscript); colour vividly
**enluminure** *nf* illuminating (manuscript); colouring
**enneigé** *adj* covered with snow
**enneigement** *nm* being covered with snow; depth of snow
**ennemi -e** *n* enemy, foe; *adj* hostile
**ennoblir** *vt* ennoble
**ennui** *nm* boredom, tediousness, tedium; worry, anxiety; **quel ~ !** what a nuisance!
**ennuyer** *vt* (7) bore, weary; annoy, worry; *coll* bother, put out; **s' ~** be bored; **s' ~ à mourir** be bored to tears; **s' ~ à ne rien faire** get fed up with doing nothing
**ennuyeux -euse** *adj* boring, tedious; annoying, unpleasant
**énoncé** *nm* statement (facts)
**énoncer** *vt* state; articulate
**énonciation** *nf* stating, expressing; enunciation
**enorgueillir** *vt* make proud; **s' ~** become proud, draw pride
**énorme** *adj* huge, enormous; outrageous
**énormément** *adv* hugely; tremendously, terribly; **~ de** a great deal of
**énormité** *nf* enormity; vastness; gravity; blunder
**enquérir (s')** *v refl* (27) inquire, ask
**enquête** *nf* inquiry, investigation; **procéder à une ~** hold an inquiry
**enquêter** *vi* make inquiries, conduct investigations
**enquiquiner** *vt coll* annoy, plague
**enraciné** *adj* deep-rooted
**enraciner** *vt* dig in; implant, establish
**enragé** *adj* furious; *coll* enthusiastic, very keen; rabid, mad (dog); **manger**

de la vache **~ e** have a hard time of it
**enrageant** *adj* maddening, infuriating
**enrager** *vi* (3) rage, fume; **faire ~ qn** tease s/o, annoy s/o
**enrayer** *vt* (7) check, slow up; stop, jam
**enrégimenter** *vt* regiment; enlist, enrol
**enregistrement** *nm* registration, recording, booking, entering up; recording (sound, etc)
**enregistrer** *vt* register, record, enter up, take note; record (sound, etc)
**enregistreur -euse** *adj* recording; registering
**enrhumer (s')** *v refl* catch a cold
**enrichi** *adj* newly rich; enriched
**enrichir** *vt* enrich
**enrichissement** *nm* enrichment
**enrober** *vt* coat, cover; disguise, wrap up
**enrôlement** *nm* enrolment; enlistment
**enrôler** *vt* enrol, recruit; enlist
**enroué** *adj* hoarse, husky
**enrouement** *nm* hoarseness, huskiness
**enrouer** *vt* make husky, hoarse
**enrouler** *vt* roll up, wind; wrap up
**enrouleur** *nm* **ceinture à ~** inertia-reel seat belt
**enrubanner** *vt* decorate, cover with ribbons
**ensabler** *vt* run aground; cover with sand, silt up
**ensanglanter** *vt* stain, cover with blood; make run with blood
**enseignant -e** *n* teacher; *adj* teaching; **corps ~** teaching profession
**enseigne** *nm* standard-bearer; *nf* sign, mark, token; sign-board; standard; **à bonne ~** on good authority; **à telle(s) ~ (s) que** so much so that, the proof being that; **être logé à la même ~** be in the same predicament
**enseignement** *nm* teaching; education; **être dans l' ~** be a teacher
**enseigner** *vt* teach; show, indicate
**ensemble** *nm* whole, entirety; group, ensemble; cohesion, unity; **avec ~** harmoniously; **dans l' ~** on the whole; **dans son ~** viewed as a whole, globally; **d' ~** general; **grand ~** large housing development; **mouvement d' ~** combined movement; **vue d' ~** general, comprehensive view; *adv* together; at the same time; **être bien ~** get on well together; **être mal ~** get on badly together
**ensemencer** *vt* (4) sow (ground); stock (with fish)
**enserrer** *vt* enclose; hem in; squeeze; fit tight
**ensevelir** *vt* bury; shroud
**ensevelissement** *nm* burial; shrouding
**ensoleillé** *adj* sunny
**ensommeillé** *adj* sleepy

105

**ensorceler** *vt* (5) bewitch, cast a spell on; captivate, charm

**ensorceleur -euse** *n* sorcerer, sorceress; charmer

**ensorcellement** *nm* witchcraft, sorcery; charm, spell

**ensuite** *adv* then, next, afterwards

**ensuivre (s')** *v refl* (43) ensue, result, follow; *coll* **et tout ce qui s'ensuit** and all the rest; **il s'ensuit que** it follows that

**entablement** *nm* entablature

**entacher** *vt* cast a slur on

**entaille** *nf* notch, nick; groove, slot; gash

**entailler** *vt* notch, nick; groove, slot; gash, cut

**entame** *nf* first slice, first piece

**entamer** *vt* cut into, open, start, break into; begin; broach (subject) **~ une réputation** taint a reputation

**entartrer** *vt* encrust, fur

**entassement** *nm* piling-up, heaping-up, pile, accumulation; crowding-in, congestion

**entasser** *vt* pile up, heap up, stack up; amass, accumulate; pack, crowd in; **s' ~** accumulate; crowd together

**entendement** *nm* understanding; capacity for comprehension

**entendeur** *nm* **à bon ~ salut** a word to the wise is enough; if the cap fits, wear it

**entendre** *vt* hear; understand; intend, mean; **~ dire que** hear that; **~ faire qch** intend to do sth; **~ parler de** hear about; **à l' ~** if one is to believe him; **donner à ~ à qn** lead s/o to believe; **faire ~** utter; **il n'entend pas la plaisanterie** he can't take a joke; **ils ne sont pas faits pour s' ~** they don't get on together; **je n'entends rien à cela** I don't understand a thing about that; **laisser ~** insinuate; **on ne s'entend pas** we can't hear ourselves speak; **qu'entendez-vous par là?** what do you mean by that?; **s' ~** agree, understand one another, get on; be good, be skilled

**entendu** *adj* agreed, decided; intelligent, sensible, business-like; **(c'est) ~ !** (it's) agreed!; **bien ~** naturally; **d'un air ~** with a knowing air; **faire l' ~** pretend to know all about sth

**entente** *nf* understanding; agreement; good relations; interpretation; **mot à double ~** word with a double meaning, double entendre

**enter** *vt* graft

**entériner** *vt* confirm, ratify

**entérite** *nf med* enteritis

**enterrement** *nm* burial; funeral; funeral procession; abandonment

**enterrer** *vt* bury; abandon (project); **il**

**nous enterrera tous** he will survive us all

**entêtant** *adj* heady

**en-tête** *nm* heading; headline

**entêté** *adj* obstinate, pig-headed, stubborn

**entêtement** *nm* obstinacy, stubbornness

**entêter (s')** *v refl* be obstinate, persist, dig one's toes in

**enthousiasme** *nm* enthusiasm

**enthousiasmer** *vt* fill with enthusiasm; **s' ~** become enthusiastic

**enthousiaste** *n* enthusiast; *adj* enthusiastic

**entiché** *adj* infatuated, crazy, keen

**enticher (s')** *v refl* become infatuated, crazy

**entier** *nm* entirety; **en ~** in full; *adj* (*f* -ière) whole, entire; complete; intact, unaltered; frank, outspoken; **nombre ~** integer; **payer place entière** pay full fare

**entièrement** *adv* wholly, entirely, utterly

**entité** *nf* entity

**entoiler** *vt* mount on canvas or linen; cover with canvas

**entomologie** *nf* entomology

**entonner** *vt* begin to sing; intone

**entonnoir** *nm* funnel; shell-hole, crater; depression, hollow

**entorse** *nf* sprain, twist; **faire une ~ à** stretch, fail to observe (law, etc)

**entortiller** *vt* wind, twist, twine, express in complicated fashion; *coll* get round

**entour** *nm* **à l' ~** round about, around; **à l' ~ de** round

**entourage** *nm* surroundings, environment; setting; circle (friends, etc)

**entourer** *vt* surround, encircle; fence in; devote attention to

**entourloupette** *nf coll* nasty trick

**entournure** *nf* arm-hole; *coll* **être gêné dans les ~s** feel awkward, ill at ease, be in difficulties

**entracte** *nm theat* interval; interlude; pause, respite

**entraide** *nf* mutual aid

**entraider (s')** *v refl* help one another

**entrailles** *nfpl* bowels, entrails; compassion, feeling, soul; **sans ~** pitiless

**entr'aimer (s')** *v refl* love one another

**entrain** *nm* briskness, go, liveliness, spirit; **avec ~** with gusto; **sans ~** listlessly, half-heartedly

**entraînant** *adj* stirring, gripping

**entraînement** *nm* dragging, carrying away; leading astray; enthusiasm; training

**entraîner** *vt* drag along, carry away, off; drive (mechanism); train, coach; seduce, lure; lead to, produce; **s' ~** train

**entraîneur** *nm* trainer, coach

**entraîneuse** *nf* night-club hostess

**entrant** *adj* incoming; newly appointed

**entr'apercevoir** *vt* glimpse, catch a glimpse of

**entrave** *nf* fetter, shackle; hobble; hindrance, impediment

**entraver** *vt* fetter, shackle; hobble; hamper, impede

**entre** *prep* between; among, amongst; ~ **amis** between friends, among friends; ~ **les deux** neither one thing nor the other; **belle** ~ **toutes** beautiful above all others; **d'** ~ of (before *pers pron*); **deux d'** ~ **eux** two of them; **femme** ~ **deux âges** middle-aged woman; **lui,** ~ **autres** he, for one; **tomber** ~ **les mains de qn** fall into the hands of s/o

**entrebâillement** *nm* small gap, chink, slit

**entrebâiller** *vt* half-open (door)

**entrechat** *nm* caper, little jump; entrechat

**entrechoquer** *vt* knock together; **s'** ~ collide, knock against one another

**entrecôte** *nf* sirloin steak

**entrecouper** *vt* interrupt

**entrecroiser** *vt* intersect, cross; interlace

**entre-déchirer (s')** *v refl* tear one another apart

**entre-deux** *nm invar* space between; intermediate state or position; insertion (dressmaking); piece of furniture (placed between two windows)

**entre-deux-guerres** *nm invar* period between the two world wars

**entredévorer (s')** *v refl* devour one another, destroy one another

**entrée** *nf* entry, entering; entrance, way in; admission, admittance; entrance hall, vestibule; *cul* entrée; beginning; ~ **interdite** no admittance; ~ **libre** admission free (= no obligation to buy); **avoir ses** ~**s** have free access; **d'** ~ **de jeu** from the word go

**entrefaite** *nf* **sur ces** ~ **s** at that moment, then

**entrefilet** *nm* short article, filler

**entregent** *nm* tact, savoir-faire

**entrelacement** *nm* interlacing, interweaving; network

**entrelacer** *vt* (4) interlace, intertwine, interweave

**entrelacs** *nm* interlacing or intertwining motif

**entrelardé** *adj* streaky (meat)

**entrelarder** *vt* lard (meat); interlard

**entremêler** *vt* intermingle, intermix, intersperse

**entremets** *nm* dessert, sweet

**entremetteur -euse** *n pej* intermediary, coupler, match-maker

**entremettre (s')** *v refl* intervene, interpose

**entremise** *nf* intervention; mediation, good offices; **par l'** ~ **de qn** through s/o

**entrepont** *nm naut* between decks

**entreposer** *vt* store, deposit

**entrepôt** *nm* warehouse, store; storehouse

**entreprenant** *adj* enterprising, bold; forward

**entreprendre** *vt* (75) undertake, embark on; contract for; try to persuade

**entrepreneur -euse** *n* contractor; ~ **(de bâtiments) (en construction)** building contractor; ~ **de pompes funèbres** undertaker

**entreprise** *nf* undertaking; concern; venture

**entrer** *vt* bring in, carry in; *vi* enter, go in, come in; be admitted; be an ingredient of; ~ **à l'université** start at university; ~ **dans le détail** examine closely; ~ **en colère** get angry; ~ **en matière** begin; ~ **en religion** take holy orders; **faire** ~ **qn** admit s/o

**entre-temps** *adv* meanwhile, in the meantime

**entretenir** *vt* (96) keep up, maintain, support; converse with; ~ **des soupçons** entertain suspicions; **femme entretenue** kept woman; **s'** ~ talk, converse

**entretien** *nm* upkeep, maintenance, support; conversation

**entre-tuer (s')** *v refl* kill one another

**entrevoir** *vt* (99) catch sight of, a glimpse of; have an inkling of

**entrevue** *nf* interview

**entrouvert** *adj* ajar, half-open

**entrouvrir** *vt* (30) open slightly

**énumérateur -trice** *n* enumerator

**énumérer** *vt* (6) enumerate

**envahir** *vt* invade, overrun, assail

**envahissant** *adj* importunate, indiscreet

**envahissement** *nm* invading; encroaching

**envahisseur** *nm* invader

**envaser** *vt* choke with mud; run into the mud

**enveloppant** *adj* enveloping; charming, seductive

**enveloppe** *nf* envelope; cover, wrapper; exterior; budget

**envelopper** *vt* envelop, wrap up, encase; close in on, surround; disguise

**envenimer** *vt* envenom, poison; aggravate, irritate; **s'** ~ fester; become nasty, unpleasant

**envergure** *nf* spread, breadth, span (wing, sail); scale, amplitude; **d'** ~ impressive, large, far-reaching

¹**envers** *nm* wrong side, reverse, back; contrary; **l' ~ de la médaille** the other side of the coin; **à l' ~** inside out; the wrong way up, upside down

²**envers** *prep* as regards, towards; **~ et contre tous** in spite of everybody

**envi (à l')** *adv phr* emulously

**envie** *nf* desire, longing; envy; birthmark; **avoir ~ de** desire, want; wish to; **faire ~ à** make envious; **porter ~ à qn** envy s/o, be jealous of s/o

**envier** *vt* envy; covet; begrudge

**envieux -ieuse** *adj* envious, jealous

**environ** *adv* about, approximately

**environnement** *nm* surroundings, environment

**environner** *vt* surround; beset

**environs** *nmpl* surroundings, neighbourhood, vicinity; **aux ~ de Pâques** round about Easter

**envisager** *vt* (3) contemplate, consider; envisage; plan

**envoi** *nm* sending, dispatch; consignment; *poet* envoy; **coup d' ~** kick-off, start

**envol** *nm* taking flight, taking off, take-off

**envolée** *nf* flight (eloquence)

**envoler (s')** *v refl* fly off, away; take off; fly (time); rise steeply (prices)

**envoûtement** *nm* spell; charm

**envoûter** *vt* cast a spell on; charm

**envoyé** *nm* envoy; messenger

**envoyer** *vt* (44) send; dispatch; throw (ball); **~ chercher qn** send for s/o; **~ dire que** send word that; *coll* **~ promener (paître) qn** tell s/o to go to hell; **réplique envoyée** telling reply; *sl* **s' ~** take, consume, appropriate, have

**envoyeur -euse** *n* sender

**éolien -ienne** *adj* Aeolian

**épagneul** *nm* spaniel

**épais -aisse** *adj* thick; dense; dull, coarse; **avoir la langue épaisse** be thick of speech; *adv* **semer ~** sow thick

**épaisseur** *nf* thickness; depth; dullness, slowness

**épaissir** *vt* thicken, make dense; *vi* become thick; **s' ~** grow stout; grow dull; grow thicker

**épaississement** *nm* thickening; growing denser; growing plumper

**épanchement** *nm* discharge, pouring out; effusion; outpouring; **~ de synovie** water on the knee

**épancher** *vt* pour out; shed (blood); **s' ~** pour out; unburden oneself, come out with everything

**épandage** *nm* spreading fertilizer, spreading manure

**épandre** *vt* spread by scattering

**épanoui** *adj* in full bloom; **visage ~** beaming face

**épanouir** *vt* cause to bloom; **s' ~** bloom, open out; bloom

**épanouissement** *nm* bloom, blooming; brightening up (face)

**épargnant -e** *n* saver

**épargne** *nf* saving, thrift; savings; **caisse d' ~** savings bank

**épargner** *vt* save, economize; be sparing with; spare; have mercy on; treat gently; dispense with

**éparpillement** *nm* scattering, dispersing

**éparpiller** *vt* scatter, disperse; dissipate (efforts)

**épars** *adj* scattered

**épatant** *adj coll* marvellous, fine, splendid

**épate** *nf coll* swank, showing off

**épaté** *adj* broad at the base; splay-footed; *coll* amazed

**épatement** *nm coll* stupefaction

**épater** *vt coll* astound, amaze

**épaulard** *nm* grampus, killer-whale

**épaule** *nf* shoulder; **donner un coup d' ~** give a helping hand; **fusil sur l' ~** rifle at the slope; **hausser les ~s** shrug one's shoulders; **par-dessus l' ~** negligently

**épauler** *vt* bring (gun) to the shoulder; take aim; help, back up

**épaulette** *nf* shoulder-strap; epaulette

**épave** *nf* wreck; abandoned or unclaimed object

**épée** *nf* sword; swordsman; **passer au fil de l' ~** put to the sword

**épeler** *vt* (5) spell, spell out

**éperdu** *adj* distracted, bewildered; desperate, wild

**éperdument** *adv* distractedly; madly

**éperlan** *nm* smelt

**éperon** *nm* spur, buttress; ram (ship)

**éperonner** *vt* put spurs on; spur on, urge on

**épervier** *nm* sparrow-hawk; *fig* hawk; sweep-net

**éphémère** *nm* may-fly, ephemera; *adj* ephemeral, short-lived, transitory

**éphéméride** *nf* tear-off calendar; almanac

**épi** *nm* ear (grain); tuft (hair), cow-lick; **stationnement en ~** fishtail parking

**épice** *nf* spice; **pain d' ~** spiced cake

**épicé** *adj* spiced, highly seasoned; spicy

**épicer** *vt* (4) spice

**épicerie** *nf* grocer's shop; groceries; grocery business; spices

**épicier -ière** *n* grocer

**épicurien -ienne** *n* epicure; Epicurean

**épidémie** *nf* epidemic

**épidémique** *adj* epidemic

**épiderme** *nm* epidermis, skin

**épier** *vt* spy on, watch closely; be on the look-out for

**épieu** *nm* pike; boar-spear
**épigastre** *nm* pit of the stomach
**épigone** *nm* imitator, follower
**épigramme** *nf* epigram
**épigraphe** *nf* inscription; epigraph
**épilation** *nf* plucking, removal of surplus hairs
**épilepsie** *nf* epilepsy
**épileptique** *n* + *adj* epileptic
**épiler** *vt* remove superfluous hairs from, pluck
**épilogue** *nm* epilogue
**épiloguer** *vi* find fault, make carping criticism; ~ **sur** comment at length on
**épinard** *nm* (*usu pl*) spinach; *coll* **mettre du beurre dans les** ~ s make life easier
**épine** *nf* thorn; thorn-bush; difficulty, snag; ~ **dorsale** spinal column, backbone; **être sur des** ~ s be on tenterhooks; **tirer une** ~ **du pied** rid of a worry
**épinette** *nf* spinet; small cage, coop; *bot* spruce
**épineux -euse** *adj* thorny, prickly; ticklish, awkward
**épingle** *nf* pin; ~ **à cheveux** hair-pin; ~ **à linge** clothes-peg; ~ **de nourrice (de sûreté)** safety-pin; **coup d'** ~ petty annoyance; *coll* **monter en** ~ give excessive importance to; **tiré à quatre** ~ s meticulously dressed, dressed up to the nines; **tirer son** ~ **du jeu** get out of a difficult situation
**épingler** *vt* pin, fasten with a pin
**épinière** *adj f* **moelle** ~ spinal cord
**épinoche** *nf* stickleback
**Épiphanie** *nf* Epiphany
**épique** *adj* epic
**épiscopat** *nm* episcopate; episcopacy
**épistolaire** *adj* epistolary
**épitaphe** *nf* epitaph
**épithète** *nf* epithet; attributive adjective
**épitomé** *nm* epitome, abridgement
**épître** *nf* epistle
**éploré** *adj* tearful, grief-stricken
**éplucher** *vt* peel, pare; clean; examine closely
**éplucheur -euse** *n* peeler; cleaner
**épluchure** *nf* (*usu pl*) peelings
**épointer** *vt* break the point of
**éponge** *nf* sponge; *coll* **passer l'** ~ **sur** forgive, say no more about
**éponger** *vt* (3) sponge up, mop up, absorb; sponge down; *econ* wipe out
**épontille** *nf* stanchion; prop, pillar
**éponyme** *n* + *adj* eponymous (hero)
**épopée** *nf* epic poem; epic
**époque** *nf* period, age, epoch; time, date; **faire** ~ be remembered, be a landmark; **meubles d'** ~ period furniture
**époumoner** (**s'**) *v refl* shout oneself

hoarse
**épouse** *nf* wife
**épouser** *vt* marry; take up, espouse; fit
**épouseur** *nm coll* suitor
**épousseter** *vt* (5) dust
**époustouflant** *adj coll* staggering, amazing
**épouvantable** *adj* dreadful, appalling
**épouvantail** *nm* scarecrow; bogey
**épouvante** *nf* terror, fright
**épouvanter** *vt* terrify; **s'** ~ become terrified
**époux** *nm* husband
**éprendre** (**s'**) *v refl* fall in love; take a fancy
**épreuve** *nf* test, trial; affliction, ordeal; proof; paper (examination); event (sport); **à l'** ~ **de** proof against; **à toute** ~ capable of withstanding anything
**épris** *adj* in love, enamoured
**éprouvant** *adj* hard, taxing
**éprouver** *vt* test, try; feel, experience; sustain; make suffer
**éprouvette** *nf* test-tube; test-piece
**épuisant** *adj* exhausting
**épuisé** *adj* exhausted; out of print; sold out
**épuisement** *nm* exhaustion; exhausting; using up; emptying, draining
**épuiser** *vt* exhaust; use up, empty, consume; tire out; **s'** ~ become exhausted; run dry, run out
**épuisette** *nf* landing-net; bailer
**épurateur** *nm* purifying apparatus, purifier
**épuration** *nf* purification; purging; expurgation
**épure** *nf* working drawing; finished design
**épurer** *vt* purify; filter; purge
**équanimité** *nf* equanimity
**équarrir** *vt* square (timber); broach (cask); quarter (carcass)
**équarrisseur** *nm* knacker
**Équateur** *nm* Ecuador
**équateur** *nm* equator
**équerre** *nf* square; ~ **à dessin** set-square; **d'** ~, **en** ~ at right angles
**équestre** *adj* equestrian
**équilibrage** *nm* balancing
**équilibre** *nm* balance; stability; **se tenir en** ~ keep one's balance
**équilibrer** *vt* balance
**équilibriste** *n* tightrope-walker, acrobat
**équin** *adj* equine
**équinoxe** *nm* equinox
**équipage** *nm* crew; equipment; retinue; attire; *coll* rig-out
**équipe** *nf* team; gang
**équipée** *nf* escapade
**équipement** *nm* equipment; fitting up; outfit

**équiper** vt equip; fit out

**équipier -ière** n member of a team or gang

**équitable** adj equitable, fair

**équitation** nf horse-riding, horsemanship

**équité** nf equity, fairness

**équivaloir** vi (95) be equivalent; be tantamount

**équivoque** nf ambiguity; uncertainty; double entendre; adj ambiguous; doubtful, questionable

**érable** nm maple-tree

**érafler** vt graze, scratch

**éraflure** nf graze

**éraillé** adj hoarse, raucous; bloodshot

**érailler** vt unravel; chafe, graze; make hoarse

**ère** nf era, epoch; **de notre ~** A.D.

**érection** nf erection; setting up

**éreintant** adj killing, tiring

**éreintement** nm violent criticism; exhaustion

**éreinter** vt exhaust, wear out; criticize violently

**ergot** nm spur (cock); stub (tree); ergot (grain)

**ergoter** vi coll quibble, split hairs

**ergoteur -euse** adj cavilling, quibbling

**ériger** vt (3) erect, set up, construct; establish; exalt; **s' ~ en** set (oneself) up as

**ermitage** nm hermitage

**ermite** nm hermit

**éroder** vt erode, eat away

**érosif -ive** adj erosive

**érotique** adj erotic

**érotisme** nm eroticism

**errant** adj wandering, roaming, rambling

**erratique** adj erratic

**erre** nf naut headway; **~s** track, spoor

**errements** nmpl erring ways

**errer** vi roam, wander; be mistaken, err

**erreur** nf mistake, slip; delusion; error; **induire en ~** mislead; **sauf ~** if I am not mistaken; **tirer qn de l' ~** undeceive someone

**erroné** adj erroneous, wrong

**ersatz** nm invar substitute

**éructer** vi eruct, belch

**érudit -e** n scholar, learned person; adj learned, erudite

**éruption** nf eruption; rash

**érysipèle** nm med erysipelas

**ès** (= **en les**) prep **docteur ~ sciences** doctor of science

**esbroufe** nf sl showing-off; **faire de l' ~** show off; **vol à l' ~** pickpocketing

**esbroufer** vt sl impress by one's airs

**escabeau** nm stool; step-ladder

**escadre** nf naut + aer squadron

**escadrille** nf naut flotilla; aer flight

**escadron** nm mil + aer squadron

**escalade** nf scaling, climbing; breaking in; escalation

**escalader** vt scale, climb

**escale** nf port of call, place at which one stops; **faire ~** put in, call; **sans ~** non-stop

**escalier** nm staircase, stairs; **~ de service** tradesmen's staircase; **~ mécanique (roulant)** escalator; **esprit de l' ~** slow wit

**escalope** nf slice (meat, etc)

**escamotable** adj disappearing, retractable

**escamoter** vt conjure away, make disappear; retract; remove subtly, filch; slur, pronounce badly; burke (question)

**escampette** nf **prendre la poudre d' ~** flee

**escarbille** nf clinker, cinder

**escarboucle** nf carbuncle

**escarcelle** nf pouch (for money)

**escargot** nm snail

**escarmouche** nf skirmish

**escarpe** nf escarp

**escarpé** adj steep, abrupt, sheer

**escarpement** nm escarpment

**escarpin** nm dancing-shoe, pump

**escarpolette** nf swing

**escarre** nf bed-sore; scab

**escient** nm **à bon ~** deliberately

**esclaffer (s')** v refl burst out laughing

**esclandre** nm scandal; quarrel; racket; **faire un ~** make a scene

**esclavage** nm slavery

**esclave** n slave

**escogriffe** nm lanky man

**escompte** nm discount, rebate; **taux d' ~** bank rate

**escompter** vt discount; count on, bank on

**escorte** nf escort; convoy

**escorter** vt escort; convoy

**escorteur** nm naut escort vessel

**escouade** nf squad, gang

**escrime** nf fencing

**escrimer (s')** v refl try hard, make every effort

**escrimeur -euse** n fencer

**escroc** nm crook, swindler

**escroquer** vt cheat, rob, swindle

**escroquerie** nf swindling; swindle

**ésotérique** adj esoteric

**espace** nm space; interval; nf typ space

**espacer** vt (4) space, space out; **s' ~** become rarer, fewer

**espadon** nm sword-fish

**espadrille** nf rope-soled shoe

**Espagnol -e** n Spaniard

**espagnol** nm Spanish (language); adj Spanish

espagnolette *nf* window fastener

espèce *nf* sort, type; species; *coll* ~ de (+*noun*) silly, stupid, blessed ...; cas d' ~ special case; en l' ~ in that case, in that matter; payer en ~ s pay in cash

espérance *nf* hope, expectation

espérer *vt* + *vi* (6) hope, hope for; ~ en trust in

espiègle *adj* mischievous, roguish

espièglerie *nf* mischievousness; prank

espion -ionne *n* spy; *nm* bugging device

espionnage *nm* spying, espionage

espionner *vt* spy on

esplanade *nf* promenade; esplanade

espoir *nm* hope

esprit *nm* spirit; ghost, sprite; mind; intellect; wit; ~ fort free thinker; bel ~ cultured, well-read person; faire de l' ~ express oneself wittily; mot d' ~ witticism; reprendre ses ~s regain consciousness; recover one's composure; Saint-Esprit Holy Ghost

esprit-de-vin *nm* alcohol

esquif *nm* skiff, small boat

esquille *nf* splinter (bone)

Esquimau -aude *n* Eskimo

esquimau *nm* choc-ice; two-piece wool garment for children

esquintant *adj coll* exhausting, killing

esquinter *vt coll* exhaust; bust up, break, spoil; criticize severely

esquisse *nf* sketch, outline; ~ d'un sourire faint smile

esquisser *vt* sketch, outline; ~ un sourire give a slight smile

esquive *nf* dodging, ducking

esquiver *vt* avoid, dodge, duck; s' ~ slip away, make oneself scarce

essai *nm* trial, test; attempt; essay; try (rugby); à l' ~ on approval, on trial

essaim *nm* swarm (bees)

essaimer *vi* swarm (bees)

essarter *vt* clear undergrowth from (after deforestation)

essayer *vt* + *vi* (7) try, attempt; test; try on; s' ~ make an attempt, try one's hand

esse *nf* S-shaped hook; S-shaped hole in violin; linchpin

essence *nf* essence, essential being; concentrate, extract; petrol, *US* gas; gist, main aspect; species (tree)

essentiel -ielle *adj* essential

esseulé *adj* lonely, solitary

essieu *nm* axle

essor *nm* flight, soaring; progress, expansion; prendre son ~ take wing

essorer *vt* spin-dry, wring

essoreuse *nm* spin-dryer

essoriller *vt* crop the ears of

essoufflement *nm* breathlessness, panting

essouffler *vt* wind, blow; s' ~ get out of breath; *fig* lose momentum, go less well

essuie-glace *nm invar* windscreen-wiper

essuie-mains *nm invar* hand-towel

essuyer *vt* (7) wipe; mop up; endure, suffer; ~ les plâtres have problems; ~ une défaite suffer a defeat

est *nm* East; *adj invar* east, eastern

estacade *nf* line of stakes; stockade; mole, breakwater

estafette *nf* courier; *mil* dispatch-rider

estafilade *nf* gash, slash (*usu* in face)

estagnon *nm* drum (for olive oil, etc)

estaminet *nm* small café

estampe *nf* print, engraving

estamper *vt* stamp; impress; *coll* swindle

estampeur -euse *n* stamper; *coll* swindler

estampille *nf* official stamp; trade-mark

estampiller *vt* stamp, mark

esthète *n* aesthete

esthétique *adj* aesthetic

estimateur -trice *n* estimator; valuer

estimatif -ive *adj* estimated; estimative

estimation *nf* estimation; valuation

estime *nf* esteem, regard; *naut* reckoning; à l' ~ by guesswork, at a rough estimation; *naut* by dead reckoning

estimer *vt* estimate, value; calculate; esteem; consider, think

estival *adj* summer, estival

estivant -e *n* summer visitor

estocade *nf* stab-wound; fatal thrust (bull-fighting)

estomac *nm* stomach; *coll* avoir de l' ~ be plucky; be cheeky; avoir l' ~ dans les talons be starving hungry

estomaquer *vt coll* stagger, amaze, astound

estomper *vt arts* stump, shade off, soften off; s' ~ become blurred

estonien -ienne *adj* Estonian

estouffade *nf* braised meat

estourbir *vt sl* kill, do in

estrade *nf* platform, stage, dais

estragon *nm* tarragon

estropier *vt* cripple, lame; ~ le français murder French

estuaire *nm* estuary

estudiantin *adj* student

esturgeon *nm* sturgeon

et *conj* and; ~ ... ~ both ... and

étable *nf* cowshed, cattle-shed

établi *nm* work-bench

établir *vt* establish, institute; install, set up; construct, put up; fix; set; prove; draw up, work out; lay down, prescribe; found; s' ~ settle; become established

établissement *nm* establishment; installing, setting up; working out; proving; drawing up; creating, instituting, founding; institution

**étage** *nm* floor, storey; tier, stage; *geol* layer, formation; rank, station

**étager** *vt* (3) range in tiers

**étagère** *nf* what-not; set of shelves; shelf

**étai** *nm* strut, prop; *naut* stay

**étain** *nm* tin; pewter

**étal** *nm* (*pl* **étals**) meat stall; market display

**étalage** *nm* show, display; ostentation; **faire ~ de** show off, display

**étalager** *vt* (3) put on display

**étalagiste** *n* window-dresser; stall-holder

**étale** *adj naut* slack (water); without headway (ship)

**étalement** *nm* display; staggering (hours, holidays)

**étaler** *vt* display, expose for sale; spread out; space out, stagger; flaunt; *naut* weather out; *coll* flatten (s/o); **s' ~** *coll* stretch out; *coll* fall over, fall down

**¹étalon** *nm* standard; **~ or** gold standard

**²étalon** *nm* stallion

**étalonner** *vt* standardize, calibrate; gauge, test

**étambot** *nm naut* stern-post

**étamer** *vt* tin-plate; galvanize; silver

**¹étamine** *nf* coarse muslin

**²étamine** *nf bot* stamen

**étampe** *nf* stamp, die

**étamper** *vt* stamp, punch; drop-forge

**étamure** *nf* metal for tinning; tin coating

**étanche** *adj* watertight

**étanchéité** *nf* watertightness

**étancher** *vt* staunch, stop the flow of; quench; make watertight

**étang** *nm* pond, pool

**étape** *nf* stage; halting-place; lap

**état** *nm* state, condition; nation; state; report, list; trade, profession; estate, social rank; **~ civil** civil status; **~ d'âme** mood, mental state; **~ des lieux** inventory of fixtures; *Fr hist* **États Généraux** States General; **ce n'est pas une affaire d'État!** it's not very important: **de son ~** by trade, by profession; **en tout ~ de cause** whatever the circumstances; *coll* **être dans tous ses ~ s** be in a terrible state; **faire ~ de qch** take sth into account; **hors d' ~ de** incapable of; **remettre qch en ~** put sth right, overhaul; **tenir en ~** maintain, keep in good repair; *Fr hist* **tiers ~** third estate

**étatiser** *vt* put under state control

**étatisme** *nm* state control; statism

**état-major** *nm* (*pl* **états-majors**) general staff; staff headquarters

**état-providence** *nm* welfare state

**États-Unis** *nmpl* United States

**étau** *nm* vice

**étayer** *vt* (7) prop up, shore up; support, back up

**¹été** *nm* summer; **~ de la Saint-Martin** Indian summer

**²été** *p part* **être**

**éteignoir** *nm* candle snuffer; *coll* kill-joy, wet blanket

**éteindre** *vt* (55) put out, extinguish; switch off; turn off; exterminate; quench (thirst); soften, fade; deaden; appease; settle (debt); **s' ~** go out; pass away

**éteint** *adj* extinct; dull, dim; toneless (voice)

**étendard** *nm* standard; flag

**étendoir** *nm* clothes-line

**étendre** *vt* spread, stretch; spread out, lay out; stretch out; extend, increase; dilute with water; **s' ~** lie down; spread, stretch

**étendu** *adj* extensive; outspread

**étendue** *nf* area, size, extent; duration, length, importance; stretch

**Éternel (l')** *nm* God, the Lord

**éternel -elle** *adj* eternal, endless, everlasting

**éterniser** *vt* perpetuate; drag out; **s' ~** *coll* stay a long time

**éternité** *nf* eternity; very long time; **de toute ~** from time immemorial

**éternuement** *nm* sneeze; sneezing

**éternuer** *vi* sneeze

**étêter** *vt* remove the head from; pollard (tree)

**éteule** *nf* stubble

**éthéré** *adj* ethereal

**Éthiopie** *nf* Ethiopia

**éthiopien -ienne** *adj* Ethiopian

**éthique** *nf* ethics; *adj* ethical

**ethnique** *adj* ethnic

**ethnologie** *nf* ethnology

**ethnologue** *n* ethnologist

**éthylisme** *nm* alcoholism

**Étienne** *nm* Stephen

**étinceler** *vi* (5) sparkle, glitter, throw out sparks

**étincelle** *nf* spark

**étincellement** *nm* sparkling, glittering; twinkling

**étiolement** *nm* drooping; fading; atrophy

**étioler** *vt* blanch; make pale; **s' ~** blanch; droop

**étique** *adj* emaciated; consumptive

**étiqueter** *vt* (5) label

**étiquette** *nf* label, docket; étiquette, ceremony, protocol

**étirer** *vt* draw out, stretch; **s' ~** stretch oneself

**étoffe** *nf* fabric, material, stuff; **il a de l' ~** he's got what it takes

**étoffé** *adj* abundant, ample, rich; plump

**étoffer** *vt* stiffen; enrich, fill out

**étoile** *nf* star; star-shaped decoration; film-star; decoration; crossing (of several roads or paths); **~ de mer** star-fish;

**~ filante** shooting star; **à la belle ~** in the open air; **né sous une bonne (mauvaise) ~** born under a lucky (unlucky) star

**étoilé** *adj* starlit, star-spangled; star-shaped

**étoiler** *vt* spangle with stars; star (glass, ice)

**étole** *nf* stole

**étonnant** *adj* surprising, astonishing; amazing

**étonnement** *nm* astonishment; amazement

**étonner** *vt* surprise, astonish; **s' ~** be surprised

**étouffant** *adj* stifling, stuffy; sweltering

**étouffée** *nf cul* **cuire à l' ~** braise

**étouffement** *nm* suffocation, smothering; breathlessness

**étouffer** *vt* suffocate, smother; stifle; stamp out; suppress; damp, deaden; hush up; *vi* choke, suffocate

**étoupe** *nf* tow

**étouper** *vt* caulk

**étourderie** *nf* thoughtlessness; blunder, oversight; **par ~** inadvertently

**étourdi** *adj* thoughtless; scatter-brained, stupid

**étourdir** *vt* stun, daze; deaden, allay; tire (with noise); **s' ~** dull oneself, stupefy oneself; intoxicate oneself

**étourdissement** *nm* giddiness, fit of dizziness; numbing, deadening

**étourneau** *nm* starling; scatter-brained person

**étrange** *adj* strange, peculiar

**étranger -ère** *n* foreigner, stranger; *adj* foreign; strange; irrelevant; **à l' ~** abroad

**étrangeté** *nf* strangeness, oddness

**étranglement** *nm* strangling; narrowing, constriction; bottle-neck

**étrangler** *vt* strangle, throttle; constrict; suppress; **~ au berceau** nip in the bud

**étrangleur -euse** *n* strangler

**étrave** *nf naut* stern-post

**être** *nm* being, existence; nature; individual; creature; *vi* (2) be, exist; go (in past); *aux* used to form past of certain verbs and passive; **~ à** belong to; **~ bien avec** be well in with; **~ de** hail from, originate from; **~ en noir** be dressed in black; **c'en est trop** it's too much; **en ~** belong to, be one of; **en ~ pour sa peine** waste one's efforts; **il en est qui** there are some people who; **il était une fois …** once upon a time there was …; **il n'est que de** one needs only to; **j'en suis là** that's what I've come to; **j'en suis pour payer son dîner** I'll have to foot the bill for his dinner; **j'y suis** I get it, I understand; **n'était sa maladie** were it not for his illness; **n' ~ plus** be dead; **nous sommes le quatorze** it's the fourteenth; **soit** so be it, that is to say

**étreindre** *vt* (56) hug, embrace; oppress (emotion)

**étreinte** *nf* hug, embrace; grasp

**étrenne** *nf* (*usu pl*) New Year gift; Christmas box; first use

**étrenner** *vt* use for the first time; wear for the first time; be the first to buy from

**étrésillon** *nm* prop, strut

**étrier** *nm* stirrup; *anat* stirrup-bone (ear); **à franc ~** at full gallop; **avoir le pied à l' ~** be ready to go; **coup de l' ~** one for the road; stirrup cup

**étrille** *nf* curry-comb

**étriller** *vt* curry-comb; beat, thrash; *coll* overcharge

**étriper** *vt* disembowel, gut

**étriqué** *adj* tight (clothing); small-minded, petty

**étroit** *adj* narrow, confined; tight; limited; close; **à l' ~** in confined quarters

**étroitesse** *nf* narrowness; tightness; closeness

**étron** *nm* turd

**étrusque** *adj* Etruscan

**étude** *nf* study; office, practice (solicitor); prep; **à l' ~** under consideration; **faire ses ~s** study

**étudiant -e** *n + adj* student

**étudié** *adj* studied; elaborate

**étudier** *vt* study; prepare, swot up; read (a subject); investigate; observe closely; *vi* study; **s' ~** strive, apply oneself; observe oneself closely

**étui** *nm* case, cover, box

**étuve** *nf* sweating-room; drying-oven; hot place

**étuvée** *nf cul* **à l' ~** steamed, braised

**étuver** *vt* braise, dry

**étymologie** *nf* etymology

**eu** *p part* avoir

**eucharistie** *nf* Eucharist, Lord's Supper

**eunuque** *nm* eunuch

**euphémisme** *nm* euphemism

**euphonie** *nf* euphony

**eurasien -ienne** *adj* Eurasian

**Européen -éenne** *n* European

**européen -éenne** *adj* European

**euthanasie** *nf* euthanasia

**eux** *pron pl* them, they

**évacuer** *vt* evacuate; drain; withdraw from; vacate

**évadé** *adj* escaped

**évader (s')** *v refl* escape, run away

**évaluation** *nf* valuation, assessment, estimate

**évaluer** *vt* value, estimate, assess; reckon

**évangélique** *adj* evangelic; evangelical

# évangéliser

**évangéliser** *vt* evangelize

**évangéliste** *nm* evangelist

**évangile** *nm* gospel

**évanouir (s')** *v refl* faint; disappear, die away

**évanouissement** *nm* fainting fit; disappearance, dying away

**évaporé** *adj* irresponsible, scatterbrained

**évaporer (s')** *v refl* evaporate, dry off

**évasé** *adj* wide-mouthed; flared

**évasement** *nm* widening out

**évaser** *vt* widen out, open out

**évasif -ive** *adj* evasive

**évasion** *nf* escape; **besoin d'** ~ need for a change

**évêché** *nm* bishopric, see; bishop's palace

**éveil** *nm* awakening; alertness; **donner l'** ~ raise the alarm; **être en** ~ be on the alert

**éveillé** *adj* awake; alert, sharp

**éveiller** *vt* awaken, wake up; arouse

**événement** *nm* event

**éventail** *nm* fan; range; **en** ~ fanshaped

**éventaire** *nm* hawker's tray; display outside shop

**éventé** *adj* stale; flat

**éventer** *vt* air, expose to the air; fan; *coll* ~ **la mèche** twig, cotton on; **s'** ~ go flat, stale

**éventrer** *vt* disembowel; gut; rip open, break open

**éventualité** *nf* possibility, eventuality

**éventuel -uelle** *adj* possible

**éventuellement** *adv* possibly; should the occasion arise

**évêque** *nm* bishop

**évertuer (s')** *v refl* try very hard, do one's utmost

**éviction** *nf* eviction, expulsion; *leg* dispossession, deprival

**évidé** *adj* hollow; cut away

**évidemment** *adv* evidently; certainly, of course, naturally

**évidence** *nf* obviousness, clearness; conspicuousness; **de toute** ~ quite obviously; **mettre en** ~ show off, display; **se rendre à l'** ~ bow to reality

**évident** *adj* obvious, plain

**évider** *vt* scoop out, hollow out; cut away

**évier** *nm* sink

**évincer** *vt* (4) eject, thrust aside, turn out; *leg* dispossess

**éviscérer** *vt* (6) eviscerate, disembowel

**évitable** *adj* avoidable

**évitement** *nm* avoidance, shunning; **voie d'** ~ siding

**éviter** *vt* avoid, keep clear of

**évocateur -trice** *adj* evocative

**évocatoire** *adj* evocatory

**évolué** *adj* developed, advanced

**évoluer** *vi* manoeuvre, go round; evolve, develop; change one's opinion(s)

**évolution** *nf mil* movement, manoeuvre; evolution, development

**évoquer** *vt* evoke, call forth, conjure up; recall

**exacerber** *vt* exacerbate

**exact** *adj* exact, accurate; correct; punctual; conscientious

**exactitude** *nf* exactness; correctness; punctuality

**ex aequo** *adv phr* equals, of equal merit

**exagération** *nf* exaggeration

**exagérer** *vt* (6) exaggerate; overstate; overrate

**exaltation** *nf* exaltation; glorifying; excitement; rapture; stimulation

**exalté** *adj* overexcited, passionate; quixotic

**exalter** *vt* exalt; extol; excite; **s'** ~ enthuse, get very excited

**examen** *nm* examination, test; investigation, scrutiny

**examinateur -trice** *n* examiner

**examiner** *vt* examine, investigate; scrutinize

**exaspération** *nf* exasperation; aggravation

**exaspérer** *vt* (6) exasperate, provoke; aggravate; **s'** ~ become exasperated

**exaucer** *vt* (4) grant the prayer of; fulfil

**excavation** *nf* digging out, excavation; pit, hole

**excaver** *vt* dig out, excavate

**excédant** *adj* surplus; exasperating, tiresome

**excédent** *nm* surplus, excess

**excédentaire** *adj* surplus

**excéder** *vt* (6) exceed; exhaust; exasperate

**excellence** *nf* excellence; excellency; **par** ~ above all

**exceller** *vi* excel

**excentrique** *adj* eccentric; outlying, remote; odd, strange

**excepté** *prep* except, but for, save

**excepter** *vt* except, exclude

**exception** *nf* exception; *leg* incidental plea; ~ **faite de, à l'** ~ **de** with the exception of; **faire** ~ be an exception; **sauf** ~ with certain exceptions

**exceptionnel -elle** *adj* exceptional

**excès** *nm* excess; *nmpl* cruel conduct; excesses

**excessif -ive** *adj* excessive, extreme, inordinate; exorbitant

**exciser** *vt* excise, cut out

**excitant** *nm* stimulant; *adj* stimulating

**excitation** *nf* excitement; incitement; encouragement

**exciter** vt excite, arouse, stimulate; incite, inflame; s' ~ get worked up

**exclamatif -ive** adj exclamatory

**exclamation** nf exclamation; **point d' ~** exclamation mark

**exclamer (s')** v refl exclaim; protest

**exclure** vt (25) exclude, leave out; be incompatible with

**exclusif -ive** adj exclusive, sole; dogmatic

**exclusivité** nf exclusiveness; sole rights; **en ~ (à, chez)** only (at)

**excommunier** vt excommunicate

**excorier** vt excoriate; peel off (skin)

**excréter** vt (6) excrete

**excroissance** nf excrescence

**excursionniste** n tripper, excursionist

**excuse** nf excuse; ~ s apology; **faire des ~ s, présenter ses (des) ~ s** apologize

**excuser** vt apologize for; excuse, let off; absolve; act as an excuse for; s' ~ apologize; excuse oneself; **se faire ~** decline; **qui s'excuse s'accuse** excuses are a sign of a guilty conscience

**exécration** nf execration; object of detestation; **avoir en ~** loathe

**exécrer** vt (6) detest, loathe

**exécutable** adj practicable, feasible

**exécutant -e** n agent; mus performer

**exécuter** vt execute, carry out, perform, fulfil; put to death; leg distrain upon; s' ~ comply, submit, oblige; pay up

**exécuteur -trice** n ~ **des hautes œuvres** executioner; leg ~ **testamentaire** executor

**exécutif -ive** adj executive

**exécution** nf execution; performance, carrying out, fulfilment; **mettre à ~** carry out, put into effect

**exécutoire** adj leg enforceable

**exégèse** nf exegesis

**exemplaire** nm pattern; specimen; copy; adj exemplary

**exemple** nm example; lesson, warning; precedent, instance; **à l' ~ de** following the example of; **par ~** for example; **par ~!** goodness!, the idea!; **sans ~** unparalleled

**exempter** vt exempt

**exercé** adj practised, experienced

**exercer** vt (4) exercise; exert; practise, pursue, carry on; s' ~ train, practise

**exercice** nm exercise; practice, carrying out; financial year; ~ **s spirituels** devotions; **en ~** practising; **entrer en ~** enter upon one's duties; **faire l' ~** drill

**exergue** nm **mettre en ~** give prominence to; use (quotation) as epigraph

**exfolier** vt exfoliate

**exhalaison** nf exhalation

**exhaler** vt exhale, give out; vent (anger); s' ~ be given off

**exhausser** vt raise, increase the height of

**exhiber** vt show, present; display, exhibit, show off; s' ~ make an exhibition of oneself, expose oneself

**exhibition** nf showing, producing; exhibition; display, flaunting

**exhorter** vt exhort, urge

**exhumer** vt exhume, disinter; bring to light, unearth

**exigeant** adj hard to please; exacting

**exigence** nf demand, requirement; need, exigency; exactingness

**exiger** vt (3) demand, require; necessitate, call for

**exigu -uë** adj tiny, exiguous; scant, slender

**exiguïté** nf exiguity, smallness; scantiness, slenderness

**exil** nm exile, banishment; place of exile

**exilé -e** n exile

**exiler** vt exile, banish

**existant** adj existing, existent

**existence** nf being; life, existence

**exister** vi exist, live; count, be important

**exocet** nm flying-fish; mil exocet (missile)

**exode** nm exodus, mass-emigration; ~ **rural** drift from the country

**exonération** nf exoneration; exemption, dispensation

**exonérer** vt (6) dispense, exempt; exonerate

**exorbité** adj **yeux ~ s** eyes popping out of the head

**exorciser** vt exorcize, cast out (devil)

**exorcisme** nm exorcizing; exorcism

**exorde** nm opening (of speech)

**exotique** adj exotic

**exotisme** nm exoticism

**expansif -ive** adj expansive

**expansion** nf expansion; expansiveness; development

**expatrier** vt expatriate; s' ~ leave one's own country

**expectative** nf expectancy, expectation

**expectorer** vt expectorate

**expédient** nm expedient, device

**expédier** vt dispatch; expedite, hasten, rush; get rid of; leg draw up

**expéditeur -trice** n sender, consigner

**expéditif -ive** adj expeditious

**expédition** nf expedition; dispatch, sending; execution; leg copy; **bulletin d' ~** way-bill

**expéditionnaire** n sender (goods); leg copying clerk; adj expeditionary

**expérience** nf experience; experiment; **faire l' ~ de** experience

**expérimental** adj experimental

**expérimentateur -trice** n experimenter

**expérimenté** adj experienced

**expérimenter** vt + vi test, try

**expert -e** n expert; connoisseur;

appraiser; *adj* expert, skilled, skilful

**expert-comptable** *nm* (*pl* **experts-comptables**) chartered accountant

**expertise** *nf* valuation, expert appraisal; expert's report

**expertiser** *vt* carry out a valuation or survey of

**expiatoire** *adj* expiatory

**expier** *vt* expiate, atone for

**expiration** *nf* breathing out, expiration; expiry

**expirer** *vt* breathe out; *vi* expire; die

**explétif** *nm* expletive

**explicatif -ive** *adj* explanatory

**explication** *nf* explanation; **avoir une ~ avec qn** have it out with s/o

**explicite** *adj* explicit, clear, plain

**expliquer** *vt* explain, elucidate; **s' ~** explain oneself; have it out; understand

**exploit** *nm* achievement, exploit; *leg* writ

**exploitable** *adj* workable; exploitable

**exploitant -e** *n* operator; cultivator

**exploitation** *nf* exploration, exploiting; working; cultivation; farm

**exploiter** *vt* exploit; operate; work; cultivate; take undue advantage of

**exploiteur -euse** *n* exploiter

**explorateur -trice** *n* explorer

**explorer** *vt* explore; examine, study, probe

**exploser** *vi* explode, blow up; *fig* overflow, develop greatly

**explosif** *nm* explosive; *adj* (*f* **-ive**) explosive

**explosion** *nf* explosion; **faire ~** explode; **moteur à ~** internal combustion engine

**exportateur -trice** *n* exporter

**exporter** *vt* export

**exposant -e** *n* exhibitor

**exposé** *nm* statement, account

**exposer** *vt* show, exhibit; expose; expound, put forward; **s' ~** expose oneself (to danger)

**exposition** *nf* exhibition, display; exposing, exposure; exposition; account; aspect (house)

**exprès -esse** *adj* express, distinct; *invar* express; *adv* intentionally, on purpose; **un fait ~** a tiresome coincidence

**express** *nm* fast train; express letter

**expressif -ive** *adj* expressive

**expression** *nf* expression; phrase; utterance

**exprimable** *adj* expressible

**exprimer** *vt* express, voice; show; **s' ~** express oneself

**exproprier** *vt* expropriate

**expulser** *vt* expel, evict, turn out

**expurger** *vt* expurgate

**exquis** *adj* exquisite; beautiful; charming, delightful

**exsangue** *adj* very pale; bloodless

**exsuder** *vt + vi* exude

**extase** *nf* ecstasy; rapture; trance; **être en ~ devant qn** be full of admiration for s/o

**extasier (s')** *v refl* go into ecstasies, be overcome with admiration

**extatique** *adj* ecstatic

**extenseur** *nm* chest-expander; *anat* extensor

**extensif -ive** *adj* extensive; tensile

**extension** *nf* extension; stretching, extending; enlargement, spreading; *med* traction; **prendre de l' ~** grow, expand

**exténuant** *adj* exhausting

**exténuer** *vt* exhaust

**extérieur** *nm* exterior, outside; **à l' ~ de** outside; *adj* exterior, outer, external

**extérieurement** *adv* outwardly, externally; on the surface

**extérioriser** *vt* exteriorize; **s' ~** show one's feelings

**exterminateur -trice** *n* exterminator; *adj* exterminating

**exterminer** *vt* exterminate

**externat** *nm* day-school; day attendance; non-residence; non-resident medical work

**externe** *n* day pupil; non-resident doctor; *adj* external

¹**extincteur** *nm* fire extinguisher

²**extincteur -trice** *adj* extinguishing

**extinction** *nf* extinction; extinguishing, putting out; suppression; **~ de voix** loss of voice

**extirper** *vt* extirpate; remove

**extorquer** *vt* extort, wring

**extra** *nm invar* extra; supplement; temporary domestic servant; *adj invar coll* extraordinarily good, very special, super

**extracteur** *nm* extractor

**extraction** *nf* extraction, drawing out; quarrying; origin, descent

**extrader** *vt* extradite

**extra-fin** *adj* superfine

**extra-fort** *nm* strong ribbon or tape

**extraire** *vt* (9) extract, pull out; quarry

**extrait** *nm* extract; excerpt; abstract; copy of legal document

**extra-muros** *adv* outside the town

**extraordinaire** *adj* extraordinary; special; unusual

**extrapoler** *vt + vi* extrapolate

**extravagance** *nf* extravagance; folly; immoderateness

**extravagant** *adj* extravagant; foolish; immoderate

**extravaguer** *vi* talk nonsense

**extraverti -e** *n* extrovert

**extrême** *nm* extreme, limit; *adj* extreme; utmost; excessive; drastic; farthest

**extrême-onction** *nf* extreme unction

**Extrême-Orient** *nm* Far East

**extrémisme** *nm* extremism

**extrémité** *nf* extremity, end; last degree; **en venir à des ~ s** give way to violence; **être à la dernière ~** be at death's door; **pousser qch à l' ~** carry sth to extremes

**extrinsèque** *adj* extrinsic

**exubérance** *nf* exuberance; superabundance

**exubérant** *adj* exuberant; superabundant

**exulter** *vi* exult, rejoice

**exutoire** *nm* outlet

# F

**fa** *nm invar mus* F, fa; **clef de ~** bass clef

**fable** *nf* fable; tale; lie; **la ~ du village** the talk of the village

**fabricant -e** *n* manufacturer; maker

**fabricateur -trice** *n* forger; fabricator

**fabrication** *nf* manufacture; forging; fabrication

**fabrique** *nf* manufacture; factory, mill; **marque de ~** trade-mark

**fabriquer** *vt* manufacture; make; forge; fabricate; *coll* **qu'est-ce que tu fabriques?** what are you up to?

**fabuleux -euse** *adj* fabulous.

**Fac** *nf coll* faculty; university

**façade** *nf* façade, front; *sl* **se refaire la ~** make up (face)

**face** *nf* face, surface, aspect; head (coin); side (dice); **~ à facing; à double ~** reversible (material); two-faced (person); **de ~** full-face; **en ~** opposite, to one's face, in the face; **en ~ de** opposite, in front of, in the presence of; **faire ~** à face up to, cope with; **pile ou ~?** heads or tails?

**face-à-main** *nm* (*pl* **faces-à-main**) lorgnette

**facétie** *nf* joke

**facétieux -ieuse** *adj* facetious

**facette** *nf* facet

**fâché** *adj* sorry; angry; on bad terms

**fâcher** *vt* anger, irritate, displease, offend; **se ~ get angry; se ~ avec** fall out with; **se ~ tout rouge** fly into a rage

**fâcheux -euse** *adj* regrettable, sad, unfortunate; tiresome, dreary

**facile** *adj* easy; easy-going; facile, fluent; **~ à vivre** easy to get on with

**facilité** *nf* easiness; facility; fluency; **~ s de paiement** easy terms, instalment plan; **solution de ~** line of least resistance, easy way out

**faciliter** *vt* facilitate

**façon** *nf* make, making; way, manner, fashion; shape, cut; **à la ~ de** after the manner of; **à sa ~** in one's own way; **de cette ~** in this (that) way, at this (that) rate; **de ~ à** so as to; **de ~ que** so that; **de toute ~** anyway, at any rate; **en aucune ~** by no means; **faire des ~ s** stand on ceremony; **sans ~** without ceremony; **sans plus de ~ s** without more ado; **tailleur à ~** bespoke tailor, *US* custom tailor

**faconde** *nf* fluency; *coll* gift of the gab

**façonner** *vt* work, fashion, shape, mould; *agr* dress

**facteur** *nm* postman, *US* mailman; porter; carrier; agent; factor

**factice** *adj* factitious, artificial

**factieux -ieuse** *adj* factious

**faction** *nf* sentry duty, guard; faction; **de (en) ~** on sentry duty

**factionnaire** *nm* sentry, sentinel

**factuel -uelle** *adj* factual

**facture** *nf* bill, invoice; structure, composition; workmanship; **suivant ~** as per invoice

**facturer** *vt* invoice

**facultatif -ive** *adj* optional; **arrêt ~** request stop

**faculté** *nf* faculty, power; option, right; faculty, department; *coll* **la Faculté** the Faculty of Medicine, doctors, medical opinion

**fada** *adj invar coll* crazy, cracked

**fadaise** *nf usu pl* nonsense, twaddle

**fade** *adj* insipid, flat, tasteless, wishy-washy

**fadeur** *nf* insipidity

**fading** *nm rad* fade

**fafiot** *nm sl* banknote

**fagot** *nm* faggot; **sentir le ~** be suspect, smack of heresy

**fagoté** *adj coll* got up, badly dressed

**faible** *nm* weakness, partiality; **les économiquement ~s** the lower-income groups, the underprivileged; *adj* feeble, weak, faint; low, slight

**faiblesse** *nf* feebleness, weakness; slightness; shortcoming, failing

**faiblir** *vi* weaken, grow weaker, abate

**faïence** *nf* earthenware; crockery; **se regarder en chiens de ~** glower at each other

**faille** *nf* fault, crack

**failli** *nm + adj* bankrupt

**faillibilité** *nf* fallibility

**faillible** *adj* fallible

**faillir** *vi* (45) fail; err; nearly do; **j'ai failli mourir** I nearly died

**faillite** *nf* failure, bankruptcy; **faire ~** go bankrupt

**faim** *nf* hunger; **avoir ~** be hungry; **manger à sa ~** eat one's fill

**faîne** *nf* beech-nut

**fainéant -e** *n* idler, lazybones; *adj* lazy, idle

**fainéantise** *nf* idleness

**faire** *vt* (46) make, create, form, beget; do, perform, cause; play, affect; imitate; travel, cover, go; do, clean, wash; be (profession, trade); **~ attention** pay attention; **~ cas de** think a great deal of; **~ comprendre** give to understand, insinuate; **~ dire** send word; **~ eau** leak; **~ entendre** hint, give to understand; **~ ~ qch** have sth done, have sth made; **~ l'affaire** be just the thing; **~ part de** notify of; **~ penser à** remind of; **~ savoir à** inform; **~ valoir** make the most of, display; **~ venir** send for; **~ voir** show; **cela ne fait rien** it doesn't matter; **il faut le ~** it takes some doing, not everyone can do it; **laisser ~** let things take their course; **pourquoi ~?** what for?; **prière de ~ suivre** please forward; **se laisser ~** put up no resistance; *vi* do, act; need; look; say; **~ bien de** do well to; **~ de son mieux** do one's best; **~ pour le mieux** act for the best; **avoir fort à ~** have one's hands full; **n'avoir que ~ de** have no need of, have no use for; **que ~?** what's to be done?; **qu'y ~?** how can it be helped?; *v impers* **il fait beau (chaud, froid, jour, nuit)** it is fine (hot, cold, light, dark); **il fait bon se reposer** it is pleasant to rest; **se ~** be made, be done; happen; become, get, grow; **cela ne se fait pas** that's not done; **comment se fait-il que ...?** how is it that ...?; **il pourrait se ~ que ...** it could be that ...; **s'en ~** worry, care;

**un bruit se fit entendre** a noise was heard

**faire-part** *nm invar* notice, announcement (birth, death, etc)

**faisable** *adj* feasible, practicable

**faisan -e** *n* pheasant

**faisandé** *adj* high (game); spicy (story, etc)

**faisander** *vt* hang (game); *sl* cheat

**faisceau** *nm* bundle; pencil (light); *mil* pile; **former les ~x** pile arms

**faiseur -euse** *n* maker, doer; *coll* swindler, crook; **bon ~** good tailor

**fait** *nm* fact, act, deed; event; matter; **~ divers** minor news item; **au ~** in fact; **au ~ de** informed about; **de (en) ~** in fact, truly; **dire son ~ à qn** give s/o a piece of one's mind; **en ~ de** with regard to; **en venir au ~** come to the point; **pris sur le ~** caught in the act; **voies de ~** assault and battery; *adj* made, done, formed, developed, accustomed; ripe (cheese); *sl* arrested, nabbed; **bien ~** shapely, well-built; **c'en est ~ de lui** it's all up with him; **c'est bien ~ pour vous** it serves you right; **tout ~** ready-made

**faîte** *nm* top, summit, ridge

**fait-tout** *nm invar* cooking-pot

**faix** *nm* burden

**falaise** *nf* cliff

**falbalas** *nmpl* flounces; showy trimmings

**fallacieux -ieuse** *adj* fallacious

**falloir** *v impers* (47) be necessary, be required; must, have to; **agir comme il faut** act correctly, suitably; **il faut partir** I (we, you, etc) must go; **il le faut** it is essential; **il lui faut ...** he must ...; he requires ...; **il m'a fallu deux heures pour venir** it took me two hours to get here; **un homme comme il faut** a well-bred man, gentleman; **s'en ~** be short, lacking; **il s'en est fallu de peu qu'il ne tombe** he came within an ace of falling; **il s'en faut de beaucoup** far from it; **il s'en faut de cinq minutes** there are five minutes to go; **peu s'en faut** very nearly

**¹falot** *nm* big lantern

**²falot** *adj* wan; tame

**falsifier** *vt* falsify, forge, adulterate

**falzar(d)** *nm sl* trousers

**famé** *adj* **mal ~** ill-famed

**famélique** *adj* hungry-looking, half-starved

**fameux -euse** *adj* famous; *coll* first-rate, terrific; **pas ~** nothing to write home about

**familial** *adj* family

**familiale** *nf* estate car

**familiariser** *vt* familiarize; **se ~ avec** master

**familiarité** *nf* familiarity, intimacy

**familier** *nm* close friend, intimate; *adj* (*f* **-ière**) familiar, intimate; well-known; colloquial

**familistère** *nm* co-operative store

**famille** *nf* family, household; **en ~** with one's family; **nom de ~** surname

**famine** *nf* famine, hunger

**fanal** *nm* lantern, light, beacon

**fanatique** *n* fanatic; *adj* fanatical

**fanatisme** *nm* fanaticism

**faner** *vt* toss, ted (hay); wither, make fade; *vi* make hay; **se ~** fade

**fanfare** *nf* fanfare, flourish; brass band

**fanfaron -onne** *n + adj* braggart

**fanfaronnade** *nf* brag, bragging

**fanfaronner** *vi* brag, boast

**fanfreluche** *nf* bauble, trifle; frill

**fange** *nf* mud, mire, filth

**fangeux -euse** *adj* muddy, miry, filthy

**fanion** *nm* pennant

**fanon** *nm* dewlap; wattle; fetlock

**fantaisie** *nf* fancy, imagination, whim; *mus* fantasia; *comm* fancy goods; **de ~** fancy

**fantaisiste** *n* capricious person; (music-hall) comedian; *adj* fanciful, whimsical

**fantasme** *nm* hallucination, phantasm

**fantasque** *adj* odd, whimsical

**fantassin** *nm* infantryman, foot-soldier

**fantastique** *adj* fantastic

**fantoche** *nm* puppet, marionette

**fantôme** *nm* ghost, phantom; *adj* imaginary; mysterious

**faon** *nm* fawn

**faquin** *nm* knave

**faramineux -euse** *adj coll* terrific, colossal

**faraud** *adj coll* snobbish, affected

**¹farce** *nf* farce; prank, practical joke

**²farce** *nf* stuffing

**farceur -euse** *n* practical joker, wag

**farcir** *vt* stuff; *sl* **se ~** treat oneself to; have it off with (a woman); put up with

**fard** *nm* make-up, paint; disguise; **parler sans ~** speak frankly

**fardeau** *nm* burden, load

**farder** *vt* paint; disguise; **se ~** make up

**farfelu** *adj* odd, crazy, hare-brained; surprising, funny

**farfouiller** *vi coll* rummage

**faribole** *nf* nonsense, idle talk

**farinacé** *adj* farinaceous

**farine** *nf* flour, meal; **~ de riz** ground rice; **gens de la même ~** birds of a feather

**farineux -euse** *adj* starchy, farinaceous

**farouche** *adj* shy, timid, unsociable; wild

**fart** *nm* wax (for skis)

**farter** *vt* wax (skis)

**fascicule** *nm* print number, part

**fascinateur -trice** *adj* fascinating, spellbinding

**fasciner** *vt* fascinate, charm

**fascisant** *adj* having fascist leanings, favouring fascism

**fascisme** *nm* fascism

**fasciste** *n + adj* fascist

**¹faste** *nm* pomp, show

**²faste** *adj* lucky, auspicious

**fastidieux -ieuse** *adj* tedious, irksome

**fastueux -ueuse** *adj* sumptuous; gaudy, showy

**fat** *nm* fop, self-satisfied individual; *adj* conceited, foppish, vain

**fatal** *adj* (*pl* **~s**) fatal; inevitable; fateful

**fatalisme** *nm* fatalism

**fataliste** *n* fatalist; *adj* fatalistic

**fatalité** *nf* fatality, fate

**fatidique** *adj* fateful

**fatigant** *adj* tiring; trying, tiresome

**fatigue** *nf* fatigue, weariness; strain; wear and tear

**fatiguer** *vt* tire, fatigue; strain, overtax; bore; mix (salad); *vi* labour; **se ~** tire, get tired

**fatras** *nm* rubbish; mess, hotch-potch

**fatuité** *nf* fatuity, self-conceit, foppishness

**faubourg** *nm* suburb

**faubourien -ienne** *adj* suburban; **accent ~** common accent

**fauché** *adj coll* broke, hard-up

**faucher** *vt* mow, scythe; mow down; *sl* pinch, knock off

**faucheur -euse** *n* mower, haymaker

**faucheuse** *nf* reaper, mowing-machine

**faucheux** *nm* daddy-long-legs

**faucille** *nf* sickle

**faucon** *nm* falcon, hawk

**faudra** *fut* **falloir**

**faufiler** *vt* tack, baste; **se ~** creep, edge, steal

**¹faune** *nm* faun

**²faune** *nf* fauna

**faussaire** *n* forger

**faussement** *adv* falsely

**fausser** *vt* falsify; bend, force, warp, distort; **~ compagnie à qn** give s/o the slip

**¹fausset** *nm* falsetto

**²fausset** *nm* spigot, *US* faucet

**fausseté** *nf* falsity; falseness; falsehood

**faut** *pres* **falloir**

**faute** *nf* fault, mistake; misdeed, transgression; lack, want, need; **~ de mieux** for want of anything better; **~ de quoi** failing which; **~ d'impression** misprint; **à qui la ~?** whose fault is it?;

faire ~ à be lacking; sans ~ without fail; se faire ~ de fail to

**fauter** *vi coll* allow oneself to be seduced

**fauteuil** *nm* arm-chair, easy-chair; *theat* ~ d'orchestre stall; ~ roulant bath-chair, wheel-chair; *coll* arriver dans un ~ win in a canter, win easily

**fauteur -trice** *n* abettor; ~ de guerre warmonger; ~ de troubles agitator

**fautif -ive** *adj* faulty, defective; guilty

**fauve** *nm* fawn (colour); large wild animal; *adj* tawny, fawn-coloured; wild

**fauvette** *nf* warbler

**¹faux** *nm* falsehood; forgery, imitation; *adj* ( *f* **fausse**) false, untrue, wrong, insincere; sham, faked; paste (jewels); counterfeit (coins); ~ col separate collar; *coll* froth on a glass of beer; ~ départ false start; ~ frais incidental expenses; ~ numéro wrong number; faire fausse route be on the wrong track; fausse clef skeleton key; fausse couche miscarriage; *adv* wrongly; *mus* out of tune; à ~ wrongly, out of true, beside the mark

**²faux** *nf* scythe

**faux-filet** *nm* sirloin

**faux-fuyant** *nm* shift, subterfuge, evasion, dodge

**faux-monnayeur** *nm* coiner, counterfeiter

**faux-semblant** *nm* false pretence; pretext

**faveur** *nf* favour, kindness; ribbon, favour; à la ~ de under cover of; billet de ~ complimentary ticket; en ~ in vogue; en ~ de in aid of; prix de ~ preferential price

**favorable** *adj* favourable, propitious

**favori -ite** *n* favourite, darling; *coll* blue-eyed boy, *US* fair-haired boy; *adj* favourite, pet

**favoris** *nmpl* side-whiskers; *coll* sideburns

**favoriser** *vt* favour

**fayot** *nm coll* haricot bean

**fébrile** *adj* feverish, febrile

**fécond** *adj* fertile, fruitful, prolific

**fécondation** *nf* fecundation; *med* impregnation; ~ artificielle artificial insemination

**féconder** *vt* fecundate; fertilize

**fécondité** *nf* fecundity; fertility

**fécule** *nf* fecula, starch

**féculent** *nm* starchy substance; starchy food

**fédérer** *vt* (6) federate; federalize

**fée** *nf* fairy; conte de ~ fairy-tale

**féerie** *nf* fairyland; fairy play

**féerique** *adj* fairy-like, enchanting

**feignant** *adj coll* idle, lazy

**feindre** *vt* (55) feign, sham, simulate,

pretend; *vi* limp (horse)

**feint** *adj* feigned, sham, mock

**feinte** *nf* feint; sham, pretence

**feinter** *vt* feint

**fêlant** *adj sl* very funny, killing

**fêlé** *adj sl* mad, cracked, crazy

**fêler** *vt* crack; se ~ crack

**félicitations** *nfpl* congratulations

**félicité** *nf* felicity, bliss

**féliciter** *vt* congratulate

**félin** *adj* feline

**félon -onne** *adj* felonious, treacherous

**félonie** *nf* felony, treason

**felouque** *nf* felucca

**fêlure** *nf* crack; *med* fracture

**femelle** *nf* + *adj* female

**féminin** *nm* + *adj* feminine

**féminisme** *nm* feminism

**féministe** *n* + *adj* feminist

**femme** *nf* woman; wife; ~ de chambre chambermaid, housemaid; ~ de ménage charwoman, daily help; ~ d'intérieur home-loving woman; ~ du monde woman who moves in fashionable society; prendre ~ marry

**femmelette** *nf* feeble, timid woman; *coll* effeminate man, cissy

**fenaison** *nf* hay-harvest, haymaking

**fendiller** *vt* crack; se ~ crack, craze

**fendoir** *nm* cleaver, chopper

**fendre** *vt* split, crack; cleave; chop; break (heart); force one's way through; se ~ lunge (fencing); *coll* se ~ de cough up, fork out, be generous; *sl* se ~ la pipe laugh like hell

**fenêtre** *nf* window

**fenil** *nm* hay-loft

**fenouil** *nm* fennel; ~ bâtard dill

**fente** *nf* crack, split, slot

**féodal** *adj* feudal

**féodalité** *nf* feudalism

**fer** *nm* iron; head, tip; sword; ferrule; ~s forceps; irons; ~ à cheval horseshoe; ~ à repasser iron (laundering); ~ à souder soldering iron; ~ de lance spearhead; ~ forgé wrought iron; fil de ~ wire; tomber les quatre ~s en l'air fall down backwards

**fer-blanc** *nm* tin; boîte en ~ tin, can; *coll* en ~ shoddy, cheap

**ferblanterie** *nf* ironmongery; ironmonger's shop

**ferblantier** *nm* tinsmith; ironmonger

**férié** *adj* jour ~ holiday

**férir** *vt* sans coup ~ without striking a blow

**ferler** *vt naut* furl

**fermage** *nm agr* rent; tenant farming

**¹ferme** *nf* farm, farmhouse; prendre à ~ rent (farm)

**²ferme** *adj* firm, fast, steady, strong; de pied ~ resolutely; terre ~ terra firma;

*adv* firmly, fast; hard; **tenez ~!** hold fast!

**fermenter** *vi* ferment

**fermer** *vt* shut, close; fasten; clench; draw (curtains); switch off; ~ **à clef** lock, lock up; ~ **boutique** shut up shop, sell up; *sl* **ferme-la!** shut up!, belt up!; ~ **la marche** bring up the rear; ~ **les yeux sur** turn a blind eye to, wink at; **ne pas ~ les yeux de la nuit** not sleep a wink all night; *vi* shut, close; **on ferme!** we're closing!, time!; **se ~** shut, close

**fermeté** *nf* firmness, steadfastness

**fermette** *nf* small farm; country cottage

**fermeture** *nf* closing, shutting; fastener; closing-time; ~ **éclair** zip, *US* zipper

**fermier -ière** *n* farmer (farmer's wife)

**fermoir** *nm* clasp, fastener

**féroce** *adj* ferocious, savage

**férocité** *nf* ferocity

**ferraille** *nf* scrap-iron, old iron; *coll* small change; **bruit de ~** rattling noise

**ferrailler** *vi* fight with swords

**ferrailleur** *nm* scrap-iron dealer

**ferré** *adj* iron-shod; hobnailed; *coll* ~ **sur** well up in; **voie ~e** railway track

**ferrer** *vt* shoe (horse)

**ferret** *nm* tag (lace)

**ferreux -euse** *adj* ferrous

**ferronnerie** *nf* decorative ironwork; place where ironwork is made or sold

**ferronnier** *nm* art ironworker

**ferroviaire** *adj* railway

**ferrugineux -euse** *adj* ferruginous

**ferrure** *nf* (piece of) ironwork; shoeing (horses)

**fertile** *adj* fertile; fruitful

**fertilisant** *adj* fertilizing

**fertiliser** *vt* fertilize

**féru** *adj* ~ **de** infatuated with; set on

**férule** *nf* ferule, cane; *bot* ferule; **sous la ~ de qn** under s/o's thumb

**fervent -e** *n* devotee; *adj* fervent, zealous

**ferveur** *nf* fervour

**fesse** *nf* buttock; ~ **s** *coll* backside, arse; **avoir chaud aux ~ s (serrer les ~ s)** be dead scared; **histoire de ~ s** bawdy story, sexy anecdote

**fessée** *nf* spanking, thrashing

**fesser** *vt* spank

**fessier** *nm* *coll* buttocks, arse

**festin** *nm* feast, banquet

**feston** *nm* festoon, garland

**festonner** *vt* festoon

**festoyer** *vi* (7) feast, booze

**fêtard** *nm* reveller, boozer

**fête** *nf* feast, festival, holiday; fête; name-day; anniversary, birthday; **Fête-Dieu** Corpus Christi; ~ **légale** bank holiday, public holiday; **faire ~ à** give a warm welcome to; **faire la ~** go on the spree; **jour de ~** feast-day,

holiday; **se faire une ~ de** look forward to; **souhaiter bonne ~ à** wish many happy returns to

**fêter** *vt* celebrate; observe; fête

**fétiche** *nm* mascot; fetish

**fétide** *adj* fetid, putrid

**fétu** *nm* wisp of straw

¹**feu** *nm* fire, heat; hearth; light; ardour; passion; ~ **arrière** rear light; ~ **de joie** bonfire; *coll* ~ **de paille** flash in the pan; ~ **x rouges** traffic lights; ~ **x (de circulation)** (traffic) lights; **mot ~ x de position** parking lights; *naut + aer* navigation lights; ~ **x rouges** traffic lights; red light; **au coin du ~** by the fireside; **au ~!** fire!; **avoir le ~ vert** get the go-ahead; **faire du ~** light a fire; **faire la part du ~** cut one's losses; **faire long ~** misfire; **je n'y vois que du ~** I can't make head or tail of it; **mettre le ~ à** set fire to; **ne pas faire long ~** not last long; **prendre ~** catch fire; **tuer à petit ~** kill by inches; *adj invar* **rouge ~** flame-coloured

²**feu** *adj* late, deceased; ~ **ma mère** my late mother; **la ~ e reine** the late queen

**feuillage** *nm* foliage

**feuille** *nf* leaf; petal; sheet; newspaper; *sl* ear; ~ **de chou** cabbage leaf; *fig* rag, small newspaper; ~ **de garde** fly-leaf; ~ **de présence** time-sheet; ~ **de route** way-bill; *mil* marching orders; *arts* ~ **de vigne** fig-leaf; ~ **volante** loose-leaf

**feuilleté** *adj* *cul* **pâte ~ e** puff-pastry

**feuilleter** *vt* (5) turn over the pages of, flick through

**feuilleton** *nm* serial; (regular) newspaper column

**feutre** *nm* felt; felt hat; felt pen, felt pencil

**feutré** *adj* felt, felty; padded; soft (footsteps)

**fève** *nf* bean

**février** *nm* February

**fi** *interj obs* for shame!; **faire ~ de** turn up one's nose at

**fiacre** *nm* cab

**fiançailles** *nfpl* betrothal, engagement

**fiancer** *vt* (4) betrothe; **se ~** become engaged

**fibre** *nf* fibre, texture

**fibreux -euse** *adj* fibrous

**fibrome** *nm* fibrous tumour

**ficelé** *adj* tied; *coll* dressed, got up

**ficeler** *vt* (5) tie up

**ficelle** *nf* string, twine; small thin loaf; *mil* (officer's) stripe; *coll* trick; trickster; **vieille ~** old hand; *adj coll* knowing, slick

**fiche** *nf* index-card, slip; peg, pin; *elect*

plug; *coll* ~ **de consolation** booby-prize

**ficher, fiche** *vt* (*p part* **fiché** + **fichu**) stick, drive; card-index (s/o); *coll* ~ **dehors** chuck out, sack; *coll* **fichez le camp!** beat it!, get out!; *coll* **fichez-moi la paix!** shut up!, leave me alone!; *coll* **ne rien** ~ not do a stroke; *coll* **se** ~ **de** not give a damn about; make fun of; *sl* **se** ~ **dedans** make a blunder, slip up

**fichier** *nm* card-index, card-index box

**fichtre** *interj obs* well, I'm blowed!, heck!

**¹fichu** *nm* scarf, square

**²fichu** *adj coll* done for, finished; awful, godforsaken; dolled up; ~ **de capable** of, up to; **bien** ~ good-looking; **mal** ~ under the weather; badly made; badly built (person)

**fictif -ive** *adj* fictitious

**fidèle** *adj* faithful, loyal; accurate

**fidélité** *nf* fidelity, faithfulness; accuracy

**fiduciaire** *adj* fiduciary; held in trust

**fieffé** *adj* arrant, absolute

**fiel** *nm* gall, bitterness

**fielleux -euse** *adj* bitter, rancorous

**fiente** *nf* droppings (*usu* birds)

**¹fier** (*f* **fière**) *adj* proud, noble, fine

**²fier (se)** *v refl* rely, trust

**fièrement** *adv* proudly; *coll* famously

**fierté** *nf* pride, dignity

**fiesta** *nf coll* spree, feast

**fièvre** *nf* fever; **avoir de la** ~ have a temperature

**fiévreux -euse** *adj* feverish

**fifre** *nm* fife; fife-player

**figé** *adj* congealed; stiff; starchy; set

**figer (se)** *v refl* (3) congeal; curdle (milk); freeze (smile)

**fignoler** *vt* take great care over

**figue** *nf* fig; ~ **de Barbarie** prickly pear; **faire la** ~ **à qn** make a vulgar gesture at s/o; **mi-**~, **mi-raisin** neither one thing nor the other

**figuier** *nm* fig-tree

**figurant -e** *n theat* walk-on; *cin* extra; inactive participant

**figuratif -ive** *adj* figurative

**figure** *nf* figure; face; air, look; court card; **faire triste** ~ cut a poor figure

**figuré** *nm* figurative sense; **au** ~ figuratively; *adj* figurative; represented; decorated

**figurer** *vt* figure, represent; *vi* figure, appear; **se** ~ imagine, fancy; picture to oneself

**fil** *nm* thread, wire; grain (wood); edge (blade); *fig* thread; ~ **à plomb** plumb-line; ~ **de fer** wire; ~**s de la Vierge** gossamer; **au bout du** ~ on the phone; **au** ~ **de l'eau** with the current; *coll* **avoir un** ~ **à la patte** be tied down; be

married, hitched; **coup de** ~ phone call; **cousu de** ~ **blanc** obvious; **de** ~ **en aiguille** step by step; **donner du** ~ **à retordre à** give a lot of trouble to

**filage** *nm* spinning

**filandreux -euse** *adj* stringy; long-drawn-out

**filant** *adj* thick, ropy; shooting (star)

**filasse** *nf* tow; **cheveux de** ~ tow-coloured hair; *adj invar* tow-coloured (hair)

**filateur** *nm* owner of spinning-mill

**filature** *nf* spinning; spinning-mill; shadowing, *US* tailing; **prendre en** ~ shadow

**file** *nf* file, queue, *US* line; **à la** ~ in file; uninterruptedly, on end

**filer** *vt* spin; pay out (cable); sustain (note); *theat* run through; shadow, *US* tail; *coll* ~ **un mauvais coton** be in poor health; *vi* smoke (lamp); shoot (star); run out (cable); ladder, run; *coll* buzz off, make off; ~ **à l'anglaise** take French leave; ~ **doux** sing small; watch one's step

**¹filet** *nm* net, network; rack (luggage); string bag; streak, trickle

**²filet** *nm cul* fillet

**filiale** *nf* subsidiary (company)

**filiation** *nf* filiation; **en** ~ **directe** in a direct line

**filière** *nf* usual channels; sequence, chain, path

**filigrane** *nm* watermark; filigree

**fille** *nf* daughter; girl; prostitute; ~**-mère** unmarried mother; **jeune** ~ girl; **rester** ~ remain single; **vieille** ~ old maid

**fillette** *nf* little girl; *coll* half-bottle

**filleul -e** *n* godson, goddaughter

**film** *nm* film; ~ **annonce** trailer, *US* preview; ~ **d'actualités** newsreel

**filmer** *vt* film

**filmothèque** *nf* film library, film collection

**filon** *nm* vein, lode; *coll* cushy job, *US* bonanza

**filou** *nm* swindler, crook

**filouter** *vt* swindle, cheat, con

**fils** *nm* son; ~ **à papa** rich man's son; ~ **de famille** young man of good family; ~ **de ses œuvres** self-made man

**filtre** *nm* filter, strainer; cup of black coffee; **bout** ~ filter-tip

**filtrer** *vt* filter, strain; *vi* percolate; leak out (news)

**¹fin** *nf* end, close, conclusion; goal, aim; death; expiration (lease); ~ **courant** at the end of the present month; ~ **de mois** monthly statement; end of the month; *leg* ~ **de non-recevoir** legal demurrer; *fig* refusal; ~ **prochain** at the end of next month; **à cette ~** with this end in view; **à la ~** in the end, at last; **à toutes ~s utiles** for whatever purpose it may serve; to whom it may concern; **en ~ de compte** when all is said and done; **mener à bonne ~** bring to a successful conclusion; **toucher à sa ~** be drawing to a close; be at the point of death

²**fin** *nm* ultimate, best; clever fellow; **jouer au plus ~** try to outsmart; **le ~ du ~** the ultimate in perfection; *adj* fine, slender, thin, delicate; sharp, shrewd, acute; keen, expert; **~e bouche** gourmet; **~e champagne** liqueur brandy; **~es herbes** herbs for seasoning; **~e mouche** shrewd customer; **au ~ fond de** in the depths of; **le ~ mot** the truth; *adv* fine, finely; **écrire ~** write small

**final** *adj* final, last

**finale** *nf sp* final

**finalité** *nf* finality

**finance** *nf* finance; money; financial circles; **ministère des Finances** = Treasury

**financement** *nm* financing

**financer** *vt* (4) finance, back

**financier** *nm* financier; *adj* (*f* **-ière**) financial

**finasser** *vi* use trickery

**finasserie** *nf* trickery; ruse

**finaud** *adj* sly

**fine** *nf* liqueur brandy

**finesse** *nf* fineness, delicacy, slenderness; finesse; shrewdness, cunning, sharpness, subtlety; nicety

**fini** *nm* finish; finite; *adj* finished, completed; done for; finite; absolute, arrant

**finir** *vt* finish, end; *vi* finish, come to an end; die; **~ mal** turn out badly, come to a bad end; **en ~ avec** have done with

**finition** *nf* finishing, finish

**Finlandais -e** *n* Finn

**finlandais** *nm* Finnish (language); *adj* Finnish

**Finlande** *nf* Finland

**finnois** *nm* Finnish (language); *adj* Finnish

**fiole** *nf* phial; *sl* head, mug

**fioriture** *nf* flourish

**firme** *nf* firm

**fisc** *nm* Inland Revenue, *US* Internal Revenue

**fiston** *nm coll* son; youngster

**fistule** *nf* fistula

**five o'clock** *nm* afternoon tea

**fixage** *nm* fixing

**fixateur** *nm* fixer; fixing bath

**fixation** *nf* fixing, settling; fixation

**fixe** *nm* fixed salary; *adj* fixed, perma-

nent; regular; set (eyes); **beau ~** set fair; **idée ~** obsession; **regard ~** stare; *interj* eyes front!

**fixé** *adj* fixed, appointed; **être ~** know where one stands; know what to think

**fixement** *adv* fixedly; **regarder ~** stare (at)

**fixer** *vt* fix; fasten, make fast; stare at; determine, appoint; **~ qn sur qch** give s/o precise information about sth; **se ~** settle; **se ~ sur qch** decide on sth

**fixité** *nf* fixity; steadiness

**flacon** *nm* bottle, flask

**fla-fla** *nm coll* show; **faire du ~** show off

**flageller** *vt* scourge, flog, whip

**flageoler** *vi* shake, tremble (legs)

**flageolet** *nm* small kidney bean

**flagorner** *vt* toady to, fawn on

**flagorneur -euse** *n* toady

**flagrant** *adj* flagrant; **en ~ délit** red-handed, in the act

**flair** *nm* scent; flair

**flairer** *vt* scent, nose out; suspect

**Flamand -e** *n* Fleming

**flamand** *nm* Flemish (language); *adj* Flemish

**flamant** *nm* flamingo

**flambant** *adj* blazing, flaming; **~ neuf** brand new

**flambé** *adj coll* done for, sunk; *cul* flambé

**flambeau** *nm* torch; candlestick

**flambée** *nf* blaze; sudden upsurge, violent upsurge

**flamber** *vt* singe; set alight; *vi* burn, blaze, blaze up

**flamboyant** *adj* flaming, blazing; flamboyant, dazzling

**flamboyer** *vi* (7) flame, blaze

**flamme** *nf* flame; pennant; *lit + obs* passion; **retour de ~** backfire; flashback

**flan** *nm* baked tart; custard tart

**flanc** *nm* flank, side; **prêter le ~ à** lay oneself open to; **sur le ~** laid up; *coll* **tirer au ~** take things easy, swing the lead

**flancher** *vi* flinch, give way

**Flandre** *nf* Flanders

**flanelle** *nf* flannel; **~ de coton** flannelette

**flâner** *vi* saunter, loiter, hang about

**flânerie** *nf* loitering; stroll

**flâneur -euse** *n* loiterer, idler

**flanquer** *vt* flank; *coll* chuck, fling; **~ à la porte** sack, kick out

**flaque** *nf* puddle

**flash** *nm* (*pl* **flashes**) *phot* flash-lamp; short interview; short news item

**flasque** *adj* flabby, flaccid

**flatter** *vt* flatter; stroke, caress

**flatterie** *nf* flattery; caress

**flatteur -euse** *n* flatterer; *adj* flattering

**fléau** nm flail; plague, scourge, pest

**fléchage** nm signposting

**flèche** nf arrow; spire; **en ~ · dead straight**; very rapidly; at the forefront, trendy; **faire ~ de tout bois** use every possible means

**flécher** vt signpost, arrow

**fléchette** nf dart

**fléchir** vt bend; move to pity; vi bend, give way

**fléchissement** nm bending, giving way

**flegmatique** adj phlegmatic, stolid

**flegme** nm phlegm, coolness

**flemmard -e** n coll slacker, lazybones; adj coll slack, lazy

**flemmarder** vi coll slack, laze

**flemme** nf coll laziness; **avoir la ~** feel lazy; **tirer sa ~** slack, laze

**flétan** nm halibut

**flétri** adj withered, faded; tarnished (reputation)

**flétrir** vt wither, blight; corrupt; stigmatize, criticize; **se ~** wither, fade

**flétrissure** nf withering, fading; stigma, condemnation

**fleur** nf flower, blossom, bloom; **~ de l'âge** prime of life; coll **la ~ des pois** the cream, pick of the bunch; **à ~ de** on a level with; **à ~ de peau** on the surface; **à ~ de tête** prominent (eyes); **arriver comme une ~** drop in unexpectedly; coll **faire une ~ à qn** do s/o an unexpected favour, show s/o a kindness

**fleurer** vt smell of

**fleuret** nm foil

**fleuri** adj in blossom, bloom; adorned with flowers; flowery

**fleurir** vt (49) decorate with flowers; vi blossom, bloom; flourish

**fleuriste** n florist

**fleuve** nm river

**flibuster** vi filibuster

**flibustier** nm filibuster, swindler

**flic** nm coll policeman, cop

**flingot** nm sl rifle, gun

**flinguer** vt sl shoot at; kill; tear a strip off, tell off

**flipper** nm pin-table machine

**flirt** nm flirting; flirtation; boy-friend, girl-friend; friendly overtures

**flirter** vi flirt; make overtures

**flocon** nm flake; flock (wool)

**floconneux -euse** adj fleecy, fluffy

**flopée** nf coll large quantity, masses

**floraison** nf flowering, blooming

**floralies** nfpl flower show

**flore** nf flora

**floréal** nm hist eighth month of the French Republican calendar (April to May)

**florissant** adj flourishing, prosperous

**flot** nm wave; flood, stream; **à ~ afloat**; **à ~ s** in torrents

**flottaison** nf floating; **ligne de ~** water-line

**flottant** adj floating; full (garment); unsteady, wavering, undecided

**flotte** nf fleet, navy; float (fishing); sl water, rain

**flottement** nm flapping; wavering

**flotter** vi float, stream; waver; sl rain

**flotteur** nm float (fishing); ball (cistern)

**flottille** nf flotilla

**flou** adj blurred, hazy, indistinct; soft, fluffy (hair)

**flouer** vt coll swindle, dupe

**flouze** nm sl money

**fluctuer** vi fluctuate

**fluet -ette** adj slender, thin and delicate; tiny (voice)

**fluide** nm + adj fluid

**fluidité** nf fluidity, fluid nature

**fluor** nm fluorine

**fluorine** nf calcium fluoride

**fluorure** nm fluoride

**¹flûte** nf flute; long loaf; flute glass; coll **~ s** long thin legs, matchsticks; **petite ~** piccolo

**²flûte** interj damn!, bother!

**flûté** adj flute-like, piping (voice)

**flûteau** nm whistle, pipe

**flûter** vi play the flute

**flûtiste** n flautist, flute-player

**Fluviale** nf **la ~** the river police

**flux** nm flow, flood, flux

**fluxion** nf inflammation; math fluxion; **~ de poitrine** inflammation, congestion of the lungs

**foc** nm naut jib

**focaliser** vt concentrate

**fofolle** adj see **fou-fou**

**foi** nf faith; belief; confidence, trust; **ajouter ~ à** believe in; **de bonne (mauvaise) ~** in good (bad) faith; **digne de ~** trustworthy; **faire ~** be authoritative; **ma ~!** well!, indeed!; **profession de ~** profession of faith; electoral manifesto

**foie** nm liver; **crise de ~** bilious attack

**foin** nm hay; coll grass (marijuana); coll **faire du ~** kick up a row; **rhume des ~ s** hay fever

**foire** nf fair; coll rumpus

**foirer** vi sl misfire, fail; sl have the shits

**fois** nf time; **à la ~** at the same time; **deux ~** twice; **encore une ~** once more; **une ~** once

**foison** nf plenty, abundance; **à ~** in abundance

**foisonnement** nm abundance

**foisonner** vi abound; teem

**fol** adj see **fou** adj

**folâtre** adj playful, frisky

**folâtrer** *vi* gambol, frolic

**folichon -onne** *adj* playful, frisky; **pas ~** unexciting, dull

**folie** *nf* madness; folly; act of folly; craze

**folklore** *nm* folklore; *fig* nonsense, pretence

**folklorique** *adj* pertaining to folklore; *fig* amusing, crazy, absurd

**folle** *n + adj see* **fou**

**follet -ette** *adj* gay, frolicsome; **feu ~** will o' the wisp

**fomenter** *vt* foment, stir up

**foncé** *adj* dark, deep (colour)

**foncer** *vt* (4) sink; drive in; darken; *vi* grow darker; rush, dash

**fonceur -euse** *n fig* determined person

**foncier -ière** *adj* fundamental, basic; landed, of the land

**fonction** *nf* function; occupation; **en ~ de** in terms of; hand in hand with; **être ~ de** be dependent on

**fonctionnaire** *n* civil servant, official

**fonctionnariser** *vt* give the status of civil servant to

**fonctionnel -elle** *adj* functional

**fonctionnement** *nm* functioning, working

**fonctionner** *vi* function, work, run

**fond** *nm* bottom; bed (sea); back, far end (room); background; foundation; basis; essence; **~ de teint** make-up foundation; **à ~** thoroughly; **à ~ de train** at top speed; **article de ~** leading article; **au ~ (dans le ~)** basically; **course de ~** long-distance race; **de ~ en comble** from top to bottom

**fondamental** *adj* fundamental, basic; radical

**fondant** *nm cul* fondant; *metal* flux; *adj* melting; juicy

**fondateur -trice** *n* founder

**fondé** *nm* **~ de pouvoir** proxy; *adj* founded; well-founded; entitled

**fondement** *nm* base, foundation; *coll* bottom; **sans ~** groundless

**fonder** *vt* found; set up; establish; base; **se ~** rest, be based

**fonderie** *nf* foundry; smelting-works; smelting

**fondeur** *nm* founder; smelter

**fondre** *vt* smelt; cast; melt; dissolve; blend; *vi* melt; dissolve; **~ en larmes** burst into tears; **~ sur** pounce on; bear down upon; **se ~** melt; dissolve; blend

**fondrière** *nf* bog, quagmire

**fonds** *nm* land, estate; fund; stock-in-trade; *pl* funds, stocks; **~ de commerce** business, goodwill; **~ publics** government stocks

**fondu** *nm + adj rad* fade

**fondue** *nf* fondue (Swiss cheese dish); **~**

**bourguignonne** meat fondue

**fongus** *nm med* fungus

**fontaine** *nf* fountain; spring

¹**fonte** *nf* melting; *metal* smelting; cast-iron

²**fonte** *nf* holster

**fonts** *nmpl* font

**footballeur, footballer -euse** *n* football player

**footing** *nm* walking

**for** *nm* **~ intérieur** heart of hearts

**forage** *nm* boring, drilling

**forain** *nm* stall-keeper; hawker; *adj* itinerant; **fête ~e** fun-fair

**forçat** *nm* convict; **mener une vie de ~** lead a life of drudgery

**force** *nf* strength, power; violence; vigour; **~s** troops, forces; **~ de frappe** nuclear strike force; **~ lui fut de** he had no option but to; **à bout de ~s** exhausted; **à ~ de** by dint of, by means of; **à toute ~** at all costs; **de ~** forcibly, willy-nilly; **la ~ de l'âge** the prime of life; *adv* many, a lot of

**forcé** *adj* strained, forced

**forcément** *adv* necessarily, inevitably; of course

**forcené** *adj* frenzied, frantic; mad

**forcer** *vt* (4) force, compel; break open; storm; **se ~** force oneself; strain oneself

**forcing** *nm* sustained pressure

**forcir** *vi* put on weight; grow strong

**forer** *vt* drill; bore

**forestier -ière** *n* forester, ranger; *adj* forest, forestry

**foret** *nm* drill, brace-bit; gimlet

**forêt** *nf* forest

**foreuse** *nf* drill

¹**forfait** *nm* serious crime

²**forfait** *nm* forfeit; **déclarer ~** give up; *sp* scratch

³**forfait** *nm* contract; agreed price; **à ~** charter, contract, by contract; **voyage à ~** package-tour

**forfaitaire** *adj* contractual; **paiement ~** lump sum

**forfaiture** *nf* forfeiture; breach

**forfanterie** *nf* bragging

**forge** *nf* forge; smithy; ironworks

**forger** *vt* (3) forge; coin, invent

**forgeron** *nm* smith, blacksmith

**forgeur** *nm* forger, smith

**formaliser (se)** *v refl* take offence, take exception

**formaliste** *n* formalist; stickler for formality; *adj* formal, stiff

**formalité** *nf* form; formality

**formateur -trice** *n* creator; *adj* formative

**formation** *nf* formation; education; **~ professionnelle** vocational training

**forme** *nf* form, shape; pattern; formality; way of proceeding; mould; **dans les ~ s** according to protocol; **par ~ de** by way of; **pour la ~** for appearance's sake; **sous (la) ~ de** in the form of

**formel -elle** *adj* formal; strict; categorical

**former** *vt* form; shape, fashion; train, teach; **se ~** take shape; be formed

**formidable** *adj* formidable, fearful; *coll* terrific, great

**formulaire** *nm* form; collection of formulae

**formule** *nf* formula; recipe; form

**formuler** *vt* formulate; put into words; write (prescription)

**forniquer** *vi* fornicate

**fors** *prep lit + obs* save, except

**fort** *nm* strong man; stronghold; forte; height (season); **~ des Halles** market porter; **~ en thème** swot; hard-working person; *adj* strong; powerful; clever; stout; high (price, wind); hard (currency); large (sum); heavy (beard, rain); **~e tête** obstinate individual; *coll* **c'est un peu ~** it's a bit thick; **esprit ~** freethinker; contester; **se faire ~ de** undertake to; *adv* very, extremely; hard, strongly; loud(ly); **y aller ~** go hard at it; exaggerate, overdo

**forteresse** *nf* fortress, stronghold

**fortifiant** *nm + adj* tonic

**fortifier** *vt* fortify; strengthen, invigorate; **se ~** fortify oneself; grow stronger

**fortin** *nm* small fort

**fortuit** *adj* chance, accidental; casual

**fortune** *nf* fortune, (piece of) luck; chance; wealth; **dîner à la ~ du pot** take pot-luck

**fortuné** *adj* fortunate; well-to-do, rich

**forum** *nm hist* forum; *fig* place for public discussion; symposium

**fosse** *nf* hole, pit; grave; den (lions); *mot* inspection pit; **~ d'aisance** latrine; **~ septique** septic tank

**fossé** *nm* ditch, trench; moat

**fossette** *nf* dimple

**fossile** *nm* fossil

**fossoyer** *vt* (7) trench, ditch

**fossoyeur** *nm* grave-digger

**fou** (*f* **folle**) *nm* lunatic, madman (madwoman); jester, fool; bishop (chess); *adj* (*m* **fou, fol,** *f* **folle**) mad, crazy, insane; foolish, silly; terrific (success); large (crowd); out of control (vehicle); **~ de** crazy about

**¹foudre** *nm* large barrel

**²foudre** *nf* thunderbolt, lightning; **coup de ~** thunderbolt; love at first sight

**foudroyant** *adj* overwhelming; lightning; crushing, withering

**foudroyer** *vt* (7) strike (lightning); strike down; dumbfound, overwhelm

**fouet** *nm* whip, lash; whisk; **coup de ~** lash; stimulus; **heurter de plein ~** collide head-on with

**fouetter** *vt* whip, flog; whisk; *vi* lash, beat (rain); **avoir d'autres chats à ~** have other fish to fry

**fou-fou** (*f* **fofolle**) *adj* foolish, silly

**fougère** *nf* fern

**fougue** *nf* spirit, dash, fire

**fougueux -euse** *adj* spirited, fiery

**fouille** *nf* excavation; search

**fouiller** *vt + vi* excavate, dig; search, ransack; *sl* **va te faire ~ !** go to hell!

**fouillis** *nm* jumble, muddle

**fouine** *nf* marten

**fouiner** *vi coll* ferret, nose about

**fouir** *vt* dig

**foulard** *nm* foulard; scarf

**foule** *nf* crowd, throng; mob; **prendre un bain de ~** (of public figures) mix with the crowd, *US* press the flesh

**foulée** *nf* tread; stride; **~s** spoor; **dans la ~ de** in the wake of; **en une seule ~** in one go

**fouler** *vt* tread, trample on; crush; sprain (joint); full (cloth); **~ aux pieds** trample underfoot; *coll* **se ~** take trouble

**foulure** *nf* sprain, wrench

**four** *nm* oven, cooker; furnace; kiln; failure, flop; **faire (un) ~** be a flop

**fourbe** *n* cheat, swindler; *adj* deceitful, crafty

**fourberie** *nf* cheating; imposture; deceit

**fourbi** *nm coll* stuff, things, thing

**fourbir** *vt* polish, rub up

**fourbu** *adj* tired out; foundered (horse)

**fourche** *nf* fork; pitchfork; **en ~** forked

**fourcher** *vt* fork (soil, etc); *vi* fork; **la langue m'a fourché** I made a slip of the tongue

**fourchette** *nf* (table) fork; wishbone; range, bracket; **c'est une belle ~** he is a big eater

**fourchu** *adj* forked; cloven (hoof)

**¹fourgon** *nm* van, wagon; luggage van, *US* baggage car

**²fourgon** *nm* poker, rake

**fourgonner** *vt* poke, rake; *vi* poke the fire; *fig* poke about

**fourgonnette** *nf* light van

**fourmi** *nf* ant; **avoir des ~s** have pins and needles

**fourmilier** *nm* ant-eater

**fourmilière** *nf* ant-hill; *fig* swarm

**fourmillement** *nm* swarming; tingling, pins and needles

**fourmiller** *vi* swarm; tingle

**fournaise** *nf* furnace

**fourneau** *nm* stove; cooker, kitchen

range; bowl (pipe); **haut ~** blast-furnace

**fournée** *nf* batch

**fourni** *adj* well-stocked; thick; bushy

**fournil** *nm* bakehouse

**fourniment** *nm* kit, equipment

**fournir** *vt* furnish, supply, equip

**fournisseur -euse** *n* supplier, purveyor; tradesman

**fourniture** *nf* supplying; supplies, equipment

**fourrage** *nm* fodder; forage

**fourrager** *vt* ravage; *vi* forage; rummage

**fourragère** *nf* hay-wagon

**fourré** *nm* thicket; *adj* furry; wooded; stuffed, filled; **porter un coup ~ à qn** deal s/o a back-handed blow

**fourreau** *nm* sheath; scabbard; sheath-dress

**fourrer** *vt* line with fur; *cul* stuff; cram, shove, thrust; **se ~** thrust, stick oneself; *coll* **~ son nez dans** poke one's nose into

**fourre-tout** *nm* hold-all

**fourreur** *nm* furrier

**fourrier** *nm* quarter-master

**fourrière** *nf* pound

**fourrure** *nf* fur; *eng* lining

**fourvoiement** *nm* going astray

**fourvoyer** *vt* (7) lead astray, mislead; **se ~** go astray, blunder

**foutaise** *nf coll* nonsense, rot

¹**foutre** *nm vulg* sperm, spunk

²**foutre** *vt coll in all meanings* do; throw, chuck; give; **~ la paix à qn** leave s/o alone; **~ le camp** get out, go away; **se ~ de** make fun of, take the piss out of; **s'en ~** not give a damn

³**foutre** *interj vulg* bugger it!, fuck me!

**foutu** *adj coll in all meanings* bloody; done for; **mal ~** out of sorts, tired; badly dressed

¹**fox** *nm* fox-terrier

²**fox** *nm* fox-trot

**foyer** *nm* hearth, fire, fireplace; *fig* home, family; firebox (engine); furnace; focus; hotbed; seat (illness); lounge (hotel); **~ des artistes** green-room; **~ des étudiants** students' hostel; students' union; **verres à double ~** bifocal lenses

**frac** *nm* dress-coat

**fracas** *nm* crash; roar; din

**fracassant** *adj fig* resounding, sensational

**fracasser** *vt* shatter, smash

**fractionnaire** *adj* fractional; **nombre ~** improper fraction

**fractionnel -elle** *adj* divisive

**fracture** *nf* breaking; fracture

**fracturer** *vt* break open; force (lock); fracture

**fragile** *adj* fragile; frail; brittle

**fragilité** *nf* fragility; frailty; brittleness

**fragment** *nm* fragment, chip; snatch (song)

**fragmentaire** *adj* fragmentary

**fragmenter** *vt* fragment, divide

**frai** *nm* spawning; spawn; fry (fish)

**fraîchement** *adv* freshly; coolly; newly, recently

**fraîcheur** *nf* freshness; coolness; bloom

**fraîchir** *vi* freshen, turn cool

¹**frais** *nm* cool, coolness; **au ~** in a cool place; *adj (f* **fraîche***)* fresh, cool; new, recent; new-laid; wet (paint); *adv* newly, just

²**frais** *nmpl* expense, expenses; .charge, charges; cost, outlay; **~ de port** (transport) carriage (freight) charges; **en être pour ses ~** get nothing for one's pains; **faire les ~ de** bear the cost of; contribute most to (conversation); **menus ~** petty expenses; **rentrer dans ses ~** cover one's costs, get one's money back; **se mettre en ~** go to great expense

¹**fraise** *nf* strawberry; strawberry mark

²**fraise** *nf* ruff; *cul* crow (lamb, calf); wattle (fowl)

³**fraise** *nf* countersink; milling cutter; (dentist's) drill

**fraiser** *vt* frill; countersink; mill; drill (tooth)

**framboise** *nf* raspberry

**framboisé** *adj* raspberry-flavoured

**framboisier** *nm* raspberry cane

**Franc** *(f* **Franque***) n* Frank

¹**franc** *nm* Frankish (language); *adj (f* **franque***)* Frankish

²**franc** *(f* **franche***) adj* candid, frank; open, free; sincere, real; downright, arrant; clear; **~ de port** postage-free; **aller ~ jeu** go about things openly; **avoir son ~-parler** be outspoken; *sp* **coup ~** free kick; **jouer ~ jeu** play a straightforward game; play fair; act fairly; **parler ~** speak frankly

**Français -e** *n* Frenchman (French-woman)

**français** *nm* French (language); *adj* French

**franchement** *adv* frankly; boldly; downright

**franchir** *vt* jump over; cross; pass through; overcome (obstacle)

**franchise** *nf* frankness; freedom (city); exemption (from charges, duty, etc)

**Franciscain -e** *n* Franciscan

**franciscain** *adj* Franciscan

**franciser** *vt* gallicize

**franc-maçon** *nm (pl* **francs-maçons***)* Freemason

**franc-maçonnerie** *nf* freemasonry

**franco** *adv* carriage free, duty paid

**francophone** *adj* native French-speaking

**franc-parler** *nm* plain-speaking

**franc-tireur** *nm* (*pl* **francs-tireurs**) franc-tireur, sniper; loner

**frange** *nf* fringe

**franger** *vt* (3) fringe

**franglais** *nm* French language with excessive content of English vocabulary

**franquette** *nf* à la bonne ~ simply, without ceremony

**frappant** *adj* striking, impressive

¹**frappe** *nf* minting; striking; stamp; touch; **faute de** ~ typing error; misprint

²**frappe** *nf sl* scoundrel, bad lot

**frapper** *vt* strike, hit; mint (money); chill (drink); impose (tax); *vi* knock; ~ **du pied** stamp one's foot; ~ **juste** strike home; **se** ~ strike oneself; *coll* worry

**frappeur -euse** *n* striker; tapper, stamper; *adj* **esprit** ~ rapping spirit

**frasque** *nf* escapade, prank

**fraternel -elle** *adj* fraternal, brotherly

**fraterniser** *vi* fraternize

**fraternité** *nf* fraternity, brotherhood

**fratricide** *adj* fratricidal

**fraude** *nf* fraud, deceit, deception; **passer en** ~ smuggle in, out

**frauder** *vt* + *vi* cheat, swindle

**fraudeur -euse** *n* defrauder; smuggler; *adj* fraudulent; bogus

**frauduleux -euse** *adj* fraudulent

**frayer** *vt* (7) open up, clear; *vi* spawn (fish); associate; **se** ~ **un chemin** clear a way for oneself

**frayeur** *nf* fright, dread, terror

**fredaine** *nf* prank, escapade

**fredonner** *vt* + *vi* hum

**freezer** *nm* ice-compartment

**frégate** *nf* frigate

**frein** *nm* brake; bit, bridle; curb, restraint; moderating influence; **donner un coup de** ~ apply the brake, put on the brakes; **mettre un** ~ **à** curb, bridle; **ronger son** ~ champ the bit

**freinage** *nm* braking

**freiner** *vt* brake; moderate; curb; slow down; *vi* brake

**frelater** *vt* adulterate

**frêle** *adj* frail, weak

**frelon** *nm* hornet

**freluquet** *nm coll* whipper-snapper; young puppy

**frémir** *vi* quiver, tremble, shudder; rustle

**frémissement** *nm* quivering, trembling, shuddering; rustling

**frêne** *nm* ash-tree

**frénésie** *nf* frenzy, madness

**frénétique** *adj* frantic, frenzied

**fréquemment** *adv* frequently

**fréquence** *nf* frequency, rate

**fréquent** *adj* frequent, rapid

**fréquentation** *nf* frequenting

**fréquenter** *vt* frequent; visit; associate with; court; *vi* visit; be courting

**frère** *nm* brother; friar

**fresque** *nf* fresco

**fret** *nm* freight, cargo

**fréter** *vt* (6) freight; charter; fit out (ship); hire (means of transport)

**frétillant** *adj* wriggling; frisky

**frétiller** *vi* wag; wriggle, fidget

**fretin** *nm* fry (fish); *fig* rubbish

**friable** *adj* crumbly

**friand** *adj* dainty; ~ **de** partial to

**friandise** *nf* titbit, delicacy

**fric** *nm sl* money, lolly

**fricassée** *nf* fricassee, hash

**fricasser** *vt* fricassee

**fric-frac** *nm sl* burglary

**friche** *nf* waste land, fallow land

**frichti** *nm coll* dish; meal; grub

**fricot** *nm coll* stew, dish

**fricoter** *vt coll* cook, stew; *fig* plot; *vi coll* cook, stew; *fig* be engaged in shady business, traffic

**fricoteur -euse** *n coll* trafficker, shady businessman (-woman)

**friction** *nf* friction; massage; *sp* rub-down

**frictionner** *vt* rub; give a rub-down to; massage

**frigidaire** *nm* refrigerator

**frigide** *adj* frigid

**frigidité** *nf* frigidity

**frigo** *nm coll* fridge, *US* ice-box; *coll* frozen meat

**frigorifier** *vt* chill, freeze

**frigorifique** *adj* refrigerating, chilling

**frileux -euse** *adj* sensitive to the cold, delicate

**frimaire** *nm hist* third month of the French Republican calendar (November to December)

**frimas** *nm* hoar-frost

**frime** *nf coll* sham, pretence, show

**frimer** *vi* bluff

**frimousse** *nf coll* face (*usu* child or girl)

**fringale** *nf coll* tremendous appetite

**fringant** *adj* frisky; smart, dashing

**fringuer** *vt sl* rig out, kit

**fringues** *nfpl sl* gear, rig-out

**friper** *vt* crumple, rumple; wrinkle; **se** ~ get crumpled; wrinkle

**fripier -ière** *n* old-clothes dealer

**fripon -onne** *n* rogue, rascal; minx; *adj* roguish

**friponnerie** *nf* (piece of) roguery

**fripouille** *nf coll* rogue, rotter

**frire** *vt* + *vi* (51) fry

frise *nf* frieze

frisé *adj* curly, frizzy

friser *vt* curl, frizz; graze; border on, verge on; *vi* curl, be curly

¹frison *nm* curl, wave

²frison -onne *adj* Friesian

frisquet -ette *adj* nippy, cold

frisson *nm* shiver, shudder; thrill

frissonnement *nm* shivering; quivering

frissonner *vi* shiver, shudder; quiver

frit *adj* fried; *coll* done for; **(pommes) frites** chips, French fried, *US* French fries

friteuse *nf* deep-fryer

friture *nf* frying; fried fish; frying fat; crackling (radio)

frivole *adj* frivolous; trifling

frivolité *nf* frivolity; trifle

froc *nm* cowl, habit, monk's gown; *sl* trousers

froid *nm* cold, coldness; **avoir ~** be cold; **battre ~ à** cold-shoulder; **coup de ~** chill; **être en ~** be on bad terms; **industrie du ~** refrigeration business; **ne pas avoir ~ aux yeux** be fearless; **prendre ~** catch cold; *adj* cold, chilly, cool, frigid; reserved, distant

froideur *nf* coldness, chilliness, frigidity; reserve

froissement *nm* rumpling; rustling; bruising; slight, annoyance

froisser *vt* rumple; bruise; offend, hurt; **se ~** get bruised; take offence

frôlement *nm* grazing, brushing

frôler *vt* graze, touch lightly, brush against; narrowly escape

fromage *nm* cheese; *fig* cushy job; **~ de tête** brawn, *US* headcheese

fromager -ère *n* cheese-maker; *adj* cheese

fromagerie *nf* cheese-factory, cheese-maker's

froment *nm* wheat

fronce *nf* crease; gather

froncement *nm* contraction, puckering; **~ des sourcils** frown

froncer *vt* (4) pucker, wrinkle; gather; **~ les sourcils** frown, scowl

frondaison *nf* foliation, foliage

fronde *nf* catapult, sling

fronder *vt* sling, catapult; criticize, sneer at

frondeur -euse *n* slinger; critic; fault-finder, grouser; *adj* fault-finding, irreverent

front *nm* forehead, brow; face; cheek, effrontery; **de ~** abreast; **faire ~ à** face up to

frontal *nm* headband; frontal bone

frontalier -ière *n* borderer; one who daily crosses a frontier to get to work; *adj* frontier

frontière *nf* frontier, border, boundary

frontispice *nm* frontispiece; title page

fronton *nm* fronton, pediment

frottée *nf* *coll* pasting, thrashing; bread rubbed with garlic

frottement *nm* rubbing; chafing; friction

frotter *vt* rub, polish; chafe; strike (match); **se ~** rub oneself; associate; **~ les oreilles à qn** box s/o's ears

frottis *nm* rubbing; *med* smear

frottoir *nm* polisher

frou-frou *nm* rustle, swish

froussard *adj* *sl* cowardly

frousse *nf* *sl* funk

fructidor *nm* *hist* twelfth month of the French Republican calendar (August to September)

fructifier *vi* bear fruit, fructify

fructueux -ueuse *adj* fruitful, profitable

frugalité *nf* frugality

fruit *nm* fruit; advantage, benefit; **~ sec** dried fruit; *fig* failure; **~s de mer** sea-food

fruité *adj* fruity

fruiterie *nf* fruit trade; fruiterer's, greengrocer's shop

fruitier -ière *n* fruiterer, greengrocer; *adj* fruit-bearing, fruit

frusques *nfpl* *sl* togs, clothes, gear

fruste *adj* worn, rough, coarse

frustrer *vt* frustrate; **~ qn de qch** deprive s/o of sth

fugace *adj* fleeting, transient

fugitif -ive *n* + *adj* fugitive

fugue *nf* fugue; *coll* flight; *coll* escapade

fuir *vt* (52) run away from, avoid, shun; *vi* run away, flee; leak

fuite *nf* flight, escape; leak, leakage; **~ des cerveaux** brain-drain; *pol* **~ en avant** precipitate action

fulgurant *adj* flashing, sharp; lightning

fuligineux -euse *adj* sooty; murky

fulmicoton *nm* gun-cotton

fulminer *vt* fulminate; *vi* fulminate, inveigh

¹fumage *nm* smoking; curing

²fumage *nm* dunging, manure-spreading

fumant *adj* smoking; *sl* smashing

fume-cigarette *nm* *invar* cigarette-holder

fumée *nf* smoke, steam; fumes

¹fumer *vt* smoke; cure; *vi* smoke, steam; fume

²fumer *vt* manure

fumet *nm* aroma; bouquet (wine)

fumeur -euse *n* smoker; curer; *nm* *coll* smoker, smoking-compartment

fumeux -euse *adj* smoky; vague

fumier *nm* dung, manure; dunghill; *sl* bastard, swine

fumiger *vt* (3) fumigate

**fumiste** *nm coll* fraud, hoaxer; heating
  engineer
**fumisterie** *nf coll* fraud, hoax; heating
  contractor's business
**fumoir** *nm* smoking-room; smoke-
  house
**funambule** *n* tight-rope walker
**funambulesque** *adj* fantastic, grotesque
**funèbre** *adj* funeral; funereal, gloomy
**funérailles** *nfpl* funeral; obsequies
**funéraire** *adj* funeral
**funeste** *adj* fatal, deadly; baleful
**funiculaire** *nm* funicular railway
**fur** *nm* au ~ et à mesure gradually,
  progressively
**furet** *nm* ferret; *fig* busybody; pass the
  slipper (game)
**fureter** *vi* (5) ferret; nose about
**fureteur -euse** *n* ferreter; *fig* Nosy
  Parker, busybody; *adj* prying
**fureur** *nf* fury, rage; frenzy, passion;
  **faire** ~ be all the rage
**furibond** *adj* furious, wild
**furie** *nf* fury, rage; passion
**furieux -ieuse** *adj* furious, mad, wild
**furoncle** *nm* boil
**furtif -ive** *adj* furtive, stealthy
**fusain** *nm* spindletree; charcoal sketch;
  charcoal pencil
**fuseau** *nm* spindle; distaff; ~ **horaire**
  time zone; *coll* **jambes en** ~ spindly
  legs; **pantalon** ~ tapered trousers, ski-
  trousers
¹**fusée** *nf* fuse; rocket; ~ **de rires** ripple
  of laughter; ~ **éclairante** flare; ~
  **gigogne** multi-stage rocket; **avion à** ~
  rocket-propelled aircraft

²**fusée** *nf* spindle
**fusée-porteuse** *nf* (*pl* **fusées-porteuses**)
  first-stage rocket
**fuselé** *adj* tapering, streamlined
**fuseler** *vt* (5) taper
**fuser** *vi* fuse, melt, run; burst out
  (laughter)
**fusible** *nm* fuse; fuse-wire
**fusil** *nm* rifle, gun; steel (tinder-box);
  whetstone; **coup de** ~ shot; *coll* very
  high charge (hotel, restaurant)
**fusilier** *nm* fusilier; ~ **marin** marine
**fusillade** *nf* fusillade; execution by
  shooting
**fusiller** *vt* shoot, execute
**fusil-mitrailleur** *nm* (*pl* **fusils-mitrail-
  leurs**) light machine-gun
**fusion** *nf* fusion, melting; merger
**fusionner** *vt* + *vi* merge, amalgamate
**fustiger** *vt* (3) flog, thrash
**fût** *nm* stock (gun); stem (tree); shaft
  (column); cask
**futaie** *nf* forest, wood
**futaille** *nf* cask, barrel
**futé** *adj coll* sharp, crafty
**futile** *adj* futile, trifling, trivial
**futilité** *nf* futility; triviality
**futur -e** *n* future husband, future wife;
  *nm gramm* future; *adj* future
**futurisme** *nm* futurism
**futuriste** *adj* futuristic
**futurologie** *nf* futurology
**futurologue** *n* futurologist
**fuyant** *adj* fleeing, fleeting; receding;
  shifty (eyes)
**fuyard -e** *n* fugitive, deserter

# G

**gabardine** *nf* raincoat, gaberdine
**gabare** *nf* lighter; barge; drag-net
**gabarier** *nm* lighterman
**gabarit** *nm* model; mould; gauge
**gabelle** *nf ar* salt-tax
**gabelou** *nm coll* customs-officer
**gabier** *nm* topman
¹**gâche** *nf* staple; wall-hook
²**gâche** *nf* trowel; *cul* spatula
**gâcher** *vt* mix (mortar); botch, bungle,
  spoil

**gâchette** *nf* trigger
**gâchis** *nm* wet mortar; mud; *fig* mess
**gaélique** *nm* Gaelic (language); *adj*
  Gaelic
**gaffe** *nf* boat-hook, gaff; *coll* blunder,
  bloomer; *coll* sentry-duty; *sl* **faire** ~
  be on the look out
**gaffer** *vt* hook, gaff; *vi* blunder, drop a
  brick, *US* pull a boner
**gaffeur -euse** *n coll* blunderer
**gaga** *nm* dodderer; *adj* doddering, senile

**gage** nm pawn, pledge; deposit, security; forfeit; stake (gambling); ~s wages, pay; **mettre en** ~ pawn

**gager** vt (3) wager, bet; stake; hire, engage; pay wages to

**gageur -euse** n better, wagerer

**gageure** nf wager, bet; challenge

**gagnant -e** n winner; adj winning

**gagne-pain** nm invar livelihood, daily bread; breadwinner

**gagner** vt gain, earn; win; reach, arrive at; win over; overtake; vi gain; improve; spread; **se** ~ be catching

**gai** adj gay, merry, jolly, cheerful

**gaieté** nf gaiety, cheerfulness, mirth

¹**gaillard** nm naut castle; ~ **d'arrière** quarter-deck; ~ **d'avant** forecastle

²**gaillard** nm fellow, chap; adj strong, jolly, merry; spicy, risky

**gaillarde** nf wench, lively girl

**gaillardise** nf jollity, liveliness; risky story

**gain** nm gain, profit; earnings; winnings

**gaine** nf sheath; case; corset, girdle

**gainer** vt sheathe

**gala** nm gala, fête; **en grand** ~ in state; **habit de** ~ full dress

**galamment** adv gallantly, courteously; gracefully

**galant** nm ladies' man; sweetheart; adj attentive to women; gallant, courteous; elegant, gay; ~ **homme** man of honour; **femme** ~e courtesan

**galanterie** nf politeness; gallantry; love affair

**galbe** nm curve, contour

**gale** nf scabies; itch; mange; scab; sl shrew

**galère** nf galley; **qu'allait-il faire dans cette** ~? what was he doing there?; **vogue la** ~! let's risk it!

**galerie** nf gallery; arcade; mot roof-rack

**galérien** nm galley-slave, convict

**galet** nm pebble, shingle; roller

**galetas** nm garret, hovel

**galette** nf cake; ship's biscuit; coll lolly, dough

**galeux -euse** adj itchy; scabby; mangy; **brebis galeuse** black sheep

¹**Galilée** nm Galileo

²**Galilée** nf Galilaea, Galilee

**galimatias** nm nonsense, gibberish; rigmarole

**Galles** nfpl **pays de** ~ Wales

**gallicisme** nm gallicism

**Gallois -e** n Welshman, Welshwoman

**gallois** nm Welsh (language); adj Welsh

**galoche** nf clog; galosh, US rubber

**galon** nm braid; stripe

**galonner** vt trim with braid, lace; braid

**galop** nm gallop; **au grand** ~ at full gallop; **au petit** ~ at a canter

**galoper** vi gallop

**galopin** nm errand-boy; urchin

**galvaniser** vt galvanize; stimulate

**galvanoplastie** nf electroplating

**galvauder** vt coll botch; sully, dishonour; **se** ~ sully one's name

**gambade** nf gambol, caper

**gambader** vi gambol, caper, romp

**gamelle** nf mess-tin, dixie

**gamin** nm boy, urchin, youngster

**gamine** nf girl, hoyden, gamine

**gamme** nf gamut, scale, range

**gammée** adj f **croix** ~ swastika

**ganache** nf lower jaw (horse); coll booby, blockhead

**gandin** nm dandy, US dude

**gangrène** nf gangrene; fig corruption

**gangrener** vt (6) gangrene; mortify; corrupt

**ganse** nf braid; piping; loop

**gant** nm glove; gauntlet

**ganterie** nf glove-trade; glove-factory; glove-shop

**gantier -ière** n glover

**garage** nm garage; parking, shunting; **voie de** ~ siding

**garagiste** nm garage proprietor; garage mechanic

**garant -e** n guarantor, surety; guarantee, bail; **se porter** ~ **de** vouch for

**garantie** nf guarantee; security; pledge

**garantir** vt guarantee; vouch for; insure; fig protect

**garce** nf sl bitch

**garçon** nm boy, lad; young man, fellow; bachelor; waiter, steward; ~ **de bureau** office messenger; ~ **d'honneur** best man

**garçonne** nf bachelor girl

**garçonnet** nm little boy

**garçonnière** nf bachelor apartment

**garde** nm guard; guardsman; keeper; watchman; ~ **champêtre** country policeman; nf guard, defence; keeping, charge; watch; nurse; flyleaf, endpaper; hilt (sword); ~ **à vous!** look out!; **prendre** ~ beware, be careful; **prendre** ~ **à** take good care to; **prendre** ~ **de** be careful not to

**garde-à-vous** nm **au** ~ at attention

**garde-barrière** nm (pl **gardes-barrières**) gatekeeper at level-crossing

**garde-boue** nm invar mudguard, US fender

**garde-chasse** nm (pl **gardes-chasses**) gamekeeper

**garde-corps** nm invar handrail; naut life-line

**garde-côte(s)** nm (pl **garde(s)-côtes**) coastguard vessel

**garde-feu** nm (pl ~ or **garde-feux**) fireguard; fender

**garde-fou** *nm invar* parapet; handrail
**garde-frein** *nm* (*pl* **gardes-freins**) brakesman
**garde-malade** *n* (*pl* ~ or **gardes-malades**) nurse
**garde-manger** *nm invar* larder, pantry; meat-safe
**garde-meuble** *nm invar* furniture store-house
**garde-nappe** *nm* (*pl* **gardes-nappes**) table-mat
**garde-pêche** *nm invar* water bailiff, river-keeper
**garde-port** *nm* (*pl* **gardes-ports**) harbour-master
**garder** *vt* guard, defend; look after; keep, preserve; nurse; observe, respect; stay in; **se** ~ protect oneself; **se** ~ **de** beware of; refrain from; take care not to
**garde-robe** *nf* wardrobe
**gardeur -euse** *n* keeper, minder
**gardien -ienne** *n* guardian; keeper; warder; caretaker; attendant; goalkeeper; ~ **de la paix** policeman; *adj* **ange** ~ guardian angel
**gardiennage** *nm* caretaking; looking after children
¹**gare** *interj* look out!, take care!; **sans crier** ~ without warning
²**gare** *nf* station; ~ **de triage** marshalling yard; ~ **maritime** harbour-station; ~ **routière** bus station
**garenne** *nf* warren
**garer** *vt* shunt; garage; park; **se** ~ shunt; pull to one side; park; take cover
**gargariser (se)** *v refl* gargle
**gargote** *nf* cheap eating-house, cook shop
**gargouille** *nf* gargoyle
**gargouiller** *vi* rumble, gurgle
**gargouillis** *nm* gurgling
**garnement** *nm coll* **mauvais** ~ scamp, rogue
**garni** *nm* furnished room(s); *adj* furnished; garnished (with vegetables); well-filled
**garnir** *vt* furnish, stock, fill; garnish, trim
**garnison** *nf* garrison
**garniture** *nf* fittings, furnishings; trimmings; lagging; *cul* garnishing; packing; *mot* lining
**garrot** *nm* tongue (saw); *med* tourniquet; garrotte
**garrotter** *vt* pinion; garrotte
**gars** *nm coll* lad, young fellow
**Gascogne** *nf* Gascony; **Golfe de** ~ Bay of Biscay
**Gascon -onne** *n* Gascon; *fig* boaster, braggart; **histoire de** ~ tall story

**gascon -onne** *adj* Gascon
**gasconnade** *nf* boasting, bragging; boast, tall story
**gas-oil** *nm* diesel oil
**gaspiller** *vt* waste, squander
**gaspilleur -euse** *n* + *adj* spendthrift
**gastrique** *adj* gastric; **embarras** ~ stomach upset
**gastrite** *nf* gastritis
**gastro-entérite** *nf* gastro-enteritis
**gastronomie** *nf* gastronomy
**gastronomique** *adj* gastronomic
**gâteau** *nm* cake, tart; ~ **de miel** honeycomb; ~ **de riz** rice-pudding; ~ **des Rois** Twelfth-Night cake; ~ **sec** biscuit; **papa** ~ doting parent
**gâter** *vt* spoil, damage, injure; taint; **se** ~ deteriorate, spoil, be spoiled
**gâterie** *nf* over-indulgence, spoiling; ~ **s** goodies, dainties
**gâteux -euse** *n* dotard, dodderer; *adj* senile, doddering
**gâtisme** *nm* senile decay, dotage
**gauche** *nf* left; *adj* left; awkward, clumsy
**gaucher -ère** *n* left-handed person; *adj* left-handed
**gaucherie** *nf* awkwardness, clumsiness
**gauchir** *vi* warp, buckle
**gauchisant** *adj* of leftist tendencies
**gauchisme** *nm* leftism
**gauchiste** *n* + *adj* leftist
**gaudriole** *nf coll* broad joke
**gaufre** *nf cul* waffle
**gaufrer** *vt* crimp, goffer; emboss; corrugate
**gaufrette** *nf* wafer
**gaufrier** *nm* waffle-iron
**Gaule** *nf* Gaul
**gaule** *nf* long pole; switch; fishing-rod
**gauler** *vt* knock down (fruit) from tree
**gaullisme** *nm* Gaullism
**gaulliste** *n* Gaullist
**Gaulois -e** *n* Gaul
**gaulois** *nm* Gallic (language); *adj* Gallic; *fig* racy, spicy
**gauloise** *nf* popular brand of French cigarette
**gausser (se)** *v refl coll* laugh, make fun
**gave** *nm* mountain stream, torrent (in Pyrenees)
**gaver** *vt* cram, stuff; **se** ~ gorge
**gavroche** *nm* urchin, street-arab
**gaz** *nm* gas; wind; ~ **hilarant** laughing-gas
**gaze** *nf* gauze
¹**gazer** *vt* cover with gauze; veil; tone down
²**gazer** *vt* gas; *vi coll* go very fast, go like a bomb
**gazette** *nf* gazette, newspaper; *fig* gossip
**gazeux -euse** *adj* gaseous; aerated, fizzy

**gazier** nm gas-fitter
**gazoduc** nm gas pipeline
**gazogène** nm gas-generator; gazogene; adj gas-producing; aerating
**gazomètre** nm gasometer
**gazon** nm grass; turf; lawn
**gazouillement** nm twittering, chirping; babbling (brook); prattling (child)
**gazouiller** vi twitter, chirp; babble; prattle
**geai** nm jay
**géant -e** n giant(ess); adj giant, gigantic
**geignard -e** n whiner, sniveller; adj whining, querulous
**geindre** vi (55) whine, complain; snivel
**gel** nm frost; freezing; blocking, stopping
**gélatineux -euse** adj gelatinous
**gelé** adj frozen; frostbitten
**gelée** nf frost; jelly
**geler** vt (5) freeze; block; vi freeze, become frozen
**gelure** nf frostbite
**Gémeaux** nmpl Gemini
**gémir** vi groan, moan, wail
**gémissement** nm groan(ing), moan(ing), wail(ing)
**gemme** nf gem; resin; bud; **sel ~** rock-salt
**gemmer** vi bud
**gênant** adj inconvenient, in the way; embarrassing, awkward
**gencive** nf gum
**gendarme** nm policeman
**gendarmerie** nf constabulary; police barracks
**gendre** nm son-in-law
**gêne** nf embarrassment; difficulty, trouble; discomfort; financial straits; **sans ~** brazen
**généalogie** nf genealogy, pedigree
**généalogique** adj genealogical, family
**gêner** vt cramp, constrict; embarrass; inconvenience, trouble; **être gêné** be short of money; **se ~** inconvenience oneself, put oneself out; be shy, stand on ceremony
**général** nm general; **~ de brigade** brigadier(-general); **~ de division** major-general; adj general
¹**générale** nf general's wife
²**générale** nf theat dress-rehearsal
**généraliser** vt generalize; **se ~** become general, spread
**généralissime** nm generalissimo, commander-in-chief
**généraliste** n general practitioner
**généralité** nf generality
**générateur -trice** n generator, dynamo; adj generating, generative
**généreux -euse** adj generous
**générique** nm credits; adj generic

**générosité** nf generosity
**genèse** nf genesis, origin
**genêt** nm bot broom
**génétique** nf genetics; adj genetic
**gêneur -euse** n intruder, spoilsport
**Genève** nf Geneva
**genévrier** nm juniper
**génial** adj inspired, brilliant
**génie** nm genius; spirit; mil engineers; **~ civil** civil engineering
**genièvre** nm juniper; gin
**génisse** nf heifer
**genou** nm knee
**genre** nm kind, sort; genus, type; gender; style; form; **le ~ humain** the human race, mankind; **se donner du ~** put on airs
**gens** npl people, folk; servants; **~ de bien** honest folk; **droit des ~** law of nations; **jeunes ~** young people; young men
**gent** nf ar race, tribe
**gentiane** nf gentian
¹**gentil** nm gentile
²**gentil -ille** adj nice; kind; amiable, pleasing; ar noble, gentle
**gentilhomme** nm (pl gentilshommes) nobleman
**gentillesse** nf graciousness; kindness; politeness; **~s** nice things
**gentiment** adv nicely; politely
**géographe** n geographer
**géographie** nf geography
**géographique** adj geographical
**geôle** nf ar gaol, prison
**geôlier -ière** n ar gaoler, warder
**géologie** nf geology
**géologue** n geologist
**géométrie** nf geometry
**géométrique** adj geometrical
**gérance** nf management; managership; board of directors
**gérant -e** n director, manager(ess); managing-director
**gerbe** nf sheaf (wheat); spray (flowers, water); shower (sparks)
**gercer** vt + vi (4) crack; chap (hands)
**gerçure** nf crack; chap (hands)
**gérer** vt (6) manage, administer
**gériatrie** nf geriatrics
**gériatrique** adj geriatric
**germain** adj first (cousin)
**germanique** adj Germanic
**germe** nm germ; eye (potato); fig seed; **dans le ~** in the bud
**germer** vi germinate; sprout, shoot
**germinal** nm hist seventh month of the French Republican calendar (March to April)
**gérondif** nm gerundive
**gérontologie** nf gerontology
**gésier** nm gizzard

**gésir** *vi* (53) lie; **ci-gît** here lies

¹**geste** *nm* gesture, motion, movement, wave

²**geste** *nf* **chanson de ~** medieval verse chronicle; **faits et ~s** exploits

**gesticuler** *vi* gesticulate

**gestion** *nf* management, administration

**gibecière** *nf* game-bag; satchel

**gibelotte** *nf cul* fricassee of rabbit or hare

**giberne** *nf* wallet; pouch

**gibet** *nm* gibbet, gallows

**gibier** *nm* game; **~ de potence** gallows bird

**giboulée** *nf* sudden shower

**giboyeux -euse** *adj* abounding in game

**gicler** *vi* splash, spurt

**gicleur** *nm* nozzle, jet

**gifle** *nf* slap in the face; box on the ear

**gifler** *vt* slap, cuff

**gigantesque** *adj* gigantic

**gigantisme** *nm* over-development, over-expansion

**gigogne** *nf* **fusée ~** multi-stage rocket; **lit ~** truckle-bed; **table ~** nest of tables

**gigot** *nm* leg of mutton or lamb

**gigoter** *vi coll* kick; jig

**gigue** *nf* hind leg, haunch; *mus* jig

**gilet** *nm* waistcoat, *US* vest; **~ de corps** singlet; **~ de sauvetage** life-jacket

**gingembre** *nm* ginger

**gingivite** *nf* gingivitis

**girafe** *nf* giraffe

**giration** *nf* gyration

**giratoire** *adj* gyratory; **sens ~** traffic flow at roundabout

**girofle** *nm* clove

**giroflée** *nf* wallflower

**giron** *nm* lap; *fig* bosom

**girouette** *nf* weathercock

**gisant** *nm* recumbent effigy; *adj* lying, recumbent

**gisement** *nm* layer, stratum, vein

**gitan -e** *n + adj* gipsy

**gîte** *nm* resting-place, lodging; lair (deer); form (hare); stratum, deposit

**gîter** *vt* lodge, shelter; *vi* lodge, lie

**givre** *nm* hoarfrost

**glabre** *adj* smooth, hairless, clean-shaven

**glaçage** *nm* glazing; *cul* icing, frosting

**glace** *nf* ice; ice-cream; icing; glass, plate-glass; mirror; window (vehicle); flaw

**glacé** *adj* frozen; icy; iced (drinks); chilled (wine); glossy; glazed

**glacer** *vt* (4) freeze; ice; chill; glaze

**glaciaire** *adj* glacial

**glacial** *adj* icy, frozen, glacial

**glacier** *nm* glacier; ice-cream man

**glacière** *nf* ice-box, freezer; *ar* ice-house;

**cette chambre est une ~** it's ice-cold in this room

**glacis** *nm* slope; glaze

**glaçon** *nm* block of ice; ice-floe; icicle; ice-cube; *fig* cold fish

**gladiateur** *nm* gladiator

**glaïeul** *nm* gladiolus

**glaire** *nf* white of egg; mucus, phlegm

**glaise** *nf* clay, loam

**glaisière** *nf* clay-pit

**glaive** *nm ar + lit* sword

**glanage** *nm* gleaning

**gland** *nm* acorn; tassel; *anat* glans

**glande** *nf* gland

**glaner** *vt* glean

**glaneur -euse** *n* gleaner

**glapir** *vi* yelp, yap; bark (fox)

**glas** *nm* knell

**glauque** *adj* glaucous, sea-green; bluish-green

**glèbe** *nf lit* land, soil

**glissade** *nf* slip, slide; sliding; glide (dancing)

**glissant** *adj* sliding; slippery

**glissement** *nm* sliding, slipping; gliding

**glisser** *vt* slip; insinuate; *vi* slip, slide; glide; *mot* skid; **~ sur** glance off; not dwell upon; **se ~** creep, steal

**glisseur -euse** *n* downhill skier

**glissière** *nf* groove, guide; **à ~s** sliding

**glissoir** *nm* slide

**glissoire** *nf* slide (ice)

**global** *adj* total, inclusive, aggregate

**globe** *nm* globe, sphere, orb, ball

**globulaire** *adj* globular

**globule** *nm* corpuscle

**gloire** *nf* glory, fame; pride; halo; **se faire ~ de** glory in

**glorieux -ieuse** *n* braggart, boaster; *adj* glorious, proud; vain, conceited

**glorifier** *vt* glorify; **se ~** boast

**gloriole** *nf* vainglory, vanity

**glose** *nf* gloss, commentary; criticism

**gloser** *vt* gloss; *vi* criticize, carp

**glossaire** *nm* glossary

**glotte** *nf* glottis

**glouglou** *nm* gurgle, gurgling; gobbling (turkey)

**glouglouter** *vi* gurgle; gobble (turkey)

**glousser** *vi* cluck; chuckle

**glouton -onne** *n* glutton; *adj* greedy, gluttonous

**gloutonnerie** *nf* gluttony

**glu** *nf* bird-lime

**gluant** *adj* sticky, gluey

**glutineux -euse** *adj* glutinous

**glycine** *nf* wistaria

**gnangnan, gnian-gnian** *n invar coll* wet (person); *adj invar* wet, feeble, namby-pamby

**gniole, gnôle** *nf sl* brandy

**go** *adv* **tout de** ~ straight off; all of a sudden

**goal** *nm* goal; goalkeeper

**gobelet** *nm* goblet, cup; **verre** ~ tumbler

**gobe-mouches** *nm invar orni* fly-catcher; *bot* fly-trap; *fig* ninny

**gober** *vt* swallow, gulp down; like enormously; ~ **des mouches** stand gaping

**gobeur -euse** *n coll* simpleton, sucker

**godasses** *nfpl sl* boots

**godet** *nm* mug, cup; flare (cloth), pucker

**godiche** *adj coll* clumsy; stupid, silly

**godille** *nf* stern-oar; scull

**godiller** *vi* scull

**godillot** *nm sl* heavy shoe; *pol* fanatical Gaullist

**goéland** *nm* seagull

**goélette** *nf* schooner

**goémon** *nm* seaweed

**¹gogo** *nm sl* mug, sucker

**²gogo (à)** *adj phr* galore

**goguenard -e** *n* mocker, jeerer; *adj* bantering, mocking

**goinfre** *nm* glutton; *adj* gluttonous

**goinfrer (se)** *v refl coll* gorge

**goinfrerie** *nf* gluttony, guzzling

**golf** *nm* golf; **culottes de** ~ plus-fours

**golfe** *nm* gulf, bay

**gomme** *nf* gum; rubber, eraser

**gommer** *vt* rub out; attenuate; eradicate

**gommeux** *nm coll* swell, *US* dude; *adj* (*f* **-euse**) gummy, sticky

**gond** *nm* hinge; *coll* **sortir de ses** ~s fly off the handle

**gondolant** *adj sl* screamingly funny

**gondole** *nf* gondola

**gondoler** *vi* warp, buckle; **se** ~ warp, buckle; *sl* split one's sides laughing

**gonflage** *nm* inflation

**gonflement** *nm* inflation, swelling

**gonfler** *vt* inflate, swell, blow up; *coll mot* hot up; *vi* **se** ~ swell, become inflated, become distended

**gonfleur** *nm* air-pump, inflator

**gordien** *adj* Gordian

**goret** *nm* piglet; *coll* dirty brat

**gorge** *nf* throat, gullet; bosom; breast; gorge, pass; **à pleine** ~ at the top of one's voice; **avoir la** ~ **serrée** have a lump in one's throat; **faire des** ~s **chaudes de** gloat over; **mal à la** ~ sore throat; **rendre** ~ disgorge, stump up; **rire à** ~ **déployée** laugh heartily

**gorgée** *nf* mouthful, gulp

**gorger** *vt* (3) gorge, cram; **se** ~ stuff oneself

**gorille** *nm* gorilla; *coll* bodyguard; *coll* secret agent

**gosier** *nm* throat, gullet; **à plein** ~ loudly

**gosse** *n coll* kid, youngster

**gothique** *nm*+*adj* Gothic

**gouailler** *vt*+*vi* chaff, banter

**gouaillerie** *nf* love of bantering

**gouailleur -euse** *adj* bantering, mocking

**gouape** *nf sl* nasty piece of work, swine

**goudron** *nm* tar

**goudronnage** *nm* tarring

**goudronner** *vt* tar

**gouffre** *nm* gulf, abyss, pit; spendthrift

**goujat** *nm* boor, cad

**¹goujon** *nm* gudgeon (fish)

**²goujon** *nm* gudgeon, stud, pin

**goulet** *nm* narrow entrance, gut; neck (bottle); gully (mountain)

**goulot** *nm* neck (bottle); *fig* bottleneck

**goulu -e** *n* glutton; *adj* greedy, gluttonous

**goupille** *nf* (linch)pin

**goupiller** *vt* pin, key; *sl* contrive, fix

**goupillon** *nm* aspergillum, holy-water sprinkler

**gourbi** *nm* hut, hovel; *mil* dugout

**gourd** *adj* numb, stiff

**gourde** *nf* gourd; water-bottle, flask; *coll* idiot, dope

**gourdin** *nm* cudgel, club

**gourer (se)** *v refl sl* be wrong

**gourmand -e** *n* gourmand, glutton; *adj* greedy, gluttonous; *fig* ~ **de** very fond of

**gourmander** *vt* scold, reprimand

**gourmandise** *nf* greediness, gluttony; ~s sweet things

**gourme** *nf* impetigo; **jeter sa** ~ sow one's wild oats

**gourmé** *adj* stiff, stuck-up

**gourmette** *nf* curb (horse); chain (watch, etc)

**gousse** *nf* shell, pod; ~ **d'ail** clove of garlic

**gousset** *nm* waistcoat pocket; gusset

**goût** *nm* taste; flavour; savour; liking; style, manner; ~ **du jour** prevailing fashion

**goûter** *nm* (afternoon) snack; *vt* taste, try; enjoy, relish; *vi* taste, try; have a snack

**¹goutte** *nf* drop; sip, dram; speck; ~ **à** ~ drop by drop; **il tombe quelques** ~s it's drizzling; **n'entendre** ~ not understand at all; **n'y voir** ~ not make anything out; **se ressembler comme deux** ~s **d'eau** be as like as two peas; **suer à grosses** ~s sweat profusely

**²goutte** *nf* gout

**goutte-à-goutte** *nm invar med* drip

**gouttelette** *nf* small drop, droplet

**goutter** *vi* drip

**goutteux -euse** *adj* gouty

**gouttière** *nf* gutter, rainspout

**gouvernail** *nm* rudder, helm

**gouvernant** *adj* governing, ruling; les ~ s the ruling class

**gouvernante** *nf* governess; housekeeper

**gouverne** *nf* guidance, direction; *aer* ~ s rudders and ailerons

**gouvernement** *nm* government; management

**gouverner** *vt* govern, control; manage; steer

**gouverneur** *nm* governor; manager; tutor

**grabat** *nm* pallet, bed, litter

**grabuge** *nm coll* squabble, row; faire du ~ kick up a row

**grâce** *nf* grace, gracefulness; favour; mercy, pardon; ~ s thanks; ~ à thanks to; action de ~ s thanksgiving; avoir bonne ~ à faire qch do sth with a good grace; de mauvaise ~ ungraciously; faire des ~ s à qn make a fuss of s/o; faire ~ à spare

**gracier** *vt* pardon, reprieve

**gracieux -ieuse** *adj* graceful, gracious; à titre ~ free, complimentary

**gracile** *adj* slender, slim

**grade** *nm* grade, rank; monter en ~ be promoted

**gradé** *nm* non-commissioned officer

**gradin** *nm* step, tier

**graduation** *nf* graduation; scale

**gradué** *adj* graduated, progressive

**graduel -uelle** *adj* gradual

**graduer** *vt* graduate, grade

**grailler** *vi* speak huskily

¹**graillon** *nm cul* bits of fat; smell of fat

²**graillon** *nm sl* gob

¹**grain** *nm* grain; seed; bean, berry; particle, speck; *coll* bee in the bonnet; ~ de beauté beauty-spot; ~ de poivre peppercorn; ~ de raisin grape; poulet de ~ free-range chicken

²**grain** *nm naut* squall

**graine** *nf* seed; *pej* ~ de likely, potential; *coll* c'est une mauvaise ~ he's a bad lot; en prendre de la ~ benefit by the example; monter en ~ go to seed; (spinster) be getting on

**grainetier -ière** *n* corn-chandler, seedsman (-woman)

**graissage** *nm* greasing, lubrication, oiling

**graisse** *nf* grease, fat; ~ de porc lard; ~ de rognon suet; ~ de rôti dripping

**graisser** *vt* grease, lubricate, oil; *coll* ~ la patte à qn grease s/o's palm

**graisseux -euse** *adj* greasy, oily

**grammaire** *nf* grammar

**grammairien -ienne** *n* grammarian

**grand** *nm* grandee; great man; adult, grown-up; big boy; *adj* great, big, large, tall; high; grand; grown-up; en ~ e partie largely, mainly; *adv* en ~ on a large scale; faire (voir) ~ do (see) things in a big way

**grand-angulaire** *nm* wide-angle lens; *adj* wide-angle

**grand-chose** *n invar* much

**Grande-Bretagne** *nf* Great Britain

**grandement** *adv* greatly, extremely; grandly, nobly

**grandeur** *nf* size; height; extent; magnitude; grandeur; Votre Grandeur Your Highness

**grandir** *vt* increase, magnify; enlarge; *vi* grow, increase; grow tall; grow up

**grand-maman** *nf* (*pl* grands-mamans) *coll* grandma, granny

**grand-mère** *nf* (*pl* grands-mères) grandmother

**grand-messe** *nf* High Mass

**grand-papa** *nm* (*pl* grands-papas) *coll* grandpa

**grand-peine (à)** *adv phr* with great difficulty

**grand-père** *nm* (*pl* grands-pères) grandfather

**grand-route** *nf* highway, high road

**grand-rue** *nf* high street, main street

**grands-parents** *nmpl* grandparents

**grange** *nf* barn; mettre en ~ garner

**granit** *nm* granite

**granulaire** *adj* granular

**granulé** *adj* granulated

**granuleux -euse** *adj* granular, granulous

**graphie** *nf* writing, way of writing

**graphique** *nm* diagram, graph; *adj* graphic

**grappe** *nf* bunch, cluster; string (onions)

**grappin** *nm* grapnel, hook; *coll* mettre le ~ sur get hold of

**gras** *nm* fat; *adj* (*f* grasse) fat, fatty; stout; greasy, oily; rich (food); thick; *fig* broad, racy

**gras-double** *nm cul* tripe

**grassement** *adv* generously, liberally

**grasseyer** *vi*(7) *phon* speak with fricative *r*

**grassouillet -ette** *adj* plump, chubby

**gratification** *nf* tip; bonus; gratification

**gratifier** *vt* bestow, confer

**gratin** *nm cul* burnt part; *fig* + *coll* upper crust; au ~ with bread-crumbs and grated cheese

**gratiné** *adj* with bread-crumbs and grated cheese; *coll* fantastic

**gratinée** *nf* onion soup with cheese

**gratte** *nf coll* pickings, perks

**gratte-ciel** *nm invar* skyscraper

**gratte-papier** *nm invar* pen-pusher

**gratte-pieds** *nm invar* shoe-scraper

**gratter** *vt* scratch, scrape; cross out (word); *coll* overtake; ça me gratte I'm itching; *vi coll* scrape

**gratuit** *adj* free; gratuitous; à titre ~ free of charge

**gratuité** *nf* gratuitousness; exemption from charge

**grave** *adj* grave, solemn; serious, severe; important; deep, low, low-pitched; *gramm* grave

**graveleux -euse** *adj* gravelly, gritty; *fig* smutty, racy

**graver** *vt* engrave, carve; ~ **à l'eau forte** etch

**graveur** *nm* engraver, carver

**gravier** *nm* gravel, grit

**gravillon** *nm* fine gravel; ~s loose chippings

**gravir** *vt* climb, ascend

**gravité** *nf* gravity; seriousness; severity; weight; deepness

**graviter** *vi* gravitate; revolve

**gravure** *nf* engraving; print; picture; ~ **à l'eau forte** etching; ~ **sur bois** wood cut

**gré** *nm* will, wish; liking; **à mon** ~ as I please; **au** ~ **de** at the mercy of; at the will of; **bon** ~, **mal** ~ willy-nilly; **de bon** ~ willingly; **de** ~ **à** ~ by mutual agreement; **de** ~ **ou de force** willy-nilly; **de mon propre** ~ of my own accord; **savoir** ~ **à qn de qch** be grateful to s/o for sth

**Grec** (*f* **Grecque**) *n* Greek

**grec** *nm* Greek (language); *adj* (*f* **grecque**) Greek; Grecian

**Grèce** *nf* Greece

**gredin** *nm* rascal, rogue

**gréement** *nm naut* rigging, gear

**gréer** *vt naut* rig

¹**greffe** *nm* office of the clerk of the court; registry

²**greffe** *nf* graft, grafting; *med* transplant

**greffer** *vt* graft; *med* transplant

**greffier** *nm* clerk of the court

**grégaire** *adj* gregarious

**grégorien -ienne** *adj* Gregorian

¹**grêle** *nf* hail; *fig* shower

²**grêle** *adj* slender, thin; shrill

**grêlé** *adj* pock-marked

**grêler** *v impers* hail

**grêlon** *nm* hailstone

**grelot** *nm* small bell; sleigh-bell; *coll* **attacher le** ~ bell the cat

**grelotter** *vi* shiver, tremble; tinkle

**grenade** *nf* pomegranate; *mil* grenade; ~ **sous-marine** depth-charge

**grenadier** *nm* pomegranate-tree; *mil* grenadier

**grenat** *nm* garnet; *adj* garnet(-red)

**grener** *vt* (6) granulate; grain; stipple; *vi* seed, corn

**grènetis** *nm* milled edge, milling

**grenier** *nm* granary; loft; attic

**grenouille** *nf* frog

**grès** *nm* sandstone; **poterie de** ~ earthenware

**grésil** *nm* sleet

**grésillement** *nm* pattering; shrivelling; crackling; sizzling

**grésiller** *vt* shrivel up; *vi* patter; crackle; sizzle; *v impers* sleet

**grève** *nf* shore, beach, strand; strike; ~ **d'avertissement** token strike; ~ **de solidarité** sympathy strike; ~ **de zèle** work to rule; ~ **perlée** go-slow; ~ **sauvage** wild-cat strike; ~ **sur le tas** sit-down strike; ~ **tournante** staggered strike; **faire** ~ be on strike; **se mettre en** ~ go on strike

**grever** *vt* (6) burden; encumber; *leg* entail

**gréviste** *n* striker

**gribouillage** *nm* scrawl, scribble

**gribouiller** *vt* + *vi* scrawl, scribble

**gribouillis** *nm* scrawl, scribble

**grief** *nm* grievance

**grièvement** *adv* severely, seriously

**griffe** *nf* claw; talon; paper-clip, clamp; signature, handwriting; label (fashion-house); *fig* ~s clutches

**griffer** *vt* scratch, claw

**griffonnage** *nm* scrawl, scribble

**griffonner** *vt* scrawl, scribble

**grignotage** *nm* eroding, rubbing away

**grignoter** *vt* nibble

**grigou** *nm coll* miser, skinflint

**gril** *nm* grill, gridiron; *fig* tenterhooks; ~ **-express** buffet-car

**grillade** *nf* grilling; grill, grilled meat

¹**grillage** *nm* grilling; toasting

²**grillage** *nm* grating; railings

**grillager** *vt* (3) surround with wire-netting; fit lattice-work to

**grille** *nf* grating; railings; grill; iron gate; *elect* grid; *mot* grille; cipher-key

¹**griller** *vt* grill; toast; roast (coffee); scorch; *vi* grill; toast; burn out (lamp)

²**griller** *vt* rail in, rail off, bar

**grillon** *nm* cricket

**grimace** *nf* grimace, wry face

**grimacer** *vi* (4) grimace, grin; make faces; simper

**grimacier -ière** *n* affected person; *adj* grimacing, grinning; simpering

**grimage** *nm theat* making-up

**grimer** *vt theat* make up; **se** ~ make up

**grimoire** *nm* magician's book; obscure book; scrawl

**grimpant** *adj* climbing, creeping; **plante** ~ **e** creeper

**grimpée** *nf* stiff climb

**grimper** *vt* + *vi* climb

**grimpeur -euse** *n* climber; *adj* climbing

**grincer** *vi* (4) grind; gnash (teeth); creak; scratch (pen)

**grincheux -euse** *n* grumbler, grouser; *adj* grumpy, surly, testy

**gringalet** *nm coll* puny individual, shrimp

**griotte** *nf* morello cherry

**grippe** *nf* influenza, flu; **prendre qn en ~** take a dislike to s/o

**grippé** *adj* suffering from influenza

**gripper** *vi* run hot; seize up; jam

**grippe-sou** *nm coll* miser, skinflint

**gris** *nm* grey; tobacco; *adj* grey; grey-haired; dull, cloudy; tipsy

**grisaille** *nf arts* grisaille; dreariness, monotony

**grisâtre** *adj* greyish

**grisbi** *nm sl* cash, dough

**griser** *vt* tint grey; intoxicate; make tipsy; **se ~** get tipsy

**griserie** *nf* tipsiness; intoxication; rapture, ecstasy

**grisonner** *vi* turn grey

**grisou** *nm* fire-damp

**grive** *nf* thrush; **faute de ~s on mange des merles** beggars can't be choosers

**grivois** *adj* broad, spicy, smutty

**grivoiserie** *nf* broad joke, smutty story

**Groënland** *nm* Greenland

**Groënlandais -e** *n* Greenlander

**groënlandais** *adj* of Greenland

**grognard** *nm* grumbler, grouser; *hist* soldier of Napoleon's Old Guard; *adj* grumbling, grousing

**grogne** *nf coll* grousing, complaining

**grognement** *nm* grunt, grunting; growl, growling; grumble, grumbling

**grogner** *vi* grunt; growl; grumble

**grognon -onne** *n* grumbler, grouser; *adj* (*f* ~ or -**onne**) grumbling, querulous

**groin** *nm* snout

**grommeler** *vi* (5) grumble, mutter

**grondement** *nm* growl, growling; rumble; roar

**gronder** *vt* scold, chide; *vi* growl; rumble; roar

**gronderie** *nf* scolding

**grondeur -euse** *n* grumbler; scold; *adj* grumbling; scolding

**groom** *nm* page-boy, *US* bell-hop; stable-lad

**gros** *nm* main part; bulk, mass; hardest part; **en ~** broadly speaking; in bulk, wholesale; *adj* (*f* **grosse**) big, large; stout, portly; thick, coarse; rough; heavy; gruff, loud; **~ mots** bad language; **femme grosse** pregnant woman

**groseille** *nf* currant (red, white); **~ à maquereau** gooseberry

**groseillier** *nm* currant-bush

**Gros-Jean** *nm* **être ~ comme devant** be back to square one

**grossesse** *nf* pregnancy

**grosseur** *nf* size, bulk, volume; thickness; *med* swelling

**grossier -ière** *adj* coarse, rough; rude;

vulgar

**grossièreté** *nf* coarseness, roughness; rudeness, vulgarity; rude remark, offensive comment

**grossir** *vt* enlarge, increase, magnify; make look fat; *vi* increase, grow bigger

**grossissant** *adj* magnifying

**grossissement** *nm* increase; swelling; magnifying, enlargement

**grossiste** *n* wholesaler

**grotte** *nf* cave; grotto

**grouiller** *vi* swarm; *coll* **se ~** look lively, hurry up

**groupe** *nm* group, party; clump (trees); cluster (stars)

**groupement** *nm* grouping, group

**grouper** *vt* group; **se ~** form a group, gather

**groupuscule** *nm pol pej* small group

**gruau** *nm* wheat flour; gruel; **~ d'avoine** oatmeal, groats

**grue** *nf orni* crane; *eng* crane; *sl* prostitute, tart

**gruger** *vt* (3) eat; crunch; *coll* sponge on, fleece

**grumeau** *nm* clot; small lump

**grumeler (se)** *v refl* (5) clot

**gué** *nm* ford

**guenille** *nf* rag, tatter

**guenon** *nf* she-monkey; *fig* ugly woman

**guépard** *nm* cheetah

**guêpe** *nf* wasp

**guêpier** *nm* wasps' nest; *fig* **tomber dans un ~** stir up a hornet's nest

**guère** *adv* **ne ... ~** hardly, scarcely; hardly ever, not much; not many

**guéret** *nm* ploughed field

**guéridon** *nm* pedestal table

**guérilla** *nf* guerrilla; guerrilla band; guerrilla warfare

**guérir** *vt* cure; heal; *vi* recover, be cured; heal, heal up

**guérison** *nf* recovery, cure; healing

**guérissable** *adj* curable

**guérisseur -euse** *n* quack; healer

**guérite** *nf* sentry-box; signal-box; watchman's hut

**guerre** *nf* war; warfare; hostilities; strife; **~ de position** trench warfare; **~ éclair** blitzkrieg; **à la ~ comme à la ~** you must take the rough with the smooth; one can't fight a war with kid-gloves; *coll* **de bonne ~** perfectly fair; **de ~ lasse** for the sake of peace and quiet; **être en ~** be at war; **se mettre en ~** go to war

**guerrier -ière** *n* warrior; *adj* warlike, war

**guerroyer** *vi* (7) wage war

**guet** *nm* watch; look-out; **au ~** on the look-out

**guet-apens** *nm* (*pl* **guets-apens**) ambush, trap

**guêtre** *nf* gaiter

**guetter** *vt* lie in wait for, look out for, watch for

**guetteur** *nm* look-out (man)

¹**gueulard** *nm* mouth (blast-furnace)

²**gueulard -e** *n* bawler; *adj* bawling

**gueule** *nf* mouth (animals); *sl* mouth, mug; muzzle (gun); *coll* **avoir de la ~** be impressive, look quite something; *sl* **avoir la ~ de bois** have a hang-over; *sl* **casser la ~ à qn** bash s/o's face in; *sl* **se casser la ~** smash oneself up; get killed; *sl* **ta ~ !** shut up!

**gueule-de-lion** *nf* (*pl* **gueules-de-lion**) antirrhinum

**gueule-de-loup** *nf* (*pl* **gueules-de-loup**) snapdragon; (chimney) cowl

**gueuler** *vt* + *vi coll* bawl, shout

**gueuleton** *nm coll* blow-out, tuck-in

**gueux -euse** *n* beggar; *adj* poor, poverty-stricken

**gui** *nm* mistletoe

**guibol(l)e** *nf sl* leg

**guiches** *nfpl* kiss-curls

**guichet** *nm* wicket-gate; entrance gate; turnstile; pay-desk; counter position; booking-office window

**guide** *nm* guide, conductor; guide-book; *nf* girl-guide; **~s** reins

**guider** *vt* guide, lead; drive, steer

**guidon** *nm* handle-bar; *mil* foresight; *naut* pennant

**guigne** *nf coll* bad luck

**guigner** *vt* ogle, peer at; look enviously at

**guignol** *nm* puppet; Punch; Punch and Judy show, puppet-show; *sl* policeman

**guignolet** *nm* cherry-brandy

**guignon** *nm coll* bad luck

**Guillaume** *nm* William

**guillemet** *nm* inverted comma, quotation mark

**guilleret -ette** *adj* brisk, perky, lively

**guillotine** *nf* guillotine; **fenêtre à ~** sash-window

**guillotiner** *vt* guillotine

**guimauve** *nf* marshmallow

**guimbarde** *nf coll* ramshackle vehicle, old crock

**guimpe** *nf* wimple

**guindé** *adj* stiff, starchy

**guindeau** *nm* windlass

**guinder** *vt* hoist; **se ~** assume a superior manner; become stilted

**Guinée** *nf* Guinea

**guinéen -éenne** *adj* Guinean

**guingan** *nm* gingham

**guingois (de)** *adv phr* askew, awry

**guinguette** *nf* open-air café where there is dancing

**guipure** *nf* point-lace, pillow-lace

**guirlande** *nf* garland, festoon

**guirlander** *vt* garland, festoon

**guise** *nf* way, manner; **à sa ~** as one pleases; **en ~ de** by way of; instead of

**guitare** *nf* guitar

**gus** *nm mil sl* soldier; bloke

**gymnase** *nm* gymnasium

**gymnaste** *n* gymnast

**gymnastique** *nf* gymnastics; *adj* gymnastic; **au pas (de) ~** at the double

**gynécologie** *nf* gynaecology

**gynécologue** *n* gynaecologist

**gypse** *nm* gypsum, plaster of Paris

# H

The letter *h* in French is never pronounced. An asterisk before a word indicates that the *h* is aspirate, i.e. that there is neither elision nor liaison

**habile** *adj* clever; skilful, expert, able; smart

**habileté** *nf* cleverness; skill; ability; smartness

**habilité** *nf* competency; *adj* entitled

**habillage** *nm* casing

**habillement** *nm* clothing; clothes

**habiller** *vt* clothe, dress; **s' ~** dress, get dressed; have one's clothes made

**habilleur -euse** *n* dresser

**habit** *nm* coat, dress-coat; *eccles* habit, frock; **~s** clothes

**habitacle** *nm aer* cockpit; *naut* binnacle; *mot* passenger compartment

**habitant -e** *n* inhabitant; dweller; occupier

**habitation** *nf* dwelling, residence

**habiter** *vt* inhabit, dwell in, occupy; *vi* live, dwell, reside

**habitude** *nf* habit, custom, use, practice; **avoir l' ~ de** be in the habit of; **comme d' ~** as usual; **d' ~** usually

**habitué -e** *n* frequenter, regular customer

**habituel -uelle** *adj* usual, habitual

**habituer** *vt* accustom, get into the habit; **s' ~** get used, become accustomed

*__**hâblerie** *nf* boasting

*__**hâbleur -euse** *n* boaster, braggart

*__**hache** *nf* axe, hatchet

*__**haché** *adj* chopped up, minced; staccato, jerky

*__**hacher** *vt* chop up, mince, hash

*__**hachis** *nm* minced meat, mince, hash

*__**hachoir** *nm* chopper, mincer; chopping-board

*__**hagard** *adj* haggard, wild-looking

*__**haie** *nf* hedge, hedgerow; hurdle; row

*__**haillon** *nm* rag, tatter

*__**haine** *nf* hate, hatred; aversion

*__**haineux -euse** *adj* spiteful, full of hatred

*__**haïr** *vt* (54) hate, detest, loathe

*__**haïssable** *adj* hateful, odious

*__**halage** *nm* towing, hauling; **chemin de ~** towpath

*__**hâle** *nm* sunburn, tan

*__**hâlé** *adj* sunburnt, tanned; weather-beaten

**haleine** *nf* breath; wind; **tenir en ~** keep in suspense

*__**haler** *vt* tow, haul, heave

*__**hâler** *vt* tan, sunburn

*__**haleter** *vi* (5) pant, gasp for breath

*__**hall** *nm* entrance hall, lounge (hotel)

*__**halle** *nf* (covered) market

*__**hallebarde** *nf* halberd; **il pleut des ~s** it's raining cats and dogs

*__**hallier** *nm* thicket, copse

*__**halte** *nf* halt, stop; resting-place

**haltère** *nm* dumb-bell

*__**hamac** *nm* hammock

*__**hameau** *nm* hamlet

**hameçon** *nm* hook; bait

*__**¹hampe** *nf* staff, pole; stem

*__**²hampe** *nf* flank of beef

*__**hanche** *nf* hip; haunch

*__**handicapé -e** *n* handicapped person

*__**handicaper** *vt* handicap

*__**hangar** *nm* outhouse, shed; hangar

*__**hanneton** *nm* cockchafer, may-bug

*__**hanter** *vt* haunt, frequent

*__**hantise** *nf* obsession

*__**happer** *vt* snap up, snatch

*__**haquet** *nm* dray

*__**haranguer** *vt* harangue, lecture

*__**haras** *nm* stud farm; stud

*__**harasser** *vt* exhaust, wear out

*__**harceler** *vt* (5) harass, pester, harry

*__**¹harde** *nf* herd; flock (birds)

*__**²harde** *nf* leash

*__**hardes** *nfpl* old clothes

*__**hardi** *adj* bold, daring, rash; impudent

*__**hardiesse** *nf* boldness, daring, rashness; impudence

*__**hareng** *nm* herring; **~ salé et fumé** kipper; **~ saur** red herring

*__**hargneux -euse** *adj* peevish, bad-tempered, surly

*__**haricot** *nm* kidney bean; **~ s d'Espagne** scarlet runners; **~s verts** French beans, *US* string beans

*__**haridelle** *nf coll* old horse, nag; *fig* tall, gawky woman

**harmonie** *nf* harmony; accord; **en ~ avec** in keeping with

**harmonieux -ieuse** *adj* harmonious; melodious; in keeping

**harmonique** *nf* harmonics; *adj* harmonic

**harmoniser** *vt* harmonize; match; **s' ~** be in keeping, blend

*__**harnachement** *nm* harness, trappings

*__**harnais** *nm* harness, saddlery; **cheval de ~** draught-horse

*__**haro** *nm* hue and cry

*__**harpe** *nf* harp

*__**harpie** *nf* harpy, shrew

*__**harpiste** *n* harpist

*__**harpon** *nm* harpoon

*__**harponner** *vt* harpoon

*__**hasard** *nm* chance, luck; risk, danger; hazard (golf); **à tout ~** on the off chance; **au ~** at random; **coup de ~** stroke of luck; fluke; **de ~** chance; **par ~** accidentally, by chance

*__**hasarder** *vt* hazard, risk, venture; **se ~** venture

*__**hasardeux -euse** *adj* hazardous, risky; daring, venturesome

*__**hâte** *nf* haste, hurry; **à la ~** in a hurry, hastily; **avoir ~ de** be in a hurry to; be eager to

*__**hâter** *vt* hasten, hurry on; expedite; force (fruit); **se ~** hurry, make haste

*__**hâtif -ive** *adj* hasty, hurried; premature; early (fruit)

*__**hauban** *nm naut* shroud

*__**hausse** *nf* rise, *US* raise; block, prop; (back-)sight (rifle); range (gun); **jouer à la ~** speculate on a rising market

*__**haussement** *nm* raising, lifting; **~ d'épaules** shrug(ging) of the shoulders

*__**hausser** *vt* raise, lift; shrug; *vi* rise; **se ~** raise oneself; lift, clear (weather)

*__**haussier** *nm comm* bull

*__**haussière** *nf* hawser

*__**haut** *nm* height; top; upper part; head (table); **de ~ en bas** downwards; from top to bottom; **en ~** above; upstairs; **les ~s et les bas** ups and downs; **tomber de son ~** fall flat on the ground; *fig* be dumbfounded; **traiter**

140

qn de (son) ~ talk down to s/o,
patronize s/o; *adj* high, tall, lofty;
raised, elevated; upper, higher; eminent, important; loud (voice); ~ e mer
open sea; les ~ s temps remote antiquity; lire à ~ e voix read aloud; mer
~ e high tide; *adv* high, up, above;
aloud, loud, loudly; back (in time); ~
les mains! hands up!
*hautain *adj* haughty, proud
*hautbois *nm* oboe
*haut-de-forme *nm* (*pl* hauts-de-forme)
top hat
*hauteur *nf* height, elevation, altitude;
eminence; hill(-top); haughtiness,
arrogance; pitch (sound); *naut* bearing; à la ~ de a match for (person);
equal to (task); *coll* être à la ~ be up to
it; *aer* prendre de la ~ climb
*haut-fond *nm* (*pl* hauts-fonds) shoal,
shallow
*haut-le-cœur *nm* invar heave (stomach); avoir un ~ retch
*haut-le-corps *nm* invar start, jump
*haut-lieu *nm* (*pl* hauts-lieux) centre,
important place
*haut-parleur *nm* loudspeaker, amplifier
*hauturier -ière *adj* of the high seas;
pilote ~ deep-sea pilot
*Havane *nf* Havana
*havane *nm* Havana (cigar); *adj* invar
brown
*hâve *adj* haggard, gaunt, emaciated
*havre *nm* haven, harbour, port
*havresac *nm* knapsack, pack
*Haye (la) *nf* The Hague
*hé *interj* hey there!; hi!; I say!; well!
*heaume *nm* hist helmet
hebdomadaire *nm* + *adj* weekly
héberger *vt* (3) lodge, put up
hébété *adj* dazed, bewildered
hébéter *vt* (6) daze, dull, stupefy
hébraïque *adj* Hebrew, Hebraic
hébraïsant -e *n* Hebraist, Hebrew scholar
hébreu *nm* Hebrew (language)
hécatombe *nf* hecatomb, slaughter
hégémonie *nf* hegemony
*hein *interj* eh?, what?; isn't it?, etc
hélas *interj* alas!
Hélène *nf* Helen
*héler *vt* (6) hail, call
hélice *nf* propeller, screw; *aer* propeller;
escalier en ~ spiral staircase
hélicoptère *nm* helicopter
hellénique *adj* Hellenic
helvétique *adj* Helvetic, Helvetian,
Swiss
hémistiche *nm* hemistich
hémoglobine *nf* haemoglobin
hémophylie *nf* haemophilia
hémorragie *nf* haemorrhage

hémorroïdes *nfpl* haemorrhoids, piles
*henné *nm* henna
*hennir *vi* neigh, whinny
Henri *nm* Henry
hépatique *n* med hepatic; *nf* bot liver-
wort; *adj* hepatic
hépatite *nf* hepatitis
heptagone *nm* heptagon; *adj* heptagonal
héraldique *nf* heraldry; *adj* heraldic
*héraut *nm* herald
herbacé *adj* herbaceous
herbage *nm* grassland; pasture; *cul*
greens
herbe *nf* herb; grass; blé en ~ corn in
the blade; en ~ budding, in embryo;
fines ~ s herbs for seasoning; manger
son blé en ~ spend one's money
before getting it; mauvaise ~ weed; *fig*
rascal
herbeux -euse *adj* grassy
herbicide *nm* weed-killer; *adj* weed-
killing
herbier *nm* herbarium
herbivore *adj* herbivorous
herboriser *vi* gather plants, botanize
herboriste *n* herbalist
herbu *adj* grassy
Hercule *nm* Hercules
hercule *nm* strong-man, strong-arm
man
herculéen -enne *adj* herculean
*hère *nm* pauvre ~ poor devil
héréditaire *adj* hereditary
hérédité *nf* heredity; hereditary right;
inheritance, succession
hérésie *nf* heresy
hérétique *n* heretic; *adj* heretical
*hérissé *adj* bristling; bristly, prickly;
shaggy
*hérisser *vt* bristle, ruffle; se ~ bristle,
bristle up, stand on end
*hérisson *nm* hedgehog; *fig* prickly
person; ~ de mer sea-urchin
héritage *nm* inheritance, heritage
hériter *vt* inherit; *vi* inherit; succeed to
héritier -ière *n* heir, heiress
hermétique *adj* hermetically sealed, airtight, water-tight
hermine *nf* ermine
*herniaire *adj* hernial; bandage ~ truss
*hernie *nf* hernia, rupture
¹héroïne *nf* heroine
²héroïne *nf* chem heroin
héroïque *adj* heroic
héroïsme *nm* heroism
*héros *nm* hero
*herse *nf* harrow; portcullis; ~ s *theat*
battens
*herser *vt* harrow
hésiter *vi* hesitate, falter; pause
hétéroclite *adj* peculiar, irregular
hétérodoxe *adj* heterodox

**hétérogène** *adj* heterogeneous, mixed
*__hêtre__ *nm* beech
**heure** *nf* hour; time; moment; o'clock; ~ H zero hour; à la bonne ~! right!, fine!; well done!; à l' ~ on time; à tout à l' ~ see you later, so long; de bonne ~ early; dernière ~ latest news, stop-press news; sur l' ~ at once; tout à l' ~ just now; in a few minutes
**heureux -euse** *adj* happy, delighted; lucky, fortunate; blessed; successful
*__heurt__ *nm* knock, bump, collision, shock; sans ~ smoothly
*__heurter__ *vt* knock against, bump into; shock, offend; clash with; *vi* strike, collide; se ~ collide; clash
*__heurtoir__ *nm* knocker; buffer
**hexagone** *nm* hexagon; l'Hexagone metropolitan France; *adj* hexagonal
**hiberner** *vi* hibernate
*__hibou__ *nm* owl
*__hic__ *nm* rub, snag
*__hideur__ *nf* hideousness
*__hideux -euse__ *adj* hideous
**hier** *adv* yesterday
*__hiérarchie__ *nf* hierarchy
*__hiérarchique__ *adj* hierarchical; voie ~ official channels
*__hiéroglyphe__ *nm* hieroglyph
**Hilaire** *nm* + *nf* Hilary
**hilarant** *adj* screamingly funny; gaz ~ laughing-gas
**hilare** *adj* hilarious
**hilarité** *nf* hilarity, mirth
**Hindou -e** *n* Hindu
**hindou** *adj* Hindu
**hindouisme** *nm* Hinduism
**hindoustani** *nm lang* Hindustani, Hindi
**hippique** *adj* equine; concours ~ horse-show; race-meeting
**hippodrome** *nm* race-course; hippodrome
**hippopotame** *nm* hippopotamus
**hirondelle** *nf* swallow
**hirsute** *adj* hairy, hirsute; shaggy
*__hisser__ *vt* hoist, lift, raise, run up; se ~ pull, hoist oneself (up)
**histoire** *nf* history; story, tale; *coll* fib, yarn; *coll* ~ de just to; faire des ~s make a fuss
**historien -ienne** *n* historian
**historier** *vt* illustrate, embellish
**historiette** *nf* anecdote, short tale
**historiographe** *n* historiographer
**historique** *nm* record, account; *adj* historic, historical
**histrionique** *adj* histrionic
**hiver** *nm* winter
**hivernage** *nm* laying up for the winter; winter season; wintering-place
**hivernal** *adj* winter, wintry
**hivernant -e** *n* winter visitor; *adj* wintering

**hiverner** *vi* winter, hibernate
**H.L.M.** *nm* = council flat, council dwelling
*__hobereau__ *nm* country squire
*__hocher__ *vt* shake, nod, toss
**hoirie** *nf* inheritance, succession
*__Hollandais -e__ *n* Dutchman, Dutch-woman
*__hollandais__ *nm* Dutch (language); *adj* Dutch
*__Hollande__ *nf* Holland
*__¹hollande__ *nm* Dutch cheese
*__²hollande__ *nf* holland (cloth)
**holocauste** *nm* holocaust; sacrifice
*__homard__ *nm* lobster
**homélie** *nf* homily
**homéopathe** *n* homoeopath; *adj* homoeopathic
**homéopathie** *nf* homoeopathy
**Homère** *nm* Homer
**homérique** *adj* Homeric
**homicide** *nm* homicide (crime); ~ involontaire manslaughter; *n* homicide (person); *adj* murderous, homicidal
**hommage** *nm* homage, tribute; token of esteem; ~s compliments, respects
**hommasse** *adj* mannish, masculine
**homme** *nm* man; mankind; *coll* husband, old man; ~ d'affaires businessman
**homme-grenouille** *nm* (*pl* hommes-grenouilles) frogman
**homme-sandwich** *nm* (*pl* hommes-sandwiches) sandwich-man
**homogène** *adj* homogeneous
**homogénéité** *nf* homogeneity
**homologue** *adj* homologous
**homologuer** *vt* sanction
**homonyme** *nm* homonym; namesake; *adj* homonymous
*__hongre__ *nm* gelding; *adj* gelded
*__hongrer__ *vt* geld
*__Hongrie__ *nf* Hungary
*__Hongrois -e__ *n* Hungarian
*__hongrois__ *nm* Hungarian (language); *adj* Hungarian
**honnête** *adj* honest, upright; decent, respectable; proper, seemly; reasonable (price)
**honnêteté** *nf* honesty; decency; respectability; fairness (price)
**honneur** *nm* honour, integrity; credit; distinction; faire ~ à honour, meet; *mil* rendre les ~s present arms
*__honnir__ *vt* disgrace, dishonour; spurn
**honorable** *adj* honourable, respectable, reputable
**honoraire** *nm* ~s fee, honorarium; *adj* honorary
**honorer** *vt* honour, respect; do credit to
**honorifique** *adj* honorary

\*honte *nf* shame; disgrace; scandal; avoir ~ be ashamed; faire ~ à put to shame; fausse ~ self-consciousness

\*honteux -euse *adj* ashamed, shame-faced; shy, bashful; disgraceful

hôpital *nm* (*pl* -aux) hospital; poor-house

\*hoquet *nm* hiccup

\*hoqueter *vi* hiccup; have the hiccups

horaire *nm* timetable; *adj* hourly

\*horde *nf* horde, pack

horloge *nf* clock

horloger -ère *n* clockmaker, watch-maker

horlogerie *nf* clockmaking, watch-making; watchmaker's shop; clock-work

\*hormis *prep* except, but, save

horreur *nf* horror; detestation; ~s atrocities; beastly things

horrible *adj* horrible, horrid

horrifier *vt* horrify

horrifique *adj* horrific, hair-raising

horripilant *adj* hair-raising; exasperating

horripiler *vt* make (s/o's) hair stand on end; exasperate

\*hors *prep* out of, outside; except, but, save; ~ circuit cut off; ~ d'affaire out of danger; ~ de combat out of action, disabled; ~ de doute beyond doubt; ~ d'ici! get out!; ~ de prix exorbitant; ~ de soi beside oneself; ~ jeu offside; ~ ligne outstanding

\*hors-bord *nm invar* speedboat

\*hors-la-loi *nm invar* outlaw

\*hors-texte *nm invar* plate (in book)

hortensia *nm* hydrangea

horticulteur *nm* horticulturist

hospice *nm* almshouse; children's home

hospitalier -ière *n* hospitaller; *adj* hospitable

hospitaliser *vt* send (admit) to hospital (home)

hospitalité *nf* hospitality

hostellerie *nf* inn

hostie *nf bibl* sacrificial victim; (eucharistic) host

hostile *adj* hostile, adverse

hostilité *nf* hostility, enmity

hôte -esse *n* host, hostess; landlord, landlady; guest, visitor

hôtel *nm* mansion, town house; hotel; ~ des ventes auction rooms; ~ de ville town hall, city hall; ~ garni, ~ meublé residential hotel, furnished lodgings; maître d'~ head waiter; butler

hôtel-Dieu *nm* (*pl* hôtels-Dieu) hospital

hôtelier -ière *n* hotel-keeper; innkeeper; landlord, landlady; *adj* hotel

hôtellerie *nf* inn, hostelry; guest rooms

(monastery); hotel trade

\*hotte *nf* basket (carried on back); (bricklayer's) hod; ~ aspirante (chimney) hood

\*houblon *nm bot* hop(s)

\*houblonnière *nf* hopfield

\*houe *nf* hoe

\*houer *vt* hoe

\*houille *nf* coal; ~ blanche hydro-electric power

\*houiller -ère *adj* coal, coal-bearing

\*houillère *nf* coal-mine, colliery

\*houilleux *adj* coal-bearing

\*houle *nf* swell, surge

\*houlette *nf* (shepherd's) crook; crozier; trowel

\*houleux -euse *adj* surging; rough (sea); *fig* stormy

\*houppe *nf* tuft, crest; powder-puff

\*houppé *adj* tufted, crested

\*houppelande *nf* great-coat, box-coat; cloak

\*houppette *nf* small tuft; powder-puff

\*hourra *interj* hurrah!; *nm* cheer

\*houspiller *vt* hustle, manhandle; *fig* abuse, insult

\*housse *nf* cover(ing); loose-cover, *US* slip-cover; dust-sheet; clothes bag; horse-cloth

\*houssine *nf* switch, riding-switch

\*houx *nm* holly

\*hoyau *nm* mattock, grubbing-hoe

\*hublot *nm* port-hole, scuttle

\*huche *nf* kneading-trough

\*hue *interj* gee-up!

\*huée *nf* boo, hoot; ~s boos, jeers

\*huer *vt* boo; *vi* boo; hoot (owl)

huilage *nm* oiling, lubrication

huile *nf* oil; *sl* les ~s the big shots

huiler *vt* oil, lubricate

huileux -euse *adj* oily, greasy

huilier *nm* oil-merchant; oil-can; *cul* oil and vinegar cruet

huis *nm* à ~ clos in camera, behind closed doors

huissier *nm* usher; sheriff's officer, bailiff

\*huit *nm* eight, eighth; *adj* eight; ~ jours a week; d'aujourd'hui en ~ today week; donner ses ~ jours à qn give s/o a week's notice

\*huitaine *nf* (about) eight; week

\*huitante *adj invar* (*Swiss, Belgian*) eighty

\*huitantième *adj* (*Swiss, Belgian*) eightieth

\*huitième *n* eighth, eighth part; *adj* eighth

huître *nf* oyster; *coll* fool, idiot

huîtrière *nf* oyster-bed

humain *nm* les ~s mankind, humanity; *adj* human; humane

humaniser *vt* humanize, civilize; s'~

become more humane
**humanisme** *nm* humanism
**humaniste** *n* humanist, classical scholar; *adj* humanist
**humanitaire** *adj* humanitarian
**humanité** *nf* humanity
**humble** *adj* humble, lowly; meek
**humecter** *vt* damp, moisten
*****humer** *vt* suck in, suck up; breathe in, sniff
**humeur** *nf* humour, mood; temper; ill-humour
**humide** *adj* damp, moist, wet, humid
**humidité** *nf* damp, dampness, moisture, humidity; **craint l' ~** to be kept dry; **taches d' ~** mildew
**humiliation** *nf* humiliation; affront
**humilier** *vt* humiliate, humble
**humilité** *nf* humility, humbleness
**humoriste** *n* humorist; *adj* humorous
**humoristique** *adj* humorous
*****hune** *nf naut* top; **~ de vigie** crow's nest
·*****hunier** *nm* topsail
*****huppe** *nf* tuft, crest
·*****huppé** *adj* tufted, crested; *coll* smart, well-dressed
*****hure** *nf* head; *cul* brawn, *US* head-cheese; *sl* head, mug
*****hurlement** *nm* howl(ing), roar(ing), yell(ing)
*****hurler** *vt* bawl out; *vi* howl, roar, yell
**hurluberlu** *nm* scatterbrain, harum-scarum
*****hussard** *nm* hussar
*****hutte** *nf* hut, shed
**hybride** *nm + adj* hybrid

**hydraulique** *nf* hydraulics; *adj* hydraulic
**hydravion** *nm* sea-plane
**hydre** *nf* hydra
**hydrogène** *nm* hydrogen
**hydroglisseur** *nm* speedboat
**hydrophile** *adj* absorbent
**hydrophobie** *nf* hydrophobia, rabies
**hydropisie** *nf* dropsy
**hyène** *nf* hyena
**hygiène** *nf* hygiene; **~ publique** public health
**hygiénique** *adj* hygienic; sanitary; **papier ~** toilet paper
**hymnaire** *nm* hymnal, hymn-book
**hymne** *nm* patriotic song; national anthem; *nf* hymn
**hyperbole** *nf* hyperbole, exaggeration
**hyperbolique** *adj* hyperbolic
**hypersensible** *adj* over-sensitive
**hypertension** *nf* high blood-pressure
**hypnose** *nf* hypnosis
**hypnotiser** *vt* hypnotize
**hypnotisme** *nm* hypnotism
**hypocondriaque** *n + adj* hypochondriac
**hypocondrie** *nf* hypochondria
**hypocrisie** *nf* hypocrisy
**hypocrite** *n* hypocrite; *adj* hypocritical
**hypodermique** *adj* hypodermic
**hypotension** *nf* low blood-pressure
**hypothécaire** *adj* mortgage
**hypothèque** *nf* mortgage
**hypothéquer** *vt* (6) mortgage
**hypothèse** *nf* hypothesis, supposition
**hypothétique** *adj* hypothetical
**hystérie** *nf* hysteria
**hystérique** *adj* hysteric, hysterical

# I

**i** *nm* the letter i; **~ grec** (the letter) y; **mettre les points sur les ~** speak plainly
**iambe** *nm* iambus, iambic
**iambique** *adj* iambic
**ibérique** *adj* Iberian
**ici** *adv* here; now; **~-bas** here on earth; **d' ~** henceforth; **d'~ là** between now and then; **d'~ peu** before long; **jusqu'~** as far as here; until now; **par ~** this way
**icône** *nf* icon

**iconoclaste** *n* iconoclast; *adj* iconoclastic
**idéal** *nm + adj* (*pl* **~ s, idéaux**) ideal
**idéaliser** *vt* idealize
**idéalisme** *nm* idealism
**idéaliste** *n* idealist; *adj* idealistic
**idée** *nf* idea, notion, view, opinion, mind; *coll* touch, small amount; **~ fixe** obsession; **~ lumineuse** brain-wave; **~ s noires** gloomy thoughts; **faire à son ~** please oneself; **il me vient à l' ~** it occurs to me; **se faire des ~ s** to

imagine things
**idem** *adv* idem, ditto
**identifier** *vt* identify; regard as identical
**identique** *adj* identical
**identité** *nf* identity
**idéogramme** *nm* ideogram, ideograph
**idéologie** *nf* ideology
**idéologique** *adj* ideological
**idéologue** *n* ideologist
**idiomatique** *adj* idiomatic
**idiome** *nm* idiom; mode of speech
**idiot -e** *n* fool, clot; *med* idiot, imbecile; *adj* idiotic, stupid, absurd; *med* idiot (child)
**idiotie** *nf* idiocy; *med* imbecility
**idiotisme** *nm* idiomatic expression
**idolâtre** *n* idolater; *adj* idolatrous
**idolâtrer** *vt* idolize, adore
**idolâtrie** *nf* idolatry
**idole** *nf* idol
**idylle** *nf* idyll
**idyllique** *adj* idyllic
**if** *nm* yew, yew-tree
**igame** *nm* high official with special powers
**ignare** *n* ignoramus; *adj* ignorant
**igné** *adj* igneous
**ignifuge** *nm* fire-proofing material; *adj* fire-proof, non-inflammable
**ignifuger** *vt* fire-proof
**ignoble** *adj* ignoble, shameful, disgraceful
**ignominie** *nf* ignominy, shame
**ignominieux -ieuse** *adj* ignominious, disgraceful
**ignorant -e** *n* ignorant person, ignoramus; *adj* ignorant, ignoramus
**ignoré** *adj* unknown
**ignorer** *vt* not know, be ignorant of; ignore
¹**il** *pron m* he, it; (ship) she
²**il** *impers pron invar* it, there; ~ était une fois once upon a time there was; ~ vient un homme there comes a man; ~ y a there is, are
**île** *nf* island, isle
**ilex** *nm invar* ilex, evergreen oak
**illégal** *adj* illegal, unlawful
**illégalité** *nf* illegality
**illégitime** *adj* illegitimate, unlawful; unwarranted
**illégitimité** *nf* illegitimacy
**illettré** *adj* uneducated, untutored
**illicite** *adj* illicit
**illico** *adv coll* at once, like a flash
**illimitable** *adj* limitless, boundless
**illimité** *adj* unlimited; **congé** ~ indefinite leave
**illisibilité** *nf* illegibility
**illisible** *adj* illegible; unreadable
**illogique** *adj* illogical
**illuminant** *adj* illuminating

**illuminateur -trice** *n* illuminator; enlightener
**illumination** *nf* lighting; ~s lights, illuminations; enlightenment, illumination
**illuminé -e** *n* visionary
**illuminer** *vt* light up, illuminate; enlighten
**illusion** *nf* illusion, delusion; ~ d'optique optical illusion; **se faire** ~, **se faire des** ~s deceive oneself
**illusionner** *vt* delude; s' ~ labour under a delusion
**illusionniste** *n* illusionist, conjurer
**illusoire** *adj* illusory, deceptive
**illustrateur -trice** *n* illustrator
**illustratif -ive** *adj* illustrative
**illustration** *nf* illustriousness; making illustrious; illustration, picture; illustrious person
**illustre** *adj* illustrious, famous
**illustré** *nm* illustrated magazine
**illustrer** *vt* make illustrious, famous; illustrate
**îlot** *nm* small island; block of houses
**ils** *pron mpl* they
**image** *nf* image, picture; mental picture; likeness, resemblance; simile, metaphor; reflection; *comm* ~ de marque public image; **sage comme une** ~ as good as gold; **se faire une** ~ de imagine
**imagé** *adj* vivid, full of imagery
**imagerie** *nf* coloured print; print factory
**imaginable** *adj* imaginable
**imaginaire** *adj* imaginary, make-believe; **malade** ~ hypochondriac
**imaginatif -ive** *adj* imaginative
**imagination** *nf* imagination; fancy
**imaginer** *vt* imagine, suppose, fancy; conceive, devise; s' ~ suppose
**imbattable** *adj* unbeatable, invincible
**imbattu** *adj* unbeaten
**imbécile** *n* imbecile, half-wit; *adj* half-witted; idiotic
**imbécillité** *nf* imbecility, feeble-mindedness; silliness; ~s nonsense
**imberbe** *adj* beardless; callow
**imbiber** *vt* soak, saturate; soak up, imbibe; imbue, impregnate; s' ~ become saturated; become steeped
**imbriqué** *adj* overlapping
**imbrisable** *adj* unbreakable
**imbrûlable** *adj* fireproof
**imbu** *adj* imbued; soaked
**imbuvable** *adj* undrinkable; *sl* insufferable
**imitateur -trice** *n* imitator
**imitatif -ive** *adj* imitative
**imitation** *nf* imitation, copying; forgery, counterfeit; forging, counterfeiting; mimicry; **à l'** ~ **de** in imitation of

**imiter** *vt* imitate, copy; mimic, model oneself on; forge (signature), counterfeit

**immaculé** *adj* immaculate, spotless, unstained

**immangeable** *adj* uneatable

**immanquable** *adj* unavoidable, certain

**immatériel -ielle** *adj* immaterial, intangible

**immatriculation** *nf* registration, inscription, enrolment; *mot* **plaque d'** ~ number-plate

**immatriculer** *vt* register, enter (s/o, sth) on a register

**immédiat** *nm* present time; *adj* immediate, instant; direct; close; *chem* **analyse** ~ **e** proximate analysis

**immense** *adj* immense, vast; boundless

**immensité** *nf* immensity, vastness; boundlessness

**immerger** *vt* (3) immerse, dip

**immérité** *adj* undeserved, unmerited

**immersion** *nf* immersion, dipping; *astron* occultation

**immesurable** *adj* immeasurable

**immeuble** *nm* building; real estate; *adj* *leg* real, immovable

**immeuble-tour** *nm* (*pl* **immeubles-tours**) high-rise building

**immigré -e** *n* immigrant

**immigrer** *vi* immigrate

**immiscer** *vt* (4) mix up, involve; s' ~ interfere

**immiscible** *adj* unmixable

**immobile** *adj* motionless, still, immobile; firm

¹**immobilier** *nm* property, *US* real estate

²**immobilier -ière** *adj* *leg* real; **agence immobilière** estate agency, *US* real estate agency; **agent** ~ estate agent; **biens** ~ **s** real estate

**immobilisation** *nf* immobilization; ~ **s** fixed assets; *leg* conversion into real estate

**immobiliser** *vt* immobilize, bring to a stop; tie up (capital); *leg* convert into real estate

**immobilisme** *nm* policy of inaction

**immobiliste** *n* die-hard

**immobilité** *nf* immobility, fixity

**immodéré** *adj* immoderate, inordinate

**immodeste** *adj* immodest, shameless

**immodestie** *nf* immodesty, shamelessness

**immoler** *vt* immolate

**immonde** *adj* filthy, disgusting, foul

**immondices** *nfpl* refuse, dirt

**immoralité** *nf* immorality

**immortaliser** *vt* immortalize

**immortalité** *nf* immortality

**immortel -elle** *n* immortal; **les Immortels** members of the French Academy;

~ **elle** everlasting flower, immortelle; *adj* immortal

**immuable** *adj* immutable, unchanging, fixed

**immuniser** *vt* immunize, make immune from

**immunité** *nf* immunity

**immutabilité** *nf* immutability

**impact** *nm* impact; effect

¹**impair** *nm* *coll* blunder, *US* goof

²**impair** *adj* odd, uneven

**impardonnable** *adj* unpardonable, unforgivable

**imparfait** *nm* imperfect tense; *adj* imperfect, defective; unfinished

**imparité** *nf* inequality, disparity; unevenness

**impartageable** *adj* indivisible; which cannot be shared

**impartial** *adj* impartial, unbiased, equitable

**impartialité** *nf* impartiality

**impartir** *vt* *leg* bestow, grant

**impasse** *nf* dead-end, cul-de-sac; deadlock; **dans une** ~ in a dilemma; (cards) **faire une** ~ finesse

**impassibilité** *nf* impassivity

**impassible** *adj* impassive, unconcerned; unimpressionable

**impatience** *nf* impatience; eagerness

**impatient** *adj* impatient; eager

**impatienter** *vt* make (s/o) lose patience, provoke, irritate; s' ~ lose patience

**impatroniser** *vt* impose, set in authority; s' ~ impose oneself, take charge

**impayable** *adj* invaluable, priceless; *coll* very funny, priceless

**impayé** *adj* unpaid, outstanding (debt)

**impeccabilité** *nf* impeccability, faultlessness

**impeccable** *adj* impeccable, faultless

**impécunieux -ieuse** *adj* impecunious

**impénétrabilité** *nf* impenetrability; inscrutability

**impénétrable** *adj* impenetrable, impervious; inscrutable

**imper** *nm* *coll* raincoat

¹**impératif** *nm* imperative

²**impératif -ive** *adj* imperative; peremptory

**impératrice** *nf* empress

**imperfection** *nf* imperfection, flaw; incompleteness

**impériale** *nf* top deck of bus; imperial beard

**impérialisme** *nm* imperialism

**impérialiste** *n* + *adj* imperialist

**impérieux -ieuse** *adj* imperious, haughty, overbearing; urgent, imperative

**impérissable** *adj* imperishable, undying

**impéritie** *nf* incapacity, inefficiency

**imperméabiliser** *vt* proof, render waterproof

**imperméable** *nm* raincoat; *adj* impermeable; impervious

**impersonnalité** *nf* impersonality

**impersonnel -elle** *adj* impersonal

**impertinence** *nf* impertinence, rudeness; irrelevance

**impertinent** *adj* impertinent, rude; irrelevant

**impétrant -e** *n leg* grantee; candidate

**impétueux -euse** *adj* impetuous, impulsive; violent

**impétuosité** *nf* impetuosity, impetuousness, impulsiveness

**impie** *adj* impious, irreligious; blasphemous

**impiété** *nf* impiety, impiousness; impious action; undutifulness

**impitoyable** *adj* pitiless, merciless

**implacable** *adj* implacable, relentless

**implanter** *vt* plant, implant; graft; s' ~ take root; *coll* s' ~ **chez qn** foist oneself on s/o

**implicite** *adj* implicit, absolute

**impliquer** *vt* implicate, involve; ~ **contradiction** imply a contradiction

**imploration** *nf* entreaty, imploring

**implorer** *vt* implore, entreat

**imployable** *adj* inflexible

**impoli** *adj* impolite, rude, uncivil

**impolitesse** *nf* impoliteness, incivility; rude, discourteous action

**impolitique** *adj* impolitic, ill-advised

**impondéré** *adj* ill-considered

**impopulaire** *adj* unpopular

**impopularité** *nf* unpopularity

**importable** *adj* unwearable; importable

**importance** *nf* importance, significance; extent, gravity, consequence; social position; **d'** ~ momentous; *adv phr* **d'** ~ soundly

**important** *nm* what matters, main point; *adj* important; considerable; consequential, self-important; **peu** ~ unimportant, trifling

**importateur -trice** *n* importer; *adj* importing

**importation** *nf* importation; import

[1]**importer** *vt* import

[2]**importer** *vi* matter, be of importance; **n'importe** no matter, never mind; **n'importe comment** no matter how; **n'importe qui** no matter who, anyone; **qu'importe?** what does it matter?

**importun** *adj* importunate; tiresome; inopportune, unreasonable

**importuner** *vt* importune; bother, be a nuisance to, pester; dun

**importunité** *nf* importunity; harassing

**imposable** *adj* taxable; rateable

**imposant** *adj* imposing, impressive; dignified

**imposé -e** *n* tax-payer; rate-payer

**imposer** *vt* impose, prescribe, lay down; tax, assess; ~ **un prix** fix a price; *vi* impress, command respect; **en** ~ **à qn** overawe s/o; deceive s/o, take s/o in; s' ~ assert oneself; be essential; s' ~ **à, chez qn** foist oneself on s/o

**imposition** *nf* imposing, prescribing; taxation, imposition of tax, assessment; tax, duty, rates

**impossibilité** *nf* impossibility; impossible thing; **être dans l'** ~ **de** be quite unable to

**impossible** *nm* what is impossible; **faire l'** ~ **pour** do one's utmost to; **par** ~ against all probability; *adj* impossible; **cela m'est** ~ I cannot; **c'est** ~ out of the question, it can't be done; **il m'est** ~ **de croire que ...** I can't believe that ...; **une idée** ~ an absurd idea

**imposteur** *nm* impostor, humbug

**imposture** *nf* imposture, deception, trickery

**impôt** *nm* tax; ~ **sur le revenu** income-tax; **frapper d'un** ~ levy a tax on

**impotence** *nf* impotence, helplessness, infirmity

**impotent -e** *n* cripple, invalid; *adj* helpless, infirm

**impraticable** *adj* impracticable, unworkable; impassable (road)

**imprécation** *nf* imprecation, curse

**imprécatoire** *adj* imprecatory

**imprécis** *adj* imprecise, inaccurate, vague

**imprécision** *nf* imprecision, vagueness

**imprégner** *vt* (6) impregnate, permeate; s' ~ become saturated, imbued

**imprémédité** *adj* unpremeditated

**imprenable** *adj* impregnable

**imprescriptible** *adj leg* imprescriptible, inalienable

**impression** *nf* impression, feeling; impressing, imprint; printing; print; ~ **en couleurs** colour-print; **à l'** ~ in the press

**impressionnable** *adj* impressionable, excitable; sensitized

**impressionnant** *adj* impressive, moving

**impressionner** *vt* impress, move, make an impression on; s' ~ be impressed

**impressionniste** *n* impressionist; *adj* impressionist, impressionistic

**imprévisible** *adj* unforeseeable

**imprévision** *nf* lack of foresight

**imprévoyable** *adj* unforeseeable

**imprévoyance** *nf* lack of foresight; improvidence

**imprévoyant** *adj* unforeseeing; improvident

**imprévu** *nm* unforeseen event; ~ **s**

unforeseen expenses, contingencies; **à moins d' ~ , sauf ~** unless something unforeseen occurs, barring accidents; **en cas d' ~** in case of emergency; *adj* unforeseen, unexpected

**imprimable** *adj* printable

**imprimante** *nf* printer (computer)

**imprimé** *nm* printed paper; printed form; cotton print, *US* calico; **~ s** printed matter

**imprimer** *vt* imprint, stamp; print; communicate (movement)

**imprimerie** *nf* printing-works, printing-press; (art of ) printing

**imprimeur** *nm* printer, master-printer; **~ -éditeur** printer and publisher

**imprimeuse** *nf* printing-machine

**improbabilité** *nf* improbability, unlikelihood

**improbable** *adj* improbable, unlikely

**improbité** *nf* improbity, dishonesty

**improductif -ive** *adj* unproductive

**impromptu** *nm* impromptu; *adj invar* impromptu, extempore; *adv* impromptu, on the spur of the moment

**imprononçable** *adj* unpronounceable

**impropre** *adj* improper, unsuitable; unfit

**impropriété** *nf* impropriety

**improvisateur -trice** *n* improvisor

**improvisation** *nf* improvisation; improvised playing, speaking

**improvisé** *adj* improvised, makeshift

**improviser** *vt* improvise; **~ un discours** make an extempore speech; *vi* improvise

**improviste (à l')** *adv phr* unexpectedly, unawares

**imprudence** *nf* imprudence, rashness; rash, incautious act

**imprudent** *adj* imprudent, rash, ill-advised, careless

**impubère** *adj* under the age of puberty

**impubliable** *adj* unpublishable

**impudence** *nf* impudence, effrontery; piece of impudence

**impudent** *adj* impudent, pert

**impudeur** *nf* shamelessness, immodesty

**impudicité** *nf* impudicity, lewdness; indecent act

**impudique** *adj* lewd, immodest

**impuissance** *nf* impotence, powerlessness; impotence (sexual)

**impuissant** *adj* impotent, powerless; unavailing; impotent (sexually)

**impulser** *vt* stimulate, animate

**impulsif -ive** *adj* impulsive

**impulsion** *nf* elect + mech impulse; *fig* impulse, stimulus

**impunément** *adv* with impunity

**impuni** *adj* unpunished

**impunité** *nf* impunity

**impur** *adj* impure, tainted; unchaste

**impureté** *nf* impurity; lewdness

**imputable** *adj* imputable; chargeable

**imputation** *nf* imputation, accusation; charging up

**imputer** *vt* impute, ascribe; charge

**in** *adj invar* in, fashionable

**inabordable** *adj* unapproachable, inaccessible; prohibitive

**inaccentué** *adj* unstressed, unaccented

**inaccessibilité** *nf* inaccessibility

**inaccessible** *adj* inaccessible; proof against

**inaccompli** *adj* unaccomplished

**inaccordable** *adj* ungrantable, inadmissible; irreconcilable

**inaccoutumé** *adj* unaccustomed; unusual

**inachevé** *adj* unfinished

**inactif -ive** *adj* inactive, indolent; *chem* inert; *comm* sluggish

**inactivité** *nf* inactivity, indolence; *chem* inertness; sluggishness

**inadaptation** *nf* maladjustment

**inadapté -e** *n* misfit; *adj* maladjusted

**inadmissibilité** *nf* inadmissibility; failure in qualifying written examination

**inadmissible** *adj* inadmissible; having failed in qualifying written examination; **c'est ~** it's out of the question

**inaliéné** *adj* inalienated

**inalliable** *adj* non-alloyable; incompatible

**inaltérable** *adj* non-deteriorating; unfailing

**inaltéré** *adj* unimpaired

**inamical** *adj* unfriendly

**inamovibilité** *nf leg* fixity of tenure; irremovability

**inamovible** *adj leg* irremovable; built-in

**inanimé** *adj* inanimate, lifeless

**inanité** *nf* inanity, futility; inane remark

**inapaisable** *adj* unappeasable; unquenchable

**inapaisé** *adj* unappeased; unquenched, unassuaged

**inaperceivable** *adj* unperceivable

**inaperçu** *adj* unperceived; **passer ~** escape notice

**inapparent** *adj* unapparent, inconspicuous

**inappliqué** *adj* lacking in application; unapplied, in abeyance

**inappréciable** *adj* imperceptible; inestimable

**inapprécié** *adj* unappreciated

**inapprêté** *adj* uncooked; unprepared; unrehearsed

**inapprivoisable** *adj* untamable

**inapprivoisé** *adj* untamed, wild

**inapte** *adj* inapt, unapt, unfit

**inaptitude** *nf* inaptitude, unfitness

**inarticulé** *adj* inarticulate; inarticulated

**inassouvi** *adj* unappeased, unsatisfied; unquenched

**inassouvissable** *adj* insatiable

**inattaquable** *adj* unassailable, unquestionable; **~ par** resistant to

**inattendu** *adj* unexpected, unforeseen

**inattentif -ive** *adj* inattentive; careless, heedless

**inattention** *nf* inattention, absent-mindedness; carelessness

**inaugurateur -trice** *n* inaugurator

**inaugurer** *vt* inaugurate; open, initiate

**inauthentique** *adj* unauthentic

**inautorisé** *adj* unauthorized

**inaverti** *adj* unwarned; inexperienced

**inavouable** *adj* unavowable; shameful

**inavoué** *adj* unavowed, unacknowledged

**incapable** *n* incapable, incompetent person; *adj* incapable, incompetent; unfit; sexually impotent

**incapacité** *nf* incapacity, incompetence; unfitness; disability

**incarcérer** *vt* (6) incarcerate, imprison

**incarnadin** *adj* incarnadine, pink

**incarnat** *nm* flesh-colour, rosiness; *adj* flesh-coloured, rosy

**incarnation** *nf* incarnation; embodiment

**incarné** *adj* incarnate; ingrowing (nail)

**incarner** *vt* incarnate, embody; *theat* play the role of; **s' ~** become incarnate; become ingrowing

**incartade** *nf* outburst, tirade; prank; swerve

**incassable** *adj* unbreakable

**incendiaire** *n* incendiary; fire-brand; *adj* incendiary, inflammatory

**incendie** *nm* fire, conflagration; **~ volontaire** arson; **bouche d' ~** hydrant; **pompe à ~** fire-engine; **poste d' ~** fire-station

**incendier** *vt* set fire to, burn down

**incertain** *adj* uncertain, doubtful; unreliable; indistinct; unsettled (weather)

**incertitude** *nf* uncertainty, doubt, indecision

**incessamment** *adv* at once, without delay; incessantly, unceasingly

**incessant** *adj* unceasing, ceaseless

**incessible** *adj* inalienable

**inceste** *nm* incest

**incestueux -ueuse** *adj* incestuous

**inchangé** *adj* unchanged

**inchoatif -ive** *adj* inceptive, inchoative

**incidence** *nf* consequence, influence

**incident** *nm* incident, happening; difficulty; **~ de parcours** hitch; *adj* incidental; *gramm* parenthetical

**incidente** *nf* subordinate clause

**incinérateur** *nm* incinerator

**incinération** *nf* incineration; cremation

**incinérer** *vt* (6) incinerate; cremate

**inciser** *vt* incise; lance

**incisif -ive** *adj* incisive; cutting

**incision** *nf* incision, cut; lancing

**incisive** *nf* incisor

**incitateur -trice** *n* inciter, agitator; *adj* inciting

**incitation** *nf* incitement

**inciter** *vt* incite, urge on

**incivil** *adj* uncivil

**incivilisé** *adj* uncivilized

**incivilité** *nf* incivility, discourtesy; act of incivility

**inclassable** *adj* unclassifiable

**inclémence** *nf* inclemency

**inclinaison** *nf* tilting, incline, slope, gradient; *naut* list; *archi* pitch; *elect* dip

**inclination** *nf* inclination, bow, nod; propensity, attachment

**incliné** *adj* inclined, tilted; bowed; disposed

**incliner** *vt* incline, slant, tilt, bend; predispose; *vi* lean, slope, list; be inclined; **s' ~** lean, slope, bend over; bow; yield

**inclure** *vt* (25) enclose; include

**inclus** *adj* enclosed; inclusive

**incolore** *adj* colourless

**incollable** *adj* impossible to catch out

**incomber** *v impers* be incumbent upon, devolve on

**incombustible** *adj* fire-proof, incombustible

**incomestible** *adj* inedible

**incommensurable** *adj math* incommensurable; *coll* large, outsize; **racine ~** irrational root

**incommodant** *adj* annoying, unpleasant

**incommode** *adj* inconvenient, incommodious, uncomfortable; awkward

**incommoder** *vt* incommode, inconvenience, bother; make unwell

**incommutable** *adj* non-transferable; **propriétaire ~** owner who cannot be dispossessed

**incompatibilité** *nf* incompatibility

**incompatible** *adj* incompatible, inconsistent

**incomplet -ète** *adj* incomplete

**incompréhensibilité** *nf* incomprehensibility

**incompréhensif -ive** *adj* lacking in understanding

**incompris** *adj* misunderstood

**inconcevable** *adj* inconceivable

**inconciliable** *adj* irreconcilable

**inconditionnel -elle** *n* die-hard; *adj* unconditional

**inconduite** *nf* immoral behaviour; *leg* misconduct

# inconfort

**inconfort** *nm* lack of comfort, discomfort

**incongru** *adj* incongruous; unbecoming, out of place

**incongruité** *nf* incongruity, incongruousness; impropriety; improper remark

**inconnaissable** *adj* unknowable

**inconnu -e** *n* unknown person; stranger; ~e *math* unknown quantity; *adj* unknown

**inconquis** *adj* unconquered

**inconscience** *nf* unconsciousness; unawareness

**inconscient** *adj* unconscious; unaware

**inconséquence** *nf* inconsequence, inconsistency; non sequitur

**inconséquent** *adj* inconsequent, inconsistent; rambling, unconnected

**inconsidéré** *adj* ill-considered; inconsiderate; thoughtless

**inconsistance** *nf* lack of cohesion, looseness; inconsistency

**inconsistant** *adj* lacking in cohesion, loose; inconsistent

**inconsolable** *adj* inconsolable; disconsolate

**inconstance** *nf* inconstancy, fickleness

**inconstitutionnel -elle** *adj* unconstitutional

**incontestable** *adj* incontestable, undeniable, incontrovertible

**incontesté** *adj* uncontested, undisputed

**incontinent** *adv* forthwith, at once

**incontrôlable** *adj* unverifiable

**incontrôlé** *adj* unverified

**inconvenance** *nf* unseemliness; indecorousness; indecency; unseemly act

**inconvenant** *adj* unseemly, indecorous, indecent

**inconvénient** *nm* disadvantage, drawback; **si vous n'y voyez pas d'** ~ if you have no objection

**inconvertissable** *adj* incorrigible; past praying for

**incorporer** *vt* incorporate; *mil* embody; s' ~ incorporate, blend

**incorrect** *adj* incorrect, wrong; indecorous

**incorrection** *nf* incorrectness, error; impropriety

**incrédule** *n* unbeliever, infidel; *adj* incredulous; unbelieving

**incrédulité** *nf* incredulousness; unbelief

**increvable** *adj mot* unpuncturable; *coll* tireless; *coll* indestructible

**incriminable** *adj* indictable, liable to be charged

**incrimination** *nf* incrimination; *leg* indictment; charge

**incriminer** *vt* condemn, blame; *leg* incriminate, charge

**incrochetable** *adj* unpickable, burglar-proof

**incroyable** *adj* incredible, unbelievable

**incroyance** *nf* unbelief

**incroyant -e** *n* unbeliever; *adj* unbelieving

**incrustation** *nf* incrustation; inlaid work; furring up (boiler)

**incruster** *vt* encrust; inlay; s' ~ become encrusted, furred up, engrained; *coll* dig oneself in

**incubateur** *nm* incubator

**incube** *nm* incubus

**inculpable** *adj* indictable, chargeable

**inculpation** *nf* indictment, charge

**inculpé -e** *n* defendant, accused

**inculper** *vt* indict, charge

**inculquer** *vt* inculcate, instil

**inculte** *adj* uncultivated; uncultured

**incurie** *nf* negligence; lack of interest

**incurieux -ieuse** *adj* incurious

**incuriosité** *nf* incuriosity

**incursion** *nf* incursion, raid; *fig* excursion

**Inde** *nf* India; **les** ~ **s** the Indies

**indébrouillable** *adj* impossible to untangle; inextricable

**indécence** *nf* indecency, immodesty; indecent act

**indécent** *adj* indecent, immodest

**indéchiffrable** *adj* indecipherable, illegible; unintelligible

**indéchirable** *adj* untearable

**indécis** *adj* undecided, hesitating; indistinct, uncertain; indecisive

**indécisif -ive** *adj* indecisive

**indéclinable** *adj* impossible to refuse; *gramm* indeclinable

**indécrottable** *n coll* oaf, hopeless clot; *adj* uncleanable; *coll* incorrigible, hopeless

**indéfendable** *adj* indefensible

**indéfini** *adj* indefinite; undefined; *gramm* indefinite

**indéfinissable** *adj* indefinable; nondescript

**indéformable** *adj* that will not lose its shape

**indéfrisable** *nf* permanent wave; *adj* that cannot come out of curl

**indélibéré** *adj* unpremeditated; undeliberated

**indélicat** *adj* indelicate, tactless, coarse; dishonest; unscrupulous

**indélicatesse** *nf* indelicacy, tactlessness, coarseness; dishonesty; unscrupulousness

**indémaillable** *adj* ladder-proof

**indemne** *adj* unhurt; undamaged; **sortir** ~ be unhurt

**indemnisation** *nf* indemnification, compensation

**indemniser** *vt* indemnify, compensate

**indemnité** *nf* indemnity, compensation; allowance, grant; ~ **de chômage** unemployment benefit; ~ **de déplacement** travelling expenses; ~ **de logement** living-out allowance; ~ **parlementaire** parliamentary stipend

**indémontrable** *adj* undemonstrable

**indémontré** *adj* undemonstrated

**indépendant** *adj* independent, free; self-contained (flat)

**indéracinable** *adj* ineradicable

**indéréglable** *adj* fool-proof, that cannot go wrong

**indescriptible** *adj* indescribable

**indéterminé** *adj* undetermined; irresolute; *math* indeterminate

**indétraquable** *adj* fool-proof, that cannot go wrong

¹**index** *nm* forefinger, index-finger; pointer

²**index** *nm* index; *eccles* Index; **mettre à l'** ~ ban, black-list

¹**indicateur** *nm* time-table, guide, directory; indicator, gauge; *mot* ~ **de vitesse** speedometer; *adj* (*f* -**trice**) indicatory, indicating; **plaque indicatrice** street-sign; **poteau** ~ sign-post

²**indicateur** -**trice** *n* informer, police-spy

¹**indicatif** *nm gramm* indicative; *rad* call-sign, signature

²**indicatif** -**ive** *adj* indicative

**indication** *nf* indication, pointing out; information, instruction; **à titre d'** ~ for guidance; **sauf** ~ **contraire** unless otherwise stated

**indice** *nm* indication, sign, clue; index; *math* index; *opt* ~ **de réfraction** refractive index

**indicible** *adj* inexpressible; unspeakable

**Indien** -**ienne** *n* + *adj* Indian

**indien** -**ienne** *adj* Indian

**indienne** *nf* printed calico; chintz

**indifféremment** *adv* indifferently, unconcernedly; indiscriminately

**indifférence** *nf* indifference, unconcern

**indifférent** -**e** *adj* indifferent, unconcerned; of no consequence, trifling; **cela m'est** ~ it doesn't matter to me

**indigence** *nf* indigence, poverty, want

**indigène** *n* native; *adj* indigenous, native

**indigent** -**e** *n* pauper; *adj* indigent, poverty-stricken

**indigeste** *adj* indigestible, stodgy; heavy, undigested

**indigne** *adj* unworthy, undeserving; shameful

**indigner** *vt* make indignant; **s'** ~ be indignant

**indignité** *nf* indignity; unworthiness; baseness

**indiquer** *vt* indicate, point out, show; fix, specify; recommend; betoken; **c'est très indiqué** it's very advisable; **c'était indiqué** it was the obvious thing to do

**indirect** *adj* indirect; oblique; *leg* circumstantial

**indiscipliné** *adj* undisciplined

**indiscret** -**ète** *n* + *adj* indiscreet, tactless (person); over-talkative (person)

**indiscrétion** *nf* indiscretion; indiscreetness, tactlessness; tactless remark; **sans** ~ without being indiscreet

**indiscutable** *adj* indisputable, unquestionable

**indisponible** *adj* unavailable; *leg* inalienable; *leg* entailed

**indisposé** *adj* indisposed, unwell; ill-disposed

**indisposer** *vt* make unwell, upset; antagonize

**indistinct** *adj* indistinct, faint, blurred, dim

**indistinctement** *adv* indistinctly, faintly; indiscriminately

**indistinguible** *adj* indistinguishable

**individu** *nm* individual, human being; *coll* (*usu pej*) chap, fellow, character

**individualiser** *vt* individualize, particularize; personalize; **s'** ~ assume individual characteristics

**individualité** *nf* individuality

**individuel** -**uelle** *adj* individual, personal; separate

**indivis** *adj* joint

**indivisibilité** *nf* indivisibility

**Indochine** *nf* Indo-China

**indocilité** *nf* indocility, untractableness

**indolence** *nf* indolence, idleness; *med* painlessness

**indolent** -**e** *adj* indolent, idle; *med* painless

**indolore** *adj* painless

**indomptable** *adj* unconquerable, untameable; indomitable

**indompté** *adj* unconquered, untamed

**Indonésie** *nf* Indonesia

**indu** *adj* undue, unwarranted; **à des heures** ~ **es** at all hours

**inductif** -**ive** *adj* inductive

**induire** *vt* (80) induce, beguile; *elect* induce

**indulgence** *nf* indulgence, leniency, forbearance

**indulgent** *adj* indulgent, lenient, forbearing

**indûment** *adv* unduly

**industrialiser** *vt* industrialize

**industrialisme** *nm* industrialism

**industrie** *nf* industry; ingenuity, dexterity; trade, manufacture; trickery; **vivre d'** ~ live by one's wits

¹**industriel** *nm* manufacturer, industrialist

²**industriel -ielle** *adj* industrial; *coll* en
quantité ~ **ielle** galore
**industrieux -ieuse** *adj* industrious
**inébranlable** *adj* unshakeable, resolute
**inéclairé** *adj* unlit; unenlightened
**inédit** *nm* unpublished work; *adj* unpublished; novel, original; unprecedented
**ineffaçable** *adj* ineffaceable, indelible
**inefficace** *adj* ineffectual, inefficacious
**inefficacité** *nf* ineffectualness, inefficacy
**inégal** *adj* unequalled
**inégalité** *nf* inequality; unevenness, roughness; capriciousness
**inemployé** *adj* unemployed, unused
**inénarrable** *adj* indescribable, untellable; *coll* hilarious
**inepte** *adj* inept, foolish, stupid
**ineptie** *nf* ineptitude, incapacity; inept remark; ~ s nonsense
**inépuisable** *adj* inexhaustible, unfailing
**inépuisé** *adj* unexhausted
**inéquitable** *adj* inequitable, unfair
**inerte** *adj* inert, sluggish, dull
**inertie** *nf* inertia, sluggishness, apathy; (force d') ~ passive resistance
**inespéré** *adj* unhoped for, unexpected
**inévitabilité** *nf* inevitability
**inévitable** *adj* inevitable, unavoidable
**inexact** *adj* inexact, incorrect; unreliable; unpunctual
**inexactitude** *nf* inexactitude, inaccuracy, mistake; unpunctuality
**inexécutable** *adj* unfeasible, unworkable
**inexécuté** *adj* unexecuted, unperformed, unfulfilled
**inexercé** *adj* unexercised, unskilled
**inexistant** *adj* non-existent
**inexpérimenté** *adj* inexperienced, unskilled; untested
**inexpié** *adj* unexpiated
**inexpliqué** *adj* unexplained, unaccounted for
**inexploité** *adj* unexploited, unworked, uncultivated
**inexploré** *adj* unexplored
**inexplosible** *adj* non-explosive
**inexpressif -ive** *adj* inexpressive, expressionless
**inexprimable** *adj* inexpressible
**inexprimé** *adj* unexpressed
**inexpugnable** *adj* inexpugnable, impregnable
**inextinguible** *adj* inextinguishable; unquenchable; irrepressible
**inextirpable** *adj* ineradicable
**infaillibilité** *nf* infallibility
**infaillible** *adj* infallible, impracticable
**infamant** *adj* defamatory; degrading, dishonourable; *leg* involving loss of civil rights
**infâme** *adj* infamous, vile, unspeakable

**infamie** *nf* infamy, disgrace; infamous deed
**infanterie** *nf* infantry
**infanticide** *nm* infanticide, childmurder; *n* child-murderer; *adj* infanticidal
**infantilisme** *nm* infantilism
**infarctus** *nm med* infarctus; ~ **du myocarde** coronary (thrombosis)
**infatigable** *adj* indefatigable, tireless
**infatuation** *nf* self-importance, smugness
**infatuer (s')** *v refl* become infatuated
**infécond** *adj* barren, sterile
**infécondité** *nf* barrenness, sterility
**infect** *adj* stinking, noisome; filthy, vile; *coll* **il est** ~ he's a shit
**infecter** *vt* infect, pollute; corrupt
**infectieux -ieuse** *adj* infectious
**infection** *nf* infection; corruption; stink, stench
**inférer** *vt* (6) infer
**inférieur -e** *n* inferior; *adj* inferior; lower; poor
**infériorité** *nf* inferiority
**infernal** *adj* infernal; diabolical, devilish; *coll* bloody
**infertilité** *nf* infertility, barrenness
**infester** *vt* infest, overrun
**infidèle** *n* infidel; *adj* unfaithful, faithless; untrue, inaccurate; dishonest
**infiltrer (s')** *v refl* infiltrate, percolate, seep
**infime** *adj* infinitesimal, minute; low, mean
**infini** *nm* infinite; à l' ~ ad infinitum, without limit; *adj* infinite, boundless, unlimited, endless
**infiniment** *adv* infinitely; *coll* terribly, awfully; **je regrette** ~ I'm terribly sorry
**infinité** *nf* infinity
**infinitif** *nm* infinitive
**infirme** *n + adj* invalid, cripple(d), disabled (person); weak (person)
**infirmer** *vt* weaken, demonstrate the weakness of; *leg* annul, quash, invalidate
**infirmerie** *nf* infirmary, hospital, sickroom
**infirmier** *nm* male nurse, hospital attendant; *mil* medical orderly
**infirmière** *nf* nurse; ~ **en chef** matron
**infirmité** *nf* infirmity; disability
**inflammabilité** *nf* inflammability
**inflammable** *adj* inflammable, *US* flammable; excitable
**inflammation** *nf* inflammation; ignition; **point d'** ~ flashpoint
**inflammatoire** *adj* inflammatory
**inflation** *nf* inflation; excessive growth
**inflationniste** *adj* inflationary

**infléchir** *vt* inflect, bend; *gramm* inflect; **s'** ~ bend, curve
**infléchissable** *adj* unbendable, rigid; inflexible
**infléchissement** *nm* modification, slight change
**inflexibilité** *nf* inflexibility
**infliger** *vt* (3) inflict, impose
**influençable** *adj* influenceable
**influence** *nf* authority, influence
**influencer** *vt* (4) influence, have an influence on, sway
**influent** *adj* influential
**influer** *vi* have an influence; ~ **sur** influence, have an effect on
**in-folio** *nm*+*adj invar* folio
**informateur -trice** *n* informant; informer
**informaticien -ienne** *n* computer scientist
**informatif -ive** *adj* informative
**information** *nf leg* investigation; ~ **s** information, news; *rad* news bulletin; **agence d'** ~ **s** news agency; *leg* **ouvrir une** ~ begin legal proceedings; *mil* **service d'** ~ **s** intelligence
**informatique** *nf*+*adj* data-processing
**informe** *adj* formless, shapeless; crude, unpolished
**informé** *nm* **jusqu'à plus ample** ~ pending further information
**informel -elle** *adj* informal
**informer** *vt* inform, tell; *vi leg* investigate; ~ **contre** lay information against; **s'** ~ make inquiries
**infortune** *nf* misfortune, trouble; **tomber dans l'** ~ fall on evil days
**infortuné** *adj* unfortunate, unlucky
**infraction** *nf* offence, infraction, infringement
**infranchissable** *adj* impassable; insuperable
**infrarouge** *adj* infra-red
**infréquenté** *adj* unfrequented
**infroissable** *adj* crease-resisting; wrinkle-proof
**infructueux -euse** *adj* unfruitful, barren; fruitless
**infus** *adj* infused; inborn; *coll* **il croit avoir la science** ~ **e** he thinks he knows it all
**infuser** *vt* infuse, steep in, instil; *vi* infuse; **s'** ~ infuse, draw (tea)
**ingambe** *adj* nimble, alert
**ingénier (s')** *v refl* strive, strain one's ingenuity
**ingénierie** *nf* engineering
**ingénieur** *nm* engineer; ~ **conseil** consulting engineer; ~ **des ponts et chaussées** government civil engineer; ~ **du son** recording engineer
**ingénieux -ieuse** *adj* ingenious, clever

**ingéniosité** *nf* ingenuity, ingeniousness
**ingénu** *adj* ingenious, artless, unsophisticated
**ingénue** *nf theat* ingenue
**ingénuité** *nf* ingenuousness, simplicity
**ingérence** *nf* interference, meddling
**ingérer** *vt* (6) *med* ingest, take (food) into the stomach; **s'** ~ interfere, meddle; **s'** ~ **dans** poke one's nose into
**ingouvernable** *adj* ungovernable, unruly, unmanageable
**ingrat -e** *n* ungrateful person; *adj* ungrateful; disagreeable; sterile; thankless; **l'âge** ~ the awkward age
**ingratitude** *nf* ingratitude; sterility; thanklessness
**inguérissable** *adj* incurable
**ingurgiter** *vt* swallow, gulp down, wolf
**inhabile** *adj* unpractised, unskilled; clumsy; *leg* incompetent
**inhabileté** *nf* lack of skill, clumsiness
**inhabilité** *nf leg* incompetence
**inhabitable** *adj* uninhabitable
**inhabité** *adj* uninhabited
**inhalateur** *nm* inhaler
**inhaler** *vt* inhale
**inharmonie** *nf* discordance
**inharmonieux -ieuse** *adj* discordant, inharmonious
**inhiber** *vt* inhibit
**inhospitalier -ière** *adj* inhospitable
**inhumain** *adj* inhuman
**inhumer** *vt* bury, inhume
**inimaginable** *adj* unimaginable
**inimitié** *nf* hostility, enmity
**inintelligence** *nf* lack of intelligence
**inintelligent** *adj* unintelligent
**inintelligible** *adj* unintelligible
**ininterrompu** *adj* uninterrupted, continuous
**inique** *adj* iniquitous
**iniquité** *nf* iniquity
**initiale** *nf* initial
**initiateur -trice** *n* initiator; *adj* initiating
**initiative** *nf* initiative; ~ **privée** private enterprise; **syndicat d'** ~ local tourist office
**initié -e** *n* initiate, someone in the know
**initier** *vt* initiate
**injecté** *adj* injected; bloodshot; congested
**injecter** *vt* inject; **s'** ~ become injected, bloodshot
**injonction** *nf* injunction, order
**injouable** *adj* unplayable; unactable
**injudicieux -ieuse** *adj* injudicious
**injure** *nf* insult; wrong; *leg* tort; ~ **s** abuse
**injurier** *vt* insult
**injurieux -ieuse** *adj* injurious, insulting, abusive
**injuste** *adj* unjust, unfair; unrighteous

**injustice** *nf* injustice, unfairness; unjust action

**injustifiable** *adj* unjustifiable

**injustifié** *adj* unjustified

**inlassable** *adj* tireless, indefatigable, untiring

**innavigable** *adj* unnavigable; unseaworthy

**inné** *adj* innate, inborn

**innocence** *nf* innocence, guiltlessness; artlessness; innocuousness

**innocent -e** *n* simple-minded person; innocent person; *adj* innocent, guiltless; simple, artless

**innocenter** *vt* prove innocent, clear; excuse

**innombrable** *adj* innumerable, countless

**innommable** *adj* unspeakable

**innom(m)é** *adj* unnamed, nameless

**innovateur -trice** *n* innovator; *adj* innovating

**innover** *vt* innovate

**inobservation** *nf* inobservance; noncompliance

**inobservé** *adj* unobserved, unnoticed; not complied with

**inoccupé** *adj* unoccupied, vacant; unemployed, idle

**inoculer** *vt* inoculate; instil into

**inodore** *adj* inodorous, odourless

**inoffensif -ive** *adj* inoffensive, harmless; innocuous

**inondable** *adj* liable to flooding

**inondation** *nf* inundation, flood

**inondé** *adj* inundated, flooded; overrun; ~ de larmes bathed in tears

**inonder** *vt* inundate, flood; overrun

**inopérant** *adj* inoperative

**inopiné** *adj* unexpected, unlooked-for

**inopportun** *adj* inopportune, ill-timed

**inorganique** *adj* inorganic

**inoubliable** *adj* unforgettable

**inouï** *adj* unheard of, unparalleled; outrageous

**inox** *nm* stainless steel

**inoxydable** *adj* inoxidizable, rustless; stainless (steel)

**inqualifiable** *adj* unqualifiable; unspeakable, infamous

**in-quarto** *nm* + *adj invar* quarto

**inquiet -iète** *adj* restless, uneasy; anxious, worried

**inquiétant** *adj* alarming, disquieting, disturbing

**inquiéter** *vt* worry, make anxious, disturb; s' ~ worry, become anxious

**inquiétude** *nf* restlessness; anxiety, disquiet, concern; éprouver des ~ s have qualms

**¹inquisiteur** *nm* inquisitor

**²inquisiteur -trice** *adj* inquisitorial

**insaisissable** *adj* impossible to seize; elusive; imperceptible; *leg* not distrainable

**insalissable** *adj* unsoilable

**insalubre** *adj* insalubrious, unhealthy

**insalubrité** *nf* insalubrity, unhealthiness

**insanité** *nf* insanity, lunacy; insane action

**insatiable** *adj* insatiable, unquenchable

**insatisfait** *adj* unsatisfied

**inscription** *nf* inscription; entry, registration, enrolment; droits d' ~ registration fee; feuille d' ~ entry form

**inscrire** *vt* (42) inscribe, write down; register, enter; s' ~, se faire ~ enter, put one's name down

**inscrit** *adj* enrolled, registered

**insecte** *nm* insect

**insécurité** *nf* insecurity

**insensé -e** *n* madman (-woman); *adj* mad, insane; foolish, crazy

**insensibiliser** *vt* anaesthetize

**insensibilité** *nf* insensibility, unconsciousness; insensitiveness; indifference

**insensible** *adj* insensible; insentient, numb; imperceptible; indifferent

**inséparable** *nm orni* love-bird; *adj* inseparable

**insérer** *vt* (6) insert

**insertion** *nf* insertion; assimilation, integration

**inserviable** *adj* disobliging

**insidieux -ieuse** *adj* insidious

**insigne** *nm* sign, badge; ~ s insignia; *adj* distinguished, noteworthy; notorious, arrant

**insignifiance** *nf* insignificance

**insignifiant** *adj* insignificant, trivial; vacuous

**insinuant** *adj* insinuating, smooth, ingratiating

**insinuer** *vt* insinuate, imply, hint at; insert; s' ~ insinuate oneself, creep

**insipide** *adj* insipid, tasteless; dull, tame

**insipidité** *nf* insipidity, tastelessness

**insistance** *nf* emphasis, insistence

**insister** *vi* insist, stress; persist, press the point; ~ auprès de qn make strong representations to s/o

**insobriété** *nf* insobriety; interference

**insociable** *adj* unsociable

**insolation** *nf* sunstroke

**insolence** *nf* insolence, impudence, impertinence; insolent remark

**insolent** *adj* insolent, impudent; arrogant, haughty

**insolite** *adj* unwonted; unexpected

**insoluble** *adj* insoluble, unsolvable

**insolvabilité** *nf* insolvency

**insolvable** *adj* insolvent

**insomnie** *nf* insomnia, sleeplessness

**insondable** *adj* unsoundable, unfathomable

**insonore** *adj* sound-proof; sound-deadening

**insonorisation** *nf* sound-proofing

**insonoriser** *vt* sound-proof, insulate

**insouciance** *nf* unconcern, heedlessness

**insouciant** *adj* unconcerned, heedless

**insoucieux -ieuse** *adj* unmindful, careless

**insoumis** *nm mil* absentee, defaulter, *US* draft dodger; *adj* unsubdued; unsubmissive, unruly, insubordinate; *mil* absent, defaulting

**insoumission** *nf* unsubmissiveness, insubordination; *mil* defaulting

**insoupçonnable** *adj* above suspicion

**insoupçonné** *adj* unsuspected

**insoutenable** *adj* untenable, indefensible; unbearable, unendurable

**inspecter** *vt* inspect, survey, examine

**inspecteur -trice** *n* inspector, inspectress; detective-inspector; ~ **d'Académie** inspector of schools ( = H.M.I.); ~ **des contributions directes** inspector of taxes; ~ **sanitaire** public health officer; ~ **du travail** factory inspector

**inspection** *nf* examination, inspection, survey; inspectorate

**inspirateur -trice** *n* inspirer, source of inspiration; *adj* inspiring; *med* inspiratory

**inspiration** *nf* inspiration, impulse; *med* inspiration, inhaling; **sous l'~ du moment** on the spur of the moment

**inspirer** *vt* inspire, encourage, prompt; *vi med* inspire, inhale; **s'~ de** draw one's inspiration from, imitate

**instabilité** *nf* instability, shakiness; inconstancy

**instable** *adj* unstable, shaky, inconstant

**installation** *nf* installation, fitting up; plant, equipment; fittings, appointments; *eccles* induction

**installer** *vt* install, fit up; equip; *eccles* install, induct; **s'~** settle down

**instamment** *adv* insistently, urgently

**instance** *nf* instancy, solicitation; *leg* suit; ~ **s entreaties; en ~ de départ** on the point of departure; **en ~ de divorce** in the process of getting a divorce; *leg* **introduire une ~** start proceedings; **tribunal de première ~** court of first instance, lower court

**instant** *nm* instant, moment; **à l'~** just now, a moment ago; at once, immediately; **un ~!** wait a moment!; *coll* hang on!; *adj* instant, urgent

**instantané** *nm* snap(shot); *adj* instantaneous, sudden

**instar (à l'~ de)** *prep phr* after the manner of, like, in imitation of

**instaurateur -trice** *n* founder

**instauration** *nf* founding, establishing

**instaurer** *vt* found, establish

**instigateur -trice** *n* instigator

**instiller** *vt* instil

**instinctif -ive** *adj* instinctive

**instituer** *vt* institute, found, establish

**institut** *nm* institute, institution; ~ **de beauté** beauty parlour

**instituteur** *nm* teacher (in primary school); founder

**institution** *nf* institution, founding; private school, academy

**institutrice** *nf* teacher (in primary school); governess; foundress

**instructeur -trice** *n* instructor; *nm mil* (drill-)instructor

**instructif -ive** *adj* instructive

**instruction** *nf* instruction; education, schooling; *mil* training; *leg* preliminary investigation of a case; **avoir de l'~** be educated; *leg* **juge d'~** examining magistrate; **sans ~** uneducated

**instruire** *vt* (80) instruct, teach; inform; *mil* train, drill; *leg* examine; **s'~** educate oneself

**instruit** *adj* educated, well-read; *mil* trained

**instrument** *nm* instrument; implement

**instrumenter** *vt mus* score; *vi leg* draw up a deed, take legal proceedings

**instrumentiste** *n* instrumentalist

**insu** *nm* ignorance; **à l'~ de** without the knowledge of; **à son ~** without his knowledge

**insubordonné** *adj* insubordinate

**insubstantiel -ielle** *adj* insubstantial

**insuccès** *nm* lack of success; failure

**insuffisance** *nf* insufficiency, inadequacy; shortage; incompetence

**insuffisant** *adj* insufficient, inadequate; incapable, incompetent

**insufflateur** *nm* throat-spray, nose-spray

**insuffler** *vt* insufflate, blow air into, inflate; *med* spray

**insulaire** *n* islander; *adj* insular

**insularité** *nf* insularity

**insuline** *nf* insulin

**insultant** *adj* insulting, offensive

**insulte** *nf* insult; **faire ~ à** insult

**insulter** *vt* insult, offend; *vi* ~ **à** jeer at, give insult to

**insupportable** *adj* unbearable, intolerable, insufferable

**insurgé -e** *n* insurgent, rebel

**insurger (s')** *v refl* (3) rise, revolt

**insurmontable** *adj* insurmountable, insuperable

**intact** *adj* intact, undamaged, whole; unblemished

**intaille** *nf* intaglio

**intangibilité** *nf* intangibility

**intarissable** *adj* inexhaustible, unfailing, perennial

**intégral** *adj* integral, full, complete; *math* **calcul ~** integral calculus; **édition ~e** unexpurgated edition; complete edition

**intégrale** *nf math* integral; complete works

**intégralité** *nf* integrality, completeness

**intégrant** *adj* integrant, integral; **partie ~e** integral part

**intègre** *adj* honest, upright

**intégrer** *vt* (6) integrate; **s'~** join, combine

**intégrité** *nf* integrity, uprightness; completeness, entirety

**intellectuel -uelle** *n* intellectual, highbrow, *US coll* egg-head; *adj* intellectual, mental

**intelligence** *nf* intelligence, intellect; comprehension, understanding; intercourse; conspiring; **~s** communications, dealings; **avoir une bonne ~ des affaires** have a good grasp of business; **d'~ avec** in collusion with; **en bonne ~ avec** on good terms with

**intelligent** *adj* intelligent, clever, brainy

**intelligibilité** *nf* intelligibility

**intelligible** *adj* intelligible, clear, understandable

**intempérant** *adj* intemperate

**intempéré** *adj* immoderate

**intempérie** *nf* inclemency; **~s** bad weather

**intempestif -ive** *adj* untimely, inopportune

**intendance** *nf* intendance, administration, management; *mil* commissariat, supply services

**intendant -e** *n* manager; (school) bursar; *nm hist* intendant

**intense** *adj* intense, severe; deep (colour); intensive; strong

**intensif -ive** *adj* intensive

**intensifier** *vt* intensify

**intensité** *nf* intensity; depth (colour); strength

**intenter** *vt leg* bring; **~ un procès contre** bring an action against, sue

**intention** *nf* intention, purpose; will, wish; *leg* intent; **~ arrêtée de** determination to; **à l'~ de** destined for, for the sake of; **à son ~** for him; **avec ~** on purpose; **dans l'~ de** with a view to; **sans ~** unintentionally

**intentionné** *adj* **bien ~** well-intentioned; **mal ~** ill-intentioned

**intentionnel -elle** *adj* intentional, deliberate

**inter** *nm tel* trunk call, long-distance call; *sp* inside-forward

**interagir** *vi* interact

**interallié** *adj* allied

**intercalaire** *nm* guide-card (card-index); *adj* intercalated, interpolated; intercalary

**intercaler** *vt* intercalate, insert

**intercéder** *vi* (6) intercede, plead

**intercepter** *vt* intercept; cut off

**intercesseur** *nm* intercessor; mediator

**interdiction** *nf* interdiction, prohibition; *leg* injunction; **~ de séjour** ban on residence (in a specified area)

**interdire** *vt* (74) forbid, prohibit, ban; amaze, disconcert; *leg* interdict, veto; **~ qn de ses fonctions** suspend s/o from his duties

**interdisciplinaire** *adj* interdisciplinary

**interdit** *nm* interdict; *adj* forbidden, prohibited, banned; amazed, speechless, disconcerted; *leg* under restraint; **~ de séjour** banned from residing (in a specified area)

**intéressant** *adj* interesting; attractive, satisfactory; **être dans un état ~** be in the family way

**intéressé** *adj* interested; concerned, involved; self-interested, calculating; **amour ~** cupboard love

**intéresser** *vt* interest, affect, concern; **~ qn dans une affaire** give s/o an interest in a business; **s'~ à** be interested in, have an interest in, concern oneself with

**intérêt** *nm* interest; advantage, benefit; attraction, charm; concern; *comm* interest, share; **~ composé** compound interest; **à ~s** interest-bearing; **avoir ~ à** be well advised to; **avoir un ~ au jeu** have a stake in the game; **il y a ~ à** it is desirable to; **ligne d'~** local branch line; **porter ~ à qn** take an interest in s/o; **sans ~** dull, boring

**interfolier** *vt* interleave

**intérieur** *nm* interior, inside; home; household affairs; *pol* interior; **à l'~** inside; **d'~** indoor; **femme d'~** home-loving woman; **ministère de l'Intérieur** = Home Office; *adj* interior, inner, inside; inward, spiritual; domestic

**intérim** *nm* interim; **assurer l'~** carry on (during vacancy or absence); **par ~** acting, deputizing

**intérimaire** *n* deputy, locum tenens; *adj* temporary, interim, provisional

**interjection** *nf gramm* interjection; *leg* lodging (appeal)

**interjeter** *vt* (5) interject, insert (remark); *leg* lodge (appeal)

**interligne** *nm* space between the lines; **double ~** double spacing

**interligner** *vt* interline, write between the lines of

**interlocuteur -trice** *n* interlocutor

**interlocutoire** *nm leg* interlocutory judgement; *adj* interlocutory, provisional

**interlope** *nm naut* blockade-runner, interloper; *adj naut* illegal, unauthorized; shady, suspect

**interloquer** *vt* disconcert, take aback; *leg* grant an interlocutory decree; s' ~ be disconcerted, be overcome by shyness

**intermède** *nm* medium, intermediary; *theat* interlude

**intermédiaire** *nm* intermediary, medium, go-between; *comm* middleman, agent; **par l' ~ de** through the medium of; *adj* intermediate, intermediary

**intermittence** *nf* intermittence; **par ~** intermittently

**intermittent** *adj* intermittent, occasional; *med* irregular (pulse)

**internat** *nm* boarding-school; boarding, living-in; *med* post of house-man, *US* internship

**interne** *n* boarder; *med* house-man, *US* intern

**internement** *nm* internment, confinement

**interner** *vt* intern, confine

**internissable** *adj* untarnishable

**interpellateur -trice** *n* interpellant, questioner

**interpellation** *nf* interpellation; (peremptory) questioning; question (in Parliament); *mil* challenge

**interpeller** *vt* question (peremptorily); put a question to (a Minister in Parliament); *mil* challenge

**interphone** *nm* intercom, *US* interphone

**interplanétaire** *adj* interplanetary, space (travel)

**interpoler** *vt* interpolate

**interposer** *vt* interpose; **par personne interposée** through an intermediary; s' ~ interpose oneself, intervene

**interposition** *nf* interposition; intervention

**interprétation** *nf* interpretation, explanation; *theat* + *mus* rendering, performance

**interprète** *n* interpreter; one who explains, expounds; *theat* + *mus* performer

**interpréter** *vt* (6) interpret; explain, expound; *theat* + *mus* perform

**interrègne** *nm* interregnum

**interrogateur -trice** *n* interrogator; *adj* interrogatory, questioning

**interrogatif -ive** *adj* interrogative

**interrogation** *nf* interrogation; **point d' ~** question-mark

**interrogatoire** *nm leg* examination, questioning; **contre- ~** cross-examination

**interroger** *vt* (3) interrogate, examine, question; consult

**interrompre** *vt* (85) interrupt, intercept; break off, suspend; break (journey); *elect* break off, cut off, switch off (current); s' ~ break off, stop (speaking)

**interrupteur -trice** *n* interrupter; *nm elect* switch, contact-breaker; *adj* interrupting

**interruption** *nf* interruption, interception; stoppage, suspension; *elect* breaking, cutting, switching off (current)

**interurbain** *adj* interurban; *tel* trunk

**intervalle** *nm* interval, gap, space; period (time); **dans l' ~** in the meantime; **par ~ s** now and then

**intervenir** *vi* (96) intervene, interfere, step in; happen, take place, arise; **faire ~** call in; *v impers* **il intervint un compromis** a compromise was made

**intervention** *nf* intervention, interference; *med* operation

**interversion** *nf* inversion, transposition

**intervertir** *vt* invert, transpose

**interviewer** *vt* interview

**interviewer** *nm* interviewer

**intestat** *adj invar* intestate

**intestin** *nm* intestine, bowel; ~ **grêle** small intestine; **gros ~** large intestine; *adj* intestine

**intimation** *nf* intimation, notification

**intime** *n* intimate, close friend; *adj* intimate, close; interior, innermost; cosy, homely

**intimé -e** *n leg* respondent

**intimer** *vt* intimate, notify; *leg* summons

**intimidant** *adj* intimidating

**intimidateur -trice** *n* intimidator; *adj* intimidating, intimidatory

**intimider** *vt* intimidate, threaten; s' ~ become nervous, shy

**intimité** *nf* intimacy, familiarity; innermost part; **dans l' ~** in private

**intitulé** *nm* heading (chapter), title (book)

**intituler** *vt* entitle, give a title to; s' ~ call oneself

**intonation** *nf* intonation; *mus* pitch, modulation

**intox(e)** *nf pol* indoctrination

**intoxicant** *adj* poisonous, toxic

**intoxication** *nf* intoxication; *pol* indoctrination

**intoxiquer** *vt* poison; *pol* indoctrinate

**intraduisible** *adj* untranslatable

**intraitable** *adj* intractable, obstinate, uncompromising; *med* untreatable

**intransigeance** *nf* intransigence; strictness

**intransigeant -e** *n* die-hard; *adj* intransigent, uncompromising; strict

**intransitif -ive** *adj* intransitive

**intraveineux -euse** *adj* intravenous

**intrépide** *adj* intrepid, bold, dauntless; **menteur** ~ brazen, bare-faced liar

**intrépidité** *nf* intrepidity, boldness, dauntlessness

**intrigant -e** *n* intriguer; *adj* intriguing, scheming

**intrigue** *nf* intrigue, plot, scheme; love-affair; *theat* plot

**intriguer** *vt* puzzle, intrigue, make curious; *vi* intrigue, scheme, plot

**intrinsèque** *adj* intrinsic

**introducteur -trice** *n* introducer

**introductif -ive** *adj* introductory

**introduction** *nf* introduction, introducing, bringing in; insertion; preface, foreword

**introduire** *vt* (80) introduce, bring in, usher in; insert; s' ~ get in, penetrate

**intronisation** *nf* enthronement; establishment

**introniser** *vt* enthrone; establish, set up; s' ~ become established; establish oneself

**introspectif -ive** *adj* introspective

**introuvable** *adj* undiscoverable

**introverti -e** *n* introvert; *adj* introverted

**intrus -e** *n* intruder; *coll* gatecrasher; *leg* trespasser; *adj* intruding

**intuitif -ive** *adj* intuitive

**inusable** *adj* hard-wearing, long-lasting

**inusité** *adj* unusual, uncommon; not in use (word, phrase)

**inutile** *adj* useless, unavailing, vain; ~ de dire needless to say; c'est ~ it's no use, don't bother

**inutilisable** *adj* unusable

**inutilisé** *adj* unused

**inutilité** *nf* inutility, uselessness; useless thing

**invaincu** *adj* unconquered

**invalide** *n* invalid; disabled person; *mil* pensioner

**invalider** *vt* invalidate, quash (election, will)

**invalidité** *nf* infirmity, disablement; *leg* invalidity

**invariabilité** *nf* invariability

**invariable** *adj* invariable; *math* constant

**invectiver** *vt* abuse, rail at; *vi* ~ contre rail against, inveigh against

**invendable** *adj* unsaleable

**invendu** *adj* unsold

**inventaire** *nm* inventory, list of stock; faire son ~ take stock

**inventer** *vt* invent, contrive, make up; *coll* il n'a pas inventé la poudre he'll never set the Thames on fire

**inventeur -trice** *n* inventor; *adj* inventive

**inventif -ive** *adj* inventive

**invention** *nf* invention, device, discovery; fabrication, lie

**inventorier** *vt* inventory, take stock

**invérifiable** *adj* unverifiable

**invérifié** *adj* unverified, unchecked

**inversable** *adj* uncapsizable

**inverse** *nm* inverse, opposite, reverse; à l' ~ de contrary to; *adj* inverse, inverted, opposite

**inverser** *vt* reverse, invert; *elect* reverse

**inverseur** *nm* reversing-device; *elect* change-over switch

**inversion** *nf* *gramm* + *math* inversion; sexual inversion; *elect* reversal (current)

**invertébré** *adj* invertebrate

**inverti -e** *n* (sexual) invert

**invertir** *vt* invert, reverse; *elect* reverse (current)

**investigateur -trice** *n* investigator; *adj* investigating, searching

**investir** *vt* invest, bestow; *comm* invest; *mil* invest, beleaguer; **investi de l'autorité** vested with power

**investisseur** *nm* investor

**invétéré** *adj* inveterate, deep-rooted; confirmed

**invétérer (s')** *v refl* (6) become inveterate, become deep-rooted

**invincibilité** *nf* invincibility

**inviolabilité** *nf* inviolability

**inviolé** *adj* inviolate

**invisibilité** *nf* invisibility

**invitation** *nf* invitation; **sans** ~ uninvited

**invite** *nf* lead (cards), call (bridge); incitement; **répondre à l'** ~ **de qn** return s/o's lead

**invité -e** *n* guest

**inviter** *vt* invite, ask; call (cards)

**invivable** *adj* *coll* unbearable, impossible to live with

**invocatoire** *adj* invocatory

**involontaire** *adj* involuntary, unintentional

**invoquer** *vt* invoke, call upon; refer to, put forward, cite

**invraisemblable** *adj* unlikely, improbable, hard to credit

**invraisemblance** *nf* unlikelihood, improbability

**invulnérabilité** *nf* invulnerability

**iode** *nm* iodine; **teinture d'** ~ tincture of iodine

**ionique** *adj* *archi* ionic

**iota** *nm* iota; *coll* jot, whit, tittle

**iouler** *vi* yodel

**irascibilité** *nf* irascibility, temper, testiness

**irascible** *adj* irascible, irritable, testy

**iris** *nm* iris (eye); prismatic halo; *bot* iris, flag

**irisation** *nf* irisation, iridescence

**irisé** *adj* iridescent

**iriser** *vt* make iridescent; **s' ~** become iridescent

**Irlandais -e** *n* Irishman (-woman)

**irlandais** *nm* Irish, Erse (language); *adj* Irish

**Irlande** *nf* Ireland

**ironie** *nf* irony

**ironique** *adj* ironic, ironical

**ironiser** *vi* speak ironically, use irony

**ironiste** *n* ironist

**irradier** *vi* irradiate, radiate, spread

**irraisonnable** *adj* irrational

**irraisonné** *adj* unreasoned

**irrationnel -elle** *adj* irrational

**irréalisable** *adj* unrealizable

**irrecevable** *adj* inadmissible; unacceptable

**irrécouvrable** *adj* irrecoverable, unrecoverable; **créance ~** bad debt

**irrécupérable** *adj* irretrievable; beyond salvation

**irrécusable** *adj* irrecusable, unimpeachable

**irréductible** *adj* indomitable, unshakeable; *math + med* irreducible

**irréel -elle** *adj* unreal

**irréfléchi** *adj* rash, unconsidered, hasty

**irréflexion** *nf* thoughtlessness

**irréformable** *adj* unalterable

**irréfuté** *adj* unrefuted

**irrégularité** *nf* irregularity; unevenness; unpunctuality

**irrégulier -ière** *adj* irregular; uneven; unpunctual

**irréligieux -ieuse** *adj* irreligious

**irrémédiable** *adj* irremediable, irreparable

**irremplaçable** *adj* irreplaceable

**irréparable** *adj* irreparable; irretrievable

**irréprochable** *adj* irreproachable, faultless

**irrésolu** *adj* irresolute, wavering; unsolved

**irrespect** *nm* disrespect

**irrespectueux -ueuse** *adj* disrespectful

**irrespirable** *adj* irrespirable, unbreathable

**irresponsabilité** *nf* irresponsibility

**irresponsable** *adj* irresponsible

**irrétrécissable** *adj* unshrinkable

**irrévérencieux -ieuse** *adj* irreverent, disrespectful

**irrigateur** *nm* hose; *med* enema

**irriguer** *vt* irrigate

**irritable** *adj* irritable, sensitive

**irritant** *nm* irritant; *adj* irritating

**irriter** *vt* irritate; **s' ~** grow angry; become inflamed

**irruption** *nf* irruption, invasion; overflowing (river); **faire ~ dans** burst into

**islamique** *adj* Islamic

**Islandais -e** *n* Icelander

**islandais** *nm* Icelandic (language); *adj* Icelandic

**Islande** *nf* Iceland

**isobare** *nf* isobar; *adj* isobaric

**isocèle** *adj* isosceles

**isolant** *nm* elect insulator; *adj* isolating; insulating; **bouteille ~ e** thermos flask; *archi* **couche ~ e** damp-course; *elect* **ruban ~** insulating tape

**¹isolateur** *nm* elect insulator

**²isolateur -trice** *adj* insulating

**isolé** *adj* isolated, detached, lonely; *elect* insulated

**isolement** *nm* isolation, loneliness; *elect* insulation

**isolément** *adv* separately, individually, singly

**isoler** *vt* isolate, detach; *elect* insulate; **s' ~** cut oneself off

**isoloir** *nm* polling-booth; *elect* insulator

**Israélien -ienne** *n* Israeli

**israélien -ienne** *adj* Israeli

**Israélite** *n* Israelite, Jew

**israélite** *adj* Israelite, Jewish

**issu** *adj* descended, born

**issue** *nf* result, upshot, issue; exit, way out; **à l' ~ de** at the end of; **chemin sans ~** dead-end, cul-de-sac; **situation sans ~** dead-lock

**isthme** *nm* isthmus

**Italie** *nf* Italy

**Italien -ienne** *n* Italian

**italien** *nm* Italian (language); *adj* (*f* **-ienne**) Italian

**italique** *nm* typ italic, italics; *adj* Italic (race)

**item** *adv* ditto, item

**itératif -ive** *adj* leg reiterated; *gramm* iterative

**itinéraire** *nm* itinerary, route; guidebook; *adj* itinerary

**itou** *adv* sl also, too

**ivoire** *nm* ivory; object made of ivory

**ivoirerie** *nf* ivory trade; ivory work

**ivoirin** *adj* ivory

**ivraie** *nf* bot darnel, tare; *bibl* tare

**ivre** *adj* drunk, intoxicated

**ivresse** *nf* drunkenness, intoxication; rapture, ecstasy; *leg* **en état d' ~ publique** drunk and disorderly

**ivrogne -esse** *n* drunkard; *coll* boozer, pub-crawler; *adj* drunken

**ivrognerie** *nf* drunkenness

# J

**jabot** *nm* frill, ruffle, jabot; crop (bird); *coll* belly; **se remplir le ~** have a good tuck-in
**jaboter** *vi coll* jabber, chatter
**jacasse** *nf coll* magpie; *coll* chatterbox (woman)
**jacasser** *vi coll* jabber, chatter
**jacasserie** *nf coll* gossip, idle chatter
**jachère** *nf* fallow, unploughed land
**jacinthe** *nf* hyacinth; **~ des bois, ~ sauvage** bluebell
**jacquerie** *nf hist* peasant rising, peasants' revolt
**Jacques** *nm* James; **Maître ~** Jack-of-all-trades, factotum
**jacquet** *nm* backgammon; backgammon board
**Jacquot** *nm* Jim, Jimmy; Poll (parrot)
**jactance** *nf* boastfulness, bragging
**jadis** *adv* formerly, of old, once upon a time
**jaillir** *vi* gush out, spout, spurt (liquids); shoot out (flames); fly (sparks); *fig* burst forth
**jaillissant** *adj* gushing, spouting; flying; **puits ~** (oil) gusher
**jaillissement** *nm* gushing out; gush, spurt; shooting out; *elect* flash, sparking
**jais** *nm* jet; **noir comme du ~** jet-black
**jalon** *nm* surveyor's staff, levelling-rod, pole; plan, preparation; **poser des ~s** prepare the way, blaze the trail
**jalonnement** *nm* marking out, staking out
**jalonner** *vt* mark out, stake out
**jalouser** *vt* envy, be jealous of
¹**jalousie** *nf* jealousy
²**jalousie** *nf* Venetian blind
³**jalousie** *nf* sweet-william
**jaloux -ouse** *adj* jealous, envious; watchful, careful; **~ de** anxious to
**Jamaïque** *nf* Jamaica
**jamais** *adv* ever (positive); never (negative); **~ de la vie!** never!, out of the question!; **ne ... ~** never
**jambage** *nm* down-stroke (writing); *archi* jamb; foundation-wall
**jambe** *nf* leg; *archi* strut, stay; *coll* **ça vous fera une belle ~!** a lot of good that'll do you!; *coll* **par dessous la ~** carelessly, perfunctorily; *coll* **prendre ses ~s à son cou** take to one's heels; **s'enfuir à toutes ~s** run away as fast as possible; *coll* **tirer dans les ~s de qn**

play a mean trick on s/o
**jambé** *adj* **bien ~** with good, well-shaped legs
**jambière** *nf mil* gaiter; *med* (elastic) stocking; *sp* shin-pad
**jambon** *nm* ham; **~ de Bayonne** = Parma ham
**jambonneau** *nm* knuckle of ham
**jante** *nf* rim
**janvier** *nm* January
**Japon** *nm* Japan
**japon** *nm* Japanese vellum; Japanese porcelain
**Japonais -e** *n* Japanese
**japonais** *nm lang* Japanese; *adj* Japanese
**japonerie** *nf* Japanese curio
**jappement** *nm* yelping, yapping
**japper** *vi* yelp, yap
**jaquette** *nf* jacket (woman); morning coat (man); dust-cover
**jardin** *nm* garden; **~ d'acclimatation** zoo; **~ d'enfants** kindergarten, nursery school; **~ potager** kitchen garden; *theat* **côté ~** prompt-side, stage right
¹**jardinage** *nm* gardening; garden produce
²**jardinage** *nm* flaw (diamond)
**jardiner** *vi* garden
**jardinet** *nm* small garden
**jardinier -ière** *n* gardener; *adj* horticultural
¹**jardinière** *nf* **~ d'enfants** kindergarten teacher
²**jardinière** *nf* flower-stand; hand-cart; *cul* mixed vegetables; vegetable soup
**jargon** *nm* jargon; cant, slang; **~ administratif** officialese; *coll* lingo
**jargonner** *vi* talk jargon
**Jarnac** *nm* **coup de ~** treacherous blow
**jarre** *nf* earthenware jar
**jarret** *nm* back of the knee; hock (horse); *cul* **~ de bœuf** shin of beef; **~ de veau** knuckle of veal; *coll* **avoir du ~** be strong in the legs; **couper le ~ à** hamstring
**jarretelle** *nf* suspender, US garter
**jarretière** *nf* garter
**jars** *nm* gander
**jaser** *vi* chatter, natter; gossip; twitter, cackle; *coll* blab, blow the gaff
**jaseur -euse** *n* chatterbox, gossip; *adj* chattering, talkative, gossiping
**jasmin** *nm* jasmine

**jaspe** *nm* jasper; marbling (bookbinding)
**jasper** *vt* marble, mottle
**jaspure** *nf* marbling
**jatte** *nf* bowl, basin
**jauge** *nf* gauge; **mot** petrol-gauge, *US* gasoline-gauge; dipstick; *naut* tonnage
**jauger** *vt* (3) gauge, measure; *fig* size up; *vi naut* draw; *naut* **~ 5.000 tonnes** be of 5,000 tons burden
**jaugeur** *nm* gauger
**jaunâtre** *adj* yellowish
**jaune** *nm* man (woman) of yellow race; *nm* yellow (colour); *coll* black-leg, scab, strike-breaker; **~ d'œuf** yolk of egg; *adj* yellow; sallow; brown (shoes); **feu ~** amber light; *pol* **livre ~** = blue book; *adv* **rire ~** give a sickly smile
**jaunir** *vi* turn yellow; fade; *vt* make yellow
**jaunisse** *nf* jaundice
**javel** *nf* eau de **~** bleach, bleaching-water
**javelot** *nm* javelin
**je** *pron* I
**Jean** *nm* John
**jean** *nm* jeans
**Jeanne** *nf* Jane, Joan, Jean
**Jeannette** *nf* Janet, Jenny
¹**jeannette** *nf* sleeve-board
²**jeannette** *nf* Brownie
**je-m'en-foutisme** *nm coll* indifference, couldn't-care-less attitude
**je-ne-sais-quoi** *nm invar* an indefinable something
**jérémiade** *nf coll* Jeremiad, lamentation
**jersey** *nm* jersey; stockinet
**jésuite** *nm* Jesuit; hypocrite; *adj coll* Jesuitical, hypocritical
**jésuitique** *adj* Jesuitical, plausible, specious
**Jésus** *nm* Jesus; **avant ~ Christ** B.C.
**jésus** *adj* imperial (paper format)
**jet** *nm* throwing, casting; throw; jet, gush, stream; burst, flush; *bot* shoot (plant); *naut* jettisoning; spout, nozzle; **~ d'eau** fountain; **à un ~ de pierre** at a stone's throw from; **d'un seul ~** at one go; **premier ~** first attempt, rough sketch
**jeté** *nm* over (knitting)
**jetée** *nf* jetty, pier; breakwater
**jeter** *vt* (5) throw, cast, fling, throw away, jettison; drop (anchor); lay (foundations); utter, let out; *med* discharge; **~ un sort** cast a spell; **le dé en est jeté** the die is cast; **se ~** throw oneself, rush; flow (river); **se ~ au cou de qn** fall on s/o's neck; **elle s'est jetée à sa tête** she threw herself at him
**jeton** *nm* counter, token; *coll* **c'est un faux ~** he's a bit of a crook
**jeu** *nm* game, play, sport; gambling, gaming; stake; *theat* acting; *mus* playing; (organ-)stop; set (chess); pack (cards); slack, looseness, play; **~ d'adresse** sleight of hand; **~ de fiches** card-index; **~ de lumière** lighting effect; **~ de mots** play on words; *theat* **~ de scène** business; **~ de société** parlour-game; **~ d'esprit** witticism; *coll* crack; **~ d'orgues** organ stop; *theat* switchboard; **avoir du ~** be loose, slack; **double ~** double-cross; **faire le ~ de qn** play into s/o's hands; **faites vos ~ x!** place your bets!; *sp* **hors ~** out of play; off-side; **jouer beau ~** play fair; **jouer gros ~** play for high stakes; **mettre qch en ~** call sth into play; **vieux ~** old-fashioned; **y aller franc ~** go right ahead
**jeudi** *nm* Thursday; **~ saint** Maundy Thursday; *coll* **la semaine des quatre ~ s** a month of Sundays
**jeun (à)** *adv phr* fasting; on an empty stomach; sober
**jeune** *n* young person, young man, young girl; *adj* young, youthful; immature, callow; *theat* **~ premier** juvenile lead; **~ première** leading lady
**jeûne** *nm* fast, fasting
**jeûner** *vi* fast
**jeunesse** *nf* youth, boyhood, girlhood; young people; *coll* girl; **il faut que ~ se passe** youth will have its fling
**jeunet -ette** *adj* youngish
**joaillerie** *nf* jewellery; jeweller's trade
**joaillier -ière** *n* jeweller
**jobard** *nm coll* simpleton, mug, dupe
**jobarder** *vt coll* dupe, fool, take (s/o) in
**jobardise** *nf coll* gullibility
**jocrisse** *nm* clown; *coll* mug, simpleton
**joie** *nf* joy, gladness, enjoyment, delight; mirth, merriment; **à cœur ~** to one's heart's content; **faire la ~ de qn** make s/o happy; **feu de ~** bonfire; *coll* **fille de ~** whore, tart
**joignant** *adj* next, adjoining; *prep* next to, adjoining
**joindre** *vt* (55) join, unite, combine; add; adjoin, be adjacent to; meet, come into contact with; enclose; clasp (hands); *eng* weld; **se ~** join, unite; be adjacent, contiguous
**joint** *nm* join, joint; *coll* solution, way out; **mot ~ de culasse** gasket; *coll* **trouver le ~** find the way; *adj* joined, united, combined; added; **ci-~** attached, enclosed; **pièces ci-~ es** enclosures
**jointé** *adj* jointed
**jointement** *nm* jointing
**jointoyer** *vt* (7) point (brickwork)
**jointure** *nf* joint; **~ des doigts** knuckles
**joli** *nm coll* **c'est du ~!** that's a fine mess!; **le ~ de l'affaire** the best of it; *adj* pretty, good-looking, nice; *coll* considerable, fair, tidy; **une ~ e somme** a tidy sum

**joliment** *adv* prettily, nicely; *coll* awfully, terribly; **vous avez ~ raison** how right you are

**jonc** *nm bot* rush; **~ marin** furze; **canne de ~** Malacca cane

**jonchée** *nf* scattering, strewing

**joncher** *vt* strew, litter

**jonction** *nf* junction, joining

**jongler** *vi* juggle

**jonglerie** *nf* juggling; trickery

**jongleur** *nm* juggler; charlatan; *lit* jongleur, minstrel

**jonque** *nf naut* junk

**jonquille** *nf* daffodil; *adj invar* pale yellow

**Jordanie** *nf* Jordan

**jouable** *adj* playable

**joue** *nf* cheek, side; **mettre en ~** aim at (with rifle, gun)

**jouer** *vt* play; stake, gamble, back; *theat* act, play part; look like, imitate, pretend to be; risk; *coll* fool, trick; *mus* play, perform; **~ pique** play, lead, spades; **~ un cheval gagnant et placé** back a horse each way; **il joue le malheureux** he is pretending to be unhappy; *vi* play (games etc); *mus+theat* play; gamble, speculate; come into play, work; be loose, have (too much) play; be operative (law, etc); **~ à la baisse** bear; **~ à la hausse** bull; *coll* **~ de la fourchette** tuck in; **~ de malheur** have a run of bad luck; **~ la comédie** play a part, put on an act; **faire ~** set going, start; **faire qch en se jouant** make child's play of sth; **se ~ de** deceive; make light of, deride

**jouet** *nm* toy, plaything

**joueur -euse** *n* player; performer; gambler; speculator; **beau (mauvais) ~** good (bad) loser; *adj* fond of gambling; playful

**joufflu** *adj* chubby

**joug** *nm* yoke (oxen); yoke, influence

**jouir** *vi* enjoy; have an orgasm, *coll* come; **~ de** enjoy possession of, own

**jouissance** *nf* enjoyment, delight, pleasure; orgasm, sexual pleasure; *leg* possession, enjoyment; **à vendre avec ~ immédiate** for sale with vacant possession

**jouisseur -euse** *n* sensualist, pleasure-seeker; *adj* sensual

**joujou** *nm coll* toy, plaything

**jour** *nm* day; daylight, light; aspect, light; opening, crack; **~ s** days, life; **~ de l'An** New Year's Day; **~ des Rois** Twelfth Night; *mil* **~ J** D-Day; **à ~** up-to-date; **attenter aux ~ s de qn** attempt to kill s/o; **au ~ le ~** from day to day; **au grand ~** in broad daylight; **au premier ~** as soon as

possible; **à un de ces ~ s!** so long!, see you soon!; **de ~** in the daytime; on day duty; **de nos ~ s** these days, in our time; **de tous les ~ s** everyday, humdrum; **donner le ~ à** give birth to; **du ~ au lendemain** soon, at any moment; **en plein ~** in broad daylight; *comm* **intérêts à ce ~** interest to date; **le ~ se lève** the sun is rising, the dawn is breaking; **mettre qch au ~** bring sth to light; **ourlet à ~ s** hemstitch; *cul* **plat du ~** today's special dish; **se faire ~** emerge, come out; **sous un ~ intéressant** in an interesting light; **sur mes vieux ~ s** in my old age

**journal** *nm* newspaper, paper, journal; diary, journal; *naut* logbook; *rad* **~ parlé, télévisé** news, *US* newscast

**journalier** *nm* day-labourer, journeyman; *adj* (*f* **-ière**) daily, everyday; changing, uncertain

**journalisme** *nm* journalism; **style de ~** journalese

**journaliste** *n* journalist, reporter

**journalistique** *adj* journalistic

**journée** *nf* day, daytime; day's work; day's march; day's wages; **à la ~** by the day; **femme de ~** charwoman, daily help

**journellement** *adv* daily, every day

**joute** *nf obs* joust; contest, tournament

**jouter** *vi obs* joust; fight, dispute

**jouvence** *nf ar* youth

**jouvenceau** *nm ar* young boy; adolescent

**jouvencelle** *nf ar* young girl

**jovial** *adj* jovial, jolly, good-humoured

**jovialité** *nf* joviality, jollity, good-humour

**joyau** *nm* jewel, precious stone

**joyeuseté** *nf* pleasantry, prank, joke; mirth

**joyeux -euse** *adj* joyful, merry, joyous

**jubé** *nm archi* rood-screen, rood-loft

**jubilé** *nm* jubilee; golden wedding

**jubiler** *vi* jubilate, glory; *coll* gloat

**juché** *adj* roosting, perched

**jucher** *vt* place high up; *vi* roost, perch; **se ~** go to roost; *coll* perch oneself

**juchoir** *nm* perch, roosting-place

**judaïque** *adj* Judaic, Jewish

**judaïsme** *nm* Judaism

**judas** *nm* traitor; betrayer; spy-hole, peep-hole (in door)

**judéo-allemand** *adj* Yiddish

**judiciaire** *adj* judicial, judiciary; legal; **police ~** = C.I.D

**judicieux -ieuse** *adj* judicious, sensible; discreet

**juge** *nm* judge, magistrate; *sp* umpire, judge; **~ d'instruction** examining magistrate; **~ de paix** police-court magistrate; ~ **de touche** touch-judge, linesman

**jugé** *nm* **au** ~ by guesswork

**jugement** *nm* judgement, opinion, discrimination; *leg* trial, award, judgement, sentence; *leg* **mettre qn en** ~ bring s/o to trial; **passer en** ~ to stand trial

**jugeote** *nf coll* gumption, nous, common-sense

**juger** *vt* (3) judge, consider, deem, estimate, think; *leg* judge, try, decide (case), pass sentence on; **mal** ~ misjudge; *vi* ~ **de** judge of; ~ **d'après** judge from; ~ **par** judge by

**jugulaire** *nf med* jugular vein; chin-strap; *adj* jugular

**juguler** *vt* strangle, throttle, jugulate

**Juif** (*f* **Juive**) *n* Jew(ess)

**juif** *nm coll* **petit** ~ funny-bone, *US* crazy-bone; *adj* (*f* **juive**) Jewish

**juillet** *nm* July

**juin** *nm* June

**juiverie** *nf pej* Jewry, the Jews; ghetto; usury

**Jules** *nm* Julius

**jules** *nm sl* chamber-pot, jerry; *sl* pimp; *sl* **mon** ~ my man

**julienne** *nf cul* vegetable soup

**jumeau -elle** *n* twin, twin-brother (sister); *adj* twin; **maison jumelle** semi-detached house

**jumelage** *nm* pairing, compiling; twinning

**jumeler** *vt* (5) pair, arrange in pairs; **ville jumelée** twinned town

**jumelles** *nfpl* binoculars, opera-glasses

**jument** *nf* mare

**junior** *adj* youthful, teenage

**jupe** *nf* skirt; *coll* **il est pendu aux** ~ **s de sa mère** he is tied to his mother's apron-strings; *sl* **il est toujours fourré dans ses** ~ **s** he's always hanging about her

**jupe-culotte** *nf* (*pl* **jupes-culottes**) culottes

**jupon** *nm* underskirt, slip; *coll* girl, woman

**juré -e** *n* juryman (-woman), juror; ~ **s** jury; *adj* sworn

**jurement** *nm* oath, swearing, bad language

**jurer** *vt* swear, take an oath; vow, promise; *vi* swear; clash, jar (colours); **il ne faut** ~ **de rien** you never can tell

**juridiction** *nf* jurisdiction; *coll* province

**juridique** *adj* juridical, judicial, legal; **texte** ~ instrument

**jurisconsulte** *nm* jurisconsult, legal expert

**juriste** *nm* jurist, legal writer

**juron** *nm* oath, swear-word

**jury** *nm* panel, board (examiners), selection committee, judges, jury

**jus** *nm* juice; *cul* gravy; *coll* electricity; *coll* petrol, *US* gas; *sl* water (*esp* dirty); *sl mil* coffee; ~ **de la treille** wine; *coll* **donner du** ~ step on the gas; *sl* **tomber dans le** ~ fall in (water)

**jusqu'auboutiste** *n* die-hard

**jusque** *prep* as far as, to, down to, up to; until; as much as; even including; **aller jusqu'à faire qch** go so far as to do sth; **jusqu'à quand?** until when?, how long for?; *conj phr* **jusqu'à ce que** until

**jusques** *prep poet* + **ar** = **jusque**

**justaucorps** *nm* jerkin

**juste** *n* just, righteous; **au** ~ exactly; *adj* just, righteous, upright; fair; right, exact; barely sufficient; tight (clothes); ~ **milieu** happy medium, middle of the road; *comm* **au plus** ~ **prix** at rock-bottom price; **c'est** ~ **!** quite so!, that's right!; **c'est tout** ~ **si je ne me suis pas blessé** I very nearly hurt myself; **le mot** ~ the right word; *adv* justly, rightly, correctly; exactly; ~ **ce qu'il fallait** just what was wanted; *coll* **ça a été** ~ **!** it was a near thing!; **comme de** ~ of course, naturally; **frapper** ~ hit the nail on the head

**justement** *adv* justly, rightly; exactly, precisely

**justesse** *nf* justness, soundness; exactness; **de** ~ barely

**justice** *nf* justice, right; *leg* justice, law, legal proceedings; *leg* **aller en** ~ go to law; **se faire** ~ commit suicide; avenge oneself; **faire** ~ **à qn** treat s/o as he deserves

**justiciable** *n* person under jurisdiction; *adj* amenable; subject

**justicier -ière** *n* pronouncer of judgements; *adj* justiciary

**justificateur -trice** *n* justifier; *adj* justifying, indicating

¹**justificatif** *nm comm* voucher

²**justificatif -ive** *adj* justificative; **pièce justificative** voucher, document of proof; *leg* relevant document

**justification** *nf* justification; *typ* indication; proof

**justifier** *vt* justify, vindicate; prove; *vi leg* ~ **de** account for; prove (identity); **se** ~ vindicate, clear oneself

**juter** *vi* be juicy; *vulg* come

¹**juteux** *nm sl mil* sergeant-major

²**juteux -euse** *adj* juicy; *sl* lucrative

**juvénilité** *nf* youthfulness, juvenility

**juxtaposer** *vt* juxtapose, place side by side

# K

**kakatoès** *nm* cockatoo
**¹kaki** *nm + adj invar* khaki
**²kaki** *nm* persimmon
**kaléidoscopique** *adj* kaleidoscopic
**kangourou** *nm* kangaroo
**keepsake** *nm* keepsake, souvenir; autograph album
**képi** *nm* peaked cap (French army), kepi
**kermesse** *nf* village fair
**kif** *nm* marijuana, *coll* pot
**kif-kif** *adj sl* all the same, much of a muchness
**kiki** *nm sl* throat, neck
**kilométrer** *vt* (6) measure in kilometres; mark off with kilometre stones
**kilométrique** *adj* kilometric

**kiosque** *nm* kiosk, stall, stand; *naut* conning-tower; ~ **à musique** bandstand; ~ **de jardin** summer-house
**klaxon** *nm* klaxon; *mot* horn, hooter; ~ **de route** horn (for open road); ~ **de ville** horn (for town)
**klaxonner** *vi mot* hoot, sound horn
**kleptomane** *n + adj* kleptomaniac
**kleptomanie** *nf* kleptomania
**Koweït** *nm* Kuwait
**krach** *nm comm* financial crash, failure, collapse
**kymrique** *adj* Cymric
**kyrielle** *nf* rigmarole, string of words
**kyste** *nm* cyst
**kysteux -euse** *adj* cystic


# L

**l'** *def art + pron* = **le** or **la** before vowel
**¹la** *def art f* the; *pron f* her; it
**²la** *nm invar mus* A, la; **donner le** ~ give the pitch
**¹là** *adv* there; then; that; **de** ~ whence; **d'ici** ~ until then; **il est un peu** ~ he's very much on the ball, he's all there; **il n'en est pas encore** ~ he's not yet come to that; **par-ci, par-** ~ here and there; **par** ~ this way; whereby
**²là** *interj* ~, ~ ! there now; gently; **oh** ~, ~ ! oh dear me!
**là-bas** *adv* over there; yonder
**labeur** *nm* work, toil
**laborantin -e** *n* laboratory assistant
**laboratoire** *nm* laboratory
**laborieux -ieuse** *adj* laborious, hardworking; laboured, heavy; hard, wearisome; **les classes laborieuses** the working classes
**labour** *nm* tilling, ploughing, tillage; ~ **s** ploughed fields
**labourable** *adj* arable
**labourage** *nm* tilling, ploughing
**labourer** *vt* plough; furrow; *naut* graze, drag (anchor)
**laboureur** *nm* ploughman
**labyrinthe** *nm* labyrinth, maze
**lac** *nm* lake; *coll* **tomber dans le** ~ fail

**lacer** *vt* (4) lace; *naut* belay; **se** ~ lace up
**lacération** *nf* laceration, tearing, mauling; defacing
**lacérer** *vt* (6) lacerate, tear; deface, slash
**lacet** *nm* shoe-lace, boot-lace; hairpin-bend; noose, snare; **route en** ~ **s** winding road; **tendre un** ~ set a snare
**lâchage** *nm* releasing, letting go; *coll* jilting, dropping
**lâche** *n* coward; *adj* cowardly, fainthearted; loose, slack; lax, perfunctory
**lâcher** *vt* release; loosen, slacken; let off; leave, drop; let down; ~ **pied** give ground; ~ **prise** let go; *coll* ~ **un juron** let out an oath; *vi* give up; run away
**lâcheté** *nf* cowardice; cowardly act; dastardliness; despicable action
**lâcheur -euse** *n coll* quitter, traitor (to friends)
**lacis** *nm* network
**laconique** *adj* laconic
**lacrymogène** *adj* tear-producing; **gaz** ~ tear gas
**lacs** *nm* noose, snare
**lacté** *adj* lacteous, milky; **voie** ~ **e** Milky Way
**lacune** *nf* lacuna, gap
**lacustre** *adj* lake-dwelling, lacustrine

**lad** *nm* stable-boy
**là-dedans** *adv* within, in there
**là-dessous** *adv* underneath, under there
**là-dessus** *adv* on that; thereupon
**ladite** *adj f see* ledit
**ladre** *n med* leper; miser; *adj med* leprous; miserly, stingy
**ladrerie** *nf* miserliness, avarice
**lagune** *nf* lagoon
**là-haut** *adv* up there
**¹lai** *nm* lit lay
**²lai** *adj eccles* lay
**laïcisation** *nf* secularization
**laïciser** *vt* secularize
**laïcisme** *nm* secularism
**laïcité** *nf* secularity
**laid** *adj* ugly, repulsive, plain; vile, mean, shabby
**laideron** *nm* plain girl, plain woman; *adj* (*f* -onne) ugly
**laideur** *nf* ugliness, plainness; meanness, shabbiness
**laie** *nf* wild sow
**lainage** *nm* woollen article; ~s woollen goods, woollens
**laine** *nf* wool; woolly hair; ~ peignée worsted
**laineux -euse** *adj* woolly, fleecy
**laïque** *n* layman, laywoman; ~s laity; *adj* lay, secular; **école** ~ state school, undenominational school
**¹laisse** *nf* leash, lead
**²laisse** *nf naut* foreshore, tide-mark
**laisser** *vt* leave, quit; leave out, omit; let, allow; let have; ~ **aller** let things slide; ~ **faire** not interfere; ~ **un bénéfice** yield a profit; ~ **voir** reveal; **je vous le laisserai pour 6.000 francs** you can have it for 6,000 francs, I will let it go for 6,000 francs; **ne pas** ~ **de** not fail to; **se** ~ let oneself; be easy to; **se** ~ **aller** let oneself go
**laisser-aller** *nm invar* abandon; neglect; slovenliness
**laisser-faire** *nm invar* laissez-faire, non-interference
**laissez-passer** *nm invar* permit, pass
**lait** *nm* milk; ~ **concentré** condensed milk; **cochon de** ~ sucking pig; **frère (sœur) de** ~ foster-brother (-sister)
**laitage** *nm* dairy produce
**laitance** *nf* soft roe
**laité** *adj* soft-roed (fish)
**laiterie** *nf* dairy; dairy farming
**laiteux -euse** *adj* milky
**laitier -ière** *n* milkman (-woman); *adj* dairy (industry); **vache laitière** milk cow
**laitière** *nf* milk-maid; milk-cart
**laiton** *nm* brass
**laitue** *nf* lettuce
**laïus** *nm coll* lengthy speech, lecture

**laïusser** *vi coll* speechify, jaw
**lambeau** *nm* rag, shred, scrap
**lambin -e** *n coll* idler, dawdler; *adj coll* idle, dawdling
**lambiner** *vi coll* dawdle, loaf
**lambrequin** *nm* valance, pelmet
**lambris** *nm* panelling, wainscoting; lining in marble; (panelled) ceiling
**lambrissage** *nm* panelling, wainscoting; lining
**lambrisser** *vt* panel, wainscot
**lame** *nf* blade (knife, sword); strip (metal); leaf (spring); wave; ~ **de fond** ground swell; **bonne** ~ good swordsman; **visage en** ~ **de couteau** hatchet-face
**lamé** *nm* ~ **d'or** gold lamé, gold spangles; *adj* spangled
**lamentable** *adj* lamentable, deplorable; dismal; pitiful, woeful
**lamentation** *nf* lamentation, lament, wailing
**lamenter (se)** *v refl* lament, wail; **se** ~ **sur** bewail, deplore
**laminer** *vt* laminate; erode
**laminoir** *nm* rolling-mill; rolling-press
**lampadaire** *nm* standard-lamp; street-lamp; candelabrum
**lampant** *adj* refined (oil)
**lampe** *nf* lamp; *rad* valve; ~ **à alcool** spirit lamp; ~ **à incandescence** fluorescent, strip lighting; ~ **à souder** blow-lamp; ~ **témoin** pilot lamp
**lampée** *nf* draught, gulp
**lamper** *vt* gulp down, swig
**lampion** *nm* fairy light; Chinese lantern
**lampiste** *nm* lamp-maker; lamp-lighter
**lamproie** *nf zool* lamprey
**lance** *nf* lance, spear, harpoon; nozzle (hose); **fer de** ~ spear-head
**lancé** *adj* started, going; launched
**lance-bombes** *nm aer* bomb-rack
**lancée** *nf* impetus; ~s shooting pains
**lance-flammes** *nm mil* flame-thrower
**lance-fusées** *nm mil* rocket-launcher
**lancement** *nm* throwing, flinging; *naut* launching; *comm* launching, floating
**lance-pierres** *nm* catapult
**lancer** *vt* (4) throw, fling; drop (bombs); start, set moving; launch; *mot* + *aer* swing (engine, propeller); set (fashion); puff out (smoke); *leg* issue (warrant); **se** ~ rush; throw oneself; **se** ~ **dans** embark on
**lance-torpilles** *nm* torpedo-tube
**lancette** *nf med* lancet
**lanceur -euse** *n* thrower; *comm* promoter, floater; initiator
**lancier** *nm* lancer
**lancinant** *adj* shooting (pain)
**landau** *nm* (*pl* ~s) pram; landau
**lande** *nf* moor, heath

**langage** *nm* language, speech; lingo

**lange** *nm* baby's napkin; ~s swaddling-clothes

**langoureux -euse** *adj* languorous, languid

**langouste** *nf* spiny lobster, crayfish

**langoustine** *nf* (large) prawn, Pacific prawn

**langue** *nf* tongue; language; style; ~ **verte** slang; **avoir la ~ bien pendue** have a glib tongue; **donner sa ~ au chat** give up (riddle, etc); **écrire une belle ~** have an elegant style; **mauvaise ~** scandal-monger, back-biter

**langueur** *nf* languor, listlessness

**languir** *vi* languish, pine; flag, drag

**languissant** *adj* languid; languishing; flagging

**lanière** *nf* thin strap, thong; lash (whip); **en ~s** in ribbons

**lanterne** *nf* lantern; **à la ~** ! hang him!, string him up!

**lanterneau** *nm* sky-light

**lanterner** *vi* linger, dawdle, shilly-shally

**lapalissade** *nf* truism, cliché

**laper** *vt* lap, lap up

**lapereau** *nm* young rabbit

**lapidaire** *nm* + *adj* lapidary

**lapider** *vt* stone; *fig* vilify

**lapin** *nm* rabbit; ~ **de garenne** wild rabbit; *coll* **poser un ~ à qn** let s/o down, fail to turn up; **un chaud ~** a lecherous character

**lapine** *nf* doe, female rabbit

**lapon -onne** *adj* Lapp

**Laponie** *nf* Lapland

**laps** *nm* ~ **de temps** lapse of time

**lapsus** *nm* slip (tongue, pen)

**laquais** *nm* lackey, footman

**laque** *nf* lac; lacquer (hair); **gomme ~** shellac; *nm or f* lacquer; ~ **de Chine** japan

**laquelle** *pron f see* **lequel**

**laquer** *vt* lacquer, japan

**larbin** *nm* flunkey

**larcin** *nm* petty theft

**lard** *nm* (pork) fat; bacon; *coll* **faire du ~** put on weight

**larder** *vt cul* lard; *fig* stab at; interlard, sprinkle

**lardon** *nm* piece of bacon; gibe, crack, taint; *sl* brat, kid

**large** *nm* breadth, width; space; *naut* open sea, offing; *naut* **au ~** in the offing; **au ~ de Marseille** off Marseilles; **de long en ~** to and fro; **dix mètres de ~** ten metres wide; **être au ~** have plenty of space; have plenty of money; **mettre le cap au ~** put out to sea; *coll* decamp, run off; **prendre le ~** clear off; *adj* wide, broad; generous, liberal; loose, ample; bold, free; con-

siderable, extensive; **avoir la main ~** be generous, open-handed; **avoir l'esprit ~** be broad-minded; **geste ~** sweeping gesture; **peinture ~** bold painting; *adv* loosely; **peindre ~** paint boldly; **s'habiller ~** wear loose clothes

**largement** *adv* broadly, widely; freely; fully, amply; **avoir ~ le temps** have plenty of time

**largesse** *nf* liberality; largesse; ~**s** gifts

**largeur** *nf* breadth, width; *naut* beam

**larguer** *vt naut* loose, let go (rope); shake out (reef); let out (sail); *aer* drop (bomb, parachutist); *fig* ditch

**larme** *nf* tear; *coll* drop; **avoir une crise de ~s, fondre en ~s** burst into tears; **pleurer à chaudes ~s** weep bitterly

**larmoyant** *adj* tearful, whimpering, lachrymose; watering (eyes); maudlin, sentimental; *coll* sloppy

**larmoyer** *vi* (7) water (eyes); snivel, whimper

**larron** *nm ar* robber, thief; **s'entendre comme ~s en foire** be as thick as thieves

**larvaire** *adj zool* larval; immature

**larve** *nf* larva, grub

**laryngite** *nf* laryngitis

**¹las** *interj obs* alas!

**²las** (*f* **lasse**) *adj* tired, weary

**lascar** *nm coll* cunning rogue

**lascif -ive** *adj* lascivious, lewd

**lasciveté** *nf* lasciviousness, lewdness

**lassant** *adj* tiring, wearisome; tedious

**lasser** *vt* tire, weary; **se ~** grow tired

**latent** *adj* latent, hidden, dormant

**latéral** *adj* lateral, sideways

**latin** *nm* Latin; ~ **de cuisine** dog-latin; *coll* **y perdre son ~** be all at sea, be unable to make head or tail of it; *adj* Latin; *naut* lateen

**latitude** *nf geog* latitude; breadth, scope, freedom

**latte** *nf* lath, batten, slat

**latter** *vt* lath, batten; lag (pipe)

**lattis** *nm* lath-work; lagging

**laudatif -ive** *adj* laudatory

**lauréat -e** *n* + *adj* laureate

**laurier** *nm bot* laurel; bay-tree; ~**s** laurels; **cueillir des ~s** win glory

**laurier-rose** *nm* (*pl* **lauriers-roses**) *bot* oleander

**lavable** *adj* washable

**lavabo** *nm* wash-stand, wash-hand basin; wash-room

**lavage** *nm* washing

**lavallière** *nf* loosely tied bow, cravat

**lavande** *nf* lavender

**lavandière** *nf obs* washerwoman

**lavasse** *nf* watery soup; *coll* dish-water, slops

**lave** nf lava

**lavé** adj washed, cleaned; washy (colour); **dessin** ~ wash-drawing

**lave-glace** nm windscreen washer

**lavement** nm med enema

**laver** vt wash, clean, wash up; bathe (wound); disculpate, clear; sl sell off; ~ **à grande eau** swill; ~ **la tête à** rebuke, haul over the coals; **se** ~ wash, wash oneself

**laverie** nf washing plant; ~ **(automatique)** launderette

**lavette** nf dish-mop; ~ **métallique** scrubber

**laveur -euse** n washer(woman)

**lave-vaisselle** nm dish-washer

**lavis** nm washing, tinting; wash-drawing

**lavoir** nm wash-house

**lavure** nf dish-water, kitchen swill; coll thin soup

**laxatif** nm laxative, aperient; adj (f -ive) laxative, aperient

**laxité** nf slackness, laxity

**layette** nf baby-linen, layette; packing-case

**lazzi** nm invar (usu pl) gibes, jokes; theat piece of comic business

**le** def art m the; pron m him; it

**léchage** nm licking

**lèche** nf coll thin slice (bread, meat); sl licking; sl **faire de la** ~ **à qn** suck up to s/o

**lèche-cul** nm invar sl arse-creeper, bum-sucker

**lèchefrite** nf cul dripping-pan

**lécher** vt (6) lick

**lécheur -euse** n coll lickspittle, toady, creep

**lèche-vitrines** nm window-shopping

**leçon** nf lesson; warning; reading, interpretation (manuscript); **faire la** ~ **à qn** give s/o a lecture

**lecteur -trice** n reader; proof-reader; (foreign) assistant at university; nm (de bande) repro head

**lecture** nf reading; ~ **sonore** sound pick-up; **abonnement de** ~s circulating library; obs **cabinet de** ~ lending library; **être d'une** ~ **agréable** make pleasant reading

**ledit** adj m (f ladite, mpl lesdits, fpl lesdites) aforesaid

**légal** adj legal, lawful, statutory

**légalisation** nf legalization, authentication

**légaliser** vt legalize, authenticate

**légalité** nf legality, lawfulness

**légat** nm legate

**légataire** n leg legatee; ~ **universel (-elle)** sole heir (heiress)

**légendaire** adj legendary

**légende** nf legend, fable; inscription, caption; key (map)

**léger -ère** adj light; slight; frivolous, flighty; mild (tobacco, beer, etc); **à la légère** lightly, thoughtlessly, flippantly; **avoir la main légère** be quick with one's hands; **propos** ~s frivolous, idle talk

**légèreté** nf lightness; slightness; levity, frivolousness; mildness

**légion** nf legion; coll host, crowd

**légionnaire** nm legionary; mil soldier of the Foreign Legion

**législateur -trice** n legislator; adj legislative

**législature** nf legislature, sitting (of law-making assembly)

**légiste** nm jurist; **médecin** ~ pathologist

**légitimation** nf legitimation, official recognition

**légitime** adj legitimate, lawful; justifiable

**légitimer** vt legitimize; justify; recognize

**légitimité** nf lawfulness

**legs** nm legacy, bequest

**léguer** vt (6) bequeath, leave

**légume** nm vegetable; nf sl **grosse** ~ bigwig

**légumier** nm vegetable dish

**Léman** nm **le lac** ~ the Lake of Geneva

**lendemain** nm next day, morrow; **du jour au** ~ overnight; **succès sans** ~ short-lived success

**lénifier** vt soften; med assuage, soothe

**lénitif -ive** adj lenitive, soothing

**lent** adj slow; dull

**lente** nf zool nit

**lenteur** nf slowness; dullness; ~s delays

**lentille** nf lentil; opt lens; naut side-light; ~ **d'eau** duck-weed

**léonin** adj leonine

**lépidoptère** nm lepidopteran; adj lepidopterous

**lèpre** nf leprosy

**lépreux -euse** n leper; adj leprous; dilapidated

**léproserie** nf leper-hospital

**lequel** rel pron (f laquelle, mpl lesquels, fpl lesquelles) (contracted with à = auquel, auxquels, auxquelles, with de = duquel, desquels, desquelles) who, whom (persons); which (things); inter pron which?; adj which

**lès, les, lez** prep (with place names) near, by, eg **Villeneuve-les-Avignon**

**lesbien -ienne** adj lesbian

**lesbienne** nf lesbian

**lesdits, lesdites** see ledit

**lèse-** adj f ~ **humanité** outrage against humanity; ~ **majesté** high treason

**léser** vt (6) injure, wrong; leg commit a tort against; **la partie lésée** the injured party

**lésine**

**lésine** *nf* stinginess, miserliness
**lésiner** *vi* be stingy, close-fisted; haggle
**lésinerie** *nf* stinginess; stingy act
**lésineur -euse** *n + adj* stingy, miserly (person)
**lésion** *nf med* lesion, injury; *leg* injury, wrong
**lesquels, lesquelles** *see* lequel
**lessivage** *nm* washing, cleaning; getting rid of; *coll* selling off, raising the wind; **~ de crâne** brain-washing
**lessive** *nf* household washing; articles washed; washing powder, washing liquid
**lessivé** *adj sl* cleaned out, broke; *sl* exhausted
**lessiver** *vt* wash (clothes, etc); scrub (floor); *coll* eliminate; *coll* sell off, raise the wind; *coll* squander, blue (money); *coll* **~ la tête à qn** rebuke s/o, tear a strip off s/o
**lessiveuse** *nf* washing-machine
**lest** *nm* (no pl) ballast; **jeter du ~** make sacrifices, cut one's losses; *naut* **navire sur ~** ship in ballast
**leste** *adj* light, nimble, smart; unscrupulous, sharp; **propos ~** dubious, broad remark
**lester** *vt naut* ballast; fill
**léthargie** *nf* lethargy
**léthargique** *adj* lethargic
**lettre** *nf* letter, character; letter, epistle; **~s** letters, literature; **à la ~**, **au pied de la ~** literally; **avant la ~** premature; **avoir des ~s** be well read; **passer comme une ~ à la poste** go through easily
**lettré -e** *n* scholar, well-read person; *adj* literate, well-read
**lettrine** *nf typ* head-letter, ornamental letter
**leu** *nm* **à la queue ~ ~** in single file, one after the other
**leucémie** *nf med* leukaemia
**leucémique** *n med* leukaemia sufferer; *adj* leukaemic
**leur** *pron* to them; *poss pron* theirs, their own; *poss adj* their
**leurre** *nm* lure, decoy; allurement, catch
**leurrer** *vt* lure, decoy; allure, deceive, delude; **se ~** delude oneself
**levage** *nm* lifting, hoisting, raising
**levain** *nm* yeast; leaven
**levant** *nm* east; *adj* rising
**levantin** *adj* Levantine
**¹levé** *nm* survey
**²levé** *adj* up, out of bed; raised; **au pied ~** impromptu, at a moment's notice; **dessin à main ~e** freehand drawing
**levée** *nf* raising, lifting; clearing (letter-box); trick (cards); dyke, embankment; levying (taxes); breaking (seals);

*mil* levy; **~ d'écrou** discharge from prison; *comm* **~ d'une option** taking up of an option; **la ~ du corps aura lieu à** the funeral will leave at
**lever** *nm* rising (from bed); levee; *theat* rise (curtain); *vt* (6) raise; remove, lift; clear (letter-box); levy (taxes); break (seals); start (hare), flush (bird); *comm* take up, exercise; **~ l'ancre** weigh anchor; *coll* **~ le pied** make oneself scarce, hop it; *coll* **~ une fille** pick up a girl; **~ un plan** draw a plan; *vi cul* rise; shoot, sprout (plant); **faire ~** rouse, wake; **se ~** get up; start up; rise (sun, wind); break (day)
**levier** *nm* lever; crow-bar; **~ de commande** control-bar; **~s de commande** reins of power
**levraut** *nm* leveret, young hare
**lèvre** *nf* lip; **rire du bout des ~s** give a forced laugh
**levrette** *nf* greyhound bitch
**lévrier** *nm* greyhound
**levure** *nf* yeast; **~ artificielle** baking powder
**lexicographe** *n* lexicographer
**lexicographie** *nf* lexicography
**lexicologie** *nf* lexicology
**lexique** *nm* lexicon, glossary; vocabulary
**lez** *prep see* lès
**lézard** *nm* lizard; *coll* **faire le ~** bask in the sun
**lézarde** *nf* crack, split, chink
**lézarder** *vt* crack, split; *vi coll* bask in the sun; **se ~** crack, split
**liage** *nm* tying, binding
**liaison** *nf* linking, joining, binding; *archi* mortar, cement; connection, communication; liaison, (love-)affair; *gramm* liaison, joining of two words; *mus* tie, slur; *cul* thickening (sauce); **effectuer la ~ avec** liaise with
**liane** *nf bot* liana, creeper
**liant** *nm* winning manner, niceness; **avoir du ~** be a good mixer; *adj* sociable, winning, engaging; good-natured; **peu ~** unsociable, standoffish
**liard** *nm* farthing
**liasse** *nf* bundle, packet; file; wad (bank-notes)
**Liban** *nm* Lebanon
**libelle** *nm* lampoon, coarse satire
**libellé** *nm* wording, lettering; *comm* trade description
**libeller** *vt* draw up, word (text, document)
**libelliste** *n* satirist, lampoonist
**libellule** *nf* dragon-fly
**libéral** *adj* liberal, generous; broad-minded, tolerant

168

**libéralité** *nf* liberality, generosity; generous act

**libérateur -trice** *n* liberator, rescuer; *adj* liberating, rescuing

**libération** *nf* liberation, freeing; release; discharge (prisoner, soldier); *comm* payment in full

**libéré** *nm* discharged prisoner, soldier

**libérer** *vt* (6) liberate, release, set free; discharge; *comm* pay up; **se ~** free oneself; *comm* pay off, redeem

**liberté** *nf* liberty, freedom; *leg* **~ sous caution** release on bail; **jour de ~** day off, free day

**libertin -e** *n* libertine, rake; *obs* free-thinker; *adj* licentious, dissolute

**libertinage** *nm* libertinage, dissoluteness; *obs* free-thinking

**libidineux -euse** *adj* libidinous, salacious, lustful

**libraire** *n* bookseller

**librairie** *nf* bookshop; booktrade, bookselling; **en ~** published

**libre** *adj* free; disengaged, unoccupied; clear, open; equivocal, loose; **~ à vous de penser** you may think what you like; **école ~** private (non-state) school (in France *usu* Catholic); **remarque un peu ~** somewhat improper remark

**libre-échange** *nm pol* free-trade

**libre-service** *nm invar* self-service (shop, restaurant)

**lice** *nf obs* lists

**licence** *nf* licence, permission; leave; licentiousness, licence; first (university) degree; **~ ès lettres** = Bachelor of Arts degree

**licencié -e** *n* graduate; licensee; **~ ès lettres, sciences** = Bachelor of Arts, Science

**licencier** *vt* disband, dismiss; lay off (workers)

**licencieux -ieuse** *adj* licentious, loose

**licher** *vt sl* lick; *coll* drink, booze

**licite** *adj* lawful, permissible, legal

**licol** *nm* halter

**licorne** *nf myth* unicorn

**lie** *nf* lees, dregs; **~ du peuple** scum, rabble

**lié** *adj* tied, bound; intimately acquainted; linked

**liège** *nm* cork

**lien** *nm* bond, tie; link

**lier** *vt* tie, fasten, bind; *cul* thicken; *gramm* link; *mus* tie; **~ connaissance avec qn** strike up an acquaintance with s/o; **se ~** make friends; *cul* thicken

**lierre** *nm* ivy

**liesse** *nf* gaiety, jollity

**lieu** *nm* place, locality; occasion, grounds, reason; **~ commun** commonplace; **~x (d'aisances)** W.C.,

privy; **au ~ de** instead of; **au ~ que** whereas; instead of; **avoir ~** take place, happen; **en aucun ~** nowhere; **en haut ~** in high places; **en quelque ~ que** wherever; **en temps et ~** in due course; **mauvais ~** shady place (often = brothel); **vider les ~x** clear out

**lieue** *nf* league

**lieur -euse** *n agr* binder (person); *adj* binding

**lieuse** *nf agr* mechanical binder

**lieutenant** *nm mil + naut* lieutenant; (air force) flying officer; *naut* **~ de vaisseau** lieutenant-commander

**lieutenant-colonel** *nm mil* (*pl* lieutenants-colonels) lieutenant-colonel; (air force) wing-commander

**lièvre** *nm zool* hare; **courir deux ~s à la fois** try to do two things at once; **prendre le ~ au gîte** catch s/o napping

**lifter** *vt* give (s/o) a face-lift

**liftier** *nm* liftman, lift boy; lift attendant

**liftière** *nf* lift girl

**lifting** *nm* face-lift

**ligature** *nf* ligature, binding, splice; *mus* tie

**ligaturer** *vt* ligature, bind, splice

**lignage** *nm* lineage, descent

**lignard** *nm coll mil* infantryman, foot-slogger

**ligne** *nf* line; row; cord; *sp* **~ de touche** touch-line; **aller à la ~** start a new paragraph, indent; *naut* **bâtiment de ~** capital ship; **descendre en ~ droite de** be a direct descendant of; **garder la ~** keep one's figure; (railway) **grande ~** main line; **hors ~** outstanding; **pilote de ~** airline pilot

**lignée** *nf* line, issue

**ligneux -euse** *adj* ligneous, woody

**ligot** *nm* bundle of firewood

**ligotage** *nm* binding, tying up

**ligoter** *vt* bind, tie up; bind hand and foot

**ligue** *nf* league

**liguer** *vt* league, bind together; **se ~** league, form a league

**lilas** *nm + adj invar* lilac

**limace** *nf* slug

**limaçon** *nm* snail; **escalier en ~** spiral staircase

**limage** *nm* (action of) filing

**limaille** *nf* filings

**limande** *nf* dab (fish)

**limbes** *nmpl* limbo

**lime** *nf* file; **~ à ongles** nail-file; **~ émeri** emery-board

**limer** *vt* file; work at, polish

**limier** *nm zool* bloodhound; *coll* sleuth, detective

**liminaire** *adj* preliminary, prefatory; **épître ~** foreword

**limitatif -ive** *adj* limiting; restrictive
**limitation** *nf* limit, limitation; marking off
**limite** *nf* limit, boundary, margin; **cas ~** borderline case; **charge ~** maximum load; **date ~** deadline; **vitesse ~** maximum speed
**limiter** *vt* limit, bound, restrict
**limitrophe** *adj* adjacent, adjoining, bordering
**limogeage** *nm mil coll* bowler-hatting
**limoger** *vt* (3) *mil coll* bowler-hat; sack
¹**limon** *nm* mud, clay, silt
²**limon** *nm bot* lime
**limonade** *nf* lemonade
**limonadier -ière** *n* dealer in soft drinks; café owner
**limoneux -euse** *adj* muddy; *geol* alluvial
**limpide** *adj* limpid, clear
**limpidité** *nf* limpidity, clarity
**lin** *nm* flax; linen; **huile de ~** linseed oil
**linceul** *nm* shroud, winding-sheet
**linéaire** *adj* linear; **dessin ~** geometrical drawing
**linge** *nm* linen; **~ de corps** underwear; **~ de table** table linen
**lingère** *nf* person in charge of linen-room
**lingerie** *nf* linen drapery; underclothing, lingerie; linen-room
**lingot** *nm* ingot
**linguiste** *n* linguist
**linguistique** *nf* linguistics; *adj* linguistic
**linon** *nm* lawn (cloth)
**linotte** *nf orni* linnet; *coll* **avoir une tête de ~** be feather-brained
**linteau** *nm* lintel
**lion** *nm* lion; *coll* celebrity
**lionceau** *nm* lion-cub
**lionne** *nf* lioness
**lippe** *nf* thick lower lip; **faire la ~** pout
**lippu** *adj* thick-lipped
**liquéfier** *vt* liquefy; **se ~** turn liquid
**liquette** *nf coll* shirt
**liqueur** *nf* liquor, alcoholic drink; liqueur; *chem* liquid solution; **~s fortes** hard liquor; **~ titrée** standard solution
**liquidateur** *nm comm* liquidator
**liquidation** *nf* liquidation, winding-up; *comm* clearance sale; settlement
**liquide** *nm* liquid; drink; *nf gramm* liquid consonant; *adj* liquid; **argent ~** ready money
**liquider** *vt* liquidate, wind up; settle up; realize (assets), sell off; *coll* liquidate, get rid of; *coll* **~ son passé** wipe out one's past; **se ~** clear oneself (debt); be settled
**liquidité** *nf* liquidity
**liquoreux -euse** *adj* like a liqueur (wine, sweet)
**lire** *vt + vi* (56) read; *mus* **~ à première**

vue sight-read; **cela se lit sur son visage** it shows on his face; **ce livre se lit facilement** this book makes easy reading
**lis, lys** *nm bot* lily; **~ d'eau** water-lily
**liseré, liséré** *nm* border, edge; piping (garment)
**liserer, lisérer** *vt* (6) border, edge; trim with piping
**liseron** *nm bot* bind-weed, convolvulus
**liseur -euse** *n* s/o fond of reading, great reader; **~ d'âmes** thought-reader; *adj* fond of reading
**liseuse** *nf* reading-lamp; book-rest; book-wrapper; bed-jacket
**lisibilité** *nf* legibility
**lisible** *adj* legible; readable
**lisière** *nf* edge, border (forest, field); list, selvedge (cloth); leading strings
**lissage** *nm* smoothing, polishing
**lisse** *adj* smooth, polished, glossy
**lisser** *vt* smooth, polish, gloss; glaze, burnish; **se ~** become smooth; **se ~ les plumes** preen feathers (bird)
**liste** *nf* list, register, roll; *pol* **scrutin de ~** voting for several candidates from a list
**lit** *nm* bed; layer; bed of river; **enfant de second ~** child of second marriage; **voiture (wagon)-~** sleeping car
**litanie** *nf* litany; *coll* rigmarole, long list
**litée** *nf* litter (animals)
**literie** *nf* bedding
**lithographe** *n* lithographer
**lithographie** *nf* lithography
**lithographier** *vt* lithograph
**litière** *nf* stretcher, litter; (stable) litter
**litige** *nm leg* litigation; legal dispute; **en ~** at issue
**litigieux -ieuse** *adj* litigious
**litote** *nf* litotes, understatement
**littéraire** *adj* literary
**littéral** *adj* literal; *leg* **preuve ~e** documentary evidence
**littérateur** *nm* man of letters, litterateur
**littérature** *nf* literature
**littoral** *nm* coastline; *adj* coastal
**liturgie** *nf* liturgy
**liturgique** *adj* liturgical
**livide** *adj* livid, ghastly
**lividité** *nf* lividity, lividness, ghastliness
**livrable** *adj comm* ready for delivery, deliverable
**livraison** *nf comm* delivery; instalment (serial)
¹**livre** *nf* pound (weight); pound (sterling)
²**livre** *nm* book; **~ à succès** bestseller; *naut* **~ de bord** log-book; **~ de poche** paper-back; *comm* **grand ~** ledger
**livrée** *nf* livery
**livrer** *vt* deliver; give up, surrender; join

(battle); hand over; betray, reveal; se ~ à surrender oneself to, indulge in; se ~ à la boisson take to drink; se ~ au travail devote oneself to work

**livresque** adj bookish, obtained from books

**livret** nm booklet; mus libretto; ~ de caisse d'épargne savings-bank book; mil ~ militaire service record

**livreur** nm comm delivery-man

**lobélie** nf bot lobelia

**lober** vt sp lob

**local** nm premises, building; adj local

**localiser** vt locate; localize; se ~ fix one's abode; become localized

**localité** nf locality, inhabited place

**locataire** n tenant; lodger

**¹locatif** nm gramm locative

**²locatif -ive** adj pertaining to letting or renting; réparations locatives tenant's repairs; valeur locative rental value

**location** nf letting, hiring; rented dwelling; booking, reserving (seats in train, theatre, etc); agent de ~ house-agent; theat bureau de ~ box-office; en ~ on hire; être en ~ live in rented accommodation; voiture en ~ coach on train with reserved seats

**location-vente** nf hire-purchase system

**loch** nm naut log

**lock-outer** vt lock out

**locomobile** nf transportable steam-engine; adj transportable; grue ~ travelling crane

**locomoteur -trice** adj med locomotor

**locomotif -ive** adj locomotive

**locomotive** nf locomotive, engine; fig energetic person, dynamic person; driving force

**locuste** nf locust

**locution** nf phrase, expression, idiom

**lof** nm naut windward side; aller au ~ sail into the wind; virer ~ pour ~ wear ship

**logarithme** nm logarithm

**loge** nf hut, cabin; lodge (porter, free-masons); theat box; theat dressing-room; fig être aux premières ~s have a front seat, be well placed

**logeable** adj inhabitable, fit for occupation

**logement** nm lodging, housing; accommodation; dwelling; mil quarters; naut berth; eng housing, socket; crise du ~ housing shortage

**loger** vt (3) lodge, house, accommodate; put up; mil quarter; put; vi lodge, live; mil be quartered; ~ en garni live in furnished lodgings; se ~ lodge; take lodgings

**logeur** nm landlord, lodging-house keeper

**logeuse** nf landlady

**logicien** nm logician

**logique** nf logic; adj logical, reasoned, consistent; c'est ~ fair enough

**logis** nm dwelling, house, abode; hostelry; corps de ~ main part of the building

**logistique** nf logistics

**loi** nf law; enactment, statute; faire la ~ à lay down the law to; projet de ~ bill (parliament); se faire une ~ de make a point of

**loin** adv far (place, time); ~ des yeux, ~ du cœur out of sight out of mind; de ~ en ~ now and then; du plus ~ que je me souvienne as far as I can recall; conj phr ~ que far from

**lointain** nm distance; adj distant, remote; far off

**loir** nm dormouse

**loisible** adj permissible, allowable, optional; il vous est ~ de you are free to

**loisir** nm leisure, spare time

**lombago** nm lumbago

**lombaire** adj lumbar; ponction ~ lumbar puncture

**lombes** nmpl med loins

**lombric** nm earthworm

**Londonien -ienne** n Londoner

**londonien -ienne** adj of London

**Londres** nm London

**londrès** nm kind of Havana (cigar)

**long** nm length; de ~ en large up and down, to and fro, up and down; deux mètres de ~ two metres long; en ~ lengthwise; étendu de tout son ~ stretched at full length; le ~ de along; naut alongside; tout au ~ all the way along; at full length; tout le ~ du jour the whole day long; adj (f longue) long; cul thin (sauce); ~ de deux mètres two metres long; comm à longue échéance long-dated; avoir les dents longues be ambitious, greedy; de longue date of long-standing; adv en dire ~ speak volumes; en savoir ~ sur know a good deal about

**longanime** adj long-suffering, forbearing, patient

**longanimité** nf forbearance, patience

**long-courrier** nm ocean-going ship, liner; intercontinental plane; adj invar ocean-going; long-distance

**longe** nf tether; thong; cul loin

**longer** vt (3) skirt, keep close to

**longévité** nf longevity

**longtemps** adv long; a long time; cela n'arrivera pas de ~ that won't happen for a long time

**longue** nf gramm long syllable; à la ~ eventually, in the long run

**longuement**

**longuement** *adv* for a long time; lengthily; slowly, deliberately
**longuet -ette** *adj coll* longish, on the long side
**longueur** *nf* length; slowness, delay; boring passage; ~ **d'onde** wavelength; **deux mètres de** ~ two metres long; **en** ~ lengthwise; *sp* **gagner d'une** ~ win by a length; **traîner en** ~ drag on
**lopin** *nm* bit, piece, plot (land)
**loquace** *adj* loquacious, talkative
**loquacité** *nf* loquacity, talkativeness
**loque** *nf* rag; (human) wreck; **en** ~ **s** in tatters, falling apart; **être comme une** ~ be worn out
**loquet** *nm* latch
**loqueteux** *nm* ragamuffin; s/o dressed in rags; *adj* (*f* **-euse**) ragged, in rags, in tatters
**lorgnade** *nf* sidelong glance
**lorgner** *vt* cast sidelong glances at, ogle; look through opera-glasses at; have one's eye on
**lorgnette** *nf* opera-glasses
**lorgnon** *nm* pince-nez; eye-glasses; lorgnette
**lors** *adv obs* then; ~ **de** at the time of; ~ **même que** even though, even when; **depuis** ~ from then on, ever since then; **dès** ~ from that time; **dès** ~ **que** since, given that
**lorsque** *conj* when
**losange** *nm* lozenge; **en** ~ diamond-shaped
**lot** *nm* share, portion, lot; batch; fate, fortune; prize (lottery); **gros** ~ first prize in lottery
**loterie** *nf* lottery; raffle; gamble, matter of chance
**loti** *adj coll* **bien** ~ well provided for, well off; **mal** ~ badly off, poor
**lotissement** *nm* dividing into lots, parcelling out; allotment, building plot; selling of building plots
**louable** *adj* laudable, praiseworthy
**louage** *nm* hiring out, hiring, engaging; **voiture de** ~ hackney carriage, cab
**louange** *nf* praise, commendation; **chanter ses propres** ~ **s** blow one's own trumpet
**louanger** *vt* (3) praise, eulogize; overpraise
**louangeur -euse** *n* praiser; flatterer; *adj* laudatory; flattering
**loubar(d)** *nm* yobbo, hoodlum
**¹louche** *nf* soup-ladle
**²louche** *adj* cross-eyed, squint-eyed; *coll* shady, suspicious, shifty; cloudy (liquid)
**loucher** *vi* squint, be cross-eyed; *coll* make eyes
**loucherie** *nf* squinting

**¹louer** *vt* hire, let out; hire, rent; book, reserve (seats)
**²louer** *vt* praise; **se** ~ be pleased, be satisfied; congratulate oneself
**¹loueur -euse** *n* hirer-out
**²loueur -euse** *n* praiser; flatterer; *adj* flattering
**loufoque** *adj coll* crazy, daft
**loufoquerie** *nf coll* daftness; eccentricity
**louis** *nm obs* gold coin (of varying value)
**loukoum** *nm* Turkish delight
**loup** *nm* wolf; sea-dace; black-velvet mask, domino; flaw, fault; *theat* fluff; *naut* ~ **de mer** old salt; **à pas de** ~ stealthily; **avoir une faim de** ~ be ravenous; **connu comme le** ~ **blanc** known to everybody; **enfermer le** ~ **dans la bergerie** set the fox to keep the geese; **il fait un froid de** ~ it's bitterly cold; **les** ~ **s ne se mangent pas entre eux** dog doesn't eat dog; *coll* **mon petit** ~ my sweet, my darling; **tenir le** ~ **par les oreilles** be in a dilemma
**loup-cervier** *nm* (*pl* **loups-cerviers**) *zool* lynx
**loupe** *nf* lens, magnifying glass; *med* wen; gnarl, lump
**louper** *vt coll* bungle, botch; miss (train, chance); *theat* fluff
**loup-garou** *nm* (*pl* **loups-garous**) werewolf
**lourd** *adj* heavy, ponderous; clumsy, ungainly; dull-witted; severe, grievous; sultry (weather); ~ **de** fraught with; **poids** ~ heavy lorry; heavy-weight boxer; *adv* heavy; *coll* **il n'en reste pas** ~ there's not much left; **ne pas peser** ~ not count for a great deal
**lourdaud -e** *n* dolt, lout; blockhead; *adj* loutish, awkward; dull-witted
**lourderie** *nf* loutishness; gross blunder
**lourdeur** *nf* heaviness, ponderousness; weight; clumsiness, dullness; sultriness
**loustic** *nm coll* wag, joker
**loutre** *nf* otter
**louve** *nf* she-wolf
**louveteau** *nm* wolf-cub; (wolf) cub (scouting)
**louvoiement** *nm* evasiveness; *naut* tacking
**louvoyage** *nm* evasiveness; *naut* tacking
**louvoyer** *vi* (7) be evasive; *naut* tack
**lover** *vt naut* coil; **se** ~ coil up (snake)
**loyal** *adj* honest, fair, dependable; sincere, straightforward
**loyalisme** *nm* loyalty, loyalism
**loyaliste** *n* loyalist
**loyauté** *nf* honesty, fairness; straightforwardness; loyalty
**loyer** *nm* rent, rental
**lu** *p part* lire
**lubie** *nf* whim, fad

**lubricité** *nf* lubricity, lust
**lubrifiant** *nm* lubricant; *adj* lubricating
**lubrifier** *vt* lubricate, grease
**lubrique** *adj* lustful, lewd
**lucarne** *nf* dormer-window; sky-light
**lucide** *adj* lucid, clear
**lucidité** *nf* lucidity, clarity
**luciole** *nf zool* firefly
**lucratif -ive** *adj* lucrative, paying
**luette** *nf med* uvula
**lueur** *nf* gleam; glimmer; flash, ray
**lugubre** *adj* lugubrious, dismal; sad, sorrowful
**luge** *nf* sleigh, toboggan
**lui** *pron* to him, to her, to it; he, he himself
**luire** *vi* (57) shine, gleam, glint
**luisant** *nm* gloss, shine, sheen; *adj* shining, shiny, glossy; **ver ~** glow-worm
**lumière** *nf* light; enlightenment; luminary; **donner de la ~** turn the light on; **la ville ~** Paris; **le siècle des ~s** the age of enlightenment; **mettre en ~** bring out, bring to light
**lumignon** *nm* candle-end; snuff; dim light
**luminaire** *nm* luminary
**lumineux -euse** *adj* luminous; brilliant; **idée lumineuse** brilliant idea; **onde lumineuse** light wave
**luminosité** *nf* luminosity, sheen
**lunaire** *adj* lunar
**lunatique** *adj* whimsical, unbalanced, capricious
**lundi** *nm* Monday
**lune** *nf* moon; *sl* behind, bum; **~ de miel** honeymoon; close understanding; **~ rousse** April moon; **clair de ~** moonlight; **dans une bonne ~** in a good humour; **être dans la ~** be day-dreaming
**luné** *adj coll* **bien, mal ~** in a good, bad, mood
**lunetier** *nm* spectacle-maker, optician
**lunette** *nf* telescope, field-glass; spy-glass; hole of W.C.; *mot* rear-window; **~s** glasses, spectacles
**lunetterie** *nf* spectacle-making; optical trade

**lupanar** *nm* brothel
**lurette** *nf* **il y a belle ~** a long time ago
**luron** *nm* big, strapping fellow; **c'est un gai ~** he's quite a lad
**luronne** *nf* strapping girl; tomboy; girl who gets around
**lustrage** *nm* glazing, glossing; shininess
**¹lustre** *nm* chandelier
**²lustre** *nm* lustre, sheen, polish; gloss
**lustré** *adj* lustrous, glossy
**luth** *nm mus* lute
**luthier** *nm mus* stringed instrument maker
**lutin** *nm* elf, goblin; imp (child)
**lutiner** *vt* tease, plague; *coll* **~ les filles** fondle the girls; *sl* snog
**lutrin** *nm eccles* lectern
**lutte** *nf* struggle, contest, strife; *sp* wrestling; *sp* **à la corde de traction** tug-of-war; **de bonne ~** by fair means; **de haute ~** by force; *leg* **les parties en ~** the contending parties
**lutter** *vi* fight, struggle; *sp* wrestle; try to resist; *sp* **~ de vitesse** race
**lutteur -euse** *n* wrestler; fighter
**luxe** *nm* luxury; wealth, profusion; **~ de précautions** excessive precautions; **se payer (se donner) le ~ de** treat oneself to
**luxer** *vt med* luxate, dislocate, put out of joint
**luxueux -ueuse** *adj* luxurious, sumptuous
**luxure** *nf* lechery, lust, lewdness
**luxurieux -ieuse** *adj* lecherous, lustful, lewd
**luzerne** *nf bot* lucerne
**lycanthropie** *nf* lycanthropy
**lycée** *nm* = state secondary grammar school
**lycéen -enne** *n* pupil at a **lycée**
**lymphatique** *adj med* lymphatic
**lymphe** *nf med* lymph
**lynchage** *nm* lynching
**lyncher** *vt* lynch
**lyrique** *adj* lyric; poet; *adj* lyrical; **théâtre ~** opera-house
**lyrisme** *nm* lyricism; *coll* enthusiasm; gush
**lys** *nm see* **lis**

# M

**ma** *poss adj f* my; *see* **mon**
**maboul** *n+adj sl* loony, idiot
**macabre** *adj* macabre, gruesome, grim; **la danse ~** the Dance of Death

**macache** *interj sl* nothing doing!, not on your life!
**macadam** *nm* macadam; macadamized road

**macadamiser** *vt* macadamize
**macaron** *nm cul* macaroon; coil (hair); *coll* decoration, medal
**macaroni** *nm cul* macaroni; *sl* Wop, Italian
**macchabée** *nm sl* corpse, stiff
**Macédoine** *nf* Macedonia
**macédoine** *nf* diced or chopped vegetables; fruit-salad; *fig* hotch-potch
**macération** *nf* maceration, steeping, soaking; mortifying (flesh)
**macérer** *vt* (6) macerate; mortify (flesh); **faire ~** steep, soak
**mâchefer** *nm* clinker, slag
**mâcher** *vt* masticate, chew; champ; tear, chew up; **ne pas ~ ses mots** not mince one's words; **~ la besogne à qn** do half s/o's work for him
**machiavélique** *adj* Machiavellian
**mâchicoulis** *nm* machicolation
**machin** *nm coll* what's-it, thingummy-jig; **Monsieur ~** Mr What's his name; *vulg* prick
**machinal** *adj* mechanical, automatic; unconscious
**machinateur -trice** *n* machinator, plotter, schemer
**machine** *nf* machine; engine; *fig* machinery; *coll* contraption; **~ s** (ship's) engines; **~ à calculer** adding-machine, calculating machine; **~ à composer** type-setting machine; **~ à coudre** sewing-machine; **~ à écrire** typewriter; **~ à laver** washing-machine; **~ à sous** one-armed bandit, fruit-machine; **~ routière** traction-engine; *theat* **pièce à ~s** play dependent on stage-effects
**machine-outil** *nf* (*pl* **machines-outils**) machine-tool
**machiner** *vt* machinate, plot, scheme, contrive; **affaire machinée d'avance** put-up job
**machinerie** *nf* machine construction; machine-shops, plant; *naut* engine-room
**machinisme** *nm* automation
**machiniste** *nm theat* stage-hand; *obs* bus-driver; **chef ~** stage-manager
**mâchoire** *nf* jaw; jaw-bone; *mot* brake-shoe; *eng* jaws (vice), flange (pulley)
**mâchonnement** *nm* chewing; mumbling
**mâchonner** *vt* chew, munch; *fig* mumble, mutter
**mâchurer** *vt* smudge, blacken; crush, bruise
**maçon** *nm* mason, bricklayer; (free-) mason
**maçonner** *vt* build; face (wall); wall up
**maçonnerie** *nf* masonry, brick-work, stone-work; freemasonry
**maçonnique** *adj* masonic

**macrobiotique** *adj* macrobiotic
**macrocéphale** *adj med* macrocephalic, large-headed
**macrocosme** *nm* macrocosm
**maculage** *nm* maculation, staining; *typ* blurring
**macule** *nf* macula, spot, stain; sun-spot; *typ* spoiled sheet
**maculer** *vt* maculate, mark with spots, stain; *typ* blur
**madame** *nf* (*pl* **mesdames**) Mrs; madam; **jouer à la ~** put on airs
**Madeleine** *nf* **pleurer comme une ~** weep bitterly, cry one's eyes out
**madeleine** *nf* sponge-cake, madeleine
**mademoiselle** *nf* (*pl* **mesdemoiselles**) Miss
**Madère** *nm* Madeira; Madeira wine
**madone** *nf* madonna
**madré** *adj* sly, wily
**madrier** *nm* beam, thick board, plank
**madrilène** *adj* of Madrid
**maestria** *nf* masterly skill, brio
**magasin** *nm* shop; warehouse; *mil* armoury; magazine (rifle, etc); **~ à succursales** chain-store; **~s généraux** bonded warehouse; **en ~** in stock; **grand ~** department store
**magasinage** *nm* storing, warehousing
**magasinier** *nm* warehouseman; *mil* storesman
**mage** *nm* Magus; seer; **les Rois ~s** the Magi, the Three Wise Men
**magicien -ienne** *n* wizard; sorcerer (sorceress); magician
**magie** *nf* magic, wizardry
**magique** *adj* magic, magical
**magistral** *adj* magisterial, skilful, masterly; *coll* first-rate, exemplary
**magistrat** *nm leg* judge; someone in judicial capacity
**magistrature** *nf leg* magistrature; **~ assise** the Judges; **~ debout** the body of public prosecutors, the law-officers of the State; **entrer dans la ~** be appointed judge or public prosecutor
**magnanime** *adj* magnanimous
**magnanimité** *nf* magnanimity
**magnat** *nm* magnate, tycoon
**magnésie** *nf* magnesia; **sulfate de ~** Epsom salts
**magnésium** *nm chem* magnesium; *obs* **lampe au ~** flash-lamp
**magnétique** *adj* magnetic
**magnétiser** *vt* magnetize; mesmerize, hypnotize
**magnétiseur** *nm* magnetizer; mesmerizer
**magnétisme** *nm* magnetism; mesmerism; *fig* magnetism
**magnéto** *nf* magneto; *nm coll* tape-recorder

**magnétophone** *nm* tape-recorder

**magnétoscope** *nm* video-tape-recorder

**magnifier** *vt* magnify; glorify

**magnifique** *adj* magnificent, splendid; sumptuous; grandiloquent, pompous; *ar* generous, liberal

¹**magot** *nm zool* Barbary ape; Chinese (grotesque) figure in porcelain

²**magot** *nm coll* hoard, pile (money)

**magouille** *nf* chicanery

**mahométan** *adj* Mohammedan, Muslim, Moslem

**mahométanisme** *nm* Mohammedanism

**mai** *nm* May

**maigre** *nm cul* lean (meat); **faire ~** abstain from meat; *adj* lean, skinny, thin; meagre, scanty, sparse; *eccles* meatless; **~ repas** scanty meal; **jour ~** fast-day; **repas ~** meatless meal

**maigrelet -ette** *adj* on the thin side, skinny

**maigreur** *nf* thinness, lankness; emaciation; scantiness, sparseness

**maigrichon -onne** *adj* on the thin side, skinny

**maigrir** *vt* make (s/o) thinner (illness); make (s/o) look thinner (garment); *vi* grow thin, lose flesh; **se faire ~** diet, slim

**mail** *nm* promenade, avenue; *ar* hammer

¹**maille** *nf* stitch; link (chain); mesh (net); **~ à l'endroit et à l'envers** plain and purl; **arrêter les ~s** cast off; **cotte de ~s** coat of mail

²**maille** *nf ar* small coin; *coll* **n'avoir ni sou ni ~** be broke; **avoir ~ à partir avec qn** have a bone to pick with s/o

**mailler** *vt* net; *naut* shackle

**maillet** *nm* mallet, maul; *sp* mallet

**maillon** *nm* link; *naut* shackle

**maillot** *nm sp* singlet, vest, jersey; *theat* tights; baby's napkin; **~ de bain** bathing-costume; *sp* **~ jaune** yellow jersey worn by winner of a stage in Tour de France cycle race; the winner of such a stage

**main** *nf* hand; hand(-writing); hand (cards); **~ courante** hand-rail; **~ de papier** quire; **à bas les ~s!** hands off!; **à ~ levée** free-hand; **avoir la haute ~ sur** have complete control of; **avoir la ~ large** be generous, open-handed; **coup de ~** raid, surprise attack; **de longue ~** for a long time past; **donner un coup de ~** give a helping hand; **en un tour de ~** in a jiffy; **en venir aux ~s** come to blows; **faire ~ basse sur** lay hands on, make a clean sweep of; **faire qch sous ~** do sth in an underhand way; **gagner haut la ~** win hands down; **haut les ~s!** hands up!; **homme de ~** thug; **je n'en mettrais pas la ~ au feu** I would not swear to it; **mariage de la ~ gauche** morganatic marriage; **mettre la ~ sur qn** get hold of s/o; **ne pas y aller de ~ morte** make no bones about it, go hard at it; **passer la ~** pass the deal (cards); **passer la ~ dans le dos de qn** soft-soap s/o, butter s/o up; **porter la ~ sur qn** lay a hand on s/o; **prêter ~ forte à** help; **se donner la ~** shake hands; **se faire la ~** get one's hand in; **se passer la ~ dans le dos** pat oneself on the back; **sous la ~** at hand

**main-d'œuvre** *nf* labour; manpower, labour-force

**mainmise** *nf leg* seizure, distraint; nefarious influence

**mainmorte** *nf leg* mortmain

**maint** *adj* many a; **à ~es reprises** time and time again

**maintenant** *adv* now; **dès ~** from now on, henceforth; *conj* **~ que** now that

**maintenir** *vt* (96) maintain, hold; hold up; keep up; affirm; **~ qn en fonction** keep s/o in office; **se ~** keep on; last, hold on; continue

**maintien** *nm* maintenance, upholding, keeping; bearing, deportment; **se donner un ~** keep countenance

**maire** *nm* mayor

**mairesse** *nf* mayoress

**mairie** *nf* town-hall; office of mayor, mayoralty

**mais** *conj* but; *adv* indeed, well, why; **~ oui!** why, certainly!, but of course!; **~ non!** not at all!; **~ vous voilà!** well you're here!; **n'en pouvoir ~** be at the end of one's tether, exhausted

**maïs** *nm* maize, Indian corn, *US* corn

**maison** *nf* house, home; household, staff; family; firm, business; dynasty; *cul* home-made; *sl* classic, prize; **~ close** brothel; **~ d'arrêt** prison; **~ de correction** approved school; **~ de fous** lunatic asylum; **~ d'habitation** dwelling-house; **~ de rapport** tenement; **~ de repos** convalescent home, mental home; **~ religieuse** convent; **à la ~** at home; **de bonne ~** of good family; **entrer en ~** go into (domestic) service; **être de la ~** be one of the family

**maisonnée** *nf* household, members of family

**maisonnette** *nf* small house, cottage

**maître** *nm* master; **Maître** (instead of **Monsieur**) applied to lawyers; *coll* **~ chanteur** blackmailer; **~ de conférences** = (university) lecturer; **~ d'école** schoolmaster; **~ de forges** iron-master, steel-manufacturer; **~ d'hôtel** head-waiter, butler; *coll* **Maître Jacques** Jack-of-all-trades, factotum;

~ queux master cook; être passé ~ en be a past master at; les ~s de la peinture the great masters; parler à qn en ~ speak authoritatively to s/o

maître-autel *nm* (*pl* maîtres-autels) *eccles* high altar

maîtresse *nf* mistress; lover; ~ d'école school-mistress; ~ de maison housewife, hostess; ~ femme very capable woman; idée ~ governing principle

maîtrise *nf* mastership; mastery; *eccles* choir-school; choir; ~ de conférences lectureship; ~ de soi self-control; agent de ~ foreman

maîtriser *vt* master, subdue, control; se ~ control oneself

majesté *nf* majesty, stateliness, grandeur; Sa Majesté His Majesty, Her Majesty

majestueux -ueuse *adj* majestic, stately

majeur *nm* second finger, longest finger; *adj* major, principal, important; of age; *mus* major; c'est un cas de force ~ e it's a case of absolute necessity, there is no choice; devenir ~ come of age, reach one's majority; Lac Majeur Lake Maggiore

majeure *nf* major premise

majolique *nf* majolica

major *nm mil* adjutant; *mil* medical officer, M.O.; mil ~ général chief of staff; (navy) ~ général Admiral Maritime Superintendent

majoration *nf* over-estimation, over-valuation; increase (price, salary); additional charge

majordome *nm* major-domo, manager of (large) household

majorer *vt* over-estimate, over-value; increase (charge, price)

majoritaire *adj* majority, pertaining to the majority

majorité *nf* majority, greater part; coming of age; *mil* adjutancy

majuscule *nf* capital letter; *adj* capital

mal *nm* (*pl* maux) evil; harm; hurt; pain; disease, illness; ~ au cœur sickness, nausea; ~ blanc gathering, sore; ~ de l'air air-sickness; ~ de mer sea-sickness; ~ du pays home-sickness; attraper du ~ catch an infection; avoir du ~ à faire qch find sth difficult to do; avoir ~ à have a pain in; il n'y a pas grand ~ there's not much harm done; ne pas penser à ~ have good intentions; prendre du ~ fall ill; prendre qch en ~ take sth amiss, take offence at sth; se donner du ~ take trouble, take pains; tourner qch en ~ put the worst construction onto sth, show up

the black side of sth; vouloir du ~ à qn wish s/o ill; *adj* bad, wrong; bon an, ~ an year in year out; bon gré, ~ gré willy-nilly, regardless; *adv* badly, ill; in bad health; on bad terms; ugly; uncomfortable; ~ léché raw, callow; aller ~ be ill, be in bad health; c'est ~ à lui de it's wrong for him to, it's too bad of him to; être au plus ~ avec qn be at daggers drawn with s/o; on n'est pas ~ ici it's not too bad here; *coll* pas ~ not bad looking; *coll* pas ~ de many, quite a lot of; prendre ~ qch take sth amiss; en être ~ be upset about sth; se mettre ~ avec qn fall out with s/o; se sentir (se trouver) ~ feel unwell; vous ne feriez pas ~ de it wouldn't be a bad idea for you to; vous ne trouverez pas ~ que you won't mind if

malade *n* invalid, sick person; patient; faire le ~ malinger; *adj* ill, unwell, sick; injured, in poor condition; ~ de ill with; en être ~ be upset about sth; être ~ du cœur, du foie have heart-trouble, liver-trouble

maladie *nf* illness, sickness, disease, malady

maladif -ive *adj* sickly, weakly; unhealthy, morbid

maladresse *nf* clumsiness, awkwardness; blunder

maladroit *n* clumsy person; blunderer; *adj* clumsy, awkward, maladroit; blundering

malais *nm* Malaysian (language); *adj* Malaysian

malaise *nm* indisposition, faintness, discomfort; uneasiness, unrest

malaisé *adj* difficult

Malaisie *nf* Malaysia

malappris -e *n* lout, boor, unmannerly person; *adj* boorish, rude, unmannerly

malard *nm zool* mallard

malavisé *adj* ill-advised, blundering, tactless

malaxage *nm* mixing (cement); kneading (dough); working (butter); *med* massage

malaxer *vt* mix (cement); knead (dough); work (butter); *med* massage

malaxeur *nm* cement-mixer; kneading machine; butter-worker

malbâti *adj* misshapen, ill-favoured

malchance *nf* bad luck; mishap; par ~ as ill luck would have it

malchanceux -euse *n + adj* unlucky, unfortunate (person)

malcommode *adj coll* inconvenient

maldonne *nf* misdeal (cards); *coll* error

mâle *nm* male; *adj* male; virile, manly, vigorous

**malédiction** *nf* curse, malediction; *interj* curse it!, damnation!

**maléfice** *nm* evil spell, malefice

**maléfique** *adj* maleficent, baleful

**malencontreux -euse** *adj* unlucky, unfortunate, untoward; ill-met

**mal-en-point** *adj invar* in a bad way, out of sorts

**malentendu** *nm* misunderstanding, misapprehension, dispute

**malfaçon** *nf* defect, bad workmanship

**malfaisant** *adj* maleficent, harmful; noxious

**malfaiteur -trice** *n* malefactor, wrongdoer; scoundrel

**malfamé** *adj* of bad repute, ill-famed, disreputable

**malgache** *nm* Madagascan (language); *adj* Madagascan, Malagasy

**malgré** *prep* in spite of, despite; ~ **moi** against my will; ~ **que** *conj phr coll* though, although; ~ **que vous en ayez** for all you can do

**malhabile** *adj* unskilful, awkward

**malheur** *nm* misfortune, bad luck; accident, calamity; **à qch ~ est bon** it's an ill wind that blows no one any good; **faire le ~ de qn** be the ruin of s/o; *coll* **faire un ~** do something desperate; **jouer de ~** be out of luck; **par ~** as ill luck would have it, unfortunately; **porter ~** bring bad luck

**malheureux -euse** *n* unfortunate person; unlucky person; *adj* unfortunate, unhappy; unlucky, ill-fated; wretched, paltry; **avoir la main malheureuse** be clumsy; be unlucky (cards); **c'est ~ que** it's a pity that; *coll* **te voici, ce n'est pas ~** ! so you are here, and about time too!

**malhonnête** *adj* dishonest, shady; impolite, rude; improper, coarse

**malhonnêteté** *nf* dishonesty; shady transaction; impoliteness; improper remark, coarse expression

**malice** *nf* mischievousness, mischief; sly remark; malevolence; **faire des ~ à** play sly tricks on; **ne pas voir ~ à qch** see nothing wrong in sth

**malicieux -ieuse** *adj* malicious; mischievous, arch, sly

**malignité** *nf* malignity; spitefulness; mischievousness; *med* malignancy

**malin -igne** *n* cunning person; *coll* sharp one; *coll* **c'est un ~**! he's pretty sharp!; *coll* **faire le ~** try to be smart; **le Malin** the Devil; *adj* malignant; malicious, wicked; mischievous; cunning, sly, shrewd; *coll* difficult; *coll* **ce n'est pas ~** that's not very clever; it's not difficult

**malingre** *adj* puny, sickly

**malintentionné** *adj* ill-intentioned

**malle** *nf* trunk, box; *mot* boot, *US* trunk; *ar* mail-boat; **faire (défaire) sa ~** pack (unpack) one's trunk

**malléable** *adj* malleable, soft; pliable, pliant

**malle-poste** *nf* (*pl* **malles-poste(s)**) mail-coach

**mallette** *nf* small suitcase, attaché-case

**malmener** *vt* (6) ill-treat, handle roughly, mishandle; harry, brow-beat

**malodorant** *adj* malodorous, evil-smelling

**malotru** *nm* boor, cad; *adj* coarse, uncouth, caddish

**malpeigné** *adj* tousled, unkempt

**malplaisant** *adj* unpleasant, displeasing

**malpropre** *adj* dirty, untidy, slovenly; smutty, dirty (remark)

**malpropreté** *nf* dirtiness, untidiness, slovenliness; smuttiness; **dire des ~s** talk smut

**malsain** *adj* unhealthy, unwholesome; pernicious, unsound

**malséant** *adj* unseemly, indecorous

**malsonnant** *adj* offensive, objectionable

**malterie** *nf* malt-house

**maltraiter** *vt* maltreat, ill-treat

**malveillance** *nf* malevolence, ill-will

**malveillant** *adj* malevolent, ill-willed; spiteful

**malvenu** *adj* ill-advised, badly placed

**maman** *nf* mother, *coll* mama, mummy; **bonne ~** grandmother, *coll* grandma, granny

**mamelle** *nf* breast; udder

**mamelon** *nm* nipple; dug, teat; *geog* hillock

**mamillaire** *adj* mamillary

**mammaire** *adj med* mammary

**mammifère** *nm zool* mammal; *adj* mammalian

**mammouth** *nm* mammoth

**mamours** *nmpl* billing and cooing; **faire des ~ à** caress, coax

**manade** *nf* herd of bulls; herd of horses

**manant** *nm ar* peasant, villager; *coll* yokel, churl, boor

**¹manche** *nf* sleeve; *sp* game, set, hand (cards); ~ **à air** *aer* windsock; *naut* ventilator; **avoir qn dans sa ~** have s/o in one's pocket; **la Manche** the Channel; **une autre paire de ~s** a different kettle of fish

**²manche** *nm* handle, haft, stock; ~ **à balai** broomstick; *aer* control-column, *coll* joy-stick; **jeter le ~ après la cognée** give up

**manchette** *nf* cuff; headline (newspaper); **boutons de ~** cuff-links; **mettre en ~** splash (newspaper)

**manchon** *nm* muff; *eng* casing, sleeve; flange; gas-mantle

¹**manchot -ote** *n* one-armed person; *adj* one-armed; *fig* clumsy; **il n'est pas ~** he's clever with his hands; he's not clumsy

²**manchot** *nm* penguin

**mandant -e** *n leg* principal; *pol* constituent

**mandarine** *nf* tangerine, mandarin

**mandarinier** *nm* tangerine orange tree

**mandat** *nm* mandate; warrant; money-order; *leg* power of attorney; **~ d'arrêt** warrant for arrest; *leg* **~ de perquisition** search-warrant; **~ du Trésor** Treasury warrant; **~ international** international money-order; **lancer un ~** issue a warrant

**mandataire** *n* proxy; *leg* representative; authorized agent

**mandat-carte** *nm* (*pl* **mandats-cartes**) (French) postcard money-order

**mandat-lettre** *nm* (*pl* **mandats-lettres**) money-order

**Mandchou -e** *n* Manchurian

**mandchou** *adj* Manchurian

**Mandchourie** *nf* Manchuria

**mandement** *nm* mandate, instructions

**mander** *vt* summon; *ar* say by letter, report

**mandibule** *nf anat* mandible, lower jaw

**mandragore** *nf* mandragora, mandrake

**mandrin** *nm eng* mandrel; punch; drift-bolt

**manécanterie** *nf* choir-school

**manège** *nm* riding-school; training (horses); roundabout, merry-go-round; *fig* trick, device

**mânes** *nmpl* manes, shades

**manette** *nf* lever; *elect* key, morse-key; *naut* spoke (wheel)

**manganèse** *nm* manganese

**mangeable** *adj* edible, eatable

**mangeoire** *nf* manger, feeding trough

**manger** *nm* food; *vt* (3) eat; eat into, away; devour, consume; spend; **~ de l'argent** squander money; *sl* **~ le morceau** squeal, blow the gaff; **~ ses mots** mumble, swallow one's words; *vi* eat; **~ à sa faim** have enough to eat; **comme quatre** eat a huge meal

**mange-tout** *nm invar* sugar pea; French bean; *ar* spendthrift

**mangeur -euse** *n* eater

**mangouste** *nf* mongoose

**mangue** *nf* mango

**manguier** *nm* mango-tree

**maniabilité** *nf* handiness; ease of handling, manoeuvrability (car, plane)

**maniable** *adj* handy; manageable, easy to handle; tractable, pliable; **peu ~** awkward, unhandy

**maniaque** *n* crank, eccentric, faddist; *med* maniac; *adj* eccentric, faddy, fussy

**manichéen -éenne** *adj* manichean

**manie** *nf* mania, craze, fad; idiosyncrasy, trick; *med* mental derangement; **avoir la ~ de** be mad about, have a craze for; have a trick of

**maniement** *nm* handling, management

**manier** *vt* handle, ply, wield; manage, use

**manière** *nf* manner, way, guise; kind; *arts* style; **~ d'être** condition, state; *arts* **à la ~ de** in the style, manner of; *coll* **de la belle ~** thoroughly; **d'une ~ ou d'une autre** in one way or another; **en ~ de** by way of; **en quelque ~** in a way; **faire des ~s** put on airs; *coll* affect reluctance; *conj phr* **de ~ à** so as to; **de ~ que** so that

**maniéré** *adj* affected, finicky; pretentious; *arts* mannered, finical

**maniérisme** *nm* mannerism

**manieur** *nm* handler, user; **~ d'argent** financier; *coll* tycoon

**manif** *nf coll* demo

**manifestant -e** *n* demonstrator

**manifestation** *nf* manifestation; public occasion; political demonstration, *sl* demo

**manifeste** *nm* manifesto; *naut* manifest; *adj* manifest, obvious, overt; palpable

**manifester** *vt* show, manifest, express; *vi* demonstrate, take part in demonstration; **se ~** appear, emerge

**manigance** *nf coll* wangling; **~s** intrigue, wiles

**manigancer** *vt* (4) *coll* wangle; intrigue, plot; *pol* gerrymander

¹**manille** *nm* Manilla cigar

²**manille** *nf* kind of card game

**manipulateur -trice** *n* manipulator, handler; *nm* sending-key (telegraphy)

**manipuler** *vt* manipulate, handle; operate; *coll* wangle

**manitou** *nm coll* bigwig, big shot

**manivelle** *nf* handle, crank; *mot* starting handle

¹**manne** *nf bibl* manna

²**manne** *nf* basket, hamper

**mannequin** *nm* tailor's dummy; manequin

**manœuvrabilité** *nf* manoeuvrability

**manœuvrable** *adj* manoeuvrable, manageable

¹**manœuvre** *nm* labourer; **travail de ~** unskilled labour

²**manœuvre** *nf* working, handling; driving; *mil* exercise, drill; move, movement; shunting; intrigue, manoeuvre, scheme; **~ électorale** vote-catching device; **fausse ~** wrong move

**manœuvrer** vt work, handle, drive; shunt; manoeuvre; vi mil+naut manoeuvre

**manoir** nm manor; country-house

**manomètre** nm manometer, pressure-gauge

**manquant** adj absent, missing; **porté ~** reported missing

**manque** nm lack, want, insufficiency; breach; **~ de cœur** heartlessness; **~ de parole** breach of faith; **par ~ de** for want of

**manqué** adj missed; unsuccessful; **c'est un acteur ~** he ought to have been an actor; **coup ~** failure, abortive attempt; **garçon ~** tomboy; **vie ~e** wasted life

**manquement** nm failure, lapse, breach; **~ à l'appel** absence from roll-call

**manquer** vt miss; vi lack, be missing, run short, fail; miss, be missing; give way; just miss, come near to; **~ à qn** be missed by s/o; be disrespectful to s/o; **~ de faire qch** nearly do something; coll **cela n'a pas manqué!** of course, it happened!; **ne ~ de rien** want for nothing; **ne pas ~ de** not fail to; v impers **il me manque une chaussette** I am one sock short; **il ne manque plus que cela!** that's the last straw!

**mansarde** nf attic, garret; dormer-window

**mansardé** adj mansard-roofed; **chambre ~e** attic-room

¹**mante** nf mantle, sleeveless cloak

²**mante** nf ent mantis

**manteau** nm overcoat; cloak; mil greatcoat; fig cloak, covering; **~ de cheminée** mantelpiece; **sous le ~** secretly, confidentially

**mantille** nf mantilla

**manucure** nf manicure

**manucurer** vt manicure

**manuel** nm manual, text-book, handbook; adj (f -**uelle**) adj manual

**manufacture** nf factory, mill, plant, works

**manufacturer** vt manufacture

**manufacturier** nm manufacturer, mill-owner; adj (f -**ière**) manufacturing

**manuscrit** nm manuscript

**manutention** nf handling; administration

**manutentionner** vt handle

**maoïsme** nm maoism

**maoïste** n maoist

**mappemonde** nf map of the world

¹**maquereau** nm mackerel

²**maquereau** nm coll pimp, ponce, procurer

**maquerelle** nf coll procuress, madam (brothel)

**maquette** nf model, mock-up; print dummy

**maquignon** nm horse-dealer; coll spiv, go-between

**maquignonner** vt sell (horses) dishonestly; coll fix, fiddle

**maquillage** nm make-up; making-up; faking

**maquiller** vt make up; fake, disguise, distort; **se ~** make up; coll paint oneself

**maquilleur -euse** n theat+cin person who does make-up

**maquis** nm bush, undergrowth (in Corsica); resistance movement; fig tangle, maze; **prendre le ~** take to the maquis, go underground

**maquisard** nm resistance fighter, partisan

**maraîcher -ère** n market-gardener; adj market-gardening (industry, produce)

**marais** nm marsh, bog; **~ salant** salt-marsh; **le Marais** the Marais district in Paris

**marasme** nm stagnation; depression, despondency

**marasquin** nm maraschino

**marâtre** nf ar step-mother; cruel, harsh step-mother

**maraudage** nm pilfering; looting

**maraude** nf thieving; marauding; coll **taxi en ~** cruising taxi

**marauder** vi pilfer; maraud; coll cruise for fares (taxi)

**marbre** nm marble, marble statue; marbling (book); typ bed of press; **livre sur le ~** book in the press

**marbré** adj marbled, mottled

**marbrer** vt marble (book); mottle

**marbrerie** nf marble work; marble-working; monumental mason's workshop

**marbrier** nm marble-cutter, monumental mason; adj (f -**ière**) marble

**marbrière** nf marble quarry

**marbrure** nf marbling (book); mottling

**marc** nm residue from fruit-pressing; kind of brandy; **~ de café** coffee-grounds

**marcassin** nm zool young wild boar

**marchand -e** n tradesman (-woman), dealer, shopkeeper; merchant; **~ au détail** retailer; **~ des quatre saisons** costermonger, barrow-boy; **~ en gros** wholesaler; adj saleable, marketable; commercial, merchant; **navire ~** merchant-ship, cargo-boat; **prix ~** market price; **valeur ~e** market value

**marchandage** nm bargaining

**marchander** vt haggle over, bargain for; grudge

**marchandise** nf merchandise, goods;

commodity; **faire valoir sa ~** present things in a favourable light

**¹marche** nf border, march, borderland

**²marche** nf step, stair; walking, gait; functioning, running; mus march; mot **~ arrière** reverse; **~ à suivre** course to be followed; **en ~** moving; **en état de ~** in working order; **fermer la ~** bring up the rear; **mettre en ~** start (engine), set moving

**marché** nm market; marketing; transaction, dealing, buying; **~ aux puces** flea-market, junk-market; **~ conclu!** it's a deal!; **~ des valeurs** stock-market; **(à) bon ~** cheap; **faire bon ~ de qch** attribute little value to sth; **faire son ~** do the shopping

**marchepied** nm mot running-board; step (railway-coach); pair of steps, step-ladder; fig stepping-stone

**marcher** nm gait, walking; vi walk, go, march; tread; function, go, work, run; coll agree; **~ à quatre pattes** walk on all fours; coll **cela n'a pas marché** it didn't work, it didn't come off; **façon de ~** gait; **faire ~ une affaire** run a business; **faire ~ une maison** run a house; **les affaires marchent** business is good; coll **on vous a fait ~** you've been had

**marcheur -euse** n walker; coll **vieux ~** old rake

**marcotte** nf hort layer; runner, sucker

**marcotter** vt hort layer

**mardi** nm Tuesday; **~ gras** Shrove Tuesday

**mare** nf pond, pool

**marécage** nm marsh, swamp, quagmire

**marécageux -euse** adj marshy, swampy

**maréchal** nm blacksmith; mil marshal; mil **~ des logis** sergeant

**maréchaussée** nf hist mounted constabulary

**marée** nf tide; fresh fish; **à ~** tidal; **la ~ monte (descend)** the tide is coming in (going out); **train de ~** fish train

**marelle** nf hopscotch

**marémoteur -trice** adj tidal (energy); **usine marémotrice** tide-power plant

**marennes** nf Marennes oyster

**mareyage** nm fish trade

**mareyeur -euse** n fishmonger

**marge** nf border, edge; margin; comm **~ bénéficiaire** profit margin; **note en ~** marginal note

**margelle** nf curb-stone of well

**margotin** nm bundle of firewood

**margoulette** nf sl mug, face; jaw

**margoulin** nm small tradesman; coll black-marketeer

**Marguerite** nf Margaret

**marguerite** nf daisy; **effeuiller la ~** play

'she loves me, she loves me not'

**marguillier** nm churchwarden

**mari** nm husband

**mariable** adj marriageable

**mariage** nm marriage, matrimony; wedding; wedlock; **acte de ~** marriage certificate; **demande en ~** proposal of marriage; **donner en ~** give away; **né en dehors du ~** born out of wedlock; **promesse de ~** engagement, betrothal

**Marie** nf Mary

**marié -e** n married person; **jeune ~** bridegroom; **jeune ~e** bride; **la ~e est trop belle** it's too good to be true

**marier** vt marry; join in marriage (priest); marry off; fig join, unite; match (colours); **fille à ~** eligible daughter; **se ~** marry, get married; **se ~ avec** get married to; fig blend, harmonize, go with

**marie-salope** nf (pl **maries-salopes**) sl slattern; mud-barge (dredger)

**marieur -ieuse** n match-maker

**marin** nm sailor; coll **~ d'eau douce** land-lubber; adj marine; **avoir le pied ~** be a good sailor (i.e. not seasick); **carte ~e** chart

**marinade** nf cul marinade, pickle

**marine** nf seamanship; sea-service; arts sea-scape; **~ (de guerre)** navy; **~ marchande** merchant navy; **terme de ~** nautical term; adj usu invar navy-blue

**mariner** vt cul marinade, pickle; vi coll be in a pickle for a long time

**marinier** nm waterman; adj (f **-ière**) marine, naval; **officier ~** petty officer

**marinière** nf jersey, blouse, tee-shirt; sp side-stroke (swimming); cul **sauce ~** onion sauce

**mariol(le)** nm sl **faire le ~** show off, talk big

**marionnette** nf puppet; **théâtre de ~s** puppet-show

**maritime** adj maritime, seaborne; **agent ~** shipping agent; **courtier ~** ship-broker

**maritorne** nf ugly slattern

**marivaudage** nm witty and sophisticated conversation; mild flirting

**marivauder** vi make witty and sophisticated conversation; flirt

**marjolaine** nf bot marjoram

**marlou** nm sl pimp

**marmaille** nf coll children, kids, brats

**marmelade** nf compote (fruit); coll hell of a mess; **~ d'oranges** marmalade; **en ~** in shreds, pounded to a jelly

**marmitage** nm coll mil (heavy) bombardment

**marmite** nf pot, pan; dixie; coll mil heavy shell; geol pot-hole

**marmiter** *vt coll mil* bombard with heavy shells, shell

**marmiton** *nm* kitchen hand, cook's boy

**marmonner** *vt* mumble, mutter (discontentedly)

**marmoréen -éenne** *adj* marmoreal, marble; cold, glacial

**marmot** *nm* brat, urchin; **croquer le ~** be kept waiting

**marmotte** *nf* marmot; **dormir comme une ~** sleep like a log

**marmotter** *vt* mumble, mutter

**marmouset** *nm coll* urchin, kid

**marne** *nf* marl

**marner** *vt* fertilize with marl, marl; *sl* work like a black

**marnière** *nf* marl-pit

**Maroc** *nm* Morocco

**Marocain -e** *n* Moroccan

**marocain** *adj* Moroccan

**maronner** *vi coll* grumble, growl

**maroquin** *nm* Morocco (leather); *coll* minister's portfolio

**maroquinerie** *nf* Morocco leather goods; fancy leather trade; shop selling fancy leather; process of dressing leather

**maroquinier** *nm* seller of fancy leather goods; dresser of Morocco leather

**marotte** *nf ar* court-jester's bauble; *coll* fad, fancy; **flatter la ~ de qn** humour s/o

**maroufle** *nf arts* mounting paste .

**maroufler** *vt arts* mount (picture)

**marquant** *adj* prominent, outstanding, striking

**marque** *nf* mark, stamp; brand, make; *fig* token; **sp à vos ~ s!** on your marks!; **~ de fabrique** trade-mark; **~ déposée** registered trade-mark; **~ d'origine** maker's signature; **personnages de ~** persons of note

**marqué** *adj* marked; unmistakeable, pronounced; **au jour ~** on the appointed day; **prix ~** list-price, price on label

**marquer** *vt* mark; label, stencil, brand; make a note of, record, put down; *sp* score; *mus* **~ la mesure** beat time; **~ le coup** celebrate (occasion); *mil* **~ le pas** mark time; *sp* **~ les points** keep the score; **~ un arbre** blaze a tree; *vi* stand out, make a mark, leave a mark; look; **~ mal** look unprepossessing; **~ son âge** look one's age

**marqueter** *vt* (5) inlay; speckle

**marqueterie** *nf* marquetry, inlaid work; *fig* patchwork

**marquise** *nf* marchioness; awning; glass roof; marquee

**marraine** *nf* godmother; sponsor

**marrant** *adj sl* side-splitting, creasing

**marre** *adv coll* **en avoir ~** be fed up, be fed to the teeth

**marrer (se)** *v refl sl* split one's sides laughing

**marri** *adj ar* sorry, sad

**¹marron** *nm* chestnut; maroon, signal-rocket; chestnut colour; *coll* blow; **~ d'Inde** horse-chestnut; *adj invar* chestnut (colour)

**²marron -onne** *adj* unlicensed, unqualified; shady; **nègre ~** runaway slave

**marronnier** *nm* chestnut-tree; **~ d'Inde** horse-chestnut-tree

**mars** *nm* March

**marsouin** *nm* porpoise

**marteau** *nm* hammer; **~ à deux mains** sledgehammer; **~ à panne fendue** claw-hammer; **~ de porte** door-knocker; *coll* **avoir un coup de ~ , être un peu ~** be cracked, barmy; **passer sous le ~** be sold under the (auctioneer's) hammer, be knocked down

**marteau-pilon** *nm* (*pl* **marteaux-pilons**) *eng* power hammer

**martelage** *nm* hammering; blazing (tree)

**martelé** *adj* hammered, wrought; **vers ~** laboured verse, chiselled verse

**marteler** *vt* (5) hammer; beat out (metal)

**martial** *adj* martial, soldierly; warlike; *mil* **cour ~ e** court martial

**martinet** *nm* strap, whip; *orni* swift, martin

**martin-pêcheur** *nm* (*pl* **martins-pêcheurs**) *orni* kingfisher

**martre** *nf zool* marten

**martyr -e** *n* martyr; *adj* martyred

**martyre** *nm* martyrdom

**martyriser** *vt* martyr; *coll* torture, make suffer

**marxisme** *nm* marxism

**marxiste** *n + adj* marxist

**maryland** *nm* Maryland tobacco

**mas** *nm* farmhouse (in S. France)

**mascarade** *nf* masquerade

**mascaret** *nm* bore, tidal wave in river

**mascotte** *nf* mascot, lucky charm

**masculin** *nm gramm* masculine (gender); *adj* masculine, male

**masochisme** *nm* masochism

**masochiste** *n* masochist

**¹masque** *nm* mask; expression of the face, features; *mil* screen (smoke); masked person (ball); **~ mortuaire** death-mask

**²masque** *nf coll* hussy, hag

**masquer** *vt* mask, disguise, hide; *naut* back (sail)

**massacrant** *adj* **d'une humeur ~ e** in a vile temper

**massacre** *nm* massacre, slaughter; **jeu de ~** Aunt Sally

**massacrer** *vt* massacre, slaughter, butcher; *fig* ruin, murder (music); botch

**massacreur -euse** *n* slayer, butcher; *fig* murderer, butcher

¹**masse** *nf* mass, heap, mound; multitude; *comm* fund, stock; *elect* mass, earth; *comm* ~ passive liabilities; **en** ~ in a body (people), in bulk (goods); *elect* **mettre à la** ~ earth

²**masse** *nf* sledge-hammer; maul; mace

**massepain** *nm* marzipan

¹**masser** *vt* mass; **se** ~ mass, form a mound

²**masser** *vt* massage

**massif** *nm* clump (shrubs); flower-bed; *geog* group of mountains; *archi* solid mass; *adj* (*f* -**ive**) massive, bulky; mass, large-scale; solid (gold, silver)

**massue** *nf* club, bludgeon

**mastic** *nm* mastic; cement; putty; *med* dental filling; *mot* puncture solution; *fig coll* mess, muddle, mix-up; *adj invar* putty-coloured

**masticage** *nm* filling, puttying

¹**mastiquer** *vt* fill (crack), putty (window)

²**mastiquer** *vt* masticate

**mastoc** *adj invar coll* heavy, lumpish

**mastodonte** *nm* mastodon

**mastoïde** *adj med* mastoid

**mastroquet** *nm coll* bar-keeper, pub-keeper

**masturber** *vt* masturbate; **se** ~ masturbate

**m'as-tu-vu** *nm invar coll* swank (person)

**masure** *nf* hovel, tumbledown cottage

¹**mat** *nm* (check)mate (chess); *adj invar* checkmated

²**mat** *adj* dull, lustreless; matt; dead, dull (sound)

**mât** *nm naut* mast; pole; *naut* ~ **d'artimon** mizzen-mast; ~ **de charge** derrick; ~ **de cocagne** greasy pole; ~ **de hune** top-mast; ~ **de misaine** fore-mast; **grand-** ~ main-mast

**matamore** *nm* braggart, swash-buckler

**matelas** *nm* mattress; cushion, padding; ~ **pneumatique** air-mattress; **toile à** ~ tick, ticking

**matelasser** *vt* pad, cushion; **porte matelassée** baize door

**matelot** *nm* sailor, seaman; ship; sailor suit; ~ **d'avant (d'arrière)** next ship ahead (astern); ~ **de première (deuxième, troisième) classe** = leading (able-bodied, ordinary) seaman

**matelote** *nf cul* fish-stew

¹**mater** *vt* mat, dull

²**mater** *vt* checkmate (chess); *fig* tame, humble, break in

**mâter** *vt naut* mast

**matérialiser** *vt* symbolize; materialize; **se** ~ materialize

**matérialisme** *nm* materialism

**matérialiste** *n* materialist; *adj* materialistic

**matériau** *nm invar* (constructional, building) material

**matériaux** *nmpl* materials

**matériel** *nm* plant, equipment; working-stock (factory); ~ **d'école** school furniture; ~ **de guerre** war material; ~ **roulant** rolling-stock; *adj* (*f* -**ielle**) material, physical; materialistic, sensual; real; *leg* **dommages** ~**s** damage to property

**maternel** -**elle** *adj* maternal, motherly

**maternelle** *nf* infant-school

**maternité** *nf* maternity, motherhood; maternity hospital

**mathématicien** -**ienne** *n* mathematician

**mathématique** *adj* mathematical

**mathématiques** *nfpl* mathematics, *coll* maths

**matière** *nf* matter, material, basis, substance; subject, topic; *med* ~ **s faeces**; ~ **s premières** raw materials; **en** ~ **de** as regards; **entrer en** ~ broach the subject; **il n'y a pas** ~ **à rire** it's no laughing matter; **table des** ~**s** table of contents

**matin** *nm* morning; **au petit** ~ in the small hours; **de bon (grand)** ~ early in the morning; **le** ~ in the morning; **un beau** ~ one of these days; *adv* early; **se lever** ~ get up early

**mâtin** *nm* mastiff, watchdog

**matinal** *adj* morning; early; **être** ~ be an early riser

**mâtiné** *adj* cross-bred, mongrel

**matinée** *nf* morning; *theat* matinée; *coll* **faire la grasse** ~ have a lie-in, sleep late

**mâtiner** *vt* cross (dogs)

**matines** *nfpl eccles* matins

**matois** *nm* crafty, artful person; **fin** ~ wily customer; *adj* crafty, artful, sly

**matou** *nm* tom-cat

**matraquage** *nm* bludgeoning: *comm* saturation publicity; *mil* heavy bombardment

**matraque** *nf* club, cosh; rubber truncheon

**matraquer** *vt* cosh, hit with truncheon; *comm* repeat (slogans, etc); *mil* bombard heavily

**matriarcal** *adj* matriarchal

**matrice** *nf anat* uterus, womb; matrix, die; master (gramophone record); standard (weights)

**matricide** *nm* matricide; *n* person committing matricide; *adj* matricidal

**matriculaire** *adj* pertaining to registration, enrolment; *mil* **feuille** ~ service record

**matricule** *nf* roll, register, list; registration certificate; *nm* official number, reference number; *mot* registration number; *mil* army number

**matriculer** *vt* register; give an official number to

**matrone** *nf* middle-aged mother; fat middle-aged woman

**mâture** *nf naut* masts, masts and spars; sheers (crane); **dans la ~** aloft

**maturité** *nf* maturity, ripeness

**maudire** *vt* (58) curse

**maudit** *nm eccles* **Le Maudit** The Evil One; **les ~s** the damned; *adj* cursed, accursed; damnable, damned

**maugréer** *vi* curse, grumble; *coll* grouse

**Maure -esque** *n* Moor, Moorish woman

**maure -esque** *adj* Moorish

**Maurice** *nm* Maurice; **l'Île ~** Mauritius

**mausolée** *nm* mausoleum

**maussade** *adj* sullen, glum, peevish, surly; dull, depressing (weather)

**mauvais -e** *nm* evil, what is bad; *adj* bad; evil, ill, wicked; poor, nasty, displeasing; faulty; wrong; rough (sea); **~e langue** malicious gossiper; **~e plaisanterie** stupid practical joke; **avoir l'air ~** look fierce; **faire ~e mine à** cold-shoulder; **prendre qch du ~ côté** put the wrong construction on sth; **prendre qch en ~e part** take exception to sth; **prendre qn par le ~ bout** rub s/o up the wrong way; **voir d'un ~ œil** bear a grudge against; *adv* **faire ~** be bad (weather); **sentir ~** smell bad

**mauve** *nm+adj* mauve, purple; *nf bot* mallow

**maxillaire** *nm* jaw-bone; *adj* maxillary

**maximal** *adj* maximum

**maxime** *nf* maxim

**maximiser** *vt* maximize

**maximum** *nm* (*pl* **maxima**, **~s**) maximum; **~ de rendement** highest efficiency; **faire son ~** do one's very best; *adj* maximum, greatest

**mazout** *nm* fuel oil

**me** *pers pron* me; to me; *refl pron* myself

**mea-culpa** *nm invar* **faire son ~** acknowledge one's faults, beat one's breast

**méandre** *nm* meander, winding (stream, path)

**mec** *nm sl* chap, bloke

**mécanicien** *nm* mechanic; engine-driver; **ingénieur ~** mechanical engineer

**mécanicienne** *nf* machinist, sewing-machine operator (factory)

**mécanique** *nf* mechanism; science of mechanics; *adj* mechanical; machine-made

**mécanisation** *nf* mechanization

**mécaniser** *vt* mechanize

**mécanisme** *nm* mechanism, works; *mus* technique

**mécano** *nm coll* mechanic

**mécanographe** *n* punch-card machine operator; business machine operator

**mécanographie** *nf* data processing; operation of business machines

**mécénat** *nm* patronage of the arts

**mécène** *nm* Maecenas, rich patron

**méchamment** *adv* wickedly, spitefully, naughtily

**méchanceté** *nf* wickedness, malice, spitefulness; spiteful act; malicious remark; naughtiness, mischievousness (child)

**méchant -e** *n* disagreeable person, spiteful person; naughty child; *adj* wicked, malicious, spiteful, ill-natured; naughty, mischievous; paltry, miserable, mean; **~ article** third-rate article; **article ~** spiteful article; **chien ~!** beware of the dog!; **un ~ billet de dix francs** a paltry ten-franc note; **un ~ pantalon** a scruffy pair of trousers

**mèche** *nf* wick; fuse; lash (whip); lock (hair); bit (drill); *coll* **être de ~ avec** be in league with, be hand in glove with; **vendre la ~** give the show away, blow the gaff

**mécompte** *nm* miscalculation, error; disappointment, foiled expectation

**méconnaissable** *adj* unrecognizable

**méconnaissance** *nf* failure to recognize, appreciate; disavowal, repudiation

**méconnaître** *vt* (68) fail to recognize, ignore; disavow, repudiate; misunderstand; underrate; **se ~** underrate oneself

**méconnu** *adj* unrecognized, unappreciated, misunderstood

**mécontent -e** *n* grumbler; malcontent; *adj* discontented, displeased

**mécontentement** *nm* discontent, displeasure

**mécontenter** *vt* displease, annoy

**mécréant -e** *n* misbeliever, unbeliever; *adj* misbelieving, unbelieving

**médaille** *nf* medal, badge; *archi* medallion; **envers de la ~** reverse side of the coin

**médaillé -e** *n mil* medal-holder; medallist, prize-winner; *adj* decorated

**médailler** *vt* decorate, give medal to

**médaillon** *nm* medallion; locket; inset (newspaper); *cul* medallion (meat)

**médecin** *nm* doctor, physician; *naut* **~ du bord** ship's doctor

**médecine** *nf* medicine; **~ de groupe** group medical practice; **faire sa ~** study medicine

**médian** *adj* median; *sp* **ligne ~e** half-way line

**médiateur -trice** *n* mediator; *adj* mediating, mediatory

**médiator** *nm mus* plectrum

**médicament** *nm* medicine, drug, medicament

**médicamenter** *vt* doctor, dose; **se ~** dose oneself

**médiéviste** *n* medievalist

**médiocre** *nm* what is mediocre, ordinary; nonentity; *adj* mediocre, indifferent, second-rate; moderate, average; unimpressive

**médiocrité** *nf* mediocrity; exiguousness (means); second-rate person, nonentity

**médire** *vi* (74) **~ de** vilify, speak ill of, run down

**médisance** *nf* slander, scandal; piece of scandal

**médisant -e** *n* slanderer, scandalmonger; *adj* slanderous, scandalmongering

**méditatif -ive** *adj* meditative

**méditation** *nf* meditation; cogitation, rumination

**méditer** *vi* meditate, muse; *vt* ponder, meditate on; contemplate, envisage, plan

**Méditerranée** *nf geog* Mediterranean

**méditerranéen -éenne** *adj* Mediterranean

**médius** *nm anat* middle finger

**méduse** *nf* jelly-fish

**méduser** *vt* petrify, paralyse with fear

**méfait** *nm* misdeed, wrong-doing; **~s** damage

**méfiance** *nf* mistrust, distrust

**méfiant -e** *adj* mistrustful, distrustful

**méfier (se)** *v refl* be on one's guard; **se ~ de** distrust, beware of

**mégalomane** *n* megalomaniac

**mégalomanie** *nf* megalomania

**mégarde** *nf* **par ~** inadvertently, through carelessness, by an oversight

**mégatonne** *nf* megaton

**mégère** *nf* shrew, termagant

**mégot** *nm coll* cigarette-end, butt

**meilleur** *nm* better; best; *adj* better; **le ~** the best; **de ~ cœur** more willingly; *adv* better; **il fera ~ demain** the weather will be better tomorrow

**méjuger** *vt* (3) misjudge; underestimate

**mélancolie** *nf* melancholy, dejection, gloom

**mélancolique** *adj* melancholy, dejected, gloomy

**mélange** *nm* mixing, blending; mixture, blend; *arts* miscellany

**mélanger** *vt* (3) mix, blend; **se ~** mix, get mixed; mingle

**mélangeur** *nm* mixing-machine; *cin+ rad* mixer

**mélasse** *nf* molasses, treacle; *sl* mess; **~ raffinée** golden syrup

**mêlé** *adj* mixed, tangled

**mêlée** *nf* conflict, scuffle; *sp* scrum

**mêler** *vt* mix, mix together; tangle, throw into confusion; involve, implicate; **~ les cartes** shuffle cards; **être mêlé à tout** have a finger in every pie; **se ~ mix,** mingle; interfere, take a hand; **mêlez-vous de vos affaires** mind your own business; **ne vous en mêlez pas!** keep out of it!, *coll* keep your nose clean!

**mélèze** *nm bot* larch

**méli-mélo** *nm coll* jumble, hotch-potch

**mélodie** *nf* melody, tune; melodiousness

**mélodieux -ieuse** *adj* melodious, tuneful

**mélodique** *adj mus* melodic

**mélodramatique** *adj* melodramatic

**mélodrame** *nm* melodrama

**mélomane** *n* music enthusiast, *coll* music fan; *adj* very keen on music, music mad

**melon** *nm bot* melon; bowler-hat, bowler

**mélopée** *nf mus* recitative; melancholy chant

**membrane** *nf* membrane, film; diaphragm; web (bird's foot)

**membrané** membranous; webbed

**membre** *nm* member, limb; *math* side (equation); *naut* timber; **~ viril** penis

**membré** *adj* limbed

**membrure** *nf* limbs; framework

**même** *adj* same; very, self; (*after pers pron*) self (as **moi-~** myself ); **c'est cela ~** that's just it; **en ~ temps** at the same time; **être la bonté ~** be kindness itself; **le jour ~** the very day; **revenir au ~** come to the same thing; *adv* even; **à ~ de** be able to, capable of; **à ~ la peau** next to the skin; **boire à ~ la bouteille** drink straight out of the bottle; **de ~ que** just as; **faire de ~** do likewise; **tout de ~** all the same

**mémento** *nm* memorandum; notebook; memento, reminder

**mémoire** *nm* memorial; report; memoir, dissertation; *leg* written statement; *comm* detailed bill; **~s** memoirs; *nf* memory; recollection, remembrance; **de ~ d'homme** within living memory; **en ~ de** in memory of; **rappeler qch à la ~ de qn** give s/o a reminder about sth; **si j'ai bonne ~** if I remember rightly

**mémorable** *adj* memorable, noteworthy; eventful

**mémorandum** *nm* memorandum; notebook

**menaçant** *adj* menacing, threatening; forbidding

**menace** *nf* menace, threat; **~s en l'air** idle threats

**menacer** *vt* (4) menace, threaten

**ménage** *nm* housekeeping; household; housework; married couple; household furniture; ~ **à trois** domestic triangle; **entrer en** ~ set up home; **faire bon (mauvais)** ~ **ensemble** get on well (badly) together; **faire le** ~ do the housework; **femme de** ~ charwoman; **un** ~ **uni** a devoted couple

**ménagement** *nm* circumspection, prudence, care; **sans** ~ bluntly, roughly

¹**ménager -ère** *adj* household; thrifty; **(Salon des) Arts** ~ **s** = Ideal Home Exhibition

²**ménager** *vt* (3) save, husband, use economically; deal tactfully with, treat considerately, humour; arrange, control

**ménagère** *nf* housewife, housekeeper; canteen of cutlery

**mendiant -e** *n* beggar; *nm cul* kind of sweet, dessert cake

**mendicité** *nf* mendicity, begging; beggary

**mendier** *vt* beg for; *vi* beg

**meneau** *nm archi* ~ **vertical** mullion; ~ **horizontal** transom

**menée** *nf* sly manoeuvre, intrigue; **déjouer les** ~ **s de** outwit, out-manoeuvre

**mener** *vt* (6) lead; conduct; take; control, manage, carry out; drive (horse, vehicle), steer (boat); *math* draw (line); ~ **plusieurs choses de front** have several irons in the fire; ~ **qch à bien** carry sth through successfully; **bien** ~ **sa barque** manage one's affairs well; **cela me mène à croire** that leads me to think; **cela peut** ~ **loin** that may have considerable consequences; *coll* **ne pas en** ~ **large** be in a jam; *vi* lead

**ménestrel** *nm* minstrel

**meneur -euse** *n* leader; ring-leader; agitator; ~ **de jeu** compère; quiz-master

**méningite** *nf* meningitis

**menotte** *nf* (child's) hand; ~ **s** handcuffs

**mensonge** *nm* lie, untruth, fib; fallacy, illusion

**mensonger -ère** *adj* lying, false, untrue; fallacious, illusory

**menstruel -uelle** *adj* menstrual

**mensualisation** *nf* changeover to monthly payment of salary

**mensualité** *nf* monthly payment; **payer par** ~ **s** pay by monthly instalments

**mensuel -uelle** *adj* monthly

**mental** *adj* mental; **calcul** ~ mental arithmetic

**mentalité** *nf* mentality

**menteur -euse** *n* liar; *adj* lying; prone to lying; deceptive, illusory

**menthe** *nf* mint; **pastilles de** ~ peppermints

**mention** *nf* mention; endorsement; distinction (examination); **reçu avec** ~ **très bien (bien)** passed with distinction (with credit)

**mentionner** *vt* mention

**mentir** *vi* (59) lie, tell lies; *coll* fib

**menton** *nm* chin

**mentonnet** *nm eng* catch, stop; tappet, lug

**mentonnière** *nf* chin-strap; chin-rest (violin)

¹**menu** *nm* menu, bill of fare; **prendre le** ~ have the set meal

²**menu** *adj* small, slender, slight; trifling, minor; ~ **e monnaie** small change; ~ **s frais** petty expenses; ~ **s propos** small talk; **le** ~ **peuple** the humbler classes; **par le** ~ in detail; *adv* small, fine; **écrire** ~ write small; **hacher** ~ chop up fine

**menuet** *nm* minuet

**menuiser** *vt* plane down, whittle (wood); *vi* do woodwork

**menuiserie** *nf* joinery, woodwork; joiner's (work)shop

**menuisier** *nm* joiner; *adj* (*f* -**ière**) **ouvrier** ~ joiner

**méplat** *nm* flat part (*esp* of face)

**méprendre (se)** *v refl* (75) be mistaken; **il n'y a pas à s'y** ~ there can be no mistake about it; **imiter qn à s'y** ~ imitate s/o to the life

**mépris** *nm* contempt, scorn; **au** ~ in contempt of; **tenir qn en** ~ despise s/o

**méprisable** *adj* contemptible, despicable

**méprisant** *adj* contemptuous, scornful

**méprise** *nf* mistake, misapprehension

**mépriser** *vt* despise, scorn

**mer** *nf* sea; *coll* **ce n'est pas la** ~ **à boire** it's not all that difficult; **en pleine** ~ on the open sea; **gens de** ~ seamen; **mal de** ~ seasickness; **pleine (basse)** ~ high (low) tide; **porter de l'eau à la** ~ carry coals to Newcastle; **prendre la** ~ put to sea

**mercanti** *nm coll* shark, profiteer

**mercantile** *adj* mercantile, commercial; mercenary, grabbing

**mercantilisme** *nm* mercantilism; mercenary spirit, money-grabbing

**mercenaire** *nm* + *adj mil* mercenary

**mercerie** *nf* haberdashery; haberdasher's shop

¹**merci** *nf* mercy; grace; **Dieu** ~ ! thank God!; **sans** ~ merciless, mercilessly

²**merci** *nm* thanks; *interj* thanks, thank you; no thank you

**mercier -ière** *n* haberdasher

**mercredi** *nm* Wednesday

**mercure** *nm* mercury

**mercuriale** *nf* reprimand, *coll* tearing off of a strip; *comm* market-price list

**mercuriel -ielle** *adj chem* mercurial

**merde** *nf vulg* shit; *interj vulg* shit!, hell!

**merdeux -euse** *n vulg* shit; conceited ass; *adj vulg* shitty; conceited

**merdier** *nm sl* mess, shambles

**mère** *nf* mother; source, origin; ~ **célibataire** unmarried mother; ~ **de tous les vices** root of all evil; *comm* **maison** ~ head-office, parent company

**méridien** *nm* meridian; *adj* (*f* **-ienne**) meridian

**méridienne** *nf* meridian line; *coll* siesta, midday nap; sofa

**Méridional -e** *n* (*mpl* **-aux**, *fpl* **-ales**) southerner

**méridional** *adj* southern, meridional

**mérinos** *nm* merino (sheep, wool, cloth)

**merise** *nf* wild cherry, merry

**merisier** *nm* wild cherry tree

**méritant** *adj* deserving, worthy (person)

**mérite** *nm* merit, desert, worth; type of award; **s'attribuer le** ~ **de** take the credit for

**mériter** *vt* merit, deserve; entitle; require, need; ~ **examen** be worth looking into

**méritoire** *adj* meritorious, deserving

**merlan** *nm* whiting; *coll* **yeux de** ~ **frit** blankly staring eyes

**merle** *nm* blackbird

**merlin** *nm* cleaving axe; *naut* marline

**merluche** *nf* hake; *cul* dried cod

**merveille** *nf* marvel, wonder; **à** ~ wonderfully, admirably; **dire des** ~**s de** speak in glowing terms of; **faire** ~ work wonders; **se porter à** ~ be wonderfully well

**merveilleux** *nm* the supernatural; *adj* (*f* **-euse**) marvellous, wonderful

**mes** *poss adj pl* my; *see* **mon**

**mésalliance** *nf* misalliance

**mésallier (se)** *v refl* marry beneath oneself

**mésange** *nf orni* tit

**mésaventure** *nf* misadventure, mishap

**mesdames** *nfpl see* **madame**

**mesdemoiselles** *nfpl see* **mademoiselle**

**mésentente** *nf* misunderstanding, disagreement

**mésestimation** *nf* underestimation, underrating

**mésestime** *nf* disesteem, low esteem

**mésestimer** *vt* underestimate, underrate; have a low opinion of

**mésintelligence** *nf* disagreement, misunderstanding; **être en** ~ **avec** be at variance with

**mesmérisme** *nm* mesmerism

**mesquin** *adj* mean, stingy; petty, narrow; **à l'esprit** ~ small-minded

**mesquinerie** *nf* meanness, stinginess; pettiness, narrow-mindedness; mean action

**messager** *nm* carrier; *n* (*f* **-ère**) messenger

**messagerie** *nf* carrying trade, transport service; ~**s aériennes** air-transport service; ~**s maritimes** sea-transport, shipping company; **bureau des** ~**s** parcels office (railway, etc)

**messe** *nf eccles* mass

**messeigneurs** *nmpl see* **monseigneur**

**messidor** *nm hist* tenth month of the French Republican calendar (June to July)

**Messie** *nm* Messiah

**messieurs** *nmpl see* **monsieur**

**mesurable** *adj* measurable

**mesure** *nf* measure, measurement, extent; arrangement; precaution, step, move; moderation; *mus* bar, time; **à** ~ in proportion; **à** ~ **que** as, in proportion as; *mus* **battre la** ~ beat time; **dans une certaine** ~ to some extent; **dépasser la** ~ overstep the bounds; **donner sa** ~ show what one is made of, capable of; **être en** ~ **de** be in a position to; **fait sur** ~ made-to-measure

**mesuré** *adj* measured; temperate, moderate

**mesurer** *vt* measure, gauge, calculate, measure out, measure off; stint, ration; ~ **qn des yeux** look s/o up and down; **se** ~ (**avec, contre**) pit oneself against, measure oneself against, try conclusions with

**mésuser** *vi* ~ **de** misuse, abuse

**métabolisme** *nm* metabolism

**métairie** *nf* small farm (where rent is paid in kind)

**métallique** *adj* metallic; **cable** ~ wire-rope; *econ* **encaisse** ~ gold and silver reserve

**métalliser** *vt* metallize

**métallo** *nm coll* metal-worker

**métallurgie** *nf* metallurgy

**métallurgique** *adj* metallurgic

**métallurgiste** *n* metallurgist

**métamorphose** *nf* metamorphosis

**métamorphoser** *vt* metamorphose, transform; **se** ~ change, be metamorphosed

**métaphore** *nf* metaphor

**métaphorique** *adj* metaphorical

**métaphysicien -ienne** *n* metaphysician

**métaphysique** *nf* metaphysics; *adj* metaphysical

**métayage** *nm* system of farm-rents paid in kind

**métayer** *nm* farmer paying rent in kind .
**métempsychose** *nf* metempsychosis
**météo** *nf coll* weather forecast; meteorological office; *nm coll* meteorologist
**météore** *nm* meteor
**météorique** *adj* meteoric
**météorologie** *nf* meteorology
**météorologique** *adj* meteorological
**météorologiste** *n* meteorologist
**métèque** *nm pej* foreigner, alien; *coll* dago, wog
**méthode** *nf* method, way, system; textbook, manual
**méthodique** *adj* methodical
**méthodisme** *nm eccles* Methodism
**méthodiste** *n eccles* Methodist
**méticuleux -euse** *adj* meticulous, painstaking, punctilious
**méticulosité** *nf* meticulousness
**métier** *nm* trade, profession, craft; skill, competence; professionalism; loom; ~ **mécanique** power-loom; **armée de** ~ regular army; **arts et** ~ **s** arts and crafts; **avoir du** ~ have experience, technique; *coll* **ce n'est pas mon** ~ that's not in my line; **corps de** ~ craft corporation; *ar* guild; **être du** ~ be in the trade; **faire** ~ **de** pride oneself on; **homme de** ~ professional; **manquer de** ~ lack experience; **ouvrage sur le** ~ work on the stocks, in progress; **parler** ~ talk shop
**métis -isse** *n* half-breed (person); crossbred (animal); *adj* half-bred, crossbred
**métisser** *vt* cross
**métonymie** *nf* metonymy
**métrage** *nm* measurement, measuring; length; *archi* quantity-surveying; *cin* footage; *cin* **court (long)** ~ short (full-length) feature film
**¹mètre** *nm* metre; metre rule; ~ **pliant** folding rule; ~ **à ruban** measuring-tape
**²mètre** *nm* metre (verse)
**métrer** *vt* (6) measure; survey
**métreur -euse** *n* quantity-surveyor
**métrique** *nf* prosody, metrics; *adj* metric (system); metrical (verse)
**métro** *nm coll* (Paris) underground (railway) = tube
**métropole** *nf* metropolis, capital; mother-country
**métropolitain** *nm* (Paris) underground railway; *adj* metropolitan
**mets** *nm* prepared food, dish
**mettable** *adj* wearable
**metteur -euse** *n* s/o who puts; *nm rad* ~ **en ondes** radio-producer; *typ* ~ **en pages** type-setter; *theat+cin* ~ **en scène** director
**mettre** *vt* (60) put, place, set, lay; put on, wear; use, take; grant, admit, suppose;

*comm* invest; spend; ~ **à contribution** press into service, oblige to co-operate; *comm* ~ **à exécution** bring into force, implement; ~ **à la voile** set sail; ~ **à mort** put to death; ~ **à nu** lay bare; ~ **aux enchères** put up for auction; ~ **bas** (of animal) give birth to; ~ **des vers en musique** set verse to music; ~ **du français en anglais** translate French into English; ~ **du temps à** take some time to; **mettez que je n'ai rien dit** I take that back; **mettons que tous les deux nous avions tort** let's admit we were both wrong; **mettons vingt francs?** shall we say twenty francs?; *coll* **on les met?** shall we go?, let's get out of here!; **y** ~ **le temps nécessaire** take all the time in the world; **se** ~ put oneself, place oneself; begin, start; become; dress; **se** ~ **à l'œuvre** get down to work; **se** ~ **à pleurer** begin to cry; **se** ~ **à table** sit down to eat; **se** ~ **au lit** go to bed; **se** ~ **au pas** fall into step; **se** ~ **de la pommade** put some ointment on; **se** ~ **en rage** lose one's temper; **se** ~ **en route** start off; **se** ~ **en short** put shorts on; **s'y** ~ get down to it; **le temps se met au beau** the weather is turning out fine
**meublant** *adj* decorative, usable for furnishing
**¹meuble** *nm* piece of furniture; ~ **s** furniture; **être dans ses** ~ **s** have one's own furniture
**²meuble** *adj* movable; *leg* **biens** ~ **s** chattels, movables; **terre** ~ light soil
**meublé** *nm* furnished apartment; *adj* furnished; *fig* stocked; **hôtel** ~ hotel not providing board
**meubler** *vt* furnish; fill, stock; *vi* be decorative; **se** ~ furnish one's home
**meuglement** *nm* lowing, mooing
**meugler** *vi* low, moo
**¹meule** *nf* millstone; grindstone; ~ **de fromage** large round cheese
**²meule** *nf* hayrick, haystack
**meuler** *vt* bore, grind
**meunerie** *nf* milling, milling trade
**meunier -ière** *n* miller
**meurt-de-faim** *nm invar* down-and-out
**meurtre** *nm leg* murder, homicide, manslaughter; *fig* crime, scandal
**meurtrier -ière** *n* murderer (murderess); *adj* murderous, deadly
**meurtrière** *nf archi* loop-hole
**meurtrir** *vt* bruise; ~ **de coups** beat
**meurtrissure** *nf* bruise
**meute** *nf* pack of hounds; crowd, mob
**mévente** *nf comm* sale at a loss; slump
**¹mi** *nm invar mus* E, mi
**²mi-** *adj invar* half, mid-, semi-; **à** ~ **-chemin** half-way; **à** ~ **-corps** to the waist; **à** ~ **-côte** half-way up the hill; **à**

~-**hauteur** half-way up; **à ~-jambes** half-way up the legs; **à ~-voix** in an undertone

**miaou** *nm* miaow, mew

**miasme** *nm* miasma

**miaulement** *nm* miawing, mewing

**miauler** *vt* wail (song, etc); *vi* miaow, mew

**mi-carême** *nf* mid-Lent

**miche** *nf* round loaf

**micheline** *nf* rail-car, autorail

**micmac** *nm coll* trick, scheming, manoeuvre, fiddle

**micocoulier** *nm* kind of elm (found in Provence)

**micro** *nm coll* microphone, mike; **parler au** ~ speak on the air

**microbe** *nm med* microbe; *coll* brat, kid

**microbien -ienne** *adj med* microbial; **guerre microbienne** bacteriological warfare

**microbiologie** *nf* microbiology

**microcosme** *nm* microcosm

**micromètre** *nm* micrometer

**microphone** *nm* microphone; ~ **à perche** boom-microphone; **au ~ électro-dynamique** moving-coil microphone

**microscopie** *nf* microscopy

**microscopique** *adj* microscopic

**microsillon** *nm* microgroove; long-playing record, *coll* L.P.

**miction** *nf med* micturition, urination

**midi** *nm* midday, twelve o'clock; noon-tide, culminating point; south; southern part of France; *coll* **chercher ~ à quatorze heures** be over-subtle, invent complications; **en plein ~** in broad daylight; **sur le ~** about midday

**midinette** *nf* dressmaker's apprentice, assistant; working girl

[1]**mie** *nf ar* sweetheart

[2]**mie** *nf* crumb; inside of loaf

**miel** *nm* honey; **lune de ~** honeymoon

**miellé** *adj* honeyed, sweetened with honey

**mielleux -euse** *adj* tasting of honey, honeyed; *fig* sugary, honeyed; bland, unctuous, oily

**mien** *nm* mine, what is mine, my property; *poss adj* (*f* **mienne**) *ar* **un ~ oncle** an uncle of mine; *poss pron* (*f* **mienne**) mine

**miette** *nf* crumb (bread); scrap, morsel, bit; *coll* **réduit en ~s** smashed to bits

**mieux** *nm* best (plan); improvement; **le ~ est l'ennemi du bien** leave well alone; *adv* better; **à qui ~ ~** vying with one another; **c'est on ne peut ~** it couldn't be better; **de ~ en ~** better and better; **être ~** be more comfortable; **il ressemble à son frère, mais en ~** he's like his brother, but better-

looking; **ne pas demander ~** be delighted; **pour ne pas dire ~** to say the least; **tant ~** so much the better; *adv phr* **le ~** best; **ce que vous avez de ~ à faire est** the best thing you can do is; **en mettant les choses au ~** at best; **être le ~ du monde avec** be on the best of terms with; **faire de son ~** do one's best; **faire pour le ~** do one's best

**mièvre** *adj* delicate, frail; affected, effete

**mièvrerie** *nf* fragility, daintiness; affectedness

**mignard** *adj* affected; *coll* dainty

**mignardise** *nf* affectation, winsomeness; affected act; prettiness (style); *bot* pink

**mignon -onne** *n* darling, pet; *nm ar* favourite, minion; *adj* dainty, delicate, tiny, sweet; **péché ~** besetting sin

**mignonnet -ette** *adj* dainty, delicate, tiny

**mignonnette** *nf* kind of lace; *bot* mignonnette

**migrateur -trice** *adj* migrant; *zoöl* migratory

**migratoire** *adj* migratory

**mijaurée** *nf* affected, pretentious woman or girl

**mijoter** *vt cul* stew slowly, let simmer; *coll* concoct, plan; *vi cul* simmer; *coll* **se ~** be brewing, be in preparation

**mil** *adj* thousand

**milan** *nm orni* kite

**mildiou** *nm* mildew

**milice** *nf* militia

**milicien -ienne** *n* member of the militia

**milieu** *nm* middle, midst; mean, middle course; milieu, environment; **~x officiels** official circles; **au beau ~ de** right in the middle of; **il n'y a pas de ~** there's no middle course, it's either one thing or the other; **juste ~** happy medium; *coll* **le ~** the underworld

**militaire** *nm* soldier, serviceman; *adj* military, soldierly; warlike; *coll* exact; **à huit heures, heure ~** at eight o'clock sharp; **marine ~** navy

**militarisation** *nf* militarization

**militariser** *vt* militarize

**militarisme** *nm* militarism

**militariste** *n* + *adj* militarist

**militer** *vi* militate; be active in; fight

[1]**mille** *nm invar* thousand; *adj invar* thousand; ~ **fois** a thousand times; *coll* time and again; very much indeed

[2]**mille** *nm* mile; *naut* nautical mile

**mille-feuille** *nm cul* kind of pastry

**millénaire** *nm* thousand years, millennium; *adj* millenary

**mille-pattes** *nm* centipede

**millésime** *nm* date on coin; date of production

**millésimé** *adj* bearing date of production (*esp* wine)

**millet** *nm bot* millet; **grains de ~** bird-seed

**milliard** *nm* milliard, thousand million

**milliardaire** *n + adj* multi-millionaire

**millième** *n + adj* thousandth

**millier** *nm* thousand, about a thousand; **par ~ s** in thousands

**millionième** *n + adj* millionth

**milord** *nm* English nobleman; my lord (form of address); *coll* very wealthy man

**mime** *nm theat* mime, pantomime; mimic

**mimer** *vt theat* mime, act in a dumb-show; mimic

**mimétisme** *nm* mimesis, mimicry

**mimique** *nf* mimicry, art of mime; *adj* mimic, mimetic

**minable** *adj* shabby, pitiable, seedy, down at heel; *eng* minable

**minauder** *vi* simper, smirk

**minauderie** *nf* simpering; **~s** mincing manner

**minaudier -ière** *n* simperer, affected person; *adj* simpering, smirking

**¹mince** *adj* thin, slender; slight, insignificant

**²mince** *interj sl* **~ alors!** well I'm damned!; *sl* **~ de** what a, what a lot of

**minceur** *nf* thinness, slenderness; slightness

**¹mine** *nf* mine; *mil + naut* mine; graphite, black lead; *fig* fund, stock; **~ de houille** coal-mine; **champ de ~ s** mine-field

**²mine** *nf* mien, appearance, look; **avoir bonne (mauvaise) ~** look well (unwell), be good-looking (ill-looking); **de bonne ~** good-looking; **faire bonne ~ à** be courteous to; **faire des ~ s** simper; **faire grise ~** look disgruntled; **faire ~ de** pretend to be, make a show of being

**miner** *vt* mine; undermine; **se ~** waste away, pine

**minérai** *nm* ore; mineral; *adj* mineral; *chem* inorganic

**minéralier** *nm* ore-carrying ship

**minéralogie** *nf* mineralogy

**minéralogique** *adj* mineralogical; *mot* **numéro ~** registration number

**minéralogiste** *n* mineralogist

**minet** *nm coll* pussy, puss; darling, sweet; camp young man

**minette** *nf coll* nymphet

**¹mineur** *nm* miner

**²mineur -e** *n* minor; *leg* infant; *adj* minor, lesser; *mus* minor

**minier -ière** *adj* mining

**minière** *nf* open-cast mine

**mini-jupe** *nf* mini-skirt

**minime** *adj* tiny; trivial

**minimum** *nm* (*pl* minima, ~s) minimum; **~ vital** subsistence wage; **au ~** at least; *adj* minimum

**ministère** *nm* help, agency; ministry; government; **~ de l'Intérieur** = Home Office; **former un ~** form a government; *leg* **le ~ public** the Public Prosecutor('s office); **par le ~ de** through the help of

**ministériel -ielle** *adj* ministerial; **crise ministérielle** cabinet crisis

**ministre** *nm* minister, secretary of state, agent; *eccles* (Protestant) minister, clergyman; **Ministre de l'Intérieur** = Home Secretary; **Ministre des Finances** = Chancellor of the Exchequer

**minium** *nm* red lead

**minois** *nm* face, pretty face

**minorité** *nf* minority; *leg* infancy

**minotaure** *nm* minotaur

**minoterie** *nf* flour-milling; flour-mill

**minotier** *nm* miller

**minuit** *nm* midnight

**minus** *n coll* half-wit, clot

**minuscule** *nf* small letter, lower-case letter; *adj* minute, small

**minus habens** *n invar coll* half-wit, clot

**¹minute** *nf* minute; **cocotte ~** pressure-cooker; **être à la ~** be punctual, be on the dot; *interj* just a minute!, hang on!

**²minute** *nf leg* draft, minute, record

**¹minuter** *vt* time

**²minuter** *vt* minute, record

**minuterie** *nf* movement (watch); *elect* time-switch (*esp* for lights on staircase, corridors)

**minutie** *nf* minute detail; attention to detail, scrupulousness; **~s** minutiae

**minutieux -ieuse** *adj* scrupulous, thorough, punctilious

**mioche** *n coll* kid, youngster, mite

**mirabelle** *nf* mirabelle plum; liqueur made from mirabelle plums

**miracle** *nm* miracle; wonder; *theat* miracle-play; **par ~** miraculously

**miraculeux -euse** *adj* miraculous

**mirador** *nm* platform; *mil* observation post

**mirage** *nm* mirage; *fig* illusion

**mire** *nf mil* foresight (rifle, etc); surveyor's pole, staff; test pattern (television); *mil* **angle de ~** angle of elevation; **point de ~** target; *fig* cynosure, centre of attention; **prendre sa ~** take aim

**mirer** *vt coll* cast one's eye on; **se ~** look at oneself (in mirror); be reflected

**mirifique** *adj coll* wonderful, terrific

**mirliton** *nm* toy musical instrument

(blown into); cream puff; **vers de ~** doggerel verse

**mirobolant** *adj coll* wonderful, staggering, terrific

**miroir** *nm* mirror; **œufs au ~** fried eggs

**miroitant** *adj* gleaming, glistening, sparkling, shimmering

**miroiter** *vi* gleam, glisten, sparkle, shimmer; **faire ~** show to advantage

**miroiterie** *nf* mirror trade; manufacture of mirrors

**miroton** *nm* beef-stew with onions

**mis** *p part* **mettre**; **bien ~** well-dressed

**misaine** *nf naut* foresail; **mât de ~** foremast

**misanthrope** *n* misanthrope; *adj* misanthropic

**misanthropie** *nf* misanthropy

**mise** *nf* placing, putting, setting in place; dress, attire; stake, outlay; ~ **à exécution** implementation; *naut* ~ **à l'eau** launching; *coll* ~ **à pied** sacking; ~ **à prix** reserve (price); ~ **au net** making a fair copy, revision of draft; ~ **au point** *mot* tuning (engine); focusing; clarification; warning; ~ **bas** dropping of young; ~ **de fonds** putting up of money; ~ **en demeure** formal notice, summons; ~ **en marche** starting (engine, motor); ~ **en ondes** radio production; *typ* ~ **en pages** lay-out; ~ **en plis** set (hair); *theat* ~ **en scène** production, staging; **être de ~** be suitable, appropriate

**miser** *vt* stake, bet (a sum); bid (a sum); *vi* stake, bet; bid (auction); ~ **sur** bank on

**misérable** *n* poor wretch; scoundrel, wretch; *adj* miserable, unhappy; unfortunate; despicable, mean, paltry

**misère** *nf* misery, misfortune, woe; need, extreme poverty; mere trifle; ~ **s** worries, troubles; ~ **noire** abject poverty; **crier** ~ complain of poverty; **être dans la** ~ be poverty-stricken; *coll* **faire des** ~ **s à qn** give s/o a rough time, tease s/o unmercifully; **reprendre le collier de la** ~ get back to the grindstone; **vêtements qui crient** ~ shabby clothes

**miséreux -euse** *n + adj* needy, destitute (person)

**miséricorde** *nf* mercy, mercifulness; *interj* mercy!, gracious me!

**miséricordieux -ieuse** *n + adj* merciful (person)

**misogyne** *n* misogynist; *adj* misogynous

**misogynie** *nf* misogyny

**missel** *nm eccles* missal

**mission** *nf* mission; (diplomatic) mission; *eccles* mission station; **en** ~ on

detached service

**missionnaire** *n + adj* missionary

**mistigri** *nm coll* puss

**mistral** *nm* violent north wind in S. France

**mitaine** *nf* mitten

**mitard** *nm sl* disciplinary cell

**mite** *nf* moth; ~ **du fromage** cheesemite

**mité** *adj* moth-eaten

**miter (se)** *v refl* get moth-eaten

**miteux -euse** *adj coll* shabby, seedy

**mitiger** *vt* (3) mitigate, soften; relax

**mitonner** *vt cul* let simmer; prepare carefully; *coll* devise, concoct; *vi* simmer

**mitoyen -enne** *adj* party; **mur** ~ party wall; **cloison** ~**enne** interior, dividing wall; **puits** ~ well used in common

**mitoyenneté** *nf* joint ownership, joint usage

**mitraille** *nf mil* machine-gun fire; *ar* grape-shot; *coll* small change

**mitrailler** *vt mil* machine-gun, tommy-gun

**mitrailleur** *nm* machine-gunner; *adj* (*f* -euse) *mil* **fusil** ~ machine-gun

**mitrailleuse** *nf mil* machine-gun

**mitre** *nm eccles* mitre; *archi* cowl (chimney pot)

**mitron** *nm* baker's apprentice

**mixage** *nm* mixing

**mixeur** *nm cul* mixer

**mixité** *nf* co-education

**mixte** *adj* mixed, joint; **assurance** ~ life and endowment assurance; **double** ~ mixed doubles (tennis); **école** ~ co-educational school; **train** ~ passenger and goods train

**mixtion** *nf* mixing; mixture

**mnémonique** *nf + adj* mnemonic

**mobile** *nm* motive; motive power; prime mover; mobile; *adj* movable; mobile; **échelle** ~ sliding-scale; *med* **rein** ~ floating kidney

**mobilier** *nm* furniture, suite of furniture; *adj* (*f* -**ière**) movable, personal; *leg* **biens** ~**s** personal estate, chattels; **valeurs mobilières** stocks and shares; **vente mobilière** furniture sale

**mobilisable** *adj* mobilizable; *comm* disposable, available

**mobilisation** *nf* mobilization; *comm* liquidation (capital), conversion

**mobiliser** *vt* mobilize; *mil* call up; *comm* free (capital), convert

**mobilité** *nf* mobility; instability, changeableness

**mobylette** *nf* moped, power-assisted bicycle

**moche** *adj coll* ugly, dowdy; poor, rotten, lousy

**modalité** *nf* modality; *pl* methods, details; ~s **de paiement** terms of payment

**mode** *nm* method, mode; *gramm* mood; *mus* mode; ~ **d'emploi** directions for use; *nf* fashion, manner; ~s millinery; **à la** ~ fashionable; **gravure de** ~ fashion-plate; **passer de** ~ go out of fashion

**modelage** *nm* modelling, moulding

**modèle** *nm* model, pattern, style; artist's model; ~ **déposé** registered pattern; ~ **réduit** small-scale model; **grand** ~ large size (garment); *adj* model

**modelé** *nm arts* relief

**modeler** *vt* (5) model, mould, shape; **se** ~ model oneself, take as pattern

**modeleur -euse** *n arts* modeller; model-maker

**modéliste** *n* dress-designer

**modérateur** *nm* regulator, governor; *n* (*f* **-trice**) moderator, restrainer; mediator; *adj* moderating, restraining

**modération** *nf* moderation, restraint; temperance

**modéré -e** *n* moderate person; *pol* moderate; *adj* moderate, temperate; gentle, subdued

**modérer** *vt* (6) moderate, lessen, restrain, soften; regulate; **se** ~ control oneself; subside (storm)

**moderne** *nm* modern, modern style; *adj* modern, up-to-date

**moderniser** *vt* modernize

**modernité** *nf* modernity

**modeste** *n* modest person; *adj* modest, unassuming; quiet, unpretentious; **prix** ~ moderate, reasonable, price

**modestie** *nf* modesty, unpretentiousness

**modicité** *nf* moderateness; paucity; lowness

**modifiant** *adj* modifying

**modificateur -trice** *n* modifier; *adj* modificatory, modifying

**modificatif -ive** *adj* modifying

**modifier** *vt* modify, qualify, alter; **se** ~ change

**modique** *adj* moderate, small, reasonable (sum, cost); slender (means)

**modulation** *nf mus* modulation; inflexion; *elect* modulation (frequency); ~ **de fréquence** V.H.F., frequency modulation

**module** *nm math* modulus; *archi* module

**moduler** *vt* modulate; *vi mus* modulate

**moelle** *nf* marrow; pith, core; *anat* medulla; *anat* ~ **épinière** spinal cord; **jusqu'à la** ~ to the bone, thoroughly

**moelleux** *nm* softness, mellowness;

juiciness; *adj* (*f* **-euse**) soft, mellow; juicy

**moellon** *nm archi* quarry-stone

**mœurs** *nfpl* morals, manners; customs; **avoir de bonnes** ~ be of good character; **être sans** ~ be unprincipled

**moi** *nm* ego, self; **culte du** ~ egotism; *pers pron* I; me; **à** ~ mine; **à** ~! help!; **de vous à** ~ between you and me

**moignon** *nm* stump (of amputated limb)

**moi-même** *refl pron* myself

**moindre** *adj* less, lesser; least, smallest

**moine** *nm* monk, friar

**moineau** *nm* sparrow; *coll* **vilain** ~ dirty dog, rat

**moins** *nm* minus, minus-sign; *adv* less, fewer; least; **à** ~ **de** unless, barring; **à** ~ **que** unless; **à tout le** ~ at least; **au** ~ not less than, at least; **de** ~ **en** ~ less and less; **du** ~ at least; **en** ~ less, missing; **en** ~ **de rien** in less than no time; **non** ~ **que** quite as much as; **rien** ~ **que** nothing less than; far from; *prep* less, minus, but for; **deux heures** ~ **vingt** twenty to two

**moins-value** *nf* depreciation, drop in value

**moire** *nf* watered silk, moiré; watering

**moiré** *nm* watered, clouded effect (on fabric or metal); *adj* watered

**moirer** *vt* water (fabric); cloud (metal)

**moirure** *nf* watered, clouded effect

**mois** *nm* month; month's pay

**moïse** *nm* cradle, basket cot

**moisi** *nm* mould, mildew, staleness; **sentir le** ~ smell musty; *adj* mouldy, mildewed, musty, stale

**moisir** *vt* make mouldy; *vi* mildew, become mouldy; **se** ~ become mouldy

**moisissure** *nf* mould, mildew; mouldiness

**moisson** *nf* harvest; harvest-time; crop

**moissonner** *vt* harvest, reap, gather; **être moissonné** be cut off, die

**moissonneur -euse** *n* harvester, reaper

**moissonneuse** *nf* reaping-machine, harvester

**moissonneuse-batteuse** *nf* (*pl* **moissonneuses-batteuses**) combine-harvester

**moite** *adj* moist, damp, clammy

**moiteur** *nf* moistness, dampness, clamminess

**moitié** *nf* half; *coll* **ma chère** ~ my better half; **se mettre de** ~ **avec qn** go halves with s/o; *adv* half; ~ **moins cher** half as dear; ~ **plus cher** half as dear again

**moka** *nm cul* Mocha coffee; coffee-flavoured cake

**mol** *adj see* **mou**

**molaire** *nf + adj* molar

**môle** *nm* mole, breakwater

**moléculaire** *adj* molecular

**moleskine** *nf* imitation leather

**molester** *vt* molest

**moleter** *vt* (5) mill, knurl

**molette** *nf* pestle; knurling-tool, cutting wheel; rowel; **clef à ~** adjustable spanner

**mollasse** *adj coll* flabby, soft; spineless; slow, lazy

**molle** *adj see* **mou**

**mollesse** *nf* softness, flabbiness; spinelessness; slackness; indolence

**¹mollet** *nm anat* calf

**²mollet -ette** *adj* soft, softest; **œuf ~** soft-boiled egg

**molletière** *adj f* **bandes ~s** puttees

**molleton** *nm* flannelette, soft wool or cotton cloth; felting (ironing-board)

**molletonné** *adj* lined with flannelette; fleece-lined (gloves)

**mollir** *vt naut* ease (helm), slacken (rope); *vi* soften, become soft; slacken, die down, flag, deteriorate

**mollusque** *nm zool* mollusc

**molosse** *nm* mastiff, watch-dog

**môme** *n sl* brat, kid; *nf sl* bird, bint

**moment** *nm* moment, instant, while; **arriver au bon ~** arrive in the nick of time; **à tout ~** constantly; at any moment; **au ~ où** just when; **au ~ voulu** at the right moment; **à un ~ donné** at a certain time; **du ~ où, du ~ que** seeing that; **d'un ~ à l'autre** at any moment; **le ~ venu** in due course; **par ~s** now and again; **sur le ~** on the spur of the moment

**momentané** *adj* momentary, temporary

**momerie** *nf* mummery

**momie** *nf* mummy; *coll* old fossil

**momification** *nf* mummification

**momifier** *vt* mummify

**mon** *poss adj m* (*f* **ma**, *pl* **mes**) my

**monacal** *adj* monastic, monkish

**monade** *nf* monad

**monarchie** *nf* monarchy

**monarchique** *adj* monarchical

**monarchisme** *nm* monarchism

**monarchiste** *n + adj* monarchist

**monarque** *nm* monarch

**monastère** *nm* monastery

**monastique** *adj* monastic

**monceau** *nm* heap, stock, pile

**mondain -e** *n* worldly person; *nm* man about town; *nf* (~e) society lady; *adj* worldly, mundane; fashionable

**mondanité** *nf* worldliness; taste for social life; ~s social events

**monde** *nm* world, earth; people; (high) society; servants, domestic staff; **ainsi va le ~** such is the way of the world, that is how things are; **aller dans le ~** move in society; **connaître son ~**

know with whom one is dealing; **être de ce ~** be alive; **être le mieux du ~ avec** be on the best of terms with; **homme (femme) du ~** man (lady) of quality; **il y a du ~** there are (lots of) people there; **le beau (grand, haut) ~** high society; **mettre au ~** give birth to; **tout le ~** everyone

**mondial** *adj* world-wide, universal; **guerre ~e** world war

**mond(i)ovision** *nf* TV satellite broadcasting

**monégasque** *adj* of Monaco

**monétaire** *adj* monetary

**monétariste** *n + adj* monetarist

**monétiser** *vt* mint

**mongolien -ienne** *n + adj med* mongol

**moniteur -trice** *n* monitor; *sp* coach, instructor

**monnaie** *nf* money, currency; change, small change; mint; *bot* ~ **du pape** honesty; ~ **forte** hard currency; **la Monnaie** the Mint; *coll* **payer qn en ~ de singe** let s/o whistle for his money

**monnayage** *nm* minting, coining

**monnayer** *vt* (7) mint, coin; *fig* exploit, cash in on

**monnayeur** *nm* maker of coins; **faux-~** counterfeiter, coiner

**monocorde** *adj* monotonous

**monogame** *adj* monogamous

**monogamie** *nf* monogamy

**monogramme** *nm* monogram

**monographie** *nf* monograph

**monokini** *nm* topless (costume)

**monolithe** *nm* monolith; *adj* monolithic

**monologuer** *vi* soliloquize, talk to oneself

**monomane** *n + adj* monomaniac

**monôme** *nm math* monomial; student's procession (single file)

**monophasé** *adj elect* single-phase, monophase

**monoplace** *n + adj aer + mot* single-seater

**monoplan** *nm* monoplane

**monopole** *nm* monopoly

**monopolisation** *nf* monopolization

**monopoliser** *vt* monopolize

**monosyllabe** *nm* monosyllable

**monosyllabique** *adj* monosyllabic

**monothéisme** *nm* monotheism

**monothéiste** *n* monotheist; *adj* monotheistic

**monotone** *adj* monotonous; humdrum

**monotonie** *nf* monotony

**monseigneur** *nm* (*pl* **messeigneurs**) (*depending on rank of person addressed or referred to*) Your Royal Highness, His Royal Highness; Your Eminence, His Eminence (cardinal); Your Grace, His Grace (archbishop, duke); my Lord, your Lordship, his Lordship (bishop); **donner du ~ à** give the title of Monseigneur to

**Monsieur** *nm* (*pl* **Messieurs**) Mr; **monsieur** gentleman; sir

**monstre** *nm* monster; monstrosity; **~ sacré** star, celebrity; *coll* **petit ~** little rascal; *adj coll* huge, colossal, terrific

**monstrueux -ueuse** *adj* monstrous, prodigious; huge; shocking, outrageous

**monstruosité** *nf* monstrosity; monstrousness, outrageousness

**mont** *nm* mount, mountain; **être toujours par ~ s et par vaux** be always on the move; **promettre ~s et merveilles** promise the earth

**montage** *nm* taking up, carrying up; assembling, mounting, setting; *cin* montage, cutting; **chaîne de ~** assembly-line

**montagnard -e** *n* mountain-dweller, highlander; *adj* mountain, highland

**montagne** *nf* mountain; mountain region; **~s russes** switchback, big dipper; **se faire une ~ de qch** exaggerate the difficulty of sth

**montagneux -euse** *adj* mountainous, hilly

**montant** *nm* upright, pole, post; riser (stair); *comm* amount, sum total; *cul* strong distinctive taste; strong smell; *sp* **~s de but** goal-posts; *adj* rising, ascending, up-hill; high (collar), high-necked (dress)

**mont-de-piété** *nm* (*pl* **monts-de-piété**) pawn-shop

**monte** *nf* covering, mounting (female animal); riding, horsemanship; *sp* **partants et ~s probables** probable starters and jockeys

**monté** *adj* mounted (soldier, photograph, gun, etc); organized, set up; provided, stocked; *theat* staged; *coll* **collet ~** prim and proper, stuffy; *coll* **coup ~** put-up job; **être ~ contre qn** be worked up against s/o

**monte-charge** *nm invar* hoist; goods-lift

**montée** *nf* rise, slope, gradient; going up, climb; *eng* up-stroke; **en ~** going upwards; *eng* **tuyau de ~** up-take pipe

**monte-en-l'air** *nm invar sl* cat-burglar

**monte-plats** *nm* service-lift, kitchen-lift

**monter** *vt* mount, climb, go up; raise, carry up; set, mount, fit on, assemble; found, set up (business, society); cover, serve (female animal); *theat* stage; *elect* wire up; **~ la tête à qn contre qn** set s/o against s/o; **~ les mailles** cast on stitches (knitting); **~ un coup** hatch a plot; *theat* **~ un décor** fit up; **~ un magasin** open a shop; *vi*

climb up, go up, mount, ascend; rise, slope up; get in, get on; *comm* amount; **~ à bicyclette** ride a bicycle; **~ en bateau** get into a boat; **~ sur un bateau** go on board ship; **~ sur la scène** go onto the stage; **faire ~ qch (qn)** have sth (s/o) brought up(stairs); **se ~** equip oneself, fit oneself out with; amount to; *coll* get worked up, get excited

**monteur -euse** *n* fitter, assembler; setter (jewellery); *comm* promoter

**montgolfière** *nf ar* hot-air balloon

**monticule** *nm* hillock, knoll

**montre** *nf* show, display; watch; *comm* shop-window, show-case; *sp* **course contre la ~** timed race; **faire ~ de** display; **mettre en ~** put in the shop-window

**montre-bracelet** *nf* (*pl* **montres-bracelet**) wrist-watch

**montrer** *vt* show, display; point out, indicate; show how, teach; **se ~** appear, show oneself; prove to be, show oneself to be

**montueux -ueuse** *adj* hilly

**monture** *nf* mount (horse, etc); setting; mounting, assembling; frame (spectacles, umbrella); stock (gun, pistol)

**monument** *nm* monument, memorial; historic building

**monumental** *adj* monumental; *coll* colossal

**moquer (se)** *v refl* mock, make fun, laugh; *coll* not care, not give a damn

**moquerie** *nf* mockery, scoffing; piece of mockery

**moquette** *nf* moquette, carpeting

**moqueur -ueuse** *n* mocker, scoffer; *adj* mocking, scoffing; sarcastic, waggish

**moral** *nm* state of mind, morale; moral faculties; **remonter le ~ de, à qn** raise s/o's morale; *adj* moral, ethical; mental, intellectual

**morale** *nf* morals, ethics; moral (of story); lecture, advice; **faire la ~ à qn** lecture s/o

**moralement** *adv* morally; virtually

**moralisateur -trice** *n* moralizer; *adj* moralizing; edifying

**moraliser** *vt* lecture, sermonize; *vi* moralize; **se ~** become moral

**moraliste** *n* moralist

**moralité** *nf* morality; morals, honesty; moral lesson; *arts* morality-play

**moratoire** *nm* moratorium; *adj leg* moratory, postponed

**morbide** *adj* morbid, unhealthy

**morbidité** *nf* morbidity, morbidness

**morbleu** *interj ar* 'sdeath!

**morceau** *nm* piece, bit, morsel; extract; piece of music; **~x choisis** selections;

**emporter le ~** win; *coll* **gober le ~** swallow the bait; *coll* **manger le ~** blow the gaff; **sucre en ~x** lump-sugar

**morceler** *vt* (5) cut up into pieces, break up, carve up

**morcellement** *nm* cutting up, parcelling out

**mordant** *nm* pungency, sharpness, pointedness; vigour, dash; *chem* corrosiveness; *adj* pungent, sharp, mordant; corrosive

**mordicus** *adv coll* stubbornly, stoutly

**mordiller** *vt* bite playfully (puppy); nibble

**mordoré** *adj* bronze, golden-brown

**mordorer** *vt* bronze (leather)

**mordorure** *nf* bronze finish

**mordre** *vt* bite; sting; *chem* eat into (acid); *coll* **s'en ~ les doigts** regret sth bitterly; *vi* bite; *arts* etch; *coll* catch on, begin to understand

**mordu** *adj* bitter; *coll* **~ de** set on, mad about

**morfondre (se)** *v refl* get bored waiting about; feel dejected

**morganatique** *adj* morganatic

**morgue** *nf* pride, arrogance, haughtiness

**moribond -e** *n* dying person; *adj* moribund, dying

**moricaud -e** *n coll* blackamoor; *adj coll* dark-skinned, dusky

**morigéner** *vt* (6) lecture, take to task; *coll* tear a strip off

**morille** *nf* morel (mushroom)

**morne** *adj* dismal, gloomy, dreary, doleful

**mornifle** *nf coll* slap

**morose** *adj* morose, gloomy, moody, sullen

**morosité** *nf* moroseness, sullenness

**morphine** *nf* morphia, morphine

**morphinomane** *n* morphine addict

**morphologie** *nf* morphology

**morphologique** *adj* morphological

**morpion** *nm coll* crab-louse, crab; *coll* brat

**mors** *nm* bit (horse); jaw (vice); **prendre le ~ aux dents** take the bit in its teeth (horse); *fig* take the bit between one's teeth (person)

**morse** *nm* walrus

**morsure** *nf* bite, biting; gnawing (hunger); nip (cold)

¹**mort** *nm* dummy (cards); **faire le ~** be dummy

²**mort -e** *n* dead person; **faire le ~** lie low; **jour des ~s** All Soul's Day; *nf* death; **à ~ X!** down with X!, death to X!; **attraper la ~** catch one's death; **avoir la ~ dans l'âme** be sick at heart; **être à l'article de la ~** be at the point of

death; **faire une bonne ~** make a good (Christian) end; **mourir de sa belle ~** die in one's bed, die a natural death; *adj* dead, lifeless; **arriver au point ~** come to a stand-still; *sp* **ballon ~** dead ball; *arts* **nature ~e** still-life; **poids-~** dead weight; *mot* **point ~** neutral

**mortaise** *nf* mortise

**mortaiser** *vt* mortise

**mortalité** *nf* mortality; number of deaths; **taux de ~** death-rate

**mort-aux-rats** *nf invar* rat-poison

**morte-eau** *nf* (*pl* **mortes-eaux**) neap-tide

**mortel -elle** *n* mortal; *adj* mortal; fatal; deadly; boring, wearisome

**mortellement** *adv* mortally, fatally; *coll* **s'ennuyer ~** be bored to death

**mortier** *nm* mortar; *mil* mortar; *eccles +leg* cap; *archi* **~ liquide** grout

**mortifiant** *adj* mortifying

**mortification** *nf* mortification, humiliation, chagrin; *cul* hanging (game)

**mortifier** *vt* mortify, humiliate; *cul* hang (game)

**mort-né -e** *n + adj* stillborn (child); *fig* abortive (project)

**mortuaire** *adj* mortuary; concerning death, burial; **acte ~** death certificate; **avis ~** announcement of death; **drap ~** pall; **extrait ~** death-certificate

**morue** *nf zool* cod; *vulg* tart; **huile de foie de ~** cod-liver oil

**morutier** *nm naut* cod-fishing boat; cod-fisherman

**morve** *nf* nasal mucus, *sl* snot; *vet* glanders

**morveux -euse** *n coll* brat; impudent puppy; *adj coll* snotty; *vet* glandered

¹**mosaïque** *nf* mosaic; test-card (television)

²**mosaïque** *adj* Mosaic

**Moscou** *n* Moscow

**moscoutaire** *adj pej* communist, *coll* red

**moscovite** *adj* Muscovite

**mosquée** *nf* mosque

**mot** *nm* word; key, clue; *mil* password; **~ à ~** word for word, literal; *mil* **~ d'ordre** password; **~s croisés** crossword; **au bas ~** at the lowest estimate; **avoir le ~ pour rire** have a good sense of humour, have funny things to say; **bon ~** witticism, *coll* crack; **comprendre à demi-~** know how to take a hint, be quick on the uptake; **dire deux ~s à qn** have a word with s/o; **dire son ~** have one's say; **écrire un ~ à qn** drop s/o a line; **faire des ~s** be witty; **gros ~** swear words, coarse language; **le fin ~** the real clue, the key; *coll* **ne pas connaître un traître ~ d'anglais** not know a single word of English; **parler à ~s couverts** hint, drop hints; **prendre qn au ~** take s/o at his word; **se donner le ~** pass the word round; **tranchons le ~** let's get this clear, let's have it out

**motard** *nm coll* motorcycle cop; motorcyclist

**mot-clé** *nm* (*pl* **mots-clé(s)**) key-word, catch-word

**moteur** *nm* mover, instigator; motor, engine; **~ à deux temps** two-stroke engine; **~ à explosion** internal combustion engine; **premier ~** prime mover; *adj* (*f* **-trice**) motive, driving

**motif** *nm* motive, incentive; pattern, motif; *leg* grounds; *mus* theme; **sans ~** groundless; *adj* (*f* **-ive**) motive

**motion** *nf* proposal, motion; **adopter une ~** carry a motion

**motiver** *vt* justify, warrant; motivate; state reasons for; *comm* account for

**moto** *nf coll* motor-bike

**moto-cross** *nm* motocross

**motocyclette** *nf* motorcycle

**motocycliste** *n* motorcyclist

**motogodille** *nf* outboard motor

**motorisation** *nf* motorization

**motoriser** *vt* motorize

**mots-croisés** *nmpl* crossword

**motte** *nf* clod, lump of earth; pat, block (butter)

**motus** *interj* not a word!, keep it dark!

**¹mou** *nm naut* slack; *cul* lights

**²mou, mol** (*f* **molle**) *adj* soft, flabby, slack; feeble, languid; lax

**mouchard -e** *n coll* sneak, tell-tale; police informer; *sl* nark

**moucharder** *vt coll* spy on; squeal on

**mouche** *nf* fly; *ar* patch (embellishment of face); tuft of hair; *sp* button (foil), bull's-eye (shooting); **~ à miel** bee; **~ bleue** blue-bottle; **~ commune** horse-fly; *sp* **faire ~** score a bull; **fine ~** sly character, slick customer; **on aurait entendu voler une ~** you could have heard a pin drop; *sp* **poids ~** fly-weight; **prendre la ~** lose one's temper; *coll* **quelle ~ vous pique?** what's biting you?

**moucher** *vt* blow (nose), wipe (child's nose); snuff, trim (candle); **se ~** blow one's nose; **il ne se mouche pas du coude** he has a great opinion of himself

**moucheron** *nm* gnat, midge; *coll* kid, brat

**moucheté** *adj* speckled, dappled, spotty

**moucheter** *vt* (5) speckle, fleck; *sp* button (foil)

**moucheture** *nf* speckle, spot

**mouchoir** *nm* handkerchief; **~ de tête** head-scarf, kerchief

**mouchure** *nf* nasal mucus; snuff (candle)

**moudre** *vt* (61) grind, mill

**moue** *nf* pout; **faire la ~** pout

**mouette** *nf* seagull

**mouffette** *nf zool* skunk

**moufle** *nf* mitten, mitt; *eng* pulley-block

**mouillage** *nm* watering, adulterating; damping; *naut* anchoring, anchorage; *naut* laying of mine; *naut* **droits de ~** harbour dues; *naut* **être au ~** ride at anchor

**mouiller** *vt* wet, moisten, damp; water down, adulterate; *naut* drop (anchor), moor; *naut* stream (buoy); *naut* lay (mine); *phon* palatalize; **se ~** get wet; water (eyes); *coll* compromise oneself; **mouillé jusqu'aux os** soaked to the skin; *coll* **poule mouillée** milksop

**mouillette** *nf cul* finger of bread

**mouilleur** *nm naut* anchor tripper; **~ de mines** mine-layer

**mouillure** *nf* wetting, damping; damp mark; wetness

**mouise** *nf sl* poverty; **dans la ~** broke, up against it

**moulage** *nm* casting, moulding; cast

**¹moule** *nm* mould, matrix; **mettre au ~** cast in a mould, run into a mould

**²moule** *nf* mussel; *coll* fat-head, clot

**moulé** *adj* moulded, cast; having a good figure; **écriture ~** e copper-plate

**mouler** *vt* mould, cast; **robe qui moule** dress that shows off the figure, skin-tight dress

**moulin** *nm* mill; grinder; *coll* **~ à paroles** chatterbox; **apporter de l'eau au ~** bring grist to the mill

**moulinet** *nm* reel (fishing-rod); twirl, flourish

**moult** *adv ar* + *joc* much, very

**moulu** *adj* ground, powdered; *coll* dead-beat, *sl* creased

**moulure** *nf archi* moulding

**mourant -e** *n* dying person; *adj* dying; *fig* faint; *coll* killing, creasingly funny

**mourir** *vi* (62) die; *fig* die away, fade, wither; **~ d'ennui** be bored to death; **~ de rire** be tickled to death; **~ d'impatience** be dying to; **se ~** be dying

**mouroir** *nm pej* old people's home

**mouron** *nm bot* chickweed

**mousquet** *nm mil* musket

**mousquetaire** *nm mil* musketeer; **gants à la ~** gauntlet gloves

**mousqueton** *nm mil ar* blunderbuss; snap-hook; carabiner (mountaineering)

**moussant** *adj* foamy, frothy

**¹mousse** *nm naut* ship's boy

**²mousse** *nf* moss; froth, foam, head (beer), lather (soap); *cul* whipped cream and eggs, mousse; **caoutchouc ~** foam rubber

**mousse**

³**mousse** *adj* blunt (knife, point)
**mousseline** *nf* muslin; ~ **de soie** chiffon; *cul* **pommes** ~ mashed potatoes
**mousser** *vi* froth, foam; sparkle, fizz (wine); lather (soap); *cul* **faire** ~ **de la crème** whip cream; *sl* **faire** ~ **qn** anger s/o; *coll* sing praise of s/o; **se faire** ~ sing one's own praises
**mousseron** *nm* kind of edible mushroom
**mousseux -euse** *adj* mossy; foaming; sparkling (wine), frothy (beer)
**mousson** *nf* monsoon
**moussu** *adj* mossy, moss-grown
**moustache** *nf* moustache; whiskers (cat)
**moustachu** *adj* moustached
**moustiquaire** *nf* mosquito-net
**moustique** *nm* mosquito
**moût** *nm* must (grapes)
**moutard** *nm* *sl* brat, kid
**moutarde** *nf* mustard
**moutardier** *nm* mustard-maker; mustard-pot
**mouton** *nm* sheep; mutton; *eng* ram, monkey (pile-driver); *naut* ~**s** white horses; **revenons à nos** ~**s** let's get back to the point; *adj* (*f* -**onne**) sheep-like
**moutonné** *adj* fleecy; covered with white horses (sea); **ciel** ~ mackerel sky; *geol* **roche** ~ **e** glaciated rock
**moutonner** *vt* curl (hair); *vi* foam, become covered with white horses (sea); **se** ~ become covered with white horses (sea); become covered with fleecy clouds (sky)
**moutonneux -euse** *adj* fleecy; foam-flecked, covered with white horses (sea)
**moutonnier -ière** *adj* ovine; sheep-like
**mouture** *nf* grinding, milling
**mouvant** *adj* moving, unstable; **sables** ~**s** quick-sands, shifting sands
**mouvement** *nm* movement, motion, activity; *comm* trend; *mus* time; mechanism, works (clock); turnover, transfer (staff); traffic; change, evolution; emotion, impulse, outburst; ~ **acquis** impetus; *geog* ~**s de terrain** hills and valleys; **chef de** ~ traffic manager (railway); **être dans le** ~ be up-to-date; **faire un faux** ~ strain a muscle; **mettre en** ~ set in motion, start (engine); **quantité de** ~ momentum
**mouvementé** *adj* animated, lively; full of incident, eventful; *geog* undulatory
**mouvementer** *vt* animate, enliven
**mouvoir** *vt* (63) move, set in motion, actuate; urge, prompt; **se** ~ move, stir
**moyen** *nm* means, way; *math* mean; **au** ~ **de** by means of; **grands** ~**s** extreme measures; **il n'y a pas** ~ nothing doing, it can't be done; **le** ~ **de savoir?**

how can one know?; *leg* **voies et** ~**s** ways and means; *adj* (*f* -**enne**) middle, average, mean; ordinary, moderate; *rad* medium; **Moyen-Âge** Middle Ages; **Moyen Orient** Middle East; **cours** ~ intermediate course (lessons); *comm* middle price; **l'homme** ~ the average man, the common man; **très** ~ middling
**moyenâgeux -euse** *adj* (quaintly) medieval; out-of-date, behind the times
**moyennant** *prep* thanks to, subject to, at the cost of; ~ **finance** for a consideration; ~ **que** provided that, on condition that; ~ **quoi** in consideration of which
**moyenne** *nf* average; pass-mark (examination); *math* mean; *mot* **faire 50 à l'heure de** ~ average fifty
**moyennement** *adv* moderately, fairly; on the average
**moyeu** *nm* hub (wheel); boss (propeller)
**muable** *adj* mutable, changeable
**mucilagineux -euse** *adj* mucilaginous, viscous
**mucosité** *nf* mucosity
**mue** *nf* moulting (bird); shedding of coat, hair, antlers, etc; breaking of voice; hen-coop
**muer** *vi* moult; shed coat, hair, antlers etc; break (voice); **se** ~ change into
**muet -uette** *n* dumb person, mute; *adj* dumb, mute; intent, speechless; *geog* **carte muette** blank map; *theat* **jeu** ~ piece of business; mime; *theat* **rôle** ~ non-speaking part, walk-on
**muette** *nf* *gramm* mute letter, unsounded letter
**mufle** *nm* muzzle, nose (animal); *coll* boor; rotter
**muflerie** *nf* *coll* boorishness; dirty trick
**muge** *nm* *zool* mullet
**mugir** *vi* low, moo (cow); roar, boom (sea); howl (wind)
**mugissement** *nm* lowing, mooing (cow); roaring, booming (sea); howling (wind)
**muguet** *nm* *bot* lily of the valley; *fig ar* dandy
**muid** *nm* large barrel, hogshead
**mulâtre** *nm* + *adj* mulatto
**mulâtresse** *nf* mulatto woman
¹**mule** *nf* (she-)mule
²**mule** *nf* slipper; *med* chilblain
**mulet** *nm* mule
**muletier** *nm* mule-driver, muleteer; *adj* (*f* -**ière**) mule; **chemin** ~ mule-track
**mulot** *nm* field-mouse
**multicolore** *adj* multicoloured, variegated
**multiforme** *adj* multiform
**multiple** *nm* *math* multiple; **le plus petit**

**commun** ~ = lowest common multiple; *adj* multiple, manifold, multifarious

**multiplicateur** *nm math* multiplier; *adj* (*f* -trice) *math* multiplying

**multiplication** *nf math* multiplication; *eng* gear-ratio; *fig* increase; **grande (petite)** ~ high (low) gear

**multiplicité** *nf* multiplicity

**multiplier** *vt math* multiply; *eng* gear up; *fig* multiply, propagate; *vi* multiply; **se** ~ multiply, increase; be in half a dozen places at once

**multitude** *nf* multitude, crowd; multiplicity, heaps

**municipalité** *nf* municipality; town council

**munir** *vt* furnish, supply, provide; **se** ~ provide oneself

**munition** *nf ar* provisioning; ~**s** *mil* ammunition; ~**s de bouche** supplies, provisions

**muqueux -euse** *adj* mucous

**muqueuse** *nf med* mucous membrane

**mur** *nm* wall, barrier; ~ **d'appui** low wall; ~ **de clôture** surrounding wall; *coll* **faire le** ~ climb out, go out without permission; **franchir le** ~ **du son** break the sound barrier; **mettre qn au pied du** ~ drive s/o into a corner; oblige s/o to come to a decision

**mûr** *adj* ripe, mellow; seasoned; mature; ready, considered; *sl* nicely drunk, mellow; *coll* worn (cloth); **femme assez** ~**e** woman well on in years

**murage** *nm* walling in, walling up

**muraille** *nf* high wall, solid wall; *naut* side (of ship)

**mural** *adj* mural; **carte** ~**e** wall-map

**mûre** *nf* mulberry; blackberry

**murer** *vt* wall in, wall up; shut up

**mûrier** *nm* mulberry-tree

**mûrir** *vt* ripen, mature; give careful thought to; work out; *med* bring to a head (abscess); *vi* ripen, become ripe; mature; *med* come to a head (abscess)

**murmurant** *adj* murmuring, muttering; sighing (wind); babbling (stream)

**murmure** *nm* murmur, murmuring; muttering; sighing (wind); babbling (stream)

**murmurer** *vt* whisper (secret); *vi* murmur, whisper; grumble, complain; mutter; sigh (wind); babble (stream)

**musaraigne** *nf zool* shrew (mouse)

**musard -e** *n coll* dawdler; *adj coll* dawdling, idling

**musarder** *vi coll* idle, dawdle

**musardise** *nf* dawdling

**musc** *nm* musk

**muscade** *nf* nutmeg

**muscadet** *nm* dry white wine from the Nantes area

**muscadier** *nm* nutmeg-tree

**muscadin** *nm ar* dandy, beau

**muscat** *nm* muscat grape; muscatel (wine); *adj* muscat (grape, wine)

**musclé** *adj* muscular, brawny, athletic; *fig* tough, brutal

**musculaire** *adj med* muscular

**musculeux -euse** *adj* brawny

**museau** *nm* muzzle, snout (animal); *coll* nose

**musée** *nm* museum

**museler** *vt* (5) muzzle (dog); *fig* muzzle, silence

**muselière** *nf* muzzle

**muser** *vi* idle, dawdle, fritter away one's time

**musette** *nf* kind of bagpipes; nose-bag (horse); *mil* haversack; **bal** ~ popular dance (one with accordeon band)

**muséum** *nm* natural history museum

**musicalité** *nf* musicality

**musicien -ienne** *n* musician; player in band; *adj* musical

**musicographe** *n* musicographer

**musicologue** *n* musicologist

**musique** *nf* music; band; *theat* incidental music; **chef de** ~ band-master; *coll* **connaître la** ~ know the ropes; **faire de la** ~ make music; study music, go in for music; *coll* **faire une** ~ **du diable** make a hell of a row

**musiquette** *nf coll* cheap music, badly played music

**musqué** *adj* musky, scented with musk; affected, lush; **bœuf** ~ musk-ox; **rat** ~ musk-rat; **rose** ~**e** musk-rose

**Musulman -e** *n* Moslem, Muslim

**musulman** *adj* Moslem, Muslim

**mutabilité** *nf* mutability

**mutation** *nf* change, alteration; transfer (job, footballers); *leg* transfer, change of ownership; *mus* + *biol* mutation

**muter** *vt* transfer (employee)

**mutilateur -trice** *n* mutilator; defacer

**mutilation** *nf* mutilation, maiming; defacement

**mutilé -e** *n* disabled soldier, disabled person; **grand** ~ badly disabled soldier (person); *adj* mutilated, disfigured; disabled

**mutiler** *vt* mutilate, maim, disfigure; deface; *fig* mangle

**mutin** *nm* mutineer; *adj* rebellious, unruly, insubordinate; *mil* + *naut* mutinous; *coll* pert, saucy

**mutiné** *nm* mutineer; *adj* rebellious, mutinous

**mutiner (se)** *v refl* revolt; be disobedient (child); *mil* + *naut* mutiny

**mutinerie** *nf* insubordination; *mil* +

*naut* mutiny; disobedience, unruliness (child)

**mutisme** *nm* muteness, dumbness; **s'enfermer dans le ~** maintain a stubborn silence

**mutualité** *nf* mutuality, reciprocity; *leg* mutual insurance

**mutuel -uelle** *adj* mutual; *sp* **pari ~** = tote; *leg* **société de secours ~ s** friendly society

**mutuelle** *nf* mutual insurance company

**mycologie** *nf bot* mycology

**myélite** *nf med* myelitis

**myocarde** *nm anat* myocardium

**myope** *n + adj* short-sighted (person)

**myopie** *nf* short-sightedness, myopia

**myosotis** *nm bot* forget-me-not

**myriade** *nf* myriad

**myrmidon** *nm coll* little man, midget

**myrrhe** *nf* myrrh

**myrte** *nm* myrtle

**myrtille** *nf* bilberry, whortleberry, *US* huckleberry

**mystère** *nm* mystery, secret; mysteriousness; *theat* mystery(-play)

**mystérieux -ieuse** *adj* mysterious

**mysticisme** *nm* mysticism

**mystificateur -trice** *n* mystifier; *coll* hoaxer, humbug; *adj* mystifying

**mystification** *nf* mystification; hoaxing, humbug

**mystifier** *vt* mystify; hoax, humbug, fool

**mystique** *n* mystic; *nf* mystical doctrine; mystique; *adj* mystical, mystic

**mythe** *nm* myth, legend

**mythique** *adj* mythical

**mythologie** *nf* mythology

**mythologique** *adj* mythological

**mythologue** *n* mythologist

**myxomatose** *nf* myxomatosis

# N

**na** *interj* there!, so there! (child language)

**nabab** *nm* nabob

**nabot -e** *n* dwarf, midget; *adj* dwarfish, tiny

**nacelle** *nf* basket (balloon); *lit* skiff

**nacre** *nf* mother of pearl

**nacré** *adj* pearly

**nage** *nf* swimming; sculling, rowing; **donner la ~** set the stroke; **être en ~** be bathed in perspiration; **traverser une rivière à la ~** swim across a river

**nageoire** *nf* fin; *sl* arm

**nager** *vi* (3) swim; float, be submerged; scull, row; *coll* be uncertain, be at a loss; **~ dans l'abondance** wallow in luxury; **~ entre deux eaux** swim under water; *coll* **savoir ~** be a smooth operator, know how to cope

**nageur -euse** *n* swimmer; oarsman; *adj* swimming

**naguère** *adv* not long ago, lately, a short while back

**naïade** *nf* naiad, water-nymph

**naïf** (*f* **naïve**) *n* simpleton; *adj* artless, naïve, ingenuous; simple, simple-minded

**nain -e** *n* dwarf, midget; *adj* dwarfish, undersized

**naissance** *nf* birth; descent; origin, beginning; *med* root (muscle, tongue, etc); **de ~ obscure** of humble birth; **prendre ~** originate

**naissant** *adj* new-born; incipient, nascent, budding

**naître** *vi* (64) be born; arise; begin, come up; **faire ~** give birth to; give rise to, cause

**naïveté** *nf* naïvety; artlessness, ingenuousness; simple-mindedness; *coll* greenness; artless remark

**naja** *nm zool* cobra

**nana** *nf coll* girl

**nanan** *nm coll obs* something good to eat, something sweet; *coll* **c'est du ~ !** yum-yum!

**nankin** *nm* nankeen

**nantir** *vt* provide, furnish; *leg* give security to, secure; **se ~** provide oneself

**nantissement** *nm leg* security, pledge, cover

**naphtaline** *nf* moth-balls; *chem* naphthaline

**naphte** *nm* naphtha

**napoléon** *nm ar* twenty-franc (gold) coin

**napolitain** adj Neapolitan

**nappe** nf tablecloth, cloth; fig sheet (water, ice, etc); ~ **d'autel** altar-cloth

**napperon** nm table-mat; tray-cloth; **petit** ~ doily

**narcisse** nm narcissus

**narcissisme** nm narcissism

**narcose** nf med narcosis

**narcotique** nm narcotic, drug; adj narcotic

**narcotiser** vt narcotize, drug

**narguer** vt taunt; snap one's fingers at; flout

**narguilé** nm hookah

**narine** nf nostril

**narquois** adj mocking, sneering, bantering

**narrateur -trice** n narrator, teller of story

**narratif -ive** adj narrative

**narration** nf narration, narrative; composition (school); gramm **infinitif de** ~ historic infinitive; gramm **présent de** ~ historic present

**narrer** vt narrate

**nasale** nf phon nasal

**nasaliser** vt nasalize

**nasalité** nf nasality

**nasarde** nf fillip, flick on the nose; fig rebuff

**naseau** nm nostril (animal)

**nasillard** adj nasal

**nasillement** nm nasal twang

**nasiller** vt say through one's nose; vi speak through one's nose, snuffle

**nasilleur -euse** n one who talks with a nasal twang

**nasse** nf trap, wicker-trap (fish); net for catching birds

**natal** (pl ~ s) adj native; natal; **ville** ~ **e** birth-place

**natalité** nf birth-rate

**natation** nf swimming

**natif -ive** n native; adj native, born; fig innate, natural; **bon sens** ~ native wit

**national** adj national; **route** ~ **e** trunk-road, = A road

**nationaliser** vt nationalize

**nationalisme** nm nationalism

**nationaliste** n nationalist; adj nationalistic

**nationalité** nf nationality

**nationaux** nmpl nationals, citizens of a country

**nativité** nf eccles nativity

**natte** nf mat, rush-matting; plait, pigtail

**natter** vt furnish (room) with mats; weave (rushes); plait (hair)

**naturalisation** nf naturalization; acclimatization; taxidermy, stuffing

**naturaliser** vt naturalize; acclimatize; stuff; **se faire** ~ become naturalized

**naturalisme** nm naturalism

**naturaliste** n naturalist; taxidermist; adj naturalist, naturalistic

**nature** nf nature, temperament, sort, kind, character; arts ~ **morte** still-life; **contre** ~ unnatural; **de** ~ **à** of such a kind as to; **payer en** ~ pay in kind; arts **peindre d'après** ~ paint from life; adj invar neat, pure; unaffected; **café** ~ black coffee; **grandeur** ~ life-size; **omelette** ~ plain omelette; **pommes** ~ boiled potatoes

**naturel** nm nature; nature, character, disposition; naturalness; **cul au** ~ boiled; **avoir un heureux** ~ have a happy disposition; **chassez le** ~, **il revient au galop** nature will tell; **voir les choses au** ~ see things as they are; adj (f **-elle**) natural; innate; simple, unaffected, plain; unfortified (wine)

**naturellement** adv naturally, by nature; of course

**naturisme** nm naturism, nudism

**naturiste** n+adj naturist, nudist

**naufrage** nm shipwreck; fig ruin; **faire** ~ be wrecked

**naufragé -e** n+adj shipwrecked (person), castaway, marooned (person)

**naufrageur** nm wrecker

**nauséabond** adj nauseous, nauseating; fig loathsome, repugnant

**nausée** nf nausea; **avoir des** ~s feel sick

**nautique** adj nautical

**nautisme** nm sailing, yachting

**naval** (pl ~ s) adj naval, nautical

**navarin** nm cul mutton stew (with carrots, onions, etc)

**navet** nm turnip; arts daub; theat+cin flop

¹**navette** nf shuttle; train on shuttle service; ~ **spatiale** space shuttle; **faire la** ~ ply to and fro (vehicle, ship, etc), go to and fro

²**navette** nf bot rape; **huile de** ~ colza oil

**navigabilité** nf navigability (river, etc); seaworthiness

**navigable** adj navigable (river, etc); seaworthy

**navigateur -trice** n navigator (sea, air); sailor; adj seafaring

**navigation** nf navigation (sea, air), sailing; ~ **de plaisance** pleasure-cruising, yachting; **compagnie de** ~ shipping company

**naviguer** vt+vi navigate, sail

**navire** *nm* ship, vessel; ~ **de ligne** capital ship

**navire-citerne** *nm* (*pl* **navires-citernes**) *naut* tanker

**navrant** *adj* heartbreaking, harrowing

**navré** *adj* heartbroken, very distressed; terribly sorry

**navrer** *vt* grieve, hurt deeply

**nazisme** *nm pol* Nazism

**ne** *adv* not, nothing (found normally as part of expressions, *eg* **ne ... pas** not; **ne ... que** only; **ne ... rien** nothing)

**né** *adj* born; **premier** ~ first-born; **bien** ~ of good family

**néanmoins** *adv* none the less, nevertheless, however, yet, still

**néant** *nm* nothingness; naught; nil, nothing

**nébuleuse** *nf astron* nebula

**nébuleux -euse** *adj* nebulous; cloudy, overcast, hazy; muddy, cloudy (liquid); *fig* confused, vague

**nébulosité** *nf* nebulosity, cloud-covering; *fig* lack of clarity

**nécessaire** *nm* what is necessary, requisite; necessaries of life; outfit, kit; ~ **à ouvrage** work-box ~ **de toilette** dressing-case; **manquer du** ~ lack the necessities of life; *adj* necessary, needful; **peu** ~ needless, unnecessary

**nécessité** *nf* necessity, need; compulsion, inevitability; *obs* poverty; **denrées de première** ~ essential foodstuffs; **il est de toute** ~ **de** it is essential to

**nécessiter** *vt* necessitate, entail

**nécessiteux -euse** *n + adj* needy (person)

**nécrologie** *nf* obituary

**nécrologique** *adj* **notice** ~ obituary notice

**nécromancie** *nf* necromancy

**nécromancien -ienne** *n* necromancer

**nécrophilie** *nf* necrophilia

**nécropole** *nf* necropolis

**nécrose** *nf med* necrosis, gangrene; *bot* canker

**Néerlandais -e** *n* Dutchman (Dutchwoman)

**néerlandais** *nm* Dutch (language); *adj* Dutch

**nef** *nf* nave; *ar* vessel, ship

**néfaste** *adj* disastrous, fatal; harmful; unlucky, ill-fated

**nèfle** *nf bot* medlar; *sl* **des** ~ **s!** nothing doing!, not on your life!

**néflier** *nm bot* medlar-tree

**négateur -trice** *n* one who denies; *adj* denying

**négatif** *nm phot* negative; *adj* (*f* **-ive**) negative

**négation** *nf* negation, denial; *gramm* negative

**négligé** *nm* négligé(e); woman's light dressing-gown; *adj* neglected, unheeded, missed; careless, slovenly, untidy

**négligeable** *adj* negligible, insignificant

**négligence** *nf* negligence, carelessness, neglect; heedlessness; slovenliness, untidiness

**négligent** *adj* negligent, careless, neglectful; heedless; untidy

**négliger** *vt* (3) neglect, omit, fail, be careless about; disregard; ~ **de faire qch** fail to do sth; **se** ~ neglect oneself, become slovenly

**négoce** *nm* trade, business

**négociabilité** *nf comm* negotiability

**négociable** *adj comm* negotiable, transferable

**négociant -e** *n* merchant

**négociateur -trice** *n* negotiator, transactor

**négociation** *nf* negotiation, negotiating; transaction

**négocier** *vt* negotiate (treaty, bill, loan); *vi* negotiate

**nègre** *nm* negro, black; ghost (writer); **faire le** ~ ghost; **petit** ~ broken French, = pidgin English; *adj* negro, black

**négresse** *nf* negress

**négrier** *nm* slave-trader; slave-ship

**négrillon -onne** *n coll* nigger-boy (-girl)

**négroïde** *adj* negroid

**neige** *nf* snow; ~ **carbonique** dry ice; ~ **fondue** slush, sleet; *cul* **blanc d'œufs battus en** ~ whipped whites of eggs; **train de** ~ skiing excursion train

**neiger** *vi* (3) snow

**neigeux -euse** *adj* snowy, snow-covered; snow-white

**nénés** *nmpl sl* tits

**nenni** *adv ar* nay!

**nénuphar** *nm* water-lily

**néolithique** *adj* neolithic

**néologisme** *nm* neologism

**Néo-Zélandais -e** *n* New Zealander

**néo-zélandais** *adj* New Zealand

**néphrétique** *adj med* nephritic, renal

**néphrite** *nf med* nephritis; *min* jade, nephrite

**népotisme** *nm* nepotism

**nerf** *nm med* nerve; sinew, tendon; *fig* nerve, sinew; *archi* rib; ~ **de bœuf** whip; *ar* pizzle; **avoir les** ~ **s à vif** be on edge, jumpy; **manquer de** ~ be flabby, lack energy; **taper (porter) sur les** ~ **s de qn** get on s/o's nerves

**nerveux -euse** *n* excitable, highly strung person; *adj med* nerve; nervous; sinewy, wiry; forceful; nervy, highly strung; *mot* lively, responsive; *bot* nervate

**nervi** *nm sl* gangster; thug, killer

**nervosité** *nf* state of nerves, excitability, irritability

**nervure** *nf archi* rib, fillet; *bot* vein, rib (leaf)

**net** *nm* **mettre qch au ~** make a fair copy of sth; *adj* (*f* **nette**) clean, spotless, neat, tidy; clear, clear-cut, distinct; unequivocal, candid, unmistakable; *comm* net; **en avoir le cœur ~** get something clear; *phot* **image nette** sharp image; **revenu ~ d'impôts** tax-free income; *adv* clearly, plainly, flatly; **mille francs ~** a clear thousand francs; **refuser ~** refuse point-blank; **s'arrêter ~** stop dead

**nettement** *adv* clearly, distinctly; definitely, decidedly; cleanly

**netteté** *nf* cleanness, cleanliness; clearness, distinctness; decidedness

**nettoiement** *nm* cleaning, cleansing (streets, town); clearing (waste land); **service du ~** refuse collection

**nettoyage** *nm* cleaning; clearing; *mil* mopping-up; **~ à sec** dry-cleaning

**nettoyer** *vt* (7) clean, scour, wash out, wash up; cleanse (wound); *mil* mop up; *coll* clean out (money); **~ à grande eau** mop; **~ à sec** dry clean; **se ~** clean oneself, wash oneself; clean; **tissu qui se nettoie bien** fabric that washes well

**nettoyeur -euse** *n* cleaner; *adj* cleaning

¹**neuf** *nm* nine; *adj* nine; ninth

²**neuf** *nm* new; **habillé de ~** dressed in new clothes; **il y a du ~** there's some news, something new has occurred; **remettre qch à ~** make sth as good as new; *adj* (*f* **neuve**) new, newly bought; fresh, inexperienced

**neurasthénie** *nf* neurasthenia

**neurasthénique** *adj* neurasthenic

**neurologie** *nf* neurology

**neurologue** *n* neurologist

**neutralisant** *nm chem* neutralizing agent; *adj chem* neutralizing

**neutraliser** *vt* neutralize

**neutralité** *nf* neutrality; *chem* neutral state

**neutre** *nm* neutral; *gramm* neuter; *adj* neutral; *gramm + zool* neuter

**neuvaine** *nf eccles* novena

**neuvième** *n* ninth; *nm* ninth part; *nf mus* ninth; *adj* ninth

**névé** *nm geog* névé, consolidated snow

**neveu** *nm* nephew

**névralgie** *nf* neuralgia

**névralgique** *adj* neuralgic; *fig* sensitive; **point ~** nerve centre

**névrite** *nf* neuritis

**névritique** *adj* neuritic

**névrose** *nf* neurosis

**névrosé -e** *n + adj* neurotic

**névrotique** *adj* neurotic

**nez** *nm* nose; bows (ship); **avoir du ~** have a sense of smell; have flair; **avoir le ~ creux** have a sharp instinct for a bargain; *sl* **avoir qn dans le ~** be unable to stand s/o; *coll* **à vue de ~** roughly speaking, at a rough estimate; **chercher du ~** nose about; **faire qch au ~ de qn** do sth under s/o's very nose; **faire un pied de ~** cock a snook; *coll* **mener qn par le bout du ~** twist s/o round one's little finger; **montrer son ~** show one's face; **piquer du ~** nosedive (aircraft), sink by the bows (ship); **rire au ~ de qn** laugh in s/o's face; **se casser le ~ à la porte de qn** find no one in; be rebuffed; *coll* **se manger le ~** quarrel (two persons); *coll* **tirer les vers du ~ de qn** worm secrets out of s/o; *naut* **vaisseau sur le ~** ship down by the bows

**ni** *conj* **ni ... ni** neither ... nor

**niais -e** *n* simpleton, fool; *adj* simple, silly, foolish

**niaiserie** *nf* simplicity, silliness, foolishness; inane remark, twaddle

¹**niche** *nf* (dog-)kennel; *archi* niche

²**niche** *nf* trick, practical joke

**nichée** *nf* brood (mice), nest (birds); *coll* brood, swarm (children)

**nicher** *vt* put in a nest; *vi* nest, build a nest; *coll* live, hang out; **se ~** nest; *coll* perch oneself, put oneself

**nichon** *nm sl* tit

**nickelage** *nm* nickel-plating

**nickeler** *vt* (5) nickel-plate; *coll* **avoir les pieds nickelés** refuse to budge, be lazy

**nid** *nm* nest; *naut* **~ de pie** crow's nest; **~ de poule** pot-hole in the road

¹**nielle** *nm* niello, inlaid enamel-work

²**nielle** *nf agr* blight

¹**nieller** *vt* inlay with niello

²**nieller** *vt agr* blight; **se ~** become blighted

¹**niellure** *nf* niello-work

²**niellure** *nf agr* blighting

**nier** *vt* deny; *leg* repudiate (debt)

**nigaud -e** *n* fool, ass, idiot, booby; *adj* silly, foolish

**nigauderie** *nf* silliness, foolishness; act of stupidity, tomfoolery

**nihilisme** *nm* nihilism

**nihiliste** *n* nihilist; *adj* nihilistic

**nimbe** *nm* nimbus, halo
**nipper** *vt coll* clothe, rig out; **se ~** *coll* rig oneself out
**nippes** *nfpl coll* togs
**Nippon -onne** *n* Japanese
**nippon -onne** *adj* Japanese
**nique** *nf* **faire la ~ à qch** despise sth, snap one's fingers at sth; **faire la ~ à qn** cock a snook at s/o
**nitouche** *nf* demure, coy girl; **sainte ~** little hypocrite; **faire la sainte ~** look as though butter wouldn't melt in one's mouth
**nitre** *nm* nitre, saltpetre
**nitreux -euse** *adj* nitrous
**nitrique** *adj* nitric
**nitrogène** *nm* nitrogen; *adj* nitrogen
**niveau** *nm* level, standard; floor; level (instrument); **~ à bulle d'air** spirit level; **mot ~ d'essence (d'huile)** petrol (oil) gauge; **~ de vie** standard of living; **au ~ de** on a level with; with regard to, in the field of; **de ~ avec** on a level with; **mettre à ~** level, level up; **passage à ~** level-crossing
**niveler** *vt* (5) survey; level, level up, even up; **se ~** become level, settle down
**niveleur -euse** *n* leveller; *adj* levelling
**nivellement** *nm* surveying; levelling
**nivôse** *nm hist* fourth month of the French Republican calendar (December to January)
**nobiliaire** *nm* peerage list; *adj* nobiliary
**noble** *n* nobleman, noblewoman *adj* noble, aristocratic; august; generous; *mech* of high technology; *theat* **père ~** heavy father
**noblesse** *nf* nobility; nobleness
**noce** *nf* wedding, wedding festivities; *coll* spree; **~s** marriage; **épouser en secondes ~s** marry for the second time; *coll* **faire la ~** go on the spree; *coll* **ne pas être à la ~** be having a bad time; **voyage de ~s** honeymoon
**noceur -euse** *n* reveller, fast liver
**nocher** *nm poet* boatman, pilot
**nocif -ive** *adj* noxious, injurious, harmful
**nocivité** *nf* noxiousness
**noctambule** *n* night-bird, one with nocturnal habits; *obs* sleepwalker; *adj* noctambulist
**nocturne** *nm mus* nocturne; *eccles* nocturn; *adj* nocturnal
**nodosité** *nf* nodosity, knottiness; nodule
**nodulaire** *adj geol* nodular
**Noé** *nm bibl* Noah; **l'arche de ~** Noah's Ark
**Noël** *nm* Christmas; Noel
**noël** *nm* Christmas carol
**nœud** *nm* knot; bow, favour; *fig* crux;

bond; nautical mile; *math + phys* node; **~s coils** (serpent); **~ coulant** slip-knot; **~ ferroviaire** railway junction; **~ papillon** bow-tie
**noir -e** *n* black man (woman); *nm* black (colour); darkness; *sp* bull's eye; **broyer du ~** be depressed, be in the dumps; **prendre le ~** go into mourning; **tourner au ~** turn dark; **voir tout en ~** look on the black side of things; *adj* black; dark; gloomy; base, foul, dirty; *sl* drunk, plastered; *cul* **au beurre ~** with browned butter sauce; **bête ~e** pet aversion; **faire ~** be dark; *theat* **four ~** dismal flop; **humour ~** macabre humour; **idées ~es** depressing thoughts, *coll* blues; **misère ~e** extreme poverty; *med* **peste ~e** bubonic plague; **travail ~** work on the side
**noirâtre** *adj* blackish
**noiraud -e** *n* dark-skinned person; *adj* swarthy, dark-skinned
**noirceur** *nf* blackness; base action; *obs* melancholy
**noircir** *vt* blacken, darken; slander; *coll* **~ du papier** write; *vi* grow dark, turn black; **se ~** grow black, grow dark; *sl* get drunk
**noircissement** *nm* blackening, darkening
**noire** *nf* black (roulette); *mus* crotchet
**noise** *nf ar* quarrel; **chercher ~ à qn** pick a quarrel with s/o
**noisetier** *nm bot* hazel-tree
**noisette** *nf bot* hazel-nut; *adj invar* nut-brown, hazel
**noix** *nm* walnut; nut; **~ de coco** coconut; **~ de terre** peanut; *sl* **à la ~** useless, lousy
**nom** *nm* name; fame, reputation; *gramm* noun, substantive; **~ de baptême** Christian name; **~ de Dieu!** for God's sake!; **~ de famille** surname; **~ de guerre** pseudonym, assumed name; **~ de jeune fille** maiden name; *comm* **~ déposé** registered trade name; **~ et prénoms** full name; **appeler les choses par leur ~** call a spade a spade; **ça n'a pas de ~!** it's unspeakable; **petit ~** Christian name; **se faire un ~** achieve fame, make a name for oneself
**nomade** *n* nomad; **~s** nomadic tribes; *adj* nomadic, wandering; migratory
**nombre** *nm* number; numbers; total; *pros* harmony; **~ de** a good many; **~ requis** quorum; **en grand ~** in large numbers; **être au ~ de** be one of, be among; **sans ~** innumerable; **tout fait ~** every little helps
**nombreux -euse** *adj* numerous, many;

large; *pros* harmonious; **peu** ~ few in number, infrequent

**nombril** *nm* navel; eye (fruit)

**nomenclature** *nf* nomenclature; nominal rate; list of words

**nominal** *adj* nominal; **appel** ~ roll-call; *comm* **valeur** ~ **e** face-value

**nominatif** *nm gramm* nominative; *adj* (*f* **-ive**) nominal; *gramm* nominative; **état** ~ nominal roll; **titres** ~**s** registered securities

**nomination** *nf* nomination, appointment; (honourable) mention; **recevoir sa** ~ be appointed

**nominativement** *adv* by name

**nommé -e** *n leg* person named; *adj* named; appointed; **à point** ~ in the nick of time, at the right moment

**nommément** *adv* by name

**nommer** *vt* name, mention by name, call; appoint, promote; **se** ~ be called, be named; state one's name

**non** *nm invar* no; **les** ~ **l'emportent** the noès have it; *adv* no; not; (in compound words) non-, un-; **mais** ~ ! oh no!; ~ **pas!** not at all!, not a bit of it!; **que** ~ ! certainly not!

**nonagénaire** *n* + *adj* nonagenarian

**non-alcoolisé** *adj* non-alcoholic

**non-aligné** *adj* non-aligned

**nonante** *adj dial* ninety

**nonce** *nm eccles* nuncio

**nonchalance** *nf* nonchalance; languidness, languor

**nonchalant** *adj* nonchalant; languid

**nonchaloir** *nm lit* nonchalance; listlessness

**non-combattant -e** *n* + *adj* non-combatant

**non-conducteur** *nm phys* non-conductor; *adj* (*f* **-trice**) *phys* non-conducting

**non-conformisme** *nm eccles* nonconformity

**non-conformiste** *n* + *adj eccles* nonconformist

**non-disponibilité** *nf* unavailability

**non-disponible** *adj* unavailable

**non-ingérence** *nf* non-intervention

**non-lieu** *nm leg* no true bill, no case to be answered; **ordonnance de** ~ dismissal of case

**nonne** *nf* nun

**nonobstant** *adv* nevertheless; *prep* notwithstanding, despite; ~ **que** although

**nonpareil -eille** *adj* nonpareil, matchless, peerless

**non-pesanteur** *nf* weightlessness

**non-recevoir** *nm* **fin de** ~ objection

**non-sens** *nm* meaningless sentence;

absurdity in translation; ludicrous notion

**non-valeur** *nf* useless object, useless person; bad debt; non-productive land

**nord** *nm* north; **au** ~ in the north; **en plein** ~ due north; **étoile du** ~ Pole star; *coll* **perdre le** ~ lose one's bearings, be all at sea; *adj invar* north, northern

**Nord-Africain -e** *n* North African

**nord-africain** *adj* North African

**nord-est** *nm* + *adj invar* north-east

**nordique** *adj* nordic

**nord-ouest** *nm* + *adj invar* north-west

**noria** *nf eng* chain-pump; bucket conveyor

**normal** *adj* normal, ordinary, habitual, standard; **école** ~ **e** teachers' training college

**normalien** *nm usu* (male) student (or ex-student) of the École Normale Supérieure in Paris; (male) student at teachers' training college

**normalienne** *nf usu* (female) student (or ex-student) of the École Normale Supérieure at Sèvres; (female) student at teachers' training college

**normalisation** *nf* normalization, standardization

**normaliser** *vt* normalize, standardize

**normalité** *nf* normality

**Normand -e** *n* Norman; **réponse de** ~ ambiguous answer

**normand** *adj* Norman; **trou** ~ glass of spirits taken in the middle of a meal

**Normandie** *nf* Normandy

**normatif -ive** *adj* normative

**norme** *nf* norm, standard; **hors de la** ~ abnormal

**¹norois, noroît** *nm naut* north-west wind

**²norois, norrois** *adj* Norse

**Norvège** *nf* Norway

**Norvégien -ienne** *n* Norwegian

**norvégien** *nm* Norwegian (language); *adj* (*f* **-ienne**) Norwegian

**nos** *poss adj pl see* **notre**

**nostalgie** *nf* homesickness; nostalgia

**nostalgique** *adj* nostalgic, yearning; homesick

**nota (nota bene)** *nm* N.B.

**notabilité** *nf* notability; important person, V.I.P.

**notable** *nm* person of note; *coll* local bigwig; *adj* notable, signal; eminent, prominent

**notaire** *nm* solicitor, notary

**notamment** *adv* notably, especially

**notarié** *adj* drawn up by a notary

**note** *nf* note, memorandum; notice, annotation; mark; tone; *comm* bill, invoice; *mus* note; *coll* **changer de ~** change one's tune; **donner la ~** set the tone; *mus* give the key; give the lead; **forcer la ~** exaggerate; **prendre bonne ~** take due note

**noter** *vt* note, take notice of; take a note of, jot down, record; **~ qn d'infamie** brand s/o with infamy; *mus* **~ un air** write down a tune; **notez bien!** mind you!; **bien (mal) noté** of good (bad) repute

**notifier** *vt* notify, intimate

**notion** *nf* notion, idea; smattering; **premières ~s** rudiments

**notoire** *adj* notorious, acknowledged; manifest

**notoriété** *nf* notoriety, notoriousness; repute, reputation; *leg* **acte de ~** certificate of identity; **de ~ publique** of common knowledge

**notre** *poss adj* ( *pl* **nos**) our

**nôtre** *nm* **le ~** our own; **les ~s** our friends, our people; **mettons-y du ~** let's help; **est-il des ~s?** is he one of us?; *poss pron* ours

**noué** *adj* knotted; stunted (mind)

**nouer** *vt* tie, knot, fasten; stiffen (joints); strike up (friendship); enter into (conversation); weave (plot of story, play); *vi bot* set (fruit); **se ~** become knotted; become stiffened (joints); *bot* set (fruit)

**noueux -euse** *adj* knotty, gnarled; arthritic

**nouille** *nf cul* noodle; *coll* idiot, ass

**nounou** *nf coll* nanny, nurse

**nourri** *adj* fed, nourished, nurtured; rich, copious, sustained; *coll* meaty; **être logé et ~** have board and lodging

**nourrice** *nf* nurse, wet-nurse; *eng* + *mot* auxiliary tank; **mettre un enfant en ~** put a child out to nurse

**nourricier -ière** *adj* nutritious, nourishing; foster; **mère nourricière** foster-mother; **père ~** foster-father

**nourrir** *vt* feed, nourish; suckle, nurse; nurture, bring up; foster, cherish; harbour, entertain (thoughts); strengthen, enrich; *arts* deepen (colour, tone); *vi* be nourishing; **se ~** feed, subsist; keep oneself

**nourrissant** *adj* nourishing

**nourrisson** *nm* infant, babe in arms

**nourriture** *nf* nourishment, feeding; suckling, nurture; food, sustenance, keep; *fig* (intellectual) nourishment

**nous** *pers pron* we; us; ourselves

**nouveau** *nm* news, something new; new boy (school); **y a-t-il du ~?** is there any news?; *adj* ( *f* **-elle**) new, recent, newly; fresh, renewed; another; **à ~** again,

afresh; **de ~** again, once more; *comm* **solde à ~** balance carried forward

**nouveau-né -e** *n* new-born child; *adj* new-born

**nouveauté** *nf* novelty, newness; change, new invention; new publication; **~s** *comm* fancy goods, linen drapery; **magasin de ~s** draper's shop

**nouvel** *adj m* form of **nouveau** before vowel or mute h

**nouvelle** *nf* news, piece of news; short novel, short story; **~s** news, tidings; **aller prendre des ~s de** go and inquire about; **envoyez-moi de vos ~s** let me hear from you, do write and tell me how you are; *coll* **vous aurez de mes ~s** you've not heard the last of this!; *coll* **vous m'en direz des ~s** you'll be delighted with it

**Nouvelle-Orléans** *nf* New Orleans

**Nouvelle-Zélande** *nf* New Zealand

**nouvelliste** *n* short-story writer

**novateur -trice** *n* innovator; *adj* innovating

**novembre** *nm* November

**novice** *n eccles* novice; beginner, apprentice; *adj* inexperienced, raw

**noviciat** *nm eccles* noviciate; apprenticeship

**noyade** *nf* drowning

**noyau** *nm* stone (fruit), kernel; *fig* nucleus, core, small group; *archi* newel; *metal* core; **~ communiste** communist cell

**noyautage** *nm fig* infiltration, creation of a nucleus; *metal* coring

**noyauter** *vt fig* infiltrate, create a nucleus

**noyé -e** *n* drowned person

¹**noyer** *nm* walnut (wood); walnut-tree

²**noyer** *vt* (7) drown; *fig* drown, submerge; dilute (wine); *mot* flood; *eng* countersink (screw); **se ~** drown, be drowned; *coll* flounder, become confused

**nu** *nm arts* nude; *adj* naked, nude, bare; plain, unvarnished; *mot* stripped; **~-tête**, **tête ~** bare-headed; **~ comme un ver** stark naked; **~ comme la main** bare as the back of your hand; **~ intégral** full frontal nudity; **mettre qch à ~** strip sth bare

**nuage** *nm* cloud; **~ de lait** drop of milk (in tea, etc); **sans ~s** cloudless; unclouded, unalloyed

**nuageux -euse** *adj* cloudy, overcast; hazy, dim, nebulous

**nuance** *nf* nuance, shade of meaning; shade of colour; *mus* slight change of tone; tinge, touch

**nuancement** *nm* blending, shading

**nuancer** *vt* (4) blend, shade; vary, make

fine differentiation in
**nubile** *adj* nubile, marriageable
**nubilité** *nf* nubility
**nucléaire** *adj* nuclear
**nudisme** *nm* nudism
**nudiste** *n* + *adj* nudist
**nudité** *nf* nudity, nakedness; bareness
**nue** *nf lit* cloud; ~ s sky, heavens; **porter aux** ~ s praise to the skies; **tomber des** ~ s be taken aback, be thunderstruck
**nuée** *nf lit* thick cloud, storm cloud; mass, multitude
**nue-propriété** *nf leg* reversion
**nuire** *vi* (65) be hurtful, be harmful, be injurious; ~ **à qn** harm s/o; ~ **aux intérêts de qn** damage s/o's interests
**nuisance** *nf* harmful environmental factor
**nuisibilité** *nf* harmfulness
**nuisible** *adj* hurtful, harmful, injurious; **bêtes** ~ s vermin
**nuit** *nf* night; night-time; darkness; **boîte de** ~ night-club; **cette** ~ last night; tonight; **de** ~ by night; **il ne passera pas la** ~ he will not live till morning; **il se fait** ~ it is getting dark; **je n'ai pas dormi de la** ~ I didn't sleep a wink all night
**nuitamment** *adv* by night; nightly
**nuitée** *nf* night's stay (at hotel)
**nul** (*f* **nulle**) *adj* no; ~ **homme ne le sait** no man knows it; *adj* useless, worthless; of no account, non-existent; *leg* invalid, worthless; *leg* ~ **et de** ~ **effet,** ~ **et non avenu** null and void; *sp* **match** ~ drawn game; *pron* no one, nobody; ~ **ne le sait** nobody knows
**nullement** *adv* not at all, in no way
**nullifier** *vt* nullify
**nullité** *nf* nullity, incapacity; incompetent person, nonentity; *leg* nullity, invalidity
**numéraire** *nm* specie; **en** ~ in cash
**numérateur** *nm math* numerator
**numérique** *adj* numerical
**numéro** *nm* number; copy, number (magazine); *theat* turn, item; *coll* odd person
**numérotage** *nm* numbering (tickets, etc); pagination
**numéroter** *vt* number (tickets, etc); paginate
**numismate** *n* numismatist
**numismatique** *nf* numismatics; *adj* numismatic
**nuptial** *adj* wedding, nuptial, bridal
**nuque** *nf* nape of the neck
**nurse** *nf* children's nurse, nanny
**nutritif -ive** *adj* nutritious, nourishing; **valeur nutritive** food value
**nymphe** *nf* nymph
**nymphéa** *nm bot* water-lily
**nymphomane** *nf* + *adj* nymphomaniac

# O

**ô** *interj* O!, oh!
**obédience** *nf eccles* obedience; *coll* submission
**obéir** *vi* obey; yield, submit; **se faire** ~ enforce obedience
**obéissance** *nf* obedience, submission
**obéissant** *adj* obedient, submissive
**obélisque** *nm* obelisk
**obérer** *vt* (6) burden (s/o) with debt; encumber (sth) with debt
**obèse** *adj* obese, stout, corpulent
**obésité** *nf* obesity, stoutness, corpulence
**obituaire** *nm eccles* obituary, register of deaths; *adj m* obituary
**objecter** *vt* object; hold against; give as a pretext
**objectif** *nm* aim, objective, target; lens, object-glass; *adj* (*f* **-ive**) objective, unbiased
**objection** *nf* objection; **faire des** ~ s argue
**objectiver** *vt* objectivize, make objective, exteriorize
**objet** *nm* object, thing; objective, purpose; *gramm* object, complement; *leg* ~ s **immobiliers** real property; ~ s **trouvés** lost property
**obligataire** *n comm* bondholder, debenture-holder
**obligation** *nf* obligation, duty; favour,

# obligatoire

gratefulness; *leg* recognizance; *comm* bond, debenture; *comm* ~ **au porteur** bearer-bond; **avoir des ~ s envers qn** be under obligation to s/o; **être dans l' ~ de** be bound to; **être d' ~** be obligatory; **se trouver dans l' ~ de** feel compelled to

**obligatoire** *adj* compulsory, obligatory, binding

**obligé -e** *n* person under obligation; *leg* obligee; *adj* obliged, bound; obligatory; grateful; inevitable

**obligeance** *nf* obligingness; **veuillez avoir l' ~ de** please be so kind as to

**obligeant** *adj* obliging, kind

**obliger** *vt* (3) oblige, constrain, compel; do a favour to; **s' ~** bind oneself, undertake

**oblique** *adj* oblique, slanting, sidelong; crooked, underhand

**obliquer** *vi* move obliquely, edge; slant

**obliquité** *nf* obliquity; crookedness

**oblitérateur** *nm* cancel (stamps, etc); *adj* (*f* -**trice**) obliterating

**oblitération** *nf* obliteration; cancelling (stamp)

**oblitérer** *vt* (6) obliterate; cancel (stamp)

**obnubiler** *vt* dim, obscure

**obole** *nf* obol; mite

**obscène** *adj* obscene, lewd, filthy

**obscénité** *nf* obscenity, lewdness; filth; ~ s filthy words, filthy expressions

**obscur** *adj* dark, gloomy, overcast; obscure, abstruse; little known, unassuming

**obscurantisme** *nm* obscurantism

**obscurcir** *vt* obscure, darken, dim; *fig* obscure, cloud, dim; **s' ~** grow dark; *fig* grow dim, wane, become obscure

**obscurcissement** *nm* darkening, dimming; black-out; *fig* obfuscation, bewildering

**obscurité** *nf* obscurity; darkness; humble situation; confusion, abstruseness

**obsédant** *adj* obsessing, haunting; pressing, urgent

**obséder** *vt* (6) obsess; worry, beset

**obsèques** *nfpl* funeral, obsequies

**obséquieux -ieuse** *adj* obsequious

**obséquiosité** *nf* obsequiousness

**observateur -trice** *n* observer, onlooker, spectator; keeper (rules); *adj* observant, observing

**observation** *nf* observation, remark; observance, fulfilment; reproof; **faire des ~ s à** reproach, find fault with

**observatoire** *nm* observatory; *mil* observation post

**observer** *vt* observe, point out, remark; watch, note; fulfil, keep; **faire ~** enforce (law); point out; **s' ~** be

circumspect; observe one another

**obsessif -ive** *adj* obsessive

**obstétrique** *nf med* obstetrics; *adj* obstetrical

**obstination** *nf* obstinacy, stubbornness

**obstiné -e** *adj* obstinate, stubborn; persistent, persevering

**obstiner (s')** *v refl* show obstinacy, become obstinate; **s' ~ à** persist in

**obstructif -ive** *adj* obstructive

**obstruction** *nf* obstruction, blocking, stopping up; *med* obstruction, stoppage

**obstruer** *vt* obstruct, block, choke; **s' ~** become blocked, choked up

**obtempérer** *vi* (6) comply, accede, obey

**obtenir** *vt* (96) obtain, get, procure; gain, achieve; ~ **de faire qch** get authorization to do sth; **s' ~** be obtained, be procurable

**obtention** *nf* obtainment, obtaining

**obturateur** *nm* closing device, stopper; *eng* stop-valve; *adj* (*f* -**trice**) obturating, closing

**obturation** *nf* obturation; filling (tooth)

**obturer** *vt* obturate, block up; fill (tooth)

**obtus** *adj* obtuse, dull; *math* obtuse

**obus** *nm mil* shell; ~ **à balles** shrapnel shell

**obusier** *nm mil* howitzer

**obvier** *vi* ~ **à** obviate

**occasion** *nf* occasion, opportunity, chance; circumstance, juncture; reason, motive, cause; bargain; **à l' ~** if the opportunity arises; at times; **avoir l' ~ de** happen to, have occasion to; **d' ~** second-hand; **en cette ~** at this juncture, in this instance; **en pareille ~** in similar circumstances; **par ~** now and again; by chance; **suivant l' ~** as occasion arises

**occasionnel -elle** *adj* fortuitous; casual

**occasionner** *vt* occasion, cause

**Occidental -e** *n* Westerner, Occidental

**occidental** *adj* western

**occire** *vt obs* (irregular and very rare) slay, kill

**occis** *obs p part* **occire** killed, slain

**occitan** *adj* of Languedoc

**occlusion** *nf med* obstruction; closure; *eng* cut off

**occulte** *adj* occult

**occulter** *vt astron* occult, eclipse

**occultisme** *nm* occultism

**occupant -e** *n* occupier, occupant

**occupation** *nf* occupation, tenure; business, job

**occuper** *vt* occupy, inhabit; fill, take up; employ; **occupé** engaged (lavatory, telephone number); ~ **qn** keep s/o busy; **être occupé à faire qch** be busy doing sth; **s' ~** keep oneself busy,

206

employ oneself; s' ~ à be busy with; s' ~ de attend to, look after; **occupez-vous de vos affaires!** mind your own business!

**occurrence** *nf* occurrence, emergency; **en l' ~** under the circumstances

**Océanie** *nf* Oceania, the South Sea Islands

**océanique** *adj* oceanic

**océanographe** *n* oceanographer

**océanographie** *nf* oceanography

**ocre** *nf* ochre

**octaèdre** *nm math* octahedron; *adj math* octahedral

**octante** *adj dial* eighty

**octobre** *nm* October

**octogénaire** *n* + *adj* octogenarian

**octogone** *nm* octagon

**octosyllabe** *nm* octosyllable; *adj* octosyllabic

**octroi** *nm* granting, concession; toll-office; local city toll, town dues

**octroyer** *vt* (7) grant, concede; s' ~ indulge in, grant oneself

**oculaire** *nm* eye-piece, ocular; *adj* ocular; **témoin ~** eye-witness

**oculiste** *n* oculist

**odeur** *nf* smell, odour; scent, perfume

**odieux -ieuse** *adj* odious, hateful; shocking, heinous

**odorant** *adj* odorous, sweet-smelling; smelly

**odorat** *nm* sense of smell

**odoriférant** *adj* fragrant, sweet-smelling, odiferous

**odyssée** *nf* odyssey

**œcuménique** *adj* ecumenical

**œdème** *nm med* oedema

**œil** *nm* (*pl* yeux) eye; sight, look; view, opinion, observation; hole; speck of fat (on soup); *typ* face; ~ **au beurre noir** black eye; **à l' ~** by eye; *sl* free, buckshee; **à mes yeux** in my view; **avoir du travail par-dessus les yeux** be up to one's eyes in work; **avoir les yeux hors de la tête** have one's eyes starting from one's head; *coll* **avoir les yeux plus gros que le ventre** bite off more than one can chew; **avoir l' ~ à tout** keep an eye on everything; **avoir l' ~ sur** have an eye on, keep tabs on; **à vue d' ~** visibly; *coll* **ça crève les yeux** it's obvious; **chercher qn des yeux** look for s/o; **coup d' ~** glance; view; *coll* **coûter les yeux de la tête** cost the earth; *comm* **donner de l' ~ à** give a bit of style to; **d'un bon (mauvais) ~** with a favourable (unfavourable) eye; *coll* **entre quatre(-z-) yeux** between you and me; **faire de l' ~ à qn** make eyes at s/o; **faire les gros yeux** look sternly; **faire les yeux doux à** look lovingly at; *coll* **faire qch pour les**

**beaux yeux de qn** do sth for love of s/o; **fermer les yeux sur qch** wink at sth, connive at sth; *naut* **l' ~ du vent** the wind eye; *sl* **mon ~ !** my foot!; **n'avoir pas froid aux yeux** be brave; *coll* **ne pas avoir les yeux dans sa poche** be all there, keep one's eyes skinned; **ne pas fermer l' ~ de la nuit** not sleep a wink at night; **sauter aux yeux** be obvious, be clear as daylight; *sl* **s'en battre l' ~** not give a damn; **se rincer l' ~** get an eyeful; **signer les yeux fermés** sign without question; *coll* **taper dans l' ~** impress; **tourner de l' ~** faint

**œil-de-bœuf** *nm* (*pl* œils-de-bœuf) bull's eye window

**œil-de-perdrix** *nm* (*pl* œils-de-perdrix) *med* soft corn

**œillade** *nf* glance; **lancer des ~s à** ogle

**œillère** *nf* blinker (horse); *med* eye-bath; *coll* **avoir des ~s** be blinkered, be narrow-minded

**œillet** *nm bot* carnation, pink; eyelet, eye-hole

**œsophage** *nm anat* oesophagus

**œstrogène** *nm* oestrogen

**œuf** *nm* egg; ovum; spawn, hard roe; ~ **à la coque** boiled egg; ~ **(à repriser)** darning egg; ~ **à thé** tea-infuser; ~ **s au lait** custard; ~ **au plat** fried egg; ~ **mollet** soft-boiled egg; **dans l' ~** in the bud; *coll* **marcher sur des ~s** be on very thin ice; **plein comme un ~** chock-full; **tondre un ~** be very miserly

**œuvre** *nm sing* complete works (of artist); *mus* opus; *archi* main work; **gros ~** main walls and foundations; **le grand ~** the philosopher's stone; *nf* work, production, finished work; action, activity, occupation; works; charitable society; ~ **de chair** sexual congress; ~ **maîtresse** masterpiece, magnum opus; *naut* ~ **s mortes** topsides; *naut* ~ **s vives** vitals; **exécuteur des hautes ~s** executioner; **faire ~** perform an action; **mettre à l' ~** set to work; **mettre en** ~ bring into play; **mise en** ~ carrying out, implementation; **se mettre à l' ~** set to work

**œuvrer** *vi* work

**offensant** *adj* offensive, insulting

**offense** *nf* offence, insult; sin, transgression; *leg* contempt

**offensé -e** *n* injured party

**offenser** *vt* offend, be offensive to, offend against; shock; s' ~ take offence

**offenseur** *nm* offender

**offensif -ive** *adj* offensive

**offertoire** *nm eccles* offertory

**office** *nm* office, duty, function; service; bureau, centre office; *eccles* service; ~ **des morts** burial service; ~ **de tourisme**

Tourist Information Bureau; **d' ~** automatically, as a matter of course; according to regulations; **faire ~ de** act as; **rendre des bons ~s à** be helpful to; *nf* servants' hall, butler's pantry

**officiant** *nm eccles* celebrant; *adj* celebrating

**officiel** *nm* official personality, authority; *adj* (*f* **-ielle**) official; **rendre ~** make publicly known; **à titre ~** officially

**Officiel (l')** *nm* (official) gazette; **être à l' ~** be gazetted

**¹officier** *nm* officer; *leg* **~ de l'état civil** municipal magistrate, registrar; **~ de la paix** police officer; **~ de santé** health officer; *ar* one authorized to practise medicine without a degree; *leg* **~ du ministère public** public prosecutor; *naut* **~ marinier** petty-officer; *leg* **~ ministériel** member of the legal profession

**²officier** *vi* officiate

**officieux -ieuse** *adj* semi-official, informal; officious

**officinal** *adj* medicinal

**officine** *nf* chemist's dispensary; *coll* den (thieves)

**offrande** *nf* offering, gift; *eccles* offertory

**offrant** *nm* **le plus ~** the highest bidder

**offre** *nf* offer, proposal; *comm* tender; **~ publique d'achat (OPA)** take-over bid; **l' ~ et la demande** supply and demand

**offrir** *vt* (30) offer, give, present; furnish; offer up; bid; **~ la main à qn** hold out one's hand to s/o; **~ un verre à qn** stand s/o a drink; **s' ~** offer oneself, volunteer; offer itself, present itself

**offusquer** *vt* offend, shock; **s' ~** take offence, be touchy

**ogive** *nf archi* ogive, gothic arch, pointed arch; **~ nucléaire** nuclear warhead

**ogresse** *nf* ogress

**ohé** *interj* hi!, hullo!

**oie** *nf* goose; **jeu de l' ~** = game like snakes and ladders

**oignon** *nm* onion; *hort* bulb; bunion; *coll* **ce n'est pas mes ~s** its nothing to do with me, it's not my cup of tea; **en rang d' ~s** in a straight line; *coll* **occupez-vous de vos ~s** mind your own business

**oindre** *vt* (55) anoint

**oint** *adj* anointed

**¹oiseau** *nm* bird; **~ de basse-cour** poultry; **à vol d' ~** as the crow flies; *coll* **drôle d' ~** queer fish; **être comme l' ~ sur la branche** be in an uncertain situation

**²oiseau** *nm* (bricklayer's) hod

**oiseau-mouche** *nm* (*pl* **oiseaux-mouches**) humming-bird

**oiseleur** *nm* fowler, bird-catcher

**oiselier** *nm* bird-seller, bird-fancier

**oisellerie** *nf* bird-catching; bird-fancier's shop; breeding of birds

**oiseux -euse** *adj* idle, useless, lazy, otiose; trivial, irrelevant

**oisif -ive** *n* idler, unemployed person; *adj* idle, lazy, unoccupied

**oisillon** *nm* fledgling

**oisiveté** *nf* idleness, laziness

**oison** *nm* gosling

**oléagineux -euse** *adj* oleaginous, oil-yielding

**oléoduc** *nm* oil pipeline

**olfactif -ive** *adj* olfactory

**olibrius** *nm coll* braggart

**oligarchie** *nf* oligarchy

**oligarchique** *adj* oligarchical

**olivaie** *nf see* **oliveraie**

**olivâtre** *adj* olive-coloured; sallow

**olive** *nf* olive; *archi* olive moulding; *adj invar* olive-coloured

**oliveraie, olivaie** *nf* olive-grove

**olivier** *nm* olive-tree

**olympiade** *nf* Olympiad, Olympic games

**olympien -ienne** *adj* Olympian

**olympique** *adj* Olympic

**ombilic** *nm* umbilicus, navel

**ombilical** *adj* umbilical

**omble** *nm zool* char

**ombrage** *nm* shade; *fig* umbrage; **prendre ~** shy (horses); *fig* take umbrage

**ombrager** *vt* give shade to, shade

**ombrageux -euse** *adj* touchy, quick to take offence; skittish (horse)

**¹ombre** *nf* shade, shadow; darkness; trace, bit; illusion; ghost; **~ d'espoir** ray of hope; *sl* **à l' ~** in jug, in prison; **à l' ~ de** in the shade of; protected by; **jeter une ~ sur** cast gloom over; **rester dans l' ~** stay in the background; **sous l' ~ de** under pretext of

**²ombre** *nm zool* grayling

**ombrelle** *nf* sunshade; *aer* umbrella, air-cover

**ombrer** *vt arts* shade, hatch; darken (eyelids)

**ombreux -euse** *adj* shady

**omelette** *nf* omelette; **faire une ~ sans œufs** make bricks without straw

**omettre** *vt* (60) omit, leave out; fail, neglect

**omnibus** *nm* omnibus; **(train) ~** stopping train

**omnium** *nm comm* general trading company; *sp* open race

**omnivore** *adj* omnivorous

**omoplate** *nf* shoulder-blade

**on** *indef pron* one, somebody; people;

I; you; he; she; we; they; ~ **demande une bonne dactylo** wanted, good typist; ~ **dit que** they say, it is alleged that; ~ **parle anglais** English spoken

**onanisme** *nm* onanism

¹**once** *nf* ounce; bit, scrap

²**once** *nf zool* snow-leopard, ounce

**oncial** *adj* uncial

**oncle** *nm* uncle

**oncques** *adv obs* never, ever

**onction** *nf* unction, anointing; unction, unctuousness

**onctueux -ueuse** *adj* greasy, oily; unctuous

**onctuosité** *nf* greasiness, oiliness; unctuousness, oiliness; watering (silk)

**onde** *nf lit* wave, billow; wavy line, corrugation; watering (silk); *rad* wave; ~ **de choc** sonic boom; **en** ~ wavy; *rad* **metteur en** ~s radio producer

**ondé** *adj* waved, wavy, undulating; watered (silk)

**ondée** *nf* heavy shower

**ondin -e** *n* water-spirit

**on-dit** *nm invar* hearsay, rumour

**ondoiement** *nm* undulation, wavy motion

**ondoyant** *adj* undulating, waving, flowing; changing, changeable

**ondoyer** *vi* (7) undulate, wave

**ondulant** *adj* undulating, waving, wavy

**ondulation** *nf* undulating, waving, flowing; wave (hair); **se faire faire une** ~ have one's hair waved

**ondulatoire** *adj* undulatory

**ondulé** *adj* undulating, wavy, corrugated

**onduler** *vt* wave (hair); **se faire** ~ have one's hair waved; *vi* undulate, wave, ripple

**onduleux -euse** *adj* wavy, sinuous

**onéreux -euse** *adj* onerous, costly; **à titre** ~ subject to payment

**ongle** *nm anat* nail; claw; talon; **coup d'** ~ scratch; **jusqu'au bout des** ~s to the fingertips; **se ronger les** ~s bite one's nails; *coll* be impatient

**onglée** *nf med* numbness, tingling of finger-tip

**onglet** *nm* nail hole on penknife; tab, thumb index (book); *carp* mitre

**onglier** *nm* manicure set

**onguent** *nm* ointment, unguent

**onomastique** *adj* onomastic

**onomatopée** *nf* onomatopoeia

**ontologique** *adj* ontological

**onze** *nm sp* eleven, team; *adj invar* eleven; eleventh

**onzième** *nm* eleventh part; *adj* eleventh

**opacité** *nf* opacity, denseness

**opale** *nf* opal

**opalin** *adj* opaline

**opéra** *nm* opera; ~ **bouffe** comic opera; ~ **comique** light opera

**opérable** *adj* operable

**opérateur -trice** *n* operator, technician; cameraman; *cin + rad* ~ **du son** sound engineer

**opératif -ive** *adj* operative

**opération** *nf* operation, process, working; transaction; surgical operation; **salle d'** ~ operating theatre

**opérationnel -elle** *adj* operational

**opéré -e** *n* patient operated on; *nm comm* deal

**opérer** *vt* (6) effect, bring out, achieve, carry out; *surg* operate on; ~ **à chaud** perform an emergency operation on; **se faire** ~ have an operation; *vi* operate, work; *surg* perform an operation; **s'** ~ take place, come about

**opérette** *nf* operetta, musical comedy

**ophtalmie** *nf* ophthalmia

**ophtalmique** *adj* ophthalmic

**ophtalmologie** *nf* ophthalmology

**ophtalmologue** *n* ophthalmologist

**opiacé** *adj* opiated

**opiner** *vi* opine, be of the opinion that; incline to the view that; ~ **de la tête** nod agreement

**opiniâtre** *adj* opinionated, stubborn, obstinate; persistent, unflagging, tenacious

**opiniâtreté** *nf* stubbornness, obstinacy; tenacity

**opinion** *nf* opinion, point of view; judgement, notion; opinion, esteem

**opiomane** *n* opium-eater, opium-addict; *adj* addicted to opium

**opportun** *adj* opportune, seasonable, timely; expedient; **en temps** ~ at the appropriate time

**opportunisme** *nm* opportunism, time-serving

**opportuniste** *n* opportunist, time-server; *adj* opportunist, time-serving

**opportunité** *nf* opportuneness, expediency, timeliness

**opposant -e** *n* opponent, antagonist; *adj* opposing

**opposé** *nm* opposite, reverse, contrary; **à l'** ~ **de** contrary to; *adj* opposite; opposed to, contrary, hostile

**opposer** *vt* oppose; set opposite to, contrast with; set against; ~ **une défense à** set up a defence against; ~ **une résistance à** put up a fight against; ~ **un véto** veto; **s'** ~ oppose, be opposed; be in conflict, be against

**opposite** *nm* **à l'** ~ **de** contrary to; opposite, facing

**opposition** *nf* opposition, resistance; contrast, clash; *leg* **faire ~ à** appeal against; *comm* **frapper d' ~** stop payment; *leg* **mettre à ~** seek an injunction against; **par ~ à** in contrast with

**oppressé** *adj* breathless, having difficulty in breathing

**oppresser** *vt* impede (breathing); be heavy on; *fig* weigh down

**oppresseur** *nm* oppressor

**oppressif -ive** *adj* oppressive

**oppression** *nf* difficulty in breathing, sense of suffocation; oppression, tyranny

**opprimé -e** *n* oppressed person, victim; *adj* oppressed, down-trodden

**opprimer** *vt* oppress, crush, trample upon

**opprobre** *nm* opprobrium, disgrace, shame, infamy

**opter** *vi* choose, decide, opt

**opticien -ienne** *n* optician

**optimal** *adj* optimum

**optimisme** *nm* optimism

**optimiste** *n* optimist; *adj* optimistic, sanguine

**option** *nf* option, choice; *comm* option

**optionnel -elle** *adj* optional

**optique** *nf* optics; *fig* perspective; *adj* optical

**opulence** *nf* opulence, wealth; *fig* richness

**opulent** *adj* opulent, wealthy; *fig* buxom

**opuscule** *nm* opuscule, monograph, pamphlet

¹**or** *nm* gold; *her* or; **~ en barre** gold ingots, bullion; *comm* **affaire en ~** excellent bargain; **à prix d' ~** extremely expensive, at a very high price; *coll* **c'est de l' ~ en barre** it's dead safe, it's as good as cash; **d' ~** golden; **livre d' ~** V.I.P. visitors' book; **rouler sur l' ~** be rolling in money; **vaisselle en ~** gold plate; *adj invar* gold (colour)

²**or** *conj* now, well, well now

**orage** *nm* thunderstorm, storm, tempest; *fig* disturbance, turmoil

**orageux -euse** *adj* stormy, tempestuous; thundery, sultry; *fig* stormy; violent

**oraison** *nf* prayer, orison; oration; **faire ses ~s** say one's prayers

**oral** *nm* oral examination, viva(-voce); *adj* oral

**orange** *nf* orange; *nm* orange (colour); *adj invar* orange-coloured

**orangé** *nm* orange (colour); *adj* orange-coloured

**oranger** *nm* orange-tree; **fleur d' ~** orange blossom

**orangerie** *nf* orangery, orange hothouse

**orateur -trice** *n* orator, speaker; spokesman (-woman); *nm eccles* preacher

**oratoire** *nm* oratory, chapel; *adj* oratorical; **art ~** oratory, public speaking

¹**orbe** *nm* orb, globe

²**orbe** *adj* **mur ~** blind wall

**orbite** *nf* orbit; eye-socket

**orbiter** *vi* orbit

**Orcades** *nfpl* Orkneys

**orchestre** *nm mus* orchestra; (dance-) band; *theat* stalls; **chef d' ~** conductor

**orchestrer** *vt mus* orchestrate, score for orchestra; *fig* harmonize; mount (campaign)

**orchidée** *nf* orchid

**ordinaire** *nm* normal practice, wont, custom; ordinary fare; normal meals; *mil* mess; *eccles* ordinary; **à l' ~**, **d' ~** usually; *adj* ordinary, usual, normal; common; humble; **expression ~** trite phrase

**ordinateur** *nm* computer

**ordonnance** *nf* order; ordering, management; ordinance, enactment; *leg* writ; *mil* orderly, batman; *med* prescription; **~ de police** police regulation; *mil* **officier d' ~** A.D.C.; *naut* flag-lieutenant

**ordonnancement** *nm* order to pay

**ordonnateur -trice** *n* organizer, arranger; director; *comm* person authorized to make payment

**ordonnée** *nf math* ordinate

**ordonner** *vt* order, command; put in order, arrange, regulate; *med* prescribe; *eccles* ordain; *vi* dispose, arrange

**ordre** *nm* order, succession; orderliness, discipline, tidiness; command, warrant, instruction; category, class, association, sort; course; decoration; **~s** holy orders; *mil* **~ d'appel** call-up papers; **~ de chevalerie** order of knighthood; **~ du jour** agenda; *mil* orders of the day; **~ monastique** monastic order; **~ public** law and order; *comm* **billet à ~** promissory note, bill payable to order; **de l' ~ de** about, of the order of; **de premier ~** first-class; *eccles* **entrer dans les ~s** take orders; **jusqu'à nouvel ~** until further notice; **l' ~ des avocats** = the Bar; **mettre bon ~ à qch** see to sth; **numéro d' ~** serial number; *mil* **porter à l' ~ du jour** mention in despatches; **rappeler qn à l' ~** call s/o to order; **rentrer dans l' ~** be in order again; **rétablir l' ~** restore order; **sans ~** untidy, untidily; **selon l' ~ des choses** in the nature of things, in the course of events; **service d' ~** police force on duty; riot-police

**ordure** *nf* excrement, dung; filth, muck, refuse, *US* trash; dirt, obscenity; **~s ménagères** refuse; *sl* **c'est une ~** he's a shit

**ordurier -ière** *adj* lewd, filthy, obscene; scurrilous, ribald

**orée** *nf* edge, border

**oreille** *nf* ear; hearing; handle, lug; **à l' ~** confidentially; *mus* **avoir de l' ~** have an ear for music; **avoir l' ~ de** have influence over, have a pull with; **avoir l' ~ fine** have good hearing; **dresser l' ~** prick up one's ears; **être dur d' ~** be hard of hearing; **faire la sourde ~** turn a deaf ear; **frotter (tirer) les ~s de qn** pull s/o up; **l' ~ basse** crest-fallen; **n'écouter que d'une ~** listen absent-mindedly; **ne pas l'entendre de cette ~** not see things in that light; **rebattre les ~s à qn de qch** drum sth into s/o; **se faire tirer l' ~** need persuading, need talking to

**oreiller** *nm* pillow

**oreillette** *nf* ear-flap; *med* auricle

**oreillons** *nmpl med* mumps

**ores** *adv obs* now; **d' ~ et déjà** here and now; from now on

**orfèvre** *nm* goldsmith

**orfèvrerie** *nf* goldsmith's trade; gold plate

**orfraie** *nf* osprey

**organe** *nm med* organ; part, component (machine); voice; agent, means, instrument; organ, mouthpiece

**organigramme** *nm* organization chart

**organique** *adj* organic

**organisateur -trice** *n* organizer; *adj* organizing

**organisation** *nf* organizing; organization, body

**organiser** *vt* organize, arrange, set up; **s' ~** become organized, get into working order, settle down

**organisme** *nm* organism; *med* physical structure, constitution; *comm* corporation

**organiste** *n* organist

**orgasme** *nm* orgasm

**orge** *nf* barley; *nm* **~ mondé** hulled barley; **~ perlé** pearl barley

**orgelet** *nm med* stye

**orgiaque** *adj* orgiastic

**orgie** *nf* orgy; profusion

**orgue** *nm mus* organ; **~ de Barbarie** barrel organ; **tenir l' ~** play the organ

**orgueil** *nm* pride, arrogance, conceit; pride, dignity; **mettre son ~ à faire qch** take a pride in doing sth

**orgueilleux -euse** *n + adj* proud, arrogant, conceited (person)

**orgues** *nfpl mus* organ; **grandes ~** church organ; *theat* **jeu d' ~** switchboard

**Orient** *nm geog* Orient, East; **Extrême- (Moyen-) ~** Far (Middle) East

**orient** *nm* orient (pearl); lodge (freemasonry)

**orientable** *adj* swivelling

**Oriental -e** *n* Oriental

**oriental** *adj* oriental, eastern

**orientalisme** *nm* orientalism

**orientaliste** *n* orientalist

**orientation** *nf* orientation; guidance, counselling; tendency, trend; *naut* trim (sails); **~ politique** political tendency; **table d' ~** panoramic landmark indicator

**orienter** *vt* orientate, orient; set, direct, guide; *naut* trim (sails); **s' ~** take one's bearings, find one's bearings; **~ vers** tend towards

**orifice** *nm* orifice, aperture, mouth; *mech* **~ d'admission** intake; **~ d'échappement** exhaust

**originaire** *adj* originating, native; innate; original, primary

**original** *nm* original, pattern, model; *n* (*f* -e) eccentric, unconventional person; *adj* original, inventive, fresh; odd, eccentric

**originalité** *nf* originality; eccentricity

**origine** *nf* origin; beginning; source; extraction, birth; **à l' ~** originally; **bureau postal d' ~** despatching post-office; **dès l' ~** from the start; *comm* **d' ~** certified genuine; **il est d' ~ française** he is French by birth

**originel -elle** *adj* original (sin); primordial

**oripeau** *nm* foil, imitation gold foil; **~ x** tawdry finery

**orme** *nm* elm

**ornement** *nm* ornament, embellishment; *mus* grace-note

**ornemental** *adj* decorative, ornamental

**orner** *vt* decorate, embellish, adorn

**ornière** *nf* rut, groove; routine

**ornithologie** *nf* ornithology

**ornithologique** *adj* ornithological

**ornithologiste** *n* ornithologist

**orographie** *nf* orography

**oronge** *nf* agaric (fungus)

**orphelin -e** *n* orphan

**orphelinat** *nm* orphanage

**orphéon** *nm* male-voice choir; brass-band

**Orsay** *nm* **Quai d' ~** French Foreign Office

**orteil** *nm* toe

**orthodoxe** *adj* orthodox; correct, normal, conventional; **peu ~** unorthodox

**orthodoxie** *nf* orthodoxy; soundness, normality

**orthographe** *nf* orthography, spelling; **faute d' ~** spelling mistake

**orthographier** *vt* spell correctly

**orthographique** *adj* orthographic

**orthopédie** *nf med* orthopaedics
**orthopédique** *adj* orthopaedic
**ortie** *nf bot* nettle
**orvet** *nm* slow-worm
**os** *nm* bone; **en chair et en ~** in the flesh
**oscillant** *adj* oscillating, fluctuating
**oscillateur** *nm* oscillator
**oscillation** *nf* oscillation, fluctuation; wavering
**oscillatoire** *adj* oscillatory
**osciller** *vi* oscillate, rock, sway; waver
**osé** *adj* bold, daring; broad, improper
**oseille** *nf bot* sorrel
**oser** *vt* dare, venture, dare to; *vi* dare
**osier** *nm* osier, wicker; **branche d' ~** withy
**osmose** *nf* osmosis
**ossature** *nf* skeleton, frame; framework
**osselet** *nm* knuckle-bone
**ossements** *nmpl* bones, remains
**osseux -euse** *adj* bony
**ossifier** *vt* ossify; **s' ~** become ossified
**ossuaire** *nm* charnel-house; heap of bones
**ostensible** *adj* conspicuous, obvious, patent
**ostensoir** *nm eccles* monstrance
**ostentation** *nf* ostentation, show, display; **faire ~ de** parade
**ostéologie** *nf med* osteology
**ostéologiste** *n med* osteologist
**ostéopathe** *n med* osteopath
**ostracisme** *nm* ostracism
**ostréiculture** *nf* oyster-breeding, ostreiculture
**Ostrogoth -e** *n* Ostrogoth; *coll* barbarian
**otage** *nm* hostage
**otarie** *nf zool* otary
**ôter** *vt* take away, take off, remove; *math* subtract; **~ qch à qn** take sth away from s/o; deprive s/o of sth; **s' ~** remove oneself, get away, get out
**otite** *nf med* otitis
**oto-rhino-laryngologiste** *n* ear, nose and throat specialist
**ottomane** *nf* ottoman, divan
**ou** *conj* or; **~ bien** or else
**où** *adv* where; to what, what; **~ en êtes-vous?** how far have you got?; **~ que** wherever; **~ voulez-vous en venir?** what are you getting at?, what do you mean?; **d' ~** from where, whence; **d' ~ que** from wherever; **jusqu' ~** how far, up to which point; **là ~** where; **n'importe ~** anywhere; **partout ~** wherever; *rel pron* where; **le jour ~ il est venu** the day when he came; **par ~** through which
**ouailles** *nfpl eccles* flock
**ouais** *interj obs* well!, my word!, I say!; *iron* yes

**ouate** *nf* cotton-wool; wadding, padding
**ouater** *vt* wad, pad; *fig* soften, deaden
**ouateux -euse** *adj* soft, fleecy
**oubli** *nm* oblivion, forgetting; forgetfulness, omission, oversight; **par ~** inadvertently
**oublier** *vt* forget, omit; overlook, pardon; let pass; **s' ~** forget oneself, lower oneself; be unmindful
**oublieux -ieuse** *adj* forgetful, unmindful
**oued** *nm geog* wadi
**ouest** *nm* west; *adj invar* west, western, westerly
**ouf** *interj* phew!, what a relief!
**oui** *adv* yes; **je crois que ~** I think so
**ouï-dire** *nm invar* hearsay
**ouïe** *nf* hearing; **~s** sound holes (violin); *zool* gills
**ouïr** *vt* (66) hear
**ouistiti** *nm* marmoset
**ouragan** *nm* hurricane; **arriver comme un ~** burst in
**Oural** *nm geog* Ural; **les monts ~** the Ural mountains
**ourdir** *vt* warp (linen, cloth); weave, hatch (plot, etc)
**ourdou** *nm* Urdu
**ourler** *vt* hem
**ourlet** *nm* hem; edge, rim; **point d' ~** hem stitch
**ours** *nm* bear; boor, uncouth person; **~ en peluche** teddy-bear; **~ mal léché** boor; **vendre la peau de l' ~** count one's chickens before they are hatched
**ourse** *nf* she-bear; *astron* **la grande Ourse** the Great Bear, Ursa Major; *astron* **la petite Ourse** the little Bear, Ursa Minor
**oursin** *nm zool* sea-urchin
**ourson** *nm* bear-cub
**oust(e)** *interj coll* get out!; **allez ~!** hop it!, get out!
**outarde** *nf orni* bustard
**outil** *nm* tool, implement
**outillage** *nm* set of tools; plant, equipment; equipping, providing with tools
**outillé** *adj* provided with tools; equipped, set up
**outiller** *vt* provide with tools; equip; **s' ~** provide oneself with tools, be equipped
**outrage** *nm* outrage, insult; offence; *leg* **~ à la pudeur** indecent exposure; *leg* **~ à magistrat (à la justice)** contempt of court; **faire subir un ~ à qn** commit an outrage against s/o
**outrageant** *adj* insulting; scurrilous
**outrager** *vt* (3) outrage, insult
**outrageux -euse** *adj* insulting; scurrilous
**outrance** *nf* excess, exaggeration; **à ~** unremittingly, to the utmost extreme

**outrancier -ière** *adj* excessive; extreme, extremist

¹**outre** *nf* goatskin bottle

²**outre** *adv* beyond, further; **en ~** besides, moreover; **passer ~** proceed further, go on regardless, disregard; *prep* in addition to, beyond, besides; **~ mesure** inordinately; **~ que** apart from the fact that

**outrecuidance** *nf* presumption, bumptiousness; insolence

**outrecuidant** *adj* presumptuous, bumptious; insolent

**outre-Manche** *adv* on the other side of the Channel

**outremer** *nm* lapis lazuli; ultramarine; *adj* ultramarine

**outre-mer** *adv* overseas

**outrepasser** *vt* exceed, go beyond (rights, authority)

**outrer** *vt* exaggerate, carry to excess; scandalize, provoke greatly

**outre-tombe** *adv* beyond the grave; **d' ~** posthumous

**ouvert** *adj* open; frank, straightforward; **grand ~** wide open

**ouverture** *nf* opening, aperture, gap; width, span; commencement; overture, proposal; *mus* overture; **~ de la chasse** first day of the shooting season; **~ d'esprit** broadmindedness; **~ d'un testament** reading of a will; *comm* **heures d' ~** business hours

**ouvrable** *adj* **jour ~** working day

**ouvrage** *nm* work, piece of work; product, production; *eng* **~ d'art** constructional work; **gros ~s** main walls (building); **sans ~** unemployed; **se mettre à l' ~** set to work, get down to work

**ouvrager** *vt* (3) work (metal, wood, etc); adorn, embroider

**ouvré** *adj* wrought, worked

**ouvre-boîte(s)** *nm* tin-opener

**ouvre-bouteille(s)** *nm* bottle-opener

**ouvrer** *vt* work (metal, wood, etc); adorn, embroider

**ouvreuse** *nf theat + cin* usherette

**ouvrier** *nm* workman, worker, craftsman, mechanic; *fig* creator, architect; **~ à façons** jobber; *adj* (*f* **-ière**) **cheville ouvrière** lynchpin; *fig* mainspring; **classe ouvrière** working class; **conflits ~s** labour disputes

**ouvrière** *nf* working woman, factory girl; worker (bee, etc); **~ lingère** seamstress

**ouvrir** *vt* (30) open, open up; start, set in train; switch on, turn on; *surg* lance; *elect* break (circuit); **~ la marche** lead the way; **~ les rideaux** draw back the curtains; *vi* open; let in; **s' ~** open, become open; begin; **s' ~ à** confide in, talk freely to

**ouvroir** *nm* sewing-room

**ovaire** *nm* ovary

**ovale** *nm + adj* oval

**ovin** *adj* ovine; **les ~s** sheep

**ovipare** *adj zool* oviparous

**ovni** *nm* UFO

**oxalique** *adj* oxalic

**oxydable** *adj* oxidizable, liable to rust

**oxydant** *nm* oxidizer; *adj* oxidizing

**oxydation** *nf* oxidization

**oxyde** *nm* oxide

**oxyder** *vt* oxidize; **s' ~** oxidize

**oxygène** *nm* oxygen

**oxygéner** *vt* (6) oxygenate; bleach; **eau oxygénée** hydrogen peroxide

**oxyton** *nm gramm* oxytone

# P

**pacage** *nm* pasture, pasturage; grazing

**pacager** *vt* (3) pasture; *vi* graze

**pacha** *nm* pasha; **vie de ~** life of luxury

**pachyderme** *nm* pachyderm

**pacificateur -trice** *n* pacifier, peacemaker; *adj* pacifying, peace-making

**pacifier** *vt* pacify, calm, appease

**Pacifique** *nm geog* Pacific

**pacifique** *adj* pacific, peaceful, quiet, calm

**pacifisme** *nm* pacifism

**pacotille** *nf* shoddy goods; **de ~** shoddy

**pacte** *nm* pact, agreement, covenant

**pactiser** *vi* enter into an agreement, compromise

**paf** *adj invar sl* **être ~** be tight; *interj*

bang!, slap!

**pagaie** *nf* paddle (canoe)

**pagaïe (pagaille)** *nf coll* muddle, shambles, mess; **en ~** in disorder; in quantity

**paganiser** *vt* paganize

**paganisme** *nm* paganism

**pagayer** *vt* (7) paddle (canoe)

**pagayeur -euse** *n* paddler (canoe)

¹**page** *nm* page(-boy)

²**page** *nf* page; **à la ~** up-to-date; in the know; *typ* **mettre en ~** make up

**paginer** *vt* paginate, page

**pagne** *nm* loin-cloth

**pagode** *nf* pagoda

**paie** *nf see* **paye**

**paiement, payement** *nm* payment

**païen -ienne** *n + adj* pagan

**paillard -e** *n* rake, debauchee; *f coll* tart; *adj* lewd, lecherous, ribald

**paillardise** *nf* lewdness, lecherousness

¹**paillasse** *nm* clown, mountebank

²**paillasse** *nf* palliasse, straw mattress; draining board; *sl* belly, guts

**paillasson** *nm* mat, door-mat; **~ à grille** wire mat; *coll* **mettre la clef sous le ~** abscond, bilk

**paille** *nf* straw; **~ de fer** wire wool; **coucher (être) sur la ~** be extremely poor; **tirer à la courte ~** draw lots; *adj invar* straw-coloured

**pailler** *vt* cane (chair); mulch (tree)

**pailleté** *adj* spangled

**paillette** *nf* spangle

**paillote** *nf* straw hut

**pain** *nm* bread; cake (soap); loaf (sugar); *sl* blow; **~ d'épice** kind of spiced cake; **~ grillé** toast; *coll* **acheter pour une bouchée de ~** buy for a mere song; **avoir du ~ sur la planche** have a lot of work on hand; **ne pas manger de ce ~-là** have no stomach for that; **petit ~** roll; **se vendre comme des petits ~s** sell like hot cakes

**pair** *nm* peer; equal; *comm* par; **de ~ avec** on a par with; *adj* even (number)

**paire** *nf* pair; **une autre ~ de manches** quite another matter

**pairesse** *nf* peeress

**pairie** *nf* peerage

**paisible** *adj* peaceful, peaceable, quiet; uneventful

**paître** *vt* (67) graze on, feed on; *vi* graze, feed; **faire ~** graze; *coll* **envoyer ~** send packing

**paix** *nf* peace; quiet, stillness, tranquillity; **faire la ~ avec** make peace with, be reconciled with; *coll* **ficher (foutre) la ~ à qn** leave s/o alone, let s/o alone, shut up

**pal** *nm* stake, pale; *her* pale

**palabre** *nm + f* palaver

**palabrer** *vi* palaver

**palace** *nm* luxury hotel

¹**palais** *nm* palace; **leg** law-court; lawyers; **terme de ~** legal jargon

²**palais** *nm* palate; **voile du ~** soft palate; **voûte du ~** hard palate

**palan** *nm naut* hoist, pulley and tackle

**palanche** *nf* yoke

**palanque** *nf* stockade

**palatale** *nf phon* palatal, front consonant, front vowel

**palatin** *adj anat* palatine

**Palatinat** *nm* Palatinate

¹**pale** *nf* blade (of oar, propeller); *mech* sluice-gate

²**pale** *nf eccles* pall

**pâle** *adj* pale, light, wan; colourless, sickly

**palefrenier** *nm* groom, ostler, stableman

**palefroi** *nm ar* palfrey

**paléographe** *n* palaeographer

**paléographie** *nf* palaeography

**paléographique** *adj* palaeographical

**paléolithique** *adj* palaeolithic

**paléontologie** *nf* palaeontology

**palet** *nm* quoit

**paletot** *nm* greatcoat, overcoat; coat

**palette** *nf* blade, paddle; ping-pong bat; *cul* shoulder of mutton; (painter's) palette

**palétuvier** *nm bot* mangrove

**pâleur** *nf* paleness, pallor, wanness

**pâlichon -onne** *adj coll* on the pale side

**palier** *nm* landing, stair-head; level, level stretch; degree, stage; *mech* bearing; **être voisins de ~** live on the same floor; **par ~s** graduated

**palière** *adj f* leading on to the landing

**palimpseste** *nm* palimpsest

**palinodie** *nf* palinode, recantation, retraction

**pâlir** *vt* bleach (colour), make pale; *vi* grow pale, pall, turn pale; fade, grow dim; be on the wane

**palis** *nm* pale, stake; enclosure

**palissade** *nf* palissade, structure; boxhedge

**palissandre** *nm* rosewood

**pâlissant** *adj* growing pale, waning

**palliatif** *nm* palliative; *adj* (*f* -**ive**) palliative

**pallier** *vt* palliate

**palmarès** *nm* prize list, honours list

**palme** *nf bot* palm-leaf; (swimming) flipper; **~s (académiques)** academic honour; **remporter la ~** bear the palm

**palmé** *adj* web-footed; *bot* palmate

**palmer** *nm* callipers

**palmeraie** *nf* palm grove

**palmette** *nf agr* fan espalier; *archi* palm-leaf, palmette

**palmier** *nm* palm-tree

**palmipède** *nm + adj zool* palmiped
**palmure** *nf* web (of web foot)
**palombe** *nf orni* ring-dove; wood-pigeon
**pâlot** *-otte adj coll* palish, peaky
**palourde** *nf zool* clam
**palpabilité** *nf* palpability
**palpe** *nm zool* palp, palpus, feeler
**palper** *vt* feel, finger; *med* palpate; *coll* receive (money)
**palpitant** *adj* palpitating, throbbing; exciting, thrilling
**palpiter** *vi* palpitate, quiver, throb; flutter (eyelid); thrill
**paltoquet** *nm* nonentity
**paludéen, -éenne** *adj* marsh; malarial, paludal
**paludisme** *nm* malaria, paludism
**palustre** *adj* marsh (plant); marshy, swampy (ground)
**pâmer (se)** *v refl* faint away, swoon; se ~ de rire die with laughter
**pâmoison** *nf* swoon, fainting fit
**pampa** *nf* pampas
**pamphlet** *nm* satirical pamphlet, lampoon
**pamphlétaire** *n* pamphleteer, lampoonist
**pamplemousse** *nm* grapefruit
**pampre** *nm* vine-branch; *archi* vine-branch motif
**¹pan** *nm* flap (garment), tail (coat, shirt); face, piece, section, side; patch (sky); wall
**²pan** *interj* bang!, clonk!
**panacée** *nf* panacea
**panache** *nm* panache, plume; wreath (smoke); dash, show, swagger
**¹panaché** *nm* lemonade shandy
**²panaché** *adj* parti-coloured, variegated; **bière ~e** shandy; **glace ~e** mixed ice-cream
**panacher** *vt* variegate; plume; *pol* spread one's votes
**panade** *nf* thin gruel made of bread, butter and water; *sl* **dans la ~** in need, in want
**panais** *nm* parsnip
**Paname** *n coll* Paris
**panard** *nm sl* foot
**panaris** *nm med* whitlow
**pancarte** *nf* bill, notice, placard, poster; show-card (shop)
**panchromatique** *adj* panchromatic
**pandit** *nm* pundit
**panégyrique** *nm + adj* panegyric
**panégyriste** *nm* panegyrist
**paner** *vt* cover with bread-crumbs
**panerée** *nf* basketful; *coll* load
**paneterie** *nf* bread-store
**panier** *nm* basket; basketful; *ar* pannier; ~ **à salade** salad-washer; *coll*

Black Maria; ~ **percé** spendthrift; **dessus du ~** elite
**panifier** *vt* turn into bread
**panique** *nf* panic, scare, stampede; *adj* panic
**paniquer** *vi* panic, flap
**¹panne** *nf* breakdown, mishap; *theat* minor part, poor part; **mot ~ d'allumage** ignition trouble; ~ **d'électricité** power failure; ~ **d'essence** running out of petrol; *coll* **être dans la ~** be reduced to poverty; **être en ~ mot** have a breakdown; *naut* be hove to; *coll* be unable to carry on; *coll* **être en ~ de qch** be lacking sth; **laisser qn en ~** leave s/o in the lurch
**²panne** *nf* plush, panne
**³panne** *nf* peen (hammer), blade; ~ **fendue** claw (hammer)
**⁴panne** *nf bui* purlin
**panné** *adj sl* broke
**panneau** *nm* panel, board, cover, boarding; net, snare, trap; *naut* ~ **d'écoutille** hatch cover; ~ **de signalisation** road sign; ~ **réclame** hoarding; **donner (tomber) dans le ~** fall into the trap
**panneton** *nm* web (key); catch (window)
**panonceau** *nm* name-plate; sign; road-sign
**panoplie** *nf* panoply; toy outfit
**panoramique** *adj* panoramic
**panse** *nf coll* paunch, pot, pot-belly; belly (vase, bottle)
**pansement** *nm* bandaging, dressing; bandage, dressing
**panser** *vt* bandage, dress; tend (patient); groom (horse)
**pansu** *adj* pot-bellied
**pantalon** *nm* trousers, pair of trousers, slacks; ~**s** *ar* woman's drawers
**pantalonnade** *nf theat* farce involving character Pantaloon; piece of humbug
**pantelant** *adj* panting, out of breath; quivering
**panthéisme** *nm* pantheism
**panthéiste** *n + adj* pantheist
**panthère** *nf zool* panther
**pantin** *nm* jumping-jack (toy); marionette, puppet; nonentity, figure of fun
**pantographe** *nm* pantograph
**pantois** *adj invar* amazed, flabbergasted, speechless
**pantomime** *nf* dumb-show, mime, pantomime; *fig* affected behaviour
**pantouflard** *adj coll* stay-at-home, home-loving
**pantoufle** *nf* slipper
**panure** *nf cul* bread-crumbs
**paon** *nm* peacock; peacock-moth
**paonne** *nf* peahen

**papa** *nm* papa, daddy; ~ **gâteau** over-indulgent father; *coll* **à la** ~ easily, without hurry; *coll* **de** ~ out of date; **fils à** ~ rich man's son, playboy

**papauté** *nf* papacy

**pape** *nm* pope

**papelard** *nm coll* bit of paper, paper; *adj* sanctimonious; hypocritical

**paperasse** *nf* useless paper; ~**s** old papers

**paperasserie** *nf* accumulation of old papers; red tape

**paperassier -ière** *adj* fond of scribbling, fond of conserving papers; given to red tape

**papeterie** *nf* paper-making; paper-mill; stationery shop

**papetier -ière** *n* paper-maker; stationer

**papier** *nm* paper; piece of paper; article; feature story; write-up; *comm* bill; ~**s** documents; ~ **à en-tête** headed paper; ~ **à lettres** writing paper; ~ **à musique** music paper; ~ **buvard** blotting-paper; ~ **calque** tracing paper; *vulg* ~ **cul** bumf, shitting-paper; ~ **de soie** tissue paper; ~ **de verre** sandpaper; ~ **hygiénique** toilet paper; ~ **journal** newsprint; ~ **peint** wall-paper; ~ **timbré** (official) stamped paper; *coll* **être dans les petits** ~ **s de qn** be in s/o's good books; **rayez cela de vos** ~**s** don't bank on that

**papillaire** *adj anat* + *bot* papillary

**papille** *nf anat* + *bot* papilla

**papillon** *nm* butterfly; bow-tie; butterfly stroke (swimming); *coll* parking-ticket; summons; *mech* butterfly-nut; *mot* butterfly-valve, throttle; inset (page), inset-map; corollary; butterfly, gaudily dressed person; changeable, unreliable person; ~ **de nuit** moth; *coll* **minute** ~! hold on!

**papillonner** *vi* flit about, flutter about; pass from one subject to another

**papillote** *nf* curl-paper; toffee-paper; *cul* greased paper

**papillotement** *nm* dazzle; flickering

**papilloter** *vi* dazzle; flicker; blink (eyes)

**papiste** *n* + *adj* papist

**papotage** *nm* chatter, gossip

**papoter** *vi* chatter, gossip

**papule** *nf bot* + *med* papula

**pâque** *nf* Jewish passover

**paquebot** *nm* liner, steamer; ~ **mixte** ship carrying both cargo and passengers

**pâquerette** *nf* daisy

**Pâques** *nfpl* Easter; ~ **fleuries** Palm Sunday; **faire ses** ~ take the sacrament at Easter; **joyeuses** ~ happy Easter; *nm sing* Easter, day of Easter; **semaine de** ~ week after Easter

**paquet** *nm* bundle, package, packet, parcel; bundle, mass; pack (rugby football); *typ* parcel; bundle; ~ **de mer** green sea; **donner (lâcher) son** ~ **à qn** give s/o a piece of one's mind; **faire son** ~ pack up; **mettre le** ~ throw everything in, use strong measures

**paquetage** *nm* parcelling; *mil* equipment (laid out for inspection)

**par** *prep* at, by, by means of; out of; per; through; in; on; ~**-ci,** ~**-là** here and there, now and then; ~ **ici** this way; ~ **là** that way; ~ **trop** far too; **de** ~ by reason of; **de** ~ **le monde** somewhere in the world; **de** ~ **le Roi** in the name of the King

**para** *nm mil* parachutist

**parabole** *nf* parable; *math* parabola

**parabolique** *adj* parabolic(al)

**parachever** *vt* (6) complete, finish off, perfect

**parachutage** *nm* parachuting

**parachuter** *vt* parachute

**parachutiste** *n* parachutist

**parade** *nf* display, parade; *mil* review; parry (fencing); sudden stop (horse); **de** ~ ostentatious, showy

**parader** *vi* parade, show off

**paradigme** *nm gramm* paradigm

**paradis** *nm* paradise; *theat* gods; ~ **fiscal** tax haven; *coll* **vous ne l'emporterez pas au (en)** ~ I'll get even with you yet

**paradoxal** *adj* paradoxical

**paradoxe** *nm* paradox

**parafe, paraphe** *nm* paraph, flourish; initials (signature)

**parafer, parapher** *vt* sign; initial

**paraffine** *nf* paraffin wax; *med* **huile de** ~ liquid paraffin

**parage** *nm ar* lineage; **de haut** ~ of high birth

**parages** *nmpl naut* area of sea; region, vicinity; district, area

**paragraphe** *nm* paragraph

**paraître** *vi* (68) appear, come into sight; look, seem; be published; come on stage; **chercher à** ~ show off; **vient de** ~ just published; *v impers* **il paraît** it seems; **à ce qu'il paraît** apparently, it would seem; **il y paraît** it's obvious; *coll* **paraît que** it looks as though

**parallaxe** *nf astron* parallax

**parallèle** *nf math* parallel; *elect* **montage en** ~ parallel connection; *nm* parallel, comparison; *geog* parallel; *adj* parallel

**parallélisme** *nm* parallelism

**paralysant** *adj* paralysing

**paralyser** *vt* paralyse, cripple

**paralysie** *nf* paralysis

**paralytique** *n* + *adj* paralytic

**paramilitaire** *adj* paramilitary

**parangon** *nm* paragon

**parangonner** *vi typ* justify different types

**paranoïaque** *adj* paranoid

**paraphe** *nm* see **parafe**

**parapher** *vt* see **parafer**

**paraphraser** *vt* paraphrase

**paraphrastique** *adj* paraphrastic

**paraplégie** *nf med* paraplegia

**paraplégique** *n + adj* paraplegic

**parapluie** *nm* umbrella

**parasitaire** *adj* parasitic

**parasite** *nm* parasite, hanger-on; *coll* sponger; *biol* parasite; *rad* interference; *adj* parasitic

**parasiter** *vt* sponge on

**parasitique** *adj* parasitic, parasitical

**parasitisme** *nm* parasitism

**paratonnerre** *nm* lightning-conductor

**paratyphoïde** *nf + adj med* paratyphoid

**paravent** *nm* screen

**parbleu** *interj* rather!, sure!

**parc** *nm* park, grounds; enclosure; bed (oysters); fold (sheep), paddock (horses), pen (cattle, sheep); *mil* depot; whole stock of vehicles possessed (by army, country); rolling-stock (railway); car-park

**parcage** *nm* parking

**parcelle** *nf* fragment, particle; plot (of land)

**parce que** *conj phr* because

**parchemin** *nm* parchment, vellum; document, title-deed; *coll* degree certificate; **papier ~** parchment paper

**parcheminé** *adj* parchment-like, shrivelled

**parcheminer (se)** *v refl* become shrivelled up

**parcimonie** *nf* parsimony

**parcimonieux -ieuse** *adj* parsimonious

**parc(o)mètre** *nm* parking meter

**parcourir** *vt* (29) go through, pass through; cover (distance), travel; look through (book), skim; **~ des yeux** glance over

**parcours** *nm* journey, trip; route; distance covered, distance to be covered (race); circuit; course (golf); **mil ~ du combattant** assault-course; **~ d'essai** trial run

**par-derrière** *adv + prep* behind

**par-dessous** *adv + prep* underneath, beneath

**pardessus** *nm* overcoat

**par-dessus** *adv + prep* over; **~ le marché** into the bargain

**par-devant** *prep* in front of, before

**pardi** *interj* indeed!

**pardieu** *interj obs* indeed!

**pardon** *nm* forgiveness, pardon; *eccles* Breton religious festival; *interj* excuse me!, sorry!

**pardonnable** *adj* pardonable, forgivable

**pardonner** *vt* excuse, forgive, pardon; **une maladie qui ne pardonne pas** incurable illness

**pare-boue** *nm invar* mud-flap

**pare-brise** *nm invar* wind-screen

**pare-chocs** *nm mot* bumper, *US* fender

**pare-étincelles** *nm* fire-guard, fire-screen

**pare-feu** *nm invar* fire-screen; fire-belt (forest)

**pare-fumée** *nm invar* smoke-shield

**parégorique** *nm + adj* paregoric

**pareil -eille** *n* equal, like, match; *coll* **c'est du ~ au même** it's all the same; **rendre la pareille** give tit for tat; **sans pareil(le)** unequalled; *adj* alike, equal, like; such; **à nul autre ~** unequalled; *adv sl* in the same way

**pareillement** *adv* also, equally, likewise, in the same way

**parement** *nm* adornment, ornament; decoration, ornamentation; adorning; dressing (stone); cuff, lapel

**parent -e** *n* kinsman, kinswoman, relative; **~s** parents; relatives; ancestors; *adj* related, similar

**parenté** *nf* kinship, relationship; affinity, analogy

**parenthèse** *nf* parenthesis, digression; bracket; **entre ~s** by the way

¹**parer** *vt* adorn, deck, embellish, ornament; attribute (qualities); prepare, dress (meat); *naut* clear, prepare; **se ~** adorn oneself, dress oneself up

²**parer** *vt* avoid, fend off, parry, ward off; *naut* round (cape); **~ à** guard against

**pare-soleil** *nm invar mot* sun-shield

**paresse** *nf* idleness, laziness; *med* sluggishness

**paresser** *vi* idle, laze

**paresseux -euse** *n* idle person, lazy person, sluggard; *adj* idle, lazy; *med* sluggish; *nm zool* sloth

**parfaire** *vt* (46) perfect

**parfait** *nm* perfection; *gramm* perfect; *cul* parfait; *adj* perfect, excellent, faultless; complete, thorough

**parfaitement** *adv* perfectly; quite so, exactly

**parfois** *adv* sometimes, occasionally

**parfum** *nm* perfume, scent; *cul* flavour; *sl* **être au ~** be in the know

**parfumer** *vt* perfume, scent; *cul* flavour

**parfumerie** *nf* perfumery

**parfumeur -euse** *n* perfumer

**pari** *nm* bet, wager; **~ mutuel** tote

**paria** *nm* pariah; outcast

**parier** *vt* bet, wager; affirm

**pariétaire** *nf bot* pellitory

217

**pariétal** *adj anat* parietal; wall (paintings)

**parieur** *nm* better, punter

**parisien -ienne** *adj* Parisian

**paritaire** *adj* composed of equal numbers

**parité** *nf* parity; *math* evenness

**parjure** *nm* perjury; *n* perjurer; *adj* perjured, forsworn

**parjurer (se)** *v refl* perjure oneself

**parking** *nm* car-park; parking (action)

**parlant** *adj* speaking, talking; expressive

**parlé** *adj* spoken; *rad* **journal ~** (radio) news

**parlement** *nm Fr hist* high court of law; parliament

**parlementaire** *n* member of parliament; *adj* parliamentary

**parlementer** *vi* parley

**parler** *nm* speaking, speech, manner of speaking; language, dialect; *vi* speak, talk; chat, confer, converse; admonish, lecture, tell; **~ pour ne rien dire** talk for the sake of talking; **il ne veut pas en entendre ~** he won't hear of it; **n'en parlons plus** let's say no more about it, that's settled; **sans ~ de** not to speak of; **trouver à qui ~** meet one's match; *sl* **tu parles!** not half!, you've said it!; some hope!

**parleur -euse** *n* speaker; confident speaker

**parloir** *nm* parlour; visiting-room (convent, prison, school)

**parlot(t)e** *nf coll* empty chatter

**parmi** *prep* amid, amidst, among, amongst

**parodie** *nf* parody; travesty

**parodier** *vt* parody; burlesque, take-off

**paroi** *nf* partition-wall; surface of wall; rock-face; *anat* + *biol* wall

**paroisse** *nf* parish

**paroissial** *adj* parochial

**paroissien -ienne** *n* parishioner; *nm* missal

**parole** *nf* word, spoken word; promise, undertaking; (faculty of) speech; eloquence; *mil* parole; **adresser la ~ à** address, speak to; **avoir la ~ facile** have the gift of the gab; **de belles ~s** promises, mere words; **demander la ~** risk leave to speak (at meeting); **histoire sans ~s** drawing or cartoon that needs no caption; **n'avoir qu'une ~** keep one's promises; **passer ~** pass (cards); **prendre la ~** begin to speak, take the floor; **rendre sa ~ à qn** release s/o from a promise

**parotide** *nf* + *adj* parotid

**paroxysme** *nm* paroxysm, climax

**parpaillot -e** *n joc* Protestant

**parpaing** *nm bui* parpen, through stone;

breeze block (cement)

**parquer** *vt* pen (animals); garrison (soldiers); coop up (people); park (car); **se ~** park (one's car); *vi* park

**'parquet** *nm Fr leg* public prosecutor's office; *collect* corps of public prosecutors

**²parquet** *nm* floor, flooring, parquet

**parqueter** *vt* (5) lay (a floor) in

**parqueteur** *nm* floor-maker, floor-layer

**parrain** *nm* godfather; sponsor (club, society)

**parrainage** *nm* function of god-parent; sponsorship, patronage

**parrainer** *vt* sponsor, support

**parsemer** *vt* (6) sprinkle, strew, stud

**'part** *nf* part, portion, share; concern, participation; allowance, consideration; *comm* share; *cul* helping, slice; *leg* portion; **à ~** aside, elsewhere; except; **autre ~** elsewhere; **d'autre ~** on the other hand, moreover; **de la ~ de** on behalf of; from; **de ~ en ~** through and through; **de toute(s) ~(s)** on all sides; **faire bande à ~** form a separate clique; **faire chambre à ~** sleep in separate rooms (of husband and wife); **faire la ~ de** make allowance for; **faire ~ de** acquaint with, inform about; **nulle ~** nowhere; **prendre qch en bonne (mauvaise) ~** take sth in good (bad) part; **quelque ~** somewhere

**²part** *nm ar* parturition; *leg* new-born child

**partage** *nm* division, partition, sharing, sharing out; portion, share; fate, lot; equality of votes; *geog* **ligne de ~ des eaux** divide, watershed

**partager** *vt* (3) divide, share, share out; **se ~** be shared, be divided up; divide; share; **amour partagé** requited love; **être mal partagé** be ill provided for

**partance** *nf* **en ~ pour** leaving for

**'partant** *nm* person departing; starter (racing)

**²partant** *adv* consequently, therefore

**partenaire** *n* partner

**parterre** *nm* flower-bed; *theat* pit, pit-audience

**parthe** *adj* Parthian; **flèche du ~** Parthian shot

**'parti** *nm* party, association, group; gang; match (marriage); choice, decision; **~ pris** bias, prejudice, obstinate view; **beau ~** desirable match, *coll* catch; **de ~ pris** deliberately, intentionally; **prendre ~** decide; **prendre son ~ de** resign oneself to; **tirer ~ de** exploit

**²parti** *adj* absent, gone; *coll* a bit drunk, lively; **bien ~** off to a good start; **mal**

~ off to a bad start, ill-conceived

**partial** *adj* partial; biased, unfair

**partialité** *nf* partiality; bias, unfairness

**participant -e** *n* participant; competitor; *adj* participating; competing

**participe** *nm gramm* participle

**participer** *vi* participate, collaborate; share, take part

**particularisation** *nf* particularization, differentiation

**particulariser** *vt* particularize, differentiate; specify; **se ~** make oneself conspicuous

**particularité** *nf* particularity; characteristic, peculiarity

**particule** *nf* particle; **avoir la ~** be of noble family (have the particle 'de' before one's name)

**particulier -ière** *n* private individual; *coll* chap, fellow; *nm* particular, specific; *adj* particular, special, strange; private; **à titre ~** in a private capacity; **en ~** in private

**partie** *nf* part, element, piece; party; game, match; *leg* party; *mus* part; **~ s** parts, genitals; **~ carrée** two couples who exchange partners; **~ de campagne** picnic; **~ de plaisir** outing, picnic; *comm* **~ double** double entry; **~ remise** pleasure to come; **faire ~ de** be part of; be a member of; *vulg* **il me casse les ~ s** he sends me up the wall; **prendre qn à ~** hold s/o responsible; **se mettre de la ~** join in

**partiel -ielle** *adj* partial, incomplete

**partir** *vi* depart, go away, leave, set off, start; come off (button, etc); go off (gun); disappear, come out (stain); **à ~ de** from, since; **faire ~** let off (gun, etc); start (engine); send (s/o) away

**partitif -ive** *adj gramm* partitive

**partition** *nf ar* partition; *mus* score

**partouse (partouze)** *nf sl* orgy

**partout** *adv* everywhere; **~ où** wherever; **trente ~** thirty all (tennis)

**parturiente** *nf* woman in labour

**parure** *nf* adornment, dress, toilette; set (jewellery, underclothes); string (pearls)

**parution** *nf* appearance, publication (book)

**parvenir** *vi* (96) attain, reach; succeed; arrive, come; manage; succeed in life

**parvenu -e** *n* parvenu, upstart; newly rich

**¹pas** *nm* pace, step, stride; footprint; step (stair); passage, strait; stage, step forward; manner of walking; *mech* pitch (propeller), thread (screw); **Pas-de-Calais** Straits of Dover; department of Pas-de-Calais; **~ de gymnastique** double; **~ de porte** key-money; **à**

**~ de loup** stealthily; **au ~** dead slow, at a walking pace; in step; **céder le ~** give way; **de ce ~** at once; **faire les cent ~** walk up and down; **faire les premiers ~** take the initiative; **faux ~** false step; blunder; *coll* black; **mauvais ~** tight corner; dangerous, exposed passage (mountaineering); **prendre le ~ sur** get in front of, precede; **salle des ~ perdus** circulating area; **se mettre au ~** get into step

**²pas** *adv* not; not any, no

**pascal** *adj* paschal

**passable** *adj* passable, fair, tolerable; **mention ~** pass (examination)

**passade** *nf* brief love affair

**passage** *nm* passage, path, way; crossing, passing over, passing through; journey by sea; fare for journey by sea; passage, extract (book); **à niveau** level-crossing; **~ clouté** pedestrian crossing; **~ protégé** sign on major road indicating that a minor road joining it is furnished with a halt sign; **~ souterrain** subway; **au ~** on the way through; **de ~** in transit, passing through

**passager -ère** *n* passenger; *adj* fleeting, momentary, transitory; migratory

**¹passant -e** *n* passer-by; *adj* busy (road, etc), well-trodden; **her** passant

**²passant** *nm* frog (on belt)

**passation** *nf leg* drawing up (act, contract); transmission (powers)

**¹passe** *nm* master-key

**²passe** *nf* passing; channel, passage, pass; thrust (fencing); pass (football); excess; **~ d'armes** passage of arms; *comm* **~ de caisse** contingency float; **être dans une bonne (mauvaise) ~** be in a strong (weak) position; **être en ~ de** be on the point of; **maison de ~** brothel; **mot de ~** password

**passé** *nm* past; *gramm* past; past life; *adj* past; faded; over-ripe; *prep* after, beyond

**passe-droit** *nm* illegitimate favour, improper promotion; *ar* injustice

**passement** *nm* thread of gold (silver, silk); braid

**passementer** *vt* trim with braid

**passe-montagne** *nm* balaclava helmet

**passe-partout** *nm invar* master-key; passe-partout, adhesive tape for framing; *adj* universally acceptable

**passe-passe** *nm invar* jugglery, juggling; **tour de ~** sleight of hand, conjuring-trick; *fig* cunning trick, deception

**passe-plat** *nm* serving-hatch

**passeport** *nm* passport

**passer** *vt* pass, cross, go over, go past; carry across, ferry; hand, pass; put on (coat, ring); go beyond, exceed, surpass; spend (time); ignore, omit, overlook; grant, pass, pass over; take (examination); survive; show (film); *mot* change (gear); connect with (on telephone); percolate, strain; *leg* conclude (agreement), enter into (contract); ~ **à tabac** beat up (*esp* of police); ~ **l'éponge sur** pass the sponge over, erase, forget, wipe out; ~ **un coup de fil à qn** ring s/o up; ~ **un mauvais quart d'heure** have a rough time, have a nasty moment; *coll* ~ **un savon à qn** tear a strip off s/o; *vi* pass, go past; call, go, pass through; undergo; pass away; die, pass away; become, be promoted; be accepted, be passed; come up (trial); fade (colour); omit, skip over; go down (food); filter through (liquid); **passe encore** very well, all right so far; *mot* ~ **en** change into (gear); ~ **outre** pass on; disregard, ignore, take no notice of; ~ **par** go through; ~ **pour** seem, be looked on as; ~ **sur** overlook; **passons!** never mind!, let's forget it!; **en passant** by the way; **en** ~ **par** put up with; *coll* **y** ~ die

**passereau** *nm* sparrow
**passerelle** *nf* foot-bridge; gangway (ship, aircraft); *naut* bridge
**passe-rose** *nf bot* hollyhock
**passe-temps** *nm invar* pastime
**passe-thé** *nm invar* (tea-)strainer
**passeur -euse** *n* ferryman, ferrywoman; smuggler (of persons across frontier)
**passible** *adj* liable; *theol* capable of suffering
**passif** *nm comm* liabilities; *gramm* passive; *adj* (*f* **-ive**) passive; *gramm* passive
**passion** *nf theol* Passion; passion; love
**passionnant** *adj* entrancing, fascinating, thrilling
**passionné** *adj* passionate, impassioned; avid, fervent
**passionnel -elle** *adj* concerning the passions; **crime** ~ crime of jealousy
**passionner** *vt* excite, interest powerfully; impassion, make passionate; **se** ~ become enthusiastic, show great interest
**passivité** *nf* passivity
**passoire** *nf cul* strainer
**pastel** *nm bot* woad; pastel shade; pastel; drawing in pastel
**pastèque** *nf* water-melon
**pasteur** *nm* shepherd; protestant clergyman, minister, pastor
**pasteurisation** *nf* pasteurization
**pasteuriser** *vt* pasteurize
**pastiche** *nm* pastiche; imitation, parody

**pasticher** *vt* pastiche; imitate, parody
**pastille** *nf* pastille, lozenge; lozenge (design)
**pastorale** *nf* pastoral play; pastoral letter
**pastorat** *nm* pastorate
**pat** *nm* + *adj invar* (chess) stalemate
**patachon** *nm* **mener une vie de** ~ lead a gay life
**patapouf** *nm coll* fat person, fat child; *interj* flop!, bump!
**pataquès** *nm* faulty liaison in pronunciation
**patate** *nf* sweet potato; *coll* potato; *coll* idiot
**patati, patata** *interj* **et patati! et patata!** and so on and so forth
**patatras** *interj* crash!
**pataud -e** *n* clumsy child; *nm* puppy with large paws; *adj* clumsy, loutish
**patauger** *vi* (3) flounder about, splash about (in mud); *fig* flounder; *coll* get bogged down
**pâte** *nf* paste; pulp (paper); *cul* pastry; ~s spaghetti, macaroni, etc; *arts* colours mixed on palette; ~ **de carton** papier-mâché; ~ **dentifrice** toothpaste; **être comme un coq en** ~ lie warm in bed; **mettre la main à la** ~ work; **vivre comme un coq en** ~ lead a very comfortable life
**pâté** *nm* pâté; pie; blot (ink); block of houses; sand-pie
**pâtée** *nf* mash (pigs, poultry), food for dogs, cats
¹**patelin** *nm coll* village, small town
²**patelin** *adj* fawning, smooth
**patenôtre** *nf ar* Lord's prayer; *iron* prayer, mumbling
**patent** *adj* evident, manifest, patent; *ar* open
**patentable** *adj* requiring a licence (trade, tradesman)
**patente** *nf* licence (to trade); *naut* ~ **de santé** bill of health
**patenté** *adj* licensed; *coll* qualified, recognized
**patenter** *vt* license
**pater** *nm invar* Lord's prayer
**patère** *nf* coat-peg, hat-peg
**paterne** *adj* benevolent, soft-spoken
**paternel -elle** *adj* paternal, fatherly
**paternité** *nf* paternity
**pâteux -euse** pasty; coated (tongue); dull, heavy
**pathétique** *nm* pathos; *adj* pathetic, touching
**pathogène** *adj med* pathogenic
**pathologie** *nf* pathology
**pathologique** *adj* pathological; abnormal, morbid
**pathologiste** *n* pathologist

**pathos** *nm* false pathos

**patibulaire** *adj* sinister (appearance); *ar* **fourches ~s** gallows

**patience** *nf* patience; long-suffering, resignation; constancy, courage; patience (cards); *mil* button-stick; **jeu de ~** jigsaw puzzle

**patient -e** *n* surgical case; patient; *adj* patient, long-suffering, persevering

**patienter** *vi* be patient

**patin** *nm* skate; flange (rail); runner (sledge); *mot* brake-shoe; **~ à roulettes** roller-skate

**patinage** *nm* skating; *mot* skidding

¹**patiner** *vi* skate; slide; skid

²**patiner** *vt* give a patina to

**patinette** *nf* scooter (child's toy)

**patineur -euse** *n* skater

**patinoire** *nf* skating-rink

**pâtir** *vi* suffer, be suffering

**pâtisserie** *nf* pastry; pastry-shop; pastry-making; **~s** cakes

**pâtissier -ière** *n* pastry-cook

**patois** *nm* patois, provincial dialect; *coll* jargon

**patouiller** *vt coll* grope, paw; *vi coll* flounder, splash about (in mud)

**patraque** *adj* off-colour, not well

**pâtre** *nm* herdsman, shepherd

**patriarche** *nm* patriarch

**patricien -ienne** *n* + *adj* patrician

**patrie** *nf* native land, fatherland, home country; nation

**patrimoine** *nm* patrimony

**patriote** *n* patriot; *adj* patriotic

**patriotique** *adj* patriotic

**patriotisme** *nm* patriotism

**patristique** *adj* patristic

¹**patron -onne** *n* patron, patroness, protector, protectress; patron saint; employer, *coll* boss; proprietor, landlord, landlady (bar, hotel); *med* clinical professor, consultant in teaching-hospital; **~ de thèse** supervisor (of thesis)

²**patron** *nm* pattern, model; stencil-plate

**patronage** *nm* patronage, support; benevolent society; youth organization; **comité de ~** list of patrons; committee running benevolent society

**patronal** *adj* pertaining to a patron-saint; pertaining to employers

**patronat** *nm* employers, body of employers

**patronner** *vt* be a patron of, patronize, protect, support

**patronnesse** *nf* + *adj* patroness; **dame ~** patroness

**patronyme** *nm* patronymic, surname

**patronymique** *adj* patronymic

**patrouille** *nf* patrol; *aer* **~ de chasse** fighter patrol

**patrouiller** *vi* patrol

**patrouilleur** *nm* member of a patrol; *aer* reconnaissance aircraft; *naut* patrol-ship, corvette

**patte** *nf* paw, leg, foot (animals, birds); *coll* leg (human), hand (human); flap (pocket); tab, strap; clamp; fluke (anchor); **~s de mouche** scrawl; **à quatre ~s** on all fours; **avoir de la ~** be skilful with one's hands; *coll* **graisser la ~** tip, bribe; *coll* **retomber sur ses ~s** fall on one's feet; **tenir qn sous sa ~** have a hold on s/o; **tirer dans les ~s de qn** cause s/o difficulties

**patte-d'oie** *nf* (*pl* **pattes-d'oie**) crow's-foot; crossroads; *bot* goose-foot

**pâturage** *nm* pasture, grazing; right of pasture

**pâture** *nf* fodder, food (animals); *fig* pabulum; pasture

**paume** *nf* palm; royal tennis, real tennis

**paumé** *adj coll* bewildered, lost; *sl* destitute, poor

**paumelle** *nf* sail-maker's palm; door-hinge

**paumer** *vt sl* lose; **se faire ~** get caught, get pinched

**paupérisme** *nm* pauperism

**paupière** *nf* eyelid

**paupiette** *nf cul* (meat-)olive

**pause** *nf* pause, stop; half-time (football, etc); rest

**pauvre** *n* poor person, pauper; beggar; *adj* poor, needy; unfortunate, wretched

**pauvresse** *nf* poor woman

**pauvret -ette** *adj* poor little

**pauvreté** *nf* poverty; humbleness; shabbiness; banality

**pavage** *nm* paving; pavement

**pavaner (se)** *v refl* strut about

**pavé** *nm* paving-stone; pavement; paved road; (stone) floor; block, chunk; long article; big book; **battre le ~** loaf about; **tenir le haut du ~** keep the best company

**paver** *vt* pave

**pavillon** *nm* detached house, lodge, villa; wing of building; horn (gramophone); bell (trumpet, etc); *naut* flag; *ar mil* pavilion, tent; **baisser ~ devant qn** yield to s/o; *naut* **battre ~ français** fly the French flag

**pavois** *nm hist mil* shield; *naut* bulwark; *naut* flags; *naut* **hisser le grand ~** dress ship overall; **hisser sur le ~** give power to, extol; *naut* **petit ~** recognition flags

**pavoisement** *nm naut* dressing ship; decking with flags

**pavoiser** *vt naut* dress ship; deck with flags, put out (flags); decorate

**pavot** *nm* poppy

**payant -e** *n* payer; *adj* paying; charged for; lucrative

**paye, paie** *nf* pay, wages; payment

**payement** *nm see* **paiement**

**payer** *vt* (7) pay, remunerate; reward; ~ **d'audace** take a risk; ~ **de sa personne** make an effort oneself, take a share in the risk; ~ **les pots cassés** repair the damage; ~ **qn de la même monnaie** pay s/o back in his own coin; ~ **qn de paroles** pay s/o with fine words; ~ **qn de retour** give tit for tat; ~ **rubis sur l'ongle** pay cash on the nail; **ça ne paie pas de mine** it's nothing to look at; **être payé pour savoir** learn to one's cost; **je suis payé pour savoir** I have good reason to know; **qui casse les verres les paie** you must pay for what you damage; **se** ~ pay oneself; buy for oneself; **se** ~ **de mots** be satisfied with mere words; *coll* **se** ~ **la tête de qn** pull s/o's leg

**payeur -euse** *n* payer

**¹pays** *nm* country, land; native land; village, small town; **être en** ~ **de connaissance** be among friends; **mal du** ~ homesickness; **voir du** ~ travel around, get about

**²pays, payse** *n coll* fellow-countryman, fellow-countrywoman

**paysage** *nm* landscape, scenery; *arts* landscape (painting)

**paysagiste** *n* landscape painter; landscape gardener

**paysan -anne** *n* peasant; farmer; *adj* peasant, rustic

**paysannat** *nm* peasantry, peasant clan

**paysannerie** *nf* peasantry; *ar* status of being a peasant; *lit* rustic novel

**Pays-Bas** *nmpl* Netherlands

**péage** *nm* toll; toll-gate; **autoroute à** ~ motorway with toll

**péager** *nm* toll collector

**peau** *nf* skin; fur; hide; peel; skin; coating, film; *sl* bag, tart; *coll* ~ **d'âne** diploma, parchment; *vulg* ~ **de vache** swine, bastard; **à fleur de** ~ superficial; *coll* **attraper qn par la** ~ **du cou (des fesses)** stop s/o at the last moment; *coll* **avoir qn dans la** ~ be infatuated with s/o; *theat* **entrer dans la** ~ **d'un personnage** get right into a part; *coll* **faire la** ~ **à qn** get s/o; **faire** ~ **neuve** cast its skin (snake); *fig* turn over a new leaf; *coll* **j'aurai sa** ~ I'll get him; *coll* **se faire crever la** ~ get oneself killed

**Peau-Rouge** *n* (*pl* **Peaux-Rouges**) Red Indian

**peausserie** *nf* skin-dressing; dressed skin

**pécari** *nm zool* peccary

**peccadille** *nf* peccadillo

**¹pêche** *nf* peach; *sl* slap

**²pêche** *nf* fishing; fishery; *leg* fishing rights; catch (of fish); **grande** ~ deep-sea fishing; **la** ~ **miraculeuse** the miraculous draught of fishes

**péché** *nm* sin, transgression; ~ **mignon** besetting sin

**pécher** *vi* (6) sin; offend

**¹pêcher** *nm* peach-tree

**²pêcher** *vt* fish for; catch (a fish); *coll* find, dig out

**pécheresse** *nf* sinner

**pêcherie** *nf* fishery

**pécheur** *nm* sinner

**pêcheur -euse** *n* fisherman, fisherwoman; *adj* fishing

**pécore** *nf coll* silly girl, stupid bitch; *ar* animal

**pectoral** *adj* pectoral; **sirop** ~ cough mixture

**pectoraux** *nmpl* pectoral muscles; cough lozenges

**pécule** *nm* nest-egg, savings; earnings (convict); gratuity (soldier)

**pécuniaire** *adj* pecuniary

**pédagogie** *nf* pedagogy, pedagogics

**pédagogique** *adj* pedagogic(al)

**pédale** *nf* pedal; *sl* pederast, queer; queer milieu; *sl* **perdre les** ~ **s** get all mixed up

**pédaler** *vi* pedal; *sl* walk fast, run; ~ **en danseuse** ride bicycle standing on the pedals

**pédaleur -euse** *n* cyclist

**pédalier** *nm* pedal-board, pedals (organ); crank gear (bicycle)

**pédalo** *nm* pedal-craft, pedalo

**pédant -e** *n* pedant; *adj* pedantic

**pédanterie** *nf* pedantry; pedantic action, pedantic phrase

**pédantisme** *nm* pedantry

**pédéraste** *nm* pederast, homosexual; *coll* queer

**pédérastie** *nf* pederasty, homosexuality

**pédestre** *adj* pedestrian, on foot

**pédiatre** *n* paediatrician, paediatrist

**pédiatrie** *nf* paediatrics

**pédicure** *n* chiropodist

**pedzouille** *n coll* ignorant provincial, rustic

**pégase** *nm* flying-fish

**pègre** *nf* crooks, underworld

**peignage** *nm* carding, combing (wool)

**peigne** *nm* comb; card (wool); *zool* pecten, scallop

**peigné** *nm* worsted; *adj* combed; carded (wool); affected (style), finicky; excessively groomed

**peignée** *nf* cardful (wool); *coll* thrashing

**peigner** *vt* comb; card (wool); **se** ~ comb one's hair; *coll* fight, have a set-to

**peignoir** *nm* lady's dressing-gown; bathing-wrap

**peinard** *adj sl* peaceful, quiet, sly

**peindre** *vt* (55) paint, coat with paint; paint, portray; **se ~** make oneself up; describe oneself; *fig* appear

**peine** *nf* penalty, punishment; affliction, distress, pain, sorrow; effort, work, trouble, difficulty; **à ~** barely, hardly, scarcely; **comme une âme en ~** alone and sadly; **donnez-vous la ~ d'entrer** be so good as to come in; **en être pour sa ~** have wasted one's time and trouble; **être en ~ de qn** be worried about s/o; **faire de la ~ à qn** grieve s/o, hurt s/o; **homme de ~** labourer; **pour votre ~** this is for you (in giving a tip); **purger sa ~** serve one's sentence; **sous ~ d'amende** under pain of a fine; **valoir la ~** be worth the trouble

**peiner** *vt* distress, grieve, pain, vex; *vi* drudge, labour, toil

**peintre** *n* painter; **~ décorateur** decorator; *theat* designer; **~ en bâtiment(s)** house-painter; **artiste ~** artist

**peinture** *nf* painting; picture; paint, colour; *lit* **~ de mœurs** portrayal of manners; **je ne peux pas le voir en ~** I can't stand him; *coll* **un vrai pot de ~** a girl with too much make-up on

**peinturer** *vt* apply a coat of paint to; paint clumsily

**peinturlurer** *vt coll* daub, paint badly in screaming colours

**péjoratif -ive** *adj* pejorative

¹**pékin** *nm* pekin (fabric)

²**pékin** *nm coll mil* civilian, civvy; **s'habiller en ~** be in civilian clothes

**pelade** *nf med* alopecia, pelade

**pelage** *nm* coat, fur, wool (animal)

**pélagique** *adj zool* pelagian, pelagic

**pelé -e** *n* bald-head; *coll* **il n'y avait que quatre ~s et un tondu** there were very few people; *adj* bald, bare, hairless

**pêle-mêle** *nm invar + adv* pell-mell

**peler** *vt* (5) peel; *vi* peel, peel off

**pèlerin -e** *n* pilgrim

**pèlerinage** *nm* pilgrimage

**pèlerine** *nf* (woman's) mantle, cape; cape with hood

**pellagre** *nf med* pellagra

**pelle** *nf* scoop, shovel; blade (oar); spade (children's); **~ mécanique** mechanical shovel; *coll* **ramasser une ~** fall; fail; **remuer l'argent à la ~** be very rich, be rolling in it

**pelletée** *nf* shovelful

**pelleter** *vt* (5) shovel, turn with a shovel

**pelleterie** *nf* pelt; preparation of furs; fur-trade

**pelleteuse** *nf* mechanical shovel

**pelletier -ière** *n* fur-trader; furrier

**pelliculaire** *adj* pellicular

**pellicule** *nf* pellicle; skin (milk); film; **~s** dandruff

**pelliculeux -euse** *adj* scurfy

**pellucide** *adj* pellucid, crystal clear, limpid

**pelotage** *nm coll* groping, pawing

**pelote** *nf* ball (string, wool); pincushion; ball used in pelota; **~ basque** game of pelota; **avoir les nerfs en ~** be on edge; *coll mil* **faire la ~** be in defaulter's squad; *coll* **faire sa ~** make one's pile

**peloter** *vt coll* grope, paw

**peloton** *nm* ball (string, wool); *mil* squad, platoon; main body of runners in a race (*esp* cycling); **~ d'exécution** firing-squad

**pelotonner** *vt* wind into a ball (string, wool); **se ~** curl oneself up, snuggle close; cluster together

**pelouse** *nf* lawn, plot of grass; public enclosure (racecourse)

**peluche** *nf* plush; speck of dust, piece of fluff

**pelucher, plucher** *vi* become fluffy, shed fluff

**pelucheux -euse, plucheux -euse** *adj* shaggy, fluffy

**pelure** *nf* peel, skin (fruit); paring (vegetable); *coll* piece of clothing, *esp* overcoat; **~ d'oignon** onion skin; name of reddish-brown wine; **papier ~** typing paper, flimsy

**pelvien -ienne** *adj anat* pelvic

**pénal** *adj* penal; *leg* **clause ~e** penalty clause

**pénalisation** *nf* penalization; free kick, penalty (football)

**pénaliser** *vt* penalize (games); *leg* inflict a penalty on

**pénalité** *nf* penalty

**pénates** *nmpl fig* home

**penaud** *adj* crestfallen, shamefaced

**penchant** *nm* inclination, propensity, tendency; affection; *ar* slope

**penché** *adj* leaning; stooping

**pencher** *vt* bend, incline, tilt; *vi* lean; slope downwards; incline towards; *naut* list; **se ~** bend, incline, stoop; **se ~ sur** interest oneself in, examine closely

**pendable** *adj* **cas ~** blameworthy action; **tour ~** dirty trick

**pendaison** *nf* hanging

**pendant** *nm* pendant, ear-drop; counterpart, match; *adj* hanging, pendant; *leg* pending; *prep* during; **~ que** while

**pendard -e** *n ar* rascal, rogue; hussy

**pendeloque** *nf* pendant; ear-drop

**pendentif** *nm archi* pendentive; pendant

**penderie** *nf* hanging-cupboard

# pendiller

**pendiller** *vi* dangle

**pendre** *vt* hang; hang up; *vi* hang, hang down; **se ~ à** hang on to, cling to

**pendu -e** *n* one who has been hanged; *adj* hanging, hung; **~ à** hanging from; **être ~ à** be stuck to

¹**pendule** *nm* pendulum; **~ de sourcier** water-diviner's rod

²**pendule** *nf* clock

**pendulette** *nf* small clock, travelling-clock

**pêne** *nm* bolt, latch

**pénétrabilité** *nf* penetrability

**pénétrable** *adj* penetrable; comprehensible

**pénétrant** *adj* penetrating, piercing, sharp; clear, perspicacious, profound, searching

**pénétration** *nf* penetration; acumen, insight, perspicacity

**pénétrer** *vt* (6) penetrate, pass through, traverse; impregnate, touch; comprehend; *vi* enter, get in; **~ dans** enter into; **faire ~** inculcate; **se ~ de** become imbued with, become impregnated with

**pénible** *adj* arduous, hard, laborious; distressing, painful, sad

**péniblement** *adv* with difficulty; with pain; barely, just

**péniche** *nf* barge, canal-boat, lighter; *ar* shallop

**pénicilline** *nf* penicillin

**péninsulaire** *adj* peninsular

**péninsule** *nf* peninsula

**pénitence** *nf* penitence, repentance; penance; punishment; forfeit; **mettre un enfant en ~** punish a child, put a child in the corner

**pénitencier** *nm* penitentiary

**pénitent -e** *n* + *adj* penitent

**pénitentiaire** *adj* penitentiary; **colonie ~** borstal

**pénitentiel -ielle** *adj* penitential

**penne** *nf* quill-feather; feather of arrow; *naut* peak

**pénombre** *nf* penumbra; half-light

**pensant** *adj* thinking; **bien ~** conventional, right-minded; **mal ~** unorthodox, subversive

¹**pensée** *nf* thought; point of view, standpoint; idea; aphorism, maxim

²**pensée** *nf bot* pansy

**penser** *vt* consider, think; admit, believe, imagine; presume, suppose; suspect; intend to, mean to; conceive; *vi* think, reflect; speculate, reason; **~ à** apply one's mind to, think about; be interested in, be concerned for; remember to

**penseur** *nm* thinker

**pensif -ive** *adj* thoughtful; meditative, preoccupied

**pension** *nf* pension, allowance; payment for board (and lodging); boarding-house; boarding-school; **~ de retraite** retirement pension; **~ d'un élève** boarding-school fees; **~ reversible** widow's pension; **~ viagère** annuity; **prendre ~** board; **prendre qn en ~** take in a lodger

**pensionnaire** *n* boarder, resident, inmate, lodger; *theat* actor (actress) at the Comédie Française; **prendre des ~s** take in lodgers

**pensionnat** *nm* boarding-school; boarders

**pensionner** *vt* pension

**pensum** *nm* imposition (school); boring task

**pentagone** *nm* pentagon; *adj* pentagonal

**pentamètre** *nm* pentameter

**Pentateuque** *nm* Pentateuch

**pente** *nf* gradient, incline, slope; inclination, propensity; **en ~** sloping; **être sur une mauvaise ~** be on a slippery slope

**Pentecôte** *nf* Whitsun, Whitsuntide

**pénultième** *adj* penultimate

**pénurie** *nf* penury, poverty; lack, shortage

**pépé** *nm coll* grandpa

**pépée** *nf sl* girl, young woman

**pépère** *nm coll* grandpa; *coll* quiet old fellow; *adj sl* big; pleasant; restful

**pépètes** *nfpl sl* money

**pépie** *nf vet* pip; **avoir la ~** be very thirsty

**pépier** *vi* chirp, tweet

¹**pépin** *nm* pip, stone; hitch, snag

²**pépin** *nm coll* umbrella

**pépinière** *nf* seed-bed, nursery; *fig* nursery, hotbed

**pépiniériste** *n* nurseryman, nurserywoman

**pépite** *nf* nugget of gold

**pepsine** *nf physiol* pepsin

**peptique** *adj physiol* peptic

**péquenaud -e** *n*, **péquenot** *nm sl* bumpkin, yokel

**perçage** *nm* boring, drilling, piercing

**perçant** *adj* keen, penetrating, piercing, sharp; high-pitched, shrill

**perce** *nf* borer, drill; *mus* hole (in wind instrument); **mettre en ~** broach (cask)

**percée** *nf* clearing, cutting, glade; *mil* breakthrough; opening (football)

**percement** *nm* boring; tunnelling

**perce-neige** *nm or f invar* snowdrop

**perce-oreille** *nm* earwig

**perce-pierre** *nf* saxifrage

¹**percepteur** *nm* tax-collector

²**percepteur -trice** *adj* discerning, perceiving

224

**perceptible** *adj* perceptible; collectable (tax)

**perceptif -ive** *adj* perceptive

**perception** *nf* perception; collection of taxes; tax-office; post of tax-collector

**percer** *vt* (4) bore, pierce; broach (cask); cut, perforate; soak through; penetrate, understand; *ar* stab; ~ **à jour** discover (secret, something hidden); *vi* break through; succeed, become famous; burst (abscess)

**perceur -euse** *n* borer, driller; *nf* drilling-machine

**percevable** *adj* perceivable; collectable, leviable (tax)

**percevoir** *vt* discern, distinguish, perceive; collect, levy

**¹perche** *nf zool* perch

**²perche** *nf* pole; *rad* microphone boom; *coll* tall thin person, maypole; *ar* perch (measure); **tendre la ~ à qn** help s/o get out of a fix

**percher** *vt coll* place high up; *vi* perch; *coll* live on upper floor; **se ~** perch

**percheron** *nm* cart-horse, percheron; *adj* (*f* **-onne**) from the Perche region

**perchoir** *nm* perch, roost

**perclus** *adj med* anchylotic; stiff; crippled; *fig* paralysed

**perçoir** *nm mech* borer, drill; awl, gimlet; punch

**percolateur** *nm* percolator

**percutant** *adj* percussive; shattering; exploding on impact; *fig* striking; energetic

**percuter** *vt* strike, tap; *med* sound; *vi* **~ contre** strike, crash into

**percuteur** *nm* hammer (gun)

**perdable** *adj* losable

**perdant -e** *n* loser; *nm* ebb-tide; *adj* losing

**perdition** *nf* perdition; *naut* **navire en ~** ship in distress

**perdre** *vt* lose; destroy, dishonour; harm; spoil; waste; **~ au change** lose by the exchange; **~ de vue** lose sight of, lose touch with; *coll* **~ le nord** lose one's bearings; *coll* **~ les pédales** get mixed up; **~ pied** lose one's footing; *naut* **~ terre** lose sight of land; **se ~** lose oneself; harm oneself; be wasted; disappear; be mixed; *vi* leak; lose, deteriorate, lose value

**perdreau** *nm* young partridge

**perdrix** *nf* partridge; **~ des neiges** ptarmigan

**perdu** *adj* lost; depraved; ruined; wasted; terminally ill; absorbed; stray (bullet); **à corps ~** recklessly; **moments ~s** leisure time

**père** *nm* father; **~ de famille** head of a family; *theat* **~ noble** heavy (father);

**le ~ X** old X

**péremptoire** *adj* peremptory, unanswerable

**pérenne** *adj* perennial

**pérennité** *nf* eternity, permanence

**perfectibilité** *nf* perfectibility

**perfectionnement** *nm* perfecting, improving

**perfectionner** *vt* perfect, improve; **se ~** improve; improve one's knowledge

**perfectionniste** *n* perfectionist

**perfide** *adj* perfidious, treacherous

**perfidie** *nf* perfidy, perfidiousness, treachery; treacherous act

**perforage** *nm* perforating, boring, drilling

**perforant** *adj* perforating

**perforateur** *nm mech* drill; punch; workman operating drill; *adj* (*f* **-trice**) boring, drilling; punching

**perforatrice** *nf mech* drilling-machine

**perforer** *vt* bore, drill; punch

**perforeuse** *nf* perforating-machine

**périanthe** *nm bot* perianth

**péricarde** *nm anat* pericardium

**péricarpe** *nm bot* pericarp

**péricliter** *vi* be in danger; be shaky, totter

**péril** *nm* peril, danger; hazard, risk; **faire qch à ses risques et ~s** do sth at one's own risk

**périlleux -euse** *adj* perilous; hazardous; **saut ~** somersault

**périmé** *adj* out-of-date; expired, lapsed

**périmer (se)** *v refl* lapse; lose validity

**périmètre** *nm* perimeter; area

**périnée** *nm anat* perineum

**¹période** *nf* period; epoch, era

**²période** *nm lit* **au plus haut ~ (au dernier ~)** at the highest point, at the height

**périodique** *nm* periodical; *adj* periodical, intermittent, recurring; *math* **fraction ~** recurring decimal

**péripatéticien -ienne** *n + adj* peripatetic; *nf coll* prostitute, tart

**péripatétique** *adj* peripatetic

**péripétie** *nf lit* peripeteia; vicissitude; **~ s** ups and downs

**périphérie** *nf* periphery, circumference; outskirts

**périphérique** *adj* peripheral; **boulevard ~** ring-road

**périphrase** *nf* periphrasis

**périphrastique** *adj* periphrastic

**périple** *nm* circumnavigation; long journey

**périr** *vi* perish, die; *fig* disappear; **faire ~** kill

**périscopique** *adj* periscopic

**périssable** *adj* perishable

**périssoire** *nf* canoe

**péritoine**

**péritoine** *nm anat* peritoneum
**péritonite** *nf med* peritonitis
**perle** *nf* pearl; *fig* pearl, treasure; *coll* blunder, howler; bead (amber, glass, etc)
**perlé** *adj* pearly; beaded; carefully executed, perfectly done; **grève ~e** go-slow
**perler** *vt* execute with care, perform perfectly; *vi* form beads (sweat, tears)
**permanence** *nf* permanence, stability; twenty-four-hour service; office always open; committee-room
**permanent** *adj* permanent, constant, stable; continuous
**permanente** *nf* permanent wave
**perméabilité** *nf* permeability
**permettre** *vt* (60) permit, allow; put up with, tolerate; **~ à** allow; enable; **permettez!** allow me!; excuse me!; **vous permettez?** may I?; *coll* **est-il permis d'être si stupide?** can anyone really be such a clot?
**permis** *nm* authorization, permission; pass; licence; **~ de séjour** certificate of registration (foreigner); **passer son ~** pass one's driving test
**permission** *nf* permission, authorization; leave
**permissionnaire** *nm* serviceman on leave
**permutation** *nf* posting, transferring; permutation
**permuter** *vt* change over, permutate; *vi* exchange posts
**pernicieux -ieuse** *adj* pernicious, harmful; corrupting
**péroné** *nm anat* fibula
**péronnelle** *nf coll* silly talkative girl
**péroraison** *nf* peroration
**pérorer** *vi* perorate; speechify
**peroxyde** *nm* peroxide
**perpendiculaire** *nf + adj* perpendicular, upright
**perpendicularité** *nf* perpendicularity
**perpète, perpette (à)** *adv phr sl* for ever, for life
**perpétrer** *vt* (6) perpetrate
**perpétuel -uelle** *adj* perpetual, everlasting; endless, incessant
**perpétuer** *vt* perpetuate; **se ~** continue, endure, become established
**perpétuité** *nf* perpetuity; **à ~** for ever, for life
**perplexe** *adj* perplexed, puzzled
**perplexité** *nf* perplexity, indecision
**perquisition** *nf leg* search, perquisition; investigation
**perquisitionner** *vi leg* conduct a search
**perroquet** *nm* parrot; *naut* topgallant
**perruche** *nf* budgerigar; female parrot; *naut* mizzen topgallant; *coll* talkative woman

**perruque** *nf* wig; old fogey, reactionary
**perruquier** *nm* wig-maker
**pers** *adj m* bluish-green, sea-green
**Persan -e** *n* Persian
**persan** *nm* Persian language; *adj* Persian
**Perse** *nf* Persia
**¹perse** *adj* Persian
**²perse** *nf* chintz
**persécuter** *vt* persecute; importune, pester
**persécuteur -trice** *n* persecutor; *adj* persecuting
**persévérant** *adj* persevering, persisting
**persévérer** *vi* (6) persevere, persist
**persienne** *nf* slatted shutter, persienne
**persifler** *vt* banter, mock, rally
**persifleur -euse** *n* banterer, mocker; *adj* mocking
**persil** *nm* parsley
**persillade** *nf* parsley sauce (*incl* garlic, vinegar); cold sliced beef with parsley sauce
**persillé** *adj* with chopped parsley; blue-veined (cheese); marbled (meat)
**persistance** *nf* persistence, determination; continuance
**persistant** *adj* persistent; continuing
**persister** *vi* persist; continue
**personnage** *nm* personage, dignitary; character, role (novel, play); figure (picture); *pej* fellow
**personnaliser** *vt* personalize
**personnalité** *nf* personality, individuality; personage, dignitary
**¹personne** *nf* person, individual; personality; personal appearance; *gramm* person
**²personne** *pron invar* anyone, anybody; **~ ne le sait** no one knows; **connaissez-vous ~ qui puisse venir?** do you know anyone who can come?; **mieux que ~** better than anyone; **ne ... ~** no one, nobody; **il n'y a ~** there is no one; **qui est là? Personne** who is there? No one
**personnel** *nm* personnel, staff; *mil* complement; *adj* (*f* **-elle**) personal, individual, private
**personnifier** *vt* personify, incarnate
**perspectif -ive** *adj* perspective
**perspective** *nf* perspective, point of view; outlook, view
**perspicace** *adj* perspicacious
**perspicacité** *nf* perspicacity
**persuader** *vt* persuade, convince; **~ (à) qn de** induce s/o to; **se ~** become convinced, decide
**persuasif -ive** *adj* persuasive, convincing
**persuasion** *nf* persuasion; belief, conviction
**perte** *nf* loss; wastage, waste; destruction, ruin; **~s** *med* excessive menstrual

226

flow; ~ **sèche** dead loss; **à ~ de vue** further than the eye can see; **en pure ~** to no purpose

**pertinemment** *adv* pertinently; **savoir ~** be precisely informed

**pertuis** *nm* sluice; *geog* narrows, strait; *ar* hole

**pertuisane** *nf hist* partisan, halberd

**perturbateur -trice** *n* disturber; *adj* disturbing

**perturbation** *nf* perturbation, agitation; disturbance (weather)

**pervenche** *nf bot* periwinkle

**pervers -e** *n + adj* perverse, depraved, vicious (person)

**perversité** *nf* perversity

**pervertir** *vt* pervert, corrupt; **se ~** become depraved, degenerate

**pesage** *nm* weighing; weighing-in (jockey); paddock (race-course)

**pesamment** *adv* heavily; slowly, with difficulty

**pesant** *adj* heavy, weighty; ponderous, sluggish

**pesanteur** *nf* weight, heaviness; *phys* gravity; dullness, sluggishness

**pèse-bébé** *nm* scales for weighing baby

**pesée** *nf* weighing; amount weighed at one time; leverage

**pèse-lettre** *nm* letter-balance

**peser** *vt* (6) weigh; *vi* be heavy; weigh; ~ **à** be hard to bear; importune, tire; ~ **sur** weigh on; press (lever, handle); **se ~** weigh oneself

**peseur -euse** *n* weigher; ~ **juré** inspector of weights and measures

**pessaire** *nm* pessary

**pessimisme** *nm* pessimism

**pessimiste** *n* pessimist; *adj* pessimistic

**peste** *nf* plague, pestilence; infernal nuisance; *coll* **c'est une petite ~** she's a little bitch

**pester** *vi* curse, storm, vociferate

**pesteux -euse** *adj* plague-infected

**pestiféré -e** *n* victim of plague; *adj* plague-infected, plague-ridden

**pestilence** *nf* pestilence; putrid smell, stink

**pestilentiel -ielle** *adj* pestilential; stinking

**pet** *nm* fart; *sl* scandal, row; *coll* **ça ne vaut pas un ~ (de lapin)** it's of no importance at all; **lâcher un ~** fart

**pétale** *nm* petal

**pétanque** *nf* variant of French bowls (played in South)

**pétarade** *nf* series of bangs; series of farts (donkey, horse); crackling (rifle fire)

**pétarader** *vi* make series of bangs; back-fire; let off farts (donkey, horse); crackle (rifles)

**pétard** *nm* cracker, banger; blast, shot (mine, quarry); detonator (railway); *coll* din, row; *sl* revolver; *sl* arse

**pétaudière** *nf* meeting out of control, bear-garden

**pet-de-nonne** *nm* (*pl* **pets-de-nonne**) *cul* kind of small cream puff

**pet-en-l'air** *nm invar coll* short jacket, bum-freezer

**péter** *vi* (6) fart; break; explode, burst; *coll* ~ **dans la soie** have very good clothes; ~ **du feu** be full of energy; *coll* ~ **plus haut que le cul** be very pretentious

**pètesec, pète-sec** *n + adj invar* disagreeably bossy (person)

**pétillant** *adj* sparkling; crackling

**pétillement** *nm* sparkling; crackling

**pétiller** *vi* bubble; sparkle; flash

**petit -e** *n* child; young animal, young bird; *nf* girl; *adj* little, small; insignificant, petty, slight, unimportant; mean, minor, paltry; small-minded; *rad* short (wave); *coll* nice little, precious; ~ **coin (endroit)** lavatory; *mil* ~ **e tenue** undress uniform; **en ~ comité** in a small group; **mon ~ Michel** dear Michael (affection); **mon ~ monsieur** my dear good sir; *adv* ~ **à ~** little by little; **en ~** in a small way

**petite-fille** *nf* (*pl* **petites-filles**) granddaughter

**petitement** *adv* meanly; humbly

**petite-nièce** *nf* (*pl* **petites-nièces**) greatniece

**petitesse** *nf* littleness; pettiness; narrowmindedness

**petit-fils** *nm* (*pl* **petits-fils**) grandson

**petit-gris** *nm* (*pl* **petits-gris**) *zool* kind of Siberian grey squirrel; fur of this grey squirrel; kind of snail

**pétition** *nf* request, petition

**petit-lait** *nm* whey

**petit-maître** *nm* (*pl* **petits-maîtres**) *hist* coxcomb, fop

**petit-nègre** *nm* incorrect (colonial) French ( = pidgin English)

**petit-neveu** *nm* (*pl* **petits-neveux**) greatnephew

**petits-enfants** *nmpl* grandchildren

**petit-suisse** *nm* (*pl* **petits-suisses**) small cream cheese

**pétoche** *nf sl* fear

**pétoire** *nf coll* (useless old) gun, pop-gun

**peton** *nm coll* little foot; tootsy-wootsy (child)

**pétrifier** *vt* petrify, turn into stone; *fig* freeze, paralyse; **se ~** turn into stone; become quite motionless

**pétrin** *nm* kneading-trough; *coll* mess, fix

**pétrir** *vt* knead; mould, shape; **pétri**

pétrissage

d'ignorance deeply ignorant; **pétri d'orgueil** consumed with pride
**pétrissage** *nm* kneading; moulding
**pétrisseur -euse** *n* kneader
**pétrochimie** *nf* petrochemistry
**pétrole** *nm* petroleum; paraffin; **bleu ~** blue-green
**pétrolette** *nf* light motorcycle
**pétrolier** *nm naut* tanker; oil-magnate; *adj* (*f* -**ière**) petrol (industry), oil (installations)
**pétrolifère** *adj* oil-bearing; **gisement ~** oil-field
**pétulance** *nf* ardour, liveliness
**pétulant** *adj* ardent, lively, sprightly
**peu** *nm* little, small quantity; **un ~** a little, a few, a bit; *adv* little, few, not enough; briefly; not very; **~ à ~** little by little; **~ de** a few, some; **~ s'en faut** very nearly; **avant ~** shortly; **de ~** narrowly; **depuis ~** lately, of late; **d'ici ~** a short time hence; **pour un ~** for two pins, for a little; **quelque ~** somewhat; **si ~ que** however little; **sous ~** shortly; **tant soit ~** just a little, the least bit
**peuh** *interj* pooh!
**peu ou prou** *adv phr see* **prou**
**peuplade** *nf* small tribe, small community
**peuple** *nm* people; nation; **bas ~** lower classes; **le ~** the people, the masses; **petit ~** humble people; *adj invar* plebeian, vulgar
**peuplement** *nm* peopling; stocking (with fish, game); afforestation
**peupler** *vt* people, populate; stock (fish, game); inhabit, throng; **se ~** become populous, fill with people
**peuplier** *nm* poplar
**peur** *nf* anguish, apprehension, fear, fright; **~ bleue** blue funk; **à faire ~** hideously; **avoir ~** be afraid; **de ~ de** for fear of; **de ~ que** lest; **en être quitte pour la ~** get off with a fright; **n'avoir pas ~ des mots** call things by their name, call a spade a spade
**peureux -euse** *adj* easily frightened, nervous, timid, timorous
**peut-être** *adv* maybe, perhaps, possibly
**pèze** *nm sl* money, dough
**phalange** *nf* phalanx; army, host; falange (Spain); finger-joint
**phalène** *nf or m* ent moth, phalena
**phallique** *adj* phallic
**phantasme** *nm see* **fantasme**
**pharamineux** *adj see* **faramineux**
**pharaon** *nm* Pharaoh; faro (card-game)
**phare** *nm* lighthouse; airport beacon; headlight; *rad* beacon; *aer* **~ d'atterrissage** landing light; *mot* **~s code** dipped headlights

**pharisien -ienne** *n* Pharisee
**pharmaceutique** *nf* pharmaceutics; *adj* pharmaceutic(al)
**pharmacie** *nf* pharmacy; chemist's shop, dispensary; medicine cupboard; contents of medicine cupboard; **~ de poche** first-aid kit
**pharmacien -ienne** *n* chemist
**pharmacologie** *nf* pharmacology
**pharmacopée** *nf* pharmacopoeia
**pharyngite** *nf* pharyngitis
**phase** *nf* phase; aspect, stage
**phénix** *nm* phoenix
**phénoménal** *adj* phenomenal; *coll* marvellous, terrific
**phénomène** *nm* phenomenon; marvel, prodigy; freak (monster); *coll* odd character, queer fish
**philanthrope** *n* philanthropist
**philanthropie** *nf* philanthropy
**philanthropique** *adj* philanthropic
**philatélie** *nf* philately
**philatélique** *adj* philatelic
**philatéliste** *n* philatelist
**philharmonie** *nf* local orchestra
**philharmonique** *adj* philharmonic
**philippique** *nf* philippic
**philistin** *nm + adj m* Philistine
**philistinisme** *nm* Philistinism
**philo** *nf coll* philosophy
**philologie** *nf* philology
**philologique** *adj* philological
**philologue** *n* philologist
**philosophale** *adj f* **pierre ~** philosopher's stone
**philosophe** *n* philosopher; thinker; *adj* philosophical; resigned, sensible, wise
**philosopher** *vi* philosophize
**philosophie** *nf* philosophy; one of the top forms in lycée
**philosophique** *adj* philosophic(al)
**phlébite** *nf med* phlebitis
**phlogistique** *nm* phlogiston
**phobie** *nf med* phobia; aversion, fear
**phonème** *nm* phoneme, phone
**phonémique** *adj* phonemic
**phonéticien -ienne** *n* phonetician
**phonétique** *nf* phonetics; *adj* phonetic
**phonique** *adj* phonic
**phonographe** *nm* gramophone; *obs* phonograph
**phonographique** *adj* phonographic
**phonologie** *nf* phonology
**phonothèque** *nf* sound archives
**phoque** *nm zool* seal
**phosphater** *vt* fertilize (soil) with phosphates
**phosphore** *nm* phosphorus
**phosphorer** *vi coll* study, swot
**phosphoreux -euse** *adj* phosphorous
**phosphure** *nm* phosphide
**photochimie** *nf* photochemistry

**photochimique** *adj* photochemical
**photocopie** *nf* photocopying; photostat
**photocopier** *vt* photocopy
**photo-électrique** *adj* photo-electric
**photogénique** *adj* photogenic
**photographe** *n* photographer
**photographie** *nf* photography; photograph
**photographier** *vt* photograph; reproduce with minute accuracy
**photographique** *adj* photographic
**photograveur** *nm* photo-engraver; block-maker
**photogravure** *nf* photo-engraving; photogravure (process, print)
**photomécanique** *adj* photomechanical
**photomètre** *nm* photometer
**photométrie** *nf* photometry
**photométrique** *adj* photometric
**photostoppeur** *nm* street photographer
**photosynthèse** *nf* photosynthesis
**photothèque** *nf* photographic archives
**phrase** *nf* sentence; *mus* phrase; **faire des ~ s** indulge in flowery language; **sans ~ s** without comment
**phraséologie** *nf* phraseology
**phraser** *vt mus* phrase
**phraseur -euse** *n* declaimer, flowery speaker
**phrénologie** *nf* phrenology
**phrénologiste** *n* phrenologist
**phrygien -ienne** *adj* Phrygian; **bonnet ~** Phrygian cap worn by revolutionaries in 1789; symbol of liberty
**phtisie** *nf med* phthisis; *ar* consumption, pulmonary consumption
**phtisique** *n + adj ar* consumptive
**phylactère** *nm* phylactery
**physicien -ienne** *n* physicist; *ar* natural philosopher
**physico-chimie** *nf* physical chemistry
**physico-chimique** *adj* physico-chemical
**physiognomonie** *nf ar* study of physiognomy
**physiologie** *nf* physiology
**physiologique** *adj* physiological
**physiologiste** *n* physiologist
**physionomie** *nf* physiognomy; face, physical features; expression; appearance, aspect
**physionomiste** *n* one who has a memory for faces; good judge of faces
**physique** *nm* physique, physical qualities; *nf* physics; *adj* physical
**piaf** *nm sl* sparrow
**piaffement** *nm* pawing the ground (horse); prancing, stamping
**piaffer** *vi* paw the ground (horse); prance, stamp
**piaillement** *nm* chirp, squawk (bird); squall, squeal
**piailler** *vi* chirp, squawk (bird); *coll* squall, squeal
**piailleur -euse** *n coll* child (person) given to squealing; *adj* chirping, squawking (bird)
**pianiste** *n* pianist
**piano** *adv mus* piano; *coll* gently
**pianoter** *vi* strum, play badly; rattle, tap
**piaule** *nf sl* room
**piauler** *vi* chirp; whimper
**¹pic** *nm* pick, pick-axe; peak; summit of mountain; *naut* peak; **à ~** sheer, vertical; *coll* at the right moment; **couler à ~** founder
**²pic** *nm* woodpecker
**pichenette** *nf* fillip
**pichet** *nm* jug, pitcher
**picoler** *vi sl* drink a lot, soak
**picorer** *vt* pick up (food) (bird); *vi* scratch about for food (of bird)
**picot** *nm* splinter (wood); pick-hammer; picot (needlework)
**picoté** *adj* pimpled, pock-marked
**picotement** *nm* prickling, tingling
**picoter** *vt* prick holes in, pit; peck; sting, cause (eyes) to smart
**picrique** *adj chem* picric
**pictural** *adj* to do with painting, pictorial
**picvert** *nm see* **pivert**
**¹pie** *nf* magpie
**²pie** *adj invar* piebald; **voiture ~** black and white police-car
**³pie** *adj f* pious
**pièce** *nf* fragment, piece; single piece, unit; head (cattle, game); coin; gun; certificate, document, papers; *theat* play; room; piece, part, patch; cask (wine); liquid measure of about forty-eight gallons; *her* ordinary; **~ à conviction** exhibit (criminal trial); **~ d'eau** ornamental lake, pond; **~ de musée** show-piece; **~ de rechange** spare part; **~ de terre** field, plot; **~ s justificatives** supporting documents; *cul* **~ montée** ornamental piece of confectionery; **deux ~ s** two-piece costume; two-roomed flat; **être tout d'une ~** be uncomplicated; be all in one piece; **faire ~ à qn** play a nasty trick on s/o; **inventé de toutes ~ s** completely untrue, totally fabricated; **six francs ~** six francs each; **travail aux ~ s (à la ~ )** piece-work
**piècette** *nf* small coin
**pied** *nm* foot; hoof; base, leg, stand; foothold; track (hunting); *hist* French unit of measurement = $12\frac{3}{4}$ inches; English foot; **~ de fer** cobbler's last; **à ~**, **à cheval et en voiture** in every possible way; **au petit ~** diminutive, pint-size; **au ~ levé** off the cuff, unprepared; **avoir le ~ marin** be a

**pied-bot**

good sailor (i.e. not seasick); *coll* **avoir
les ~ s nickelés** refuse to budge, be
lazy; *coll* **casser les ~ s** bother, be a
bloody nuisance; *coll* **comme un ~**
very badly; **coup de ~** kick; **coup de
~ de pénalité** penalty (football); **de
~ en cap** from tip to toe; **de ~ ferme**
with determination; **en ~** full-length
(portrait); **faire des ~ s et des mains**
use every possible means; **faire du ~ à
qn** give warning kick to s/o; play foot-
sie with s/o; **faire les ~ s à** teach, give
experience to; **fouler aux ~ s** trample
(underfoot); **lâcher ~** give ground;
**lever le ~** run off with the cash-box;
**marcher sur les ~ s de qn** treat s/o
without consideration; try to supplant
s/o; **mettre les ~ s dehors** go outside;
**mettre qn à ~** give s/o the sack;
**mettre qn au ~ du mur** call for a
straightforward answer from s/o; **ne
pas savoir sur quel ~ danser** be undecided, be uncertain what line to take;
**se lever du ~ gauche** get out of bed on
the wrong side; **y mettre les ~ s** set foot
there

**pied-bot** *nm see* **bot**
**pied-d'alouette** *nm* (*pl* **pieds-d'alouette**)
*bot* delphinium, larkspur
**pied-de-biche** *nm* (*pl* **pieds-de-biche**)
cabriole leg; kind of bell-pull or door
knocker; *mech* nail-claw; guide on
sewing-machine
**pied-de-poule** *nm* (*pl* **pieds-de-poule**)
+ *adj invar* broken check (cloth)
**piédestal** *nm* pedestal
**pied-noir** *nm* (*pl* **pieds-noirs**) *coll* French
colonist in Algeria
**piège** *nm* snare, trap; ambush, hidden
danger
**piéger** *vt* (6, 3) trap; arm (mine)
**pie-grièche** *nf* (*pl* **pies-grièches**) *orni*
shrike; *coll* harpy, shrew
**pierraille** *nf* rubble, small stones
**pierre** *nf* stone; rock; *med* stone; precious stone; **~ à aiguiser** whetstone; **~
à briquet** lighter-flint; **~ à fusil**
gun-flint; **~ bleue** washing blue; **~ de
taille** ashlar; **~ levée** raised stone
(druidical, etc); **apporter sa ~ à
l'édifice** contribute one's mite; **faire
d'une ~ deux coups** kill two birds with
one stone
**pierreries** *nfpl* jewels, precious stones
**pierreux -euse** *adj* stony; in stone; gritty
(pear)
**pierrot** *nm* sparrow; pierrot, clown
**piété** *nf* piety, devotion; affection, respect, tenderness
**piétinement** *nm* stamping, trampling;
sound of stamping crowd; marking
time, stagnation

**piétiner** *vt* stamp on, trample on; **~ un
cadavre** insult the memory of dead
person; *vi* stamp one's feet, mark time;
stamp along; *fig* make little or no progress
**piétisme** *nm hist* pietism
**piéton** *nm* + *adj* (*f* **-onne**) pedestrian
**piètre** *adj lit* mediocre, miserable,
wretched
¹**pieu** *nm* post, stake; *eng* pile
²**pieu** *nm sl* bed, kip
**pieuter** *vi sl* turn in, kip down
**pieuvre** *nf* octopus, devil-fish; *fig* limpet
**pieux -euse** *adj* devout, pious; *lit* devoted
**pif** *nm sl* big nose, nose, conk
**pifer, piffer** *vt sl* put up with, stand
**pige** *nf* measuring-rod; *sl* year (of age);
*coll* payment by the line (journalist); *sl*
**faire la ~ à** go one better than
**pigeon** *nm* pigeon; *coll* dupe; **~ ramier**
wood-pigeon; **~ voyageur** carrier
pigeon, homing pigeon
**pigeonneau** *nm* young pigeon
**pigeonner** *vt coll* dupe
**pigeonnier** *nm* pigeon-loft, dovecot
**piger** *vt* (3) *sl* cotton on to, understand;
pay; *ar* catch, get hold of
**pigmentaire** *adj* pigmentary
**pigmenté** *adj* pigmented
**pigne** *nf* pine-cone
**pignocher** *vi coll* peck at one's food;
paint with small finicky brush-strokes
¹**pignon** *nm* gable, gable-end; **avoir ~
sur rue** have a flourishing business situated in a good position; *ar* have a house
of one's own
²**pignon** *nm mech* pinion
³**pignon** *nm bot* pine-seed
**pignouf** *nm sl* uncouth bastard, lout
**pilastre** *nm* pilaster
¹**pile** *nf* heap, pile; pier (bridge); battery;
pile (atomic)
²**pile** *nf coll* thrashing; crushing defeat
³**pile** *nf* **~ ou face** heads or tails; **jouer à
~ ou face** toss up
⁴**pile** *adv coll* exactly; **ça tombe ~** just
what's wanted; **s'arrêter ~** stop dead
**piler** *vt* crush, grind, pound; *coll* thrash;
defeat
**pileux -euse** *adj* pilose, hairy
**pilier** *nm* column, pillar; *fig* support;
prop-forward (rugby football); **~ de
cabaret** s/o always to be found propping up the bar
**pillage** *nm* looting, pillage
**pillard -e** *n* looter, pillager; plagiarist; *adj*
looting, pillaging
**piller** *vt* loot, pillage; plagiarize
**pilleur -euse** *n* looter, pillager; plagiarist
**pilon** *nm* pestle; earth-rammer; steam-
hammer; *cul* drumstick; wooden leg;
**mettre un livre au ~** pulp a book

**pilonnage** *nm* crushing; heavy bombardment

**pilonner** *vt* crush; bombard heavily

**pilori** *nm* pillory; **mettre au ~** pillory, put in the pillory

**pilosité** *nf* pilosity, hairiness

**pilot** *nm eng* pile

**pilotage** *nm* piloting

**pilote** *nm* pilot; driver; pilot-fish; *adj* pilot, experimental, model

**piloter** *vt* pilot; drive; guide

**pilotis** *nm eng* piling

**pilou** *nm* flannelette

**pilule** *nf* pill

**pimbêche** *nf* uppish and disagreeable woman; *coll* affected bitch

**piment** *nm* capsicum, pimento; red pepper; *fig* seasoning, spice

**pimenter** *vt* season with red pepper; *fig* give spice to

**pimpant** *adj* smart, spruce

**pimprenelle** *nf bot* pimpernel

**pin** *nm* pine-tree

**pinacle** *nm archi* pinnacle; *fig* exalted position; **porter qn au ~** praise s/o to the skies

**pinard** *nm sl* wine

**pince** *nf* pincers, pliers, tongs; clip; *sl* hand; pleat, tuck; claw (crab, lobster); **~ à linge** clothes-peg; *sl* **aller à ~** s go on foot

**pincé** *adj* affected, constrained, prim; thin

**pinceau** *nm* (artist's) paint-brush; painting; technique of painter; beam (light); *sl* foot

**pincée** *nf* pinch

**pince-fesse(s)** *nm invar sl* cheap dance-hall

**pincement** *nm* pinching; *mus* plucking; pruning, topping; **~ au cœur** spasm of anguish

**pince-monseigneur** *nf* (*pl* **pinces-monseigneur**) (burglar's) jemmy

**pincer** *vt* (4) nip, pinch; *mus* pluck; pinch off; prune, top; *coll* catch, cop, nab; *coll* **ça pince** it's very cold; **en ~ pour qn** be in love with s/o

**pince-sans-rire** *n invar + adj* unsmilingly ironical (person)

**pincette** *nf* small pincers, tweezers; **~ s** fire-tongs; **il n'est pas à prendre avec des ~ s** he is filthy dirty; he is extremely bad-tempered

**pinçon** *nm* mark left by pinch

**pine** *nf vulg* penis, prick

**pinède** *nf* pine-wood

**pingouin** *nm* auk; penguin

**pingre** *n* miser; *adj* miserly

**pingrerie** *nf* miserliness

**pinot** *nm* kind of vine

**pinson** *nm* finch; **gai comme un ~** happy as a lark

**pintade** *nf* guinea-fowl

**pintadeau** *nm* young guinea-fowl

**pinte** *nf ar* (French) pint ( = $1\frac{3}{4}$ English pints); glass containing a pint; (English) pint

**pinter** *vi sl* drink hard, soak

**piochage** *nm* digging; *fig* hard study, swotting

**pioche** *nf* pick, pickaxe; mattock; *coll* **une tête de ~** a very obstinate person

**piocher** *vt* dig up; *coll* swot at; *vi coll* swot

**piocheur** *nm* navvy; *n* (*f* **-euse**) *coll* swot; hard worker

**piocheuse** *nf* scarifier

**piolet** *nm* ice-axe

**pion** *nm* pawn (chess); piece (draughts); *coll* junior master

**pioncer** *vi* (4) *sl* sleep, snooze

**pionne** *nf* junior mistress

**pionnier** *nm* pioneer

**pioupiou** *nm ar* young infantryman, tommy

**pipe** *nf* pipe; large cask; *ar* reed pipe, tube; pipeful; *sl* **casser sa ~** die; *sl* **par tête de ~** per person; **se fendre la ~** burst with laughter

**pipeau** *nm* reed-pipe, shepherd's pipe

**pipelet -ette** *n sl* concierge

**piper** *vt* snare (birds); load (dice); *vi* **ne pas ~** say not a word

**piperade** *nf cul* Basque dish (eggs, tomatoes, peppers)

**pipi** *nm coll* (or child's term) pee, piss; **faire ~** pee, piss; **~ de chat** nasty wine

**pipistrelle** *nf zool* small bat

**piquage** *nm* stitching (with sewing machine); piercing, making small holes

**piquant** *nm* prickle, thorn; quill, spine; *fig* piquancy; *adj* pricking, stinging; pungent; stimulating; wounding

¹**pique** *nf* pike (weapon); wounding word, phrase

²**pique** *nm* spade (cards)

**piqué** *nm* piqué, quilting; nose-dive; **bombardement en ~** dive-bombing; *adj* quilted; stitched; fly-blown, mildewed; sour (wine); *mus* staccato; *coll* cracked, round the bend

**pique-assiette** *n invar* sponger, parasite

**pique-feu** *nm invar* poker

**pique-nique** *nm* picnic

**pique-niquer** *vi* picnic

**pique-niqueur -euse** *n* picnicker

**pique-notes** *nm invar* spike-file

**piquer** *vt* goad; prick, puncture; bite, sting; sew, stitch; inoculate; pin up, stitch; impress; nettle, pique; quilt; *coll* pinch, steal, acquire, take; *coll* arrest;

have an attack of; *mus* play staccato; ~ **au vif** cut to the quick; ~ **des deux** go at full gallop; ~ **une tête** rush head first, take a dive; ~ **un fard (un soleil)** blush; **ça me pique** that itches, I'm itching; **quelle mouche te pique?** what's biting you?; *vi* gallop; dive, fall; **se ~** prick oneself; give oneself an injection; become mildewed; become sour (wine); become angry; **se ~ de** claim to be; *coll* **se ~ le nez** get drunk

**piquet** *nm* picket, post, stake; *mil* picket; punishment of standing in the corner; ~ **de grève** strike picket

**piqueter** *vt* (5) mark out with stakes; dot with

**piquette** *nf* beverage made from fermented marc with water; sharp, poor wine; **ce n'est pas de la ~** it's not a trifling matter

**piqueur -euse** *n* stitcher; *nm* whipper-in (hunting); stable-lad; platelayer (railway); road engineer; workman using pneumatic drill

**piqûre** *nf* bite, sting; stitching, quilting; puncture, small hole; worm-hole; injection; patch of mildew

**pirate** *nm* pirate; *fig* unscrupulous businessman; shark, swindler; ~ **de l'air** hijacker; *rad* **poste radio ~** pirate station

**pirater** *vi* be a pirate

**piraterie** *nf* piracy; swindle

**pire** *nm* **le ~** the worst; **au ~** at the worst; *adj* worse; worst

**pirogue** *nf* dug-out canoe

**pirouetter** *vi* pirouette

¹**pis** *nm* teat, udder

²**pis** *nm* **le ~** the worst; *adj invar lit* worse; **dire ~ que pendre de qn** say the most appalling things about s/o; *adv* worse; worst; **au ~ aller** if the worst comes to the worst

**pis-aller** *nm invar* last resource, makeshift

**pisciculteur** *nm* one who breeds fish

**piscine** *nf* swimming-bath, swimming-pool

**pissaladière** *nf cul* Provençal dish like Italian pizza

**pisse** *nf vulg* piss

**pisse-froid** *nm invar coll* boring, morose individual

**pissenlit** *nm bot* dandelion; *coll* **manger les ~s par la racine** push up the daisies

**pisser** *vt* piss (out); cause to flow; leak; *vi vulg* piss; *coll* **il pleut comme vache qui pisse** it's pissing with rain; **c'est comme si on pissait dans un violon** it's a complete waste of time, it's a quite pointless thing to do

**pisseur -euse** *n vulg* pisser; *nf coll* little girl; ~ **de copie** hack journalist

**pisseux -euse** *adj coll* impregnated with, smelling of urine; of the colour of urine

**pissoir** *nm coll* urinal

**pissotière** *nf coll* urinal

**pistache** *nf + adj invar* pistachio (nut)

**piste** *nf* track; cycle-track, race-track, running-track; *aer* runway; ring (circus); rink (skating); dance-floor; ~ **sonore** sound-track

**pister** *vt* track; shadow

**pistolet** *nm* pistol; spray-gun; bread roll (in Belgium); *naut* davit; *coll* queer fish; **pistolet-mitrailleur** *nm* (*pl* **pistolets-mitrailleurs**) sub-machine gun

**piston** *nm* piston; *mus* valve; *fig* influence, wire-pulling

**pistonner** *vt* back, pull strings for

**pistou** *nm cul* **soupe de (au) ~** Provençal soup with chopped basil

**pitchpin** *nm* pitch-pine

**piteux -euse** *adj* piteous, pitiable, woeful; derisory; **en ~ état** in a bad way

**pitié** *nf* compassion, pity; **faire ~** arouse pity; **par ~** for pity's sake

**piton** *nm* ring, bolt; sharp peak; piton

**pitoyable** *adj* pitiable; paltry

**pitre** *nm* clown; buffoon

**pitrerie** *nf* clowning; buffoonery

**pittoresque** *nm* picturesqueness; brilliance, vividness; *adj* picturesque; brilliant, vivid

**pituitaire** *adj anat* pituitary

**pivert, picvert** *nm orni* green woodpecker

**pivoine** *nf bot* peony

**pivot** *nm* pivot, pin, swivel; *fig* centre; tap-root

**pivoter** *vi* pivot, swing round, wheel

**placage** *nm* facing (marble, stone), plating, veneering; tackle (rugby, football)

**placard** *nm* built-in cupboard; placard, poster; large advertisement in paper; *print* galley proof

**placarder** *vt* post up, stick up; placard; print (a galley proof)

**place** *nf* place, position; square (in town); garrison town; *comm* market; seat; room, space; job, situation; ~ **entière** full fare; ~ **forte** fortress; *comm* **avoir du crédit sur la ~** be thought a sound man financially; **demi-~** half fare; **être à sa ~** be in the right place; **être en ~** have a job; **faire la ~** do the rounds (as commercial traveller); **mise en ~** arrangement, installing; **remettre qn à sa ~** put s/o in his place; **rester en ~** keep still; **sur ~** on the spot; **voiture de ~** taxi, hire-car

**placement** *nm* investing, investment; placing; seating (at table); **bureau de ~** employment agency

**placer** *vt* (4) lay, place, put, set down; find (s/o) a job; locate, situate (story); insert (remark); sell; invest; seat (guests); post (sentries); land (blow); marry (daughter); **se ~** seat oneself; place oneself; take a job

**placeur -euse** *n* steward (meeting); usher (theatre); head of employment agency

**placide** *adj* placid

**placidité** *nf* placidity

**placier -ière** *n* agent, canvasser, seller

**plafond** *nm* ceiling; maximum; *aer* ceiling; *mot* maximum speed

**plafonnage** *nm* installation of ceiling; *archi* ceiling work

**plafonner** *vt* instal a ceiling in; *vi* reach ceiling (aircraft, price)

**plafonnier** *nm* ceiling light, ceiling fitting

**plage** *nf* beach, shore; seaside resort; *naut* freeboard deck; band (on gramophone record)

**plagiaire** *n* plagiarist

**plagiat** *nm* plagiarism, plagiary

**plagier** *vt* plagiarize; imitate

**plaid** *nm* travelling-rug

**plaidant** *adj* leg pleading

**plaider** *vt* plead (case); allege, put forward; *vi* leg go to law; plead

**plaideur -euse** *n* leg litigant

**plaidoirie** *nf* leg counsel's speech; plea

**plaidoyer** *nm* leg speech in defence; *fig* defence

**plaie** *nf* wound; cut, sore; *fig* wound, running sore; *fig* curse

**plaignant -e** *n* leg plaintiff; complainer; *adj* leg **partie ~ e** plaintiff

**plain** *adj ar* level

**plain-chant** *nm* (*pl* **plains-chants**) plainsong

**plaindre** *vt* (55) pity; **se ~** complain, protest

**plaine** *nf* plain, flat country

**plain-pied** *adv* **de ~** on the same level; *fig* with no trouble; **être de ~ avec qn** get on well with s/o

**plainte** *nf* groan, moan, sigh; complaint; *leg* complaint, indictment; **déposer une ~** (**dresser ~** , **porter ~** ) bring an action

**plaintif -ive** *adj* plaintive; complaining, querulous

**plaire** *vi* (69) charm, content, fascinate, please, satisfy; be pleasant; be loved; **se ~** be pleased with oneself; take pleasure; enjoy oneself; like one another; flourish (plant); **s'il vous plaît** please; I'd have you note; **plaît-il?** pardon?, what did you say?

**plaisamment** *adv* agreeably, pleasantly; absurdly, ridiculously

**plaisance** *nf ar lit* pleasure; **bateau de ~** pleasure craft; **maison de ~** country retreat

**plaisant** *nm* amusing side, what is amusing; jester, joker; **mauvais ~** practical joker; one who makes jokes in bad taste; *adj* pleasant, agreeable; amusing, funny; absurd, ridiculous

**plaisanter** *vt* banter, chaff; *vi* jest, joke, not be serious

**plaisanterie** *nf* joke; joking; absurdity; something very easy; push-over; **mauvaise ~** silly joke, nasty trick

**plaisir** *nm* contentment, delight, enjoyment, pleasure; satisfaction; well-being; amusement; sexual pleasure; **à ~** as much as one wants; wantonly; **au ~ de vous revoir** (*coll* **au ~** ) until we meet again (see you soon); *joc* **menus ~ s** minor amusements; **vous me ferez ~ de** you would be doing me a kindness by

¹**plan** *nm* plane, surface; *cin* take; *cin* **gros ~** close-up; **premier ~** foreground; *theat* downstage; *theat* **second ~** up-stage; **sur le ~ de** as regards; *adj* flat, smooth; plane

²**plan** *nm* plan; blue-print, drawing; street map; design, plan, project; **~ horizontal** ground-plan; **laisser qn en ~** leave s/o in the lurch; **laisser son travail en ~** stop working; **lever un ~** draw up a plan

**planche** *nf* board, plank; block, engraving, plate; strip of land; *coll* ski; **~ s** *theat* boards, stage; *naut* gang-plank; **~ à roulettes** skate-board; **~ à voile** wind-surf board; *aer* **~ de bord** instrument panel; **~ de salut** last resort, sheet anchor; **être cloué entre quatre ~ s** be in one's coffin; **faire la ~** float on one's back

**planchéier** *vt* board over, floor

**plancher** *nm* floor; **~ des vaches** terra firma; *coll* **débarrasser le ~** run for it, clear out; *coll mot* **mettre le pied au ~** put one's foot down; **prix ~** minimum authorized price

**planchette** *nf* small plank, shelf; plane-table

**plancton** *nm zool* plankton

**plané** *adj vol* **~** glide; *coll* **faire un vol ~** fall, tumble

¹**planer** *vt* plane

²**planer** *vi* glide; float in the air, soar; *fig* be in the air, threaten

**planétaire** *adj* planetary

**planète** *nf* planet

¹**planeur -euse** *n* planisher; *nf* **planeuse** planing machine

²**planeur** *nm* glider

**planifier** *vt* plan

**planning** *nm* work schedule

**planque** *nf coll* cushy job; *sl* hideout, hiding-place

**planquer** vt sl hide; sl **se ~** hide, lie low

**plant** nm hort (nursery) plantation (trees); bed (plants); slip (seedling)

**plantaire** adj anat plantar

**plantation** nf planting; plantation; theat fit-up

¹**plante** nf plant; **~s potagères** vegetables; **jardin des ~s** botanical gardens

²**plante** nf sole (of the foot)

**planté** adj stuck; **bien ~** well set up; **rester ~** remain standing

**planter** vt plant; stick in; set up; knock in (nail); theat fit up; establish (character); **~ là qn** leave s/o standing; **se ~** be planted; stand stock still

**planteur** nm planter (esp tropics)

**planteuse** nf potato planting machine

**plantoir** nm dibble

**planton** nm mil orderly; orderly duty; coll **faire le ~** stand waiting

**plantureux -euse** adj abundant, copious; buxom

**plaquage** nm tackle (rugby, football); sl **~ de** walking out on (girl)

**plaque** nf plate, sheet; badge, plaque, sign; patch, blotch; **~ d'identité** identity plate, identity disc; **mot ~ d'immatriculation (minéralogique)** number plate; **~ tournante** turntable; important centre

**plaqué** nm (metal) plating; plated metal; **montre ~ or** gold-plated watch

**plaquer** vt plate, plaster, veneer; tackle (rugby, football); mus hold (chord); coll abandon, walk out on; push; thrust; **se ~** lie flat; plaster (hair)

**plaquette** nf small plate, tablet; booklet, opuscule

**plaqueur -euse** n plater

**plasmatique** adj plasmatic

**plastic** nm plastic explosive

**plasticage, plastiquage** nm bomb outrage

**plasticité** nf plasticity

**plastique** nm plastic; nf plastic art; adj plastic; malleable

**plastiquer** vt blow up with plastic explosive

**plastron** nm breastplate; fencing jacket; shirt front, bodice front

**plastronner** vt protect (with breastplate); vi pose, strut, throw out one's chest

¹**plat** nm flat, flat part; board (bookbinding); coll **faire du ~ à qn** flatter s/o; adj even, flat, level; lank, straight (hair); low (heel); thin; dull; flat, mediocre; **angle ~** angle of 180°; **à ~** horizontally; **à ~ ventre** flat on one's face; obsequiously; **être à ~** be exhausted; be broke; have a flat tyre; lit

**rimes ~es** couplets with alternating masculine and feminine rhymes

²**plat** nm dish, plate; cul course, dish; **~ garni** meat (or fish) with vegetables; **mettre les petits ~s dans les grands** take a lot of trouble over entertaining s/o, bring out the red carpet; coll **mettre les pieds dans le ~** drop a brick; **œufs au ~**, **œufs sur le ~** fried eggs; **servir à qn un ~ de sa façon** tear s/o apart, tell s/o off

**platane** nm bot plane-tree

**plat-bord** nm (pl plats-bords) naut gunwale

**plateau** nm salver; tray; board (cheese); turntable (record player); geog plateau; platform; theat stage; cin set; **~ continental** continental shelf

**plate-bande** nf (pl **plates-bandes**) flower-bed; archi flat moulding; flat lintel; **marcher sur les ~s de qn** encroach on s/o's preserves, tread on s/o's toes

**platée** nf dishful

**plate-forme** nf (pl **plates-formes**) platform, terrace; mil gun-platform; open wagon (railway); pol programme

¹**platine** nm platinum; adj invar platinum (coloured)

²**platine** nf plate (lock, watch); typ platen; stage (microscope)

**platiné** adj platinum-plated; dyed platinum

**platiner** vt plate with platinum

**platitude** nf flatness, mediocrity; banality, platitude; servility; servile act

**platonicien -ienne** adj Platonist

**platonique** adj Platonic; platonic; pure; theoretical

**platonisme** nm Platonism

**plâtrage** nm plastering; plaster-work

**plâtras** nm debris of plaster-work; rubble; weight (on stomach)

**plâtre** nm plaster; plaster-cast; **~s** plaster-work; **~ à mouler** plaster of Paris; **battre qn comme ~** flatten s/o, reduce s/o to pulp; **essuyer les ~s** be the first occupant; suffer the initial consequences; **pierre à ~** gypsum

**plâtrer** vt plaster, plaster up; put into plaster; lime (field); plaster (wine); coll make (one's face) up badly

**plâtrerie** nf plastering; plaster works

**plâtrier** nm plasterer

**plâtrière** nf gypsum quarry; gypsum kiln

**plausibilité** nf plausibility

**plèbe** nf plebs

**plébéien -ienne** n + adj plebeian

**plébiscite** nm plebiscite, referendum

**plébisciter** vt approve (sth), elect (s/o) by referendum; approve (sth) or elect (s/o) by overwhelming majority

**plein** *nm* fill; bull's eye; downstroke (handwriting); **battre son** ~ be at its height (tide); *fig* be in full swing; **donner son** ~ give of one's best; *mot* **faire le** ~ fill up with petrol; *adj* full; crowded; massive, solid; plump (cheeks); complete, total; fresh (air); ~ **e** pregnant (animal); ~ **aux** as very rich, rolling in it; **à** ~ fully, totally; **à** ~ **e gorge** at the top of one's voice; **avoir le nez** ~ have one's nose blocked up; **en avoir** ~ **la bouche de** be always talking about; *coll* **en avoir** ~ **le dos** be fed up with; *coll* **en avoir** ~ **les bottes** be tired out from walking; **en** ~ fully, totally; in the midst; **en** ~ **dans (sur)** exactly in (on), right in (on); **en** ~ **jour** in broad daylight; *sl* **être** ~ be drunk, be pissed; *coll* **un gros** ~ **de soupe** a very fat man; *adv* **sonner** ~ give out clear, full sound; *coll* **tout** ~ very

**plein-emploi** *nm invar* full employment

**plénier -ière** *adj* plenary

**plénipotentiaire** *nm* plenipotentiary

**plénitude** *nf* plenitude, fullness; ampleness

**plénum** *nm* plenary session

**pléonasme** *nm* pleonasm

**pléonastique** *adj* pleonastic

**plésiosaure** *nm* plesiosaurus

**pléthore** *nf* plethora, superabundance

**pléthorique** *adj* abundant, overcrowded; *med* plethoric

**pleur** *nm* tear; ~ **s** tears, weeping

**pleurard -e** *n coll* weeper, whimperer; *adj* tearful, whimpering

**pleurer** *vt* mourn, regret; weep; *coll* ~ **misère** complain; *vi* cry, shed tears, whine; water (eyes); ~ **à chaudes larmes** weep bitterly; ~ **comme une vache** (*coll* **comme un veau**) weep buckets; **à** ~ (**à faire** ~) extremely

**pleurésie** *nf* pleurisy

**pleurétique** *n* + *adj* pleuritic (patient)

**pleureur -euse** *n* weeper, person given to whining; *adj* tearful, weeping, whining; *bot* with drooping branches; **saule** ~ weeping willow

**pleurnichement** *nm,* **pleurnicherie** *nf coll* snivelling, whining

**pleurnicher** *vi coll* snivel, whine

**pleurnicheur -euse** *n* sniveller; *adj* snivelling, whining

**pleutre** *nm* coward; *adj* cowardly

**pleuvasser, pleuvoter** *vi* rain intermittently

**pleuviner, pluviner** *vi* drizzle

**pleuvoir** *vi* (70) *impers* rain; *vi* rain down, fall down; **il pleut à verse (à flots, à seaux, à torrents)** it's raining cats and dogs, it's raining buckets; *sl* **il**

**pleut des cordes** it's pouring with rain

**pleuvoter** *vi see* pleuvasser

**plèvre** *nf anat* pleura

**pli** *nm* fold, pleat; wrinkle; crease; fall, hang (of garment); cover, envelope; habit; trick (cards); *geol* fold; **faux** ~ crease; **mise en** ~ **s** setting (hair); **prendre un** ~ acquire a habit

**pliable** *adj* easily folded, pliable

**pliage** *nm* folding

**pliant** *nm* camp-stool, folding stool; *adj* collapsible, folding

**plie** *nf zool* plaice

**plier** *vt* fold, fold up; roll up; strike (tent); bend; *fig* cause to bend, make obey; *vi* bend; give way; **se** ~ **à** give in to, give way to, obey, yield to

**plinthe** *nf* plinth

**plioir** *nm* folding machine; paper-knife; winder (fishing-line)

**plissage** *nm* folding, putting in creases

**plissé** *nm* pleating; *adj* folded, creased; pleated

**plissement** *nm* corrugation, creasing, wrinkling; *geog* folding

**plisser** *vt* fold, crease; pleat; *vi* crease, crumple; **se** ~ crease, be creased, wrinkle

**pliure** *nf* crease, mark made by crease; *typ* folding

**ploiement** *nm* bending, folding

**plomb** *nm* lead; *naut* lead; lead shot; leaden seal; *elect* fuse; *typ* type; **à** ~ upright, vertical; **n'avoir pas de** ~ **dans la tête** be feather-brained; **soldats de** ~ tin soldiers; **sommeil de** ~ deep sleep·

**plombage** *nm* sheathing with lead; applying of leaden seals, sealing; filling (tooth)

**plombagine** *nf* plumbago, black lead; graphite

**plombé** *adj* sheathed with lead; sealed; leaden (colour); filled (tooth)

**plomber** *vt* sheath with lead; seal; plumb (wall); fill (tooth); leaden (colour); **se** ~ take on leaden colour

**plomberie** *nf* lead industry; lead works; plumbing (installation)

**plombier** *nm* plumber

**plombières** *nf cul* ice-cream with candied fruit in it

**plonge** *nf coll* dish-washing

**plongeant** *adj* plunging

**plongée** *nf* dive, diving; submersion (submarine); downward view

**plongement** *nm* immersion

**plongeoir** *nm* diving-board

**¹plongeon** *nm orni* diver, loon

**²plongeon** *nm* dive, plunge; *coll* **faire le** ~ be in financial trouble

**plonger** *vt* (3) dip, immerse, plunge; *vi*

dive, plunge; *naut* dive, submerge; plunge into, look down into; slope downwards; **se ~ dans** be plunged in, be immersed in, immerse oneself in

**plongeur -euse** *n* dish-washer, washer-up; plunger; diver; *nm orni* diver

**plot** *nm elect* contact

**plouf** *interj* plop!

**ploutocrate** *nm* plutocrat

**ploutocratie** *nf* plutocracy

**ploutocratique** *adj* plutocratic

**ployer** *vt* (7) bend; tame; *vi* bend, bow; give way, yield

**plucher** *vi*, **plucheux** *adj see* **pelucher, pelucheux**

**pluie** *nf* rain; **en ~** in drops; **ennuyeux comme la ~** deeply boring; **faire la ~ et le beau temps** have a lot of influence; **parler de la ~ et du beau temps** make polite conversation

**plumage** *nm* plumage, feathers; plucking

**plumard** *nm sl* bed

**plumasserie** *nf* feather trade

**plume** *nf* feather, plume; pen; quill pen; *coll* **y laisser des ~ s** sustain a loss

**plumeau** *nm* feather duster; tuft of feathers

**plumer** *vt* pluck; *coll* fleece; *vi* feather (rowing)

**plumet** *nm* plume

**plumeur -euse** *n* plucker

**plumeux -euse** *adj* feathery

**plumier** *nm* pen-case, pencil-box

**plumitif** *nm coll* pen-pusher; bureaucrat, petty official; hack writer

**plupart** *nf* greater part, greatest part, majority, most, most part; **la ~ du temps** normally

**pluralisme** *nm* pluralism

**pluraliste** *adj* pluralist

**pluralité** *nf* plurality

**pluriel** *nm gramm* plural; **~ de majesté** royal we; *adj* plural

¹**plus** *nm* more; most; **le ~ de** the greatest amount of; **au ~, tout au ~** at the most

²**plus** *adv* (1. *comparative*) more, the more; **~ il criait, ~ je ris** the more he shouted, the more I laughed; **beaucoup ~, bien ~** much more; **de ~** moreover; **de ~ en ~** more and more; **en ~** and in addition; **en ~ beau** more beautifully; **on ne peut ~ stupide** impossibly stupid, more stupid than one can imagine; **qui ~ est** and what is more; **sans ~** and nothing more, without ado; (2. *superlative*) **le, la, les ~** most, the most; **ce que j'ai de ~ précieux** the most precious thing I have; **des ~** among the most; (3. *negative*) **je ne veux ~ le voir** I don't want to see

him any more; **non ~, ne ... ~** no more; **pas ~ grand que moi** no bigger than I; **Vous ne partez pas? Moi non ~** You're not going? Nor am I

³**plus** *conj* plus; **deux ~ trois font cinq** two plus three make five

**plusieurs** *adj* several; **~ personnes** several people; *pron pl* several

**plus-que-parfait** *nm gramm* pluperfect

**plus-value** *nf* appreciation, increment, capital gain; budget surplus; increased payment

**plutonique** *adj geol* plutonic

**plutôt** *adv* rather, sooner, somewhat; **ou ~** or to be more exact

**pluvial** *adj* pluvial; rainy (season)

**pluvier** *nm orni* plover

**pluvieux -ieuse** *adj* rainy, wet

**pluviner** *vi see* **pleuviner**

**pluviomètre** *nm* rain-gauge

**pluviométrique** *adj* pluviometric

**pluviôse** *nm hist* fifth month of the French Republican calendar (January to February)

**pluviosité** *nf* raininess; rainfall

**pneu** *nm* tyre; express letter (Paris, sent by pneumatic tube)

**pneumatique** *nm* tyre; express letter (Paris, sent by pneumatic tube); *adj* pneumatic

**pneumologue** *n* lung specialist

**pneumonie** *nf* pneumonia

**pochade** *nf* quick sketch (painting or writing)

**pochard -e** *n coll* drunkard; *adj coll* drunken

**poche** *nf* pocket; bag, sack; pouch; sac; bagginess (trousers); *sl* **c'est dans la ~** it's in the bag; **en être de sa ~** sustain a loss; **mettre qn dans sa ~** overcome s/o; **mettre sa fierté dans sa ~** pocket one's pride; **n'avoir pas les yeux dans sa ~** be observant; **n'avoir pas sa langue dans sa ~** have plenty to say

**poché** *adj* black (eye); poached (egg)

**pocher** *vt* black (s/o's eye); poach (egg); sketch rapidly

**pochette** *nf* envelope, folder; book (matches); compendium (paper and envelopes); pocket handkerchief; (gramophone) record sleeve

**pochoir** *nm* stencil

**podagre** *nf* gout; *n + adj* gouty (person)

¹**poêle** *nm eccles* funeral pall

²**poêle** *nm* stove

³**poêle** *nm* frying-pan; *coll* **tenir la queue de la ~** be in control of sth

**poêler** *vt* fry; pot-roast

**poêlon** *nm* pan; casserole

**poème** *nm* poem

**poésie** *nf* poetry; poem

**poète** *nm* + *adj* poet
**poétesse** *nf* poetess
**poétique** *nf* poetics; *adj* poetic(al)
**poétiser** *vt* poeticize
**pognon** *nm sl* money
**poids** *nm* weight; heaviness; load; burden; importance, influence, moment; weight (boxing); ~ **coq** bantamweight; ~ **léger** light-weight; ~ **lourd** heavy-weight; long, heavy vehicle; ~ **mi-lourd** light heavy-weight; ~ **mi-moyen** welter-weight; ~ **mouche** fly-weight; ~ **moyen** middleweight; ~ **plume** feather-weight; ~ **spécifique** specific gravity; ~ **utile** payload; **ne pas faire le** ~ not make the weight (boxing); lack the necessary qualities
**poignant** *adj* poignant, heart-searching, gripping
**poignard** *nm* dagger
**poignarder** *vt* stab
**poigne** *nf* grasp, grip; command, energy, firmness; **à** ~ firm, strong
**poignée** *nf* handful; grip, handle; ~ **de main** hand-shake
**poignet** *nm* wrist; cuff; **à la force du** ~ by one's own efforts
**poil** *nm* coat, fur, hair (animals); bristle; nap (cloth), pile (velvet); ~**s** hairs (human being); *coll* **à** ~ naked; **à un** ~ **près** very nearly; ~ **coll au** ~ fine, super!; *coll* **avoir un** ~ **dans la main** be lazy; **de tout** ~ **(de tous** ~**s)** of all kinds; *coll* **être de bon (mauvais)** ~ be in a good (bad) temper; *coll* **ne pas avoir un** ~ **de sec** sweat profusely; **reprendre du** ~ **de la bête** recover oneself
**poiler (se)** *v refl* roar with laughter
**poilu** *nm* soldier (in First World War); *adj* hairy
**poinçon** *nm* awl, bradawl, pricker, stabber; punch (tickets); die; hallmark; *bui* king-post
**poinçonnage, poinçonnement** *nm* perforating; punching; hall-marking
**poinçonner** *vt* perforate; punch; hallmark, stamp
**poinçonneur -euse** *n* puncher; ticket-puncher
**poinçonneuse** *nf* punching machine, stamping machine
**poindre** *vt* (71) hurt, wound; *vi* appear (dawn); come up, sprout (plants)
**poing** *nm* fist; **coup de** ~ punch; **coup de** ~ **américain** knuckle-duster; **dormir à** ~**s fermés** sleep deeply; **serrer les** ~**s** summon up one's courage
¹**point** *nm* point, spot; *naut* position; moment, point; situation, state; argument; aspect; degree; question; reason;

lace, needlework, stitch; full-stop; dot (dice); score (game); mark (school); *leg* point of law; *naut* base; ~ **de côté** stitch (in side); ~ **d'exclamation** exclamation mark; ~ **d'interrogation** question mark; ~ **d'orgue** rest; ~ **du jour** dawn; **mot** ~ **mort** neutral; ~ **noir** blackhead; *fig* problem; **à** ~ at the right moment; in the right state; *cul* to a turn; **à** ~ **nommé** at the right moment; **à ce** ~ **que** to such an extent; **à ce** ~ **que** so much so that; **au** ~ ready, right; **de** ~ **en** ~ literally; **faire le** ~ sum up the position; *aer* + *naut* take a fix; **mal en** ~ in a bad way; **mettre au** ~ adjust, regulate; *mot* tune; **mettre les** ~**s sur les i** dot the i's and cross the t's; **mise au** ~ adjustment; summing-up of situation
²**point** *adv* not at all
**pointage** *nm* checking, checking in; *mil* aiming, laying; *naut* marking up (chart); pointing (telescope)
**pointe** *nf* extremity; head, point, spike; cape, headland; pointed object; point (compass); triangular scarf; *mil* advance, sally; wedge; pointed remark, sally; touch, trace; spurt; peak (period); ~ **des pieds** tip-toe; *lit* ~ **du jour** dawn; *arts* ~ **sèche** dry-point etching, etching; **en** ~ pointed; **faire des** ~**s** execute points (ballet); **heure de** ~ peak-hour, rush-hour
**pointeau** *nm mech* centre-punch; *mot* needle (carburettor)
**pointer** *vt* prod, sharpen; prick up (ears); stitch; *vi* point, soar; advance, sally forth; dawn; **(se)** ~ clock on
**pointeur -euse** *n* checker, tally-clerk; timekeeper (athletics); *mil* gun-layer
**pointillé** *nm* dotting, stippling; dotted line; perforation (paper)
**pointiller** *vt* dot; *vi* make dots, stipple
**pointilleux -euse** *adj* captious, finicky, fussy, fastidious, particular
**pointu** *adj* pointed; sharp, shrill; unpleasant; touchy
**pointure** *nf* size (shoes, etc)
**point-virgule** *nm* (*pl* **points-virgules**) semi-colon
**poire** *nf* pear; pear-shaped object; *elect* pear-switch; *coll* head, nut; *coll* dupe, idiot; *coll* **couper la** ~ **en deux** split the difference; **garder une** ~ **pour la soif** keep something in reserve
**poiré** *nm* perry
**poireau, porreau** *nm bot* leek; *med* wart; *coll* **faire le** ~ wait, hang around
**poireauter** *vi coll* wait, hang around
**poirée** *nf* white beet
**poirier** *nm* pear-tree
**pois** *nm* pea; polka dot, spot; ~ **cassés**

237

split peas; ~ **chiche** chick pea; ~ **de senteur** sweet pea

**poison** *nm* poison; *coll* damn nuisance; *n coll* pest

**poissard** *adj* low-life, vulgar

**poissarde** *nf* fish-wife

**poisse** *nf coll* bad luck

**poisser** *vt* coat with pitch, dirty, soil; *coll* arrest, catch, nab; **vin poissé** resinated wine, retsina

**poisseux -euse** *adj* sticky

**poisson** *nm* fish; ~ **d'avril** April fool; ~ **rouge** goldfish; *coll* **engueuler qn comme du ~ pourri** tear a strip off s/o; **être (heureux) comme un ~ dans l'eau** be in one's element; *mot* **faire une queue de ~ à qn** cut in on s/o; **finir en queue de ~** fizzle out

**poissonnerie** *nf* fish trade; fish market; fish shop

**poissonneux -euse** *adj* full of fish

**poissonnier -ière** *n* fish merchant

**poissonnière** *nf* fish kettle

**poitevin** *adj* of Poitou; of Poitiers

**poitrail** *nm* breast; *bui* breast-summer

**poitrinaire** *n + adj* consumptive (patient)

**poitrine** *nf* chest; breasts (woman); *cul* breast (meat)

**poivrade** *nf cul* sauce with pepper and vinegar; **à la ~** with salt and pepper

**poivre** *nm* pepper; ~ **et sel** dark hair streaked with white

**poivré** *adj* peppered, peppery; *fig* improper, spicy

**poivrer** *vt* pepper, season with pepper; *coll* **se ~** get drunk

**poivrier** *nm bot* pepper plant; pepper-pot

**poivrière** *nf* pepper plantation; pepper-pot; *archi* (conical) turret

**poivron** *nm bot* capsicum, pepper

**poivrot -e** *n sl* drunkard

**poix** *nf* pitch, resin

**poker** *nm* poker (game); four of a kind (at poker); ~ **d'as** poker-dice

**polaire** *adj geog + math* polar

**Polaque** *nm hist* Polack; *coll pej* Pole

**polariser** *vt* polarize

**polariseur** *nm* polarizer

**polarité** *nf* polarity

**pôle** *nm* pole; polar regions

**polémique** *nf* polemic, controversy; *adj* polemical

**polémiste** *n* polemist

¹**poli** *nm* gloss, polish; *adj* polished, smooth; burnished

²**poli** *adj* polite, civil, courteous, well-behaved

¹**police** *nf* police, police-force; policing; discipline; **des mœurs** vice squad; ~ **judiciaire** = C.I.D.; ~ **parallèle** secret police; **appeler ~ secours** = dial

999, call the police; **commissariat (poste) de ~** police-station; *mil* **salle de ~** guardroom

²**police** *nf* insurance policy; ~ **tous risques** comprehensive policy

**policer** *vt* (4) *lit* civilize

**polichinelle** *nm* Punch, Punchinello; buffoon, puppet; **secret de ~** no secret; public knowledge

**policier** *nm* policeman; detective, private detective; *adj* (*f* **-ière**) police; **régime ~** police state; **roman ~** detective story

**policlinique** *nf* out-patient clinic; clinical training

**poliment** *adv* politely, courteously

**polio** *n med* polio patient; *nf* polio

**poliomyélite** *nf med* poliomyelitis

**polir** *vt* burnish, polish, shine; file

**polissable** *adj* polishable

**polissage** *nm* burnishing, polishing, shining

**polisseur -euse** *n* polisher (person); gem-polisher

**polisson -onne** *n* naughty child, scamp; *adj* improper, smutty, lascivious; sexy (glance)

**polissonner** *vi* be naughty (child); *ar* behave indecently

**polissonnerie** *nf* mischievousness, prank (child); dirty remark; lewd act

**politesse** *nf* politeness, courtesy, good manners; polite action; polite remark; **brûler la ~** leave abruptly, go without saying goodbye; **échange de ~s** exchange of compliments; **faire des ~s** be civil, be polite

**politicard** *nm pej* (unscrupulous) politician

**politicien -ienne** *n often pej* politician; *adj pej* typical of a politician

**politique** *nm* political figure, statesman; s/o with statesmanlike qualities; *nf* politics, policy; *adj* political; politic, prudent

**politiser** *vt* make politically aware, make political

**pollinisation** *nf* pollinization

**polluer** *vt* defile, pollute

**polo** *nm* polo; open-necked sports shirt

**Polonais -e** *n* Pole

**polonais** *nm* Polish (language); *adj* Polish

**polonaise** *nf mus* polonaise; *cul* kind of meringue (containing candied fruit)

**poltron -onne** *n* coward; *ar* poltroon; *adj* cowardly, faint-hearted, fearful

**poltronnerie** *nf* cowardice

**polyandre** *adj* having several husbands; *bot* polyandrous

**polyandrie** *nf* polyandry; *bot* polyandria

238

**polychrome** *adj* polychrome, polychromatic

**polyclinique** *nf* general clinic, general hospital

**polycopie** *nf* cyclostyling, duplicating, mimeographing, stencilling

**polycopié** *nm* cyclostyled document; **cours** ~ cyclostyled course of lectures

**polycopier** *vt* cyclostyle, duplicate

**polyculture** *nf* mixed farming

**polyèdre** *nm* polyhedron

**polyédrique** *adj* polyhedral

**polygame** *n* polygamist; *adj* polygamous

**polygamie** *nf* polygamy

**polyglotte** *n* + *adj* polyglot

**polygone** *nm* polygon; *mil* fortified place; artillery range

**polymorphe** *adj* polymorphous

**polype** *nm zool* polyp; *med* polypus, soft tumour

**polyphasé** *adj elect* multiphase, polyphase

**polyphonie** *nf mus* polyphony

**polyphonique** *adj mus* polyphonic

**polysyllabe, polysyllabique** *adj* polysyllabic

**polytechnicien -ienne** *n* student, former student, of the Paris École Polytechnique

**Polytechnique** *nf* École Polytechnique in Paris

**polytechnique** *adj* polytechnic

**polythéisme** *nm* polytheism

**polythéiste** *n* + *adj* polytheist

**polyvalence** *nf* polyvalency

**pomiculteur** *nm* fruit-grower (apples, pears)

**pommade** *nf* ointment; *ar* pomade, pomatum; ~ **rosat** lip salve; **passer de la** ~ **à qn** flatter s/o grossly

**pommader** *vt joc* + *pej* plaster (hair)

**pomme** *nf* apple; knob (bedstead, walking-stick); head (cabbage, lettuce); potato; rose (hose-pipe, shower); ~ **de pin** fir-cone, pine-cone; ~ **de terre** potato; ~**s frites** chips; *coll* **aux** ~**s** fine, splendid; **compote de** ~**s** stewed apples; apple sauce; apple jam; *sl* **ma** ~ , **sa** ~ myself, himself; *coll* **tomber dans les** ~**s** faint

**pommeau** *nm* knob (walking-stick); pommel

**pommelé** *adj* dappled (horse); dappled, mottled

**pommeler (se)** *v refl* (5) become dappled; become rounded

**pommer** *vi bot* form a head

**pommette** *nf* cheek-bone

**pommier** *nm* apple-tree

**pomoculture** *nf* fruit-growing (apples, pears)

**pompage** *nm* pumping

**¹pompe** *nf* ceremony, pomp; ~**s funèbres** funeral arrangements; **conducteur (entrepreneur, ordonnateur) des** ~**s funèbres** undertaker

**²pompe** *nf* pump; *sl* shoe; ~ **à incendie** fire engine; ~ **à vide** vacuum pump; *coll* **à toute** ~ at full speed; *sl* **avoir un coup de** ~ feel whacked; **Château-la-Pompe** tap-water

**pomper** *vt* pump, suck in; *sl* drink; *sl* exhaust; *fig* attract, draw

**pompette** *adj coll* slightly drunk, merry

**pompeux -euse** *adj pej* declamatory, high-flown, pompous; *ar* dignified, solemn; imposing, stately

**¹pompier** *nm* fireman

**²pompier** *nm coll* bombastic writer or painter; *adj* (*f* **-ière**) *coll* bombastic, pretentious

**pompiste** *n* petrol-pump attendant

**pompon** *nm* pompom, tassel, tuft; **avoir le** ~ succeed, win

**pomponner** *vt* doll up, dress up, trick out; **se** ~ doll oneself up, dress up

**ponant** *nm lit* west

**ponce** *nf* pumice; *arts* pounce bag

**¹ponceau** *nm bot* poppy, poppy colour; *adj invar* poppy-coloured, flaming-red

**²ponceau** *nm* culvert

**poncer** *vt* (4) pumice; pounce (drawing)

**poncif** *nm* pounce (pattern); *arts* + *lit* banal work, conventional work

**ponction** *nf surg* puncture

**ponctionner** *vt surg* puncture

**ponctualité** *nf* punctuality; assiduity, exactitude

**ponctuel -uelle** *adj* punctual; assiduous, exact

**ponctuer** *vt* punctuate

**pondérable** *adj* ponderable, weighable

**pondérateur -trice** *adj* balancing

**pondération** *nf* balance; level-headedness

**pondéré** *adj* calm, level-headed

**pondérer** *vt* (6) balance, weigh up

**pondeur** *nm coll* prolific writer

**pondeuse** *nf* layer (eggs); *coll* prolific woman; *adj* egg-laying

**pondre** *vt* lay (eggs); *sl pej* give birth to; *coll* give birth to (article, book)

**poney** *nm* pony

**pont** *nm* bridge; *naut* deck; *mot* transmission; flap (hat, trousers); *fig* link; ~ **aérien** air-lift; *mot* ~ **de graissage** inspection-hoist; *naut* ~ **d'envol** flight-deck; ~ **en dos d'âne** hump-backed bridge; ~ **roulant** travelling crane; **Ponts et Chaussées** = Highways Department; **être solide comme le Pont-Neuf** be very strong and active; **faire le** ~ take an extra day off between two

ponte

public holidays; **faire un ~ d'or à qn**
offer s/o inducement of higher salary;
*naut* **faux ~** orlop deck; *comm* **sur ~**
f.o.b., free on board

¹**ponte** *nf* (egg-)laying; number of eggs
laid at one sitting; *physiol* **~ ovarienne**
ovulation

²**ponte** *nm* gambler not holding the bank
(baccara, roulette, etc); *coll* big-shot

**ponté** *adj naut* decked

**ponter** *vt* wager; *vi* gamble against the
bank

**pontife** *nm* pontiff; *coll often iron*
pundit

**pontifiant** *adj* pontificating

**pontificat** *nm* pontificate; papacy

**pontifier** *vi* pontificate

**pont-levis** *nm* (*pl* **ponts-levis**) drawbridge

**ponton** *nm* floating platform, pontoon;
flat-bottomed barge; hulk

**pontonnier** *nm mil* bridge-builder, pioneer

**popeline** *nf* poplin

**popote** *nf mil coll* officers' mess; *coll*
cooking; *adj coll* too home-loving,
stay-at-home

**popotin** *nm sl* arse, backside

**populace** *nf pej* rabble, riff-raff

**populacier -ière** *adj* coarse, low, vulgar

**populaire** *nm ar* people; *adj* of the
people; folk (culture, tradition); familiar, popular (expression, style); popular, well-liked

**populariser** *vt* popularize, vulgarize

**popularité** *nf* popularity

**populeux -euse** *adj* populous

**populo** *nm coll* people, populace; crowd

**poquet** *nm hort* seed-hole

**porc** *nm* pig; pork; pig-skin; *fig* hog, pig;
*fig* dirty old man

**porcelaine** *nf* porcelain, china; object
made of porcelain

**porcelet** *nm* piglet

**porc-épic** *nm* (*pl* **porcs-épics**) porcupine

**porche** *nm* porch; vestibule

**porcher -ère** *n* swineherd

**porcherie** *nf* piggery

**porcin** *nm* pig; *adj* porcine

**poreux -euse** *adj* porous

**porion** *nm* foreman (in mine)

**pornographe** *nm* pornographer

**pornographie** *nf* pornography

**pornographique** *adj* pornographic

**priorité** *nf* priority

**porphyre** *nm* porphyry

**porreau** *nm see* poireau

¹**port** *nm* harbour, port; haven, shelter;
sea-port town; *naut* **~ d'attache** port
of registry; **arriver à bon ~** come safe
into port, arrive safely

²**port** *nm* carrying; wearing; bearing

(name); transporting; price of transport; postage; bearing, deportment;
*mil* **~ d'armes** presenting arms; *mus*
**~ de voix** glide, portamento; **franc de
~ (franco de ~)** post-paid, carriage-
paid

**portable** *adj* portable; wearable

**portail** *nm* portal

**portant** *nm* trunk handle; *elect* armature
(magnet); *theat* flat; batten, spot-bar;
*naut* rowlock; *bui* mullion; *adj* supporting; bearing, carrying; **à bout ~**
point-blank; **bien (mal) ~** in good
(bad) health

**portatif -ive** *adj* portable; **glace portative** ice-cream to be consumed elsewhere

¹**porte** *nf* gate, gateway (town); door,
doorway, gate; *geog* defile; **~ à ~**
door-to-door selling, door-to-door
canvassing; **de ~ en ~** door to door,
house to house; **entrer (passer) par la
grande ~** be appointed straight to a
high post; **frapper à la bonne (mauvaise) ~** go to the right (wrong)
place; get on to the right (wrong)
person; **interdire sa ~ à qn** refuse to
admit s/o, be not at home to s/o;
**mettre qn à la ~** dismiss s/o; throw
s/o out

²**porte** *adj anat* portal

**porte-à-faux** *nm bui* overhang; **en ~**
overhanging, overhung; *fig* uncertain,
unstable

**porte-aiguilles** *nm* needle-case

**porte-allumettes** *nm* match-holder,
match-box

**porte-amarre** *nm naut* life-saving
rocket, apparatus

**porte-avions** *nm* aircraft-carrier

**porte-bagages** *nm* luggage-rack; lug-
gage-grid

**porte-balais** *nm elect* brush-holder
(dynamo)

**porte-billets** *nm* note-case, small wallet

**porte-bonheur** *nm invar* amulet, lucky
charm

**porte-bouteilles** *nm* bottle-rack, wine-
bin

**porte-carte, porte-cartes** *nm* small
wallet (for identity papers etc); map-
case

**porte-chapeaux** *nm* hat-stand

**porte-cigares** *nm invar* cigar-case

**porte-cigarettes** *nm* cigarette-case

**porte-clefs, porte-clés** *nm invar* key-
ring; *ar* turnkey, warder

**porte-couteau** *nm* knife-rest

**porte-crayon** *nm* pencil-holder

**porte-documents** *nm invar* flat briefcase

**porte-drapeau** *nm mil* + *fig* standard-
bearer

**portée** *nf* litter; *naut* load; *archi* bearing; span (arch, bridge); *mus* stave; reach; range; comprehension, import; *naut* ~ **lourde** dead-weight; **à (la)** ~ **de** within range of; accessible to; understandable by; **hors de (la)** ~ **de** inaccessible to; beyond the understanding of

**porte-épée** *nm invar* frog

**porte-étendard** *nm invar mil* standard-bearer

**porte-faix, portefaix** *nm invar ar* porter

**porte-fenêtre** *nf* (*pl* **portes-fenêtres**) French window

**portefeuille** *nm* portfolio (ministerial); *comm* portfolio; wallet, *US* billfold; *lit* **en** ~ apple-pie bed

**porte-greffe** *nm hort* plant, tree on which a graft is placed

**porte-jarretelles** *nm* suspender-belt

**portemanteau** *nm* coat (and hat) stand; *naut* davit

**porte-menu** *nm invar* menu-holder

**porte-mine, portemine** *nm* propelling pencil

**porte-monnaie** *nm invar* purse

**porte-musique** *nm invar* music-case

**porte-objet** *nm* (microscope) object slide

**porte-parapluies** *nm* umbrella-stand

**porte-parole** *nm invar* spokesman; spokeswoman; mouthpiece

**porte-plume** *nm invar* pen-holder, pen

**porter** *vt* carry, support; bear, have; hold up, raise; wear; convey; give (blow); enter, inscribe, put down; refer, concern; deliver; register (complaint); show (age); incline, induce; feel; nominate, propose; *her* carry; ~ **à** bring to; incite; **être porté à be** inclined to; **être porté sur** have a taste for; **être porté sur la chose** be of amorous temperament, like making love; **il n'est pas bien porté de** it is not done to, the best people do not; *vi* carry (sound); be effective, have effect; ~ **sur** lie on, weigh on; strike against; be about, concern; *coll* **cela me porte sur les nerfs** that gets on my nerves; **se** ~ go, proceed; be worn (clothes); be (ill, well); present oneself (as candidate)

**porte-savon** *nm invar* soap-dish

**porte-serviettes** *nm* towel-rail

**porteur -euse** *n* porter; messenger; holder; *comm* bearer; *med* carrier; *adj* bearing, carrying

**porte-voix** *nm* speaking-tube; megaphone, speaking trumpet

**portier -ière** *n* doorkeeper, janitor; hotel porter; *ar* concierge

**portière** *nf* door (vehicle); door curtain

**portillon** *nm* gate; ~ **automatique** automatic barrier

**portion** *nf* portion; share (inheritance); helping (food)

**portionner** *vt* portion out, apportion

**portique** *nm* porch, portico; crossbar; gantry (crane); (airport) magnetic check-point

**porto** *nm* port (wine)

**portraitiste** *n* portrait-painter

**portrait-robot** *nm* (*pl* **portraits-robots**) identikit picture

**port-salut** *nm* kind of mild, soft cheese

**portuaire** *adj* port, harbour

**Portugais -e** *n* Portuguese

**portugais** *nm* Portuguese (language); *adj* Portuguese

**pose** *nf* fitting up, installing, laying down, setting up; pose; position (body); affectation, pretention; *phot* exposure

**posé** *adj* calm, sober, steady; even (voice)

**posément** *adv* calmly, deliberately, gently

**poser** *vt* place, put, set down; fit, install, set up; establish; formulate; put forward, state (candidature); abandon, set down; *sl* ~ **culotte** have a shit; *vi* lie on, rest on; pose (artist's model); pose, attitudinize; **se** ~ alight, land; arise (question); **se** ~ **en** set oneself up as

**poseur -euse** *n* layer (carpets, floors, rails, etc); poseur, prig; *adj* posing, affected

**positif** *nm mus* choir-organ; positive, rational; *adj* (*f* **-ive**) positive; actual, real; certain, sure; affirmative, favourable; constructive

**position** *nf* position, disposition; job, situation; attitude, point of view, standpoint; statement (bank); *naut* **feu de** ~ navigation light; *mot* **feux de** ~ parking lights; **rester sur ses** ~ **s** remain unconvinced; maintain the same attitude

**positivement** *adv* positively; really, exactly

**positivisme** *nm philos* positivism

**positiviste** *n* + *adj philos* positivist

**posologie** *nf med* posology, dosage

**possédant -e** *n* + *adj* moneyed, propertied (person)

**possédé -e** *n* + *adj* possessed (person)

**posséder** *vt* (6) have, hold, possess; know well (subject); have, possess (sexually); *sl* fool, trick; **se** ~ control oneself, possess oneself; *coll* **se faire** ~ be had

**possesseur** *nm* possessor, owner, proprietor

**possessif** *nm gramm* possessive; *adj* (*f* **-ive**) *gramm* possessive

possession

**possession** *nf* possession; self-possession; *leg* ~ **vaut titre** possession is nine points of the law

**possibilité** *nf* possibility

**possible** *nm* possible, what is possible; **au** ~ extremely, as can be; *adj* possible, allowable; conceivable; eventual; acceptable; *adv coll* maybe, perhaps

**postdater** *vt* post-date

**¹poste** *nf* post, postal services; post-office; *ar* relay (horses); **grande** ~ main post-office

**²poste** *nm mil* post; police-station; job; post; shift; *rad* set; transmitting station; *mil* guardroom; *comm* ledger entry; *naut* ~ **de combat** action stations

**poster** *vt* post; place, position; **se** ~ place oneself

**postérieur** *nm coll* backside, buttocks; *adj* posterior, subsequent, behind

**postérité** *nf* posterity; descendants; future generations

**posthume** *adj* posthumous

**postiche** *nm* postiche, hair-piece; *adj* false, imitation, sham; bogus, false

**postier -ière** *n* post-office employee

**postillon** *nm* postillion; *coll* speck of saliva

**postillonner** *vi coll* spit, splutter when speaking

**postopératoire** *adj med* post-operative

**postscolaire** *adj* after-school, continuation

**post-scriptum** *nm* postscript

**postulant -e** *n* applicant, candidate; *eccles* postulant

**postulat** *nm* assumption, postulate

**postuler** *vt* apply for; postulate; *vi leg* plead

**posture** *nf* posture; position, situation; **en bonne (mauvaise)** ~ well (badly) placed

**pot** *nm* can, jar, jug, pot; cooking pot, casserole; potful; *coll* good luck, luck; *sl* arse, backside; pot, potty (child); *coll* drink, glass; *coll* canteen, refectory; ~ **de chambre** chamber-pot; *mot* ~ **d'échappement** exhaust-pipe; silencer; **découvrir le** ~ **aux roses** find out the truth about sth; **payer les** ~s **cassés** pay for the damage, take the blame; **sourd comme un** ~ deaf as a post; **tourner autour du** ~ beat about the bush; cunningly seek an advantage

**potable** *adj* drinkable, fit to drink; *coll* all right, passable

**potache** *nm coll* schoolboy

**potage** *nm* soup; *lit* **pour tout** ~ all in all

**potager** *nm* kitchen-garden; *adj* (*f* -ère) vegetable

**potasse** *nf* potash

**potasser** *vt coll* study hard, swot

**potasseur** *nm coll* swot

**potassique** *adj* potassic

**pot-au-feu** *nm invar cul* stew of boiled beef and vegetables, hot-pot; *adj invar coll* home-loving, stay-at-home

**pot-de-vin** *nm* (*pl* **pots-de-vin**) bribe, graft

**pote** *nm sl* friend, mate

**poteau** *nm* pole, post, stake; stake (execution); *sl* friend, mate; ~ **d'arrivée (de départ)** winning (starting) post (race); ~ **indicateur** signpost; **au** ~! death!

**potée** *nf* kind of meat and vegetable stew; founder's clay

**potelé** *adj* chubby, plump

**potence** *nf* gallows, gibbet; death by hanging; bracket, support

**potentat** *nm* potentate

**potentialité** *nf* potentiality

**potentiel** *nm* potential; *adj* (*f* -ielle) potential

**poterie** *nf* pottery, earthenware (objects)

**poterne** *nf* postern

**potiche** *nf* large (porcelain) vase (*esp* oriental); figure-head, man of straw

**potier** *nm* potter

**potin** *nm* din, row; ~s gossip

**potiner** *vi* gossip

**potiron** *nm* pumpkin

**potron-jaquet, potron-minet** *nm invar coll* dawn, first light

**pou** *nm* louse; ~ **de mouton** tick; **chercher des** ~x **dans la tête de qn (à qn)** nag s/o; *coll* **être laid comme un** ~ be as ugly as sin

**pouah** *interj coll* ugh!

**poubelle** *nf* dustbin; *coll* **jeter à la** ~ reject scornfully

**pouce** *nm* thumb; big toe; inch; **donner le coup de** ~ add finishing touch; **donner un coup de** ~ **à qn** help s/o on (career); *sl* **et le** ~! and a bit more on top!; **manger un morceau sur le** ~ eat a hasty snack; **mettre les** ~s give in, throw in the sponge; **tourner ses** ~s, **se tourner les** ~s be idle, twiddle one's thumbs

**poucier** *nm* thumb-stall; thumb-piece (door latch)

**pouding, pudding** *nm* pudding

**poudingue** *nm geol* conglomerate, pudding stone

**poudrage** *nm agr* spraying of powder

**poudre** *nf* dust; powder; (cosmetic) powder; explosive, gunpowder; **cela sent la** ~ there is a threat of trouble; **il n'a pas inventé la** ~ he's not very bright; **jeter de la** ~ **aux yeux de qn** throw dust in s/o's eyes; **mettre le feu**

242

aux ~s cause a disaster, provoke violent reactions

**poudrer** vt powder

**poudrerie** nf gunpowder factory

**poudreux -euse** adj dusty, powdery; ar dust-covered

**poudrier** nm powder-case, compact

**poudrière** nf powder-magazine

**poudrin** nm naut spindrift

**poudroiement** nm dust-haze

**poudroyer** vi (7) form clouds of dust

**¹pouf** nm pouffe; bustle

**²pouf** interj plop!; faire ~ fall (children's phrase)

**pouffer** vi ~ de rire burst out laughing

**pouffiasse, poufiasse** nf sl tart; old bag

**pouilleux -euse** n+adj verminous (person); miserable (place); adj geog sterile

**poulailler** nm hen-house; coll theat gallery

**poulain** nm colt, foal; novice, promising newcomer, trainee; skid (for unloading barrels)

**poularde** nf cul chicken fattened for the table

**poulbot** nm urchin

**poule** nf hen; hen bird; coll tart; coll bird, girl; darling, dear; (gambling) pool; knock-out competition; orni ~ d'eau wader; ~ mouillée coward; chair de ~ goose-flesh; mère ~ over-fussy mother; quand les ~ s auront des dents when pigs can fly; tuer la ~ aux œufs d'or kill the goose that lays the golden eggs

**poulet** nm chicken; coll love-letter; coll letter; coll parking ticket; darling; coll policeman

**poulette** nf coll girl, young woman; darling; ar young hen; cul sauce (à la) ~ sauce made of butter, yolk of egg and vinegar

**pouliche** nf filly

**poulie** nf pulley; block

**pouliner** vi vet foal (mare)

**poulinière** nf+adj f (jument) ~ broodmare

**poulpe** nm zool octopus

**pouls** nm pulse; tâter le ~ de qn (de qch) sound out s/o (sth)

**poumon** nm lung; ~ d'acier iron lung; à pleins ~s at the top of one's voice; avoir des ~s have a powerful voice; have plenty of stamina

**poupard** nm plump baby; adj chubby

**poupe** nf naut stern; avoir le vent en ~ forge ahead, be doing fine

**poupée** nf doll; coll bird, girl; bandaged finger

**poupin** adj doll-like

**poupon** nm baby, small child

**pouponner** vi give cuddles

**pouponnière** nf crèche; nursery

**pour** nm le ~ et le contre the pros and cons; prep for; in exchange for, in place of; as; on behalf of; on account of; in favour of; as for, regarding; per (cent); about; for, at the price of; meant for; because; during; to, for, in order to; for, by; though; ~ ce qui est de as far as (that) is concerned; coll ~ de bon for good (and all); sl ~ de vrai honest, really, truly; ~ lors then; ~ peu que however little; ~ que for, in order that; ~ ... que however; sl c'est fait ~ it's meant, it's done, for that; en tout et ~ tout once and for all; et ~ cause! for obvious reasons!; être ~ be in favour of; être ~ + infin be on the point of; n'être pas ~ not be calculated to

**pourboire** nm tip, gratuity

**pourceau** nm ar+lit pig; hog, swine

**pourcentage** nm percentage, proportion

**pourchasser** vt pursue, track down; se ~ pursue one another

**pourfendeur** nm ar+joc slayer

**pourfendre** vt lit destroy; ar cleave in twain

**pourlécher** vt (6) complete, polish up; se ~ lick one's lips

**pourparler** nm (usu pl) diplomatic negotiation, parley

**pourpoint** nm doublet

**pourpre** nm crimson; nf purple; cloth of purple; hist consular dignity; royal dignity; cardinalate; adj crimson, purple; hêtre ~ copper beech

**pourpré** adj crimson, purple, purplish

**pourquoi** nm invar cause, reason; question; adv+conj why

**pourri** adj rotted, rotten; corrupt, corrupted; dank (weather); coll full

**pourrir** vt rot; corrupt; infect; spoil (child); vi decompose, go bad, rot, decay; addle (egg); se ~ rot away; become worse

**pourrissant** adj rotting

**pourrissement** nm deterioration, rotting

**pourriture** nf decay, putrefaction, rotting; corruption, rottenness; corrupt person

**poursuite** nf pursuit, seeking after; continuation; leg often pl action, lawsuit

**poursuivant -e** n pursuer; leg plaintiff; ar her poursuivant

**poursuivre** vt (92) pursue, chase, follow; harass; obsess; continue, go on with, proceed with; leg proceed against, prosecute, sue

**pourtant** adv however, nevertheless, none the less, still, yet

# pourtour

**pourtour** *nm* circumference, periphery, surround

**pourvoi** *nm leg* appeal; ~ **en grâce** petition for clemency

**pourvoir** *vt* (72) furnish, give, provide; endow, equip, provide for; *leg* **se** ~ appeal to higher court; **se** ~ **de** provide oneself with

**pourvoyeur -euse** *n* provider, purveyor

**pourvu que** *conj phr* provided that, so long as; it is to be hoped that

**pousse** *nf* growth; short sprout

**poussé** *adj* deep, profound (study); exaggerated; *mot moteur* ~ hotted-up engine

**pousse-café** *nm invar* brandy, liqueur; chaser

**poussée** *nf* impulse, pressure, pushing; *archi* thrust; push, shove; eruption (skin); attack (fever); growth (plant)

**pousse-pousse (pousse)** *nm invar* rickshaw

**pousser** *vt* push, shove; open; close; drive, impel; prolong, pursue; utter; heave (sigh); sing; put out (foliage); cut (teeth); attack (fever); growth (plant); ~ **l'aiguille** sew; **à la va comme je te pousse** anyhow, in any manner; *vi* push, push on, push out; go further on; grow (plant); **se** ~ push oneself forward; get on, make one's way, make progress; get out of the way, make way; push one another

**poussette** *nf* push-chair (child)

**poussier** *nm* coal-dust

**poussière** *nf* dust; powder; human remains; **réduire en** ~ pulverize; annihilate; **tomber en** ~ disintegrate, fall apart

**poussiéreux -euse** *adj* dusty

**poussif -ive** *adj vet* broken-winded (horse); short of breath, wheezy; uninspired

**poussin** *nm* child; *cul* spring chicken

**poussinière** *nf* coop; incubator

**poussoir** *nm* push-button; *mech* rod

**poutrage** *nm* framework of beams

**poutre** *nf* beam; girder

**poutrelle** *nf* small steel girder

**pouvoir** *nm* power; force, clout; means; authority, competence, competency; sovereignty; *leg* authority, power of attorney; ~ **d'achat** purchasing power; **fondé de** ~ agent, proxy; manager, managing director; *vt* (73) be able to, be in a position to; *vi* be able to, be capable of; be allowed to, have permission to; be possible; **il peut (il pourra)** there may be; **n'en** ~ **plus** be exhausted; **on ne peut mieux** best possible; **on ne peut plus** as much as possible; **puissiez-vous être ...** may you

be ...; **se** ~ be possible; *coll* **ça se peut** maybe

**pragmatique** *adj* pragmatic

**pragmatisme** *nm* pragmatism

**pragmatiste** *n + adj* pragmatist

**prairial** *nm hist* ninth month of the French Republican calendar (May to June)

**prairie** *nf* meadow, grassland; prairie

**praline** *nf* burnt almond

**praliné** *adj* browned in sugar; containing burnt almonds; **chocolat** ~ nut chocolate

**praliner** *vt* brown in sugar

**praticabilité** *nf* practicability

**praticable** *nm theat* ros; platform; *adj* practicable, feasible; possible; negotiable; suitable for vehicles

**praticien -ienne** *n med* practitioner; practical exponent

**pratiquant -e** *n + adj* practising (Christian, Mohammedan, etc)

**pratique** *nf* experience, practice; practising; habit; observance; business custom; customer; *leg* procedure; religious observances; *adj* practical; realistic; utilitarian; ingenious, useful

**pratiquer** *vt* observe, practise, put into practice, exercise; perform; construct; contrive; cut (opening); frequent (author); **se** ~ be the custom

**pré** *nm* field, meadow; **aller sur le** ~ fight a duel

**préalable** *nm* necessary condition, precondition; preliminary; **au** ~ to begin with, as a first step; *adj* preliminary, previous

**préalpin** *adj* pre-alpine

**préambule** *nm* preamble

**préau** *nm* playground, covered part of playground; inner courtyard (prison, hospital, monastery, etc)

**préavis** *nm* previous warning; notice (of dismissal); **appel avec** ~ personal call (telephone)

**prébende** *nf eccles* prebend; sinecure

**prébendier** *nm eccles* prebendary; holder of sinecure

**précaire** *adj* precarious, uncertain; delicate, fragile

**précarité** *nf* precariousness

**précaution** *nf* precaution; care, caution, circumspection, wariness; *coll* **prendre ses** ~ **s** go to the lavatory as a precautionary measure

**précautionner** *vt ar* caution against, warn against; **se** ~ **contre** take one's precautions against; **se** ~ **de** furnish oneself with

**précautionneux -euse** *adj* prudent, wary

**précédemment** *adv* already, before, previously

244

**précédent** *nm* precedent; **sans ~** un-heard of; *adj* preceding, previous
**précéder** *vt* (6) go before, precede; have precedence over
**précellence** *nf lit* supreme excellence
**précepte** *nm* precept
**précepteur -trice** *n* (private) tutor, (*f*) governess
**prêche** *nm eccles* sermon; boring moral discourse
**prêcher** *vt eccles* preach (gospel, sermon); advocate, preach; *eccles* evangelize (s/o); *coll* try to persuade; *vi eccles* preach; moralize boringly; **~ d'exemple (par l'exemple)** practise what one preaches
**prêcheur -euse** *n* moralizer, sermonizer; *adj eccles* preaching (friar); moral-izing, preaching, sermonizing
**prêchi, prêcha, prêchi-prêcha** *nm invar coll* tedious moralizing
**précieuse** *nf Fr lit hist* précieuse, expo-nent of preciosity
**précieux -ieuse** *adj* precious, valuable, invaluable; affected, over-refined, pre-cious
**préciosité** *nf* preciosity, affectation, over-refinement
**précipitamment** *adv* hastily, headlong, precipitately
**précipitation** *nf* haste, hurry, precipita-tion
**précipité** *nm chem* precipitate; *adj* fast, rapid; hasty, hurried
**précipiter** *vt* hurl down, precipitate, throw down; force, push; hasten, hurry, precipitate; **se ~** hurl oneself down; fall down; rush; hasten, hurry
**précis** *nm* précis, abstract, epitome; short manual; *adj* clear, precise; de-tailed, explicit
**précisément** *adv* clearly, precisely; in fact
**préciser** *vt* express precisely; specify; determine, establish; emphasize; make clear; **se ~** become clearer
**précision** *nf* accuracy, exactness, preci-sion, clarity; **~ s** details, precise facts
**précité** *adj* above, previously mentioned
**préclassique** *adj* pre-classical
**précoce** *adj* precocious; *hort* early
**précocité** *nf* precociousness, precocity
**précompter** *vt comm* deduct beforehand
**préconception** *nf* preconception, pre-conceived idea; prejudice
**préconçu** *adj* preconceived, pre-estab-lished; prejudiced
**préconiser** *vt* advocate, recommend
**précontraint** *nm + adj eng* pre-stressed (concrete)
**précontrainte** *nf eng* pre-stressing
**précurseur** *nm* forerunner, precursor;

*adj m* precursory, premonitory
**prédateur** *nm + adj* predatory (animal, insect)
**prédestiné -e** *n theol* elect; *adj theol* predestined, preordained
**prédestiner** *vt theol* predestine; destine
**prédéterminer** *vt* predetermine
**prédicant** *nm* protestant preacher; *adj* moralizing
**prédicat** *nm gramm* predicate
**prédicateur** *nm* preacher
**prédication** *nf* preaching; sermon
**prédiction** *nf* forecast, prediction; prophecy
**prédigéré** *adj* predigested
**prédilection** *nf* predilection, preference; **de ~** favourite
**prédire** *vt* (74) forecast, foretell, predict
**prédisposer** *vt* incline, predispose; influ-ence
**prédisposition** *nf* predisposition, ten-dency; aptitude, gift
**prédominant** *adj* predominant
**prédominer** *vi* predominate
**prééminence** *nf* pre-eminence
**prééminent** *adj* pre-eminent
**préemption** *nf leg* pre-emption, first refusal
**préexistant** *adj* pre-existent
**préexistence** *nf* pre-existence
**préexister** *vi* pre-exist
**préfabriqué** *adj* prefabricated; arranged in advance
**préfacer** *vt* (4) preface
**préfectoral** *adj* prefectorial
**préfecture** *nf* prefecture; area adminis-tered by a prefect; **~ de police** (Paris) police headquarters; **~ maritime** naval port
**préférable** *adj* preferable; wiser
**préféré -e** *n + adj* favourite
**préférence** *nf* preference; predilection, weakness; privilege; **de ~** preferably; **de ~ à** rather than
**préférentiel -ielle** *adj* preferential
**préférer** *vt* (6) like better, prefer; adopt, choose
**préfet** *nm Rom hist* prefect; (French administration) prefect; priest in charge of discipline in French Catholic school; **~ de police** chief of Paris police; **~ maritime** admiral com-manding naval district
**préfète** *nf* wife of prefect
**préfigurer** *vt* prefigure
**préfixe** *nm gramm* prefix; dialling code (telephone)
**préfixer** *vt* prefix
**prégnant** *adj* having implicit meaning, significant; *gramm* pregnant
**préhellénique** *adj* prehellenic
**préhistoire** *nf* prehistory

**préhistorique** *adj* prehistoric
**préjudice** *nm* detriment, wrong; *leg* tort; **porter ~ à** injure, wrong; **sans ~ de** without prejudice to, without referring to
**préjudiciable** *adj* detrimental, injurious, prejudicial
**préjugé** *nm* presumption; bias, preconception, prejudice
**préjuger** *vt* (3) *lit* prejudge; **~ de** prejudge
**prélart** *nm* tarpaulin
**prélasser (se)** *v refl* loll about; *ar* give oneself airs
**prélat** *nm* prelate
**prélèvement** *nm* taking of a part of sth, taking of a sample; appropriation; quantity appropriated
**prélever** *vt* (6) take a part of, take a sample of; appropriate, extract, remove; remove in advance
**préliminaire** *adj* preliminary
**préliminaires** *nmpl* preliminaries
**préluder** *vi mus* prelude; **~ à** lead up to; try out
**prématuré** *adj* premature, untimely
**préméditation** *nf* premeditation; *leg* **avec ~** with malice aforethought
**préméditer** *vt* premeditate; calculate; **~ de** plan to
**prémices** *nfpl hist* first-fruit (offering); *lit* beginning
**premier -ière** *n* first, the first; first (of month); British prime minister; first syllable in charade; **en ~** first of all, of first rank; *theat* **jeune ~** juvenile lead; **le ~ venu** anyone at all, no matter who; *adj* first, initial; prime (quality); former, original, pristine; best, highest; essential; primordial; *math+ philos* prime; **~ ministre** prime minister; **première nouvelle!** first I've heard of it!, I'd no idea!; **au (du) ~ coup** at the first attempt; **au ~ plan** in the foreround; **enfant d'un ~ lit** child of first marriage; **enseignement du ~ degré** primary education; *math* **facteurs ~ s** prime factors; *theat* **grand ~ rôle** lead; **matières premières** raw materials; *math* **nombre ~** prime number
**première** *nf* first night; sixth form (school); first-class ticket; first-class cabin; first-class seat (train); *mot* first gear
**premier-né** (*f* **première-née**) *n+adj* (*pl* **premiers-nés, premières-nées**) first-born (child)
**prémisse** *nf philos* premise, premises; affirmation
**prémonitoire** *adj* premonitory
**prémunir** *vt* protect from, warn against; **se ~** arm oneself, protect oneself

**prenable** *adj* seizable, takeable
**prenant** *adj* prehensile; captivating, engaging, interesting; *leg* **partie ~e** payee
**prendre** *vt* (75) take, take hold of; pick up, seize; go and get; carry, take along; consider, think about; enjoy, feel; accept (responsibility); assume, take on; drink, eat, take; ask, charge (a price); buy (seat, ticket); arrest, capture, catch; deceive, take; have, obtain; have, possess (woman); catch out; *coll* put up with; receive (blow); *coll* come over one; **~ au passage** intercept; **~ de l'âge** be getting old; **~ du poids** put on weight; **~ du ventre** develop a paunch; **~ en grippe** take a strong dislike to; **~ froid** catch a cold; **~ goût à** begin to like; develop a taste for; *naut* **~ le large (la mer)** put out to sea; **~ la parole** speak at a meeting; **prenez la peine de** be so good as to; **~ l'eau** leak (boat); **~ le deuil** go into mourning; **~ le lit** take to one's bed; **~ les armes** take up arms; **~ le voile** go into a convent; **~ mal** take badly; fall ill; **~ qch à qn** take sth from s/o; **~ qch sur soi** take sth upon oneself; **~ sur soi** take it upon oneself to; **~ sur son compte** take full responsibility; **~ un baiser** steal a kiss; **à tout ~** in short, when all is said and done; *coll* **ça vous prend souvent?** do you often behave like this?; **c'est à ~ ou à laisser** it's take it or leave it; *coll* **c'est autant de pris** that's something anyway; **on ne sait pas où le ~** he's very touchy; *coll* **qu'est-ce qui vous prend?** what's biting you?, what's the matter?; *vi* congeal, curdle; freeze, set, take; stick (to pan); begin to burn (fire); succeed, catch on (fashion, habit); go in a given direction; **~ à gauche** turn left; **se ~** be taken; be caught; catch oneself out; freeze (water); hold one another; make love together; take from one another; **se ~ à** begin to; **se ~ de** begin to feel (affection, etc); **se ~ pour** think oneself to be; **s'en ~ à** hold responsible for; **s'y ~** go about sth; **se ~ aux cheveux** quarrel
**preneur -euse** *n* taker; purchaser; *comm* payee; *leg* lessee, lease-holder; **je suis ~ à 2.000 francs** my offer is 2,000 francs
**prénom** *nm* Christian name, first name
**prénommé -e** *n+adj* above named
**prénommer** *vt* give a first name to; **se ~** be called
**préoccupation** *nf* preoccupation, obsession, absorption; anxiety, care

**préoccupé** *adj* preoccupied, absorbed; anxious, concerned

**préoccuper** *vt* preoccupy, absorb, engross; disturb, make worried; **se ~ de** attend to, see to, take trouble over; worry about

**préparateur -trice** *n* research assistant (sciences); dispenser (chemist's shop)

**préparatifs** *nmpl* arrangements, preparations

**préparation** *nf* preparation, preparing; dressing (skins); **mil ~ d'artillerie** barrage; **annoncer sans ~** blurt out

**préparatoire** *adj* preparatory

**préparer** *vt* get ready, organize; fit, train; study for (examination); dress (skins); **se ~** get ready; be about to happen, be imminent

**prépondérant** *adj* preponderant; decisive, dominant; **voix ~ e** casting vote

**préposé -e** *n* minor official (customs officer, postman, etc); attendant

**préposer** *vt* appoint, entrust with

**prépositif -ive** *adj* gramm prepositional

**préraphaélisme** *nm* preraphaelitism

**préromantique** *adj* preromantic

**préromantisme** *nm* preromanticism

**près** *adv* close, close by, near, nearby; **~ de** close to, near to; by the side of; beside; nearby; *naut* **~ du vent** close-hauled; **à beaucoup ~** far from it, nothing near; **à cela ~** excepting; **à peu ~** about; **à peu de chose(s) ~** very nearly; **à ... ~** approximately, nearly, save; *naut* **au plus ~** close-hauled; **de ~** closely, carefully

**présage** *nm* omen, portent, presage

**présager** *vt* (3) presage; foresee

**pré-salé** *nm* (*pl* **prés-salés**) salt-meadow sheep; salt-meadow mutton

**presbyte** *n + adj* long-sighted (person)

**presbytéral** *adj* priestly; **conseil ~** presbytery (Protestant)

**presbytère** *nm* presbytery (Catholic); (also used for) vicarage (Anglican), manse (non-conformist)

**presbytérianisme** *nm* presbyterianism

**presbytérien -ienne** *n + adj* presbyterian

**presbytie** *nf* med long-sightedness

**prescience** *nf* theol divine prescience; foreknowledge

**prescription** *nf* prescription; regulation; instruction

**prescrire** *vt* (42) indicate, prescribe, recommend; med prescribe; *leg* bar, prescribe; acquire by prescription

**préséance** *nf* precedence

**présélection** *nf* pre-selection

**présence** *nf* presence; existence; actuality; personality; **en ~** face to face; **en ~ de** before, in front of; **faire acte de ~** be formally present

**¹présent** *nm* present; *gramm* present (tense); *adj* present; at hand, on hand; current; *gramm* present; **à ~** at this moment, now; **à ~ que** now that; **d'à ~ concurrent**, of this time, present

**²présent** *nm* lit gift, present

**présentateur -trice** *n* presenter; promoter; *rad* compère

**présentation** *nf* presentation; introduction; *coll* appearance; presenting; launching (exhibition, novel); manner of presentation

**présenter** *vt* present; introduce; propose (for employment); put in (candidate for examination); put up (candidate for election); display, exhibit; convey (congratulations, sympathy); describe, show; appear to have; *vi coll* **~ bien (mal)** have a good (bad) appearance; **se ~** appear, arrive, call on; introduce oneself; make oneself known; apply, be a candidate, present oneself; come to mind

**préservateur -trice** *adj* preserving

**préservatif -ive** *adj* sheath; *coll* French letter

**préserver** *vt* preserve, protect, save, shelter; **se ~** protect oneself

**présidence** *nf* presidency; duration of presidency; presidential residence; chairmanship

**président** *nm* pol president; president (society); chairman (company, examiners, magistrates); **~ -directeur général (P.D.G.)** chairman and managing director; **~ du conseil** (French) prime minister, head of government

**présidentiel -ielle** *adj* presidential

**présider** *vt* preside over; take the chair at; direct, watch over; *vi* preside

**présomptif -ive** *adj* presumptive; **héritier ~** heir apparent

**présomption** *nf* presumption, conjecture; supposition; pretentiousness

**présomptueux -ueuse** *adj* presumptuous, pretentious

**presque** *adv* almost, nearly; near; hardly, scarcely

**presqu'île** *nf* peninsula

**pressage** *nm* pressing

**pressant** *adj* pressing, urgent

**presse** *nf* crowd, press; press; (printing) press; press (newspapers); peak period, rush; **~ du cœur** women's magazines; **~ monétaire** minting press; **mettre sous ~** begin to print, go to press

**pressé** *nm* **aller au plus ~** deal with the most urgent thing first; *adj* pressed; in a hurry, pressed; pressing, urgent

**presse-bouton** *adj* invar push-button

**presse-citron** *nm* invar lemon squeezer

**pressée** *nf* pressing (fruit, etc)

# pressentiment

**pressentiment** *nm* foreboding, intuition, presentiment

**pressentir** *vt* have a presentiment of; be aware of; sound out

**presse-papiers** *nm* paper-weight

**presser** *vt* press, squeeze; assail, beset, harass; expedite, hurry (s/o) on, quicken (step); clasp, embrace; encourage, urge; *vi* be urgent; **se ~** press oneself; hasten, hurry

**presse-raquette** *nm invar* racket-press (tennis)

**presseur -euse** *n* presser; *adj* pressing, which presses

**pressing** *nm* cleaner's (shop)

**pression** *nf* pressure; **bière à la ~** draught-beer; **sous ~** pressurized; under pressure; under steam

**pressoir** *nm* cider-press, oil-press, wine-press; building housing cider-press, etc

**pressurer** *vt* press (fruit, etc); pressurize; exact money from; *coll* **se ~ le cerveau** torment oneself

**pressuriser** *vt* pressurize

**prestance** *nf* bearing, demeanour, imposing presence

**prestation** *nf hist + leg* taking of an oath; *mil* allowance; benefit (health service, insurance); war indemnity; *theat* turn, number; **~ en espèces (en nature)** benefits in cash (in kind)

**preste** *adj* agile, alert, nimble, quick; **avoir la main ~** be adroit

**prestidigitateur -trice** *n* conjuror

**prestidigitation** *nf* conjuring, sleight of hand

**prestige** *nm* glamour, prestige

**prestigieux -ieuse** *adj lit* glamorous, remarkable, wonderful

**présumé** *adj* presumed, supposed

**présumer** *vt* presume, suppose; guess, infer, think; **~ trop de** over-estimate

**présupposer** *vt* presuppose

**présure** *nf* rennet

**présurer** *vt* curdle (milk)

**¹prêt** *nm* lending, loan; *mil* pay; advance (of salary)

**²prêt** *adj* prepared, ready; **~ à** ready to, willing to; about to

**prétantaine** *nf see* **prétentaine**

**prêt-à-porter** *nm collect* ready-made clothes

**prêté** *nm* **c'est un ~ pour un rendu** it's tit for tat; *adj* lent

**prétendant -e** *n* claimant, pretender (throne); *nm* suitor

**prétendre** *vt* affirm, declare, maintain; intend, mean to; claim; **~ à** aspire to, lay claim to; **à ce qu'il prétend** according to him; **en prétendant que** on the pretext that; **se ~** maintain that one is

**prétendu -e** *n* intended (fiancé, fiancée); *adj* alleged, so-called, would-be

**prête-nom** *nm* agent, proxy; *pej* man of straw

**prétentaine, prétantaine** *nf* **courir la ~** get into scrapes; gad about, have a lot of love affairs, lead a wild life

**prétentieux -ieuse** *adj* affected, mannered; pretentious, vain

**prétention** *nf* pretentiousness, vanity; claim, demand; ambition, pretension; condition, request

**prêter** *vt* lend; give, grant; ascribe, attribute; *vi* give, stretch (material); **à** give rise to; **~ attention** pay attention; **~ la main** help; **~ sa voix à** speak for; **~ serment** take an oath; **se ~ à** agree to; indulge in; be adapted to

**prétérit** *nm gramm* preterite

**préteur** *nm Rom hist* praetor

**prêteur -euse** *n* lender, money-lender; **~ sur gages** pawnbroker; *adj* disposed to lend, willing to lend

**prétexte** *nm* pretext; excuse, reason; **sous aucun ~** under no circumstances

**prétexter** *vt* allege, plead

**prétoire** *nm* court, court-room; *Rom hist* praetorium

**prétorien** *nm + adj* (*f* **-ienne**) praetorian

**prêtre** *nm* priest

**prêtresse** *nf* priestess

**prêtrise** *nf* priesthood

**preuve** *nf* proof; evidence, justification, sign, token; **~ d'une opération** cross-check; *hist* **~ par jugement de Dieu** trial by ordeal; **~ par l'absurde** reductio ad absurdum; *hist* **~ par le combat** trial by combat; *coll* **à ~** example, witness; **à ~ que** the proof is that; **faire ~ de** show; **faire ses ~s** show one's mettle, prove oneself

**preux** *nm* champion, valiant knight; *adj m* brave, valiant

**prévaloir** *vi* (76) prevail, succeed, win; **se ~ de** take advantage of; pride oneself on

**prévaricateur -trice** *n* culpably negligent administrator or judge; *adj* culpably negligent

**prévarication** *nf* culpable negligence; breach of trust

**prévariquer** *vi leg* be guilty of culpable negligence; be guilty of breach of trust

**prévenance** *nf* consideration, kindness, kindly act

**prévenant** *adj* considerate, kindly, thoughtful

**prévenir** *vt* (96) anticipate, avert, forestall, ward off; bias, influence; apprise, inform, tell, warn

**préventif -ive** *adj* precautionary, preventive

248

**prévention** *nf* bias, preconceived idea, prejudice; prepossession; prevention; *leg* imprisonment awaiting trial; ~ **routière** road safety organization

**prévenu -e** *n* accused, prisoner; *adj* biased, prejudiced

**prévisible** *adj* foreseeable

**prévision** *nf* estimate, expectation, forecast; **en** ~ **de** in expectation of

**prévoir** *vt* (77) forecast, foresee; estimate, make provision for; plan ahead for; **être prévu pour** be designed for, be meant for

**prévôt** *nm hist* provost; *mil* officer of the military police; privileged prisoner

**prévôté** *nf hist* provostship; *hist* + *mil* (service of) military police

**prévoyance** *nf* foresight, forethought; **société de** ~ provident society

**prévoyant** *adj* foreseeing, prudent, far-sighted

**prévu** *adj* anticipated, expected, foreseen; allowed for, provided for

**prie-Dieu** *nm invar* prayer-stool

**prier** *vt* pray to; beg, request; invite; **je vous prie** please; **je vous en prie** it doesn't matter in the least, not at all; **sans se faire** ~ willingly; without trouble; **se faire** ~ agree after persuasion; *vi* pray

**prière** *nf* prayer; entreaty, request; ~ **de** you are asked to

**prieur -e** *n* prior(ess)

**prieuré** *nm* priory; priory church

**primaire** *nm* primary education; *elect* primary current; narrow-minded individual; dimwit; person ruled by primitive instincts; *adj* primary; narrow-minded, pedantic; dim; primitive

**primat** *nm eccles* primate; primacy

**primauté** *nf* pre-eminence, primacy, supremacy

**prime** *nf comm* premium; bonus, subsidy; free gift; expenses; *eccles* prime; prime (fencing); **marché à** ~ option market; *adj math* prime; *ar* first; ~ **jeunesse** earliest youth; **de** ~ **abord** right from the start

**primer** *vt* award a prize to, give a bonus to; *vi* excel, take the lead

**primerose** *nf* hollyhock

**primesautier -ière** *n* + *adj* impulsive, spontaneous (person)

**primeur** *nf* novelty; *ar* newness; ~ **s** early vegetables, fruit before season

**primevère** *nf bot* primrose

**primitif -ive** *n anthrop* + *arts* primitive; *adj* primitive; initial, original; primary (colour, tense); crude, primitive

**primo** *adv* firstly, in the first place

**primordial** *adj* primordial; essential, of prime importance

**primulacées** *nfpl bot* primulaceae

**prince** *nm* prince; **être bon** ~ be generous and kindly

**prince de Galles** *nm invar* kind of woollen cloth

**princeps** *adj* **édition** ~ first edition (of old, rare work)

**princesse** *nf* princess; **aux frais de la** ~ expenses paid

**princier -ière** *adj* princely

**principal** *nm* essential, main thing; principal (college, etc); main principal, capital sum; *adj* chief, leading, main, principal

**principauté** *nf* principality

**principe** *nm* principle; first principle; hypothesis, premise, proposition; cause, mainspring; principle, rule, rule of conduct; ~ **s** rudiments; moral principles; **de** ~ a priori; **en** ~ in theory; **par** ~ on principle, a priori; **pour le** ~ on principle

**printanier -ière** *adj* spring, spring-like; youthful

**printemps** *nm* spring, springtime; *ar* **avoir quinze** ~ be fifteen years old

**prioritaire** *n* + *adj* priority (holder)

**priorité** *nf* priority; *mot* right of way; *mot* ~ **à droite** (road sign) give way to traffic coming from the right; *comm* **action de** ~ preference share; *mot* **route à** ~ major road

**pris** *adj* caught, taken; engaged, occupied; affected; coagulated, set; **bien** ~ svelte, slender

**prise** *nf* grasp, grip; hold; capture, catching, taking; catch (fish); pinch (snuff); take; coagulation, setting; means of catching, means of taking; *elect* plug; socket; *naut* prize; ~ **d'armes** military parade; ~ **d'eau** tap; hydrant; ~ **de bec** altercation, dispute; *leg* ~ **de corps** arrest; *elect* ~ **de courant** plug; socket; *med* ~ **de sang** blood-test; taking of blood from donor; ~ **de son** recording; *cin* ~ **de vue(s)** take; *mot* ~ **directe** direct transmission; **avoir** ~ **sur** have a hold over; **donner** ~ **à** give a handle to, give an opening to; **être aux** ~ **s avec** be struggling with; *mot* **être en** ~ be in top gear; **lâcher** ~ let go; abandon; **mettre aux** ~ **s** set by the ears

¹**priser** *vt* admire, prize, rate highly, value; **se** ~ think well of oneself

²**priser** *vt* + *vi* take (snuff)

¹**priseur -euse** *n* snuff-taker

²**priseur** *nm see* **commissaire-priseur**

**prismatique** *adj* prismatic

**prisme** *nm* prism

**prison** *nf* gaol, jail, prison; imprisonment; prison-like building; *coll* **aim-**

# prisonnier

**able comme une porte de ~** very disagreeable

**prisonnier -ière** *n* prisoner; *adj* captive, imprisoned

**privatif** *nm* + *adj* (*f* -**ive**) *gramm* privative (prefix)

**privation** *nf* deprivation, lack; privation

**privatiser** *vt* privatize

**privautés** *nfpl* familiarity, liberties

**privé** *nm* private life; *coll* private industry; *adj* private; intimate, personal; individual, particular

**priver** *vt* deprive; debar; **se ~** deny oneself; impose privations on oneself

**privilège** *nm* privilege; exclusive right; *leg* lien, preference; *Fr hist* authorization from the king to publish a book; grant, licence, preferential right

**privilégié** *adj* privileged; *comm* preference (shares); exceptionally gifted, favoured

**prix** *nm* cost, price, value; rate, tariff; importance, value, weight; prize, reward; **~ de détail** retail price; **~ de gros** wholesale price; **~ de revient** cost price; **~ fixe** fixed price; fixed price meal; **à aucun ~** on no account; **à tout ~** at all costs; **attacher du ~ à** regard as important; **au ~ de** at the cost of; **au ~ fort** at a very high price; **à vil ~** at a very low price; **de ~** valuable; **dernier ~** final price; last word; **donner du ~ à** cause to be valued; **être sans ~** be priceless, be very valuable; **hors de ~** extremely expensive; **mise à ~** reserve price (auction)

**probabilisme** *nm philos* probabilism

**probabilité** *nf* probability, likelihood; conjecture

**probant** *adj* conclusive; *leg* probative

**probe** *adj* honest, upright

**probité** *nf* probity; uprightness

**problématique** *adj* problematical, questionable

**problème** *nm* problem, puzzle; sum

**procédé** *nm* method, process; *pej* stereotyped method; behaviour, conduct, dealing, method of handling; cue-tip (billiards); **échange de bons ~ s** mutual help; exchange of courtesies

**procéder** *vi* (6) proceed; originate; act, behave, proceed; **~ à** *leg* execute; proceed with

**procédure** *nf leg* procedure, proceedings; legal practice

**procédurier -ière** *n* compulsive litigant; *adj* fond of chicanery, pettifogging

**procès** *nm* case, cause; trial; *anat* process; **être en ~ avec qn** be fighting a case against s/o; **faire le ~ de** criticize; **intenter un ~ à** bring an action against; **sans autre forme de ~**

without further ado; **soutenir un ~** bring an action

**processif -ive** *adj* litigious

**procession** *nf* religious procession; stream of persons

**processionnel -elle** *adj* processional

**processus** *nm* development method; *anat* process

**procès-verbal** *nm* (*pl* **procès-verbaux**) formal (police) report; minutes, proceedings; **~ de contravention (P.V.)** (police) ticket; **dresser (un) ~** draw up a report; take particulars

**prochain -e** *n* fellow-creature, neighbour; *adj* near, nearest, neighbouring; approaching (in time), following, next; proximate; **à la ~ e!** be seeing you!

**proche** *adj* near, neighbouring; closely related; *adv* near, nearby; **de ~ en ~** by degrees, step by step

**proclamer** *vt* proclaim; announce, publish; affirm

**proclitique** *adj gramm* proclitic

**proconsulaire** *adj* proconsular

**proconsulat** *nm* proconsulate

**procréateur -trice** *n ar* + *joc* parent; *adj* procreating

**procréer** *vt* engender, procreate

**procurateur** *nm hist* procurator

**procuration** *nf leg* procuration, proxy; power of attorney; **par ~** by proxy

**procurer** *vt* procure; provide; cause; **se ~** acquire

**¹procureur -atrice** *n leg* proxy

**²procureur** *nm* law officer; **~ de la république** public prosecutor

**prodigalité** *nf* prodigality; extravagance

**prodige** *nm* marvel, prodigy, wonder; **enfant ~** infant prodigy

**prodigieux -ieuse** *adj* extraordinary, prodigious, wonderful

**prodigue** *n* prodigal, spendthrift; *adj* prodigal, wasteful; generous, lavish

**prodiguer** *vt* give too readily, give generously, be lavish with; **se ~** exert oneself generously

**prodrome** *nm* preamble, preliminary; *med* premonitory symptom

**producteur -trice** *n* producer; *cin* producer; *adj* producing, productive

**productible** *adj* producible

**productif -ive** *adj* productive

**production** *nf* production, producing, formation; yield; output, manufacturing; product(s)

**productivité** *nf* productivity

**produire** *vt* (80) bring forth, engender, produce; adduce, bring out, show; yield; generate, manufacture; cause; **se ~** happen, occur; *ar* appear

**produit** *nm* product; takings; yield; **~ s** goods, produce

**proéminence** *nf* protuberance; prominence

**proéminent** *adj* protuberant; prominent

**prof** *n coll* teacher

**profanateur -trice** *n* profaner; *adj* profaning

**profane** *n* uninitiated person; ignoramus; *adj* profane; ignorant; uninitiated

**profaner** *vt* desecrate, profane; degrade, violate

**proférer** *vt* (6) emit, pour forth, utter

**professer** *vt* teach, declare; profess

**professeur** *nm* master, mistress, teacher; lecturer; professor

**profession** *nf* business, calling, occupation; profession; ~ **de foi** *pol* (electoral) manifesto

**professionalisme** *nm* professionalism

**professionnel -elle** *n + adj* professional; *nf coll* whore

**professoral** *adj* concerning teaching; professoral

**professorat** *nm* teaching, teaching profession; status of teacher or professor

**profil** *nm* profile; contour, outline, silhouette; *archi* section; **de** ~ from the side, side-face

**profiler** *vt* profile, draw in profile; shape, streamline; outline sharply; **se** ~ be outlined, be silhouetted

**profit** *nm* advantage, benefit, enrichment, profit; **au** ~ **de** in aid of; **être à** ~ be showing a profit; **faire son** ~ **de** take advantage of; **mettre à** ~ use profitably; **tirer** ~ **de** derive benefit from

**profiter** *vi* profit; *coll* become stronger, develop; ~ **à** benefit from, derive profit from; bring profit to, be useful to; ~ **de** benefit by, profit by; avail oneself of, take advantage of; ~ **de qch pour** use sth as a pretext for

**profiteur -euse** *n pej* profiteer

**profond** *nm* depth; *adj* deep, deep-seated, profound; penetrating; impenetrable; downright; *adv* deep

**profondément** *adv* deeply, profoundly; intensely; intimately; extremely

**profondeur** *nf* depth; profoundness, profundity

**profus** *adj* profuse

**profusion** *nf* profusion, abundance; prodigality; **à** ~ in abundance

**progéniture** *nf* offspring, progeny

**prognathe** *adj anthrop* prognathous, protruding

**programmateur -trice** *n rad* programme-planner; *adj* programming (computer, etc)

**programmation** *nf cin + rad* programme-planning, programming

**programme** *nm* programme; syllabus;

intention, project; (computer) program

**programmer** *vt + vi* programme

**programmeur -euse** *n* (computer) programmer

**progrès** *nm* improvement, progress; development, progress; worsening (disease)

**progresser** *vi* advance, improve, progress; develop, make progress; worsen (disease)

**progressif -ive** *adj* progressive; developing; gradual, graduated

**progression** *nf* advancement, forward movement, progress, progression; aggravation; *math + mus* progression

**progressiste** *n + adj* progressive

**progressivité** *nf* progressiveness

**prohiber** *vt* forbid, prohibit

**prohibitif -ive** *adj* prohibitory; prohibitive

**prohibitionnisme** *nm* protection (by customs duties); *US hist* prohibitionism

**proie** *nf* prey, quarry; victim; **de** ~ predatory; **en** ~ **à** tormented by, tortured by, obsessed by

**projecteur** *nm* projector; floodlight; spotlight

**projectionniste** *n cin* operator, projectionist

**projet** *nm* design, intention, plan, project; blue-print, preliminary plan; ~ **de loi** bill; **à l'état de** ~ at the planning stage; provisional

**projeter** *vt* (5) project; cast, throw, hurl; design, intend, plan

**prolapsus** *nm path* prolapse

**prolétaire** *nm* proletarian

**prolétarien -ienne** *adj* proletarian

**prolifère** *adj bot* proliferous

**proliférer** *vi* (6) proliferate; increase, multiply

**prolifique** *adj* prolific

**prolixe** *adj* prolix, verbose, wordy

**prolixité** *nf* prolixity

**prolongation** *nf* extension, prolongation, protraction; *mus* holding; *sp* **jouer les** ~ **s** play extra time

**prolongé** *adj* continued, prolonged, protracted; *coll* ~ **e** not yet married (girl)

**prolongement** *nm* extension, lengthening, prolongation; consequence; development

**prolonger** *vt* (3) extend, lengthen, prolong, protract; **se** ~ go on, last longer than expected

**promenade** *nf* avenue, promenade, public walk; excursion, outing; stroll, walk; ~ **à bicyclette**, ~ **à cheval** ride; ~ **à pied** walk; ~ **en bateau** row, sail; ~ **en voiture** drive

**promener** vt (6) show round, take about; take for a drive, ride, run, sail, walk; move, run up and down (fingers, hand); carry about; se ~ walk; go for a drive, ride, run, sail, walk; **allez vous ~ !** go to hell!; coll **envoyer ~ qn** send s/o packing, turn s/o out; **envoyer tout ~** abandon everything, give up

**promeneur -euse** n stroller, walker; nf children's nurse

**promenoir** nm ambulatory, courtyard (convent, prison, etc); theat foyer

**promesse** nf assurance, pledge, promise, undertaking; hope, promise

**prometteur -euse** adj promising

**promettre** vt (60) assure, pledge, promise, undertake; announce, predict, promise; ~ **la lune,** ~ **monts et merveilles** promise the earth; se ~ count on, hope for; promise one another; se ~ de plan to

**promis -e** n betrothed, fiancé(e); adj promised; ~ à destined for

**promiscuité** nf promiscuity

**promontoire** nm promontory

**promoteur -trice** n author, creator, instigator, promoter; property developer

**promotion** nf advancement, preferment, promotion; collect successful candidates in competitive examination or at end of course

**promouvoir** vt (78) promote; encourage, foster

**prompt** adj immediate, prompt; diligent; adroit, quick; **avoir la main ~ e** be always ready to strike

**promptitude** nf promptitude, readiness; rapidity

**promu -e** n + adj promoted (person)

**promulguer** vt promulgate; issue, publish

**prône** nm eccles homily, sermon

**prôner** vt extol, praise highly; advocate, recommend

**pronom** nm gramm pronoun

**prononcé** nm leg (text of) judgement; adj declared, pronounced; definite, marked, pronounced

**prononcer** vt (4) announce; deliver (judgement); pronounce (sentence); articulate, say, utter; deliver, give (speech); vi take a decision; come down in favour; give judgement; se ~ be pronounced, become pronounced

**prononciation** nf pronunciation; delivery of judgement

**pronostic** nm med prognosis; forecast, prediction, prognostication

**pronostiquer** vt med forecast, predict, prognosticate

**pronostiqueur -ueuse** n forecaster

**propagande** nf propaganda; publicity

**propagandiste** n + adj propagandist

**propagateur -trice** n propagator

**propager** vt (3) propagate; se ~ spread (ideas, illness)

**propédeutique** nf introductory study at university

**propension** nf inclination, propensity, tendency

**prophète** nm prophet, augur

**prophétesse** nf prophetess

**prophétie** nf prophecy; prophesying; prediction, forecast

**prophétique** adj prophetic, prophetical

**prophétiser** vt prophesy; foretell, predict

**prophylactique** adj prophylactic

**prophylaxie** nf prophylaxis

**propice** adj auspicious, favourable, propitious

**propitiatoire** adj propitiatory

**proportion** nf percentage, proportion, ratio; harmony, scale; ~ s dimensions, size; à ~ (en ~) in proportion, proportionately; à ~ de according to; à ~ que as, in proportion as

**proportionné** adj proportioned; well-proportioned; proportionate

**proportionnel -elle** adj proportional; **impôt ~** ad valorem tax; math **moyenne ~ elle** geometrical mean

**proportionner** vt adapt, adjust, proportion

**propos** nm purpose, resolution; matter, subject; pl remarks, words; à ~ by the way; at the right moment; appropriately enough; à ~ de concerning; à ce ~ with regard to this; à quel ~ ? about what?; à tout ~ all the time, incessantly; hors de ~ inappropriate; mal à ~ inopportune, unfortunate

**proposer** vt offer, propose; show; present, propound, submit; announce; set (question, subject); propose (candidate); vi form a plan, propose; se ~ propose oneself, submit one's candidature; have as one's aim, intend, mean

**proposition** nf proposal, proposition; offer; motion; math + philos proposition; sur ~ de at the suggestion of, on a motion of

**propre** nm characteristic, property; au ~ in the literal sense, literally; coll **c'est du ~** it's disgraceful, it's disgusting; en ~ in one's own right; adj own, particular, personal; proper (name); appropriate, apt, very; clean, neat; correct, immaculate; honest, honourable; house-trained (pet); ~ à conducive to, suitable for; apt; ~ à rien good for nothing; **être ~** be in a fix, be in a fine mess; **mettre au ~** make a clean copy; **sens** ~ exact meaning; correct usage

**proprement** *adv* correctly, properly; exactly, precisely, truly; carefully; cleanly; *coll* decently; **à** ~ **parler** to be quite precise; ~ **dit** properly speaking

**propret-ette** *adj* nice and clean, neat

**propreté** *nf* cleanliness, neatness, tidiness; *arts* cleanness of execution

**propriétaire** *n* proprietor, proprietress; owner, landlord (landlady) (house); ~ **foncier** landed proprietor

**propriété** *nf* ownership, possession; property; estate, holding; house; spacious house in own grounds; characteristic, specific quality; correctness, propriety

**propulser** *vt* propel

**propulseur** *nm* propeller, propelling mechanism; *adj invar* propelling, propulsive

**propulsif -ive** *adj* propelling, propulsive

**prorata** *nm invar* **au** ~ **de** in proportion to

**prorogatif -ive** *adj pol* proroguing

**prorogation** *nf* extension, postponement; *pol* prorogation

**proroger** *vt* (3) extend, postpone; *pol* prorogue

**prosaïque** *adj* inelegant, ordinary, prosaic, vulgar

**prosaïsme** *nm* flatness, ordinariness, vulgarity

**prosateur** *nm* prose-writer

**proscription** *nf* banishment, outlawry, proscription; condemnation; rejection

**proscrire** *vt* (42) banish, outlaw, proscribe; condemn; reject

**proscrit -e** *n* exile, outlaw; *adj* banished, outlawed

**prosélytisme** *nm* proselytizing

**prosodie** *nf* prosody

**prosodique** *adj* prosodic, prosodical

**prospecter** *vt* prospect; do market research on

**prospecteur -trice** *n* prospector; *fig* explorer

**prospectif -ive** *adj* prospective

**prospective** *nf* study of future trends

**prospection** *nf* prospection (minerals); *comm* canvassing, sounding

**prospectus** *nm* publicity hand-out; brochure, handbill; *lit* prospectus

**prospère** *adj* flourishing; prosperous

**prospérer** *vi* (6) flourish, prosper, thrive

**prospérité** *nf* prosperity, well-being

**prostatique** *n* + *adj med* prostatic (patient)

**prosternement** *nm* prostrate position; *fig* humiliation

**prosterner** *vt* prostrate; **se** ~ prostrate oneself; *fig* behave humbly, be servile

**prostitué -e** *n* prostitute

**prostituer** *vt* prostitute; make into a prostitute; *fig* degrade; **se** ~ be a prostitute; prostitute oneself; *fig* degrade oneself

**prostitution** *nf* prostitution; degradation

**prostration** *nf* lying prone, prostration; exhaustion

**prostré** *adj* exhausted; prostrate

**protagoniste** *nm* protagonist

**prote** *nm* foreman, owner (in factory works)

**protecteur -trice** *n* protector, protectress; patron, patroness; lover (maintaining a mistress); *adj* protecting; *econ* protectionist; condescending, protective

**protection** *nf* aid, protection; encouragement, patronage; *mil* armour plating; condescension

**protectionnisme** *nm econ* protectionism

**protectorat** *nm* protectorate

**protégé -e** *n* protégé(e); dependant

**protège-dents** *nm* boxer's gum shield

**protège-oreilles** *nm* scrum-cap (rugby football)

**protège-parapluie** *nm invar* umbrella cover

**protéger** *vt* (6, 3) help, protect; defend; shelter, shield; encourage, favour, patronize; give support to

**protéine** *nf* protein

**protestantisme** *nm* Protestantism

**protestataire** *n* objector, protester; *adj* protesting

**protestation** *nf* protest, protestation; assertion, profession; *leg* declaration of protest

**protester** *vt* + *vi* protest; ~ **de** assert, maintain

**protêt** *nm leg* protest

**prothèse** *nf med* prosthesis; ~ **dentaire** false teeth; **appareils de** ~ artificial limbs

**protocolaire** *adj* in accordance with protocol; regarding formal etiquette

**protocole** *nm* protocol; ceremonial; etiquette; *fig* social convention; *typ* list of conventional signs in proof correcting

**protoplasma, protoplasme** *nm* protoplasm

**protoxyde** *nm* nitrous oxide; laughing gas

**protubérance** *nf* protuberance; *med* bump

**prou** *adv lit* **peu ou** ~ more or less

**proue** *nf naut* bows, prow

**prouesse** *nf* bravery, prowess, valour; exploit

**prouver** *vt* demonstrate, establish,

prove, show; indicate, reveal; **se ~** demonstrate to oneself

**provenance** *nf* origin, provenance, source; **~ s** imported goods; **en ~ de** (coming) from

**Provençal -e** *n* inhabitant of Provence

**provençal** *nm* Provençal language; *adj* Provençal; *cul* **à la ~ e** cooked with garlic and parsley

**provende** *nf* fodder; *ar* provender

**provenir** *vi* (96) come; originate

**proverbe** *nm* proverb; *theat* comedy illustrating a proverb; **passer en ~** become proverbial

**providence** *nf* providence; one who brings succour, protection, saviour; **être la ~ de qn** be the cause of s/o's happiness

**providentiel -ielle** *adj* providential

**province** *nf* province; **la ~** the provinces

**provincialisme** *nm lang* provincialism; *pej* provincialism

**proviseur** *nm* **~ de lycée** headmaster of French lycée

**provision** *nf* provision, store, supply; **~ s** food, provisions, supplies; *leg* interim payment (to creditor); advance, retainer; *comm* cover, deposit; **chèque sans ~** cheque referred to drawer; **faire ~ de** stock up with; **faire ses ~ s** do one's shopping

**provisionnel -elle** *adj leg* provisional; **acompte ~** advance instalment of tax (based on previous year's assessment)

**provisoire** *nm* what is provisional, provisional state of affairs; *leg* interim judgement; *adj* provisional; temporary, transitory; acting; **à titre ~** for the time being

**provocant** *adj* aggressive, provocative; alluring, tempting

**provocateur -trice** *n* (rare) instigator; person used to incite to crime or violence; *adj* instigating, inciting, provocative

**provocation** *nf* provocation, incitement; challenge, defiance

**provoquer** *vt* incite, provoke; excite (sexually); bring about, cause, give rise to, provoke

**proxénète** *n* go-between (in love affair); *nm* procurer; pimp

**proxénétisme** *nm* living off immoral earnings

**proximité** *nf* nearness, proximity; approach, imminence; **à ~ de** near, nearby

**prude** *adj* prudish; *ar* virtuous

**prudence** *nf* caution, discretion, prudence

**prudent** *adj* careful, cautious, prudent; judicious, sensible

**pruderie** *nf* prudery, prudishness

**prud'homme** *nm* arbitrator in labour dispute; **conseil des ~ s** conciliation tribunal

**prudhommesque** *adj* pompously banal

**pruine** *nf* bloom (on fruit)

**prune** *nf* plum; *coll* **des ~ s!** not on your life!; *coll* **pour des ~ s** for no reason, for nothing; *adj invar* plum-coloured

**pruneau** *nm* dried plum, prune; *sl* bullet

**¹prunelle** *nf bot* sloe; sloe gin

**²prunelle** *nf* pupil (eye); **~ de ses yeux** apple of one's eye; **jouer de la ~** make eyes at

**prunier** *nm* plum-tree

**prurigineux -euse** *adj path* itching

**prurit** *nm path* pruritus; *lit* longing, urge

**Prussien -ienne** *n* Prussian

**prussien -ienne** *adj* Prussian

**prussique** *adj m chem* prussic

**prytanée** *nm* school for the sons of servicemen

**psalmodie** *nf eccles* psalmody; *lit* monotonous declamation or singing

**psalmodier** *vt + vi eccles* intone; *fig* speak monotonously

**psaume** *nm eccles* psalm; musical setting of psalm

**psautier** *nm* psalter

**pseudonyme** *nm* pseudonym; *adj* pseudonymous

**psittacose** *nf path* psittacosis

**psychanalyse** *nf* psychoanalysis; psychoanalytic treatment

**psychanalyser** *vt* psychoanalyse

**psychanalyste** *n* psychoanalyst

**psychanalytique** *adj* psychoanalytic

**psyché** *nf* cheval-glass; *psych* psyche

**psychédélique** *adj* psychedelic

**psychiatre** *n* psychiatrist

**psychiatrie** *nf* psychiatry

**psychiatrique** *adj* psychiatric

**psychique** *adj* psychic, psychical

**psychisme** *nm* psychic phenomena

**psycholinguistique** *nf* psycholinguistics; *adj* psycholinguistic

**psychologie** *nf* psychology; *coll* mentality

**psychologique** *adj* psychological

**psychologue** *n* psychologist

**psychopathe** *n* psychopath

**psychopathie** *nf* psychopathic state

**psychopathologie** *nf* psychopathology

**psychophysique** *nf* psychophysics

**psychose** *nf* psychosis; obsession

**psychosomatique** *adj* psychosomatic

**psychothérapie** *nf* psychotherapy

**psychotique** *n + adj* psychotic

**ptérodactyle** *nm* pterodactyl

**puant** adj evil-smelling, stinking; fig conceited, pretentious

**puanteur** nf bad smell, stink

**pubère** adj pubescent

**puberté** nf puberty

**pubien -ienne** adj pubic

**publiable** adj publishable

**public** nm public; audience; adj (f -ique) public; generally known; notorious

**publicitaire** n publicist; coll adman; adj advertising

**publicité** nf advertising, publicity; advertising matter

**publier** vt publish; write; issue (order)

**puce** nf flea; coll midget (person); jeu de ~ tiddly-winks; (marché aux) ~s flea-market; mettre la ~ à l'oreille de qn intrigue s/o; make s/o suspicious; coll sac à ~s bed; secouer les ~s à qn reprimand s/o; coll tear a strip off s/o; secouer ses ~s stretch oneself on waking; adj invar puce (colour)

**puceau** nm (male) virgin

**pucelage** nm coll maidenhead, virginity

**pucelle** nf virgin

**puceron** nm ent greenfly; coll tiny child

**pucier** nm sl bed

**puddler** vt eng puddle

**pudeur** nf modesty; delicacy, reserve; attentat à la ~ indecent assault

**pudibond** adj prudish; easily shocked

**pudibonderie** nf prudishness; false modesty

**pudicité** nf modesty; modest nature

**pudique** adj chaste, modest; discreet, reserved

**puer** vt give off a disgusting smell of, stink of; vi smell, stink

**puéricultrice** nf children's nurse

**puériculture** nf rearing of children; medical care of small children

**puéril** adj childish, puerile

**puérilisme** nm med infantilism

**puérilité** nf puerility

**puerpéral** adj med puerperal

**pugilat** nm fight, set-to; ar pugilism

**pugiliste** nm lit boxer; ar pugilist

**pugilistique** adj lit pugilistic

**pugnace** adj lit combative, pugnacious

**pugnacité** nf lit pugnaciousness, pugnacity

**puîné -e** n + adj younger (son, daughter)

**puis** adv after that, next, then; besides; further on; et ~ moreover; et ~ ?, coll et ~ après?, et ~ quoi? well?; coll so what?

**puisard** nm sunk draining trap; mech sump; naut bilges

**puisatier** nm well-sinker

**puiser** vt draw, ladle out (liquid); vi ~ dans dig into (sack, wallet); derive inspiration from, draw on

**puisque** conj as, considering that, seeing that, since

**puissamment** adv powerfully; coll extremely

**puissance** nf power, strength, ability, capacitv; philos possibility; authority, force, sovereignty; nation, state; volume (sound); phys energy; mot ~ administrative, ~ fiscale horse-power (for purpose of licensing); en ~ potential; volonté de ~ urge to dominate

**puissant** nm powerful individual; adj mighty, powerful, strong; effective

**puits** nm well; (mine-)shaft, pit; fig fount; ~ de pétrole oil-well; ~ naturel pothole

**pull** nm pullover

**pullulation** nf, **pullulement** nm multiplication, pullulation; swarming

**pulluler** vi pullulate; swarm; abound

**pulmonaire** nf bot lungwort; adj pulmonary

**pulpe** nf pulp; fleshy part of finger-tip

**pulpeux -euse** adj pulpy

**pulsative** adj f med douleur ~ throbbing pain

**pulvérisable** adj reducible to powder or fine clay

**pulvérisateur** nm atomizer, spray, vaporizer

**pulvérisation** nf pulverization; spraying, vaporizing

**pulvériser** vt pulverize, grind into powder; spray, vaporize; coll crush, destroy; coll beat easily, flatten

**pulvériseur** nm agr pulverizer

**punaise** nf ent bed-bug; bug; drawing-pin

**punch** nm (of boxer) ability to punch; coll dynamism, energy, go; (drink) punch

**punique** adj Punic

**punir** vt punish

**punissable** adj punishable

**punitif -ive** adj punitive

**punition** nf punishing, punishment

**pupe** nf ent pupa

**¹pupille** n leg pupil, ward; orphan

**²pupille** nf anat pupil

**pupitre** nm desk (school); music-stand; lectern

**pur** adj pure; unalloyed, undiluted; spotless, unsullied; impeccable, perfect; chaste, innocent; mere, sheer

**purée** nf cul purée, mash; mashed potatoes; coll poverty; sl ~ ! what a shambles!; ~ de pois pea-souper, thick fog; sl être dans la ~ be in the soup, be hard up

**purement** adv purely; entirely

**pureté** nf pureness, purity; innocence;

correctness (language, style); clearness

**purgatif** *nm* laxative, purge; *adj* (*f* -**ive**) purgative

**purgatoire** *nm* purgatory

**purge** *nf* purge, purging; draining, draining-off; *leg* redemption; cleaning (raw fabrics)

**purger** *vt* (3) purge; give laxative to; drain off; purify; get rid of, sweep away; *leg* redeem (mortgage); serve (sentence); **se ~** take a laxative

**purifiant** *adj* purifying

**purificateur -trice** *adj* purifying

**purifier** *vt* purify; clean, cleanse, refine

**purin** *nm* liquid manure; **fosse à ~** manure-pit (in farmyard)

**purisme** *nm* purism

**puriste** *n* + *adj* purist

**puritain -e** *n* Puritan; *adj* puritan, puritanical

**puritanisme** *nm* Puritanism

**purotin** *nm sl* s/o who is broke, hard-up

**purpurin** *adj* crimson, purplish

**pur-sang** *nm invar* thoroughbred (horse)

**purulent** *adj* festering, purulent; reprehensible

**pusillanime** *adj* faint-hearted, pusillanimous

**pusillanimité** *nf* faint-heartedness, pusillanimity

**pustuleux -euse** *adj* pustular

**putain** *nf sl* whore; *vulg as interj* shit!; *sl* ~ **de** bloody

**putatif -ive** *adj* putative

**pute** *nf sl* tart, whore

**putois** *nm zool* polecat

**putréfiable** *adj* liable to putrefy

**putréfier** *vt* decompose, putrefy, rot; **se ~** decompose, rot

**putrescible** *adj* liable to putrefy; corruptible

**putridité** *nf* putridness

**puy** *nm geog* peak (Auvergne)

**pygmée** *nm* pygmy

**pyjama** *nm* pyjamas

**pylône** *nm* pylon; *archi* pillar, pylon

**pylore** *nm anat* pylorus

**pyorrhée** *nf med* pyorrhoea

**pyramide** *nf* pyramid

**pyrénéen -éenne** *adj geog* Pyrenean

**pyrèthre** *nm bot* feverfew, pyrethrum; **poudre de ~** pyrethrum powder, insect powder

**pyrexie** *nf path* feverish condition, pyrexia

**pyrite** *nf chem* pyrites

**pyromane** *n* incendiary, fire-raiser, arsonist

**pyromanie** *nf* pyromania

**pyrotechnie** *nf* pyrotechnics

**pyrotechnique** *adj* pyrotechnic

**pyrrhonien -ienne** *n* + *adj philos* sceptic

**pyrrhonisme** *nm philos* doctrine of Pyrrho, scepticism

**pythagoricien -ienne** *n* + *adj* Pythagorean

**pythagorique** *adj* Pythagorean

**pythonisse** *nf* prophetess, clairvoyante

# Q

**quadragénaire** *n* + *adj* quadragenarian

**quadrangulaire** *adj* quadrangular

**quadratique** *adj* quadratic

**quadrilatère** *nm* quadrilateral

**quadrillage** *nm* cross-ruling; chequerwork; partitioning (area, for policing operations)

**quadriller** *vt* rule in squares; partition (area, for policing operations)

**quadrimoteur** *nm* four-engined aircraft; *adj m* four-engined

**quadrupède** *nm* quadruped

**quadrupler** *vt* + *vi* quadruple

**quai** *nm* quay, wharf; embankment; platform; **Quai d'Orsay** French Foreign Office

**qualifiable** *adj* describable

**qualificatif -ive** *adj* qualifying

**qualification** *nf* naming, calling; qualifying; name; qualification

**qualifier** *vt* qualify; call, term; describe; **crime qualifié** aggravated crime; **ouvrier qualifié** skilled worker; **se ~** call oneself

**qualitatif -ive** *adj* qualitative

**qualité** *nf* quality; excellence; property; capacity, qualification; rank; **en ~ de** as, in the capacity of

**quand** *adv* when; ~ **même** nevertheless;

à ~ votre départ? when is your departure?; de ~ est sa lettre? when does his letter date from?; n'importe ~ at any time; *conj* when; whenever; even if; *coll* ~ je vous le disais! didn't I tell you so!

quant à *prep* as to, as regards

quant-à-soi *nm* reserve, dignity; rester sur son ~ stand on one's dignity

quantifier *vt* quantify

quantitatif -ive *adj* quantitative

quantité *nf* quantity; large number

quantum *nm* (*pl* quanta) amount, proportion; *phys* quantum

quarantaine *nf* about forty; age of forty; quarantine; mettre qn en ~ send s/o to Coventry; put s/o in quarantine

quarante *adj* forty; les Quarante the members of the French Academy; *sl* s'en ficher comme de l'an ~ not care a damn about s/o (sth)

quarantième *adj* fortieth

quart *nm* quarter; *naut* watch; carafe, mug (holding quarter of a litre); *sl* police station; aux trois ~s largely, mainly; moins le (un) ~ a quarter to; *coll* passer un mauvais ~ d'heure have a few nasty moments; *adj ar* fourth

quarteron *nm* small number

quartier *nm* quarter; district; ~s quarters; ~ général headquarters; bureau de ~ branch office

quartier-maître *nm* (*pl* quartiers-maîtres) *mil* quartermaster

¹quasi *nm* chump-end (of loin)

²quasi *adv* almost

quasiment *adv coll* almost

Quasimodo *nf eccles* Low Sunday

quatorze *nm* fourteen; fourteenth; *adj* fourteen

quatre *nm* four; fourth; *adj* four; ~ à ~ four at a time; à ~ pas very near; à ~ pattes on all fours; manger comme ~ eat greedily; ne pas y aller par ~ chemins get straight to the point; se mettre en ~ do one's utmost; un de ces ~ matins one of these days

quatre-saisons *nf invar* variety of strawberry; marchand des ~ costermonger

quatre-vingts *nm*+*adj* eighty

quatrième *nm* fourth floor; *nf* third-year class (at secondary school); *adj* fourth

quatuor *nm mus* quartet; quatuor

que *rel pron* whom, that; that which; as; *inter pron* whom?, what?; *adv* why?; how?; what a lot; only; ne ... ~ only; *conj* that; lest; may ..., let ...; so that; before, until; since; when; as; than; whether; *coll* ~ si! yes, surely

quel (*f* quelle) *pron* who, what; ~ que

whoever, whatever; *adj* which, what; what a ...!

quelconque *adj* any; *coll* ordinary, commonplace

quelque *adj* any, some; whatsoever, whatever; ~s a few, some; ~ chose something, anything; ~ part somewhere; *adv* about, some; ~ ... que however

quelquefois *adv* sometimes, occasionally

quelques-uns (*f* quelques-unes) *pron pl* a few, some

quelqu'un (*f* quelqu'une) *pron* one (or other); somebody, someone, anyone; *coll* se prendre pour ~ think oneself important

quémander *vt* beg for; *vi* beg

qu'en-dira-t-on *nm invar* gossip

quenelle *nf* fish ball, meat ball

quenotte *nf coll* child's tooth

quenouille *nf* distaff

querelle *nf* quarrel; controversy; ~ d'Allemand trumped-up quarrel; chercher ~ à qn try to pick a quarrel with s/o

quereller *vt* quarrel with (s/o); se ~ quarrel

querelleur -euse *adj* quarrelsome

quérir *vt* (79) fetch

qu'est-ce que *inter pron* what?; ~ c'est que ça? what's that?; *coll* qu'est-ce qu'il fait froid! how cold it is!

qu'est-ce qui *inter pron* what?

question *nf* question, query; point; matter; torture (judicial); être ~ de be a matter of; mettre en ~ question, challenge; ne pas faire ~ be beyond doubt; poser une ~ ask a question

questionnaire *nm* list of questions, questionnaire

questionner *vt* question

quête *nf* collection, fund-raising; *ar* search

quêter *vt* angle for, fish for; *vi* collect (alms), take collection

quêteur -euse *n* collector of alms

queue *nf* tail; queue; handle (pan); stalk; train (dress); pigtail; pin (brooch); cue (billiards); *vulg* prick; à la ~ leu leu one behind the other; en ~ at the rear; faire la ~ queue up; *mot* faire une ~ de poisson à qn cut in on s/o; finir en ~ de poisson fizzle out; piano à ~ grand piano

queue-d'aronde *nf* (*pl* queues-d'aronde) *carp* dovetail

queue-de-pie *nf* (*pl* queues-de-pie) *coll* tails

queue-de-rat *nf* (*pl* queues-de-rat) rat-tailed file

queux *nm ar* maître ~ cook, chef

**qui** *rel pron* who, which, that; whom, which; he who; him who; that which, what; ~ ... ~ one ... another; ~ **que vous soyez** whoever you may be; *inter pron* who?; whom?

**quia (à)** *adv phr* at a loss, in a quandary

**quiche** *nf* kind of savoury flan

**quiconque** *pron* whoever, whosoever, anyone who; anyone else

**quidam** *nm* someone, individual

**qui est-ce que** *inter pron* whom?

**qui est-ce qui** *inter pron* who?

**quiétude** *nf* quietude, peace of mind

**quignon** *nm* chunk of bread

¹**quille** *nf* skittle, ninepin; *sl* demob

²**quille** *nf* keel

**quincaillerie** *nf* ironmongery; hardware shop

**quincaillier** *nm* ironmonger

**quinconce** *nm* quincunx; **en** ~ quincuncial

**quinquagénaire** *adj* fifty years old

**quinquennal** *adj* five-year, quinquennial

**quinquet** *nm* kind of lamp; *sl* ~ **s** eyes

**quinquina** *nm* Peruvian . bark; chinchona

**quinte** *nf mus* fifth, quint; quint (cards, fencing); ~ **de toux** fit of coughing

**quintessencié** *adj* oversubtle

**quinteux -euse** *adj* capricious

**quintupler** *vt* + *vi* increase fivefold

**quintuplés -ées** *npl* quintuplets

**quinzaine** *nf* about fifteen; fortnight

**quinze** *nm* fifteen, fifteenth; rugby fifteen; *adj* fifteen; ~ **jours** a fortnight

**quinzième** *n* + *adj* fifteenth

**quiproquo** *nm* mistake, misunderstanding

**quittance** *nf* receipt

**quittancer** *vt* (4) receipt

**quitte** *adj* free, quit, rid; quits; ~ **à** at the risk of; **en être** ~ **pour** get off with; **tenir** ~ dispense

**quitter** *vt* leave, quit; give up; take off (clothing); **ne quittez pas** hold the line; **se** ~ part, separate

**qui-vive** *nm invar mil* sentry's challenge; **être sur le** ~ be on the alert

**quoi** *rel pron* what, which; *pron* ~ **que** whatever; ~ **que ce soit** anything; whatever it may be; ~ **qu'il en soit** be that as it may; *coll* **comme** ~ which goes to show that; **de** ~ the wherewithal, enough to, something with which to; **il n'y a pas de** ~ don't mention it; *inter pron* what?; **à** ~ **bon?** what's the use?; **en** ~ **est-il?** what is it made of?; **un je ne sais** ~ an indefinable something; *interj* what!

**quoique** *conj* although

**quolibet** *nm* gibe, coarse joke

**quote-part** *nf* (*pl* **quotes-parts**) portion, quota

**quotidien** *nm* daily newspaper; *adj* (*f* **-ienne**) daily

**quotité** *nf* quota, amount of share

# R

**ra** *nm invar* drum-roll

**rabâchage** *nm* tiresome repetition

**rabâcher** *vt* + *vi* repeat again and again

**rabais** *nm* price reduction; **au** ~ on the cheap, cheap

**rabaisser** *vt* lower; reduce; depreciate, disparage; humble

**rabat** *nm* bands (clergy, magistrates); flap

**rabat-joie** *nm invar* killjoy, spoilsport

**rabattage** *nm* beating up (game)

**rabatteur -euse** *n* tout (for customers); beater (shoot)

**rabattre** *vt* fold down, fold back; flatten; put down; shut down; turn down; reduce, diminish; beat up (game); **en** ~ be less demanding, climb down; **se** ~ fall back; fold back

**rabbin** *nm* rabbi

**rabelaisien -ienne** *adj* Rabelaisian

**rabiot** *nm coll* extra work, overtime; *sl mil* surplus rations, surplus; *mil* extra service

**rabique** *adj* rabid

**râble** *nm cul* back, saddle

**râblé** *adj* strapping; broad-backed

**rabot** *nm* plane

**raboter** *vt* plane, plane down

**raboteux -euse** *adj* uneven, rough

**rabougri** *adj* stunted

**rabouter** *vt* join end to end

**rabrouer** *vt* scold

**racaille** *nf* riff-raff

**raccommodage** *nm* mending, repairing; mend

**raccommodement** *nm* reconciliation

**raccommoder** *vt* mend, repair; reconcile; **se ~ avec qn** make it up with s/o

**raccompagner** *vt* escort back; run back

**raccord** *nm* join; joint, connection

**raccordement** *nm* joining, linking-up; junction

**raccorder** *vt* join, link up, connect; **se ~** connect, fit together

**raccourci** *nm* foreshortening; epitome; short cut

**raccourcir** *vt* shorten; abridge; *vi* become shorter, shrink; **à bras raccourcis** violently, vigorously

**raccourcissement** *nm* shortening, shrinking

**raccoutumer (se)** *v refl* reaccustom oneself

**raccroc** *nm* fluke; **par ~** by chance

**raccrocher** *vt* hang up again, hook up again; *vi* hang up, ring off; recover

**race** *nf* race; species; strain; breed; **chasser de ~** be true to type; **cheval de ~** thoroughbred horse; **chien de ~** pedigree dog

**racé** *adj* thoroughbred; distinguished, well-bred

**rachat** *nm* buying back; redemption; atonement

**racheter** *vt* (5) buy back; buy again; redeem; atone for; ransom; **se ~** atone

**rachitique** *adj* rachitic

**rachitisme** *nm* rickets

**racine** *nf* root; cause, origins; base

**racisme** *nm* racialism, racism

**raciste** *n* racialist, racist

**raclée** *nf coll* thrashing, hiding

**racler** *vt* scrape; rake over; **~ du violon** play the violin badly; **se ~ la gorge** clear one's throat

**raclette** *nf* scraper; *cul* melted cheese dish

**racolage** *nm* recruiting; touting; soliciting

**racoler** *vt* recruit, impress; catch, bring in; solicit

**racontar** *nm* piece of gossip

**raconter** *vt* relate, tell, tell about; **en ~** tell wild tales

**raconteur -euse** *n* narrator, story-teller; raconteur, raconteuse

**racornir** *vt* make hard as horn; **se ~** become hard; *coll* shrivel up

**radariste** *n* radar technician

**rade** *nf naut* roads; natural harbour

**radeau** *nm* raft

**radiateur** *nm* radiator

**radiation** *nf* erasing, striking off; erasure

**¹radier** *nm bui* frame, bed, floor

**²radier** *vt* erase, strike out; strike off, cross off

**radieux -ieuse** *adj* radiant; beaming

**radin** *adj coll* stingy

**radio** *nf* radio; X-ray; **passer à la ~** broadcast; X-ray

**radio-actif -ive** radio-active

**radio-activité** *nf* radio-activity

**radiodiffuser** *vt* broadcast

**radiodiffusion** *nf* radio broadcasting

**radiogramme** *nm* radio message

**radiographie** *nf* X-ray photograph

**radiographier** *vt* make an X-ray of

**radiologie** *nf* X-ray treatment, radiology

**radiophonique** *adj* radiophonic

**radio-reportage** *nm* radio-reporting, commentary on the radio

**radioscopie** *nf* radioscopy

**radiothérapie** *nf* radiotherapy

**radis** *nm* radish; *coll* **n'avoir pas un ~** not have a halfpenny, be broke

**radotage** *nm* nonsense, drivel; rambling

**radoter** *vi* drivel, talk nonsense

**radoteur -euse** *n* dotard

**radoub** *nm naut* refit, repair; **bassin de ~** dry dock

**radouber** *vt naut* repair the hull of; repair (net)

**radoucir** *vt* calm; make milder; mollify, assuage, appease; **se ~** become milder; calm down

**rafale** *nf* squall; burst of fire

**raffermir** *vt* make firmer, harden; strengthen, fortify

**raffinage** *nm* refining process

**raffiné** *adj* refined; subtle

**raffinement** *nm* refining; refinement

**raffiner** *vt + vi* refine; **~ sur** split hairs over

**raffinerie** *nf* refinery

**raffineur -euse** *n* refiner

**raffoler** *vi* be very fond, dote

**raffut** *nm coll* shindy, row

**rafiot** *nm coll* poor boat, old tub

**rafistolage** *nm coll* repairing, patching up

**rafistoler** *vt coll* repair, patch up

**rafle** *nf* looting, cleaning out; round-up, police raid

**rafler** *vt* carry off, take away; round up

**rafraîchir** *vt* refresh, cool; revive; do up, renovate; trim (hair); touch up; **se ~** become cooler, fresher; refresh oneself, have a drink

**rafraîchissant** *adj* refreshing, cooling

**rafraîchissement** *nm* cooling; cooling down; reviving, freshening up; refreshing; cool drink; **~ s** refreshments

**ragaillardir** *vt* cheer up; give strength to

**rage** *nf* rage, fury; violent pain; passion,

mania; rabies; **faire ~** rage, be raging

**rageant** *adj* infuriating

**rager** *vi* (3) fume, be furious, be wild with anger

**rageur -euse** *adj* choleric; angry

**ragot** *nm coll* piece of gossip

**ragoût** *nm* stew

**ragoûtant** *adj* appetizing; attractive

**raid** *nm* raid; long-distance run, flight

**raide, roide** *adj* stiff; steep; obstinate; starchy; **c'est un peu ~** it's a bit thick; *adv* violently, hard; **~ mort** stone dead

**raideur, roideur** *nf* stiffness; steepness; starchiness; inflexibility

**raidillon** *nm* short steep path

**raidir, roidir** *vt* stiffen; tauten

**raidissement** *nm* stiffening

¹**raie** *nf* line, stroke; stripe; parting (hair); ridge (between furrows)

²**raie** *nm* skate (fish), ray

**raifort** *nm* horseradish

**rail** *nm* rail; railway

**railler** *vt* laugh at, jeer at; *vi* speak lightly, in jest

**railleur -euse** *adj* mocking, bantering

**rainer** *vt* groove, slot

**rainette** *nf* tree-frog

**rainure** *nf* furrow, groove

**raisin** *nm* grape; **~ de Corinthe** currant; **~** see raisin

**raisiné** *nm* jam made with grape juice and other fruit

**raison** *nf* reason; motive, ground; good sense; argument; proof; **~ de plus** all the more reason; **~ sociale** name under which a firm trades; **âge de ~** age of discretion; **à plus forte ~** all the more reason; **à ~ de** at the rate of; **avoir ~ de** get the better of; **comme de ~** as one could expect; **demander ~ de** ask for satisfaction for; **en ~ de** in consideration of; **entendre ~** listen to reason; **perdre la ~** take leave of one's senses; **ramener qn à la ~** bring s/o back to his senses; **rendre ~ de qch** give an explanation of sth; **se faire une ~** resign oneself to the inevitable

**raisonnable** *adj* reasonable, sensible; adequate

**raisonnement** *nm* reasoning; argument; objection

**raisonner** *vt* reason out, consider; reason with; *vi* reason, argue; be argumentative

**raisonneur -euse** *n* argumentative person; *adj* reasoning; argumentative

**rajeunir** *vt* rejuvenate; make look younger; *vi* grow young again

**rajeunissement** *nm* rejuvenation

**rajouter** *vt* add (something further)

**rajuster** *vt* readjust; set right; modify; **se**

~ adjust one's clothing

¹**râle** *nm* rattle; **~ de la mort** death-rattle

²**râle** *nm orni* rail

**ralenti** *nm* slow motion; **au ~** slowly; *mot* **tourner au ~** idle

**ralentissement** *nm* slowing down, slowing up

**râler** *vi* rattle; gasp; *coll* grumble

**ralliement** *nm* rally, rallying

**rallier** *vt* rally, assemble; rejoin; win over; get to; **se ~** rally; adhere

**rallonge** *nf* extension; extra leaf (table); *coll* supplement; *coll* rise; **nom à ~** double-barrelled name

**rallonger** *vt* (3) lengthen, make longer

**rallumer** *vt* light again; revive; **se ~** light up again, be relit; flare up again

**rallye** *nm* rally

**ramage** *nm* warbling; floral design, branch design

**ramassage** *nm* picking up; collecting; **~ scolaire** school transport

**ramassé** *adj* thick-set, stocky; concise, compact

**ramasse-miettes** *nm* crumb-scoop

**ramasse-poussière** *nm invar* dust-pan

**ramasser** *vt* pick up; gather, collect, gather up; condense (style); *coll* make (money); *coll* take in, arrest; **se ~** crouch; gather oneself; *sl* pick oneself up

**ramassis** *nm pej* pile, heap, collection

¹**rame** *nf* oar, scull

²**rame** *nf* ream (paper); string, group (carriages, barges); **~ de métro** tube train

**rameau** *nm* small branch; twig; branch, subdivision; **dimanche des Rameaux** Palm Sunday

**ramée** *nf ar* branches, twigs

**ramener** *vt* (6) bring back, bring again; win over, bring round

**ramequin** *nm* cheese tart; baking vessel

**ramer** *vi* row

**rameur -euse** *n* rower, oarsman (oarswoman)

**rami** *nm* rummy (cards)

**ramier** *adj* **pigeon ~** wood pigeon

**ramifier (se)** *v refl* branch out, divide

**ramolli** *adj* soft; *coll* dull-witted

**ramollir** *vt* soften; weaken

**ramollissement** *nm* softening

**ramonage** *nm* chimney-sweeping

**ramoner** *vt* sweep (chimney); climb (rock chimney)

**ramoneur** *nm* chimney-sweep

**rampant** *adj* creeping, crawling; subservient, grovelling; *her* rampant

**rampe** *nf* ramp; slope; *theat* footlights; handrail; **~ de lancement** launching pad; *coll* **lâcher la ~** die; *theat* **passer**

la ~ get across

**ramper** *vi* creep, crawl; grovel

**ramure** *nf* branches; antlers

**rancart** *nm* mettre au ~ put aside, get rid of

**rance** *adj* rancid

**rancir** *vi* go rancid

**rancœur** *nf* bitterness, rancour

**rançon** *nf* ransom; price

**rançonner** *vt* ransom, hold to ransom

**rancune** *nf* rancour, malice, spite, resentment; **garder** ~ harbour resentment; **sans** ~ no ill feelings

**rancunier -ière** *adj* vindictive, spiteful

**randonnée** *nf* trip, outing, excursion

**rang** *nm* line, row; rank; station; **en** ~ **d'oignons** in a line; **rompre les** ~**s** disperse; **se mettre en** ~**s** fall in; **se mettre sur les** ~**s** put in for; **serrer les** ~**s** close up; **sortir du** ~ rise from the ranks; make one's name

**rangé** *adj* tidy; steady; **bataille** ~**e** pitched battle

**rangée** *nf* row, line

**ranger** *vt* (3) arrange; draw up; put away, tidy; set in order; range, rank; put aside, set aside; subjugate; go alongside; **se** ~ line up; side, take sides; stand aside, get out of the way; calm down, settle down

**ranimer** *vt* revive, restore to life; **se** ~ revive, come to life again

**rapace** *adj* rapacious, grasping; predacious

**rapaces** *nmpl* birds of prey

**rapacité** *nf* rapacity

**rapatriement** *nm* repatriation

**rapatrier** *vt* repatriate, send home

**râpe** *nf* grater; rasp

**râpé** *adj* grated; worn out, threadbare; *coll* failed

**râper** *vt* grate; rasp

**rapetasser** *vt coll* patch up

**rapetisser** *vt* make smaller; make appear smaller; diminish the merit of; *vi* become smaller, shorter

**râpeux -euse** *adj* rough

**raphia** *nm* raffia

**rapiat** *adj coll* stingy, miserly

**rapide** *nm* express, fast train; rapids; *adj* fast, rapid; steep

**rapidité** *nf* speed, swiftness; steepness

**rapiécer** *vt* (6, 4) patch

**rapin** *nm ar* art student; dauber

**rapiner** *vt* + *vi* pillage

**rapière** *nf* rapier

**raplapla** *adj coll invar* washed out, exhausted

**raplatir** *vt* flatten again

**rappel** *nm* recall; reminder; *eng* return; back payment; **battre le** ~ call to arms

**rappeler** *vt* (5) recall, call back; bring back; remind of, bring to mind; **se** ~ remember

**rappliquer** *vi sl* come back; come

**rapport** *nm* report; return, yield; relations, relationship, connection; proportion; *sl* ~ **à** regarding; **avoir** ~ **à** relate to; **avoir des** ~ **s avec** be in touch with; have sexual relations with; **en** ~ **avec** in keeping with; **mettre en** ~ **avec** put in touch with; **par** ~ **à** in relation to; **sous ce** ~ in this respect

**rapportage** *nm coll* tale-bearing, sneaking

**rapporter** *vt* bring back, carry back; bring in, yield; report; repeat; annul, call off; ascribe; *vi* sneak; **se** ~ agree, tally; refer, relate; **s'en** ~ **à** rely on, leave things to

**rapporteur -euse** *n* tale-bearer; *nm* reporter, recorder; *math* protractor

**rapproché** *adj* near, nearly

**rapprochement** *nm* bringing together; reconciling, reconciliation; comparing; bringing nearer, coming nearer

**rapprocher** *vt* bring nearer, bring closer, bring near again; compare; bring together; reconcile; **se** ~ draw nearer

**rapt** *nm* abduction

**raquette** *nf* racket; snow-shoe; prickly pear

**rare** *adj* rare; exceptional, uncommon; sparse, thin

**raréfaction** *nf* rarefaction; depletion

**raréfier** *vt* rarefy; deplete

**rareté** *nf* rarity, scarcity, dearth; singularity; rare occurrence; rare object

**rarissime** *adj* very rare

¹**ras** *nm see* raz

²**ras** *adj* cut short, close-shaven; **à poil** ~ short-haired; **à** ~ **bord** to the brim; **à (au)** ~ **de** level with; *sl* **en avoir** ~ **le bol** be fed up to the teeth; **en** ~ **e campagne** in the open country; **faire table** ~ **e** make a clean sweep; *adv* close; **couper** ~ cut very short

**rasade** *nf* full glass

**rasage** *nm* shaving

**rasant** *adj* low-lying; low (shooting); *coll* boring, tiresome

**rascasse** *nf* hog-fish

**rase-mottes** *nm invar* vol en ~ very low flight, hedge-hopping

**raser** *vt* shave, shave off; raze; skim over, graze; keep close to, hug; *coll* bore, annoy; **se** ~ shave; *coll* be bored

**raseur -euse** *n coll* bore

**rasibus** *adv sl* very close

¹**rasoir** *nm* razor; ~ **de sûreté** safety razor

²**rasoir** *adj coll* boring, tiresome

**rassasier** *vt* satisfy (hunger); sate, surfeit; **se** ~ eat one's fill

**rassemblement** *nm* assembling, gathering; *mil* fall-in; crowd; political grouping

**rassembler** *vt* assemble, gather together; muster; collect; **se ~** assemble; *mil* fall in

**rasseoir** *vt* (15) replace; **se ~** sit down again

**rasséréner** *vt* (6) make calm again; **se ~** become calm again; clear up

**rassis** *adj* calm, staid, sedate; **pain ~** stale bread

**rassortir** *vt see* **réassortir**

**rassurant** *adj* reassuring

**rassurer** *vt* reassure, cheer

**rasta(quouère)** *nm coll* flashy foreigner

**rat** *nm* rat; *coll* miserly person; *coll* **~ de bibliothèque** book-worm; **~ de cave** wax taper; **~ d'église** regular churchgoer; **~ d'hôtel** hotel thief; **~ de l'Opéra** ballet pupil at the Opéra; **être fait comme un ~** be caught out

**rata** *nm sl mil* grub

**ratafia** *nm* ratafia (liqueur)

**rataplan** *nm* rat-tat (of drum)

**ratatiner** *vt* shrivel up, diminish; **se ~** shrivel up

**ratatouille** *nf coll* stew; poor cooking; **~ niçoise** Provençal vegetables cooked in olive oil

**rate** *nf anat* spleen; *coll* **dilater la ~** make laugh; *coll* **se fouler la ~** make an effort

**raté -e** *n* failure, flop, unsuccessful person

**râteau** *nm* rake

**râteler** *vt* (5) rake up

**râtelier** *nm* rack (stable); rack; row of teeth; *coll* false teeth, dentures; *coll* **manger à plusieurs (tous les) ~s** have two strings to one's bow; have a foot in both camps

**rater** *vt* miss; fail in; *vi* misfire, fail to go off; miscarry, fail

**ratiboiser** *vt coll* pinch, snaffle; clean out (at gambling)

**ratier** *nm* ratter (dog)

**ratière** *nf* rat-trap

**ratification** *nf* ratification; confirmation

**ratifier** *vt* ratify; confirm

**ratine** *nf* ratteen, petersham

**ratiociner** *vi* cavil, ratiocinate

**rationaliser** *vt* rationalize

**rationalisme** *nm* rationalism

**rationnel -elle** *adj* rational

**rationnement** *nm* rationing

**rationner** *vt* ration

**ratisser** *vt* rake, rake over; rake in (stakes); *mil* search and destroy; hook (rugby football)

**raton** *nm* young rat; *coll+pej* wog; **~ laveur** raccoon

**rattacher** *vt* tie up, fasten; tie again; bind; link up

**rattraper** *vt* catch again, recapture; catch up; correct, make good; **se ~** catch hold; compensate oneself; catch up, make up lost time

**rature** *nf* crossing out

**raturer** *vt* cross out, strike out

**rauque** *adj* hoarse, raucous, harsh

**ravage** *nm* damage; destruction; deterioration

**ravager** *vt* (3) ravage, lay waste; play havoc with; undermine, take a toll of

**ravalement** *nm* resurfacing, cleaning up

**ravaler** *vt* swallow again; clean up, resurface (wall); reduce the height of; humble; **se ~** degrade oneself

**ravaudage** *nm* mending, darning

**ravauder** *vt* mend, patch, darn

**rave** *nf bot* rape

**ravenelle** *nf* wallflower; wild radish

**ravi** *adj* delighted

**ravier** *nm* hors-d'œuvres dish

**ravigoter** *vt coll* revive, refresh

**ravin** *nm* ravine

**raviner** *vt* gulley, hollow out, channel

**ravir** *vt* carry off, ravish; delight, ravish; **à ~** delightful; delightfully, admirably

**raviser (se)** *v refl* change one's mind

**ravissant** *adj* delightful; entrancing

**ravissement** *nm* rapture, delight; *ar* carrying off

**ravisseur -euse** *n* kidnapper; ravisher

**ravitaillement** *nm* provisioning; provisions, food

**ravitailler** *vt* provision, revictual; supply with food, fuel

**raviver** *vt* revive; brighten up

**ravoir** *vt* (1) get again, recover

**rayé** *adj* striped; scratched

**rayer** *vt* (7) scratch, score; strike out; exclude; rifle

**¹rayon** *nm* ray, beam; spoke; radius; *hort* drill, small furrow; **~ d'action** range, scope

**²rayon** *nm* shelf; department (shop); **~ de miel** honeycomb

**rayonnant** *adj* radiant; beaming

**rayonne** *nf* rayon

**rayonnement** *nm* radiance

**rayonner** *vi* radiate; beam, shine

**rayure** *nf* stripe, streak; striking off; erasure

**raz, ras** *nm* strong sea current; **~ de marée** bore; tidal wave; upheaval

**razzia** *nf* raid, foray

**ré** *nm invar mus* D, re

**réabonner** *vt* renew (s/o's) subscription; **se ~** renew one's subscription

**réacteur** *nm* reactor; jet-engine

**réaction** *nf* reaction; **avion à ~** jet plane

**réactionnaire** *n+adj* reactionary

**réactiver** vt reactivate

**réaffirmer** vt reaffirm

**réagir** vi react; fig resist

**réalisateur -trice** n cin director; rad producer

**réaliser** vt realize; effect, execute, carry out; make (film, etc)

**réalisme** nm realism

**réaliste** n realist; adj realist, realistic

**réalité** nf reality; **en ~** in actual fact; **prendre ses désirs pour des ~s** entertain illusions

**réanimation** nf reanimation; **centre de ~** intensive care unit

**réanimer** vt revive, reanimate

**réapparaître** vi (68) reappear

**réapparition** nf reappearance

**réassortir** vt replenish, restock; **se ~** replenish one's stocks

**rébarbatif -ive** adj forbidding, grim; surly

**rebattre** vt (16) beat again; coll **~ les oreilles à qn de qch** tell s/o the same thing over and over again

**rebattu** adj hackneyed; **avoir les oreilles ~es de qch** have heard sth over and over again

**rebelle** n rebel; adj rebellious, unruly; stubborn; difficult to control

**rebeller (se)** v refl rebel

**rébellion** nf rebellion, revolt

**rebiffer (se)** v refl jib, kick

**reboiser** vt replant (with trees)

**rebond** nm bounce

**rebondi** adj plump; chubby

**rebondir** vi rebound; bounce; start up again

**rebondissement** nm new development; recurrence

**rebord** nm edge, rim; ledge; hem

**rebours** nm **à ~** against the grain; **à ~ de** contrary to; **compte à ~** countdown

**rebouteur, rebouteux -euse** n coll bonesetter

**reboutonner** vt button up again; **se ~** button one's clothes up again; adjust one's dress

**rebrousse-poil (à)** adv phr the wrong way; against the grain

**rebrousser** vt turn or brush up the wrong way; **~ chemin** retrace one's steps

**rebuffade** nf rebuff, snub

**rébus** nm picture puzzle; punning riddle

**rebut** nm throw-out, reject; dregs; **de ~** low-grade

**rebutant** adj disheartening, off-putting; tiresome

**rebuter** vt rebuff, repulse; discourage; put off, repel

**récalcitrant** adj recalcitrant

**recaler** vt coll fail; plough (candidate)

**récapituler** vt recapitulate, sum up

**recel** nm receiving; concealment

**receler, recéler** vt (5) receive; conceal; harbour; contain

**receleur -euse** n receiver

**récemment** adv recently, lately

**recensement** nm census; counting

**recenser** vt make a census of; count; check off

**récépissé** nm receipt; acknowledgement

**récepteur** nm receiver (phone); collector, recipient; adj (f -trice) receiving

**réceptif -ive** adj receiving

**réception** nf receipt, receiving; welcome; reception; reception-desk

**réceptionner** vt check and sign for goods on their arrival

**réceptionniste** n receptionist

**recette** nf receipts, takings; collection (of money due); office of tax-collector; tax-collector's function; receipt; **faire ~** be a draw

**recevable** adj allowable, receivable; leg admissible

**receveur -euse** n receiver; tax-collector; conductor (bus)

**recevoir** vt receive, get; welcome; admit; absorb; **être reçu à un examen** pass an examination; **être reçu médecin** qualify as a doctor; vi entertain, have visitors; **se ~** land (after a jump)

**rechange** nm replacement; **de ~** spare, replacement

**rechaper** vt retread (tyre)

**réchapper** vi escape

**recharge** nf recharging; refill

**rechargement** nm recharging; reloading; refilling

**recharger** vt (3) recharge; reload; make up (fire); charge again; re-metal (road)

**réchaud** nm small portable stove; plate warmer

**réchauffé** nm warmed-up food; coll rehash

**réchauffer** vt warm up, heat up; rekindle; warm; **se ~** warm oneself up; become warmer

**rechausser** vt put shoes on again; archi bank up

**rêche** adj rough; cross-grained; difficult to get on with

**recherche** nf search, pursuit; refinement; affectation, studied elegance; research; **à la ~ de** in search of

**recherché** adj select, rare; in great demand; affected, mannered

**rechercher** vt search for; inquire into; look for again; seek after

**rechigné** adj sour-tempered, sour-faced

**rechigner** vi jib, show bad grace

**rechute** nf relapse

**récidive** nf backsliding; relapse into

crime; recurrence (of illness)

**récidiver** *vi* repeat the same crime; recur (of illness)

**récidiviste** *n* habitual criminal, old offender

**récif** *nm* reef

**récipiendaire** *n* new member (of learned body)

**récipient** *nm* container, receptacle

**réciprocité** *nf* reciprocity

**réciproque** *nf* rendre la ~ à qn get even with s/o; *adj* reciprocal

**récit** *nm* narration, narrative, relation

**récitant -e** *n* narrator

**récitation** *nf* recitation, reciting

**réciter** *vt* recite

**réclamation** *nf* complaint, objection

**réclame** *nf* advertising; advertisement; en ~ at a reduced price; faire de la ~ advertise

**réclamer** *vt* demand, claim; ask for, clamour for; beg for; *vi* protest, complain; intercede; se ~ de qn appeal to s/o, call s/o to witness

**reclassement** *nm* fresh classification; rearrangement

**reclasser** *vt* reclassify; rearrange

**reclus -e** *n* recluse

**réclusion** *nf* imprisonment, detention

**recoin** *nm* nook; recess

**récoler** *vt* leg verify, check; read out witness's testimony

**recoller** *vt* stick, glue again

**récolte** *nf* harvesting; harvest; collection

**récolter** *vt* harvest; get, receive

**recommandable** *adj* commendable, estimable; advisable

**recommandation** *nf* recommendation; advice; injunction; (postal) registration

**recommander** *vt* recommend; urge, enjoin; register (letter, etc); se ~ à qn ask for s/o's assistance, protection; se ~ de qn invoke s/o's assistance; give s/o as a reference

**recommencer** *vt* + *vi* begin again, start again

**récompense** *nf* reward, recompense

**réconciliateur -trice** *n* reconciler

**réconcilier** *vt* reconcile

**reconduction** *nf* renewal, continuation

**reconduire** *vt* (80) escort back; show out

**réconfort** *nm* comfort, consolation

**réconfortant** *adj* strengthening; comforting

**réconforter** *vt* strengthen; comfort

**reconnaissance** *nf* recognition; gratitude; acknowledgement; reconnoitring

**reconnaissant** *adj* grateful

**reconnaître** *vt* (68) recognize; acknowledge, admit; reconnoitre; be grateful for; je ne m'y reconnais plus

I'm at sea, I'm lost; je vous reconnais là that's just like you; se faire ~ make oneself known

**reconquérir** *vt* (27) reconquer; regain

**reconquête** *nf* reconquest

**reconstituant** *nm* + *adj* tonic

**reconstituer** *vt* reconstitute; reconstruct; restore

**reconstruire** *vt* (80) reconstruct, rebuild

**reconversion** *nf* changing over

**reconvertir** *vt* change over, convert; se ~ train for another job

**recopier** *vt* copy again; make a clean copy of

**recorder** *vt* re-string; rope up again

**recordman, recordwoman** *nm* (*pl* recordmen, recordwomen) record-holder

**recouper** *vt* cut again; blend (wines); corroborate

**recourber** *vt* bend back; bend again

**recourir** *vi* (29) run again; have recourse, address oneself, resort

**recours** *nm* recourse, resort; leg ~ en grâce appeal for mercy; en dernier ~ as a last resort; il n'y a aucun ~ contre cela that is irremediable; sans ~ unavoidable

**¹recouvrement** *nm* recovery; collection

**²recouvrement** *nm* covering

**recouvrer** *vt* recover, regain, retrieve; collect

**recouvrir** *vt* (30) cover again; cover, cover entirely; conceal

**récréation** *nf* recreation; amusement; break (in school); cour de ~ playground

**récréer** *vt* entertain, amuse; refresh

**récrier (se)** *v refl* exclaim

**récriminer** *vi* recriminate

**recroquevillé** *adj* curled up, shrivelled

**recroqueviller (se)** *v refl* shrivel up, curl up, crumple up

**recru** *adj* exhausted, worn out

**recrue** *nf* recruit; new member

**recrutement** *nm* recruiting, recruitment

**recruter** *vt* recruit, enlist

**recta** *adv* coll punctually

**rectangle** *nm* rectangle; *adj* right-angled

**rectangulaire** *adj* rectangular

**recteur** *nm* head of university; *eccles* rector; parish priest (Brittany)

**rectification** *nf* rectification; straightening; correction; adjustment

**rectifier** *vt* rectify, correct, amend; straighten; adjust; re-distil (alcohol)

**rectiligne** *adj* rectilinear

**rectitude** *nf* straightness; rectitude; rightness; integrity, uprightness

**rectoral** *adj* rectorial

**rectorat** *nm* rectorate, rectorship

**reçu** *nm* receipt

**recueil** *nm* collection

**recueillement** *nm* meditation, contemplation; veneration

**recueilli** *adj* contemplative

**recueillir** *vt* (33) draw, gather, get; collect, gather up; take in, give refuge to; **se ~** reflect, meditate; turn one's thoughts to God

**recul** *nm* retreat; backing; recoil, kick; step back; position of detachment

**reculé** *adj* remote, distant

**reculer** *vt* move back, push back, draw back; defer, postpone; *vi* move back, fall back, back; recoil, kick; **ne ~ devant rien** shrink from nothing

**reculons (à)** *adv phr* backwards

**récupération** *nf* recovery; recoupment; recuperation

**récupérer** *vt* (6) recover; recoup; *vi* get one's strength back

**récurer** *vt* scour

**récusable** *adj leg* untrustworthy (witness); exceptionable

**récuser** *vt leg* object to, take exception to; impugn (evidence); **se ~** disclaim competence

**recyclage** *nm* recycling

**recycler** *vt* recycle

**rédacteur -trice** *n* writer, drafter; sub-editor; **~ en chef** editor

**rédaction** *nf* drawing up, drafting, writing; editing; composition, essay

**reddition** *nf* surrender; presenting of accounts

**redemander** *vt* ask for again

**rédempteur -trice** *n* redeemer

**redevable** *adj* indebted

**rédiger** *vt* (3) draw up, draft, write; edit

**redingote** *nf* frock-coat; woman's coat

**redire** *vt* (38) say again, repeat; **trouver à ~ à** find fault with

**redite** *nf* frequent and useless repetition

**redondance** *nf* wordiness; superfluity; redundance

**redondant** *adj* wordy; pleonastic

**redonner** *vt* give again; restore

**redorer** *vt* gild again; **~ son blason** (of poor nobleman) marry a rich woman

**redoublement** *nm* redoubling; starting the year in the same class as last

**redoubler** *vt* redouble, increase; **~ une classe** do a second year in the same class; *vi* redouble; **~ d'efforts** try harder than ever

**redoutable** *adj* formidable, redoubtable

**redoute** *nf* redoubt

**redouter** *vt* fear, dread

**redressement** *nm* setting up again, re-erecting; straightening; rectification; righting; recovery

**redresser** *vt* set up again, re-erect; straighten; rectify, right, redress; **se ~**

sit up again; right oneself; draw oneself up

**réducteur -trice** *adj* reducing

**réductible** *adj* reducible

**réduction** *nf* cutting down, reduction; conquest, capture

**réduire** *vt* (80) reduce; **se ~ à** confine oneself to; amount to

**¹réduit** *nm* corner, retreat; fortress, redoubt

**²réduit** *adj* reduced; cheap

**rééditer** *vt* republish

**réel** *nm* reality; *adj* (*f* **réelle**) actual, real

**réélection** *nf* re-election

**réellement** *adv* really, actually

**réexpédier** *vt* send on, forward; send back

**réexporter** *vt* re-export

**refaire** *vt* (46) remake, make again; do again; do differently; repair; do up, restore; *sl* trick, dupe; **se ~** get one's health back, pick up

**réfection** *nf* remaking, rebuilding; doing up, restoration

**référé** *nm leg* summary procedure; injunction

**référence** *nf* reference, referring; recommendation; **~s** references

**référendaire** *nm leg* verifying magistrate

**référer** *vt + vi* (6) refer; **se ~** refer; **je m'en réfère à votre avis** I refer the matter to you

**refiler** *vt sl* pass on, slip, give

**réfléchi** *adj* thoughtful; considered; reflexive

**réfléchir** *vt* reflect; *vi* reflect, consider, ponder; **donner à ~** give food for thought, make one think

**réflecteur** *nm* reflector

**reflet** *nm* reflection; echo

**refléter** *vt* (6) reflect

**réflexe** *nm* reflex, reflex action

**réflexion** *nf* reflection; thought; **(toute) ~ faite** on thinking it over

**refluer** *vi* flow back, surge back

**reflux** *nm* flowing back, ebb

**refondre** *vt* melt again; recast

**refonte** *nf* melting again; recasting

**réformateur -trice** *n* reformer

**réforme** *nf* reformation, reform; *mil* invaliding out; exemption from military service (on physical grounds)

**réformé -e** *n + adj* Protestant

**réformer** *vt* reform; amend; discharge from military service, exempt from military service

**réformiste** *n + adj* reformist

**refoulé** *adj* repressed

**refoulement** *nm* forcing back, thrusting back; repression

**refouler** *vt* force back, drive back; compress, repress, suppress

**réfractaire** *adj* refractory, rebellious; resistant; heat-resistant

**réfracter** *vt* refract

**réfracteur -trice** *adj* refracting

**refrain** *nm* refrain; **toujours le même ~** always the same old story

**refréner** *vt* (6) bridle, curb

**réfrigérant** *adj* refrigerating, cooling; icy

**réfrigérateur** *nm* refrigerator; **mettre qch au ~** put sth on ice

**réfrigération** *nf* refrigeration, chilling

**réfrigérer** *vt* (6) refrigerate, cool

**refroidir** *vt* cool; dampen; *vi* grow cool, cool off; **se ~** grow cool; catch cold

**refroidissement** *nm* cooling; chill

**refuge** *nm* shelter, refuge; street island

**réfugié -e** *n* refugee

**réfugier (se)** *v refl* take refuge

**refus** *nm* refusal; **ce n'est pas de ~** I won't say no

**refuser** *vt* refuse; reject, turn down; deny; turn away; **se ~** object, decline

**réfuter** *vt* refute, disprove

**regagner** *vt* regain, win back, recover; get back to

**régal** *nm* feast; treat

**régalade** *nf* **boire à la ~** pour drink down one's throat

**régaler** *vt* regale, feast; **se ~** eat well, feast

**regard** *nm* glance, look; man-hole, inspection-hole; **au ~ de** in comparison with; **chercher qn du ~** look round for s/o; *leg* **droit de ~** right of inspection; **en ~ de** opposite; in comparison with

**regardant** *adj* careful, stingy

**regarder** *vt* look at; look towards; face; regard; *vi* consider; **~ à un franc** think twice before spending a franc; **y ~ à deux fois** consider carefully; **y ~ de près** be very particular

**regarnir** *vt* regarnish; re-stock; retrim

**régate** *nf* regatta; (neck-)tie

**régence** *nf* regency

**régénérateur -trice** *n* regenerator

**régénérer** *vt* (6) regenerate

**régent -e** *n* regent

**régenter** *vt* lord it over, give orders to

**régie** *nf* public administration, state management; state corporation; theatre administration; excise; excise personnel; **en ~** under state control; **salle de ~** control room

**regimber** *vi* kick; jib

**régime** *nm* diet, regimen; form of government; organization, system; running, operation; flow; **être au ~** be on a diet

**régiment** *nm* regiment; *coll* mass of people; **au ~** in the army

**régimentaire** *adj* regimental

**région** *nf* region, area

**régionalisme** *nm* regionalism

**régir** *vt* govern, rule; direct; *gramm* govern

**régisseur** *nm* manager; steward; *theat* stage-manager

**registre** *nm* register; account-book

**réglable** *adj* adjustable

**réglage** *nm* ruling; adjusting, regulating, setting

**règle** *nf* ruler; rule; **~s** menstrual periods; **agir dans les ~s** act according to the rules; **en ~** in order

**réglé** *adj* ruled; regular

**règlement** *nm* adjustment, settlement; payment; regulation

**réglementaire** *adj* regular, prescribed

**réglementation** *nf* making of rules; regulating

**réglementer** *vt* regulate

**régler** *vt* (6) rule (paper); regulate; settle, put in order; pay

**réglisse** *nf* liquorice

**régnant** *adj* ruling, dominating

**règne** *nm* reign, rule

**régner** *vi* (6) reign, rule; be prevalent, prevail

**regorger** *vi* (3) overflow, brim over; abound; be crowded

**régresser** *vi* regress; diminish

**régressif -ive** *adj* regressive

**régression** *nf* regression

**regret** *nm* regret; **à ~** regretfully; **avoir le ~ de** regret; **être au ~ (de)** regret, be sorry (for, that)

**regretter** *vt* regret, be sorry about; miss

**regrouper** *vt* assemble, group together; group again

**régularisation** *nf* regularizing; putting in order

**régulariser** *vt* regularize; put in order

**régularité** *nf* regularity; evenness; punctuality

**régulateur** *nm* regulator; *adj* (*f* -**trice**) regulating

**régulation** *nf* regulation, adjustment, setting

**régulier -ière** *adj* regular; punctual; even, equable

**régulièrement** *adv* regularly; evenly; normally

**régurgiter** *vt* regurgitate

**réhabilitation** *nf* rehabilitation; discharge (of bankrupt)

**réhabiliter** *vt* rehabilitate; discharge

**rehausser** *vt* raise; enhance; heighten

**réimpression** *nf* reprinting; reprint

**réimprimer** *vt* reprint

**rein** *nm* *anat* kidney; **avoir les ~s solides** be sturdy; *coll* be rich

266

**reine** nf queen

**reine-claude** nf (pl **reines-claudes**) greengage

**reine-marguerite** nf (pl **reines-marguerites**) china aster

**reinette** nf rennet (apple)

**réinstaller** vt reinstall

**réintégrer** vt (6) restore, reinstate; return to

**réitérer** vt (6) repeat; reiterate

**reître** nm brutal soldier

**rejaillir** vi spurt back, gush out; be reflected

**rejet** nm throwing out; casting up; rejection; displacement

**rejeter** vt (5) throw back; cast out; reject; shift, transfer; **se ~** fall back

**rejeton** nm shoot, sucker; offspring, descendant

**rejoindre** vt (55) rejoin; join, overtake; **se ~** meet

**réjoui** adj joyous, jolly

**réjouir** vt gladden, delight, amuse; **se ~** rejoice; look forward, be glad

**réjouissance** nf rejoicing

**réjouissant** adj cheering

**¹relâche** nm + nf slackening; theat no performance

**²relâche** nf naut call, putting in; **faire ~ à un port** put into a port

**relâché** adj slack, relaxed; loose, lax

**relâchement** nm relaxing, slackening; falling off; looseness

**relâcher** vt slacken, relax; loosen; release, set free; **se ~** slacken; abate; flag, fall off, diminish

**relais** nm relay; shift; stage, stopping-point; **~ gastronomique** good restaurant worth stopping at; **~ routier** service station with restaurant; **prendre le ~** take over

**relance** nf giving new life, boosting, recrudescence

**relancer** vt (4) throw back, throw again; start again (quarry); coll pester, pursue assiduously

**relaps -e** n relapsed heretic

**relater** vt relate, state

**relatif -ive** adj relative

**relation** nf relation; connection; report, account

**relax(e)** nm relaxation; adj relaxed

**relaxation** nf leg release, discharge; reduction (of sentence)

**relaxer** vt leg discharge, release

**relayer** vt (7) relay; relieve; **se ~** take over from each other, turn and turn about

**relégation** nf relegation; transportation (to a penal settlement)

**reléguer** vt (6) relegate; transport (to a penal settlement)

**relent** nm musty smell; trail

**relève** nf relief (troops), changing (guard); relief troops

**¹relevé** nm account, statement

**²relevé** adj raised; exalted, noble

**relèvement** nm raising up, raising again; picking up; restoring; recovery; relieving (sentry); rise

**relever** vt (6) raise up again, lift up again; pick up; rebuild; enhance, set off; point out; relieve; release; read (meter); vi depend; **~ de maladie** have just recovered from an illness; **se ~** get up again; revive, recover

**relier** vt tie again; connect; bind (book)

**relieur** nm book-binder

**religieuse** nf nun; kind of chocolate éclair

**religieux** nm monk, friar; adj (f **-euse**) religious, sacred

**religiosité** nf religiosity

**reliquaire** nm reliquary, shrine

**reliquat** nm remainder, residue; after-effects (of illness)

**relique** nf relic (of saint)

**relire** vt (56) re-read

**reliure** nf bookbinding; binding (book)

**reluire** vi (57) shine, glisten, gleam

**reluisant** adj shining; **peu ~** poor, mediocre

**reluquer** vt coll eye, ogle; have one's eye on

**remâcher** vt dwell on

**remailler** vt re-mesh; mend a ladder (in stocking)

**remaniement** nm change, modification

**remanier** vt change, alter, recast; re-handle

**remarquable** adj remarkable; distinguished

**remarque** nf remark; note; **digne de ~** noteworthy; **faire la ~ que** remark that

**remarquer** vt remark, notice; mark again; **faire ~ à qn** point out to s/o; **se faire ~** attract attention

**remballer** vt re-pack

**rembarquer** vt + vi re-embark

**rembarrer** vt coll tell off; contradict sharply

**remblai** nm filling material; mound, bank; filling up; banking up

**remblayer** vt (7) fill up; bank up

**remboîter** vt set (bone); re-bind (book)

**rembourrer** vt stuff; upholster

**remboursement** nm reimbursement, repayment

**rembourser** vt reimburse, refund, repay

**rembrunir** vt darken; make sad; **se ~** grow dark; grow sad

**remède** nm cure, remedy; **sans ~** beyond remedy; **il n'y a pas de ~**

there's no help for it

**remédier** *vi* ~ **à** remedy, put right

**remembrement** *nm* ~ **des terres** regrouping of land

**remembrer** *vt* regroup (land into larger plots)

**remémorer** *vt* bring back to mind; **se** ~ recall

**remerciement** *nm* thanking; thanks; **se confondre en** ~ **s** thank effusively

**remercier** *vt* thank; dismiss; refuse

**remettre** *vt* (60) put back (again); put on again; deliver, hand over; remit; postpone; set, put back into place; recall; ~ **ça** have another go; ~ **en état** repair; ~ **qn** recall s/o; ~ **son âme à Dieu** commit one's soul to God; *coll* **en** ~ do too much; say too much; **partie remise** pleasure deferred; **se** ~ put oneself back again; start again; recover; **s'en** ~ **à qn** rely on s/o

**remise** *nf* putting back into place; handing over, delivery; reduction (in price); remission; award; remittance; postponement; shed, coach-house

**remiser** *vt* put in a shed; put away

**rémission** *nf* remission; **sans** ~ relentlessly; uninterruptedly

**remontant** *nm* tonic

**remonte** *nf* going upstream; remounting

**remontée** *nf* climb

**remonte-pente** *nm* ski-lift

**remonter** *vt* take up again; go up again; raise, elevate; wind up; remount; reassemble; refurbish; ~ **qn** cheer s/o up; *vi* go up again; go back

**remontoir** *nm* winder

**remontrance** *nf* remonstrance, reprimand

**remontrer** *vt* show again; point out; **en** ~ **à qn** give advice to s/o; be superior to s/o

**rémora** *nm* remora, sucking-fish; pilot-fish

**remords** *nm* remorse, compunction

**remorque** *nf* towing; trailer; tow-line

**remorquer** *vt* tow, pull, draw

**remorqueur** *nm* tug (boat)

**rémoulade** *nf cul* sauce made with mustard, oil, garlic, etc

**rémouleur** *nm* knife-grinder

**remous** *nm* eddy, swirl, backwash

**rempailler** *vt* re-seat, re-bottom (chair)

**rempailleur -euse** *n* chair-mender

**rempart** *nm* rampart; bulwark

**rempiler** *vt* pile up again; *vi sl* re-engage for military service

**remplaçant -e** *n* substitute

**remplacement** *nm* replacement; **de** ~ substitute, spare

**remplacer** *vt* (4) replace; take the place of

**rempli** *nm* tuck (in a dress); *adj* full, filled

**remplier** *vt* make a tuck in

**remplir** *vt* fill up; fill in; occupy; fulfil, perform

**remplissage** *nm* filling; padding

**remplumer (se)** *v refl* get new feathers; *coll* pick up again; regain weight

**remporter** *vt* carry back, take away, carry off; ~ **la victoire** be victorious

**rempoter** *vt* repot (plant)

**remuant** *adj* restless

**remue-ménage** *nm invar* bustle, stir

**remuer** *vt* stir; move; *vi* move, change places; fidget; **se** ~ bestir oneself

**remugle** *nm* musty smell

**rémunérateur -trice** *adj* remunerative, profitable

**rémunération** *nf* payment, remuneration

**rémunérer** *vt* (6) remunerate; reward

**renâcler** *vi* snort; draw back, be reluctant

**renaître** *vi* (64) be born again; spring up again, revive

**renard** *nm* fox; cunning fellow

**renarde** *nf* viven

**renchérir** *vi* get dearer; outbid; outdo

**renchérissement** *nm* rise in price

**rencogner** *vt coll* drive into a corner; **se** ~ retreat into a corner

**rencontre** *nf* meeting; encounter; skirmish; occasion; **aller à la** ~ **de** go to meet

**rencontrer** *vt* meet; run across; **se** ~ meet; occur; tally

**rendement** *nm* yield, return, profit; productivity; **à plein** ~ at maximum output

**rendez-vous** *nm* appointment; meeting-place; **prendre** ~ make an appointment

**rendormir (se)** *v refl* fall asleep again

**rendre** *vt* give back, return; repay; deliver; vomit; surrender; express; reproduce; make; produce, give out; ~ **grâce à** give thanks to; ~ **la justice** dispense justice; ~ **l'âme** die, pass away; ~ **les armes** admit defeat; **se** ~ go, proceed; surrender

¹**rendu** *nm* rendering

²**rendu** *adj* exhausted; arrived

**rêne** *nf* rein

**renégat -e** *n* renegade

**renfermé** *nm* close smell, musty odour; *adj* uncommunicative

**renfermer** *vt* shut up again; lock up; contain, include; **se** ~ **dans le silence** withdraw into silence

**renflement** *nm* swelling, bulging

**renfler** *vt* + *vi* swell out, enlarge

**renflouer** *vt* refloat; set up again

**renfoncement** *nm* hollow, cavity, recess

**renfoncer** *vt* (4) knock in, drive in further

**renforcer** *vt* (4) strengthen, reinforce; intensify

**renfort** *nm* reinforcement; backing, stiffening piece; **à grand ~ de** with the help of plenty of

**renfrogné** *adj* frowning, sullen

**renfrogner (se)** *v refl* scowl, knit one's brows

**rengaine** *nf coll* old story; refrain

**rengainer** *vt* sheathe; suppress, bottle up

**rengorger (se)** *v refl* strut, swagger

**reniement** *nm* denial, repudiation; disavowal

**renier** *vt* disown; disavow

**reniflard** *nm mech* snifting valve; breather

**reniflement** *nm* sniffing; sniff

**renifler** *vt* + *vi* sniff

**renne** *nm* reindeer

**renom** *nm* renown, fame

**renommé** *adj* renowned, famous

**renommée** *nf* renown, fame; rumour

**renommer** *vt* re-appoint, re-elect

**renoncement** *nm* renouncing, renouncement; self-denial, renunciation

**renoncer** *vi* (4) **~ à** renounce, give up; **y ~** give it up as a bad job

**renonciateur -trice** *n* renouncer

**renonciation** *nf* renunciation

**renoncule** *nf* buttercup, ranunculus

**renouer** *vt* tie up again; renew, resume

**renouveau** *nm* springtide; renewal

**renouveler** *vt* (5) renew, renovate; revive; **se ~** be renewed; happen again

**renouvellement** *nm* renewal, replacement; renovation

**rénovateur -trice** *n* renovator

**rénovation** *nf* renovation, renewing

**renseignement** *nm* piece of information, indication; **prendre des ~s** make inquiries

**renseigner** *vt* inform; **se ~** find out, make inquiries

**rentabilité** *nf* profitability

**rentable** *adj* profitable, paying

**rente** *nf* revenue; pension, allowance; **vivre de ses ~s** live on one's (private) income

**rentier -ière** *n* person of independent means

**rentoiler** *vt* back (painting)

**rentrant** *adj* re-entrant (angle)

**rentré** *adj* sunken, hollow

**rentrée** *nf* return, home-coming; beginning of term, end of holidays; taking in, encashment; gathering in

**rentrer** *vt* bring in, take in; bottle up, suppress; *vi* re-enter, go in again, come back; come home; go home, return; resume, re-open; **~ dans ses droits**

recover one's rights; **~ dedans** bang into sth, crash into sth; **~ en grâce** be forgiven; **faire ~** call in (debt)

**renversant** *adj coll* staggering, astounding

**renverse** *nf* **à la ~** backwards

**renversé** *adj* reversed; upset; **crême ~e** sweet made of eggs and cream

**renversement** *nm* inversion, reversal; overthrow, upsetting

**renverser** *vt* reverse, invert; upset, overturn; overthrow; **se ~** fall down; tip over, capsize

**renvoi** *nm* return, sending back, throwing back; dismissal, discharge; postponement; referring; reference mark; belch; *mus* repeat mark

**renvoyer** *vt* (7) send back, return, throw back; turn away; dismiss, discharge; postpone; refer

**réorganiser** *vt* reorganize

**réouverture** *nf* re-opening; resumption

**repaire** *nm* den, nest, haunt

**repaître** *vt* (81) feed (animal); **se ~** feed; eat one's fill

**répandre** *vt* pour out; shed; spread, scatter, broadcast; give off; **se ~** spread, gain ground; spill; **se ~ en excuses** apologize profusely

**répandu** *adj* widespread, prevalent; widely known

**reparaître** *vi* (68) reappear; turn up again

**réparateur -trice** *n* repairer; *adj* restorative

**réparation** *nf* reparation; repairing, repair; redress; **en ~** under repair

**réparer** *vt* repair, mend; restore; make amends for; rectify

**reparler** *vi* speak again

**repartie** *nf* retort

**repartir** *vt* (89) retort; *vi* set out again

**répartir** *vt* share out, distribute; allocate

**répartiteur** *nm* distributor; assessor of taxes

**répartition** *nf* sharing out, distribution; allocation; assessment (of taxes)

**repas** *nm* meal

**repassage** *nm* ironing; sharpening

**repasser** *vt* pass by again, cross again; go over again, look over again; sharpen; iron; *vi* pass by again; call again

**repasseuse** *nf* ironer; ironing machine

**repêcher** *vt* fish out again, pick up; give a bare pass to (exam candidate)

**repeindre** *vt* (55) repaint, paint over

**repenser** *vt* re-examine

**repenti** *adj* repentant

¹**repentir** *nm* repentance

²**repentir (se)** *v refl* (59) repent, be sorry

**repérage** *nm* locating, marking

**répercussion** *nf* repercussion; consequence

répercuter

**répercuter** *vt* reflect back, reflect, reverberate; **se ~** have repercussions
**repère** *nm* mark, reference; **point de ~** landmark; guide mark
**repérer** *vt* (6) locate, spot; mark with guide marks; **se ~** take one's bearings
**répertoire** *nm* list, table; repertory
**répertorier** *vt* index, make a reference table for; enter in an index
**répéter** *vt* (6) repeat; do again; rehearse; **ne pas se faire ~ qch** not need to be told sth twice
**répétiteur -trice** *n* tutor, private coach; part-time teacher
**répétition** *nf* repetition; reproduction; rehearsal; lesson; **montre à ~** repeater watch
**repeupler** *vt* repopulate; restock; replant
**repiquer** *vt* prick again, sting again; plant out, transplant; restitch; nab again
**répit** *nm* respite, breathing-space
**replacer** *vt* (4) put back in place; reinvest; give another job to
**replâtrer** *vt* replaster; *coll* patch up
**replet -ète** *adj* stout
**réplétion** *nf* repletion; corpulence
**repli** *nm* retreat; crease; recess; meander, winding
**replier** *vt* fold again; fold up, coil up; tuck in; **se ~** turn back; fold up; bend; retreat
**réplique** *nf* rejoinder, answer; *theat* cue; **argument sans ~** unanswerable argument
**répliquer** *vt* + *vi* retort, answer back
**répondant** *nm* *eccles* server; *n* (*f* -**e**) *leg* surety, referee
**répondre** *vt* answer; *eccles* **~ la messe** make the responses at mass; *vi* answer; respond, comply; correspond; be answerable; **je vous en réponds** take my word for it
**répons** *nm* *eccles* response
**réponse** *nf* answer, reply; response
**report** *nm* carrying forward; sum carried forward; contango; postponement; transfer
**reportage** *nm* reporting; report
**reporter** *vt* carry back, take back; postpone; carry forward; **se ~** refer
**repos** *nm* rest; pause; peace; **~!** stand at ease!; **au ~** laid off; **de tout ~** absolutely safe
**reposant** *adj* restful
**reposé** *adj* rested; calm; **à tête ~e** deliberately, at leisure
**reposer** *vt* put back, place back, replace; rest; *vi* rest; lie buried; **~ sur** be founded on; **se ~** rest, have a rest; settle again; rely
**reposoir** *nm* temporary altar

**repoussant** *adj* repulsive, loathsome
**repousse** *nf* fresh growth (hair)
**repoussé** *adj* embossed; repoussé
**repousser** *vt* push back, drive off, repulse, repel; put aside; reject; emboss; work in repoussé; throw out (shoots); delay, postpone; *vi* grow again, sprout again
**repoussoir** *nm* *carp, etc* starting-punch; cuticle remover; *fig* foil; ugly person
**reprendre** *vt* (75) take again, take back, recapture; resume; revive (play); criticize; *vi* start again, revive; improve, pick up; **se ~** correct oneself; recover oneself; **se ~ à faire qch** begin again to do sth
**représailles** *nfpl* reprisals; **user de ~** carry out reprisals
**représentant -e** *n* representative; (commercial) traveller
**représentatif -ive** *adj* representative
**représentation** *nf* representation; *theat* performance; *comm* agency; protest; (official) state display; **frais de ~** entertainment expenses
**représenter** *vt* present again, reintroduce; represent; portray; *theat* perform; point out; *vi* have a good presence; **se ~** present oneself again; reappear; occur again; imagine
**répressif -ive** *adj* repressive
**réprimande** *nf* reprimand
**réprimander** *vt* reprimand, reprove
**réprimer** *vt* repress, check, quell
**repris** *nm* **~ de justice** old offender, habitual criminal
**reprise** *nf* retaking, recapture; renewal; revival, resumption; acceleration; round (boxing); darn; deduction (in part-exchange transaction); taking over of fittings (with flat); **à plusieurs ~s** repeatedly; on several occasions
**repriser** *vt* darn
**réprobateur -trice** *adj* reproachful
**reproche** *nm* reproach; **sans ~** blameless
**reprocher** *vt* reproach; grudge
**reproducteur -trice** *n* animal kept for breeding purposes; *adj* reproductive
**reproductif -ive** *adj* reproductive
**reproduire** *vt* (80) reproduce; **se ~** happen again; breed
**reprographie** *nf* reprography, duplicating of documents
**réprouvé -e** *n* outcast; damned
**réprouver** *vt* disapprove of; reject; damn
**reps** *nm* rep(p)
**repu** *adj* sated, full
**républicain -e** *n* + *adj* republican
**républicanisme** *nm* republicanism
**république** *nf* republic; **la ~ des lettres**

270

writers, literary men

**répudier** *vt* repudiate; renounce

**répugnance** *nf* repugnance, dislike, aversion

**répugnant** *adj* loathsome

**répugner** *vi* feel repugnance; be reluctant; inspire loathing

**répulsif -ive** *adj* repulsive

**réputation** *nf* reputation, repute; **perdre qn de ~** ruin s/o's reputation

**réputé** *adj* well-known

**réputer** *vt* repute, consider, think

**requérant -e** *n leg* plaintiff, petitioner

**requérir** *vt* (27) ask for, demand; call upon

**requête** *nf* request, petition, suit; **à la ~ de** at the suit of

**requin** *nm* shark; greedy person (business)

**requinquer** *vt* pep up; **se ~** smarten oneself up; recover

**requis** *adj* required, necessary

**réquisition** *nf* requisitioning; requisition

**réquisitionner** *vt* requisition, commandeer

**réquisitoire** *nm* indictment; violent reproach

**R.E.R.** *see* réseau

**rescapé -e** *n* survivor; *adj* saved

**rescinder** *vt leg* annul, rescind

**rescousse** *nf* **à la ~** to the rescue

**réseau** *nm* network, system; **~ express régional (R.E.R.)** fast train service between Paris and outer suburbs

**réséda** *nm* mignonette

**réséquer** *vt* (6) *med* resect (bone)

**réservation** *nf* reservation, reserving; reserve; **~ légale** part of inheritance that must go to heirs; **à la ~ de** except for; **de ~** reserve; **sans ~** without prejudice

**réserve** *nf* reserve; **sous ~ de** subject to

**réservé** *adj* discreet, reserved

**réserver** *vt* reserve, set aside, keep in store; **se ~** hold back, wait

**réserviste** *nm* reservist

**réservoir** *nm* reservoir; tank, container

**résidence** *nf* residence; residing; luxury housing development, luxury block of flats

**résident, -e** *n* foreign resident

**résider** *vi* reside, dwell

**résidu** *nm* residue

**résiduel -uelle** *adj* residual

**résignation** *nf* resignation; submissiveness

**résigner** *vt* resign; give up; **se ~** submit, resign oneself

**résiliation** *nf* cancellation, annulment

**résilience** *nf* resilience

**résilier** *vt* annul, cancel

**résille** *nf* hair-net

**résine** *nf* resin

**résiner** *vt* dip in resin; extract the resin from

**résineux -euse** *adj* resinous

**résistance** *nf* resistance, opposition; endurance; resistance movement; **pièce de ~** principal dish; main feature

**résistant -e** *n* resistance fighter, member of resistance movement; *adj* resistant, strong

**résister** *vi* **~ à** resist, withstand

**résolu** *adj* resolute, determined

**résoluble** *adj* solvable; terminable

**résolument** *adv* courageously

**résolution** *nf* resolution; solution; annulment; **adopter une ~** pass a resolution

**résonnement** *nm* resonance, reverberation

**résonner** *vi* resound, reverberate

**résorber** *vt* reabsorb, absorb

**résoudre** *vt* (82) resolve; dissolve; annul; clear up, solve, settle; persuade, induce; **se ~** determine, resolve; dissolve

**respect** *nm* respect, regard; **~ humain** fear of public opinion; **sauf votre ~** with all due respect; **tenir en ~** keep at a respectful distance; keep in awe

**respectabilité** *nf* respectability

**respecter** *vt* respect, treat with regard; **se ~** have self-respect

**respectif -ive** *adj* respective

**respectueuse** *nf* prostitute

**respectueux -ueuse** *adj* respectful

**respiratoire** *adj* respiratory

**respirer** *vt* + *vi* breathe, inhale

**resplendir** *vi* shine, be resplendent

**resplendissant** *adj* shining, resplendent

**responsabilité** *nf* responsibility; liability; **engager sa ~ personnelle** assume personal responsibility

**responsable** *adj* responsible, answerable

**resquiller** *vi coll* get in without paying; gate-crash

**resquilleur -euse** *n* person who avoids paying (train, cinema, etc); uninvited guest

**ressac** *nm* undertow; surf

**ressaisir** *vt* seize again; **se ~** regain one's self-control

**ressasser** *vt coll* repeat ceaselessly

**ressaut** *nm* projection

**ressemblance** *nf* resemblance, likeness

**ressemblant** *adj* like; faithful (portrait)

**ressembler** *vi* **~ à** resemble, look like; **ça ne ressemble à rien** it's like nothing on earth; *coll* **ça ne vous ressemble pas** that's not a bit like you

**ressemelage** *nm* re-soling

**ressemeler** *vt* (5) re-sole

**ressentiment** *nm* resentment

**ressentir** *vt* (59) feel; experience; resent; **se ~ de** feel the effects of

**resserre** *nf* store-room

**resserrer** *vt* tighten; tie again; contract; restrain, confine; put away again; draw closer; **se ~** shrink, contract; retrench

**resservir** *vt* serve again; *vi* be used again, be of use again

**¹ressort** *nm* spring; elasticity, springiness; motive, cause; **avoir du ~** be resilient

**²ressort** *nm* scope, competence; **cela n'est pas de mon ~** that's not within my competence; **en dernier ~** in the last resort

**¹ressortir** *vi* (83) go out again, come out again; stand out, be evident

**²ressortir** *vi* (83) come under the jurisdiction

**ressortissant -e** *n* national

**ressource -e** *nf* resource; resourcefulness; expedient; **~s means**

**ressuer** *vi* sweat (walls)

**ressusciter** *vt + vi* resuscitate; revive

**restant** *nm* remainder; *adj* remaining

**restaurateur -trice** *n* restorer; restaurant-keeper

**restauration** *nf* restoration, restoring; restaurant business

**restaurer** *vt* restore; refresh; **se ~** take refreshment

**reste** *nm* remainder, rest; **~s** remains; **au ~** moreover; **de ~** over, remaining; **du ~** moreover; **être en ~** be under an obligation; **jouir de son ~** make the most of what is left to one; **ne pas demander son ~** clear out; have enough

**rester** *vi* remain, stay; be left; **en ~ là** stop at that point; **il n'en reste pas moins que** nevertheless; **reste à savoir si** it remains to be seen whether

**restituer** *vt* restore; hand back, return

**restitution** *nf* restoration; restitution

**restoroute** *nm* motorway restaurant

**restreindre** *vt* (55) restrict, curtail; **se ~** cut down on one's expenses

**restreint** *adj* restricted, limited

**restrictif -ive** *adj* restrictive, limitative

**résultante** *nf math + mech* resultant

**résultat** *nm* result, outcome

**résulter** *vi* result, arise; **il en résulte que** consequently

**résumé** *nm* summary, abstract; **en ~** to sum up

**résumer** *vt* summarize, sum up; **se ~** sum up

**résurrection** *nf* resurrection; revival

**retable** *nm* reredos, altar-piece

**rétablir** *vt* re-establish, restore; reinstate; bring back into force; **se ~** get well again

**rétablissement** *nm* re-establishment; restoration; recovery

**rétamer** *vt* re-tin; re-silver

**rétameur** *nm* tinker

**retape** *nf sl* **faire la ~** solicit (prostitute)

**retaper** *vt coll* do up, touch up, mend; *coll* **se ~** get well again

**retard** *nm* delay, slowness; **avoir du ~** be late; **en ~** late, behind

**retardataire** *n* late-comer, late arrival, straggler; *adj* late, behindhand

**retardateur -trice** *adj* retarding

**retarder** *vt* delay, retard, hold up; put off, put back; *vi* be late, be slow; lag, be behind

**retenir** *vt* (96) hold back, keep back, detain; retain; engage, reserve; curb, check; carry (numbers); **~ l'attention** hold the attention; **se ~** hold on; restrain oneself

**rétention** *nf med* retention; carrying (number)

**retentir** *vi* resound, echo, reverberate

**retentissant** *adj* resounding

**retentissement** *nm* reverberation; resounding noise; repercussion

**retenue** *nf* deduction; detention (at school); confinement; discretion, reserve, restraint, holding back; damming; **mettre un élève en ~** keep a pupil in

**réticence** *nf* reserve, reticence

**réticule** *nm* hand-bag; *opt* reticle

**rétif -ive** *adj* stubborn, recalcitrant

**rétine** *nf anat* retina

**retiré** *adj* remote; retired

**retirer** *vt* pull out; withdraw; take away; get, obtain; **se ~** retire; withdraw; subside, recede, ebb

**retombée** *nf* falling down; **~s radio-actives** radio-active fall-out

**retomber** *vi* fall down again; fall; hang down; *coll* **~ sur ses pieds** land on one's feet

**retordre** *vt* wring out again, twist again; **donner du fil à ~** give trouble

**rétorquer** *vt* retort

**retors** *adj* twisted; crafty; cunning

**rétorsion** *nf* retorting

**retouche** *nf* slight alteration; retouch; *phot* retouching

**retoucher** *vt* touch up, retouch

**retour** *nm* return; turn, twist; vicissitude, reversal; **~ d'âge** menopause; **~ de conscience** qualms of conscience; **~ de flamme** blow-back; **être de ~** be back; **être sur le ~** be on the way home; be past one's prime; **faire un ~ sur soi-même** think seriously about one's conduct; **par ~ du courrier** by return of post; **payer de ~** requite

**retourne** *nf* turned-up card

**retourner** *vt* turn inside out; return, send back; turn up, turn over; examine thoroughly; *coll* upset; *vi* return, go back; revert; **de quoi retourne-t-il?** what's it all about?; **se ~** turn over, overturn; look round, turn round; devise means; **se ~ contre** round on; **s'en ~** return

**retracer** *vt* (4) retrace, trace again

**rétracter** *vt* retract; draw in; **se ~** recant, retract

**retrait** *nm* withdrawal; shrinkage; **en ~** set back; recessed

**retraite** *nf* retreat; tattoo; retirement; (retirement) pension; place of retirement; haunt; **battre en ~** beat a retreat; **caisse de ~** pension fund

**retraité -e** *n* retired person; *adj* retired

**retranchement** *nm* docking, cutting off; excision; entrenchment

**retrancher** *vt* cut off, retrench; strike out; fortify; **se ~** entrench oneself

**retransmettre** *vt* (60) retransmit, pass on; *rad* relay

**rétrécir** *vt + vi* narrow, contract, shrink; **se ~** shrink

**rétrécissement** *nm* narrowing, shrinking

**retremper** *vt* soak again; retemper; **se ~** acquire new strength

**rétribuer** *vt* remunerate, pay

**rétribution** *nf* remuneration, salary; reward

**rétro** *nm abbr* **rétroviseur**

**rétroactif -ive** *adj* retroactive

**rétrocéder** *vt* (6) reassign

**rétrocession** *nf leg* retrocession

**rétrofusée** *nf* retro-rocket

**rétrograder** *vi* move backwards; change down (gear)

**rétrospectif -ive** *adj* retrospective

**rétrospective** *nf* chronological exhibition of artist's work

**retrousser** *vt* turn up, roll up; curl up; tuck up

**retrouver** *vt* find again; find; meet, join; **se ~** meet again; meet; find one's bearings; be where one was before

**rétroviseur** *nm* driving-mirror

**rets** *nm ar* net; trap, ruse

**réunion** *nf* reunion; joining up again, junction; meeting, coming together

**réunir** *vt* reunite; unite, join together; **se ~** get together, meet; join forces

**réussi** *adj* successful

**réussir** *vt* make a success of; *vi* succeed, do well; **tout lui réussit** everything turns out well for him

**réussite** *nf* success, successful result; patience (cards)

**revaloir** *vt* (95) pay back, return in kind

**revaloriser** *vt* revalue

**revanche** *nf* revenge; return match; **en ~** on the other hand

**rêvasser** *vi* day-dream, muse

**rêvasserie** *nf* day-dreaming, musing

**rêve** *nm* dream; day-dream; **c'est le ~!** it's all one could wish

**revêche** *adj* cross-grained, difficult

**réveil** *nm* waking; re-awakening; alarm-clock; **sonner le ~** sound reveille

**réveille-matin** *nm invar* alarm-clock

**réveiller** *vt* wake, awake; stir up, rouse; **se ~** wake up; revive

**réveillon** *nm* midnight supper (on Christmas Eve and New Year's Eve)

**réveillonner** *vi* have a **réveillon**

**révélateur -trice** *n* revealer, indicator; *adj* revealing

**révélation** *nf* revelation, disclosure

**révéler** *vt* (6) reveal; show; betray; **se ~** reveal oneself; come to light

**revenant** *nm* ghost; s/o who has been away

**revendeur -euse** *n* second-hand dealer; retailer

**revendication** *nf* claim, demand; claiming

**revendiquer** *vt* claim, demand

**revenez-y** *nm* return; renewal; *coll* **goût de ~** appetizing taste

**revenir** *vi* (96) return, come back; start again; **~ à** cost, come to; **~ à soi** regain consciousness; **~ au même** come to the same thing; **~ de loin** have been at death's door; have escaped a great danger; **~ de ses craintes** get over one's fears; **~ sur ses pas** retrace one's footsteps; **ça me revient maintenant** I remember it now; **cela revient à dire** that is tantamount to saying; **cul faire ~ brown**; **je n'en reviens pas** I can't get over it; **son visage ne me revient pas** I don't like his face; **y ~** return to a subject

**revente** *nf* resale

**revenu** *nm* income, yield; drawing the temper (out of steel)

**rêver** *vt* dream of; *vi* dream

**réverbère** *nm* street lamp; reflector

**réverbérer** *vt* (6) reverberate, reflect

**reverdir** *vi* grow green again; grow young again

**révérence** *nf* reverence; bow, curtsey; **tirer sa ~** bow, drop a curtsey; *coll* go off

**révérenciel -ielle** *adj* reverential

**révérencieux -ieuse** *adj* ceremonious, over-polite

**révérer** *vt* (6) revere

**rêverie** *nf* dreaming, musing

**revers** *nm* reverse side, other side; lapel; turn-over; reverse; back-hand stroke; **~ de la médaille** other side of the coin;

à ~ in the rear

**reverser** *vt* pour again; transfer

**réversible** *adj* reversible; revertible

**reversoir** *nm* weir

**revêtement** *nm* coating, covering, surface (road); revetment

**revêtir** *vt* (97) reclothe; dress; put on, don; face, coat; invest (with office, honour); ~ **l'aspect de** assume the appearance of

**rêveur -euse** *n* dreamer; *adj* dreamy, dreaming

**revient** *nm* **prix de** ~ cost price

**revirement** *nm* sudden change, change of direction

**réviser** *vt* revise; re-examine; overhaul

**réviseur** *nm* reviser; *typ* proof-reader

**révision** *nf* revising; re-examination; *typ* proof-reading; inspection; *mot* servicing, overhauling; **conseil de** ~ medical examination (for army recruits)

**révisionniste** *adj* revisionist

**revivre** *vi* (98) live again; revive; relive

**révocable** *adj* revocable; removable

**révocation** *nf* revocation; repeal; dismissal

**revoici** *prep* + *adv coll* me ~ ! here I am again!

**revoilà** *prep* + *adv coll* le ~ ! there he is again!

**revoir** *nm invar* seeing again; **au** ~ good-bye; *vt* (99) see again; revise; re-examine

**révoltant** *adj* revolting, sickening

**révolte** *nf* revolt, rebellion

**révolté -e** *n* insurgent

**révolter** *vt* arouse indignation, revolt; se ~ revolt

**révolu** *adj* completed

**révolution** *nf* revolution; upheaval

**révolutionnaire** *n* + *adj* revolutionary

**révolutionner** *vt* revolutionize

**révoquer** *vt* revoke, repeal; dismiss; recall

**revue** *nf* review, survey; magazine; *theat* revue; *coll* **être de la** ~ have one's hopes dashed; **passer en** ~ revue

**révulser** *vt* overturn, upset; **les yeux révulsés** eyes turned upwards

**révulsif -ive** *adj* revulsive, counter-irritating

· **rez-de-chaussée** *nm invar* ground floor, *US* first floor

**rhabiller** *vt* repair, mend; dress again; se ~ get dressed again

**rhabilleur** *nm* repairer

**rhapsodie** *nf* rhapsody

**rhénan** *adj* Rhenish

**rhétoricien -ienne** *n* rhetorician

**rhétorique** *nf* rhetoric; *ar* class in lycée = lower sixth

**Rhin** *nm* Rhine

**rhodanien -ienne** *adj* of the Rhône

**rhombe** *nm* rhombus

**rhomboïde** *adj* rhomboid

**rhubarbe** *nf* rhubarb

**rhum** *nm* rum

**rhumatisant** *adj* rheumatic; afflicted with rheumatism

**rhumatismal** *adj* rheumatic

**rhumatisme** *nm* rheumatism

**rhume** *nm* cold; ~ **de cerveau** head cold

**riant** *adj* smiling; cheerful; pleasant

**ribambelle** *nf coll* string, swarm, collection

**ribote** *nf sl* drinking orgy

**ribouldingue** *nf sl* feasting

**ricanement** *nm* sneering

**ricaner** *vi* sneer, mock

**ricaneur -euse** *n* sneerer; *adj* sneering

**richard -e** *n coll* rich person

**riche** *adj* rich, wealthy; fertile; ~ **à millions** enormously wealthy

**richesse** *nf* wealth, riches; fertility; sumptuousness

**richissime** *adj* very wealthy

**ricin** *nm* castor-oil plant; **huile de** ~ castor oil

**ricocher** *vi* rebound, glance off; ricochet

**ricochet** *nm* rebound; ricochet

**rictus** *nm* grin; *anat* rictus

**ride** *nf* wrinkle; ripple

**ridé** *adj* wrinkled

**rideau** *nm* curtain; screen; ~ **de fer** iron curtain; *theat* safety curtain; **tirer le** ~ **sur** draw a veil over

**rider** *vt* wrinkle, line; shrivel; ripple; se ~ grow wrinkled; ripple

**ridicule** *nm* absurdity; ridiculous touch; **tomber dans le** ~ make oneself ridiculous; **tourner en** ~ hold up to ridicule; *adj* laughable, ridiculous

**ridiculiser** *vt* ridicule

**rien** *nm* trifle, mere nothing; tiny quantity; *indef pron* anything; very little; nothing, not anything; ~ **moins que** far from; ~ **que** nothing but, only; **ce n'est pas** ~ it's quite something; **de** ~ don't mention it; **en** ~ in no way; **il n'en est** ~ nothing of the kind; **un homme de** ~ a man of no account

**rieur -euse** *n* person who laughs; *adj* fond of laughter

**rififi** *nm sl* fight

¹**riflard** *nm* plastering-trowel, paring-chisel; coarse file

²**riflard** *nm coll* umbrella

**rigaudon** *nm see* **rigodon**

**rigide** *adj* rigid, inflexible; tense

**rigidité** *nf* rigidity; tenseness

**rigodon, rigaudon** *nm* rigadoon

**rigolade** *nf coll* lark, fun

**rigole** *nf* drain, gutter, channel; trickle

**rigoler** *vi coll* laugh

**rigolo -ote** *n coll* amusing person; *nm coll* revolver; *adj coll* comical, funny
**rigoriste** *adj* strict (as regards morals)
**rigoureux -euse** *adj* rigorous
**rigueur** *nf* severity, harshness; strictness, exactness; **à la ~** if necessary; **de ~** compulsory, indispensable; **user de ~** be severe
**rikiki** *nm see* **riquiqui**
**rillettes** *nfpl* potted minced pork (cooked)
**rimailler** *vi* write poor poetry
**rime** *nf* rhyme
**rimer** *vt* put into rhyme; *vi* rhyme; write verse; *coll* **cela ne rime à rien** there's no sense in that
**rimeur -euse** *n* rhymester
**rince-doigts** *nm* finger-bowl
**rincer** *vt* (4) rinse, rinse out
**rincette** *nf coll* nip (in bottom of glass or coffee cup)
**ringard** *nm* poker, fire-iron
**ripaille** *nf coll* feasting; **faire ~** feast
**riper** *vt* scrape, polish; slip (chain); shift; *vi* scrape; skid
**ripoliner** *vt* paint with gloss paint
**riposte** *nf* riposte; counter; retort
**riposter** *vi* counter; retort
**riquiqui** *nm coll* tiny thing, tiny person
**rire** *nm* laughter, laughing; laugh; *vi* (84) laugh; joke; have a laugh; **~ de** make fun of; scorn; **à mourir de ~** killingly funny; **avoir le mot pour ~** tell good jokes; **histoire de ~** for fun, as a joke; **il n'y a pas de quoi ~** it's no laughing matter; **pour ~** for fun; **prêter à ~** give cause for laughter; **rira bien qui rira le dernier** he who laughs last laughs best; **vous voulez ~!** you're joking; **se ~ de** mock
¹**ris** *nm naut* reef
²**ris** *nm* **~ de veau** sweetbread
¹**risée** *nf* mockery; laughing-stock
²**risée** *nf* light squall
**risette** *nf* laugh (*usu* child); **fais ~!** smile!
**risible** *adj* laughable, ludicrous
**risque** *nm* risk; **assurance tous ~s** comprehensive insurance policy; **à vos ~s et périls** at your own risk
**risquer** *vt* risk, chance; *coll* **~ de** be likely to; **~ le coup** chance it
**risque-tout** *nm invar* dare-devil
**rissoler** *vt cul* brown
**ristourne** *nf* refund; rebate; rake-off, commission
**ristourner** *vt* refund; return; give as commission
**ritournelle** *nf mus* ritornelle; *coll* same old story
**ritualiste** *adj* ritualistic
**rituel -uelle** *adj* ritual

**rivage** *nm* bank, shore
**rivaliser** *vi* rival, compete
**rivalité** *nf* rivalry
**rive** *nf* bank, shore; edge, border
**rivelaine** *nf* miner's pick
**river** *vt* rivet; attach, fix; **~ son clou à qn** shut s/o up
**riverain -e** *n* riverain; resident; *adj* waterside, riverside; bordering
**riveter** *vt* (5) rivet
**rivière** *nf* river, stream; **~ de diamants** diamond necklace
**rivoir** *nm* riveting-machine; riveting-hammer
**rixe** *nf* brawl, scuffle
**riz** *nm* rice
**rizière** *nf* rice-plantation, rice-paddy
**rob, robre** *nm* rubber (cards)
**robe** *nf* dress, frock, gown; legal profession; skin, husk; coat (animal); **~ de chambre** dressing-gown; **pommes de terre en ~ de chambre (des champs)** potatoes in their jackets
**robinet** *nm* tap, *US* faucet
**robinetterie** *nf* taps and fittings
**robot** *nm* robot; automatic kitchen gadget
**robre** *nm see* **rob**
**robuste** *adj* robust, sturdy, hardy
**robustesse** *nf* sturdiness, hardiness
**roc** *nm* rock
**rocade** *nf* by-pass
**rocaille** *nf* rockery; rubble
**rocailleux -euse** *adj* rocky, stony; harsh, rugged
**rocambolesque** *adj* fantastic
**roche** *nf* rock; **clair comme de l'eau de ~** crystal clear; **il y a anguille sous ~** there's something brewing
**rocher** *nm* rock
**rochet** *nm* rachet
**rocheux -euse** *adj* rocky, stony
**rodage** *nm* grinding; running in; wearing; **en ~** running in
**roder** *vt* grind; polish; run in
**rôder** *vi* prowl, wander about
**rôdeur -euse** *n* prowler
**rodomontade** *nf* blustering, swaggering
**Rogations** *nfpl eccles* Rogation-days
**rogatons** *nmpl coll* scraps (food)
**rogne** *nf coll* anger; **être en ~** be angry
**rogner** *vt* clip, trim, cut back
**rognon** *nm cul* kidney
**rognures** *nfpl* cuttings, clippings
**rogomme** *nm coll* spirits, liquor; **voix de ~** husky voice
**rogue** *adj* arrogant, haughty
**roi** *nm* king; **morceau de ~** dish fit for a king; **Nuit des Rois** Twelfth Night
**roide** *adj + adv see* **raide**
**roideur** *nf see* **raideur**
**roidir** *vt see* **raidir**

**roitelet** *nm* king of tiny country; wren
**rôle** *nm* roll, list, register; *theat* part, rôle; **à tour de** ~ in turn
**Romain -e** *n* Roman
**romain** *adj* Roman
¹**romaine** *nf* steelyard
²**romaine** *nf* cos lettuce
**roman** *nm* novel, (medieval) romance; romance language, Romanic; *adj archi* romanesque; Norman (in England)
**romance** *nf* sentimental song
**romancer** *vt* give a romantic turn to
**romanche** *nm* Romansh
**romancier -ière** *n* novelist
**romand** *adj* Suisse ~ **e** French Switzerland
**romanesque** *adj* romantic; of the novel
**roman-feuilleton** *nm* (*pl* **romans-feuilletons**) serial
**romanichel -elle** *n* gipsy
**romaniste** *n* student of Romance languages
**roman-photo** *nm* (*pl* **romans-photos**) story told in photographs
**romantique** *adj* of the Romantic school; romantic
**romantisme** *nm* Romanticism
**romarin** *nm bot* rosemary
**rombière** *nf* pretentious old bag
**rompre** *vt* (85) break, snap, break off; ~ **la tête (les oreilles) à qn** deafen s/o; weary s/o; **à tout** ~ noisily, frantically; *vi* break off, cease relations; **se** ~ break, break off; **se** ~ **à** accustom oneself to
**rompu** *adj* broken; experienced
**romsteck, rumsteak** *nm* rump steak
**ronce** *nf* bramble
**ronceraie** *nf* ground overgrown with brambles
**ronchonner** *vi coll* grouse, grumble
**rond** *nm* circle, ring, round; disk, washer; *sl* penny, dime; **en** ~ in a ring; in circles; **faire des** ~**s de jambe** be obsequious; *adj* round; plump; straightforward; *adv* **tourner** ~ run true, run smoothly (engine); *coll* **ne pas tourner** ~ not function properly; be unwell
**rond-de-cuir** *nm* (*pl* **ronds-de-cuir**) *pej* bureaucrat; clerk
**ronde** *nf* round; beat; round-hand; round dance; **à la** ~ around; **chemin de** ~ sentry's watch (on battlements); **faire la** ~ go the rounds
**rondeau** *nm* rondo
**rondelet -ette** *adj* plumpish; **somme rondelette** tidy sum
**rondelle** *nf* washer; small round slice
**rondement** *adv* promptly, smartly, briskly; **y aller** ~ go about things briskly

**rondeur** *nf* roundness; frankness
**rondin** *nm* billet, log; cudgel
**rondouillard** *adj coll* plump
**rond-point** *nm* (*pl* **ronds-points**) circus (roads); roundabout
**ronflant** *adj* snoring; booming, rumbling
**ronflement** *nm* snore; snoring; booming; humming
**ronfler** *vi* snore; roar, boom; hum
**ronfleur -euse** *n* snorer
**ronger** *vt* (3) gnaw, nibble; eat away, corrode; ~ **son frein** chafe
**rongeur** *nm* rodent; *adj* (*f* **-euse**) rodent, gnawing
**ronron** *nm* purr, purring; hum, whirr
**ronronner** *vi* purr; hum, whirr
**roquefort** *nm* Roquefort cheese
**roquer** *vi* castle (in chess)
**roquet** *nm* yapping little dog; grumpy little fellow
**roquette** *nf* rocket
**rosace** *nf* rose-window
**rosacé** *adj* rosaceous
**rosaire** *nm* rosary
**rosâtre** *adj* pinkish
**rosbif** *nm* roast beef
**rose** *nf* rose; rose-window; ~ **des vents** compass card; *adj* pink; rosy; **voir tout en** ~ see everything through rose-tinted spectacles
**rosé** *adj* roseate; rosé
**roseau** *nm* reed
**rosée** *nf* dew
**roseraie** *nf* rose-garden
**rosette** *nf* bow (of ribbon); rosette; ~ **de Lyon** particular type of **saucisson**
**rosier** *nm* rose-tree, rose-bush
**rosière** *nf* virtuous maiden
**rosir** *vi* turn pink
**rosse** *nf coll* nag, sorry steed; *coll* unpleasant person; *adj coll* nasty, ill-natured, spiteful
**rossée** *nf* thrashing
**rosser** *vt coll* thrash
**rosserie** *nf coll* nasty trick; nastiness
**rossignol** *nm* nightingale; skeleton key; *coll* piece of junk; white elephant
**rot** *nm coll* belch
**rôt** *nm ar* roast meat
**rotatif -ive** *adj* rotary
**rotation** *nf* rotary motion; rotation
**rotative** *nf* rotary printing-press
**roter** *vi coll* belch
**rôti** *nm* roast
**rôtie** *nf* toast
**rôtir** *vt* + *vi* roast, toast; dry up
**rôtisserie** *nf* eating-house; grill-room
**rôtisseur -euse** *n* meat-roaster
**rôtissoire** *nf* small portable oven
**rotonde** *nf* rotunda
**rotondité** *nf* rotundity; roundness; plumpness

**rotule** nf knee-cap; mech knee-joint
**roturier -ière** n commoner
**rouable** nm fire-rake
**rouage** nm wheel; cog
**rouan -anne** adj roan
**roublard** adj coll artful, cunning
**roublardise** nf coll cunning; piece of trickery
**roucouler** vi coo
**roue** nf wheel; ~ **de secours** spare wheel; **cinquième** ~ **d'un carrosse** useless person, useless thing; **faire la** ~ spread its tail (peacock); swagger, show off; do cartwheels; **pousser à la** ~ lend a helping hand
**roué -e** n rake, profligate; adj cunning
**rouelle** nf round slice
**rouer** vt ar break on the wheel; ~ **de coups** beat, thrash
**rouerie** nf piece of trickery
**rouet** nm spinning-wheel; pulley wheel
**rouflaquette** nf coll lovelock
**rouge** nm red; rouge; coll red wine; **porter un métal au** ~ make a metal red hot; adj red; adv **se fâcher tout** ~ become furious
**rougeâtre** adj reddish
**rougeaud** adj red-faced
**rouge-gorge** nm (pl **rouges-gorges**) robin (redbreast)
**rougeole** nf measles
**rougeoyer** vi (7) turn reddish
**rouge-queue** nm (pl **rouges-queues**) red-start
**rouget** nm red-mullet; swine disease
**rougeur** nf redness; blush; redspot
**rougir** vt redden; vi turn red; blush; ~ **de qch** be ashamed of sth
**rouille** nf rust; agr mildew, blight
**rouiller** vt rust; agr mildew; **se** ~ become rusty; agr become mildewed
**rouillure** nf rust; agr blight
**roulade** nf mus roulade; rolled slice of meat or fish
**roulage** nm rolling; cartage, haulage
**roulant** adj rolling; moving; travelling; smooth; coll funny; **matériel** ~ rolling stock
**rouleau** nm roller; roll; coil; spool; ~ **compresseur** steam-roller; **être au bout de son (du)** ~ have no more to say; have tried everything; be absolutely exhausted; be near the end; be broke
**roulement** nm rolling; rumbling; rattle; taking turns, alternation; ~ **à billes** ball-bearing; ~ **de fonds** circulation of capital; **fonds de** ~ working capital
**rouler** vt roll; coll trick, swindle; turn over (project); vi roll, roll along; drive, cruise along; rumble; roam, rove; ~ **sur l'or** be rolling in money
**roulette** nf caster, small wheel, tracing-wheel; roulette; **patins à** ~**s** roller-skates
**rouleur** nm good long-distance cyclist
**rouleuse** nf sl prostitute
**roulis** nm naut rolling
**roulotte** nf caravan
**roulure** nf cupshake; sl prostitute
**Roumain -e** n Romanian
**roumain** nm Romanian (language); adj Romanian
**Roumanie** nf Romania
¹**roupie** nf rupee
²**roupie** nf drop (on person's nose)
**roupiller** vi coll sleep
**roupillon** nm coll sleep
**rouquin -e** n redhead; adj red-haired
**rouspéter** vi (6) coll grumble
**rouspéteur -euse** adj grumbling
**rousseur** nf redness; **taches de** ~ freckles
**roussi** nm smell of burning; **ça sent le** ~ there's a smell of burning; coll there's trouble brewing
**roussin** nm cob (horse)
**roussir** vt redden, turn brown; cul brown; singe; vi turn brown
**routage** nm routing (mail, papers)
**route** nf road, track; way, route; ~ **nationale** main road; **code de la** ~ highway code; **en** ~! off we go!; off you go!; **faire fausse** ~ lose one's way; take the wrong course; **mettre en** ~ start, start up; **se mettre en** ~ set out
**router** vt route (mail, papers)
**routier** nm long-distance lorry-driver; road racer (cyclist); **vieux** ~ old stager; adj (f **-ière**) road, roadside; **carte routière** road map; **relai** ~ roadside restaurant, pull-up
**routinier -ière** adj routine
**rouvrir** vt + vi (30) reopen
¹**roux** nm russet; cul brown sauce
²**roux** (f **rousse**) adj red, russet, brown; red-haired
**royal** adj royal, regal, kingly
**royaliste** n + adj royalist
**royaume** nm kingdom; ~ **des cieux** kingdom of heaven
**royauté** nf royalty
**ru** nm little stream
**ruade** nf kicking out (horse)
**ruban** nm ribbon; metal strip; tape; ~ **bleu** Blue Riband
**rubéole** nf German measles, rubella
**rubicond** adj rubicund
**rubis** nm ruby
**rubrique** nf heading; imprint; column (newspaper)
**ruche** nf bee-hive
**rude** adj rough, coarse; harsh, rugged; uncouth; arduous; tough; redoubtable
**rudement** adv harshly; roughly, coarsely

**rudesse** nf roughness, coarseness; harshness, severity

**rudimentaire** adj rudimentary

**rudoyer** vt (7) treat roughly

**rue** nf street; **grand' ~ , grande ~** high street

**ruée** nf onrush; rush

**ruelle** nf alley, back street; space between the bed and the wall

**ruer** vi kick, lash out; **se ~** rush, fling oneself

**rugir** vi roar

**rugissement** nm roar

**rugosité** nf ruggedness, rugosity; wrinkle

**rugueux -ueuse** adj rough, rugged; gnarled

**ruine** nf ruin; downfall

**ruiner** vt ruin, destroy

**ruineux -euse** adj ruinous

**ruisseau** nm stream, brook; gutter

**ruisseler** vi (5) stream, run, run down, trickle

**rumeur** nf confused murmur; rumour; **~ publique** opinion of the crowd

**ruminer** vt ruminate; coll ponder over; vi chew the cud

**rumsteak** nm see romsteck

**rupin** adj sl rich, luxurious

**rupteur** nm elect contact breaker, make-and-break

**rupture** nf breaking, rupture; bursting; breaking off; breach

**ruse** nf trick, dodge, ruse

**rusé** adj crafty, cunning, wily

**ruser** vi use cunning

**Russe** n Russian

**russe** nm Russian (language); adj Russian

**Russie** nf Russia

**rustaud** adj boorish

**rusticité** nf rusticity; primitiveness; hardiness (plant)

**rustique** adj rustic; hardy (plant)

**rustre** adj boorish, coarse

**rustrerie** nf boorishness

**rut** nm rutting

**rutabaga** nm swede

**rutilant** adj glowing red; gleaming

**rutiler** vi glow red; gleam

**rythme** nm rhythm

**rythmer** vt give rhythm to

**rythmique** adj rhythmic

# S

**s** nm **sentier en ~** winding path

**sa** poss adj see son

**sabayon** nm cul zabaglione

**sabbat** nm Sabbath; witches' sabbath; coll row, shindy

**sabbatique** adj sabbatical

**sabir** nm lingo; Mediterranean lingua franca

**sable** nm sand; **~s mouvants** quicksands; **le marchand de ~ a passé** he (she) is nodding off

**sablé** nm kind of shortbread

**sabler** vt sand; **~ le champagne** drink champagne (to celebrate an occasion)

**sableux -euse** adj mixed with sand

**sablier** nm hour-glass; egg-timer

**sablière** nf gravel-pit, sand-pit; sand-box (locomotive)

**sablonner** vt sprinkle with sand; sand

**sablonneux -euse** adj sandy, gritty

**sablonnière** nf sand-pit

**sabord** nm naut (gun-)port

**saborder** vt scuttle

**sabot** nm clog, wooden shoe; hoof; whipping-top; shoe (brake); useless tool or machine

**sabotage** nm clog-making; botching; sabotage

**saboter** vt botch; damage, sabotage

**saboteur -euse** n saboteur; botcher

**sabotier -ière** n clog-maker

**sabrer** vt sabre, hack down; cut drastically; coll criticize

**¹sac** nm sack, bag; sackful; sackcloth; **~ à dos** rucksack; **~ à main** handbag; **~ à vin** drunkard; coll **~ percé** spendthrift; coll **l'affaire est dans le ~** it's in the bag, the affair is as good as settled; coll **prendre qn la main dans le ~** catch s/o red-handed; **vider son ~** hold nothing back, unbosom oneself

**²sac** nm sacking, pillaging

**saccade** nf jolt, jerk; **par ~s** in jerks

**saccadé** adj jerky, abrupt

**saccager** *vt* (3) pillage; ransack; *coll* put in disorder
**sacerdoce** *nm* priesthood; calling
**sacerdotal** *adj* priestly
**sachée** *nf* sackful
**sachet** *nm* small bag
**sacoche** *nf* satchel; wallet
**sacquer** *vt coll* sack, dismiss
**sacramental -elle** *adj* sacramental
**sacre** *nm* consecration; coronation
¹**sacré** *adj* sacred, consecrated; *coll* blessed, confounded; inviolable; **feu ~ zeal**
²**sacré** *adj anat* sacral
**sacrement** *nm* sacrament; marriage
**sacrer** *vt* consecrate; anoint, crown; *vi coll* swear
**sacrificateur -trice** *n* sacrificer
**sacrificatoire** *adj* sacrificial
**sacrifier** *vt* sacrifice; give
**sacrilège** *nm* sacrilege; *adj* sacrilegious
**sacripant** *nm* scoundrel, rascal
**sacristain** *nm* sacristan, sexton
**sacristi, sapristi** *interj coll* Lord!
**sacristie** *nf eccles* vestry
**sacro-saint** *adj* sacrosanct
**sadique** *n* sadist; *adj* sadistic
**sadisme** *nm* sadism
**safran** *nm* saffron
**sagace** *adj* sagacious
**sagacité** *nf* sagacity, shrewdness
**sagaie** *nf* assegai
**sage** *adj* wise; discreet, judicious; well-behaved, good; chaste; **~ comme une image** as good as gold
**sage-femme** *nf* (*pl* sages-femmes) midwife
**sagesse** *nf* wisdom; discretion, prudence; good behaviour; chasteness
**sagou** *nm* sago
**sagouin** *nm* squirrel-monkey; *coll* dirty, slovenly person
**saignant** *adj* bleeding; underdone (meat)
**saignée** *nf* bleeding, bloodletting; bend (of the arm); trench; drain (resources)
**saigner** *vt* bleed; draw blood from; *vi* bleed; **se ~** make great sacrifices
**saillant** *nm* salient; *adj* projecting; striking, outstanding
**saillie** *nf* projection, ledge; flash of wit; **en ~** projecting
**saillir** *vt* (86) cover, mount; *vi* jut out, project
**sain** *adj* healthy; sound; wholesome; **~ et sauf** safe and sound
**saindoux** *nm* lard
**saint -e** *n* saint; **~e nitouche** little hypocrite; **ne plus savoir à quel ~ se vouer** not know where to turn; **prêcher pour son ~** have an eye to one's own interest; *adj* holy; godly, saintly; *coll* **toute la ~e journée** the whole

wretched day; **vendredi saint** Good Friday
**Saint-Esprit** *nm* Holy Ghost
**sainteté** *nf* holiness, saintliness; sanctity
**saint-frusquin** *nm invar sl* **tout le ~** the whole damn lot
**saint-glinglin (à la)** *adv phr coll* never
**saint-honoré** *nm* kind of cream cake
**Saint-Office** *nm* Holy Office; *hist* Inquisition
**Saint-Siège** *nm* Holy See
**Saint-Sylvestre** *nf* New Year's Eve
**saisie** *nf* seizure; *leg* distraint, attachment
**saisir** *vt* seize; take hold of, grasp, grip; *leg* distrain, attach; *leg* place before (court); understand; *cul* seal; **être saisi d'étonnement** be startled; **se ~ de** lay hands on, take possession of
**saisissement** *nm* sudden chill; seizure
**saison** *nf* season; **de ~** in season; timely; **hors de ~** out of place, inopportune
**saisonnier -ière** *n* seasonal worker; *adj* seasonal
**salace** *adj* salacious
**salade** *nf* salad; *coll* jumble
**saladier** *nm* salad-bowl
**salage** *nm* salting (roads)
**salaire** *nm* wage, pay; reward
**salaison** *nf* salting; curing; **~s** provisions
**salamalec** *nm coll* salaam, deep bow
**salamandre** *nf* salamander; slow-combustion stove
**salant** *adj* salt-producing; **marais ~s** salt marshes
**salarial** *adj* concerning wages
**salariat** *nm* wage-earning; wage-earners
**salarié -e** *n* wage-earner
**salarier** *vt* pay, give a wage to
**salaud** *nm sl* swine, shit
**sale** *adj* dirty, filthy; rotten, nasty, beastly; dishonest; **~ comme un peigne** filthy
**salé** *nm* salt pork; **petit ~** cooked salt pork; *adj* salt; salted; salty; spicy; *coll* exaggerated, exorbitant; **prés ~s** saltings
**salement** *adv* dirtily; *sl* very, extremely
**saler** *vt* salt; cure (pork); *coll* punish excessively; sell at an excessive price
**saleté** *nf* dirt, filth; dirtiness; rubbish; obscenity; nasty trick
**salière** *nf* salt-cellar; hollow above collar-bone (in skinny person)
**saligaud** *nm sl* swine, shit
**salin** *nm* salt-marsh; *adj* saline, salt-bearing
**saline** *nf* salt-pan
**salinité** *nf* saltness
**salique** *adj* Salic
**salir** *vt* dirty; defile; tarnish

**salissant** *adj* dirty, messy; easily dirtied

**salissure** *nf* stain

**salivaire** *adj* salivary

**salive** *nf* saliva, spittle; *coll* **perdre sa ~** waste one's breath

**saliver** *vi* salivate

**salle** *nf* hall; large room; audience, house; **~ à manger** dining-room; **~ d'armes** fencing school; **~ d'attente** waiting-room; **~ de bains** bathroom; **~ des fêtes** local hall; **~ des pas perdus** waiting-hall; **~ des ventes** auction rooms

**salmigondis** *nm* mixed stew; *coll* miscellany

**salmis** *nm cul* salmi, game stew

**saloir** *nm* salting-tub

**salon** *nm* drawing-room; art exhibition; show, exhibition; **~ de thé** tea-room; **fréquenter les ~s** move in society

**salopard** *nm sl* bastard, shit

**salope** *nf sl* slut

**saloper** *vt sl* botch

**saloperie** *nf sl* filthiness; dirt; trash, rubbish; dirty trick

**salopette** *nf* overalls, dungarees.

**salpêtre** *nm* saltpetre

**salsifis** *nm* salsify

**saltimbanque** *n* tumbler, circus acrobat

**salubre** *adj* salubrious, healthy, wholesome

**salubrité** *nf* salubriousness, healthiness, wholesomeness

**saluer** *vt* salute; greet; hail; acclaim

**salure** *nf* saltness; tang

**salut** *nm* salvation; safety; saving; salute; greeting; *eccles* evening service; **~!** hullo!; **Armée du Salut** Salvation Army; **faire son ~** seek salvation

**salutaire** *adj* salutary, beneficial

**salutation** *nf* greeting

**salutiste** *n* member of the Salvation Army

**salve** *nf* salvo; **~ d'applaudissements** burst of applause

**samaritain** *adj* Samaritan

**samedi** *nm* Saturday

**sanctificateur -trice** *n* sanctifier; *adj* sanctifying

**sanctifier** *vt* sanctify, make holy, hallow

**sanction** *nf* sanction; approval, consent; punishment; consequence; **prendre des ~s** take repressive measures

**sanctionner** *vt* sanction; approve; *coll* punish

**sanctuaire** *nm* sanctuary

**sandale** *nf* sandal

**sang** *nm* blood; race; *coll* **avoir du ~ dans les veines** be energetic; **avoir le ~ chaud** be quick-tempered; **bon ~!** Heavens!, Good God!; **coup de ~**

stroke; **pur ~** thoroughbred; **se faire du mauvais ~** worry; **suer ~ et eau** slave away

**sang-froid** *nm invar* composure, calm

**sanglant** *adj* bloody; blood-stained; cruel, scathing

**sangle** *nf* strap; **lit de ~s** camp bed

**sangler** *vt* girth (horse); strap

**sanglier** *nm* wild boar

**sanglot** *nm* sob

**sangloter** *vi* sob

**sangsue** *nf* blood-sucker, leech

**sanguin** *adj* of the blood; full-blooded

**sanguinaire** *adj* sanguinary, bloody; bloodthirsty

**sanguine** *nf* red chalk; drawing in red chalk; bloodstone; blood orange

**sanguinolent** *adj* tinged with blood

**sanie** *nf med* pus

**sanieux -ieuse** *adj med* purulent

**sanitaire** *nm* plumbing installation; *adj* sanitary

**sans** *prep* without; but for; **~ cela** otherwise; **~ mentir** to tell the truth; **~ plus** nothing more; **~ quoi** otherwise; **être ~ le sou** be penniless; **je ne suis pas ~ le savoir** I do know; *conj* **~ que** without

**sans-abri** *n invar* homeless person

**sans-cœur** *n invar coll* heartless person

**sans-façon** *nm invar* straightforwardness; *adj invar* homely

**sans-filiste** *n* wireless enthusiast, radio ham

**sans-gêne** *nm invar* excessive familiarity; cheek; *adj invar* unceremonious, rude

**sans-le-sou** *n invar coll* penniless person

**sans-logis** *n* homeless person

**sansonnet** *nm* starling

**sans-souci** *n invar* carefree person

**sans-travail** *n invar* unemployed person

**santal** *nm* sandalwood-tree

**santé** *nf* health; **maison de ~** mental home

**santon** *nm* small painted clay figure of saint

**saoul** *adj* see **soûl**

**saouler** *vt* see **soûler**

**sape** *nf* undermining, sapping

**saper** *vt* undermine, sap

**saperlipopette** *interj obs* Good Lord!

**sapeur** *nm mil* sapper

**sapeur-pompier** *nm* (*pl* **sapeurs-pompiers**) fireman

**saphir** *nm* sapphire

**sapin** *nm* fir-tree; **bois de ~** deal; *coll* **sentir le ~** not have long to live

**sapinière** *nf* fir plantation

**sapristi** *interj* see **sacristi**

**saquer** *vt* see **sacquer**

**sarabande** *nf* sarabande

**sarbacane** *nf* blow-pipe
**sarcasme** *nm* taunt, piece of sarcasm
**sarcastique** *adj* sarcastic
**sarcelle** *nf* teal
**sarcler** *vt* + *vi* hoe, weed
**sarcloir** *nm* hoe
**sarcome** *nm* sarcoma
**sarcophage** *nm* sarcophagus
**Sardaigne** *nf* Sardinia
**sardane** *nf* Catalan dance
**sarde** *adj* Sardinian
**sardine** *nf* sardine; pilchard; *mil coll* stripe
**sardinier** *nm* sardine-boat; sardine-net
**sardonique** *adj* sardonic
**sargasse** *nf* gulf-weed, sargasso
**sarment** *nm* climbing stem; vine-shoot
**¹sarrasin** *nm* buckwheat
**²sarrasin** *adj* Saracen
**sarrasine** *nf* portcullis
**sarrau** *nm* (*pl* **sarraus** or **sarraux**) smock
**sas** *nm* sieve, riddle; air lock; flooding chamber
**sasser** *vt* sift; screen (flour); lock (boat)
**satané** *adj coll* damned, confounded
**satanique** *adj* satanic, diabolical
**satelliser** *vt* put into orbit
**satiété** *nf* satiety; surfeit
**satiner** *vt* give a glossy surface to
**satinette** *nf* sateen
**satirique** *adj* satirical
**satiriser** *vt* satirize
**satisfaction** *nf* satisfaction; reparation
**satisfaire** *vt* (46) satisfy; gratify; *vi* satisfy; make amends; meet; fulfil
**satisfaisant** *adj* satisfying; acceptable
**satisfait** *adj* satisfied
**saturer** *vt* saturate; sate
**saturnin** *adj* saturnine
**satyre** *nm* satyr; *coll* sex-maniac
**sauce** *nf* sauce; soft black crayon; accompaniment; manner; **mettre qn à toutes les ~s** use s/o in all kinds of ways
**saucée** *nf coll* shower
**saucer** *vt* (4) dip in the sauce; drench
**saucier** *nm* sauce-cook
**saucière** *nf* sauce-boat, gravy-boat
**saucisse** *nf* sausage; observation balloon; *coll* **ne pas attacher son chien avec des ~s** be careful with one's money
**saucisson** *nm* French salami
**¹sauf, sauve** *adj* safe, unhurt
**²sauf** *prep* except, save, but for; saving; **~ avis contraire** unless I (you, we, etc) hear to the contrary; **~ imprévu** barring any unforeseen occurrence
**sauf-conduit** *nm* safe-conduct, pass
**sauge** *nf bot* sage
**saugrenu** *adj* preposterous, absurd
**saule** *nm* willow; **~ pleureur** weeping willow

**saumâtre** *adj* brackish, briny
**saumon** *nm* salmon
**saumoné** *adj* **truite ~ e** salmon-trout
**saumure** *nf* brine (for pickling)
**saunier** *nm* salt-maker
**saupiquet** *nm cul* spiced sauce
**saupoudrer** *vt* sprinkle, dust; *fig* disperse (resources)
**saur** *adj m* **hareng ~** bloater
**saurer** *vt* cure, bloat
**saurien** *adj* saurian
**saut** *nm* jump, leap; waterfall; **~ en hauteur** high jump; **~ en longueur** long jump; **~ périlleux** somersault in mid-air; **au ~ du lit** on getting out of bed; **faire le ~** take the plunge; **faire un ~ chez** pop over to
**saut-de-lit** *nm* (*pl* **sauts-de-lit**) dressing gown
**saut-de-loup** *nm* (*pl* **sauts-de-loup**) deep ditch
**saute** *nf* sudden change, jump
**sauté** *adj* fried, sauté
**saute-mouton** *nm invar* leap-frog
**sauter** *vt* jump over, clear; leave out, skip; *vi* jump, leap; explode, blow up; change (wind); **~ au plafond** be very surprised; be furious; **faire ~** make (s/o) jump; blow up; burst; **faire ~ qn** deprive s/o of his turn; **se faire ~ la cervelle** blow one's brains out
**sauterelle** *nf* grasshopper; *carp* bevel square
**sauterie** *nf coll* hop, dance
**saute-ruisseau** *nm invar* errand boy, messenger boy
**sauteuse** *nf* shallow saucepan (for frying); *coll* trollop, tart
**sautiller** *vi* hop about, jump about
**sautoir** *nm* long chain necklace; **en ~** crosswise; over the shoulder
**sauvage** *n* savage; *adj* savage, wild; uncivilized; barbarous; shy; unsociable; wild-cat (strike)
**sauvageon -onne** *n* shy, unsociable child; *nm* wild stock
**sauvagerie** *nf* unsociable nature; savagery
**sauvagine** *nf* waterfowl
**sauvegarde** *nf* safeguard, safekeeping; *naut* life-line
**sauvegarder** *vt* safeguard
**sauve-qui-peut** *nm invar* panic flight; stampede
**sauver** *vt* save, rescue; preserve; **se ~** escape, flee; clear off; boil over
**sauvetage** *nm* rescue, life-saving; **bateau de ~** lifeboat; **ceinture de ~** life-belt
**sauveteur** *nm* rescuer, life-saver
**sauvette (à la)** *adv phr* hastily; **marchand ~** illicit street vendor

**savamment** *adv* knowingly; learnedly

**savane** *nf* savanna

**savant** *nm* scientist; scholar; *adj* learned, scholarly; clever, skilful

**savate** *nf* old shoe, old slipper; *coll* **traîner la ~** be poor; be idle

**savetier** *nm ar* cobbler

**saveur** *nf* taste, savour, flavour

**savoir** *nm* knowledge, learning; *vt* (87) know, be aware of; learn, get to know; know how to, be able to; **à ~** namely, that is to say; **en ~ long sur** know a lot about; **faire ~** inform; **il ne veut rien ~** he won't hear of it; **je ne sache pas I** am not aware; **je ne saurais** I can't; **que je sache** that I know of; **que sais-je!** goodness knows!; **reste à ~** it remains to be seen; **un je ne sais quoi** something

**savoir-faire** *nm invar* ability

**savoir-vivre** *nm invar* knowledge of the world, good manners

**savon** *nm* soap; *coll* reprimand

**savonner** *vt* soap, wash

**savonnerie** *nf* soap-works; soap-trade

**savonnette** *nf* cake of toilet-soap

**savonneux -euse** *adj* soapy

**savourer** *vt* enjoy, relish

**savoureux -euse** *adj* tasty, savoury; rich (story, joke)

**savoyard** *adj* of Savoy

**saynète** *nf* playlet

**sbire** *nm pej* hired thug; tough policeman

**scabieux -ieuse** *adj* scabby

**scabreux -euse** *adj* ticklish, difficult; indelicate; improper

**scalper** *vt* scalp

**scandale** *nm* scandal, disgrace; **faire ~** shock

**scandaleux -euse** *adj* disgraceful, scandalous

**scandaliser** *vt* scandalize; **se ~** be indignant

**scander** *vt* scan (verse); stress, emphasize

**scandinave** *adj* Scandinavian

**scaphandre** *nm* diving-suit; space-suit; **~ autonome** aqualung

**scaphandrier** *nm* (deep-sea) diver

**scapulaire** *nm eccles* scapular; *adj anat* scapular

**scarabée** *nm* beetle; scarab

**scare** *nm* parrot-fish

**scarificateur** *nm agr* scarifier; *surg* scarificator

**scarifier** *vt agr* + *surg* scarify

**scarlatine** *nf* scarlet fever

**scarole** *nf bot* endive

**scatologique** *adj* scatological

**sceau** *nm* seal; mark, stamp; **Garde des Sceaux** = Lord Chancellor

**scélérat -e** *n* villain, scoundrel; *adj* villainous; crafty

**sceller** *vt* seal, seal up; confirm

**scellés** *nmpl* **apposer (mettre) les ~** affix the seals

**scénario** *nm* scenario, script

**scénariste** *n* script-writer

**scène** *nf* stage; scene; row; *theat* **mettre en ~** produce; *theat* **mise en ~** production

**scénique** *adj* scenic; theatrical

**scepticisme** *nm* scepticism

**sceptique** *n* sceptic; *adj* sceptical

**schéma** *nm* diagram, sketch-plan

**schématique** *adj* schematic, diagrammatic

**schisme** *nm* schism

**schiste** *nm* schist, shale

**schizophrénie** *nf* schizophrenia

**schlass** *adj invar sl* drunk

**schnaps** *nm coll* spirits

**schuss** *nm* direct descent (skiing)

**sciatique** *nf* sciatica; *adj* sciatic

**scie** *nf* saw; *coll* bore; **~ à découper** fret-saw; **~ à métaux** hack-saw

**sciemment** *adv* knowingly, wittingly

**science** *nf* knowledge, learning; science

**scientifique** *adj* scientific

**scier** *vt* saw, saw off

**scierie** *nf* saw-mill

**scieur** *nm* sawyer

**scinder** *vt* split up, divide

**scintiller** *vi* sparkle, scintillate, twinkle

**scission** *nf* split, scission; secession

**sciure** *nf* sawdust

**scléreux -euse** *adj* sclerosed, hard

**sclérose** *nf* sclerosis; hardening

**scléroser** *vt* harden; **se ~** harden

**sclérotique** *nf* sclera

**scolaire** *adj* school; **groupe ~** (large) school

**scolariser** *vt* provide with schools; give schooling to

**scolastique** *adj* scholastic

**scoliose** *nf* scoliosis

**scolopendre** *nf* scolopendra, centipede; *bot* hart's tongue

**sconse** *nm* skunk

**scorbut** *nm* scurvy

**scorbutique** *adj* scurvied

**scorie** *nf usu pl* slag, cinders

**scorsonère** *nf* black salsify

**scotch** *nm* (Scotch) whisky; adhesive tape

**scoutisme** *nm* Boy Scout movement

**script** *nm* script handwriting, copperplate

**scripte** *nf* continuity girl

**scrofule** *nf* scrofula

**scrofuleux -euse** *adj* scrofulous

**scrupule** *nm* scruple; **se faire ~** scruple

**scrupuleux -euse** *adj* scrupulous

**scrutateur -trice** *n* teller, scrutineer; *adj* searching, scrutinizing

**scruter** *vt* scrutinize, examine closely

**scrutin** *nm* poll, voting; **procéder au ~** take the votes; divide

**scull** *nm* double-sculler

**sculpter** *vt* sculpture, carve

**sculpteur** *nm* sculptor

**scythe** *adj* Scythian

**se** *refl pron* oneself; himself; herself; themselves; each other; one another

**séance** *nf* session; meeting; sitting; performance; seance; **lever la ~** close the meeting

**¹séant** *nm* bottom, behind, posterior

**²séant** *adj* becoming, fitting

**seau** *nm* pail; pailful; **~ hygiénique** sanitary pail; **pleuvoir à ~x** rain very hard

**sébacé** *adj* sebaceous

**sébile** *nf* wooden bowl

**sec** (*f* **sèche**) *adj* dry; lean, gaunt; dull; brusque; **à ~** dry; broke; **boire ~** drink hard; have one's drink neat; **coup ~** sharp blow; **mettre à ~** dry, dry up; **parler ~** speak frankly; **perte sèche** dead loss

**sécateur** *nm* pruning scissors, secateurs

**sèche-cheveux** *nm* hair-drier

**sèchement** *adv* drily, curtly

**sécher** *vt* + *vi* (6) dry, dry up; *coll* cut (lecture); fail to answer

**sécheresse** *nf* drought; dryness; leanness; curtness; lack of feeling

**sécherie** *nf* drying establishment, drying-place

**séchoir** *nm* drier; clothes-horse; drying-place

**second -e** *n* second; *nm* second floor; assistant, second-in-command; **sans ~** peerless, unparalleled; *adj* second

**secondaire** *nm* secondary education; *adj* secondary; minor, accessory

**seconde** *nf* second; jiffy

**seconder** *vt* help, support

**secouer** *vt* shake; shake up; shake down; **se ~** shake oneself; *coll* buck up, bestir oneself

**secourable** *adj* helpful

**secourir** *vt* (29) help

**secourisme** *nm* first-aid

**secouriste** *n* first-aid worker

**secours** *nm* help, assistance, relief; **au ~!** help!; **sortie de ~** emergency exit

**secousse** *nf* shake, shaking; jolt, jerk; shock; tremor

**secret** *nm* secret; secrecy; hidden spring; *adj* (*f* **-ète**) secret; hidden

**secrétaire** *n* secretary; *nm* writing-desk; secretary-bird

**secrétariat** *nm* secretariat; office of secretary

**sécréter** *vt* (6) secrete

**sectaire** *adj* sectarian

**sectarisme** *nm* sectarianism

**secte** *nf* sect

**secteur** *nm* district; sector

**section** *nf* cutting; section; branch; department; platoon; subdivision

**sectionner** *vt* cut, sever; divide into sections

**séculaire** *adj* century-old; occurring once a century; secular

**séculariser** *vt* secularize; deconsecrate

**séculier -ière** *adj* secular

**secundo** *adv* secondly

**sécurité** *nf* security; safety

**sédatif** *nm* sedative; *adj* (*f* **-ive**) sedative

**sédentaire** *adj* sedentary; stationary, fixed

**sédimentaire** *adj* sedimentary

**séditieux -ieuse** *adj* seditious; rebellious

**sédition** *nf* mutiny; sedition

**séducteur -trice** *n* seducer; *adj* seductive

**séduction** *nf* seduction; charm; leading astray

**séduire** *vt* (80) charm, captivate; seduce; lead astray

**segmenter** *vt* segment, divide into segments

**ségrégation** *nf* segregation; isolation

**seiche** *nf* cuttle-fish

**seigle** *nm* rye

**seigneur** *nm* lord; master; **le Seigneur** God, the Lord; **faire le grand ~** give oneself airs

**seigneurie** *nf* domain, manor; lordship

**seille** *nf dial* bucket

**sein** *nm* breast, bosom; *fig* heart; **donner le ~ à** suckle

**seing** *nm leg* **acte sous ~ privé** simple contract, private agreement

**séisme** *nm* earthquake, seism

**seize** *nm* + *adj* sixteen; sixteenth

**seizième** *n* + *adj* sixteenth

**séjour** *nm* stay; place, residence

**séjournant -e** *n* holiday-maker

**séjourner** *vi* stay, stop, sojourn

**sel** *nm* salt; *fig* wit; **~ gemme** rock-salt; **~s** smelling-salts

**sélectif -ive** *adj rad* selective

**sélection** *nf* choice, selection

**self** *nm coll* self-service restaurant; *nf elect* inductance coil

**selle** *nf* saddle; *med* stool; **être bien en ~** be firmly established

**seller** *vt* saddle

**sellette** *nf* small seat, stool; stool for accused; **être sur la ~** be accused; be in the hot seat

**sellier** *nm* saddler

**selon** *prep* according to; **~ que** according as; **c'est ~** it all depends

**semailles** *nfpl* sowing; sowing-time

**semaine** *nf* week; week's wages; ~ **anglaise** five-day week; **prêter à la petite ~** lend money on a weekly interest basis

**semainier -ière** *n* person on duty for a week; *nm* bracelet with seven links; piece of furniture with seven drawers

**sémantique** *nf* semantics; *adj* semantic

**sémaphore** *nm* semaphore

**semblable** *n* equal, like; fellow-man; *adj* similar, like; such

**semblant** *nm* appearance, semblance; **faire ~ de** pretend; **faux ~** pretence; **sans faire ~ de rien** surreptitiously; pretending not to be aware of anything

**sembler** *vi* seem, appear; **à ce qu'il me semble** as it strikes me; **que vous en semble?** what do you think of it?

**semelle** *nf* sole; *bui* ground-sill; *coll* **battre la ~** stamp (to warm one's feet); *coll* **ne pas reculer d'une ~** not yield an inch

**semence** *nf* seed

**semer** *vt* (6) sow; disseminate, scatter, spread; *sl* shake off; ~ **son argent** spend one's money freely

**semestre** *nm* semester; half-year; six months' pay

**semestriel -ielle** *adj* half-yearly

**semeur -euse** *n* sower; disseminator

**semi-circulaire** *adj* semi-circular

**sémillant** *adj* bright, sprightly

**séminaire** *nm* seminary; seminar; **petit ~** Catholic school

**séminariste** *nm* seminarist

**sémiotique** *nf* semiotics

**semis** *nm* sowing; sowing-plot; seedlings

**sémitique** *adj* Semitic

**semoir** *nm* seed-bag; sowing-machine

**semonce** *nf* reprimand; **verte ~** good dressing-down

**semoule** *nf* semolina

**sempiternel -elle** *adj* never-ending

**sénat** *nm* senate; senate-house

**sénateur** *nm* senator; **train de ~** slow, solemn walk

**séné** *nm* senna

**séneçon** *nm* groundsel

**sénégalais** *adj* Senegalese

**sénevé** *nm* *bot* mustard

**sénilité** *nf* senility

**sens** *nm* sense; intelligence, judgement; meaning; direction; ~ **dessus dessous** upside down; ~ **devant derrière** back to front; ~ **interdit** no entry; ~ **unique** one-way (street); **abonder dans le ~ de qn** be in agreement with s/o, be of the same opinion as s/o; **à mon ~** to my way of thinking; **en dépit du bon ~** against all reason

**sensass** *adj invar coll* terrific, super

**sensation** *nf* feeling, sensation; excite-ment; **faire ~** create a sensation

**sensationnel -elle** *adj* sensational; *coll* terrific

**sensé** *adj* sensible

**sensibilisateur** *nm phot* sensitizer

**sensibiliser** *vt* make aware, arouse (opinion); *phot* sensitize

**sensibilité** *nf* sensibility; sensitiveness; compassion

**sensible** *adj* sensitive, susceptible; perceptible; tender, sore; **d'une manière ~** appreciably

**sensiblement** *adv* appreciably

**sensiblerie** *nf* sentimentalism

**sensitif -ive** *adj* sensitive; sensory

**sensoriel -ielle** *adj* relating to the senses

**sensualisme** *nm* sensualism

**sensualité** *nf* sensuality

**sensuel -uelle** *adj* sensual

**sente** *nf* footpath, little path

**sentence** *nf* maxim; judgement, sentence

**sentencieux -ieuse** *adj* sententious

**senteur** *nf* perfume, aroma

**senti** *adj* strongly felt

**sentier** *nm* path

**sentiment** *nm* feeling; sensation; opinion; **faire du ~** sentimentalize

**sentimentalité** *nf* sentimentality

**sentine** *nf naut* bilge; *fig* cess-pit

**sentinelle** *nf* sentry, sentinel

**sentir** *vt* (59) feel; be aware of; smell; **faire ~** make felt; *vi* smell of; smack of; ~ **bon (mauvais)** smell nice (bad); **se ~** feel; **il ne se sent pas de joie** he is beside himself with joy; **il se sent du courage** he feels brave; **se ~ de qch** be affected by sth

**seoir** *vi* (88) suit, become

**séparateur** *nm* separator; *elect* separating-plate

**séparatif -ive** *adj* separating, separative

**séparation** *nf* separation, parting; dispersal; ~ **de biens** separate ownership (in marriage); ~ **de corps** legal separation

**séparatisme** *nm* separatism

**séparé** *adj* separate, distinct; separated

**séparément** *adv* separately

**séparer** *vt* separate, part; keep apart; **se ~** separate, part; divide; disperse, break up

**sépia** *nf* cuttle-fish; sepia (colour)

**sept** *nm + adj* seven; seventh

**septante** *adj* seventy (in Belgium and Switzerland)

**septembre** *nm* September

**septennal** *adj* septennial

**septentrional** *adj* northern

**septicémie** *nf* septicaemia

**septième** *n + adj* seventh

**septique** *adj* septic

**septuagénaire** *n + adj* septuagenarian

**Septuagésime** *nf* Septuagesima
**septuor** *nm* septet
**septupler** *vt* multiply by seven
**sépulcral** *adj* sepulchral
**sépulcre** *nm* sepulchre
**sépulture** *nf* burial, interment; burial-place
**séquelle** *nf usu pl* results, consequences (of illness)
**séquence** *nf* sequence
**séquentiel -ielle** *adj* sequential
**séquestration** *nf* isolation; sequestration; seclusion
**séquestre** *nm* leg sequestration
**séquestrer** *vt* sequestrate; seclude, isolate
**sérail** *nm* seraglio
**séraphin** *nm* seraph
**séraphique** *adj* seraphic
**serein** *adj* calm, serene; cheerful
**sérénité** *nf* serenity, calmness
**séreux -euse** *adj* serous
**serf** (*f* **serve**) *n* serf; *adj* in bondage
**serfouette** *nf* combined hoe and fork tool
**sergent** *nm* sergeant; *ar* ~ **de ville** policeman
**sériciculture** *nf* silkworm breeding
**série** *nf* series, succession; line (samples); **fabrication en** ~ mass production; **fin de** ~ remnant, oddment; **hors** ~ specially manufactured; exceptional
**sérier** *vt* arrange in series
**sérieux -euse** *nf* seriousness, gravity; **manque de** ~ irresponsibility; *adj* (*f* -**ieuse**) serious, grave; serious-minded; earnest, sincere; important; reliable
**serin** *nm* canary
**seriner** *vt coll* repeat ad nauseam
**seringue** *nf* syringe
**seringuer** *vt* syringe; squirt
**serment** *nm* oath; **prêter** ~ swear an oath, be sworn
**sermonner** *vt* sermonize, lecture; reprimand
**sérosité** *nf* serosity
**serpe** *nf* bill-hook
**serpent** *nm* snake, serpent; spiteful, cunning person
**serpenter** *vi* wind, meander
**serpentin** *nm* coil of tubing; paper streamer; *adj* serpentine
**serpette** *nf* pruning-knife
**serpillière** *nf* floor cloth; sacking
**serpolet** *nm* wild thyme
¹**serre** *nf* greenhouse
²**serre** *nf* grip, squeezing; claw, talon
**serré** *adj* tight, close, dense; **avoir le cœur** ~ be sad; *adv* **jouer** ~ play carefully; act cautiously
**serre-livres** *nm* book-end

**serrement** *nm* squeezing; ~ **de cœur** pang
**serrer** *vt* squeeze, grasp; tighten, screw up; close; put away, shut away; clench; keep close to, hug; ~ **la main à qn** shake hands with s/o; ~ **les freins** apply the brakes; **se** ~ crowd together; tighten
**serre-tête** *nm invar* headband
**serrure** *nf* lock
**serrurerie** *nf* locksmith's trade; metal-work
**serrurier** *nm* locksmith
**sertir** *vt* set (jewel, etc); *metal* crimp
**sertissure** *nf* setting
**servage** *nm* serfdom
**servant** *adj m* **chevalier (cavalier)** ~ faithful admirer
**servante** *nf* servant-girl, servant-woman
**serveur** *nm* waiter
**serveuse** *nf* waitress
**serviabilité** *nf* obliging nature
**serviable** *adj* obliging
**service** *nm* service; **chef de** ~ head of department; **entrée de** ~ staff entrance; **être de** ~ be on duty; **hors de** ~ out of action; **offrir ses** ~s offer one's good offices; **premier** ~ first sitting (meal); **rendre (un)** ~ **à qn** do s/o a good turn
**serviette** *nf* table napkin; towel; brief-case
**serviette-éponge** *nf* (*pl* **serviettes-éponges**) Turkish towel
**servilité** *nf* servility; slavishness
**servir** *vt* (89) serve; wait on; serve up; help, be of service to; satisfy; ~ **la messe** serve at mass; ~ **une rente** pay out a yearly income; *vi* serve, be of use; ~ **à qch** be useful for some purpose; **cela ne sert à rien de ...** it's no use ...; **rien ne sert de ...** it's no use ...; **se** ~ help oneself; supply oneself; **se** ~ **de** use, make use of
**serviteur** *nm* servant; **votre** ~ your obedient servant
**servitude** *nf* servitude, slavery; charge, financial obligation
**servofrein** *nm* servo-assisted brake
**ses** *poss adj see* **son**
**session** *nf* sitting, session
**sétacé** *adj* bristly, setaceous
**seuil** *nm* threshold; door-step; *geog* shelf
**seul** *adj* single, only; alone; mere, very; ~ **et unique** one and only; **parler** ~ **à** ~ **à qn** speak to s/o alone, with no one else present
**seulement** *adv* only; even
**sève** *nf* sap; vigour
**sévère** *adj* strict; severe; stern
**sévérité** *nf* severity; strictness

sévices

**sévices** *nmpl* brutality, ill-treatment
**sévir** *vi* inflict severe punishment; rage, be rife
**sevrer** *vt* (6) wean; deprive
**sexagénaire** *n* + *adj* sexagenarian
**sexe** *nm* sex; sexual organ
**sexisme** *nm* sexism
**sexiste** *n* + *adj* sexist
**sexologie** *nf* sexology
**sextupler** *vt* increase sixfold
**sexualité** *nf* sexuality
**sexué** *adj* sexed
**sexuel -uelle** *adj* sexual
**seyant** *adj* becoming, attractive
**shampooing** *nm* shampoo
**shooter** *vi* kick (football)
¹**si** *nm invar mus* B, ti, te
²**si** *adv* so; so much; such; yes (after *neg*); ~ **bien que** with the result that; ~ **fait** yes; ~ **grand qu'il soit** however big he may be; **que** ~ yes, of course (after *neg*)
³**si** *conj* if; whether; how much; what if; ~ **ce n'est** but for; ~ **je le connais!** of course I know him!; ~ **tant est que** + *subj* if indeed ...
**siamois** *adj* Siamese
**sibylle** *nf* sibyl
**sibyllin** *adj* sybilline
**siccatif -ive** *adj* quick-drying
**sicilien -ienne** *adj* Sicilian
**SIDA** *nm med* Aids
**sidéral** *adj* sidereal
**sidérant** *adj* staggering
**sidéré** *adj* amazed, staggered
**sidérer** *vt* (6) dumbfound, amaze
**sidérurgie** *nf* metallurgy of iron and steel
**sidérurgique** *adj* **industrie** ~ iron and steel industry
**sidi** *nm pej* North African
**siècle** *nm* century; period; *theol* world; **le Grand Siècle** the age of Louis XIV
**siège** *nm* seat; centre; siege; chair; ~ **social** registered office; **bain de** ~ hip bath; **état de** ~ martial law; **lever le** ~ raise the siege; **mettre le** ~ lay siege; **Saint-Siège** Holy See
**siéger** *vi* (6,3) sit, be in session; be seated; have a seat
**sien** (*f* **sienne**) *n* one's own; **faire des siennes** be up to one's tricks; **les** ~ **s** one's friends; one's kin; **y mettre du** ~ make one's contribution; *pron* his; hers; its; one's
**sieste** *nf* siesta
**sieur** *nm leg* Mr
**sifflant** *adj* hissing, whistling
**sifflement** *nm* whistling, whistle
**siffler** *vt* whistle; whistle for; boo; *sl* swig down; *vi* whistle; hiss; wheeze; boo
**sifflet** *nm* whistle; **coup de** ~ whistle blast; *sl* **couper le** ~ **à qn** cut s/o's throat; shut somebody up

**siffleur -euse** *n* whistler; *adj* whistling; hissing; wheezing
**siffloter** *vi* whistle legently, whistle to oneself
**sigle** *nm* set of initials
**signal** *nm* signal; **donner le** ~ **de** cause, start
**signalement** *nm* description (person), particulars
**signaler** *vt* point out; draw attention to; report; signal; give a description of; **se** ~ distinguish oneself, attract notice
**signalétique** *adj* descriptive; **fiche** ~ police record card
**signaleur** *nm* signaller
**signalisation** *nf* signalling; signalling system
**signataire** *n* signatory
**signature** *nf* signing; signature
**signe** *nm* sign; indication, mark; symbol; gesture; **en** ~ **de** as a sign of; **faire** ~ **à qn** beckon to s/o, motion to s/o; **placé sous le** ~ **de** the theme (keynote) of which is
**signer** *vt* sign; **se** ~ cross oneself
**signet** *nm* book-mark
**significatif -ive** *adj* significant
**signification** *nf* meaning, significance, sense; *leg* notification
**signifier** *vt* mean, signify; notify quite clearly; give notice of
**silence** *nm* silence; **faire** ~ be quiet, stop talking; **passer qch sous** ~ fail to mention sth
**silencieux** *nm mot* silencer; *adj* (*f* **-ieuse**) silent; taciturn; peaceful
**silex** *nm* flint
**silhouetter** *vt* silhouette, outline
**silice** *nf* silica
**sillage** *nm* wake, wash; slipstream
**sillon** *nm* furrow; drill; track, trace; groove (record); ~ **s** wrinkles; **faire (creuser) son** ~ carry out one's self-allotted task
**sillonner** *vt* furrow; streak; wrinkle
**silurien -ienne** *adj* Silurian
**simagrée** *nf coll* pretence; **faire des** ~ **s** mince; make a fuss
**simien -ienne** *adj* Simian
**simiesque** *adj* monkey-like
**similaire** *adj* similar, like
**similarité** *nf* similarity
**simili** *nm* half-tone block; *coll* imitation; *pref* imitation
**similigravure** *nf* process engraving, half-tone
**similitude** *nf* resemblance, likeness; similitude
**simonie** *nf* simony
**simoun** *nm* simoon
**simple** *nm* singles (tennis); ~ **s** medicinal herbs; *adj* simple; single; unaffected;

straightforward, easy; plain; ordinary; naïve, ingenuous; ~ **comme bonjour** simple as can be; ~ **d'esprit** stupid; ~ **soldat** private soldier; **corps** ~ element; **passé** ~ past definite, past historic
**simplet -ette** *adj coll* naïve, a bit simple
**simplicité** *nf* simplicity
**simplificateur -trice** *n* simplifier; *adj* simplifying
**simplifier** *vt* simplify
**simplisme** *nm* over-simplification; superficial argumentation
**simpliste** *adj* over-simple
**simulacre** *nm* semblance, appearance, show
**simulateur -trice** *n* shammer; *nm* simulator
**simuler** *vt* sham, feign
**simultané** *adj* simultaneous
**sinapiser** *vt* add mustard to
**sinapisme** *nm* mustard poultice; mustard plaster
**sincère** *adj* sincere; frank; genuine
**sincérité** *nf* sincerity; frankness; genuineness
**singe** *nm* monkey, ape
**singer** *vt* (3) ape, mimic
**singerie** *nf* monkey trick, antic; clumsy mimicry; monkey-house
**singulariser** *vt* make conspicuous
**singularité** *nf* singularity; peculiarity; oddness
**singulier -ière** *adj* singular; remarkable; peculiar, strange; **combat** ~ single combat
**sinistre** *nm* disaster, calamity; *adj* sinister, ominous
**sinistré -e** *n* victim of a disaster; *adj* distressed, destroyed by a disaster
**sinologie** *nf* sinology
**sinologue** *n* China specialist
**sinon** *conj* otherwise, or else; except
**sinueux -ueuse** *adj* winding, sinuous, meandering
**sinuosité** *nf* winding, sinuosity; bend (river)
**sinusite** *nf* sinusitis
**sioniste** *n* + *adj* Zionist
**siphon** *nm* siphon; trap (sink-pipe)
**siphonner** *vt* siphon
**sire** *nm ar* sir, Lord; sire; **un triste** ~ a miserable rogue
**sirène** *nf* siren, hooter; mermaid
**sirop** *nm* syrup
**siroter** *vt* sip
**sis** *adj* situated
**sismique** *adj* seismic
**sismographie** *nf* seismography
**site** *nm* site; beauty spot
**sitôt** *adv* straightaway, so soon; **de** ~ soon; ~ **que** as soon as

**situation** *nf* situation; position, site; condition, state; job
**situer** *vt* situate
**sixième** *n* + *adj* sixth
**Sixtine** *adj* Sistine
**sizain** *nm* six-line stanza
**ski** *nm* ski; skiing; **faire du** ~ go skiing
**skieur, skieuse** *n* skier
**slave** *adj* Slav, Slavonic
**slip** *nm* briefs; *naut* slipway; ~ **de bain** bathing trunks
**slovaque** *adj* Slovakian
**smala** *nf coll* large family; Arab chief's household
**smicard -e** *n* minimum wage-earner
**smoking** *nm* dinner-jacket
**snack** *nm coll* snack-bar
**snober** *vt* treat with disdain
**sobre** *adj* moderate; abstemious; sparing; simple, sober
**sobriété** *nf* moderation; temperateness; sobriety, simplicity
**sobriquet** *nm* nickname
**soc** *nm* ploughshare
**sociabilité** *nf* sociableness
**social** *adj* social; **capital** ~ registered capital; **raison** ~**e** name of company; **siège** ~ head office
**socialisant** *adj* with socialist tendencies
**socialiser** *vt* socialize
**socialisme** *nm* socialism
**socialiste** *n* + *adj* socialist
**sociétaire** *n* member
**société** *nf* society; community; company; association; ~ **à responsabilité limitée** limited (liability) company; ~ **par actions** joint-stock company
**sociologie** *nf* sociology
**socle** *nm* base, pedestal; stand
**socque** *nm* clog, patten
**socquette** *nf* ankle-sock
**sodomie** *nf* sodomy
**sœur** *nf* sister; ~ **de lait** foster-sister; **bonne** ~ nun
**soi** *pron* oneself; himself, herself, itself; **aller de** ~ create no problem, present no obstacle
**soi-disant** *adj invar* so-called; self-styled; *adv* allegedly
**soie** *nf* silk; pig's bristle; **papier de** ~ tissue paper
**soierie** *nf* silk article; silk factory
**soif** *nf* thirst; **avoir** ~ be thirsty; **avoir** ~ **de** be eager for; **boire à sa** ~ slake one's thirst
**soigné** *adj* carefully done, polished
**soigner** *vt* take care of, look after; nurse; take care with; **se** ~ take care of oneself; *coll* do oneself well
**soigneur** *nm* second (boxing)
**soigneux -euse** *adj* painstaking, meticulous, careful

**soin**

soin *nm* care; charge; attention, trouble;
~ s medical attention; avoir ~ de faire
qch take good care to do sth; avoir ~
de qch take care of sth; être aux petits
~ s pour qn be full of attentions for
s/o; premiers ~ s first aid; prendre ~
de take care of; sans ~ careless, untidy; untidily
soir *nm* evening; à ce ~! see you
tonight!
soirée *nf* evening; social evening; ~
dansante dancing-party
soit *adv* so be it, agreed; suppose; *conj*
~ ... ~ either ... or; ~ que ... ~ que
whether ... or; tant ~ peu very little
soixantaine *nf* about sixty; the sixties
(age)
soixante *nm* + *adj* sixty
soixante-dix *nm* + *adj* seventy
soixantième *n* + *adj* sixtieth
¹sol *nm* ground, earth
²sol *nm invar mus* G, so(h)
sol-air *adj invar* ground-to-air
solaire *adj* solar; cadran ~ sundial
soldat *nm* soldier; ~ de plomb tin
soldier
soldatesque *nf pej* soldiery; *adj* barrack-
room
¹solde *nf* soldier's pay; être à la ~ de qn
be in s/o's pay
²solde *nm comm* balance; sale; ~ s
goods sold in sale
solder *vt* settle the balance of, pay off
(account); sell off cheap; remainder;
se ~ par have as a result
solécisme *nm* solecism
soleil *nm* sun; sunshine; sunflower;
catherine-wheel; ~ couchant setting
sun; ~ levant rising sun; avoir du bien
au ~ have landed property; faire (du)
~ be sunny; grand ~ bright sunshine;
*coll* piquer un ~ go red, blush
solennel -elle *adj* solemn; grave
solenniser *vt* solemnize
solennité *nf* solemnity; solemn ceremony
solénoïde *nm elect* solenoid
solfège *nm* rudiments of music
solidaire *adj* interdependent; *leg* jointly
responsible
solidariser (se) *v refl* make common cause
solidarité *nf* solidarity; interdependence; *leg* joint responsibility
solide *nm* solid body; *adj* solid; resistant, strong
solidifier *vt* solidify; se ~ become solid
solidité *nf* solidity; soundness; stability
soliloque *nm* soliloquy
soliste *n* soloist
solitaire *nm* hermit; solitaire; old male
boar; *adj* solitary, lonely
solive *nf* beam, joist

soliveau *nm* small beam
sollicitation *nf* entreaty, solicitation
solliciter *vt* solicit, beg for; apply for;
attract, provoke
solliciteur -euse *n* solicitant, petitioner
sollicitude *nf* anxiety, concern; solicitude
solubiliser *vt* make soluble
solubilité *nf* solubility
solutionner *vt* solve
solvabilité *nf* solvency
solvable *adj* solvent
somatique *adj* somatic
sombre *adj* dark; gloomy; dull; dismal
sombrer *vi* sink, go down; fall
sommaire *nm* summary; *adj* concise,
summary; hasty
sommation *nf leg* summons; demand,
urgent request
¹somme *nf* amount, sum, sum total; ~
toute when all's said and done; en ~ in
short
²somme *nf* bête de ~ beast of burden
³somme *nm* nap, short sleep; faire un ~
take a nap
sommeil *nm* sleep; sleepiness; inactivity;
avoir le ~ léger be a light sleeper;
avoir le ~ lourd be a sound sleeper;
avoir ~ be sleepy
sommeiller *vi* doze, sleep lightly; be
dormant
sommelier *nm* wine-waiter; cellarman
sommer *vt* call on; summon
sommes *first pers pl pres ind* être
sommet *nm* summit, top; crest; pinnacle; conférence au ~ summit conference
sommier *nm* box-mattress; lintel
sommité *nf* top, extremity; top personality
somnambule *n* sleep-walker; *adj* som-
nambulistic
somnambulisme *nm* sleep-walking
somnifère *nm* soporific, sleeping tablet;
*adj* sleep-inducing
somnolent *adj* drowsy, sleepy
somnoler *vi* doze
somptueux -ueuse *adj* sumptuous
somptuosité *nf* sumptuousness
¹son (*f* sa, *pl* ses) *adj* his, her, its, one's
²son *nm* sound; mur du ~ sound barrier
³son *nm* bran; taches de ~ freckles
sonate *nf* sonata
sonatine *nf* sonatina
sondage *nm* sounding; boring; investigation; ~ d'opinion opinion poll
sonde *nf* sounding-line; probe; sound-
ing-rod
sonder *vt* sound; probe, examine; ~ le
terrain try to find out what is going on
sondeur *nm* pollster
songe *nm* dream

288

**songe-creux** *nm* dreamer, visionary

**songer** *vi* (3) dream; day-dream; think; remember; intend

**songerie** *nf* day-dreaming; reverie

**songeur -euse** *adj* dreamy; thoughtful

**sonnant** *adj* **espèces ~ es** hard cash; **horloge ~ e** striking clock; **huit heures ~ es** eight o'clock precisely

**sonné** *adj* announced by a bell; *sl* crazy, barmy; **il est midi ~** it has struck twelve

**sonner** *vt* ring, ring for; play (trumpet, etc); *coll* bash, knock out; *vi* sound; strike, ring

**sonnerie** *nf* ringing; set of bells; chiming mechanism

**sonnette** *nf* little bell, hand bell; house bell; **coup de ~** ring; **serpent à ~ s** rattlesnake

**sonneur** *nm* bell-ringer

**sonore** *adj* sonorous, loud; resonant, resounding; **bande ~** sound track; **consonne ~** voiced consonant; **fond ~** sound background

**sonoriser** *vt* sound; add sound to; equip for sound reproduction

**sonorité** *nf* sonorousness, sound quality

**sont** *third pers pl pres ind* être

**sophisme** *nm* sophism

**sophistication** *nf* sophistication; adulteration

**soporifique** *adj* soporific; *coll* tedious

**sorbet** *nm* water-ice, sorbet

**sorbetière** *nf* freezer (for making sorbets)

**sorbier** *nm bot* sorb, service-tree

**sorcellerie** *nf* witchcraft

**sorcier** *nm* wizard, sorcerer; *adj coll* (*f* **-ière**) clever

**sorcière** *nf* witch, sorceress

**sordide** *adj* filthy, sordid

**sordidité** *nf* sordidness

**Sorlingues** *nfpl* Isles of Scilly

**sornettes** *nfpl obs* nonsense

**sort** *nm* destiny, fate; lot; chance; spell; **faire un ~ à** show to advantage; *coll* finish with; **jeter un ~** cast a spell; **tirer au ~** draw lots

**sortable** *adj* presentable, decent

**sortant** *adj* going out; outgoing; retiring; **numéro ~** winning number

**sorte** *nf* kind, sort; manner, way; **de la ~** like that, in that way; **de ~ que** so that; **en quelque ~** as it were; **en ~ que** so that

**sortie** *nf* exit, way out; going out, departure; excursion, outing, sally; outburst; *theat* exit

**sortie-de-bain** *nf* (*pl* **sorties-de-bain**) bathgown

**sortilège** *nm* spell, charm

**sortir** *nm* **au ~ de** on coming out of, on leaving; at the end of; *vt* (59) take out, bring out; *vi* go out; come out; get out;

protrude, stick out; spring from, be descended from; turn up (lottery number); **~ de faire qch** have just done sth; **~ d'embarras** escape from an awkward situation; **d'où sors-tu?** wherever have you been?; **faire ~** take out; send out; **laisser ~** let out; **ne pas ~ de là** persist in one's opinion; **s'en ~** get out of a jam

**sosie** *nm* double (person)

**sot, sotte** *n* fool; *adj* stupid, silly; embarrassed; absurd

**sottise** *nf* stupidity; foolish act, stupid word; insult

**sou** *nm* five centimes piece, sou; **cent ~ s** five francs; **être près de ses ~ s** be very careful with money; **être sans le ~** be penniless; **machine à ~ s** fruit-machine; **n'avoir pas le ~** be penniless; **pas ...** **pour deux ~ s** not in the least ...; **question de gros ~ s** matter of hard cash

**soubassement** *nm* base, sub-foundation (building)

**soubresaut** *nm* leap, bound; sudden movement, jerk

**soubrette** *nf coll* maid; *theat* maid, waiting-maid

**souche** *nf* stump, stock; founder (family); counterfoil, stub; stack (chimney); **faire ~** found a family; *coll* **rester comme une ~** remain inactive

¹**souci** *nm* care; worry, anxiety

²**souci** *nm* marigold

**soucier** *vt* worry; **se ~** worry

**soucieux -ieuse** *adj* anxious, concerned

**soucoupe** *nf* saucer

**soudage** *nm* soldering, welding

**soudain** *adj* sudden; *adv* suddenly, all of a sudden

**soudaineté** *nf* suddenness

**soudard** *nm ar* mercenary soldier, professional soldier; old trooper, coarse fighting man

**soude** *nf* soda

**souder** *vt* solder, weld; **se ~** fuse together, join together, knit

**soudoyer** *vt* (7) hire, bribe

**soudure** *nf* soldering, welding; soldering joint; join; solder

**soue** *nf* pigsty

**soufflage** *nm* blowing; glass-blowing

**souffle** *nm* breath; blast; puff; breathing; *coll* **avoir du ~** have a cheek; **couper le ~ à qn** wind s/o; take s/o's breath away; **effet de ~** blast (explosion); **être à bout de ~** be exhausted; **manquer de ~** be short of breath; be short of (poetic) inspiration

**souffler** *vt* blow, blow up; blow out; utter, breathe (word); *theat* prompt; suggest; *coll* **~ qch à qn** do s/o out of sth; *vi* blow; breathe; puff, pant; ~ **comme un bœuf** breathe heavily

**soufflerie** *nf* blower; bellows

¹**soufflet** *nm* bellows; vestibule (railway coach)

²**soufflet** *nm* blow, box on the ear; affront

**souffleter** *vt* (5) slap, deal a blow to

¹**souffleur -euse** *n theat* prompter; *theat* **trou du** ~ prompt-box

²**souffleur** *nm* glass-blower

**soufflure** *nf* blister, bubble

**souffrance** *nf* suffering; **en** ~ in abeyance; held up in transit

**souffrant** *adj* suffering; unwell, indisposed

**souffre-douleur** *nm invar* butt

**souffreteux -euse** *adj* sickly, weak

**souffrir** *vt* (30) suffer; endure, put up with; allow, brook; *vi* suffer, be in pain; feel ill effects

**soufre** *nm* sulphur

**soufrer** *vt* treat with sulphur, sulphur

**soufrière** *nf* sulphur-mine

**souhait** *nm* wish, desire; **à** ~ according to one's desire; **à vos** ~**s!** bless you!

**souhaitable** *adj* desirable

**souhaiter** *vt* wish, desire

**souiller** *vt* dirty, make filthy; defile; tarnish (reputation)

**souillon** *n* filthy person; slattern

**souillure** *nf* stain; blemish

**soûl -e** *adj* drunk; glutted, surfeited; **tout son** ~ as much as one can, as much as one wants

**soulagement** *nm* relief; comfort

**soulager** *vt* (3) relieve; lighten the burden of; alleviate; **se** ~ obtain relief; *coll* relieve oneself

**soûlard -e** *n sl* drunkard

**soûler** *vt coll* make drunk, intoxicate; *coll* **se** ~ get drunk; surfeit oneself

**soûlerie** *nf sl* drinking-bout; drunkenness

**soulèvement** *nm* rising, heaving; uprising, revolt; surge of indignation; ~ **de cœur** nausea

**soulever** *vt* (6) raise; lift, lift up; arouse, excite; stir up, rouse; ~ **le cœur** disgust; **se** ~ rise; lift oneself; revolt

**soulier** *nm* shoe; *coll* **être dans ses petits** ~**s** be in an awkward situation

**souligner** *vt* underline; emphasize, stress

**soumettre** *vt* (60) subdue; submit; subject; **se** ~ submit, give in

**soumis** *adj* submissive; dutiful; subject

**soumission** *nf* submission; obedience; submissiveness; tender

**soumissionnaire** *n* party or person making a tender

**soumissionner** *vt* tender

**soupape** *nf* valve; ~ **d'admission** inlet valve; ~ **d'échappement** outlet valve; ~ **de sûreté** safety valve; ~ **en tête**

overhead valve; ~ **latérale** side valve

**soupçon** *nm* suspicion; conjecture; slight appearance, trace; *coll* small quantity, dash

**soupçonner** *vt* suspect; surmise

**soupçonneux -euse** *adj* distrustful, of a suspicious nature

**soupe** *nf* soup; bread soaked in broth; *coll* grub, meal; ~ **au lait** ·bread and milk; ~ **populaire** soup kitchen; **à la** ~ ! grub's up!

**soupente** *nf* garret; recess (under stairs)

**souper** *nm* supper; *vi* have supper, sup; *sl* **avoir soupé de qch** be fed up with sth

**soupeser** *vt* (6) weigh, feel the weight of

**soupière** *nf* soup-tureen

**soupir** *nm* sigh; crotchet rest; **pousser un** ~ heave a sigh

**soupirail -aux** *nm* air-hole, ventilator

**soupirant** *nm obs* iron wooer, gallant, suitor

**soupirer** *vi* sigh; ~ **après qch** long for sth

**souple** *adj* supple; flexible; lithe; pliant, tractable

**souplesse** *nf* suppleness; flexibility; litheness; pliancy, tractability

**souquer** *vt naut* haul taut; *vi* row hard

**source** *nf* source; spring, well; cause, origin; **couler de** ~ be the natural result

**sourcier** *nm* water-diviner

**sourcil** *nm* eyebrow

**sourciller** *vi* frown, knit one's brows; flinch; **sans** ~ without turning a hair

**sourcilleux -euse** *adj* haughty; fussy

**sourd -e** *n* deaf person; **crier comme un** ~ shout one's head off; *adj* deaf; dull, muffled; secret; veiled; ~ **comme un pot** deaf as a post; **consonne** ~ **e** voiceless consonant; **faire la** ~ **e oreille** pretend not to hear

**sourdement** *adv* with a dull sound; secretly

**sourdine** *nf mus* mute; **en** ~ secretly, unobtrusively; **mettre une** ~ **à** tone down, be less noisy with

**sourd-muet** *n* (*f* **sourde-muette**, *mpl* **sourds-muets**, *fpl* **sourdes-muettes**) deaf mute; *adj* deaf and dumb

**sourdre** *vi* (90) well up; spring, arise

**souriant** *adj* smiling; cheerful

**souricier** *nm* mouse-catcher

**souricière** *nf* mouse-trap; trap, police-trap

**sourire** *nm* smile; *vi* (84) smile; be favourable, be attractive

¹**souris** *nf* mouse; knuckle-end of leg of mutton; *coll* girl

²**souris** *nm obs* smile

**sournois** *adj* sly, crafty, cunning

**sournoiserie** *nf* craftiness, cunning

**sous** *prep* under, beneath, below; within the time of; ~ **ce rapport** in this respect;

**~ clef** under lock and key; **~ le nom de** by the name of; **~ mes yeux** before my eyes; **~ peine de** on pain of; **~ peu** in a short time; **~ un mauvais jour** in a bad light; **être ~ les drapeaux** serve with the colour

**sous-alimentation** *nf* malnutrition

**sous-alimenté** *adj* undernourished

**sous-bois** *nm* undergrowth

**sous-chef** *nm* deputy chief, assistant head

**sous-comité** *nm* sub-committee

**sous-commission** *nf* sub-commission

**souscripteur -trice** *n* subscriber

**souscription** *nf* signing; subscription, signature; contribution

**souscrire** *vt* (42) sign, execute; take out a subscription; contribute; **~ à** subscribe to; agree, consent to

**sous-cutané** *adj* subcutaneous

**sous-développé** *adj* underdeveloped, developing (nation)

**sous-diacre** *nm* sub-deacon

**sous-directeur -trice** *n* assistant manager, assistant manageress; vice-principal

**sous-emploi** *nm* underemployment

**sous-entendre** *vt* imply

**sous-entendu** *nm* implication

**sous-équipé** *adj* under-equipped

**sous-estimer** *vt* underestimate

**sous-exposer** *vt phot* under-expose

**sous-garde** *nf* trigger-guard

**sous-genre** *nm* sub-group

**sous-jacent** *adj* underlying

**sous-jupe** *nf* underslip, underskirt

**sous-lieutenant** *nm* sub-lieutenant, second lieutenant

**sous-locataire** *n* subtenant

**sous-location** *nf* sub-letting; sub-let

**sous-louer** *vt* sub-let

**sous-main** *nm invar* blotting-pad; **en ~** secretly

**sous-marin** *nm* submarine; *adj* submarine, underwater, deep-sea

**sous-maxillaire** *adj* submaxillary

**sous-nappe** *nf* under-tablecloth

**sous-œuvre** *nm bui* underpinning

**sous-off** *nm coll* non-commissioned officer

**sous-officier** *nm* non-commissioned officer; petty officer

**sous-ordre** *nm* subordinate

**sous-peuplé** *adj* under-populated

**sous-pied** *nm* under-strap (gaiters); trouser-strap

**sous-préfecture** *nf* sub-prefecture; town where the sub-prefect resides

**sous-préfet** *nm* sub-prefect

**sous-préfète** *nf* sub-prefect's wife

**sous-production** *nf* under-production

**sous-produit** *nm* by-product

**sous-secrétaire** *nm* under-secretary

**sous-seing** *nm invar* private contract

**soussigné** *adj* undersigned

**soussigner** *vt* sign, undersign

**sous-sol** *nm* basement; subsoil

**sous-station** *nf* sub-station

**sous-titre** *nm* subtitle

**soustractif -ive** *adj* subtractive

**soustraction** *nf* taking away, removal; subtraction

**soustraire** *vt* (9) take away, withdraw; shield, preserve; subtract; **se ~ à** escape, avoid

**sous-traitant** *nm* sub-contractor

**sous-traiter** *vt* sub-contract

**sous-verre** *nm invar* passe-partout picture

**sous-vêtement** *nm* undergarment

**soutache** *nf* braid

**soutacher** *vt* braid

**soutane** *nf* cassock; **prendre la ~** go into the priesthood

**soute** *nf naut* store-room, bunker

**soutenable** *adj* bearable; tenable, arguable

**soutènement** *nm* supporting, propping, holding up; **mur de ~** retaining wall

**souteneur** *nm* pimp; *obs* upholder

**soutenir** *vt* (96) support, sustain; hold up; back, help; maintain, uphold; affirm, assert; bear; withstand; **se ~** stand on one's feet; hold oneself up; support one another; continue, last

**soutenu** *adj* sustained; constant, unflagging

**souterrain** *nm* underground passage; vault; *adj* underground

**soutien** *nm* support; supporter; **~ de famille** bread-winner

**soutien-gorge** *nm* (*pl* **soutiens-gorge**) brassière, bra

**soutier** *nm naut* coal-trimmer

**soutirer** *vt* draw off, tap; squeeze, wheedle (money out of s/o)

**souvenance** *nf* **avoir ~ de** remember

**souvenir** *nm* memory, recollection; memento, souvenir; **veuillez me rappeler au bon ~ de Jean** please remember me to John; *v impers* **il me souvient que** I remember; **se ~** *v refl* (96) remember

**souvent** *adv* often, frequently

**souverain -e** *n* sovereign, ruler; *adj* sovereign

**souverainement** *adv* highly, extremely

**souveraineté** *nf* sovereignty; supreme authority

**soviétique** *adj* Soviet

**soyeux -euse** *adj* silky

**spacieux -ieuse** *adj* roomy, spacious

**spadassin** *nm* bravo, ruffian

**sparadrap** *nm med* adhesive plaster

**sparte** *nm* esparto grass

**Sparte** *nf* Sparta

**Spartiate** *n* Spartan

**spartiate** *nf* sandal; *adj* Spartan

**spasme** *nm* spasm

**spasmodique** *adj* spasmodic

**spath** *nm min* spar

**spatule** *nf* spatula

**speaker** (*f* **speakerine**) *n* speaker, announcer

**spécialisé** *adj* specialized; **ouvrier ~** semi-skilled worker

**spécialiser** *vt* specialize; **se ~** specialize

**spécialiste** *n* specialist

**spécialité** *nf* speciality; special feature

**spécieux -ieuse** *adj* specious

**spécifier** *vt* specify; determine

**spécifique** *nm + adj* specific

**spéciosité** *nf* speciousness

**spectacle** *nm* sight, spectacle; *theat* play, show; display; **pièce à grand ~** spectacular; **salle de ~** theatre; **se donner en ~** make an exhibition of oneself

**spectaculaire** *adj* spectacular

**spectateur -trice** *n* spectator; onlooker, beholder

**spectral** *adj* spectral, ghost-like; **couleurs ~ es** colours of the spectrum

**spectre** *nm* ghost, spectre; spectrum

**spéculaire** *adj* specular; **écriture ~** mirror writing

**spéculateur -trice** *n* speculator

**spéculatif -ive** *adj* speculative

**spéculation** *nf* speculation; theory

**spéculer** *vi* speculate; cogitate

**spéléologie** *nf* speleology

**spéléologue** *n* speleologist

**spencer** *nm* short jacket

**spermatozoïde** *nm* spermatozoon

**sperme** *nm* sperm

**sphère** *nf* sphere; globe; orbit, field

**sphérique** *adj* spherical

**sphinx** *nm* sphinx; hawk-moth

**spirale** *nf* spiral

**spirante** *nf ling* spirant consonant, fricative

**spire** *nf* whorl; twirl

**spirite** *n + adj* spiritualist

**spiritisme** *nm* spiritualism

**spiritualiser** *vt* spiritualize

**spiritualisme** *nm philos* spiritualism

**spiritualiste** *n + adj* spiritualist

**spirituel -uelle** *adj* spiritual; religious; witty

**spiritueux** *nm* alcoholic spirit; *adj* (*f* **-ueuse**) spirituous

**spirochète** *nm biol* spirochaeta

**splendeur** *nf* splendour; brilliance; grandeur

**splendide** *adj* splendid; brilliant, magnificent

**splénique** *adj* splenic

**spoliateur -trice** *n* despoiler

**spolier** *vt* despoil, rob, plunder

**spongieux -ieuse** *adj* spongy

**spongiosité** *nf* sponginess

**spontané** *adj* spontaneous

**spontanéité** *nf* spontaneity

**sporadique** *adj* sporadic

**sport** *nm* sport; *adj invar* sportsmanlike; *coll* sporty

**sportif -ive** *n* lover of sport; *adj* sporting

**sportsman** *nm* (*pl* **sportsmen**) racegoer

**spot** *nm* spotlight, spot; television commercial

**spumeux -euse** *adj* foamy, frothy

**squale** *nm* dog-fish

**squame** *nf* scale (skin)

**squelette** *nm* skeleton; framework; bare outline

**squelettique** *adj* skeletal

**squirr(h)e** *nm med* scirrhus

**stabilisateur** *nm* stabilizer; *adj* (*f* **-trice**) stabilizing

**stabiliser** *vt* stabilize; **se ~** become stable

**stabilité** *nf* stability, steadiness; firmness

**stable** *adj* stable, steady; firm; lasting, durable

**stabulation** *nf* stabling (horses), stalling (cattle)

**stade** *nm* stadium, sports-ground; stage

**stage** *nm* period of training

**stagiaire** *n + adj* trainee

**stalle** *nf* stall (church); box (stable)

**staminé** *adj bot* staminate

**stance** *nf* stanza

**stand** *nm* shooting-stand; booth, stall, stand (exhibition)

**standard** *nm* standard; switchboard

**standardiser** *vt* standardize

**standing** *nm* social status; **(de) grand ~** luxurious, luxury

**staphylocoque** *nm biol* staphylococcus

**star** *nf* film-star

**starlette** *nf* starlet

**starter** *nm mot* choke; *sp* starter

**station** *nf* station; standing; stop, halt; stage; position; **~ thermale** spa; **en ~** stationed

**stationnaire** *adj* stationary

**stationnement** *nm* stopping; parking

**stationner** *vi* park; stop

**statique** *adj* static

**statisticien -ienne** *n* statistician

**statuaire** *n + adj* statuary

**statuer** *vi* ordain, decree; **~ sur** pronounce on, settle

**statufier** *vt coll* erect a statue to

**statu quo** *nm invar* status quo

**statut** *nm* statute; rule; status

**statutaire** *adj* statutory

**stéarique** *adj* stearic (acid)

**stèle** *nf* stele, column

**stellaire** *adj* stellar

**sténo** *nf coll* shorthand; *coll* shorthand-writer

**sténodactylo(graphe)** *nf* shorthand-typist

**sténodactylo(graphie)** *nf* shorthand and typing

**sténographe** *n* shorthand-writer

**sténographie** *nf* shorthand

**sténographier** *vt* take down in shorthand

**sténotypie** *nf* shorthand-typing

**stercoraire** *adj* stercoraceous

**stère** *nm* cubic metre of wood

**stéréophonie** *nf* stereophony

**stéréophonique** *adj* stereophonic

**stéréotypé** *adj* stereotyped, ordinary, hackneyed

**stéréotyper** *vt* stereotype

**stérile** *adj* barren, sterile; fruitless, unprofitable

**stérilet** *nm* loop, coil (contraception)

**stérilisateur** *nm* sterilizer

**stériliser** *vt* sterilize

**stérilité** *nf* sterility

**sternutation** *nf* sneezing

**sternutatoire** *adj* causing sneezing

**stéroïde** *nm* + *adj* steroid

**stick** *nm* swagger-stick

**stigmate** *nm* stigma; trace, stain, mark; stigmata

**stigmatiser** *vt* stigmatize; brand; stain

**stimulant** *nm* stimulant; stimulus, incentive; *adj* stimulating

**stimulateur -trice** *adj* stimulative

**stimuler** *vt* stimulate, incite

**stipendié -e** *n* + *adj* mercenary

**stipendier** *vt* have in one's pay

**stipuler** *vt* stipulate

**stockage** *nm* stocking, laying in stocks

**stocker** *vt* stock; stock-pile

**stockiste** *nm* stocker; wholesale warehouseman

**stoïcisme** *nm* stoicism

**stoïque** *n* + *adj* stoic

**stolon** *nm bot* runner, sucker

**stomacal** *adj* gastric, stomachal

**stop** *nm* stop; stop-sign; *coll* hitch-hiking

**stoppage** *nm* invisible mending

¹**stopper** *vt* repair by invisible mending

²**stopper** *vt* stop; check; *vi* stop

¹**stoppeur -euse** *n* invisible mender

²**stoppeur -euse** *n coll* hitch-hiker

**store** *nm* blind

**strabique** *adj* squint-eyed

**strabisme** *nm* squinting

**strapontin** *nm* folding seat

**stratagème** *nm* stratagem

**stratège** *nm* strategist

**stratégie** *nf* strategy

**stratégique** *adj* strategic

**stratifier** *vt* stratify

**streptocoque** *nm biol* streptococcus

**strette** *nf mus* stretto

**strict** *adj* severe, strict; **le ~ nécessaire** the barest essential

**stridence** *nf* harshness, stridency

**striduler** *vi* chirr, stridulate

**strie** *nf* scratch, ridge

**strié** *adj* striped, scored

**strier** *vt* score, scratch; groove

**strige** *nf* vampire

**striure** *nf* scratch; groove

**strophe** *nf* verse, stanza

**structuralisme** *nm* structuralism

**structurer** *vt* give a structure to

**stuc** *nm* stucco

**studieux -ieuse** *adj* studious

**studio** *nm* studio; one-room flat

**stupéfaction** *nf* stupefaction, amazement

**stupéfait** *adj* stupefied, amazed

**stupéfiant** *nm* narcotic, drug

**stupéfier** *vt* stupefy; amaze, astound

**stupeur** *nf* stupor; amazement

**stupide** *adj* stupid, silly; stunned, bemused

**stupidité** *nf* stupidity; piece of stupidity

**stupre** *nm* debauchery

**stuquer** *vt* stucco

**stygien -ienne** *adj* Stygian

**style** *nm* style; stylus

**styler** *vt* train

**stylet** *nm* stiletto; *surg* probe

**styliser** *vt* stylize

**styliste** *n* stylist

**stylistique** *nf* stylistics

**stylo** *nm* fountain-pen; **~ à bille** ball-point pen

**styptique** *nm* + *adj* styptic

**su** *nm* **au vu et au ~ de** known to

**suaire** *nm* shroud, winding-sheet

**suave** *adj* pleasant, sweet

**suavité** *nf* sweetness; suavity

**subalterne** *adj* subordinate, minor, inferior

**subconscient** *nm* + *adj* subconscious

**subdiviser** *vt* subdivide

**subéreux -euse** *adj bot* corky

**subir** *vt* undergo; suffer, sustain; **faire ~** inflict, put through

**subit** *adj* sudden, unexpected

**subito** *adv coll* suddenly

**subjectif -ive** *adj* subjective

**subjonctif** *nm* subjunctive; *adj* (*f* -ive) subjunctive

**subjuguer** *vt* subjugate, subdue; dominate; charm

**sublimé** *nm chem* sublimate

**sublimer** *vt* sublimate

**sublimité** *nf* sublimity

**submerger** *vt* (3) submerge; flood; swamp; *coll* overwhelm

**submersible** *nm obs* submarine; *adj* submersible; sinkable

**subordonné** *adj* subordinate (clause)

**subordonner** *vt* subordinate

**suborner** *vt* suborn, instigate

**subreptice** *adj* surreptitious, clandestine

**subrogation** *nf leg* substitution, delegation

**subroger** *vt* (3) *leg* subrogate, appoint as deputy

**subside** *nm* subsidy

**subsidiaire** *adj* subsidiary, auxiliary

**subsistance** *nf* subsistence, maintenance; keep; ~s provisions

**subsistant** *adj* subsisting, remaining in existence

**subsister** *vi* subsist, remain in existence; ~ **de** live on

**substance** *nf* substance; material; **en ~** substantially

**substantiel -ielle** *adj* substantial, important; nourishing

**substantif** *nm* noun, substantive; *adj* (*f* -ive) substantive; substantial

**substituer** *vt* substitute; *leg* ~ **un héritier** appoint an heir in another's place; **se ~ à qn** take s/o else's place

**substitut** *nm leg* deputy magistrate; substitute

**substrat** *nm* substratum

**subtil** *adj* subtle; tenuous; shrewd, discerning; acute

**subtiliser** *vt coll* pinch, sneak

**subtilité** *nf* subtlety; shrewdness; subtle argument

**suburbain** *adj* suburban

**subvenir** *vi* (96) come to the help; supply, provide

**subvention** *nf* subsidy, grant

**subventionner** *vt* subsidize

**subversif -ive** *adj* subversive

**suc** *nm* sap; juice; essence

**succédané** *nm* substitute

**succéder** *vi* (6) succeed, come after

**succès** *nm* happy issue; success

**successeur** *nm* successor

**successif -ive** *adj* successive

**succession** *nf* succession; sequence; inheritance; **droits de ~** estate duty; **prendre la ~ de** succeed; take over from

**succin** *nm* yellow amber

**succion** *nf* suction

**succomber** *vi* succumb; yield; die

**succube** *nm* succubus

**succursale** *nf* branch; sub-office; **magasin à ~s multiples** chain store

**sucer** *vt* (4) suck; *coll* suck dry

**sucette** *nf* baby's dummy; lollipop

**suçoir** *nm ent + bot* sucker

**suçon** *nm* kiss-mark (on skin); love-bite

**suçoter** *vt* suck away at

**sucre** *nm* sugar; ~ **cristallisé** granulated sugar; ~ **en poudre** caster sugar

**sucré** *adj* sweet; sugared, sweetened; sugary

**sucrer** *vt* sweeten, sugar; *coll* **se ~** take a good cut, do well out of s/o

**sucrerie** *nf* sugar-refinery

**sucrier** *nm* sugar-basin; sugar-manufacturer

**sud** *nm* south; *adj invar* southern, southerly

**sudation** *nf med* sweating

**sud-est** *nm* south-east; *adj invar* south-east

**Sudiste** *n US* southerner

**sud-ouest** *nm* south-west; *adj invar* south-west

**Suède** *nf* Sweden

**Suédois -e** *n* Swede

**suédois** *nm* Swedish (language); *adj* Swedish

**suée** *nf coll* sweating

**suer** *vi* sweat; perspire; exude, ooze; *coll* reek; be steeped; *sl* **faire ~ qn** annoy s/o; *vt coll* ~ **sang et eau** make tremendous efforts

**sueur** *nf* sweat, perspiration; **être en ~** be sweating

**suffire** *vi* (91) suffice, be enough; **suffit!** that'll do!; **à chaque jour suffit sa peine** sufficient unto the day is the evil thereof; **il suffit de ...** all that is needed is to ...; **il suffit d'une fois** once is enough; **se ~** be self-sufficient, support oneself

**suffisance** *nf* sufficiency; conceit; **à ~** in plenty

**suffisant** *adj* sufficient, enough; conceited, self-important, presumptuous

**suffixe** *nm* suffix

**suffocant** *adj* stifling, suffocating

**suffoquer** *vt* suffocate, stifle; *coll* astonish; *vi* suffocate, choke

**suffragant** *nm + adj eccles* suffragan

**suffrage** *nm* vote, suffrage

**suggérer** *vt* (6) suggest

**suggestibilité** *nf* suggestibility

**suggestif -ive** *adj* suggestive

**suicidé -e** *n* suicide

**suicider (se)** *v refl* commit suicide

**suie** *nf* soot

**suif** *nm* tallow

**suint** *nm* wool grease

**suinter** *vi* ooze, seep; leak, run

**suis** *first pers sing pres ind* être

**Suisse** *nf* Switzerland; *n* (*f* Suissesse) Swiss (person)

**¹suisse** *adj* Swiss

**²suisse** *nm* hall porter; church official; **boire en ~** drink alone; **petit ~** small cream cheese

**suite** *nf* continuation; train, retinue; sequence, series; result; *mus* suite; **à la**

~ **de** following, after; **avoir de la ~ dans les idées** be capable of perseverance; **de ~** in succession, on end; **donner ~ à** carry out; give effect to; **esprit de ~** methodical perseverance; **et ainsi de ~** and so on; **par la ~** later on, subsequently; **par ~** consequently; **sans ~** incoherent; **tout de ~** immediately

**suivant -e** *n* follower; *adj* next, following; **au ~** ! and the next!; *prep* according to; **~ que** according as

**suivi** *adj* connected; sustained; continuous

**suivre** *vt* (92) follow; escort; pursue; succeed, come after; keep up with; result; **à ~** to be continued; **faire ~ une lettre** forward a letter

**sujet** *nm* topic, subject; cause, reason; individual; **au ~ de** concerning; **bon ~** good chap; **mauvais ~** bad lot; *n* (*f* **-ette**) subject; *adj* (*f* **-ette**) subject; prone, liable

**sujétion** *nf* subjection, servitude; obligation

**sulfate** *nm* sulphate

**sulfater** *vt* sulphate; treat with copper sulphate

**sulfure** *nm* sulphide

**sulfuré** *adj* sulphuretted

**sulfureux -euse** *adj* sulphureous; sulphurous

**sulfurique** *adj* sulphuric

**sultane** *nf* sultana

**summum** *nm* height, highest degree

¹**super** *nm abbr* **supercarburant**

²**super** *adj coll* terrific, first-rate

³**super** *vt* suck in (pump)

**superbe** *nf lit* + *obs* pride; *adj* superb, splendid, magnificent; *lit* + *obs* arrogant, proud

**supercarburant** *nm* high-octane petrol

**supercherie** *nf* deceit, fraud

**supérette** *nf* small supermarket

**superfétation** *nf* superfluity; redundancy

**superficie** *nf* surface; area; superficial aspect

**superficiel -ielle** *adj* superficial; shallow

**superfin** *adj* superfine; of very fine quality

**superflu** *nm* superfluity; *adj* superfluous, unnecessary

**superfluité** *nf* superfluity

**supérieur** *nm* superior, head; *adj* upper; superior; higher

**supériorité** *nf* superiority

**superlatif** *nm* superlative; *adj* (*f* **~ive**) superlative

**supermarché** *nm* supermarket

**superposer** *vt* superimpose, place on top of

**superposition** *nf* superimposition

**supersonique** *adj* supersonic

**superstitieux -ieuse** *adj* superstitious

**superviser** *vt* supervise, check

**supin** *nm gramm* supine

**supplanter** *vt* supplant, supersede

**suppléance** *nf* temporary post, interim post

**suppléant -e** *n* substitute; deputy; *adj* acting, temporary

**suppléer** *vt* make up, supply; take the place of; *vi* make up, compensate

**supplément** *nm* supplement; extra payment, additional charge, excess fare; extra; **en ~** additional, extra

**supplémentaire** *adj* supplementary, additional, extra; **heures ~s** overtime

**suppliant -e** *n* supplicant; *adj* suppliant, imploring, pleading

**supplice** *nm* torture, punishment; violent pain; **être au ~** suffer agony, be on the rack; **mettre au ~** torture

**supplicié -e** *n* executed criminal; criminal under torture

**supplicier** *vt* put to the torture, torture; execute by torture

**supplier** *vt* implore, beseech; **je vous en supplie** I beg of you

**supplique** *nf* petition

**support** *nm* prop, support; stand, mount, holder; backing, back-up material

**supportable** *adj* bearable, endurable

**supporter** *vt* support; hold up; bear, endure; stand, put up with, tolerate

**supposer** *vt* suppose, assume; imply, presuppose; **supposé que** supposing that

**suppositoire** *nm* suppository

**suppôt** *nm* tool, agent; **~ de Satan** fiend, wicked person

**suppression** *nf* suppression; discontinuance, cancellation

**supprimer** *vt* suppress, abolish; leave out; cut out; kill; withhold, conceal; **~ qch à qn** deprive s/o of sth

**suppurer** *vi* run, ooze pus, suppurate

**supputation** *nf* calculation

**supputer** *vt* compute, calculate

**supraliminaire** *adj psych* supraliminal

**suprématie** *nf* supremacy

**suprême** *adj* supreme; highest; last; **moment (heure) ~** moment (hour) of death

¹**sur** *adj* sour, tart

²**sur** *prep* on, upon; towards; over, above; about; out of; by; after, upon; **~ ce, ~ quoi** whereupon

**sûr** *adj* sure; safe, secure; reliable, trustworthy; certain; **~ et certain** absolutely certain; **à coup ~** certainly, without fail; **avoir le pied ~** be sure-footed; **bien ~!** of course!; **jouer au plus ~** play safe; **peu ~** unsafe;

uncertain; *coll* pour ~ ! to be sure!

**surabondance** *nf* superabundance, excess

**surabondant** *adj* superabundant

**surabonder** *vi* be very abundant

**suraigu -uë** *adj* very shrill, very high-pitched

**surajouter** *vt* add extra

**suralimentation** *nf* feeding up; overfeeding; supercharging

**suralimenter** *vt* feed up; overfeed; supercharge

**suranné** *adj* out-of-date, old-fashioned

**surbaissé** *adj mot* low-slung; *archi* depressed

**surboum** *nf coll* party

**surcharge** *nf* overloading; extra load; excess luggage weight; overcharge; weight-handicap; additional charge, surcharge

**surcharger** *vt* (3) overload; overcharge; overtax; surcharge

**surchauffe** *nf* overheating; overheating of economy; superheat

**surchauffer** *vt* overheat; superheat

**surchauffeur** *nm mech* superheater

**surchoix** *nm* best quality

**surclasser** *vt* outclass

**surcomposé** *adj gramm* double-composed

**surcompression** *nf mech* supercharging

**surcomprimé** *adj mech* supercharged

**surcontre** *nm* redouble (bridge)

**surcontrer** *vt* redouble (bridge)

**surcouper** *vt* overtrump

**surcroît** *nm* increase; **par ~** into the bargain, in addition

**surdité** *nf* deafness

**sureau** *nm* elder; **baie de ~** elderberry

**surélévation** *nf* heightening, raising; additional floor

**surélever** *vt* (6) heighten, raise

**sûrement** *adv* certainly, surely; confidently; steadily; safely

**surenchère** *nf* overbid; outbidding

**surenchérir** *vi* bid higher, overbid; go one higher; promise too much

**surérogation** *nf* supererogation

**surestimer** *vt* overestimate, overvalue; overrate

**suret -ette** *adj* slightly sour, tart

**sûreté** *nf* safety, security; sureness; guarantee, surety; **La Sûreté =** Criminal Investigation Department; **être en ~** be in a safe place; **pour plus de ~** to make absolutely sure; **rasoir de ~** safety razor

**surexcitation** *nf* agitation, excitement

**surexciter** *vt* excite; over-stimulate

**surexposer** *vt phot* over-expose

**surexposition** *nf phot* over-exposure

**surface** *nf* surface; **grande ~** supermarket

**surfaire** *vt* (46) overprice, overcharge; overrate, overestimate

**surfiler** *vt* oversew

**surfin** *adj* of very fine quality

**surgeler** *vt* (6) deep-freeze, *US* quick-freeze

**surgeon** *nm* hort sucker

**surgir** *vi* rise, loom, come into view

**surhausser** *vt* heighten, raise; cant; bank; force up (price)

**surhomme** *nm* superman

**surhumain** *adj* superhuman

**surimposer** *vt* increase the tax on; over-tax; *ar* superimpose

**surimposition** *nf* superimposition; increase of taxation; over-taxation

**surintendance** *nf hist* stewardship

**surintendant** *nm hist* overseer, steward

**surir** *vi* turn sour

**surjet** *nm* overcasting; overcast seam

**surjeter** *vt* (5) overcast, whip (seam)

**sur-le-champ** *adv* immediately

**surlendemain** *nm* next day but one

**surmenage** *nm* overworking

**surmener** *vt* (6) overwork; **se ~** overwork, work too hard

**surmonter** *vt* surmount, overcome, get over; **se ~** control one's feelings

**surmultiplié** *adj vitesse* **~e** overdrive

**surnager** *vi* (3) float on the surface; subsist, survive

**surnaturel -elle** *adj* supernatural; extraordinary

**surnom** *nm* nickname

**surnombre** *nm* excess number, number over the regulation number; **en ~** in excess

**surnommer** *vt* name; nickname

**surnuméraire** *adj* supernumerary

**suroffre** *nf* better offer

**suroît** *nm naut* south-west wind, sou'wester

**surpasser** *vt* surpass; exceed, outdo; **se ~** excel oneself

**surpaye** *nf* extra pay

**surpayer** *vt* (7) overpay

**surpeuplé** *adj* overpopulated

**surpeuplement** *nm* overpopulation; overcrowding

**surplis** *nm* surplice

**surplomb** *nm* overhang; **être en ~** overhang

**surplomber** *vt* overhang; *vi* jut out, overhang

**surplus** *nm* excess, surplus; **au ~** besides, after all

**surpopulation** *nf* overpopulation

**surprenant** *adj* surprising, astonishing

**surprendre** *vt* (75) surprise, catch unawares; catch in the act; come upon unexpectedly, take by surprise; aston-

ish; overhear; take advantage of; disconcert; **se ~ à faire qch** catch oneself doing sth
**surpression** *nf* high pressure, excessive pressure
**surpris** *adj* surprised, amazed
**surprise** *nf* surprise, astonishment; unexpected present
**surprise-partie** *nf* bottle-party
**surproduction** *nf* overproduction
**surréalisme** *nm* surrealism
**surréaliste** *n + adj* surrealist
**surrénal** *adj* suprarenal; **les glandes ~es** adrenal glands
**sursalaire** *nm* supplementary wage, extra pay
**sursaturer** *vt* supersaturate
**sursaut** *nm* start, jump; **en ~** with a start
**sursauter** *vi* start; **faire ~ qn** startle s/o
**surseoir** *vi* (93) **~ à** defer, delay, put off
**sursis** *nm* leg delay, stay of proceedings; reprieve, deferment; **deux ans de prison avec ~** two years' suspended sentence
**surtaux** *nm* excessive rate
**surtaxe** *nf* surcharge; extra tax
**surtension** *nf elect* surge of voltage
¹**surtout** *nm* overcoat; centre-piece (table)
²**surtout** *adv* particularly, especially
**surveillance** *nf* supervision; watch, watching
**surveillant -e** *n* supervisor, overseer; teacher on duty
**surveiller** *vt* supervise; tend; watch over, look after
**survenir** *vi* (96) happen, occur; arise; arrive unexpectedly
**survêtement** *nm* warm overgarment
**survie** *nf* survival; life after death
**survireur -euse** *adj mot* with a tendency to over-steer
**survivance** *nf* survival; relic; reversion
**survivant -e** *n* survivor
**survivre** *vi* (98) survive
**survol** *nm* flying over; flight over
**survoler** *vt* fly over
**survolter** *vt elect* boost
**survolteur** *nm elect* booster
**sus (en)** *adv phr* in addition, extra
**susceptibilité** *nf* susceptibility; irritability
**susceptible** *adj* susceptible; sensitive; touchy; **~ de** liable to; capable of
**susciter** *vt* give rise to; rouse
**suscription** *nf* address (on letter)
**susdit** *adj* aforesaid
**susmentionné** *adj* above-mentioned
**susnommé** *adj* above-named
**suspect** *nm* suspect; *adj* suspicious, doubtful, suspect

**suspecter** *vt* suspect, doubt
**suspendre** *vt* suspend; hang up; postpone, adjourn; interrupt
**suspendu** *adj* suspended, hanging; **bien ~** well sprung; **pont ~** suspension bridge
**suspens** *nm* **en ~** in suspense, in uncertainty; in abeyance
**suspension** *nf* suspension, hanging; interruption, discontinuance; hanging lamp; *mot* springs
**sustentation** *nf* sustenance; support
**sustenter** *vt* sustain, support, nourish
**susurrement** *nm* murmuring; rustling
**susurrer** *vi* murmur, whisper
**suture** *nf anat* suture, join; **point de ~** stitch
**suturer** *vt* stitch, stitch up (wound)
**suzeraineté** *nf* suzerainty
**svastika** *nm* swastika
**svelte** *adj* slim, slender
**sveltesse** *nf* slimness, slenderness
**sycomore** *nm* sycamore
**sycophante** *nm* sycophant
**syllabe** *nf* syllable
**syllabique** *adj* syllabic
**syllepse** *nf* syllepsis
**syllogisme** *nm* syllogism
**sylphe** *nm* sylph
**sylphide** *nf* sylph; lovely woman
**sylvestre** *adj* woodland
**sylviculture** *nf* forestry
**symbiose** *nf* symbiosis
**symbole** *nm* symbol; conventional sign; creed
**symbolique** *adj* symbolic
**symboliser** *vt* symbolize
**symbolisme** *nm* symbolism
**symétrie** *nf* symmetry
**symétrique** *adj* symmetrical
**sympathie** *nf* sympathy; attraction; **avoir de la ~ pour qn** like s/o
**sympathique** *nm anat* **le grand ~** the sympathetic nerve; *adj* likeable, attractive, congenial; **encre ~** invisible ink
**sympathiser** *vi* have friendly feelings; sympathize
**symphonie** *nf* symphony
**symphonique** *adj* symphonic
**symptomatique** *adj* symptomatic
**symptôme** *nm* symptom; sign, indication
**synchroniser** *vt* synchronize
**syncope** *nf med* syncope, faint, swoon; *mus* syncopation; **tomber en ~** swoon
**syncoper** *vt mus* syncopate
**syndic** *nm* syndic, representative
**syndical** *adj* trade-union; syndical
**syndicalisme** *nm* trade-unionism; trade unions; trade-union action
**syndicat** *nm* (trade) union; syndicate; **~**

**d'initiative** local tourist office; ~
**ouvrier** trade union, *US* labor union
**syndiquer** *vt* enrol in a union; syndicate;
  **syndiqué** belonging to a union; **se ~**
  combine; form a trade union
**synecdoque** *nf* synecdoche
**synode** *nm eccles* synod
**synonyme** *nm* synonym; *adj* synonymous
**synoptique** *adj* synoptic
**synovie** *nf anat* synovia
**syntaxe** *nf* syntax
**syntaxique** *adj* syntactical

**synthèse** *nf* synthesis
**synthétique** *adj* synthetic
**synthétiser** *vt* synthesize
**Syrie** *nf* Syria
**syrien -ienne** *adj* Syrian
**systématique** *adj* systematic; dogmatic,
hide-bound
**systématiser** *vt* systematize
**système** *nm* system; scheme, method;
  *coll* ~ **D** resourcefulness; *sl* **il me tape
  sur le ~** he gets on my nerves; **par ~** in a
  set way, deliberately

# T

**ta** *poss adj f see* **ton**
**tabac** *nm* tobacco; tobacconist's shop;
  ~ **à priser** snuff; **bureau (débit) de ~**
  tobacconist's shop; *coll* **passer qn à ~**
  grill s/o, treat s/o roughly
**tabagie** *nf* place that reeks of tobacco
smoke
**tabasser** *vt coll* beat up
**tabatière** *nf* snuff-box
**tabellion** *nm leg + ar* scrivener
**tablature** *nf mus* notation
**table** *nf* table; eating, board; slab;
  tablet; list; ~ **d'écoute** bugging
  device; ~ **de nuit** bedside table; ~ **de
  toilette** dressing table; ~ **roulante** tea
  (dinner) trolley; **la sainte ~** the communion table; **mettre la ~** lay the
  table; **se mettre à ~** sit down to dinner
  (or lunch); **service de (par) petites ~s**
  separate tables
**tableau** *nm* board; notice-board; painting; list, table; ~ **d'avancement** promotion list; ~ **de bord** fascia;
  instrument panel; ~ **de chasse** bag
  (hunting); ~ **de contrôle** control
  panel; ~ **noir** blackboard
**tableautin** *nm* small picture
**tablée** *nf* group of people seated round
a table
**tabler** *vi* ~ **sur qch** count on sth
**tablette** *nf* shelf; sill; slab; bar (chocolate); ~ **s** tablets; **mettre qch sur ses
  ~s** make a note of sth
**tabletterie** *nf* fancy-goods industry;
inlaid ware
**tablier** *nm* apron; smock; blower (fire-

place); steel shutter; superstructure;
roadway (on bridge); *coll* **rendre son
~** stop doing one's job
**tabou** *nm* taboo
**tabouret** *nm* stool; footstool
**tabulateur** *nm* tabulator
**tabulatrice** *nf* punch-card machine
**tac** *nm* click; **répondre du ~ au ~**
answer quickly in the same vein
**tache** *nf* stain, spot; blemish, flaw; blot;
  **faire ~** jar, stand out as a blemish
**tâche** *nf* task; **à la ~** on piece-work;
  **prendre à ~ de** make every effort to
**tacher** *vt* stain; blemish, sully
**tâcher** *vi* try, endeavour
**tâcheron** *nm* hard-worker; *bui* jobber,
sub-contractor
**tacheter** *vt* (5) stain with spots; fleck,
speckle
**tachycardie** *nf med* tachycardia, rapid
heart-beat
**tachygraphe** *nm* tachograph
**tachymètre** *nm* tachometer, speedometer
**tacite** *adj* tacit, implied, understood
**taciturne** *adj* taciturn, uncommunicative
**taciturnité** *nf* taciturnity
**tacot** *nm coll* old crock (car)
**tact** *nm* touch; tact; **manquer de ~** be
tactless, act tactlessly
**tacticien -ienne** *n* tactician
**tactique** *nf* tactics; *adj* tactical
**tadorne** *nm orni* sheldrake
**taffetas** *nm* taffeta
**taïaut** *interj* tally-ho!

**taie** nf ~ d'oreiller pillow-case; speck (in eye), leucoma

**taillable** adj hist liable to pay the taille; ~ et corvéable à merci exploited on all sides

**taillade** nf cut, gash

**taillader** vt slash, gash

**taillanderie** nf edge-tool industry

**taillandier** nm edge-tool maker

**taillant** nm cutting edge

**taille** nf cutting; pruning, trimming; cut; edge (sword); trees growing again (after being cut); stature, height; waist; tally; hist direct tax; être de ~ à be strong enough to; pierre de ~ rough-hewn stone; tour de ~ waist measurement

**taillé** adj ready, prepared; ~ pour suitable for, made for; bien ~ well built

**taille-crayon** nm (pl invar or taille-crayons) pencil-sharpener

**taille-douce** nf copper-plate engraving

**tailler** vt cut; hew; prune, trim, clip; ~ une armée en pièces hack an army to pieces; sl se ~ clear off

**tailleur** nm tailor; cutter; hewer; (costume) ~ woman's suit; s'asseoir en ~ sit cross-legged

**tailleuse** nf dressmaker

**taillis** nm coppice, copse

**tailloir** nm trencher

**tain** nm silvering (mirror)

**taire** vt (69) keep silent about, suppress, hush up; faire ~ qn silence s/o; se ~ be silent, say nothing

**talc** nm French chalk; talc; poudre de ~ talcum powder

**talé** adj bruised (fruit)

**talent** nm talent, gift; avoir du ~ be gifted, be talented

**talentueux -euse** adj coll talented

**talkie-walkie** nm (pl talkies-walkies) walkie-talkie

**talle** nf agr+hort sucker

**taller** vi agr+hort throw out suckers

**taloche** nf coll cuff, clout

**talon** nm heel; crust; counterfoil; être sur les ~s de qn dog s/o's footsteps; montrer (tourner) les ~s clear off, run away

**talonner** vt follow closely, dog; spur on; sp heel

**talonnette** nf heel-piece; reinforcement (for bottom of trouser-leg)

**talonneur** nm sp hooker

**talonnière** nf heel-wing

**talquer** vt cover or sprinkle with talcum powder

**talus** nm slope; bank, embankment

**tamarinier** nm tamarind(-tree)

**tamaris** nm bot tamarisk

**tambour** nm drum; drummer; winding-drum, barrel; revolving door; ~ de basque tambourine; ~ de frein brake-drum; ~ de ville town-crier; coll mener qn ~ battant jolly s/o along; sans ~ ni trompette without fuss; secretly

**tambourin** nm long narrow drum; tambourine

**tambouriner** vt make known by beating on a drum; make known; vi beat a drum; drum, beat a tattoo

**tambour-major** nm (pl tambours-majors) drum-major

**tamia** nm chipmunk

**tamis** nm sieve; riddle; passer au ~ sift

**Tamise** nf Thames

**tamiser** vt sift, bolt (flour); strain, filter

**tampon** nm stopper, plug, bung; wad, plug; rubber-stamp; pad; wall-plug; buffer; ~ hygiénique tampon, sanitary towel

**tamponnement** nm collision; plugging; dabbing

**tamponner** vt bang into, run into; plug; dab

**tam-tam** nm tom-tom; coll faire du ~ make a great noise

**tan** nm tanner's bark

**tancer** vt (4) reprimand, scold

**tanche** nf tench

**tandis que** conj phr whereas; whilst

**tangage** nm pitching (ship)

**tangente** nf tangent; coll s'échapper par la ~ dodge the question; slip away

**tangentiel -ielle** adj tangential

**tango** nm tango; adj invar orange-coloured

**tanguer** vi naut pitch

**tanière** nf den, lair

**tanin** nm tannin

**tanne** nf blackhead

**tanné** nm tan; adj tanned (leather, face)

**tannée** nf spent tan; coll thrashing

**tanner** vt tan; coll bore, pester; sl thrash

**tannerie** nf tannery

**tanneur** nm tanner

**tannique** adj tannic

**tant** adv so much; as much; as long; ~ et plus ever so many; ever so much; ~ mieux! so much the better!, good!; ~ pis so much the worse; it can't be helped; coll ~ qu'à faire while one's about it; ~ que as long as; ~ s'en faut que far from; ~ soit peu ever so little; en ~ que in the capacity of, qua; in so far as; faire ~ et si bien que work to such good effect that; si ~ est que if indeed; coll vous m'en direz ~! you don't say so!

**tante** nf aunt; sl homosexual; coll ma ~ pawnshop

**tantième** nm share, percentage

**tantinet** *nm coll* small quantity, tiny bit, dash, touch

**tantôt** *nm coll* afternoon; *adv* soon, presently; a short time ago, just now; ~ ... ~ at one time ... at another time; **à** ~ see you presently, so long

**taon** *nm* horse-fly

**tapage** *nm* noise, din; *leg* ~ **nocturne** disturbing of the peace at night

**tapageur -euse** *adj* rowdy, noisy; showy, flashy

**tapant** *adj* striking; **à midi** ~ on the stroke of noon

¹**tape** *nf* tap, pat, rap

²**tape** *nf* stopper, plug

**tapé** *adj* dried (fruit); *coll* **bien** ~ successful

**tape-à-l'œil** *adj invar coll* flashy

**tapecul** *nm* see-saw; boneshaking carriage

**tapée** *nf sl* large quantity, mass

**taper** *vt* strike, pat; type; *coll* borrow money from; *sl* **se** ~ **qch** get oneself sth; *vi* ~ **sur** hit; *coll* ~ **dans** help oneself from; ~ **sur qn** slang s/o

**tapette** *nf* mallet; swatter; carpet-beater; *coll* tongue; *sl* queer, fairy

**tapin** *nm sl* **faire le** ~ walk the street (prostitute)

**tapinois (en)** *adv phr* stealthily

**tapir (se)** *v refl* cower, squat, crouch

**tapis** *nm* carpet; cover; ~ **roulant** conveyor belt; ~ **vert** gaming table; **aller au** ~ get knocked down (boxing); **amuser le** ~ keep the company amused; **être sur le** ~ be under discussion; **mettre qch sur le** ~ bring sth up for discussion

**tapis-brosse** *nm* door-mat

**tapisser** *vt* hang with tapestry; paper (wall); plaster (with adverts)

**tapisserie** *nf* tapestry, hangings; tapestry-making; wallpaper; **faire** ~ be a wall-flower (at a dance)

**tapissier -ière** *n* tapestry-worker; paper-hanger; upholsterer

**tapoter** *vt coll* pat, thrum

**taquet** *nm* bracket; angle-block

**taquin** *adj* fond of teasing

**taquiner** *vt* tease

**taquinerie** *nf* teasing; teasing nature

**tarabiscoté** *adj* heavily ornamented; affected

**tarabuster** *vt* plague, pester

**tarare** *nm* winnowing-machine

**taratata** *interj* fiddlesticks!

**taraud** *nm mech* tap

**tarauder** *vt mech* tap, thread

**tard** *nm* **sur le** ~ late in life; at a late hour; *adv* late

**tarder** *vi* delay; be a long time; ~ **à faire qch** be a long time doing sth; defer

doing sth; **il me tarde de** I am longing to; **sans** ~ without delay

**tardif -ive** *adj* belated, late; slow, tardy

**tardiveté** *nf* lateness, backwardness

**tare** *nf* defect, blemish; allowance for weight, tare; **faire la** ~ allow for the tare

**taré** *adj* tainted, blemished, spoilt

**tarentelle** *nf* tarantella

**tarentule** *nf* tarantula

**tarer** *vt comm* tare, ascertain (weight of packing)

**targette** *nf* small (flat) bolt

**targuer (se)** *v refl* boast, pride oneself

**tarière** *nf* auger; drill; *ent* terebra

**tarif** *nm* price-list, tariff; charge, price; *coll* **c'est le** ~ that's what it costs; that's what you must expect

**tarifer** *vt* fix the price of

**tarir** *vt* dry up; exhaust; *vi* run dry; stop, cease; **ne pas** ~ **sur** not cease talking about

**tarse** *nm anat + zool* tarsus

**tartine** *nf* slice of bread and butter; *coll* long speech

**tartiner** *vt* spread (with butter); **fromage à** ~ cheese spread

**tartre** *nm* tartar; scale, fur

**tartreux -euse** *adj* tartarous

**tartrique** *adj* tartaric (acid)

**tartuf(f)e** *nm* hypocrite

**tartuf(f)erie** *nf* hypocrisy

**tas** *nm* pile, heap; *coll* great deal, lot; **dans le** ~ from the mass; *fig* **sur le** ~ at work; **tirer dans le** ~ fire at random

**tasse** *nf* cup; cupful

**tassé** *adj* abundant, slap-up; strong

**tasseau** *nm* cleat, batten; bracket; lug

**tasser** *vt* compress, squeeze together, pack; **se** ~ settle, subside; *coll* settle down, calm down

**taste-vin, tâte-vin** *nm invar* pipette or cup for tasting wine

**tâter** *vt* feel, touch, handle; ~ **de (à)** sample, try; ~ **le terrain** sound out the ground; **se** ~ examine oneself; *coll* hesitate

**tatillon -onne** *adj* fussy, finicky, meddlesome

**tâtonner** *vi* grope, feel one's way

**tâtons (à)** *adv phr* gropingly

**tatouage** *nm* tattooing

**tatouer** *vt* tattoo

**taudis** *nm* hovel, miserable lodging

**taule, tôle** *nf sl* room; *sl* prison

**taulier -ière, tôlier -ière** *n sl* hotel-keeper

**taupe** *nf* mole

**taupé** *adj* **feutre** ~ velours felt

**taupier** *nm* mole-catcher

**taupière** *nf* mole-trap

**taupinière** *nf* mole-hill

**taureau** *nm* bull

**taurillon** nm bull-calf
**tauromachie** nf bull-fighting
**tautologie** nf tautology
**taux** nm rate, fixed price
**taveler** vt (5) speckle, spot
**taverne** nf café; café with old-world décor
**taxateur** nm taxer, assessor
**taxation** nf fixing (prices, wages); taxing; assessment
**taxe** nf fixed price; fixed rate; charge; tax, duty; taxing; ~ à (sur) la valeur ajoutée (T.V.A.) value added tax (V.A.T.)
**taxer** vt regulate (price, rate); charge; tax, accuse
**taxidermie** nf taxidermy
**taximètre** nm taximeter, coll clock
**taxiphone** nm public telephone
**tchécoslovaque** adj Czechoslovak
**Tchécoslovaquie** nf Czechoslovakia
**Tchèque** n Czech
**tchèque** nm Czech (language); adj Czech
**te** (t' before vowel) pers pron you; to you; thee, thyself
¹**té** interj (S. France) Well!, Fancy!
²**té** nm T-shaped object; T-square; T-bracket
**technicien -ienne** n qualified person, technician
**technique** nf technics; technique; adj technical
**technocrate** n technocrat; partisan of technocracy
**technologie** nf technology
**technologique** adj technological
**teck, tek** nm teak
**teckel** nm dachshund
**tectonique** nf tectonics; adj tectonic
**teigne** nf moth; scalp disease; coll nasty person, pest
**teigneux -euse** n + adj (person) suffering from scalp disease
**teiller** vt strip (flax)
**teindre** vt (55) dye; se ~ dye one's hair
**teint** nm dye; complexion
**teinte** nf shade, hue; slight touch, tinge
**teinter** vt tint
**teinture** nf dyeing; tinting; dye, colour, hue; tincture
**teinturerie** nf dyeing; dry-cleaners
**teinturier -ière** n dry-cleaner; dyer
**tek** nm see teck
**tel** (f telle) adj such; so great; like, as; ~ quel just as it is; de ~ le sorte que so that, in such a way that; pron such a one, such; ~ et ~ this man and that; ~ qui he who; un ~ so-and-so
**télé** nf abbr coll television
**télébenne** nf see télécabine
**télécabine** nf cable-car; cable railway

**télécommande** nf remote control
**télécommander** vt control by remote control
**téléférique, téléphérique** nm cable-car railway
**télégénique** adj that looks good on the TV screen
**télégramme** nm telegram
**télégraphe** nm telegraph
**télégraphie** nf telegraphy; ~ sans fil wireless telegraphy
**télégraphier** vt + vi telegraph, wire
**télégraphique** adj telegraphic
**télégraphiste** n telegraphist
**téléguidage** nm remote control, radio control
**téléguider** vt guide by remote control, radio control; engin téléguidé guided missile
**téléimprimeur** nm teleprinter, US teletypewriter
**télémécanique** nf telemechanics
**télémètre** nm range-finder
**téléobjectif** nm telescopic lens
**téléologie** nf teleology
**télépathie** nf telepathy
**télépathique** adj telepathic
**téléphérique** nm see téléférique
**téléphone** nm telephone; ~ arabe bush telegraph, grape-vine; ~ rouge hot line (White House–Kremlin); coup de ~ phone call
**téléphoner** vt + vi telephone, US call
**téléphonie** nf telephony
**téléphonique** adj telephonic
**téléphoniste** n telephonist
**télescopage** nm telescoping
**télescoper** vt + vi telescope
**télescopique** adj telescopic
**téléscripteur** nm teleprinter, US teletypewriter
**télésiège** nm chairlift
**téléski** nm ski-lift
**téléspectateur -trice** n viewer
**télétype** nm teleprinter, US teletypewriter
**téléviser** vt televize
**téléviseur** nm television set
**tellement** adv so, in such a way, to such an extent; coll a lot, a great deal
**tellurien -ienne** adj tellurian, earth
**téméraire** adj rash, reckless, foolhardy
**témérité** nf temerity, foolhardiness
**témoignage** nm testimony, evidence; mark, token; en ~ de as a token of; rendre ~ à bear grateful witness to; give evidence in favour of
**témoigner** vt testify, bear witness to; vi testify, bear witness; ~ de bear witness to; show, display
**témoin** nm witness; sign, proof; boundary-mark; sp baton; appartement ~

show (model) flat; **barre des ~ s** witness box; *leg* **en ~ de quoi** in witness whereof; **lampe ~** pilot light; **prendre qn à ~** call s/o to witness

**tempe** *nf anat* temple

**tempérament** *nm* temperament; constitution; **avoir du ~** be lusty; **vente à ~** hire-purchase

**tempérance** *nf* moderation, temperance; abstinence (from drink)

**tempérant** *adj* moderate, temperate

**température** *nf* temperature

**tempéré** *adj* mild, temperate; restrained

**tempérer** *vt* (6) moderate, temper

**tempête** *nf* storm, tempest

**tempêter** *vi* rage, fulminate

**tempêtueux -ueuse** *adj* tempestuous, stormy

**temple** *nm* temple; Protestant church; **Ordre du Temple** Order of the Knights Templars

**templier** *nm hist* Templar

**temporaire** *adj* temporary, provisional

**temporel -elle** *adj* temporal, secular

**temporisateur -trice** *n* temporizer

**temporiser** *vi* temporize

**temps** *nm* time; weather; *gramm* tense; *mus* beat; **à ~** in good time; **avant le ~** prematurely; **avec le ~** in the course of time; **avoir fait son ~** be worn out; **de ~ à autre (de ~ en ~)** from time to time; **en même ~** at the same time; **en ~ et lieu** at the appropriate time and place; **gros ~** stormy weather at sea; **il est grand ~ de** it is high time to; **le ~ de m'habiller, je descends** just give me time to dress, and I'll come down; **marquer un ~** pause; **moteur à deux ~** two-stroke engine; **par tous les ~** in all kinds of weather; *coll* **se donner du bon ~** enjoy oneself, have a good time

**tenable** *adj* bearable

**tenace** *adj* tough; tenacious, persistent, stubborn

**ténacité** *nf* tenacity; toughness; adhesiveness

**tenaille** *nf usu pl* pincers

**tenancier -ière** *n* lessee manager(ess)

**tenant** *nm* champion, supporter (opinion); *sp* holder (title); **d'un seul ~** in one block; **les ~ s et les aboutissants** adjacent parts; full details, all relevant details; *adj* **séance ~ e** immediately

**tendance** *nf* tendency, propensity

**tendancieux -ieuse** *adj* tendentious

¹**tendeur -euse** *n* layer; hanger

²**tendeur** *nm* stretcher, tightener; elastic strap (for luggage); chain-adjuster (bicycle)

**tendoir** *nm* drying-line

¹**tendre** *vt* stretch; set, fix up; hold out; pitch (tent); paper (room); **~ l'oreille** prick up one's ears; *vi* tend, conduce

²**tendre** *adj* tender, soft, delicate; early (age); affectionate, loving

**tendresse** *nf* tenderness, fondness

**tendron** *nm cul* gristle (veal)

**tendu** *adj* tense; taut, tight

**ténèbres** *nfpl* darkness, gloom; *fig* ignorance

**ténébreux -euse** *adj* gloomy, dark; mysterious

**teneur** *nf* purport, tenor; content, amount

**ténia** *nm* tapeworm

**tenir** *vt* (96) hold; take up, occupy; keep, maintain; contain; run, manage; restrain, hold back; **~ la chambre** be confined to one's room; **~ la (sa) droite (gauche)** keep to the right (left); **~ qch de qn** have sth from s/o; **tenez-vous le pour dit** I shan't tell you again; **tiens!** fancy!, well!; *vi* hold, stick fast; be contained, fit into; **~ à** be fond of, be keen on; value; result from; **~ à ce qu'on fasse qch** be insistent that sth should be done; **~ bon** hold fast, stand fast; **~ de qn** take after s/o; **~ pour** be in favour of; **il ne tient qu'à vous** it all depends on you; **ne pas ~ en place** be restless; **qu'à cela ne tienne!** never mind that!; **un tiens vaut mieux que deux tu l'auras** a bird in the hand is worth two in the bush; **se ~** remain; contain oneself; **se ~ tranquille** keep quiet; **ne pas savoir à quoi s'en ~** not know what to believe; **s'en ~ à qch** abide by sth, want nothing more; **tenez-vous bien** mind out, watch it; **tiens-toi** behave yourself

**tension** *nf* tension; stretching; tightness; tenseness

**tentaculaire** *adj* tentacular

**tentacule** *nm* tentacle

**tentant** *adj* tempting, alluring

**tentateur -trice** *n* tempter (temptress); *adj* tempting

**tentatif -ive** *adj* tentative

**tentation** *nf* temptation

**tentative** *nf* attempt

**tente** *nf* tent

**tenter** *vt* tempt; try, attempt

**tenture** *nf* hangings, tapestry

**tenu** *adj* kept; neat, tidy; **être ~ de (à)** be obliged to; **mal ~** neglected, untidy

**ténu** *adj* tenuous, slender

**tenue** *nf* keeping, maintaining; behaviour, bearing; dress; *mus* sustained note; **~ de livres** book-keeping; **~ de route** road-holding; **avoir de la ~** have good manners; **d'une seule ~** without interruption; **en grande ~** in full dress; *coll* **en petite ~** scantily dressed; **en ~** in uniform; **tout d'une ~** without interruption

**ténuité** *nf* tenuity; slenderness; fineness

**ter** *adv* three times

**tératologie** *nf* teratology

**térébenthine** *nf* turpentine

**tergiverser** *vi* beat about the bush, tergiversate

**terme** *nm* term; end, limit; appointed time; date for paying (rent, etc); rent, payment; expression, word; **~s** terms, footing; conditions; wording; **à court ~** short-term; short-dated; **à long ~** long-term; long-dated; **marché à ~** forward transaction; **mettre un ~ à** put an end to; **né avant ~** premature

**terminaison** *nf* termination, ending

**terminale** *nf* last year at secondary school ( = Upper Sixth)

**terminer** *vt* terminate, finish, conclude; complete; **se ~** come to an end

**terminologie** *nf* terminology

**ternaire** *adj* ternary

¹**terne** *nm* tern, set of three

²**terne** *adj* dull, flat, colourless

**ternir** *vt* tarnish; dull; **se ~** grow dull; become tarnished

**terrain** *nm* ground; plot, piece of ground; *sp* field; **connaître le ~** know the people one has to deal with; **être sur son ~** be on familiar ground; **véhicule tout ~** cross-country vehicle

**terrasse** *nf* terrace; **en ~** terraced

**terrassement** *nm* banking; terracing; earthwork

**terrasser** *vt* crush, knock down, beat; dismay

**terrassier** *nm* navvy

**terre** *nf* earth; world; land, ground; soil; **~s** property, estate; **~ à ~** matter-of-fact, down-to-earth; ordinary; **~ cuite** terra cotta; **être sur ~** be alive, exist; *elect* **mettre à la ~** earth; **par ~** on the ground; to the ground; **porter qn en ~** bury s/o

**terreau** *nm* vegetable mould

**Terre-Neuve** *nf* Newfoundland

**terre-neuve** *nm invar* Newfoundland dog

**terre-plein** *nm* terrace, earth platform

**terrer** *vt* earth up; cover with earth; **se ~** go to ground, hide below ground; hide, stay concealed

**terrestre** *adj* terrestrial; earthly, worldly

**terreur** *nf* terror, dread

**terreux -euse** *adj* earthy; dirty; sickly, ashy

**terrible** *adj* terrible; *coll* marvellous, terrific

**terrien -ienne** *n* earth-dweller; land-dweller; *adj* land-owning; of the land

**terrier** *nm* burrow, earth, hole; terrier

**terrifiant** *adj* terrifying

**terrifier** *vt* terrify

**terrine** *nf* earthenware pot; earthenware vessel; terrine

**territoire** *nm* territory

**terroir** *nm* soil; **sentir le ~** betray one's native origins

**terroriser** *vt* terrorize

**terrorisme** *nm* terrorism

**terroriste** *n* terrorist

**tertiaire** *adj* tertiary

**tertre** *nm* hillock, mound

**tes** *poss adj pl see* **ton**

**tesson** *nm* piece (broken glass, etc), shard

**test** *nm see* **têt**

**testament** *nm* will, testament; **mettre (coucher) qn sur son ~** mention s/o in one's will

**testamentaire** *adj* testamentary

**testateur -trice** *n* testator (testatrix)

¹**tester** *vi* make one's will

²**tester** *vt* test, examine

**testicule** *nm* testicle

**têt, test** *nm chem* small fire-clay cup, crucible

**tétanique** *adj med* tetanic

**tétanos** *nm med* tetanus, lock-jaw

**têtard** *nm* tadpole; pollard

**tête** *nf* head; top; beginning; front; brains, imagination; leader; *coll* face; **~ baissée** rashly, headlong; **~ brûlée** desperate character; **~ de bielle** big end; **~ de lecture** repro head; **~ de ligne** rail-head; starting point; **~ de mort** skull; **avoir mal à la ~** have a headache; **courber la ~** submit; *coll* **en avoir par-dessus la ~** be fed up; **en faire à sa ~** have one's way, do as one likes; **faire une ~** pull a long face; **femme de ~** capable woman; **forte ~** unruly character; **ne pas savoir où donner de la ~** not know where to turn; **se casser la ~** rack one's brains; **signe de ~** nod; **tenir ~ à qn** stand up to s/o; **tourner la ~ à qn** drive s/o mad

**tête-à-queue** *nm invar mot* **faire un ~** spin right round

**tête-à-tête** *nm invar* private conversation; **en ~** alone together

**tête-bêche** *adv* head to foot (alongside)

**tête-de-loup** *nf* ( *pl* **têtes-de-loup**) long-handled brush, wall-broom

**tête-de-nègre** *nm + adj invar* dark brown

**tétée** *nf* suck, feeding; milk drunk at one feed

**téter** *vt + vi* (6) suck, feed

**têtière** *nf* head-stall; head-rest; anti-macassar

tétin *nm* nipple
tétine *nf* dug, udder; teat
téton *nm coll* tit, nipple
tétrarchie *nf* tetrarchy
tétras *nm* grouse
tette *nf* dug, teat
têtu *adj* stubborn, obstinate
teuf-teuf *nm invar coll* vintage car
teutonique *adj* Teutonic
texte *nm* text
textuel -uelle *adj* textual
thaumaturge *nm* miracle-worker
thé *nm* tea; tea-party
théâtral *adj* theatrical
théâtre *nm* theatre; scene, stage; dramatic art; dramatic works; **coup de ~** dramatic turn of events, startling event; **faire du ~** act; **pièce de ~** play
thébaïde *nf* wilderness; solitary retreat
théière *nf* tea-pot
théisme *nm* theism
théiste *n* theist; *adj* theistic
thématique *adj* thematic
thème *nm* topic, theme; prose composition; **fort en ~** swot, bookworm
théocratie *nf* theocracy
théologal *adj* relating to theology
théologie *nf* theology
théologien *nm* theologian
théologique *adj* theological
théorème *nm* theorem
théoricien -ienne *n* theorist
théorie *nf* theory; group in procession
théorique *adj* theoretical
théoriser *vi* theorize
théosophie *nf* theosophy
thérapeutique *nf* therapeutics; *adj* therapeutic
thermes *nmpl* hot springs, thermal baths; Roman baths
thermidor *nm hist* eleventh month of the French Republican calendar (July to August)
thermie *nf* therm
thermique *adj* thermic
thermo-dynamique *nf* thermodynamics
thermogène *adj* heat-producing
thermomètre *nm* thermometer
thésauriser *vt* pile up, hoard (money)
thèse *nf* thesis; argument, proposition
thibaude *nf* coarse hair-cloth, underlay
thon *nm* tunny, tuna
thoracique *adj* thoracic
thrombose *nf* thrombosis
thuriféraire *nm* incense-bearer; flatterer
thym *nm* thyme
thyroïde *nf* thyroid gland
tiare *nf* tiara
Tibétain -e *n* Tibetan
tibétain *nm* Tibetan (language); *adj* Tibetan
tic *nm* twitching, tic; mannerism, trick

ticket *nm* ticket, voucher, coupon, slip; **~ modérateur** part-payment of French health service charges; *coll* **avoir un (le) ~ avec** be a hit with
tic-tac *nm invar* tick-tock, ticking
tiède *adj* tepid, lukewarm
tiédeur *nf* tepidity, lukewarmness; lack of enthusiasm
tiédir *vt* make lukewarm; *vi* become lukewarm
tien (*f* tienne) *n* yours; thine; your property; **les ~s** your family and relatives; *pron* yours; thine
tiens *interj* fancy!; well!; hullo!
tierce *nf mus* third; tierce (fencing); run of three cards; *print* final proof
tiercé *nm* bet (to forecast first three horses in race)
tiercelet *nm* male falcon
tiers *nm* third; third party, third person; **~ provisionnel** third of income tax (to be paid in advance); **le ~ et le quart** anybody; *adj* (*f* tierce) ar third; *hist* **~ état** third estate, bourgeoisie; **~ monde** third world
tige *nf* stalk, stem; spindle, shaft
tignasse *nf* mop of hair
tigré *adj* striped; speckled
tigresse *nf* tigress
tillac *nm naut ar* upper deck
tilleul *nm* lime-tree; lime-blossom tea; **vert ~** lime-coloured
tilt *nm coll* **faire ~** have a shock effect
timbale *nf* kettledrum; metal mug; circular pie-dish; kind of vol-au-vent
timbrage *nm* franking
timbre *nm* bell; timbre (voice); (postage-)stamp; stamp duty; shell (helmet); **~ de la poste** postmark
timbré *adj* stamped; *coll* cracked, crackbrained; sonorous
timbrer *vt* stamp
timide *adj* timid; timorous; shy
timidité *nf* timidity
timon *nm* pole (cart, etc); *naut + ar* rudder
timonier *nm naut* helmsman; wheelhorse
timoré *adj* fearful, timorous
tin *nm naut* chock, stocks
tinette *nf* soil-tub; *coll* lavatory
tintamarre *nm coll* racket, din
tintement *nm* ringing
tinter *vt* ring, toll; *vi* tinkle; chink; ring
tintin *nm sl* nothing at all
tintinnabuler *vi* tinkle
tintouin *nm coll* worry, trouble; din
tique *nf ent* tick
tiquer *vi coll* show surprise, show annoyance
tiqueté *adj* speckled, mottled

**tiqueur -euse** *n* person with a manner-ism
**tir** *nm* shooting; gunnery; firing; shooting-gallery, rifle-range; **à ~ rapide** quick-firing
**tirade** *nf* declamation, long speech; tirade
**tirage** *nm* pulling; draught; drawing; draw; number of copies printed; *print + phot* printing off; circulation
**tiraillement** *nm* tugging; *coll* quarrel-ling, wrangling
**tirailler** *vt* pull, tug; *fig* pester; (pain) stab at; *vi* shoot wildly
**tirailleur** *nm* sharp-shooter
**tirant** *nm* purse-string; boot-tag; sinew (meat); tie-beam, tie-rod; *naut* **~ d'eau** displacement
**tire** *nf* **voleur à la ~** pickpocket
**tiré** *adj* drawn, haggard
**tire-au-cul** *nm invar sl* shirker
**tire-au-flanc** *nm invar coll* shirker
**tire-botte** *nm* boot-jack
**tire-bouchon** *nm* corkscrew
**tire-bouton** *nm* button-hook
**tire-d'aile (à)** *adv phr* swiftly, flying fast
**tire-fesses** *nm coll* ski-lift
**tire-fond** *nm invar* long bolt; ring (screwed into ceiling)
**tire-laine** *nm invar obs* robber, footpad
**tire-larigot (à)** *adv phr coll* abundantly, copiously
**tire-ligne** *nm* drawing-pen; scribing awl
**tirelire** *nf* money-box; *sl* stomach
**tirer** *vt* pull, tug, haul; stretch, pull out; extract; pull off; draw; print off; fire, let off; gain; **~ d'embarras** get out of an awkward situation; **~ parti de qch** take advantage of sth; *vulg* **~ un coup** have it off; **~ une conséquence** con-clude; *vi* pull; tend, verge; draw (chim-ney); shoot; **~ à sa fin** draw to an end; *sl* **se ~** scram, clear off; **se ~ de** extricate oneself from
**tiret** *nm* dash
**tirette** *nf* flue damper; tablet, sliding shelf
**tireur -euse** *n* drawer; marksman; **tireuse de cartes** fortune-teller
**tiroir** *nm* drawer; slide-valve
**tiroir-caisse** *nm* (*pl* **tiroirs-caisses**) till, cash register
**tisane** *nf* herb tea
**tison** *nm* fire-brand; fusee
**tisonner** *vt* poke, stir (fire)
**tisonnier** *nm* poker
**tisser** *vt* weave
**tisserand -e** *n* weaver
**tisseur -euse** *n* weaver
**tissu** *nm* tissue; cloth, fabric; *adj ar* woven; mixed
**tissu-éponge** *nm* (*pl* **tissus-éponge**) towelling
**tissure** *nf* texture
**titane** *nm* titanium
**titi** *nm sl* urchin, cheeky little fellow
**titiller** *vt* titillate; tickle
**titrage** *nm chem* titration; assaying; sizing
**titre** *nm* title; diploma, certificate; claim; heading; right; grade (ore); titre, strength (chemical solution); **~ s** stocks and shares; **à juste ~** rightly; **à quel ~?** by what right?; **à ~ de** by right of; **en ~** titular
**titré** *adj* titled; titrated, standard (solution)
**titrer** *vt* give a title to; titrate; assay; size; give sub-titles to
**tituber** *vi* stagger, reel about
**titulaire** *n* holder; incumbent; bearer; *adj* titular
**titulariser** *vt* establish, confirm the appointment of
**toboggan** *nm* toboggan; slide, chute; temporary overpass
**¹toc** *nm coll* cheap imitation (jewellery, etc)
**²toc** *interj* tap!
**tocante** *nf see* **toquante**
**tocard** *nm* poor race-horse; *sl* useless individual; *adj coll* ugly, poor
**toge** *nf* toga; gown, robe (judge)
**tohu-bohu** *nm* confusion; hubbub
**toi** *pers pron* you; thou
**toile** *nf* linen, cloth; canvas; oil paint-ing; sail; **~ d'araignée** spider's web; **~ de coton** calico; **~ de fond** back-cloth
**toilette** *nf* wash-stand; toilet-table, dressing-table; washing, dressing; toilet; dress, costume; tailor's wrap-per; **~ s** lavatory; **en grande ~** in full dress
**toi-même** *pers pron* yourself; thyself
**toise** *nf* measuring instrument; *ar* fathom
**toiser** *vt* measure; size up, eye from head to foot
**toison** *nf* fleece; mop of hair
**toit** *nm* roof; house, home; **crier qch sur les ~ s** shout sth all over the place, broadcast sth
**toiture** *nf* roofing, roof
**¹tôle** *nf* sheet-metal, sheet-iron; **~ ondulée** corrugated iron
**²tôle** *nf see* **taule**
**tolérable** *adj* bearable, tolerable
**tolérance** *nf* tolerance; toleration; **maison de ~** brothel
**tolérer** *vt* (6) tolerate; wink at, close one's eyes to
**tôlerie** *nf* sheet-iron; sheet-iron works
**tolet** *nm naut* thole-pin

¹**tôlier** *nm* sheet-iron dealer; sheet-iron worker; *mot* panel-beater

²**tôlier -ière** *n see* **taulier -ière**

**tollé** *nm* furious cries, hue and cry

**tomate** *nf* tomato

**tombal** *adj* relating to tombs; **pierre ~ e** tombstone

**tombant** *adj* falling; drooping; **à la nuit ~ e** at nightfall

**tombée** *nf* fall

**tomber** *nm* **au ~ du jour** at nightfall; *vt sl* throw to the ground, make fall; *sl* seduce; *coll* **~ la veste** take off one's jacket; *vi* fall, fall down, drop down; abate, drop, decline; fail; hang down, hang; lapse; **~ bien** come at the right time; **~ de sommeil** be dead-tired; **~ sous le sens** be evident; **~ sur** attack, fall upon; light on, meet; **faire ~ qn** knock s/o down, knock s/o over; **laisser ~** drop; *coll* **laisser ~ qn** drop s/o; **se laisser ~** drop, sink

**tombereau** *nm* tip-cart, tumbril

**tombeur** *nm* wrestler who overthrows his opponent; *coll* seducer

**tombola** *nf* lottery

**tomme** *nf* fat cheese from S.E. France

**tom-pouce** *nm invar coll* tiny man; small collapsible umbrella

¹**ton** *nm* tone; intonation; breeding, manners; *mus* pitch; *mus* key; colour, tint; **bon ~** good form; **donner le ~** set the fashion; **faire baisser le ~ à qn** make s/o sing small, take s/o down a peg

²**ton** *poss adj* (*f* **ta**, *pl* **tes**) your; thy

**tonalité** *nf* tonality; shade; dialling tone

**tondeur -euse** *n* shearer, clipper

**tondeuse** *nf* lawn-mower; hair-clippers; shears, shearing machine

**tondre** *vt* shear, clip; mow; *coll* fleece, rook

**tonifiant** *adj* tonic, bracing

**tonifier** *vt* brace, tone up, invigorate

**tonique** *nm* tonic; tonic accent; *nf mus* key-note; *adj* tonic

**tonitruant** *adj* stentorian, thunderous

**tonne** *nf* (metric) ton; tun

**tonneau** *nm* barrel, cask; *naut* ton; somersault; *aer* roll

**tonnelet** *nm* small barrel

**tonnelier** *nm* cooper

**tonnelle** *nf* arbour, bower

**tonner** *vi* thunder; boom; fulminate

**tonnerre** *nm* thunder; thunderbolt, lightning; rumble; *coll* **c'est du ~** it's terrific; **coup de ~** thunderclap

**tonsurer** *vt* tonsure

**tonte** *nf* sheep-shearing; shearing-time; clip

**tonton** *nm coll* uncle

**tonus** *nm* tone (muscle); *coll* energy

**top** *nm rad* pip

**topaze** *nf* topaz

**toper** *vi* agree, shake hands on it; **tope!** done!, agreed!

**topinambour** *nm* Jerusalem artichoke

**topique** *nm* topical remedy; commonplace; *adj med* topical

**topo** *nm* speech, exposé; plan, sketchplan

**topographe** *nm* topographer

**topographie** *nf* topography

**topographique** *adj* topographical

**toponymie** *nf* toponymy

**toquade** *nf coll* passing fancy, infatuation

**toquante** *nf sl* watch

**toque** *nf* cap, toque

**toqué** *adj coll* crazy, mad; **être ~ de qn** be infatuated with s/o

**toquer (se)** *v refl coll* **~ de qn** become infatuated with s/o

**torche** *nf* torch; twist of straw

**torcher** *vt* wipe, wipe clean; *coll* botch, skimp

**torchère** *nf* candelabrum; standard-lamp

**torchis** *nm bui* daub

**torchon** *nm* dish-cloth, floor-cloth, duster, rag; **le ~ brûle** they are quarrelling

**torchonner** *vt coll* botch, skimp

**tordant** *adj coll* screamingly funny

**tord-boyaux** *nm coll* strong spirits, rot-gut

**tordre** *vt* twist; wring; **se ~** writhe, twist; **se ~ de rire** split one's sides with laughter; **se ~ les mains** wring one's hands

**tordu** *adj* twisted; *coll* strange; *coll* crazy

**toréer** *vi* engage in bull-fighting

**torgnole** *nf coll* slap, blow, cuff

**tornade** *nf* tornado

**torpédo** *nf mot* open tourer

**torpeur** *nf* torpor

**torpille** *nf* torpedo

**torpiller** *vt* torpedo

**torpilleur** *nm* torpedo-boat; torpedo man

**torréfaction** *nf* roasting (coffee, etc)

**torréfier** *vt* roast (coffee, etc); scorch

**torrentiel -ielle** *adj* torrential

**torrentueux -ueuse** *adj* torrent-like

**torride** *adj* torrid; scorching

**tors** *adj* twisted

**torsade** *nf* twisted fringe; cable moulding; **~ de cheveux** coil of hair

**torsader** *vt* twist

**torse** *nm* bust

**torsion** *nf* twisting, torsion

**tort** *nm* wrong, fault; harm, injury; **à ~** wrongly; **à ~ et à travers** without rhyme or reason, indiscriminately;

**tourner**

avoir ~ be wrong; **donner** ~ **à qn** decide against s/o; **faire** ~ **à** harm, injure; **se mettre dans son** ~ put oneself in the wrong

**torticolis** *nm* crick in the neck, stiff neck

**tortillage** *nm* quibbling

**tortillard** *nm* slow local train (on light railway)

**tortiller** *vt* twist; *vi* quibble, prevaricate; **se** ~ writhe, wriggle

**tortillon** *nm* pad (for carrying loads on the head); twist (rag, paper)

**tortionnaire** *nm* torturer, tormentor; *adj* torturing

**tortu** *adj* crooked

**tortue** *nf* tortoise; ~ **marine** turtle

**tortueux -euse** *adj* winding, tortuous; crooked, underhand

**torturer** *vt* torture; twist (meaning)

**torve** *adj* regard ~ menacing look

**toscan** *adj* Tuscan

**tôt** *adv* early; ~ **ou tard** sooner or later; **le plus** ~ **sera le mieux** the sooner the better

**totalement** *adv* totally, wholly

**totalisateur** *nm* adding-machine; *adj* (*f* -**trice**) adding, calculating

**totaliser** *vt* totalize

**totalitaire** *adj* totalitarian

**totalité** *nf* totality, whole

**totémisme** *nm* totemism

**toton** *nm* teetotum, small top

**toubib** *nm coll* doctor

**touchant** *adj* touching, affecting; *prep* concerning, about

**touche** *nf* touch, touching; key (piano, typewriter); dab; goad; manner (painter); hit (fencing); appearance; *coll* **faire (avoir) une** ~ **avec** make a hit with

**touche-à-tout** *nm invar* busybody, meddler

**toucher** *nm* touch; *vt* touch; move, affect; concern; draw, receive (money); touch on, allude to; *vi* touch; ~ **à** be in touch with; be close to, border on; start, make a start on; change, alter; meddle, interfere; **je lui en toucherai un mot** I'll mention it to him; **n'avoir pas l'air d'y** ~ put on an innocent air

**touchette** *nf* fret (guitar)

**toue** *nf* flat-bottomed barge; towing

**touer** *vt* tow

**touffe** *nf* tuft; clump

**touffeur** *nf* suffocating heat

**touffu** *adj* bushy, thick; involved, obscure

**touiller** *vt coll* stir

**toujours** *adv* always, ever; still; just the same, nevertheless, all the same; ~ **est-il que ...** the fact remains that...; **allez** ~ go on, go ahead; **pour** ~ for ever

**toundra** *nf* tundra

**toupet** *nm* tuft of hair, quiff; toupet; *coll* cheek, nerve

**toupie** *nf* top, spinning-top; milled cutter; **vieille** ~ old trout, trump

**toupiller** *vt* shape (wood); *vi coll* spin round

**¹tour** *nf* tower; castle (chess); tall block (flats)

**²tour** *nm* turn; revolution; trip; stroll; circuit, circumference; lathe; adornment; trick, feat; turn of phrase; shape; course, turn (of events); ~ **à** ~ by turns, alternately; ~ **de main** knack; ~ **de poitrine** chest measurement; **à qui le** ~? whose turn is it?; **à** ~ **de bras** hard, with all one's might; **à** ~ **de rôle** in turn; **donner un** ~ **de clef à** lock; **en un** ~ **de main** in an instant; **faire le** ~ **de** go round; **faire un** ~ go for a walk

**tourangeau -elle** *adj* of Tours; of Touraine

**tourbe** *nf* peat

**tourbeux -euse** *adj* peaty

**tourbière** *nf* peat-bog

**tourbillon** *nm* whirlwind; whirlpool, eddy; bustle, whirl

**tourbillonner** *vi* whirl, swirl

**tourelle** *nf* small tower; gun-turret

**tourie** *nf* carboy

**tourisme** *nm* tourism; touring

**touriste** *n* tourist; **classe** ~ economy class

**touristique** *adj* touristic

**tourment** *nm* torture; torment, anguish

**tourmente** *nf* storm, tempest; turmoil

**tourmenté** *adj* irregular; tormented; laboured (style)

**tourmenter** *vt* torture; torment; worry, trouble; pester, plague; **se** ~ worry

**tournage** *nm* turning (on lathe); *cin* shooting

**tournailler** *vi* prowl about, wander round and round

**tournant** *nm* turning; bend, corner; turning point; *adj* turning; revolving

**tourné** *adj* turned; **bien** ~ well set up; well disposed; **mal** ~ cross-grained; soured

**tournebroche** *nm* roasting-jack; turn-spit

**tourne-disque** *nm* record-player

**tournedos** *nm* fillet steak

**tournée** *nf* tour, round; **payer une** ~ stand a round of drinks

**tournemain** *nm* **en un** ~ in a trice

**tourner** *vt* turn; shape, fashion; revolve, rotate; shoot (film); act in (film); convert; evade, get round; ~ **la tête à qn** arouse s/o's admiration; arouse s/o's affections; *vi* revolve, go round; turn,

307

turn off; result, turn out; ~ **autour de qn** hang around s/o; ~ **autour du pot** beat about the bush; ~ **court** stop suddenly, stop short, finish inconclusively; *coll* ~ **de l'œil** die; ~ **en ridicule** hold up to ridicule; **mal** ~ go to the bad; turn out badly; **se** ~ turn, turn round

**tournesol** *nm* sunflower

**tourneur -euse** *n* lathe-operator; *adj* **derviche** ~ dancing dervish

**tourne-vent** *nm invar* chimney-cowl

**tournevis** *nm* screwdriver

**tourniole** *nf* whitlow

**tourniquer** *vi* wander about

**tourniquet** *nm* turnstile; turn-buckle; whirligig; *surg* tourniquet

**tournis** *nm vet* staggers

**tournoi** *nm* tournament

**tournoiement** *nm* whirling

**tournoyer** *vi* (7) whirl, swirl, turn round and round

**tournure** *nf* turn, course; figure, appearance; *metal* turnings; bustle (dress); turn (mind, phrase)

**tourte** *nf* tart; *sl* fool, idiot

**tourteau** *nm* round loaf; oil-cake; edible crab; *her* roundel

**tourtereau** *nm* young turtle-dove; *fig* ~ **x** love-birds

**tourterelle** *nf* turtle-dove

**tourtière** *nf* pie-dish; baking-tin

**tous** *pron* + *adj see* **tout**

**Toussaint** *nf* All Saints' day

**tousser** *vi* cough

**toussoter** *vi* cough slightly and frequently

**tout** *nm* whole; total; **risquer le** ~ **pour le** ~ stake everything; *pron* (*pl* **tous, toutes**) all, everything; **c'est** ~ **dire** I needn't say more; *adj* (*pl* **tous, toutes**) all, every; any; all the, the whole; ~ **autre que vous** anyone other than yourself; ~ **le monde** everyone; **à** ~ **e vitesse** at full speed; **à** ~ **prendre** all things considered; **c'est** ~ **e une histoire** it's a long story; **de** ~ **e beauté** extremely beautiful; **le Tout-Paris** fashionable Paris society; **somme** ~ **e** all in all, all things considered; **tous (les) deux** both; **tous les** every; **tous les deux jours** every other day; *adv* quite, wholly, entirely; very; ~ **à fait** quite, utterly; ~ **agréable qu'elle est** however pleasant she is; ~ **au moins** at least; ~ **au plus** at most; ~ **droit** straight on; quite straight; **c'est** ~ **le portrait de son père** he (she) is the living image of his (her) father

**tout-à-l'égout** *nm invar* mains drainage

**toutefois** *adv* nevertheless, yet, however

**toute-puissance** *nf* omnipotence

**toutou** *nm* doggie

**Tout-Paris** *nm* fashionable Paris society

**Tout-Puissant** *nm* **le** ~ the Almighty

**tout-puissant** *adj* (*f* **toute-puissante**) all-powerful, almighty

**toux** *nf* cough

**toxémie** *nf* blood-poisoning, toxaemia

**toxicité** *nf* toxic nature, toxicity

**toxicologie** *nf* toxicology

**toxicomane** *n* drug-addict

**toxicomanie** *nf* drug addiction

**toxine** *nf* toxin

**toxique** *nm* poison; *adj* toxic

**trac** *nm* stage-fright; **tout à** ~ thoughtlessly

**traçage** *nm* tracing

**traçant** *adj* running, creeping; **balle** ~ **e** tracer bullet

**tracas** *nm* trouble, worry, bother

**tracasser** *vt* worry, bother; **se** ~ worry

**tracasserie** *nf* worry; pestering

**tracassier -ière** *adj* pestering; vexatious; bothersome; fussy

**trace** *nf* trace; trail, track; mark, scar; impression; **marcher sur les** ~ **s de qn** follow in s/o's footsteps

**tracé** *nm* tracing, plotting; outline; lay-out; diagram, sketch

**tracer** *vt* (4) trace; lay out, mark out, plot; write out, describe; set out

**traceur -euse** *adj* tracer

**trachée** *nf* trachea, windpipe

**trachée-artère** *nf* (*pl* **trachées-artères**) trachea, windpipe

**trachéen -éenne** *adj anat* trachean

**trachéotomie** *nf* tracheotomy

**trachome** *nm* trachoma

**tractation** *nf* dealing, bargaining

**tracteur** *nm* tractor

**tractif -ive** *adj* tractive

**traction** *nf* traction; pulling; draught; ~ **(avant)** front-wheel drive car

**tradition** *nf* tradition; *leg* handing over

**traditionnel -elle** *adj* traditional, customary

**traducteur -trice** *n* translator

**traduction** *nf* translating; translation

**traduire** *vt* (80) translate; interpret, explain, express; ~ **en justice** prosecute

**traduisible** *adj* translatable

**trafic** *nm* trafficking, illegal trading; trading; traffic

**trafiquant -e** *n* trafficker

**trafiquer** *vi* traffic, deal

**tragédie** *nf* tragedy

**tragédien -ienne** *n* tragic actor, tragedian

**tragi-comédie** *nf* tragi-comedy

**tragi-comique** *adj* tragi-comic

**tragique** *nm* tragic side; tragic art; tragic author; **prendre qch au** ~ make a tragedy of sth; *adj* tragic

**trahir** *vt* betray; reveal, disclose; distort; let down

**trahison** *nf* treason, betrayal

**train** *nm* train; string, line; pace, rate; ~ **d'atterrissage** landing gear; ~ **de derrière** hindquarters; ~ **de maison** household expenses; ~ **de vie** style of living; **à fond de** ~ at full speed; **aller bon** ~ go at a good speed; **être en** ~ be in good form; **être en** ~ **de faire qch** be doing sth, be occupied in doing sth; **être mal en** ~ be out of sorts, be in poor shape; **mener bon** ~ hustle along; **mener grand** ~ live on a grand scale; **mettre en** ~ get ready, start, get going

**traînage** *nm* hauling; dragging

**traînant** *adj* trailing; languid; drawling

**traînard -e** *n coll* straggler, dawdler

**traînasser** *vi* loiter, dawdle

**traîne** *nf* dawdling; being dragged; drag-net; train (dress); **à la** ~ in tow; *coll* in disorder, in disarray; **pêcher à la** ~ troll

**traîneau** *nm* sledge, sleigh

**traînée** *nf* trail; ground-line (fishing); *coll* slut

**traîner** *vt* pull, drag, haul, draw; drag out; drawl; *vi* trail; lag, trail behind; lie around; loiter, dawdle; drag; ~ **en longueur** drag on and on; ~ **la jambe** limp

**traîneur -euse** *n* straggler

**train-train** *nm coll* routine

**traire** *vt* (9) milk

**trait** *nm* pulling; trace (harness); line, stroke; draught, gulp; deed; *mus* brilliant passage; ~**s** features; ~ **d'esprit** flash of wit; ~ **de génie** stroke of genius; ~ **d'union** hyphen; **avaler d'un** ~ swallow at one go; **avoir** ~ **à** be relevant to, have reference to; **partir comme un** ~ be off like a flash

**traitable** *adj* manageable, tractable

**traitant** *adj* **médecin** ~ doctor treating a case; family doctor

**traite** *nf* stretch, stage; trading; *comm* draft, bill of exchange; milking; ~ **des blanches** white slave traffic; ~ **des noirs** slave trade; **d'une** ~ at a stretch, at one stretch

**traité** *nm* treaty; treatise

**traitement** *nm* treatment; salary, remuneration

**traiter** *vt* treat; negotiate; deal with; ~ **d'un sujet** deal with a subject, write about a subject; ~ **qn de voleur** call s/o a thief

**traiteur** *nm* caterer

**traître -esse** *n* traitor (traitress); **en** ~ treacherously; *adj* treacherous; **ne pas**

**dire un** ~ **mot** not say a single word

**traîtreusement** *adv* treacherously

**traîtrise** *nf* treachery

**trajectoire** *nf* trajectory

**trajet** *nm* journey, trip; *anat* course (nerve, vessel)

**tralala** *nm coll* fuss, exaggerated ceremony

**trame** *nf* woof, weft; plot, intrigue; *fig* web, thread

**tramer** *vt* weave; plot; **se** ~ be afoot, be brewing

**tramontane** *nf* north wind from the mountains

**tranchant** *nm* cutting edge; *adj* cutting, sharp; trenchant

**tranche** *nf* slice; block, group; instalment; slab; edge (book); round (beef); **livre doré sur** ~ gilt-edged book; *coll* **s'en payer une** ~ have a fling

**tranchée** *nf* trench; cutting

**trancher** *vt* cut, slice; decide, settle; ~ **le mot** speak out, speak plainly; *vi* decide; contrast strongly, stand out clearly

**tranchet** *nm* paring knife

**tranchoir** *nm* cutting-board

**tranquille** *adj* calm, quiet, still; peaceful, undisturbed; unworried, untroubled

**tranquillisant** *nm* tranquillizer

**tranquilliser** *vt* reassure, set at rest

**tranquillité** *nf* tranquillity, quiet, calm

**transactionnel -elle** *adj* transactional

**transalpin** *adj* transalpine

**transat** *nm abbr* deck-chair

**transatlantique** *nm* transatlantic liner; deck-chair; *adj* transatlantic

**transbordement** *nm* trans-shipment; transfer of goods

**transborder** *vt* trans-ship; transfer (goods)

**transbordeur** *nm* **(pont)** ~ transporter bridge

**transcendance** *nf* transcendency

**transcendant** *adj* transcendent, surpassing

**transcendantal** *adj* transcendental; speculative

**transcender** *vt* transcend, be superior to

**transcripteur** *nm* transcriber

**transcription** *nf* transcribing, transcription; copy, transcript

**transcrire** *vt* (42) transcribe, write out

**transe** *nf* trance; anxiety; **entrer en** ~ get all worked up

**transférer** *vt* (6) transfer; move, shift

**transfert** *nm* transfer; transference; making over, assignment, conveyance

**transfigurer** *vt* transfigure

**transformateur** *nm* transformer; *adj* (*f* -**trice**) transforming

**transformer** *vt* transform, change, convert; **se ~** change, turn
**transfuge** *nm* deserter; *n* turncoat
**transfuser** *vt* transfuse
**transgresser** *vt* transgress, contravene
**transhumance** *nf* movement of cattle to mountain pastures
**transhumer** *vt* move to mountain pastures
**transi** *adj* numb with cold
**transiger** *vi* (3) compromise
**transir** *vt* chill; paralyse (with fear, cold)
**transit** *nm* transit, passage of goods; through traffic
**transitaire** *nm* forwarding agent; *adj* through which goods are conveyed
**transiter** *vt* send through (goods); *vi* pass through (goods)
**transitif -ive** *adj* transitive
**transitoire** *adj* transient
**translation** *nf* leg transferring, conveyance
**translucide** *adj* translucent
**translucidité** *nf* translucence
**transmetteur** *nm* transmitter
**transmettre** *vt* (60) transmit; pass on; *leg* transfer
**transmigrer** *vi* transmigrate
**transmission** *nf* transmission; passing on; handing down; *mot* transmission (gear); *leg* making over, assignment; communication; **arbre de ~** driving-shaft
**transmuer, transmuter** *vt* transmute
**transparaître** *vi* (68) show through, appear
**transparence** *nf* transparency
**transpercer** *vt* (4) pierce, transfix
**transpiration** *nf* perspiring; perspiration; *bot* transpiration
**transpirer** *vi* perspire; transpire
**transplanter** *vt* transplant
**transport** *nm* transport, conveyance; troop transport, troop-ship; *leg* transfer, making over; rapture, outburst; **~s en commun** public transport, *US* public transportation
**transporter** *vt* transport, convey; *leg* transfer; enrapture; **se ~** betake oneself
**transporteur** *nm* carrier, forwarding agent; transporter; conveyor
**transposer** *vt* transpose
**transsexuel -uelle** *adj* transsexual
**transsuder** *vi* ooze through
**transvaser** *vt* decant
**transvider** *vt* pour into another container
**trapèze** *nm* trapeze; trapezium
**trappe** *nf* trap; trap-door
**trappeur** *nm* trapper
**trappiste** *nm* Trappist monk
**trapu** *adj* thickset, stocky

**traquenard** *nm* trap, pitfall, ambush
**traquer** *vt* hunt down, track down; beat up (game)
**traqueur** *nm* beater; tracker
**traumatique** *adj* traumatic
**traumatiser** *vt* traumatize
**traumatisme** *nm* traumatism
**travail** *nm* (*pl* **-aux**) work; labour; working; piece of work; workmanship; craftsmanship; employment; fermenting; **travaux forcés** hard labour; **attention travaux!** road works ahead!; **avoir le ~ facile** work easily; **sans ~** out of work; **se mettre au ~** get down to work
**travaillé** *adj* wrought; elaborate
**travailler** *vt* work, shape, fashion; torment, obsess; stir up, work up; *vi* work, toil; make efforts; ferment; warp; perform (animals)
**travailleur -euse** *n* worker; *adj* hard-working
**travailleuse** *nf* work-table
**travaillisme** *nm pol* Labour doctrine
**travailliste** *n pol* member of Labour party, Labour supporter; *adj* Labour
**travée** *nf span; archi* bay; row of seats
**travers** *nm* fault, quirk, bad habit; **à ~** through; across; **au ~ de** through, right through; **de ~** the wrong way; amiss; **en ~** athwart; **prendre qch de ~** take sth wrongly, put a bad construction on sth; **regarder qn de ~** look askance at s/o
**traverse** *nf* cross-piece, cross-bar; sleeper (railway); **~s** obstacles; **chemin de ~** short cut; **se mettre à la ~** oppose, provide obstacles
**traversée** *nf* crossing, passage
**traverser** *vt* cross, pass through, traverse, go through; span
**traversier -ière** *adj* cross, crossing
**traversin** *nm* bolster
**traversine** *nf* cross-bar; cross-beam
**travesti** *nm* disguise; *theat* man playing woman's part or vice versa; transvestite
**travestir** *vt* disguise; travesty, parody; **bal travesti** fancy-dress ball; **se ~** dress up (*esp* as member of opposite sex)
**travestisme** *nm* transvestism
**travestissement** *nm* disguise; transvestism
**trayeur -euse** *n* milker
**trayeuse** *nf* milking machine
**trébuchant** *adj* stumbling; **espèces sonnantes et ~es** hard cash
**trébucher** *vt* test for weight (coin); *vi* stumble, totter
**tréfilerie** *nf* wire-works
**trèfle** *nm* clover, trefoil; clubs (cards); **(carrefour en) ~** motorway intersection
**tréfonds** *nm* deepest part, heart; subsoil
**treillage** *nm* trellis-work, lattice-work
**treillager** *vt* (3) trellis

treille *nf* vine-arbour; climbing-vine; *coll* jus de la ~ wine

treillis *nm* trellis; grating; sacking

treillisser *vt* trellis

treize *nm + adj* thirteen; thirteenth

treizième *n + adj* thirteenth

tréma *nm* diaeresis

tremblant *adj* trembling, quivering; unsteady; flickering

tremble *nm* aspen

tremblé *adj* shaky (handwriting); trembling (voice)

tremblement *nm* trembling, shaking; tremor; ~ de terre earthquake; *coll* tout le ~ the whole caboodle

trembler *vi* tremble, shake; quake; quiver

trembleur *nm elect* trembler, vibrator

tremblote *nf* avoir la ~ have the shivers; quake with fear

trembloter *vi* tremble slightly, quiver

trémie *nf* mill-hopper; loading funnel; hopper

trémière *adj f* rose ~ holly-hock

trémousser (se) *v refl* jump up and down; fidget

trempe *nf* soaking, dipping; tempering; temper (steel); quality; *coll* scolding

tremper *vt* soak, steep, drench; dilute with water; harden, temper; ~ sa soupe put bread in one's soup; *vi* soak; ~ dans dabble in; trempé jusqu'aux os soaked to the skin

trempette *nf* faire ~ take a quick dip; dip (bread, biscuit, etc) in milk, wine, etc

tremplin *nm* spring-board; diving-board

trentaine *nf* about thirty; thirties (age)

trente *nm + adj* thirty; thirtieth; *coll* se mettre sur son ~ et un put on one's best clothes

trentième *n + adj* thirtieth

trépan *nm* rock-drill; trepan

trépanation *nf* trepanning

trépaner *vt* bore, drill; trepan

trépas *nm obs + lit* death

trépasser *vi obs + lit* die; les trépassés the dead

trépidant *adj* agitated, bustling

trépidation *nf* agitation, flurry

trépider *vi* shake, vibrate

trépied *nm* tripod; three-legged stool

trépigner *vi* stamp (with rage)

trépointe *nf* welt (shoe)

très *adv* very, very much; most

Très-Haut *nm* Almighty

trésor *nm* treasure; treasure-house; le Trésor national financial resources

trésorerie *nf* treasury; office of treasurer

trésorier -ière *n* treasurer

tressaillement *nm* start, quiver

tressaillir *vi* (14) start, jump; shudder, quiver

tressauter *vi* start, jump

tresse *nf* plait, braid

tresser *vt* plait, braid, weave

tréteau *nm* trestle, support; ~x stage, boards

treuil *nm* winch

trêve *nf* truce; *coll* ~ de enough of; sans ~ unremittingly

tri *nm* sorting, sorting out

triade *nf* triad

triage *nm* sorting; sorting place; gare de ~ marshalling yard

triangulaire *adj* triangular

tribalisme *nm* tribalism

tribord *nm naut* starboard

tribu *nf* tribe

tribun *nm Rom hist* tribune; popular orator

tribunal *nm* law-court; tribunal; bar (public opinion); en plein ~ in open court

tribune *nf* tribune, platform; forum; gallery (church); ~s stands

tribut *nm* tribute

tributaire *adj* tributary

tricentenaire *nm + adj* tercentenary

tricher *vi* cheat

tricherie *nf* cheating, trickery

tricheur -euse *n* cheat; *adj* cheating

tricolore *nm* tricolour; *adj* tricolour, three-coloured

tricorne *nm* three-cornered hat

tricot *nm* knitting; jumper; ~ (de corps) (under)vest

tricoter *vt + vi* knit; *vi sl* walk very fast; pedal

tricoteuse *nf* knitting-machine; knitter

trictrac *nm* backgammon

triennal *adj* triennial; lasting three years

trier *vt* sort, sort out

trifouiller *vi coll* rummage

trigonométrie *nf* trigonometry

trilingue *adj* trilingual

trille *nm mus* trill

triller *vi mus* trill

trilogie *nf* trilogy

trimarder *vi sl* tramp, be a vagabond

trimardeur *nm sl* vagabond

trimbaler *vt coll* cart around, carry

trimer *vi coll* work hard, slave away

trimestre *nm* three-month period, trimester; (school) term; termly pay; termly fees

trimestriel -ielle *adj* three-monthly

tringle *nf* rod, metal rod; *coll* se mettre la ~ go without

trinité *nf* trinity

trinquer *vi* clink glasses; *coll* drink; *sl* get the worst of things

trinqueur *nm coll* drinker

triolet *nm* triolet; *mus* triplet

triomphal *adj* triumphal

**triomphant** *adj* triumphant

**triomphe** *nm* triumph; **arc de ~** triumphal arch; **porter qn en ~** carry s/o shoulder high

**triompher** *vi* triumph; exult; **~ de qch** overcome sth; **~ de qn** get the better of s/o

**tripaille** *nf coll* offal

**tripatouiller** *vt coll* tamper with; paw, mishandle

**tripe** *nf* tripe; *coll* bowel; inside of cigar; *coll* **~s** innards; **avoir la ~ royaliste** be a royalist at heart

**triperie** *nf* tripe-shop

**tripette** *nf sl* **ne pas valoir ~** be worthless

**triphasé** *adj elect* three-phase

**tripier -ière** *n* tripe-dealer

**triple** *adj* treble, triple; *coll* very great, extreme

**tripler** *vt + vi* treble, triple

**triplicata** *nm* third copy

**triporteur** *nm* carrier-tricycle

**tripot** *nm* gambling den

**tripotage** *nm* shady dealing; *coll* fiddling about

**tripotée** *nf coll* thrashing; great quantity

**tripoter** *vt coll* handle, paw; fiddle with; *vulg* touch up; *vi coll* fiddle around; engage in shady dealing

**tripoteur -euse** *n coll* shady dealer

**triptyque** *nm* triptych; *mot* triptyque

**trique** *nf* cudgel, truncheon

**trisaïeul -e** *n* (*mpl* **trisaïeuls** or **trisaïeux**) great-great-grandfather (great-great-grandmother)

**trisannuel -uelle** *adj* triennial, three yearly

**trisser** *vi sl* go away; *sl* **se ~** clear off, escape

**triste** *adj* sad, sorrowful; poor, wretched; vile; unhappy; gloomy; **c'est une ~ affaire** it's a bad business; **faire ~ mine** look sad; **faire ~ mine à qn** give s/o a poor reception

**tristesse** *nf* sadness; gloom; dullness, dreariness

**triturer** *vt* triturate, reduce to powder; handle roughly

**triumvirat** *nm* triumvirate

**trivial** *adj* low, coarse

**trivialité** *nf* coarseness, vulgarity

**troc** *nm* barter, exchange

**troène** *nm bot* privet

**trogne** *nf coll* ruddy, bloated face

**trognon** *nm* stump (cabbage, etc); core (apple); *sl* **jusqu'au ~** completely

**Troie** *nf* Troy

**trois** *nm + adj* three; third

**trois-étoiles** *nm* three-star (hotel, restaurant); **Monsieur ~** Mr X

**troisième** *n* third; *nm* third floor; *nf* fourth form; third class; *adj* third

**trois-mâts** *nm* three-masted vessel

**trois-quarts** *nm* child's violin; three-quarter-length coat; *sp* three-quarter

**trolley** *nm coll* trolleybus

**trombe** *nf* whirlwind; **~ d'eau** torrential downpour; **arriver (passer) en ~** arrive (go past) at lightning speed

**trombine** *nf sl* face

**tromblon** *nm* blunderbuss

**trombone** *nm* trombone; trombone-player; paper-clip

**trompe** *nf* horn; trunk, proboscis; *anat* tube; *eng* aspirator

**trompe-la-mort** *n invar* person who escapes death, dare-devil

**trompe-l'œil** *nm invar art* trompe l'œil; dummy window; illusion, eyewash

**tromper** *vt* deceive; cheat; be unfaithful to, betray; outwit; while away; **se ~** be wrong, be mistaken; **se ~ de chemin** take the wrong way

**tromperie** *nf* deception, deceit; fraud

**trompeter** *vt* (5) trumpet abroad; shout from the rooftops

**trompette** *nf* trumpet; *nm* trumpeter

**trompettiste** *n* trumpet-player

**trompeur -euse** *adj* deceptive, misleading

**tronc** *nm* trunk; stem, body; drum (column); offertory-box; **~ commun** common curriculum (in early years at French secondary school)

**tronçon** *nm* stub, broken end, stump; section, stage

**tronçonner** *vt* cut into sections, cut into lengths

**tronçonneuse** *nf* chain saw

**trône** *nm* throne

**trôner** *vi* be enthroned; sit in state; *coll* lord it

**tronquer** *vt* truncate; mutilate; curtail

**trop** *nm* excess; too much, too many; *adv* too, too much; **de ~** too much; *coll* **en ~** in excess; **être de ~** be unwelcome; be superfluous; *coll* **par ~** too much

**trophée** *nm* trophy

**tropique** *nm* tropic

**trop-plein** *nm* excess liquid; excess; overflow

**troquer** *vt* exchange, barter

**trotte** *nf coll* stretch, distance to walk

**trotter** *vi* trot; *coll* walk fast; *sl* **se ~** clear off

**trotteur -euse** *n* trotter; trotting horse

**trottiner** *vi* trot about; toddle; walk fast with short steps

**trottinette** *nf* scooter; *coll* little car

**trottoir** *nm* pavement, footpath, *US* sidewalk; **faire le ~** walk the streets (prostitute)

**trou** *nm* hole; cavity; *coll* dump, backwater; **~ d'air** air pocket; **~ du souffleur** prompter's box; **avoir un ~ de mémoire** have a lapse of memory; **boucher un ~** pay back a debt

**troublant** *adj* disturbing, disquieting

**trouble** *nm* confusion; agitation, anxiety; *med* trouble; **~s** uprising, revolt; **jeter le ~ dans** upset, disturb; *adj* cloudy, turbid; dim; murky; confused; *adv* **voir ~** not see clearly

**trouble-fête** *n invar* spoil-sport, kill-joy

**troubler** *vt* make cloudy; blur; perturb, worry; disturb, upset; interrupt, interfere with; **se ~** become cloudy; cloud over; go dim, become blurred; falter; get confused

**trouée** *nf* opening; breach; *geog* gap

**trouer** *vt* make a hole in, perforate

**troufignon** *nm vulg* arse

**troufion** *nm sl* soldier

**trouille** *nf sl* funk, fear

**trou-madame** *nm* (*pl* **trous-madame**) kind of bagatelle

**troupe** *nf* company, band; troupe of actors; soldiery; troup (scouts)

**troupeau** *nm* herd, flock

**troupier** *nm ar* soldier; *coll* trooper

**trousse** *nf* case, kit; **être aux ~s de qn** be on s/o's heels

**trousseau** *nm* outfit, trousseau; **~ de clefs** bunch of keys

**trousser** *vt* tuck up, turn up; truss (fowl); *coll* dispatch, get through fast; *coll* seduce; *coll* **bien troussé** well done, well executed; **se ~** tuck up one's clothes

**trouvaille** *nf* lucky find, windfall

**trouver** *vt* find, discover; invent; feel; consider, think; **~ à qui parler** meet one's match; **~ à redire** find fault; **~ bon (mauvais)** approve (disapprove); **~ la mort** be killed; **~ le temps long** get bored; **aller ~ qn** go and look s/o up, go and see s/o; **bien trouvé** felicitous, clever; **il se trouve que** it so happens that; *coll* **la ~ mauvaise** dislike sth, disapprove of sth; **objets trouvés** lost property; **se ~** be, be situated; turn out, happen; **se ~ mieux** feel better

**trouvère** *nm* minstrel (N. France)

**troyen -enne** *adj* Trojan

**truand** *nm* rogue, crook; vagabond (in Middle Ages)

**trublion** *nm* trouble-maker

**truc** *nm coll* knack, skill; trick; thing; what's-it, thingummy

**trucage** *nm see* **truquage**

**truchement** *nm* intermediary, go-between

**truelle** *nf* trowel

**truffe** *nf* truffle; end of dog's nose

**truffer** *vt* stuff with truffles; fill, pack

**truie** *nf* sow

**truisme** *nm* truism

**truite** *nf* trout

**truité** *adj* speckled; crackled; spotted

**trumeau** *nm* pier-glass; chimney-breast, panel; leg of beef

**truquage, trucage** *nm* faking; *cin* trick picture

**truquer** *vt* fake

**tsar** *nm* czar

**tsé-tsé** *nf* (**mouche**) **~** tsetse fly

**tu** *pers pron* you; thee; **être à ~ et à toi avec qn** be on familiar terms with s/o

**tuant** *adj* exhausting; trying

**tuba** *nm* diver's respiration tube

**tube** *nm* tube; *sl* top-hat; duct; hit (song, record)

**tubercule** *nm bot* tuber; *med* tubercle

**tuberculeux -euse** *n* tuberculosis sufferer; *adj* tubercular

**tuberculose** *nf* tuberculosis

**tubéreuse** *nf* tuberose

**tubéreux -euse** *adj* tuberous

**tubulaire** *adj* tubular

**tubulure** *nf* tubulature; pipe; nozzle

**tudesque** *adj* Germanic

**tue-mouche(s)** *adj* (**papier**) **~** fly-paper

**tuer** *vt* kill, slay, slaughter; tire out

**tuerie** *nf* slaughter, carnage

**tue-tête (à)** *adv phr* **crier ~** bawl out, shout at the top of one's voice

**tueur -euse** *n* killer; *nm* slaughterman

**tuf** *nm* tufa; bed-rock, foundation

**tuffeau, tufeau** *nm* calcareous tufa

**tuile** *nf* tile; *coll* misfortune, piece of bad luck

**tuilerie** *nf* tile-works

**tulipe** *nf* tulip; tulip-shaped ornament

**tuméfaction** *nf* swelling, tumefaction

**tuméfier** *vt* tumefy, make swell

**tumeur** *nf* tumour, growth

**tumulaire** *adj* tumular; sepulchral

**tumulte** *nm* uproar, tumult, hubbub

**tumultueux -ueuse** *adj* tumultuous, noisy

**tungstène** *nm* tungsten

**tunique** *nf* tunic

**Tunisie** *nf* Tunisia

**Tunisien -ienne** *n* Tunisian

**tunisien -ienne** *adj* Tunisian

**turbidité** *nf* turbidity, cloudiness

**turbin** *nm sl* work

**turbiner** *vi sl* work

**turbo-alternateur** *nm elect* turbo-alternator

**turbocompresseur** *nm* turbocompressor

**turbomoteur** *nm* turbine; steam turbine

**turbotrain** *nm* train driven by gas turbine

**turbulence** *nf* unruliness; boisterousness; turbulence

turbulent *adj* unruly, restless; boisterous; turbulent

Turc (*f* Turque) *n* Turk; **fort comme un ~** strong as a horse; **tête de ~** whipping-boy

turc *nm* Turkish (language); *adj* (*f* turque) Turkish

turf *nm* race-course

turfiste *n* race-goer

turlupiner *vt coll* worry, torment

turlutaine *nf* constant theme

turlututu *interj* fiddlesticks!

turne *nf sl* squalid digs; *coll* room, study

turnep(s) *nm* kohl-rabi

Turquie *nf* Turkey

turquin *nm* kind of blue marble

tussilage *nm bot* coltsfoot

tussor *nm* tussore (silk)

tutélaire *adj* tutelary

tutelle *nf* guardianship, tutelage; protection

tuteur -trice *n* guardian, tutor; *nm hort* support, stake

tutoyer *vt* (7) address (s/o) as **tu**, be on familiar terms with

tutu *nm* ballet skirt

tuyau *nm* pipe; barrel (quill); stalk (corn); tubing, tube; *coll* tip; **~ d'arrosage** hose-pipe; **~ d'incendie** fire-hose

tuyauter *vt* goffer; *coll* inform, give a tip to

tuyauterie *nf* pipes, pipes and fittings

tuyère *nf metal* twyer, blast-pipe, nozzle

tympan *nm* ear-drum; *archi* tympanum

type *nm* type; pattern; personality; *sl* fellow, bloke

typhoïde *nf + adj* typhoid

typhon *nm* typhoon

typique *adj* typical

typographe *n* typographer

typographie *nf* typography

typographique *adj* typographical

tyran *nm* tyrant

tyranneau *nm* petty tyrant

tyrannie *nf* tyranny

tyrannique *adj* tyrannical

tyranniser *vt* tyrannize

tyrolien -ienne *adj* Tyrolean

# U

ubiquité *nf* ubiquity

ukase *nm* edict, ukase

ukrainien -ienne *adj* Ukrainian

ulcère *nm* ulcer

ulcéré *adj* embittered; ulcerated

ulcérer *vt* (6) ulcerate; embitter

ulcéreux -euse *adj* ulcerous

ultérieur *adj* ulterior; subsequent, later; farther

ultérieurement *adv* subsequently, later on

ultime *adj* final, ultimate

ultra *n pol* extremist; *adv* (*usu* with hyphen) extremely, very, ultra-

ululement *nm* hooting, hoot (owl)

ululer *vi* hoot (owl)

Ulysse *nm* Ulysses

un (*f* -une) *indef art* (*pl* des), *num adj*, *pron* a, an; one; some, someone; **~ à ~** one by one; **~ d'entre nous** one of us; **~ par ~** one by one; *coll* **c'est d'~ fini!** it really is most polished!; **c'est tout ~** it all comes to the same; **chambre à ~ lit** single (bed)room; *coll*

**en savoir plus d'~ e** know a thing or two; *coll* **et d'~ (e)!** so much for that one!, that's one done (gone)!; **il n'a fait ni ~ e ni deux** he didn't hesitate a moment; **ils sont d'~ égoïsme!** they are incredibly selfish!; **la ~ e** front page of the newspaper(s); **les ~ s ... les autres** some ... others; **le ~** number one; **l'~ et l'autre** both; **l'~ l'autre** each other; *coll* **ne faire qu'~** be one and the same, be indistinguishable; be hand in glove

unanime *adj* unanimous

unanimité *nf* unanimity; **à l'~** unanimously

uni *adj* united; even, level, smooth; plain, uniform; equable, calm

unicorne *nm* unicorn

unième *adj* vingt (trente, etc) **-et-~** twenty-(thirty-, etc)first

unificateur -trice *n* unifier; *adj* unifying

unification *nf* unification; standardization; amalgamation

**unifier** *vt* unify; consolidate; standardize; s' ~ become united, unite

**uniforme** *nm* uniform; **grand** ~ full-dress uniform; *coll* **quitter l'** ~ leave the service; *adj* uniform, even, unvarying; consistent

**uniformément** *adv* uniformly; consistently

**uniformisation** *nf* standardization

**uniformiser** *vt* make uniform, standardize

**uniformité** *nf* uniformity

**unijambiste** *n + adj* one-legged (person)

**unilatéral** *adj* one-sided, unilateral

**uniment** *adv* smoothly, evenly, plainly

**union** *nf* union, association; combination; unity; agreement; marriage; **l'** ~ **fait la force** unity is strength

**unionisme** *nm pol* unionism

**unioniste** *adj* unionist

**unipersonnel** *adj gramm* impersonal

**unique** *adj* only, single, sole; unique, matchless, unrivalled; *coll* priceless; **rue à sens** ~ one-way street; **seul et** ~ one and only

**unir** *vt* unite, combine, join; level, smoothe; ~ **le geste à la parole** suit the action to the word; **s'** ~ unite, join forces; become level; **s'** ~ **à qn** marry s/o

**unisexe** *adj invar* unisex

**unisexué** *adj biol* unisexual

**unisson** *nm* unison; **à l'** ~ in unison; in keeping

**unitaire** *adj* unitary; *eccles* Unitarian

**unitarisme** *nm* unitarianism

**unité** *nf* unity, one; unit; consistency, uniformity; (examination) ~ **de valeur** credit; **prix de l'** ~ price per article

**univers** *nm* universe, world

**universaliser** *vt* universalize, make universal

**universalité** *nf* universality

**universel -elle** *adj* universal, worldwide; **homme** ~ man who knows everything; **légataire** ~ residuary legatee

**universitaire** *n* academic; *adj* university, academic; **cité** ~ students' halls of residence

**université** *nf* university

**upériser** *vt* uperize

**urbain** *adj* urban, town; urbane; **central** ~ local telephone exchange

**urbanisation** *nf* town planning, urbanization

**urbaniser** *vt* urbanize; **zone à** ~ area destined for residential occupation; **s'** ~ become polite, become more polished

**urbanisme** *nm* town planning

**urbaniste** *n* town planner; *adj* urban

**urbanité** *nf* urbanity

**urée** *nf* urea

**urémie** *nf med* uraemia

**uretère** *nm anat* ureter

**urétral** *adj anat* urethral

**urètre** *nm anat* urethra

**urgence** *nf* urgency, urgent nature; emergency (hospital) case; **état d'** ~ state of emergency; **être appelé d'** ~ receive an urgent call; **salle des** ~s emergency ward; **transporter d'** ~ **un malade à l'hôpital** rush a patient to hospital

**urger** *vi* (3) *coll* be urgent

**urinaire** *adj* urinary

**uriner** *vi* urinate

**urinoir** *nm* urinal

**urique** *adj* uric

**urne** *nf* urn; ~ **de scrutin** ballot box; **aller aux** ~s go to the polls

**urologie** *nf* urology

**urologue** *n* urologist

**urticaire** *nf* nettle-rash

**us** *nmpl obs* customs; **les** ~ **et coutumes** the ways and customs

**usage** *nm* custom, practice; use, employment; ~ **du monde** good breeding; **à l'** ~ with use; **à l'** ~ **de** for the use of; **à** ~s **multiples** multi-purpose; **d'** ~ customary, usual; **faire** ~ **de** make use of; **garanti à l'** ~ guaranteed to wear well; **hors d'** ~ worn out; **manquer d'** ~ be lacking in breeding; **à** ~ **externe** for external use only

**usagé** *adj* used, worn; secondhand; **non** ~ new

**usager -ère** *n* user; *adj* everyday, for common use

**usé** *adj* worn, worn-out, shabby; hackneyed, stale

**user** *nm* wear; **être d'un bon** ~ wear well; *vt* use up; wear out; *vi* ~ **de** use, make use of, have recourse to; ~ **de force** resort to force; ~ **de son droit** exercise one's rights; **en** ~ **bien (mal) avec qn** treat s/o well (badly); **s'** ~ wear, wear away, wear out

**usinage** *nm* machining

**usine** *nf* factory, works, plant, mill

**usiner** *vt* machine, machine-finish; manufacture

**usinier -ière** *n* manufacturer, mill owner

**usité** *adj* used, in current use; **peu** ~ rarely used

**ustensile** *nm* utensil, tool, implement

**usuel -uelle** *adj* usual, customary, everyday

**usufruit** *nm leg* usufruct, life interest

**usuraire** *adj* usurious, exorbitant

¹**usure** *nf* usury

²**usure** *nf* wear and tear; ~ **en magasin** shelf depreciation; *coll* **avoir qn à l'** ~ wear s/o down; **guerre d'** ~ war of

attrition; **résister à l'** ~ be resistant to wear

**usurier -ière** *n* usurer; *adj* usurious

**usurpateur -trice** *n* usurper; *adj* usurping

**usurpatoire** *adj* usurpatory

**usurper** *vt* usurp, encroach upon; *vi* ~ **sur** encroach upon

**ut** *nm invar mus* C, do(h)

**utérin** *adj* uterine; **frère** ~ half-brother

**utile** *nm* utility; **joindre l'** ~ **à l'agréable** combine business with pleasure; *adj* useful, of use, serviceable; advisable **charge** ~ carrying capacity; **en temps** ~ in good time; duly; **être** ~ **à qn** be of service to s/o; **prendre toutes les dispositions** ~s take all the necessary steps

**utilement** *adv* usefully, profitably, advantageously

**utilisable** *adj* usable, fit for use, utilizable

**utilisateur -trice** *n* user

**utiliser** *vt* use, utilize, make use of; turn to account, make the best of

**utilitaire** *adj* utilitarian

**utilitarisme** *nm* utilitarianism

**utilité** *nf* utility, usefulness; service; advisability; *theat* bit part; **d'** ~ **publique** of public interest; **n'être d'aucune** ~ be of no earthly use

**utopie** *nf* utopia

**utopique** *adj* utopian

**utopiste** *n* dreamer

**uvulaire** *adj phon* uvular

**uvule** *nf anat* uvula

# V

**va** *third pers pres indic* **aller**

**vacance** *nf* vacancy, vacant post; (mind) vacuity; ~s holidays, vacation; ~s **de neige** winter holidays in the mountains; **entrer en** ~s break up; **en** ~s on holiday; **les grandes** ~s the summer holidays

**vacancier -ière** *n* holiday-maker

**vacarme** *nm* din, noise, row, uproar

**vacation** *nf* sitting (of public officials); *leg* recess; (rights) abeyance; *leg* ~s fees

**vaccin** *nm* vaccine

**vaccine** *nf* cowpox; cowpox vaccination

**vacciner** *vt* vaccinate

**vache** *nf* cow; cowhide; *sl* fat woman; *sl fig* swine; *sl* pig (policeman); ~ **à lait** milch-cow; sucker; *sl* **être** ~ be a swine; *coll* **le plancher des** ~s dry land, terra firma; **manger de la** ~ **enragée** have a rough time; *naut* **nœud de** ~ granny knot; **parler français comme une** ~ **espagnole** speak dreadful French; **pleurer comme une** ~ cry one's eyes out; *adj sl* mean, disgusting, swinish

**vachement** *adv sl* bloody, damned, tremendously

**vacher** *nm* cowherd; cowman

**vachère** *nf* cowgirl

**vacherie** *nf ar* cowshed; *sl* dirty trick

**vacherin** *nm* type of sweet made with ice-cream and meringue; type of cheese

**vachette** *nf* young cow; calfskin (leather)

**vacillant** *adj* vacillating, wavering; unsteady, uncertain; flickering

**vacillation** *nf* vacillation, wavering; unsteadiness; flickering

**vacillement** *nm see* **vacillation**

**vaciller** *vi* vacillate, waver; be unsteady; be undecided; flicker; stagger, wobble

**va-comme-je-te-pousse (à la)** *adv phr* haphazardly

**vacuité** *nf* vacuity, emptiness

**vadrouille** *nf naut* deck-swab; *coll* **aller en** ~ go on the spree

**vadrouiller** *vi coll* gallivant, knock around, gad about

**vadrouilleur -euse** *n* roamer

**va-et-vient** *nm invar* coming and going; to-and-fro movement, swinging movement; *elect* two-way wiring; *elect* **commutateur** ~ two-way switch; **faire le** ~ **entre** ply between; **porte** ~ swing door

**vagabond -e** *n* tramp, vagrant, vagabond; *adj* vagrant, roving

**vagabondage** *nm* vagrancy

**vagabonder** *vi* tramp, rove, roam, wander

**vagin** *nm anat* vagina

**vagir** *vi* wail, cry

**vagissement** *nm* wailing

¹**vague** *nf* wave; *coll* **faire des ~s** shock, scandalize

²**vague** *nm* vagueness, imprecision; *adj* vague, indefinite; hazy, dim; sketchy; **quelque ~ ...** some ... or other

³**vague** *nm* emptiness; *adj* empty, vacant; **terrain ~** waste land

**vaguelette** *nf* little wave

**vaguer** *vi* wander, roam

**vaillamment** *adv* valiantly, bravely, courageously

**vaillance** *nf* valour, bravery, courage

**vaillant** *adj* valiant, brave, courageous

**vain** *adj* vain, fruitless, useless; unreal, empty, sham; conceited; **~e gloire** vainglory; **en ~** in vain

**vaincre** *vt* (94) conquer, vanquish, defeat, beat; master, get the better of; **s'avouer vaincu** admit defeat; **se laisser ~ par** give way to; *vi* conquer

**vaincu -e** *n* vanquished person; *adj* vanquished

**vainement** *adv* vainly, fruitlessly, to no purpose

**vainqueur** *nm* victor, conqueror; *sp* winner; *adj m* conquering, victorious

**vair** *nm* her vair; (Cinderella) **pantoufle de ~** glass slipper

**vairon** *nm* minnow; *adj* **aux yeux ~s** with eyes of different colours

**vaisseau** *nm* ship, vessel; receptacle; (blood) vessel; nave; **~ amiral** flagship; **le ~ fantôme** the Flying Dutchman

**vaisseau-école** *nm* (*pl* **vaisseaux-écoles**) training ship

**vaisselier** *nm* dresser

**vaisselle** *nf* crockery, plates and dishes; **~ d'or (d'argent)** gold (silver) plate; **eau de ~** dishwater; **faire la ~** wash up; **machine à laver la ~** dishwasher

**val** *nm* (*pl* **~s** *or* **vaux**) valley, vale, dale; **par monts et par vaux** up hill and down dale

**valable** *adj* valid, good, cogent

**valence** *nf* *chem* valency

**valériane** *nf* valerian

**valet** *nm* valet, manservant; support, stand; jack (cards); weight (door); clamp; **~ de chambre** manservant; **~ d'écurie** groom; **~ de ferme** farm-hand; **âme de ~** servile nature; **tel maître tel ~** like master like man

**valetaille** *nf pej* menials, varletry

**valétudinaire** *n + adj* valetudinarian

**valeur** *nf* value, worth, price; meaning, import; courage, valour; *comm* **~s** securities; **avoir de la ~** be of value; *fig* carry weight; **homme de ~** man of ability, man of merit; **mettre en ~** show to advantage; develop, exploit;

**objets de ~** valuables; **sans ~** worthless

**valeureux -euse** *adj* gallant, brave

**valide** *adj* able-bodied, fit; valid

**valider** *vt* validate, authenticate

**validité** *nf* validity

**valise** *nf* suitcase, grip; **~ diplomatique** diplomatic bag

**vallée** *nf* valley

**vallon** *nm* small valley

**vallonné** *adj* undulating

**vallonnement** *nm* foothills; laying out in dells

**valoir** *vt + vi* (95) be worth; deserve, merit; be equal to, be as good as; be valid, hold good; procure, gain; **~ mieux** be better; **à ~ on** account; **autant vaut** one may as well; *coll* **ça se vaut** it's the same either way; *coll* **ça vaut le coup** it's worth it; it's worth trying; **cela ne vaut rien** that's no use, that's not worth anything, that's no good; **cela vaut pour** that goes for; **(en) ~ la peine** be worth it; **faire ~ que** point out that; **faire ~ qch** make the most of sth, set sth to advantage; show off sth, set off sth; emphasize sth; **mieux vaut tard que jamais** better late than never; **ne pas ~ cher** not be worth much; *coll* not be much good; **rien qui vaille** nothing worth mentioning; **se faire ~** make the most of oneself; put oneself forward; **vaille que vaille** for better or for worse

**valoriser** *vt* valorize; stabilize

**valse** *nf* waltz

**valser** *vi* waltz; *coll* **faire ~ qch** send sth flying; **faire ~ qn** do the waltz with s/o; *coll fig* lead s/o a dance

**valseur -euse** *n* waltzer; *nfpl sl* testicles

**valve** *nf* valve

**valvulaire** *adj* valvular

**vamper** *vt coll* vamp

**van** *nm* winnowing-basket; winnowing-machine

**vandale** *n* vandal

**vandalisme** *nm* vandalism

**vanille** *nf* vanilla

**vanillé** *adj* vanilla-flavoured

**vanité** *nf* vanity; conceit; futility, emptiness; **sans ~** without wanting to boast; **tirer ~ de qch** take an empty pride in sth

**vaniteux -euse** *adj* vain, conceited

**vannage** *nm* winnowing

**vanne** *nf* sluice, flood-gate; **~ de décharge** overflow weir; **~ d'entrée** inlet valve; **~ de réglage** regulating valve; **lever les ~s** open the floodgates

**vanneau** *nm* lapwing, peewit

¹**vanner** *vt* winnow; sift; *coll* exhaust, tire out

²**vanner** vt fit sluices to, sluice

**vannerie** nf basket-making; basket-work

**vanneur -euse** n winnower

**vannier** nm basket-maker

**vannure** nf chaff, winnowings

**vantail** nm leaf (of door)

**vantard -e** n boaster, braggart; adj boasting

**vantardise** nf bragging, boasting; boast

**vanter** vt praise, extol, vaunt; se ~ brag, boast; **il ne s'en vante pas** he keeps quiet about it

**vanterie** nf bragging, boasting

**va-nu-pieds** n beggar, barefooted vagabond

**vapeur** nm steamship; nf vapour; steam; haze; ~s fumes; obs vapours; à la ~ by steam; à toute ~ at full speed; bateau à ~ steamship; cul cuire à la ~ steam; machine à ~ steam engine

**vaporeux -euse** adj vaporous; misty; hazy; nebulous

**vaporisateur** nm atomizer, spray

**vaporiser** vt vaporize; atomize, spray; se ~ vaporize, turn to vapour; spray oneself

**vaquer** vi be vacant; be in recess; ~ à attend to, concern oneself with, go about

**varappe** nf rock-climbing

**varapper** vi climb rock-faces

**varappeur** nm rock-climber

**varech** nm seaweed, wrack

**vareuse** nf sailor's jersey, jumper; mil tunic

**variabilité** nf variability, changeableness

**variable** adj variable, changeable

**variant** adj variable, fickle

**variante** nf variant

**varice** nf varicose vein

**varicelle** nf chicken-pox

**varié** adj varied, varying; variegated; miscellaneous

**varier** vt vary, change; diversify; variegate; vi vary, change; differ in opinion

**variété** nf variety, diversity; choice, range; **spectacle de** ~ s variety show

**variole** nf smallpox

**variolé** adj pock-marked

**variqueux -euse** adj varicose

**Varsovie** nf Warsaw

**vasculaire** adj vascular

¹**vase** nm vase; vessel, receptacle; ~ de nuit chamber pot; en ~ clos in isolation

²**vase** nf mud, slime, sludge

**vasectomie** nf vasectomy

**vaseux -euse** adj muddy, slimy; sl washed-out, off-colour; woolly

**vasistas** nm fanlight

**vasomoteur -trice** adj vasomotor

**vasouiller** vi sl be at sea, be all confused

**vasque** nf basin (fountain); bowl

**vaste** adj vast, immense; spacious

**vaticiner** vi lit + pej prophesy

**va-tout** nm invar one's whole stake; **jouer son** ~ stake one's all

**vaudou** nm voodoo

**vau-l'eau (à)** adv phr with the stream; **aller** ~ go to rack and ruin, degenerate

**vaurien -ienne** n good-for-nothing, layabout

**vautour** nm vulture

**vautrer (se)** v refl wallow, sprawl

**va-vite (à la)** adv phr **fait** ~ rushed, botched

**veau** nm calf; veal; calf-leather; sl fool; ~ **marin** seal; **le** ~ **gras** the fatted calf; **pleurer comme un** ~ blubber, cry like a baby; **reliure en** ~ calf binding; **ris de** ~ sweetbread; **s'étendre comme un** ~ sprawl, loll about

**vecteur** nm carrier (disease); vehicle

**vécu** p part **vivre**; adj experienced; true-to-life

**vedette** nf sentry, scout; cin star; motor-boat, patrol boat, launch; **en** ~ in the limelight; **imprimer en** ~ print in bold type, make stand out; **mettre en** ~ highlight

**végétal** nm plant; adj vegetable, plant

**végétarien -ienne** n + adj vegetarian

**végétarisme** nm vegetarianism

**végétatif -ive** adj vegetative; cabbage-like (existence)

**végétation** nf vegetation; coll ~ s adenoids

**végéter** vi (6) vegetate

**véhémence** nf vehemence

**véhément** adj vehement, violent

**véhiculaire** adj vehicular

**véhicule** nm vehicle

**véhiculer** vt transport, carry

**veille** nf watching, sitting up, staying up; late night, vigil; eve, day before; coll **ce n'est pas demain la** ~ not likely, it won't be for ages; **être à la** ~ **de** be on the brink of; **la** ~ **au soir** the evening before

**veillée** nf evening; watching, night nursing, vigil

**veiller** vt watch over, sit up with, attend to; ~ **un mort** keep vigil over a dead body; vi sit up, stay awake, keep watch; ~ **à** see to, watch over; ~ **à ses intérêts** attend to one's interests

**veilleur** nm watcher, guard; ~ **de nuit** night watchman

**veilleuse** nf night-light; pilot-light (heater, etc); **mettre en** ~ turn low (gas); dim (lights); shelve, put off (plans, etc)

**veinard -e** *n coll* lucky person; *adj* lucky
**veine** *nf* vein; seam; inspiration; *fig* luck;
**avoir de la ~** be lucky; **avoir une ~ de
cocu** have the devil's own luck; **c'est
bien ma ~!** just my luck!; **coup de
~** stroke of luck; **être en ~ de faire
qch** be in the mood for sth; **porter ~ à**
bring good luck to
**veiner** *vt* vein, grain
**veineux -euse** *adj* veinous, veined
**veinure, vêlement** *nf* veining
**vêlage** *nm* calving
**vélaire** *adj ling* velar
**vêlement** *nm see* **vêlage**
**vêler** *vi* calve
**vélin** *nm* vellum
**velléitaire** *adj* erratic, hesitant
**velléité** *nf* whim, fancy, impulse; slight
desire; half-hearted attempt
**vélo** *nm coll* bike; **aller à (en) ~** cycle;
**faire du ~** cycle
**véloce** *adj lit* swift
**vélocité** *nf* speed, velocity
**vélodrome** *nm* cycle-racing track
**vélomoteur** *nm* light motor-cycle
**vélomotoriste** *n* rider of light motor-
cycle
**vélo-pousse** *nm* bicycle rickshaw
**velours** *nm* velvet; **~ côtelé (à côtes)**
corduroy velvet; **~ de coton** velveteen;
**c'est du ~** it's delicious; *sl* it's a
pushover; **faire patte de ~** draw in
claws (cat); *fig* show the velvet glove;
**jouer sur le ~** take no risks, act
without risks
**velouté** *nm* velvet quality, softness;
bloom (fruit); *cul* thick soup; *adj*
velvety, downy
**velouter** *vt* make like velvet, give a
velvety appearance to
**velouteux -euse** *adj* velvety
**veloutier** *nm* velvet-maker
**Velpeau** *nm* **bande ~** crape bandage
**velu** *adj* hairy, shaggy
**vélum, vélum** *nm* awning
**venaison** *nf* venison
**vénal** *adj* venal; mercenary
**vénalité** *nf* venality
**venant** *nm* **à tous ~s (à tout ~)** to all
and sundry
**vendable** *adj* saleable, marketable
**vendange** *nf* grape-harvest; vintage;
**faire les ~s (la ~)** gather in the grapes
**vendanger** *vt + vi* (3) gather, harvest
(grapes)
**vendangeur -euse** *n* wine-harvester; *nf*
aster
**vendémiaire** *nm hist* first month of the
French Republican calendar (September to October)
**vendeur -euse** *n* seller, vendor; salesman
(saleswoman), shop assistant, *US* sales

clerk
**vendre** *vt* sell; *fig* betray, give away; **à ~**
for sale; **se ~** sell, be sold; **se ~
comme des petits pains** sell like hot
cakes
**vendredi** *nm* Friday; **~ saint** Good
Friday
**vendu** *nm* traitor; *sl* double-crosser
**venelle** *nf* alley
**vénéneux -euse** *adj* poisonous
**vénérer** *vt* (6) venerate, reverence
**vénerie** *nf* venery, hunting
**vénérien -ienne** *adj* venereal
**vengeance** *nf* revenge; retribution; **crier
~** cry aloud for vengeance; **tirer ~ de**
be revenged for
**venger** *vt* (3) avenge; **se ~** take revenge,
be revenged
**vengeur -euse** *n* avenger; *adj* avenging
**venimeux -euse** *adj* poisonous; spiteful
**venin** *nm* venom, poison; spite
**venir** *vi* (96) come; originate; occur,
happen; grow, thrive; *fig* **~ à** happen
to; **~ au monde** be born; *fig* **~ de** have
just; **d'où vient que ...?** how is it that
...?; **en ~ à faire qch** come to the point
of doing sth; be reduced to doing sth;
**en ~ aux mains** come to blows; **faire
~** summon, call, send for; (crops)
grow; **je vous vois ~** I see what your
game is; **la semaine qui vient** next
week; **ne faire qu'aller et ~** be right
back, be just a moment; **où veut-il en
~?** what is he driving at?; *fig* **voir ~**
wait and see
**Venise** *nf* Venice
**vénitien -ienne** *adj* Venetian
**vent** *nm* wind; scent; *med* flatulence; **~
debout** head wind; **~ du nord (du sud,
etc)** north (south, etc) wind; **aller
(faire) ~ arrière** sail before the wind;
**au ~** in the wind; **au ~ de** to the
leeward of; *fig* **avoir le ~ en poupe** be on
a successful course; *coll* have everything going for one; **avoir ~ de** get
wind of; suspect; **ce n'est que du ~** it's
all hot air; **côté du ~** weather side;
**coup de ~** gust of wind; **donner ~ à**
give vent to; **en coup de ~** hurriedly;
**en plein ~** in the open air; **être dans le
~** be with it, be up-to-date; **faire du ~**
be windy; **mettre au ~** hang out to dry;
**prendre le ~** catch the wind; *coll* see
how the land lies; **quel bon ~ vous
amène?** how nice to see you!; **tomber
sous le ~** drop to leeward; **virer à tout
~** be a weathercock
**vente** *nf* sale, selling; tree-felling;
timber; **~ aux enchères** auction; **~
par correspondance** mail-order business; **en ~** for sale; **en ~ chez** for sale
at; **en ~ libre** unrationed; **mettre en ~**

put up for sale, put on sale; **point de ~** sales outlet; **salle des ~s** auction rooms

**venter** *v impers* blow, be windy

**venteux -euse** *adj* windy

**ventilateur** *nm* ventilator; **~ électrique** electric fan

**ventiler** *vt* ventilate, air

**ventôse** *nm hist* sixth month of the French Republican calendar (February to March)

**ventouse** *nf med* cupping-glass; suction pad; air-hole, air-vent; **faire ~** adhere by suction; *coll* **voiture ~** car that stays parked in one spot

**ventre** *nm* abdomen, belly; paunch; womb; bulge; **~ à terre** at full speed, at full tilt; **à plat ~** flat on one's face, flat on the ground; **avoir le ~ creux** have an empty stomach; **avoir mal au ~** have a bellyache; *coll* **avoir qch dans le ~** have guts; **faire ~** bulge out; **prendre du ~** grow stout; **se mettre à plat ~ devant qn** grovel before s/o; **serrer le ~** tighten one's belt

**ventricule** *nm* ventricle

**ventriloque** *n* ventriloquist

**ventru** *adj* portly, corpulent

**venu -e** *n* comer; **le dernier ~** the last to arrive; **le premier ~** the first arrival; anybody; **un nouveau ~** a newcomer; *adj* **bien ~** sturdy; pleasing; **mal ~** stunted, displeasing

**venue** *nf* coming, arrival; growth

**vêpres** *nfpl eccles* vespers, evensong

**ver** *nm* worm; maggot, grub, mite; **~ à soie** silkworm; **~ de terre** earthworm; **~ luisant** glow-worm; **~ solitaire** tapeworm; **nu comme un ~** stark naked; **rongé (piqué) des ~s** worm-eaten; **tirer les ~s du nez à qn** worm secrets out of s/o

**véracité** *nf* veracity, truthfulness

**verbalement** *adv* verbally, by word of mouth

**verbalisation** *nf leg* entry of charge; *coll* taking down of particulars

**verbaliser** *vi* draw up an official report; *coll* take down particulars; verbalize

**verbe** *nm* tone of voice, speech; verb; **avoir le ~ haut** talk in a loud voice; talk in a peremptory manner

**verbeux -euse** *adj* verbose, wordy, prolix

**verbomanie** *nf* verbal diarrhoea

**verbosité** *nf* verbosity

**verdâtre** *adj* greenish

**verdelet -ette** *adj* tart (wine); hale and hearty

**verdeur** *nf* greenness; tartness; vigour

**verdier** *nm* greenfinch

**verdir** *vt* make green, colour green; *vi* grow green, turn green

**verdissement** *nm* turning green, going green

**verdoiement** *nm* turning green

**verdoyant** *adj* green, verdant

**verdoyer** *vi* (7) become green

**verdure** *nf* greenness, greenery; vegetables for salad

**véreux -euse** *adj* worm-eaten, maggoty; *coll* fishy, dubious

**verge** *nf* switch, wand, rod, cane; shank (anchor); *anat* penis; *coll bot* **~ d'or** golden rod

**vergé** *adj* laid (paper); worm-eaten

**verger** *nm* orchard

**vergette** *nf* small cane, switch

**verglacé** *adj* icy

**verglas** *nm* coating of ice, black ice

**vergogne** *nf obs* shame; **sans ~** shameless(ly)

**vergue** *nf naut* yard

**véridique** *adj* truthful, veracious

**vérificateur -trice** *n* checker, examiner, verifier

**vérification** *nf* inspection, check, checking, examination

**vérifier** *vt* check, verify, examine, inspect; *comm* audit; confirm, prove

**vérin** *nm mech* jack

**véritable** *adj* true; genuine, real

**vérité** *nf* truth; fact; authenticity; likeness; **à la ~** as a matter of fact; **c'est la ~** it's the truth; it's a fact; **dire ses (quatre) ~s à qn** tell s/o a few home truths; **en ~** actually, verily; truly; **être en dessous de la ~** fall short of the truth

**verjus** *nm* verjuice

**vermeil** *nm* silver-gilt; *adj* (*f* **-eille**) vermilion, rosy, bright red

**vermicelle** *nm* vermicelli

**vermicide** *nm* vermicide; *adj* vermicidal

**vermiculé** *adj* vermiculated

**vermillon** *nm* vermilion, bright red

**vermine** *nf* vermin

**vermineux -euse** *adj* infested with vermin, verminous

**vermoulu** *adj* worm-eaten; decrepit

**vermoulure** *nf* worm-hole

**vermout(h)** *nm* vermouth

**verni** *adj* varnished; (leather) patent; *coll* lucky

**vernir** *vt* varnish, lacquer, japan

**vernis** *nm* varnish, polish, gloss; veneer; **~ à ongles** nail varnish; **~ au tampon** French polish; **~ gras** oil varnish

**vernissage** *nm* varnishing; japanning; private viewing at opening of exhibition

**vernisser** *vt* glaze

**vernisseur -euse** *n* varnisher

**vernissure** *nf* varnishing; glazing

**vérole** *nf coll* syphilis, pox; **petite ~** smallpox

**véronique** *nf* veronica

**verre** *nm* glass; glassful; lens; ~ **à boire** drinking glass, tumbler; ~ **à dents** tooth glass; ~ **à glace** plate glass; ~ **à pied** stemmed glass; ~ **ballon** brandy balloon; ~ **dépoli** frosted glass; ~ **grossissant** magnifying glass; **boire un** ~ have a drink; **papier de** ~ sand-paper; **porter des** ~s wear glasses

**verrerie** *nf* glassware; glass-works

**verrier** *nm* glassmaker, glassblower; artist in stained glass

**verrière** *nf* glass casing; glass roof; glass wall

**verroterie** *nf* glass trinkets, glass beads

**verrou** *nm* bolt, bar; **être sous les** ~s be in custody; **fermer au** ~ bolt

**verrouillage** *nm* bolting, locking; stop

**verrouiller** *vt* bolt, lock; stop; lock up

**verrue** *nf* wart, verruca

**verruqueux -euse** *adj* warty

[1]**vers** *nm* verse, line of verse; *pl* poetry

[2]**vers** *prep* towards; approximately, about (time); in the area of

**versant** *nm* slope, hill-side, bank

**versatile** *adj* fickle, changing, changeable

**versatilité** *nf* inconstancy, fickleness

**verse** *nf* beating down (corn); **pleuvoir à** ~ pour with rain

**versé** *adj* versed, experienced

**Verseau** *nm astrol* Aquarius

**versement** *nm* pouring; payment, deposit

**verser** *vt* pour, pour out; spill; shed (blood, tears); overturn, upset; pay in, deposit; flatten, beat down (corn); *mil* incorporate; *vi* overturn; be laid flat (corn); ~ **dans** drift into, fall into

**verset** *nm* verse (Bible)

**verseur** *adj m* pouring

**verseuse** *nf* coffee-pot

**versificateur -trice** *n* versifier

**versifier** *vt* + *vi* versify

**version** *nf* version, account; translation, unseen; ~ **anglaise** (film) dubbed into English

**verso** *nm* reverse, back, verso; **voir au** ~ see overleaf

**vert** *nm* green; **prendre qn sans** ~ catch s/o napping; *adj* green; unripe; vigorous; sharp; acid, tart (wine); unroasted (coffee); **en raconter des** ~es tell some crude stories; **en voir des** ~es **et des pas mûres** have a rough time; **langue** ~e slang

**vert-de-gris** *nm* verdigris

**vertébral** *adj* vertebral; **colonne** ~e spine

**vertèbre** *nf anat* vertebra

**vertébré** *adj* vertebrate

**vertical** *adj* vertical, perpendicular, up-right

**verticale** *nf* vertical; vertical position

**vertige** *nm* vertigo; dizziness, giddiness; **avoir le** ~ feel dizzy; have no head for heights; **cela me donne le** ~ it makes me feel giddy

**vertigineux -euse** *adj* vertiginous, dizzy; breakneck

**vertigo** *nm vet* staggers

**vertu** *nf* virtue; chastity; property; *obs* valour; *coll* **ce n'est pas une** ~ she's no angel; **en** ~ **de** by virtue of; **faire de nécessité** ~ make a virtue of necessity

**vertueux -ueuse** *adj* virtuous; chaste

**verve** *nf* animation, zest, verve; **être en** ~ be in excellent form

**verveine** *nf* verbena

**verveux -euse** *adj* lively, animated

**vésicule** *nf* vesicle, bladder; ~ **biliaire** gall-bladder

**vespasienne** *nf* public urinal

**vessie** *nf* bladder; **prendre des** ~s **pour des lanternes** believe the moon is made of green cheese

**vestale** *nf* vestal virgin

**veste** *nf* jacket; **retourner sa** ~ be a turncoat; *coll* **tomber la** ~ take off one's jacket

**vestiaire** *nm* cloak-room; changing-room; clothes-locker

**vestibule** *nm* hall, lobby, vestibule

**vestige** *nm* trace, vestige; remains

**vestimentaire** *adj* vestimentary

**veston** *nm* jacket; ~ **croisé (droit)** double-breasted (single-breasted) jacket; **complet** ~ lounge suit

**Vésuve** *nm* Vesuvius

**vêtement** *nm* garment, article of clothing; ~s clothes

**vétérinaire** *n* veterinary surgeon, *coll* vet; *adj* veterinary

**vétille** *nf* trifle, bagatelle

**vêtir** *vt* (97) clothe, dress; **se** ~ get dressed

**vétuste** *adj* decrepit, ancient

**vétusté** *nf* decrepitude, decay

**veuf** *nm* widower; *adj* (*f* **veuve**) widowed

**veule** *adj* soft, flabby, weak, sluggish

**veulerie** *nf* slackness, sluggishness

**veuvage** *nm* widowhood; widowerhood

**veuve** *nf* widow

**vexant** *adj* annoying, provoking

**vexation** *nf* humiliation, mortification

**vexatoire** *adj* vexatious, oppressive

**vexer** *vt* annoy, vex, provoke, irritate; **se** ~ **de qch** be annoyed, offended about sth

**viabilisé** *adj* **terrain** ~ site with roads, mains, drainage, etc

**viabiliser** *vt* put in roads, drains, etc (on site)

[1]**viabilité** *nf* viability

321

²**viabilité** *nf* practicability (road); development (site)
¹**viable** *adj* capable of living, viable
²**viable** *adj* fit for traffic
**viaduc** *nm* viaduct
**viager** *nm* life interest, life annuity; **mettre en ~** invest so as to bring in annuity for life; *adj* (*f* -ère) for life
**viande** *nf* meat, flesh
**viatique** *nm eccles* last sacrament
**vibrant** *adj* vibrating, vibrant; stirring, rousing
**vibrateur** *nm* vibrator
**vibratoire** *adj* vibratory
**vibrer** *vi* vibrate
**vibromasseur** *nm* vibrator (massage)
**vicaire** *nm* curate; **~ de Dieu** vicar of Christ, Pope
**vicariat** *nm* vicariate; = curacy
**vice** *nm* vice, depravity; defect; fault
**vice-amiral** *nm* vice-admiral
**vice-chancelier** *nm* vice-chancellor
**vice-gérant -e** *n* assistant manager
**vice-présidence** *nf* vice-presidency
**vice-roi** *nm* viceroy
**vicié** *adj* vitiated, corrupt, tainted; polluted
**vicier** *vt* corrupt, spoil, pollute
**vicieux -ieuse** *adj* depraved; faulty, imperfect; restive (horse)
**vicinal** *adj* local (road, path)
**vicomte** *nm* viscount
**vicomtesse** *nf* viscountess
**victime** *nf* victim
**victoire** *nf* victory; **crier (chanter) ~** triumph, crow victory; **remporter la ~** gain the victory
**victorien -ienne** *adj* Victorian
**victorieux -ieuse** *adj* victorious
**victuailles** *nfpl* victuals
**vidage** *nm* emptying; gutting
**vidange** *nf* emptying, draining; *mot* oil-change; **~ s** night-soil; sludge
**vidanger** *vt* (3) empty, drain
**vidangeur** *nm* cesspool-emptier
**vide** *nm* empty space, vacuum, blank, void; **à ~** empty; **emballage sous ~** vacuum packing; *coll* **faire le ~ autour de qn** isolate s/o; **regarder dans le ~** stare into space; **son départ laisse un ~** his departure creates a gap; **taper dans le ~** miss the mark; *adj* empty; vacant, unoccupied; void; **~ de sens** devoid of meaning; **revenir les mains ~ s** return empty-handed
**vide-ordures** *nm invar* rubbish-chute
**vide-poches** *nm invar* receptacle (for odds and ends)
**vider** *vt* empty; clear out; vacate; drain; end, settle; draw (poultry); clean (fish); *coll* exhaust; *coll* dismiss, chuck out; ruin; *coll* **~ les lieux** clear out; *coll*

**~ son sac** get sth off one's chest; **se ~** become empty, empty
**vie** *nf* life, existence; lifetime; living; **à ~** for life; **avoir la ~ dure** be hard to kill, die hard; **changer de ~** change one's way of life; **de toute sa ~** all his life; **donner la ~ à** give birth to; **en ~** alive; **faire la ~** lead a fast life; **femme de mauvaise ~** prostitute; **il y va de la ~** it's a matter of life and death; **jamais de la ~!** never!, not on your life!; **mener la grande ~** live it up; **niveau de ~** standard of living; **rendre la ~ dure à qn** make things tough for s/o; **sans ~** lifeless
**vieil** *adj see* vieux
**vieillard** *nm* old man
**vieille** *adj see* vieux
**vieillerie** *nf* old thing, out-of-date thing, old junk
**vieillesse** *nf* old age; *coll* old people; **bâton de ~** support in old age
**vieilli** *adj* grown old; old-looking; old-fashioned
**vieillir** *vt* make old; age, make look old; *vi* grow old; age; become out-of-date
**vieillissement** *nm* growing old, ageing; making old
**vieillot -otte** *adj* quaint, old-fashioned
**vielle** *nf ar* ancient stringed instrument
**Vienne** *nf* Vienna (Austria); Vienne (France)
**viennois** *adj* Viennese
**vierge** *nf* virgin, maid; **la Sainte Vierge** the Blessed Virgin; *adj* virgin; unsoiled, pure; empty, blank
**vietnamien -ienne** *adj* Vietnamese
**vieux** (*f* **vieille**) *n* old man (old woman); *coll* father (mother); **mon ~** old chap; **un ~ de la vieille** one of the old brigade; *adj* (**vieil**) (*f* **vieille**) old, elderly, aged; ancient; **~ jeu** old-fashioned; *coll* **prendre un coup de ~** get old all of a sudden; **se faire ~** be getting on in years; **une vieille fille** an old maid; **un ~ garçon** a bachelor; **vivre ~** live to a ripe old age
**vif** *nm* leg living person; quick; **avoir les nerfs à ~** be all on edge; **blessé au ~** stung to the quick; **le ~ de la question** the heart of the matter; **pêcher au ~** fish with live bait; **sur le ~** from (real) life; *adj* (*f* **vive**) alive, living; animated; quick, lively, bright; vivid; keen, intense; brisk, sharp, hasty; **chaux vive** quicklime; **de vive voix** by word of mouth; **eau vive** running water, spring water; **haie vive** quickset hedge
**vif-argent** *nm invar* quicksilver, mercury
**vigie** *nf* look-out; watch-tower; observation box

**vigilant** *adj* vigilant, alert, watchful
**vigile** *nm* watchman; *nf eccles* vigil
**vigne** *nf* vine; vineyard; ~ **vierge** Virginia creeper; *coll* **être dans les** ~ **s du Seigneur** be drunk
**vigneron -onne** *n* vine-grower
**vignette** *nf* vignette; text illustration; small label; *mot* tax label
**vignoble** *nm* vineyard; vine-growing area
**vigogne** *nf* vicuna; vicuna wool
**vigoureux -euse** *adj* vigorous, strong, sturdy
**vigueur** *nf* vigour, strength; **entrer en** ~ come into effect; **en** ~ in force
**vil** *adj* low, mean, base; cheap; **à** ~ **prix** dirt cheap
**vilain -e** *n* rogue, villain; naughty boy (girl); *hist* villein; *coll* **il y aura du** ~ there's trouble brewing; *adj* ugly; nasty, unpleasant; low, mean; shabby, sordid; **il fait (un)** ~ **(temps)** the weather's filthy; *sl* **un** ~ **coco** a nasty piece of work
**vilebrequin** *nm* brace, brace and bit; *mech* crankshaft
**vilenie** *nf* mean trick, vile action
**vilipender** *vt* vilify, abuse; run down
**villageois -e** *n* villager; *adj* village, country
**ville** *nf* town, city; ~ **d'eaux** spa; **à la** ~ in town (as opposed to country); **costume de** ~ lounge suit; **dîner en** ~ dine out; **en** ~ in town; **hôtel de** ~ town hall
**ville-dortoir** *nf* (*pl* **villes-dortoirs**) dormitory town
**villégiature** *nf* stay in the country, holiday in the country; **en** ~ on holiday
**ville-satellite** *nf* (*pl* **villes-satellites**) satellite town
**vin** *nm* wine; ~ **cacheté** better-quality wine; ~ **chaud** mulled wine; ~ **cuit** aperitif wine; ~ **de marque** fine wine, vintage wine; ~ **de messe** communion wine; ~ **mousseux** sparkling wine; ~ **ouvert** carafe wine; **avoir le** ~ **triste (gai)** be sad (merry) when drunk; **cuver son** ~ sleep it off; **entre deux** ~ **s** half seas over, tight; **être pris de** ~ be drunk; **quand le** ~ **est tiré, il faut le boire** it's too late to draw back now; **mettre de l'eau dans son** ~ water one's wine; *coll fig* reduce one's expectations; **offrir un** ~ **d'honneur à qn** hold a reception in s/o's honour; **tache de** ~ strawberry mark
**vinaigre** *nm* vinegar
**vinaigrer** *vt* add vinegar to
**vinaigrerie** *nf* vinegar factory; vinegar trade

**vinaigrette** *nf* French dressing, oil and vinegar
**vinaigrier** *nm* vinegar manufacturer; vinegar-cruet
**vinasse** *nf coll* poor wine
**vindas** *nm naut* windlass
**vindicatif -ive** *adj* vindictive
**viner** *vt* fortify, add alcohol to
**vineux -euse** *adj* the colour of red wine; wine-flavoured
**vingt** *nm + adj invar* twenty, a score; **le** ~ **mars** 20 March; **les années** ~ the twenties; **trois heures moins** ~ twenty to three; *coll* ~ **-deux (les flics)!** look out!
**vingtaine** *nf* a score, about twenty
**vingtième** *n + adj* twentieth
**vinicole** *adj* wine-growing, wine-producing
**vinyle** *nm* vinyl
**vinylique** *adj* of vinyl
**vioc, vioque** *adj sl* old
**viol** *nm* rape; violation
**violacé** *adj* purplish-blue
**violateur -trice** *n* infringer, transgressor; violator
**violation** *nf* violation; infringement
**violâtre** *adj* purplish
**viole** *nf mus* viol
**violemment** *adv* violently
**violence** *nf* violence, force; **faire** ~ **à qch** violate sth; **faire** ~ **à qn** do violence to s/o; **faire subir des** ~ **s à une femme** assault a woman; **se faire une douce** ~ agree willingly to sth after a show of resistance; **se faire** ~ go against one's feelings
**violenter** *vt* do violence to; rape
**violer** *vt* violate; transgress; break (oath); rape
**violet** *nm* violet colour; *adj* (*f* **-ette**) violet, purple
**violette** *nf bot* violet
**violeur** *nm* rapist
**violiste** *n* viol-player
**violon** *nm* violin; violin-player; *sl* lock-up cells; ~ **d'Ingres** sideline; *fig* **accordez vos** ~ **s** make sure you all agree on your story; *sl* **c'est comme si on pissait dans un** ~ it's a waste of breath; **payer les** ~ **s** pay the piper
**violoncelle** *nm* cello; cello-player
**violoncelliste** *n* cellist
**violoneux** *nm* fiddler
**violoniste** *n* violinist
**viorne** *nf bot* viburnum
**vipère** *nf* viper, adder; *coll fig* snake
**vipérin** *adj* viperish
**virage** *nm* curve, turning, bend; cornering, swinging round; changing of colour; *naut* tacking; change of opinion

**virée** *nf coll* trip, outing

**virement** *nm* turning; *naut* tacking; transfer (banking)

**virer** *vt* turn over; transfer (banking); *phot* tone; *coll* chuck out; *vi* turn; *naut* tack, veer; change colour; bank (plane)

**virevolte** *nm* spinning round, half turn; *fig* volte-face

**virevolter** *vi* spin round, wheel round suddenly

**virginité** *nf* virginity, maidenhood

**virgule** *nf* comma; decimal point

**viril** *adj* virile; male; **l'âge ~** manhood; **parties ~es** male sex organs

**viriliser** *vt* make virile

**virilité** *nf* virility; manhood; manliness

**virole** *nf* ferrule; *mech* collar, sleeve

**virtuel -uelle** *adj* virtual

**virtuose** *n* virtuoso

**virtuosité** *nf* virtuosity

**vis** *nf* screw; **~ à droite (à gauche)** right-handed (left-handed) screw; **~ à papillon** wing screw; **~ de réglage** adjusting screw; **mot ~ platinées** contact points; **~ sans tête** grub screw; **escalier à ~** spiral staircase; **pas de ~** thread; *fig* **serrer la ~ à qn** be very strict with s/o

**visa** *nm* visa; certificate

**visage** *nm* face, countenance; aspect; **à deux ~s** two-faced; **à ~ découvert** with one's face uncovered; barefacedly; **faire bon ~** smile in adversity; **faire bon ~ à qn** be amiable with s/o; **se faire le ~** make one's face up; **voir les choses sous leur vrai ~** see things in their true light

**visagiste** *n* beautician

**vis-à-vis** *nm* person opposite; partner (cards); *adv* opposite; *prep* **~ de** facing, opposite; with regard to, with respect to

**viscéral** *adj* visceral; deep-seated

**viscères** *nmpl* viscera, entrails

**viscosité** *nf* viscosity, stickiness

**visée** *nf* aiming; aim, end; **homme à grandes ~s** ambitious man

**¹viser** *vt* aim at, take aim at; refer to; take a sight on; *fig* aspire to; *sl* look at; *vi* aim

**²viser** *vt* put a visa in; countersign; stamp

**viseur** *nm* sight; viewfinder

**visibilité** *nf* visibility

**visible** *adj* visible; obvious, perceptible; *coll* able to receive visitors

**visière** *nf* vizor, eye-shade; peak (cap); gun-sight; **mettre sa main en ~** shade one's eyes with one's hand; **rompre en ~ à (avec) qn** quarrel violently with s/o; contradict s/o violently

**vision** *nf* vision, eyesight; dream, fancy; sight, view; *cin* **en première ~** first showing

**visionnaire** *n* visionary, dreamer

**visionner** *vt cin* view, preview

**visionneuse** *nf cin + phot* viewer

**visite** *nf* visit; call; inspection, examination; **~ dirigée (accompagnée)** conducted tour; **carte de ~** visiting card; **leg droit de ~** right of access; *naut* right of search; **être en ~ chez qn** be visiting s/o; **faire la ~** go on a tour of inspection, inspect; **heures de ~** visiting hours; **passer la ~** have one's medical; **recevoir des ~s** have visitors; **rendre (faire) ~ à qn** pay s/o a visit; **trou de ~** manhole

**visiter** *vt* visit; call on; examine, inspect; search

**visiteur -euse** *n* visitor; examiner, inspector; **infirmière visiteuse** district nurse

**vison** *nm* mink; mink coat

**visqueux -euse** *adj* viscous, sticky

**visser** *vt* screw, screw on, screw down; *coll fig* treat severely; **être vissé sur sa chaise** be sitting glued to one's chair

**visualiser** *vt cin* translate into visual terms

**visuel -uelle** *adj* visual; appealing to the eye; **champ ~** field of vision

**vitalité** *nf* vitality

**vitamine** *nf* vitamin

**vite** *adj* fast (sport); *adv* quickly, fast, rapidly; soon; **au plus ~** as quickly as possible; **avoir ~ fait de faire qch** be quick about doing sth; **faites ~!** look sharp!; **on a ~ fait de** it's easy to

**vitesse** *nf* speed, quickness, rapidity; **à toute ~** at full speed; *mot* **boîte de ~s** gear-box; *mot* **changer de ~** change gear; **en ~** speedily, in haste; **être en perte de ~** be slowing down, be flagging; **excès de ~** exceeding the speed limit; **faire de la ~** speed; **gagner (prendre) qn de ~** outstrip s/o; **grande (petite) ~** by passenger (goods) train (rail freight); *mot* **passer les ~s** go through the gears; **prendre de la ~** gather speed

**viticole** *adj* wine-growing

**viticulteur** *nm* wine-grower

**viticulture** *nf* wine-growing

**vitrage** *nm* glazing; glass windows

**vitrail** *nm* stained glass window

**vitre** *nf* pane, window-pane; *mot* **~ arrière** rear window; *mot* **~ avant** windscreen; *fig* **casser les ~s** kick up a row

**vitrer** *vt* glaze; **porte vitrée** glass door

**vitreux -euse** *adj* glassy, glazed, vitreous

**vitrier** *nm* glazier

**vitrifier** *vt* vitrify; coat with transparent plastic

**vitrine** *nf* shop-window; glass case, show case

**vitrioler** *vt* throw vitriol at; add sulphuric acid to

**vitupérateur -trice** *n* vituperator; *adj* vituperative

**vitupérer** *vi* (6) vituperate, protest

**vivable** *adj coll* that can be lived (in); bearable; *coll* **elle n'est pas ~** she's impossible

**vivace** *adj* long-lived; hardy; persistent, tenacious

**vivacité** *nf* vivacity, liveliness; spirit; promptness; hastiness; acuteness of feeling

**vivandière** *nf mil + hist* canteen-keeper

**vivant** *nm* lifetime; living person; **bon ~** person who enjoys life; **de son ~** during his lifetime; **du ~ de** during the lifetime of; *adj* living, alive; animated, lively; life-like

**vivat** *nm* cheer, hurrah; *interj obs* hurrah!

**¹vive** *nf* weaver-fish

**²vive** *see* **¹vivre**

**vivement** *adv* briskly, sharply; suddenly; keenly, acutely; *interj* **~ les vacances!** roll on the holidays!; **~ qu'il arrive!** I wish he'd arrive!

**viveur** *nm* pleasure-seeker

**vivier** *nm* fish-pond; fish-tank

**vivifiant** *adj* bracing, invigorating

**vivifier** *vt* quicken, vitalize; invigorate

**vivipare** *adj* viviparous

**vivoter** *vi* live sparely, subsist; just manage, struggle along

**¹vivre** *nm usu pl* supplies, provisions; *fig* **couper les ~s à qn** stop s/o's allowance

**²vivre** *vt* (98) live, live through, experience; **~ sa vie** live one's own life; **~ une expérience unique** live through a unique experience; *vi* live, be alive; survive; **~ bien** eat well; **~ de** live on, live by means of; live off; **apprendre à ~ à qn** teach s/o manners; **avoir de quoi ~** have enough to live on; **elle a beaucoup vécu** she has seen life; **facile à ~** easy to get on with; **faire ~ les siens** support one's family; **ne rencontrer âme qui vive** not meet a soul; **mil qui vive?** who goes there?; **qui vivra verra** time will show; **savoir ~** know how to behave; **se laisser ~** take life easy; **vive la joie!** let's all be merry!; **vive le roi!** long live the King!

**vizir** *nm* vizier

**vlan, v'lan** *interj* wham!, bang!, smack!

**vocabulaire** *nm* vocabulary; word list, short dictionary

**vocalement** *adv* vocally, orally

**vocalique** *adj* vocalic

**vocalise** *nf mus* vocalization exercise

**vocaliser** *vt + vi* vocalize

**vocatif** *nm* vocative

**vocation** *nf* calling, vocation; inclination

**vociférer** *vi* (6) vociferate, cry out, yell

**vœu** *nm* vow; wish; **accomplir un ~** fulfil a vow; **émettre un ~** express a wish; **faire des ~x pour** wish ardently for; **faire (le) ~ de faire qch** vow to do sth

**vogue** *nf* fashion, vogue; **en ~** in fashion; **mettre en ~** bring into fashion

**voguer** *vi* sail; **vogue la galère!** let's risk it; come what may!

**voici** *prep* here is, here are; this is, these are; **~ l'heure!** it's time!; **~ pourquoi** this is the reason; **~ quatre ans qu'il est parti** he's been gone four years; **~ qui est facile** here's something easy; **~ qu'il se met à chanter** and now he's started to sing; **en ~ bien d'une autre** here's something new; **la dame que ~** this lady here; **la ~ qui vient!** here she comes!; **le ~!** here he is!; **les ~!** here they are!

**voie** *nf* way, road, route; track, line; means, course; passage, duct; *chem* process; **~ de garage** railway siding; *fig* dead end; **~ ferrée** railway; **~ publique** public thoroughfare; **~s de fait** acts of violence; **en ~ de** in the process of; nearing; **être en bonne ~ de** be in a fair way to; **faire ~ d'eau** spring a leak; **mettre qn sur la ~** put s/o on the right track; **par la ~ des airs** by air; **pays en ~ de développement** developing country

**voilà** *prep* there is, there are; **~!** there!; **~ ce que c'est que d'aller trop vite** that's what you get for going too fast; **~, monsieur!** coming, sir!; **~ qui est fait!** that's done!; **~ qu'il se met à hurler** there he goes and starts shouting; **~ tout** that's all; **~ trois jours qu'il est parti** he's been gone for three days; **comme vous ~ beau!** how nice you look!; **en ~ assez!** that'll do!, no more of that!; **en ~ des manières!** what bad manners!; **le ~ bien!** that's him all over; **le ~ qui vient!** here he comes!; **me ~!** here I am!

**¹voile** *nm* veil; *phot* fog; *anat* **~ du palais** velum; **avoir un ~ devant les yeux** have a mist before one's eyes; **prendre le ~** take holy orders; **sous le ~ de** under the guise of

**²voile** *nf* sail; **bateau à ~s** sailing boat; **faire de la ~** sail, go sailing; **faire ~** set sail

**voilé** *adj* veiled; clouded; dim, obscure; husky

¹**voiler** *vt* veil; cloud, obscure; disguise, conceal; muffle; *phot* fog; **se ~** wear a veil; grow dim

²**voiler** *vt naut* equip with sails; *vi obs* warp; **se ~** warp

**voilette** *nf* veil (hat)

**voilier** *nm* sailing boat; sailmaker

**voilure** *nf* sails, canvas

**voir** *vt* (99) see; inspect; visit; understand; attend to; look after; look into; regard; **~ du pays** travel; **~ venir qn** see what s/o is after; **à le ~** judging by his appearance; **aller ~** go and see; **c'est à ~** that's worth seeing; that remains to be seen; *coll* **écoutez ~** just listen; *coll* **en faire ~ à qn** lead s/o a dance; **faire ~** show; **je ne peux pas le ~** I can't stand him; **je n'y vois rien** I can't see a thing; **je vois ça d'ici** I can visualize what it's like; **ni vu ni connu** without anyone being any the wiser; **se faire mal ~** get a bad reputation; *vi* see; **~ c'est croire** seeing is believing; **cela n'a rien à ~ avec** that has nothing to do with; **on verra bien** we'll see; **voyez un peu** just look; **voyons!** look here!; now, now!; **se ~** see oneself; see one another (each other); **cela se voit** that's obvious

**voire** *adv* indeed, even, nay; **~ même** and even

**voirie** *nf* public highway; administration of public thoroughfare; refuse-dump

**voisin -e** *n* neighbour; *adj* neighbouring, next-door; adjoining, next; akin

**voisinage** *nm* neighbourhood, vicinity; proximity, nearness

**voisiner** *vi obs* visit one's neighbours; **~ avec** be sitting next to

**voiture** *nf* carriage, conveyance, vehicle; (motor-)car; cart, wagon; railway coach; **~ cellulaire** prison van; **~ de livraison** delivery van; **~ de malade** invalid chair; **~ d'enfant** pram; **~ de place** cab; **en ~!** all aboard!; take your seats!; *comm* **lettre de ~** waybill

**voiture-pie** *nf* (*pl* **voitures-pies**) police car, = panda car

**voiturer** *vt* transport by car

**voiture-restaurant** *nf* (*pl* **voitures-restaurants**) restaurant-car, dining-car

**voiturette** *nf* small car; small cart, trap

**voiturier** *nm* carter, carrier

**voix** *nf* voice; tone; vote; *gramm* voice; speech; **à haute ~** aloud; **à portée de ~** within earshot; **à ~ basse** softly, in an undertone; **de vive ~** by word of mouth; **donner de la ~** give tongue; **d'une commune ~** by common consent; **mettre aux ~** put to the vote; **n'avoir pas ~ au chapitre** have no say in the matter

¹**vol** *nm* flight; flying; flock (of birds); **à ~ d'oiseau** as the crow flies; **de haut ~** high-class; lofty; **en plein ~** in full flight; **prendre son ~** take flight; **saisir l'occasion au ~** jump at the opportunity

²**vol** *nm* theft, stealing, larceny; robbery; **~ à la tire** bag-snatching, purse-snatching; **~ à l'étalage** shop-lifting; **~ à main armée** armed robbery; **~ avec agression** robbery with violence; **~ avec effraction** housebreaking; **~ qualifié** aggravated theft; *coll* **c'est un ~ manifeste** it's daylight robbery

**volage** *adj* fickle, flighty, inconstant

**volaille** *nf* poultry

¹**volant** *nm* shuttlecock; flounce, frill; *mech* flywheel; *mot* steering-wheel; tear-off leaf; **être tué au ~** be killed in a car accident; **jouer au ~** play at battledore and shuttlecock; **tenir le ~** drive

²**volant** *adj* flying; movable; loose; fluttering; **table ~e** occasional table; **vivre en camp ~** live in makeshift accommodation, camp out

**volatil** *adj* volatile

**volatile** *nm* winged creature, bird; farmyard bird

**volatiliser** *vt* volatilize; **se ~** fade away, vanish

**volatilité** *nf* volatility

**volcan** *nm* volcano

**volcanique** *adj* volcanic

**volcanologue** *n* vulcanologist

**vole** *nf* **faire la ~** win all the tricks (cards)

**volée** *nf* flight; flock, bevy, brood; volley, salvo; peal of bells; hail of blows; rank; **à la ~** in flight, on the wing; **de haute ~** of high rank; **lancer à toute ~** hurl; **semer à la ~** broadcast seed; **sonner à toute ~** ring out loudly

¹**voler** *vt* steal; rob; swindle, cheat; **il ne l'a pas volé** it serves him right; **je suis volé** I've been swindled

²**voler** *vi* fly; *fig* rush, go very fast; *fig* **entendre ~ une mouche** hear a pin drop; **faire ~ qch** send sth flying

**volet** *nm* shutter; sorting-board; *aer* flap; *coll* **trié sur le ~** hand-picked

**voleter** *vi* (5) flutter, flutter about

**voleur -euse** *n* thief; robber; burglar; **~ à la tire** bag-snatcher; **~ à l'étalage** shop-lifter; **~ de grand chemin** highway robber; **au ~!** stop thief!; *adj* thieving

**volière** *nf* aviary

**volige** *nf bui* batten

**voliger** *vt* (3) *bui* batten; lath

**volontaire** *n* volunteer; *adj* voluntary; headstrong, self-willed

**volonté** *nf* will; will-power; pleasure, wish; **à ~** at will; ad lib; **dernières ~s** last will and testament; **faire ses quatre ~s** do as one pleases; **mauvaise ~** unwillingness; **n'en faire qu'à sa ~** refuse to listen to reason

**volontiers** *adv* willingly, gladly; readily

**volte-face** *nf invar* turning about, volte-face; **faire ~** face about, turn right about

**voltige** *nf* acrobatics (rope, trapeze); *aer* aerobatics

**voltiger** *vi* (3) flit, hover, fly about; perform acrobatics (rope, trapeze)

**voltigeur -euse** *n* acrobat (rope, trapeze); *nm ar* light infantryman

**volubile** *adj* voluble

**volubilis** *nm bot* convolvulus

**volubilité** *nf* volubility

**volume** *nm* bulk, volume, mass; tome; volume, sound level; capacity

**volumétrique** *adj* volumetric

**volumineux -euse** *adj* voluminous

**volupté** *nf* voluptuousness; pleasure, delight

**voluptueux -ueuse** *adj* voluptuous

**volute** *nf* volute, scroll; wreath (smoke); whorl; curl (wave)

**vomir** *vt* vomit, belch out, spew up; *vi* vomit, be sick; **c'est à ~** it's enough to make one sick

**vomissement** *nm* vomiting

**vomissure** *nf* vomit

**vomitif** *nm* emetic

**vorace** *adj* voracious, ravenous

**voracité** *nf* voracity

**vos** *poss adj pl see* **votre**

**votant -e** *n* voter

**votation** *nf* voting

**vote** *nm* vote, voting, suffrage; **droit de ~** franchise

**voter** *vt* pass, carry; *vi* vote

**votif -ive** *adj* votive

**votre** *poss adj* (*pl* **vos**) your; **vos père et mère** your father and mother

**vôtre** *pron* yours; **à la ~!** your very good health!; **il faut y mettre du ~** you must do your bit; *comm* **j'ai reçu la ~ du 15 avril** I am in receipt of yours of 15 April

**vouer** *vt* vow, dedicate, devote; **ne pas (plus) savoir à quel saint se ~** not know which way to turn; **voué à l'échec** destined to fail

**vouloir** *nm* will; **de son bon ~** of one's own accord; *vt* (100) want, wish; desire, wish for; require; **combien en veut-il?** how much is he asking for it?; **en veux-tu en voilà** as much as you like; **en ~ à qn** bear s/o a grudge; **il l'a voulu** he wanted it; he asked for it; **que lui voulez-vous?** what do you want of

him?; **que voulez-vous?** what do you want?; what do you expect?; **que voulez-vous que j'y fasse?** how can I help it?; **qu'il le veuille ou non** willy-nilly; **sans le ~** unintentionally; **s'en ~** be annoyed with oneself; **se ~** claim; *vi* will; want; wish; be willing; **~ c'est pouvoir** where there's a will there's a way; **~ de qch** want sth; **~ dire** mean; **c'est comme vous voudrez** as you please; **Dieu veuille** God grant, please to God; **il en veut à mon argent** he has designs on my money; **je ne veux pas de ça** I want none of that; **je veux bien** willingly; **je veux bien que tu l'aies vu** you may well have seen him; **je veux qu'il vienne** I want him to come; **voulez-vous bien me passer le sel** please (kindly) pass me the salt

**voulu** *adj* required, requisite; intentional, deliberate

**vous** *pron* you; yourself; to you; one; **c'est à ~** it's yours; it's your turn; **de ~ à moi** between ourselves

**vous-même** *pron* yourself

**voussure** *nf* curve of arch

**voûte** *nf* vault, arch

**voûté** *adj* vaulted, arched; bent, stooping

**voûter (se)** *v refl* become round-shouldered, grow bent

**vouvoiement** *nm* use of 'vous' in addressing people

**vouvoyer** *vt* (7) use 'vous' in addressing people

**voyage** *nm* journey, voyage; travel; *coll* trip; **~ accompagné** conducted tour; **~ d'agrément** pleasure trip; **~ de noces** honeymoon; **bon ~!** have a good journey!; **être en ~** be travelling; be away; **partir en ~** set off on a journey

**voyager** *vi* (3) travel; *coll* have a trip

**voyageur -euse** *n* traveller; passenger; fare (taxi); **~ (de commerce)** (commercial) traveller; **pigeon ~** carrier pigeon

**¹voyant** *nm* signal, mark; signal light, indicator light; *adj* gaudy, garish, showy, loud

**²voyant -e** *n* seeing person; clairvoyant

**voyelle** *nf* vowel

**voyou** *nm* hooligan, layabout

**voyouterie** *nf* hooliganism; gutter wit

**vrac** *nm* **en ~** loose (goods)

**vrai** *nm* truth; reality; **être dans le ~** be in the right; **il y a du ~ là-dedans** there's some truth in that; *adj* true, real; genuine; correct; realistic; **pour de ~** really, seriously; *adv* truly, indeed, really; *coll* **~ de ~** really and truly; **à ~ dire** to tell the truth

**vraiment** *adv* really, truly
**vraisemblable** *adj* probable, likely; plausible; **au delà du ~** beyond the bounds of probability
**vraisemblance** *nf* probability, likelihood; plausibility
**vrille** *nf* tendril; *eng* gimlet, borer; *aer* spin; **tomber en ~** come down in a spin
**vrillé** *adj* curled; twisted; *bot* with tendrils
**vrillée** *nf coll bot* bindweed
**vriller** *vt* bore; *vi* whirl; *aer* climb in a spiral; snarl, shrink
**vrillette** *nf* deathwatch beetle
**vrombir** *vi* buzz, zoom, hum, purr
**vrombissement** *nm* buzzing, zooming, humming, purring
**vu** *nm* **au ~ et au su de tous** openly; *p part* **voir**; *prep* considering, seeing, in view of
**vue** *nf* sight, eyesight; view, aspect, prospect; intention; opinion; view; slide; **~ d'oiseau** bird's eye view; **à la ~ de** at the sight of; **à première ~** at first sight; **avoir des ~s sur** have designs on; **avoir la ~ basse (longue)** be short-sighted (long-sighted); **à ~ de nez** at a rough guess; **à ~ d'œil** visibly; **du point de ~ de** with regard to; **en mettre plein la ~ à qn** try to impress s/o; **entrer dans les ~s de qn** agree with s/o; **en ~ de** with an eye to; **être très en ~** be very much in the public eye; **garder à ~** keep in sight; **payable à ~** payable on sight; **perdre de ~** lose sight of
**vulcaniser** *vt* vulcanize
**vulcanologie** *nf* vulcanology
**vulgaire** *nm obs* the common people; *adj* vulgar, common; ordinary; **la langue ~** the vernacular
**vulgarisateur -trice** *n* popularizer
**vulgarisation** *nf* popularization, vulgarization
**vulgariser** *vt* popularize; make vulgar
**vulgarité** *nf* vulgarity
**vulnérabilité** *nf* vulnerability
**vulve** *nf anat* vulva

# W

**wagnérien -ienne** *adj* Wagnerian
**wagon** *nm* carriage, coach, car; wagon, truck; wagon-load; **~ à bagages** luggage-van, *US* baggage car; **~ à caisse** goods-truck, *US* freight-car; **~ à chevaux** horse-box, *US* horse-car; **~ de marchandises** goods-wagon, *US* freight-car; **~ en plate-forme** flat goods-truck, *US* flat-car; **~ frein** brake-van; **~ frigorifique** refrigerator-car; **~ rail-route** road railer
**wagon-citerne** *nm* (*pl* **wagons-citernes**) tank-car, tank-wagon
**wagon-foudre** *nm* (*pl* **wagons-foudres**) tank-car, tank-wagon
**wagon-lit** *nm* (*pl* **wagons-lits**) sleeping-car, *coll* sleeper
**wagonnet** *nm* tip-truck, tip-wagon
**wagon-poste** *nm* (*pl* **wagons-poste**) mail-van
**wagon-restaurant** *nm* (*pl* **wagons-restaurants**) restaurant-car, dining-car
**wallon -onne** *adj* Walloon
**waters** *nmpl coll* water-closet, W.C., *coll* loo
**wattman** *nm obs* tram-driver
**western** *nm* cowboy film, western

# X

**X** *nm invar* **avoir les jambes en ~** be knock-kneed; **l' ~** the École Polytechnique; **rayons ~** X-rays
**xénophobie** *nf* xenophobia

**Xérès** *nm* sherry
**xérographie** *nf* xeroxing
**xylographie** *nf* wood-engraving; woodcut

# Y

**y** *adv* there; here; thither; **il ~ a** there is, there are; *coll* **je n' ~ suis pas du tout** I'm all at sea; *coll fig* **j' ~ suis!** I've got it!; *coll* **j' ~ suis, j' ~ reste!** here I am and here I stay!; *pron invar* at it, to it, about it, of it, etc; **ça ~ est!** it's done!, that's it!, all right!; **il ~ est pour quelque chose** he has a hand in it; **je n' ~ manquerai pas** I shall not fail to do so; **je n' ~ suis pour personne** I'm not at home to anyone; **je n' ~ suis pour rien** it is none of my doing; **pendant que j' ~ suis** while I'm about it; **pensez-~** think of it; **rien n' ~ fait** it's no good; **vas-~!** go there!, get on with it!

**yaourt** *nm* yogurt; *coll* **mot pot de ~** bubble-car
**yeuse** *nf* ilex, holm-oak, holly-oak
**yeux** *nmpl* eyes (*pl* of œil)
**yé-yé** *n* with-it teenager, hipster, raver
**yole** *nf naut* yawl
**yougoslave** *adj* Yugoslav
**Yougoslavie** *nf* Yugoslavia
**youpin -e** *n sl pej* Yid
**youyou** *nm* dinghy
**ypérite** *nf chem* yperite, mustard-gas
**ypréau** *nm* broad-leaved elm; white poplar

# Z

**zazou** *nm* teddy-boy
**zèbre** *nm* zebra; *coll* chap
**zébré** *adj* striped
**zébrer** *vt* (6) mark with stripes; streak

**zébrure** *nf* stripe; series of stripes; zebra-markings
**zélateur -trice** *n* zealot; *adj* zealous
**zèle** *nm* zeal, ardour; **brûler de ~** be fired

with enthusiasm; *coll* **faire du** ~ be over-zealous

**zélé** *adj* zealous

**zélote** *nm* zealot

**zéro** *nm* cipher, nought; *coll sp* nil, love; **c'est un** ~ he's a nobody; **partir de** ~ start from scratch

**zeste** *nm cul* zest, outer skin (of orange, lemon); *coll* very small quantity

**zézaiement** *nm* lisping, lisp

**zézayer** *vi* (7) lisp

**zibeline** *nf zool* (**martre**) ~ sable

**zig, zigue** *nm sl* fellow, chap; **un bon** ~ a decent fellow

**zigoteau, zigoto** *nm sl* fellow, chap

**zigouiller** *vt sl* kill, murder, knife

**zigzag** *nm* zigzag; **éclair en** ~ forked lightning

**zigzaguer** *vi* zigzag; drive erratically

**zinc** *nm* zinc; *coll* counter (of a bar); *coll* café, bar; **pommade à l'oxyde de** ~ zinc ointment

**zinguer** *vt* cover with zinc; *metal* galvanize

**zingueur** *nm* zinc-worker; zinc-roofer

**zinzin** *nm coll* thing; *adj coll* barmy

**zizanie** *nf* discord

**zizi** *nm coll* thing; *sl* penis; *sl* vagina

**zob** *nm vulg* penis

**zodiaque** *nm* zodiac

**zona** *nm med* shingles, zona

**zone** *nf* zone; sphere, area; *coll* outskirts of Paris; *mot* ~ **bleue** area of restricted parking; *meteor* ~ **de dépression** trough of low pressure; *geog* ~ **des alizés** trade wind belt; *mil* ~ **des armées** war zone; ~ **verte** green belt

**zoologie** *nf* zoology

**zoologique** *adj* zoological; **jardin** ~ zoological garden, zoo

**zoologiste** *n* zoologist

**zouave** *nm mil* zouave; *coll* **faire le** ~ play the fool

**zozoter** *vi coll* lisp

**zut** *interj* blast!; oh, hell!; ~ **pour vous!** go to blazes!

**zyeuter, zieuter** *vt sl* stare at, have a look at

# ENGLISH-FRENCH

# A

**a** *n* (la lettre) a; *mus* la *m*; **A 1** en parfait état

**a, an** *indef art* un (*f* une)

**aback** *adv naut* masqué, pris vent debout; **taken ~** dérouté, décontenancé

**abacus** *n* abaque *m*, boulier compteur *m*; *archi* abaque *m*

**abaft** *adv naut* vers l'arrière; *prep naut* derrière

**abandon** *n* nonchalance *f*, abandon *m*, laisser-aller *m invar*; *vt* abandonner, lâcher, délaisser; **~ oneself** s'abandonner, se livrer

**abandonment** *n* abandon *m*; (casualness) laisser-aller *m invar*; renonciation *f*

**abase** *vt* humilier, mortifier, abaisser

**abasement** *n* humiliation *f*, abaissement *m*

**abash** *vt* déconcerter, confondre

**abate** *vt* diminuer; (price) rabattre; (lessen) affaiblir; *leg* annuler; *vi* diminuer, s'affaiblir

**abatement** *n* diminution *f*; rabais *m*; *leg* annulation *f*

**abattoir** *n* abattoir *m*

**abbatial** *adj* abbatial

**abbess** *n* abbesse *f*

**abbey** *n* abbaye *f*; (church) (église) abbatiale *f*

**abbot** *n* abbé *m*, supérieur *m* d'un monastère

**abbreviate** *vt* abréger, écourter

**abbreviation** *n* abréviation *f*

**ABC** *n* alphabet *m*; **ABC** *m*, rudiments *mpl* de connaissances

**abdicate** *vt* abdiquer, renoncer à; *vi* abdiquer

**abdication** *n* abdication *f*

**abdomen** *n* abdomen *m*

**abdominal** *adj* abdominal

**abduct** *vt* enlever, kidnapper

**abduction** *n* enlèvement *m*, rapt *m*; (minor) détournement *m*; *med* abduction *f*

**abductor** *n* ravisseur -euse; *med* (muscle) abducteur *m*

**abeam** *adj naut* par le travers

**abed** *adv* au lit

**aberrance** *n* aberrance *f*

**aberrant** *adj* aberrant

**aberration** *n* aberration *f*, déviation *f*, égarement *m*

**abet** *vt* inciter, aiguillonner, encourager;

**aid and ~** être complice de, prendre part à

**abetter, abettor** *n* complice

**abeyance** *n* suspension *f*; **fall into ~** tomber en désuétude

**abhor** *vt* détester, exécrer, abhorrer

**abhorrence** *n* exécration *f*, horreur *f*

**abhorrent** *adj* détestable, exécrable

**abidance** *n* persistance *f*; conformité *f*

**abide** *vt* (wait for) attendre; souffrir; supporter; *vi* durer, continuer; **~ by** rester fidèle à, respecter

**abiding** *adj* permanent, constant

**ability** *n* compétence *f*, capacité *f*; (cleverness) habileté *f*

**abiogenesis** *n* génération spontanée

**abject** *adj* abject, ignoble, répugnant

**abjection** *n* abjection *f*, avilissement *m*, indignité *f*

**abjuration** *n* abjuration *f*

**abjure** *vt* abjurer

**ablation** *n* geol + surg ablation *f*

**ablative** *n gramm* ablatif *m*; *adj gramm* ablatif -ive

**ablaze** *adj* embrasé, en feu, en flammes; *fig* excité, enflammé

**able** *adj* intelligent, habile; capable, compétent; *med* sain; *leg* compétent

**able-bodied** *adj* robuste, fort; **~ seaman** matelot *m* de deuxième classe

**ablution** *n* ablution *f*

**abnegate** *vt* (responsibility) renier; (rights) renoncer à

**abnegation** *n* abnégation *f*; renoncement *m*

**abnormal** *adj* anormal, singulier -ière; exceptionnel -elle; insolite

**abnormality** *n* anomalie *f*, singularité *f*; (oddness) bizarrerie *f*

**abnormity** *n* anomalie *f*; monstruosité *f*

**aboard** *adv* à bord; **take ~** embarquer; *prep* à bord de

**abode** *n* habitation *f*, domicile *m*, demeure *f*

**abolish** *vt* abolir, supprimer

**abolition** *n* abolition *f*, suppression *f*

**abolitionist** *n* abolitionniste

**A-bomb** *n* bombe *f* atomique

**abominable** *adj* abominable, monstrueux -ueuse

**abominate** *vt* abominer, exécrer, détester

**abomination** *n* abomination *f*, exécration *f*

## aboriginal

**aboriginal** *n* aborigène, indigène; *adj* aborigène, indigène
**aborigines** *npl* aborigènes *pl*, indigènes *pl*
**abort** *vt* faire avorter; *mil* (operation) interrompre; *vi* avorter; échouer
**abortion** *n* avortement *m*; (creature) avorton *m*
**abortionist** *n* avorteur -euse; *coll* faiseuse *f* d'anges
**abortive** *adj* prématuré, avorté; rudimentaire
**aboulia, abulia** *n* aboulie *f*
**abound** *vi* abonder, foisonner, regorger; *coll* grouiller
**about** *adv* de tous côtés, çà et là; (around) environ; à peu près, vers; (near) près; (all round) autour; (opposite direction) à rebours; *mil* ~ **turn!** demi-tour, marche!; **be ~ to** être sur le point de; *naut* **go ~** virer de bord; **out and ~** sur pied; **put sth ~** lancer un canard, faire courir un bruit; *prep* (near to) autour de, aux alentours de; (concerning) au sujet de, à propos de; (concerned with) occupé à; **how ~ a walk?** si l'on allait se promener?; **what's ~** ? de quoi s'agit-il?; **while I'm ~** it pendant que j'y suis
**above** *adv* (higher up) au-dessus, en haut, plus haut; (heaven) au ciel; (in text) plus haut; (more than) à partir de; **over and ~** en sus de; *prep* (higher than) au-dessus de, plus haut que; (more than) plus de; (upstream) en amont de; (better) supérieur à
**above-board** *adj* franc (*f* franche), ouvert; *adv* ouvertement
**abrade** *vt* gratter, racler, user en frottant; éroder
**abrasion** *n* abrasion *f*; érosion *f*; (scratch) écorchure *f*
**abreast** *adv* de front, côte à côte; ~ **of** à la hauteur de; **keep ~ of** se tenir au courant de
**abridge** *vt* abréger, résumer; (lessen) diminuer; *leg* priver
**abridgement** *n* abrégé *m*, résumé *m*; diminution *f*; *leg* privation *f*
**abroach** *adv* + *adj* (cask) en perce
**abroad** *adv* (in another country) à l'étranger; (outside) dehors, à l'extérieur; (far and wide) au loin
**abrogate** *vt* abroger
**abrupt** *adj* brusque; (style) décousu; abrupt, escarpé
**abruptness** *n* brusquerie *f*; (haste) précipitation *f*; (slope) raideur *f*
**abscess** *n* abcès *m*
**abscond** *vi* filer, se sauver, s'enfuir; *coll* déguerpir; décamper
**absence** *n* absence *f*; (lack) manque *m*;

leg défaut *m*; ~ **of mind** distraction *f*; **in the ~ of** faute de; *mil* **leave of ~** permission *f*
**absent** *vt* ~ **oneself** s'absenter; *adj* absent; manquant; distrait
**absentee** *n* absent -e, absentéiste
**absenteeism** *n* absentéisme *m*
**absent-minded** *adj* distrait, absent, rêveur -euse, étourdi
**absent-mindedness** *n* distraction *f*, absence *f*, étourderie *f*
**absinth** *n* absinthe *f*
**absolute** *n* absolu *m*; *adj* absolu, complet -ète, parfait; entier -ière, intransigeant; indépendant
**absolutely** *adv* absolument, parfaitement; entièrement; *coll* (agreed) d'accord, oui
**absolution** *n* absolution *f*
**absolutism** *n* absolutisme *m*
**absolve** *vt* absoudre; *leg* acquitter
**absonant** *adj* discordant; *mus* dissonant
**absorb** *vt* absorber, assimiler; (noise, shock) amortir
**absorbent** *n* absorbant *m*; *adj* absorbant
**absorber** *n* **shock ~** amortisseur *m*
**absorbing** *adj* absorbant; *fig* passionnant
**absorption** *n* absorption *f*; (sounds) amortissement *m*
**abstain** *vi* s'abstenir; ~ **from** se priver de, renoncer à
**abstainer** *n* *pol* abstentionniste; **total ~** personne *f* qui ne boit jamais d'alcool
**abstemious** *adj* sobre, frugal, modéré
**abstention** *n* abstention *f*
**abstinence** *n* privation *f*; *eccles* abstinence *f*
**abstinent** *adj* sobre, frugal, modéré
**abstract** *n* résumé *m*, abrégé *m*; *philos* abstrait *m*; abstraction *f*; *vt* abstraire; *euph* soustraire, voler; *adj* abstrait
**abstracted** *adj* distrait, rêveur -euse; dégagé
**abstraction** *n* abstraction *f*; (absentmindedness) distraction *f*; *euph* vol *m*; *leg* soustraction *f*
**abstruse** *adj* abstrus
**absurd** *n* absurde *m*; ridicule *m*; *adj* absurde, déraisonnable; ridicule
**absurdity** *n* absurdité *f*
**abundance** *n* abondance *f*, profusion *f*; foisonnement *m*; richesse *f*
**abundant** *adj* abondant, foisonnant; (lavish) plantureux -euse, riche
**abuse** *n* abus *m*, excès *m*; (verbal) injure *f*, insulte *f*; *vt* maltraiter, faire mauvais usage de; (verbally) injurier, insulter; (privilege) abuser de
**abusive** *adj* injurieux -ieuse, insultant; abusif -ive
**abut** *vi* être contigu -üe, être limitrophe

334

**abysmal** *adj* insondable; *coll* exécrable; (ignorance) profond
**abyss** *n* abîme *m*; *geog* abysse *m*
**abyssal** *adj* abyssal
**acacia** *n* acacia *m*
**academic** *n* personne *f* exerçant une fonction dans l'enseignement supérieur (universitaire); *adj* académique; (learned) savant, érudit; *pej* pédant, théorique; universitaire
**academician** *n* membre *m* d'une académie savante
**academy** *n* académie *f*
**acanthus** *n* acanthe *f*
**accede** *vi* accéder, atteindre; (agree to) accepter, agréer
**accelerate** *vt* + *vi* accélérer, hâter, presser; activer
**acceleration** *n* accélération *f*
**accelerator** *n* accélérateur *m*; *coll* mot champignon *m*
**accent** *n* accent *m*; inflexion *f*, intonation *f*; *ling* accent *m* tonique; *vt* accentuer; intensifier
**accentual** *adj* accentuel -uelle
**accentuate** *vt* accentuer; augmenter, intensifier
**accentuation** *n* accentuation *f*
**accept** *vt* accepter; (agree to) accueillir, agréer; adhérer à; se résigner à, souffrir; (adopt) adopter, approuver
**acceptable** *adj* acceptable, recevable, satisfaisant; (welcome) opportun, bienvenu
**acceptance** *n* acceptation *f*; consentement *m*, agrément *m*
**acceptation** *n* acceptation *f*
**acceptor** *n comm* accepteur *m*
**access** *n* accès *m*, abord *m*; entrée *f*, ouverture *f*; *med* accès *m*, crise *f*
**accessary** *n* complice; adjoint -e; *adj* accessoire
**accessible** *adj* accessible; abordable; compréhensible; ouvert
**accession** *n* accession *f*; (joining) adhésion *f*; *leg* accession *f*; (addition) accroissement *m*
**accessory** *n* (person) complice; *theat* + *comm* accessoire *m*; *adj* accessoire, secondaire, auxiliaire
**accidence** *n gramm* morphologie *f*; rudiments *mpl*
**accident** *n* accident *m*; chance *f*, hasard *m*
**accidental** *n mus* accident *m*, signe accidentel; *adj* accidentel -elle, contingent, fortuit; accessoire; extrinsèque; *mus* accidentel -elle
**acclaim** *n* acclamation *f*; *vt* acclamer, applaudir; (announce) proclamer
**acclamation** *n* acclamation *f*
**acclimatization** *n* acclimatation *f*

**acclimatize** *vt* acclimater, habituer; *vi* s'acclimater, s'habituer
**acclivity** *n* montée *f*
**accolade** *n* accolade *f*; *mus* accolade *f*
**accommodate** *vt* accommoder, adapter, ajuster; harmoniser, mettre d'accord, réconcilier; (arrange) agencer, disposer; (assist) aider, rendre service à; (put up) loger, abriter
**accommodating** *adj* obligeant, serviable; (helpful) accommodant, débonnaire, complaisant
**accommodation** *n* accommodation *f*, ajustement *m*; adaptation *f*; accommodement *m*, arrangement *m*, compromis *m*; (lodging) logement *m*; (train, ship, etc) place *f*; (hotel) chambre *f*; (loan) prêt *m* d'argent; *naut* ~ **ladder** échelle *f* de coupée
**accompaniment** *n* accompagnement *m*
**accompanist** *n* accompagnateur -trice
**accompany** *vt* accompagner
**accomplice** *n* complice
**accomplish** *vt* accomplir, achever, terminer; exécuter, réaliser
**accomplished** *adj* accompli, consommé, incomparable
**accomplishment** *n* accomplissement *m*, réalisation *f*; (success) réussite *f*; ~s talents *mpl*; (social) talents *mpl* de société
**accord** *n* accord *m*, consentement *m*; harmonie *f*; (agreement) traité *m*; *vt* accorder; ajuster; octroyer; (bring to agreement) mettre d'accord; *vi* s'accorder, être d'accord
**accordance** *n* accord *m*, compatibilité *f*, conformité *f*; **in ~ with** suivant, selon, conformément à
**accordant** *adj* conforme
**according** *adv conj phr* ~ **as** selon que, suivant que; *prep phr* ~ **to** suivant, selon, conformément à
**accordingly** *adv* donc; en conséquence
**accordion** *n* accordéon *m*
**accordionist** *n* accordéoniste
**accost** *vt* accoster, aborder; *coll* draguer; racoler
**account** *n* compte *m*; (part payment) acompte *m*; (narrative) récit *m*, description *f*, relation *f*; (significance) estime *f*, égard *m*, importance *f*; ~s comptabilité *f*, écritures *fpl*; **bank ~** compte *m* en banque; **by all ~s** de l'avis général; **call s/o to ~** demander des comptes à qn; **current ~** compte courant; **give a good ~ of oneself** se défendre bien; **keep the ~s** tenir la comptabilité; **on ~** à valoir; **on ~ of** à cause de; *vt* estimer, considérer; *vi* ~ **for** rendre compte de, expliquer, justifier; **there's no ~ing for tastes** des

goûts et des couleurs on ne dispute pas

**accountable** *adj* responsable, comptable; explicable

**accountant** *n* comptable, agent comptable; **chartered** ~ = expert *m*+*f* comptable

**accoutre** *vt lit* accoutrer

**accoutrement** *n* accoutrement *m*

**accredit** *vt* accréditer, attribuer

**accrete** *vt* accroître; *vi* adhérer, s'accroître, s'attacher

**accretion** *n* accroissement *m*

**accrue** *vi* revenir, échoir; s'accroître

**accumulate** *vt* accumuler, amasser, amonceler, entasser; *vi* s'accumuler, s'entasser

**accumulation** *n* accumulation *f*, entassement *m*, amoncellement *m*; (capital) accroissement *m*; *leg* cumul *m*

**accumulative** *adj* (person) qui accumule; (miserly) avare; qui s'accumule; *comm* cumulatif -ive

**accumulator** *n* accumulateur *m*; *coll* accu *m*

**accuracy** *n* exactitude *f*, précision *f*

**accurate** *adj* exact, précis

**accursed** *adj* maudit; détestable

**accusal** *n* accusation *f*

**accusation** *n* accusation *f*; *leg* (indictment) acte *m* d'accusation

**accusative** *n gramm* accusatif *m*; *adj* à l'accusatif

**accusatory** *adj* accusateur -trice; *leg* accusatoire

**accuse** *vt* accuser, inculper, incriminer

**accuser** *n* accusateur -trice

**accustom** *vt* accoutumer, habituer; *vi* s'accoutumer, s'habituer

**accustomed** *adj* accoutumé, habitué; habituel -uelle

**ace** *n* as *m*; **within an** ~ **of** à deux doigts de

**acephalous** *adj* acéphale

**acerbity** *n* acerbité *f*, aigreur *f*

**acetate** *n* acétate *m*

**acetic** *adj* acétique

**acetify** *vt* acétifier; *vi* aigrir

**acetone** *n* acétone *f*

**acetylene** *n* acétylène *m*

**ache** *n* mal *m*, douleur *f*; peine *f*; *vi* avoir mal, souffrir; ~ **for** désirer, avoir envie de; **my head** ~**s** j'ai mal à la tête

**achieve** *vt* accomplir, achever; effectuer, exécuter; atteindre, mener à bien

**achievement** *n* accomplissement *m*, exécution *f*; réalisation *f*; (success) réussite *f*

**aching** *adj* endolori, douloureux -euse; **have an** ~ **heart** avoir le cœur gros

**achromatic** *adj opt* + *biol* achromatique

**acid** *n* acide *m*; *adj* acide; (bitter) aigre; (criticism) acerbe

**acidify** *vt* acidifier; *vi* s'acidifier

**acidosis** *n med* acidose *f*

**acidulated** *adj* acidulé

**acidulous** *adj* acidulé, aigrelet -ette

**acknowledge** *vt* reconnaître, admettre, avouer; accuser réception de; (gift) remercier de *or* pour

**acknowledg(e)ment** *n* reconnaissance *f*; accusé *m* de réception; *comm* récépissé *m*; aveu *m*; remerciement *m*

**acme** *n* acmé *f*, comble *m*, summum *m*

**acne** *n* acné *f*

**acolyte** *n* acolyte *m*

**aconite** *n* aconit *m*

**acorn** *n* gland *m*

**acoustic** *adj* acoustique

**acoustics** *npl* acoustique *f*

**acquaint** *vt* renseigner, informer, aviser; **be** ~**ed with** connaître

**acquaintance** *n* (person) connaissance *f*, relation *f*; (knowledge) familiarité *f*; **have some** ~ **with** avoir une certaine connaissance de; **make the** ~ **of** faire la connaissance de; **upon further** ~ en connaissant mieux

**acquiesce** *vi* acquiescer, accepter, consentir, déférer

**acquiescence** *n* acquiescement *m*, assentiment *m*, consentement *m*

**acquire** *vt* acquérir, gagner; (learn) apprendre

**acquired** *adj* acquis

**acquisition** *n* acquisition *f*

**acquisitive** *adj* avide, cupide, âpre au gain

**acquit** *vt* acquitter, payer; absoudre, acquitter; ~ **oneself well** se comporter bien

**acquittal** *n* acquittement *m*; (duty) exécution *f*

**acquittance** *n* acquittement *m*; *leg* quittance *f*; *comm* acquit *m*

**acre** *n* acre *f*, arpent *m*, demi-hectare *m*; ~**s of** des hectares de; **God's** ~ cimetière *m*

**acrid** *adj* acre; acerbe, sarcastique, caustique

**acrimonious** *adj* acrimonieux -ieuse

**acrimony** *n* acrimonie *f*

**acrobat** *n* acrobate

**acrobatic** *adj* acrobatique

**across** *adv* en travers, de l'autre côté; *prep* à travers, au travers de; de l'autre côté de; **come** ~ (person) rencontrer; (thing) tomber sur; **get sth** ~ faire comprendre qch; **put sth** ~ s/o faire marcher qn

**acrostic** *n* acrostiche *m*

**act** *n* acte *m*; action *f*; (law) loi *f*, décret *m*; (acting turn) numéro *m*; ~ **of God** force majeure; **caught in the** ~ pris en flagrant délit; **in the** ~ **of** en train de;

**put on an** ~ jouer la comédie, feindre; *vt theat* jouer; (pretend) feindre, simuler; *vi* agir; (behave) se comporter, se tenir; ~ **for** représenter

**acting** *n* action *f*; *theat* jeu *m*, art *m* de jouer, métier *m* d'acteur; *adj* suppléant, intérimaire, provisoire

**actinic** *adj* actinique

**action** *n* action *f*; acte *m*, fait *m*; influence *f*; activité *f*, effort *m*; *leg* action *f*, procès *m*; *mil* **go into** ~ aller au feu; *mil* **killed in** ~ mort au champ d'honneur; **out of** ~ hors d'usage, en panne; **put into** ~ mettre à exécution; **take** ~ prendre des mesures; *leg* **take** ~ **against** citer, poursuivre; *vt leg* actionner

**actionable** *adj leg* donnant matière à procès

**activate** *vt* activer, accélérer, hâter; rendre radio-actif -ive

**active** *adj* actif -ive; travailleur -euse, efficace, diligent

**activism** *n* activisme *m*

**activist** *n* activiste

**activity** *n* activité *f*; occupation *f*; dynamisme *m*

**actor** *n* acteur *m*, comédien *m*

**actress** *n* actrice *f*, comédienne *f*

**actual** *adj* réel -elle, concret -ète; actuel -uelle

**actuality** *n* réalité *f*, fait *m*, actualité *f*; circonstances actuelles

**actualize** *vt* réaliser; décrire avec réalisme

**actually** *adv* de fait, vraiment; (right now) pour l'instant, actuellement; même; (really) véritablement

**actuary** *n* actuaire

**actuate** *vt* actionner; faire agir, pousser

**acuity** *n* acuité *f*

**acumen** *n* pénétration *f*, sagacité *f*, perspicacité *f*

**acuminate** *vt* aiguiser; *adj bot* acuminé

**acupuncture** *n* acuponcture *f*, acupuncture *f*

**acute** *adj* aigu -üe, pointu; (clever) perspicace, avisé, pénétrant

**acuteness** *n* acuité *f*, intensité *f*; pénétration *f*, sagacité *f*, perspicacité *f*

**ad** *n coll abbr* réclame *f*

**adage** *n* adage *m*, maxime *f*

**Adam** *n* Adam *m*; ~**'s apple** pomme *f* d'Adam; **not to know from** ~ ne pas connaître ni d'Ève ni d'Adam

**adamant** *adj* inflexible

**adamantine** *adj* adamantin

**adapt** *vt* adapter, accommoder; mettre en harmonie

**adaptability** *n* souplesse *f*, maniabilité *f*

**adaptable** *adj* adaptable, souple

**adaptation** *n* adaptation *f*; *mus* arrangement *m*

**adapter, adaptor** *n* adapteur -trice; *elect* prise *f* multiple

**add** *vt* ajouter; ~ **to** augmenter, accroître; ~ **up** additionner; ~ **up to** se résumer à, signifier; ~**ed to which** au surplus; *vi* **that** ~**s up** cela concorde

**addendum** *n* (*pl* **addenda**) addenda *mpl*

**adder** *n* vipère *f*

**addict** *n* drogué -e, toxicomane; *fig* fanatique; *vt* vouer, consacrer; ~ **oneself** se vouer à

**addiction** *n* toxicomanie *f*; (taste) goût *m*, penchant *m*

**addictive** *adj* qui mène à la toxicomanie; qui crée une dépendance

**addition** *n* addition *f*; (increase) augmentation *f*; (of collaborators) adjonction *f*

**additional** *adj* additionnel -elle, supplémentaire

**additive** *n* additif *m*; *adj* additif -ive

**addle** *vt* brouiller, troubler; (egg) pourrir; *vi* se pourrir

**addled** *adj* (egg) pourri; *fig* brouillé, confus, troublé

**address** *n* adresse *f*, domicile *m*; (speech) discours *m*, allocution *f*; (skill) habileté *f*, dextérité *f*; (flair) doigté *m*; **form of** ~ titre *m*; **of no fixed** ~ sans domicile; **pay** ~**es to** faire la cour à; *vt* adresser; apostropher; mettre l'adresse sur; (encounter) aborder; (talk to) s'adresser à

**addressee** *n* destinataire

**adduce** *vt* citer, alléguer, mettre en avant

**adducent** *adj med* adducteur *m*

**adduction** *n* allégation *f*; *med* adduction *f*

**adductor** *n med* adducteur *m*

**adenoidal** *adj* adénoïde

**adenoids** *npl* végétations *fpl* adénoïdes

**adept** *n* expert *m*; *ar* initié -e; *adj* expert

**adequacy** *n* à-propos *m*, justesse *f*

**adequate** *adj* adéquat, juste, congru; (all right) suffisant

**adhere** *vi* adhérer, tenir; persister, maintenir

**adherent** *n* adhérent -e, membre *m*; *adj* adhérent

**adhesion** *n* (support) adhésion *f*; (sticking) adhérence *f*; *med* adhérence *f*

**adhesive** *adj* adhésif -ive, collant

**adieu** *n* + *interj* adieu *m*

**adipose** *adj* adipeux -euse

**adiposity** *n* adiposité *f*

**adit** *n* entrée *f*; accès *m*

**adjacent** *adj* adjacent, attenant, contigu -üe

**adjectival** *adj* adjectif -ive

**adjective** *n* adjectif *m*, épithète *f*

**adjoin** *vt* adjoindre, joindre; toucher à; être adhérent à

**adjoining** *adj* limitrophe

**adjourn** *vt* ajourner, différer, renvoyer; *vi* s'ajourner; se déplacer

**adjournment** *n* ajournement *m*, renvoi *m*; suspension *f*

**adjudge** *vt leg* juger; condamner; (reward) décerner, adjuger

**adjudicate** *vt* juger; *leg* décider, arrêter

**adjudication** *n leg* décision *f*; jugement *m*

**adjudicator** *n* juge *m*

**adjunct** *n* (person) adjoint -e; (thing) accessoire *m*; *gramm* complément *m*; *adj* accessoire, ajouté

**adjuration** *n* adjuration *f*

**adjure** *vt* adjurer

**adjust** *vt* ajuster, régler, arranger

**adjustable** *adj* ajustable, réglable; ~ **spanner** clef *f* à molette

**adjutant** *n mil* = adjudant-major *m* (*pl* adjudants-major)

**ad lib** *vt + vi coll theat* improviser; *adj* improvisé, impromptu; *adv* à volonté

**adman** *n coll* publicitaire *m*, publiciste *m*

**admass** *n comm* clientèle *f* influençable (par la publicité)

**administer** *vt* administrer; gérer; (oath) faire prêter

**administration** *n* administration *f*, gestion *f*

**administrative** *adj* administratif -ive

**admirable** *adj* admirable, merveilleux -euse

**admiral** *n* amiral *m*; *ent* vulcain *m*

**Admiralty** *n* amirauté *f*; = ministère *m* de la Marine

**admiration** *n* admiration *f*

**admire** *vt* admirer; estimer

**admirer** *n* admirateur -trice; soupirant *m*

**admissibility** *n* admissibilité *f*, acceptabilité *f*

**admissible** *adj* admissible, acceptable

**admission** *n* admission *f*; (way in) accès *m*, entrée *f*; (confession) aveu *m*, acceptation *f*; **by his own ~** de son propre aveu; **free ~** entrée gratuite

**admit** *vt* admettre, avouer; laisser entrer; accepter, reconnaître, concéder; **~ bearer** laissez passer; **~ of** permettre; **one must ~** on doit avouer; *vi* admettre

**admittance** *n* admission *f*; *elect* admittance *f*

**admittedly** *adv* de l'aveu général

**admix** *vt* mélanger; *vi* se mélanger

**admixture** *n* mélange *m*, dosage *m*

**admonish** *vt* admonester, réprimander; avertir

**admonition** *n* admonition *f*, admonestation *f*, réprimande *f*

**admonitory** *adj* qui admoneste

**ado** *n* agitation *f*; difficulté *f*, embarras *m*; **much ~ about nothing** beaucoup de bruit pour rien; **without further ~** sans plus d'histoires

**adobe** *n* adobe *m*

**adolescence** *n* adolescence *f*

**adolescent** *n + adj* adolescent -e

**adopt** *vt* adopter; choisir

**adoption** *n* adoption *f*

**adoptive** *adj* adopté; adoptif -ive

**adorable** *adj* adorable

**adoration** *n* adoration *f*

**adore** *vt* adorer

**adorer** *n* adorateur -trice

**adorn** *vt* orner, parer

**adornment** *n* ornement *m*, parure *f*

**adrenal** *adj med* surrénal

**adrenalin** *n* adrénaline *f*

**adrift** *adj* à la dérive, en dérive; *fig* **be ~** divaguer

**adroit** *adj* adroit

**adroitness** *n* adresse *f*

**adulate** *vt* aduler, flatter, flagorner

**adulation** *n* adulation *f*, flagornerie *f*

**adulator** *n* adulateur -trice

**adulatory** *adj* adulateur -trice, flatteur -euse

**adult** *n + adj* adulte

**adulterate** *vt* adultérer, frelater; *adj* adultéré, frelaté; (child) adultérin

**adulteration** *n* altération *f*, frelatage *m*

**adulterer** *n* adultère *m*

**adulteress** *n* adultère *f*

**adulterine** *adj* adultérin

**adulterous** *adj* adultère

**adultery** *n* adultère *m*

**adumbrate** *vt* esquisser; prédire

**adumbration** *n* esquisse *f*

**advance** *n* avance *f*, progression *f*; (rise) hausse *f*; (salary) acompte *m*; paiement anticipé; *vt* avancer, faire progresser; (money) prêter; faire avancer; (price) augmenter; *vi* avancer, progresser; s'avancer; augmenter

**advance-guard** *n* avant-garde *f*

**advancement** *n* avance *f*, avancement *m*

**advantage** *n* avantage *m*, supériorité *f*; gain *m*, profit *m*; *sp* avantage *m*; **show to ~** avantager; **take ~ of** profiter de; *pej* abuser de; **turn to ~** tirer parti de; *vt* avantager, favoriser

**advantageous** *adj* avantageux -euse, favorable; profitable, intéressant

**advent** *n* arrivée *f*, venue *f*; **Advent** *eccles* Avent *m*, Avènement *m*

**adventitious** *adj* adventice

**adventure** *n* aventure *f*, risque *m*; *vt* aventurer, risquer; *vi* s'aventurer

**adventurer** *n* aventurier *m*

338

adventuresome *adj* aventureux -euse
adventuress *n* aventurière *f*
adventurous *adj* aventureux -euse
adverb *n* adverbe *m*
adverbial *adj* adverbial
adversary *n* adversaire
adverse *adj* adverse, hostile, contraire
adversity *n* adversité *f*, malheur *m*
¹advert *n coll abbr* annonce *f*, réclame *f*
²advert *vi* faire allusion
advertise *vt* faire de la publicité pour, faire de la réclame pour; afficher, annoncer; *vi* faire de la publicité; (in paper) mettre une annonce
advertisement *n* annonce *f*; (poster) affiche *f*; (classified) petite annonce; publicité *f*
advertiser *n* annonceur *m*
advice *n* avis *m*, conseils *mpl*; *comm* avis *m*; act on s/o's ~ suivre les conseils de qn; piece of ~ conseil *m*; seek ~ from demander conseil à
advisable *adj* recommandable; prudent; opportun
advise *vt* conseiller; (inform) aviser; *vi* conseiller
advised *adj* avisé; délibéré
advisedly *adv* délibérément, en pleine connaissance de cause
adviser *n* conseiller -ère
advisory *adj* consultatif -ive
advocacy *n* profession *f* d'avocat; (plea) plaidoyer *m*, justification *f*
advocate *n* avocat -e, défenseur *m*; devil's ~ avocat *m* du diable; *vt* recommander, préconiser
adze *n* (h)erminette *f*
aegis *n* égide *f*
aeolian *adj* éolien -ienne
aerate *vt* aérer; (liquids) gazéifier; ~d water eau gazeuse
aeration *n* aération *f*
aerial *n rad* antenne *f*; *adj* aérien -ienne
aerie *n see* eyrie
aerify *vt* aérifier
aerobatics *npl* acrobatie aérienne
aerobic *adj* aérobique
aerodrome *n* aérodrome *m*
aerodynamic *adj* aérodynamique
aerodynamics *npl* aérodynamique *f*
aerolite, aerolith *n* aérolit(h)e *m*
aerology *n* aérologie *f*
aeronaut *n* aéronaute
aeronautics *npl* aéronautique *f*
aeroplane *n* avion *m*, aéroplane *m*
aerosol *n* aérosol *m*, bombe *f*
aerostat *n* aérostat *m*
aerostatics *npl* aérostatique *f*
aertex *n* cellular *m*
aesthete *n* esthète
aesthetic *adj* esthétique
aestheticism *n* esthétisme *m*
aesthetics *npl* esthétique *f*

aestivation *n zool* estivation *f*
aestival, estival *adj* estival
aether *n see* ether
aetiology *n* étiologie *f*
afar *adv* loin
affability *n* affabilité *f*
affable *adj* affable
affair *n* (business) affaire *f*, occupation *f*; (matter) affaire *f*, question *f*; (love) affaire *f* de cœur, liaison *f*
¹affect *vt* (assume) affecter, adopter; (like) affectionner; (pretend) feindre
²affect *vt* affecter, influencer; (change) affecter, modifier; (move) affecter, toucher, émouvoir; *med* affecter, intéresser
affectation *n* affectation *f*
affected *adj* affecté, maniéré; (put on) feint; (moved) ému, touché
affecting *adj* émouvant, touchant
affection *n* affection *f*, tendresse *f*; état *m* d'âme, émotion *f*; *med* maladie *f*
affectionate *adj* affectueux -euse
affectionately *adv* affectueusement
affective *adj* affectif -ive
afferent *adj physiol* afférent
affiance *vt* fiancer
affidavit *n leg* déclaration *f* sous serment
affiliate *vt* affilier; *leg* attribuer la paternité; ~ oneself s'affilier
affiliation *n* affiliation *f*; *leg* attribution *f* de paternité; ~ order jugement *m* en constatation de paternité
affinity *n* affinité *f*; ressemblance *f*; attrait *m*
affirm *vt* affirmer, maintenir, soutenir; *vi* affirmer
affirmation *n* affirmation *f*, assertion *f*; *leg* confirmation *f*
affirmative *n* affirmatif *m*; *adj* affirmatif -ive
affix *n* prolongement *m*; *gramm* affixe *m*; *vt* (signature) apposer; ajouter; attacher
afflatus *n poet* inspiration divine
afflict *vt* affliger
affliction *n* affliction *f*, détresse *f*; (disaster) désastre *m*
affluence *n* richesse *f*; abondance *f*
¹affluent *n geog* affluent *m*
²affluent *adj* riche, prospère; abondant
afflux *n* afflux *m*
afford *vt* (give, bestow) fournir, procurer; (be able to pay for) avoir les moyens d'acheter, pouvoir s'offrir; (time) avoir le temps
afforest *vt* boiser, reboiser
afforestation *n* boisement *m*, reboisement *m*
affranchise *vt* affranchir
affray *n* bagarre *f*, rixe *f*
affright *n poet* effroi *m*; *vt poet* effrayer
affront *n* affront *m*, insulte *f*; *vt* insulter; (confront) braver, affronter
afield *adv* au loin; far ~ très loin

**afire** *adj* + *adv lit* enflammé, en feu

**aflame** *adj* + *adv lit* embrasé, en flammes

**afloat** *adv* sur l'eau, à flot; en mer; *fig* (rumour) en circulation; *fig comm* à flot, hors de dettes; **keep ~** maintenir à flot

**afoot** *adv* en voie de préparation, imminent; (on foot) à pied; **there is sth ~** il se prépare qch

**aforementioned, aforesaid** *adj* susdit, susmentionné

**aforethought** *adj* prémédité; **leg with malice ~** avec préméditation criminelle

**afraid** *adj* effrayé, pris de peur, apeuré; **be ~ to** avoir peur de; **be ~ that** (regret) regretter, être désolé

**afresh** *adv* de nouveau, encore, de plus belle

**Africa** *n* Afrique *f*

**African** *n* Africain -e; *adj* africain

**Afrikaaner** *n* Afrikander

**Afrikaans** *n* afrikans *m*

**afro** *adj coll* afro *invar*

**Afro-Asian** *adj* afro-asiatique

**aft** *adv naut* à l'arrière; vers l'arrière

**after** *adj* (time) subséquent; *naut* arrière; *adv* après, ensuite; d'après; *prep* après; **be ~ s/o** chercher qn; *US* **half ~ six** six heures et demie; **take ~** ressembler à; **what are you ~?** que voulez-vous?; *conj* après, après que

**afterbirth** *n* arrière-faix *m*, placenta *m*

**after-care** *n* postcure *f*

**after-effect** *n med* séquelle *f*; répercussion *f*

**afterglow** *n* (sunset) dernières lueurs

**afterlife** *n* vie future

**aftermath** *n* suites *fpl*, conséquences *fpl*

**afternoon** *n* après-midi *m* + *f invar*

**afters** *npl coll* dessert *m*

**after-sales** *adj* après-vente *invar*

**aftershave** *n* after-shave *m*, lotion *f* après-rasage

**aftertaste** *n* arrière-goût *m*

**afterthought** *n* pensée *f* après coup

**afterwards** *adv* plus tard, après, ensuite

**again** *adv* encore, de nouveau, encore une fois; (in addition) une fois de plus; (moreover) d'ailleurs; **~ and ~** maintes et maintes fois, à plusieurs reprises; **and there ~** et puis alors; **as much ~** deux fois plus; **never ~** jamais plus; **not ~!** encore!; **now and ~** de temps en temps

**against** *prep* contre, à l'encontre de; (bump) sur; (in preparation for) en vue de, en prévision de; **over ~** en face de

**¹agape** *n hist eccles* agape *f*

**²agape** *adv* bouche bée

**agaric** *n bot* agaric *m*

**agate** *n* agate *f*

**age** *n* âge *m*; (period) époque *f*, ère *f*; *coll*

(long time) éternité *f*, siècle *m*; **come of ~** atteindre sa majorité; **middle ~** un certain âge; **old ~** vieillesse *f*; **over ~** trop vieux (*f* vieille); **under ~** trop jeune; *vt* vieillir; *vi* vieillir, prendre de l'âge; (metal) fatiguer

**age-bracket** *n* tranche *f* d'âge

**aged** *npl* gens âgés; *adj* (old) âgé, vieux (*f* vieille); (of the age of) âgé de; (grown old) vieilli

**age-group** *n* groupe *m* de personnes du même âge

**ageless** *adj* sans âge

**age-long** *adj* pérenne

**agency** *n* (means) entremise *f*, intermédiaire *m*; *comm* agence *f*, bureau *m*

**agenda** *n* ordre *m* du jour

**agent** *n* agent *m*; (for product) concessionnaire

**age-old** *adj* antique

**agglomerate** *n* agglomérat *m*; *vt* agglomérer; *vi* s'agglomérer

**agglomeration** *n* agglomération *f*

**agglutinant** *n* agglutinant *m*; *adj* agglutinant

**agglutinate** *vt* agglutiner; *vi* s'agglutiner; *adj* agglutiné

**agglutination** *n* agglutination *f*

**aggrandize** *vt* agrandir

**aggrandizement** *n* agrandissement *m*

**aggravate** *vt* aggraver; (quarrel) envenimer; (irritate) irriter, exaspérer

**aggravating** *adj* aggravant; (irritating) agaçant, exaspérant

**aggravation** *n* aggravation *f*; (irritation) agacement *m*, exaspération *f*

**aggregate** *n* total *m*, ensemble *m*; *geol* + *phys* agrégat *m*; **in the ~** au total; *vt* agréger, rassembler; *vi* s'agréger; *adj* total, global; *geol* agrégé

**aggress** *vi* être l'agresseur

**aggression** *n* agression *f*

**aggressive** *adj* agressif -ive; *mil* offensif -ive

**aggressor** *n* agresseur *m*

**aggrieved** *adj* blessé, affligé

**aggro** *n sl* agressivité *f*, violence *f*; grabuge *m*

**aghast** *adj* ahuri, abasourdi, atterré

**agile** *adj* agile, leste

**agility** *n* agilité *f*, souplesse *f*

**agio** *n* agio *m*

**agiotage** *n* agiotage *m*

**agitate** *vt* (stir) agiter, remuer; (emotion) troubler, émouvoir; *vi* faire de l'agitation, exciter l'opinion publique, attirer l'attention publique

**agitated** *adj* troublé; inquiet -iète

**agitation** *n* agitation *f*; (emotion) trouble *m*, agitation *f*

**agitator** *n* agitateur -trice; *mech* agitateur *m*

aglow *adj* embrasé; (person) rayonnant
agnostic *n + adj* agnostique
agnosticism *n* agnosticisme *m*
ago *adv* il y a; **ten years** ~ il y a dix ans
agog *adj + adv* en émoi
agonize *vi* (try) s'efforcer; être au supplice, souffrir le martyre
agonizing *adj* déchirant, agonisant
agony *n* angoisse *f*; (physical pain) paroxysme *m*; (death) agonie *f*; (newspaper) ~ **column** rubrique *f* des messages personnels; *coll* **pile on the** ~ en rajouter, exagérer
agrarian *n + adj hist* agrarien -ienne
agree *vt* accepter, consentir à; (opinion) convenir de; (admit) avouer; *vi* être d'accord, être du même avis; (come to terms) se mettre d'accord; (coincide) concorder, correspondre; *gramm* s'accorder; ~ **to differ** rester sur ses positions; (health) ~ **with** être bon (*f* bonne) pour
agreeable *adj* agréable, aimable; (willing) consentant; **be** ~ **to** vouloir bien
agreed *adj* d'accord, entendu; *coll* d'accord
agreement *n* accord *m*, harmonie *f*; *comm* contrat *m*; *leg* accommodement *m*; *gramm* accord *m*; **be in** ~ être d'accord; **by mutual** ~ d'un commun accord; **enter into an** ~ signer un accord
agricultural *adj* agricole
agriculturalist *n* agronome; (farmer) agriculteur *m*
agriculture *n* agriculture *f*
agronomics *npl* agronomie *f*
agronomist *n* agronome *m*
aground *adj naut* échoué
ague *n* fièvre intermittente
ah *interj* ah!
aha *interj* eh voilà!, tiens!
ahead *adv* en avant, devant; (time) en avance, d'avance; ~ **of** (time) avant; (place) devant; **draw** ~ gagner de l'avant; **get** ~ avancer; **go** ~ prendre de l'avance; **look** ~ considérer l'avenir
ahoy *interj naut* ohé!
aid *n* aide *f*, assistance *f*, secours *m*; (person) aide, assistant -e; **deaf** ~ appareil *m* acoustique; **first** ~ secours *mpl* d'urgence; **in** ~ **of** à l'appui de; (charity) au profit de; **legal** ~ assistance *f* judiciaire; *coll* **what's this in** ~ **of?** qu'est-ce que ça signifie?; *vt* aider, assister, secourir; *leg* ~ **and abet** être complice de, avoir part à
aide-de-camp *n* aide *m* de camp
Aids *n med* SIDA *m*
aigrette *n* aigrette *f*
ail *vt ar + poet* affliger; *vi* souffrir

aileron *n* aileron *m*
ailing *adj* souffrant, en mauvaise santé
ailment *n* indisposition *f*
aim *n* action *f* de viser; (purpose) but *m*, objet *m*, visées *fpl*; **take** ~ viser; *vt* (gun) braquer; (blow) allonger; (remark) diriger; *vi* (intend) viser, aspirer; ~ **high** être ambitieux -ieuse; ~ **to** aspirer à
aimless *adj* sans but; futile
ain't *dial + sl abbr* = **am not, are not, is not, has not, have not**
air *n* air *m*, atmosphère *f*; (breeze) brise *f*; *fig* air *m*, aspect *m*, mine *f*; *mus* air *m*; ~ **s** minauderies *fpl*; ~ **traffic control** contrôle *m* de la circulation aérienne; **be in the** ~ être à l'état de projet; **by** ~ par avion; **give oneself (put on)** ~ **s** se donner de grands airs; **have an** ~ **about one** avoir de l'allure; *coll* **hot** ~ blablabla *m*; **on the** ~ à la radio, sur les ondes; **open** ~ plein air; **there's sth in the** ~ le bruit court; **tread on** ~ être aux anges; *vt* aérer, sécher; (opinions) exprimer, faire connaître
air-base *n* base aérienne, base *f* d'aviation
air-bed *n* matelas *m* pneumatique
airborne *adj* aéroporté; (plane) **be** ~ avoir décollé
air-brake *n* frein *m* à air comprimé; *aer* aérofrein *m*
airbus *n* airbus *m*, aérobus *m*
air-chamber *n* chambre *f* à air
Air-Chief-Marshal *n* = général *m* d'armée aérienne
Air-Commodore *n* = général *m* de brigade aérienne
air-conditioned *adj* climatisé
air-conditioning *n* climatisation *f*
air-cooled *adj* à refroidissement par air
air-cooling *n* refroidissement *m* par air
aircraft *n* avion *m*
aircraft-carrier *n* porte-avions *m*
aircraft(s)man *n* = soldat *m* de deuxième classe (de l'armée de l'air)
air-crew *n* équipage *m* (d'un avion)
air-cushion *n* coussin *m* pneumatique
airdrome *n US see* aerodrome
airdrop *n* parachutage *m*
air-ferry *n* avion transbordeur
airfield *n* terrain *m* d'aviation, aérodrome *m*
air-filter *n* filtre *m* à air
air-force *n* = armée *f* de l'air
air-gun *n* fusil *m* à air comprimé
air-hole *n* soupirail *m*
air-hostess *n* hôtesse *f* de l'air
airily *adv* légèrement, d'un ton dégagé, avec désinvolture
airiness *n* aération *f*; (behaviour)

désinvolture *f*, insouciance *f*

**airing** *n* aération *f*; (problem) discussion *f*

**air-lane** *n* couloir *m* de navigation aérienne

**airless** *adj* mal ventilé, privé d'air

**airline** *n* compagnie *f* d'aviation

**airliner** *n* avion *m* de ligne

**airlock** *n* bulle *f* d'air; (caisson) sas *m*

**airmail** *n* poste aérienne; *adj* + *adv* par avion

**airman** *n* aviateur *m*; soldat *m* de l'armée de l'air

**Air-Marshal** *n* = général *m* de corps aérien

**air-mattress** *n* matelas *m* pneumatique

**airplane** *n US see* **aeroplane**

**air-pocket** *n* trou *m* d'air

**airport** *n* aéroport *m*

**air-pressure** *n* pression *f* atmosphérique

**air-pump** *n* compresseur *m*

**air-raid** *n* attaque aérienne; ~ **precautions** défense aérienne passive

**air-screw** *n* hélice *f*

**airshaft** *n min* puits *m* d'aérage

**airship** *n* dirigeable *m*

**air-sickness** *n* mal *m* de l'air

**air-space** *n* espace aérien; (room) cubage *m* d'air

**airstrip** *n* piste *f* d'atterrissage

**airtight** *adj* étanche, hermétique

**air-to-air** *adj* avion-avion *invar*

**air-to-ground** *adj* air-sol *invar*

**Air-Vice-Marshal** *n* = général *m* de division aérienne

**airway** *n* (shaft) conduit *m* d'air; (route) voie aérienne

**airwoman** *n* aviatrice *f*; = auxiliaire *f* de l'armée de l'air

**airworthiness** *n* navigabilité *f*; **certificate of** ~ certificat *m* de navigabilité

**airworthy** *adj* navigable; muni d'un certificat de navigabilité

**airy** *adj* (ventilated) aéré; (light) léger -ère; (casual) désinvolte

**aisle** *n* nef latérale, bas-côté *m*; allée centrale, passage *m*, couloir *m*

**ajar** *adj* entrebâillé, entr'ouvert

**akimbo** *adv* **arms** ~ les mains *fpl* sur les hanches

**akin** *adj* apparenté; ~ **to** qui ressemble à

**alabaster** *n* albâtre *m*; *adj* d'albâtre

**alack** *interj poet* hélas!

**alacrity** *n* entrain *m*, empressement *m*, alacrité *f*

**alarm** *n* alarme *f*, alerte *f*; (fear) alarme *f*, agitation *f*; inquiétude *f*; *joc* ~ **s and excursions** branle-bas *m* de combat; *vt* alarmer, alerter; faire peur à

**alarm-bell** *n* sonnerie *f* d'alarme

**alarm-clock** *n* réveil *m*, réveille-matin *m invar*

**alarming** *adj* déconcertant, alarmant

**alarmist** *n* + *adj* alarmiste

**alas** *interj* hélas!

**alb** *n eccles* aube *f*

**albatross** *n* albatros *m*

**albeit** *conj lit* encore que, bien que

**albino** *n* albinos

**album** *n* album *m*

**albumen, albumin** *n* (egg) albumen *m*, blanc *m* de l'œuf; *physiol* albumine *f*

**albuminous** *adj* albumineux -euse

**alchemic** *adj* alchimique

**alchemist** *n* alchimiste *m*

**alchemy, alchymy** *n* alchimie *f*

**alcohol** *n* alcool *m*

**alcoholic** *n* alcoolique; *adj* alcoolique; (drink) alcoolisé

**alcoholism** *n* alcoolisme *m*

**alcove** *n* alcôve *f*; (summerhouse) tonnelle *f*

**aldehyde** *n chem* aldehyde *m*

**alder** *n* aulne *m*, aune *m*

**alderman** *n* = conseiller -ère municipal -e (ou) général -e d'une certaine ancienneté; *hist* échevin *m*

**Alderney** *n geog* Aurigny *f*

**ale** *n* bière *f*, ale *f*

**aleatory** *adj* aléatoire

**alembic** *n* alambic *m*

**alert** *n* alerte *f*; *adj* alerte, vigilant; (sharp) éveillé; *vt* alerter, éveiller l'attention de

**alexandrine** *n lit* alexandrin *m*

**alexia** *n* cécité verbale, alexie *f*

**alfa** *n* alfa *m*

**alfalfa** *n* luzerne *f*

**alfresco** *adv* en plein air

**alga** *n* (*pl* **algae**) algue(s) *f*(*pl*)

**algebra** *n* algèbre *f*

**algebraic** *adj* algébrique

**algebrist** *n* algébriste

**Algeria** *n geog* Algérie *f*

**alias** *n* nom *m* d'emprunt; *adv* alias

**alibi** *n* alibi *m*

**alien** *n* + *adj* étranger -ère

**alienable** *adj leg* aliénable

**alienate** *vt* aliéner

**alienation** *n* *leg* + *med* aliénation *f*; éloignement *m*; désaffection *f*

**alienist** *n* aliéniste

¹**alight** *vi* descendre, mettre pied à terre

²**alight** *adj* en feu, allumé

**align** *vt* aligner, mettre en ligne; *vi* s'aligner

**alignment** *n* alignement *m*

**alike** *adj* semblable, pareil -eille; *adv* pareillement, de même; de la même façon

**aliment** *n* aliment *m*; *vt* alimenter, nourrir

**alimentary** *adj* alimentaire; ~ **canal** tube digestif

**alimentation** *n* alimentation *f*
**alimony** *n leg* pension *f* alimentaire
**alive** *adj* vivant, en vie; (lively) vif (*f* vive); (sensitive) sensible; (alert) alerte, actif -ive; ~ **with** grouillant de; **keep** ~ maintenir, préserver
**alkali** *n* alcali *m*
**alkaline** *adj* alcalin
**alkaloid** *n* alcaloïde *m*
**all** *n* tout *m*; (everyone) tous les hommes, tout le monde, tous (*f* toutes); ~ **clear signal** *m* de fin d'alerte; ~ **in** ~ à tout prendre; **after** ~ après tout; **at** ~ du tout; **for good and** ~ pour toujours; **in** ~ en tout; **once for** ~ une fois pour toutes; *sp* **three** ~ (tennis) trois partout; (other games) trois à trois; *pron* tout (*mpl* tous, *fpl* toutes); *adj* tout (*mpl* tous, *fpl* toutes); (utmost) le plus possible; ~ **the** tout le (*f* toute la, *mpl* tous les, *fpl* toutes les); **for** ~ **that** malgré tout; **on** ~ **fours** à quatre pattes; *adv* tout, tout à fait, entièrement; ~ **at once** tout d'un coup; ~ **but** presque; ~ **over** (finished) fini; (everywhere) partout; ~ **right** bien, très bien; (health) en bonne santé; (agreement) d'accord; ~ **the better** tant mieux; *coll* ~ **there** intelligent, malin (*f* maligne); *coll* ~ **up with** ruiné, fichu
**allay** *vt* apaiser, calmer, modérer; (suspicion) dissiper
**allegation** *n* allégation *f*
**allege** *vt* alléguer, prétendre
**alleged** *adj* prétendu; (criminal) présumé
**allegiance** *n hist* allégeance *f*; fidélité *f*, obéissance *f*
**allegoric, allegorical** *adj* allégorique
**allegory** *n* allégorie *f*
**allegretto** *n* allegretto *m*; *adv* allegretto
**allegro** *n* allegro *m*; *adv* allegro
**alleluia, hallelujah** *interj* alléluia!
**allemande** *n mus* allemande *f*
**allergic** *adj* allergique
**allergy** *n med* allergie *f*
**alleviate** *vt* alléger, calmer, soulager
**alley** *n* (in garden) allée *f*; (between buildings) ruelle *f*; **blind** ~ cul-de-sac *m* (*pl* culs-de-sac), impasse *f*; *fig* impasse *f*; **bowling** ~ bowling *m*
**alleyway** *n* ruelle *f*
**alliance** *n* alliance *f*, pacte *m*
**allied** *adj* allié; (related) apparenté
**alligator** *n* alligator *m*
**all-in** *adj coll* épuisé; ~ **(insurance) policy** police *f* (d'assurances) tous risques; ~ **wrestling** lutte *f* libre, catch *m*; *adv* tout compris
**alliteration** *n* allitération *f*
**alliterative** *adj* allitératif -ive

**all-night** *adj* de nuit, durant toute la nuit
**allocate** *vt* allouer, attribuer, affecter
**allocation** *n* allocation *f*; (sum) affectation *f*; (amount) part *f*; (distribution) répartition *f*
**allocution** *n* allocution *f*
**allopathy** *n* allopathie *f*
**allot** *vt* (share out) répartir; (assign) attribuer, assigner
**allotment** *n* répartition *f*, assignation *f*; (share) part *f*; *mil* délégation *f* de solde; (plot of land) lopin de terre loué pour la culture
**allotropic** *adj chem* allotropique
**allotropy** *n chem* allotropie *f*
**all-out** *adj* total; *coll* tous azimuts; *coll* ~ **effort** effort *m* maximum; *adv coll* **go** ~ faire son possible, mettre toutes ses forces
**allow** *vt* permettre; (admit) admettre, concéder; (grant) allouer, accorder; ~ **for** tenir compte de
**allowable** *adj* admissible, permis
**allowance** *n* allocation *f*, rente *f*, pension *f*; (rent, lodging, etc) indemnité *f*; (discount) rabais *m*, réduction *f*; *mech* tolérance *f*; **make** ~ **for s/o** se montrer indulgent à l'égard de qn; **make** ~ **for sth** prendre qch en considération
**allowed** *adj* permis; (true) reconnu, accepté; **not** ~ interdit
**alloy** *n* alliage *m*; *vt* allier; *fig* altérer, corrompre
**all-round** *adj* complet -ète, sur toute la ligne
**all-rounder** *n coll esp sp* qn ayant des talents (sportifs) très variés
**all-star** *adj* (cast) de vedettes
**all-time** *adj coll* sans précédent, inouï
**allude** *vi* faire allusion
**allure** *n* charme *m*, attirance *f*; *vt* séduire, charmer, attirer
**allurement** *n* attrait *m*, fascination *f*
**alluring** *adj* séduisant, attrayant
**allusion** *n* allusion *f*
**allusive** *adj* allusif -ive
**alluvial** *adj* alluvial
**alluvium** *n* alluvion *f*
**ally** *n* allié -e; *hist* **the Allies** les Alliés; *vt* allier; ~ **oneself with** s'allier avec
**almanac** *n* almanach *m*
**almighty** *n* **the Almighty** le Tout-Puissant; *adj* tout-puissant, omnipotent; *coll* extrême, énorme, fameux -euse
**almond** *n* amande *f*; (tree) amandier *m*; *adj* en amande
**almoner** *n* (in a hospital) assistant -e social -e
**almost** *adv* presque, à peu près
**almshouse** *n* hospice *m*; maison *f* de retraite
**aloe** *n* aloès *m*; ~ **s** aloès médicinal

**aloft** adv en haut, en l'air; naut dans la mâture

**alone** adj seul; **let s/o** ~ laisser qn tranquille; **let well** ~ le mieux est l'ennemi du bien; adv seulement; conj **let** ~ sans parler de

**along** adv en avant; ~ **with** avec; **all** ~ (time) du début à la fin; (space) d'un bout à l'autre; **come** ~ allons; **get** ~ se débrouiller, s'arranger; **get** ~ **with you!** sans blague!; **move** ~ ! circulez!; prep le long de

**alongside** adv naut bord à bord; prep le long de, à côté de, près de; **come** ~ naut accoster

**aloof** adj distant, réservé; adv à distance; **stand** ~ **from** se tenir à l'écart de

**aloofness** n réserve f

**aloud** adv à haute voix, à voix haute, tout haut

**alp** n (mountain pasture) alpe f, pâturage m de montagne; **the Alps** les Alpes fpl

**alpaca** n alpaga m

**alpha** n alpha m; (mark at school, university) = très bonne note; ~ **particle** particule f alpha

**alphabet** n alphabet m

**alphabetical** adj alphabétique

**alpine** adj alpin

**already** adv déjà

**alright** see all right

**Alsatian** n Alsacien -ienne; ~ (dog) chien m loup, berger allemand; adj alsacien -ienne, d'Alsace

**also** adv aussi, d'ailleurs, également

**also-ran** n sp cheval non classé; fig raté -e

**altar** n autel m; **high** ~ maître-autel m (pl maîtres-autels); **lead to the** ~ épouser

**altar-bread** n hostie f

**altar-cloth** n nappe f d'autel

**altar-piece** n retable m

**altar-rail(s)** n balustre m du chœur

**alter** vt changer, modifier; (touch up) retoucher, remanier; vi changer

**alterable** adj modifiable, transformable

**alterant** n altérogène m; adj altérant

**alteration** n changement m, modification f

**altercation** n altercation f

**alter ego** n alter ego m

**alternate** adj alterné, alternatif -ive; (every other) tous les deux; vt faire alterner; vi alterner

**alternating** adj alternant; **elect** ~ **current** courant alternatif

**alternation** n alternance f

**alternative** n alternative f, choix m; adj alternatif -ive, autre

**alternator** n elect alternateur m

**although** conj quoique, bien que, encore que

**altimeter** n altimètre m

**altitude** n altitude f, hauteur f

**alto** n mus (male voice) haute-contre f (pl hautes-contre); (female voice) contralto m

**altogether** adv tout à fait, entièrement, absolument; (on the whole) tout compte fait, au total; (in total) en tout

**altruism** n altruisme m

**altruist** n altruiste

**altruistic** adj altruiste

**alum** n alun m

**aluminium** n aluminium m

**aluminum** n US see aluminium

**alumna** n (pl alumnae) US ancienne élève (d'une école, d'une université)

**alumnus** n (pl alumni) US ancien élève (d'une école, d'une université)

**alveolar** adj alvéolaire

**alveole, alveolus** n alvéole m or f

**always** adv toujours

**am** see be

**amain** adv ar poet violemment, de toutes ses forces, à toute vitesse

**amalgam** n amalgame m

**amalgamate** vt amalgamer, unifier; vi s'amalgamer, s'unifier

**amalgamation** n amalgamation f, unification f, fusion f

**amanuensis** n (pl amanuenses) secrétaire, copiste

**amaranth** n bot amarante f

**amaranthine** adj amarante invar

**amaryllis** n amaryllis f

**amass** vt amasser, accumuler, amonceler

**amateur** n amateur m; adj d'amateur

**amateurish** adj pej d'amateur, de dilettante

**amatory** adj amoureux -euse; lascif -ive

**amaze** vt ébahir, étonner, frapper de stupeur

**amazement** n ébahissement m, étonnement m, stupeur f

**amazing** adj ahurissant, étonnant; merveilleux -euse

**Amazon** n myth Amazone f; sp athlète f

**ambassador** n ambassadeur m

**ambassadress** n ambassadrice f

**amber** n ambre m; adj d'ambre; (colour) ambré; mot ~ **light** feu m jaune

**ambergris** n ambre gris

**ambidextrous** adj ambidextre

**ambience** n ambiance f

**ambient** adj ambiant

**ambiguity** n ambiguïté f, équivoque f

**ambiguous** adj ambigu -uë, équivoque; obscur

**ambiguousness** n ambiguïté f, équivoque f

**ambit** *n* pourtour *m*, limites *fpl*; étendue *f*, sphère *f* d'influence

**ambition** *n* ambition *f*

**ambitious** *adj* ambitieux -ieuse

**ambivalence** *n* ambivalence *f*

**ambivalent** *adj* ambivalent

**amble** *vi* (horse) ambler, aller l'amble; (person) flâner

**ambrosia** *n* ambroisie *f*

**ambrosial** *adj* au parfum d'ambroisie

**ambulance** *n* ambulance *f*

**ambulant** *adj* ambulant

**ambulatory** *n* cloître *m*; (apse) abside *f*; *adj* ambulatoire

**ambuscade** *n* embuscade *f*; *vt* embusquer; *vi* s'embusquer

**ambush** *n* embuscade *f*, guet-apens *m* (*pl* guets-apens); *vt* attirer dans une embuscade

**ameliorate** *vt* améliorer; *vi* s'améliorer

**amen** *n* amen *m invar*; *interj* amen!

**amenable** *adj* (responsive) sensible, raisonnable, maniable; (responsible) responsable

**amend** *vt* amender, corriger, modifier; *vi* s'amender

**amendment** *n* amendement *m*, rectification *f*

**amends** *npl* réparation *f*, compensation *f*; **make ~** faire réparation; (admit wrong) faire amende honorable; **make ~ to** dédommager

**amenity** *n* agrément *m*, charme *m*; (place, district) **amenities** commodités *fpl*, agréments *mpl*

**America** *n* Amérique *f*

**American** *n* Américain -e; *adj* américain

**americanism** *n* américanisme *m*

**americanize** *vt* américaniser

**amethyst** *n* améthyste *f*

**Amharic** *n ling* amharique *m*

**amiability** *n* amabilité *f*, gentillesse *f*

**amiable** *adj* aimable, gentil -ille

**amicable** *adj* amical

**amice** *n eccles* amict *m*

**amid** *prep* parmi, au milieu de

**amidships** *adv naut* au milieu du navire

**amidst** *prep* parmi, au milieu de

**amino-acid** *n* amino-acide *m*, acide aminé

**amiss** *adj* incorrect, mal à propos; *adv* mal, mal à propos, incorrectement; **it wouldn't come ~** ça ne ferait pas de mal; **take sth ~** prendre qch en mauvaise part; **there is sth ~** il y a qch qui cloche

**amity** *n* amitié *f*, concorde *f*

**ammeter** *n elect* ampèremètre *m*

**ammonia** *n* ammoniac *m*; **~ solution** ammoniaque *f*

**ammoniac** *adj* ammoniac -aque

**ammunition** *n* munitions *fpl*; *fig* armes *fpl*

**amnesia** *n* amnésie *f*

**amnesic** *adj* amnésique

**amnesty** *n* amnistie *f*; *vt* amnistier

**amoeba** *n* amibe *f*

**amoebic** *adj* amibien -ienne

**amok** *adv see* **amuck**

**among(st)** *prep* parmi; (between) au milieu de

**amoral** *adj* amoral

**amorous** *adj* amoureux -euse, lascif -ive

**amorousness** *n* lasciveté *f*

**amorphous** *adj* amorphe; *fig* sans forme, mal organisé

**amortization** *n* amortissement *m*

**amortize** *vt* amortir

**amount** *n* quantité *f*; (sum) montant *m*, somme *f*, total *m*; (meaning) signification *f*; **any ~ of** des quantités de; *vi* **~ to** s'élever à, se chiffrer à; (be equivalent to) se réduire à, se ramener à; **it ~ s to the same thing** ça revient au même

**amour** *n* liaison *f*, intrigue amoureuse

**amperage** *n elect* intensité *f* d'un courant exprimé en ampères

**ampere** *n* ampère *m*

**ampersand** *n* esperluète *f*

**amphetamine** *n* amphétamine *f*

**amphibia** *npl zool* amphibiens *mpl*, batraciens *mpl*

**amphibian** *n zool* amphibie *m*; *mil* char *m* amphibie, avion *m* amphibie; *adj* amphibie

**amphibious** *adj* amphibie

**amphitheatre** *n* amphithéâtre *m*; *coll* amphi *m*

**amphora** *n* (*pl* **amphorae**) amphore *f*

**ample** *adj* abondant, sans bornes; (garment) ample; bien assez de; **have ~ means** avoir une grosse fortune; **have ~ time** avoir largement le temps

**amplification** *n* amplification *f*

**amplifier** *n* amplificateur *m*, *coll* ampli *m*

**amplify** *vt* amplifier, augmenter; (view) développer

**amplitude** *n* amplitude *f*

**amply** *adv* amplement, largement

**ampoule** *n* ampoule *f*

**amputate** *vt* amputer

**amputation** *n* amputation *f*

**amuck, amok** *adv* **run ~** s'abandonner à l'amok, être pris d'un accès de folie meurtrière; *fig* perdre tout contrôle de soi-même

**amulet** *n* amulette *f*

**amuse** *vt* amuser, divertir, faire rire

**amusement** *n* amusement *m*, divertissement *m*; (pastime) distraction *f*, amusement *m*; **~ arcade** luna-park *m*

**amusing** *adj* amusant, drôle, divertissant

**amusingly** *adv* drôlement, d'une manière amusante

**amyl** *n* amyle *m*; ~ **alcohol** alcool *m* amylique

¹**an** *indef art see* **a**

²**an** *conj ar* si

**Anabaptist** *n* anabaptiste

**anabolism** *n physiol* anabolisme *m*

**anachronism** *n* anachronisme *m*

**anachronistic** *adj* anachronique

**anacoluthon** *n* (*pl* **anacolutha**) anacoluthe *f*

**anaconda** *n* anaconda *m*

**anacreontic** *adj* anacréontique

**anaemia** *n* anémie *f*

**anaemic** *adj* anémique

**anaesthesia** *n* anesthésie *f*

**anaesthetic** *n* anesthésique *m*; *adj* anesthésique

**anaesthetist** *n* anesthésiste

**anaesthetize** *vt* anesthésier

**anagram** *n* anagramme *f*

**anal** *adj* anal

**analgesia** *n* analgésie *f*

**analgesic** *n* analgésique *m*; *adj* analgésique

**analog** *n US see* **analogue**

**analogical** *adj* analogique

**analogous** *adj* analogue

**analogue** *n* analogue *m*; ~ **computer** calculateur *m* analogique

**analogy** *n* analogie *f*

**analyse, analyze** *vt* analyser, faire l'analyse de; *gramm* faire l'analyse logique de; *psych* psychanalyser

**analysis** *n* (*pl* **analyses**) analyse *f*; *psych* psychanalyse *f*

**analyst** *n chem* analyste; *psych* psychanalyste

**analytic, analytical** *adj* analytique

**analytics** *n* analytique *f*

**anapaest** *n pros* anapeste *m*

**anaphrodisiac** *n* anaphrodisiaque *m*; *adj* anaphrodisiaque

**anarchic, anarchical** *adj* anarchique

**anarchism** *n* anarchisme *m*

**anarchist** *n* + *adj* anarchiste

**anarchy** *n* anarchie *f*

**anathema** *n eccles* + *fig* anathème *m*

**anathematize** *vt* frapper d'anathème, maudire

**anatomical** *adj* anatomique

**anatomist** *n* anatomiste

**anatomize** *vt* disséquer; examiner minutieusement

**anatomy** *n* anatomie *f*; *fig* analyse détaillée

**ancestor** *n* ancêtre *m*, aïeul *m* (*pl* aïeux)

**ancestral** *adj* ancestral

**ancestress** *n* aïeule *f*

**ancestry** *n* ascendance *f*, ancêtres *mpl*

**anchor** *n* ancre *f*; *fig* soutien *m*; **cast** ~,

**come to** ~ jeter l'ancre, mouiller; **weigh** ~ lever l'ancre; *vt* mettre à l'ancre; *fig* ancrer; *vi* mouiller, se mettre à l'ancre

**anchorage** *n* mouillage *m*, ancrage *m*; (dues) droits *mpl* de mouillage

**anchored** *adj* ancré

**anchorite** *n* anachorète *m*

**anchovy** *n* anchois *m*

**anchylosis** *n* ankylose *f*

**anchylotic** *adj* ankylosé

**ancient** *n* **the** ~**s** les anciens; *adj* (antiquity) antique; (dated) ancien -ienne

**ancillary** *adj* auxiliaire

**and** *conj* et; ~ **so forth**, ~ **so on** et ainsi de suite; **faster** ~ **faster** de plus en plus vite; **go** ~ **ask** allez demander; **more** ~ **more** de plus en plus; **one hundred** ~ **ten** cent dix; **wait** ~ **see** attendez voir

**andante** *n mus* andante *m*

**andiron** *n* chenet *m*

**androgynous** *adj* androgène

**anecdotal** *adj* anecdotique

**anecdote** *n* anecdote *f*

**anemometer** *n* anémomètre *m*

**anemone** *n* anémone *f*; **sea** ~ actinie *f*, anémone *f* de mer

**aneroid** *n* baromètre *m* anéroïde; *adj* anéroïde

**aneurism** *n path* anévrisme *m*

**anew** *adv* encore, de nouveau

**angel** *n* ange *m*; *coll* amour *m*

**angel-fish** *n* ange *m* de mer

**angelic** *adj* angélique

**angelica** *n* angélique *f*

**angelical** *adj* angélique

**angelus** *n* angélus *m*

**anger** *n* colère *f*, fureur *f*; *lit* courroux *m*; *vt* irriter, mettre en colère; *lit* courroucer

**angina** *n* angine *f*; ~ **pectoris** angine *f* de poitrine

¹**angle** *n* angle *m*; *fig* point *m* de vue, aspect *m*, angle *m*; **at an** ~ de biais; *vt coll* (news, information) présenter avec parti-pris, donner des renseignements tendancieux

²**angle** *vi* pêcher à la ligne; *fig* manœuvrer

**angler** *n* pêcheur -euse à la ligne

**Angles** *npl hist* Angles *mpl*

**Anglican** *n* + *adj* anglican -e

**Anglicanism** *n* anglicanisme *m*

**anglicism** *n* anglicisme *m*

**anglicize** *vt* angliciser

**angling** *n* pêche *f* à la ligne

**anglomania** *n* anglomanie *f*

**anglophile** *n* + *adj* anglophile

**anglophobe** *n* + *adj* anglophobe

**anglophobia** *n* anglophobie *f*

**Anglo-Saxon** *n* (person) Anglo-Saxononne; *ling* anglo-saxon *m*; *adj* anglo-saxon -onne

**angora** *n* (wool) laine *f* angora, angora *m*; (animal) chat *m* angora, lapin *m* angora, chèvre *f* angora

**angostura, angustura** *n* angusture *f*; ~ **bitters** bitter *m* à base d'angusture

**angry** *adj* en colère, furieux -ieuse, irrité, fâché; *med* enflammé, irrité

**anguish** *n* angoisse *f*, anxiété *f*; *vt* angoisser, inquiéter

**angular** *adj* anguleux -euse, pointu

**aniline** *n* aniline *f*; *adj* à base d'aniline

**animadversion** *n* animadversion *f*, observation *f* hostile

**animadvert** *vi* blâmer, critiquer

**animal** *n* animal *m*, bête *f*; *adj* animal; ~ **magnetism** hypnotisme *m*; ~ **spirits** vivacité *f*, entrain *m*

**animality** *n* animalité *f*

**animalize** *vt* brutaliser, animaliser

**animate** *adj* vivant; (lively) vivace; *vt* animer, stimuler, encourager

**animated** *adj* animé; ~ **cartoon** dessin animé

**animation** *n* animation *f*, vivacité *f*, entrain *m*

**animator** *n* animateur -trice

**animism** *n* animisme *m*

**animist** *n* + *adj* animiste

**animosity** *n* animosité *f*, hostilité *f*

**animus** *n see* animosity

**anise** *n* anis *m*

**aniseed** *n* graine *f* d'anis

**ankle** *n* cheville *f*

**anklet** *n* bracelet *m* de cheville

**annalist** *n* annaliste *m*

**annals** *npl* annales *fpl*

**anneal** *vt metal* recuire

**annex, annexe** *n* annexe *f*; *vt* annexer, incorporer

**annexation** *n* incorporation *f*

**annexe** *n see* annex

**annihilate** *vt* annihiler, anéantir

**annihilation** *n* annihilation *f*, anéantissement *m*

**anniversary** *n* anniversaire *m*

**annotate** *vt* annoter

**annotation** *n* annotation *f*

**announce** *vt* annoncer, proclamer; faire savoir; (birth, death, etc) faire part de

**announcement** *n* annonce *f*, avis *m*; (birth, death, etc) faire-part *m invar*

**announcer** *n rad* + *TV* speaker -ine

**annoy** *vt* ennuyer, vexer, agacer, contrarier, irriter

**annoyance** *n* contrariété *f*, irritation *f*, ennui *m*

**annoying** *adj* ennuyeux -euse, agaçant, fâcheux -euse, contrariant

**annual** *n* publication annuelle; *bot* plante annuelle; *adj* annuel -elle

**annuity** *n* annuité *f*, rente viagère, viager *m*

**annul** *vt* annuler; *leg* abroger

**annular** *adj* annulaire

**annulary** *n* annulaire *m*

**annulment** *n* annulation *f*; *leg* abrogation *f*

**Annunciation** *n* Annonciation *f*

**anode** *n elect* anode *f*

**anodize** *vt* anodiser

**anodyne** *n* analgésique *m*; *adj* analgésique, calmant; *fig* inoffensif -ive

**anomalous** *adj* irrégulier -ière, anormal

**anomaly** *n* anomalie *f*

¹**anon** *adv ar joc* bientôt, tout à l'heure

²**anon** *adj abbr* anonyme

**anonymity** *n* anonymat *m*

**anonymous** *adj* anonyme

**anopheles** *n ent* anophèle *m*

**anorak** *n* anorak *m*

**anorexia** *n* anorexie *f*

**another** *adj* (one more) encore un(e), un(e) de plus; (different) un(e) autre; *pron* un(e) autre, encore un(e)

**answer** *n* (reply) réponse *f*; (solution) solution *f*; *vt* répondre à, répliquer à; (prayer) exaucer; ~**ing machine** répondeur *m* téléphonique ~ **the door** aller ouvrir la porte; *vi* répondre; *coll* ~ **back** donner une réponse impertinente

**answerable** *adj* responsable; (question) susceptible de réponse

**ant** *n* fourmi *f*

**antacid** *n* antiacide *m*, alcalin *m*; *adj* anti-acide, alcalin

**antagonism** *n* antagonisme *m*

**antagonist** *n* antagoniste, adversaire

**antagonize** *vt* contrarier, éveiller l'hostilité de

**Antarctic** *n* Antarctique *m*; *adj* antarctique, austral

**Antarctica** *n* Antarctique *m*, Terres Australes

**ante-** *pref* anté-, anti-

**ant-eater** *n* fourmilier *m*

**antecede** *vt* précéder

**antecedent** *n* antécédent *m*; ~ **s** (person) passé *m*; *adj* antérieur

**antechamber** *n* antichambre *f*

**antedate** *vt* antidater; (precede) précéder

**antediluvian** *adj* antédiluvien -ienne

**antelope** *n* antilope *f*

**antenatal** *adj* prénatal

**antenna** *n* (*pl* antennae) antenne *f*

**antepenultimate** *adj* antépénultième

**anterior** *adj* antérieur

**anteroom** *n* antichambre *f*

**ant-heap** *n* fourmilière *f*

**anthem** *n* motet *m*, hymne *m* + *f*; **national** ~ hymne national

**ant-hill** *n* fourmilière *f*
**anthologist** *n* éditeur -trice d'anthologie
**anthology** *n* anthologie *f*
**anthracite** *n* anthracite *m*
**anthrax** *n biol* anthrax *m*; *vet* charbon *m*
**anthropocentric** *adj* anthropocentrique
**anthropoid** *n* anthropoïde *m*; *adj* anthropoïde
**anthropological** *adj* anthropologique
**anthropologist** *n* anthropologiste, anthropologue
**anthropology** *n* anthropologie *f*
**anthropometry** *n* anthropométrie *f*
**anthropomorphic** *adj* anthropomorphique
**anthropomorphism** *n* anthropomorphisme *m*
**anthropophagi** *npl* anthropophages *mpl*, cannibales *mpl*
**anthropophagous** *adj* anthropophage, cannibale
**anthropophagy** *n* anthropophagie *f*, cannibalisme *m*
**anti-** *pref* anti-; *adv coll* contre
**anti-aircraft** *adj* antiaérien -ienne; ~ **defence** défense *f* contre avions
**antibiotic** *n* antibiotique *m*; *adj* antibiotique
**antibody** *n* anticorps *m*
**antic** *adj* grotesque; ~**s** *npl* cabrioles *fpl*, gambades *fpl*; *fig* bouffonneries *fpl*
**anti-carbon** *n* ~ **additive** décalaminant *m*
**Antichrist** *n* Antéchrist *m*
**antichristian** *adj* antichrétien -ienne
**anticipate** *vt* prévoir, s'attendre à; prévenir, devancer
**anticipation** *n* attente *f*, pressentiment *m*; **in** ~ d'avance
**anticlerical** *adj* anticlérical
**anticlericalism** *n* anticléricalisme *m*
**anticlimax** *n* chute *f*, déception *f*
**anticlinal** *adj* anticlinal
**anticline** *n* anticlinal *m*
**anti-clockwise** *adj* dans le sens inverse des aiguilles d'une montre
**anticoagulant** *n* anticoagulant *m*; *adj* anticoagulant
**anticyclone** *n* anticyclone *m*
**anti-dazzle** *adj mot* anti-éblouissant
**antidemocratic** *adj* antidémocratique
**antidote** *n* antidote *m*, contrepoison *m*
**antifreeze** *n mot* antigel *m*
**antigen** *n* antigène *m*
**antihistamine** *n* antihistaminique *m*
**anti-icer** *n aer* antigivrant *m*
**anti-knock** *n mot* produit antidétonant
**antilogarithm** *n* antilogarithme *m*
**antimacassar** *n* têtière *f*
**antimony** *n* antimoine *m*
**antinomy** *n* antinomie *f*
**anti-particle** *n* antiparticule *f*

**antipathetic, antipathetical** *adj* antipathique
**antipathy** *n* antipathie *f*, aversion *f*
**anti-personnel** *adj mil* antipersonnel *invar*
**antiphlogistic** *adj med* antiphlogistique
**antiphon** *n* antienne *f*
**antiphonal** *n* antiphonaire *m*; *adj* antiphoné
**antiphony** *n* chant *m* d'antiennes
**antipodal, antipodean** *adj* antipodal
**antipodes** *npl* antipode *m*
**antipope** *n eccles* antipape *m*
**anti-proton** *n* antiproton *m*
**antiquarian** *n* amateur *m* d'antiquités; (dealer) antiquaire; *adj* d'antiquaire; ~ **bookseller** libraire spécialisé en vieilles éditions
**antiquary** *n* archéologue; collectionneur -euse d'antiquités
**antiquated** *adj* vieilli, vieillot -otte
**antique** *n* objet *m* d'époque; (furniture) meuble *m* d'époque, meuble ancien; *adj* (old) ancien -ienne; (antiquity) antique
**antiquity** *n* antiquité *f*; **antiquities** antiquités *fpl*, objets *mpl* d'art antiques
**antirrhinum** *n* muflier *m*, gueule-de-loup *f* (*pl* gueules-de-loup)
**antiscorbutic** *adj* antiscorbutique
**anti-semite** *n* antisémite
**anti-semitic** *adj* antisémite, antisémitique
**anti-semitism** *n* antisémitisme *m*
**antisepsis** *n* antisepsie *f*
**antiseptic** *n* antiseptique *m*; *adj* antiseptique
**antisocial** *adj* antisocial
**anti-tank** *adj* antichar
**antithesis** *n* antithèse *f*; contraire *m*
**antithetic, antithetical** *adj* antithétique
**antitoxic** *adj* antitoxique
**antitoxin** *n* antitoxine *f*
**anti-vivisectionist** *n* adversaire de la vivisection; *adj* contre la vivisection
**antler** *n* andouiller *m*; ~**s** ramure *f*, bois *mpl*
**antonym** *n* antonyme *m*
**antrum** *n* (*pl* **antra**) *anat* antre *m*
**anus** *n* anus *m*
**anvil** *n* enclume *f*
**anxiety** *n* (worry) anxiété *f*, inquiétude *f*, souci *m*; (eagerness) grand désir
**anxious** *adj* (worried) anxieux -ieuse, soucieux -ieuse, troublé, inquiet -iète; (eager) anxieux -ieuse, désireux -euse, impatient
**any** *adj* (no matter what) n'importe quel (*f* quelle), tout, quelconque; (some) un peu de, quelque; (with neg) aucun; ~ **person who** toute personne qui; **at** ~ **moment** à tout moment; **have you** ~

**comments to make?** avez-vous des remarques à faire?; **I haven't ~ reason to think** je n'ai aucune raison de croire; *pron* (no matter who) n'importe qui; (no matter which) n'importe lequel (*f* laquelle); (some) en; (someone) quelconque; (with neg) aucun; **have you ~ ?** en avez-vous?; **if ~ of you know** si quelconque d'entre vous sait; *adv* (a little) un peu; (not at all) nullement, aucunement; **at ~ rate, in ~ case** en tout cas; **can you walk ~ faster?** pouvez-vous marcher un peu plus vite?; **he is not ~ cleverer than you** il n'est nullement plus intelligent que vous

**anybody** *pron* (somebody) quelqu'un, n'importe qui; (with *neg*) personne

**anyhow** *adv* (in any case) en tout cas, de toute façon; (carelessly) n'importe comment, tant bien que mal

**anyone** *pron see* **anybody**

**anything** *pron* (no matter what) n'importe quoi; *inter* quelque chose; (with *neg*) rien

**anywhere** *adv* n'importe où, partout; *inter* quelque part; (with *neg*) nulle part

**aorist** *n* aoriste *m*

**aorta** *n* aorte *f*

**apace** *adv lit* vite, rapidement

**Apache** *n* Apache; **apache** *obs* apache *m*, voyou *m*

**apanage, appanage** *n* apanage *m*

**apart** *adv* à distance, à l'écart, de côté, à part; (separately) séparément; (in pieces) en morceaux; **~ from** en dehors de; **come ~** se détacher; **live ~** être séparé; **take ~** démonter; **tell ~** distinguer

**apartheid** *n* apartheid *m*

**apartment** *n* (room) pièce *f*; *US* appartement *m*; **~s** logement (meublé); **~ house** immeuble (divisé en appartements), maison *f* de rapport

**apathetic** *adj* apathique, indifférent

**apathy** *n* apathie *f*, indifférence *f*

**ape** *n* (grand) singe; *vt* singer

**aperient** *n* laxatif *m*; *adj* laxatif -ive

**aperitif** *n* apéritif *m*

**aperture** *n* trou *m*, orifice *m*; *phot* ouverture *f*

**apex** *n* (*pl* apices) sommet *m*

**aphasia** *n* aphasie *f*

**aphis** *n* (*pl* aphides) aphis *m*

**aphonia, aphony** *n* aphonie *f*

**aphonic** *adj* aphone

**aphorism** *n* aphorisme *m*

**aphrodisiac** *n* aphrodisiaque *m*; *adj* aphrodisiaque

**aphtha** *n* aphte *m*

**apiarist** *n* apiculteur *m*

**apiary** *n* rucher *m*

**apiculture** *n* apiculture *f*

**apiece** *adv* (person) par personne, par tête, chacun; (thing) chacun, la pièce

**apish** *adj* comme un singe, singeant

**aplomb** *n* sang-froid *m invar*, aplomb *m*, assurance *f*

**Apocalypse** *n* Apocalypse *f*

**apocalyptic** *adj* apocalyptique

**apocope** *n* apocope *f*

**Apocrypha** *n* apocryphes *mpl*

**apocryphal** *adj* apocryphe

**apogee** *n* apogée *m*

**apologetic** *adj* d'excuse, plein de déférence; *eccles* apologétique

**apologetics** *npl* apologétique *f*

**apologia** *n* apologie *f*

**apologist** *n* apologiste

**apologize** *vi* s'excuser

**apologue** *n* apologue *m*, fable *f*

**apology** *n* excuses *fpl*; expédient *m*; apologie *f*

**apoplectic** *n* + *adj* apoplectique; **~ fit** attaque *f* d'apoplexie

**apoplexy** *n* apoplexie *f*

**apophthegm, apothegm** *n* maxime *f*, apophtegme *m*

**apostasy** *n* apostasie *f*

**apostate** *n* apostat *m*; *adj* apostat

**apostatic** *adj* apostatique

**apostatize** *vi* apostasier

**a posteriori** *adv* a posteriori

**apostle** *n* apôtre *m*; **~'s creed** symbole *m* des apôtres

**apostrophe** *n* apostrophe *f*

**apostrophize** *vt* apostropher

**apothecary** *n ar* apothicaire *m*

**apothegm** *n see* **apophthegm**

**apotheosis** *n* apothéose *f*

**appal** *vt* consterner, choquer

**appalling** *adj* consternant, choquant; horrible, épouvantable

**appanage** *n see* **apanage**

**apparatus** *n* appareil *m*, mécanisme *m*

**apparel** *n* habillement *m*; *vt* habiller

**apparent** *adj* apparent; (obvious) apparent, évident; **heir ~** héritier -ière présomptif -ive

**apparition** *n* apparition *f*

**appeal** *n* appel *m*; (request) supplication *f*; (attraction) attrait *m*; **Court of Appeal** cour *f* d'appel; *vi* (for money) lancer un appel; (request) faire appel; *leg* se pourvoir en appel; (attract) plaire, attirer

**appealing** *adj* émouvant, attendrissant; (attractive) attirant; (asking) implorant

**appear** *vi* (become visible) apparaître, se montrer, arriver; *leg* comparaître; (book) paraître, sortir; (actor) jouer; (seem) sembler, paraître

**appearance** *n* (action of appearing) apparition *f*, arrivée *f*; (look) apparence *f*, aspect *m*, mine *f*; *leg* comparution *f*; (book) parution *f*; **at first** ~ au premier abord; **keep up** ~**s** sauver les apparences; **judge by** ~**s** se fier aux apparences; **make one's first** ~ débuter

**appease** *vt* apaiser, calmer, assouvir

**appeasement** *n* apaisement *m*, assouvissement *m*, conciliation *f*

**appellant** *n leg* appelant -e; *adj* appelant

**appellate** *adj leg* d'appel

**appellation** *n* appellation *f*

**append** *vt* ajouter, joindre

**appendage** *n* appendice *m*, prolongement *m*

**appendicitis** *n* appendicite *f*

**appendix** *n* (*pl* **appendices**) appendice *m*

**appertain** *vi* appartenir, faire partie, relever

**appetence** *n* appétence *f*

**appetite** *n* appétit *m*

**appetizer** *n* (liquid) apéritif *m*; (food) amuse-gueule *m invar*

**appetizing** *adj* appétissant, alléchant

**applaud** *vt* applaudir, approuver

**applause** *n* applaudissements *mpl*, acclamation *f*

**apple** *n* pomme *f*; **be the** ~ **of s/o's eye** être le chouchou de qn

**apple-brandy** *n* eau-de-vie *f* (*pl* eaux-de-vie) de pommes; (Normandy) calvados *m*

**apple-cart** *n coll* **upset the** ~ tout ficher en l'air

**apple-dumpling** *n* pomme *f* au four

**applejack** *n US* eau-de-vie *f* (*pl* eaux-de-vie) de pommes

**apple-pie** *n* tarte *f* aux pommes; ~ **bed** lit *m* en portefeuille; ~ **order** ordre parfait

**apple-tree** *n* pommier *m*

**appliance** *n* appareil *m*, dispositif *m*

**applicable** *adj* applicable

**applicant** *n* candidat -e, demandeur -euse

**application** *n* (request) demande *f*; (post, etc) candidature *f*; (use) application *f*; (ointment) enduit *m*; (hard work) assiduité *f*

**applied** *adj* appliqué

**appliqué** *n* application *f*, travail *m* d'application

**apply** *vt* (put on) appliquer, mettre; ~ **the brakes** freiner; ~ **pressure** faire pression; *vi* s'adresser; (refer) s'appliquer; ~ **for** faire une demande de, poser sa candidature pour; ~ **oneself** s'appliquer

**appoggiatura** *n mus* appoggiature *f*

**appoint** *vt* (elect) nommer, désigner; (fix) fixer, désigner; **well** ~**ed** bien aménagé

**appointment** *n* (meeting) rendez-vous *m*; (election) nomination *f*, désignation *f*; (post) emploi *m*, poste *m*; **by** ~ **to** fournisseur *m* de; (fitments) ~**s** ameublement *m*, mobilier *m*

**apportion** *vt* répartir, partager, assigner

**apposite** *adj* juste, à propos

**apposition** *n* apposition *f*

**appraisal** *n* évaluation *f*, appréciation *f*

**appraise** *vt* évaluer

**appreciable** *adj* appréciable, considérable

**appreciate** *vt* (esteem) apprécier, goûter; (value) évaluer, estimer; (gratitude) être sensible à, être reconnaissant de; *vi* monter, s'apprécier, augmenter de valeur

**appreciation** *n* (judgement) appréciation *f*, évaluation *f*; (gratitude) reconnaissance *f*; *fin* hausse *f*

**appreciative** *adj* sensible; reconnaissant

**apprehend** *vt* (understand) comprendre, percevoir; (arrest) arrêter, appréhender

**apprehension** *n* appréhension *f*, crainte *f*; (arrest) arrestation *f*; (understanding) compréhension *f*

**apprehensive** *adj* appréhensif -ive, craintif -ive

**apprentice** *n* apprenti -e, élève; *vt* mettre en apprentissage

**apprenticeship** *n* apprentissage *m*

**apprise** *vt* informer, prévenir

**approach** *n* approche *f*, arrivée *f*; (access) abord *m*, voie *f* d'accès; **make** ~ **es to s/o** faire des avances à qn; *vt* approcher de; s'adresser à; *vi* approcher, s'approcher; **be easy to** ~ être d'un abord facile

**approachable** *adj* avenant, approchable, accessible

**approbation** *n* approbation *f*

**appropriate** *adj* juste, opportun, convenable, approprié; *vt* s'approprier, s'emparer de

**appropriateness** *n* justesse *f*, à-propos *m*

**appropriation** *n* appropriation *f*

**approval** *n* approbation *f*, assentiment *m*; **on** ~ à l'essai

**approve** *vt* approuver, confirmer, ratifier, homologuer; *vi* approuver

**approved** *adj* approuvé, estimé; ~ **school** centre *m* d'éducation surveillée

**approving** *adj* approbateur -trice

**approximate** *adj* approximatif -ive; *vi* se rapprocher, s'approcher

**approximation** *n* approximation *f*

**appurtenance** *n usu pl* dépendances *fpl*, accessoires *mpl*, installations *fpl*

**apricot** *n* abricot *m*; (tree) abricotier *m*; ~ **tart** tarte *f* aux abricots

**April** *n* avril *m*; ~ **fool** poisson *m* d'avril; ~ **shower** giboulée *f* de mars

**a priori** *adv* a priori
**apron** *n* tablier *m*; *theat* avant-scène *f*; *aer* aire *f* de stationnement
**apron-strings** *npl* **tied to his mother's ~** pendu aux jupes de sa mère
**apropos** *adj* opportun; *adv* à propos, opportunément
**apse** *n* abside *f*
**apsidal** *adj* absidal
**apt** *adj* (suitable) approprié, juste; (intelligent) doué, intelligent; **~ to** enclin à, porté à
**aptitude** *n* aptitude *f*
**aptly** *adv* avec justesse, à propos
**aptness** *n* justesse *f*
**aqualung** *n* scaphandre *m* autonome
**aquamarine** *n* (stone) aigue-marine *f* (*pl* aigues-marines); (colour) bleu-vert *m invar*
**aquaplane** *n* aquaplane *m*; *vi* faire de l'aquaplane
**aquarelle** *n* aquarelle *f*
**aquarium** *n* aquarium *m*
**Aquarius** *n astrol* le Verseau
**aquatic** *adj* aquatique; *sp* nautique
**aquatint** *n* aquatinte *f*
**aqueduct** *n* aqueduc *m*
**aqueous** *adj* aqueux -euse
**aquiline** *adj* aquilin
**Arab** *n* Arabe; cheval *m* arabe; *adj* arabe; **street arab** gamin -e des rues
**arabesque** *n* arabesque *f*
**Arabia** *n* Arabie *f*
**Arabian** *adj* arabe; **~ Gulf** golfe *m* Arabique; **the ~ Nights** les Mille et Une Nuits
**Arabic** *n ling* arabe *m*; *adj* arabe; **~ numerals** chiffres *mpl* arabes
**Arabist** *n* arabisant -e
**arable** *adj* arable, cultivable
**arachnid** *n* ~ s arachnides *mpl*
**Aramaic** *n ling* araméen *m*; *adj* araméen -enne
**arbiter** *n* arbitre *m*, juge *m*
**arbitrariness** *n* arbitraire *m*
**arbitrary** *adj* arbitraire
**arbitrate** *vt* arbitrer, juger; *vi* arbitrer
**arbitration** *n* arbitrage *m*
**arbitrator** *n* arbitre *m*, juge *m*
**arboreal** *adj* arboricole
**arborescent** *adj* arborescent
**arboretum** *n* (*pl* **arboreta**) arboretum *m*
**arboriculture** *n* arboriculture *f*
**arborist** *n* arboriculteur -trice
**arbour** *n* tonnelle *f*, charmille *f*
**arc** *n* arc *m*; **~ lamp** lampe *f* à arc; **~ welding** soudure *f* à arc (voltaïque)
**arcade** *n* arcade *f*; (shops) galerie marchande, passage *m*
**Arcadian** *adj* arcadien -ienne
**arcanum** *n* (*pl* **arcana**) arcane *m*
**¹arch** *n archi* voûte *f*, arc *m*, cintre *m*;

(bridge) arche *f*; *anat* arcade *f*, cambrure *f*; *vt* arquer, cambrer; *vi* s'arquer
**²arch** *adj* espiègle; malicieux -ieuse
**³arch-** *pref* archi-
**Archaean** *adj geol* archéen -éenne
**archaeological** *adj* archéologique
**archaeologist** *n* archéologue
**archaeology** *n* archéologie *f*
**archaic** *adj* archaïque
**archaism** *n* archaïsme *m*
**archangel** *n* archange *m*
**archbishop** *n* archevêque *m*
**archbishopric** *n* archevêché *m*
**archdeacon** *n* archidiacre *m*
**archdiocese** *n* archidiocèse *m*
**archduchess** *n* archiduchesse *f*
**archduchy** *n* archiduché *m*
**archduke** *n* archiduc *m*
**archer** *n* archer *m*
**archery** *n* tir *m* à l'arc
**archetypal** *adj* archétype
**archetype** *n* archétype *m*
**archiepiscopal** *adj* archiépiscopal
**archimandrite** *n* archimandrite *m*
**archipelago** *n* archipel *m*
**architect** *n* architecte *m*
**architectonic** *adj* architectonique
**architectural** *adj* architectural
**architecture** *n* architecture *f*
**architrave** *n archi* architrave *f*; (frame) encadrement *m*
**archival** *adj* archivistique
**archives** *npl* archives *fpl*
**archivist** *n* archiviste
**archness** *n* espièglerie *f*, malice *f*
**archway** *n* passage voûté; voûte *f*, porche *m*
**Arctic** *adj* arctique
**ardent** *adj* ardent; passionné, fervent
**ardour** *n* ardeur *f*, ferveur *f*
**arduous** *adj* ardu, laborieux -ieuse, pénible
**arduously** *adv* laborieusement, péniblement
**arduousness** *n* difficulté *f*, peine *f*
**are** *see* **be**
**area** *n* superficie *f*; région *f*, zone *f*; (scope) domaine *m*, champ *m*; **dining ~** coin *m* salle-à-manger; *adj* **~ manager** directeur régional, chef *m* de secteur; **~ office** agence régionale
**arena** *n* arène *f*
**arete** *n geog* arête *f*
**Argentina** *n* Argentine *f*
**Argentine** *adj* argentin
**Argentinian** *n* Argentin -e; *adj* argentin
**argillaceous** *adj* argileux -euse
**argon** *n* argon *m*
**Argonaut** *n* Argonaute *m*
**argosy** *n ar* galion *m*
**arguable** *adj* discutable; **it is ~ that** on peut soutenir que

**argue** *vt* (debate) discuter, débattre; (denote) dénoter, indiquer; (maintain) soutenir; (persuade) persuader; (dissuade) dissuader; (case) présenter; *vi* raisonner, argumenter; (dispute) se disputer; **don't ~!** pas de discussion!; **that ~ s well for you** cela parle en votre faveur

**argument** *n* (reason) argument *m*; (discussion) discussion *f*, débat *m*; (synopsis) sommaire *m*, résumé *m*, argument *m*

**argumentation** *n* argumentation *f*

**argumentative** *adj* raisonneur -euse; logique

**aria** *n mus* aria *f*

**Arian** *n* Arien -ienne; *adj* arien -ienne

**Arianism** *n* arianisme *m*

**arid** *adj* aride

**aridity** *n* aridité *f*

**Aries** *n astrol* le Bélier

**aright** *adv* correctement, bien

**arise** *vi* (get up) se lever; (come about, appear) survenir, se présenter; (problem, question) se poser; (result) résulter, provenir; **~ out of** résulter de; **arising from that** à partir de cela; **if the question ~ s** le cas échéant; **should the need ~** en cas de besoin

**aristocracy** *n* aristocratie *f*

**aristocrat** *n* aristocrate

**aristocratic** *adj* aristocratique

**arithmetic** *n* arithmétique *f*

**arithmetical** *adj* arithmétique

**arithmetician** *n* arithméticien -ienne

**ark** *n* arche *f*; **Ark of the Covenant** arche *f* d'alliance, arche sainte; **Noah's ~** arche *f* de Noé

**¹arm** *n* (limb) bras *m*; **~ in ~** bras dessus bras dessous; **child in ~ s** enfant au berceau; **keep at ~ 's length** tenir à distance; **with open ~ s** à bras ouverts

**²arm** *n* (weapon) arme *f*; (military career) **~ s** armes *fpl*; **her arms** *fpl*, armoiries *fpl*; **~ s race** course *f* aux armements; **be up in ~ s against** s'insurger contre; **lay down one's ~ s** se rendre, déposer les armes; **take up ~ s** prendre les armes; *vt* (person) armer; (missile) munir d'une ogive; *vi* s'armer

**armada** *n* armada *f*

**armament** *n* armement *m*; matériel *m* de guerre; (preparation for war) armement *m*

**armature** *n mil* armure *f*; (armour-plating) blindage *m*; *elect* armature *f*; *zool* carapace *f*

**arm-band** *n* brassard *m*

**armchair** *n* fauteuil *m*

**armed** *adj* armé

**armful** *n* brassée *f*

**arm-hole** *n* emmanchure *f*

**armistice** *n* armistice *m*

**armless** *adj* sans bras

**armlet** *n* brassard *m*

**armorial** *n* armorial *m*; *adj* armorial

**armory** *n US* fabrique *f* d'armes

**armour** *n hist* armure *f*; (plating) blindage *m*; (armoured forces) forces blindées

**armour-bearer** *n hist* écuyer *m*

**armoured** *adj* blindé; **~ car** voiture blindée

**armourer** *n* armurier *m*

**armour-piercing** *adj* (gun) antichar (*f invar*; *mpl*+*fpl* antichars); (shell, bullet) perforant

**armour-plate** *n* blindage *m*

**armour-plated** *adj* blindé

**armoury** *n* dépôt *m* d'armes

**armpit** *n* aisselle *f*

**arm-rest** *n* accoudoir *m*

**army** *n* armée *f*; *fig* foule *f*, multitude *f*; **join the ~** s'engager

**army-corps** *n* corps *m* d'armée

**army-list** *n* annuaire *m* militaire

**arnica** *n* arnica *f*

**aroma** *n* arôme *m*

**aromatic** *n* aromate *m*; *adj* aromatique

**aromatize** *vt* aromatiser

**around** *adv* autour; (near) alentour, dans les parages; **be ~** être dans les parages; *prep* autour de; (about) environ, à peu près

**arouse** *vt* éveiller, réveiller; (cause) susciter, provoquer

**arpeggio** *n mus* arpège *m*

**arraign** *vt leg* poursuivre en justice, accuser, blâmer

**arraignment** *n leg* assignation *f*; critique *f*, attaque *f*

**arrange** *vt* arranger, aménager; organiser; régler; *vi* s'arranger, prendre des mesures

**arrangement** *n* arrangement *m*; aménagement *m*, disposition *f*; (agreement) accommodement *m*, entente *f*; **~ s** mesures *fpl*, préparations *fpl*; **by ~ with** avec l'accord de, avec l'autorisation de

**arrant** *adj* notoire, fieffé

**arras** *n* tapisserie *f*

**array** *n* ordre *m*, rang *m*; *vt mil* ranger, déployer

**arrears** *npl* arriéré *m*; **be in ~** s'arriérer, être en retard

**arrest** *n* arrestation *f*; *leg* (judgement) suspension *f*; **close ~** arrêts *mpl* de rigueur; **house ~** assignation *f* à domicile; **open ~** arrêts *mpl* simples; **under ~** en état d'arrestation; *mil* aux arrêts; *vt* arrêter, appréhender

**arresting** *adj* frappant, impressionnant

arrival *n* arrivée *f*; (person) arrivant -e; on ~ à l'arrivée; (letter) to await ~ prière de ne pas faire suivre
arrive *vi* arriver; *fig* réussir
arrogance *n* arrogance *f*, morgue *f*
arrogant *adj* arrogant
arrogate *vt* (claim wrongly) s'arroger, revendiquer à tort; (attribute unfairly) attribuer injustement
arrogation *n* usurpation *f*
arrow *n* flèche *f*
arrow-head *n* pointe *f* de flèche
arrowroot *n* arrow-root *m*
arse *n sl* cul *m*; *vi sl* ~ about, around faire l'imbécile
arse-hole *n sl* trou *m* du cul
arsenal *n* arsenal *m*
arsenic *n* arsenic *m*
arsenical *adj* arsenical
arson *n* incendie criminel
arsonist *n* incendiaire
art *n* art *m*; (cunning) ruse *f*, artifice *m*; (skill) adresse *f*, habileté *f*; black ~ s magie noire; fine ~ s beaux arts
artefact *n* objet fabriqué
arterial *adj* artériel -ielle; ~ road voie *f* à grande circulation
arteriosclerosis *n* artériosclérose *f*
artery *n* artère *f*
artesian *adj* artésien -ienne
art-form *n* moyen *m* d'expression artistique
artful *adj* malin -igne, astucieux -ieuse, rusé; ingénieux -ieuse
arthritic *adj* arthritique
arthritis *n* arthrite *f*
arthropoda *npl* arthropodes *mpl*
artichoke *n* artichaut *m*; Jerusalem ~ topinambour *m*
article *n* article *m*; objet *m*; *vt* mettre en apprentissage; *leg* stipuler
articulate *vt + vi* articuler; *adj* articulé; (speech) bien articulé
articulation *n* articulation *f*
artifice *n* artifice *m*, stratagème *m*
artificer *n* artisan *m*
artificial *adj* artificiel -ielle, synthétique; (affected) affecté, factice
artificiality *n* insincérité *f*, manque *m* de naturel
artillery *n* artillerie *f*
artillery-man *n* artilleur *m*
artisan *n* artisan *m*
artist *n* artiste
artistic *adj* artistique
artistry *n* talent *m* artistique, art *m*
artless *adj* (simple) ingénu; (crude) grossier -ière
artlessness *n* (simplicity) ingénuité *f*; grossièreté *f*
art-silk *n* rayonne *f*
arty *adj coll* qui affecte le genre artistique

arty-crafty, *US* artsy-craftsy *adj coll pej* artisanal
Aryan *n* Aryen -enne; *adj* aryen -enne
as *adv* si, aussi; *conj* comme; (time) alors que, tandis que; (since) puisque, étant donné que; (in the capacity of ) en tant que; ~ for, ~ to quant à; ~ good ~ aussi bon que; ~ long ~ pourvu que; (time) aussi longtemps que; ~ many ~ autant que; (all who) tous ceux qui; ~ well ~ aussi bien que; be dressed ~ être habillé en; much ~ en dépit du fait que
asbestos *n* amiante *f*, asbeste *m*
ascend *vt* gravir, monter; *vi* monter, s'élever
ascendancy *n* ascendant *m*, emprise *f*
ascendant *n astrol* ascendant *m*; be in the ~ monter; *adj astrol* ascendant; dominant
ascension *n* ascension *f*
ascent *n* montée *f*, ascension *f*
ascertain *vt* établir, vérifier; s'informer de
ascetic *n* ascète; *adj* ascétique
asceticism *n* ascétisme *m*
ascorbic *adj* ascorbique, antiscorbutique; ~ acid acide *m* ascorbique, vitamine *f* C
ascribable *adj* attribuable, imputable
ascribe *vt* attribuer, imputer
ascription *n* attribution *f*, imputation *f*
asdic *n mil* asdic *m*
asepsis *n* asepsie *f*
aseptic *adj* aseptique
asexual *adj* asexué
asexuality *n* asexualité *f*
¹ash *n* frêne *m*; mountain ~ sorbier *m*
²ash *n* cendre *f*; ~ es (cremated body) cendres *fpl*; ~ blond blond cendré; sackcloth and ~ es le sac et la cendre; turn to dust and ~ es être anéanti
ashamed *adj* honteux -euse, confus
ash-bin, ash-can *n* poubelle *f*, boîte *f* à ordures
¹ashen *adj* cendreux -euse, terreux -euse
²ashen *adj* (wood) en frêne
ashlar *n* pierre *f* de taille
ashore *adv* à terre; go ~ débarquer; run ~ échouer
ash-pan *n* cendrier *m*
ash-tray *n* cendrier *m*
Ash-Wednesday *n* mercredi *m* des Cendres
ashy *adj* cendré; (pale) cendreux -euse; couvert de cendres
Asia *n* Asie *f*
Asian *n* Asiatique; *adj* asiatique
Asiatic *n* Asiatique; *adj* asiatique
aside *n* aparté *m*; *adv* de côté, à part; *leg* set ~ casser
asinine *adj* idiot, sot (*f* sotte)
ask *vt* (inquire, request) demander;

(invite) inviter; (prices) vouloir; *vi* demander; **~ after (about)** demander des nouvelles de; **~ for s/o** demander à voir qn; *sl* **~ for it** chercher des ennuis; **~ for sth** demander qch; **~ for sth back** demander qu'on rende qch; **~ s/o in** prier qn d'entrer; **~ out** inviter à sortir

**askance** *adv* de côté, de biais; **look ~** regarder de travers, regarder d'un œil désapprobateur

**askew** *adv* de travers, obliquement

**aslant** *adv* de biais, de travers

**asleep** *adj* endormi; (limb) engourdi; **fall ~** s'endormir

**asp** *n* aspic *m*

**asparagus** *n* asperge *f*

**aspect** *n* aspect *m*, air *m*; (question) aspect *m*, angle *m*; (building) orientation *f*, exposition *f*; *gramm + astrol* aspect *m*

**aspen** *n* tremble *m*

**asperge** *n* asperger

**aspergillum** *n* goupillon *m*

**asperity** *n* aspérité *f*, dureté *f*; (person) rudesse *f*

**aspersion** *n* calomnie *f*

**asphalt** *n* asphalte *m*; *vt* asphalter

**asphodel** *n* asphodèle *m*

**asphyxia** *n* asphyxie *f*

**asphyxiate** *vt* asphyxier; *vi* s'asphyxier

**asphyxiation** *n* asphyxie *f*

**aspic** *n cul* gelée *f*

**aspidistra** *n* aspidistra *m*

**aspirant** *n* aspirant -e

**aspirate** *n* consonne aspirée; *adj* aspiré; *vt* aspirer

**aspiration** *n* aspiration *f*

**aspirator** *n* aspirateur *m*

**aspire** *vi* aspirer, viser, ambitionner

**aspirin** *n* aspirine *f*; (tablet) comprimé *m* d'aspirine

**aspiring** *adj* ambitieux -ieuse

¹**ass** *n* âne *m* (*f* ânesse); *coll* idiot -e, imbécile

²**ass** *n US vulg* cul *m*

**assail** *vt* assaillir, attaquer

**assailant** *n* aggresseur *m*

**assassin** *n* assassin *m*

**assassinate** *vt* assassiner

**assassination** *n* assassinat *m*

**assault** *n mil* assaut *m*; *leg* agression *f*; **~ and battery** voies *fpl* de fait; **~ course** parcours *m* du combattant; **~ craft** chaland *m* de débarquement; **indecent ~** attentat *m* à la pudeur; *vt mil* attaquer; *leg* agresser

**assay** *n* essai *m*; *vt* essayer

**assemblage** *n* assemblage *m*, montage

*m*; (people) réunion *f*, foule *f*

**assemble** *vt* assembler; (people) réunir; *vi* s'assembler, se réunir

**assembly** *n* assemblée *f*, réunion *f*

**assent** *n* assentiment *m*, consentement *m*; *vi* consentir

**assert** *vt* affirmer, soutenir; (maintain) défendre; (claim) revendiquer; **~ oneself** faire valoir ses droits, se pousser

**assertion** *n* assertion *f*, affirmation *f*

**assertive** *adj* péremptoire, tranchant

**assess** *vt* estimer, évaluer; (payment) fixer

**assessment** *n* estimation *f*, évaluation *f*, détermination *f*

**assessor** *n leg* assesseur *m*

**asset** *n* avantage *m*, atout *m*; (possession) avoir *m*; **~s** biens *mpl*; *comm* actif *m*

**asseverate** *vt* affirmer solennellement, déclarer

**asseveration** *n* affirmation solennelle, déclaration *f*

**assiduity** *n* assiduité *f*, zèle *m*

**assiduous** *adj* assidu

**assiduousness** *n* assiduité *f*

**assign** *n leg* ayant-droit *m* (*pl* ayants-droit); *vt* assigner, fixer; attribuer; (appoint) nommer, affecter; *leg* céder

**assignation** *n* (meeting) rendez-vous *m*; attribution *f*; *leg* cession *f*

**assignee** *n leg* cessionaire, mandataire

**assignment** *n* (task) mission *f*; attribution *f*, allocation *f*; *leg* cession *f*

**assimilable** *adj* assimilable

**assimilate** *vt* assimiler; *vi* s'assimiler

**assimilation** *n* assimilation *f*, rapprochement *m*

**assist** *vt* assister, aider, secourir; *vi* aider

**assistance** *n* assistance *f*, aide *f*, secours *m*

**assistant** *n* assistant -e, aide, auxiliaire; *adj* auxiliaire; (deputy) adjoint; sous-

**assize** *n obs* **~s** assises *fpl*

**associate** *n* associé -e, collègue; (crime) complice; (club, society) membre *m*; *adj* associé; *US* **~ professor** = maître *m* de conférences; *vt* associer; *vi* **~ with** s'associer avec, fréquenter

**association** *n* association *f*; fréquentation *f*

**assonance** *n* assonance *f*

**assonant** *adj* assonant

**assort** *vt* ranger, classer, assortir; *vi* s'assortir, s'accorder; **~ with** fréquenter

**assorted** *adj* assorti

**assortment** *n* assortiment *m*, collection *f*

**assuage** *vt* assouvir, calmer, soulager, apaiser

**assume** *vt* assumer, endosser, prendre sur soi; (accept) présumer, supposer; (air) prendre

**assumed** *adj* faux (*f* fausse); **~ name** nom *m* d'emprunt

**assuming** *conj* en supposant que

**assumption** *n* supposition *f*; hypothèse *f*; *eccles* **Assumption** Assomption *f*

**assurance** *n* assurance *f*; (promise) promesse *f*; affirmation *f*; (cheek) toupet *m*

**assure** *vt* assurer, affirmer; convaincre; (life) assurer

**assured** *adj* assuré

**assuredly** *adv* assurément, certainement

**aster** *n* aster *m*

**asterisk** *n* astérisque *m*; *vt* marquer d'un astérisque

**astern** *adv naut* en poupe, à l'arrière; **go ~** faire marche arrière

**asteroid** *n* astéroïde *m*

**asthenia** *n med* asthénie *f*

**asthenic** *adj med* asthénique

**asthma** *n* asthme *m*

**asthmatic** *n* + *adj* asthmatique

**astigmatic** *adj* astigmate

**astigmatism** *n* astigmatisme *m*

**astir** *adv* en mouvement; **be ~** être levé; **set ~** mettre en branle

**astonish** *vt* étonner, ébahir, ahurir

**astonishing** *adj* étonnant, ahurissant

**astonishingly** *adv* incroyablement, remarquablement

**astonishment** *n* étonnement *m*, ahurissement *m*

**astound** *vt* ébahir, abasourdir

**astounding** *adj* ahurissant

**astragal** *n anat* + *archi* astragale *m*

**astrakhan** *n* astrakan *m*

**astral** *adj* astral

**astray** *adv* égaré; **go ~** s'égarer; **lead ~** dévoyer

**astride** *adv* à califourchon; *prep* à califourchon sur

**astringency** *n* astringence *f*

**astringent** *adj* astringent

**astrolabe** *n* astrolabe *m*

**astrologer** *n* astrologue *m*

**astrology** *n* astrologie *f*

**astronaut** *n* astronaute

**astronautics** *npl* astronautique *f*

**astronomer** *n* astronome *m*

**astronomic, astronomical** *adj* astronomique

**astronomy** *n* astronomie *f*

**astrophysics** *npl* astrophysique *f*

**astute** *adj* astucieux -ieuse, malin (*f* maligne), rusé; (mind) pénétrant

**astuteness** *n* astuce *f*, ruse *f*

**asunder** *adv* en morceaux; éloigné, à distance

**asylum** *n* asile *m*, refuge *m*; (mental) asile *m* d'aliénés

**asymmetrical** *adj* asymétrique

**at** *prep* (place, time, price) à; (at the house of) chez; (towards) vers;

(because of) à propos de, à cause de; **~ all events** tout de même; **~ first** d'abord; **~ his request** sur sa demande; **~ home** chez soi, à la maison; **~ night** la nuit; **~ once** tout de suite, immédiatement; **~ one** en accord; **~ sea** en mer; *fig* perdu; *coll* **~ that** encore; **~ the same time** en même temps; **be ~** être occupé à; **be hard ~ it** travailler ferme; **he's always ~ me** il me casse les pieds tout le temps; **while you're ~ it** pendant que vous y êtes

**ataraxy** *n* ataraxie *f*

**atavism** *n* atavisme *m*

**atavistic** *adj* atavistique

**ataxia, ataxy** *n* ataxie *f*

**ate** *see* eat

**atheism** *n* athéisme *m*

**atheist** *n* athée

**atheistic, atheistical** *adj* athée

**athlete** *n* athlète

**athletic** *adj* athlétique

**athletics** *n pl* athlétisme *m*

**athwart** *adv* en travers; *naut* par le travers; *prep* en travers de

**Atlantic** *n* Atlantique *m*; *adj* atlantique

**atlas** *n* atlas *m*

**atmosphere** *n* atmosphère *f*; *fig* atmosphère *f*, ambiance *f*

**atmospheric** *adj* atmosphérique

**atmospherics** *npl rad* parasites *mpl*

**atoll** *n* atoll *m*

**atom** *n* atome *m*; *fig* grain *m*, brin *m*; **smash to ~s** réduire en miettes

**atom-bomb** *n* bombe *f* atomique

**atomic** *adj* atomique

**atomicity** *n* atomicité *f*

**atomize** *vt* atomiser, vaporiser

**atomizer** *n* atomiseur *m*

**atonal** *adj* atonal

**atonality** *n* atonalité *f*

**atone** *vi* expier, racheter

**atonement** *n* expiation *f*

**atonic** *adj pros* atone; *anat* atonique

**atrocious** *adj* atroce; *coll* horrible, affreux -euse

**atrociousness** *n* conduite *f* atroce

**atrocity** *n* atrocité *f*

**atrophy** *n* atrophie *f*; *vt* atrophier; *vi* s'atrophier

**atropine** *n* atropine *f*

**attach** *vt* (fasten) attacher, joindre, lier; (appoint) affecter, attacher; *fig* attribuer; *leg* (person) arrêter; saisir; **be ~ed to** être attaché à; *vi* être imputé à

**attaché** *n* attaché -e

**attaché-case** *n* mallette *f*, attaché-case *m invar*

**attachment** *n* (fastening) fixation *f*; (accessory) accessoire *m*; (feelings) attachement *m*, affection *f*; *leg* (person) arrestation *f*; (goods) saisie *f*; (appointment) affectation *f*; (temporary work) stage *m*; action *f* d'attacher

**attack** *n* attaque *f*; *med* crise *f*, attaque *f*; *vt* attaquer, assaillir; (tackle) s'attaquer à

**attacker** *n* agresseur *m*, attaquant *m*, assaillant *m*

**attain** *vt* atteindre, parvenir à, arriver à

**attainable** *adj* susceptible d'être atteint

**attainment** *n* (accomplishment) travail *m*, réalisation *f*, accomplissement *m*; (knowledge) acquisition *f*

**attempt** *n* tentative *f*, effort *m*, essai *m*; (attack) attentat *m*; *vt* essayer, tenter; *mil* attaquer; (difficult task) entreprendre, s'attaquer à

**attend** *vt* (look after) servir; accompagner; (doctor) soigner; (be present at) assister à; (church, school) aller à, fréquenter; *vi* faire attention; ~ **to** s'occuper de

**attendance** *n* présence *f*; (audience) assistance *f*; **dance ~ on** être aux petits soins pour

**attendant** *n* domestique, suivant -e; (guide) gardien -ienne; *adj* qui accompagne, qui suit; concomitant

**attention** *n* attention *f*; (care) attentions *fpl*; *mil* garde-à-vous *m*; **stand at ~** être au garde-à-vous

**attentive** *adj* attentif -ive; (careful) empressé

**attenuate** *vt* atténuer, modérer; (make thin) amincir; (dilute) raréfier; *vi* s'atténuer, diminuer; *adj* atténué, raréfié; mince

**attenuation** *n* atténuation *f*, diminution *f*

**attest** *vt* attester, témoigner de; *leg* (signature) légaliser; (put on oath) faire prêter serment à; *vi* prêter serment; (vouch for) témoigner de

**attestation** *n* attestation *f*, témoignage *m*; *leg* (signature) légalisation *f*

**¹attic** *n* grenier *m*; ~ **room** mansarde *f*

**²attic** *adj* attique

**attire** *n* vêtements *mpl*; *vt* vêtir, parer

**attitude** *n* attitude *f*, disposition *f*; **strike an ~** poser

**attitudinize** *vi* poser, prendre un air affecté

**attorney** *n leg* mandataire *m*, *US* avoué *m*; **Attorney General** = Procureur Général; *US* = Garde *m* des Sceaux; **power of ~** procuration *f*

**attract** *vt* attirer; *fig* plaire à, séduire; charmer

**attraction** *n* attraction *f*; ~ **s** attractions *fpl*, attraits *mpl*

**attractive** *adj* attirant, attrayant;

charmant; (price) intéressant; *phys* attractif -ive

**attractiveness** *n* attraction *f*, attrait *m*, charme *m*

**attribute** *n* attribut *m*; *gramm* épithète *f*; *vt* attribuer, imputer, prêter

**attribution** *n* attribution *f*, imputation *f*

**attributive** *n* attribut *m*; *gramm* épithète *f*; *adj* attributif -ive; *gramm* qualicatif -ive

**attrition** *n* usure *f*, attrition *f*

**attune** *vt* mettre à l'unisson, accorder

**atypical** *adj* atypique

**aubade** *n* aubade *f*

**aubergine** *n* aubergine *f*

**auburn** *adj* auburn *invar*

**auction** *n* vente *f* aux enchères; **Dutch ~** enchères *fpl* au rabais; *vt* vendre aux enchères

**auctioneer** *n* adjudicateur -trice, commissaire-priseur *m* (*pl* commissaires-priseurs)

**audacious** *adj* audacieux -ieuse, hardi; impudent, effronté

**audacity** *n* audace *f*, hardiesse *f*; impudence *f*, effronterie *f*

**audibility** *n* audibilité *f*

**audible** *adj* audible

**audience** *n* (entertainment) spectateurs *mpl*, public *m*; *theat* salle *f*; (lecture) assistance *f*; *rad* auditeurs *mpl*; (television) téléspectateurs *mpl*; (hearing) audience *f*; *rad+TV* ~ **rating** indice *m* d'audience

**audio-visual** *adj* audio-visuel -elle; ~ **aids** moyens audio-visuels

**audit** *n* vérification *f*; *vt* vérifier, apurer

**audition** *n* audition *f*; *vt+vi theat* auditionner

**auditive** *adj* auditif -ive

**auditor** *n* (listener) auditeur -trice; *comm* expert-comptable *m* (*pl* experts-comptables), vérificateur *m* (de comptes)

**auditorium** *n* auditorium *m*; *theat* salle *f*

**auditory** *adj* auditif -ive

**auger** *n* vrille *f*

**aught** *n lit* quoi que ce soit *m*, quelque chose *m*; *adv* **for ~ I know** pour autant que je sache

**augment** *vt* augmenter, accroître; *vi* augmenter, s'accroître

**augmentation** *n* augmentation *f*, accroissement *m*

**augur** *n* augure *m*; *vt* prédire, présager; *vi* ~ **well (ill)** être de bon (de mauvais) augure

**augury** *n* augure *m*, présage *m*

**August** *n* août *m*

**august** *adj* auguste

**Augustan** *adj hist* d'Auguste; (neo-classical) néo-classique

**Augustinian** *n* augustin -e
**auk** *n orni* guillemot *m*; **little** ~ mergule *m*
**aunt** *n* tante *f*; ~ **Sally** (game) jeu *m* de massacre; (person) tête *f* de turc
**auntie** *n coll* tatie *f*
**au pair** *adj* + *adv* au pair
**aura** *n* aura *f*, ambiance *f*
**aural** *adj* auriculaire
**aureola, aureole** *n* auréole *f*
**auricle** *n anat* (heart) oreillette *f*; (ear) pavillon *m* auriculaire
**auricular** *adj* auriculaire
**aurochs** *n* aurochs *m*
**aurora borealis** *n* aurore boréale
**auroral** *adj* auroral
**auscultation** *n* auscultation *f*
**auspice** *n* augure *m* favorable; ~ **s** auspices *mpl*, patronage *m*
**auspicious** *adj* propice, de bon augure
**Aussie** *n* + *adj coll see* **Australian**
**austere** *adj* austère, sévère
**austerity** *n* austérité *f*, sévérité *f*; (wartime) restrictions *fpl*; *adj* d'austérité, de restrictions
**austral** *adj* austral (*pl* -als)
**Australasia** *n* Australasie *f*
**Australia** *n* Australie *f*
**Australian** *n* Australien -ienne; *adj* australien -ienne
**authentic** *adj* authentique
**authenticate** *vt* vérifier, valider
**authentication** *n* authentification *f*
**author** *n* auteur *m*; (writer) écrivain *m*
**authoress** *n* femme *f* auteur, femme *f* écrivain
**authoritarian** *n* partisan -e de l'autorité; *adj* autoritaire
**authoritarianism** *n* tyrannie *f*, despotisme *m*
**authoritative** *adj* autoritaire; (definitive) qui fait autorité
**authority** *n* autorité *f*, pouvoir *m*, compétence *f*; (right) autorisation *f*; (person, book, etc) autorité *f*; **authorities** autorités *fpl*, administration *f*
**authorization** *n* autorisation *f*; *leg* mandat *m*
**authorize** *vt* autoriser, sanctionner
**authorship** *n* paternité *f*; (profession) métier *m* d'écrivain
**autism** *n* autisme *m*
**autistic** *adj* autistique
**autobahn** *n* autoroute *f*
**autobiographical** *adj* autobiographique
**autobiography** *n* autobiographie *f*
**autocade** *n US* cortège *m* d'automobiles
**autochthon** *n* + *adj* autochtone
**autoclave** *n* autoclave *m*
**autocracy** *n* autocratie *f*
**autocrat** *n* autocrate *m*

**autocratic** *adj* autocratique
**auto-cycle** *n* cyclomoteur *m*; ~ **rider** cyclomotoriste
**auto-da-fé** *n* (*pl* **autos-da-fé**) autodafé *m*
**auto-erotism** *n* auto-érotisme *m*
**autograph** *n* autographe *m*; ~ **album** album *m* d'autographes; *vt* autographier, dédicacer
**autography** *n* autographie *f*
**auto-intoxication** *n* auto-intoxication *f*
**autolysis** *n bioch* autolyse *f*
**automate** *vt* automatiser
**automated** *adj* automatisé
**automatic** *n* automatique *m*; ~ **s** automatique *f*; *adj* automatique
**automation** *n* automatisation *f*
**automatism** *n* automatisme *m*
**automaton** *n* (*pl* **automata**) automate *m*, robot *m*
**automobile** *n* automobile *f*, auto *f*; *US* voiture *f*
**autonomist** *n* autonomiste
**autonomous** *adj* autonome
**autonomy** *n* autonomie *f*
**autopsy** *n* autopsie *f*
**auto-suggestion** *n* autosuggestion *f*
**autumn** *n* automne *m*; *adj* d'automne
**autumnal** *adj* d'automne
**auxiliary** *n* auxiliaire; *gramm* auxiliaire *m*; *adj* auxiliaire, subsidiaire
**avail** *n* secours *m*, utilité *f*, avantage *m*; **be of little** ~ ne pas servir à grand-chose; **be to no** ~ ne servir à rien; **of no** ~ sans résultats; *vt* aider, secourir; ~ **oneself of** utiliser; *vi* être utile, être efficace
**availability** *n* disponibilité *f*
**available** *adj* disponible
**avalanche** *n* avalanche *f*; *vi* tomber en avalanche
**avant-garde** *n* avant-garde *f*
**avarice** *n* avarice *f*
**avaricious** *adj* avare
**avariciousness** *n* avarice *f*
**avatar** *n* avatar *m*
**avaunt** *interj lit* hors d'ici!
**ave** *n* avé *m*, avé Maria *m*
**avenge** *vt* venger; ~ **oneself on** prendre sa revanche sur
**avenue** *n* avenue *f*, boulevard *m*; *fig* possibilité *f*
**aver** *vt* affirmer; *leg* démontrer
**average** *n* moyenne *f*; *adj* moyen -enne; *vt* faire la moyenne de; ~ **out at** revenir à la moyenne de
**averse** *adj* peu disposé, ennemi, opposé
**aversion** *n* aversion *f*, dégoût *m*, répugnance *f*; objet *m* d'aversion
**avert** *vt* éviter, prévenir; (eyes) détourner
**aviary** *n* volière *f*

**aviation** *n* aviation *f*
**aviator** *n* aviateur -trice
**aviculture** *n* aviculture *f*
**avid** *adj* avide
**avidity** *n* avidité *f*
**avionics** *npl* avionique *f*
**avocado** *n* avocat *m*
**avocation** *n* métier *m*, profession *f*; passe-temps *m*, violon *m* d'Ingres
**avoid** *vt* éviter, échapper à, esquiver; *leg* résilier, annuler
**avoidance** *n* réserve *f*, attitude distante, évitement *m*; évasion *f*
**avoirdupois** *n* poids commercial; (over-weight) excès *m* de poids, embonpoint *m*
**avouch** *vt* se porter garant de, garantir; affirmer; *vi* confesser
**avow** *vt* avouer, confesser
**avowal** *n* aveu *m*
**avowed** *adj* déclaré
**avowedly** *adv* nettement
**avuncular** *adj* avunculaire
**await** *vt* attendre; être réservé à
**awake** *adj* éveillé, réveillé; en éveil; *vt* éveiller, réveiller; *vi* s'éveiller, se réveiller
**awaken** *vt* réveiller; *vi* s'éveiller
**awakening** *n* réveil *m*
**award** *n* prix *m*, récompense *f*; *leg* décision *f*; (scholarship) bourse *f*; *vt* décerner, attribuer
**aware** *adj* conscient, averti; (knowledgeable) avisé
**awareness** *n* conscience *f*
**awash** *adj* *naut* à fleur d'eau
**away** *adj* *sp* ~ **match** match *m* à l'extérieur; *adv* au loin, très loin; (continuously) sans arrêt; *interj* hors d'ici!; ouste!; *coll* be ~ être absent; **be** ~ **well** être parti; **far and** ~ de beaucoup; **twenty kilometres** ~ à

vingt kilomètres de distance; **we must** ~ nous devons partir
**awe** *n* crainte *f*, effroi *m*; *vt* inspirer de la crainte à
**awe-inspiring** *adj* imposant, terrible
**awesome** *adj* mystérieux -ieuse, étrange, épouvantable
**awestruck** *adj* frappé de terreur; épouvanté
**awful** *adj* affreux -euse, terrible, horrible; ~ **cheek!** quel culot!
**awfully** *adv* terriblement; *coll* très, vraiment, comme tout, rudement
**awhile** *adv* un instant; quelque temps
**awkward** *adj* peu commode, difficile, peu maniable; gênant, embarrassant; (clumsy) gauche, maladroit; ~ **age** âge ingrat; ~ **customer** type *m* pas commode
**awkwardness** *n* gaucherie *f*, maladresse *f*; (circumstance) embarras *m*
**awl** *n* poinçon *m*
**awning** *n* taud *m*; store *m*
**awry** *adj* de travers, de guingois
**axe,** *US* **ax** *n* hache *f*; *coll* (money) coupe *f* sombre; *coll* **have an** ~ **to grind** prêcher pour son saint, agir dans un but intéressé
**axiom** *n* axiome *m*
**axiomatic, axiomatical** *adj* axiomatique
**axis** *n* axe *m*
**axle** *n* axe *m*; *mot* essieu *m*, pont *m*
**axle-box** *n* boîte *f* d'essieu
**axle-pin** *n* clavette *f* d'essieu
**aye** *n* *pol* vote *m* pour; **the** ~ **s have it** les oui l'emportent; *interj* oui; *dial* toujours
**azalea** *n* azalée *f*
**azimuth** *n* azimut *m*
**azote** *n* azote *m*
**Aztec** *n* Aztèque; *adj* aztèque
**azure** *n* azur *m*; *adj* azuré, d'azur

# B

**baa** *n* bêlement *m*; *vi* bêler
**babble** *n* babil *m*, babillage *m*, bavardage *m*; (stream) gazouillement *m*; *vt* débiter; (secrets) divulguer; *vi* babiller; (stream) gazouiller, murmurer
**babbler** *n* babillard -e, bavard -e

**babe** *n* bébé *m*; naïf -ive; débutant -e
**baboon** *n* babouin *m*
**babouche** *n* babouche *f*
**baby** *n* bébé *m*; enfant, gosse; *US coll* chérie *f*; *sl* **hold the** ~ payer les pots cassés; *adj* de bébé; petit, de taille

réduite; **~ grand (piano)** crapaud *m*, (piano *m*) demi-queue *m invar*

**babyhood** *n* première enfance

**babyish** *adj* enfantin, puéril

**baby-sit** *vi* faire du baby-sitting

**baby-sitter** *n* baby-sitter

**baby-sitting** *n* baby-sitting *m*

**baby-talk** *n* langage enfantin

**baccalaureate** *n* baccalauréat *m*

**bacchic** *adj* bachique

**bachelor** *n* célibataire *m*; *hist* bachelier *m*; **Bachelor of Arts** licencié -e

**bachelor-girl** *n* célibataire *f*

**bachelorhood** *n* célibat *m*

**bacillary** *adj* bacillaire

**bacillus** *n* bacille *m*

**back** *n* (human being, animal, knife, book, etc) dos *m*; (head, building) derrière *m*; (chair) dossier *m*; (cloth, mountain range) envers *m*; (coin, medal) revers *m*; (page) verso *m*; (hall, theatre) fond *m*; *sp* arrière *m*; *naut* quille *f*; **~ to ~** dos à dos; **at the ~ of beyond** au fin fond du bled; **be on one's ~** être sur le flanc; *fig* **break one's ~** s'éreinter; **break the ~ of sth** en faire le plus dur; **put one's ~ into** donner un coup de collier à, en mettre un coup à; **put s/o's ~ up** vexer qn, froisser qn; **turn one's ~ on s/o** tourner le dos à qn; **with one's ~ to the wall** au pied du mur, acculé au mur; *vt* faire reculer; (bet) parier pour; financer; (plan) avaliser; épauler, encourager; **~ up** soutenir; *vi* reculer, faire marche arrière; *naut* (tide, wind) renverser; **~ down, ~ out** se retirer, lâcher la partie; *adj de* derrière, arrière *invar*; (out-of-date) arriéré; **~ seat** siège *m* arrière; **~-seat driver** personne *f* prodigue de conseils superflus; **take a ~ seat** être au second plan; *adv* en arrière; plus tôt, au passé; (from journey) de retour; **~ and forth** en allant et venant; **answer ~** rétorquer, objecter; **go ~ on** (principle) répudier; (promise) violer; (friend) trahir; **pay s/o ~** payer qn de retour; **take ~** rétracter

**back-bench(es)** *n*(*pl*) (British Parliament) banc(s) *m*(*pl*) où s'assoient les députés qui n'ont pas de position ministérielle

**back-bencher** *n* (British Parliament) député *m* sans portefeuille

**backbite** *vt* dénigrer, décrier; *vi* médire

**backbiter** *n* médisant *m*

**backbone** *n* épine dorsale, colonne vertébrale; *fig* pivot *m*; *fig* caractère *m*, courage *m*

**back-breaking** *adj* épuisant, éreintant

**back-chat** *n coll* réplique impertinente

**back-cloth** *n theat* + •g toile *f* de fond

**backdoor** *adj* secret; louche

**back-drop** *n theat* toile *f* de fond

**backer** *n comm* commanditaire *m*; soutien *m*; *sp* parieur -ieuse, turfiste

**backfire** *n mot* pétarade *f*, retour *m* de flamme; *vi mot* pétarader, avoir des retours de flamme; *coll fig* échouer

**backgammon** *n* trictrac *m*

**background** *n* arrière-plan *m*, fond *m*; (person) origines *fpl*; (experience) acquis *m*; (epoch) climat culturel; *adj* de fond

**backhand** *n* (tennis, etc) revers *m*; (writing) écriture renversée; *adj* de revers; renversé

**backhanded** *adj* (writing) renversé; *fig* (compliment) douteux -euse, équivoque

**backhander** *n* (blow) revers *m*; reproche *m*; *coll* (bribe) dessous *m* de table

**backing** *n* soutien *m*; (going backwards) recul *m*

**backlash** *n mech* secousse *f*; *pol* réaction brutale

**backlog** *n* arriéré *m*

**back-number** *n* (newspaper, etc) ancien numéro; *fig* personne *f* qui ne compte plus

**back-pedal** *vi* rétropédaler; *fig* faire machine arrière

**back-room** *adj* **~ boy** expert *m* (qui travaille à l'arrière-plan)

**back-scratcher** *n* gratte-dos *m invar*

**backside** *n* derrière *m*, *sl* cul *m*

**backsight** *n* cran *m* de mire

**backslapping** *n* grandes démonstrations d'amitié

**backslide** *vi* rechuter, récidiver

**backslider** *n* récidiviste

**backstage** *adj* + *adv theat* en coulisse

**backstairs** *n* escalier *m* de service; *adj fig* louche, clandestin

**backstays** *npl* haubans *mpl*

**backstitch** *n* point *m* arrière

**backstroke** *n* nage *f* sur le dos

**backward** *adj* en arrière; (outmoded) arriéré; (child) retardé

**backward(s)** *adv* (motion) en arrière; à rebours, à l'envers; **know sth ~** connaître qch à fond

**backwardness** *n* retard *m*; *med* arriération *f*, faiblesse *f* d'esprit

**backwash** *n* remous *m*

**backwater** *n* (river) bras mort; *fig* trou *m* de province, bled *m*

**backwoods** *npl* forêt *f* vierge

**backwoodsman** *n* bûcheron *m*; *pej* rustre *m*

**bacon** *n* lard *m*, bacon *m*

**bacterial** *adj* bactérien -ienne

**bactericide** *n* produit *m* bactéricide

**bacteriological** *adj* bactériologique

**bacteriologist**

**bacteriologist** *n* bactériologiste
**bacteriology** *n* bactériologie *f*
**bacterium** *n* (*pl* **-ia**) bactérie *f*
**bad** *n* mauvais *m*; (evil) mal *m*; **be £500 to the ~** être en déficit de £500; **go to the ~** mal tourner; *adj* mauvais; défectueux -euse, imparfait; inférieur; (behaviour) méchant, vicieux -ieuse, cruel -elle; (food) avarié, pourri; (harmful) désagréable, nuisible; (ill) malade; (word, language) grossier -ière; (mistake, cold) gros (*f* grosse); **~ blood** hostilité *f*; **~ debt** dette *f* irrécouvrable; **~ form** manque *m* d'éducation; **be ~ at** ne pas réussir à; **be ~ for** ne rien valoir à; **go ~** se gâter, tourner; **in a ~ way** en mauvaise posture; **look ~** faire mauvaise impression; **too ~!** dommage!, tant pis!
**baddish** *adj* assez mauvais
**badge** *n* insigne *m*, badge *m*
¹**badger** *n* blaireau *m*
²**badger** *vt* taquiner, harceler; importuner
**badinage** *n* badinage *m*
**badly** *adv* mal; cruellement; (hopelessly) désespérément; (very much) beaucoup; **~ beaten** battu à plate(s) couture(s); **do ~** mal réussir
**badminton** *n* badminton *m*
**badness** *n* mauvaise qualité, mauvais état; (evil) méchanceté *f*
¹**baffle** *n* déflecteur *m*; *rad* baffle *m*
²**baffle** *vt* confondre, dérouter; frustrer
**baffling** *adj* déroutant, déconcertant
**bag** *n* sac *m*; sacoche *f*; (purse) bourse *f*; (eye) poche *f*; *sp* tableau *m* de chasse; *sl* putain *f*, vioquarde *f*; **~s** *coll obs* pantalon *m*; **~ and baggage** tout le bazar; **~ of bones** paquet *m* d'os; **be in the ~** être dans le sac; **diplomatic ~** valise *f* diplomatique; **let the cat out of the ~** vendre la mèche; **sleeping ~** sac *m* de couchage; *vt* mettre en sac, ensacher; *sp* tuer à la chasse; *coll* mettre le grappin sur; *vi* (garment) bouffer, faire des poches
**bagatelle** *n* bagatelle *f*, fadaise *f*; *mus* divertissement *m*; (game) espèce *f* de jeu de billard
**baggage** *n* bagages *mpl*; *coll* traînée *f*
**baggy** *adj* bouffant, gonflé; (trousers) faisant poche
**bagpipe(s)** *n* cornemuse *f*
**bah** *interj* bah!
¹**bail** *n* *leg* caution *f*, cautionnement *m*; (person) répondant *m*, caution *f*, garant -e; **go ~ for** s/o se porter caution pour qn; *vt* *leg* cautionner, se rendre caution pour; *leg* **~ s/o out** obtenir moyennant caution la liberté

provisoire de qn; *fig* tirer qn d'une situation difficile
²**bail** *n* *naut* écope *f*; *vt* *naut* écoper
**bailiff** *n* bailli *m*; *leg* huissier *m*; *agr* intendant *m*
**bairn** *n* *dial* enfant
**bait** *n* amorce *f*, appât *m*; *fig* tentation *f*; **rise to the ~** mordre à l'hameçon; *vt* (hook) appâter; (horse) donner à manger à; *fig* harceler
**baize** *n* (green) tapis vert
**bake** *vt* cuire au four; (skin) bronzer; *vi* cuire
**bakehouse** *n* boulangerie *f*
**Bakelite** *n* Bakélite *f*
**baker** *n* boulanger -ère; **~'s dozen** treize
**bakery** *n* boulangerie *f*
**baking** *n* cuisson *f*; (bread) fournée *f*; *adj* très chaud; **~ powder** levure *f*
**baksheesh, bakshish** *n* bakchich *m*
**balaclava** *n* passe-montagne *m*
**balalaika** *n* balalaïka *f*
**balance** *n* balance *f*; contrepoids *m*; (clock, watch) balancier *m*; *comm* balance *f*; *fig* équilibre *m*, accord *m*; **~ of payments** balance *f* des paiements; **~ sheet** bilan *m*; **hang in the ~** être en balance; **on ~** tout considéré; *vt* mettre en équilibre, balancer; équilibrer; *comm* balancer, équilibrer; *vi* balancer, hésiter; se balancer
**balcony** *n* balcon *m*
**bald** *adj* chauve; (statement, style) simple, sec (*f* sèche)
**balderdash** *n* balivernes *fpl*
**baldness** *n* calvitie *f*; *fig* simplicité *f*, sécheresse *f*
¹**bale** *n* balle *f*, ballot *m*; *vt* emballotter
²**bale** *vi* *aer* **~ out** faire un saut en parachute
**baleful** *adj* nuisible; sinistre, funeste
**balk, baulk** *n* *bui* solive *f*; *agr* billon *m*; *fig* obstacle *m*, pierre *f* d'achoppement; *vt* éviter, esquiver; (thwart) entraver, contrecarrer; *vi* (horse) se dérober; **~ at sth** reculer devant qch
**Balkan** *adj* balkanique
**Balkans** *npl* Balkans *mpl*
¹**ball** *n* (golf, tennis) balle *f*; (football) ballon *m*; (billiards) bille *f*; (hockey, snow) boule *f*; *cul* boulette *f*; (eye) prunelle *f*; (wool) pelote *f*; *sl* **~s** couilles *fpl*; *sl* **~s!** conneries! *fpl*; *fig* **be on the ~** être dégourdi; **keep the ~ rolling** soutenir la conversation; faire le boute-en-train; **play ~** coopérer, être de mèche; *vt* (wool) peloter; *sl* **~ up** embrouiller, bousiller
²**ball** *n* bal *m*; **fancy-dress ~** bal costumé; *US coll* **have a ~** s'amuser énormément, rire aux éclats
**ballad** *n* ballade *f*; poème narratif; *mus*

romance *f*

**ballast** *n naut + aer* lest *m*; (railway) ballast *m*; *fig* pondération *f*; *vt* lester; empierrer

**ball-bearing** *n eng* bille *f*

**ball-cock** *n* flotteur *m* (de chasse d'eau)

**ballerina** *n* ballerine *f*

**ballet** *n* ballet *m*

**ballistic** *adj* balistique

**ballistics** *npl* balistique *f*

**ballocks** *npl sl* couilles *fpl*; *sl* conneries! *fpl*

**balloon** *n* ballon *m*; ~ **barrage** ballons *mpl* de protection, ballons *mpl* de barrage; ~ **glass** verre *m* ballon; *vt* ballonner; *vi* monter en ballon

**ballot** *n* (paper) bulletin *m* de vote; (method of voting) scrutin *m*; *pol* scrutin *m*; (lots) tirage *m* au sort; *vi* voter au scrutin; ~ **for** élire par scrutin

**ballot-box** *n* urne électorale

**ball-point** *n* stylo *m* à bille

**ballroom** *n* salle *f* de bal; *adj* ~ **dancing** danse *f* de salon

**balls-up** *n sl* make a ~ of bousiller

**ballyhoo** *n* (publicity) battage *m*; (nonsense) bobard *m*

**balm** *n* baume *m*

**balmy** *adj* embaumé, parfumé; *fig* calmant; (weather) doux (*f* douce); *coll* cinglé

**balsa** *n* balsa *m*

**balsam** *n med + fig* baume *m*; *bot* balsamine *f*

**balsamic** *adj* balsamique

**baluster** *n* balustre *m*; ~ **s** rampe *f*, main courante

**balustrade** *n* balustrade *f*

**bamboo** *n* bambou *m*

**bamboozle** *vt coll* embobiner, rouler

**ban** *n* interdiction *f*, exclusive *f*; *eccles* interdit *m*, excommunication *f*; *vt* interdire, défendre, proscrire

**banal** *adj* insignifiant, banal (*pl* banals)

**banality** *n* banalité *f*

**banana** *n* banane *f*

**¹band** *n* (cloth, paper, metal, *rad*, etc) bande *f*

**²band** *n* (group) bande *f*; *mil* troupe *f*; *mus* orchestre *m*; **brass** ~ fanfare *f*; **military** ~ musique *f* militaire

**³band** *vt* bander; grouper; *vi* se grouper

**bandage** *n* pansement *m*, bandage *m*; *vt* bander, mettre un pansement à

**bandeau** *n* bandeau *m*

**banderole, banderol** *n* banderole *f*

**bandit** *n* bandit *m*; **one-armed** ~ machine *f* à sous

**bandmaster** *n* chef *m* de musique

**bandolier** *n* bandoulière *f*, cartouchière *f*

**band-saw** *n* scie *f* sans fin

**bandstand** *n* kiosque *m* à musique

**bandwagon** *n US* char *m* (de carnaval) portant des musiciens; *coll* **climb on the** ~ se mettre du côté du manche

**¹bandy** *vt* renvoyer, relancer; ~ **words** ergoter, se disputer; *usu pej* **have one's name bandied about** défrayer la chronique

**²bandy** *adj* tors, tordu; ~ **legged** bancal (*pl* bancals)

**bane** *n* ruine *f*, fléau *m*; *ar* poison *m*; **be the** ~ **of s/o's life** empoisonner la vie de qn

**baneful** *adj* injurieux -ieuse; (poisonous) vénéneux -euse

**¹bang** *n* détonation *f*, explosion *f*; coup *m*; bruit sec; (supersonic) bang *m*; *vulg* **have a** ~ baiser; **with a** ~ avec grand succès, précisément, exactement; *vt* cogner, marteler; (door) claquer; *vi* faire un bruit sec; *adv phr coll* ~ **on** juste, exact; *interj* ~! paf!

**²bang** *n* (hair) frange *f*

**bangle** *n* bracelet *m*

**banian, banyan** *n bot* banian *m*

**banish** *vt* exiler, bannir; expulser, chasser

**banishment** *n* exil *m*, bannissement *m*

**banister, bannister** *n* rampe *f* (d'escalier)

**banjo** *n* banjo *m*

**¹bank** *n* (mound) talus *m*, remblai *m*; (river, lake) bord *m*, berge *f*, rive *f*; (sand, cloud) banc *m*; (camber) bombement *m*; *vt* remployer; (heap up) amonceler; *vi* s'amonceler, s'entasser; *aer* virer sur l'aile

**²bank** *n* (galley) banc *m* des rameurs; (oars) rangée *f*; *mus* clavier *m*

**³bank** *n* banque *f*; ~ **card** carte *f* d'identité bancaire; **Bank Holiday** fête légale; ~ **rate** taux *m* d'escompte; **break the** ~ faire sauter la banque; *vt* déposer en banque; *vi* ~ **on**, ~ **upon** compter sur; ~ **with** avoir un compte en banque à

**bank-book** *n* carnet *m* de banque

**banker** *n* banquier *m*

**¹banking** *n* finance *f*, banque *f*

**²banking** *n* remblai *m*; (camber) bombement *m*; *aer* virage *m* sur l'aile

**bank-note** *n* billet *m* de banque

**bankrupt** *n* failli -e; **fraudulent** ~ banqueroutier -ière; *vt* faire faire faillite à; *adj* failli, en faillite; *fig* ~ **of** privé de; **go** ~ faire faillite

**bankruptcy** *n* faillite *f*; **fraudulent** ~ banqueroute *f*

**banner** *n* bannière *f*; étendard *m*; ~ **headline** titre *m* sur cinq colonnes à la une

**bannister** *n see* **banister**

**bannock** *n* (espèce *f* de) galette *f*

**banns** *npl* bans *mpl*

**banquet** *n* banquet *m*; *vt* régaler; *vi* banqueter

**bantam** *n* coq *m*; *sp* ~ **weight** poids *m* coq

**banter** *n* plaisanterie *f*, badinerie *f*; *vt* railler, plaisanter; *vi* plaisanter, badiner

**ban-the-bomb** *adj* ~ **campaign** campagne *f* contre la bombe atomique

**banyan** *n see* **banian**

**baobab** *n* baobab *m*

**baptism** *n* baptême *m*; ~ **of fire** baptême *m* du feu

**baptismal** *adj* baptismal

**Baptist** *n* baptiste

**baptistery** *n* baptistère *m*

**baptize** *vt* baptiser

**¹bar** *n* (wood, metal, etc) barre *f*; (gate, window) barreau *m*; (for drinking) bar *m*; *leg* barreau *m*; *naut* barre *f*; *mus* barre *f*; *fig* obstacle *m*; entrave *f*; *her* bande *f*; *her* ~ **sinister** barre *f* de bâtardise; *leg* **be called to the** ~ être inscrit au barreau; *vt* barrer; fermer; (stripe) rayer; (exclude) exclure; *leg* interdire; *prep* sauf; ~ **none** sans exception

**²bar** *n zool* bar *m*

**barb** *n zool* + *bot* barbe *f*; (hook, arrow) pointe *f*; *fig* pointe *f*, flèche *f*; *vt* aiguiser, effiler

**barbarian** *n* + *adj* barbare

**barbaric** *adj* barbare, rude; de mauvais goût, inculte

**barbarism** *n* barbarie *f*; brutalité *f*; *ling* barbarisme *m*

**barbarity** *n* barbarie *f*, brutalité *f*

**barbarize** *vt* rendre barbare; *ling* corrompre

**barbarous** *adj* barbare, sauvage; cruel -elle; *ling* barbare, inculte; grossier -ière, bruyant

**barbecue** *n* barbecue *m*; *vt* griller sur barbecue

**barbed** *adj* barbelé; *fig* mordant, acéré

**barbel** *n zool* (fish) barbeau *m*; *zool* (bristle) barbillon *m*

**barber** *n* coiffeur *m*; *ar* barbier *m*

**barbican** *n* barbacane *f*

**barbitone** *n* véronal *m*

**barbiturates** *npl chem* dérivés *mpl* de l'acide barbiturique, somnifères *mpl*

**barbituric** *adj* barbiturique

**barcarole, barcarolle** *n* barcarolle *f*

**¹bard** *n poet* barde *m*

**²bard** *n cul* barde *f*; *vt cul* barder

**bare** *adj* nu, dénudé; dégarni; (empty) vide; simple, peu orné; à peine suffisant; **earn a** ~ **living** gagner à peine de quoi vivre; *vt* dénuder, mettre à nu; (sword) dégainer; *fig* révéler, montrer

**bareback** *adj* ~ **rider** cavalier -ière à cru; *adv* à cru, à poil

**barefaced** *adj* à visage découvert; *fig* effronté, éhonté

**barefoot** *adj* + *adv* nu-pieds; *adj phr* + *adv phr* pieds nus

**bare-headed** *adj* nu-tête *invar*

**barely** *adv* à peine, juste; pauvrement

**bargain** *n comm* marché *m*, accord *m*; (cheap purchase) occasion *f*; **into the** ~ par-dessus le marché; aussi; *vi* marchander; ~ **for** s'attendre à

**bargain-basement** *n* rayon *m* des soldes

**barge** *n* péniche *f*, chaland *m*; (navy) canot *m* major; *vi coll* ~ **in** arriver comme un chien dans un jeu de quilles; s'immiscer dans; *coll* ~ **into** se cogner contre, se heurter contre

**bargee** *n* marinier *m*; **swear like a** ~ jurer comme un charretier

**baritone** *n* baryton *m*; *adj* de baryton

**barium** *n chem* baryum *m*

**¹bark** *n* (tree) écorce *f*; *vt* (tree) écorcer; (skins) tanner; *coll* s'écorcher

**²bark** *n* aboiement *m*; *coll* toux *f*; **his** ~ **is worse than his bite** tous les chiens qui aboient ne mordent pas; *vi* aboyer; *coll* tousser; ~ **up the wrong tree** se tromper, se tromper de but

**³bark** *n see* **barque**

**barley** *n* orge *f*; **pearl** ~ orge perlé

**barley-sugar** *n* sucre *m* d'orge

**barley-water** *n* infusion *f* d'orge perlé, orgeat *m*

**barmaid** *n* barmaid *f*, serveuse *f* de bar

**barman** *n* barman *m*

**barmy** *adj coll* toqué

**barn** *n* grange *f*; *coll* **a** ~ **of a place** une grande baraque

**barnacle** *n* (shellfish) anatife *m*, bernache *f*; (goose) bernacle *f*; *coll fig* crampon *m*, importun *-e*

**barn-door** *n* porte *f* d'une grange; *coll* cible si grande qu'on ne peut pas la manquer

**barn-owl** *n* effraie *f*

**barn-stormer** *n theat* cabotin *-e*

**barograph** *n* baromètre *m* à cadran

**barometer** *n* baromètre *m*

**baron** *n* baron *m*; ~ **of beef** double aloyau *m*

**baronage** *n collect* noblesse *f*; *hist* Gotha *m*

**baroness** *n* baronne *f*

**baronet** *n* baronnet *m*

**baronial** *adj* de baron

**barony** *n* baronnie *f*

**baroque** *n* baroque *m*; *adj* baroque

**barque, bark** *n naut* trois-mâts carré

**barrack** *vt* + *vi sp* applaudir ironiquement

**barracking** n sp applaudissements mpl
ironiques
**barrack(s)** n mil caserne f; fig grande
baraque; mil **barrack room** chambrée
f; vt **barrack** caserner
**barrage** n eng barrage m; mil tir m de
barrage
**barratry** n leg baraterie f
**barrel** n (small) baril m; (larger) barrique f, tonneau m; (herring) caque f;
(firearm) canon m; (watch, clock, lock)
barillet m; ~ **vault** archi arc m en
berceau
**barrel-organ** n orgue m de Barbarie
**barren** adj med stérile; stérile, inculte,
aride; fig sans intérêt, sans idées
**barrenness** n med stérilité f; aridité f; fig
manque m d'idées
**barricade** n barricade f; vt barricader
**barrier** n barrière f; fig obstacle m,
empêchement m
**barring** prep sauf, excepté
**barrister** n leg = avocat -e
¹**barrow** n arch tumulus m
²**barrow** n charrette f à bras; **wheel** ~
brouette f
**barrow-boy** n marchand m des quatre-
saisons
**barter** n troc m; vt troquer; fig échanger;
~ **away** vendre, faire trafic de
**basalt** n geol basalte m
**bascule** n eng bascule f
¹**base** n base f; archi assise f, fondation f;
phil racine f; fig point m de départ,
principe m; vt baser, fonder, appuyer;
~ **oneself on** se baser sur
²**base** adj (birth) de basse extraction; vil,
abject, bas (f basse)
**baseball** n US base-ball m
**baseless** adj sans fondement
**basement** n sous-sol m
**baseness** n bassesse f, abjection f
**bash** n coll coup m; coll **have a** ~
essayer; vt coll cogner; ~ **in** enfoncer;
coll ~ **up** tabasser; vi ~ **on** continuer,
se résigner
**bashful** adj timide, transi
**bashfulness** n timidité f
**basic** adj de base; chem basique
**basil** n bot basilic m
**basilica** n basilique f
**basilisk** n basilic m
**basin** n bassin m, cuvette f; (for food)
bol m; geog+naut bassin m; geol
cuvette f; **wash** ~ lavabo m
**basinful** n pleine cuvette; coll **have a** ~
en avoir ras le bol
**basis** n base f, fondement m
**bask** vi ~ **in the sun** paresser au soleil,
coll lézarder; fig se plaire
**basket** n panier m, corbeille f
**basketball** n sp basket-ball m, basket m

**basketful** n panier m
**basket-work, basketry** n vannerie f
**Basque** n Basque; (language) basque m;
adj basque
**bas-relief, bass-relief** n bas-relief m
¹**bass** n mus basse f; adj mus de basse,
grave
²**bass** n (freshwater) perche f; (sea)
bar m
**basset** n basset m
**basset-horn** n mus cor m de basset
**bassoon** n basson m
**bassoonist** n basson m, bassoniste
**bastard** n bâtard -e, enfant naturel -elle;
sl fig salaud m; sl (nuisance) emmerdement m; sl fig **stupid** ~ ! crétin!; adj
bâtard, illégitime; fig faux (f fausse),
anormal
**bastardize** vt déclarer illégitime
**bastardy** n bâtardise f
**baste** vt cul arroser
**bastion** n bastion m
¹**bat** n chauve-souris f (pl chauves-
souris); fig **have** ~**s in the belfry** avoir
une araignée au plafond
²**bat** n sp batte f; (table-tennis) raquette
f; **off one's own** ~ sans aide; vt (eyelid)
cligner; vi sp manier la batte
**batch** n (baking) fournée f; tas m;
(persons) groupe m
**bate** vt baisser; vt diminuer; **with** ~**d
breath** anxieusement
**bath** n baignoire f; (action of taking a
bath) bain m; ~**s** établissement m de
bains; **have a** ~ prendre un bain; vt
baigner, donner un bain à; vi prendre
un bain
**bath-chair** n fauteuil roulant (pour
malade)
**bathe** n bain m, baignade f; vt baigner;
(flood) inonder; vi se baigner
**bather** n baigneur -euse
**bathetic** adj rhet qui tombe dans le
ridicule
**bathing** n baignade f, bain m de mer (de
rivière)
**bathing-costume** n maillot m de bain;
slip m
**bath-mat** n tapis m de bain
**bathos** n rhet chute f dans le ridicule
**bathroom** n salle f de bains
**bath-towel** n serviette f de bain
**bathtub** n baignoire f
**bathyscaphe** n bathyscaphe m
**bathysphere** n bathysphère f
**batiste** n batiste f
**batman** n mil ordonnance f or m
**baton** n mus bâton m; (police) matraque
f
**bats** adj coll cinglé, toqué
**battalion** n bataillon m
¹**batten** n planche f, latte f; theat herse f;

**batten**

*vt* latter; *naut* ~ **down hatches** fermer les écoutilles

²**batten** *vi* s'engraisser; *fig* ~ **on** prospérer aux dépens de

¹**batter** *n cul* pâte *f* à frire; *print* caractère écrasé

²**batter** *vt* rouer de coups; *sl* tabasser; (deform) cabosser, bosseler; *mil* battre en brèche; ~ **down** démolir; ~ **in** défoncer

**battering-ram** *n mil ar* bélier *m*

**battery** *n leg* voie *f* de fait; *mil* + *elect* + *agr* batterie *f*; ~ **hen** poulet *m* de batterie; **dry** ~ pile (sèche)

**battle** *n* bataille *f*, combat *m*; **give** ~ livrer bataille; **killed in** ~ mort au champ d'honneur; *vi* ~ **against** lutter contre; ~ **for** bataile pour, combattre pour

**battle-axe** *n hist* hache *f* d'armes; *fig* mégère *f*

**battle-cruiser** *n naut* croiseur lourd

**battle-cry** *n* cri *m* de guerre; *fig* slogan *m*

**battle-dress** *n mil* tenue *f* de combat, tenue *f* de campagne

**battlefield** *n* champ *m* de bataille

**battlement** *n* créneau *m*

**battleship** *n naut* cuirassé *m*

**batty** *adj coll* cinglé, toqué

**bauble** *n hist* marotte *f*; *fig* babiole *f*, colifichet *m*

**baulk** *n* + *vt* + *vi see* **balk**

**bauxite** *n min* bauxite *f*

**bawd** *n obs* proxénète *m*

**bawdry** *n* grivoiseries *fpl*

**bawdy** *n* gauloiserie *f*; *adj* gaulois, grivois, leste

**bawdy-house** *n obs* bordel *m*

**bawl** *n* braillement *m*; *vt* brailler, beugler; *vi* brailler, beugler; *coll* ~ **out** engueuler

¹**bay** *n* golfe *m*; baie *f*, anse *f*

²**bay** *n bot* laurier *m*

³**bay** *n archi* travée *f*; ~ **window** bay-window *f*, oriel *m*; *naut* **sick** ~ hôpital *m* de bord

⁴**bay** *n* aboiement *m*; abois *mpl*; **at** ~ aux abois; **keep at** ~ tenir en échec; *vi* aboyer

⁵**bay** *adj* (horse) bai

**bayonet** *n* baïonnette *f*; *vt* donner un coup de baïonnette à

**bazaar, bazar** *n* (department store) bazar *m*; vente *f* de charité; (oriental) souk *m*, bazar *m*

**bazooka** *n mil* bazooka *m*

**be** *vi* (exist) être, exister, se trouver; (come, go) être, venir, aller; (well, ill) aller, se porter; (age) avoir; (feel) avoir; (remain) rester; *math* faire; (have to) devoir; (cost) coûter, valoir; **here is** voici; **how are you?** comment

allez-vous?, comment vous portez-vous?; **how long are you here for?** vous restez combien de temps ici?; **how much is this hat?** combien coûte-t-il, ce chapeau?, combien vaut-il, ce chapeau?; **I am afraid** j'ai peur; **I am here** je suis ici; **I am hot** j'ai chaud; **I am to say** je dois dire; **I am twenty years old** j'ai vingt ans; **I have been to London** je suis allé à Londres; **no one has been here today** personne n'est venu ici aujourd'hui; **there is** il y a; *lit* il est; (pointing out) voilà; **two and two are four** deux et deux font quatre; *v aux* être; *v impers* (weather) **it is fine** il fait beau; **it is time to go** il est temps de partir

**beach** *n* plage *f*, grève *f*; *vt naut* échouer

**beachcomber** *n obs* (Pacific Islands) colon blanc appauvri; (wave) lame déferlante

**beachhead** *n mil* tête *f* de pont

**beacon** *n* signal lumineux; fanal *m*; phare *m*; *naut* balise *f*; *vt naut* baliser

**bead** *n* perle *f*; (rosary) grain *m*; (sweat) goutte *f*; *mil* cran *m* de mire; *archi* baguette *f*; ~**s** collier *m*; *eccles* chapelet *m*; **draw a** ~ **on** viser; **tell one's** ~**s** égrener son chapelet; *vt* enfiler; orner de perles

**beading** *n carp* baguette *f*; garniture *f* de perles

**beady** *adj* (eye) perçant

**beagle** *n* beagle *m*; *vi* chasser avec des beagles

**beagling** *n* chasse *f* avec des beagles

**beak** *n* bec *m*; *sl* nez crochu; *sl* magistrat *m*, juge *m*

**beaked** *adj* pointu

**beaker** *n lit* coupe *f*; *chem* vase *m*

**be-all** *n* ~ **and end-all** le fin fond

**beam** *n* (light) rayon *m*, faisceau *m*; *bui* poutre *f*; (plough) timon *m*; *naut* largeur *f*; *naut* (side) travers *m*; (scales) fléau *m*; *phys* + *rad* + *aer* + *naut* faisceau *m*; *fig* grand sourire, sourire rayonnant; ~ **navigation** navigation *f* radiogonométrique; **on the port (starboard)** ~ par le travers bâbord (tribord); *vt* émettre, diriger; *vi* sourire; rayonner

**beaming** *adj* rayonnant; *phys* + *rad* directionnel -elle

**bean** *n* haricot *m*; fève *f*; *coll* sou *m*; **broad** ~ fève *f*; **runner** ~ haricot vert; *coll* **spill the** ~**s** vendre la mèche

¹**bear** *n zool* + *fig* ours *m*; (Stock Exchange) baissier *m*; *astron* **Great Bear** Grande Ourse; **Little Bear** Petite Ourse; *vi* jouer à la baisse

²**bear** *vt* porter, transporter; (endure) supporter, tolérer, endurer;

(child) porter, enfanter, accoucher; (responsibility) porter; (remembering) mériter; (grudge) éprouver, ressentir; (relation) avoir rapport à; ~ **away** enlever, emmener; ~ **out** confirmer; ~ **with** supporter avec patience; ~ **witness** témoigner; *vi* ~ **down on** foncer sur; *naut* s'approcher rapidement de; ~ **hard on** peser sur; *naut* ~ **off** prendre le large, s'éloigner de; ~ **right** prendre à droite; ~ **up** montrer du courage, faire preuve de courage

**bearable** *adj* supportable, tolérable

**beard** *n* barbe *f*; *vt* tirer par la barbe; confronter, défier

**bearded** *adj* barbu

**beardless** *adj* imberbe

**bearer** *n* porteur *m*; *comm* porteur *m*, titulaire *m*; *adj* ~ **bond** titre *m* au porteur

**bear-garden** *n* pétaudière *f*

**bearing** *n* port *m*, allure *f*; (behaviour) maintien *m*; (relevance) rapport *m*, portée *f*; (endurance) endurance *f*, patience *f*; (child) enfantement *m*; (direction) relèvement *m*; *archi* appui *m*, portée *f*; *eng* cône *m*, galet *m*; *her* pièce *f* honorable; **lose one's** ~ **s** s'égarer, perdre le nord

**bearish** *adj* bourru, grincheux -euse; (Stock Exchange) tendant à la baisse

**beast** *n* bête *f*; *fig* brute *f*; *coll* abruti -e, vache *f*; ~ **s** bétail *m*, bestiaux *mpl*

**beastliness** *n* méchanceté *f*; obscénité *f*; *coll* saloperie *f*

**beastly** *adj* dégoûtant, infect; brutal; abominable

¹**beat** *n* battement *m*; coup *m*; *mus* temps *m*, battement *m*; (hunting) battue *f*; (policeman) secteur *m*, ronde *f*; *vt* battre, frapper; (defeat) battre, vaincre; *mus* + *cul* battre; *mil* ~ **a retreat** se retirer; (price) ~ **down** faire rabattre; ~ **in** enfoncer; *coll* ~ **it** foutre le camp; ~ **off** repousser; ~ **out** marteler; ~ **time** battre la mesure; ~ **up** rosser; *coll* **that** ~ **s me!** ça me dépasse; *vi naut* louvoyer; ~ **about the bush** tergiverser

²**beat** *adj coll* beatnik

**beaten** *adj* battu; (metal) martelé; (exhausted) éreinté

**beater** *n* batteur -euse; (carpet) battoir *m*; *sp* rabatteur -euse

**beatific** *adj* béatifique

**beatification** *n eccles* béatification *f*

**beatify** *vt eccles* béatifier

**beating** *n* battement *m*; *naut* louvoiement *m*; volée *f* de coups; défaite *f*; **take a** ~ se faire battre à plate(s) couture(s); **take some** ~ être difficile à battre

**beatitude** *n* béatitude *f*

**beatnik** *n* + *adj* beatnik (*f sing invar*, *m* + *fpl* beatniks)

**beau** *n* dandy *m*, élégant *m*

**beauteous** *adj* beau (*f* belle)

**beautician** *n US* esthéticien -ienne

**beautiful** *n* **the** ~ le beau; *adj* beau (*f* belle), admirable

**beautify** *vt* rendre beau (*f* belle)

**beauty** *n* beauté *f*; **the** ~ **of it is...** le plus beau, c'est que...; **the Sleeping Beauty** la Belle au bois dormant

**beauty-parlour** *n* institut *m* de beauté

**beauty-sleep** *n* sommeil *m* d'avant minuit

**beauty-spot** *n* grain *m* de beauté; (patch) mouche *f*; endroit *m* de beauté naturelle

**beaver** *n* castor *m*; *coll* **eager** ~ personne *f* qui fait du zèle; *vi coll* ~ **away** travailler avec persévérance

**be-bop** *n* be-bop *m*

**becalm** *vt* calmer; *naut* **be** ~ **ed** être encalminé

**because** *conj* parce que; ~ **of** en raison de, à cause de

**béchamel** *n cul* béchamel *f*

**beck** *n* signe *m*, geste *m*; **at the** ~ **and call of** prêt à obéir à; *vt* + *vi see* **beckon**

**beckon** *vt* faire signe à; *vi* faire signe

**become** *vt* (suit) convenir à; *vi* devenir, se faire

**becoming** *adj* convenable; (clothes, etc) seyant

**bed** *n* lit *m*; *lit* couche *f*; (plants) plate-bande *f* (*pl* plates-bandes), parterre *m*; *geol* couche *f*, gisement *m*; (base) assiette *f*; *fig* rapport sexuel; ~ **and board** le logement et la nourriture, pension complète; **be brought to** ~ accoucher; **double** ~ grand lit; **get out of** ~ **on the wrong side** se lever du pied gauche; **go to** ~ se coucher, aller se coucher; **put to** ~ coucher; **take to one's** ~ s'aliter; *vt* planter, repiquer; *bui* asseoir; *sl* baiser; *vi bui* s'asseoir

**bedaub** *vt* barbouiller

**bed-bug** *n* punaise *f*

**bed-clothes** *npl* draps *mpl* et couvertures *fpl*

**bedding** *n* literie *f*; *agr* litière *f*; (plants) repiquage *m*; *geol* stratification *f*

**bedeck** *vt* orner, parer

**bedevil** *vt* abîmer, gâter; harceler; tourmenter; (bewitch) envoûter

**bedevilment** *n* (confusion) désordre *m*; (bewitching) envoûtement *m*

**bedfellow** *n* compagnon *m* de lit; *fig* associé *m*

**bedim** *vt* obscurcir

**bedlam** *n obs* maison *f* de fous; *fig* tumulte *m*

# bed-linen

**bed-linen** n draps mpl de lit et taies fpl d'oreiller

**Bedouin** n Bédouin -e

**bed-pan** n bassin m (hygiénique)

**bedpost** n (of four-poster) colonne f; coll **between you and me and the ~** strictement entre nous deux

**bedraggle** vt crotter, tacher de boue

**bedridden** adj alité

**bed-rock** n geol soubassement m (rocheux); fig fondement m

**bedside** n chevet m; **~ lamp** lampe f de chevet; (doctor) **have a good ~ manner** savoir inspirer confiance à un malade

**bedsitter, bedsit** n coll, **bedsitting room** n studio m, chambre meublée

**bed-socks** npl chaussettes fpl de nuit

**bedsore** n escarre f

**bedspread** n couvre-lit m

**bedstead** n châlit m, bois m de lit

**bedtime** n heure f de se coucher

**bedwetting** n incontinence f nocturne

**bee** n abeille f; fig personne affairée; **have a ~ in one's bonnet** avoir une marotte, avoir une araignée au plafond

**beech** n hêtre m

**beef** cul bœuf m; fig force f musculaire, vigueur f

**beef-steak** n bifteck m

**beefy** adj musculaire

**beehive** n ruche f

**bee-keeper** n apiculteur m

**bee-keeping** n apiculture f

**bee-line** n **make a ~ for** se diriger tout droit vers

**beer** n bière f; **small ~** petite bière; (person) personne f sans importance

**beer-mat** n dessous m de verre (de bière)

**beery** adj qui sent la bière; un peu parti

**beeswax** n cire f d'abeille

**beet** n betterave f; US **red ~** betterave (potagère)

**¹beetle** n maillet m, masse f

**²beetle** n coléoptère m, cafard m; (scarab) scarabée m

**³beetle** vi (cliff) surplomber; coll **~ off** s'en aller; adj surplombant

**beetling** adj surplombant; proéminent

**beetroot** n betterave (potagère)

**befall** vt arriver à; vi arriver

**befit** vt convenir à, être digne de

**befog** vt brouiller, embrouiller

**before** adv devant, en avant; (time) avant, auparavant; (in the past) déjà; **~ day** veille f; prep (place) devant; (time) avant de; de préférence à; leg pardevant; conj avant que; (rather than) plutôt que de

**beforehand** adv d'avance, préalablement

**befoul** vt souiller; fig salir

**befriend** vt nouer une amitié avec; aider

**beg** vt mendier; (request) solliciter, demander; (urge) prier, supplier; **~ off** s/o solliciter la grâce de qn; **~ the question** présumer vrai ce qui est en question; vi mendier, demander l'aumône; (dog) faire le beau; **~ to** avoir l'honneur de

**beget** vt engendrer, procréer; fig produire

**beggar** n mendiant -e; coll type m; vt ruiner, réduire à la mendicité; fig dépasser

**beggarly** adj pauvre, misérable, sordide

**beggary** n mendicité f

**begin** vt commencer, entamer; inaugurer; vi commencer, s'y mettre; **~ at the beginning** commencer par le commencement; **~ by doing** commencer par faire; **to ~ with** d'abord

**beginner** n débutant -e

**beginning** n commencement m, début m; (origin) principe m, origine f

**begonia** n bégonia m

**begrudge** vt envier; donner à contre-cœur

**beguile** vt tromper; (trick out of) soutirer; charmer, ensorceler; (time) passer agréablement

**behalf** n **on ~ of** au nom de; pour le compte de; (representing) de la part de

**behave** vi se conduire, se comporter; **~ oneself** se conduire bien, se comporter bien

**behaviour** n comportement m, conduite f, façon f d'agir; mech fonctionnement m

**behead** vt décapiter

**behest** n obs ordre m, commandement m

**behind** n derrière m; coll cul m; adv en arrière, derrière; (time) dans le passé; (late) en retard; **fall ~** rester en arrière, se laisser distancer; **put ~ one** refuser de considérer; **stay ~** rester; prep derrière, en arrière de; (time) en retard sur; **~ the scenes** en coulisse; **~ the times** arriéré, suranné; **~ time** en retard

**behindhand** adj **be ~** être en retard; (old-fashioned) être suranné; adv en retard; (payment) en retard

**behold** vt + vi regarder, contempler; voir; **~!** regardez!, voyez!

**beholden** adj obligé, redevable

**beholder** n spectateur -trice

**behove** v impers incomber

**beige** n tissu écru; (colour) beige m; adj beige

**being** n être m, créature f; vie f, existence f

**bel** n phys bel m

**belabour** vt rouer de coups; (words) invectiver

**belated** adj tardif -ive; (not on schedule) en retard, retardé

**belay** n (mountaineering) point m

d'appui; *vt naut* amarrer; ~ ! ferme!, stop!

**belaying-pin** *n naut* cabillot *m*

**belch** *n* éructation *f*, *sl* rot *m*; *vt fig* cracher, vomir; *vi* éructer, *sl* rôter

**beleaguer** *vt* assiéger, investir, bloquer

**belfry** *n* beffroi *m*, clocher *m*

**Belgian** *n* Belge; *adj* belge

**Belgium** *n* Belgique *f*

**belie** *vt* (misrepresent) mentir au sujet de; (mislead) donner une impression fausse de; (hopes) décevoir, démentir

**belief** *n* croyance *f*, conviction *f*; (confidence) confiance *f*; foi (religieuse)

**believable** *adj* croyable

**believe** *vt* croire, penser; ajouter foi à; *vi* croire; ~ **in** croire à

**believer** *n eccles* croyant -e; partisan -e

**belittle** *vt* rapetisser; déconsidérer, dénigrer

**bell** *n* cloche *f*; (hand-bell, electric bell) sonnette *f*; (bicycle, typewriter) timbre *m*; (on harness) grelot *m*; *mus* (trumpet, trombone, etc) pavillon *m*; *naut* ~ s coups *mpl* de cloche; **ring a** ~ faire penser à qch, faire souvenir de qch; **ring the** ~ gagner un prix; **sound as a** ~ en parfaite santé; *vt* mettre une cloche à; ~ **the cat** attacher le grelot

**belladonna** *n bot* belladone *f*

**bell-bottomed** *adj* (trousers) à patte d'éléphant

**bell-boy** *n* chasseur *m*, groom *m*

**belle** *n* belle *f*, beauté *f*

**bell-founder** *n* fondeur *m* de cloches

**bell-hop** *n US* chasseur *m*, groom *m*

**bellicose** *adj* belliqueux -euse

**belligerence** *n* belligérance *f*

**belligerent** *n* belligérant -e; *adj* belligérant

**bellow** *n* (animal) beuglement *m*, mugissement *m*; hurlement *m*; *vt* beugler; *vi* beugler, mugir; hurler

**bellows** *npl* soufflet *m*; *mus* (organ) soufflerie *f*

**belly** *n* ventre *m*; estomac *m*, abdomen *m*; *lit* (womb) sein *m*; *mus* table *f* d'harmonie; *vi* se gonfler, s'enfler

**belly-ache** *n* colique *f*, mal *m* de ventre; *vi sl* rouspéter, ronchonner

**belly-button** *n sl* nombril *m*

**bellyflop** *n* plat-ventre *m*

**bellyful** *n* quantité plus que suffisante; *coll* **have a** ~ en avoir plein le dos, *sl* en avoir ras le bol

**bellyland** *vi aer* atterrir sur le ventre

**bellylanding** *n aer* atterrissage *m* sur le ventre

**belong** *vi* appartenir; faire partie (born in) être originaire de; (fit in with) aller ensemble, s'accorder ensemble; ~ **with** dépendre de, relever de

**belongings** *npl* possessions *fpl*, biens *mpl*

**beloved** *n* bien-aimé -e; *adj* bien-aimé, chéri

**below** *adv* au-dessous, en bas; (lower) plus bas; en dessous; (downstream) en aval; (in book) ci-dessous, infra; (on earth) sur terre; (in hell) en enfer; *naut* en bas; *prep* au-dessous de; inférieur à

**belt** *n* ceinture *f*; *mech* courroie *f*; *mil* ceinturon *m*; (machine-gun) bande *f* de mitrailleuse; *geog* zone *f*; **conveyor** ~ chaîne *f* de fabrication, chaîne *f* de montage; **green** ~ ceinture verte; **blow below the** ~ coup *m* de Jarnac; *aer* + *mot* **seat** ~ ceinture *f* de sécurité; **tighten one's** ~ faire des économies, réduire ses dépenses; *vt* ceinturer; donner une raclée à; *vi sl* ~ **on** courir vite; *sl* ~ **up** se taire

**belting** *n coll* raclée *f*; *collect* ceintures *fpl*; courroies *fpl*

**belvedere** *n* belvédère *m*

**bemoan** *vt* + *vi* pleurer, lamenter

**bemuse** *vt* hébéter; déconcerter

**bench** *n* banc *m*; (work) établi *m*, table *f*; *leg* banc *m* des magistrats, banc *m* d'un juge; *leg collect* juges *mpl*, magistrats *mpl*; *pol* **front** ~ banc *m* des ministres

**bench-mark** *n* repère *m* de niveau

**bend** *n* courbe *f*; (road) virage *m*; *her* bande *f*; *naut* nœud *m*; ~ s maladie *f* des caissons; *her* ~ **sinister** barre *f*; *coll* **round the** ~ cinglé; *vt* courber, ployer, plier; (gaze) diriger; (stretch) tendre; *fig* faire plier, faire dévier; tendre; *naut* (rope, etc) amarrer; *naut* (sail) enverguer; **be bent upon** s'acharner à; *vi* se courber, s'incliner, (se) plier; (road) faire un coude

**benediction** *n* bénédiction *f*; (grace at meal) bénédicité *m*

**benefaction** *n* (gift) don *m*; (good deed) bienfait *m*

**benefactor** *n* donateur *m*, bienfaiteur *m*

**benefactress** *n* donatrice *f*, bienfaitrice *f*

**benefice** *n eccles* bénéfice *m*

**beneficence** *n* bienfaisance *f*

**beneficent** *adj* bienfaisant

**beneficial** *adj* salutaire; avantageux -euse, favorable; utile

**beneficiary** *n* bénéficiaire; *eccles* possesseur *m* d'un bénéfice

**benefit** *n* profit *m*, avantage *m*, bénéfice *m*; *leg* bénéfice *m*; *eccles hist* privilège *m*; (social) allocation *f*; *theat* représentation *f* au profit d'une œuvre; *vt* faire du bien à; profiter à; *vi* profiter, bénéficier

**Benelux** *n* Bénélux *m*

**benevolence** *n* bienveillance *f*, bonté *f*, générosité *f*

**benighted**

benighted *adj* surpris par la nuit; *fig* ignorant, arriéré

benign *adj* bon (*f* bonne), gentil -ille, affable; (favorable) propice; *med* bénin (*f* bénigne)

benignant *adj* bon (*f* bonne), affable; bienveillant

¹bent *n* disposition *f*, aptitude *f*; **follow one's ~** poursuivre ses propres intérêts; **to the top of one's ~** au maximum possible

²bent *adj* tordu, courbé; *sl* (crooked) malhonnête; *sl* (stolen) volé; *sl* homosexuel -elle

benumb *vt* engourdir, paralyser

benzine *n* benzine *f*

bequeath *vt* léguer

bequest *n* legs *m*

berate *vt* morigéner

bereave *vt* priver, déposséder; priver (par la mort)

bereaved *n* the ~ la famille du disparu

bereavement *n* perte *f*; dépossession *f*; isolement *m*

beret *n* béret *m*

bergamot *n* *bot* (tree) bergamotier *m*; (fruit) bergamote *f*; (oil) essence *f* de bergamote

bergschrund *n* rimaye *f*

beriberi *n* *path* béribéri *m*

berlin *n* berline *f*

berry *n* baie *f*; (coffee) grain *m*; (roe) œuf *m*; **brown as a ~** tout bronzé; *vi* produire des baies; cueillir des baies

berserk *adj* frénétique; **go ~** devenir fou furieux

berth *n* *naut* mouillage *m*; (travel) lit *m*; (folding) couchette *f*; (job) poste *m*; **give a wide ~ to** éviter soigneusement; *vt* *naut* amarrer; *vi* *naut* mouiller

beryl *n* béryl *m*

beryllium *n* *chem* béryllium *m*

beseech *vt* implorer, supplier, conjurer

beset *vt* assiéger, serrer de près; *fig* assaillir; (adornments) parsemer

besetting *adj* habituel -elle; **~ sin** péché mignon

beside *prep* à côté de, près de; (like) comparé à; (irrelevant to) sans rapport avec; (wide of) loin de; **~ oneself** hors de soi, furieux -ieuse

besides *adv* en outre, de plus; (moreover) d'ailleurs, d'autre part; (else) d'autre; *prep* outre, en dehors de; (except) hormis

besiege *vt* assiéger

besieger *n* assiégeant -e

besmear *vt* souiller; *fig* calomnier

besmirch *vt* salir; ternir; *fig* salir, flétrir

besom *n* balai *m* (de brindilles)

besotted *adj* saoul, hébété; *fig* entiché, épris; idiot

bespatter *vt* éclabousser; crotter; *fig* salir

bespeak *vt* commander, réserver; indiquer, suggérer

bespoke *adj* fait sur commande

best *n* mieux *m*; meilleur -e; **~ man** garçon *m* d'honneur; **at ~** au mieux; **be at one's ~** être en excellente forme; **do one's ~** faire de son mieux; **for the ~** pour le mieux; **have the ~ of it** l'emporter; **look one's ~** être en beauté; **make the ~ of** s'arranger de; **make the ~ of a bad job** faire contre mauvaise fortune bon cœur; **to the ~ of my knowledge** autant que je sache; *adj superl* meilleur, plus grand; sans égal; plus beau (*f* belle); **it would be ~ to** le mieux serait de; *adv superl* mieux, le mieux; **as ~ I can** de mon mieux; **you know ~** vous êtes le mieux placé pour savoir; *vt* vaincre, battre

bestial *adj* bestial

bestiality *n* bestialité *f*

bestiary *n* bestiaire *m*

bestir *vt* **~ oneself** se remuer, se démener

bestow *vt* conférer, accorder; ranger, placer; loger

bestowal *n* don *m*

bestrew *vt* joncher, éparpiller

bestride *vt* être à cheval sur; (horse) enfourcher; (stride across) enjamber

best-seller *n* best-seller *m*

bet *n* pari *m*; *vt* + *vi* parier; *coll* **you ~!** pour sûr

beta *n* bêta *m*

betake *vt* (place, person) **~ oneself** se rendre

betatron *n* *phys* bêtatron *m*

bethink *vt* **~ oneself** réfléchir

betimes *adv* de bonne heure; (quickly) vite

betoken *vt* présager; indiquer, révéler

betray *vt* trahir, livrer; révéler; (trust, hope) décevoir; (emotion) manifester, montrer

betrayal *n* trahison *f*; traîtrise *f*

betroth *vt* fiancer

betrothal *n* fiançailles *fpl*

betrothed *n* fiancé -e

¹better *n* ~(s) supérieur(s) *m(pl)*; **get the ~ of** avoir le dessus sur, avoir l'avantage sur; *vt* améliorer; **~ oneself** s'améliorer; *adj comp* meilleur, supérieur; plus grand; plus convenable; (health) mieux, guéri; *coll* (wife) **~ half** moitié *f*; **be ~ than** valoir mieux que; **hope for ~ things** espérer mieux; *adv comp* mieux, plus; **~ and ~** de mieux en mieux; **~ still** encore mieux; (illness) **be ~** aller mieux; **be ~ off** être plus riche; **know ~** en savoir plus long; **make sth ~**

améliorer qch; **think ~ of sth** se raviser, changer d'avis; **you had ~ leave** vous feriez mieux de partir

²**better** *n* parieur -ieuse

**betterment** *n* amélioration *f*

**betting** *n* activité *f* de parieur; *adj* ~ **shop** bureau *m* de paris

**between** *adv* entre; au milieu; ~ **whiles** entretemps; **betwixt and** ~ entre les deux; *prep* entre, au milieu de

**betwixt** *adv* + *prep see* **between**

**bevel** *n* biseau *m*; *vt* biseauter, couper en biais; *adj* biseauté

**beverage** *n* boisson *f*, *esp* boisson non-alcoolisée

**bevy** *n* essaim *m* (de jeunes filles); (birds) vol *m*

**bewail** *vt* lamenter, déplorer; *vi* se lamenter

**beware** *vt* prendre garde à, se méfier de; *vi* prendre garde, se méfier; ~ ! attention!

**bewilder** *vt* déconcerter, dérouter

**bewildering** *adj* déconcertant, déroutant

**bewilderment** *n* ahurissement *m*, confusion *f*

**bewitch** *vt* ensorceler; *fig* fasciner, ensorceler

**beyond** *n* au-delà *m*; **at the back of** ~ au fin fond; *adv* là-bas; (on the other side) de l'autre côté; (further off) plus loin; *prep* au delà de, de l'autre côté de; outre; hors de; (more than) au dessus de; (time) plus de; ~ **belief** incroyable; **it's ~ me** cela me dépasse; **that's ~ a joke** cela dépasse les bornes

**bezel** *n* (chisel) biseau *m*; (setting of jewel) chaton *m*; (face of jewel) facette *f*; *vt* biseauter

**bezique** *n* bésigue *m*

**biannual** *adj* (twice a year) semestriel -ielle; (every two years) biennal

**bias** *n* inclination *f*, préjugé *m*, penchant *m*; (cloth) biais *m*; *sp* (bowls) déviation *f*; *vt* influencer; ~ **against** prévenir contre

**biased, biassed** *adj* influencé

¹**bib** *n* bavette *f*; **best ~ and tucker** habits *mpl* du dimanche

²**bib** *vt* + *vi* boire, *coll* biberonner

**bible** *n* bible *f*; livre *m* qui fait autorité

**biblical** *adj* biblique

**bibliographer** *n* bibliographe

**bibliography** *n* bibliographie *f*

**bibliophile** *n* bibliophile

**bibulous** *adj* adonné à la boisson

**bicarbonate** *n* bicarbonate *m*

**bicentenary** *n* bicentenaire *m*

**bicephalous** *adj* bicéphale

**biceps** *n* biceps *m*

**bicker** *vi* se disputer, se chamailler

**bickering** *n* prise *f* de bec, querelle *f*

**bicycle** *n* bicyclette *f*, vélo *m*; *vi* aller à bicyclette, faire du vélo

**bicyclist** *n* cycliste

**bid** *n* offre *f*, enchère *f*; (bridge) annonce *f*; *fig* effort *m*, tentative *f*; *vt* inviter, prier; (order) ordonner, commander; (auction) offrir; (bridge) annoncer; *vi* faire une offre; enchérir; ~ **fair to** paraître devoir

**biddable** *adj* soumis, docile

**bidder** *n* enchérisseur *m*

**bidding** *n* enchères *fpl*; (bridge) annonces *fpl*; (order) ordre *m*

**bide** *vt* tolérer; ~ **one's time** attendre, patienter; *vi* tolérer

**bidet** *n* bidet *m*

**biennial** *n* *bot* plante bisannuelle; *adj* biennal, bisannuel -uelle

**bier** *n* civière *f*

**biff** *n* *coll* tape *f*; *sl* gnon *m*; *vt* *coll* cogner, taper

**bifocal** *adj* bifocal

**bifocals** *npl* lunettes bifocales, verres *mpl* à double foyer

**bifurcate** *vt* faire bifurquer; *vi* bifurquer; *adj* bifurqué

**bifurcation** *n* bifurcation *f*

**big** *adj* grand; (bulk) gros (*f* grosse); (powerful) fort; *fig* important; noble; *coll* généreux -euse; *sl* ~ **bug**, ~ **noise**, ~ **shot** grosse légume; ~ **business** grosses affaires; ~ **game** gros gibier; ~ **with child** enceinte; **earn ~ money** gagner gros; **talk ~** se vanter, faire l'important; **too ~ for one's boots** vaniteux -euse, prétentieux -ieuse

**bigamist** *n* bigame

**bigamous** *adj* bigame

**bigamy** *n* bigamie *f*

**big-end** *n* *mot* tête *f* de bielle

**big-head** *n* *coll* vaniteux -euse

**big-headed** *adj* *coll* vaniteux -euse

**bight** *n* *geog* baie *f*; (river) boucle *f*; *naut* (knot) boucle *f*

**bigot** *n* bigot -e; fanatique

**bigoted** *adj* bigot; fanatique

**bigwig** *n* *coll* grosse légume, huile *f*

**bijou** *n* bijou *m*; *adj* (often *iron*) petit; élégant

**bike** *n* *coll* vélo *m*; *vi* *coll* aller en vélo

**bikini** *n* bikini *m*

**bilateral** *adj* bilatéral

**bilberry** *n* myrtille *f*

**bile** *n* bile *f*; *fig* bile *f*, colère *f*

**bilge** *n* *naut* sentine *f*; eaux *fpl* de sentine; (cask) fond *m*; *coll* *fig* absurdité *f*, *sl* connerie *f*

**biliary** *adj* *med* biliaire

**bilingual** *adj* bilingue

**bilious** *adj* bilieux -ieuse; *fig* colérique; ~ **attack** crise *f* de foie

**bilk** *vt* escroquer; (taxi, hotel, etc) filer

**bill**

sans payer; frauder, tromper
¹**bill** *n* facture *f*; (restaurant, etc) addition *f*, note *f*; *pol* projet *m* de loi; *leg* plainte *f*; (poster) affiche *f*; *comm* billet *m*, effet *m*; ~ **of exchange** effet *m* de commerce, lettre *f* de change; ~ **of fare** menu *m*; *naut* ~ **of health** patente *f* de santé; *naut* ~ **of lading** connaissement *m*; *bui* ~ **of quantities** devis descriptif; **fill the** ~ être au niveau requis, convenir; **foot the** ~ solder; *coll* payer les pots cassés
²**bill** *n* *zool* + *naut* bec *m*; *geog* cap *m*; *vi* ~ **and coo** se bécoter
³**bill** *n* *hist* hallebarde *f*; *agr* serpe *f*; *vt* élaguer
⁴**bill** *vt* afficher; *theat* annoncer en vedette
**billboard** *n* panneau *m* d'affichage
**billet** *n* *mil* logement *m* chez l'habitant; *mil* billet *m* de logement; *fig* emploi *m*, poste *m*; *vt* *mil* loger
**bill-hook** *n* serpe *f*
**billiards** *npl* jeu *m* de billard
**billiard-table** *n* billard *m*
¹**billing** *n* *fig* ~ **and cooing** roucoulements *mpl*
²**billing** *n* *theat* star ~ mise *f* en vedette
**billion** *n* billion *m*; *US* milliard *m*
**billow** *n* *poet* lame *f*; *vi* onduler
**bill-poster, bill-sticker** *n* colleur *m* d'affiches
**billy-can** *n* gamelle *f*
**billy-goat** *n* bouc *m*
**bimetallism** *n* bimétallisme *m*
**bimonthly** *adj* bi-mensuel -elle
**bin** *n* huche *f*; coffre *m*; (wine) casier *m*; ~ **end** fin *f* de série; *vt* mettre dans un coffre; (wine) mettre dans un casier
**binary** *adj* binaire
**bind** *n* *mus* ligature *f*; *sl* embêtement *m*; corvée *f*; *sl* (person) crampon *m*; *vt* lier, lier ensemble; (tie) attacher, ficeler; (prisoner) ligoter; (book) relier; constiper; (agreement) ratifier; engager; *leg* obliger; *vi* durcir; *mech* se coincer; **bound up in** absorbé dans
**binder** *n* *agr* (person) lieur (*f* lieuse); (machine) lieuse *f*; relieur -ieuse
**binding** *n* reliure *f*; action *f* de lier; *adj* qui lie; obligatoire; *med* constipant
**bind-weed** *n* liseron *m*
**binge** *n* *sl* bombe *f*
**bingo** *n* loto *m*
**binnacle** *n* habitacle *m*
**binocular** *adj* binoculaire
**binoculars** *npl* jumelle *f*
**binomial** *n* *math* binôme *m*; *adj* binôme
**biochemistry** *n* biochimie *f*
**biographer** *n* biographe
**biographic, biographical** *adj* biographique
**biography** *n* biographie *f*

**biological** *adj* biologique
**biologist** *n* biologiste
**biology** *n* biologie *f*
**biometrics** *npl*, **biometry** *n* biométrie *f*
**biophysics** *npl* biophysique *f*
**biopsy** *n* *med* biopsie *f*
**bipartite** *adj* biparti
**biped** *n* bipède *m*; *adj* bipède
**bipolar** *adj* bipolaire
**birch** *n* *bot* bouleau *m*; (for punishment) faisceau *m* de verges; *vt* fouetter (avec des verges)
**bird** *n* oiseau *m*; *sl* fille *f*, poule *f*; ~ **of passage** oiseau migrateur; *fig* voyageur -euse, vagabond -e; *pej* ~ **s of a feather** gens *mpl* du même acabit; **a little** ~ **told me** mon petit doigt me l'a dit; **give s/o the** ~ *theat* huer qn, siffler qn; envoyer paître qn; *cul* **veal** ~ paupiette *f* de veau
**bird-cage** *n* cage *f*; (large) volière *f*
**bird-fancier** *n* oiselier -ière
**bird-lime** *n* glu *f*
**bird-nesting, bird's nesting** *n* go ~ aller dénicher des oiseaux
**bird's-eye** *adj* ~ **view** vue *f* à vol d'oiseau; *fig* résumé *m*
**bird's-nest** *n* nid *m* d'oiseau
**bird's-nester** *n* dénicheur -euse d'oiseaux
**bird-watcher** *n* ornithologiste, ornithologue
**biretta** *n* *eccles* barrette *f*
**Biro** *n* stylo *m* à bille; pointe *f* Bic
**birth** *n* naissance *f*; origine *f*, extraction *f*; *med* accouchement *m*; *fig* commencement *m*, genèse *f*
**birth-control** *n* contrôle *m* des naissances
**birthday** *n* anniversaire *m*; **in one's** ~ **suit** tout nu, dans la tenue d'Adam
**birthmark** *n* tache *f* de vin, envie *f*
**birthplace** *n* lieu *m* de naissance; pays natal; maison natale
**birth-rate** *n* natalité *f*
**birthright** *n* droit *m* d'aînesse; patrimoine *m*
**Biscay** *n* *geog* **Bay of** ~ golfe *m* de Gascogne
**biscuit** *n* biscuit *m*, gâteau sec
**bisect** *vt* couper en deux; *vi* bifurquer
**bisection** *n* division *f* en deux parties; *geom* bissection *f*
**bisector** *n* *geom* bissecteur -trice
**bisexual** *adj* bisexuel -elle
**bisexuality** *n* bisexualité *f*
**bishop** *n* évêque *m*; (chess) fou *m*
**bishopric** *n* (diocese) évêché *m*; (office) épiscopat *m*
**bisk** *n* *cul* bisque *f*
**bissextile** *n* année *f* bissextile; *adj* bissextile

**bistoury** *n surg* bistouri *m*

**bit** *n* morceau *m*, bout *m*, bribe *f*; (food) bouchée *f*; (time) petit moment; *coll* fille *f*; *mech* mèche *f*; (bridle) mors *m*; *vt* mettre le mors à; *fig* brider; *adj theat* ~ **part** petit rôle, panne *f*

**bitch** *n* chienne *f*; *coll* chipie *f*, femme *f* acariâtre; *vi US* rouspéter

**bite** *n* morsure *f*; (insect) piqûre *f*; (mouthful) bouchée *f*; (action) coup *m* de dents; (fishing) touche *f*; *vt* mordre; (insect) piquer; *fig* prendre, attraper; *mot* adhérer; (cold) piquer, mordre; ~ **the dust** tomber par terre, être vaincu; *vi* mordre; (insect) piquer

**biting** *adj* (cold) âpre, mordant; (irony) caustique, cinglant

**bitter** *n* bière blonde; *adj* amer -ère; *fig* cruel -elle; (violent); (style) mordant, acéré; (criticism) acerbe; (wind) cinglant

**bittern** *n zool* butor *m*

**bitters** *npl* bitter *m*

**bitter-sweet** *adj* aigre-doux (*f* aigre-douce)

**bitumen** *n* bitume *m*

**bituminous** *adj* bitumineux -euse

**bivalent** *adj chem* bivalent

**bivalve** *n* bivalve *m*; *adj* bivalve

**bivouac** *n* bivouac *m*; *vi* bivouaquer

**bizarre** *adj* bizarre, grotesque; excentrique

**blab** *vt* divulguer; *vi* cancaner; *sl* manger le morceau

**black** *n* noir *m*; (mourning) deuil *m*; (person) noir -e, nègre (*f* négresse); *adj* noir; sombre, obscur; (dirty) sale; *fig* mortel -elle; infâme; (angry) menaçant; ~ **and blue** fortement ecchymosé, plein de bleus; ~ **art** nécromancie *f*; ~ **eye** œil *m* au beurre noir; *coll* **Black Maria** panier *m* à salade; ~ **market** marché noir; **in** ~ **and white** par écrit; *vt* noircir; (shoes) cirer; *fig* calomnier

**blackball** *vt* blackbouler; évincer

**black-beetle** *n* blatte *f*, cafard *m*

**blackberry** *n* mûre *f*; *vi* cueillir des mûres

**blackbird** *n* merle *m*

**blackboard** *n* tableau noir

**blackcurrant** *n* cassis *m*

**blacken** *vt* + *vi* noircir

**blackguard** *n* vaurien *m*, malfaiteur *m*; *vt* vilipender, injurier

**blackhead** *n* point noir

**blacking** *n* cirage noir

**blacklead** *n* graphite *m*

**blackleg** *n* jaune *m*

**blacklist** *n* liste noire; *vt* porter sur la liste noire

**blackmail** *n* chantage *m*; *vt* faire chanter

**blackmailer** *n* maître chanteur

**blackout** *n med* étourdissement *m*; *theat* noir *m*; (wartime) black-out *m*; (lighting

failure) panne *f* d'électricité; (news) censure *f*; *vt* (wartime) faire le black-out de

**black-pudding** *n* boudin *m*

**blackshirt** *n* fasciste

**blacksmith** *n* forgeron *m*

**blackthorn** *n* prunellier *m*

**bladder** *n* (urinary) vessie *f*; (vesicle) vésicule *f*; (football) vessie *f* (de ballon); **gall** ~ vésicule *f* biliaire

**blade** *n* (grass) brin *m*; (sword) épée *f*, lame *f*; (of knife) lame *f*; (oar, propeller) pale *f*; *coll obs* gandin *m*, dandy *m*

**blamable** *adj* blâmable

**blame** *n* blâme *m*; responsabilité *f*; *vt* blâmer, reprocher à; **be to** ~ être responsable, mériter le blâme

**blameless** *adj* irréprochable, sans tache

**blameworthy** *adj* blâmable, méritant le blâme

**blanch** *vt* blanchir; (hair) faire blanchir; *vi* blémir, pâlir

**bland** *adj* suave, poli; (ingratiating) doucereux -euse; (weather, drink) doux (*f* douce)

**blandish** *vt* cajoler, flatter

**blandishment** *n* cajolerie *f*, flatterie *f*

**blank** *n* blanc *m*, vide *m*; *mil* cartouche *f* à blanc; **draw a** ~ ne pas réussir; *adj* blanc (*f* blanche), vide; (page) vierge; (cartridge) à blanc; (verse) blanc; (cheque) en blanc; *fig* catégorique, total, absolu; (look) vide, morne

**blanket** *n* couverture *f*; (layer) couche *f*; **wet** ~ éteignoir *m*, rabat-joie *m invar*; *adj* intégral, complet -ète; *vt* couvrir d'une couverture; couvrir

**blankly** *adv* sans expression; (boldly) carrément

**blare** *n* tintamarre *m*; (trumpet) sonnerie *f*; *vi* corner; sonner de la trompette; ~ **out** (music) faire retentir; (news) claironner

**blarney** *n coll* boniment *m*; *vt coll* flagorner; *vi* bonimenter

**blaspheme** *vt* + *vi* blasphémer

**blasphemer** *n* blasphémateur -trice

**blasphemous** *adj* blasphématoire

**blasphemy** *n* blasphème *m*

**blast** *n* (wind) rafale *f*, souffle *m*; (trumpet, horn) sonnerie *f*; explosion *f*; *vt* (explosive) faire sauter; (shatter) fracasser; flétrir; ruiner

**blasted** *adj* désolé; *coll* sacré; (hopes) anéanti

**blast-furnace** *n* haut fourneau

**blasting** *n* (quarry) action *f* de faire sauter, tir *m* de mines

**blast-off** *n* (rocket, spacecraft) lancement *m*

**blatancy** *n* vulgarité criarde

**blatant** *adj* criard, vulgaire; flagrant

**¹blaze** n flambée f, flamboiement m; feu m; (fire) incendie m; (light) éclat m; coll **go to ~s!** diable!; coll **like ~s** vigoureusement; vi flamber, flamboyer; briller, étinceler; **~ away** tirer sans arrêt; fig travailler avec acharnement; **~ up** s'embraser; fig s'emporter

**²blaze** n (horse) étoile f; (tree) encoche f; vt marquer; **~ the trail** frayer la piste

**blazer** n blazer m

**blazing** adj flamboyant; éblouissant; fig furieux -euse

**blazon** n blason m; vt blasonner; **~ abroad** proclamer

**bleach** n eau f de Javel; vt + vi blanchir

**¹bleak** n zool ablette f

**²bleak** adj (bare) nu; (cold) froid; (dreary) morne, désolé

**bleary** adj **~-eyed** aux yeux chassieux

**bleat** n bêlement m; vi bêler; fig geindre

**bleb** n (blister) ampoule f; (bubble) bulle f

**bleed** vt saigner; vi saigner; (colour) déteindre; bot suinter; **my heart ~s** je suis désolé

**bleeder** n hémophile; coll salaud m

**bleeding** n saignement m; perte f de sang; (blood-letting) saignée f; adj saignant; coll sacré

**bleep** n top m; vt biper

**blemish** n tache f; vt entacher, gâter, endommager

**blench** vi broncher, reculer

**blend** n mélange m; vt mélanger; vi se mêler, se mélanger

**bless** vt bénir; être reconnaissant à; favoriser, douer

**blessed, blest** adj béni; doué; coll sacré

**¹lessing** n bénédiction f; (luck) chance f; avantage m; **~ in disguise** avantage inattendu

**blight** n nielle f; fig fléau m; vt nieller; fig flétrir, miner

**blighter** n sl salaud m

**blind** n (window) store m; coll soûlerie f; **the ~ les** aveugles; **Venetian ~** store vénitien; adj aveugle; (dark) sombre, obscur; (door, window) aveugle, faux (f fausse); aer sans visibilité; coll saoul; **~ alley** rue f sans issue, impasse f; (job) poste m sans avenir; **~ spot** angle mort; **turn a ~ eye** faire semblant de ne pas voir; vt aveugler; **~ oneself** s'aveugler; vi sl mot foncer à l'aveuglette

**blindfold** adj aux yeux bandés; adv les yeux bandés; vt bander les yeux à, aveugler

**blinding** adj éblouissant

**blindness** n cécité f; fig aveuglement m

**blind-side** n côté m de l'angle mort; fig point m faible

**blink** n lueur f, clignotement m; vi cligner des yeux; (light) clignoter; vaciller

**blinker(s)** n(pl) œillère(s) f(pl)

**blinking** adj coll euph sacré

**bliss** n félicité f, joie f, contentement m

**blissful** adj bienheureux -euse; coll merveilleux -euse

**blister** n ampoule f; cloque f; coll emmerdeur -euse; vt provoquer des ampoules sur; fig flétrir; vi développer des ampoules

**blistering** n (skin) formation f d'ampoules; (paint) boursouflure f; adj (heat) étouffant; (attack) cinglant

**blithe** adj heureux -euse, gai, folâtre

**blithering** adj coll **~ idiot** crétin -e

**blitz** n bombardement aérien; vt bombarder

**blizzard** n tourmente f de neige; (polar) blizzard m

**¹bloat** vt (herring) fumer

**²bloat** vt gonfler, enfler, bouffir; vi enfler

**bloated** adj gonflé, boursouflé; (face) bouffi

**bloater** n hareng saur

**blob** n tache f; (ink) pâté m

**bloc** n pol bloc m

**block** n bloc m; (tree) souche f; (scaffold, cobbler, ship-yard) billot m; (butcher) hachoir m; (pulley) chape f; (hatter) forme f; (buildings) îlot m, pâté m; print planche f; fig obstacle m, blocage m, obstruction f; **~s** jeu m de cubes; vt bloquer, barrer, boucher; entraver; **~ out** (obstruct) boucher; (sketch out) ébaucher; adj **~ grant** subvention f fixe; **~ letters** lettres fpl majuscules

**blockade** n blocus m; **raise the ~** lever le blocus; **run the ~** forcer le blocus; vt faire le blocus de

**blockbuster** n coll bombe f de gros calibre; (film, etc) superproduction f

**blockhead** n crétin -e

**blockhouse** n blockhaus m

**bloke** n coll type m

**blond** n blond m; adj blond

**blonde** n blonde f

**blood** n sang m; (bloodshed) meurtre m, mort f; (relationship) parenté f, race f, descendance f; tempérament m, colère f; coll obs dandy m; **bad ~** haine f, malveillance f; **blue ~** sang bleu; **first ~** avantage initial; **flesh and ~** parents mpl; **in cold ~** délibérément; **make s/o's ~ boil** faire bouillir le sang à qn; **one's ~ is up** on est en colère; vt faire une saignée à; fig initier; adj **~ bank** banque f du sang; **~ count** numération f globulaire; **~ feud** vendetta f; **~ orange** sanguine f; **~ pressure** tension artérielle; **~ sports** chasse f

**blood-bath** n massacre m, bain m de sang

blurb

**blood-curdling** adj horrible, à faire frémir
**blood-donor** n donneur -euse de sang
**blood-group** n groupe sanguin
**bloodhound** n limier m; fig limier m, détective m
**bloodless** adj med exsangue; pâle; sans vitalité; sans effusion de sang
**blood-letting** n saignée f
**bloodlust** n désir m de sang, soif f de sang
**blood-money** n prix m du sang
**blood-poisoning** n med empoisonnement m du sang
**blood-pudding** n boudin m
**blood-red** adj rouge sang invar
**blood-relation** n parent -e par le sang
**bloodshed** n meurtre m, carnage m, effusion f de sang
**bloodshot** adj injecté de sang
**blood-stained** adj taché de sang
**bloodstock** n pur-sang m invar
**bloodstone** n sanguine f, héliotrope m
**blood-sucker** n sangsue f
**blood-test** n examen m du sang
**blood-thirsty** adj sanguinaire
**blood-transfusion** n transfusion sanguine
**blood-vessel** n vaisseau sanguin
**bloody** adj ensanglanté; (battle) sanguinaire; coll sacré, foutu
**bloody-mary** n vodka f au jus de tomate
**bloody-minded** adj coll hargneux -euse
**bloody-mindedness** n coll hargne f
**bloom** n fleur f; (flowering) floraison f; (certain fruit) velouté m; vi fleurir; fig être resplendissant
**bloomer** n coll gaffe f
**bloomers** npl obs culotte bouffante
**blooming** n floraison f; adj fleuri, épanoui, rayonnant; coll sacré
**blossom** n fleur f; vi fleurir; s'épanouir; fig ~ out s'épanouir; avoir du succès
**blot** n pâté m, tache f; vt (stain) tacher; (dry) sécher (au buvard); fig tacher; ~ out effacer
**blotch** n tache f; vt couvrir de taches
**blotchy** adj taché, tacheté
**blotter** n buvard m
**blotting-paper** n papier m buvard, buvard m
**blotto** adj coll parti, ivre
**blouse** n blouse f
¹**blow** n coup m; choc m
²**blow** n coup m de vent; souffle m; vt souffler; faire souffler; (trumpet, etc) sonner de; elect faire sauter; ~ one's own trumpet se vanter; ~ the gaff révéler des secrets, vendre la mèche; ~ the lid off exposer; vi souffler, venter; mus sonner; ~ hot and cold vaciller, souffler le chaud et le froid; coll ~ off steam exprimer ses sentiments; ~ up

faire sauter; fig exagérer; coll phot élargir; vi ~ over se calmer, s'apaiser; ~ up exploser; coll devenir furieux
**blower** n (fireplace) tablier m; coll bigophone m
**blow-hole** n évent m
**blow-lamp** n chalumeau m
**blow-out** n (tyre) éclatement m; coll gueuleton m; elect there's a ~ les plombs ont sauté
**blow-pipe** n chalumeau m; (weapon) sarbacane f
**blow-up** n phot coll agrandissement m
**blowzy** adj échevelé, malpropre; (face) rougeâtre
**blub** vi coll chialer
¹**blubber** n graisse f de baleine
²**blubber** vi pleurnicher, pleurer
³**blubber** adj (lips) lippu
**bludgeon** n matraque f; trique f; vt matraquer
**blue** n bleu m, azur m; adj bleu; fig misérable, malheureux -euse; sl grivois, obscène, porno; ~ chip shares valeurs fpl de tout repos; coll ~ funk frousse f; once in a ~ moon tous les trente-six du mois; true ~ fidèle, loyal; vt (laundry) passer au bleu; coll (money) gaspiller
**bluebell** n jacinthe f des bois
**blue-book** n pol livre bleu
**bluebottle** n mouche bleue; coll flic m
**blue-eyed** adj coll préféré, favori -ite
**bluejacket** n matelot m
**blue-pencil** vt censurer, couper; (delete) barrer
**blueprint** n plan m, épure f; fig schéma m
**blues** npl mus blues m; fig cafard m, idées noires
**blue-stocking** n bas-bleu m
¹**bluff** n escarpement m; adj à pic, escarpé; fig brusque, franc (f franche)
²**bluff** n bluff m; coll call s/o's ~ relever le défi de qn, mettre qn au pied du mur; vt + vi bluffer
**bluffer** n bluffeur-euse
**bluish** adj bleuâtre
**blunder** n erreur f, bévue f, balourdise f, gaffe f; (social) impair m; vt gâcher; vi faire une gaffe; ~ on avancer à l'aveuglette; ~ upon découvrir par hasard
**blunderbuss** n hist tromblon m
**blunderer** n balourd -e; coll gaffeur -euse
**blunt** vt émousser; épointer; fig émousser, engourdir; adj émoussé; épointé; (mind) lourd; (speech) brusque, cassant
**bluntness** n épointement m; brusquerie f
**blur** n tache f; barbouillage m; aspect indistinct; vt brouiller, barbouiller, ternir; vi se brouiller
**blurb** n coll bande f publicitaire, texte m de lancement

**blurt** *vt* dire spontanément, dire sans réfléchir; (secret) ~ **out** révéler

**blush** *n* rougeur *f*; couleur *f* rose; lueur *f*; **at the first** ~ au premier regard; *vi* rougir, devenir rouge

**blushing** *adj* rougissant; *fig* timide

**bluster** *n* fracas *m*; fanfaronnade *f*; *vi* (wind) souffler fort, mugir; *fig* déblatérer, tonitruer

**blusterer** *n* fanfaron -onne

**blustering, blustery** *adj* (wind, sea) furieux -ieuse; (manner) fanfaron-onne

**boa** *n* boa *m*

**boar** *n* (hog) verrat *m*; (wild) sanglier *m*

**¹board** *n* planche *f*; (notices) panneau *m*; (blackboard) tableau noir; (cardboard) carton *m*; *theat obs* ~ s scène *f*, plateau *m*; *vt* planchéier

**²board** *n* nourriture *f*, pension *f*; table *f* avec couverts; (directors, etc) conseil *m* (d'administration); **above** ~ honnête, juste; **sweep the** ~ tout gagner; *vt* nourrir; *vi* être en pension

**³board** *n naut* bord *m*; **go by the** ~ tomber à l'eau; **on** ~ à bord; *vt* (ship) monter à bord de; (train, bus) monter dans; *fig* monter

**boarder** *n* (lodging-house) pensionnaire; (school) interne

**boarding** *n* planchéiage *m*; *aer* ~**ing card** carte *f* d'accès à bord

**boarding-house** *n* pension *f* de famille

**boarding-school** *n* pensionnat *m*, internat *m*

**boast** *n* vantardise *f*; hâblerie *f*; objet *m* d'orgueil; *vt* se vanter de; se faire gloire de posséder; *vi* se vanter

**boastful** *adj* vantard

**boastfulness** *n* vantardise *f*

**boat** *n* bateau *m*; (small) canot *m*, embarcation *f*; (steamer) paquebot *m*; *cul* saucière *f*; **be in the same** ~ être dans le pétrin ensemble, être logé à la même enseigne; **burn one's** ~ s s'engager à fond; *coll* **miss the** ~ manquer le coche

**boater** *n* canotier *m*

**boatful** *n* cargaison *f*, plein bateau

**boathook** *n* gaffe *f*

**boat-house** *n* hangar *m* à canots

**boating** *n* canotage *m*

**boatman** *n* batelier *m*; (hirer) loueur *m* de canots

**boatswain** *n naut* maître *m* d'équipage

**¹bob** *n* (horse) queue écourtée; hair-style) coiffure *f* à la Jeanne d'Arc; (curl) boucle *f*; (pendulum) poids *m*; *vt* (hair) écourter

**²bob** *n* tape *f*; *vt* taper, faire taper

**³bob** *n* (curtsy) révérence *f*; *vi* faire une révérence

**⁴bob** *n coll obs* shilling *m*

**⁵bob, bob-sled, bobsleigh** *n sp* traîneau *m*, bobsleigh *m*, bob *m*

**bobbed** *adj* (hair) à la Jeanne d'Arc

**bobbin** *n* bobine *f*; fuseau *m*

**bobby** *n coll* flic *m*

**bobbysoxer** *n US coll* minette *f*

**bob-sled, bobsleigh** *n see* bob⁵

**bobstay** *n naut* sous-barbe *f*

**bob-tail** *n* (horse) queue écourtée; *pej* **rag-tag and** ~ quatre pelés et un tondu

**Boche** *n pej* Boche *m*; *adj* boche

**bode** *vt* présager; *vi* ~ **well (ill)** être de bon (mauvais) augure

**bodice** *n* corsage *m*

**bodily** *adj* corporel -elle, physique; *adv* en personne, en chair et en os; en masse, tout ensemble

**bodkin** *n* poinçon *m*

**body** *n* corps *m*; (dead) cadavre *m*; *mot* carrosserie *f*; (bodice) corsage *m*; (main part) corps *m*; (people) groupe *m*, masse *f*; (organization) corps *m*, corporation *f*, groupement *m*; (solidity) consistance *f*; (wine) corps *m*; *coll* type *m*; ~ **politic** l'État *m*; ~ **(repair) shop** atelier *m* de carrosserie; **heavenly** ~ corps *m* céleste

**body-builder** *n mot* carrossier *m*; (food) aliment nourrissant; appareil *m* pour développer les muscles

**bodyguard** *n* garde *m* du corps; *coll* barbouze *f*

**body-snatcher** *n ar* déterreur *m* de cadavres

**bodywork** *n mot* carrosserie *f*

**boffin** *n coll* chercheur *m* (à la solde des forces armées)

**bog** *n* marais *m*; *sl* latrines *fpl*; *vulg* chiottes *fpl*; *vt* embourber; **get bogged down** s'embourber

**bogey, bogie, bogy** *n* épouvantail *m*

**boggle** *vi* hésiter; avoir peur; ~ **at** avoir des scrupules concernant; **the mind** ~ s on croit rêver

**boggler** *n* peureux -euse; (stickler) tatillon -onne

**boggy** *adj* marécageux -euse

**bogie, bogey, bogy** *n* (railway) bogie *m*

**bogus** *adj* factice, faux (*f* fausse)

**¹boil** *n* furoncle *m*; *coll* clou *m*

**²boil** *n* ébullition *f*; *vt* faire bouillir; (egg) faire bouillir à la coque; *vi* bouillir; *fig* bouillonner

**boiled** *adj* bouilli; (egg) à la coque; *coll* ~ **shirt** plastron *m*

**boiler** *n* chaudière *f*; (kettle) bouilloire *f*; (chicken) poule *f* à bouillir

**boiler-suit** *n* bleu *m* de travail

**boiling** *n* ébullition *f*; *coll* **the whole** ~ tout le bazar; *adj* bouillonnant

**boiling-point** *n* température *f* de bouillonnement

**boisterous** *adj* turbulent, tapageur -euse; exubérant; (sea) houleux -euse

**bold** *adj* courageux -euse, hardi, brave, audacieux -ieuse; impudent, effronté; (cliff) à pic, escarpé; **make so ~ as to** présumer

**bold-face** *n print* gras *m*

**boldness** *n* courage *m*, audace *f*; impudence *f*, effronterie *f*

**bollard** *n naut* bitte *f* d'amarrage, bollard *m*; *mot* borne (lumineuse)

**Bolshevik** *n* Bolchevik, Bolcheviste; *adj* bolchevique

**Bolshevism** *n* bolchevisme *m*

**Bolshy** *adj coll* bolchevique

**bolshy** *adj coll* pas commode, difficile

**bolster** *n* traversin *m*; *bui* traverse *f*; *mech* coussin *m*; *vt* soutenir, étayer; ~ **up** soutenir; couvrir, protéger

**bolt** *n* (lock) verrou *m*, pêne *m*; (screw) boulon *m*; (thunderbolt) coup *m* de foudre; (cloth) coupe *f*, pièce *f*; *mil* culasse *f* mobile; départ *m* brusque; ~ **from the blue** coup de tonnerre; **shoot one's ~** faire un dernier effort; *vt* verrouiller; (food) engloutir; *vi* partir brusquement; (horse) s'emballer; *adv* ~ **upright** droit comme un i

**bolt-hole** *n* terrier *m*

**bomb** *n* bombe *f*; *coll* **cost a ~** coûter les yeux de la tête; *vt* bombarder; ~**ed out** sinistré (par bombardement)

**bombard** *vt* bombarder

**bombardier** *n mil* caporal *m* d'artillerie

**bombast** *n* emphase *f*, grandiloquence *f*

**bombastic** *adj* emphatique, ampoulé, grandiloquent

**Bombay duck** *n cul* poisson salé (dans un curry)

**bomb-disposal** *n* désamorçage *m* (de bombes)

**bombe** *n cul* bombe *f*

**bomber** *n* aer + *mil* bombardier *m*

**bomb-proof** *adj* blindé, protégé contre les bombes

**bombshell** *n mil* obus *m*; *fig* surprise ahurissante

**bomb-sight** *n* viseur *m* de bombardement

**bomb-site** *n* lieu bombardé

**bona fide** *adj* de bonne foi; authentique

**bonanza** *n min* filon *m* riche; *fig* aubaine *f*

**bond** *n* lien *m*; *leg* engagement *m*; contrat *m*; *comm* titre *m*, valeur *f*; (customs) entrepôt *m*; *bui* appareil *m*; *vt* lier; (customs) entreposer; *bui* appareiller; *adj* en esclavage

**bondage** *n* esclavage *m*, asservissement *m*

**bonded** *adj* entreposé; ~ **warehouse** entrepôt *m*

**bondsman, bondswoman** *n* esclave

**bone** *n* os *m*; (fish) arête *f*; (whale) fanon *m*; ~ **s** corps *m*, cadavre *m*; (dice) *mpl*; (castanets) castagnettes *fpl*; ~ **of contention** pomme *f* de discorde; **have a ~ to pick with** avoir maille à partir avec; **make no ~s** ne pas hésiter; **to the ~** jusqu'à l'os; (roots) jusqu'au minimum; *vt* désosser; *sl* voler; *coll* ~ **up on** potasser, bûcher

**bone-dry** *adj* complètement sec (*f* sèche)

**bone-head** *n sl* crétin -e

**bone-idle** *adj* extrêmement paresseux -euse

**boneless** *adj* sans os, désossé; *fig* faible

**bonemeal** *n* engrais *m* d'os (broyés)

**bone-setter** *n* rebouteux *m*

**bonfire** *n* feu *m* de joie; feu *m* de jardin

**bonhomie** *n* bonhomie *f*

**bonkers** *adj coll* cinglé

**bonnet** *n* bonnet *m*; (chimney) capuchon *m*; *mot* capot *m*

**bonny** *adj* joli, beau (*f* belle)

**bonus** *n* prime *f*, gratification *f*; *fig* aubaine *f*; **cost of living ~** indemnité *f* de vie chère; **no-claim ~** bonification *f* pour non-sinistre

**bony** *adj* osseux -euse

**bonze** *n* bonze *m*

**boo** *interj* hou!; *vt* huer, chahuter; *vi* pousser des huées

**boob** *n sl* idiot -e, crétin -e; *sl* (breast) néné *m*; *vi sl* gaffer

**booby** *n* idiot -e, crétin -e, benêt *m*

**booby-prize** *n* prix *m* de consolation

**booby-trap** *n* attrape-nigaud *m*; *mil* objet piégé

**boodle** *n sl* fric *m*

**boogie-woogie** *n* boogie-woogie *m*

**book** *n* livre *m*, bouquin *m*; *mus* livret *m*; (exercise book) cahier *m*; *sp* livre *m* de paris; *comm* registre *m*; **bring s/o to ~** demander des comptes à qn; **in s/o's good (bad) ~s** bien (mal) vu de qn; **keep the ~s** tenir la comptabilité; **suit one's ~** convenir à qn, plaire à qn; **take a leaf out of s/o's ~** imiter qn; *vt* inscrire; (seat, place) louer, retenir, réserver; (performer, speaker) engager; *sp* (referee) prendre le nom de; *US* (police) donner une contravention à

**bookbinder** *n* relieur *m*

**bookbinding** *n* reliure *f*

**bookcase** *n* bibliothèque *f*

**book-ends** *npl* serre-livres *mpl*

**booking** *n* inscription *f*; location *f*, réservation *f*; *sp* **he got a ~ from the referee** l'arbitre a pris son nom

**booking-office** *n* guichet *m*

**bookish** *adj* studieux -euse; livresque

**book-keeper** *n* comptable

**book-keeping** *n* comptabilité *f*

**book-learning** *n* connaissances *fpl* livresques

**booklet** *n* livret *m*

**bookmaker** *n* bookmaker *m*

**bookmark** *n* signet *m*

**bookmobile** *n* US bibliobus *m*

**book-plate** *n* ex-libris *m*

**bookseller** *n* libraire

**bookshop** *n* librairie *f*

**bookstall** *n* kiosque *m*; (station) bibliothèque *f* de gare

**bookstore** *n* librairie *f*

**book-token** *n* chèque-livre *m* (*pl* chèques-livres)

**bookworm** *n coll fig* rat *m* de bibliothèque

¹**boom** *n* (harbour) estacade *f*; *naut* gui *m*; *rad* perche *f*; (crane) flèche *f*

²**boom** *n* grondement *m*, mugissement *m*; *vi* gronder, mugir

³**boom** *n comm* boom *m*; *vi* prospérer, augmenter brusquement de valeur

**boomerang** *n* boomerang *m*; *vi fig* faire boomerang

**boon** *n* aubaine *f*; *ar* faveur *f*; *adj* ~ **companion** joyeux compère, grand copain

**boor** *n* paysan -anne; *fig* butor *m*

**boorish** *adj* balourd, rustre

**boost** *n coll* aide *f*; *coll* éloge *m* publicitaire; *vt* élever, prôner, faire de la réclame pour; *augmenter*; *elect* survolter

**booster** *n elect* survolteur *m*; fusée *f* gigogne; *med* piqûre *f* supplémentaire, rappel *m*

¹**boot** *n* botte *f*; (ankle boot) botillon *m*; (buttoned) bottine *f*; *mot* coffre *m*; **bet one's ~s** être sûr de; **get the ~** être licencié; **the ~ is on the other foot** les rôles sont renversés; *vt* donner un coup de pied à; *coll* ~ **out** licencier; flanquer à la porte

²**boot** *n* **to ~** d'ailleurs, par surcroît

**booth** *n* baraque *f*; (election) isoloir *m*; (telephone) cabine *f*

**bootlace** *n* lacet *m*

**bootleg** *vt US* vendre ou importer en contrebande; *vi* faire de la contrebande (d'alcools)

**bootlegger** *n US hist* bootlegger *m*

**bootless** *adj* sans profit, inutile; (without boots) sans bottes

**boots** *n* garçon *m* d'hôtel

**booty** *n* butin *m*

**booze** *n coll* boisson *f* alcoolique; *vi* boire beaucoup

**boozed** *adj coll* saoul, parti

**boozer** *n coll* (person) ivrogne; *coll* bar *m*, bistro *m*

**bop** *n* bop *m*, be-bop *m*

**boracic** *adj chem* borique

**borage** *n bot* bourrache *f*

**borax** *n chem* borax *m*

**border** *n* bord *m*, côté *m*; marge *f*; frontière *f*; (garden) bordure *f*; (dress) galon *m*; *vt* border, entourer; ~ **on** être contigu à; ressembler à, avoisiner, friser

**borderer** *n* frontalier -ière

**borderland** *n* zone *f* frontière

**borderline** *n* frontière *f*; ligne *f* de démarcation; *adj* douteux -euse, incertain; ~ **case** cas *m* limite

¹**bore** *n* (gun) calibre *m*; *mot* alésage *m*; *vt* vriller, percer, perforer, creuser; forer; *mot* aléser

²**bore** *n* fâcheux -euse; *coll* raseur -euse, casse-pieds; (thing) barbe *f*, scie *f*; *vt* ennuyer; *coll* ~ **s/o stiff** casser les pieds à qn

³**bore** *n* (river) mascaret *m*

**boreal** *adj* boréal

**boredom** *n* ennui *m*

**borehole** *n* trou *m* de sondage

**borer** *n* vrille *f*; foret *m*; insecte térébrant

**boric** *adj chem* borique

**boring** *adj* ennuyeux -euse; *coll* barbant, assommant

**born** *adj* né; (innate) inné; naturel -elle

**boron** *n chem* bore *m*

**borough** *n* ville *f*; (England) ville administrée par un maire et un conseil municipal; (England) **parliamentary ~** ville *f* formant une circonscription électorale

**borrow** *vt* emprunter

**borrower** *n* emprunteur -euse

**borrowing** *n* emprunt *m*

**borsch, bortsch** *n cul* bortsch *m*

**bosh** *n coll* idiotie *f*, absurdité *f*; *interj* avec ça!

**bosk, bosket, bosquet** *n* bosquet *m*, fourré *m*

**bosky** *adj* touffu

**bosom** *n* sein *m*; ~ **of the family** intimité familiale; *adj* familier -ière, intime

¹**boss** *n* bosse *f*, bossage *m*; *vt* bosseler

²**boss** *n coll* patron *m*; (foreman) contremaître *m*; *US coll* manitou *m* politique; *vt* contrôler, gérer; *coll* dominer; ~ **about** régenter

³**boss** *vt sl* bousiller

**boss-eyed** *adj coll* louche, bigle; *fig* tortueux -ueuse

**boss-shot** *n coll* bousillage *m*

**bossy** *adj* autoritaire

**botanic, botanical** *adj* botanique

**botanist** *n* botaniste

**botanize** *vi* faire de la botanique, herboriser

**botany** *n* botanique *f*

**botch** n défaut m, tache f; travail bâclé; vt coll bousiller, bâcler

**both** pron tous (f toutes) les deux, l'un (f l'une) et l'autre; adj les deux; adv à la fois, aussi bien; ~ ... **and** non seulement ... mais aussi

**bother** n ennui m; tracas m, souci m; coll embêtement m; vt ennuyer, importuner; (worry) tracasser; coll embêter; vi se tourmenter, se tracasser; ~! zut!

**botheration** n tracas m; coll embêtement m; ~! zut!

**bothersome** adj gênant, agaçant

**bottle** n bouteille f; (child) biberon m; (hot-water) bouillotte f; (beer) boisson f, habitude f de boire; ~ **party** réunion f intime où chacun apporte à boire; vt embouteiller, mettre en bouteille; ~ **up** retenir, contenir

**bottled** adj en bouteille; ~ **by** mis en bouteille par

**bottle-green** adj vert bouteille invar

**bottleneck** n mot bouchon m; goulot m

**bottle-washer** n plongeur m; **head cook and** ~ factotum m

**bottom** n fond m; (hill, tree) pied m; (page) bas m; fig fondement m, base f; coll derrière m, cul m; naut quille f; naut navire m; **be at the** ~ **of** être la cause de; **get to the** ~ **of** examiner en détail; adj le plus bas; (last) dernier -ière; ~ **gear** première vitesse; ~ **half** deuxième moitié; vt mettre un fond à; vi toucher le fond

**bottomless** adj sans fond; insondable

**boudoir** n boudoir m

**bough** n rameau m

**bouillon** n bouillon m

**boulder** n roche f, bloc m; geol roche f erratique; geol ~ **clay** dépôt argileux; geol ~ **period** période f glaciaire

**boulevard** n boulevard m

**bounce** n bond m, rebondissement m; (ball) rebond m; coll jactance f; élasticité f; vt faire rebondir; vi rebondir, sauter, bondir; coll (cheque) être retourné sans provision

**bouncer** n (lie) mensonge éhonté; (liar) hâbleur -euse; coll videur m

**bouncing** adj qui rebondit; fig plantureux -euse, robuste

¹**bound** n limite f, borne f; **out of** ~ **s** accès interdit; vt borner, limiter; vi être limitrophe de, avoir ses limites

²**bound** n bond m, saut m; vi bondir, rebondir

³**bound** adj prêt à partir; naut en partance

⁴**bound** adj ~ **to** obligé à

**boundary** n limite f, frontière f

**bounden** adj ar ~ **duty** devoir absolu

**bounder** coll obs salaud m

**boundless** adj sans limite, infini

**bounteous** adj généreux -euse; abondant

**bounteousness** n générosité f; abondance f

**bountiful** adj généreux -euse, libéral; **lady** ~ dame patronnesse

**bounty** n générosité f, libéralité f; prime f

**bouquet** n (flower, wine) bouquet m

**Bourbon** n (espèce f de) whisky américain

**bourdon** n bourdon m

**bourgeois** n + adj bourgeois -e

**bourgeoisie** n bourgeoisie f

**bout** n coup m; (boxing, wrestling, etc) match m; med accès m; période f; coll (drink) cuite f

**boutique** n boutique f

**bovine** adj bovin

¹**bow** n arc m; mus archet m; (knot) boucle f; coll **draw the long** ~ exagérer; **have many strings to one's** ~ avoir plusieurs cordes à son arc; vi mus tirer l'archet

²**bow** n salut m, inclination f de la tête; **make one's** ~ apparaître; (withdraw) se retirer; vt incliner, courber; (knee) fléchir; faire ployer; vi saluer, s'incliner; fléchir, se courber; ~ **and scrape** faire des courbettes; ~ **down** se baisser; ~ **out** tirer sa révérence

³**bow(s)** n naut avant m, proue f

**bowdlerize** vt expurger

**bowel(s)** n(pl) intestin(s) m(pl); ~ **s** fig entrailles fpl; lit émotions fpl; ~ **s of mercy** sentiments mpl de piété

¹**bower** n tonnelle f; poet boudoir m; maison f rustique

²**bower** n naut ancre f

¹**bowl** n bol m; (wine) coupe f; (washing) cuvette f; assiette f à soupe, assiette creuse; (pipe) fourneau m

²**bowl** n boule f; vt rouler, faire rouler, lancer; fig ~ **out** battre; ~ **over** renverser; fig déconcerter, décontenancer; vi ~ **along** rouler

**bow-legged** adj bancal

**bowler** n sp joueur -euse de boules

**bowler(-hat)** n (chapeau m) melon m

**bowline** n nœud m de chaise

**bowling** n jeu m de boules

**bowling-alley** n bowling m

**bowling-green** n boulingrin m

**bowls** n jeu m de boules

**bowsprit** n naut beaupré m

**bow-wow** n aboiement m; (child language) toutou m

¹**box** n boîte f; (cardboard) carton m; (sizable) caisse f; theat loge f, baignoire f; (horse) box m; leg (jury, press) banc m; (witness) barre f (des témoins); mot (gears, differential) carter m; sl télé f; (railway) ~ **car** fourgon m; ~ **number**

boîte postale; **Christmas** ~ étrennes *fpl*; *vt* mettre en boîte, mettre en caisse; *leg* déposer; ~ **in** cerner; *fig* circonscrire; ~ **off** circonscrire; ~ **up** mettre en boîte

²**box** *n* claque *f*, gifle *f*, soufflet *m*; *vt* boxer; souffleter; *vi* boxer

³**box** *n bot* buis *m*

**box-calf** *n* box-calf *m*

¹**boxer** *n* boxeur *m*

²**boxer** *n* (dog) boxer *m*

**boxing** *n* boxe *f*

**Boxing-Day** *n* le lendemain de Noël

**box-office** *n theat* bureau *m* de location

**box-spanner** *n* clef *f* en tube

**box-tree** *n* buis *m*

**boy** *n* garçon *m*; jeune homme *m*; (servant) boy *m*; ~ **friend** petit ami, amoureux *m*; **old** ~ ancien élève; *coll* mon vieux

**boycott** *n* boycottage *m*; *vt* boycotter

**boyhood** *n* enfance *f*; adolescence *f*

**boyish** *n* d'un garçon; *fig* puéril

**bra** *n coll* soutien-gorge *m* (*pl* soutiens-gorge)

**brace** *n* étai *m*, attache *f*; *bui* étrésillon *m*; (tool) vilebrequin *m*; (pair) couple *m*, paire *f*; ~**s** bretelles *fpl*; *vt* attacher; appuyer; étayer; *naut* brasser; revigorer, tonifier; ~ **oneself up** rassembler ses forces; *coll* prendre un petit verre

**bracelet** *n* bracelet *m*; *coll* ~**s** menottes *fpl*

**bracken** *n* fougère *f*

**bracket** *n bui* support *m*, poterne *f*, tasseau *m*; *print* (square) crochet *m*; (round) parenthèse *f*; *vt* mettre entre crochets; mettre entre parenthèses; *mil* encadrer; *fig* grouper ensemble

**brackish** *adj* saumâtre

**bradawl** *n* poinçon *m*

**brag** *n* vanterie *f*, hâblerie *f*; *vi* se vanter

**braggart** *n*+*adj* hâbleur -euse

**Brahmin, Brahman** *n* brahmane *m*

**braid** *n* (plait) tresse *f*; (trimming) soutache *f*; *mil* galon *m*; *vt* tresser; soutacher; galonner

**Braille** *n* braille *m*

**brain** *n* cerveau *m*; *fig* as *m*; ~**s** intelligence *f*; *cul* cervelle *f*; **blow out one's** ~ **s** se brûler la cervelle; **have something on the** ~ être obsédé par quelque chose; **pick s/o's** ~ **s** utiliser les idées d'un autre; **rack one's** ~ **s** se creuser la cervelle; *vt* défoncer le crâne à

**brain-child** *n* invention personnelle

**brain-drain** *n* brain-drain *m*, émigration *f* des cerveaux (des chercheurs)

**brain-fever** *n med* fièvre cérébrale, méningite *f*

**brainless** *adj* stupide, crétin

**brain-storm** *n* congestion cérébrale, transport *m* au cerveau; *fig* idée géniale

**brains-trust** *n coll* brain-trust *m*

**brainwash** *vt* faire un lavage de cerveau à

**brainwashing** *n* lavage *m* de cerveau

**brainwave** *n coll* trouvaille *f*, idée géniale

**brainy** *adj* intelligent

**braise** *vt cul* braiser

¹**brake** *n* frein *m*; *vt* freiner

²**brake** *n ar* break *m*

³**brake** *n bot* fougère *f*

**brake-drum** *n mot* tambour *m* de frein

**bramble** *n* ronce *f*; mûre *f*

**bran** *n* son *m*

**branch** *n* branche *f*; (railway) embranchement *m*; *comm* succursale *f*; (river) affluent *m*; *mil* arme *f*; **root and** ~ entièrement, complètement; *vi bot* pousser des branches; ~ **out** se ramifier, se séparer

**brand** *n* brandon *m*, tison *m*; fer *m* à marquer; *fig* flétrissure *f*; *comm* marque *f*; *vt* marquer au fer rouge; *fig* dénoncer; *fig* ~ **on the memory** graver dans la mémoire

**brandish** *vt* brandir

**brand-new** *adj* tout à fait neuf (*f* tout à fait neuve), flambant neuf (*f* flambant neuve)

**brandy** *n* eau-de-vie *f* (*pl* eaux-de-vie); *usu* cognac *m*

**brash** *adj* outrecuidant, impudent, vulgaire

**brass** *n* laiton *m*; bronze *m*; *mus* cuivres *mpl*; *fig* impudence *f*, effronterie *f*; *coll* (money) fric *m*; *mil sl* **top** ~ huiles *fpl*; ~ **tacks** réalités *fpl*

**brassard** *n* brassard *m*

**brass-band** *n* fanfare *f*

**brass-hat** *n coll* officier supérieur

**brassière** *n* soutien-gorge *m* (*pl* soutiens-gorge)

**brassy** *adj* de bronze; *fig* effronté

**brat** *n* moutard *m*; *cont* morveux -euse

**bravado** *n* bravade *f*; *ar* spadassin *m*

**brave** *adj* courageux -euse, brave; élégant, beau (*f* belle); *vt* braver, défier

**bravery** *n* courage *m*, bravoure *f*

**bravo** *interj* bravo!

**brawl** *n* bagarre *f*, rixe *f*; *vi* beugler; se bagarrer; (stream) bruire

**brawler** *n* braillard -e; bagarreur *m*

**brawling** *adj* braillard, gueulard

**brawn** *n cul* fromage *m* de tête; muscle *m*; *fig* force *f*

**brawny** *adj* musclé, costaud, fort

¹**bray** *n* braiment *m*; *vi* braire

²**bray** *vt* (crush) broyer

**brazen** adj d'airain, de bronze; (sound) cuivré; fig impudent, effronté

**brazen-faced** adj impudent, effronté

**brazier** n brasero m

**Brazil** n Brésil m

**Brazilian** n Brésilien -ienne; adj brésilien -ienne

**breach** n rupture f, cassure f; mil brèche f; leg infraction f, violation f; fig rupture f, brouille f; ~ **of promise** rupture f d'un mariage; ~ **of the peace** désordre m; ~ **of trust** abus m de confiance; vt ouvrir une brèche dans, percer

**bread** n pain m; fig subsistance f, gagne-pain m invar; eccles hostie f; sl fric m; ~ **and butter** tartine (beurrée); fig gagne-pain m invar; **earn one's** ~ **and butter** gagner son pain

**bread-basket** n corbeille f à pain; sl estomac m, bide m

**breadcrumb** n miette f; cul ~s chapelure f

**breadth** n largeur f; fig largeur f, ampleur f; tolérance f

**break** n cassure f, rupture f; (gap) trou m; interruption f; (rest) repos m, répit m, pause f; (school) récréation f; (hiatus) solution f de continuité; (billiards) série f; (prison) évasion f; sl (luck) veine f; sl (bad luck) malchance f; vt briser, casser, rompre; (burst) crever, faire éclater; séparer; (law) violer, enfreindre; (news) annoncer; (journey) interrompre; mil (resistance) rompre; (enemy) anéantir; (promise) manquer à; (reduce to ranks) casser; (promise) manquer à; (bank in gambling) faire sauter; fig briser, anéantir; ~ **down** démolir, abattre; (analyse) analyser, compartimenter; ~ **in** défoncer; (animal) mater; ~ **into** cambrioler; fig percer; ~ **in upon** interrompre; ~ **off** casser; fig rompre, faire cesser; ~ **open** ouvrir avec violence; ~ **through** percer; ~ **up** démolir; (soil) ameublir; faire disperser, dissoudre; vi se briser, se casser, se rompre; (day) poindre; (health) se détériorer, s'altérer; (voice) muer; ~ **down** (actor, speaker) s'interrompre, coll sécher; mot avoir une panne; ~ **even** couvrir ses frais; ~ **in** interrompre; (building) entrer par effraction; ~ **off** s'interrompre, cesser; rompre avec; ~ **out** s'évader; (war, fire, storm, epidemic, scandal, etc) éclater; (disease) se répandre, faire éruption; (skin) ~ **out into** se couvrir de; ~ **up** se disperser; (school) fermer pour les vacances; ~ **with** rompre avec

**breakable** adj fragile, cassable

**breakage** n casse f; objets cassés; dégâts mpl

**breakdown** n mot + med panne f; (negotiation) rupture f; (health) effondrement m, dépression nerveuse; analyse f; (dividing up) compartimentage m; ~ **service** service m de dépannage

**breaker** n naut brisant m; (person) casseur m; elect interrupteur m; naut baril m

**breakfast** n petit déjeuner; **English** ~ breakfast m; vi prendre le petit déjeuner

**breakneck** adj (speed) à se casser le cou, dangereux -euse

**break-out** n (prison) évasion f, cavale f

**breakthrough** n mil percée f; fig découverte majeure

**break-up** n désintégration f; effondrement m; (ice) dégel m; (school) fin f des cours

**breakwater** n brise-lames m invar, môle m

**bream** n zool brème f

**breast** n anat poitrine f; (woman) sein m; fig cœur m; **make a clean** ~ **of it** tout avouer; vt affronter, faire face à; opposer; (crest) surmonter

**breast-feed** vt nourrir au sein

**breast-feeding** n allaitement m au sein

**breast-plate** n hist plastron m

**breast-stroke** n brasse f

**breast-work** n mil parapet m

**breath** n souffle m, haleine f; respiration f; fig vie f; souffle m, brise f; **catch one's** ~ retenir son souffle; **draw** ~ respirer; **draw one's last** ~ rendre le dernier soupir; **hold one's** ~ retenir son souffle; **out of** ~ essoufflé; **take s/o's** ~ **away** alarmer qn, surprendre qn; **under one's** ~ à voix basse

**breathalyser** n mot alcoo(l)test m

**breathe** vt respirer; (out) exhaler; murmurer; (courage, desire) insuffler; vi respirer; être vivant; soupirer; fig ~ **freely** n'avoir plus peur, être soulagé

**breather** n bol m d'air; moment m de répit

**breathing** n respiration f

**breathing-space** n moment m de répit

**breathless** adj essoufflé, haletant; sans vie, inanimé

**breathlessness** n essoufflement m

**bred** adj engendré; élevé; **well** ~ de bonne souche

**breech** n culasse f; cul m; ~ **es** culotte f, coll pantalon m

**breech-block** n bloc m de culasse

**breed** n espèce f, race f; (kind) type m; vt produire, porter; engendrer, procréer; (animals) faire l'élevage de; vi se reproduire; avoir des enfants; (animal) avoir des petits

**breeder** n éleveur m

**breeding** n élevage m; éducation f; bonnes manières

**breeze** n brise f; coll dispute f; vi coll ~ **in** entrer en coup de vent

**breeze-block** n bui parpaing m

**breezy** adj aéré; fig désinvolte

**Bren** n mil (espèce f de) mitrailleuse légère

**brethren** npl frères mpl

**Breton** n Breton -onne; adj breton -onne

**breve** n mus carrée f

**brevet** n brevet m

**breviary** n bréviaire m

**brevity** n brièveté f, concision f

**brew** n breuvage m; (beer) brassin m; vt (beer) brasser; (tea) faire (infuser); fig tramer, mijoter; vi infuser; (beer) fermenter; fig se préparer, se mijoter

**brewer** n brasseur -euse

**brewery** n brasserie f

**brewing** n brassage m

¹**briar** n bot églantier m; ~ **s** ronces fpl

²**briar** n (pipe) pipe f en racine de bruyère

**bribable** adj corruptible

**bribe** n pot-de-vin m (pl pots-de-vin); vt corrompre, acheter; vi donner des pots-de-vin

**bribery** n corruption f

**brick** n brique f; coll brave type m; ~ **s** (toy) jeu m de construction; coll **drop a** ~ faire une gaffe; vt murer de briques

**brickbat** n fig critique f

**bricklayer** n ouvrier m maçon

**brickwork** n briquetage m

**brickyard** n briqueterie f

**bridal** n poet noce f; adj (bed) conjugal; nuptial, de mariée

**bride** n (jeune) mariée f, promise f

**bridegroom** n (jeune) marié m, promis m

**bridesmaid** n demoiselle f d'honneur

¹**bridge** n pont m; (gangway) passerelle f; mus chevalet m; (nose) dos m; (dentistry) bridge m; vt faire un pont sur; fig faire la soudure entre

²**bridge** n (cards) bridge m

**bridgehead** n mil tête f de pont

**bridle** n bride f; vt brider, freiner; vi se rebiffer

**bridle-path** n sentier m

¹**brief** n leg dossier m, résumé m, cause f; eccles bref m; leg+fig **hold a** ~ **for** plaider pour; **hold no** ~ **for** ne pas être du côté de; leg **take a** ~ accepter une cause; vt leg confier une cause à; mil donner des instructions à; fig documenter

²**brief** adj bref (f brève), prompt, court, concis; **in** ~ bref

**briefcase** n serviette f

**briefing** n briefing m

**briefness** n brièveté f

**briefs** npl coll slip m

**brig** n naut brick m

**brigade** n brigade f

**brigadier** n mil général m de brigade

**brigand** n brigand m

**brigandage** n brigandage m

**brigantine** n naut brigantin m

**bright** adj brillant, vif (f vive); (shiny) luisant; (light) clair; intelligent, doué

**brighten** vt faire briller; fig ranimer, raviver; vi s'animer; (weather) s'éclaircir

**brightness** n éclat m, brillant m; intelligence f; vivacité f

**brill** n zool barbue f

**brilliance** n éclat m, brillant m; intelligence f; excellence f

**brilliant** adj brillant, éclatant, scintillant

**brilliantine** n brillantine f

**brim** n bord m; vi être plein à déborder; ~ **over** déborder

**brimful** adj plein à déborder; tout à fait plein

**brimstone** n soufre m; bibl **fire and** ~ les feux mpl de l'enfer

**brine** n saumure f

**bring** vt (person, animal) amener, faire venir, conduire; (object) apporter; (cause) causer, entraîner, engendrer; persuader; ~ **about** causer; ~ **back** (memories) rappeler; (person) ramener; ~ **down** abattre; faire tomber; ~ **forward** avancer; (figures) reporter; ~ **in** (money) rapporter; coll ~ **off** réussir; ~ **on** causer; ~ **out** (qualities) faire valoir; (book) publier; (emphasize) souligner; ~ **round** ranimer; rallier; ~ **to** naut mettre en panne; med ranimer; ~ **up** soulever; (children) élever; (idea) avancer; (food) vomir; naut mettre en panne

**brink** n bord m

**briny** n coll obs mer f; adj saumâtre

**brio** n brio m

**briquette** n briquette f

**brisk** adj vif (f vive); alerte, animé; (business, trade) actif -ive; mil (fire) nourri; vt animer, activer

**brisket** n cul poitrine f

**bristle** n poil m; vi (animal) se hérisser; fig se fâcher; (problems) être rempli

**Bristol-board** n bristol m

**Britain** n Grande-Bretagne f

**Britannia** n metall métal anglais; poet Albion f

**Britannic** adj britannique

**British** npl Anglais mpl, Britanniques mpl; adj britannique

**Britisher** n US Anglais -e

**Briton** n Anglais -e; hist Celte, Breton -onne

**buck**

**Brittany** n Bretagne f
**brittle** adj fragile
**broach** n mech foret m, perçoir m; (leather) alène f; cul broche f; vt entamer, ouvrir; percer; fig aborder, entamer
**broad** n sl poule f; adj large, vaste, étendu; (accent) fort, prononcé; fig clair, manifeste; tolérant; (improper) sale, grivois; ~ **bean** fève f; **have a ~ back** avoir bon dos; coll **it's as ~ as it's long** c'est kif-kif, cela revient au même
**broadcast** n rad transmission f, émission f; vt rad diffuser, émettre; fig diffuser, répandre; (seed) semer à la volée; adj rad diffusé; fig diffusé, répandu; (seed) semé à la volée
**broadcaster** n quelqu'un qui parle à la radio; (announcer) speaker m (f speakerine), annonceur m
**broadcasting** n radiodiffusion f; télévision f
**broaden** vt élargir; vi s'élargir
**broad-minded** adj large d'esprit, tolérant
**broadsheet** n placard m, affiche f
**broadside** n naut (salvo) bordée f; fig sortie f, invective f; ~ **on** naut par le travers
**brocade** n brocart m; vt brocher
**broccoli** n brocoli m
**brochure** n brochure f, dépliant m
**broil** vt cul griller; fig cuire, rôtir
**broiler** n cul gril m; cul poulet m à rôtir
**broke** adj coll fauché
**broken** adj brisé, cassé; (ground) accidenté; (speech) incorrect, défectueux -euse; fig brisé, rompu; (humble) ruiné; (voice) mué
**broken-down** adj délabré; med en panne; fig infirme
**broken-hearted** adj au cœur brisé, inconsolable
**broker** n courtier m; brocanteur m
**brokerage** n courtage m
**broking** n courtage m
**bromide** n chem bromure f; sédatif m; fig (person) raseur -euse; (remark) platitude f
**bromine** n chem brome m
**bronchial** adj bronchique
**bronchitis** n bronchite f
**broncho-pneumonia** n bronco-pneumonie f
**brontosaurus** n brontosaure m
**bronze** n bronze m; ~ **age** âge m de bronze; vt bronzer; vi se bronzer
**brooch** n broche f
**brood** n (birds) couvée f, nichée f; (children) nichée f, coll couvée f; vi (hen) couver; fig couver, ruminer, broyer du noir; ~ **on (over)** ruminer
**broody** adj (hen) prête à couver; fig cafardeux -euse

**¹brook** n ruisseau m
**²brook** vt supporter, tolérer
**broom** n balai m; bot genêt m; **a new ~ sweeps clean** tout nouveau tout beau
**broomstick** n manche m à balai
**broth** n bouillon m
**brothel** n bordel m
**brother** n frère m; camarade m, compagnon m
**brotherhood** n fraternité f, confraternité f; eccles confrérie f
**brother-in-law** n beau-frère m ( pl beaux-frères)
**brotherly** adj fraternel -elle
**brow** n sourcil m; front m; (hill) sommet m
**browbeat** vt malmener, rudoyer, rabrouer
**brown** n brun m; adj brun; (person) bronzé, hâlé; ~ **bread** pain bis; ~ **study** rêverie f; vt brunir; (person) bronzer; cul dorer; coll ~ **ed off** cafardeux -euse
**brownish** adj brunâtre
**browse** vi brouter; (book) lire au hasard; (bookshop) bouquiner
**bruise** n contusion f, ecchymose f; coll bleu m; vt meurtrir, contusionner; vi être meurtri, se meurtrir
**bruit** vt ébruiter
**brunette** n brune f
**brunt** n choc m; attaque principale
**brush** n brosse f; coup m de brosse; (painter) pinceau m; elect balai m; (undergrowth) broussailles fpl; (verbal) prise f de bec; mil + fig escarmouche f; ~ **work** (painter) peinture f; **shaving ~** blaireau m; vt brosser; effleurer; ~ **aside** écarter; ~ **away** balayer; coll ~ **off** liquider; ~ **up** donner un coup de brosse à; réviser; fig rafraîchir; vi ~ **past** frôler en passant
**brush-off** n coll refus m
**brushwood** n broussailles fpl
**brusque** adj brusque
**brusqueness** n brusquerie f
**Brussels** n Bruxelles m; ~ **sprouts** choux mpl de Bruxelles
**brutal** adj brutal
**brutality** n brutalité f, férocité f
**brutalize** vt abrutir; brutaliser
**brute** n brute f; coll salaud m; adj brutal; ~ **force** vive force
**bubble** n bulle f; fig chimère f; vi faire des bulles; ~ **over** bouillonner
**bubbly** n coll obs champagne m; adj plein de bulles, pétillant
**bubo** n med bubon m
**bubonic** adj bubonique
**buccaneer** n flibustier m
**buck** n daim m, chevreuil m; mâle m (du lapin, du lièvre, de l'antilope, du chamois, etc); fig dandy m; coll US dollar m;

381

*sl* **pass the ~** esquiver une obligation; *vt*
*coll* **~ s/o up** remonter qn, encourager
qn; *vi* (horse) ruer; *coll* **~ up** se hâter
**bucket** *n* seau *m*; (dredger) godet *m*; *sl*
**kick the ~** mourir, crever; *vt* (horse)
surmener; *vi* **~ about** être ballotté
**bucketful** *n* plein seau
**bucket-shop** *n* bureau *m* de courtier
marron
**buckle** *n* boucle *f*; *vt* boucler; *vi* (bend)
se voiler; *coll* **~ down to** s'y mettre
**buckled** *adj* bouclé; (bent) voilé, faussé
**buckler** *n* bouclier *m*
**buckram** *n* bougran *m*
**buckshee** *n sl* ce qu'on n'a pas payé; *adj*
aux frais de la princesse, à l'œil, gratuit
**buckskin** *n* peau *f* de daim
**buckwheat** *n* sarrasin *m*, blé noir
**bucolic** *adj* bucolique
**bud** *n* bourgeon *m*, bouton *m*; *fig* **nip in
the ~** tuer dans l'œuf; *vt* écussonner;
*vi* bourgeonner
**Buddha** *n* Bouddha *m*
**Buddhism** *n* bouddhisme *m*
**Buddhist** *n* Bouddhiste; *adj* bouddhiste
**budding** *n* bourgeonnement *m*; *adj*
bourgeonnant; *fig* en herbe
**buddy** *n coll US* copain *m*; *sl* pote *m*
**budge** *vt* faire bouger; *vi* bouger
**budgerigar** *n* perruche *f*
**budget** *n* budget *m*; *vi* estimer; **~ for**
inscrire à son budget
**buff** *n* peau *f* de buffle; (colour) chamois
*m*; *coll fig* **to the ~** tout nu (*f* toute
nue); *vt* polir
**buffalo** *n* buffle *m*; bison *m*
¹**buffer** *n* (railway) tampon *m*; pare-
chocs *m*; **~ state** état *m* tampon
²**buffer** *n coll* croulant *m*
¹**buffet** *n* (punch) coup *m* de poing,
bourrade *f*; *fig* malheur *m*, coup *m* du
sort; *vt* souffleter, bourrer de coups;
(waves) **~ed by** ballotté par
²**buffet** *n* (refreshment bar, sideboard)
buffet *m*; **~ car** gril-express *m*; **~
lunch** lunch *m*
**buffeting** *n* série *f* de coups
**buffoon** *n* pitre *m*
**bug** *n zool* punaise *f*; *coll* virus *m*; *coll*
**big ~** grosse légume; *vt* mettre sur
écoute, brancher sur table d'écoute
**bugbear** *n* épouvantail *m*
**bugger** *n leg* sodomite *m*; *coll* idiot *m*;
(silly) crétin *m*; *vt leg* sodomiser; *sl*
enculer; *vi sl* **~ off** foutre le camp
**buggery** *n leg* sodomie *f*
**bugle** *n mil* clairon *m*
**bugler** *n mil* clairon *m*
**build** *n* (person) carrure *f*, charpente *f*;
structure *f*; *vt* bâtir, construire, élever;
*fig* bâtir, établir, développer; *fig* **~ on**
se baser sur; **~ up** développer, amé-

liorer, fortifier; construire, bâtir
**builder** *n* entrepreneur *m* (en bâtiments)
**building** *n* bâtiment *m*, édifice *m*, immeuble *m*; **~ society** société *f* qui
accorde des prêts pour l'achat d'une
maison (d'un appartement)
**build-up** *n coll mil* préparatifs *mpl* pour
une offensive; *coll fig* campagne *f* publicitaire
**built-in** *adj* (cupboards, etc) encastré; *fig*
garanti
**built-up** *adj* **~ area** agglomération *f*
**bulb** *n bot* bulbe *m*, oignon *m*; *elect*
ampoule *f*
**bulbous** *adj* bulbeux -euse
**bulge** *n* bosse *f*; *mil* saillant *m*; *vi*
bomber
**bulging** *adj* gonflé, archi-plein
**bulk** *n* masse *f*; (person) corpulence *f*;
volume *m*; majeure partie; **in ~** en
gros; *naut* en vrac); *vt* entasser (en
vrac); *vi* tenir de la place; *fig* sembler
important, apparaître signifiant
**bulkhead** *n naut* cloison *f*
**bulky** *adj* encombrant, volumineux
-euse; (person) corpulent
¹**bull** *n* taureau *m*; mâle *m* (de l'éléphant,
de la baleine, etc); *comm* haussier *m*;
(target) noir *m*, mille *m*; *mil sl* astiquage *m*; *sl* baliverne *fpl*; **~ in a china
shop** éléphant *m* dans un magasin de
porcelaine; **take the ~ by the horns**
prendre le taureau par les cornes; *vt*
essayer de faire hausser le cours de; *vi*
jouer à la hausse
²**bull** *n eccles* bulle *f*
**bull-calf** *n* jeune taureau *m*
**bulldog** *n* bouledogue *m*
**bulldoze** *vt* passer au bulldozer; *fig US*
intimider, persuader de force
**bulldozer** *n* bulldozer *m*
**bullet** *n* balle *f*
**bulletin** *n* bulletin *m*, communiqué *m*
**bullet-proof** *adj* blindé
**bullfight** *n* course *f* de taureaux, corrida *f*
**bullfighter** *n* matador *m*, torero *m*
**bullfinch** *n orni* bouvreuil *m*
**bullfrog** *n* grosse grenouille (d'Amérique)
**bullion** *n* (gold) or *m* en barre, or *m* en
lingot(s); (silver) argent *m* en barre,
argent *m* en lingot(s)
**bullish** *adj comm* tendant à la hausse
**bullock** *n* bœuf *m*
**bull-ring** *n* arène *f* (de corrida), arènes
*fpl*
**bull's-eye** *n* (target) mille *m*; (sweet)
bonbon *m* à la menthe; *bui* œil-de-
bœuf *m* (*pl* œils-de-bœuf); **get a ~**
faire mouche
**bullshit** *n sl mil* astiquage *m*; *sl* balivernes *fpl*

¹**bully** n tyranneau m; vt brimer, persécuter, intimider

²**bully** adj coll ar épatant, sensas invar

³**bully (beef)** n coll singe m; (viande f de) bœuf m en conserve

**bulrush** n jonc m

**bulwark** n rempart m; naut pavois m; brise-lames m invar; fig défense f; protecteur m

¹**bum** n sl fesses fpl, cul m

²**bum** n sl US (idler) flemmard m; (vagrant) clochard m; vt sl US écornifler; vi sl US vivre aux crochets des autres; ~ around fainéanter

**bumble-bee** n bourdon m

**bumf** n sl torche-cul m; coll paperasses fpl

**bump** n choc m, coup m; bosse f; vt (strike) cogner; (bump into) tamponner; vi (car) être cahoté; sl ~ off descendre, démolir

**bumper** n mot pare-chocs m invar; plein verre; adj abondant

**bumpkin** n pej péquenot m

**bumptious** adj satisfait, suffisant, arrogant

**bumpy** adj (surface) bosselé; (ride) cahoteux -euse

**bun** n (espèce f de) brioche f; (hair) chignon m; coll have a ~ in the oven avoir un polichinelle dans le tiroir

**bunch** n groupe m; (flowers) bouquet m; (keys) trousseau m; (grapes) grappe f; sl bande f; vt grouper; nouer; vi se grouper, se serrer

**bundle** n ballot m; paquet m; (papers) liasse f; (asparagus, carrots) botte f; vt empaqueter, emballer; ~ away (off, out) expédier, renvoyer; vi coll ~ away décamper; ~ in s'entasser

**bung** n bonde f; vt mettre une bonde à; sl jeter; ~ up (pipe) obstruer; ~ed up (eyes) gonflé; (nose) bouché

**bungalow** n bungalow m

**bungle** vt bâcler, brouiller; vi travailler d'une façon incompétente

**bunion** n oignon m

¹**bunk** n (ship, train) couchette f; sl do a ~ foutre le camp; vi sl foutre le camp; ~ down se coucher

²**bunk** n sl balivernes fpl

**bunker** n naut soute f à charbon; mil bunker m, casemate f; vt naut (coal, oil) mettre en soute; (coal) charbonner; (oil) mazouter

**bunkum** n coll sornettes fpl, balivernes fpl

**bunny** n (child's language) lapin m

**Bunsen-burner** n bec m Bunsen

¹**bunting** n (cloth) étamine f; (flag) drapeau m; collect drapeaux mpl

²**bunting** n orni bruant m

**buoy** n naut bouée f; vt baliser; fig ~ up soutenir, épauler

**buoyancy** n flottabilité f; fig gaieté f, animation f; comm (prices) fermeté f

**buoyant** n flottable; fig gai, animé; comm (prices) ferme

¹**bur(r)** n bot bardane f; coll (person) crampon m

²**bur(r)** n grasseyement m

**burble** n gloussement m; vi glousser, bafouiller

**burden** n fardeau m, faix m; naut tonnage m; fig fardeau m, charge f; ~ of proof obligation f de faire la preuve; beast of ~ bête f de somme; vt charger; opprimer

**burdensome** adj lourd, pesant

**burdock** n bot bardane f

**bureau** n (desk) bureau m; US commode f; (office) bureau m

**bureaucracy** n bureaucratie f

**bureaucrat** n bureaucrate

**bureaucratic** adj bureaucratique

**burglar** n cambrioleur -euse

**burglary** n cambriolage m; leg cambriolage m nocturne

**burgle** vt cambrioler

**Burgundy** n geog Bourgogne f; (wine) bourgogne m

**burial** n enterrement m

**burial-ground** n cimetière m

**burin** n burin m

**burlap** n toile f d'emballage

**burlesque** n burlesque m, parodie f; adj burlesque; vt satiriser, parodier

**burly** adj costaud, solide

¹**burn** n ruisseau m

²**burn** n brûlure f; vt brûler; consumer; (set fire to) incendier, mettre la flamme à; (acid) corroder; (put to death) brûler vif (f vive), faire mourir sur le bûcher; ~ one's fingers se brûler les doigts; vi brûler, être en flammes, flamber; (feel hot) avoir très chaud; sl ~ up se fâcher tout rouge

**burner** n brûleur m, bec m

**burning** n incendie m; adj brûlant, enflammé, en feu; fig ardent, brûlant; ~ bush buisson ardent

**burnish** n lustre m; cati m; vt brunir, polir

**burnt** adj brûlé; (colour) jaune foncé

**burp** n sl rot m; vi sl roter

**burr** n see bur(r)

**burrow** n terrier m; vt creuser

**bursar** n (school, university) économe, intendant -e

**bursary** n (grant) bourse f; bureau m de l'économe

**burst** n éclatement m, explosion f; (pipe) fuite f; mil (fire) rafale f; (flames) jaillissement m; fig élan m; (enthusiasm) accès *m*; (applause) tonnerre *m*; *sp* (speed) sprint *m*, emballage *m*; *vt* crever; (explode) faire sauter; (banks) déborder; (break) rompre; ~ **in** (door, etc) enfoncer; *vi* sauter, éclater, exploser; crever; déborder; ~ **into flower** s'épanouir

**burton** *n sl* **gone for a** ~ mort, crevé

**bury** *vt* ensevelir, enterrer, inhumer; dissimuler, celer; (quarrel) oublier; ~ **oneself in** se plonger dans; ~ **the hatchet** se réconcilier

**bus** *n* autobus *m*; (coach) car *m*; *coll mot* bagnole *f*; ~ **station** gare routière; *vt US* transporter en car; *vi coll* aller en autobus

¹**bush** *n* buisson *m*; (undergrowth) broussailles *fpl*; (Africa, Australia) brousse *f*; (Corsica) maquis *m*; ~ **telegraph** téléphone *m* arabe; **beat about the** ~ tergiverser; *vi* pousser en broussailles

²**bush** *n eng* bague *f*

**bushel** *n* boisseau *m*; **hide one's light under a** ~ être trop modeste

**bushy** *adj* broussailleux -euse, touffu

**business** *n* (task) affaire *f*; (trade) affaires *fpl*; métier *m*, travail *m*, profession *f*; (commercial undertaking) commerce *m*, maison *f*, entreprise *f*; *fig* affaire *f*, question sérieuse; *theat* jeux *mpl* de scène

**businesslike** *adj* méthodique, efficace

**businessman** *n* homme *m* d'affaires, businessman *m*

**busman** *n* (driver) conducteur *m* d'autobus; (conductor) receveur *m* d'autobus

¹**bust** *n* buste *m*; *anat* poitrine *f*; (woman) gorge *f*

²**bust** *vt sl* briser, rompre; *sl* (catch) prendre sur le fait; (arrest) arrêter; *adj sl* fauché

**bustard** *n zool* outarde *f*

¹**bustle** *n* tournure *f*

²**bustle** *n* remue-ménage *m invar*; *vt* bousculer; activer; *vi* s'affairer, s'empresser, se démener

**bust-up** *n sl* bagarre *f*

**busy** *n sl* flic *m*; *adj* occupé, affairé; (day) chargé; (street, town, etc) animé; *pej* officieux -ieuse, important; *vt* ~ **one-self with** s'activer à, se mêler de

**busybody** *n* officieux -ieuse; *sl* emmerdeur -euse

**but** *n* mais *m*; **ifs and** ~ **s** les si et les mais; *adv* seulement, ne ... que; **could you** ~ **understand!** si seulement vous pouviez comprendre!; **it is** ~ **a short distance away** ce n'est qu'à deux pas d'ici; *prep* sauf, excepté; sans, sinon; **no one** ~ **you could do that** personne sauf (excepté) vous ne pourrait faire

cela; **no one came** ~ **him of course** bien sûr personne n'est venu sinon lui; **you could have gone** ~ **for me** sans moi vous seriez parti; *conj* mais

**butane** *n* butane *m*

**butch** *n sl* gouine *f*; homosexuel -uelle actif (*f* active)

**butcher** *n* boucher -ère; *fig* boucher -ère, assassin -e; *vt* massacrer

**butchery** *n* (slaughter-house) abattoir *m*; métier *m* de boucher; (massacre) boucherie *f*

**butler** *n* maître d'hôtel *m*

¹**butt** *n* bout *m*; (rifle) crosse *f*; (cigarette) mégot *m*; *coll US* derrière *m*

²**butt** *n* barrique *f*

³**butt** *n mil* ouvrage *m* de terre devant les cibles d'un champ de tir; *fig* bouc *m* émissaire, victime *f*; *mil* ~ **s** champ *m* de tir

⁴**butt** *n* coup *m* de corne, coup *m* de tête; *vt* encorner, donner un coup de corne (de tête) à; *vi* donner des cornes, donner de la tête; ~ **in** intervenir, dire son mot

**butt-end** *n* extrémité inférieure, gros bout

**butter** *n* beurre *m*; *fig* flatterie *f*; *vt* beurrer; *fig* ~ **s/o up** flatter qn

**buttercup** *n* bouton d'or *m*

**butter-dish** *n* beurrier *m*

**butterfly** *n* papillon *m*; *fig* dandy *m*; *adj* frivole

**buttermilk** *n* babeurre *m*, lait *m* de beurre

**butter-muslin** *n* étamine *f*

**butterscotch** *n* (espèce *f* de) caramel *m* au beurre

**buttock** *n* fesse *f*

**button** *n* bouton *m*; ~ **mushroom** champignon *m* de Paris; *vt* boutonner; *vi* se boutonner; *coll* ~ **up** ne plus rien dire

**button-hole** *n* boutonnière *f*; fleur *f*; *vt* faire une boutonnière à; *fig* retenir, importuner; *coll* cramponner

**buttress** *n* contrefort *m*; *fig* pilier *m*, soutien *m*; (mountain) contrefort *m*; **flying** ~ arc-boutant *m* (*pl* arcs-boutants)

**buxom** *adj* plantureux -euse, dodu, bien en chair

**buy** *n coll* achat *m*; (bargain) occasion *f*; *vt* acheter; acquérir; *sl* accepter, adapter; ~ **dear** payer cher; ~ **in** racheter; ~ **s/o off** acheter qn, soudoyer qn; ~ **s/o out** acheter les droits de qn; ~ **up** acheter en bloc

**buyer** *n* acheteur -euse; acquéreur *m*

**buzz** *n* bourdonnement *m*; *coll* (rumour) canard *m*, bruit *m*; *coll* (telephone) coup *m* de fil; *vt coll* (rumour) répandre;

*coll* lancer; *coll* téléphoner; *aer* frôler; *vi* bourdonner; *coll* ~ **off** se barrer, filer
**buzzard** *n* buse *f*, busard *m*
**buzzer** *n* (factory) sirène *f*; *elect* vibrateur *m*
**by** *adv* près, auprès; ~ **the** ~ à propos; **put** ~ mettre de côté; *prep* par, de; près de; (time) à, pendant, vers; (measure) à, de, sur; ~ **and** ~ bientôt; ~ **chance** par hasard; ~ **day** pendant le jour; ~ **far** de beaucoup; ~ **means of** au moyen de; ~ **oneself** tout seul (*f* toute seule); ~ **the minute** à la minute; ~ **then** avant ce moment; ~ **the ton** à la tonne; **near** ~ tout près; **ten** ~ **six** dix sur six
**by-election** *n* élection partielle

**bygone** *n* événement passé; **let** ~ **s be** ~ **s!** oubliez et pardonnez!; *adj* du passé, d'autrefois, du temps jadis
**by-law** *n leg* arrêté administratif local
**by-pass** *n* mot bretelle *f* de contournement; voie *f* de dérivation, by-pass *m*; *mech* conduit *m* de dérivation; *elect* dérivation *f*; *vt* contourner, éviter
**bypath** *n* chemin écarté
**by-play** *n theat* jeux *mpl* de scène en aparté
**by-product** *n* sous-produit *m*, dérivé *m*
**byre** *n* étable *f*
**bystander** *n* spectateur -trice
**by-way** *n* route *f* secondaire; *fig* à-côté *m*
**by-word** *n* dicton *m*; objet *m* de dérision; **become a** ~ passer en proverbe

# C

**cab** *n ar* fiacre *m*; taxi *m*; (railway, lorry) cabine *f*; ~ **rank** station *f* de taxis
**cabal** *n* cabale *f*, intrigue *f*; *vi* comploter, intriguer
**cabala, cabbala** *n* cabale *f*
**cabaret** *n obs* estaminet *m*, bistrot *m*; cabaret *m*, café-concert *m* (*pl* cafés-concerts), boîte *f* de nuit
**cabbage** *n* chou *m*; *coll* lourdaud -e; ~ **butterfly** papillon blanc
**cabby** *n obs coll* chauffeur *m* de taxi
**cab-driver** *n* chauffeur *m* de taxi
**cabin** *n* cabine *f*; (hut) cabane *f*; *naut* ~ **class** deuxième classe *f*
**cabin-boy** *n* mousse *m*
**cabinet** *n* cabinet *m*, bureau *m*; (furniture) cabinet *m*; *pol* conseil *m* des ministres; **filing** ~ classeur *m*
**cabinet-maker** *n* ébéniste *m*
**cable** *n* câble *m*; *naut* (distance) encablure *f*; *vt* + *vi* télégraphier, câbler
**cablegram** *n* télégramme *m*
**cable-railway** *n* funiculaire *m*; (carried on pylons) téléférique *m*
**caboodle** *n coll* **the whole** ~ tout le bazar
**cabotage** *n naut* cabotage *m*
**cab-rank** *n* station *f* de taxis
**cacao** *n* cacao *m*
**cache** *n* cache *f*; cachette *f*; objet caché;

*vt* cacher, mettre en réserve
**cachet** *n* cachet *m*
**cachou** *n* cachou *m*
**cackle** *n* caquet *m*; gloussement *m*; **cut the** ~! en voilà assez!; *vi* caqueter; glousser
**cacophonous** *adj* discordant
**cacophony** *n* discordance *f*
**cactus** *n* cactus *m*
**cad** *n* goujat *m*, malotru *m*
**cadaver** *n* corps *m*, mort -e
**cadaveric, cadaverous** *adj* cadavérique; (pale) blême
**caddie, caddy** *n* (golf) cadet *m*, caddie *m*
**caddish** *n coll* grossier -ière, de goujat
**caddy** *n* boîte *f* à thé
**cadence** *n* cadence *f*
**cadet** *n* cadet *m*; *mil* aspirant *m*
**cadge** *vt* écornifler, quémander; *vi* quémander
**cadger** *n* écornifleur -euse
**cadmium** *n chem* cadmium *m*
**cadre** *n* cadre *m*
**caecum** *n anat* caecum *m*
**Caesarean, Caesarian** *n surg* césarienne *f*; *adj surg* (operation) césarienne; *hist* césarien -ienne
**caesura** *n* césure *f*
**café** *n* café *m*, café-restaurant *m* (*pl*

cafés-restaurants)

**cafeteria** *n* cafétéria *f*, cafeteria *f*, (restaurant *m*) libre-service *m* (*pl* libres-services); *coll* self *m*

**caffeine** *n chem* caféine; **~-free** décaféiné

**caftan, kaftan** *n* caftan *m*, cafetan *m*

**cage** *n* cage *f*; *vt* mettre en cage; encager

**cagey** *adj coll* prudent, finaud

**caginess** *n coll* prudence *f*, finauderie *f*

**cahoot** *n coll* **in ~ s** de mèche

**cairn** *n* cairn *m*

**Cairo** *n* Le Caire

**caisson** *n* caisson *m*

**cajole** *vt* cajoler

**cajolery** *n* cajolerie *f*

**cake** *n* gâteau *m*, galette *f*; *agr* tourteau *m*; (soap) pain *m*; *coll* **a piece of ~** du gâteau; *coll* **take the ~** être la fin des haricots; *vt* durcir, coaguler, couvrir d'une croûte; *vi* se coaguler, faire croûte

**calamine** *n chem* calamine *f*

**calamitous** *adj* calamiteux -euse

**calamity** *n* calamité *f*, catastrophe *f*; malheur *m*

**calcareous** *adj* calcaire

**calcedony** *n see* **chalcedony**

**calcification** *n* calcification *f*

**calcify** *vt* calcifier; *vi* se calcifier

**calcine** *vt* calciner; *vi* se calciner

**calcium** *n chem* calcium *m*

**calculable** *adj* calculable

**calculate** *vt* calculer; régler, organiser; *vi* calculer, faire des calculs; **~ on** compter sur

**calculated** *adj* calculé; réfléchi, délibéré

**calculating** *adj* prudent; calculateur -trice; **~ machine** calculatrice *f*

**calculation** *n* calcul *m*

**calculator** *n* (person) calculateur -trice; (machine) calculatrice *f*

**calculous** *adj med* calculeux -euse

**calculus** *n med* + *math* calcul *m*

**calendar** *n* calendrier *m*; *leg* rôle *m*; *vt* classer, indexer

**calends, kalends** *npl Rom hist* calendes *fpl*; **at the Greek ~** aux calendes grecques

¹**calf** *n* (*pl* **calves**) veau *m*; (seal, whale, buffalo, etc) petit *m*; *fig* blanc-bec *m* (*pl* blancs-becs); (leather) veau *m*, box(-calf) *m*

²**calf** *n* (*pl* **calves**) (muscle) mollet *m*

**calfskin** *n* cuir *m* de veau

**calibrate** *vt* calibrer

**calibration** *n* calibrage *m*

**calibre** *n* calibre *m*

**calico** *n* calicot *m*

**calif, caliph** *n* calife *m*

**calipers** *n see* **callipers**

**calisthenics, callisthenics** *npl* gymnas-

tique *f* rythmique

**calix** *n* (*pl* **calices**) *biol* calice *m*

¹**calk** *n* crampon *m* (à glace); *vt* ferrer

²**calk** *vt* calquer, décalquer

³**calk** *vt see* **caulk**

**call** *n* (shout) cri *m*; appel *m*; appel *m* téléphonique, communication *f*; vocation *f*; *leg* sommation *f*; courte visite; (need) besoin *m*; (cards) demande *f*; *theat* (curtain) rappel *m*; *comm* appel *m* de fonds; *mil* sonnerie *f*; *naut* escale *f*; *comm* **~ option** option *f*; **on ~** disponible, prêt; *comm* payable à vue; **within ~** tout près; *vt* appeler, faire venir; (wake) réveiller; (cards) annoncer; appeler par téléphone; (meeting) convoquer; **~ a halt to** mettre fin à; **~ aside** prendre à part; **~ attention to** attirer l'attention sur; **~ for** demander, réclamer; **~ forth** faire naître, soulever; **~ in** faire entrer; *comm* faire rentrer, rappeler; **~ in question** mettre en question; **~ into play** faire agir; **~ it a day** cesser le travail pour la journée; **~ names** dénigrer, bafouer; **~ off** annuler; **~ out** (duel) provoquer; (workers) faire mettre en grève; *mil* faire intervenir; **~ over** faire appel; **~ over the coals** réprimander; *eccles* **~ the banns** proclamer les bans; **~ to mind** rappeler; **~ to the bar** inscrire au barreau; *mil* **~ up** appeler, mobiliser; *vi* appeler, crier; (visit) passer; *naut* faire escale; **~ out** appeler

**call-box** *n* cabine *f* téléphonique

**caller** *n* visiteur -euse; (telephone) personne *f* qui appelle

**call-girl** *n* prostituée *f* qu'on retient par téléphone, call-girl *f*

**calligraphist** *n* calligraphe

**calligraphy** *n* calligraphie *f*

**calling** *n* profession *f*, vocation *f*; (meeting) convocation *f*

**callipers, calipers** *n* compas *m*

**callosity** *n* callosité *f*

**callous** *adj* (skin) calleux -euse; *fig* dur, brutal, insensible

**callousness** *n* dureté *f*, brutalité *f*, insensibilité *f*

**callow** *adj zool* sans plumes; *fig* naïf -ïve, inexpérimenté

**call-up** *n mil* appel *m*

**callus** *n med* cal *m* (*pl* **cals**), durillon *m*

**calm** *n* calme *m*, tranquillité *f*; *adj* calme, tranquille; *vt* calmer; *vi* se calmer; **~ down** s'apaiser, se calmer

**calmness** *n* calme *m*, sang-froid *m invar*

**calomel** *n med* calomel *m*

**calorie** *n* calorie *f*

**calorific** *adj* calorifique

**calorimeter** *n phys* calorimètre *m*

**calumniate** *vt* calomnier

calumniator *n* calomniateur -trice
calumnious *adj* calomnieux -ieuse
calumny *n* calomnie *f*
calvary *n* calvaire *m*
calve *vt zool* mettre bas; *vi* vêler
Calvinism *n* calvinisme *m*
Calvinist *n* + *adj* calviniste
calypso *n* calypso *m*
calyx *n* (*pl* calyces) *bot* calice *m*
cam *n mech* came *f*
camber *n* (road) bombement *m*; *archi* cambrure *f*; *vt* bomber; cambrer; *vi* se bomber; se cambrer
Cambrian *adj* gallois; *geol* cambrien -ienne
cambric *n* batiste *f*
camel *n* chameau *m* (*f* chamelle); *naut* chameau *m*; (colour) couleur *f* fauve; *mil* Camel Corps = méharistes *mpl*
camel-driver *n* chamelier *m*
camel-hair *n* poil *m* de chameau
camellia *n* camélia *m*
cameo *n* camée *m*
camera *n* appareil *m* de photo; (film, television) caméra *f*; leg in ~ à huis clos
camisole *n obs* camisole *f*
camomile *n bot* camomille *f*; ~ tea camomille *f*
camouflage *n* camouflage *m*; *vt* camoufler
¹camp *n* camp *m*, campement *m*; *fig* vie *f* militaire; faction *f*, parti *m*; strike ~ lever le camp; *vi* camper; go ~ing faire du camping
²camp *adj sl* affecté, efféminé; *theat* cabotin; *vi sl theat* ~ it up faire le cabotin, cabotiner
campaign *n mil* campagne *f*; *vi* faire campagne, militer
campaigner *n* militant -e; *mil* old ~ vétéran *m*
campanile *n* campanile *m*
campanology *n* art *m* de sonner les cloches; art *m* de la fonte des cloches
campanula *n bot* campanule *f*
camp-bed *n* lit *m* de camp
camp-chair *n* chaise pliante
camper *n* campeur -euse
camp-follower *n mil hist* cantinière *f*; personne *f* qui vit aux crochets d'une armée; prostituée *f*
camphor *n* camphre *m*
camphorated *adj* camphré
camping *n* camping *m*; ~ site (terrain *m* de) camping *m*
camp-stool *n* pliant *m*
campus *n* campus *m*
camshaft *n mech* arbre *m* à cames
¹can *n* boîte *f* en fer blanc, boîte *f* de conserve; (milk, petrol) bidon *m*; (oil) burette *f*; (beer) canette *f*; *sl* carry the

~ payer les pots cassés; *vt* mettre en conserve; *coll rad* enregistrer; *sl* ~ it! ta gueule!
²can *v aux* pouvoir; (allow oneself to) se permettre de; avoir la permission de; (know how to) savoir
Canada *n* Canada *m*
canal *n* canal *m*
canalization *n* canalisation *f*
canalize *vt* canaliser
canary *n* canari *m*, serin *m*; *adj* ~ yellow jaune serin *invar*
canasta *n* canasta *f*
can-can *n* cancan *m*
cancel *vt* annuler; oblitérer; (delete) barrer, rayer; (arrangement) décommander; (will) révoquer; *vi* ~ out s'annuler
cancellation *n* annulation *f*; contre-ordre *m*
cancer *n* cancer *m*; Cancer Cancer *m*
cancerous *adj med* cancéreux -euse
candelabrum, candelabra *n* candélabre *m*
candid *adj* franc (*f* franche)
candidate *n* candidat -e, postulant -e
candidature *n* candidature *f*
candied *adj cul* candi *adj m*, confit
candle *n* (wax) bougie *f*; (tallow) chandelle *f*; *eccles* cierge *m*; burn the ~ at both ends brûler la chandelle par les deux bouts; not fit to hold a ~ to très inférieur à; *coll* the game is not worth the ~ ça ne vaut pas le coup
candlelight *n* lumière *f* d'une chandelle (des chandelles)
candlepower *n obs phys* bougie *f*
candlestick *n* chandelier *m*
candour *n* candeur *f*, franchise *f*, sincérité *f*
candy *n* sucre *m* candi; *US* bonbon(s) *m*(*pl*); *vt* confire, candir; *vi* se candir
candy-floss *n* barbe *f* à papa
cane *n* canne *f*, bâton *m*; férule *f*; (plant) tige; get the ~ être fouetté; *vt* fouetter; (chair) canner
canine *adj* canine *f*; *adj* canin
caning *n* volée *f* de coups de bâton
canister *n* (tea, coffee, etc) boîte *f* métallique
canker *n med* ulcère *m*, chancre *m*; gangrène *f*; *bot* + *fig* chancre *m*; *vt* ulcérer, ronger, gangrener; *vi* se gangrener
cankered *adj fig* ulcéré, aigri
cannabis *n* marihuana *f*, marijuana *f*; cannabis *m*
canned *adj* en conserve; *coll mus* enregistré; *coll* ivre, parti
cannery *n* conserverie *f*
cannibal *n* cannibale
cannibalism *n* cannibalisme *m*
cannibalize *vt mech* démonter pour

obtain des pièces de rechange
¹**cannon** *n* canon *m*; ~ **fodder** chair *f* à canon
²**cannon** *n* (billiards) carambolage *m*; *vi* caramboler; *fig* ~ **into** se heurter contre, heurter
**cannonade** *n* canonade *f*; *vi* tirer un canon contre
**cannon-ball** *n hist* boulet *m* (de canon)
**cannot** = **can not** *see* **can**
**canny** *adj* rusé, finaud
**canoe** *n* canoë *m*; (Africa, S.E. Asia) pirogue *f*; *vi* faire du canoë
**canoeist** *n* canoéiste
¹**canon** *n* (church law) canon *m*; critère *m*, règle *f*; *mus* canon *m*; œuvre *m* authentique
²**canon** *n* (cathedral) chanoine *m*
**canonical** *adj* canonique
**canonicals** *npl* vêtements *mpl* sacerdotaux
**canonization** *n eccles* canonisation *f*
**canonize** *vt eccles* canoniser
**canonry** *n* canonicat *m*
**canoodle** *vt sl* peloter; *vi sl* se peloter
**can-opener** *n* ouvre-boîte(s) *m*
**canopy** *n* baldaquin *m*, dais *m*, ciel *m* de lit; *fig* voûte *f*; *vt* surmonter d'un baldaquin, d'un dais, etc
¹**cant** *n* surface inclinée; inclinaison *f*; (bevel) biseau *m*; (movement) poussée déviatrice; *vt* pencher, incliner; biseauter; *vi* pencher, s'incliner
²**cant** *n* jargon *m*; hypocrisie *f*; *vi* employer un jargon; parler hypocritement
**cantaloup(e)** *n* cantaloup *m*
**cantankerous** *adj* revêche, hargneux -euse
**cantankerousness** *n* hargne *f*, mauvaise humeur
**cantata** *n mus* cantate *f*
**canteen** *n* cantine *f*; *mil* (mess-tin) gamelle *f*; *mil* (water-bottle) bidon *m*; (cutlery) ménagère *f*
**canter** *n* canter *m*; **win in a** ~ gagner facilement; *coll* arriver dans un fauteuil; *vt* mener au canter; *vi* aller au canter
**canticle** *n* cantique *m*
**cantilever** *n eng* cantilever *m*; *adj* cantilever *invar*
**canto** *n* chant *m*
**canton** *n* canton *m*
**cantonment** *n mil* cantonnement *m*
**canvas** *n* grosse toile; (tapestry) canevas *m*; *arts* tableau *m*, toile *f*; *fig* canevas *m*; **under** ~ sous la tente; *naut* sous voiles
**canvass** *n pol* campagne électorale; campagne *f* publicitaire; *vt pol* (elector) solliciter la voix de; (customer) visiter; *vi pol* solliciter des voix; *comm* visiter

la clientèle
**canvassing** *n pol* démarchage électoral
**canyon** *n* cañon *m*
**cap** *n* (baby, lace, bathing) bonnet *m*; (judge, fur) toque *f*; (officer, jockey, schoolboy) casquette *f*; (bottle, tube) capsule *f*; *eccles* calotte *f*; (fountain pen) capuchon *m*; *mot* bouchon *m*; ~ **in hand** humblement; **percussion** ~ amorce *f*; **set one's** ~ **at** jeter son dévolu sur; *vt* (person) coiffer; (bottle) capsuler; *sp* choisir pour l'équipe nationale; couvrir; *fig* surpasser; renchérir sur
**capability** *n* compétence *f*, capacité *f*; **capabilities** moyens *mpl*, possibilités *fpl*
**capable** *adj* capable, compétent; ~ **of** capable de; (likely) susceptible de
**capacious** *adj* spacieux -ieuse, vaste
**capaciousness** *n* grande capacité
**capacity** *n* capacité *f*, faculté *f*; aptitude *f*, talent *m*; (size) capacité *f*, contenance *f*; (position) qualité *f*
¹**cape** *n* cape *f*, pèlerine *f*
²**cape** *n geog* cap *m*, promontoire *m*
¹**caper** *n* (shrub) câprier *m*; *cul* câpre *f*
²**caper** *n* cabriole *f*, entrechat *m*; *vi* cabrioler, gambader
**capillary** *n* capillaire *m*; *adj* capillaire
¹**capital** *n archi* chapiteau *m*
²**capital** *n geog* capitale *f*; (letter) majuscule *f*; *comm* capital *m*, capitaux *mpl*; **working** ~ fonds *mpl* de roulements; *adj* (crime) capital; important, signifiant, essentiel -ielle; (mistake) désastreux -euse, fatal (*pl* fatals); *coll* au poil; *naut* ~ **ship** cuirassé *m*
**capitalism** *n* capitalisme *m*
**capitalist** *n* capitaliste
**capitalization** *n* capitalisation *f*
**capitalize** *vt* capitaliser; *fig* tourner à son avantage
**capitation** *n* capitation *f*
**capitulate** *vi* capituler
**capitulation** *n* capitulation *f*
**capon** *n* chapon *m*
**caprice** *n* caprice *m*
**capricious** *adj* capricieux -ieuse
**capriciousness** *n* caprice *m*, inconstance *f*
**Capricorn** *n* Capricorne *m*
**capsize** *n* chavirement *m*; *vt* faire chavirer; *vi* chavirer
**capstan** *n naut* cabestan *m*
**capsular** *adj* capsulaire
**capsule** *n med* + *anat* capsule *f*; (bottle) capsule *f*
**captain** *n mil* + *sp* + *naut* capitaine *m*; (navy) capitaine *m* de vaisseau; *comm* chef *m*; *vt mil* commander; *fig* diriger
**captaincy** *n mil* grade *m* de capitaine

caption *n* (title-heading) en-tête *m*; (illustration) légende *f*; (film) sous-titre *m*
captious *adj* (person) vétilleux -euse, pointilleux -euse; (argument) critique
captivate *vt* fasciner, captiver, séduire
captivating *adj* fascinant, enchanteur (*f* enchanteresse)
captive *n* captif -ive, prisonnier -ière; *adj* captif -ive, prisonnier -ière
captivity *n* captivité *f*
captor *n* personne *f* qui capture
capture *n* capture *f*, prise *f*; *vt* capturer
car *n* voiture *f*, automobile *f*; (railway) wagon *m*, voiture *f*; ~ **licence** = carte grise; ~ **park** parking *m*; ~ **sleeper train** *m* autocouchettes
carafe *n* carafe *f*
caramel *n* caramel *m*
carat *n* carat *m*
caravan *n* (desert) caravane *f*; (gipsy) roulotte *f*; *mot* caravane *f*
caraway *n* cumin *m*, carvi *m*
carbide *n* chem carbure *m*
carbine *n* carabine *f*
carbohydrate *n* chem hydrate *m* de carbone, glucide *m*
carbolic *adj* chem phénique; ~ **acid** phénol *m*
carbon *n* chem + elect carbone *m*; graphite *m*; (typing) (papier *m*) carbone *m*
carbon-copy *n* double *m* au carbone, carbone *m*
carbonic *adj* chem carbonique
carboniferous *adj* carbonifère
carbonize *vt* carboniser
carborundum *n* carborundum *m*
carboy *n* bonbonne *f*
carbuncle *n* (jewel) escarboucle *f*; (boil) anthrax *m invar*
carburettor, carburetter *n* mot carburateur *m*
carcass, carcase *n* carcasse *f*
carcinoma *n* med carcinome *m*
¹card *n* carte *f*; carte postale; carte *f* de visite; (compass) rose *f* des vents; *coll* (person) numéro *m*, original -e; **get one's ~ s** être licencié; **on the ~ s** probable; **play one's ~ s well** manœuvrer habilement; **put one's ~ s on the table** jouer cartes sur table, jouer franc jeu
²card *n* carde *f*; *vt* carder
cardboard *n* carton *m*; *adj fig* factice; raide
cardiac *adj* cardiaque
cardigan *n* cardigan *m*
¹cardinal *n* eccles cardinal *m*
²cardinal *adj* cardinal; (colour) rouge vif *invar*
card-index *n* fichier *m*, catalogue *m* sur fiches
cardiogram *n* cardiogramme *m*

cardiograph *n* cardiographe *m*
cardiography *n* cardiographie *f*
cardiology *n* cardiologie *f*
cardsharper *n* bonneteur *m*, tricheur -euse
card-table *n* table *f* de jeu
care *n* attention *f*, soin *m*, sollicitude *f*; précaution *f*; (anxiety) souci *m*; ~ **of** aux bons soins de; **take** ~ faire attention, prendre garde; **take** ~ **of** prendre soin de; *vi* se soucier; ~ **for** avoir de l'affection pour, avoir de la sympathie pour; prendre soin de; **I couldn't** ~ **less** je m'en fiche; **not** ~ être indifférent
careen *vt naut* caréner; *vi naut* donner de la bande
careenage *n naut* carénage *m*
career *n* carrière *f*, profession *f*; course *f*; *vi* aller à toute vitesse, se ruer
careerist *n* arriviste
carefree *adj* insouciant, sans souci
careful *adj* attentif -ive; prudent, circonspect; (work) soigné; (worker) soigneux -euse
careless *adj* insouciant, sans souci; négligent, inattentif -ive; naturel -elle, spontané
caress *n* caresse *f*; *vt* caresser; (soothe) câliner, cajoler
caressing *adj* caressant
caretaker *n* gardien -ienne, concierge
car-ferry *n* car-ferry *m*
cargo *n* cargaison *f*
cargo-boat *n* cargo *m*
caribou *n* caribou *m*
caricature *n* caricature *f*; *vt* caricaturer
caries *n med* carie *f*
carillon *n* carillon *m*
carious *adj med* carié
carmine *n* carmin *m*; *adj* carmin *invar*
carnage *n* carnage *m*
carnal *adj* charnel -elle, sensuel -elle; sexuel -elle; ~ **knowledge** rapports sexuels
carnality *n* sensualité *f*
carnation *n bot* œillet *m*; (colour) incarnat *m*; *adj* incarnat
carnival *n* carnaval *m* (*pl* carnavals), fête *f*
carnivore *n* carnivore *m*
carnivorous *adj* carnivore, carnassier -ière
carol *n mus* chant *m* allègre; (Christmas) noël *m*; *vt* chanter; *vi* chanter allègrement
carotid *n anat* carotide *f*; *adj* carotide
carousal *n* beuverie *f*
carouse *n* beuverie *f*; *vi* faire la noce
¹carp *n zool* carpe *f*
²carp *vi* critiquer, trouver à redire
carpenter *n* charpentier *m*; (joiner)

menuisier *m*; *vi* faire de la menuiserie

**carpentry** *n* charpenterie *f*; menuiserie *f*

**carpet** *n* tapis *m*; **on the ~** (under discussion) sur le tapis; *coll* (rebuke) sur la sellette; *vt* recouvrir d'un tapis; *coll* mettre sur la sellette

**carpet-slipper** *n* pantoufle *f*

**carpet-sweeper** *n* balai *m* mécanique

**carping** *n* chicanerie *f*; *adj* chicanier -ière

**carriage** *n* transport *m*; port *m*; (charges) frais *mpl* de port; (bearing) maintien *m*, posture *f*; wagon *m*, voiture *f*; (typewriter) chariot *m*; (gun) affût *m*; **~ forward** port dû; **~ paid** port payé

**carriageway** *n* chaussée *f*

**Carribean** *n* mer *f* des Antilles (des Caraïbes)

**carrier** *n* roulier *m*, voiturier *m*; *med* porteur *m* de microbes, vecteur *m*; (bicycle) porte-bagages *m*

**carrier-bag** *n* sac *m* en papier (en plastique)

**carrier-pigeon** *n* pigeon voyageur

**carrion** *n* chair *f* en putréfaction

**carrot** *n* carotte *f*

**carroty** *adj* roux (*f* rousse)

**carry** *n* (ball, bullet) portée *f*; *vt* porter, transporter, charrier; *mil* (capture) enlever, emporter; (bear child) porter; (include) comporter; *archi* supporter, soutenir; (pipe) amener; *math* reporter; **~ all before one** marcher en vainqueur; **~ down** descendre; *comm* **~ forward**, **~ over** reporter; **~ in** rentrer; **~ off** (s/o) enlever; (sth) emporter; (prize) remporter; **~ off well** se tirer d'affaire avec aisance; **~ on** poursuivre, continuer; (trade, business) exercer; **~ out** emporter; exécuter, accomplir; **~ the day** gagner la bataille; **~ through** mener à terme; **~ up** monter; **~ weight** avoir de l'influence; *vi* effectuer des transports; (voice) porter; **~ on** continuer, persister; *coll* se comporter d'une façon idiote; flirter; **~ oneself** se tenir

**carry-cot** *n* lit d'enfant portatif

**cart** *n* charrette *f*; **hand ~** charrette *f* à bras; **put the ~ before the horse** mettre la charrue devant les bœufs

**carte (à la)** *adv phr* à la carte

**carte-blanche** *n* carte blanche

**cartel** *n* cartel *m*

**carthorse** *n* cheval *m* de trait

**Carthusian** *n* chartreux -euse

**cartilage** *n anat* cartilage *m*

**cartographer** *n* cartographe

**cartography** *n* cartographie *f*

**cartomancy** *n* cartomancie *f*

**carton** *n* carton *m*; (target) blanc *m*, mouche *f*

**cartoon** *n arts* carton *m*; caricature *f*; dessin *m* satirique; *cin* dessin animé

**cartoonist** *n* caricaturiste

**cartridge** *n* (small-arms) cartouche *f*; (gun) gargousse *f*; (record player) cellule *f*; **blank ~** cartouche *f* à blanc

**cartridge-paper** *n* papier *m* à cartouche

**cart-track** *n* chemin muletier

**cart-wheel** *n* roue *f* de charrette; (somersault) roue *f*

**carve** *vt* sculpter, ciseler, tailler; *cul* découper; **~ out** tailler; **~ up** dépecer

**carving** *n* sculpture *f*; *cul* découpage *m*

**carving-knife** *n* couteau *m* à découper

**caryatid** *n* cariatide *f*

**cascade** *n* cascade *f*; *vi* cascader

**¹case** *n* cas *m*, fait *m*, circonstance *f*; (plight) état *m*, position *f*; argument *m*; *leg* affaire *f*, procès *m*; *med* **~ history** dossier médical; **~ in point** bon exemple; **as the ~ may be** selon le cas; **in any ~** en tout cas; **in ~** au besoin; dans le cas où; **in ~ of** en cas de; **in that ~** dans ce cas, si cela arrive; **put the ~ that** supposez que

**²case** *n* caisse *f*, boîte *f*; (casing) enveloppe *f*; (cigarettes, glasses) étui *m*; (jewels) écrin *m*; (display) vitrine *f*; *print* casse *f*; *print* **lower ~** bas *m* de casse; *print* **upper ~** haut *m* de casse; *vt* mettre en caisse

**casein** *n* caséine *f*

**case-law** *n leg* précédents *mpl*

**casemate** *n mil* casemate *f*

**casement** *n bui* fenêtre *f* à battants

**cash** *n* argent *m* liquide (comptant), espèces *fpl*; *coll* fric *m*; **~ on delivery**, **c.o.d.** livraison *f* contre remboursement; **pay ~ down** payer comptant; *coll* payer cash; **~** (cheque) encaisser, toucher; **~ in on** profiter de

**cash-book** *n* livre *m* de caisse

**cash-flow** *n* cash-flow *m*

**¹cashier** *n* caissier -ière

**²cashier** *vt mil* casser; renvoyer

**cashmere** *n* cachemire *m*

**cash-register** *n* caisse enregistreuse

**casing** *n* enveloppe *f*; *mech* revêtement *m*

**casino** *n* casino *m*

**cask** *n* barrique *f*, tonneau *m*

**casket** *n* écrin *m*, coffret *m*

**cassava** *n* manioc *m*

**casserole** *n cul* (pot) cocotte *f*; (food) ragoût *m* en cocotte

**cassock** *n* soutane *f*

**cast** *n* lancement *m*, jet *m*; (dice) coup *m*; (angling) lancer *m*; *theat* distribution *f*; (metal) fonte *f*; (mould) moule *m*; *med* plâtre *m*; *med* strabisme *m*; (snake) dépouille *f*; *fig* trempe *f*; disposition *f*; *vt* lancer, jeter; (glance, anchor; jeter; (shed) perdre; *arts+eng* mouler; *theat* distribuer les rôles de; ~ **aside** mettre de côté, rejeter; ~ **away** rejeter, repousser; ~ **off** rejeter; (knitting) arrêter (les mailles); *naut* larguer; ~ **out** chasser, expulser; ~ **up** (sea) rejeter; vomir; (eyes) lever au ciel; ~ **a vote** voter; *vi* (angling) jeter la ligne; (eyes) loucher; ~ **about for how to** chercher le moyen de; ~ **off** *naut* larguer les amarres; (knitting) arrêter les mailles

**castanets** *npl* castagnettes *fpl*

**castaway** *n* naufragé -e

**caste** *n* caste *f*; *fig* élite *f*

**castellated** *adj* crénelé

**caster, castor** *n* (salt, sugar, etc) saupoudroir *m*; (furniture) roulette *f*; ~ **sugar** sucre *m* en poudre

**castigate** *vt* châtier, punir

**castigation** *n* châtiment *m*, punition *f*

**casting** *n mech* fonte *f*; *mech* pièce fondue; *arts* moulage *m*; *theat* distribution *f* des rôles

**casting-vote** *n* voix prépondérante

**cast-iron** *n* fonte *f*; *adj fig* de fer, certain

**castle** *n* château fort; (chess) tour *f*; ~ **s in the air, ~ s in Spain** châteaux *mpl* en Espagne; *vi* (chess) roquer

**cast-off** *n* ~ **s** (clothes) frusques *fpl*; *adj* rejeté

¹**castor** *n see* **caster**

²**castor** *n zool* castor *m*

**castor-oil** *n* huile *f* de ricin

**castrate** *vt* châtrer, émasculer, castrer

**castration** *n* castration *f*

**casual** *adj* (chance) fortuit, de hasard; (uncaring) insouciant, désinvolte; (clothes) de sport; ~ **labourer** travailleur *m* temporaire; ~ **ward** asile *m* de nuit

**casualty** *n med* accidenté -e; victime *f*; *mil* **casualties** pertes *fpl*; *mil* ~ **list** état *m* des pertes; ~ **(ward)** service *m* des urgences

**casuist** *n* casuiste

**casuistic** *adj* de casuiste

**casuistry** *n* casuistique *f*

**cat** *n* chat *m* (*f* chatte); *zool* félin -e; *coll pej* (woman) chipie *f*; *naut* bossoir *m*; *sl* joueur *m* de swing; *abbr* (cat o' nine tails) chat *m* à neuf queues; **a ~ may look at a king** même les plus humbles ont des droits; **enough to make a ~ laugh** extrêmement drôle; *coll* **it's raining ~ s and dogs** il pleut à verse; **see which way the ~ jumps** attendre le déroulement des événements; **when the ~ 's away the mice will play** quand le chat n'est pas là les souris dansent; *vt naut* lever (l'ancre) au bossoir; *vi sl* dégueuler

**cataclysm** *n* cataclysme *m*

**catacomb** *n* catacombe *f*

**catafalque** *n* catafalque *m*

**catalepsy** *n* catalepsie *f*

**cataleptic** *adj* cataleptique

**catalogue** *n* catalogue *m*; *vt* cataloguer

**Catalonia** *n* Catalogne *f*

**catalysis** *n chem* catalyse *f*

**catalyst** *n chem* catalyseur *m*

**catamaran** *n naut* catamaran *m*

**cataplasm** *n* cataplasme *m*

**catapult** *n* catapulte *f*; *vt* catapulter

**cataract** *n geog+med* cataracte *f*; cascade *f*; torrent *m*; trombe *f*, déluge *m*

**catarrh** *n* catarrhe *m*

**catarrhal** *adj* catarrheux -euse

**catastrophe** *n* catastrophe *f*

**catastrophic** *adj* catastrophique, désastreux -euse

**cat-burglar** *n* cambrioleur -euse; *sl* monte-en-l'air *m invar*

**catcall** *n* sifflet *m*, huée *f*

**catch** *n* prise *f*, capture *f*; (buckle) ardillon *m*; (lock) loquet *m*; (window) loqueteau *m*; (cog-wheel) cliquet *m*; (fish) pêche *f*; *mus* chanson *f* à reprises; (trick) attrape *f*; (snag) hic *m*, difficulté *f*; *coll* (marriage) beau parti; *vt* attraper; (seize) prendre, capturer, saisir; (deceive) attraper, prendre; (surprise) surprendre; (attention) saisir, attirer; (glance) apercevoir; *coll* ~ **it** écoper; *coll* ~ **me doing that again!** on ne m'y reprendra plus; ~ **out** surprendre, prendre; ~ **up** rattraper; *vi* s'accrocher; s'enchevêtrer; (key) accrocher; (fire) prendre; *cul* attacher; *coll* ~ **on** piger; prendre, devenir à la mode

**catching** *adj* contagieux -ieuse; (appealing) prenant

**catchment** *n* captage *m*; ~ **area** *geog* bassin *m*; *fig* aire *f*

**catchword** *n print* réclame *f*; slogan *m*

**catchy** *adj* (tune) facile à retenir; (question) insidieux -ieuse

**catechism** *n* catéchisme *m*

**catechist** *n* catéchiste

**catechize** *vt* catéchiser; endoctriner

**categorical** *adj* catégorique

**categorize** *vt* ranger par catégories

**category** *n* catégorie *f*

**cater** *vi* approvisionner; ~ **for** pourvoir à

**caterer** *n* traiteur *m*

**catering** *n* activité *f* de traiteur

**caterpillar** *n* chenille *f*

**caterwaul** *vi* (cat) miauler; (person) brailler

**catgut** *n surg* catgut *m*; corde *f* à violon; *sp* corde *f* de raquette

**catharsis** *n med+lit* purgation *f*

**cathartic** *adj* purgatif -ive

**cathead** n naut bossoir m
**cathedral** n cathédrale f; adj cathédral
**catherine-wheel** n soleil m; (somersault) roue f; bui rosace f
**catheter** n cathéter m, sonde creuse
**cathode** n elect cathode f; adj cathodique; ~ **ray tube** tube m cathodique
**catholic** n catholique; adj universel -elle; libéral, large d'esprit; (Roman) catholique; **Catholic church** Église catholique (romaine)
**catholicism** n catholicisme m
**catholicity** n universalité f, compréhension f; catholicité f
**catkin** n bot chaton m
**catlick** n toilette f de chat
**cat-like** adj félin
**catnap** n petit somme
**cat-o'-nine-tails** n chat m à neuf queues
**cat's-eyes** npl clous mpl à catadioptre
**cats-paw** n coll dupe f; naut vent léger, bouffée f
**cattle** n bétail m; bestiaux mpl; ~ **crossing** passage m de troupeaux
**catty** adj méchant, rosse
**caucus** n groupe m de pression
**caudal** adj caudal
**cauldron** n cul chaudron m
**cauliflower** n chou-fleur m (pl choux-fleurs)
**caulk, calk** vt calfeutrer; naut calfater
**causal** adj causal
**causality** n causalité f
**causation** n causalité f
**cause** n cause f, raison f; motif m; give ~ **for** donner lieu à; have ~ **for** avoir lieu de; **make common** ~ agir de concert; vt causer, produire, provoquer; ~ **s/o to do sth** faire faire qch à qn
**causeway** n digue f, chaussée f
**caustic** n caustique m; adj caustique; acerbe, moquant
**cauterization** n cautérisation f
**cauterize** vt cautériser
**cautery** n cautère m
**caution** n prudence f, circonspection f; avertissement m; ~ **money** cautionnement m; vt avertir, donner des conseils de prudence à, mettre en garde
**cautionary** adj avertisseur -euse; moral
**cautious** adj prudent, circonspect
**cautiousness** n prudence f, circonspection f
**cavalcade** n cavalcade f
**cavalier** n cavalier m; hist partisan m du roi Charles 1er d'Angleterre; adj sans souci, libre; dédaigneux -euse
**cavalry** n cavalerie f
**cave** n caverne f; vi ~ **in** s'effondrer; coll fig se soumettre, céder
**cave** interj coll pet!
**caveat** n avertissement m; leg notification f d'opposition
**cave-man** n homme m des cavernes
**cavern** n caverne f
**cavernous** adj caverneux -euse
**caviar, caviare** n caviar m
**cavil** n ergoterie f, chicane f; vi chicaner, ergoter
**cavity** n cavité f, creux m, trou m (pl trous)
**cavort** vi coll cabrioler
**caw** n croassement m; vi croasser
**cayenne** n cul poivre m de Cayenne
**cease** n without ~ sans cesse; vt cesser, arrêter; vi cesser, s'arrêter
**cease-fire** n mil cessez-le-feu m invar
**cedar** n cèdre m
**cede** vt céder
**cedilla** n gramm cédille f
**ceiling** n plafond m
**celebrant** n eccles célébrant m
**celebrate** vt célébrer, solenniser, fêter; vi célébrer; coll s'amuser
**celebrated** adj célèbre, éminent
**celebration** n célébration f, commémoration f; coll bringue f
**celebrity** n célébrité f; coll grosse légume
**celeriac** n céleri-rave m
**celerity** n célérité f
**celery** n céleri m
**celesta** n mus célesta m
**celestial** adj céleste
**celibacy** n célibat m
**celibate** n+adj célibataire
**cell** n cellule f
**cellar** n cave f
**cellist** n mus violoncelliste
**cello** n mus violoncelle m
**cellophane** n cellophane f
**cellular** adj cellulaire
**celluloid** n celluloïd m
**cellulose** n cellulose f; adj en (de) cellulose
**Celt** n Celte
**Celtic** n celtique m; adj celtique, celte
**cement** n ciment m; vt cimenter
**cement-mixer** n bétonnière f
**cemetery** n cimetière m
**cenotaph** n cénotaphe m
**censer** n eccles encensoir m
**censor** n censeur m; vt censurer
**censorial** adj censorial
**censorious** adj pointilleux -euse, désapprobateur -trice, dénigreur -euse
**censorship** n censure f
**censure** n blâme m, réprobation f; critique f, censure f; vt censurer, blâmer
**census** n recensement m
**centaur** n centaure m
**centenarian** n+adj centenaire
**centenary** n centenaire m
**centigrade** adj centigrade
**centigramme** n centigramme m

centilitre *n* centilitre *m*

centimetre *n* centimètre *m*

centipede *n* mille-pattes *m invar*

central *adj* central

centralization *n* centralisation *f*

centralize *vt* centraliser; *vi* se centraliser

centre *n* centre *m*; foyer *m*; *sp* ~ **for-ward** avant-centre *m* (*pl* avants-centres); *sp* ~ **half** demi-centre *m*; ~ **of attraction** point *m* de mire; ~ **of gravity** centre *m* de gravité; *adj* central; *vt* centrer; (hopes, etc) concentrer; *vi* se concentrer; (converge) se rassembler

centre-board *n naut* quille *f* mobile, dérive *f*

centric *adj* central

centrifugal *adj* centrifuge

centrifuge *n* centrifugeur *m*, centrifugeuse *f*

centripetal *adj* centripète

centuple *adj* centuple; *vt* centupler

centurion *n* centurion *m*

century *n* siècle *m*

ceramic *adj* céramique

ceramics *npl arts* céramique *f*

cereal *n* céréale *f*; ~ **s** (breakfast food) flocons *mpl* de céréales

cerebellum *n anat* cervelet *m*

cerebral *adj* cérébral

cerebration *n* activité *f* du cerveau; *coll* **do a little** ~ se creuser la cervelle

cerebro-spinal *adj* cérébro-spinal

cerebrum *n* cerveau *m*

ceremonial *n* cérémonial *m* (*pl* cérémonials); *eccles* rituel *m*; *adj* de cérémonie

ceremonious *adj* cérémonieux -ieuse

ceremony *n* cérémonie *f*; **stand on** ~ faire des façons

cert *n sl* bon tuyau; **it's a (dead)** ~ c'est du tout cuit

certain *adj* certain, sûr; assuré; précis; indiscutable, indéniable; (quantity) certain, appréciable; **for** ~ assurément; **make** ~ **of** s'assurer de

certainly *adv* certainement, sans doute; ~ **!** mais bien sûr!

certainty *n* certitude *f*; conviction *f*; ce qui est sûr d'arriver, fait certain

certifiable *adj* certifiable; *coll* dingue

certificate *n* certificat *m*; (examination) diplôme *m*; **bankrupt's** ~ concordat *m*; *vt* donner un certificat à; diplômer

certify *vt* certifier; garantir; *med* interner

certitude *n* certitude *f*

cessation *n* cessation *f*; interruption *f*

cession *n leg* cession *f*

cesspit, cesspool *n* fosse *f* d'aisance

cetacean *n zool* cétacé *m*

chaconne *n mus* chaconne *f*

chafe *n* éraflure *f*, écorchure *f*; *fig* irritation *f*; *vt* frotter; érafler, irriter; *vi*

s'érafler, s'écorcher; *fig* s'irriter; ~ **against** s'érafler contre

chaff *n* balle *f*; paille hâchée; *coll* taquinerie *f*; *fig* vétille *f*; *vt* taquiner

chaffer *n* marchandage *m*; *vi* marchander

chaffinch *n* pinson *m*

chafing-dish *n cul* chaufferette *f*

chagrin *n* chagrin *m*, contrariété *f*; irritation *f*; déception *f*; *vt* chagriner, contrarier

chain *n* chaîne *f*; (fetters) ~ **s** fers *mpl*; *vt* enchaîner; barrer à l'aide d'une chaîne

chain-bridge *n* pont suspendu

chain-drive *n eng* transmission *f* par chaîne

chain-gang *n* forçats *mpl* à la chaîne

chain-mail *n* armure *f* de mailles

chain-reaction *n* réaction *f* en chaîne

chain-saw *n* scie *f* à chaînette

chain-smoker *n* fumeur -euse invétéré -e

chain-store *n* magasin *m* à succursales multiples

chair *n* chaise *f*, siège *m*; (university) chaire *f*; (meeting) fauteuil *m* du président; *US coll* chaise *f* électrique; *vt* porter en triomphe; (meeting) présider

chairman *n* (meeting, company) président -e; **Madam** ~ Madame la présidente

chairmanship *n* présidence *f*

chairperson *n* président -e

chalcedony, calcedony *n* calcédoine *f*

chalet *n* chalet *m*

chalice *n eccles* + *bot* calice *m*; coupe *f*

chalk *n* craie *f*; (piece) bâton *m* de craie; **by a long** ~ de beaucoup, de loin; **French** ~ talc *m*; **not know** ~ **from cheese** ne pas savoir distinguer entre le jour et la nuit; *vt* marquer à la craie; ~ **out** tracer; ~ **up** (tally) porter sur l'ardoise

chalk-pit *n* carrière *f* de craie

chalky *adj* crayeux -euse

challenge *n* défi *m*; *sp* challenge *m*; *mil* sommation *f*; *leg* récusation *f*; *fig* provocation *f*, épreuve *f*; *vt* défier; provoquer en duel; mettre en question, contester; *mil* faire une sommation à; *leg* récuser

challenger *n* provocateur -trice; *sp* challenger *m*

challenging *adj* qui provoque

chamber *n* chambre *f*; salle *f*; (firearm) chambre *f*; *med* chambre *f*, cavité *f*; *leg* ~ **s** cabinet *m* de juge (ou d'avocat); *vt* évider

chamberlain *n hist* chambellan *m*

chambermaid *n* femme *f* de chambre

chamber-music *n* musique *f* de chambre

chamber-pot *n* pot *m* de chambre, vase *m* de nuit

**chameleon** *n* caméléon *m*
**chamfer** *n* chanfrein *m*; *vt* chanfreiner
**chammy-leather** *n* chamois *m*
**chamois** *n* *zool* chamois *m*; (leather)
chamois *m*; ~ **leather** peau *f* de
chamois
**champ** *vt* + *vi* mâchonner, mâcher; ~ **at
the bit** ronger son frein
**champagne** *n* champagne *m*
**champion** *n* champion -ionne; défenseur
*m*; *adj* *coll* de première classe,
suprême; *coll* fantastique, fameux
-euse, au poil; *vt* défendre comme
champion; *fig* défendre, soutenir
**championship** *n* championnat *m*; *fig*
défense *f*
**chance** *n* chance *f*, hasard *m*; bonne
chance; possibilité *f*, occasion *f*; risque
*m*; **take one's** ~ courir sa chance; **the
main** ~ possibilité *f* de gain personnel;
*adj* fortuit, accidentel -elle; *vt* risquer,
courir la chance de; *vi* (happen) arriver; avoir l'occasion de; ~ **upon** trouver par hasard, rencontrer par hasard
**chancel** *n* *eccles* chœur *m*
**chancellery** *n* chancellerie *f*
**chancellor** *n* chancelier *m*; *pol* **Chancellor of the Exchequer** = ministre *m*
des Finances
**chancery** *n* *leg* section *f* de la Haute Cour
en Angleterre
**chancre** *n* *med* chancre *m*
**chancy** *adj* *coll* incertain, douteux -euse,
chanceux -euse
**chandelier** *n* lustre *m*
**chandler** *n* marchand *m* de chandelles;
*naut* **ships'** ~ marchand *m* de fournitures pour bateaux
**change** *n* changement *m*; variété *f*, distraction *f*; (replacement) rechange *m*;
échange *m*; (money) monnaie *f*; vicissitudes *fpl*, hauts *mpl* et bas *mpl*; ~ **of
life** retour *m* d'âge, ménopause *f*; **get
no** ~ **out of** ne pouvoir rien tirer de; **it
makes a** ~ ça vous change les idées;
**just for a** ~ pour changer un peu; **big
ring the** ~s répéter en variant; *vt*
transformer; modifier; échanger;
changer; (clothes) changer de; *mot* ~
**gear** changer de vitesse; *vi* changer; se
transformer, se modifier; *mot* ~ **down**
rétrograder; ~ **over** passer de; *mot* ~
**up** passer à une vitesse supérieure
**changeability** *n* inconstance *f*
**changeable** *adj* changeant, variable,
inconstant
**changeless** *adj* constant, immuable
**channel** *n* (river-bed) lit *m*; *naut* chenal
*m*; *geog* détroit *m*; (groove) cannelure
*f*; canal *m*, conduit *m*; *rad* (television)
chaîne *f*; voie *f* de communication; **the
English Channel** la Manche; **usual** ~ **s**

voie *f* hiérarchique; *vt* creuser des
canaux dans; canaliser; canneler
**chant** *n* *eccles* psalmodie *f*, plain-chant
*m* (*pl* plains-chants); chant *m* monotone; *vt* *eccles* psalmodier; (verse)
réciter; (celebrate) chanter
**chaos** *n* chaos *m*
**chaotic** *adj* chaotique
**¹chap** *n* *coll* type *m*
**²chap** *n* gerçure *f*; *vt* gercer; *vi* se gercer
**chapel** *n* chapelle *f*; (non-conformist)
temple *m*; *typ* association syndicale
**chaperon** *n* chaperon *m*; *hist* duègne *f*;
*vt* chaperonner
**chaplain** *n* *eccles* chapelain *m*; *mil*
aumônier *m*
**chapped** *adj* gercé
**chaps** *npl* mâchoire *f*
**chapter** *n* chapitre *m*; *eccles* chapitre *m*;
~ **of accidents** suite *f* de malheurs;
**give** ~ **and verse** citer ses autorités
**¹char** *n* *zool* ombre *m*, omble *m*
**²char** *n* *coll* thé *m*
**³char** *n* *coll* femme *f* de ménage; *vi* *coll*
faire des ménages
**⁴char** *vt* charbonner; roussir; *vi* roussir
**charabanc** *n* *obs* car *m*, autocar *m*
**character** *n* caractère *m*, naturel *m*,
nature *f*, tempérament *m*; (writing)
caractère *m*, écriture *f*; *print* lettre *f*;
(type) genre *m*, caractéristique *f*; fermeté *f*, volonté *f*, énergie *f*; réputation
*f*; personnalité *f*; (literature) personnage *m*; *coll* type *m*, numéro *m*; (testimonial) certificat *m* (de bonnes
mœurs), attestation *f*; *theat* ~ **part**
rôle *m* de composition; **in** ~ typique
**characteristic** *n* caractéristique *f*; *adj*
caractéristique, typique
**characterization** *n* caractérisation *f*
**characterize** *vt* caractériser; décrire;
dépeindre
**characterless** *adj* sans caractère; sans
certificat
**charade** *n* charade *f*
**charcoal** *n* charbon *m* de bois; (colour)
gris foncé
**charge** *n* charge *f*; (burden) faix *m*, fardeau *m*; responsabilité *f*; soin *m*;
recommandation *f*; fonction *f*, emploi
*m*; (cost) coût *m*, prix *m*; **give in** ~
livrer à la police; **in** ~ **of** responsable
de; **in the** ~ **of** confié aux soins de; *vt*
charger; faire responsable; *leg* accuser,
inculper; (price) compter, faire payer;
*fig* imputer; *vi* *mil* charger; donner
l'ordre
**chargeable** *adj* imputable, à la charge;
*leg* accusable
**¹charger** *n* grand plat
**²charger** *n* cheval *m* de bataille
**chariness** *n* prudence *f*

394

**chariot** n chariot m; char m

**charisma** n charisme m

**charitable** adj charitable; indulgent

**charity** n charité f; indulgence f, bienveillance f; générosité f; (alms) aumône f; œuvre f de bienfaisance; **cold as ~** insensible, négligent; adj charitable; de charité

**charlady** n femme f de ménage

**charlatan** n charlatan m

**charlatanism** n charlatanisme m

**charlotte** n cul charlotte f

**charm** n charme m; (spell) enchantement m; séduction f; plan m; amulette f, talisman m; (on bracelet) breloque f; **like a ~** parfaitement; vt charmer, enchanter; calmer; plaire à

**charmer** n charmeur -euse; enchanteur m (f enchanteresse)

**charming** adj charmant, enchanteur (f enchanteresse)

**charnel-house** n charnier m

**chart** n naut carte f; plan m; graphique m; med courbe f; **organization ~** organigramme m; vt naut (position) établir

**charter** n charte f; leg statuts mpl; vt (plane, ship, etc) affréter; accorder une charte à; **~ ed accountant** expert-comptable m (pl experts-comptables)

**charter-flight** n (vol m) charter m

**charter-party** n naut charte-partie f (pl chartes-parties)

**chartreuse** n chartreuse f

**charwoman** n femme f de ménage

**chary** adj prudent; (frugal) chiche

¹**chase** n chasse f, poursuite f; vt chasser, poursuivre; fig dissiper; **~ after** courir après

²**chase** vt enchâsser, ciseler

**chasm** n gouffre m; abîme m

**chassis** n châssis m

**chaste** adj chaste, pudique; fig pur, raffiné

**chasten** vt châtier, éprouver; modérer

**chastening** n châtiment m; adj qui corrige; purifiant

**chastise** vt battre, fouetter; punir

**chastisement** n correction f

**chastity** n chasteté f; hist **~ belt** ceinture f de chasteté

**chasuble** n eccles chasuble f

**chat** n bavardage m, causette f; **~ show** entretien radiodiffusé (télévisé); vi bavarder, causer; coll **~ up** flatter, amadouer

**chattels** npl possessions fpl; leg biens mpl meubles; **goods and ~** biens mpl et effets mpl

**chatter** n bavardage m; babil m; (teeth) claquement m; vi bavarder, babiller; (teeth) claquer

**chatterbox** n bavard -e; coll moulin m à paroles

**chatty** adj bavard, causeur -euse, familier -ière

**chauffeur** n chauffeur m

**chauvinism** n chauvinisme m

**cheap** adj bon marché, pas cher (f chère), avantageux -euse; pej sans valeur, de pauvre qualité; (person) vulgaire; **dirt ~** vraiment pas cher; **on the ~** au rabais; adv à bon marché

**cheapen** vt baisser le prix de; **~ oneself** se déconsidérer; vi baisser

**cheapness** n bon marché; fig médiocrité f, vulgarité f

**cheat** n trompeur -euse, filou m, escroc m; tricheur -euse; vt tromper, duper, rouler, escroquer; vi tromper, tricher

**check** n arrêt m, obstacle m; contrôle m, vérification f; (cloakroom, baggage) ticket m; (pattern) carreau m, damier m; US chèque m; US (bill) note f; (restaurant) addition f; adj à carreaux, à damiers; vt arrêter, enrayer; vérifier, contrôler; examiner; (chess) faire échec à; US **~ out** vérifier; **~ up** vérifier; vi s'arrêter; hésiter; **~ in** (hotel) s'inscrire; (airport) présenter son billet; (hotel) **~ out** payer sa note; **~ up on** se renseigner sur

**checkbook** n US see **cheque-book**

**check-list** n liste f de contrôle

**checkmate** n (chess) échec m et mat m; fig échec m, défaite f; vt (chess) mater; frustrer, circonvenir

**check-out** n (supermarket) caisse f

**checkpoint** n contrôle m

**check-room** n US vestiaire m

**check-up** n contrôle m, vérification f; med check-up m invar, bilan m de santé

**cheek** n joue f; coll toupet m, effronterie f; coll (buttock) fesse f; **~ by jowl with** s/o côte à côte avec qn

**cheekbone** n pommette f

**cheeky** adj effronté, impudent

**cheep** n gazouillis m; vi gazouiller

**cheer** n gaieté f, allégresse f; état m d'esprit; (food) chère f, nourriture f; (solace) soulagement m; acclamations fpl; **of good ~** heureux -euse, content; vt encourager, réconforter; acclamer, applaudir; égayer; **~ up** réconforter; vi encourager; applaudir; **~ up** s'égayer

**cheerful** adj gai, allègre, heureux -euse

**cheeriness** n gaieté f, allégresse f, bonne humeur

**cheering** n acclamations fpl, applaudissements mpl; adj réconfortant, réjouissant

**cheerio** interj coll au revoir!, ciao!

cheerless *adj* morne, triste, misérable
cheers *interj coll* à la vôtre!
cheery *adj* animé, gai, allègre; *pej* trop empressé
¹cheese *n* fromage *m*
²cheese *vt sl* ~ it ta gueule!; halte-là!
cheesecake *n* tarte *f* au fromage blanc; *coll* photo *f* de pin-up
cheesed *coll* ennuyé, emmerdé
cheesemonger *n* marchand -e de fromages
cheeseparing *n* avarice *f*, pingrerie *f*; *adj* avare, pingre
cheesy *adj* caséeux -éeuse
cheetah *n zool* guépard *m*
chef *n* chef *m*, cuisinier *m*, chef *m* de cuisine
chef-d'œuvre *n* (*pl* chefs-d'œuvre) chef-d'œuvre *m* (*pl* chefs-d'œuvre)
chemical *n* produit *m* chimique; *adj* chimique
chemise *n* (for women) chemise *f*
chemist *n* (researcher) chimiste; (dispenser) pharmacien -ienne
chemistry *n* chimie *f*
chemotherapy *n* chimiothérapie *f*
cheque *n* chèque *m*
cheque-book *n* carnet *m* de chèques, chéquier *m*
chequer *n* carreau *m*, damier *m*; *vt* orner de carreaux (de damiers), quadriller; diversifier; ~ed career vie mouvementée, vie *f* avec des hauts et des bas
cherish *vt* chérir; *fig* entretenir; nourrir
cherry *n* cerise *f*; (tree) cerisier *m*; *adj* (colour) cerise *invar*
cherry-brandy *n* cherry-brandy *m*, liqueur *f* de cerises
cherub *n* chérubin *m*
cherubic *adj* de chérubin; (child) dodu, sage
chervil *n bot* cerfeuil *m*
chess *n* échecs *mpl*
chessboard *n* échiquier *m*
chessmen *npl* pièces *fpl* de jeu d'échecs
chest *n* caisse *f*, boîte *f*, coffre *m*; *anat* poitrine *f*; ~ of drawers commode *f*
chesterfield *n* sofa capitonné
chestnut *n* châtaigne *f*, marron *m*; (horse-chestnut) marron *m* d'Inde; (colour) châtain *m*; (horse) alezan *m*; *coll* (joke) anecdote archi-connue; *adj* châtain *invar*
chevalier *n* chevalier *m*
chevron *n* chevron *m*
chew *n* mâchonnement *m*; *vt* mâcher, mâchonner; (tobacco) chiquer; *vi* chiquer; *fig* ~ over ruminer, ressasser
chewing-gum *n* chewing-gum *m*, gomme *f* à mâcher
chiaroscuro *n* clair-obscur *m* (*pl* clairs-obscurs)

chic *n* chic *m*; *adj* chic *invar*
chicane *n* chicane *f*; *vt* + *vi* chicaner
chicanery *n* chicane *f*, chicanerie *f*, ergoterie *f*
chichi *adj coll pej* délicat, affecté
chick *n* (chicken) poussin *m*; (young bird) oisillon *m*; *coll US* nana *f*
chicken *n* poulet *m*, poularde *f*, poule *f*; *fig* naïf -ïve, tendron *m*; *sl* lâche; no ~ d'un certain âge
chicken-feed *n* pâtée *f*; *coll fig* qch sans aucune valeur
chicken-hearted *adj* peureux -euse
chickenpox *n* varicelle *f*
chicken-run *n* cage *f* à poules
chickweed *n bot* mouron *m*
chicory *n* chicorée *f*; (vegetable) endive *f*
chide *vt* + *vi* gronder
chiding *n* grondement *m*
chief *n* chef *m*; *coll* patron -onne; *adj* principal, en chef, plus grand
chiefly *adv* surtout, principalement
chieftain *n* chef *m*
chiffon *n* mousseline *f* de soie
chignon *n* chignon *m*
chilblain *n* engelure *f*
child *n* enfant *m*; *fig* disciple *m*
childbearing *n* gestation *f*; (state) grossesse *f*
childbirth *n* accouchement *m*
childhood *n* enfance *f*; second ~ gâtisme *m*, affaiblissement *m*, sénilité *f*
childish *adj* enfantin, puéril
childishness *n* enfantillage *m*
childless *adj* sans enfants
childlike *adj* innocent, candide
chill *n* refroidissement *m*; froid *m*; *adj* froid, transi, glacé; *vt* refroidir, transir; congeler; *vi* se refroidir
chilled *adj* refroidi; congelé
chilli, chili *n* piment *m*
chilliness *n* froid *m*; froideur *f*
chilly *adj* frais (*f* fraîche), frisquet -ette; froid, glacial
chime *n* carillon *m*; mélodie *f*; *vt* carillonner; (hour) sonner; *vi* carillonner; *fig* s'accorder
chimera *n* chimère *f*
chimerical *adj* chimérique
chimney *n* cheminée *f*; (lamp) verre *m*
chimney-breast *n* trumeau *m*
chimney-corner *n* coin *m* du feu
chimney-piece *n* manteau *m* de cheminée
chimney-pot *n* pot *m* de cheminée, cheminée *f*
chimney-stack *n* cheminée *f*; cheminée *f* d'usine
chimpanzee *n* chimpanzé *m*
chin *n* menton *m*
China *n* Chine *f*

**china** n porcelaine f; vaisselle f; adj de porcelaine
**china-clay** n kaolin m
**Chinaman** n Chinois m
**chinchilla** n chinchilla m
**chin-chin** interj coll à la vôtre!
¹**chine** n ravin m
²**Chine** n échine f
**Chinese** n (language) chinois m; adj chinois; ~ **lantern** lanterne vénitienne
¹**chink** n (crack) fente f, lézarde f
²**chink** n (sound) tintement m; vt faire tinter; vi tinter
**chinstrap** n mentonnière f
**chintz** n perse f, cretonne imprimée
**chip** n fragment m, copeau m, éclat m; (crack) brèche f; (gambling) jeton m; (potatoes) ~s pommes frites; US chips mpl; ~ **off the old block** digne rejeton; **have a ~ on one's shoulder** en vouloir à tout le monde; **pass in one's ~s** mourir; **silicon ~** plaquette f de silicium; vt (wood) faire des copeaux; (glass, plate) ébrécher, écorner, tailler, sculpter; vi s'ébrécher, s'écorner; coll ~ **in** (conversation) intervenir; (cost) contribuer aux frais; (participate) coopérer dans une entreprise
**chippings** npl gravillons mpl
**chiromancy** n chiromancie f
**chiropodist** n pédicure
**chiropractic** n chiropraxie f, chiropractie f
**chiropractor** n chiropracteur m
**chirp** n gazouillis m, pépiement m; vi gazouiller, pépier
**chirpy** adj coll allègre
**chisel** n ciseau m; (engraving) burin m; vt ciseler; (engrave) buriner; fig sl escroquer
**chiselled** adj ciselé, buriné; (clear-cut) précis, clair
**chiseller** n sl escroc m
¹**chit** n coll gamine f
²**chit** n note f, certificat m
**chitchat** n bavardage m
**chitterlings** npl tripes fpl de porc
**chivalric** adj chevaleresque
**chivalrous** adj chevaleresque
**chivalry** n chevalerie f; qualités fpl chevaleresques
**chive** n cul ciboulette f, cive f, civette f
**chivvy, chivy** vt harceler
**chloral** n chem chloral m
**chlorate** n chem chlorate m
**chloric** adj chem chlorique m
**chloride** n chem chlorure m
**chlorinate** n javelliser
**chlorination** n javellisation f
**chlorine** n chem chlore m
**chloroform** n med chloroforme m; vt chloroformer

**chlorophyll** n bot chlorophylle f
**chlorosis** n chlorose f
**chlorotic** adj chlorotique
**choc-ice** n esquimau m
**chock** n cale f; vt caler, coincer
**chock-a-block** adj plein à craquer
**chock-full** adj bondé, plein à craquer
**chocolate** n chocolat m; adj au chocolat; (colour) brun foncé
**choice** n choix m; assortiment m; **Hobson's ~** aucun choix; adj choisi, raffiné; comm de première qualité, sélectionné
**choir** n mus chœur m, chorale f; mus + eccles maîtrise f; archi chœur m
**choirboy** n enfant m de chœur
**choke** n étranglement m, étouffement m; obstruction f; mot starter m; sl taule f; vt étouffer, étrangler; boucher, obstruer; coll ~ **off** envoyer promener, décourager; ~ **up** obstruer; vi étouffer, s'étrangler
**choker** n (necklace) collier m; (scarf) foulard m
**choky** adj étouffant, suffocant
**choler** n ar bile f; colère f
**cholera** n med choléra m
**choleric** adj colérique, coléreux -euse
**cholesterol** n med cholestérol m
**choose** vt choisir; élire; vi choisir, décider; **I cannot ~ but** je ne peux faire autrement que; **pick and ~** sélectionner, choisir avec attention
**choosy** adj difficile à plaire, chichiteux -euse
¹**chop** n (tree) coup m de hache; (butcher) coup m de hachoir; cul côtelette f; coll **get the ~** être licencié; vt trancher; (tree) donner un coup de hache à; (butcher) donner un coup de hachoir à, hacher; ~ **down** abattre; vi donner un coup de hache (de hachoir)
²**chop** vt changer; ~ **and change** changer souvent; ~ **logic** ergoter, discutailler; vi (wind) varier
**chopper** n hache f, hachoir m; coll hélicoptère m
**choppy** adj (sea) agité
**chops** npl mâchoires fpl
**chopstick** n baguette f
**chopsuey** n ragoût m à la chinoise
**choral** adj choral
**chorale** n mus choral m (pl chorals)
**chord** n corde f; mus accord m; fig **strike a ~** toucher la corde, faire vibrer la corde
**chore** n corvée f; ~s travaux mpl domestiques
**choreographer** n chorégraphe
**choreographic** adj chorégraphique
**choreography** n chorégraphie f
**chorister** n enfant m de chœur

**chortle** n gloussement m; vi glousser
**chorus** n theat + mus chœur m; (in song) refrain m; fig chœur m, concert m
**chorus-girl** n girl f
**chosen** adj choisi; élu; **the ~ people** les Juifs, le peuple élu
**chough** n zool crave m
**chow** n zool chow-chow m
**chowder** n US cul (sorte f de) soupe f de poissons
**Christ** n Christ m
**christen** vt baptiser; donner le nom de
**Christendom** n chrétienté f
**christening** n baptême m
**Christian** n chrétien -ienne; adj chrétien -ienne; fig charitable, bienfaisant, indulgent; **~ name** nom m de baptême, prénom m; **~ Science** scientisme chrétien
**Christianity** n christianisme m
**christianize** vt christianiser
**Christlike** adj semblable au Christ
**Christmas** n Noël m, jour m de Noël; **~ card** carte f de Noël; **Father ~** père m Noël
**Christmas-box** n cadeau m de Noël (en espèces), = étrennes fpl
**Christmastide, Christmas-time** n temps m de Noël, saison f de Noël
**Christmas-tree** n arbre m de Noël
**Christology** n christologie f
**chromatic** adj chromatique
**chromatics** n chromatique f
**chrome** n chrome m, chromate m de plomb; **~ steel** acier chromé
**chromic** adj chem chromique
**chromium** n chem chrome m; **~ plating** chromage m
**chromosome** n biol chromosome m
**chronic** adj med chronique, invétéré; fig chronique; sl terrible
**chronicle** n chronique f; vt écrire (des chroniques), enregistrer (des faits)
**chronicler** n chroniqueur m, historien m
**chronological** adj chronologique
**chronology** n chronologie f
**chronometer** n chronomètre m
**chrysalis** n ent chrysalide f
**chrysanthemum** n bot chrysanthème m
**chrysolite** n chrysolithe f
**chrysoprase** n chrysoprase f
**chub** n zool chevesne f, chevaine f
**chubby** adj joufflu
**¹chuck** n (under the chin) petite tape; action f de lancer; sl **give s/o the ~** balancer qn; vt tapoter; coll lancer, jeter; coll **~ it!** en voilà assez!, ça suffit!; coll **~ out** vider; coll **~ up** renoncer à
**²chuck** n coll (endearment) poulet m, poule f
**chucker-out** n sl videur m

**chuckle** n glousssement m; vi glousser
**chuckling** n gloussements mpl
**chuffed** adj sl vain, content
**chug** n halètement m; teuf-teuf m (pl teufs-teufs); vi haleter, faire teuf-teuf
**chum** n coll copain m; vi coll **~ up with** se lier d'amitié avec
**chummy** adj liant, sociable
**chump** n souche f, bloc m de bois; gros bout; coll idiot -e, balourd -e; **~ chop** côte première de mouton; sl **off one's ~** dingue
**chunk** n gros morceau; (bread) quignon m
**church** n église f; (protestant) temple m; clergé m, ordres mpl; **enter the ~** devenir prêtre, devenir pasteur
**church-goer** n pratiquant -e
**church-service** n office m, service m, culte m
**churchwarden** n marguillier m
**churchyard** n cimetière m
**churl** n malotru -e; avare
**churlish** adj (bad-mannered) grossier -ière; (surly) revêche, grincheux -euse; (mean) avaricieux -ieuse
**churn** n bidon m; (butter-making) baratte f; vt (milk) baratter; battre; fig brasser, agiter; **~ out** produire abondamment; vi bouillonner
**chute** n (river) rapide m; (water overflow) chenal m; (snow) glissoire f
**chutney** n condiment m (à base de fruits, etc), chutney m
**cicada** n zool cigale f
**cicatrice** n cicatrice f
**cicatrize** vt cicatriser; vi se cicatriser
**cider** n cidre m
**cigar** n cigare m
**cigarette** n cigarette f
**cigarette-case** n porte-cigarettes m invar
**cigarette-end** n mégot m
**cigarette-holder** n fume-cigarette m invar
**cinch** n US coll **it's a ~!** c'est du tout cuit!
**cinder** n cendre f; (furnace) scories fpl
**Cinderella** n Cendrillon f
**cinder-path, cinder-track** n piste cendrée
**cine-camera** n caméra f
**cinema** n cinéma m
**Cinemascope** n cinémascope m
**cinematic** adj du cinéma, relatif -ive au cinéma
**cinematograph** n cinématographe m
**cinematography** n cinématographie f
**cine-projector** n projecteur m (de cinéma)
**Cinerama** n cinérama m
**cinerary** adj cinéraire f
**Cingalese** adj see Sing(h)alese
**cinnabar** n chem cinabre m

**cinnamon** n (tree) cinnamome m, cannelier m; (spice) cannelle f
**cipher** n math chiffre m arabe; zéro m; (code) chiffre m; monogramme m; vt chiffrer; vi calculer
**circa** adv autour; prep autour de
**circle** n cercle m; theat (premier) balcon; fig cercle m, sphère f; theat upper ~ deuxième balcon m; **vicious** ~ cercle vicieux; vt encercler, entourer; vi tourner autour (de)
**circs** npl coll circonstances fpl
**circuit** n circuit m, tour m; (line or distance round) pourtour m; leg tournée f; **elect** circuit m; **closed** ~ circuit fermé; **short** ~ court circuit; vt **short** ~ court-circuiter
**circuitous** adj indirect, qui fait un détour; fig détourné
**circular** n circulaire f; adj circulaire
**circularize** vt envoyer des circulaires à
**circulate** vt faire circuler; vi circuler
**circulation** n circulation f; (newspaper) tirage m
**circumambient** adj ambiant
**circumcise** vt circoncire
**circumcision** n circoncision f
**circumference** n circonférence f
**circumflex** n gramm accent m circonflexe
**circumlocution** n périphrase f, circonlocution f
**circumnavigate** vt faire le tour de
**circumnavigation** n circumnavigation f
**circumscribe** vt circonscrire; encercler
**circumscription** n circonscription f; délimitation f; (coin) légende f
**circumspect** adj prudent, avisé, circonspect
**circumspection** n prudence f, circonspection f
**circumstance** n circonstance f, événement m; détail m, fait m; pompe f; ~ s situation f de fortune
**circumstantial** adj circonstancié, détaillé
**circumstantiate** vt fournir des détails comme preuve de
**circumvent** vt circonvenir
**circumvention** n finesse f, duperie f; mise f en échec
**circumvolution** n enroulement m, circonvolution f
**circus** n cirque m; (roads) rond-point m (pl ronds-points)
**cirque** n cirque m
**cirrhosis** n med cirrhose f
**cirro-cumulus** n cirro-cumulus m
**cirro-stratus** n cirro-stratus m
**cirrus** n cirrus m
**cisalpine** adj cisalpin
**cissy, sissy** n coll efféminé m

**cistern** n réservoir m; (W.C.) chasse f d'eau
**citadel** n citadelle f
**citation** n citation f
**cite** vt citer
**citizen** n citoyen -enne; leg ressortissant -e, sujet -ette
**citizenship** n nationalité f
**citrate** n chem citrate m
**citric** adj chem citrique
**citron** n bot cédrat m; (tree) cédratier m
**citronella** n bot citronnelle f
**citrous** adj relatif -ive aux agrumes
**citrus** n citrus mpl
**city** n ville f, cité f; **the City** la Cité de Londres
**civet** n civette f
**civic** adj civique; ~ **centre** bâtiments municipaux
**civics** npl instruction f civique
**civil** adj civil; ~ **defence** défense passive; ~ **law** droit civil; (in England) ~ **list** sommes votées par le Parlement anglais pour le maintien de la famille royale; ~ **servant** fonctionnaire; **the Civil Service** la fonction publique
**civilian** n civil -e; adj civil
**civility** n civilité f
**civilization** n civilisation f
**civilize** vt civiliser
**civvies** npl coll vêtements mpl de pékin
**civvy** adj coll civil, de pékin; ~ **street** vie civile
**clack** n claquement m; mech clapet m; vi jacasser
**clad** adj vêtu
**claim** n revendication f; demande f, réclamation f; leg droit m, titre m; **disputed** ~ s **office** contentieux m; vt revendiquer, exiger; prétendre à; affirmer
**claimant** n leg requérant -e
**clairvoyance** n voyance f
**clairvoyant** n voyant -e
**clam** n zool palourde f; coll fig taciturne
**clamber** vi grimper
**clammy** adj humide, suintant
**clamorous** adj criard, braillard
**clamour** n clameur f; revendication f; vi clamer, vociférer
¹**clamp** n crampon m, serre-joint(s) m, sergent m, pince f; vt serrer, cramponner; fig ~ **down on** supprimer; (expenditure) freiner
²**clamp** n piétinement m; trépignement m; vt piétiner; vi trépigner
**clan** n clan m
**clandestine** adj clandestin
**clang** n bruit m métallique; son m de cloche; vt faire retentir, faire résonner; vi retentir, résonner

clanger

**clanger** n coll bévue f, gaffe f; ~ coll **drop a ~ gaffer**

**clank** n cliquetis m; vt faire cliqueter; vi cliqueter

**clannish** adj ayant l'esprit de clan

**¹clap** n claquement m; battement m; battements mpl de mains; tape f; (thunder) coup m; vt battre, claquer; applaudir; ~ **eyes on** voir; ~ **on** surajouter, coller sur; vi applaudir, battre des mains

**²clap** n sl chaude-pisse f

**clapper** n qui applaudit; (bell) battant m

**claptrap** n boniment m, baratin m

**claque** n claque f

**claret** n (vin m de) bordeaux m rouge

**clarification** n clarification f

**clarify** vt clarifier, éclaircir; vi se clarifier, s'éclaircir

**clarinet** n clarinette f

**clarion** n mus clairon m; ~ **call** appel vibrant

**clarity** n clarté f

**clash** n choc m, heurt m; fracas m; bruit m métallique, cliquetis m; fig conflit m, clash m; (colours) disparate f, discordance f; vt heurter, choquer; faire cliqueter; vi se heurter; cliqueter; (colours) jurer, détonner; fig se heurter

**clasp** n agrafe f, fermoir m; (person) étreinte f; (hands) serrement m; vt agrafer, fermer; étreindre, serrer

**clasp-knife** n couteau m de poche

**class** n classe f, catégorie f; (school) classe f; (order of merit) classement m; fig qualité f; adj de haute qualité; vt classer, classifier

**class-conscious** adj ayant l'esprit de classe

**class-consciousness** n esprit m de classe

**class-distinction** n sens m des différences de classe

**classic** n classique m; (studies) ~ **s** études fpl de l'antiquité grecque et latine; adj classique

**classical** adj classique

**classicism** n classicisme m

**classicist** n humaniste

**classification** n classification f

**classified** adj classé, classifié; mil secret -ète

**classify** vt classifier, classer

**classless** adj sans classe; dénué d'esprit de classe

**class-war** n lutte f des classes

**classy** adj coll chic invar

**clatter** n fracas m; (talk) brouhaha m; vt choquer; vi cliqueter; (talk) jacasser

**clause** n gramm membre m de phrase; leg disposition f; pol clause f

**claustrophobia** n claustrophobie f

**clavichord** n clavecin m

**clavicle** n anat clavicule f

**clavier** n mus clavier m

**claw** n (bird) serre f; (lobster, etc) pince f; (cat, etc) griffe f; carp arrache-clou m; vt griffer; vi s'agripper; naut louvoyer au vent

**claw-hammer** n pied-de-biche m (pl pieds-de-biche), arrache-clou m

**clay** n argile f, glaise f; fig terre f; cadavre m; ~ **pigeon shoot** ball-trap m

**clean** adj propre, lavé, net (f nette); fig honnête, pur; (skilful) adroit, achevé; **come** ~ avouer; adv absolument; vt nettoyer, laver; (brush) brosser; (polish) polir; ~ **out** nettoyer; coll plumer, dépouiller; ~ **up** nettoyer

**clean-cut** adj précis, bien défini

**cleaner** n dégraisseur -euse; femme f de ménage; détergent m, détersif m

**cleaning** n nettoyage m; adj détersif -ive

**clean-limbed** adj bien bâti

**clean-living** adj chaste; honnête

**cleanly** adj propre, net (f nette); adv proprement

**cleanness** n propreté f, netteté f

**clean-out** n nettoyage m, déblaiement m

**cleanse** vt nettoyer, décrotter; fig purifier

**cleansing** n nettoiement m; fig purification f

**clean-up** n nettoyage m; fig épuration f, assainissement m; (person) débarbouillage m

**clear** n be in the ~ être au-dessus de tout soupçon; adj clair, brillant; (sky) dégagé; (complexion) frais (f fraîche); transparent; distinct; (free) libre; évident, manifeste; (entire) entier -ière, absolu; (lucid) lucide; innocent; vt clarifier, éclairer; (obstruction) débarrasser; leg innocenter, disculper; (obstacle) sauter, franchir; (cheque) solder; ~ **away** dégager; ~ **off** liquider; ~ **out** désencombrer; ~ **up** ranger; (resolve) élucider; vi (sky) se dégager, s'éclaircir; ~ **off** se libérer; s'en aller, sl foutre le camp; ~ **out** s'en aller; ~ **up** (weather) s'éclaircir

**clearage** n naut dédouanement m

**clearance** n débarras m; naut dédouanement m; mech dégagement m, jeu m

**clear-cut** adj précis, bien défini

**clearing** n clairière f; (weather) éclaircie f; dédouanement m

**clearing-house** n comm chambre f de compensation (de clearing)

**clearing-station** n mil poste m de secours

**clearness** n clarté f

**clear-out** n see clean-out

**clear-sighted** adj qui voit clair; qui prévoit

clearway *n* mot voie *f* à stationnement interdit

cleat *n naut* taquet *m*

cleavage *n* clivage *m*; scission *f*; (woman) décolleté *m*

¹cleave *vt* cliver, fendre; *vi* se fendre

²cleave *vi* coller, adhérer; *fig* s'attacher

cleaver *n* (butcher's) hachoir *m*, couperet *m*

clef *n mus* clef *f*, clé *f*

cleft *n* fissure *f*, fente *f*; *adj* fendu, fourbu

cleft-palate *n anat* palais fendu

clematis *n bot* clématite *f*

clemency *n* clémence *f*; (gentleness) douceur *f*

clement *adj* clément; (gentle) doux (*f* douce)

clench *vt* crisper, serrer; *mech* rabattre, river; (bargain, deal) conclure; *vi* se crisper; se rabattre

clerestory *n archi* claire-voie *f* (*pl* claires-voies)

clergy *n* clergé *m*

clergyman *n* pasteur *m*, clergyman *m*

cleric *n* clerc *m*, ecclésiastique *m*

clerical *adj* clérical

clericalism *n* cléricalisme *m*

clerihew *n lit* = petit poème (quatre vers) satirique ou fantaisiste

clerk *n* commis *m*, employé -e; *eccles* ecclésiastique *m*; *ar* érudit *m*; (solicitor's) clerc *m*

clever *adj* intelligent, astucieux -ieuse; adroit, habile; savant

cleverness *n* intelligence *f*, habileté *f*

clew *n* (thread) pelote *f*; *naut* point *m* d'écoute; *vt* pelotonner; *naut* carguer

cliché *n* cliché *m*, poncif *m*; *typ* cliché *m*

click *n* déclic *m*, claquement *m*; (tongue) clappement *m*; *vt* claquer; (tongue) clapper de; *vi* cliqueter, claquer; *sl* faire une touche

client *n* client -e

clientele *n collect* clientèle *f*

cliff *n* falaise *f*; paroi *f*

cliff-hanging *adj coll* (story) à suspense

climacteric *n* climatérique *f*; ménopause *f*

climactic *adj* à son apogée

climate *n* climat *m*

climatic *adj* climatique

climatology *n* climatologie *f*

climax *n* apogée *m*, sommet *m*; orgasme *m*

climb *n* montée *f*, ascension *f*; *vt* grimper, escalader, gravir; monter; *vi* grimper; monter

climber *n* grimpeur -euse; alpiniste; *bot* plante grimpante; *fig* arriviste

climbing *n* alpinisme *m*; (rock-climbing) varappe *f*; *adj* grimpeur -euse; *bot* grimpant

clinch *n* (boxing) corps à corps *m*; (grip) étreinte *f*; (riveting) rivetage *m*; (rivet) rivet *m*; *vt* (nail) river; *fig* boucler; (bargain) conclure; *vi* s'accrocher, se prendre corps à corps

cling *vi* s'accrocher, se cramponner; adhérer, se coller; *fig* rester attaché, se maintenir

clinging *adj* collant; tenace; possessif -ive

clinic *n* clinique *f*

clinical *adj* clinique; ~ thermometer thermomètre médical

¹clink *n* tintement *m*; *vt* faire tinter; *vi* tinter

²clink *n sl* taule *f*

clinker *n* mâchefer *m*

clinometer *n* clinomètre *m*

¹clip *n* attache *f*, pince *f*, agrafe *f*; (paper) trombone *m*; *cin* séquence *f*; (jewel) clip *m*; *vt* agrafer, serrer; *vi* être agrafé

²clip *n* (wool) tonte *f*; (blow) coup *m*; *sl* pas *m* rapide; *vt* tondre, couper; (wings) rogner; (words) manger; (ticket) poinçonner

clip-joint *n coll* restaurant *m*, etc où l'on vous assassine, restaurant *m*, etc coup de fusil

clipper *n naut* clipper *m*; (sheep) tondeur *m*; (tool) tondeuse *f*

clippie *n coll* receveuse *f* (d'autobus)

clipping *n* coupe *f*, tonte *f*; coupure *f* de presse

clique *n* clique *f*, coterie *f*

cliquish *adj* exclusif -ive

clitoris *n* clitoris *m*

cloaca *n* cloaque *m*

cloak *n* capote *f*, manteau *m*; *fig* apparence *f*; ~ and dagger story roman *m* de cape et d'épée; *vt* couvrir d'un manteau; déguiser

cloakroom *n theat* vestiaire *m*; (railway) consigne *f*

clobber *vt sl* arrêter; attaquer; rouer de coups

cloche *n* cloche *f*

¹clock *n* horloge *f*; (small) pendule *f*; *vt sp* chronométrer; *vi* ~ in (on) (se) pointer

²clock *n* (stocking) baguette *f*

clockwise *adj* dans le sens des aiguilles d'une montre

clockwork *n* mouvement *m* d'horlogerie; mécanisme *m*; like ~ précis, régulier -ière; *adj* mécanique

clod *n* motte *f*; *coll* balourd *m*

clod-hopper *n* rustre *m*, cul-terreux *m* (*pl* culs-terreux)

clog *n* sabot *m*; *fig* entrave *f*; *vt* entraver; obstruer

**cloisonné** adj cloisonné

**cloister** n cloître m; vt cloîtrer; ~ **one-self** se cloîtrer

¹**close** n (enclosure) enclos m; (cathedral) enceinte f; (quadrangle) cour f; adj proche; intime; clos; (reticent) renfermé; (compact) serré; étroit; concis, précis; (thorough) minutieux -ieuse; (stingy) avaricieux -ieuse; (weather) lourd, étouffant; ~ **season** période f où l'on n'a pas le droit de chasser; ~ **vowel** voyelle fermée; **have a ~ call (shave)** l'échapper belle; adv près; ~ **by** tout près; ~ **on** tout près

²**close** n fin f, conclusion f; vt fermer, clore; elect fermer; (finish) achever, terminer; ~ **down** finir, fermer; ~ **in** cerner, envelopper; ~ **up** boucher, bloquer; vi fermer, finir, clore; se fermer; (agree) s'accorder, se mettre d'accord; ~ **down** rad cesser de transmettre; fermer; ~ **in** s'approcher; (night) tomber

**closed** adj fermé; limité; (blocked) barré; ~ **circuit** circuit fermé; ~ **shop** atelier m (usine f) qui n'engage que des employés syndiqués, monopole m d'embauche (d'un syndicat); **road ~** route barrée

**close-down** n fermeture f; rad fin f des émissions

**close-fisted** adj grippe-sou invar

**close-hauled** adj naut au plus près

**closely** adv de près, étroitement

**closeness** n (weather) lourdeur f; intimité f; (miserliness) pingrerie f

**close-quarters** npl mil contact m avec l'ennemi; espace restreint; **come to ~ with** en venir aux mains avec

**close-stool** n chaise percée

**closet** n (room) cabinet m; (cupboard) penderie f

**closeted** adj en petit comité

**close-up** n cin gros plan

**closing** n fermeture f, clôture f

**closing-time** n heure f de fermeture

**closure** n (business, etc) fermeture f; (debate, parliament) clôture f; vt clôturer

**clot** n caillot m; coll idiot -e, lourdaud -e; vi cailler, coaguler

**cloth** n tissu m, étoffe f, drap m; theat toile f; (cleaning) chiffon m, torchon m; **the ~** le clergé

**clothe** vt habiller, vêtir; fig revêtir, couvrir

**clothes** npl vêtements mpl, habits mpl; **in plain ~** en civil

**clothes-basket** n panier m à linge

**clothes-brush** n brosse f à habits

**clothes-horse** n séchoir m

**clothes-line** n étendoir m

**clothes-peg** n pince f à linge

**clothier** n (marchand m) drapier m

**clothing** n vêtements mpl

**clotted** adj coagulé

**cloud** n nuage m; lit nuée f, nue f; (mirror) buée f; fig ombre f; **have one's head in the ~s** être dans les nuages; **under a ~** soupçonné, en butte aux soupçons; vt couvrir de nuages, obscurcir; (reputation) ternir; vi se couvrir de nuages; s'obscurcir; (reputation) se ternir

**cloudburst** n pluie battante, déluge m; trombe f d'eau

**clouded** adj couvert de nuages; obscurci; fig terne, mélancolique

**cloudiness** n aspect nuageux; (liquid) aspect m trouble

**cloudless** adj sans nuages, serein

**cloudy** adj nuageux -euse, couvert, sombre; (liquid) trouble; fig sombre; vague, nébuleux -euse

**clout** n torchon m; morceau m d'étoffe; coll gifle f, soufflet m, torgnole f; coll (power) pouvoir m; influence f; vt gifler; rapiécer

¹**clove** n gousse f

²**clove** n bot clou m de girofle

**cloven** adj fendu, fourchu; ~ **foot** pied fourchu

**clover** n trèfle m; **be in ~** être comme un coq en pâte

**cloverleaf** n mot échangeur m

**clown** n pitre m; (circus) clown m; ar bouffon m; rustre m; vi bouffonner, faire le clown

**clowning** n bouffonnerie f, pitrerie f

**clownish** adj gauche, balourd

**cloy** vt rassasier, blaser; fig lasser; vi se blaser

**club** n (weapon) matraque f, trique f, gourdin m; club m, société f, cercle m, association f; (cards) trèfle m; (golf) crosse f; vt matraquer; vi se réunir; ~ **together** cotiser

**clubbable** adj sociable

**club-foot** n pied-bot m (pl pieds-bot)

**club-room** n salle f de réunion

**cluck** n gloussement m; vi glousser

**clue** n indice m; **not have a ~** n'en avoir pas la moindre idée

**clueless** adj coll crétin; incapable; **he's ~** il ne sait jamais rien

**clump** n touffe f, massif m, bosquet m; (footsteps) bruit m de pas; coll coup m, gifle f; vt grouper en massif; coll gifler; vi marcher d'un pas lourd

**clumsiness** n gaucherie f, maladresse f; lourdeur f; manque m de tact

**clumsy** adj gauche, maladroit; lourd, incommode; inélégant

**cluster** n (fruit) grappe f; (flowers)

bouquet *m*; (trees) massif *m*; groupe *m*; (houses) pâté *m*; *vi* se grouper

¹**clutch** *n mot* embrayage *m*; (grasp) étreinte *f*, prise *f*; (snatch) griffe *f*; *vt* saisir, étreindre; *vi* se cramponner, s'accrocher

²**clutch** *n* (eggs) couvée *f*

**clutter** *n* désordre *m*, *coll* pagaïe *f*; *vt* mettre en désordre, *coll* mettre en pagaïe

**clyster** *n* clystère *m*

**coach** *n* carrosse *m*; coche *m*; (railway) wagon *m*, voiture *f*; *mot* car *m*; *sp* entraîneur *m*; (tutor) répétiteur -trice; *vt sp* entraîner; (teach) préparer (à un examen)

**coachbuilder** *n mot* carrossier *m*

**coach-built** *adj mot* à carrosserie hors série

**coaching** *n sp* entraînement *m*; enseignement *m*, préparation *f*

**coachman** *n* cocher *m*

**coachwork** *n mot* carrosserie *f*

**coagulant** *n* coagulant *m*; *adj* coagulant

**coagulate** *vt* coaguler; *vi* se coaguler

**coal** *n* charbon *m*, houille *f*; **carry ~ s to Newcastle** apporter de l'eau à la mer; **haul s/o over the ~ s** réprimander qn; **heap ~ s of fire on s/o's head** rendre le bien pour le mal; *vt naut* fournir en charbon; *vi naut* s'approvisionner en charbon

**coalblack** *adj* noir comme du charbon

**coal-bunker** *n naut* soute *f* à charbon

**coal-cellar** *n* cave *f* à charbon

**coalesce** *vi* (substances) se souder, fusionner; *fig* s'unir

**coal-face** *n* banc *m* de houille

**coalfield** *n* bassin houiller

**coal-gas** *n* gaz *m* de houille

**coaling** *n naut* approvisionnement *m* en charbon

**coalition** *n* coalition *f*

**coal-mine** *n* houillère *f*, mine *f* de charbon

**coal-miner** *n* mineur *m*

**coal-pit** *n* houillère *f*, mine *f* de charbon

**coal-scuttle** *n* seau *m* à charbon

**coal-tar** *n* coaltar *m*, goudron *m*

**coarse** *adj* vulgaire, commun; (substance) grossier -ière, rude; (joke) indécent

**coarsen** *vt* rendre vulgaire; (substance) rendre grossier -ière; *vi* devenir vulgaire; (substance) devenir grossier -ière

**coarseness** *n* vulgarité *f*; grossièreté *f*

**coast** *n* côte *f*; littoral *m*; **the ~ is clear** il n'y a pas de danger; *vi* (vehicle) descendre en roue libre

**coastal** *adj* côtier -ière

**coaster** *n naut* caboteur *m*

**coastguard** *n* garde-côte *m*

**coastline** *n* littoral *m*

**coat** *n* habit *m*; veste *f*, veston *m*; (overcoat) manteau *m*, pardessus *m*; (tails) habit *m*; (layer) couche *f*; (animal) pelage *m*; *anat* membrane *f*; **~ of arms** blason *m*, armoiries *fpl*; *vt* enduire, couvrir; *cul + med* enrober

**coax** *vt* cajoler, amadouer, entortiller

**coaxer** *n* cajoleur -euse, flatteur -euse

**co-axial** *adj math* coaxial

**coaxing** *adj* cajoleur -euse

**cob** *n* (coal) tête *f* de moineau; (maize) épi *m*; (nut) noisette *f*; (horse) bidet *m*; *zool* cygne *m* mâle; *vt coll* frapper, battre

**cobalt** *n* cobalt *m*

¹**cobble** *n* pavé rond; *vt* paver

²**cobble** *vt* réparer (des chaussures); rafistoler

**cobbler** *n* cordonnier *m*, savetier *m*

**cobble-stone** *n* pavé rond

**co-belligerent** *n* cobelligérant *m*; *adj* cobelligérant

**cob-loaf** *n* pain arrondi, boule *f*

**cob-nut** *n* noisette *f*

**cobra** *n* cobra *m*, naja *m*

**cobweb** *n* toile *f* d'araignée

**Coca-Cola** *n* Coca-Cola *m*

**cocaine** *n* cocaïne *f*

**coccyx** *n anat* coccyx *m*

**cochineal** *n* cochenille *f*

**cock** *n* coq *m*; oiseau *m* mâle, mâle *m*; (tap) robinet *m*; (rifle) chien *m*; (balance) aiguille *f*; (sundial) style *m*; (weather-vane) girouette *f*; *agr* meulon *m*; *coll* type *m*, bonhomme *m*; *sl* (penis) queue *f*, bite *f*; **~ of the walk** coq *m* du village; **go off at half ~** commencer prématurément; *coll* **old ~** mon vieux; *sl* **talk ~** déconner; *vt* dresser, redresser; (rifle) armer; *sl* **~ up** bousiller

**cockade** *n* cocarde *f*

**cock-a-hoop** *adj* triomphant, allègre; *adv* allègrement, triomphalement

**cockatoo** *n zool* cacatoès *m*

**cockatrice** *n* basilic *m*

**cock-crow** *n* aube *f*

**cocked** *adj* (rifle) armé; (ears) dressé; **~ hat** chapeau *m* à cornes

**cocker** *n* (dog) cocker *m*

**cockerel** *n* coquelet *m*

**cock-eyed** *adj coll* louche, bigle; *sl* (crooked) de travers; (drunk) ivre

**cock-fight** *n* combat *m* de coqs

**cockiness** *n* suffisance *f*

**cockle** *n zool* coque *f*; (boat) coquille *f* de noix; **warm the ~ s of one's heart** réconforter

**Cockney** *n* Cockney; *adj* cockney

**cockpit** *n naut + aer* cockpit *m*; *fig* arène *f*

**cockroach** *n zool* blatte *f*, cafard *m*
**cockscomb** *n* crête *f* de coq; *bot* crête-de-coq *f* (*pl* crêtes-de-coq)
**cock-sparrow** *n* moineau *m* (mâle); *fig pej* freluquet *m*
**cocksure** *adj* suffisant
**cocktail** *n* (drink) cocktail *m*; (horse) courtaud -e; ~ **party** cocktail *m*
**cock-up** *n sl* pagaïe *f*, pagaille *f*
**cocky** *adj* arrogant, suffisant
**coco** *n bot* cocotier *m*
**cocoa** *n* cacao *m*
**coconut, cocoanut** *n* noix *f* de coco; ~ **butter** beurre *m* de coco; ~ **matting** tapis *m* de fibre (de noix de coco)
**cocoon** *n* cocon *m*
**cod** *n* morue *f*
**coda** *n mus* coda *f*
**coddle** *vt* dorloter, choyer; *cul* faire mijoter
**code** *n* code *m*; (cypher) chiffre *m*; (telephone) indicatif *m*; *vt* coder
**codeine** *n med* codéine *f*
**codfish** *n zool* morue *f*
**codger** *n coll* croulant *m*
**codicil** *n leg* codicille *m*
**codification** *n* codification *f*
**codify** *vt* codifier
**co-director** *n* (managing) codirecteur -trice; coadministrateur -trice
**cod-liver-oil** *n* huile *f* de foie de morue
**co-ed** *n US coll* étudiante *f* dans un collège mixte
**co-education** *n* éducation *f* mixte
**co-educational** *adj* mixte
**coefficient** *n* coefficient *m*
**coerce** *vt* contraindre
**coercion** *n* contrainte *f*
**coercive** *adj* coercitif -ive
**coeval** *n* contemporain -e; *adj* contemporain, du même âge
**coexist** *vi* coexister
**coexistence** *n* coexistence *f*
**coffee** *n* café *m*; **black** ~ café *m* nature; **white** ~ café au lait, café crème
**coffee-bean** *n* grain de café
**coffee-grounds** *n* marc de café
**coffee-mill** *n* moulin *m* à café
**coffee-pot** *n* cafetière *f*
**coffee-table** *n* table basse; ~ **book** grand livre illustré
**coffer** *n* coffre *m*, caisse *f*; *eng* caisson *m*; ~ **s** ressources financières
**coffin** *n* cercueil *m*, bière *f*
**¹cog** *n* dent *f*; *carp* tenon *m*
**²cog** *vt* (dice) manipuler en trichant; *vi* tricher
**cogency** *n* puissance *f*, bien-fondé *m*
**cogent** *adj* puissant, convaincant, péremptoire
**cogitate** *vt* + *vi* méditer
**cogitation** *n* méditation *f*, réflexion *f*

**cognac** *n* cognac *m*
**cognate** *n leg* cognat *m*; *gramm* analogue *m*; *adj leg* parent; *gramm* analogue
**cognition** *n* perception *f*; *philo* cognition *f*
**cognizance** *n* connaissance *f*; *leg* compétence *f*, ressort *m*
**cognizant** *adj* instruit, ayant connaissance
**cognomen** *n* nom *m* de famille; (nickname) surnom *m*
**cog-wheel** *n* roue *f* à dents
**cohabit** *vi* cohabiter
**cohere** *vi* se tenir; adhérer
**coherence** *n* cohérence *f*
**coherent** *adj* cohérent, logique
**cohesion** *n* cohésion *f*
**cohesive** *adj* cohésif -ive
**cohort** *n* cohorte *f*
**coiffure** *n* coiffure *f*
**coil** *n* rouleau *m*, tour *m*; (hair) chignon *m*; *elect* bobine *f*; (contraceptive) stérilet *m*; *vt* enrouler; *elect* bobiner; *vi* s'enrouler
**coin** *n* pièce *f* (de monnaie); numéraire *m*; **pay s/o in his own** ~ rendre à qn la monnaie de sa pièce; *vt* frapper; (words) inventer; *coll* ~ **money** s'enrichir
**coinage** *n* monnaie *f*; frappe *f*; (words) invention *f*
**coincide** *vi* coïncider
**coincidence** *n* coïncidence *f*
**coincident** *adj* coïncident
**coincidental** *adj* de coïncidence
**coiner** *n* faux-monnayeur *m*
**coitus, coition** *n* coït *m*
**¹coke** *n* coke *m*; *vt* cokéfier
**²coke** *n sl* cocaïne *f*; *coll* coca *m*
**col** *n* col *m*
**colander** *n* passoire *f*
**cold** *n* froid *m*; *med* rhume *m*; **catch** ~ s'enrhumer; **out in the** ~ négligé, à l'écart; *fig* froid, indifférent, détaché; ~ **comfort** maigre consolation *f*; ~ **sweat** sueur froide; ~ **war** guerre froide; **have** ~ **feet** avoir peur; **in** ~ **blood** de sang-froid; *coll* **it leaves me** ~ ça ne me fait aucun effet, ça ne m'intéresse point; **throw** ~ **water on** refroidir, décourager
**cold-blooded** *adj zool* à sang froid; *fig* cruel -elle, insensible, dur
**cold-chisel** *n* burin *m*, ciseau *m* à froid
**cold-cream** *n* cold-cream *m*
**cold-frame** *n agr* châssis *m*
**cold-front** *n meteor* masse *f* d'air froid
**coldish** *adj* frisquet -ette, frais (*f* fraîche)
**coldness** *n* froideur *f*
**cold-shoulder** *n* indifférence voulue,

rebuffade *f*; *vt* faire grise mine à

**cold-storage** *n* conservation *f* en congélateur; *fig* **put into** ~ différer sine die

**coleslaw** *n* salade *f* de chou cru

**colibri** *n* colibri *m*

**colic** *n med* colique *f*; *adj med* du côlon; de colique

**colitis** *n med* colite *f*

**collaborate** *vi* collaborer

**collaboration** *n* collaboration *f*

**collaborator** *n* collaborateur -trice

**collage** *n* collage *m*

**collapse** *n* chute *f*, effondrement *m*, écroulement *m*; *med* collapsus *m*; *vi* s'effondrer, s'écrouler, tomber

**collapsible** *adj* pliant

**collar** *n* col *m*, collet *m*; (detachable) faux col; (blouse) collerette *f*; (dog) collier *m*; *mech* collet *m*; *vt coll* saisir, prendre au collet; *coll* rafler

**collar-bone** *n anat* clavicule *f*

**collate** *vt* collationner; *eccles* nommer

**collateral** *n* nantissement *m*; *adj* parallèle; *leg* collatéral; secondaire; *comm* subsidiaire

**collation** *n* collation *f*

**colleague** *n* collègue

¹**collect** *n eccles* collecte *f*; *US* ~ **call** appel *m* en P.C.V.

²**collect** *vt* grouper, rassembler, réunir; collectionner; (pick up) ramasser; (gather) recueillir; *vi* se rassembler; ~ **oneself** se recueillir

**collected** *adj* groupé, ramassé; (calm) calme, recueilli; ~ **works** œuvres complètes

**collection** *n* collection *f*; *eccles* quête *f*, collecte *f*; (group) groupement *m*, rassemblement *m*; (mail) levée *f*

**collective** *adj* collectif -ive

**collectivism** *n* collectivisme *m*

**collectivization** *n* collectivisation *f*

**collector** *n* collectionneur -euse; (tax) percepteur *m*, receveur *m*; (railway ticket) contrôleur -euse

**college** *n* collège *m*; (school) école privée; **electoral** ~ collège électoral; **military** ~ école *f* militaire; **naval** ~ école navale; **technical** ~ collège *m* technique

**collegial** *adj* de collège

**collegiate** *adj* de collège; *eccles* collégial; ~ **church** collégiale *f*

**collide** *vi* se heurter, se tamponner; ~ **with** heurter, tamponner; *fig* se heurter contre, être en conflit avec

**collie** *n* colley *m*

**collier** *n* mineur *m*; *naut* charbonnier *m*

**colliery** *n* mine *f* de charbon, houillère *f*

**collision** *n* collision *f*, choc *m*, heurt *m*, tamponnement *m*; *fig* conflit *m*

**collocate** *vt* arranger, juxtaposer

**collocation** *n* arrangement *m*, juxtaposition *f*

**collodion** *n chem* collodion *m*

**colloquial** *adj* familier -ière, parlé

**colloquialism** *n* tournure familière

**colloquy** *n* colloque *m*; dialogue *m*

**collude** *vi* agir de connivence

**collusion** *n* collusion *f*, complicité *f*

**collusive** *adj* collusoire, complice

**collywobbles** *n coll* mal *m* d'estomac, coliques *fpl*

¹**colon** *n anat* côlon *m*

²**colon** *n gramm* deux-points *mpl*

**colonel** *n* colonel *m*

**colonial** *n* colonial -e; *adj* colonial

**colonialism** *n* colonialisme *m*

**colonic** *adj* du côlon; ~ **irrigation** lavement *m*

**colonist** *n* colon *m*

**colonization** *n* colonisation *f*

**colonize** *vt* coloniser

**colony** *n* colonie *f*

**Colorado** *n* Colorado *m*; *zool* ~ **beetle** doryphore *m*

**coloration** *n* coloration *f*, coloris *m*

**colossal** *adj* colossal

**colossus** *n* colosse *m*

**colour** *n* couleur *f*, teinte *f*, coloris *m*; teinture *f*; (complexion) teint *m*; *mus* ton *m*, timbre *m*; *fig* aspect *m*; vivacité *f*; ~**s** *sp* couleurs *fpl*; *mil* drapeau *m*; ~ **problem** problème racial; **change** ~ changer de visage; **off** ~ malade, souffrant; **with flying** ~**s** triomphalement; *vt* colorer; (dye) teindre; (paint) colorier, peindre; *fig* colorer; (distort) dénaturer; *vi* se colorer, changer de couleur; (flush) rougir

**colourable** *adj* spécieux -ieuse, plausible

**colour-bar** *n* discrimination raciale

**colour-blind** *adj* daltonien -ienne

**colour-blindness** *n* daltonisme *m*

**coloured** *adj* coloré; (person) de couleur; *fig* dénaturé; influencé

**colourful** *adj* éclatant, vif (*f* vive); *fig* pittoresque, original, gai

**colouring** *n* pigment *m*; (hue) coloration *f*; complexion *f*; *fig* aspect *m*, apparence *f*

**colourist** *n* coloriste

**colourless** *adj* incolore; *fig* fade, terne

¹**colt** *n* poulain *m*

²**colt** *n* colt *m*, pistolet *m*

**coltish** *adj* fringant; inexpérimenté

**columbine** *n bot* colombine *f*

**column** *n* colonne *f*

**columnist** *n* (newspaper) collaborateur -trice régulier -ière d'un journal

**coma** *n* coma *m*

**comatose** *adj* comateux -euse

**comb** *n* peigne *m*; (wool) carde *f*; (cock) crête *f*; (honey) rayon *m*; *vt* peigner;

combat

carder; *fig* fouiller; ~ **out** démêler; sélectionner

**combat** *n* combat *m*; *vt* combattre; *vi* se battre

**combatant** *n + adj* combattant -e

**combative** *adj* combatif -ive

**comber** *n* (person) peigneur -euse; (machine) peigneuse *f*; (wave) vague déferlante

**combination** *n* combinaison *f*; association *f*; (garment) combinaison *f*; **motor-cycle** ~ side-car *m*

**combine** *n comm* trust *m*, consortium *m*; *agr* moissonneuse-batteuse *f* (*pl* moissonneuses-batteuses); *vt* combiner, unir; *vi* s'unir, se grouper ensemble

**combine-harvester** *n* moissonneuse-batteuse *f* (*pl* moissonneuses-batteuses)

**combustible** *n* combustible *m*; *adj* combustible

**combustion** *n* combustion *f*

**come** *vi* venir, approcher; arriver, paraître; (happen) se produire, advenir; arriver, survenir; (cause) être causé par; *coll* jouer le rôle de; *sl* (orgasm) jouir, juter; ~! voyons!, tout de même!; ~ **about** arriver, advenir; *naut* virer; ~ **across** rencontrer, trouver par hasard; *sl* ~ **across with** (lend) prêter; (cough up) casquer; ~ **along** avancer rapidement, se presser; ~ **at** attaquer, atteindre; ~ **away** s'en aller, partir; se détacher; ~ **back** retourner; *sl* riposter; ~ **between** séparer, brouiller; ~ **by** obtenir; *coll* ~ **clean** avouer; ~ **down** descendre; *fig* tomber bas; (be transmitted) se transmettre; ~ **down on** blâmer, gronder; ~ **forward** offrir de l'aide; se proposer, s'offrir; ~ **from** venir de, provenir de; ~ **in** entrer, arriver; devenir à la mode; *coll* ~ **in for** obtenir; encourir; ~ **into** hériter; ~ **off** réussir; advenir, avoir lieu; se détacher; ~ **off it!** dis la vérité!; ~ **on** avancer, faire des progrès; (pain) commencer; *theat* entrer en scène, faire une entrée; ~ **out** être révélé, se divulguer; sortir, paraître; (book) paraître, être publié; (in society) débuter; (strike) se mettre en grève; ~ **out with** (words) lâcher; ~ **over** passer à l'autre camp; (feel) se sentir; ~ **round** *med* revenir à soi, se ranimer; (accept) se résigner, donner son accord; *coll* visiter, faire un saut; ~ **through** survivre; ~ **to** *med* revenir à soi; (bill, amount) revenir à; ~ **under** (list) se trouver sous la mention de; être sous l'autorité de; ~ **up** (plant) pousser, pointer; (conversation) être mentionné, venir sur le tapis; monter; ~

**upon** (on) trouver par hasard, tomber sur; ~ **up to** égaler; ~ **up with** (catch up) rejoindre; (idea) proposer

**come-back** *n coll* rentrée *f*; *coll* riposte *f*

**comedian** *n* (music-hall) comique; *theat* acteur -trice comique; comédien -ienne

**come-down** *n* déchéance *f*, humiliation *f*

**comedy** *n* comédie *f*; **musical** ~ opérette *f*

**comeliness** *n* beauté *f*, charme *m*, grâce *f*

**comely** *adj* avenant, beau (*f* belle)

**comestible** *n* comestible *m*; *adj* comestible

**comet** *n* comète *f*

**comfort** *n* confort *m*; aises *fpl*; (consolation) réconfort *m*, encouragement *m*; (ease) bien-être *m*, aisance *f*; ~ **station** *US* toilettes *fpl* publiques; *vt* consoler, soulager; encourager, réconforter

**comfortable** *adj* confortable, commode; (thought) rassurant; (money) aisé

**comforter** *n* consolateur -trice; (scarf) cache-nez *m*; (child) sucette *f*

**comfortless** *adj* sans confort, incommode; (cheerless) triste

**comfy** *adj coll* confortable, douillet -ette

**comic** *n coll* (performer) comique; *coll* (magazine, strip) bande(s) dessinée(s); *adj* comique; amusant

**comical** *adj* comique, drôle; (absurd) cocasse

**comic-strip** *n* bande dessinée

**Cominform** *n pol* Cominform *m*

**coming** *n* venue *f*, arrivée *f*; *eccles* événement *m*; *adj* à venir, futur; (week, month, year) prochain; (promising) qui promet, d'avenir

**comity** *n* courtoisie *f*; *pol* ~ **of nations** nations *fpl* ayant de bons rapports entre elles

**comma** *n* virgule *f*; **inverted** ~ (s) guillemet(s) *m*(*pl*)

**command** *n* ordre *m*; autorité *f*; *mil* commandement *m*; *mil* troupes *fpl*; *mil* **high** ~ haut commandement; *vt* ordonner; (respect) exiger; (control) commander, dominer, contrôler; (overlook) donner sur; (price) atteindre; (respect) inspirer

**commandant** *n mil* commandant *m*

**commandeer** *vt* réquisitionner

**commander** *n* chef *m*, commandant *m*, *naut* = capitaine *m* de frégate; *aer* chef *m* de bord; ~ **in chief** commandant *m* en chef

**commanding** *adj* (tone, etc) de commandement; (presence) imposant; (height, position) dominant, élevé; *mil* ~ **officer** commandant *m*

**commandment** *n* ordre *m*; *eccles* commandement *m*

406

commando *n mil* commando *m*
commemorate *vt* commémorer
commemoration *n* commémoration *f*
commence *vt + vi* commencer
commencement *n* commencement *m*
commend *vt* louer; (recommend) recommander; (entrust) confier; ~ oneself se recommander; ~ itself (idea, plan) faire bonne impression
commendable *adj* louable
commendation *n* louange *f*, approbation *f*
commendatory *adj* laudatif -ive, approbatif -ive
commensurability *n* commensurabilité *f*
commensurable *adj* commensurable
commensurate *adj* de même mesure, proportionné; en accord
comment *n* commentaire *m*, observation *f*, remarque *f*; (note) annotation *f*; *vi* faire des remarques
commentary *n* commentaire *m*; *rad* running ~ reportage *m* en direct
commentate *vt* commenter; *vi* faire un reportage
commentator *n* commentateur -trice; *rad* radio-reporter *m*
commerce *n* commerce *m*
commercial *n* spot *m* publicitaire; *adj* commercial, de commerce; ~ traveller voyageur *m* de commerce
commercialism *n pej* esprit *m* mercantile; pratique *f* du commerce
commercialize *vt* commercialiser
commination *n* commination *f*
comminatory *adj* comminatoire
commingle *vt* mélanger; *vi* se mélanger
commiserate *vi* avoir de la commisération, compatir aux malheurs
commiseration *n* commisération *f*
commissariat *n mil* intendance *f*; ravitaillement *m*
commissary *n* commissaire *m*
commission *n* commission *f*, comité *f*; *mil* brevet *m*; (artist) commande *f*; *comm* commission *f*; *naut* armement *m*; *eccles* commission *f*; *vt* donner pouvoir à, déléguer; (artist) passer une commande à; *naut* armer
commissionaire *n* commissionaire *m* d'hôtel (de restaurant, etc)
commissioner *n* membre *m* d'une commission
commit *vt* commettre, perpétrer; (entrust) confier, livrer; *leg* écrouer; ~ oneself s'engager
commitment *n* engagement *m*; (handing over) action *f* de confier; perpétration *f*; *leg* incarcération *f*; *leg* mandat *m* de dépôt; engagement financier
committal *n* action *f* de perpétrer; ~ to the earth enterrement *m*

committee *n* comité *m*, commission *f*
committee-room *n* salle *f* de réunion; (electoral) permanence *f*
commode *n* commode *f*; chaise percée
commodious *adj* spacieux -ieuse
commodity *n* denrée *f*, produit *m*
commodore *n* commodore *m*; président *m* d'un yacht-club
common *n* (city) espace vert; (village) terrain communal; *adj* commun; (widespread) général, public (*f* publique); (well-known) familier -ière, habituel -uelle, ordinaire; fréquent, normal; (low) vulgaire, bas (*f* basse); *gramm + math* commun; *mus* parfait; ~ decency simple politesse *f*; ~ ground faits incontestés; *leg* ~ law droit coutumier; ~ people commun *m*; ~ sense sens commun, bon sens; ~ soldier simple soldat *m*
commonalty *n* commun *m*; gens *mpl* du peuple
commoner *n* roturier -ière
commonly *adv* généralement, ordinairement
commonness *n* vulgarité *f*
commonplace *n* cliché *m*, lieu commun, banalité *f*; *adj* banal, ordinaire, quelconque
commons *npl* gens *mpl* du peuple, commun *m*; (rations) quantité *f* fixe de vivres; House of Commons Chambre *f* des Communes; short ~ portion congrue
commonweal *n* bien public
commonwealth *n* nation *f* démocratique; confédération *f* de nations; the Commonwealth le Commonwealth (britannique)
commotion *n* commotion *f*, agitation *f*; tumulte *m*
communal *adj* communal; commun
¹commune *n* commune *f*
²commune *vi* communier, converser; *US eccles* communier; ~ with oneself se recueillir
communicable *adj* communicable
communicant *n eccles* communicant -e; informateur -trice
communicate *vt* communiquer, transmettre; *vi* communiquer, se mettre en rapport; *eccles* communier
communication *n* communication *f*; transmission *f*; message *m*, information *f*, renseignement *m*; ~ s système *m* de transmission de messages; moyens *mpl* de communication; (railway) ~ cord signal *m* d'alarme; ~ satellite satellite-relais *m* (*pl* satellites-relais)
communicative *adj* communicatif -ive, expansif -ive
communicator *n* communicateur -trice, transmetteur -trice

## communion

**communion** *n* communion *f*, communion *f* d'idées; relations *fpl* intimes; *eccles* communion *f*

**communiqué** *n* communiqué *m*

**communism** *n* communisme *m*

**communist** *n+adj* communiste

**communistic** *adj* communiste; (tendency) communisant

**community** *n* communauté *f*, collectivité *f*; société *f*; *eccles* communauté *f*, ordre *m*; *leg* communauté *f* (de biens)

**commutability** *n* permutabilité *f*

**commutable** *adj* permutable

**commutation** *n* permutation *f*, commutation *f*

**commute** *vt* échanger; *leg* commuer; *elect* modifier; *vi* faire la navette

**commuter** *n* personne *f* qui fait la navette; ~ **belt** grande banlieue

**¹compact** *n* accord *m*, contrat *m*, convention *f*

**²compact** *n* poudrier *m*

**³compact** *n US* petite voiture; *adj* compact, dense; *fig* concis, bref (*f* brève); *vt* rendre compact, tasser, comprimer

**compacted** *adj* comprimé, tassé

**compactness** *n* densité *f*; concision *f*

**¹companion** *n* compagnon *m*, compagne *f*; dame *f* de compagnie; (book) guide *m*, manuel *m*; (pair) pendant *m*; *adj* qui se fait pendant; *vt* accompagner

**²companion** *n naut* capot *m*; ~ **hatch** écoutille *f*; ~ **ladder** échelle *f* des cabines

**companionable** *adj* sociable

**companionship** *n* camaraderie *f*

**company** *n* compagnie *f*; (guests) invités -ées *pl*; camaraderie *f*; **bad** ~ mauvaises fréquentations; **be good** ~ être très agréable; **keep** ~ **with** frayer avec; **keep s/o** ~ tenir compagnie à qn; **part** ~ **with** se séparer de; ne plus être d'accord avec

**comparable** *adj* comparable

**comparative** *adj* comparatif -ive; relatif -ive; *gramm* comparatif -ive; (literature, linguistics, etc) comparé

**compare** *n* comparaison *f*; **beyond** ~ incomparable; *vt* comparer, mettre en comparaison; *vi* se comparer

**comparison** *n* comparaison *f*

**compartment** *n* compartiment *m*

**compass** *n naut*, *etc* boussole *f*; *fig* étendue *f*; (scope) champ *m*, rayon *m*; *mus* portée *f*; *math* ~**es** compas *m*; *vt* faire le tour de; entourer; (scheme) projeter, comploter; (achieve) réaliser, accomplir

**compass-card** *n* rose *f* des vents

**compassing** *adj* entourant; (achieving) accomplissant

**compassion** *n* compassion *f*

**compassionate** *adj* compatissant

**compatibility** *n* compatibilité *f*

**compatible** *adj* compatible

**compatriot** *n* compatriote

**compel** *vt* obliger, contraindre, forcer

**compelling** *adj* irrésistible

**compendious** *adj* compendieux -ieuse, succinct

**compendium** *n* abrégé *m*

**compensate** *vt* compenser, indemniser; *mech* compenser; *vi* ~ **for** être une compensation de

**compensation** *n* compensation *f*, dédommagement *m*, indemnité *f*; *mech* compensation *f*

**compensatory** *adj* compensateur -trice, compensatoire

**compete** *vi* concourir; (rival) faire concurrence; participer

**competence** *n* compétence *f*, capacité *f*; aisance *f*; *leg* compétence *f*

**competent** *adj* compétent, capable; qualifié; *leg* compétent, habile

**competition** *n* compétition *f*, concurrence *f*; (contest) concours *m*

**competitive** *adj comm* compétitif -ive; de concours

**competitor** *n* concurrent -e

**compilation** *n* compilation *f*

**compile** *vt* compiler, recueillir

**complacence, complacency** *n* satisfaction *f*, contentement *m* de soi, suffisance *f*

**complacent** *adj* satisfait, suffisant

**complain** *vi* se plaindre, se lamenter; formuler une plainte

**complainant** *n leg* plaignant -e

**complaint** *n* plainte *f*, lamentation *f*; (grievance) grief *m*, réclamation *f*; maladie *f*; *leg* plainte *f*

**complaisance** *n* complaisance *f*, obligeance *f*; (courtesy) courtoisie *f*

**complaisant** *adj* complaisant, obligeant; (polite) courtois

**complement** *n* complément *m*; *mil* +*naut* effectif *m*; *gramm* complément *m*, attribut *m*; *vt* compléter, complémenter

**complementary** *adj* complémentaire

**complete** *adj* complet -ète, entier -ière; (finished) achevé, fini; *coll* parfait, consommé; *vt* achever, finir; compléter

**completeness** *n* plénitude *f*

**completion** *n* achèvement *m*; réalisation *f*; plénitude *f*

**complex** *n* complexe *m*; *adj* complexe

**complexion** *n* complexion *f*; *fig* aspect *m*, nature *f*

**complexity** *n* complexité *f*, complication *f*

**compliance** *n* acquiescement *m*;

(conformity) conformité *f*; (submission) complaisance *f*; **in ~ with** conformément à

**compliant** *adj* accommodant, complaisant; servile

**complicate** *vt* compliquer

**complication** *n* complication *f*

**complicity** *n* complicité *f*

**compliment** *n* compliment *m*, louange *f*; **~ s** compliments *mpl*, hommages *mpl*; vœux *mpl*; *vt* complimenter, féliciter

**complimentary** *adj* flatteur -euse, élogieux -ieuse; (free) gratuit; **~ copy** (book) exemplaire offert en hommage; **~ ticket** billet *m* de faveur

**compline** *n eccles* complies *fpl*

**comply** *vi* céder, se plier; **~ with** se conformer à, observer

**component** *n* élément *m*; *chem* composant *m*; *adj* composant

**comport** *vt* **~ oneself** se comporter, se conduire; *vi* s'accorder

**compose** *vt* composer, constituer, former; (calm) arranger, apaiser; (order) disposer, organiser

**composed** *adj* composé; calme, tranquille

**composer** *n* compositeur -trice

**composite** *n* composé *m*; *bot* composée *f*; *archi* composite *m*; *adj* composite, divers, hétéroclite; mixte

**composition** *n* composition *f*, œuvre *f*; rédaction *f*, dissertation *f*; *leg* accommodement *m*, compromis *m*; *fig* composé *m*, nature *f*

**compositor** *n print* compositeur -trice

**compos mentis** *adj phr* sain d'esprit

**compost** *n* compost *m*

**composure** *n* calme *m*, flegme *m*

**compote** *n cul* compote *f*

**¹compound** *n* enclos *m*

**²compound** *n* composé *m*; *chem* composé *m*; *adj* composé, complexe; *med* **~ fracture** fracture compliquée; **~ interest** intérêts composés; *gramm* **~ sentence** phrase *f* complexe; **~ word** mot composé

**³compound** *vt* mêler, mélanger; *chem* composer; *leg* régler à l'amiable; *leg* (felony) pactiser avec; *vi* composer; transiger; s'arranger à l'amiable

**comprehend** *vt* comprendre; inclure, contenir

**comprehensibility** *n* compréhensibilité *f*, intelligibilité *f*

**comprehensible** *adj* compréhensible, intelligible

**comprehension** *n* compréhension *f*, intelligence *f*; inclusion *f*

**comprehensive** *n* = C.E.S. (Collège *m* d'Enseignement Secondaire); *adj* compréhensif -ive, large, ample

**compress** *n med* compresse *f*; *vt* comprimer

**compressed** *adj* comprimé; (made smaller) réduit; (terse) concis

**compressible** *adj* compressible

**compression** *n* compression *f*; concision *f*, concentration *f*

**compressive** *adj* compressif -ive

**compressor** *n* compresseur *m*

**comprise** *vt* contenir, comprendre, comporter

**compromise** *n* compromis *m*, arrangement *m*; *vt* transiger, régler par un compromis; (endanger) compromettre, mettre en danger; **~ oneself** se compromettre; *vi* transiger

**compulsion** *n* contrainte *f*; *psych* compulsion *f*

**compulsive** *adj* irrésistible; *psych* compulsif -ive

**compulsory** *adj* obligatoire, forcé; (required) exigé

**compunction** *n* remords *m*; hésitation *f*, scrupule *m*; *eccles* componction *f*

**computable** *adj* calculable

**computation** *n* calcul *m*, évaluation *f*

**compute** *vt* calculer, évaluer

**computer** *n* ordinateur *m*

**computerize** *vt* calculer au moyen d'un ordinateur; équiper d'un ordinateur

**comrade** *n* camarade

**comradeship** *n* camaraderie *f*

**¹con** *vt* étudier; apprendre par cœur

**²con** *vt naut* gouverner

**³con** *n sl* escroquerie *f*; **~ man** escroc *m*; *vt sl* escroquer

**concatenate** *vt* enchaîner

**concatenation** *n* enchaînement *m*

**concave** *adj* concave

**concavity** *n* concavité *f*; (hollow) creux *m*

**conceal** *vt* celer, cacher; garder secret -ète

**concealment** *n* action *f* de cacher; (place) cachette *f*; *fig* dissimulation *f*

**concede** *vt* concéder, admettre, reconnaître; *vi* céder

**conceit** *n* suffisance *f*, vanité *f*, prétention *f*; *lit* trait *m* d'esprit; **~ s** concetti *mpl*

**conceited** *adj* suffisant, vaniteux -euse

**conceivable** *adj* concevable, imaginable

**conceive** *vt* concevoir, imaginer; exprimer, formuler; (child) concevoir; *vi* penser; concevoir

**concentrate** *n* concentré *m*; *vt* concentrer; *vi* se concentrer

**concentration** *n* concentration *f*; **~ camp** camp *m* de concentration

**concentric** *adj* concentrique

**concept** *n* concept *m*, idée *f*

**conception** *n* conception *f*

**conceptive** *adj philos* capable de concevoir

**conceptual** *adj* conceptuel -elle

**conceptualize** *vt* former un concept au sujet de

**concern** *n* souci *m*, inquiétude *f*; (business) affaire *f*; responsabilité *f*; soin *m*; *comm* entreprise *f*, firme *f*, établissement *m*; *vt* concerner, regarder; intéresser; (upset) affliger, inquiéter; ~ **oneself** s'inquiéter; (take trouble) se donner du mal

**concerned** *adj* intéressé; impliqué; inquiet -iète, soucieux -ieuse

**concerning** *prep* concernant, regardant, à propos de, au sujet de

**concert** *n* concert *m*; concorde *f*, harmonie *f*, accord *m*; *vt* concerter, arranger, organiser

**concerted** *adj* concerté; *mus* orchestré

**concert-grand** *n mus* piano *m* de concert

**concertina** *n mus* concertina *m*

**concerto** *n mus* concerto *m*

**concert-pitch** *n mus* diapason *m* de concert; **at** ~ *mus* au diapason; *fig* en pleine forme

**concession** *n* concession *f*

**concessionaire** *n* concessionnaire

**concessionary** *adj* concessionnaire

**conch** *n zool* + *anat* conque *f*

**conchology** *n* conchyliologie *f*

**conciliate** *vt* concilier; gagner, amener

**conciliation** *n* conciliation *f*

**conciliatory** *adj* conciliatoire

**concise** *adj* concis

**conciseness, concision** *n* concision *f*

**conclave** *n eccles* conclave *m*; discussion secrète

**conclude** *vt* conclure, finir, achever, terminer; (deduce) conclure, déduire; *vi* conclure; se terminer, s'achever; décider

**conclusion** *n* conclusion *f*, fin *f*; déduction *f*; décision *f*; **foregone** ~ affaire réglée d'avance; **in** ~ finalement; **try** ~ **s with** se mesurer contre

**conclusive** *adj* conclusif -ive, concluant

**concoct** *vt cul* confectionner; *fig* inventer, fabriquer

**concoction** *n* mélange *m*, confection *f*; *pej* médicament *m* désagréable

**concomitant** *n* fait concomitant; *adj* concomitant

**concord** *n* concorde *f*, entente *f*; harmonie *f*; *gramm* + *mus* accord *m*

**concordance** *n* concordance *f*; index *m*

**concordant** *adj* concordant, harmonieux -ieuse

**concordat** *n eccles* concordat *m*

**concourse** *n* concours *m*; affluence *f*, foule *f*; *US* (street) boulevard *m*; (station) salle *f* des pas perdus, hall *m*

**concrete** *n* béton *m*; **reinforced** ~ béton armé; *adj* concret -ète; *bui* en béton; ~ **mixer** bétonnière *f*; ~ **music** musique concrète; *vt* bétonner; solidifier; *vi* se solidifier

**concreteness** *n* concrétion *f*; solidité *f*

**concretion** *n med* calcul *m*

**concubinage** *n* concubinage *m*

**concubine** *n* concubine *f*

**concupiscence** *n* concupiscence *f*

**concupiscent** *adj* concupiscent

**concur** *vi* être d'accord; concourir, coïncider

**concurrence** *n* accord *m*, assentiment *m*; concurrence *f*, concours *m*, coïncidence *f*

**concurrent** *n* circonstance concourante; *adj* simultané, courant; (agreeing) concordant, d'accord; convergent

**concuss** *vt* secouer, frapper; *med* commotionner

**concussion** *n med* commotion cérébrale; choc *m*, secousse *f*

**condemn** *vt* condamner; blâmer, censurer; (building) déclarer inhabitable; (food) interdire la consommation de

**condemnation** *n* condamnation *f*

**condemnatory** *adj* condamnatoire

**condensation** *n* condensation *f*

**condense** *vt* condenser, concentrer; résumer; ~ **d milk** lait condensé

**condenser** *n* condensateur *m*; *phys* condenseur *m*

**condescend** *vi* daigner, condescendre; s'abaisser, descendre

**condescending** *adj* condescendant

**condescension** *n* condescendance *f*

**condign** *adj* mérité, juste

**condiment** *n cul* condiment *m*

**condition** *n* condition *f*, stipulation *f*; (state) état *m*, circonstance *f*; (rank) rang *m*, position *f*; ~ **s** circonstances *fpl*, ambiance *f*; **on** ~ pourvu que; *vt* stipuler; (influence) conditionner, déterminer

**conditional** *n gramm* conditionnel *m*; *adj* conditionnel -elle, dépendant; *gramm* conditionnel -elle; **be** ~ **on** dépendre de

**conditioned** *adj* conditionné, déterminé; *psych* ~ **reflex** réflexe conditionné; **well** ~ en bonne condition, en bonne forme

**conditioning** *n psych* modification *f* des réflexes

**condole** *vi* prendre part à la douleur, offrir ses condoléances

**condolence** *n* condoléance *f*

**condom** *n* préservatif *m*; *coll* capote anglaise

**condominium** *n pol* condominium *m*

**condone** vt pardonner; (adultery) passer sous silence

**condor** n zool condor m

**conduce** vi ~ **to** tendre à, produire

**conducive** adj tendant, contribuant

**conduct** n (management, behaviour) conduite f, comportement m, attitude f; **safe** ~ sauf-conduit m; vt conduire, mener; (guide) diriger; mus diriger; elect conduire; ~ **oneself** se conduire, se comporter; ~ **ed tour** visite guidée

**conductance** n elect conductance f

**conductibility** n phys conductibilité f

**conductible** adj phys conductible

**conduction** n phys + physiol conduction f

**conductive** adj elect + phys conducteur -trice

**conductor** n conducteur -trice; (bus) receveur m; mus chef m d'orchestre; phys + elect conducteur m

**conductress** n (bus) receveuse f

**conduit** n conduit m, tuyau m, tube m

**cone** n math + geol cône m; bot pomme f de pin; (ice-cream) cornet m

**cone-bearing** adj conifère

**confabulation** n discussion amicale

**confection** n fabrication f; cul friandise f, petit gâteau; article m de Paris

**confectioner** n confiseur -euse

**confectionery** n confiserie f

**confederacy** n confédération f; fédération f; conspiration f

**confederate** n confédéré m; complice; adj confédéré, allié; vt confédérer; vi se confédérer

**confederation** n confédération f

**confer** vt conférer, accorder; vi conférer, s'entretenir

**conference** n congrès m, assemblée f, conférence f

**conferment** n action f de conférer, octroi m

**confess** vt avouer, confesser, admettre; eccles confesser (qn); vi passer aux aveux; eccles confesser, se confesser

**confession** n aveu m; confession f; eccles confession f; secte f

**confessional** n eccles confessionnal m; adj confessionnel -elle

**confessor** n eccles confesseur m

**confetti** n confetti mpl

**confidant** n confident m; ~ **e** confidente f

**confide** vt confier; vi ~ **in** se fier à, s'ouvrir à

**confidence** n confiance f, espoir m, assurance f; secret m, confidence f; ~ **trick** escroquerie f; **in** ~ confidentiel -ielle

**confidential** adj confidentiel -ielle, intime, particulier -ière; (trustworthy)

de confiance; ~ **secretary** secrétaire particulier -ière

**confiding** adj confiant

**configuration** n configuration f

**confine** vt confiner, enfermer; emprisonner; limiter, retenir; med be ~ **d** être en couches

**confinement** n emprisonnement m, réclusion f; med couches fpl

**confines** npl confins mpl, bornes fpl; fig limites fpl

**confirm** vt confirmer, corroborer; affirmer, renforcer; ratifier; eccles confirmer

**confirmation** n confirmation f; ratification f

**confirmative, confirmatory** adj qui confirme

**confirmed** adj confirmé; (inveterate) invétéré, durci; (habitual) habituel -elle

**confiscate** vt confisquer; adj leg confisqué

**confiscation** n confiscation f

**conflagration** n conflagration f; incendie m

**conflict** n conflit m, combat m; désaccord m; vi s'opposer, se heurter

**confluence** n geog + fig confluence f

**confluent** n geog affluent m; adj qui se rejoignent

**conform** vt conformer; adapter; vi se conformer, s'adapter

**conformation** n conformation f, configuration f, structure f

**conformist** n conformiste

**conformity** n conformité f; accord m; (submission) soumission f

**confound** vt confondre, brouiller, rendre confus; (overthrow) détruire; coll ~ **it!** diable!

**confounded** adj confus; (abashed) déconcerté; coll sacré

**confoundedly** adv coll extrêmement, très, diablement

**confraternity** n confraternité f, confrérie f

**confront** vt affronter, braver; (compare texts) collationner; confronter, mettre en présence

**confrontation** n confrontation f

**Confucian** n confucianiste; adj confucianiste

**confuse** vt (bewilder) effarer, obscurcir; (mix) brouiller, mêler; (fail to distinguish) confondre, ne pas distinguer; embarrasser

**confused** adj ahuri, embarrassé; confus

**confusion** n confusion f, désordre m; embarras m, désarroi m

**confutation** n réfutation f

**confute** vt réfuter

**congeal** vt (freeze) congeler; (blood)

coaguler; (milk) cailler; (oil) figer; *vi* (freeze) se congeler; (blood) se coaguler; (milk) se cailler; (oil) se figer

**congelation** *n* congélation *f*

**congenial** *adj* sympathique, aimable, agréable; approprié, de même tempérament

**congenital** *adj* congénital

**conger** *n zool* ~ (eel) congre *m*

**congest** *vt* (pack) entasser; (crowd) encombrer, congestionner; *med* congestionner

**congestion** *n* encombrement *m*; (traffic) embouteillage *m*; *med* congestion *f*

¹**conglomerate** *n geol* + *fig* conglomérat *m*

²**conglomerate** *vt* conglomérer; *vi* se conglomérer

**conglomeration** *n* conglomération *f*

**congratulate** *vt* féliciter, congratuler

**congratulation** *n* félicitation *f*, congratulation *f*; ~ s! félicitations!

**congregate** *vt* rassembler, réunir; *vi* se rassembler, se réunir

**congregation** *n* assemblée *f*; *eccles* congrégation *f*

**congregationalism** *n eccles* (protestant) congrégationalisme *m*

**congress** *n* congrès *m*; *US* **Congress** Congrès *m*

**congressman** *n US* membre *m* du Congrès

**congruence** *n* accord *m*, conformité *f*; *math* congruence *f*

**congruent** *adj* d'accord, en conformité; convenable; *math* congru

**congruous** *adj* convenable, approprié, consistant

**conic** *adj* conique; *math* ~ **section** section *f* conique

**conical** *adj* conique

**conifer** *n* conifère *m*

**coniferous** *adj* conifère

**conjectural** *adj* conjectural

**conjecture** *n* conjecture *f*, supposition *f*; *vt* conjecturer, supposer; *vi* conjecturer, faire des conjectures

**conjoin** *vt* adjoindre, conjoindre; *vi* s'unir

**conjoint** *adj* uni, combiné, joint

**conjugal** *adj* conjugal

**conjugate** *adj* conjugué; *vt gramm* conjuguer; *vi* se conjuguer

**conjugation** *n* conjugaison *f*

**conjunction** *n* conjonction *f*; jonction *f*, union *f*

**conjunctive** *adj* unissant; *gramm* + *med* conjonctif -ive

**conjunctivitis** *n med* conjonctivite *f*

**conjuncture** *n* conjoncture *f*, circonstance *f*; crise *f*

¹**conjure** *vt* conjurer

²**conjure** *vt* escamoter; ~ **up** faire apparaître

**conjurer, conjuror** *n* prestidigitateur -trice

**conjuring** *n* prestidigitation *f*; *adj* de passe-passe

¹**conk** *n coll* nez *m*; *coll* gnon *m* (sur le nez)

²**conk** *vi mot* ~ **out** caler, rester en panne

**connect** *vt* joindre, unir; relier; *elect* connecter; *vi* se relier, se raccorder; (train) correspondre

**connecting-rod** *n eng* bielle *f*

**connection, connexion** *n* union *f*, connexion *f*; (relationship) rapport *m*, lien *m*, association *f*; rapports sexuels; *elect* prise *f*, connexion *f*; (railway) correspondance *f*

**conning** *n naut* commandement *m*; *adj* ~ **tower** tourelle *f* de commandement

**connivance** *n* connivence *f*, complicité *f*

**connive** *vi* ~ **at** être de connivence dans; (pretend not to notice) fermer les yeux sur

**connoisseur** *n* connaisseur -euse

**connotation** *n* implication *f*, associations *fpl*; *philos* connotation *f*

**connote** *vt* impliquer, suggérer; *coll* signifier

**connubial** *adj* conjugal

**conquer** *vt* vaincre, battre; subjuguer; (overcome) surmonter, conquérir

**conqueror** *n* vainqueur *m*, conquérant -e

**conquest** *n* conquête *f*

**consanguineous** *adj* consanguin

**consanguinity** *n* consanguinité *f*

**conscience** *n* conscience *f*

**conscientious** *adj* consciencieux -ieuse; ~ **objector** objecteur *m* de conscience

**conscious** *adj* conscient; intentionnel -elle; embarrassé, gêné

**conscript** *n* conscrit *m*; *adj* conscrit; *vt mil* enrôler par conscription

**conscription** *n mil* conscription *f*

**consecrate** *adj eccles* consacré; *vt* consacrer; (king, bishop) sacrer

**consecration** *n* consécration *f*; (king, bishop) sacre *m*

**consecutive** *adj* consécutif -ive, successif -ive

**consensus** *n* accord général, consensus *m*

**consent** *n* consentement *m*, assentiment *m*, accord *m*; permission *f*; **age of** ~ nubilité *f*, âge *m* nubile; *vi* consentir, acquiescer

**consequence** *n* conséquence *f*; effet *m*; importance *f*, valeur *f*

**consequent** *n philos* conséquent *m*; *adj* conséquent, résultant; logique

**consequential** *adj* résultant, dérivé; (pompous) suffisant, prétentieux -ieuse

**conservancy** *n* = administration *f* des eaux et forêts; protection *f* écologique

**conservation** *n* conservation *f*, préservation *f*

**conservatism** n conservatisme m; pol (Britain) idées fpl du parti conservateur

**conservative** n pol (Britain) membre m du parti conservateur; adj conservateur -trice; prudent, modéré

**conservatoire** n conservatoire m

**conservatory** n serre f; conservatoire m

**conserve** n ( jam) confiture f; fruits confits; vt conserver, préserver

**conshy, conshie, conchy** n coll obs mil objecteur m de conscience

**consider** vt considérer, examiner; estimer, respecter; peser; vi réfléchir, méditer

**considerable** adj considérable, notable; important, remarquable

**considerate** adj attentionné, prévenant

**considerateness** n égards mpl, gentillesse f, humanité f

**consideration** n considération f; réflexion f, étude f; estime f; (money) compensation f, dédommagement m; sollicitude f

**considered** adj pondéré, réfléchi; estimé

**considering** prep vu, étant donné; en raison de; adv coll quand on y pense

**consign** vt consigner, confier, remettre; expédier

**consignation** n expédition f; consignation f

**consignee** n destinataire

**consigner, consignor** n expéditeur -trice, consignateur -trice

**consignment** n envoi m; (despatch) expédition f; quantité f de marchandises

**consist** vi ~ in consister en; ~ of consister de, se composer de; ~ with être consistant avec

**consistence, consistency** n consistance f; (unchanging character) stabilité f, fermeté f, uniformité f

**consistent** adj consistant, stable, logique, régulier -ière; ~ with compatible avec, en accord avec

**consistory** n eccles consistoire m

**consolable** adj consolable

**consolation** n consolation f

**consolatory** adj consolateur -trice

¹**console** n archi + mus + rad console f

²**console** vt consoler

**consolidate** vt consolider; fusionner, joindre; vi se consolider

**consolidation** n consolidation f

**consols** n consolidés mpl

**consommé** n cul consommé m

**consonance** n accord m; harmonie f; mus consonance f

¹**consonant** n gramm consonne f

²**consonant** adj d'accord, en harmonie; mus consonant

¹**consort** n conjoint -e; naut navire m

voyageant de conserve

²**consort** vi s'associer, frayer; (agree) s'accorder

**consortium** n consortium m

**conspectus** n sommaire m, tableau m synoptique

**conspicuous** adj évident, très visible; frappant, remarquable; insigne, exceptionnel -elle; pej voyant; **make oneself** ~ se faire remarquer

**conspiracy** n conspiration f, conjuration f

**conspirator** n conspirateur -trice, conjuré -e

**conspire** vi conspirer, comploter

**constable** n hist connétable m; (Britain) constable m; agent m de police, gendarme m; **chief** ~ = préfet m de police

**constabulary** n police f; agents mpl de police (d'une ville, d'une région)

**constancy** n constance f, fermeté f, fidélité f; stabilité f

**constant** n math constante f; adj constant, fidèle, ferme; stable

**constantly** adv fréquemment, constamment; fidèlement

**constellation** n constellation f

**consternation** n atterrement m, désarroi m

**constipate** vt constiper

**constipation** n constipation f

**constituency** n circonscription f

**constituent** n (component) élément m, composant m; pol électeur -trice; adj constituant, composant

**constitute** vt établir, constituer, former; (make up) composer; (appoint) désigner, instituer

**constitution** n constitution f; pol + med constitution f; tempérament m; leg statuts mpl

**constitutional** n promenade f; adj constitutionnel -elle

**constitutionally** adv constitutionnellement; naturellement

**constrain** vt contraindre, réprimer; forcer; (restrict) restreindre

**constrained** adj embarrassé, gêné; gauche, contraint

**constraint** n contrainte f, force f; embarras m

**constrict** vt comprimer, serrer; (contract) rétrécir; (inhibit) retenir, restreindre

**constriction** n constriction f

**constrictor** n anat constricteur m; zool boa constricteur

**construct** n construction f; vt construire, édifier, bâtir

**construction** n construction f; édifice m, bâtiment m; interprétation f

**constructional** adj de construction

413

**constructive** *adj* constructif -ive, créateur -trice; inféré, déduit; implicite

**constructor** *n* constructeur -trice

**construe** *vt gramm* faire l'analyse grammaticale de; traduire mot à mot; *fig* interpréter; *vi* faire une analyse grammaticale

**consubstantial** *adj* consubstantiel -ielle

**consubstantiation** *n theol* consubstantiation *f*

**consul** *n* consul *m*

**consular** *adj* consulaire

**consulate** *n* consulat *m*

**consult** *vt* consulter, demander l'avis de; (book) se référer à; (take into account) considérer, prendre en considération; *vi* conférer; se consulter

**consultant** *n med* médecin consultant; *leg* avocat *m* conseil; *eng* ingénieur *m* conseil

**consultation** *n* consultation *f*

**consultative** *adj* consultatif -ive

**consulting** *adj med* consultant; conseil *invar*

**consumable** *adj* consommable

**consume** *vt* consumer, brûler; user, gaspiller; (food, drink) consommer; *fig* obséder, consumer; *vi* se consumer

**consumer** *n* consommateur -trice; ~ **durables** appareils ménagers; ~ **goods** denrées *fpl* de consommation; ~ **research** études *fpl* de marchés

**consummate** *vt* (marriage) consommer; (complete) achever, parfaire; *adj* achevé; parfait, consommé

**consummation** *n* consommation *f*; achèvement *m*, fin *f*; perfection *f*; résultat *m*

**consumption** *n* consommation *f*; *med* tuberculose *f*

**consumptive** *n + adj med* tuberculeux -euse, phtisique

**contact** *n* contact *m*; (person) relation *f*; (relationship) rapport *m*; ~ **lenses** verres *mpl* de contact; *vt coll* contacter

**contact-breaker** *n* interrupteur *m*, conjoncteur *m*

**contagion** *n* contagion *f*

**contagious** *adj* contagieux -ieuse

**contagiousness** *n* contagiosité *f*

**contain** *vt* contenir, renfermer; *math* être divisible par; *fig* contenir, réprimer; se contenir

**container** *n* (goods) containeur *m*; boîte *f*; récipient *m*

**containment** *n* endiguement *m*, limitation *f*

**contaminate** *vt* contaminer

**contamination** *n* contamination *f*

**contango** *n* report *m*

**contemplate** *vt* contempler; envisager, considérer; (plan) projeter; *vi* méditer, réfléchir

**contemplation** *n* contemplation *f*; (deep thought) méditation *f*

**contemplative** *adj* pensif -ive, méditatif -ive, songeur -euse; *eccles* contemplatif -ive

**contemporaneous** *adj* contemporain

**contemporary** *n + adj* contemporain -e

**contempt** *n* mépris *m*; dédain *m*; ~ **of court** outrage *m* à magistrat

**contemptibility** *n* ignominie *f*, bassesse *f*

**contemptible** *adj* méprisable, indigne

**contemptuous** *adj* méprisant, dédaigneux -euse

**contemptuousness** *n* mépris *m*, dédain *m*

**contend** *vi* lutter; (argue) discuter, disputer; (maintain) maintenir, assurer

¹**content** *n* contenu *m*; capacité *f*, volume *m*; sens *m*, signification *f*; ~ **s** contenu *m*; **table of ~ s** table *f* des matières

²**content** *n* contentement *m*, satisfaction *f*; *adj* content, satisfait, heureux -euse; *vt* contenter, satisfaire; ~ **oneself** se contenter, être satisfait

**contention** *n* contention *f*, controverse *f*, démêlé *m*; affirmation *f*, prétention *f*

**contentious** *adj* querelleur -euse, ergoteur -euse; (issue) controversé; *leg* contentieux -ieuse

**contentment** *n* contentement *m*

**conterminous, co-terminous** *adj* contigu -üe, limitrophe; (time) de même durée; (space) de même étendue

**contest** *n* lutte *f*, compétition *f*; conflit *m*; *sp* épreuve *f*; *vt* contester, discuter; disputer

**contestant** *n* contestant -e

**contestation** *n* contestation *f*

**context** *n* contexte *m*

**contiguity** *n* contiguïté *f*

**contiguous** *adj* contigu -üe, adjacent, limitrophe

**continence** *n* continence *f*, retenue *f*

¹**continent** *n* continent *m*; *coll* (continent *m* d') Europe *f*

²**continent** *adj* continent; sobre

**continental** *n* Européen -éenne; *adj* continental; ~ **breakfast** café complet

**contingency** *n* éventualité *f*; *philos* contingence *f*

**contingent** *adj* éventuel -uelle, imprévu; *philos* contingent; **be ~ (up)on** dépendre de

**continual** *adj* continuel -uelle

**continuance** *n* continuation *f*; durée *f*

**continuation** *n* continuation *f*, prolongement *m*, extension *f*

**continuator** *n* continuateur -trice

**continue** *vt* continuer, poursuivre;

persister; prolonger; (start again) reprendre; *vi* continuer; (remain) rester, demeurer, persister

**continued** *adj* continu; prolongé; (restarted) repris

**continuing** *adj* durable

**continuity** *n* continuité *f*

**continuity-girl** *n cin* scripte *f*

**continuous** *adj* continu; *cin* permanent

**contort** *vt* tordre; déformer; dénaturer

**contortion** *n* torsion *f*, contorsion *f*

**contortionist** *n* contorsionniste

**contour** *n* contour *m*; profil *m*; *geog* ~ (line) courbe *f* de niveau; courbe *f* hypsométrique; ~ **map** carte *f* hypsométrique; *vt* dessiner le contour de

**contra** *n* contrepartie *f*; *prep* contre

**contraband** *n* contrebande *f*; *adj* de contrebande

**contrabandist** *n* contrebandier -ière

**contrabass** *n mus* contrebasse *f*

**contraception** *n* contraception *f*

**contraceptive** *n* contraceptif *m*, préservatif *m*; *adj* contraceptif -ive, anticonceptionnel -elle

¹**contract** *n* contrat *m*; (agreement) accord *m*, pacte *m*; contrat *m* de mariage; ~ **bridge** bridge *m* contrat; ~ **work** travail *m* à forfait; *vt* contracter; *vi* s'engager; ~ **in** (out) accepter (refuser) de participer; ~ **to do sth** s'engager à faire qch

²**contract** *vt* contracter, crisper; (shorten) écourter; *vi* se contracter, se crisper

**contractible** *adj* qui peut être contracté

**contractile** *adj* contractile

**contracting** *adj* contractant; *pol* high ~ **powers** hautes parties contractantes

**contraction** *n* contraction *f*

**contractor** *n* entrepreneur *m*; contractant *m*; *anat* muscle *m* contractile

**contractual** *adj* contractuel -uelle

**contracture** *n med* contracture *f*

**contradict** *vt* contredire; (rumour) démentir

**contradiction** *n* contradiction *f*

**contradictory** *adj* contradictoire, inconsistant

**contradistinction** *n* contraste *m*

**contra-indicate** *vt med* contre-indiquer

**contra-indication** *n med* contre-indication *f*

**contralto** *n mus* contralto *m*

**contraption** *n coll* truc *m*, machin *m*, gadget *m*

**contrapuntal** *adj* en contrepoint

**contrariety** *n* opposition *f*; (setback) entrave *f*

**contrarily** *adv* contrairement; (perversely) avec perversité

**contrariness** *n coll* esprit *m* de contradiction

**contrariwise** *adv* en sens contraire

¹**contrary** *n* contraire *m*, opposé *m*; **on the** ~ pas du tout, au contraire; **unless you hear to the** ~ sauf avis contraire; *adj* contraire, opposé; hostile, défavorable

²**contrary** *adj* contrariant, obstiné

**contrast** *n* contraste *m*, opposition *f*; *vt* faire contraster; contraster, opposer; *vi* faire contraste, contraster

**contravene** *vt* violer, désobéir à; contredire

**contretemps** *n* contretemps *m*

**contribute** *vt* contribuer, donner; (articles) écrire; *vi* souscrire, contribuer

**contribution** *n* contribution *f*, souscription *f*, cotisation *f*; (paper) article *m*

**contributor** *n* collaborateur -trice, auteur *m*; (subscriber) souscripteur -trice

**contributory** *adj* qui contribue; accessoire

**contrite** *adj* contrit

**contrition** *n* contrition *f*

**contrivance** *n* invention *f*; dispositif *m*, machin *m*; plan *m*, procédé *m*; idée ingénieuse

**contrive** *vt* réussir, concevoir; arranger, organiser; *fig* machiner, combiner

**control** *n* autorité *f*; restriction *f*, limitation *f*; contrôle *m*; réglementation *f*; (spiritualism) esprit *m* contrôleur; *mech* commande *f*; ~**s** instruments *mpl* de commande; *vt* commander, diriger; contrôler, vérifier; régler; (restrain) maîtriser, contenir

**controller, comptroller** *n* contrôleur *m*

**controversial** *adj* controversable

**controversy** *n* controverse *f*; dispute *f*

**controvert** *vt* contredire, opposer, argumenter, disputer

**controvertible** *adj* controversable, contestable

**contumacious** *adj* rebelle, réfractaire; *leg* contumace

**contumacy** *n* insubordination *f*; *leg* contumace *f*

**contumely** *n* injure *f*, insolence *f*; (scorn) mépris *m*, dédain *m*

**contuse** *vt med* contusionner, meurtrir

**contusion** *n med* contusion *f*, meurtrissure *f*

**conundrum** *n* devinette *f*

**conurbation** *n* conurbation *f*

**convalesce** *vi* être en convalescence, se remettre

**convalescence** *n* convalescence *f*

**convalescent** *adj* convalescent

**convection** *n* convection *f*

**convector** *n* appareil *m* de chauffage à convection

**convene** *vt* convoquer; *vi* se réunir

**convenience** *n* convenance *f*, opportunité *f*; (usefulness) utilité *f*; (comfort) commodité *f*, confort *m*; (lavatory) toilettes *fpl*; **at one's ~** à loisir; **at your earliest ~** dans les meilleurs délais
**convenient** *adj* commode; acceptable; loisible; *coll* tout près
**convent** *n* couvent *m*
**convention** *n* convention *f*, usage *m*; (meeting) assemblée *f*
**conventional** *adj* de convention, conventionnel -elle; **~ weapons** armes *fpl* classiques
**conventionality** *n* bienséance *f*; usage conventionnel
**conventionalize** *vt* rendre conventionnel
**conventual** *n* + *adj eccles* conventuel -elle
**converge** *vt* faire converger; *vi* converger
**convergence** *n* convergence *f*
**convergent** *adj* convergent
**conversable** *adj* sociable, causeur -euse
**conversant** *adj* familier -ière; (experienced) versé, expérimenté, compétent
**conversation** *n* conversation *f*, entretien *m*
**conversational** *adj* de conversation; (style) coulant, facile
**conversationalist** *n* causeur -euse; raconteur -euse
¹**converse** *n* conversation *f*, entretien *m*; *vi* converser, s'entretenir
²**converse** *n* contraire *m*, inverse *m*; *adj* contraire, inverse
**conversion** *n* conversion *f*, transformation *f*, mutation *f*; (building) aménagement *m*
**convert** *n* converti -e; *vt* transformer, convertir, changer
**converter** *n mech* + *elect* convertisseur *m*
**convertible** *n mot* voiture *f* décapotable; *adj* convertissable; *comm* convertible
**convex** *adj* convexe
**convexity** *n* convexité *f*
**convey** *vt* transporter, porter; amener; transmettre, communiquer; exprimer, rendre; *leg* aliéner, transférer
**conveyance** *n* transport *m*; moyen *m* de transport, véhicule *m*; *leg* cession *f*, transfert *m*
**conveyancer** *n leg* personne *f* qui opère un transfert
**conveyancing** *n leg* cession *f* de biens, transfert *m*, aliénation *f*
**conveyer, conveyor** *n* (person) porteur *m*; (thing) transporteur *m*, convoyeur *m*; **~ belt** convoyeur *m*, tapis roulant
**convict** *n* condamné -e, forçat *m*; *vt* condamner, déclarer coupable
**conviction** *n* conviction *f*, croyance *f*; *leg* condamnation *f*
**convince** *vt* convaincre, persuader

**convincing** *adj* convaincant, plausible
**convivial** *adj* sociable, jovial; *coll* un peu parti
**convocation** *n* convocation *f*; *eccles* synode *m*
**convoke** *vt* convoquer
**convolute, convoluted** *adj* convoluté
**convolution** *n* convolution *f*
**convolvulus** *n bot* volubilis *m*
**convoy** *n naut* convoi *m*; *vt naut* convoyer
**convulse** *vt* convulsionner; *med* convulser; **~ with laughter** faire tordre de rire
**convulsion** *n* convulsion *f*; agitation *f*
**convulsive** *adj* convulsif -ive
**cony** *n* lapin *m*; (fur) fourrure *f* de lapin
**coo** *n* roucoulement *m*; *vi* roucouler; **bill and ~** se bécoter; *interj coll* tiens!
**cook** *n* cuisinier -ière; chef *m*; *vt* cuire, faire cuire; *coll* (fake) cuisiner, falsifier; **~ s/o's goose** ruiner qn; **~ up** inventer, falsifier; *vi* cuisiner, faire la cuisine; cuire
**cooker** *n* cuisinière *f*; **pressure ~** cocotte *f* minute, autocuiseur *m*
**cookery** *n* cuisine *f*; **~ book** livre *m* de cuisine
**cook-house** *n mil* cuisine *f*
**cookie** *n* petit gâteau
**cooking** *n* cuisine *f*; (process) cuisson *f*
**cool** *n* fraîcheur *f*; *sl* calme *m*; **keep one's ~** garder son sang-froid, rester calme; *adj* frais (*f* fraîche); calme, froid, indifférent, tiède; *coll* sans gêne; (with it) chic *invar*; (no less than) au moins; *vt* rafraîchir, refroidir; *sl* **~ it** se calmer; **~ one's heels** être obligé d'attendre; *vi* se refroidir
**cooler** *n* glacière *f*; (apparatus) refroidisseur *m*; *sl* taule *f*
**coolie** *n* coolie *m*
**coolness** *n* fraîcheur *f*; calme *m*; (estrangement) froideur *f*
**coombe** *n* combe *f*
**coon** *n zool* laveur raton *m*; *obs pej* nègre (*f* négresse)
**coop** *n* poulailler *m*, mue *f*; *vt* enfermer; mettre en cage; **~ up** enfermer
**cooper** *n* tonnelier *m*
**co-operate** *vi* coopérer, contribuer
**co-operation** *n* coopération *f*
**co-operative** *n* coopérative *f*; *adj* coopératif -ive
**co-opt** *vt* coopter
**co-option** *n* cooptation *f*
**co-ordinate** *n math* coordonnées *fpl*; *adj* coordonné; *vt* coordonner
**co-ordination** *n* coordination *f*
**coot** *n zool* foulque *f*; *coll* idiot -e; **bald as a ~** chauve comme un œuf
**cop** *n sl* (policeman) flic *m*; *sl* prise *f*; **it's not much ~** ça ne vaut pas grand-

chose; *vt sl* coincer; ~ **it** être puni

¹**cope** *n eccles* chape *f*; *vt* couvrir d'une chape; *archi* chaperonner

²**cope** *vi* se débrouiller; ~ **with** se charger de; (successfully) venir à bout de

**coper** *n* maquignon *m*

**copier** *n* copiste; machine *f* à photocopier

**co-pilot** *n* copilote *m*

**coping** *n bui* chaperon *m*

**coping-stone** *n archi* couronnement *m*

**copious** *adj* copieux -ieuse, abondant

**copiousness** *n* abondance *f*, profusion *f*

¹**copper** *n* cuivre *m*; (small coin) sou *m*; couleur *f* cuivre; (cauldron) chaudron *m*; *adj* de cuivre, cuivré; *vt* cuivrer

²**copper** *n sl* flic *m*

**copper-beech** *n* hêtre *m* pourpre

**copper-bottomed** *adj fig* absolument sûr

**copperplate** *n* plaque *f* de cuivre; (engraving) taille-douce *f* (*pl* tailles-douces); (writing) écriture moulée

**coppersmith** *n* fabricant *m* de dinanderie

**coppery** *adj* cuivré

**coppice, copse** *n* taillis *m*, bosquet *m*

**copra** *n* copra *m*

**copse** *n see* **coppice**

**copula** *n gramm* copule *f*

**copulate** *vi* copuler

**copulation** *n* copulation *f*, coït *m*

**copulative** *adj* copulatif -ive

**copy** *n* copie *f*, imitation *f*; reproduction *f*, transcription *f*; (book) exemplaire *m*; (journalism) copie *f*; *leg* **certified** ~ copie *f* conforme; *vt* copier, imiter; reproduire, transcrire; *vi* copier, faire une copie

**copy-book** *n* cahier *m* (d'écriture); **blot one's** ~ endommager sa réputation

**copyist** *n* copiste

**copyright** *n* copyright *m*, propriété *f* littéraire; *adj* aux droits réservés; *vt* réserver les droits de reproduction de

**copywriter** *n* personne *f* qui compose des textes publicitaires, publiciste

**coquet, coquette** *vi* flirter

**coquetry** *n* coquetterie *f*

**coquette** *n* coquette *f*

**cor** *interj sl* mince alors!

**coral** *n* corail *m*; couleur *f* corail; *adj* de corail, en corail; couleur de corail

**coralline** *adj* corallien -ienne; *obs* corallin

**coral-reef** *n* récif *m* de corail

**cor anglais** *n mus* cor anglais, hautbois *m* alto

**corbel** *n archi* corbeau *m*, console *f*; *vt* soutenir par une console

**cord** *n* corde *f*; ~**s** (corduroy) pantalon *m* de velours côtelé; **spinal** ~ moelle

épinière; *vt* encorder, lier

**cordage** *n naut* cordages *mpl*

**corded** *adj* ligoté; (cloth) côtelé

**cordial** *n* cordial *m*; *adj* cordial

**cordiality** *n* cordialité *f*

**cordite** *n* cordite *f*

**cordon** *n* cordon *m*; *archi* + *mil* cordon *m*; *joc* ~ **bleu** cordon-bleu *m* (*pl* cordons-bleus); *vt* établir un cordon autour de; ~ **off** isoler

**corduroy** *n* velours côtelé; *adj* en velours côtelé

**core** *n* cœur *m*; (fruit) trognon *m*; *elect* noyau *m*; *med* (boil) bourbillon *m*; *fig* cœur *m*, tréfonds *m*; **hard** ~ ceux que l'on ne peut pas convaincre; **rotten to the** ~ pourri jusqu'à la moelle; *vt* enlever le cœur de, évider

**co-religionist** *n* coreligionnaire

**co-respondent** *n* partenaire d'un homme (d'une femme) adultère

**coriander** *n bot* coriandre *f*

**cork** *n* (substance) liège *m*; (bottle) bouchon *m*; *adj* de liège; *vt* (bottle) boucher; *fig* enrayer; noircir au bouchon

**corked** *adj* (wine) qui sent le bouchon

**corker** *n coll* (lie) craque *f*; argument *m* massue; (person) type *m* formidable; (girl) beau morceau (de fille)

**corking** *adj coll* énorme, formidable

**corkscrew** *n* tire-bouchon *m*; *adj* en tire-bouchon, spiral; *vi* se tire-bouchonner, se tortiller

**cork-tree** *n bot* chêne-liège *m* (*pl* chênes-lièges)

**cormorant** *n zool* cormoran *m*

¹**corn** *n* grain *m*; (wheat) blé *m*; (oats) avoine *f*; *US* maïs *m*; *coll* banalité *f*, cliché *m*

²**corn** *n med* cor *m*

**corn-chandler** *n* grainetier *m*

**corn-cob** *n* épi *m* de maïs

**corn-crake** *n orni* râle *m*

**cornea** *n anat* cornée *f*

**corned-beef** *n* bœuf *m* en conserve; *coll* singe *m*

**cornelian** *n* cornaline *f*

**corner** *n* coin *m*, angle *m*; *comm* accaparement *m*; *sp* (football, hockey) corner *m*; **drive into a** ~ coincer, mettre au pied du mur; **round the** ~ tout près; **turn the** ~ commencer à se remettre; *vt* mettre dans un coin; mettre au pied du mur, coincer; *mot* prendre un virage; *comm* accaparer

**cornered** *adj* à coins; acculé

**corner-stone** *n* pierre *f* angulaire

**cornet** *n mus* cornet *m* à pistons; (ice-cream) cornet *m*; *eccles* (nun's head-dress) cornette *f*; *mil ar* cornette *f*

**cornflakes** *npl* cornflakes *fpl*

**cornflour** *n* maïzena *f*

cornice *n archi* corniche *f*
cornucopia *n* corne *f* d'abondance
corny *adj coll* banal (*pl* banals)
corolla *n bot* corolle *f*
corollary *n* corollaire *m*; *adj* corollaire
corona *n astron* couronne *f*, halo *m*; (tooth) couronne *f*
coronary *adj med* coronaire; ~ **thrombosis** thrombose *f* coronaire
coronation *n* couronnement *m*
coroner *n* coroner *m*
coronet *n* diadème *m*, couronne *f*
¹corporal *n mil* caporal *m*
²corporal *adj* corporel -elle; ~ **punishment** châtiment corporel
corporate *adj* constitué
corporation *n* corporation *f*; = conseil municipal; *coll* (paunch) bide *m*
corporeal *adj* corporel -elle; matériel -ielle; tangible
corps *n mil* corps *m*; ~ **de ballet** corps *m* de ballet
corpse *n* cadavre *m*
corpulence *n* corpulence *f*
corpulent *adj* corpulent
corpus *n* corpus *m*, recueil *m*; *comm* capital *m*; **Corpus Christi** Fête-Dieu *f*
corpuscle *n med* corpuscule *m*; *phys* molécule *f*
corpuscular *adj med* corpusculaire; *phys* moléculaire
corral *n* corral *m*
correct *adj* correct, exact, juste; *vt* corriger, redresser; améliorer; rectifier
correction *n* correction *f*, rectification *f*; (punishment) peine *f*, châtiment *m*; **house of** ~ maison *f* de correction
corrective *adj* correctif -ive
correctness *n* exactitude *f*; (propriety) correction *f*, convenance *f*, justesse *f*
corrector *n* correcteur -trice; *print* corrigeur -euse
correlate *n* corrélatif *m*; *vt* mettre en corrélation avec; *vi* être en corrélation avec
correlation *n* corrélation *f*
correlative *n* corrélatif *m*; *adj* corrélatif -ive
correspond *vi* correspondre, communiquer; correspondre, être conforme
correspondence *n* correspondance *f*; corrélation *f*; ~ **column** (newspaper) rubrique *f* des lettres; ~ **course** cours *m* par correspondance
correspondent *n* + *adj* correspondant -e
corresponding *adj* correspondant
corridor *n* corridor *m*, couloir *m*
corrigendum *n* erratum *m*
corroborate *vt* corroborer
corrode *vt* corroder; *vi* se corroder
corrosion *n* corrosion *f*
corrosive *n* corrosif *m*; *adj* corrosif -ive

corrugate *vt* onduler; (wrinkle) rider; *vi* onduler; se rider
corrugated *adj* ondulé; ~ **iron** tôle ondulée
corrupt *adj* corrompu, pourri; (bribed) acheté; *vt* corrompre; soudoyer, acheter; *vi* se corrompre; pourrir
corrupter *n* corrupteur -trice
corruptible *adj* corruptible
corrupting *adj* corrupteur -trice
corruption *n* corruption *f*; putréfaction *f*; (depravation) avilissement *m*
corruptly *adv* d'une façon corrompue
corruptness *n* corruption *f*
corsage *n* corsage *m*
corsair *n* corsaire *m*
corset *n* corset *m*, gaine *f*
cortège *n* cortège *m*
cortex *n bot* écorce *f*; *anat* cortex *m*
cortical *adj bot* + *anat* cortical
cortisone *n med* cortisone *f*
corundum *n* corindon *m*
coruscate *vi* scintiller
coruscation *n* scintillement *m*
corvette *n naut* corvette *f*
coryza *n med* coryza *m*
¹cos *n bot* romaine *f*
²cos *n abbr math* cosinus *m*
cosecant *n geom* cosécante *f*
cosh *n coll* matraque *f*, trique *f*; *vt coll* matraquer
co-signatory *n* + *adj* cosignataire
cosily *adv* douillettement
cosine *n math* cosinus *m*
cosiness *n* confort *m*
cosmetic *n* cosmétique *m*; ~ s produits *mpl* de beauté; *adj* cosmétique
cosmetician *n* esthéticien -ienne
cosmic *adj* cosmique
cosmogony *n* cosmogonie *f*
cosmographer *n* cosmographe
cosmography *n* cosmographie *f*
cosmology *n* cosmologie *f*
cosmonaut *n* cosmonaute
cosmopolitan *n* + *adj* cosmopolite
cosmos *n* cosmos *m*
Cossack *n* cosaque *m*
cosset *vt* choyer, dorloter
cost *n* prix *m*, coût *m*, frais *mpl*; ~ s *fig leg* dépens *mpl*; *leg* frais *mpl* judiciaires; ~ **of living** coût *m* de la vie; ~ **price** prix coûtant; **at the** ~ **of** aux dépens de; **to one's** ~ à ses dépens; *vt* coûter, valoir
coster, costermonger *n* marchand -e des quatre-saisons
costing *n* établissement *m* d'un devis
costive *adj* constipé; *fig* lent, indolent
costly *adj* cher -ère, coûteux -euse; (valuable) de prix
costume *n* costume *m*; deux-pièces *m*; ~ **jewellery** bijoux *mpl* en toc; *vt* costumer

418

**costumier** *n* costumier -ière

**cosy** *n* petit lainage qu'on met sur une théière, ou sur un œuf à la coque (pour conserver la chaleur); *adj* douillet -ette, confortable, chaud

¹**cot** *n* lit *m* d'enfant, petit lit; *naut* cadre *m*

²**cot** *n poet* cabane *f*

**cotangent** *n math* cotangente *f*

**coterie** *n* coterie *f*

**co-terminous** *adj see* **conterminous**

**cotillion** *n* cotillon *m*

**cottage** *n* petite maison rustique; ~ **industry** artisanat *m; cul* ~ **pie** mélange *m* de viande hachée et pommes purée cuit au four; **country** ~ cottage *m;* **thatched** ~ chaumière *f*

**cottager** *n* campagnard -e

**cotter** *n* clavette *f;* ~ **pin** goupille fendue

**cotton** *n* coton *m;* (fabric) cotonnade *f;* (plant) cotonnier *m; adj* de coton; *vi* aimer, avoir bonne impression; ~ **on** comprendre; *coll* piger

**cotton-cake** *n agr* tourteau *m*

**cotton-print** *n* percale *f,* indienne *f*

**cotton-wool** *n* ouate *f;* coton *m* hydrophile; **wrap in** ~ dorloter

¹**couch** *n* (bed) couche *f;* divan *m; vt* coucher; *fig* (words) exprimer, rédiger

²**couch, couch-grass** *n* chiendent *m*

**couchant** *adj her* couchant

**cough** *n* toux *f; vi* tousser; ~ **up** cracher, expectorer (en toussant); *coll* (money) casquer; *coll* (information) révéler

**cough-drop** *n* pâte pectorale

**could** *see* **can** *v aux*

**coulomb** *n elect* coulomb *m*

**council** *n* conseil *m,* assemblée *f; eccles RC* concile *m; fig* conseil *m,* débat *m*

**council-chamber** *n* salle *f* de réunion (d'un conseil municipal)

**council-flat** *n* = appartement *m* H.L.M. (habitation *f* à loyer modéré)

**council-house** *n* maison louée à la municipalité

**councillor** *n* conseiller -ère (municipal -e)

**council-school** *n* école *f* primaire, école communale

**counsel** *n* conseil *m,* avis *m;* consultation *f;* = avocat -e; ~ **of perfection** conseil idéal mais peu pratique; *vt* conseiller

**counsellor** *n* conseiller -ère; (social services, etc) orienteur *m*

¹**count** *n* compte *m,* calcul *m; leg* chef *m* d'accusation; *sp* (boxing) compte *m;* **on all** ~ **s** de tous les points de vue; **take no** ~ **of** négliger; *vt* compter, calculer, dénombrer; *fig* tenir pour, considérer; ~ **in** inclure; ~ **out** ajourner; *sp* déclarer K.O.; *coll* exclure; *vi* compter; avoir de l'importance; ~ **down** faire le compte à rebours; ~ **for** être considéré comme; ~ **on** se fier à

²**count** *n* (title) comte *m*

**count-down** *n* compte *m* à rebours

**countenance** *n* visage *m,* air *m,* expression *f;* (bearing) contenance *f;* appui *m,* encouragement *m;* **keep one's** ~ cacher ses sentiments; **lose** ~ se décontenancer; **out of** ~ déconcerté; *vt* approuver, encourager; tolérer

¹**counter** *n* (machine) compteur *m;* jeton *m;* **revolution** ~ compte-tours *m*

²**counter** *n* (shop, etc) comptoir *m;* **under the** ~ subrepticement, furtivement; illégalement

³**counter** *n* (horse) poitrail *m; naut* poupe *f*

⁴**counter** *adj* contraire, opposé; *adv* à l'encontre, à contresens, contrairement; *vt* contrarier, contrer; déjouer; *vi* contrer

**counteract** *vt* neutraliser, contrecarrer; limiter

**counteraction** *n* contre-mesure *f,* neutralisation *f*

**counter-attack** *n mil* contre-attaque *f; vt* contre-attaquer

**counter-attraction** *n* attraction rivale

**counterbalance** *n* contrepoids *m; vt* contrebalancer

**counterblast** *n* riposte *f*

**countercharge** *n leg* contre-accusation *f*

**counter-espionage** *n* contre-espionnage *m*

**counterfeit** *n* contrefaçon *f; adj* faux (*f* fausse); *vt* contrefaire; simuler

**counterfeiter** *n* faux-monnayeur *m*

**counterfoil** *n* (cheque, receipt, etc) talon *m*

**countermand** *vt* révoquer, annuler

**countermarch** *n* contremarche *f; vi* faire une contremarche

**countermine** *n mil* contre-mine *f; vt* contreminer

**counter-offensive** *n mil* contre-offensive *f*

**counterpane** *n* couvre-lit *m*

**counterpoint** *n mus* contrepoint *m*

**counterpoise** *n* contrepoids *m; vt* contrebalancer; *vi* faire contrepoids à

**counter-productive** *adj* qui produit un résultat opposé (à celui désiré)

**counter-revolution** *n* contre-révolution *f*

¹**countersign** *n mil* mot *m* d'ordre, consigne *f*

²**countersign** *vt* contresigner; ratifier, confirmer

**countersink** *n mech* fraise *f; vt* fraiser

**counter-tenor** *n* (voice) haute-contre *f;* (singer) haute-contre *m*

**countess** *n* comtesse *f*

**countless** *adj* innombrable, sans nombre

**countrified** *adj* campagnard, provincial

**country** *n* pays *m,* nation *f,* patrie *f;* (landscape) contrée *f;* (countryside) campagne *f;* ~ **cousin** provincial -e; **go to**

## country-dance

the **~** consulter la nation; *US* **God's own ~** les États-Unis; *adj* campagnard, rustique, provincial

**country-dance** *n* contredanse *f*, quadrille *m*

**countryman** *n* compatriote *m*; paysan *m*, campagnard *m*

**country-seat** *n* manoir *m*

**countryside** *n* campagne *f*, paysage *m*

**countrywoman** *n* compatriote *f*; paysanne *f*, campagnarde *f*

**county** *n* (England) comté *m*; (people) aristocratie terrienne; **~ town** chef-lieu *m* (*pl* chefs-lieux) de comté; *adj coll* snob

**coup** *n* coup *m*

**coupé** *n* coupé *m*

**couple** *n* couple *m*, paire *f*; mari *m* et femme *f*; (hounds) laisse *f*; *vt* coupler; accoupler; *fig* associer; *vi* s'accoupler

**coupler** *n mech* coupleur *m*; personne *f* qui couple

**couplet** *n* distique *m*

**coupling** *n* accouplement *m*, union *f*; *elect* couplage *m*; (railway) chaîne *f* d'attelage

**coupon** *n* coupon *m*, ticket *m*

**courage** *n* courage *m*

**courageous** *adj* courageux -euse

**courier** *n* courrier *m*

**course** *n* (time) cours *m*, progrès *m*; (direction) route *f*, voie *f*, direction *f*; développement *m*; (studies) programme, cours *m*; *cul* service *m*, plat *m*; *sp* terrain *m*; (bricks) assise *f*; *naut* route *f*; **in due ~** en temps voulu; **of ~** certainement, bien sûr; *vt* faire courir, courir; *vi* courir; couler

**coursing** *n* chasse *f* au lièvre

**court** *n* cour *f*; *leg* cour *f*; *sp* terrain *m*; (tennis) court *m*; (courtyard) cour *f*; **out of ~** en défaveur; *vt* courtiser, faire la cour à; (risk) courir; chercher; *vi* faire la cour; **be ~ing** sortir ensemble, se fréquenter

**court-card** *n* figure *f*

**courteous** *adj* courtois

**courtesan** *n* courtisane *f*, cocotte *f*, prostituée *f*

**courtesy** *n* courtoisie *f*, politesse *f*; **by ~ of** avec la permission de

**courtier** *n* courtisan *m*

**courting** *adj* **~ couple** couple *m* d'amoureux

**courtly** *adj* courtois, distingué, poli

**court-martial** *n* conseil *m* de guerre, tribunal *m* militaire; *vt* traduire en conseil de guerre

**courtship** *n* cour *f*

**courtyard** *n* cour *f*

**cousin** *n* cousin -e; **first ~** cousin -e germain -e; **second ~** cousin -e issu -e de germains

**¹cove** *n geog* anse *f*, crique *f*; *archi* cintre *m*

**²cove** *n coll* type *m*

**covenant** *n* pacte *m*, convention *f*

**cover** *n* couverture *f*; (lid) couvercle *m*; (chair) housse *f*, enveloppe *f*; (at table) couvert *m*; (shelter) abri *m*; *leg* nantissement *m*; *comm* couverture *f*; (journalism) reportage *m*; **break ~** déboucher; **take ~** se mettre à l'abri; **under ~ of** protégé par, caché par; (pretence) sous prétexte de; **under separate ~** sous pli séparé; *vt* couvrir; protéger, abriter; (distance) couvrir, parcourir; (hide) cacher, dissimuler; (subject) comprendre, traiter; (journalism) faire un reportage sur; (firearm) mettre en joue; **~ in** remplir; **~ over** couvrir, envelopper; **~ up** couvrir, envelopper; cacher, déguiser

**coverage** *n* reportages *mpl*; (insurance) risques couverts

**cover-charge** *n* couvert *m*

**cover-girl** *n* cover-girl *f*

**covering** *n* couverture *f*; protection *f*; *adj* qui couvre; **~ letter** lettre explicative

**coverlet** *n* couvre-lit *m*

**¹covert** *n* fourré *m*; gîte *m*, terrier *m*

**²covert** *adj* secret -ète, déguisé

**covet** *vt* convoiter

**covetous** *adj* avide; avaricieux -ieuse

**covetousness** *n* convoitise *f*; avidité *f*, avarice *f*

**¹cow** *n* vache *f*; femelle *f*; *coll* (woman) vache *f*, salope *f*

**²cow** *vt* intimider, mater

**coward** *n* lâche, couard -e, poltron -onne

**cowardice** *n* lâcheté *f*, couardise *f*, poltronnerie *f*

**cowardly** *adj* lâche, poltron -onne

**cowboy** *n* cowboy *m*

**cower** *vi* s'accroupir; s'aplatir

**cowherd** *n* vacher *m*

**cowhide** *n* cuir *m* de vache; (whip) fouet *m*

**cowl** *n* capuchon *m*, cagoule *f*; *archi* mitre *f*

**cow-pox** *n* vaccine *f*

**cowslip** *n bot* coucou *m*

**cox** *n* barreur -euse

**coxcomb** *n ar* casquette *f* de bouffon; *obs* dandy *m*, fat *m*

**coxswain** *n* patron *m* de barque; barreur *m*

**coy** *adj* timide, effarouché

**coyness** *n* timidité *f*

**cozen** *vt* filouter, escroquer; *vi* tricher

**¹crab** *n* crabe *m*; *astron* cancer *m*; (louse) morpion *m*; *vi* pêcher le crabe; *aer* dériver

²**crab** *n* pomme *f* sauvage; (person) grincheux -euse; *vt* déblatérer contre; *vi* rouspéter
**crabbed** *adj* grincheux -euse, acariâtre; (writing) griffonné, gribouillé
**crab-louse** *n* morpion *m*
**crab-pot** *n* casier *m*, nasse *f*
**crack** *n* (noise) craquement *m*, bruit sec; fissure *f*, fêlure *f*, fente *f*; *coll* effort *m*, essai *m*; *coll* riposte *f*, bon mot; *coll* (expert) crack *m*; ~ **of dawn** moment *m* de l'aube; ~ **of doom** Jugement dernier; *adj coll* expert, formidable; *vt* fendre, fêler; (bone) fracturer; (skin) crevasser; (wall) lézarder; faire craquer; faire claquer; casser; (joke) débiter; (problem) résoudre; (bottle) boire; *sl* ~ **a crib** cambrioler une maison; ~ **down on** mettre un frein à; ~ **up** louer beaucoup; *vi* (noise) craquer; (whip) claquer; (split) se fendre, se fêler; (bone) se fracturer; (skin) se crevasser; (wall) se lézarder; (voice) muer; *naut* ~ **on** mettre (toutes les voiles); *coll* ~ **up** s'effondrer, flancher; *coll* **be** ~ **ed** être fêlé, être toqué
**crack-brained** *adj coll* fêlé, toqué
**cracked** *adj* fêlé, plein de fissures; (voice) cassé; *coll* fêlé, toqué
**cracker** *n* (firework) pétard *m*; (paper) diablotin *m*; (biscuit) craquelin *m*; *US* biscuit *m*; ~ **s** casse-noisettes *m*
**crackers** *adj coll* fêlé, toqué
¹**cracking** *n chem* cracking *m*, craquage *m*
²**cracking** *adj* très rapide; *adv* remarquablement
**crackle** *n* crépitement *m*; *vi* crépiter
**crackling** *n* crépitement *m*; *cul* couenne *f*
**cradle** *n* berceau *m*; *med* arceau *m*; *naut* ber *m*, bers *m*; *fig* enfance *f*; *vt* bercer; coucher dans un berceau; *vi* bercer
**craft** *n* adresse *f*, habileté *f*, dextérité *f*; (cunning) ruse *f*, astuce *f*; art manuel, métier *m*; *naut* bâtiment *m*, embarcation *f*; *aer* appareil *m*
**craftily** *adv* habilement, astucieusement
**craftiness** *n* habileté *f*, astuce *f*
**craftsman** *n* artisan *m*
**craftsmanship** *n* artisanat *m*
**crafty** *adj* habile, astucieux -ieuse
**crag** *n* rocher *m*
**craggy** *adj* escarpé, à pic
**cragsman** *n* varappeur -euse
**cram** *n* (examination) bachotage *m*; *coll* mensonge *m*; *vt* bourrer, bonder; (poultry) gaver, gorger; (subject) potasser; *vi* se bourrer, se gaver; (examination) bachoter
**crammer** *n coll* bachoteur -euse; répétiteur -trice; ~ **'s boîte** *f* à bachot
¹**cramp** *n med* crampe *f*; (spasm) crispation *f*; *vt* donner des crampes à

²**cramp** *n* crampon *m*, étau *m*; *vt* cramponner; *fig* comprimer, restreindre
**cramped** *adj* resserré, comprimé; restreint; (writing) illisible
**crampon** *n* crampon *m*
**cranberry** *n* airelle *f*
**crane** *n orni* + *mech* grue *f*; *vt* + *vi* tendre (le cou)
**cranial** *adj anat* cranien -ienne
**cranium** *n anat* crâne *m*
**crank** *n mech* manivelle *f*; bizarrerie *f* de langage; (person) excentrique; *vt* couder; faire partir à la manivelle
**crankiness** *n* excentricité *f*
**cranky** *adj* eccentrique, fêlé, toqué
**cranny** *n* fissure *f*, petit trou
**crap** *n vulg* merde *f*; *sl fig* balivernes *fpl*; *vi vulg* chier
**crapulence** *n* crapule *f*
**crash** *n* fracas *m*; heurt *m*, collision *f*, impact *m*; *comm* krach *m*; *fig* ruine *f*, effondrement *m*; *vt* fracasser; *vi* s'écraser; retentir avec fracas; s'effondrer; ~ **into** percuter, tamponner
**crash-helmet** *n* casque *m* (de motocycliste)
**crashing** *n* fracas *m*; *adj* écrasant; *coll* total
**crash-landing** *n aer* atterrissage forcé
**crass** *adj* épais (*f* épaisse); crasse, grossier -ière; stupide
**crate** *n* cageot *m*, caisse *f*; *vt* mettre dans un cageot, emballer
**crater** *n* cratère *m*; (bomb) entonnoir *m*
**cravat** *n* foulard *m*
**crave** *vt* souhaiter, désirer beaucoup; solliciter
**craven** *n* + *adj* lâche, poltron -onne
**craving** *n* désir *m* intense, aspiration *f*; *adj* intense, dévorant
**crawfish** *n see* crayfish
**crawl** *n* rampement *m*; (snake) reptation *f*; allure lente; *sp* crawl *m*; *vi* ramper, se traîner (à quatre pattes); avancer lentement; (insects, etc) grouiller, fourmiller; *coll fig* s'aplatir
**crawler** *n* (baby-clothes) barboteuse *f*; *coll fig* (idler) paresseux -euse; flatteur -euse
**crawling** *adj* rampant; (swarming) grouillant, foisonnant
**crayfish, crawfish** *n* (freshwater) écrevisse *f*; (sea) langouste *f*
**crayon** *n* fusain *m*, pastel *m*; *vt* dessiner au fusain, crayonner
**craze** *n* manie *f*, mode *f*; *vt* rendre cinglé; *vi* devenir cinglé
**crazed** *adj* cinglé, toqué
**crazy** *adj* fou (*f* folle), toqué; *coll* enthousiaste; ~ **paving** dalles irrégulières
**creak** *n* grincement; *vi* grincer

**creaky** *adj* grinçant
**cream** *n* crème *f*; *fig* crème *f*, élite *f*; **cold ~** cold-cream *f*; *vt* écrémer; (butter, etc) battre
**cream-cake** *n* pâtisserie *f* à la crème
**cream-cheese** *n* fromage blanc
**creamer** *n* écrémeuse *f*; (pot) pot *m* à la crème
**creamery** *n* (shop) crémerie *f*; (dairy) laiterie *f*
**creamy** *adj* crémeux -euse
**crease** *n* pli *m*; (unintentional) faux pli; *vt* plisser, froisser; *vi* se plisser
**create** *vt* créer; *vi coll* rouspéter
**creation** *n* création *f*
**creative** *adj* créateur -trice
**creativeness, creativity** *n* pouvoir créateur
**creator** *n* créateur -trice; **the Creator** Dieu *m*
**creature** *n* créature *f*, animal *m*; personne *f*; **~ comforts** confort matériel
**crèche** *n* crèche *f*
**credence** *n* créance *f*
**credentials** *npl* lettre *f* de créance
**credibility** *n* crédibilité *f*
**credible** *adj* croyable, plausible
**credit** *n* crédit *m*; réputation *f*; honneur *m*; (balance) crédit *m*; *cin + TV* **~s** générique *m*; **do ~ to** faire honneur à; **letter of ~** accréditif *m*; *vt* créditer; croire; attribuer à, imputer
**creditable** *adj* louable; estimable
**creditor** *n* créancier -ière; (bookkeeping) compte créditeur
**credo** *n* foi *f*, credo *m*
**credulity** *n* crédulité *f*
**credulous** *adj* crédule
**creed** *n* foi *f*, credo *m*; **apostle's ~** symbole *m* des apôtres
**creek** *n* crique *f*, anse *f*; *sl* **be up the ~** être en difficulté
**creep** *n sl* salaud *m*; **~s** chair *f* de poule; *vi* ramper, se faufiler, se glisser; *bot* grimper; (flesh) avoir la chair de poule; *fig* s'abaisser, ramper
**creeper** *n* personne *f* qui rampe; *bot* plante grimpante; *coll* flatteur -euse; **~s** chaussures *fpl* à semelle de caoutchouc
**creepiness** *n* effroi *m*
**creeping** *n* (serpent) reptation *f*; action *f* de ramper; *adj* rampant
**cremate** *vt* incinérer
**cremation** *n* incinération *f*, crémation *f*
**crematorium** *n* four *m* crématoire, crématoire *m*
**crematory** *adj* crématoire
**crenellated** *adj* crénelé
**crenellation** *n* créneau *m*
**creole** *n + adj* créole
**creosote** *n* créosote *f*

**crêpe** *n* crêpe *m*; **~ de Chine** crêpe *m* de Chine; **~ paper** papier gaufré; **~ rubber** crêpe *m*; **~ sole** semelle *f* de crêpe
**crepitate** *vi* crépiter
**crepuscular** *adj* crépusculaire
**crescendo** *n* crescendo *m*; *adv* crescendo
**crescent** *n* croissant *m*; rue *f* en demi-lune; *adj* croissant, en croissant
**cresol** *n* crésol *m*
**cress** *n* cresson *m*
**crest** *n* crête *f*; (helmet) panache *m*, cimier *m*; *her* écusson *m*; *vt* orner d'un panache; atteindre la crête de; *vi* (wave) moutonner
**crestfallen** *adj* penaud, mortifié
**cretin** *n* crétin -e
**cretinism** *n* crétinisme *m*
**cretinous** *adj* crétin
**cretonne** *n* cretonne *f*
**crevasse** *n* crevasse *f*
**crevice** *n* fissure *f*
**crew** *n* équipage *m*; *sp* équipe *f*; *coll* bande *f*; *vt naut* faire partie de l'équipage de
**crew-cut** *n* coupe *f* en brosse
**crib** *n* (manger) mangeoire *f*; (cradle) berceau *m*; *eccles* crèche *f*; *coll* (school) traduction *f* juxtalinéaire; *vt coll* copier, plagier; *vi* (examination) tricher
**crick** *n* (neck) torticolis *m*; (back) lumbago *m*; *vt* **~ one's neck (back)** causer un torticolis (un lumbago)
**¹cricket** *n zool* grillon *m*
**²cricket** *n sp* cricket *m*; **not ~** pas de jeu
**crier** *n* crieur *m*; *leg* huissier *m*; **town ~** crieur public
**crime** *n* crime *m*
**criminal** *n* criminel -elle; malfaiteur *m*; *adj* criminel -elle; *leg* **~ conversation** adultère *m*
**criminality** *n* criminalité *f*
**criminologist** *n* criminologiste
**criminology** *n* criminologie *f*
**crimp** *n* pli *m*; *vt* gaufrer, crêper; (hair) friser; *cul* (fish) taillader
**crimson** *n* cramoisi *m*, pourpre *m*; *adj* cramoisi, pourpre; *vt* teindre en pourpre; *vi* s'empourprer
**cringe** *vi* s'abaisser, s'aplatir, faire des courbettes
**crinkle** *n* ride *f*, ondulation *f*; *vt* onduler, plisser; *vi* onduler, se plisser, se chiffonner
**crinoline** *n* crinoline *f*
**cripple** *n* estropié -e, infirme; *vt* estropier; *fig* paralyser, endommager
**crisis** *n* crise *f*
**crisp** *n cul* **potato ~s** pommes *fpl* chips; *adj* sec (*f* sèche); (air) vif (*f* vive); *cul* croustillant, croquant; (hair) crépu; *fig* net (*f* nette), précis, alerte; *vt* crêper;

*cul* rendre croustillant; *vi* se crêper; *cul* devenir croustillant

**criterion** *n* (*pl* **criteria**) critérium *m*, critère *m*

**critic** *n* critique *m*; (hostile) censeur *m*

**critical** *adj* critique; (demanding) exigeant, difficile; (situation) dangereux -euse, crucial, délicat

**criticism** *n* critique *f*; (reproach) blâme *m*; **textual ~** examen *m* critique de manuscrits

**criticize** *vt* critiquer; analyser, juger

**critique** *n* critique *f*

**croak** *n* (frog) coassement *m*; (raven) croassement *m*; *vt* dire d'une voix enrouée; *vi* (frog) coasser; (raven) croasser; *fig* grommeler, grogner; *sl* crever

**croaker** *n* grognon -onne; pessimiste, rabat-joie *m invar*

**croaky** *adj* rauque, enroué

**crochet** *n* crochet *m*; *vt* faire au crochet; *vi* faire du crochet

**crock** *n* cruche *f*; (horse) rosse *f*; *coll* (person) débris *m*; (car) guimbarde *f*; *vt* claquer; *vi* se claquer

**crockery** *n* vaisselle *f*

**crocodile** *n* crocodile *m*; *coll* groupe *m* d'élèves marchant deux par deux; *adj* de crocodile

**crocus** *n* crocus *m*; (colour) safran *m*

**croft** *n* clos *m*; petite ferme

**crofter** *n* fermier *m*

**cromlech** *n* cromlech *m*

**crone** *n* vieille rətatinée

**crony** *n* compagnon *m*, ami *m*; *coll* copain *m*

**crook** *n* houlette *f*; *eccles* crosse *f*; (hook) croc *m*; (bend) virage *m*; *coll* escroc *m*; *adj* fourbe, malhonnête; *vt* recourber; *vi* se recourber

**crooked** *adj* courbé, recourbé; tordu, tors; sinueux -euse; tortueux -euse, malhonnête

**croon** *vt* + *vi* (sing softly) fredonner

**crooner** *n* chanteur -euse de charme

**crop** *n* récolte *f*; *zool* jabot *m*; (whip) manche *m*; (hair) coupe *f*; *geol* affleurement *m*; *fig* quantité *f*; **neck and ~** totalement; *vt* (graze) brouter; (cut) couper, tondre; (plant) semer de; *vi* produire; *geol* ~ **out**, ~ **up** affleurer; *coll* ~ **up** paraître à l'imprévu

**crop-eared** *adj* essorillé

**cropper** *n* plante productrice; (person) agriculteur *m*; *coll* **come a ~** tomber lourdement, ramasser une pelle; (fail) manquer

**croquet** *n* croquet *m*

**croquette** *n* *cul* croquette *f*

**crosier, crozier** *n* *eccles* crosse *f*

**cross** *n* croix *f*; (race) croisement *m*, métis -isse; *hist* **take the ~** devenir croisé;

**take up one's ~** supporter patiemment ses malheurs; *adj* transversal, en biais; (breed) croisé, métis -isse; (angry) fâché, en colère; (opposite) contraire; *vt* croiser; (intersect) couper; rencontrer; (go across) traverser; (thwart) contrecarrer; *eccles* signer; (letter t) barrer; (cheque) barrer; ~ **one's fingers** conjurer le sort; ~ **one's heart** jurer ses grands dieux; ~ **one's mind** *impers* venir en tête; ~ **the palm of** graisser la patte de; ~ **the path of** rencontrer; *vi* se croiser; *eccles* se signer; ~ **off** barrer, biffer

**crossbar** *n* traverse *f*

**crossbeam** *n* traverse *f*

**cross-bow** *n* arbalète *f*

**crossbred** *adj* métissé

**crossbreed** *n* métis -isse; *vt* métisser

**cross-channel** *adj* (service) à travers la Manche

**cross-check** *vt* recouper; *vi* se recouper

**cross-country** *adj* ~ **race** cross-country *m*

**crosscut** *n* coupe *f* en travers; ~ **saw** scie *f* à deux mains; *vt* couper en travers

**cross-examination** *n* *leg* interrogatoire *m*

**cross-examine** *vt* *leg* interroger

**cross-eyed** *adj* louche, bigle

**cross-fire** *n* *mil* feu croisé

**cross-grained** *adj* (wood) à fibres torses; (person) grincheux -euse

**cross-hatch** *vt* hacher, hachurer

**cross-hatching** *n* hachure *f*

**crossing** *n* croisement *m*; (sea, desert, etc) traversée *f*; **level ~** passage *m* à niveau; **pedestrian ~**, **zebra ~** passage clouté

**crossness** *n* irritation *f*, mauvaise humeur

**cross-over** *n* (road) passage supérieur

**crosspatch** *n* grincheux -euse, chipie *f*

**crosspiece** *n* entretoise *f*, entrait *m*

**cross-purpose** *n* but opposé; **be at ~ s** être en désaccord

**cross-question** *vt* *leg* interroger

**cross-reference** *n* renvoi *m*

**crossroad** *n* carrefour *m*, intersection *f*

**cross-section** *n* coupe transversale; tranche *f*

**cross-stitch** *n* point *m* de croix

**cross-talk** *n* *coll* répliques *fpl*

**crossways, crosswise** *adv* en croix; en travers

**crossword** *n* mots croisés *pl*

**crotch** *n* fourche *f*

**crotchet** *n* *mus* noire *f*

**crotchety** *adj* grincheux -euse

**crouch** *n* accroupissement *m*; *vi* s'accroupir

**¹croup** *n* *med* croup *m*

**²croup** *n* (horse) croupe *f*

**croupier** *n* croupier *m*

**¹crow** *n* corbeau *m*, corneille *f*; **as the ~**

flies à vol d'oiseau, en ligne droite

²**crow** *n* cocorico *m*; (baby) gazouillis *m*, gazouillement *m*; *vi* faire cocorico; (baby) gazouiller; *fig* exulter, triompher

**crowbar** *n* barre *f* de fer, levier *m*

**crowd** *n* foule *f*, cohue *f*, presse *f*; masse *f*; *coll* bande *f*; *vt* assembler, attrouper; (pile) entasser, empiler; (fill) bonder, encombrer; ~ **out** repousser faute de place; *vi* s'assembler, s'attrouper

**crown** *n* couronne *f*; monarchie *f*; (hill) sommet *m*; (garland) guirlande *f*, diadème *m*; (road) axe *m*; (head) tête *f*; (tooth) couronne *f*; *fig* couronnement *m*; *adj* de la Couronne; *vt* couronner; (reward) récompenser, combler; (dentist) couronner; (complete) achever; *sl* cogner

**crown-court** *n* (England) = cour *f* d'assises

**crowned** *adj* couronné

**crowning** *n* couronnement *m*; *adj* le plus haut, parfait

**crown-wheel** *n* couronne *f*

**crow's-feet** *npl* patte-d'oie *f* (*pl* pattes-d'oie)

**crow's-nest** *n naut* nid *m* de pie

**crozier** *n see* **crosier**

**crucial** *adj* décisif -ive, critique, capital, crucial

**crucible** *n* creuset *m*

**crucifix** *n* crucifix *m*

**crucifixion** *n* crucifixion *f*

**cruciform** *adj* cruciforme

**crucify** *vt* crucifier, mettre en croix; *fig* torturer; mortifier

**crude** *adj* cru; brut; (vulgar) grossier -ière; brutal; (botched) sommaire

**crudity, crudeness** *n* crudité *f*; grossièreté *f*

**cruel** *adj* cruel -elle; (painful) douloureux -euse; *adv coll* mal

**cruelty** *n* cruauté *f*

**cruet** *n cul* poivrier *m*, salière *f* et pot *m* de moutarde; *eccles* burette *f*

**cruise** *n* croisière *f*; *vi naut* croiser; (taxi) marauder; ~ **along** rouler tranquillement; **cruising speed** vitesse *f* de croisière

**cruiser** *n naut* croiseur *m*

**crumb** *n* miette *f*; (inside of loaf) mie *f*; (scrap) brin *m*

**crumble** *vt* émietter, effriter; *vi* s'émietter, s'effriter; *fig* se désagréger

**crumbly** *adj* friable

**crump** *n* bruit *m* d'explosion; *vi* faire un bruit d'explosion

**crumpet** *n* crêpe beurrée; *sl* poule *f*

**crumple** *vt* froisser, chiffonner; *fig* flancher, céder; *vi* se froisser, se chiffonner

**crunch** *n* craquement *m*; *coll fig* moment décisif; *vt* broyer, écraser; (chew) croquer; *vi* mâchonner

**crupper** *n* croupe *f*; (harness) croupière *f*

**crusade** *n* croisade *f*; *vi* partir en croisade; ~ **for** militer pour

**crusader** *n* croisé *m*

**crush** *n* presse *f*, foule *f*; (act of crushing) écrasement *m*; *coll* béguin *m*; *vt* écraser, broyer; *fig* écraser, dominer, mater, réprimer; *vi* s'écraser, se tasser

**crushing** *adj* total, absolu; (overwhelming) écrasant, accablant

**crust** *n* croûte *f*, croûton *m*; (wine) dépôt *m*; couche *f*; *geol* écorce *f* terrestre; *vt* former croûte sur; *vi* former croûte

**crustacea** *npl* crustacés *mpl*

**crustacean** *n* crustacé *m*; *adj* crustacé

**crusted** *adj* couvert d'une croûte; (wine) ayant un dépôt; *fig* vieux (*f* vieille)

**crusty** *adj* croquant; *fig* grincheux -euse

**crutch** *n* béquille *f*; support *m*; *anat* fourche *f*

**crux** *n* point crucial, nœud *m*

**cry** *n* cri *m*; (call) appel *m*; (tears) larmes *fpl*, crise *f* de larmes; (request) prière *f*, demande *f*; slogan *m*; (hounds) clabaudage *m*; **a far** ~ une grande distance, loin; **in full** ~ acharné; *vt* crier; pleurer; implorer; proclamer, publier; ~ **down** dénigrer; *vi* crier; s'écrier; (tears) pleurer; (hounds) clabauder; ~ **for** solliciter, demander; ~ **off** se décommander, se retirer; ~ **out** crier, pousser des cris

**cry-baby** *n* (enfant) pleurnicheur -euse

**crying** *adj* criant; *fig* notoire, patent

**crypt** *n* crypte *f*

**cryptic** *adj* cryptique, abscons, abstrus

**cryptogam** *n bot* cryptogame *m* or *f*

**cryptogram** *n* cryptogramme *m*

**cryptographer** *n* cryptographe

**crystal** *n* cristal *m*; *adj* de cristal, cristallin

**crystal-gazing** *n* art *m* de la voyante

**crystalline** *adj* cristallin

**crystallization** *n* cristallisation *f*

**crystallize** *vt* cristalliser

**crystallography** *n* cristallographie *f*

**crystalloid** *n* cristalloïde *m*; *adj* cristalloïde

**cub** *n* petit *m*; (fox) renardeau *m*; (wolf) louveteau *m*; (lion) lionceau *m*; (bear) ourson *m*; (scout movement) louveteau *m*; *coll* gosse *m*; *vi* chasser des renardeaux; (give birth) mettre bas

**cubby-hole** *n* taule *f*

**cube** *n* cube *m*; *cul* bouillon *m* cube; *adj* ~ **root** racine *f* cubique; *vt* cuber

**cubic** *adj* cubique; cube

**cubicle** *n* box *m*, alcôve *f*; (baths) cabine *f*

**cubism** n cubisme m

**cuckold** n cocu m; vt faire cocu; sl cocufier

**cuckoldry** n cocuage m

**cuckoo** n coucou m; adj coll toqué; ~ **clock** pendule f à coucou

**cuckoo-flower** n bot cardomine m des prés

**cucumber** n concombre m; **cool as a ~** très maître de soi

**cud** n chew the ~ ruminer

**cuddle** n enlacement m, étreinte f; vt caresser, peloter; vi s'entrelacer; ~ **up** se pelotonner, coucher dans les bras l'un de l'autre

**cuddly** adj coll qu'on a envie de caresser

**cudgel** n matraque f; **take up the ~ s for** défendre vigoureusement; vt matraquer; ~ **one's brains** se creuser la cervelle

¹**cue** n theat réplique f; mus signal m d'entrée; fig indication f, mot m d'ordre; vt theat donner la réplique à

²**cue** n (billiards) queue f

¹**cuff** n poignet m, manchette f; US revers m de pantalon; sl ~ s menottes fpl; coll **off the ~** à l'improviste

²**cuff** n gifle f, calotte f; vt gifler, calotter

**cuff-link** n bouton m de manchette

**cuirass** n mil cuirasse f

**cuirassier** n mil cuirassier m

**cuisine** n cuisine f

**cul-de-sac** n impasse f, cul-de-sac m (pl culs-de-sac)

**culinary** adj culinaire

**cull** vt cueillir, sélectionner; (animals) tuer pour diminuer le nombre

**cullander** n see colander

**culminate** vi culminer

**culmination** n culmination f

**culpability** n culpabilité f

**culprit** n coupable; leg prévenu -e

**cult** n culte m; mode f

**cultivate** vt cultiver

**cultivated** adj cultivé; raffiné

**cultivation** n culture f

**cultivator** n cultivateur -trice; (machine) cultivateur m

**cultural** adj agr cultural; arts culturel -elle

**culture** n culture f

**culvert** n conduit m

**cumbersome** adj encombrant, lourd

**cumbrous** adj encombrant, lourd

**cumin** n bot cumin m

**cummerbund** n large ceinture f (en étoffe)-

**cumulate** vt accumuler; leg cumuler; vi s'accumuler

**cumulation** n accumulation f; leg cumul m

**cumulative** adj qui s'ajoute; leg cumulatif -ive; (vote) plural; (interest) composé

**cumulo-nimbus** n cumulo-nimbus m

**cumulus** n cumulus m

**cuneiform** adj cunéiforme

**cunning** n ruse f, astuce f, fourberie f; ar adresse f; adj rusé, astucieux -ieuse, fourbe; habile, adroit, malin (f maligne)

**cunt** n vulg + sl fig con m

**cup** n tasse f; (prize) coupe f; eccles + bot calice m; mélange m de vin et de fruits; fig (pleasant) coupe f; (unpleasant) calice m; surg ventouse f; **in one's ~ s** ivre; coll **one's ~ of tea** ce qu'on aime; vt ~ **one's hands** mettre ses mains en coupe

**cupboard** n placard m, armoire f; ~ **love** amour intéressé

**cupful** n tasse f

**cupidity** n cupidité f

**cupola** n coupole f, dôme m

**cupper, cuppa** n coll tasse f de thé

**cupric** adj cuprique

**cupro-nickel** n cupro-nickel m

**cup-tie** n match m (de football) éliminatoire

**cur** n chien bâtard; coll clebs m; fig salaud m

**curaçoa, curaçao** n curaçao m

**curacy** n eccles vicariat m

**curare** n curare m

**curate** n eccles vicaire m

**curative** adj curatif -ive

**curator** n conservateur -trice

**curb** n (harness) gourmette f; frein m; (pavement) bord m du trottoir; vt restreindre, freiner, contraindre

**curd** n lait caillé, caillebotte f; vt cailler; vi se cailler

**curdle** vt cailler; coaguler; vi se cailler; se coaguler; **make s/o's blood ~** terrifier qn, effrayer qn

**cure** n (remedy) remède m; (treatment) cure f; guérison f; eccles charge f; vt guérir; cul saler; cul fumer; fig remédier à; (rubber) vulcaniser

**curfew** n couvre-feu m

**curia** n eccles curie f

**curio** n bibelot m, objet curieux

**curiosity** n curiosité f; bizarrerie f; objet curieux, rareté f

**curious** adj curieux -ieuse; étrange, singulier -ière; avide de savoir, indiscret -ète; extraordinaire

**curl** n boucle f; spirale f, volute f; vt boucler, faire boucler, friser; vi boucler, friser; ~ **up** (person) se pelotonner; s'enrouler; coll s'effondrer

**curler** n bigoudi m

**curlew** n zool courlis m

¹**curling** adj à friser; qui frise; ~ **irons**, ~ **tongs** fer m à friser; ~ **pin** bigoudi m

²**curling** n sp curling m
**curl-paper** n papillote f
**curly** adj frisé, bouclé
**curmudgeon** n grincheux m
**currant** n raisin m de Corinthe; groseille f; **black~** cassis m; **red~** groseille rouge
**currency** n circulation f; monnaie f ayant cours; devise f; (general acceptance) cours m; **foreign ~** devises étrangères
**current** n (stream, air) courant m; (water) cours m; adj courant, commun; (accepted) admis; reçu; en cours; **comm ~ account** compte courant; **~ events** actualités fpl
**curriculum** n programme m scolaire; **~ vitae** curriculum vitae m, abbr C.V.
¹**curry** n curry m, cari m; vt assaisonner au cari
²**curry** vt (horse) étriller; (leather) corroyer; **~ favour with s/o** amadouer qn par flatterie
**curse** n malédiction f; (oath) juron m, imprécation f; eccles excommunication f; fig désastre m, calamité f; coll (period) règles fpl; vt maudire; eccles excommunier; vi jurer, blasphémer
**cursed, curst** adj maudit, abominable, odieux -ieuse; coll sacré, irritant; obstiné
**cursive** n cursive f; adj cursif -ive
**cursoriness** n hâte f, rapidité f
**cursory** adj sommaire, superficiel -ielle, hâtif -ive, rapide
**curt** adj brusque, sec (f sèche), cassant
**curtail** vt écourter, raccourcir; réduire, diminuer
**curtailment** n raccourcissement m; diminution f
**curtain** n rideau m; fig voile m; mil courtine f; mil **~ of fire** tir m de barrage; fig **draw a ~ over** cacher, ne plus rien dire sur; **iron ~** rideau m de fer; **it's ~s** c'est la fin; vt garnir de rideaux; **~ off** cacher par un rideau
**curtain-call** n theat rappel m
**curtain-raiser** n theat lever m de rideau
**curtness** n brusquerie f
**curtsey, curtsy** n révérence f; vi faire la (une) révérence
**curvature** n courbure f
**curve** n courbe f; mot virage m; **~s** rondeurs fpl; vt courber; vi se courber; décrire une courbe
**cushion** n coussin m; (billiards) bande f; **air ~** matelas m d'air; vt orner de coussins; (stuff) matelasser; fig amortir
**cushy** adj coll pépère
**cusp** n geom sommet m; archi lobe m; astron corne f
**cuspidor** n crachoir m

**cuss** n coll juron m; coll type m; vt + vi jurer
**cussed** adj coll obstiné; (annoying) emmerdant
**cussedness** n esprit m de contradiction
**custard** n cul crème anglaise
**custodian** n gardien -ienne; concierge
**custody** n garde f; état m d'arrestation; **take into ~** écrouer
**custom** n coutume f, usage m, habitude f; **~s** douane f; (officials) douaniers -ières; **~s duty** droits mpl de douane
**customary** adj normal, habituel -elle, coutumier -ière
**custom-built, custom-made** adj US fait sur commande; (clothes) fait sur mesure
**customer** n client -e; coll type m
**custom-house** n douane f
**cut** n coupe f; coupure f, entaille f; (wound) plaie f; incision f; (slash) estafilade f; (slice) tranche f; (abridgement) coupure f, réduction f, passage coupé; sl pot-de-vin m (pl pots-de-vin), pourcentage m; **a ~ above** supérieur à; **short ~** raccourci m; adj divisé, coupé; gravé; réduit; coupé en tranches; (castrated) châtré; **~ and dried** préparé d'avance; vt couper, trancher, tailler; (notch) entailler, encocher; croiser, traverser; (chisel) ciseler; (reduce) réduire, censurer; (castrate) couper; sp couper; coll (class, lesson) sécher; **~ a dash** faire de l'épate; (argument) **~ both ways** être à double tranchant; **~ down** tuer; (reduce) réduire, raccourcir; (trees) abattre; (text) tronquer; coll **~ fine** laisser peu de temps, laisser peu de marge; coll **~ it out!** en voilà assez!, ta gueule!; **~ no ice** rester sans effet, ne rien changer; **~ off** couper, découper; prélever; surg amputer; elect couper le courant à; **~ off with a shilling** déshériter; **~ out** couper, tailler, émonder; sculpter; coll évincer, supplanter; **~ short** abréger; **~ s/o dead** faire semblant de ne pas voir qn; **~ up** découper; (criticize) éreinter; **be ~ off** être coupé; **be ~ out for** avoir l'étoffe de; **have one's work ~ out** avoir du mal vers; vi **~ back to** revenir sur ses pas à; **~ in** interrompre; **~ in on** (cards, dance) prendre la place de; mot faire une queue de poisson à; **~ loose** rompre avec, jeter sa gourme; **~ out** eng découpler; mot caler; **~ up rough** se fâcher
**cutaneous** adj cutané
**cute** adj coll malin (f maligne), déluré; US mignon -onne, charmant
**cuteness** n coll finesse f; US gentillesse f
**cuticle** n bot cuticule f; anat épiderme m

**cutlass** *n* coutelas *m*
**cutler** *n* coutelier *m*
**cutlery** *n* coutellerie *f*
**cutlet** *n* côtelette *f*
**cut-off** *n eng* obturateur *m*, valve *f*; (rifle) cran *m* de sûreté
**cut-out** *n elect* coupe-circuit *m invar*; *mot* échappement *m* libre; (wood, etc) découpage *m*
**cut-price** *adj* au rabais
**cutter** *n* (tailor) coupeur -euse; (stone) tailleur *m*; *naut* cotre *m*, canot *m*
**cut-throat** *n* assassin *m*; *coll* rasoir *m* à main; *adj* meurtrier -ière
**cutting** *n* action *f* de couper; coupe *f*; percement *m*; *hort* bouture *f*; (wood) percée *f*; (newspaper) coupure *f*; *cin* découpage *m*; (railway, road) tranchée *f*; *adj* coupant, tranchant; (rain) cinglant; (cold) piquant; (words) blessant, mordant
**cuttle-fish** *n zool* seiche *f*
**cutwater** *n naut* étrave *f*
**cyanide** *n chem* cyanure *m*
**cyanosis** *n med* cyanose *f*
**cybernetics** *n* cybernétique *f*
**cyclamen** *n bot* cyclamen *m*
**cycle** *n* cycle *m*; *lit* cycle *m*; bicyclette *f*, vélo *m*; *elect* cycle *m*; *vi* revenir par cycles; faire de la bicyclette
**cyclic, cyclical** *adj* cyclique
**cycling** *n* cyclisme *m*

**cyclist** *n* cycliste
**cyclometer** *n* compteur *m* kilométrique
**cyclone** *n* cyclone *m*
**cyclonic** *adj* cyclonal
**cyclopean** *adj* cyclopéen -éenne
**Cyclops** *n* Cyclope *m*
**cyclostyle** *n* duplicateur *m* à stencils; *vt* reproduire, polycopier
**cyclotron** *n phys* cyclotron *m*
**cygnet** *n zool* jeune cygne *m*
**cylinder** *n* cylindre *m*
**cylindrical** *adj* cylindrique
**cymbal** *n mus* cymbale *f*
**cynic** *n philos* cynique; sceptique
**cynical** *adj* cynique
**cynicism** *n* scepticisme *m*; causticité *f*
**cynosure** *n* point *m* de mire; centre *m* d'attraction
**cypress** *n bot* cyprès *m*
**Cypriot** *n* Cypriote
**Cyprus** *n* Chypre *f*
**cyst** *n* kyste *m*
**cystitis** *n med* cystite *f*
**cystotomy** *n surg* cystotomie *f*
**cytology** *n* cytologie *f*
**czar, tzar** *n* tsar *m*, czar *m*
**czarina** *n* tsarine *f*
**Czech** *n* Tchèque; *adj* tchèque
**Czechoslovak** *n* Tchécoslovaque; *adj* tchécoslovaque
**Czechoslovakia** *n* Tchécoslovaquie *f*

# D

**d** *n mus* ré *m*; **D-day** le jour J
**¹dab** *n* tape *f*; tache *f*; *coll* ~ s empreintes digitales; *vt* tapoter; tamponner
**²dab** *n zool* limande *f*
**³dab** *adj coll* calé, expert; **be a ~ hand at** être doué pour
**dabble** *vi* ~ **in** (at) donner dans, s'occuper un peu de
**dabbler** *n* amateur *m*; (writer) écrivailleur *m*
**dachshund** *n* dachshund *m*
**dactyl** *n* dactyle *m*
**dad, daddy** *n coll* papa *m*
**daddy-long-legs** *n zool* tipule *f*
**dado** *n* lambris *m*; (pedestal) dé *m*; plinthe *f*

**daffodil** *n* jonquille *f*; *adj* (colour) jonquille *invar*
**daft** *adj* toqué, cinglé; faible d'esprit
**dagger** *n* dague *f*; poignard *m*; *print* croix *f*; **at ~ s drawn** à couteaux tirés; **look (speak) ~ s** regarder (parler) avec haine
**dahlia** *n bot* dahlia *m*
**daily** *n* (newspaper) quotidien *m*; (maid) femme *f* de journée; *adj* quotidien -ienne, journalier -ière; *adv* tous les jours, quotidiennement, journellement
**daintiness** *n* délicatesse *f*, raffinement *m*; élégance *f*; finesse *f*
**dainty** *n cul* friandise *f*, mets fin; *adj*

délicat, raffiné; élégant, fin, choisi

**dairy** *n* (installation) laiterie *f*; (shop) crémerie *f*, laiterie *f*; *adj* laitier -ière

**dairy-cattle** *npl* vaches laitières

**dairy-farm** *n* laiterie *f*

**dairymaid** *n* laitière *f*

**dairyman** *n* laitier *m*

**daïs** *n* estrade *f*

**daisy** *n* paquerette *f*, marguerite *f*

**dale** *n* vallée *f*

**dalliance** *n* (amorous) badinage *m*; (sophisticated) marivaudage *m*, *pej* libertinage *m*

**dally** *vi* (amorously) badiner; jouer; (idly) flâner, traînasser; ~ **with** considérer, envisager

**dalmatic** *n eccles* dalmatique *f*

**daltonism** *n* daltonisme *m*

¹**dam** *n* barrage *m* (de retenue); reversoir *m*; *vt* construire un barrage sur

²**dam** *n zool* femelle *f*

**damage** *n* dommage *m*; (material) dégâts *mpl*; *coll* **what's the** ~? ça fait combien?; *leg* ~ **s** dommages-intérêts *mpl*; *vt* endommager; *fig* léser; *vi* causer des dégâts

**damageable** *adj* dommageable

**damascene** *vt* damasquiner

**Damascus** *n* Damas *f*

**damask** *n* damas *m*; (colour) incarnat *m*; *adj* (fabric) damassé; (steel) damasquiné; *vt* damasquiner

**dame** *n US coll* femme *f*

**damn** *n* juron *m*; **not care a** ~ s'en ficher totalement; *adj* damné, sacré; *vt* condamner; maudire; *eccles* damner; *fig* désapprouver; *interj* zut!

**damnable** *adj* exécrable

**damnation** *n* damnation *f*; *interj* malheur!

**damned** *n eccles* damnés *mpl*; *adj eccles* damné; maudit; *coll* sacré

**damning** *adj* accablant, écrasant

**damp** *n* humidité *f*; (mining) grisou *m*; *fig* découragement *m*, abattement *m*; *adj* humide, mouillé; *vt* humecter, mouiller; (fire) étouffer; (sound) étouffer, amortir; *fig* décourager, déprimer

**damp-course** *n bui* couche isolante

**dampen** *vt see* **damp** *vt*

**damper** *n* (stamps) mouilleur *m*; (piano) étouffoir *m*; (stove) registre *m*; *fig* (person) rabat-joie *m invar*; **put a** ~ **on** jeter un froid sur

**dampness** *n* humidité *f*

**damp-proof** *adj* imperméable

**damsel** *n* jeune fille *f*, demoiselle *f*

**damson** *n* prune *f* de Damas

**dance** *n* danse *f*; bal *m*; ~ **of death** danse *f* macabre; **lead s/o a** ~ en faire voir à qn, faire des difficultés à qn; **St Vitus's** ~ danse *f* de Saint-Guy; *vt* + *vi* danser;

~ **attendance on** faire l'empressé auprès de, être au petits soins avec

**dance-band** *n* orchestre *m* de danse

**dance-hall** *n* dancing *m*

**dancer** *n* danseur -euse

**dancing** *n* danse *f*

**dandelion** *n bot* pissenlit *m*

**dandle** *vt* faire sauter

**dandruff** *n* pellicules *fpl*

**dandy** *n* dandy *m*; fat *m*; *adj* bien habillé; *coll* au poil

**dandyism** *n* dandysme *m*

**Dane** *n* Danois -e

**danger** *n* danger *m*, péril *m*; **be in** ~ **of** risquer de

**danger-money** *n* prime *f* de risque

**dangerous** *adj* dangereux -euse, périlleux -euse

**dangle** *vt* laisser pendiller; *vi* pendiller, brimbaler

**Danish** *n* (language) danois *m*; *adj* danois

**dank** *adj* humide

**dankness** *n* humidité *f*

**dapper** *adj* pimpant; actif -ive

**dapple** *vt* tacheter

**dapple-grey** *adj* gris pommelé *invar*

**dare** *n coll* défi *m*; *vt* oser; (challenge) défier; *vi* oser; **I** ~ **say** cela se peut bien, il me semble que, très probablement

**daredevil** *n* casse-cou *m invar*; *adj* audacieux -ieuse

**daring** *n* courage *m*, audace *f*; *adj* courageux -euse, audacieux -ieuse

**dark** *n* obscurité *f*; noir *m*, nuit *f*; *fig* ignorance *f*; *adj* obscur, sombre, noir; (colour) foncé; (hair) noir, brun; *fig* lugubre, sinistre; mystérieux -ieuse; *hist* **Dark Ages** première partie du Moyen Âge; *fig* ~ **horse** outsider *m*; **keep** ~ tenir secret -ète; **keep s/o in the** ~ laisser qn dans l'ignorance

**darken** *vt* obscurcir; (colour) foncer; *fig* obscurcir, assombrir; noircir; *vi* s'obscurcir; (colour) foncer; *fig* s'obscurcir, s'assombrir, se rembrunir

**darkling** *adj* qui devient sombre; lugubre

**darkly** *adv* d'un air sombre, d'un air lugubre; mystérieusement

**darkness** *n* obscurité *f*; ténèbres *fpl*; *fig* ignorance *f*

**darling** *n* chéri -e; *adj* bien aimé

**darn** *n* reprise *f*; *vt* repriser

**darning** *n* ravaudage *m*

**darning-ball** *n* œuf *m* à repriser

**darning-needle** *n* aiguille *f* à repriser

**dart** *n* javelot *m*; *sp* fléchette *f*; (insect) dard *m*; (movement) brusque élan *m*; *vt* lancer; *vi* foncer, avancer vite

**dartboard** *n* cible *f* du jeu de fléchettes

**darts** *npl* jeu *m* de fléchettes

**dash** *n* ruée *f*; (punctuation, Morse) trait *m*; (liquid) goutte *f*; (colour) touche *f*;

428

*fig* élan *m*; entrain *m*, énergie *f*; **cut a ~** faire de l'effet, sembler important; **make a ~** prendre ses jambes à son cou; *vt* lancer, jeter avec violence; *fig* (hopes) abattre; (person) démoraliser; **~ off** bâcler, enlever; *vi* s'élancer, se précipiter, se ruer; **~ away, ~ off** partir vite

**dashboard** *n mot* tableau *m* de bord

**dashing** *adj* fringant, élégant, dynamique

**dastard** *n obs* lâche, poltron -onne

**dastardly** *adj* lâche, couard, infâme

**data** *npl* données *fpl*

**data-bank** banque *f* de données

**datable** *adj* datable

**¹date** *n* date *f*; époque *f*; *coll* rendez-vous *m*; **out of ~** démodé; **up to ~** moderne, à la page; *vt* dater; *coll US* fixer un rendez-vous avec; *vi* dater; être démodé

**²date** *n* datte *f*

**date-line** *n* méridien *m* 180°; (newspaper, etc) date *f* de publication

**date-palm** *n* dattier *m*

**dative** *n gramm* datif *m*

**datum** *n* (*pl* **data**) donnée *f*; (mark, line) repère *m*

**daub** *n* badigeonnage *m*, enduit *m*; *arts* croûte *f*; *vt* badigeonner, enduire; *arts* barbouiller

**dauber** *n* peintre *m* médiocre, barbouilleur *m*

**daughter** *n* fille *f*

**daughter-in-law** *n* belle-fille *f* (*pl* belles-filles), bru *f*

**daunt** *n* décourager, abattre

**dauntless** *adj* courageux -euse, intrépide

**dauphin** *n* dauphin *m*

**davit** *n naut* bossoir *m* d'embarcations, portemanteau *m*

**daw** *n orni* choucas *m*

**dawdle** *vi* flâner, traîner

**dawdler** *n* flâneur -euse

**dawn** *n* aube *f*, aurore *f*; *fig* aube *f*, commencement *m*; *vi* poindre, se lever; *fig* naître, commencer; **~ upon** devenir clair à

**dawning** *n* aube *f*, aurore *f*; *fig* commencement *m*, naissance *f*; *adj* naissant

**day** *n* (*usu* unit of time) jour *m*; (*usu* daylight hours, working) journée *f*; **~s** jours *mpl*, époque *f*; **~ by ~** tous les jours; **~s of grace** délai *m* de grâce; **any ~ now** d'un jour à l'autre; **call it a ~** cesser le travail; **every other ~** tous les deux jours; **name the ~** fixer la date d'un mariage, prendre la décision de se marier; **one of these ~s** bientôt; **pass the time of ~** saluer, faire un bout de conversation; **the good old ~s**

le bon vieux temps; *adj* de jour; (ticket, etc) valable un jour seulement

**day-bed** *n* divan *m*

**day-boy** *n* (school) externe *m*

**daybreak** *n* aube *f*, point *m* du jour

**daydream** *n* rêverie *f*; *vi* rêver, rêvasser

**day-girl** *n* (school) externe *f*

**day-labour** *n* travail *m* à la journée

**day-labourer** *n* journalier -ière

**daylight** *n* jour *m*, lumière *f* du jour; **in broad ~** en plein jour; **see ~** commencer à comprendre

**day-nursery** *n* crèche *f*, garderie *f* (d'enfants)

**day-school** *n* externat *m*

**day-shift** *n* équipe *f* de jour

**day-time** *n* jour *m*, journée *f*

**daze** *n* étourdissement *m*, abrutissement *m*; *vt* étourdir, abrutir

**dazzle** *n* éblouissement *m*; *vt* éblouir, aveugler

**dazzling** *adj* éblouissant

**deacon** *n eccles* diacre *m*

**deaconess** *n eccles* diaconesse *f*

**dead** *n collect* morts *mpl*; *fig* **~ of night** milieu *m* de la nuit; *adj* mort, sans vie; crevé; (numbed) engourdi; (colour) terne, neutre; (sound) sourd, assourdi; *coll* total; *elect* à plat; (calm) plat; *bui* (door, window) faux (*f* fausse), condamné; **~ end** impasse *f*, cul-de-sac *m* (*pl* culs-de-sac); *mil* **~ ground** angle mort; *sp* **~ heat** égalité *f*; **~ letter** (mail) rebut *m*; **~ loss** perte sèche; *coll* (useless person) bon (*f* bonne) à rien; **~ march** marche *f* funèbre; *coll* **~ men** bouteilles *fpl* vides; *naut* **~ reckoning** estime *f*; **~ set** attaque poussée; *coll* effort *m* de séduction; **~ shot** tireur *m* hors ligne; *adv* absolument, très; **~ slow** au pas

**dead-and-alive** *adj* (place) triste, mort; (person) sans entrain

**dead-beat** *n US coll* écornifleur -euse; *adj coll* épuisé, éreinté

**dead-centre** *n eng* point mort

**deaden** *vt* amortir; (sound) assourdir; (blunt) émousser; ternir

**dead-end** *n* impasse *f*; *adj* **~ job** métier *m* sans avenir

**deadline** *n* date *f* limite

**deadlock** *n* impasse *f*

**deadly** *adj* mortel -elle, fatal; (weapon) meurtrier -ière; *coll* rasant; *adv coll* extrêmement

**deadly-nightshade** *n bot* belladone *f*

**deadness** *n* mort *f*; stagnation *f*, engourdissement *m*; apathie *f*

**deadpan** *n* visage *m* sans expression; *adj* sans expression

**dead-weight** *n* poids mort, masse lourde

**deaf** *n collect* sourds *mpl*; *adj* sourd; *fig*

indifférent, insensible; ~ **and dumb** sourd-muet (*pl* sourds-muets) (*f* sourde-muette, *pl* sourdes-muettes); ~ **as a post** sourd comme un pot

**deaf-aid** *n* prothèse auditive, appareil *m* acoustique

**deafen** *vt* assourdir; étouffer

**deaf-mute** *n* sourd-muet *m* (*pl* sourds-muets), sourde-muette *f* (*pl* sourdes-muettes)

**deafness** *n* surdité *f*

¹**deal** *n* quantité *f*; affaire *f*, transaction *f*; (cards) donne *f*; *vt* distribuer, répartir; (blow) asséner, allonger; (cards) donner; *vi* (cards) donner; ~ **in** faire le commerce de; ~ **with** concerner, s'agir de; discuter avec; (resolve) résoudre, maîtriser; *comm* (order) régler; être client de

²**deal** *n* bois blanc, sapin *m*

**dealer** *n* marchand -e, négociant -e; (cards) joueur -euse qui donne les cartes

**dealing** *n* comportement *m*, manière *f* d'agir; commerce *m*

**dean** *n* doyen -enne

**deanery** *n eccles* doyenné *m*

**dear** *n* cher (*f* chère), chéri -e; *coll* amour *m*; *adj* cher (*f* chère), aimé, chéri; précieux -ieuse; (cost) cher (*f* chère), coûteux -euse; *adv* trop cher; *interj* mon Dieu!

**dearly** *adv* affectueusement; cher, chèrement

**dearness** *n* affection *f*, attachement *m*; (price) cherté *f*, coût élevé

**dearth** *n* manque *m*; pénurie *f*

**death** *n* mort *f*; *lit* trépas *m*; décès *m*; *fig* fin *f*; **at** ~ **'s door** à l'article de la mort; **be in at the** ~ (hunting) être présent à la mise à mort; *fig* assister à la phase finale, voir le dénouement; *coll* **catch one's** ~ attraper la crève

**deathbed** *n lit m* de mort; *adj* in extremis

**death-blow** *n* coup mortel

**death-duties** *n leg* droits *mpl* de succession

**death-knell** *n* glas *m*

**deathless** *adj* immortel -elle

**deathlike** *adj* de mort, cadavéreux -euse

**deathly** *adj* mortel -elle, de mort; *adv* mortellement; ~ **pale** pâle comme la mort

**death-mask** *n* masque *m* mortuaire

**death-rate** *n* mortalité *f*

**death-rattle** *n* râle *m*

**death-roll** *n* liste *f* des morts; nombre *m* de morts

**death's-head** *n* tête *f* de mort; ~ **moth** sphinx *m*, tête *f* de mort

**death-trap** *n* casse-cou *m invar*

**death-watch (beetle)** *n* vrillette *f*

**debacle** *n* débâcle *f*

**debar** *vt* exclure; (prevent) interdire, empêcher

**debark** *vt* + *vi* débarquer

**debase** *vt* avilir; (coinage) déprécier

**debatable** *adj* discutable

**debate** *n* débat *m*; discussion *f*, controverse *f*; *vt* débattre, discuter; examiner; *vi* discuter; réfléchir

**debater** *n* argumentateur -trice

**debauch** *n* débauche *f*, partie *f* de débauche; *vt* débaucher, corrompre

**debauchee** *n* débauché -e

**debauchery** *n* débauche *f*, luxure *f*

**debenture** *n* obligation *f*

**debilitate** *vt* débiliter

**debilitating** *adj* débilitant

**debility** *n* débilité *f*

**debit** *n* débit *m*; *vt* débiter

**debonair** *adj* gai, riant; affable

**debouch** *vi* déboucher

**debris** *n* débris *mpl*, décombres *mpl*

**debt** *n* dette *f*; **in** ~ endetté

**debtor** *n* débiteur -trice

**debunk** *vt coll* dégonfler, déboulonner

**début, debut** *n* début *m*

**débutante** *n* débutante *f*

**decade** *n* décennie *f*

**decadence** *n* décadence *f*

**decadent** *adj* décadent

**décalogue** *n bibl* décalogue *m*

**decamp** *vi* décamper

**decant** *vt* décanter

**decanter** *n* carafe *f*, carafon *m*

**decapitate** *vt* décapiter

**decapitation** *n* décapitation *f*

**decarbonize** *vt mot* décalaminer

**decasyllable** *n* décasyllabe *m*

**decay** *n* décomposition *f*, pourriture *f*; (teeth) carie *f*; désintégration *f*; déclin *m*, déchéance *f*; *vi* se détériorer, pourrir; décliner; (teeth) se carier

**decease** *n* décès *m*; *vi* décéder

**deceased** *n* défunt -e; *adj* décédé, défunt

**deceit, deceitfulness** *n* duperie *f*, supercherie *f*, duplicité *f*

**deceitful** *adj* trompeur -euse, fourbe; illusoire

**deceive** *vt* tromper, duper; *vi* se tromper

**deceiver** *n* trompeur -euse, fourbe

**decelerate** *vt* + *vi* ralentir

**deceleration** *n* décélération *f*, ralentissement *m*

**December** *n* décembre *m*

**decency** *n* décence *f*, modestie *f*; (seemliness) convenance *f*, bienséance *f*

**decent** *adj* décent, modeste, respectable; (seemly) convenable, bienséant; *coll* passable; (nice) gentil -ille

**decentralization** *n* décentralisation *f*

**decentralize** *vt* décentraliser

**deception** *n* duperie *f*, supercherie *f*,

duplicité *f;* (trick) leurre *m*

**deceptive** *adj* trompeur -euse; décevant

**deceptiveness** *n* apparence trompeuse

**decibel** *n* décibel *m*

**decide** *vt* décider, déterminer; (arrange) résoudre, régler; *vi* se décider, se résoudre, décider

**decided** *adj* défini, déterminé; décidé, résolu; précis, net (*f* nette)

**decidedly** *adv* nettement, incontestablement

**decider** *n sp* belle *f*

**deciduous** *adj bot* (tree) à feuilles caduques

**decimal** *n* décimale *f; adj* décimal; ~ **point** virgule *f;* **recurring** ~ fraction *f* périodique; **two** ~ **five** deux virgule cinq

**decimate** *vt* décimer

**decimation** *n* décimation *f*

**decipher** *vt* déchiffrer

**decision** *n* décision *f;* détermination *f,* résolution *f*

**decisive** *adj* décisif -ive, còncluant, probant; (determined) résolu, ferme

**decisiveness** *n* décision *f,* fermeté *f*

**¹deck** *n naut* pont *m;* (cards) jeu *m* de cartes; **aer** *coll* sol *m;* **clear the** ~ **s** *naut* faire lc branle-bas; *fig* se préparer à agir; **top** ~ (bus) impériale *f*

**²deck** *vt* orner, parer; *naut* ponter

**deck-chair** *n* transat *m,* transatlantique *m*

**declaim** *vt* + *vi* déclamer

**declamation** *n* déclamation *f*

**declamatory** *adj* déclamatoire

**declarable** *adj* à déclarer

**declaration** *n* déclaration *f*

**declarative** *adj* explicatif -ive

**declaratory** *adj* déclaratoire; explicatif -ive

**declare** *vt* déclarer, assurer; faire connaître, proclamer; ~ **for** prendre parti pour; *vi* se déclarer

**declared** *adj* déclaré, ouvert

**déclassé** *adj* déclassé

**declension** *n* déclin *m,* détérioration *f; gramm* déclinaison *f*

**declinable** *adj gramm* déclinable

**declination** *n* inclination *f,* pente *f; astron* déclinaison *f*

**decline** *n* déclin *m,* baisse *f; fig* déclin *m,* décadence *f; vt* décliner; *vi* pencher, s'incliner; baisser, décliner

**declivity** *n* déclivité *f*

**declutch** *vi mot* débrayer

**decoction** *n* décoction *f*

**decode** *vt* déchiffrer, décoder

**decoder** *n* déchiffreur -euse; appareil *m* qui décode

**decoke** *vt mot coll* décalaminer

**décolleté** *n* décolleté *m; adj* décolleté

**decolorant** *n* décolorant *m*

**decolour, decolourize** *vt* décolorer

**decompose** *vt* décomposer; analyser; *vi* se décomposer

**decomposition** *n* décomposition *f*

**decompress** *vt* décomprimer

**decompression** *n* décompression *f*

**deconsecrate** *vt eccles* séculariser, désaffecter

**decontaminate** *vt* décontaminer

**decontamination** *n* décontamination *f*

**decontrol** *vt* libérer de contrôle

**décor** *n theat* décor *m*

**decorate** *vt* décorer, orner; (medal) décorer

**decoration** *n* décoration *f*

**decorative** *adj* décoratif -ive; joli

**decorator** *n* décorateur -trice, ensemblier *m;* (painter) peintre *m*

**decorous** *adj* bienséant, comme il faut

**decorum** *n* décorum *m,* tenue *f;* bienséance *f*

**decoy** *n* appeau *m,* leurre *m;* (person) compère *m; vt* leurrer, piper; attirer dans un piège

**decrease** *n* décroissance *f,* diminution *f; vt* + *vi* diminuer, décroître

**decree** *n* arrêt *m,* décret *m,* ordonnance *f; eccles* décret *m; leg* ~ **nisi** jugement *m* provisoire (de divorce); *vt* décréter; *vi* faire un décret

**decrepit** *adj* décrépit, délabré

**decrepitude** *n* décrépitude *f*

**decretal** *n eccles* décrétale *f*

**decry** *vt* décrier, dénigrer

**decuple** *adj* décuple; *vt* décupler

**dedicate** *vt eccles* dédier, consacrer; (devote) dédier, vouer; (book) dédier

**dedication** *n* dédicace *f;* (devotion) dévouement *m*

**dedicatory** *adj* dédicatoire

**deduce** *vt philos* déduire

**deduct** *vt math* déduire, soustraire, défalquer

**deduction** *n math* + *philos* déduction *f;* (money) défalcation *f*

**deductive** *adj* déductif -ive

**¹deed** *n* action *f,* exploit *m*

**²deed** *n leg* contrat *m,* acte notarié

**deem** *vt* croire, juger, estimer; *vi* avoir une opinion

**deep** *n* ce qui est profond; *poet* océan *m;* (abyss) gouffre *m,* abîme *m;* ~ **s** profondeurs *fpl; adj* profond; (colour) foncé, riche; (sound) grave; *fig* sérieux -ieuse, intense, profond; obscur; extrême, total; *coll* malin (*f* maligne), fourbe; ~ **in** absorbé par, enfoncé dans; **go off the** ~ **end** s'emballer, se mettre en colère; **in** ~ **water** en difficulté; *adv* profondément

**deep-dyed** *adj fig* profondément coupable

**deepen** *vt* approfondir; intensifier; *mus* rendre plus grave; *vi* s'approfondir; (colour) se foncer; s'intensifier

**deep-freeze** *n* congélateur *m*, freezer *m*; *vt* surgeler, congeler

**deep-fry** *vt* faire cuire en friteuse

**deep-laid** *adj* bien préparé

**deep-rooted** *adj* profondément enraciné

**deep-sea** *adj* au grand large; de haute mer

**deep-seated** *adj* profondément enraciné, ancré

**deer** *n* (species) cervidé *m*; (red) cerf *m*; (fallow) daim *m*; (roe) chevreuil *m*

**deerskin** *n* daim *m*

**deface** *vt* défigurer, lacérer; (make illegible) effacer, rendre illisible

**defacement** *n* lacération *f*; effacement *m*

**de facto** *adj* de facto

**defalcate** *vt* détourner

**defamation** *n* diffamation *f*

**defamatory** *adj* diffamatoire

**defame** *vt* diffamer

**default** *n* défaut *m*; *leg* défaut *m*, non-comparution *f*, contumace *f*; **in ~ of** dans l'absence de, faute de; **judgement by ~** jugement *m* par contumace; *vt leg* condamner par défaut; *vi leg* faire défaut; (debt) manquer à ses engagements

**defaulter** *n leg* contumace, défaillant -e; *mil* réfractaire *m*, puni *m*

**defeat** *n* défaite *f*; (setback) échec *m*; *vt* vaincre, défaire; faire échec à; *pol* mettre en minorité

**defeatism** *n* défaitisme *m*

**defecate** *vi* déféquer

**defecation** *n* défécation *f*

**defect** *n* défaut *m*, défectuosité *f*, imperfection *f*; *vt* abandonner, déserter

**defection** *n* défection *f*, abandon *m*

**defective** *adj* défectueux -euse; *gramm* défectif -ive; *med* déficient

**defence** *n* défense *f*; *mil* ~s défenses *fpl*, ouvrages défensifs, fortifications *fpl*; *psych* ~ **mechanism** réflexe *m* de défense

**defenceless** *adj* sans défense

**defencelessness** *n* impuissance *f*

**defend** *vt* défendre, protéger; *leg* défendre

**defendant** *n leg* défendeur *m*, défenderesse *f*

**defensible** *adj* défendable

**defensive** *n* défensive *f*; *adj* défensif -ive

¹**defer** *vt* différer, remettre; *vi* différer, atermoyer

²**defer** *vi* déférer, accéder

**deference** *n* déférence *f*, respect *m*

**deferential** *adj* déférent, humble; *pej* servile

**deferment** *n* sursis *m*

**deferred** *adj* différé; *mil* ajourné

**defiance** *n* défi *m*, bravade *f*; **in ~ of** au mépris de

**defiant** *adj* intraitable; (reply) provocant

**deficiency** *n* déficience *f*; *comm* défaut *m*; ~ **disease** avitaminose *f*

**deficient** *adj* déficient, insuffisant; **be ~ in** manquer de; **mentally ~** déficient

**deficit** *n* déficit *m*, découvert *m*

¹**defile** *n geog* défilé *m*

²**defile** *vt* polluer, souiller; *fig* violer

³**defile** *vi mil* défiler

**definable** *adj* définissable

**define** *vt* définir; (limit) délimiter

**definite** *adj* défini, explicite; (clear) clair, précis; délimité; sûr; *gramm* ~ **article** article défini; *gramm* **past ~** passé défini

**definitely** *adv* définitivement, avec précision; (surely) assurément, certainement

**deflagration** *n* déflagration *f*

**deflate** *vt* dégonfler

**deflation** *n* dégonflement *m*; déflation *f*

**deflationary** *adj* déflationniste

**deflect** *vt* détourner, dévier; *vi* dévier, se détourner

**deflection** *n* déviation *f*, détournement *m*

**deflector** *n* déflecteur *m*

**defloration** *n bot* défloraison *f*; (woman) défloration *f*

**deflower** *vt bot* défleurir; (woman) déflorer

**defoliation** *n* défoliation *f*

**deforest** *vt* déboiser

**deforestation** *n* déboisement *m*

**deform** *vt* déformer, contrefaire; enlaidir

**deformation** *n* déformation *f*

**deformity** *n* difformité *f*, laideur *f*

**defraud** *vt* frauder, escroquer

**defray** *vt* payer, couvrir (les frais)

**defreeze** *vt* (food) décongeler

**defrock** *vt eccles* défroquer

**defrost** *vt* dégivrer; (food) décongeler

**deft** *adj* adroit, habile

**deftness** *n* adresse *f*, habileté *f*, dextérité *f*

**defunct** *n* défunt -e; *adj* défunt

**defuse** *vt* désamorcer

**defy** *vt* défier, mettre au défi; braver; désobéir à

**degeneracy** *n* dégénérescence *f*

**degenerate** *n* dégénéré -e; *adj* dégénéré; *vi* dégénérer, détériorer

**degeneration** *n* dégénération *f*

**degradation** *n* dégradation *f*, avilissement *m*

**degrade** *vt* dégrader, avilir

**degrading** *adj* dégradant, avilissant
**degree** *n* degré *m*, rang *m*; (university) grade *m*; diplôme *m*; *math+gramm+phys+geog* degré *m*; **by ∼ s** peu à peu; **third ∼** passage *m* à tabac; **to a ∼** considérablement
**degression** *n* dégrèvement *m*
**degressive** *adj* dégressif -ive
**dehumanize** *vt* déshumaniser
**dehydrate** *vt* déshydrater
**dehydration** *n* déshydratation *f*
**de-ice** *vt* dégivrer
**deify** *vt* déifier
**deign** *vt* daigner
**deism** *n* déisme *m*
**deist** *n* déiste
**deity** *n* déité *f*, divinité *f*
**déjà-vu** *n* illusion *f* d'avoir déjà vu
**deject** *vt* déprimer
**dejection** *n* déjection *f*; abattement *m*
**de jure** *adj+adv* de jure
**delate** *vt* *leg* dénoncer
**delation** *n* *leg* délation *f*
**delay** *n* délai *m*, retard *m*; (waiting) attente *f*; *vt* retarder, différer
**delectable** *adj* délicieux -ieuse, agréable; *cul* délectable
**delectation** *n* délectation *f*
**delegacy** *n* commission *f*, délégation *f*
**delegate** *n* délégué -e; *vt* déléguer
**delegation** *n* commission *f*, délégation *f*; (act of delegating) délégation *f*
**delete** *vt* biffer, rayer, supprimer
**deleterious** *adj* délétère, nocif -ive
**deletion** *n* rature *f*; suppression *f*
**deliberate** *adj* délibéré, pondéré; voulu, intentionnel -elle; prudent; (slow) lent; *vt* délibérer de, décider; *vi* délibérer, réfléchir
**deliberation** *n* délibération *f*; (consideration) réflexion *f*, pondération *f*; (slowness) lenteur *f*
**deliberative** *adj* délibérant; (with power to decide) délibératif -ive
**delicacy** *n* (food) friandise *f*; (tact) délicatesse *f*, finesse *f*, tact *m*; modestie *f*, sensibilité *f*
**delicate** *adj* délicat; fin; (colour) pâle, tendre; fragile, frêle; (refined) raffiné, sensible
**delicatessen** *n* (shop) épicerie fine; (food) produits *mpl* d'épicerie fine
**delicious** *adj* délicieux -ieuse
**delight** *n* délice *m*, plaisir *m*; **Turkish ∼** loukoum *m*; *vt* charmer, ravir; *vi* se délecter
**delightful** *adj* délicieux -ieuse, charmant, agréable; (sight) ravissant
**delimit** *vt* délimiter
**delimitation** *n* délimitation *f*
**delineate** *vt* esquisser, ébaucher; décrire
**delineation** *n* esquisse *f*; description *f*

**delinquency** *n* délinquance *f*
**delinquent** *n* délinquant -e
**deliquesce** *vi* *chem* se liquéfier
**deliquescence** *n* déliquescence *f*
**deliquescent** *adj* déliquescent
**delirious** *adj* délirant
**delirium** *n* *med* délire *m*; *fig* délire *m*, transport *m*, excitation *f*; **∼ tremens** délirium *m* tremens
**deliver** *vt* délivrer, libérer; (mail) distribuer; transmettre; (speech) prononcer; (goods) livrer; *med* délivrer; *leg* signifier; **be ∼ed of** accoucher de; **stand and ∼ !** la bourse ou la vie!
**deliverance** *n* délivrance *f*, libération *f*; *leg* déclaration *f*
**deliverer** *n* libérateur -trice
**delivery** *n* (mail) distribution *f*; (goods) livraison *f*; (speech) débit *m*; *leg* prononcé *m*; (manner of speech) élocution *f*; *med* accouchement *m*, délivrance *f*
**dell** *n* vallon *m*
**delouse** *vt* épouiller
**delousing** *n* épouillage *m*
**delphinium** *n* dauphinelle *f*, pied *m* d'alouette
**delta** *n* *geog* delta *m*; *aer* **∼ wing** aile *f* (en) delta
**deltoid** *n* *anat* deltoïde *m*; *adj* deltoïde
**delude** *vt* tromper
**deluge** *n* déluge *m*; *vt* inonder, submerger
**delusion** *n* illusion *f*; *psych* hallucination *f*
**delusive** *adj* décevant, irréel -elle, trompeur -euse
**delusory** *adj* illusoire
**delve** *vt* bêcher; *vi* bêcher; **∼ into** creuser, fouiller (dans)
**demagogic** *adj* démagogique
**demagogue** *n* démagogue *m*
**demand** *n* demande *f*; exigence *f*; (claim) prétention *f*; **in great ∼** très recherché; **payable on ∼** payable sur demande; *vt* exiger, réclamer; avoir besoin de
**demarcate** *vt* délimiter, démarquer
**demarcation** *n* démarcation *f*, délimitation *f*
**demarche, démarche** *n* démarche *f*
**demean** *v* *refl* (degrade) s'abaisser, s'avilir
**demeanour** *n* comportement *m*, conduite *f*
**demented** *adj* fou (*f* folle)
**dementia** *n* *med* démence *f*; **∼ praecox** schizophrénie *f*
**demerara** *n* cassonade *f*
**demesne** *n* domaine *m*
**demi-john** *n* dame-jeanne *f* (*pl* dames-jeannes)
**demilitarize** *vt* démilitariser
**demise** *n* décès *m*; *leg* cession *f* par legs;

## demission

*vt leg* (estate) léguer; (honour, sovereignty) transmettre
**demission** *n* démission *f*
**demister** *n* mot dispositif *m* antibuée
**demiurge** *n* démiurge *m*
**demo** *n coll* manif *f*
**demobilization** *n mil* démobilisation *f*
**demobilize** *vt mil* démobiliser
**democracy** *n* démocratie *f*
**democrat** *n* démocrate
**democratic** *adj* démocratique
**demodé, démodé** *adj* démodé
**demographic** *adj* démographique
**demography** *n* démographie *f*
**demolish** *vt* démolir; *coll* bouffer
**demolition** *n* démolition *f*
**demon** *n* démon *m*
**demonetization** *n* démonétisation *f*
**demonetize** *vt* démonétiser
**demoniac** *n + adj* démoniaque
**demoniacal** *adj* démoniaque
**demonic** *adj* possédé
**demonism** *n* démonisme *m*
**demonology** *n* démonologie *f*
**demonstrable** *adj* démontrable
**demonstrably** *adv* indiscutablement
**demonstrate** *vt* démontrer; *vi* (in public) manifester
**demonstration** *n* démonstration *f*; (public) manifestation *f*
**demonstrative** *adj* probant; (feelings) démonstratif -ive; *gramm* démonstratif -ive
**demonstrator** *n* démonstrateur -trice; *sci* préparateur -trice; (in public) manifestant -e
**demoralization** *n* démoralisation *f*, découragement *m*
**demoralize** *vt* démoraliser, décourager; (pervert) corrompre
**demote** *vt* rétrograder
**demotic** *adj* démotique
**demotion** *n* rétrogradation *f*
**demur** *n* hésitation *f*; objection *f*; *vi* hésiter; soulever des objections; *leg* opposer une exception
**demure** *adj* pudique, réservé; *pej* d'une modestie affectée
**demureness** *n* air *m* pudique, réserve *f*; *pej* modestie affectée
**den** *n* antre *m*, tanière *f*; (thieves) repaire *m*; *coll* piaule *f*
**denationalize** *vt* dénationaliser
**denaturalize** *vt* dénaturaliser
**denature** *vt* dénaturer
**dene** *n* ravin *m*, ravine *f*
**denial** *n* démenti *m*, dénégation *f*; (disavowal) reniement *m*; refus *m*
**denigrate** *vt* dénigrer
**denigration** *n* dénigrement *m*
**denim** *n* toile *f* de jean, treillis *m*; ~s (trousers) jean(s) *m (pl)*; (overalls) bleu

*m* (de travail); *mil* treillis *m*
**denizen** *n* habitant -e; étranger -ère ayant un permis de séjour; *bot* plante acclimatée; *zool* animal naturalisé; *gramm* mot *m* d'emprunt
**denominate** *vt* dénommer
**denomination** *n* dénomination *f*, appellation *f*; (money) valeur *f*; *eccles* confession *f*
**denominational** *adj eccles* confessionnel -elle
**denominative** *adj* dénominatif -ive
**denominator** *n math* dénominateur *m*; **common** ~ *math* facteur commun; *fig* ce que les membres d'un groupe ont en commun
**denotation** *n* dénotation *f*, notation *f*, signe *m*; symbole *m*; sens *m*
**denouement, dénouement** *n* dénouement *m*
**denounce** *vt* dénoncer; critiquer, condamner
**dense** *adj* dense, tassé; épais (*f* épaisse); *phot* opaque; *coll* lourd, stupide
**density** *n* densité *f*, épaisseur *f*
**dent** *n* bosse *f*, creux *m*; *vt* bosseler, cabosser
**dental** *n phon* dentale *f*; *adj med* dentaire; *phon* dental
**dentate** *adj* denté, dentelé
**dentifrice** *n* dentifrice *m*
**dentine** *n anat* dentine *f*
**dentist** *n* dentiste
**dentistry** *n* chirurgie *f* dentaire
**dentition** *n* dentition *f*
**denture** *n* dentier *m*, *coll* râtelier *m*
**denudation** *n* mise *f* à nu
**denude** *vt* dénuder; (deprive) dépouiller
**denunciation** *n* dénonciation *f*; critique violente; condamnation *f*
**denunciator** *n* dénonciateur -trice
**deny** *vt* nier; (declare untrue) démentir; (faith) renier; (refuse) refuser; (deprive) priver; **there's no** ~**ing it** c'est indéniable
**deodorant** *n* désodorisant *m*, déodorant *m*; *adj* désodorisant, déodorant
**deodorize** *vt* désodoriser
**deodorizer** *n* désodorisant *m*, déodorant *m*
**depart** *vi* partir, s'en aller; (deviate) s'écarter; (die) mourir
**departed** *n* mort -e; **the** ~ **les morts** *mpl*; *adj* (finished) disparu, achevé; (dead) mort
**department** *n* section *f*; (administration) service *m*; *pol* ministère *m*; *pol + comm* département *m*; (shop) rayon *m*; ~ **store** grand magasin
**departmental** *adj* départemental; d'un service

**departmentalism** *n* méthodes *fpl* bureaucratiques

**departure** *n* départ *m*; déviation *f*; innovation *f*

**depend** *vi* ~ **on** dépendre de; (rely on) se fier à; *leg* être pendant; ~ **on it** vous pouvez compter là-dessus; **that** ~ **s** peut-être

**dependable** *adj* de confiance, sûr

**dependant, dependent** *n* protégé -e; subordonné -e, domestique

**dependence** *n* dépendance *f*; subordination *f*; confiance *f*

**dependency** *n* dépendance *f*

**dependent** *adj* dépendant, subordonné; (for support) à charge; (hanging) pendant

**depending** *adj* (hanging on) pendant; dépendant; *leg* pendant

**depersonalize** *vt* dépersonnaliser; *vi* se dépersonnaliser

**depict** *vt* dépeindre, peindre; décrire

**depiction** *n* peinture *f*; description *f*

**depilatory** *n* dépilatoire *m*; *adj* dépilatoire

**deplete** *vt* (exhaust) épuiser; (empty) vider, dégarnir; *med* décongestionner

**deplorable** *adj* déplorable, lamentable

**deplore** *vt* déplorer, désapprouver

**deploy** *vt mil* déployer; *vi* se déployer

**deployment** *n mil* déploiement *m*

**depone** *vi leg* déposer

**¹deponent** *n leg* déposant -e

**²deponent** *n gramm* déponent *m*; *adj* déponent

**depopulate** *vt* dépeupler; *vi* se dépeupler

**depopulation** *n* dépeuplement *m*

**deport** *vt* expulser, déporter; ~ **oneself** se comporter

**deportation** *n* expulsion *f*, déportation *f*

**deportee** *n* déporté -e

**deportment** *n* (behaviour) comportement *m*; (bearing) port *m*, maintien *m*

**depose** *vt* déposer, détrôner; *vi leg* déposer

**deposit** *n* (money) dépôt *m*; (security) cautionnement *m*; (on account) arrhes *fpl*; (sediment) dépôt *m*; *geol* gisement *m*; *vt* déposer, verser

**depositary** *n* (person) dépositaire

**deposition** *n* déposition *f*; *eccles* descente *f* de croix; (sediment) dépôt *m*

**depositor** *n* déposant -e

**depository** *n* entrepôt *m*; lieu *m* de dépôt

**depot** *n* dépôt *m*, entrepôt *m*; *mil* caserne *f*; (bus, locomotive) dépôt *m*; *US* gare *f*

**depravation, depravity** *n* dépravation *f*, corruption *f*

**deprave** *vt* dépraver, pervertir, corrompre

**deprecate** *vt* désapprouver, déplorer

**deprecatory** *adj* désapprobateur -trice

**depreciate** *vt* déprécier, dévaloriser; dénigrer; *vi* se déprécier

**depreciation** *n* dépréciation *f*; *fig* dénigrement *m*

**depredate** *vt* piller, dévaster

**depredation** *n* déprédation *f*, dévastation *f*, pillage *m*

**depress** *vt* (lower) baisser; (pedal, handle) appuyer sur, abaisser; (person) déprimer, abattre; (price) faire baisser

**depressant** *n med* sédatif *m*

**depressed** *adj* (person) déprimé, découragé; (business) en crise; ~ **area** région *f* pauvre ayant beaucoup de chômeurs

**depressing** *adj* morne, déprimant

**depression** *n* dépression *f*; *econ* crise *f*

**depressive** *adj* dépressif -ive

**depressor** *n anat* abaisseur *m*

**deprivation** *n* privation *f*; (loss) perte *f*; (office, rank) destitution *f*

**deprive** *vt* priver, déposséder, destituer

**depth** *n* profondeur *f*; *mus* gravité *f*; *fig* profondeur *f*, intensité *f*; (night, winter) milieu *m*; **in** ~ en profondeur; (thoroughly) de façon approfondie; **in the** ~ **s of** au fin fond de; *fig* au comble de; **out of one's** ~ ayant perdu pied; *fig* dépassé

**depth-charge** *n naut* grenade sous-marine

**depth-gauge** *n* sondeur *m*

**deputation** *n* députation *f*

**depute** *vt* députer; déléguer

**deputize** *vt* députer; *vi* assurer l'intérim

**deputy** *n* suppléant -e; *pol* député *m*

**deracinate** *vt* déraciner

**derail** *vt* faire dérailler; *vi* dérailler

**derange** *vt* déranger, bouleverser; distraire

**derangement** *n* maladie mentale

**derelict** *n naut* + *leg* + *fig* épave *f*; *adj* abandonné, délaissé

**dereliction** *n* abandon *m*; (duty) négligence *f*, manquement *m* au devoir

**derequisition** *vt* déréquisitionner

**deride** *vt* tourner en dérision, ridiculiser; traiter avec mépris; faire peu de cas de

**derision** *n* dérision *f*

**derisive** *adj* railleur -euse, moqueur -euse

**derisory** *adj* dérisoire

**derivation** *n* dérivation *f*

**derivative** *n* dérivé *m*; *adj* dérivé

**derive** *vt* tirer, trouver, puiser; *vi* tracer son origine; ~ **from** émaner de

**dermatitis** *n* dermatite *f*, dermite *f*

**dermatologist** *n* dermatologiste, dermatologue

**dermatology** *n* dermatologie *f*

**derogate** *vi* amoindrir, nuire à, déroger à

**derogation** *n* dénigrement *m*, diminution *f*; amoindrissement *m*

**derogatory** *adj* dénigrant, irrespectueux -euse, qui abaisse

**derrick** *n* (oil) derrick *m*; *naut* mât *m* de charge, palan *m*

**derv** *n* gas-oil *m*

**dervish** *n* derviche *m*

**descale** *vt* détartrer

**descant** *n mus* déchant *m*; *vi mus* exécuter un déchant

**descend** *vt* descendre; *vi* descendre; (originate) être issu; dégénérer; ~ **upon** se jeter sur; visiter à l'improviste; ~ **to** s'abaisser à

**descendant** *n* descendant -e

**descent** *n* descente *f*; pente *f*; (lineage) descendance *f*; attaque *f*

**describe** *vt* décrire, relater; tracer

**description** *n* description *f*, récit *m*; sorte *f*, espèce *f*; (personal) signalement *m*

**descry** *vt* apercevoir, discerner de loin

**desecrate** *vt* profaner

**desecration** *n* profanation *f*

¹**desert** *n* désert *m*, région *f* désertique; *adj* désertique, inculte, inhabité

²**desert** *n* mérite *m*; ~ **s dû** *m*

³**desert** *vt* abandonner, quitter; *mil* déserter; *vi* déserter

**desertion** *n* abandon *m*; *mil* désertion *f*

**deserve** *vt* + *vi* mériter

**deservedly** *adv* à bon droit, à juste titre

**deserving** *adj* digne, méritoire, méritant

**desiccate** *vt* dessécher

**desiccation** *n* dessèchement *m*, dessiccation *f*

**desiderata** *npl* desiderata *mpl*

**design** *n* dessein *m*, projet *m*, plan *m*; intention *f*; *theat* décors *mpl*; *pej* dessein *m* sinistre; (painting) dessin *m*, motif *m*; (sketch) esquisse *f*; *comm* modèle *m*; **by** ~ délibérément; *vt* (sketch) esquisser, ébaucher; faire le plan de; avoir l'intention de, projeter de; *vi* créer des modèles; (sketch) faire des esquisses

**designate** *adj* désigné; *vt* désigner, nommer; spécifier

**designation** *n* désignation *f*

**designer** *n* dessinateur -trice; *theat* décorateur -trice

**designing** *n* dessin *m*, création *f* de modèles; *theat* création *f* de maquettes, création *f* de décors; *adj* intrigant

**desirable** *adj* désirable, souhaitable

**desire** *n* désir *m*; envie *f*; concupiscence *f*; vœu *m*; demande *f*; *vt* désirer, souhaiter; (covet) convoiter; (ask) demander

**desirous** *adj* désireux -euse; ambitieux -ieuse

**desist** *vi* désister

**desk** *n* bureau *m*, secrétaire *m*; (school) pupitre *m*; *mus* pupitre *m*; (cash) caisse *f*; *US* ~ **clerk** réceptionniste

**desolate** *adj* désolé, ravagé; inhabité, désert; seul, affligé; *vt* dépeupler; rendre désert; (sadden) désoler, rendre malheureux -euse

**desolation** *n* désolation *f*, dévastation *f*; (abandonment) abandon *m*, solitude *f*

**despair** *n* désespoir *m*; *vi* désespérer

**despatch, dispatch** *n* (message) dépêche *f*; (sending) expédition *f*, envoi *m*; (speed) rapidité *f*, promptitude *f*; (newspaper) reportage *m*; (killing) exécution *f*; ~ **box** valise *f* qui contient des documents, valise officielle; ~ **rider** estafette *f* (à motocyclette); *vt* (messenger) dépêcher; (letter) envoyer; (goods) acheminer; (hasten) expédier; (kill) achever

**desperado** *n* bandit *m*, desperado *m*

**desperate** *adj* capable de tout, acharné; (without hope) désespéré; (illness) mortel -elle; *coll* terrible, énorme

**desperation** *n* désespoir *m*

**despicable** *adj* méprisable

**despise** *vt* mépriser, dédaigner

¹**despite** *n* dépit *m*; dédain *m*; **in** ~ **of** malgré

²**despite** *prep* malgré, en dépit de

**despoil** *vt* dépouiller, spolier

**despoliation** *n* dépouillement *m*, spoliation *f*

**despond** *n ar* désespoir *m*; *vi* perdre courage, être déprimé

**despondency** *n* découragement *m*, dépression *f*

**despondent** *adj* découragé, déprimé

**despot** *n* despote *m*, tyran *m*

**despotic** *adj* despotique, tyrannique

**despotism** *n* despotisme *m*, tyrannie *f*

**dessert** *n* dessert *m*

**dessert-spoon** *n* cuillère *f* à dessert

**destination** *n* destination *f*

**destine** *vt* destiner, prédestiner; déterminer, fixer; ~ **d for** voué à

**destiny** *n* destinée *f*; (fate) destin *m*

**destitute** *adj* dénué, dépourvu, indigent

**destroy** *vt* détruire, démolir; ruiner

**destroyer** *n naut* destroyer *m*, contre-torpilleur *m*; (person) destructeur -trice

**destructible** *adj* destructible

**destruction** *n* destruction *f*, perte *f*; démolition *f*

**destructive** *adj* destructif -ive; destructeur -trice

**destructor** *n* incinérateur *m*

**desuetude** *n* désuétude *f*

**desultory** *adj* décousu, sans suite, sans méthode

**detach** vt détacher, séparer

**detached** adj détaché, séparé; impartial

**detachment** n détachement m

**detail** n détail m; mil détachement m; **in ~** en détail, dans le détail; vt détailler; mil détacher

**detailed** adj détaillé; mil détaché

**detain** vt détenir; (delay) retarder, retenir

**detainee** n leg détenu

**detainer** n leg détention f; leg mandat m de dépôt

**detect** vt déceler, découvrir, détecter; se rendre compte de

**detection** n découverte f, détention f

**detective** n inspecteur m de police, détective m; adj policier -ière; **~ story** roman policier

**detector** n détecteur m

**detente, détente** n détente f

**detention** n détention f; (school) retenue f; mil **~ barracks** prison f militaire

**deter** vt détourner, décourager

**detergent** n détergent m, détersif m; adj détersif -ive, détergent

**deteriorate** vt détériorer, déprécier; vi se détériorer, baisser, dégénérer; empirer

**deterioration** n détérioration f, altération f; (worsening) aggravation f

**determent** n détournement m; dissuasion f

**determinable** adj déterminable

**determinant** n math + gramm déterminant m; adj déterminant

**determinate** adj déterminé, fixé; (conclusive) établi, définitif -ive

**determination** n détermination f, résolution f; décision f, résolution f; délimitation f; leg résiliation f

**determinative** n gramm + math déterminant m; adj déterminant

**determine** vt déterminer, décider, résoudre; (set limits to) délimiter; (fix) régler; leg résilier; vi se déterminer, se résoudre; leg expirer

**determined** adj déterminé, résolu; fixe

**determinism** n déterminisme m

**determinist** n déterministe

**deterrence** n dissuasion f, découragement m

**deterrent** n mil forces fpl de dissuasion; **act as a ~** avoir un effet dissuasif; adj de dissuasion, dissuasif -ive

**detest** vt détester

**detestable** adj détestable

**detestation** n détestation f; objet m d'horreur

**dethrone** vt détrôner

**detonate** vt faire éclater, faire détoner; vi éclater, détoner

**detonation** n détonation f, explosion f

**detonator** n détonateur m, amorce f;

(railway) pétard m

**detour** n détour m

**detract** vt ôter; vi **~ from** diminuer

**detraction** n détraction f, dénigrement m, calomnie f

**detractor** n détracteur -trice, accusateur -trice

**detrain** vt + vi esp mil débarquer (d'un train)

**detriment** n détriment m, dommage m, préjudice m

**detrimental** adj préjudiciable, nuisible

**detrition** n détrition f

**detritus** n geol détritus mpl, roches fpl détritiques; fig détritus mpl

**deuce** n (tennis) égalité f, quarante à; interj diable!

**deuced** adj coll du diable; adv coll diablement

**deuterium** n chem deutérium m

**devaluate** vt dévaluer

**devaluation** n dévaluation f

**devalue** vt + vi dévaluer

**devastate** vt dévaster

**devastating** adj dévastateur -trice; coll foudroyant, efficace

**devastation** n dévastation f

**develop** vt développer; (set forth) exposer, élaborer; (strengthen) développer, fortifier; (exploit) mettre en valeur, exploiter; (habit, disease) contracter; (skill) faire preuve de, manifester; vi se développer, s'amplifier, évoluer, progresser; **~ing country** pays m en voie de développement

**developer** n phot révélateur m

**development** n développement m; évolution f, extension f, progrès m; exposé m; mus développement m; **~ area** zone f à urbaniser en priorité (Z.U.P. f)

**deviate** vi dévier

**deviation** n déviation f, divergence f, écart m; (compass, traffic, math) déviation f

**deviationist** n + adj pol déviationniste

**device** n expédient m, moyen m; (trick) truc m, astuce f; mech dispositif m, appareil m, invention f; her dévise f; **leave s/o to his own ~s** laisser qn se débrouiller tout seul, laisser qn suivre sa pente

**devil** n diable m, démon m; (lawyer's) apprenti m; (printer, writer) nègre m; **~'s advocate** avocat m du diable; **be a ~!** laissez-vous tenter!; **between the ~ and the deep blue sea** entre l'enclume et le marteau; **go to the ~** être ruiné; interj foutez-moi le camp!; **play the ~ with** ruiner, léser; **poor ~** pauvre diable m; **raise the ~** faire un bruit de tous les diables; **talk of the ~**

quand on parle du loup on en voit la
queue; **there'll be the ~ to pay** ça nous
(vous, etc) coûtera cher; *vt cul* griller en
ajoutant beaucoup d'épices; *vi* faire le
nègre

**devilish** *adj* diabolique; *adv coll* extrêmement, diablement

**devil-may-care** *adj* téméraire; insouciant

**devilment** *n* diablerie *f*

**devilry** *n* (black magic) magie noire;
satanisme *m*; (wickedness) méchanceté
*f*, cruauté *f*; (daring) témérité *f*

**devious** *adj* tortueux -euse

**devise** *vt* concevoir, inventer; (plot)
manigancer

**devitalization** *n* dévitalisation *f*

**devitalize** *vt* dévitaliser

**devoid** *adj* dépourvu, dénué

**devolution** *n* transmission *f*, délégation
*f*; *biol* dégénérescence *f*; *pol* décentralisation *f*

**devolve** *vt* transmettre, déléguer; *vi* ~ **on**
incomber à; *leg* être dévolu à

**devote** *vt* vouer, consacrer; ~ **oneself**
s'adonner, se livrer, se consacrer

**devoted** *adj* dévoué, fidèle; (dedicated)
voué, consacré

**devotee** *n* fervent -e, partisan -e

**devotion** *n* eccles dévotion *f*, piété *f*;
dévouement *m*, attachement *m*; ~ **s**
dévotions *fpl*

**devour** *vt* dévorer

**devout** *adj* (person) pieux (*f* pieuse),
dévot; (prayer, etc) fervent

**dew** *n* rosée *f*

**dewdrop** *n* goutte *f* de rosée

**dewlap** *n* fanon *m*; (human) double
menton *m*

**dewy** *adj* humide de rosée

**dewy-eyed** *adj* aux grands yeux ingénus

**dexter** *adj* dextre

**dexterity** *n* dextérité *f*

**dexterous, dextrous** *adj* habile, adroit,
plein de dextérité

**dextrose** *n chem* dextrose *m*

**diabetes** *n* diabète *m*

**diabetic** *n* + *adj* diabétique

**diabolic, diabolical** *adj* diabolique; (evil)
méchant; *coll* difficile, désagréable

**diabolism** *n* satanisme *m*; (sorcery) sorcellerie *f*; action *f* diabolique

**diachronic** *adj ling* diachronique

**diaconal** *adj eccles* diaconal

**diaconate** *n eccles* diaconat *m*

**diacritic, diacritical** *adj* diacritique

**diadem** *n* diadème *m*

**diaeresis** *n phon* diérèse *f*

**diagnose** *vt* diagnostiquer

**diagnosis** *n* diagnostic *m*; *biol* diagnose
*f*

**diagnostic** *adj* diagnostique

**diagnostician** *n* diagnostiqueur *m*

**diagonal** *n* diagonale *f*; *adj* diagonal,
oblique

**diagram** *n geom* figure *f*; diagramme *m*,
plan *m*, schéma *m*

**diagrammatic** *adj* schématique

**dial** *n* (sun) cadran *m* solaire; (clock,
gauge, telephone, etc) cadran *m*; *coll*
(face) gueule *f*; *vt* (telephone number)
composer

**dialect** *n* dialecte *m*; (regional) patois
*m*

**dialectal** *adj* dialectal

**dialectic** *n* dialectique *f*; *adj* dialectique

**dialectical** *adj* dialectique; ~ **materialism** matérialisme *m* marxiste

**dialectician** *n* dialecticien -ienne

**dialling** *n* action *f* de composer un
numéro de téléphone; ~ **tone** tonalité
*f*; **subscriber trunk** ~ (**S.T.D.**) automatique *m*

**dialogue** *n* dialogue *m*

**diameter** *n* diamètre *m*

**diametric, diametrical** *adj* diamétral;
(opposite) opposé

**diametrically** *adv* diamétralement; *fig*
tout à fait, absolument

**diamond** *n* diamant *m*; *math* losange *m*;
(cards) carreau *m*; (baseball) terrain *m*;
~ **drill** diamant *m* (de vitrier, de miroi-
tier); ~ **jubilee** soixantième anniversaire *m* de l'accession au trône; ~
**wedding** noces *fpl* de diamant; **be a
rough** ~ avoir bon cœur et mauvais
caractère; **black** ~ charbon *m*; *adj* de
diamant, en diamant; *vt* diamanter

**diamonded** *adj* diamanté

**diapason** *n mus* registre *m*, diapason *m*;
(tuning fork) diapason *m*; *fig* harmonie
majestueuse

**diaper** *n* (baby) couche *f*; *archi* décoration *f* en losanges; *her* losange *m*; *vt*
décorer de losanges

**diaphanous** *adj* diaphane, transparent

**diaphragm** *n* diaphragme *m*

**diarist** *n* personne *f* qui tient un journal
intime

**diarrhoea** *n* diarrhée *f*; **verbal** ~ verbomanie *f*

**diary** *n* journal *m*; carnet *m*; agenda *m*

**diatonic** *adj mus* diatonique

**diatribe** *n* diatribe *f*

**dibber** *n agr* plantoir *m*

**dibble** *n agr* plantoir *m*; *vt* trouer au
plantoir; *vi* se servir d'un plantoir

**dice** *npl* dés *mpl*; *vt cul* couper en dés; *vi*
jouer aux dés

**dice-box** *n* cornet *m* à dés

**dicey** *adj coll* pas sûr, dangereux -euse

**dichotomous** *adj* divisé en deux

**dichotomy** *n* dichotomie *f*

**dicing** *n* activité *f* de jouer aux dés; *cul*
action *f* de couper en dés

dick *n coll obs* type *m*; *sl obs* détective *m*; *vulg obs* bite *f*

dickens *interj coll* diable!

¹dicky, dickey *n mot obs* spider *m*; (shirt front) plastron *m*

²dicky *adj coll* peu sûr; (unwell) un peu malade; (financially) peu solide

dicky-bird *n* (child language) oiseau *m*

dictaphone *n* dictaphone *m*

dictate *n pol* diktat *m*; *vt* dicter; ordonner; *vi* donner des ordres, s'imposer

dictation *n* dictée *f*

dictator *n* dictateur *m*

dictatorial *adj* dictatorial

dictatorship *n* dictature *f*

diction *n* diction *f*, élocution *f*; choix *m* de mots; **poetic** ~ langage *m* de la poésie

dictionary *n* dictionnaire *m*

dictum *n* dicton *m*; maxime *f*; (statement) affirmation *f*

didactic *adj* didactique; pédantesque

didacticism *n*, didactics *npl* didactique *f*

diddle *vt coll* carotter, escroquer; *vi* tricher

¹die *n* (*pl* dice) dé *m*; (*pl* ~ s) (minting) coin *m*; **the** ~ **is cast** les jeux sont faits

²die *vi* mourir, expirer; disparaître, s'éteindre; ~ **away** se dissiper, s'éteindre; ~ **back** se flétrir; ~ **down** diminuer; ~ **hard** avoir la vie dure; ~ **in harness** mourir en plein travail; ~ **off** mourir un à un; ~ **out** s'éteindre; ~ **the death** souffrir la peine de mort; **be dying to** mourir d'envie de

diehard *n* + *adj* réactionnaire; intransigeant -e

diesel *n* diesel *m*; ~ **oil** gas-oil *m*

¹diet *n* régime *m*; (normal food) alimentation *f*; *vt* mettre au régime; *vi* suivre un régime

²diet *n pol* diète *f*

dietary *n* régime *m*; *adj* de régime

dietetic *adj* diététique

dietetics *npl* diététique *f*

dietician *n* diététicien -ienne

differ *vi* différer, se différencier, être différent; (quarrel) se brouiller; **agree to** ~ rester sur ses positions

difference *n* différence *f*, divergence *f*, disparité *f*; (gap) écart *m*; querelle *f*, dispute *f*; **split the** ~ couper la poire en deux

different *adj* différent, dissemblable; varié, divers

differential *n elect* + *eng* différentiel *m*; *math* différentielle *f*; *adj* différentiel -ielle

differentiate *vt* différencier; *vi* se différencier

differing *adj* contradictoire

difficult *adj* difficile

difficulty *n* difficulté *f*; obstacle *m*; objection *f*; (trouble) ennui *m*; **be in difficulties** avoir des problèmes; **make difficulties** soulever des objections

diffidence *n* manque *m* d'assurance, timidité *f*

diffident *adj* dépourvu d'assurance, timide, embarrassé

diffraction *n* diffraction *f*

diffuse *adj* diffus; *vt* diffuser; *vi* se diffuser

diffusible *adj* diffusible

diffusion *n* diffusion *f*

diffusive *adj* qui diffuse; (verbose) verbeux -euse, bavard, prolixe

dig *n* bêchage *m*; *arch* fouilles *fpl*; *coll* sarcasme *m*, brocard *m*; ~ **s** logement *m*; *vt* bêcher, piocher; creuser; excaver; extraire; (vegetables) arracher; (nails) enfoncer; *fig* découvrir; *coll* brocarder; *sl* comprendre; approuver; aimer; *sl* travailler; *vi* creuser; faire des fouilles; *sl* loger; *sl* comprendre; ~ **in** enterrer; *mil* se creuser un abri; s'incruster; *coll* ~ **into** travailler dur à; ~ **out**, ~ **up** découvrir, trouver

¹digest *n* digest *m*; résumé *m*; *hist leg* digeste *m*

²digest *vt* digérer; assimiler; (summarize) abréger, résumer; *vi* être digéré

digestible *adj* digestible

digestion *n* digestion *f*

digestive *n* digestif *m*; *adj* digestif -ive

digger *n* (person) bêcheur -euse; chercheur *m* d'or; *mech* plantoir *m*; *agr* arrachoir *m*; *sl* Australien -ienne

digit *n* chiffre *m*; *anat* + *astron* doigt *m*

digital *adj* digital

digitalin *n med* digitaline *f*

digitalis *n bot* digitale *f*; *med* digitaline *f*

dignified *adj* solennel -elle, digne, imposant

dignitary *n* dignitaire *m*

dignity *n* dignité *f*, gravité *f*; rang *m*, dignité *f*

digress *vi* faire une digression; (deviate) dévier

digression *n* digression *f*

digressive *adj* décousu, avec des digressions

digs *n coll* logement *m*

dihedral *n* dièdre *m*; *adj* dièdre

dike *n* + *vt see* dyke

dilapidate *vt* abîmer, dégrader, délabrer; (fortune) dilapider; *vi* se délabrer

dilapidation *n* délabrement *m*, dégradation *f*; (fortune) dilapidation *f*

dilatable *adj* dilatable, expansible

dilatation *n* dilatation *f*

dilate *vt* dilater

dilation *n* dilatation *f*

dilator *n med* dilatant *m*; dilatateur *m*

439

**dilatory** adj dilatoire

**dilemma** n dilemme m; **on the horns of a** ~ enfermé dans un dilemme

**dilettante** n (pl **dilettanti**) + adj dilettante

**dilettantism** n dilettantisme m

¹**diligence** n diligence f, application f; persévérance f

²**diligence** n (coach) diligence f

**diligent** adj diligent

**dill** n bot fenouil m

**dilly-dally** vi vaciller, lambiner

**diluent** n dissolvant m

**dilute** vt diluer, noyer; (wine) couper, baptiser; fig affaiblir; adj dilué, affaibli

**dilution** n dilution f; affaiblissement m

**diluvial** adj diluvial; diluvien -ienne

**diluvium** n geol diluvium m

**dim** adj terne, faible, pâle; (sight) trouble; (sound) sourd; indistinct, confus; coll bête, stupide; coll (boring) ennuyeux -euse, sl emmerdant; vt ternir, obscurcir; (sight) troubler; (sound) assourdir; mot baisser, mot mettre en code; vi (glory) se ternir, s'obscurcir

**dime** n US (pièce f de) dix cents mpl

**dimension** n dimension f

**diminish** vt diminuer, réduire; raccourcir; vi diminuer, décliner

**diminuendo** n mus diminuendo m

**diminution** n diminution f

**diminutive** n gramm diminutif m; adj minuscule, tout petit

**dimness** n aspect m terne; (weakness) faiblesse f; coll stupidité f, bêtise f

**dimple** n fossette f

**dimwit** n coll crétin -e, idiot -e

**din** n potin m, boucan m; bruit m; vt rabâcher; vi faire du potin

**dine** vi inviter à dîner; vi dîner

**diner** n dîneur -euse; US wagon-restaurant m (pl wagons-restaurants); coll restaurant m

**diner-out** n mondain -e

**ding** n son m de cloche; vi résonner

**ding-dong** n son m de cloche; adj à qui mieux mieux

**dinghy** n naut canot m, youyou m

**dinginess** n aspect m minable

**dingle** n vallon m

**dingy** adj terne, minable

**dining-car** n wagon-restaurant m (pl wagons-restaurants)

**dining-hall** n réfectoire m

**dining-room** n salle f à manger

**dining-table** n table f de salle à manger

**dinky** adj col chou invar, chouette

**dinner** n dîner m; ~ **dress** robe longue; ~ **jacket** smoking m; ~ **time** heure f du dîner

**dinosaur** n dinosaure m

**dint** n bosse f, creux m; **by** ~ **of** à force

de; vt bosseler, cabosser

**diocesan** n diocésain m; adj diocésain

**diocese** n diocèse m

**diode** n elect diode f

**dioxide** n chem bioxyde m

**dip** n (bathe) baignade f; (immersion) plongée f; (incline) déclivité f, inclinaison f; vt tremper, plonger; mot baisser; vi plonger, se plonger; mot se mettre en code

**diphase** adj elect diphasé

**diphtheria** n med diphtérie f

**diphthong** n phon diphtongue f

**diploma** n diplôme m

**diplomacy** n diplomatie f

**diplomat** n diplomate m

**diplomatic** adj diplomatique; ~ **corps** corps m diplomatique

**diplomatics** npl diplomatique f

**dipper** n plongeur -euse; cul louche f; orni merle m; mot basculeur m; (fair) montagnes fpl russes

**dipsomania** n dipsomanie f

**dipsomaniac** n dipsomane

**dipstick** n mot jauge f (d'huile)

**diptera** npl zool diptères mpl

**diptych** n diptyque m

**dire** adj terrible, désastreux -euse

**direct** adj direct; (straight) droit; (frank) net (f nette), franc (f franche), immédiat; absolu, complet -ète; elect continu; gramm direct; ~ **action** recours m à la grève; ~ **input** entrée directe; adv directement, tout droit; vt diriger; (lead) mener, conduire; (point) braquer; administrer; theat mettre en scène; cin réaliser; (letters) adresser

**direction** n direction f, conduite f, administration f; sens m, orientation f; (letter) adresse f; theat mise f en scène; cin réalisation f; ~ **s** instructions fpl; **in the ~ of** vers; rad ~ **finder** radiogoniomètre m; mot ~ **indicator** (winker) clignotant m; (pointer) flèche f

**directional** adj rad directionnel -elle; directeur -trice

**directive** n directive f, instruction f; adj directeur -trice

**directly** adv directement, immédiatement; conj dès que

**directness** n netteté f, franchise f

**director** n directeur -trice

**directorate** n conseil m d'administration

**directorial** adj directorial

**directorship** n direction f, présidence f

**directory** n annuaire m; US conseil m d'administration; adj directeur -trice

**directress** n directrice f

**direful** adj terrible, désastreux -euse

**dirge** n lamentation f; hymne m funèbre; mélodie f triste

**dirigible** n dirigeable m; adj dirigeable

440

**dirk** *n obs* poignard *m*

**dirt** *n* saleté *f*, crasse *f*; (mud) boue *f*, fange *f*; (dust) poussière *f*; obscénité *f*, pornographie *f*, ordures *fpl*; ~ **cheap** pour rien, à vil prix; *sl* **do ~ to** escroquer, jouer un sale tour à; **throw ~ at** traîner dans la boue

**dirtiness** *n* saleté *f*

**dirt-track** *n* piste *f*; *sp* cendrée *f*

**dirty** *adj* sale, crasseux -euse; boueux -euse, crotté; obscène, grossier -ière, ordurier -ière; (weather) vilain, sale; *coll* **do the ~ on** jouer un sale tour à; *vt* salir; *vi* se salir

**disability** *n* incapacité *f*; invalidité *f*

**disable** *vt* estropier; rendre inapte; (put out of action) mettre hors d'état; *naut* désemparer; *leg* frapper d'incapacité

**disablement** *n* incapacité *f* physique

**disabuse** *vt* désabuser

**disaccord** *n* désaccord *m*; *vi* différer

**disadvantage** *n* désavantage *m*; *vt* désavantager

**disadvantageous** *adj* désavantageux -euse

**disaffect** *vt* aliéner, mécontenter

**disaffected** *adj* mécontent, mal disposé, dissident

**disaffectedness, disaffection** *n* désaffection *f*

**disagree** *vi* différer, ne pas être d'accord; (argue) se disputer, se quereller; ~ **with** ne pas convenir à, rendre malade

**disagreeable** *adj* désagréable

**disagreeableness** *n* hargne *f*

**disagreement** *n* désaccord *m*; dispute *f*, querelle *f*; (discrepancy) discordance *f*

**disallow** *vt* rejeter, repousser; défendre

**disappear** *vi* disparaître

**disappearance** *n* disparition *f*

**disappoint** *vt* décevoir, désappointer; (thwart) faire échouer, contrecarrer

**disappointment** *n* déception *f*, désappointement *m*; (hitch, snag) contretemps *m*

**disapprobation** *n* désapprobation *f*

**disapproval** *n* désapprobation *f*

**disapprove** *vt* désapprouver, condamner; *vi* trouver à redire

**disarm** *vt* désarmer

**disarmament** *n* désarmement *m*

**disarming** *adj* désarmant, touchant

**disarrange** *vt* déranger, bouleverser

**disarrangement** *n* dérangement *m*, bouleversement *m*

**disarray** *n* désordre *m*, confusion *f*, désarroi *m*; négligé *m*; *vt* mettre en désordre, bouleverser; dévêtir

**disassociate** *vt* dissocier

**disassociation** *n* dissociation *f*

**disaster** *n* désastre *m*, catastrophe *f*

**disastrous** *adj* désastreux -euse, catastrophique

**disavow** *vt* désavouer

**disband** *vt* disperser; *mil* licencier; *vi* se disperser; *mil* se débander

**disbandment** *n mil* licenciement *m*

**disbar** *vt leg* exclure du barreau

**disbelief** *n* incrédulité *f*

**disburden** *vt* décharger

**disburse** *vt* + *vi* débourser

**disbursement** *n* déboursement *m*

**disc, disk** *n* disque *m*; **slipped ~** hernie discale; *rad* ~ **jockey** présentateur -trice de disques

**discal** *adj* discal

**discard** *n* action *f* de jeter; (cards) écart *m*; *vt* jeter, mettre de côté, écarter; (clothes) enlever, ôter, rejeter; (cards) écarter, se défausser de; *vi* se défausser

**discern** *vt* discerner, percevoir, distinguer

**discernible** *adj* discernable, perceptible

**discerning** *adj* judicieux -ieuse, pénétrant, fin

**discernment** *n* discernement *m*, discrimination *f*

**discharge** *n* (dismissal) renvoi *m*, congédiement *m*; (unloading) déchargement *m*; libération *f*; *mil* démobilisation *f*, licenciement *m*; (firearm) décharge *f*; *elect* décharge *f*; *med* suppuration *f*; *leg* acquittement *m*; *comm* (debt) règlement *m*; *eng* débit *m*; (duty) exercice *m*; (prisoner) élargissement *m*; *vt* (dismiss) renvoyer, congédier; (unload) décharger; libérer; *mil* (weapon) décharger; (soldier) démobiliser, licencier; (unfit soldier) réformer; *elect* décharger; *leg* acquitter; *comm* régler; (prisoner) élargir; *eng* débiter; (duty) accomplir; *vi med* suppurer; se déverser

**disciple** *n* disciple *m*

**disciplinable** *adj* disciplinable

**disciplinarian** *n* personne *f* très sévère en matière de discipline

**disciplinary** *adj* disciplinaire, de discipline

**discipline** *n* discipline *f*; *vt* discipliner, punir

**disclaim** *vt* rejeter, désavouer; *leg* renoncer à

**disclaimer** *n* désaveu *m*, déni *m*; *leg* désistement *m*, renonciation *f*

**disclose** *vt* découvrir, révéler, divulguer

**disclosure** *n* révélation *f*

**discoid** *adj* discoïde

**discoloration, discolouration** *n* décoloration *f*

**discolour** *vt* décolorer

**discomfit** *vt* déconcerter, décontenancer; *mil* battre

**discomfiture** *n* déconvenue *f*, déconfiture *f*, échec *m*; *mil* défaite *f*

**discomfort** *n* inconfort *m*; *med* malaise *m*; *vt* incommoder

**discommode** *vt* incommoder, gêner

**discompose** *vt* troubler, bouleverser

**discomposure** *n* trouble *m*; embarras *m*, gêne *f*

**disconcert** *vt* déconcerter, décontenancer; (embarrass) gêner; frustrer

**disconnect** *vt* disjoindre, séparer; (telephone) couper; *elect* débrancher

**disconnected** *adj* séparé; incohérent

**disconnection, disconnexion** *n* séparation *f*; *elect* débranchement *m*

**disconsolate** *adj* triste, inconsolable, misérable

**discontent** *n* mécontentement *m*; *adj* mécontent; *vt* mécontenter

**discontented** *adj* mécontent

**discontinuance** *n* interruption *f*, discontinuation *f*

**discontinuation** *n* interruption *f*, discontinuation *f*

**discontinue** *vt* discontinuer, interrompre, cesser; *vi* prendre fin

**discontinuity** *n* discontinuité *f*

**discontinuous** *adj* discontinu

**discophile** *n* + *adj* discophile

**discord** *n* discorde *f*, division *f*; discordance *f*; *mus* dissonance *f*

**discordance, discordancy** *n* discorde *f*; désaccord *m*

**disco(theque)** *n* disco(thèque) *f*

**discount** *n* escompte *m*; rabais *m*, réduction *f*; **at a ~** au rabais; (unimportant) de peu de valeur; *vt* rabattre, décompter; escompter; faire peu de cas de, ne pas tenir compte de

**discourage** *vt* décourager, rebuter; dissuader

**discouragement** *n* découragement *m*

**discourse** *n* discours *m*; conversation *f*; dissertation *f*; *vi* discourir, disserter; s'entretenir

**discourteous** *adj* discourtois, impoli

**discourtesy** *n* discourtoisie *f*, impolitesse *f*

**discover** *vt* découvrir, trouver; *ar* révéler

**discovery** *n* découverte *f*

**discredit** *n* discrédit *m*; doute *m*; *vt* discréditer; mettre en doute, douter de

**discreditable** *adj* honteux -euse

**discreet** *adj* discret -ète, circonspect, réservé

**discrepance, discrepancy** *n* contradiction *f*, discordance *f*

**discrete** *adj* séparé, discontinu; *med* + *bot* discret -ète

**discretion** *n* discrétion *f*, prudence *f*; jugement *m*, discernement *m*; latitude *f*; **at the ~ of** selon l'avis de; **years of ~** âge *m* de raison

**discretionary** *adj* discrétionnaire

**discriminate** *adj* distinct, discriminatoire; *vt* discriminer, distinguer; *vi* établir une discrimination

**discriminating** *adj* judicieux -ieuse, avisé, perceptif -ive; (tariff) différentiel -ielle

**discrimination** *n* discrimination *f*; discernement *m*

**discriminatory** *adj* discriminatoire

**disculpate** *vt* disculper

**discursive, discursory** *adj* décousu, incohérent

**discus** *n sp* disque *m*

**discuss** *vt* discuter, s'entretenir de

**discussion** *n* discussion *f*

**disdain** *n* dédain *m*, mépris *m*; *vt* dédaigner, mépriser

**disease** *n* maladie *f*, mal *m*; *fig* mal *m*

**disembark** *vt* + *vi* débarquer

**disembarkation** *n* débarquement *m*

**disembodiment** *n* séparation *f* du corps

**disembody** *vt mil* licencier; séparer du corps

**disembowel** *vt* étriper, éviscérer

**disenchant** *vt* désenchanter; désillusionner

**disenchantment** *n* désenchantement *m*, désillusion *f*

**disencumber** *vt* désencombrer

**disenfranchise** *vt see* **disfranchise**

**disengage** *vt* dégager, détacher; *vi* se dégager

**disengagement** *n* dégagement *m*

**disentangle** *vt* démêler, débrouiller; dénouer; *coll* dépêtrer; *vi* se dénouer; *coll* se dépêtrer

**disentanglement** *n* démêlage *m*; dénouement *m*

**disequilibrium** *n* déséquilibre *m*, instabilité *f*

**disestablish** *vt* (church) séparer de l'état

**disestablishment** *n* (church) séparation *f* de l'état

**disesteem** *n* défaveur *f*; *vt* mésestimer

**disfavour** *n* défaveur *f*; disgrâce *f*, déconsidération *f*; *vt* désapprouver, ne pas aimer

**disfiguration** *n see* **disfigurement**

**disfigure** *vt* défigurer, enlaidir

**disfigurement** *n* défiguration *f*, enlaidissement *m*

**disfranchise, disenfranchise** *vt* priver des droits civiques, priver du droit de vote

**disfranchisement** *n* privation *f* des droits civiques, privation *f* du droit de vote

**disgorge** *vt* dégorger; (give back) rendre; (river) déverser

**disgrace** *n* disgrâce *f*; déshonneur *m*, honte *f*; *vt* disgracier, déshonorer

# disorder

**disgraceful** *adj* honteux -euse, déshonorant

**disgruntled** *adj* mécontent, de mauvaise humeur

**disguise** *n* déguisement *m*, travesti *m*; *fig* travestissement *m*, faux-semblant *m*; *vt* déguiser, travestir; dissimuler

**disgust** *n* dégoût *m*, écœurement *m*; *vt* dégoûter, écœurer

**disgusting** *adj* dégoûtant, écœurant; révoltant, indigne

**dish** *n* (plate, food, plateful) plat *m*; *cul* mets *m*; (hollow) cuvette *f*; *sl* homme *m*, femme *f* ayant du chien; *vt cul* apprêter, servir (un plat); *coll* (spoil) couler, enfoncer; ~ **out** servir à manger; *coll* distribuer; ~ **up** servir à table dans un plat; *coll* présenter avec goût

**dish-cloth** *n* torchon *m*

**dish-cover** *n* couvercle *m*

**dishearten** *vt* décourager, démoraliser, déprimer

**disheartening** *adj* décourageant, déprimant

**dished** *adj* concave; *mot* désaxé; *coll* cuit, fichu

**dishevelled** *adj* (hair) échevelé, ébouriffé; (person) mal tenu, débraillé

**dishful** *n* plat *m*, platée *f*

**dish-mat** *n* dessous-de-plat *m invar*

**dishonest** *adj* malhonnête

**dishonesty** *n* malhonnêteté *f*

**dishonour** *n* déshonneur *m*, disgrâce *f*, honte *f*, ignominie *f*; *vt* déshonorer; (woman) séduire; insulter; *comm* (cheque) refuser d'honorer; (bill) protester; (promise) ne pas tenir; ~ **ed cheque** chèque *m* sans provision

**dishonourable** *adj* honteux -euse, déshonorant

**dishwasher** *n* plongeur -euse

**dish-water** *n* eau *f* de vaisselle; *coll pej* (soup, coffee, etc) lavasse *f*

**dishy** *adj sl* excitant, sexy

**disillusion** *n* désillusion *f*; *vt* désillusionner

**disillusionment** *n* désillusionnement *m*

**disincentive** *n* qch qui décourage l'action ou l'initiative

**disinclination** *n* répugnance *f*, aversion *f*

**disincline** *vt* rendre peu enthousiaste; *vi* devenir peu enthousiaste

**disinfect** *vt* désinfecter

**disinfectant** *n* désinfectant *m*

**disinfection** *n* désinfection *f*

**disinfest** *vt* dératiser; (lice) épouiller

**disinfestation** *n* dératisation *f*; (lice) épouillage *m*

**disingenuous** *adj* insincère, faux (*f* fausse)

**disingenuousness** *n* insincérité *f*, finasserie *f*

**disinherit** *vt* déshériter

**disinheritance** *n leg* exhérédation *f*

**disintegrate** *vt* désintégrer, désagréger; *vi* se désagréger

**disintegration** *n* désintégration *f*, désagrégation *f*

**disinter** *vt* déterrer, exhumer; *fig* révéler

**disinterested** *adj* désintéressé; impartial; *sl* ennuyé

**disinterestedness** *n* désintéressement *m*; impartialité *f*

**disinterment** *n* déterrement *m*, exhumation *f*

**disjoin** *vt* disjoindre, désunir

**disjoint** *vt* disloquer; désunir, détraquer

**disjointed** *adj* disloqué; *fig* incohérent, décousu

**disjunction** *n* disjonction *f*, séparation *f*

**disjuncture** *n gramm* disjonctive *f*; *adj* disjonctif -ive

**disk** *n see* **disc**

**dislike** *n* antipathie *f*, aversion *f*; dégoût *m*; *vt* ne pas aimer; avoir de l'aversion pour

**dislocate** *vt* disloquer; *med* désarticuler; désorganiser, bouleverser

**dislocation** *n* dislocation *f*; *med* luxation *f*; dérangement *m*; désorganisation *f*

**dislodge** *vt* déloger; (object) déplacer, faire bouger

**disloyal** *adj* déloyal; infidèle

**disloyalty** *n* déloyauté *f*

**dismal** *adj* morne, terne, sombre

**dismantle** *vt mil* démanteler; *naut* dégréer; *mech* démonter

**dismast** *vt naut* démâter

**dismay** *n* consternation *f*, atterrement *m*; effroi *m*; *vt* consterner, atterrer; effrayer

**dismember** *vt* démembrer

**dismemberment** *n* démembrement *m*

**dismiss** *vt* congédier, renvoyer; (official) révoquer; *leg* (case) classer; (appeal) rejeter; *fig* cesser de considérer; *mil* ~ ! rompez!

**dismissal** *n* renvoi *m*; (official) révocation *f*

**dismissive** *adj* qui signifie un renvoi; méprisant

**dismount** *vt* faire descendre, démonter, désarçonner; *vi* descendre de, mettre pied à terre

**disobedience** *n* désobéissance *f*

**disobedient** *adj* désobéissant

**disobey** *vt + vi* désobéir

**disoblige** *vt* désobliger; (offend) offenser, peiner

**disobliging** *adj* désobligeant, désagréable

**disorder** *n* désordre *m*, tumulte *m*; désordres *mpl*; *med* maladie *f*, trouble *m*;

443

## disorderliness

*vt* mettre en désordre; mettre en confusion; rendre malade

**disorderliness** *n* désordre *m*; esprit *m* de désordre

**disorderly** *adj* en désordre, désordonné; (mob) turbulent; ~ **house** maison *f* de prostitution, bordel *m*; (gambling) maison *f* de jeu

**disorganization** *n* désorganisation *f*

**disorganize** *vt* désorganiser

**disorientate** *vt* désorienter

**disorientation** *n* égarement *m*, désorientation *f*

**disown** *vt* désavouer; nier

**disparage** *vt* dénigrer; discréditer, déprécier

**disparagement** *n* dénigrement *m*, dépréciation *f*

**disparate** *adj* disparate

**disparity** *n* disparité *f*

**dispassionate** *adj* sans émotion, calme, froid; (unbiased) sans préjugés

**dispatch** *n* + *vt see* **despatch**

**dispel** *vt* dissiper, chasser

**dispensable** *adj* superflu, dont on peut se passer; dispensable; *eccles* pardonnable

**dispensary** *n* dispensaire *m*; (chemist's shop) officine *f*

**dispensation** *n* distribution *f*; *leg* + *eccles* dispense *f*; (decree) décret *m*; disposition providentielle

**dispense** *vt* distribuer, administrer; *med* préparer; dispenser, exempter; *vi* se dispenser, se passer

**dispenser** *n* (person) pharmacien -ienne; (device) distributeur *m*

**dispersal** *n* dispersion *f*

**disperse** *vt* disperser, éparpiller; dissiper; (spread) répandre; *opt* décomposer; *vi* se disperser

**dispersion** *n* dispersion *f*; *opt* décomposition *f*

**dispirit** *vt* déprimer, décourager

**displace** *vt* déplacer; (from office) remplacer, évincer

**displaced** *adj* déplacé; ~ **person** réfugié -e

**displacement** *n* déplacement *m*; (from office) remplacement *m*; destitution *f*; *naut* + *phys* déplacement *m*; *geol* faille *f*

**display** *n* (spreading) étalement *m*, déploiement *m*; manifestation *f*; (show) étalage *m*, exposition *f*; parade *f*; *print* mise *f* eh vedette; *vt* étaler, déployer; manifester; mettre à l'étalage, étaler; *print* mettre en vedette

**displease** *vt* mécontenter; déplaire à; *vi* déplaire

**displeasure** *n* déplaisir *m*, mécontentement *m*

**disport** *vt* ~ **oneself** s'ébattre, s'amu-

ser; *vi* jouer

**disposable** *adj* à jeter

**disposal** *n* action *f* de disposer; (selling) vente *f*; *leg* cession *f*; (rubbish) enlèvement *m*; (ordering) arrangement *m*; (bomb) désamorçage *m*; **at one's** ~ à sa disposition

**dispose** *vt* disposer, arranger; (regulate) régler; (make willing) disposer, incliner; préparer; *vi* disposer; ~ **of** disposer de; (settle) régler; *comm* céder, vendre; *coll* (food) manger; ~ **of s/o** se débarrasser de qn

**disposition** *n* disposition *f*, arrangement *m*; *leg* disposition *f* testamentaire; disposition *f* entre vifs; droit *m* de disposition; (nature) tempérament *m*, disposition *f*, caractère *m*; tendance *f*, inclination *f*

**dispossess** *vt* déposséder; (oust) faire sortir; *leg* exproprier

**dispossession** *n* dépossession *f*; *leg* expropriation *f*

**dispraise** *n* blâme *m*, dénigrement *m*; *vt* blâmer, dénigrer

**disproof** *n* réfutation *f*

**disproportion** *n* disproportion *f*; *vt* rendre disproportionné

**disproportional, disproportionate** *adj* disproportionné

**disprove** *vt* réfuter; démontrer la fausseté de

**disputable** *adj* discutable, douteux -euse

**disputant** *n* interlocuteur -trice; contradicteur -trice; *eccles* controversiste

**disputation** *n* débat *m*, discussion *f*; *hist* + *theol* dispute *f*

**disputatious** *adj* ergoteur -euse; raisonneur -euse

**dispute** *n* querelle *f*, dispute *f*; discussion *f*, débat *m*; **beyond** ~ incontestable, réglé; **in** ~ en discussion, incertain; **industrial** ~ conflit industriel; *vt* discuter, disputer, débattre; (oppose) contester; *vi* discuter, disputer; se disputer

**disqualification** *n* inaptitude *f*, incapacité *f*; *sp* disqualification *f*

**disqualify** *vt* *sp* disqualifier; rendre inapte; *mot* retirer le permis à

**disquiet** *n* inquiétude *f*; agitation *f*, trouble *m*; *vt* inquiéter, troubler

**disquieting** *adj* inquiétant, troublant

**disquietude** *n* inquiétude *f*

**disquisition** *n* traité *m*, étude *f*, dissertation *f*

**disregard** *n* négligence *f*; déconsidération *f*; *leg* violation *f*; (danger) insouciance *f*; *vt* déconsidérer; négliger; manquer d'égards envers; (danger) mépriser

**disrepair** *n* délabrement *m*, état *m* de

délabrement; **fall into** ~ se délabrer

**disreputable** *adj* louche; peu estimable; mal famé; (action) honteux -euse

**disrepute** *n* discrédit *m*; mauvaise réputation

**disrespect** *n* manque *m* de respect, irrespect *m*; impolitesse *f*

**disrespectful** *adj* irrespectueux -euse; impoli

**disrobe** *vt* dévêtir; *vi* se dévêtir

**disrupt** *vt* faire éclater; disloquer; interrompre, disperser

**disruption** *n* éclatement *m*; dislocation *f*; interruption *f*

**disruptive** *adj* qui cherche à disloquer, perturbateur -trice

**dissatisfaction** *n* insatisfaction *f*; mécontentement *m*

**dissatisfied** *adj* insatisfait, mécontent

**dissatisfy** *vt* mécontenter

**dissect** *vt* découper; *anat* disséquer; *fig* analyser, dépouiller

**dissection** *n* découpement *m*; *anat* dissection *f*; *fig* analyse *f*, dépouillement *m*

**dissector** *n* *anat* (person) disséqueur *m*; (instrument) scalpel *m*

**dissemble** *vt* dissimuler, déguiser; *vi* dissimuler

**dissembler** *n* dissimulateur -trice

**disseminate** *vt* disséminer

**dissemination** *n* dissémination *f*

**dissension** *n* dissension *f*, désaccord *m*

**dissent** *n* désaccord *m*, dissentiment *m*; dissidence *f*; *eccles hist* non-conformisme *m*; *vi* être d'un avis contraire, ne pas être d'accord; *eccles* être dissident

**dissenter** *n* *eccles* (England, Scotland) non-conformiste

**dissentient** *n* dissident -e; *adj* dissident; minoritaire

**dissertation** *n* dissertation *f*, mémoire *m*, étude *f*

**disserve** *vt* desservir

**disservice** *n* mauvais service

**dissident** *n* dissident -e; *adj* dissident

**dissimilar** *adj* dissemblable

**dissimilarity** *n* dissemblance *f*

**dissimilate** *vt* différencier

**dissimulate** *vt* + *vi* dissimuler

**dissimulation** *n* dissimulation *f*

**dissimulator** *n* dissimulateur -trice

**dissipate** *vt* dissiper; chasser, disperser; (waste) gaspiller; *vi* se dissiper; se livrer à la débauche

**dissipation** *n* dissipation *f*; dispersion *f*; vie dissipée, débauche *f*

**dissociate** *vt* dissocier, séparer, désagréger; ~ **oneself from** se séparer de, se désolidariser de; se désintéresser de

**dissociation** *n* séparation *f*; disassociation *f*

**dissolute** *adj* dissolu, débauché

**dissolution** *n* dissolution *f*, désagrégation *f*; (in liquid) fonte *f*; *leg* résiliation *f*

**dissolve** *n* *cin* + *TV* fondu (enchaîné); *vt* dissoudre, faire fondre; dissiper, disperser; *leg* résilier; *vi* se dissoudre, fondre; *cin* enchaîner

**dissolvent** *n* dissolvant *m*; *adj* dissolvant

**dissonance** *n* *mus* dissonance *f*; désaccord *m*

**dissonant** *adj* *mus* dissonant; *adj* en désaccord

**dissuade** *vt* dissuader; déconseiller

**dissuasion** *n* dissuasion *f*

**distaff** *n* quenouille *f*; ~ **side** côté maternel

**distance** *n* distance *f*, éloignement *m*; lointain *m*; *mus* intervalle *m*; *fig* distance *f*, froideur *f*; **at a** ~, **in the** ~ loin, distant; **keep at a** ~ traiter avec froideur; **keep one's** ~ tenir ses distances; *vt* distancer; éloigner; (painting) reculer, donner un effet de profondeur

**distant** *adj* distant, séparé, éloigné; *fig* froid

**distantly** *adv* de loin; avec froideur

**distaste** *n* dégoût *m*, aversion *f*

**distasteful** *adj* dégoûtant, répugnant

**distastefulness** *n* dégoût *m*, sens *m* d'aversion

**¹distemper** *n* maladie *f* de Carré; *obs* malaise *m*; *fig* mécontentement *m*; désordre *m*

**²distemper** *n* (paint) détrempe *f*, badigeon *m*; *vt* peindre en détrempe

**distend** *vt* distendre; *vi* se distendre

**distension** *n* distension *f*

**distil** *vt* distiller; faire couler goutte à goutte; *fig* distiller, répandre, épancher; *vi* se distiller, couler goutte à goutte

**distillation** *n* distillation *f*; *fig* essence *f*

**distiller** *n* distillateur *m*; (home) bouilleur *m* de cru

**distillery** *n* distillerie *f*

**distinct** *adj* distinct, séparé; précis, net (*f* nette)

**distinction** *n* distinction *f*; discrimination *f*; (honour) décoration *f*; (refinement) raffinement *m*; (quality) valeur *f*

**distinctive** *adj* distinctif -ive

**distinctly** *adv* distinctement; (undoubtedly) nettement, indubitablement

**distinctness** *n* netteté *f*, clarté *f*

**distingué** *adj* distingué

**distinguish** *vt* distinguer; différencier; caractériser; apercevoir

**distinguishable** *adj* perceptible; que l'on peut distinguer

**distinguished** *adj* distingué

**distort** vt déformer, dénaturer; (twist) tordre

**distortion** n déformation f, contorsion f; dénaturation f; (sound) distorsion f; (TV picture) déformation f

**distract** vt distraire; (divert) détourner; (drive mad) rendre fou (f folle)

**distracted** adj affolé, perplexe; (mad) fou (f folle); (absent-minded) distrait

**distraction** n distraction f; inattention f; diversion f, amusement m; folie f

**distrain** n leg ~ **upon s/o's goods** saisir les biens de qn

**distraint** n leg saisie f

**distraught** adj affolé, égaré; fou (f folle)

**distress** n détresse f, angoisse f, désarroi m; (poverty) misère f; péril m, danger m; leg droit m de saisie; ~ **gun** canon m porte-amarre invar; ~ **signal** signal m de détresse; naut **in** ~ en perdition; vt affliger, désoler; leg saisir

**distressed** adj troublé, affolé; (exhausted) épuisé; misérable

**distressful** adj (painful) douloureux -euse; (unpleasant) pénible; angoissant

**distressing** adj pénible, pitoyable, lamentable

**distribute** vt distribuer, dispenser; (divide out) répartir

**distribution** n distribution f; (dividing out) répartition f; (newspaper) diffusion f

**distributive** adj qui distribue; gramm distributif -ive

**distributor** n distributeur -trice; comm concessionnaire; mot distributeur m

**district** n district m; région f; unité administrative; ~ **nurse** infirmière visiteuse

**distrust** n défiance f; (suspicion) méfiance f; vt se méfier de; soupçonner

**distrustful** adj méfiant; soupçonneux -euse

**disturb** vt troubler, déranger; (disquiet) inquiéter, rendre perplexe

**disturbance** n trouble m, dérangement m; (anxiety) inquiétude f; (riot) soulèvement m, désordre m

**disturbing** adj inquiétant

**disunite** vt désunir; vi se désunir

**disunity** n désunion f

**disuse** n abandon m, désuétude f; vt ne plus utiliser

**disyllabic, dissyllabic** adj dissyllabique

**ditch** n fossé m; **die in the last** ~ défendre une position jusqu'à la fin; vt creuser des fossés dans; entourer d'un fossé; coll jeter, abandonner; coll aer (plane) faire descendre en mer; coll mot faire verser dans un fossé; vi creuser des fossés; coll mot verser dans le fossé

**ditch-water** n eau stagnante, eau bourbeuse; **as dull as** ~ assommant au possible; **clear as** ~ obscur

**dither** n coll tremblotement m, agitation f; vi coll s'agiter; trembler; hésiter, tergiverser

**dithyrambic** adj dithyrambique

**ditto** adv idem; **say** ~ **to** être d'accord avec

**ditty** n petite chanson

**diuresis** n med diurèse f

**diuretic** n med diurétique m; adj med diurétique

**diurnal** n eccles diurnal m; adj diurne

**diva** n (opera) diva f

**divagate** vi divaguer; (wander) errer; (digress) s'écarter du sujet

**divagation** n divagation f

**divan** n divan m

**dive** n sp plongeon m; plongée f; aer piqué m; coll bistrot m, gargote f; (gambling den) maison f de jeu; vi plonger; aer piquer; se plonger; se précipiter

**dive-bomb** vt + vi bombarder en piqué

**dive-bomber** n avion m qui bombarde en piqué

**dive-bombing** n bombardement m en piqué

**diver** n sp plongeur -euse; (deep sea) scaphandrier m; orni plongeon m

**diverge** vi bifurquer; dévier

**divergence** n divergence f

**divergent** adj divergent

**divers** adj pl plusieurs, divers

**diverse** adj divers, différent; varié

**diversification** n diversification f

**diversify** vt diversifier

**diversion** n déviation f; mil diversion f; diversion f, divertissement m

**diversity** n diversité f

**divert** vt détourner, dévier; distraire, divertir; mot dévier

**diverting** adj divertissant, amusant

**divest** vt dépouiller; priver, déposséder

**divide** n geog ligne f de partage des eaux; vt diviser; séparer; (share) partager; (distribute) répartir, distribuer; (parliament) faire voter; vi se diviser; se séparer, se partager; math être divisible; voter, procéder au scrutin

**divided** adj divisé

**dividend** n dividende m

**dividers** npl compas m

**divination** n divination f

**divinatory** adj divinatoire

**divine** n eccles théologien m; coll prêtre m, pasteur m; adj divin; vt + vi deviner

**diviner** n (water) sourcier -ière; devin m, devineresse f

**diving-bell** n caisson m, cloche f à plongeur

**diving-board** n plongeoir m
**diving-suit** n scaphandre m
**diving-rod** n baguette f de sourcier
**divinity** n divinité f; théologie f
**divisible** adj divisible
**division** n division f; séparation f; (partition) cloison f; (sharing out) partage m, distribution f; section f, subdivision f; désaccord m, dissension f; (parliament, meeting) scrutin m, vote m; mil division f; math ~ sign signe conventionnel de division
**divisive** adj qui entraîne la division, qui cause le désaccord
**divisor** n math diviseur m
**divorce** n divorce m; fig séparation f; vt divorcer d'avec; vi divorcer
**divorcee** n divorcé -e
**divulge** vt révéler, divulguer
**dixie** n gamelle f
**dizziness** n vertige m; étourdissement m
**dizzy** adj pris de vertige, ayant un vertige; (height) vertigineux -euse; coll stupide; vt donner le vertige à, faire tourner la tête à
**djinn, jinn** n djinn m
¹**do** n coll réception f; réunion f, soirée f; (trick) escroquerie f; **fair** ~s parts égales; vt faire; (perform) accomplir, effectuer; (work at) travailler à, étudier; (distance) faire, parcourir; (speed) faire, atteindre; (destroy) ruiner, éreinter; (finish) terminer, finir; (harm) faire, causer; (hair) arranger; (shoes) polir, nettoyer; (nails) couper; (tour) faire, visiter; (justice) faire, rendre; (suit) convenir; theat (play) monter; (time in prison) faire; coll (cheat) escroquer; coll (hit) frapper, battre; ~ **down** coll rouler; ~ **in** coll éreinter, épuiser; sl descendre, zigouiller; ~ **out** nettoyer; ~ **s/o out of sth** escroquer qch à qn; ~ **over** coll décorer, enduire; sl passer à tabac; ~ **s/o in the eye** escroquer qn; ~ **to death** tuer; ~ **up** ficeler, emballer; (refurbish) refaire, remettre à neuf; cul accommoder, réchauffer; vi+v aux (behave) agir, se comporter; (suffice) suffire; (health) aller, se porter; ~ **away with** abolir, supprimer, tuer; ~ **badly** aller mal; ~ **by** agir aux égards de; coll ~ **for** détruire, tuer; (char) tenir le ménage de; ~ **go away!** partez, je vous prie!; ~ **well** prospérer, progresser; ~ **with** sth (need) avoir besoin de qch; tolérer qch; ~ **without** se passer de; **did he come?** est-il venu?; **have to** ~ **with** avoir affaire à; **he did come** il est venu en effet; **he did not come** il n'est pas venu; **he drank that wine faster than I could have done** il a bu ce vin plus vite

que je n'aurais pu le faire; **He drinks a lot of wine. – Does he?** Il boit beaucoup de vin. – Vraiment?; **I could** ~ **with** j'ai besoin de; **make** ~ se débrouiller; **nothing** ~**ing!** rien à faire!; **nothing to** ~ **with** rien à voir avec; **you** ~ **love me, don't you?** vous m'aimez, n'est-ce pas?; **you don't love me,** ~ **you?** vous ne m'aimez pas, n'est-ce pas?
²**do** n mus do m, ut m
³**do** adv abbr idem
**docile** adj docile
**docility** n docilité f
¹**dock** n naut bassin m, dock(s) m(pl); (quayside) quai m; (landing-stage) embarcadère m; **dry** ~, **graving** ~ cale sèche; **floating** ~ dock flottant; **tidal** ~ bassin ouvert; vt (bring to quayside) mettre à quai; (put in dock) faire entrer au(x) dock(s); vi naut (come alongside quay) se mettre à quai; (go in dock) entrer au(x) dock(s); coll mot **be in** ~ être en réparation
²**dock** n bot patience f
³**dock** n (tail) tronçon m; (harness) trousse-queue m invar; vt (tail) écourter, couper; (wages) retrancher, rogner
⁴**dock** n leg banc m des accusés
**docker** n docker m
**docket** n fiche f; (abstract) bordereau m; leg registre m des jugements; récépissé m de douane; vt résumer; faire une fiche pour; attacher une fiche à
**dockyard** n chantier naval (pl navals); **naval** ~ arsenal m
**doctor** n med médecin m, docteur m, femme f médecin; (law, letters, music, philosophy, etc) docteur m; vt med soigner, traiter; donner des remèdes à; fig falsifier, truquer; coll (domestic animal) châtrer
**doctoral** adj doctoral
**doctorate** n doctorat m
**doctrinaire** n+adj doctrinaire
**doctrinal** adj doctrinal
**doctrine** n doctrine f
**document** n document m; vt documenter
**documentary** n cin documentaire m; adj documentaire
**documentation** n documentation f
**dodder** vi chanceler, flageoler, tituber
**dodderer** n gâteux -euse
**dodecagon** n geom dodécagone m
**dodecahedron** n geom dodécaèdre m
**dodge** n coll tour m, truc m; mouvement m de côté; vt esquiver, éluder; (task, etc) éviter; vi se jeter de côté; (disappear) s'esquiver; (trick) biaiser
**dodgem** n coll auto tamponneuse f
**dodger** n coll roublard -e; (military

service) embusqué *m*

**dodgy** *adj* malin (*f* maligne); *sl* difficile

**doe** *n* (deer) daine *f*; (hare) hase *f*; (rabbit) lapine *f*

**doer** *n* personne active; (action) auteur *m*

**doeskin** *n* daim *m*

**doff** *vt* ôter, enlever

**dog** *n* chien *m*; *pej* salaud *m*, lâche *m*; *coll* type *m*; (live wire) boute-en-train *m invar*; *mech* crampon *m*; (fire) ~ s chenet *m*; ~ eat ~ rivalité acharnée; ~ in the manger chien *m* du jardinier; a hair of the ~ that bit you un petit verre pour guérir la gueule de bois; be top ~ avoir le dessus; die like a ~ mourir comme un chien; every ~ has his day à chacun vient sa chance; *coll* go and see a man about a ~ aller faire pipi; go to the ~ s mal tourner, dégénérer; hot ~ hot-dog *m*; lead a ~'s life avoir une vie de chien; let sleeping ~ s lie il ne faut pas réveiller le chat qui dort; lucky ~ veinard -e; the ~ s courses *fpl* de levrettes; *vt* suivre de très près, filer; ~ s/o's footsteps talonner qn

**dog-collar** *n* collier *m* de chien; *coll* col *m* d'ecclésiastique

**dog-days** *npl* canicule *f*

**doge** *n* doge *m*

**dog-eared** *adj* corné

**dogfight** *n* *aer* duel aérien

**dogfish** *n* *zool* chien *m* de mer

**dogged** *adj* obstiné; déterminé

**doggedness** *n* persévérance *f*, obstination *f*

**doggerel** *n* vers *mpl* de mirliton; *adj* de mirliton

**doggie, doggy** *n* *coll* toutou *m*

**dogginess** *n* ressemblance *f* aux chiens; amour *m* des chiens

**doggo** *adv* sans mouvement

**doggone** *adj* US *coll* sacré

**dog-house** *n* chenil *m*; *sl* in the ~ en disgrâce

**dog-latin** *n* latin *m* de cuisine

**dogma** *n* dogme *m*

**dogmatic, dogmatical** *adj* dogmatique

**dogmatism** *n* dogmatisme *m*

**dogmatist** *n* dogmatiseur *m*

**dogmatize** *vi* dogmatiser

**dog-rose** *n* (flower) églantine *f*; (bush) églantier *m*

**dogsbody** *n* *sl* souillon *f*, factotum *m*

**dog-show** *n* exposition canine

**dog-star** *n* *astron* Sirius *m*

**dog-tired** *adj* fourbu, vanné

**dog-watch** *n* *naut* petit quart

**doily** *n* napperon *m*

**doings** *npl* activités *fpl*; (behaviour) façons *fpl*, conduite *f*; *coll* truc *m*, machin *m*

**doldrums** *npl* *naut* zone *f* des calmes; *fig* cafard *m*, dépression *f*

**dole** *n* charité *f*; (unemployment) allocation *f* de chômage; be on the ~ être au chômage, toucher l'allocation de chômage; *vt* ~ out distribuer parcimonieusement

**doleful** *adj* morne, lugubre, triste, mélancolique

**dolefulness** *n* mélancolie *f*, tristesse *f*

**doll** *n* (toy) poupée *f*; *coll* (pretty girl) poupée *f*; *sl* (girl) nana *f*, pépée *f*; *vt* orner; ~ oneself up se bichonner

**dollar** *n* dollar *m*

**dollop** *n* *coll* tas *m*, gros morceau

**dolly** *n* poupée *f*; (laundry) agitateur *m*; (sailing) plate-forme *f*; (filming) chariot *m*; *vi* (filming) se servir d'un chariot; ~ in se rapprocher; ~ out se distancer

**dolmen** *n* dolmen *m*

**dolomite** *n* *min* dolomite *f*; **Dolomites** *npl* Dolomites *fpl*

**dolorous** *adj* lugubre; (painful) douloureux -euse

**dolour** *n* affliction *f*, chagrin *m*

**dolphin** *n* dauphin *m*

**dolt** *n* crétin -e; *sl* andouille *f*

**domain** *n* domaine *m*

**dome** *n* dôme *m*, coupole *f*; *coll* tête *f*

**domestic** *n* domestique; *adj* domestique, ménager -ère; (home-loving) casanier -ière

**domesticate** *vt* domestiquer

**domestication** *n* domestication *f*

**domesticity** *n* vie *f* de famille, amour *m* du foyer

**domicile** *n* domicile *m*

**dominance, dominancy** *n* prédominance *f*, autorité *f*

**dominant** *n* *mus* dominante *f*; *adj* dominant

**dominate** *vt* dominer

**domination** *n* domination *f*

**domineer** *vi* dominer tyranniquement; se conduire avec arrogance

**Dominican** *n* + *adj* *eccles* dominicain -e

**dominion** *n* dominion *m*

**domino** *n* domino *m*; ~ es jeu *m* de dominos

¹**don** *n* (academic) professeur *m*

²**don** *vt* revêtir, mettre, enfiler

**donate** *vt* donner, faire don de; (blood) donner

**donation** *n* donation *f*

**donator** *n* donateur -trice

**done** *adj* fini, achevé; (cooked) cuit; (worn out) usé; *coll* (exhausted) fourbu; *sl* (tricked) escroqué; ~ for ruiné; ~ in, ~ up épuisé, fourbu; mourant; ~ up fini, ruiné; have ~ with

# double-jointed

renoncer à, en finir avec; **not ~** contre les bonnes manières; **the ~ thing** ce qui se fait

**donkey** *n* âne *m*, baudet *m*; *coll* crétin -e, idiot -e; *coll* **~ work** travail *m* de routine; *coll* **for ~ 's years** très longtemps

**donnish** *adj* professoral; pédant

**donor** *n* donateur -trice; donneur -euse; **blood ~** donneur -euse de sang

**doodle** *vi* gribouiller

**doodle-bug** *n hist* bombe volante

**doom** *n leg+eccles* jugement *m*; destin *m*; mort *f*; ruine *f*; **crack of ~** fin *f* du monde; *vt* condamner; vouer à une fin terrible

**doomsday** *n* jour *m* du jugement dernier

**door** *n* porte *f*; (large) portail *m*; (car, train) portière *f*; **~ to** porte à porte; **answer the ~** ouvrir la porte à un visiteur; **lay sth at s/o's ~** imputer qch à qn; **lie at the ~ of** être imputable à; **next ~** la maison voisine; **next ~ to** à côté de; (almost) presque; *fig* **open the ~ to** ouvrir la voie à; **out of ~s** au dehors, en plein air; **show s/o the ~** congédier qn, chasser qn

**doorbell** *n* sonnette *f*

**door-frame** *n* chambranle *m*

**door-handle** *n* poignée *f* de porte

**door-keeper** *n* portier -ière; (flats) concierge

**door-knob** *n* bouton *m* de porte

**doorman** *n* portier *m*

**doormat** *n* paillasson *m*

**door-plate** *n* plaque *f* de propreté

**doorstep** *n* seuil *m*; *coll* tranche épaisse de pain

**door-stop** *n* butoir *m*

**doorstrip** *n* bourrelet *m*

**doorway** *n* ouverture *f* de porte; moyen *m* d'accès

**dope** *n coll* drogue *f*, stupéfiant *m*; *sp* doping *m*; *coll* (information) tuyau *m*, détails *mpl*; *aer* enduit *m*, laque *f*; *phot* révélateur *m*; *sl* crétin -e, idiot -e; *US sl* (drug-addled) drogué -e; *vt aer* enduire, laquer; *coll* doper; calmer; **~ oneself** se droguer

**dopey, dopy** *adj coll* drogué; (stupid) lent, abruti

**dorado** *n zool* daurade *f*

**Doric** *adj archi* dorique

**Dorien** *adj geog+mus* dorien -ienne

**dormant** *adj* dormant, assoupi

**dormer** *n archi* lucarne *f*

**dormitory** *n* dortoir *m*; **~ suburb** banlieue-dortoir *f* (*pl* banlieues-dortoirs); **~ town** ville-dortoir *f* (*pl* villes-dortoirs)

**dormouse** *n* loir *m*

**dorsal** *adj* dorsal

**dosage** *n* dosage *m*; posologie *f*

**dose** *n* dose *f*; *sl* maladie vénérienne; *vt* donner un médicament à; *vi* mesurer une dose; prendre un médicament

**doss** *n sl* lit *m* dans un asile de nuit; *vi sl* dormir dans un asile de nuit; *coll* **~ down** dormir dans un lit de fortune

**doss-house** *n* asile *m* de nuit

**dossier** *n* dossier *m*

**dot** *n* point *m*; **in the year ~** il y a très longtemps; *coll* **on the ~** pile, recta; *vt* mettre un point sur; (line) pointiller; (scatter) éparpiller, parsemer; *mus* pointer; *coll* frapper; *coll* **~ and carry one** clopiner; **~ one's i's** *fig* être très méticuleux -euse; mettre les points sur les i; **sign on the ~ted line** donner son accord; accepter aveuglément

**dotage** *n* radotage *m*

**dotard** *n* gâteux -euse, radoteur -euse

**dote** *vi* être gâteux -euse; **~ on** raffoler de

**doting** *adj* qui adore, entiché; gâteux -euse, sénile

**dotty** *adj coll* cinglé, toqué; pointillé

**double** *n* double *m*, sosie *m*; (bridge) contre *m*; (running) pas *m* de gymnastique; *theat* doublure *f*; (tennis) **~s** double *m*; *adj* double; doublé, redoublé; (room) à deux, pour deux personnes; *fig* ambigu; fourbe, à deux faces; **~ bed** grand lit; **~ time** tarif *m* heures supplémentaires; **play a ~ game** jouer double jeu; *adv* double; à deux; *vt* doubler; (fold) doubler, plier en deux, replier; (speed) redoubler; *theat* doubler; (bridge) contrer; *vi* doubler, se doubler; (run) prendre le pas de course; **~ back** (return) revenir sur ses pas; **~ up** se plier en deux; *coll* partager une chambre, partager un lit

**double-barrelled** *adj* à deux coups; (name) à tiroirs

**double-bass** *n* contrebasse *f*

**double-breasted** *adj* croisé

**double-chin** *n* double menton *m*

**double-cross** *n* escroquerie *f*; *vt* rouler, trahir

**double-dealer** *n* fourbe

**double-dealing** *n* duplicité *f*, fourberie *f*

**double-decker** *n* autobus *m* à impériale

**double-declutch** *vi mot* faire un double débrayage

**double-Dutch** *n coll* baragouin *m*, charabia *m*

**double-edged** *adj* à double tranchant

**double-entry** *n* comptabilité *f* en partie double

**double-faced** *adj* à double face, hypocrite

**double-glazing** *n* **put in ~** poser des doubles fenêtres

**double-jointed** *adj* désarticulé

449

**double-lock** *vt* fermer à double tour

**double-park** *vi* se garer en double file

**double-quick** *adj* très vite; au pas de gymnastique

**double-stop** *vi mus* jouer à double corde

**doublet** *n hist* pourpoint *m*; *ling* doublet *m*

**double-talk** *n* balivernes *fpl*; *pol* slogans *mpl* vides

**doublethink** *n* acceptation simultanée de deux notions contradictoires

**doubling** *n* multiplication *f* par deux; (fold) pli *m*; (lining) doublure *f*

**doubly** *adv* doublement, deux fois plus

**doubt** *n* doute *m*, incertitude *f*; (worry) inquiétude *f*; **beyond ~** sans aucun doute; **give s/o the benefit of the ~** accorder à qn le bénéfice du doute; **in ~** incertain; **without ~** sans aucun doute; *vt* douter de, mettre en doute; *vi* douter, être incertain, se demander

**doubtful** *adj* douteux -euse, incertain, problématique; hésitant; (unclear) peu clair, ambigu -uë; (suspect) équivoque, louche

**doubtless** *adv* sans doute; probablement

**douceur** *n* (tip) pourboire *m*; (bribe) pot-de-vin *m* (*pl* pots-de-vin)

**douche** *n med* injection *f*; douche *f*; **cold ~ surprise** *f* désagréable; découragement *m*; *vt* doucher; donner une injection à; *vi* prendre une douche, se doucher

**dough** *n cul* pâte *f*; *sl* fric *m*

**dough-boy** *n US coll* soldat américain

**doughnut** *n cul* sorte *f* de beignet

**doughty** *adj* vaillant

**doughy** *adj cul* pâteux -euse

**dour** *adj* obstiné; (gloomy) austère, sombre

**dourness** *n* obstination *f*; austérité *f*, humeur *f* sombre

**douse, dowse** *vt* arroser, tremper; *coll* (light) éteindre

**dove** *n zool* + *fig* colombe *f*

**dove-colour** *adj* gorge-de-pigeon *invar*

**dovecot** *n* colombier *m*

**dovetail** *n carp* queue-d'aronde *f* (*pl* queues-d'aronde); *vt* assembler à queue-d'aronde; *fig* joindre facilement; *vi* se raccorder, s'engrener; *fig* s'accorder

**dowager** *n* douairière *f*

**dowdiness** *n* manque *m* d'élégance

**dowdy** *adj* (woman) mal habillée, mal fichue; (clothes) (shabby) fripé; (out of fashion) démodé

**dower** *n* (wife) dot *f*; (widow) douaire *m*; *vt* doter; assigner un douaire à

**¹down** *n* duvet *m*

**²down** *n* colline dénudée

**³down** *n* infortune *f*; *coll* antipathie *f*;

**have a ~ on** avoir une dent contre; *adj* qui descend; *mus* (beat) fort; (sad) triste, déprimé; (train) d'aller; (tyre) à plat; **~ payment** acompte *m*; *adv* en bas; vers le bas; (time) le long de; **~ and out** sans le sou; **~ at heel** minable; pauvre; misérable; **~ in the mouth** la mine longue, avec triste mine; **~ on** en colère contre, hostile à; **~ on one's luck** en difficulté; à court d'argent; **~ to the ground** entièrement; *coll* **~ under** en Australie, en Nouvelle Zélande; **~ with** souffrant de; **~ with!** à bas!; *prep* au bas de; en descendant; le long de; **~ stream** en aval; **~ wind** au vent

**downbeat** *n mus* temps frappé

**downcast** *adj* abattu, triste; (look) baissé

**down-draught** *n* courant *m* d'air descendant

**downfall** *n* chute *f*; *fig* effondrement *m*

**downgrade** *n* descente *f*; déchéance *f*; **on the ~** sur le déclin; *vt* rétrograder, mettre (réduire) à un niveau inférieur

**downhearted** *adj* découragé

**downhill** *n* pente *f*, descente *f*; *adj* en pente, descendant; *adv* en pente; sur le déclin

**downpipe** *n* tuyau *m* de descente

**downpour** *n* pluie battante

**downright** *adj* franc (*f* franche); complet -ète, total; absolu; *adv* carrément, nettement; tout à fait

**downstairs** *n* rez-de-chaussée *m invar*; *adj* du bas; *adv* en bas de l'escalier; au rez-de-chaussée

**downstream** *adv* en aval

**downtrodden** *adj* piétiné; *fig* opprimé, subjugué

**downward** *adj* (slope) descendant; (time) postérieur

**downward(s)** *adv* en bas, vers le bas

**downy** *adj* duveté; *sl* avisé, pas con

**dowry** *n* dot *f*

**¹dowse** *vt see* **douse**

**²dowse** *vi* faire le sourcier

**dowsing-rod** *n* baguette *f* de sourcier

**doxology** *n* doxologie *f*

**doxy** *n sl* putain *f*, traînée *f*

**doyen** *n* doyen *m*, doyenne *f*

**doyenne** *n* doyenne *f*

**doze** *n* petit somme; *vi* somnoler

**dozen** *n* douzaine *f*; **baker's ~** treize; **daily ~** gymnastique quotidienne; **talk nineteen to the ~** parler vite et sans arrêt

**doziness** *n* somnolence *f*

**dozy** *adj* somnolent

**¹drab** *n ar* prostituée *f*, souillon *f*

**²drab** *n* (fabric) bure *f*; *adj* terne, monotone; (colour) fauve

**drabble** *vt* crotter, salir; *vi* se crotter

**drabness** *n* monotonie *f*; (colour) grisaille *f*

# drawbridge

drachm *n* drachme *f*

drachma *n* drachme *f*

draconian *adj* draconien -ienne

draft *n* brouillon *m*; (sketch) esquisse *f*; *comm* traite *m*; *mil* contingent *m*; *vt* faire un brouillon de; esquisser; *mil* affecter; *US* appeler

draftee *n US mil* conscrit *m*

draftsman *n see* draughtsman

drag *n aer* ralentissement *m*; (brake) frein *m*; *naut* gaffe *f*; *agr* herse *f*; *ar* calèche *f*, drag *m*; (hindrance) entrave *f*; *coll* (bore) emmerdement *m*; *coll* bouffée *f* de cigarette; *sl* in ~ en travesti; *vt* traîner, tirer, entraîner; (river) draguer; *agr* herser; *naut* ~ **anchor** chasser sur l'ancre; *coll* (conversation) ~ in introduire (un sujet) mal à propos; ~ **one's feet** hésiter, ne pas montrer d'entrain; (children) ~ **up** élever plutôt mal; *vi* traîner à terre; se traîner; *naut* (anchor) chasser; ~ **on** traîner

draggle *vt* traîner dans la boue, crotter; *vi* se crotter; traîner

drag-net *n* seine *f*

dragon *n* dragon *m*; *coll* (woman) dragon *m* de vertu

dragon-fly *n* libellule *f*

dragon's teeth *npl mil* fortifications *fpl* antichar

dragoon *n mil* dragon *m*; *vt* gendarmer; (compel) contraindre

drain *n* tuyau *m* d'écoulement; *agr* fosse *f* d'écoulement; *med* drain *m*; *comm* (money) drainage *m*; *fig* perte *f*, écoulement *m*, fuite *f*; (drink) goutte *f*; ~ s (dregs) lie *f*; *vt* faire écouler; (glass) vider; (marsh) assécher, assainir; *mot* (sump) vidanger; *med* drainer; *fig* épuiser; *coll* ~ **s/o dry** saigner qn à blanc; *vi* s'écouler

drainage *n agr* drainage *m*, assainissement *m*; *med* drainage *m*; réseau *m* d'égouts; eaux *fpl* d'égout; *geol* drainage *m*

drainer *n cul* égouttoir *m*

draining-board *n* paillasse *f*, égouttoir *m*

draining-rack *n* égouttoir *m*

drainpipe *n* tuyau *m* de vidange; (rainwater) descente *f*; *sl* ~ s pantalon collant, pantalon *m* cigarette

drake *n* canard *m*

dram *n* drachme *f*; *coll* petit verre, goutte *f*

drama *n* drame *m*; théâtre *m*, art *m* dramatique

dramatic *adj* dramatique; théâtral; excitant

dramatics *npl* activité théâtrale; *coll* (histrionics) comédie *f*

dramatist *n* auteur *m* dramatique

dramatization *n* adaptation théâtrale; *fig* dramatisation *f*

dramatize *vt* dramatiser; adapter pour le théâtre (le cinéma, la télévision)

dramaturge, dramaturgist *n* dramaturge *m*

drape *n* (cloth) façon *f* de pendre; *theat* toile *f*; ~ s tentures *fpl*; *US* rideaux *mpl*; *vt* draper; *vi* se draper

draper *n* drapier *m*, marchand -e de draps

drapery *n* draperie *f*; commerce *m* de draperie; métier *m* de drapier

drastic *adj* énergique, violent; efficace; *med* (purge) drastique; (measure) draconien -ienne

drat *interj coll* zut!

dratted *adj coll* misérable, sacré

draught *n* traction *f*; (drinking) trait *m*, gorgée *f*; (chimney) tirage *m*; (current of air) courant *m* d'air, vent *m* coulis; *naut* tirant *m* d'eau; (fish) coup *m* de filet, pêche *f*; *med* potion *f*; (game) ~ s dames *fpl*; ~ **beer** bière *f* à la pression; *coll fig* feel the ~ rencontrer des difficultés

draught-board *n* damier *m*

draught-excluder *n* bourrelet *m*

draughtiness *n* présence *f* de courants d'air

draughtsman, draftsman *n* dessinateur industriel; (documents) rédacteur *m*; (game) pion *m*

draughty *adj* plein de courants d'air

draw *n* loterie *f*, tirage *m* au sort; *sp* match nul; *theat* pièce *f* à succès; *coll* attraction *f*; *vt* tirer, traîner; (water, strength, information) puiser; (pull out) extraire, arracher; (lots) tirer au sort, tirer à la courte paille; (cheque, money) tirer; (sword) dégainer; (sketch) dessiner; (map) dresser; (write) tracer; *cul* (bird) vider; (tea) faire infuser; (abscess) faire mûrir; (attract) attirer; (conclusion) tirer; (comparison) établir; (face) contracter; ~ **a blank** faire un coup nul, faire chou blanc; être déçu; ~ **breath** respirer; ~ **down** encourir; ~ **in** entraîner; (liquid) ~ **off** tirer; ~ **oneself up** se tenir droit; ~ **out** faire parler; ~ **the line** avoir des scrupules; *fig* ~ **the longbow** exagérer, mentir; ~ **the teeth of** rendre inoffensif -ive; ~ **up** (document) rédiger; (account) établir; (troops) aligner; *vi* tirer; (sketch) dessiner; (chimney) tirer; *naut* (sails) porter; (tea) infuser; (abscess) mûrir; ~ **aside** s'écarter; ~ **back** se retirer; ~ **in** (days) raccourcir; s'approcher; ~ **level** arriver à la même hauteur; ~ **near** se rapprocher; ~ **on** (time) avancer; ~ **out** devenir plus long, se prolonger; ~ **up** s'arrêter

drawback *n* inconvénient *m*; *comm* drawback *m*

drawbridge *n hist* pont-levis *m* (*pl* ponts-levis), pont basculant

## drawer

**drawer** n (cheque) tireur m; (sketch) dessinateur -trice; (furniture) tiroir m; **~ s** (man) caleçon m; (woman) culotte f; **chest of ~ s** commode f

**drawing** n dessin m; metal étirage m

**drawing-board** n planche f à dessin

**drawing-pin** n punaise f

**drawing-room** n salon m, living m

**drawl** n manière de parler traînante; vt dire d'un ton traînant; vi parler d'un ton traînant

**drawn** adj (weapon) dégainé, tiré; sp nul (f nulle); (appearance) fatigué, tendu; (disembowelled) éviscéré

**dray** n haquet m

**dray-horse** n cheval m de trait

**dread** n épouvante f, effroi m; appréhension f; adj redoutable, terrifiant; vt redouter, craindre

**dreadful** adj terrible, redoutable; coll terrible, épouvantable

**dreadfully** adv d'une manière terrible; coll très

**dream** n rêve m, songe m; (daydream) rêverie f; idéal m, ambition f; **wet ~** émission f nocturne; adj coll idéal; vt rêver, songer; imaginer; coll **~ up** inventer, concevoir; vi rêver, faire un rêve; songer; imaginer, se figurer

**dreamer** n rêveur -euse; idéaliste; songe-creux m invar

**dreamland** n pays m des songes

**dreamless** adj (sleep) sans rêves

**dreamlike** adj comme un rêve; irréel -elle, vague

**dreamy** adj rêveur -euse, songeur -euse; vague, distrait

**drear** adj see dreary

**dreariness** n tristesse f, mélancolie f; aspect m lugubre

**dreary, drear** adj terne, morne, mélancolique, lugubre

**¹dredge** n naut drague f; vt + vi draguer

**²dredge** n cul saupoudreuse f; vt saupoudrer

**dregs** npl lie f

**drench** n vet breuvage médicinal; vt tremper, inonder; vet faire boire

**drencher** n vet entonnoir m; coll saucée f

**drenching** adj **~ rain** pluie battante

**Dresden** n (china) porcelaine f de Saxe; geog Dresde

**dress** n habits mpl, vêtements mpl, habillement m; (woman) robe f; (formal) tenue f, mise f; theat **~ circle** corbeille f, premier balcon; **~ coat** habit m, frac m; theat **~ rehearsal** générale f; **~ suit** tenue f de soirée, smoking m; **evening ~** tenue f de soirée; **morning ~** jaquette f et pantalon rayé; vt habiller, vêtir; (decorate) orner, parer, décorer; mil aligner; carp

dégrossir; (stone) équarrir; préparer, apprêter; cul apprêter; (poultry, fish, etc) habiller, accommoder; (salad) assaisonner; med panser; **~ a window** faire l'étalage; **~ down** (horse) panser; coll arranger, engueuler; **~ up** parer, attifer; déguiser; vi s'habiller; mil s'aligner; **~ up** s'habiller avec soin; pej se déguiser; (Sunday best) s'endimancher; (fancy dress) se costumer

**dressage** n dressage m

**¹dresser** n habilleur -euse; theat habilleuse f; surg assistant -e; mech équarrissoir m

**²dresser** n buffet m de cuisine, dressoir m

**dressing** n toilette f; action f de s'habiller; cul assaisonnement m; sauce f; (salad) mayonnaise f; med pansement m; mil alignement m; préparation f, apprêt m

**dressing-case** n nécessaire m de toilette

**dressing-down** n coll savon m, engueulade f

**dressing-gown** n robe f de chambre

**dressing-room** n vestiaire m; theat loge f

**dressing-table** n coiffeuse f

**dressmaker** n couturier -ière

**dressy** adj chic invar, à la mode

**dribble** n (saliva) bave f; (liquid) égouttement m; sp dribble m; vt faire couler goutte à goutte, faire dégoutter; sp dribbler; vi couler goutte à goutte, dégoutter; (saliva) baver; sp dribbler

**driblet** n petite quantité

**dribs and drabs** n **in ~** au compte-gouttes

**drier** n séchoir m; (substance) siccatif m

**drift** n poussée f, traînée f; naut + aer dérive f; tendance f; (meaning) sens m, portée f, intention f; (pile) tas m, amoncellement m; (snow) congère f; (mining) galerie f; vt charrier, entraîner; faire entasser, faire amonceler; vi naut + aer aller à la dérive, dériver; s'amonceler, s'entasser; se laisser aller; coll flâner

**drift-anchor** n naut ancre flottante

**driftwood** n bois flotté

**¹drill** n mech foret m; (bit) mèche f; (machine) foreuse f, perforatrice f; (dentist) roulette f, fraise f; vt forer, percer; (dentist) fraiser; vi se servir d'un foret, d'une foreuse, etc

**²drill** n mil exercice m, drill m; entraînement m physique; (lesson repeated) drill m; vt mil faire faire l'exercice à; vi mil faire l'exercice

**³drill** n agr sillon m; (machine) semoir m; vt semer; creuser des sillons dans

**⁴drill** n (fabric) coutil m, treillis m

**drill-sergeant** n mil sergent instructeur m

**drily** adv see dryly

**drink** n boisson f; (glass of sth alcoholic) verre m, petit verre, drink m; (soft) boisson non-alcoolisée; sl (sea) mer f; **drive to** ~ pousser à la boisson; **take to** ~ s'adonner à la boisson; vt (soup) manger; fig boire, absorber; ~ **in** (words) boire; ~ **like a fish** boire comme un trou; ~ **off** vider; ~ **to** porter un toast à, boire à la santé de; vi boire; boire beaucoup; (customer) consommer

**drinkable** adj (good) buvable; (safe) potable

**drinker** n buveur -euse

**drinking** n boire m; (habit) boisson f, ivrognerie f; adj qui boit

**drinking-bout** n beuverie f

**drinking-fountain** n fontaine publique

**drinking-song** n chanson f à boire

**drinking-water** n eau f potable

**drip** n goutte f, égouttement m; med goutte-à-goutte m invar; sl nouille f; archi larmier m; vt faire couler goutte à goutte, faire égoutter; vi couler goutte à goutte, égoutter, dégoutter

**drip-dry** adj ne nécessitant aucun repassage

**drip-feed** vt med nourrir au goutte-à-goutte, alimenter par perfusion

**dripping** n égouttement m, gouttes fpl; cul graisse f (de viande); adj ~ **wet** mouillé jusqu'à l'os

**drive** n coup violent; dynamisme m, énergie f, allant m, entrain m; mech transmission f; mot promenade f en voiture; comm campagne f; (road) voie privée; sp drive m; mot **front-wheel** ~ traction f avant; **rear-wheel** ~ propulsion f arrière; **right-hand** ~ conduite f à droite; vt pousser, chasser; propulser; mech faire marcher, actionner; mot conduire, transporter; comm (bargain) passer, conclure; fig obliger, forcer; (push) pousser, amener; (overwork) surmener; sp (ball) renvoyer, driver; ~ **back** refouler; (nail) ~ **in** enfoncer; ~ **mad** rendre fou (f folle); ~ **off**, ~ **out** chasser; vi avancer vigoureusement; mot conduire, rouler; fig s'acharner, s'atteler; ~ **at** avoir comme but; (mean) vouloir dire; ~ **home** insister sur; ~ **off** partir en voiture

**drive-in** n drive-in m invar

**drivel** n radotage m, balivernes fpl; vi baver, radoter

**driver** n (car, taxi) chauffeur m; (car, bus, train, etc) conducteur -trice; (train) mécanicien m; (carriage) cocher m

**driving** n conduite f; adj qui transmet le mouvement; (rain) battant

**driving-licence** n permis m de conduire

**driving-school** n auto-école f

**driving-wheel** n mech roue motrice

**drizzle** n bruine f, crachin m; vi bruiner

**droll** n bouffon m; adj drôle, bizarre

**drollery** n drôlerie f, bouffonnerie f

**dromedary** n dromadaire m

**drone** n zool abeille f mâle, faux bourdon; fig oisif m, parasite m; (sound) bourdonnement m; (speech) ronronnement m; vt dire sur un ton monotone; vi (bees) bourdonner; fig bourdonner, ronronner

**drool** n radotage m, balivernes fpl; vi dire des bêtises; baver; (drivel) radoter; (lick lips) s'en lécher les babines

**droop** n (eyelids) abaissement m; (spirits) abattement m; vt pencher, baisser; vi se pencher, se baisser; fig languir, s'affaiblir

**drop** n goutte f; pendant m; (chandelier) pendeloque f; (sweet) bonbon m; (descent) dénivellation f; précipice m; hauteur f de chute; (price, number, temperature) baisse f; coll (drink) goutte f, doigt m; a ~ **in the ocean** une quantité insignifiante, une goutte d'eau dans la mer; **at the** ~ **of a hat** tout de suite, sans hésiter; vt laisser tomber, faire tomber, lâcher; (let fall in drops) laisser tomber goutte à goutte; (eyes, voice) baisser; (omit) omettre; (set down) déposer; math abaisser; coll abandonner, délaisser; (animal) mettre bas; fig laisser, cesser, interrompre; coll laisser tomber; coll ~ **a brick** faire une gaffe; ~ **down on** gronder, morigéner; ~ **it!** en voilà assez!, laisse tomber!; ~ **s/o a line** envoyer un mot à qn; **let** ~ dire en passant, faire savoir; vi couler goutte à goutte, s'égoutter; tomber; (wind, voice, price) baisser; fig cesser, prendre fin; ~ **away** diminuer; ~ **behind** se laisser devancer; ~ **in** entrer en passant; ~ **off** piquer un somme, s'endormir; (diminish) diminuer; sl ~ **out** renoncer, abandonner; sp drop(p)er; ~ **out of** sortir de, disparaître de

**drop-kick** n sp drop m

**drop-leaf** n volet m de table

**droplet** n gouttelette f

**drop-out** n sl drop-out, dropé -e

**dropping** n chute f; aer parachutage m; ~ **s** fiente f, crottes fpl

**dropsical** adj med hydropique

**dropsy** n med hydropisie f

**dross** n scories fpl; immondices fpl, ordures fpl; fig camelote f, toc m

**drought** n sécheresse f

**drove** n troupeau m en marche

**drover** n toucheur m

**drown** vt noyer; fig inonder, submerger;

(sound) étouffer, assourdir; *vi* se noyer

**drowning** *n* noyade *f*; *adj* qui se noie

**drowse** *n* somme *m*, somnolence *f*; *vt* assoupir; *vi* somnoler, s'assoupir

**drowsiness** *n* somnolence *f*

**drowsy** *adj* somnolent

**drub** *vt* battre; rosser; (abuse) engueuler

**drubbing** *n* volée *f* de coups, raclée *f*; *coll* tripotée *f*

**drudge** *n* domestique surmené -e; *vi* trimer

**drudgery** *n* travail dur et monotone

**drug** *n* produit *m* pharmaceutique, médicament *m*, drogue *f*; (addictive) drogue *f*, stupéfiant *m*; ~ **addict** toxicomane; ~ **addiction** toxicomanie *f*; *fig* ~ **on the market** article *m* invendable; *vt* droguer; administrer un narcotique à; *vi* se droguer

**druggist** *n* pharmacien -ienne

**drugstore** *n* US drugstore *m*

**druid** *n* druide *m*

**druidic** *adj* druidique

**drum** *n* *mus* tambour *m*; *anat* tympan *m*; *mech* tambour *m*, cylindre *m*; (container) baril *m*, bidon *m*; *archi* tambour *m*; *elect* bobine *f*; *mus* **big** ~ grosse caisse; *vt* *mus* tambouriner, pianoter; ~ **into** enseigner à force de répétitions; *mil* ~ **up** battre le rappel de; (support) faire du battage pour; *vi* battre du tambour

**drum-major** *n* tambour-major *m* (*pl* tambours-majors)

**drummer** *n* *mus* tambour *m*; US commis-voyageur *m*

**drumstick** *n* baguette *f* de tambour; *cul* pilon *m*

**drunk** *n* ivrogne; *sl* soulard -e; *adj* saoul, ivre; *fig* ivre, enivré

**drunkard** *n* ivrogne *m*, ivrognesse *f*

**drunkenness** *n* ivrognerie , saoulerie *f*

**dry** *adj* sec (*f* sèche); desséché; (answer, style, humour) froid; US à régime sec; ~ **battery** pile sèche; ~ **goods** textiles *mpl*, nouveautés *fpl*; ~ **land** terre *f* ferme; ~ **rot** pourriture sèche; ~(-**stone**) **wall** mur *m* en pierres sèches; *vt* faire sécher; essuyer; *vi* sécher, se sécher; tarir; *theat* sécher; ~ **up** se sécher; *coll* cesser de parler

**dryad** *n* dryade *f*

**dry-clean** *vt* nettoyer à sec

**dry-cleaning** *n* nettoyage *m* à sec

**dry-dock** *n* cale sèche

**dryer** *n* *see* **drier**

**dry-eyed** *adj* sans larmes

**dry-ice** *n* *chem* neige *f* carbonique

**dryly, drily** *adv* sèchement; ironiquement

**dryness** *n* sécheresse *f*

**dry-shod** *adj* à pied sec

**dual** *adj* double, à deux, jumelé

**dual-carriageway** *n* *mot* route *f* à deux voies

**dualism** *n* dualisme *m*

**dualistic** *adj* dualiste

**duality** *n* dualité *f*

**dual-purpose** *adj* utilisable de deux façons, à double usage

**dub** *vt* conférer le titre de chevalier à; donner un surnom à; *cin* doubler; (recording) copier; (leather) graisser

**dubbing** *n* *cin* doublage *m*; (recording) copie *f*

**dubious** *adj* douteux -euse; hésitant; discutable, vague; suspect, louche; (unclear) ambigu -uë

**ducal** *adj* ducal

**ducat** *n* ducat *m*

**duchess** *n* duchesse *f*

**duchy** *n* duché *m*

**¹duck** *n* canard *m*; (female) cane *f*; *coll* chou *m*, chéri -e; *coll* *mil* camion *m* amphibie; **lame** ~ canard boiteux; **like a** ~ **takes to water** naturellement, facilement; **like a dying** ~ **in a thunderstorm** faible, impuissant, inerte; **like water off a** ~'**s back** sans faire la moindre impression; **play** ~**s and drakes** faire des ricochets sur l'eau; **play** ~**s and drakes with one's money** gaspiller son argent; **wild** ~ canard *m* sauvage; *vt* (head) baisser vivement; ~ **s/o** plonger qn dans l'eau; *vi* se courber, s'esquiver en se courbant; se plonger

**²duck** *n* toile *f*; ~ **s** pantalon *m* de toile

**duck-bill** *n* ornithorynque *m*

**duck-board** *n* caillebotis *m*

**ducking** *n* bain forcé

**duckling** *n* caneton *m*

**duckweed** *n* *bot* lentille *f* d'eau

**duct** *n* conduite *f*; *anat* canal *m*, conduit *m*; canalisation *f*

**ductile** *adj* (metal) ductile; *fig* souple, influençable

**ductless** *adj* *anat* à sécrétion interne; ~ **gland** glande endocrine

**dud** *n* *coll* *mil* obus non éclaté; objet *m* inutile, rossignol *m*; (coin) pièce fausse; (person) raté -e; *adj* inutile, qui ne marche pas; ~ **cheque** chèque *m* sans provision

**dude** *n* US *sl* poseur *m*, gommeux *m*

**dude-ranch** *n* hôtel *m* ranch

**dudgeon** *n* colère *f*, ressentiment *m*

**due** *n* dû *m*; ~ **s** droits *mpl*; *adj* dû (*f* due); (fallen due) échu; juste, mérité; (arrival) attendu, prévu; ~ **to** à cause de; *adv* ~ **north, east, etc** plein nord, est, etc

**duel** *n* duel *m*; *vi* se battre en duel

**dueller, duellist** *n* duelliste *m*

**duenna** n duègne f

**duet** n mus duo m

**duffel, duffle** n molleton m; ~ **coat** duffel-coat m

**duffer** n coll (schoolboy) cancre m; crétin -e, gourde f

**dug** n tétine f; (cow) pis m

**dugout** n naut pirogue f; mil abri souterrain

**duke** n duc m

**dukedom** n duché m; titre m de duc

**dulcet** adj mélodieux -ieuse, doux (f douce)

**dulcimer** n mus tympanon m

**dull** adj lourd, lent, bête, borné; (colour) terne, morne; (appearance) sans éclat; (sound) sourd, mat; (weather) couvert; (boring) ennuyeux -euse, insipide; (inactive) sans entrain; (bored) ennuyé; (pain) sourd; (blunt) émoussé; vt alourdir, hébéter; (blunt) émousser; (colour) ternir; (sound) assourdir; (pain) amortir; vi s'alourdir; se ternir; s'assourdir; s'émousser; s'amortir

**dullard** n baloud -e, crétin -e

**dullness** n lourdeur f, lenteur f; aspect m terne; (appearance) manque m d'éclat; caractère m insipide; insipidité f

**duly** adv dûment, correctement

**dumb** adj muet -ette; silencieux -ieuse; coll borné, gourde, crétin; ~ **blonde** blonde évaporée; ~ **show** pantomime f

**dumb-bell** n haltère m

**dumbfound** vt ébahir, désarçonner, étonner

**dumbness** n mutisme m

**dumb-waiter** n table roulante; (stand) plateau tournant; US monte-plats m invar

**dum-dum** n mil dum-dum f invar

**dummy** n simulacre m; (draper's model) mannequin m; (cards) mort m; (baby) sucette f; mech ~ **run** essai m; tailor's ~ mannequin m; sl m'as-tu vu m invar, m'as-tu vue f invar

**dump** n (rubbish) dépotoir m; (pile) tas m, amas m; mil dépôt m; coll trou m; vt décharger, déverser; comm faire du dumping pour; coll se débarrasser de; vi se décharger

**dumpling** n cul boulette f de pâte; **apple** ~ pomme entourée de pâte

**dumps** npl cafard m

**dumpy** adj courtaud, rondouillard

¹**dun** n couleur f gris-foncé; adj gris foncé invar

²**dun** n huissier m; vt (debtor) relancer

**dunce** n cancre m, âne m

**dune** n dune f

**dung** n fiente f, crotte f; **cow** ~ bouse f;

**horse** ~ crottin m; vt fumer

**dungaree** n treillis m; ~ **s** bleu m de travail, coll salopette f

**dungeon** n cachot m, oubliette f; hist donjon m

**dunghill** n tas m de fumier

**dunk** vt tremper

**duo** n mus duo m

**duodecimal** adj math duodécimal

**duodecimo** n (book) in-douze m invar

**duodenal** adj med duodénal

**duodenum** n anat duodénum m

**duologue** n dialogue m

**dupe** n dupe f; vt duper

**duplex** n US ~ **apartment** appartement m à deux étages, duplex m; adj double; elect + rad duplex

**duplicate** n double m, copie exacte; adj double, en double; vt faire en double exemplaire; reproduire

**duplication** n reproduction f par duplicateur

**duplicator** n duplicateur m

**duplicity** n duplicité f

**durability** n durabilité f

**durable** adj durable

**duralumin** n duralumin m

**duration** n durée f

**duress** n emprisonnement m, captivité f; leg contrainte f

**during** prep pendant, durant

**dusk** n crépuscule m; obscurité f, ombre f; adj poet sombre; vt poet assombrir; vi poet s'assombrir

**dusky** adj sombre; (complexion) hâlé, brun

**dust** n poussière f; poudre f; (corpse) cendres fpl; **gold** ~ poudre f d'or; **lick the** ~ ramper; **shake the** ~ **(of a place) off one's feet** quitter dédaigneusement un endroit; **throw** ~ **in the eyes** jeter de la poudre aux yeux; vt épousseter; (sprinkle) saupoudrer; vi enlever la poussière

**dustbin** n poubelle f, boîte f à ordures

**dust-bowl** n région f à sol dénudé, désert m de poussière

**dust-cart** n camion m des boueux

**dust-cover** n (book) couvre-livre m; (furniture) housse f

**duster** n chiffon m

**dusting** n époussetage m; coll raclée f; med poudre f antiseptique

**dust-jacket** n couvre-livre m

**dustman** n boueux m, éboueur m

**dustpan** n pelle f à ordures, pelle f à poussière

**dust-proof** adj protégé contre la poussière

**dust-sheet** n housse f

**dust-up** n coll bagarre f, querelle f

**dust-wrapper** n couvre-livre m

**dusty** *adj* poussiéreux -euse, poudreux -euse; *sl* **not so ~** pas si moche
**Dutch** *n* hollandais *m*; *adj* hollandais, néerlandais; **~ cap** pessaire *m*; **~ courage** courage *m* d'ivrogne; *coll* **~ treat** repas *m* où l'on partage les frais; *coll* **double ~** charabia *m*, baragouin *m*; *coll* **go ~** partager les frais; **talk to s/o like a ~ uncle** réprimander qn, tancer qn
**Dutchman** *n* Hollandais *m*
**Dutchwoman** *n* Hollandaise *f*
**duteous** *adj* obéissant; respectueux -euse
**dutiable** *adj* sujet -ette aux droits de douane
**dutiful** *adj* respectueux -euse, déférent; obéissant; consciencieux -ieuse
**duty** *n* devoir *m*, obligation *f*; déférence *f*; (tax) droits *mpl*; **duties** fonctions *fpl*; **do ~ for** remplacer; *mil* **on ~** de service
**duty-free** *adj* en franchise, exempt de droits de douane
**dwarf** *n* nain -e; *adj* nain; (stunted) rabougri; *vt* rapetisser; éclipser; *bot* rabougrir, étioler
**dwarfish** *adj* rabougri; minuscule
**dwell** *vi* habiter, demeurer; rester; **~ on** réfléchir sur; insister sur
**dweller** *n* habitant -e
**dwelling** *n* habitation *f*, demeure *f*; **~ place** demeure *f*
**dwindle** *vi* diminuer; s'étioler; perdre de l'importance

**dye** *n* teinture *f*; teinte *f*; *vt* teindre; *vi* se teindre
**dyeing** *n* teinture *f*; teinturerie *f*
**dyer** *n* teinturier -ière
**dyestuffs** *npl* teintures *fpl*
**dying** *adj* mourant
¹**dyke, dike** *n* digue *f*; (ditch) fossé *m*; *geol* filon *m*, dyke *m*; *vt* endiguer
²**dyke** *n sl* (lesbian) gouine *f*
**dynamic** *adj phys* dynamique; *med* fonctionnel -elle; *fig* dynamique, énergique
**dynamics** *npl phys* dynamique *f*
**dynamism** *n philos* dynamisme *m*
**dynamite** *n* dynamite *f*; *vt* faire sauter à la dynamite, dynamiter
**dynamiter** *n* dynamiteur -euse
**dynamo** *n* dynamo *f*; **human ~** personne *f* énergique
**dynamometer** *n* dynamomètre *m*
**dynast** *n ar* dynaste *m*, souverain *m* héréditaire
**dynastic** *adj* dynastique
**dynasty** *n* dynastie *f*
**dyne** *n phys* dyne *f*
**dysentery** *n med* dysenterie *f*
**dyslexia** *n med* dyslexie *f*
**dyslexic** *n* + *adj med* dyslexique
**dyspepsia** *n* dyspepsie *f*
**dyspeptic** *adj med* dyspepsique, dyspeptique; *fig* lugubre

# E

**each** *adj* chaque; *pron* chacun -e; **~ other** l'un l'autre; **ten francs ~** dix francs pièce, dix francs chaque
**eager** *adj* ardent, impatient; enthousiaste; avide; *coll* **~ beaver** personne *f* qui fait du zèle
**eagerness** *n* impatience *f*; zèle *m*, enthousiasme *m*
**eagle** *n* aigle *m*; **golden ~** aigle royal
**eagle-eyed** *adj* perspicace, qui voit tout
**eaglet** *n* aiglon *m*
¹**ear** *n* oreille *f*; (hearing) ouïe *f*; **be all ~s** être tout oreilles; **keep one's ~s to the ground** être aux écoutes; **play by ~** (music) jouer à l'oreille; *fig* improviser

le moment venu; **set by the ~s** semer le désaccord; **turn a deaf ~** faire la sourde oreille; *coll* **up to the ~s** extrêmement, jusqu'au cou
²**ear** *n bot* épi *m*; *vi* épier
**earache** *n* mal *m* d'oreilles, mal *m* aux oreilles
**eardrum** *n* tympan *m*
**earl** *n* = comte *m*
**earldom** *n* = comté *m*
**early** *adj* de bonne heure, matinal; *bot* précoce, de primeur; *hist* primitif -ive; *coll* **~ bird** personne *f* qui se lève de bonne heure; personne *f* qui arrive tôt; **~ closing day** jour *m* où les magasins

sont fermés l'après-midi; ~ times passé lointain; in the ~ nineteenth century au début du dix-neuvième siècle; *adv* tôt, de bonne heure; au début; (right from) as ~ as dès; as ~ as possible le plus tôt possible

**earmark** *n* (sheep) marque *f* à l'oreille; *fig* signe distinctif, caractéristique *f*; *vt* (sheep) marquer à l'oreille; réserver, affecter

**earn** *vt* (money) gagner; (interest) rapporter; *fig* mériter

**¹earnest** *n* arrhes *fpl*; gage *m*

**²earnest** *n* sérieux *m*; in ~ sérieusement; *adj* sérieux -ieuse; sincère; (assiduous) empressé, zélé

**earnings** *npl* (salary) appointements *mpl*, salaire *m*; (wages) gages *mpl*; (profits) bénéfices *mpl*

**earphone** *n* écouteur *m*

**earring** *n* boucle *f* d'oreille

**earshot** *n* portée *f* de la voix

**ear-splitting** *adj* assourdissant

**earth** *n* terre *f*, monde *m*; (soil) terre *f*, sol *m*; (burrow) terrier *m*; down to ~ réaliste; run to ~ se terrer; where on ~? où diable?; *vt* couvrir de terre; *elect* mettre à la terre

**earth-born** *adj* mortel -elle

**earth-bound** *adj* terrestre; prosaïque; *eccles* mondain

**earthen** *adj* en terre, de terre

**earthenware** *n* faïence *f*

**earthly** *adj* terrestre; *eccles* mondain; profane, matériel; *coll* possible; no ~ use sans aucune utilité; *sl* not an ~ rien à faire

**earthly-minded** *adj* profane, matérialiste

**earthquake** *n* tremblement *m* de terre

**earthwork** *n* *eng* terrassement *m*; *mil* ouvrage *m* de terre

**earthworm** *n* ver *m* de terre

**earthy** *n* terreux -euse; (crude) grossier -ière

**ear-trumpet** *n* cornet *m* acoustique

**earwax** *n* cérumen *m*

**earwig** *n* perce-oreille *m*

**ease** *n* (well-being) bien-être *m*; confort *m*, aises *fpl*; (facility) aisance *f*; at ~ à l'aise; *mil* repos!; *vt* apaiser, alléger; réconforter; *naut* mollir; *vi* se détendre

**easel** *n* chevalet *m*

**easily** *adv* facilement; (possibly) bien

**easiness** *n* facilité *f*, aisance *f*; confort *m*; nonchalance *f*

**east** *n* est *m*, levant *m*; Orient *m*; Far East Extrême-Orient *m*; Middle East Moyen-Orient *m*; *adj* à l'est, de l'est; *adv* à l'est

**Easter** *n* Pâques *fpl* or *m sing*; ~ egg œuf *m* de Pâques

**easterly** *adj* d'est; *adv* de l'est

**eastern** *adj* face à l'est; oriental; de l'Orient

**eastward, eastwards** *adv* vers l'est

**easy** *adj* facile, aisé, simple; (chair, clothes) confortable; (relaxed) à l'aise; (understanding) souple; tolérant; tranquille, calme; *comm* peu demandé; ~ on the eye bien balancé; by ~ stages par petites étapes; in ~ circumstances prospère; *adv* à l'aise, sans effort; *coll* ~ does it! doucement!, ôn a le temps!; *coll* take it ~ se la couler douce

**easy-chair** *n* fauteuil *m*

**easy-going** *adj* tolérant, accommodant, facile à vivre

**eat** *vt* manger; dévorer; *fig* manger; ronger; *sl* tracasser, irriter; ~ away dévorer peu à peu; corroder; ~ one's heart out se consumer de chagrin; ~ one's words se rétracter; ~ out of s/o's hand faire les quatre volontés de qn; ~ up dévorer; tout manger; *vi* manger; ~ into ronger, corroder, pénétrer dans; be ~en se manger

**eatable** *adj* mangeable, comestible

**eatables** *npl* victuailles *fpl*

**eater** *n* mangeur -euse

**eating** *n* manger *m*; *adj* comestible; ~ apple pomme *f* à couteau

**eating-house** *n* restaurant pas cher

**eau-de-Cologne** *n* eau *f* de Cologne

**eau-de vie** *n* eau-de-vie *f* (*pl* eaux-de-vie)

**eaves** *npl* avant-toit *m*

**eavesdrop** *vi* écouter aux portes

**eavesdropper** *n* écouteur -euse aux portes

**ebb** *n* reflux *m*; *fig* déclin *m*, diminution *f*; *vi* refluer; *fig* décliner

**ebb-tide** *n* jusant *m*, reflux *m*

**ebonist** *n* ébéniste *m*

**ebonite** *n* ébonite *f*

**ebony** *n* ébène *f*; *adj* d'ébène; tout à fait noir

**ebullience, ebulliency** *n* ébullition *f*; exubérance *f*

**ebullient** *adj* bouillonnant; exubérant

**ebullition** *n* ébullition *f*; *fig* éclatement *m*, débordement *m*

**eccentric** *n* original -e; *adj* eccentrique

**eccentricity** *n* eccentricité *f*

**ecchymosis** *n* ecchymose *f*

**ecclesiastic** *n* ecclésiastique *m*; *adj* ecclésiastique

**echelon** *n* *mil* échelon *m*

**echo** *n* écho *m*; *vt* répéter; *vi* faire écho

**éclair** *n* *cul* éclair *m*

**eclectic** *n* + *adj* éclectique

**eclecticism** *n* éclectisme *m*

**eclipse** *n* éclipse *f*; *vt* éclipser; *vi* s'éclipser

**eclogue** *n* églogue *f*

**ecological** *adj* écologique
**ecologist** *n* écologiste
**ecology** *n* écologie *f*
**economic** *adj* économique
**economical** *adj* économique; (person) économe
**economics** *npl* économique *f*; économie *f* politique
**economist** *n* économiste; personne *f* économe
**economize** *vt* économiser; *vi* faire des économies, économiser
**economy** *n* économie *f*; système *m* économique
**ecstasy** *n* extase *f*, joie *f* intense, ravissement *m*, transport *m*
**ecstatic** *adj* extatique
**ectoplasm** *n* ectoplasme *m*
**Ecuador** *n* Équateur *m*
**ecumenical, oecumenical** *adj* œcuménique
**ecumenism, oecumenism** *n* œcuménisme *m*
**eczema** *n med* eczéma *m*
**eddy** *n* remous *m*, tourbillon *m*; *vi* tourbillonner
**edema** *n see* oedema
**Eden** *n* Éden *m*, paradis *m* terrestre
**edge** *n* (blade) tranchant *m*, fil *m*; (border) bord *m*, extrémité *f*, marge *f*; *geog* arête *f*; *fig* enthousiasme *m*, mordant *m*; **have the ~ on** devancer mais de peu; **on ~** crispé, irrité, exaspéré; **set the teeth on ~** irriter, agacer; **take the ~ off** émousser; *vt* (sharpen) aiguiser, affiler; border, ourler; **~ out** évincer; *vi* **~ away** s'éloigner peu à peu; **~ into** s'insinuer dans
**edgeways, edgewise** *adv* de biais, de côté; **be unable to get a word in ~** ne pouvoir placer un mot
**edging** *n* bordure *f*
**edgy** *adj* tranchant; *fig* crispé, nerveux -euse; *arts* sans contours accusés
**edible** *adj* comestible, mangeable
**edict** *n* édit *m*, décret *m*
**edification** *n* édification *f*
**edifice** *n* édifice *m*
**edify** *adj* édifier
**edifying** *adj* édifiant
**Edinburgh** *n* Édimbourg
**edit** *vt* (text, book) éditer, préparer pour la publication; (newspaper) diriger, être le rédacteur -trice en chef de
**edition** *n* édition *f*; (number of copies) tirage *m*
**editor** *n* (text) éditeur -trice; (newspaper) rédacteur -trice en chef; (department of newspaper) rédacteur -trice
**editorial** *n* éditorial *m*, article *m* de fond
**editorship** *n* (publishing) profession *f* d'éditeur -trice; (newspaper) profession *f* de rédacteur -trice en chef
**educable** *adj* éducable
**education** *n* éducation *f*; (teaching) enseignement *m*, instruction *f*
**educational** *adj* éducateur -trice, éducatif -ive
**educationalist, educationist** *n* pédagogue
**educator** *n* éducateur -trice
**edulcorate** *vt* édulcorer
**eel** *n* anguille *f*
**eerie, eery** *adj* sinistre, effrayant; mystérieux -ieuse
**efface** *vt* effacer; **~ oneself** s'effacer
**effacement** *n* effacement *m*
**effect** *n* effet *m*, résultat *m*; influence *f*; impression *f*, sens *m*; **~s** effets *mpl*; *theat + cin* (sound) bruitage *m*; (visual) truquage *m*; **put into ~** mettre en application; **to no ~** en vain; **to the same ~** dans le même sens; *vt* causer, effectuer; accomplir
**effective** *n mil* effectif *m*; *adj* efficace, efficient; *mil* effectif -ive
**effectiveness** *n* efficacité *f*
**effectual** *adj* efficace; (valid) valable
**effectuate** *vt* effectuer
**effeminacy** *n* caractère efféminé; manque *m* de virilité
**effeminate** *n* efféminé *m*; *adj* efféminé
**effervesce** *vi* être en effervescence, bouillonner
**effervescence** *n* effervescence *f*
**effervescent** *adj* effervescent
**effete** *adj* épuisé; sans force; stérile
**effeteness** *n* épuisement *m*; faiblesse *f*
**efficacious** *adj* efficace
**efficaciousness, efficacy** *n* efficacité *f*
**efficiency** *n* efficacité *f*; (productivity) capacité *f* de rendement; compétence *f*; *phys + mech + econ* rendement *m*
**efficient** *adj* efficace, efficient; capable, compétent
**effigy** *n* effigie *f*
**effloresce** *vi bot* être en fleurs; *chem* effleurir
**efflorescence** *n bot* floraison *f*; *chem* efflorescence *f*
**efflorescent** *adj bot* en fleurs; *chem* efflorescent
**effluent** *n* effluent *m*
**effluvium** *n* effluve *m*
**efflux** *n* écoulement *m*
**effort** *n* effort *m*; *coll* accomplissement *m*
**effortless** *adj* sans effort; facile, naturel -elle, aisé
**effrontery** *n* effronterie *f*, audace *f*
**effulgence** *n* éclat *m* (de lumière)
**effulgent** *adj* éclatant, rayonnant
**effusion** *n* effusion *f*, déversement *m*, épanchement *m*; *lit* flot *m* de paroles;

écrit plein d'épanchements; *med* effusion *f*

**effusive** *adj* exubérant, démonstratif -ive

**effusiveness** *n* effusion *f*, épanchement *m*

**egalitarian** *adj* égalitaire

**egalitarianism** *n* égalitarisme *m*

**egality** *n* égalité *f*

¹**egg** *n* œuf *m*; *biol* ovule *m*; *coll* good ~ brave type *m*; **hard-boiled** ~ œuf dur; **soft-boiled** ~ œuf *m* à la coque

²**egg** *vt* inciter, pousser; ~ **on** pousser

**egg-cup** *n* coquetier *m*

**egg-flip** *n* lait *m* de poule

**egg-head** *n* + *adj sl cont US* intellectuel -elle

**egg-nog** *n* flip *m*

**egg-plant** *n* aubergine *f*

**eggshell** *n* coquille *f* d'œuf

**egg-timer** *n* sablier *m*

**egg-whisk** *n cul* fouet *m*

**eglantine** *n bot* églantine *f*

**ego** *n* ego *m*, moi *m*

**egocentric** *adj* égocentrique

**egoism** *n* égoïsme *m*; suffisance *f*

**egoist** *n* égoïste; égotiste

**egoistic** *adj* égoïste

**egotism** *n* égotisme *m*

**egregious** *adj* terrible, très mauvais, no-toire

**egress , egression** *n* sortie *f*

**Egypt** *n* Égypte *f*

**Egyptian** *n* Égyptien -ienne; *adj* égyptien -ienne

**egyptologist** *n* égyptologue

**egyptology** *n* égyptologie *f*

**eh** *interj* hé!, hein?

**eider** *n zool* eider *m*

**eiderdown** *n* édredon *m*, duvet *m*

**eight** *n* huit *m invar*; *sp* (rowing) équipe *f* de huit personnes; (skating) **figure of** ~ huit *m*; *sl* **have one over the** ~ boire un coup de trop; *adj* huit *invar*

**eighteen** *n* dix-huit *m invar*; *adj* dix-huit *invar*

**eighteenth** *n* dix-huitième; (date) dix-huit *m*; *adj* dix-huitième

**eighth** *n* huitième; (date) huit *m*; *adj* huitième

**eightieth** *n* + *adj* quatre-vingtième

**eighty** *n* quatre-vingts *m*; *adj* quatre-vingts

**either** *adj* + *pron* l'un ou l'autre; **not** ~ **of them** ni l'un ni l'autre; *adv* non plus; *conj* ~ ... **or** ou ... ou, soit ... soit

**ejaculate** *vt* (cry) pousser (un cr.); *vi* s'exclamer, s'écrier; *physiol* éjaculer

**ejaculation** *n* exclamation *f*; *physiol* éjaculation *f*

**eject** *vt* éjecter; émettre, lancer; (person) chasser, expulser

**ejection** *n* éjection *f*; expulsion *f*

**ejector** *n* éjecteur *m*; *aer* ~ **seat** siège *m*

éjectable

**eke** *vt* ~ **out** augmenter, supplémenter; faire durer

**elaborate** *adj* compliqué; soigné; *vt* élaborer

**elaboration** *n* élaboration *f*

**elan** *n* élan *m*

**elapse** *vi* (time) passer, s'écouler

**elastic** *n* élastique *m*; *adj* élastique, souple

**elasticity** *n* élasticité *f*

**elate** *vt* exciter, ravir, enthousiasmer

**elation** *n* ravissement *m*, transport *m*, enivrement *m*

**elbow** *n* coude *m*; **at one's** ~ à portée de la main; **out at the** ~s déguenillé; *vt* coudoyer; pousser du coude; frayer à coups de coude; ~ **one's way through** se frayer un passage à travers; *vi* jouer des coudes

**elbow-grease** *n* huile *f* de coude, travail *m* physique

**elbow-room** *n* espace *m*; **have** ~ avoir les coudées franches

¹**elder** *n* aîné -e; supérieur *m*; *adj* plus âgé, aîné; plus ancien -ienne; ~ **states-man** ancien ministre qu'on consulte toujours

²**elder** *n bot* sureau *m*

**elderly** *adj* mûr; vieux (*f* vieille)

**eldest** *adj* aîné, le plus âgé

**elect** *n* élu -e; *adj* élu; *vt* élire; (choose) choisir

**election** *n* élection *f*

**electioneer** *vi* faire une campagne élec-torale, faire de la propagande élec-torale

**electioneering** *n* campagne électorale, propagande électorale

**elective** *adj* électif -ive

**elector** *n* électeur -trice

**electoral** *adj* électoral

**electorate** *n* corps électoral; (consti-tuency) circonscription électorale

**electric** *adj* électrique; *fig* chargé d'émo-tion; ~ **blue** bleu *m* métallique; *zool* ~ **eel** gymnote *m*; ~ **field** champ *m* électrique; ~ **shock** décharge *f* élec-trique

**electrical** *adj* électrique

**electrician** *n* électricien *m*

**electricity** *n* électricité *f*

**electrification** *n* électrification *f*; (charge) électrisation *f*

**electrify** *vt* électrifier, électriser; *fig* éton-ner, exciter, électriser

**electrocardiogram** *n med* électrocardio-gramme *m*

**electrocute** *vt* électrocuter

**electrocution** *n* électrocution *f*

**electrode** *n* électrode *f*

**electrolysis** *n* électrolyse *f*

459

**electromagnet** n électro-aimant m
**electromagnetic** adj électromagnétique
**electromagnetism** n électromagnétisme m
**electron** n électron m; ~ **microscope** microscope m électronique
**electronic** adj électronique
**electronics** npl électronique f
**electroplate** n plaqué m; vt plaquer par électrolyse
**electroscope** n électroscope m
**electrostatic** adj électrostatique
**electrotherapy** n électrothérapie f
**elegance** n élégance f
**elegant** adj élégant
**elegiac, elegical** adj élégiaque
**elegy** n élégie f
**element** n élément m; elect résistance f; ~**s** éléments mpl, rudiments mpl; eccles espèces fpl
**elemental** adj des éléments; primordial, fondamental, simple
**elementary** adj élémentaire, rudimentaire; ar ~ **school** école primaire
**elephant** n éléphant m; fig **white** ~ rossignol m
**elephantiasis** n med éléphantiasis f
**elephantine** adj éléphantin, très lourd
**elevate** vt élever, hausser; (rank, morals) élever; exalter
**elevation** n élévation f, érection f; promotion f, dignité f, noblesse f; éloquence f; exaltation f; geog altitude f
**elevator** n monte-charge m invar, élévateur m; US ascenseur m
**eleven** n onze m invar; sp équipe f de onze personnes; adj onze invar
**elevenses** npl coll snack m vers onze heures du matin
**eleventh** n onzième; (date) onze m; adj onzième; ~ **hour** dernière minute
**elf** n elfe m, génie m; fig jeune enfant grêle
**elfin** adj féerique
**elfish** adj féerique; espiègle
**elicit** vt dévoiler, (draw out) arracher, tirer; (facts) tirer au clair
**elide** vt gramm élider
**eligibility** n éligibilité f
**eligible** adj éligible; ~ **man** bon parti
**eliminate** vt éliminer
**elimination** n élimination f
**elision** n gramm élision f
**élite** n élite f
**elixir** n élixir m
**Elizabethan** n Élisabéthain -e; adj élisabéthain
**elk** n zool élan m
**ell** n ar aune f
**ellipse** n geom ellipse f
**ellipsis** n gramm ellipse f
**elliptic, elliptical** adj elliptique

**elm** n orme m
**elocution** n diction f; élocution f
**elocutionist** n diseur -euse; professeur m de diction
**elongate** vt allonger; vi s'allonger
**elongation** n élongation f, allongement m
**elope** vi partir avec un amant (une amante)
**elopement** n fugue amoureuse
**eloquence** n éloquence f
**eloquent** adj éloquent
**else** adv autre, d'autre; **anywhere** ~ ailleurs; **everything** ~ tout autre chose; **or** ~ autrement, sinon; **what** ~? quoi d'autre?; **who** ~? qui d'autre?
**elsewhere** adv ailleurs, autre part
**elucidate** vt élucider
**elucidation** n élucidation f
**elude** vt éluder; éviter, esquiver
**elusive, elusory** adj évasif -ive; difficile à saisir; difficile à comprendre
**Elysian** adj élyséen -éenne; ~ **fields** Champs-Élysées mpl
**Elysium** n Élysée m
**emaciate** vt amaigrir, émacier; creuser; vi s'émacier
**emaciation** n émaciation f
**emanate** vi émaner
**emanation** n émanation f
**emancipate** vt émanciper, affranchir, libérer
**emancipated** adj libéré, émancipé; coll émancipé, affranchi
**emancipation** n émancipation f, libération f
**emancipator** n libérateur -trice
**emasculate** vt émasculer
**emasculation** n émasculation f
**embalm** vt embaumer; fig conserver pieusement le souvenir de; parfumer
**embankment** n (river) digue f; (road, railway) remblai m
**embargo** n embargo m; **under an** ~ sous séquestre; vt mettre l'embargo sur
**embark** vt embarquer; vi s'embarquer
**embarkation** n embarquement m
**embarrass** vt embarrasser, gêner; (disconcert) décontenancer; fig (financial) mettre en difficulté
**embarrassment** n embarras m; difficulté f, anicroche f
**embassy** n ambassade f
**embattle** vt ranger en bataille
**embed** vt fixer; mech emboîter, encastrer
**embellish** vt embellir
**embellishment** n embellissement m
**ember** n tison m, braise f
**embezzle** vt détourner
**embezzlement** n détournement m de fonds

**embitter** vt (quarrel) envenimer, aggraver; (person) aigrir
**emblazon** vt blasonner
**emblem** n emblème m; her devise f
**emblematic** adj emblématique
**embodiment** n incorporation f, incarnation f
**embody** vt incorporer, incarner
**embolden** vt enhardir
**embolism** n med embolisme m
**emboss** vt (leather) gaufrer; (metal) bosseler, estamper
**embossment** n (leather) gaufrage m; (metal) bosselage m
**embrace** n embrassement m, étreinte f; vt embrasser, étreindre; (comprise) embrasser, englober, contenir; (perceive) saisir; (adopt) adopter
**embrasure** n embrasure f
**embrocation** n embrocation f
**embroider** vt broder; fig enjoliver
**embroidery** n broderie f; fig enjolivement m
**embroil** vt (affairs) embrouiller; (person) brouiller
**embroilment** n (confusion) embrouillement m; (discord) brouille f
**embryo** n embryon m; adj embryonnaire
**embryology** n embryologie f
**embryonic** adj embryonnaire
**embus** vt mil faire monter en car; vi monter en car
**emend** vt corriger
**emendation** n correction f
**emerald** n émeraude f; adj émeraude invar
**emerge** vi émerger, surgir, sortir; (appear) apparaître, se faire jour
**emergence** n émergence f
**emergency** n état m d'urgence, crise f, situation f critique; in case of ~ en cas d'urgence; rise to the ~ être à la hauteur des circonstances; adj d'urgence; de secours; (temporary) de fortune, provisoire; ~ exit sortie f de secours
**emeritus** adj émérite, honoraire
**emersion** n émersion f
**emery** n émeri m; ~ board lime f en carton; ~ cloth toile f émeri; ~ paper papier m d'émeri
**emetic** n émétique m; adj émétique
**emigrant** n émigrant -e
**emigrate** vi émigrer
**emigration** n émigration f; (persons) émigrants mpl, émigrantes fpl
**émigré** n Fr hist émigré -e
**eminence, eminency** n éminence f; (ground) élévation f; (position) grandeur f; anat saillie f
**eminent** adj éminent
**emir** n émir m

**emissary** n émissaire m
**emission** n émission f
**emit** vt émettre; (fumes) dégager; (smell) exhaler; (water) décharger
**emollient** n émollient m; adj émollient
**emolument** n traitement m, émoluments mpl, appointements mpl
**emote** vi coll s'épancher excessivement
**emotion** n émotion f, émoi m
**emotional** adj émotif -ive; émotionnable, impressionnable; psych émotionnel -elle
**emotionalism** n émotivité f, impressionnabilité f; pej sensiblerie f
**emotionalize** vt traiter avec (un excès d')émotion
**emotive** adj émotif -ive, émouvant
**empanel, impanel** vt leg - a jury dresser la liste des jurés; inscrire sur la liste des jurés
**empathy** n psych intuition f psychologique; coll état m d'être sur la même longueur d'ondes,. communion f d'idées
**emperor** n empereur m; ent paon m de nuit; ~ penguin manchot m empereur
**emphasis** n force f, intensité f; gramm accent m, accentuation f; fig importance f, poids m
**emphasize** vt mettre en valeur, souligner; gramm accentuer
**emphatic** adj catégorique, formel -elle; gramm accentué
**empire** n empire m; adj empire invar
**empiric** n med empirique m; adj empirique
**empirical** adj empirique
**empiricism** n empirisme m
**empiricist** n + adj empiriste
**emplacement** n position f; mil emplacement m
**employ** n emploi m, service m; vt employer, utiliser, faire usage de
**employable** adj utilisable, employable
**employee** n employé -e
**employer** n employeur -euse, patron -onne; ~'s union syndicat patronal
**employment** n emploi m, travail m, occupation f
**emporium** n grand magasin; centre commercial
**empower** vt autoriser; rendre capable; leg nantir d'un pouvoir, habiliter
**empress** n impératrice f
**emptiness** n vide m, néant m
**empty** n coll (bottle) bouteille f vide; (case) caisse f vide; adj vide; vt vider; vi se vider
**empty-handed** adj les mains vides, bredouille
**empty-headed** adj à la tête creuse, sans cervelle

**empyrean** *n* empyrée *m*

**emu** *n* orni émeu *m*, émou *m*

**emulate** *vt* être l'émule de, rivaliser avec, tenter d'égaler

**emulation** *n* émulation *f*

**emulator** *n* émule

**emulous** *adj* plein d'émulation, rivalisant; ambitieux -ieuse

**emulsifier** *n* (apparatus) émulseur *m*; (substance) émulsifiant *m*

**emulsify** *vt* émulsionner

**emulsion** *n* émulsion *f*

**enable** *vt* rendre capable, mettre à même, permettre; *leg* habiliter

**enabling** *adj leg* habilitant

**enact** *vt* décréter; *leg* promulguer; (perform) accomplir; *theat* représenter

**enactment** *n* décret *m*; *leg* promulgation *f*

**enamel** *n* émail *m*; vernis *m*; (paint) peinture laquée, ripolin *m*; *adj* émaillé, vernissé; *vt* émailler, vernisser

**enamelling** *n* émaillage *m*, vernissage *m*

**enamour** *vt* enamourer, captiver; **be ~ed of** être épris de

**encamp** *vt mil* mettre dans un camp; *vi* camper, dresser des tentes

**encampment** *n* campement *m*

**encase** *vt* encaisser, enfermer; (box) mettre dans un étui; (machinery) blinder

**encash** *vt* encaisser

**encashment** *n* encaissement *m*

**encaustic** *n* encaustique *f*; *adj* encaustique

**encephalic** *adj* encéphalique

**encephalitis** *n* encéphalite *f*

**enchain** *vt* enchaîner; *fig* captiver

**enchant** *vt* enchanter; *fig* captiver, enchanter

**enchanter** *n* enchanteur *m*, enchanteresse *f*; magicien -ienne

**enchanting** *adj* enchanteur (*f* enchanteresse); charmant

**enchantment** *n* enchantement *m*

**enchantress** *n* enchanteresse *f*; sorcière *f*

**enchase** *vt* enchâsser

**encircle** *vt* encercler

**encirclement** *n* encerclement *m*

**enclave** *n* enclave *f*

**enclitic** *n gramm* enclitique *m*

**enclose, inclose** *vt* enclore, enfermer; (surround) entourer; (put inside) inclure, joindre; **~d** sous ce pli, ci-joint

**enclosure, inclosure** *n* (act) clôture *f*; (space) enclos *m*, enceinte *f*; (fence) clôture *f*; (in letter) pièce jointe

**encomium** *n* panégyrique *m*

**encompass** *vt* encercler, entourer, contenir

**encore** *n theat* bis *m*; *vt* bisser; *interj* bis!

**encounter** *n* rencontre *f*; *mil* combat *m*; *vt* rencontrer, rencontrer par hasard, tomber sur

**encourage** *vt* encourager, aider, soutenir; (urge) pousser, stimuler

**encouragement** *n* encouragement *m*

**encouraging** *adj* encourageant

**encroach** *vi* empiéter; **~ on** empiéter sur

**encrust, incrust** *vt* encroûter, incruster

**encrustation, incrustation** *n* incrustation *f*, encroûtement *m*

**encumber** *vt* encombrer, gêner, obstruer; *leg* grever

**encumbrance** *n* encombrement *m*, gêne *f*; *leg* charge *f*

**encyclical, encyclic** *n eccles* encyclique *f*; *adj* encyclique

**encyclop(a)edia** *n* encyclopédie *f*

**encyclop(a)edic** *adj* encyclopédique

**encyclop(a)edist** *n* encyclopédiste *m*

**end** *n* fin *f*, bout *m*; limite *f*; conclusion *f*, terme *m*; (death) mort *f*; (purpose) but *m*, intention *f*; **at a loose ~** désœuvré; **be at an ~** être terminé; **bring to an ~** achever, terminer; **come to an ~** s'achever, se terminer; **get hold of the wrong ~ of the stick** comprendre de travers; **go off the deep ~** s'emporter, se mettre en colère; **keep one's ~ up** tenir bon; **latter ~** (old age) vieillesse *f*; (death) mort *f*; **make an ~ of** mettre fin à; **make ~s meet** joindre les deux bouts; **coll no ~** extrêmement, à n'en plus finir, à gogo; **no ~ of** un tas de; **on ~** debout; (without stopping) de suite; **there's no ~ to it** cela n'en finit plus; **with that ~ in view** dans ce but; *vt* finir, terminer, achever; *vi* finir, se terminer, prendre fin; mourir

**end-all** *n* fin *f* de tout; but final

**endanger** *vt* mettre en péril, exposer au danger

**endear** *vt* rendre cher (*f* chère); **~ one-self to** se faire aimer de

**endearing** *adj* attachant

**endearment** *n* affection *f*, caresse *f*; **~s** (words) paroles *fpl* tendres

**endeavour** *n* effort *m*, tentative *f*; *vi* essayer, tâcher, s'efforcer

**endemic** *adj* endémique

**end-game** *n* fin *f* de partie

**ending** *n* fin *f*, conclusion *f*; *gramm* désinence *f*, terminaison *f*; **happy ~** dénouement heureux

**endive** *n* (straight) endive *f*; (curly) chicorée *f*

**endless** *adj* sans fin, infini; continuel -elle, incessant; (too long) interminable

**endocardium** *n anat* endocarde *m*

**endocrine** *n anat* glande *f* endocrine; *adj* endocrine

**endorse, indorse** *vt* (cheque) endosser; *fig* soutenir, approuver; (passport) viser; *mot* **~ a driving licence** (in England) inscrire les détails d'un délit au verso d'un permis de conduire

**endorsee, indorsee** *n* endossataire

**endorsement, indorsement** *n* endos *m*, aval *m*; *fig* soutien *m*, appui *m*; *mot* (in England) contravention portée sur un permis de conduire

**endow** *vt* faire une dotation à; *fig* douer, pourvoir

**endowment** *n* dotation *f*; *fig* don *m*, qualité *f*

**endpapers** *npl* feuilles *fpl* de garde

**end-product** *n* résultat final

**endue** *vt* douer, investir

**endurable** *adj* endurable, supportable

**endurance** *n* endurance *f*, résistance *f*

**endure** *vt* endurer, souffrir, subir; supporter; *vi* (last) durer; (hold out) endurer

**enduring** *adj* durable; éternel -elle

**endways, endwise** *adv* debout

**enema** *n* lavement *m*, clystère *m*

**enemy** *n* ennemi -e; *adj* ennemi

**energetic** *adj* énergique, vigoureux -euse

**energize** *vt* stimuler, donner de l'énergie à

**energy** *n* énergie *f*, force *f*, vigueur *f*, fermeté *f*; *adj* énergétique

**enervate** *vt* abattre, amollir, affaiblir

**enervation** *n* amollissement *m*, affaiblissement *m*

**enfeeble** *vt* affaiblir

**enfilade** *n* *mil* tir *m* d'enfilade; *vt* prendre en enfilade

**enfold** *vt* enrouler, envelopper; embrasser

**enforce** *vt* imposer par la force; (law) faire respecter, appliquer

**enforcement** *n* contrainte *f*; (law) application *f*

**enfranchise** *vt* donner le droit de vote à; (slave) affranchir; (landed property) affranchir

**enfranchisement** *n* octroi *m* du droit de vote; affranchissement *m*

**engage** *vt* engager; (reserve) louer, retenir; (betroth) fiancer; (employ) embaucher, employer; (attract) attirer, séduire; *mil* attaquer, engager le combat contre; *mech* engager; *vi* s'engager; (pledge) promettre; *mech* s'engager, s'embrayer

**engaged** *adj* (betrothed) fiancé; (telephone, lavatory, etc) occupé; (employee) embauché

**engagement** *n* engagement *m*; (betrothal) fiançailles *fpl*; (appointment) engagement *m*, rendez-vous *m*; *mil* engagement *m*, bataille *f*; *mech* embrayage *m*, engrenage *m*

**engaging** *adj* attirant, engageant, charmant

**engender** *vt* engendrer, produire

**engine** *n* machine *f*; *mot* moteur *m*; (railway) locomotive *f*; *mil hist* engin *m*

**engine-driver** *n* mécanicien *m*

**engineer** *n* ingénieur *m*; *mil* officier *m* du génie, soldat *m* du génie; *rad sound ~* ingénieur *m* du son; *vt* construire; exécuter; *pej* manigancer

**engineering** *n* ingénierie *f*, génie *m*; *fig pej* machinations *fpl*; **civil ~** génie civil; **military ~** génie *m* militaire; **production ~** technique *f* de la production

**engine-room** *n* salle *f* des machines

**English** *n* (language) anglais *m*; (people) Anglais *mpl*; *adj* anglais; *vt* traduire en anglais; angliciser

**Englishism** *n* anglicisme *m*

**Englishman** *n* Anglais *m*

**Englishwoman** *n* Anglaise *f*

**engorge** *vt* engloutir, dévorer

**engraft** *vt* greffer; *fig* implanter

**engrain** *vt* teindre

**engrained** *adj see* ingrained

**engrave** *vt* graver

**engraver** *n* graveur *m*

**engraving** *n* gravure *f*

**engross** *vt* absorber, accaparer; *leg* grossoyer

**engrossing** *adj* absorbant, passionnant

**engrossment** *n* accaparement *m*; *leg* grosse *f*

**engulf** *vt* engouffrer

**enhance** *vt* rehausser, intensifier, relever

**enhancement** *n* rehaussement *m*

**enigma** *n* énigme *f*

**enigmatic, enigmatical** *adj* énigmatique

**enjambment** *n pros* enjambement *m*

**enjoin** *vt* ordonner à, enjoindre à

**enjoy** *vt* prendre plaisir à, jouir de, aimer; (have use of) jouir de, posséder; **~ oneself** s'amuser, prendre du plaisir

**enjoyable** *adj* agréable

**enjoyment** *n* plaisir *m*, agrément *m*; *leg* possession *f*, jouissance *f*

**enkindle** *vt* allumer; *fig* enflammer

**enlace** *vt* enlacer

**enlarge** *vt* agrandir, développer; *phot* agrandir; *vi* s'agrandir; **~ upon** développer, s'étendre sur

**enlargement** *n* agrandissement *m*; accroissement *m*

**enlarger** *n phot* agrandisseur *m*

**enlighten** *vt* éclairer, édifier

**enlightenment** *n* lumières *fpl*, édification *f*; *lit hist* **the Enlightenment** le Siècle des lumières

**enlist** *vt mil* enrôler; *fig* gagner, obtenir; *vi* s'enrôler

**enlistment** *n* enrôlement *m*

**enliven** *vt* animer, stimuler

**enmesh** *vt* prendre au filet; *fig* enchevêtrer, embrouiller

**enmity** *n* inimitié *f*, hostilité *f*

**ennoble** vt anoblir; *fig* ennoblir, élever
**ennoblement** n anoblissement m; *fig* ennoblissement m
**ennui** n ennui m
**enormity** n monstruosité f; atrocité f; (size) énormité f
**enormous** adj énorme, immense
**enough** n suffisance f; adj assez de, suffisant; adv assez, suffisamment; *interj* assez!, en voilà assez!, ça suffit!
**enounce** vt prononcer; proclamer
**enquire** vt + vi *see* inquire
**enquiry** n *see* inquiry
**enrage** vt enrager, rendre furieux -ieuse
**enrapture** vt ravir, enchanter
**enrich** vt enrichir; (soil) fertiliser
**enrichment** n enrichissement m
**enrol** vt porter sur une liste, enrôler
**enrolment** n inscription f sur une liste, enrôlement m
**ensconce** vt placer, mettre en sûreté; ~ oneself bien s'installer
**ensemble** n ensemble m
**enshrine** vt *eccles* enchâsser; *fig* révérer
**enshrinement** n *eccles* enchâssement m
**enshroud** vt ensevelir (dans un linceul); (conceal) cacher; (veil) voiler
**ensign** n (badge) insigne m; *naut* pavillon m; *ar mil* enseigne m; *US naut* enseigne m de vaisseau
**enslave** vt réduire en esclavage, asservir
**enslavement** n asservissement m
**ensnare** vt prendre au piège, piéger
**ensue** vi résulter, s'ensuivre
**ensure** vt assurer, rendre certain
**entablature** n *archi* entablement m
**entail** n *leg* substitution f d'héritiers; *leg* bien substitué; vt entraîner, occasionner; *leg* substituer
**entangle** vt enchevêtrer, embrouiller; *fig* compliquer
**entanglement** n enchevêtrement m, embrouillement m; *mil* réseau m de barbelés; *fig* complication f
**entente** n entente f
**enter** vt entrer dans, pénétrer (dans); (join) s'inscrire à, s'enrôler à; (name, etc) inscrire; *leg* intenter; (cargo) déclarer; (protest) formuler; vi entrer, pénétrer; *theat* entrer en scène; ~ for s'inscrire pour; ~ into prendre part à, participer à; (start) entamer; ~ upon commencer, entreprendre; prendre possession de
**enteric** adj intestinal
**enteritis** n entérite f
**enterprise** n entreprise f; esprit m d'entreprise
**enterprising** adj entreprenant, aventureux -euse
**entertain** vt divertir, amuser; (guest) recevoir; (idea) considérer; (doubt,

hope) nourrir; vi recevoir, donner une réception
**entertainer** n amuseur m, diseur -euse, comique m
**entertaining** adj divertissant, amusant
**entertainment** n réception f; hospitalité f; (amusement) divertissement m, distraction f; *theat* spectacle m
**enthral, enthrall** vt captiver, fasciner; *ar* asservir
**enthralling** adj captivant, fascinant
**enthrone** vt *eccles* introniser; (king) placer sur le trône
**enthuse** vi *coll* s'enthousiasmer
**enthusiasm** n enthousiasme m
**enthusiast** n enthousiaste, fervent -e
**enthusiastic** adj enthousiaste, fervent
**entice** vt tenter, séduire; (attract) attirer
**enticement** n attrait m; tentation f
**enticing** adj attirant, alléchant, séduisant
**entire** adj entier -ière, complet -ète
**entirety** n entièreté f, totalité f
**entitle** vt intituler; donner droit à
**entity** n entité f
**entomb** vt enterrer; *fig* ensevelir
**entomological** adj entomologique
**entomologist** n entomologiste
**entomology** n entomologie f
**entourage** n entourage m
**entr'acte** n *theat* entracte m
**entrails** npl intestins mpl; *lit fig* entrailles fpl
**entrain** vt mettre dans un train; *mil* faire monter dans un train; emporter; vi monter dans un train
**entrance** n entrée f; ~ fee prix m d'entrée; tradesman's ~ entrée f de service
**entrance** vt ravir, transporter
**entrancement** n ravissement m
**entrancing** adj ravissant
**entrant** n *sp* participant -e; (examination) candidat -e
**entrap** vt prendre au piège
**entreat** vt supplier, conjurer
**entreaty** n supplication f
**entrechat** n entrechat m
**entrée** n entrée f
**entremets** n *cul* entremets m
**entrench** vt *mil ar* retrancher; *fig* ~ oneself s'établir; se défendre
**entrenchment** n retranchement m
**entrepot** n entrepôt m
**entrepreneur** n entrepreneur m
**entrepreneurial** adj d'entrepreneur
**entrust** vt (person) charger; (thing) confier
**entry** n entrée f; (list) inscription f; *leg* entrée f en possession, jouissance f; double ~ partie f double; no ~ entrée interdite; single ~ partie f simple

entwine *vt* enlacer, entrelacer; *vi* s'entre-lacer
enumerate *vt* énumérer
enumeration *n* énumération *f*
enunciate *vt* énoncer, articuler; pro-clamer, formuler
enunciation *n* énonciation *f*, articula-tion *f*; proclamation *f*
enuresis *n* énurésie *f*
envelop *vt* envelopper
envelope *n* enveloppe *f*
envelopment *n* enveloppement *m*; (wrapper) enveloppe *f*
envenom *vt* envenimer, empoisonner; (embitter) aigrir
enviable *adj* enviable
envious *adj* envieux -ieuse, jaloux -ouse
environ *vt* environner, entourer
environment *n* environnement *m*; milieu *m*
environmental *adj* écologique; environ-nemental
environs *npl* alentours *mpl*, environs *mpl*
envisage *vt* envisager, considérer
envoy *n poet* envoi *m*; émissaire *m*, plénipotentiaire *m*
envy *n* envie *f*; *vt* envier
enwrap *vt* envelopper
enzyme *n* enzyme *f*
eon *n* éon *m*
epaulet, epaulette *n mil* épaulette *f*
epergne *n* milieu *m* de table, surtout *m*
ephemera *n ent* éphémère *m*
ephemeral *adj* éphémère
epic *n* épopée *f*, poème *m* épique; *adj* épique
epicene *n* hermaphrodite *m*; *adj* herma-phrodite; *gramm* épicène
epicentre *n* épicentre *m*
epicure *n* gourmet *m*; épicurien -ienne
epicurean *n* + *adj* épicurien -ienne
epicureanism *n* épicurisme *m*
epicycle *n* épicycle *m*
epidemic *n* épidémie *f*; *adj* épidémique
epidermal *adj* épidermique
epidermis *n* épiderme *m*
epidiascope *n* épidiascope *m*
epiglottis *n anat* épiglotte *f*
epigram *n* épigramme *m*
epigrammatic(al) *adj* épigrammatique
epigrammatist *n* auteur *m* d'épi-grammes
epigraph *n* épigraphe *f*
epigraphy *n* épigraphie *f*
epilepsy *n* épilepsie *f*
epileptic *n* + *adj* épileptique; ~ fit crise *f* d'épilepsie
epilogue *n* épilogue *m*
Epiphany *n eccles* Épiphanie *f*, jour *m* des Rois; epiphany *fig* moment tran-scendant

episcopacy *n* épiscopat *m*
episcopal *adj* épiscopal
episcopalian *adj* épiscopalien -ienne
episcopate *n* épiscopat *m*
episode *n* épisode *m*
episodic *adj* épisodique
epistemology *n* épistémologie *f*
epistle *n* épître *f*
epistolary *adj* épistolaire
epitaph *n* épitaphe *f*
epithalamium *n* épithalame *m*
epithelium *n biol* + *bot* épithélium *m*
epithet *n* épithète *f*
epitome *n* abrégé *m*, résumé *m*
epitomize *vt* abréger, faire un résumé de
epoch *n* époque *f*
epoch-making *adj* qui fait époque; très important
eponymous *adj* éponyme
Epsom salts *npl* sulfate *m* de magnésie
equability *n* uniformité *f*; sérénité *f*
equable *adj* uniforme; serein
equal *n* égal -e; *adj* égal; (capable) à la hauteur, de force; other things being ~ toutes choses égales; *vt* égaler, être l'égal de
equality *n* égalité *f*
equalization *n* égalisation *f*
equalize *vt* égaliser; *vi sp* égaliser
equally *adv* également, au même degré
equanimity *n* équanimité *f*, égalité *f* d'âme
equate *vt* égaler, donner comme équiva-lent; *math* mettre en équation
equation *n* égalisation *f*; *math* + *chem* + *astron* équation *f*
equator *n* équateur *m*
equatorial *adj* équatorial
equerry *n* officier *m* de la maison du roi; *ar* écuyer *m*
equestrian *n* cavalier -ière; *adj* équestre
equidistant *adj* équidistant
equilateral *n geom* figure équilatérale; *adj geom* équilatéral
equilibrate *vt* équilibrer; *vi* s'équilibrer
equilibration *n* équilibrage *m*
equilibrist *n* équilibriste
equilibrium *n* équilibre *m*, aplomb *m*
equine *adj* équin
equinoctial *adj* équinoxial, d'équinoxe
equinox *n* équinoxe *m*
equip *vt* équiper
equipment *n* équipement *m*, matériel *m*; (action) équipement *m*, aménage-ment *m*; (tools) outillage *m*; *naut* armement *m*
equipoise *n* équilibre *m*; (object) contre-poids *m*
equitable *adj* équitable
equitation *n* équitation *f*
equity *n* équité *f*; *comm* equities actions *fpl* ordinaires

**equivalence** *n* équivalence *f*

**equivalent** *adj* équivalent

**equivocal** *adj* équivoque, ambigu -uë, douteux -euse; (conduct) louche

**equivocate** *vi* équivoquer, biaiser

**equivocation** *n* ambiguïté *f*, faux-fuyant *m*

**equivocator** *n* ergoteur -euse

**era** *n* ère *f*

**eradicate** *vt* déraciner, extirper; (destroy) supprimer, détruire

**eradication** *n* éradication *f*; extirpation *f*

**erase** *vt* effacer, raturer, gommer

**eraser** *n* gomme *f*

**erasure** *n* rature *f*

**ere** *prep* + *adv poet* avant; *conj* avant que

**erect** *adj* droit, debout, dressé; *vt* dresser, mettre debout; *archi* ériger, construire; *math* élever

**erectile** *adj* érectile

**erection** *n* érection *f*; (building) bâtiment *m*

**erector** *n mech* ajusteur-monteur *m* (*pl* ajusteurs-monteurs); *anat* muscle érecteur

**erg** *n* erg *m*

**ergonomics** *npl* ergonomie *f*

**ergot** *n bot* ergot *m*

**ermine** *n* hermine *f*

**erode** *vt* éroder; corroder

**erosion** *n* érosion *f*

**erotic** *adj* érotique

**erotica** *npl* littérature *f* érotique

**eroticism** *n* érotisme *m*

**err** *vi* errer, se tromper; (sin) pécher

**errand** *n* course *f*, commission *f*

**errand-boy** *n* garçon *m* de courses

**errant** *adj* errant

**erratic** *adj* (odd) fantasque, excentrique, original; (results, performance) irrégulier -ière; *geol* + *med* erratique

**erratum** *n* (*pl* **errata**) erratum *m* (*pl* errata)

**erroneous** *adj* erroné, incorrect

**error** *n* erreur *f*, méprise *f*; opinion fausse; (sin) errement *m*, faute *f*; **in ~** par méprise; **printer's ~** coquille *f*; **see the ~ of one's ways** revenir de ses erreurs

**ersatz** *n* ersatz *m*

**Erse** *n* erse *m*, gaélique *m*

**erstwhile** *adj ar* d'autrefois; *adv ar* autrefois, jadis

**erubescence** *n* érubescence *f*

**erubescent** *adj* érubescent

**eruct, eructate** *vi* éructer

**eructation** *n* éructation *f*

**erudite** *adj* érudit

**erudition** *n* érudition *f*

**erupt** *vi* (volcano) faire éruption; *fig* se déchaîner; (teeth) percer

**eruption** *n* (volcano) éruption *f*; *fig* explosion *f*; (teeth) percée *f*; *med* éruption *f*

**eruptive** *adj* éruptif -ive

**erysipelas** *n med* érysipèle *m*

**escalade** *vt* escalader

**escalate** *vt* augmenter; intensifier; *vi* faire escalade; augmenter

**escalation** *n* escalade *f*

**escalator** *n* escalier roulant, escalier *m* mécanique

**escapade** *n* escapade *f*

**escape** *n* évasion *f*, action *f* d'échapper, fuite *f*; (leak) fuite *f*, échappement *m*; (pipe) tuyau *m* d'échappement; *leg* **~ clause** échappatoire *f*; *vt* échapper à, fuir; *vi* s'échapper, s'enfuir, s'évader; (leak) s'échapper, fuir

**escapee** *n* évadé -e

**escapement** *n mech* échappement *m*

**escapism** *n fig* évasion *f*

**escapist** *n* personne *f* qui fuit la réalité; *adj* d'évasion

**escarpment** *n* escarpement *m*

**eschatology** *n theol* eschatologie *f*

**eschew** *vt* éviter, se détourner de

**escort** *n* escorte *f*; (male companion) cavalier *m*; *vt* escorter, accompagner

**escritoire** *n* secrétaire *m*

**escutcheon** *n her* + *naut* écusson *m*; **blot on one's ~** tache *f* sur son nom

**Eskimo** *n* Esquimau -aude; *adj* esquimau -aude

**esoteric** *adj* ésotérique

**espalier** *n* espalier *m*

**esparto** *n* spart(e) *m*, alfa *m*

**especial** *adj* spécial, particulier -ière

**especially** *adv* en particulier; (very) très, fort, spécialement

**Esperantist** *n* + *adj* espérantiste

**Esperanto** *n* espéranto *m*

**espionage** *n* espionnage *m*

**esplanade** *n* esplanade *f*, promenade *f*

**espousal** *n* épousailles *fpl*; *fig* ralliement *m*

**espouse** *vt* épouser; *fig* adopter, se rallier à

**espresso** *n* (café *m*) express *m*

**espy** *vt* discerner, apercevoir

**Esquire** *n* (*abbr* **Esq.**) (après le nom de famille sur une adresse) = Monsieur

**essay** *n* dissertation *f*, rédaction *f*, composition *f*; (attempt) essai *m*, tentative *f*; *vt* essayer; éprouver, mettre à l'essai

**essayist** *n* essayiste

**essence** *n* essence *f*

**essential** *n* essentiel *m*; *adj* essentiel -ielle

**essentially** *adv* essentiellement, au fond

**establish** *vt* établir, fonder, installer; *fig* établir, prouver, démontrer, faire reconnaître

**establishment** *n* établissement *m*, fondation *f*; institution *f*; *fig* établissement *m*, démonstration *f*; *coll pej* **the Establishment** l'establishment *m*, les gens *mpl* en place

**estate** *n* (land) propriété *f*, domaine *m*; (rank) état *m*; *leg* (possessions) biens *mpl*; *coll* **the fourth** ~ la presse; **man's** ~ l'âge *m* d'homme; **real** ~ propriété foncière; *hist* **the Third Estate** le Tiers État

**estate-agency** *n* agence immobilière

**estate-agent** *n* agent immobilier

**estate-car** *n* break *m*

**esteem** *n* estime *f*; *vt* estimer, priser, considérer

**ester** *n chem* ester *m*

**esthete** *n see* **aesthete**

**esthetic** *adj see* **aesthetic**

**estimable** *adj* estimable, respectable

**estimate** *n* estimation *f*, évaluation *f*; *comm* devis *m*; *pol* ~s crédits *mpl* budgétaires, budget *m*; *vt* estimer, évaluer; calculer; *fig* estimer, jauger

**estimation** *n* estimation *f*; (opinion) avis *m*, jugement *m*; (esteem) estime *f*

**estrange** *vt* s'aliéner l'estime (l'affection) de; détourner; **they have become** ~**d** ils sont brouillés

**estrangement** *n* désaffection *f*, éloignement *m*, brouille *f*

**estuary** *n* estuaire *m*

**etcetera** *n* (*abbr* etc) et caetera (cetera) *m invar*; ~**s** extras *mpl*

**etch** *vt* graver

**etching** *n* gravure *f*

**eternal** *adj* éternel -elle, sans fin; (without change) éternel -elle, immuable; (endless) éternel -elle, incessant; **Eternal City** = Rome *f*; ~ **triangle** ménage *m* à trois

**eternalize** *vt* éterniser; rendre immortel -elle

**eternity** *n* éternité *f*

**ethane** *n chem* éthane *m*

**ether** *n chem* + *phys* éther *m*; *fig ar* ciel *m* (*pl* cieux)

**ethereal** *adj* éthéré, céleste, léger -ère; *chem* éthéré

**etherealize** *vt* rendre éthéré, spiritualiser

**etherize** *vt* éthériser

**ethic** *n* éthique *f*, morale *f*; *adj* éthique

**ethical** *adj* éthique, moral

**ethics** *npl* éthique *f*

**Ethiopian** *n* Ethiopien -ienne; *adj* éthiopien -ienne

**ethnic(al)** *adj* ethnique

**ethnographer** *n* ethnographe

**ethnographic** *adj* ethnographique

**ethnography** *n* ethnographie *f*

**ethnological** *adj* ethnologique

**ethnologist** *n* ethnologue

**ethnology** *n* ethnologie *f*

**ethology** *n* éthologie *f*

**ethos** *n* caractéristiques morales (d'un groupe, d'une société)

**ethyl** *n chem* éthyle *m*

**ethylene** *n chem* éthylène *m*

**etiolate** *vt* étioler

**etiology** *n* étiologie *f*

**etiquette** *n* étiquette *f*, protocole *m*; bonnes manières; **medical** ~ déontologie médicale

**Eton crop** *n phr* coiffure *f* à la garçonne

**etymological** *adj* étymologique

**etymologize** *vi* étudier l'étymologie; proposer une étymologie

**etymology** *n* étymologie *f*

**etymon** *n* étymon *m*

**eucalyptus** *n* eucalyptus *m*

**Eucharist** *n* Eucharistie *f*

**Euclidean** *adj* euclidien -ienne

**eugenic** *adj* eugénique

**eugenics** *npl* eugénique *f*

**eugenist** *n* eugéniste

**eulogist** *n* panégyriste

**eulogistic** *adj* laudatif -ive

**eulogize** *vt* louer hautement, exalter

**eulogy** *n* panégyrique *m*

**eunuch** *n* eunuque *m*

**euphemism** *n* euphémisme *m*

**euphemistic** *adj* euphémique

**euphemize** *vt* exprimer par un euphémisme; *vi* se servir d'euphémismes

**euphonious** *adj* euphonique

**euphonium** *n* saxhorn *m*

**euphony** *n* euphonie *f*

**euphorbia** *n bot* euphorbe *f*

**euphoria** *n* euphorie *f*

**euphoric** *adj* euphorique

**euphuism** *n* euphuisme *m*

**Eurasia** *n* Eurasie *f*

**Eurasian** *n* Eurasien -ienne; *adj* eurasien -ienne

**eurhythmics** *npl* gymnastique *f* rythmique

**Europe** *n* Europe *f*

**European** *n* Européen -éenne; *adj* européen -éenne

**Eurovision** *n* Eurovision *f*; **on** ~ en Eurovision

**Eustachian** *adj anat* ~ **tube** trompe *f* d'Eustache

**euthanasia** *n* euthanasie *f*

**evacuate** *vt* évacuer

**evacuation** *n* évacuation *f*

**evacuee** *n* évacué -e

**evade** *vt* éviter, éluder, échapper à

**evaluate** *vt* évaluer

**evaluation** *n* évaluation *f*

**evanesce** *vi* disparaître

**evanescence** *n* évanescence *f*

**evanescent** *adj* évanescent

**evangelic, evangelical** *adj* évangélique

**evangelical** *n* protestant -e évangélique

**evangelism** *n* évangélisme *m*

**evangelist** *n* évangéliste *m*

**evangelize** *vt* évangéliser

**evaporate** *vt* évaporer, faire évaporer; *vi* s'évaporer; *fig* disparaître

**evaporation** *n* évaporation *f*

**evaporator** *n* évaporateur *m*

**evasion** *n* évasion *f*, dérobade *f*; (excuse) faux-fuyant *m*

**evasive** *adj* évasif -ive

**evasiveness** *n* (reply) caractère évasif

**eve** *n* veille *f*

¹**even** *n ar* soir *m*

²**even** *adj* (smooth) uni, plat; (equal) uniforme, égal; (calm) tranquille, calme, serein, équilibré; (like) semblable, identique; (right) juste, équitable; *math* pair; *adv* même; ~ **so** précisément; *vt* aplanir, unifier, égaliser

**even-handed** *adj* impartial, équitable

**evening** *n* soir *m*; soirée *f*; ~ **dress** tenue *f* de soirée; ~ **gown** robe *f* de soirée; **the** ~ **before** la veille au soir

**evenness** *n* égalité *f*, uniformité *f*

**evensong** *n eccles* = vêpres *fpl*

**event** *n* événement *m*; conséquence *f*, résultat *m*; *sp* épreuve *f*; **after the** ~ après coup; **at all** ~ **s** en tout cas; **in the** ~ **of** au cas où

**even-tempered** *adj* calme, placide, d'humeur égale

**eventful** *adj* mémorable, important; (full of incidents) mouvementé

**eventide** *n poet* soir *m*

**eventual** *adj* final; éventuel -elle

**eventuality** *n* éventualité *f*

**ever** *adv* jamais; toujours; *coll* ~ **so** très; *coll* ~ **so much** beaucoup; **for** ~ pour toujours, sans cesse; **if** ~ **there was one** s'il en fut jamais; **what** ~ **can I say?** qu'est-ce que je peux bien dire?; **when** ~ **?** quand donc?; **yours** ~ bien cordialement vôtre

**evergreen** *n* arbre toujours vert; *adj* toujours vert

**everlasting** *adj* éternel -elle, sans fin; (repeated) perpétuel -uelle, incessant

**evermore** *adv* toujours

**every** *adj* chaque, chacun de, tout; tous (*f* toutes) les; ~ **now and then de** temps en temps; ~ **other** tous (*f* toutes) les deux

**everybody** *n* chacun, tout le monde, tous

**everyday** *adj* de tous les jours; habituel -elle

**everyone** *n* chacun, tout le monde, tous

**everything** *n* tout *m*, toutes choses

**everyway** *adv* de toutes manières

**everywhere** *adv* partout

**evict** *vt leg* expulser

**eviction** *n leg* éviction *f*

**evidence** *n leg* déposition *f*, témoignage *m*, preuve *f*; (clearness) évidence *f*; (sign) marque *f*; **circumstantial** ~ preuves indirectes; **turn queen's (king's)** ~ témoigner contre un complice

**evident** *adj* évident, clair

**evidently** *adv* évidemment, manifestement

**evil** *n* mal *m*; malheur *m*, désastre *m*; *adj* mauvais, méchant; (causing harm) néfaste, nuisible; **the Evil One** le Malin

**evil-doer** *n* malfaiteur *m*, méchant -e

**evilly** *adv* mal

**evil-minded** *adj* malintentionné, malveillant

**evince** *vt* montrer, démontrer

**eviscerate** *vt* éviscérer, éventrer; *fig* affaiblir, vider de sa substance

**evocation** *n* évocation *f*

**evocative** *adj* évocateur -trice

**evoke** *vt* évoquer, rappeler

**evolution** *n* évolution *f*, développement *m*

**evolutionary** *adj* d'évolution

**evolutionism** *n* évolutionnisme *m*

**evolve** *vt* faire évoluer, développer; *vi* évoluer, se développer

**ewe** *n* brebis *f*

**ewer** *n* broc *m*

**exacerbate** *vt* exacerber, exaspérer, irriter

**exacerbation** *n* exacerbation *f*

¹**exact** *adj* exact, précis, juste, rigoureux -euse

²**exact** *vt* exiger, demander; extorquer

**exacting** *adj* (person) exigeant; (task) ardu, dur, pénible

**exaction** *n* exaction *f*, extorsion *f*

**exactitude** *n* exactitude *f*, précision *f*

**exactly** *adv* exactement, précisément; *interj* parfaitement!

**exactness** *n* exactitude *f*

**exaggerate** *vt* + *vi* exagérer; (fashion, etc) outrer

**exaggeration** *n* exagération *f*

**exalt** *vt* exalter, glorifier, porter aux nues

**exaltation** *n* exaltation *f*, glorification *f*; (excitement) transport *m*, excitation *f*

**exalted** *adj* noble, élevé; (elated) exalté

**exam** *n coll abbr* examen *m*

**examination** *n* examen *m*; inspection *f*, contrôle *m*; *leg* instruction *f*; (customs) visite *f*; *leg* **cross-** ~ interrogatoire *m*; **medical** ~ visite médicale

**examine** *vt* examiner, inspecter, contrôler; *leg* (case) instruire, (witness) interroger; (baggage) visiter

**examinee** *n* candidat -e

**examiner** *n* examinateur -trice, membre *m* du jury (d'examen)

**example** *n* exemple *m*; **for** ~ par exemple; **make an** ~ **of** punir de façon exemplaire; **set an** ~ donner

l'exemple; **without ~** sans précédent
**exasperate** *vt* exaspérer; aggraver
**exasperating** *adj* exaspérant, énervant
**exasperation** *n* exaspération *f*; fureur *f*
**excavate** *vt* creuser; *vi arch* faire des fouilles
**excavation** *n* creusement *m*; *arch* fouilles *fpl*
**excavator** *n* personne *f* qui creuse; (machine) excavateur *m*, excavatrice *f*
**exceed** *vt* excéder, dépasser, surpasser; *vi* dépasser les bornes
**exceeding** *adj* très grand
**exceedingly** *adv* extrêmement
**excel** *vt* surpasser, dépasser; *vi* exceller
**excellence** *n* excellence *f*, supériorité *f*, mérite *m*
**excellency** *n* excellence *f*
**excellent** *adj* excellent
**except** *vt* excepter; *prep* excepté, hormis, sauf; **~ for** sauf; *conj ar* à moins que, sauf que
**excepting** *prep* hormis, sauf, à l'exception de
**exception** *n* exception *f*; **take ~** élever des objections, trouver à redire; **with certain ~s** sauf exceptions
**exceptionable** *adj* critiquable, blâmable
**exceptional** *adj* exceptionnel -elle, rare, remarquable
**excerpt** *n* extrait *m*, fragment *m*, morceau choisi; *vt* extraire, choisir
**excess** *n* excès *m*; (quantity) excédent *m*; (charge) supplément *m*; *adj* excédentaire
**excessive** *adj* excessif -ive
**exchange** *n* échange *m*, troc *m*; (telephone) central *m*; (currency) change *m*; **Stock Exchange** Bourse *f*; *vt* échanger, troquer; (currency) changer; *vi* s'échanger
**exchequer** *n hist* échiquier *m*; trésor public; **Chancellor of the Exchequer** = ministre *m* des Finances
**excisable** *adj* imposable
**¹excise** *n* impôt indirect; *vt* imposer
**²excise** *vt* exciser, retrancher
**exciseman** *n* employé *m* des contributions indirectes
**excision** *n* excision *f*; *fig* rejet *m*
**excitable** *adj* excitable
**excitant** *n* excitant *m*
**excitation** *n* excitation *f*
**excite** *vt* exciter, agiter; inciter, stimuler, émouvoir; **get ~d** s'exciter
**excitement** *n* excitation *f*, agitation *f*, fièvre *f*
**exciting** *adj* excitant, émouvant, passionnant, impressionnant
**exclaim** *vi* s'écrier, s'exclamer; **~ against** protester contre
**exclamation** *n* exclamation *f*; **~ mark**

point *m* d'exclamation
**exclamatory** *adj* exclamatif -ive
**exclude** *vt* exclure, rejeter; (prevent) empêcher
**excluding** *prep* à l'exclusion de
**exclusion** *n* exclusion *f*
**exclusive** *adj* exclusif -ive; snob *invar*; (keeping others out) fermé, select (no *f*); **~ of** sans compter; **mutually ~** incompatible
**exclusiveness** *n* exclusivité *f*
**excogitate** *vt* imaginer, combiner
**excommunicate** *vt* excommunier
**excommunication** *n* excommunication *f*
**excoriate** *vt* excorier, écorcher
**excoriation** *n* excoriation *f*, écorchure *f*
**excrement** *n* excrément *m*
**excremential** *adj* excrémentiel -ielle
**excrescence** *n* excroissance *f*
**excrescent** *adj* qui forme une excroissance, superflu
**excreta** *npl* excrétions *fpl*
**excrete** *vt* excréter; (plant) sécréter
**excretion** *n* excrétion *f*; (plant) sécrétion *f*
**excretory** *adj* excréteur -trice
**excruciate** *vt* torturer, mettre au supplice
**excruciating** *adj* très douloureux -euse; atroce
**excruciation** *n* supplice *m*, torture *f*
**exculpate** *vt* disculper
**exculpation** *n* disculpation *f*
**excursion** *n* excursion *f*; *obs mil* sortie *f*; *fig* digression *f*; *fig* **alarms and ~s** confusion *f*, commotion *f*
**excursionist** *n* excursionniste
**excursive** *adj* décousu, digressif -ive
**excursus** *n* digression *f*, appendice *m*
**excusable** *adj* excusable
**excuse** *n* excuse *f*, prétexte *m*; *vt* excuser; pardonner; dispenser, exempter; **~ me** pardon, permettez
**execrable** *adj* exécrable, abominable
**execrate** *vt* exécrer, détester
**execration** *n* exécration *f*, détestation *f*
**executant** *n* exécutant -e
**execute** *vt* exécuter, accomplir; (criminal, will, etc) exécuter
**execution** *n* exécution *f*, accomplissement *m*; *leg* (criminal, will, etc) exécution *f*
**executioner** *n* bourreau *m*; *hist* exécuteur *m* des hautes œuvres
**executive** *n* (pouvoir *m*) exécutif *m*; (person) administrateur -trice; *adj* exécutif -ive
**executor** *n leg* exécuteur *m* testamentaire
**executrix** *n leg* exécutrice *f* testamentaire
**exegesis** *n* exégèse *f*
**exegetic** *adj* exégétique
**exegetics** *npl* exégétique *f*

469

**exemplar** n modèle m
**exemplary** adj exemplaire, parfait; (warning) exemplaire
**exemplification** n exemple m, illustration f au moyen d'exemples; leg ampliation f
**exempt** adj exempt; vt exempter
**exemption** n exemption f
**exercise** n exercice m; (task) devoir m; vt exercer; (puzzle) rendre perplexe; vi s'exercer, faire de l'exercice
**exert** vt employer, déployer, exercer; ~ oneself se dépenser, se donner du mal, se remuer
**exertion** n effort m; emploi m, usage m
**exfoliate** vt exfolier
**exfoliation** n exfoliation f
**exhalation** n exhalaison f; émanation f, effluve m
**exhale** vt exhaler, émettre, évaporer; vi expirer
**exhaust** n échappement m; tuyau m d'échappement; vt épuiser, exténuer; (use up) épuiser, vider; fig (subject) épuiser
**exhaustible** adj épuisable
**exhausting** adj exténuant, épuisant
**exhaustion** n épuisement m, grande fatigue
**exhaustive** adj exhaustif -ive
**exhaust-pipe** n tuyau m d'échappement
**exhibit** n objet exposé; leg document m; vt exhiber, exposer, montrer; leg exhiber; vi faire une exposition
**exhibition** n exposition f; leg exhibition f; (education) bourse f
**exhibitionism** n exhibitionnisme m
**exhibitor** n exposant -e
**exhilarate** vt animer, vivifier, émoustiller
**exhilarating** adj vivifiant, émoustillant
**exhilaration** n gaieté f de cœur, animation f, joie f de vivre
**exhort** vt exhorter, inciter; recommander; avertir
**exhortation** n exhortation f
**exhumation** n exhumation f
**exhume** vt exhumer
**exigence, exigency** n exigence f, urgence f; nécessité f
**exigent** adj urgent, exigeant
**exiguity** n exiguïté f
**exiguous** adj exigu -uë
**exiguousness** n exiguïté f
**exile** n exil m, bannissement m; (person) exilé -e; vt exiler, bannir
**existence** n existence f
**existent** adj existant
**existential** adj existentiel -ielle
**existentialism** n philos existentialisme m
**existentialist** n + adj philos existentialiste
**exit** n sortie f; vi sortir; fig mourir

**exodus** n exo᳚ᵃᵘ˘ m
**ex-officio** adj nommé d'office; adv ex officio, d'office
**exonerate** vt exonérer, dispenser; (blame) disculper
**exoneration** n exonération f, dispense f; (blame) disculpation f
**exorbitance** n extravagance f
**exorbitant** adj exorbitant, extravagant
**exorcism** n exorcisme m
**exorcist** n exorciste
**exordium** n exorde m
**exoteric** adj exotérique, populaire
**exotic** adj exotique
**expand** vt étendre, élargir; développer; physiol dilater; vi s'étendre, s'élargir; se développer, s'épanouir; physiol se dilater
**expander** n extenseur m
**expanse** n étendue f
**expansible** adj expansible, extensible
**expansion** n expansion f, extension f; élargissement m; fig développement m
**expansionism** n expansionnisme m
**expansive** adj expansible; phys expansif -ive; fig expansif -ive, démonstratif -ive
**expatiate** vi disserter, discourir, s'étendre
**expatiation** n long discours, dissertation f
**expatriate** n + adj expatrié -e; vt expatrier, exiler
**expatriation** n expatriation f
**expect** vt attendre, compter sur; coll supposer, présumer; coll be ~ing être enceinte; know what to ~ savoir à quoi s'en tenir
**expectancy** n attente f, expectative f; (possession) espérance f
**expectant** adj d'attente, d'expectative, expectant; ~ mother femme enceinte
**expectation** n expectative f; perspective f, probabilité f; espérance f; ~ of life espérance f de vie
**expectorant** n expectorant m; adj expectorant
**expectorate** vt expectorer, cracher; vi cracher
**expectoration** n expectoration f
**expedience, expediency** n convenance f, à-propos m; opportunité f; opportunisme m
**expedient** n expédient m; adj expédient, politique; avantageux -euse
**expedite** vt accélérer, activer; expédier
**expedition** n expédition f
**expeditionary** adj mil expéditionnaire
**expeditious** adj prompt, expéditif -ive
**expel** vt expulser, refouler; (school) renvoyer
**expend** vt dépenser
**expendable** adj remplaçable, de

consommation; *mil* à sacrifier
**expenditure** *n* dépense *f*
**expense** *n* dépense *f*; prix *m*; *fig* dépens *mpl*; ~ s frais *mpl*; ~ **account** frais *mpl* de représentation; **at the ~ of** aux dépens de
**expensive** *adj* coûteux -euse, cher (*f* chère)
**experience** *n* expérience *f*; *vt* éprouver, faire l'expérience de
**experiment** *n* expérience *f*; *vi* expérimenter, faire une expérience
**experimental** *adj* expérimental
**experimentalist** *n* expérimentateur -trice
**experimenter** *n* expérimentateur -trice
**expert** *n* expert *m*, spécialiste; *adj* expert, habile, adroit
**expertise** *n* expertise *f*
**expertly** *adv* de façon experte
**expertness** *n* adresse *f*, habileté *f*
**expiable** *adj* expiable
**expiate** *vt* expier
**expiation** *n* expiation *f*
**expiatory** *adj* expiatoire
**expiration** *n* expiration *f*
**expiratory** *adj* expirateur -trice
**expire** *vt* + *vi* expirer
**expiry** *n* expiration *f*
**explain** *vt* expliquer, élucider; expliquer, donner l'explication de; ~ **away** justifier, rendre raison de; ~ **oneself** s'expliquer
**explanation** *n* explication *f*, éclaircissement *m*
**explanatory** *adj* explicatif -ive
**expletive** *n* juron *m*; *gramm* explétif *m*; *adj* superflu; *gramm* explétif -ive
**explicable** *adj* explicable
**explicate** *vt* expliquer, élucider
**explication** *n* explication *f*, élucidation *f*
**explicative**, **explicatory** *adj* explicatif -ive
**explicit** *adj* explicite, défini, clair; (outspoken) catégorique
**explicitness** *n* précision *f*, caractère *m* explicite
**explode** *vt* faire exploser, faire sauter, faire détoner; *fig* réfuter, discréditer; *vi* exploser, sauter
¹**exploit** *n* exploit *m*, haut fait
²**exploit** *vt* exploiter
**exploitable** *adj* exploitable
**exploitation** *n* exploitation *f*
**exploiter** *n* (developer, cultivator) exploitant -e; *pej* exploiteur -euse
**exploration** *n* exploration *f*
**exploratory** *adj* de recherche, de découverte; exploratoire
**explore** *vt* explorer; *vi* faire des explorations
**explorer** *n* explorateur -trice
**explosion** *n* explosion *f*

**explosive** *n* explosif *m*; *phon* explosive *f*; *adj* explosif -ive
**exponent** *n* interprète, explicateur -trice; *math* exposant *m*
**export** *n* exportation *f*; (goods) article *m* d'exportation; *adj* d'exportation; *vt* exporter
**exportable** *adj* exportable
**exportation** *n* exportation *f*
**exporter** *n* exportateur -trice
**expose** *vt* exposer, mettre au jour; (crime, scandal) dévoiler
**exposé** *n* exposé *m*, relation *f*; révélation *f*, mise *f* à jour
**exposed** *adj* exposé, ouvert, sans protection; révélé, dévoilé
**exposition** *n* exposition *f*; explication *f*, exposé *m*
**expositor** *n* commentateur -trice, interprète
**expository** *adj* descriptif -ive
**expostulate** *vi* protester
**expostulation** *n* remontrance *f*
**exposure** *n* exposition *f*; *phot* pose *f*; *fig* révélation *f*; *phot* ~ **meter** posemètre *m*; **indecent** ~ attentat *m* à la pudeur
**expound** *vt* expliquer, interpréter, exposer
¹**express** *n* (railway) rapide *m*; (letter) exprès *m*; *adj* exprès (*f* expresse); (railway) rapide; *adv* par exprès; très rapidement
²**express** *vt* exprimer, émettre, formuler, communiquer; ~ **oneself** s'exprimer
**expressible** *adj* exprimable
**expression** *n* expression *f*
**expressionism** *n* expressionnisme *m*
**expressionist** *n* + *adj* expressionniste
**expressionistic** *adj* expressionniste
**expressive** *adj* expressif -ive, significatif -ive
**expressly** *adv* expressément, explicitement, exprès
**expropriate** *vt* déposséder; *leg* exproprier
**expropriation** *n* expropriation *f*
**expulsion** *n* expulsion *f*; (school, etc) renvoi *m*
**expunge** *vt* effacer, supprimer
**expurgate** *vt* expurger
**expurgation** *n* expurgation *f*
**expurgator** *n* celui (celle) qui expurge
**exquisite** *n* dandy *m*; *ar* petit-maître (*pl* petits-maîtres); *adj* exquis, délicat, parfait, raffiné
**exquisiteness** *n* perfection *f*, délicatesse *f*
**ex-serviceman** *n* ancien combattant
**extant** *adj* existant, qui existe encore, subsistant
**extemporaneous**, **extempory**, **extempore** *adj* improvisé, impromptu
**extemporaneously**,        **extemporarily**,

extempore *adv* impromptu, à l'improviste

extemporization *n* improvisation *f*

extemporize *vt* + *vi* improviser

extend *vt* étendre, allonger, prolonger; *fig* (help, comfort) apporter, offrir; (sympathy) manifester; *vi* s'étendre; se prolonger

extendible, extensible, extensile *adj* extensible

extension *n* extension *f*, étendue *f*, prolongement *m*; (building) annexe *f*; (time) prolongation *f*; (telephone) poste *m*; *carp* rallonge *f*; ~ ladder échelle *f* à coulisse

extensive *adj* étendu, vaste; compréhensif -ive

extensor *n anat* extenseur *m*

extent *n* étendue *f*; (dimension) grandeur *f*, longueur *f*; (degree) mesure *f*, portée *f*; to some ~ dans une certaine mesure; to such an ~ that à tel point que; to the full ~ entièrement, le maximum possible

extenuate *vt* diminuer, atténuer, minimiser

extenuating *adj* ~ circumstances circonstances atténuantes

extenuation *n* diminution *f*, atténuation *f*

exterior *n* extérieur *m*; *adj* extérieur, du dehors

exteriorize *vt psych* extérioriser

exterminate *vt* exterminer

extermination *n* extermination *f*

exterminator *n* exterminateur -trice

exterminatory *adj* exterminateur -trice

external *n* extérieur *m*; ~s apparences *fpl*; *adj* extérieur, du dehors; visible; superficiel -ielle; *med* externe

externalization *n* extériorisation *f*

externalize *vt* extérioriser

extinct *adj* éteint, disparu

extinction *n* extinction *f*

extinguish *vt* éteindre

extinguisher *n* (fire) extincteur *m*; (candle) éteignoir *m*

extirpate *vt* extirper, déraciner

extirpation *n* extirpation *f*, déracinement *m*

extirpator *n agr* extirpateur *m*, scarificateur *m*

extol *vt* exalter, porter aux nues

extort *vt* extorquer, soutirer; arracher

extortion *n* extorsion *f*, exaction *f*

extortionate *adj* exorbitant, excessif -ive

extra *n* extra *m*, supplément *m*; (newspaper) édition spéciale; *theat* + *cin* figurant -e; *adj* supplémentaire; *adv* en plus, en sus, en supplément; extra, d'extra

extract *n* extrait *m*; *cul* extrait *m*, concentré *m*; *vt* extraire; (money) extorquer, soutirer; (promise) arracher

extractable *adj* qu'on peut extraire

extraction *n* extraction *f*

extractor *n* extracteur *m*

extraditable *adj* susceptible d'extradition

extradite *vt* extrader

extradition *n* extradition *f*

extramural *adj* extra-muros *invar*; (course) hors faculté

extraneous *adj* étranger -ère

extraordinariness *n* extraordinaire *m*

extraordinary *adj* extraordinaire, rare, remarquable, exceptionnel -elle

extrapolate *vt* + *vi* extrapoler

extrapolation *n* extrapolation *f*

extrasensory *adj* extra-sensoriel -ielle

extra-special *adj coll* très spécial, extra

extraterritorial *adj* d'extra-territorialité

extraterritoriality *n* extra-territorialité *f*

extravagance *n* extravagance *f*; prodigalité *f*; dévergondage *m*

extravagant *adj* extravagant; prodigal; dévergondé

extravaganza *n theat* + *mus* fantaisie *f*; débauche *f* d'imagination; histoire abracadabrante

extravasation *n med* extravasation *f*

extraversion *n see* extroversion

extravert *n* + *adj see* extrovert

extreme *n* extrême *m*; (extremity) extrémité *f*; plus haut point *m*; go to ~ s pousser les choses à l'extrême; in the ~ à l'extrême; *adj* extrême; dernier -ière, le plus éloigné; intense; excessif -ive, abusif -ive; rigoureux -euse, sévère; ~ penalty peine *f* de mort; ~ unction extrême-onction *f*

extremely *adv* extrêmement, très

extremism *n* extrémisme *m*

extremist *n* + *adj* extrémiste

extremity *n* extrémité *f*

extricate *vt* dégager, libérer

extrication *n* dégagement *m*, libération *f*

extrinsic *adj* extrinsèque

extroversion, extraversion *n* extroversion *f*, extraversion *f*

extrovert, extravert *n* + *adj* extraverti -e, extroverti -e

extrude *vt mech* refouler; expulser

extrusion *n mech* extrusion *f*

exuberance, exuberancy *n* exubérance *f*

exuberant *adj* exubérant; luxuriant, abondant

exude *vt* + *vi* exsuder

exult *vi* exulter, se réjouir

exultancy *n* exultation *f*

exultant *adj* exultant, triomphant

exultation *n* exultation *f*

eye *n* œil *m* (*pl* yeux); vision *f*; estimation *f*, faculté *f* d'observation; *fig* point *m* de vue, jugement *m*; (needle) chas *m*; *elect*+*bot*+*zool* œil *m*; (loop) œillet *m*; *mil* ~s front! fixe!; *mil* ~s right! tête à droite!; *coll* all my ~ balivernes!; be in the public ~ être très en vue; *sl* do in the ~ gâcher; *coll* easy on the ~ agréable à reluquer; glad ~ regard lascif; have an ~ for remarquer; être bon juge de; *naut* in the ~ of the wind contre le vent; keep an ~ on surveiller; protéger; keep one's ~s open (skinned, peeled) ouvrir l'œil; make ~s at faire de l'œil à; *sl* my ~! mince alors!; (contradiction) mon œil!; open the ~s of s/o faire comprendre à qn; see ~ to ~ with être complètement d'accord avec; see with half an ~ voir facilement; sheep's ~s yeux *mpl* de merlan frit, regards amoureux; the mind's ~ l'imagination *f*; turn a blind ~ to ignorer; up to the ~s in très occupé avec, débordé de; with an ~ to en prévision de; *vt* dévisager; regarder souvent

**eyeball** *n* globe *m* de l'œil, globe *m* oculaire; ~ to ~ face à face

**eye-bath** *n* bain *m* oculaire, œillère *f*

**eyebrow** *n* sourcil *m*; not raise an ~ ne pas sourciller

**eyeful** *n* ce qu'on peut voir d'un regard; *coll* get an ~ se rincer l'œil, s'en mettre plein la vue

**eye-glass** *n* monocle *m*; ~es pince-nez *m*

**eyelash** *n* cil *m*

**eyelet** *n* œillet *m*

**eyelid** *n* paupière *f*

**eye-opener** *n* *coll* révélation surprenante

**eyepiece** *n* oculaire *m*

**eyeshade** *n* visière *f*

**eyeshadow** *n* rimmel *m*

**eyeshot** *n* portée *f* du regard

**eyesight** *n* vue *f*

**eyesore** *n* objet déplaisant, ce qui blesse la vue; *coll* horreur *f*

**eye-tooth** *n* (dent) canine *f*; cut one's eye-teeth sortir de l'enfance

**eyewash** *n* *med* collyre *m*; *coll* boniment *m*, bourrage *m* de crâne

**eye-witness** *n* témoin *m* oculaire

**eyot** *n* ilôt *m*

**eyrie** *n* aire *f*, nid *m* d'aigle

# F

**fa** *n* *mus* fa *m*

**fab** *adj* *sl* sensas

**fable** *n* fable *f*; légende *f*, mythe *m*; invention *f*

**fabled** *adj* légendaire, fabuleux -euse; inventé

**fabric** *n* structure *f*, charpente *f*; (cloth) tissu *m*, étoffe *f*; *archi* édifice *m*; *fig* base *f*

**fabricate** *vt* construire, fabriquer; inventer; *pej* fabriquer, forger

**fabrication** *n* invention *f*; *pej* fabrication *f*

**fabricator** *n* constructeur *m*; *pej* fabricateur -trice, faussaire

**fabulist** *n* fabuliste *m*

**fabulous** *adj* fabuleux -euse; *coll* merveilleux -euse, sensationnel -elle

**façade** *n* façade *f*

**face** *n* visage *m*, figure *f*, face *f*; expression *f*, mine *f*, contenance *f*; grimace *f*; (impudence) effronterie *f*, toupet *m*; apparence *f*; (surface) surface *f*, plat *m*, face *f*; (clock) cadran *m*; *typ* œil *m*; (coal) front *m* de taille; ~ to ~ face à face; ~ value valeur nominale; fly in the ~ of défier; have the ~ to avoir le toupet (culot) de; in the ~ of opposé à, au nez de; keep a straight ~ garder son sérieux; look s/o in the ~ faire face à qn; lose ~ perdre contenance, perdre la face; make (pull) a ~ grimacer; on the ~ of it apparemment; pull (wear) a long ~ faire triste mine; put a bold ~ on faire bonne contenance devant; save one's ~ sauver les apparences (la face); set one's ~ against opposer résolument; show one's ~ faire une apparition; to one's ~ ouvertement; *vt* faire face à, regarder; affronter, faire front à, se trouver devant; (surface) revêtir; (stone) aplanir; (window) donner sur; ~ both ways ménager la chèvre et le chou; ~ out payer d'audace; ~ **the music** répondre de ses actions; *vi* être tourné vers; être orienté à; *US mil* ~ **about** faire demi-tour; ~ **up to** faire face à

**face-ache** *n* névralgie faciale

**face-cloth** *n* gant *m* de toilette

**face-cream** *n* crème *f* de toilette

**faceless** *adj pej* anonyme

**face-lifting** *n* chirurgie *f* esthétique du visage, lifting *m*

**face-pack** *n* masque *m* anti-rides

**face-powder** *n* poudre *f* de riz

**facer** *n coll* (blow) gifle *f*; problème *m*, difficultés *fpl*

**facet** *n* facette *f*; *fig* aspect *m*

**facetious** *adj* facétieux -ieuse

**facetiousness** *n* bouffonnerie *f*, humeur facétieuse

**facial** *n* traitement *m* anti-rides (du visage); *adj* facial, du visage

**facile** *adj* facile, aisé; influençable, accommodant; (talk) patelin, coulant; superficiel -ielle

**facilitate** *vt* faciliter

**facility** *n* facilité *f*, aisance *f*; talent *m*, aptitude *f*; dextérité *f*; **facilities** facilités *fpl*, possibilités *fpl*

**facing** *n bui* revêtement *m*; ~ **s** parements *mpl*

**facsimile** *n* fac-similé *m*

**fact** *n* fait *m*; réalité *f*, vérité *f*; *leg* fait *m*; ~ **and fiction** le vrai et le faux; **as a matter of** ~, **in point of** ~ de fait, à vrai dire, en réalité; **know for a** ~ savoir de source sûre; **stick to the** ~ **s** s'en tenir aux faits; **the** ~ **of the matter is that** le fait est que; **the** ~ **remains that** le fait est que

**fact-finding** *adj* qui enquête

**faction** *n* faction *f*

**factious** *adj* factieux -ieuse, séditieux -ieuse

**factiousness** *n* esprit *m* de faction

**factitious** *adj* factice

¹**factor** *n* facteur *m*; *math* **common** ~ facteur commun

²**factor** *n comm* agent *m* de vente; (Scotland) intendant *m*

**factorial** *adj math* factoriel -ielle

**factory** *n* usine *f*, fabrique *f*; (trading-post) comptoir *m*

**factotum** *n* factotum *m*

**factual** *adj* effectif -ive, réel -elle, positif -ive

**facultative** *adj* facultatif -ive

**faculty** *n* faculté *f*; (ability) don *m*; *eccles* dispense *f*

**fad** *n* marotte *f*, manie *f*

**faddy** *adj* capricieux -ieuse

**fade** *n rad* fading *m*; *cin* fondu *m*; *vt* faner, flétrir, décolorer; *vi* se faner, se flétrir; (colours) déteindre, pâlir; *fig*

s'évanouir, disparaître; ~ **away** mourir, s'éteindre

**fadeless** *adj* (cloth) bon teint *invar*

**faecal, fecal** *adj med* fécal

**faeces, feces** *npl med* fèces *fpl*

**faerie, faery** *n lit* pays *m* des fées; *adj* féerique

**fag** *n coll* corvée *f*; fatigue *f*; *sl* cigarette *f*, clope *m*, sèche *f*; (school) petit *m* (qui fait des corvées pour les grands); *vt* éreinter, fatiguer; *vi* s'éreinter, se fatiguer

**fag-end** *n* mégot *m*; *fig* bout *m*

**fagged** *adj* crevé

**faggot** *n* fagot *m*; *bui* + *mil* fascine *f*; *cul* boulette *f* de foie; *sl* pédé *m*; *vt* fagoter

**Fahrenheit** *n* Fahrenheit *m*; *adj* Fahrenheit *invar*

**faience** *n* faïence *f*

**fail** *n* échec *m*; faute *f*; **without** ~ sans faute; *vt* (test, examination) échouer à, *coll* rater; (candidate) refuser, *coll* coller; (let down) manquer à; (omit) omettre, négliger; *vi* manquer, faillir; négliger, omettre; échouer; baisser, diminuer; *comm* faire faillite; *mech* tomber en panne; ~ **to do sth** ne pas réussir à faire qch

**failing** *n* faiblesse *f*, défaut *m*, faute *f*; *prep* sans, à défaut de, faute de

**failsafe** *adj* à sûreté intégrée

**failure** *n* échec *m*; (person) raté -e; négligence *f*; manque *m*; *mech* panne *f*

**fain** *adj ar* prêt, disposé; ~ **to** obligé à; *adv* heureusement

**faint** *n* évanouissement *m*, pâmoison *f*; *adj* faible, sans vigueur, timide; vague, indistinct, peu clair; défaillant, prêt à s'évanouir; *vi* s'évanouir; (weaken) s'affaiblir

**faint-hearted** *adj* peureux -euse, pusillanime, timide

**fainting** *n* évanouissement *m*

**faintly** *adv* faiblement; vaguement; *coll* un peu

**faintness** *n* faiblesse *f*; malaise *m*

¹**fair** *n* foire *f*, foire commerciale; (amusement) fête foraine

²**fair** *adj* beau (*f* belle); (weather) clair, ensoleillé; (colour) clair, blond; (honest) juste, impartial, franc (*f* franche), honnête, équitable; *fig* pur, prometteur -euse; plausible; passable, moyen -enne; (wind) propice; ~ **and square** direct, honorable; ~ **copy** copie *f* au net; ~ **enough** ça va!, d'accord!; ~ **game** proie *f* légitime; ~ **play** franc-jeu *m*, fair-play *m*; **in a** ~ **way to** de nature à; (barometer) **set** ~ au grand beau (temps); *adv* honorablement, bien, convenablement,

carrément, franchement; **bid ~ to** avoir des chances de

**fairground** n champ m de foire

**fair-haired** adj aux cheveux blonds

**fairly** adv assez, justement; complètement

**fair-minded** adj équitable, juste

**fairness** n équité f, droiture f, franchise f, loyauté f; blancheur f, beauté f, clarté f

**fair-spoken** adj poli, avenant; plausible

**fairway** n naut chenal m navigable, passe f; (golf) parcours normal

**fair-weather** adj des beaux jours

**fairy** n fée f; sl pédé m, tapette f; adj féerique, enchanteur (f enchanteresse)

**fairy-lamp** n lampion m

**fairyland** n royaume m des fées

**fairy-like** adj féerique

**fairy-story** n conte m de fées

**faith** n foi f, croyance f; loyauté f, honneur m, fidélité f, parole f; confiance f; promesse f; **bad ~** mauvaise foi; **in good ~** sincèrement

**faithful** n collect fidèles mpl; adj fidèle, loyal, digne; juste, exact

**faithfully** adv fidèlement; loyalement; exactement; **yours ~** veuillez agréer l'expression de mes sentiments les plus distingués

**faithfulness** n fidélité f; loyauté f; exactitude f

**faith-healing** n guérison f par la foi

**faithless** adj infidèle, inconstant, déloyal; eccles infidèle, incroyant

**fake** n imitation f, faux m, falsification f; adj faux (f fausse), truqué, falsifié; vt truquer, falsifier

**fakir** n fakir m

**falcon** n faucon m

**falconer** n fauconnier m

**falconry** n fauconnerie f

**fall** n chute f, tombée f; (decline) baisse f; mil chute f, reddition f; comm baisse f, dépréciation f; theat (curtain) baisser m; fig chute f, défaite f; (sin) péché m; (waterfall) cascade f; US automne m; **head for a ~** courir à l'échec; **try a ~ with** se mesurer contre; vi tomber; lit choir; (collapse) s'écrouler; (ground) s'incliner, descendre; (river) déboucher, se jeter; (event) arriver, survenir; (categories) se diviser, se classer; (value, health, sight) baisser, diminuer, être en baisse; (night) tomber, approcher; (face) s'allonger; (star) filer; (sea, wind) se calmer; fig tomber, déchoir; décroître; (morally) pécher, succomber, s'avilir; (blame) retomber; sl **~ about** rire aux éclats; **~ away** (ground) s'affaisser; (follower, soldier) déserter; theol apostasier; (thin) s'amaigrir; **~**

**back** se replier; **~ back on** se rabattre sur; **~ behind** rester en arrière; (payment) s'arriérer; coll **~ down (on)** (fail) échouer; (go wrong) faire une grande erreur; **~ flat** faillir, ne produire aucun effet; **~ for** donner dans, se laisser prendre à; (love) s'amouracher de; **~ foul of** naut entrer en collision avec; fig se heurter à; **~ in** mil former les rangs; (collapse) s'effondrer; (lease) expirer; (debt) échoir; **~ in with** consentir à; (meet) rencontrer par hasard; **~ off** baisser, diminuer; naut ne pas obéir à la barre; **~ on** attaquer; (incumbent) incomber à; **~ out** advenir, arriver; mil rompre les rangs; (quarrel) se brouiller; **~ over backwards** se mettre en quatre; **~ short** rester en deçà, être insuffisant; **~ short of** ne pas être à la hauteur de; **~ through** tomber à l'eau; **~ to** commencer, entamer; attaquer; commencer à manger; **~ under** être classé comme

**fallacious** adj fallacieux -ieuse

**fallacy** n opinion fausse, raisonnement erroné; argument fallacieux; philos sophisme m

**fallen** adj coupable, déchu; **~ woman** prostituée f; **the ~** les morts mpl au champ d'honneur

**fall-guy** n US bouc m émissaire

**fallibility** n faillibilité f

**fallible** adj faillible

**Fallopian** adj anat de Fallope; **~ tube** trompe f de Fallope

**fall-out** n retombée(s) radioactive(s)

¹**fallow** n agr jachère f, friche f; adj agr en jachère, en friche; fig inculte; vt agr laisser en jachère

²**fallow** adj fauve

**fallow-deer** n daim m

**false** adj faux (f fausse), erroné; (lying) menteur -euse, trompeur -euse; traître -esse; (sham) factice, contrefait; artificiel -ielle, postiche; **~ bottom** double fond m; **~ position** situation fausse; **~ pretences** prétextes frauduleux; **~ step** faux pas; adv **play s/o ~** tromper qn

**false-hearted** adj déloyal, traître -esse

**falsehood** n (lie) mensonge m; (falseness) fausseté f

**falseness** n fausseté f

**falsetto** n mus fausset m; adj mus de fausset

**falsies** npl sl seins mpl postiches

**falsification** n falsification f

**falsify** vt falsifier; déformer, dénaturer

**falsity** n fausseté f; mensonge m; malhonnêteté f, traîtrise f

**falter** vi (trip) trébucher; (wobble) vaciller, chanceler; hésiter, balancer; (speech) bredouiller, balbutier

**fame** n réputation f, gloire f; renom m,

renommée *f*; *ar* bruit *m* qui court; **house of ill ~** bordel *m*

**famed** *adj* renommé, célèbre

**familiar** *n* (friend) familier -ière, intime; (demon) esprit familier; *eccles* familier *m*; *adj* familier -ière, amical, intime; impudent, libre; ordinaire, commun; (well-known) connu; **be ~ with** être au courant de

**familiarity** *n* familiarité *f*

**familiarize** *vt* familiariser

**family** *n* famille *f*; **~ allowance** allocation familiale; **~ man** homme *m* d'intérieur; **her ~ tree** arbre *m* généalogique; **in the ~ way** enceinte; *adj* familial

**famine** *n* famine *f*, disette *f*

**famish** *vt* affamer; *vi* être réduit à la famine; **be ~ed** avoir très faim

**famous** *adj* célèbre, fameux -euse; *coll* excellent, fameux -euse

**famously** *adv coll* très bien

**¹fan** *n* éventail *m*; (mechanical) ventilateur *m*; *agr* van *m*; **~ vaulting** voûte *f* en éventail; *vt* éventer; (flames) souffler sur; (fire) attiser; *agr* vanner; *fig* exciter, attiser, envenimer; *vi* se déployer en éventail

**²fan** *n* fan, admirateur -trice; **~ mail** courrier *m* des fans

**fanatic** *n* fanatique, fervent -e, enthousiaste, *coll* fana; *adj* fanatique, coll fana

**fanatical** *adj* fanatique, fervent, *coll* fana

**fanaticism** *n* fanatisme *m*

**fanaticize** *vt* fanatiser

**fancier** *n* amateur -trice, connaisseur -euse; (animals, birds, etc) éleveur -euse, marchand -e

**fanciful** *adj* imaginatif -ive, rêveur -euse; capricieux -ieuse, fantaisiste; fantastique, étrange

**fancy** *n* chimère *f*, illusion *f*; caprice *m*, lubie *f*; goût *m*, inclination *f*; *lit* fantaisie *f*, imagination *f*; **take a ~ to** (person) se sentir attiré par, *coll* avoir le béguin pour; (thing) se sentir du goût pour; **take the ~ of** attirer, plaire à; **the ~ took him** il a eu envie; *adj* de fantaisie; fantaisiste, extravagant; de luxe, cher (*f* chère); imaginatif -ive; **~ dress** travesti *m*, déguisement *m*; **~ goods** articles *mpl* de Paris; *sl* **~ man** proxénète *m*, maquereau *m*; **~ woman** maîtresse *f*; prostituée *f*; **~ work** broderie *f*; *vt* imaginer, s'imaginer; avoir du goût pour, *coll* avoir le béguin pour; supposer, croire; **~ oneself** avoir bonne opinion de soi

**fancy-free** *adj* libre, avec le cœur libre

**fandango** *n* fandango *m*

**fanfare** *n* fanfare *f*

**fang** *n* (animal) croc *m*; (snake) crochet *m* (à venin); (of tooth) racine *f*

**fanlight** *n* imposte *f* (en éventail)

**fanny** *n sl* cul *m*; *vulg* con *m*

**fantasia** *n mus* fantaisie *f*

**fantastic, fantastical** *adj* fantastique, grotesque; imaginaire, chimérique; fantasque; *coll* sensationnel -elle

**fantasy, phantasy** *n* fantaisie *f*, caprice *m*, lubie *f*; illusion *f*; *mus* + *lit* fantaisie *f*

**far** *adj* éloigné, lointain, distant; (other) autre, plus éloigné; **~ cry** grande distance; **Far East** Extrême Orient *m*; **~ side** autre côté *m*; *adv* loin; (much) beaucoup; **~ and away** de beaucoup; **~ and wide** partout; **~ back** loin dans le passé; **~ be it from me to** loin de moi l'idée de; **~ from it!** tant s'en faut!; **~ gone** bien parti, avancé; **~ into** très avant dans; **~ off** au loin; **by ~** de loin; *fig* **go ~** réussir; **go ~ towards** beaucoup contribuer à; **go too ~** aller trop loin, dépasser les bornes; **how ~ is it to London?** Londres est à quelle distance?; **in so ~ as** dans la mesure où; **thus ~** jusqu'ici; (time) jusqu'à présent

**faraway** *adj* lointain, éloigné; *fig* rêveur -euse, vague

**farce** *n* farce *f*; *vt cul* farcir

**farcical** *adj* de farce; bouffon -onne; grotesque

**fare** *n* (bus, train, aircraft) prix *m* de la place, prix *m* du voyage; (taxi) prix *m* de la course; (taxi passenger) client -e; *cul* nourriture *f*, chère *f*; **excess ~** supplément *m*; **full ~** plein tarif; *vi* aller, se trouver; advenir, résulter; *cul* se nourrir, manger; *ar* voyager

**farewell** *n* adieu *m*; *interj* adieu!

**far-fetched** *adj* recherché, tiré par les cheveux

**far-flung** *adj* vaste, très étendu

**farinaceous** *adj* farinacé

**farm** *n* ferme *f*, exploitation *f* agricole; *vt* cultiver, exploiter; **~ out** (work) confier, affermer; (children) donner à garder; **~ out work** céder un travail en sous-traitance; *vi* être fermier -ière

**farmer** *n* fermier -ière, exploitant -e agricole, cultivateur -trice

**farm-hand** *n* ouvrier *m* agricole

**farm-house** *n* maison *f* de ferme

**farming** *n* agriculture *f*, culture *f*; (rearing) élevage *m*; **~ out** affermage *m*; (sub-contracting) sous-traitance *f*

**farm-labourer** *n* ouvrier *m* agricole

**farmstead** *n* ferme *f*

**farmyard** *n* cour *f* de ferme, basse-cour *f* (*pl* basses-cours)

**farrago** *n* fouillis *m*, méli-mélo *m* (*pl* mélis-mélos)

**far-reaching** *adj* de grande envergure

476

**farrier** *n* maréchal-ferrant *m* (*pl* maréchaux-ferrants)

**farrow** *n* portée *f* de cochons; *vt* mettre bas (des cochons); *vi* cochonner

**far-sighted** *adj* presbyte; *fig* prévoyant

**fart** *n vulg* pet *m*; *vi* péter

**farther** *adj* plus éloigné; plus avancé; *adv* plus loin; (moreover) de plus

**farthermost** *adj* le plus éloigné

**farthest** *adj* le plus éloigné; *adv* le plus loin

**farthing** *n obs* le quart d'un ancien penny; *fig* sou *m*

**fascicule** *n* fascicule *m*

**fascinate** *vt* fasciner, charmer, éblouir

**fascination** *n* fascination *f*, enchantement *m*

**Fascism** *n* fascisme *m*

**Fascist** *n* + *adj* fasciste

**fashion** *n* habitude *f*, coutume *f*; mode *f*, vogue *f*; (way) façon *f*, manière *f*; (garment) forme *f*; ~ **magazine** journal *m* de mode; **after a** ~ tant bien que mal; **in** ~ à la mode; **out of** ~ démodé; *vt* façonner, former; **fully** ~**ed** diminué, proportionné

**fashionable** *adj* à la mode, élégant, chic *invar*

**fashion-plate** *n* gravure *f* de mode; *coll* élégant -e

¹**fast** *n* jeûne *m*, période *f* de jeûne; *vi* jeûner; (partially) faire maigre

²**fast** *adj* solide, ferme; rapide, prompt; (colour) bon teint *invar*; (clock) en avance; *fig* loyal, fidèle; (dissipated) dévergondé, émancipé; ~ **train** rapide *m*; *coll* **pull a** ~ **one on** s/o avoir qn; *adv* solidement, fermement; rapidement, vite, promptement; (thoroughly) complètement; **be** ~ **asleep** dormir à poings fermés; *naut* **make** ~ amarrer; **play** ~ **and loose with** s/o se jouer de qn; **stand** ~ tenir bon

**fasten** *vt* fixer, attacher; (bind) lier; (clasp) agrafer; ~ **on** saisir; imputer à, rejeter sur; *vi* se fixer, s'attacher, s'agrafer

**fastener** *n* attache *f*, fermeture *f*; (clasp) agrafe *f*; **paper** ~ trombone *m*

**fastening** *n* attache *f*

**fastidious** *adj* délicat, difficile

**fastidiousness** *n* délicatesse exagérée; (food) goût *m* difficile

**fasting** *n* jeûne *m*

**fast-living** *adj* dissolu

**fastness** *n* forteresse *f*; fermeté *f*, solidité *f*; rapidité *f*

**fat** *n* graisse *f*; (meat) gras *m*; *chem* glycéride *f*; **live off the** ~ **of the land** vivre comme un coq en pâte; **the** ~ **is in the fire** on a mis le feu aux poudres; *adj* gros (*f* grosse), corpulent; (greasy) gras (*f* grasse); (soil) fertile, riche; (salary)

élevé; *coll* lourd, idiot; *coll* **a** ~ **lot** beaucoup; (ironical) rien du tout

**fatal** *adj* fatal, inévitable; funeste, désastreux -euse; mortel -elle

**fatalism** *n* fatalisme *m*

**fatalist** *n* fataliste

**fatality** *n* mort accidentelle; calamité *f*; fatalité *f*

**fate** *n* destin *m*, sort *m*, destinée *f*; (death) mort *f*; *myth* **Fates** Parques *fpl*

**fated** *adj* destiné, voué; décrété par le destin

**fateful** *adj* décisif -ive, important; fatal, mortel -elle

**fat-head** *n* idiot -e, imbécile

**father** *n* père *m*; *fig* créateur *m*, fondateur *m*; *eccles* (title) père *m*; **from** ~ **to son** de père en fils; **the Father** Dieu *m* le père; **Holy-Father** Saint-Père; *vt* engendrer, être le père de; *fig* créer, inventer, enfanter; prendre la responsabilité de; ~ **sth on** s/o attribuer la responsabilité de qch à qn

**fatherhood** *n* paternité *f*

**father-in-law** *n* beau-père *m* (*pl* beaux-pères)

**fatherland** *n* patrie *f*

**fatherless** *adj* orphelin -e de père, sans père

**fatherly** *adj* paternel -elle

**fathom** *n naut* = brasse *f*; *ar* toise *f*; *vt* sonder; *fig* comprendre

**fathomless** *adj* insondable; incompréhensible

**fatigue** *n* fatigue *f*, épuisement *m*; *mil* corvée *f*; *mech* fatigue *f*; *vt* fatiguer

**fatness** *n* grosseur *f*, embonpoint *m*; fertilité *f*; abondance *f*

**fatted** *adj* ~ **calf** veau gras

**fatten** *vt* + *vi* engraisser

**fatty** *adj* graisseux -euse

**fatuous** *adj* sot (*f* sotte), idiot

**faucet** *n* (barrel) cannelle *f*; *US* robinet *m*

**fault** *n* défaut *m*, imperfection *f*; (sin) faute *f*, péché *m*; erreur *f*; *geol* faille *f*; **be at** ~ être fautif -ive, être en défaut; **find** ~ **with** critiquer, trouver à redire à; *vt* blâmer, critiquer; *geol* provoquer une faille; **I can't** ~ **him** je ne peux pas le prendre en défaut; *vi* relever une faute, noter une erreur; *geol* présenter une faille

**fault-finder** *n* critiqueur -euse, mécontent -e

**fault-finding** *n* critique *f*

**faultiness** *n* imperfection *f*

**faultless** *adj* sans défaut, sans faille

**faulty** *adj* défectueux -euse, imparfait

**faun** *n* faune *m*, faunesse *f*

**fauna** *n* faune *f*

**favour** *n* faveur *f*; (kindness) service *m*, considération *f*; approbation *f*, aide *f*;

(partiality) bienfait *m*, décision indulgente; préférence *f*; (token) faveur *f*, ruban *m* souvenir; *comm* lettre *f*; ~ s (sexual) faveurs *fpl*, complaisances *fpl*; **as a** ~ pour rendre service; *coll* **do me a** ~ ! je t'en prie!; **in** ~ **of** pour; *vt* considérer favorablement, être pour; favoriser; aider, appuyer, préférer; faciliter

**favourable** *adj* favorable, bien disposé; approbateur -trice

**favoured** *adj* avantagé, privilégié; favorisé; (lucky) fortuné

**favouring** *adj* favorable, propice

**favourite** *n* favori -ite, préféré -e; *adj* favori -ite, préféré

**favouritism** *n* favoritisme *m*

¹**fawn** *n zool* faon *m*; *adj* fauve

²**fawn** *vi* ramper, s'aplatir; *fig* ~ (up)on s/o flatter qn, lécher les bottes de qn

**fear** *n* peur *f*, crainte *f*; **for** ~ **of** de peur de; *coll* **no** ~ ! jamais de la vie!; **put the** ~ **of God into** s/o passer à qn une semonce qu'il n'oubliera pas de sitôt; (alarm) faire une peur bleue à qn; *vt* craindre, avoir peur de, redouter; *vi* avoir peur, craindre; **never** ~ ne vous en faites pas

**fearful** *adj* craintif -ive, peureux -euse, effrayé; (terrible) effrayant, terrible

**fearfulness** *n* crainte *f*, timidité *f*; caractère *m* terrible

**fearless** *adj* sans peur, intrépide, courageux -euse

**fearlessness** *n* intrépidité *f*, courage *m*

**fearsome** *adj* effrayant, terrible

**feasibility** *n* praticabilité *f*, possibilité *f*; plausibilité *f*

**feasible** *adj* faisable, praticable; probable

**feast** *n eccles* fête *f*; banquet *m*, festin *m*; *fig* fête *f*, régal *m*; *vt* fêter, régaler; *vi* banqueter, se régaler; *fig* se délecter

**feast-day** *n* jour *m* de fête

**feat** *n* haut fait, exploit *m*

**feather** *n* plume *f*; (arrow) penne *f*; **a** ~ **in one's cap** de quoi être fier; **birds of a** ~ gens *mpl* du même acabit; **in high** ~ vigoureux -euse, en pleine forme; de bonne humeur; **show the white** ~ avoir la frousse, être lâche; *vt* emplumer, empenner; (rowing) ramener à plat; ~ **one's nest** s'enrichir, se remplir les poches; *vi* mettre les plumes

**feather-bed** *n* lit *m* de plume(s); *fig* délice *m*; ~ **industry** compagnie (industrie) protégée et subventionnée par le gouvernement; *vt* favoriser, dorloter

**feather-brained** *adj* sans cervelle, écervelé, étourdi

**feathered** *adj* emplumé, garni de plumes; **our** ~ **friends** les oiseaux *mpl*

**feathering** *n* plumage *m*; (rowing) nage plate

**feather-weight** *n sp* poids *m* plume

**feathery** *adj* couvert de plumes; plumeux -euse; très léger -ère

**feature** *n* trait *m*, trait *m* caractéristique; (facial trait) trait *m* du visage, particularité *f*; *cin* grand film, long métrage; (newspaper) article *m* (à sensation); *vt* caractériser, marquer; dépeindre; *cin* + *rad* + *theat* présenter, mettre en vedette

**feature-length** *adj cin* de long métrage

**featureless** *adj* monotone, terne, uniforme

**febrile** *adj* fébrile; *fig* agité

**February** *n* février *m*

**fecal** *adj*, **feces** *npl see* **faecal, faeces**

**feckless** *adj* insouciant, irréfléchi, étourdi; incapable, mou (*f* molle)

**feculence** *n* féculence *f*; crasse *f*

**feculent** *adj* crasseux -euse, fétide, féculent

**fecund** *adj* fécond

**fecundate** *vt* féconder

**fecundity** *n* fécondité *f*

**federal** *adj* fédéral

**federalism** *n* fédéralisme *m*

**federalize** *vt* fédérer; *vi* se fédérer

**federate** *vt* fédérer; *vi* se fédérer

**federation** *n* fédération *f*

**fee** *n* émoluments *mpl*; (doctor, lawyer) honoraires *mpl*; (actor) cachet *m*; (school) frais *mpl* (de scolarité); (entrance) droits *mpl* (d'entrée); *hist* fief *m*; *vt* payer des droits à, louer

**feeble** *adj* faible, débile, timide; influençable; fragile; *fig* irrésolu; (joke, story) piètre

**feeble-minded** *adj* d'esprit faible, pauvre d'esprit

**feed** *n* action *f* de nourrir; alimentation *f*; *agr* fourrage *m*, pacage *m*; (poultry) pâtée *f*; *coll* gueuleton *m*; *vt* nourrir, donner à manger à; alimenter; *agr* faire paître, engraisser; *theat* donner la réplique à; *fig* alimenter, satisfaire; ~ **on** manger habituellement; ~ **up** engraisser; *vi* se nourrir, manger; *agr* paître; *coll* **be fed up with** en avoir marre de, en avoir ras-le-bol de

**feedback** *n elect* feed-back *m invar*, rétroaction *f*; *fig* feed-back *m invar*

**feeder** *n* mangeur -euse; (for baby) biberon *m*; (tributary river) affluent *m*; (road) route *f* secondaire; *elect* feeder *m*

**feed-pipe** *n* tuyau *m* d'alimentation

**feel** *n* toucher *m*; sensation *f*; attouchement *m*; *vt* sentir, avoir la sensation de; (touch) palper, tâter, manier; éprouver, ressentir, être affecté par; *coll* tripoter; ~ **one's way** tâtonner; *vi* (think)

478

penser, considérer, trouver, avoir le sentiment; se sentir ému; (state) se sentir, se trouver; ~ **for** éprouver de la pitié pour; ~ **like** avoir envie de; ~ **up to** se sentir le courage de

**feeler** n antenne f, palpe m; fig ballon m d'essai

**feeling** n toucher m, tact m; (act) palpage m; sensation f; sentiment m, sensibilité f, gentillesse f; susceptibilité f; (hostile) irritation f, ressentiment m; intuition f, conviction f; adj sensible, émotionné

**fee-simple** n leg pleine propriété; bien m en toute propriété

**feet** npl see **foot**

**feign** vt feindre, simuler; vi feindre

**feint** n feinte f; vi faire semblant

**feldspar, felspar** n min feldspath m

**felicitate** vt féliciter

**felicitation** n félicitation f

**felicitous** adj heureux -euse

**felicity** n félicité f

**feline** n félin m; adj félin

¹**fell** n colline rocheuse

²**fell** adj poet féroce, cruel -elle, meurtrier -ière

³**fell** vt abattre, faire tomber

**fellah** n fellah m

**fellatio** n fellation f

**fellow** n camarade m, compagnon m, coll copain m; complice m; homme m, individu m, quidam m, coll type m; professeur m (à Oxford ou à Cambridge); membre m (d'une académie savante); adj pareil -eille, égal

**fellow-feeling** n sentiment m réciproque, sympathie f

**fellowship** n camaraderie f, fraternité f, solidarité f; compagnie f, association f; poste m de professeur (à Oxford ou à Cambridge); titre m de membre (d'une académie savante)

**fellow-traveller** n compagnon m (f compagne) de voyage; pol communisant -e

¹**felon** n criminel -elle; adj poet vil

²**felon** n panaris m

**felonious** adj criminel -elle; vil

**felony** n crime m

**felspar** n see **feldspar**

**felt** n feutre m; adj de feutre; vt feutrer; vi se feutrer

**felting** n feutrage m; étoffe feutrée

**felucca** n felouque f

**female** n femelle f; femme f; joc femelle f

**feminine** n gramm féminin m; adj féminin

**femininity** n féminité f

**feminism** n féminisme m

**feminist** n féministe f

**feminize** vt féminiser; vi se féminiser

**femoral** adj anat fémoral

**femur** n anat fémur m

**fen** n marais m, marécage m

**fence** n clôture f, claie f, palissade f, barrière f; sl (receiver) receleur -euse; mech garde f; **be on the other side of the** ~ ne pas être du même bord; **sit on the** ~ ménager la chèvre et le chou; vt clôturer, enclore; protéger; ~ **off** parer; vi faire de l'escrime; sl (stolen goods) receler; fig ~ **with** esquiver, se dérober

**fencer** n escrimeur -euse

**fencing** n palissade f, clôture f, barrière f; sp escrime f; sl (stolen goods) recel m

**fend** vt repousser, parer; vi ~ **for oneself** se débrouiller, s'arranger tout seul

**fender** n garde-feu m invar; naut défense f; US mot pare-chocs m

**fennel** n fenouil m

**feoff** n see **fief**

¹**feral** adj fatal; funèbre

²**feral** adj sauvage; féroce

**ferment** n ferment m, levure f; fermentation f; fig agitation f, excitation f; vt faire fermenter; fig exciter, agiter; vi fermenter

**fermentation** n fermentation f

**fern** n fougère f

**ferocious** adj féroce, cruel -elle

**ferociousness** n férocité f, cruauté f

**ferocity** n férocité f

**ferrate** n chem ferrate m

**ferreous** adj ferreux (no f)

**ferret** n furet m; vt prendre au furet; ~ **out** détecter, dénicher; vi chasser au furet; ~ **about** fureter, fouiner

**ferrety** adj de furet, fureteur -euse

**ferric** adj ferrique

**ferro-concrete** n béton armé

**ferrous** adj ferreux -euse

**ferruginous** adj ferrugineux -euse

**ferrule** n bout ferré; virole f

**ferry** n (river) bac m; (sea) ferry m; (place) lieu m de passage en bac; vt (passengers, cars, etc) faire traverser en bac, faire traverser en bateau

**ferryman** n passeur m

**fertile** adj fertile

**fertility** n fertilité f

**fertilization** n fertilisation f

**fertilize** vt agr fertiliser; biol + bot féconder

**fertilizer** n engrais m

**ferule** n férule f

**fervency** n ferveur f

**fervent** adj passionné, fervent; brûlant, incandescent

**fervid** adj passionné, intense

**fervour** n ferveur f, ardeur f; chaleur f intense

**festal** adj de fête

**fester** n pustule f; vt med rendre

479

purulent; gâter, envenimer; *vi med + fig* s'envenimer

**festival** *n* festival *m*; *eccles* fête *f*; *adj* gai

**festive** *adj* gai, de fête

**festivity** *n* fête *f*; festival *m*; **festivities** festivités *fpl*

**festoon** *n* feston *m*, guirlande *f*; *vt* festonner

**fetch** *n coll* ruse *f*; *vt* (s/o) amener; (sth) apporter, ramener, chercher; (induce) tirer; (blows) asséner, flanquer; *comm* atteindre, rapporter; *coll* séduire, attirer; *fig* ~ **and carry for** s/o faire des courses pour qn, être aux ordres de qn; *naut* ~ **away** larguer; ~ **back** ramener; ~ **out** faire sortir; *coll* ~ **up** vomir; *coll naut* ~ **up at** arriver à

**fetching** *adj coll* séduisant

**fête** *n* festival *m*, fête *f*; *vt* fêter

**fetich** *n see* fetish

**fetid, foetid** *adj* fétide, puant

**fetish, fetich** *n* fétiche *m*

**fetishism** *n* fétichisme *m*

**fetlock** *n* (joint) boulet *m*; (hair) fanon *m*

**fetter** *vt* mettre aux fers; *fig* entraver

**fetters** *npl* fers *mpl*

**fettle** *n* condition *f*, état *m*; santé *f*

**feud** *n* inimitié *f*, vendetta *f*

**feudal** *adj* féodal

**feudalism** *n* féodalité *f*

**feudalistic** *adj* féodal

**feudality** *n* féodalité *f*

**feudalize** *vt* inféoder

**feudatory** *n* feudataire; *adj* féodal

**fever** *n* fièvre *f*

**feverish** *adj* fiévreux -euse; fébrile

**few** *n* minorité *f*, peu *m* de gens; **a good** ~ un assez grand nombre de, *coll* pas mal de; *adj* peu de, quelques; ~ **and far between** rares; **every** ~ **days** à quelques jours d'intervalle; **some** ~ quelques; **with** ~ **exceptions** à quelques exceptions près

**fey** *adj* voué à la mort; *coll* farfelu

**fez** *n* fez *m*

**fiancé** *n* fiancé *m*

**fiancée** *n* fiancée *f*

**fiasco** *n* fiasco *m*

**fiat** *n* autorisation *f*; ordre *m*, décret *m*

**fib** *n* petit mensonge, craque *f*; *vi* en conter

**fibre** *n* fibre *f*; *fig* trempe *f*

**fibre-glass** *n* plexiglas(s) *m*, altuglas *m*

**fibrous** *adj* fibreux -euse

**fibula** *n anat* péroné *m*

**fichu** *n* fichu *m*

**fickle** *adj* inconstant, volage, capricieux -ieuse

**fickleness** *n* inconstance *f*

**fiction** *n* fiction *f*; invention *f*; **legal** ~ fiction légale

**fictitious** *adj* fictif -ive, imaginaire; faux (*f* fausse), simulé

**fictive** *adj* fictif -ive

**fid** *n naut* épissoir *m*

**fiddle** *n mus + naut* violon *m*; *sl* combine *f*; **as fit as a** ~ en pleine santé; **play second** ~ **to** jouer en sous-fifre auprès de, jouer un rôle secondaire auprès de; *vt coll* truquer, maquiller; *vi* jouer du violon, violonner

**fiddler** *n* violoniste; *coll* escroc *m*, filou *m*

**fiddlestick** *n mus* archet *m*; ~ **s!** balivernes!

**fiddling** *adj* insignifiant, sans valeur; (annoying) tâtillon -onne

**fidelity** *n* fidélité *f*; **high** ~ haute fidélité

**fidget** *n* agité -e; **be a** ~ avoir la bougeotte; *vt* agacer, irriter; *vi* s'agiter, se démener, se trémousser

**fidgety** *adj* agité, remuant; impatient, nerveux -euse

**fiduciary** *n* fiduciaire *m*; *adj* fiduciaire

**fie** *interj* fi!

**fief, feoff** *n hist* fief *m*

**field** *n* champ *m*; terrain *m*; (extent) étendue *f*; (oil, mineral, etc) gisement *m*; *sp* **a strong** ~ beaucoup de concurrents valables; **hold the** ~ se maintenir en position; être maître du champ; *mil* **in the** ~ en campagne; **take the** ~ se mettre en campagne; *vt mil* mettre en campagne; *sp* faire jouer (une équipe); (ball) attraper

**field-artillery** *n mil* artillerie *f* de campagne

**field-battery** *n mil* batterie *f* de campagne

**field-day** *n mil* jour *m* de manœuvres; *fig* jour *m* de grands succès

**field-gun** *n mil* canon *m* de campagne

**field-hospital** *n mil* antenne chirurgicale

**field-marshal** *n mil* maréchal *m*

**field-mouse** *n* mulot *m*

**field-officer** *n mil* (in British army) officier *m* au-dessus du rang de capitaine

**field-sports** *npl* sports *mpl* de plein air; la chasse et la pêche

**field-work** *n mil* ouvrage *m* de campagne; travaux *mpl* pratiques; *geol* recherches *fpl* sur le terrain

**fiend** *n* démon *m*, diable *m*; *coll* (drugs, etc) intoxiqué -e

**fiendish** *adj* diabolique

**fierce** *adj* féroce; (desire) ardent, brûlant; acharné; violent, furieux -ieuse; *mot* (clutch) brutal

**fierceness** *n* férocité *f*; violence *f*

**fiery** *adj* flamboyant, embrasé; (person) ardent, fougueux -euse, enflammé; (temper) bouillant

**fife** *n* fifre *m*

**fifteen** *n* quinze *m invar*; *sp* (rugby) quinze *m*; *adj* quinze *invar*

**fifteenth** *n* quinzième; (date) quinze *m*; *adj* quinzième

**fifth** *n* cinquième; (date) cinq *m*; *mus* quinte *f*; *adj* cinquième

**fiftieth** *n* + *adj* cinquantième

**fifty** *n* cinquante *m invar*; **the fifties** (epoch) les années cinquante; (age) la cinquantaine; *adj* cinquante *invar*

**fifty-fifty** *adj* + *adv* kif-kif *invar*, fifty-fifty *invar*; **go** ~ partager également

**fig** *n* figue *f*; (tree) figuier *m*; **I don't give a** ~ ça m'est égal, je m'en fous

**fight** *n* combat *m*, lutte *f*, bataille *f*; (fighting spirit) combativité *f*; **free** ~ bagarre *f*; **put up a good** ~ se défendre bien; **show** ~ accepter le conflit; *vt* combattre, se battre contre, lutter pour; (battle) livrer; ~ **down** réprimer, écraser; ~ **off** lutter contre; chasser; ~ **one's way** avancer; *vi* se battre, combattre, lutter; ~ **back** se défendre bien; ~ **it out** lutter jusqu'au bout

**fighter** *n* combattant -e; batailleur -euse; *aer* chasseur *m*

**fighting** *n* lutte *f*, bataille *f*; rixe *f*; *adj* combatif -ive, agressif -ive; qui se bat; *fig* (speech) enflammé

**fig-leaf** *n bot* feuille *f* de figuier; (statue) feuille *f* de vigne

**figment** *n* invention *f*

**fig-tree** *n* figuier *m*

**figuration** *n* figuration *f*; configuration *f*, forme *f*

**figurative** *adj* figuratif -ive; symbolique; (style) imagé

**figure** *n* forme *f*; figure *f*, apparence *f*; (important) personnage *m*; représentation *f*, imitation *f*; *arts* motif *m*, dessin *m*, illustration *f*; symbole *m*, emblème *m*; (money) somme *f* d'argent; *math* chiffre *m*; (shape of body) ligne *f*; *astrol* horoscope *m*; **at a low (high)** ~ bon marché (cher, *f* chère); **have no head for** ~**s** ne rien comprendre aux chiffres; *vt* figurer, représenter, dépeindre; décorer; *US* calculer, penser; ~ **out** calculer, penser; *vi* figurer; *coll* **that doesn't** ~ ça ne tient pas debout

**figured** *adj* figuré, à dessins; *mus* chiffré

**figurehead** *n naut* figure *f* de proue; *fig* personnalité majeure, figure *f* de proue

**figure-of-eight** *n* huit *m invar*

**figurine** *n* figurine *f*

**filament** *n* filament *m*; *bot* filet *m*

**filature** *n* filature *f*; (machine) dévidoir *m*

**filbert** *n* (tree) avelinier *m*; (nut) aveline *f*, noisette *f*

**filch** *vt* chiper, chaparder

**filcher** *n* chapardeur -euse

¹**file** *n* (documents, etc) classeur *m*, casier *m*; (card-index) fichier *m*; archives *fpl*, dossier *m*; *vt* classer; *leg* ~ **one's petition** déposer son bilan

²**file** *n* (tool) lime *f*; *vt* limer

³**file** *n* file *f*, colonne *f*; **Indian** ~ file indienne; **in** ~ en file, à la file; **the rank and** ~ *mil* les hommes *mpl* de troupe; le commun, les gens *mpl* ordinaires; *vt mil* faire défiler; *vi* défiler

**filial** *adj* filial

**filiation** *n* filiation *f*

**filibuster** *n* (pirate) flibustier *m*; *pol* tactique *f* obstructionniste; *vi* flibuster; *pol* faire de l'obstructionnisme

**filiform** *adj* filiforme

**filigree** *n* filigrane *m*

¹**filing** *n* classement *m*; *adj* ~ **cabinet** classeur *m*

²**filing** *n* limage *m*; (particle) limaille *f*

**fill** *n* quantité *f* pour remplir; ce qu'il faut (pour remplir); (enough) saoul *m*, soûl *m*; **I've had my** ~ **of that** j'en ai assez de cela; *vt* remplir, emplir; (gap) combler; (post, office) occuper; (vacancy) pourvoir à; (balloon) gonfler; (tooth) plomber, obturer; *naut* (sails) mettre le vent dans; ~ **in** (form) remplir; (hole) combler; *coll* ~ **the bill** être à la hauteur; ~ **up** remplir tout à fait; (form) remplir; *vi* se remplir, s'emplir; ~ **out** grossir; se gonfler; ~ **up** s'emplir

**filler** *n* (person) remplisseur -euse; (funnel) entonnoir *m*; (painting) mastic *m*

**fillet** *n* (meat, fish, etc) filet *m*; (hair) bandeau *m*, serre-tête *m invar*; *vt* lever les filets de; (bone) désosser; (head) orner d'un bandeau

**filling** *n* remplissage *m*; (teeth) plombage *m*, obturation *f*; *cul* farce *f*

**filling-station** *n* station-service *f* (*pl* stations-service), poste *m* d'essence

**fillip** *n* chiquenaude *f*; *fig* stimulant *m*, encouragement *m*; *vt* donner une chiquenaude à; *fig* stimuler, encourager; *vi* donner une chiquenaude

**filly** *n* pouliche *f*; *coll* (girl) jeune fille alléchante

**film** *n* film *m*; (coating) pellicule *f*, couche *f*; *phot* pellicule *f*; *vt* filmer; couvrir d'une pellicule; *vi* se couvrir d'une pellicule

**filmic** *adj* du cinéma, filmique

**film-star** *n* vedette *f*, star *f*

**filmy** *adj* couvert d'une pellicule

**filter** *n* filtre *m*; *vt* + *vi* filtrer

**filter-paper** *n* papier-filtre *m* (*pl* papiers-filtres)

**filter-tip** *n* bout *m* filtre

**filth**

**filth** *n* ordure *f*, immondices *mpl*; *fig* obscénité *f*

**filthy** *adj* sale; ordurier -ière, obscène

**filtrate** *n* filtrat *m*; *vt* filtrer

**filtration** *n* filtration *f*

**fin** *n* (fish) nageoire *f*; (shark) aileron *m*; *aer* aileron *m*; *mech* ailette *f*

**final** *n sp* finale *f*; ~ s = examens *mpl* de dernière année; *adj* final, ultime; déterminant, conclusif -ive; définitif -ive

**finale** *n* conclusion *f*; *mus* finale *m*

**finalist** *n* finaliste

**finality** *n* caractère définitif; *philos* finalité *f*

**finalization** *n* règlement *m*, arrangement définitif

**finalize** *vt* régler définitivement, conclure

**finance** *n* finance *f*; *vt* financer, commanditer

**financial** *adj* financier -ière

**financier** *n* financier -ière, commanditaire *m*

**finch** *n* pinson *m*

**find** *n* découverte *f*, trouvaille *f*; *vt* trouver, découvrir; constater, établir; considérer, estimer; (supply) fournir, pourvoir; ~ out découvrir, apprendre, venir à savoir; ~ s/o out démasquer qn; *vi leg* rendre un verdict; *leg* ~ for s/o retourner un verdict en faveur de qn

**finder** *n* trouveur -euse; *phot* viseur *m*; *astron* chercheur *m*

**finding** *n* découverte *f*; *leg* verdict *m*; décision *f*, conclusion *f*

¹**fine** *n* amende *f*; (key-money) pas *m* de porte; *vt* infliger une amende à, mettre à l'amende

²**fine** *adj* beau (*f* belle), superbe, excellent, splendide; (sharp) aigu -uë, fin; (pure) fin, pur; délicat, élégant, raffiné; (distinction) subtil; (weather) beau (*f* belle); *coll* + *iron* joli; ~ arts beaux arts; *coll* one ~ day un de ces jours, un de ces quatre matins; *adv coll* bien; cut it ~ y arriver de justesse; *vt* (gold) affiner; (liquid) clarifier; *fig* affiner; *vi* s'affiner

**fine-draw** *vt* stopper; (wire) étirer

**fine-drawn** *adj* stoppé; (wire) étiré; *fig* subtil, délié; (athlete) amaigri

**fine-looking** *adj* beau (*f* belle)

**finely** *adv* admirablement; (small pieces) menu

**fineness** *n* beauté *f*, finesse *f*, subtilité *f*, délicatesse *f*

¹**finery** *n* atours *mpl*

²**finery** *n mech* fourneau *m* d'affinage

**fine-spun** *adj* ténu, fragile; *fig* trop subtil

**finesse** *n* finesse *f*, habileté *f*; (bridge) impasse *f*; *vi* (bridge) ~ against faire l'impasse à

**finger** *n* doigt *m*; (bread) mouillette *f*; first ~ index *m*; have a ~ in sth y être pour qch; lay a ~ on toucher, faire du mal à; middle ~ médius *m*; not lift a ~ to ne pas remuer le petit doigt pour; put one's ~ on mettre le doigt sur; ring ~ annulaire *m*; *coll* take one's ` ~ out faire un effort; twist s/o round one's little ~ dominer qn, influencer qn, mener qn par le bout du nez; *vt* manier du doigt, toucher du doigt, palper; *mus* (instrument) toucher de; *mus* (give fingering) doigter

**finger-alphabet** *n* alphabet *m* des sourds-muets

**fingerboard** *n mus* (violin, etc) touche *f*; (piano) clavier *m*

**fingerbowl** *n* rince-doigts *m*

**fingering** *n mus* doigté *m*; (handling) maniement *m*

**fingernail** *n* ongle *m*

**fingerplate** *n* plaque *f* de propreté

**fingerpost** *n* poteau indicateur

**fingerprint** *n* empreinte digitale

**fingerstall** *n med* doigtier *m*

**fingertip** *n* bout *m* du doigt; have at one's ~ s savoir sur le bout des doigts

**finical, finicking, finicky** *adj* précieux -ieuse, pointilleux -euse, difficile

**fining** *n* clarification *f*; (metal) affinage *m*

**finis** *n* fin *f*

**finish** *n* fin *f*; (polish, paint) fini *m*; fight to the ~ combat *m* à l'outrance; *vt* finir, terminer, achever, compléter, accomplir; (perfect) perfectionner, parachever; ~ off achever; donner le dernier coup de main à; ~ up finir; *vi* finir, achever; cesser, s'achever, prendre fin

**finished** *adj* fini, terminé; parfait, soigné, achevé; (done for) fichu

**finisher** *n mech* finisseur -euse; *coll* coup *m* de grâce

**finishing** *n* parachèvement *m*, finissage *m*; *adj* qui finit, dernier -ière; ~ touch coup *m* de fion

**finite** *adj* fini

**fink** *n US sl* salaud *m*, mouchard -e, salope *f*; *vt* moucharder contre; *vi* moucharder

**Finland** *n* Finlande *f*

**Finn** *n* Finlandais -e

**finnan** *n* haddock fumé

**Finnish** *n* (language) finnois *m*; *adj* finnois

**finny** *adj* à nageoires; poissonneux -euse

**fiord, fjord** *n* fjord *m*

**fir** *n* sapin *m*

**fire** *n* feu *m*; (conflagration) incendie *m*; *mil* feu *m*; *fig* flamme *f*, énergie *f*, passion *f*; (glow) lueur *f*; be under ~ essuyer le feu; catch ~ prendre feu; go through ~ and water faire face à de grands périls; hang ~ (guns) faire long feu; (project, etc) traîner en longueur;

lay a ~ préparer le feu; on ~ en feu, en flammes; **open** ~ ouvrir le feu; **play with** ~ jouer avec le feu; *mil* **running** ~ tir *m* rapide; **set** ~ **to, set on** ~ allumer; lancer; **set the Thames on** ~ inventer la poudre; *vt* mettre le feu à, incendier; (firearm) tirer; (rocket) lancer; (explosive, mine) faire exploser; (pottery) cuire; *fig* enflammer, exciter; *coll* (employee) balancer; (questions) lancer; *vi* prendre feu; *mot*+*mech* marcher, tourner; *fig* s'enflammer; ~ **up** s'emporter

**fire-alarm** *n* avertisseur *m* d'incendie; signal *m* d'incendie

**firearm** *n* arme *f* à feu

**firebox** *n* foyer *m*

**firebrand** *n* tison *m*, brandon *m*; *fig* boutefeu *m*

**firebreak** *n* (forest) pare-feu *m invar*

**firebrick** *n* brique *f* réfractaire

**fire-brigade** *n* corps *m* des sapeurs-pompiers, pompiers *mpl*

**fire-bug** *n* luciole *f*; *sl* (arsonist) incendiaire

**fireclay** *n* argile *f* réfractaire, terre *f* réfractaire

**firedamp** *n* grisou *m*

**firedog** *n* chenet *m*

**fire-eater** *n* avaleur *m* de feu; *fig* grognon -onne, batailleur -euse

**fire-engine** *n* pompe *f* à incendie

**fire-escape** *n* échelle *f* d'incendie

**fire-extinguisher** *n* extincteur *m*

**fire-fighter** *n* pompier *m*

**firefly** *n* luciole *f*

**fireguard** *n* garde-feu *m invar*

**fire-insurance** *n* assurance *f* contre l'incendie

**fire-irons** *npl* garniture *f* de foyer

**fireless** *adj* sans feu

**firelight** *n* lumière *f* du feu

**firelighter** *n* allume-feu *m invar*

**fireman** *n* pompier *m*; (stoker) chauffeur *m*

**fireplace** *n* âtre *m*, cheminée *f*

**fire-plug** *n* bouche *f* d'incendie

**fireproof** *adj* ininflammable, ignifuge

**fire-raiser** *n* pyromane *m*

**fire-raising** *n* pyromanie *f*

**fire-screen** *n* écran *m*

**fireside** *n* coin *m* du feu, foyer *m*

**fire-station** *n* caserne *f* de pompiers, poste *m* d'incendie

**firewater** *n coll* gnôle *f*

**firewood** *n* bois *m* de chauffage

**firework** *n* pièce *f* d'artifice; ~s feu *m* d'artifice

**firing** *n mil* fusillade *f*; *mech* chauffage *m*, chauffe *f*; (pottery) cuite *f*, cuisson *m*; (fuel) combustible *m*; mise *f* à feu, allumage *m*; ~ **line** ligne *f* de feu; ~

**party,** ~ **squad** peloton *m* d'exécution

**firkin** *n* barillet *m*

¹**firm** *n comm* compagnie *f*, maison *f*, firme *f*

²**firm** *adj* ferme, solide, résolu; stable, fort; déterminé

**firmament** *n* firmament *m*

**firmness** *n* fermeté *f*

**first** *n* premier -ière; commencement *m*, début *m*; *adj* premier -ière; principal; le plus haut; unième; original, primordial; ~ **thing** en premier lieu, tout de suite; ~ **thing in the morning** dès le matin; *adv* premièrement, au début, d'abord; plutôt

**first-aid** *n* premiers secours

**firstborn** *n*+*adj* premier-né (*f* première-née)

**first-class** *adj* de première classe, excellent, de premier ordre; *adv* très bien

**first-floor** *n* premier étage; *US* rez-de-chaussée *m invar*

**first-fruits** *npl* prémices *fpl*

**first-hand** *adj* de première main

**first-night** *n theat* première *f*

**first-rate** *adj* de première classe, excellent, de premier ordre; *adv* très bien

**firth** *n* estuaire *m*, bras *m* de mer

**fiscal** *n Scots* = procureur *m* de la République); *adj* fiscal

¹**fish** *n* poisson *m*; *coll* type *m*; **cry stinking** ~ se déprécier; *coll* **feed the** ~**es** (drown) se noyer; (be seasick) avoir le mal de mer; *coll fig* **have other** ~ **to fry** avoir d'autres chats à fouetter; *coll fig* **pretty kettle of** ~ jolie affaire, beau gâchis; *vt* pêcher; *coll* ~ **for** pêcher, quêter; ~ **out** repêcher, tirer de l'eau; *vi* pêcher; *fig* ~ **in troubled waters** pêcher en eau trouble

²**fish** *n naut* jumelle *f*; *vt* jumeler

**fishball, fishcake** *n* boulette *f* de poisson

**fisher** *n* pêcheur *m*; (boat) bateau *m* de pêche

**fisherman** *n* pêcheur *m*; (boat) bateau *m* de pêche

**fisherwoman** *n* pêcheuse *f*

**fishery** *n* pêche *f*; (fishing ground) pêcherie *f*; **leg** droit *m* de pêche

**fish-glue** *n* colle *f* de poisson

**fish-hook** *n* hameçon *m*

**fishiness** *n* goût *m* de poisson; odeur *f* de poisson; *coll fig* caractère *m* louche

**fishing** *n* pêche *f*; droit *m* de pêche; ~ **boat** bateau *m* de pêche

**fish-kettle** *n cul* poissonnière *f*

**fish-knife** *n* couteau *m* à poisson

**fishmonger** *n* marchand -e de poisson

**fishpaste** *n* pâté *m* d'anchois, pâté *m* de saumon, pâté *m* de homard, pâté *m* de crabe

**fishplate** *n* éclisse *f*

483

**fish-slice** *n* truelle *f* à poisson
**fishwife** *n* marchande *f* de poisson; *fig* harengère *f*
**fishy** *adj* de poisson; *fig* louche, véreux -euse
**fissile** *adj* fissile
**fission** *n* fission *f*
**fissionable** *adj* fissible
**fissure** *n* fissure *f*; *vt* fissurer; *vi* se fissurer
**fist** *n* poing *m*; *coll* écriture *f*; *vt* cogner; *naut* empoigner
**fistful** *n* poignée *f*
**fisticuffs** *npl* rixe *f* à coups de poing
**fistula** *n path* fistule *f*
**¹fit** *n* accès *m*, attaque *f*, crise *f*; (coughing) quinte *f*; *fig* accès *m*, caprice *m*; ~ s convulsions *fpl*; by ~ s and starts par à-coups, par saccade; *coll* throw a ~ piquer une crise
**²fit** *n* ajustement *m*; this coat is a good ~ for me ce veston est à ma taille; *adj* convenable, approprié; apte, propre; en bonne santé, dispos; ~ as a fiddle en pleine forme; *vt* (clothes) aller à; (suit) être propre à; adapter, ajuster; (match) répondre à; (clothes) ~ on essayer; ~ out équiper; *naut* armer; ~ up équiper, aménager; *vi* s'ajuster, s'adapter; (clothes) aller bien; ~ in with s'adapter à, accorder avec
**fitful** *adj* irrégulier -ière, changeant, capricieux -ieuse
**fitment** *n* meuble *m* à demeure; *mech* accessoire *m*, pièce *f*
**fitness** *n* aptitude *f*; (appropriateness) justesse *f*, à-propos *m*; (health) santé *f*, bonne forme
**fitter** *n* ajusteur *m*, monteur *m*; (clothes) essayeur -euse
**fitting** *n* ajustage *m*, ajustement *m*; montage *m*; (clothes) essayage *m*; *adj* convenable, approprié; (proper) bienséant
**fit-up** *n theat* pose *f* des décors
**five** *n* cinq *m invar*; *adj* cinq *invar*
**five-fold** *adj* quintuple; *adv* au quintuple
**fiver** *n coll* billet *m* de cinq livres
**fives** *npl sp* jeu anglais semblable à la pelote basque
**fivescore** *n* cent *m*
**fix** *n coll* embarras *m*, difficulté *f*; *naut*+*aer* détermination *f*; position déterminée; *sl* piqûre *f* de drogue; be in a ~ être dans le pétrin; *vt* fixer; (arrange) arrêter, décider; *US* arranger, préparer; (repair) réparer; (bribe) soudoyer; (election) truquer
**fixate** *vt* fixer
**fixation** *n* fixation *f*
**fixative** *n* fixatif *m*; *adj* fixatif -ive
**fixed** *adj* fixe, arrêté; constant, invariable; ~ idea idée *f* fixe

**fixer** *n* personne *f* qui arrange les choses; *phot* fixateur *m*
**fixing** *n* fixation *f*; *phot* fixage *m*; *coll* ~ s accessoires *mpl*
**fixity** *n* fixité *f*
**fixture** *n* meuble *m* à demeure, meuble *m* fixe; *sp* engagement *m*, match prévu; *leg* ~ s biens *mpl* par destination
**fizz** *n* pétillement *m*; effervescence *f*; *coll* champagne *m*; boisson gazeuse; *vi* pétiller
**fizzle** *n* pétillement *m*; *coll* fiasco *m*; *vi* pétiller; ~ out finir en queue de poisson, avorter
**fizzy** *adj* pétillant, gazeux -euse
**fjord** *n see* fiord
**flabbergast** *vt coll* abasourdir, étonner; déconcerter, dérouter
**flabbiness** *n* mollesse *f*
**flabby** *adj* mou (*f* molle), flasque, avachi
**flaccid** *adj* flasque
**flaccidity** *n* flaccidité *f*
**¹flag** *n* drapeau *m*; *naut* pavillon *m*; (small) fanion *m*; (bookmarker) signet *m*; *coll* show the ~ se manifester, être présent; yellow ~ pavillon *m* de quarantaine; white ~ parlementaire *m*; *vt* pavoiser; transmettre par signaux (au moyen de fanions); faire signe à; ~ down faire signe de s'arrêter à
**²flag** *n bot* iris *m*
**³flag** *n* (stone) dalle *f*; *vt* daller
**⁴flag** *vi* (hang down) pendre mollement; (weaken) s'affaiblir, diminuer; (zeal) défaillir, fléchir; (interest) faiblir; (plant) languir
**flag-day** *n* jour *m* de quête
**flagellant** *n* flagellant *m*
**flagellate** *vt* flageller, fouetter
**flagellation** *n* flagellation *f*
**flageolet** *n mus* flageolet *m*
**¹flagging** *n* dallage *m*, carrelage *m*
**²flagging** *adj* languissant
**flagitious** *adj* infâme, abominable, vil
**flag-lieutenant** *n naut* lieutenant *m* de pavillon
**flag-officer** *n naut* officier général
**flagon** *n* grande bouteille; pot *m* (pour le vin)
**flagrance, flagrancy** *n* énormité *f*, caractère scandaleux; *leg* flagrance *f*
**flagrant** *adj* flagrant, énorme, scandaleux -euse
**flagship** *n naut* vaisseau *m* amiral
**flagstaff** *n* mât *m* (de drapeau)
**flagstone** *n* dalle *f*
**flagwagging** *n coll mil*+*naut* signalisation *f* (au moyen de fanions); *coll fig* chauvinisme *m*, patriotisme exagéré
**flail** *n* fléau *m*; *vt* battre au fléau
**flair** *n* flair *m*, don *m*; perspicacité *f*
**flake** *n* (snow, etc) flocon *m*; (layer)

écaille *f*, lamelle *f*; *cul* feuillette *f*; (soap) paillette *f*; *vi* s'écailler

**flake-white** *n* blanc *m* de céruse

**flaky** *adj* floconneux -euse; lamellé; *cul* feuilleté

**flamboyance** *n* caractère flamboyant; panache *m*

**flamboyant** *adj* flamboyant

**flame** *n* flamme *f*; *fig* flamme *f*, ardeur *f*, passion *f*; *coll* béguin *m*, flirt *m*, amoureux -euse; *vi* flamber, flamboyer; s'enflammer

**flamenco** *n* flamenco *m*

**flame-thrower** *n mil* lance-flammes *m*

**flaming** *adj* flambant, flamboyant; *fig* ardent, passionné; *coll* sacré

**flamingo** *n* flamant *m*

**flammable** *adj* inflammable

**flan** *n* flan *m*

**flange** *n* (wheel) boudin *m*; (tube) collerette *f*; (pulley) joue *f*; *vt* brider

**flank** *n* flanc *m*; *vt* flanquer; *mil* prendre de flanc; *vi* être aux flancs, être à côté

**flannel** *n* flanelle *f*; (face-cloth) gant *m* de toilette; **~s** pantalon *m* de flanelle; *vi coll* baratiner

**flannelette** *n* finette *f*

**flap** *n* (movement) battement *m*; (pocket, envelope) rabat *m*; (table) battant *m*; *coll fig* panique *f*; *coll* **be in a ~** s'affoler; *vt* (wings) battre; *vi* battre, claquer; *coll fig* paniquer

**flapjack** *n* crêpe épaisse

**flapper** *n* (fly-whisk) émouchoir *m*; *ar* adolescente *f*

**flare** *n* flamboiement *m*; (signal) feu *m*, signal lumineux; *mil* fusée éclairante; (dress) évasement *m*; *vi* flamber, flamboyer; (dress) s'évaser

**flare-path** *n aer* rampe *f* de balisage

**flare-up** *n* flamboiement *m*, flambée soudaine; *fig* altercation *f*

**flash** *n* éclat *m*; (lightning, inspiration) éclair *m*; (camera, news) flash *m*; *mil* parement *m*; **~ in the pan** feu *m* de paille; **in a ~** tout de suite, en un clin d'œil; *adj coll* (showy) voyant, criard; (suspect) louche; *vt* (light) projeter; (news, etc) transmettre (par radio, etc); *mot* **~ one's headlights** faire une appel de phares; *pej* (display) étaler; *sl* (look) reluquer; *vi* (bright object) étinceler; *mot* (lights) clignoter; **~ past** passer comme un éclair

**flashback** *n* retour *m* en arrière

**flasher** *n mot* clignotant *m*; exhibitionniste *m*

**flashiness** *n* clinquant *m*

**flashlight** *n* (torch) lampe *f* électrique; *phot* flash *m*

**flashpoint** *n* point *m* d'ignition

**flashy** *adj* clinquant, voyant

**flask** *n* flacon *m*; *chem* fiole *f*

**flat** *n* appartement *m*; (mud) marécage *m*; *mus* bémol *m*; *theat* portant *m*; (racing) plat *m*; *adj* plat, monotone; *mus* faux (*f* fausse); (beer, lemonade) éventé; (categorical) net (*f* nette); (tyre) crevé; *coll* (absolute) net (*f* nette),. catégorique; *coll* **~ broke** fauché; **~ race** course *f* de plat; *mus* **A ~ A** bémol; *coll* **be in a ~ spin** être dans tous ses états; **fall ~ on one's face** tomber sur le nez; *coll* **that's ~** un point c'est tout; *adv* à plat; *coll* (definitely) carrément, sans ambages; *mus* faux; **be ~ out** être à plat; *coll* **go ~ out** (runner) courir à fond de train; (car) être à sa vitesse de pointe; *fig* donner son maximum; **work ~ out** travailler d'arrache-pied

**flatfish** *n* poisson plat

**flat-footed** *adj* aux pieds plats; *fig* balourd

**flat-iron** *n* fer *m* à repasser

**flatlet** *n* studio *m*

**flatly** *adv* carrément; (deny) catégoriquement

**flatness** *n* égalité *f*, aspect plat; (dullness) monotonie *f*

**flatten** *vt* (smooth) aplanir; (press, hammer) aplatir; (crops) coucher; (trees) abattre; *vi* **~ out** s'aplanir; *aer* se redresser

**flatter** *vt* flatter; **~ oneself** se flatter

**flatterer** *n* flatteur -euse

**flattery** *n* flatterie *f*

**flattish** *adj* assez plat

**flatulence, flatulency** *n* flatulence *f*

**flaunt** *vt* étaler, faire étalage de; *pej* faire parade de

**flautist** *n* flûtiste *f*

**flavour** *n* arôme *m*, goût *m*, saveur *f*; (ice-cream, etc) parfum *m*; (meat) fumet *m*; *fig* atmosphère *f*; *vt* donner du goût à; (season) assaisonner; (sweet, ice-cream, etc) parfumer

**flavouring** *n* (seasoning) assaisonnement *m*; (sweet, ice-cream, etc) parfum *m*

**flaw** *n* défaut *m*, imperfection *f*; *leg* vice *m* de forme; *fig* (blemish) faille *f*; (snag) inconvénient *m*; *vt* abîmer

**flawed** *adj* imparfait

**flawless** *adj* parfait, sans faille, impeccable

**flax** *n* lin *m*

**flaxen** *adj* de lin

**flay** *vt* écorcher; (beat) fouetter, battre; (criticize) éreinter

**flea** *n* puce *f*; *fig* **~ in one's ear** rebuffade *f*

**flea-bag** *n coll* sac *m* de couchage

**flea-bite** *n* piqûre *f* de puce; *fig* vétille *f*, broutille *f*

**flea-bitten** *adj* mordu par les puces; *coll* moche, miteux -euse

**flea-pit** *n coll* (cinema) ciné miteux

**fleck** *n* particule *f*, petite tache; *vt* tacheter, moucheter, pommeler

**flection** *n see* **flexion**

**fledged** *adj* **fully ~** (bird) qui a toutes ses plumes; *fig* qualifié, diplômé; adulte

**fledgeling** *n* oiselet *m*; (novice) blanc-bec *m* (*pl* blancs-becs)

**flee** *vt* fuir, s'enfuir de; *vi* fuir, s'enfuir

**fleece** *n* toison *f*; *vt* (sheep) tondre; *fig* escroquer, filouter

**fleecy** *adj* (wool) laineux -euse; (clouds) floconneux -euse

**¹fleet** *n* flotte *f*

**²fleet** *adj* rapide

**fleet-footed** *adj* au pied léger

**Fleming** *n* Flamand -e

**Flemish** *n* (language) flamand *m*; *adj* flamand

**flesh** *n* chair *f*; (fruit) pulpe *f*; *cul* viande *f*; *poet* être humain; **go the way of all ~** payer le tribut de la nature; **in the ~** en chair et en os; **make one's ~ creep** donner la chair de poule à qn; **one's own ~ and blood** sa famille; **pound of ~** dû *m*

**flesh-coloured** *adj* couleur chair *invar*

**fleshly** *adj* charnel -elle

**fleshpots** *npl* bonne chère

**fleshy** *adj* charnu

**¹flex** *n* fil *m* (souple)

**²flex** *vt* fléchir; (muscles) bander

**flexibility** *n* flexibilité *f*, souplesse *f*

**flexible** *adj* flexible, souple; *fig* (person) accommodant, souple

**flexion** *n* flexion *f*, courbure *f*

**flexor** *n anat* fléchisseur *m*

**flibbertigibbet** *n* hurluberlu *m*, écervelé -e, tête *f* de linotte

**flick** *n* (finger) chiquenaude *f*; (light blow) petit coup; *coll* **~s** ciné *m*; *vt* donner un petit coup à; **~ off** enlever d'une chiquenaude; (book, etc) **~ through** feuilleter, lire en diagonale

**flicker** *n* vacillement *m*; (hope) lueur *f*; *vi* vaciller, trembloter, danser

**flick-knife** *n* couteau *m* à cran d'arrêt

**flier** *n see* **flyer**

**¹flight** *n* vol *m*; (bullet, etc) trajectoire *f*; (fancy) essor *m*, envol *m*; (birds) vol *m*, volée *f*; (planes) escadrille *f*; (stairs) volée *f*; **in the first (top) ~** de pointe; **two ~s up** (on second floor) au deuxième étage; deux étages plus haut

**²flight** *n* fuite *f*; **put to ~** mettre en fuite; **take to ~** s'enfuir

**flight-deck** *n naut* pont *m* d'envol; *aer* poste *m* de pilotage

**flight-lieutenant** *n* = capitaine *m* de l'armée de l'air

**flighty** *adj* volage, capricieux -ieuse

**flimsiness** *n* fragilité *f*, minceur *f*; (excuse) faiblesse *f*

**flimsy** *n coll* papier *m* pelure *invar*; *adj* mince; (excuse) faible, piètre

**flinch** *vi* broncher, reculer

**flinders** *npl* éclats *mpl*

**fling** *n* action *f* de lancer; mouvement *m* brusque; *fig* (taunt) raillerie *f*; *coll* **have a ~** faire la noce; **youth must have its ~** il faut que jeunesse se passe; *vt* jeter, lancer; **~ away** jeter; **~ in s/o's teeth** reprocher à qn; *fig* **~ off** se débarrasser de; **~ oneself at s/o** se jeter à la tête de qn; **~ oneself into** se lancer à corps perdu dans; **~ out** jeter, se débarrasser de; **~ up** jeter en l'air; *vi* se précipiter

**flint** *n* silex *m*; (cigarette lighter) pierre *f* (à briquet); *adj* de pierre

**flinty** *adj* à silex; *fig* dur, de pierre

**flip** *n* chiquenaude *f*, pichenette *f*; *sl* petit tour en zinc; *adj coll* désinvolte; (record) **~ side** autre face *f* (d'un disque); *vt* donner une chiquenaude à; **~ over**, **~ through** (book) feuilleter

**flippancy** *n* désinvolture *f*

**flippant** *adj* désinvolte

**flipper** *n* (animal) nageoire *f*; **~s** (swimmer) palmes *fpl*

**flipping** *adj coll* maudit

**flirt** *n* flirteur -euse; *vi* flirter

**flirtation** *n* flirt *m*, amourette *f*

**flirtatious** *adj* flirteur -euse, flirt *invar*

**flit** *n* déménagement *m*; **do a moonlight ~** déménager à la cloche de bois; *vi* voleter, voltiger; (move house) déménager à la cloche de bois

**flitch** *n cul* flèche *f*

**flitting** *n* déménagement *m*

**flivver** *n coll* bagnole *f*, tacot *m*, guimbarde *f*

**float** *n* (fishing, seaplane, carburettor) flotteur *m*; (raft) radeau *m*; (cart) char *m*; *theat* **~s** rampe *f*; *vt* (boat) faire flotter; (company) créer, fonder; (loan, idea) lancer; *vi* flotter, être à flot; (swimmer) faire la planche; **~ around** circuler; **~ away** partir à la dérive

**floatation** *n* flottaison *f*; *comm* lancement *m*

**floating** *adj* flottant; *fig* instable; **~ assets** capitaux courants; **~ voter** électeur -trice indécis -e

**flocculent** *adj* floconneux -euse

**¹flock** *n* (animals, geese) troupeau *m*; (birds) vol *m*; (people) foule *f*; *eccles* ouailles *fpl*; *vi* affluer, venir en masse; **~ round** se grouper autour de; **~ together** s'assembler

**²flock** *n* bourre *f* (de laine, de coton)

**floe** *n* banquise *f*

**flog** vt fouetter, fustiger; coll (sell) vendre; fig ~ **a dead horse** enfoncer une porte ouverte, perdre sa peine

**flogging** n flagellation f; leg fouet m

**flood** n inondation f; (spate) crue f; (tide) flux m; fig flot m, déluge m, torrent m; fig **at the** ~ au moment le plus propice; eccles **the Flood** le déluge; vt inonder, submerger; mot noyer; vi (river) déborder; (crowd) affluer

**floodgate** n vanne f; fig **open the** ~**s** ouvrir les vannes

**flooding** n inondation f

**floodlight** n projecteur m; vt illuminer, éclairer; fig mettre en lumière

**floodlighting** n illumination f, éclairage m

**floodtide** n flux m

**floor** n plancher m; parquet m; (tiled) carrelage m; (storey) étage m; (sea-bed) fond m; (dance) piste f; fig comm plancher m; **on the** ~ par terre, sur le sol; **take the** ~ prendre la parole; vt plancheier, parqueter; (knock to the ground) terrasser, envoyer au tapis; coll réduire au silence, déconcerter

**floorboard** n planche f, latte f

**floorcloth** n (cleaning) serpillière f; (covering) revêtement m de sol

**floor-polish** n encaustique f

**floor-polisher** n cireuse f

**floor-show** n attractions fpl

**floosie, floozy** n sl poule f

**flop** n floc m; fig (disaster) four m, fiasco m; **be a** ~ échouer; vi (collapse) s'effondrer, s'affaler; theat faire un four; (scheme) être un fiasco

**flop-house** n US asile m de nuit

**floppy** adj flottant, flou

**flora** n flore f

**floral** adj floral

**florescence** n floraison f

**florescent** adj en fleurs

**floriculture** n floriculture f

**florid** adj (complexion) rubicond, rougeaud; (style) fleuri

**florist** n fleuriste

**floss** n bourre f de soie

**flotation** n see **floatation**

**flotilla** n flotille f

**flotsam** n épave flottante

¹**flounce** n mouvement m brusque; vi avoir des mouvements vifs, faire un mouvement brusque; ~ **in** entrer brusquement; ~ **out** sortir brusquement

²**flounce** n volant m; vt garnir de volants

¹**flounder** n flet m, plie f, carrelet m

²**flounder** vi patauger, barboter; (struggle) se débattre; fig hésiter, bredouiller

**flour** n farine f; vt fariner; (face) enfariner

**flourish** n fioriture f, ornement m; mus fanfare f; vt (stick) brandir; vi fleurir, prospérer; (develop) s'épanouir, bien venir

**flourishing** adj florissant, prospère; (health) en bonne santé

**floury** adj enfariné; (foodstuff) farineux -euse

**flout** n moquerie f; vt se moquer de, faire fi de

**flow** n (liquid) écoulement m; (words) flot m; (current) courant m; (tide) flux m; vi couler; (current) circuler; (tide) monter; fig résulter; (hair) flotter

**flower** n fleur f; floraison f; fig (best part) crème f, élite f; ~ **people** hippies mpl; vt faire fleurir; vi fleurir

**flowerbed** n plate-bande f (pl plates-bandes), parterre m

**flowered** adj fleuri

**flowering** n floraison f; adj en fleurs

**flowerpot** n pot m à fleurs

**flower-shop** n boutique f de fleuriste

**flower-show** n floralies fpl

**flowery** adj fleuri, couvert de fleurs; (style) orné

**flowing** adj coulant; (tide) montant; (beard) long (f longue); (movement) gracieux -ieuse

**flu** n coll grippe f

**fluctuate** vi fluctuer, varier

**fluctuating** adj variant, vacillant

**fluctuation** n fluctuation f, variation f

¹**flue** n conduit m de cheminée, tuyau m de cheminée

²**flue** vt évaser; vi s'évaser

**fluency** n aisance f, facilité f

**fluent** adj aisé, coulant; **speak** ~ **French** parler couramment le français

**fluently** adv couramment

**fluff** n peluche f; (bird, etc) duvet m; sl (girl) nénette f; vt ébouriffer; theat (line) louper; vi theat louper

**fluffy** adj duveteux -euse

**fluid** n fluide m, liquide m; adj fluide, liquide

**fluidity** n fluidité f

¹**fluke** n coup m de veine

²**fluke** n naut patte f (d'ancre)

³**fluke** n (fish) carrelet m

**flummery** n coll flagornerie f

**flummox** vt coll déconcerter

**flunk** vt US (examination) être collé à

**flunkey** n laquais m; fig larbin m

**fluoresce** vi devenir fluorescent

**fluorescence** n fluorescence f

**fluorescent** adj fluorescent

**fluoride** n chem fluorure m

**fluorine** n chem fluor m

**fluorite** n chem fluorine f

**flurry** n (wind) rafale f; fig agitation f; vt agiter, effarer

¹**flush** n (redness) rougeur f; (shy)

rougeoiement *m*; (blood) flux *m*; (lavatory) chasse *f* (d'eau); *fig* (excitement) élan *m*, ivresse *f*; (health) éclat *m*; *med* **hot** ~ bouffée *f* de chaleur; *vt* nettoyer à grande eau; ~ **the lavatory** tirer la chasse (d'eau); *vi* rougir, s'empourprer

²**flush** *n* (birds) envolée *f*; *vt* (birds) lever

³**flush** *n* (cards) flush *m*

⁴**flush** *adj* (full) plein à déborder; (level) au même niveau, à ras; *coll* ~ **with money** plein de fric; *adv* de niveau, à ras; *vt* mettre au niveau

**fluster** *n* trouble *m*, agitation *f*, énervement *m*; **in a** ~ énervé; *vt* troubler, agiter, énerver

**flute** *n* flûte *f*; (player) flûtiste *m*; *archi* cannelure *f*; *vt archi* canneler; *vi* jouer de la flûte; chanter d'un ton flûté

**fluted** *adj archi* cannelé

**fluting** *n archi* cannelure *f*

**flutist** *n see* **flautist**

**flutter** *n* (movement) battement *m*; (heart) palpitation *f*; (worry) agitation *f*, émoi *m*; *coll* **have a** ~ (bet) parier de petites sommes; (speculation) boursicoter; *vt* (wings, eyelids) battre de; *vi* (fly) voleter, voltiger; (wings) battre; (heart) palpiter; (flag) flatter; (person) virevolter, être agité

**fluvial** *adj* fluvial

**flux** *n* (flow) flot *m*, flux *m*; (change) vicissitudes *fpl*, fluctuation *f*; *med +phys* flux *m*; **be in a state of** ~ changer sans arrêt

**fluxion** *n med* fluxion *f*

¹**fly** *n* (insect, fishing) mouche *f*; *fig* ~ **in the ointment** hic *m*, ennui *m*; *coll* **there are no flies on him** il n'est pas né d'hier; *adj coll* malin (*f* maligne), rusé

²**fly** *n* (flying) vol *m*; (trousers) braguette *f*; (tent) auvent *m*; (flag) battant *m*; (carriage) fiacre *m*; *theat* **flies** cintres *mpl*; *coll* (trousers) braguette *f*; *vt* (aircraft) piloter; (passenger, goods) transporter en avion; ~ **a kite** faire voler un cerf-volant; *fig* lancer un ballon d'essai; ~ **the country** s'enfuir du pays; *naut* ~ **the French flag** battre pavillon français; *vi* (bird, aircraft, etc) voler; (passenger) voyager en avion; (time) passer vite; (flee) fuir, s'enfuir; (move fast) se précipiter, courir; (spark) jaillir; ~ **at** attaquer violemment; *coll* ~ **high** être ambitieux -ieuse; ~ **in the face of** lancer un défi à; ~ **into a rage** s'emporter, se mettre en colère; ~ **off the handle** sortir de ses gonds, s'emporter; ~ **out at** insulter violemment; ~ **over** survoler; **I must** ~ il faut que je file; **let** ~ **at** s/o prendre qn violemment à partie

**flyaway** *adj* (hair) intraitable

**flyblown** *adj* couvert de chiures de mouche; *fig* gâté

**fly-button** *n* bouton *m* de braguette

**fly-by-night** *n* débiteur -trice qui décampe en douce

**fly-catcher** *n orni* gobe-mouches *m*; *bot* plante *f* carnivore; (trap) attrape-mouches *m*

**flyer, flier** *n aer* aviateur -trice; *fig* doué -e

**fly-fishing** *n* pêche *f* à la mouche

**fly-half** *n sp* demi *m* d'ouverture

**flying-boat** *n* hydravion *m*

**flying-bomb** *n* bombe volante

**flying-buttress** *n* arc-boutant *m* (*pl* arcs-boutants)

**flying-fish** *n* poisson volant

**flying-saucer** *n* soucoupe volante

**flying-squad** *n* brigade volante de la police judiciaire

**flyleaf** *n* page *f* de garde

**fly-over** *n* autopont *m*, toboggan *m*; *US* défilé aérien

**fly-paper** *n* papier *m* tue-mouches

**fly-past** *n* défilé aérien

**fly-sheet** *n* feuille volante

**fly-swatter** *n* tapette *f*

**flyweight** *n sp* poids *m* mouche

**fly-wheel** *n* volant *m*

**foal** *n* (horse) poulain *m*; (ass) ânon *m*; *vi* mettre bas

**foam** *n* (sea) écume *f*; (beer) mousse *f*; ~ **rubber** caoutchouc *m* mousse; ~ **sprayer** extincteur *m* à mousse; *vi* (sea) écumer, moutonner; (soapy water) mousser; (sparkling wine) mousser, pétiller; ~ **at the mouth** (animal) baver; *fig* (person) écumer de rage

**foamy** *adj* (sea) écumeux -euse; (beer) mousseux -euse

**fob** *n ar* gousset *m*; *vt* tricher; ~ **s/o off with promises** payer qn de promesses; ~ **sth off on** s/o refiler qch à qn

**focal** *adj* focal; ~ **length** distance focale; ~ **point** foyer *m*; *fig* point central

**focus** *n* foyer *m*; *fig* centre *m*; **in** ~ au point; *vt fig* concentrer; *vi* (light, rays) converger

**fodder** *n* fourrage *m*

**foe** *n* ennemi -e

**foehn, föhn** *n* foehn *m*, föhn *m*

**foetal** *adj* fœtal

**foetid** *adj see* **fetid**

**foetus** *n* fœtus *m*

**fog** *n* brouillard *m*; *naut* brume *f*; *phot* voile *m*; *vt* (windows, glasses, etc) embuer; *phot* voiler; *fig* obscurcir; *vi* (windows, glasses, etc) s'embuer; (landscape) s'embrunir; *phot* se voiler

**fogbank** *n* banc *m* de brume

**fogbound** *adj* pris dans le brouillard

**fogey, fogy** *n coll old* ~ vieux bonze, vieille baderne

**foggy** *adj* brumeux -euse; *fig* (idea) vague, confus; **I haven't the foggiest idea!** aucune idée!

**foghorn** *n* sirène *f* de brume

**foglamp** *n mot* phare *m* antibrouillard

**fog-signal** *n* (railway) pétard *m*

**fogy** *n see* fogey

**föhn** *n see* foehn

**foible** *n* marotte *f*, petite manie

**¹foil** *n* feuille *f* de métal, lame *f* de métal; (mirror) tain *m*; *cul* papier *m* d'aluminium; *archi* lobe *m*; *fig* (contrast) repoussoir *m*

**²foil** *n sp* fleuret *m*

**³foil** *vt* contrecarrer, déjouer

**foist** *vt* refiler, repasser; ~ **oneself on** s'imposer à

**¹fold** *n* (sheep) parc *m* à moutons; *eccles* bercail *m*; *vt* (sheep) parquer

**²fold** *n* pli *m*; *geol* plissement *m*; (hollow) repli *m*; *vt* plier; (wrap) envelopper, entourer; ~ **in two** plier en deux; ~ **one's arms** se croiser les bras; ~ **s/o in one's arms** étreindre qn; *vi* (chair, table, etc) se replier; *coll theat* faire un four, tomber; (business) fermer ses portes; ~ **up** (business) échouer

**folder** *n* (file) chemise *f*; (circular) brochure *f*, dépliant *m*

**folding** *adj* pliant; ~ **door** porte *f* en accordéon; ~ **seat** pliant *m*; *mot* + *theat* strapontin *m*

**foliage** *n* feuillage *m*

**foliate** *adj bot* folié; *vt* (book) folioter; *archi* décorer de lobes

**foliation** *n bot* foliation *f*, feuillaison *f*; (book) foliotage *m*

**folio** *n* folio *m*; (book) in-folio *m*

**folk** *n* (people) gens *mpl*; (people in general) les gens *mpl*; **old** ~ les vieux; **young** ~ les jeunes; *coll* ~ **s** (relatives) parents *mpl*, famille *f*; *adj* traditionnel -elle, populaire, folklorique

**folk-dance, folk-dancing** *n* danse *f* folklorique, danse *f* rustique

**folklore** *n* folklore *m*

**folk-music** *n* musique *f* folklorique; (contemporary) musique *f* folk

**folksinger** *n* chanteur -euse de musique folklorique (de musique folk)

**folksong** *n* chanson *f* folklorique

**folksy** *adj coll* populaire, rustique; (person) gentil -ille

**folktale** *n* conte *m* populaire, conte *m* folklorique

**follicle** *n* follicule *m*

**follow** *vt* suivre, marcher derrière; (pursue) poursuivre; (suspect) filer; (profession) suivre, exercer; (understand) suivre, comprendre; (fashion) se conformer à, suivre; ~ **out** poursuivre jusqu'au bout; ~ **suit** fournir une carte; *fig* faire de même; (inquiries) ~ **up** poursuivre, continuer; *vi* suivre; (understand) suivre, comprendre; (result) s'ensuivre; ~ **on** suivre; résulter; (meal) **what's to** ~ ? qu'est-ce qu'il y a après?

**follower** *n* disciple *m*, partisan -e; (retainer) suivant -e; *coll ar* admirateur *m*, amoureux *m*

**following** *n* suite *f*; partisans *mpl* (*fpl* partisanes), adeptes *pl*; *adj* suivant, ce qui suit

**follow-up** *n* suite *f*; (circular) rappel *m*; *med* ~ **care** soins post-hospitaliers; ~ **study** étude *f* complémentaire

**folly** *n* folie *f*, absurdité *f*, sottise *f*; *archi* folie *f*

**foment** *vt* fomenter

**fomentation** *n* fomentation *f*

**fond** *adj* tendre, affectueux -euse; (doting) trop indulgent; (hope) fervent; (belief) naïf (*f* naïve); **be** ~ **of** aimer, aimer beaucoup

**fondle** *vt* caresser

**fondly** *adv* affectueusement; (credulously) naïvement

**fondness** *n* (people) affection *f*, tendresse *f*; (things) penchant *m*, prédilection *f*

**font** *n* fonts baptismaux

**food** *n* nourriture *f*, aliment *m*, de quoi manger; (cattle) pâture *f*; (poultry, domestic animals, etc) pâtée *f*; *fig* nourriture *f*, pâture *f*; ~ **s** aliments *mpl*; ~ **chain** chaîne *f* alimentaire; ~ **for thought** matière *f* à réflexion; ~ **shop** magasin *m* d'alimentation; ~ **supplies** ravitaillement *m*; **convenience** ~ **s** aliments *mpl* à préparation rapide

**foodstuff** *n* denrée *f* alimentaire; ~ **s** denrées *fpl* alimentaires, vivres *mpl*, comestibles *mpl*

**¹fool** *n* imbécile, idiot -e, sot (*f* sotte); (jester) bouffon *m*; ~ **'s paradise** bonheur *m* illusoire; **make a** ~ **of** duper; **make a** ~ **of oneself** se rendre ridicule; **play the** ~ faire l'idiot -e; *vt* duper, berner, *coll* avoir; *vi* faire l'imbécile; ~ **about** perdre son temps, faire l'idiot

**²fool** *n cul* mousse *f* de fruits

**foolery** *n* ânerie *f*, bêtises *fpl*, bouffonnerie *f*

**foolhardiness** *n* témérité *f*, imprudence *f*

**foolhardy** *adj* téméraire, imprudent

**foolish** *adj* bête, idiot, stupide; (rash) imprudent, insensé; (simple) simple d'esprit; (behaviour) **be** ~ faire l'idiot -e

**foolishly** *adv* bêtement, sottement

**foolishness** *n* bêtise *f*, sottise *f*

**foolscap** *n* papier écolier, papier *m* ministre

**foot**

foot *n* (*pl* feet) pied *m*; (animal) patte *f*; *mil* infanterie *f*; (page) bas *m*; (table, bed) bout *m*; *fig* **at one's feet** fasciné; **fall on one's feet** avoir de la chance; **find one's feet** trouver le joint; **get off on the wrong** ~ commencer mal; **get one's** ~ **in the door** établir un premier contact; *coll* **my** ~**!** balivernes!; **one** ~ **in the grave** un pied dans la tombe; **put one's best** ~ **forward** allonger le pas, faire de son mieux; **put one's** ~ **down** faire acte d'autorité; *mot* appuyer sur le champignon; *coll* **put one's** ~ **in it** mettre ses pieds dans le plat; **set on** ~ mettre en train; *vt* (stocking) rempiéter; ~ **it** aller à pied; *coll* ~ **the bill** casquer

**footage** *n cin* = métrage *m*

**foot-and-mouth (disease)** *n* fièvre aphteuse

**football** *n* ballon *m*; (game) football *m*

**footballer** *n* joueur *m* de football

**footboard** *n* marchepied *m*

**foot-bridge** *n* passerelle *f*

**footfall** *n* pas *m*; (sound) bruit *m* de pas

**footgear** *n* chaussures *fpl*

**foothill** *n* contrefort *m*

**foothold** *n* prise *f* de pied, point *m* d'appui; *fig* pied *m*

**footing** *n* prise *f* de pied, point *m* d'appui; *fig* (status) position *f*, situation *f*; (contact) relation *f*

**footle** *vi coll* faire l'âne

**footlights** *npl theat* rampe *f*

**footling** *adj coll* futile

**foot-loose** *adj* libre comme l'air

**footman** *n* valet *m* de pied

**footmark** *n* empreinte *f* (de pied)

**footnote** *n* note *f* en bas de la page; *vt* annoter

**footpad** *n ar* voleur *m* de grands chemins

**footpath** *n* sentier *m*

**footplate** *n* plate-forme *f* (*pl* plates-formes) (d'une locomotive)

**footprint** *n* empreinte *f* (de pied)

**foot-slog** *vi coll* marcher d'un pas lourd

**footsore** *adj* aux pieds endoloris

**footstep** *n* pas *m*; **follow in the** ~**s of** imiter

**footstool** *n* tabouret *m*

**footway** *n* sentier *m*

**footwear** *n* chaussures *fpl*

**footwork** *n* jeu *m* de jambes

**fop** *n* dandy *m*, petit-maître *m* (*pl* petits-maîtres), fat *m*

**foppery** *n* fatuité *f*

**foppish** *adj* dandy *invar*

**for** *prep* pour; au profit de; (because of) pour, en raison de; (instead of) à la place de; (time) pour, pendant, depuis; (distance) pendant, sur; (considering) pour; (in spite of) malgré; (towards) dans la direction de, vers; ~ **all that** malgré tout; ~ **my part** quant à moi; **be all** ~ être tout à fait pour; **what** ~? pourquoi?; **what is that** ~? à quoi ça sert?; **you're** ~ **it!** qu'est-ce que tu vas prendre!; *conj* car

**forage** *n* fourrage *m*; *vi* fourrager, fouiller

**forage-cap** *n mil* calot *m*

**forasmuch** *conj* ~ **as** vu que, étant donné que

**foray** *n* raid *m*, razzia *f*, incursion *f*; *vi* faire un raid

¹**forbear, forebear** *n* ancêtre *m*

²**forbear** *vi* s'abstenir; ~ **to** se garder de

**forbearance** *n* tolérance *f*, longanimité *f*, patience *f*

**forbearing** *adj* tolérant, patient

**forbid** *vt* défendre, interdire; (refuse access) interdire l'accès de; **God** ~**!** j'espère bien que non!

**forbidden** *adj* défendu, interdit; ~ **fruit** fruit défendu

**forbidding** *adj* menaçant, sombre; (person) rebutant, sévère

**force** *n* force *f*, violence *f*, énergie *f*, vigueur *f*; (influence) influence *f*; *mil* force *f*; *mil* ~**s** forces armées; **brute** ~ violence *f* physique; **by brute** ~ de vive force; **by sheer** ~ **of** à force de; **in** ~ en vigueur; **police** ~ forces *fpl* de police; *vt* contraindre, forcer, obliger; (lock, entry) forcer; (rape) violer; (extort) arracher, extorquer; *hort* forcer, hâter; (push) pousser; ~ **back** faire reculer, repousser; (aircraft) ~ **down** forcer à atterrir; ~ **in** faire entrer de force; ~ **out** faire sortir de force

**forced** *adj* forcé, contraint, artificiel -ielle

**force-feed** *vt* nourrir de force

**forceful** *adj* puissant; vigoureux -euse, énergique

**forcemeat** *n cul* farce *f*, hâchis *m*

**forceps** *n* forceps *m*

**forcible** *adj* de force, par force; (forceful) puissant; (language) vigoureux -euse

**ford** *n* gué *m*; *vt* passer à gué

**fordable** *adj* guéable

**fore** *n naut* avant *m*; **to the** ~ en évidence; *adj* à l'avant, antérieur; *naut* ~ **and aft** (rig, sail) aurique; *adv* à l'avant

**forearm** *n* avant-bras *m*

**forebear** *n see* ¹**forbear**

**forebode** *vt* annoncer, prédire; présager

**foreboding** *n* prémonition *f*

**forecast** *n* prévision *f*; *sp* pronostic *m*; **weather** ~ bulletin *m* météorologique, prévisions *fpl* météorologiques, *coll* météo *f*; *vt* prévoir

**forecastle** *n naut* gaillard *m* d'avant, poste *m* d'équipage

**foreclose** *vt leg* saisir; ~ **on a mortgage** saisir un bien hypothéqué

**foreclosure** *n leg* saisie *f*

**forecourt** *n* avant-cour *f*; (petrol station) devant *m*

**forefather** *n* ancêtre *m*

**forefinger** *n* index *m*

**forefoot** *n* (large animal) pied antérieur; (dog, etc) patte antérieure, patte *f* de devant

**forefront** *n* premier rang; (progress) avant-garde *f*

**foregather, forgather** *vi* s'assembler, se réunir

**forego, forgo** *vt* se priver de, renoncer à, se passer de

**foregoing** *adj* précédent; déjà cité

**foregone** *adj* déjà réglé; ~ **conclusion** qch de réglé à l'avance

**foreground** *n* premier plan

**forehand** *n sp* coup droit

**forehead** *n* front *m*

**foreign** *adj* étranger -ère; (trade) extérieur

**foreigner** *n* étranger -ère

**foreknowledge** *n* préconnaissance *f*

**foreland** *n* promontoire *m*, cap *m*

**foreleg** *n* (large animal) jambe antérieure; (dog, etc) patte antérieure, patte *f* de devant

**forelock** *n* mèche *f*; **take time by the** ~ sauter sur l'occasion; **touch one's** ~ saluer obséquieusement

**foreman** *n* contremaître *m*; (jury) président *m*

**foremast** *n naut* mât *m* de misaine

**forementioned** *adj* déjà cité, précité

**foremost** *adj* principal, le plus en vue; *adv* **first and** ~ avant tout

**forenoon** *n* matinée *f*

**forensic** *adj leg* du barreau; ~ **evidence** expertise médico-légale; ~ **medicine** médecine légale

**forerunner** *n* précurseur *m*

**foresail** *n naut* voile *f* de misaine

**foresee** *vt* prévoir

**foreseeable** *adj* prévisible

**foreshadow** *vt* présager, annoncer, augurer

**foreshore** *n* laisse *f* de mer; *leg* lais *m*

**foreshorten** *vt phot* faire un raccourci de

**foreshortening** *n phot* raccourci *m*

**foresight** *n* prévoyance *f*

**foreskin** *n* prépuce *m*

**forest** *n* forêt *f*

**forestall** *vt* anticiper, devancer

**forester** *n* garde forestier

**forestry** *n* sylviculture *f*

**foretaste** *n* avant-goût *m*

**foretell** *vt* prédire

**forethought** *n* prévoyance *f*

**forever** *adv* toujours, sans cesse

**forewarn** *vt* prévenir, avertir

**foreword** *n* avant-propos *m*, préface *f*

**forfeit** *n* peine *f*; (game) ~**s** gages *mpl*; *vt* perdre, payer de

**forfeiture** *n* perte *f* par confiscation

**forgather** *vi see* **foregather**

**forge** *n* forge *f*; *vt* (metal, alliance, friendship) forger; (counterfeit) contrefaire, faire un faux de; *vi* ~ **ahead** pousser de l'avant

**forger** *n* faussaire

**forgery** *n* contrefaçon *f*, falsification *f*; (thing forged) faux *m*

**forget** *vt* oublier; (leave behind) oublier, laisser; ~ **it!** n'y pensez plus!; ~ **oneself** se comporter mal; *vi* oublier; **not forgetting** sans oublier

**forgetful** *adj* distrait, étourdi

**forgetfulness** *n* étourderie *f*, distraction *f*

**forging** *n* falsification *f*

**forgivable** *adj* pardonnable

**forgive** *vt* pardonner

**forgiveness** *n* pardon *m*; miséricorde *f*

**forgiving** *adj* indulgent, clément

**forgo** *vt see* **forego**

**forgotten** *adj* oublié

**fork** *n agr* fourche *f*; (cutlery) fourchette *f*; (junction) fourche *f*, embranchement *m*, bifurcation *f*; *anat* fourche *f*; *vt* fourcher; *vi* bifurquer; *coll* ~ **out** casquer

**forked** *adj* fourchu; ~ **lightning** éclair *m* en zigzag

**fork-lift** *n* ~ **truck** chariot *m* de levage, chariot élévateur

**forlorn** *adj* délaissé, abandonné, triste; ~ **hope** mince espoir *m*; (last effort) tentative désespérée

**form** *n* forme *f*, genre *m*; (document to be filled in) formule *f*, formulaire *m*; (fitness) forme *f*, condition *f*; (school) classe *f*; (bench) banc *m*; **be good (bad)** ~ se faire (ne pas se faire); (racing) **study** ~ établir un pronostic; *coll* **what's the** ~? qu'est-ce qu'on doit faire?; *vt* former, modeler, construire, façonner; (train) former, éduquer, contracter; (organize) constituer, composer; *mil* se mettre, s'aligner; *vi* prendre forme, se former; ~ **up** se mettre en ligne

**formal** *adj* formel -elle, officiel -ielle, explicite; (stiff) austère, guindé; (ceremonial) cérémonieux -ieuse; (superficial) de forme, pour la forme

**formaldehyde** *n chem* formaldéhyde *m*

**formalin** *n chem* formol *m*

**formalism** *n* formalisme *m*

**formality** *n* formalité *f*; (stiffness)

**formalize**

raideur *f*, cérémonie *f*
**formalize** *vt* formaliser
**formally** *adv* officiellement; cérémonieusement
**format** *n* format *m*
**formation** *n* formation *f*; création *f*, organisation *f*
**formative** *adj* formateur -trice
**forme** *n* print forme *f*
**former** *adj* précédent, ancien -ienne; (first mentioned) premier -ière; *pron* celui-là (*f* celle-là, *mpl* ceux-là, *fpl* celles-là)
**formerly** *adv* autrefois, jadis
**formic** *adj* chem formique
**Formica** *n* Formica *m*
**formidable** *adj* redoutable, terrible, énorme
**formless** *adj* informe
**formula** *n* formule *f*
**formularize** *vt* formuler
**formulate** *vt* formuler
**formulation** *n* formulation *f*
**formulize** *vt* formuler
**fornicate** *vi* forniquer
**fornication** *n* fornication *f*
**fornicator** *n* fornicateur *m*
**fornicatress** *n* fornicatrice *f*
**forrard** *adv* naut vers le devant
**forsake** *vt* délaisser, quitter; (give up) renoncer à
**forsaken** *adj* délaissé
**forsooth** *adv ar* + *joc* en vérité; *interj* par exemple!
**forswear** *vt* abjurer, renoncer à, désavouer; ~ **oneself** se parjurer
**forsworn** *adj* parjure
**forsythia** *n* bot forsythia *m*
**fort** *n* fort *m*
¹**forte** *n* fort *m*
²**forte** *adv mus* forte
**forth** *adv* en avant; **and so** ~ et ainsi de suite; **from this day (time, moment)** ~ dorénavant, désormais; **go back and** ~ aller et venir; **hold** ~ parler longuement; **set** ~ se mettre en route
**forthcoming** *adj* à paraître, à venir; (available) disponible; (frank) ouvert, accueillant, avenant
**forthright** *adj* direct, franc (*f* franche), carré
**forthwith** *adv* aussitôt, sur-le-champ
**fortieth** *n* + *adj* quarantième
**fortification** *n* fortification *f*
**fortify** *vt* fortifier, armer; (food) renforcer en vitamines; (drink) augmenter la teneur en alcool de
**fortitude** *n* courage *m*, force *f* d'âme
**fortnight** *n* quinzaine *f*, quinze jours *mpl*
**fortnightly** *adj* bimensuel -elle; *adv* tous les quinze jours
**fortress** *n* fort *m*, forteresse *f*

**fortuitous** *adj* fortuit, imprévu
**fortuitousness** *n* chance *f*, hasard *m*
**fortunate** *adj* heureux -euse, favorable, propice
**fortune** *n* fortune *f*, chance *f*; (wealth) fortune *f*, richesse *f*
**fortune-hunter** *n* coureur *m* de dot
**fortune-teller** *n* diseur -euse de bonne aventure
**forty** *n* quarante *m invar*; **the forties** les années quarante; *geog* **the roaring forties** les quarantièmes rugissants; *adj* quarante *invar*; *coll* ~ **winks** petit somme
**forum** *n* forum *m*, tribune *f*
**forward** *n* sp avant *m*; *vt* favoriser; (goods, etc) expédier, faire suivre; *adj* en avant; (well advanced) en avance, précoce; (presumptuous) effronté, insolent; (long-term) à long terme; *naut* vers le devant; *mot* ~ **gears** vitesses *fpl* avant; *adv* en avant
**forwarding** *adj* ~ **address** adresse *f* pour faire suivre le courrier; ~ **agent** transitaire *m*
**forward-looking** *adj* progressif -ive, tourné vers l'avenir
**forwardness** *n* précocité *f*; *pej* audace *f*, effronterie *f*
**forwards** *adv see* forward *adv*
**fossil** *n* fossile *m*; *coll* croulant *m*; *adj* fossile; ~ **fuel** combustible *m* fossile
**fossilize** *vt* fossiliser; *vi* se fossiliser
¹**foster** *vt* nourrir, élever; *fig* encourager, chérir; (harbour) entretenir
²**foster** *adj* adoptif -ive, nourricier -ière, de lait
**foster-brother** *n* frère adoptif, frère *m* de lait
**foster-father** *n* père adoptif
**foster-mother** *n* mère adoptive
**foster-parent** *n* parent adoptif
**foster-sister** *n* sœur adoptive, sœur *f* de lait
**foul** *n* sp coup irrégulier; *adj* infect, immonde, crasseux -euse; (smell) fétide; (air) vicié; *fig* vil, infâme, abominable; (language) grossier -ière, ordurier -ière; ~ **play** meurtre *m*, assassinat *m*; **fall** ~ **of** *naut* aborder, entrer en collision avec; *fig* attirer l'hostilité de; *vt* polluer, infecter; (block) obstruer; *naut* aborder, entrer en collision avec; (entangle) embrouiller, entortiller; *vi* (rope, etc) s'emmêler, s'embrouiller
**foul-mouthed** *adj* (language) ordurier -ière; (person) au langage ordurier
**foulness** *n* saleté *f*
¹**found** *vt* fonder, créer, établir
²**found** *vt metal* fondre
**foundation** *n* fondation *f*, création *f*,

établissement *m*; (basis) base *f*, fondement *m*; (make-up) fond *m* de teint;
*bui* ~s fondations *fpl*; ~ **garment**
gaine *f*, combiné *m*; ~ **stone** pierre
commémorative
¹**founder** *n* fondateur -trice
²**founder** *n* metal fondeur *m*
³**founder** *vi* (horse) se mettre à boiter;
(ship) sombrer, chavirer; *fig* s'effondrer, échouer
**foundling** *n* enfant trouvé -e
**foundry** *n* fonderie *f*
**fount** *n* source *f*; *typ* fonte *f*
**fountain** *n* fontaine *f*, jet *m* d'eau;
(drinking) source *f* d'eau potable, fontaine publique
**fountain-head** *n* source *f*, origine *f*
**fountain-pen** *n* stylo *m*
**four** *n* quatre *m invar*; **in** ~ **figures** dans
les milliers; **on all** ~**s** à quatre pattes;
*adj* quatre *invar*
**four-door** *adj mot* à quatre portes
**four-engined** *adj* ~ **plane** quadrimoteur
*m*
**four-figure** *adj* ~ **salary** traitement *m* de
plus de mille livres
**four-fold** *adj* quadruple; *adv* au quadruple
**four-letter** *adj* ~ **word** obscénité *f*,
parole grossière
**four-poster (bed)** *n* lit *m* à baldaquin
**fourscore** *n* quatre-vingts *m*
**four-seater** *n* voiture *f* à quatre places
**foursome** *n sp* partie *f* à quatre; deux
couples *mpl*; partie carrée
**foursquare** *adj* carré *f*; *fig* ferme, inébranlable
**fourteen** *n* quatorze *m invar*; *adj* quatorze *invar*
**fourth** *n* quatrième; (fraction) quart *m*;
*adj* quatrième
**four-wheel** *adj* ~ **drive** propulsion *f* à
quatre roues motrices
**fowl** *n* volatile *m*, volaille *f*; *collect* volaille *f*, oiseaux *mpl* de basse-cour; *cul*
**roast** ~ poulet rôti; *vt* (birds) chasser
**fowling-piece** *n* fusil de chasse léger
**fox** *n* renard; *fig* rusé *m*, malin *m*; *vt coll*
mystifier; (fool) berner
**fox-cub** *n* renardeau *m*
**fox-earth** *n* terrier *m* de renard
**foxed** *n* (paper) marqué de rousseurs;
*coll* mystifié
**foxglove** *n bot* digitale *f*
**foxhole** *n* terrier *m* de renard; *mil* petite
tranchée, gourbi *m*
**foxhound** *n* foxhound *m*
**foxhunt** *n* chasse *f* au renard
**foxhunter** *n* chasseur *m* (de renard)
**foxhunting** *n* chasse *f* au renard; *adj*
adonné à la chasse au renard
**fox-terrier** *n* fox *m*

**fox-trot** *n* slow *m*, slow-fox *m*
**foxy** *adj* rusé, finaud
**foyer** *n* foyer *m*, hall *m*
**fracas** *n* fracas *m*
**fraction** *n* fraction *f*, partie *f*
**fractional** *adj* infime; *math* fractionnaire; *chem* fractionné
**fractionally** *adv* un tout petit peu
**fractious** *adj* grincheux -euse, hargneux
-euse
**fracture** *n* fracture *f*; *vt* fracturer; *vi* se
casser, se fracturer
**fragile** *adj* fragile, frêle, précaire
**fragility** *n* fragilité *f*
**fragment** *n* fragment *m*, morceau *m*;
**reduce to** ~**s** réduire en miettes; *vt*
fragmenter; *vi* se fragmenter
**fragmental** *adj* fragmentaire; *geol* clas-
tique
**fragmentary** *adj* fragmentaire
**fragmentation** *n* fragmentation *f*
**fragrance** *n* parfum *m*, senteur *f*
**fragrant** *adj* parfumé; *fig* doux (*f* douce)
**frail** *adj* fragile, frêle, délicat
**frailty** *n* fragilité *f*, faiblesse *f*
**frame** *n* (picture) cadre *m*; (window, car)
châssis *m*; (door) encadrement *m*;
(spectacles) monture *f*; *hort* châssis *m*,
cloche *f*; *cin* image *f*; (bone structure)
ossature *f*, charpente *f*; *fig* ~ **of mind**
disposition *f*; *vt* (surround) encadrer;
(construct) bâtir; (plan, etc) formuler,
concevoir; *coll* monter un coup contre
**frame-house** *n* maison *f* à charpente de
bois
**frame-rucksack** *n* sac *m* à dos à armature
**frame-up** *n coll* coup monté
**framework** *n* cadre *m*, ossature *f*, structure *f*
**franc** *n* franc *m*
**France** *n* France *f*
**franchise** *n* droit *m* de suffrage
**Franciscan** *n* franciscain *m*; *adj* franciscain
**francophile** *n* + *adj* francophile
**francophobe** *n* + *adj* francophobe
**frangipane** *n* frangipane *f*
**Frank** *n hist* Franc *m* (*f* Franque)
¹**frank** *adj* franc (*f* franche), ouvert, sincère
²**frank** *vt* affranchir
**frankfurter** *n* saucisse *f* de Francfort
**frankincense** *n* encens *m*
**Frankish** *adj* franc (*f* franque)
**frankness** *n* franchise *f*, sincérité *f*
**frantic** *adj* frénétique, effréné; (person)
hors de soi, fou (*f* folle)
**fraternal** *adj* fraternel -elle
**fraternity** *n* fraternité *f*; *US* (students)
confrérie *f*
**fraternization** *n* fraternisation *f*

493

**fraternize** vi fraterniser

**fratricidal** adj fratricide

**fratricide** n fratricide m

**fraud** n (money) escroquerie f; (crime) imposture f, tromperie f, fraude f; (person) imposteur m, charlatan m; (cheat) escroc m; coll **he's a bit of a ~** c'est un fumiste

**fraudulence, fraudulency** n caractère frauduleux

**fraudulent** adj frauduleux -euse; leg **~ conversion** malversation f

**fraught** adj plein, chargé; fig lourd, tendu; risqué

¹**fray** n rixe f, conflit m; fig **enter the ~** entrer en lice

²**fray** vt effilocher; (cuff) effranger; naut (rope) raguer; fig exaspérer; vi s'effilocher, s'effiler; naut se raguer

**frazzle** n **to a ~** complètement, tout à fait; vt US coll éreinter, crever

**freak** n monstre m, phénomène m; (whim) lubie f; (behaviour) caprice m; sl dingue; adj anormal, insolite, bizarre; vi (also **~ out**) sl (drugs) se défoncer; (drop out) se défouler, devenir hippie

**freakish** adj insolite, anormal, bizarre, saugrenu

**freckle** n tache f de rousseur, tache f de son; vt marquer de taches de rousseur; vi se couvrir de taches de rousseur

**freckled** adj taché de son, couvert de taches de rousseur

**free** adj libre; indépendant, autonome; (without payment) gratuit, libre; (lavish) généreux -euse, prodigue; **~ and easy** décontracté; **~ church** église f nonconformiste; **~ fight** mêlée f, rixe f; **~ hand** carte blanche; sp **~ kick** coup franc; comm **~ on board (f.o.b.)** franco à bord; coll **feel ~!** sers-toi!, fais ce que tu veux!; coll **for ~** à l'œil; **get ~ of** se débarrasser de; **give ~ rein to** donner libre cours à; **go ~** être relâché; **make ~ with** se permettre des libertés avec; vt libérer, affranchir; (exempt) exempter, exonérer; (burden) soulager

**freeboard** n naut franc-bord m (pl francs-bords)

**freebooter** n pirate m, flibustier m

**freeborn** adj né libre

**freedom** n liberté f; (exemption) franchise f

**free-for-all** n foire f d'empoigne

**free-hand** adj à main levée

**free-handed** adj généreux -euse, large

**free-hearted** adj ouvert, généreux -euse

**freehold** n propriété foncière libre; adj tenu en propriété perpétuelle et libre

**freeholder** n propriétaire foncier -ière

sans obligation

**freelance** n + adj indépendant -e

**freeman** n hist homme m libre; **~ of a city** citoyen -enne d'honneur d'une ville

**Freemason** n franc-maçon m (pl francs-maçons)

**freemasonry** n franc-maçonnerie f

**free-range** adj **~ eggs** œufs mpl de ferme; **~ poultry** poulets mpl de ferme

**freesia** n bot freesia m

**free-spoken** adj franc (f franche); (forthright) carré

**free-standing** adj non encastré

**freestone** n pierre f de taille

**freestyle** adj sp **~ swimming** nage f libre

**freethinker** n libre-penseur -euse (mpl libres-penseurs, fpl libres-penseuses)

**freethinking** n libre pensée f; adj libre-penseur (pl libres-penseurs)

**free-thought** n libre pensée f

**freeway** n US autoroute f (sans péage)

**free-wheel** n (bicycle) roue f libre; vi (bicycle) être en roue libre; mot rouler au point mort

**free-will** n philos libre arbitre m; adj volontaire

**freeze** n gel m, temps m de gel; vt geler; (food) congeler; (prices) bloquer, stabiliser; (credit) geler; **~ out** exclure; vi geler; fig se figer; US coll **~!** ne bouge pas!; coll **~ on to s/o** se cramponner à qn; **~ to death** mourir de froid; **~ up** se prendre en glace; mot (windscreen) se givrer

**freezer** n congélateur m; (compartment in refrigerator) freezer m

**freeze-up** n grand gel

**freezing** adj glacial; **~ cold** froid m de canard; **~ mixture** antigel m; **~ point** point m de congélation

**freight** n fret m, cargaison f; transport m; (chartering of ship) affrètement m; **air ~** fret m par avion; **by ~** par petite vitesse; adj US **~ car** wagon m de marchandises; **~ train** train m de marchandises; vt (ship) affréter, charger

**freightage** n fret m

**freighter** n naut cargo m; aer avion m de fret

**French** n (language) français m; **the ~** les Français; adj français; **~ bean** haricot vert; **~ Canadian** Canadien -ienne français -e; **~ chalk** craie f de tailleur; cul **~ dressing** vinaigrette f; **~ fried**, US **~ fries** pommes frites; **~ horn** cor m d'harmonie; coll **~ letter** capote anglaise; **~ polish** vernis m à l'alcool; **~ window** porte-fenêtre f (pl portes-fenêtres); **take ~ leave** filer à l'anglaise

**frenchify** vt franciser
**Frenchman** n Français m
**French-speaking** adj francophone
**Frenchwoman** n Française f
**frenetic** adj frénétique, effréné
**frenzied** adj frénétique, effréné; (enthusiastic) délirant
**frenzy** n frénésie f; (delight) transport m de joie
**frequency** n fréquence f; ~ **modulation** modulation f de fréquence
**frequent** adj fréquent, courant; vt fréquenter
**frequentation** n fréquentation f
**fresco** n fresque f
**fresh** adj frais (f fraîche); (new) nouveau (f nouvelle); (colour) gai; (lively) fringant, plein d'entrain; coll familier -ière, culotté; inexpérimenté, naïf (f naïve); ~ **as a daisy** frais (f fraîche) comme une rose; adv ~ **from** frais émoulu de, fraîchement arrivé de
**freshen** vt rafraîchir, débarbouiller; rendre plus clair; vi (wind) fraîchir; ~ **up** faire un brin de toilette; (woman) se refaire une beauté
**fresher, freshman** n coll (student) conscrit m, bleu m, bizuth m
**freshness** n fraîcheur f; fig franchise f, spontanéité f; nouveauté f
**freshwater** adj d'eau douce
**¹fret** n anxiété f, tension nerveuse; vt corroder; (wind) rider; vi se tourmenter, se tracasser; (baby) geindre
**²fret** n (guitar) touchette f; (design) motif m; vt découper, chantourner
**fretful** adj pleurnicheur -euse, mécontent, geignard
**fretfulness** n pleurnicherie f
**fret-saw** n scie f à découper
**fretwork** n découpage m
**Freudian** adj freudien -ienne
**friability** n friabilité f
**friable** adj friable
**friar** n religieux m, frère m
**fricassee** n fricassée f
**fricative** n fricative f; adj fricatif -ive
**friction** n friction f, frottement m; désaccord m
**Friday** n vendredi m; **Good** ~ vendredi saint; **man** ~ fidèle serviteur m
**fridge** n abbr frigo m, frigidaire m
**friend** n ami -e; (school, work, etc) camarade, copain m, copine f; **a** ~ **in need is a** ~ **indeed** c'est dans le besoin qu'on connaît ses vrais amis; **boy-** petit ami; **girl** ~ petite amie; **have** ~ **s at court** avoir des amis influents; (parliament) **my honourable** ~, leg **my learned** ~ mon honorable confrère; **Society of Friends** Quakers mpl
**friendless** adj seul, sans amis

**friendliness** n bienveillance f, amabilité f
**friendly** adj amical, gentil -ille, affectueux -ueuse; bienveillant
**friendship** n amitié f
**¹frieze** n archi frise f, bordure f
**²frieze** n ratine f
**frigate** n naut frégate f
**fright** n effroi m, peur f; coll (person) horreur f, épouvantail m; **give s/o a** ~ effrayer qn; **have a** ~ avoir peur; **take** ~ s'épouvanter, s'effrayer
**frighten** vt effrayer, faire peur à, épouvanter; ~ **away**, ~ **off** effaroucher
**frightened** adj effrayé; **don't be** ~ n'ayez pas peur
**frightful** adj épouvantable, effroyable
**frightfully** adv épouvantablement, affreusement; coll terriblement; **be** ~ **sorry** être absolument désolé
**frightfulness** n atrocité f, horreur f
**frigid** adj glacial, froid, glacé; (woman) frigide
**frigidity** n froideur f; (sexual) frigidité f
**frigorific** adj frigorifique
**frill** n ruche f; (shirt) jabot m; fig fanfreluche f; coll ~s façons fpl, manières fpl
**frilly** adj à fanfreluches
**fringe** n (edging, hair) frange f; (border) bord m, lisière f; **on the** ~ **of** en marge de; adj sur le bord de la légalité; peu orthodoxe; ~ **benefits** avantages mpl accessoires, petits bénéfices; ~ **group** groupe marginal
**frippery** n colifichets mpl; fig préciosité f
**frisk** vt fouiller; vi gambader, folâtrer
**friskiness** n animation f, vivacité f
**frisky** adj animé, vif (f vive)
**¹fritter** n cul beignet m
**²fritter** vt ~ **away** gaspiller, perdre
**frivolity** n frivolité f
**frivolous** adj frivole
**frivolousness** n frivolité f
**frizz** n boucles désordonnées; vt faire friser
**¹frizzle** vt (hair) faire friser
**²frizzle** vt faire griller; vi grésiller; ~ **d up** calciné
**frizzy** adj crépu, crêpelé
**fro** adv to and ~ de long en large; **go to and** ~ **between** faire la navette entre
**frock** n robe f; (monk) froc m
**frock-coat** n ar redingote f
**frog** n grenouille f; coll pej Français -e; (loop) brandebourg m; (in throat) chat m
**frogman** n homme-grenouille m (pl hommes-grenouilles)
**frog-march** vt amener (qn) de force; (carry) amener (qn) en le prenant par les quatre membres
**frolic** n ébats mpl, réjouissances fpl;

(prank) espièglerie f; vi folâtrer, gambader

**frolicsome** adj folâtre, gai

**from** prep de; (beginning at) à partir de; (person) de la part de, d'après; (price) à partir de; (time) depuis; (keep, take) à; ~ **a novel by Balzac** d'après un roman de Balzac; ~ **150 francs a day** à partir de 150 francs par jour; ~ **now on** à partir de maintenant; ~ **the mayor** de la part du maire; **take that glass** ~ **the child** enlevez ce verre à l'enfant

**frond** n fronde f

**front** n devant m, avant m; (first row) premier rang; (beginning) début m; mil front m; (seaside) bord m de mer; (promenade) front m de mer; (figurehead) homme m de paille; (cover) couverture f; theat salle f; (shirt) plastron m; coll effronterie f; **be in** ~ mener, être en tête; fig **come to the** ~ percer; **put on a bold** ~ faire bonne contenance; adj de devant, premier -ière; de face; ~ **door** porte f d'entrée; archi ~ **elevation** élévation frontale; **have a** ~ **seat** avoir une place au premier rang; fig être aux premières loges; adv par devant; mil **eyes** ~ ! fixe!; vt bui donner une façade à; vi ~ **on to** faire face à, donner sur

**frontage** n (shop) devanture f; (house) façade f

**frontal** adj med frontal; mil de front; **full** ~ **nude** nu(e) de face

**frontier** n frontière f; adj de frontière

**frontiersman** n frontalier m

**frontispiece** n frontispice m

**front-page** adj ~ **news** nouvelles importantes; **be** ~ **news** être à la une

**frontwards** adv vers l'avant, en avant

**front-wheel** adj mot ~ **drive** traction f avant

**frost** n gel m, gelée f, givre m; coll four m; vt geler; (glass) givrer; US (cake) glacer

**frostbite** n gelure f

**frostbitten** adj gelé

**frosted** adj givré; ~ **glass** verre dépoli

**frosting** n US cul glaçage m

**frosty** adj glacial

**froth** n écume f, mousse f; fig vent m, futilités fpl; vi écumer, mousser

**frothy** adj écumeux -euse, mousseux -euse; (clothing) vaporeux -euse; fig creux (f creuse)

**frown** n froncement m de sourcils; vi froncer les sourcils, se renfrogner; ~ **upon** désapprouver

**frowsty, frowzy** adj qui sent le renfermé

**frozen** adj gelé, glacé; (food) congelé

**fructification** n fructification f

**fructify** vt faire fructifier; vi fructifier

**frugal** adj économe; (meal) frugal

**frugality** n frugalité f; (thrift) parcimonie f, économie f

**frugally** adv parcimonieusement, simplement, sobrement

**fruit** n fruit m; fig bear ~ porter fruit; ~ **machine** machine f à sous; ~ **salad** salade f de fruits; ~ **salts** sels purgatifs; vi (tree) donner, porter des fruits

**fruit-cake** n cake m

**fruiterer** n marchand -e de fruits, fruitier -ière

**fruitful** adj fécond, fertile; (useful) fructueux -euse, profitable

**fruitfulness** n fécondité f, fertilité f; fig utilité f, profit m

**fruitiness** n caractère fruité

**fruitless** adj infécond, stérile; fig stérile, vain

**fruitlessness** n infécondité f, stérilité f; fig stérilité f

**fruity** adj fruité; (voice) moelleux -euse; coll corsé

**frump** n bonne femme mal fagotée

**frustrate** vt frustrer, tromper; (foil) contrecarrer, déjouer

**frustration** n frustration f, déception f

¹**fry** n (fish) fretin m; (unimportant people) le menu fretin; (children) marmaille f

²**fry** n friture f; vt frire, faire frire; **fried egg** œuf m sur le plat; vi frire

**fryer** n poêle f à frire; **deep** ~ friteuse f

**frying-pan** n poêle f à frire; **out of the** ~ **into the fire** de Charybde en Scylla

**fuchsia** n bot fuchsia m

**fuck** n vulg baisage m; **she's a good** ~ elle baise bien; vt vulg baiser; ~ !, ~ **it!** putain f de merde!; ~ **me!** merde alors!; vi ~ ! va te faire foutre!; **feel** ~ **ed** être mal foutu; vi vulg baiser; ~ **about** déconner; ~ **off** foutre le camp; ~ **up** foutre la merde dans

**fuck-all** n vulg rien m de rien

**fucking** adj vulg putain f de; ~ **hell** putain f de bordel; **this** ~ **car** cette putain de voiture

**fuddled** adj brouillé, confus; (tipsy) éméché, gris

**fuddy-duddy** n vieux machin; sl croulant -e

**fudge** n cul fondant m; (newspaper) dernières nouvelles; interj balivernes!; vt monter, truquer; (work) bâcler

**fuel** n combustible m; mot carburant m; fig **add** ~ **to the flames** jeter de l'huile sur le feu; vt alimenter, ravitailler en combustible

**fuelling** n combustible m; ravitaillement m en combustible

**fuel-oil** n mazout m

**fug** n odeur f de renfermé

**fugitive** n fugitif -ive, fuyard -e; adj fugitif -ive; fig éphémère
**fugue** n mus+psych fugue f
**fulcrum** n pivot m, point m d'appui
**fulfil** vt accomplir, réaliser, satisfaire; (prayer) exaucer
**fulfilment** n accomplissement m, réalisation f, satisfaction f; (prayer) exaucement m
**full** n in ~ en toutes lettres; intégralement; to the ~ tout à fait, pleinement; adj plein, rempli; (crowded) comble; (clothes) large, ample; (plump) rondelet -ette; (hotel) complet -ète; (face) rond, joufflu; coll (having eaten) rempli, rassasié; ~ dress mil grande tenue; tenue f de soirée; ~ face portrait portrait m de face; ~ fare place entière; ~ house theat salle f comble; (cards) full m; ~ of préoccupé de; ~ of oneself satisfait; (punctuation) ~ stop point m; arrêt complet; ~ up plein à craquer; (noise) at ~ blast à pleins tubes; at ~ speed à toute vitesse; be in ~ swing battre son plein; fall ~ length tomber de tout son long; in ~ blast très actif -ive; in ~ cry suivant de très près; adv complètement, directement; ~ in the face en plein visage; go ~ out aller à toute vitesse
**fullback** n sp arrière m
**full-blooded** adj vigoureux -euse, robuste
**full-bodied** adj corpulent; (wine) corsé
**full-dress** adj (clothes) de cérémonie; (discussion, etc) dans les règles
**fuller** n fouleur -euse
**fuller's earth** n terre f à foulon
**full-fledged** adj US see fully-fledged
**full-grown** adj grand, adulte
**full-length** adj étendu; cin de long métrage; (portrait) en pied
**fullness** n abondance f, ampleur f; in the ~ of time (eventually) avec le temps; (at the appointed time) en temps et lieu
**full-scale** adj grandeur nature invar; de grande envergure
**full-time** n sp fin f de match; adj à plein temps
**fully** adv entièrement, pleinement; (at least) au moins, largement
**fully-fashioned** adj entièrement diminué
**fully-fledged** adj (bird) ayant toutes ses plumes; fig qualifié; (entire) à part entière
**fulmar** n orni fulmar m
**fulminant** adj fulminant
**fulminate** n chem fulminate m; vi exploser; fig fulminer, pester
**fulmination** n explosion f; fig fulmination f

**fulsome** adj exagéré, plein d'effusions
**fumarole** n fumerolle f
**fumble** vt manier maladroitement; vi fouiller; (grope) chercher à tâtons; ~ for words chercher ses mots
**fume** n ~s fumées fpl, exhalaisons fpl; vi exhaler des vapeurs; fig être furieuse -ieuse, rager
**fumigate** vt fumiger
**fumigation** n fumigation f
**fumigator** n fumigateur m
**fun** n amusement m, divertissement m; (joke) plaisanterie f; euph rapport sexuel; be ~ être amusant; for ~ pour rire; have good ~ s'amuser bien; in ~ par plaisanterie; sl like ~ iron pas du tout; très vite; make ~ of se moquer de; adj coll marrant
**funambulist** n funambule
**function** n fonction f, charge f; (meeting) réunion f, réception f; vi fonctionner, marcher; ~ as jouer le rôle de
**functional** adj fonctionnel -elle
**functionary** n (public) fonctionnaire; employé -e
**fund** n fonds m, caisse f; (charity, etc) souscription f; fig (stock) fond m, quantité f; capitaux mpl; ~s (public) fonds publics; vt consolider; financer
**fundament** n fesses fpl; anus m
**fundamental** n mus fondamental m; principe essentiel; adj fondamental, de principe, de base
**fundamentalist** n fondamentaliste
**funeral** n enterrement m, obsèques fpl; (large-scale) funérailles fpl; state ~ funérailles nationales; coll that's your ~! tant pis pour toi!; adj funèbre
**funerary** adj funéraire
**funereal** adj funèbre, lugubre, sépulcral
**fun-fair** n fête foraine
**fungoid** adj med fongueux -euse; bot cryptogamique
**fungus** n champignon m; (mould) moisissure f; med fungus m; joc moustaches fpl et barbe f
**funicular** n funiculaire m; adj funiculaire
**funk** n coll froussard -e, poltron -onne; be in a blue ~ avoir la frousse; vt avoir peur de; vi se dégonfler, caner
**funky** adj coll froussard
**funnel** n entonnoir m; (ship) cheminée f; vt faire passer dans un entonnoir; fig canaliser
**funnily** adv drôlement; (curiously, oddly) curieusement, bizarrement; ~ enough c'est drôle
**funny** adj drôle, amusant, comique; (odd) curieux -ieuse, bizarre, drôle de; (slightly unwell) indisposé, drôle; ~ business qch de louche; don't try to be

~ ce n'est pas le moment de faire de
l'esprit

**funnybone** *n coll* petit juif

**fur** *n* poil *m*, fourrure *f*; (clothing) four-
rure(s) *f(pl)*; (kettle) incrustation *f*;
**have ~ on one's tongue** avoir la langue
empâtée; **make the ~ fly** faire du grabuge; *vt* revêtir de fourrures; *vi* ~ **up**
s'incruster; (tongue) être chargée

**furbelow** *n* falbala *m*; fanfreluches *fpl*

**furbish** *vt* (rust) dérouiller; astiquer, remettre à neuf

**furious** *adj* furieux -ieuse; (raging)
déchaîné; (struggle) acharné; (speed)
fou (*f* folle)

**furiousness** *n* fureur *f*

**furl** *vt naut* ferler; (umbrella, flag)
rouler

**furlong** *n* = 200 mètres (à peu près)

**furlough** *n* congé *m*, permission *f*

**furnace** *n* fourneau *m*; *fig* fournaise *f*

**furnish** *vt* (house, etc) meubler; (supply)
fournir, munir

**furnisher** *n* marchand -e de meubles

**furnishing** *n* installation *f* de meubles;
~s mobilier *m*, meubles *mpl*, ameublement *m*

**furniture** *n* mobilier *m*, meubles *mpl*,
ameublement *m*; **piece of ~** meuble *m*;
~ **remover** déménageur *m*; ~ **shop**
magasin *m* de meubles; ~ **store** garde-
meuble *m*; ~ **van** camion *m* de
déménagement

**furore**, *US* **furor** *n* débordement *m*
d'enthousiasme, admiration *f* sans
bornes

**furrier** *n* fourreur *m*

**furrow** *n* sillon *m*, rayon *m*; (wrinkle)
ride *f*; *vt* sillonner; (face) rider

**furry** *adj* à poil; (toy) en peluche

**further** *adj* plus éloigné; additionnel
-elle, supplémentaire; (education)
post-scolaire; **until ~ notice** jusqu'à
nouvel ordre; **without ~ delay** sans
plus attendre; *adv* plus loin; (more)
davantage, plus; (moreover) de plus,
d'ailleurs; *comm* ~ **to your letter** par
suite à votre lettre; *vt* avancer, favoriser

**furtherance** *n* avancement *m*

**furthermore** *adv* en outre, par ailleurs,
de plus

**furthermost** *adj* le plus éloigné

**furthest** *adj* le plus éloigné; *adv* le plus
loin

**furtive** *adj* furtif -ive, sournois

**fury** *n* fureur *f*, furie *f*; *myth* furie *f*; *fig*
mégère *f*; **like ~** d'arrache-pied

**furze** *n* ajoncs *mpl*

**fuse** *n elect* fusible *m*, plomb *m*; *min*
cordeau *m*, mèche *f*; (bomb) amorce *f*,
détonateur *m*; *vt* (metal) fondre,
mettre en fusion; *fig* fusionner, unifier;
*elect* faire sauter; (bomb) amorcer; *vi*
(metal) fondre; *fig* s'unifier, fusionner;
*elect* sauter

**fuse-box** *n elect* coupe-circuit *m invar*

**fuselage** *n* fuselage *m*

**fusel-oil** *n* huile *f* de fusel

**fuse-wire** *n elect* fusible *m*

**fusibility** *n* fusibilité *f*

**fusible** *adj* fusible

**fusilier** *n* fusilier *m*

**fusillade** *n* fusillade *f*

**fusion** *n* (metal) fonte *f*, fusion *f*; *phys*
fusion *f*; *fig* fusionnement *m*

**fuss** *n* agitation *f*, tapage *m*; embarras
*m*; *coll* **kick up a ~** faire un tas d'histoires; **make a ~ about** faire des histoires pour; **make a ~ of** être aux
petits soins pour; *vt* ennuyer, embêter;
*vi* s'agiter; (worry) se tracasser, s'en
faire; ~ **about** s'affairer

**fuss-pot** *n coll* enquiquineur -euse,
coupeur -euse de cheveux en quatre

**fussy** *adj* pointilleux -euse, tâtillon
-onne; enquiquinant; (over elegant)
tarabiscoté; **I'm not ~** ça m'est égal,
je ne suis pas difficile

**fustian** *n* futaine *f*

**fustigate** *vt joc* fouetter, fustiger

**fusty** *adj* de moisi, renfermé; *fig* suranné

**futile** *adj* futile

**futility** *n* futilité *f*

**future** *n* avenir *m*; *gramm* futur *m*;
*comm* ~s marchandises achetées à
terme; *adj* futur, à venir

**futureless** *adj* sans avenir

**futurism** *n* futurisme *m*

**futuristic** *adj* futuriste

**futurity** *n* avenir *m*

**fuzz** *n* cheveux crépus; (on body) duvet
*m*; *sl* **the ~** la flicaille

**fuzzy** *adj* (hair) crépu; (blurred) flou;
(muddled) déconcerté; (drunk) un peu
parti; **feel ~** avoir la tête qui tourne

# G

**G** *n mus* sol *m*
**gab** *n coll* tapette *f*, loquacité *f*; *coll* bec *m*, gueule *f*; **have the gift of the ~** avoir la langue bien pendue; *vi* bavarder, bonimenter
**gabble** *n* bredouillement *m*, jacasserie *f*; *vt* bredouiller; *vi* bredouiller, jacasser
**gabbler** *n* bredouilleur -euse
**gable** *n* pignon *m*; **~ end** pignon *m*; *vt* mettre des pignons à; *vi* être à pignons
**gabled** *adj* à pignons
¹**gad** *n* aiguillon *m*; (spear) pointe *f*
²**gad** *n* flâne *f*, balade *f*; *vi* vadrouiller; courailler
**gadabout** *n* vadrouilleur -euse; coureur -euse
**gadfly** *n* taon *m*
**gadget** *n* truc *m*, machin *m*; (device) dispositif *m*, gadget *m*
**Gaelic** *n* (language) gaélique *m*; *adj* gaélique
¹**gaff** *n* gaffe *f*; harpon *m*; *naut* corne *f*; *vt* gaffer
²**gaff** *n coll* **blow the ~** manger le morceau, vendre la mèche
**gaffer** *n* vieux *m*; *coll* croulant *m*; (foreman) contremaître *m*; (boss) patron *m*
**gag** *n* bâillon *m*; *theat* gag *m*, lazzi *m*; *vt* bâillonner, museler; *vi coll theat* improviser; *theat* faire des gags
**gaga** *adj coll* gaga, gâteux -euse; cinglé
**gage** *n* gage *m*; *leg* nantissement *m*; *ar* défi *m*; *vt* donner en gage
**gaggle** *n* troupeau *m* (d'oies); *vi* cacarder
**gaiety** *n* gaieté *f*, allégresse *f*, enjouement *m*
**gaily** *adv* gaiement, allègrement, avec entrain
**gain** *n* profit *m*, gain *m*, bénéfice *m*; accroissement *m*; avantage *m*, amélioration *f*; (clock) avance *f*; *vt* gagner; atteindre; acquérir; (information) obtenir; **~ ground** gagner du terrain, faire des progrès; **~ time** gagner du temps, se procurer un sursis; *vi* gagner; augmenter; (clock) avancer; **~ by** trouver avantage à; **~ on** prendre de l'avance sur, rattraper, gagner du terrain sur
**gain-control** *n rad* bouton *m* de puissance
**gainer** *n* celui *m* (*f* celle) qui gagne
**gainful** *adj* rémunérateur -trice, rentable
**gainfully** *adv* **~ employed** ayant un emploi rémunérateur
**gainsay** *vt* contredire
**gait** *n* démarche *f*, manière *f* de marcher, allure *f*
**gaiter** *n* guêtre *f*
**gaitered** *adj* guêtré
**galactic** *adj* galactique; *med* lactaire
**galaxy** *n astron* galaxie *f*; *fig* constellation *f*; pléiade *f*
**gale** *n* vent violent, tempête *f*
**galena** *n* galène *f*
**Galilean** *n* Galiléen -éenne; *adj* galiléen -éenne
**galiot** *n see* **galliot**
¹**gall** *n med* bile *f*; (of animals) fiel *m*; *fig* amertume *f*, fiel *m*
²**gall** *n* écorchure *f*; enflure *f*; *vet* (*esp* of horse) gale *f*, rouvieux *m*; *bot* galle *f*; *vt* écorcher, excorier; *fig* irriter
**gallant** *n* galant *m*; soupirant *m*, élégant *m*; *adj* courageux -euse, vaillant; élégant, noble; galant; *vi* faire le galant, faire la cour
**gallantly** *adv* courageusement, vaillamment; galamment
**gallantry** *n* courage *m*, vaillance *f*; galanterie *f*; propos flatteur, compliment *m*, douceur *f*
**gall-bladder** *n* vésicule *f* biliaire
**galleon** *n* galion *m*
**gallery** *n* galerie *f*, tribune *f*; *eng* galerie *f*; musée *m*, galerie *f*; *theat* paradis *m*, galerie *f*, *coll* poulailler *m*; **play to the ~** poser pour la galerie
**galley** *n naut* (ship) galère *f*; (rowing-boat) yole *f*; (ship's kitchen) coquerie *f*; *print* placard *m*
**galley-proof** *n print* placard *m*
**galley-slave** *n* galérien *m*
**galliard** *n* gaillarde *f*
**Gallic** *adj* gaulois
**gallic** *adj chem* gallique
**gallicism** *n* gallicisme *m*
**gallicize** *vt* franciser
**gallimaufry** *n* salmigondis *m*, galimatias *m*
**gallinaceous** *adj* gallinacé
**galling** *adj* irritant, mortifiant
**galliot, galiot** *n naut* galiote *f*
**gallivant** *vi* vadrouiller; courailler; flirter
**gallon** *n* gallon *m* ( = 4.54 litres)
**gallop** *n* galop *m*; *vt* faire galoper; *vi* galoper; courir vite, aller vite; faire vite

499

**gallows** n gibet m, potence f; peine f de mort; ~ **bird** gibier m de potence; ~ **tree** gibet m, potence f

**gall-stone** n med calcul m biliaire

**galop** n galop m; vi danser un galop

**galore** adv à foison, à profusion, en quantité; coll à gogo

**galoshes** npl botillons mpl de caoutchouc, caoutchoucs mpl

**galumph** vi coll gambader, caracoler

**galvanic** adj elect galvanique; fig convulsif -ive; frénétique

**galvanism** n elect galvanisme m; med galvanisation f

**galvanization** n galvanisation f, zingage m

**galvanize** vt galvaniser, zinguer; fig électriser, galvaniser

**galvanometer** n galvanomètre m

**gambit** n (chess) gambit m; ruse f, astuce f

**gamble** n action f de miser; fig entreprise risquée; **it's a** ~ c'est un risque; vt jouer, miser; risquer; vi jouer; prendre des risques

**gambler** n joueur -euse

**gambling** n jeu m

**gamboge** n gomme-gutte f (pl gommes-guttes)

**gambol** n gambade f, cabriole f; vi gambader, cabrioler, sautiller

¹**game** n jeu m, amusement m; match m, partie f; (hunting) gibier m; cul gibier m; fig jeu m, manège m, manigance f, artifice m; **big** ~ grands fauves; **fair** ~ proie f légitime; **make** ~ **of** se moquer de; **one** ~ **all** un partout; **paying** ~ entreprise lucrative; **play a good** ~ jouer bien; **play the** ~ jouer franc jeu; **the** ~ **is up** tout est raté; vi (gamble) jouer

²**game** adj estropié; coll brave, crâne, culotté; prêt, disposé; **be** ~ **for anything** n'avoir peur de rien, avoir du cran

**game-bag** n gibecière f

**game-cock** n coq m de combat

**gamekeeper** n garde-chasse m (pl gardes-chasse(s))

**game-laws** n code m de la chasse

**gamely** adv courageusement

**gameness** n crânerie f

**gamesmanship** n utilisation f d'astuces pour gagner

**gamester** n joueur -euse

**gaming** n (gambling) jeu m

¹**gammon** n quartier de porc fumé; jambon fumé; vt (pork, ham) fumer

²**gammon** n coll baliverne f, bourde f; vt mettre en boîte, tromper; vi coll dire des balivernes, dire des bourdes

**gammy** adj coll estropié

**gamut** n mus gamme f; fig gamme f, étendue f

**gamy** adj faisandé; coll crâne, culotté

**gander** n jars m; niais m; coll coup m d'œil

**gang** n bande f, équipe f, clan m, clique f; (criminals) gang m; (tools) jeu m; vi coll former une bande; ~ **up on** se liguer contre

**ganger** n contremaître m

**gangling** adj dégingandé

**ganglionique** adj ganglionnaire

**gang-plank** n naut planche f

**gangrene** n gangrène f; vt gangrener; vi se gangrener

**gangrenous** adj gangreneux -euse

**gangster** n gangster m, bandit m, malfaiteur m

**gangway** n passage m; (in seats) couloir m; naut passerelle f; interj dégagez!

**gannet** n orni fou m

**gantry** n eng portique m; (railway) portique m à signaux; (barrels) chantier m

**gaol, jail** n prison f

**gaol-bird** n récidiviste, cheval m de retour

**gaoler, jailer** n geôlier -ière, gardien -ienne

**gaol-fever** n typhus m

**gap** n trou m, vide m; (between mountains, in hedge, etc) brèche f; (time) intervalle m; fig trou m, lacune f, interruption f, hiatus m, solution f de continuité; **bridge the** ~ faire la soudure, combler le vide; **credibility** ~ crise f de confiance

**gape** n bâillement m; ouverture f; vi bâiller; béer, bayer aux corneilles; fig s'ouvrir, rester ouvert; ~ **at** regarder bouche bée

**garage** n garage m; vt mettre au garage, garer

**garb** n accoutrement m, costume m; vt accoutrer, vêtir

**garbage** n ordures fpl, détritus mpl; saleté f

**garble** vt dénaturer, fausser

**garden** n jardin m; ~s jardin public; **flower** ~ jardin m d'agrément; **kitchen** ~ potager m; **market** ~ maraîcher m; **lead s/o up the** ~(-path) duper qn, berner qn; adj (plants) de jardin; (tools) de jardinage; vi jardiner

**garden-city** n cité-jardin f (pl cités-jardins)

**gardener** n jardinier -ière

**gardenia** n gardénia m

**gardening** n jardinage m

**gargantuan** adj gargantuesque

**gargle** n gargarisme m; vi se gargariser

**gargoyle** n gargouille f

**garish** adj (colour, appearance) criard, voyant; (light) cru

gaudy

garishness *n* aspect criard, couleur criarde; (light) crudité *f*
garland *n* guirlande *f*, feston *m*; *fig* palme *f*; *vt* enguirlander; *fig* couronner
garlic *n* ail *m*
garment *n* vêtement *m*; ~s habillement *m*
garner *n* grenier *m*, fenil *m*, grange *f*; anthologie *f*; *vi* engranger, accumuler
garnet *n* grenat *m*
garnish *n* ornementation *f*; *cul* garniture *f*; *vt* orner, garnir, parer; *cul* garnir
garnishing *n* ornementation *f*; *cul* garniture *f*
garniture *n* ornementation *f*
garret *n* mansarde *f*, grenier *m*
garrison *n* garnison *f*; *vt* (town) installer une garnison dans; (troops) mettre en garnison
garrotte *n* garrot *m*; *vt* étrangler
garrulity *n* loquacité *f*
garrulous *adj* loquace, bavard
garrulousness *n* loquacité *f*
garter *n* jarretière *f*
garth *n* cour *f*, enclos *m*
gas *n* gaz *m*; *US* essence *f*; *coll* bavardage *m*, baratin *m*; coal ~ gaz *m* de houille; laughing ~ gaz hilarant; marsh ~ gaz *m* du marais, méthane *m*; natural ~ gaz naturel, gaz *m* du pétrole; poison ~ gaz asphyxiant; *coll* step on the ~ accélérer, *coll* appuyer sur le champignon; tear ~ gaz *m* lacrymogène; *vt mil* gazer; asphyxier; *vi coll* bavarder, baratiner
gas-bag *n* enveloppe *f* d'un aérostat; *coll* baratineur -euse
gas-bracket *n* applique *f* à gaz
gas-burner *n* bec *m* de gaz
gas-chamber *n* chambre *f* à gaz
gas-cooker *n* cuisinière *f* à gaz
gaseous *adj* gazeux -euse
gas-fire *n* radiateur *m* à gaz
gas-fitter *n* gazier *m*
gas-fittings *npl* installations *fpl* de gaz
gash *n* balafre *f*, entaille *f*, estafilade *f*, taillade *f*; *vt* balafrer, entailler, taillader
gasification *n* gazéification *f*
gasify *vt* gazéifier; *vi* passer à l'état de gaz
gas-jet *n* bec *m* de gaz
gasket *n mot* joint *m* de culasse; *naut* raban *m* de ferlage
gaslight *n* lumière *f* de gaz
gas-main *n* conduite *f* de gaz
gas-mantle *n* manchon *m* à incandescence
gas-mask *n* masque *m* à gaz
gas-meter *n* compteur *m* à gaz
gasoline *n* gazoline *f*; *US* essence *f*
gasometer *n* gazomètre *m*

gasp *n* halètement *m*, souffle *m*; at the last ~ au bout des forces, sur le point de mourir, à l'agonie; *vt* parler en soufflant; *vi* haleter, souffler
gasper *n sl* sèche *f*
gasping *n* halètement *m*; *adj* essoufflé, spasmodique
gas-ring *n* réchaud *m* à gaz
gas-station *n US* poste *m* d'essence, station-service *f* (*pl* stations-service)
gas-stove *n* (cooker) cuisinière *f* à gaz; (heater) fourneau *m* à gaz
gassy *adj* gazeux -euse; *coll* loquace
gasteropod *n zool* gastéropode *m*
gastric *adj med* gastrique
gastritis *n med* gastrite *f*
gastro-enteritis *n med* gastro-entérite *f*
gastronome, gastronomer, gastronomist *n* gastronome *m*
gastronomic *adj* gastronomique
gastronomy *n* gastronomie *f*
gas-works *npl* usine *f* à gaz
gat *n US coll* revolver *m*, *coll* pétard *m*
gate *n* porte *f*, (in field) barrière *f*, (*usu* metal) grille *f*; (lock, dock) vanne *f*; *geog* porte *f*, défilé *m*; (crowd at match) entrées *fpl*, public *m*; (money paid by crowd at match) entrées *fpl*, recette *f*; (slalom) porte *f*; *vt* (student) consigner
gate-crash *vt* assister à (une réception ou réunion privée) sans être invité; (without paying) resquiller
gate-crasher *n* intrus -e qui assiste (à une réception ou réunion privée) sans être invité -e; (without paying) resquilleur -euse
gate-house *n* loge *f*; *mil* corps *m* de garde
gate-keeper *n* portier -ière, concierge
gate-legged *adj* (table) à battants
gate-post *n* montant *m*
gateway *n* porte *f*, portail *m*; *fig* porte *f*
¹gather *n* (pleat) fronce *f*
²gather *vt* assembler, grouper, rassembler, recueillir; acquérir, prendre, reprendre; (flowers, fruit) cueillir; (corn) récolter; (skirt) froncer; *typ* (pages) assembler; ~ breath reprendre haleine; ~ speed prendre de la vitesse; *vt* conclure, déduire, induire, inférer; *vi* s'assembler, se grouper, se rassembler, se réunir; (increase) augmenter, s'entasser, grandir; *med* (boil, abscess) mûrir
gathering *n* assemblage *m*, rassemblement *m*, réunion *f*, assemblée *f*; *med* abcès *m*
gatling *n obs* mitrailleuse *f*
gaud *n* colifichet *m*, babiole *f*
gaudiness *n* éclat *m* vulgaire, clinquant *m*
¹gaudy *n* banquet *m* d'anciens élèves

501

²**gaudy** *adj* voyant, criard; éclatant, rutilant

**gauge** *n* étalon *m*; (bore) calibre *m*; (fluid level) jauge *f*; (railway) écartement *m*; indicateur *m*, mesureur *m*; *fig* étendue *f*; portée *f*, capacité *f*; *naut* point *m*; (railway) **loading** ~ gabarit *m*; (railway) **narrow** ~ voie étroite; **petrol** ~ jauge *f* à essence; **pressure** ~ manomètre *m*; **rain** ~ pluviomètre *m*; **wind** ~ anémomètre *m*; *vt* mesurer, calibrer, jauger; *fig* mesurer, estimer, jauger

**gauger** *n* jaugeur *m*

**Gaul** *n geog* Gaule *f*; (inhabitant) Gaulois -e

**gaunt** *adj* décharné, anguleux -euse; sévère, lugubre

¹**gauntlet** *n* gantelet *m*; *sp* + *mot* gant *m* à crispin; **take up the** ~ relever un défi, relever le gant; **throw down the** ~ lancer un défi, jeter le gant

²**gauntlet** *n* **run the** ~ *hist* passer par les baguettes; *fig* essuyer des critiques

**gauntness** *n* maigreur *f* extrême

**gauze** *n* (film) gaze *f*; (metal) toile *f* métallique

**gauzy** *adj* diaphane

**gavel** *n* marteau *m*

**gawk** *n coll* lourdaud -e, balourd -e, maladroit -e

**gawkiness** *n* lourdeur *f*, balourdise *f*

**gawky** *adj* lourdaud, balourd, maladroit

**gay** *n* homosexuel -elle; *adj* gai, joyeux -euse; (colour) vif (*f* vive), éclatant, gai; frivole; homosexuel -elle, *coll* de la pédale

**gaze** *n* regard *m* fixe; *vi* regarder fixement, fixer du regard

**gazebo** *n* belvédère *m*

**gazette** *n* journal officiel; journal *m*, revue *f*; **the London Gazette** = l'Officiel; *vt* publier à l'Officiel

**gazetteer** *n* dictionnaire *m* géographique

**gear** *n* équipement *m*, outils *mpl*, ustensiles *mpl*; (harness) harnachement *m*; (clothing) habillement *m*; *mech* engrenage *m*; *mot* vitesse *f*; **change** ~ changer de vitesse; **first** ~ première vitesse; **in** ~ engrené, enclenché; **out of** ~ *mot* au point mort, déclenché; *fig* détraqué; **reverse** ~ marche *f* arrière; *vt* engrener, équiper; *fig* ~ **to** adapter à, lier à; *vi* s'engrener

**gear-box** *n* boîte *f* de vitesse

**gearing** *n* engrenage *m*

**gear-lever** *n* levier *m* de vitesse

**gear-wheel** *n* roue *f* d'engrenage; (bicycle) pignon *m*

**gee** *interj* hue!; *US* tiens!

**gee-gee** *n* (child's language) dada *m*

**gee-up** *interj* hue!

**geezer** *n sl* type *m*, zèbre *m*, zig *m*, zigue *m*

**gehenna** *n* géhenne *f*, enfer *m*

**Geiger counter** *n* compteur *m* Geiger

**gel** *n chem* colloïde *m*; *vi* se coaguler

**gelatine** *n* gélatine *f*

**gelatinous** *adj* gélatineux -euse

**geld** *vt* châtrer

**gelding** *n* castration *f*; animal châtré; (horse) hongre *m*

**gelid** *adj* gelé, transi

**gelidity, gelidness** *n* froid *m* intense

**gelignite** *n* gélignite *f*

**gem** *n min* gemme *f*; pierre précieuse, joyau *m*, bijou *m*; *fig* joyau *m*, bijou *m*, perle *f*; *vt* orner de pierres précieuses

**geminate** *vt* géminer; *adj* géminé

**Gemini** *n astron* Gémeaux *mpl*

**gemma** *n bot* bourgeon *m*, gemme *f*

**gemmate** *vi bot* bourgeonner, gemmer

**gemmation** *n* gemmation *f*

**gen** *n coll* vérité vraie, tuyau *m*, coordonnées *fpl*; *vt* ~ **s/o up on** mettre qn au parfum de; *vi* ~ **up on sth** se rencarder sur qch

**gender** *n gramm* genre *m*; *coll* sexe *m*

**gene** *n biol* gène *m*

**genealogical** *adj* généalogique; ~ **tree** arbre *m* généalogique

**genealogist** *n* généalogiste

**genealogy** *n* généalogie *f*

¹**general** *n mil* + *eccles* général *m*; *coll* bonne *f* à tout faire

²**general** *adj* général; non spécialisé; ~ **election** élections législatives; **in** ~ en général

**generalissimo** *n* généralissime *m*

**generality** *n* généralité *f*, majorité *f*, commun *m*

**generalization** *n* généralisation *f*

**generalize** *vt* généraliser, rendre général; *vi* généraliser

**generally** *adv* généralement, en général, pour la plupart

**generalship** *n mil* (rank) généralat *m*; habileté *f* stratégique, compétence *f* tactique

**generate** *vt* engendrer, causer, produire

**generating** *adj* générateur -trice; ~ **station** centrale *f* électrique

**generation** *n* engendrement *m*; génération *f*

**generative** *adj* générateur -trice, producteur -trice

**generator** *n* générateur -trice; *elect* génératrice *f*

**generic, generical** *adj* générique

**generosity** *n* générosité *f*; acte généreux

**generous** *adj* généreux -euse, charitable, libéral; brave, élevé, humain; (wine) généreux -euse, corsé

**genesis** *n* genèse *f*

**genet** *n zool* genette *f*

**genetic, genetical** *adj* génétique

**genetics** *npl* génétique *f*

**Geneva** *n* Genève *f*; **lake of ~** Lac *m* Léman, Lac *m* de Genève

**geneva** *n* genièvre *m*

**genial** *adj* bienveillant, amical, cordial, ouvert; (climate) doux (*f* douce), favorable, mitigé

**geniality** *n* bienveillance *f*, cordialité *f*, bonhomie *f*

**genic** *adj* génétique

**genie** *n* génie *m*, djinn *m*

**genista** *n bot* genêt *m*

**genital** *adj* génital

**genitalia, genitals** *npl* parties génitales

**genitive** *n gramm* génitif *m*

**genius** *n* (*pl* **geniuses**) (characteristic) génie *m*, aptitude *f* remarquable, caractère distinctif; (person) génie *m*; (*pl* **genii**) génie *m*, lutin *m*, démon *m*; **evil ~** mauvais génie

**genocide** *n* génocide *m*

**genre** *n* genre *m*

**gent** *n coll* chic type *m*

**genteel** *adj* ar bien élevé, distingué; *pej* distingué, délicat

**gentian** *n bot* gentiane *f*

**gentile** *n* gentil *m*; *adj* des gentils

**gentility** *n* bonne naissance, distinction *f*; *pej* distinction *f*, délicatesse *f*

¹**gentle** *adj* doux (*f* douce), aimable, modéré, tendre, docile; *obs* bien né, noble; *her* ayant droit aux armoiries

²**gentle** *n* asticot *m*

**gentlefolk** *npl* gens *mpl* comme il faut, gens bien nés

**gentleman** *n* gentleman *m*, homme *m* du monde, galant homme, monsieur *m*; *ar* noble *m*, gentilhomme *m*; **~ 's agreement** convention *f* tacite

**gentleman-at-arms** *n* gentilhomme *m* de la garde royale

**gentleman-farmer** *n* gentleman-farmer *m* (*pl* gentlemen-farmers)

**gentlemanlike, gentlemanly** *adj* (behaviour) courtois, poli, de bon ton; (person) bien élevé, bien né

**gentleness** *n* douceur *f*; amabilité *f*, tendresse *f*, docilité *f*

**gentlewoman** *n* dame *f*, demoiselle *f*, dame *f* du monde; *obs* grande dame

**gently** *adv* doucement, aimablement, tendrement, docilement

**genuflect** *vi* faire une génuflexion

**genuflection, genuflexion** *n* génuflexion *f*

**genuine** *adj* vrai, authentique, véridique; sincère, franc (*f* franche); *zool* de pure race

germination

**genuineness** *n* authenticité *f*; sincérité *f*, franchise *f*

**genus** *n biol* genre *m*

**geocentric, geocentrical** *adj* géocentrique

**geodesic** *adj* géodésique

**geodesy** *n* géodésie *f*

**geographer** *n* géographe

**geographic, geographical** *adj* géographique

**geography** *n* géographie *f*; topographie *f*, configuration *f*; livre *m* de géographie

**geological** *adj* géologique

**geologist** *n* géologue

**geologize** *vt* étudier la géologie de; *vi* faire de la géologie

**geology** *n* géologie *f*

**geometer** *n* géomètre *m*

**geometric, geometrical** *adj* géométrique; *fig* régulier -ière, symétrique, angulaire

**geometrician** *n* géomètre

**geometry** *n* géométrie *f*

**geophysical** *adj* géophysique

**geophysics** *npl* géophysique *f*

**geopolitical** *adj* géopolitique

**geopolitics** *npl* géopolitique *f*

**George** *n* Georges *m*; **by ~!** mon Dieu!

**georgette** *n* crêpe *m* georgette

**georgic** *adj* géorgique *f*

**geranium** *n bot* géranium *m*

**gerfalcon** *n orni* gerfaut *m*

**geriatric** *adj* gériatrique

**geriatrics** *npl* gériatrie *f*

**germ** *n med* bacille *m*, microbe *m*, germe *m*; *fig* source *f*, origine *f*, germe *m*; **~ warfare** guerre *f* bactériologique

**German** *n* Allemand -e; *hist* Germain -e; (language) allemand *m*; *adj* allemand, germanique; *hist* germain; **~ measles** rubéole *f*

**german** *adj* (cousin) germain

**germane** *adj* apparenté; **~ to** se rapportant à

**Germanic** *n* germanique *m*; *adj* germanique

**Germanism** *n* germanisme *m*

**Germanist** *n* germaniste

**Germanize** *vt* germaniser

**German silver** *n* argentan *m*, maillechort *m*

**Germany** *n* Allemagne *f*

**germen** *n bot* germe *m*

**germicidal** *adj* germicide, bactéricide, microbicide

**germicide** *n* microbicide *m*; *adj* germicide, bactéricide, microbicide

**germinal** *adj biol* germinal; en germe

**germinant** *adj* qui germe

**germinate** *vt* faire germer; *vi* germer

**germination** *n* germination *f*

503

germon

**germon** *n* germon *m*, thon blanc
**gerontology** *n* gérontologie *f*
**gerrymander** *n* modification *f* de cir-
conscriptions pour des raisons électorales, *coll* cuisine électorale; *vt*
truquer (une élection), *coll* cuisiner
(une élection)
**gerrymandering** *n* action *f* de truquer
une élection
**gerund** *n gramm* (English) substantif
verbal; (Latin, French) gérondif *m*
**gerundive** *n gramm* (English) adjectif
formé d'après un substantif verbal
**gestalt** *n* gestaltisme *m*
**gestation** *n* gestation *f*
**gestatory** *adj* gestatoire
**gesticulate** *vi* gesticuler, faire des gestes
**gesticulation** *n* gesticulation *f*, geste *m*
**gesticulatory** *adj* gesticulant
**gesture** *n* geste *m*, signe *m*; acte *m*; *vt*
exprimer par gestes; *vi* gesticuler, faire
des gestes
**get** *vt* obtenir, acquérir; recevoir; (bring)
amener, apporter; (succeed in doing)
réussir, atteindre; (illness) attraper;
(cause to do) faire faire; (cause) engendrer; *coll* (understand) piger; (notice)
remarquer; (annoy) irriter; (impress)
impressionner; *sl* exciter; *coll* (kill)
tuer; (stop) arrêter; ~ **across**
faire comprendre; communiquer; ~
**away** entraîner, faire partir; ~ **back**
recouvrer, faire revenir; ~ **back into**
faire rentrer dans; ~ **down** descendre,
faire descendre; (food) avaler; (on
paper) noter; (depress) décourager; ~
**in** faire entrer, introduire, rentrer;
(word) placer; (harvest) rentrer, engranger; *coll* ~ **it** piger, comprendre; ~
**off** ôter, enlever; *leg* faire acquitter;
(send) expédier; *naut* (refloat) renflouer; ~ **on** mettre, enfiler; faire progresser; ~ **oneself up** s'attifer, se
déguiser; ~ **one's hand in** se faire la
main; ~ **one's own back** prendre sa
revanche; ~ **out** enlever; (cork) tirer;
(tooth) enlever; (book) sortir; (account) dresser; (list) établir; (problem)
résoudre; ~ **over** en finir avec; ~
**round** persuader; ~ **s/o into trouble**
causer des ennuis à qn; (girl) faire un
enfant à; ~ **s/o out of trouble** tirer qn
du pétrin; *coll* ~ **s/o's back up** agacer
qn, emmerder qn; ~ **sth on the brain**
n'avoir que ça dans la tête; ~ **through**
(law) faire adopter; (pupil) faire réussir; ~ **up** (person) faire monter,
obliger à se lever; (thing) monter; (role,
part) apprendre, préparer; (play)
monter; ~ **with child** engrosser; he

~ s **me down** il me tape sur les nerfs;
**have got** posséder; **have got to** être
obligé de; *vi* (become) devenir; (be) être;
~ **about** (person) se déplacer, circuler;
(news) s'ébruiter; ~ **ahead** prospérer,
faire des progrès, prendre de l'avance;
~ **along** s'en aller, avancer; (manage)
se débrouiller; ~ **along with** s'accorder avec; ~ **along with you!** allez!,
c'est ridicule!; *coll* ~ **around**
s'amuser; être connu; (news) se disséminer; ~ **at** parvenir à, atteindre,
toucher; *coll* (bribe) acheter, corrompre; ~ **away** partir, se sauver; sortir
indemne, s'en tirer; *coll* ~ **away with
you!** pas vrai!; ~ **back** revenir, retourner; ~ **back at** rendre la pareille à; ~
**by** se débrouiller, se tirer d'affaire; ~
**cracking** démarrer; ~ **down** descendre; ~ **down to** se mettre à; ~ **hold
of** obtenir; (understand) comprendre;
~ **home** rentrer à la maison; ~ **in**
entrer, rentrer; *pol* être élu; (examination) être reçu; ~ **into** (clothes)
mettre; (enter) pénétrer dans; ~ **into
the habit of** prendre l'habitude de; ~
**into trouble** s'attirer des ennemis; (girl)
fauter; ~ **in** with s/o entrer dans les
bonnes grâces de qn; *coll* ~ **it** piger; ~
**nowhere** ne faire aucun progrès; ~ **off**
(dismount) descendre; (accusation) se
tirer d'affaire; *coll* ~ **off with** faire une
touche avec; ~ **on** continuer, poursuivre, avancer; (vehicle) monter dans;
(agree) s'entendre; (make progress)
progresser, réussir; ~ **on one's feet** se
lever, se mettre debout; *coll* ~ **on s/o's
nerves** taper sur les nerfs de qn; ~ **on
top** vaincre, être à la hauteur; ~ **on to**
s/o (telephone) avoir qn; ~ **on with**
s'entendre avec; ~ **out** sortir,
descendre; (rumour, news) s'ébruiter,
se propager; *coll* ~ **out!** fous le camp!;
~ **out of sth** se tirer d'affaire, se soustraire à qch; ~ **over** se remettre de, se
rétablir de, se faire à; (obstacle) franchir; ~ **past** passer; ~ **round** faire le
tour de, contourner; ~ **there** réussir;
~ **through** passer à travers; (examination) être reçu; (money, task) arriver
au bout de; ~ **through to** établir la
communication avec; ~ **together**
s'assembler, se réunir; ~ **under** passer
par-dessous; *naut* ~ **under way** appareiller; ~ **up** monter; (from bed, chair,
etc) se lever; (sea) grossir; (wind) se
lever; ~ **up to** faire; ~ **wind of** avoir
vent de; *coll* **tell s/o where he** ~ s **off**
remettre qn à sa place; **what are you**
~ **ting at?** où voulez-vous en venir?
**get-at-able** *adj coll* accessible

504

**getaway** n coll fuite f, départ m; mot démarrage m

**get-out** n coll échappatoire m

**get-together** n réunion f

**get-up** n coll accoutrement m, habillement m

**gewgaw** n colifichet m, babiole f

**geyser** n geol geyser m; (water heater) chauffe-bain m

**ghastliness** n aspect m sinistre; extrême pâleur f

**ghastly** adj effroyable, atroce; (pale) blême

**gherkin** n cornichon m

**ghetto** n ghetto m

**ghost** n spectre m, fantôme m, revenant m; (soul) âme f; phys image f secondaire; fig ombre f, soupçon m, trace f; (writer) nègre m; give up the ~ rendre l'âme; **Holy Ghost** Saint Esprit

**ghostliness** n aspect spectral

**ghostly** adj spectral

**ghoul** n goule f; déterreur m de cadavres

**ghoulish** adj morbide, macabre

**giant** n géant m; adj géant, énorme

**giantess** n géante f

**gib** n + vi see **jib**

**gibber** vi baragouiner; émettre des sons inarticulés

**gibberish** n baragouinage m, charabia m

**gibbet** n gibet m, potence f

**gibbon** n gibbon m

**gibbose, gibbous** adj gibbeux -euse, bossu

**gibe, jibe** n moquerie f, raillerie f; vi se moquer, railler

**giblets** npl abattis mpl

**giddiness** n vertige m, étourdissement m; fig frivolité f, légèreté f

**giddy** adj pris de vertige, étourdi; (height) vertigineux -euse; (whirling) giratoire; fig frivole, léger -ère

**gift** n don m, cadeau m; fig don m, talent m; comm prime f; coll aubaine f

**gifted** adj doué

**gift-horse** n look a ~ in the mouth faire le difficile

**gig** n cabriolet m; naut yole f

**gigantic** adj gigantesque, géant, colossal

**gigantism** n med gigantisme m

**giggle** n gloussement m; vi glousser

**gigolo** n gigolo m

**gigue** n gigue f

¹**gild** n see **guild**

²**gild** vt dorer; fig embellir, illuminer; ~ **the lily** ajouter des ornements superflus; ~ **the pill** dorer la pilule

**gilded** adj doré; ~ **youth** jeunesse dorée

**gilding** n dorure f

**gill** n (fish) branchie f; ~s ouïes fpl

**gillyflower** n giroflée f

**gilt** n feuille f d'or, peinture f d'or; éclat m, brillant m; adj doré

**gilt-edged** adj (book) doré sur tranche; ~ **security** rente f à intérêts fixes; fig placement m de tout repos

**gimcrack** n babiole f; adj de camelote

**gimlet** n vrille f

**gimmick** n truc m, dispositif m; (advertising) astuce f publicitaire

¹**gin** n gin m

²**gin** n obs piège m, collet m; eng chèvre f

**ginger** n gingembre m; (colour) roux m; fig entrain m; ~ **group** groupe m de pression; adj (colour) roux (f rousse), coll rouquin; vt parfumer au gingembre; fig ~ **up** animer, secouer

**ginger-ale, ginger-beer** n boisson gazeuse au gingembre

**gingerbread** n gâteau m au gingembre; **take the gilt off the** ~ enlever l'attraction

**gingerly** adj prudent, circonspect; adv prudemment, avec circonspection

**ginger-nut** n biscuit m au gingembre

**ginger-wine** n boisson alcoolisée au gingembre

**gingery** adj ayant un goût de gingembre; (colour) roux (f rousse); fig irascible, coléreux -euse

**gingham** n (cloth) vichy m

**gingival** adj gingival

**gingivitis** n gingivite f

**gipsy, gypsy** n bohémien -ienne, gitan -e; fig vagabond -e, coquin -e; adj de bohémien, gitan

**giraffe** n girafe f

**girandole** n girandole f

**gird** vt ceindre, entourer, cercler

**girder** n poutre f métallique, poutrelle f, longeron m

¹**girdle** n ceinture f; (corset) gaine f; vt ceinturer, entourer

²**girdle** n see **griddle**

**girl** n fille f, jeune fille f; (little) fillette f; (servant) bonne f; ~ **friend** petite amie; (school) old ~ ancienne élève; old ~! ma vieille!

**girlhood** n enfance f, jeunesse f

**girlish** adj de jeune fille, de petite fille

**girlishness** n enfance f, jeunesse f

**girth** n tour m de taille; circonférence f; (horse) sangle f

**gist** n fond m, essentiel m

**give** n élasticité f, flexibilité f; ~ **and take** échange m de bons procédés; vt donner, offrir; occasionner, causer, provoquer; exécuter, formuler, faire; conférer, infliger; concéder; payer; (shout) pousser; (judgement) rendre; ~ **away** donner; (prizes) distribuer; coll (betray) moucharder, dénoncer; (secret) trahir; (oneself) se trahir; ~ **back** rendre, restituer; ~ **chase** poursuivre; ~ **forth** annoncer, proclamer; ~ **ground** céder, reculer, battre en retraite; ~ **in** remettre; *coll* ~ **it to** punir; (scold) engueuler; ~ **off** émettre, dégager; ~ **oneself out for** s'intituler, se dire; ~ **oneself up** se rendre, se constituer prisonnier -ière; ~ **oneself up to** s'adonner à; ~ **out** distribuer; (announce) faire connaître, proclamer; ~ **place to** être remplacé par; ~ **rise to** causer, provoquer; ~ **s/o best** reconnaître la supériorité de qn; ~ **s/o out for** faire passer qn pour; *med* ~ **s/o up** condamner; ~ **tongue** parler fort; (dog) aboyer; ~ **up** abandonner, délaisser; renoncer à, cesser de; (post) se démettre de; (seat) céder; *vi* donner; céder; ~ **and take** transiger, faire des concessions mutuelles; ~ **in** renoncer, abandonner; ~ **into** donner accès à, donner sur; ~ **in to s/o** céder à qn; ~ **onto** donner sur; ~ **out** faire défaut, venir à manquer; finir; ~ **over** renoncer; *coll* arrêter; ~ **up** renoncer, abandonner

**given** *adj* donné, déterminé; *Scots+US* ~ **name** prénom *m*; ~ **to** adonné à, enclin à, porté à

**giving** *n* action *f* de donner; *adj* généreux -euse; flexible

**gizzard** *n* gésier *m*

**glabrous** *adj* glabre

**glacé** *adj* glacé

**glacial** *adj* glacial; *geol* glaciaire

**glaciation** *n* glaciation *f*

**glacier** *n* glacier *m*

**glacis** *n* glacis *m*

**glad** *adj* content, heureux -euse, joyeux -euse, enchanté; *coll* **give the ~ eye to** reluquer, faire de l'œil à; *coll* ~ **rags** beaux atours

**gladden** *vt* réjouir, rendre heureux -euse

**glade** *n* clairière *f*

**gladiator** *n* gladiateur *m*

**gladiatorial** *adj* de gladiateur

**gladiolus** *n* (*pl* **gladioli**) glaïeul *m*

**gladly** *adv* avec plaisir, volontiers, de bon cœur; avec joie

**gladness** *n* contentement *m*, joie *f*

**gladsome** *adj ar* joyeux -euse

**glair** *n cul* blanc *m* d'œuf; matière blanche et visqueuse; *med* glaire *f*; *vt* glairer

**glamorize** *vt* exalter; porter aux nues

**glamorous** *adj* romantique, séduisant; enchanteur -eresse, ensorcelant

**glamour** *n* éclat *m*, enchantement *m*; sex-appeal *m*; ensorcellement *m*

**glance** *n* coup *m* d'œil; (blow) coup *m* de biais; **have a ~ at** jeter un coup d'œil à; *vi* regarder rapidement, jeter un coup d'œil; (glint) étinceler, briller; ~ **off** effleurer; être dévié; (book) ~ **at**, ~

**through** feuilleter

**glancing** *adj* (blow) oblique

**gland** *n* glande *f*

**glanders** *npl vet* morve *f*

**glandular** *adj* glandulaire; ~ **fever** mononucléose infectieuse

**glandule** *n* glandule *f*; tumeur *f*

**glare** *n* lumière crue, éclat éblouissant; (look) regard furieux; *vi* briller; (look) jeter un regard furieux

**glaring** *adj* (light) éblouissant, aveuglant; (colour) éclatant, criard; (mistake) manifeste, flagrant

**glass** *n* verre *m*; (drinking) verre *m*; baromètre *m*; (mirror) glace *f*, miroir *m*; télescope *m*; ~**es** lunettes *fpl*; **cut ~** cristal taillé; **hour ~** sablier *m*; **looking ~** glace *f*, miroir *m*; **magnifying ~** loupe *f*; **opera ~es** jumelles *fpl*; **pane of ~** carreau *m*, vitre *f*; *adj* de verre, en verre; (door) vitré

**glassblower** *n* souffleur *m*

**glass-cloth** *n* essuie-verres *m*

**glasscutter** *n* vitrier *m*; (tool) diamant *m*

**glass-frame** *n hort* châssis *m*

**glassful** *n* verre *m*, plein verre

**glasshouse** *n* serre *f*; *coll* prison *f* militaire

**glass-paper** *n* papier *m* de verre

**glassware** *n* verrerie *f*, articles *mpl* de verre

**glass-wool** *n* laine *f* de verre

**glass-works** *n* verrerie *f*

**glassy** *adj* vitreux -euse; (smooth) uni, lisse

**glauber's salt** *n med* sulfate *m* de soude

**glaucoma** *n med* glaucome *m*

**glaucous** *adj* glauque

**glaze** *n* vernis *m*, glaçure *f*, enduit *m*; *cul* glace *f*; *vt* (insert glass) vitrer; *obs* vernisser; (tiles) vitrifier; *cul* glacer; *vi* (expression) devenir impassible; (eye) devenir vitreux

**glazed** *adj* vitré; vernissé; *cul* glacé

**glazier** *n* vitrier *m*

**glazing** *n* (trade) vitrerie *f*; (inserting glass) pose *f* des vitres; vernissage *m*; vernis *m*, enduit *m*; *cul* glace *f*; **double ~** double vitrage *m*

**gleam** *n* lueur *f*; *vi* luire

**gleaming** *adj* luisant

**glean** *vt* glaner

**gleaner** *n* glaneur -euse

**gleanings** *npl* glanure *f*

**glebe** *n* lit glèbe *f*

**glee** *n* allégresse *f*, joie *f*; *mus* chant à plusieurs voix non accompagné

**gleeful** *adj* allègre, joyeux -euse

**glen** *n* ravin *m*, petite vallée

**glib** *adj* plausible, spécieux -ieuse; facile

**glibness** *n* plausibilité *f*; facilité *f*

**glide** *n* glissement *m*, glissade *f*;

**go**

(dancing) glissade *f*, glissé *m*
**glider** *n aer* planeur *m*
**gliding** *n* glissement *m*; *aer* vol *m* à voile, vol plané
**glimmer** *n* lueur *f*; *vi* jeter une lueur; vaciller
**glimmering** *n* lueur *f*; *adj* vacillant
**glimpse** *n* coup *m* d'œil; *vt* entrevoir
**glint** *n* lueur *f*, reflet *m*; *vi* luire
**glissade** *n* glissade *f*
**glisten** *vi* étinceler, scintiller; briller, miroiter
**glistening** *adj* étincelant, scintillant; brillant, miroitant
**glister** *n* + *vi obs see* glitter
**glitter** *n* scintillement *m*; *fig* éclat *m*, brillant *m*; *vi* briller, chatoyer, étinceler; (sea) brasiller
**glittering** *adj* brillant, chatoyant, étincelant
**gloaming** *n* crépuscule *m*
**gloat** *vi* triompher; *coll* faire des gorges chaudes
**global** *adj* global, universel -elle, achevé
**globe** *n* globe *m*; sphère *f*; *geog* mappemonde *f*; (glass) bocal *m* sphérique
**globe-trotter** *n* globe-trotter *m*
**globular** *adj* globulaire, globuleux -euse
**globule** *n med* globule *m*; gouttelette *f*
**globulin** *n* globuline *f*
**glockenspiel** *n mus* glockenspiel *m*
**glomerate** *adj* congloméré
**gloom, gloominess** *n* obscurité *f*, noir *m*; *fig* mélancolie *f*, dépression *f*
**gloominess** *n see* gloom
**gloomy** *adj* obscur, sombre, ténébreux -euse; *fig* mélancolique, sombre
**gloria** *n eccles* gloria *m invar*
**glorification** *n* glorification *f*
**glorify** *vt* glorifier, célébrer; (adorn) enrichir, parer
**gloriole** *n* auréole *f*
**glorious** *adj* glorieux -ieuse, illustre; célèbre, magnifique; (weather) radieux -ieuse; *coll* fameux -euse, épatant
**gloriously** *adv* glorieusement; magnifiquement; *coll* fameusement
**glory** *n* gloire *f*, magnificence *f*, splendeur *f*; (halo) auréole *f*; **be in one's ~** se savoir bon gré, triompher; **Old Glory** drapeau *m* des États-Unis
**glory-hole** *n* débarras *m*; *naut* cambuse *f*
¹**gloss** *n* glose *f*, commentaire *m*; *vt* gloser, commenter; **~ over** atténuer, justifier tant bien que mal
²**gloss** *n* brillant *m*, éclat *m*, lustre *m*; *fig* vernis *m*; apparence trompeuse; *vt* lustrer, polir
**glossary** *n* glossaire *m*
**glossiness** *n* brillant *m*, lustre *m*
**glossy** *adj* brillant, lustré, vernissé; *phot* glacé; *coll* **~ magazine** magazine chic

(imprimé sur papier glacé)
**glottal** *adj* glottique, glottal; **~ stop** coup *m* de glotte
**glottis** *n anat* glotte *f*
**glove** *n* gant *m*; **be hand in ~** s'entendre comme larrons en foire; **fit like a ~** aller comme un gant; **throw down the ~** lancer un défi; **with ~s off** à outrance
**glove-maker** *n* gantier -ière
**glover** *n* gantier -ière
**glow** *n* rougeur *f*, embrasement *m*; *fig* ardeur *f*; (well-being) bien-être *m*; *vi* rougeoyer; (fire) couver; *fig* sentir une chaleur; être radieux -ieuse, rayonner
**glower** *vi* se renfrogner, faire grise mine
**glowing** *adj* rougeoyant, embrasé; (complexion) rouge; *fig* chaleureux -euse, enthousiaste
**glow-lamp** *n* lampe *f* à incandescence
**glow-worm** *n* ver luisant
**glucose** *n* glucose *m*
**glue** *n* colle *f*; *vt* coller
**gluey** *adj* collant, gluant
**glum** *adj* morose, renfrogné, sombre
**glumness** *n* humeur chagrine, morosité *f*
**glut** *n* excès *m*; *comm* surabondance *f*; *vt comm* saturer; rassasier
**glutinosity** *n* viscosité *f*
**glutinous** *adj* glutineux -euse, visqueux -euse
**glutton** *n* glouton -onne, goinfre *m*; *fig* enthousiaste
**gluttonous** *adj* glouton -onne, goinfre, goulu
**gluttony** *n* gloutonnerie *f*, goinfrerie *f*
**glycerine** *n* glycérine *f*, glycérol *m*
**glycerol** *n chem* glycérol *m*, glycérine *f*
**glycogen** *n chem* glycogène *m*
**glycol** *n chem* glycol *m*
**gnarl** *n bot* nœud *m*
**gnarled** *adj* noueux -euse; rugueux -euse
**gnash** *vt* **~ one's teeth** grincer des dents
**gnashing** *n* grincement *m*
**gnat** *n* moucheron *m*
**gnaw** *vt* ronger, grignoter
**gnawing** *n* grignotement *m*, rongement *m*; *adj* rongeur -euse
**gneiss** *n geol* gneiss *m*
**gnome** *n* gnome *m*, homme petit et contrefait
**gnomic** *adj* gnomique
**gnosis** *n* gnose *f*
**Gnostic** *n* gnostique
**gnostic** *adj* gnostique
**gnosticism** *n* gnosticisme *m*
**gnu** *n zool* gnou *m*
**go** *n* mouvement *m*, action *f*; (attempt) essai *m*, coup *m*, tentative *f*; dynamisme *m*, énergie *f*, allant *m*, entrain *m*; **at one ~** d'un seul coup; **be always on the ~** être toujours sur la brèche;

**goad**

have a ~ ! allez-y toujours!; *coll* it's all
the ~ c'est le dernier cri; it's your ~
c'est votre tour; make a ~ of it réussir
qch; no ~ rien à faire; that was a near
~ on l'a échappé belle; *vi* aller,
marcher; (depart) partir, s'en aller;
(road) conduire; (yield) céder, se
casser; (work) marcher, fonctionner;
(eyesight) baisser; (evolve) se
présenter, se développer, tourner;
(become) devenir; (time) s'écouler,
passer; (disappear) disparaître; (wear
out) s'user; ~ **about** voyager;
(rumour) courir; (undertake) vaquer à;
*naut* virer de bord; ~ **after** courir
après, poursuivre; ~ **against** s'opposer à; (current) remonter; ~ **ahead**
avancer, progresser; (start) commencer; ~ **(all) out for** s'efforcer d'obtenir; ~ **along** continuer, avancer; ~
**along with** accompagner; *coll* accepter;
~ **and get** aller chercher; ~ **at** attaquer; ~ **away** s'en aller, partir; ~
**back** retourner en arrière; (memory)
remonter; ~ **back on one's word** manquer à sa parole; *leg* ~ **bail for** se
porter caution pour; ~ **beyond** dépasser; ~ **by** passer; (time) s'écouler;
(name) être connu sous (le nom de); ~
**down** descendre; (wind) tomber; (ship)
sombrer, couler; (in history) être per-
pétué; (university) quitter l'université,
finir ses études; ~ **for** aller chercher;
(sale) être vendu pour; *coll* attaquer;
(fall for) être entiché de; ~ **for one
another** se prendre aux cheveux; ~
**forward** avancer; (plan) être en voie de
réalisation; **going! going! gone!** une
fois, deux fois, trois fois, adjugé!
(vendu!); ~ **hard with** aller mal pour;
~ **in** entrer; (sun) se cacher; ~ **in for**
se présenter à, affronter; (habit)
s'adonner à; *pej* se livrer à; ~ **into**
entrer en, entrer dans, se lancer dans;
(examine) approfondir; ~ **into hiding**
se cacher; ~ **into mourning** prendre le
deuil; ~ **off** s'en aller, partir; (food)
s'abîmer, se gâter; (milk) tourner;
*theat* faire une sortie; ~ **on** continuer,
poursuivre, avancer; (take place) se
dérouler; *theat* faire une entrée; ~ **on
at** harceler, gronder; ~ **on for** (be
nearly) approcher; ~ out sortir, quitter; (light) s'éteindre; (fashion) passer
de mode; ~ out of office quitter le
pouvoir; (heart) ~ out to sympathiser
avec; ~ **over** verser, basculer; (check)
vérifier, repasser, revoir; ~ **round**
faire le tour; ~ **through** traverser;
(book) dépouiller; (endure) subir,
souffrir; ~ **through with** mener à
bien, achever; ~ **to** aller à, aller

trouver, s'adresser à; ~ **together** aller
ensemble; ~ **to show** servir à montrer;
~ **to the country** en appeler à la
nation, provoquer des élections législatives; ~ **to the trouble of** se donner la
peine de; ~ **towards** aller vers; (fund)
être une contribution à; ~ **under** sombrer, couler; ~ **up** monter, augmenter; (university) entrer dans;
(price) ~ **up to** aller jusqu'à; *coll* ~
**west** être foutu; (die) crever; ~ **with**
(match) aller avec, s'assortir avec; (accompany) accompagner; ~ **without** se
passer de; ~ **without saying** aller de
soi, aller sans dire; be ~ing to être sur
le point de; **let** ~ laisser aller, lâcher
prise, relâcher; **let oneself** ~ se laisser
aller, s'abandonner; **the meat will** ~
**round** il y aura assez de viande pour
tout le monde

**goad** *n* aiguillon *m*; *fig* stimulant *m*; *vt*
aiguillonner; *fig* stimuler, aiguillonner,
provoquer

**go-ahead** *n* signal *m* du départ; autorisation *f* du départ; *adj* entreprenant

**goal** *n* but *m*

**goal-keeper** *n* gardien *m* de but

**goal-line** *n* ligne *f* de but

**goal-post** *n* montant *m* (de but)

**goat** *n* bouc *m*, chèvre *f*; *fig* satyre *m*;
*coll* idiot -e; *coll* **act the (giddy)** ~ sl
faire des conneries; *coll* **get s/o's** ~
irriter qn, emmerder qn

**goatee** *n* (beard) bouc *m*

**goatherd** *n* chevrier -ière

**goatish** *adj* de bouc; *fig* libidineux -euse,
lubrique

**gob** *n sl* (mouth) gueule *f*; *sl* (spit) glaviot
*m*; *US sl* matelot *m*

**gobbet** *n* morceau *m*

**gobble** *vt* engloutir, dévorer; *vi*
se gaver, s'empiffrer; (turkey) glouglouter

**gobbledygook** *n sl* charabia *m*, baragouin *m*

**go-between** *n* intermédiaire; (pimp)
entremetteur *m*

**goblet** *n* gobelet *m*

**goblin** *n* lutin *m*

**go-by** *n* **give s/o the** ~ éviter qn

**go-cart** *n* poussette *f*; chariot *m* d'enfant; charrette *f* à bras

**god** *n* dieu *m*; **God** Dieu *m*; **God's acre**
cimetière *m*; *leg* **act of God** cas *m* de
force majeure; **house of God** église *f*;
*coll theat* **the** ~s le paradis, le poulailler; *coll* **tin** ~ tyranneau *m*

**godchild** *n* filleul -e

**goddam** *adj* damné, maudit

**goddaughter** *n* filleule *f*

**goddess** *n* déesse *f*

**godfather** *n* parrain *m*

**godfearing** adj pieux (f pieuse), religieux -ieuse

**godforsaken** adj sinistre, désert, misérable; (wicked) mauvais; coll ~ **place** trou perdu

**godhead** n divinité f

**godless** adj impie, irréligieux -ieuse, athée

**godlessness** n impiété f, irréligion f, athéisme m

**godlike** adj divin, comme un dieu

**godly** adj pieux (f pieuse), dévot, religieux -ieuse

**godmother** n marraine f; **fairy ~** bienfaitrice f, protectrice f

**godparent** n parrain m, marraine f

**godsend** n aubaine f

**godson** n filleul m

**god-speed** n bonne chance

**goer** n personne qui va; cheval m (voiture f, etc) qui va vite; coll as m

**gofer** n US factotum m

**goffer** n tuyauté m; vt (clothes) tuyauter; (paper, leather) gaufrer

**goffering** n tuyauté m

**go-getter** n coll arriviste, ambitieux -ieuse

**goggle** vi bayer aux corneilles, ouvrir de grands yeux; (eye) être saillant

**goggle-eyed** adj aux yeux saillants

**goggles** npl lunettes fpl de protection, lunettes fpl de motocycliste; coll lunettes fpl, besicles fpl

**going** n action f d'aller, action f de partir, départ m; (ground) état m du terrain; **while the ~ is good** pendant que les circonstances sont favorables; adj prospère, en bon ordre; en état de marche

**going-over** n coll interrogatoire m; passage m à tabac; correction f

**goings-on** npl coll pej manigance f, micmac m

**goitre** n goitre m

**goitrous** adj goitreux -euse

**gold** n or m; fig richesses fpl; ~ **standard** étalon-or m; adj en or

**goldbearing** adj aurifère

**goldbeater** n batteur m d'or

**gold-digger** n chercheur m d'or; coll femme f qui cherche un mari riche

**gold-dust** n poudre f d'or

**golden** adj en or; d'or, doré; ~ **age** âge m d'or; ~ **syrup** mélasse raffinée

**gold-field** n terrain m aurifère

**goldfinch** n chardonneret m

**goldfish** n poisson m rouge

**gold-foil** n feuille f d'or

**gold-lace** n galon m d'or

**gold-leaf** n feuille f d'or

**gold-mine** n mine f d'or

**gold-plate** n vaisselle f d'or

**gold-rush** n ruée f vers l'or

**goldsmith** n orfèvre m

**golf** n golf m; vi faire du golf

**golf-club** n (object) club m, canne f, crosse f (de golf); (place) golf m

**golf-course, golf-links** n terrain m de golf

**golfer** n golfeur -euse

**golliwog** n poupée f représentant un nègre

**golly** interj coll ciel!, mon Dieu!, ça alors!

**golosh** n (usu pl) botillons mpl de caoutchouc, caoutchoucs mpl

**gonad** n biol gonade f

**gondola** n gondole f; (airship) nacelle f

**gondolier** n gondolier m

**gone** adj parti; coll perdu; sl foutu; (dead) mort; coll ~ **on** entiché de

**goner** n sl homme foutu, type perdu

**gonfalon** n gonfalon m

**gong** n gong m; sl médaille f; vt appeler par un coup de gong; vi frapper sur un gong

**gonorrhoea** n blennorragie f

**goo** n sl pej douceur mielleuse, sentimentalité f

**good** n bon m, bien m; vertu f; avantage m, profit m; ~**s** marchandises fpl, biens mpl; **be up to no ~** préparer un mauvais coup; coll **deliver the ~s** remplir une promesse; (perform satisfactorily) prouver ses capacités; **for ~** pour de bon; **it's no ~ doing that** inutile de faire cela; **so much to the ~** autant de gagné; (object) **that's no ~** cela ne vaut rien; **the ~** (persons) les bons; **what's the ~ of?** à quoi bon?; adj bon (f bonne), brave; bien invar; (fine) beau (f belle), joli; (kind) bienveillant, aimable; (child) sage; (beneficial) salutaire; compétent, expert; (worthy) honorable, digne; (saintly) pieux (f pieuse); **Good Friday** vendredi saint; ~ **turn** service m; **a ~ deal** beaucoup; **a ~ many** beaucoup; **a ~ while** longtemps; **as ~ as** pour ainsi dire, pratiquement; **be as ~ as** valoir; coll **be on to a ~ thing** trouver le filon; **have a ~ time** s'amuser bien; **in ~ time** bien à l'heure; **make ~** prospérer; (mend) réparer; (loss) compenser; (promise) remplir, tenir

**goodbye** n + interj adieu m, au revoir m

**good-for-nothing** n + adj bon (f bonne) à rien

**good-humoured** adj de bonne humeur, allègre, gai

**goodish** adj assez bon (f bonne)

**good-looking** adj beau (f belle), coll bien invar

**goodly** adj beau (f belle); gracieux

-ieuse, avenant; (sizable) grand, considérable

**good-natured** *adj* aimable, sympathique

**goodness** *n* bonté *f*; gentillesse *f*; *interj* mon Dieu!, vraiment!: ~ **gracious!**, ~ **me!, my** ~ **!** mon Dieu!

**good-tempered** *adj* de bon caractère, de caractère égal

**goodwill** *n* bienveillance *f*; bonne volonté; *leg* réputation *f* d'une maison de commerce

**goody** *n* (*usu pl*) friandise *f*

**goody-goody** *n coll* petit -e saint -e, dévot -e

**gooey** *adj* gluant; *coll fig* sentimental

**goof** *n* toqué -e; *vt* ~ **up** bousiller; *vi* faire une gaffe

**goofy** *adj sl* idiot

**goon** *n coll* bouffon *m*

**goose** *n* oie *f*; *coll* imbécile; (girl) oie *f*, pécore *f*; *coll* **cook s/o's** ~ régler son compte à qn

**gooseberry** *n* groseille *f* à maquereau; *coll* chaperon *m*; *coll* **play** ~ être le tiers incommode

**gooseflesh** *n* chair *f* de poule

**goose-neck** *n eng* col *m* de cygne

**goose-step** *n mil* pas *m* de l'oie

¹**gore** *n* sang *m*

²**gore** *n* godet *m*; *vt* mettre un godet dans

³**gore** *vt* corner, donner un coup de corne à

**gorge** *n geog* + *physiol* gorge *f*; **my** ~ **rises at it** cela m'écœure; *vt* gorger, rassasier; *vi* se gorger, s'empiffrer

**gorgeous** *adj* fastueux -euse, somptueux -euse; *coll* splendide, épatant; (woman) plantureux -euse

**gorgeousness** *n* magnificence *f*, faste *m*, splendeur *f*

**Gorgon** *n myth* Gorgone *f*; *fig* mégère *f*

**gorilla** *n* gorille *m*

**gormandize** *vi* s'empiffrer, se bourrer

**gormless** *adj coll* lourdaud

**gorse** *n* ajonc *m*

**gory** *adj* ensanglanté; *fig* sanglant

**gosh** *interj* ça alors!, pas possible!

**goshawk** *n* autour *m*

**gosling** *n* oison *m*

**go-slow** *n* travail *m* au ralenti; (work to rule) grève perlée

**gospel** *n* évangile *m*; *bibl* Évangile *m*; ~ **truth** parole *f* d'évangile

**gospeller** *n* évangéliste *m*, prédicateur *m*

**gossamer** *n* (cobweb) fils *mpl* de la vierge; gaze légère

**gossip** *n* commérage *m*, cancans *mpl*; (person) bavard -e; *ar* compère *m*, commère *f*; *vi* caqueter; *pej* cancaner

**gossipy** *adj* (person) cancanier -ière; (conversation) de commérages

**Goth** *n* Goth *m*; *fig* barbare *m*

**Gothic** *n* gothique *m*; *adj* gothique

**gouache** *n* gouache *f*

**gouge** *n* gouge *f*

**goulash** *n cul* goulasch (goulache) *m* or *f*

**gourd** *n* gourde *f*

**gourmand** *n* gourmand -e

**gourmet** *n* gourmet *m*

**gout** *n* goutte *f*

**gouty** *adj* goutteux -euse

**gov** *n sl* patron *m*; (address) m'sieu *m*

**govern** *vt* gouverner; (affairs) administrer, diriger; *fig* régler, déterminer, guider; *gramm* régir; (temper) maîtriser, dominer; *vi* gouverner

**governable** *adj* gouvernable

**governess** *n* préceptrice *f*, institutrice *f* à domicile

**governing** *adj* gouvernant; ~ **body** conseil *m* d'administration, conseil *m* de gestion; ~ **idea** idée dominante

**government** *n* gouvernement *m*; régime *m*; conseil *m* des ministres, cabinet gouvernemental

**governmental** *adj* gouvernemental, du gouvernement

**governor** *n* (country, province, bank) gouverneur *m*; (in general) administrateur *m*; *mech* régulateur *m*; *coll* père *m*; *coll* patron *m*

**governor-general** *n* gouverneur général

**governorship** *n* fonction *f* de gouverneur

**gown** *n* robe *f*; (official, academic) toge *f*

**grab** *n* mouvement *m* pour saisir; empoigne *f*; *mech* pelle *f* mécanique; *vt* empoigner, agripper; (acquire) accaparer, saisir; usurper

**grace** *n* grâce *f*, distinction *f*; (favour) faveur *f*; (forgiveness) pardon *m*, clémence *f*; (before meal) bénédicité *m*; (after meal) grâces *fpl*; *leg* act of ~ amnistie *f*; **airs and** ~**s** manières affectées; **in the bad (good)** ~**s of** mal (bien) vu de; **with bad (good)** ~ de mauvaise (bonne) grâce; *vt* orner, honorer

**graceful** *adj* gracieux -ieuse, élégant

**gracefulness** *n* grâce *f*, élégance, distinction *f*

**graceless** *adj* sans grâce, gauche, inélégant; *eccles* hors de l'état de grâce

**gracelessness** *n* manque *m* de grâce, gaucherie *f*, inélégance *f*

**grace-note** *n mus* agrément *m*

**gracile** *adj* gracile, mince

**gracious** *adj* gracieux -ieuse, aimable, bienveillant; condescendant; *interj* mon Dieu!, vraiment!

**graciousness** *n* grâce *f*, amabilité *f*, bienveillance *f*; condescendance *f*

**gradation** *n* gradation *f*

**grade** *n* degré *m*, rang *m*, grade *m*; qualité *f*; catégorie *f*; *US* (school)

classe *f*; (mark) note *f*; **make the ~**
réussir, se montrer à la hauteur; *vt*
classifier, classer, trier; graduer; *US*
(school) noter

**gradient** *n* pente *f*

**gradual** *adj* graduel -elle, progressif -ive

**gradually** *adv* peu à peu, petit à petit,
progressivement

**gradualness** *n* progression *f*, lent développement

**graduate** *n* (university) diplômé -e, licencié -e; *vt* classer en grades; graduer;
*vi* (university) obtenir sa licence; se
changer graduellement

**graduation** *n* graduation *f*; (university)
obtention *f* de licence

**graffiti** *npl* graffiti *mpl*

**graft** *n* greffe *f*, greffon *m*; *coll* pot-de-vin
*m* (*pl* pots-de-vin), tripotage *m*; *sl*
boulot *m*; *vt* greffer; *vi coll* tripoter; *sl*
travailler dur

**grafter** *n* (person) greffeur *m*; (instrument) greffoir *m*; *coll* tripoteur *m*

**grafting** *n* greffage *m*

**grail** *n* graal *m*

**grain** *n* (small particle) grain *m*; (corn)
blé *m*; (cloth, paper, etc) grain *m*;
(weight) grain *m*; (wood) fibres *fpl*;
**against the ~** à rebours; *vt* granuler,
grener, marbrer

**graining** *n* grain *m*, marbrure *f*

**gram** *n* gramme *m*

**graminaceous** *adj* graminé

**grammar** *n* grammaire *f*; **~ school** =
collège *m*, lycée *m*

**grammarian** *n* grammairien -ienne

**grammatic(al)** *adj* grammatical

**gramme** *n* gramme *m*

**gramophone** *n* phonographe *m*, électrophone *m*

**grampus** *n zool* épaulard *m*; *coll*
(person) poussif *m*

**granary** *n* grenier *m*

**grand** *n coll US* mille dollars *mpl* ; *coll*
piano *m* à queue; **baby ~** piano *m*
demi-queue; *adj* splendide, imposant,
important, magnifique, grandiose;
(duke, cross, master) grand; (main)
principal; prétentieux -ieuse; *coll*
épatant; **~ piano** piano *m* à queue

**grandchild** *n* petit-fils *m* (*f* petite-fille, *pl*
petits-enfants)

**grand-dad, grandad** *n coll* grand-père *m*
(*pl* grands-pères), bon papa

**granddaughter** *n* petite-fille *f* (*pl* petites-
filles)

**grandee** *n* grand *m* d'Espagne; noble *m*

**grandeur** *n* grandeur *f*; splendeur *f*, magnificence *f*

**grandfather** *n* grand-père *m* (*pl* grands-
pères); **~ clock** horloge *f* de parquet

**grandiloquence** *n* grandiloquence *f*,

emphase *f*

**grandiloquent** *adj* grandiloquent

**grandiose** *adj* grandiose, imposant,
prétentieux -ieuse

**grandiosity** *n* prétention *f*

**grandly** *adv* avec grandeur; grandiose-
ment

**grandma** *n coll* grand-maman *f* (*pl*
grands-mamans), mémé *f*

**grandmother** *n* grand-mère *f* (*pl* grands-
mères)

**grand-nephew** *n* petit-neveu *m* (*pl*
petits-neveux)

**grandness** *n* grandeur *f*

**grand-niece** *n* petite-nièce *f* (*pl* petites-
nièces)

**grandpapa, grandpa** *n coll* grand-papa
*m* (*pl* grands-papas), pépé *m*

**grandparent** *n* grand-père *m* (*f* grand-
mère, *pl* grands-parents)

**grandson** *n* petit-fils *m* (*pl* petits-fils)

**grandstand** *n* tribune *f*

**grand-uncle** *n* grand-oncle *m* (*pl* grands-
oncles)

**grange** *n* manoir *m*; *ar* grenier *m*

**granite** *n* granit(e) *m*; *adj* de granit(e)

**granitic** *adj* granitique

**granny** *n coll* grand-maman *f* (*pl*
grands-mamans), mémé *f*; **~ knot**
nœud plat fait incorrectement, nœud
*m* de vache

**grant** *n* don *m*; allocation *f*; subvention
*f*; concession *f*; *leg* cession *f*, acte *m* de
donation; bourse *f* (d'études); *vt*
donner; accorder, octroyer; *leg* céder;
(admit) admettre, concéder; **~ed that**
étant donné que

**grantee** *n leg* donataire

**grantor** *n leg* donateur -trice

**granular** *adj* granuleux -euse, granulaire

**granulate** *vt* granuler; *vi* se granuler

**granulated** *adj* granuleux -euse, granulé;
(sugar) cristallisé

**granulation** *n* granulation *f*

**granule** *n* granule *m*

**granulous** *adj* granuleux -euse

**grape** *n* grain *m* de raisin; **~s** raisin *m*,
raisins *mpl*

**grapefruit** *n* pamplemousse *m*

**grapeshot** *n* mitraille *f*

**grape-sugar** *n* glucose *m*, sucre *m* de
raisin

**grapevine** *n* vigne *f*, treille *f*; *coll* téléphone *m* arabe

**graph** *n* graphique *m*, courbe *f*

**graphic(al)** *adj* graphique; *fig* pittoresque, expressif -ive

**graphics** *npl* procédés *mpl* graphiques

**graphite** *n* graphite *m*, plombagine *f*

**graphology** *n* graphologie *f*

**grapnel** *n naut* grappin *m*

**grapple** *n naut* grappin *m*; (struggle)

corps à corps *m*; *vt naut* saisir au grappin; (clutch) empoigner à bras le corps, agripper; *vi* lutter corps à corps, lutter à bras le corps; *fig* se débattre; *naut* jeter le grappin

**grappling-iron** *n naut* grappin *m*

**grasp** *n* étreinte *f*, poigne *f*; *fig* compréhension *f*, entendement *m*; *vt* empoigner, saisir; *fig* comprendre, saisir; *vi* ~ **at** essayer de saisir

**grasping** *adj* avide (de gain, de pouvoir), âpre (au gain); avare, cupide

**grass** *n* herbe *f*; pelouse *f*; (pasture) pâturage *m*, herbage *m*; *sl* (marijuana) herbe *f*; *sl* (informer) mouchard *m*; **out to** ~ en pâture; *coll* au repos; *vt* mettre en herbe, gazonner; (cattle) faire paître; (prey) abattre; (fish) prendre, gaffer; *coll* descendre, abattre; *vi sl* ~ **on** moucharder sur

**grass-cutter** *n* tondeuse *f* à gazon

**grass-green** *adj* vert pré *invar*

**grasshopper** *n* sauterelle *f*

**grassland** *n* herbage *m*; prairie *f*

**grass-plot** *n* pelouse *f*

**grass-roots** *npl fig* électeurs moyens; (workers) base *f*

**grass-snake** *n* couleuvre *f*

**grass-widow** *n* femme *f* dont le mari est absent

**grass-widower** *n* mari *m* dont la femme est absente

**grassy** *adj* herbeux -euse

**¹grate** *n* grille *f* en fonte (de cheminée); foyer *m*

**²grate** *vt* râper; *vi* grincer; *fig* ~ **on** agacer

**grateful** *adj* reconnaissant

**gratefully** *adv* avec reconnaissance

**gratefulness** *n* reconnaissance *f*, gratitude *f*

**grater** *n* râpe *f*

**gratification** *n* gratification *f*, contentement *m*, cause *f* de contentement; *ar+ joc* (tip) pourboire *m*

**gratify** *vt* (person) faire plaisir à, satisfaire; (wish) contenter

**gratifying** *adj* satisfaisant, acceptable; agréable

**gratin** *n cul* gratin *m*

**¹grating** *n* grille *f*, grillage *m*

**²grating** *n* (sound) grincement *m*; *adj* grinçant

**gratis** *adv* gratis, gratuitement

**gratitude** *n* gratitude *f*, reconnaissance *f*

**gratuitous** *adj* gratuit, bénévole, gracieux -ieuse; *fig* gratuit, arbitraire

**gratuity** *n* pourboire *m*; gratification *f*, prime *f*; *mil* pécule *m*

**¹grave** *n* fosse *f*, tombe *f*; tombeau *m*

**²grave** *adj* grave, sérieux -ieuse, solennel -elle; important; *phon* grave

**³grave** *vt naut* radouber

**grave-digger** *n* fossoyeur *m*

**gravel** *n* gravier *m*, gravillon *m*; *med* gravelle *f*; *vt* couvrir de gravier; *fig* déconcerter

**gravelly** *adj* de gravier

**gravely** *adv* gravement, sérieusement

**graven** *adj ar* gravé, sculpté

**graver** *n* (person) graveur *m*; (tool) outil *m* de graveur, burin *m*

**gravestone** *n* pierre tombale

**graveyard** *n* cimetière *m*

**gravid** *adj* enceinte; (female animal) pleine

**graving-dock** *n* bassin *m* de radoub

**gravitate** *vi* graviter; être attiré

**gravitation** *n* gravitation *f*

**gravity** *n* gravité *f*

**gravy** *n* jus *m*, sauce *f*

**gravy-boat** *n* saucière *f*

**gray** *n* + *adj* + *vi see* grey

**grayling** *n zool* ombre *m*

**¹graze** *vt* (grass) paître, brouter; (cattle) faire paître, paître; *vi* paître, brouter

**²graze** *n* effleurement *m*, frôlement *m*; (scratch) égratignure *f*, éraflure *f*; *vt* effleurer, frôler; (scratch) égratigner, érafler

**grazing** *n* pâturage *m*

**grease** *n* graisse *f*, lubrifiant *m*; (wool) suint *m*; *coll* (bribe) pot-de-vin *m* (*pl* pots-de-vin); *coll* flatterie *f*; *vt* graisser; *coll* (bribe) graisser la patte à; *coll* flatter, lécher les bottes à

**greasepaint** *n theat* fard *m*

**greaseproof** *adj* résistant à la graisse; (paper) sulfurisé

**greaser** *n* graisseur *m*; *US coll* Mexicain -e; Sud-américain -e

**grease-remover** *n* (substance) dégraissant *m*; (person) dégraisseur -euse

**greasiness** *n* graisse *f*; *fig* flagornerie *f*

**greasy** *adj* graisseux -euse; glissant; *fig* onctueux -euse

**great** *adj* grand, important, nombreux -euse, principal, excellent, grandiose, supérieur; éminent, haut placé, illustre, noble; *coll* agréable, épatant, fameux -euse; ~ **at** expert en; **Great Dane** (chien) danois *m*; **Greater London** l'agglomération londonienne; ~ **on** s'intéressant beaucoup à, connaissant fort bien

**great-aunt** *n* grand-tante *f* (*pl* grand(s)-tantes)

**great-coat** *n* pardessus *m*; *mil* capote *f*

**great-grandchild** *n* arrière-petit-fils *m* (*f* arrière-petite-fille, *pl* arrière-petits-enfants)

**great-granddaughter** *n* arrière-petite-fille *f* (*pl* arrière-petites-filles)

**great-grandfather** *n* arrière-grand-père

*m* (*pl* arrière-grands-pères), bisaïeul *m*
**great-grandmother** *n* arrière-grand-mère *f* (*pl* arrières-grands-mères), bisaïeule *f*
**great-grandparent** *n* arrière-grand-père *m* (*f* arrière-grand-mère, *pl* arrière-grands-parents), bisaïeul -e (*pl* bisaïeuls)
**great-grandson** *n* arrière-petit-fils *m* (*pl* arrière-petits-fils)
**great-hearted** *adj* magnanime, généreux -euse
**greatly** *adv* beaucoup, très, fort, grandement, énormément
**great-nephew** *n* petit-neveu *m* (*pl* petits-neveux)
**greatness** *n* grandeur *f*
**great-niece** *n* petite-nièce *f* (*pl* petites-nièces)
**grebe** *n orni* grèbe *m*
**Grecian** *adj* grec (*f* grecque)
**Greece** *n* Grèce *f*
**greed** *n* avidité *f*; (eating) gloutonnerie *f*
**greedily** *adv* avidement; (eating) gloutonnerie
**greediness** *n* avidité *f*; (eating) gloutonnerie *f*
**greedy** *adj* avide; (eating) glouton -onne
**greedy-guts** *n sl* goinfre *m*
**Greek** *n* Grec (*f* Grecque); (language) grec *m*; **it's all ~ to me** c'est de l'hébreu pour moi; *adj* grec (*f* grecque)
**green** *n* vert *m*; verdure *f*; (lawn) gazon *m*; **~ s** légumes verts; *adj* vert, verdoyant; (unripe) vert, pas mûr; (complexion) vert, blême; *fig* jaloux -ouse, envieux -ieuse; *coll* inexpérimenté, naïf -ïve; *fig* florissant, vivace; **~ belt** ceinture verte; *mot* **~ light** feu vert
**greenback** *n US coll* billet *m* de banque
**greenery** *n* verdure *f*, feuillage *m*
**greenfinch** *n* verdier *m*
**greenfly** *n* puceron *m*
**greengage** *n* reine-claude *f* (*pl* reines-claudes)
**greengrocer** *n* marchand -e de fruits et légumes, fruitier -ière
**greengrocery** *n* fruiterie *f*; (wares) fruits *mpl* et légumes *mpl*
**greenhorn** *n* blanc-bec *m* (*pl* blancs-becs), débutant -e; dupe *f*
**greenhouse** *n* serre *f*
**greenish** *adj* verdâtre
**greenness** *n* verdeur *f*
**green-room** *n theat* foyer *m* des artistes
**green-sickness** *n med* chlorose *f*
**greenstick** *n med* **~ fracture** fracture incomplète
**greenstuff** *n* légumes verts, verdure *f*
**greensward** *n ar* tapis *m* de verdure, pelouse *f*
**greet** *vt* saluer, accueillir; envoyer des vœux à

**greeting** *n* salut *m*, accueil *m*; **~ s card** carte *f* de vœux
**gregarious** *adj* grégaire
**gregariousness** *n* grégarisme *m*
**Gregorian** *adj* grégorien -ienne; **~ chant** chant grégorien
**grenade** *n* grenade *f*
**grenadier** *n* grenadier *m*
**grenadine** *n* grenadine *f*
**grey, gray** *n* gris *m*; (horse) cheval gris; *adj* gris; *coll* (person) fade, incolore; **~ matter** matière grise; *vi* (hair) grisonner
**grey-beard** *n* grison *m*, barbon *m*
**greyhound** *n* lévrier *m*
**greyish** *adj* grisâtre
**greyness** *n* grisaille *f*, teinte grise
**grid** *n* grille *f*, grillage *m*; *cul* + *naut* + *theat* gril *m*; réseau *m* électrique
**griddle, girdle** *n* plaque *f* de four
**griddle-cake** *n* galette *f*
**gridiron** *n cul* gril *m*
**grief** *n* affliction *f*, chagrin *m*; **come to ~** avoir un accident
**grievance** *n* grief *m*
**grieve** *vt* affliger, chagriner, peiner; *vi* s'affliger, se désoler
**grievous** *adj* atroce, cruel -elle, douloureux -euse, pénible; **charged with causing ~ bodily harm** inculpé pour coups et blessures
**grievousness** *n* gravité *f*
**griffin, griffon, gryphon** *n her* + *myth* + *orni* griffon *m*
**grill** *n cul* gril *m*; (food) grillade *f*; grill-room *m*, rôtisserie *f*; (grating) grille *f*; *vt cul* griller, faire griller; *coll* (question) cuisiner, passer à tabac; *vi cul* griller
**grille** *n* grille *f*
**grill-room** *n* grill-room *m*, rôtisserie *f*
**grim** *adj* austère, sévère; lugubre, sinistre; *coll* désagréable
**grimace** *n* grimace *f*; *vi* grimacer
**grime** *n* crasse *f*, saleté *f*; *vt* encrasser, noircir, salir
**griminess** *n* crasse *f*, saleté *f*
**grimness** *n* caractère *m* sinistre, sévérité *f*
**grimy** *adj* crasseux -euse, sale
**grin** *n* (smile) large sourire *m*; (forced) grimace *f*; (hostile) ricanement *m*; *vi* (smile) sourire franchement; (forced) grimacer; (hostile) ricaner **~ and bear it** supporter un malheur en souriant
**grind** *n* broyage *m*, trituration *f*; *coll* (hard work) corvée *f*; *vt* broyer, moudre, triturer; polir, buriner; (teeth) grincer de; (barrel-organ) moudre; **~ down** opprimer; *vi* se broyer, se moudre; (teeth) grincer; *coll* (study) bûcher, potasser; *coll* (work) boulonner
**grindstone** *n* meule *f*; **keep one's nose to the ~** travailler ferme

**grip** n étreinte f; poigne f; fig compréhension f; (control) emprise f; (tool, handle) prise f, poignée f; (suitcase) petite valise, mallette f; **get to ~ s with** se mettre à; **in the ~ of** en proie à; fig **lose one's ~** baisser; vt saisir, empoigner; fig comprendre

**gripe** n colique aiguë; vt provoquer des coliques; vi avoir des coliques; sl ronchonner

**gripping** adj saisissant, excitant

**grisliness** n macabre m; horreur f

**grisly** adj macabre, sinistre; horrible

**grist** n blé m à moudre; **it is all ~ to my mill** je fais flèche de tout bois

**gristle** n cartilage m

**gristly** adj cartilagineux -euse

**grit** n gravier m; gros sable; (courage) cran m; vt sabler; **~ one's teeth** serrer les dents; fig tenir bon

**gritstone** n geol grès m

**gritty** adj graveleux -euse, sablonneux -euse

¹**grizzle** n (colour) gris m

²**grizzle** vi coll pleurnicher; se plaindre

**grizzled** adj grisonnant; (hair) poivre et sel invar

¹**grizzly** n zool ours gris

²**grizzly** adj (hair) grisonnant

**groan** n gémissement m, geignement m; (complaint) grognement m; vi gémir, geindre; (complain) grogner

**grocer** n épicier -ière

**grocery** n épicerie f, magasin m d'alimentation; **groceries** épicerie f

**grog** n grog m

**grogginess** n coll faiblesse f; défaillance f

**groggy** adj coll chancelant, titubant, défaillant

**groin** n aine f; archi arête f, nervure f

**grommet, grummet** n naut anneau m de cordage

**groom** n valet m d'écurie, palefrenier m; (bridegroom) marié m; vt (horse) panser, étriller; soigner, parer; **~ oneself** se soigner

**groove** n rainure f, cannelure f; (pulley) gorge f; (record) sillon m; coll **get into a ~** s'encroûter; sl **in the ~** en pleine forme; vt canneler, rainer

**groovy** adj sl dans le vent; sexy

**grope** vt chercher à tâtons; sl peloter; vi tâtonner

**groping** n tâtonnement m; adj tâtonnant

¹**gross** n grosse f

²**gross** n tout m; majorité f; adj gros (f grosse), lourd; vulgaire, grossier -ière; total, brut; flagrant, évident; vt totaliser

**grotesque** n grotesque m; adj grotesque, bizarre

**grotesqueness** n grotesque m

**grotto** n grotte f

**grotty** adj sl moche

**grouch** n coll grognement m; vi coll grogner

**ground** n terre f, sol m, terrain m; (basis) fond m, base f; (picture) champ m; **~ s** raison f, motif m; leg considérants mpl; parc m; (coffee) marc m; **~ floor** rez-de-chaussée m invar; **~ landlord** propriétaire foncier; (airport) **~ staff** personnel m au sol; **break new ~** faire les premiers pas; **common ~** point acquis; **down to the ~** complètement; **get in on the ~ floor** être d'une affaire dès le début; **give ~** lâcher du terrain; **on the ~ s that** sous prétexte que; **stand one's ~** se défendre; adj broyé, concassé; poli; (coffee, etc) moulu; vt (base) fonder, baser; mettre à terre; aer empêcher de voler; naut échouer; vi naut (s')échouer

**ground-bass** n mus basse continue

**grounding** n action f de mettre qch à terre; naut échouage m; aer interdiction f de voler; fig base f, connaissance f élémentaire

**groundless** adj dénué de fondement, mal fondé

**groundling** n hist spectateur -trice du parterre; fig personne f inculte

**groundnut** n arachide f

**ground-plan** n archi plan horizontal; fig plan m de base

**ground-rent** n redevance foncière; rente foncière

**groundsel** n bot séneçon m

**groundsheet** n tapis m de sol

**groundsman** n responsable m d'un terrain de sport, gardien m de stade

**groundswell** n lame f de fond

**groundwork** n fondement m, base f; travail m préliminaire; (painting) fond m

**group** n groupe m; (mountains) massif m; aer **~ captain** colonel m d'aviation; adj de groupe; vt grouper, classifier; vi se grouper

**grouping** n groupement m

¹**grouse** n orni coq m de bruyère, grouse f

²**grouse** n coll grief m, rogne f; vi rouspéter

**grouser** n rouspéteur -euse

**grout** n mortier m, gâchis m; vt remplir de mortier

**grove** n bosquet m

**grovel** vi se vautrer, s'aplatir; courber l'échine, s'humilier

**groveller** n personne f qui s'humilie

**grovelling** adj abject; rampant

**grow** vt faire pousser, faire croître, cultiver; vi croître, grandir, pousser; se développer, augmenter; (become) devenir; ~ **on** plaire de plus en plus à; ~ **out of** (clothes) devenir trop grand pour; (habits) perdre en grandissant; ~ **to** en venir à; ~ **up** devenir adulte; (spread) se répandre

**grower** n cultivateur -trice, producteur -trice

**growing** n croissance f; agr culture f

**growl** n grognement m; vt + vi grogner, gronder

**growler** n ronchonneur -euse

**grown** adj adulte

**grown-up** n adulte m, grande personne; adj adulte

**growth** n croissance f; (plant) pousse f; (wine) crû m; med tumeur f, (external) excroissance f; fig développement m, expansion f

**groyne** n naut brise-lames m

¹**grub** n larve f, asticot m; (drudge) gratte-papier m invar; sl (food) boustifaille f

²**grub** vt fouiller; ~ **up** déraciner, extirper; vi fouiller; (work) trimer

**grubber** n (person) défricheur m; (tool) scarificateur m

**grubbiness** n crasse f, saleté f

**grubby** adj crasseux -euse, sale; (fruit) véreux -euse

**grudge** n rancune f; grief m; **bear s/o a** ~ en vouloir à qn; vt donner à contrecœur à; envier à; reprocher à

**grudging** adj donné à regret, donné à contrecœur; pingre, avare

**gruel** n gruau m; coll punition f

**gruelling** n sl raclée f; adj coll éreintant; sévère

**gruesome** adj horrible, macabre, horrifiant

**gruff** adj bourru, brusque; (voice) éraillé, rauque

**gruffness** n brusquerie f

**grumble** n grief m, grognement m, bougonnement m; vi grogner, bougonner; coll ronchonner, rouspéter; ~ **about** se plaindre de

**grumbler** n grogneur -euse, coll rouspéteur -euse

**grumbling** n grognement m, bougonnement m; adj grognon -onne, mécontent, ronchon -onne; (pain) intermittent

**grummet** n see **grommet**

**grumpiness** n grogne f, maussaderie f

**grumpy** adj grincheux -euse, grognon -onne, maussade

**grunt** n grognement m; vt + vi grogner

**gryphon** n see **griffin**

**g-string** n cache-sexe m invar

**guana** n zool iguane m

**guano** n guano m

**guarantee, guaranty** n caution f, garantie f; (person) garant -e; vt cautionner, garantir; fig (answer for) répondre de

**guarantor** n leg garant -e

**guaranty** n see **guarantee** n

**guard** n garde f, protection f; (person) garde m; mil sentinelle f; (railway) chef m de train; (fire) garde-feu m invar; **be caught off one's** ~ être pris au dépourvu; **be on one's** ~ être sur ses gardes; mil **on** ~ en garde; vt garder, protéger; vi se garder, se prémunir

**guarded** adj gardé; fig circonspect

**guardedly** adv prudemment, avec circonspection

**guardhouse** n mil corps m de garde

**guardian** n gardien -ienne, protecteur -trice; leg tuteur -trice; adj gardien -ienne, protecteur -trice

**gudgeon** n goujon m; mech tourillon m; mot ~ **pin** goupille f

**guelder-rose** n bot boule-de-neige f (pl boules-de-neige)

**Guernsey** n Guernesey m

**guerrilla** n guérillero m, franc-tireur m (pl francs-tireurs); ~ **band** guérilla f; ~ **warfare** guérilla f

**guess** n conjecture f, supposition f; **at a** ~ au jugé; **at a rough** ~ à vue de nez; **have a** ~ deviner; **have a** ~! devinez!; **my** ~ **is** d'après moi; vt deviner; conjecturer, supposer; (calculate) estimer, évaluer; US (believe) croire, penser, avoir l'impression; vi deviner; ~ **right** deviner juste; ~ **wrong** tomber à côté; **keep s/o** ~ **ing** laisser qn dans le doute

**guesswork** n conjecture f, hypothèse f; **by** ~ par flair

**guest** n hôte, invité -e; (meal) convive; (hotel) client -e; ~ **room** chambre f d'amis

**guest-house** n pension f

**guff** n coll bêtises fpl

**guffaw** n gros rire; vi s'esclaffer

**guidance** n conduite f, direction f

**guide** n (person, book) guide m; indication f; mech glissière f; **girl** ~ guide f; vt guider, diriger

**guided** adj (missile) téléguidé

**guidelines** npl directives fpl

**guild, gild** n hist guilde f; corporation f

**guilder** n gulden m

**guildhall** n hôtel m de ville

**guile** n astuce f, ruse f; (deceit) fourberie f

**guileful** adj astucieux -ieuse, rusé; (deceitful) fourbe

**guileless** adj candide, naïf -ïve; franc (f franche)

**guilelessness** n candeur f, naïveté f; franchise f

**guillemot** *n* guillemot *m*
**guillotine** *n* guillotine *f*; *vt* guillotiner
**guilt** *n* culpabilité *f*
**guiltiness** *n* culpabilité *f*
**guiltless** *adj* innocent
**guiltlessness** *n* innocence *f*
**guilty** *adj* coupable; ~ **conscience** mauvaise conscience
**guinea** *n ar* guinée *f*
**guinea-fowl** *n* pintade *f*
**guinea-pig** *n zool* + *fig* cobaye *m*
**guise** *n* apparence *f*, aspect *m*; costume *m*
**guitar** *n* guitare *f*
**guitarist** *n* guitariste
**gulch** *n US* ravin *m*
**gules** *n her* gueules *fpl*
**gulf** *n* golfe *m*; *fig* abîme *m*, gouffre *m*
**¹gull** *n orni* goéland *m*, mouette *f*
**²gull** *n* dupe *f*, imbécile; *sl* poire *f*; *vt* duper, rouler
**gullet** *n* œsophage *m*, gosier *m*
**gulley** *n see* gully
**gullibility** *n* crédulité *f*
**gullible** *adj* crédule
**gully, gulley** *n* rigole *f*; (mountain) couloir *m*; *vt* creuser une rigole dans
**gulp** *n* action *f* d'avaler; (liquids) gorgée *f*; (food) bouchée *f*; serrement *m* de gorge; *vt* avaler, engloutir; ~ **sth out** dire qch la gorge serrée
**¹gum** *n* gencive *f*
**²gum** *n* gomme *f*, colle *f*, résine *f*; **chewing** ~ chewing-gum *m*; *vt* gommer, coller; *coll* ~ **up** bousiller, rendre inutilisable
**gumboil** *n* abcès *m* aux gencives
**gumboots** *npl* bottes *fpl* en caoutchouc
**gummy** *adj* gommeux -euse, collant, gluant
**gumption** *n coll* bon sens, jugeotte *f*, initiative *f*
**gum-tree** *n bot* gommier *m*; *sl* **up a** ~ foutu, perdu
**gun** *n mil* canon *m*; (rifle) fusil *m*; fusil *m* de chasse; revolver *m*; (spraying) pistolet *m*; ~ **dog** chien *m* d'arrêt, retriever *m*; *coll* **big** ~ grosse légume; **stick to one's** ~ **s** ne pas fléchir, ne pas démordre; *vt* + *vi* chasser, tirer; *vi sl* ~ **for s/o** viser qn, chercher qn
**gunboat** *n* canonnière *f*
**gun-carriage** *n* affût *m* (de canon)
**gun-cotton** *n* coton-poudre *m* (*pl* cotons-poudre), fulmicoton *m*
**gun-fire** *n* tir *m* d'artillerie
**gunman** *n* bandit armé, gangster *m*
**gunner** *n mil* artilleur *m*, canonnier *m*
**gunnery** *n* balistique *f*; tir *m* d'artillerie
**gunpowder** *n* poudre *f* (à canon)
**gunrunner** *n* contrebandier *m* d'armes
**gunrunning** *n* contrebande *f* d'armes
**gunshot** *n* coup *m* de feu; **within** ~ à

portée de canon; *adj* (wound) causé par un projectile
**gunsmith** *n* armurier *m*
**gun-stock** *n* fût *m*
**gunwale** *n naut* plat-bord *m* (*pl* platsbords)
**gurgle** *n* gargouillement *m*, glouglou *m*; *vi* gargouiller, glouglouter
**gush** *n* jaillissement *m*, ruissellement *m*, flot *m*; *fig* effusion sentimentale, épanchement *m*; *vi* jaillir, ruisseler; *fig pej* s'épancher
**gushing** *adj* jaillissant, ruisselant; *fig pej* trop expansif -ive
**gusset** *n* (clothes) soufflet *m*; (bracket) tasseau *m*
**gust** *n* coup *m* de vent; *fig* accès *m*
**gustatory** *adj* gustatif -ive
**gusto** *n* entrain *m*
**gusty** *adj* venteux -euse; *fig* émotif -ive
**gut** *n* boyaux *mpl*, intestin *m*; *mus* corde *f*; ~ **s** ventre *m*; *coll fig* cran *m*; *vt* étriper, vider; (fire) ravager
**gutta-percha** *n* gutta-percha *f*
**gutter** *n* (roof) gouttière *f*; (street) caniveau *m*, ruisseau *m*; (groove) rainure *f*; *fig* boue *f*, pauvreté *f* sordide; ~ **press** presse *f* à sensation; *vt* mettre des gouttières à; rainer; *vi* (candle) couler
**guttering** *n* gouttières *fpl*
**guttersnipe** *n* gamin -e des rues, petit voyou
**guttural** *n* gutturale *f*; *adj phon* guttural; rauque
**¹guy** *n naut* hauban *m*, étai *m*; (tent) corde *f* d'attache; *vt naut* haubaner
**²guy** *n* (strangely dressed person) épouvantail *m*; *coll* type *m*
**³guy** *vt* ridiculiser, tourner en ridicule
**guy-rope** *n* corde *f* de tente
**guzzle** *vt* manger gloutonnement; *coll* bâfrer; *vi* se goinfrer, s'empiffrer
**guzzler** *n* glouton -onne, goinfre *m*
**gybe** *vi naut* empanner
**gym** *n* (place) gymnase *m*; (activity) gymnastique *f*
**gymnasium** *n* gymnase *m*
**gymnast** *n* gymnaste
**gymnastic** *adj* gymnastique
**gymnastics** *npl* gymnastique *f*
**gynaecological** *adj* gynécologique
**gynaecologist** *n* gynécologue
**gynaecology** *n* gynécologie *f*
**gypsum** *n* gypse *m*
**gypsy** *n* + *adj see* gipsy
**gyrate** *vi* tournoyer
**gyration** *n* giration *f*, rotation *f*
**gyratory** *adj* giratoire, rotatif -ive
**gyrocompass** *n* gyrocompas *m*
**gyroscope** *n* gyroscope *m*
**gyrostat** *n* gyrostat *m*

# H

**ha** *interj* ha!

**haberdasher** *n* mercier -ière

**haberdashery** *n* mercerie *f*

**¹habit** *n* habitude *f*; coutume *f*

**²habit** *n ar + eccles* habit *m*

**habitability** *n* habitabilité *f*

**habitable** *adj* habitable

**habitat** *n* habitat *m*

**habitation** *n* habitation *f*

**habitual** *adj* habituel -elle

**habituate** *vt* habituer

**habitué** *n* habitué -e

**hachures** *npl* hachure *f*

**¹hack** *n* coupure *f*, entaille *f*; (kick) coup *m* de pied (à la jambe); *med* toux sèche; (tool) pioche *f*; *vt* couper, entailler, taillader; (kick) donner un coup de pied (à la jambe); piocher

**²hack** *n* cheval *m* de louage; cheval *m* de selle; *coll* canasson *m*; *fig* forçat *m* du travail; (writer) écrivailleur -euse; *vi* aller au petit trot

**hacking** *adj* (cough) sec (*f* sèche)

**hackle** *n orni* plumes *fpl* du cou; **with ~ s up** sur ses ergots; *fig* en colère

**hackney** *n* cheval *m* de louage; cheval *m* de selle

**hackney-carriage** *n* voiture *f* de louage, voiture *f* de place

**hackneyed** *adj* banal (*pl* banals), insignifiant, plat

**hacksaw** *n* scie *f* à métaux

**hackwork** *n* travail *m* monotone

**hack-writer** *n* écrivailleur -euse

**haddock** *n* haddock *m*, aiglefin *m*

**haemoglobin** *n* hémoglobine *f*

**haemophilia** *n med* hémophilie *f*

**haemorrhage, hemorrhage** *n* hémorragie *f*

**haemorrhoid, hemorrhoid** *n* hémorroïde *f*

**haft** *n* manche *m*, poignée *f*

**¹hag** *n* sorcière *f*; *coll* vieille bique

**²hag** *n* (marsh) fondrière *f*; (peat) tourbière *f*

**haggard** *adj* hagard; défait, hâve

**haggle** *vi* marchander

**haggler** *n* marchandeur -euse

**hagiarchy** *n* gouvernement *m* par des prêtres; hiérarchie *f* des saints

**hagiographer** *n* hagiographe

**hagiographic** *adj* hagiographique

**hagiography** *n* hagiographie *f*

**hagiology** *n* littérature *f* hagiographique

**hag-ridden** *adj* obsédé; sujet -ette à des cauchemars

**Hague (The)** *n* La Haye

**¹hail** *n* grêle *f*; *vt* déverser, décharger; *vi* grêler; tomber rapidement

**²hail** *n* appel *m*; salut *m*; **within ~** à portée de voix; *vt* appeler, héler; saluer; *vi naut + coll* **~ from** venir de, être en provenance de

**³hail** *interj* salut!

**hailstone** *n* grêlon *m*

**hailstorm** *n* tempête *f* de grêle

**hair** *n* (human body, animal) poil *m*; (human head) cheveu *m*; (human head) cheveux *mpl*, chevelure *f*; (animal) pelage *m*; **do one's ~** se coiffer; *coll* **keep one's ~ on** rester calme; **let one's ~ down** parler sans gêne; agir sans inhibitions; **make s/o's ~ stand on end** faire dresser les cheveux sur la tête de qn; **not turn a ~** ne pas broncher; **put one's ~ up** se coiffer en toupet; **split ~ s** couper les cheveux en quatre; **tear one's ~** s'arracher les cheveux; **to a ~** exactement, tout à fait

**hairbreadth** *n* épaisseur *f* d'un cheveu; **by a ~** de justesse; *adj* de l'épaisseur d'un cheveu, très étroit

**hairbrush** *n* brosse *f* à cheveux

**haircloth** *n* tissu *m* de crin

**hair-cut** *n* coupe *f* de cheveux; **have a ~** se faire couper les cheveux

**hair-do** *n coll* coiffure *f*

**hairdresser** *n* coiffeur -euse

**hairdressing** *n* coiffure *f*

**hairiness** *n* (head) aspect chevelu; (body) aspect poilu

**hairline** *n* ligne *f* très mince; naissance *f* des cheveux; **~ fracture** fêlure *f*

**hairnet** *n* résille *f*

**hairpin** *n* épingle *f* à cheveux; **~ bend** virage *m* en épingle à cheveux

**hair-raising** *adj* horrifique, effrayant

**hair-shirt** *n* haire *f*, cilice *m*

**hair-slide** *n* barrette *f*

**hair-splitting** *n* ergotage *m*

**hairspring** *n* spiral *m* (de montre)

**hairy** *adj* (head) chevelu; (body, animal) poilu, velu

**hake** *n* merlu *m*, colin *m*

**halberd** *n* hallebarde *f*

**halberdier** *n* hallebardier *m*

**halcyon** *adj* serein, tranquille; **~ days** temps *m* de paix et de bonheur

**¹hale** *adj* costaud, vigoureux -euse

**²hale** *vt* tirer, traîner

**half** n moitié f, demi m, demie f; sp demi m; (match) mi-temps f; joc **better ~** moitié f; **by halves** partiellement; **go halves** être de moitié, partager; **too clever by ~** trop habile de moitié, beaucoup trop habile; adj demi (invar before noun); adv demi-, à demi; coll **not ~!** certainement!, bien sûr!; coll **not ~ bad** pas mal du tout, très bien

**half-and-half** adv moitié-moitié

**half-back** n demi m

**half-baked** adj à demi-cuit; fig (person) étourdi; (idea) inconsidéré

**half-breed** n métis -isse, sang-mêlé invar; (horse) demi-sang m invar; adj métis -isse

**half-brother** n demi-frère m

**half-caste** n + adj métis -isse

**half-cock** n **go off at ~** exploser prématurément; fig mal partir

**half-crown** n obs demi-couronne f

**half-dollar** n US demi-dollar m; coll ar demi-couronne f

**half-fare** n demi-place f; adj à demi-tarif

**half-hearted** adj peu empressé, peu enthousiaste

**half-heartedness** n manque m d'enthousiasme

**half-hitch** n naut demi-clef f

**half-holiday** n congé m d'une demi-journée

**half-length** n portrait m en buste; adj en buste

**half-light** n demi-jour m

**half-mast** n **at ~** en berne

**half-moon** n demi-lune f

**half-nelson** n sp clef f du cou

**half-pay** n mil demi-solde f; adj mil en demi-solde

**halfpenny** n demi-penny m, sou m

**half-seas-over** adj sl parti, éméché

**half-sister** n demi-sœur f

**half-timbered** adj aux poutres apparentes

**half-time** n sp mi-temps f; (work) **be on ~** travailler (être) à mi-temps

**half-tone** n arts demi-teinte f; mus demi-ton m

**half-track** n half-track m

**half-truth** n demi-vérité f

**half-volley** n demi-volée f

**halfway** adj + adv à mi-chemin

**half-wit** n coll crétin -e, idiot -e

**halibut** n flétan m

**halitosis** n med mauvaise haleine

**hall** n salle f, grande salle; (dining) réfectoire m; (hotel) hall m; (house) vestibule m; (students' hostel) maison f d'étudiants, pavillon m; **town ~** hôtel m de ville

**hallelujah** interj alléluia!

**halliard** n see **halyard**

**hallmark** n (gold, silver) poinçon m de garantie; fig preuve f de grande qualité, garantie f

**hallo, hello, hullo** interj hola!; allo!

**hallow** vt sanctifier, bénir

**Hallowe'en** n veille f de la Toussaint

**hallucination** n hallucination f

**hallucinatory** adj hallucinatoire

**halo** n auréole f, nimbe m; astron halo m; vt auréoler; astron entourer d'un halo

**halogen** n chem halogène m

¹**halt** n halte f, arrêt m; interj halte!; vt arrêter, faire arrêter; vi faire halte, s'arrêter

²**halt** npl ar estropiés mpl; adj boiteux -euse; vi boiter, clopiner; (speech) balbutier

**halter** n licol m, licou m; vt mettre un licou à

**halting** adj boiteux -euse; hésitant

**halve** vt diviser en deux, partager entre deux

**halyard, halliard** n naut drisse f

**ham** n jambon m; theat cabotin -e; coll radio-amateur m; **~s** fesses fpl; vt theat charger; vi theat cabotiner

**hamburger** n hamburger m; US **~ meat** viande hachée

**ham-fisted** adj maladroit

**ham-handed** adj maladroit

**hamlet** n hameau m

**hammer** n marteau m; (firearm) percuteur m; **~ and tongs** avec acharnement; **come under the ~** être vendu aux enchères; vt marteler, pilonner; frapper fort; coll attaquer, battre; (Stock Exchange) proclamer comme failli; **~ in** enfoncer à coups de marteau; fig faire apprendre à force de répéter; **~ out** résoudre; vi **~ away at** s'acharner à

**hammer-head** n tête f de marteau; zool (shark) requin m marteau

**hammock** n hamac m

**hammy** adj coll theat cabotin

¹**hamper** n banne f, manne f, panier m

²**hamper** vt entraver, gêner, obstruer

**hamster** n hamster m

**hamstring** n tendon m de jarret; vt couper le jarret à; fig couper les moyens à

**hand** n main f; (share) part f; (person) ouvrier m, travailleur m; naut marin m; agr valet m de ferme; (handwriting) écriture f; (dial) aiguille f; (measure) palme f; (help) aide f; (cards held) jeu m; (card game) partie f; (card player) joueur -euse; (applause) applaudissements mpl; **~ in glove** comme larrons en foire, coll de mèche; **~ in ~** la main dans la main; **~s off!** pas d'intervention!; *coll* bas les pattes!; ~ over ~ avec une main après l'autre; ~ to ~ corps à corps; ~s up! haut les mains!; at first ~ de première main; at ~ à proximité; by ~ à la main; par livraison personnelle; cash in ~ encaisse *f*; change ~s changer de mains; come to ~ être arrivé, être retrouvé; eat out of s/o's ~ être totalement soumis à qn; from ~ to ~ de la main à la main; from ~ to mouth au jour le jour; get one's ~ in se faire la main; have a free ~ avoir carte blanche; have a ~ in avoir un doigt dans; in ~ sur le chantier, en train; keep one's ~ in s'entretenir la main; lay ~s on saisir; (find) mettre la main sur; *eccles* laying on ~s imposition *f* des mains; lend a ~ donner un coup de main; lost with all ~s péri corps et biens; not to do a ~'s turn ne rien faire de ses dix doigts; off one's ~s n'étant plus sa responsabilité; old ~ vétéran *m*; on all ~s de tous côtés; on one's ~s sur les bras; on the one ~ ... on the other ~ d'une part ... d'autre part; out of ~ de suite, sans hésitation; hors des gonds; play into the ~s of faire le jeu de; shake ~s with serrer la main à; show one's ~ dévoiler son jeu; take a ~ in participer à; take in ~ s'occuper de; upper ~ dessus *m*; wash one's ~s of se laver les mains de; win ~s down gagner facilement; with a heavy ~ avec poigne; with a high ~ autoritairement; *adj* fait (à la) main; à main, qu'on tient dans la main; *vt* passer, donner, transmettre; ~ down (inheritance, tradition) transmettre; ~ in remettre; *sl* ~ it to tirer son chapeau à; ~ on transmettre, envoyer; ~ out distribuer; ~ over livrer; ~ round distribuer

**handbag** *n* sac *m* à main

**handbarrow** *n* brouette *f*; charrette *f* à bras

**handbell** *n* clochette *f*, sonnette *f*

**handbill** *n* prospectus *m*, avis *m*

**handbook** *n* (instruction) manuel *m*; (guide) guide *m*

**handbrace** *n mech* vilebrequin *m*

**handbrake** *n mot* frein *m* à main

**handcart** *n* charrette *f* à bras

**handcuff** *vt* mettre les menottes à

**handcuffs** *npl* menottes *fpl*

**handful** *n* poignée *f*; *fig* petit nombre; that child is a real ~ cet enfant est une vraie peste

**hand-glass** *n* miroir *m* à main, glace *f* à main

**hand-grenade** *n* grenade *f* à main

**handgrip** *n* poignée *f* de main; prise *f*

**handhold** *n* prise *f*

**handicap** *n* handicap *m*, désavantage *m*; *vt* handicaper, désavantager

**handicraft** *n* travail *m* d'artisanat

**handicraftsman** *n* artisan *m*

**handily** *adv* adroitement; commodément

**handiness** *n* (skill) adresse *f*; (convenience) commodité *f*; proximité *f*

**handiwork** *n* travail fait à la main; objet fait à la main; *fig* œuvre *f*, ouvrage *m*

**handkerchief** *n* mouchoir *m*

**handle** *n* (basket) anse *f*; (door) poignée *f*; (axe, broom, knife, etc) manche *m*; (pan) queue *f*; *coll* fly off the ~ sortir de ses gonds; give a ~ to donner prise à; have a ~ to one's name avoir un nom à particule; *vt* manier, manipuler; contrôler; *comm* trafiquer de; (subject) traiter; I can ~ him je sais le prendre

**handlebar(s)** *n* guidon *m*; ~ moustache moustache *f* en croc

**handling** *n* maniement *m*; traitement *m*

**handmade** *adj* fait (à la) main

**handmaid** *n ar* servante *f*; *fig* subordonnée *f*, aide *f*

**hand-me-down** *adj US* (ready-made) de confection; (cheap) bon marché; (secondhand) d'occasion

**hand-mill** *n cul* moulin *m*

**handout** *n* (statement) communiqué *m*; *US* aumône *f*

**hand-picked** *adj* sélectionné (à la main)

**handrail** *n* main courante

**handsaw** *n* scie *f* à main

**handshake** *n* poignée *f* de main

**handsome** *adj* beau (*f* belle); généreux -euse; *coll* come down ~ être généreux

**handsomeness** *n* beauté *f*; générosité *f*

**handspring** *n* saut périlleux

**handwork** *n* travail fait à la main

**handwriting** *n* écriture *f*

**handy** *adj* (near) accessible, sous la main; (convenient) commode, pratique; (skilled) adroit, habile; *adv* tout près

**handyman** *n* bricoleur *m*

**hang** *n* (clothes, curtains, etc) drapé *m*; *coll* get the ~ of comprendre; *vt* pendre; accrocher, suspendre; (drape) tendre; (painting) exposer; (wallpaper) poser; (execute) pendre; ~ fire (firearm) faire long feu; *fig* être retardé; ~ oneself se pendre; ~ one's head baisser la tête; ~ out étendre, suspendre au dehors, (flag) arborer; ~ up accrocher, suspendre; (telephone) raccrocher; ~ upon s'appuyer sur; (words) écouter avidement; *vi* pendre, être accroché; (curtains) tomber; (recline) pencher, s'incliner; (on gallows) être pendu; ~ about (around) traîner, musarder; ~ back hésiter; rester en arrière; ~ by a

**thread** ne tenir qu'à un fil; ~ **on** s'accrocher; *fig* tenir bon; *coll* attendre; ~ **out** pendre dehors; *coll* habiter, percher; ~ **together** se tenir les coudes; (story, etc) tenir debout; **be hung up** être retardé

**hangar** *n* hangar *m*

**hangdog** *adj* ~ **look** air *m* coupable

**hanger** *n* crochet *m*; (coat) cintre *m*, portemanteau *m*; (on hat stand) patère *f*; (handwriting) jambage *m*

**hanger-on** *n* parasite *m*

**hanging** *n* pendaison *f*; accrochage *m*; (wallpaper) pose *f*; ~ **s** draperies *fpl*; *adj* pendant, suspendu, tombant; ~ **garden** jardin suspendu; ~ **matter** cas *m* pendable

**hangman** *n* bourreau *m*

**hangover** *n* gueule *f* de bois

**hang-up** *n* complexe *m*

**hank** *n* écheveau *m*

**hanker** *vi* ~ **after, for** avoir envie de, soupirer après

**hankering** *n* envie forte, grand désir

**hanky** *n coll* mouchoir *m*

**hanky-panky** *n coll* roublardise *f*

**Hansard** *n* le Hansard, transcription *f* des débats du parlement britannique

**Hanseatic** *adj hist* hanséatique

**hansom** *n obs* cab *m*

**ha'penny** *n see* halfpenny

**haphazard** *adj* fortuit, au hasard

**hapless** *adj* infortuné, malchanceux -euse

**haplessness** *n* infortune *f*, malchance *f*

**happen** *vi* arriver, advenir, avoir lieu, se produire, survenir; ~ **along** arriver par hasard; ~ **on (upon)** trouver par hasard; ~ **to be** se trouver par hasard

**happening** *n* événement *m*

**happiness** *n* bonheur *m*, contentement *m*, satisfaction *f*

**happy** *adj* heureux -euse, content, enchanté, satisfait

**happy-go-lucky** *adj* insouciant, nonchalant

**hara-kiri** *n* harakiri *m*; **commit** ~ faire harakiri

**harangue** *n* harangue *f*, *coll* laïus *m*; *vt* haranguer; *vi* prononcer une harangue; *coll* faire un laïus

**harass** *vt* harceler, tourmenter, tracasser

**harassment** *n* harcèlement *m*, tourment *m*, tracas *m*

**harbinger** *n* avant-coureur *m*, annonciateur -trice

**harbour** *n* port *m*; *vt* abriter, héberger; (criminal) receler; (feelings) nourrir; *vi* se mettre à l'abri, se réfugier

**harbour-bar** *n naut* barre *f*

**harbour-master** *n* capitaine *m* de port

**hard** *n naut* quai *m*, cale *f*; *coll* travaux forcés; *vulg* **have a** ~ **on** bander; *adj* dur, solide; difficile; ardu, fatigant, pénible, rude; brutal; exigeant, implacable, sévère; (words) amer -ère, violent; (fate) injuste; (weather) inclément, rigoureux -euse; (water) calcaire; ~ **and fast** inflexible, ferme; ~ **cash** liquide *m*; ~ **court** tennis asphalté; ~ **currency** devises fortes; ~ **drinking** beuverie *f*; ~ **labour** travaux forcés; ~ **lines!** dommage!, tant pis!; ~ **luck** malchance *f*; ~ **of hearing** dur d'oreille; ~ **up** fauché; **be** ~ **on** traiter durement; *adv* dur, durement, ferme, fort; énergiquement, sévèrement, violemment; ~ **by** tout près; ~ **hit** très affecté; **die** ~ **by** mettre longtemps à disparaître; **it will go** ~ **with you** vous aurez bien des ennuis

**hardback** *n* livre relié

**hard-baked** *adj* cuit longuement au four; *coll fig* dur, endurci

**hard-bitten** *adj* implacable, inexorable

**hardboard** *n* carton-cuir *m*

**hard-boiled** *adj* (egg) dur; *coll* implacable, inexorable; (shrewd) astucieux -ieuse

**hardcore** *n bui* blocaille *f*

**hard-core** *adj* impénitent, inébranlable

**hard-earned** *adj* durement gagné

**harden** *vt* durcir, rendre dur, endurcir; *med* indurer, scléroser; (steel) tremper; *vi* durcir, se durcir, s'endurcir; *med* s'indurer, se scléroser; (prices) monter

**hardened** *adj fig* impénitent, invétéré

**hardening** *n* durcissement *m*; *med* induration *f*, sclérose *f*; (steel) trempe *f*

**hard-faced, hard-favoured, hard-featured** *adj* aux traits durs; *sl* pète-sec *invar*

**hard-fisted** *adj* pingre

**hard-headed** *adj* perspicace; pratique, terre à terre

**hard-hearted** *adj* cruel -elle, insensible

**hardihood** *n* courage *m*, hardiesse *f*

**hardily** *adv* audacieusement, fermement

**hardiness** *n* audace *f*, hardiesse *f*; résistance *f*

**hard-liner** *n* faucon *m*, dur *m*

**hardly** *adv* à peine, guère, tout juste; durement, rudement

**hardness** *n* dureté *f*, rigueur *f*, sévérité *f*; ~ **of heart** sécheresse *f* de cœur

**hard-pressed** *adj* aux prises *fpl* avec des problèmes; (short of money) gêné

**hard-set** *adj* (cement, etc) durci; *fig* obstiné, têtu

**hardship** *n* épreuve *f*, privation *f*, rigueur *f*

**hardtop** *n mot* hard-top *m*

**hardware** *n* quincaillerie *f*; (computers)

hardware *m*; (communication, teaching) audio-visuel *m*; *US* ~ **store** quincaillerie *f*

**hardwood** *n* bois dur

**hardy** *adj* résistant, robuste; hardi, intrépide

**hare** *n* lièvre *m*; *sl* projet *m* chimérique; **start a** ~ intervenir mal à propos dans un argument; *vi coll* courir vite; ~ **off** détaler

**harebell** *n bot* campanule *f*

**hare-brained** *adj* écervelé, étourdi

**hare-lip** *n* bec-de-lièvre *m* (*pl* becs-de-lièvre)

**harem** *n* harem *m*, sérail *m*

**haricot** *n bot* haricot blanc; *cul* navarin *m*

**hark** *vi* écouter; ~ **back to** revenir sur

**harken** *vi see* hearken

**Harlequin** *n* Arlequin *m*

**harlequin** *adj* bigarré, d'arlequin

**harlequinade** *n* arlequinade *f*

**harlot** *n* prostituée *f*, putain *f*

**harlotry** *n* prostitution *f*

**harm** *n* dommage *m*, mal *m*, préjudice *m*, tort *m*; *vt* endommager, faire du mal à, nuire à; *leg* léser

**harmful** *adj* malfaisant, néfaste, nocif -ive, nuisible

**harmless** *adj* anodin, inoffensif -ive

**harmlessness** *n* innocuité *f*

**harmonic** *n* harmonique *m or f*; ~ **s** harmonique *m or f*; *adj* harmonique; ~ **series** série *f* harmonique

**harmonica** *n* harmonica *m*

**harmonious** *adj* harmonieux -ieuse, mélodieux -ieuse; (pleasant) plaisant; bien arrangé, bien construit

**harmoniousness** *n* harmonie *f*

**harmonist** *n* harmoniste

**harmonium** *n* harmonium *m*

**harmonization** *n* harmonisation *f*

**harmonize** *vt* harmoniser; *vi* s'harmoniser

**harmony** *n* harmonie *f*; *fig* concordance *f*, entente *f*

**harness** *n* harnachement *m*, harnais *m*; (parachute) ceinture *f*; **die in** ~ travailler jusqu'à la mort; **get back in** ~ reprendre le collier; *vt* harnacher; (river) aménager; (energy, etc) exploiter

**harp** *n* harpe *f*; *vi mus* jouer de la harpe; ~ **on** rabâcher

**harpist** *n* harpiste

**harpoon** *n* harpon *m*; *vt* harponner

**harpsichord** *n* clavecin *m*

**harpy** *n myth* harpie *f*; *fig* mégère *f*

**harquebus, arquebus** *n hist* arquebuse *f*

**harridan** *n* vieille sorcière, vieille chipie

**harrier** *n* (bird) busard *m*; (dog) braque *m*; (runner) coureur *m* de fond, coureur *m* de cross

**harrow** *n agr* herse *f*; *vt agr* herser; *fig* affliger, tourmenter

**harrowing** *adj* affligeant, angoissant

**harry** *vt* dévaster, piller; (pester) harceler

**harsh** *adj* sévère, cruel -elle; (touch) rêche, rugueux -euse; (voice) rauque; (sound) discordant; (colour) criard; (taste) râpeux -euse

**harshness** *n* sévérité *f*, cruauté *f*; (touch) rudesse *f*, rugosité *f*; (sound) discordance *f*; (colour) aspect criard; (taste) âpreté *f*

**hart** *n* cerf *m*

**harum-scarum** *n + adj* écervelé -e

**harvest** *n* moisson *f*, récolte *f*; ~ **festival** service *m* d'action de grâces au moment de la récolte; ~ **moon** pleine lune de l'équinoxe d'automne; *vt* moissonner, récolter; *vi* faire la moisson

**harvester** *n* (person) moissonneur -euse; (machine) moissonneuse *f*; ~ **bug** aoûtat *m*

**harvest-home** *n* rentrée *f* de la moisson; festin *m* de la moisson

**harvest-mouse** *n* mulot *m*

**has-been** *n coll* croulant *m*

**hash** *n cul* hachis *m*; *coll* (mess) gâchis *m*, pagaïe *f*; *coll* (repetition) rabâchage *m*; *coll* haschisch *m*; *coll* **settle s/o's** ~ régler son compte à qn; *vt cul* hacher; *coll* (mess up) gâcher

**hashish** *n* hachisch *m*, haschisch *m*

**haslets** *npl* fressure *f*

**hasp** *n* (door, lock) loquet *m*, moraillon *m*; (window) espagnolette *f*; (thread) écheveau *m*; *vt* fermer au loquet

**hassock** *n* coussin *m* (d'agenouilloir)

¹**haste** *n* hâte *f*; précipitation *f*

²**haste** *vt + vi see* hasten

**hasten** *vt* hâter, presser; *vi* se hâter, se dépêcher, se presser

**hastily** *adv* hâtivement, à la hâte; à la légère

**hastiness** *n* hâte *f*, précipitation *f*; brusquerie *f*

**hasty** *adj* hâtif -ive, précipité; inconsidéré, irréfléchi

**hat** *n* chapeau *m*; *coll* **keep it under your** ~ n'en dites pas un mot; **my** ~ ! vraiment!; *coll* **talk through one's** ~ dire n'importe quoi

**hatband** *n* ruban *m* de chapeau

¹**hatch** *n* trappe *f*; *naut* écoutille *f*; *coll* **down the** ~! à la vôtre!; **serving** ~ passe-plat *m*; *naut* **under** ~ **es** dans la cale; *fig* emprisonné

²**hatch** *n* (arts) hachure *f*; *vt* hachurer

³**hatch** *n* éclosion *f*; couvée *f*; *vt* couver; *fig* ourdir, tramer; *vi* éclore

**hatcher** *n* couveuse *f*

**hatchery** *n* alevinier *m*

**hatchet** n hachette f; ~ **face** visage m en lame de couteau; ~ **man** tueur m à gages; **bury the** ~ faire la paix

**hatchway** n naut écoutille f

**hate** n haine f, exécration f; (person) objet m de haine; vt haïr, détester, exécrer

**hateful** adj détestable, haïssable, odieux -ieuse

**hatefulness** n aspect m détestable, aspect m haïssable

**hatpin** n épingle f à chapeau

**hatrack** n porte-chapeaux m

**hatred** n haine f, exécration f

**hatstand** n porte-chapeaux m

**hatted** adj coiffé d'un chapeau

**hatter** n chapelier m; **mad as a** ~ complètement cinglé

**haughtiness** n hauteur f, morgue f

**haughty** adj altier -ière, hautain

**haul** n traction f; naut bordée f; (fish) prise f; vt + vi haler, tirer, traîner

**haulage** n halage m; (road) camionnage m; ~ **contractor** entrepreneur m de transport, transporteur m

**haulier** n (coal-mining) herscheur m; transporteur m

**haunch** n hanche f; cul (venison) cuissot m

**haunt** n lieu m de prédilection; (den) repaire m; vt fréquenter, visiter souvent; (ghost) hanter; fig hanter, obséder

**haunted** adj hanté

**haunting** adj fascinant, inoubliable, qui hante

**hautboy** n ar hautbois m

**have** n coll attrape f; ~s riches mpl; **the** ~**s and the** ~**-nots** les riches et les pauvres; vt avoir, posséder; (hold) tenir, saisir; (feel) éprouver, sentir; (undergo) subir; (take) prendre; (drink) boire; (eat) manger; (get) obtenir; (cause) faire; (allow) permettre, supporter, tolérer; coll (trick) avoir, duper; vulg faire l'amour avec, baiser; v aux avoir; ~ **better** faire mieux; coll ~ **had it** être cuit; sl être foutu; (die) mourir, crever; ~ **in** inviter (à la maison); coll ~ **it in for** en vouloir à, garder une dent contre; ~ **it out** s'expliquer; ~ **just** venir de; ~ **s/o on** canuler qn; ~ **sth done** faire faire qch; ~ **sth on** avoir qch à faire; ~ **to** avoir à, devoir, être obligé de; ~ **to do with** avoir à faire à; coll ~ **up** faire passer en correctionnelle, poursuivre en justice

**haven** n port m; fig asile m, havre m

**have-not** n pauvre m, démuni -e

**haver** vi hésiter; Scots déraisonner

**haversack** n havresac m

**havoc** n dévastation f

¹**haw** n bot fleur m d'aubépine

²**haw** vi hum and ~ see **hum**

¹**hawk** n faucon m; fig escroc m; pol faucon m; vi chasser au faucon

²**hawk** vi expectorer

³**hawk** vt colporter

**hawker** n colporteur m; (fruit, vegetables) marchand -e des quatre saisons

**hawk-eyed** adj aux yeux de lynx

**hawkmoth** n sphinx m

**hawser** n naut haussière f, câble m

**hawthorn** n aubépine f

**hay** n foin m; coll **hit the** ~ aller se coucher; **make** ~ faner; **make** ~ **of** embrouiller; **make** ~ **while the sun shines** saisir l'occasion

**hay-fever** n rhume m des foins

**haymaker** n faneur -euse

**haymaking** n fanage m

**hayrick** n meule f de foin

**haystack** n meule f de foin

**haywire** adj coll fou (f folle); embrouillé, en pagaïe

**hazard** n hasard m, chance f; obstacle m; péril m, risque m; vt hasarder, risquer; exposer à un risque

**hazardous** adj hasardeux -euse; périlleux -euse, risqué

¹**haze** n brume f, brouillard m; fig incertitude f

²**haze** vt brimer, railler; naut accabler de corvées

**hazel** n bot coudrier m, noisetier m; couleur f noisette; adj (couleur) noisette invar

**hazel-nut** n noisette f

**hazy** adj brumeux -euse; fig nébuleux -euse, vague

**H-bomb** n bombe f H

¹**he** n mâle m; adj mâle

²**he** pron 3rd pers sing masc nom il; lui; ~ **is** il est, c'est; ~ **who** celui qui

³**he** n tête f; fig chef m, directeur -trice; (front) devant m; (top) haut m; geog cap m, promontoire m; (section, heading) partie f, chef m; (boil, pimple) tête f; (froth) mousse f, faux-col m; (steam) pression f; fig idée f, intelligence f, raison f; coll mal m de tête; (coin) ~s face f; ~ **and shoulders above** loin au-dessus; ~ **of water** hauteur f de chute; ~ **over heels** cul pardessus tête; **above one's** ~ trop difficile à comprendre; **be off one's** ~ être cinglé; **bring matters to a** ~ amener une crise; **come to a** ~ aboutir à une crise; (boil, pimple) mûrir; **give s/o his** ~ donner carte blanche à qn; **keep one's** ~ rester calme; **keep one's** ~ **above water** surnager, se maintenir; **lose one's** ~ perdre la tête, s'affoler; **not make** ~ **or tail of it** n'y comprendre rien; **put** ~s

**together** conférer; **talk** s/o's ~ **off** casser la tête à qn; **turn** s/o's ~ tourner la tête à qn; **under that** ~ sous cette rubrique; *adj* principal; *vt* (direct) diriger, mener; (article, chapter) intituler, mettre en tête de; (football) donner un coup de tête à; (lead) être à la tête de, venir en tête de; ~ **off** détourner, faire dévier; *vi* ~ **for se -diriger vers, courir vers; *naut* mettre le cap sur; ~ **for disaster** aller vers la ruine

**headache** n mal m de tête; *coll fig* casse-tête m invar

**headband** n bandeau m

**head-dress** n coiffure f

**headed** *adj* à tête; (paper) à en-tête

**header** n (dive) plongeon m; (football) coup m de tête; *bui* boutisse f

**head-first, head-foremost** *adv* la tête la première, tête baissée; impétueusement, témérairement

**headgear** n coiffure f

**head-hunter** n chasseur m de têtes

**headiness** n excitation f, ivresse f

**heading** n (writing-paper) en-tête m; (title) intitulé m; (article) rubrique f

**headlamp** n phare m

**headland** n cap m, promontoire m

**headlight** n phare m; **drive with dipped** ~ s rouler en code

**headline** n en-tête m, titre m; *coll* **hit the** ~ s défrayer la chronique

**headlong** *adj* impétueux -euse, précipité, téméraire; *adv* la tête la première, tête baissée; impétueusement

**headman** n chef m; contremaître m

**headmaster** n directeur m; (French lycée) proviseur m

**headmistress** n directrice f

**head-office** n siège central

**head-on** *adj* + *adv* de front

**headphone** n écouteur m; ~ s casque m

**headpiece** n coiffure f, couvre-chef m; *coll* tête f, cervelle f

**headquarters** npl quartier général; *comm* siège social

**headrest** n appui-tête m invar

**headroom** n hauteur f libre, dégagement m

**headship** n poste m de chef (school); poste m de directeur (proviseur, directrice)

**headsman** n bourreau m

**headstone** n pierre tombale; *archi* pierre f angulaire

**headstrong** *adj* entêté, têtu; impétueux -euse

**headway** n progrès m; *archi* hauteur f libre, dégagement m

**headwind** n *naut* vent m debout, vent m contraire

**headword** n mot m souche

**heady** *adj* capiteux -euse, enivrant, excitant; impétueux -euse

**heal** *vt* (person) guérir; (wound) cicatriser; *fig* réparer; apaiser; *vi* (person) se guérir; (wound) se cicatriser; *fig* s'apaiser

**healer** n guérisseur m

**healing** n guérison f; (wound) cicatrisation f; *fig* apaisement m; *adj* curatif -ive; apaisant

**health** n santé f; hygiène f; toast m; ~ **insurance** assurance f maladie; ~ **resort** station f climatique; **drink** s/o's ~ boire à la santé de qn, porter un toast à qn

**healthiness** n salubrité f

**healthy** *adj* sain; (climate, etc) salubre; (beneficial) salutaire; (prosperous) florissant; (appetite) robuste

**heap** n tas m, amas m, amoncellement m; ~ s beaucoup; *coll* **struck all of a** ~ bouleversé, étonné; *vt* amonceler, entasser; (bestow) combler

**heaps** *adv coll* beaucoup

**hear** *vt* entendre; (listen to) écouter; (learn) apprendre, entendre dire; (concert, lecture, etc) assister à; ~ **out** entendre jusqu'au bout; *vi* entendre; ~ **about** avoir connaissance de, entendre parler de; ~ **from** recevoir des nouvelles de, recevoir une lettre de; ~ **of** entendre parler de; **he will not** ~ **of it** il ne veut rien savoir

**hear! hear!** *interj* bravo!, d'accord!

**hearer** n auditeur -trice

**hearing** n ouïe f; (action) audition f; *leg* audience f; **in my** ~ en ma présence; **within** ~ à portée de voix

**hearing-aid** n prothèse auditive, appareil m acoustique

**hearken, harken** *vi* écouter attentivement

**hearsay** n ouï-dire m invar; *adj* par ouï-dire

**hearse** n corbillard m

**heart** n cœur m; affection f, émotion f, sentiment m; humanité f; courage m, énergie f; (soul) âme f, for intérieur; centre m, noyau m; (artichoke) cœur m, fond m; ~ **and soul** corps et âme; ~ **to** ~ **intime; after my own** ~ selon mon cœur; **at** ~ au fond du cœur; **break** s/o's ~ briser le cœur à qn; **by** ~ par cœur; **eat one's** ~ **out** se ronger; **have at** ~ attacher grande importance à; **have one's** ~ **in one's mouth** être plein d'appréhension; **have one's** ~ **in the right place** avoir le cœur bien placé; **have the** ~ **to** être assez dur pour; **in his** ~ **of** ~ s au plus profond de son cœur (de lui-même); **lose one's** ~ **to** tomber amoureux -euse de; **set one's** ~ **on** désirer fort, se résoudre à obtenir; **take** ~ prendre courage; **to one's** ~ **'s content** à cœur joie; **with all one's** ~ de tout son cœur

**heartache** *n* chagrin persistant, peine *f* de cœur

**heartbeat** *n* battement *m* de cœur

**heartbreak** *n* déchirement *m* de cœur, déception amère

**heartbreaking** *adj* déchirant; *coll* épuisant

**heartbroken** *adj* le cœur brisé, navré

**heartburn** *n med* pyrosis *m*, brulûres *fpl* d'estomac

**heartburning** *n* envie dissimulée; amertume *f*

**hearten** *vt* encourager

**heartening** *adj* encourageant

**heartfelt** *adj* sincère

**hearth** *n* âtre *m*, foyer *m*; (home) foyer *m*

**hearthstone** *n* foyer *m*, dalle *f* de foyer

**heartiness** *n* cordialité *f*, empressement *m*; vigueur *f*

**heartless** *adj* sans cœur, cruel -elle, dur

**heartlessness** *n* manque *m* de cœur, cruauté *f*, dureté *f*

**heart-rending** *adj* touchant, qui fend le cœur

**heart-searching** *n* examen *m* de conscience

**heart-strings** *npl fig* sentiments profonds

**heart-throb** *n sl* béguin *m*

**hearty** *n sl* sportif -ive; *pej* béotien -ienne; *adj* cordial, empressé; vigoureux -euse; (appetite) gros (*f* grosse); (meal) copieux -ieuse; *pej* béotien -ienne

**heat** *n* chaleur *f*; (race) manche *f*; *fig* ardeur *f*, enthousiasme *m*; (temper) colère *f*, indignation *f*; (animal) rut *m*; ~ **stroke** coup *m* de chaleur; ~ **wave** vague *f* de chaleur; *sp* **dead** ~ deadheat *m*; **on** ~ en chaleur, en rut; *fig* **turn the** ~ **on s/o** exercer une pression sur qn; *vt* + *vi* chauffer

**heated** *adj* chaud, chauffé; *fig* animé, excité; (word) vif (*f* vive); **become** ~ s'échauffer

**heater** *n* appareil *m* de chauffage, radiateur *m*; **water** ~ chauffe-eau *m invar*

**heath** *n* lande *f*; bruyère *f*

**heathen** *n* païen -ïenne; *coll* agnostique; barbare; *adj* païen -ïenne; *coll* agnostique; barbare

**heathenish** *adj* païen -ïenne; *coll* barbare

**heathenism** *n* paganisme *m*

**heather** *n* bruyère *f*

**heating** *n* chauffage *m*; ~ **engineer** installateur *m* de chauffage; *adj* chauffant

**heave** *n* soulèvement *m*; *med* nausée *f*; *vt* soulever; (throw) jeter, lancer; (sigh) pousser; *naut* haler; *vi* se gonfler, se soulever; *med* avoir des nausées; *naut* ~ **to** se mettre en panne

**heaven** *n* ciel *m*, paradis *m*; *coll* félicité *f*;

**Heaven** Dieu *m*; ~ **s** ciel *m*; **for** ~ **'s sake!** pour l'amour de Dieu!; **move** ~ **and earth** remuer ciel et terre

**heavenly** *adj* céleste, du ciel; *coll* divin, épatant

**heavenward** *adj* + *adv* vers le ciel

**heaver** *n* déchargeur *m*

**heavily** *adv* lourdement; fortement; **rain** ~ pleuvoir dru

**heaviness** *n* lourdeur *f*, pesanteur *f*; *fig* appesantissement *m*, abattement *m*

**heavy** *adj* lourd, pesant; (eater, rain, cold, etc) gros (*f* grosse); (sea) houleux -euse; (sky) couvert; (weather) lourd, orageux -euse; (gunfire) violent; (drinker) grand; (soil) gras (*f* grasse); *fig* lourd, pénible, triste; (day) chargé; ~ **with young** grosse; *adv* lourd, lourdement

**heavy-handed** *adj* gauche, maladroit

**heavy-laden** *adj* chargé; opprimé

**heavyweight** *n* poids lourd

**Hebraic** *adj* hébraïque

**Hebraism** *n* judaïsme *m*; culture *f* hébraïque; (idiom) hébraïsme *m*

**Hebrew** *n* (person) Hébreu *m*, Juif -ive, Israélite; (language) hébreu *m*; *adj* hébreu (*m* only), juif -ive

**hecatomb** *n* hécatombe *f*

**heck** *interj* diable!

**heckle** *vt* interpeller; *vi* porter la contradiction

**heckler** *n* interpellateur -trice

**hectare** *n* hectare *m*

**hectic** *adj* fiévreux -euse, mouvementé

**hectogram** *n* hectogramme *m*

**hectolitre** *n* hectolitre *m*

**hectometre** *n* hectomètre *m*

**hector** *vt* rudoyer; *vi* faire l'autoritaire

**hedge** *n* haie *f*; *fig* protection *f*; *vt* entourer d'une haie; ~ **in** entourer, restreindre; *coll* ~ **one's bets** placer des paris secondaires comme assurance; prendre ses précautions; *vi* planter une haie; *coll* refuser de se déclarer, parler (agir) d'une manière équivoque

**hedgehog** *n* hérisson *m*

**hedge-hop** *vi coll aer* voler en rasemottes

**hedgerow** *n* haie *f*

**hedonic** *adj* hédoniste

**hedonism** *n* hédonisme *m*, recherche *f* du plaisir

**hedonist** *n* hédoniste

**hedonistic** *adj* hédoniste

**heed** *n* attention *f*, soin *m*; prudence *f*; (obedience) obéissance *f*; **take** ~ faire attention; *vt* faire attention à, noter; *vi* faire attention, prendre garde

**heedful** *adj* circonspect, prudent; attentif -ive; obéissant

**heedfulness** *n* circonspection *f*,

prudence *f*; attention *f*; obéissance *f*

**heedless** *adj* étourdi, insouciant; inattentif -ive

**heedlessness** *n* étourderie *f*, insouciance *f*; inattention *f*

**hee-haw** *n* hi-han *m*; *vi* braire

¹**heel** *n* talon *m*; *coll US* canaille *f*, salaud *m*; **Achilles'** ~ talon *m* d'Achille; **at (upon)** s/o's ~s juste derrière qn; **come to** ~ (dog) venir à côté de son maître; *fig* se soumettre; **cool (kick) one's** ~s être obligé d'attendre, faire le pied de grue; **down at** ~ minable; **lay by the** ~s attraper, capturer; **out at** ~ minable; **show a clean pair of** ~s détaler; **take to one's** ~s prendre ses jambes à son cou; *vt* talonner

²**heel** *vi naut* gîter, donner de la bande; pencher

**heel-tap** *n* fond *m* de verre

**hefty** *adj coll* costaud; *fig* considérable

**heftiness** *n coll* force *f*

**hegemony** *n* hégémonie *f*

**heifer** *n* génisse *f*

**height** *n* hauteur *f*; altitude *f*; (person) taille *f*; *fig* apogée *m*, comble *m*

**heighten** *vt* rehausser, relever; (increase) augmenter; *vi* s'élever, se rehausser

**heinous** *adj* exécrable, odieux -ieuse

**heinousness** *n* énormité *f*

**heir** *n* héritier *m*; ~ **apparent** héritier assuré; ~ **presumptive** héritier présomptif

**heiress** *n* héritière *f*

**heirloom** *n* objet reçu en héritage; bijou *m* de famille

**helical** *adj* hélicoïdal

**helicopter** *n* hélicoptère *m*

**heliocentric** *adj* héliocentrique

**heliography** *n* héliographie *f*

**heliotrope** *n bot* héliotrope *m*

**heliport** *n* héliport *m*

**helium** *n chem* hélium *m*

**helix** *n* hélice *f*, spirale *f*; *anat* + *zool* hélix *m*

**hell** *n* enfer *m*; *coll* **a** ~ **of** a un sacré; *coll* **for the** ~ **of it** pour rire, pour s'amuser; *coll* **give** ~ **to** rudoyer, faire passer un mauvais quart d'heure à; **go** ~ **for leather** aller ventre à terre; *coll* **like** ~ beaucoup, énormément, *iron* pas du tout, mais non

**hellbent** *adj US* acharné

**hellcat** *n* harpie *f*

**hellebore** *n bot* ellébore *m*

**Hellene** *n* Hellène *m*; *adj* hellène

**Hellenic** *adj* (language) hellénique; (race) hellène

**Hellenism** *n* hellénisme *m*

**Hellenist** *n* helléniste

**Hellenistic** *adj* hellénistique

**hellhound** *n* suppôt *m* d'enfer

**hellish** *adj* infernal; *coll* très désagréable; *adv coll* très désagréablement; extrêmement

**hellishly** *adv* infernalement

**hello** *interj* + *vi* see **hallo**

¹**helm** *n naut* barre *f*, gouvernail *m*; *fig* contrôle *m*

²**helm** *n hist* heaume *m*

**helmet** *n* casque *m*

**helmeted** *adj* casqué

**helmsman** *n* timonier *m*, homme *m* de barre

**helot** *n* ilote

**help** *n* aide *f*, assistance *f*, secours *m*; remède *m*; (person) aide; (household) femme *f* de ménage; *vt* aider, assister, secourir, venir en aide à; (ease) faciliter; (at table) servir; (avoid, prevent) éviter, empêcher; ~ **oneself to** prendre, se servir de; ~ **out** aider, *coll* dépanner; **I can't** ~ **it** je n'y peux rien; *vi* aider

**helper** *n* aide, assistant -e, auxiliaire

**helpful** *adj* secourable, serviable; salutaire, utile

**helpfulness** *n* serviabilité *f*

**helping** *n* portion *f*; *adj* secourable; **lend a** ~ **hand** donner un coup de main

**helpless** *adj* impuissant, incapable; incompétent; sans protection

**helplessness** *n* impuissance *f*, incapacité *f*; manque *m* de protection

**helpmate, helpmeet** *n* collaborateur -trice; (wife) moitié *f*

**helter-skelter** *adj* débridé, désordonné; *adv* pêle-mêle, à la débandade

¹**hem** *n* bord *m*, ourlet *m*; *vt* border, ourler; ~ **in** encercler, entourer

²**hem, hum, h'm** *interj* hem!, hum!; *vi* faire hem, faire hum

**he-man** *n coll* costaud *m*

**hemicycle** *n* hémicycle *m*

**hemiplegia** *n med* hémiplégie *f*

**hemisphere** *n* hémisphère *m*

**hemistich** *n* hémistiche *m*

**hem-line** *n* hauteur *f* (du sol) d'une jupe

**hemlock** *n bot* ciguë *f*

**hemorrhage** *n see* **haemorrhage**

**hemorrhoid** *n see* **haemorrhoid**

**hemp** *n* (plant, fibre) chanvre *m*; (drug) ha(s)chich *m*, *coll* kif *m*

**hempen** *adj* de chanvre

**hemstitch** *n* ourlet *m* à jour; *vt* ourler à jour

**hen** *n* poule *f*; (birds in general) femelle *f*; *coll* mijaurée *f*

**hence** *adv* (therefore) donc, ainsi, d'où; (place) d'ici; (time) dorénavant; *interj ar* allez!, partez!

**henceforth, henceforward** *adv* désormais, dorénavant

**henchman** *n* suivant *m*; partisan *m* fidèle

**hen-coop, hen-house** *n* poulailler *m*
**henna** *n* henné *m*
**hen-party** *n* réunion *f* de femmes
**henpeck** *vt* (wife) dominer
**hep** *adj sl* qui aime le swing; à la page
**hepatic** *adj* hépatique; jaune, olivâtre
**hepatitis** *n med* hépatite *f*
**hep-cat** *n sl* fanatique du swing; joueur -euse de swing
**heptagon** *n* heptagone *m*
**heptagonal** *adj* heptagonal
**her** *poss adj* son (*f* sa, *mpl*+*fpl* ses); *pron* elle; la; lui; celle; **give ~ the book** donnez-lui le livre; **I see ~** je la vois; **I thought of ~** j'ai pensé à elle; **to ~ who came** à celle qui est venue
**herald** *n* héraut *m*; messager *m*; *vt* proclamer; annoncer
**heraldic** *adj* héraldique
**heraldry** *n* blason *m*, science *f* héraldique
**herb** *n* herbe *f*; **~s** *cul* fines herbes; *med* herbes médicinales
**herbaceous** *adj* herbacé; **~ border** parterre *m* de plantes herbacées
**herbage** *n* herbage *m*; *leg* (droit *m* de) pâturage *m*
**herbal** *n* traité *m* de botanique; *adj* d'herbes
**herbalist** *n* botaniste; *med* herboriste
**herbarium** *n* herbier *m*
**herbivorous** *adj* herbivore
**Herculean** *adj* herculéen -éenne
**Hercules** *n* Hercule *m*; *fig* hercule *m*
**herd** *n* troupeau *m*; (people) foule *f*; *vt* mettre en troupeau, rassembler en troupeau; *vi* s'attrouper, se rassembler
**herdsman** *n* bouvier *m*, pâtre *m*
**here** *adv* ici, en ce lieu; **~ and there** ça et là; **neither ~ nor there** hors de propos; **~ goes!** allons-y donc!; **~ I am!** me voici!; **~'s to vive**; **~ you are** voici ce qu'il vous faut
**hereabout(s)** *adv* près d'ici, aux alentours
**hereafter** *n* au-delà *m*; vie future; *adv* plus tard; dans l'autre monde
**hereby** *adv* en ceci, par ceci, par ces moyens; *leg* par les présentes
**hereditament** *n leg* bien *m* transmissible, patrimoine *m*
**hereditary** *adj* héréditaire; **~ factor** gène *m*
**heredity** *n* hérédité *f*
**herein** *adv* en ceci, sur ce point; dans ce bien, ici; (enclosed) ci-inclus
**hereof** *adv* de ceci
**heresy** *n* hérésie *f*
**heretic** *n* hérétique
**heretical** *adj* hérétique
**hereunder** *adv* ci-après, ci-dessous
**hereupon** *adv* sur ce point; (then) sur ce;

(above) ci-dessus
**herewith** *adv* avec ceci, ci-joint
**heritage** *n* héritage *m*
**hermaphrodite** *n* hermaphrodite *m*; *adj* hermaphrodite
**hermetic** *adj* hermétique
**hermit** *n* ermite *m*, solitaire *m*; **~ crab** bernard-l'(h)ermite *m invar*
**hermitage** *n* ermitage *m*
**hernia** *n med* hernie *f*
**hernial** *adj med* herniaire
**hero** *n* héros *m*; **~ worship** culte *m* des héros
**heroic** *adj* héroïque; (style) grandiloquent; **~ age** temps *mpl* héroïques; **~ couplet** deux décasyllabes rimés; **~ verse** vers *mpl* héroïques, vers *mpl* épiques; **mock ~** héroï-comique, burlesque
**heroical** *adj* héroïque
**heroics** *npl* emphase *f*, grandiloquence *f*
**heroin** *n* héroïne *f*
**heroine** *n* héroïne *f*
**heroism** *n* héroïsme *m*
**heron** *n* héron *m*
**herring** *n* hareng *m*; **red ~** argument *m* hors de propos servant à détourner l'attention
**herring-bone** *n* arête *f* de hareng; *adj* (stitch) au point de chausson; *archi* en épi
**hers** *pron* le sien (*f* la sienne), à elle
**herself** *refl pron* se; *emph* elle-même; **by ~** toute seule
**Hertzian** *adj* hertzien -ienne
**hesitance, hesitancy** *n* hésitation *f*, incertitude *f*, indécision *f*
**hesitant** *adj* hésitant, indécis
**hesitate** *vi* hésiter; balancer, osciller
**hesitation** *n* hésitation *f*, indécision *f*
**hessian** *n* toile *f* d'emballage, toile *f* de jute
**heterodox** *adj* hétérodoxe
**heterodoxy** *n* hétérodoxie *f*
**heterogeneity** *n* hétérogénéité *f*
**heterogeneous** *adj* hétérogène
**heterosexual** *adj* hétérosexuel -elle
**heterosexuality** *n* hétérosexualité *f*
**het-up** *adj coll* excité, énervé; tourmenté
**hew** *vt* tailler, taillader; (stone) équarrir
**hewer** *n* tailleur *m*
**hewn** *adj* taillé
**hexagon** *n* hexagone *m*
**hexagonal** *adj* hexagonal
**hexameter** *n* hexamètre *m*
**hexametric(al)** *adj* hexamètre
**hey** *interj* hé!, ohé!
**heyday** *n* apogée *m*, comble *m*; (youth) fleur *f*
**hi** *interj* hé!, ohé!
**hiatus** *n* hiatus *m*; lacune *f*, solution *f* de continuité

hibernal *adj* hivernal

hibernate *vi* hiverner, hiberner; *fig* somnoler

hibernation *n* hibernation *f*; *fig* somnolence *f*

hibiscus *n* hibiscus *m*

hiccup, hiccough *n* hoquet *m*; *vt* dire en hoquetant; *vi* avoir le hoquet, hoqueter

hick *n US sl* péquenot *m*

hickory *n* hickory *m*

hidalgo *n* hidalgo *m*

¹hide *n* cuir *m*, peau *f*; *coll* have a thick ~ être insensible; tan the ~ off s/o rosser qn; *vt* écorcher; *coll* rosser

²hide *n* cachette *f*; *mil* observatoire caché; *vt* cacher, tenir secret -ète; *vi* se cacher

hide-and-seek *n* cache-cache *m invar*

hidebound *adj* conservateur -trice, réactionnaire; (limited) borné

hideous *adj* hideux -euse, horrible; (crime) abominable, atroce

hideousness *n* hideur *f*; (crime) atrocité *f*

hideout *n* cachette *f*, *sl* planque *f*

¹hiding *n* action *f* de cacher; ~ place cachette *f*; in ~ caché

²hiding *n* volée *f* de coups

hierarchal, hierarchic, hierarchical *adj* hiérarchique

hierarchy *n* hiérarchie *f*

hieroglyphic *adj* hiéroglyphique

hieroglyphics *npl* écriture *f* hiéroglyphique

hi-fi *n* hi-fi *f*, haute fidélité

higgledy-piggledy *adj + adv* en désordre

high *adj* haut, grand, de haute taille; élevé; (rank) élevé, puissant, supérieur; (main) principal; excellent; (voice, note) aigu -guë; (meat) faisandé; *coll* (drunk) saoul, parti; (drugged) exalté; (life) luxueux -euse, mondain; (words) violent; ~ altar maître-autel *m* (*pl* maîtres-autels); ~ and dry *naut* échoué; *fig* abandonné; (safe) en sûreté; ~ and low partout; ~ colour teint fleuri; ~ court haute cour; ~ explosive explosif puissant; ~ living grand train de vie, luxe *m*; ~ noon midi exactement; ~ priest grand prêtre; ~ school école *f* d'enseignement secondaire; ~ seas haute mer; ~ street rue principale, grand-rue *f*; ~ tea repas substantiel servi vers six heures du soir; ~ tide marée haute; be ~ and mighty se donner de grands airs; get on one's ~ horse monter sur ses grands chevaux, prendre qch de haut; it is ~ time c'est le moment, ce n'est pas trop tôt; the Most High le Très-Haut; *adv* haut, en haut; de haut

highball *n US coll* whisky *m* soda, fine *f*

à l'eau de Seltz

highborn *adj* de haute naissance

highbrow *n coll pej* intellectuel -uelle; *adj coll* intellectuel -uelle

high-class *adj* chic *invar*; de classe; de haute qualité

highday *n* jour *m* de fête

highfalutin *adj coll* prétentieux -ieuse; déclamatoire

high-fidelity *adj* haute fidélité

high-flier *n* ambitieux -ieuse

highflown *adj* prétentieux -ieuse

high-frequency *adj elect* à haute fréquence

high-grade *adj* de qualité supérieure; ~ petrol super *m*

high-handed *adj* arbitraire, autoritaire

high-hat *n + adj US coll* snob

high-jump *n* saut *m* en hauteur; *coll* he's for the ~ ça va aller très mal pour lui

highland(s) *n(pl)* pays *m* de montagne; hautes terres

high-life *n* vie *f* du monde, vie mondaine

highlight *n* (painting, etc) rehaut *m*; *fig* trait marquant; *vt* rehausser, éclairer

highly *adv* fort, hautement, extrêmement

highly-strung *adj* nerveux -euse, surexcitable

high-mettled *adj* courageux -euse

high-minded *adj* noble, d'âme noble, d'esprit noble

high-mindedness *n* noblesse *f* d'âme

highness *n* élévation *f*, hauteur *f*; (title) altesse *f*

high-pitched *adj* (voice) aigu -uë; *archi* pointu; *fig* noble

high-powered *adj* puissant; efficace

high-pressure *adj* à haute pression; *fig* dynamique, énergique

high-principled *adj* honorable

high-rise *adj* ~ building tour *f* d'habitation

highroad *n* route principale

high-sounding *adj* grandiloquent; *coll* ronflant; *pej* ampoulé

high-spirited *adj* intrépide; animé, gai; (horse) fougueux -euse

high-up *n coll* personnage important, grosse légume

high-water *n* marée haute; ~ mark limite atteinte par la marée haute; *fig* apogée *m*

highway *n* voie publique; grande route

highwayman *n* voleur *m* de grand chemin

hijack *vt* (plane) détourner; *US coll* (person) détrousser; *orig* voler des spiritueux de contrebande

hijacker *n* pirate *m* de l'air; *US coll* détrousseur *m*

**hijacking** *n* piraterie *f* de l'air; *US coll* vol *m*

**hike** *n* randonnée *f* à pied; *vt* traîner; *vi* faire une randonnée à pied

**hiker** *n* excursionniste à pied

**hiking** *n* marche *f*

**hilarious** *adj* hilare, très gai

**hilarity** *n* hilarité *f*

**hill** *n* colline *f*, coteau *m*; (slope) côte *f*, descente *f*, montée *f*; *mil* côte *f*; **old as the ~s** vieux (*f* vieille) comme le monde

**hillbilly** *n* + *adj US coll* montagnard -e

**hillock** *n* mamelon *m*

**hillside** *n* flanc *m* de coteau

**hilly** *adj* accidenté, vallonné

**hilt** *n* garde *f*, poignée *f*; **up to the ~** jusqu'à la garde; *fig* complètement

**him** *pron* le; lui; celui; **I see ~** je le vois; **I thought of ~** j'ai pensé à lui; **show ~ the book** montrez-lui le livre; **to ~ who came** à celui qui est venu

**himself** *refl pron* se; *emph* lui-même; **by ~** tout seul

**¹hind** *n zool* biche *f*

**²hind** *adj* postérieur, de derrière

**hinder** *vt* entraver, gêner, retarder, retenir

**hindmost** *n* dernier -ière; *adj* dernier -ière, ultime

**hindquarters** *npl* arrière-train *m*; fesses *fpl*

**hindrance** *n* empêchement *m*, entrave *f*, obstacle *m*

**hindsight** *n* sagesse rétrospective; (rifle, gun) hausse *f*

**Hindu** *n* Hindou -e; *adj* hindou

**Hinduism** *n* hindouisme *m*

**Hindustani** *n* (language) hindi *m*; Hindou -e; *adj* hindou

**hinge** *n* charnière *f*, gond *m*; *fig* plaque tournante; *vt* (door) mettre dans ses gonds; *vi* pivoter; *fig* **~ on** dépendre de, être axé sur

**hint** *n* allusion *f*, insinuation *f*; (advice) conseil *m*; *fig* nuance *f*, soupçon *m*; *vt* insinuer, laisser entendre, suggérer; *vi* **~ at** faire allusion à

**hinterland** *n* arrière-pays *m*

**¹hip** *n* hanche *f*; *bui* arête *f*; **~ and thigh** sans merci; *coll* **on the ~** acculé, en mauvaise posture

**²hip** *n bot* gratte-cul *m invar*

**hip-bath** *n* bain *m* de siège

**hip-bone** *n anat* os coxal; (os *m* de) la hanche

**hipped** *adj coll* démoralisé, emmerdé

**hippo** *n coll* hippopotame *m*

**hippocampus** *n zool* hippocampe *m*

**hippopotamus** *n* hippopotame *m*

**hippy** *n* hippie

**hire** *n* location *f*; (payment) prix *m* de location; *US* embauchage *m*; *vt* louer; *US* embaucher

**hireling** *n* mercenaire

**hire-purchase** *n* achat *m* à crédit (à tempérament)

**hirsute** *adj* hirsute

**his** *poss adj* son (*f* sa, *mpl* + *fpl* ses); *poss pron* le sien (*f* la sienne); à lui

**Hispanic** *adj* hispanique

**hiss** *n* sifflement *m*; *theat* sifflet *m*; *vt* + *vi* siffler

**hissing** *n* sifflement *m*

**histamine** *n med* histamine *f*

**histological** *adj* histologique

**histology** *n* histologie *f*

**historian** *n* historien -ienne

**historic** *adj* célèbre, historique

**historical** *adj* historique

**historiographer** *n* historiographe *m*

**history** *n* histoire *f*; (story) récit *m*; (play) drame *m* historique; **~ book** livre *m* d'histoire; **make ~** entrer dans l'histoire, créer un précédent

**histrionic** *adj* théâtral

**histrionics** *npl* technique *f* du jeu théâtral; *pej* cabotinage *m*

**hit** *n* coup *m*; (fencing) touche *f*; (success) succès *m*, réussite *f*; **make a ~ with** impressionner, *coll* accrocher avec; *vt* battre, frapper; (knock against) heurter; (reach) atteindre, toucher; (hurt) blesser, toucher; **~ and run driver** chauffard *m*; *coll* **~ it** deviner correctement; *sl* foutre le camp; *coll* **~ it off with** s'entendre bien avec; **~ off** (likeness) attraper, saisir; (imitate) imiter; *vi* **~ at** attaquer, condamner; **~ back** riposter; **~ out at** cogner sur, s'attaquer à; **~ upon (on)** trouver par hasard, tomber sur

**hitch** *n* secousse *f*; (setback) accroc *m*, contretemps *m*, obstacle *m*; *naut* demi-clef *f*; *coll* trajet *m* en auto-stop; *vt* accrocher, attacher, fixer; *naut* amarrer; *vi* s'accrocher; *coll* faire de l'auto-stop; *coll* **~ up with** épouser

**hitched** *adj coll* marié

**hitch-hike** *vi* faire de l'auto-stop, faire du stop

**hitch-hiker** *n* auto-stoppeur -euse

**hitch-hiking** *n* auto-stop *m*

**hither** *adv* ici; **~ and thither** çà et là

**hitherto** *adv* jusqu'ici, jusqu'à présent

**hit-or-miss** *adj* fortuit, au hasard

**hitter** *n* personne *f* qui frappe

**hive** *n* ruche *f*; *vt* mettre dans une ruche, recevoir dans une ruche; **~ off** séparer; *vi* entrer dans une ruche, être dans une ruche; **~ off** se séparer

**hoar** *n* givre *m*, gelée blanche; *adj* givré

**hoard** *n* accumulation *f*, amas *m*; trésor *m*; *vt* accumuler, amasser, entasser; *vi* économiser, thésauriser

**hoarder** *n* personne *f* qui amasse

¹**hoarding** *n* accumulation *f*, thésaurisation *f*

²**hoarding** *n* panneau *m* (d'affichage); clôture *f* en bois

**hoarfrost** *n* givre *m*, gelée blanche

**hoarse** *adj* enroué, rauque

**hoarseness** *n* enrouement *m*

**hoary** *adj* ayant les cheveux gris (blancs); grisonnant; *fig* vénérable

**hoax** *n* attrape *f*, canular *m*; *vt* duper, attraper, berner

**hoaxer** *n* personne *f* qui monte une attrape (un canular)

**hobble** *vt* (horse) entraver; *vi* boiter, clocher

**hobby** *n* hobby *m*, passe-temps *m*, violon *m* d'Ingres

**hobby-horse** *n* cheval *m* de bois; (toy) tête de cheval en bois montée sur un bâton; *fig* manie *f*, dada *m*

**hobgoblin** *n* lutin *m*

**hobnail** *n* caboche *f*

**hobnailed** *adj* ferré (de caboches)

**hobnob** *vi* frayer; boire ensemble; bavarder ensemble

**hobo** *n* US *coll* clochard *m*

¹**hock** *n* (animal) jarret *m*; *vt* couper le jarret à

²**hock** *n* vin blanc allemand, vin *m* du Rhin

³**hock** *n* US *sl* in ~ (pawn) au clou; (prison) en taule; *vt* US *sl* mettre au clou

**hockey** *n* hockey *m*

**hocus-pocus** *n* charabia *m*; mystification *f*, tour *m* de passe-passe

**hod** *n* hotte *f*; seau *m* à charbon

**hodge-podge** *n* see **hotchpotch**

**hoe** *n* binette *f*, houe *f*; *vt + vi* biner, houer

**hog** *n* cochon *m*, porc *m*, pourceau *m*; *coll fig* goinfre *m*; *coll* **go the whole ~** y aller à fond; **road ~** chauffard *m*; *vt* prendre pour soi-même, monopoliser; *vi* se goinfrer

**hogback, hogsback** *n* dos *m* d'âne

**hoggish** *adj* glouton -onne, goinfre; égoïste

**hogmanay** *n* Scots nuit *f* de la nouvelle année, Saint-Sylvestre *f*; réveillon *m*

**hogshead** *n* barrique *f*

**hogwash** *n* pâtée *f*; *coll* (gossip) cancan *m*, ragot *m*; *sl* vinasse *f*

**hoick** *vt* soulever abruptement; *vi* se soulever abruptement

**hoist** *n* action *f* de hisser; *naut* palan *m*; *mech* monte-charge *m invar*; *vt* hisser, remonter

**hoity-toity** *adj* arrogant, hautain

¹**hold** *n* naut cale *f*

²**hold** *n* prise *f*, étreinte *f*; contrôle *m*, autorité *f*; **get ~ of** obtenir; **have a ~ on** avoir prise sur; avoir un moyen de faire du chantage à; *vt* tenir; (contain) contenir; (hold back) retenir; (support) soutenir; (seize) saisir; (preserve) conserver; (mass) célébrer; (funds) détenir; (post) occuper, remplir; (court) présider; (record) détenir; (attention) retenir; (deem) estimer, juger, considérer; ~ **back** retenir; ~ **down** tenir baissé, subjuguer; ~ **in** retenir; ~ **it!** ne bougez pas!; ~ **off** tenir éloigné; (postpone) retarder; ~ **on** maintenir, saisir; ~ **one's own** se défendre bien; ~ **one's tongue** ne rien dire; ~ **out** tendre; tenir, offrir; ~ **over** ajourner, différer; *coll* ~ **the baby** payer les pots cassés; ~ **the line!** ne quittez pas!; *ar* ~ **them up!** haut les mains!; ~ **up** relever, soutenir; retenir; (delay) différer; (rob) dévaliser; (as example) citer; *fig* ~ **water** tenir debout; *vi* tenir, rester ferme, se maintenir; (last) demeurer, durer; continuer, persister; (believe) croire, être de l'avis de; ~ **back** rester en arrière, se retenir; ~ **forth** faire un discours, pérorer; ~ **good** être valable, être vrai; ~ **hard!** attendez!, doucement!; ~ **off** se tenir éloigné; *naut* tenir le large; ~ **on** se cramponner, se maintenir; (resist) tenir bon, tenir le coup; ~ **on!** attendez!, minute!; ~ **out** tenir, résister; ~ **out on** cacher l'essentiel à; ~ **to** maintenir; ~ **with** approuver

**holdall** *n* sac *m* de voyage, fourre-tout *m invar*

**holder** *n* qn qui tient; qch qui contient; (office) titulaire; (record) détenteur -trice; (funds, stocks) détenteur -trice

**holding** *n* action *f* de tenir; possession *f*; (investments) portefeuille *m*, fonds *mpl*

**hold-up** *n* attaque *f* à main armée, hold-up *m invar*; (delay) entrave *f*, retard *m*

**hole** *n* trou *m*; (hollow) creux *m*; excavation *f*, fosse *f*; brèche *f*; orifice *m*; ouverture *f*; *bui* boulin *m*; (button) œillet *m*; (rabbit) terrier *m*; (argument) défaut *m*; (awkward situation) embarras *m*; *coll* trou perdu; *coll* **make a ~ in** entamer; **pick ~s in** relever les points faibles; *vt* faire un trou dans, percer; (clothes) trouer; *vi* se trouer

**hole-and-corner** *adj* furtif -ive, fait en sous-main

**holiday** *n* jour *m* de congé, congé *m*; *eccles* fête *f*, jour *m* de fête; ~**s** vacances *fpl*; **Bank (public) ~** jour férié; ~**s with pay** congés payés; *adj* de fête;

allègre; *vi* passer des vacances
**holiday-maker** *n* estivant -e; touriste
**holiness** *n* sainteté *f*; **His Holiness** Sa
Sainteté
**Holland** *n* Hollande *f*
**holland** *n* (cloth) hollande *f*
**hollandaise** *n cul* sauce hollandaise
**holler** *vi* crier, hurler
**hollow** *n* creux *m*; vallon *m*; cavité *f*,
cuvette *f*; *adj* creux (*f* creuse); (eye)
cave; (voice) caverneux -euse; (sound)
sourd; *fig* faux (*f* fausse), vain, vide;
*adv coll* **to beat ~** battre à plate(s) cou-
ture(s); *vt* creuser
**hollowness** *n* creux *m*; *fig* fausseté *f*, vide
*m*
**holly** *n* houx *m*
**hollyhock** *n* rose trémière
**holocaust** *n* holocauste *m*
**holster** *n* étui *m* de revolver
**holy** *adj* (Alliance, City, Father, Land,
person, Scriptures, Spirit, Trinity,
Week) saint; (sacred) sacré; (water)
bénit; **Holy Ghost** Saint Esprit; *coll* ~
**terror** enfant terrible; personne *f* redoutable; **Holy Writ** la Bible, les
Saintes Écritures
**holy-day** *n eccles* fête *f*
**holystone** *n naut* brique *f*
**homage** *n* hommage *m*; **pay ~** rendre
hommage
**home** *n* demeure *f*, maison *f*; chez-soi *m*
*invar*, foyer *m*, home *m*; intérieur *m*;
famille *f*; pays natal; (institution) asile
*m*, hospice *m*; (sailors, students, etc)
foyer *m*; **at ~** à la maison; *fig* à son
aise; **be at ~** recevoir (des visiteurs);
**make oneself at ~** faire comme chez
soi; *coll* **nothing to write ~ about** peu
intéressant; *adj* de famille, familial;
domestique; fait à la maison; du pays,
national; **~ counties** = environs *mpl*
de Londres; **Home Office** = ministère
*m* de l'Intérieur; *adv* à la maison, chez
soi; au pays; (fully) à fond; **bring ~ to**
faire comprendre pleinement à; **drive**
**sth ~** souligner qch; **go ~** rentrer chez
soi; *fig* (argument, idea) porter; **send**
**~** renvoyer à la maison; rapatrier; *vi*
revenir chez soi; (pigeon) revenir au
colombier
**homecoming** *n* retour *m* au pays, retour
*m* chez soi
**homeland** *n* pays natal
**homeless** *adj* sans abri, sans foyer
**homeliness** *n* manque *m* de façons, simplicité *f*; *US* manque *m* d'attraits
**homely** *adj* sans façons, simple; *US*
sans attraits
**home-made** *adj* fait à la maison; (fait)
maison *invar*
**Homeric** *adj* homérique

**homesick** *adj* nostalgique
**homesickness** *n* mal *m* du pays, nostalgie *f*
**homespun** *n* homespun *m*; *adj* filé à la
main; *fig* sans façons, simple
**homestead** *n* manoir *m*
**homestretch** *n* dernière partie d'une
course
**home-thrust** *n* botte enfoncée; *fig*
(remark) flèche *f*
**homeward** *adj* de retour; *adv* vers la
maison, vers la patrie; **~ bound** sur le
chemin du retour
**homework** *n* devoirs *mpl* (du soir)
**homey** *adj see* homy
**homicidal** *adj* homicide
**homicide** *n* homicide *m*
**homily** *n* homélie *f*
**homing** *adj* (pigeon) voyageur; (missile)
à tête chercheuse
**hominy** *n US* bouillie *f* de farine de maïs
**homo** *n sl* homosexuel -elle, inverti -e,
(male) pédé *m*, (female) lesbienne *f*;
*adj sl* homosexuel -elle, inverti
**homoeopath** *n* homéopathe
**homoeopathic, homeopathic** *adj* ho-
méopathique
**homoeopathy, homeopathy** *n* homéopathie *f*
**homogeneity** *n* homogénéité *f*
**homogeneous** *adj* homogène
**homogenize** *vt* homogénéiser
**homologous** *adj* homologue
**homologue** *n* homologue *m*
**homonym** *n* homonyme *m*
**homosexual** *n* homosexuel -elle; *adj*
homosexuel -elle
**homosexuality** *n* homosexualité *f*
**homy, homey** *adj* familial, comme à la
maison; intime
**hone** *n* pierre *f* à aiguiser, meule *f* à
aiguiser; *vt* affiler, affûter, aiguiser
**honest** *adj* honnête, intègre, loyal,
probe; franc (*f* franche), sincère;
(woman) chaste; **make an ~ woman of**
épouser
**honestly** *adv* honnêtement; *coll* franchement, vraiment
**honest-to-goodness** *adj coll* véritable
¹**honesty** *n* honnêteté *f*, intégrité *f*, probité *f*; franchise *f*, sincérité *f*, vertu *f*;
(woman) chasteté *f*
²**honesty** *n bot* lunaire *f*, monnaie-du-
pape *f* (*pl* monnaies-du-pape)
**honey** *n* miel *m*; *coll* chéri -e; *adj*
de miel
**honey-bee** *n* abeille *f*
**honeycomb** *n* rayon *m* de miel; motif
hexagonal; *vt* cribler, percer de trous
**honeydew** *n bot* miellée *f*; *poet* ambroisie *f*
**honeyed** *adj* couvert de miel; *fig*

mielleux -euse, doucereux -euse

**honeymoon** *n* lune *f* de miel; *vi* passer sa lune de miel

**honeysuckle** *n* chèvrefeuille *m*

**honk** *n* coup *m* de klaxon; *vi* klaxonner

**honky-tonk** *n US sl* bastringue *m*, boîte *f*

**honorarium** *n* (*pl* **honoraria**) honoraires *mpl*

**honorary** *adj* honoraire, honorifique, d'honneur

**honorific** *adj* honorifique

**honour** *n* honneur *m*, estime *f*; gloire *f*, réputation *f*; distinction *f*, titre *m* honorifique; dignité *f*; privilège *m*; honnêteté *f*, pudeur *f*; **do the ∼s** faire les honneurs, faire les présentations; **maid of ∼** demoiselle *f* d'honneur; **on one's ∼** sur son honneur, engagé d'honneur; *vt* honorer, rendre honneur à; estimer, respecter, révérer; *comm* honorer, acquitter

**honourable** *adj* honorable, digne, estimable, respectable

**hooch** *n US sl* whisky *m*

**hood** *n* capuchon *m*; (monk) capuchon *m*, cagoule *f*; (university, etc) épitoge *f*; *US* mot capot *m*; *mot* capote *f*; *bui* (fireplace) hotte *f*, (cowl) capot *m*; *vt* couvrir d'un capuchon

**hoodlum** *n US sl* voyou *m*

**hoodoo** *n* porte-malheur *m invar*; (bad luck) malchance *f*; *coll* guigne *f*, guignon *m*; *vt* porter malchance à; (curse) maudire

**hoodwink** *vt fig* berner, duper

**hoof** *n* (*pl* **hooves**) *zool* sabot *m*; *joc* pied *m*; (cattle) **on the ∼** vivant; *vt sl* **∼ it** marcher, danser; **∼ out** chasser, vider

**hoo-ha** *n coll* bruit *m*; dispute *f*; (fuss) histoires *fpl*

**hook** *n* crochet *m*; croc *m*, grappin *m*; (meat) pendoir *m*; (fishing) hameçon *m*; (boxing) crochet *m*; (clothes) agrafe *f*; **∼, line and sinker** absolument tout; **by ∼ or by crook** par n'importe quel moyen; *coll* **let s/o off the ∼** épargner qn; *vt* accrocher, agrafer; (fish) prendre; (boxing) donner un crochet à; (rugby football) talonner; *fig* agripper, happer, saisir; *sl* **∼ it** déguerpir; *coll* **get ∼ed** se marier; être drogué; *sl* **get ∼ed on** prendre goût à; *vi* s'accrocher; **∼ on to** se cramponner à

**hookah** *n* houka *m*, narguilé *m*

**¹hooker** *n* (rugby) talonneur *m*; *US sl* putain *f*

**²hooker** *n coll naut* navire *m*

**hookey** *n US coll* **play ∼** faire l'école buissonnière

**hookup** *n rad* relais *m*

**hookworm** *n* ankylostome *m*

**hooligan** *n* voyou *m*, crapule *f*

**hooliganism** *n* conduite *f* de voyou

**¹hoop** *n* cerceau *m*, cercle *m*; (croquet) arceau *m*; *coll* **go through the ∼** passer un mauvais quart d'heure

**²hoop, whoop** *n* quinte *f*; (shout) cri *m* rauque; *vi* avoir une quinte (de toux); (shout) pousser un cri rauque

**hooping-cough, whooping-cough** *n* coqueluche *f*

**hooray** *vi* pousser des hourras; *interj* hourra!

**hoot** *n* huée *f*; (bird) (h)ululement *m*; (siren) mugissement *m*; *mot* coup *m* de klaxon; (train) coup *m* de sifflet; *sl* qch de très drôle; *coll* **not care a ∼ about** se ficher de; *vt* huer; *vi* huer; (bird) (h)ululer; (siren) mugir; *mot* klaxonner; (train) siffler

**hooter** *n* sirène *f*; *mot* klaxon *m*, avertisseur *m*

**Hoover** *n* aspirateur *m*

**hoover** *vt* passer l'aspirateur sur

**¹hop** *n* sautillement *m*, saut *m*; *coll* sauterie *f*; *aer* étape *f*; **on the ∼** au dépourvu, à l'improviste; *vt* sauter; *coll* **∼ it!** fiche le camp!; *vi* sautiller, sauter, sauter à cloche-pied; **∼ across** to faire un saut à

**²hop** *n bot* houblon *m*; fleur *f* de houblon

**hope** *n* espérance *f*, espoir *m*; *coll* **what a ∼!** aucune chance!; *vi* espérer, avoir de l'espoir; **∼ against ∼** espérer contre toute attente

**hopeful** *n joc* **young ∼** jeune espoir *m*, poulain *m*; *adj* optimiste, plein d'espoir; encourageant, prometteur -euse

**hopefulness** *n* espoir *m*, espérance *f*

**hopeless** *adj* désespérant, désespéré, navrant; *coll* incorrigible

**hopelessly** *adv* sans espoir, désespérément, irrémédiablement

**hopelessness** *n* désespoir *m*; vanité *f*

**hopper** *n* sauteur *m*; *med* trémie *f*; (railway) wagon *m* à fond ouvrant

**hop-picker** *n* cueilleur -euse de houblon

**hopscotch** *n* marelle *f*

**horde** *n* horde *f*; *coll* des tas *mpl*, des masses *fpl*

**horizon** *n* horizon *m*; *geol* **scil ∼** horizon *m* du sol; *astron* **true ∼** horizon *m* astronomique

**horizontal** *adj* horizontal

**hormone** *n* hormone *f*

**horn** *n* corne *f*; (deer) bois *m*; (shoehorn) chausse-pied *m*; *mot* avertisseur *m*, klaxon *m*; *cul* cornet *m* de pâtisserie; *mus* cor *m*; **∼ of plenty** corne *f* d'abondance; **draw in one's ∼s** faire des économies; **English ∼** cor anglais; **on the ∼s of a dilemma** enfermé dans un dilemme; **take the bull by the ∼s**

prendre le taureau par les cornes; *adj* de corne; *vt* encorner; *coll* ~ **in on** s'immiscer dans, mettre son grain de sel dans

**hornbeam** *n bot* charme *m*

**hornblende** *n* hornblende *f*

**horned** *adj* cornu

**hornet** *n* frelon *m*; *coll* **stir up a** ~ **'s nest** tomber dans un guêpier

**hornpipe** *n* matelote *f*

**hornrimmed** *adj* à monture de corne

**horny** *adj* corné, cornu, en corne; (hands) calleux -euse; *US vulg* excité

**horoscope** *n* horoscope *m*

**horrible** *adj* horrible, abominable, affreux -euse, atroce, hideux -euse, monstrueux -ueuse

**horrid** *adj* horrible, horrifiant, répugnant, révoltant; *coll* désagréable

**horrific** *adj* horrible, terrifiant

**horrify** *vt* horrifier

**horror** *n* horreur *f*, épouvante *f*, peur *f*; abomination *f*, répugnance *f*; infamie *f*; ~ **comic** comique *m* d'épouvante; ~ **s** peur irrationnelle

**horror-stricken** *adj* frappé d'horreur, effrayé

**hors d'œuvre** *n* hors-d'œuvre *m invar*

**horse** *n* cheval *m*; (stallion) étalon *m*; (gymnasium) cheval *m* d'arçons; *mil* cavalerie *f*; séchoir *m* à lessive; chevalet *m*; ~ **of another colour** une toute autre question; **back the wrong** ~ faire un mauvais choix; **dark** ~ outsider *m*; **eat like a** ~ manger comme quatre; **flog a dead** ~ vouloir ranimer une vieille controverse; **hold your** ~ **s!** du calme!, rien ne presse!; **on one's high** ~ sur ses grands chevaux; (waves) **white** ~ **s** moutons *mpl*; *adj* de cheval; *mil* (guards, artillery) monté

**horseback** *n* dos *m* de cheval; **on** ~ à cheval

**horsebox** *n* wagon (camion) affecté au transport des chevaux

**horse-chestnut** *n* marron *m* d'Inde; (tree) marronier *m* d'Inde

**horse-cloth** *n* housse *f*, couverture *f* de cheval

**horse-coper** *n* maquignon *m*

**horsedrawn** *adj* hippomobile

**horseflesh** *n* viande *f* de cheval; *collect* chevaux *mpl*

**horsefly** *n* taon *m*

**horsehair** *n* crin *m* de cheval

**horse-laugh** *n coll* gros rire

**horseman** *n* cavalier *m*, écuyer *m*

**horsemanship** *n* équitation *f*

**horseplay** *n* tapage *m*, jeu turbulent

**horse-power** *n* puissance *f* en chevaux; *mot* cheval-vapeur *m* (*pl* chevaux-vapeur)

**horse-race** *n* course *f* de chevaux

**horse-racing** *n* courses *fpl* de chevaux

**horseradish** *n* raifort *m*

**horse-sense** *n* bon sens, finesse *f*

**horseshoe** *n* fer *m* à cheval

**horseshow** *n* concours *m* hippique

**horsetail** *n* queue *f* de cheval

**horsewhip** *n* cravache *f*; *vt* cravacher

**horsewoman** *n* amazone *f*, cavalière *f*

**horsy** *adj* passionné de chevaux; *joc* + *pej* ayant des traits chevalins

**hortative, hortatory** *adj* persuasif -ive, encourageant

**horticultural** *adj* horticole

**horticulturalist** *n* horticulteur *m*

**horticulture** *n* horticulture *f*

**hosanna** *n* hosanna *m*

¹**hose** *n* tuyau *m* d'arrosage; *vt* arroser

²**hose** *n ar* chausses *fpl*; (stockings) bas *m*

**hosepipe** *n* tuyau *m* d'arrosage

**hosier** *n* bonnetier -ière

**hosiery** *n* bonneterie *f*

**hospice** *n* asile *m*, hospice *m*

**hospitable** *adj* hospitalier -ière, accueillant

**hospitableness** *n* disposition hospitalière, générosité *f*

**hospital** *n* hôpital *m*; hospice *m*

**hospitality** *n* hospitalité *f*

**hospitalization** *n* hospitalisation *f*

**hospitalize** *vt* hospitaliser

¹**host** *n bibl* armée *f*; foule *f*

²**host** *n* hôte *m*; aubergiste *m*

³**host** *n eccles* hostie *f*

**hostage** *n* otage *m*

**hostel** *n* maison *f* d'étudiants, maison *f* du marin, maison *f* du soldat; **youth** ~ auberge *f* de (la) jeunesse

**hosteller** *n* touriste fréquentant les auberges de (la) jeunesse, *coll* ajiste

**hostelry** *n* auberge *f*

**hostess** *n* hôtesse *f*; **air** ~ hôtesse *f* de l'air

**hostile** *adj* hostile

**hostility** *n* hostilité *f*

**hot** *adj* chaud; *fig* ardent, impétueux -euse, passionné, violent; (sauce) piquant; (jazz) hot; *sl* (clever) calé, expert; *sl* sexy; ~ **air** balivernes *fpl*; ~ **dog** hot-dog *m*; ~ **favourite** grand favori; ~ **line** téléphone *m* rouge; ~ **news** dernières nouvelles, information sensationnelle; ~ **on the track of** serrant de près; *coll* ~ **stuff** formidable; (get near) **get** ~ brûler; *coll* **have got into** ~ **water** être dans le pétrin; *coll* **not so** ~ pas fameux -euse; *adv* chaleureusement, chaudement; vigoureusement; coléreusement; **blow** ~ **and cold** être indécis; *vt coll* ~ **up** chauffer, animer; (engine) surcomprimer; *vi coll* ~ **up** chauffer, s'échauffer, s'animer

**hotbed** n hort couche f; fig (intrigue, etc) foyer m
**hot-blooded** adj au sang chaud, passionné
**hotchpotch, hodge-podge** n cul+fig salmigondis m; coll fig méli-mélo m (pl mélis-mélos)
**hotel** n hôtel m
**hotelier** n hôtelier -ière
**hotfoot** adv hâtivement, précipitamment
**hot-head** n exalté -e, tête brûlée
**hot-headed** adj exalté, à tête brûlée
**hot-house** n serre chaude; adj cultivé en serre chaude; fig fragile
**hotly** adv chaleureusement, chaudement; vigoureusement; coléreusement
**hot-plate** n (cooker) plaque chauffante; (dishes) chauffe-plats m
**hotpot** n pot-au-feu m invar
**hound** n chien courant; ~s meute f; fig vaurien m; vt poursuivre, s'acharner sur
**hour** n heure f; at the eleventh ~ au dernier moment, in extremis; in the small ~s au petit matin; keep good (late) ~s se coucher tôt (tard); office ~s heures fpl de bureau; the ~ has come le moment est venu
**hour-glass** n sablier m
**hour-hand** n aiguille f des heures
**hourly** adj à chaque heure, de toutes les heures; qui dure une heure; fig fréquent, incessant; adv toutes les heures; fréquemment
**house** n maison f, demeure f, habitation f; hôtel m, pension f; famille f; (household) maisonnée f, ménage m; (parliament) chambre f; ~ of ill-fame maison close, bordel m; ~ to ~ canvassing porte-à-porte m; bring the ~ down provoquer rires et applaudissements; theat full (good) ~ salle f comble; keep ~ tenir le ménage; keep open ~ être très hospitalier -ière; like a ~ on fire très vite; fameusement; coll on the ~ aux frais de la princesse; safe as ~s tout à fait sûr; set one's ~ in order mettre de l'ordre dans ses affaires (dans sa vie); vt héberger, loger; vi loger, habiter, se loger
**house-agent** n agent immobilier
**houseboat** n péniche f
**housebound** adj obligé de rester à la maison
**housebreaker** n cambrioleur m; démolisseur m
**housebreaking** n cambriolage m
**housecoat** n robe f d'intérieur
**house-dog** chien m de garde
**houseful** n maisonnée f
**household** n maison f, maisonnée f;

famille f; gens mpl de maison; adj domestique, de ménage, du ménage; mil Household Troops régiments mpl de la garde royale anglaise; ~ word mot très répandu; nom très connu
**householder** n chef m de famille; occupant -e
**housekeeper** n gouvernante f; (large household) intendante f
**housekeeping** n ménage m; (money) sous mpl du ménage, économie f domestique
**housemaid** n bonne f, domestique f; ~'s knee épanchement m de synovie
**house-party** n invités réunis dans une maison de campagne
**house-physician** n interne
**houseproud** adj coll popote invar
**houseroom** n logement m, place f
**house-surgeon** n chirurgien m interne
**house-trained** adj (animal) propre
**house-warming** n pendaison f de crémaillère
**housewife** n maîtresse f de maison; ménagère f; (sewing) trousse f à couture
**housewifery** n soins mpl du ménage
**housework** n travaux ménagers
**housing** n logement m; ~ estate cité f; (council) groupe m de H.L.M.; ~ shortage crise f du logement
**hovel** n baraque f, bouge m, taudis m
**hover** vi planer, voltiger; fig s'attarder, tourner autour; hésiter
**hovercraft** n aéroglisseur m, hovercraft m
**how** n comment m, manière f; adv (manner) comment, de quelle façon; (extent) combien; comme; que; coll ~ come? comment ça se fait?; ~ far is it to X? combien de kilomètres y a-t-il d'ici à X?; ~ he talks! comme il parle!; ~ long has he been here? depuis combien de temps est-il ici?; ~ long is the journey? le voyage dure combien de temps?; ~ long is the ship? de quelle longueur est le navire?; ~ many? combien?; ~ much? combien?; ~ often? combien de fois?; ~ old is he? quel âge a-t-il?; ~ pleased I am! que je suis content!
**how-do-you-do, how-d'ye-do** n coll here's a fine ~! en voilà une histoire!
**however** adv de quelque façon (manière) que; quelque ... que, pour ... que, si ... que; inter comment?; ~ good he is quelque bon qu'il soit, si bon qu'il soit; conj cependant, néanmoins, pourtant, toutefois
**howitzer** n obusier m
**howl** n hurlement m; huées fpl; (laughter) éclat m de rire; vi hurler; ~ down huer

**howler** n hurleur m; coll bourde f, perle f

**howling** n hurlement m; adj hurlant; coll énorme, fantastique

**howsoever** adv + conj see however

**hoy** interj ohé!

**hoyden** n garçon manqué

**hub** n moyeu m; fig centre m, pivot m

**hubbub** n brouhaha m, tumulte m, vacarme m

**hubby** n coll époux m, mari m

**hub-cap** n mot enjoliveur m

**hubris** n arrogance f, insolence f

**huckleberry** n US bot myrtille f

**huckster** n colporteur m; vi marchander

**huddle** n foule f, tas m; **go into a ~** discuter en petit comité; vt empiler, entasser; vi s'empiler, s'entasser

¹**hue** n teinte f

²**hue** n — **and cry** haro m; poursuite acharnée; protestation f

**huff** n bouderie f, irritation f; accès m de mauvaise humeur; **be in a ~** bouder; vt brimer, malmener; insulter, offenser; (draughts) souffler; vi (breathing) souffler; bouder, se formaliser, s'offusquer; s'emporter

**huffiness, huffishness** n mauvaise humeur, irritation f

**huffish, huffy** adj de mauvaise humeur, irrité

**hug** n embrassement m, étreinte f; (wrestling) prise f; vt embrasser, étreindre, serrer dans ses bras; fig chérir; (ship) **~ the coast** serrer la côte

**huge** adj énorme, immense, vaste

**hugeness** n immensité f

**Huguenot** n Huguenot -e; adj huguenot

**hulk** n naut ponton m; **~ s** galères fpl; coll lourdaud m

**hulking** adj lourdaud; encombrant, énorme

¹**hull** n naut coque f

²**hull** n bot cosse f, gousse f; vt écosser

**hullabaloo** n coll tapage m, vacarme m

**hullo** interj + vi see hallo

¹**hum** n bourdonnement m; (music) fredonnement m; (engine) ronflement m; (aircraft) vrombissement m; vt (tune) fredonner; vi bourdonner; (engine) ronfler; (aircraft) vrombir; **~ and haw** bafouiller, bredouiller; **make things ~** activer les choses; coll **things are humming** ça gaze

²**hum** vi sl puer, schlinguer

³**hum** interj see 'hem

**human** n être humain; adj humain

**humane** adj humain, bon (f bonne), gentil -ille; humaniste

**humaneness** n humanité f, bonté f

**humanism** n humanisme m

**humanist** n humaniste

**humanistic** adj humaniste

**humanitarian** n + adj humanitaire

**humanity** n humanité f; genre humain; bonté f; **humanities** études fpl classiques; études fpl littéraires

**humanization** n humanisation f

**humanize** vt + vi humaniser, civiliser

**humanly** adv humainement; avec humanité

**humble** adj humble, effacé, modeste, obscur; vt abaisser, humilier, rabaisser

**humble-bee** n bourdon m

**humble-pie** n eat **~** s'humilier, s'excuser humblement

**humbly** adv humblement

**humbug** n hypocrisie f, insincérité f; charlatanisme m; (person) blagueur m, charlatan m; cul bonbon m à la menthe; vt duper hypocritement; entortiller

**humdinger** n US sl it's a real **~** c'est sensationnel

**humdrum** adj monotone, ordinaire; ennuyeux -euse

**humectation** n med humectage m

**humeral** adj anat huméral

**humerus** n anat humérus m

**humid** adj humide

**humidification** n humidification f

**humidifier** n humidificateur m

**humidify** vt humidifier

**humiliate** vt abaisser, humilier, rabaisser

**humiliation** n humiliation f, mortification f; disgrâce f

**humility** n humilité f

**humming** n (insects) bourdonnement m; (tune) fredonnement m; (engine) ronflement m; (aircraft) vrombissement m; adj bourdonnant; fredonnant; ronflant; vrombissant

**humming-bird** n colibri m, oiseau-mouche m (pl oiseaux-mouches)

**hummock** n mamelon m, monticule m, tertre m

**humorist, humourist** n humoriste

**humoristic** adj comique, humoristique

**humorous** adj amusant, comique, divertissant; (person) humoriste; (account) humoristique

**humorousness** n comique m, humour m

**humour** n humour m, amusement m; disposition f, humeur f; med ar humeur f; **out of ~** fâché, irrité; vt ménager, passer les caprices à, ne plus contrarier

**humourless** adj dépourvu de sens de l'humour

**hump** n bosse f; geog monticule m; coll mauvaise humeur; vt arrondir, voûter; sl charger sur son dos

**humpback** *n* bossu -e; *zool* baleine *f* à bosse

**humpbacked** *adj* bossu

**humph** *interj* hum!

**humpy** *adj* bosselé, bossu

**humus** *n* humus *m*

**Hun** *n hist* Hun *m*; *sl obs* Boche *m*

**hunch** *n* bosse *f*; (chunk) morceau *m*; *coll* intuition *f*, pressentiment *m*; *vt* arrondir, voûter

**hunchback** *n* bossu -e

**hunchbacked** *adj* bossu

**hundred** *n* centaine *f*; *hist* (England) canton *m*; ~ s grand nombre; *adj* cent

**hundredfold** *adv* au centuple

**hundredth** *n* + *adj* centième

**hundredweight** *n* mesure de poids anglaise (environ cinquante kilogrammes)

**Hungarian** *n* Hongrois -e; (language) hongrois *m*; *adj* hongrois

**Hungary** *n* Hongrie *f*

**hunger** *n* faim *f*; famine *f*; *fig* désir *m*; soif *f*; ~ **strike** grève *f* de la faim; *vi* avoir faim; ~ **after** désirer, avoir soif de

**hungry** *adj* ayant faim; affamé; (soil) infertile; *fig* avide

**hunk** *n* morceau *m*; (bread) quignon *m*

**hunt** *n* chasse *f*; *vt* chasser; (area) battre, courir; *fig* pourchasser, poursuivre; ~ **down** traquer; ~ **out** dénicher, déterrer; *vi* chasser; *mech* vibrer excessivement

**hunter** *n* chasseur *m*; cheval *m* de chasse

**hunting** *n* chasse *f*

**hunting-box** *n* pavillon *m* de chasse

**hunting-crop** *n* cravache *f*

**hunting-ground** *n* terrain *m* de chasse; *fig* terrain *m* riche; *fig* **happy** ~ terrain *m* propice, lieu *m* propice

**hunting-lodge** *n* pavillon *m* de chasse

**huntress** *n* chasseuse *f*, *lit* chasseresse *f*

**huntsman** *n* chasseur *m*; veneur *m*

**hurdle** *n* claie *f*; (athletics) haie *f*; *fig* obstacle *m*; *vt* entourer de claies; *vi* (athletics) faire une course de haies

**hurdler** *n* (athletics) coureur -euse de course de haies

**hurdy-gurdy** *n* orgue *m* de barbarie

**hurl** *vt* jeter violemment, lancer

**hurling** *n* lancement *m*

**hurly-burly** *n* hâte *f*, empressement *m*; brouhaha *m*; confusion *f*, tohu-bohu *m*

**hurrah, hurray** *n* hourra *m*; *interj* hourra!

**hurricane** *n* ouragan *m*

**hurricane-lamp** *n* lampe-tempête *f* (*pl* lampes-tempête)

**hurried** *adj* précipité, rapide

**hurry** *n* hâte *f*, empressement *m*, précipitation *f*; **in a** ~ empressé, impatient; **there's no** ~ rien ne presse; *vt* hâter, précipiter, presser; *vi* se dépêcher, se presser; ~ **up** se hâter

**hurt** *n* mal *m*, blessure *f*; *fig leg* dommage *m*, tort *m*; *adj* blessé; *fig* affligé, attristé, navré; *vt* blesser, faire du mal à; *fig* affliger, attrister; *leg* faire du tort à; léser; *vi* faire mal, faire souffrir

**hurtful** *adj* nocif -ive; blessant, offensant

**hurtfulness** *n* nocivité *f*; ce qui cause du chagrin

**hurtle** *vi* s'élancer, se lancer, voler

¹**husband** *n* époux *m*, mari *m*

²**husband** *vt* économiser, ménager

**husbandry** *n* agriculture *f*; économie *f*; bonne gestion

**hush** *n* silence *m*, tranquillité *f*; *vt* faire taire, tranquilliser; ~ **up** étouffer; *vi* se taire; *interj* chut!

**hush-hush** *adj coll* secret -ète

**hush-money** *n* argent obtenu par chantage; prix *m* du silence

**husk** *n* (cereals) balle *f*; *vt* décortiquer

**huskiness** *n* enrouement *m*

¹**husky** *n* chien esquimau

²**husky** *adj* enroué, rauque; *US* costaud

**hussar** *n mil* hussard *m*

**hussy** *n pej* chipie *f*; garce *f*; *sl* salope *f*, traînée *f*

**hustings** *npl* estrade *f* en plein air pour réunions électorales

**hustle** *n* bousculade *f*; *vt* bousculer, forcer, pousser; faire avancer; *vi* se dépêcher, se hâter, se précipiter

**hustler** *n* personnage *m* dynamique; *sl* (male) prostitué *m*

**hut** *n* cabane *f*, hutte *f*; *mil* baraquement *m*

**hutch** *n* (rabbit) clapier *m*; wagonnet *m*; coffre *m*, huche *f*

**hutment** *n mil* baraquement *m*

**hyacinth** *n* jacinthe *f*; (stone) hyacinthe *f*

**hyaena** *n see* **hyena**

**hybrid** *n* + *adj* (person) métis -isse; hybride

**hydra** *n myth* + *zool* hydre *f*; *fig* monstre *m*

**hydrangea** *n* hortensia *m*

**hydrant** *n* bouche *f* d'incendie

**hydrate** *n chem* hydrate *m*; *vt* hydrater; *vi* s'hydrater

**hydration** *n* hydratation *f*

**hydraulic** *adj* hydraulique

**hydric** *adj chem* hydrogéné

**hydro** *n* établissement thermal

**hydrocarbon** *n chem* hydrocarbure *m*

**hydrocephalic** *adj* hydrocéphale

**hydrocephalus, hydrocephaly** *n med* hydrocéphalie *f*

**hydrochloric** *adj* chlorhydrique

**hydrodynamic** *adj* hydrodynamique

**hydrodynamics** *npl* hydrodynamique *f*

**hydro-electric** *adj* hydro-électrique

**hydro-electricity** *n* énergie *f* hydro-électrique
**hydrofoil** *n* hydrofoil *m*
**hydrogen** *n* hydrogène *m*; ~ **peroxide** eau oxygénée; **sulphuretted** ~ sulfure *m* d'hydrogène
**hydrogenation** *n* hydrogénation *f*
**hydrogen-bomb** *n* bombe *f* à hydrogène
**hydrogenize** *vt* hydrogéner
**hydrogenous** *adj* hydrogéné
**hydrographer** *n* hydrographe
**hydrographic** *adj* hydrographique
**hydrography** *n* hydrographie *f*
**hydrology** *n* hydrologie *f*
**hydrolysis** *n* hydrolyse *f*
**hydrometer** *n* hydromètre *m*
**hydrometry** *n* hydrométrie *f*
**hydropathic** *adj* hydrothérapique
**hydropathy** *n* hydrothérapie *f*
**hydrophobe** *n* hydrophobe
**hydrophobia** *n* hydrophobie *f*
**hydrophobic** *adj* hydrophobe
**hydropic** *adj* hydropique
**hydroplane** *n* *naut* bateau glisseur; *aer* hydravion *m*; (submarine) barre *f* de plongée
**hydrosphere** *n* hydrosphère *f*
**hydrostat** *n* indicateur *m* de niveau d'eau
**hydrostatic** *adj* hydrostatique
**hydrostatics** *n* hydrostatique *f*
**hydrous** *adj* aqueux -euse
**hydroxide** *n* *chem* hydroxyde *m*
**hyena, hyaena** *n* *zool* + *fig* hyène *f*
**hygiene** *n* hygiène *f*
**hygienic** *adj* hygiénique
**hygrometer** *n* hygromètre *m*
**hygroscope** *n* hygroscope *m*
**hygroscopic** *adj* hygroscopique
**hymen** *n* hymen *m*
**hymn** *n* *eccles* hymne *m* or *f*, cantique *m*; *lit* hymne *m*; *vt* célébrer, chanter, glorifier; *vi* chanter des hymnes
**hymnal** *n* recueil *m* d'hymnes
**hymn-book** *n* recueil *m* d'hymnes
**hype** *n* *coll* battage *m* publicitaire, publicité *f* tapageuse
**hyperbola** *n* *geom* hyperbole *f*
**hyperbole** *n* *rhet* hyperbole *f*
**hyperbolic, hyperbolical** *adj* hyperbolique

**hyperborean** *adj* *lit* hyperboréen -éenne
**hypercritical** *adj* hypercritique
**hyperphysical** *adj* surnaturel -elle
**hypersensitive** *adj* hypersensible
**hypersonic** *adj* hypersonique
**hypertension** *n* *med* hypertension *f*
**hyperthyroidism** *n* *med* hyperthyroïdie *f*
**hypertrophied** *adj* hypertrophié
**hypertrophy** *n* hypertrophie *f*
**¹hyphen** *n* trait *m* d'union
**²hyphen, hyphenate** *vt* mettre un trait d'union à
**hypnosis** *n* hypnose *f*; hypnotisme *m*
**hypnotic** *n* hypnotique *m*; sujet *m* hypnotique; *adj* hypnotique; *coll* fascinant
**hypnotism** *n* hypnotisme *m*; *fig* fascination *f*
**hypnotist** *n* hypnotiseur *m*
**hypnotize** *vt* hypnotiser; *fig* éblouir, fasciner
**hypo** *n* *chem* hyposulfite *m* de soude; *phot* fixateur *m*
**hypochondria** *n* hypocondrie *f*
**hypochondriac** *n* + *adj* hypocondriaque
**hypocrisy** *n* hypocrisie *f*
**hypocrite** *n* hypocrite
**hypocritical** *adj* hypocrite
**hypodermic** *n* piqûre *f* hypodermique; seringue *f* hypodermique; *adj* hypodermique
**hypodermis** *n* hypoderme *m*
**hypostasis** *n* *med* + *philos* + *theat* hypostase *f*
**hypotenuse** *n* *geom* hypoténuse *f*
**hypothesis** *n* hypothèse *f*
**hypothesize** *vt* supposer; *vi* émettre une hypothèse
**hypothetic, hypothetical** *adj* hypothétique
**hypothyroidism** *n* *med* hypothyroïdie *f*
**hypsometer** *n* hypsomètre *m*
**hyssop** *n* *bibl* hysope *f*
**hysterectomy** *n* *surg* hystérectomie *f*
**hysteria** *n* hystérie *f*
**hysteric, hysterical** *adj* hystérique
**hysterics** *npl* crise *f* hystérique
**hysterotomy** *n* *surg* hystérotomie *f*, césarienne *f*

# I

**I** *pron* je, (before vowel) j'; (stressed) moi; ~ **myself think** moi je pense; **you and** ~ vous et moi
**iambic** *n* iambe *m*; *adj* iambique
**Iberia** *n* Ibérie *f*
**Iberian** *n* Ibérien -ienne; (language) ibérien *m*; *adj* ibérien -ienne
**ibex** *n* ibex *m*, bouquetin *m*
**ibid(em)** *adv* ibid(em)
**ibis** *n* orni ibis *m*
**ice** *n* glace *f*; (ice-cream) glace *f*; **be on thin** ~ être sur la corde raide; **black** ~ verglas *m*; **break the** ~ briser la glace; *fig* commencer une démarche délicate; **cut no** ~ **with** laisser froid, ne faire aucun effet sur; **keep sth on** ~ mettre qch à la glacière; *fig* mettre qch en attente; *vt* (chill) rafraîchir; (cake) glacer; ~ **up** (windscreen, etc) givrer; *vi* ~ **over** (lake, river) geler; ~ **up** (windscreen, etc) givrer
**ice-age** *n* période *f* glaciaire
**ice-axe** *n* piolet *m*
**iceberg** *n* iceberg *m*
**icebound** *adj* (ship) pris dans les glaces; (port) fermé par les glaces
**icebox** *n* glacière *f*; *US* frigidaire *m*; **this room is like an** ~ on gèle dans cette pièce
**ice-breaker** *n* brise-glaces *m*
**ice-cap** *n* calotte *f* glaciaire
**ice-cream** *n* glace *f*
**ice-field** *n* champ *m* de glace
**ice-floe** *n* banquise *f*
**ice-house** *n* glacière *f*
**Iceland** *n* Islande *f*
**Icelander** *n* Islandais -e
**Icelandic** *n* (language) islandais *m*; *adj* islandais
**iceman** *n US* livreur *m* de glace, marchand *m* de glace
**ice-pack** *n* banquise *f*
**ice-rink** *n* patinoire *f*
**ice-skate** *n* patin *m* à glace; *vi* patiner sur glace
**ice-skating** *n* patinage *m* sur glace
**ichthyology** *n* ichtyologie *f*
**icicle** *n* glaçon *m*
**icily** *adv* (speech) d'un ton glacial; (manner) d'un air glacial
**iciness** *n* air glacial; (road, etc) verglas *m*
**icing** *n* (windscreen, aircraft) givre *m*; *cul* glaçage *m*; ~ **sugar** sucre *m* glace
**icon, ikon** *n* icône *f*
**iconoclasm** *n* iconoclasme *m*

**iconoclast** *n* iconoclaste
**iconoclastic** *adj* iconoclaste
**iconographer** *n* iconographe
**iconography** *n* iconographie *f*
**icy** *adj* glacial, glacé
**id** *n psych* ça *m*
**idea** *n* idée *f*; (vague) notion *f*; (thought) pensée *f*; (opinion) opinion *f*, avis *m*; plan *m*; **I've got the general** ~ j'ai compris à peu près; **that's the** ~! c'est ça!; **the** ~ **is to** il s'agit de; **the very** ~! quelle idée!; *coll* **what's the big** ~? qu'est-ce que c'est que cette histoire?
**ideal** *n* idéal *m*; *adj* idéal, parfait
**idealism** *n* idéalisme *m*
**idealist** *n* + *adj* idéaliste
**idealize** *vt* idéaliser
**ideally** *adv* idéalement, d'une manière idéale
**idem** *adv* idem
**identical** *adj* identique; ~ **twins** vrais jumeaux, vraies jumelles
**identifiable** *adj* identifiable
**identification** *n* identification *f*
**identify** *vt* identifier, établir l'identité de; *vi* ~ **oneself with** s'identifier avec
**identikit** *adj* ~ **portrait** portrait-robot *m* (*pl* portraits-robots)
**identity** *n* identité *f*; ~ **card** carte *f* d'identité
**ideogram, ideograph** *n* idéogramme *m*
**ideological** *adj* idéologique
**ideologist** *n* idéologue
**ideology** *n* idéologie *f*
**ides** *n Rom hist* ides *fpl*
**idiocy** *n* idiotie *f*, stupidité *f*, imbécillité *f*
**idiom** *n* (phrase) idiotisme *m*; (mode of language) idiome *m*
**idiomatic** *adj* idiomatique; (colloquial) de la langue populaire; ~ **expression** idiotisme *m*
**idiosyncrasy** *n* caractéristique *f*, particularité *f*, excentricité *f*
**idiosyncratic** *adj* caractéristique, particulier -ière
**idiot** *n* imbécile, crétin -e
**idiotic** *adj* imbécile, crétin, bête, stupide
**idle** *adj* paresseux -euse, fainéant, oisif -ive; (unemployed) en chômage; (unoccupied) désœuvré, sans occupation; (trivial) oiseux -euse, frivole, futile; *mech* ~ **wheel** roue folle; *vi mech* tourner au ralenti; ~ **(about)** fainéanter, paresser; ~ **away one's time**

gaspiller son temps

**idleness** *n* paresse *f*, oisiveté *f*, désœuvrement *m*

**idler** *n* fainéant -e, oisif -ive, paresseux -euse; *mech* (wheel) roue folle

**idly** *adv* paresseusement; (without thinking) négligemment

**idol** *n* idole *f*

**idolater** *n* idolâtre

**idolatrous** *adj* idolâtre

**idolatry** *n* idolâtrie *f*

**idolize** *vt* idolâtrer, adorer

**idyll** *n* idylle *f*

**idyllic** *adj* idyllique

**if** *n* ~ s and buts les si *mpl* et les mais *mpl*; *conj* si; **as** ~ comme si

**igloo** *n* igloo *m*, iglou *m*

**igneous** *adj* igné

**ignitable** *adj* inflammable

**ignite** *vt* mettre le feu à, enflammer; *vi* prendre feu, s'enflammer

**ignition** *n* ignition *f*; *mot* allumage *m*

**ignoble** *adj* ignoble, infâme, vil

**ignominious** *adj* ignominieux -ieuse, honteux -euse

**ignominy** *n* ignominie *f*

**ignoramus** *n* ignorant -e, ignare

**ignorance** *n* ignorance *f*

**ignorant** *adj* ignorant

**ignore** *vt* (make no mention of) passer sous silence, ne pas relever; (person) faire semblant de ne pas reconnaître; (rule) ne pas respecter

**iguana** *n* iguane *m*

**ikon** *n see* **icon**

**ilex** *n* yeuse *f*; (genus) houx *m*

**ilk** *adj* Scots of that ~ de cet acabit

**ill** *n* mal *m*; *adj* (unwell) malade, souffrant; (evil) méchant, mauvais; ~ **luck** malchance *f*; **it's an** ~ **wind that blows nobody any good** à quelque chose malheur est bon; *adv* mal; ~ **at ease** mal à l'aise; **speak** ~ **of** dire du mal de

**ill-advised** *adj* malavisé, peu judicieux -ieuse

**ill-affected** *adj* mal disposé

**ill-bred** *adj* mal élevé; (birth) mal né

**ill-breeding** *n* manque *m* d'éducation, manque *m* de savoir-vivre

**ill-conditioned** *adj* mal conditionné

**illegal** *adj* illégal

**illegality** *n* illégalité *f*

**illegally** *adv* illégalement

**illegible** *adj* illisible

**illegitimacy** *n* illégitimité *f*

**illegitimate** *adj* illégitime; (wrongful) erroné; illogique

**ill-fated** *adj* malheureux -euse, infortuné; (occasion) néfaste, fatal

**ill-favoured** *adj* laid, déplaisant, répugnant

**ill-gotten** *adj* mal acquis

**ill-humoured** *adj* maussade, de mauvaise humeur

**illiberal** *adj* (petty) mesquin; intolérant; (miserly) ladre

**illicit** *adj* illicite

**illimitable** *adj* illimité, sans bornes

**illiteracy** *n* analphabétisme *m*

**illiterate** *n* analphabète, illettré -e; *adj* analphabète, illettré

**ill-judged** *adj* peu judicieux -ieuse, malavisé

**ill-mannered** *adj* impoli, mal élevé, grossier -ière

**ill-natured** *adj* désagréable, fruste, revêche

**illness** *n* maladie *f*; (ill-health) mauvaise santé

**illogical** *adj* illogique

**illogicality** *n* illogisme *m*

**ill-omened** *adj* de mauvais augure

**ill-starred** *adj* désastreux -euse, néfaste; (person) infortuné

**ill-tempered** *adj* grincheux -euse, de mauvaise humeur

**ill-timed** *adj* malencontreux -euse, inopportun, mal à propos

**ill-treat** *vt* malmener, maltraiter, brutaliser

**ill-treatment** *n* mauvais traitement

**illuminate** *vt* illuminer, éclairer; *fig* éclairer, faire la lumière sur; (manuscript) enluminer

**illuminating** *adj* révélateur -trice, éclairant

**illumination** *n* (lighting) éclairage *m*; (flood-lighting) illumination *f*; (manuscript) enluminure *f*; *fig* lumière *f*, inspiration *f*; ~ s illuminations *fpl*

**illumine** *vt* éclairer, faire la lumière sur

**ill-usage** *n* mauvais traitement

**illusion** *n* illusion *f*; **be under an** ~ se faire des illusions

**illusionist** *n* illusionniste

**illusive** *adj* qui cause une illusion; (caused by illusion) illusoire; (deceptive) trompeur -euse

**illustrate** *vt* illustrer; *fig* illustrer, éclairer

**illustration** *n* illustration *f*; *fig* illustration *f*, exemple *m*

**illustrative** *adj* qui illustre, explicatif -ive

**illustrator** *n* illustrateur -trice

**illustrious** *adj* illustre, célèbre, glorieux -ieuse

**illustriousness** *n* gloire *f*, renommée *f*

**ill-will** *n* malveillance *f*, hostilité *f*

**image** *n* image *f*; (mirror, sth) réflexion *f*; (public impression of sth) image *f* de marque; *coll* **he is the spit** ~ **of his father** c'est son père tout craché; *vt* imager; refléter; imaginer

**imagery** *n* images *fpl*

**imaginable** *adj* imaginable

**imaginary** *adj* imaginaire, fictif -ive
**imagination** *n* imagination *f*
**imaginative** *adj* imaginatif -ive, plein d'imagination
**imaginativeness** *n* imagination *f*, esprit créateur
**imagine** *vt* (suppose) supposer, imaginer, croire; (to oneself) s'imaginer, se figurer
**imbalance** *n* déséquilibre *m*
**imbecile** *n* imbécile, idiot -e; *adj* imbécile, idiot, stupide
**imbecility** *n* imbécillité *f*, stupidité *f*
**imbibe** *vt* boire, absorber; *fig* assimiler; *vi coll* lever le coude, picoler
**imbricate** *vt* imbriquer; *vi* s'imbriquer; *adj* imbriqué
**imbroglio** *n* imbroglio *m*
**imbue** *vt* imprégner; *fig* imprégner, inculquer
**imitable** *adj* imitable
**imitate** *vt* imiter
**imitation** *n* imitation *f*; (counterfeit) contrefaçon *f*
**imitative** *adj* imitatif -ive; peu original
**imitator** *n* imitateur -trice
**immaculate** *adj* (pure) immaculé; (clean) tout propre; (faultless) irréprochable, impeccable; *theol* immaculé; **the Immaculate Conception** l'Immaculée Conception
**immanence, immanency** *n* immanence *f*
**immanent** *adj* immanent
**immaterial** *adj* insignifiant, négligeable, sans importance; (spiritual) immatériel -ielle
**immateriality** *n* insignifiance *f*
**immature** *adj* (person) jeune, peu avancé; (fruit) vert, pas mûr; **be ~** manquer de maturité
**immaturity** *n* manque *m* de maturité, immaturité *f*
**immeasurability** *n* incommensurabilité *f*
**immeasurable** *adj* incommensurable; énorme, vaste
**immediacy** *n* caractère immédiat
**immediate** *adj* immédiat, direct, instantané
**immemorial** *adj* immémorial
**immense** *adj* immense, vaste, énorme; *sl* épatant
**immensely** *adv* immensément, extrêmement
**immensity** *n* immensité *f*
**immensurable** *adj* incommensurable
**immerse** *vt* immerger, plonger; (baptism) baptiser par immersion; *fig* **~ oneself in** se plonger dans, être absorbé dans
**immersion** *n* immersion *f*; (baptism) baptême *m* par immersion; **~ heater** chauffe-eau *m invar* à élément chauffant

**immigrant** *n* immigrant -e; *adj* immigré
**immigrate** *vi* immigrer
**immigration** *n* immigration *f*
**imminence** *n* imminence *f*
**imminent** *adj* imminent
**immobile** *adj* immobile
**immobility** *n* immobilité *f*
**immobilize** *vt* immobiliser
**immoderate** *adj* excessif -ive, immodéré
**immoderation** *n* immodération *f*, excès *m*
**immodest** *adj* immodeste, impudique; arrogant, présomptueux -euse
**immodesty** *n* immodestie *f*, impudeur *f*; arrogance *f*, présomption *f*
**immolate** *vt* immoler
**immolation** *n* immolation *f*
**immoral** *adj* immoral
**immorality** *n* immoralité *f*; acte immoral
**immortal** *n* immortel -elle; *adj* immortel -elle, impérissable
**immortality** *n* immortalité *f*
**immortalize** *vt* immortaliser
**immortelle** *n bot* immortelle *f*
**immovability** *n* (officials) inamovibilité *f*; (immutability) immuabilité *f*; fixité *f*
**immovable** *adj* fixe; (resolution) inébranlable, immuable, impossible à déplacer; *leg* immobilier -ière; **~ s** *npl* immeubles *mpl*
**immune** *adj* immunisé, à l'abri
**immunity** *n* immunité *f*
**immunization** *n* immunisation *f*
**immunize** *vt* immuniser
**immure** *vt* emmurer, enfermer; **~ oneself** s'isoler
**immutability** *n* immutabilité *f*, immuabilité *f*
**immutable** *adj* immuable, inaltérable
**imp** *n* lutin *m*, diablotin *m*; (child) petit espiègle
**impact** *n* impact *m*, choc *m*; *vt* enfoncer; **~ ed tooth** dent incluse
**impair** *vt* (senses) affaiblir, abîmer; (injure) détériorer, diminuer
**impale** *vt* empaler
**impalpable** *adj* impalpable
**impanel** *v see* empanel
**impart** *vt* communiquer, transmettre, faire connaître
**impartial** *adj* impartial, objectif -ive
**impartiality** *n* impartialité *f*
**impassable** *adj* infranchissable
**impasse** *n* impasse *f*
**impassibility** *n* impassibilité *f*
**impassible** *adj* impassible
**impassion** *vt* exalter
**impassioned** *adj* exalté, fervent, passionné
**impassive** *adj* impassible
**impassivity** *n* impassibilité *f*

**impatience** *n* impatience *f*; intolérance *f*

**impatient** *adj* impatient; intolérant

**impeach** *vt pol* + *leg* mettre en accusation, entamer la procédure de destitution contre; (discredit) mettre en doute; *leg* ~ **a witness** récuser un témoin

**impeachment** *n pol* + *leg* mise *f* en accusation; (character) dénigrement *m*

**impeccable** *adj* impeccable, irréprochable

**impecuniosity** impécuniosité *f*, indigence *f*

**impecunious** *adj* impécunieux -ieuse, nécessiteux -euse

**impede** *vt* empêcher, gêner, entraver

**impediment** *n* (speech) défaut *m* de prononciation, défaut *m* d'élocution; obstacle *m*, entrave *f*

**impedimenta** *npl* bagages *mpl*

**impel** *vt* pousser, faire avancer; *fig* obliger, forcer, pousser

**impend** *vi* être imminent; planer

**impending** *adj* imminent, prochain; menaçant

**impenetrability** *n* impénétrabilité *f*

**impenetrable** *adj* impénétrable

**impenitence** *n* impénitence *f*

**impenitent** *adj* impénitent

**imperative** *n* exigence *f*, impératif *m*; *gramm* impératif *m*; *adj* impératif -ive, urgent, pressant; autoritaire

**imperceptibility** *n* imperceptibilité *f*

**imperceptible** *adj* imperceptible, minuscule

**imperceptive** *adj* peu perspicace

**imperfect** *n gramm* imparfait *m*; *adj* imparfait, incomplet -ète, défectueux -euse; *gramm* imparfait

**imperfectibility** *n* imperfectibilité *f*

**imperfectible** *adj* imperfectible

**imperfection** *n* imperfection *f*, défectuosité *f*

**imperforate** *adj* non perforé

**imperial** *n* (beard) barbe *f* à l'impériale; *adj* impérial; grandiose

**imperialism** *n* impérialisme *m*

**imperialist** *n* impérialiste

**imperialistic** *adj* impérialiste

**imperil** *vt* mettre en péril

**imperious** *adj* impérieux -ieuse, autoritaire; (need) urgent, pressant

**imperishable** *adj* impérissable; immortel -elle

**impermanence** *n* caractère *m* éphémère

**impermanent** *adj* éphémère, transitoire

**impermeable** *adj* imperméable, étanche; *fig* impénétrable

**impersonal** *adj* impersonnel -elle

**impersonality** *n* impersonnalité *f*

**impersonate** *vt* imiter; se faire passer pour; *leg* usurper l'identité de

**impersonation** *n* imitation *f*; *leg* usurpation *f* d'identité

**impersonator** *n* imitateur -trice; *leg* usurpateur -trice d'identité; **female** ~ travesti *m*

**impertinence** *n* impertinence *f*, insolence *f*; (irrelevance) manque *m* de rapport

**impertinent** *adj* impertinent, insolent; (irrelevant) sans rapport, hors de propos

**imperturbability** *n* imperturbabilité *f*

**imperturbable** *adj* imperturbable

**impervious** *adj* imperméable, étanche; ~ **to** sourd à

**impetigo** *n* impétigo *m*

**impetuosity, impetuousness** *n* impétuosité *f*, imprudence *f*, fougue *f*

**impetuous** *adj* impétueux -ueuse, imprudent, fougueux -euse

**impetuousness** *n see* impetuosity

**impetus** *n* force *f* d'impulsion; (momentum) élan *m*, vitesse *f*; *fig* élan *m*, impulsion *f*

**impiety** *n* impiété *f*

**impinge** *vi* ~ **on** toucher, affecter; (encroach) empiéter sur; (strike) frapper

**impingement** *n* empiétement *m*

**impious** *adj* impie

**impish** *adj* espiègle

**impishness** *n* espièglerie *f*

**implacability** *n* implacabilité *f*

**implacable** *adj* implacable

**implant** *n med* implant *m*; *vt* implanter; *fig* inculquer, inspirer

**implantation** *n* implantation *f*

**implausibility** *n* invraisemblance *f*

**implausible** *adj* invraisemblable, peu plausible

**implement** *n* outil *m*, instrument *m*; ~ **s** matériel *m*; *vt* exécuter, accomplir; (complete) achever

**implementation** *n* exécution *f*, accomplissement *m*

**implicate** *vt* impliquer, compromettre

**implication** *n* implication *f*; insinuation *f*

**implicit** *adj* implicite, tacite; (absolute) absolu, aveugle

**implied** *adj* sous-entendu, tacite

**implode** *vt* causer l'implosion de; *vi* imploser

**implore** *vt* implorer, supplier

**imploring** *adj* implorant, suppliant

**implosion** *n* implosion *f*

**imply** *vt* impliquer, suggérer, laisser entendre, insinuer

**impolite** *adj* impoli

**impoliteness** *n* impolitesse *f*

**impolitic** *adj* impolitique, malavisé

**imponderability** *n* impondérabilité *f*

**imponderable** *n* impondérable *m*; *adj* impondérable

**import** *n comm* importation *f*; (meaning) sens *m*, signification *f*; importance *f*; ~ **duty** droit *m* d'entrée; *comm* ~s articles *mpl* d'importation; *vt comm* importer; (meaning) signifier
**importable** *adj* importable
**importance** *n* importance *f*
**important** *adj* important
**importantly** *adv* d'un air important
**importation** *n* importation *f*
**importer** *n* importateur -trice
**importunate** *adj* importun; (insistent) harcelant
**importune** *vt* importuner; harceler; (prostitute) racoler; *vi* (prostitute) racoler
**importunity** *n* importunité *f*
**impose** *vt* imposer; (tax) imposer, taxer; (penalty) infliger; *vi* ~ **on** (upon) (mislead) tromper, duper; (take advantage of) abuser de
**imposing** *adj* imposant, impressionnant
**imposition** *n* imposition *f*, taxe *f*; (school) punition *f*
**impossibility** *n* impossibilité *f*
**impossible** *n* impossible *m*; *adj* impossible; (person) impossible, insupportable; *coll* invivable
**impost** *n* impôt *m*
**impostor** *n* imposteur *m*, charlatan *m*
**imposture** *n* imposture *f*
**impotence** *n* impuissance *f*, faiblesse *f*; (sexual) impuissance *f*; *med* impotence *f*
**impotent** *adj* impuissant, faible
**impound** *vt* saisir, confisquer; (confine) enfermer
**impoverish** *vt* appauvrir
**impoverishment** *n* appauvrissement *m*
**impracticability** *n* impraticabilité *f*
**impracticable** *adj* impraticable, impossible
**impractical** *adj* (person) peu pratique; (thing) pas pratique
**imprecation** *n* imprécation *f*, malédiction *f*
**imprecatory** *adj* imprécatoire
**impregnable** *adj* imprenable, inexpugnable; *fig* invincible
**impregnate** *vt* féconder; (saturate) imprégner
**impregnation** *n* fécondation *f*; imprégnation *f*
**impresario** *n* impresario *m*
**imprescriptible** *adj leg* imprescriptible
**impress** *n* empreinte *f*, marque *f*; *vt* (mark) imprimer, marquer; (make impression) impressionner, faire impression sur
**impression** *n* impression *f*; (mark) empreinte *f*, trace *f*; **be under the** ~ avoir une vague idée, avoir l'impression

**impressionability** *n* impressionnabilité *f*
**impressionable** *adj* impressionnable, sensible
**impressionism** *n* impressionnisme *m*
**impressionist** *n* + *adj* impressionniste
**impressionistic** *adj* impressionniste; subjectif -ive
**impressive** *adj* impressionnant, frappant, imposant
**impressiveness** *n* caractère impressionnant
**imprimatur** *n* imprimatur *m*
**imprint** *n* empreinte *f*, marque *f*; **under the** ~ **of** édité chez; *vt* imprimer, marquer
**imprison** *vt* emprisonner
**imprisonment** *n* emprisonnement *m*; **one month's** ~ un mois de prison
**improbability** *n* improbabilité *f*, invraisemblance *f*
**improbable** *adj* improbable, invraisemblable
**impromptu** *n* impromptu *m*; *adj* + *adv* impromptu
**improper** *adj* malséant, de mauvais goût; indécent, scabreux -euse; (dishonest) malhonnête
**impropriety** *n* inconvenance *f*
**improvable** *adj* susceptible d'amélioration
**improve** *vt* améliorer, perfectionner; (fortune, knowledge) augmenter, accroître; (land) bonifier; (landscape) embellir; (make good use of) tirer parti de, profiter de; *vi* s'améliorer; augmenter, s'accroître; ~ **on** faire mieux que
**improvement** *n* amélioration *f*, perfectionnement *m*; progrès *m*
**improvidence** *n* imprévoyance *f*
**improvident** *adj* imprévoyant; (spendthrift) prodigue
**improving** *adj* édifiant, moralisant
**improvisation** *n* improvisation *f*
**improvise** *vt* + *vi* improviser
**imprudence** *n* imprudence *f*
**imprudent** *adj* imprudent
**impudence** *n* impudence *f*, effronterie *f*
**impudent** *adj* impudent, effronté
**impudicity** *n* impudeur *f*
**impugn** *vt* attaquer, critiquer
**impulse** *n* impulsion *f*, élan *m*; (thrust) poussée *f*; **rash** ~ coup *m* de tête
**impulsion** *n* impulsion *f*
**impulsive** *adj* impulsif -ive, spontané, primesautier -ière; (force) irrésistible
**impulsively** *adv* sur impulsion
**impulsiveness** *n* impulsivité *f*
**impunity** *n* impunité *f*; **with** ~ impunément
**impure** *adj* impur; (immoral) impudique
**impurity** *n* impureté *f*; (immorality) impudicité *f*

**imputable**

**imputable** *adj* imputable
**imputation** *n* imputation *f*, accusation *f*
**impute** *vt* imputer, attribuer
**in** *n* the ~ s and outs les tenants et les
aboutissants; *prep* (place) dans, en, à;
(during) en, dans, pendant; (after)
dans, au bout de; (made of) en; (dress)
en, de; (towns) à; (countries) en, au(x);
~ **a week's time** dans une semaine, au
bout d'une semaine; ~ **cotton** en
coton; ~ **England** en Angleterre; ~
**Portugal** au Portugal; ~ **Rome** à
Rome; ~ **shorts** en short; ~ **so far as**
dans la mesure où; ~ **spring** au printemps; ~ **the country** à la campagne;
~ **the evening** le soir, dans la soirée,
pendant la soirée; ~ **the house** dans la
maison; ~ **town** en ville; ~ **winter** en
hiver; ~ **writing** par écrit; **dressed** ~
**wool** vêtu de laine; *adv* dedans, à
l'intérieur; **be** ~ (at home) être chez
soi, être là; (government) être au pouvoir; (candidate) être élu; *coll* être à la
mode; **be** ~ **for** aller avoir; (candidature) être candidat pour; *coll* **be** ~ **for**
**it** aller écoper; **be** ~ **on sth** (informed)
être au courant de qch; être dans le
coup; **be well** ~ **with** être en bons
termes avec; *coll* **have it** ~ **for** s/o
avoir une dent contre qn; *adj* intérieur
**inability** *n* incapacité *f*, impuissance *f*
**inaccessibility** *n* inaccessibilité *f*
**inaccessible** *adj* inaccessible; (person)
inabordable
**inaccuracy** *n* inexactitude *f*, imprécision
*f*
**inaccurate** *adj* inexact, imprécis; (wrong)
incorrect
**inaction** *n* inaction *f*, inactivité *f*;
paresse *f*
**inactive** *adj* inactif -ive; inerte
**inactivity** *n* inactivité *f*
**inadaptability** *n* incapacité *f* de
s'adapter
**inadaptable** *adj* incapable de s'adapter
**inadequacy** *n* insuffisance *f*, médiocrité
*f*, incompétence *f*
**inadequate** *adj* insuffisant, médiocre, incompétent; *psych* mal adapté
**inadmissibility** *n* inadmissibilité *f*
**inadmissible** *adj* inadmissible, inacceptable; *leg* (evidence) irrecevable
**inadvertence, inadvertency** *n* inattention *f*, inadvertence *f*, mégarde *f*
**inadvertent** *adj* inattentif -ive, par mégarde
**inadvisability** *n* inopportunité *f*
**inadvisable** *adj* inopportun, peu recommandable
**inalienable** *adj* inaliénable
**inane** *adj* stupide, inepte, vide; ~
**remark** ineptie *f*

**inanimate** *adj* inanimé
**inanition** *n* inanition *f*
**inanity** *n* ineptie *f*
**inappetence** *n* inappétence *f*, indifférence *f*
**inapplicability** *n* impossibilité *f* d'être
mis en vigueur (pratique); (relevance)
manque *m* de rapport
**inapplicable** *adj* inapplicable
**inapplication** *n* inapplication *f*, défaut
*m* d'application
**inapposite** *adj* sans rapport, hors de
propos
**inappreciable** *adj* inappréciable
**inapproachable** *adj* réservé, distant
**inappropriate** *adj* inopportun, mal à
propos
**inappropriateness** *n* inopportunité *f*
**inapt** *adj* inapte, incapable
**inaptitude, inaptness** *n* inaptitude *f*,
incapacité *f*
**inarticulate** *adj* (speech) mal prononcé,
inarticulé; (person) incohérent, qui
s'exprime avec difficulté; *anat* inarticulé
**inarticulateness** *n* incohérence *f*
**inartistic** *adj* peu artistique; (person)
peu artiste
**inasmuch** *adv* ~ **as** vu que, attendu que
**inattention** *n* inattention *f*, manque *m*
d'attention
**inattentive** *adj* inattentif -ive, distrait
**inaudibility** *n* imperceptibilité *f*
**inaudible** *adj* inaudible
**inaugural** *adj* inaugural
**inaugurate** *vt* inaugurer; (person) investir de ses fonctions
**inauguration** *n* inauguration *f*; (person)
investiture *f*
**inauspicious** *adj* de mauvais augure, peu
propice; (unfavourable) malencontreux -euse
**inboard** *adj naut* intérieur; *adv naut* à
bord, à l'intérieur
**inborn** *adj* inné
**inbred** *adj* inné; (engendering) né de
parents consanguins
**inbreed** *vt* croiser; *vi* être croisé
**inbreeding** *n* unions consanguines
**incalculable** *adj* incalculable, imprévisible
**incandescence** *n* incandescence *f*
**incandescent** *adj* incandescent
**incantation** *n* incantation *f*
**incapability** *n* incapacité *f*
**incapable** *adj* incapable, incompétent;
(physically helpless) impotent; *leg* incapable; ~ **of proof** impossible à
prouver
**incapacitate** *vt* rendre incapable; *leg*
frapper d'incapacité
**incapacitation** *n* incapacité *f*

incapacity *n* incapacité *f*, incompétence *f*; (helplessness) impotence *f*; *leg* incapacité *f*

incarcerate *vt* incarcérer

incarceration *n* incarcération *f*, emprisonnement *m*

incarnadine *adj* incarnat

incarnate *adj* incarné; *vt* incarner

incarnation *n* incarnation *f*

incautious *adj* imprudent, inconsidéré

incautiousness *n* imprudence *f*

incendiarism *n* incendie criminel

incendiary *n* (person) incendiaire; (bomb) bombe *f* incendiaire; *fig* agitateur -trice; *adj* incendiaire

¹incense *n* encens *m*; *vt* encenser

²incense *vt* exaspérer, rendre furieux -ieuse, mettre en colère

incensory *n* encensoir *m*

incentive *n* motivation *f*, bonne raison; *comm* **provide** ~ s donner des primes; *adj* stimulant, encourageant; ~ **bonus** prime *f* d'encouragement; (pieceworker) prime *f* de rendement

incertitude *n* incertitude *f*, doute *m*

incessant *adj* incessant, ininterrompu, continu

incest *n* inceste *m*

incestuous *adj* incestueux -ueuse

inch *n* pouce *m*; ~ es hauteur *f*; ~ by ~ , by ~ es petit à petit; be every ~ an artist être artiste jusqu'au bout des ongles; within ~ es of à deux doigts de; *vt* ~ sth forward faire avancer qch peu à peu; *vi* ~ forward avancer peu à peu

inchoate *adj* naissant, débutant; (undeveloped) rudimentaire; *vt* + *vi* commencer

inch-tape *n* = centimètre *m*

incidence *n* fréquence *f*; *phys* incidence *f*

incident *n* incident *m*, événement *m*; (fiction) épisode *m*; *adj* associé; *leg* attaché

incidental *n* chose fortuite; *adj* fortuit, accidentel -elle; (subordinate) accessoire; ~ **expenses** frais *mpl* accessoires; ~ **music** *theat* musique *f* de scène; *cin* musique *f* de film

incidentally *adv* incidemment; (by the way) à propos

incinerate *vt* incinérer

incineration *n* incinération *f*

incinerator *n* incinérateur *m*

incipient *adj* naissant, commençant

incise *vt* inciser; (engrave) graver

incision *n* incision *f*, coupure *f*; *surg* incision *f*; *fig* tranchant *m*

incisive *adj* incisif -ive, acéré, tranchant; lucide

incisiveness *n* tranchant *m*, pénétration *f*, lucidité *f*

incisor *n* incisive *f*

incitation *n* incitation *f*

incite *vt* inciter, pousser, encourager

incitement *n* incitation *f*

incivility *n* incivilité *f*, impolitesse *f*

inclemency *n* inclémence *f*, rigueur *f*

inclement *adj* inclément, rigoureux -euse

inclination *n* inclination *f*, pente *f*, inclinaison *f*; (liking) inclination *f*, penchant *m*

incline *n* inclination *f*, pente *f*; *vt* incliner, pencher; *vi* s'incliner, pencher, se courber; be ~ d to incliner à, être enclin à; be well ~ d towards s/o être bien disposé à l'égard de qn

inclose *v see* enclose

inclosure *n see* enclosure

include *vt* inclure, comprendre, englober; *sl* ~ out exclure

including *prep* inclus, y compris; ~ service service compris

inclusion *n* inclusion *f*

inclusive *adj* inclus, compris; ~ charge prix *m* tout compris

incognito *n* incognito *m*; *adj* dans l'incognito; *adv* incognito

incoherence *n* incohérence *f*

incoherent *adj* incohérent

incoherently *adv* d'une façon incohérente

incohesive *adj* sans cohésion

incombustibility *n* incombustibilité *f*

incombustible *adj* incombustible

income *n* revenu *m*; (unearned) rente(s) *f*(*pl*); ~ tax impôt *m* sur le revenu; ~ tax collector percepteur *m* des contributions directes; ~ s policy politique *f* des revenus; taxable ~ revenu *m* imposable

incomer *n* arrivant -e; (immigrant) immigrant -e

incoming *adj* entrant, qui arrive, nouveau (*f* nouvelle); ~ tide marée montante

incommensurable *adj* incommensurable

incommensurate *adj* sans rapport, disproportionné; (inadequate) insuffisant; incommensurable

incommode *vt* incommoder, gêner

incommodious *adj* incommode; (small) trop petit

incommodity *n* incommodité *f*

incommunicable *adj* incommunicable

incommunicado *adj* tenu au secret; *adv* au secret

incomparable *adj* incomparable, sans pareil -eille

incompatibility *n* incompatibilité *f*

incompatible *adj* incompatible

incompetence *n* incompétence *f*, incapacité *f*

incompetent *adj* incompétent, incapable

**incomplete** *adj* incomplet -ète, inachevé
**incompleteness** *n* état incomplet
**incomprehensibility** *n* incompréhensibilité *f*
**incomprehensible** *adj* incompréhensible; (hand-writing) indéchiffrable
**incomprehension** *n* incompréhension *f*
**incomprehensive** *adj* incompréhensif -ive; incomplet -ète
**inconceivable** *adj* inconcevable
**inconceivably** *adv* à un degré inconcevable
**inconclusive** *adj* peu concluant; sans résultat
**incongruity** *n* incongruité *f*, inconvenance *f*, disproportion *f*
**incongruous** *adj* incongru, déplacé; (unsuitable) peu convenable; absurde; incompatible, disparate
**inconsequence** *n* inconséquence *f*
**inconsequent** *adj* inconséquent, illogique
**inconsequential** *adj* inconséquent, sans importance
**inconsiderable** *adj* insignifiant
**inconsiderate** *adj* (person) qui manque d'égards; (action, speech) inconsidéré, irréfléchi
**inconsistency** *n* inconsistance *f*, inconséquence *f*
**inconsistent** *adj* inconsistant, inconséquent
**inconsolable** *adj* inconsolable
**inconspicuous** *adj* peu voyant, qui passe inaperçu
**inconstancy** *n* inconstance *f*
**inconstant** *adj* inconstant, changeant; (fickle) volage
**incontestability** *n* incontestabilité *f*
**incontestable** *adj* incontestable, indiscutable
**incontinence** *n* incontinence *f*
**incontinent** *adj* incontinent; qui ne peut se retenir
**incontrollable** *adj* irrésistible, qui ne peut être contenu
**incontrovertible** *adj* indéniable, irréfutable
**inconvenience** *n* inconvénient *m*, désagrément *m*; (trouble) dérangement *m*; *vt* déranger, incommoder
**inconvenient** *adj* inopportun, gênant; (uncomfortable) incommode
**inconvertibility** *n econ* non-convertibilité *f*, inconvertibilité *f*
**inconvertible** *adj econ* inconvertible
**incorporate** *adj* incorporel -elle; uni; *vt* incorporer, contenir; *leg* ~ **with** former une société avec; *vi leg* se constituer en société
**incorporation** *n* incorporation *f*
**incorporeal** *adj* incorporel -elle

**incorrect** *adj* incorrect, inexact, erroné; (conduct) incorrect, déplacé
**incorrectness** *n* incorrection *f*, inexactitude *f*, erreur *f*
**incorrigible** *adj* incorrigible
**incorruptibility** *n* incorruptibilité *f*
**incorruptible** *adj* incorruptible
**increase** *n* augmentation *f*; (growth) croissance *f*, accroissement *m*, agrandissement *m*; **on the** ~ en augmentation; *vt* augmenter, accroître, agrandir; *vi* augmenter, croître, monter
**increasing** *adj* croissant
**increasingly** *adv* de plus en plus
**incredibility** *n* incrédibilité *f*
**incredible** *adj* incroyable, inimaginable; *coll fig* extraordinaire, fantastique
**incredulity** *n* incrédulité *f*
**incredulous** *adj* incrédule
**incredulousness** *n* incrédulité *f*
**increment** *n* (salary) augmentation *f*
**incremental** *adj* par augmentation; ~ **scale** échelle *f* des salaires
**incriminate** *vt* incriminer; accuser d'un crime
**incrimination** *n* incrimination *f*; accusation *f*
**incriminatory** *adj* compromettant
**incrust** *v see* encrust
**incrustation** *n see* encrustation
**incubate** *vt* couver, incuber; *vi* couver
**incubation** *n* incubation *f*
**incubator** *n* incubateur *m*, couveuse *f*
**incubus** *n* incube *m*; (anxiety) poids *m*; (nightmare) cauchemar *m*
**inculcate** *vt* inculquer
**inculcation** *n* inculcation *f*
**inculpate** *vt* (accuse) inculper; incriminer
**inculpation** *n* inculpation *f*
**incumbency** *n eccles* charge *f*
**incumbent** *n eccles* titulaire *m* (d'une charge); *adj* obligatoire; **be** ~ **on s/o** incomber à qn
**incunabula** *npl* incunables *mpl*
**incur** *vt* (be liable to) encourir, s'attirer; (debts) contracter
**incurability** *n* incurabilité *f*
**incurable** *n* incurable; *adj* incurable, inguérissable
**incurious** *adj* incurieux -ieuse, sans curiosité
**incursion** *n* incursion *f*
**indebted** *adj* redevable
**indebtedness** *n* dette(s) *f* (*pl*)
**indecency** *n* indécence *f*; *leg* outrage *m* à la pudeur
**indecent** *adj* indécent; (unseemly) malséant; *leg* ~ **assault** attentat *m* à la pudeur; *leg* ~ **exposure** outrage *m* à la pudeur

**indecipherable** *adj* indéchiffrable
**indecision** *n* indécision *f*
**indecisive** *adj* indécisif -ive, irrésolu, incertain
**indeclinable** *adj gramm* indéclinable
**indecorous** *adj* inconvenant, peu convenable
**indecorousness** *n* inconvenance *f*
**indecorum** *n* inconvenance *f*, manquement *m* aux usages
**indeed** *adv* (truly) vraiment; (corroboration) en effet; *interj* (corroboration) en
effet!; mais certainement!; *iron* vraiment?
**indefatigable** *adj* infatigable, inlassable
**indefeasible** *adj leg* qui ne peut pas être
annulé
**indefensible** *adj* indéfendable, injustifiable, insoutenable
**indefinable** *adj* indéfinissable
**indefinite** *adj* indéfini, incertain, vague;
(unlimited) illimité
**indelibility** *n* indélébilité *f*
**indelible** *adj* indélébile; *fig* ineffaçable
**indelicacy** *n* indélicatesse *f*; (words)
grossièreté *f*
**indelicate** *adj* indélicat; (coarse) grossier
-ière; indécent
**indemnification** *n* indemnisation *f*; (sum)
indemnité *f*, dédommagement *m*
**indemnify** *vt* indemniser, dédommager;
(safeguard) garantir
**indemnity** *n* indemnité *f*, dédommagement *m*; (insurance) garantie *f*, assurance *f*
**indent** *n* (notch) encoche *f*; (dent) bosselure *f*; (edge) dentelure *f*; *comm* commande *f*; *leg see* **indenture**; *vt* encocher;
bosseler; denteler; *vi comm* ~ **for**
commander
**indentation** *n* (notch) encoche *f*; (dent)
bosselure *f*; (edge) dentelure *f*; (imprint) empreinte *f*; *comm* acte *m* de
passer une commande
**indenture** *n leg* contrat *m* synallagma-
tique; (apprentice) contrat *m* d'apprentissage; *vt leg* lier par contrat
(d'apprentissage)
**independence** *n* indépendance *f*, autonomie *f*
**independent** *n pol* député non inscrit;
*adj* indépendant, autonome; (uninflu-
enced) original; **have** ~ **means** vivre de
ses rentes, avoir une fortune personnelle
**indescribable** *adj* indescriptible; inexprimable, indicible
**indestructibility** *n* indestructibilité *f*
**indestructible** *adj* indestructible
**indeterminable** *adj* indéterminable
**indeterminate** *adj* indéterminé; vague,
incertain

**indetermination** *n* indétermination *f*,
irrésolution *f*, hésitation *f*
**index** *n* (*pl* **indices, indexes**) (book)
index *m*, table *f* des matières; (library)
catalogue *m*; (pointer) aiguille *f*, index
*m*; *math* exposant *m*; *fig* indice *m*,
signe *m*; *ar eccles* **the Index** l'Index *m*;
*vt* (book) mettre un index à; (word)
mettre dans l'index
**index-finger** *n* index *m*
**India** *n* Inde *f*, les Indes *fpl*
**Indian** *n* Indien -ienne; (American)
Indien -ienne d'Amérique; **Red** ~
Peau-Rouge (*pl* Peaux-Rouges); *adj*
indien -ienne; (American) amérindien
-ienne; ~ **club** massue *f* de gymnastique; ~ **corn** maïs *m*; ~ **file** file
indienne; ~ **ink** encre *f* de Chine; ~
**summer** été *m* de la Saint-Martin
**india-paper** *n* papier *m* bible
**indiarubber** *n* (substance) caoutchouc
*m*; (eraser) gomme *f*
**indicate** *vt* indiquer, montrer; (reveal)
révéler, dénoter; (be a sign of) dénoter,
être l'indice de; (make known) faire
connaître, signaler; *med* indiquer
**indication** *n* indication *f*, indice *m*, signe
*m*
**indicative** *n gramm* indicatif *m*; *adj*
indicatif -ive
**indicator** *n* indicateur *m*; (pointer)
aiguille *f*, index *m*; *mot* clignotant *m*
**indict** *vt leg* accuser, mettre en accusation; *fig* porter une accusation contre
**indictable** *adj leg* ~ **offence** délit pénal
**indictment** *n leg* acte *m* d'accusation; *fig*
accusation *f*
**indifference** *n* indifférence *f*
**indifferent** *adj* indifférent; médiocre,
quelconque
**indigence** *n* indigence *f*
**indigenous** *adj* indigène, autochtone
**indigent** *adj* indigent, très pauvre
**indigestible** *adj* indigeste
**indigestion** *n* indigestion *f*, dyspepsie *f*;
**attack of** ~ indigestion *f*
**indignant** *adj* indigné, furieux -ieuse;
**grow** ~ s'indigner
**indignation** *n* indignation *f*
**indignity** *n* indignité *f*, affront *m*
**indigo** *n* indigo *m*; *adj* indigo *invar*
**indirect** *adj* indirect; (route, etc) détourné; ~ **taxes** contributions indirectes
**indirectness** *n* caractère indirect
**indiscernible** *adj* indiscernable, imperceptible
**indiscipline** *n* indiscipline *f*
**indiscreet** *adj* indiscret -ète; imprudent
**indiscretion** *n* indiscrétion *f*; imprudence *f*; **youthful** ~ péché *m* de jeunesse
**indiscriminate** *adj* qui manque de

discernement; (without distinctions) fait au hasard; confus

**indispensable** *adj* indispensable, essentiel -ielle

**indispose** *vt* mécontenter, indisposer; rendre malade

**indisposed** *adj* souffrant, indisposé

**indisposition** *n* indisposition *f*, malaise *m*; (unwillingness) manque *m* de bonne volonté

**indisputable** *adj* indiscutable, incontestable

**indissoluble** *adj* indissoluble; *chem* insoluble

**indistinct** *adj* indistinct, peu clair; vague, confus, faible

**indistinguishable** *adj* qu'on ne distingue pas; imperceptible, insaisissable

**individual** *n* individu *m*; *adj* individuel -elle; original, particulier -ière

**individualism** *n* individualisme *m*

**individualist** *n* + *adj* individualiste

**individuality** *n* individualité *f*

**individualize** *vt* individualiser

**individually** *adv* individuellement, séparément

**indivisibility** *n* indivisibilité *f*

**indivisible** *adj* indivisible

**Indo-China** *n* Indo-Chine *f*

**indocile** *adj* indocile

**indoctrinate** *vt* endoctriner

**indoctrination** *n* endoctrinement *m*

**Indo-European** *n* *ling* indo-européen *m*; *adj* indo-européen -éenne

**indolence** *n* indolence *f*, nonchalance *f*

**indolent** *adj* indolent, nonchalant, paresseux -euse

**indomitable** *adj* indomptable, invincible

**Indonesian** *n* Indonésien -ienne; (language) indonésien *m*; *adj* indonésien -ienne

**indoor** *adj* d'intérieur; (swimming-pool) couvert; (game) pratiqué en intérieur

**indoors** *adv* à l'intérieur, à la maison

**indorse** *v see* endorse

**indorsee** *n see* endorsee

**indorsement** *n see* endorsement

**indubitable** *adj* indubitable, incontestable

**induce** *vt* persuader; causer, provoquer, amener; *philos* induire, conclure; *elect* produire par induction; *med* ~ **labour** déclencher l'accouchement

**inducement** *n* motif *m*, encouragement *m*; (incentive) motivation *f*; (bribe) pot-de-vin *m* (*pl* pots-de-vin)

**induct** *vt* installer; *US mil* incorporer

**induction** *n* *philos* + *elect* induction *f*; *eccles* installation *f*; *psych* provocation *f*; *elect* ~ **coil** bobine *f* d'induction

**inductive** *adj* inductif -ive; *elect* inducteur -trice

**inductor** *n* inducteur *m*

**indulge** *vt* (spoil) gâter; (yield to) céder à; (desire) satisfaire, donner libre cours à; *vi* ~ **in** s'adonner à, se permettre

**indulgence** *n* indulgence *f*, complaisance *f*, satisfaction *f*; *eccles* indulgence *f*

**indulgent** *adj* indulgent, complaisant, compréhensif -ive, accommodant

**indurate** *vt* *med* indurer; *vi* *med* s'indurer

**induration** *n* *med* induration *f*

**industrial** *adj* industriel -ielle; (disease) professionnel -elle; ~ **action** action revendicative, grève *f*; ~ **medicine** médecine *f* du travail

**industrialism** *n* industrialisme *m*

**industrialist** *n* industriel *m*

**industrialization** *n* industrialisation *f*

**industrialize** *vt* industrialiser

**industrious** *adj* travailleur -euse, industrieux -ieuse, courageux -euse

**industriousness** *n* assiduité *f*

**industry** *n* industrie *f*; (hard work) assiduité *f*, zèle *m*

**inebriate** *n* ivrogne, alcoolique; *adj* saoul, ivre; *vt* saouler, griser

**inebriation, inebriety** *n* ébriété *f*, ivresse *f*

**inedible** *adj* non comestible; (disgusting) immangeable

**ineffable** *adj* inexprimable, indicible

**ineffaceable** *adj* ineffaçable, indélébile

**ineffective, ineffectual, inefficacious** *adj* inefficace, sans effet; inutile, plat; incompétent

**inefficacy** *n* inefficacité *f*

**inefficiency** *n* inefficacité *f*, incompétence *f*

**inefficient** *adj* inefficace, incompétent, incapable

**inelastic** *adj* inélastique; rigide

**inelasticity** *n* inélasticité *f*

**inelegance** *n* inélégance *f*, manque *m* d'élégance

**inelegant** *adj* inélégant, sans élégance

**ineligibility** *n* inéligibilité *f*

**ineligible** *adj* inéligible; (without rights) n'ayant pas droit

**ineluctable** *adj* inéluctable, inévitable

**inept** *adj* inepte, stupide, absurde

**ineptitude** *n* ineptie *f*, sottise *f*

**inequality** *n* inégalité *f*

**inequitable** *adj* inéquitable, injuste

**inequity** *n* inéquité *f*, injustice *f*

**ineradicable** *adj* indéracinable, tenace

**inerrable** *adj* infaillible

**inert** *adj* inerte

**inertia** *n* inertie *f*, apathie *f*; ~ **reel belt** ceinture *f* de sécurité à enrouleurs; *comm* ~ **selling** vente *f* par envoi forcé

**inescapable** *adj* inévitable, inéluctable

**inessential** *adj* non-essentiel -ielle, superflu

**inestimable** *adj* inestimable, incalculable

**inevitability** *n* inévitabilité *f*

**inevitable** *adj* inévitable, inéluctable

**inexact** *adj* inexact, erroné

**inexactitude** *n* inexactitude *f*

**inexcusable** *adj* inexcusable, impardonnable

**inexhaustible** *adj* inépuisable

**inexhaustive** *adj* peu approfondi

**inexorability** *n* inexorabilité *f*

**inexorable** *adj* inexorable

**inexpedient** *adj* malavisé

**inexpensive** *adj* peu cher (*f* chère), bon marché

**inexperience** *n* inexpérience *f*, manque *m* d'expérience

**inexperienced** *adj* inexpérimenté

**inexpert** *adj* inexpert, maladroit

**inexpiable** *adj* inexpiable

**inexplicable** *adj* inexplicable

**inexpressible** *adj* inexprimable

**inexpugnable** *adj* inexpugnable; invincible

**inextinguishable** *adj* inextinguible

**inextricable** *adj* inextricable

**infallibility** *n* infaillibilité *f*

**infallible** *adj* infaillible

**infamous** *adj* infâme, abominable

**infamy** *n* infamie *f*

**infancy** *n* petite enfance, bas âge; *leg* minorité *f*

**infant** *n* (baby) nouveau-né (*f* -née), bébé *m*; *leg* mineur -e; *adj* infantile

**infanta** *n* infante *f*

**infante** *n* infant *m*

**infanticide** *n* infanticide *m*; (person) infanticide

**infantile** *adj* infantile, enfantin, puéril; ~ **paralysis** poliomyélite *f*

**infantilism** *n* infantilisme *m*

**infantry** *n* infanterie *f*

**infantryman** *n* fantassin *m*

**infatuate** *vt* tourner la tête à

**infatuated** *adj* entiché; **be ~ with** (person) avoir le béguin pour; (idea) s'engouer de

**infatuation** *n* béguin *m*; (idea) engouement *m*

**infect** *vt* infecter, contaminer; (disease) transmettre; *fig* corrompre

**infection** *n* infection *f*, contamination *f*, contagion *f*; **ear ~** otite *f*; **throat ~** angine *f*

**infectious** *adj* infectieux -ieuse, contagieux -ieuse

**infectiousness** *n med* nature infectieuse; *fig* contagion *f*

**infective** *adj* infectueux -euse

**infelicitous** *adj* malheureux -euse; (inappropriate) mal à propos; fâcheux -euse

**infelicity** *n* malheur *m*; inopportunité *f*, maladresse *f*

**infer** *vt* inférer, conclure, déduire

**inference** *n* inférence *f*, conclusion *f*, déduction *f*

**inferential** *adj* déductif -ive

**inferior** *n* inférieur -e; (rank) subalterne; *adj* inférieur

**inferiority** *n* infériorité *f*; ~ **complex** complexe *m* d'infériorité

**infernal** *adj* infernal, diabolique; ~ **machine** bombe *f* à retardement; objet piégé

**inferno** *n* enfer *m*

**infertile** *adj* infertile, infécond, stérile

**infest** *vt* infester

**infestation** *n* infestation *f*

**infidel** *n* infidèle, païen -ienne

**infidelity** *n* infidélité *f*

**infighting** *n* corps à corps *m*; *fig* luttes *fpl* internes

**infiltrate** *vt* (liquid) infiltrer; (troops) faire s'infiltrer; (spy, etc) noyauter

**infiltration** *n* infiltration *f*; *pol* noyautage *m*

**infinite** *n* infini *m*; *adj* infini, sans bornes

**infinitesimal** *adj* infinitésimal, infime

**infinitive** *n gramm* infinitif *m*; *adj* infinitif -ive

**infinitude** *n* infinité *f*

**infinity** *n* infinité *f*

**infirm** *adj* infirme; (hesitant) irrésolu, indécis

**infirmary** *n* hôpital *m*; (sick bay) infirmerie *f*

**infirmity** *n* infirmité *f*; (disease) maladie *f*; (hesitation) irrésolution *f*, indécision *f*

**infix** *vt* insérer

**inflame** *vt* enflammer, mettre en feu; *med* enflammer; *fig* envenimer, exacerber; *vi* s'enflammer, prendre feu; *med* s'enflammer; *fig* s'échauffer

**inflammable** *adj* inflammable; *US* ignifuge

**inflammation** *n* inflammation *f*

**inflammatory** *adj* incendiaire; *med* inflammatoire

**inflate** *vt* (air, gas) gonfler; (prices) hausser; *econ* augmenter la quantité de (monnaie en circulation); *fig* enfler

**inflated** *adj* (air, gas) gonflé; (prices) gonflé, exagéré; (style) enflé, boursouflé

**inflation** *n* (air, gas) gonflement *m*; (prices) hausse *f*; *econ* inflation *f*

**inflationary** *adj* inflationniste

**inflationism** *n* politique *f* inflationniste

**inflationist** *adj* inflationniste

**inflect** *vt* (bend) courber, fléchir; (voice) moduler; *gramm* modifier la désinence de; *vi gramm* prendre une désinence

**inflection** *n see* **inflexion**

inflectional

**inflectional** *adj see* **inflexional**
**inflexibility** *n* rigidité *f*; *fig* inflexibilité *f*
**inflexible** *adj* rigide; *fig* inflexible
**inflexion, inflection** *n* (voice) modulation *f*; *gramm* (process) modification *f* de désinence; (ending) désinence *f*
**inflexional, inflectional** *adj ling* flexionnel -elle, désinentiel -ielle
**inflict** *vt* infliger, faire subir
**infliction** *n* infliction *f*
**inflow** *n* afflux *m*
**influence** *n* influence *f*; (drink, drugs, etc) **under the ~ of** sous l'effet de, sous l'empire de; *vt* influencer, influer sur, persuader
**influential** *adj* influent
**influenza** *n* grippe *f*
**influx** *n* afflux *m*, flot *m*; (confluence) confluent *m*
**info** *n sl abbr* tuyaux *mpl*
**inform** *vt* informer, avertir, aviser, tenir au courant; *vi* ~ **against** dénoncer, informer contre
**informal** *adj* simple, sans façons; informel -elle, dénué de formalité; (unofficial) officieux -ieuse; ~ **dress** tenue *f* de ville
**informality** *n* simplicité *f*, absence *f* de formalité
**informant** *n* informateur -trice
**information** *n* information(s) *f(pl)*, renseignements *mpl*; (knowledge) connaissances *fpl*; *leg* dénonciation *f*; **for your ~** à titre de renseignement
**informative, informatory** *adj* instructif -ive
**informed** *adj* informé; (enlightened) éclairé
**informer** *n* dénonciateur -trice, délateur -trice; (police) indicateur -trice
**infra** *adv* au-dessous; *coll* ~ **dig** au-dessous de sa dignité
**infraction** *n* infraction *f*
**infrangible** *adj* incassable
**infra-red** *adj* infrarouge
**infrequency** *n* rareté *f*
**infrequent** *adj* peu fréquent, rare; peu normal
**infringe** *vt* enfreindre, transgresser, contrevenir à
**infringement** *n* infraction *f*, contravention *f*; ~ **of patent** contrefaçon *f* d'une fabrication brevetée
**infuriate** *vt* rendre furieux -ieuse, exaspérer
**infuriating** *adj* exaspérant
**infuse** *vt* infuser; *fig* inspirer, insuffler
**infusion** *n* infusion *f*
**ingenious** *adj* ingénieux -ieuse, astucieux -ieuse
**ingenue** *n* ingénue *f*
**ingenuity** *n* ingéniosité *f*

**ingenuous** *adj* ingénu, naïf (*f* naïve); (candid) sincère, ouvert
**ingenuousness** *n* ingénuité *f*, naïveté *f*; sincérité *f*
**ingest** *vt* ingérer
**ingestion** *n* ingestion *f*
**ingle-nook** *n* coin *m* du feu
**inglorious** *adj* peu glorieux -ieuse, honteux -euse
**ingot** *n* lingot *m*
**ingrained** *adj* invétéré, enraciné, ancré
**ingratiate** *vt* ~ **oneself with s/o** s'insinuer dans les bonnes grâces de qn
**ingratiating** *adj* insinuant
**ingratitude** *n* ingratitude *f*
**ingredient** *n* ingrédient *m*
**ingress** *n* entrée *f*
**ingrowing** *adj* ~ **nail** ongle incarné
**ingurgitate** *vt* ingurgiter, avaler
**inhabit** *vt* habiter
**inhabitable** *adj* habitable
**inhabitant** *n* habitant -e
**inhabitation** *n* habitation *f*
**inhalation** *n* inhalation *f*, aspiration *f*
**inhale** *vt* aspirer, inhaler, avaler; *vi* (smoking) avaler la fumée
**inhaler** *n* inhalateur *m*
**inharmonious** *adj* inharmonieux -ieuse, discordant
**inhere** *vi* être inhérent
**inherence** *n* inhérence *f*
**inherent** *adj* inhérent
**inherently** *adv* en soi
**inherit** *vt* hériter, hériter de; *vi* hériter
**inheritable** *adj* qu'on peut recevoir en héritage
**inheritance** *n* héritage *m*, patrimoine *m*; (process of inheriting) succession *f*
**inheritor** *n* héritier -ière
**inhibit** *vt* entraver, empêcher; (desire) maîtriser; *psych* inhiber; (forbid) interdire
**inhibited** *adj* inhibé, ayant des inhibitions
**inhibition** *n* inhibition *f*; *leg* interdiction *f*
**inhibitory** *adj* inhibiteur -trice; *leg* prohibitif -ive
**inhospitable** *adj* (climate, etc) inhospitalier -ière; (person) peu accueillant, désagréable
**inhuman** *adj* inhumain
**inhumane** *adj* cruel (*f* cruelle), inhumain, brutal
**inhumanity** *n* inhumanité *f*, cruauté *f*, brutalité *f*
**inhumation** *n* inhumation *f*, enterrement *m*
**inhume** *vt* inhumer, enterrer
**inimical** *adj* inamical, hostile, ennemi
**inimitable** *adj* inimitable; *coll* impayable

548

**iniquitous** *adj* inique
**iniquity** *n* iniquité *f*
**initial** *n* (lettre) initiale *f*; ~s initiales *fpl*; *adj* initial, premier -ière; *vt* parafer, parapher
**initially** *adv* au début, au commencement, initialement
**initiate** *n* initié -e; *adj* initié; *vt* (admit) initier; (originate) inaugurer, lancer, amorcer; *leg* intenter
**initiation** *n* (admission) initiation *f*, admission *f*; (beginning) commencement *m*, début *m*
**initiative** *n* initiative *f*
**initiator** *n* initiateur -trice
**inject** *vt* injecter, faire une piqûre à (qn); *fig* insuffler
**injection** *n* injection *f*, piqûre *f*
**in-joke** *n coll* plaisanterie comprise seulement par les initiés
**injudicious** *adj* malavisé, peu judicieux -ieuse
**injunction** *n leg* injonction *f*; ordre *m*
**injure** *vt* (hurt) blesser; (wrong) faire un tort à; *leg* léser
**injured** *adj* blessé; *fig* offensé; *leg* lésé
**injurious** *adj* nuisible, préjudiciable
**injury** *n* blessure *f*; (wrong) tort *m*; *leg* lésion *f*
**injustice** *n* injustice *f*
**ink** *n* encre *f*; *vt* encrer; ~ **in** repasser à l'encre
**inkling** *n* soupçon *m*, idée *f* vague; **have no** ~ ne pas avoir la moindre idée
**inkstand** *n* encrier *m*
**inkwell** *n* encrier *m* (de pupitre)
**inky** *adj* taché d'encre; (darkness) noir comme de l'encre
**inland** *adj* intérieur; ~ **revenue** fisc *m*; (money received) contributions directes; *adv* à l'intérieur
**in-laws** *npl* belle famille
**inlay** *n* incrustation *f*; (wood) marqueterie *f*; (floor) parquet *m*; *vt* incruster; marqueter; parqueter
**inlet** *n* crique *f*, bras de mer; *mech* arrivée *f*; ~ **pipe** tuyau *m* d'arrivée
**inly** *adv* secrètement, intimement
**inmate** *n* (hospital) hospitalisé -e; (asylum) interné -e; (prison) détenu -e
**inmost** *adj* le plus profond, le plus secret (*f* la plus secrète)
**inn** *n* auberge *f*; **Inns of Court** écoles *fpl* de droit à Londres
**innards** *npl coll* entrailles *fpl*
**innate** *adj* inné, naturel -elle
**innateness** *n* innéité *f*
**inner** *n* (target) zone *f* autour du mille; *adj* intérieur, interne; *fig* intime, secret -ète; *mot* ~ **tube** chambre *f* à air
**innermost** *adj* le plus profond, le plus secret (*f* la plus secrète)

**innings** *n sp* tour *m* de batte; *fig* tour *m*, période *f*
**innkeeper** *n* aubergiste
**innocence** *n* innocence *f*; (simplicity) naïveté *f*, candeur *f*
**innocent** *n* innocent -e; *adj* innocent; (simple) naïf (*f* naïve), candide; ~ **of** dépourvu de
**innocuous** *adj* inoffensif -ive
**innovate** *vi* innover
**innovation** *n* innovation *f*, changement *m*
**innovator** *n* innovateur -trice, novateur -trice
**innuendo** *n* insinuation (malveillante), allusion (malveillante)
**innumerable** *adj* innombrable, sans nombre
**inobservance** *n* manque *m* d'observance
**inoculate** *vt* inoculer, vacciner; *fig* inculquer
**inoculation** *n* inoculation *f*
**inodorous** *adj* inodore
**inoffensive** *adj* inoffensif -ive
**inoperable** *adj* inopérable
**inoperative** *adj* inopérant
**inopportune** *adj* inopportun, déplacé, intempestif -ive
**inordinate** *adj* excessif -ive, démesuré, immodéré
**inorganic** *adj* inorganique
**in-patient** *n* malade hospitalisé -e
**input** *n elect* puissance *f*; (computer) données *fpl*
**inquest** *n leg* enquête *f* judiciaire
**inquietude** *n* inquiétude *f*
**inquire, enquire** *vt* demander, s'enquérir, poser des questions; *vi* demander, s'enquérir, s'informer; (health) ~ **after** demander des nouvelles de; ~ **into** faire des recherches sur, enquêter sur
**inquiring, enquiring** *adj* curieux -ieuse; interrogateur -trice
**inquiry, enquiry** *n* demande *f* (de renseignements); (official) enquête *f*, investigation *f*
**inquisition** *n* enquête *f*, investigation *f*; *eccles* **the Inquisition** l'Inquisition *f*
**inquisitive** *adj* curieux -ieuse; *pej* trop curieux -ieuse
**inquisitiveness** *n* curiosité *f*; *pej* indiscrétion *f*
**inquisitor** *n* enquêteur *m*; *eccles* inquisiteur *m*
**inquisitorial** *adj* inquisitorial
**inroad** *n* incursion *f*; **make** ~s **upon** empiéter sur, entamer
**insalubrious** *adj* insalubre, malsain
**insalubrity** *n* insalubrité *f*
**insalutary** *adj* qui n'est pas salutaire
**insane** *n med* **the** ~ *npl* les aliénés *mpl*;

*adj* fou (*f* folle); *med* aliéné, dément; *fig* insensé

**insanitary** *adj* insalubre, malsain

**insanity** *n* folie *f*, insanité *f*; *med* aliénation *f*, démence *f*

**insatiable** *adj* insatiable

**inscribe** *vt* inscrire, graver; (dedicate) dédicacer

**inscription** *n* inscription *f*; (dedication) dédicace *f*

**inscrutability** *n* impénétrabilité *f*

**inscrutable** *adj* impénétrable

**insect** *n* insecte *m*; ~ **spray** aérosol *m* insecticide, bombe *f* insecticide

**insecticide** *n* insecticide *m*; *adj* insecticide

**insecure** *adj* (object) peu solide, qui tient mal; (future) incertain; (worried) anxieux -ieuse; (unsafe) peu sûr

**insecurity** *n* insécurité *f*

**inseminate** *vt* inséminer

**insemination** *n* insémination *f*

**insensate** *adj* insensé; (not alive) inanimé

**insensibility** *n* insensibilité *f*, indifférence *f*; *med* inconscience *f*

**insensible** *adj* insensible, indifférent; *med* inconscient

**insensitive** *adj* insensible

**insensitiveness** *n* insensibilité *f*

**inseparable** *adj* inséparable

**insert** *n typ* encart *m*; (newspaper) insertion *f*; *vt* insérer; *typ* encarter; (jewel) incruster

**insertion** *n* insertion *f*

**inset** *n typ* encart *m*; (map, diagram, etc, inserted on page) carte *f* (schéma *m*) en cartouche; *vt* insérer (en cartouche); (jewel) incruster

**inshore** *adj* côtier -ière; *adv* près de la côte, vers la côte

**inside** *n* dedans *m*, intérieur *m*; *coll* ventre *m*; ~ **out** à l'envers, sens dessus dessous; (completely) à fond; *adj* intérieur, d'intérieur; (secret) secret -ète; ~ **information** renseignements obtenus à la source; *coll* ~ **job** coup monté de l'intérieur; *mot* ~ **lane** (in England) voie *f* de gauche; (in France) voie *f* de droite; ~ **leg measurement** hauteur *f* d'entre-jambes; *adv* dedans, au-dedans, à l'intérieur; (in prison, in taule; *prep* à l'intérieur de, dans; (time) en moins de

**inside-forward** *n sp* intérieur *m*

**insider** *n* initié -e

**insidious** *adj* insidieux -ieuse, spécieux -ieuse

**insight** *n* perspicacité *f*

**insignia** *npl* insignes *mpl*

**insignificance** *n* insignifiance *f*

**insignificant** *adj* insignifiant

**insincere** *adj* insincère, de mauvaise foi

**insincerity** *n* insincérité *f*, manque *m* de sincérité, mauvaise foi

**insinuate** *vt* insinuer, laisser entendre; *vi* s'insinuer

**insinuation** *n* insinuation *f*, allusion *f*

**insipid** *adj* insipide, fade

**insipidity** *n* insipidité *f*, fadeur *f*

**insist** *vt* insister, affirmer, maintenir; *vi* insister

**insistence** *n* insistance *f*

**insistent** *adj* insistant, pressant, persistant

**insobriety** *n* ivrognerie *f*

**insofar** *adv* à tel point

**insolation** *n* exposition *f* au soleil; (sunstroke) insolation *f*

**insole** *n* semelle *f*

**insolence** *n* insolence *f*

**insolent** *adj* insolent

**insolubility** *n* insolubilité *f*

**insoluble** *adj* insoluble

**insolvency** *n* insolvabilité *f*, faillite *f*

**insolvent** *adj* insolvable, en faillite; **become** ~ faire faillite; **declare oneself** ~ déposer son bilan

**insomnia** *n* insomnie *f*

**insomniac** *n* insomniaque

**insomuch** *adv* à tel point; ~ **as** d'autant que

**insouciance** *n* insouciance *f*

**inspect** *vt* inspecter, examiner, vérifier; *med* passer en revue

**inspection** *n* inspection *f*, examen *m*, vérification *f*; *mil* inspection *f*, revue *f*

**inspector** *n* inspecteur -trice; (bus, train) contrôleur -euse

**inspectorate** *n* corps *m* des inspecteurs

**inspiration** *n* inspiration *f*

**inspire** *vt* inspirer, stimuler

**inst** *adj abbr comm* courant

**instability** *n* instabilité *f*

**install** *vt* installer, établir

**installation** *n* installation *f*

**instalment** *n comm* acompte *m*, versement partiel; (serial) épisode *m*; **buy on the** ~ **plan** acheter à tempérament; **pay by** ~ **s** payer par traites échelonnées

**instance** *n* cas *m*, exemple *m*; circonstance *f*; *leg* demande *f*, instance *f*; **for** ~ par exemple; **in the first** ~ en premier lieu; *vt* donner en exemple, illustrer

**instant** *n* instant *m*, moment *m*; **this** ~ tout de suite; *adj* immédiat, instantané; ~ **coffee** café *m* soluble; ~ **soup** potage instantané en poudre

**instantaneous** *adj* instantané

**instanter** *adv* immédiatement

**instantly** *adv* immédiatement

**instate** *vt* installer

**instead** *adv* au lieu de cela, à la place de

cela, plutôt; ~ of à la place de, au lieu de

**instep** n cou-de-pied m (pl cous-de-pied); (shoe) cambrure f

**instigate** vt inciter, pousser

**instigation** n instigation f, incitation f

**instigator** n instigateur -trice

**instil** vt insuffler, inculquer, instiller

**instillation** n instillation f

**instilment** n instillation f

**instinct** n instinct m

**instinctive** adj instinctif -ive

**institute** n institut m; vt instituer, établir; (found) fonder, créer; leg ~ **proceedings** entamer un procès

**institution** n institution f, fondation f, établissement m; leg mise f en train; (hospital) hôpital m; (mental hospital) hôpital m psychiatrique; (workhouse) asile m

**institutional** adj institutionnel -elle

**institutionalize** vt institutionnaliser; (person) garder dans un établissement (dans un hôpital, dans un asile, etc)

**instruct** vt (teach) instruire, enseigner; (order) donner des ordres à; leg ~ **counsel** confier une cause à un(e) avocat(e)

**instruction** n instruction f, enseignement m; ~ s (directions) directives fpl, instructions fpl; indications fpl; mil (orders) consigne f; (method of use) mode m d'emploi

**instructive** adj instructif -ive, révélateur -trice

**instructor** n maître m; mil instructeur m; sp moniteur m

**instructress** n maîtresse f; sp monitrice f

**instrument** n instrument m, outil m, ustensile m; vt orchestrer

**instrumental** adj mus instrumental; be ~ **in** être pour quelque chose dans

**instrumentalist** n instrumentiste

**instrumentation** n orchestration f

**insubordinate** adj insubordonné, indiscipliné, rebelle

**insubordination** n insubordination f, rébellion f

**insubstantial** adj irréel -éelle; peu substantiel -ielle, sans substance

**insufferable** adj insupportable, intolérable

**insufficiency** n insuffisance f

**insufficient** adj insuffisant

**insufflate** vt insuffler

**insufflation** n insufflation f

**insular** adj insulaire; fig étroit

**insularity** n insularité f; étroitesse f

**insulate** vt isoler; (sound) insonoriser; (heat) calorifuger; fig isoler, séparer

**insulation** n isolation f; (sound) insonorisation f; (heat) calorifugeage m; (substance) isolant m

**insulator** n (substance) isolant m; (device) isolateur m

**insulin** n insuline f; ~ **shock** choc m insulinique

**insult** n insulte f, injure f, affront m; **add** ~ **to injury** porter l'insulte à son comble; vt insulter, injurier

**insulting** adj injurieux -ieuse, insultant

**insuperable** adj insurmontable

**insupportable** adj insupportable

**insurable** adj assurable

**insurance** n assurance f, garantie f; **comprehensive** ~ assurance f tous risques; **fire** ~ assurance-incendie f (pl assurances-incendie); **life** ~ assurance-vie f (pl assurances-vie); **take out** ~ s'assurer; **third-party** ~ assurance f au tiers

**insure** vt assurer; (make sure) garantir, assurer

**insurer** n assureur m

**insurgency** n rébellion f

**insurgent** n insurgé -e, rebelle; adj insurgé, en révolte

**insurmountable** adj insurmontable

**insurrection** n insurrection f, rébellion f, émeute f

**insurrectionary** adj insurrectionnel -elle

**insusceptibility** n insensibilité f

**insusceptible** adj insensible, peu susceptible

**intact** adj intact

**intake** n (school, etc) admission(s) f (pl); mil contingent m; (inlet, tube, etc) prise f, adduction f; (food, liquid) consommation f; mech ~ **valve** soupape f d'admission

**intangible** adj intangible

**integer** n nombre entier

**integral** n math intégrale f; adj intégral, complet -ète; (essential) intégrant; ~ **part** partie intégrante

**integrate** vt intégrer, compléter, coordonner; US (school) imposer la déségrégation raciale

**integration** n intégration f; US déségrégation raciale

**integrity** n intégrité f, probité f; (wholeness) intégrité f, totalité f, intégralité f

**integument** n tégument m

**intellect** n intellect m; intelligence f, esprit m; (person) intelligence f, esprit m

**intellectual** n + adj intellectuel -uelle

**intellectualism** n intellectualisme m

**intellectuality** n intellectualité f

**intellectualize** vt intellectualiser

**intelligence** n intelligence f; (news) information(s) f (pl), renseignement(s) m (pl); mil renseignements mpl; ~ **service** service m de renseignements; ~ **test** test m d'aptitude intellectuelle

**intelligent** adj intelligent

**intelligentsia** n élite intellectuelle

**intelligibility** *n* intelligibilité *f*
**intelligible** *adj* intelligible
**intemperance** *n* excès *m*, manque *m* de modération, intempérance *f*; (drunkenness) ivrognerie *f*
**intemperate** *adj* immodéré, excessif -ive; (drunken) adonné à la boisson; (climate) rigoureux -euse
**intend** *vt* avoir l'intention de, penser, projeter; destiner
**intended** *n coll* (future husband, future wife) promis -e, futur -e; *adj* intentionnel -elle, voulu, délibéré
**intense** *adj* intense, extrême; ardent; violent, excessif -ive
**intensification** *n* intensification *f*
**intensify** *vt* intensifier; *vi* s'intensifier
**intensity** *n* intensité *f*; puissance *f*
**intensive** intensif -ive; *med* ~ **care unit** service *m* de réanimation
¹**intent** *n* intention *f*, dessein *m*, but *m*; **to all ~ s and purposes** virtuellement, en fait
²**intent** *adj* résolu, absorbé, attentif -ive
**intention** *n* intention *f*, but *m*, dessein *m*
**intentional** *adj* intentionnel -elle, voulu, délibéré
**interact** *vi* réagir réciproquement
**interaction** *n* interaction *f*
**interbreed** *vt* croiser; *vi* se croiser
**intercalary** *adj* intercalaire
**intercalate** *vt* intercaler
**intercalation** *n* intercalation *f*
**intercede** *vi* intercéder
**intercept** *vt* intercepter; (halt) arrêter au passage
**interception** *n* interception *f*
**interceptor** *n* intercepteur *m*
**intercession** *n* intercession *f*
**intercessor** *n* intercesseur *m*
**interchange** *n* échange *m*; (alteration) alternance *f*; *mot* (motorway) échangeur *m*; *vt* échanger, faire alterner; (exchange places) changer de place
**interchangeable** *adj* interchangeable
**intercom** *n* interphone *m*
**intercommunicate** *vi* communiquer réciproquement
**intercommunication** *n* intercommunication *f*
**intercommunion** *n eccles* intercommunion *f*
**interconnect** *vt* connecter; *vi* communiquer
**intercontinental** *adj* intercontinental
**intercostal** *adj anat* intercostal
**intercourse** *n* commerce *m*, rapports *mpl*, relations *fpl*; **sexual ~** rapports sexuels, copulation *f*
**interdenominational** *adj eccles* interconfessionnel -elle

**interdepend** *vi* dépendre l'un de l'autre (les uns des autres)
**interdependence** *n* interdépendance *f*
**interdependent** *adj* interdépendant
**interdict** *n leg* interdiction *f*; *eccles* interdit *m*; *vt leg* interdire; *eccles* jeter l'interdit sur
**interdiction** *n* interdiction *f*
**interest** *n* intérêt *m*; (benefit) avantage *m*, profit *m*; *comm* (share in) intérêts *mpl*, participation *f*; (on capital) intérêt(s) *m(pl)*; (hobby) passe-temps *m*; *vt* intéresser, s'intéresser à; (concern) intéresser, concerner, toucher, préoccuper
**interested** *adj* intéressé; *leg* ~ **party** ayant-droit *m* (*pl* ayants-droit)
**interesting** *adj* intéressant; *coll obs* **in an ~ condition** enceinte
**interface** *n* interface *f*
**interfere** *vi* s'occuper, s'ingérer, s'immiscer, se mêler; *phys* interférer; ~ **with** empêcher, contrecarrer; (molest) importuner; *leg* (sexually) attenter à la pudeur de
**interference** *n* ingérance *f*, intrusion *f*; *phys* interférence *f*; *rad* parasites *mpl*
**interfering** *adj* importun
**interim** *n* intérim *m*; (dividend) dividende *m* intérimaire; *adj* provisoire, intérimaire; ~ **payment** acompte *m*
**interior** *n* intérieur *m*; *arts* (tableau *m* d')intérieur *m*; *adj* intérieur
**interject** *vt* placer, lancer
**interjection** *n* interjection *f*
**interlace** *vt* entrelacer, entrecroiser; *vi* s'entrelacer, s'entrecroiser
**interlard** *vt* entrelarder
**interleave** *vt* interfolier
**interline** *vt typ* interligner; (clothing) mettre une doublure intermédiaire à
**interlinear** *adj* interlinéaire
**interlining** *n* doublure *f* intermédiaire
**interlock** *vt* enclencher; *vi* s'enclencher
**interlocutor** *n* interlocuteur -trice
**interlocutory** *adj* interlocutoire
**interloper** *n* intrus -e; *comm* commerçant -e marron -onne
**interlude** *n mus* interlude *m*; (interval) intervalle *m*; *theat* intermède *m*
**intermarriage** *n* mariage *m* entre personnes de races (religions, nationalités) différentes; mariage *m* entre membres de la même famille, de la même tribu
**intermarry** *vi* se marier avec une personne de race (religion, nationalité) différente; se marier avec une personne de la même famille, de la même tribu
**intermediary** *n + adj* intermédiaire
**intermediate** *adj* intermédiaire
**interment** *n* enterrement *m*, inhumation *f*

552

**intermezzo** n mus intermezzo m; inter-mède m

**interminable** adj interminable

**intermingle** vt entremêler, mélanger; vi s'entremêler, se mélanger

**intermission** n interruption f, trêve f, pause f; theat entracte m; med inter-mission f

**intermittent** adj intermittent

¹**intern** n US interne

²**intern** vt interner

**internal** adj interne, intérieur; (intrinsic) intrinsèque; ~ **combustion engine** moteur m à combustion interne

**international** n sp (match, player) inter-national m; adj international; ~ **date line** ligne f de changement de date

**Internationale** n the ~ l'Internationale f

**internationalism** n internationalisme m

**internationalize** vt internationaliser

**internecine** adj de destruction mutuelle

**internee** n interné -e

**internment** n internement m

**interpellate** vt interpeller

**interpellation** n interpellation f

**interpenetrate** vt interpénétrer

**interpenetration** n interpénétration f

**interphone** n interphone m

**interplanetary** adj interplanétaire

**interplay** n effet m réciproque

**interpolate** vt (text) corrompre; (insert) interpoler

**interpolation** n interpolation f

**interpose** vt intercaler, insérer; (veto) objecter; vi s'interposer, intervenir

**interposition** n interposition f, interven-tion f

**interpret** vt interpréter; vi interpréter, faire l'interprète

**interpretation** n interprétation f

**interpretative** adj interprétatif -ive

**interpreter** n ínterprète

**interracial** adj entre races différentes

**interregnum** n interrègne m

**interrelate** vt mettre en corrélation

**interrelation** n corrélation f

**interrogate** vt interroger

**interrogation** n interrogation f; (grilling) interrogatoire m

**interrogative** n gramm interrogatif m; adj interrogateur -trice; gramm inter-rogatif -ive

**interrogator** n interrogateur -trice

**interrogatory** n interrogatoire m; adj interrogateur -trice

**interrupt** vt interrompre, couper; (ob-struct) gêner, cacher

**interruption** n interruption f

**intersect** vt couper, croiser; math inter-secter; vi s'entrecouper, s'entrecroiser

**intersection** n croisement m, carrefour m; math intersection f

**intersperse** vt parsemer, répandre

**interstellar** adj interstellaire

**interstice** n interstice m

**intertwine** vt entrelacer; vi s'entrelacer

**interurban** adj interurbain

**interval** n intervalle m, pause f; theat entrácte m; (space) intervalle m, écarte-ment m; **at** ~ **s** par intervalles

**intervene** vi intervenir; (occur) survenir, arriver; (time) passer, s'écouler

**intervention** n intervention f

**interview** n entrevue f; (media) interview f; vt avoir une entrevue avec; (media) interviewer

**interviewer** n (media) interviewer m; (opinion poll, etc) enquêteur -euse

**interweave** vt tisser ensemble, entre-lacer; fig entremêler; vi s'entrelacer

**intestacy** n état produit quand quelqu'un meurt intestat

**intestate** adj intestat invar

**intestinal** adj intestinal

**intestine** n intestin m; **large** ~ gros intestin; **small** ~ intestin m grêle; adj fig interne, intestin

**intimacy** n intimité f; rapports sexuels, rapports mpl intimes

¹**intimate** n intime, familier -ière; adj intime, proche; (knowledge) appro-fondi; **be** ~ **with** avoir des rapports sexuels (intimes) avec

²**intimate** vt faire savoir, annoncer; (hint) suggérer, laisser entendre

**intimation** n annonce f, avis m; (hint) indice m, indication f

**intimidate** vt intimider

**intimidation** n intimidation f

**into** prep dans, en; coll **be** ~ donner dans; **far** ~ très avant dans; (dividing) **two** ~ **ten** dix divisé par deux

**intolerable** adj intolérable, insuppor-table

**intolerance** n intolérance f

**intolerant** adj intolérant

**intonation** n intonation f

**intone** vt + vi psalmodier

**intoxicant** n boisson f alcoolique; adj enivrant

**intoxicate** vt saouler; fig griser, enivrer

**intoxication** n ivresse f; med intoxica-tion f; fig ivresse f, griserie f

**intractability** n opiniâtreté f

**intractable** adj intractable, opiniâtre, indocile

**intramural** adj intra-muros invar

**intransigence** n intransigeance f

**intransigent** n intransigeant -e; adj in-transigeant

**intransitive** n gramm intransitif m; adj gramm intransitif -ive

**intravenous** adj intraveineux-euse

553

**intrepid** *adj* intrépide
**intrepidity** *n* intrépidité *f*
**intricacy** *n* complexité *f*
**intricate** *adj* complexe
**intrigue** *n* intrigue *f*; (love affair) liaison *f*; *vt* intriguer, intéresser; *vi* intriguer, comploter
**intrinsic** *adj* intrinsèque
**introduce** *vt* (bring in) introduire; (socially) présenter; (put into) introduire, insérer; (bring into use) établir, faire adopter; (bill in parliament) déposer; (make known) initier, faire connaître, lancer
**introduction** *n* introduction *f*; (social) présentation *f*; (book) introduction *f*, avant-propos *m*; (elementary textbook) introduction *f*, manuel *m* élémentaire, cours *m* de base
**introductory** *adj* préliminaire, préalable
**introit** *n eccles* introït *m*
**introspection** *n* introspection *f*
**introspective** *adj* introspectif -ive
**introversion** *n* introversion *f*
**introvert** *n* introverti -e; *adj* introverti; *vt* (turn inwards) tourner sur soi-même
**intrude** *vt* entrer de force; entrer sans permission; (views) imposer; *vi* (person) s'imposer; ~ **on** s'ingérer dans, s'immiscer dans; (encroach) empiéter sur
**intruder** *n* intrus -e; avion (navire) isolé
**intrusion** *n* intrusion *f*, imposition *f*
**intrusive** *adj* importun, gênant
**intuition** *n* intuition *f*
**intuitive** *adj* intuitif -ive
**intumescence** *n* intumescence *f*
**inundate** *vt* inonder
**inundation** *n* inondation *f*
**inure, enure** *vt* accoutumer, endurcir
**inutility** *n* inutilité *f*
**invade** *vt* envahir
**invader** *n* envahisseur -euse
¹**invalid** *n* malade; *adj* malade, infirme; ~ **chair** fauteuil *m* de malade; *vt mil* ~ **out** démobiliser pour blessures (pour raisons de santé)
²**invalid** *adj* non valable; (ticket) périmé
**invalidate** *vt* invalider, annuler; *leg* casser
**invalidation** *n* invalidation *f*
**invalidity** *n* invalidité *f*, état périmé
**invaluable** *adj* inestimable, hors de prix
**invariable** *adj* invariable
**invariably** *adv* invariablement, toujours
**invasion** *n* invasion *f*, envahissement *m*; (rights) empiètement *m*
**invective** *n* invective *f*
**inveigh** *vi* ~ **against** invectiver contre, tonner contre
**inveigle** entraîner, cajoler, attirer
**invent** *vt* inventer

**invention** *n* invention *f*; (lie) invention *f*, mensonge *m*
**inventive** *adj* inventif -ive
**inventiveness** *n* esprit *m* d'invention
**inventor** *n* inventeur -trice
**inventory** *n* inventaire *m*; stock *m*; *vt* inventorier
**inverse** *n* inverse *m*; *adj* inverse; **in** ~ **ratio to** en raison inverse de
**inversion** *n* inversion *f*; *mus* renversement *m*
**invert** *n* inverti -e; *vt* intervertir, renverser; ~ **ed commas** guillemets *mpl*
**invertebrate** *n* invertébré *m*; *adj* invertébré
**invest** *vt* (money) investir, placer; *mil* investir; *fig* (clothes) revêtir; (endow) investir; *vi* (money) placer de l'argent, investir
**investigate** *vt* examiner, sonder, enquêter sur
**investigation** *n* examen *m*, enquête *f*, investigation *f*
**investigator** *n* investigateur -trice
**investiture** *n* investiture *f*
**investment** *n* investissement *m*, placement *m*; *mil* investissement *m*; investiture *f*
**investor** *n* investisseur *m*; (shareholder) actionnaire
**inveterate** *adj* invétéré, acharné; ~ **liar** fieffé menteur
**invidious** *adj* propre à susciter la jalousie; (task) ingrat
**invigilate** *vt* (examination) surveiller; *vi* être de surveillance à un examen
**invigilation** *n* surveillance *f* d'un examen
**invigilator** *n* surveillant -e à un examen
**invigorate** *vt* revigorer, fortifier, tonifier, vivifier
**invigorating** *adj* tonifiant
**invigoration** *n* revigoration *f*
**invincibility** *n* invincibilité *f*
**invincible** *adj* invincible
**inviolability** *n* inviolabilité *f*
**inviolable** *adj* inviolable
**inviolate** *adj* inviolé
**invisibility** *n* invisibilité *f*
**invisible** *adj* invisible; ~ **ink** encre *f* sympathique; ~ **mending** stoppage *m*
**invitation** *n* invitation *f*
**invite** *n coll* invitation *f*; *vt* inviter; (seek) demander, solliciter; (provoke) appeler, chercher; ~ **in** inviter à entrer; ~ **out** inviter à sortir; ~ **over** inviter à venir
**inviting** *adj* invitant, attrayant, engageant; (food) alléchant, appétissant
**invocation** *n* invocation *f*
**invocatory** *adj* invocatoire
**invoice** *n* facture *f*; *vt* facturer
**invoke** *vt* invoquer; demander l'aide de; (spirits) évoquer

**involuntary** *adj* involontaire
**involve** *vt* (entangle) impliquer, entraîner, mêler; (imply) entraîner, nécessiter
**involved** *adj* compliqué, complexe; **be
~** être en jeu; **be ~ in** être mêlé à
**involvement** *n* participation *f*; (commitment) engagement *m*, rôle *m*
**invulnerability** *n* invulnérabilité *f*
**invulnerable** *adj* invulnérable
**inward** *adj* intérieur; (mind, soul)
intime; (towards the interior) vers l'intérieur; *adv* **~s** vers l'intérieur; **turn
~s upon oneself** rentrer en soi-même
**inwardly** *adv* intérieurement, au-dedans, à l'intérieur; (privately) secrètement
**inwards** *adv see* **inward**
**iodine** *n* iode *m*; **tincture of ~** teinture *f*
d'iode
**iodize** *vt* ioder
**iodoform** *n* iodoforme *m*
**ion** *n phys* ion *m*
**Ionian** *adj* ionien -ienne
**Ionic** *adj archi* ionique
**ionic** *adj phys* ionique
**ionization** *n* ionisation *f*
**ionize** *vt* ioniser
**ionosphere** *n* ionosphère *f*
**iota** *n* iota *m*, brin *m*
**I.O.U.** *n* reconnaissance *f* de dette(s)
**ipecacuanha** *n* ipéca *m*
**Iran** *n* Iran *m*
**Iranian** *n* Iranien -ienne; (language)
iranien *m*; *adj* iranien -ienne
**Iraq** *n* Iraq *m*
**Iraqi** *n* Irakien -ienne; *adj* irakien -ienne
**irascibility** *n* irascibilité *f*
**irascible** *adj* irascible, colérique
**irate** *adj* courroucé, furieux -ieuse
**ire** *n* courroux *m*, colère *f*, ire *f*
**Ireland** *n* Irlande *f*; **Northern ~** Irlande
*f* du Nord; **Republic of ~** République *f*
d'Irlande
**iridescence** *n* chatoiement *m*
**iridescent** *adj* irisé
**iridium** *n* iridium *m*
**iris** *n bot* + *anat* iris *m*
**Irish** *n* (language) irlandais *m*; **the ~** les
Irlandais; *adj* irlandais; **~ stew** ragoût
*m* de mouton à l'irlandaise
**Irishman** *n* Irlandais *m*
**Irishwoman** *n* Irlandaise *f*
**irk** *vt* ennuyer, contrarier, embêter
**irksome** *adj* ennuyeux -euse, assommant
**iron** *n* fer *m*; (tool) fer *m*; (clothes) fer *m*
à repasser; (golf) fer *m*; *sl* pétard *m*; **~ s**
(fetters) fers *mpl*, chaînes *fpl*; (for legs)
entraves *fpl*; **have many ~ s in the fire**
avoir beaucoup d'affaires en train; **man
of ~** homme *m* de fer; **scrap ~** ferraille
*f*; **strike while the ~ is hot** battre le fer
pendant qu'il est chaud; **the ~ has**

entered his soul (bitterness) il est plein
d'amertume; (grief) il a la mort dans
l'âme; *adj* de fer; *chem* ferreux -euse;
**the Iron Age** l'âge *m* de fer; *pol* **~ curtain** rideau *m* de fer; **~ lung** poumon *m*
d'acier; **~ rations** vivres *mpl* de réserve; *vt* repasser; donner un coup de fer
à; **~ out** (creases) faire disparaître au
fer; *fig* (difficulties) aplanir, faire disparaître
**ironclad** *n naut* cuirassé *m*
**iron-founder** *n* fondeur *m*
**iron-grey** *n* + *adj* gris fer *invar*
**ironic, ironical** *adj* ironique
**ironing** *n* repassage *m*; **~ board** planche
*f* à repasser
**ironist** *n* ironiste
**ironmaster** *n* maître *m* de forges
**ironmonger** *n* quincaillier; **~'s shop**
quincaillerie *f*
**ironmongery** *n* quincaillerie *f*
**ironware** *n* quincaillerie *f*
**ironwork** *n* ferronerie *f*; **wrought ~** ferronerie *f* d'art; **~s** usine *f* sidérurgique
**irony** *n* ironie *f*
**irradiate** *vt* (expose to radiation) irradier; *fig* illuminer; *vi* irradier, émettre
de la lumière
**irradiation** *n* irradiation *f*, illumination *f*
**irrational** *adj* irrationnel -elle; (person)
pas rationnel -elle; (belief) déraisonnable, absurde
**irrationality** *n* irrationalité *f*
**irrationalize** *vt* rendre irrationnel -elle
**irrealizable** *adj* irréalisable
**irreclaimable** *adj* incorrigible; (land) in-
cultivable
**irrecognizable** *adj* impossible à reconnaître
**irreconcilable** *adj* irréconciliable; (hostile) implacable; incompatible
**irrecoverable** *adj* irrécupérable; irréparable
**irrecusable** *adj* irrécusable
**irredeemable** *adj* irrémédiable; *comm*
non remboursable
**irredentism** *n* irrédentisme *m*
**irreducible** *adj* irréductible
**irrefutable** *adj* irréfutable, irrécusable
**irregular** *adj* irrégulier -ière, asymétrique; (conduct) déréglé
**irregularity** *n* irrégularité *f*, asymétrie *f*
**irrelevance** *n* manque *m* d'à-propos,
manque *m* de rapport
**irrelevant** *adj* sans rapport, hors de
propos
**irreligion** *n* irreligion *f*
**irreligious** *adj* irreligieux -ieuse
**irremediable** *adj* irrémédiable
**irremovable** *adj* immuable; (official,
judge) inamovible
**irreparable** *adj* irréparable

555

**irreplaceable** *adj* irremplaçable
**irrepressible** *adj* irrépressible, irrésistible
**irreproachable** *adj* irréprochable
**irresistibility** *n* état *m* d'être irrésistible
**irresistible** *adj* irrésistible
**irresolute** *adj* irrésolu, indécis
**irresoluteness, irresolution** *n* irrésolution *f*, hésitation *f*
**irresolvable** *adj* qu'on ne peut pas résoudre
**irrespective** *adj* ~ of sans tenir compte de
**irresponsibility** *n* irresponsabilité *f*
**irresponsible** *adj* irréfléchi, inconsidéré; irresponsable
**irresponsive** *adj* qui réagit peu; peu aimable
**irresponsiveness** *n* réserve *f*; manque *m* d'amabilité
**irretrievable** *adj* irréparable, irrémédiable; (lost) introuvable
**irreverence** *n* irrévérence *f*
**irreverent** *adj* irrévérencieux -ieuse
**irreversibility** *n* irréversibilité *f*
**irreversible** *adj* irréversible
**irrevocability** *n* irrévocabilité *f*
**irrevocable** *adj* irrévocable
**irrigable** *adj* irrigable
**irrigate** *vt* irriguer
**irrigation** *n* irrigation *f*
**irrigator** *n* (machine) irrigateur *m*
**irritability** *n* irritabilité *f*, irascibilité *f*
**irritable** *adj* irritable, irascible, coléreux -euse
**irritant** *n* irritant *m*; *adj* irritant
**irritate** *vt* irriter, agacer
**irritating** *adj* irritant, agaçant
**irritation** *n* irritation *f*
**irruption** *n* irruption *f*
**isinglass** *n cul* gélatine *f*
**Islam** *n* Islam *m*
**Islamic** *adj* islamique
**island** *n* île *f*; **small** ~ îlot *m*; **traffic** ~ refuge *m*; *adj* insulaire
**islander** *n* insulaire, habitant -e d'une île
**isle** *n* île *f*
**islet** *n* îlot *m*
**ism** *n pej* théorie *f*, doctrine *f*
**isobar** *n* isobare *f*
**isolate** *vt* isoler
**isolation** *n* isolement *m*; solitude *f*
**isolationism** *n* isolationnisme *m*
**isolationist** *n* isolationniste
**isosceles** *adj* isocèle
**isotherm** *n* isotherme *f*
**isotope** *n* isotope *m*
**Israel** *n* Israël *m*
**Israeli** *n* Israélien -ienne; *adj* israélien -ienne
**Israelite** *n* Israélite

**issue** *n* (publication) sortie *f*, parution *f*; (distributing) livraison *f*, émission *f*; (copy) numéro *m*; (problem, question) problème *m*, question *f*, sujet *m*; (result) issue *f*, résultat *m*; *med* écoulement *m*; *leg* descendance *f*, progéniture *f*; **at** ~ sous discussion; **cloud the** ~ brouiller les cartes; **evade the** ~ prendre la tangente; **join** ~ **with** engager une controverse avec; **make an** ~ **of sth** monter qch en épingle; **point at** ~ point controversé; *vt* (book) publier, faire paraître; (give out) distribuer, mettre en circulation, émettre, fournir; *vi* (originate) émaner, descendre
**isthmus** *n* isthme *m*
**it** *n coll* perfection *f*, idéal *m*; *sl* sex-appeal *m*; (game) **you're** ~ c'est toi le chat; *coll abbr* vermouth italien; *pron* il, elle; (accusative case) le, la, (before vowel) l'; (dative case) lui; *impers* il, ce, cela, ça; **above** ~ au-dessus; **below** ~ au-dessous; *coll* **be with** ~ être dans le vent; *coll* **have had** ~ être fichu; *coll* **have** ~ **in for s/o** avoir une dent contre qn; *coll* **have what** ~ **takes** être à la hauteur; **let's face** ~ regardons les choses en face, pour dire vrai; **of** ~ en; **to** ~ y; *coll* **you'll catch** ~ , **you're for** ~ tu vas écoper
**Italian** *n* Italien -ienne; (language) italien *m*; *adj* italien -ienne
**italic** *adj* *print* italique; *npl* ~**s** italique *m*
**italicize** *vt* mettre (imprimer) en italique
**itch** *n* démangeaison *f*; désir *m*, envie *f*; *vi* éprouver des démangeaisons; avoir très envie
**itchy** *adj* qui démange; *coll* **have** ~ **feet** avoir la bougeotte; *coll* **have** ~ **fingers** avoir les doigts collants
¹**item** *n* (article) article *m*; (in programme) numéro *m*; (agenda) question *f*, numéro *m*
²**item** *adv* de plus; *comm* item
**itemize** *vt* détailler, spécifier
**iterate** *vt* répéter
**iterative** *adj* itératif -ive
**itinerant** *adj* itinérant, errant
**itinerary** *n* itinéraire *m*
**its** *poss adj* son (*f* sa, *pl* ses)
**itself** *pron* lui-même *m*, elle-même *f*
**ivory** *n* ivoire *m*; (colour) ivoire *m*; *coll* **ivories** (piano) touches *fpl*; *sl* dents *fpl*; *sl* (dice) dés *mpl*; *sl* (billiard balls) boules *fpl* de billard; **Ivory Coast** Côte *f* d'Ivoire; *coll* **black** ~ esclaves *pl* de l'Afrique noire
**ivy** *n* lierre *m*; *US* **Ivy League** ensemble *m* de certaines grandes universités de l'est des États-Unis
**izard** *n* isard *m*

556

# J

**jab** *n* coup *m* de pointe; *coll* piqûre *f*; (boxing) coup droit; *vt* pousser, donner un coup de doigt à; (stab) poignarder; (boxing) lancer un coup droit à

**jabber** *vi* jacasser, bavarder

**jabbering** *n* jacasserie *f*, bavardage *m*

**jabot** *n* jabot *m*

**jacaranda** *n bot* jacaranda *m*

**jack** *n* mot cric *m*; (cards) valet *m*; (bowls) cochonnet *m*; *elect* fiche *f* d'alimentation; (flag) drapeau *m*; ~ **of all trades** homme *m* à tout faire; **Jack Tar** matelot *m*; **before you can say Jack Robinson** tout de suite, en un clin d'œil; **every man** ~ chacun, tous; **Union Jack** drapeau *m* britannique; *vt* ~ **up** soulever avec un cric; (prices) faire monter; *coll* renoncer, plaquer

**jackal** *n* chacal *m* (*pl* chacals)

**jackanapes** *n* polisson *m*

**jackass** *n* âne *m*; *coll* crétin *m*

**jackboot** *n* botte *f* à l'écuyère

**jackdaw** *n* choucas *m*

**jacket** *n* (man) veston *m*, veste *f*; (woman) jaquette *f*; (book) couverture *f*; (boiler, tank, etc) enveloppe *f*; (potato) peau *f*, pelure *f*; **potatoes baked in their** ~s pommes de terre *fpl* en robe de chambre

**jack-in-office** *n coll pej* petit fonctionnaire satisfait, rond-de-cuir *m* (*pl* ronds-de-cuir) qui joue à l'important

**jack-in-the-box** *n* diable *m* à ressort

**jack-knife** *n* couteau *m* de poche; (dive) saut *m* de carpe; *vi* (trailer) se mettre en travers

**jack-o'-lantern** *n* feu follet

**jackpot** *n* (cards) pot *m*; gros lot; *coll* **hit the** ~ gagner le gros lot, avoir de la veine

**Jacobean** *adj* de l'époque de Jacques I^er (d'Angleterre)

**Jacobite** *n* Jacobite

**jactation** *n* vantardise *f*

**¹jade** *n* (horse) haridelle *f*; (whore) prostituée *f*

**²jade** *n* jade *m*; *adj* (colour) jade; ~ **green** vert jade *invar*

**jag** *n* pointe *f*, saillie *f*; *sl* cuite *f*; *vt* déchirer, déchiqueter

**jagged** *adj* déchiqueté, dentelé

**jaguar** *n* jaguar *m*

**jail** *n see* **gaol**

**jailer** *n see* **gaoler**

**jalopy** *n coll* vieux tacot

**jalousie** *n* jalousie *f*

**¹jam** *n* confiture *f*; ~ **jar** pot *m* à confiture; ~ **roll** roulé *m* à la confiture; *vt* **session** séance *f* de jazz improvisé; ~ **tart** tarte *f* à la confiture; **money for** ~ de l'argent gagné sans peine

**²jam** *n* foule *f*; (traffic) embouteillage *m*, bouchon *m*; *coll* (tight spot) pétrin *m*; ~ **full** plein à craquer; *vt* (squeeze) serrer, écraser; (wedge) coincer; (block) bloquer; (gun) enrayer; (thrust into) enfoncer, fourrer; (obstruct) encombrer; (with traffic) embouteiller; *rad* brouiller; ~ **the brakes on** bloquer les freins; *vi* (crowd) s'entasser; (become stuck) se bloquer, se coincer; (gun) s'enrayer

**Jamaica** *n* Jamaïque *f*

**Jamaican** *n* Jamaïquain -e; *adj* jamaïquain

**jamb** *n bui* jambage *m*, montant *m*

**jamboree** *n* (scouts) jamboree *m*; grande fête

**jamming** *n rad* brouillage *m*

**jangle** *n* cliquetis *m*, bruit confus; dispute *f*; *vt* faire cliqueter, faire faire un bruit de ferraille à; *vi* retentir avec un bruit de ferraille

**janissary** *n* janissaire *m*

**janitor** *n* portier *m*, gardien *m*; concierge

**Jansenism** *n* jansénisme *m*

**January** *n* janvier *m*

**Jap** *n coll abbr* Japonais -e

**Japan** *n* Japon *m*

**japan** *n* laque *f*; *vt* laquer

**Japanese** *n* Japonais -e; (language) japonais *m*; *adj* japonais

**jape** *n coll* farce *f*, blague *f*

**japonica** *n* cognassier *m* du Japon

**¹jar** *n* pot *m*; (earthenware) jarre *f*; (glass) bocal *m*

**²jar** *n* (sound) son discordant; (shock) choc *m*, secousse *f*; *vt* (shake) ébranler; ~ **on** agacer, irriter; *vi* (sound) faire un bruit discordant, grincer; (vibrate) vibrer; (colour) jurer; *mus* détonner; (ideas) se heurter

**jargon** *n* jargon *m*; charabia *m*

**jarring** *adj* discordant, rauque; irritant; (colour) qui jure

**jasmine** *n* jasmin *m*

**jasper** *n* jaspe *m*

**jaundice** *n* jaunisse *f*; *fig* amertume *f*, jalousie *f*

557

**jaundiced** adj amer -ère, aigri; jaloux -ouse; **have a ~ view of things** voir les choses en noir; **with a ~ eye** d'un mauvais œil

**jaunt** n balade f; vi aller se balader

**jauntiness** n désinvolture f, insouciance f; (swagger) crânerie f

**jaunty** adj désinvolte, insouciant; (swaggering) crâneur -euse

**javelin** n javelot m

**jaw** n mâchoire f; sl (sermon) laïus m; coll (chat) causette f; ~s gueule f; mech mâchoires fpl; vt coll sermonner; vi coll faire un sermon; coll (chat) bavarder

**jaw-bone** n (os m) maxillaire m

**jay** n geai m

**jay-walker** n piéton indiscipliné

**jazz** n jazz m; adj de jazz; vt arranger en style de jazz; ~ **up** animer, rajeunir; vi danser sur un rythme de jazz

**jazzy** adj de jazz; (colour) tapageur -euse

**jealous** adj jaloux -ouse; (watchful) vigilant

**jealousness** n jalousie f

**jealousy** n jalousie f

**jeans** n blue-jean m, jean m; (overalls) bleu m de travail

**jeep** n jeep f

**jeer** n sarcasme m, raillerie f; vt huer; vi railler, huer; ~ **at** insulter, se moquer de

**jeering** adj railleur -euse, moqueur -euse

**Jehovah** n Jéhovah m; ~'**s witness** témoin m de Jéhovah

**jejune** adj ennuyeux -euse; (meagre) maigre

**jell** vi cul épaissir; coll prendre tournure

**jellied** adj en gelée

**jelly** n cul gelée f; sl gélignite f

**jelly-fish** n méduse f

**jemmy** n pince-monseigneur f (pl pinces-monseigneur)

**jeopardize** vt mettre en danger, exposer à des risques, compromettre

**jeopardy** n danger m, péril m; **in ~** menacé, en péril

**jeremiad** n jérémiade f

**jerk** n secousse f, saccade f; med crispation nerveuse; sl pauvre type m; coll **physical ~s** gymnastique f; vt secouer, donner une secousse à; vi cahoter; ~ **along** avancer par saccades

**jerkily** adv par saccades

**jerkin** n blouson m; hist justaucorps m

**jerky** adj saccadé

**Jerry** n coll Fritz m invar

**jerry** n coll Jules m, pot m de chambre

**jerry-builder** n constructeur m de maisons en carton-pâte

**jerry-built** adj construit en carton-pâte

**jerry-can** n jerrycan m

**Jersey** n Jersey f

**jersey** n tricot m; vache f de Jersey

**Jerusalem** n Jérusalem f; ~ **artichoke** topinambour m

**jest** n plaisanterie f; **in ~** pour rire; vi plaisanter

**jester** n hist bouffon m; plaisantin m

**Jesuit** n Jésuite m

**jesuitical** adj jésuitique

¹**jet** n jais m; adj de jais

²**jet** n (spurt) jet m, giclée f; aer avion m à réaction, jet m; (burner) brûleur m; mot gicleur m; ~ **engine** moteur m à réaction, réacteur m; ~ **fighter** chasseur m à réaction; ~ **lag** décalage m horaire; ~ **set** clientèle f des jets; vt faire gicler, faire jaillir; vi gicler, jaillir; voyager en jet

**jet-black** adj noir comme (du) jais

**jet-propelled** adj à réaction

**jet-propulsion** n propulsion f à réaction

**jetsam** n naut objets jetés à la mer (pour alléger un navire); fig rebut m

**jettison** vt naut jeter par dessus bord, se délester de; aer larguer; fig abandonner, se délester de

**jetty** n embarcadère m, débarcadère m, jetée f

**Jew** n Juif (f Juive); coll pej avare m, grippe-sou m (pl grippe-sou(s))

**jewel** n bijou m, joyau m; (watch) rubis m; fig perle f, trésor m; vt sertir

**jeweller** n bijoutier m, joaillier m; ~'**s shop** bijouterie f, joaillerie f

**jewellery** n bijouterie f, bijoux mpl

**Jewess** n Juive f

**jew's harp** n guimbarde f

¹**jib** n naut foc m; coll **the cut of one's ~** sa tournure

²**jib** vi renâcler, répugner; (horse) se refuser

**jib-boom** n naut gui m de beaupré, boutdehors m (pl bouts-dehors) de foc

**jibe** n + vi see gibe

**jiffy** n coll instant m; coll **in a ~** en moins de deux

**jig** n (dance) gigue f; mech (template) gabarit m; (sieve) tamis m; vt mech tamiser; vi danser la gigue, sautiller

¹**jigger** n mech tamis m

²**jigger** n zool pou m des sables

**jiggered** adj coll étonné; **well! I'll be ~!** ça alors!

**jiggery-pokery** n manigances fpl

**jiggle** vt secouer légèrement

**jigsaw** n mech scie f à chantourner; (puzzle) puzzle m

**jilt** vt laisser tomber, rompre avec

**Jim Crow** n US politique f raciste envers les noirs; obs pej nègre m

**jimjams** npl coll délirium m tremens;

**have the** ~ avoir les chocottes, avoir le trac

**jingle** *n* (noise) tintement *m*, cliquetis *m*; (verse) petit couplet; (advertising) couplet *m* publicitaire; *vt* faire tinter; *vi* tinter

**jingo** *n* chauvin *m*; *coll* **by** ~ **!** nom d'une pipe!

**jingoism** *n* chauvinisme *m*

**jingoistic** *adj* chauvin

**jink** *vi* se faufiler; *sp* faire une esquive

**jinks** *npl coll* **high** ~ ébats bruyants

**jinx** *n coll* porte-guigne *m invar*

**jitney** *n US coll* pièce *f* de cinq cents; *adj US coll* bon marché

**jitter** *vi coll* avoir la frousse

**jitterbug** *n* boogie-woogie *m*; *fig* froussard -e; *vi* danser le boogie-woogie

**jitters** *npl coll* frousse *f*, trac *m*

**jittery** *adj coll* froussard

**jiu-jitsu** *n see* **ju-jutsu**

**jive** *n* swing *m*; *vi* danser le swing

**job** *n* (piece of work) travail *m*, tâche *f*; (employment) poste *m*, travail *m*, *coll* boulot *m*; (difficulty) mal *m*, peine *f*; *coll* (criminal act) combine *f*, vol *m*; ~ **lot** objets divers; *coll* ~ **s for the boys** des planques *fpl* pour les petits copains; **a good** ~ **!** à la bonne heure!; **have a** ~ **doing sth** avoir du mal à faire qch; **just the** ~ **!** juste ce qu'il faut!; **it's a bad** ~ c'est une sale affaire; **it's a good** ~ **that** c'est une chance que; **know one's** ~ connaître son affaire; *coll* **on the** ~ occupé; **out of a** ~ en chômage; **put up** ~ coup monté; *sl* **the blonde** ~ **over there isn't bad** elle n'est pas mal la nana blonde en face; *vt* (work) sous-traiter; *vi* travailler à la pièce, faire de petits travaux; faire le courtier en bourse; (peculate) détourner des fonds publics

**jobber** *n* (Stock Exchange) intermédiaire *m*; (piece-worker) ouvrier -ière à la pièce; *pej* tripoteur -euse

**jobbery** *n* tripotage *m* (de fonds publics)

**jobbing** *n* travail *m* à la pièce; tripotage *m* (de fonds publics); (Stock Exchange) activité *f* de courtier; ~ **gardener** jardinier -ière à la journée

**jockey** *n* jockey *m*; **Jockey Club** Jockey-Club *m*; *vt* manœuvrer; *vi* intriguer, manœuvrer

**jock-strap** *n* suspensoir *m*

**jocose** *adj* enjoué, facétieux -ieuse, jovial

**jocular** *adj* enjoué, facétieux -ieuse, jovial

**jocularity** *n* jovialité *f*

**jocund** *adj* jovial, joyeux -euse

**jocundity** *n* jovialité *f*

**jodhpurs** *n* jodhpurs *mpl*, culotte *f* de cheval

**jog** *n* secousse *f*, cahot *m*; (elbow) coup *m* de coude; *vt* secouer, pousser; ~ **s/o's memory** rafraîchir la mémoire de qn; *vi sp* faire du jogging; ~ **along** aller son chemin

**jogging** *n sp* jogging *m*

**joggle** *vt* secouer; *vi* branler

**jog-trot** *n* petit trot

**John** *n* Jean *m*; ~ **Bull**, *US* ~ **Doe** = Monsieur Dupont, Monsieur Durand

**john** *n US* cabinets *mpl*

**join** *n* ligne *f* de raccord; (sewing) couture *f*; *vt* joindre, unir, relier; (become member of) devenir membre de, s'inscrire à, adhérer à; (meet) rejoindre; (go into the company of) aller avec; *vi* se joindre, s'unir, se rejoindre

**joiner** *n* menuisier *m*

**joinery** *n* menuiserie *f*

**joint** *n anat* + *carp* articulation *f*; *cul* rôti *m*; *coll* (bar, restaurant, etc) bistrot *m*, boîte *f*; (night club) boîte *f* de nuit; *sl* (drugs) joint *m*; **clip** ~ endroit *m* (boîte *f*) où l'on se fait estamper; *anat* **out of** ~ démis, luxé; *fig* disloqué; **put s/o's nose out of** ~ défriser qn, évincer qn; *adj* commun, réuni; *vt* joindre, articuler

**jointed** *adj* articulé; (rod, etc) démontable; **double** ~ désarticulé

**jointly** *adv* en commun, conjointement

**joint-stock** *n* ~ **company** société *f* par actions

**jointure** *n* douaire *m*

**joist** *n* solive *f*

**joke** *n* plaisanterie *f*, blague *f*; (trick) tour *m*; (laughing-stock) risée *f*; **no** ~ une affaire sérieuse; **practical** ~ farce *f*; **the** ~ **is that** le plus drôle c'est que; *vi* plaisanter, blaguer; *coll* **you must be joking!** tu veux rire!, tu plaisantes!

**joker** *n* blagueur -euse; (cards) joker *m*

**jollification** *n* réjouissances *fpl*

**jollity** *n* gaieté *f*

**jolly** *adj* gai, enjoué; agréable; *adv coll* drôlement; *sl* vachement; *vt* enjôler, flatter

**jolt** *n* secousse *f*, choc *m*, coup *m*; *vt* secouer, cahoter; *vi* cahoter

**Jonah** *n* Jonas *m*; porte-malheur *m invar*

**jonquil** *n bot* jonquille *f*, narcisse *m*

**josh** *n US coll* mise *f* en boîte; canular *m*; *vt* mettre en boîte; faire un canular à; *vi* blaguer

**joss-stick** *n* bâton *m* d'encens

**jostle** *n* bousculade *f*; *vt* bousculer; *vi* se bousculer, se cogner

**jot** *n* iota *m*, brin *m*; *vt* ~ **down** noter

**jotter** *n* cahier *m*, bloc-notes *m invar*

**jottings** *npl* notes *fpl*

**journal** n (diary) journal m; (newspaper) journal m; (periodical) revue f; naut livre m de bord
**journalese** n pej jargon m journalistique
**journalism** n journalisme m
**journalist** n journaliste
**journalistic** adj journalistique
**journey** n voyage m; (distance travelled) trajet m, parcours m; vi voyager
**journeyman** n compagnon m
**joust** n joute f; vi jouter
**Jove** n Jupiter m; coll by ~! mon Dieu!, sapristi!
**jovial** adj jovial, enjoué
**joviality** n jovialité f
**jowl** n (jaw) mâchoire f; (cheek) joue f; (flabby cheek) bajoue f; (cattle) fanon m; **cheek by ~** côte à côte
**joy** n joie f, bonheur m; ~**s** plaisirs mpl; **get no ~** ne rien gagner; iron **I wish you ~** je vous souhaite bien du plaisir
**joyful** adj joyeux -euse
**joyless** adj morne, sans joie
**joyous** adj joyeux -euse
**joyousness** n joie f, bonheur m
**joy-ride** n coll virée f, balade f
**joystick** n aer manche m à balai
**jubilant** adj radieux -ieuse, débordant de joie, triomphant, allègre
**jubilate** vi se réjouir, triompher
**jubilation** n jubilation f, exultation f, allégresse f
**jubilee** n eccles jubilé m; **diamond ~** soixantième anniversaire m; **golden ~** cinquantième anniversaire m; **silver ~** vingt-cinquième anniversaire m
**Judaic** adj judaïque
**Judaism** n judaïsme m
**Judas** n Judas m; traître m, judas m
**judas** n (peephole) judas m
**judge** n juge m; connaisseur m; **be a good ~ of** s'y connaître en; **sober as a ~** pas ivre du tout; vt juger, estimer, considérer; vi juger, penser
**judicatory** n tribunal m, cour f; adj judiciaire
**judicature** n justice f; (judges) magistrature f; (system) organisation f judiciaire
**judicial** adj leg judiciaire; fig juste, impartial; ~ **murder** assassinat légal
**judicious** adj judicieux -ieuse
**judo** n judo m
**jug** n pot m, cruche f, broc m; sl (prison) taule f; vt cul cuire à l'étuvée; coll (imprison) coffrer; ~**ged hare** civet m de lièvre
**jugful** n contenu m d'un pot
**juggernaut** n (lorry) mastodonte m; fig force meurtrière
**juggins** n niais -e, cruche f
**juggle** vt jongler avec; vi jongler

**juggler** n jongleur -euse, prestidigitateur -trice
**jugglery** n jonglerie f, tours mpl de passe-passe
**Jugoslav, Yugoslav** n Yougoslave; adj yougoslave
**Jugoslavia, Yugoslavia** n Yougoslavie f
**jugular** n jugulaire f; adj jugulaire
**juice** n jus m; physiol suc m; coll elect courant m
**juiciness** n jutosité m
**juicy** adj juteux -euse; (story) savoureux -euse; (spicy story) salé
**jujube** n jujube m
**ju-jutsu, jiu-jitsu** n jiu-jitsu m
**jukebox** n juke-box m
**julep** n sirop m; US mint ~ bourbon glacé à la menthe
**July** n juillet m
**jumble** n mélange m, fouillis m; ~ **sale** vente f d'objets usagés; vt mélanger, brouiller
**jumbo** n (child language) éléphant m; ~ **jet** avion géant, Boeing m 747
**jump** n saut m; (nervous movement) sursaut m; vt sauter, franchir d'un bond; vi bondir; (nervousness) sursauter, tressauter; ~ **at** sauter sur; ~ **down** descendre d'un bond; ~ **on** s/o prendre qn à partie; ~ **the gun** partir avant le départ; mot ~ **the lights** passer au rouge; ~ **the rails** dérailler; ~ **up and down** sautiller
**jumped-up** adj parvenu, prétentieux -ieuse
**jumper** n pullover m; naut vareuse f
**jumpy** adj nerveux -euse
**junction** n jonction f; (road) bifurcation f; (crossroads) carrefour m; (railway) embranchement m; (rivers) confluent m; (station) gare f de correspondance; elect ~ **box** boîte f de dérivation
**juncture** n jointure f; fig conjoncture f; **at this ~** maintenant
**June** n juin m
**jungle** n jungle f
**junior** n cadet -ette; adj plus jeune, cadet -ette; (subordinate) subalterne; US **John Smith ~** John Smith fils
**juniper** n genévrier m
¹**junk** n ferraille f, vieilleries fpl, bric-à-brac m invar; fig âneries fpl; sl (drugs) came f
²**junk** n (boat) jonque f
**junket** n cul lait caillé
**junketing** n bringue f; US voyage m (banquet m) aux frais de la princesse
**junkie** n sl drogué -e, camé -e, toxicomane
**junta** n junte f
**Jurassic** adj jurassique
**juridical** adj juridique

**jurisdiction** *n* juridiction *f*
**jurisprudence** *n* jurisprudence *f*
**jurist** *n* juriste *m*, légiste *m*
**juror** *n* juré *m*, femme jurée
¹**jury** *n* jury *m*, jurés *mpl*
²**jury** *adj naut* improvisé, de fortune
¹**just** *adj* juste, équitable, mérité, légitime
²**just** *adv* exactement, juste, parfaitement, précisément; (nearly) de justesse; (quite) juste; (simply) tout simplement; (absolutely) tout simplement; ~ **about here** à peu près ici; ~ **as** tout aussi; ~ **look!** regardez un peu ça!; ~ **now** tout à l'heure; en ce moment; ~ **the same** tout de même; **have** ~ venir de; **it's** ~ **as well!** heureusement!; **it's** ~ **one of those things** c'est la vie; **that's** ~ **the point!**

justement!
**justice** *n* justice *f*; équité *f*; (magistrate) juge *m*; **do oneself** ~ se montrer à sa juste valeur
**justiciary** *n* justicier -ière
**justifiable** *adj* justifiable
**justification** *n* justification *f*
**justificative** *adj* justificatif -ive
**justify** *vt* justifier, légitimer, prouver
**justly** *adv* avec raison
**jut** *vi* faire saillie, dépasser; ~ **out** dépasser, saillir
**jute** *n* jute *m*
**juvenile** *n* adolescent -e, jeune; *adj* juvénile; *pej* puéril; ~ **delinquency** délinquence *f* juvénile
**juvenilia** *n* œuvres *fpl* de jeunesse
**juxtapose** *vt* juxtaposer
**juxtaposition** *n* juxtaposition *f*

# K

**Kaffir** *n* Cafre
**kale** *n* chou frisé (d'Écosse)
**kaleidoscope** *n* kaléidoscope *m*
**kaleidoscopic** *adj* kaléidoscopique
**kangaroo** *n* kangourou *m*
**kaolin** *n geol* kaolin *m*
**kapok** *n* kapok *m*, capoc *m*
**karate** *n* karaté *m*
**kedge** *n* ancre *f* de touée
**keel** *n* quille *f*; *fig* navire *m*; *vi* ~ **over** chavirer
**keen** *adj* aiguisé, affilé, tranchant; (cold, mind, feelings) vif (*f* vive); *fig* ardent, acharné, intense; enragé; ~ **appetite** appétit dévorant; *coll* **be** ~ **on s/o** avoir le béguin pour qn; **be** ~ **on sth** être enthousiaste de qch; **have a** ~ **ear** avoir l'ouïe fine
**keenly** *adv* avidement, vivement
**keenness** *n* acuité *f*; (cold) âpreté *f*; ardeur *f*, enthousiasme *m*; (mind) finesse *f*
**keep** *n* donjon *m*; nourriture *f*; *coll* **for** ~ **s** pour de bon; **300 francs a week and his** ~ 300 francs par semaine logé et nourri; *vt* garder; (promise) tenir; (rules, etc) suivre, observer; (preserve) préserver, protéger, défendre; (festival) célébrer; (maintain) maintenir, en-

tretenir; (retain) conserver; (reserve) retenir, réserver; (prevent) empêcher; (delay) retarder; ~ **an appointment** aller à un rendez-vous; (not to miss) ne pas manquer à un rendez-vous; ~ **away** tenir éloigné; ~ **back** retenir; (hide) cacher; ~ **company with** fréquenter; ~ **down** réprimer; (prices) maintenir bas; ~ **from** empêcher de; ~ **in** tenir enfermé; (school) mettre en retenue; ~ **off** éloigner; (repel) repousser; ~ **on** (retain) garder; ~ **one's hand in** s'entretenir la main; ~ **one's temper** ne pas s'emporter; ~ **out** empêcher d'entrer; ~ **s/o waiting** faire attendre qn; ~ **sth from s/o** cacher qch à qn; ~ **under** tenir dans la soumission; ~ **up** (hold up) soutenir; (price) maintenir; (appearances) sauver; (maintain) entretenir; (keep from going to bed) faire veiller; *vi* (last) se garder, se conserver; (stay) rester, se tenir; *coll* ~ **at it** travailler ferme; ~ **away** rester éloigné; ~ **back** rester en arrière; ~ **down** se tapir; ~ **from** s'abstenir de; ~ **off** se tenir à l'écart; ~ **off the grass** défense de marcher sur le gazon; ~ **on** (doing) continuer (à faire); (go forward) avancer; (stay

**keeper**

fixed on) tenir; ~ **out** rester dehors; ~ **straight on** continuer tout droit; ~ **to** s'en tenir à, se conformer à; ~ **together** rester ensemble; ~ **to one-self** faire bande à part, se tenir à l'écart; ~ **to the right** tenir la droite; ~ **up with** marcher de front avec; suivre; ~ **up with the times** être de son temps

**keeper** n garde f, gardien m; surveillant m; (museum) conservateur m

**keeping** n garde f; **in** ~ **with** en rapport avec; **in safe** ~ sous bonne garde

**keepsake** n souvenir m

**keg** n caque f, baril m; (beer) (bière f) pression f

**kelp** n varech m

**ken** n connaissance f

**kennel** n niche f; (dogs' home) ~**s** chenil m

**kerb** n rebord m du trottoir; bord m, bordure f

**kerbstone** n rebord m du trottoir

**kerchief** n fichu m

**kernel** n amande f; fig noyau m

**kerosene** n kérosène m

**kestrel** n crécerelle f

**ketch** n ketch m

**ketchup** n ketchup m

**kettle** n bouilloire f; **a pretty** ~ **of fish!** voilà une belle affaire!

**kettledrum** n timbale f

¹**key** n clef f, clé f; (piano, typewriter) touche f; mus ton m; mech clavette f; ~ **money** pas m de porte; **under lock and** ~ sous clef; adj essentiel -ielle; ~ **person** personnage m clef; vt mus ~ **up** accorder; ~**ed up** tendu

²**key** n ilôt m à fleur d'eau

**keyboard** n clavier m

**keyhole** n trou m de serrure

**keynote** n ton m; fig idée principale

**key-ring** n porte-clefs m invar

**keystone** n clef f de voûte

**khaki** n kaki m; adj kaki invar

**kibbutz** n (pl kibbutzim) kibboutz m

**kibosh** n sl bêtises fpl; sl **put the** ~ **on** mettre fin à

**kick** n coup m de pied; (gun) recul m; (thrill) plaisir violent; **for** ~**s** histoire de rire; **free** ~ coup franc; **penalty** ~ coup m de pénalité; vt donner un coup de pied à; ~ **a goal** marquer un but; ~ **one's heels** poireauter; ~ **out** chasser à coups de pied; sl ~ **s/o up the arse** botter les fesses à qn; coll ~ **the bucket** mourir, coll crever; ~ **up a row** faire du tapage; vi donner des coups de pied; (gun) reculer; (horse, etc) ruer; ~ **against** regimber contre; ~ **off** donner le coup d'envoi

**kick-off** n coup m d'envoi

¹**kid** n chevreau m; coll (child) gosse,

mioche m; ~ **brother** petit frère: **handle s/o with** ~ **gloves** ménager qn

²**kid** vt coll faire marcher, tromper

**kid-glove** adj délicat

**kidnap** vt enlever, kidnapper

**kidnapper** n ravisseur -euse, kidnappeur -euse

**kidnapping** n enlèvement m, vol m d'enfant

**kidney** n anat rein m; cul rognon m; **of the same** ~ du même acabit

**kidney-bean** n haricot m

**kill** n mise f à mort; (hunting) tableau m (de chasse); vt tuer, abattre; (destroy) détruire; (sound) amortir; ~ **off** exterminer; ~ **or cure remedy** remède m héroïque; ~ **two birds with one stone** faire d'une pierre deux coups; coll **be dressed to** ~ être en grand tralala

**killer** n tueur -euse; meurtrier -ière

**killer-whale** n épaulard m

**killing** n tuerie f; (Stock Exchange) **make a** ~ faire un grand bénéfice; adj meurtrier -ière; (work) tuant; (joke) tordant; coll crevant

**killjoy** n rabat-joie m invar, trouble-fête m invar

**kiln** n four m

**kilo** n kilo m

**kilocycle** n rad + elect kilohertz m

**kilogram(me)** n kilogramme m, kilo m

**kilolitre** n kilolitre m

**kilometre** n kilomètre m

**kilowatt** n kilowatt m

**kilowatt-hour** n kilowatt-heure m (pl kilowatts-heures)

**kilt** n kilt m

**kimono** n kimono m

**kin** n parents mpl; parenté f, famille f; **inform the next of** ~ prévenir la famille

¹**kind** n genre m, sorte f, espèce f; (nature) nature f; coll ~ **of** en quelque sorte; **in a** ~ **of way** en quelque sorte; **nothing of the** ~ rien de la sorte; **of its** ~ dans son genre; **pay in** ~ payer en nature; **repay s/o in** ~ rendre à qn la monnaie de sa pièce

²**kind** adj bon (f bonne), aimable, gentil -ille, bienveillant; **give my** ~ **regards to** faites mes amitiés à; **it's very** ~ **of you** c'est très aimable à vous

**kindergarten** n école maternelle, jardin m d'enfants

**kind-hearted** adj bienveillant; **be** ~ avoir bon cœur

**kindle** vt allumer, enflammer; susciter; vi prendre feu, s'enflammer

**kindling** n allumage m; bois m d'allumage

**kindly** adj bon (f bonne), aimable, bienveillant; adv avec bonté; ~ **close the**

**door** veuillez fermer la porte
**kindness** *n* bonté *f*, amabilité *f*; service *m*
**kindred** *n* parenté *f*, parents *mpl*; *adj* du même genre, apparenté; ~ **spirit** âme *f* sœur
**kinetic** *adj* cinétique
**kinetics** *npl* cinétique *f*
**king** *n* roi *m*; (draughts) dame *f*
**kingdom** *n* royaume *m*; **animal** ~ règne animal; **United Kingdom** Royaume-Uni
**kingfisher** *n* martin-pêcheur *m* (*pl* martins-pêcheurs)
**kingly** *adj* royal, de roi
**king-pin** *n* cheville ouvrière
**kingship** *n* royauté *f*
**king-size(d)** *adj* géant
**kink** *n* nœud *m*; faux pli; lubie *f*
**kinky** *adj* (rope) noué; (hair) crépu; *coll* (person) bizarre, pas normal
**kinsfolk** *npl* parents *mpl*
**kinship** *n* parenté *f*
**kinsman** *n* parent *m*
**kinswoman** *n* parente *f*
**kiosk** *n* kiosque *m*
**kip** *n coll* plumard *m*; *vi* se pieuter
**kipper** *n* kipper *m*
**kirk** *n Scots* église *f*
**kiss** *n* baiser *m*; ~ **of life** bouche à bouche *m*; *vt* embrasser, donner un baiser à, baiser; ~ **the dust** mordre la poussière
**kiss-curl** *n* accroche-cœur *m*
**kisser** *n sl* gueule *f*
**kissing** *n* baisers *mpl*, embrassement *m*
**kit** *n* effets *mpl*; *mil* équipement *m*; bagage *m*; outils *mpl*; (assembly) kit *m*; **repair** ~ nécessaire *m* de réparation
**kit-bag** *n* sac *m* de voyage; *mil* ballot *m*
**kitchen** *n* cuisine *f*; ~ **utensils** batterie *f* de cuisine; **soup** ~ soupe *f* populaire; **thieves'** ~ repaire *m* de voleurs
**kitchenette** *n* petite cuisine
**kitchen-garden** *n* jardin potager
**kitchen-maid** *n* fille *f* de cuisine
**kite** *n orni* milan *m*; cerf-volant *m* (*pl* cerfs-volants); *fig* **fly a** ~ lancer un ballon d'essai, tâter le terrain
**kith** *n* ~ **and kin** amis *mpl* et parents *mpl*, famille *f*
**kitten** *n* chaton *m*; petit(e) chat(te)
¹**kitty** *n see* **kitten**
²**kitty** *n* cagnotte *f*
**klaxon** *n* klaxon *m*
**kleptomania** *n* kleptomanie *f*
**kleptomaniac** *n* kleptomane
**knack** *n* don *m*; chic *m*; tour *m* de main
**knacker** *n* abatteur *m* de chevaux, équarisseur *m*
**knapsack** *n* havresac *m*
**knave** *n* fripon *m*, coquin *m*; (cards)

**valet** *m*
**knavery** *n* fourberie *f*
**knavish** *adj* fourbe, de coquin
**knead** *vt* pétrir; (clay) travailler
**kneading-trough** *n* pétrin *m*
**knee** *n* genou; **on one's** ~**s** à genoux; *vt* pousser du genou
**knee-breeches** *npl* culotte courte
**knee-cap** *n anat* rotule *f*
**knee-deep** *adj* + *adv* jusqu'aux genoux, à hauteur du genou
**kneel** *vi* s'agenouiller, se mettre à genoux
**kneeler** *n eccles* agenouilloir *m*
**kneeling** *n* agenouillement *m*; *adj* agenouillé
**knell** *n* glas *m*
**knickerbockers** *npl* culotte bouffante; knickerbockers *mpl*
**knickers** *npl* culotte *f*; pantalon *m* de femme
**knick-knack** *n* (cheap) colifichet *m*; bibelot *m*
**knife** *n* couteau *m*; *surg* bistouri *m*; **have one's** ~ **into** s/o s'acharner contre (après) qn; **war to the** ~ guerre *f* à outrance; *vt* donner un coup de couteau à; poignarder
**knife-edge** *n* arête *f* en lame de couteau
**knife-grinder** *n* rémouleur *m*
**knife-rest** *n* porte-couteau *m*
**knife-sharpener** *n* affiloir *m*, fusil *m*
**knight** *n* chevalier *m*; (chess) cavalier *m*; *vt* créer chevalier
**knight-errant** *n* chevalier errant
**knighthood** *n* chevalerie *f*; titre *m* de chevalier
**knightly** *adj* chevaleresque
**knit** *vt* tricoter; joindre, unir; ~ **one's brows** froncer les sourcils; *vi* tricoter; ~ **together** se souder
**knitting** *n* tricot *m*; tricotage *m*; soudure *f*
**knitting-machine** *n* machine *f* à tricoter
**knitting-needle** *n* aiguille *f* à tricoter
**knob** *n* bosse *f*; bouton *m*; (door) poignée *f*; (walking-stick) pomme *f*
**knobb(l)y** *adj* noueux -euse
**knock** *n* coup *m*, heurt *m*; **hear a** ~ entendre frapper; *vt* frapper, heurter; *coll* critiquer; ~ **about** maltraiter, malmener; *sl* ~ **back** s'envoyer; ~ **down** renverser, abattre; (at auction) adjuger; ~ **in** enfoncer; défoncer; ~ **off** faire tomber de; achever; *sl* faucher; ~ **out** faire sortir; supprimer; mettre knock-out; éliminer; ~ **over** renverser, faire tomber; *coll* ~ **up** construire rapidement; (awaken) réveiller; *vi* frapper, taper; cogner; ~ **about** bourlinguer; ~ **against** se heurter contre; *coll* ~ **off** débrayer

# knockabout

**knockabout** n bateleur m, clown m; adj bruyant, violent
**knock-down** adj (price) minimum; de réclame
**knocker** n marteau m (de porte)
**knock-kneed** adj cagneux -euse
**knock-out** n knock-out m
**knoll** n tertre m, monticule m
**knot** n nœud m; groupe m; vt nouer, faire un nœud à; vi se nouer
**knotty** adj noueux -euse; difficile
**know** vt (facts) savoir; connaître; reconnaître; distinguer; ~ **best** être le meilleur juge de; ~ **better than to** se garder de, être trop avisé pour; ~ **how to do sth** savoir faire qch; ~ **of** connaître; connaître de réputation; avoir entendu parler de; **don't I ~ it!** à qui le dites-vous!; **get to** ~ apprendre à connaître; faire la connaissance de; **let s/o** ~ faire savoir à qn; **not that I** ~ pas que je sache
**knowable** adj connaissable; reconnaissable
**know-all** n personne f qui prétend tout savoir
**know-how** n connaissance f technique

**knowing** adj malin (f maligne), rusé; **without my** ~ à mon insu
**knowingly** adv sciemment, à bon escient
**knowledge** n connaissance f; savoir m, connaissances fpl; **not to my** ~ pas que je sache; **without my** ~ à mon insu
**knowledgeable** adj bien informé
**¹knuckle** n jointure f du doigt; ~ **of veal** jarret m de veau
**²knuckle** vi ~ **down** s'y mettre; ~ **under** se soumettre
**knucklebone** n osselet m
**knuckleduster** n coup-de-poing (pl coups-de-poing) américain
**knurl** n mech molette f
**koala, koolah** n zool koala m
**kohlrabi** n bot chou-rave m (pl choux-raves)
**Koran** n Coran m
**Korean** adj coréen -éenne
**kosher** adj kascher invar, cascher invar
**kow-tow** vi se prosterner, s'aplatir
**Kremlin** n Kremlin m
**kudos** n gloire f, gloriole f
**kummel** n kummel m

# L

**la** n mus la m
**lab** n labo m
**label** n étiquette f; vt étiqueter
**labial** adj labial
**laboratory** n laboratoire m; ~ **assistant** laborantin -e
**laborious** adj laborieux -ieuse, travailleur -euse; pénible
**labour** n travail m, labeur m, peine f; main d'œuvre f; pol Labour les travaillistes; ~ **exchange** bureau public de placement; US **labor union** syndicat (ouvrier); adj pol travailliste; vt ~ **a point** s'étendre sur qch; vi travailler, peiner; ~ **under a delusion** être victime d'une illusion
**laboured** adj pénible; travaillé
**labourer** n travailleur m; manœuvre m
**labouring** adj ouvrier -ière
**labour-saving** adj qui allège le travail
**labrador** n terre-neuve m invar
**laburnum** n bot cytise m

**labyrinth** n labyrinthe m, dédale m
**lace** n dentelle f; (shoe) lacet m; galon m; vt lacer; garnir de dentelles; (drink) arroser
**lacerate** vt lacérer, déchirer
**laceration** n lacération f, déchirure f
**lachrymose** adj larmoyant
**lack** n manque m, défaut m; **for** ~ **of** faute de; vt manquer de; vi manquer
**lackadaisical** adj apathique, languissant
**lackey** n laquais m
**lacking** adj dépourvu (de), dénué (de)
**laconic** adj laconique
**lacquer** n laque f, peinture laquée; vt laquer; vernir
**lacrosse** n crosse canadienne
**lacuna** n lacune f
**lad, laddie** n garçon m, jeune homme m
**ladder** n échelle f; (stocking) maille f qui file
**ladder-proof** adj indémaillable
**laddie** n see lad

**lade** *vt naut* charger

**laden** *adj* chargé

**la-di-da** *adj coll* affecté

**lading** *n naut* bill of ~ connaissement *m*

**ladle** *n* louche *f*; *vt* ~ out servir

**lady** *n* dame *f*; dame bien élevée; **Lady Day** Fête *f* de l'Annonciation; ~ **doctor** femme *f* médecin; **ladies and gentlemen!** mesdames, mesdemoiselles, messieurs!; **ladies' man** homme galant; **Our Lady** Notre-Dame *f*, la Sainte Vierge; **young** ~ demoiselle *f*, jeune femme *f*

**ladybird**, *US* **lady-bug** *n* coccinelle *f*; *coll* bête *f* à bon Dieu

**lady-in-waiting** *n* dame *f* d'atour

**lady-killer** *n* tombeur *m* de femmes

**ladylike** *adj* distingué, comme il faut, de dame

**ladyship** *n* **your (her)** ~ madame la comtesse (marquise, etc)

**¹lag** *n coll old* ~ repris *m* de justice

**²lag** *vi* traîner, rester en arrière; retarder

**³lag** *vt* garnir, envelopper

**lager** *n* bière blonde allemande

**laggard** *n* traînard -e; *adj* lent, paresseux -euse

**lagging** *n* enveloppe *f*, garniture *f*; enveloppe isolante

**lagoon** *n* lagune *f*; (coral) lagon *m*

**laid** *adj coll* ~ **back** calme, imperturbable

**lair** *n* repaire *m*, tanière *f*

**laissez-faire, laisser-faire** *n* laisser-faire *m invar*

**laity** *n* les laïques *mpl*

**lake** *n* lac *m*

**lake-dwelling** *adj* lacustre

**lakeland** *n* la Région des Lacs (en Angleterre)

**lama** *n* lama *m*

**lamb** *n* agneau *m*; ~ **chop** côtelette *f* d'agneau; *bot* ~**'s lettuce** mâche *f*; *vi* mettre bas

**lame** *adj* boiteux -euse; (crippled) estropié; (excuse) faible, pauvre; **be** ~ boiter; *vt* rendre boiteux -euse; estropier

**lameness** *n* boitement *m*; (excuse) faiblesse *f*

**lament** *n* lamentation *f*; *vt* pleurer; *vi* se lamenter

**lamentable** *adj* lamentable, déplorable

**lamentation** *n* lamentation *f*

**lamented** *adj* late ~ regretté

**laminate** *vt* laminer; diviser en lamelles

**lamination** *n* laminage *m*

**lamp** *n* lampe *f*; *mot* phare *m*; (cycle) lanterne *f*; **ceiling** ~ plafonnier *m*; **table** ~ lampe *f* de table; **wall** ~ applique *f*

**lamp-bracket** *n* applique *f*

**lamp-holder** *n* douille *f*

**lamplighter** *n* allumeur *m* de réverbères

**lampoon** *n* libelle *m*, satire *f*; *vt* lancer des satires contre

**lamp-post** *n* réverbère *m*

**lamprey** *n* lamproie *f*

**lampshade** *n* abat-jour *m invar*

**lance** *n* lance *f*; *vt med* (abscess) percer

**lancer** *n mil* lancier *m*

**lancet** *n med* lancette *f*, bistouri *m*

**land** *n* terre *f*; (country) pays *m*; (ground) terrain *m*, sol *m*; **dry** ~ terre *f* ferme; **native** ~ patrie *f*; *vt* mettre à terre, débarquer; ~ **a blow** porter un coup; **be** ~**ed with sth** rester avec qch sur les bras; *vi* atterrir; descendre à terre, débarquer; tomber, retomber; (on moon) alunir; ~ **on one's feet** retomber sur ses pieds

**land-agent** *n* intendant *m* d'un domaine

**landed** *adj* (proprietor) terrien -ienne; (property) foncier -ière

**landfall** *n naut* arrivée *f* en vue de terre

**land-girl** *n* femme *f* agriculteur

**landing** *n naut* débarquement *m*; mise *f* à terre; *aer* atterrissage *m*; (on sea) amerrissage *m*; (on moon) alunissage *m*

**landing-craft** *n* péniche *f* de débarquement

**landing-ground** *n* terrain *m* d'atterrissage

**landing-net** *n* épuisette *f*

**landing-stage** *n* débarcadère *m*; ponton *m*

**landlady** *n* propriétaire *f*; logeuse *f*; hôtelière *f*; patronne *f*

**land-line** *n* câble aérien, câble *m* téléphonique

**landlocked** *adj* enfermé dans les terres

**landlord** *n* propriétaire *m*; aubergiste *m*; hôtelier *m*

**landlubber** *n* terrien -ienne; marin *m* d'eau douce

**landmark** *n* point *m* de repère; borne *f*, limite *f*; *fig* événement marquant

**landowner** *n* propriétaire foncier

**land-rover** *n* voiture *f* tout-terrain *invar*; tout-terrain *m invar*

**landscape** *n* paysage *m*

**landscape-painter** *n* paysagiste *m*

**landslide** *n* éboulement *m*; *pol* victoire écrasante

**landslip** *n* glissement *m* de terrain

**lane** *n* chemin *m*; ruelle *f*; *naut* route *f* de navigation; (for traffic) voie *f*; **three-** ~ **motorway** autoroute *f* à trois voies

**lang syne** *n Scots* le temps jadis; *adv* jadis, autrefois

**language** *n* langue *f*; (expression) langage *m*; **bad** ~ langage grossier; **modern** ~**s** langues vivantes

**languid** *adj* languissant, langoureux -euse

**languish** *vi* languir

**languishing** *adj* languissant

**languor** *n* langueur *f*

**lank** *adj* maigre; pendant; (animal) efflanqué

**lanky** *adj* maigre, grand et maigre

**lantern** *n* lanterne *f*; *naut* fanal *m*; **Chinese ~** lampion *m*; **magic ~** lanterne *f* magique

**lanyard** *n* aiguillette *f*; *naut* cordon *m*

¹**lap** *n* giron *m*; (clothing) pan *m*, basque *f*; **in the ~ of the gods** impossible à prévoir; **on s/o's ~** sur les genoux de qn

²**lap** *n* tour *m* de piste, circuit *m*

³**lap** *vt* laper; **~ up** avaler; *vi* clapoter

⁴**lap** *vt* **~ over** recouvrir; **~ round** enrouler autour; *vi* **~ over** chevaucher

**lapdog** *n* chien *m* d'appartement; bichon -onne

**lapel** *n* revers *m*

**lapidary** *n* lapidaire *m*; *adj* lapidaire

**Lapp** *n* Lapon -one; *adj* lapon -one

**lapse** *n* (time) cours *m*; laps *m* de temps; (mistake) erreur *f*, faute *f*; *leg* déchéance *f*; *vi* manquer à ses devoirs; faire un faux pas; *leg* tomber en désuétude

**lapsed** *adj* déchu; (ticket) périmé; *leg* périmé; caduc (*f* caduque)

**lapwing** *n* vanneau *m*

**larceny** *n* larcin *m*, vol *m*

**larch** *n bot* mélèze *m*

**lard** *n* saindoux *m*; *vt* larder

**larder** *n* garde-manger *m invar*

**large** *adj* grand; gros (*f* grosse); (extensive) étendu; considérable; (numerous) nombreux -euse; **~ sum** forte somme; **at ~** libre, en liberté; **grow ~** grandir; grossir; **in (a) ~ measure** en grande partie; **on a ~ scale** en grand; **set at ~** élargir

**largely** *adv* en grande partie

**large-scale** *adj* grand

**largess(e)** *n* largesse *f*

**lariat** *n* lasso *m*

¹**lark** *n orni* alouette *f*; **sing like a ~** chanter comme un rossignol

²**lark** *n coll* rigolade *f*; **for a ~** pour s'amuser, histoire de rigoler; *vi coll* rigoler; faire des farces

**larkspur** *n bot* pied-d'alouette *m* (*pl* pieds-d'alouette)

**larva** *n* larve *f*

**laryngitis** *n med* laryngite *f*

**larynx** *n anat* larynx *m*

**lascivious** *adj* lascif -ive

**lasciviousness** *n* lasciveté *f*

**laser** *n phys* laser *m*

¹**lash** *n* coup *m* de fouet; (of whip) lanière *f*; (eye) cil *m*; *vt* fouetter, cingler; *vi* ~

out (animal) ruer; **~ out against s/o** se déchaîner contre qn

²**lash** *vt* attacher, lier, ligoter; *naut* amarrer

¹**lashing** *n* coups *mpl* de fouet; **~ s of** des masses de, des tas de; *adj* cinglant

²**lashing** *n naut* amarrage *m*

**lass** *n esp Scots* jeune fille *f*

**lassitude** *n* lassitude *f*

**lasso** *n* lasso *m*; *vt* prendre au lasso

¹**last** *n* (shoe) forme *f*

²**last** *adj* dernier -ière; **~ but one** avant-dernier -ière; **~ night** hier soir; (in the night) cette nuit; **~ year** l'année passée (dernière); **at ~** enfin; **in the ~ resort** en dernier ressort; **the ~ straw** le bouquet; *fig* **the ~ word** le dernier cri; **to the ~** jusqu'au bout; **we shall never hear the ~ of it** on ne nous le laissera pas oublier; *adv* la dernière fois

³**last** *vi* durer; **it will ~ me six months** ça me fera six mois

**lasting** *adj* durable; résistant

**lastly** *adv* en dernier lieu

¹**latch** *n* loquet *m*

²**latch** *vi coll* **~ on to sth** piger qch

**latch-key** *n* clef *f* de maison

**late** *adj* tard; (not on time) en retard; (delayed) tardif -ive; récent; (deceased) décédé, feu; (former) ancien -ienne; **it is getting ~** il se fait tard; **latest** dernier -ière; **of ~** dernièrement; *adv* tard; en retard; **get up ~** faire la grasse matinée; **see you later!** à tout à l'heure!; **sooner or later** tôt ou tard

**late-comer** *n* retardataire

**lately** *adv* dernièrement

**lateness** *n* retard *m*; heure tardive; arrivée tardive; (fruit) tardiveté *f*

**latent** *adj* latent; caché

**lateral** *adj* latéral

**latex** *n bot* latex *m*

**lath** *n bui* latte *f*

**lathe** *n* tour *m*

**lather** *n* mousse *f* de savon; (horse) écume *f*; *vt* savonner; *vi* mousser

**Latin** *n* (language) latin *m*; *adj* latin

**latitude** *n* latitude *f*

**latrine** *n* latrines *fpl*

**latter** *adj* dernier -ière; second; *pron* **the ~** celui-ci (*f* celle-ci, *mpl* ceux-ci)

**latterly** *adv* dernièrement

**lattice-window** *n* fenêtre treillagée

**lattice(-work)** *n* treillis *m*; *vt* treillisser, treillager

**Latvian** *adj* letton -on(n)e

**laud** *vt* louer

**laudable** *adj* louable, digne d'éloges

**laudanum** *n* laudanum *m*

**laudatory** *adj* élogieux -ieuse

**laugh** *n* rire *m*; **with a ~** en riant; *vi* rire; **~ at s/o** se moquer de qn; **~ at sth** rire de qch; ~ **heartily** rire de bon cœur; ~ **in s/o's face** rire au nez de qn; ~ **sth off** tourner qch en plaisanterie; ~ **to oneself** rire tout bas; **burst out** ~**ing** éclater de rire; **don't make me** ~! laissez-moi rire!

**laughable** *adj* risible, ridicule

**laughing** *adj* rieur (*f* rieuse); ~ **gas** gaz hilarant; **it's no** ~ **matter** il n'y a pas de quoi rire

**laughing-stock** *n* risée *f*

**laughter** *n* rire *m*, rires *mpl*; **roar with** ~ rire aux éclats

¹**launch** *n* chaloupe *f*

²**launch** *vt* lancer; ~ **an attack** déclencher une attaque; *vi* ~ **out into** se lancer dans

**launching** *n* lancement *m*

**launching-pad** *n* aire *f* de lancement

**launder** *vt* blanchir

**launderette** *n* laverie *f* (automatique)

**laundering** *n* blanchissage *m*

**laundress** *n* blanchisseuse *f*

**laundry** *n* blanchisserie *f*; (linen, etc) linge *m*; (wash-place) buanderie *f*

**laureate** *n* + *adj* lauréat -e

**laurel** *n bot* laurier *m*; **rest on one's** ~ **s** se reposer sur ses lauriers

**lava** *n* lave *f*

**lavatory** *n obs* cabinet *m* (de toilette), lavabo *m*; (W.C.) waters *mpl*, cabinets *mpl*, toilettes *fpl*

**lavender** *n* lavande *f*; ~ **water** eau *f* de lavande

**lavish** *adj* prodigue; abondant, somptueux -euse; *vt* prodiguer

**lavishness** *n* prodigalité *f*

**law** *n* loi *f*; (system of laws, profession) droit *m*; ~ **and order** ordre public; ~ **court** tribunal *m*; **be a** ~ **unto oneself** n'en faire qu'à sa tête; **be at** ~ être en procès; **common** ~ droit coutumier; **go to** ~ avoir recours (recourir) à la justice; **lay down the** ~ faire la loi; **she thinks she's above the** ~ elle se croit tout permis; **study** ~ étudier le droit, faire son droit

**law-abiding** *adj* respectueux -euse des lois

**law-breaker** *n* transgresseur *m*

**lawful** *adj* légal; licite, permis; légitime

**lawgiver** *n* législateur -trice

**lawless** *adj* sans loi; déréglé

**lawlessness** *n* dérèglement *m*, anarchie *f*

¹**lawn** *n* pelouse *f*, gazon *m*

²**lawn** *n* (textile) batiste *f*

**lawn-mower** *n* tondeuse *f*

**lawn-tennis** *n* tennis *m*, lawn-tennis *m*

**lawsuit** *n* procès *m*

**lawyer** *n* homme *m* de loi; juriste *m*; (solicitor) notaire *m*; (barrister) avocat -e

**lax** *adj* (person) négligent; (behaviour) relâché; (authority) mou (*f* molle); (limp) flasque; **become** ~ se relâcher

**laxative** *n* laxatif *m*; *adj* laxatif -ive

**laxity** *n* relâchement *m*

¹**lay** *n* lai *m*, chanson *f*

²**lay** *adj* laïque

³**lay** *vt* mettre, poser, placer; coucher; (eggs) pondre; (dust) abattre; (bet) parier; (fire) préparer; *sl* coucher avec; ~ **aside** mettre de côté; ~ **bare** mettre à nu; ~ **down** déposer, poser; (arms) rendre; (give up) renoncer à; (rules) établir; (ship) mettre en chantier; ~ **down the law** faire la loi; ~ **hold of** saisir; ~ **in** faire provision de; *fig* ~ **it on thick** y aller fort; ~ **off** licencier, congédier; ~ **out** arranger, disposer; (spend) dépenser; (corpse) faire la toilette de; *coll* étendre d'un coup; ~ **the table** mettre la table (le couvert); ~ **up** amasser; mettre en réserve; (car) remiser; (ship) désarmer; **be laid up** être alité; *vi coll* ~ **off** cesser

**layabout** *n* fainéant -e

**layby** *n* terre-plein *m* de stationnement; (railway) voie *f* de garage

¹**layer** *n* (stratum) couche *f*; (hen) pondeuse *f*; (plant) marcotte *f*; poseur -euse

²**layer** *vt hort* marcotter

**layman** *n* laïc *m*, laïque *m*

**lay-off** *n* mise *f* en chômage technique

**layout** *n* disposition *f*, arrangement *m*

**laze** *vi* paresser

**laziness** *n* paresse *f*

**lazy** *adj* paresseux -euse, indolent

**lazybones** *n* fainéant -e

¹**lead** *n* (metal) plomb *m*; sonde *f*; (pencil) mine *f*; *coll* **swing the** ~ tirer au flanc

²**lead** *n* conduite *f*; *theat* premier rôle *m*; (dog) laisse *f*; *elect* câble *m*, branchement *m*; **give the** ~ montrer la voie

³**lead** *vt* conduire, mener; guider; diriger, commander; (induce) porter; (cards) jouer; ~ **astray** égarer; ~ **away** emmener; ~ **back** ramener; ~ **on** entraîner; ~ **the way** montrer le chemin; ~ **to** amener à; *vi* mener; (cards) jouer le premier (*f* la première); ~ **onto** donner sur

**leaden** *adj* de plomb

**leader** *n* conducteur -trice; guide *m*; chef *m*; (agitator) meneur -euse; (newspaper) article *m* de fond

**leadership** *n* direction *f*; conduite *f*

**leading** *adj* principal; premier -ière; ~ **article** article *m* de fond; ~ **idea** idée maîtresse; *theat* ~ **man** premier rôle

**leaf** *n* (*pl* **leaves**) feuille *f*; (book) feuillet *m*; (door) battant *m*; (table) rallonge *f*;

**leafless**

take a ~ out of s/o's book prendre exemple sur qn; turn over a new ~ changer de conduite; turn over the leaves of a book feuilleter un livre

**leafless** adj sans feuilles

**leaflet** n feuillet m; (advertising) papillon m; pol tract m

**leafy** adj couvert de feuilles; feuillu

**¹league** n ligue f; hist League of Nations Société f des Nations; be in ~ with être ligué (de coalition) avec

**²league** n (distance) lieue f

**³league** vi ~ together se liguer

**leak** n fuite f; (water) écoulement m; infiltration f; have a ~ fuir; coll pisser; spring a ~ faire (une voie d')eau; vt (news) laisser filtrer; vi fuir, avoir une fuite; (ship) faire eau; prendre l'eau; ~ out s'ébruiter

**leakage** n fuite f; perte f

**leaky** adj qui fuit; (ship) qui fait eau; qui laisse entrer l'eau

**¹lean** vt appuyer; vi s'appuyer; se pencher; s'adosser; ~ back in one's chair se renverser dans son fauteuil; ~ forward se pencher en avant; fig ~ over backwards faire le maximum de concessions

**²lean** adj maigre; (animal) efflanqué

**leaning** n penchant m; inclination f; adj penché

**leanness** n maigreur f

**lean-to** n appentis m

**leap** n saut m, bond m; vi sauter, bondir; ~ over franchir d'un bond

**leap-frog** n saute-mouton m; vi jouer à saute-mouton

**leap-year** n année f bissextile

**learn** vt apprendre; savoir

**learned** adj savant, érudit, instruit

**learner** n débutant m

**learning** n science f, savoir m

**lease** n bail m (pl baux); concession f; take on a new ~ of life renaître à la vie; vt louer; (land) affermer

**leasehold** n tenure f à bail; adj tenu à bail

**lease-lend** n prêt-bail m

**leash** n laisse f; vt mettre à l'attache

**leasing** n location f à bail; (land) affermage m

**least** adj moindre, plus petit; le moins important; at the very ~ tout au moins; not in the ~ pas le moins du monde; to say the ~ pour le moins; adv le moins

**leather** n cuir m; (fancy) ~ goods maroquinerie f; vt garnir de cuir; (thrash) rosser

**leatherette** n similicuir m

**leather-neck** n US sl fusilier marin

**leathery** adj qui ressemble au cuir; (meat) coriace

**leave** n permission f, autorisation f; congé m; by your ~ avec votre permission; sick ~ congé m de maladie; take French ~ filer à l'anglaise; take ~ of s/o prendre congé de qn; take one's ~ prendre congé; vt quitter; laisser; partir de; (desert) abandonner; (deposit) déposer; (bequeath) léguer; ~ about laisser traîner; ~ behind laisser; oublier; ~ go lâcher; ~ it to me laissez-moi faire; be left rester; I ~ it to you je m'en remets à vous; three from ten ~s seven dix moins trois égale (reste) sept; vi partir

**leaven** n levain m; vt faire lever

**leavings** npl restes mpl

**Lebanese** n Libanais -e; adj libanais

**Lebanon** n Liban m

**lecher** n débauché m

**lecherous** adj lascif -ive, débauché

**lechery** n lasciveté f

**lectern** n lutrin m

**lecture** n conférence f; coll semonce f; give a ~ faire une conférence; vt sermonner; faire la morale à; vi faire une conférence (des conférences); faire un cours

**lecturer** n conférencier -ière; (university) maître m de conférences, chargé -e de cours

**ledge** n rebord m; saillie f; (building) corniche f

**ledger** n grand livre m

**lee** n abri m; naut côté m sous le vent

**leech** n sangsue f

**leek** n poireau m

**leer** n mauvais regard m; vi regarder d'un air méchant; lancer des œillades

**lees** npl lie f; fig rebut m

**leeward** adj + adv sous le vent

**leeway** n naut dérive f; retard m; liberté f d'action

**left** n gauche f; keep to the ~ tenir la gauche; on the ~ à gauche; adj gauche

**left-hand** adj gauche; ~ drive conduite f à gauche

**left-handed** adj gaucher -ère; ~ compliment compliment douteux

**leftist** n + adj gauchiste

**left-luggage office** n consigne f

**leftward** adv vers la gauche

**left-wing** adj pol de gauche

**leg** n jambe f; (animal) patte f; (chicken) cuisse f; (mutton) gigot m; (furniture) pied m; be on one's ~s être sur pied, être debout; pull s/o's ~ faire marcher qn

**legacy** n legs m

**legal** adj légal; licite; ~ department service m du contentieux; ~ document acte m authentique; take ~ advice consulter un avocat

**legality** n légalité f
**legalize** vt légaliser, rendre légal
**legate** n légat m
**legatee** n légataire
**legation** n légation f
**legend** n légende f; inscription f; explication f
**legendary** adj légendaire
**legerdemain** n tour m de passe-passe; prestidigitation f
**leggings** npl jambières fpl, guêtres fpl
**legibility** n lisibilité f
**legible** adj lisible
**legion** n légion f; **they are ~** ils sont innombrables
**legislate** vi légiférer, faire des lois
**legislation** n législation f
**legislative** adj législatif -ive
**legislator** n législateur m
**legislature** n législature f
**legitimacy** n légitimité f
**legitimate** adj légitime
**legitimatize, legitimize** vt légitimer
**leg-pull** n mystification f
**leguminous** adj légumineux -euse
**leg-up** n give s/o a ~ faire la courte échelle à qn; aider qn à monter en selle
**leisure** n loisir m; ~ **hours** heures fpl de loisir, moments perdus
**leisurely** adj (person) qui n'est pas pressé; lent, mesuré
**leitmotiv** n leitmotiv m
**lemon** n citron m; ~ **sole** limande f; ~ **squash** citronnade f
**lemonade** n citronnade f; **fizzy ~** limonade f
**lemon-drop** n bonbon acidulé au citron
**lemon-squeezer** n presse-citron m invar
**lend** vt prêter; ~ **a hand** prêter secours; ~ **an ear** prêter l'oreille; ~ **oneself to** se prêter à
**lender** n prêteur -euse
**lending-library** n bibliothèque f de prêt
**lend-lease** n prêt-bail m
**length** n longueur f; (time) durée f; (string) bout m; (material) métrage m; **at ~** enfin; **at full ~** d'un bout à l'autre; **at some ~** assez longuement; **fall full ~** tomber de tout son long; **go to great ~s** pousser les choses bien loin; **go to the ~ of doing sth** aller jusqu'à faire qch
**lengthen** vt allonger; rallonger; (time) prolonger; vi s'allonger; croître, grandir
**lengthways, lengthwise** adv en longueur; en long
**lengthy** adj long (f longue); qui traîne en longueur
**leniency** n indulgence f; clémence f
**lenient** adj indulgent; clément
**lens** n lentille f; phot objectif m

**Lent** n carême m
**Lenten** adj de carême
**lentil** n lentille f
**leopard** n léopard m; **American ~** jaguar m
**leopardess** n léoparde f
**leper** n lépreux -euse
**leprechaun** n lutin m
**leprosy** n lèpre f
**leprous** adj lépreux -euse
**lesbian** n lesbienne f; adj lesbien -ienne
**lesion** n lésion f
**less** adj moindre; plus petit; adv moins; ~ **and ~** de moins en moins; **grow ~** diminuer, s'amoindrir; **he continued none the ~** il n'en continua pas moins; **nothing ~ than** rien moins que
**lessee** n locataire; tenancier -ière
**lessen** vt diminuer, amoindrir; vi diminuer, s'amoindrir, s'atténuer
**lesser** adj moindre; petit
**lesson** n leçon f; **let that be a ~ to you** que cela vous serve de leçon; **object ~** (school) leçon f de choses; exemple m; **private ~** leçon particulière
**lest** conj de peur (de crainte) que … ne
¹**let** n ar empêchement m; (tennis, etc) balle f de filet
²**let** n location f; vt (allow) permettre, laisser; (hire out) louer; ~ **alone** laisser tranquille; ~ **down** laisser; laisser descendre; fig faire faux bond à; ~ **go** lâcher, lâcher prise; ~ **him come** qu'il vienne; ~ **in** faire entrer; laisser passer; ~ **off** (pardon) faire grâce à; (gun) tirer; (firework) faire partir; (cry) laisser échapper; coll ~ **on about sth** aller dire qch; ~ **oneself in for sth** s'engager à qch; ~ **out** laisser sortir; (release) lâcher; (secret) trahir; (hire) louer; (fire) laisser éteindre; ~ **s/o do sth** permettre à qn de faire qch; ~ **s/o into the secret** mettre qn dans le secret; ~ **s/o off from doing sth** dispenser qn de faire qch; ~ **'s see** voyons; ~ **up** diminuer; ~ **us go** allons; ~ **us hear about it** racontez-nous cela; ~ **us know** faites-nous savoir
**let-down** n déception f
**lethal** adj mortel -elle; ~ **weapon** arme meurtrière
**lethargic** adj léthargique
**lethargy** n léthargie f
**letter** n lettre f; caractère m; **capital ~** majuscule f; **man of ~s** homme m de lettres; **small ~** minuscule f; vt mettre des lettres sur, graver avec des lettres
**letter-box** n boîte f aux lettres
**letter-card** n carte-lettre f (pl cartes-lettres)
**letterhead** n en-tête m
**lettering** n lettrage m

**letter-press** *n* impression *f* typographique; texte *m*

**lettuce** *n* laitue *f*, salade verte

**let-up** *n* diminution *f*

**leukaemia** *n med* leucémie *f*

**Levant** *n* Levant *m*

**level** *n* niveau *m*; **at eye ~** à la hauteur des yeux; **at ministerial ~** à l'échelon ministériel; **come down to s/o's ~** se mettre au niveau de qn; **on a ~ with** à la hauteur de; *archi* de plain-pied avec; **on the ~** à plat; *coll* de bonne foi; *mot* **speed on the ~** vitesse *f* en palier; *adj* de niveau, horizontal; (ground) uni; **~ with** à fleur de, au ras de; **be ~** être de niveau; **do one's ~ best** faire tout son possible; **keep a ~ head** garder son sang-froid; *vt* niveler, aplanir; (gun) pointer; (direct) diriger; (raze) raser; **~ an accusation** lancer une accusation; **~ out** égaliser

**level-crossing** *n* passage *m* à niveau

**level-headed** *adj* qui a la tête bien équilibrée

**levelling** *n* nivellement *m*

**lever** *n* levier *m*; **gear ~** levier *m* de vitesse; *vt* soulever (manœuvrer) au moyen d'un levier

**leverage** *n* force *f* de levier

**leveret** *n* levraut *m*

**leviathan** *n* Léviathan *m*

**levity** *n* légèreté *f*

**levy** *n* levée *f*; (tax) impôt *m*; *vt* lever; (tax) percevoir

**lewd** *adj* impudique; ignoble

**lewdness** *n* impudicité *f*

**lexicographer** *n* lexicographe

**lexicography** *n* lexicographie *f*

**liability** *n* responsabilité *f*; (tendency) susceptibilité *f*, tendance *f*; **liabilities** dettes *fpl*, obligations *fpl*; **assets and liabilities** actif *m* et passif *m*; **be a ~** être un poids mort

**liable** *adj* responsable; sujet -ette, exposé; (likely) susceptible; **~ to tax** soumis à l'impôt

**liaise** *vi* effectuer la liaison, établir le contact

**liaison** *n* liaison *f*

**liar** *n* menteur -euse

**libel** *n* diffamation *f*; écrit *m* diffamatoire; *vt* diffamer

**libellous** *adj* diffamatoire

**liberal** *adj* libéral; d'esprit large; généreux -euse, prodigue; (plentiful) abondant; **Liberal** *n* + *adj pol* libéral -e

**liberalism** *n* libéralisme *m*

**liberality** *n* libéralité *f*; générosité *f*

**liberalize** *vt* libéraliser

**liberally** *adv* libéralement

**liberate** *vt* libérer; mettre en liberté, lâcher

**liberation** *n* libération *f*

**liberator** *n* libérateur -trice

**libertine** *n* libertin *m*, débauché *m*

**liberty** *n* liberté *f*; **at ~** en liberté; **be at ~ to do sth** être libre de faire qch; **take liberties** prendre des libertés; **take the ~ of doing sth** se permettre de faire qch

**libido** *n* libido *f*

**librarian** *n* bibliothécaire

**library** *n* bibliothèque *f*; **photographic ~** photothèque *f*; **public ~** bibliothèque municipale; **record ~** discothèque *f*

**libretto** *n* livret *m*

**licence** *n* permis *m*; (trade) patente *f*; (permission) permission *f*, autorisation *f*; (freedom) licence *f*; (immorality) débauche *f*; **car ~** carte grise; **driving ~** permis *m* de conduire; **game ~** permis *m* de chasse; **marriage ~** dispense *f* de bans

**license** *vt* accorder un permis (une patente) à; autoriser; **~d** patenté

**licensee** *n* détenteur -trice d'une patente; (pub, café) patron -onne

**licentious** *adj* licencieux -ieuse, dévergondé

**licentiousness** *n* licence *f*, dévergondage *m*

**lichen** *n* lichen *m*

**licit** *adj* licite

**lick** *n* coup *m* de langue; *coll* **at a great ~** à grande vitesse; *vt* lécher; *coll* battre; **~ up** laper; **that's got me ~ed** ça me dépasse

**licking** *n* léchage *m*; *coll* raclée *f*, défaite *f*

**lid** *n* couvercle *m*; (eye) paupière *f*; *coll* **that puts the ~ on it!** ça c'est le comble!

**lido** *n* lido *m*, piscine *f* en plein air

**¹lie** *n* mensonge *m*; **give s/o the ~** donner un démenti à qn; **tell ~s** mentir; **white ~** mensonge innocent; *vi* mentir

**²lie** *n* position *f*, disposition *f*; **~ of the land** configuration *f* du terrain; *vi* être couché (étendu); (be situated) se trouver; (consist) résider; **~ about** traîner; **~ asleep** être endormi; *naut* **~ at anchor** être à l'ancre; **~ down** se coucher, s'étendre; (rest) se reposer; **~ in** faire la grasse matinée; **~ in ambush** se tenir en embuscade; **~ in wait** guetter; **~ over** rester en suspens; *coll* **~ up** garder le lit; *ar* **~ with** coucher avec; **a great future ~s before him** un grand avenir s'ouvre devant lui; **here ~s** ci-gît; **take sth lying down** se laisser faire; **the difference ~s in that …** la différence réside en ceci que …; **time**

lay heavy on his hands le temps lui pesait

**lie-detector** *n* machine *f* à déceler le mensonge

**liege** *n hist* seigneur *m*; *adj* lige

**lie-in** *n coll* have a ~ faire la grasse matinée

**lieutenant** *n* lieutenant *m*

**life** *n* (*pl* lives) vie *f*; (object) durée *f*; biographie *f*; ~ and soul of the party boute-en-train *m invar* de la compagnie; ~ imprisonment prison *f* à perpétuité; a matter of ~ and death une question de vie ou de mort; at my time of ~ à mon âge; early ~ enfance *f*; flee for one's ~ se sauver à toutes jambes; for ~ à vie; from ~ d'après nature; high ~ grande vie; *coll* how's ~? que devenez-vous?; lay down one's ~ donner sa vie; not on your ~! jamais de la vie!; put new ~ into ranimer; run for your lives! sauve qui peut!; save s/o's ~ sauver la vie à qn; such is ~ c'est la vie, ainsi va la vie; take one's ~ se suicider; the prime of ~ la fleur de l'âge; true to ~ tout à fait naturel -elle

**lifebelt** *n* ceinture *f* de sauvetage

**life-blood** *n fig* âme *f*

**lifeboat** *n* canot *m* de sauvetage

**lifebuoy** *n* bouée *f* de sauvetage

**life-cycle** *n* cycle *m* d'évolution

**life-giving** *adj* vivifiant

**life-guard** *n* garde *m* du corps

**life-jacket** *n* gilet *m* de sauvetage

**lifeless** *adj* sans vie, mort; sans vigueur, sans entrain

**lifelike** *adj* vivant, ressemblant

**lifelong** *adj* de toute la vie

**life-preserver** *n* casse-tête *m invar*; *US* ceinture *f* de sauvetage

**life-size** *adj* de grandeur naturelle

**lifetime** *n* vie *f*; in my ~ de mon vivant

**lift** *n* haussement *m*; (in building) ascenseur *m*; ~ attendant liftier -ière; give s/o a ~ faire monter qn (dans sa voiture); goods ~ monte-charge *m invar*; hitch (thumb) a ~ faire de l'auto-stop; *vt* lever, soulever, élever; *agr* lever, arracher; *coll* voler; ~ one's hand against s/o lever la main contre qn; ~ sth down descendre qch; ~ up one's head redresser la tête; *vi* (fog) se disperser, se lever

**liftboy, liftman** *n* liftier *m*

**lift-off** *n* lancement *m*

**ligament** *n anat* ligament *m*

**¹light** *n* lumière *f*; (day) jour *m*; lueur *f*; lampe *f*, bougie *f*; (match) feu *m*; (window) fenêtre *f*; (skylight) lucarne *f*; according to one's ~s selon ses lumières; against the ~ à contre-jour;

by the ~ of à la lumière de; give ~ éclairer; in this ~ sous cet angle; it is ~ il fait jour; navigation ~s feux *mpl* de bord; parking ~s feux *mpl* de stationnement (position); throw ~ on a matter éclairer une question; traffic ~s feux *mpl* rouges, signaux lumineux; *adj* clair; bien éclairé; (hair) blond; *vt* allumer; illuminer, éclairer; *vi* s'allumer; prendre feu; s'éclairer; ~ up (face) s'éclairer; *coll* allumer sa pipe; *coll* lit up éméché

**²light** *adj* léger -ère; (wind) faible; (easy) facile; be a ~ sleeper avoir le sommeil léger; make ~ of faire peu de cas de, traiter à la légère

**³light** *vi* se poser; ~ on trouver, rencontrer, tomber sur

**¹lighten** *vt* éclairer; *vi* s'éclairer; (lightning) faire des éclairs

**²lighten** *vt* alléger; (relieve) soulager

**¹lighter** *n* briquet *m*; (person) allumeur -euse

**²lighter** *n naut* chaland *m*, péniche *f*

**light-fingered** *adj* aux doigts agiles

**light-headed** *adj* étourdi, écervelé

**light-hearted** *adj* enjoué, au cœur gai

**lighthouse** *n* phare *m*

**lighting** *n* éclairage *m*, allumage *m*

**lightness** *n* légèreté *f*

**lightning** *n* éclairs *mpl*, foudre *f*; ~ conductor paratonnerre *m*; ~ strike grève *f* surprise; flash of ~ éclair *m*; *adj* rapide, foudroyant, éclair *invar*

**lights** *npl cul* mou *m*

**lightship** *n* bateau-phare *m* (*pl* bateaux-phares)

**lightweight** *n* (boxing) poids léger; *adj* léger -ère; *fig* insignifiant

**light-year** *n* année-lumière *f* (*pl* années-lumières)

**¹like** *n* pareil *m*; chose *f* semblable; *adj* semblable, pareil -eille; tel (*f* telle); (portrait) ressemblant; ~ father, ~ son tel père, tel fils; *coll* ~ hell! jamais de la vie!; a man ~ him un homme tel que lui; do the ~ en faire autant; he's ~ that il est ainsi; I never saw anything ~ that je n'ai jamais rien vu de pareil; look ~ ressembler à; nothing ~ as loin de; sth ~ ten à peu près dix; that's just ~ a man voilà bien les hommes; that's just ~ him c'est bien lui; there's nothing ~ a good holiday rien ne vaut de bonnes vacances; very ~, ~ enough probablement; what's he ~? comment est-il?; what's it ~? comment est-ce?; *adv* comme; probablement; *prep* comme

**²like** *n* ~s *mpl*, préférences *fpl*; *vt* aimer; (person) aimer bien; (food) trouver bon; ~ it or not bon gré, mal gré; ~ **to do sth** aimer (à) faire qch; **as much as you** ~ tant (autant) que vous voudrez; **do as one** ~**s** en faire à sa tête; **he would** ~ **nothing better** il ne demande pas mieux; **how do you** ~ **it?** comment le trouvez-vous?; **if you** ~ si vous voulez; **I** ~ **him** il me plaît, je le trouve sympathique

**likeable** *adj* sympathique, agréable

**likelihood** *n* probabilité *f*

**likely** *adj* probable, vraisemblable; ~ **to** susceptible de; **coll that's a** ~ **one!** en voilà une bonne!; *adv* **most** ~ très probablement

**like-minded** *adj* du même avis, partageant le même point de vue

**liken** *vt* comparer

**likeness** *n* ressemblance *f*; portrait *m*

**likewise** *adv* également, aussi, pareillement, de même

**liking** *n* goût *m*; penchant *m*; **acquire a** ~ **for sth** prendre goût à qch; **take a** ~ **to s/o** prendre qn en amitié

**lilac** *n* lilas *m*

**lilt** *n* rythme *m*, cadence *f*

**lily** *n* lis *m*; *US sl* tapette *f*; ~ **of the valley** muguet *m*; **water** ~ nénuphar *m*

**lily-livered** *adj* poltron *-onne*

**lily-white** *adj* blanc (*f* blanche) comme le lis

**limb** *n* membre *m*; (tree) branche *f*; ~ **of the law** homme *m* de loi; agent *m* de police; **coll out on a** ~ en plan

¹**limber** *n* avant-train *m*

²**limber** *vi* ~ **up** se dégourdir

**limbless** *adj* sans membres, sans bras ni jambes

**limbo** *n* limbes *mpl*; **descend into** ~ tomber dans l'oubli

¹**lime** *n* chaux *f*; **bird** ~ glu *f*; *vt* gluer

²**lime** *n* (tree) tilleul *m*; (fruit) lime *f*

**lime-kiln** *n* four *m* à chaux

**limelight** *n* **in the** ~ *fig* très en vue; sous les feux de la rampe

**limerick** *n* poème comique, souvent scabreux, en cinq vers

**limestone** *n* pierre *f* à chaux

**limey** *n* *US* (English sailor) marin anglais; *Aust sl* (Englishman) Anglais *m*

**limit** *n* limite *f*, borne *f*; *eng* tolérance *f*; **coll that's the** ~ **!** ça c'est le comble!; *vt* limiter, borner

**limitation** *n* limitation *f*, restriction *f*

**limited** *adj* (mind, view) borné; ~ **edition** édition *f* à tirage restreint; ~ **liability company** compagnie *f* à responsabilité limitée

**limousine** *n* limousine *f*

¹**limp** *adj* flasque, mou (*f* molle)

²**limp** *n* boitement *m*; *vi* boiter, clopiner

**limpet** *n* patelle *f*; **coll fig cling like a** ~ être crampon *f invar*

**limpid** *adj* limpide

**limpidity** *n* limpidité *f*

**limpness** *n* mollesse *f*

**linchpin** *n* eng esse *f*, clavette *f* de bout d'essieu; *fig* clef *f* de voûte

**linctus** *n* sirop *m* pharmaceutique, sirop *m* pour la toux

**linden(-tree)** *n* tilleul *m*

¹**line** *n* ligne *f*; (wire) fil *m*; (row) rang *m*, rangée *f*; corde *f*; file *f*; (wrinkle) ride *f*; (drawing) trait *m*; (stroke) raie *f*; (transport) service *m*, ligne *f*; (railway) voie *f*; (poetry) vers *m*; (note) mot *m*; *geog* équateur *m*; spécialité *f*, genre *m*; queue *f*, file *f*; ~ **drawing** dessin *m* au trait; ~ **of argument** raisonnement *m*; ~ **of business** partie *f*; **draw the** ~ **at sth** ne pas aller jusqu'à; **drop s/o a** ~ envoyer un petit mot à qn; **fall into** ~ **with** se conformer à; (paragraph) **first** ~ alinéa *m*; **leading** ~ article *m* de réclame; **main** ~ grande ligne; **marriage** ~**s** acte *m* de mariage; *vt* (paper) régler; (face) rider; ~ **up** aligner; *vi* ~ **up** s'aligner; faire la queue

²**line** *vt* doubler, fourrer; (edge) border; (pockets) remplir; garnir

**lineage** *n* lignée *f*

**lineament** *n* trait *m*

**linear** *adj* linéaire

**linen** *n* toile *f* (de lin); linge *m*; **table** ~ linge *m* de table; *adj* de toile

**liner** *n* transatlantique *m*, paquebot *m*

**linesman** *n* (sport) arbitre *m* de lignes; (railway) poseur *m* de lignes

**line-up** *n* alignement *m*, mise *f* en rangs

**linger** *vi* s'attarder, tarder; traîner; (sick person) languir, traîner; ~ **on** subsister

**lingerie** *n* lingerie *f*

**lingering** *adj* lent, languissant; ~ **death** mort lente; ~ **look** regard prolongé

**lingo** *n* langue *f* du pays; baragouin *m*

**lingua franca** *n* sabir *m*

**linguist** *n* linguiste

**linguistic** *adj* linguistique

**linguistics** *n* linguistique *f*

**liniment** *n* liniment *m*

**link** *n* chaînon *m*, maillon *m*; (chain) anneau *m*; lien *m*; *vt* relier, enchaîner; *vi* ~ **on to sth** s'unir à qch

**links** *npl* terrain *m* de golf

**linnet** *n* orni linotte *f*

**lino, linoleum** *n* linoléum *m*

**linseed** *n* graine *f* de lin; ~ **oil** huile *f* de lin

**lint** *n* tissu *m* de pansement, charpie *f*

**lintel** *n* linteau *m*

**lion** *n* lion *m*; *coll* célébrité *f*; ~ **cub** lionceau *m*

**lioness** *n* lionne *f*

**lion-hearted** *adj* au cœur de lion
**lionize** *vt coll* traiter comme une personne célèbre
**lip** *n* lèvre *f*; (animal) babine *f*; (cup) bord *m*; (jug) bec *m*; *coll* toupet *m*, insolence *f*; saillie *f*, rebord *m*; **hang on s/o's ~ s** boire les paroles de qn; **he never opened his ~ s** il n'a pas desserré les dents; **keep a stiff upper ~** rester impassible; **smack one's ~ s** se lécher les babines
**lip-read** *vi* lire sur les lèvres
**lip-reading** *n* lecture *f* sur les lèvres
**lip-service** *n* **pay ~** payer de paroles
**lipstick** *n* bâton *m* de rouge; rouge *m* à lèvres
**liquefy** *vt* liquéfier; *vi* se liquéfier
**liqueur** *n* liqueur *f*
**liquid** *n* liquide *m*; *adj* liquide
**liquidate** *vt* liquider
**liquor** *n* boisson *f* alcoolique; *cul* eau *f* de cuisson; *US* alcool *m*; **in ~** ivre
**liquorice, licorice** *n* réglisse *f*
**Lisbon** *n* Lisbonne *f*
**lisp** *n* zézaiement *m*; *vt* + *vi* zézayer
**lissom** *adj* souple, agile
**¹list** *n* liste *f*, rôle *m*; **be on the danger ~** être dans un état grave; **mailing ~** liste *f* d'envoi; **waiting ~** liste *f* d'attente; *vt* cataloguer
**²list** *n naut* bande *f*; **have a ~** donner de la bande; *vi* donner de la bande
**listen** *vi* écouter; faire attention; **~ to** écouter
**listener** *n* auditeur -trice
**listless** *adj* apathique; nonchalant
**lists** *npl* lice *f*
**litany** *n* litanie *f*
**literacy** *n* aptitude *f* à lire et écrire
**literal** *adj* littéral; **in the ~ sense of the word** au sens propre du mot
**literally** *adv* littéralement; **take sth ~** prendre qch au pied de la lettre
**literary** *adj* littéraire
**literate** *adj* qui sait lire et écrire; (well-read) lettré
**literature** *n* littérature *f*; documentation *f*
**lithe** *adj* agile, souple
**litheness** *n* souplesse *f*
**lithograph** *n* lithographie *f*; *vt* lithographier
**Lithuania** *n* Lithuanie *f*
**Lithuanian** *n* Lithuanien -ienne; *adj* lithuanien -ienne
**litigate** *vi* plaider
**litigation** *n* litige *m*
**litre** *n* litre *m*
**litter** *n* (straw, vehicle) litière *f*; (refuse) papiers *mpl* sales; désordre *m*; (animals) portée *f*; *vt* mettre en désordre; **~ed with** encombré de

**litter-bin** *n* boîte *f* à ordures
**little** *n* peu, peu de; **a ~** un peu (de); **a ~ more** encore un peu; **think ~ of sth** faire peu de cas de qch; *adj* petit; **~ ways** manières *fpl*; **I know his ~ game** je sais ce qu'il manigance; **tiny ~** tout petit; *adv* peu; **~ by ~** peu à peu; **a ~** un peu; **for a ~ (while)** pendant un certain temps
**littleness** *n* petitesse *f*
**littoral** *n* littoral *m*
**liturgic(al)** *adj* liturgique
**liturgy** *n* liturgie *f*
**livable, liveable** *adj* vivable; (house, etc) habitable
**live** *vt* **~ a life of** mener une vie de; *coll* **~ it up** mener grand train; *vi* vivre; (dwell) demeurer, habiter; **~ on** continuer à vivre; **~ on sth** se nourrir de qch; **~ sth down** faire oublier qch; **~ well** faire bonne chère; **enough to ~ on** de quoi vivre; **one ~ s and learns** qui vivra verra; *adj* vivant, en vie; *elect* en charge, sous tension; **~ broadcast** émission *f* en direct; **~ cartridge** cartouche chargée; *fig* **he's a ~ wire** il est dynamique
**livelihood** *n* vie *f*; gagne-pain *m invar*
**liveliness** *n* vivacité *f*, animation *f*
**livelong** *adj* **the ~ day** toute la journée
**lively** *adj* vif (*f* vive), animé, gai; **take a ~ interest in** s'intéresser vivement à
**¹liver** *n anat* foie *m*
**²liver** *n* personne *f* qui vit
**liveried** *adj* en livrée
**livery** *n* livrée *f*
**livid** *adj* livide, blême
**living** *n* vie *f*; *eccles* bénéfice *m*; **make a good ~** gagner bien sa vie; *adj* vivant, en vie; **~ or dead** mort ou vif; **~ wage** salaire minimum vital; **no one ~** personne au monde
**living-room** *n* salle *f* de séjour, living (-room) *m*
**living-space** *n* espace vital
**lizard** *n* lézard *m*
**llama** *n* lama *m*
**load** *n* charge *f*; (burden) fardeau *m*; **have a ~ on one's conscience** avoir un poids sur la conscience; **~ s of** des quantités de; **that's a ~ off my mind** c'est un grand soulagement pour moi; **we have ~ s of time** nous avons largement le temps; *vt* charger; (dice) piper; *vi* **~ up** prendre un chargement
**loaded** *adj* chargé; **~ question** question *f* piège; **~ up with** encombré de; **~ with cares** accablé de soucis
**loader** *n* chargeur *m*
**loadstone, lodestone** *n* aimant (naturel)
**¹loaf** *n* pain *m*, miche *f* (de pain); *coll*

tête f; coll use your ~! réfléchis un peu!
²**loaf** vi flâner; ~ **about** faire le (la)
fainéant -e
**loafer** n fainéant -e, flâneur -euse; (shoe)
mocassin m
**loam** n terre grasse, terre végétale
**loan** n prêt m; (borrowing) emprunt m;
**on** ~ **from** prêté par; vt US + coll prêter
**loan-word** n mot m d'emprunt
**loath** adj be ~ **to do sth** répugner à faire
qch; **nothing** ~ très volontiers
**loathe** vt détester, avoir horreur de
**loathsome** adj odieux -ieuse, répugnant
**lob** n lob m; vt lober
**lobby** n vestibule m; (parliament) couloir
m; pol groupe m de pression; US trust
m; vt pol chercher à influencer; vi pol intriguer dans les couloirs de la Chambre
**lobe** n lobe m
**lobelia** n bot lobélie f
**lobster** n homard m
**lobster-pot** n casier m à homards
**local** n habitant -e de l'endroit (du pays);
coll bistrot m du coin; adj local; ~
**government** administration locale; ~
**road** route départementale
**locality** n localité f, voisinage m; caractère local
**localize** vt localiser
**locate** vt découvrir; situer; localiser
**location** n (locating) repérage m; emplacement m, situation f; (S. Africa)
réserve f indigène; cin be on ~ tourner
hors des studios
**loch** n Scots lac m
¹**lock** n mèche f (de cheveux)
²**lock** n serrure f; (padlock) cadenas m;
mot angle m de braquage; (wrestling)
étreinte f; (waterway) écluse f; (gun)
platine f; ~, **stock and barrel** tout sans
exception; **under** ~ **and key** sous clef;
(person) sous les verrous; vt fermer à
clef; (wheels) bloquer; ~ **in** enfermer (à
clef); ~ **out** empêcher d'entrer (en fer-
mant la porte à clef); (industry) lock-
outer; ~ **up** mettre sous clef, enfermer;
fermer à clef; (capital) immobiliser
**locker** n coffre m
**locket** n médaillon m
**lockjaw** n tétanos m, trismus m
**lock-keeper** n éclusier -ière
**locksmith** n serrurier m
**locomotion** n locomotion f
**locomotive** n locomotive f
**locum(-tenens)** n remplaçant -e;
(doctor) suppléant -e
**locust** n criquet m
**locution** n locution f
**lode** n filon m
**lodestar** n étoile f polaire
**lodge** n loge f; **shooting (hunting)** ~
pavillon m de chasse; vt loger, héberger;

(deposit) placer; ~ **a complaint** porter
plainte; vi se loger; ~ **with** s/o
demeurer chez qn
**lodge-keeper** n concierge
**lodger** n locataire
**lodging** n logement m; ~s logement m,
appartement meublé; **let** ~s louer des
chambres; **live in furnished** ~s habiter
en garni
**lodging-house** n hôtel garni
**loft** n grenier m, soupente f
**loftiness** n hauteur f; élévation f
**lofty** adj haut, élevé; (manner) hautain
¹**log** n (fire) bûche f; (timber) bille f; naut
loch m
²**log** n logarithme m
³**log** vt noter, porter au journal
**loganberry** n ronce-framboise f (pl ron-
ces-framboises)
**logarithm** n logarithme m
**log(-book)** n mot carnet m de route; (in
France) carte grise; (ship) journal m de
bord
**log-cabin** n cabane f en rondins
**loggerhead** n be at ~s **with** s/o être en
désaccord avec qn
**loggia** n loggia f
**logic** n logique f
**logical** adj logique; (person) qui a de la
logique
**logician** n logicien -ienne
**logistics** npl logistique f
**loin** n (lamb, veal) filet m; longe f (de
veau); ~s reins mpl
**loin-cloth** n pagne m
**loiter** vi traîner, flâner; (linger) s'attarder
**loiterer** n flâneur -euse
**loitering** n flânerie f; vagabondage m
**loll** vt (head) laisser pendre; vi ~ **about** se
vautrer; ~ **back** se renverser; ~ **out**
pendre
¹**lolly, lollipop** n sucette f
²**lolly** n sl argent m; sl pognon m, sl fric m
**London** n Londres m; **Greater** ~ l'agglomération londonienne; adj londonien -ienne, de Londres
**Londoner** n Londonien -ienne
**lone** adj solitaire, seul; **be a** ~ **wolf** aimer
agir seul
**loneliness** n solitude f
**lonely** adj solitaire, isolé
**lonesome** adj solitaire
¹**long** n **before** ~ avant peu; **for** ~ pendant longtemps; adj long (f longue); **a**
~ **time** longtemps; **be two metres** ~
avoir deux mètres de long; **get** ~er rallonger; **how** ~ **is their garden?** quelle
est la longueur de leur jardin?; **how** ~
**are the holidays?** quelle est la durée des
vacances?; **in the** ~ **run** à la longue;
**that's a** ~ **time ago** il y a longtemps de
cela; adv longtemps; ~ **live the Queen!**

vive la Reine!; **as ~ as** tant que; **don't be ~** dépêchez-vous, ne me faites pas attendre; **how ~ has he been here?** depuis combien de temps est-il ici?; **she won't be ~** elle ne tardera pas; **so ~!** à bientôt!; **so ~ as** pourvu que; **they were not ~ in doing sth** ils eurent vite fait de faire qch

²**long** vi **~ for sth** avoir grande envie de qch; **~ to do sth** avoir bien envie de faire qch

**long-distance** adj **~ runner** coureur -euse de fond; **~ telephone** (téléphone) interurbain m

**longevity** n longévité f

**longhand** n écriture courante

**longing** n grande envie

**longish** adj assez long (f longue)

**longitude** n longitude f

**long-jump** n saut m en longueur

**long-playing** adj **~ record** (disque m) microsillon m

**long-range** adj à longue portée

**long-sighted** adj presbyte; fig prévoyant

**long-standing** adj de longue date

**long-suffering** adj patient; indulgent

**long-term** adj à longue échéance

**longways** adv en long

**long-winded** adj interminable; (boring) ennuyeux -euse

**loo** n coll cabinets mpl

**look** n regard m; air m, mine f; aspect m; coup m d'œil; **good ~s** belle mine; **have a ~ at sth** regarder qch; vi regarder; (appear) paraître, avoir l'air, sembler; **~ about one** regarder autour de soi; **~ after** s'occuper de; (nurse) soigner; **~ at** regarder; **~ away** détourner les yeux (le regard); **~ back** regarder en arrière; (turn round) se retourner; **~ down** baisser les yeux; **~ down on s/o** mépriser qn; **~ for** chercher; **~ forward to sth** attendre qch avec plaisir; **~ here!** écoutez!; **~ in** passer, s'arrêter (chez qn) en passant; **~ into sth** examiner qch; **~ like** ressembler à; **~ on** regarder; **~ out** regarder au dehors; (take care) faire attention; **~ out!** attention!; **~ out for** être à la recherche de; **~ out on** donner sur; **~ over** examiner; **~ sharp!** dépêchez-vous!; **~ s/o up and down** toiser qn; **~ the part** avoir le physique de l'emploi; **~ through** parcourir, examiner; **~ to s/o** compter sur qn; **~ to sth** s'occuper de qch; **~ up** lever les yeux; chercher; (call on) passer chez; (improve) reprendre; **~ up to s/o** respecter qn; **~ well** avoir bonne mine; **it ~s like rain** on dirait qu'il va pleuvoir; **not be much to ~ at** ne pas payer de mine; **to ~ at him** à le regarder

**looker-on** n spectateur -trice; curieux -ieuse

**look-in** n he won't get a **~** il n'a aucune chance

**looking-glass** n glace f, miroir m

**look-out** n guet m; poste m d'observation; (person) guetteur m; **be on the ~** être sur ses gardes; **keep a good ~** faire bonne garde; **that's a poor ~!** voilà une triste perspective!; **that's his ~** c'est son affaire

**look-see** n sl coup m d'œil rapide

¹**loom** n métier m

²**loom** vi se dessiner; **~ ahead** menacer; **~ up** surgir

**loony** n + adj fou (f folle), timbré -e

**loop** n boucle f; (stream) méandre m; vt boucler; **~ the ~** boucler la boucle

**loophole** n (fortress) meurtrière f; fig ouverture f, trou m; fig **find a ~** trouver une échappatoire

**loose** adj (slack) lâche, mal assujetti; détaché; (escaped) évadé; (page) détaché; (morals) relâché; (knot) défait; (screw) desserré; (vague) vague; (tooth, etc) branlant; (translation) approximatif- ive; **at a ~ end** désœuvré; **come ~** se détacher; **let ~** lâcher; vt délier, détacher; (knot) dénouer; (arrow) décocher

**loose-leaf** adj à feuilles mobiles

**loose-limbed** adj démanché, dégingandé

**loosen** vt détacher, relâcher; (screw) desserrer; (untighten) détendre; vi se délier, se défaire

**looseness** n relâchement m; (clothes) ampleur f; (play) jeu m; imprécision f

**loot** n butin m, pillage m

**lop** vt élaguer

**lope** vi **~ along** courir à petits bonds

**lop-eared** adj aux oreilles pendantes

**lop-sided** adj déjeté, de guingois

**loquacious** adj loquace

**loquacity** n loquacité f

**lord** n seigneur m, maître m; **~ of the manor** châtelain m; **live like a ~** vivre en seigneur; **the Lord** le Seigneur; **the Lord's Prayer** le Pater invar, l'oraison dominicale; vt **~ it over s/o** agir en maître avec qn

**lordly** adj majestueux -euse; hautain

**lordship** n suzeraineté f; **your ~** votre Seigneurie; (to nobleman) monsieur le comte, etc

**lore** n savoir m

**lorgnette** n face-à-main m (pl faces-à-main)

**lorry** n camion m; **heavy ~** poids lourd

**lorry-driver** n routier m

**lorryload** n a **~ of** un plein camion de

**lose** vt perdre, égarer; (waste) gaspiller; **~ face** perdre la face; **~ oneself**

s'égarer; ~ **one's temper** se mettre en colère; ~ **sight of s/o** perdre qn de vue; **my watch** ~**s five minutes a day** ma montre retarde de cinq minutes par jour; *vi* perdre; ~ **out** ne pas réussir

**loser** *n* perdant -e; **good (bad)** ~ bon (mauvais) joueur, bonne (mauvaise) joueuse

**losing** *adj* perdant; ~ **game** partie perdue d'avance

**loss** *n* perte *f*; ~ **of voice** extinction *f* de voix; **be at a** ~ être embarrassé, ne savoir que faire; **dead** ~ perte sèche; **sell at a** ~ vendre à perte

**lost** *adj* perdu, égaré; ~ **property office** bureau *m* (service *m*) des objets trouvés; **be** ~ **in thought** être absorbé dans ses pensées

**lot** *n* sort *m*, destin *m*; (share) partage *m*; quantité *f*; beaucoup; (auction, ground) lot *m*; **a** ~ beaucoup, bien; **draw** ~**s** tirer au sort; **it fell to my** ~ **to ...** le sort voulut que je ...; **such a** ~ tellement, tant, un si grand nombre; **what a** ~ **of ...!** que de ...!

**lotion** *n* lotion *f*

**lottery** *n* loterie *f*

**lotto** *n* loto *m*

**lotus, lotos** *n* lotus *m*

**loud** *adj* bruyant; (voice) fort, haut; (colours) voyant, criard; **in a** ~ **voice** à haute voix; *adv* haut

**loudhailer** *n* porte-voix *m*

**loudly** *adv* à voix haute, haut

**loudmouthed** *adj sl* fort en gueule

**loudspeaker** *n* haut-parleur *m*

**lounge** *n* flânerie *f*; salon *m*; (hotel) hall *m*; **sun** ~ véranda *f*; *vi* flâner; (in chair) s'étaler

**lounger** *n* flâneur -euse

**lounge-suit** *n* complet *m*, costume *m*

**lour** *vi see* **lower** *vi*

**louse** *n* (*pl* lice) pou *m*; *sl* salaud *m*

**lousy** *adj* pouilleux -euse; *sl* miteux -euse, moche

**lout** *n* rustre *m*, lourdaud *m*

**lovable** *adj* aimable; sympathique

**love** *n* amour *m*; affection *f*, tendresse *f*; chéri -e; (tennis) zéro *m*; ~ **game** jeu blanc; **fall in** ~ **with** s'éprendre de; **give my** ~ **to** faites mes amitiés à; **make** ~ faire l'amour; **not for** ~ **nor money** à aucun prix; **play for** ~ jouer pour le plaisir; *vt* aimer; **(be in love with)** aimer d'amour; adorer; affectionner

**love-affair** *n* affaire *f* de cœur, aventure amoureuse

**love-bird** *n* perruche *f*; *fig* ~**s** tourtereaux *mpl*

**love-child** *n* enfant naturel -elle

**loveless** *adj* sans amour

**love-letter** *n* billet doux

**love-life** *n* vie sentimentale; vie sexuelle

**loveliness** *n* beauté *f*, charme *m*

**love-lorn** *adj* délaissé

**lovely** *adj* beau (*f* belle); ravissant

**love-making** *n* amour *m*; (courtship) cour amoureuse

**love-match** *n* mariage *m* d'amour

**lover** *n* amoureux -euse; fiancé -e; amant -e; *arts* amateur *m*

**lovesick** *adj* malade d'amour

**love-story** *n* histoire *f* d'amour; roman *m* d'amour

**loving** *adj* tendre, affectueux -euse

¹**low** *n* **all-time** ~ point le plus bas; *adj* bas (*f* basse); (deep) profond; (spirits) abattu; (voice) grave; (vulgar) vulgaire; (dress) décolleté; **lie** ~ rester caché; ~**est price** dernier prix; **the Low Countries** les Pays-Bas; **the** ~**est of the** ~ le dernier des derniers; *adv* bas; à voix basse

²**low** *vi* meugler

**low-born** *adj* de basse naissance

**lowbrow** *adj* peu intellectuel -elle

**low-down** *n coll* **give s/o the** ~ **on** renseigner qn sur

¹**lower** *adj* inférieur, plus bas (*f* basse); *geog* bas (*f* basse); **the** ~ **regions** les régions infernales; *vt* baisser; abaisser; (lessen) diminuer, réduire; rabattre; (bring down) descendre; ~ **oneself** s'abaisser

²**lower** *vi* froncer les sourcils; (sky) s'assombrir, se couvrir, menacer

¹**lowering** *adj* menaçant, sombre

²**lowering** *adj* dégradant, humiliant

**lowing** *n* meuglement *m*

**lowland** *n* plaine basse; ~**s** pays plat

**lowliness** *n* humilité *f*

**lowly** *adj* humble, modeste

**low-lying** *adj* situé en bas, bas (*f* basse)

**lowness** *n* situation basse; (moral) bassesse *f*; (spirits) abattement *m*; (sound) gravité *f*; (volume) faiblesse *f*; (price) modicité *f*

**low-pitched** *adj* grave

**low-priced** *adj* bon marché *invar*

**low-spirited** *adj* triste, abattu

**loyal** *adj* fidèle, dévoué, loyal

**loyalist** *n* loyaliste

**loyalty** *n* fidélité *f*

**lozenge** *n* pastille *f*; (shape) losange *m*

**lubber** *n* lourdaud *m*

**lubricant** *n* lubrifiant *m*; *adj* lubrifiant

**lubricate** *vt* lubrifier; graisser

**lubrication** *n* graissage *m*

**lucid** *adj* lucide, clair

**lucidity** *n* (mind) lucidité *f*; transparence *f*

**luck** *n* chance *f*, hasard *m*; (favourable) bonheur *m*, bonne fortune; **as** ~

would have it par bonheur; **bad ~**
mauvaise chance, déveine *f*; **be in ~**
avoir de la chance; **be out of ~** jouer
de malheur; **good ~!** bonne chance!;
**hard ~!** pas de chance!, tant pis!;
**stroke of ~** coup *m* de chance; **worse
~!** tant pis!
**luckily** *adv* par bonheur, heureusement
**luckless** *adj* malheureux -euse, infortuné
**lucky** *adj* heureux -euse; chanceux -euse;
(bringing luck) porte-bonheur *invar*;
*coll* **~ dog** veinard *m*
**lucrative** *adj* lucratif -ive
**lucre** *n* lucre *m*; **for filthy ~** par amour
du gain
**ludicrous** *adj* risible, grotesque
**luff** *vi naut* lofer
¹**lug** *n coll* + *mech* oreille *f*
²**lug** *vt* tirer, traîner, trimbaler
**luggage** *n* bagages *mpl*
**luggage-rack** *n* porte-bagages *m invar*;
. *mot* galerie *f*
**luggage-van** *n* fourgon *m*
**lugubrious** *adj* lugubre
**lukewarm** *adj* tiède
**lull** *n* moment *m* de calme; (weather)
accalmie *f*; *vt* bercer, endormir; calmer
**lullaby** *n* berceuse *f*
**lumbago** *n* lumbago *m*
**lumbar** *adj* lombaire
**lumber** *n* fatras *m*; *US* bois *m* de charpente; *vt* encombrer, embarrasser; *vi*
**~ along** avancer lourdement
**lumbering** *adj* lourd
**lumberjack,** *US* **lumberman** *n* bûcheron
*m*
**lumber-room** *n* débarras *m*, grenier *m*
**luminous** *adj* lumineux -euse
¹**lump** *n* (piece) morceau *m*; (swelling)
bosse *f*; (earth) motte *f*; masse *f*; (in
soup, etc) grumeau *m*; *med* grosseur *f*;
*sl* (person) pataud *m*; **~ sugar** sucre *m*
en morceaux; **~ sum** somme globale;
*vt* **~ together** mettre ensemble, réunir
²**lump** *vt coll* **he can ~ it!** tant pis pour
lui!, qu'il s'arrange!
**lumpish** *adj* lourd
**lumpy** *adj* (soup, etc) grumeleux -euse;
(soil) rempli de mottes; (person)
difforme, gros (*f* grosse)
**lunacy** *n* folie *f*, démence *f*
**lunar** *adj* lunaire; **~ landing** alunissage
*m*

**lunatic** *n* fou (*f* folle), aliéné -e; **~
asylum** asile *m* d'aliénés; *adj* de fou (*f*
folle)
**lunch** *n* déjeuner *m*; **have ~** déjeuner;
*vt* offrir à déjeuner à; *vi* déjeuner
**luncheon** *n* déjeuner *m*
**lunch-hour** *n* heure *f* du déjeuner
**lung** *n* poumon *m*; **iron ~** poumon *m*
d'acier
**lunge** *n* mouvement *m* en avant; (fencing) botte *f*; *vi* (fencing) se fendre; **~
forward** se précipiter en avant; **~ out
at s/o** allonger un coup de poing à qn
**lupin** *n* lupin *m*
¹**lurch** *n* **leave s/o in the ~** planter là qn
²**lurch** *n* embardée *f*; *mot* cahot *m*; *vi*
(person) tituber; faire une embardée
**lure** *n* leurre *m*, piège *m*; attrait *m*; *vt*
leurrer; attirer
**lurid** *adj* sinistre, effrayant; (sky) rougeoyant
**lurk** *vi* se cacher, rôder
**luscious** *adj* délicieux -ieuse, succulent
**lush** *adj* plein de sève; *coll* abondant;
*coll* agréable, confortable
**lust** *n* luxure *f*; convoitise *f*; *vi* **~ after**
convoiter; **~ for** avoir soif de, avoir
envie de
**lustful** *adj* lascif -ive
**lustily** *adv* vigoureusement
**lustiness** *n* vigueur *f*
**lustre** *n* éclat *m*, splendeur *f*, brillant *m*
**lustrous** *adj* éclatant, brillant
**lusty** *adj* vigoureux -euse, robuste, fort
**lute** *n* luth *m*
**Lutheran** *adj* luthérien -ienne
**luxate** *vt* luxer
**luxuriance** *n* exubérance *f*, luxuriance *f*
**luxuriant** *adj* luxuriant
**luxurious** *adj* luxueux -euse
**luxury** *n* luxe *m*; objet *m* de luxe
¹**lying** *n* mensonge *m*; *adj* faux (*f* fausse)
²**lying** *adj* couché, étendu
**lying-in** *n* accouchement *m*
**lymph** *n anat* lymphe *f*; *med* vaccin *m*
**lymphatic** *adj* lymphatique
**lynch** *vt* lyncher
**lynx** *n* lynx *m*
**lyre** *n* lyre *f*
**lyric** *n* poème *m* lyrique; chanson *f*; **~ s**
couplets *mpl* de chanson; *adj* lyrique
**lyrical** *adj* lyrique
**lyricism** *n* lyrisme *m*

577

# M

ma *n coll* maman *f*
ma'am *n see* madam
mac *n imper m*
macabre *adj* macabre
macadam *n* macadam *m*
macaroni *n cul* macaroni(s) *m(pl)*
macaroon *n* macaron *m*
¹mace *n* masse *f*; *hist* (weapon) massue *f*
²mace *n* (spice) macis *m*
Macedonia *n* Macédoine *f*
macerate *vt + vi* macérer
mach *n aer* mach *m*
machiavellian *adj* machiavélique
machinate *vi* comploter
machination *n* complot *m*, machination *f*
machine *n* machine *f*, appareil *m*; organisation *f*; *vt* façonner; (sewing) piquer à la machine
machine-gun *n* mitrailleuse *f*; *vt* mitrailler
machinery *n* mécanisme *m*, machines *fpl*; *fig* rouages *mpl*
machine-tool *n* machine-outil *f* (*pl* machines-outils)
machinist *n* machiniste
mackerel *n* maquereau *m*
mackintosh *n* imperméable *m*; *obs* manteau *m* en caoutchouc
macrocosm *n* macrocosme *m*
mad *adj* fabriqué, fait; ~-up (face) maquillé; (story) inventé; *US coll* have it ~ avoir réussi; ready-~ confectionné
drive s/o ~ rendre qn fou (*f* folle); go ~ devenir fou (*f* folle); raving ~ fou furieux (*f* folle furieuse), fou (*f* folle) à lier
madam, ma'am *n* madame *f*
madcap *n + adj* écervelé -e
madden *vt* rendre fou (*f* folle), exaspérer
made *adj* fabriqué, fait; ~-up (face) maquillé; (story) inventé; *US coll* have it ~ avoir réussi; ready-~ confectionné
madhouse *n* maison *f* de fous, asile *m* d'aliénés; the place is like a ~ on se croirait chez les fous
madly *adv* follement; furieusement
madman *n* fou *m*
madness *n* folie *f*, démence *f*
madonna *n* madone *f*
madrigal *n* madrigal *m*
madwoman *n* folle *f*
maelstrom *n* maelström *m*; tourbillon *m*

maestro *n* maître *m*, maestro *m*
mafia *n* maf(f)ia *f*
magazine *n* revue *f*, magazine *m*; (rifle) magasin *m*; *mil* magasin *m* d'armes
magenta *n + adj* rouge violacé
maggot *n* ver *m*, asticot *m*
Magi *n* the ~ les Rois *mpl* mages
magic *n* magie *f*, enchantement *m*; *adj* magique
magical *adj* magique
magician *n* magicien -ienne
magisterial *adj* magistral
magistracy *n* magistrature *f*
magistrate *n* magistrat *m*
magnanimity *n* magnanimité *f*
magnanimous *adj* magnanime
magnate *n* magnat *m*
magnesium *n* magnésium *m*
magnet *n* aimant *m*
magnetic *adj* magnétique; ~ tape bande *f* magnétique
magnetism *n* magnétisme *m*
magnetize *vt* magnétiser
magneto *n* magnéto *f*
magnification *n* grossissement *m*
magnificence *n* magnificence *f*
magnificent *adj* magnifique; somptueux -euse
magnifier *n* loupe *f*
magnify *vt* grossir; *phot* agrandir; amplifier; ~ing glass loupe *f*
magnitude *n* grandeur *f*
magnolia *n* magnolia *m*
magnum *n* magnum *m*
magpie *n* pie *f*
mahogany *n* acajou *m*
Mahometan *n + adj see* Mohammedan
maid *n* jeune fille *f*, vierge *f*; (servant) bonne *f*, servante *f*; ~ of all work bonne *f* à tout faire; ~ of honour demoiselle *f* d'honneur; lady's ~ femme *f* de chambre; old ~ vieille fille; the Maid of Orleans la Pucelle d'Orléans
maiden *n* jeune fille *f*, vierge *f*; ~ aunt tante non mariée; ~ lady demoiselle *f*; ~ name nom *m* de jeune fille; ~ voyage premier voyage
maidenhead *n* hymen *m*
maidenhood *n* virginité *f*
maidenly *adj* modeste; de jeune fille
maidservant *n* servante *f*, bonne *f*
¹mail *n* courrier *m*; ~ boat courrier postal; ~ train train-poste *m* (*pl* trains-poste); *vt* envoyer par la poste

578

**malign**

²**mail** *n* maille *f*
**mailbag** *n* sac postal
**mail-box** *n* US boîte *f* aux lettres
**mail-coach** *n* *obs* malle-poste *f* (*pl* malles-poste)
**mailing-list** *n* liste *f* d'adresses
**mail-man** *n* US facteur *m*
**mail-order** *n* commande *f* par poste; ~ **firm** maison *f* de vente par correspondance
**maim** *vt* estropier, mutiler
**main** *n* conduite principale; *lit* (sea) océan *m*; *elect* ~ s câble *m* de distribution; ~ s **water** eau *f* de la ville; **in the** ~ en général; **with might and** ~ de toutes ses forces; *adj* principal, essentiel -ielle; ~ **dish** plat *m* de résistance; ~ **line** voie principale, grande ligne; ~ **road** grande route, route principale; **the** ~ **body** le gros; **the** ~ **point** le point capital, l'essentiel *m*
**mainland** *n* continent *m*; *adj* continental
**mainline** *adj coll* important, essentiel -ielle
**mainly** *adv* principalement, surtout
**mainmast** *n* grand mât
**mainspring** *n* grand ressort; *fig* mobile essentiel
**mainstay** *n* soutien principal
**mainstream** *adj* important, essentiel -ielle
**maintain** *vt* maintenir, soutenir; (affirm) prétendre; (keep) conserver, entretenir; (attitude) garder
**maintenance** *n* maintien *m*; (upkeep, family) entretien *m*; (machine) maintenance *f*; (money allowance) pension *f* alimentaire
**maisonnette** *n* appartement *m* dans une maison; duplex *m*; maisonnette *f*
**maize** *n* maïs *m*
**majestic** *adj* majestueux -euse
**majesty** *n* majesté *f*
¹**major** *n mil* commandant *m*
²**major** *adj* majeur; (older) aîné; ~ **road** route *f* à priorité
³**major** *vi* US ~ **in** obtenir sa licence en
**Majorca** *n* Majorque *f*
**major-domo** *n* majordome *m*
**majority** *n* majorité *f*; plupart *f*, plus grande partie; **be in the** ~ être en majorité; *adj* majoritaire
**make** *n* construction *f*, fabrication *f*; (brand) marque *f*; *coll* **on the** ~ intéressé; *vt* faire, créer, construire; (manufacture) fabriquer; (clothes) confectionner; (render) rendre; (force) forcer, faire; (gain) gagner; (reach) atteindre; (estimate) estimer; (friends) se faire; ~ **fast** amarrer; ~ **good** réparer; ~ **it** réussir; ~ **it up to s/o** dédommager qn; ~ **it up with s/o** se

réconcilier avec qn; ~ **oneself up** se maquiller, *theat* se maquiller, se grimer; ~ **over** céder; ~ **s/o out** comprendre qn; ~ **sth into sth** transformer qch en qch; ~ **sth out** (recognize) distinguer qch; (prove) prouver qch; ~ **the best of** s'accommoder de; ~ **the most of** tirer le meilleur parti de; ~ **up** compléter; (deficit) combler; (invent) inventer; (face) maquiller; (actor) grimer; (prescription) préparer; ~ **up one's mind** se décider; **what do you** ~ **the time?** quelle heure avez-vous?; **what do you** ~ **of it?** qu'en pensez-vous?; *vi* ~ **away** s'éloigner; ~ **away with** (kill) détruire, supprimer; (escape with) disparaître avec; ~ **for** se diriger vers; (tend) contribuer à; ~ **good** réussir; ~ **off** filer, se sauver; ~ **up for lost time** rattraper le temps perdu; *coll* ~ **up to s/o** faire des avances à qn
**make-and-break** *n elect* conjoncteur-disjoncteur *m* (*pl* conjoncteurs-disjoncteurs)
**make-believe** *n* semblant *m*; trompe-l'œil *m invar*
**maker** *n* faiseur -euse; (manufacturer) fabricant *m*, constructeur *m*; **Maker** Créateur *m*
**makeshift** *n* pis-aller *m invar*, moyen *m* de fortune; *adj* de fortune, de rencontre
**make-up** *n* maquillage *m*, fard *m*; (composition) composition *f*
**makeweight** *n* complément *m* de poids; **he's there as a** ~ il est là pour faire le nombre
**making** *n* création *f*, fabrication *f*; construction *f*; (clothes) façon *f*; ~ s petits profits; **have the** ~ s **of** avoir (tout) ce qu'il faut pour faire
**maladjusted** *adj* inadapté
**maladministration** *n* mauvaise administration
**maladroit** *adj* maladroit
**malady** *n* maladie *f*, mal *m*
**malaise** *n* malaise *m*
**malaria** *n* paludisme *m*, malaria *f*
**malcontent** *n* + *adj* mécontent -e
**male** *n* mâle *m*; *adj* mâle
**malediction** *n* malédiction *f*
**malefactor** *n* malfaiteur -trice
**malevolence** *n* malveillance *f*
**malevolent** *adj* malveillant
**malformation** *n* malformation *f*
**malice** *n* malveillance *f*, méchanceté *f*; **bear** ~ **towards s/o** en vouloir à qn; **with** ~ **aforethought** avec préméditation
**malicious** *adj* méchant, malveillant; rancunier -ière
¹**malign** *adj* nuisible

579

²**malign** *vt* diffamer, calomnier

**malignancy, malignity** *n* malignité *f*

**malignant** *adj* méchant; malin (*f* maligne)

**malignity** *n see* **malignancy**

**malinger** *vi* faire le (*f* la) malade

**malingerer** *n* faux (*f* fausse) malade

**malleable** *adj* malléable

**mallet** *n* maillet *m*

**malnutrition** *n* sous-alimentation *f*

**malodorous** *adj* malodorant

**malpractice** *n* méfait *m*; (doctor) négligence *f*; *leg* malversation *f*

**malt** *n* malt *m*

**Maltese** *n* Maltais -e; *adj* maltais

**maltreat** *vt* maltraiter

**maltreatment** *n* mauvais traitement

**mammal** *n* mammifère *m*

**mammoth** *n* mammouth *m*; *adj* géant, énorme

**man** *n* homme *m*; (workman) ouvrier *m*; (servant) domestique *m*, valet *m*; (chess) pièce *f*; (draughts) pion *m*; ~ proposes, God disposes l'homme propose, Dieu dispose; ~ to ~ d'homme à homme; come on, old ~ viens, mon vieux; he's a big ~ c'est qn; he's not the ~ for that il n'est pas fait pour cela; the ~ in the street l'homme moyen; they died to a ~ ils moururent jusqu'au dernier; *vt naut* équiper, (gun) servir; pourvoir de main-d'œuvre

**manacle** *n* ~ s menottes *fpl*; *vt* mettre les menottes à

**manage** *vt* gérer, diriger, administrer; (handle) manier; (person) mater; (animal) maîtriser; (business) arranger; (cope with) venir à bout de; can you ~ another cup? pouvez-vous en boire encore une tasse?; I can ~ him je sais le prendre; I can't ~ any more money je ne peux plus payer d'argent; *vi* s'en tirer, s'y prendre, se débrouiller; ~ to do réussir à faire; how do you ~ to ...? comment faites-vous pour ...?; I'll ~ je m'arrangerai

**manageable** *adj* maniable; (person) docile, traitable; (possible) faisable

**management** *n* conduite *f*, direction *f*, administration *f*; (property) gestion *f*; (things, men) maniement *m*

**manager** *n* directeur *m*; gérant *m*; (property) régisseur *m*; *sp* manager *m*; (household) ménagère *f*

**manageress** *n* directrice *f*; gérante *f*

**managing** *adj* directeur -trice; ~ director administrateur directeur, directeur général = P.D.G. *m*

¹**mandarin** *n* (person) mandarin *m*

²**mandarin(e)** *n* (fruit) mandarine *f*

**mandate** *n* mandat *m*; *vt* mandater

**mandatory** *adj* mandataire

**mandolin(e)** *n* mandoline *f*

**mane** *n* crinière *f*

**man-eater** *n* (cannibal) anthropophage *m*; (animal) mangeur *m* d'hommes

**manful** *adj* viril, vaillant, courageux -euse

**manganese** *n* manganèse *m*

**mange** *n* gale *f*

**manger** *n* mangeoire *f*, crèche *f*; the dog in the ~ le chien du jardinier

¹**mangle** *n* essoreuse *f*; *vt* (clothes) essorer

²**mangle** *vt* mutiler; (tear) déchirer; (language) estropier

**mango** *n* mangue *f*

**mangrove** *n bot* manglier *m*

**mangy** *adj* galeux -euse; (poor) minable; *coll* moche

**manhandle** *vt* manutentionner; *coll* malmener

**manhater** *n* misanthrope

**manhole** *n* trou *m* de visite; ~ cover plaque *f* d'égout

**manhood** *n* humanité *f*; âge *m* d'homme, âge viril

**man-hour** *n* heure *f* de main-d'œuvre

**manhunt** *n* chasse *f* à l'homme

**mania** *n* manie *f*; folie *f*; have a ~ for doing sth avoir la passion de faire qch

**maniac** *n* + *adj* fou furieux (*f* folle furieuse); maniaque

**manic** *adj* atteint de manie

**manicure** *n* soin *m* des mains; *vt* soigner les mains à

**manicurist** *n* manucure

**manifest** *n* manifeste *m*; *adj* manifeste, évident; *vt* manifester, témoigner; *naut* déclarer

**manifestation** *n* manifestation *f*

**manifesto** *n* manifeste *m*

**manifold** *n mot* tubulure *f* d'échappement; *adj* divers, varié; *vt obs* polycopier

**manipulate** *vt* manipuler; manœuvrer

**manipulation** *n* manipulation *f*; manœuvre *f*

**mankind** *n* le genre humain, les hommes *mpl*

**manly** *adj* viril, d'homme

**man-made** *adj* artificiel -ielle

**manna** *n* manne *f*

**mannequin** *n* mannequin *m*

**manner** *n* manière *f*, façon *f*; (bearing) air *m*, maintien *m*; (sort) sorte *f*, espèce *f*; ~ s (customs) mœurs *fpl*; in a ~ of speaking pour ainsi dire; in such a ~ that de telle sorte que; in this ~ de cette façon (manière)

**mannered** *adj* maniéré; (style) précieux -ieuse

**mannerism** *n* affectation *f*; maniérisme *m*

**mannerless** adj sans éducation

**mannerly** adj poli, bien élevé, courtois

**mannish** adj hommasse

**manoeuvre** n manœuvre f; vt ma-nœuvrer

**man-of-war** n vaisseau m de guerre

**manor** n manoir m, château seigneurial

**manpower** n main-d'œuvre f (pl mains-d'œuvre), effectifs mpl

**manservant** n domestique m

**mansion** n (in country) château m; (in town) hôtel (particulier)

**manslaughter** n homicide m involon-taire

**mantelpiece** n cheminée f; tablette f de cheminée

**mantelshelf** n tablette f de cheminée

**mantilla** n mantille f

**mantis** n mante f; **praying ~** mante reli-gieuse

**mantle** n cape f, pèlerine f; (covering) manteau m; (gas) manchon m; vt cou-vrir d'un manteau; vi se répandre

**manual** n manuel m; adj manuel -elle

**manufacture** n fabrication f; (clothes) confection f; (article) produit manu-facturé; vt fabriquer

**manure** n engrais m; (farmyard) fumier m; **liquid ~** purin m; vt fumer, en-graisser

**manuscript** n manuscrit m

**many** n un grand nombre, une multi-tude; adj + adv beaucoup (de), bien des, un grand nombre (de); **~ a** maint; **~ of you** beaucoup d'entre vous; **as ~** autant (de); **how ~** combien (de); **one too ~** un (f une) de trop; **so ~** tant (de); **too ~** trop (de)

**many-sided** adj complexe; (object) à plusieurs côtés; (person) aux talents variés

**map** n carte f (géographique); (town) plan m; **put sth on the ~** mettre qch en vedette; vt dresser une carte (un plan) de; **~ out** tracer

**maple** n érable m

**mar** vt gâter, gâcher; **make or ~ matters** tout arranger ou tout gâcher

**marathon** n marathon m

**maraud** vt piller; vi marauder

**marauder** n maraudeur -euse

**marble** n marbre m; (toy) bille f; **play ~s** jouer aux billes

**marcasite** n marcassite f

**March** n mars m; **in ~** au mois de mars

¹**march** n marche f; **quick ~** pas ca-dencé; vi marcher; **~ along** marcher; **~ in** entrer; **~ off** se mettre en marche; coll décamper; **quick ~!** en avant, marche!

²**march** n ar marche f; vi ar **~ with** être

limitrophe de

**marchioness** n marquise f

**march-past** n défilé m

**mare** n jument f; **~ 's nest** découverte f illusoire

**margarine** n margarine f

**margin** n marge f, bord m; (divergence) écart m; vt annoter en marge; faire une marge à

**marginal** adj en marge, marginal

**marguerite** n marguerite f

**marigold** n souci m

**marijuana, marihuana** n marihuana f, marijuana f

**marina** n marina f

**marinade** n marinade f; vt + vi mariner

**marine** n marine f; mil fusilier marin; **tell that to the ~s!** à d'autres!; adj marin

**mariner** n marin m

**marionette** n marionnette f

**marital** adj marital, matrimonial

**maritime** adj maritime

**marjoram** n marjolaine f, origan m

¹**mark** n marque f; (sign) signe m, témoignage m; (aim) but m, cible f; (school) note f, point m; (for signature) croix f; **as a ~ of my esteem** en témoi-gnage de mon estime; **be up to the ~** être à la hauteur; (health) être dans son assiette; **be wide of the ~** être loin du compte; **make one's ~** se distinguer, se faire une réputation; vt marquer; in-diquer; (note) observer, noter; (under-line) souligner; **~ down** baisser le prix de; (note) inscrire; **~ my words!** écou-tez bien ce que je dis!; vous verrez!; (on list) **~ off** cocher; **~ out** délimiter; dis-tinguer; **~ time** marquer le pas; **~ up** augmenter le prix de

²**mark** n (coin) mark m

**marked** adj marqué, évident, prononcé

**marker** n marqueur -euse; (book) signet m; repère m

**market** n marché m; (covered) halle f, halles fpl; (price) cours m; **~ square** place f du marché; **be in the ~ for** être acheteur -euse de; **find a ~ for** trouver un débouché pour; vt lancer sur le marché, vendre

**market-garden** n jardin maraîcher

**market-gardener** n maraîcher -ère

**marketing** n marketing m

**market-price** n prix courant

**marking** n marquage m; marque f, tache f; (school) correction f

**marksman** n bon tireur

**marl** n marne f

**marmalade** n confiture f d'oranges

**marmot** n marmotte f

¹**maroon** n marron m; adj marron invar

²**maroon** vt abandonner sur une île dé-

serte; **~ ed by floods** isolé par les inondations

**marquee** n grande tente

**marquis, marquess** n marquis m

**marriage** n mariage m; **~-lines** acte m de mariage; **~ service** bénédiction nuptiale; **by ~** par alliance

**marriageable** adj (girl) nubile; mariable

**married** adj marié; **~ couple** ménage m; **~ name** nom m de femme mariée

**marrow** n moelle f; cul amourettes fpl; (vegetable) courge f

**marry** vt épouser, se marier avec; (priest) marier; **~ money** faire un mariage d'argent; vi se marier

**marsh** n marais m, marécage m

**marshal** n maréchal m; US commissaire m de police; vt ranger, placer en rang; (rolling-stock) trier

**marshalling-yard** n gare f de triage

**marshmallow** n guimauve f

**marshy** adj marécageux -euse

**marsupial** n marsupial m; adj marsupial

**marten** n martre f

**martial** adj martial; **declare ~ law** proclamer l'état de siège

**martin** n **house ~** hirondelle f (de toit, de fenêtre)

**martinet** n officier m sévère; sl pète-sec m invar

**martyr** n martyr -e; vt martyriser

**martyrdom** n martyre m

**marvel** n merveille f; vi s'émerveiller

**marvellous** adj merveilleux -euse

**Marxism** n marxisme m

**Mary** n Marie f

**marzipan** n massepain m

**mascara** n mascara m

**mascot** n mascotte f, porte-bonheur m invar

**masculine** adj masculin, mâle

**masculinity** n masculinité f

**mash** n purée f, pâte f; (farm animals) pâtée f; vt brasser, mélanger, écraser; (potatoes) mettre en purée

**mask** n masque m; (velvet) loup m; **throw off the ~** lever le masque; vt masquer; cacher, voiler

**masochism** n masochisme m

**mason** n maçon m; (freemason) francmaçon m (pl francs-maçons)

**masonic** adj maçonnique

**masonry** n maçonnerie f

**masque** n masque m

**masquerade** n mascarade f

**¹mass** n eccles messe f; **high ~** grandmesse f; **low ~** messe basse

**²mass** n masse f; (people) foule f, multitude f; (majority) majorité f, plus grande partie; **the ~es** les masses m; vt masser; vi se masser

**massacre** n massacre m; vt massacrer

**massage** n massage m; vt masser

**masseur** n masseur m

**masseuse** n masseuse f

**massif** n massif m

**massive** adj massif -ive

**mass-produce** vt fabriquer en série

**mass-production** n fabrication f en série

**¹mast** n naut mât m; pylône m

**²mast** n (beech) faîne f; (oak) gland m

**master** n maître m; (teacher) professeur m; (boss) patron m; (ship) capitaine m; **~-card** carte maîtresse; **~ of foxhounds** grand veneur; **be a past ~** être passé maître; **be ~ of a subject** posséder à fond un sujet; **form ~** professeur principal; **old ~** tableau m de maître; vt maîtriser, dompter; (learn well) apprendre à fond; **~ a difficulty** surmonter une difficulté

**masterful** adj autoritaire, impérieux -ieuse

**master-key** n passe-partout m invar; coll passe m

**masterly** adj magistral, de maître

**mastermind** n esprit supérieur; vt organiser

**masterpiece** n chef-d'œuvre m (pl chefsd'œuvre)

**masterstroke** n coup m de maître

**mastery** n maîtrise f, domination f; (of a subject) connaissance approfondie; (skill) grande habileté; **gain the ~ over** l'emporter sur

**masticate** vt mâcher, mastiquer

**mastication** n mastication f

**mastiff** n mâtin m

**mastodon** n mastodonte m

**mastoid** adj mastoïde

**mastoids** n mastoïdite f

**masturbate** vi se masturber

**¹mat** n natte f, paillasson m; carpette f; (table) dessous m de plat; **be on the ~** être sur la sellette; vt natter, tresser; (hair) emmêler

**²mat** adj mat

**matador** n matador m

**¹match** n allumette f; **safety ~** allumette suédoise; **strike a ~** frotter une allumette

**²match** n égal -e, pareil -eille; sp match m, partie f, lutte f; (marriage) alliance f, mariage m; **be a good ~** aller bien ensemble; **be a ~ for s/o** être de force à lutter avec qn; **make a good ~** faire un beau mariage; vt égaler, être l'égal de; (oppose) opposer; (pairs) apparier; (colours) assortir; vi s'assortir, s'harmoniser

**matchbox** n boîte f à allumettes

**matchet** n machette f

**matchless** adj incomparable; sans pareil -eille

**matchmaker** *n* marieur -ieuse
**matchwood** *n* bois *m* d'allumettes;
**smashed to ~** brisé en petits morceaux
¹**mate** *n* camarade, compagnon *m* (*f*
compagne); *coll* copain *m* (*f* copine);
(couple) époux (*f* épouse); (animals)
mâle *m*, femelle *f*; *naut* officier *m*; *vt*
accoupler; unir; *vi* s'accoupler; **mating
season** saison *f* des amours
²**mate** *n see* **checkmate**
**material** *n* matière *f*, matériau *m*; (textile) tissu *m*, étoffe *f*; **~s** fournitures
*fpl*; **raw ~s** matières premières; *adj*
matériel -ielle; grossier -ière, terre-à-
terre *invar*; (important) essentiel -ielle,
important; (germane) pertinent
**materialism** *n* matérialisme *m*
**materialist** *n* + *adj* matérialiste
**materialize** *vt* matérialiser; *vi* se réaliser;
(appear) apparaître
**materially** *adv* matériellement, essentiellement
**maternal** *adj* maternel -elle
**maternity** *n* maternité *f*; **~ hospital**
maternité *f*
**matey** *adj coll* amical
**mathematical** *adj* mathématique
**mathematician** *n* mathématicien -ienne
**mathematics** *npl* mathématiques *fpl*
**maths** *npl* math(s) *fpl*
**matins** *npl* matines *fpl*
**matriarch** *n* matrone *f*
**matricide** *n* matricide *m*; (person) matricide
**matriculate** *vi* (university) se faire inscrire
**matriculation** *n* (university) inscription
*f*
**matrimonial** *adj* matrimonial, conjugal
**matrimony** *n* mariage *m*
**matrix** *n* matrice *f*
**matron** *n* matrone *f*, mère *f* de famille;
(hospital) infirmière *f* en chef; (institution) intendante *f*
**matronly** *adj* opulent, de matrone, plantureux -euse
**matter** *n* matière *f*; (business) affaire *f*;
(subject) sujet *m*; (case) cas *m*; (thing)
chose *f*; *med* pus *m*; **as a ~ of course**
cela va sans dire; **as a ~ of fact** en fait;
**as if nothing was the ~** comme si de
rien n'était; **for that ~** quant à cela;
**hanging ~** cas *m* pendable; **it's no
laughing ~** il n'y a pas de quoi rire; **no
~ how much you try** vous avez beau
essayer; **printed ~** imprimé *m*; **reading
~** de quoi lire, lecture *f*; **sth must be
the ~** il doit y avoir qch; **what's the
~?** qu'est-ce qu'il y a?; **what's the
with you?** qu'avez-vous?; *vi* importer;
avoir de l'importance; *med* suppurer;
**it doesn't ~** cela ne fait rien, n'im-

porte; **what does it ~?** qu'importe?
**matter-of-fact** *adj* positif -ive
**matting** *n* nattes *fpl*
**mattock** *n* pioche *f*
**mattress** *n* matelas *m*; **air ~** matelas *m*
pneumatique
**maturation** *n* maturation *f*
**mature** *adj* mûr, mûri; *vt* mûrir; *vi*
mûrir; (bill) arriver à échéance
**maturity** *n* maturité *f*
**maudlin** *adj* larmoyant, pleurard;
(drink) **be ~** avoir le vin triste
**maul** *vt* malmener, meurtrir
**maunder** *vi* divaguer
**mausoleum** *n* mausolée *m*
**mauve** *n* mauve *m*; *adj* mauve
**maverick** *n coll* non-conformiste
**maw** *n* (animal) estomac *m*; (bird) jabot
*m*; (jaws) gueule *f*
**mawkish** *adj* insipide, fade; excessivement sentimental
**maxi** *adj* maxi
**maxim** *n* maxime *f*
**maximize** *vt* exploiter à fond
**maximum** *n* maximum *m* (*pl* maximums
*or* maxima); *adj* maximum (*f* maximum *or* maxima, *pl* maximums *or*
maxima)
¹**may** *n* (hawthorn) aubépine *f*; **May** mai
*m*
²**may** *v aux* (*p* **might**) **~ he never know!**
puisse-t-il ne jamais savoir!; **~ I come
in?** puis-je entrer?; **be that as it ~** quoi
qu'il en soit; **he ~ come tonight** il peut
venir ce soir; **I might try** je pourrais
essayer; **it ~ be that ...** il se peut que
...; **it ~ rain** il peut pleuvoir; **it might
be that ...** il se pourrait que ...; **long ~
you wait!** puissiez-vous attendre longtemps!; **that's as ~ be** c'est selon; **they
~ have phoned** ils ont pu téléphoner;
**they might have phoned** ils auraient pu
téléphoner; **whoever it ~ be** qui que ce
soit; **you might say good morning** vous
pourriez bien dire bonjour
**maybe** *adv* peut-être
**may-bug** *n* hanneton *m*
**May-day** *n* le premier mai; **~!** = signal
international de détresse
**may-fly** *n* éphémère *m*
**mayhem** *n US* **commit ~ on** s/o se livrer
à des voies de fait contre qn
**mayonnaise** *n* mayonnaise *f*
**mayor** *n* maire *m*; **deputy ~** maire adjoint
**mayoress** *n* mairesse *f*, femme *f* du
maire; (holder of office) Madame le
Maire
**maze** *n* labyrinthe *m*, dédale *m*
**mazurka** *n* mazurka *f*
**me** *pron* me; moi; **dear ~!** mon Dieu!;
**tell him from ~** dites-lui de ma part

**mead**

mead *n* hydromel *m*
meadow *n* pré *m*, prairie *f*
meagre *adj* maigre, peu copieux -ieuse
¹meal *n* repas *m*; make a ~ of it en faire son repas; *coll* make a ~ of s/o ne faire qu'une bouchée de qn
²meal *n* farine *f*
mealy *adj* farineux -euse
mealy-mouthed *adj* doucereux -euse, patelin
¹mean *n* milieu *m*; (average) moyenne *f*; ~s moyen *m*; (resources) moyens *mpl*; by all ~s! mais certainement!; by fair ~s honnêtement; by ~s of au moyen de; by no ~s pas du tout; find ~s to do sth trouver le moyen de faire qch; live beyond one's ~s vivre au-dessus de ses moyens; man of ~s homme aisé; private ~s fortune personnelle; there's no ~s of doing it il n'y a pas moyen de le faire; *adj* moyen -enne
²mean *adj* misérable, mesquin; (avaricious) avare; (low) bas (*f* basse); ~ trick vilain tour
³mean *vt* signifier, vouloir dire; (intend) avoir l'intention de, entendre; (destine) destiner; ~ s/o harm vouloir du mal à qn; ~ well avoir de bonnes intentions; be meant to être censé; do you really ~ it? êtes-vous vraiment sérieux -ieuse?; he didn't ~ to do it il ne l'a pas fait exprès; he ~s no harm il ne pense pas à mal; that ~s nothing to me cela ne me dit rien; what do you ~ by that? qu'entendez-vous par cela?; you don't ~ it! vous plaisantez!
meander *n* méandre *m*; *vi* serpenter, faire des méandres
meaning *n* signification *f*, sens *m*; *adj* significatif -ive
meaningful *adj* significatif -ive
meaningless *adj* dénué de sens
meanness *n* avarice *f*; (character) bassesse *f*, mesquinerie *f*; (poorness) pauvreté *f*, médiocrité *f*
means-test *n* enquête *f* sur la situation (de fortune)
meantime, meanwhile *adv* en attendant
measles *npl* rougeole *f*; German ~ rubéole *f*
measly *adj coll* misérable
measurable *adj* mesurable
measure *n* mesure *f*; (step) démarche *f*; *math* diviseur *m*; (bound) limite *f*; beyond ~ outre mesure; in great ~ en grande partie; in some ~ jusqu'à un certain point, en partie; made to ~ fait sur mesure; *vt* mesurer; (tailor) prendre la mesure de; ~ one's words peser ses mots; ~ out distribuer
measured *adj* mesuré, déterminé; (language) modéré

measureless *adj* infini
measurement *n* mesurage *m*; (size) dimension *f*, mesure *f*
meat *n* viande *f*; (food) aliment *m*, nourriture *f*
meatless *adj* maigre
meat-safe *n* garde-manger *m invar*
meaty *adj* charnu; *fig* plein de substance
Mecca *n* la Mecque
mechanic *n* mécanicien -ienne, monteur -euse
mechanical *adj* mécanique; (action) machinal, automatique
mechanism *n* mécanisme *m*; appareil *m*
mechanization *n* mécanisation *f*
mechanize *vt* mécaniser
medal *n* médaille *f*
medallion *n* médaillon *m*
medallist *n* médailleur *m*; *sp* gagnant -e de médaille(s)
meddle *vi* ~ in s'immiscer dans; ~ with toucher à, se mêler de
meddler *n* officieux -ieuse, touche-à-tout *m invar*
meddlesome *adj* intrigant
media *npl* media *mpl*, média *mpl*; mass ~ mass-media *mpl*
mediate *vi* s'interposer, servir de médiateur -trice
mediation *n* médiation *f*
mediator *n* médiateur -trice
medical *adj* médical; ~ inspection visite médicale; ~ officer médecin *m* du travail; ~ profession corps médical; ~ student étudiant -e en médecine
medicate *vt* médicamenter
medicinal *adj* médicinal
medicine *n* médecine *f*, médicament *m*; (remedy) remède *m*
medicine-chest *n* pharmacie *f*
medicine-man *n* sorcier guérisseur
medieval, mediaeval *adj* médiéval, du moyen âge
mediocre *adj* médiocre
mediocrity *n* médiocrité *f*
meditate *vt* + *vi* méditer
meditation *n* méditation *f*
meditative *adj* méditatif -ive
Mediterranean *n* Méditerranée *f*; *adj* méditerranéen -éenne
medium *n* milieu *m*; véhicule *m*; (intermediary) intermédiaire *m*, agent *m*; (spirit) médium *m*; happy ~ juste milieu *m*; *adj* moyen -enne
medlar *n bot* nèfle *f*
medley *n* mélange *m*; *mus* pot-pourri *m* (*pl* pots-pourris)
meek *adj* humble, doux (*f* douce)
meekness *n* humilité *f*, soumission *f*
¹meet *n* rendez-vous *m* de chasseurs; *vt* rencontrer; (first time) faire la connaissance de; (join) rejoindre; (problem,

584

demand) faire face à; (death) trouver; (danger) affronter; (requirement) satisfaire à; ~ s/o half-way faire des concessions à qn; **arrange to** ~ s/o donner rendez-vous à qn; **go and** ~ s/o aller au devant de qn; **my eyes met his** nos regards se croisèrent; **pleased to** ~ **you** enchanté de faire votre connaissance; **there's more here than** ~s **the eye** il y a quelque anguille sous roche; *vi* se rencontrer, se voir, se réunir; ~ **with** rencontrer; ~ **with a loss** essuyer une perte; **make both ends** ~ joindre les deux bouts; **till we** ~ **again!** au revoir!

²**meet** *adj lit* convenable, à propos; **as is** ~ comme il convient

**meeting** *n* rencontre *f*; réunion *f*, assemblée *f*; *sp+pol* meeting *m*; (roads) croisement *m*

**meeting-house** *n* (Quakers) temple *m*

**meeting-place** *n* lieu *m* de réunion; lieu *m* de rendez-vous

**megalomania** *n* mégalomanie *f*, folie *f* des grandeurs

**megaphone** *n* porte-voix *m invar*

**megaton** *n* mégatonne *f*

**melancholic** *adj* mélancolique

**melancholy** *n* mélancolie *f*; *adj* mélancolique

**mellifluous** *adj* mielleux -euse, doucereux -euse

**mellow** *adj* mûr; (wine) moelleux -euse; (voice) doux (*f* douce); (drunk) gris; *vt* mûrir, faire mûrir; (wine) rendre moelleux -euse; adoucir; *vi* mûrir; (character) s'adoucir

**melodic** *adj* mélodique

**melodious** *adj* mélodieux -ieuse, harmonieux -ieuse

**melodrama** *n* mélodrame *m*

**melodramatic** *adj* mélodramatique

**melody** *n* mélodie *f*, air *m*

**melon** *n* melon *m*

**melt** *vt* fondre, faire fondre; *fig* attendrir, émouvoir; ~ **down** fondre; *vi* fondre; se fondre, se dissoudre; (crowd) se disperser; ~ **into tears** fondre en larmes

**melting** *n* fonte *f*, fusion *f*; *fig* attendrissement *m*; *adj* fondant

**melting-point** *n* point *m* de fusion

**melting-pot** *n* creuset *m*

**member** *n* membre *m*, adhérent -e; *anat* membre *m*, organe *m*; **Member of Parliament** = député *m*

**membership** *n* qualité *f* de membre; (total) nombre *m* des membres; ~ **card** carte *f* de membre (d'adhérent -e)

**membrane** *n* membrane *f*; **mucous** ~ muqueuse *f*

**memento** *n* souvenir *m*

**memo** *n* mémorandum *m*

**memoir** *n* étude *f*; ~s mémoires *fpl*, autobiographie *f*

**memorable** *adj* mémorable

**memorandum** *n* mémorandum *m*, note *f*

**memorial** *n* monument (commémoratif); **war** ~ monument *m* aux morts; *adj* commémoratif -ive

**memorialist** *n* mémorialiste

**memorize** *vt* apprendre par cœur

**memory** *n* (faculty) mémoire *f*; souvenir *m*; **from** ~ de mémoire; **have a good** ~ avoir de la mémoire, avoir une bonne mémoire; **in** ~ **of** en souvenir de, en mémoire de; **to the best of my** ~ autant que je m'en souvienne; **within living** ~ de mémoire d'homme

**menace** *n* menace *f*; *coll* **he's a** ~ il est terrible; *vt* menacer

**menagerie** *n* ménagerie *f*

**mend** *n* (clothes) reprise *f*; **be on the** ~ (patient) être en voie de guérison; (business) reprendre; *vt* (clothes) repriser, raccommoder; réparer; (rectify) corriger, rectifier; (matters) arranger; ~ **one's ways** changer de conduite; *vi* (health) se rétablir; (weather) se remettre; (reform) s'amender; (improve) s'améliorer

**mendacious** *adj* mensonger -ère

**mendacity** *n* penchant *m* au mensonge

**mender** *n* raccommodeur -euse; (machines, etc) réparateur -trice; **invisible** ~ stoppeur -euse

**mendicant** *n+adj* mendiant -e

**mending** *n* raccommodage *m*; **invisible** ~ stoppage *m*

**menfolk** *npl* les hommes *mpl* (de la famille)

**menhir** *n* menhir *m*

**menial** *n* domestique; *adj* servile; domestique

**meningitis** *n* méningite *f*

**menopause** *n* ménopause *f*

**menstrual** *adj* menstruel -elle

**menstruate** *vi* avoir ses règles

**mental** *adj* mental; *coll* fou (*f* folle); ~ **case** aliéné -e; ~ **defective** minus habens *m*; ~ **home** hospice *m* d'aliénés; ~ **hospital** hôpital *m* psychiatrique; ~ **specialist** médecin *m* aliéniste

**mentality** *n* mentalité *f*

**mention** *n* mention *f*; *vt* mentionner, faire mention de; (quote) citer; **don't** ~ **it!** il n'y a pas de quoi!; **not to** ~ sans parler de; **not worth** ~ing sans aucune importance

**menu** *n* menu *m*

**mercantile** *adj* mercantile, marchand

**mercenary** *n+adj* mercenaire

**merchandise** *n* marchandises *fpl*

**merchant** *n* négociant -e, commerçant

-e, marchand -e; *coll* type *m*; *adj* marchand, de commerce; ~ **bank** banque *f* d'affaires
**merciful** *adj* miséricordieux -ieuse
**merciless** *adj* impitoyable
**mercurial** *adj* vif (*f* vive); inconstant
**mercury** *n* mercure *m*
**mercy** *n* miséricorde *f*, grâce *f*, pitié *f*; **ask for** ~ demander grâce; **at the** ~ **of** à la merci de; **for** ~**'s sake!** par pitié!; **Sister of Mercy** sœur *f* de la Charité; **what a** ~! quelle chance!
¹**mere** *n* lac *m*, étang *m*, mare *f*
²**mere** *adj* pur, simple, seul
**merely** *adv* simplement, seulement
**merge** *vt* fondre; amalgamer; ~ **into** englober dans; *vi* se fondre, se confondre; (firms) fusionner
**merger** *n* fusion *f*, amalgamation *f*
**meridian** *n* méridien *m*
**meringue** *n* meringue *f*
**merino** *n* mérinos *m*
**merit** *n* mérite *m*, valeur *f*; *vt* mériter
**meritorious** *adj* méritoire; (person) méritant
**mermaid** *n* sirène *f*
**merriment** *n* gaieté *f*, hilarité *f*
**merry** *adj* gai, joyeux -euse; ~ **Christmas!** joyeux Noël!; *coll* **be** ~ être éméché; **make** ~ s'amuser; **the more the merrier** plus on est de fous, plus on rit
**merry-go-round** *n* chevaux *mpl* de bois, carrousel *m*
**merry-making** *n* réjouissances *fpl*
**mesh** *n* maille *f*; *mech* engrenage *m*, prise *f*; (tangle) rets *mpl*; *vt* prendre au filet; *mech* engrener
**mesmerize** *vt* hypnotiser
**mess** *n* (muddle) gâchis *m*, fouillis *m*; (dirt) saleté *f*; *mil* (officers) mess *m*, (men) popote *f*; *ar* (dish) plat *m*; **be in a** ~ (person) être dans de beaux draps; (room) être en désordre; **make a** ~ **of** (dirty) salir; (create confusion) gâcher; *vt* gâcher; salir; *vi mil* faire popote; ~ **about** bricoler; faire l'idiot -e; ~ **about with** (girl) tripoter
**message** *n* message *m*; (phone) communication *f*; (writer) enseignement *m*; *coll* **get the** ~ piger; **give the** ~ faire la commission; **leave a** ~ laisser un mot
**messenger** *n* messager -ère; commissionnaire *m*; (hotel) chasseur *m*; garçon *m* de bureau
**Messiah** *n* Messie *m*
**messmate** *n* camarade *m* de table
**Messrs** *npl* Messieurs *mpl*
**mess-tin** *n* gamelle *f*
**mess-up** *n* gâchis *m*; (misunderstanding) malentendu *m*
**messy** *adj* malpropre, sale

**metal** *n* métal *m*; *vt* ~ **a road** empierrer une route
**metallic** *adj* métallique
**metallurgy** *n* métallurgie *f*
**metamorphosis** *n* métamorphose *f*
**metaphor** *n* métaphore *f*
**metaphoric** *adj* métaphorique
**metaphysical** *adj* métaphysique
**metaphysics** *n* métaphysique *f*
**mete** *vt* ~ **out** assigner, distribuer
**meteor** *n* météore *m*
**meteoric** *adj* météorique; atmosphérique
**meteorite** *n* météorite *m* or *f*
**meteorological** *adj* météorologique
**meteorology** *n* météorologie *f*
**meter** *n* compteur *m*; **parking** ~ parcomètre *m*, compteur *m*
**methane** *n* méthane *m*
**method** *n* méthode *f*; (manner) manière *f*; procédé *m*
**methodical** *adj* méthodique
**Methodism** *n* méthodisme *m*
**methodology** *n* méthodologie *f*
**methylated** *adj* ~ **spirit** alcool *m* à brûler
**meticulous** *adj* méticuleux -euse
**metonymy** *n* métonymie *f*
¹**metre** *n pros* mètre *m*, mesure *f*
²**metre** *n* mètre *m*
**metric, metrical** *adj* métrique
**metro** *n* métro *m*
**metronome** *n* métronome *m*
**metropolis** *n* métropole *f*
**metropolitan** *n eccles* métropolitain *m*; *adj* métropolitain
**mettle** *n* courage *m*, ardeur *f*; **be on one's** ~ se piquer d'honneur; **show one's** ~ faire preuve de courage
¹**mew** *n* (bird) mouette *f*
²**mew** *n* + *vi see* **miaow**
**mews** *n* écuries *fpl*; (street) ruelle *f*; écuries transformées en habitations
**Mexican** *n* Mexicain -e; *adj* mexicain
**Mexico** *n* le Mexique
**mezzanine** *n* entresol *m*
**mi** *n mus* mi *m*
**miaow, mew** *n* miaulement *m*, miaou *m*; *vi* miauler
**miasma** *n* miasme *m*
**mica** *n* mica *m*
**Michael** *n* Michel *m*
**Michaelmas** *n* la Saint-Michel; ~ -**daisy** aster *m*, marguerite *f* d'automne
**mickey** *n coll* **take the** ~ **out of** s/o se payer la tête de qn
**microbe** *n* microbe *m*
**microbiology** *n* microbiologie *f*
**microcosm** *n* microcosme *m*
**microfilm** *n* microfilm *m*
**microgroove** *n* microsillon *m*
**microphone** *n* microphone *m*
**microscope** *n* microscope *m*

**mìcroscopic** *adj* microscopique

**mid** *adj* du milieu, mi-; **in ~ -air** (high) en plein ciel; en l'air; **in ~ -July** à la mi-juillet; **in ~ -winter** au cœur de l'hiver

**midday** *n* midi *m*; *adj* de midi

**middle** *n* milieu *m*, centre *m*; **be in the ~ of doing sth** être en train de faire qch; **in the ~ of** au milieu de; *adj* du milieu, central; (intermediate) moyen -enne; **Middle Ages** moyen âge; **~ class** bourgeoisie *f*; **Middle East** Moyen-Orient *m*; **~ finger** médius *m*; **~-sized** de grandeur moyenne; **take a ~ course** prendre le parti moyen

**middle-aged** *adj* d'un certain âge

**middleman** *n* intermédiaire *m*

**middle-weight** *n sp* poids moyen

**middling** *adj* médiocre, passable; (health) pas mal, comme ci comme ça; (quality) de qualité moyenne; *adv* passablement

**midge** *n* moucheron *m*

**midget** *n* nain -e; *adj* tout petit, minuscule

**midnight** *n* minuit *m*; *adj* de minuit

**midriff** *n* diaphragme *m*

**midshipman** *n* = aspirant *m* (de marine)

**midst** *n* milieu *m*; **in our ~** parmi nous; **in the ~ of** en plein milieu de; **in the ~ of doing sth** en train de faire qch; **in the ~ of winter** en plein hiver, au cœur de l'hiver

**midstream** *n* **in ~** au milieu du courant

**midsummer** *n* cœur *m* de l'été

**midway** *adv* à mi-chemin

**midwife** *n* (*pl* **midwives**) sage-femme *f* (*pl* sages-femmes)

**midwifery** *n* obstétrique *f*

**midwinter** *n* fort *m* de l'hiver, cœur *m* de l'hiver

**mien** *n* mine *f*, air *m*

**might** *n* force *f*, puissance *f*; **~ is right** la raison du plus fort est toujours la meilleure; **with all one's ~** de toutes ses forces; *vi see* **may**

**mighty** *adj* puissant, fort; (big) grand, vaste; *adv* fort, bien, extrêmement

**mignonette** *n* réséda *m*

**migraine** *n* migraine *f*

**migrant** *n* + *adj* migrateur -trice

**migrate** *vi* émigrer

**migration** *n* migration *f*

**migratory** *adj* migrateur -trice

**mild** *adj* doux (*f* douce); léger -ère; (illness) bénin (*f* bénigne); modéré; **~ beer** bière brune

**mildew** *n* (wheat) rouille *f*; (vine) mildiou *m*; moisissure *f*

**mildness** *n* douceur *f*; (illness) bénignité *f*; (weather) clémence *f*

**mile** *n* mille *m*

**mileage** *n* distance *f* en milles

**milestone** *n* borne *f* milliaire; = borne *f* kilométrique

**milieu** *n* milieu *m*

**militancy** *n* attitude militante, esprit militant

**militant** *n* + *adj* militant -e

**militarism** *n* militarisme *m*

**military** *n* **the ~** les militaires *mpl*; *adj* militaire; **~ age** âge *m* de servir

**militate** *vi* militer

**militia** *n* milice *f*

**milk** *n* lait *m*; **~ and water** lait coupé d'eau; **land flowing with ~ and honey** pays *m* de cocagne; **malted ~** farine lactée; *vt* traire; *fig* exploiter

**milk-bar** *n* milk-bar *m*

**milk-float** *n* voiture *f* de laitier

**milkiness** *n* couleur laiteuse

**milking** *n* traite *f*

**milk-jug** *n* pot *m* à lait

**milkmaid** *n* laitière *f*

**milkman** *n* laitier *m*

**milksop** *n coll* poule mouillée

**milk-tooth** *n* dent *f* de lait

**milky** *adj* laiteux -euse

**mill** *n* moulin *m*; (modern) minoterie *f*; (factory) usine *f*, manufacture *f*; (spinning) filature *f*; *vt* moudre; (cloth) fouler; *mech* fraiser; *vi* (crowd) fourmiller

**millennium** *n* millénaire *m*, mille ans *mpl*

**miller** *n* meunier *m*; minotier *m*; *mech* (person) fraiseur *m*; (machine) fraiseuse *f*

**millet** *n* millet *m*, mil *m*

**milligram(me)** *n* milligramme *m*

**millimetre** *n* millimètre *m*

**milliner** *n* modiste *f*

**millinery** *n* articles *mpl* de mode

**million** *n* million *m*

**millionaire** *n* millionnaire

**millionth** *n* millionième; (fraction) millionième *m*; *adj* millionième

**millipede, millepede** *n* mille-pattes *m*

**millstone** *n* meule *f*; (encumbrance) boulet *m*

**mime** *n* mime *m*; *vt* mimer

**mimic** *n* mime *m*, imitateur -trice; *adj* mimique; *vt* imiter, mimer; (ape) singer

**mimicry** *n* imitation *f*

**mimosa** *n* mimosa *m*

**minaret** *n* minaret *m*

**mince** *n* hachis *m*; *vt* hacher; **~ one's words** parler du bout des lèvres; **not to ~ one's words** ne pas mâcher ses mots; *vi* minauder; marcher à petits pas

**mincemeat** *n* (meat) hachis *m*; espèce *f* de compote anglaise; *fig* **make ~ of** détruire

**mince-pie** *n* tartelette *f* contenant du mincemeat

**mincer** *n* hachoir *m*

**mincing-machine** *n* hachoir *m*, hache-viande *m invar*

**mind** *n* esprit *m*, âme *f*; (memory) souvenir *m*, mémoire *f*; (thought) pensée *f*, idée *f*; (intention) intention *f*, envie *f*; **bear in ~** ne pas oublier; **be in one's right ~** avoir toute sa raison; **be in two ~s about sth** être indécis sur qch; **be out of one's ~** avoir perdu la raison; **call to ~** se rappeler; **change one's ~** changer d'avis; **give s/o a piece of one's ~** dire son fait à qn; **have a good ~ to** avoir envie de; **have sth in ~** avoir qch en vue; **he has sth on his ~** il a qch qui le préoccupe (tracasse); **it came to my ~ that** il m'est venu à l'esprit que; **it went out of my ~** cela m'est sorti de l'esprit; **know one's own ~** savoir ce qu'on veut; **make up one's ~** prendre son parti, se décider; **sound of ~** sain d'esprit; **put sth out of one's ~** ne plus penser à qch; **speak one's ~** dire ce qu'on pense; **to my ~** à mon avis; **turn of ~** tour *m* d'esprit; *vt + vi* faire attention à; (look after) veiller sur, garder; (be concerned with) s'occuper de, se mêler de; (take care of) avoir soin de; (worry over) se soucier de; **~ (out)!** attention!; **~ the step** attention à la marche; **~ you** remarquez; **~ you don't fall** prenez garde de tomber; **~ your own business** mêlez-vous de ce qui vous regarde; **I don't ~** cela m'est égal; **I wouldn't ~ a chocolate** je prendrais volontiers un chocolat; **never ~** n'importe, tant pis; **never ~ the money** ne regardez pas à l'argent; **Will you have a cake? – I don't ~ if I do** Voulez-vous prendre un gâteau? – Je veux bien; **would you ~ moving on a bit?** voudriez-vous avancer un peu?

**minded** *adj* disposé

**mindful** *adj* attentif -ive

**mindless** *adj* insouciant, indifférent; (stupid) imbécile, stupide

**mind-reader** *n* liseur -euse de pensées

¹**mine** *n* mine *f*; **lay ~s** mouiller des mines; *vt* miner

²**mine** *poss pron* le mien (*f* la mienne, *mpl* les miens, *fpl* les miennes); **a brother of ~** un de mes frères; **this chair is ~** cette chaise est à moi

**minefield** *n* champ *m* de mines

**mine-layer** *n* mouilleur *m* de mines

**miner** *n* mineur *m*

**mineral** *n* minéral *m*; (ore) minerai *m*; *adj* minéral; **~ water** eau minérale

**mineralogy** *n* minéralogie *f*

**minesweeper** *n* dragueur *m* de mines

**mingle** *vt* mêler, mélanger; *vi* se mêler, se mélanger

**mingy** *adj coll* misérable, pauvre

**mini** *n + adj* mini

**mini-** *prefix* mini-

**miniature** *n* miniature *f*; **~ painter** miniaturiste; *adj* en miniature, (de) petit format

**minibus** *n* minibus *m*

**minim** *n* (measure) goutte *f*; *mus* blanche *f*

**minimal** *adj* minimal

**minimize** *vt* réduire au minimum, minimiser

**minimum** *n* minimum *m* (*pl* minimums *or* minima); *adj* minimum (*f* minimum *or* minima, *pl* minimums *or* minima)

**mining** *n* exploitation minière; *adj* minier -ière

**minion** *n* favori -ite; (subject) subordonné -e

**minister** *n* ministre *m*; *eccles* pasteur *m*; *vi* **to s/o's needs** soigner qn, pourvoir aux besoins de qn

**ministerial** *adj* ministériel -ielle; exécutif -ive; *eccles* sacerdotal

**ministry** *n* ministère *m*; (good offices) entremise *f*

**mink** *n* vison *m*

**minnow** *n* vairon *m*

**minor** *n* mineur -e; *adj* moindre, mineur; (unimportant) peu important, petit

**Minorca** *n* Minorque *f*

**minority** *n* minorité *f*; *adj* minoritaire

**minster** *n* cathédrale *f*

**minstrel** *n hist* ménestrel *m*; poète *m*, musicien *m*

¹**mint** *n* **the Mint** la Monnaie; **be worth a ~ of money** (person) rouler sur l'or; (thing) valoir des millions; **fresh from the ~** tout battant neuf (*f* neuve); **make a ~ of money** gagner un argent fou; *adj* **in ~ condition** tout neuf (*f* toute neuve); *vt* (money) battre; (gold) monnayer; (invent) inventer

²**mint** *n bot* menthe *f*; **~-sauce** vinaigrette *f* à la menthe

**minuet** *n* menuet *m*

**minus** *n* (sign) moins *m*; **~ quantity** quantité négative; *prep* moins

¹**minute** *n* minute *f*; (moment) moment *m*; (note) note *f*; **~s of a meeting** procès-verbal *m* d'une séance; **he is due any ~** il doit arriver d'un instant à l'autre; **I shan't be a ~** j'en ai pour une seconde; **ten ~s past three** trois heures dix; **ten ~s to three** trois heures moins dix; **this very ~** à l'instant même; *vt* minuter

²**minute** *adj* tout petit, minuscule;

(precise) minutieux -ieuse

**minute-book** *n* registre *m* des procès-verbaux

**minute-hand** *n* grande aiguille

**minutely** *adv* minutieusement; en détail

**minuteness** *n* petitesse *f*; (exactitude) minutie *f*

**minutiae** *npl* petits détails

**minx** *n* coquine *f*

**miracle** *n* miracle *m*

**miraculous** *adj* miraculeux -euse; extra-ordinaire

**mirage** *n* mirage *m*

**mire** *n* bourbier *m*; (mud) boue *f*; *fig* fange *f*; **sink into the ~** s'embourber

**mirror** *n* miroir *m*, glace *f*; **driving-~** rétroviseur *m*; *vt* refléter

**mirth** *n* gaieté *f*, allégresse *f*

**mirthful** *adj* joyeux -euse, gai

**mirthless** *adj* triste, sans gaieté

**misadventure** *n* mésaventure *f*

**misalliance** *n* mésalliance *f*

**misanthrope** *n* misanthrope

**misanthropic** *adj* misanthropique

**misanthropist** *n see* **misanthrope**

**misanthropy** *n* misanthropie *f*

**misapply** *vt* mal appliquer, mal employer; (funds) détourner

**misapprehend** *vt* mal comprendre

**misapprehension** *n* malentendu *m*, méprise *f*

**misappropriate** *vt* détourner

**misappropriation** *n* détournement *m*

**misbegotten** *adj* (child) illégitime; *fig* misérable

**misbehave** *vi* se conduire mal

**misbehaviour** *n* mauvaise conduite.

**miscalculate** *vt* mal calculer

**miscalculation** *n* mauvais calcul

**miscall** *vt* mal nommer

**miscarriage** *n* (failure) insuccès *m*; *med* fausse couche; (loss) égarement *m*; **~ of justice** erreur *f* judiciaire

**miscarry** *vi* (go astray) s'égarer; *med* faire une fausse couche; (fail) échouer

**miscellaneous** *adj* divers, varié

**miscellany** *n* mélange *m*

**mischance** *n* mauvaise chance; mésaventure *f*, malheur *m*

**mischief** *n* (harm) mal *m*, tort *m*; (child) espièglerie *f*; malice *f*; **be up to some ~** méditer un mauvais coup; **keep s/o out of ~** empêcher qn de faire des sottises; **make ~** semer la discorde

**mischief-maker** *n* brandon *m* de discorde

**mischievous** *adj* méchant; (thing) nuisible; (child) espiègle; malicieux -ieuse

**misconceive** *vt* mal concevoir

**misconception** *n* malentendu *m*; conception fausse

**misconduct** *n* (business) mauvaise gestion; (person) mauvaise conduite; (adultery) adultère *m*; *vt* mal gérer; **~ oneself** se conduire mal

**misconstruction** *n* fausse interprétation

**misconstrue** *vt* mal interpréter

**miscount** *n* erreur *f* d'addition; *pol* erreur *f* dans le dépouillement du scrutin; *vt* mal compter

**miscreant** *n* scélérat -e

**misdeal** *n* maldonne *f*; *vt* maldonner

**misdeed** *n* méfait *m*

**misdemeanour** *n leg* délit *m*; écart *m* de conduite

**misdirect** *vt* (letter) mal adresser; (aim) mal viser; (direction) mal diriger; (misinform) mal renseigner

**miser** *n* avare

**miserable** *adj* misérable, malheureux -euse, triste

**miserly** *adj* avare

**misery** *n* misère *f*, détresse *f*; (suffering) supplice *m*

**misfire** *vi* rater, faire long feu; (engine) avoir des ratés; (joke) manquer šon effet

**misfit** *n* vêtement manqué; (social) inadapté -e

**misfortune** *n* malheur *m*, infortune *f*

**misgiving** *n* pressentiment *m*, doute *m*; (fear) crainte *f*

**misgovern** *vt* mal gouverner

**misguided** *adj* peu judicieux -ieuse, mal avisé, malencontreux -euse

**mishandle** *vt* maltraiter; (business) mal conduire

**mishap** *n* contretemps *m*, accident *m*, mésaventure *f*

**misinform** *vt* mal renseigner

**misinterpret** *vt* mal interpréter

**misinterpretation** *n* fausse interprétation

**misjudge** *vt* mal juger; méconnaître

**mislay** *vt* égarer

**mislead** *vt* tromper; (lead astray) égarer

**misleading** *adj* trompeur -euse

**mismanage** *vt* mal conduire; mal gérer

**mismanagement** *n* mauvaise gestion

**misname** *vt* mal nommer

**misnomer** *n* erreur *f* de nom; fausse appellation

**misogynist** *n* misogyne

**misplace** *vt* mal placer; **~d remark** remarque déplacée

**misprint** *n* faute *f* d'impression, coquille *f*; *vt* faire une faute d'impression dans

**mispronounce** *vt* mal prononcer

**mispronunciation** *n* faute *f* de prononciation, mauvaise prononciation

**misquotation** *n* citation incorrecte

**misquote** *vt* citer à faux

**misread** *vt* mal lire; (misinterpret) mal interpréter

**misrepresent** vt mal représenter; (facts) dénaturer, travestir

**misrule** n mauvais gouvernement; désordre m; vt mal gouverner

**Miss** n Mademoiselle f; ~ **World** Miss Monde; **miss** demoiselle f

**miss** n coup manqué; **give sth a** ~ omettre qch; vt manquer, rater; (omit) omettre, passer; (not see) ne pas voir; remarquer l'absence de; coll fig ~ **the bus** rater l'occasion; ~ **the point** ne pas comprendre; **he** ~**ed his wallet** il ne trouva pas son portefeuille; **I** ~**ed my footing** le pied me manqua; **I** ~ **my mother** ma mère me manque; **my pen is** ~**ing** mon stylo a disparu; **narrowly** ~ **doing sth** faillir faire qch; coll **you haven't** ~**ed much** vous n'avez pas raté grand-chose; **we** ~ **the car** nous regrettons la voiture; vi ~ **out** échouer

**missal** n eccles missel m

**misshapen** adj difforme

**missile** n projectile m; mil missile m; **guided** ~ engin téléguidé

**missing** adj absent, manquant; ~ **link** forme intermédiaire disparue

**mission** n mission f

**missionary** n + adj missionnaire

**missive** n missive f, lettre f

**misspell** vt mal épeler

**misspent** adj mal employé

**misstate** vt rapporter incorrectement

**misstatement** n rapport inexact

**missus** n coll **the** ~ la vieille, la bourgeoise

**mist** n brume f; (on glass) buée f; **the** ~**s of time** la nuit des temps; vt couvrir de buée; vi disparaître sous la brume; se couvrir de buée

**mistakable** adj facile à confondre

**mistake** n erreur f, méprise f, faute f; **make a** ~ se tromper; **there's no** ~ **about it** c'est bien le cas de dire, il n'y a pas à dire; vt mal comprendre; (intentions) se méprendre sur; ~ **one's way** se tromper de chemin; ~ **s/o for s/o else** prendre qn pour qn d'autre

**mistaken** adj (idea) erroné; (misunderstood) mal compris; **be** ~ se tromper, faire erreur; **if I am not** ~ sauf erreur

**Mister** n see **Mr**

**mistime** vt faire à contretemps; mal calculer

**mistimed** adj inopportun

**mistiness** n état brumeux

**mistletoe** n gui m

**mistranslate** vt mal traduire

**mistreat** vt maltraiter

**mistress** n maîtresse f; (teacher) institutrice f; (boss) patronne f; **be one's own** ~ être indépendante

**mistrust** n méfiance f, manque m de confiance; vt se méfier de

**misty** adj brumeux -euse; (eye) voilé

**misunderstand** vt mal comprendre, mal interpréter; méconnaître

**misunderstanding** n malentendu m; (quarrel) mésentente f, brouille f

**misuse** n abus m, mauvais usage; vt abuser de, faire un mauvais usage de; (use wrongly) employer incorrectement; (ill-treat) maltraiter

**mite** n (small gift) obole f; (insect) mite f; (child) mioche; (small quantity) miette f

**mitigate** vt adoucir, atténuer, amoindrir; (heat) tempérer; **mitigating circumstances** circonstances atténuantes

**mitigation** n adoucissement m; amoindrissement m; (penalty) atténuation f

**mitre** n mitre f

**mitten** n mitaine f

**mix** n mélange m, proportions fpl; vt mêler, mélanger; (drink) préparer; (salad) retourner; ~ **ed up in sth** être mêlé à une affaire; **he** ~**es everything up** il embrouille tout; vi se mêler, se mélanger; ~ **with people** fréquenter les gens

**mixed** adj mêlé, mélangé; (school, bathing, etc) mixte; (colours) assorti

**mixer** n mélangeur m, mixe(u)r m; rad opérateur m des sons; **be a good (bad)** ~ être (peu) sociable

**mixture** n mélange m; (pharmacy) mixture f

**mix-up** n confusion f, embrouillement m; coll pagaille f; (fight) coll bagarre f

**mnemonic** n mnémonique f; adj mnémonique

**moan** n gémissement m, plainte f; vi gémir

**moat** n douve f

**mob** n (crowd) foule f; (rabble) populace f; vt malmener; (fans) assiéger; vi s'attrouper

**mobile** n mobile m; adj mobile; (character) changeant

**mobility** n mobilité f

**mobilization** n mobilisation f

**mobilize** vt mobiliser; vi entrer en mobilisation

**moccasin, moccassin** n mocassin m

**mock** n **make a** ~ **of s/o** se moquer de qn; adj faux (f fausse), contrefait, d'imitation; vt se moquer de; narguer; tromper; (mimic) imiter, singer

**mockery** n moquerie f, raillerie f; (pretence) semblant m; objet m de dérision

**mock-up** n maquette f

**mod** n sl jeune homme (fille) habillé(e) avec recherche (à motocyclette); adj sl moderne

**mode** n (manner) façon f, mode m,

manière *f*; (fashion) mode *f*

**model** *n* modèle *m*; maquette *f*; (dress-making) patron *m*; **scale ~** modèle réduit; *adj* modèle; *vt* modeler; *vi* (fashions) être mannequin

**modelling** *n* modelage *m*

¹**moderate** *adj* modéré; médiocre, ordinaire; (character) raisonnable; (price) modique

²**moderate** *vt* modérer, tempérer; présider, arbitrer; *vi* se modérer

**moderation** *n* modération *f*, mesure *f*; **in ~** modérément

**moderator** *n* président *m*

**modern** *adj* moderne; **~ languages** langues vivantes

**modernism** *n* modernisme *m*; nouveauté *f*

**modernistic** *adj* moderniste

**modernity** *n* modernité *f*

**modernize** *vt* moderniser

**modest** *adj* modeste; (prudish) pudique

**modesty** *n* modestie *f*; (prudery) pudeur *f*; (expense) modicité *f*; (demand) modération *f*; absence *f* de prétention

**modicum** *n* petite quantité

**modification** *n* modification *f*; (attenuation) atténuation *f*

**modify** *vt* modifier; (attenuate) atténuer

**modish** *adj* élégant, à la mode

**modulate** *vt* moduler

**modulation** *n* modulation *f*

**module** *n* module *m*; **command ~** module *m* de commande; **service ~** module *m* de service

**mohair** *n* mohair *m*

**Mohammedan, Mahometan** *n* Musulman -e; *adj* musulman, mahométan

**moil** *vi* **toil and ~** travailler dur

**moist** *adj* humide, mouillé; (skin) moite

**moisten** *vt* humecter, mouiller

**moisture** *n* humidité *f*; (skin) moiteur *f*

**molar** *n* molaire *f*; *adj* molaire

**molasses** *npl* mélasse *f*

¹**mole** *n zool* taupe *f*

²**mole** *n* (pier) môle *m*, jetée *f*

³**mole** *n* (spot) envie *f*, grain *m* de beauté

**molecular** *adj* moléculaire

**molecule** *n* molécule *f*

**molehill** *n* taupinière *f*

**molest** *vt* molester; rudoyer

**mollify** *vt* apaiser, adoucir

**mollusc** *n* mollusque *m*

**mollycoddle** *vt* dorloter, choyer

**molten** *adj* fondu

**molybdenum** *n* molybdène *m*

**moment** *n* moment *m*, instant *m*; **a ~ ago** il y a un moment; **at the present ~** en ce moment; **from the ~ when …** dès l'instant où …; **I have just this ~ arrived** j'arrive à l'instant, je viens tout

juste d'arriver; **it all happened in a ~** cela se passa en un clin d'œil; **just one ~, please** un petit instant, s'il vous plaît; **not for one ~** ! jamais de la vie!; **of great ~** de (d'une) grande importance; **the ~ he arrives** dès qu'il viendra

**momentary** *adj* passager -ère, momentané

**momentous** *adj* important, capital

**momentum** *n* vitesse acquise, élan *m*; *phys* quantité *f* de mouvement

**monarch** *n* monarque *m*

**monarchist** *n* + *adj* monarchiste

**monarchy** *n* monarchie *f*

**monastery** *n* monastère *m*

**monastic(al)** *adj* monastique

**monasticism** *n* monachisme *m*, vie *f* monastique

**Monday** *n* lundi *m*

**monetary** *adj* monétaire

**money** *n* argent *m*, monnaie *f*; **be coining ~** ramasser l'argent à la pelle; **be rolling in ~** rouler sur l'or; **bring in big ~** rapporter gros; **buy sth with one's own ~** acheter qch de ses propres deniers; **come into ~** hériter d'une fortune; **get one's ~ back** être remboursé; **have one's ~'s worth** en avoir pour son argent; *coll* **have pots of ~** *sl* être plein aux as; **paper ~** papier-monnaie *m*; **part with one's ~** débourser *m*; **pocket ~** argent *m* de poche; **ready ~** argent *m* liquide; **there's ~ in it** c'est une bonne affaire; **your ~ or your life!** la bourse ou la vie!

**money-box** *n* tirelire *f*

**money-changer** *n* changeur *m*, cambiste *m*

**moneyed** *adj* riche

**money-grubber** *n* grippe-sou *m* (*pl* grippe-sou(s))

**money-lender** *n* prêteur -euse d'argent

**money-market** *n* marché *m* monétaire

**money-order** *n* mandat *m*

**money-spinner** *n coll* chose *f* qui rapporte beaucoup d'argent; personne *f* qui gagne beaucoup d'argent

**mongol** *n* + *adj* mongolien -ienne

**Mongolian** *n* Mongol -e; *adj* mongol

**mongoose** *n* mangouste *f*

**mongrel** *n* + *adj* (human) métis -isse; (dog) bâtard *m*

**monitor** *n* moniteur -trice; *rad* opérateur -trice d'interception; **~ screen** écran *m* témoin; **~ speaker** haut-parleur *m* témoin; *vt* contrôler

**monk** *n* moine *m*, religieux *m*

**monkey** *n* singe *m*; **female ~** guenon *f*; *sl* **get one's ~ up** piquer une colère; *coll* **I'm not having any ~ business** on ne va pas me la faire; *vi* **~ about** faire l'idiot -e; ~ **about with** tripoter; toucher à

**monkey-nut** n cacahouète f

**monkey-puzzle** n bot araucaria m

**monkey-wrench** n clef f (clé f) à molette, US clef (clé) anglaise

**mono** adj coll mono

**monochrome** n monochrome m; adj monochrome

**monocle** n monocle m

**monogamy** n monogamie f

**monogram** n monogramme m

**monograph** n monographie f

**monolith** n monolithe m

**monologue** n monologue m

**monomania** n monomanie f

**monoplane** n monoplan m

**monopolist** n monopolisateur -trice

**monopolize** vt monopoliser

**monopoly** n monopole m

**monorail** n monorail m

**monosyllable** n monosyllabe m

**monotone** n bruit m monotone, son m monotone

**monotonous** adj monotone; ennuyeux -euse, fastidieux -ieuse

**monotony** n monotonie f

**monsoon** n mousson f

**monster** n monstre m; adj énorme, colossal

**monstrosity** n monstruosité f; monstre m; énormité f

**monstrous** adj monstrueux -euse

**montage** n montage m

**month** n mois m; **by the** ~ au mois; **calendar** ~ mois m du calendrier; **get one's** ~ **'s pay** toucher son mois; **in the** ~ **of** au mois de; **once a** ~ une fois par mois

**monthly** adj mensuel -elle; (ticket, etc) valable (pour) un mois; ~ **pay** mois m; ~ **payment** (instalment) mensualité f; physiol ~ **period** règles fpl; adv mensuellement, par mois; **be paid** ~ être payé au mois

**monument** n monument m; pierre tombale

**monumental** adj monumental; ~ **mason** marbrier m

**moo** n meuglement m, beuglement m; vi meugler, beugler; interj meuh!

**mooch** vi ~ **about** flâner, rôder

**mood** n humeur f, disposition f; gram mode m; **be in a good (bad)** ~ être de bonne (mauvaise) humeur; **be in no** ~ **for** n'avoir aucune envie de; **be in the** ~ **for** être d'humeur à; **have** ~ s être lunatique

**moodiness** n humeur changeante

**moody** adj d'humeur incertaine

**moon** n lune f; **landing on the** ~ alunissage m; **land on the** ~ alunir; **many** ~ s

**ago** il y a longtemps; **once in a blue** ~ tous les trente-six du mois; vi ~ **about** muser

**moonbeam** n rayon m de lune

**moonlight** n clair m de lune; **in the** ~ au clair de la lune

**moonlit** adj éclairé par la lune

**moonshine** n clair m de lune; (nonsense) balivernes fpl, blague f; US alcool m de contrebande

**moonshot** n envoi m d'une fusée vers la lune

**moonstruck** adj coll toqué

**moony** adj rêveur -euse

**Moor** n Maure m, Mauresque f

[1]**moor** n lande f, bruyère f

[2]**moor** vt amarrer; vi s'amarrer

**moorhen** n poule f d'eau

**mooring** n amarrage m; **ship at her** ~ s navire m sur ses amarres

**moorland** n lande f

**moose** n élan m du Canada

[1]**moot** adj discutable

[2]**moot** vt (question) soulever; **be** ~ **ed** être mis sur le tapis

**mop** n balai m à franges, balai m à laver; ~ **of hair** tignasse f; vt essuyer; ~ **one's brow** s'éponger le front; ~ **up** éponger; (absorb) absorber

**mope** vi être triste; s'ennuyer

**moped** n cyclomoteur m, vélomoteur m

**mopping-up** n épongeage m, essuyage m

**moral** n morale f, moralité f; ~ s moralité f, mœurs fpl; adj moral; (morally good) conforme aux bonnes mœurs

**morale** n moral m

**moralist** n moraliste

**morality** n moralité f; (good conduct) bonnes mœurs

**moralize** vi moraliser, faire de la morale

**morally** adv moralement

**morass** n marais m, fondrière f

**moratorium** n moratoire m

**morbid** adj morbide

**morbidity** n morbidité f

**more** n davantage, plus; encore; ~ **than five** plus de cinq; **a little** ~ encore un peu; **be no** ~ être mort; **one** ~ un de plus, encore un; **say no** ~ n'en parlez plus; **the** ~ **he tries, the** ~ **he loses** plus il essaie, plus il perd; **what is** ~ qui plus est; adj plus de; adv plus, davantage; ~ **and** ~ de plus en plus; **all the** ~ d'autant plus; **don't come any** ~ ne venez plus; **once** ~ encore une fois

**moreover** adv d'ailleurs, du reste, de plus

**morgue** n morgue f

**moribund** adj moribond

**Mormon** n + adj mormon -e

**morning** n matin m; matinée f; **all the** ~ toute la matinée; **early in the** ~ de bon matin; **good** ~ ! bonjour!; **in the** ~ le

592

matin; **the ~ before** la veille au matin; **the next ~** le lendemain matin; **two o'clock in the ~** deux heures du matin; *adj* matinal, du matin

**Morocco** *n* le Maroc; (leather) maroquin *m*

**moron** *n* idiot -e; minus habens *m invar*

**morose** *adj* morose

**morphia, morphine** *n* morphine *f*

**morphinomaniac** *n* + *adj* morphinomane

**morphology** *n* morphologie *f*

**morris-dance** *n* danse folklorique anglaise

**morse** *n* (code) morse *m*

**morsel** *n* morceau *m*, petit morceau

**mortal** *adj* mortel -elle

**mortality** *n* mortalité *f*

**mortar** *n* mortier *m*

**mortar-board** *n* planche *f* à mortier

**mortgage** *n* hypothèque *f*; *vt* hypothéquer

**mortification** *n* mortification *f*

**mortify** *vt* mortifier; humilier; *med* gangrener

**mortuary** *n* morgue *f*; (hospital) salle *f* mortuaire

**mosaic** *n* mosaïque *f*; *adj* en mosaïque

**Moscow** *n* Moscou *m*

**Moslem, Muslim** *n* Mahométan -e, Musulman -e; *adj* mahométan, musulman

**mosque** *n* mosquée *f*

**mosquito** *n* moustique *m*

**mosquito-net** *n* moustiquaire *f*

**moss** *n bot* mousse *f*; (bog) marais *m*

**mossy** *adj* moussu

**most** *n* le plus; la plupart, la majeure partie; **~ of them** la plupart d'entre eux; **at the ~** tout au plus; **make the ~ of sth** tirer le meilleur parti possible de qch, profiter au maximum de qch; (eke out) ménager le plus possible qch; *adj* le plus de; **~ people** la plupart des gens; **for the ~ part** pour la plupart; *adv* le plus; (very much) très, fort, bien, on ne peut plus, tout ce qu'il y a de plus

**motel** *n* motel *m*

**moth** *n* (clothes) mite *f*; papillon *m* de nuit

**moth-ball** *n* boule *f* de naphtaline

**moth-eaten** *adj* mité, mangé des mites; *fig* miteux -euse

**mother** *n* mère *f*; **~ country** mère patrie *f*; **~ naked** nu comme un ver; **~ of five** mère *f* de cinq enfants; **Mother's Day** la fête des Mères; **~ tongue** langue maternelle; **every ~'s son** tous sans exception; **unmarried ~** mère *f* célibataire, *pej* fille-mère *f* (*pl* filles-mères); *vt* servir de mère à; (fuss over) dorloter

**motherhood** *n* maternité *f*

**mother-in-law** *n* belle-mère *f* (*pl* belles-mères)

**motherland** *n* patrie *f*

**motherless** *adj* sans mère, orphelin de mère

**motherly** *adj* maternel -elle

**mother-of-pearl** *n* nacre *f*

**moth-killer** *n* antimite *m*

**mothproof** *adj* antimite(s)

**motion** *n* mouvement *m*; déplacement *m*; (sign) signe *m*, geste *m*; (proposal) proposition *f*, motion *f*; *med* évacuation *f*; **~-picture** film *m*; **carry a ~** adopter une motion; **go through the ~s of doing sth** faire semblant de faire qch; **propose a ~** faire une proposition; **set in ~** mettre en mouvement; *vt* faire signe à

**motionless** *adj* immobile

**motivate** *vt* motiver

**motivation** *n* motivation *f*

**motive** *n* motif *m*; (action) mobile *m*; ressort *m*; *adj* moteur -trice

**motley** *adj* (colours) bariolé; (varied) divers

**motor** *n* moteur *m*; (car) auto *f*, voiture *f*; **~-coach** autocar *m*; **~ show** salon *m* de l'auto; *vi* voyager en automobile

**motorbike** *n* motocyclette *f*

**motorboat** *n* canot *m* automobile

**motorcade** *n US* défilé *m* de voitures

**motorcar** *n* auto *f*, voiture *f*

**motorcycle** *n* motocyclette *f*

**motoring** *n* automobilisme *m*; **school of ~** auto-école *f*

**motorist** *n* automobiliste *f*

**motorize** *vt* motoriser

**motor-scooter** *n* scooter *m*

**motorway** *n* autoroute *f*

**mottle** *n* tache *f*; (marbling) marbrure *f*; *vt* tacheter, marbrer; **~d** (sky, horse) pommelé; (skin) marbré

**motto** *n* devise *f*

¹**mould** *n* (soil) terre *f*, terreau *m*

²**mould** *n* (mildew) moisi *m*, moisissure *f*; *vi* moisir

³**mould** *n* (shape) moule *m*; *vt* mouler; former

**moulder** *vi* tomber en poussière; moisir

**mouldiness** *n* moisissure *f*

**moulding** *n* moulage *m*; (character) formation *f*; (decoration, etc) moulure *f*

**mouldy** *adj* moisi; **go ~** moisir; **smell ~** sentir le moisi

**moult** *vi* muer

**moulting** *n* mue *f*

**mound** *n* butte *f*, tertre *m*

¹**mount** *n* mont *m*, montagne *f*

²**mount** *n* (horse) monture *f*; montage *m*, support *m*; (photo) carton *m*; (machine) armement *m*; (stamp) charnière *f*; *vt* monter, monter sur; **~ guard**

monter la garde; *vi* monter; (horse) monter à cheval; (rise) s'élever, augmenter; **~ed** à cheval; **~ up** augmenter

**mountain** *n* montagne *f*; **~ range** chaîne *f* de montagnes; **make ~s out of molehills** se noyer dans un verre d'eau; *adj* (mountainous) montagneux -euse; de montagne, montagnard

**mountaineer** *n* alpiniste; *vi* faire de l'alpinisme

**mountaineering** *n* alpinisme *m*

**mountainous** *adj* montagneux -euse

**mountebank** *n* saltimbanque *m*; (quack) charlatan

**mourn** *vt* pleurer, prendre le deuil pour; *vi* pleurer

**mourner** *n* personne *f* qui suit le cortège funèbre

**mournful** *adj* lugubre, triste

**mourning** *n* deuil *m*; (clothes) habits *mpl* de deuil; **be in ~ for** porter le deuil de; **go into ~** prendre le deuil; **in deep ~** en grand deuil

**mouse** *n* souris *f*; *vi* chasser les souris

**mouse-colour** *n* gris *m* de souris

**mouse-hole** *n* trou *m* de souris

**mouse-like** *adj* insignifiant

**mouse-trap** *n* souricière *f*; *coll* fromage *m* de qualité inférieure

**mousse** *n* mousse *f*

**moustache** *n* moustache *f*

**mousy** *adj* gris souris *invar*; timide

**mouth** *n* bouche *f*; (animal) gueule *f*; (opening) ouverture *f*; (river) embouchure *f*; (bottle) goulot *m*; **by word of ~** de vive voix; **down in the ~** triste; **make s/o's ~ water** faire venir l'eau à la bouche de qn; **put words into s/o's ~** attribuer des paroles à qn; *vt* déclamer; grimacer

**mouthful** *n* bouchée *f*; (liquid) gorgée *f*; (swimming) **swallow a ~** boire la tasse

**mouth-organ** *n* harmonica *m*

**mouthpiece** *n* (instrument) embouchure *f*; (person) porte-parole *m invar*

**movable** *adj* mobile; **~s** *npl* biens mobiliers

**move** *n* (house) déménagement *m*; mouvement *m*; (chess) coup *m*; (intervention) démarche *f*; **be on the ~** être en mouvement; **get a ~ on** *coll* se dépêcher; *sl* se grouiller; **it's your ~** (c'est) à vous de jouer; **make a ~** (game) jouer; (depart) se mettre en route, partir; **make the first ~** faire le premier pas; *vt* déplacer; bouger, remuer; (goods) transporter; (furniture) déménager; (feelings) toucher, émouvoir; (opinion) faire changer d'avis à; (resolution) proposer; **~ back** faire reculer; **~ forward** faire

avancer; **~ heaven and earth** faire des pieds et des mains; **~ on** faire circuler; **~ out** déloger, faire sortir; **~ over** écarter; **~ s/o to anger** provoquer la colère de qn; **~ s/o to do sth** inciter qn à faire qch; *vi* se déplacer; bouger; **~ away** s'éloigner; **~ back** reculer; **~ forward** avancer; (house) **~ in** emménager; **~ off** s'en aller; **~ on** circuler; aller plus loin; **~ out** sortir; (house) déménager; **~ over** s'écarter

**movement** *n* mouvement *m*; (shift) déplacement *m*; **watch s/o's ~s** surveiller les allées et venues de qn

**mover** *n* moteur *m*; auteur *m*

**movie** *n coll US* film *m*; **go to the ~s** aller au cinéma

**moving** *adj* en mouvement; mobile; (feeling) touchant, émouvant; (force) moteur -trice

**mow** *vt* (lawn) tondre; (field) faucher

**mower** *n* (person) faucheur -euse; (lawn) tondeuse *f*

**Mr** *n* M., Monsieur *m*

**Mrs** *n* Mme, Madame *f*

**much** *n* une bonne (grande) partie; beaucoup, grand-chose; **~ has happened** il s'est passé beaucoup de choses; **he's not ~ of a teacher** ce n'est pas un très bon professeur; **I don't think ~ of him** je ne l'estime pas beaucoup; **I don't think ~ of it** j'en fais peu de cas; **make ~ of sth** faire grand cas de qch; vanter qch; **that's not up to ~** cela ne vaut pas grand-chose; **this is too ~!** c'est trop fort!; **twice as ~ as** deux fois plus que; *adj* beaucoup de, bien du (de la, des); **as ~** autant de; **how ~?** combien de?; **so ~** tant de; **too ~** trop de; *adv* beaucoup, bien; **~ to his surprise** à son grand étonnement; **~ the best** de beaucoup le meilleur; **~ the same** à peu près la même chose; **as ~** autant; **as ~ as to say** avec l'air de vouloir dire; **how ~?** combien?; **it doesn't matter ~** cela n'a pas grande importance; **so ~** tant; **too ~** trop; **very ~** beaucoup

**muchness** *n* **much of a ~** pareil -eille; *coll* kif-kif *invar*

**muck** *n* fumier *m*; (mire) fange *f*; (animal) crotte *f*; (filth) ordures *fpl*; *coll fig* cochonneries *fpl*; bêtises *fpl*; *vt* salir, crotter; **~ up sth** gâcher qch; (work) cochonner; *vi* **~ about** flâner; *sl* **~ in with s/o** partager la chambre de qn, partager les repas de qn

**muckiness** *n* saleté *f*

**muck-raking** *n* publication *f* de scandales; colportage *m* de potins

**mucky** *adj* sale, crotté

**mud** *n* boue *f*; bourbe *f*; (mire) fange *f*; (liquid) vase *f*; **drag s/o's name in the**

~ traîner qn dans la boue; **stuck . ï the ~** embourbé

**muddle** *n* fouillis *m*, confusion *f*; **be in a ~** être en désordre; (person) avoir les idées brouillées; **get into a ~** s'embrouiller; *vt* embrouiller, brouiller; *vi* ~ **through** se débrouiller, s'en tirer tant bien que mal

**muddle-headed** *adj* à l'esprit confus; (idea) embrouillé

**muddler** *n* brouillon -onne

**muddy** *adj* boueux -euse, crotté, couvert de boue

**mudguard** *n* garde-boue *m invar*

**mud-slinging** *n* médisance *f*

¹**muff** *n* manchon *m*

²**muff** *n* (person) empoté -e; *vt* rater, louper

**muffin** *n* sorte *f* de galette

**muffle** *vt* emmitoufler, envelopper; (sound) étouffer; (bell) assourdir; *vi* ~ **up** s'emmitoufler

**muffler** *n* cache-nez *m invar*

¹**mug** *n* pot *m*, chope *f*; grosse tasse; gobelet *m*; *sl* (face) binette *f*, gueule *f*

²**mug** *n sl* nigaud -e, andouille *f*

³**mug** *vt* dévaliser, agresser et dévaliser; *coll* ~ **up** bûcher, piocher

**muggy** *adj* lourd, mou ( *f* molle)

**mulberry** *n* mûre *f*; ~ **-tree** mûrier *m*

**mulch** *n hort* paillis *m*; *vt* pailler

**mulct** *vt* frapper d'une amende; priver de

¹**mule** *n* mulet *m*, mule *f*

²**mule** *n* (slipper) mule *f*

**muleteer** *n* muletier *m*

**mulish** *adj* têtu, entêté

¹**mull** *vt* chauffer avec des épices

²**mull** *vt* ~ **over** réfléchir sur

**mullet** *n* muge *m*; **red ~** rouget *m*

**mulligatawny** *n* potage *m* au curry

**mullion** *n* meneau *m*

**multicoloured** *adj* multicolore

**multifarious** *adj* divers, multiple

**multilateral** *adj* multilatéral

**multimillionaire** *n* multimillionnaire *m*; *adj* multimillionnaire

**multiple** *n* multiple *m*; *adj* multiple

**multiplication** *n* multiplication *f*

**multiplicity** *n* multiplicité *f*

**multiply** *vt* multiplier; *vi* se multiplier

**multitude** *n* multitude *f*, foule *f*; multiplicité *f*

**multitudinous** *adj* innombrable, nombreux -euse

¹**mum** *n coll* maman *f*

²**mum** *interj* chut!; ~ **'s the word!** motus!; **keep ~** ne pas souffler mot

**mumble** *vt* + *vi* marmonner, marmotter

**mumbo-jumbo** *n* baragouin *m*; culte superstitieux

**mummify** *vt* momifier

¹**mummy** *n* momie *f*

²**mummy** *n coll* maman *f*

**mumps** *n* oreillons *mpl*

**munch** *vt* mâcher, mâchonner

**mundane** *adj* mondain

**municipal** *adj* municipal

**municipality** *n* municipalité *f*

**munificence** *n* munificence *f*

**munificent** *adj* libéral, généreux -euse

**munitions** *npl* munitions *fpl*

**mural** *n* peinture murale; *adj* mural

**murder** *n* meurtre *m*, assassinat *m*; *vt* assassiner; (song) massacrer; (language) estropier

**murderer** *n* meurtrier *m*, assassin *m*

**murderess** *n* meurtrière *f*

**murderous** *adj* meurtrier -ière

**murk, mirk** *n* obscurité *f*

**murkiness** *n* obscurité *f*

**murky** *adj* obscur, sombre; *fig* ténébreux -euse

**murmur** *n* murmure *m*; *vt* + *vi* murmurer, susurrer

**muscatel** *n* muscat *m*

**muscle** *n* muscle *m*

**muscular** *adj* musculaire

¹**muse** *n* muse *f*

²**muse** *vi* rêver, méditer

**museum** *n* musée *m*; ~ **-piece** pièce *f* de musée

**mush** *n coll* bouillie *f*; *rad* friture *f*

**mushroom** *n* champignon *m*; ~ **spawn** blanc *m* de champignon; *vi* proliférer, se propager

**mushroom-bed** *n* champignonnière *f*

**mushroom-grower** *n* champignonniste

**mushrooming** *n* **go ~** aller cueillir des champignons

**mushy** *adj* (ground) détrempé; (fruit) blet ( *f* blette); *fig* plein de sensiblerie

**music** *n* musique *f*; *fig* **face the ~** accepter les conséquences de ses actes; tenir tête à l'orage; **programme ~** musique *f* de genre; **set to ~** mettre en musique

**musical** *n* opérette *f*; *adj* musical; (person) musicien -ienne; harmonieux -ieuse; ~ **box** boîte *f* à musique; ~ **comedy** opérette *f*

**musically** *adv* du point de vue musical

**music-hall** *n* music-hall *m*

**musician** *n* musicien -ienne

**music-stand** *n* pupitre *m* à musique

**music-stool** *n* tabouret *m* à piano

**musk** *n* musc *m*

**musket** *n* mousquet *m*

**musky** *adj* musqué

**Muslim** *n* + *adj see* **Moslem**

**muslin** *n* mousseline *f*

**musquash** *n* rat musqué

**mussel** *n* moule *f*

¹**must** *n* moisi *m*

²**must** *n* (wine) moût *m*

³**must** *n coll* **it's a ~** c'est absolument

essentiel, c'est une nécessité; *vi* (necessity) falloir; devoir; **I ~ go now** il faut que je parte maintenant; **she ~ have seen him** elle a dû le voir, elle l'aura vu; **that ~ be my mother** ce doit être ma mère

**mustang** *n* mustang *m*

**mustard** *n* moutarde *f*

**mustard-gas** *n* ypérite *f*

**mustard-plaster** *n* sinapisme *m*

**mustard-pot** *n* moutardier *m*

**muster** *n* (assembly) rassemblement *m*; *mil* revue *f*; **pass ~** être passable; *vt* rassembler; (comprise) compter; *mil* passer en revue; **~ one's strength** rassembler ses forces; *vi* se rassembler, se réunir

**mustiness** *n* remugle *m*, odeur *f* de moisi

**musty** *adj* **~ smell** remugle *m*, odeur *f* de moisi; **smell ~** sentir le moisi; (room) sentir le renfermé

**mutable** *adj* muable, variable, changeant

**mutate** *vi* subir une mutation

**mutation** *n* mutation *f*; changement *m*

**mute** *n* + *adj* muet -ette; *n* (funeral attendant) croque-mort *m*; *mus* sourdine *f*; *vt* amortir, étouffer

**mutilate** *vt* mutiler, estropier

**mutilation** *n* mutilation *f*

**mutineer** *n* mutin *m*, rebelle *m*

**mutinous** *adj* mutin, rebelle

**mutiny** *n* révolte *f*, mutinerie *f*; *vi* se mutiner, se révolter

**mutt** *n* *coll* imbécile

**mutter** *vt* + *vi* marmonner, marmotter

**mutton** *n* mouton *m*; **dead as ~** tout à fait mort; **leg of ~** gigot *m*; **roast ~**
rôti *m* de mouton

**mutual** *adj* réciproque, mutuel -elle; **~ benefit society** société *f* de secours mutuels; **~ friend** ami -e commun -e

**mutuality** *n* mutualité *f*

**Muzak** *n* musique enregistrée et continue

**muzzle** *n* museau *m*; (for dogs) muselière *f*; (gun) bouche *f*; *vt* museler, bâillonner

**muzzy** *adj* (idea) confus, vague; (person) brouillé dans ses idées; (outline) flou; (dazed) hébété; (weather) brumeux -euse; (tipsy) gris

**my** *adj* mon (*f* ma, *pl* mes); **~ arm hurts** le bras me fait mal; (emphatic) **~ car** ma voiture à moi; **I have broken ~ arm** je me suis cassé le bras

**myopic** *adj* myope

**myriad** *n* myriade *f*

**myrrh** *n* myrrhe *f*

**myrtle** *n* myrte *m*

**myself** *pron* moi-même; **all by ~** (moi) tout seul (*f* toute seule)

**mysterious** *adj* mystérieux -ieuse

**mystery** *n* mystère *m*; **make a ~ of sth** faire mystère de qch

**mystic** *n* + *adj* mystique

**mystical** *adj* mystique

**mysticism** *n* mysticisme *m*

**mystification** *n* mystification *f*; embrouillement *m*

**mystify** *vt* mystifier, dérouter

**mystique** *n* mystique *f*

**myth** *n* mythe *m*

**mythical** *adj* mythique

**mythological** *adj* mythologique

**mythology** *n* mythologie *f*

**myxomatosis** *n* myxomatose *f*

# N

**nab** *vt* *coll* pincer; (thing) chiper; **get ~ bed** se faire pincer

**nabob** *n* nabab *m*

**nadir** *n* nadir *m*

**¹nag** *n* bidet *m*, canasson *m*

**²nag** *vt* gronder, quereller

**nagging** *adj* hargneux -euse, querelleur -euse; (pain) agaçant

**naiad** *n* naïade *f*

**nail** *n* (metal) clou *m*; (finger) ongle *m*;
**bite one's ~s** se ronger les ongles; **he's hard as ~s** c'est un dur; il est sans pitié; **hit the ~ on the head** tomber juste; **pay on the ~** payer comptant; *vt* clouer; (shoes, etc) clouter; **~ down** clouer; *coll* attraper

**nail-brush** *n* brosse *f* à ongles

**nail-file** *n* lime *f* à ongles

**nail-scissors** *n* ciseaux *mpl* à ongles, coupe-ongles *m*

**nail-varnish** *n* vernis *m* à ongles

**naïve** *adj* naïf (*f* naïve), ingénu

**naïvety** *n* naïveté *f*

**naked** *adj* nu; dégarni, dénudé; **~ truth** vérité *f* sans fard; **stark ~** nu comme un ver

**nakedness** *n* nudité *f*

**namby-pamby** *n+adj* maniéré -e, minaudier -ière

**name** *n* nom *m*; réputation *f*; (firm) raison sociale; **~-day** fête *f*; **call s/o ~ s** dire des injures à qn; **Christian ~**, **first ~**, *US* **given ~** prénom *m*; **in the ~ of** au nom de; **know s/o by ~** connaître qn de nom; **maiden ~** nom *m* de jeune fille; **mention no ~s** ne nommer personne; **my ~ is** je m'appelle; **put down one's ~** s'inscrire; (be a candidate) poser sa candidature; **what is your ~?** comment vous appelez-vous?; *vt* nommer; désigner; (quote) citer; (day) fixer

**nameless** *adj* sans nom, inconnu; (anonymous) anonyme; (horrible) inexprimable, indicible; **a person who shall be ~** une personne dont je tairai le nom

**namely** *adv* à savoir, c'est-à-dire

**nameplate** *n* plaque *f*

**namesake** *n* homonyme *m*

**nancy, nancy-boy** *n sl* homosexuel *m*

**nankeen** *n* nankin *m*

**nanny** *n* nurse *f*, bonne *f* d'enfants, nounou *f*

**nanny-goat** *n* chèvre *f*, *coll* bique *f*

**¹nap** *n* petit somme; *vi* sommeiller; **catch s/o ~ping** prendre qn au dépourvu

**²nap** *n* (cloth) poil *m*; **against the ~** à rebrousse-poil; *vt* garnir, gratter

**³nap** *n* (cards) nap *m*

**napalm** *n* napalm *m*

**nape** *n* nuque *f*

**naphtha** *n* naphte *m*

**naphthalene** *n* naphtaline *f*

**napkin** *n* serviette *f*; (baby) couche *f*; **~-ring** rond *m* de serviette

**Napoleonic** *adj* napoléonien -ienne

**nappy** *n* couche *f*

**narcissus** *n* (*pl* **narcissi**) narcisse *m*

**narcosis** *n* narcose *f*

**narcotic** *n* stupéfiant *m*, narcotique *m*; *adj* narcotique

**nark** *n sl* mouchard *m*; *vt* (annoy) irriter; **~ it!** fiche-nous la paix!; *vi sl* moucharder

**narrate** *vt* raconter, narrer

**narration** *n* narration *f*

**narrative** *n* récit *m*

**narrator** *n* narrateur -trice; *adj* narratif -ive

**narrow** *adj* étroit, resserré; (ideas) borné; **~ majority** faible majorité *f*; **have a ~ escape** l'échapper belle; *vt* limiter, restreindre; rétrécir; *vi* devenir plus étroit, se rétrécir, se resserrer

**narrowly** *adv* étroitement; (only just) tout juste; (closely) de près

**narrow-minded** *adj* à l'esprit étroit, borné

**narrows** *npl* passe étroite; (river) étranglement *m*

**nasal** *adj* nasal; **~ twang** accent nasillard

**nascent** *adj* naissant

**nasturtium** *n* capucine *f*

**nasty** *adj* désagréable, sale, vilain; **~ piece of work** sale type *m*; **~ trick** vilain tour; **have a ~ mind** avoir l'esprit mal tourné

**natality** *n* natalité *f*

**nation** *n* nation *f*; **the United Nations** les Nations Unies

**national** *n* ressortissant -e; *adj* national; **~ service** service *m* militaire

**nationalism** *n* nationalisme *m*

**nationalist** *n+adj* nationaliste

**nationality** *n* nationalité *f*

**nationalization** *n* nationalisation *f*

**nationalize** *vt* nationaliser

**nationally** *adv* du point de vue national, nationalement

**nationwide** *adj* répandu dans tout le pays

**native** *n* natif -ive, indigène, originaire; *adj* (place) natal; natif -ive, naturel -elle, inné; (language) maternel -elle; (indigenous) originaire, indigène

**nativity** *n* nativité *f*

**Nato** *n* Otan *f* (*abbr* Organisation *f* du Traité de l'Atlantique du Nord)

**natter** *n* causette *f*; *vi* jacasser, bavarder

**natty** *adj* (dress) coquet -ette; (woman) pimpant

**natural** *n mus* note naturelle; *adj* naturel -elle; (inherent) inhérent, inné; **as is ~** comme de raison

**naturalism** *n* naturalisme *m*

**naturalist** *n* naturaliste

**naturalization** *n* naturalisation *f*

**naturalize** *vt* naturaliser; (plant) acclimater

**naturally** *adv* naturellement; (by nature) de nature; **die ~** mourir de sa belle mort

**nature** *n* nature *f*; (character) caractère *m*; (kind) sorte *f*, espèce *f*; **by ~** par tempérament; **draw from ~** dessiner d'après nature

**nature-study** *n* histoire naturelle

**naught** *n* néant *m*, rien *m*

**naughtiness** *n* méchanceté *f*, mauvaise conduite

**naughty** *adj* méchant, vilain; (story) grivois

**nausea** *n* nausée *f*; *fig* dégoût *m*
**nauseate** *vt* écœurer, dégoûter
**nauseating** *adj* dégoûtant, nauséabond
**nauseous** *adj see* **nauseating**
**nautical** *adj* nautique, marin; ~ **term** terme *m* de navigation
**naval** *adj* naval (*pl* navals); *mil* ~ **forces** marine *f*; ~ **officer** officier *m* de marine
**nave** *n* (church) nef *f*
**navel** *n* nombril *m*
**navigable** *adj* navigable
**navigate** *vt* (ship) gouverner; naviguer sur; *vi* naviguer
**navigation** *n* navigation *f*; (ship) conduite *f*
**navigator** *n* navigateur *m*
**navvy** *n* terrassier *m*
**navy** *n* marine *f* (militaire); **merchant** ~ marine marchande
**navy-blue** *adj* bleu marine *invar*
**nay** *adv ar* non
**Nazi** *n* Nazi -e
**neap** *adj* ~ **tide** morte-eau *f* (*pl* mortes-eaux)
**near** *adj* proche, voisin; (friend) cher (*f* chère); (stingy) parcimonieux -ieuse, chiche; ~ **offer** offre approchante; *mot* **on the** ~ ~ **side** du côté du trottoir; **that was a** ~ **thing for us** nous l'avons échappé belle; **the** ~**est way** le chemin le plus court; **to the** ~**est centimetre** à un centimètre près; *adv* près, de près; (almost) presque; ~ **-by** tout près; **as** ~ **as I can remember** autant que je puisse m'en souvenir; **be** ~ **to doing sth** être sur le point de faire qch; **she came** ~ **to being killed** elle a failli être tuée; *vt* (s')approcher de; *prep* près de, auprès de; ~ **death** près de mourir
**near-by** *adj* proche, voisin
**nearly** *adv* presque, à peu près, peu s'en faut; **I** ~ **fell** j'ai manqué (de) tomber, j'ai failli tomber; **it is** ~ **six** il est bientôt six heures; **pretty** ~ peu s'en faut, à peu de chose près; **they are not** ~ **so rich as you** ils sont loin d'être aussi riches que vous
**nearness** *n* proximité *f*; (accuracy) exactitude *f*
**near-sighted** *adj* myope
**neat** *adj* (person) ordonné; (tidy) soigné, propre, bien rangé; (drink) sec (*f* sèche); (writing) net (*f* nette); (style) élégant
**neatly** *adv* (tidily) avec ordre; (skilfully) adroitement; (dressing) avec soin
**neatness** *n* simplicité *f*; (dress) bon goût; (tidiness) bon ordre; (skill) adresse *f*; (writing) netteté *f*
**nebulous** *adj* nébuleux -euse
**necessary** *n* nécessaire *m*; *adj* nécessaire;

**do everything** ~ faire (tout) ce qu'il faut; **if** ~ s'il le faut; **make all the** ~ **arrangements** prendre toutes les dispositions utiles
**necessitate** *vt* nécessiter, rendre nécessaire
**necessitous** *adj* nécessiteux -euse
**necessity** *n* nécessité *f*, besoin *m*; obligation *f*; (poverty) indigence *f*; **bare necessities** strict nécessaire; **case of absolute** ~ cas *m* de force majeure; **of** ~ de nécessité; **out of** ~ par nécessité
**neck** *n* cou *m*; (bottle) goulot *m*; (vase) col *m*; (land) langue *f*; (violin) manche *m*; (horse) encolure *f*; ~ **and** ~ à égalité; ~ **measurement** encolure *f*; **be up to one's** ~ **in work** avoir du travail par-dessus la tête; **fling one's arms round s/o's** ~ sauter au cou de qn; **get it in the** ~ écoper; *coll* **he's a pain in the** ~ il est casse-pieds; **it's** ~ **or nothing** il faut jouer le tout pour le tout; **low** ~ décolleté *m*; **save one's** ~ sauver sa peau; **stiff** ~ torticolis *m*; *vi coll* se peloter, se faire des mamours
**neckerchief** *n* fichu *m*
**necking** *n* pelotage *m*
**necklace** *n* collier *m*
**necktie** *n* cravate *f*
**necromancy** *n* nécromancie *f*
**necropolis** *n* nécropole *f*
**nectar** *n* nectar *m*
**nectarine** *n* brugnon *m*
**née** *adj f* née
**need** *n* besoin *m*; (poverty) embarras *m*, adversité *f*, indigence *f*; **be in** ~ **of** avoir besoin de; **have no** ~ **to do sth** n'avoir que faire de faire qch; **if** ~ **be** au besoin, en cas de besoin; **what** ~ **is there to see her?** à quoi bon la voir?; *vt* avoir besoin de; (thing) demander, exiger; **I** ~ **n't go** je ne suis pas tenu d'y aller; **it** ~ **s a screwdriver** il faut un tournevis; **no** ~ **to** inutile de; **you only knock** vous n'avez qu'à frapper
**needful** *n coll* argent *m*; *adj* nécessaire
**needle** *n* aiguille *f*; (carburettor) pointeau *m*; *vt* piquer d'une aiguille; *coll* chiner, irriter
**needless** *adj* inutile; ~ **to say** ... il va sans dire que ...
**needlewoman** *n* couturière *f*
**needlework** *n* travaux *mpl* à l'aiguille; couture *f*
**needs** *adv* **if** ~ **must** s'il le faut; **I must** ~ **go** je suis obligé de partir
**needy** *adj* nécessiteux -euse, besogneux -euse
**ne'er** *adv poet* jamais
**ne'er-do-well** *n* propre à rien
**nefarious** *adj* infâme, scélérat
**negate** *vt* nier; (law) nullifier

**negation** *n* négation *f*

**negative** *n* négative *f*; *gramm* négation *f*; *phot* négatif *m*; **answer in the ~** répondre de façon négative; *adj* négatif -ive; *vt* réfuter; nier; (reject) rejeter; (cancel) annuler

**neglect** *n* négligence *f*; manque *m* de soins; manque *m* d'égards; (machine) mauvais entretien; *vt* négliger; manquer de soins pour; manquer d'égards envers; **~ an opportunity** laisser échapper une occasion; **~ to do sth** négliger de faire qch

**neglectful** *adj* négligent

**négligé** *n* négligé *m*

**negligence** *n* négligence *f*; manque *m* de soins

**negligent** *adj* négligent

**negligible** *adj* négligeable

**negotiable** *adj* négociable; (track, etc) praticable

**negotiate** *vt* négocier; (obstacle) franchir; (difficulty) surmonter; **~ a bend** prendre un virage

**negotiation** *n* négociation *f*; (obstacle) franchissement *m*; **enter into ~s with s/o** entamer des négociations avec qn; **price by ~** prix *m* à débattre; **under ~** en négociation

**negotiator** *n* négociateur -trice

**Negress** *n* négresse *f*

**Negro** *n* nègre *m*

**negroid** *adj* négroïde

**neigh** *n* hennissement *m*; *vi* hennir

**neighbour** *n* voisin -e; *bibl* prochain -e

**neighbourhood** *n* voisinage *m*, proximité *f*; (locality) quartier *m*; (district) environs *mpl*

**neighbouring** *adj* voisin, avoisinant

**neighbourly** *adj* (person) amical; **in a ~ fashion** en bon voisin (*f* en bonne voisine)

**neither** *adj*+*pron* aucun (*f* aucune), ni l'un ni l'autre; *adv* non plus; *conj* ni; **~ ... nor** ni ... ni

**neologism** *n* néologisme *m*

**neon** *n* néon *m*; **~ lighting** éclairage *m* au néon

**neophyte** *n* *eccles* néophyte; débutant -e

**nephew** *n* neveu *m*

**nephritis** *n* néphrite *f*

**nepotism** *n* népotisme *m*

**Neptune** *n* Neptune *m*

**nerve** *n* nerf *m*; (courage) audace *f*; (cheek) toupet *m*; **it gets on my ~s** ça me porte (tape) sur les nerfs; **strain every ~** to déployer tous ses efforts pour; *vt* **~ oneself to** s'armer de courage pour

**nerveless** *adj* sans force, sans vigueur

**nerve-racking** *adj* énervant, horripilant

**nervous** *adj* (frightened) peureux -euse,

timide; (worried) inquiet -iète; (excitable) excitable; *anat* nerveux -euse; **it makes me ~** cela m'intimide

**nervy** *adj* irritable, énervé; (action) nerveux -euse; peureux -euse

**nest** *n* nid *m*; (den) repaire *m*; (eggs) nichée *f*; **~ of shelves** casier *m*; **~ of tables** table *f* gigogne; *vi* faire son nid, nicher

**nest-egg** *n* (savings) magot *m*, pécule *m*

**nestle** *vi* se nicher, se blottir; **~ close up to s/o** se serrer contre qn

**nestling** *n* oisillon *m*

**net** *n* filet *m*; (fabric) tulle *m*; *vt* prendre au filet; (ball) envoyer dans le filet

**net(t)** *adj* net (*f* nette); **~ cash** argent comptant; *vt* (person) toucher net; (deal) rapporter net

**netball** *n* basket *m*

**nether** *adj* inférieur

**Netherlands** *npl* Pays-Bas *mpl*

**netting** *n* filet *m*; (fabric) tulle *m*; pose *f* de filet

**nettle** *n* ortie *f*

**nettle-rash** *n* urticaire *f*

**network** *n* réseau *m*; **railway ~** réseau *m* ferroviaire; **road ~** réseau routier

**neural** *adj* neural

**neuralgia** *n* névralgie *f*

**neuralgic** *adj* névralgique

**neurasthenia** *n* neurasthénie *f*

**neuritis** *n* névrite *f*

**neurologist** *n* neurologue

**neurology** *n* neurologie *f*

**neurosis** *n* névrose *f*

**neurotic** *adj* névrosé

**neuter** *adj* neutre; *vt* châtrer

**neutral** *n*+*adj* neutre

**neutrality** *n* neutralité *f*

**neutralize** *vt* neutraliser

**never** *adv* jamais, ne ... jamais; **~!** jamais de la vie!; **~ again** (ne ...) plus jamais, jamais plus (... ne); **I ~ expected this** je ne m'attendais aucunement à cela; **~ mind** n'importe; **well I ~!** par exemple!

**never-ending** *adj* interminable

**nevermore** *adv* (ne ...) plus jamais, jamais plus (... ne)

**nevertheless** *adv* néanmoins, pourtant, quand même

**new** *adj* (unused) neuf (*f* neuve); (changed) nouveau (*f* nouvelle); **~ bread** pain frais; **New Year** Nouvel An; **as ~** à l'état de neuf; **brand ~** tout neuf (*f* toute neuve)

**newborn** *adj* nouveau-né

**newcomer** *n* nouveau venu (*f* nouvelle venue), nouvel arrivé (*f* nouvelle arrivée)

**newfangled** *adj* d'un moderne outré

**Newfoundland** *n* Terre-Neuve *f*

**new-laid** adj du jour; frais (f fraîche)
**newly** adv récemment, nouvellement; fraîchement
**newly-weds** npl nouveaux mariés
**newness** n nouveauté f; (inexperience) inexpérience f; (article) état neuf
**news** npl nouvelle f, nouvelles fpl; (broadcasting) informations fpl; **film** film m d'actualités; **be in the ~** défrayer la chronique; **make ~** faire sensation
**news-agency** n agence f d'informations
**newsagent** n marchand -e de journaux
**newscaster** n speaker m, speakerine f
**newspaper** n journal m, quotidien m; **~-stall** kiosque m; **weekly ~** hebdomadaire m
**newsprint** n papier m de journal
**newsreel** n film m d'actualités
**news-room** n salle f de rédaction
**news-sheet** n feuille f
**news-stand** n kiosque m
**news-theatre** n ciné-actualités m
**newsy** adj plein de nouvelles
**newt** n triton m
**next** adj prochain; (following) suivant; (neighbouring) voisin; (nearest) le (f la) plus proche; (adjacent) attenant; **door** (d')à côté; **~ week** la semaine prochaine; **and the ~** au suivant; **for ~ to nothing** pour presque rien; **the ~ day** le lendemain; **the ~ morning** le lendemain matin; **the ~ week** la semaine suivante; **what ~!** par exemple!; **who's ~?** à qui le tour?; adv ensuite, après; prep à côté de; **~ to me** à côté de moi
**next of kin** n famille f, proche parenté f
**nib** n bec m de plume
**nibble** n grignotement m; vt + vi grignoter, mordiller
**nice** adj bon (f bonne); joli, agréable; (person) gentil -ille, sympathique, aimable; (particular) difficile; (question) délicat; (respectable) convenable; **~ and ... bien ...; a ~ sum** une somme rondelette; **be ~ to s/o** se montrer aimable envers qn
**nice-looking** adj beau (f belle), avenant
**nicely** adv joliment, bien, gentiment; **get on ~** (patient) faire des progrès; (business) marcher bien; **that will do ~** cela fera bien mon affaire
**nicety** n précision f; subtilité f; **niceties** minuties fpl; **to a ~** exactement, à la perfection
**niche** n niche f
**nick** n cran m, entaille f; sl taule f; **in the ~ of time** juste à temps; vt encocher, entailler; coll pincer, faucher; vi **~ in** s'insinuer
**nickel** n nickel m; US pièce f de cinq

cents; vt nickeler
**nickname** n sobriquet m; vt surnommer
**nicotine** n nicotine f
**niece** n nièce f
**nifty** adj coll adroit, agile; (smelly) puant
**niggardly** adj (person) pingre, chiche; (sum) mesquin
**nigger** n pej nègre (f négresse); **there's a ~ in the woodpile** il y a quelque anguille sous roche
**niggle** vi couper les cheveux en quatre; **~ over trifles** s'attarder à des détails insignifiants
**niggling** adj (detail) insignifiant; (person) tatillon -onne
**nigh** adj lit + ar proche; adv près, proche; prep près de
**night** n nuit f; (evening) soir m; **at ~** la nuit; **by ~** de nuit; **eleven o'clock at ~** onze heures du soir; theat **first ~** première f; **have a good (bad) ~** dormir bien (mal); **have a late ~** aller se coucher tard; **in the ~** la nuit; **it is ~** il fait nuit; **last ~** hier (au) soir; **make a ~ of it** continuer toute la nuit; **the ~ before last** avant-hier (au) soir; **the ~ train** le train de nuit; **tomorrow ~** demain soir
**night-bird** n oiseau m de nuit
**night-blindness** n héméralopie f
**nightcap** n bonnet m de nuit; boisson prise avant de se coucher
**night-club** n boîte f de nuit
**night-dress** n chemise f de nuit
**nightfall** n tombée f de la nuit; **at ~** à la nuit tombante
**nightgown** n chemise f de nuit
**nightingale** n rossignol m
**nightjar** n engoulevent m
**night-light** n veilleuse f
**nightly** adj nocturne, de nuit; (every night) (de) tous les soirs, (de) chaque nuit; adv tous les soirs, toutes les nuits
**nightmare** n cauchemar m
**night-school** n cours mpl du soir
**nightshade** n morelle noire; **deadly ~** belladone f
**night-shift** n équipe f de nuit
**nightshirt** n chemise f de nuit
**night-soil** n vidanges fpl
**night-time** n nuit f
**nightwatchman** n veilleur m, gardien m de nuit
**nigritude** n négritude f
**nihilism** n nihilisme m
**nihilist** n nihiliste f
**nil** n rien m, zéro m, néant m
**Nile** n Nil m
**nimble** adj agile, leste; (mind) subtil, prompt
**nimbus** n auréole f; meteor nimbus m

**nincompoop** *n* niais -e, nigaud -e, imbécile

**nine** *n* neuf *m invar*; *adj* neuf *invar*

**nineteen** *n* dix-neuf *m invar*; *adj* dix-neuf *invar*

**nineteenth** *n* dix-neuvième; (date) dix-neuf *m*; *adj* dix-neuvième

**ninetieth** *n* + *adj* quatre-vingt-dixième

**ninety** *n* quatre-vingt-dix *m invar*; *adj* quatre-vingt-dix *invar*

**ninny** *n coll* imbécile, niais -e

**ninth** *n* neuvième; (date) neuf *m*; *adj* neuvième

¹**nip** *n* pincement *m*; (bite) morsure *f*; *vt* pincer; mordre; *vi* ~ **in** passer en courant; ~ **off** filer; ~ **out** sortir un instant; ~ **round to s/o's (house)** courir chez qn

²**nip** *n* goutte *f*, petit coup

**nipper** *n* pince *f*; *coll* gosse, gamin -e

**nippers** *npl* pinces *fpl*, tenailles *fpl*

**nipple** *n* mamelon *m*; (feeding bottle) tétine *f*

**nippy** *adj coll* leste, vif (*f* vive); (air) âpre; **be ~ about it!** *sl* grouillez-vous!

**nirvana** *n* nirvāna *m*

¹**nit** *n ent* lente *f*

²**nit** *n coll* andouille *f*

**nitrate** *n* nitrate *m*

**nitrogen** *n* azote *m*

**nitroglycerin(e)** *n* nitroglycérine *f*

**nitwit** *n coll* andouille *f*, crétin -e

**nix** *n coll* rien *m* du tout

**no** *n* non; **not take ~ for an answer** ne pas admettre le refus; **the ~ es have it** le vote est contre; *adj* (ne ...) nul (*f* nulle), pas de, (ne ...) aucun (*f* aucune); ~ **admittance** entrée interdite; ~ **doubt** sans doute; ~ **longer** (ne ...) plus; ~ **matter** n'importe; ~ **more** (ne ...) plus; ~ **nonsense!** pas de bêtises!; ~ **one** (ne ...) personne; ~ **smoking** défense de fumer; **he is ~ teacher** il n'est pas professeur; il n'a aucune des qualités voulues pour être professeur; **in less than ~ time** en moins de rien; **of ~ importance** sans importance; **this is ~ easy problem** ce problème n'est pas facile du tout; *adv* non; ~ **better than I** pas mieux que moi

**Noah** *n* Noé *m*; ~ **'s ark** l'arche *f* de Noé

**nobble** *vt coll* (horse) écloper; (person) soudoyer; (pinch) chiper; (approach) aborder; (catch) pincer

**nobility** *n* noblesse *f*

**noble** *n* noble *m*; *adj* noble

**nobleman** *n* noble *m*, gentilhomme *m*

**noblewoman** *n* aristocrate *f*

**nobly** *adv* noblement, magnifiquement

**nobody** *n* zéro *m*, nullité *f*; *pron* (ne ...) personne, nul (ne ...), (ne ...) aucun

**nocturnal** *adj* nocturne

**nocturne** *n* nocturne *m*

**nod** *n* signe de tête affirmatif; **give a ~** faire un signe de tête (affirmatif); **on the ~** à l'œil; *vt* + *vi* faire un signe de tête; (with sleep) somnoler; (make mistake) se tromper; ~ **to s/o** faire un signe de tête à qn

**nodule** *n* nodule *m*

**noggin** *n* petit pot; (drink) petit coup

**no-good** *n* vaurien -ienne; *adj* d'aucune valeur

**noise** *n* bruit *m*; tapage *m*, fracas *m*; *coll* **he's a big ~** c'est un grand manitou; *vt* ~ **abroad** ébruiter, répandre

**noiseless** *adj* silencieux -ieuse, sans bruit

**noisiness** *n* vacarme *m*; (children) turbulence *f*

**noisome** *adj* nuisible, nocif -ive; (smell) fétide, malsain; (work) désagréable

**noisy** *adj* bruyant; (child) turbulent

**nomad** *n* nomade

**nomadic** *adj* nomade

**no-man's-land** *n mil* zone *f* neutre; terrain *m* vague

**nom de plume** *n* pseudonyme *m*

**nomenclature** *n* nomenclature *f*

**nominal** *adj* nominal

**nominate** *vt* nommer, désigner; (candidate) présenter

**nomination** *n* nomination *f*; (candidate) présentation *f*

**nominative** *n gramm* nominatif *m*; *adj* nominatif -ive

**nominee** *n* candidat -e désigné -e

**non-acceptance** *n* non-acceptation *f*

**nonagenarian** *n* + *adj* nonagénaire

**non-aggression** *n* non-agression *f*

**non-alcoholic** *adj* non-alcoolique

**non-appearance** *n* non-comparution *f*

**non-attendance** *n* absence *f*

**nonchalance** *n* nonchalance *f*

**nonchalant** *adj* indifférent, nonchalant

**non-combatant** *n* non-combattant *m*; *adj* non-combattant

**non-commissioned** *adj* ~ **officer** sous-officier *m*

**non-committal** *adj* qui n'engage à rien

**non-conformist** *adj eccles* dissident

**non-denominational** *adj* n'adhérant à aucune confession

**nondescript** *adj* indéfinissable; (ordinary) quelconque

**none** *pron* (ne ...) aucun (*f* aucune); ~ **but he** ... il n'y a que lui qui ..., lui seul ...; ~ **can say** personne ne le sait; ~ **of this is correct** rien de ceci n'est juste; ~ **of you** aucun (*f* aucune) (personne) d'entre vous; ~ **the less** néanmoins; **I have ~** je n'en ai point (pas); **it was ~ other than his father** ce n'était autre que son père; **these apples are ~ of the best** ces pommes ne sont pas des meilleures; *adv* ~ **too** ... (far from) rien moins que; (not very) pas très; ~ **too soon** juste à temps; **he is** ~ **the richer for that** il n'en est pas plus riche

**nonentity** *n* personne insignifiante, nullité *f*

**non-essential** *adj* non essentiel -ielle

**non-existent** *adj* inexistant, non-existant

**non-fiction** *n* documentaire *m*

**non-fulfilment** *n* non-exécution *f*

**non-intervention** *n* non-intervention *f*

**non-payment** *n* non-paiement *m*

**nonplus** *vt* embarrasser

**non-resident** *n* + *adj* non-résident -e

**non-returnable** *adj* non repris

**nonsense** *n* non-sens *m*, absurdité *f*, sottise *f*; ~ ! pas possible!; **no** ~ ! pas de bêtises!; **piece of** ~ bêtise *f*; **talk** ~ dire des bêtises

**nonsensical** *adj* absurde

**non sequitur** *n* illogicité *f*

**non-skid** *adj* antidérapant

**non-smoker** *n* non-fumeur *m*; (railway) compartiment *m* non-fumeurs

**non-smoking** *adj* ~ **compartment** compartiment *m* non-fumeurs

**non-stop** *adj* direct; *adv* (air travel) sans escale; (train) sans arrêt

**non-violence** *n* non-violence *f*

¹**noodle** *n coll* nigaud -e, andouille *f*

²**noodle** *n cul* nouille *f*

**nook** *n* coin *m*, recoin *m*

**noon** *n* midi *m*

**noose** *n* nœud coulant; (snare) lacet *m*

**nor** *conj* ni; ~ **do I wish** ... de plus, je ne souhaite pas ...; ~ **you neither** ni vous non plus; **neither** ... ~ ni ... ni; **they don't know,** ~ **do they care** ils ne savent pas et ils ne s'en soucient pas

**Nordic** *adj* nordique, scandinave

**norm** *n* norme *f*

**normal** *adj* normal, régulier -ière

**normalcy** *n US* normalité *f*

**normality** *n* normalité *f*

**normalize** *vt* normaliser

**normally** *adv* normalement; *coll* régulièrement

**Norman** *n* Normand -e; *adj* normand; ~ **architecture** (in England) architecture romane; (in Normandy) architecture normande

**Normandy** *n* Normandie *f*

**normative** *adj* normatif -ive

**north** *n* nord *m*; **to the** ~ **of** au nord de; *adj* nord *invar*, septentrional; (north-facing) exposé au nord; ~ **wind** vent *m* du nord; *adv* du nord

**north-east** *n* nord-est *m*; *adj* nord-est *invar*

**northerly** *adj* du nord; (direction) vers le nord

**northern** *adj* du nord, septentrional; ~

lights aurore boréale

**northernmost** *adj* le plus au nord

**northward** *adj* au nord, du nord, vers le nord

**northwards** *adv* vers le nord

**north-west** *n* nord-ouest *m*; *adj* nord-ouest *invar*

**Norway** *n* Norvège *f*

**Norwegian** *n* Norvégien -ienne; (language) norvégien *m*; *adj* norvégien -ienne

**nose** *n* nez *m*; (animals) museau *m*; (sense of smell) odorat *m*; **blow one's** ~ se moucher; **lead s/o by the** ~ mener qn par le bout du nez; **look down one's** ~ **at** regarder avec mépris; (fowl) **parson's** ~ croupion *m*; **pay through the** ~ payer le prix fort; **poke one's** ~ **into** fourrer son nez dans; **speak through the** ~ nasiller, parler du nez; **turn up one's** ~ **at** faire fi de; **under his very** ~ à son nez; *vt* flairer, sentir; ~ **out** flairer, dépister; *vi* ~ **about** fureter, fouiner

**nosebag** *n* musette *f*

**nose-bleed** *n* saignement *m* de nez

**nose-cone** *n* (rocket) ogive *f*

**nose-dive** *n* piqué *m*; *vi* descendre en piqué

**nosey, nosy** *adj* fouinard; ~ **parker** indiscret -ète

**nosh** *n sl* boustifaille *f*; *vt sl* bouffer, boulotter

**nostalgia** *n* nostalgie *f*

**nostalgic** *adj* nostalgique

**nostril** *n* narine *f*; (animal) naseau *m*

**nosy** *adj see* **nosey**

**not** *adv* (ne ...) pas, (ne ...) point; ~ **a few** pas mal de; ~ **at all** pas du tout; *sl* ~ **half!** tu parles!, et comment!; ~ **that** ... non (pas) que ...; *coll* ~ **to worry!** ne vous en faites pas!; **am I** ~ ? (aren't I?, aren't you?, isn't he?, etc) n'est-ce pas?; **I think** ~ je crois que non; **Thank you very much. – Not at all** Merci beaucoup. – De rien; **why** ~ ? pourquoi pas?

**notability** *n* notabilité *f*

**notable** *adj* notable, considérable; (person) éminent

**notation** *n* notation *f*

**notch** *n* entaille *f*, encoche *f*, cran *m*; (blade) brèche *f*; *US* défilé *m*; *vt* entailler, encocher; (blade) ébrécher

**note** *n* note *f*; (mark) marque *f*, signe *m*; (piano) touche *f*; *comm* bordereau *m*; (short letter) mot *m*, billet *m*; (bank-note) billet *m*; **credit** ~ note *f* de crédit; **make a** ~ **of sth** prendre note de qch; **man of** ~ homme *m* de renom; **nothing of** ~ rien d'important; **take** ~ **of** constater, remarquer; **take** ~ **s**

prendre des notes; *vt* noter, constater, remarquer; (mistake) relever; ~ sth down inscrire qch, noter qch
**notebook** *n* carnet *m*
**noted** *adj* éminent, célèbre, distingué
**notepad** *n* bloc-notes *m* (*pl* blocs-notes)
**notepaper** *n* papier *m* à lettres (à écrire)
**noteworthy** *adj* remarquable, digne d'attention
**nothing** *n* néant *m*, zéro *m*, rien *m*; ~ at all rien du tout; ~ but rien que; ~ doing! rien à faire!; ~ else rien d'autre; ~ much pas grand-chose; ~ new rien de nouveau; ~ to do rien à faire; come to ~ aboutir à rien; do ~ but ne faire que; get ~ out of sth en être pour ses frais; I have ~ to do with it je n'y suis pour rien; it's ~ to do with me cela ne me regarde pas; that has ~ to do with my work cela n'a rien à voir avec mon travail; that's ~ to me cela m'est égal; there's ~ for it but to go il n'y a qu'à partir; there's ~ more to be said il n'y a plus rien à dire; think ~ of doing sth ne pas se faire scrupule de faire qch; think ~ of sth ne faire aucun cas de qch; *adv* aucunement, nullement
**nothingness** *n* néant *m*
**notice** *n* avis *m*, notification *f*; (poster) affiche *f*; (newspaper) annonce *f*; (book) revue *f*; at a day's ~ du jour au lendemain; at short ~ à bref délai; attract ~ se faire remarquer; at two days' ~ dans un délai de deux jours; bring to the ~ of porter à l'attention de; give ~ that prévenir que; give one's ~ donner son congé; give s/o ~ donner son congé à qn; he takes no ~ il n'y prend pas garde; public ~ avis *m* au public; take ~ of tenir compte de; until further ~ jusqu'à nouvel avis; without ~ sans préavis; *vt* remarquer, observer, s'apercevoir de; (take notice) prendre garde à; get oneself ~ d attirer l'attention sur soi
**noticeable** *adj* perceptible; (not inconsiderable) digne d'attention
**notice-board** *n* écriteau *m*; (institution) tableau *m* d'annonces
**notification** *n* avis *m*, annonce *f*, notification *f*
**notify** *vt* notifier, déclarer, faire savoir
**notion** *n* idée *f*, notion *f*; opinion *f*; (whim) caprice *m*; *US* ~s mercerie *f*; have a ~ that avoir dans l'idée que; have a ~ to do sth s'aviser de faire qch
**notional** *adj* imaginaire; spéculatif -ive; *econ* fictif -ive
**notoriety** *n* notoriété *f*
**notorious** *adj* insigne; (place) mal famé
**notwithstanding** *adv* quand même, tout de même, pourtant; *prep* malgré, en

dépit de
**nougat** *n* nougat *m*
**nought** *n* zéro *m*
**noun** *n* nom *m*, substantif *m*
**nourish** *vt* nourrir, alimenter; (hope) entretenir
**nourishment** *n* nourriture *f*
**nous** *n* coll intelligence *f*
**¹novel** *n* roman *m*
**²novel** *adj* nouveau -elle; original
**novelist** *n* romancier -ière
**novelty** *n* nouveauté *f*, innovation *f*
**November** *n* novembre *m*
**novena** *n* eccles neuvaine *f*
**novice** *n* débutant -e; *eccles* novice
**noviciate, novitiate** *n* noviciat *m*
**now** *adv* maintenant, à présent, en ce moment, actuellement; (not referring to time) or; (meaning 'then', in narrative) alors, à ce moment-là; ~ and then de temps en temps, de temps à autre; ~ ... ~ tantôt ... tantôt; ~ then! allons!; ~ and then d'ici là; by ~ à l'heure qu'il est; even ~ même à cette heure tardive; in three days from ~ d'ici trois jours; right ~ tout de suite; until ~ jusqu'ici; *conj* maintenant que, à présent que
**nowadays** *adv* de nos jours, aujourd'hui, au jour d'aujourd'hui
**noway(s)** *interj coll* pas du tout
**nowhere** *adv* nulle part; ~ else nulle part ailleurs; ~ near loin d'être
**noxious** *adj* nuisible, nocif -ive; malfaisant
**nozzle** *n* jet *m*; (pipe) lance *f*; (spout) bec *m*; (jet) ajutage *m*
**nuance** *n* nuance *f*
**nub** *n* (coal, etc) petit morceau; (question) essentiel *m*
**nubile** *adj* nubile
**nuclear** *adj* nucléaire
**nucleus** *n* noyau *m*
**nude** *n* (drawing) nu *m*; in the ~ nu; *adj* nu
**nudge** *n* coup *m* de coude; *vt* pousser du coude
**nudism** *n* nudisme *m*
**nudist** *n* nudiste
**nudity** *n* nudité *f*
**nugget** *n* pépite *f*
**nuisance** *n* désagrément *m*; *coll* peste *f*, fléau *m*; *leg* dommage *m*; be a ~ to s/o embêter qn; what a ~! que c'est embêtant!
**null** *adj* ~ and void nul et non avenu
**nullify** *vt* nullifier, annuler
**nullity** *n* nullité *f*
**numb** *adj* engourdi; *vt* engourdir
**number** *n* (quantity) nombre *m*; (symbol) numéro *m*; *math* nombre *m*, chiffre *m*; *theat* numéro *m*; a large ~ of

beaucoup de; **a** ~ **of times** plusieurs fois; **back** ~ vieux numéro; **few in** ~ peu nombreux -euse; **five in** ~ au nombre de cinq; *coll* **his** ~'**s up** il est fichu; **in small** ~**s** en petit nombre; *coll* **look after** ~ **one** prendre soin de sa petite personne; **one of our** ~ un (*f* une) d'entre nous; **swell the** ~ faire nombre; **without** ~ innombrable; *vt* numéroter; (count) compter; (amount to) se monter à, compter; **his days are** ~**ed** il n'a plus longtemps à vivre

**numberless** *adj* innombrable

**number-plate** *n* plaque *f* minéralogique, plaque *f* d'immatriculation

**numbness** *n* engourdissement *m*; (mind) torpeur *f*

**num(b)skull** *n* nigaud -e, idiot -e, *coll* cornichon *m*

**numeral** *n* chiffre *m*, nombre *m*; *adj* numéral

**numerate** *adj* connaissant les éléments de l'arithmétique

**numerical** *adj* numérique

**numerous** *adj* nombreux -euse

**numismatics** *npl* numismatique *f*

**nun** *n* religieuse *f*, nonne *f*

**nuncio** *n* nonce *m*

**nunnery** *n* couvent *m*

**nuptial** *adj* nuptial

**nurse** *n* (wet-nurse) nourrice *f*; (children's nurse) bonne *f* d'enfants, nurse *f*; (hospital) infirmière *f*; (sick-nurse) garde-malade *f* (*pl* gardes-malades); **male** ~ infirmier *m*; *vt* soigner, garder; (grief, etc) nourrir, entretenir; (child) bercer; (fondle) dorloter

**nursemaid** *n* bonne *f* d'enfants

**nursery** *n* nursery *f*, chambre *f* des enfants; (public) crèche *f*; (plants) pépinière *f*; ~ **rhyme** chanson *f* de nourrice; ~ **school** maternelle *f*

**nurseryman** *n* pépiniériste *m*

**nursing** *n* (medical) soins *mpl*; (profession) profession *f* de garde-malade (d'infirmière); **take up** ~ se faire infirmière

**nursing-home** *n* clinique *f*, hôpital privé

**nursling** *n* nourrisson *m*

**nurture** *n* nourriture *f*; éducation *f*; *vt* nourrir; élever

**nut** *n* noix *f*; (hazel-nut) noisette *f*; *mech* écrou *m*; *sl* tête *f*, *coll* caboche *f*; **be** ~ **s** être timbré; **be off one's** ~ être timbré; **he's a tough** ~ c'est un dur; **you can't play for** ~ **s** vous ne savez pas jouer du tout

**nut-brown** *adj* couleur noisette *invar*

**nutcracker** *n* casse-noisette(s) *m*

**nutmeg** *n* muscade *f*

**nutriment** *n* nourriture *f*

**nutrition** *n* nutrition *f*

**nutritious** *adj* nutritif -ive, nourrissant

**nutritive** *adj* nutritif -ive, nourrissant

**nutshell** *n* coquille *f* de noix; **in a** ~ en un mot

**nutty** *adj* ayant le goût de noix; *sl* timbré, toqué

**nuzzle** *vi* (animal) mettre son museau contre; (person) se blottir contre; (pig) fouiller avec le groin

**nylon** *n* nylon *m*

**nymph** *n* nymphe *f*

**nymphomaniac** *n* nymphomane *f*

# O

**o** *interj* ô!, oh!

**oaf** *n* lourdaud -e

**oak** *n* chêne *m*

**oaken** *adj* de chêne, en chêne

**oakum** *n* étoupe *f*

**oar** *n* aviron *m*, rame *f*; **put (stick) one's** ~ **in** intervenir

**oarsman** *n* rameur *m*

**oasis** *n* oasis *f*

**oath** *n* serment *m*; (curse) juron *m*; **on** ~ sous serment; **take the** ~ prêter serment

**oatmeal** *n* farine *f* d'avoine

**oats** *n* avoine *f*; **sow one's wild** ~ faire des fredaines

**obduracy** *n* entêtement *m*, opiniâtreté *f*

**obdurate** *adj* têtu, opiniâtre; inflexible

**obedience** *n* obéissance *f*

**obedient** *adj* obéissant, soumis

**obeisance** *n* révérence *f*; *hist* hommage *m*

**obelisk** *n* obélisque *m*

**obese** *adj* obèse

**obesity** *n* obésité *f*

**obey** *vt* obéir à; *vi* obéir

**obituary** *n* notice *f* nécrologique; *adj* nécrologique

**¹object** *n* objet *m*, chose *f*; (aim) but *m*; (reason) raison *f*; *gramm* complément *m* d'objet; **~ lesson** leçon *f*, exemple *m*; **expense is no ~ for me** je ne regarde pas à la dépense; **there's no ~ in going there** cela ne sert à rien d'y aller; **with this ~ in view** dans ce but

**²object** *vt* objecter; *vi* s'opposer, trouver à redire, faire objection; **~ to doing sth** se refuser à faire qch

**objection** *n* objection *f*; inconvénient *m*; **have no ~ to** ne pas s'opposer à; **if you have no ~** si cela ne vous fait rien; **raise an ~** soulever une objection; **see no ~ to sth** ne voir aucun inconvénient à qch

**objectionable** *adj* répréhensible; désagréable; choquant

**objective** *n* but *m*, objectif *m*; *adj* objectif -ive

**objectivity** *n* objectivité *f*

**objector** *n* protestataire, contestataire; **conscientious ~** objecteur *m* de conscience

**obligate** *vt* imposer une obligation à

**obligation** *n* obligation *f*; **be under an ~ to s/o** devoir de la reconnaissance à qn; **fail to meet one's ~s** manquer à ses engagements; **put s/o under an ~ to do sth** imposer à qn l'obligation de faire qch

**obligatory** *adj* obligatoire

**oblige** *vt* obliger; (do a favour) rendre service à; **can you ~ me with a match?** voudriez-vous me donner du feu?; **do sth to ~** faire qch par complaisance; **he is ~d to go away** il faut qu'il parte; **I am much ~d to you** je vous suis très reconnaissant

**obliging** *adj* complaisant, serviable

**oblique** *adj* oblique; indirect; *vi* obliquer

**obliterate** *vt* oblitérer, effacer; (ticket) composter

**oblivion** *n* oubli *m*

**oblivious** *adj* oublieux -ieuse; **be ~ of** ignorer

**oblong** *adj* oblong (*f* oblongue)

**obnoxious** *adj* odieux -ieuse, détestable, exécrable

**oboe** *n* hautbois *m*

**obscene** *adj* obscène

**obscenity** *n* obscénité *f*

**obscurantism** *n* obscurantisme *m*

**obscure** *adj* obscur, peu clair; *vt* obscurcir

**obscurity** *n* obscurité *f*

**obsequies** *npl* obsèques *fpl*, funérailles *fpl*

**obsequious** *adj* obséquieux -ieuse

**observable** *adj* visible, perceptible

**observance** *n* observance *f*

**observant** *adj* observateur -trice

**observation** *n* observation *f*; remarque *f*; **~ car** voiture *f* panoramique; **under ~** en observation

**observatory** *n* observatoire *m*

**observe** *vt* observer, regarder, apercevoir; (note) noter; (say) dire, faire remarquer; (rule, etc) se conformer à

**observer** *n* observateur -trice

**obsess** *vt* obséder

**obsession** *n* obsession *f*, hantise *f*, idée *f* fixe

**obsessive** *adj* obsédant

**obsolescence** *n* vieillissement *m*

**obsolescent** *adj* qui tombe en désuétude

**obsolete** *adj* désuet -ète, suranné, tombé en désuétude

**obstacle** *n* obstacle *m*; **be an ~ to** faire obstacle à

**obstetric** *adj* obstétrique, obstétrical

**obstetrician** *n* médecin accoucheur; obstétricien -ienne

**obstetrics** *n* obstétrique *f*

**obstinacy** *n* entêtement *m*, obstination *f*

**obstinate** *adj* entêté, obstiné, opiniâtre

**obstreperous** *adj* bruyant, tapageur -euse; (unruly) indiscipliné, turbulent

**obstruct** *vt* obstruer, encombrer; (block) boucher; (hinder) gêner; (prevent) empêcher; **~ the traffic** entraver la circulation

**obstruction** *n* obstacle *m*, empêchement *m*; *med* obstruction *f*, occlusion *f*; *mot* stationnement gênant; (navigation) entrave *f*; *pol* obstruction *f*

**obstructionism** *n* *pol* obstructionnisme *m*

**obstructive** *adj* obstructif -ive; *pol* obstructionniste

**obtain** *vt* obtenir, se procurer; *vi* (prevail) prévaloir; avoir cours, régner; être en vigueur

**obtainable** *adj* qu'on peut se procurer

**obtrude** *vt* mettre en avant, imposer; *vi* s'imposer; **~ oneself on s/o** importuner qn

**obtrusion** *n* importunité *f*; intrusion *f*

**obtrusive** *adj* importun, indiscret -ète

**obtuse** *adj* obtus

**obtuseness** *n* stupidité *f*

**obverse** *n* avers *m*, obvers *m*, face *f*

**obviate** *vt* éviter, obvier à

**obvious** *adj* évident, clair; **it's the ~ thing to do** c'est la chose à faire, cela s'impose

**occasion** *n* cause *f*, occasion *f*, raison *f*; (need) besoin *m*; occurrence *f*; **as ~ requires** au besoin; **have no ~ to**

**complain** n'avoir aucun sujet de se plaindre; **have ~ to** avoir à; **on ~** à l'occasion; **on several ~s** plusieurs fois, à plusieurs reprises; **on such an ~** en pareille occasion; **on the ~ of** à l'occasion de; **should (the) ~ arise** le cas échéant; *vt* occasionner, provoquer

**occasional** *adj* qui se produit de temps en temps; (chance) fortuit

**occasionally** *adv* de temps en temps

**occidental** *adj* occidental

**occlude** *vt* boucher, fermer

**occlusion** *n* occlusion *f*

**occult** *n* the ~ le surnaturel; *adj* occulte

**occupancy** *n* occupation *f*, habitation *f*

**occupant** *n* habitant -e; (tenant) locataire; (post) titulaire

**occupation** *n* occupation *f*; (job) emploi *m*, métier *m*; (possession) possession *f*

**occupational** *adj* professionnel -elle; ~ **hazards** risques *mpl* du métier

**occupier** *n* locataire, occupant -e, habitant -e

**occupy** *vt* occuper; (house) habiter; (time) employer

**occur** *vi* avoir lieu, arriver, se produire; (be found) se trouver; **don't let it ~ again!** que cela n'arrive plus!; **if the opportunity ~s** si l'occasion se présente; **it ~s to me** il me vient à l'esprit

**occurrence** *n* (event) événement *m*; (circumstance) occurrence *f*; **be of frequent ~** arriver souvent

**ocean** *n* océan *m*

**ocean-going** *adj* ~ **ship** navire *m* au long cours

**Oceania** *n* Océanie *f*

**oceanic** *adj* océanique

**oceanography** *n* océanographie *f*

**ochre** *n* ocre *f*; (colour) ocre *m*

**o'clock** *adv* **one (two) ~** une (deux) heure(s)

**octagon** *n* octogone *m*

**octagonal** *adj* octogonal

**octane** *n* octane *m*

**octave** *n* octave *f*

**octavo** *n* in-octavo *m invar*

**octet** *n mus* octuor *m*

**October** *n* octobre *m*

**octogenarian** *n + adj* octogénaire

**octopus** *n* pieuvre *f*, poulpe *m*

**ocular** *adj* oculaire

**oculist** *n* oculiste

**odd** *adj* (number) impair; (unmatched) dépareillé; (single) seul; (queer) singulier -ière, drôle, curieux -ieuse, bizarre; ~ **job man** homme *m* à tout faire; ~ **moments** moments perdus; **a hundred ~** une centaine; **at ~ times** à diverses reprises; **be ~ man out** rester en surnombre; **the ~ game** (cards) la

belle; **twenty pounds ~** vingt et quelques livres

**oddity** *n* singularité *f*; (person) original -e

**oddly** *adv* singulièrement; ~ **enough** chose curieuse

**oddments** *npl* fins *fpl* de série; restes *mpl*

**odds** *n* avantages *mpl*, chances *fpl*; (difference) différence *f*, inégalité *f*; ~ **and ends** petits bouts, restes *mpl*; **be at ~ with s/o** (quarrel) être brouillé avec qn; (differ) ne pas être d'accord avec qn; **it doesn't make the slightest ~** cela ne fait rien du tout; **lay ~** parier; **the ~ are that** il y a à parier que

**ode** *n* ode *f*

**odious** *adj* odieux -ieuse, détestable

**odium** *n* détestation *f*, réprobation *f*

**odorous** *adj* odorant

**odour** *n* odeur *f*, parfum *m*

**odourless** *adj* inodore

**Odyssey** *n* odyssée *f*

**oecumenical** *adj see* **ecumenical**

**oedema, edema** *n* œdème *m*

**Oedipus** *n* ~ **complex** complexe *m* d'Œdipe

**oesophagus** *n* œsophage *m*

**of** *prep* de; ~ **a Saturday** le samedi; ~ **late** dernièrement; ~ **necessity** obligatoirement; ~ **old** d'autrefois; ~ **the hundred ten were useless** sur les cent dix étaient inutilisables; **all ~ a sudden** tout à coup; *US* **a quarter ~ six** six heures moins le (un) quart; **I'm a friend ~ his** je suis de ses amis; **it's very good ~ you** c'est très gentil de votre part; **she's one ~ us** elle est des nôtres; **the fifth ~ June** le cinq juin; **what ~ it?** et alors?, et après?

**off** *adv* (away) éloigné de; (aside) à l'écart; (cancelled) annulé, rompu; (removed from) détaché, séparé; (food) pas frais (*f* fraîche), avarié; *naut* au large; (tap, etc) fermé; (current) coupé; ~ **he goes!** le voilà parti; **be badly ~** être dans la gêne; **beef is ~** il n'y a plus de bœuf; **be ~** partir, se sauver; **be ~!** allez-vous-en!, va-t'en!; **be well ~** être riche (aisé); **be worse ~** être moins bien qu'avant; **come ~** se détacher; **far ~** très éloigné; **go ~ to sleep** s'endormir; **hats ~!** chapeaux bas!; **have a day ~** avoir un jour de congé; *coll* **have it ~ with** faire l'amour avec; **keep ~** se tenir éloigné; (abstain) s'abstenir; **leave ~** cesser; **on and ~** de temps à autre; **straight ~** tout de suite; *prep* de; *naut* au large de; **be ~ one's food** n'avoir pas d'appétit; **be ~ work** être malade, ne pas pouvoir travailler; **eat ~ a plate** manger dans une assiette

**offal** *n* (rubbish) ordures *fpl*; (waste)

déchets *mpl*; (animal) abats *mpl*

**offbeat** *adj coll* original; *mus* syncopé

**off-chance** *n* vague possibilité *f*; **on the ~**
à tout hasard

**off-colour** *adj coll* peu bien; *sl* grivois,
grossier -ière

**off-day** *n* mauvais jour

**offence** *n* offense *f*, faute *f*; (crime) délit *m*;
**give ~ to s/o** offenser (blesser) qn;
**mean no ~** ne vouloir offenser personne; **second ~** récidive *f*; **take ~** se
froisser

**offend** *vt* offenser, déplaire à, froisser; **~
the eye** choquer la vue; **be easily ~ed**
être très susceptible; **be ~ed at sth** se
fâcher de qch

**offender** *n* délinquant -e; offenseur *m*;
(guilty person) coupable; **old ~** repris
*m* de justice

**offensive** *n* offensive *f*; *adj mil* offensif -ive;
choquant, désagréable, repoussant

**offensively** *adv mil* offensivement;
désagréablement

**offer** *n* offre *f*, proposition *f*; **~ of marriage** demande *f* en mariage; *vt* offrir,
présenter; **~ an opinion** avancer une
opinion; *vi* s'offrir; **~ to do sth** offrir de
faire qch

**offering** *n* offre *f*

**offertory** *n* (part of service) offertoire *m*;
(collection) quête *f*

**off-hand, off-handed** *adj* désinvolte,
cavalier -ière; spontané, impromptu

**office** *n* bureau *m*; (public position)
charge *f*, fonctions *fpl*; (lawyer) étude *f*;
(duty) devoir *m*; *eccles* office *m*; **~
hours** heures *fpl* de bureau; **be in ~**
(government) être au pouvoir; **head ~**
siège social; **hold ~** remplir un emploi;
**Home Office** = ministère *m* de
l'Intérieur; **through the good ~s of**
grâce aux bons offices de

**office-boy** *n* garçon *m* de bureau

**officer** *n* officier *m*; (public) fonctionnaire *m*; (police) agent *m* de police

**official** *n* fonctionnaire; employé -e; *adj*
officiel -ielle

**officialdom** *n* bureaucratie *f*; administration *f*

**officialese** *n coll* jargon administratif

**officialism** *n* bureaucratie *f*

**officially** *adv* officiellement

**officiate** *vi* officier

**officious** *adj* (meddlesome) empressé;
autoritaire; (unofficial, informal)
officieux -ieuse

**offing** *n naut* large *m*; *fig* **in the ~** en
perspective

**off-licence** *n* débit *m* de boissons

**off-peak** *adj* **~ hours** heures creuses

**off-putting** *adj coll* déconcertant, rébarbatif -ive

**off-season** *n* morte-saison *f* (*pl* mortes-
saisons)

**offset** *n* compensation *f*; *hort* rejeton *m*;
*typ* offset *m*; *vt* compenser; *vi hort* pousser des rejetons

**offshoot** *n* rejeton *m*

**offshore** *adj* éloigné de la côte, qui se
trouve au large

**off-side** *n sp* hors-jeu *m invar*; *adv sp* hors
jeu; *mot* du côté de la route

**offspring** *n* rejeton *m*, descendant *m*; *coll*
progéniture *f*

**offstage** *adv* dans les coulisses

**off-white** *n* blanc cassé; *adj* blanc cassé
*invar*, quasi-blanc (*f* quasi-blanche)

**oft** *adv poet* mainte fois, souvent

**often** *adv* souvent, fréquemment; **every
so ~** de temps en temps; **how ~?** combien de fois?

**ogle** *vt* lorgner, lancer des œillades à

**ogre** *n* ogre *m*

**ogress** *n* ogresse *f*

**oh** *interj* oh!

**oil** *n* huile *f*; (mineral) pétrole *m*; (fuel)
mazout *m*; **~ industry** industrie pétrolière; *mot* **change the ~** faire la
vidange; *vt* huiler, graisser, lubrifier

**oil-bearing** *adj geol* pétrolifère

**oil-can** *n* (pouring) burette *f* à huile;
(storing) bidon *m* à huile

**oil-cloth** *n* toile cirée

**oil-colour, oil-paint** *n* couleur *f* à l'huile

**oil-field** *n* gisement *m* pétrolifère

**oil-fired** *adj* **~ heating** chauffage *m* au
mazout

**oil-gauge** *n* jauge *f* de niveau d'huile

**oiliness** *n fig* onctuosité *f*

**oil-lamp** *n* lampe *f* à huile (pétrole)

**oil-paint** *n see* **oil-colour**

**oil-painting** *n* peinture *f* à l'huile

**oilskin** *n* toile cirée; **~ cape** cape *f* en toile
cirée

**oil-stove** *n* (heater) réchaud *m* à pétrole;
(cooker) fourneau *m* à pétrole

**oil-tanker** *n* pétrolier *m*

**oil-well** *n* puits *m* à (de) pétrole

**oily** *adj* huileux -euse, graisseux -euse,
gras (*f* grasse); *fig* onctueux -euse

**ointment** *n* pommade *f*, onguent *m*; **fly in
the ~** ombre *f* au tableau

**O.K., okay, okey-doke** *n coll* approbation *f*, feu vert; *adj invar* + *interj coll*
O.K., très bien; *vt coll* approuver

**old** *adj* vieux, vieil (*f* vieille), âgé;
(former) ancien -ienne; **~ age** vieillesse
*f*; **~ age pension** retraite *f* de vieillesse;
**~ boy** ancien élève; **~ chap** mon
vieux; **~ man** vieillard *m*, vieil homme;
*coll* mari *m*; **~ salt** loup *m* de mer; **~
woman** vieille *f*; *coll* femme *f*; **anything** la première chose venue; **be an ~
hand** avoir une longue expérience; **be**

~ **enough to do sth** être d'âge à (en âge de) faire qch; **good ~ age** âge avancé; **grow ~** vieillir; **how ~ are you?** quel âge avez-vous?; **I am ~er than you** je suis votre aîné, je suis plus âgé que vous; **she is five years ~** elle a cinq ans; **the good ~ days** le bon vieux temps; **the ~ man** (dad) papa; (boss) patron *m*; *naut* capitaine *m*

**olden** *adj* **in ~ times** au temps jadis

**old-fashioned** *adj* (out-of-date) démodé, suranné; à l'ancienne mode

**old-world** *adj* de l'ancien temps

**oleander** *n bot* laurier-rose *m* (*pl* lauriers-roses)

**oligarchy** *n* oligarchie *f*

**olive** *n* olive *f*; (tree) olivier *m*; *cul* **meat-~** paupiette *f*; *adj* olive *invar*, olivâtre

**olive-branch** *n* rameau *m* d'olivier

**olive-green** *adj* couleur d'olive

**olive-oil** *n* huile *f* d'olive

**Olympian** *adj* olympien -ienne

**Olympic** *n* **the ~s** les Jeux *mpl* olympiques; *adj* olympique

**ombudsman** *n* = haut fonctionnaire chargé d'enquêter dans les cas d'injustice bureaucratique

**omelet(te)** *n* omelette *f*

**omen** *n* présage *m*, augure *m*

**ominous** *adj* de mauvais augure, sinistre, menaçant

**omission** *n* omission *f*; négligence *f*, oubli *m*

**omit** *vt* omettre; (not mention) passer sous silence

**omnibus** *n* autobus *m*

**omnipotence** *n* toute-puissance *f*, omnipotence *f*

**omnipotent** *adj* omnipotent, tout-puissant (*f* toute-puissante)

**omnipresence** *n* omniprésence *f*

**omnipresent** *adj* omniprésent

**omniscient** *adj* omniscient

**omnivorous** *adj* omnivore

**on** *adv* (forward) en avant; (light) allumé; (tap) ouvert; (engine) en marche; **and so ~** et ainsi de suite; (actor) **be ~** être sur scène; **from then ~** à partir de ce moment; **go ~** continuer; (happen) se passer; **go ~!** pas vrai!; **have nothing ~** être tout(e) nu(e); *fig* ne pas avoir de projet; *coll* être libre; **have sth ~** porter qch; (plan) projeter qch; *coll* **it's not ~** il n'y a pas moyen; **keep ~ doing sth** continuer à faire qch; **later ~** plus tard; **put ~** mettre; **what's ~?** *cin* qu'est-ce qui se donne?; *theat* qu'est-ce qu'on joue?; *prep* sur; à, de, en; ~ **arrival** en arrivant; ~ **foot** à pied; ~ **Friday** vendredi; ~ **horseback** à cheval; ~ **page two** à la page

deux; ~ **pain of** sous peine de; ~ **purpose** exprès; ~ **sale** en vente; ~ **strike** en grève; ~ **the left** (right) à gauche (droite); ~ **the other side** de l'autre côté; ~ **the phone** au téléphone; ~ **the train** dans le train; **be ~ the staff** faire partie du personnel; **just ~ two years ago** il y a à près de deux ans

**onanism** *n* onanisme *m*

**once** *adv* une fois; (formerly) autrefois; ~ **again** encore une fois; ~ **a week** une fois par semaine; **at ~** tout de suite; (simultaneously) en même temps; **just for ~** pour cette fois-ci; *conj* aussitôt que

**once-over** *n coll* examen *m* rapide

**one** *n* un *m* (*f* une); **it's all ~ to me** ça m'est égal; **the good ~** le bon (*f* la bonne); **you're a ~!** vous alors!; *adj* seul, unique; ~ **hundred and ~ cent** un; *coll* **be ~ up on** avoir l'avantage sur; **have ~ drink too many** boire un verre de trop; *sl* **number ~** soi-même; **twenty-~** vingt-et-un; *pron* on; ~ **another** les un(e)s les autres; ~ **Mr X** un certain Monsieur X; ~ **'s** son (*f* sa, *pl* ses); **that ~** celui-là (*f* celle-là); **the ~ who** celui (*f* celle) qui; **this ~** celui-ci (*f* celle-ci); **which ~?** lequel (*f* laquelle)?

**one-armed** *adj* manchot; *coll* ~ **bandit** machine *f* à sous

**one-eyed** *adj* borgne

**one-horse** *adj US coll* misérable, de rien

**oneness** *n* unité *f*, accord *m*

**onerous** *adj* onéreux -euse

**oneself** *pron* soi, soi-même; se; **be beside ~** être hors de soi

**one-sided** *adj* unilatéral; (partial) partial, injuste; (lop-sided) de biais, asymétrique

**one-track** *adj* ~ **mind** esprit obsédé par une seule idée

**one-upmanship** *n coll* art *m* de surpasser les autres

**one-way** *adj* à sens unique; *US* ~ **ticket** billet *m* simple

**onion** *n* oignon *m*; *coll* **know one's ~s** connaître son affaire; **spring ~** ciboule *f*; **string of ~s** chapelet *m* d'oignons

**onlooker** *n* spectateur -trice, assistant -e

**only** *adj* seul, unique; ~ **child** enfant unique; **the ~ one** le seul (*f* la seule); *adv* seulement, ne ... que; ~ **this morning** pas plus tard que ce matin; ~ **to imagine it** rien que de l'imaginer; ~ **you can say** seul vous êtes à même de le dire; **he has ~ to ask** il n'a qu'à demander; **he ~ tried** il n'a fait qu'essayer; *conj* mais

**onomatopoeia** *n* onomatopée *f*

**onrush** *n* ruée *f*, attaque *f*
**onset** *n* assaut *m*, attaque *f*; choc *m*; **at the first** ~ de prime abord
**onslaught** *n* assaut *m*, attaque *f*
**onto** *prep* sur
**onus** *n* responsabilité *f*, charge *f*
**onward** *adj* progressif -ive
**onwards** *adv* en avant; **from now** ~ à partir de maintenant
**onyx** *n* onyx *m*
**oodles** *npl coll* une grande quantité, des masses
**ooze** *n* (oozing) suintement *m*; (mud) limon *m*; *vi* suinter
**opal** *n* opale *f*
**opaque** *adj* opaque
**open** *adj* ouvert; (bottle) débouché; (frank) franc (*f* franche); (question) discutable; (disposed) disposé, prêt; (public) manifeste; (unobstructed) libre; ~ **to the winds** exposé au vent; **break** ~ éventrer; **half** ~ entrouvert; **in the** ~ **air** en plein air; **in the** ~ **country** en pleine campagne; **it is** ~ **to you to** il vous est loisible de; **keep** ~ **house** tenir table ouverte; **lay oneself** ~ **to** s'exposer à; **wide** ~ grand ouvert; *vt* ouvrir; (bottle) déboucher; (parcel) défaire; (uncover) découvrir, exposer; (begin) commencer; (legs) écarter; (hole) percer; ~ **out** ouvrir; (orifice, sleeve) évaser; ~ **up** ouvrir; *vi* s'ouvrir; (shop) ouvrir (ses portes); (begin) commencer, débuter; (flowers) s'épanouir; ~ **on to** donner sur; ~ **out** s'élargir; **half** ~ entrouvrir
**open-cast** *adj* à ciel ouvert
**open-eared** *adj* attentif -ive
**opener** *n* ouvreur -euse; (tin) ouvre-boîte(s) *m*
**open-eyed** *adj* qui voit clair; vigilant
**open-handed** *adj* généreux -euse
**open-hearted** *adj* franc (*f* franche); (sympathetic) compatissant
**opening** *n* ouverture *f*; (beginning) commencement *m*; (wood) clairière *f*; (clouds) éclaircie *f*; (opportunity) occasion *f* favorable; *comm* débouché *m*; (flower) épanouissement *m*; (uncorking) débouchage *m*; *adj* inaugural, d'ouverture, de début
**openly** *adv* ouvertement, franchement
**open-minded** *adj* impartial, sans parti pris
**open-mouthed** *adj* bouche bée
**openness** *n* franchise *f*; aspect découvert
**open-plan** *adj* sans cloisons
**opera** *n* opéra *m*
**operable** *adj* opérable
**opera-glasses** *npl* jumelles *fpl*, lorgnette *f*
**opera-house** *n* opéra *m*

**operate** *vt* effectuer; faire fonctionner, faire manœuvrer, actionner; *vi* opérer; agir; fonctionner; ~ **on s/o** opérer qn
**operatic** *adj* d'opéra
**operating** *adj med* d'opération
**operation** *n* opération *f*; *surg* intervention *f*; (functioning) fonctionnement *m*; **be in** ~ (rule) être en vigueur; (machine) fonctionner, être en marche; **undergo an** ~ se faire opérer, subir une intervention (chirurgicale)
**operational** *adj* opérationnel -elle
**operative** *n* ouvrier -ière; *adj* opératif -ive, actif -ive; **become** ~ entrer en vigueur
**operator** *n* opérateur -trice; **telephone** ~ standardiste
**operetta** *n* opérette *f*
**ophthalmic** *adj* ophtalmique
**ophthalmology** *n* ophtalmologie *f*
**opinion** *n* opinion *f*, avis *m*; **ask s/o's** ~ consulter qn; **form an** ~ se faire une opinion; **I am of the** ~ **that** je suis d'avis que; **in my** ~ à mon avis
**opinionated** *adj* imbu de ses opinions
**opium** *n* opium *m*; ~ **den** fumerie *f*
**opponent** *n* adversaire *m*
**opportune** *adj* opportun, à propos
**opportunely** *adv* à propos
**opportuneness** *n* opportunité *f*
**opportunism** *n* opportunisme *m*
**opportunity** *n* occasion *f* (favorable); **at the earliest** ~ à la première occasion; **take the** ~ profiter de l'occasion
**oppose** *vt* (resist) s'opposer à; (contrast) opposer
**opposed** *adj* opposé, hostile; **as** ~ **to** par opposition à
**opposite** *n* opposé *m*, contraire *m*; *adj* opposé; (facing) vis-à-vis, en face; (contrary) contraire; **in the** ~ **direction** en sens inverse; **on the** ~ **side** de l'autre côté; **their** ~ **neighbours** leurs voisins d'en face; *adv* vis-à-vis, en face; *prep* en face de; (level with) à la hauteur de
**opposition** *n* opposition *f*; résistance *f*; *comm* concurrence *f*
**oppress** *vt* opprimer; (mind) oppresser
**oppression** *n* oppression *f*; (mind) accablement *m*
**oppressive** *adj* oppressif -ive, tyrannique; (weather) lourd
**oppressor** *n* oppresseur *m*, opprimant *m*
**opprobrious** *adj* injurieux -ieuse
**opprobrium** *n* opprobre *m*
**opt** *vi* opter
**optic** *adj* optique
**optical** *adj* optique; ~ **illusion** illusion *f* d'optique; ~ **instrument** instrument *m* d'optique
**optician** *n* opticien -ienne

**optics** n optique f
**optimism** n optimisme m
**optimist** n optimiste
**optimistic** adj optimiste
**optimize** vt + vi tirer le meilleur parti (de)
**optimum** n optimum m (pl optimums or optima); adj optimum (f optimum or optima, pl optimums or optima)
**option** n option f, choix m
**optional** adj facultatif -ive
**opulence** n opulence f
**opulent** adj opulent
**opus** n mus opus m
**opuscule** n opuscule m
**or** conj ou; (with neg) ni; ~ **else** ou bien; **a kilometre** ~ **so** environ un kilomètre; **either...**~ ou ... ou; **without...**~ sans ... ni
**oracle** n oracle m
**oracular** adj équivoque; d'oracle
**oracy** n capacité f de s'exprimer
**oral** adj oral; ~ **examination** (examen m) oral m; ~ **vaccine** vaccin buccal
**orally** adv oralement, de vive voix; med par voie buccale
**orange** n orange f; **blood** ~ sanguine f; **Seville** ~ orange amère; adj orange
**orangeade** n orangeade f
**orange-blossom** n fleurs fpl d'oranger
**orange-house** n orangerie f
**orange-peel** n pelure f d'orange
**orang-outang, orang-utan** n orang-outang m (pl orangs-outangs)
**orate** vi pej pérorer
**oration** n discours m, allocution f
**orator** n orateur -trice
**oratorical** adj oratoire; (speech) verbeux -euse
**oratorio** n oratorio m
**¹oratory** n éloquence f
**²oratory** n eccles oratoire m
**orb** n orbe m, sphère f
**orbit** n orbite f; vt décrire une orbite autour de, orbiter autour de
**orchard** n verger m
**orchestra** n orchestre m; ~ **stalls** fauteuils mpl d'orchestre
**orchestral** adj orchestral
**orchestrate** vt orchestrer
**orchid** n orchidée f
**orchitis** n med orchite f
**ordain** vt ordonner, décréter; eccles ordonner
**ordeal** n épreuve f
**order** n ordre m; comm commande f; (rule) règlement m; (sequence) suite f, succession f; mil commandement m; eccles ~ s ordres mpl; **call s/o to** ~ rappeler qn à l'ordre; **in good** ~ en bon état; (affairs) en règle; **in** ~ dans les règles; **in** ~ **that** pour que, afin que; **in** ~ **to** pour, afin de; **made to** ~ fait

sur commande; **out of** ~ (machine) détraqué; (on public notice) en panne; (telephone) en dérangement; (irregular) irrégulier -ière; **postal** ~ , **money** ~ mandat-poste m (pl mandats-poste); **the lower** ~ s les classes inférieures; **the old** ~ l'ancien régime; **until further** ~ s jusqu'à nouvel ordre; vt ordonner; comm commander; (tidy) ranger, arranger; ~ **about** envoyer à droite et à gauche; (posting) ~ **s/o to** envoyer qn à; ~ **s/o to do sth** ordonner (commander) à qn de faire qch; **just what the doctor** ~ ed tout à fait ce qu'il faut
**ordering** n mise f en ordre, disposition f
**orderliness** n bon ordre; habitude f d'ordre
**orderly** n mil ordonnance f; (hospital) infirmier m; adj ordonné, méthodique; (life) tranquille, rangé
**ordinal** adj ordinal
**ordinance** n ordonnance f
**ordinary** n ordinaire m; **out of the** ~ exceptionnel -elle; adj ordinaire; normal, habituel -elle; pej quelconque
**ordination** n arrangement m; eccles ordination f
**ordnance** n artillerie f; ~ **survey map** carte f d'état-major
**ordure** n ordure f, excrément m; saleté f
**ore** n minerai m
**organ** n anat organe m; mus orgue m, orgues fpl; (publication) journal m; **barrel (street)** ~ orgue m de Barbarie; **preside at the** ~ tenir l'orgue (les orgues)
**organdie** n organdi m
**organ-grinder** n joueur -euse d'orgue de Barbarie
**organic** adj organique
**organism** n organisme m
**organist** n organiste
**organization** n organisation f; pol organisme m
**organize** vt organiser
**organizer** n organisateur -trice
**orgasm** n orgasme m
**orgiastic** adj orgiaque
**orgy** n orgie f
**Orient** n Orient m
**Oriental** n Oriental -e; adj oriental, d'Orient
**orientate** vt orienter
**orientation** n orientation f
**orienteering** n sp traversée f de terrain en se servant de moyens d'orientation
**orifice** n ouverture f, orifice m
**origin** n origine f, provenance f
**original** n original m; adj (primitive) originel -elle, primitif -ive, originaire; original

**originality** *n* originalité *f*

**originally** *adv* à l'origine, originairement; (at first) originalement

**originate** *vt* être l'auteur de, donner naissance à; *vi* avoir son origine, provenir, tirer son origine

**originator** *n* créateur -trice, auteur *m*; initiateur -trice

**ormolu** *n* chrysocale *m*, similor *m*

**ornament** *n* ornement *m*; *vt* orner, décorer

**ornamental** *adj* ornemental

**ornamentation** *n* décoration *f*, embellissement *m*

**ornate** *adj* surchargé (d'ornements); (style) fleuri

**ornithologist** *n* ornithologiste, ornithologue

**ornithology** *n* ornithologie *f*

**orphan** *n* orphelin -e; *vt* rendre orphelin -e

**orphanage** *n* orphelinat *m*

**orthodox** *adj* orthodoxe

**orthodoxy** *n* orthodoxie *f*

**orthography** *n* orthographe *f*

**orthopaedic** *adj* orthopédique

**Oscar** *n cin* Oscar *m*

**oscillate** *vt* faire osciller; *vi* osciller

**oscillation** *n* oscillation *f*

**osmosis** *n* osmose *f*

**osprey** *n* orfraie *f*

**ossify** *vt* ossifier; *vi* s'ossifier

**ostensible** *adj* prétendu, feint

**ostensibly** *adv* en apparence

**ostentation** *n* ostentation *f*, apparat *m*; bravade *f*

**ostentatious** *adj* fastueux -euse

**osteopath** *n* chiropracteur *m*

**osteopathy** *n* chiropraxie *f*

**ostler** *n* garçon *m* d'écurie

**ostracism** *n* ostracisme *m*

**ostracize** *vt* frapper d'ostracisme

**ostrich** *n* autruche *f*

**other** *adj* autre; ~ **people** d'autres; ~ **things being equal** toutes choses égales; **each** ~ l'un (*f* l'une) l'autre; **every week** toutes les deux semaines; **the habits of** ~ **people** les mœurs *fpl* d'autrui; **the** ~ **ones** les autres; **the three** les trois autres; *pron* autre; **has he any** ~**s?** en a-t-il d'autres?; **one or** ~ **of us** l'un (*f* l'une) de nous; **some...** ~**s** les uns (*f* les unes)... les autres; *adv* autrement

**otherwise** *adv* autrement; dans le cas contraire; ~ **, he is quite normal** sous d'autres égards, il est tout à fait normal; **be** ~ **engaged** être occupé à faire autre chose; **except where** ~ **stated** sauf indication contraire

**otherworldly** *adj* détaché de ce monde

**otiose** *adj* inutile, superflu

**otter** *n* loutre *f*

**Ottoman** *n* Ottoman -e; *adj* ottoman

**ottoman** *n* ottomane *f*

**ouch** *interj* aïe!

**ought** *vi* devoir, falloir; **my father** ~ **to know** mon père est bien placé pour le savoir; **one** ~ **to keep calm** il faut rester calme; **you** ~ **not to have left** vous n'auriez pas dû partir; **you really to try it** vous devriez vraiment l'essayer

**ounce** *n* once *f*

**our** *adj* notre (*pl* nos)

**ours** *pron* le (la) nôtre; **a friend of** ~ un de nos amis (*f* une de nos amies); **that's** ~ c'est à nous

**ourselves** *pron* nous-mêmes; *refl pron* nous

**oust** *vt* déloger; (take the place of ) évincer, supplanter

**out** *adj* ~ **tray** corbeille *f* pour le courrier à expédier, corbeille *f* dépant; *vt coll* sortir, mettre à la porte; *adv* dehors; (away from home) sorti; (fire, etc) éteint; (book) paru; (on strike) en grève; (discovered) découvert; *sp* hors jeu; (aloud) à haute voix; (plant, etc) en fleur; ~ **at sea** au large; ~ **of** parmi, de; ~ **with it!** dites-le!; *mot* **all** ~ à toute vitesse; **be** ~ **and about** être sur pied; **before the year is** ~ avant la fin de l'année; **be** ~ **in one's reckoning** être loin du compte; **far** ~ loin; **go all** ~ **to** mettre tout en œuvre pour; **go** ~ sortir; **have an evening** ~ faire une sortie le soir; **have a tooth** ~ se faire arracher une dent; **have it** ~ **with** s/o avoir une explication (des explications) avec qn; **hear s/o** ~ écouter qn jusqu'au bout; **mil lights** ~ extinction *f* des feux; *fig* **put s/o** ~ dérouter qn; **that's** ~ (excluded) c'est exclu; (old-fashioned) c'est vieux jeu; **the journey** ~ l'aller *m*; **the sun is** ~ il fait du soleil; **you are far** ~ vous vous trompez de beaucoup; *prep* ~ **of** hors de, au dehors de; ~ **of doors** dehors; ~ **of gear** débrayé; ~ **of patience** à bout de patience; ~ **of print** épuisé; ~ **of respect** par respect; ~ **of sight** hors de vue; ~ **of sight,** ~ **of mind** loin des yeux, loin du cœur; ~ **of tune** (singing) faux (*f* fausse); (instrument) désaccordé; **be** ~ **of it** ne pas être de la partie; être laissé à l'écart; **be** ~ **of one's mind** avoir perdu la raison; **drink** ~ **of a glass** boire dans un verre; **it's** ~ **of the question!** jamais de la vie!; **look** ~ **of the window** regarder par la fenêtre; **turn** ~ **of doors** mettre à la porte

**out-and-out** *adj* consommé, achevé

611

**outbid**

**outbid** vt enchérir sur; (outdo) surpasser

**outboard** adj ~ **motor** moteur m hors-bord invar; ~ **motor boat** hors-bord m invar

**outbreak** n (riot) révolte f, émeute f; (illness) épidémie f; (from confinement) éruption f; (feelings) explosion f

**outbuilding** n dépendance f; (shed) hangar m

**outburst** n éruption f; (laughter) éclat m; (anger) déchaînement m

**outcast(e)** n + adj proscrit -e, exilé -e, expulsé -e

**outclass** vt surclasser

**outcome** n résultat m, conséquence f

**outcrop** n geol affleurement m

**outcry** n clameur f, cri m, cri m d'indignation

**outdated** adj démodé, suranné

**outdistance** vt distancer

**outdo** vt surpasser, l'emporter sur

**outdoor** adj extérieur, au grand air

**outdoors** adv dehors, en plein air

**outer** adj extérieur

**outermost** adj le plus à l'extérieur

**outface** vt dévisager

**outfit** n (gear) équipement m, attirail m; (clothes) trousseau m; (kit) trousse f; coll organisation f

**outfitter** n confectionneur -euse

**outflank** vt détourner, déborder

**outflow** n écoulement m; décharge f

**outgoing** n sortie f; ~ s dépenses fpl; adj sortant; (official) démissionnaire

**outgrow** vt dépasser en croissance, devenir plus grand que; (clothes) devenir trop grand pour; (habit) perdre

**outgrowth** n excroissance f

**outhouse** n dépendance f; (shed) hangar m

**outing** n sortie f, excursion f, promenade f

**outlandish** adj bizarre, étrange; (place) retiré

**outlast** vt durer plus longtemps que, survivre à

**outlaw** n proscrit m, hors-la-loi m invar; vt proscrire

**outlay** n frais mpl, dépenses fpl; (first expense) mise f de fonds

**outlet** n issue f, sortie f; comm débouché m

**outline** n contour m, silhouette f; (sketch) dessin m, esquisse f; (rough idea) aperçu m; vt esquisser, ébaucher

**outlive** vt survivre à

**outlook** n vue f, perspective f

**outlying** adj écarté

**outmanoeuvre** vt déjouer

**outmatch** vt surpasser

**outmoded** adj démodé

**outnumber** vt être plus nombreux -euses que, surpasser en nombre

**out-of-date** adj passé de mode, vieilli; (ticket, etc) périmé

**out-of-door** adj en plein air, de plein air

**out-of-school** adj extra-scolaire

**out-of-the-way** adj (situation) écarté; (unusual) peu ordinaire

**outpace** vt dépasser, devancer

**out-patient** n malade qui vient consulter à l'hôpital

**outplay** vt jouer mieux que

**outpost** n avant-poste m

**outpouring** n épanchement m; (feeling) effusion f

**output** n rendement m; production f; (author) débit m

**outrage** n outrage m; attentat m; vt outrager

**outrageous** adj outrageant; (price) excessif -ive; immodéré

**outrider** n piqueur m

**outrigger** n outrigger m

**outright** adj (manner) franc (f franche); absolu, total; adv complètement, tout à fait; **kill s/o** ~ tuer qn raide

**outrun** vt dépasser, distancer

**outset** n commencement m, début m; **at the** ~ dès le début

**outshine** vt éclipser, dépasser

**outside** n extérieur m, dehors m; **at the** ~ tout au plus; adj extérieur, du dehors; (price) maximum (f maximum or maxima, pl maximums or maxima); adv dehors, en dehors, en dehors; prep à l'extérieur de, en dehors de

**outsider** n étranger -ère; (racing) outsider m

**outsize** adj pointure f (taille f) hors série; (very big) géant

**outskirts** npl (town) faubourgs mpl, banlieue f; (forest) lisière f; (surroundings) abords mpl

**outsmart** vt déjouer les intentions de, duper

**outspoken** adj franc (f franche); **be** ~ ne pas mâcher ses mots

**outspokenness** n franchise f

**outspread** adj étendu; (wings) déployé

**outstanding** adj (jutting) saillant; (excellent) éclatant; (person) marquant, éminent; (debt) dû, à payer; (matter) en suspens

**outstay** vt rester plus longtemps que

**outstretched** adj étendu; (wings) déployé

**outstrip** vt dépasser, devancer; surpasser

**outvote** vt obtenir la majorité sur; **be** ~ d être mis en minorité

**outward** adj extérieur; en dehors, de dehors; ~ **journey** voyage m d'aller

**outwardly** adv à l'extérieur; en apparence

**outwards** *adv* au dehors; vers l'extérieur

**outweigh** *vt* peser plus que; *fig* avoir plus d'influence que, l'emporter sur

**outwit** *vt* duper, déjouer les intentions de

**outwork** *n mil* ouvrage avancé

**outworn** *adj* démodé

**oval** *n* ovale *m*; *adj* oval

**ovary** *n* ovaire *m*

**ovation** *n* ovation *f*

**oven** *n* four *m*

**ovenware** *n* vaisselle *f* allant au four

**over** *adv* par-dessus; (finished) fini, passé; (remaining) de reste; (too much) trop; (more) davantage; ~ **and above** en outre; ~ **and** ~ à maintes reprises; ~ **there** là-bas; **all** ~ partout; **it's all** ~ **with us** c'en est fait de nous; **that's you all** ~ c'est typique de vous; *prep* sur; par-dessus; au-dessus de; (more than) plus de; (on the other side of) de l'autre côté de; (during) au cours de; ~ **the way** en face; **all** ~ **England** partout en Angleterre

**overact** *vt + vi theat* charger, outrer

**overall** *n* blouse *f*; ~s salopette *f*, bleus *mpl*; *adj* global, total

**overawe** *vt* intimider

**overbalance** *vt* renverser; *vi* perdre l'équilibre

**overbearing** *adj* arrogant, impérieux -ieuse

**overblown** *adj* trop épanoui

**overboard** *adv* par-dessus bord

**overburden** *vt* surcharger, accabler

**overcast** *adj* couvert, obscurci; *vt* obscurcir

**overcharge** *n* prix excessif; *elect* surcharge *f*; *vt* (battery) surcharger; ~ s/o faire payer qn trop cher

**overcloud** *vt* couvrir de nuages; *fig* obscurcir

**overcoat** *n* pardessus *m*

**overcome** *adj* accablé; *vt* (enemy) vaincre; (difficulty) surmonter

**overconfidence** *n* confiance excessive

**overconfident** *adj* trop confiant de soi, trop assuré

**overcrowd** *vt* trop remplir; (with people) surpeupler

**overcrowded** *adj* (vehicle) bondé; (place) surpeuplé

**overdo** *vt* exagérer, outrer; *cul* faire trop cuire; ~ **it** se surmener; (exaggerate) exagérer

**overdose** *n* dose trop forte; dose mortelle

**overdraft** *n* découvert *m*

**overdraw** *vt* mettre à découvert

**overdress** *vt* habiller avec trop de recherche; *vi* s'habiller avec trop de recherche

**overdrive** *n mot* vitesse surmultipliée *f*

**overdue** *adj* en retard; (account) arriéré

**overeat** *vi* trop manger

**overestimate** *vt* surestimer

**overexcite** *vt* surexciter

**overexcitement** *n* surexcitation *f*

**over-expose** *vt* surexposer

**overfeed** *vt* suralimenter

**overflow** *n* débordement *m*; trop-plein *m*; (cistern) déversoir *m*; *vi* déborder

**overgrow** *vt* couvrir, envahir

**overgrown** *adj* couvert

**overhang** *n* surplomb *m*; *vt* surplomber

**overhanging** *adj* en surplomb, surplombant

**overhaul** *n* révision *f*, remise *f* en état; *vt* examiner à fond; *mech* réviser, remettre en état; (overtake) rattraper

**overhead** *adj* aérien -ienne; ~ **expenses**, ~s frais généraux; ~ **valves** soupapes *fpl* en tête; *adv* en haut, au-dessus

**overhear** *vt* entendre par hasard; (conversation) surprendre

**overheat** *vt* surchauffer; ~ **oneself** s'échauffer; *vi* trop chauffer

**overjoyed** *adj* ravi, rempli de joie

**overladen** *adj* surchargé

**overland** *adj* ~ **route** voie *f* de terre; *adv* par voie de terre

**overlap** *n* chevauchement *m*; (duplication) double emploi *m*; *vt + vi* chevaucher, recouvrir

**overlay** *n* matelas *m*; *vt* recouvrir, couvrir

**overleaf** *adv* au verso

**overload** *vt* surcharger

**overlook** *vt* dominer, donner sur; (forgive) laisser passer, pardonner; (forget) oublier; (not see) ne pas voir; (neglect) négliger; (watch) surveiller

**overlord** *n* suzerain *m*

**overmuch** *adv* trop, par trop

**overnight** *adj* de nuit; *adv* (pendant) la nuit; la veille au soir; (until next day) jusqu'au lendemain; (suddenly) du jour au lendemain

**overpaid** *adj* trop payé

**overpass** *n* viaduc routier

**overpopulate** *vt* surpeupler

**overpower** *vt* maîtriser, vaincre; *fig* accabler

**overpowering** *adj* accablant, écrasant

**overproduction** *n* surproduction *f*

**overrate** *vt* surestimer, surfaire

**overreach** *vt* (deceive) duper; ~ **oneself** aller trop loin

**override** *vt* outrepasser; (horse) surmener

**overrider** *n mot* banane *f*

**overrule** *vt* annuler, rejeter

**overrun** *vt* envahir; (infest) infester; (go past) dépasser; *typ* reporter à la ligne (page) suivante

**overseas** *adj* d'outre-mer; *adv* outre-mer, par delà les mers

**oversee** *vt* surveiller

**overseer** *n* surveillant *m*

**overshadow** *vt* ombrager; *fig* éclipser

**overshoe** *n* galoche *f*; **rubber ~ s** caoutchoucs *mpl*

**overshoot** *vt* dépasser; **~ the mark** dépasser le but

**oversight** *n* oubli *m*, inadvertance *f*; (supervision) surveillance *f*

**oversleep** *vi* dormir trop longtemps

**overspend** *vi* dépenser trop

**overspill** *n* déversement *m* de population

**overstate** *vt* exagérer

**overstatement** *n* exagération *f*

**overstay** *vt* dépasser

**oversteer** *vi* *mot* survirer

**overstep** *vt* dépasser, outrepasser

**overstock** *vt* encombrer, surcharger

**overstrain** *vt* surmener

**overstrung** *adj* énervé

**overt** *adj* évident, manifeste

**overtake** *vt* (catch up) rattraper; (pass) doubler, dépasser; (surprise) surprendre; (happen to) arriver à

**overtax** *vt* trop exiger de; **~ one's strength** se surmener

**overthrow** *n* renversement *m*; (defeat) défaite *f*; *vt* renverser; (enemy) vaincre

**overtime** *n* heures *fpl* supplémentaires; **work ~** faire des heures supplémentaires

**overtire** *vt* surmener

**overtly** *adv* ouvertement

**overtone** *n* *mus* harmonique *m* or *f*; *fig* nuance *f*

**overture** *n* ouverture *f*

**overturn** *vt* renverser; (boat) faire chavirer; *vi* se renverser; (boat) chavirer

**overvalue** *vt* surévaluer, surestimer

**overweening** *adj* outrecuidant, présomptueux -ueuse

**overweight** *n* surpoids *m*, excédent *m*; **be ~** être trop lourd; être trop gros (*f* grosse)

**overwhelm** *vt* accabler; (with kindness) combler; (surprise) étonner

**overwork** *n* surmenage *m*; *vt* surmener; *vi* se surmener

**overwrought** *adj* surmené, excédé

**ovine** *adj* ovin

**owe** *vt* devoir, être redevable de

**owl** *n* hibou *m*

**owlish** *adj* de hibou

**¹own** *n* all one's **~** original; **be (all) on one's ~** être tout seul (*f* toute seule); **come into one's ~** entrer en possession de son bien; **do sth on one's ~** faire qch tout seul (*f* toute seule); (taking responsibility for) faire qch de son propre chef; **my ~** à moi, le mien (*f* la mienne); *adj* propre

**²own** *vt* posséder; (confess) avouer; (acknowledge) reconnaître

**owner** *n* propriétaire

**owner-driver** *n* conducteur *m* propriétaire

**owner-occupier** *n* propriétaire qui habite sur place

**ownership** *n* possession *f*, droit *m* de propriété

**ox** *n* bœuf *m*

**oxide** *n* oxyde *m*

**oxidize** *vt* oxyder

**oxtail** *n* queue *f* de bœuf

**oxyacetylene** *adj* oxyacétylénique

**oxygen** *n* oxygène *m*

**oxygen-mask** *n* masque *m* à oxygène

**oxygen-tent** *n* tente *f* à oxygène

**oyster** *n* huître *f*

**oyster-bed** *n* parc *m* à huîtres, banc *m* d'huîtres

**oyster-shell** *n* écaille *f* d'huître

**ozone** *n* ozone *m*

# P

**pace** *n* pas *m*; (speed) train *m*, allure *f*; **at a good ~** à vive allure; **at a walking ~** au pas; **keep ~ with** marcher de pair avec; **put s/o through his ~ s** mettre qn à l'épreuve; **set the ~** mener le train; *vt* arpenter; *vi* **~ up and down** faire les cent pas

**pacemaker** *n* entraîneur *m*; *med* stimulateur *m* cardiaque

**pacific** *adj* pacifique

**pacification** *n* pacification *f*, apaisement *m*

**pacifism** n pacifisme m
**pacifist** n pacifiste
**pacify** vt pacifier, apaiser
**pack** n paquet m; (group) bande f; (collection) tas m; (cards) jeu m; (hounds) meute f; sp mêlée f; (wool) balle f; med emplâtre m; vt emballer; (luggage) faire; (cram) serrer, tasser, bourrer; ~ed hall salle f comble; ~ s/o off expédier qn; send s/o ~ing envoyer promener qn; the train was ~ed le train était bondé; vi se tasser, se presser; ~ up plier bagage; fig cesser
**package** n paquet m, colis m; ~ tour voyage organisé, voyage m à forfait; vt conditionner
**packaging** n conditionnement m
**packer** n emballeur -euse
**packet** n paquet m, colis m; obs (boat) paquebot m
**packhorse** n cheval m de somme
**pack-ice** n glace f de banquise
**packing** n emballage m; (snow) tassement m
**packing-case** n boîte f (caisse f) d'emballage
**packing-paper** n papier m d'emballage
**pact** n pacte m
**¹pad** n (cushion, stuffing) coussinet m, bourrelet; mech tampon m; mot (bearing) coussinet m; (paper) bloc m; (blotter) sous-main m invar; (certain animals) patte f; sl (bed) pieu m; sl (room) piaule f
**²pad** vt rembourrer; capitonner; ~ out délayer
**³pad** vi aller à pied
**padding** n rembourrage m; fig remplissage m; (speech) délayage m; (substance) bourre f, ouate f; (writing) cheville f
**paddle** n pagaie f; (steamship) aube f; vt+vi pagayer; vi (wade) barboter, patauger
**paddle-steamer** n vapeur m (navire m) à aubes
**paddle-wheel** n roue f à aubes
**paddock** n enclos m; (horse-racing) paddock m, pesage m
**paddyfield** n rizière f
**padlock** n cadenas m; vt cadenasser
**padre** n aumônier m
**paederast, pederast** n pédéraste m
**paederasty, pederasty** n pédérastie f
**paediatrician, pediatrician** n pédiatre m
**paediatrics, pediatrics** n pédiatrie f
**paeony** see peony
**pagan** n+adj païen -ïenne
**paganism** n paganisme m
**¹page** n page m; (hotel) chasseur m; vt (call) appeler
**²page** n page f; vt paginer, numéroter

**pageant** n spectacle m
**pageantry** n pompe f, apparat m
**pagination** n pagination f
**pagoda** n pagode f
**pail** n seau m
**pailful** n seau m, plein seau
**pain** n douleur f, souffrance f; (mental) peine f; be a ~ in the neck être enquiquinant; be in ~ souffrir, avoir mal; have a ~ in avoir mal à; on ~ of sous peine de; take ~s to se donner du mal pour; vt (mental) faire de la peine à; (physical) faire souffrir
**pained** adj peiné
**painful** adj douloureux -euse
**pain-killer** n calmant m, analgésique m
**painless** adj sans douleur
**painstaking** adj soigneux -euse; (work) soigné
**paint** n peinture f; vt peindre; (describe) dépeindre; med badigeonner; ~ one's face se farder; ~ the town red faire une noce du tonnerre
**paint-box** n boîte f de couleurs
**paint-brush** n pinceau m
**¹painter** n peintre m
**²painter** n naut amarre f
**painting** n peinture f; (picture) tableau m, peinture f
**paint-remover** n décapant m
**paint-sprayer** n pistolet m (à peindre)
**Pakistan** n Pakistan m
**Pakistani** n Pakistanais -e; adj pakistanais
**pal** n coll copain m (f copine)
**palace** n palais m; (of bishop) évêché m
**palatable** adj agréable au goût
**palate** n palais m
**palatial** adj magnifique, grandiose
**palaver** n palabre m
**¹pale** n pieu m, pal m; beyond the ~ au ban de la société
**²pale** adj pâle, blême; ~ blue bleu pâle invar; turn ~ pâlir; vi pâlir
**paleness** n pâleur f
**Palestinian** n Palestinien -ienne; adj palestinien -ienne
**palette** n palette f
**paling** n palissade f, clôture f à claire-voie
**palisade** n palissade f
**¹pall** n drap m mortuaire, poêle m
**²pall** vi devenir fade, s'affadir
**pallbearer** n porteur m d'un cordon du poêle
**palliate** vt pallier, atténuer
**palliative** n palliatif m; adj palliatif -ive
**pallid** adj pâle, blafard, blême
**pallor** n pâleur f
**pally** adj coll be ~ with être copain (f copine) avec
**¹palm** n (tree) palmier m; (branch) palme

**palm**

*f*; **Palm Sunday** le dimanche des
Rameaux
²**palm** *n* (hand) paume *f*; **grease s/o's
~** graisser la patte à qn
³**palm** *vt* (card) escamoter; **~ off** refiler
**palmist** *n* chiromancien -ienne
**palmistry** *n* chiromancie *f*
**palpability** *n* palpabilité *f*; évidence *f*
**palpable** *adj* palpable; clair, évident
**palpate** *vt med* palper
**palpitate** *vi* palpiter
**palsy** *n* paralysie *f*
**paltry** *adj* misérable, mesquin
**pamper** *vt* dorloter, choyer
**pamphlet** *n* brochure *f*; (scurrilous)
pamphlet *m*
¹**pan** *n* casserole *f*, poêlon *m*; (scales)
plateau *m*; (lavatory) cuvette *f*
²**pan** *vt coll* éreinter
**panacea** *n* panacée *f*
**panache** *n* panache *m*, bravoure *f*
**Panama** *n* Panama *m*
**panama** *n* panama *m*
**pancake** *n* crêpe *f*; **~ day** mardi gras;
*aer* **~ landing** atterrissage *m* sur le
ventre
**panchromatic** *adj* panchromatique
**pancreas** *n* pancréas *m*
**panda** *n* panda *m*
**pandemonium** *n* vacarme *m*, pandémo-
nium *m*
**pander** *n* entremetteur -euse; *vi* **~ to**
encourager; (person) flatter bassement
**pane** *n* carreau *m*, vitre *f*
**panegyric** *n* panégyrique *m*
**panel** *n* panneau *m*; *leg* liste *f* du jury,
jury *m*; *vt* diviser en panneaux; recouvrir de panneaux, lambrisser
**panel-beater** *n* tôlier *m*
**panel-game** *n* jeu *m* de groupe
**panelist** *n* membre *m* d'un groupe (dans
un jeu, une discussion)
**panelling** *n* division *f* en panneaux; lambris *m*, boiserie *f*
**pang** *n* douleur *f*; angoisse subite; **~s of
death** affres *fpl* de la mort
**panic** *n* panique *f*, terreur *f*, affolement
*m*; *vt* remplir de panique; *vi* s'affoler,
paniquer
**panicky** *adj* (person) sujet -ette à la panique
**panic-stricken** *adj* affolé, pris de panique
**pannier** *n* panier *m*
**panoply** *n* panoplie *f*
**panorama** *n* panorama *m*
**panoramic** *adj* panoramique
**pansy** *n* pensée *f*; *sl* (homosexual)
tapette *f*
**pant** *vi* haleter; (heart) palpiter; **~ for
sth** soupirer après qch
**pantechnicon** *n* camion *m* de déménagement; (store) garde-meuble *m* (*pl*

garde-meuble(s))
**pantheism** *n* panthéisme *m*
**pantheon** *n* panthéon *m*
**panther** *n* panthère *f*
**panties** *npl* slip *m*
**pantomime** *n* pantomime *f*; revue-féerie
*f* (*pl* revues-féeries) (en Grande-Bretagne à l'époque de Noël)
**pantry** *n* garde-manger *m invar*; **butler's
~ office** *f*
**pants** *npl* caleçon *m*; (short) slip *m*
(d'homme); *US* (trousers) pantalon *m*;
**be caught with one's ~ down** se trouver en mauvaise posture; **kick in the ~**
coup *m* de pied au derrière; *US* **short
~s** culotte *f*, short *m*
**pap** *n* bouillie *f*
**papa** *n* papa *m*
**papacy** *n* papauté *f*
**papal** *adj* papal
**paper** *n* papier *m*; (newspaper) journal
*m*; (essay) article *m*; (exam) composition *f*, épreuve *f*; (learned) mémoire *m*;
**~ bag** sac *m* en papier; **~ money**
billets *mpl* de banque; **it looks good on
~** cela paraît bien en théorie; **old ~s**
paperasse *f*; **read a ~** faire un exposé;
*vt* (room) tapisser; **~ up** recouvrir de
papier
**paperback** *n* livre *m* de poche
**paper-boy** *n* garçon *m* livreur de journaux
**paper-chase** *n* rallye-paper *m*
**paper-clip** *n* trombone *m*
**paper-fastener** *n* agrafe *f*
**paper-knife** *n* coupe-papier *m invar*
**papermill** *n* fabrique *f* de papier, papeterie *f*
**paperweight** *n* presse-papiers *m invar*
**papier-mâché** *n* papier mâché
**papist** *n* papiste
**paprika** *n* paprika *m*
**papyrus** *n* papyrus *m*
**par** *n* pair *m*, égalité *f*; **above (below) ~**
au-dessus (au-dessous) du pair; **at ~**
au pair; **be on a ~ with** aller de pair
avec; **feel below ~** ne pas être dans son
assiette
**parable** *n* parabole *f*
**parabola** *n* parabole *f*
**parachute** *n* parachute *m*; *vt* + *vi* parachuter
**parachutist** *n* parachutiste
**parade** *n* parade *f*; (procession) défilé *m*;
*mil* rassemblement *m*; promenade *f*,
esplanade *f*; **on ~** à l'exercice; *vt* faire
parade de, afficher; *mil* faire défiler; *vi*
parader; défiler
**parade-ground** *n* place *f* d'armes
**paradigm** *n* paradigme *m*
**paradise** *n* paradis *m*
**paradox** *n* paradoxe *m*

616

**paradoxical** *adj* paradoxal
**paraffin** *n* pétrole *m*; *med* paraffine *f*; ~ **lamp** lampe *f* à pétrole; **liquid** ~ huile *f* de paraffine
**paragon** *n* modèle *m*, parangon *m*
**paragraph** *n* paragraphe *m*; *vt* diviser en paragraphes
**parakeet, paroquet** *n* perruche *f*
**parallax** *n astron* parallaxe *f*
**parallel** *adj* parallèle; (similar) semblable, pareil -eille; *vt* égaler
**parallelism** *n* parallélisme *m*
**parallelogram** *n* parallélogramme *m*
**paralyse** *vt* paralyser
**paralysis** *n* paralysie *f*; **creeping** ~ paralysie progressive; **infantile** ~ poliomyélite *f*
**paralytic** *adj* paralytique
**para-military** *adj* paramilitaire
**paramount** *adj* souverain, éminent; **of** ~ **importance** de première importance
**paranoia** *n* paranoia *f*
**paranoiac** *n* + *adj* paranoïaque
**parapet** *n* parapet *m*; (safety wall) garde-fou *m*
**paraphernalia** *npl* attirail *m*, effets *mpl*; **all the** ~ tout le bataclan
**paraphrase** *n* paraphrase *f*; *vt* paraphraser
**paraplegic** *adj* paraplégique
**parasite** *n* parasite *m*; (sponger) pique-assiette *m invar*
**parasitic(al)** *adj* parasite; (illness) parasitaire
**parasol** *n* ombrelle *f*, parasol *m*
**paratrooper** *n* (soldat *m*) parachutiste *m*
**paratroops** *npl* (soldats *mpl*) parachutistes *mpl*
**paratyphoid** *n* paratyphoïde *f*
**parcel** *n* paquet *m*, colis *m*; (ground) parcelle *f*; ~ **post** service *m* des colis postaux; **send sth by** ~ **post** envoyer qch comme colis postal; *vt* ~ **out** partager, morceler; ~ **up** emballer, empaqueter
**parch** *vt* sécher, dessécher; **be** ~**ed with thirst** avoir une soif terrible; *vi* se dessécher
**parchment** *n* parchemin *m*
**pardon** *n* pardon *m*; **I beg your** ~ je vous demande pardon; *vt* (crime, etc) pardonner; ~ **s/o** pardonner à qn; *leg* gracier qn
**pardonable** *adj* pardonnable, excusable
**pare** *vt* (nails) rogner; (fruit, etc) éplucher, peler; ~ **down** rogner
**parent** *n* (father) père *m*; (mother) mère *f*; ~ **s** père *m* et mère *f*; ~ **establishment** maison *f* mère
**parentage** *n* naissance *f*, origine *f*
**parental** *adj* des parents, paternel -elle, maternel -elle

**parenthesis** *n* parenthèse *f*
**parenthood** *n* paternité *f*, maternité *f*
**pariah** *n* paria *m*
**paring** *n* rognage *m*; ~**s** rognures *fpl*
**Paris** *n* Paris *m*
**parish** *n* paroisse *f*; (civil) commune *f*; ~ **priest** (catholic) curé *m*; (protestant) pasteur *m*
**parishioner** *n* paroissien -ienne
**parish-pump** *adj* d'intérêt local
**Parisian** *n* Parisien -ienne; *adj* parisien -ienne
**parity** *n* égalité *f*, parité *f*
**park** *n* parc *m*, jardin public; **car** ~ parc *m* de stationnement, parking *m*; *vt* enfermer dans un parc; *mot* garer, parquer; ~ **oneself** s'installer; *vi* stationner, se garer
**parking** *n* stationnement *m*; ~ **attendant** gardien *m* d'autos; ~ **lights** feux *mpl* de position; ~ **lot** (place) parc *m* de stationnement; ~ **ticket** papillon *m*
**parking-meter** *n* parc(o)mètre *m*
**Parkinson** *n* ~ **'s disease** maladie *f* de Parkinson
**parlance** *n* langage *m*
**parley** *n* pourparlers *mpl*; *vi* parlementer
**parliament** *n* parlement *m*
**parliamentarian** *n* + *adj* parlementaire
**parliamentary** *adj* parlementaire
**parlour** *n* petit salon, parloir *m*; *US* salon *m*
**parlous** *adj* précaire, dangereux -euse; alarmant
**parochial** *adj eccles* paroissial; communal; *pej* provincial
**parochialism** *n* esprit *m* de clocher
**parody** *n* parodie *f*, pastiche *m*
**parole** *n* parole *f* (d'honneur); **be put on** ~ être libéré sur parole
**paroquet** *n see* **parakeet**
**paroxysm** *n* paroxysme *m*, crise *f*
**parquet** *n* parquet *m*
**parricide** *n* (person) parricide; (crime) parricide *m*
**parrot** *n* perroquet *m*
**parry** *vt* parer, détourner
**parsimonious** *adj* parcimonieux -ieuse
**parsimony** *n* parcimonie *f*
**parsley** *n* persil *m*
**parsnip** *n* panais *m*
**parson** *n* (protestant) pasteur *m*
**parsonage** *n* presbytère *m*
**¹part** *n* partie *f*; (share) part *f*; (side) parti *m*; (district) quartier *m*; (region) région *f*; *theat* rôle *m*; ~ **and parcel** partie intégrante; **a man of** ~**s** un homme très doué; **for my** ~ quant à moi; **have no** ~ **in sth** n'y être pour rien; **in** ~ partiellement, en partie; **in these** ~**s** dans cette région; **take** ~ **in** prendre part à; **take sth in good** ~ prendre qch

en bonne part; *adv* partiellement, en partie

²**part** *vt* séparer (en deux); (divide) diviser; ~ one's hair se faire une raie; *vi* se séparer, se diviser, se quitter; (break) céder; ~ with céder

**partake** *vi* ~ of (in) sth participer à qch

**partial** *adj* partiel -ielle; (unjust) partial; be ~ to aimer bien

**partiality** *n* (bias) partialité *f*; (fondness) prédilection *f*

**partially** *adv* en partie; (unjustly) partialement

**participant** *n* + *adj* participant -e

**participate** *vi* participer, prendre part

**participation** *n* participation *f*

**participle** *n* participe *m*

**particle** *n* particule *f*

**parti-coloured** *adj* bigarré

**particular** *n* détail *m*; ~s détails *mpl*, renseignements *mpl*; (personal) coordonnées *fpl*; *adj* particulier -ière, spécial; (fussy) difficile; (careful) minutieux -ieuse, méticuleux -euse; (exact) précis, exact; a ~ friend un ami (*f* une amie) intime; he's very ~ about it il y tient beaucoup; nothing ~ rien de spécial

**particularity** *n* particularité *f*

**particularize** *vt* particulariser

**parting** *n* séparation *f*; (leaving) départ *m*; (farewell) adieux *mpl*; (hair) raie *f*; *adj* d'adieu; (last) dernier -ière

**partisan, partizan** *n* partisan *m*; *adj* de parti pris

**partition** *n* partage *m*; (wall) cloison *f*; *vt* partager, morceler; ~ a room cloisonner une pièce

**partly** *adv* partiellement, en partie

**partner** *n* associé -e; (games) partenaire; (dance, outing) cavalier -ière, danseur -euse; sleeping ~ commanditaire *m*; *vt* être associé à; *sp* être le (*f* la) partenaire de

**partnership** *n* association *f*; take s/o into ~ prendre qn comme associé

**part-owner** *n* copropriétaire

**partridge** *n* perdrix *f*; (young) perdreau *m*

**part-song** *n* chanson *f* à plusieurs voix

**part-time** *n* + *adj* ~ work travail *m* à mi-temps; be on ~ être en chômage partiel

**party** *n* parti *m*; (pleasure) partie *f*; (group) bande *f*, groupe *m*; (accomplice) complice *m*; (telephone) ~ line ligne partagée; ~ politics politique *f* de partis; ~ wall mur mitoyen; a third ~ un tiers; be a small ~ être peu nombreux -euse; be no ~ to sth ne pas s'associer à qch; private ~ réunion *f* intime; third ~ insurance assurance *f*

au tiers

¹**pass** *n* (mountain) col *m*, défilé *m*

²**pass** *n* passe *f*; (permit) permis *m*, laissez-passer *m invar*; come to a pretty ~ être dans un bel état; *coll* make a ~ at faire des avances à; obtain a ~ obtenir la moyenne; *fig* sell the ~ vendre la mèche

³**pass** *vt* passer; franchir; (overtake) dépasser; *mot* doubler; (from opposite direction) croiser; (exam) être reçu à; (candidate) recevoir; (approve) approuver; (law) adopter; (hand over) transmettre, donner; ~ a remark faire une observation; ~ off for faire passer pour; ~ sentence prononcer le jugement; ~ sth on répéter qch; (hand on) transmettre qch; ~ sth round faire circuler qch; *coll* ~ the buck se débrouiller sur le voisin; ~ through traverser; ~ water uriner; *vi* passer; (time) s'écouler; (storm) se dissiper; ~ along! circulez!, avancez!; ~ away (die) mourir; disparaître; ~ off se passer; ~ on passer son chemin; ~ out s'évanouir; come to ~ arriver; that will never ~ ça ne prendra jamais

**passable** *adj* passable; (road) praticable

**passage** *n* passage *m*; (sea) traversée *f*; (corridor) couloir *m*, corridor *m*; (small street) ruelle *f*; (fare) prix *m* du billet; (music) morceau *m*; have a rough (sea) ~ faire une mauvaise traversée; *fig* avoir beaucoup de mal

**pass-book** *n* carnet *m* de banque

**passé** *adj* passé de mode; (faded) défraîchi

**passenger** *n* (by sea or air, in car) passager -ère; (by train) voyageur -euse; *coll* be a ~ être la cinquième roue du carrosse

**passer-by** *n* passant -e

**passion** *n* passion *f*; (love) amour *m*; (fury) emportement *m*, colère *f*; fly into a ~ se mettre en colère

**passionate** *adj* passionné; (angry) emporté, irascible

**passion-flower** *n* fleur *f* de la passion

**passive** *n gramm* passif *m*; *adj* passif -ive

**passivity** *n* passivité *f*

**pass-key** *n* passe-partout *m invar*; *coll* passe *m*

**Passover** *n* Pâque *f* (des Juifs)

**passport** *n* passeport *m*

**password** *n* mot *m* de passe

¹**past** *n* passé *m*; be a thing of the ~ ne plus exister; in the ~ autrefois, au passé; *adj* passé, ancien -ienne; (recent) dernier -ière; for some time ~ depuis quelque temps

²**past** *prep* au-delà de; (more than) plus de; *coll* be ~ caring s'en ficher

complètement; *coll* **be ~ it** être trop
vieux (*f* vieille), ne plus y arriver; **five
~ four** quatre heures cinq; **go ~**
passer devant; **half ~ five** cinq heures
et demie; **it's ~ belief** c'est incroyable;
**I wouldn't put it ~ him** il en est bien
capable; **just ~ the house** un peu plus
loin que la maison
**paste** *n* (glue) colle *f*; pâte *f*; **tooth ~**
pâte *f* dentifrice; *vt* coller
**pastel** *n* pastel *m*; crayon *m* pastel,
couleur *f* pastel
**pasteurize** *vt* pasteuriser
**pastiche** *n* pastiche *m*
**pastille** *n* pastille *f*
**pastime** *n* passe-temps *m invar*
**past-master** *n* expert *m*
**pastor** *n* pasteur *m*
**pastoral** *n* pastorale *f*; poème pastoral;
*adj* pastoral
**pastry** *n* pâtisserie *f*; (for cooking) pâte
*f*; *US* **~ shop** pâtisserie *f*
**pastry-cook** *n* pâtissier -ière *f*
**pasture** *n* pâturage *m*; *vt* faire paître; *vi*
paître
¹**pasty** *n* petit pâté
²**pasty** *adj* pâteux -euse; pâle
¹**pat** *n* tape *f*; caresse *f*; (butter) coquille
*f*; *fig* **give s/o a ~ on the back** encourager qn; *vt* taper, tapoter; caresser;
(animal) flatter
²**pat** *adv* à propos; **answer ~** répondre
sur-le-champ
**patch** *n* pièce *f*; (land) parcelle *f*; (tyre)
pastille *f*; (colour) tache *f*; (vegetable)
carré *m*; **strike a bad ~** être en déveine;
**that's not a ~ on mine** ce n'est rien à
côté du mien (*f* de la mienne); *vt* rapiécer, raccommoder; **~ up** rafistoler
**patchiness** *n* manque *m* d'harmonie
**patchwork** *n* rapiéçage *m*; ouvrage fait
de pièces et de morceaux d'étoffe
**patchy** *adj* inégal
**pâté** *n* pâté *m*
**patent** *n* brevet *m* d'invention; (thing
patented) invention brevetée; **take out
a ~ on sth** faire breveter qch; *adj* (obvious) manifeste; (patented) breveté;
**~ leather** cuir verni; **~ medicine**
spécialité *f* pharmaceutique; *vt* faire
breveter
**patently** *adv* manifestement
**paternal** *adj* paternel -elle
**paternalism** *n* paternalisme *m*
**paternally** *adv* paternellement
**paternity** *n* paternité *f*
**path** *n* chemin *m*, sentier *m*; (garden)
allée *f*; (route) route *f*; (course) course
*f*, trajectoire *f*; (orbit) orbite *f*
**pathetic** *adj* touchant, pathétique; *coll*
pitoyable
**pathfinder** *n* pionnier *m*

**pathological** *adj* pathologique
**pathologist** *n* pathologiste; *leg* médecin
*m* légiste
**pathology** *n* pathologie *f*
**pathos** *n* pathétique *m*
**pathway** *n* sentier *m*
**patience** *n* patience *f*; (cards) réussite *f*;
**his ~ is exhausted** il est à bout de patience; **play ~** faire des réussites
**patient** *n* malade, patient -e; *adj* patient
**patina** *n* patine *f*
**patio** *n* patio *m*
**patois** *n* patois *m*
**patriarch** *n* patriarche *m*
**patrician** *n* patricien -ienne
**patricide** *n* (person) parricide; (crime)
parricide *m*
**patrimony** *n* patrimoine *m*
**patriot** *n* patriote
**patriotic** *adj* patriote
**patriotism** *n* patriotisme *m*
**patrol** *n* patrouille *f*; *US* **~ wagon** voiture *f* cellulaire; *vt* faire la patrouille
dans; *vi* patrouiller
**patrol-car** *n* voiture policière, voiture pie
*f* (*pl* voitures pie)
**patron** *n* protecteur *m*; (arts) mécène *m*;
(charity) patron *m*; (customer) client
-e; **~ saint** patron -onne
**patronage** *n* protection *f*, patronage *m*;
(of establishment) clientèle *f*
**patroness** *n* (arts) protectrice *f*; (charity)
patronnesse *f*
**patronize** *vt* patronner; (artist) protéger;
(shop) accorder sa clientèle à; (be condescending) traiter d'un air protecteur
**patronymic** *n* nom *m* patronymique,
patronyme *m*; *adj* patronymique
¹**patter** *n* petit bruit de pas; (rain) fouettement *m*; *vi* trottiner; (rain) fouetter
²**patter** *n* (fast sales talk) boniment *m*, *sl*
baratin *m*; (chatter) bavardage *m*; *vi*
bavarder sans arrêt, caqueter
**pattern** *n* modèle *m*; (design) dessin *m*;
(sample) échantillon *m*; (paper) patron
*m*; *vt* façonner, modeler
**paucity** *n* manque *m*, rareté *f*
**paunch** *n* ventre *m*, panse *f*, *coll* bedaine
*f*
**pauper** *n* indigent -e
**pause** *n* pause *f*; hésitation *f*; **give ~ to**
faire hésiter; *vi* faire une pause,
s'arrêter (un instant); hésiter; **make s/o
~** donner à réfléchir à qn
**pave** *vt* paver; **~ the way** ouvrir la voie,
préparer le terrain
**pavement** *n* trottoir *m*; pavé *m*; *US*
chaussée *f*
**pavilion** *n* pavillon *f*
**paving** *n* dallage *m*; **~ stone** pavé *m*
**paw** *n* patte *f*; *sl* **~s off!** bas les pattes!; *vt*
(horse) piaffer; *coll pej* tripoter, peloter

**pawl** n mech cliquet m

**¹pawn** n gage m; vt mettre en gage, engager

**²pawn** n (chess) pion m

**pawnbroker** n prêteur -euse sur gages

**pawnshop** n mont-de-piété m (pl monts-de-piété), établissement m de prêt sur gages

**pawn-ticket** n reconnaissance f (de dépôt sur gages)

**pay** n paie f, salaire m, traitement m; (wages) gages mpl; mil solde f; US ~ phone téléphone public; US ~ station cabine f téléphonique; holidays with ~ congés payés; in the ~ of à la solde de; vt payer; (visit) faire, rendre; (bill) régler, acquitter; ~ attention faire attention; ~ back rembourser, rendre; ~ dearly payer cher; ~ for sth payer qch; ~ in (to bank) verser; ~ off (debts) acquitter; (dismiss) congédier; ~ one's way se suffire, joindre les deux bouts; ~ out débourser; coll ~ through the nose payer le prix fort; I'll ~ him for that je le lui paierai; it ~s him to ... il gagne à ...; vi payer, être rentable

**payable** adj payable

**pay-as-you-earn** n (système m de) retenue f de l'impôt à la source

**pay-day** n jour m de paie

**payee** n bénéficiaire

**pay-envelope** n US enveloppe f contenant la paie de la semaine

**pay-load** n charge commerciale

**payment** n paiement m; (instalment) versement m; (settlement) règlement m

**pay-off** n paiement (versement) final; fig le fin mot de l'histoire

**pay-packet** n enveloppe f contenant la paie de la semaine

**pay-roll** n liste f des employé(e)s (d'une compagnie, etc); he is on the ~ il émarge au budget

**pay-slip** n feuille f de paie

**pea** n pois m; be as like as two ~s se ressembler comme deux gouttes d'eau; green ~s petits pois; split ~s pois cassés

**peace** n paix f; (of mind) tranquillité f; at ~ en paix; break the ~ troubler l'ordre public; hold one's ~ se taire, garder le silence; sleep in ~ dormir tranquille

**peaceable** adj pacifique

**peaceful** adj paisible, calme

**peacemaker** n pacificateur -trice

**peace-offering** n cadeau m de réconciliation

**¹peach** n pêche f; (tree) pêcher m

**²peach** vi sl moucharder

**peacock** n paon m

**pea-green** adj vert feuille invar

**peahen** n paonne f

**peak** n cime f, pic m; (cap) visière f; (high point) pointe f, apogée f; ~ hours heures fpl de pointe; ~ load charge f maximum

**peaked** adj à visière

**peal** n (bells) carillon m; (thunder) coup m, grondement m; ~ of laughter éclat m de rire; vt sonner à toute volée; vi (bells) carillonner; (thunder) gronder

**peanut** n arachide f, cacahouète f; coll ~s rien du tout

**pear** n poire f; (tree) poirier m

**pearl** n perle f; mother of ~ nacre f

**pearl-barley** n orge perlé

**pearl-diver** n pêcheur -euse de perles

**peasant** n paysan -anne, campagnard -e

**pea-shooter** n sarbacane f

**pea-souper** n brouillard m jaune

**peat** n tourbe f

**peat-bog** n tourbière f

**pebble** n caillou m; (on beach) galet m; fig you're not the only ~ on the beach vous n'êtes pas unique au monde

**pebble-dash** n crépi m

**pebbly** adj caillouteux -euse; ~ beach plage f de galets

**peccadillo** n peccadille f, vétille f

**peck** n coup m de bec; (kiss) bise f, bécot m; vt donner des coups (un coup) de bec à; (bird) picoter

**peckish** adj be ~ avoir faim; feel ~ avoir le ventre creux

**pectoral** adj pectoral

**peculation** n détournement m de fonds

**peculiar** adj particulier -ière, spécial; (unusual) étrange, singulier -ière; (odd) bizarre

**peculiarity** n particularité f, singularité f; (oddness) bizarrerie f

**pecuniary** adj pécuniaire

**pedagogic** adj pédagogique

**pedagogue** n pédagogue; pej pédant -e

**pedagogy** n pédagogie f

**pedal** n pédale f; vi pédaler

**pedant** n pédant -e

**pedantic** adj (person) pédant; (thing) pédantesque

**pedantry** n pédantisme m

**peddle** vt colporter; vi faire le (du) colportage

**pederast** n see paederast

**pederasty** n see paederasty

**pedestal** n piédestal m, socle m

**pedestrian** n piéton m; adj pédestre; fig prosaïque; ~ crossing passage clouté

**pediatrician** n see paediatrician

**pediatrics** n see paediatrics

**pedigree** n généalogie f; (tree) arbre m généalogique; (certificate) pedigree m; adj de race

**pedlar** *n* colporteur *m*; **drug ~** trafiquant *m* en stupéfiants

**pee** *vi coll* faire pipi

**peek** *n* + *vi see* ¹**peep**

**peel** *n* pelure *f*, écorce *f*, peau *f*; *cul* zeste *m*; *vt* peler, éplucher; **~ off one's clothes** se déshabiller; *vi* peler; (paint) s'écailler

**peeler** *n* (person) éplucheur -euse; (thing) éplucheur *m*

**peelings** *npl* épluchures *fpl*

¹**peep** *n* coup *m* d'œil; **at ~ of day** au point du jour; *vi* donner un coup d'œil; **~ at sth** regarder quelque chose à la dérobée; **~ out** se montrer, se laisser entrevoir

²**peep** *n* pépiement *m*; *vi* (bird) pépier; (mouse) crier

**peep-hole** *n* judas *m*

¹**peer** *n* pair *m*; (equal) pareil -eille

²**peer** *vi* **~ at** scruter du regard

**peerage** *n* (rank) pairie *f*; *collect* noblesse *f*

**peeress** *n* pairesse *f*

**peerless** *adj* sans pareil -eille, incomparable

**peeve** *vt* irriter, vexer, fâcher

**peevish** *adj* grognon -onne, grincheux -euse

**peevishness** *n* mauvaise humeur

**peewit** *see* pewit

**peg** *n* cheville *f*; (for clothes) patère *f*; épingle *f*; *coll* (drink) coup *m*; **be a square ~ in a round hole** n'être pas dans son emploi; **clothes off the ~** vêtements *mpl* de confection; **take s/o down a ~** remettre qn à sa place; *vt* cheviller; (prices) stabiliser; *vi* **~ away at sth** persévérer à qch, travailler ferme à qch; *coll* **~ out** casser sa pipe

**pejorative** *adj* péjoratif -ive

**pekinese, pekingese** *n* (chien *m*) pékinois *m*

**pelican** *n* pélican *m*

**pellet** *n* boulette *f*; *med* pilule *f*; (lead shot) grain *m* de plomb

**pell-mell** *adj* en désordre; *adv* pêle-mêle

**pellucid** *adj* transparent, pellucide, clair, lucide

**pelmet** *n* lambrequin *m*

¹**pelt** *n* peau *f*, fourrure *f*

²**pelt** *n* **at full ~** à toute vitesse; *vt* lancer à, lancer contre; *vi* tomber à verse; **~ along** aller à toute vitesse; **~ing rain** pluie battante

**pelvis** *n* bassin *m*

**pemmican** *n* pemmican *m*

¹**pen** *n* enclos *m*, parc *m*; *US* (cattle) étable *f*, (pigs) porcherie *f*; *vt* (animals) parquer; (people) confiner

²**pen** *n* plume *f*; **make a living by one's ~** vivre de sa plume; *vt* écrire

**penal** *adj* (law) pénal; (crime) qui entraîne une pénalité; **~ servitude** travaux forcés

**penalize** *vt sp* pénaliser; infliger une peine à

**penalty** *n* peine *f*, pénalité *f*; (fine) amende *f*; (rugby) pénalité *f*; (soccer) penalty *m* (*pl* penalties); **death ~** peine *f* de mort

**penance** *n* pénitence *f*

**penchant** *n* penchant *m*

**pencil** *n* crayon *m*; **~ of light** faisceau lumineux; **in ~** au crayon; **propelling ~** porte-mines *m invar*; *vt* marquer au crayon; (draw) dessiner au crayon; **~ a note** crayonner un billet

**pencil-sharpener** *n* taille-crayon(s) *m invar*

**pendant, pendent** *n* (necklace) pendentif *m*; (lamp) pendeloque *f*; (counterpart) pendant *m*; *adj* suspendu

**pending** *adj leg* en instance; *prep* en attendant

**pendulous** *adj* pendant; (swinging) oscillant

**pendulum** *n* pendule *m*, balancier *m*

**penetrability** *n* pénétrabilité *f*

**penetrable** *adj* pénétrable

**penetrate** *vt* + *vi* pénétrer

**penetrating** *adj* pénétrant

**penetration** *n* pénétration *f*; perspicacité *f*

**pen-friend** *n* correspondant -e

**penguin** *n* pingouin *m*

**pen-holder** *n* porte-plume *m invar*

**penicillin** *n* pénicilline *f*

**peninsula** *n* péninsule *f*, presqu'île *f*

**penis** *n* pénis *m*

**penitence** *n* pénitence *f*

**penitent** *n* + *adj* pénitent -e

**penitential** *adj* pénitentiel -ielle

**penitentiary** *n* pénitencier *m*, prison *f*

**penitently** *adv* d'un air contrit

**penknife** *n* canif *m*

**penmanship** *n* calligraphie *f*

**pen-name** *n* pseudonyme *m*

**pennant** *n* flamme *f*

**penniless** *adj* sans le sou

**penny** *n* penny *m*; *fig* deux sous *mpl*; **~ dreadful** roman *m* à quatre sous; **cost a pretty ~** coûter cher; **he's a bad ~** c'est un mauvais sujet; **spend a ~** faire pipi; *coll* **the ~ has dropped** ça y est, il a compris (elle a compris, etc)

**penny-in-the-slot (machine)** *n* distributeur *m* automatique; (entertainment) machine *f* à sous

**penny-wise** *adj* qui fait des économies de bouts de chandelle

**pension** *n* pension *f*, retraite *f*; (boarding-house) pension *f* (de famille); **old-age ~** retraite *f* de vieillesse (des vieux); retire on a ~ prendre sa retraite; *vt* pensionner; ~ off mettre à la retraite

**pensionable** *adj* ayant droit à une pension

**pensioner** *n* retraité -e, titulaire d'une pension

**pensive** *adj* pensif -ive, songeur -euse

**pent** *adj* ~ up enfermé

**pentagon** *n* pentagone *m*

**pentathlon** *n* pentathlon *m*

**Pentecost** *n* la Pentecôte

**penthouse** *n* appentis *m*; ~ flat appartement *m* sur le toit, entouré d'une terrasse; ~ roof auvent *m*

**penultimate** *adj* avant-dernier -ière, pénultième

**penumbra** *n* pénombre *f*

**penurious** *adj* (poor) pauvre; (stingy) mesquin, parcimonieux -ieuse

**penury** *n* (poverty) indigence *f*; (shortage) pénurie *f*

**peony, paeony** *n* pivoine *f*

**people** *n* (of a country) nation *f*, peuple *m*; gens *mpl* or *fpl*; (citizens) citoyens *mpl*, habitants *mpl*; (persons) personnes *fpl*; (crowd) monde *m*; *coll* (relatives) parents *mpl*; ~ say on dit; *vt* peupler

**pep** *n coll* allant *m*, entrain *m*; *vt* ~ s/o up ragaillardir qn; ~ sth up donner de l'entrain à qch

**pepper** *n* poivre *m*; *vt* poivrer; *fig* cribler

**peppercorn** *n* grain *m* de poivre; ~ rent loyer nominal

**pepper-mill** *n* moulin *m* à poivre

**peppermint** *n* bonbon *m* à la menthe

**pepper-pot** *n* poivrier *m*

**peppery** *adj* poivré; *fig* irascible

**pep-talk** *n* petit discours d'encouragement

**peptic** *adj* peptique

**per** *prep* par; ~ annum par an; ~ capita par tête; ~ cent pour cent; as ~ conformément à

**perambulate** *vt* parcourir, inspecter; *vi* se promener

**perambulator** *n* voiture *f* d'enfant, landau *m*

**perceivable** *adj* perceptible

**perceive** *vt* percevoir; (notice) s'apercevoir de

**percentage** *n* pourcentage *m*, proportion *f*

**perceptibility** *n* perceptibilité *f*

**perceptible** *adj* perceptible

**perception** *n* perception *f*; (sensitiveness) sensibilité *f*

**perceptive** *adj* perceptif -ive

**perceptivity** *n* perceptivité *f*

¹**perch** *n* perchoir *m*; *vi* (se) percher, jucher

²**perch** *n* (fish) perche *f*

**percipient** *n* sujet *m* télépathique; *adj* percepteur -trice

**percolate** *vt* filtrer, passer; *vi* filtrer, percoler

**percolator** *n* filtre *m* à café

**percussion** *n* percussion *f*; ~ cap amorce *f*; *mus* ~ instruments batterie *f*

**perdition** *n* perdition *f*, ruine *f*, perte *f*

**peregrination** *n* pérégrination *f*

**peremptoriness** *n* intransigeance *f*

**peremptory** *adj* péremptoire; (total) absolu

**perennial** *n bot* plante *f* vivace; *adj* (constant) perpétuel -elle; *bot* vivace

**perfect** *n gramm* parfait *m*; in the ~ (tense) au parfait; *adj* parfait; *coll* (first-rate) impeccable; *vt* achever, parachever; (make perfect) perfectionner, rendre parfait; (device) mettre au point

**perfectibility** *n* perfectibilité *f*

**perfectible** *adj* perfectible

**perfection** *n* perfection *f*; (finishing) achèvement *m*, accomplissement *m*; to ~ à la perfection

**perfectionism** *n* perfectionnisme *m*

**perfectly** *adv* parfaitement; tout à fait

**perfidious** *adj* perfide, traître -esse

**perfidy** *n* perfidie *f*

**perforate** *vt* percer; *med* perforer

**perforation** *n* perforation *f*; (piercing) percement *m*; (little hole) petit trou

**perforce** *adv* forcément

**perform** *vt* accomplir, exécuter, effectuer; (ceremony) célébrer; *theat* jouer, représenter; (dance) exécuter; (role) remplir

**performance** *n mus* exécution *f*; *theat* représentation *f*; *cin* séance *f*; (task) accomplissement *m*; (action) action *f*, exploit *m*; *sp* performance *f*; (ceremony) célébration *f*; (machine) fonctionnement *m*, marche *f*; afternoon ~ matinée *f*; *cin* continuous ~ spectacle permanent; evening ~ soirée *f*; no ~ relâche *f*

**performer** *n* artiste; *theat* acteur -trice; *mus* exécutant -e

**perfume** *n* parfum *m*; *vt* parfumer

**perfunctory** *adj* (person) négligent, léger -ère; (examination) fait pour la forme

**perhaps** *adv* peut-être

**peril** *n* péril *m*, danger *m*; at one's own ~ à ses risques et périls

**perilous** *adj* périlleux -euse, dangereux -euse

**perimeter** *n* périmètre *m*

**period** *n* période *f*, durée *f*; (school) cours *m*, heure *f* de cours; époque *f*, âge *m*; *gramm* point *m*; *med* ~ (s) règles *fpl*; *US* I'm not going, ~ je n'y vais pas, un point c'est tout

**periodic** *adj* périodique

**periodical** *n* publication *f* périodique, périodique *m*; *adj* périodique

**periodicity** *n* périodicité *f*

**peripatetic** *adj* péripatéticien -ienne, péripatétique

**peripheral** *adj* périphérique

**periphery** *n* périphérie *f*

**periphrasis** *n* périphrase *f*

**periscope** *n* périscope *m*

**perish** *vi* mourir, périr; (substance) se détériorer

**perishable** *adj* périssable

**perished** *adj* détérioré

**perishing** *adj coll* it's ~ cold il fait un froid de canard

**peritonitis** *n* péritonite *f*

¹**periwinkle** *n bot* pervenche *f*

²**periwinkle** *n* bigorneau *m*

**perjure** *vt* ~ oneself se parjurer

**perjurer** *n* parjure

**perjury** *n* parjure *m*; commit ~ faire (rendre) un faux témoignage

¹**perk** *n sl* avantage *m*, casuel *m*

²**perk** *vt* ~ s/o up requinquer qn; *vi* ~ up se ranimer, redresser la tête

**perky** *adj* éveillé

**perm** *n coll* permanente *f*; *vt coll* have one's hair ~ed se faire faire une permanente

**permanence** *n* permanence *f*, stabilité *f*

**permanency** *n* emploi permanent

**permanent** *adj* permanent; ~ address résidence *f* fixe

**permeability** *n* perméabilité *f*

**permeable** *adj* perméable

**permeate** *vt* pénétrer, s'insinuer dans; *vi* pénétrer, s'insinuer

**permissible** *adj* permis, autorisé

**permission** *n* permission *f*, autorisation *f*

**permit** *n* permis *m*, autorisation *f*; (customs) passavant *m*; *vt* permettre, autoriser; ~ s/o to do sth permettre à qn de faire qch; *vi* this ~s of no reply cela n'admet pas de réplique

**permutation** *n* permutation *f*

**pernicious** *adj* pernicieux -ieuse

**pernickety** *adj* (person) pointilleux -euse, difficile; (task) délicat

**perorate** *vi* pérorer

**peroration** *n* péroraison *f*

**peroxide** *n* peroxyde *m*, eau oxygénée

**perpendicular** *n* fil *m* à plomb; (line) perpendiculaire *f*; *adj* perpendiculaire

**perpetrate** *vt* perpétrer, commettre

**perpetrator** *n* auteur *m*

**perpetual** *adj* perpétuel -elle, éternel -elle

**perpetuate** *vt* perpétuer

**perpetuation** *n* perpétuation *f*

**perpetuity** *n* perpétuité *f*

**perplex** *vt* embarrasser

**perplexed** *adj* perplexe

**perplexity** *n* embarras *m*, perplexité *f*

**perquisite** *n* avantage *m*, casuel *m*

**perry** *n* cidre *m* de poire

**persecute** *vt* persécuter; tourmenter

**persecution** *n* persécution *f*

**persecutor** *n* persécuteur -trice

**perseverance** *n* persévérance *f*

**persevere** *vi* persévérer

**persevering** *adj* assidu, persévérant

**Persian** *n* Persan -e; *adj* persan; ~ Gulf golfe *m* Persique

**persimmon** *n bot* kaki *m*

**persist** *vi* persister, s'obstiner; (continue) continuer

**persistence, persistency** *n* persistance *f*, obstination *f*

**persistent** *adj* persistant, tenace

**person** *n* personne *f*; (often *pej*) individu *m*; ~s gens *mpl*; in ~ en personne

**personable** *adj* qui présente bien, bien fait de sa personne

**personage** *n* personnage *m*, personnalité *f*

**personal** *adj* personnel -elle; ~ property biens mobiliers; don't be ~ ne faites pas de personnalités; make a ~ application se présenter en personne

**personality** *n* personnalité *f*, personnage *m*

**personalize** *vt* (personify) personnifier; personnaliser

**personally** *adv* personnellement; (for my part) pour moi, quant à moi

**personalty** *n leg* biens meubles *mpl*

**personification** *n* personnification *f*

**personify** *vt* personnifier; she is stupidity personified elle est la stupidité même

**personnel** *n* personnel *m*

**perspective** *n* perspective *f*; see a matter in its true ~ voir une affaire sous son vrai jour

**perspex** *n* perspex *m*

**perspicacious** *adj* perspicace

**perspicacity** *n* perspicacité *f*, discernement *m*

**perspicuity** *n* clarté *f*, lucidité *f*

**perspicuous** *adj* lucide, clair

**perspiration** *n* transpiration *f*; bathed in ~ trempé de sueur

**perspire** *vi* transpirer

**persuade** *vt* persuader, convaincre; ~ s/o to do sth persuader qn de faire qch

**persuasion** *n* persuasion *f*; (conviction) croyance *f*, conviction *f*; (religious) confession *f*

**persuasive** *adj* persuasif -ive

**pert** *adj* effronté, impertinent

**pertain** *vi* appartenir; ~ **ing to** ayant rapport à
**pertinacious** *adj* obstiné, entêté, opiniâtre
**pertinacity** *n* obstination *f*, entêtement *m*, opiniâtreté *f*
**pertinence, pertinency** *n* pertinence *f*, à-propos *m*
**pertinent** *adj* pertinent, à propos
**pertly** *adv* avec impertinence, d'un air effronté
**pertness** *n* effronterie *f*, impertinence *f*
**perturb** *vt* inquiéter, troubler
**perturbation** *n* inquiétude *f*, trouble *m*
**Peru** *n* Pérou *m*
**perusal** *n* lecture *f*, examen *m*
**peruse** *vt* lire attentivement, examiner
**pervade** *vt* pénétrer, s'infiltrer dans, se répandre dans
**pervasion** *n* pénétration *f*, infiltration *f*
**pervasive** *adj* pénétrant
**perverse** *adj* pervers, méchant; (wayward) contrariant
**perverseness, perversity** *n* perversité *f*; (contrariness) caractère *m* revêche
**perversion** *n* perversion *f*; ~ **of justice** travestissement *m* de la vérité
**perversity** *n see* perverseness
**pervert** *n* perverti -e; *vt* pervertir; dépraver; détourner
**perverter** *n* pervertisseur -euse
**pessary** *n* pessaire *m*
**pessimism** *n* pessimisme *m*
**pessimist** *n* pessimiste
**pessimistic** *adj* pessimiste
**pest** *n ent* insecte *m* nuisible; (plague) fléau *m*, peste *f*; **he's an absolute** ~ ! quel casse-pieds, celui-là!
**pester** *vt* tourmenter, ennuyer, importuner
**pesticide** *n* pesticide *m*
**pestiferous** *adj* pestifère; nuisible
**pestilence** *n* peste *f*
**pestilential** *adj* pestilentiel -ielle; (disease) contagieux -ieuse; (idea) pernicieux -ieuse
**pestle** *n* pilon *m*
**¹pet** *n* animal familier; enfant gâté, enfant choyé; **my** ~ mon petit chou; *adj* favori, choyé; ~ **aversion** bête noire; ~ **name** nom *m* d'amitié; *vt* choyer, chouchouter; *coll* peloter
**²pet** *n* accès *m* de mauvaise humeur
**petal** *n* pétale *m*
**Peter** *n* Pierre *m*
**peter** *vi* ~ **out** s'épuiser, disparaître; (plan) s'en aller en fumée
**petite** *adj* petite *f*
**petition** *n* pétition *f*, supplique *f*, requête *f*; ~ **for divorce** demande en divorce; *vt* présenter (adresser) une pétition (requête) à

**petrel** *n* pétrel *m*; *fig* **stormy** ~ émissaire *m* de discorde
**petrify** *vt* pétrifier; *vi* se pétrifier
**petrochemical** *adj* pétrochimique
**petrol** *n* essence *f*; **premium grade** ~ supercarburant *m*, *coll* super *m*; ~ **station** station *f* d'essence; **run out of** ~ avoir une panne d'essence
**petrol-can** *n* bidon *m* à essence
**petroleum** *n* pétrole *m*; ~ **industry** industrie pétrolière; ~ **jelly** vaseline *f*
**petticoat** *n* jupon *m*
**pettifogging** *adj* chicanier -ière, avocassier -ière
**pettiness** *n* mesquinerie *f*, petitesse *f*
**petty** *adj* (mean) mesquin; (trifling) insignifiant, sans importance; ~ **cash** petite caisse; ~ **expenses** menus frais; *naut* ~ **officer** sous-officier *m*
**petulance** *n* irritabilité *f*
**petunia** *n* pétunia *m*
**pew** *n* banc *m* d'église
**pewit, peewit** *n* vanneau *m*
**pewter** *n* étain *m*
**phalanx** *n* phalange *f*
**phallic** *adj* phallique
**phallus** *n* phallus *m*
**phantasmagoria** *n* fantasmagorie *f*
**phantom** *n* fantôme *m*, spectre *m*
**Pharaoh** *n* Pharaon *m*
**Pharisee** *n* Pharisien -ienne
**pharmaceutical** *adj* pharmaceutique
**pharmaceutics** *npl* pharmaceutique *f*
**pharmacist** *n* pharmacien -ienne
**pharmacology** *n* pharmacologie *f*
**pharmacy** *n* pharmacie *f*
**pharynx** *n* pharynx *m*
**phase** *n* phase *f*
**pheasant** *n* faisan *m*
**phenol** *n* phénol *m*
**phenomenal** *adj* phénoménal
**phenomenon** *n* phénomène *m*
**phial** *n* fiole *f*, flacon *m*
**philander** *vi* flirter, conter fleurette à
**philanderer** *n* galant *m*; flirteur *m*
**philanthropic** *adj* philanthropique; (person) philanthrope
**philanthropist** *n* philanthrope
**philanthropy** *n* philanthropie *f*
**philatelist** *n* philatéliste
**philately** *n* philatélie *f*
**philharmonic** *adj* philharmonique
**Philistine** *n* Philistin *m*
**philological** *adj* philologique
**philology** *n* philologie *f*
**philosopher** *n* philosophe
**philosophic(al)** *adj* philosophique
**philosophize** *vi* philosopher
**philosophy** *n* philosophie *f*
**phlebitis** *n* phlébite *f*
**phlegm** *n* flegme *m*
**phlegmatic** *adj* flegmatique

**phlox** *n* bot phlox *m*
**phobia** *n* phobie *f*
**phoenix** *n* phénix *m*
**phone** *n* coll téléphone *m*; **be on the ~**
(have the ~) avoir le téléphone; (be
speaking) être au téléphone; *vt* téléphoner à; *vi* téléphoner
**phoneme** *n* phonème *m*
**phonetic** *adj* phonétique
**phonetician** *n* phonéticien -ienne
**phonetics** *n* phonétique *f*
**phoney, phony** *n* coll imposteur *m*; *adj*
*coll* faux (*f* fausse); **~ war** drôle de
guerre *f*
**phonograph** *n* US phonographe *m*
**phonology** *n* phonologie *f*
**phosgene** *n* phosgène *m*
**phosphate** *n* phosphate *m*
**phosphorescence** *n* phosphorescence *f*
**phosphorous** *adj* phosphoreux -euse
**phosphorus** *n* phosphore *m*
**photo** *n* photo *f*
**photocopier** *n* photocopieur *m*; photo-
copieuse *f*
**photocopy** *n* photocopie *f*
**photoelectric** *adj* photo-électrique
**photo-finish** *n* photo *f* à l'arrivée
**photogenic** *adj* photogénique
**photograph** *n* photographie *f*; *vt* photographier, prendre en photo
**photographer** *n* photographe *m*
**photographic** *adj* photographique
**photography** *n* photographie *f*
**photostat** *n* photocopie *f*, photostat *m*;
*vt* photocopier
**phrase** *n* expression *f*, locution *f*; *vt*
exprimer; *mus* phraser
**phraseology** *n* phraséologie *f*
**phrenetic** *adj* frénétique
**phrenology** *n* phrénologie *f*
**phut** *adv* coll **go ~** claquer
**physical** *adj* physique; **~ impossibility**
impossibilité matérielle
**physician** *n* médecin *m*
**physicist** *n* physicien -ienne
**physics** *n* physique *f*
**physiognomy** *n* physionômie *f*
**physiological** *adj* physiologique
**physiologist** *n* physiologue
**physiology** *n* physiologie *f*
**physique** *n* physique *m*
**pianist** *n* pianiste
**piano** *n* piano *m*
**pianola** *n* pianola *m*
**piano-stool** *n* tabouret *m* de piano
**picaresque** *adj* picaresque
**piccalilli** *n* pickles *mpl* à la moutarde
**piccolo** *n* piccolo *m*
¹**pick** *n* pioche *f*, pic *m*
²**pick** *n* choix *m*; élite *f*; *vt* (gather)

cueillir; (choose) choisir; (lock) crocheter; **~ a bone** enlever la chair d'un os;
**~ and choose** se montrer difficile; **~ a
quarrel with s/o** chercher querelle à qn;
**~ off** descendre; **~ one's teeth** se curer
les dents; **~ on s/o** accuser qn; **~ out**
choisir, sélectionner; (spot) repérer; **~
pockets** pratiquer le vol à la tire; **~ up**
ramasser; (learn) apprendre; (buy
cheaply) acheter à bon marché; (s/o)
prendre, rejoindre; *sl* (s/o) draguer;
**have a bone to ~ with s/o** avoir maille
à partir avec qn; *vi* **~ up** (recover) se
rétablir, se ressaisir; (engine) reprendre
**pickaback** *adv* sur le dos, sur les épaules
**pickax(e)** *n* pioche *f*
**picker** *n* cueilleur -euse, récolteur -euse
**picket** *n* piquet *m*; *mil* poste *m*; **~ fence**
palissade *f*; **strike ~** piquet *m* de grève;
*vt* mettre au piquet; (factory, etc) installer (poster) des piquets de grève
devant
**picking** *n* (fruit) cueillette *f*; (birds) pico-
tage *m*; (selecting) triage *m*; **~s** (remainder) restes *mpl*; **fat ~s** beaux
bénéfices
**pickle** *n* marinade *f*; (brine) saumure *f*;
**~s** pickles *mpl*, conserves *fpl* au vinaigre; *coll* **be in a (pretty) ~** être dans de
beaux draps; *vt* conserver dans du
vinaigre
**pick-me-up** *n* coll remontant *m*
**pickpocket** *n* voleur *m* à la tire, pickpocket *m*
**pick-up** *n* (recovery) reprise *f*; (record-
player) pick-up *m invar*
**picnic** *n* pique-nique *m*; *vi* pique-niquer
**picnicker** *n* pique-niqueur -euse
**pictorial** *adj* illustré; (description) pittoresque
**picture** *n* image *f*; (painting) tableau *m*,
peinture *f*; (engraving) gravure *f*; (likeness) portrait *m*; *cin* film *m*; **be a ~ of
health** respirer la santé; *coll* **be in the ~**
être au courant, être au parfum; **put
s/o in the ~** mettre qn au courant; *vt*
représenter, dépeindre; **~ to oneself** se
figurer
**picture-book** *n* livre *m* d'images
**picture-frame** *n* cadre *m*
**picture-postcard** *n* carte postale illustrée
**picturesque** *adj* pittoresque
**piddling** *adj* coll sans importance
**pidgin, pigeon** *n* **~ English** pidgin *m*;
**~ talk** parler petit nègre
**pie** *n* (meat) pâté *m*; tarte *f*
**piebald** *adj* (horse) pie; (motley) bigarré
**piece** *n* morceau *m*, bout *m*; (part) partie
*f*; (chip) éclat *m*; (land) parcelle *f*; fragment *m*; (from book) passage *m*; (coin)
pièce *f*; *coll* fille *f*; **~ of advice** conseil
*m*; **~ of clothing** vêtement *m*; **~ of**

luggage valise *f*, colis *m*; ~ of news nouvelle *f*; ~ of work ouvrage *m*; all of a ~ tout d'une pièce; fall into ~s s'en aller en morceaux; fly into ~s voler en éclats; *fig* give s/o a ~ of one's mind dire son fait à qn; take to ~s démonter; tear to ~s déchirer; (argument) démolir; *vt* rapiécer; ~ together raccommoder, rassembler

piecemeal *adv* par morceaux, pièce à pièce

piece-work *n* travail *m* à la pièce; be on ~ être payé à la pièce, *coll* être aux pièces

pie-crust *n* croûte *f* de pâté

pied *adj* bigarré

pied-à-terre *n* pied-à-terre *m invar*

pie-dish *n* plat *m* allant au four, terrine *f*; tourtière *f*

pier *n* jetée *f*, digue *f*; (at resort) jetée *f* promenade; (for landing) débarcadère *m*; *bui* pilier *m*

pierce *vt* percer, transpercer, pénétrer

piercing *adj* perçant, pénétrant; (shout) aigu

piety *n* piété *f*

piffle *n coll* bêtises *fpl*

pig *n* cochon *m*, porc *m*, pourceau *m*; *metal* gueuse *f*; bleed like a ~ saigner comme un bœuf; buy a ~ in a poke acheter un chat en poche; make a ~ of oneself manger gloutonnement

¹pigeon *n* pigeon *m*; carrier (homing) ~ pigeon voyageur; *coll* that's my ~ c'est mon affaire; wood ~ pigeon ramier

²pigeon *n see* pidgin

pigeon-hole *n* case *f*; *vt* classer, caser

pigeon-house, pigeon-loft *n* colombier *m*, pigeonnier *m*

pigeon-toed *adj* qui marche les pieds tournés en dedans

piggery *n* porcherie *f*

piggish *adj* désagréable; (dirty) sale

piggy *n* (child's language) petit cochon

pigheaded *adj* entêté, têtu

pig-iron *n* fer *m* en fonte

piglet *n* porcelet *m*, cochon *m* de lait

pigment *n* colorant *m*, pigment *m*

pigmy *n see* pygmy

pigskin *n* peau *f* de porc

pigsty *n* porcherie *f*; *coll* bauge *f*; *fig* taudis *m*

pigtail *n* natte *f*; (tobacco) tabac *m* en corde

¹pike *n* pique *f*

²pike *n* (fish) brochet *m*

pikestaff *n* plain as a ~ parfaitement clair

pilaf *n* pilaf *m*

pilchard *n* (espèce *f* de) sardine *f*

¹pile *n* pieu *m*; built on ~s bâti sur pilotis

²pile *n* (heap) tas *m*, pile *f*, monceau *m*; (arms) faisceau *m*; (funeral) bûcher *m*; (atomic) pile *f*; édifice *m*; make one's ~

faire sa pelote; *vt* entasser, amasser; empiler; *coll* ~ it on exagérer; *vi* ~ up s'amonceler, s'accumuler

³pile *n* (carpet) poil *m*

pile-driver *n* sonnette *f*

piles *npl* hémorroïdes *fpl*

pile-up *n* mot accident *m* multiple

pilfer *vt* chaparder, chiper

pilfering *n* chapardage *m*

pilgrim *n* pèlerin -e

pilgrimage *n* pèlerinage *m*

pill *n* pilule *f*; sugar the ~ dorer la pilule

pillage *n* pillage *m*; *vt* piller, saccager

pillar *n* pilier *m*, colonne *f*

pillar-box *n* boîte *f* aux lettres

pill-box *n* boîte *f* à pilules; *mil* réduit *m* en béton armé, blockhaus *m*

pillion *n* (motor-cycle) siège *m* arrière; ride ~ monter derrière

pillory *n* pilori *m*; *vt* mettre au pilori

pillow *n* oreiller *m*

pillow-case, pillow-slip *n* taie *f* d'oreiller

pilot *n* pilote *m*; *vt* piloter, conduire

pilot-boat *n* bateau *m* pilote

pilotless *adj* sans pilote; ~ plane avion *m* robot

pilot-light *n* veilleuse *f*

pilot-officer *n* sous-lieutenant *m* aviateur

pimento *n* piment *m*

pimp *n* proxénète *m*, *coll* maquereau *m*

pimpernel *n* mouron *m*

pimple *n* bouton *m*

pimply *adj* boutonneux -euse

pin *n* épingle *f*; *carp* cheville *f*; *mech* goupille *f*; *coll* ~s jambes *fpl*; ~s and needles fourmillements *mpl*; hear a ~ drop entendre voler une mouche; not care two ~s about it s'en moquer comme de l'an quarante; safety ~ épingle *f* de sûreté (nourrice); *vt* épingler; *carp* cheviller; (fasten) attacher, fixer; (nail) clouer; ~ one's faith in s/o se fier à qn; be ~ned down être (se trouver) pris

pinafore *n* tablier *m*

pince-nez *n* pince-nez *m*, lorgnon *m*

pincers *npl* tenailles *fpl*, pince *f*; *zool* pinces *fpl*

pinch *n* action *f* de pincer; (small amount) pincée *f*; (snuff) prise *f*; at a ~ au besoin; *vt* pincer; (shoe) blesser; *coll* (steal) chiper, faucher; *coll* (arrest) pincer; ~ and scrape se priver

pincushion *n* pelote *f* à épingles

¹pine *n* pin *m*; bois *m* de pin

²pine *vi* languir, dépérir

pineapple *n* ananas *m*

pine-cone *n* pomme *f* de pin

pine-needle *n* aiguille *f* de pin

**ping-pong** *n* tennis *m* de table, ping-pong *m*

**pinhead** *n* tête *f* d'épingle; *coll* crétin -e

**pinhole** *n* trou *m* d'épingle

¹**pinion** *n* aileron *m*; *poet* aile *f*; *vt* rogner les ailes à; (tie up) lier

²**pinion** *n mech* pignon *m*

¹**pink** *n bot* œillet *m*; (colour) rose *m*; **in the ~** en parfaite santé; *adj* rose

²**pink** *vt* toucher; (dressmaking) denteler les bords de

³**pink** *vi mot* cliqueter

**pinnace** *n* pinasse *f*

**pinnacle** *n* sommet *m*; *archi* pinacle *m*; *fig* faîte *m*, apogée *m*

**pinpoint** *n* pointe *f* d'épingle; *vt* mettre le doigt sur; définir de façon précise

**pinprick** *n* piqûre *f* d'épingle; *fig* tracasserie *f*; **it's a mere ~** ce n'est rien

**pin-stripe** *n* **~ trousers** pantalon rayé

**pint** *n* pinte *f*

**pin-table** *n* flipper *m*, billard *m* électrique

**pint-sized** *adj coll* tout petit

**pin-up** *n* pin-up *f invar*

**pioneer** *n* pionnier *m*; *vt* introduire, être à l'avant-garde dans

**pious** *adj* pieux (*f* pieuse)

¹**pip** *n* (poultry disease) pépie *f*; *coll* **give s/o the ~** donner le cafard à qn

²**pip** *n* (fruit) pépin *m*

³**pip** *n* (cards) point *m*; *mil* galon *m*

⁴**pip** *n* (time signal) top *m*

⁵**pip** *vt* vaincre; (exam) échouer à

**pipe** *n* tuyau *m*, conduit *m*; *mus* pipeau *m*, chalumeau *m*; (smoking) pipe *f*; (birdsong) chant *m*; *vt* jouer (un air); (water, etc) canaliser; *vi* jouer du chalumeau; *coll* **~ down** *sl* la boucler; *coll* **~ up** se faire entendre

**pipe-cleaner** *n* cure-pipe *m*

**pipe-dream** *n* rêve *m* impossible, chimère *f*

**pipeful** *n* **~ (of tobacco)** pipe *f* (de tabac)

**pipeline** *n* canalisation *f*, conduite *f*; (oil) oléoduc *m*, pipe-line *m*

**pipe-organ** *n* grand orgue

**piper** *n* joueur -euse de chalumeau; **he who pays the ~ calls the tune** celui qui paie a le droit de choisir; **pay the ~** payer les violons

**pipette** *n* pipette *f*

**piping** *n* son *m* du chalumeau (de la cornemuse); (whistle) sifflement *m*; (pipes) canalisation *f*, tuyauterie *f*; **~ cord** ganse *f*, passepoil *m*; *adj* (voice) flûté; **~ hot** tout chaud (*f* toute chaude)

**pipit** *n* pipi *m*, pipit *m*

**pippin** *n* (pomme *f*) reinette *f*

**pip-squeak** *n coll* rien *m* du tout *invar*

**piquancy** *n* piquant *m*

**piquant** *adj* piquant

**pique** *n* pique *f*, ressentiment *m*

**piracy** *n* piraterie *f*; (plagiarism) plagiat *m*

**pirate** *n* pirate *m*; (book) plagiaire

**piratical** *adj* de pirate; (book) de plagiaire

**pirouette** *n* pirouette *f*; *vi* pirouetter

**piss** *n sl* urine *f*; (animal) pissat *m*; *vt coll* pisser; *sl* **~ed** ivre; *vi* uriner, pisser, *coll* faire pipi; *vulg* **~ off** foutre le camp

**pistachio** *n* pistache *f*

**pistol** *n* pistolet *m*

**piston** *n* piston *m*

**pit** *n* fosse *f*, trou *m*; (stomach) creux *m*; *theat* parterre *m*; (quarry) carrière *f*; (mine-shaft) puits *m*; *vt* (acid) piquer, trouer; *med* marquer; **~ s/o against s/o** opposer qn à qn

**pit-a-pat** *adv* **go ~** (heart) palpiter; (rain) crépiter; (feet) trottiner

¹**pitch** *n* poix *f*, bitume *m*, goudron *m*; *vt* enduire de poix

²**pitch** *n* (throwing) lancement *m*; (street-vendor) place *f*; *naut* tangage *m*; *sp* terrain *m*; (degree) point *m*, degré *m*; *mus* diapason *m*; **reach the highest ~** atteindre son comble; **to such a ~ that** à tel point que; *vt* (throw) lancer, jeter; (tent) dresser; *coll* **~ a yarn** débiter une histoire; *mus* **~ one's voice higher (lower)** hausser (baisser) le ton de sa voix; **~ed battle** bataille rangée; *vi* (ship) tanguer; **~ into** s'attaquer à; (criticize) dire son fait à

**pitch-black** *adj* noir comme poix

**pitchblende** *n* pechblende *f*

**pitch-dark** *adj* très noir; **it is ~** il fait nuit noire

¹**pitcher** *n* lanceur -euse

²**pitcher** *n* (vessel) cruche *f*

**pitchfork** *n* fourche *f*; *vt* lancer avec la fourche; *coll fig* bombarder

**pitch-pine** *n* pitchpin *m*

**piteous** *adj* pitoyable, piteux -euse

**pitfall** *n* piège *m*

**pith** *n* moelle *f*; *fig* vigueur *f*, ardeur *f*; (book) essence *f*

**pit-head** *n* carreau *m*

**pithy** *adj* plein de moelle; *fig* vigoureux -euse, nerveux -euse, concis

**pitiable** *adj* pitoyable

**pitiful** *adj* pitoyable; (compassionate) compatissant; *pej* lamentable

**pitiless** *adj* sans pitié, impitoyable, cruel -elle

**pit-prop** *n* poteau *m* de mine

**pittance** *n* maigre salaire *m*

**pitter-patter** *n* (rain) fouettement *m*

**pituitary** *n* hypophyse *f*; *adj* hypophisaire

**pity** *n* pitié *f*, compassion *f*; **out of ~**

par pitié; **take ~ on s/o** prendre pitié
de qn; **that's a ~** c'est dommage; **what
a ~!** quel dommage!; *vt* avoir pitié de,
plaindre
**pivot** *n* pivot *m*; *vi* pivoter, tourner
**pixie** *n* fée *f*, lutin *m*
**pizzicato** *n* pizzicato (*pl* pizzicati *or*
pizzicatos); *adj + adv* pizzicato
**placard** *n* écriteau *m*, affiche *f*, panneau
*m*; *vt* afficher
**placate** *vt* calmer, apaiser
**place** *n* endroit *m*, lieu *m*, localité *f*;
(seat) place *f*; (rank) position *f*; (employment) place *f*, poste *m*, emploi *m*;
(home) demeure *f*, domicile *m*; (at
meal) couvert *m*; **all over the ~** partout; **at my ~** chez moi; **be out of ~**
ne pas être à sa place; *fig* être mal à
propos; **change ~s with** changer de
place avec; **give ~ to** faire place à; **in
high ~s** en haut lieu; **in my ~** à ma
place; **in the first ~** d'abord; **it's not
his ~ to** ce n'est pas à lui de; **put s/o in
his (her) ~** remettre qn à sa place; **take
~** avoir lieu; *vt* placer, mettre, poser;
donner un rang à; (recognize) remettre;
**~ an order** passer une commande; *sp*
**be ~d** être classé; (horse) être placé
**place-kick** *n* coup placé
**placement** *n* placement *m*, arrangement
*m*
**placenta** *n* placenta *m*
**placid** *adj* placide, calme, tranquille
**placidity** *n* placidité *f*, calme *m*
**placidly** *adv* tranquillement, avec calme
**plagiarism** *n* plagiat *m*
**plagiarist** *n* plagiaire
**plagiarize** *vt* plagier
**plague** *n* peste *f*; *fig* fléau *m*; **the ten ~s**
les dix plaies *fpl*; *vt* tourmenter; (bore)
embêter, raser
**plaice** *n* carrelet *m*, plie *f*
**plaid** *n* plaid *m*
**plain** *n* plaine *f*; *adj* simple; (clear) évident, clair; (smooth) uni; (face) sans
attraits; (ugly) laid; (frank) franc (*f*
franche); **~ cooking** cuisine *f* simple;
**~ dealing** procédés *mpl* honnêtes; **in
~ clothes** en civil; **that's as ~ as daylight** c'est clair comme le jour; *adv*
clairement, distinctement
**plain-chant** *n* plain-chant *m*
**plainness** *n* (simplicity) simplicité *f*;
(clearness) clarté *f*, netteté *f*; (frankness) franchise *f*; (features) manque *m*
d'attraits
**plain-song** *n* plain-chant *m*
**plain-spoken** *adj* franc (*f* franche)
**plaintiff** *n* demandeur -eresse, plaignant
-e
**plaintive** *adj* plaintif -ive
**plait** *n* natte *f*, tresse *f*; *vt* natter, tresser

**plan** *n* plan *m*, projet *m*; **go according to
~** marcher selon les prévisions; **your
best ~ is to go away** le mieux serait que
vous partiez; *vt* faire le plan de;
(intend) projeter, arranger
¹**plane** *n* (tool) rabot *m*; *vt* raboter
²**plane** *n coll* avion *m*
³**plane, plane-tree** *n* platane *m*
⁴**plane** *n* (surface) plan *m*; *adj* plan, uni,
plat
**planet** *n* planète *f*
**plane-table** *n* planchette *f*
**planetarium** *n* planétarium *m*
**planetary** *adj* planétaire
**plank** *n* planche *f*, madrier *m*; *vt* planchéier; *coll* **~ down** jeter, déposer
**planking** *n* (action) planchéiage *m*;
(planks) planches *fpl*
**plankton** *n* plancton *m*
**planning** *n* organisation *f*, planification
*f*; **family ~** contrôle *m* des naissances
**plant** *n* plante *f*; *mech* matériel *m*; **~ life**
vie végétale; *vt* planter; **~ a bomb** déposer une bombe; **~ an idea** implanter
une idée
**plantation** *n* plantation *f*
**planter** *n* planteur *m*; propriétaire *m*
d'une plantation
**plaque** *n* plaque *f*
**plasma** *n biol* plasma *m*
**plaster** *n* plâtre *m*; *med* emplâtre *m*; *med*
**adhesive ~** sparadrap *m*; **~ cast** moulage *m* au plâtre, plâtre *m*; **~ of Paris**
plâtre *m*; *vt* plâtrer; *med* mettre un
emplâtre sur; (hair) **~ down** plaquer;
**~ up** plâtrer
**plastered** *adj* plâtré; *coll* ivre
**plasterer** *n* plâtrier *m*
**plastic** *n* matière *f* plastique, plastique
*m*; (explosive) plastic *m*; *adj* plastique;
malléable, souple; **~ surgery** chirurgie
*f* plastique
**Plasticine** *n* pâte *f* à modeler
**plasticity** *n* plasticité *f*
**plastics** *n* matières *fpl* plastiques; industrie *f* plastique
**plate** *n* assiette *f*; (metal, etc) plaque *f*,
feuille *f*; (book) planche *f*; (gold, silver) vaisselle *f* d'or (d'argent); (dental)
dentier *m*; **dinner ~** assiette plate; **hot
~** plaque chauffante; *mot* **number ~**
plaque *f* minéralogique; *phot* **sensitive
~** plaque *f* sensible; **soup ~** assiette
creuse; *vt* plaquer; blinder
**plateau** *n* plateau *m*
**plateful** *n* assiettée *f*
**plate-glass** *n* glace *f*, verre *m* à vitre
**platform** *n* plate-forme *f* (*pl* plates-
formes), terrasse *f*; (railway) quai *m*;
(public) estrade *f*, tribune *f*; *pol* programme *m*, plate-forme *f* (*pl* plates-
formes)

**plating** *n* revêtement *m* en métal; plaquage *m*

**platinum** *n* platine *m*

**platitude** *n* platitude *f*

**platitudinous** *adj* (style) banal, plat; (person) qui débite des banalités

**Platonic** *adj* (love) platonique; *philos* platonicien -ienne

**platoon** *n* mil section *f*

**platter** *n* assiette *f* (en bois); *US* plat *m*

**platypus** *n* ornithorynque *m*

**plaudit** *n* applaudissement *m*

**plausibility** *n* plausibilité *f*

**plausible** *adj* plausible, vraisemblable; (specious) spécieux -ieuse; (person) enjôleur -euse

**play** *n* jeu *m*; *theat* pièce *f* (de théâtre), spectacle *m*; (fun) amusement *m*; ~ on words calembour *m*; come into ~ entrer en jeu; give full ~ to donner libre cours à; *sp* (ball) out of ~ hors jeu; *vt* jouer; (game) jouer à; (instrument) jouer de; (direct) diriger; (match) disputer; (fish) manœuvrer; ~ along with coopérer avec; ~ back faire repasser; *coll* ~ ball marcher; ~ down minimiser; ~ s/o off against s/o opposer qn à qn; ~ the fool faire l'imbécile; ~ up (annoy) agacer; *vi* jouer; (animals) gambader; s'amuser; ~ fair jouer franc jeu; (cards) ~ first entamer; ~ on continuer de jouer; ~ on s/o's credulity abuser de la crédulité de qn; ~ out jouer jusqu'au bout; ~ up (try) faire de son mieux

**playable** *adj* qu'on peut jouer; (ground) sur lequel on peut jouer

**play-act** *vi* jouer la comédie

**playback** *n* play-back *m*, lecture *f* sonore

**play-bill** *n* affiche *f*, annonce *f* de spectacle

**playboy** *n* play-boy *m*, bon vivant

**player** *n* joueur -euse; *theat* acteur -trice, comédien -ienne; *mus* exécutant -e

**playfellow** *n* camarade de jeu

**playful** *adj* enjoué, badin

**playgoer** *n* amateur *m* de théâtre

**playground** *n* cour *f* (terrain *m*) de récréation

**playing** *n* jeu *m*; *theat* interprétation *f*; *mus* exécution *f*

**playing-card** *n* carte *f* (à jouer)

**playing-field** *n* terrain *m* de jeux (sport)

**playmate** *n* camarade de jeu

**play-off** *n* belle *f*

**playpen** *n* parc *m* pour enfants

**plaything** *n* jouet *m*, *coll* joujou *m*

**playtime** *n* récréation *f*

**playwright** *n* auteur *m* dramatique, dramaturge *m*

**plea** *n* excuse *f*, prétexte *m*; *leg* défense *f*; on the ~ of sous prétexte de; submit the ~ that plaider que

**plead** *vt* (cause) plaider; (allege) invoquer, alléguer; *vi* plaider; *leg* ~ (not) guilty plaider (non) coupable; ~ with plaider auprès de

**pleading** *n* art *m* de plaider; plaidoirie *f*, supplication *f*

**pleasant** *adj* agréable, aimable

**pleasantry** *n* plaisanterie *f*

**please** *vt* plaire à, faire plaisir à; (satisfy) contenter; ~ d satisfait, content; ~ do! je vous en prie!; ~ God! plaise à Dieu!; ~ yourself faites à votre guise; as you ~ comme vous voudrez; be as ~ d as Punch être heureux comme un roi; be ~ d to être heureux -euse de; be ~ d with être content de; do as one ~ s n'en faire qu'à sa tête; hard to ~ difficile; if you ~ s'il vous plaît; *adv + interj* s'il vous (te) plaît

**pleasing** *adj* agréable

**pleasurable** *adj* agréable

**pleasure** *n* plaisir *m*; (wish) volonté *f*, bon plaisir; at your ~ à votre gré; take ~ in éprouver du plaisir à

**pleasure-loving** *adj* qui aime le plaisir

**pleasure-trip** *n* voyage *m* d'agrément

**pleat** *n* pli *m*; *vt* plisser

**plebeian** *adj* plébéien -ienne

**plebiscite** *n* plébiscite *m*

**plectrum** *n* plectre *m*

**pledge** *n* gage *m*; (promise) promesse *f*, vœu *m*; take the ~ faire vœu de tempérance; *vt* mettre en gage, engager; (toast) boire à la santé de

**plenary** *adj* entier -ière, complet -ète; ~ assembly assemblée plénière; ~ powers pleins pouvoirs

**plenipotentiary** *n* plénipotentiaire; *adj* plénipotentiaire

**plenitude** *n* plénitude *f*

**plenteous** *adj* abondant

**plentiful** *adj* abondant, copieux -ieuse

**plenty** *n* abondance *f*; ~ of bien assez de, beaucoup de; land of ~ pays *m* de cocagne; live in ~ vivre très à l'aise; *adv coll* ~ big enough bien assez gros (*f* grosse)

**plethora** *n* pléthore *f*, surabondance *f*

**pleurisy** *n* pleurésie *f*

**pliability** *n* flexibilité *f*; (character) souplesse *f*

**pliable, pliant** *adj* flexible; (character) souple, complaisant

**pliers** *npl* pinces *fpl*

**plight** *n* condition *f*, état *m*; be in a sorry ~ être dans de beaux draps; *vt lit* ~ one's troth engager sa foi

**Plimsoll** *n* ~ line ligne *f* de Plimsoll

**plimsolls** *npl* chaussures *fpl* de gymnastique

**plinth** *n* plinthe *f*

**plod** vi marcher péniblement, marcher lourdement; ~ **away at sth** travailler laborieusement à qch; ~ **on** persévérer

**plodder** n piocheur -euse

**¹plonk** n bruit sourd; vt ~ **sth down** déposer qch bruyamment

**²plonk** n coll vin m ordinaire, coll pinard m

**plop** vi tomber en faisant plouf; interj plouf!

**plot** n (conspiracy) complot m; (story) intrigue f, action f; (ground) parcelle f, lopin m; vt comploter, conspirer; tracer, faire le plan de; (record) relever; vi comploter

**plotter** n conspirateur -trice; traceur m

**plough** n charrue f; astron **the Plough** le Chariot; vt labourer; (ship) sillonner; coll (candidate) recaler; ~ **back profits** reverser des bénéfices dans une affaire; ~ **into the ground** enterrer en labourant; coll **be ~ ed** échouer à un examen

**ploughman** n laboureur m

**ploughshare** n soc m de charrue

**ploy** n coll (dodge) tour m, truc m

**pluck** n courage m, cran m; vt (flower) cueillir; (feathers) arracher; (hairs) épiler; ~ **out** arracher; ~ **up courage** s'armer de courage

**plucky** adj courageux -euse; coll crâne

**plug** n tampon m, bouchon m; elect fiche f; sl coup m de poing; (lavatory) chasse f d'eau; coll (advertising) réclame f; mot bougie f; **wall** ~ prise f de courant; vt boucher, tamponner; coll (advertise) faire une campagne de publicité pour; sl (shoot) tirer sur; sl (punch) donner un coup de poing à; ~ **in** brancher; vi ~ **away** persévérer

**plum** n prune f; coll (job) meilleur poste

**plumage** n plumage m

**plumb** n plomb m; aplomb m; adj droit, d'aplomb; ~ **in the middle** en plein milieu; adv US complètement; vt sonder, plomber

**plumber** n plombier m

**plumbing** n plomberie f

**plumb-line** n fil m à plomb

**plume** n plume f; (ornamental) panache m; vt orner de plumes; (bird) ~ **itself** se lisser les plumes; (person) ~ **oneself on sth** se piquer de qch

**plummet** n plomb m; vi descendre à pic

**¹plump** adj rebondi, grassouillet -ette, dodu, potelé; vt + vi engraisser

**²plump** n bruit sourd

**³plump** vt flanquer; vi tomber lourdement; ~ **for** choisir; pol voter pour un seul candidat

**plum-pudding** n plum-pudding m

**plum-tree** n prunier m

**plunder** n pillage m; (booty) butin m; vt piller, dépouiller

**plunderer** n pillard m

**plunge** n plongeon m; **take the** ~ faire le plongeon; vt plonger, immerger; vi plonger; (penetrate) s'enfoncer; (rush) se précipiter; ~ **forward** s'élancer en avant

**plunger** n plongeur m; coll (gaming) joueur effréné; coll (speculator) risque-tout m invar

**plural** n pluriel m; **in the** ~ au pluriel; adj pluriel -ielle; ~ **vote** vote plural

**plurality** n pluralité f

**plus** n plus m; quantité positive; adj positif -ive; prep plus

**plus-fours** npl culotte f de golf

**plush** n peluche f; adj sl rupin

**plushy** adj peluché; sl rupin

**plutocracy** n ploutocratie f

**plutocrat** n ploutocrate m

**plutocratic** adj ploutocratique

**plutonium** n plutonium m

**¹ply** n (fold) pli m; (thickness) épaisseur f; (strand) fil m, brin m

**²ply** vt (use) manier énergiquement; (trade) exercer; (person) presser; vi faire le service, faire la navette

**plywood** n contre-plaqué m

**pneumatic** adj pneumatique; ~ **drill** foreuse f (perceuse f) à air comprimé

**pneumonia** n pneumonie f, fluxion f de poitrine

**¹poach** vt cul pocher

**²poach** vt (game) braconner

**poacher** n braconnier m

**pock** n pustule f

**pocket** n poche f; (bag) sac m, sacoche f; **air** ~ trou m d'air; **be out of** ~ y être de sa poche; **breast** ~ poche intérieure; fig **I've got him in my** ~ je le tiens; **line one's** ~s faire sa pelote; vt empocher, mettre dans sa poche; pej chiper; (billiards) blouser; (insult) avaler; ~ **one's pride** mettre son orgueil dans sa poche

**pocket-book** n carnet m de poche

**pocket-handkerchief** n mouchoir m de poche

**pocket-knife** n couteau m de poche, canif m

**pocket-money** n argent m de poche

**pock-marked** adj variolé

**pod** n cosse f, gousse f

**podgy** adj boulot -otte; (finger) boudiné

**podium** n (dais) podium m

**poem** n poème m, poésie f

**poet** n poète m

**poetess** n poétesse f

**poetic(al)** adj poétique

**poetry** n poésie f

**po-faced** adj sl à l'air solennel

**pogrom** n pogrom m

630

**poignancy** *n* (grief) acuité *f*; (feeling) violence *f*; (satire) mordant *m*

**poignant** *adj* (feeling) vif (*f* vive); (thoughts) angoissant; piquant

**point** *n* point *m*; (sharp end) pointe *f*; (decimal) virgule *f*; (question) question *f*; (feature) trait *m*, détail *m*; *elect* prise *f* de courant; (railway) ~s aiguilles *fpl*; ~ **of the compass** aire *f* de vent; ~ **of view** point *m* de vue; **a case in** ~ un cas topique; **a sore** ~ un endroit sensible; **at the** ~ **of death** à l'article de la mort; **be on the** ~ **of doing sth** être sur le point de faire qch; **beside the** ~ hors de propos, sans rapport; **from every** ~ **of view** sous tous les rapports; **gain one's** ~ atteindre son but; **in** ~ **of fact** en fait, par le fait; **make a** ~ **of doing sth** s'obliger à faire qch; **off the** ~ hors de propos; **on this** ~ à cet égard; **score** ~s marquer des points; **see the** ~ comprendre (la signification); **stretch a** ~ faire une exception (concession); **there's no** ~ **in** inutile de; **to the** ~ à propos; **up to a** ~ jusqu'à un certain point; **what's the** ~? à quoi bon?; *vt* (sharpen) tailler (en pointe), aiguiser; (way) indiquer, montrer; (gun) braquer; (wall) jointoyer; (dot) marquer de points; ~ **out a fact** faire ressortir un fait; ~ **sth out** montrer qch du doigt; *vi* (gun) pointer; ~ **at** (to) **sth** indiquer qch du doigt; ~ **towards** être tourné vers; ~ **up** souligner; **this** ~s **to his guilt** cela laisse supposer qu'il est coupable

**point-blank** *adj* direct; *adv* (shooting) à bout portant; **ask** ~ demander à brûle-pourpoint; **refuse** ~ refuser net

**point-duty** *n* **be on** ~ être de service à point fixe

**pointed** *adj* pointu; (answer) mordant; (reference) direct

**pointer** *n* (dog) chien *m* d'arrêt; (on dial) aiguille *f*; (stick) baguette *f*; (information) renseignement *m*, *coll* tuyau *m*

**pointing** *n* ponctuation *f*; (gun) braquage *m*; *bui* jointoiement *m*

**pointless** *adj* (remark) qui ne rime à rien; (joke) fade; (futile) futile, inutile

**poise** *n* équilibre *m*, aplomb *m*; *vt* équilibrer, balancer

**poison** *n* poison *m*; *vt* empoisonner, intoxiquer; *fig* corrompre

**poisonous** *adj* toxique; empoisonné; (animal) venimeux -euse; (plant) vénéneux -euse; *fig* (tongue) venimeux -euse

**poke** *n* poussée *f*; (elbow) coup *m* de coude; (finger) coup *m* du bout du doigt; (poker) coup *m* de tisonnier; **buy a pig in a** ~ acheter un chat en poche; *vt* pousser du doigt (du coude); (fire) attiser, tisonner; (push) passer, fourrer; ~ **fun at s/o** se moquer de qn; ~ **one's head out of the window** passer la tête par la fenêtre; *vi* ~ **about** fureter, farfouiller; ~ **at sth** tâter qch

¹**poker** *n* tisonnier *m*

²**poker** *n* (card game) poker *m*

**poker-face** *n* visage *m* impassible

**poky** *adj* étroit, misérable; (job) mesquin

**Poland** *n* Pologne *f*

**polar** *adj* polaire

**polarity** *n* polarité *f*

**polarization** *n* polarisation *f*

**polarize** *vt* polariser; *vi* se polariser

**Pole** *n* Polonais -e

¹**pole** *n* perche *f*; (telegraph) poteau *m*; (mast) mât *m*; (cart) timon *m*; *coll* **be up the** ~ être timbré, être toqué

²**pole** *n geog* pôle *m*; **Pole Star** étoile *f* polaire

**pole-axe** *n* assommoir *m*

**polecat** *n* putois *m*

**pole-jump, pole-vault** *n* saut *m* à la perche; *vi* sauter à la perche

**polemic** *n* polémique *f*; *adj* polémique

**pole-vault** *n* + *vi see* **pole-jump**

**police** *n* police *f*; (rural) gendarmerie *f*; ~ **constable** agent *m* de police; ~ **station** poste *m* de police, commissariat *m* de police; (rural) gendarmerie *f*; *adj* policier -ière; *vt* policer, maintenir l'ordre dans

**policeman** *n* agent *m* de police; (rural) gendarme *m*

**policewoman** *n* femme-agent *f* (de police) (*pl* femmes-agents)

¹**policy** *n* politique *f*; **think it** ~ **to** juger prudent de

²**policy** *n* (insurance) police *f*; **take out a** ~ s'assurer, prendre une police

**polio** *n* polio *f*

**poliomyelitis** *n* poliomyélite *f*

**Polish** *n* (language) polonais *m*; *adj* polonais

**polish** *n* poli *m*, brillant *m*; (shoe) cirage *m*; (nail) vernis *m*; (floor) encaustique *f*; (manners) politesse *f*; *vt* polir; (shoes) cirer; (floor) encaustiquer; *coll* ~ **off** (work) expédier, bâcler; (person) régler le compte de; (food) ne rien laisser de; ~ **up** astiquer; ~ **up one's French** dérouiller son français

**polisher** *n* (person) polisseur -euse; (machine) cireuse *f*; (tool) polissoir *m*

**polite** *adj* poli, courtois

**politeness** *n* politesse *f*

**politic** *adj* avisé, politique; (skilful) adroit, habile

**political** *adj* politique

**politician** *n* homme *m* politique

# politics

**politics** *n* politique *f*

**polka** *n* polka *f*

**poll** *n* vote *m*, scrutin *m*; (opinion) sondage *m*; **declare the** ~ proclamer le résultat du scrutin; **go to the** ~**s** aller aux urnes; *vt* (votes) réunir; (horns) écorner; (tree) étêter; *vi* voter

**pollen** *n* pollen *m*

**pollinate** *vt* polliniser

**pollination** *n* pollinisation *f*

**polling-booth** *n* isoloir *m*

**polling-station** *n* bureau *m* de vote

**pollster** *n* sondeur *m*

**pollute** *vt* polluer, souiller; (corrupt) corrompre

**pollution** *n* pollution *f*

**polo** *n* polo *m*

**polonaise** *n* polonaise *f*

**polo-neck** *n* col roulé

**poltergeist** *n* esprit frappeur

**polygamist** *n* polygame

**polygamous** *adj* polygame

**polygamy** *n* polygamie *f*

**polyglot** *n* + *adj* polyglotte

**polymath** *n* homme très savant

**polymer** *n chem* polymère *m*

**polyp** *n* polype *m*

**polystyrene** *n* polystyrène *m*

**polysyllabic** *adj* polysyllabique

**polytechnic** *n* (école *f*) polytechnique; *adj* polytechnique

**polythene** *n* polyéthylène *m*

**pomegranate** *n* grenade *f*

**pommel, pummel** *n* pommeau *m*; *vt* bourrer de coups

**pomp** *n* pompe *f*, faste *m*, éclat *m*

**pompon** *n* pompon *m*

**pomposity** *n* suffisance *f*

**pompous** *adj* (person) suffisant; (style) pompeux -euse

**poncho** *n* poncho *m*

**pond** *n* étang *m*, mare *f*; (artificial) pièce *f* d'eau

**ponder** *vt* réfléchir sur, peser; *vi* méditer

**ponderous** *adj* pesant, lourd

**pong** *n sl* mauvaise odeur; *vi sl* puer, schlinguer

**pontiff** *n* pontife *m*

**pontifical** *adj* pontifical

**pontificate** *vi* pontifier; faire l'important

**¹pontoon** *n* ponton *m*

**²pontoon** *n* (cards) vingt-et-un

**pontoon-bridge** *n* pont *m* de bateaux

**pony** *n* poney *m*; *sl* (glass) petit verre

**pony-tail** *n* queue *f* de cheval

**poodle** *n* caniche *m*

**poof** *n sl* tapette *f*

**pooh-pooh** *vt* faire peu de cas de; (advice) repousser

**¹pool** *n* mare *f*; (swimming) piscine *f*; (puddle) flaque *f*

**²pool** *n* (cards) poule *f*, cagnotte *f*;

(game) billard américain; *pol*+*econ* pool *m*; **typing** ~ équipe *f* de dactylos; *vt* mettre en commun

**poop** *n* poupe *f*

**poor** *adj* pauvre; (bad) mauvais; (wretched) malheureux -euse; (quality) médiocre; (weak) faible; ~ **quality** basse qualité

**poor-box** *n eccles* tronc *m*

**poorhouse** *n* hospice *m*, asile *m* des pauvres

**poorly** *adj* indisposé, souffrant

**poorness** *n* pauvreté *f*

**poor-spirited** *adj* pusillanime

**¹pop** *n coll* papa *m*

**²pop** *adj coll* populaire; ~ **music** musique *f* pop

**³pop** *n* bruit sec; *coll* (drink) boisson gazeuse; *vt* (put) mettre, fourrer; (burst) crever; (cork) faire sauter; *sl* (put in pawn) mettre au clou; ~ **one's head out of the window** passer la tête par la fenêtre; *vi* péter, éclater; ~ **in** entrer en passant; ~ **out** sortir; ~ **over** passer; ~ **round** faire un saut; ~ **up** surgir, apparaître; *interj* crac!, pan!

**popcorn** *n* maïs éclaté, pop-corn *m*

**Pope** *n* Pape *m*

**popery** *n pej* papisme *m*

**pop-eyed** *adj coll* aux yeux protubérants

**popgun** *n* pistolet *m* d'enfant

**poplar** *n* peuplier *m*

**poplin** *n* popeline *f*

**poppy** *n* pavot *m*; **field** ~ coquelicot *m*

**poppycock** *n coll* bêtises *fpl*

**pop-singer** *n* chanteur -euse pop

**popsy** *n coll* fille *f*

**populace** *n* peuple *m*; *pej* populace *f*

**popular** *adj* populaire, du peuple; en vogue; (error) courant

**popularity** *n* popularité *f*

**popularization** *n* popularisation *f*; (knowledge) vulgarisation *f*

**popularize** *vt* populariser; (knowledge) vulgariser

**popularly** *adv* de façon courante, couramment

**populate** *vt* peupler

**population** *n* population *f*

**populous** *adj* populeux -euse

**porcelain** *n* porcelaine *f*

**porch** *n* porche *m*, portique *m*; *US* véranda *f*

**porcupine** *n* porc-épic *m* (*pl* porcs-épics)

**¹pore** *n* pore *m*

**²pore** *vi* ~ **over** regarder attentivement; ~ **over a book** s'absorber dans la lecture d'un livre

**pork** *n* porc *m*, viande *f* de porc; ~ **chop** côte *f* (côtelette *f*) de porc; ~ **pie** pâté *m* de porc

**pork-butcher** *n* charcutier -ière; ~ **'s**

shop charcuterie *f*

**porker** *n* jeune porc gras

**porky** *adj coll* gras (*f* grasse), gros (*f* grosse)

**pornographer** *n* pornographe *m*

**pornographic** *adj* pornographique

**pornography** *n* pornographie *f*

**porosity** *n* porosité *f*

**porous** *adj* poreux -euse

**porpoise** *n* marsouin *m*

**porridge** *n* porridge *m*, bouillie *f* d'avoine

¹**port** *n* port *m*; (ship) bâbord *m*; ~ **charges** droits *mpl* de port; ~ **of call** port *m* d'escale, escale *f*; **come into** ~ entrer au port; **naval** ~ port *m* militaire; **put into** ~ faire escale; *vt* mettre à bâbord; *vi* venir sur bâbord

²**port** *n naut* (for guns) sabord *m*; (port-hole) hublot *m*

³**port** *n* (wine) porto *m*

⁴**port** *vt mil* porter; ~ **arms** présenter les armes pour l'inspection

**portable** *adj* portatif -ive, transportable

**portage** *n* transport *m*, port *m*; (charges) frais *mpl* de port

**portal** *n* portail *m*, portique *m*

**portcullis** *n* herse *f*

**portend** *vt* présager, augurer

**portent** *n* mauvais présage

**portentous** *adj* de mauvais augure, sinistre; (marvellous) prodigieux -ieuse

¹**porter** *n* (house) portier *m*, concierge *m*; ~ **'s lodge** loge *f* du concierge

²**porter** *n* (station) porteur *m*; *obs* portefaix *m*; (market) fort *m* des Halles

³**porter** *n* (beer) bière brune, porter *m*

**porterhouse** *n* ~ **steak** filet *m* de bœuf

**portfolio** *n* (brief-case) serviette *f*; *pol* + *comm* portefeuille *m*

**porthole** *n* hublot *m*

**portion** *n* portion *f*; (part) partie *f*; (destiny) destinée *f*; (inheritance) part *f*; **marriage** ~ dot *f*; *vt* répartir, distribuer

**portliness** *n* corpulence *f*, embonpoint *m*

**portly** *adj* corpulent, ventru

**portmanteau** *n obs* valise *f*

**portrait** *n* portrait *m*; **full-length** ~ portrait *m* en pied

**portraiture** *n* art *m* du portrait; portrait *m*

**portray** *vt* (paint) peindre, faire le portrait de; (describe) dépeindre

**portrayal** *n* peinture *f*, description *f*

**Portugal** *n* le Portugal

**Portuguese** *n* Portugais -e; (language) portugais *m*; *adj* portugais

**pose** *n* pose *f*; attitude *f*; (affectation) affectation *f*; *vt* (question) poser; *vi* (model) poser; se donner des airs affectés; ~ **as** se faire passer pour

**poser** *n* question *f* difficile, *coll* colle *f*

**posh** *adj coll* chic (*f invar*); *vi* ~ **oneself up** se faire beau (*f* belle)

**position** *n* position *f*; attitude *f*; (place) place *f*, situation *f*; (employment) poste *m*, emploi *m*; (order) rang *m*, classement *m*; ~ **of trust** poste *m* de confiance; **be in a** ~ **to** être à même de; **he's in a better** ~ **to** il est mieux placé pour; **in a high** ~ haut placé; **in** ~ en place; **keep up one's** ~ tenir son rang; **put yourself in my** ~ mettez-vous à ma place; **take up a** ~ prendre position; *vt* placer, mettre en position; (find) déterminer la position de, situer

**positive** *adj* positif -ive; (sure) certain, assuré, convaincu; (absolute) absolu

**positively** *adv* positivement; (certainly) certainement, sûrement, absolument

**positiveness** *n* certitude *f*, assurance *f*; (manner) ton décisif

**positivism** *n* positivisme *m*

**posse** *n* (crowd) foule *f*, troupe *f*, bande *f*; (police) détachement *m*

**possess** *vt* posséder, être en possession de; ~ **oneself of sth** s'emparer de qch; **be ~ed of a quality** être doué d'une qualité; **be ~ed with** être obsédé de; **whatever ~ed you to ...?** qu'est-ce qui vous a pris de ...?

**possession** *n* possession *f*; (property) jouissance *f*; ~ **s** biens *mpl*, avoir *m*; **be in** ~ **of** disposer de, posséder; **enter into** ~ **of** entrer en possession de; **take** ~ **of** s'emparer de

**possessive** *adj* qui aime posséder entièrement; *gramm* possessif -ive

**possessor** *n* possesseur *m*, propriétaire

**possibility** *n* possibilité *f*; (possible event) éventualité *f*; **within the range of** ~ dans la limite du possible

**possible** *adj* possible; **as early as** ~ le plus tôt possible; **as far as** ~ dans la mesure du possible, autant que possible; le plus loin possible; **do everything** ~ faire tout son possible; **if** ~ si possible, si c'est possible; **it's just** ~ il y a une chance

**possibly** *adv* peut-être; **do all one** ~ **can** faire tout son possible; **I can't** ~ **come** je ne peux absolument pas venir

¹**post** *n* (wooden) poteau *m*; (door) montant *m*, pilier *m*; **as deaf as a** ~ sourd comme un pot; *fig* **be left at the** ~ manquer le départ; *vt* placarder, coller, afficher; ~ **no bills** défense d'afficher

²**post** *n* (duty) poste *m*; (employment) situation *f*, emploi *m*; **take up one's** ~ entrer en fonctions; *vt* poster; (sentinel) mettre en faction; **be ~ed to a command** être affecté à un commandement

³**post** *n* (letters) courrier *m*; (postal

organization) poste *f*; ~ **office** bureau *m* de poste; ~ **office clerk** employé(e) des postes; **Post Office Savings Bank** = Caisse Nationale d'Épargne; ~ **paid** port payé, franco; **by** ~ par la poste; **by return of** ~ par retour du courrier; **first-class** ~ = tarif normal; **miss the** ~ manquer le courrier; manquer la levée; **open one's** ~ dépouiller son courrier; **second-class** ~ = tarif réduit; **the (General) Post Office** = les Postes *fpl* et Télécommunications *fpl*; **the** ~ **has come** le facteur est passé; *vt* mettre à la poste, poster; ~ **sth to s/o** envoyer qch à qn par la poste; **keep s/o** ~ **ed** tenir qn au courant

⁴**post** *n mil* **last** ~ sonnerie *f* aux morts

**postage** *n* port *m*, affranchissement *m*

**postage-stamp** *n* timbre-poste *m* ( *pl* timbres-poste); timbre *m*

**postal** *adj* postal; ~ **order** mandat-poste *m* ( *pl* mandats-poste)

**postbag** *n* (mail) courrier *m*; sac postal

**post-box** *n* boîte *f* aux lettres

**postcard** *n* carte postale

**post-date** *vt* postdater

**poster** *n* affiche *f*

**poste restante** *n* poste restante

**posterior** *n* postérieur *m*, derrière *m*; *adj* postérieur

**posterity** *n* postérité *f*

**postern** *n* poterne *f*

**post-free** *adj* franc de port *invar*

**post-graduate (student)** *n* licencié -e qui poursuit ses études

**post-haste** *adv* en toute hâte

**posthumous** *adj* posthume

**postman** *n* facteur *m*

**postmark** *n* cachet *m* de la poste

**postmaster** *n* receveur *m* (des Postes)

**postmistress** *n* receveuse *f* (des Postes)

**post-mortem** *n* ~ **(examination)** autopsie *f*; *adj* après décès

**postpone** *vt* remettre, ajourner, différer, reporter (à plus tard)

**postponement** *n* ajournement *m*, renvoi *m*

**postscript** *n* post-scriptum *m invar*

**postulant** *n eccles* postulant -e

**postulate** *vt* postuler

**posture** *n* attitude *f*, posture *f*; (state) état *m*; *vi* prendre une posture

**post-war** *adj* d'après-guerre; **the** ~ **period** l'après-guerre *m*

**posy** *n* petit bouquet

**pot** *n* pot *m*; (cooking) marmite *f*; *coll* marihuana *f*; ~ **s and pans** batterie *f* de cuisine; *coll* ~ **s of money** des tas *mpl* d'argent; *coll* **go to** ~ aller à la ruine; *vt* mettre en pot; *coll* (shoot) tirer, abattre; (billiards) blouser; (child) mettre sur le pot; *vi* ~ **at** tirer un coup de fusil sur

**potash** *n* potasse *f*

**potassium** *n* potassium *m*

**potato** *n* ( *pl* ~ **es**) pomme *f* de terre; ~ **crisps**, *US* ~ **chips** pommes *fpl* chips; **boiled** ~ **es** pommes *fpl* (de terre) à l'anglaise; **baked** ~ **es** pommes *fpl* de terre au four; **chipped (French fried)** ~ **es** pommes (de terre) frites, *coll* frites *fpl*; **mashed** ~ **es** purée *f* de pommes de terre; **roast** ~ **es** pommes *fpl* de terre au four

**pot-belly** *n* panse *f*, bedon *m*

**pot-boiler** *n* œuvre *f* qui fait bouillir la marmite

**potency** *n* force *f*, puissance *f*; (medicine) efficacité *f*; *physiol* virilité *f*

**potent** *adj* (drug, etc) puissant, efficace; (argument, etc) convaincant; viril

**potentate** *n* potentat *m*

**potential** *n* potentiel *m*; *adj* potentiel -ielle; latent, en puissance

**potentiality** *n* potentialité *f*

**potently** *adv* puissamment

**pothole** *n* trou *m* dans une route, *coll* nid *m* de poule; *geol* gouffre *m*

**potholer** *n* spéléologue

**potholing** *n* spéléologie *f*

**pot-hook** *n* crémaillère *f*; (writing) bâton *m*

**potion** *n* potion *f*, dose *f*

**potluck** *n* **take** ~ manger à la fortune du pot

**pot-pourri** *n* pot-pourri *m* ( *pl* pots-pourris)

**pot-shot** *n coll* **take a** ~ **at sth** tirer au petit bonheur un coup de fusil sur qch; *fig* faire qch au petit bonheur

**potted** *adj* en pot, conservé *f* de

¹**potter** *n* potier *m*; ~ **'s wheel** tour *m* de potier

²**potter** *vi* ~ **about** (do odd jobs) bricoler; (wander) flâner; ~ **along** aller son petit bonhomme de chemin

**pottery** *n* poterie *f*

**potting** *n hort* mise *f* en pots; (jam, etc) mise *f* en conserve

¹**potty** *n coll* pot *m* de chambre

²**potty** *adj coll* (mad) timbré, toqué; (small) petit

**pouch** *n* petit sac; (animal) poche (ventrale); (under eyes) poche *f*

**pouf, pouffe** *n* (furniture) pouf *m*; (dress) bouffant *m*

**poulterer** *n* marchand -e de volaille

**poultice** *n* cataplasme *m*; *vt* mettre un cataplasme sur

**poultry** *n* volaille *f*

**pounce** *vi* ~ **on** s'abattre sur, se jeter sur

¹**pound** *n* (money, weight) livre *f*; ~ **sterling** livre *f* sterling; **by the** ~ à la livre

²**pound** *n* (animals) fourrière *f*

³**pound** vt broyer, piler; vi ~ **on** frapper sur

**pour** vt verser; vi (rain) tomber à verse; ~ **in** (people) affluer; ~ **into** (liquid) entrer à flots dans; (people) entrer en foule dans; **it is ~ing** il pleut à verse; **it never rains but it ~s** un malheur ne vient jamais seul

**pourer** n verseur -euse

**pout** n moue f; vi faire la moue

**poverty** n pauvreté f; (lack) pénurie f; ~ **of ideas** dénuement m d'idées

**poverty-stricken** adj indigent, dans la misère

**powder** n poudre f; vt (face) poudrer; (sprinkle with) saupoudrer; pulvériser; coll fig ~ **one's nose** aller aux toilettes

**powder-box** n poudrier m

**powder-compact** n poudrier m

**powderpuff** n houppe f (à poudre)

**powder-room** n toilette f pour dames

**power** n pouvoir m; (nation, machine) puissance f; (ability) faculté f, capacité f; (strength) force f, vigueur f; (authority) autorité f; **a ~ of good** grand bien; **all in my ~** tout ce qui est en mon pouvoir; **come to ~** arriver au pouvoir; **it's beyond my ~** cela ne m'est pas possible; **the ~s that be** les autorités fpl; vt fournir d'énergie

**power-driven** adj automoteur -trice

**powered** adj mû (f mue); **high-(low-)~** de haute (faible) puissance

**powerful** adj puissant, fort

**power-house** n see power-station

**powerless** adj impuissant

**powerlessness** n impuissance f

**power-mower** n tondeuse f à moteur

**power-point** n prise f de courant

**power-station, power-house** n centrale f électrique

**pox** n vérole f, syphilis f

**practicability** n praticabilité f

**practicable** adj praticable, faisable, pratique

**practical** adj pratique; ~ **consideration** considération f d'ordre pratique; ~ **joke** farce f; ~ **joker** farceur -euse

**practicality** n (plan, etc) caractère m pratique

**practically** adv pratiquement; (almost) presque, pour ainsi dire

**practicalness** n sens m pratique

**practice** n pratique f; (usage) habitude f, coutume f; (exercise) exercice m; (clients) clientèle f; ~ **makes perfect** c'est en forgeant qu'on devient forgeron; ~ **match** match m d'entraînement; **be in ~** être entraîné; **do sth for ~** faire qch pour s'exercer; **put into ~** mettre en pratique

**practise** vt pratiquer; (profession) exercer; (train at) s'exercer à; ~ **what one preaches** prêcher d'exemple; vi mus s'exercer; sp s'entraîner; (doctor, lawyer) exercer

**practised** adj expérimenté, exercé

**practising** adj qui exerce, exerçant; (religion) pratiquant

**practitioner** n praticien -ienne

**pragmatic(al)** adj pragmatique

**prairie** n prairie f

**praise** n louange f, éloge m; ~ **be to God!** Dieu soit loué!; **be loud in s/o's ~** prodiguer des éloges à qn; **beyond all ~** au-dessus de tout éloge; vt louer, faire l'éloge de; ~ **to the skies** porter aux nues

**praiseworthy** adj digne d'éloges; (work) méritoire

**pram** n voiture f d'enfants

**prance** vi (person) se pavaner; (horse) caracoler

**prank** n tour m, farce f; (mischief) frasque f, fredaine f; **play a ~ on** s/o jouer un tour à qn, faire une farce à qn

**prate** vi bavarder, jaser

**prattle** n babil m, babillage m; vi (esp child) babiller; (chatter) jaser, bavarder

**prattler** n babillard -e; bavard -e

**prawn** n bouquet m

**pray** vt + vi prier, supplier, implorer; ~ **come in** veuillez entrer; **be past ~ing for** être perdu sans retour; coll être incorrigible

**prayer** n prière f; **say one's ~s** faire ses dévotions; **the Lord's Prayer** l'oraison dominicale, le Pater

**preach** vt + vi prêcher

**preacher** n prédicateur m; pej prêcheur -euse

**preaching** n prédication f; pej prêcherie f

**preamble** n préambule m

**prebend** n prébende f

**precarious** adj précaire

**precaution** n précaution f

**precautionary** adj de précaution

**precede** vt précéder; (bring before) faire précéder; (have precedence) avoir la préséance sur

**precedence** n préséance f, priorité f

**precedent** n précédent m

**precentor** n eccles maître m de chapelle

**precept** n précepte m

**precinct** n enceinte f, enclos m; ~**s** pourtour m, limite f; **shopping ~** centre commercial (interdit à la circulation)

**preciosity** n préciosité f

**precious** adj précieux -ieuse; (style) affecté; adv ~ **few** très peu

**precipice** n précipice m

**precipitance, precipitancy** n précipita-

# precipitate

tion f, empressement m

**precipitate** adj précipité, irréfléchi; vt (cast down) précipiter; (hurry) hâter, accélérer, précipiter

**precipitation** n précipitation f

**precipitous** adj escarpé

**précis** n précis m, résumé m, abrégé m

**precise** adj précis, exact; (person) pointilleux -euse, méticuleux -euse

**precision** n précision f

**preclude** vt exclure, empêcher

**precocious** adj précoce

**precociousness, precocity** n précocité f

**precognition** n préconnaissance f

**preconceive** vt préconcevoir

**preconception** n préconception f; (bias) préjugé m

**precondition** n condition f préalable

**precursor** n précurseur m, devancier m

**pre-date** vt antidater; (come before) venir avant

**predatory** adj rapace

**predecessor** n prédécesseur m

**predestination** n prédestination f

**predestine** vt prédestiner, destiner d'avance

**predetermine** vt déterminer d'avance

**predicament** n embarras m, situation f difficile

**predicate** n gramm attribut m

**predict** vt prédire

**predictable** adj prévisible, qui peut être prédit

**prediction** n prédiction f

**predilection** n prédilection f

**predispose** vt prédisposer

**predisposition** n prédisposition f

**predominance** n prédominance f

**predominant** adj prédominant

**predominate** vi prédominer

**pre-eminence** n prééminence f

**pre-eminent** adj prééminent

**pre-empt** vt préempter; acquérir d'avance

**pre-emption** n (droit m de) préemption f

**pre-emptive** adj préemptif -ive; préventif -ive

**preen** vt (bird) lisser, nettoyer; ~ one-self se bichonner; fig se montrer satisfait

**prefab** n coll maison préfabriquée

**prefabricate** vt préfabriquer

**preface** n préface f, avant-propos m; introduction f; vt préfacer; préluder

**prefatory** adj préliminaire

**prefect** n préfet m; (school) élève qui aide à maintenir la discipline, moniteur -trice

**prefer** vt préférer; (promote) nommer; ~ a complaint déposer une plainte

**preferable** adj préférable

**preference** n préférence f; econ ~ stock actions privilégiées; in ~ to de préférence à

**preferential** adj préférentiel -ielle, de préférence

**preferment** n avancement m

**prefigure** vt préfigurer

**pregnancy** n grossesse f

**pregnant** adj enceinte, grosse

**prehensile** adj préhensile

**prehistoric** adj préhistorique

**prehistory** n préhistoire f

**prejudge** vt préjuger; (condemn in advance) condamner d'avance

**prejudice** n prévention f, préjugé m; (injury) préjudice m; have a ~ against être prévenu contre; without ~ sous toutes réserves; vt prévenir, prédisposer; (injure) nuire à, porter préjudice à

**prejudiced** adj prévenu

**prejudicial** adj préjudiciable, nuisible

**prelate** n prélat m

**preliminary** n prélude m; **preliminaries** préliminaires mpl; adj préliminaire, préalable

**prelude** n prélude m; vt préluder à, précéder; vi préluder

**premarital** adj avant le mariage

**premature** adj prématuré

**prematurely** adv prématurément, de façon prématurée; (birth) avant terme

**prematureness, prematurity** n prématurité f

**premeditate** vt préméditer

**premeditation** n préméditation f

**premier** n premier ministre; adj premier -ière

**premiership** n fonction f de premier ministre

**premise** n log prémisse f; ~s local m, locaux mpl; on the ~s sur les lieux; vt poser en principe; citer en guise d'introduction

**premium** n (prize) prix m, récompense f; (insurance) prime f; (initial payment) droit m; be at a ~ (be scarce) être très recherché; (be expensive) se vendre très cher; (stock) faire prime; put a ~ on donner une prime à

**premolar** n prémolaire f

**premonition** n pressentiment m, prémonition f

**prenatal** adj prénatal

**preoccupation** n préoccupation f

**preoccupy** vt préoccuper, absorber

**pre-ordain** vt ordonner d'avance

**prep** n coll étude f; ~ school école f préparatoire

**pre-packed** adj préconditionné

**preparation** n préparation f; (school) devoirs mpl; ~s préparatifs mpl

636

**preparatory** adj préparatoire

**prepare** vt préparer; (dish) accommoder; ~ **a surprise for s/o** ménager une surprise à qn; vi se préparer, s'apprêter; ~ **for an examination** préparer un examen

**prepared** adj préparé, prêt; **be ~ for** être prêt à, s'attendre à

**prepay** vt payer d'avance (à l'avance); (letter) affranchir

**preponderance** n prépondérance f

**preponderant** adj prépondérant

**preponderate** vi l'emporter, emporter la balance

**preposition** n préposition f

**prepossessing** adj agréable, prévenant

**preposterous** adj absurde, déraisonnable

**prerequisite** n nécessité f préalable

**prerogative** n prérogative f, privilège m

**presage** n présage m, pressentiment m; vt présager; (person) prédire

**Presbyterian** n+adj presbytérien -ienne

**Presbyterianism** n presbytérianisme m

**presbytery** n presbytère m, cure f; (chancel) chœur m

**prescience** n prescience f

**prescribe** vt prescrire, ordonner

**prescription** n prescription f; med ordonnance f; **make out a ~** rédiger une ordonnance

**presence** n présence f; (person) air m; (impressive) prestance f, allure f; ~ **of mind** sang-froid m, présence f d'esprit; **in the ~ of** en la présence de; ar **saving your ~** sauf votre respect

¹**present** n présent m; **at ~** à présent; **for the ~** pour le moment; adj présent; actuel -elle; **all those ~** toute l'assistance, tous les assistants; **at the ~ time** à l'époque actuelle; **be ~ at** être présent à, assister à; **the ~ tense** le (temps) présent

²**present** n don m, cadeau m, présent m; **is it for a ~?** c'est pour offrir?; **make s/o a ~ of sth** faire cadeau de qch à qn; vt présenter, offrir, donner

**presentable** adj présentable; (clothing) portable

**presentation** n présentation f

**present-day** adj actuel -elle, d'aujourd'hui

**presentiment** n pressentiment m

**presently** adv bientôt, tout à l'heure; US maintenant

**preservation** n conservation f; (from danger, etc) préservation f

**preservative** n agent m de conservation; adj préservatif -ive

**preserve** vt conserver; (from danger, etc) préserver; (peace) maintenir; ~ **appearances** sauver les apparences

**preside** vi présider; ~ **over** présider (à)

**presidency** n présidence f

**president** n président -e

**presidential** adj présidentiel -ielle

**press** n (papers) presse f; (crowd) foule f; (pressure) pression f; (printing) imprimerie f; (grapes) pressoir m; ~ **conference** conférence f de presse; ~ **release** communiqué m de presse; **have a good ~** avoir bonne presse; **in the ~** sous presse; vt presser; (press on) appuyer sur, peser sur; (squeeze out) exprimer; (squash) pressurer; (clothes) repasser; ~ **down** enfoncer; ~ **for a reply** insister sur une réponse; ~ **into service** enrôler; ~ **one's advantage** poursuivre son avantage; vi se serrer, se presser; ~ **back** refouler; ~ **on** avancer, continuer

**press-agency** n agence f de presse

**press-agent** n agent m de publicité

**press-box** n stand m pour la presse

**press-button** adj presse-bouton invar

**press-clipping, press-cutting** n coupure f de journal

**pressed** adj pressé, serré, comprimé; ~ **for time** très pressé; **be very ~** être débordé; **hard ~** serré de près

**press-gallery** n tribune f de la presse

**pressing** adj urgent, pressant

**press-stud** n bouton-pression m (pl boutons-pression)

**pressure** n pression f; ~ **of business** poids m des affaires; **act under ~** agir par contrainte; **blood ~** tension artérielle; **bring ~ to bear** exercer une pression

**pressure-cooker** n autocuiseur m, cocotte f minute

**pressure-gauge** n jauge f de pression

**pressurize** vt pressuriser

**prestige** n prestige m

**prestigious** adj prestigieux -ieuse

**presumable** adj présumable

**presume** vt présumer; vi ~ **to do sth** se permettre de faire qch, présumer de faire qch

**presuming** adj présomptueux -euse

**presumption** n présomption f; arrogance f

**presumptuous** adj présomptueux -euse

**presuppose** vt présupposer

**presupposition** n présupposition f

**pretence** n semblant m, prétexte m; (claim) prétention f; **make a ~ of doing sth** faire semblant de faire qch; **on the ~ of** sous prétexte de; **under false ~s** par des moyens frauduleux

**pretend** vt simuler, feindre; (claim) prétendre; vi faire semblant; (act) jouer la comédie; ~ **to be deaf** jouer le sourd

**pretended**

(*f* la sourde); ~ **to do sth** faire semblant de faire qch

**pretended** *adj* simulé, feint, faux (*f* fausse); (person) prétendu, supposé

**pretender** *n* (to the throne, etc) prétendant; simulateur -trice

**pretension** *n* prétention *f*

**pretentious** *adj* prétentieux -ieuse

**preterite** *n gramm* prétérit *m*

**preternatural** *adj* surnaturel -elle

**pretext** *n* prétexte *m*; **on the ~ of** sous prétexte de; *vt* prétexter, alléguer comme prétexte

**prettily** *adv* joliment, gentiment

**prettiness** *n* gentillesse *f*

**pretty** *adj* joli, gentil -ille; ~ **as a picture** joli à croquer; *coll* **be sitting ~** avoir la bonne place; **cost a ~ penny** coûter assez cher; **this is a ~ state of affairs!** c'est du joli!; *adv* assez, passablement; ~ **nearly** à peu près

**pretzel** *n cul* bretzel *m*

**prevail** *vi* (win) prévaloir; (dominate) prédominer; (be prevalent) régner; ~ **upon s/o to do sth** décider qn à faire qch; **be ~ed upon to do sth** se laisser persuader de faire qch

**prevailing** *adj* dominant; (fashion) en vogue

**prevalence** *n* prédominance *f*

**prevalent** *adj* général, répandu; dominant

**prevaricate** *vi* équivoquer, biaiser

**prevarication** *n* tergiversation *f*; (lies) mensonge *m*

**prevaricator** *n* tergiversateur -trice; (liar) menteur -euse

**prevent** *vt* empêcher; (forestall) prévenir, éviter; ~ **s/o from doing sth** empêcher qn de faire qch

**preventable** *adj* évitable

**preventative** *adj* préventif -ive

**prevention** *n* empêchement *m*

**preventive** *n* empêchement *m*; *med* médicament préventif; *adj* préventif -ive

**preview** *n cin* + *theat* avant-première *f*; (art gallery) vernissage *m*

**previous** *adj* préalable, antérieur; *coll* trop pressé; **the ~ day** la veille, le jour précédent; *adv* ~ **to** avant, antérieurement à

**previously** *adv* préalablement, auparavant

**prewar** *adj* d'avant-guerre

**prey** *n* proie *f*; **be a ~ to** être en proie à; **beasts of ~** carnassiers *mpl*; **birds of ~** oiseaux *mpl* de proie; **fall a ~ to** tomber en proie à; *vi* ~ **upon** faire sa proie de; (mind) tourmenter, travailler, ronger

**price** *n* prix *m*; **at any ~** à tout prix, coûte que coûte; **at a reduced ~** au rabais; **cost ~** prix coûtant; **fixed ~**

prix *m* fixe; **not at any ~** pour rien au monde; **what ~ ...?** que dites-vous de ...?; *vt* fixer le prix de; estimer, évaluer; (inquire) s'informer du prix de; (show price) marquer le prix de; **be ~d at ten francs** être marqué dix francs

**priceless** *adj* inestimable, hors de prix; *coll fig* inouï, (person) impayable

**price-list** *n* tarif *m*, prix courant

**pricey** *adj coll* coûteux -euse, cher (*f* chère)

**prick** *n* piqûre *f*; coup *m* d'épingle; *sl* queue *f*; **kick against the ~s** regimber; *vt* piquer; (conscience) causer des remords; *hort* ~ **out** repiquer; ~ **up one's ears** (person) tendre l'oreille; (animal) dresser les oreilles; *vi* picoter

**pricking** *n* piquage *m*; ~ **s of conscience** remords *mpl* de conscience

**prickle** *n* piquant *m*, épine *f*; *vt* piquer, picoter; *vi* fourmiller

**prickling** *n* picotement *m*, fourmillement *m*

**prickly** *adj* (plant) épineux -euse; (animal) armé de piquants; ~ **pear** figue *f* de Barbarie

**pride** *n* orgueil *m*, fierté *f*; (self-esteem) amour-propre *m* (*pl* amours-propres); (zenith) comble *m*; **be the ~ of** faire l'orgueil de; **take ~ in doing sth** faire qch avec amour; *vt* ~ **oneself on sth** se piquer de qch, s'enorgueillir de qch

**priest** *n* prêtre *m*

**priestess** *n* prêtresse *f*

**priesthood** *n* sacerdoce *m*, prêtrise *f*

**prig** *n* poseur -euse; petit saint (*f* petite sainte)

**priggish** *adj* poseur -euse; bégueule

**prim** *adj* guindé; (person) collet monté *invar*

**primacy** *n* primauté *f*

**prima donna** *n* prima donna *f invar*

**primaeval** *adj see* **primeval**

**prima facie** *adj* + *adv* à première vue, de prime abord

**primarily** *adv* principalement; primitivement

**primary** *n US* élection *f* préliminaire qui permet de choisir les candidats à la présidence; *adj* premier -ière, originel -elle; primaire; (chief) principal; ~ **product** produit *m* de base

**primate** *n eccles* primat *m*; *zool* primate *m*

¹**prime** *n* perfection *f*; commencement *m*; (best) choix *m*; **be past one's ~** être sur le retour; **in the ~ of life** dans la force (fleur) de l'âge; *adj* premier -ière, principal; (quality) de première qualité; primitif -ive; (very important) primordial; ~ **minister** premier ministre

²**prime** *vt* (gun, pump) amorcer;

638

(instruct) mettre au courant; (surface) apprêter

**primeval, primaeval** adj primitif -ive, primordial; ~ **forest** forêt f vierge

**primitive** adj primitif -ive

**primly** adv d'un air guindé

**primness** n air m collet monté

**primogeniture** n primogéniture f; **right of** ~ droit m d'aînesse

**primordial** adj primordial

**primrose** n primevère f

**primula** n primevère f

**primus** n ~ **(stove)** réchaud m à pétrole

**prince** n prince m

**princely** adj princier -ière, de prince; fig magnifique

**princess** n princesse f

**principal** n directeur -trice; (boss) chef m, patron -onne; (money) capital m; leg auteur m; theat rôle principal; adj principal

**principality** n principauté f

**principally** adv principalement

**principle** n principe m; **do sth as a matter of** ~ faire qch par principe; **on** ~ par principe

**prink** vt (bird) ~ **its feathers** se lisser les plumes; vi prendre des airs

**print** n (finger, foot) empreinte f; (engraving) gravure f, estampe f; (printed matter) imprimé m, matière imprimée; phot épreuve f, copie f; (cloth) indienne f, cotonnade f; **be in** ~ être imprimé; **large (small)** ~ gros (petits) caractères; **out of** ~ épuisé; vt imprimer; (make impression) marquer d'une empreinte; phot tirer; ~**ed matter** imprimés mpl; ~ **off a newspaper** tirer un journal; ~ **out** imprimer

**printable** adj imprimable

**printer** n imprimeur m; (workman) (ouvrier m) typographe m; (computer) printer; ~**'s error** faute f d'impression, coquille f; ~**'s ink** encre f d'imprimerie; ~**'s reader** correcteur -trice d'épreuves

**printing** n impression f; (art) imprimerie f; phot tirage m

**printing-press** n presse f (d'imprimerie)

¹**prior** n eccles prieur m

²**prior** adj préalable, antérieur, précédent; adv ~ **to** avant, antérieurement à

**prioress** n eccles prieure f

**priority** n priorité f; **according to** ~ selon l'ordre de priorité; adj prioritaire

**priory** n prieuré m

**prise, prize** vt ~ **open** forcer; ~ **up** soulever à l'aide d'un levier

**prism** n prisme m

**prismatic** adj prismatique

**prison** n prison f; **have been in** ~ avoir

fait de la prison

**prison-camp** n camp m de prisonniers

**prisoner** n prisonnier -ière; détenu -e; ~ **at the bar** prévenu -e, accusé -e; **take** ~ faire prisonnier

**prison-van** n voiture f cellulaire, coll panier m à salade

**pristine** adj premier -ière, primitif -ive

**privacy** n vie privée; retraite f; intimité f; **have no** ~ n'être jamais seul

**private** n mil simple soldat m; ~**s** parties (génitales); **in** ~ (meeting) en séance privée; dans l'intimité, en famille; adj privé; (personal) particulier -ière, personnel -elle; (secret) secret -ète; ~ défense d'entrer, entrée interdite; ~ **lesson** leçon particulière; ~ **opinion** avis personnel; ~ **person** particulier m; ~ **residence** domicile particulier

**privation** n privation f

**privet** n bot troène m

**privilege** n privilège m, prérogative f

**privy** n leg partie intéressée; ar (toilet) cabinets mpl; adj privé; **Privy Council** = Conseil m du Roi; **be** ~ **to sth** avoir connaissance de qch

¹**prize** n prix m; (lottery) lot m; (navy) prise f; vt priser, estimer, évaluer; ~ **highly** faire grand cas de

²**prize** vt see prise

**prize-fight** n match m de boxe (professionnelle)

**prize-winner** n lauréat -e

¹**pro** n sp pro, professionel -elle

²**pro** n **the** ~**s and cons** le pour et le contre; prep ~ **forma** pour la forme

**probability** n probabilité f; (plausibility) vraisemblance f; **in all** ~ selon toute probabilité

**probable** adj probable; (plausible) vraisemblable

**probate** n (will) homologation f

**probation** n temps m d'épreuve; liberté f sous surveillance; **be on** ~ être mise à l'épreuve, être en liberté surveillée; ~ **officer** délégué -e à la liberté surveillée

**probationary** adj d'épreuve; (person) stagiaire

**probationer** n stagiaire; eccles novice; leg personne f en liberté surveillée

**probe** n sonde f; coup m de sonde; (inquiry) enquête f; **space** ~ sonde f cosmique; vt sonder, explorer; fouiller, examiner

**probity** n probité f

**problem** n problème m; ~ **child** enfant difficile

**problematic(al)** adj problématique

**procedure** n procédé m, manière f d'agir; leg procédure f

**proceed** vi aller; (go on) avancer, passer, poursuivre son chemin; (continue) continuer; (act) procéder; ~ **against** s/o procéder contre qn; ~ **from** provenir de; **be** ~**ing** être en cours, suivre son train

**proceeding** n procédé m, façon f d'agir; ~s (meeting) séance f; (deliberation) débats mpl; **take** ~s **against** s/o intenter un procès contre qn

**proceeds** n produit m; (money) recette f

¹**process** n processus m; (method) procédé m, méthode f; (work) travail m; **in the** ~ **of** en cours de; **in the** ~ **of time** avec le temps; vt traiter, transformer

²**process** vi coll aller en cortège

**processing** n traitement m d'une matière première; **data** ~ traitement m des informations; **food** ~ industrie f alimentaire; **information** ~ informatique f

**procession** n cortège m; (religious) procession f

**proclaim** vt proclamer, déclarer

**proclamation** n proclamation f, déclaration f

**proclivity** n penchant m, tendance f

**procrastinate** vi temporiser, remettre les choses à plus tard

**procrastinator** n temporisateur -trice

**procreate** vt procréer

**procreation** n procréation f

**procurable** adj procurable

**procuration** n acquisition f; leg procuration f

**procure** vt obtenir, procurer; ~ **sth (for oneself)** se procurer qch; vi (prostitution) faire le métier de proxénète

**procurement** n acquisition f

**procurer** n acquéreur -euse; (for s/o else) personne f qui procure; (prostitution) proxénète m

**prod** n coup m; vt donner un petit coup à; fig stimuler, aiguillonner

**prodigal** n + adj prodigue

**prodigality** n prodigalité f

**prodigious** adj prodigieux -ieuse

**prodigy** n prodige m, merveille f; **infant** ~ enfant prodige

**produce** n produit m; (production) rendement m; vt produire; (show) présenter; (industry) fabriquer; cin + theat mettre en scène; (create) créer; (profit) rapporter

**producer** n producteur -trice; theat metteur m en scène; cin + TV réalisateur -trice; rad metteur m en ondes

**producible** adj productible

**product** n produit m

**production** n production f; (showing) présentation f; (manufacture) fabrication f; theat mise f en scène; rad mise f en ondes; (show, film, etc) réalisation f

**productive** adj productif -ive; (land) fécond

**productivity** n productivité f

**profanation** n profanation f

**profane** adj profane; impie; vt profaner, polluer

**profess** vt professer; (profession) exercer; ~ **oneself** se déclarer; (falsely) se faire passer pour

**professed** adj déclaré; (falsely) prétendu, soi-disant

**profession** n profession f, métier m; déclaration f; **by** ~ de profession

**professional** n professionnel -elle; adj professionnel -elle; expert; ~s gens mpl du métier; ~ **classes** membres mpl des professions libérales

**professionalism** n professionnalisme m

**professor** n professeur m (titulaire d'une chaire)

**professorial** adj professoral

**professorship** n chaire f; **obtain a** ~ être nommé à une chaire

**proffer** vt offrir, présenter

**proficiency** n compétence f, capacité f

**proficient** adj compétent, capable

**profile** n profil m, silhouette f; (newspaper) portrait m; **maintain a low** ~ se comporter avec réserve; vt profiler

**profit** n profit m, bénéfice m; avantage m; ~ **and loss** profits mpl et pertes fpl; **sell at a** ~ vendre à profit; vt profiter à; vi bénéficier, profiter

**profitability** n rentabilité f

**profitable** adj profitable, avantageux -euse

**profiteer** n profiteur m

**profitless** adj sans profit

**profit-sharing** n participation f aux bénéfices

**profligacy** n libertinage m, débauche f

**profligate** n + adj débauché -e, libertin -e

**profound** adj profond, approfondi

**profundity, profoundness** n profondeur f

**profuse** adj prodigue; abondant

**profusion** n profusion f, abondance f

**progenitor** n ancêtre m

**progeniture** n progéniture f

**progeny** n progéniture f; (descendants) descendants mpl, lignée f

**prognosis** n med diagnostic m, pronostic m

**prognostic** n pronostic m, présage m; adj pronostique

**prognosticate** vt pronostiquer, prédire

**prognostication** n pronostication f, prédiction f

**programme,** US **program** n programme m; vt programmer

**programme-music** n musique f de genre

**programmer** n programmeur -euse

**progress** n progrès m; (movement) marche f en avant; **in ~** en cours; **make ~** faire des progrès; vi s'avancer; (improve) faire des progrès; (illness) progresser

**progression** n progression f

**progressive** adj progressif -ive

**prohibit** vt interdire, défendre; **smoking ~ed** défense f de fumer

**prohibition** n interdiction f, défense f, prohibition f; US hist prohibition f

**prohibitive** adj prohibitif -ive; **~ price** prix m inabordable

**project** n projet m; vt projeter; (throw) lancer, projeter; vi s'avancer, faire saillie

**projectile** n projectile m

**projecting** adj en saillie

**projection** n projection f; (jutting out) saillie f, avancement m; cin **~ room** cabine f de projection

**projectionist** n projectionniste

**projector** n projecteur m; cin appareil m de projection

**proletarian** n prolétaire m; adj prolétarien -ienne

**proletariat(e)** n prolétariat m

**proliferate** vi proliférer

**proliferation** n prolifération f

**prolific** adj prolifique, fécond

**prolix** adj diffus, prolixe

**prolixity** n prolixité f

**prologue** n prologue m

**prolong** vt prolonger

**prolongation** n prolongation f

**prom** n coll (seaside) esplanade f; US bal m d'étudiants; = **promenade concert**

**promenade** n (walk) promenade f; lieu m de promenade, esplanade f; theat promenoir m; **~ concert** concert m où une partie des auditeurs restent debout; vt promener; vi se promener; parader

**promenade-deck** n pont m promenade

**prominence** n proéminence f; fig distinction f, éminence f

**prominent** adj saillant, proéminent; (noteworthy) remarquable; (famous) éminent; **~ personality** personnage m très en vue; **play a ~ part** jouer un rôle important

**promiscuity** n promiscuité f

**promiscuous** adj mêlé, confus; (indiscriminate) sans distinction; **be ~** coucher avec tout le monde

**promise** n promesse f; **break one's ~** manquer à sa promesse; **full of ~** qui promet; vt promettre; vi promettre; **~ well** s'annoncer bien

**promising** adj prometteur -euse, qui promet bien

**promissory** adj **~ note** billet m à ordre

**promontory** n promontoire m

**promote** vt (person) donner de l'avancement à, nommer; (arts) encourager; (company) lancer, fonder; (interests) avancer; (make easier) faciliter; (advertise) faire de la publicité (réclame) pour

**promoter** n instigateur -trice; comm promoteur m

**promotion** n avancement m; promotion f; (arts) encouragement m; comm lancement m

**prompt** adj prompt, exact; (quick) rapide; (immediate) immédiat; adv promptement, à l'heure

**prompt** n suggestion f; vt theat souffler; (urge) exciter; (inspire) inspirer; **~ s/o to do sth** suggérer qch à qn, inciter qn à faire qch; **be ~ed by sth** être mû (f mue) par qch

**prompt-box** n theat trou m du souffleur

**prompt-corner** n theat côté m jardin

**prompter** n instigateur -trice; theat souffleur m; **~'s box** trou m du souffleur

**promptitude** n promptitude f, empressement m

**promptly** adv promptement; immédiatement

**promulgate** vt promulguer; (news, idea) répandre

**promulgation** n promulgation f; (news, idea) dissémination f

**prone** adj (person) couché sur le ventre, couché la face contre terre; (inclined) enclin, disposé

**proneness** n disposition f, inclination f

**prong** n fourchon m; (fork) dent f

**pronged** adj à dents

**pronoun** n pronom m

**pronounce** vt prononcer; (declare) déclarer

**pronounceable** adj prononçable

**pronounced** adj marqué, prononcé, très fort

**pronouncement** n déclaration f

**pronunciation** n prononciation f

**proof** n (evidence) preuve f; (test) épreuve f; phot + print épreuve f; **give (show) ~ of** faire preuve de; **in ~ of** en preuve de; **put to the ~** mettre à l'épreuve; adj résistant; **~ against sth** à l'épreuve de qch

**proof-reader** n correcteur -trice

**prop** n (support) appui m, support m, étai m; (plant) tuteur m; vt **~ up** soutenir; étayer

**prop** n theat accessoire m

**prop** n coll (propeller) hélice f

**propaganda** n propagande f

**propagandize** vt soumettre à la propagande

**propagate** *vt* propager; (ideas) répandre, disséminer; *vi* se propager, se reproduire

**propagation** *n* propagation *f*, reproduction *f*

**propagator** *n* propagateur -trice

**propane** *n* propane *m*

**propel** *vt* propulser; donner une impulsion à

**propellant** *n* combustible *m*; *adj* propulseur (no *f*)

**propeller** *n* (screw) hélice *f*; propulseur *m*

**propensity** *n* penchant *m*, tendance *f*, inclination *f*

**proper** *adj* propre; (suitable) convenable, juste, approprié; (correct) correct, comme il faut; (real) vrai; ~ to sth particulier -ière à qch; at the ~ time en temps utile; do as you think ~ faites comme bon vous semble; *adv coll* vraiment

**properly** *adv* proprement; (correctly) correctement; (well) bien, comme il faut; (very much) absolument

**property** *n* propriété *f*; biens *mpl*; *theat* accessoire *m*; landed ~ biens fonciers; lost ~ objets trouvés

**prophecy** *n* prophétie *f*

**prophesy** *vt* prophétiser, prédire

**prophet** *n* prophète *m*

**prophetess** *n* prophétesse *f*

**prophetic(al)** *adj* prophétique

**prophylactic** *n* prophylactique *m*; *adj* prophylactique

**prophylaxis** *n* prophylaxie *f*

**propinquity** *n* proximité *f*

**propitiate** *vt* rendre propice; (appease) apaiser

**propitiation** *n* propitiation *f*; apaisement *m*

**propitiator** *n* propitiateur -trice

**propitiatory** *adj* propitiatoire

**propitious** *adj* propice, favorable

**proportion** *n* proportion *f*, partie *f*; in ~ as à mesure que; in ~ to en proportion à; out of ~ mal proportionné; out of ~ to disproportionné à; *vt* proportionner; (ingredients) doser

**proportional** *adj* proportionnel -elle, en proportion

**proportionate** *adj* proportionné

**proposal** *n* proposition *f*; offre *f*; (marriage) demande *f* en mariage

**propose** *vt* proposer, offrir; ~ s/o's health proposer un toast à qn; *vi* (intend) compter; (marriage) faire une demande en mariage; ~ to do sth se proposer (avoir l'intention) de faire qch

**proposition** *n* proposition *f*; (business) affaire *f*; a tough ~ un problème difficile

**propound** *vt* proposer; (idea) émettre; (question) poser

**proprietary** *adj* de propriétaire, de propriété; ~ article article breveté; ~ medicine spécialité *f* pharmaceutique

**proprietor** *n* propriétaire *m*

**proprietress** *n* propriétaire *f*

**propriety** *n* (suitability) propriété *f*; bienséance *f*, décence *f*; (correctness) justesse *f*, correction *f*, rectitude *f*

**propulsion** *n* propulsion *f*

**prorogation** *n* prorogation *f*

**prorogue** *vt* proroger

**prosaic** *adj* prosaïque

**proscenium** *n theat* avant-scène *f*, proscenium *m*

**proscribe** *vt* proscrire; (forbid) interdire, défendre

**prose** *n* prose *f*; (translation into foreign language) thème *m*

**prosecute** *vt* poursuivre en justice

**prosecution** *n leg* poursuites *fpl*; (continuation) continuation *f*; (execution) exercice *m*; the Prosecution (state) le ministère public; (private) les plaignants *mpl*; witness for the ~ témoin *m* à charge

**prosecutor** *n* plaignant *m*, demandeur *m*; Public Prosecutor procureur *m* de la République

**proselyte** *n* prosélyte

**proselytize** *vt* convertir

**prosiness** *n* prosaïsme *m*; (person) verbosité *f*

**prosody** *n* prosodie *f*

**prospect** *n* vue *f*; *fig* perspective *f*; (prospects) espérances *fpl*, avenir *m*; (chance) chance *f*; *vt* + *vi* prospecter

**prospecting** *n* recherche *f*

**prospective** *adj* prospectif -ive, en perspective

**prospector** *n* prospecteur -trice, chercheur -euse

**prospectus** *n* prospectus *m*

**prosper** *vi* prospérer, réussir

**prosperity** *n* prospérité *f*

**prosperous** *adj* prospère; (favourable) favorable

**prostate** *n* prostate *f*

**prostitute** *n* prostituée *f*; *vt* prostituer

**prostitution** *n* prostitution *f*

**prostrate** *adj* prosterné; *fig* abattu, accablé; *vt* abattre; ~ oneself se prosterner

**prostration** *n* prostration *f*; *fig* abattement *m*

**prosy** *adj* prosaïque; (person) ennuyeux -euse; (wordy) verbeux -euse

**protagonist** *n* protagoniste *m*

**protect** *vt* protéger, défendre; (interests) sauvegarder

**protection** *n* protection *f*, défense *f*;

(interests) sauvegarde *f*; (patronage) patronage *m*; (shelter) abri *m*

**protective** *adj* protecteur -trice

**protector** *n* protecteur -trice

**protectorate** *n* protectorat *m*

**protégé** *n* protégé -e

**protein** *n* protéine *f*

**protest** *n* protestation *f*; **raise a ~** élever une protestation; **under ~** en protestant; *vt* + *vi* protester

**Protestant** *n* + *adj* protestant -e

**Protestantism** *n* protestantisme *m*

**protestation** *n* protestation *f*; (affirmation) déclaration *f*

**protocol** *n* protocole *m*

**protoplasm** *n* protoplasme *m*

**prototype** *n* prototype *m*

**protract** *vt* prolonger, traîner en longueur

**protraction** *n* prolongation *f*

**protractor** *n geom* rapporteur *m*

**protrude** *vi* s'avancer, faire saillie

**protruding** *adj* saillant

**protrusion** *n* saillie *f*

**protuberance** *n* protubérance *f*

**protuberant** *adj* protubérant

**proud** *adj* fier (*f* fière), orgueilleux -euse; (haughty) hautain; *coll* **do oneself ~** ne se priver de rien; *coll* **do s/o ~** se mettre en frais pour qn

**provable** *adj* prouvable, démontrable

**prove** *vt* prouver, démontrer; (test) éprouver; (check) vérifier; *leg* homologuer; **~ oneself** faire ses preuves; **to ~ my case** comme preuve à l'appui; *vi* se montrer, être; (turn out to be) s'avérer

**provender** *n* fourrage *m*

**proverb** *n* proverbe *m*

**proverbial** *adj* proverbial

**provide** *vt* fournir, munir, nantir; **~ s/o with sth** fournir qch à qn; *vi* **~ against** se prémunir contre; **~ for oneself** se suffire; (feeding) se nourrir; **~ for s/o** pourvoir aux besoins de qn; **~ for sth** prévoir qch

**provided** *adj* pourvu, muni; *conj* **~ that** pourvu que

**providence** *n* providence *f*; (foresight) prévoyance *f*; (economy) économie *f*

**provident** *adj* prévoyant; (thrifty) économe

**providential** *adj* providentiel -ielle

**province** *n* province *f*; (sphere) ressort *m*, domaine *m*

**provincial** *adj* provincial, de province

**provincialism** *n* provincialisme *m*

**provision** *n* provision *f*; stipulation *f*; *comm* prestation *f*; (law) clause *f*; **~ s** vivres *mpl*, provisions *fpl*; (in shop) produits *mpl* d'alimentation; **come within the ~ s of the law** tomber sous le coup de la loi; **make ~ against** prendre

des mesures contre; **make ~ for s/o** pourvoir aux besoins de qn; **make ~ for sth** pourvoir à qch; *vt* ravitailler, approvisionner

**provisional** *adj* provisoire, temporaire

**proviso** *n* condition *f*, stipulation *f*

**provisory** *adj* conditionnel -elle; provisoire

**provocation** *n* provocation *f*

**provocative** *adj* provocateur -trice; provocant; (annoying) agaçant

**provoke** *vt* provoquer, inciter; (annoy) irriter, contrarier, agacer; (curiosity) exciter

**provoking** *adj* irritant, exaspérant

**prow** *n* proue *f*

**prowess** *n* prouesse *f*

**prowl** *n* **be on the ~** rôder; *vi* rôder

**prowl-car** *n US* voiture *f* de patrouille

**prowler** *n* rôdeur -euse

**proximity** *n* proximité *f*

**proxy** *n leg* procuration *f*; (person) fondé -e de pouvoir(s), délégué -e

**prude** *n* prude *f*; *adj* prude, *coll* bégueule

**prudence** *n* prudence *f*, sagesse *f*

**prudent** *adj* prudent, sage

**prudery** *n* pruderie *f*, *coll* bégueulerie *f*

**prudish** *adj* prude, pudibond, *coll* bégueule

¹**prune** *n* pruneau *m*

²**prune** *vt* tailler, élaguer

**pruning** *n* taille *f*

**pruning-knife** *n* serpette *f*

**prurience, pruriency** *n* lasciveté *f*, luxure *f*

**prurient** *adj* lascif -ive

**Prussian** *n* Prussien -ienne; *adj* prussien -ienne

**prussic** *adj* prussique

**pry** *vi* fureter, fouiller, *coll* fourrer le nez

**prying** *adj* trop curieux -ieuse

**psalm** *n* psaume *m*

**psalmist** *n* psalmiste *m*

**psalmody** *n* psalmodie *f*

**psalter** *n* psautier *m*

**pseudo** *adj coll* fumiste

**pseudonym** *n* pseudonyme *m*

**psyche** *n* psyché *f*

**psychedelic** *adj* psychédélique

**psychiatric** *adj* psychiatrique

**psychiatrist** *n* psychiatre

**psychiatry** *n* psychiatrie *f*

**psychic(al)** *adj* psychique

**psychoanalyse** *vt* psychanalyser

**psychoanalysis** *n* psychanalyse *f*

**psychoanalyst** *n* psychanalyste

**psychological** *adj* psychologique

**psychologist** *n* psychologue

**psychology** *n* psychologie *f*

**psychopath** *n* psychopathe

**psychosis** *n* psychose *f*

**psychosomatic** *adj* psychosomatique

psychotherapy *n* psychothérapie *f*
psychotic *n* + *adj* psychotique
ptarmigan *n* lagopède *m*
ptomaine *n chem* ptomaïne *f*
pub *n coll* pub *m*, bar *m*
pub-crawl *n* tournée *f* des bistrots
puberty *n* puberté *f*
pubescent *adj* pubère
pubic *adj* pubien -ienne; ~ hair poils *mpl* (du pubis)
public *n* public *m*; in ~ en public; the general ~ le grand public; *adj* public (*f* publique); ~ holiday fête légale; ~ library bibliothèque municipale; ~ ownership nationalisation *f*; ~ school = lycée indépendant et privé d'une certaine catégorie; *US* école *f* d'état; ~ spirit civisme *m*; ~ transport transports publics, transports *mpl* en commun
publican *n* patron -onne de café (de bistrot), aubergiste
publication *n* publication *f*; (of book) parution *f*; (decree) promulgation *f*
public-house *n* café *m*, bistrot *m*, pub *m*
publicity *n* publicité *f*; ~ department service *m* de presse
publicize *vt* faire connaître au public; *comm* faire de la publicité autour de
publicly *adv* publiquement, en public
publish *vt* publier; (book) faire paraître, sortir; just ~ed vient de paraître
publishable *adj* publiable
publisher *n* éditeur -trice
publishing *n* publication *f*; (trade) édition *f*
puce *n* puce *m*; *adj* puce *invar*
puck *n* (ice-hockey) palet *m*
pucker *n* plissement *m*; *vt* rider; (crease) plisser; (sewing) faire goder; *vi* ~ up faire des plis
pudding *n* pudding *m*, pouding *m*; black ~ boudin (noir); rice ~ riz *m* au lait
puddle *n* flaque *f* (d'eau); *vt* (clay) corroyer; (metal) puddler
pudgy *adj* boulot -otte, grassouillet -ette
puerile *adj* puéril
puerility *n* puérilité *f*
puff *n* souffle *m*; (air) bouffée *f*; (dress) bouffant *m*; *cul* gâteau feuilleté; (publicity) boniment *m*; *vt* (swell) gonfler, faire gonfler; (exaggerate) faire mousser; ~ a cigarette fumer une cigarette (par petites bouffées); *vi* souffler; lancer des bouffées; (shirt) bouffer; ~ and blow haleter
puffin *n* macareux *m*
puffiness *n* boursouflure *f*, enflure *f*
puff-pastry *n* pâte feuilletée
puffy *adj* (swollen) bouffi, boursouflé; (wind) qui souffle par bouffées

¹pug *n* (dog) carlin *m*, roquet *m*
²pug *n* (clay) argile malaxée; *vt* malaxer, corroyer
pugilism *n* pugilat *m*, boxe *f*
pugilist *n* pugiliste *m*, boxeur *m*
pugnacious *adj* batailleur -euse, querelleur -euse
pugnacity *n* humeur batailleuse
pug-nose *n* nez épaté
puke *vi* vomir; *sl* dégobiller
pull *n* traction *f*, tirage *m*; (advantage) avantage *m*; *coll* (influence) piston *m*; (rowing) coup *m* d'aviron; *coll* (drink) gorgée *f*; (magnet) force *f* d'attraction; *vt* tirer; ~ about tirailler; ~ a face faire une grimace; ~ apart détacher, séparer; ~ away arracher; ~ down faire descendre; (illness) affaiblir; (topple) renverser; (demolish) démolir; ~ in rentrer; *coll* (police) arrêter; *coll* (succeed) ~ it off réussir; ~ off enlever, arracher, retirer; *sp* gagner; ~ oneself together se reprendre; ~ out sortir, tirer, retirer; (tooth) arracher; ~ round ranimer; (after illness) remettre sur pied; ~ s/o back empêcher qn de progresser; (restrain) retenir; ~ s/o's leg taquiner qn, faire marcher qn; ~ s/o through aider qn à se remettre; ~ up remonter; (tell off) réprimander; *coll* ~ up one's socks s'activer; *coll* he ~ed a fast one on me il m'a eu; *vi* tirer; ~ ahead se détacher, prendre de l'avance; ~ at tirer sur; ~ away s'éloigner; ~ in (train) entrer en gare; *mot* se ranger près du trottoir; *mot* ~ out démarrer; prendre le milieu de la chaussée; sortir pour doubler; *coll* (give up) *sl* se dégonfler; abandonner; ~ out of se retirer de; *mot* ~ over se ranger; ~ round se ranimer; (after illness) se remettre, guérir; ~ through s'en tirer; ~ together se mettre d'accord; (agree) s'entendre; ~ up *mot* s'arrêter; (recover) se rattraper
puller *n* tireur -euse
pullet *n* poularde *f*, poulette *f*
pulley *n* poulie *f*
pull-in *n* parking *m*; restaurant routier, café *m* pour routiers
Pullman *n* (voiture *f*) pullman *m*; *US* wagon-lit *m* (*pl* wagons-lits)
pullover *n* pullover *m*
pulmonary *adj* pulmonaire
pulp *n* pulpe *f*, (paper) pâte *f* (à papier); *vt* réduire en pulpe
pulp-fiction *n US* roman *m* à quatre sous
pulpit *n* chaire *f*
pulpy *adj* pulpeux -euse, charnu
pulsate *vi* battre; palpiter
pulsation *n* pulsation *f*
pulse *n* pouls *m*, battement *m* du cœur;

feel s/o 's ~ tâter le pouls à qn; vi battre, palpiter
**pulverize** vt pulvériser, réduire en poudre; fig réduire à néant
**puma** n puma m
**pumice-stone** n pierre f ponce
**pummel** n + vt see **pommel**
**pump** n pompe f; **petrol** ~ pompe f à essence; vt pomper; (person) sonder, faire causer; ~ **up** faire monter en pompant; (tyre) gonfler; vi pomper
**pumpkin** n potiron m, citrouille f
**pump-room** n (at a spa) pavillon m de la source
**pun** n calembour m, jeu m de mots; vi faire des jeux de mots
¹**punch** n (tool) poinçon m; vt poinçonner; (pierce) percer; ~ **in** enfoncer; ~ **out** découper à l'emporte-pièce
²**punch** n coup m de poing; fig énergie f; vt donner un coup de poing à
³**punch** n (drink) punch m
**Punch** n ~ **and Judy show** théâtre m de guignol
**punch-ball** n punching-ball m
**punch-bowl** n bol m à punch; geog cuvette f
**punch-card** n carte perforée
**punch-drunk** adj abruti de coups
**punch-line** n mot m de la fin
**punch-up** n bagarre f
**punctilious** adj pointilleux -euse
**punctual** adj ponctuel -elle, exact, à l'heure
**punctuality** n ponctualité f, exactitude f
**punctually** adv ponctuellement, exactement
**punctuate** vt ponctuer
**punctuation** n ponctuation f; ~ **mark** signe m de ponctuation
**puncture** n (tyre) crevaison f; perforation f; surg ponction f
**pundit** n pandit m; coll ponte m
**pungency** n goût piquant; (smell) odeur forte; (speech) âcreté f; (tale) saveur f
**pungent** adj (smell, taste) fort, piquant; (feeling) poignant
**punish** vt punir, châtier; (child) corriger; ~ **an engine** forcer un moteur
**punishable** adj punissable
**punishment** n punition f, châtiment m; **as a** ~ par punition; **capital** ~ peine capitale, peine f de mort; **corporal** ~ châtiment corporel
**punitive** adj punitif -ive
¹**punt** n bateau m à fond plat; vt transporter dans un bateau à fond plat; vi pousser un bateau à la perche
²**punt** n (rugby) coup m (de pied) de volée
³**punt** vi (racing) parier; (cards) ponter
**punter** n (racing) parieur -ieuse; (cards) ponte m

**puny** adj chétif -ive; (tiny) menu, petit; (wretched) mesquin
**pup** n petit chien, chiot m
¹**pupil** n élève, écolier -ière; leg (ward) pupille
²**pupil** n anat pupille f
**puppet** n marionnette f; (person) pantin m, fantoche m
**puppet-show** n spectacle m de marionnettes; théâtre m de marionnettes
**puppy** n petit chien, jeune chien m, chiot m
**purblind** adj myope; fig obtus
**purchase** n achat m, acquisition f; (leverage) prise f; **take** ~ **on** prendre appui sur; vt acheter, acquérir
**purchaser** n acheteur -euse, acquéreur -euse
**pure** adj pur
**purgation** n purgation f
**purgative** adj purgatif -ive
**purgatory** n purgatoire m
**purge** n purge f; épuration f, nettoyage m; vt purger; (clean) nettoyer; épurer
**purification** n purification f, épuration f
**purificatory** adj purificatoire
**purify** vt purifier, épurer
**purism** n purisme m
**purist** n puriste
**Puritan** n + adj puritain -e
**Puritanism** n puritanisme m
**purity** n pureté f
**purl** n (lace) picot m; ~ **stitch** maille f à l'envers; vt (knitting) tricoter à l'envers; **knit one,** ~ **one** une maille à l'endroit, une maille à l'envers
**purloin** vt soustraire, détourner; voler, dérober
**purple** n pourpre f, violet m; adj violet -ette; ~ **passage** morceau m de bravoure
**purport** n sens m, signification f; vt impliquer, vouloir dire; ~ **to be** avoir la prétention d'être
**purpose** n but m, dessein m, intention f, fin f; **answer the** ~ répondre au but; **for the** ~ **of** dans le but de; **for this** ~ à cet effet; **on** ~ à dessein, exprès; **serve no** ~ ne servir à rien; **speak to the** ~ parler à propos; **to no** ~ en vain, inutile; **to some** ~ utilement; **to what** ~ ? à quoi bon?; vt avoir l'intention
**purposeful** adj (person) tenace; (act) prémédité, réfléchi
**purposeless** adj inutile
**purposely** adv exprès, à dessein
**purr** n ronron m; (engine) ronflement m; vi ronronner; (engine) ronfler
¹**purse** n porte-monnaie m invar, bourse f; sp prix m; **well-lined** ~ bourse bien garnie
²**purse** vt ~ **one's lips** pincer les lèvres

645

**purser**

**purser** n naut commissaire m
**purse-strings** npl fig **hold the ~** tenir les cordons de la bourse
**pursue** vt poursuivre; (continue) continuer; (course) suivre; (seek) rechercher; **~ a profession** exercer une profession
**pursuer** n poursuivant -e
**pursuit** n poursuite f; (knowledge) recherche f; (occupation) occupation f; **in ~ of** en quête de, à la recherche de; **set out in ~ of** se mettre à la poursuite de
**purulence** n purulence f
**purulent** adj purulent
**purvey** vt fournir, pourvoir
**purveyor** n fournisseur -euse, pourvoyeur -euse
**purview** n limites fpl, portée f
**pus** n pus m
**push** n poussée f; impulsion f; effort m; (go) allant m, dynamisme m; mil attaque f; coll **at a ~** au besoin; **when it comes to the ~** à l'instant critique; vt pousser; (goods) pousser la vente de; (advantage) poursuivre; (urge) presser; (push about) bousculer; (use influence for) pistonner; **~ away** repousser, éloigner; **~ forward** pousser en avant, faire avancer; **~ in** enfoncer; **~ oneself forward** se mettre en avant; **~ out** pousser au dehors, faire sortir; **~ through** faire passer à travers; (complete) terminer, mener à bien; **~ up** relever; **be ~ed for money** être à court d'argent; vi pousser; **~ forward** avancer; **~ off** coll s'en aller; naut pousser au large; **~ on** se remettre en route; continuer
**push-bike** n vélo m, bécane f
**push-button** n bouton m de contact
**push-cart** n charrette f à bras, poussette f
**push-chair** n fauteuil roulant
**pusher** n personne f qui pousse; (drugs) trafiquant -e; coll arriviste
**pushing, pushy** adj entreprenant
**pushover** n coll **it's a ~** c'est du gâteau
**pusillanimity** n pusillanimité f
**pusillanimous** adj pusillanime
**puss, pussy** n minet m; **Puss in Boots** le Chat Botté
**pussy** n US vulg con m
**pustule** n pustule f
¹**put** vt mettre; (lay down) poser, déposer; (place) placer; (question) poser; (apply) appliquer; (express) dire; (estimate) évaluer; (resolution) présenter; naut **~ about** virer; **~ a matter right** arranger une affaire; **~ aside** mettre de côté; (save) économiser; **~ away** (tidy) ranger; (save) économiser; **~ by**

(money) mettre de côté; (store up) mettre en réserve; **~ down** déposer; (write) noter, mettre par écrit; (ascribe) attribuer; (person) humilier; (animal) endormir, abattre; **~ forward** proposer; avancer; **~ in** insérer, introduire; **~ in a word** placer un mot; **~ it to s/o** présenter la chose à qn; **~ money on sth** parier sur qch; **~ off** ôter, retirer; (postpone) remettre, différer; (disconcert) déconcerter; (discourage) décourager; **~ on** mettre; (add) ajouter; (clock) avancer; (flesh) prendre; (light) allumer; (assume) prendre; (play) monter; **~ out** mettre dehors, faire sortir; (hand) tendre; (fire) éteindre; (disturb) déranger, gêner; (upset) contrarier, vexer; (leaves, shoots) pousser; **~ out one's tongue** tirer la langue; coll **~ s/o on to sth** donner un tuyau à qn; **~ the weight** lancer le poids; **~ through** (complete) mener à bonne fin; (telephone) mettre en communication, passer; **~ together** mettre ensemble, rassembler; (machine) monter; (compare) comparer; **~ up** relever, lever; (install) installer; (fix) fixer; (lodge) loger; (offer) offrir, faire; (price) augmenter; (umbrella) ouvrir; **~ up for sale** mettre en vente; **be hard ~ to it to** avoir fort à faire à; **I ~ it to you** je vous le demande; **to ~ it bluntly** pour parler franc; vi naut **~ back** revenir au port; naut **~ in** faire relâche; **~ in for** poser sa candidature pour, postuler; **~ into port** entrer au port, faire escale dans un port; naut **~ off** pousser au large; **~ to sea** prendre le large; **~ up** loger; (at a hotel) descendre; **~ up with s/o** supporter qn; **~ up with sth** se résigner à qch
²**put** vt see **put(t)**
**putative** adj putatif -ive
**putrefaction** n putréfaction f
**putrefy** vt putréfier; vi se putréfier, pourrir
**putrescence** n putrescence f
**putrid** adj putride
**putsch** n putsch m
**put(t)** vt (golf) frapper très doucement
**puttees** npl bandes molletières fpl
**putty** n mastic m; vt mastiquer
**put-up** adj coll **~ job** coup monté
**puzzle** n (mystery) énigme f; (dilemma) embarras m, perplexité f; (jigsaw) puzzle m; (problem) problème m, devinette f; (crossword) problème m de mots croisés; vt intriguer; (confuse) embarrasser; **~ out** éclaircir, déchiffrer, trouver la solution de; vi **~ over sth** se creuser la tête pour comprendre qch

646

**puzzler** *n* question embarrassante; casse-tête *m invar*; (school) colle *f*
**pygmy, pigmy** *n* pygmée *m*
**pyjamas** *npl* pyjama *m*
**pylon** *n* pylône *m*
**pyorrhea** *n* pyorrhée *f*

**pyramid** *n* pyramide *f*
**pyre** *n* bûcher *m*
**pyrex** *n* pyrex *m*
**pyrotechnic** *adj* pyrotechnique
**python** *n* python *m*
**pyx** *n eccles* ciboire *m*

# Q

**qua** *adv* comme
¹**quack** *n* coin-coin *m invar*; *vi* faire coin-coin
²**quack** *n* (doctor) charlatan *m*
**quad** *n abbr* quadrangle; *abbr* quadruplet
**quadragenarian** *n* quadragénaire
**quadrangle** *n geom* quadrilatère *m*; (school) cour *f*
**quadrant** *n* quart *m* de cercle, quadrant *m*
**quadratic** *adj* quadratique
**quadrille** *n* quadrille *m*
**quadruped** *n* quadrupède *m*
**quadruple** *adj* quadruple
**quadruplet** *n* quadruplé -e
**quaff** *vt* boire à grands traits; *coll* lamper
**quagmire** *n* fondrière *f*, marécage *m*
¹**quail** *n* caille *f*
²**quail** *vi* fléchir, faiblir, trembler
**quaint** *adj* bizarre, étrange; (old) vieillot -otte
**quake** *n* tremblement *m*; *coll* tremblement *m* de terre; *vi* trembler, frémir
**Quaker** *n* quaker -eresse *m*
**qualification** *n* qualification *f*; (for a post) qualité *f*, compétence *f*, aptitude *f*; (modification) réserve *f*, restriction *f*
**qualified** *adj* qualifié; diplômé; (authorised) autorisé; **be ~ to do sth** avoir les capacités pour faire qch
**qualify** *vt* qualifier; (make reservations) apporter des réserves à; (modify) modifier; **~ oneself for sth** acquérir la compétence nécessaire pour faire qch; **~ s/o to do sth** rendre qn propre à faire qch; *vi* se qualifier; **~ for (as)** passer l'examen de
**qualitative** *adj* qualitatif -ive
**quality** *n* qualité *f*; **~ products** produits *mpl* de qualité
**qualm** *n* scrupule *m*, remords *m*; (worry)

inquiétude *f*; nausée *f*; **without any ~ s** sans le moindre scrupule
**quandary** *n* embarras *m*, dilemme *m*; **be in a ~** ne trop savoir que faire
**quantify** *vt* quantifier; déterminer la quantité de
**quantitative** *adj* quantitatif -ive
**quantity** *n* quantité *f*
**quantity-surveyor** *n* métreur (vérificateur)
**quantum** *n* quantum *m*; **~ theory** théorie *f* des quanta
**quarantine** *n* quarantaine *f*; *vt* mettre en quarantaine
**quarrel** *n* querelle *f*, dispute *f*, brouille *f*; **have no ~ with s/o** n'avoir rien à reprocher à qn; **I have no ~ with that** je ne trouve rien à redire à cela; **pick a ~ with s/o** chercher querelle à qn; *vi* se quereller, se disputer; (find fault) trouver à redire
**quarrelsome** *adj* querelleur -euse, batailleur -euse
¹**quarry** *n* (pit) carrière *f*; *vt* tirer de la carrière; *vi* creuser une carrière
²**quarry** *n* (prey) proie *f*
**quart** *n* quart *m* (de gallon)
**quarter** *n* quart *m*; (district) quartier *m*; (three months) trimestre *m*; (meat, moon) quartier *m*; **~ s** logement *m*, appartements *mpl*; **~ of an hour** quart *m* d'heure; **a ~ past five** cinq heures et quart; **a ~ to four** quatre heures moins le (un) quart; **ask for ~** demander quartier; **at close ~ s** de près; **divide into ~ s** diviser en quartiers; **from all ~ s** de tous (les) côtés, de partout, de toutes parts; **give ~** faire quartier; **take up one's ~ s** s'installer; *vt* diviser en quatre; *mil* cantonner, loger; **leg + her** écarteler
**quarter-day** *n* jour *m* du terme, terme *m*

647

**quarter-deck** n gaillard m d'arrière
**quarterly** adj trimestriel -ielle
**quartermaster** n mil maréchal m des logis; naut quartier-maître m (pl quartiers-maîtres); US ~ corps service m de l'intendance
**quartet(te)** n quatuor m
**quarto** n in-quarto m invar
**quartz** n quartz m
**quasar** n astron quasar m
**quash** vt casser, annuler; (suppress) écraser
**quatrain** n quatrain m
**quaver** n mus croche f; mus (tremor) trille f; (trembling) tremblement m; vi (voice) trembloter, chevroter; (singer) faire des trilles
**quay** n quai m, appontement m
**queasy** adj sujet -ette à des nausées
**queen** n reine f; (cards) dame f; coll homosexuel m; ~ bee reine f des abeilles; beauty ~ reine f de beauté; vi coll ~ it faire la reine
**queenly** adj de reine
**¹queer** n coll homosexuel m, sl tapette f; adj étrange, bizarre, drôle; (unwell) peu bien; (suspicious) suspect; coll homosexuel -elle
**²queer** vt ~ the pitch for s/o faire échouer les plans de qn, mettre les bâtons dans les roues à qn
**quell** vt réprimer; (feeling) calmer; (passion) étouffer
**quench** vt (thirst) étancher; (fire) éteindre; fig refroidir
**querulous** adj plaintif -ive, maussade
**query** n question f; vt mettre en question, mettre en doute
**quest** n recherche f; in ~ of à la recherche de
**question** n question f; (doubt) doute m; ask a ~ poser une question; beyond ~ hors de question; it is a ~ of il s'agit de; out of the ~ impossible, exclu; that's not the ~ il ne s'agit pas de cela; without ~ sans aucun doute; vt questionner, interroger; (doubt) mettre en doute, mettre en question
**questionable** adj discutable; douteux -euse
**question-mark** n point m d'interrogation
**question-master** n rad + TV meneur m de jeu
**questionnaire** n questionnaire m
**queue** n queue f; form a ~ faire la queue; vi ~ up faire la queue
**quibble** n chicane f; vi chicaner, ergoter
**quibbling** n chicane f
**quick** n vif m; cut s/o to the ~ blesser qn au vif; the ~ les vivants mpl; adj rapide; prompt; (sharp) vif (f vive), éveillé; as

~ as lightning comme un éclair; be ~ faire vite, se dépêcher; have a ~ ear avoir l'oreille fine; have a ~ temper s'emporter facilement; the ~ est way le chemin le plus court; adv vite, rapidement
**quicken** vt (hasten) hâter, presser; (bring (back) to life) (r)animer; (stimulate) stimuler, exciter; vi (hope, etc) s'animer; (pace) devenir plus rapide; (foetus) donner des signes de vie
**quick-firing** adj à tir rapide
**quicklime** n chaux vive
**quickly** adv vite, rapidement
**quickness** n rapidité f, vitesse f; (ear) finesse f; (eye) acuité f; (mind) vivacité f
**quicksand** n sable mouvant
**quickset** adj ~ hedge haie vive
**quicksilver** n vif-argent m, mercure m
**quickstep** n (dance) fox-trot m
**quick-tempered** adj coléreux -euse
**quick-witted** adj à l'esprit prompt
**¹quid** n coll livre f
**²quid** n (tobacco) chique f
**quiescence** n repos m, tranquillité f
**quiescent** adj tranquille, en repos
**quiet** n tranquillité f; repos m, calme m; adj tranquille, calme; (silent) silencieux -ieuse; (character) doux (f douce); (unassuming) simple, sobre; (without worry) tranquille, sans inquiétude; be ~! taisez-vous!; keep ~ se tenir tranquille; on the ~ en cachette, à la dérobée
**quiet(en)** vt calmer, apaiser, faire taire; (fears) dissiper
**quietly** adv tranquillement, doucement, silencieusement; be married ~ se marier dans l'intimité
**quietness** n see quiet n
**quietude** n quiétude f
**quiff** n mèche f
**quill** n (pen) plume f; (porcupine) piquant m
**quilt** n couvre-pieds m invar, couverture piquée; vt capitonner, ouater, piquer
**quince** n coing m; (tree) cognassier m
**quinine** n quinine f
**quinquennial** adj quinquennal
**quins** npl quintuplé(e)s
**quinsy** n angine f
**quintessence** n quintessence f
**quintet(te)** n quintette m
**quintuple** adj quintuple
**quintuplet** n quintuplé -e
**quip** n repartie f, raillerie f, sarcasme m
**quire** n (paper) main f
**quirk** n équivoque f; (character) bizarrerie f de caractère
**quirky** adj have ~ habits avoir des habitudes vraiment bizarres
**¹quit** adj quitte; be ~ for en être quitte

pour; **be** ∼ **of s/o (sth)** être débarrassé
de qn (qch)
²**quit** *vt* quitter; (acquit) ∼ **oneself** se
comporter; *vi coll* abandonner; *US*
∼ **doing sth** cesser de faire qch;
**notice to** ∼ congé *m*
**quite** *adv* tout à fait, tout, entièrement;
(at least) bien, au moins; (fairly) assez;
∼ **as much** tout autant; ∼ **a surprise**
une vraie surprise; ∼ **right** tout à fait,
très bien, très juste; ∼ **so** parfaitement; **it's been** ∼ **a day!** quelle
journée!
**quits** *adj* **we are** ∼ nous sommes quittes
**quitter** *n coll* lâcheur -euse
¹**quiver** *n* (arrows) carquois *m*
²**quiver** *n* tremblement *m*, frémissement
*m*; (eyelid) battement *m*; *vi* trembler,

frémir
**quixotic** *adj* exalté
**quiz** *n* quiz *m*; *vt* poser des colles à
**quizmaster** *n* *rad*+*TV* meneur *m* de
jeu
**quizzical** *adj* (laughable) risible; (mocking) railleur -euse
**quod** *n sl* taule *f*
**quoit** *n* palet *m*
**quorum** *n* quorum *m*
**quota** *n* quote-part *f* (*pl* quotes-parts)
**quotable** *adj* citable
**quotation** *n* citation *f*; (price) prix *m*,
cours *m*
**quote** *n coll* quotation *f*; *vt* citer; ∼ **an**
**example** fournir un exemple; ∼ **a price**
fixer (établir) un prix
**quotient** *n math* quotient *m*

# R

**rabbi** *n* rabbin *m*
**rabbit** *n* lapin *m*; (person) poltron *m*;
**tame** ∼ lapin *m* domestique; **wild** ∼
lapin *m* de garenne
**rabbit-hole** *n* terrier *m* de lapin
**rabbit-hutch** *n* clapier *m*
**rabbit-warren** *n* garenne *f*
**rabble** *n* cohue *f*; (populace) canaille *f*,
populace *f*
**rabble-rouser** *n* agitateur -trice
**rabid** *adj* furieux -ieuse, acharné; (dog)
enragé
**rabies** *n* *vet* rage *f*
¹**race** *n* course *f*; (water) raz *m*; **arms** ∼
course *f* aux armements; **long-distance**
∼ course *f* de fond; **run a** ∼ disputer
une course; *vt* (person) lutter de vitesse
avec; (horse) faire courir; *mot*+*eng*
emballer; *vi* (go fast) filer à toute
vitesse; faire la course; *mot*+*eng* s'emballer; ∼ **along** aller grand train
²**race** *n* (breed) race *f*, espèce *f*; (lineage)
descendance *f*, lignée *f*; ∼ **relations**
rapports *mpl* entre les races
**racecourse** *n* champ *m* de courses
**racegoer** *n* turfiste
**racehorse** *n* cheval *m* de course
**racer** *n* coureur -euse; (horse) cheval
*m* de course; (car) voiture *f* de
course

**race-track** *n* piste *f*
**racial** *adj* racial; de race
**racialism** *n* racisme *m*
**racily** *adv* d'une façon piquante
**raciness** *n* (style) piquant *m*; (wine) bouquet *m*
**racing** *n* course *f*, courses *fpl*; (engine)
emballement *m*; ∼ **car** voiture *f* de
course
**racist, racialist** *n*+*adj* raciste
**rack** *n* (stable) râtelier *m*; (for coats)
portemanteau *m*; (railway carriage)
filet *m*; (car) porte-bagages *m*, galerie
*f*; chevalet *m* (de torture); ∼ **and**
**pinion** crémaillère *f*; **be on the** ∼ être
au supplice; **go to** ∼ **and ruin** tomber
en ruine; *vt* tourmenter, torturer; (extort) extorquer; ∼ **one's brains** se
creuser le cerveau
¹**racket** *n sp* raquette *f*
²**racket** *n* (din) vacarme *m*, tapage *m*;
(swindle) escroquerie *f*; (crime) racket
*m*; **stand the** ∼ subir les conséquences;
*coll* payer les pots cassés; *vi* ∼ **about**
faire du tapage
**racketeer** *n* gangster *m*, racketter *m*
**raconteur** *n* raconteur *m*
**racy** *adj* (person) vif (*f* vive); ∼ **anec-**
**dote** anecdote savoureuse; ∼ **style**
style plein de verve

**radar** *n* radar *m*; ~ **screen** écran *m* de radar

**raddled** *adj* grossièrement fardé

**radial** *n* (radial-ply tyre) pneu *m* à armature (carcasse) radiale; *adj* radial

**radiance, radiancy** *n* rayonnement *m*, éclat *m*

**radiant** *adj* rayonnant; (brilliant) radieux -ieuse

**radiate** *vt* (emit) émettre, dégager; *vi* rayonner

**radiation** *n* rayonnement *m*; (subjecting to) irradiation *f*; (emitting of rays) radiation *f*

**radiator** *n* radiateur *m*; mot ~ cap bouchon *m* de radiateur

**radical** *n* radical *m*; *adj* radical

**radio** *n* radio *f*, T.S.F. *f*; ~ **set** poste *m* de radio, radio *f*; ~ **station** poste émetteur (de) radio; *vt* radiotélégraphier, envoyer par radio

**radioactive** *adj* radio-actif -ive

**radioactivity** *n* radio-activité *f*

**radio-astronomy** *n* radio-astronomie *f*

**radio-control** *n* téléguidage *m*

**radio-controlled** *adj* téléguidé

**radiogram** *n* poste *m* de radio avec tourne-disques (pick-up)

**radiography** *n* radiographie *f*

**radiology** *n* radiologie *f*

**radiotherapy** *n* radiothérapie *f*

**radish** *n* radis *m*

**radium** *n* radium *m*

**radius** *n* rayon *m* (de cercle); *anat* radius *m*; **within a** ~ **of** dans un rayon de

**raffia** *n* raphia *m*

**raffle** *n* loterie *f*, tombola *f*; *vt* mettre en loterie

**raft** *n* radeau *m*

**rafter** *n* chevron *m*

**¹rag** *n* chiffon *m*; *coll* (newspaper) feuille *f* de chou; ~**s** haillons *mpl*, guenilles *fpl*, loques *fpl*; **be in** ~**s** être en guenilles; **the** ~ **trade** l'industrie *f* de l'habillement

**²rag** *n* chahut *m*, farce *f*; (student) monôme *m*; *vt* (teacher) chahuter; (fellow-student) brimer; *vi* chahuter

**ragamuffin** *n* gueux -euse; (rascal) mauvais garnement

**rag-and-bone** *n* ~ **man** chiffonnier *m*

**rag-bag** *n* *fig* mélange *m*

**rage** *n* rage *f*, fureur *f*; (mania) manie *f*; **be all the** ~ faire fureur; **fly into a** ~ s'emporter, se mettre en colère; *vi* être furieux -ieuse, rager; (wind) faire rage; (epidemic) sévir

**ragged** *adj* (person) en haillons; (torn) déchiré, en lambeaux; (disorderly) en désordre

**raging** *n* rage *f*, fureur *f*; *adj* furieux -ieuse; ~ **thirst** soif ardente

**ragtime** *n* rag-time *m*

**raid** *n* raid *m*, incursion *f*; (police) rafle *f*, descente *f* de police; (bandits) razzia *f*; *vt* (police) faire une rafle dans; faire une incursion dans; ~ **the larder** aller se servir dans le garde-manger

**raider** *n* pillard *m*; (plane) avion *m* en raid

**¹rail** *n* (bar) barre *f*; (stairs) rampe *f*; (railing) grille *f*; (railway) rail *m*; (parapet) garde-fou *m*, parapet *m*; (balcony) balustrade *f*; **British Rail** Chemins *mpl* de Fer Britanniques; **go off the** ~**s** dérailler; **live** ~ rail conducteur (de contact); **send sth by** ~ envoyer qch par chemin de fer (par le rail); **travel by** ~ voyager en chemin de fer; *vt* ~ **in** fermer avec une grille, griller; entourer d'une grille; ~ **off** protéger par une grille; séparer avec une grille

**²rail** *vi* proférer des injures; ~ **at s/o** crier contre qn, s'en prendre à qn

**railhead** *n* tête *f* de ligne

**railing** *n* (abuse) injures *fpl*

**railing(s)** *n* grille *f*, palissade *f*

**raillery** *n* raillerie *f*

**railroad** *n* voie ferrée; *vt US* forcer; (bill) faire voter en vitesse

**railway** *n* chemin *m* de fer

**railwayman** *n* employé *m* des chemins de fer, cheminot *m*

**raiment** *n* habillement *m*

**rain** *n* pluie *f*; **driving** ~ pluie battante; **it looks like** ~ le temps est à la pluie; *vt* + *vi* pleuvoir; ~ **hard** pleuvoir à verse; **it is** ~**ing** il pleut

**rainbow** *n* arc-en-ciel *m* (*pl* arcs-en-ciel)

**raincoat** *n* imperméable *m*

**raindrop** *n* goutte *f* de pluie

**rainfall** *n* précipitation *f*

**rain-gauge** *n* pluviomètre *m*

**rainproof** *adj* imperméable; *vt* imperméabiliser

**rainy** *adj* pluvieux -ieuse; ~ **season** saison *f* des pluies; **put sth by for a** ~ **day** garder une poire pour la soif

**raise** *n US* augmentation *f* (de salaire); *vt* lever, élever; (lift up) soulever; (pole, ladder, etc) dresser; (erect) ériger; (build) bâtir; (breed, bring up) élever; (produce) produire; (plants) cultiver; (cry) pousser; (prices, salary) augmenter; (money) se procurer; (dead) ressusciter; (hopes) faire naître; (objection) soulever; (spirit) évoquer; ~ **an army** lever une armée; ~ **one's glass to one's lips** porter son verre à ses lèvres; ~ **one's voice** élever la voix

**raisin** *n* raisin sec

**¹rake** *n* viveur *m*, noceur *m*

**²rake** *n* (slope) inclinaison *f*

**³rake** *n* (tool) râteau *m*; (fire) fourgon

*m*; **thin as a** ~ maigre comme un clou; *vt* (leaves) ratisser; (soil) râteler; (guns) prendre en enfilade; (money) ~ **in** amasser; ~ **out the ashes** retirer les cendres du feu; ~ **up the past** revenir sur le passé

**rake-off** *n* gratte *f*

**¹rakish** *adj* dissolu, libertin; ~ **appearance** air *m* bravache

**²rakish** *adj naut* élancé

**¹rally** *n* ralliement *m*; *mot* rallye *m*; (health) reprise *f* des forces, retour *m* d'énergie; (prices) reprise *f*; *vt* rallier; *vi* se rallier; (health) reprendre des forces; (team) se reprendre

**²rally** *vt ar* (mock) railler

**ram** *n* bélier *m*; *naut* éperon *m*; *vt* cogner, heurter; (ship) éperonner; (stake) enfoncer; ~ **down** (soil) tasser; (stake) enfoncer

**ramble** *n* excursion *f* à pied, promenade *f*, balade *f*; *vi* (wander) errer à l'aventure; faire des excursions à pied; (speech) divaguer

**rambler** *n* promeneur -euse; (rose) rosier grimpant

**rambling** *adj* vagabond, errant; (speech) décousu; ~ **house** grande maison pleine de recoins

**ramification** *n* ramification *f*

**ramify** *vi* se ramifier

**¹ramp** *n* (on road) rampe *f*; (slope) pente *f*

**²ramp** *n comm* coup monté, combine *f*

**rampage** *n* **be on the** ~ agir comme un fou (*f* une folle); *vi* se conduire comme un fou (*f* une folle)

**rampant** *adj* (person) déchaîné, violent; *her* rampant; (disease) **be** ~ sévir

**rampart** *n* rempart *m*

**ramrod** *n* baguette *f* (de fusil); (cannon) écouvillon *m*; **straight as a** ~ droit comme un piquet

**ramshackle** *adj* délabré

**ranch** *n US* ranch *m*; ferme *f* d'élevage

**rancid** *adj* rance

**rancorous** *adj* rancunier -ière

**rancour** *n* rancune *f*

**random** *n* **at** ~ au hasard; *adj* fait (tiré) au hasard

**randy** *adj coll* porté sur la bagatelle, lascif -ive; *Scots* bruyant

**range** *n* (extent) étendue *f*; (reach) portée *f*; (mountain) chaîne *f*; (spread) gamme *f*; (plane) rayon *m* d'action, autonomie *f*; (salary) éventail *m*; *US* grand pâturage; (shooting) champ *m* de tir; (kitchen) fourneau *m*, cuisinière *f*; **at long** ~ à longue portée; **out of** ~ hors d'atteinte, hors de portée; *vt* ranger, aligner; (order) disposer en ordre;

(scan) parcourir; ~ **oneself with s/o** se ranger du côté de qn; *vi* (extend) s'étendre; (wander) errer; (vary) varier; ~ **over** (roam) parcourir; (cover) s'étendre sur

**range-finder** *n* télémètre *m*

**ranger** *n* garde forestier; gardien *m*; *US* ranger *m*

**¹rank** *n* rang *m*; (social) classe *f*; *mil* grade *m*; (taxis) station *f*; **close** ~**s** serrer les rangs; *mil* **other** ~**s** simples soldats *mpl*; **the** ~ **and file** *mil* les simples soldats *mpl*; le commun des mortels; *vt* ranger, compter; *vi* se ranger, être classé; **he** ~**s among the finest writers** il compte parmi les meilleurs écrivains

**²rank** *adj* (growth) luxuriant; (fierce) violent, fort; (smell) répugnant; (downright) vrai; (rancid) rance

**rankle** *vi* rester sur le cœur, ronger le cœur

**ransack** *vt* saccager, piller; (search) fouiller (dans)

**ransom** *n* rançon *f*; **hold s/o to** ~ rançonner qn; *vt* racheter, payer la rançon de; (hold to ransom) mettre à rançon, rançonner

**rant** *n* déclaration extravagante, rodomontade *f*; *vi* déclarer avec extravagance

**¹rap** *n* tape *f*, petit coup; *vt* frapper, donner un petit coup à; *vi* ~ **at** donner un (petit) coup à

**²rap** *n coll* **not care a** ~ s'en ficher

**rapacious** *adj* rapace

**rapacity** *n* rapacité *f*

**rape** *n* viol *m*; *vt* violer

**²rape** *n bot* colza *m*

**rapid** *n geog* rapide *m*; *adj* rapide

**rapidity** *n* rapidité *f*, vitesse *f*

**rapidly** *adv* rapidement

**rapier** *n* rapière *f*

**rapist** *n* auteur *m* d'un viol, violeur *m*

**rapprochement** *n* rapprochement *m*

**rapt** *adj* (delighted) ravi; (absorbed) absorbé

**rapture** *n* ravissement *m*; **go into** ~**s over** s'extasier sur

**rapturous** *adj* d'extase, frénétique

**¹rare** *adj* rare; *coll* (famous) fameux -euse

**²rare** *adj* (steak) saignant

**rarebit** *n* **Welsh** ~ **(rabbit)** fondue *f* au fromage sur canapé

**rarefy** *vt* raréfier

**rarely** *adv* rarement

**rareness** *n* rareté *f*

**rarity** *n* rareté *f*; (thing) chose *f* rare

**rascal** *n* coquin -e, fripon -onne

**rascally** *adj* vilain, de coquin

**¹rash** *n* éruption *f*

²**rash** adj téméraire, imprudent, ir-réfléchi

**rasher** n tranche f de lard

**rashness** n témérité f, imprudence f, étourderie f

**rasp** n râpe f; vt râper; vi grincer; fig irriter

**raspberry** n framboise f; fig rebuffade f; **give s/o a ~** engueuler qn

**rat** n rat m; **~ poison** mort f aux rats; **smell a ~** flairer un piège, soupçonner quelque anguille sous roche; vi faire la chasse aux rats; coll fig abandonner son parti (ses amis); **~ on s/o** vendre qn

**ratable** adj see **rateable**

**rat-catcher** n preneur m de rats

**ratchet** n cliquet m

¹**rate** n (speed) vitesse f, allure f; nombre proportionnel, taux m; (exchange) cours m; **~s** impôts locaux; **~ of interest** taux m d'intérêt; **at that ~** à ce taux-là, à ce compte-là; **at the ~ he's going** au train où il va; **at the ~ of** à raison de; **bank ~** taux m d'escompte; **birth ~** (taux m de la) natalité f; **growth ~** taux m de croissance; vt estimer, évaluer; (assess) taxer; (consider) considérer; vi être classé

²**rate** vt (scold) tancer, gronder

**rateable, ratable** adj imposable

**rate-collector** n receveur municipal

**ratepayer** n contribuable

**rather** adv plutôt; (somewhat) un peu, assez; (preferably) de préférence; **I would ~** j'aimerais mieux; **I would ~ not** veuillez m'excuser; interj et comment!, pour sûr!

**ratification** n ratification f

**ratify** vt ratifier

**rating** n évaluation f; classement m; sp classe f; (scolding) semonce f; (navy) classe f; (navy) **~s** les matelots mpl et gradés

**ratio** n proportion f, rapport m

**ration** n ration f; vt rationner

**rational** adj raisonnable; (able to think) doué de raison; (reasoned) raisonné

**rationale** n analyse raisonnée

**rationalism** n rationalisme m

**rationalist** n rationaliste

**rationality** n rationalité f

**rationalization** n rationalisation f

**rationalize** vt rationaliser

**rationally** adv raisonnablement

**ration-book** n carte f d'alimentation

**rat-race** n coll foire f d'empoigne, course f au bifteck

**rattle** n crécelle f, (child's toy) hochet m; (noise) bruit m, fracas m; (metal) cliquetis m; (death) râle m; vt agiter avec bruit; (metal) faire cliqueter; (shake) secouer; coll fig consterner; vi (metal) cliqueter; (windows) trembler; (be noisy) faire du bruit; med râler

**rattler, rattlesnake** n serpent m à sonnettes

**rattling** n bruit m, fracas m; (metal) cliquetis m; adj bruyant; (fine) épatant; coll **at a ~ pace** à vive allure

**ratty** adj infesté de rats; coll fâché

**raucous** adj rauque

**ravage** n ravage m; vt ravager, dévaster

**rave** n coll louange f enthousiaste; sl béguin m; **~ notices** (review) critique très élogieuse; vi être en délire; coll battre la campagne; **~ about sth** s'extasier sur qch; **~ at s/o** pester (tempêter) contre qn

**ravel** vt embrouiller, emmêler; vi s'embrouiller

**raven** n corbeau m

**ravenous** adj vorace; **be ~** avoir une faim de loup

**ravine** n ravin m

**raving** adj **~ mad** fou furieux (f folle furieuse)

**ravioli** n ravioli mpl

**ravish** vt ravir; (kidnap) enlever; (rape) violer

**ravishing** adj ravissant, enchanteur -eresse

**raw** adj cru; (inexperienced) sans expérience; (wound) à vif; (uncouth) grossier -ière; (weather) froid et humide; (commodity) brut; **~ materials** matières premières; **it's a ~ deal** c'est dur à avaler; **touch s/o on the ~** piquer qn au vif

**raw-boned** adj décharné, maigre

**rawhide** n cuir vert; adj en cuir vert

¹**ray** n rayon m

²**ray** n (fish) raie f

**rayon** n rayonne f

**raze** vt raser, démolir

**razor** n rasoir m; **~ blade** lame f de rasoir; **safety ~** rasoir m de sûreté

**razor-edge** n fil m du rasoir

**reach** n (of hand) extension f; (extent) étendue f; portée f, atteinte f; **out of ~** (range) hors de portée; (safety) hors d'atteinte; **within easy ~ of** tout près de, à proximité de; **within one's ~** à sa portée; **within ~ of everyone** accessible à tous; vt (place) arriver à; (goal) atteindre; (give) passer, donner; vi (extend) s'étendre; **~ down to** descendre jusqu'à; **~ out (with one's hand) for sth** avancer la main pour prendre qch; **~ to** arriver à; **~ up to** monter jusqu'à

**reach-me-downs** npl coll costume m de confection; coll **wear ~** s'habiller au décrochez-moi-ça

react *vi* réagir
reaction *n* réaction *f*
reactionary *adj* réactionnaire
reactor *n* réacteur *m*
read *n* have a quiet ~ lire tranquillement; *vt* lire; (study at university) étudier; ~ aloud lire à haute voix; ~ into
trouver un sens caché dans; ~ law
faire son droit; ~ on continuer de lire;
~ the gas meter relever le compteur à
gaz; ~ through parcourir; ~ up étudier; *vi* ~ to s/o faire la lecture à qn;
this story ~ s like a poem cette histoire
fait l'effet d'un poème
readable *adj* lisible
readdress *vt* (letter) faire suivre; changer
l'adresse de
reader *n* liseur -euse, lecteur -trice;
(proofs) correcteur -trice; (book) livre
*m* de lecture; (university) = maître *m* de
conférences ·
readership *n* nombre *m* de lecteurs,
public *m*
readily *adv* volontiers, avec empressement
readiness *n* empressement *m*; promptitude *f*; (ease) facilité *f*
reading *n* lecture *f*; (interpretation) interprétation *f*; (meter) relevé *m*; (instruments) observation *f*
reading-desk *n* pupitre *m*
reading-lamp *n* lampe *f* de bureau
reading-room *n* salle *f* de lecture
readjust *vt* rajuster; (ways) réadapter; *vi*
se réadapter
readmission, readmittance *n* réadmis-
sion *f*
readmit *vt* réadmettre
readmittance *n see* readmission
ready *n sl* fric *m*; *adj* prêt; (and willing)
disposé; (eager) empressé; (finished)
fini; (quick) prompt; (near) sous la
main; (meal) servi; (prone) porté; ~
money argent comptant; ~ reckoner
barème *m*; make ~ se préparer, s'apprêter
ready-made *adj* tout fait; (clothes) de
confection
ready-to-wear *adj* prêt-à-porter
reaffirm *vt* réaffirmer
real *adj* réel -elle; (true) vrai; (genuine)
véritable, authentique; ~ estate propriété immobilière; ~ silk soie naturelle; *adv US coll* très
realism *n* réalisme *m*
realist *n* réaliste
realistic *adj* réaliste
reality *n* réalité *f*
realizable *adj* réalisable; imaginable
realization *n* réalisation *f*
realize *vt* (achieve) réaliser; (understand) se rendre compte de, bien com-

prendre, prendre conscience de
really *adv* vraiment, réellement
realm *n* royaume *m*; *fig* domaine *m*
realty *n US* propriété immobilière
¹ream *n* rame *f*
²ream *vt metal* aléser
reap *vt* moissonner, récolter; *fig* recueillir; (advantage) retirer; we ~ as we
sow on recueille ce qu'on a semé
reaper *n* moissonneur -euse
reappear *vi* réapparaître, reparaître
reappoint *vt* réintégrer dans ses fonctions
¹rear *n* arrière *m*, derrière *m*; (end) dernier rang *m*, queue *f*; *mil* arrière-garde
*f*; *mil* bring up the ~ fermer la marche;
*adj* de derrière, arrière; at the ~ end of
the train en queue du train
²rear *vt* élever; (plants) cultiver; *vi*
(horse) se cabrer
rear-admiral *n* contre-amiral *m*
rearguard *n* arrière-garde *f*
rearm *vt* réarmer
rearmament *n* réarmement *m*
rearmost *adj* dernier -ière
rearrange *vt* réarranger, arranger de
nouveau
rear-view *adj mot* ~ mirror rétroviseur
*m*
rearward *adj* situé à l'arrière
rearwards *adv* à l'arrière; vers l'arrière
rear-window *n mot* lunette *f* arrière
reason *n* raison *f*, cause *f*; motif *m*;
(good sense) bon sens; all the more ~
for doing it raison de plus pour le faire;
by ~ of à cause de; for no ~ sans
motif; for the same ~ au même titre;
for (very) good ~ et pour cause; have
~ to be glad avoir sujet d'être content;
it stands to ~ cela va de soi; listen to
~ entendre raison; with good ~ à bon
droit, à juste titre; within ~ jusqu'à un
certain point, raisonnablement; *vi* raisonner, arguer; try to ~ with him essayez de le raisonner
reasonable *adj* raisonnable
reasoning *n* raisonnement *m*; *adj* doué
de raison
reassemble *vt* rassembler, assembler de
nouveau; (machine) remonter; *vi* se
rassembler
reassert *vt* réaffirmer
reassessment *n* réévaluation *f*
reassurance *n* action *f* de rassurer
reassure *vt* rassurer, tranquilliser
rebate *n* rabais *m*; (refund) remboursement *m*, ristourne *f*
rebel *n* rebelle, insurgé -e; *adj* insurgé,
rebelle; *vi* se rebeller, se révolter
rebellion *n* rébellion *f*, révolte *f*
rebellious *adj* rebelle
rebirth *n* renaissance *f*

**rebore** n mech réalésage m; vt mech réaléser

**reborn** adj né de nouveau

**rebound** n rebondissement m; vi rebondir

**rebuff** n rebuffade f; (setback) échec m; vt repousser

**rebuild** vt reconstruire, rebâtir

**rebuilding** n reconstruction f

**rebuke** n réprimande f; vt réprimander

**rebus** n rébus m

**rebut** vt réfuter

**rebuttal** n réfutation f

**recalcitrance** n récalcitrance f

**recalcitrant** adj récalcitrant

**recall** n rappel m; **beyond ~** irrévocablement; vt rappeler; (remember) se rappeler; (evoke) évoquer

**recant** vt rétracter, abjurer; vi se rétracter

**recantation** n rétractation f, abjuration f

**recap** n coll récapitulation f; vt + vi coll récapituler

**recapitulate** vt récapituler

**recapitulation** n récapitulation f

**recapture** n reprise f; vt reprendre

**recast** vt metal refondre; theat faire une nouvelle distribution des rôles de

**recce** n coll mil reconnaissance f

**recede** vi s'éloigner, se retirer

**receding** adj qui s'éloigne; **~ forehead** front fuyant

**receipt** n réception f; (for money) reçu m, quittance f, récépissé m; US cul recette f; **~s** recettes fpl; **acknowledge ~ of** accuser réception de; **on ~ of** au reçu de; **pay on ~** payer à la réception

**receive** vt recevoir; (stolen goods) receler; **~d with thanks** pour acquit

**receiver** n personne f qui reçoit; (letters) destinataire; (administration) receveur -euse; (stolen goods) receleur -euse; (telephone) récepteur m; rad poste m (récepteur de radio)

**recent** adj récent

**receptacle** n récipient m

**reception** n réception f; (welcome) accueil m; **~ centre** centre m d'accueil; (hotel) **~ desk** réception f; **~ room** salle f de réception; (flat, house) pièce f

**receptionist** n réceptionniste

**receptive** adj réceptif -ive

**receptivity** n réceptivité f

**recess** n (building, wall) recoin m, enfoncement m; (window) embrasure f; (holiday) vacances fpl; vt pratiquer un enfoncement dans

**recession** n (withdrawing) recul m, retraite f; econ récession f

**recharge** n recharge f; vt recharger

**recidivism** n rechute f, récidive f

**recipe** n recette f

**recipient** n personne f qui reçoit; (letter) destinataire; (gift) donataire

**reciprocal** adj réciproque

**reciprocate** vt (feeling) payer de retour; (service) se rendre mutuellement; vi retourner le compliment; rendre la pareille

**reciprocation** n action f de payer de retour, retour m

**reciprocity** n réciprocité f

**recital** n (story) narration f, récit m; (poetry) récitation f; mus récital m

**recitative** n mus récitatif m

**recite** vt réciter, raconter

**reciter** n déclamateur m

**reckless** adj (bold) téméraire; (careless) insouciant; (incautious) imprudent

**recklessness** n insouciance f; manque m de précaution

**reckon** vt + vi compter, calculer; (estimate) estimer, juger; **~ up** additionner, calculer; vi **~ with s/o** compter avec qn

**reckoner** n (person) calculateur -trice; barème m

**reckoning** n compte m, calcul m; (bill) note f; fig expiation f

**reclaim** vt (person) réformer; (land) défricher

**reclamation** n (persons) réforme f; (land) défrichement m; réclamation f

**recline** vt appuyer, reposer; vi être couché, être appuyé

**reclining** adj étendu, allongé; **~ seat** siège m réglable

**recluse** n + adj reclus -e, solitaire

**recognition** n reconnaissance f; **beyond ~** méconnaissable

**recognizable** adj reconnaissable

**recognize** vt reconnaître; (admit) admettre, avouer

**recoil** n recul m; mouvement m de recul; vi reculer; (spring) se détendre; fig retomber

**recollect** vt se rappeler, se souvenir de

**recollection** n souvenir m, mémoire f; **to the best of my ~** autant que je m'en souvienne

**recommence** vt recommencer

**recommend** vt recommander; **have little to ~ one** n'avoir pas grand-chose pour soi; **not to be ~ed** à déconseiller

**recommendable** adj recommandable

**recommendation** n recommandation f

**recompense** n récompense f; (damage) dédommagement m; vt récompenser; dédommager; (service) payer de retour

**recompose** vt recomposer

**reconcilable** adj conciliable

**reconcile** vt réconcilier; (facts) concilier; **~ oneself** se résigner; **~ s/o to sth** faire accepter qch à qn

**reconciliation** n réconciliation f; (opinions, facts) conciliation f

**recondite** adj abstrus; (obscure) mystérieux -ieuse; (style) obscur

**recondition** vt rénover, remettre à neuf

**reconnaissance** n reconnaissance f

**reconnoitre** vt mil reconnaître; vi faire une reconnaissance

**reconsider** vt reconsidérer, considérer de nouveau; (problem) repenser; (decision) revenir sur

**reconstitute** vt reconstituer

**reconstruct** vt reconstruire, rebâtir; (crime) reconstituer

**reconstruction** n reconstruction f

**reconversion** n reconversion f

**record** n enregistrement m; (written) registre m; (mention) mention f; sp record m; (gramophone) disque m; (of sth) souvenir m; .(police) dossier m; (career) carrière f, passé m; **break the ~** battre le record; **have a clean ~** avoir un casier judiciaire vierge; **hold the ~** détenir le record; **make a ~ of sth** noter qch; **off the ~** à titre confidentiel; entre nous; **Public Record Office** = Archives Nationales; adj record invar; vt enregistrer; (note down) consigner par écrit; (report) rapporter

**record-breaking** adj qui bat tous les records

**recorder** n magnétophone m; mus flûte f à bec; archiviste; leg magistrat m

**record-holder** n recordman (f recordwoman)

**recording** n enregistrement m; **~ head** tête enregistreuse

**record-player** n tourne-disque m, électrophone m

**recount** vt (narrate) raconter

**re-count** n (votes) nouveau dépouillement du scrutin; vt recompter

**recoup** vt rembourser, dédommager; **~ one's losses** se rattraper de ses pertes

**recourse** n recours m; **have ~ to sth** courir à qch

**recover** vt (get back) recouvrer, regagner; (appetite) retrouver; **~ lost ground** reprendre le terrain perdu; **~ lost time** rattraper le temps perdu; **~ one's balance** retrouver son équilibre; **~ one's breath** reprendre haleine; **~ one's health** se rétablir, guérir; vi (health) se rétablir, se remettre, guérir; (prices) se relever

**re-cover** vt recouvrir; (upholstery) regarnir

**recoverable** adj recouvrable

**recovery** n (getting back) recouvrement m; (health) rétablissement m, guérison f; econ redressement m; **be past ~** être dans un état désespéré

**recreant** n apostat m

**re-create** vt recréer

**recreation** n récréation f, divertissement m

**recreational, recreative** adj récréatif -ive

**recriminate** vi récriminer

**recrimination** n récrimination f

**recriminatory** adj récriminatoire

**recrudescence** n recrudescence f

**recruit** n recrue f; vt recruter

**recruiting-officer** n officier recruteur

**recruitment** n recrutement m

**rectal** adj rectal

**rectangle** n rectangle m

**rectangular** adj rectangulaire

**rectifiable** adj rectifiable

**rectification** n rectification f

**rectifier** n rectificateur m

**rectify** vt rectifier, corriger; (omission) réparer

**rectilineal** adj rectiligne

**rectitude** n rectitude f; (character) droiture f

**recto** n recto m

**rector** n (priest) curé m; Scots (headmaster) directeur m

**rectum** n rectum m

**recumbent** adj couché

**recuperable** adj recouvrable

**recuperate** vt remettre, rétablir; vi se remettre, se rétablir

**recuperation** n récupération f

**recuperative** adj (beneficial) restauratif -ive; **~ powers** pouvoirs mpl de rétablissement

**recur** vi revenir; (event) se reproduire; (opportunity) se représenter

**recurrence** n réapparition f, retour m

**recurrent, recurring** adj périodique, qui revient souvent

**red** n rouge m; coll **be in the ~** avoir une balance (un compte) déficitaire; adj rouge; (hair) roux (f rousse); (lips) vermeil -eille; fig **~ tape** paperasserie f; tracasseries administratives; **go (turn) ~** rougir; coll see **~** voir rouge

**red-blooded** adj (person) vigoureux -euse

**redbreast** n rouge-gorge m (pl rouges-gorges)

**red-cap** n coll mil soldat m de la police militaire

**redden** vt + vi rougir

**reddish** adj rougeâtre

**redecorate** vt repeindre

**redeem** vt (buy back) racheter; (from pawn) retirer, dégager; (promise) tenir; (debt) amortir

**redeemable** adj rachetable, amortissable, remboursable

**Redeemer** n Rédempteur m

**redemption** n rédemption f; remboursement *m*, amortissement *m*; rachat *m*

**red-haired** *adj* roux (*f* rousse)

**red-handed** *adj* **be caught** ~ être pris en flagrant délit, être pris la main dans le sac

**red-head** *n* rouquin -e

**red-hot** *adj* (chauffé au) rouge; *fig* ardent; (person) acharné

**redirect** *vt* (letter) faire suivre

**rediscover** *vt* redécouvrir

**redistribute** *vt* redistribuer

**redistribution** *n* redistribution *f*

**red-lead** *n* minium *m*

**red-letter** *adj* ~ **day** jour *m* mémorable

**redness** *n* rougeur *f*; (hair) rousseur *f*

**redo** *vt* refaire

**redolence** *n* parfum *m*, odeur *f* suave

**redolent** *adj* odorant, parfumé; *fig* ~ **of** évocateur -trice de

**redouble** *vt* + *vi* redoubler

**redoubt** *n* redoute *f*

**redoubtable** *adj* redoutable, formidable

**redound** *vi* contribuer, résulter

**redress** *n* réparation *f*, redressement *m*; (abuse) réforme *f*; **seek** ~ demander justice; *vt* (balance) rétablir; (wrong) réparer; (abuse) réformer

**redskin** *n* peau-rouge (*pl* peaux-rouges)

**reduce** *vt* réduire, diminuer; (length) raccourcir; (attenuate) atténuer; (humiliate) ravaler; ~ **speed** ralentir; *mil* ~ **to the ranks** casser; **be** ~ **d to doing sth** en être réduit à faire qch; *vi* maigrir

**reducible** *adj* réductible

**reduction** *n* réduction *f*, diminution *f*; (making smaller) rapetissement *m*; (temperature) baisse *f*; *comm* rabais *m*, remise *f*

**redundance, redundancy** *n* surabondance *f*, surplus *m*, excédent *m*; (style) redondance *f*; (unemployment) licenciement *m*

**redundant** *adj* surabondant; (style) redondant; (person) **be** ~ être en surnombre; (unemployed) être licencié, être au chômage

**reduplicate** *vt* redoubler, répéter

**reduplication** *n* redoublement *m*

**redwood** *n bot* séquoia *m*

**re-echo** *vt* (repeat) répéter; *vi* retentir, résonner

**reed** *n bot* roseau *m*; (pipe) chalumeau *m*; *mus* anche *f*

**re-edit** *vt* rééditer

**re-educate** *vt* rééduquer

**reedy** *adj* plein de roseaux, couvert de roseaux; ~ **voice** voix flûtée

¹**reef** *n* récif *m*; **submerged** ~ écueil *m*

²**reef** *n naut* ris *m*; *vt* prendre un ris dans

**reefer** *n sl* cigarette *f* de marijuana

**reef-knot** *n* nœud plat

**reek** *n* exhalaison *f*; odeur forte; *vi* fumer; exhaler une mauvaise odeur; ~ **of sth**

puer (empester) qch

¹**reel** *n* (cotton, etc) bobine *f*; (winder) dévidoir *m*; (fishing-line) moulinet *m*; (film) rouleau *m*; *vt* (wind) dévider, bobiner; *fig* ~ **off sth** réciter qch d'un trait

²**reel** *n* (dance) danse écossaise; *vi* tournoyer; (totter) chanceler, tituber; **my head** ~ **s** la tête me tourne

**re-elect** *vt* réélire

**re-embark** *vt* + *vi* rembarquer

**re-enact** *vt* reproduire; (law) remettre en vigueur

**re-engage** *vt* rengager

**re-enter** *vt* rentrer dans; (on document) réinscrire; *vi* rentrer

**re-entry** *n* rentrée *f*

**re-establish** *vt* rétablir

**re-examination** *n* nouvel examen,

**re-examine** *vt* examiner à nouveau

**re-export** *vt* réexporter

**ref** *n coll* arbitre *m*

**reface** *vt* (building) ravaler

**refashion** *vt* refaçonner

**refectory** *n* réfectoire *m*

**refer** *vt* rapporter; (send back) renvoyer; (submit) soumettre; ~ **a matter to s/o** s'en référer à qn d'une question; ~ **s/o to s/o** adresser qn à qn; *vi* se référer; (be relevant) se rapporter, avoir trait; (allude) faire allusion; **I won't** ~ **to it again** je n'en reparlerai plus

**referee** *n* arbitre *m*; (sponsor) répondant *m*; *vt* ~ **a match** arbitrer un match

**reference** *n* référence *f*; renvoi *m*; (allusion) allusion *f*; (relation) rapport *m*; **give s/o as a** ~ se recommander de qn; **terms of** ~ mandat *m*; **with** ~ **to** en ce qui concerne; **with** ~ **to my letter of** comme suite à ma lettre de; **work of** ~ ouvrage *m* à consulter, instrument *m* de travail

**referendum** *n* référendum *m*, referendum *m*

**refill** *n* objet *m* de rechange; (pen) recharge *f*; (battery) pile *f* de rechange; (pencil) mine *f* de rechange; (file) feuilles *fpl* de rechange; *vt* remplir (à nouveau)

**refine** *vt* raffiner, affiner; (purify) épurer

**refined** *adj* raffiné; (person) distingué

**refinement** *n* (action) raffinage *m*; (taste) raffinement *m*; (person) distinction *f*, raffinement *m*

**refinery** *n* raffinerie *f*

**refit** *n* rajustement *m*; *naut* radoub *m*; *vt* rajuster; *naut* radouber, réarmer; (factory) réaménager

**reflect** *vt* refléter, réfléchir; *vi* réfléchir, méditer

**reflection, reflexion** *n* réflexion *f*; reflet *m*, image *f*; **cast a** ~ **on s/o** critiquer qn;

on ~ réflexion faite; **that's a ~ on his honour** cela porte atteinte à son honneur

**reflective** *adj* réfléchissant; (person) réfléchi

**reflector** *n* réflecteur *m*; *mot US* (on road) cataphote *m*

**reflex** *n* réflexe *m*; *adj* réflexe

**reflexion** *n see* reflection

**reflexive** *adj gramm* réfléchi

**refloat** *vt* renflouer

**reform** *n* réforme *f*; *vt* réformer, corriger; *vi* se réformer, se corriger

**re-form** *vt* reformer; *vi* se reformer

**reformation** *n* réformation *f*; *eccles* réforme *f*

**reformative** *adj* ~ **measures** mesures *fpl* de réforme

**reformatory** *n* maison *f* de correction

**reformer** *n* réformateur -trice

**refract** *vt* réfracter

**refraction** *n* réfraction *f*

**refractory** *adj* réfractaire, indocile, insoumis

¹**refrain** *n* refrain *m*

²**refrain** *vi* se retenir, s'abstenir; **he can't ~ from talking** il ne peut s'empêcher de bavarder

**refresh** *vt* rafraîchir; (rest) délasser

**refresher** *n* chose *f* qui rafraîchit; (fees) supplément *m* d'honoraires; ~ **course** cours *m* de perfectionnement

**refreshing** *adj* rafraîchissant; *fig* agréable

**refreshment** *n* rafraîchissement *m*; (rest) délassement *m*; (railway) ~ **room** buffet *m*

**refrigerate** *vt* réfrigérer, frigorifier

**refrigeration** *n* réfrigération *f*, frigorification *f*

**refrigerator** *n* réfrigérateur *m*, frigidaire *m*, *coll* frigo *m*

**refuel** *vt* réapprovisionner en combustible (en essence, en fuel); *vi* se réapprovisionner en combustible (en fuel); *mot* prendre de l'essence, faire le plein d'essence

**refuge** *n* refuge *m*, abri *m*; lieu *m* de refuge; **seek ~** chercher refuge; **take ~** se réfugier

**refugee** *n* réfugié -e

**refulgence** *n* éclat *m*, splendeur *f*

**refulgent** *adj* éclatant, resplendissant

**refund** *n* remboursement *m*; (rebate) ristourne *f*; *vt* rembourser; (rebate) ristourner; restituer; ~ **s/o** rembourser qn

**refurbish** *vt* remettre à neuf

**refurnish** *vt* remeubler

**refusal** *n* refus *m*; **a flat ~** un refus net; **meet with a ~** essuyer un refus

¹**refuse** *n* rebut *m*, déchets *mpl*, ordures *fpl*; ~ **bin** poubelle *f*; ~ **dump** décharge (publique); **household ~** ordures ménagères

²**refuse** *vt* refuser; (reject) rejeter; ~ **s/o sth** refuser qch à qn; ~ **to do sth** refuser de faire qch; *vi* refuser

**refutation** *n* réfutation *f*

**refute** *vt* réfuter

**regain** *vt* regagner; (health) recouvrer; ~ **consciousness** reprendre connaissance

**regal** *adj* royal

**regale** *vt* régaler

**regalia** *n* insignes *mpl* de la royauté; *joc* atours *mpl*

**regally** *adv* royalement

**regard** *n* (consideration) égard *m*; (esteem) respect *m*, estime *f*; **give my kind ~s to** faites mes amitiés à; **have no ~ for** faire peu de cas de; **having ~ to** eu égard à; **in this ~** à cet égard; **out of ~ for** par égard pour; **with ~ to** pour ce qui concerne; *vt* considérer; (take into consideration) tenir compte de; (concern) concerner; **as ~s** en ce qui concerne

**regarding** *prep* quant à, à l'égard de, concernant

**regardless** *adj* inattentif -ive; peu soigneux -euse; ~ **of** sans se soucier de; ~ **of expense** sans regarder à la dépense

**regatta** *n* régates *fpl*

**regency** *n* régence *f*

**regenerate** *vt* régénérer

**regeneration** *n* régénération *f*

**regent** *n* régent -e

**regicide** *n* (person) régicide; (crime) régicide *m*

**régime** *n* régime *m*

**regimen** *n* régime *m*

**regiment** *n* régiment *m*; *vt* enrégimenter

**regimental** *adj* du régiment, régimentaire

**regimentation** *n* réglementation *f*

**region** *n* région *f*; **in the ~ of five hundred francs** dans les cinq cents francs

**regional** *adj* régional

**register** *n* registre *m*; matricule *f*; ~ **of voters** liste électorale; *vt* enregistrer; (name) inscrire; (letter) recommander; (births, etc) déclarer; (emotion) témoigner; (patent) déposer; (luggage) enregistrer; *vi* (fit) coïncider exactement; (in hotel) s'inscrire sur le registre; *coll* être compris, pénétrer

**registrar** *n* *leg* greffier *m*; (births, etc) officier *m* de l'état civil

**registration** *n* enregistrement *m*; inscription *f*; (patent) dépôt *m*; (vehicle) immatriculation *f*; (letter) recommandation *f*; ~ **number** numéro *m* matri-

# registry

cule; ~ **plate** plaque *f* minéralogique

**registry** *n* enregistrement *m*; bureau *m* d'enregistrement; bureau *m* de l'état civil; (employment) bureau *m* de placement

**registry-office** *n* bureau *m* de l'état civil

**regress** *n* retour *m* en arrière; *vi* régresser

**regression** *n* régression *f*

**regressive** *adj* régressif -ive

**regret** *n* regret *m*; **much to my ~** à mon grand regret; **with ~** à regret; *vt* regretter

**regretful** *adj* (person) plein de regrets; (thing) à regretter

**regrettable** *adj* regrettable

**regroup** *vt* regrouper; reclasser

**regular** *n* (customer) habitué -e, bon client (*f* bonne cliente); (at pub, café) *coll* pilier *m* de café; *mil* ~ **s** troupes *fpl* de l'active; *adj* régulier -ière; (correct) en règle, dans les règles; (character) réglé, rangé; (usual) ordinaire; (downright) vrai, véritable

**regularity** *n* régularité *f*

**regularize** *vt* régulariser

**regularly** *adv* régulièrement

**regulate** *vt* régler, ajuster; (business) diriger; (make rules) fixer les règles pour

**regulation** *n* règlement *m*, réglementation *f*; (technical) réglage *m*; *adj* réglementaire

**regulator** *n* (person) régulateur -trice; (device) régulateur *m*

**regurgitate** *vt* régurgiter

**regurgitation** *n* régurgitation *f*

**rehabilitate** *vt* réhabiliter; réadapter

**rehabilitation** *n* réhabilitation *f*; (injured) rééducation *f*; (refugees) réadaptation *f*; ~ **centre** centre *m* de rééducation professionnelle

**rehash** *n* réchauffé *m*; *fig + pej* resucée *f*; *vt* réchauffer

**rehearsal** *n* répétition *f*; **dress ~** répétition générale

**rehearse** *vt* répéter; (go over) énumérer

**rehouse** *vt* reloger

**reign** *n* règne *m*; **in the ~ of** sous le règne de; *vi* régner

**reimburse** *vt* rembourser

**reimbursement** *n* remboursement *m*

**reimport** *vt* réimporter

**rein** *n* rêne *f*, guide *f*; **give ~ to** lâcher la bride à; *fig* donner libre cours à; **keep a tight ~ on** s/o tenir la bride serrée à qn; *vt* ~ **in a horse** serrer la bride à un cheval; *vi* ~ **in** ramener son cheval au pas

**reincarnate** *vt* réincarner

**reincarnation** *n* réincarnation *f*

**reindeer** *n* renne *m*

**reinforce** *vt* renforcer; (request) appuyer; ~ **d concrete** béton armé

**reinforcement** *n* renforcement *m*; *mil* ~ **s** renforts *mpl*

**reinstate** *vt* réintégrer

**reinsure** *vt* réassurer

**reinvest** *vt* replacer, trouver un nouveau placement pour

**reissue** *n* nouvelle édition; *vt econ* émettre de nouveau; (book) publier une nouvelle édition de

**reiterate** *vt* réitérer, répéter

**reiteration** *n* réitération *f*, répétition *f*

**reiterative** *adj* réitératif -ive

**reject** *n* pièce *f* de rebut; **export ~** article *m* impropre à l'exportation; *vt* rejeter, repousser; (applicant) refuser

**rejection** *n* rejet *m*; refus *m*

**rejoice** *vt* réjouir; *vi* se réjouir

**rejoicing** *n* réjouissance *f*, allégresse *f*; *adj* réjouissant

**rejoin** *vi* répliquer, répondre

**re-join** *vt* rejoindre, réunir; *mil* rallier; *vi* se rejoindre, se réunir

**rejoinder** *n* réplique *f*, repartie *f*

**rejuvenate** *vt* rajeunir

**rejuvenation** *n* rajeunissement *m*

**rekindle** *vt* rallumer; (hope) ranimer; *vi* se rallumer; (hope) se ranimer

**relapse** *n* rechute *f*; *vi med* faire une rechute; retomber; ~ **into crime** retomber dans le crime

**relate** *vt* raconter; (connect) rapporter, rattacher; *vi* avoir rapport, se rapporter

**related** *adj* ayant rapport; (person) apparenté; (by marriage) allié

**relation** *n* (kin) parent -e; (story) récit *m*; (connection) rapport *m*, relation *f*; **bear a ~ to** avoir rapport à; **break off ~ s with** cesser tout rapport avec; **public ~ s** relations publiques; **this bears no ~ to** ceci n'a rien à voir avec

**relationship** *n* (connection) rapport *m*; (kin) parenté *f*

**relative** *n* parent -e; *adj* relatif -ive

**relatively** *adv* relativement

**relativism** *n* relativisme *m*

**relativity** *n* relativité *f*

**relax** *vt* relâcher, détendre; (mind) délasser; (hold) desserrer; *vi* (muscles) se relâcher; (person) se détendre, se décontracter

**relaxation** *n* (discipline, muscles) relâchement *m*; (from work) délassement *m*, détente *f*, repos *m*

**relaxing** *adj* délassant, décontractant; (climate) débilitant

**relay** *n* relais *m*; *vt* relayer

**release** *n* délivrance *f*; (from obligation) libération *f*; (from debt) décharge *f*; (film) mise *f* en circulation; (gas) dégagement *m*; (spring) déclenchement *m*; **press ~** communiqué *m* de presse; *vt* libérer; (from obligation) acquitter,

658

décharger; (let go) lâcher; (film) mettre en circulation; (mechanism) déclencher; ~ **one's hold** lâcher prise

**relegate** vt reléguer

**relegation** n leg + sp relégation f; (putting aside) mise f à l'écart

**relent** vi s'attendrir; revenir sur une décision

**relentless** adj implacable, impitoyable

**re-let** vt relouer; (sublet) sous-louer

**relevance, relevancy** n pertinence f, à-propos m

**relevant** adj applicable, pertinent; ~ **to** qui touche à, qui a rapport à

**reliability** n sûreté f, honnêteté f; (statement) crédibilité f; (machine) sécurité f de fonctionnement, régularité f de marche

**reliable** adj sûr; (person) digne de confiance; (friend) solide; (machine) d'un fonctionnement sûr

**reliance** n confiance f; **place** ~ **on** s/o se fier à qn, compter sur qn

**reliant** adj confiant

**relic** n eccles relique f; (remnant) reste m

**¹relief** n (pain) soulagement m; (from distress) allégement m; (help) secours m; mil (guard) relève f; (siege) dégagement m; leg réparation f; ~ **train** train m supplémentaire; **go to** s/o's ~ aller au secours de qn

**²relief** n relief m; **stand out in** ~ **against sth** se détacher sur qch

**relieve** vt (pain) soulager; (help) aider, secourir; (rid) débarrasser, délester; mil (soldiers) relever, (town) dégager; ~ **boredom** dissiper l'ennui; ~ **oneself** faire ses besoins; ~ **one's feelings** se décharger le cœur

**religion** n religion f; (denomination) confession f

**religious** adj religieux -ieuse, pieux (f pieuse)

**re-line** vt (clothes) remettre une doublure à; (brakes) regarnir

**relinquish** vt abandonner; (claim, plan, etc) renoncer à; (let go) lâcher

**relish** n saveur f, goût m; **do sth with** ~ se plaire (se délecter) à faire qch; **eat with** ~ manger de bon appétit; vt savourer, goûter; (give taste to) relever le goût de; ~ **doing sth** trouver du plaisir à faire qch

**relive** vt revivre

**reluctance** n répugnance f; **with** ~ à contre-cœur

**reluctant** adj qui agit à contre-cœur; **be** ~ **to do sth** être peu disposé à faire qch

**rely** vi ~ **on** compter sur

**remain** vi rester, demeurer; ~ **behind** ne pas partir; **I** ~, **Sir, yours faithfully**

agréez, Monsieur, mes salutations distinguées; **it** ~ **s to be seen whether** reste à savoir si; **the fact** ~ **s that** il n'en est pas moins vrai que

**remainder** n restant m, reste m; (book) livre soldé; **the** ~ les autres; vt (books) solder

**remains** npl restes mpl; débris mpl; **mortal** ~ dépouille mortelle

**remake** n cin remake m; vt refaire

**remand** n leg renvoi m à une autre audience; ~ **home** maison f de correction; vt leg renvoyer à une autre audience

**remark** n remarque f, observation f, commentaire m; vt remarquer, observer; (point out) faire observer; vi faire une remarque

**remarkable** adj remarquable, frappant

**remarry** vi se remarier

**remediable** adj remédiable

**remedial** adj (treatment) curatif -ive, réparateur -trice

**remedy** n remède m; leg recours m; vt remédier à

**remember** vt se rappeler, se souvenir de; ~ **doing sth** se souvenir d'avoir fait qch; ~ **me to Mr X** rappelez-moi au bon souvenir de Monsieur X; ~ **what I told you** n'oubliez pas ce que je vous ai dit; **as far as I can** ~ autant qu'il m'en souvienne (souvient); **if I** ~ **rightly** si j'ai bonne mémoire

**remembrance** n souvenir m, mémoire f

**remind** vt faire penser à, rappeler; ~ **me to tell him** faites-moi penser à lui dire; ~ s/o **of sth** rappeler qch à qn; **that** ~ **s me!** à propos!

**reminisce** vi raconter des souvenirs

**reminiscence** n réminiscence f

**reminiscent** adj ~ **of** qui rappelle, qui fait penser à

**remiss** adj négligent

**remission** n rémission f; (punishment) remise f

**remit** vt remettre; (sins) pardonner; leg renvoyer; vi diminuer d'intensité

**remittance** n remise f, envoi m de fonds

**remitter** n comm remetteur m

**remnant** n reste m, restant m; (cloth) coupon m; (shop) ~ **s** soldes mpl

**remodel** vt remodeler; (work) remanier, refondre

**remonstrance** n remontrance f

**remonstrate** vi faire des remontrances, protester

**remorse** n remords m

**remorseful** adj plein de remords

**remorseless** adj sans remords; impitoyable

**remote** adj éloigné, lointain, écarté; (hazy) vague; ~ **control** télécom-

mande *f*; **not the ~st chance** pas la moindre chance
**remoteness** *n* éloignement *m*
**remould** *n* mot pneu rechapé
**remount** *n* cheval *m* de remonte; *vt* remonter à cheval; *vi* remonter à cheval; (bicycle) enfourcher son vélo à nouveau
**removal** *n* enlèvement *m*; (house) déménagement *m*; (abuse) suppression *f*; (dismissal) révocation *f*, renvoi *m*; (pain) soulagement *m*
**remove** *n* distance *f*; **at one ~** tout près; *vt* (take away) enlever; (take off) ôter; (suppress) supprimer; (furniture) déménager; (dismiss) renvoyer, révoquer; (objection) résoudre; *vi* déménager
**remunerate** *vt* rémunérer
**remuneration** *n* rémunération *f*
**remunerative** *adj* rémunérateur -trice
**renaissance** *n* renaissance *f*
**renal** *adj* rénal
**rename** *vt* rebaptiser
**rend** *vt* déchirer; **a cry rent the air** un cri fendit l'air
**render** *vt* rendre; (translate) traduire; (interpret) interpréter
**rendering** *n* (work) interprétation *f*; (translation) traduction *f*; (surrender, giving) reddition *f*
**rendez-vous** *n* rendez-vous *m*
**rendition** *n* reddition *f*; *US* traduction *f*
**renegade** *n* renégat *m*
**renegotiate** *vt* renégocier
**renew** *vt* renouveler; (begin again) recommencer; **~ acquaintance with s/o** renouer connaissance avec qn; **~ a subscription** se réabonner
**renewable** *adj* renouvelable
**renewal** *n* renouvellement *m*; **~ of subscription** réabonnement *m*
**renounce** *vt* renoncer à, abandonner; (treaty) dénoncer; (child) renier; (belief) répudier
**renovate** *vt* rénover, remettre à neuf
**renovation** *n* rénovation *f*, remise *f* à neuf
**renovator** *n* rénovateur -trice
**renown** *n* renommée *f*, célébrité *f*
**renowned** *adj* renommé, célèbre
**¹rent** *n* (tear) déchirure *f*
**²rent** *n* (lodging) loyer *m*, location *f*; *vt* (let, hire) louer; (hire) prendre en location
**rental** *n* loyer *m*, prix *m* de location
**rent-free** *adj* **live ~** habiter sans payer (sans avoir à payer) de loyer
**renunciation** *n* renoncement *m*, renonciation *f*
**reopen** *vt* rouvrir; **~ hostilities** reprendre les hostilités; *vi* rouvrir; (wound) se rouvrir

**reorganization** *n* réorganisation *f*
**reorganize** *vt* réorganiser; *vi* se réorganiser
**reorientation** *n* réorientation *f*
**¹rep** *n* reps *m*
**²rep** *n* *theat abbr* **repertory**; *abbr* **representative**
**repaint** *vt* repeindre
**¹repair** *vi* (go) se rendre
**²repair** *n* réparation *f*; *naut* radoub *m*; **be under ~** être en réparation; **in bad ~** mal entretenu; **in good ~** en bon état; *vt* réparer; (machine) remettre en état; (clothing) raccommoder; *naut* radouber
**repairer** *n* réparateur -trice
**re-paper** *vt* retapisser
**reparable** *adj* réparable
**reparation** *n* réparation *f*
**repartee** *n* repartie *f*
**repartition** *n* répartition *f*
**repast** *n* *lit* repas *m*
**repatriate** *vt* rapatrier
**repatriation** *n* rapatriement *m*
**repay** *vt* (money) rembourser, rendre; (reward) récompenser; (person) rembourser; **~ an obligation** s'acquitter d'une obligation; **~ s/o's kindness** payer de retour la bonté de qn; **~ s/o with ingratitude** payer qn d'ingratitude; **how can I ever ~ you?** comment pourrai-je jamais m'acquitter envers vous?
**repayable** *adj* remboursable
**repayment** *n* remboursement *m*; (for service) récompense *f*
**repeal** *n* abrogation *f*, révocation *f*; *vt* abroger, annuler, révoquer
**repeat** *n* reprise *f*; *adj* repris, renouvelé; *vt* répéter, réitérer; (renew) renouveler; (class) redoubler
**repeater** *n* (watch) montre *f* à répétition
**repel** *vt* repousser
**repellent** *adj* répulsif -ive, repoussant
**repent** *vi* se repentir
**repentance** *n* repentir *m*
**repentant** *adj* repenti, repentant
**repercussion** *n* répercussion *f*, contrecoup *m*
**repertoire** *n* répertoire *m*
**repertory** *n* *theat* théâtre *m* de répertoire
**repetition** *n* répétition *f*; (music-playing) reprise *f*; (effort) renouvellement *m*
**repetitive** *adj* (person) qui se répète; (book) plein de répétitions
**replace** *vt* (put back) remettre en place, replacer; remplacer; **~ the receiver** raccrocher (le récepteur)
**replacement** *n* (action) remise *f* en place; remplacement *m*, substitution *f*; **~s** pièces *fpl* de rechange
**replant** *vt* replanter

**replay** *n sp* match rejoué; *vt* rejouer

**replenish** *vt* remplir (à nouveau); (stock) réapprovisionner

**replenishment** *n* remplissage *m*; réapprovisionnement *m*

**replete** *adj* rempli, plein

**repletion** *n* réplétion *f*

**replica** *n* reproduction *f*, copie *f*; (picture) réplique *f*

**reply** *n* réponse *f*; *vt + vi* répondre, répliquer

**reply-coupon** *n* coupon-réponse *m* (*pl* coupons-réponse)

**repoint** *vt bui* repointoyer

**repopulate** *vt* repeupler

**report** *n* rapport *m*, compte rendu; (rumour) bruit *m*; (détonation *f*, coup *m* de fusil (de canon); (repute) réputation *f*; *comm* **annual ~** rapport *m* de gestion; **policeman's ~** procès-verbal *m*; **weather ~** bulletin *m* météorologique; *vt* rapporter, rendre compte de; (notify) signaler; (media) faire un reportage sur; (denounce) dénoncer; **nothing to ~** rien à signaler; *vi* **~ sick** se porter malade; **~ to a place** se présenter à un endroit

**reportage** *n* reportage *m*

**reporter** *n* reporter *m*, journaliste

¹**repose** *n* repos *m*; calme *m*; *vi* se reposer; dormir

²**repose** *vt* **~ one's trust in s/o** mettre sa confiance en qn

**repository** *n* dépôt *m*, entrepôt *m*; (information) répertoire *m*; (of secret) dépositaire; **furniture ~** garde-meuble *m*

**reprehend** *vt* réprimander, blâmer

**reprehensible** *adj* répréhensible, blâmable

**represent** *vt* représenter; (play) jouer; (indicate) faire remarquer, signaler

**representation** *n* représentation *f*; **make ~s** faire une démarche; protester

**representative** *n* représentant -e; délégué -e; *US pol* = député *m*; *adj* représentatif -ive

**repress** *vt* réprimer; *psych* refouler

**repressed** *adj* réprimé, contenu; *psych* refoulé

**repression** *n* répression *f*; *psych* refoulement *m*

**repressive** *adj* répressif -ive

**reprieve** *n* sursis *m*; répit *m*; commutation *f* de la peine capitale; *vt* accorder un délai à; donner du répit à; accorder une commutation de la peine capitale à

**reprimand** *n* réprimande *f*; *vt* réprimander; *leg* blâmer publiquement

**reprint** *n* réimpression *f*, nouveau tirage; *vt* réimprimer

**reprisals** *npl* représailles *fpl*; **carry out ~** user de représailles

**reproach** *n* reproche *m*; (shame) honte *f*, opprobre *m*; *vt* faire des reproches à, blâmer

**reproachful** *adj* réprobateur -trice

**reprobate** *n* vaurien -ienne

**reproduce** *vt* reproduire, copier; *vi* se reproduire

**reproduction** *n* reproduction *f*

**reproductive** *adj* reproducteur -trice, reproductif -ive

**reproof** *n* reproche *m*, réprimande *f*

**reprove** *vt* réprimander, reprendre, condamner, blâmer

**reptile** *n* reptile *m*

**reptilian** *adj* reptilien -ienne

**republic** *n* république *f*

**republican** *n + adj* républicain -e

**republicanism** *n* républicanisme *m*

**republish** *vt* rééditer

**repudiate** *vt* répudier, désavouer

**repudiation** *n* répudiation *f*, désaveu *m*; (debt) reniement *m*

**repugnance** *n* répugnance *f*, antipathie *f*

**repugnant** *adj* répugnant

**repulse** *n* échec *m*; (refusal) refus *m*; (rebuff) rebuffade *f*; *vt* repousser, refouler

**repulsion** *n* répulsion *f*, aversion *f*

**repulsive** *adj* répulsif -ive, repoussant

**repurchase** *n* rachat *m*; *vt* racheter

**reputable** *adj* honorable, estimé

**reputation** *n* réputation *f*, renom *m*

**repute** *n* réputation *f*, renom *m*

**reputed** *adj* réputé, supposé; **be ~ rich** passer pour riche, avoir la réputation d'être riche

**request** *n* demande *f*; **~ stop** arrêt facultatif; **at the ~ of** à la demande de; **on ~** sur demande; *vt* demander, prier; **~ s/o to do sth** demander à qn de faire qch; **~ sth of s/o** demander qch à qn

**requiem** *n* requiem *m invar*; **~ mass** messe *f* des morts

**require** *vt* demander, réclamer; (desire) vouloir; (necessitate) nécessiter; (need) avoir besoin de; **if ~d** s'il le faut; **the ~d sum** la somme nécessaire; **what does he ~ of me?** que veut-il de moi?

**requirement** *n* besoin *m*, exigence *f*; demande *f*; nécessité *f*

**requisite** *n* chose *f* nécessaire; **toilet ~s** accessoires *mpl* de toilette; *adj* nécessaire, requis, indispensable

**requisition** *n* demande *f*; *mil* réquisition *f*

**requital** *n* récompense *f*; (revenge) revanche *f*

**requite** *vt* récompenser; (revenge) venger; **~ s/o's love** répondre à l'amour de qn

**reredos** *n* retable *m*

**resale** n revente f; ~ **price maintenance** système m de prix imposés

**rescind** vt annuler; (law) abroger

**rescue** n délivrance f; (at sea) sauvetage m; ~ **team** équipe f de secours; **come to s/o's** ~ venir au secours de qn

**rescuer** n naut sauveteur m; libérateur -trice

**research** n recherche f; ~ **work** travaux mpl de recherche; recherches fpl; ~ **worker** chercheur -euse; vi faire des recherches

**reseat** vt rasseoir, faire rasseoir; (chair) refaire un fond à

**resell** vt revendre

**resemblance** n ressemblance f

**resemble** vt ressembler à

**resent** vt s'offenser de; être froissé de

**resentful** adj rancunier -ière; irrité, froissé

**resentment** n ressentiment m, rancœur f

**reservation** n réserve f; (seat) place retenue (louée), location f (des places); **have you a** ~ ? avez-vous retenu?

**reserve** n réserve f; (land) terrain réservé; restriction f; (sale) mise f à prix; (aloofness) discrétion f; vt réserver; (seat) retenir; ~ **the right to do sth** se réserver le droit de faire qch

**reserved** adj réservé

**reservist** n mil réserviste m

**reservoir** n réservoir m

**reset** vt replacer, remettre en place; (jewels) remonter; (limb) remettre; (watch) remettre à l'heure

**resettle** vt réinstaller; vi se réinstaller

**resettlement** n transfert m de population; nouvelle colonisation

**reshuffle** n remaniement m; (cards) nouveau battement m; vt (cards) rebattre; (posts, people) remanier

**reside** vi résider

**residence** n demeure f, résidence f; leg domicile m; (stay) séjour m

**resident** n résident -e, habitant -e; adj résidant; ~ **population** population f fixe

**residential** adj résidentiel -ielle

**residual** adj résiduel -elle

**residue** n fig + chem résidu m; reste m

**residuum** n résidu m

**resign** vt résigner, se démettre de; (give up) abandonner; ~ **oneself to doing sth** se résigner à faire qch; ~ **sth to s/o** céder qch à qn; vi démissionner; ~ ! démission!

**resignation** n (from office) démission f; (rights) abandon m; (submission) résignation f

**resigned** adj résigné; **become** ~ **to sth** prendre son parti de qch

**resilience, resiliency** n (thing) élasticité f; (person) ressort m

**resilient** adj élastique; (person) **be** ~ avoir du ressort

**resin** n résine f

**resinous** adj résineux -euse

**resist** vt résister à; **not be able to** ~ **doing sth** ne (pas) pouvoir s'empêcher de faire qch

**resistance** n résistance f; ~ **fighter** résistant -e

**resistant** adj résistant

**resistless** adj irrésistible

**re-sole** vt (shoes) ressemeler

**resolute** adj résolu, déterminé

**resolutely** adv résolument

**resoluteness** n résolution f

**resolution** n résolution f; décision f

**resolvable** adj résoluble

**resolve** vt résoudre; (doubt) dissiper; vi se résoudre; ~ **to do sth** se décider à faire qch

**resolved** adj décidé, résolu

**resonance** n résonance f

**resonant** adj résonnant; (voice) sonore

**resort** n recours m, ressource f; (meeting-place) (lieu m de) rendez-vous m; (holiday, etc) station f; **in the last** ~ en dernier ressort; vi avoir recours, recourir; ~ **to a place** (go) se rendre à un endroit; (frequent) fréquenter

**resound** vi résonner, retentir

**resounding** adj résonnant, retentissant

**resource** n ressource f

**resourceful** adj habile, plein de ressources; coll débrouillard

**respect** n respect m; (reference) rapport m, égard m; **command** ~ se faire respecter; **give my** ~**s to** présentez mes hommages à; **in every** ~ à tous égards; **in some** ~**s** en quelque sorte, sous certains rapports; **pay one's** ~**s to** présenter ses respects à; **with** ~ **to** quant à

**respectability** n respectabilité f

**respectable** adj respectable, honorable, digne de respect; (decent) convenable

**respecter** n **be no** ~ **of persons** ne se laisser impressionner par personne

**respectful** adj respectueux -euse

**respecting** prep quant à, relativement à, à l'égard de

**respective** adj respectif -ive

**respectively** adv respectivement

**respiration** n respiration f

**respirator** n respirateur m; masque m à gaz

**respiratory** adj respiratoire

**respire** vt + vi respirer

**respite** n répit m, sursis m; vt accorder un sursis à; (sentence) différer

**resplendence, resplendency** n splendeur f

**resplendent** adj resplendissant, éblouissant

**respond** vi répondre; ~ **to affection** être sensible à l'affection; ~ **to music** apprécier la musique

**respondent** n leg défenseur -eresse; adj qui répond, répondant

**response** n réponse f, réplique f; eccles répons m; (reaction) réaction f; **meet with a warm** ~ être très bien accueilli

**responsibility** n responsabilité f

**responsible** adj (capable) capable, compétent; (answerable) responsable, chargé; (post) important, plein de responsabilités; (trustworthy) sérieux -ieuse; **be** ~ **for one's actions** être maître (f maîtresse) de ses actes; **be** ~ **for sth** avoir la charge de qch; être cause de qch; **be** ~ **for sth to s/o** avoir à rendre compte à qn de qch

**responsive** adj sensible, impressionnable

**rest** n (repose) repos m; (support) appui m, support m; (shelter) abri m, asile m; mus pause f, silence m; ~ **home** maison f de repos; US ~ **room** toilettes fpl; **at** ~ au repos; (stopped) à l'arrêt; **come to** ~ s'arrêter, s'immobiliser; **have a good night's** ~ passer une bonne nuit; **have a little** ~ se reposer un peu (un moment); **set s/o's mind at** ~ dissiper les inquiétudes de qn; vt reposer; (lean) appuyer; (base) baser; vi se reposer, reposer; (lean) s'appuyer; ~ **in God** s'en remettre à Dieu; **it** ~s **with you to** c'est à vous de; **the matter** ~s **there** l'affaire en reste là; **we won't let it** ~ **there** nous ne permettrons pas que la chose se passe ainsi; **you may** ~ **assured that** soyez sûr (assuré) que

**restate** vt réaffirmer; exposer de nouveau

**restatement** n réaffirmation f

**restaurant** n restaurant m; (railway) ~ **car** wagon-restaurant m (pl wagons-restaurants)

**rest-cure** n cure f de repos

**restful** adj reposant, paisible; (quiet) tranquille

**resting-place** n lieu m de repos; **last** ~ dernière demeure

**restitution** n restitution f

**restive** adj (person) inquiet -iète; rétif -ive, indocile

**restless** adj agité, troublé; (night) sans repos; (child) remuant; (worried) inquiet -iète; **become** ~ s'impatienter, s'énerver

**restlessness** n agitation f; (worry) inquiétude f; nervosité f

**restock** vt repeupler; (goods) réapprovisionner; (river) rempoissonner

**restoration** n (building, monarch) restauration f; (giving back) restitution f; (health) rétablissement m

**restorative** n med fortifiant m; adj fortifiant

**restore** vt (building, monarch) restaurer; (give back) restituer, rendre; (freedom, order, health, etc) rétablir; (place) remettre

**restorer** n restaurateur -trice

**restrain** vt (check) réprimer, retenir, restreindre; (prevent) empêcher; (bottle up) contenir; (slow down) freiner

**restrained** adj contenu, mesuré

**restraining** adj restrictif -ive

**restraint** n contrainte f, entrave f; **lack of** ~ manque m de réserve; **speak without** ~ parler en toute liberté

**restrict** vt limiter, restreindre

**restriction** n restriction f; (reduction) réduction f

**restrictive** adj restrictif -ive

**result** n résultat m, suite f; **as a** ~ **of** par suite de; vi résulter; aboutir; ~ **in nothing** ne mener à rien

**resultant** adj résultant

**resume** vt (continue) reprendre, continuer; (sum up) résumer; ~ **work** se remettre au travail; vi reprendre

**résumé** n résumé m

**resumption** n reprise f, continuation f

**resurface** vt ~ **a road** refaire le revêtement d'une route; vi faire surface, revenir à la surface

**resurgence** n résurrection f

**resurrect** vt ressusciter, faire revivre

**resurrection** n résurrection f

**resuscitate** vt + vi ressusciter

**resuscitation** n ressuscitation f

**retail** n détail m, vente f au détail; ~ **dealer** détaillant -e; ~ **price** prix m de détail; **sell** ~ vendre au détail; vt détailler, vendre au détail; (repeat) colporter, répéter

**retailer** n détaillant -e; (of gossip) colporteur -euse

**retain** vt retenir, conserver, garder; (maintain) maintenir; (engage) engager; (remember) garder en mémoire

**retainer** n dispositif m de retenue; (fee) arrhes fpl; leg honoraires mpl; ~ s gens mpl, suite f

**retaining** adj ~ **dam** barrage m de retenue; ~ **fee** provision f; ~ **wall** mur m de soutènement

**retake** n reprise f; cin réplique f; vt reprendre

**retaliate** vi rendre la pareille

**retaliation** n représailles fpl

**retaliatory** adj de représailles

**retard** vt retarder

663

**retardation** n retardement m, retard m, ralentissement m

**retch** vi faire des efforts pour vomir

**retention** n conservation f, maintien m; med rétention f

**retentive** adj (memory) fidèle

**rethink** vt repenser

**reticence** n réticence f

**reticent** adj réticent, peu communicatif -ive

**reticular** adj réticulaire

**retina** n rétine f

**retinue** n suite f

**retire** vt mettre à la retraite; vi se retirer; (give up post) se démettre de ses fonctions; (on a pension) prendre sa retraite; (withdraw) abandonner; ~ to bed aller se coucher; ~ into oneself se replier sur soi-même

**retired** adj retiré; (person) retraité, en (à la) retraite

**retirement** n retraite f

**retiring** adj (person) réservé; (from office) sortant

¹**retort** n réplique f, riposte f; vt répliquer, riposter

²**retort** n chem cornue f

**retouch** n retouche f; vt retoucher

**retrace** vt (past) reconstituer; remonter à l'origine de; ~ one's steps revenir sur ses pas

**retract** vt rétracter; vi se rétracter

**retractable** adj rétractable; (undercarriage) escamotable

**retraction** n retrait m, rétraction f

**retranslate** vt retraduire

¹**retread** vt fouler de nouveau; ~ the same path repasser par le même chemin

²**retread** n (tyre) pneu rechapé; vt (tyre) rechaper

**retreat** n retraite f; (shelter) abri m; (home) asile m; vi se retirer, s'éloigner; mil battre en retraite

**retrench** vt retrancher; (expenses) réduire, restreindre

**retrenchment** n retranchement m; (expenses) réduction f

**retrial** n leg nouveau procès

**retribution** n châtiment m

**retributive** adj vengeur -eresse

**retrievable** adj recouvrable; (mistake) réparable

**retrieve** vt (get back) recouvrer; (fetch back) rapporter; (find) retrouver; (restore) rétablir; (mistake) réparer

**retriever** n (dog) retriever m

**retroactive** adj rétroactif -ive

**retrograde** adj rétrograde

**retrogress** vi rétrograder

**retrogression** n mouvement m rétrograde

**retrogressive** adj rétrogressif -ive, rétrograde

**retro-rocket** n rétrofusée f

**retrospect** n examen rétrospectif; in ~ en regardant dans le passé

**retrospection** n rétrospection f

**retrospective** adj rétrospectif -ive

**retry** vt leg juger à nouveau

**return** n retour m; (home, after holidays) rentrée f; (sending back) renvoi m; (giving back) restitution f; (profit) profit m, bénéfice m; (receipts) recettes fpl; (account) rapport m; (election) élection f; (putting back) remise f; (election) ~ s résultat m du scrutin; ~ match revanche f; ~ ticket billet m aller et retour; by ~ par retour du courrier; in ~ for (exchange) en échange de; (reward) en récompense de; many happy ~ s (of the day) meilleurs vœux pour votre anniversaire; on his ~ à son retour; vt (give back) rendre; (send back) renvoyer; (money) rembourser; (put back) remettre; (candidate) élire; (stolen object) restituer; (report) déclarer, rapporter; (answer) répliquer, répondre; ~ s/o's feelings répondre aux sentiments de qn; vi (come back) revenir; (go back) retourner; (home, after holidays) rentrer

**returnable** adj restituable; ~ bottle bouteille consignée; ~ goods marchandises fpl de retour

**reunion** n réunion f, assemblée f; coll a touching ~ de touchantes retrouvailles

**reunite** vt unir de nouveau, réunir; vi se réunir

**rev** n abbr **revolution** coll mot tour m; vt coll mot faire tourner (plus) vite; vi ~ up tourner vite, s'emballer

**revaluation** n réévaluation f

**reveal** vt révéler, faire connaître, laisser voir

**revealing** adj révélateur -trice

**reveille** n mil diane f

**revel** n usu pl réjouissances fpl, orgie f; vi se réjouir; coll faire bombance; ~ in se délecter à, aimer beaucoup

**revelation** n révélation f; (the Book of) **Revelations** l'Apocalypse f (de Jean)

**reveller** n joyeux -euse convive, noceur -euse

**revelry** n festin m, bombance f

**revenge** n vengeance f; have one's ~ se venger; take ~ for sth on s/o se venger de qch sur qn; vt venger; ~ oneself se venger

**revengeful** adj vindicatif -ive

**revenue** n revenu m, rentes fpl; excise ~ contributions indirectes; the Inland Revenue = le fisc

**reverberant** adj retentissant, réverbérant

664

**reverberate** *vi* (light) réverbérer; (sound) résonner, retentir

**reverberation** *n* (light) réverbération *f*; (sound) répercussion *f*

**revere** *vt* révérer, vénérer

**reverence** *n* révérence *f*, vénération *f*; *vt* révérer

**reverend** *adj* révérend

**reverent** *adj* respectueux -euse

**reverential** *adj* révérenciel -ielle

**reverie** *n* rêverie *f*

**reversal** *n* *leg* annulation *f*; renversement *m*, inversion *f*

**reverse** *n* contraire *m*, opposé *m*; (other side) revers *m*, dos *m*; (page) verso *m*; (defeat) échec *m*; *mot* go (get) into ~ faire (mettre en) marche arrière; *mot* in ~ en marche arrière; *adj* contraire, inverse, opposé; ~ **charge call** communication *f* en P.C.V.; **in ~ order** en ordre inverse; *vt* renverser; (order) invertir; (clothing) retourner; *leg* révoquer, annuler; *vi mot* faire marche arrière; (go backwards) reculer

**reversed** *adj* renversé; contraire, opposé

**reversible** *adj* réversible

**reversion** *n* réversion *f*, retour *m*

**revert** *vi* revenir, retourner

**review** *n* revue *f*; (book) critique *f*, analyse *f*; *leg* révision *f*; *vt* réviser; (troops) passer en revue; (book) faire la critique de

**reviewer** *n* critique *m* littéraire

**revile** *vt* injurier, insulter

**revise** *n* *typ* épreuve *f* de révision; *vt* revoir, relire; (correct) corriger; (laws) réviser; ~ **a lesson** revoir une leçon

**revision** *n* révision *f*

**revisionist** *n* révisionniste

**revisit** *vt* revisiter, visiter de nouveau

**revitalize** *vt* revivifier

**revival** *n* retour *m* à la vie; (arts) renaissance *f*; (religion) réveil *m*; (play, business) reprise *f*; (renewal) renouvellement *m*

**revive** *vt* faire revivre, ressusciter; (renew) renouveler; (hope) ranimer, faire renaître; (desire) réveiller; (play) reprendre; *vi* reprendre connaissance, ressusciter; (feelings) renaître, se ranimer; (custom) reprendre

**revivify** *vt* revivifier

**revocable** *adj* révocable

**revocation** *n* révocation *f*

**revoke** *vt* révoquer; (promise) rétracter

**revolt** *n* révolte *f*; *vt* révolter, indigner; *vi* se révolter, se rebeller

**revolting** *adj* révoltant, dégoûtant

**revolution** *n* révolution *f*; (motor) tour *m*; ~ **counter** compte-tours *m*

**revolutionary** *n* + *adj* révolutionnaire

**revolutionize** *vt* révolutionner

**revolve** *vt* faire tourner; (thoughts) ruminer; *vi* tourner

**revolver** *n* revolver *m*

**revolving** *adj* en rotation; ~ **chair** fauteuil pivotant; ~ **door** porte *f* à tambour

**revue** *n* *theat* revue *f*

**revulsion** *n* revirement *m*; *med* révulsion *f*

**reward** *n* récompense *f*; *vt* récompenser

**rewarding** *adj* (money) rémunérateur -trice; qui en vaut la peine

**rewind** *vt* rebobiner; (film) réembobiner; (clock) remonter à nouveau

**rewire** *vt* refaire toute la canalisation électrique de

**reword** *vt* recomposer

**rewrite** *n* remaniement *m*; *cin* rewriting *m*; *vt* récrire, remanier

**rhapsodize** *vi* ~ **over sth** s'extasier sur qch

**rhapsody** *n* rhapsodie *f*

**rheostat** *n* *elect* rhéostat *m*

**rhesus** *n* rhésus *m*

**rhetoric** *n* rhétorique *f*, éloquence *f*

**rhetorical** *adj* de rhétorique; ~ **question** question *f* pour la forme

**rhetorician** *n* rhétoricien -ienne

**rheumatic** *n* rhumatisant -e; *adj* (pain) rhumatismal; (person) rhumatisant; ~ **fever** rhumatisme articulaire aigu

**rheumatism** *n* rhumatisme *m*

**Rhine** *n* Rhin *m*

**rhinoceros** *n* rhinocéros *m*

**Rhodesia** *n* Rhodésie *f*

**rhododendron** *n* rhododendron *m*

**rhombus** *n* *geom* losange *m*, rhombe *m*

**rhubarb** *n* rhubarbe *f*

**rhumba** *n* see **rumba**

**rhyme, rime** *n* rime *f*; **in ~** en vers; *vt* faire rimer; *vi* rimer

**rhythm** *n* rythme *m*, cadence *f*

**rhythmic(al)** *adj* rythmique, cadencé

**rib** *n* *anat* côte *f*; (support) support *m*; (umbrella) baleine *f*; (ship) membrure *f*; *vt* garnir de côtes; *coll* (tease) taquiner

**ribald** *adj* grossier -ière, licencieux -ieuse

**ribaldry** *n* grivoiseries *fpl*

**ribbon** *n* ruban *m*; **tear sth to ~s** mettre qch en lambeaux

**rice** *n* riz *m*; ~ **pudding** riz *m* au lait; **ground ~** farine *f* de riz

**rice-paper** *n* papier *m* de riz

**rice-plantation** *n* rizière *f*

**rich** *adj* riche; (soil) fertile; (food) difficile à digérer; (story) impayable

**riches** *npl* richesse *f*

**richly** *adv* richement, abondamment; (very) bien

---

665

## richness

**richness** *n* richesse *f*, abondance *f*; (soil) fertilité *f*

**¹rick** *n* (hay) meule *f*

**²rick** *n* entorse *f*; ~ **in the neck** torticolis *m*; *vt* ~ **one's ankle** se fouler la cheville; ~ **oneself** se donner une entorse

**rickets** *npl* rachitisme *m*

**rickety** *adj* (chair) bancal; (stair) branlant; *med* rachitique

**rickshaw** *n* pousse-pousse *m invar*

**ricochet** *n* ricochet *m*; *vi* ricocher

**rid** *vt* débarrasser, délivrer; ~ **oneself of sth** se débarrasser de qch; **get** ~ **of** se débarrasser de; (sack) renvoyer; (suppress) faire disparaître

**riddance** *n* **good** ~ ! bon débarras!

**¹riddle** *n* énigme *f*, devinette *f*

**²riddle** *n* (sieve) crible *m*; *vt* cribler, passer au crible

**ride** *n* promenade *f* à cheval (en auto, à bicyclette, etc); trajet *m*, course *f*; **take s/o for a** ~ (kidnap) enlever qn; (dupe) duper qn; *vt* monter; (waves) voguer sur; ~ **down** écraser; ~ **out the storm** *naut* étaler la tempête; *fig* surmonter la crise; *vi* se promener (aller) à cheval (en auto, à bicyclette, etc); (astride) chevaucher; ~ **at anchor** être mouillé; ~ **away** partir; (horse) ~ **behind** monter en croupe; ~ **by** passer; ~ **up** arriver à cheval; ~ **well** monter bien à cheval, être bon cavalier (*f* bonne cavalière); *fig* **be riding for a fall** courir à un échec

**rider** *n* cavalier -ière *f*; (racing) jockey *m*; (document) annexe *f*

**riderless** *adj* sans cavalier

**ridge** *n* (mountains) crête *f*, arête *f*; (roof) faîte *m*; *agr* billon *m*

**ridicule** *n* moquerie *f*, dérision *f*; **hold s/o up to** ~ se moquer de qn; **lay oneself open to** ~ s'exposer au ridicule; *vt* se moquer de, tourner en ridicule

**ridiculous** *adj* (absurd) absurde; ridicule

**riding** *n* équitation *f*

**riding-school** *n* manège *m*

**riding-whip** *n* cravache *f*

**rife** *adj* **be** ~ sévir, régner

**riff-raff** *n* canaille *f*, racaille *f*

**¹rifle** *n* fusil *m*; (hunting) carabine *f*; ~ **s** (soldiers) fusiliers *mpl*; **magazine** ~ fusil *m* à répétition; *vt* rayer

**²rifle** *vt* (rob) piller; (empty) vider

**rifling** *n* rayure *f*

**rift** *n* fente *f*, fissure *f*; ~ **in the clouds** éclaircie *f*

**¹rig** *n naut* gréement *m*; *coll* toilette *f*; équipement *m*

**²rig** *vt naut* gréer; équiper; ~ **out** équiper; *coll* attifer

**³rig** *vt* truquer; ~ **the market** provoquer une hausse (ou une baisse) factice

**rigging** *n naut* gréement *m*

**right** *n* droit *m*; bien *m*; justice *f*; (of possession) titre *m*; (side) côté droit, droite *f*; (boxing) coup *m* du droit; ~ **s** droits *mpl*; **be in the** ~ avoir raison; **be within one's** ~ **s** être dans son droit; **by** ~ **s** en toute justice; **by what** ~ ? de quel droit?; **have a** ~ **to sth** avoir droit à qch; **on the** ~ à droite; **set things to** ~ **s** rétablir les choses; *adj* droit; (proper) bon (*f* bonne), juste; (correct) correct, juste, exact; (true) vrai; (required) qu'il faut, bon (*f* bonne), voulu; ~ **side up** à l'endroit; *sl* **a bit of all** ~ qch d'épatant; (girl) un beau brin de fille; **all** ~ ! très bien!, à la bonne heure!; (enough) c'est bon!; **as** ~ **as rain** en parfait état; **be in one's** ~ **mind** avoir toute sa raison; **be in the** ~ **place** (well placed) être bien placé; (correct place) être à sa place; **be** ~ avoir raison; *coll* **come** ~ s'arranger; **more than is** ~ plus que de raison; **put** ~ corriger, rectifier, réparer; **put s/o** ~ (direct) mettre qn sur le bon chemin; (correct) détromper qn; **set things** ~ rétablir les choses; **that's** ~ ! c'est bien cela!; **the** ~ **time** l'heure exacte; **think it** ~ **to** croire bon de; *adv* droit; (well) bien; (correctly) correctement; (to the right) à droite; ~ **away** tout de suite, sur-le-champ; ~ **in the middle** au beau milieu; ~ **now**, *US* ~ **off** tout de suite; ~ **round** tout autour; ~ **to the end** jusqu'au bout; **do** ~ bien agir; **go** ~ réussir; **it's** ~ **here!** le voilà!; **see** ~ voir juste; *vt* redresser, réparer; (mistake) corriger, rectifier

**right-about** *n* demi-tour *m* à droite; **turn** ~ faire demi-tour

**right-angled** *adj* à angle droit

**righteous** *adj* juste, droit; vertueux -euse

**righteousness** *n* droiture *f*

**rightful** *adj* légitime, juste

**right-hand** *adj* de droite; (thumb, etc) de la main droite; ~ **man** bras droit

**right-handed** *adj* (person) droitier -ière

**right-ho** *interj coll* d'accord!

**rightly** *adv* légitimement; (correctly) correctement; ~ **or wrongly** à tort ou à raison; ~ **act** ~ bien agir

**right-minded** *adj* sensé; *pej* bien pensant

**rightness** *n* rectitude *f*; justesse *f*

**right-of-way** *n* droit *m* de passage

**right-wing** *adj* de droite

**right-winger** *n* (football) ailier droit; *pol* homme *m* de droite

**rigid** *adj* rigide, raide; (behaviour) strict

**rigidity** *n* rigidité *f*, raideur *f*; sévérité *f*

**rigmarole** *n* discours *m* sans suite, galimatias *m*

**rigor** *n med* (fever) frissons *mpl*; ~

mortis rigidité *f* cadavérique

**rigorous** *adj* rigoureux -euse

**rigour** *n* rigueur *f*, sévérité *f*; exactitude *f*; (religion) austérité *f*

**rig-out** *n coll* toilette *f*

**rile** *vt* agacer, énerver

**rim** *n* bord *m*; (wheel) jante *f*; (spectacles) monture *f*

**rime** *n see* **rhyme** *n*

**rind** *n* écorce *f*; (fruit) peau *f*, pelure *f*; (cheese) croûte *f*; (bacon) couenne *f*

**¹ring** *n* anneau *m*; (finger) bague *f*; (serviette) rond *m*; (circle) cercle *m*; (clique) coterie *f*, groupe *m*; (round eyes) cerne *m*; (boxing) ring *m*; *comm* cartel *m*; (circus) piste *f*; **form a ~** se former en cercle; **in a ~** en rond; *coll* **make ~s round s/o** se montrer nettement supérieur à qn; *vt* (bird) baguer

**²ring** *n* sonnerie *f*; (sound) son *m*; (voice) timbre *m*, intonation *f*; (bell) coup *m* de sonnette; (telephone) coup *m* de téléphone; *vt* sonner, faire sonner; *coll* that **~s a bell** cela me rappelle qch; *vi* sonner, tinter; **~ for the maid** sonner la bonne; **~ off** raccrocher (l'appareil); **~ out** retentir; **~ up s/o** téléphoner à qn, appeler qn au téléphone; **that does not ~ true** cela sonne faux

**ringer** *n* sonneur *m*

**ring-finger** *n* annulaire *m*

**ringing** *n* son *m*; tintement *m*; retentissement *m*; *adj* (bell) qui tinte; (cheers, etc) retentissant

**ringleader** *n* meneur *m*, chef *m*

**ringlet** *n* (hair) boucle *f*

**ringmaster** *n* maître *m* de manège

**ring-road** *n* route *f* de ceinture; (round Paris) boulevard *m* périphérique

**ringside** *n* **have a ~ seat** avoir une place au premier rang

**ringworm** *n* teigne *f*

**rink** *n* (skating) patinoire *f*

**rinse** *n* rinçage *m*; *vt* rincer

**riot** *n* émeute *f*, bagarre *f*; (abundance) orgie *f*; *coll* **it's a ~** (funny) c'est tordant; **run ~** se déchaîner; *vi* s'ameuter, faire une émeute; (be noisy) faire du vacarme

**rioter** *n* émeutier -ière

**riotous** *adj* tumultueux -euse, turbulent; (person) bruyant; **~ living** vie dissipée

**rip** *n* fente *f*, déchirure *f*; *vt* fendre, déchirer; **~ off** arracher; **~ open** éventrer, ouvrir en déchirant; **~ up** éventrer, arracher; *vi* se déchirer, se fendre; *coll* **~ along** aller bon train, aller à toute vitesse; *coll mot* **let her ~** laissez-la filer; *coll* **let ~** être déchaîné, laisser déchaîner sa colère

**rip-cord** *n* cordelette *f* de déclenchement

**ripe** *adj* mûr; (cheese) bien fait; **a ~ old age** un bel âge

**ripen** *vt* faire mûrir, mûrir; *vi* mûrir; (cheese) se faire

**ripeness** *n* maturité *f*

**rip-off** *n coll* coup *m* de fusil

**riposte** *n* riposte *f*

**ripper** *n* éventreur *m*

**ripping** *adj coll fig* épatant

**ripple** *n* (water) ride *f*; (sound) murmure *m*; *vt* rider; *vi* (water) se rider; onduler

**rise** *n* ascension *f*; (road, hill) montée *f*; (price) hausse *f*; (water) crue *f*; (increase) augmentation *f*; (promotion) avancement *m*; *coll* **get a ~ out of s/o** se payer la tête de qn; **give ~ to** faire naître, donner lieu à, provoquer; *vi* (get up) se lever; (price) monter, augmenter; (building, etc) se dresser, s'élever; (go upwards) monter; (revolt) se soulever; (river) prendre (sa) source; (spring) naître; (cake, etc) lever; (from the dead) ressusciter; **~ in price** augmenter de prix; **~ in the world** faire son chemin; **~ to it (the occasion)** se montrer à la hauteur de l'occasion

**riser** *n* (step) contremarche *f*; **be an early ~** être matinal

**risible** *adj* (laughable) risible; enclin au rire

**rising** *n* lever *m*; (revolt) soulèvement *m*; (water) crue *f*; *adj* (sun) levant; (anger) croissant; (going upwards) montant

**risk** *n* risque *m*, péril *m*; **at your own ~** à vos risques et périls; *coll* **not be worth the ~** ne pas valoir le coup; **run the ~** courir le risque; *vt* risquer, hasarder

**risky** *adj* risqué, hasardeux

**risotto** *n* risotto *m*

**risqué** *adj* risqué, scabreux -euse

**rissole** *n* croquette *f*

**rite** *n* rite *m*, cérémonie *f*; **last ~s** derniers sacrements

**ritual** *n* rites *mpl*; *adj* rituel -elle

**ritualism** *n* ritualisme *m*

**ritualistic** *adj* ritualiste

**ritually** *adv* selon les rites

**rival** *n* rival -e; *comm* concurrent -e; *adj* rival; *comm* concurrentiel -ielle

**rivalry** *n* rivalité *f*

**river** *n* fleuve *m*; (tributary) rivière *f*; **down ~** en aval; *coll* **sell s/o down the ~** trahir qn; **up ~** en amont

**river-bed** *n* lit *m* de rivière

**river-side** *n* rive *f*, bord *m* de l'eau; *adj* situé au bord de la rivière

**rivet** *n* rivet *m*; *vt* riveter, river; (attention) capter

**rivulet** *n* ruisseau *m*

**roach** *n* gardon *m*

**road** *n* (main) route *f*; (secondary) chemin *m*, voie *f*; *fig* voie *f*; (roadway) chaussée *f*; (street) rue *f*; *naut* **~s** rade *f*; **be on the right** ~ être sur la bonne voie; **be on the** ~ être en route; (commercial traveller) être en tournée; *adj* routier -ière

**roadblock** *n* barrage (routier)

**road-hog** *n* chauffard *m*

**roadhouse** *n* relais *m*

**road-map** *n* carte routière

**road-sense** *n* sens *m* pratique des dangers de la route

**roadside** *n* bord *m* de la route; *adj* situé au bord de la route

**road-user** *n* usager *m* de la route

**roadway** *n* chaussée *f*

**roadworthy** *adj* mot en état de marche

**roam** *vt* parcourir; *vi* errer, rôder; ~ **about the world** rouler sa bosse

**roan** *n* (cheval) rouan *m*

**roar** *n* (animal) rugissement *m*; (thunder) grondement *m*; (person) hurlement *m*; (laughter) éclat *m*; *vt* vociférer; *vi* (animal) rugir; (thunder) gronder; (person) hurler; (engine) ronfler, vrombir; ~ **with laughter** éclater de rire

**roaring** *n see* **roar** *n*; *adj coll* **do a** ~ **trade** faire faire des affaires d'or

**roast** *n* rôti *m*; (beef) rosbif *m*; *vt* faire rôtir, rôtir; (coffee) griller; *vi* rôtir

**roaster** *n* (machine) rôtissoire *f*; (poultry) poulet *m* à rôtir, volaille *f* à rôtir

**rob** *vt* voler, dévaliser; ~ **s/o of sth** voler qch à qn

**robber** *n* voleur -euse

**robbery** *n* vol *m*, vol qualifié; **armed** ~ vol *m* à main armée; **highway** ~ vol *m* de grand chemin; *fig* escroquerie *f*

**robe** *n* robe *f*; (clothing) vêtement *m*; **bath** ~ peignoir *m* de bain

**robin** *n* rouge-gorge *m* (*pl* rouges-gorges)

**robot** *n* robot *m*, automate *m*

**robust** *adj* robuste, vigoureux -euse

**robustness** *n* robustesse *f*

**rock** *n* rocher *m*, roche *f*, roc *m*; *fig* **be on the** ~**s** être dans la dèche; (drink) **on the** ~**s** avec des glaçons; *vt* (cradle, child) bercer, balancer; (tip over) basculer; *fig* ~ **the boat** créer des ennuis; *vi* balancer; (person) se balancer; ~ **with laughter** se tordre de rire

**rock-and-roll, rock-n-roll** *n* rock and roll *m*

**rock-bottom** *n* fond rocheux; ~ **price** prix le plus bas; **reach** ~ toucher le fond, tomber au plus bas

**rock-cake** *n* petit gâteau aux raisins secs

¹**rocker** *n* bascule *f*; *eng* culbuteur *m*; *sl* **be off one's** ~ être un peu toqué

²**rocker** *n* (youth) blouson noir

**rockery** *n* rocaille *f*, jardin *m* de rocaille

**rocket** *n* fusée *f*; *mil* roquette *f*; *vi* se lancer; monter comme une fusée;

(prices) monter en flèche; ~ **to fame** devenir célèbre du jour au lendemain

**rocket-launcher** *n* lance-fusées *m*, lance-roquettes *m*

**rock-fall** *n* chute *f* de pierres, éboulement *m*

**rock-garden** *n* jardin *m* de rocaille

**rocking** *n* branlement *m*, balancement *m*; *adj* (unsteady) branlant; oscillant

**rocking-chair** *n* fauteuil *m* à bascule

**rocking-horse** *n* cheval *m* à bascule

¹**rocky** *adj* rocheux -euse, rocailleux -euse; (of rock) de roche

²**rocky** *adj coll* chancelant

**rococo** *n* rococo *m*; *adj* rococo *invar*

**rod** *n* baguette *f*, verge *f*; (fishing) canne *f* (à pêche); (curtain) tringle *f*; *eng* tige *f*; **fish with a** ~ **and line** pêcher à la ligne; **rule s/o with a** ~ **of iron** mener qn à la baguette; **spare the** ~ **and spoil the child** qui aime bien châtie bien

**rodent** *n* rongeur *m*; *adj* rongeur -euse

**rodeo** *n* rodéo *m*

¹**roe** *n* (deer) chevreuil *m*; (female) chevrette *f*

²**roe** *n* (hard) œufs *mpl* de poisson; (soft) laitance *f*

**rogue** *n* coquin -e, fripon -onne; *adj* (animal) solitaire

**roguery** *n* coquinerie *f*, friponnerie *f*

**roguish** *adj* coquin, fripon -onne; (mischievous) espiègle

**roisterer** *n* fêtard -e

**roistering** *adj* tapageur -euse

**role** *n* rôle *m*

**roll** *n* rouleau *m*; (list) liste *f*, état *m*; (bread) petit pain; (film) bobine *f*; (ship) roulis *m*; (thunder) grondement *m*; (drum) roulement *m*; ~ **of fat** bourrelet *m*; **call the** ~ faire l'appel; *vt* rouler; ~ **off** (print) imprimer; ~ **one's r's** rouler les r; ~ **over** retourner; ~ **up** enrouler, rouler; (sleeves) retrousser; *vi* rouler; (thunder) gronder; ~ **about** rouler çà et là; ~ **back** rouler en arrière; ~ **by** passer en roulant; ~ **down** (tears) couler; ~ **on** continuer de rouler; (time) s'écouler; *coll* ~ **on tomorrow** vivement demain; ~ **over** se retourner; *coll* ~ **up** arriver; ~ **up into a ball** se mettre en boule; **be** ~**ing in money** rouler sur l'or

**roll-call** *n* appel *m*

**roller** *n* rouleau *m*; (road) rouleau compresseur; *eng* galet *m*

**roller-coaster** *n* montagnes *fpl* russes

**roller-skate** *n* patin *m* à roulettes; *vi* faire du patin à roulettes

**roller-towel** *n* essuie-mains *m* à rouleau

**rollicking** *n* jovial, rigoleur -euse, exubérant

**rolling** *n* roulement *m*; (ship) roulis *m*;

*adj* roulant; (sea) houleux -euse; (countryside) accidenté; **a ~ stone gathers no moss** pierre qui roule n'amasse pas mousse

**rolling-pin** *n* rouleau *m* à pâtisserie

**rolling-stock** *n* matériel roulant

**roll-top** *adj* **~ desk** bureau *m* à cylindre

**roly-poly** *adj coll* boulot -otte

**Roman** *n* Romain -e; *adj* romain; **~ Catholic** catholique

**romance** *n* (medieval) roman *m*; (story) histoire *f* romanesque; (affair) idylle *f*; *vi* exagérer

**romancer** *n pej* brodeur -euse

**Romania** *n*, **Romanian** *n + adj see* **Roumania, Roumanian**

**romantic** *adj* romanesque, romantique

**romanticism** *n* romantisme *m*

**romp** *n* gambades *fpl*; *vi* s'ébattre; *coll* **~ home** gagner haut la main; *coll fig* **~ through** réussir facilement

**rompers** *npl* barboteuse *f*

**roneo** *n* ronéo *f*; *vt* ronéotyper, polycopier

**roof** *n* toit *m*, toiture *f*; (tunnel) voûte *f*; (mouth) dôme *m* du palais; *fig* **raise the ~** (be noisy) faire du vacarme; (applaud) applaudir à tout casser; *mot* **sunshine ~** toit ouvrant; *vt* couvrir (recouvrir) d'un toit

**roof-garden** *n* jardin *m* sur le toit

**roofing** *n* toiture *f*

**roofless** *adj* sans toit; (person) sans abri

**roof-light** *n mot* plafonnier *m*

¹**rook** *n* corneille *f*

²**rook** *n* (chess) tour *f*

³**rook** *vt coll* rouler, refaire

**rookery** *n* colonie *f* de corneilles

**room** *n* (space) espace *m*, place *f*; (in house) pièce *f*; (bedroom) chambre *f*; (large) salle *f*; (grounds) lieu *m*; **~s** appartement *m*; **double ~** chambre *f* à deux personnes; **single ~** chambre *f* à une personne; **take up ~** prendre de la place; **there is ~ for improvement** cela laisse à désirer; *vi US* loger, vivre en garni

**roomful** *n* salle pleine, chambrée *f*

**roominess** *n* dimensions spacieuses

**rooming-house** *n US* maison *f* où on loue des chambres meublées

**room-mate** *n* compagnon (*f* compagne) de chambre

**roomy** *adj* spacieux -ieuse

**roost** *n* perchoir *m*, juchoir *m*; *fig* **come home to ~** se retourner contre son auteur; **go to ~** se jucher; *coll* aller coucher; **rule the ~** être le maître chez soi; *vi* se percher, se jucher

**rooster** *n* coq *m*

¹**root** *n* racine *f*; (origin) source *f*; **~ and branch** de fond en comble; **~ cause**

cause première; **lie at the ~ of** être à la source de; **pull up by the ~s** déraciner; **take ~** prendre racine; *vt* enraciner; **~ up** déraciner; *vi* s'enraciner

²**root, rout** *vt* **~ out** dénicher, déterrer; *vi* **~ among** fouiller parmi

**rooted** *adj* ancré, enraciné

**rope** *n* corde *f*; *naut* cordage *m*; (onions) chapelet *m*; *fig* **give s/o plenty of ~** lâcher la bride à qn; *fig* **know the ~s** connaître son affaire; *fig* **show s/o the ~s** mettre qn au courant; *vt* corder, attacher avec une corde; **~ in** entourer de cordes; (catch) prendre; (enrol) embrigader; *vi* (mountaineering) **~ up** s'encorder

**rope-ladder** *n* échelle *f* de corde

**ropey** *adj coll* pas fameux -euse, assez moche

**rosary** *n* chapelet *m*, rosaire *m*

**rose** *n* rose *f*; (colour) rose *m*; (watering-can) pomme *f* (d'arrosoir); **ceiling ~** rosace *f* de plafond; **under the ~** en cachette, en confidence; **wild ~** églantine *f*

**rosebud** *n* bouton *m* de rose

**rose-bush** *n* rosier *m*

**rose-coloured** *adj* rose, rosé; **see things through ~ spectacles** voir tout en rose

**rose-garden** *n* roseraie *f*

**rosemary** *n* romarin *m*

**rose-tree** *n* rosier *m*

**rosette** *n* cocarde *f*, rosette *f*

**rosewood** *n* palissandre *m*

**rosiness** *n* teint rosé

**roster** *n* liste *f*; *mil* tableau *m* de service

**rostrum** *n* tribune *f*

**rosy** *adj* rose, rosé; **~ cheeks** joues vermeilles; **he has a ~ future** il a un bel avenir

**rot** *n* pourriture *f*; *fig* démoralisation *f*; (trees) carie *f*; (vine) mildiou *m*; *coll* (nonsense) bêtises *fpl*; **dry ~** carie sèche; **stop the ~** enrayer une progression dangereuse; **wet ~** carie *f* humide; *vt* faire pourrir, décomposer; *vi* pourrir, se décomposer

**rota** *n* liste *f*, tableau *m* de service

**rotary** *n US* rond-point *m* (*pl* ronds-points); *adj* rotatif -ive; **Rotary Club** Rotary Club *m*; **~ press** rotative *f*

**rotate** *vt* faire tourner; *agr* alterner; *vi* tourner, pivoter

**rotation** *n* rotation *f*; mouvement *m* rotatoire; **in ~** à tour de rôle

**rote** *n* **by ~** par cœur

**rotor** *n* rotor *m*

**rotten** *adj* pourri, carié; *coll* mâuvais, moche, misérable

**rotter** *n coll* sale type *m*

**rotund** *adj* rond, arrondi

**rotunda** *n* rotonde *f*

**rotundity** *n* rondeur *f*, rotondité *f*

**rouble** *n* rouble *m*

**rouge** *n* rouge *m*, fard *m*

**rough** *n* (person) voyou *m*; (ground) terrain accidenté; **in the ~** à l'état brut; **take the ~ with the smooth** prendre le bénéfice avec les charges; *adj* rude; (coarse) grossier -ière; (surface) rugueux -euse, inégal; (conduct) brutal, brusque; (weather) gros (*f* grosse); (wind) violent; (sea) agité; (approximate) approximatif -ive; (voice) rauque; (unpolished) brut; (path) raboteux -euse; *coll* **~ customer** type violent; **~ draft** (work) brouillon *m*; **~ sketch** ébauche *f*; **be ~ with s/o** brutaliser qn; **give s/o a ~ handling** malmener qn; *coll* **have a ~ time** en baver; *adv see* **roughly**; *vt coll* **~ it** vivre à la dure; (have a bad time) en voir de dures; **~ up** (hair) ébouriffer; (glass) dépolir; *coll* (ill-treat) malmener

**roughage** *n* genre *m* d'aliments stimulant l'intestin

**rough-and-ready** *adj* (work) fait à la hâte; (person) sans façon

**rough-and-tumble** *n* bagarre *f*, mêlée *f*

**rough-cast** *n* crépi *m*

**roughen** *vt* rendre rude

**rough-handle** *vt* malmener

**rough-hew** *vt* dégrossir; **~ n stone** pierre *f* de taille

**rough-house** *n* bagarre *f*

**roughish** *adj* assez rude; (surface) rugueux -euse; (sea) assez houleux -euse

**roughly** *adv* rudement; (coarsely) grossièrement; brutalement; (about) approximativement, à peu près

**roughness** *n* rudesse *f*; (surface) rugosité *f*, aspérité *f*; (coarseness) grossièreté *f*; (manner) brusquerie *f*; (taste) âpreté *f*; (sea) agitation *f*; (roads) état raboteux; (violence) violence *f*

**roughshod** *adj* (horse) ferré à glace; *fig* **ride ~ over s/o** traiter qn sans ménagement

**rough-spoken** *adj* au langage grossier

**roulette** *n* roulette *f*

**Roumania, Romania** *n* Roumanie *f*

**Roumanian, Romanian** *n* Roumain -e; (language) roumain *m*; *adj* roumain

**round** *n* cercle *m*, rond *m*; tour *m*, circuit *m*; (patrol) ronde *f*; (ladder) échelon *m*; (applause) salve *f*; (boxing) round *m*, reprise *f*; (golf, drinks, postman) tournée *f*; **~ of toast** rôtie *f*; **daily ~** train-train quotidien; **fire a ~** tirer un coup; **go on (make) one's ~s** faire sa tournée; *adj* rond, circulaire; **~ dance** ronde *f*; **~ robin** pétition revêtue de signatures en rond; **~ shoul-**ders épaules voûtées; **~ sum** forte somme; *US* **~ trip** aller et retour *m*; **a ~ dozen** une bonne douzaine; **in ~ figures** en chiffres ronds; **make ~** arrondir; *adv* en rond; **~ about** tout autour, alentour; **all the year ~** pendant toute l'année; **a long way ~** un grand détour; **ask s/o ~** inviter qn (à venir chez soi); **bring ~** apporter; *fig* ranimer; **come ~** (visit) passer; (recover) reprendre connaissance; (return) revenir; **fifty metres ~** cinquante mètres de tour; **get ~ a problem** résoudre un problème; **get ~ s/o** enjôler qn; **get ~ to doing sth** finir par faire qch; **go ~** tourner; (call) passer, y aller; **hand ~** faire passer; **turn ~ and ~** tournoyer; **walk ~** faire le tour de; *prep* autour de; (near) aux abords de, près de; **go ~ sth** tourner autour de qch; (avoid) contourner qch; (visit) visiter qch; *coll* **go ~ the bend** devenir fou (*f* folle); **take s/o ~ a place** faire visiter un endroit à qn; *vt* arrondir; (cape) doubler; (obstacle) contourner; **~ off** arrondir; *fig* finir; **~ up** rassembler; (police) rafler; *vi* s'arrondir; *coll* **~ on s/o** s'en prendre brusquement à qn

**roundabout** *n* manège *m*, carrousel *m*, chevaux *mpl* de bois; (road) rond-point *m* (*pl* ronds-points); *adj* détourné, indirect; **~ way** détour *m*; **in a ~ way** de façon détournée

**rounders** *npl* balle *f* au camp

**roundly** *adv* rondement, vivement

**roundness** *n* rondeur *f*

**round-shouldered** *adj* au dos voûté

**roundsman** *n* livreur *m*

**round-table** *adj* **~ conference** table ronde

**round-up** *n* (cattle) rassemblement *m*; (police) rafle *f*

**rouse** *vt* (awaken) réveiller; (provoke) provoquer; (indignation) soulever; (stimulate) exciter; (admiration) susciter; (from idleness) secouer; **~ oneself** se secouer; **~ s/o to action** inciter qn à l'action; **be ~d** être monté, être furieux -ieuse

**rousing** *adj* (cheers) chaleureux -euse; (speech) vibrant, émouvant

**¹rout** *n* déroute *f*; **put to ~** mettre en déroute; *vt* mettre en déroute, disperser

**²rout** *see* **²root**

**route** *n* itinéraire *m*; route *f*, voie *f*; (bus) ligne *f*

**routine** *n* routine *f*; **~ questions** questions *fpl* d'usage; **daily ~** train-train quotidien

**roux** *n* cul roux *m*

**rove** *vt* parcourir; *vi* rôder, errer

**rover** *n* rôdeur -euse, vagabond -e; *naut* écumeur *m* de mer

**roving** *n* vagabondage *m*; *adj* vagabond, nomade

¹**row** *n* rang *m*, rangée *f*, ligne *f*; (figures) colonne *f*; (cars) file *f*; **in** ~ **s** par rangs; **in the front** ~ au premier rang

²**row** *n* (on water) promenade *f* en barque (en canot); *vt* conduire à l'aviron; ~ **s/o across** transporter qn en barque à l'autre rive; *vi* ramer, faire du canotage; *naut* nager

³**row** *n* (noise) tapage *m*, chahut *m*, vacarme *m*; (quarrel) scène *f*, dispute *f*; **get into a** ~ se faire attraper; *coll* se faire passer un savon; **kick up a** ~ faire du chahut; *vi* se quereller

**rowdy** *n* (troublemaker) voyou *m*; (noisy person) chahuteur *m*; *adj* tapageur -euse

**rowdyism** *n* chahutage *m*

**rowing** *n* (sport) canotage *m*

**rowing-boat** *n* bateau *m* à rames, barque *f* à rames

**rowlocks** *npl* tolets *mpl*

**royal** *adj* royal

**royalist** *n* + *adj* royaliste

**royally** *adv* royalement

**royalty** *n* royauté *f*; (author's) **royalties** droits *mpl* d'auteur

**rub** *n* frottement *m*; (dusting) coup *m* de torchon; (snag) hic *m*; *vt* frotter; (massage) frictionner; ~ **away** user en frottant; ~ **down** frotter; (person) frictionner; ~ **out** (off) effacer; ~ **shoulders with** frayer avec; *fig* ~ **s/o up the wrong way** prendre qn à rebrousse-poil; ~ **up** donner un coup de torchon à; *vi* frotter; (person) se frotter; ~ **along** se débrouiller

¹**rubber** *n* (instrument) frottoir *m*; (person) frotteur -euse

²**rubber** *n* (substance) caoutchouc *m*; (eraser) gomme *f*; *US* ~ **s** caoutchoucs *mpl*; ~ **band** élastique *m*; ~ **gloves** gants *mpl* en caoutchouc; ~ **stamp** tampon *m*; **foam** ~ caoutchouc *m* mousse

³**rubber** *n* (cards) robre *m*

**rubberize** *vt* caoutchouter

**rubberneck** *n US coll* badaud -e

**rubbery** *adj* caoutchouteux -euse

**rubbing** *n* frottement *m*; friction *f*

**rubbish** *n* détritus *mpl*; (household) ordures *fpl*; (old things) vieilleries *fpl*; (nonsense) bêtises *fpl*; (valueless) camelote *f*; **talk** ~ dire des bêtises; *vt coll* dénigrer

**rubbish-dump** *n* décharge publique

**rubbishy** *adj* sans valeur

**rubble** *n* (in ruins) décombres *mpl*; *bui* moellons *mpl*; (for roads) blocaille *f*

**rub-down** *n* friction *f*

**rubicund** *adj* rubicond

**rubric** *n* rubrique *f*

**ruby** *n* rubis *m*; *adj* couleur de rubis

¹**ruck** *n* (racing) peloton *m*; **the** ~ le commun du peuple

²**ruck** *n* faux pli; *vt* froisser, chiffonner; *vi* se chiffonner

**rucksack** *n* sac *m* à dos

**ructions** *npl coll* **there will be** ~ il y aura du grabuge

**rudder** *n* gouvernail *m*; *aer* palonnier *m*

**rudderless** *adj* sans gouvernail

**ruddiness** *n* rougeur *f*

**ruddy** *adj* (cheeks) vermeil -eille; (complexion) coloré; *coll* sacré

**rude** *adj* (crude) primitif -ive, rude; (impolite) impoli, mal élevé; (vulgar) grossier -ière; (obscene) obscène; (sudden) brusque

**rudeness** *n* rudesse *f*; (person) impolitesse *f*; (coarseness) grossièreté *f*

**rudiment** *n* rudiment *m*; (basic knowledge) ~ **s** premières notions

**rudimentary** *adj* rudimentaire, élémentaire

¹**rue** *n bot* rue *f*

²**rue** *vt* regretter amèrement, se repentir de

**rueful** *adj* triste, lugubre

**ruff** *n* fraise *f*, collerette *f*

**ruffian** *n* bandit *m*, brute *f*

**ruffianly** *adj* brutal

**ruffle** *n* (wrist) manchette *f* en dentelle; (neck) fraise *f*; (chest) jabot plissé; *vt* (hair) ébouriffer; (vex) irriter; (dress) plisser; (water) troubler, rider

**rug** *n* couverture *f*; (floor) carpette *f*; (bedside) descente *f* (de lit)

**rugby** *n* rugby *m*

**rugged** *adj* (ground) raboteux -euse, accidenté; (bark) rugueux -euse; (person) rude

**rugger** *n coll* rugby *m*

**ruin** *n* ruine *f*; *vt* ruiner; (spoil) abîmer; (seduce) séduire

**ruination** *n* ruine *f*, perte *f*

**ruinous** *adj* ruineux -euse; (in ruins) délabré

**rule** *n* règle *f*; gouvernement *m*, autorité *f*; *leg* décision *f*; ~ **of the road** code *m* de la route; ~ **of thumb** méthode *f* empirique; ~ **s and regulations** règlements *mpl*; **as a** ~ en général; **do things by** ~ faire les choses selon les règles; **hard and fast** ~ règle rigoureuse; *vt* gouverner; *leg* décider; (lines) régler, tracer; *vi* (prices) se pratiquer

**ruler** *n* souverain -e; gouverneur *m*; (for lines) règle *f*

**ruling** *adj* dominant; ~ **classes** classes dirigeantes

**¹rum** n rhum m

**²rum** adj coll bizarre, drôle

**rumba, rhumba** n rumba f

**rumble** n (traffic) roulement m; (thunder) grondement m; (stomach) gargouillement m; US mot spider m; vi (traffic) rouler; (thunder) gronder; (stomach) gargouiller

**rumbling** n see **rumble**

**rumbustious** adj chahuteur -euse, bruyant

**ruminant** n ruminant m

**ruminate** vt + vi ruminer

**rumination** n rumination f

**ruminative** adj méditatif -ive

**rummage** n fouille f; (things) vieilleries fpl de rebut; vt + vi fouiller

**rummage-sale** n vente f d'objets usagés

**rumour** n rumeur f, bruit m; ~ **has it that** le bruit court que

**rumoured** adj allégué, présumé; **it is** ~ **that** le bruit court que

**rump** n (animal) croupe f; (person) derrière m; cul (beef) culotte f; fig reste m

**rumple** vt chiffonner, froisser

**rumpsteak** n romsteck m, rumsteck m

**rumpus** n coll vacarme m, chahut m

**run** n course f; (train) trajet m; naut parcours m; (outing) promenade f, tour m; (course) cours m; (rush to buy) descente f; (duration) durée f; (succession) suite f; (generality) commun m; mus roulade f; **an hour's** ~ **from** à une heure de; **at a** ~ au pas de course; **break into a** ~ se mettre à courir; **give s/o a** ~ **for his money** en donner à qn pour son argent; **have a long** ~ tenir longtemps; theat rester longtemps à l'affiche; **have a** ~ **of luck** être en veine; **have the** ~ **of the house** avoir libre accès dans la maison; **in the long** ~ à la longue; (criminal) **on the** ~ recherché par la police; **there's a** ~ **on sugar** tout le monde achète du sucre; **trial** ~ cours m d'essai; vt (risk) courir; (animal) faire courir; (wires, pipes) faire passer; (drive) conduire; (engine) faire marcher; (organization, service) diriger; (errand) faire; (house, car) entretenir; (shop, hotel) tenir; (liquid) verser, faire couler; (train, bus) mettre en service; ~ **down** (run over) écraser; (knock over) renverser; (find) dépister; fig dénigrer; ~ **in** conduire au poste (de police); (engine) roder; ~ **off** réciter; (liquid) faire couler; (letter) taper; ~ **one's car into a tree** heurter un arbre avec sa voiture; ~ **one's eye over sth** jeter un coup d'œil sur qch; (rope) ~ **out** laisser filer; ~ **over** (document) parcourir; (search) fouiller; (with vehicle) écraser; ~ **s/o**

through transpercer qn, passer son épée à travers le corps de qn; ~ **s/o to the station** conduire qn à la gare; ~ **up debts** laisser accumuler des dettes; vi courir; (escape) se sauver, filer; (machine) marcher, fonctionner; (liquid) couler; (leak) fuir; (bus, train) circuler; (eyes) pleurer; (rope) glisser; (nose) couler; (wound) suppurer; (play) se jouer, tenir l'affiche; (colour) déteindre; ~ **about** courir de côté et d'autre; ~ **across** traverser en courant; ~ **across** s/o tomber sur qn; ~ **after** courir après; ~ **aground** échouer; ~ **along** (flank) longer; (go away) filer; ~ **at** se jeter sur; ~ **away** se sauver, s'enfuir; ~ **away with** (kidnap) enlever; **away with the idea that** aller s'imaginer que; ~ **down** descendre en courant; (flow) ruisseler; (battery) se décharger; ~ **for sth** courir chercher qch; (sea) ~ **high** être grosse; ~ **into** (figures) s'élever à; (collide) heurter; ~ **into debt** s'endetter; ~ **into s/o** tomber sur qn; ~ **off** fuir; ~ **out** sortir en courant; (time) expirer; (supplies) s'épuiser; ~ **through** traverser en courant; (read quickly) parcourir; (money) dissiper; ~ **up** monter en courant

**runabout** n mot petite voiture; (person) vagabond -e

**runaway** n + adj fugitif -ive; ~ **marriage** mariage clandestin; ~ **victory** victoire f facile

**run-down** n résumé m; diminution f d'activité; adj épuisé, affaibli; (battery) à plat

**rune** n rune f

**rung** n échelon m; (chair) bâton m

**runic** adj runique

**runnel** n ruisseau m

**runner** n coureur -euse; (sledge) patin m; (messenger) messager m; **scarlet** ~ **bean** haricot m d'Espagne

**runner-up** n second -e

**running** n course f; (machine) fonctionnement m; (hotel, etc) direction f; (water) ruissellement m; (wound) suppuration f; **be out of the** ~ n'avoir plus aucune chance; **make the** ~ mener la course; adj courant; (wound) qui suppure; (continuous) continu; ~ **cold** rhume m de cerveau; ~ **commentary** reportage m en direct; ~ **expenses** dépenses courantes; ~ **jump** saut m avec élan; **in** ~ **order** en état de fonctionnement

**running-board** n mot marchepied m

**runny** adj liquide; (nose) qui coule

**runt** n bœuf m de petite race; coll nabot m

**run-through** n répétition f

**runway** *n aer* piste *f* d'envol; *eng* chemin *m* de roulement

**rupture** *n* rupture *f*; (hernia) hernie *f*; *vt* rompre; **be ~ d** avoir une hernie; *vi* se rompre

**rural** *adj* rural

**ruse** *n* ruse *f*, stratagème *m*

**¹rush** *n* jonc *m*

**²rush** *n* ruée *f*, course précipitée; (people) presse *f*, bousculade *f*; (haste) hâte *f*; *cin* ~ es projection *f* d'essai; ~ **hour** heure *f* d'affluence (de pointe); ~ **job** travail urgent; *vt* (person) entraîner, faire dépêcher; (transport) transporter d'urgence; (invade) envahir; *coll* (charge high price) estamper; ~ **up** (build) bâtir à la hâte; *vi* se précipiter, s'élancer; ~ **at s/o** se jeter sur qn; ~ **into** se précipiter dans; ~ **out** sortir précipitamment; ~ **through** traverser à toute vitesse; ~ **to conclusions** conclure hâtivement

**rusk** *n* biscotte *f*

**russet** *n* (apple) reinette (grise); *adj* (colour) roussâtre

**Russia** *n* Russie *f*

**Russian** *n* Russe; (language) russe *m*; *adj* russe

**rust** *n* rouille *f*; *vt* rouiller; *vi* se rouiller, rouiller

**rustic** *n* paysan -anne; *pej* rustre; *adj* rustique

**rusticate** *vt* (student) renvoyer temporairement; *vi* habiter à la campagne; se retirer à la campagne

**rustication** *n* (student) renvoi *m* temporaire; résidence *f* à la campagne

**rusticity** *n* rusticité *f*

**rustle** *n* (leaves, etc) bruissement *m*; (paper) froissement *m*; (silk) frou-frou *m*; *vt* (leaves, etc) faire bruire; (paper) froisser; (silk) faire froufrouter; *US* (steal cattle) voler du bétail; *coll* ~ **up** se débrouiller pour trouver (pour faire); *vi* (leaves, etc) bruire; (silk) faire frou-frou; (paper) produire un bruissement

**rustless** *adj* (rustproof) inoxydable; (not rusted) sans rouille

**rust-preventive** *n* anti-rouille *m*

**rustproof** *adj* inoxydable

**rusty** *adj* rouillé; (colour) couleur de rouille; (voice) rauque, éraillé; **get ~** se rouiller

**¹rut** *n* ornière *f*; *vt* sillonner d'ornières

**²rut** *n* (of animals) chaleur *f*; *vt* couvrir; *vi* être en chaleur

**ruthless** *adj* impitoyable, sans merci

**rye** *n* seigle *m*

**rye-grass** *n* ray-grass *m*

# S

**Sabbath** *n* sabbat *m*

**sabbatical** *adj eccles* sabbatique; ~ **year** année *f* de congé

**sable** *n* (animal) zibeline *f*

**sabotage** *n* sabotage *m*; *vt* saboter

**saboteur** *n* saboteur -euse

**sabre** *n* sabre *m*

**sabre-rattling** *n* menaces *fpl* de guerre

**saccharin** *n* saccharine *f*

**sacerdotal** *adj* sacerdotal

**sachet** *n* sachet *m*

**¹sack** *n* sac *m*; *coll* **get the ~** recevoir son congé; *coll* **give s/o the ~** congédier qn; *vt* mettre en sac; *coll* (fire) congédier

**²sack** *n* (pillage) pillage *m*, sac *m*; *vt* saccager, mettre à sac

**sackcloth** *n* toile *f* à sac

**sackful** *n* plein sac *m*

**¹sacking** *n* mise *f* en sac; *coll* (firing) congédiement *m*

**²sacking** *n* (pillage) sac *m*

**sacrament** *n* sacrement *m*

**sacramental** *adj* sacramentel -elle

**sacred** *adj* sacré, saint; ~ **to** consacré à

**sacredness** *n* sainteté *f*

**sacrifice** *n* sacrifice *m*; (giving up) renoncement *m*; (offering) victime *f*; **at a great ~** au prix de grands sacrifices; *vt* sacrifier; (giving up) renoncer à

**sacrificial** *adj* sacrificatoire

**sacrilege** *n* sacrilège *m*

**sacrilegious** *adj* sacrilège

**sacristan** *n* sacristain *m*

**sacristy** *n* sacristie *f*

**sacrosanct** *adj* sacro-saint

**sacrum** *n* sacrum *m*

**sad** *adj* triste; (regrettable) déplorable; (loss) cruel -elle; (place) morne; **make s/o ~** attrister qn

**sadden** *vt* attrister, affliger

**saddle** *n* selle *f*; (mountain) col *m*; (mutton) selle *f*; (hare) râble *m*; **in the ~ en selle**; *vt* seller; *coll* **~ s/o with sth** mettre qch sur le dos de qn

**saddle-bag** *n* sacoche *f* de selle

**saddler** *n* bourrelier *m*, sellier *m*

**saddlery** *n* bourrellerie *f*, sellerie *f*

**sadism** *n* sadisme *m*

**sadist** *n* sadiste

**sadistic** *adj* sadique

**sadly** *adv* tristement; (greatly) beaucoup, vraiment

**sadness** *n* tristesse *f*

**safari** *n* safari *m*

¹**safe** *n* coffre-fort *m* (*pl* coffres-forts)

²**safe** *adj* (in safety) en sûreté; (place) sûr; (not dangerous) sans danger; (out of danger) hors de danger; **~ and sound** sain et sauf; **be on the ~ side** être du bon côté; **get home ~** rentrer sans accident; **in a ~ place** en lieu sûr; **it's quite ~ to** il n'y a aucun danger à

**safe-conduct** *n* sauf-conduit *m*

**safeguard** *n* sauvegarde *f*; *vt* sauvegarder, protéger

**safekeeping** *n* bonne garde

**safely** *adv* sans accident; sûrement; (without risk) sans danger; (securely) en sûreté

**safety** *n* sûreté *f*, sécurité *f*; **~ device** dispositif *m* de sûreté; **~ first!** soyez prudents!; **~ road** sécurité routière

**safety-belt** *n* *mot* ceinture *f* de sécurité

**safety-catch** *n* cran *m* de sécurité

**safety-lamp** *n* lampe *f* de sûreté

**safety-match** *n* allumette suédoise

**safety-pin** *n* épingle *f* de sûreté (de nourrice)

**safety-razor** *n* rasoir *m* de sûreté

**safety-valve** *n* soupape *f* de sûreté

**saffron** *n* safran *m*

**sag** *n* affaissement *m*, fléchissement *m*; *vi* s'affaisser, fléchir; (lean over) pencher d'un côté; (cord, cable) se détendre

**saga** *n* *lit* saga *f*; suite *f* d'événements extraordinaires

**sagacious** *adj* sagace, perspicace, avisé

**sagacity, sagaciousness** *n* sagacité *f*

¹**sage** *n* sage *m*, philosophe *m*; *adj* sage

²**sage** *n* *bot* sauge *f*

**sago** *n* sagou *m*

**Sahara** *n* the **~** le Sahara

**sail** *n* voile *f*; (windmill) aile *f*; (trip) promenade *f* à la voile, promenade *f* en mer; **hoist ~** hisser une voile; **lower ~** amener une voile; **set ~** appareiller,

prendre la mer; **under full ~** toutes voiles dehors; *vt* manœuvrer, naviguer sur; (sea) parcourir; *vi* faire de la voile, naviguer; (glide) planer; (leave) partir; **~ at five knots** filer cinq nœuds; **~ down** descendre

**sailing** *n* navigation *f*; (departure) départ *m*; **he likes ~** il aime la voile; **it's plain ~** cela va tout seul

**sailing-boat** *n* canot *m* à voiles

**sailing-ship** *n* voilier *m*, bateau *m* à voiles

**sailor** *n* marin *m*, matelot *m*; **be a bad ~** être sujet -ette au mal de mer; **be a good ~** avoir le pied marin

**saint** *n* saint -e; **All Saints' Day** la Toussaint; *adj* saint

**saintly** *adj* saint

¹**sake** *n* cause *f*; **art for art's ~** l'art pour l'art; **for God's ~** pour l'amour de Dieu; **for his ~** à cause de lui; **for pity's ~!** pour l'amour de Dieu!; **for the ~ of** à cause de, pour l'amour de

²**sake** *n* (drink) saké *m*, saki *m*

**salacious** *adj* lubrique

**salad** *n* salade *f*; **~ days** années *fpl* de jeunesse; **fruit ~** macédoine *f* de fruits; **mixed ~** salade panachée

**salad-bowl** *n* saladier *m*

**salad-dressing** *n* vinaigrette *f*

**salamander** *n* salamandre *f*

**salami** *n* salami *m*

**salaried** *adj* rétribué, rémunéré, salarié

**salary** *n* traitement *m*, appointements *mpl*

**sale** *n* vente *f*; (clearance) solde *m*; (auction) vente *f* aux enchères; *US* **~ s clerk** vendeur -euse; **~s promotion** campagne *f* de vente; **for ~** à vendre; **on ~** en vente; **put up for ~** mettre en vente

**saleable** *adj* vendable

**sale-price** *n* prix *m* de solde

**saleroom** *n* salle *f* des ventes

**salesgirl** *n* vendeuse *f*

**salesman** *n* vendeur *m*

**salesmanship** *n* art *m* de vendre

**sales-resistance** *n* hésitation *f* à acheter; **there is a lot of ~** la clientèle boude

**sales-talk** *n* boniment *m*

**saleswoman** *n* vendeuse *f*

**salient** *n* *mil* saillant *m*; *adj* saillant; *fig* frappant

**saline** *n* marais *m* salant; (saltworks) saline *f*; *med* sel purgatif; *adj* salin, salé

**salinity** *n* salinité *f*

**saliva** *n* salive *f*

**salivary** *adj* salivaire

**salivate** *vi* saliver

**salivation** *n* salivation *f*

**sallow** *adj* jaune, jaunâtre

**sally** *n* *mil* sortie *f*; (wit) saillie *f*; *vi* *mil* faire une sortie; ~ **forth** se mettre en route

**salmon** *n* saumon *m*; *adj* saumon *invar*

**salmon-trout** *n* truite saumonée

**salon** *n* salon *m*; **beauty** ~ institut *m* de beauté

**saloon** *n* salle *f*, salon *m*; *mot* conduite intérieure; *US* bar *m*; ~ **deck** pont *m* de première classe

**saloon-bar** *n* = bar plus cher dans un pub anglais

**salt** *n* sel *m*; **an old** ~ un loup de mer; **kitchen** ~ gros sel; **not worth one's** ~ inutile; **rock** ~ sel *m* gemme; **spirits of** ~ esprit *m* de sel; **with a pinch of** ~ avec un grain de sel; *adj* salé; *vt* saler

**salt-cellar** *n* salière *f*

**saltiness** *n* salinité *f*, salure *f*

**salt-marsh** *n* marais salant

**saltpetre** *n* salpêtre *m*

**salt-tax** *n hist* gabelle *f*

**salt-water** *adj* de mer

**salty** *adj* salé

**salubrious** *adj* salubre

**salutary** *adj* salutaire

**salutation** *n* salutation *f*

**salute** *n* salut *m*, salutation *f*; **fire a** ~ tirer une salve; **take the** ~ passer les troupes en revue; *vt* saluer

**salvage** *n* sauvetage *m*; (money) prime *f* de sauvetage; (things) objets sauvés; (materials) récupération *f*; *vt* sauver; effectuer le sauvetage de; (waste materials) récupérer

**salvation** *n* salut *m*; **Salvation Army** Armée *f* du Salut

**salve** *n* pommade *f*, baume *m*; *vt* adoucir, apaiser

**salver** *n* plateau *m*

**salvo** *n* salve *f*

**samba** *n* samba *f*

**same** *adj* + *pron* même; ~ **here!** moi aussi!; **and the** ~ **to you** à vous de même; **at the** ~ **time** en même temps; (simultaneously) à la fois; **do the** ~ en faire autant; **he looks just the** ~ il n'a pas changé du tout; **in the** ~ **way** de même; **it comes to the** ~ **thing** cela revient au même; **it's all the** ~ c'est tout un; **it's all the** ~ **to me** cela m'est égal; *adv* de même; **all the** ~ malgré tout, quand même

**sameness** *n* identité *f*; monotonie *f*

**sample** *n* échantillon *m*; **as a** ~ à titre d'échantillon; *vt* échantillonner; (taste) déguster, goûter; (try out) essayer

**sanatorium** *n* (*pl* sanatoria) sanatorium *m*; (school) infirmerie *f*

**sanctification** *n* sanctification *f*

**sanctify** *vt* sanctifier, consacrer

**sanctimonious** *adj* papelard, cagot

**sanctimoniousness, sanctimony** *n* cagoterie *f*, papelardise *f*

**sanction** *n* sanction *f*; *vt* sanctionner, approuver

**sanctity** *n* sainteté *f*

**sanctuary** *n* sanctuaire *m*; *fig* refuge *m*; **right of** ~ droit *m* d'asile; **take** ~ chercher asile

**sanctum** *n* sanctuaire *m*; (private room) cabinet privé

**sand** *n* sable *m*; ~ **s** plage *f*; *vt* sabler; *vi* ~ **up** s'ensabler

**sandal** *n* sandale *f*

**sandbag** *n* sac *m* de sable, sac *m* de terre; *vt* protéger avec des sacs de sable

**sandbank** *n* banc *m* de sable

**sand-blast** *n* jet *m* de sable; *vt* passer au jet de sable

**sandcastle** *n* château *m* de sable

**sand-dune** *n* dune *f*

**sandiness** *n* nature sablonneuse

**sandman** *n* the ~ **is coming** le marchand de sable passe

**sandpaper** *n* papier *m* de verre; *vt* frotter au papier de verre

**sandstone** *n* grès *m*

**sandstorm** *n* tempête *f* de sable

**sandwich** *n* sandwich *m* (*pl* sandwiches); *vt* intercaler; **be** ~ **ed between** être pris entre

**sandwichman** *n* homme-sandwich *m* (*pl* hommes-sandwiches)

**sandy** *adj* sableux -euse, sablonneux -euse; (hair) roux (*f* rousse)

**sane** *adj* sain d'esprit, sensé

**sanguinary** *adj* sanguinaire

**sanguine** *adj* (temperament) sanguin; (complexion) rubicond; (optimistic) optimiste, confiant

**sanitary** *adj* sanitaire, hygiénique; ~ **towel** serviette *f* hygiénique

**sanitation** *n* hygiène *f*; système *m* sanitaire; (in house) sanitaire *m*

**sanity** *n* santé *f* d'esprit; bon sens

**Sanskrit** *n* sanskrit *m*

**Santa Claus** *n* le Père Noël

¹**sap** *n bot* sève *f*

²**sap** *n coll* idiot -e, nigaud -e

³**sap** *vt* miner, saper

**sapless** *adj* sans sève, desséché

**sapling** *n* jeune arbre *m*

**sapper** *n mil* sapeur *m*

**sapphire** *n* saphir *m*

**sappy** *adj* plein de sève

**saraband** *n mus* sarabande *f*

**sarcasm** *n* sarcasme *m*, ironie *f*

**sarcastic** *adj* sarcastique, mordant

**sarcoma** *n med* sarcome *m*

**sardine** *n* sardine *f*; **packed like** ~ **s** serrés comme des harengs

**sardonic** *adj* sardonique

**sari, saree** *n* sari *m*

**sarong** n sarong m
**sartorial** adj de tailleur
**¹sash** n écharpe f, ceinture f
**²sash** n (window) châssis m
**sash-window** n fenêtre f à guillotine
**Satan** n Satan m
**satanic** adj diabolique, satanique
**satchel** n (bag) sacoche f; (school) cartable m
**sate** vt assouvir, rassasier
**satellite** n satellite m; ~ **town** ville f satellite
**satiate** vt rassasier
**satiety** n satiété f
**satin** n satin m; adj de satin; (like satin) satiné
**satire** n satire f
**satiric(al)** adj satirique
**satirist** n auteur m satirique
**satirize** vt satiriser
**satisfaction** n satisfaction f; (payment) paiement m, acquittement m; (reparation) réparation f; (passion) assouvissement m; (reason for satisfaction) motif m de satisfaction; **give s/o** ~ faire réparation à qn; **to his** ~ de manière à le satisfaire
**satisfactorily** adv de façon satisfaisante
**satisfactory** adj satisfaisant
**satisfied** adj content, satisfait; (convinced) convaincu
**satisfy** vt satisfaire, contenter; (convince) convaincre; (condition) remplir; (honour) satisfaire à; (make reparation to) faire réparation à; (desire) assouvir; **done to** ~ **one's conscience** fait par acquit de conscience
**saturate** vt saturer, tremper
**saturation** n saturation f
**Saturday** n samedi m
**Saturn** n Saturne m
**saturnine** adj taciturne, sombre
**satyr** n satyre m
**sauce** n sauce f; coll (impertinence) culot m, toupet m; **what is** ~ **for the goose is** ~ **for the gander** ce qui est bon pour l'un est bon pour l'autre
**sauce-boat** n saucière f
**saucepan** n casserole f
**saucer** n soucoupe f; **flying** ~ soucoupe volante
**saucy** adj impertinent; (roguish) fripon -onne
**Saudi Arabia** n Arabie Saoudite f
**sauerkraut** n choucroute f
**sauna** n sauna m
**saunter** vi flâner, se balader; ~ **up** s'approcher sans se presser
**sausage** n saucisse f; (dry) saucisson m
**sausage-meat** n chair f à saucisse
**sausage-roll** n saucisse enrobée de pâte
**sauté** adj cul sauté; vt faire sauter

**savage** n sauvage; adj sauvage, barbare; (animal) féroce; vt attaquer
**savagery, savageness** n sauvagerie f, barbarie f, brutalité f
**savant** n savant -e
**¹save** n sp arrêt m; vt sauver; (save up) économiser; (put aside) mettre de côté; (time) gagner; (protect) protéger; (avoid) éviter; (look after) ménager; (reserve) réserver; (from danger, etc) préserver; ~ **appearances** sauvegarder (sauver) les apparences; ~ **oneself for sth** se ménager pour qch; ~ **s/o the trouble of doing sth** épargner à qn la peine de faire qch
**²save** prep excepté, sauf
**saveloy** n cervelas m
**saver** n (saviour) sauveur m; (rescuer) sauveteur m; (economiser) personne f économe
**¹saving** n (rescue) sauvetage m; (freeing) délivrance f; (souls) salut m; (money) économie f; ~ **s** économies fpl
**²saving** prep sauf
**savings-bank** n caisse f d'épargne
**saviour** n sauveur m
**savory** n bot sarriette f
**savour** n saveur f, goût m; (trace) trace f; vt savourer; ~ **of sth** tenir de qch
**savoury** n entremets non sucré; adj savoureux -euse, succulent
**¹saw** n scie f; power ~ scie f mécanique; (for trees) tronçonneuse f; vt scier; ~ **the air** battre l'air; ~ **up** débiter
**²saw** n ar (saying) dicton m, maxime f
**sawdust** n sciure f
**saw-mill** n scierie f
**sawyer** n scieur m
**saxifrage** n saxifrage f
**Saxon** n Saxon -onne; adj saxon -onne
**Saxony** n Saxe f
**saxophone** n saxophone m
**say** n parole f, mot m; **have one's** ~ dire ce qu'on a à dire; **have no** ~ **in the matter** ne pas avoir voix au chapitre; vt dire; (prayers) faire; ~ **no more!** n'en dites pas davantage!; **didn't I** ~ **so!** quand je vous le disais!; **have plenty to** ~ **for oneself** ne pas avoir la langue dans sa poche; **I must** ~ **that** j'avoue que; **it is said that** on dit que; **let's** ~ **five pounds** disons cinq livres; **so to** ~ pour ainsi dire; **that is to** ~ c'est à dire; **there's much to be said for doing this** il y a de bonnes raisons pour faire cela; **to** ~ **nothing of** sans parler de; **what did you** ~? comment?, que dites-vous?; **what do you** ~ **to a walk?** si on faisait une promenade?; **without** ~**ing a word** sans mot dire; vi **as one might** ~ comme qui dirait; **I** ~! dites donc!; **so to** ~ pour ainsi dire; **that is to** ~ c'est

676

à dire; **you don't ~!** pas possible!, par exemple!

**saying** n dicton m; (action) énonciation f

**scab** n (disease) gale f; (over wound) croûte f; coll (workman refusing to strike) jaune m; vi former une croûte

**scabbard** n fourreau m, gaine f

**scabby** adj galeux -euse; (sore) croûteux -euse; coll (worthless) méprisable

**scabies** n gale f

**scabious** n bot scabieuse f

**scabrous** adj rugueux -euse; (story, etc) scabreux -euse

**scaffold** n échafaud m; (for speaker) estrade f

**scaffolding** n échafaudage m

**scald** n échaudure f; vt échauder, ébouillanter

**scalding** n échaudage m; adj bouillant

¹**scale** n (fish, skin) écaille f; (deposit) dépôt m; (on teeth) tartre m; vt écailler; (teeth) détartrer; vi s'écailler; (boiler) s'incruster

²**scale** n (of balance) plateau m; **~s** balance f; **bathroom- ~s** pèse-personne m (pl pèse-personne(s)); **letter ~s** pèse-lettre m; **tip the ~s at** peser plus de; fig **turn the ~s** faire pencher la balance; vi peser

³**scale** n échelle f; (extent) étendue f; mus gamme f; **on a large (small) ~** en grand (petit); **on the ~ of** à l'échelle de; vt (climb) escalader; (map) tracer à l'échelle; **~ up (down)** augmenter (réduire) à l'échelle

**scalene** adj scalène

**scaliness** n squamosité f

**scallop** n zool pétoncle m, coquille f Saint-Jacques; (needlework) feston m; vt faire cuire en coquille; festonner

**scallywag** n coll propre à rien

**scalp** n cuir chevelu; vt scalper

**scalpel** n scalpel m

**scaly** adj écailleux -euse; (boiler) tartreux -euse

**scamp** n mauvais garnement, vaurien -ienne; **young ~** petit galopin; vt bâcler

**scamper** vi courir allègrement; **~ away (off)** détaler, se sauver à toutes jambes

**scampi** npl scampi mpl

**scan** vt scruter, examiner; (verse) mesurer; cin + TV balayer; (read quickly) parcourir rapidement

**scandal** n scandale m, honte f; (slander) médisance f; **create a ~** faire un scandale; **talk ~** cancaner

**scandalize** vt scandaliser

**scandalmonger** n médisant -e, mauvaise langue

**scandalous** adj scandaleux -euse, honteux -euse

**Scandinavian** n Scandinave; adj scandinave

**scanner** n scrutateur -trice; elect appareil explorateur; **radar ~** déchiffreur m de radar

**scansion** n scansion f

**scant** adj insuffisant, peu abondant

**scanty** adj insuffisant; (meal) maigre; (news, hair) rare

**scapegoat** n bouc m émissaire

**scar** n cicatrice f; (face) balafre f; vt laisser une cicatrice sur; balafrer; vi se cicatriser

**scarce** adj rare, peu abondant; **grow ~** se faire rare; coll **make oneself ~** filer

**scarcely** adv à peine; **~ ever** presque jamais; **he can ~ walk** c'est à peine s'il peut marcher; **he ~ goes out** il ne sort guère; **I can ~ believe it** j'ai de la peine à le croire

**scarcity, scarceness** n pénurie f, manque m, rareté f

**scare** n panique f, alarme f; **give s/o a ~** faire peur à qn; vt effrayer, alarmer, faire peur à; **~ away** effaroucher; vi s'effrayer, s'alarmer

**scarecrow** n épouvantail m

**scaremonger** n alarmiste

**scarf** n écharpe f; (woman's) fichu m; (silk) foulard m; (man's) cache-col m invar

**scarifier** n scarificateur m

**scarify** vt scarifier

**scarlet** n écarlate f; adj écarlate; **~ fever** scarlatine f

**scarred** adj portant des cicatrices; balafré

**scary** adj coll épouvantable, effrayant

**scat** interj file!, filez!

**scathing** adj mordant, cinglant

**scatological** adj scatologique

**scatology** n scatologie f

**scatter** n dispersion f; vt disperser; (put to flight) mettre en fuite; (clouds) dissiper; (seeds) semer à la volée; (throw about) éparpiller; vi (mob) se disperser; (clouds) se dissiper; s'éparpiller

**scatter-brain** n étourdi -e

**scattered** adj dispersé, épars

**scattering** n dispersion f; éparpillement m; (small number) petite quantité

**scatty** adj coll étourdi, timbré

**scavenge** vt + vi balayer, nettoyer

**scavenger** n boueur m, balayeur m des rues; (creature) animal m nécrophage

**scenario** n scénario m

**scene** n scène f; (event) théâtre m, lieu m; (theatre set) décor m; (landscape) paysage m; sl ambiance f; **behind the ~s** dans la coulisse (les coulisses); **make a ~** faire une scène; **on the ~ of the accident** sur les lieux de l'accident

**scenery** n (landscape) paysage m; *theat* décors mpl

**scenic** adj scénique; théâtral

**scent** n odeur f, parfum m, senteur f; (track) piste f, trace f; (sense) odorat m; (dog) flair m; **be on the right ~** être sur la piste; vt (smell out) flairer; (perfume) parfumer, embaumer

**scented** adj parfumé; (air) embaumé

**scentless** adj sans odeur, inodore

**sceptic** n sceptique

**sceptical** adj sceptique

**scepticism** n scepticisme m

**sceptre** n sceptre m

**schedule** n liste f; (timetable) horaire m; (to law) annexe f; note explicative; (inventory) inventaire m; (taxes) cédule f; (plan) plan m d'exécution; **according to ~** selon les provisions; **be behind ~** être en retard sur l'horaire prévu; **on ~** à l'heure; **up to ~** comme prévu, à la date voulue; vt (law) ajouter comme annexe; (put on list) inscrire sur une liste; (plan) dresser le programme de; *aer* **~d service** vol régulier

**schema** n (pl **schemata**) schéma m

**schematic** adj schématique

**scheme** n plan m, projet m; arrangement m; *pej* intrigue f, machination f; vt combiner, machiner; vi intriguer, comploter

**schemer** n intrigant -e

**scheming** adj intrigant

**scherzo** n scherzo m

**schism** n schisme m

**schismatic** adj schismatique

**schizoid** adj schizoïde

**schizophrenia** n schizophrénie f

**schizophrenic** adj schizophrène

**schmaltzy** adj coll d'un sentimentalisme exagéré

**schnap(p)s** n schnaps m

**schnorkel** n see **snorkel**

**scholar** n écolier -ière, élève; (learned) savant -e, érudit -e; (holder of scholarship) boursier. -ière

**scholarly** adj savant, érudit

**scholarship** n savoir m, érudition f; (for studies) bourse f

**scholastic** adj scolastique, érudit

**scholasticism** n scolastique f

**¹school** n école f, groupe m scolaire; (grammar) lycée m, collège m; (boarding) pension f, pensionnat m; (schooling) études fpl scolaires, les classes fpl; (higher education) académie f, institut m; **~ year** année f scolaire; **church ~** = école f libre; **comprehensive ~** = collège m d'enseignement secondaire (C.E.S.); **go to ~** aller en classe; **independent ~** collège privé; **night ~** cours mpl du soir; **public ~** collège privé; *US* école f d'état; **state ~** école f d'état; vt discipliner, former, instruire; **~ed in** habitué à

**²school** n (fish) banc m, bande f

**schoolbook** n livre m scolaire

**schoolboy** n écolier m, élève m

**schoolday** n jour m de classe; **in my ~s** pendant mes années d'école

**schoolfellow** n camarade d'école

**schoolgirl** n écolière f, élève f

**schooling** n éducation f, instruction f

**schoolmarm** n coll maîtresse f d'école

**schoolmaster** n (secondary) professeur m; (primary) instituteur m

**schoolmate** n copain (f copine) d'école

**schoolmistress** n (secondary) professeur m; (primary) institutrice f

**schoolroom** n salle f de classe

**schoolteacher** n (secondary) professeur m; (primary) instituteur -trice

**schoolteaching** n enseignement m scolaire

**schooner** n naut schooner m, goélette f; grand verre (à Xérès)

**sciatic** adj sciatique

**sciatica** n sciatique f

**science** n science f

**science-fiction** n science-fiction f

**scientific** adj scientifique

**scientist** n savant -e, homme m de science, scientifique

**Scilly Isles** npl Sorlingues fpl

**scimitar** n cimeterre m

**scintillate** vi scintiller, étinceler

**scion** n descendant -e; *bot* rejeton m

**scissors** npl ciseaux mpl

**sclerosis** n sclérose f; **multiple ~** sclérose f en plaques

**sclerotic** adj sclérosé

**¹scoff** vi se moquer; **~ at** se moquer de

**²scoff** vt bouffer

**scold** n mégère f; vt + vi gronder, réprimander

**sconce** n bougeoir m

**scone** n pain m au lait

**scoop** n (shovel) pelle f; (spoon) grande cuiller; (news) scoop m; vt (scoop out) évider; (liquid) écoper; (news) faire un scoop de

**scoot** vi coll décamper, filer

**scooter** n (child's) trottinette f; (motor-scooter) scooter m

**scope** n (extent) étendue f, portée f; (space) espace m; (freedom) liberté f; **fall within the ~ of a work** rentrer dans le plan d'un ouvrage; **give ~ for** donner carrière à; **have full ~ to** avoir toute latitude pour

**scorbutic** adj scorbutique

**scorch** vt roussir, brûler; (sun) rôtir, dessécher; vi coll **~ along** brûler le pavé, rouler comme un fou

scorcher *n coll* journée *f* torride;
(remark) riposte cinglante

scorching *adj* brûlant; (weather) torride

score *n* (notch) entaille *f*, encoche *f*;
(game) nombre *m* de points, score *m*;
(twenty) vingtaine *f*; *mus* partition *f*;
(subject) question *f*, point *m*; ~s of
people des masses de gens; keep ~
marquer les points; *coll* know the ~
s'y connaître; on that ~ à cet égard;
pay off old ~s régler de vieux comptes;
pay one's ~ régler son compte; *vt*
(scratch) érafler, rayer; (notch) entailler, cocher; (goal, point) marquer; *mus*
noter; (success) remporter; *vi* (game)
marquer un but (un point); ~ off s/o
marquer des points aux dépens de qn;
~ over s/o l'emporter sur qn

scorer *n* marqueur *m*

scoria *n* scorie *f*, scories *fpl*

scorn *n* dédain *m*, mépris *m*

scornful *adj* méprisant, dédaigneux
-euse

scorpion *n* scorpion *m*

Scot *n* Écossais -e

Scotch *adj* écossais

¹scotch *n* (whisky) scotch *m*

²scotch *vt* (plan) faire avorter, déjouer

scotfree *adj* get off ~ s'en tirer indemne

Scotland *n* Écosse *f*

Scots *n* dialecte écossais; *adj* écossais

Scotsman *n* Écossais *m*

Scotswoman *n* Écossaise *f*

Scottish *adj* écossais

scoundrel *n* scélérat *m*, gredin *m*, voyou
*m*

scour *n* nettoyage *m*, récurage *m*; *vt* nettoyer, frotter; (greasy object) dégraisser; (saucepan) récurer; (country)
battre, parcourir

scourer *n* nettoyeur -euse, récureur
-euse; (for pans) éponge *f* métallique

scourge *n* fléau *m*; *vt* fouetter; *fig* châtier

¹scout *n* éclaireur *m*; *vi* aller en reconnaissance

²scout *vt* repousser avec mépris

scoutmaster *n* chef *m* de troupe

scowl *n* air renfrogné; *vi* froncer les
sourcils, se renfrogner

scrabble *vi* ~ about gratter; (search)
chercher à quatre pattes

scrag *n* (person) personne *f* maigre;
(animal) bête efflanquée; ~ of mutton
collet *m* de mouton; *vt* tordre le cou à

scraggy *adj* maigre, décharné

scram *vi coll* filer, ficher le camp, se débiner

scramble *n* (walking) marche *f* pénible;
(struggle) mêlée *f*, bousculade *f*; *vt*
brouiller; *vi* avancer péniblement; ~
for sth se bousculer pour avoir qch; ~

up grimper à quatre pattes

scrambler *n* (telephone) brouilleur *m*

¹scrap *n* petit morceau, bout *m*, fragment *m*; (land) parcelle *f*; (conversation) bribe *f*; (comfort) brin *m*;
(newspaper) coupure *f*; ~s (left-overs)
restes *mpl*; (materials) déchets *mpl*; *vt*
mettre au rebut; (plan, etc) mettre au
rancart

²scrap *n coll* bagarre *f*; *vi* se battre

scrapbook *n* album *m*

scrape *n* coup *m* de grattoir; *coll* mauvais pas, embarras *m*; (violin) grincement *m*; *coll* mince couche *f* de beurre
(de margarine); get into a ~ se mettre
dans le pétrin; get out of a ~ se tirer
d'affaire; *vt* gratter, racler; (flesh) écorcher; (shoes) décrotter; ~ away (off)
enlever en raclant; (violin) ~ the bow
faire grincer l'archet; ~ together
amasser; *vi* gratter, racler; ~ against
(passing by) raser; (rubbing) frotter
contre; ~ on the violin racler du
violon; ~ through passer tout juste;
(exam) réussir de justesse

scraper *n* (tool) grattoir *m*, racloir *m*

scrap-heap *n* tas *m* de ferraille

scraping *n* éraflement *m*, raclage *m*;
bowing and ~ courbettes *fpl*

scrap-iron *n* ferraille *f*

scrap-merchant *n* marchand *m* de ferraille

scrappy *adj* hétérogène, disparate;
(speech) décousu

¹scratch *n* égratignure *f*; (with nail) coup
*m* d'ongle; (with claw) coup *m* de griffe;
(on surface) rayure *f*; (sound) gratte-
ment *m*, grincement *m*; (sport) scratch
*m*; come up to ~ se montrer à la hauteur de l'occasion; start from ~ partir
de zéro; *vt* griffer, égratigner, donner
un coup de griffe à; (skin) écorcher;
(surface) rayer; (body) gratter; (sport)
scratcher; ~ one's head se gratter la
tête; ~ out rayer; ~ the surface of a
problem ne pas aller jusqu'au fond
d'un problème; *vi* grincer, gratter

²scratch *adj* improvisé

scratchy *adj* qui gratte, qui grince;
(rough) rugueux -euse

scrawl *n* gribouillage *m*, griffonnage *m*;
*vt* + *vi* gribouiller, griffonner

scrawny *adj* maigre, décharné

scream *n* cri *m*, cri perçant; *coll fig*
chose amusante; ~ of laughter éclat *m*
de rire; give a ~ pousser un cri; *coll*
he's a ~ il est tordant; *vi* pousser des
cris, crier; ~ with laughter rire aux
éclats

screaming *n* cris *mpl*, hurlements *mpl*;
*adj* criard

scree *n* éboulis *m*; (rocky) clapier *m*

**screech** n cri perçant; vi pousser des cris perçants

**screech-owl** n chouette f

**screed** n longue liste

**screen** n écran m; (folding) paravent m; (trees) rideau m; (sieve) crible m; (profession) cinéma m; vt (give screen to) munir d'un écran; (hide) cacher, masquer; (protect) abriter, protéger; (sift) passer au crible; (film) mettre à l'écran

**screenplay** n scénario m

**screw** n vis f; (propeller) hélice f; (with screwdriver) coup m de tournevis; coll (miser) avare, grippe-sou m (pl grippe-sou(s)); coll (wages) salaire m, gages mpl; sl (warder) gardien m; vt visser; sl baiser; ~ **down** visser; ~ **off** dévisser; ~ **on** visser, fixer; coll ~ **sth out of** s/o tirer qch de qn; ~ **up one's courage** prendre son courage à deux mains; ~ **up one's face** faire la (une) grimace; ~ **up sth** resserrer qch, visser qch à fond; vi se visser

**screwball** n US cinglé -e, loufoque

**screw-cap** n bouchon vissé

**screwdriver** n tournevis m

**screwed** adj coll ivre; US coll fichu

**screwy** adj US coll timbré, cinglé

**scribble** n griffonnage m; vt griffonner

**scribbler** n griffonneur -euse; coll (office clerk) gratte-papier m (pl gratte-papier(s))

**scribe** n scribe m

**scrimmage** n mêlée f, bousculade f

**scrimp** vi faire des économies de bouts de chandelle

**scrip** n ar besace f; (Stock Exchange) ~ **issue** émission f d'actions gratuites

**script** n manuscrit m; (exam) copie f; cin + TV scénario m; (handwriting) écriture f

**scriptural** adj scriptural

**Scripture** n (Holy) ~ (s) Écriture Sainte

**script-writer** n cin + TV scénariste

**scroll** n rouleau m (de papier, de parchemin)

**scrotum** n anat scrotum m

**scrounge** n coll **be on the** ~ être à la recherche de choses à chiper; vt coll chiper, chaparder; vi coll ~ **on** s/o vivre aux crochets de qn

**scrounger** n coll chapardeur -euse, rabioteur -euse

¹**scrub** n brousse f, broussailles fpl

²**scrub** n friction f, nettoyage m; vt (floor) frotter; (pan) récurer; coll (cancel) annuler

**scrubbing-brush** n brosse dure

**scrubby** adj (stunted) rabougri; (ground) couvert de broussailles

**scruff** n nuque f; peau f de la nuque; by

**the** ~ **of the neck** par la peau du cou

**scruffy** adj coll mal soigné

**scrum, scrummage** n coll bousculade f; (rugby) mêlée f

**scrum-half** n demi m de mêlée

**scrummage** n see scrum

**scrumptious** adj coll délicieux -ieuse, excellent

**scruple** n scrupule m; vi ~ **to do sth** avoir des scrupules à faire qch

**scrupulous** adj scrupuleux -euse; (very careful) méticuleux -euse

**scrupulousness** n scrupules mpl

**scrutinize** vt scruter, examiner minutieusement

**scrutiny** n examen minutieux; (votes) vérification f

**scud** n (squall) rafale f; vi courir vite, filer; ~ **away** s'enfuir

**scuff** vt racler avec les pieds; vi traîner les pieds

**scuffle** n mêlée f, rixe f; vi se battre

**scull** n (oar) aviron m; (stern) godille f; vi ramer, godiller

**sculler** n rameur m de couple; (boat) scull m

**scullery** n arrière-cuisine f; ~ **maid** laveuse f de vaisselle

**sculpt** vt + vi sculpter

**sculptor** n sculpteur m

**sculptress** n femme f sculpteur

**sculpture** n sculpture f; vt sculpter; (decorate) orner de sculptures

**scum** n écume f, mousse f; coll rebut m; vt + vi écumer

**scummy** adj écumeux -euse

**scupper** n naut dalot m; vt naut saborder; coll ruiner; saboter

**scurf** n (dandruff) pellicules fpl

**scurfy** adj (head) pelliculeux -euse; (hair) plein de pellicules

**scurrility** n grossièreté f

**scurrilous** adj (person) ignoble; (language) grossier -ière

**scurry** n débandade f; vi courir à toutes jambes; ~ **off** détaler

¹**scurvy** n scorbut m

²**scurvy** adj vilain, misérable, indigne

¹**scuttle** n (coal) seau m à charbon

²**scuttle** n naut écoutille f; (porthole) hublot m; vt naut saborder

³**scuttle** vi ~ **off** déguerpir, détaler

**scythe** n faux f; vt faucher

**sea** n mer f; fig infinité f, multitude f; fig **be at** ~ être perdu, ne pas y être du tout; **beyond the** ~ outre-mer; **by** ~ par voie de mer; **by the** ~ au bord de la mer; **go to** ~ se faire marin; **on the high** ~s en pleine mer; **the open** ~ le large, la haute mer

**sea-anemone** n actinie f

**seabird** n oiseau m de mer

**seaboard** n littoral m
**sea-breeze** n brise f de mer
**sea-captain** n capitaine m au long cours
**sea-coast** n côte f, littoral m
**sea-dog** n loup m de mer, vieux marin
**seafarer** n marin m
**seafaring** adj ~ **man** marin m
**seafood** n fruits mpl de mer
**sea-front** n esplanade f
**sea-going** adj de haute mer
**sea-green** adj vert de mer invar, glauque
**seagull** n mouette f
**sea-horse** n hippocampe m
¹**seal** n zool phoque m
²**seal** n sceau m; (letter) cachet m; leg
affix (remove) the ~ s poser (lever) les
scellés; vt (deeds, etc) sceller; (letter)
cacheter; (decide) décider; ~ **a bargain**
confirmer une affaire; ~ **up** fermer
hermétiquement; **his fate is ~ed** c'en
est fait de lui
**sea-legs** npl have one's ~ avoir le pied
marin
**sea-level** n niveau m de la mer
**sealing-wax** n cire f à cacheter
**sea-lion** n otarie f
**sealskin** n peau f de phoque
**seam** n couture f; min couche f, gisement m; (face) ride f; vt coudre
**seaman** n matelot m, marin m
**seamanship** n navigation f, manœuvre f
**sea-mile** n mille marin
**seamless** adj sans couture
**sea-monster** n monstre marin (des mers)
**seamstress, sempstress** n ouvrière couturière f
**seamy** adj the ~ **side of life** le mauvais
côté de la vie
**séance** n séance f de spiritisme
**seaplane** n hydravion m
**seaport** n port m de mer
**sea-power** n puissance f maritime
**sear** adj desséché, sec (f sèche); vt dessécher, flétrir; (wound) cautériser
**search** n recherche f; leg perquisition f;
(customs) visite f; **in** ~ **of** à la recherche de; vt chercher dans, fouiller; leg
perquisitionner dans; (customs) visiter; vi leg faire une perquisition; ~ **for**
chercher
**searcher** n chercheur -euse
**searching** adj (look) pénétrant; (examination) minutieux -ieuse
**searchlight** n projecteur m
**search-party** n expédition f de secours
**search-warrant** n mandat m de perquisition
**seascape** n marine f
**sea-serpent** n serpent m de mer
**sea-shell** n coquillage m
**sea-shore** n rivage m, plage f.
**sea-sick** adj be ~ avoir le mal de mer

**sea-sickness** n mal m de mer
**seaside** n bord m de la mer; adj (resort)
balnéaire; (place) situé au bord de la
mer
**season** n saison f; (period) temps m,
période f; (abbr season-ticket) abonnement m; **be in** ~ être en saison;
(animal) être en chaleur; **for a** ~ pendant quelque temps; **holiday** ~ saison
f des vacances; **off** ~ morte-saison f;
**remark in** ~ remarque faite à propos;
**remark out of** ~ remarque déplacée;
vt assaisonner, relever; (timber)
sécher; (allow to mature) mûrir;
(person) acclimater, endurcir; (temper)
tempérer
**seasonable** adj de saison; (opportune) à
propos
**seasonal** adj saisonnier -ière, des saisons
**seasoned** adj assaisonné; (wood) sec (f
sèche); **become** ~ s'aguerrir
**seasoning** n assaisonnement m; (wood)
séchage m; (person) acclimatement m
**season-ticket** n abonnement m
**seat** n siège m; (vehicle) banquette f;
(chair) chaise f; (seat-space) place f;
(sitting part of chair, trousers) fond m;
(bench) banc m; (illness) foyer m; (residence) château m; ~ **belt** ceinture f de
sécurité; ~ **in the House** siège m au
Parlement (à la Chambre); **take a** ~
s'asseoir; vt faire asseoir; asseoir,
placer; (chair) mettre un fond à; (find
room for) trouver une place pour;
(have room for) tenir; **please be** ~**ed**
veuillez vous asseoir
**seating** n allocation f des places; (accommodation) nombre m des places;
(seats) bancs mpl, sièges mpl; (machine) lit m de pose
**sea-trout** n truite saumonée
**sea-wall** n digue f
**seaward** adj (tide) qui porte au large;
adv vers la mer
**seawards** adv vers la mer, vers le large
**seaweed** n algue f, varech m
**seaworthiness** n bon état de navigabilité
**seaworthy** adj en bon état de navigabilité
**secant** n math sécante f
**secateurs** npl sécateur m
**secede** vi se séparer, faire sécession
**secession** n sécession f
**seclude** vt tenir éloigné
**secluded** adj retiré, écarté
**seclusion** n retraite f, solitude f
¹**second** n (time) seconde f; moment m,
instant m
²**second** n second -e, deuxième; (duel)
témoin m; (boxing) second m; ~ **s** articles mpl de deuxième qualité; adj
second, deuxième; (other) autre,

nouveau (*f* nouvelle); (dates, kings) deux; *US* (floor) premier; **every ~ day** tous les deux jours; **take ~ place** passer second; **the ~ nicest house** la plus belle maison sauf une; *vt* (support) seconder, appuyer; *mil* détacher; **~ a motion** appuyer une proposition

**secondary** *adj* secondaire

**second-best** *n* **be ~** être un pis-aller; **come off ~** être battu; *adj* numéro deux; (everyday) de tous les jours

**second-class** *adj* (quality) de deuxième qualité; (traveller) de seconde (classe); de second ordre, de deuxième rang; **~ mail rate** = tarif réduit; *adv* **travel ~** voyager en seconde

**seconder** *n* **be the ~ of** appuyer

¹**second-hand** *n* aiguille *f* des secondes

²**second-hand** *adj* d'occasion; (news) de seconde main; **~ dealer** brocanteur -euse

**secondly** *adv* deuxièmement, en second lieu

**second-rate** *adj* inférieur, médiocre

**secrecy** *n* secret *m*, discrétion *f*; **in ~** en secret

**secret** *n* secret *m*; **in ~** en secret; **make a ~ of sth** faire mystère de qch; **open ~** secret *m* de Polichinelle; *adj* secret -ète, caché; **the Secret Service** = le Deuxième Bureau; **top ~** très secret -ète

**secretarial** *adj* de secrétaire

**secretariat** *n* secrétariat *m*

**secretary** *n* secrétaire; *pol* ministre *m*; **Secretary of State** secrétaire *m* d'État; *US* Ministre *m* des Affaires étrangères; **principal private ~** (of minister) chef *m* de cabinet; **private ~** secrétaire particulier -ière

¹**secrete** *vt* (exude) sécréter

²**secrete** *vt* (hide) cacher

**secretion** *n* sécrétion *f*

**secretive** *adj* cachottier -ière, dissimulé

**secretly** *adv* secrètement, en secret

**sect** *n* secte *f*

**sectarian** *n* + *adj* sectaire

**section** *n* section *f*, division *f*, tranche *f*; (drawing) coupe *f*, profil *m*; *vt* diviser en sections, sectionner

**sectional** *adj* (drawing) en coupe; en sections

**sector** *n* secteur *m*

**secular** *adj* séculier -ière; (school) laïc (*f* laïque); (time) séculaire

**secularization** *n* laïcisation *f*

**secularize** *vt* séculariser; (school) laïciser

**secure** *adj* sûr, assuré; (safe) en sûreté, sauf (*f* sauve); (well fixed) solide, ferme, bien fixé; **~ against** à l'abri de; *vt* mettre en sûreté, mettre à l'abri; (fasten) fixer, assujettir; (window) fermer bien; (guard) garder; (obtain) se

procurer; (get possession of) s'emparer de; (debt) garantir

**security** *n* sécurité *f*, sûreté *f*; (protection) sauvegarde *f*; *comm* caution *f*, garantie *f*; **securities** valeurs *fpl*, titres *mpl*; **Security Council** Conseil *m* de sécurité; **~ device** dispositif *m* de sûreté; **~ police** police secrète; **~ risk** personne *f* présentant des risques pour la sécurité de l'État; **give sth as ~** donner qch comme gage; **government securities** fonds *mpl* d'État

**sedan** *n US* (voiture *f* à) conduite intérieure

**sedan-chair** *n* chaise *f* à porteurs

**sedate** *adj* (person) posé; (bearing) composé; (mind) rassis

**sedation** *n* sédation *f*

**sedative** *n* calmant *m*; *adj* sédatif -ive

**sedentary** *adj* sédentaire

**sedge** *n* laîche *f*

**sediment** *n* dépôt *m*, sédiment *m*; (wine) lie *f*

**sedimentary** *adj* sédimentaire

**sedimentation** *n* sédimentation *f*

**sedition** *n* sédition *f*

**seditious** *adj* séditieux -ieuse

**seduce** *vt* séduire; (corrupt) corrompre

**seducer** *n* séducteur -trice

**seduction** *n* séduction *f*; corruption *f*; attraction *f*, charme *m*

**seductive** *adj* séduisant

**sedulity, sedulousness** *n* assiduité *f*, diligence *f*

**sedulous** *adj* assidu, diligent, appliqué

¹**see** *n eccles* siège épiscopal, évêché *m*

²**see** *vt* voir; (visit) visiter; (notice) remarquer; (doctor) consulter; (understand) comprendre; (make sure) s'assurer; (judge) juger, apprécier; **~ fit to judge** convenable de; **~ s/o home** reconduire qn chez lui; **~ s/o off** accompagner qn (jusqu') à la porte; **~ s/o to the station** accompagner qn jusqu'à la gare; **~ sth out** mener qch à bonne fin; voir la fin de qch; **~ you soon!** à bientôt!; **he can't ~ a joke** il n'entend pas la plaisanterie; **nothing to be ~ n** rien à voir; **what can you ~ in her?** qu'est-ce que vous lui trouvez?; *vi* voir; **~ about sth** s'occuper de qch; **~ into** examiner; **~ through** s/o pénétrer les intentions de qn; **~ to it that** veiller à ce que; **~ to read** voir assez clair pour lire; **as far as the eye can ~** à perte de vue; **I'll ~ about it** j'y réfléchirai, je verrai; **let me ~!** (show) faites voir!; *fig* attendez un peu!

**seed** *n agr* + *bot* graine *f*; collect + *fig* semence *f*; (descendants) lignée *f*; **go to ~** monter en graine; *vt* semer, ensemencer; *sp* sélectionner, trier; **~ ed**

**players** têtes *fpl* de série; *vi* (plant) monter en graine; (cereal) s'égrener
**seedbed** *n* couche *f* de semis
**seedcake** *n* gâteau *m* au carvi (cumin)
**seediness** *n* coll apparence *f* minable; (state) malaise *m*
**seedless** *adj* (fruit) sans pépins
**seedling** *n* jeune plant *m*
**seedy** *adj* (full of seeds) plein de graines; *coll* (shabby) râpé; *coll* miteux -euse; *coll* (out of sorts) mal en train, peu bien
**seeing** *n* vue *f*, vision *f*; ~ **is believing** voir c'est croire; **that is worth** ~ cela vaut la peine d'être vu
**seeing that** *conj phr* vu que
**seek** *vt* chercher, rechercher; (request) demander; *vi* ~ **after** rechercher, poursuivre; ~ **to do sth** essayer de faire qch
**seeker** *n* chercheur -euse
**seem** *vi* sembler, paraître, avoir l'air; **how does it** ~ **to you?** que vous en semble?; **it** ~ **s that** il semble que; **so it** ~ **s** à ce qu'il paraît
**seeming** *adj* apparent, soi-disant
**seemingly** *adv* en apparence
**seemly** *adj* convenable, bienséant
**seep** *vi* suinter, filtrer
**seepage** *n* suintement *m*, infiltration *f*
**seer** *n* prophète *m*
**see-saw** *n* bascule *f*, balançoire *f*, tape-cul *m*; *adj* de bascule; *vi* basculer, osciller
**seethe** *vi* bouillonner; (mass) grouiller
**segment** *n* segment *m*; *vt* partager en segments
**segmentation** *n* segmentation *f*
**segregate** *vt* isoler, séparer; *vi* se mettre à part
**segregation** *n* ségrégation *f*; séparation *f*
**segregationist** *n* partisan -e de la ségrégation raciale
**seismic** *adj* séismique, sismique
**seismograph** *n* sismographe *m*
**seismology** *n* sismologie *f*
**seize** *vt* saisir, s'emparer de; (person) appréhender; (capture) capturer; **be** ~ **d with** être pris de; *vi mech* gripper; ~ **on** se saisir de; ~ **up** caler
**seizure** *n* leg (things) saisie *f*; leg (persons) appréhension *f*; confiscation *f*; med attaque *f*
**seldom** *adv* rarement
**select** *adj* choisi, de choix, d'élite; (circle) fermé; *vt* choisir; sélectionner
**selection** *n* choix *m*, sélection *f*; (extracts) morceaux choisis
**selective** *adj* sélectif -ive
**selectivity** *n* sélectivité *f*
**selector** *n* sélecteur *m*
**self** *n* moi *m*; **be one's old** ~ **again** être rétabli; **one's better** ~ notre meilleur

côté; **pay** ~ payez à moi-même; *pron* (compounded with *adj*: **my** ~ , **your** ~ etc) -même; **by my** ~ , **your** ~ , **him** ~ , etc tout seul (*f* toute seule); **everyone for him** ~ chacun pour soi; **he is kindness it** ~ il est la bonté même; *refl pron* **my** ~ , **your** ~ , etc me, te, etc
**self-abuse** *n* masturbation *f*, onanisme *m*
**self-accusation** *n* auto-accusation *f*
**self-adjusting** *adj* à autoréglage
**self-assertion** *n* caractère impérieux, autoritarisme *m*
**self-assertive** *adj* autoritaire
**self-assurance** *n* assurance *f*, aplomb *m*
**self-centred** *adj* égocentrique
**self-closing** *adj* à fermeture automatique
**self-complacent** *adj* satisfait, content de soi
**self-conceit** *n* vanité *f*, suffisance *f*
**self-confidence** *n* assurance *f*, confiance *f* en soi
**self-conscious** *adj* gêné, embarrassé; (manners) contraint
**self-contained** *adj* (person) réservé; indépendant; (flat) ayant son entrée particulière
**self-control** *n* maîtrise *f* de soi
**self-deception** *n* illusion *f*
**self-defence** *n* défense personnelle; *leg* légitime défense *f*
**self-denial** *n* abnégation *f*; (economy) frugalité *f*
**self-determination** *n* auto-détermination *f*
**self-drive** *adj* ~ **car hire** location *f* de voitures sans chauffeur
**self-educated** *adj* autodidacte
**self-effacing** *adj* modeste
**self-employed** *adj* indépendant
**self-esteem** *n* amour-propre *m*
**self-evident** *adj* évident, qui saute aux yeux
**self-explanatory** *adj* qui s'explique de soi-même
**self-expression** *n* expression *f* de soi-même
**self-governing** *adj* autonome
**self-government** *n* autonomie *f*
**self-importance** *n* suffisance *f*, présomption *f*
**self-indulgence** *n* sybaritisme *m*
**self-interest** *n* égoïsme *m*, intérêt personnel
**selfish** *adj* égoïste, intéressé
**selfless** *adj* désintéressé
**self-made** *adj* qui est arrivé par lui-même (*f* elle-même)
**self-opinionated** *adj* opiniâtre
**self-pity** *n* pitié *f* pour soi-même

**self-portrait** n autoportrait m, portrait m de l'artiste par lui-même (f elle-même)

**self-possessed** adj maître (f maîtresse) de soi

**self-preservation** n conservation f de soi-même

**self-propelled** adj autopropulsé

**self-propulsion** n autopropulsion f

**self-raising** adj ~ **flour** farine préparée à la levure chimique

**self-reliant** adj confiant en soi, indépendant

**self-respect** n amour-propre m, respect m de soi

**self-respecting** adj qui se respecte

**self-restraint** n retenue f; **exercise** ~ faire preuve de modération

**self-righteous** adj pharisaïque

**self-sacrifice** n abnégation f de soi

**self-same** adj identique, exactement le (la) même

**self-satisfied** adj content de soi, suffisant

**self-seeking** adj égoïste, intéressé

**self-service** n libre-service m invar; ~ **store (restaurant)** magasin m (restaurant m) libre-service, libre-service (pl libres-services), self-service m (pl self-services), coll self m

**self-starter** n mot démarreur m

**self-styled** adj soi-disant

**self-sufficiency** n indépendance f

**self-sufficient** adj indépendant

**self-supporting** adj qui vit de son travail; indépendant

**self-taught** adj autodidacte

**self-willed** adj obstiné, entêté, volontaire

**self-winding** adj à remontage automatique

**sell** n (swindle) escroquerie f; coll déception f; vt vendre; coll (trick) duper; ~ **off** solder, liquider; ~ **out** vendre tout son stock de; ~ **short** vendre à découvert; ~ ~ **sth for ten francs** vendre qch dix francs; coll **be sold on sth** être entiché de qch; **sold out** épuisé; (person) avoir tout vendu; **to be sold** à vendre; vi se vendre; ~ **up** vendre tout

**seller** n vendeur -euse, marchand -e; **be a good** ~ se vendre bien

**selling** n vente f; comm écoulement m

**sell-out** n trahison f

**semantic** adj sémantique

**semantics** n sémantique f

**semaphore** n sémaphore m; vt + vi transmettre par sémaphore

**semblance** n semblant m, apparence f

**semeiology** n sém(é)iologie f

**semen** n semence f, sperme m

**semester** n semestre m

**semi** n (house) maison jumelle (jumelée)

**semi-** pref semi-

**semibreve** n mus ronde f

**semicircle** n demi-cercle m

**semicircular** adj demi-circulaire, semi-circulaire

**semicolon** n point-virgule m (pl points-virgules)

**semi-conscious** adj à demi conscient

**semi-detached** adj ~ **house** maison jumelle (jumelée)

**semi-final** n demi-finale f

**seminal** adj séminal

**seminar** n séminaire m

**seminary** n séminaire m

**semi-official** adj officieux -ieuse, semi-officiel -ielle

**semi-precious** adj (stones) fin

**semiquaver** n mus double croche f

**Semitic** adj sémitique

**semitone** n demi-ton m

**semi-tropical** adj subtropical

**semolina** n semoule f

**senate** n sénat m

**senator** n sénateur m

**send** vt envoyer; (dispatch) expédier; sl exciter; ~ **away** renvoyer; (person) congédier; ~ **back** renvoyer; ~ **down** (person) faire descendre; (student) expulser; ~ **for** envoyer chercher; ~ **forth** (give off) répandre; jeter; ~ **in** envoyer; présenter, soumettre; ~ **off** envoyer, expédier; ~ **on** faire suivre; ~ **out** (person) faire sortir; (things) expédier; (emit) émettre; ~ **round** faire circuler; (person) envoyer; ~ **s/o packing** envoyer promener qn; ~ **up** faire monter; coll se moquer de, parodier; ~ **word** faire dire, faire savoir

**sender** n expéditeur -trice

**send-off** n fête f d'adieu; **give s/o a good** ~ être nombreux -euses au départ de qn

**senescence** n sénescence f

**senile** adj sénile

**senility** n sénilité f

**senior** n aîné -e; doyen -enne; (pupil) grand; US étudiant -e en dernière année; adj aîné; (rank) supérieur; **she is two years** ~ **to me** elle est mon aînée de deux ans; **the Senior Service** la marine

**seniority** n ancienneté f, priorité f d'âge

**senna** n séné m

**sensation** n sensation f; sentiment m, impression f; **create a** ~ faire sensation

**sensational** adj sensationnel -elle

**sensationalism** n recherche f du sensationnel

**sense** n sens m; (feeling) sentiment m; (meaning) signification f; bon sens, intelligence f; ~ **of humour** sens m de l'humour; **bring s/o to his** ~s ramener qn à la raison; **common** ~ bon sens,

sens commun; **have the good ~ to** avoir l'intelligence de; **in a ~** d'un certain point de vue; **in the literal ~** au sens propre; **lose one's ~ s** perdre connaissance; **make ~** avoir un sens; **make ~ of** comprendre; **take leave of one's ~ s** perdre la tête (la raison); **talk ~** parler raison; *vt* percevoir, sentir intuitivement; (in advance) pressentir; (understand) comprendre

**senseless** *adj* (person) sans connaissance, inanimé; (silly) absurde, insensé

**sensibility** *n* sensibilité *f*

**sensible** *adj* (reasonable) sensé, raisonnable; (aware) sensible; (perceptible) perceptible; (appreciable) appréciable; (clothing) pratique

**sensibly** *adv* raisonnablement; perceptiblement; sensiblement

**sensitive** *adj* sensible; (touchy) susceptible; **~ plant** sensitive *f*

**sensitivity, sensitiveness** *n* sensibilité *f*; (touchiness) susceptibilité *f*

**sensitize** *vt* sensibiliser

**sensory** *adj* sensoriel -ielle

**sensual** *adj* sensuel -elle; voluptueux -euse

**sensualism** *n* sensualisme *m*

**sensuality** *n* sensualité *f*

**sensuous** *adj* voluptueux -euse; (charm) capiteux -euse

**sentence** *n gramm* phrase *f*; *leg* jugement *m*, sentence *f*; (punishment) peine *f*; **serve one's ~** purger sa peine; *vt leg* condamner

**sententious** *adj* sentencieux -ieuse

**sentient** *adj* sensible

**sentiment** *n* sentiment *m*; (opinion) avis *m*; (mawkish) sensiblerie *f*

**sentimental** *adj* sentimental

**sentimentalism** *n* sensiblerie *f*

**sentimentalist** *n* personne sentimentale

**sentimentality** *n* sensiblerie *f*

**sentimentalize** *vt* apporter du sentiment à; *vi* faire du sentiment

**sentinel** *n* sentinelle *f*, factionnaire *m*; **stand ~** monter la garde

**sentry** *n* sentinelle *f*, factionnaire *m*; **be on ~-go** être de faction, monter la garde

**sentry-box** *n* guérite *f*

**separability** *n* séparabilité *f*

**separable** *adj* séparable

**separate** *adj* séparé, détaché; (distinct) distinct; (room, etc) individuel -elle, particulier -ière; *vt* séparer, détacher; (disunite) désunir; *vi* se séparer, se détacher; (part) se quitter

**separation** *n* séparation *f*; (gap) écart *m*

**separatist** *n* + *adj* séparatiste

**separator** *n* séparateur *m*; (cream) écrémeuse *f*

**sepia** *n* sépia *f*

**sepsis** *n med* septicémie *f*; putréfaction *f*

**September** *n* septembre *m*

**septet** *n mus* septuor *m*

**septic** *adj* septique; *sl* infecte; **~ tank** fosse *f* septique

**septicaemia** *n* septicémie *f*

**septuagenarian** *n* + *adj* septuagénaire

**Septuagesima** *n eccles* Septuagésime *f*

**sepulchral** *adj* sépulcral

**sepulchre** *n* sépulcre *m*

**sequel** *n* suite *f*

**sequence** *n* suite *f*, succession *f*, chaîne *f*; **~ of tenses** concordance *f* des temps; **in ~** en série

**sequential** *adj* consécutif -ive

**sequester** *vt* séquestrer, mettre sous séquestre

**sequestered** *adj* retiré, isolé; *leg* sous séquestre

**sequestrate** *vt* séquestrer

**sequestration** *n* retraite *f*; *leg* mise *f* sous séquestre

**sequin** *n* sequin *m*

**seraglio** *n* sérail *m*

**seraph** *n* séraphin *m*

**seraphic** *adj* séraphique

**Serbia** *n* Serbie *f*

**Serbo-Croat(ian)** *n* (language) serbo-croate *m*

**serenade** *n* sérénade *f*; *vt* donner une sérénade à

**serendipity** *n* don *m* de faire des trouvailles; *coll* veine *f*

**serene** *adj* serein, calme; (title) sérénissime

**serenity** *n* sérénité *f*, calme *m*

**serf** *n* serf (*f* serve)

**serfdom** *n* servage *m*

**serge** *n* serge *f*

**sergeant** *n* sergent *m*

**sergeant-major** *n* adjudant *m*

**serial** *n* feuilleton *m*, roman-feuilleton *m* (*pl* romans-feuilletons); **~ rights** droits *mpl* de reproduction en feuilleton; **~ writer** feuilletoniste *m*; *adj* **~ number** numéro *m* de série

**serialize** *vt* publier en feuilleton; (film) passer en feuilleton

**serially** *adv* en série

**series** *n* série *f*, suite *f*

**serious** *adj* sérieux -ieuse; (wound, illness) grave

**seriousness** *n* sérieux *m*; (illness) gravité *f*

**sermon** *n* sermon *m*; *fig* remontrance *f*

**sermonize** *vt* sermonner, chapitrer; *vi* sermonner

**serous** *adj* séreux -euse

**serpent** *n* serpent *m*

**serpentine** *adj* serpentin, sinueux -euse

**serrate** *vt* denteler

**serrated** *adj* en dents de scie, dentelé

**serried** *adj* serré

**serum** *n* sérum *m*

**servant** *n* domestique; serviteur *m* ( *f* servante); (maid) bonne *f*; (employee) employé -e; **civil** ~ fonctionnaire

**serve** *vt* servir; (suffice) suffire à; (treat) traiter; (bus, train, etc) desservir; (breeding) couvrir; ~ **one's apprenticeship** faire un apprentissage; ~ **out** distribuer; ~ **s/o with sth** servir qch à qn; ~ **the purpose** faire l'affaire; ~ **time** faire de la prison; ~ **up** servir; **are you being** ~ **d?** est-ce qu'on vous sert?; *mil* **he has** ~**d twenty years** il a vingt ans de service; **I'll** ~ **you out for that** vous me le payerez; **it** ~**s him right** c'est bien fait pour lui; *vi* ~ **as** servir de; ~ **to** servir à

**service** *n* service *m*; (employ) emploi *m*; *eccles RC* office *m*; *eccles* (Protestant) culte *m*; (usefulness) utilité *f*; ~ **charge** service *m*; **be at s/o's** ~ être à la disposition de qn; **be of** ~ **to** être utile à; **be in** ~ être en condition; **be in the civil** ~ être fonctionnaire (de l'État); **do good** ~ faire bon usage; **postal** ~**s** Postes *fpl* et Télécommunications *fpl*; **the armed** ~**s** les forces armées; **the public service** l'administration *f*; *vt mot* entretenir et réparer

**serviceable** *adj* pratique, utile; (usable) utilisable; (durable) durable; (person) serviable

**service-flat** *n* appartement *m* avec service

**service-hatch** *n* passe-plat *m*

**service-station** *n mot* station-service ( *pl* stations-service)

**servicing** *n mot* entretien *m*, maintenance *f*

**serviette** *n* serviette *f* de table

**servile** *adj* servile

**servility** *n* servilité *f*

**servitude** *n* servitude *f*, esclavage *m*; **penal** ~ travaux forcés

**servobrake** *n* servofrein *m*

**servomechanism** *n* servomécanisme *m*

**sesame** *n bot* sésame *m*

**session** *n* séance *f*, session *f*; trimestre *m* (année *f*) scolaire (universitaire)

**sestet** *n see* **sextet**

**set** *n* série *f*, assortiment *m*, collection *f*; (china) service *m*; (buttons, ornaments) garniture *f*; (jewels) parure *f*; (false teeth) dentier *m*; (people) bande *f*, clique *f*, société *f*; *rad* + *TV* poste *m*; (hairdressing) mise *f* en plis; *cin* + *theat* décor *m*; (chess) jeu *m*; (tennis) set *m*; *coll* **make a dead** ~ **at** s/o attaquer qn furieusement; *theat* **on the** ~ sur le plateau; **the smart** ~ le monde élégant;

*adj* (firm) résolu, ferme; (prices) fixe; (time) fixe, fixé; (speech) préparé; (motionless) immobile; (expression) figé; (fruit) noué; (imposed) imposé, assigné; ~ **book** livre *m* au programme; ~ **fair** au beau fixe; ~ **phrase** expression consacrée; **be dead** ~ **against sth** être totalement opposé à qch; **be** ~ **on sth** être résolu à qch, tenir à qch; *vt* (put) poser, mettre, placer; (task) imposer; (bone) remettre; (watch) régler; (example) donner; (trap) tendre, dresser; (tool) affiler, affûter; (signature) apposer; (jewels) sertir; (sail) déployer; ~ **aside** mettre de côté; (reject) rejeter; (will) annuler; ~ **down** déposer; ~ **down** **(forth) in writing** coucher par écrit; ~ **eyes on** s/o voir qn, apercevoir qn; ~ **fire to sth** mettre le feu à qch; ~ **limits to** assigner des limites à; ~ **off** faire ressortir; (debt) compenser; (show to advantage) faire valoir; ~ **oneself against sth** s'opposer à qch; ~ **oneself up as** se poser en; ~ **one's teeth** serrer les dents; ~ **out** (display) étaler; (arrange) ranger; (reasons) présenter; ~ **right** arranger; rectifier; ~ **s/o doing sth** mettre qn à faire qch; ~ **sth going** mettre qch en train; ~ **the dog on** s/o lancer le chien contre qn; ~ **to music** mettre en musique; ~ **up** monter, dresser, établir; (type) composer; *coll US* (frame) faire accuser faussement; **have one's hair** ~ se faire faire une mise en plis; *vi* (sun) se coucher; (jelly, etc) prendre; (flowers) se nouer; ~ **about doing sth** se mettre à faire qch; ~ **about** s/o attaquer qn; ~ **forth** se mettre en route; ~ **in** commencer; ~ **off** se mettre en route, partir; ~ **on** **(upon)** s/o attaquer qn; ~ **out for** partir pour; ~ **to** s'y mettre, se mettre au travail; *coll* (fight) en venir aux mains; ~ **up as** s'établir

**setback** *n* échec *m*, revers *m* de fortune; (business) recul *m*; (illness) rechute *f*

**set-square** *n* équerre *f*

**settee** *n* canapé *m*, causeuse *f*

**setter** *n* (person) monteur *m*; (jewels) sertisseur *m*; (dog) setter *m*

**setting** *n* mise *f*, pose *f*; (arrangement) disposition *f*, arrangement *m*; (sun) coucher *m*; (jewels) monture *f*; (type) composition *f*; *mech* réglage *m*; (hair) mise *f* en plis; (sharpening) aiguisage *m*; (tools) affûtage *m*; (task) imposition *f*; (fracture) réduction *f*; (cement, jelly) prise *f*; (story) cadre *m*

**settle** *vt* établir, installer; (fix) fixer; (dispute) arranger; (accounts) régler, payer; (question) résoudre, décider;

(quieten) calmer; (country) coloniser; **~ property on s/o** assigner des biens à qn; **it's all ~d** tout est réglé; **that ~s it!** c'est réglé; cela me décide; *vi* (residence) s'établir, s'installer; (perch) se poser; (sink) se précipiter; (weather) se remettre au beau; (quieten) se calmer; *fig* (ground) se tasser; **~ down** se ranger; (marry) entrer en ménage; *coll* (get quieter) se tasser; **~ down to work** se mettre au travail; **~ in** s'installer; **~ up** régler un compte; **~ upon sth** se décider pour qch; **~ with s/o** s'arranger avec qn

**settlement** *n* établissement *m*, installation *f*; (colony) colonie *f*; (accounts) règlement *m*; (question) résolution *f*; (subsidence) tassement *m*; **deed of ~** acte *m* de disposition; **marriage ~** contrat *m* de mariage; **reach a ~** arriver à un accord amical

**settler** *n* colon *m*

**set-to** *n coll* combat *m*, empoignade *f*; **have a ~** en venir aux mains

**set-up** *n coll* arrangement *m*, organisation *f*

**seven** *n* sept *m invar*; *adj* sept *invar*

**seventeen** *n* dix-sept *m invar*; *adj* dix-sept *invar*

**seventeenth** *n* dix-septième; (date) dix-sept *m*; *adj* dix-septième

**seventh** *n* septième; (date) sept *m*; *adj* septième

**seventieth** *n + adj* soixante-dixième

**seventy** *n* soixante-dix *m invar*; *adj* soixante-dix; (Belgium, Switzerland) septante

**sever** *vt* (divide) désunir; (break off) rompre; (cut) couper, trancher, sectionner

**several** *adj* différent, séparé; *pl* plusieurs, divers; *pron* plusieurs

**severally** *adv* séparément

**severance** *n* séparation *f*, rupture *f*; **~ pay** indemnité *f* de départ

**severe** *adj* sévère; rigoureux -euse; (weather) dur; (pain) vif (*f* vive)

**severity** *n* sévérité *f*; (illness) gravité *f*; (weather) rigueur *f*; (pain) violence *f*

**sew** *vt* coudre; (bookbinding) brocher

**sewage** *n* eaux *fpl* d'égout; **~ farm** champ *m* d'épandage; **~ system** système *m* du tout à l'égout; **~ works** usine *f* d'épuration

¹**sewer** *n* (person) personne *f* qui coud, couseuse *f*; (bookbinding) brocheuse *f*

²**sewer** *n* (drain) égout *m*

**sewerage** *n* système *m* d'égouts

**sewing** *n* couture *f*; (bookbinding) brochage *m*; **~ cotton** fil *m* à coudre; **~ needle** aiguille *f* à coudre

**sewing-machine** *n* machine *f* à coudre

**sex** *n* sexe *m*; amour *m* physique, coïtion *f*; **have ~ with s/o** coucher avec qn; **the fair ~** le beau sexe; *vt* déterminer le sexe de

**sexagenarian** *n + adj* sexagénaire

**sex-appeal** *n* sex-appeal *m*, *coll* chien *m*

**sexed** *adj* sexué; **be highly ~** avoir du tempérament

**sexily** *adv* de manière très sexy

**sexless** *adj* asexué; *coll* froid

**sex-maniac** *n* obsédé sexuel (*f* obsédée sexuelle)

**sextant** *n* sextant *m*

**sextet** *n* sextuor *m*

**sexton** *n* sacristain *m*; (bell-ringer) sonneur *m* de cloches; (gravedigger) fossoyeur *m*

**sextuple** *adj* sextuple; *vt* sextupler

**sexual** *adj* sexuel -elle

**sexuality** *n* sexualité *f*

**sexually** *adv* d'une manière sexuelle

**sexy** *adj* sexy, excitant, aguichant; **be ~** (attractive) avoir du chien; (highly sexed) avoir du tempérament

**sh** *interj* chut!

**shabby** *adj* (clothes) râpé, usé; (mean) mesquin; (poor) pauvre; *coll* moche

**shack** *n* hutte *f*, cabane *f*; *vi* **~ up with** *coll* cohabiter avec; *coll* partager un logement avec

**shackle** *vt* mettre les fers à

**shackles** *npl* fers *mpl*; *fig* entraves *fpl*

**shade** *n* ombre *f*; (tree) ombrage *m*; (colour, meaning) nuance *f*; (lamp) abat-jour *m invar*; *US* (blind) store *m*; **a ~ better** un tout petit peu mieux; **put s/o in(to) the ~** éclipser qn; **the Shades** les enfers; *vt* ombrager; (protect) abriter, mettre à l'abri de; (drawing) ombrer; *vi* **~ into** se fondre en

**shadiness** *n* ombre *f*, ombrage *m*; (suspicious character) aspect *m* louche

**shading** *n* projection *f* d'une ombre; (drawing) ombres *fpl*

**shadow** *n* ombre *f*; **~ government** gouvernement *m* fantôme; **be reduced to a ~** être un pâle reflet de soi-même; **cast a ~** projeter une ombre; **have ~s under one's eyes** avoir les yeux cernés; **in the ~ of** à l'ombre de; *vt* (follow) filer

**shadowy** *adj* (plan) indécis, vague; chimérique

**shady** *adj* (shaded) ombragé; (giving shade) ombreux -euse; (suspicious) louche

¹**shaft** *n* (spear, arrow) hampe *f*; (handle) manche *m*; (spear) bois *m*; (arrow) flèche *f*, trait *m*; (light) rayon *m*; *mech* arbre *m*; (cart) brancard *m*

²**shaft** *n* (mine) puits *m*; (lift) cage *f*

**shag** *n coll* tabac fort

**shagged** *adj sl* crevé
**shaggy** *adj* poilu; (beard) touffu; (eyebrows) en broussailles
**shah** *n* chah *m*
**shake** *n* secousse *f*; (hand) poignée *f* (de main); (trembling) tremblement *m*; (head) hochement *m* de tête; *mus* trille *m*; *coll* ~ s ne pas valoir grand-chose; *coll* **be no great** ~ s *m* délirium *m* tremens; *vt* secouer, agiter; (make weaker) ébranler; (frighten) effrayer; (rouse) réveiller; ~ **down** faire tomber; ~ **hands on sth** toper; ~ **hands with s/o** serrer la main à qn; ~ **off** secouer; (get rid of) se débarrasser de; ~ **one's fist at s/o** menacer qn du poing; ~ **out** secouer; (empty) vider (en secouant); ~ **up** remuer, secouer; *coll* stimuler; *vi* trembler; (totter) branler, chanceler; (voice) trembloter; ~ **all over** trembler de tout son corps; ~ **down** s'installer
**shake-down** *n coll* lit improvisé
**shaken** *adj* secoué, ébranlé; **be** ~ **by sth** se ressentir de qch
**shaker** *n* trembleur *m*; **cocktail** ~ shaker *m*; **salad** ~ panier *m* à salade
**shake-up** *n* remaniement *m*
**shakily** *adv* (weakly) faiblement; (unsteadily) à pas chancelants; (writing) d'une main tremblante
**shakiness** *n* tremblement *m*; manque *m* de stabilité; (voice) chevrotement *m*
**shaky** *adj* (building, etc) peu solide; (health) faible; (legs) chancelant; (voice) mal assuré; **feel** ~ se sentir patraque; **his maths are** ~ il est faible en mathématiques
**shale** *n* schiste argileux
**shall** *aux v fut* **I** ~ **give** je donnerai; (immediate *fut*) **I** ~ **be with you in a minute** je vais être chez vous dans un instant; (obligation) devoir; ~ **I come?** dois-je venir?; **should I come?** devrais-je venir?; (strong obligation) **all boys** ~ **be dressed in blue** tous les garçons sont tenus d'être habillés en bleu; (must) **they** ~ **not do this** il ne faut pas qu'ils fassent cela; (polite request) ~ **I help you?** voulez-vous que je vous aide?; (in answers) **Will you go?** – **I** ~ (**I shan't**) Irez-vous? – Oui (Non)
**shallot** *n* échalote *f*
**shallow** *n* bas-fond *m*; *adj* peu profond; (dish) plat; (person) superficiel -ielle
**shallowness** *n* manque *m* de profondeur; (person) caractère superficiel
**sham** *n* feinte *f*; *coll* chiqué *m*; imposture *f*; *adj* simulé, feint, faux (*f* fausse); *vt* feindre, simuler
**shamble** *vi* ~ **along** marcher (aller) à pas traînants
**shambles** *n* abattoir *m*; *coll* désordre *m*, pagaille *f*

**shame** *n* honte *f*; **for** ~ ! fi donc!; **it's a** ~ ! c'est honteux!; **put s/o to** ~ faire honte à qn; **what a** ~ ! quel dommage!; *vt* faire honte à, humilier
**shamefaced** *adj* penaud, honteux -euse, timide
**shameful** *adj* honteux -euse, scandaleux -euse
**shameless** *adj* (person) éhonté, effronté; (action) honteux -euse
**shampoo** *n* shampooing *m*; **dry** ~ friction *f*; *vt* faire un shampooing à
**shamrock** *n* trèfle *m*
**shandy** *n* bière panachée
**shanghai** *vt naut* enlever après avoir enivré (drogué); forcer
**shank** *n* tige *f*; *coll* ~ s jambes *fpl*, *coll* quilles *fpl*; **go on** ~ **'s pony** aller à pied
¹**shanty** *n* baraque *f*, cabane *f*
²**shanty** *n sea* ~ chanson *f* de bord
**shantytown** *n* bidonville *m*
**shape** *n* forme *f*; (clothes) coupe *f*; (style) façon *f*; (mould) moule *m*; **be in good (bad)** ~ être en bonne (mauvaise) forme; **keep in** ~ garder sa forme; **out of** ~ déformé; **take** ~ prendre forme, se dessiner; *vt* façonner, former; (plan) inventer; ~ **one's course** diriger ses pas; *vi* se développer; ~ **well** promettre, prendre bonne tournure
**shaped** *adj* façonné, taillé, en forme de
**shapeless** *adj* sans forme, difforme
**shapely** *adj* bien fait, bien tourné
**shard** *n* tesson *m*
**share** *n* portion *f*, part *f*; (contribution) contribution *f*, écot *m*; (Stock Exchange) action *f*, titre *m*; ~ **in the profits** participation *f* aux bénéfices; **go** ~ s partager; **have** ~ s **in** être intéressé dans; *vt* partager; (profits) avoir part à; ~ **out** répartir; *vi* ~ **in** participer à
**shareholder** *n* actionnaire
**share-out** *n* partage *m*, répartition *f*
**shark** *n* requin *m*; (cheat) escroc *m*, filou *m*; *vt* escroquer
**sharkskin** *n* peau *f* de requin; peau *f* de chagrin
¹**sharp** *n mus* dièse *m*
²**sharp** *adj* tranchant; (point) pointu, aigu -uë; (taste) acide, aigre; (cold) vif (*f* vive); (features) anguleux -euse; (clever) intelligent, éveillé; (cunning) rusé, fin; (sound) perçant, acerbe; (pain) violent; (hearing) fin; (distinct) net (*f* nette); (glance) pénétrant; ~ **corner** tournant *m* brusque; *mot* virage serré; ~ **practice** procédé *m* peu honnête; ~ **tongue** langue acérée; **at seven** ~ à sept heures précises; **keep a** ~ **look-out** avoir l'œil bien ouvert

**sharpen** vt aiguiser, affiler, affûter; (pencil) tailler; (wits) dégourdir; cul relever; vi s'aiguiser; (sound) devenir plus aigu -uë

**sharpener** n (instrument) dispositif m d'affûtage

**sharper** n coll escroc m, tricheur -euse

**sharp-eyed** adj aux yeux perçants

**sharpish** adv coll plus vite que ça

**sharply** adv (clearly) nettement; (suddenly) brusquement; (briskly) vivement

**sharpshooter** n tirailleur m

**sharp-sighted** adj à la vue perçante

**sharp-witted** adj éveillé, dégourdi

**shatter** vt fracasser, briser; fig be ~ed être bouleversé; vi se fracasser

**shave** vt acte m de raser; have a ~ se raser; (at barber's) se faire raser; coll have a close (narrow) ~ l'échapper belle; vt raser; (graze) friser, effleurer, frôler; (clip) rogner, tondre; vi se raser

**shaver** n rasoir m; (person) raseur m; coll gosse m; sl moutard m

**shaving** n action f de (se) raser; (wood) copeau m; (metal) rognure f

**shaving-brush** n blaireau m

**shaving-cream** n crème f à raser

**shaving-soap** n savon m à barbe

**shawl** n châle m

**she** n+adj femelle f; pron elle; there ~is! la voilà!

**sheaf** n gerbe f; (papers) liasse f

**shear** vt tondre, couper

**shearing** n (sheep) tonte f; (hedge) taille f

**shear-legs** n grue f de chargement

**shears** npl cisailles fpl, grands ciseaux

**sheath** n (sword) fourreau m; (case) étui m; (knife) gaine f; anat enveloppe f; (contraceptive) condom m, coll capote anglaise

**sheathe** vt rengainer, (re)mettre au fourreau; (cover) recouvrir

¹**shed** n (store) hangar m; (lean-to) appentis m; (garden, tools) remise f; (cattle) étable f

²**shed** vt (tears, blood, etc) verser; (light, etc) répandre; (leaves) perdre; (skin) jeter; ~ light on sth éclairer une affaire

**shedding** n perte f, chute f; (skin) mue f; (blood) effusion f

**sheen** n éclat m, lustre m

**sheep** n mouton m; fig black ~ brebis galeuse; feel like a lost ~ se sentir dépaysé; lost ~ brebis égarée; make ~'s eyes at s/o regarder qn tendrement

**sheepdog** n chien m de berger

**sheepfold** n parc m à moutons; fig bercail m

**sheepish** adj penaud

**sheep-shearing** n tonte f

**sheepskin** n peau f de mouton

¹**sheer** adj pur, véritable; (cliff, etc) à pic; (transparent) transparent; a ~ impossibility une impossibilité absolue; a ~ waste of time une pure perte de temps; adv tout à fait, complètement

²**sheer** vi naut ~ off prendre le large; larguer les amarres; coll s'écarter

¹**sheet** n (bed) drap m; (paper) feuille f; coll (newspaper) journal m; (water) nappe f; (snow) couche f; have a clean ~ avoir une conduite impeccable

²**sheet** n naut écoute f

³**sheet** vt couvrir d'un drap

**sheet-anchor** n naut ancre f de veille; fig planche f de salut

**sheeting** n toile f pour draps de lit

**sheet-iron** n tôle f

**sheet-lightning** n éclairs mpl en nappe

**sheet-steel** n tôle f d'acier

**sheikh** n cheik m

**shelf** n rayon m, tablette f; (ledge) rebord m; (rock) corniche f; ~ space rayonnage m; coll be on the ~ être au rancart; (spinster) avoir coiffé Sainte-Catherine; continental ~ plateau continental

**shell** n coquille f; (crab, etc) carapace f; (oyster) écaille f; (ship) coque f; (peas, beans) cosse f, gousse f; (boat) canot m de course; (cannon) obus m; come out of one's ~ sortir de sa coquille; retire into one's ~ rentrer dans sa coquille; vt (peas) écosser; (nuts) écaler; mil bombarder; coll ~ out débourser; vi coll ~ out payer la note

**shellac** n laque f en plaques

**shellfish** n coquillage m, crustacé m

**shell-hole** n trou m d'obus

**shelling** n (prawns) épluchage m; (peas) égrenage m; mil bombardement m

**shell-shock** n psychose f traumatique

**shelter** n abri m, asile m, lieu m de refuge; take ~ se mettre à l'abri; under ~ à l'abri; vt abriter; (fugitive) donner asile à; vi s'abriter, se mettre à l'abri

¹**shelve** vt (defer) remettre, ajourner; (put aside) mettre au rancart

²**shelve** vi (slope) aller en pente, être en pente

**shelving** n (deferring) ajournement m; (putting aside) mise f au rancart; (shelves) rayonnage m, rayons mpl

**shepherd** n berger m; ~'s pie hachis aux pommes de terre cuit au four; vt garder; (guide) piloter

**shepherdess** n bergère f

**sherbet** n sorbet m

**sheriff** n shérif m; US chef m de la police; ~'s officer huissier m

**sherry** n xérès m, vin m de Xérès

**shew** vt see **show** vt

689

**shibboleth** *n* mot *m* d'ordre

**shield** *n* bouclier *m*; *her* écusson *m*; *mech* garde *f*; *fig* défense *f*; *vt* protéger, défendre

**shift** *n* changement *m* (de position); (means) expédient *m*, moyen *m*; (workmen) équipe *f*; (clothing) chemise *f*; ~ **work** travail *m* par équipes; **make ~ to do sth** trouver moyen de faire qch; **make ~ with** s'accommoder de; **make ~ without sth** se passer de qch; *vt* changer de place, déplacer; *vi* changer de place, se déplacer; (wind) tourner, virer; ~ **for oneself** se débrouiller

**shiftiness** *n* sournoiserie *f*

**shifting** *adj* qui se déplace; (scene) changeant; ~ **sands** sables mouvants

**shift-key** *n* (typewriter) touche *f* de majuscule

**shiftless** *adj* peu débrouillard; (lazy) paresseux -euse

**shifty** *adj* sournois, louche

**shilling** *n obs* shilling *m*

**shilly-shally** *n* vacillation *f*, hésitation *f*; *vi* barguigner, vaciller

**shimmer** *n* lueur *f*, chatoiement *m*; *vi* miroiter, chatoyer, luire

**shin** *n* devant *m* du tibia; (beef) jarret *m*; ~ **bone** tibia *m*; *vi* ~ **up** grimper à

**shindy** *n coll* chahut *m*, tapage *m*

**shine** *n* éclat *m*, brillant *m*; **give a ~ to** faire reluire; **rain or ~** par tous les temps; *vt* faire briller; (shoes) cirer, polir; *vi* briller, luire, reluire, rayonner; **his face is shining with joy** sa figure rayonne de joie; **the sun is shining** il fait du soleil

**¹shingle** *n bui* bardeau *m*

**²shingle** *n* (pebbles) galets *mpl*, cailloux *mpl*

**shingles** *n med* zona *m*

**shiny** *adj* luisant, brillant

**ship** *n* navire *m*, bateau *m*, vaisseau *m*; (war) bâtiment *m*; **on board ~** à bord; *vt* embarquer, mettre à bord; (send) expédier; (oars) armer, rentrer; *vi* s'embarquer

**shipbuilder** *n* constructeur *m* de navires

**shipbuilding** *n* construction navale

**shipload** *n* cargaison *f*, chargement *m*

**shipmate** *n* camarade *m* de bord

**shipment** *n* (load) chargement *m*; (shipping) expédition *f*

**shipowner** *n* armateur *m*

**shipper** *n* chargeur *m*, expéditeur *m*

**shipping** *n* (loading) embarquement *m*; (sending by ship) expédition *f*; (ships) navires *mpl*; (merchant) marine marchande

**shipping-company** *n* compagnie *f* maritime

**shipshape** *adj* en bon ordre

**shipwreck** *n* naufrage *m*; *vt* faire naufrager

**shipwrecked** *adj* naufragé; **be ~** faire naufrage

**shipwright** *n* charpentier *m* de navires

**shipyard** *n* chantier *m* de constructions navales

**shire** *n* comté *m*

**shirk** *vt* se dérober à, esquiver

**shirker** *n mil* embusqué *m*, tire-au-flanc *m invar*

**shirt** *n* chemise *f*; **in one's ~ sleeves** en bras de chemise; *coll* **keep your ~ on** ne vous fâchez pas

**shirt-front** *n* plastron *m*

**shirt-maker** *n* chemisier -ière

**shirty** *adj coll* irritable

**shit** *n vulg* merde *f*; (person) salaud *m*; *vi vulg* chier

**¹shiver** *n* éclat *m*, fragment *m*; *vt* fracasser; *vi* voler en éclats

**²shiver** *n* frisson *m*, frissonnement *m*; *vi* frissonner, trembler, grelotter

**shivery** *adj* tremblant, grelottant; **feel ~** avoir des frissons, grelotter de froid

**¹shoal** *n* haut-fond *m* (*pl* hauts-fonds)

**²shoal** *n* (fish) banc *m*; (large amount) tas *m*, grande quantité; *vi* se réunir (voyager) en bancs

**¹shock** *n* choc *m*, heurt *m*; (blow) coup *m*; (electric) secousse *f*; *med* commotion *f*; ~ **troops** troupes *fpl* d'assaut; **it gave me a terrible ~** cela m'a porté un coup terrible; *vt* choquer, scandaliser, bouleverser; ~ **the ear** blesser l'oreille

**²shock** *n* (hair) tignasse *f*

**³shock** *n agr* meulette *f*

**shock-absorber** *n* amortisseur *m*

**shocker** *n coll* (thing) chose affreuse; (person) personne affreuse

**shock-headed** *adj* à tignasse

**shocking** *adj* choquant, révoltant; (frightful) affreux -euse

**shock-proof** *adj* antichoc *invar*

**shoddy** *adj* de camelote, de pacotille

**shoe** *n* soulier *m*, chaussure *f*; (horse) fer *m*; (wood) sabot *m*; **court ~** escarpin *m*; *mot* **Denvèr ~** sabot *m* de Denver; *fig* **step into s/o's ~s** prendre la place de qn; *vt* chausser; (horse) ferrer

**shoeblack** *n* cireur *m*

**shoehorn** *n* chausse-pied *m*

**shoe-lace** *n* lacet *m*

**shoemaker** *n* (mender) cordonnier *m*; (maker) bottier *m*; (manufacturer) fabricant *m* de chaussures

**shoe-polish** *n* cirage *m*

**shoestring** *n coll* **on a ~** à peu de frais, avec des moyens réduits

**shoe-tree** *n* forme *f*

**shoot** *n bot* rejeton *m*, pousse *f*; (rubbish) dépôt *m*; (hunt) partie *f* de chasse; (spout) gouttière *f*; (chute) glissière *f*; *coll* **the whole** ~ tout le bataclan; *vt* tirer; (kill) tuer; (hit) atteindre; (animal) abattre; (firing squad) fusiller; (throw) précipiter, lancer; (rays) darder; (gun, rubbish) décharger; (football) shooter; (arrow) décocher; (glance) lancer; *coll* ~ **a line** exagérer son importance, crâner; *coll* ~ **one's mouth off** bavarder indiscrètement; *mot* ~ **the lights** brûler les feux; ~ **s/o** (kill) tuer qn d'un coup de revolver (fusil); ~ (hit) atteindre qn d'un coup de revolver (fusil); ~ **up** tirer des coups de feu sur, mitrailler; *vi* tirer; (rush) se précipiter, se lancer; (star) filer; (plant) pousser; (bud) bourgeonner; ~ **ahead** aller rapidement en avant; ~ **at s/o** tirer sur qn; ~ **off** filer, partir d'un trait; ~ **out** sortir précipitamment; ~ **past** passer comme un éclair; ~ **straight** bien viser; ~ **up** (flame) jaillir; (grow) grandir rapidement; **go** ~**ing** aller à la chasse

**shooter** *n* tireur -euse; *US coll* revolver *m*, arme *f* à feu

**shooting** *n* tir *m*; (hunting) chasse *f*; (firing) fusillade *f*; (wound) élancement *m*; (discharging) déchargement *m*; (rapids) franchissement *m*; (arrow) décochement *m*; *cin* tournage *m*; **beginning of the** ~ **season** ouverture *f* de la chasse; *adj* (pain) lancinant; (star) filant; ~ **war** guerre chaude

**shooting-box** *n* pavillon *m* de chasse
**shooting-brake** *n* mot break *m*
**shooting-range** *n* champ *m* de tir
**shooting-star** *n* étoile filante
**shooting-stick** *n* canne-siège *f* (*pl* cannes-sièges)

**shop** *n* magasin *m*, boutique *f*; *coll* **be all over the** ~ être en désordre; **closed** ~ atelier (usine) fermé(e) aux ouvriers non-syndiqués; **go round the** ~**s** courir les magasins; **on the** ~ **floor** dans l'atelier, dans l'usine; *coll* **talk** ~ parler métier; *vi* faire des achats; ~ **around** comparer les prix dans les magasins

**shop-assistant** *n* vendeur -euse, employé -e de magasin
**shop-front** *n* devanture *f* (de magasin)
**shop-girl** *n* vendeuse *f*
**shopkeeper** *n* commerçant -e, marchand -e
**shopkeeping** *n* commerce *m*
**shoplifter** *n* voleur -euse à l'étalage
**shoplifting** *n* vol *m* à l'étalage
**shopper** *n* acheteur -euse
**shopping** *n* achats *mpl*, emplettes *fpl*; **go** ~ faire ses (des) emplettes, faire ses courses

**shopsoiled** *adj* défraîchi
**shop-steward** *n* délégué -e syndical -e
**shop-walker** *n* inspecteur -trice (du magasin)
**¹shore** *n* rivage *m*, littoral *m*, bord *m*; **in** ~ près de la côte; **keep close to the** ~ côtoyer; **off** ~ au large; **on** ~ à terre
**²shore** *n bui* étai *m*; *vi* ~ **up** étayer
**short** *n cin* court métrage; *elect abbr* court-circuit *m* (*pl* courts-circuits); *coll* (drink) petit verre; ~ **s** short *m*, culotte *f*; **the long and the** ~ **of it** le fin mot de l'affaire; *adj* court; (brief) bref (*f* brève); (insufficient) insuffisant; (person) de courte taille; (abrupt) brusque; (tone) cassant; ~ **cut** raccourci *m*; ~ **pastry** pâte brisée; ~ **story** conte *m*, nouvelle *f*; **be** ~ **of sth** manquer de qch; **for a** ~ **time** pour (pendant) peu de temps; **for** ~ pour abréger; **get** ~**er** raccourcir; **give** ~ **weight** ne pas donner le poids; **go** ~ **of sth** se priver de qch; **in a** ~ **time** sous peu; **in** ~ bref; **make** ~ **work of sth** mener rondement les choses; **nothing** ~ **of a bomb will move him** seule une bombe le fera bouger; **this is little** ~ **of madness** cela tient de la folie; **we are** ~ **of one person** il nous manque une personne; *adv* ~ **of going the whole way** à moins d'aller jusqu'au bout; **cut s/o** ~ couper la parole à qn; **fall** ~ **of** ne pas répondre à; **stop** ~ s'arrêter pile; *vt elect* court-circuiter
**shortage** *n* manque *m*, insuffisance *f*; (materials) crise *f*, pénurie *f*; (scarcity) disette *f*
**shortbread, shortcake** *n* sablé *m*
**shortchange** *vt* rendre une monnaie insuffisante à
**short-circuit** *n* court-circuit *m* (*pl* courts-circuits); *vt* court-circuiter
**shortcoming** *n* défaut *m*, imperfection *f*
**shorten** *vt* raccourcir; (abridge) abréger; *naut* ~ **sail** réduire la voilure; *vi* raccourcir
**shortfall** *n* déficit *m*
**shorthand** *n* sténographie *f*, *coll* sténo *f*; ~ **typist** sténodactylo *f*
**shorthanded** *adj* à court de personnel (de main d'œuvre)
**short-list** *n* liste choisie
**short-lived** *adj* (person) qui est mort jeune; (animal) qui vit peu de temps; (not lasting) éphémère, de courte durée, passager -ère
**shortly** *adv* (soon) bientôt; (briefly) brièvement; (abruptly) brusquement; ~ **after(wards)** peu (de temps) après
**shortness** *n* peu *m* de longueur; (stature) petitesse *f*; (brevity) brièveté *f*, courte

durée; (abruptness) brusquerie *f*; (lack) manque *m*, insuffisance *f*

**short-sighted** *adj* myope

**short-spoken** *adj* brusque

**short-tempered** *adj* irascible

**short-winded** *adj* à l'haleine courte, poussif -ive

**shot** *n* coup *m* de feu; (bullet) balle *f*; (hunting) plomb *m*; (football) shoot *m*; (go) coup *m*; *cin* prise *f* de vue; *coll* (injection) piqûre *f*; *coll* (stimulant) coup *m* de fouet; *fig* ~ **in the arm** encouragement *m*; **at a** ~ d'un coup; **be a good** ~ être bon (*f* bonne) tireur -euse; **be off like a** ~ partir comme un trait; **big** ~ gros bonnet; *coll* **have a** ~ essayer; **like a** ~ très vite, avec empressement; *coll* **long** ~ coup *m* à tenter; *adj* (cloth) chatoyant; (colour) ~ **with** parsemé de; *coll* **be** ~ **of** être débarrassé de

**shotgun** *n* fusil *m* de chasse; ~ **wedding** mariage forcé

**shot-silk** *n* taffetas changeant

**shoulder** *n* épaule *f*; (mountain) contrefort *m*; (road) bas-côté *m*; **give the cold** ~ **to** battre froid à; **I let him have it straight from the** ~ je ne le lui ai pas envoyé dire; **over (across) the** ~ en bandoulière; **put one's** ~ **to the wheel** pousser à la roue; **stand head and** ~**s above** s/o dépasser qn de la tête; *vt* **mettre** (charger) sur l'épaule; (arms) porter; (responsibility) endosser; ~ **one's way through** se frayer un chemin à coups d'épaule

**shoulder-blade** *n* omoplate *f*

**shoulder-strap** *n* bretelle *f*, bandoulière *f*

**shout** *n* cri *m*, hurlement *m*; (laughter) éclat *m*; ~**s of applause** acclamations *fpl*; *vt* crier; *vi* crier, pousser des cris; ~ **down** huer; ~ **out** s'écrier, crier

**shove** *n coll* coup *m* d'épaule; *vt coll* pousser; *coll* ~ **aside** écarter; *coll* ~ **back** repousser; *naut* ~ **off** pousser au large; *vi coll* se frayer un chemin; *coll* ~ **off** s'en aller

**shovel** *n* pelle *f*; *vt* peller, pelleter, prendre à la pelle; ~ **away** enlever à la pelle; ~ **up** ramasser à la pelle

**shovelful** *n* pelletée *f*

**show** *n* spectacle *m*; (exhibition) exposition *f*; (appearance) semblant *m*, apparence *f*; (display) étalage *m*; (competition) concours *m*; (motor) salon *m*; (ostentation) parade *f*; *cin* séance *f*; (fashion) collection *f*; *agr* comice *m*; ~ **flat (house)** appartement *m* (maison *f*) témoin; ~ **of friendship** démonstration *f* d'amitié; ~ **of hands** vote *m* à main levée; *coll* **give the** ~ **away** vendre la mèche; *coll* **good** ~**!** très

bien!, bravo!; **go to a** ~ aller au spectacle; **make a poor** ~ faire triste figure; **make a** ~ **of oneself** se donner en spectacle; *coll* **put up a good** ~ se comporter bien; *coll* **run the** ~ diriger l'affaire; *vt* montrer, faire voir; indiquer; (feeling) témoigner, faire preuve de; (prove) prouver; (exhibit) exposer; *cin* projeter; (passport) présenter; ~ **off** faire valoir, faire parade de; ~ **oneself** (put in appearance) faire acte de présence; ~ **one's face** se montrer; ~ **one's hand** jouer cartes sur table; (reveal intentions) dévoiler ses intentions; ~ **s/o into a room** faire entrer qn dans une pièce; ~ **s/o out** reconduire qn; ~ **s/o to his room** conduire qn à sa chambre; ~ **s/o up** (expose) démasquer qn; ~ **s/o up (upstairs)** faire monter qn; ~ **sth up** (schoolwork) donner; (relief) mettre en relief; ~ **the time** indiquer l'heure; **time will** ~ qui vivra verra; *vi* paraître, se montrer; (stick out) dépasser; ~ **off** poser; ~ **through** transparaître; ~ **to advantage** faire bonne figure; ~ **up** (turn up) arriver, se présenter; (stand out) ressortir, se détacher; *coll* ~ **willing** faire preuve de bonne volonté

**show-case** *n* vitrine *f*, montre *f*

**show-down** *n* confrontation *f*; **have a** ~ en venir au fait

**shower** *n* (rain) averse *f*, ondée *f*; (toilet) douche *f*; *fig* pluie *f*; *vt* faire pleuvoir, verser; ~ **blows on s/o** rouer qn de coups

**shower-bath** *n* douche *f*

**showery** *adj* pluvieux -ieuse

**showgirl** *n* girl *f*

**showily** *adv* d'une façon prétentieuse

**showiness** *n* prétention *f*, clinquant *m*

**showing** *n* exposition *f*; *cin* **first** ~ première exclusivité; **on your own** ~ à ce que vous dites vous-même

**show-jumping** *n* concours *m* de monte à l'obstacle

**showman** *n* animateur -trice; (circus) forain *m*; **be a great** ~ savoir attirer l'attention sur soi-même

**showmanship** *n* art *m* de la mise en scène; talent *m* d'animateur -trice

**show-off** *n* poseur -euse

**showpiece** *n* article *m* d'exposition; objet *m* de grand intérêt

**show-place** *n* endroit *m* d'intérêt touristique

**showroom** *n* magasin *m*, salon *m* (salle *f*) d'exposition

**showy** *adj* voyant; (person) prétentieux -ieuse; *coll* tape-à-l'œil *invar*

**shrapnel** *n* shrapnel *m*, éclats *mpl* d'obus

**shred** *n* brin *m*; (cloth) lambeau *m*; **there isn't a** ~ **of evidence** il n'y a pas l'ombre d'une preuve (la moindre preuve); vt (paper) déchirer en lambeaux; (cloth) effilocher; (vegetables) couper en languettes

¹**shrew** n mégère f, femme f acariâtre

²**shrew** n zool musaraigne f

**shrewd** adj rusé, sagace; ~ **blow** coup bien placé; **I have a ~ idea** je suis porté à croire que

**shrewdness** n perspicacité f, finesse f

**shrewish** adj acariâtre

**shriek** n cri perçant; vi pousser des cris perçants; ~ **with laughter** éclater de rire

**shrill** adj aigu -uë, strident

**shrimp** n crevette f; coll fig gringalet m; vi faire la pêche aux crevettes

**shrine** n châsse f, reliquaire m; (tomb) tombeau m; chapelle f; lieu saint; fig sanctuaire m

**shrink** vt rétrécir; vi rétrécir; ~ **away** s'éloigner timidement; ~ **from doing sth** répugner à faire qch; ~ **from sth** reculer devant qch; ~ **in the wash** rétrécir au lavage

**shrinkage, shrinking** n (cloth) rétrécissement m; contraction f

**shrinking** n see shrinkage

**shrivel** vt ratatiner, rider; (plants) brûler; vi se ratatiner, se rider

**shroud** n linceul m, suaire m; vt ensevelir, envelopper d'un linceul; fig voiler; ~**ed in mystery** enveloppé de mystère

**Shrove Tuesday** n mardi gras

**shrub** n arbuste m, arbrisseau m

**shrubbery** n bosquet m, plantation f d'arbustes

**shrug** n haussement m d'épaules; vt ~ **one's shoulders** hausser les épaules; ~ **off** faire peu de cas de

**shucks** interj US allons donc!

**shudder** n frisson m, frémissement m; vi frissonner, frémir

**shuffle** n marche traînante; (cards) battement m; (evasion) détours mpl, tergiversation f; vt mêler; (cards) battre; vi traîner les pieds; tergiverser; ~ **off** s'en aller en traînant le pas

¹**shun** vt éviter, fuir

²**shun** interj abbr mil ( = attention!) garde à vous!

**shunt** n manœuvre f; elect shunt m; ~ **line** voie f de garage; vt manœuvrer; elect shunter

**shut** vt fermer; ~ **down** fermer; ~ **in** enfermer; (enclosure) entourer; ~ **off** couper; séparer; ~ **out** exclure; ~ **up** enfermer; (silence) faire taire; sl ~ **your trap!** (ferme) ta gueule!; vi (se) fermer; coll ~ **up** se taire

**shut-down** n fermeture f

**shut-eye** n coll somme m

**shutter** n volet m; phot obturateur m

**shuttle** n navette f; ~ **service** navette f; vi faire la navette

**shuttlecock** n volant m

¹**shy** adj timide, sauvage; (animal) farouche; (horse) ombrageux -euse; **fight ~ of sth** se méfier de qch

²**shy** vi (horse) faire un écart; ~ **at sth** prendre ombrage de qch

³**shy** vt + vi coll lancer

**shyness** n timidité f, réserve f

**Siamese** n Siamois -e; adj siamois

**Siberia** n Sibérie f

**sibilant** n sifflante f; adj sifflant

**sibling** n frère m, sœur f

**Sicily** n Sicile f

**sick** adj malade; **be ~** vomir; (ill) être malade; coll **be ~ of sth** être dégoûté de qch; **feel ~** avoir mal au cœur; **I'm ~ of it!** j'en ai marre!; **report ~** se faire porter malade; **the ~** les malades

**sick-bay** n infirmerie f

**sick-bed** n lit m de douleur

**sicken** vt rendre malade; dégoûter; vi tomber malade; **be ~ing for an illness** couver une maladie

**sickening** adj coll écœurant

**sickle** n faucille f

**sick-leave** n congé m de maladie

**sickliness** n pâleur f; état maladif f; (taste) fadeur f; (feeling) sentimentalité f

**sick-list** n rôle m des malades

**sickly** adj maladif -ive; (taste) douceureux -euse, fade; (smile) pâle; (light) faible; (unhealthy) insalubre

**sickness** n maladie f; (feeling) nausées fpl, mal m au cœur; **air ~** mal m de l'air; **car ~** mal m de voiture; **sea ~** mal m de mer; **sleeping ~** maladie f du sommeil

**sick-pay** n (benefit) allocation f de maladie; (salary) traitement m pendant la maladie

**side** n côté m; (flank) flanc m; (edge, ship) bord m; (river) rive f; (team) équipe f; (party) parti m; (slope) pente f; ~ **by** côte à côte; **by my ~** à côté de moi; **hear both ~s of a question** entendre le pour et le contre d'une question; **on all ~s** de tous côtés; **on both ~s** des deux côtés; **on the other ~** de l'autre côté; coll **put on ~** faire de l'épate; **put sth on (to) one ~** mettre qch à l'écart; (cloth) **right ~** endroit m; **see the bright ~** voir le bon côté; **take ~s** prendre parti; **time is on our ~** le temps travaille pour nous; **wrong ~ up** sens dessus dessous; adj latéral, de côté; ~ **issue** question f d'intérêt secondaire; vi ~ **with s/o** se ranger du côté de qn

# sideboard

**sideboard** *n* buffet *m*

**sidecar** *n* sidecar *m*

**side-drum** *n* caisse *f*

**side-effect** *n* résultat *m* secondaire

**side-face** *n* profil *m*

**side-kick** *n* US coll subordonné -e

**sidelight** *n* mot feu *m* de position

**side-line** *n* (occupation) violon *m* d'Ingres, occupation *f* secondaire; *comm* article *m* à côté; (sport) ligne *f* de touche

**sidelong** *adj* oblique

**sidereal** *adj* sidéral

**side-saddle** *n* ride ~ monter en amazone

**sideshow** *n* spectacle forain; *coll fig* affaire *f* d'importance secondaire

**side-splitting** *adj* tordant; *sl* marrant

**side-step** *vt* éviter; *vi* faire un pas de côté

**sidestroke** *n* nage *f* sur le côté

**sidetrack** *vt fig* détourner l'attention de; (train) garer

**side-view** *n* vue *f* de côté, vue *f* de profil

**sidewalk** *n* US trottoir *m*

**sideward** *adj* latéral, de côté

**sidewards** *adv* de côté

**sideways** *adv* de côté, latéralement, en travers

**siding** *n* voie *f* de garage

**sidle** *vi* marcher de biais; ~ **along** s'avancer de côté; ~ **up to s/o** se couler auprès de qn

**siege** *n* siège *m*; **lay ~ to** assiéger

**siesta** *n* sieste *f*

**sieve** *n* crible *m*, tamis *m*; *vt* passer au crible, tamiser

**sift** *vt* passer au crible (au tamis), tamiser; *fig* examiner minutieusement; *vi* filtrer

**sifter** *n* cribleur *m*, tamiseur *m*; (thing) crible *m*, tamis *m*

**sigh** *n* soupir *m*; *vi* soupirer

**sight** *n* vue *f*; (spectacle) spectacle *m*; (gun) cran *m* de mire, guidon *m*; (sight) monuments *mpl* et curiosités *fpl*; **at first ~** au premier abord; **at (on) ~** à vue; **catch ~ of s/o** apercevoir qn; **come into ~** apparaître; *coll* **I can't bear the ~ of him** je ne peux pas le sentir; **keep s/o in ~** ne pas perdre qn de vue; **know s/o by ~** connaître qn de vue; **lose ~ of** perdre de vue; **love at first ~** coup *m* de foudre; **out of ~, out of mind** loin des yeux, loin du cœur; **short ~** myopie *f*; *vt* apercevoir; (gun) viser

**sightless** *adj* aveugle

**sightly** *adj* agréable à voir, avenant

**sight-reading** *n* lecture *f* à vue

**sightseeing** *n* visite *f* touristique; **go ~** visiter les curiosités (touristiques)

**sightseer** *n* touriste

**sign** *n* signe *m*; (advert) réclame *f*; (shop, etc) enseigne *f*; (indication) indice *m*; (trace) trace *f*; (omen) présage *m*; symbole *m*; **road ~s** signalisation routière; **show no ~ of life** ne donner aucun signe de vie; **there's no ~ of him** il reste invisible (introuvable); *vt* signer; (indicate) indiquer; ~ **away** céder par écrit; ~ **on (up)** embaucher, engager; *vi* ~ **off** (work) pointer au départ; (programme) terminer l'émission; ~ **on (up)** s'engager

**signal** *n* signal *m*; *rad* indicatif *m*; **traffic ~s** feux *mpl* de circulation; *adj* insigne, remarquable; *vt* signaler; *vi* donner un signal; ~ **to s/o to do sth** faire signe à qn de faire qch

**signal-box** *n* poste *m* d'aiguillage

**signalize** *vt* signaler, marquer

**signaller** *n* signaleur *m*

**signally** *adv* remarquablement

**signalman** *n* aiguilleur *m*

**signatory** *n* + *adj* signataire

**signature** *n* signature *f*; ~ **tune** indicatif musical

**signboard** *n* (notice-board) écriteau *m*; (shop) enseigne *f*; (advert) réclame *f*

**signet** *n* sceau *m*, cachet *m*

**signet-ring** *n* chevalière *f*

**significance** *n* signification *f*, importance *f*

**significant** *adj* significatif -ive; (important) important

**signification** *n* signification *f*

**signify** *vt* signifier, vouloir dire; (declare) déclarer; *vi* importer

**signing** *n* signature *f*

**signpost** *n* poteau indicateur

**Sikh** *n* Sikh -e

**silage** *n* fourrage ensilé

**silence** *n* silence *m*; **dead ~** silence absolu; **pass over in ~** passer sous silence; *vt* faire taire, réduire au silence; (complaints) étouffer

**silencer** *n* mot pot *m* d'échappement; (gun) silencieux *m*; amortisseur *m* de son

**silent** *adj* silencieux -ieuse; **keep ~** garder le silence

**silhouette** *n* silhouette *f*; *vt* silhouetter

**silicon** *n* silicium *m*; ~ **chip** plaquette *f* de silicium

**silk** *n* soie *f*; (sewing) fil *m* de soie; ~ **handkerchief** foulard *m*; ~ **hat** (chapeau *m*) haut-de-forme *m* (*pl* hauts-de-forme); **oiled ~** taffetas *m* imperméable

**silken** *adj* soyeux -euse, de soie

**silkiness** *n* nature soyeuse

**silkworm** *n* ver *m* à soie

**silky** *adj* soyeux -euse, de soie

**sill** *n* (window) rebord *m*; (door) seuil *m*

**silliness** *n* sottise *f*

**silly** *n* (person) idiot -e; *adj* sot (*f* sotte), niais; ~ **ass** imbécile *m*; ~ **thing** bêtise *f*; **knock s/o** ~ assommer qn

**silo** *n* silo *m*; **launching** ~ puits *m* de lancement

**silt** *n geol* limon *m*; *vt* ~ **up** ensabler; *vi* s'ensabler

**silver** *n* argent *m*; (plate) argenterie *f*; *adj* d'argent, en argent; ~ **coin** pièce *f* d'argent; ~ **fox** renard argenté; *fig* ~ **lining** consolation *f*; ~ **paper** papier *m* d'argent; *vt* argenter; (mirror) étamer

**silver-gilt** *n* vermeil *m*

**silver-haired** *adj* aux cheveux argentés

**silver-plated** *adj* argenté

**silverside** *n* gîte *m* à la noix

**silversmith** *n* orfèvre *m*

**silverware** *n* argenterie *f*

**silvery** *adj* argenté; (laugh) argentin

**simian** *adj* simiesque

**similar** *adj* semblable, pareil -eille

**similarity** *n* ressemblance *f*, similarité *f*

**simile** *n* comparaison *f*

**similitude** *n* similitude *f*

**simmer** *vt* faire mijoter; *vi* (liquid) frémir; (food) mijoter; *fig* ~ **down** s'apaiser peu à peu, se calmer

**simony** *n eccles* simonie *f*

**simper** *n* sourire affecté; *vi* minauder

**simple** *n med* simple *m*; *adj* simple; (person) naturel -elle, sans affectation; *pej* naïf (*f* naïve), crédule

**simple-minded** *adj* naïf (*f* naïve)

**simpleness** *n see* **simplicity**

**simpleton** *n* nigaud -e

**simplicity** *n* simplicité *f*, candeur *f*; *pej* niaiserie *f*; **be** ~ **itself** être simple comme bonjour

**simplification** *n* simplification *f*

**simplify** *vt* simplifier

**simply** *adv* simplement; ~ **marvellous** absolument (tout à fait) merveilleux -euse

**simulate** *vt* simuler, feindre

**simulation** *n* simulation *f*, feinte *f*

**simulator** *n* simulateur -trice; *aer* simulateur *m* de vol

**simultaneity** *n* simultanéité *f*

**simultaneous** *adj* simultané

**sin** *n* péché *m*; (offence) offense *f*; **original** ~ péché originel; **ugly as** ~ laid comme un singe; *vi* pécher

**since** *adv* depuis; **long** ~ il y a longtemps; **many years** ~ il y a bien des années; *prep* depuis; *conj* depuis que; (reason) puisque; **it's a year** ~ **he arrived** il y a un an qu'il est arrivé

**sincere** *adj* sincère

**sincerity** *n* sincérité *f*

**sine** *n math* sinus *m*

**sinecure** *n* sinécure *f*

**sinew** *n* tendon *m*; ~ **s** nerfs *mpl*; **the** ~ **s**

**of war** le nerf de la guerre

**sinewy** *adj* (arm) musclé; (meat) tendineux -euse

**sinful** *adj* pécheur (*f* pécheresse); *coll fig* scandaleux -euse

**sing** *vt* + *vi* chanter; *vi* (ears) bourdonner, tinter; (wind) siffler; *US* (inform) moucharder

**singe** *n* légère brûlure; *vt* brûler légèrement, roussir; (poultry) passer à la flamme; ~ **hair** brûler la pointe des cheveux

**singer** *n* chanteur -euse; (opera) cantatrice *f*

**Sing(h)alese, Cingalese** *adj* cingalais

**singing** *n* chant *m*

**single** *n* (ticket) aller *m* (simple), billet *m* simple; (record) 45 tours *m sing*; *sp* simple *m*, partie *f* simple; *adj* unique, seul; (not married) célibataire, pas marié; (character) simple, honnête; ~ **bed** lit *m* pour une personne; ~ **bedroom** chambre *f* à un lit; ~ **ticket** billet *m* simple; *vt* ~ **out** choisir; (for distinction) distinguer

**single-breasted** *adj* (jacket) droit

**single-handed** *adj* seul, sans aide

**single-minded** *adj* qui ne vise qu'un but

**singleness** *n* sincérité *f*; (one mind) unicité *f*; (celibacy) célibat *m*

**single-seater** *adj* à une place

**singlet** *n* gilet *m* de corps; (sport) maillot fin

**singly** *adv* séparément, un à un; (alone) seul

**singsong** *n* chant *m* monotone; *coll* chants *mpl* en chœur; *adj* ~ **voice** voix *f* monotone

**singular** *n gramm* singulier *m*; *adj* singulier -ière, bizarre; (remarkable) remarquable

**singularity** *n* singularité *f*

**singularize** *vt* singulariser

**singularly** *adv* singulièrement, remarquablement

**sinister** *adj* sinistre; dangereux -euse, traître -esse

**¹sink** *n* évier *m*; *fig* cloaque *m*

**²sink** *vt* (ship) couler, faire sombrer; (lower) baisser; (push down) enfoncer; (dig) creuser; (money) placer, *pej* engloutir; (objection) supprimer; *vi* (ship) couler, sombrer; (in chair) se laisser tomber, s'affaisser; (into ground) s'enfoncer; (sun) baisser; ~ **down** s'affaisser; ~ **in** pénétrer; ~ **to one's knees** tomber à genoux; **my heart sank** le cœur me manqua

**sinker** *n* plomb *m*; **hook, line and** ~ à fond, totalement

**sinking** *n* enfoncement *m*; (ground, etc) affaissement *m*; (weakening) défaillance f, affaiblissement m; (well) creusage m

**sinless** adj innocent, sans péché

**sinner** n pécheur (f pécheresse)

**sinologist** n sinologue

**sinology** n sinologie f

**sinuosity** n sinuosité f

**sinuous** adj sinueux -euse; (supple) souple

**sinus** n sinus m

**sinusitis** n sinusite f

**sip** n petite gorgée, petit coup; vt boire à petits coups, siroter

**siphon** n siphon m; vt siphonner

**sir** n monsieur m; (letters) dear Sir Monsieur; mil yes, ~ oui, mon capitaine (général, etc); naut ay, aye, aye, ~ oui, mon commandant (amiral, etc); vt ~ s/o donner du Monsieur à qn

**sire** n sire m; (father) père m; vt engendrer

**siren** n sirène f; (vamp) femme fatale

**sirloin** n aloyau m, faux-filet m

**sisal** n sisal m

**sissy** n coll garçon (homme) efféminé; (coward) poule mouillée

**sister** n sœur f; (nurse) infirmière f en chef

**sisterhood** n communauté religieuse; union fraternelle

**sister-in-law** n belle-sœur f (pl belles-sœurs)

**sisterly** adj de sœur

**sit** vt asseoir; ~ out ne pas prendre part à; (wait till end) rester assis jusqu'à la fin de; vi (sit down) s'asseoir; (be sitting) être assis; (assembly, M.P.) siéger; (committee, council) se réunir; (photo) poser; (hen) couver; (garment) aller, tomber; ~ back in one's chair se renverser dans sa chaise; coll fig se relaxer; ~ down s'asseoir; ~ down to a meal se mettre à table; coll fig ~ on s/o rabrouer qn; coll fig ~ on sth laisser dormir qch; ~ tight (resist) tenir ferme (bon); (stay put) ne pas bouger de sa place; ~ up se redresser, se tenir droit dans sa chaise; (stay up) veiller; ~ up for s/o attendre qn; ~ with s/o tenir compagnie à qn; (sick person) veiller qn

**sit-down** adj ~ strike grève f sur le tas

**site** n emplacement m; archi site m; building ~ chantier m de construction; camping ~ camping m, terrain m de camping; vt situer

**sit-in** n ~ strike grève f sur le tas

**siting** n (situation) emplacement m; choix m de l'emplacement

**sitter** n personne assise; (art) modèle; baby-~ baby-sitter

**sitting** n posture assise; (session) séance f; (court) audience f; (hen) couvaison f; (lunch) service m; adj assis; (court) en séance; coll fig ~ duck cible f facile; be ~ pretty avoir trouvé le filon

**sitting-room** n salle f de séjour, living(-room m) m

**situate** vt situer

**situated** adj situé; awkwardly ~ dans une position embarrassante

**situation** n situation f, position f; (post) place f, emploi m; ~s vacant offres fpl d'emploi; ~s wanted demandes fpl d'emploi

**six** n six m invar; at ~ es and sevens en désordre; it is ~ of one and half a dozen of the other c'est bonnet blanc et blanc bonnet; adj six

**sixteen** n seize m invar; adj seize invar

**sixteenth** n seizième; (date) seize m; adj seizième

**sixth** n sixième; (date) six m; adj sixième

**sixtieth** n + adj soixantième

**sixty** n soixante m invar; he is in his sixties il a passé soixante ans; the sixties les années soixante; adj soixante invar

**siz(e)able** adj assez grand

**¹size** n grandeur f; (person) taille f; (bulk) grosseur f; (volume) volume m; (books) format m; (shoes, gloves) pointure f; (collar, neck) encolure f; full (life) ~ grandeur naturelle; small ~ petit modèle; vt classer par grosseur; ~ up jauger; (person) juger

**²size** n (glue) colle f, apprêt m; (textiles) apprêt m; vt coller, apprêter

**sizzle** n grésillement m; vi grésiller

**¹skate** n patin m; vi patiner

**²skate** n (fish) raie f

**skateboard** n planche f à roulettes, skateboard m

**skater** n patineur -euse

**skating** n patinage m

**skating-rink** n patinoire f

**skedaddle** vi coll filer, se sauver à toutes jambes

**skein** n écheveau m

**skeletal** adj squelettique

**skeleton** n squelette m; (framework) charpente f, carcasse f; ~ in the cupboard secret honteux de la famille

**skeleton-key** n (master-key) passe-partout m invar; (locksmith's) crochet m

**sketch** n croquis m, esquisse f; (short play) sketch m, saynète f; (outline) exposé m; vt esquisser, croquer

**sketch-book** n cahier m de croquis, album m

**sketch-map** n carte-croquis f (pl cartes-croquis), coll topo m

**sketchy** adj imprécis, plutôt vague

**skew** adj biais, de biais; on the ~ de biais; adv en biais, de travers; vi obliquer, biaiser

**skewer** *n* brochette *f*; *vt* brocheter, embrocher

**ski** *n* ski *m*; **on ~ s** à skis; *vi* faire du ski, skier

**skid** *n* dérapage *m*; *vi* déraper, faire une embardée

**skidding** *n* dérapage *m*

**skid-lid** *n* coll casque *m* (de motocycliste)

**skid-pan** *n* mot piste savonnée

**skier** *n* skieur (*f* skieuse)

**skiff** *n* esquif *m*, skiff *m*

**skiffle** *n* jazz basé sur des chansons folkloriques

**skiing** *n* ski *m*; **water ~** ski *m* nautique

**ski-jump** *n* saut *m* à skis

**skilful** *adj* habile, adroit

**ski-lift** *n* téléski *m*, remonte-pente *m*

**skill** *n* habileté *f*, dextérité *f*; **lack of ~** maladresse *f*

**skilled** *adj* habile; (experienced) expérimenté; **~ worker** ouvrier spécialisé

**skillet** *n* poêlon *m* à long manche

**skim** *vt* écumer; (milk) écrémer; (soup) dégraisser; (surface) effleurer, raser; **~ over (through)** parcourir rapidement; *vi* **~ along** passer légèrement

**skimmer** *n* (soup) écumoire *f*; (milk) écrémeuse *f*

**skimp** *vt* (be sparing of) lésiner sur; *coll* bâcler, saboter

**skimpy** *adj* (insufficient) maigre; (garment) étriqué

**skin** *n* peau *f*; (hide) cuir *m*; *fig* **by the ~ of one's teeth** de justesse; *fig* **have a thin (thick) ~** être (peu) susceptible; *fig* **I've got her under my ~** je l'ai dans la peau; **next to one's ~** à même la peau; **wet to the ~** mouillé jusqu'aux os; *vt* écorcher, dépouiller; (fruit) peler, éplucher

**skin-deep** *adj* superficiel -ielle

**skin-disease** *n* maladie *f* de (la) peau

**skin-diving** *n* plongée *f* autonome

**skinflint** *n* grippe-sou *m*

**skinful** *n* pleine outre de vin; *sl* cuite *f*

**skin-graft** *n* greffe *f* de peau

**skin-grafting** *n* greffe cutanée

**skinny** *adj* maigre, décharné

**skint** *adj sl* sans argent, *sl* fauché

**skin-tight** *adj* collant

**¹skip** *n* benne *f*; panier *m*

**²skip** *n* petit saut, bond *m*, gambade *f*; *vt* sauter, passer; *sl* **~ it!** ça suffit!; *vi* sauter, gambader; (with rope) sauter à la corde

**¹skipper** *n naut* patron *m*; *sl* chef *m*

**²skipper** *n* sauteur -euse

**skipping-rope** *n* corde *f* à sauter

**skirmish** *n mil* escarmouche *f*; échauffourrée *f*; *vi* escarmoucher

**¹skirt** *n* jupe *f*; *sl* femme *f*; **~ s** lisière *f*, bordure *f*

**²skirt** *vt* contourner; longer, serrer

**skirting-board** *n* plinthe *f*

**skit** *n* satire *f*; *theat* pièce *f* satirique

**skitter** *vi* raser l'eau

**skittish** *adj* (woman) volage, folâtre; (horse) ombrageux -euse

**skittle** *n* quille *f*

**skittle-alley** *n* jeu *m* de quilles

**skivvy** *n sl* bonne *f* à tout faire

**skulduggery** *n* coll manœuvres *fpl* louches

**skulk** *vi* (hide) se tenir caché; (creep about) rôder furtivement

**skull** *n* crâne *m*; **~ and crossbones** tête *f* de mort (et tibias)

**skull-cap** *n* calotte *f*

**skunk** *n* mouffette *f*; (fur) sconse *m*, skunks *m*; *coll* rosse *f*

**sky** *n* ciel *m*; (climate) climat *m*; **praise s/o to the skies** porter qn aux nues; *coll* **the ~ is the limit** il n'y a pas de limite; **under the open ~** au grand air; (at night) à la belle étoile; *vt* (ball) lancer en chandelle

**sky-blue** *adj* bleu ciel *invar*, azuré

**sky-high** *adv* jusqu'aux nues

**skylark** *n* alouette *f*; *vi coll* faire le fou (*f* la folle), rigoler, faire du chahut

**skylight** *n* lucarne *f*

**skyline** *n* horizon *m*, ligne *f* d'horizon

**skyscraper** *n* gratte-ciel *m invar*

**skyward(s)** *adv* vers le ciel

**slab** *n* (stone) dalle *f*; (metal) plaque *f*; (cake) grosse tranche; (chocolate) tablette *f*

**slack** *n* (rope) mou *m*; *mech* jeu *m*; **take up the ~ in a cable** mettre un câble au raide; *adj* (loose) lâche, mou (*f* molle), mal tendu; (screw) desserré; (careless) négligent; (not lively) peu vif (*f* vive); **~ period** accalmie *f*; (during day) heure(s) creuse(s); **~ season** mortesaison *f* (*pl* mortes-saisons); *naut* **water** *mer f* étale; **be ~ in doing sth** être lent à faire qch; **business is ~** les affaires vont mal; *vt* relâcher, détendre; *vi* (sail) prendre du lâche; *coll* se relâcher

**slacken** *vt* (loosen) relâcher, détendre; (screw) desserrer; (pace) ralentir; *vi* (speed) ralentir; (abate) diminuer; (wind) tomber; (person) devenir négligent, se relâcher

**slacker** *n* paresseux -euse, fainéant -e; *coll* flemmard -e

**slackness** *n* relâchement *m*, négligence *f*; (laziness) paresse *f*, manque *m* d'énergie; (slowness) lenteur *f*; (unpunctuality) inexactitude *f*; (looseness) détente *f*; (rope) mou *m*; *comm* stag-

slacks

nation *f*, marasme *m*
**slacks** *npl* pantalon *m*
**slag** *n* scories *fpl*
**slag-heap** *n* crassier *m*
**slake** *vt* ~ **one's thirst** étancher sa soif
**slalom** *n* slalom *m*
¹**slam** *n* (door) claquement *m*; *vt* + *vi* claquer; *sl* éreinter, blâmer
²**slam** *n* (cards) chelem (schelem) *m*
**slander** *n* calomnie *f*, médisance *f*, diffamation *f*; *vt* calomnier, médire de, diffamer
**slanderous** *adj* calomnieux -ieuse, diffamatoire
**slang** *n* argot *m*; *vt coll* injurier; *sl* engueuler
**slangy** *adj* argotique; (person) qui aime à employer des termes d'argot
**slant** *n* pente *f*, inclinaison *f*; biais *m*; (opinion) point *m* de vue; *vt* incliner; *vi* être en pente; être oblique
**slanting** *adj* (sloping) en pente, incliné; (direction) oblique
**slap** *n* claque *f*, tape *f*; (on face) gifle *f*; *fig* affront *m*; *adv* en plein; ~ **in the middle** en plein milieu; *vt* frapper avec la main; (child) donner une fessée à; (on face) gifler; *coll* ~ **s/o down** remettre qn à sa place; *vi* claquer
**slap-bang** *adv see* **slap** *adv*
**slapdash** *adj* sans soin; ~ **work** travail bâclé; *adv* sans soin
**slap-happy** *adj coll* fou-fou (*f* fofolle)
**slapstick** *n* farce bouffonne, burlesque *m*
**slap-up** *adj coll* fameux -euse
**slash** *n* entaille *f*; (face) balafre *f*; *vt* taillader; (face) balafrer; (strike wildly) frapper à droite et à gauche; *coll* (criticize) éreinter; *coll* (reduce) diminuer, réduire
**slashing** *adj* (criticism) mordant; (rain) cinglant
**slat** *n* lame *f*, planchette *f*
¹**slate** *n* ardoise *f*; *US pol* liste *f* provisoire de candidats; **clean** ~ passé *m* irréprochable; **wipe the** ~ **(clean)** passer l'éponge sur le passé; *vt* ardoiser
²**slate** *vt coll* réprimander, tancer; (book, play) éreinter
**slating** *n coll* (telling off) savon *m*; (criticism) éreintement *m*
**slatted** *adj* à planchettes; ~ **shutters** persiennes *fpl*
**slattern** *n* souillon *f*
**slatternly** *adj* mal soigné, malpropre
**slaughter** *n* massacre *m*; (cattle) abattage *m*; *vt* massacrer, tuer; (cattle) abattre
**slaughterer** *n* tueur *m*, égorgeur *m*
**slaughterhouse** *n* abattoir *m*
**Slav** *n* Slave; *adj* slave
**slave** *n* esclave; *vi* travailler dur, peiner;

~ **away at sth** s'éreinter à (faire) qch
**slave-driver** *n fig* patron dur (*f* patronne dure)
**slave-labour** *n* travail *m* d'esclave
**slavery** *n* esclavage *m*
**slave-trade**, **slave-traffic** *n* traite *f* des noirs, commerce *m* des esclaves; **white** ~ traite *f* des blanches
**Slavic** *adj* slave
**slavish** *adj* d'esclave, servile
**Slavonic** *adj* (language) slave
**slay** *vt* tuer
**sleazy** *adj* léger -ère; *coll* sordide
**sledge, sled** *n* traîneau *m*
**sledge-hammer** *n* marteau *m* à deux mains
**sleek** *adj* lisse, luisant; (manner) onctueux -euse
**sleep** *n* sommeil *m*; **drop (go) off to** ~ s'endormir; **not have a wink of** ~ ne pas fermer l'œil; **put to** ~ endormir; **walk in one's** ~ être somnambule; *vi* dormir; (at hotel) coucher; ~ **in** être logé dans l'établissement (la maison); (get up late) faire la grasse matinée; ~ **lightly** avoir le sommeil léger; ~ **like a log (top)** dormir sur les deux oreilles (à poings fermés); ~ **out** découcher; ~ **with s/o** coucher avec qn
**sleeper** *n* dormeur -euse; (rail track) traverse *f*; (sleeping-car) wagon-lit *m* (*pl* wagons-lits); **be a light (heavy)** ~ avoir le sommeil léger (profond)
**sleepily** *adv* d'un air endormi
**sleepiness** *n* somnolence *f*; léthargie *f*
**sleeping** *n* sommeil *m*; ~ **accommodation** logement *m*; *adj* dormant; (asleep) endormi; ~ **partner** (associé *m*) commanditaire *m*; ~ **sickness** maladie *f* du sommeil; **let** ~ **dogs lie** ne réveillez pas le chat qui dort
**sleeping-bag** *n* sac *m* de couchage
**sleeping-car** *n* wagon-lit *m* (*pl* wagons-lits), voiture-lit *f* (*pl* voitures-lits)
**sleeping-pill, sleeping-draught** *n* somnifère *m*
**sleeping-quarters** *npl* dortoir *m*
**sleepless** *adj* sans sommeil
**sleeplessness** *n* insomnie *f*
**sleepwalker** *n* somnambule
**sleepwalking** *n* somnambulisme *m*
**sleepy** *adj* somnolent, endormi; **be (feel)** ~ avoir sommeil
**sleepyhead** *n coll* endormi -e
**sleet** *n* grésil *m*, neige *f* à moitié fondue; *US* grêle *f*; *vi* grésiller
**sleeve** *n* manche *f*; *mech* manchon *m*; (record) pochette *f*
**sleeve-board** *n* jeannette *f*
**sleeveless** *adj* sans manches
**sleigh** *n* traîneau *m*
**sleight-of-hand** *n* prestidigitation *f*;

(trick) tour *m* de passe-passe

**slender** *adj* mince; (person) svelte; (hope) faible; (not much) modeste

**slenderize** *vt US* amincir

**sleuth** *n* (dog) limier *m*; *coll* (detective) détective *m*

**slew** *vi* pivoter, virer; *mot* faire un tête-à-queue

**slewed** *adj sl* ivre

**slice** *n* tranche *f*; (sausage, etc) rondelle *f*; ~ **of bread and butter** tartine *f*; ~ **of luck** coup *m* de veine; *vt* découper en tranches; (cut) couper, trancher

**slicer** *n* machine *f* à trancher

¹**slick** *n* nappe *f* d'huile

²**slick** *adj* lisse; *coll* habile, astucieux -ieuse; **look ~ about it** dépêchez-vous un peu; *vt US* (hair) lisser; mettre en ordre

**slicker** *n sl* escroc adroit, filou *m*

**slide** *n* glissade *f*, glissement *m*; (groove) coulisse *f*; (ice) glissoire *f*; (slipway) glissière *f*; *phot* diapositive *f*; (hair) barrette *f*; *vt* + *vi* glisser, couler; *vi* ~ **down** descendre en glissant; *coll* ~ **off** filer; *coll* **let a thing ~** se désintéresser de qch

**slide-rule** *n* règle *f* à calcul

**sliding** *adj* glissant, coulissant; ~ **door** porte coulissante; ~ **scale** échelle *f* mobile

¹**slight** *n* affront *m*, manque *m* de respect; *vt* manquer d'égards à; négliger

²**slight** *adj* mince, léger -ère; (figure) menu, frêle

**slightest** *adj* le (la) moindre; **not in the ~** pas le moins du monde

**slighting** *adj* exprimant le mépris; (air) de mépris

**slightly** *adv* légèrement, un peu, faiblement

**slightness** *n* minceur *f*; (figure) sveltesse *f*; légèreté *f*; peu *m* d'importance

**slim** *adj* svelte, élancé, mince; (hope, etc) léger -ère; *sl* rusé; *vt* amincir; *vi* se faire maigrir

**slime** *n* vase *f*, limon *m*; (snail) bave *f*

**sliminess** *n* viscosité *f*; *fig* servilité *f*

**slimming** *n* amaigrissement *m*; *adj* amaigrissant

**slimness** *n* sveltesse *f*, taille *f* mince

**slimy** *adj* limoneux -euse; (sticky) visqueux -euse; *fig* servile

¹**sling** *n* fronde *f*; (arm) écharpe *f*; *mech* élingue *f*, courroie *f*; *vt* lancer, jeter; (suspend) suspendre; *naut* élinguer; ~ **over one's shoulder** mettre en bandoulière

²**sling** *n* (drink) grog *m*

**slink** *vi* ~ **away** partir furtivement, s'éclipser

**slinking** *adj* furtif -ive

**slinky** *adj coll* svelte; (alluring) séduisant; (clothes) collant

**slip** *n* glissade *f*, glissement *m*; (mistake) erreur *f*; (underskirt) combinaison *f*, jupon *m*; (behaviour) écart *m* de conduite; (dog lead) laisse *f*; (briefs, bathing) slip *m*; *naut* cale *f*; (pathway) sentier *m*; *hort* bouture *f*; (paper) bande *f*, fiche *f*; (note) billet *m*; ~ **of the tongue** lapsus *m*; **detachable ~** volant *m*; **fine ~ of a girl** beau brin de fille; **give s/o the ~** faire faux bond à qn; **gym ~** tunique *f*; **pillow ~** taie *f* d'oreiller; *vt* glisser, couler; (escape from) se dégager de; (cable) filer; ~ **off** ôter; ~ **on** mettre; **it has ~ped my memory** cela m'a échappé; *vi* (se) glisser, couler; ~ **away** (**off**) s'esquiver, s'échapper; (time) s'écouler; ~ **out** sortir; (escape) s'échapper; ~ **over** (**round**) **to the shops** faire un saut jusqu'aux magasins; ~ **up** tomber; *fig* se tromper; **let ~** laisser échapper

**slip-knot** *n* nœud coulant

**slipper** *n* pantoufle *f*

**slippered** *adj* en pantoufles

**slipperiness** *n* nature glissante; *fig* caractère rusé

**slippy** *adj coll* **look ~** se dépêcher

**slip-road** *n* petite route de déviation

**slipshod** *adj* (work) négligé; (person) mal soigné, négligent

**slip-up** *n coll* erreur *f*, *coll* gaffe *f*

**slipway** *n* cale *f* de lancement

**slit** *n* fente *f*, fissure *f*; *surg* incision *f*; *vt* fendre; *surg* faire une incision dans; ~ **s/o's throat** égorger qn

**slither** *vi* glisser; (snake) ramper

**slithery** *adj* glissant

**sliver** *n* tranche *f*; (wood) éclat *m*

**slob** *n coll* goujat *m*, manant *m*

**slobber** *vi* baver; (sob) larmoyer

**sloe** *n bot* prunelle *f*

**slog** *n coll* (blow) coup violent; *coll* (hard work) corvée *f*; *vt coll* frapper violemment; *vi coll* (work hard) boulonner, turbiner

**slogan** *n* devise *f*; *pol* slogan *m*

**sloop** *n* sloop *m*

**slop** *n* boue *f*; liquide renversé; ~ **s** (for invalids) aliments *mpl* liquides; (dishwater) eaux ménagères; *vt* répandre; *vi* ~ **over** se répandre, déborder

**slop-basin** *n* petit bol pour recevoir les fonds de tasses de thé

¹**slope** *n* pente *f*, inclinaison *f*; (bank) talus *m*; (mountain) versant *m*; (railway) rampe *f*; (road) côte *f*; (rifle) arme *f*; **at the ~** sur l'épaule; **on a (the) ~** en pente; *vt* incliner; *mil* mettre (l'arme) sur l'épaule; *vi* incliner, être en pente; ~ **down** descendre; ~ **up(wards)** monter

²**slope** *vi sl* ~ **off** filer

**sloping** *adj* en pente, incliné; ~ **shoulders** épaules tombantes

**slop-pail** *n* seau *m* hygiénique

**sloppy** *adj* détrempé; (character) mou (*f* molle); (work) bâclé, négligé; (dress) mal ajusté, négligé; (feeling) larmoyant

**slosh** *vt coll* flanquer un coup à

**sloshed** *adj sl* soûl (saoul), paf *invar*

**slot** *n* entaille *f*, fente *f*, rainure *f*; *vt* tailler une fente dans, entailler; ~ **in** insérer par une fente; *fig* trouver une place pour

**sloth** *n* paresse *f*, indolence *f*; *zool* paresseux *m*

**slothful** *adj* paresseux -euse, indolent

**slot-machine** *n* distributeur *m* automatique

**slouch** *n* démarche lourde; épaules arrondies; *vi* traîner le pas, avoir une allure lourde

¹**slough** *n* bourbier *m*

²**slough** *n* (snake) dépouille *f*; *vi* se dépouiller, muer

**sloven** *n* personne mal soignée (malpropre)

**slovenliness** *n* manque *m* de tenue

**slovenly** *adj* mal soigné, mal peigné

**slow** *adj* lent; (dull) lourd; (clock) en retard; *mech* ~ **running** ralenti *m*; ~ **train** train omnibus *m*; **be a** ~ **speaker** avoir la parole lente; (clock) **be** ~ retarder; **in a** ~ **oven** à feu doux; **not be** ~ **in doing sth** ne pas tarder à faire qch; *vt* + *vi* ralentir; *adv* lentement

**slowcoach** *n coll* lambin -e

**slowly** *adv* lentement

**slow-motion** *n* **in** ~ au ralenti

**slowness** *n* lenteur *f*; (mind) lourdeur *f*; (clock) retard *m*

**slowpoke** *n US coll* lambin -e

**slow-worm** *n* orvet *m*

**sludge** *n* fange *f*; (sewage) vidanges *fpl*

**slug** *n zool* limace *f*; (air-gun) balle *f*; *min* + *typ* lingot *m*; *vt coll* assommer

**sluggard** *n* paresseux -euse, fainéant -e

**sluggish** *adj* léthargique, lourd; (river, pulse) lent; (engine) peu nerveux -euse; (digestion) paresseux -euse

**sluice** *n* écluse *f*; *vt* vanner; ~ **out** laver à grande eau; *vi* ~ **out** couler à flots

**sluice-gate** *n* vanne *f*

**slum** *n* bas quartier; (street) rue *f* sordide; (hovel) taudis *m*; **the** ~ **s** les basfonds *mpl*; *vi* **go** ~ **ming** *coll pej* fréquenter un milieu inférieur; *ar* faire des visites de charité dans les quartiers pauvres

**slumber** *n* sommeil *m*; *vi* dormir paisiblement

**slumber-wear** *n* vêtements *mpl* de nuit

**slum-clearance** *n* suppression *f* des taudis

**slummy** *adj* ~ **district** quartier *m* de taudis

**slump** *n* effondrement *m*; *econ* crise *f*; ~ **in sales** mévente *f*; *vi* tomber lourdement, s'écrouler; (prices, etc) baisser tout à coup, s'effondrer

**slur** *n* affront *m*, tache *f*; (speech) mauvaise articulation; **cast a** ~ **on s/o's reputation** porter atteinte à la réputation de qn; *vt* ne pas articuler clairement, bredouiller; *mus* lier; ~ **over** passer légèrement sur

**slush** *n* neige à demi fondue; (mud) fange *f*; *coll* sensiblerie *f*

**slushy** *adj* boueux -euse; détrempé par la neige; *coll* d'une sentimentalité exagérée

**slut** *n* souillon *f*; *coll* coureuse *f*

**sluttish** *adj* sale, malpropre

**sly** *adj* rusé, sournois, fin; (mischievous) malicieux -ieuse, espiègle; **on the** ~ à la dérobée

**slyness** *n* sournoiserie *f*; espièglerie *f*

¹**smack** *n* (flavour) petit goût; soupçon *m*; *vi* ~ **of** avoir un léger goût de

²**smack** *n naut* bateau *m* pêcheur

³**smack** *n* claquement *m*; (hand) claque *f*; ~ **in the face** gifle *f*; *adv* ~ **in the middle** en plein milieu; ~ **into a tree** en plein dans un arbre; *vt* faire claquer; (hit) frapper; *coll* ~ **one's lips** se lécher les babines; *vi* claquer

**smacker** *n sl* (smack) gifle retentissante; (kiss) gros baiser; (pound note) livre *f*, billet *m* d'une livre; *US* dollar *m*

**small** *n* ~ **of the back** creux *m* (chute *f*) des reins; ~ **s** sous-vêtements *mpl*; *adj* petit, menu; (figure) de petite taille; (weak) faible; (in numbers) peu nombreux -euse; (unimportant) peu important; (petty) mesquin; ~ **change** petite (menue) monnaie; ~ **letter** minuscule *f*; ~ **matter** bagatelle *f*; **in a** ~ **way** en petit; *fig* **look** ~ avoir l'air penaud; **make s/o look** ~ humilier qn; *adv* menu, en morceaux

**small-arms** *npl* armes portatives

**small-holding** *n* petite ferme

**small-minded** *adj* à l'esprit mesquin

**smallpox** *n* petite vérole, variole *f*

**small-talk** *n* bavardage *m*, banalités *fpl*

**small-time** *adj US* de troisième ordre

**smarmy** *adj coll* doucereux -euse

**smart** *n* douleur aiguë; *adj* (alert) vif (*f* vive), alerte; (blow) fort, sec (*f* sèche); *fig* (sharp) éveillé, à l'esprit alerte; *pej* malin (*f* maligne), finaud; (dress) chic *invar*; ~ **pace** vive allure; **look** ~ se dépêcher; *vi* cuire, brûler; ~ **under an injustice** souffrir sous le coup d'une injustice; **he will make us** ~ **for it** il nous le fera payer cher

**smarten** *vt* (pace) accélérer; faire beau (*f* belle); ~ **oneself up** dégourdir qn; *vi* ~ **up** s'animer, se dégourdir

**smartly** *adv* vivement, promptement; (cleverly) habilement; (dressed) élégamment

**smartness** *n* (liveliness) vivacité *f*; (cleverness) finesse *f*, habileté *f*; (dress) élégance *f*

**smash** *n* fracas *m*; (accident) accident *m*, collision *f*, sinistre *m*; (disaster) débâcle *f*; *comm* faillite *f*; (tennis) smash *m*; ~ **hit** succès fou; *adv* go ~ faire faillite; *vt* briser, écraser; (tennis) smasher; ~ **in** défoncer; ~ **open the door** enfoncer la porte; ~ **s/o's face in** casser la figure à qn; ~ **sth against sth** heurter qch contre qch; ~ **up** briser en morceaux; *vi* (break) éclater en morceaux, se briser; *comm* faire faillite; ~ **against** (se) heurter (contre) qch; ~ **into** rentrer dans, heurter

**smash-and-grab (raid)** *n* vol *m* après bris de vitrine

**smasher** *n* coup écrasant; *coll* she's a ~! elle est drôlement bien!

**smashing** *adj* écrasant; *coll* formidable

**smash-up** *n* (accident) collision *f*; (destruction) destruction totale; (bankruptcy) banqueroute *f*

**smattering** *n* légère connaissance

**smear** *n* tache *f*, souillure *f*; *med* frottis *m*; *coll* ~ **campaign** campagne *f* de diffamation; *vt* barbouiller, salir; *fig* diffamer

**smell** *n* odeur *f*, parfum *m*, senteur *f*; (sense) odorat *m*; *vt* sentir; (animal) flairer; ~ **out** flairer, dépister; *vi* sentir; ~ **nice (nasty)** sentir bon (mauvais); ~ **of sth** sentir qch

**smelliness** *n* puanteur *f*

**smelling-salts** *npl* sels *mpl*

**smelly** *adj* malodorant

**¹smelt** *vt* fondre

**²smelt** *n* éperlan *m*

**smelting** *n* fonte *f*

**smile** *n* sourire *m*; **be all** ~**s** être tout souriant; *vi* sourire

**smiling** *adj* souriant; *fig* serein, paisible

**smirch** *n* tache *f*; *vt* tacher, souiller

**smirk** *n* sourire satisfait; *vi* sourire d'un air satisfait

**smite** *vt* frapper; *coll* **be smitten with** être épris de

**smith** *n* forgeron *m*

**smithereens** *npl* **smash to** ~ réduire en miettes, briser en éclats

**smithy** *n* forge *f*

**smock** *n* blouse *f*, sarrau *m*

**smog** *n coll* brouillard enfumé, brouillard industriel

**smoke** *n* fumée *f*; (something to smoke) qch à fumer, cigarette *f*, pipe *f*, cigare *m*; *fig* (plan) **go up in** ~ n'aboutir à rien; **have a** ~ fumer; *vt + vi* fumer; ~ **out** enfumer

**smoke-bomb** *n* bombe *f* fumigène

**smokeless** *adj* sans fumée

**smoker** *n* fumeur -euse; *see* **smoking-compartment**

**smokescreen** *n* rideau *m* de fumée

**smokestack** *n* cheminée *f*

**smokiness** *n* condition fumeuse, atmosphère enfumée

**smoking** *n* émission *f* de fumée; (curing) fumage *m*; action *f* de fumer; **no** ~ défense *f* de fumer

**smoking-compartment, smoker** *n* compartiment *m* fumeurs

**smoking-jacket** *n* veston *m* d'intérieur

**smoky** *adj* fumeux -euse; (room) enfumé

**smooth** *adj* lisse; (level) uni; (soft) doux (*f* douce); (polished) poli; (calm) calme; (manner) doucereux -euse; (person) à l'air doucereux; *vt* lisser; (level) égaliser; (calm) calmer, apaiser; (brow) dérider; ~ **down** lisser; ~ **out** défroisser; ~ **over** aplanir; ~ **the way** aplanir le chemin

**smoothly** *adv* sans inégalités; (steadily) sans secousses; (softly) doucement

**smoothness** *n* (surface) égalité *f*; (softness) douceur *f*; (sea) calme *m*; (person) air doucereux

**smooth-spoken, smooth-tongued** *adj* aux paroles doucereuses

**smoothy** *n coll* personne trop polie

**smother** *vt* étouffer; (cover) recouvrir; *vi* étouffer, suffoquer

**smoulder** *vi* brûler lentement; *fig* couver

**smudge** *n* tache *f*; bavure *f* de plume; *vt* tacher, salir, barbouiller

**smudgy** *adj* taché, souillé, barbouillé

**smug** *adj* satisfait de soi-même; (air) suffisant

**smuggle** *vt* passer en fraude (en contrebande); *vi* faire de la contrebande

**smuggler** *n* contrebandier *m*, fraudeur *m*

**smuggling** *n* contrebande *f*, fraude *f*

**smugly** *adv* d'un air suffisant

**smugness** *n* suffisance *f*

**smut** *n* tache *f* de suie, flocon *m* de suie; *coll* grivoiseries *fpl*

**smutty** *adj* noirci de suie; *fig* grivois

**snack** *n* snack *m*, casse-croûte *m invar*; **have a** ~ casser la croûte, manger sur le pouce

**snack-bar** *n* snack-bar *m*, snack *m*

**snaffle** *vt* chiper

**snag** *n* (hitch) accroc *m*, anicroche *f*; (tree-stump) chicot *m*; **strike a** ~ se heurter à un obstacle; **that's the ~!** voilà le hic!

**snail** *n* escargot *m*, limaçon *m*

**snake** *n* serpent *m*; *fig* individu traître *m*; (game) **~ s and ladders** = le jeu de l'ôie; *vi* serpenter

**snake-charmer** *n* charmeur *m* de serpent

**snaky** *adj* de serpent; (road) serpentant

**snap** *n* coup *m* de dents; (noise) bruit sec; (fingers) claquement *m*; (break) cassure *f*; (fastener) fermoir *m*, agrafe *f*, bouton-pression *m* (*pl* boutons-pression); *coll* (energy) vivacité *f*, énergie *f*; *coll phot* instantané *m*; *cul* petit biscuit croquant; **cold ~** période *f* de temps froid; *adj* imprévu, soudain; **make a ~ decision** prendre une décision sur le coup; *adv* crac; *vt* (bite) happer; (fingers) faire claquer; (break) casser, rompre; *phot* prendre un instantané de; **~ one's fingers at s/o** narguer qn; **~ up a bargain** saisir une occasion; *vi* (break) se casser (net); (fingers, whip) claquer; (dog, etc) chercher à mordre; **~ off** se détacher brusquement; **~ out of it** se grouiller

**snapdragon** *n* bot gueule *f* de loup

**snap-judgement** *n* décision soudaine, jugement *m* rapide

**snappish** *adj* hargneux -euse, irritable

**snappy** *adj* irritable; (lively) vif (*f* vive); *coll* (dress) chic *invar*; **make it ~!** grouillez-vous!

**snapshot** *n* instantané *m*

**snare** *n* piège *m*, collet *m*, lacet *m*; *fig* piège *m*; *fig* **be caught in a ~** être pris au piège; *vt* prendre au collet, attraper

**¹snarl** *n* grognement *m*, grondement *m*; *vi* grogner, gronder

**²snarl** *n* enchevêtrement *m*; (traffic) embouteillage *m*; *vt* enchevêtrer; *mot* **~ ed up** pris dans un embouteillage

**snatch** *n* mouvement vif pour saisir qch; (conversation) bribe *f*; (fragment) morceau *m*; (theft) vol exécuté rapidement; *vt* saisir, empoigner; *sl* kidnapper; **~ sth from s/o** arracher qch à qn

**snatchy** *adj* décousu, interrompu

**snazzy** *adj sl* voyant, *coll* tape-à-l'œil *invar*

**sneak** *n* (mean person) pleutre *m*; *coll* mouchard -e, rapporteur -euse; *vi coll* moucharder; **~ away** partir furtivement; **~ in (out)** entrer (sortir) furtivement

**sneakers** *npl US* chaussures *fpl* en toile à semelles de caoutchouc, souliers *mpl* de gymnastique

**sneaking** *adj* furtif -ive, sournois; **~ feeling** sentiment inavoué

**sneak-thief** *n* chapardeur -euse

**sneer** *n* ricanement *m*, sourire moqueur; *vi* ricaner, sourire d'un air moqueur; **~ at sth** dénigrer qch

**sneeze** *n* éternuement *m*; *vi* éternuer; *coll* **not to be ~ d at** pas à dédaigner

**snick** *n* encoche *f*, petite entaille; *vt* faire une entaille dans

**snicker** *n + vi see* **snigger**

**snide** *adj sl* (mocking) ricanant, narquois; **~ remark** remarque offensante

**sniff** *n* reniflement *m*; *vt + vi* renifler; **not to be ~ ed at** pas à dédaigner

**sniffle** *n* léger reniflement; *vi* renifler légèrement; (cry) pleurnicher

**sniffy** *adj* coll dédaigneux -euse; (sniffing) morveux -euse

**snigger, snicker** *n* léger ricanement; *vi* rire sous cape, ricaner tout bas

**snip** *n* coup *m* de ciseaux; (bit) petit morceau, petit bout; *coll* certitude *f*; *coll* (racing) gagnant sûr; *vt* couper (avec des ciseaux)

**¹snipe** *n orni* bécassine *f*

**²snipe** *vi* **~ at** *coll* canarder

**sniper** *n* tireur caché (embusqué)

**snippet** *n* petit bout, morceau coupé; (short passage) court extrait

**snitch** *vi sl* moucharder

**snivel** *vi* pleurnicher

**snob** *n* snob, poseur -euse

**snobbery** *n* snobisme *m*, morgue *f*

**snobbily** *adv* d'une manière snob

**snobbish** *adj* snob, poseur -euse

**snook** *n* coll pied *m* de nez; **cock a ~ at** s/o faire un pied de nez à qn

**snooker** *n* sorte *f* de jeu de billard

**snoop** *vi* fouiner

**snooper** *n* fouineur -euse

**snooty** *adj sl* prétentieux -ieuse

**snooze** *n* petit somme, *sl* roupillon *m*; *vi* faire un petit somme, *sl* roupiller

**snore** *n* ronflement *m*; *vi* ronfler

**snorkel, schnorkel** *n* (submarine) schnorchel (schnorkel) *m*; (swimmer) masque sous-marin

**snort** *n* reniflement *m*; (horse) ébrouement *m*; *vi* renifler; (horse) s'ébrouer

**snorty** *adj coll* désapprobateur -trice

**snot** *n sl* morve *f*

**snotty** *adj sl* morveux -euse

**snout** *n* museau *m*; (pig) groin *m*

**snow** *n* neige *f*; *sl* (cocaine) cocaïne *f*; **~ flurry** rafale *f* de neige; *vi* neiger; *coll* **be ~ ed under with work** être submergé de travail; **~ ed up** bloqué par la neige

**snowball** *n* boule *f* de neige; *vt* lancer des boules de neige à; *vi* faire boule de neige

**snowblind** *adj* atteint de la cécité des neiges

**snowbound** *adj* bloqué par la neige; (person) retenu par la neige

**snowcapped** *adj* couronné de neige

snowdrift *n* amas *m* (amoncellement *m*) de neige, congère *f*

snowdrop *n* perce-neige *f invar*

snowfall *n* chute *f* de neige; quantité *f* de neige

snow-field *n* champ *m* de neige

snowflake *n* flocon *m* de neige

snowline *n* limite *f* des neiges perpétuelles

snowman *n* bonhomme *m* de neige

snow-plough *n* chasse-neige *m invar*

snow-shoes *npl* raquettes *fpl*

snowstorm *n* tempête *f* de neige

snowy *adj* neigeux -euse

¹snub *n* rebuffade *f*; *vt* infliger un affront à

²snub *adj* retroussé, camus

snub-nosed *adj* au nez retroussé

¹snuff *n* tabac *m* (à priser); take ~ priser

²snuff *vt* moucher, éteindre (avec des mouchettes)

snuff-box *n* tabatière *f*

snuffle *n* reniflement *m*; (speech) ton nasillard; *vi* renifler; (speech) nasiller

snug *n see* snuggery; *adj* (house, etc) confortable; (person) bien, bien au chaud

snuggery *n coll* petite pièce confortable et chaude

snuggle *vi* se pelotonner

snugly *adv* confortablement

snugness *n* confort *m*

so *adv* (thus) de cette façon (manière), ainsi; (to such degree) si, tellement; ~ do I moi aussi; ~ long! à bientôt!; ~ long as tant que; ~ much tant, tellement; ~ nice a person une personne si aimable; ~ saying ce disant; ~ to say (speak) pour ainsi dire; ~ what? et alors?, et puis quoi?; and ~ on et ainsi de suite; fifty or ~ environ cinquante; how ~? comment cela?; if ~ s'il en est ainsi; not ~ pas du tout; not ~ bad pas si mal, pas trop mal; why ~? pourquoi cela?; *conj* donc, ainsi; *conj phr* ~ as to afin de; ~ that de sorte que; (purpose) afin que

soak *n* trempe *f*; *sl* (drunkard) ivrogne *m*, soûlard *m*; *sl* beuverie *f*; *vt* tremper; *coll* (charge heavily) écorcher, faire payer; ~ up absorber; ~ed to the skin trempé jusqu'aux os; *vi* tremper, baigner; *sl* (drink) boire comme un trou; ~ into s'infiltrer dans; ~ through s'infiltrer à travers

soaking *adj* trempé; ~ wet trempé jusqu'aux os

so-and-so *n coll* ceci et cela; Mr (Mrs) Monsieur (Madame) un tel (une telle); old ~ vieux salaud

soap *n* savon *m*; *sl* ~ opera feuilleton mélodramatique et sentimental; cake

of ~ savonnette *f*; household ~ savon *m* de Marseille; *vt* savonner

soap-box *n* caisse *f* à savon; *fig* estrade *f*

soap-bubble *n* bulle *f* de savon

soap-flakes *npl* savon *m* en paillettes

soapiness *n* caractère savonneux; goût *m* (odeur *f*) de savon; *fig pej* onction *f*

soapsuds *npl* eau *f* de savon, eau savonneuse

soapy *adj* savonneux -euse; (person) onctueux -euse

soar *vi* prendre son essor, s'élancer, s'élever; (prices) monter en flèche

sob *n* sanglot *m*; *vi* sangloter; ~ one's heart out pleurer à chaudes larmes

sober *adj* sobre, modéré, posé, calme; (not drunk) pas ivre; (colour) peu voyant; in ~ fact en réalité; *vt* dégriser; *vi* ~ down se dégriser

sober-minded *adj* sérieux -ieuse, pondéré

soberness, sobriety *n* sobriété *f*, tempérance *f*; (calm) tranquillité *f*

sob-stuff *n coll* sentimentalité exagérée

so-called *adj* soi-disant, prétendu

soccer *n* football *m*

sociability *n* sociabilité *f*

sociable *adj* sociable

social *n* réunion amicale; *adj* social; ~ (gathering) soirée *f*; ~ insurance assurances sociales; ~ worker assistant(e) social(e)

socialism *n* socialisme *m*

socialist *n + adj* socialiste

socialistic *adj* socialiste

socialite *n coll* habitué -e du beau monde

socialize *vt* socialiser; *vi* ~ with frayer avec

socially *adv* socialement

society *n* société *f*; compagnie *f*; (fashionable) monde *m*; (high) haute société, beau monde; go into (move in) ~ aller dans le monde

sociological *adj* sociologique

sociologist *n* sociologue

sociology *n* sociologie *f*

¹sock *n* chaussette *f*; (in shoe) semelle intérieure; ankle ~s socquettes *fpl*; *coll fig* pull up one's ~s se dégourdir

²sock *n sl* coup *m*; *vt* donner un coup de poing à

socket *n* (eye) orbite *m*; (tool) douille *f*; (lamp) bec *m*; (candle) bobèche *f*; (tooth) alvéole *f*; *elect* prise *f* de courant

¹sod *n* gazon *m*; (piece of turf) motte *f*

²sod *n vulg* sodomite *m*; *coll* salaud *m*

soda *n* soude *f*; US ~ fountain bar *m* pour rafraîchissements, milk bar *m*

sodality *n eccles* confrérie *f*

soda-water *n* soda *m*, eau *f* de seltz

**sodden** *adj* trempé, détrempé
**sodium** *n* sodium *m*
**sodomite** *n* pédéraste *m*, sodomite *m*
**sodomy** *n* pédérastie *f*, sodomie *f*
**sofa** *n* sofa *m*
**soft** *adj* doux (*f* douce); (to touch) mou
 (*f* molle); (tender) tendre; *coll* (simple)
 simple, niais; ~ **currency** devises *fpl*
 faibles; ~ **drink** boisson non alcoolisée; ~ **job** emploi *m* pépère;
 **become** ~ se ramollir; **have a** ~ **spot**
 **for** avoir un faible pour
**soften** *vt* amollir, ramollir; adoucir; (appease) apaiser; *vi* se ramollir; (feeling)
 s'attendrir
**softener** *n* substance amollissante; *coll*
 pot-de-vin *m* (*pl* pots-de-vin)
**softening** *n* amollissement *m*, ramollissement *m*; adoucissement *m*; (feeling) attendrissement *m*
**soft-hearted** *adj* au cœur tendre
**softly** *adv* doucement; tendrement; mollement
**softness** *n* douceur *f*; mollesse *f*; (stupidity) niaiserie *f*
**soft-pedal** *vt fig* atténuer, diminuer l'importance de; *vi fig* y aller doucement
**soft-sell** *n* promotion (de vente) discrète,
 publicité subtile
**soft-soap** *n* savon noir; *fig* flatterie *f*; *vt*
 *fig* flatter
**soft-spoken** *adj* doucereux -euse
**software** *n* (computer) software *m*,
 logiciel *m*
**softwood** *n* bois *m* tendre
**softy** *n* *coll* (simple-minded) niais -e;
 efféminé
**soggy** *adj* détrempé; (bread) pâteux
 -euse
**¹soil** *n* sol *m*, terre *f*
**²soil** *n* (mark) tache *f*; *vt* souiller, salir
**sojourn** *n* *lit* séjour *m*; lieu *m* de séjour;
 *vi lit* séjourner
**solace** *n* consolation *f*; *vt* consoler
**solar** *adj* solaire; ~ **plexus** plexus *m*
 solaire
**solder** *n* soudure *f*; *vt* souder
**soldering-iron** *n* fer *m* à souder
**soldier** *n* soldat *m*, militaire *m*; **foot** ~
 fantassin *m*; **private** ~ simple soldat
 *m*; **tin** (toy) ~ soldat *m* de plomb; *vi*
 faire le métier de soldat; ~ **on** persévérer, aller de l'avant
**soldiering** *n* métier *m* de soldat
**soldierly** *adj* de soldat
**¹sole** *n* (foot) plante *f*; (shoe) semelle *f*; *vt*
 mettre une semelle à; ressemeler
**²sole** *n* (fish) sole *f*
**³sole** *adj* seul, unique; (legatee) universel
 -elle; ~ **agent** agent exclusif; ~ **right**
 droit exclusif
**solecism** *n* solécisme *m*

**solely** *adv* uniquement
**solemn** *adj* solennel -elle; (person)
 sérieux -ieuse
**solemnity** *n* solennité *f*; (bearing) gravité
 *f*; (ceremony) fête solennelle
**solemnize** *vt* solenniser; (celebrate)
 célébrer
**solemnly** *adv* solennellement; gravement
**solenoid** *n* *elect* solénoïde *m*
**sol-fa** *n* *mus* solfège *m*
**solicit** *vt* solliciter; (prostitute) racoler
**solicitation** *n* sollicitation *f*; (prostitute)
 racolage *m*
**soliciting** *n* (prostitute) racolage *m*
**solicitor** *n* *leg* = avoué *m*
**solicitous** *adj* (eager) désireux -euse;
 (anxious) inquiet -iète
**solicitude** *n* sollicitude *f*, préoccupation
 *f*, souci *m*
**solid** *n* solide *m*; *adj* solide; massif -ive;
 ~ **oak** chêne massif; ~ **state** état *m*
 solide; **become** ~ se solidifier; **six**
 **hours** ~ six heures d'affilée
**solidarity** *n* solidarité *f*
**solidify** *vt* solidifier; *vi* se solidifier, se
 figer
**solidity** *n* solidité *f*
**solidly** *adv* solidement
**soliloquize** *vi* monologuer
**soliloquy** *n* soliloque *m*, monologue *m*
**solitaire** *n* solitaire *m*
**solitary** *n* solitaire; *adj* solitaire; (place)
 retiré
**solitude** *n* solitude *f*, isolement *m*;
 (place) lieu *m* solitaire
**solo** *n* *mus* solo *m*; **violin** ~ solo *m* de
 violon; *adv* solo; *mus* **play** ~ jouer en
 solo
**soloist** *n* soliste
**solstice** *n* solstice *m*
**solubility** *n* solubilité *f*
**soluble** *adj* soluble
**solution** *n* solution *f*
**solve** *vt* résoudre
**solvency** *n* solvabilité *f*
**solvent** *n* dissolvant *m*; *adj* solvable
**somatic** *adj* somatique
**sombre** *adj* sombre, triste, morne
**sombrero** *n* sombrero *m*
**some** *adj* du, de la, de l', des; (unknown)
 quelque, quelconque; ~ **way or other**
 d'une manière ou d'une autre; *coll* he's
 ~ **teacher** c'est un professeur formidable; **I'll do it** ~ **day** je le ferai un de
 ces jours; *coll* **this is** ~ **place** c'est un
 endroit vraiment bien; **we'll be there**
 **for** ~ **time** nous y serons un certain
 temps; *pron pl* certains (*f* certaines),
 quelques-uns (*f* quelques-unes); en; ~
 **of them** certains (quelques-uns) d'entre
 eux (*f* certaines (quelques-unes)

d'entre elles); ~ ... **others (some)** les uns (*f* les unes) ... les autres; **pass me ~ of that cake** passez-moi de ce gâteau; **we have ~** nous en avons; *adv* environ, quelque; *US* **this surprises me ~** cela m'étonne assez

**somebody, someone** *pron* quelqu'un, on; **~ or other** je ne sais qui

**somehow** *adv* d'une manière ou d'une autre; **~, I can't find it** je ne sais pas pourquoi, mais je ne le trouve pas

**someone** *pron see* **somebody**

**somersault** *n* culbute *f*; **do a ~** (accidental) faire une culbute; (gym) faire une cabriole

**something** *n + pron* quelque chose *m*; **~ else** autre chose; **~ good** quelque chose de bon; **~ of a mystery** plus ou moins (un peu) mystérieux; **~ or other** une chose ou une autre, je ne sais quoi; **that's ~, anyway** en tout cas, c'est toujours quelque chose; **there's ~ in that boy** ce garçon a du bon; **there's ~ in what she says** il y a un fond de vérité dans ce qu'elle dit; **there's ~ the matter with her** elle a qch; *adv* quelque peu, un peu; **~ like** un peu semblable à

**sometime** *adj* **my ~ friend** autrefois mon ami; *adv* tôt ou tard; **~ last week** au cours de la semaine passée; **~ soon** bientôt

**sometimes** *adv* quelquefois, parfois; **~ good, ~ bad** tantôt bon (*f* bonne), tantôt mauvais -e

**somewhat** *adv* un peu, quelque peu; **do it ~ like he said** faites-le à peu près comme il a dit

**somewhere** *adv* quelque part; **~ else** ailleurs, autre part; **~ or other** je ne sais où

**somnambulism** *n* somnambulisme *m*

**somnambulist** *n* somnambule *m*

**somnolence** *n* somnolence *f*

**somnolent** *adj* somnolent

**son** *n* fils *m*

**sonar** *n* sonar *m*

**sonata** *n* sonate *f*

**song** *n* chant *m*, chanson *f*; *eccles* cantique *m*; **buy sth for a ~** acheter qch pour un morceau de pain; **make a (great) ~ and dance about sth** faire un foin de tous les diables au sujet de qch

**song-bird** *n* oiseau chanteur

**song-book** *n* recueil *m* de chansons

**songster** *n* chanteur -euse; (bird) oiseau chanteur

**sonic** *adj* sonique; **~ barrier** mur *m* du son; **~ boom** bang *m*

**son-in-law** *n* beau-fils *m* (*pl* beaux-fils)

**sonnet** *n* sonnet *m*

**sonny** *n coll* mon petit, jeune homme *m*

**sonority** *n* sonorité *f*

**sonorous** *adj* sonore

**soon** *adv* bientôt; (early) tôt; (quickly) vite; **~ er or later** tôt ou tard; **as ~ as** aussitôt que; **as ~ as possible** le plus tôt possible; **how ~?** dans combien de temps?; en combien de temps?; **none too ~** juste à temps; **no ~er had they arrived than I left** à peine furent-ils arrivés que je partis; **see you (again) ~!** à bientôt!; **so ~** si tôt; **the ~er the better** le plus tôt sera le mieux; **too ~** trop tôt; **we would ~er die** nous aimerions mieux mourir

**soot** *n* suie *f*; *vt* **~ up** encrasser

**soothe** *vt* calmer, apaiser

**soothing** *adj* calmant, apaisant

**sooty** *adj* couvert de suie, noir de suie

**sop** *n* morceau (de pain) trempé; *fig* concession *f*; *vt* tremper; **~ up** éponger

**sophism** *n* sophisme *m*

**sophist** *n* sophiste

**sophistic(al)** *adj* sophistique

**sophisticated** *adj* blasé; recherché, subtil; (device) compliqué

**sophistication** *n* sophistication *f*; (behaviour) usage *m* du monde

**sophistry** *n* sophistique *f*; sophismes *mpl*

**sophomore** *n US* étudiant -e de deuxième année

**soporific** *n* somnifère *m*; *adj* soporifique

**sopping** *adj* **~ wet** tout trempé

**soppy** *adj* détrempé; *coll* (person) mou (*f* molle); *coll* (sloppily sentimental) larmoyant

**soprano** *n* soprano

**sorbet** *n* sorbet *m*

**sorcerer** *n* sorcier *m*

**sorceress** *n* sorcière *f*

**sorcery** *n* sorcellerie *f*

**sordid** *adj* sordide; (filthy) crasseux -euse; (base) vil, bas (*f* basse)

**sore** *n* plaie *f*, blessure *f*; (ulcer) ulcère *m*; *fig* souvenir *m* pénible; *adj* douloureux -euse, endolori; (sorry) chagriné; *US* (irritated) irrité, vexé; **~ point** sujet *m* pénible; **be in ~ need of sth** avoir grandement besoin de qch; **be like a bear with a ~ head** être d'une humeur massacrante; **have a ~ throat** avoir mal à la gorge; **that's a ~ point** c'est une question délicate

**sorely** *adv* gravement, fortement; (wounded) grièvement

**soreness** *n* endolorissement *m*; (sorrow) chagrin *m*; (grudge) sentiment *m* de rancune

**sorority** *n US* cercle féminin

**sorrel** *n bot* oseille *f*

**sorrow** *n* chagrin *m*, peine *f*, douleur *f*, tristesse *f*; *vi* être affligé; **~ after s/o** pleurer qn

**sorrowful** *adj* affligé, triste; (bringing

sorrow) attristant

**sorry** adj fâché, chagriné, désolé; (poor) misérable, pauvre; **be ~** regretter; **be ~ for** s/o plaindre qn; **look ~ for oneself** avoir l'air malheureux; **so ~!** pardon!

**sort** n sorte f, espèce f, genre m; coll **he's a good ~** c'est un brave type; **I shall do nothing of the ~** je n'en ferai rien; coll **I ~ of** told him to go away je lui ai plus ou moins dit de partir; **it was a meal of ~s** c'était un soi-disant repas; **nothing of the ~** (not at all) pas du tout; (nothing like it) rien de semblable; **out of ~s** peu bien, indisposé; **sth of the ~** qch comme cela; vt trier; classifier; (match) assortir

**sorter** n trieur (f trieuse); (machine) trieuse f

**sortie** n sortie f

**S.O.S.** n S.O.S. m

**so-so** adj médiocre; adv comme ci comme ça

**sot** n ivrogne m, alcoolique

**soufflé** n soufflé m

**sough** n murmure m; vi murmurer

**soul** n âme f; **not a ~** pas un chat; **poor ~!** le (la) pauvre!; **without meeting a living ~** sans rencontrer âme qui vive

**soulful** adj sentimental, expressif -ive

**soulless** adj sans âme; (job) abrutissant

¹**sound** n son m, bruit m; rad **~ engineer** ingénieur m du son; **I don't like the ~ of that** je n'aime pas du tout cela; **not a ~** pas le moindre bruit; vt sonner; (pronounce) prononcer; med ausculter; (praises) chanter; naut sonder; vi résonner, sonner, retentir; (seem) paraître, avoir l'air; sl **~ off** râler

²**sound** n (strait) détroit m

³**sound** adj (healthy) sain; (in good condition) en bon état; (construction) solide; (sleep) profond; (argument) valide, juste; (reliable) sérieux -ieuse; **safe and ~** sain et sauf (f saine et sauve); adv **sleep ~** dormir profondément

**sound-barrier** n mur m du son

**sound-effects** npl bruitage m

**sounding** n résonnement m, retentissement m; med auscultation f; naut + fig sondage m

**sounding-board** n abat-voix m; mus table f d'harmonie

**soundless** adj silencieux -ieuse

**soundly** adv sainement; (sleep) profondément; (reason) judicieusement

**soundness** n bon état; (mind) état sain; solidité f; (judgement) justesse f

**sound-proof** adj insonore; (material) isolant; vt insonoriser

**sound-track** n bande f sonore

**sound-wave** n onde f sonore

¹**soup** n potage m, soupe f; coll **be in the ~** être dans le pétrin; **clear ~** consommé m; **vegetable ~** potage m de légumes, julienne f

²**soup** vt **~ed-up engine** moteur poussé

**soup-kitchen** n soupe f populaire

**soup-plate** n assiette creuse, assiette f à soupe

**soup-spoon** n cuiller f à potage (à soupe)

**soupy** adj qui ressemble à de la soupe; coll sentimental

**sour** adj aigre, acide; (person) revêche; (not ripe) vert; (wine) suret -ette; **that's ~ grapes** c'est pur dépit; **turn sth ~** aigrir qch; vt + vi aigrir

**source** n source f; fig origine f

**sourly** adv avec aigreur; d'un air revêche

**sourness** n aigreur f, acidité f

**souse** n cul marinade f; (drenching) saucée f; vt cul faire mariner; immerger, plonger; vi mariner

**south** n sud m; adj sud invar, du midi, du sud, méridional; adv au sud; vers le sud

**southbound** adj qui va vers le sud

**south-east** n sud-est m; adj du sud-est; adv vers le sud-est

**south-easterly** adj du sud-est

**south-eastern** adj du sud-est

**southerly** adj du sud; qui se dirige vers le sud

**southern** adj du midi, méridional; astron **the Southern Cross** la Croix du Sud

**southerner** n (in France) Méridional -e; habitant -e du sud; US hist sudiste

**southernmost** adj le plus au sud

**southward** adj au sud, du sud

**southwards** adv vers le sud

**south-west** n sud-ouest m; adj du sud-ouest; adv vers le sud-ouest

**south-westerly** adj du sud-ouest

**south-western** adj du sud-ouest

**south-westward** n sud-ouest m

**souvenir** n souvenir m

**sou'wester** n naut vent m du sud-ouest; (hat) chapeau m imperméable

**sovereign** n + adj souverain -e

**sovereignty** n souveraineté f

**Soviet** n soviet m; adj soviétique; **~ Union** Union f Soviétique

¹**sow** vt (seed, rumour) semer; (ground) ensemencer

²**sow** n truie f

**sower** n semeur -euse

**soya** n soja m, soya m

**sozzled** adj coll ivre

**spa** n ville f d'eau, station thermale

**space** n espace m; (room) place f; (extent) étendue f; (between two things) intervalle m, écartement m;

(empty) vide *m*; (on form) case *f*; *adj* spatial; *vt* ~ (out) espacer

**spacecraft** *n* astronef *m*, navire spatial

**space-flight** *n* vol spatial, voyage spatial

**spaceman** *n* cosmonaute *m*, astronaute *m*

**space-probe** *n* sonde *f* interplanétaire

**space-rocket** *n* fusée *f* interplanétaire

**space-saving** *adj* compact

**spaceship** *n* astronef *m*, vaisseau spatial

**space-shuttle** *n* navette spatiale

**space-suit** *n* scaphandre *m* (d'astronaute)

**space-travel** *n* navigation *f* interplanétaire

**spacing** *n* espacement *m*; (typing) double ~ double interligne *m*; single ~ interligne *m* simple

**spacious** *adj* spacieux -ieuse, vaste

¹**spade** *n* bêche *f*; (small) pelle *f*; *sl* nègre *m*, négresse *f*

²**spade** *n* (cards) pique *m*

**spadeful** *n* pelletée *f*

**spade-work** *n fig* travaux *mpl* préliminaires

**spaghetti** *n* spaghetti *mpl*

**Spain** *n* Espagne *f*

**span** *n* (hand) empan *m*; (wing) envergure *f*; (between supports) portée *f*; (arch) largeur *f*; (bridge) travée *f*; (short time) courte durée; *vt* (bridge) franchir, enjamber; mesurer à l'empan

**spangle** *n* paillette *f*; *vt* pailleter

**Spaniard** *n* Espagnol -e

**spaniel** *n* épagneul *m*

**Spanish** *n* (language) espagnol *m*; *adj* espagnol

**spank** *vt* fesser

¹**spanking** *n* fessée *f*

²**spanking** *adj coll* go at a ~ pace filer à toute allure

**spanner** *n* clef *f* (à écrous); adjustable ~ clef anglaise, clef à molette; *coll* throw a ~ in the works mettre le bâton dans les roues

¹**spar** *n naut* espar *m*

²**spar** *vi* (boxing) faire un assaut de boxe amical (d'entraînement)

**spare** *n mech* pièce *f* de rechange; *adj* (thin) maigre, sec (*f* sèche); (in reserve) de réserve; (left over) de reste; ~ parts (~s) pièces *f* de rechange; ~ room chambre *f* d'ami; ~ time loisir *m*, temps *m* disponible; *mot* ~ tyre pneu *m* de rechange; *mot* ~ wheel roue *f* de secours; *vt* épargner, ménager; (do without) se passer de; (lend, give) prêter, donner; (show mercy to) faire grâce à; (respect) respecter; ~ no pains ne pas ménager sa peine; ~ s/o a few moments accorder quelques moments (d'entretien) à qn; have enough to ~

avoir plus qu'il n'en faut; **have nothing to** ~ n'avoir que le strict nécessaire; **have no time to** ~ n'avoir pas de temps libre; **I can** ~ **him** je n'ai pas besoin de lui

**spare-rib** *n* côte découverte de porc

**sparing** *adj* économe, ménager -ère

¹**spark** *n* étincelle *f*; *fig* (trace) trace *f*, trait *m*; *fig* (intelligence) intelligence *f*, vivacité *f*; *fig* ~**s will fly** il y aura du grabuge; *vt* ~ **off** déclencher; *vi* émettre des étincelles

²**spark** *n* élégant *m*; **gay** ~ joyeux luron

**sparking-plug** *n* (*US* **spark plug**) *mot* bougie *f*

**sparkle** *n* étincellement *m*, pétillement *m*; *fig* éclat *m*; *vi* étinceler, scintiller; (wine) pétiller; *fig* briller

**sparkler** *n sl* diamant *m*

**sparklet** *n* petite étincelle; (soda) sparklet *m*

**sparkling** *n* étincellement *m*, pétillement *m*; *adj* étincelant; (wine) mousseux -euse; *fig* brillant; (drinks) gazeux -euse

**sparring** *n* boxe amicale

**sparrow** *n* moineau *m*

**sparrow-hawk** *n* épervier *m*

**sparse** *adj* épars, clairsemé

**spartan** *adj fig* spartiate; *fig* frugal

**spasm** *n* accès *m*, spasme *m*

**spasmodic** *adj* spasmodique, convulsif -ive

**spastic** *n med* handicapé -e moteur (*pl* handicapé(e)s moteur); *adj med* spasmodique; (person) handicapé -e moteur (*pl* handicapé(e)s moteur)

**spate** *n* crue *f*

**spatial** *adj* spatial

**spats** *npl* guêtres *fpl*

**spatter** *vt* éclabousser

**spatula** *n* spatule *f*

**spawn** *n* (fish) frai *m*; (mushroom) blanc *m* (de champignon); *coll pej* (offspring) progéniture *f*; *vi* (fish) frayer; (multiply) se multiplier

**spay** *vt vet* châtrer

**speak** *vt* (say) dire; (express) exprimer; (language) parler; *vi* parler; (at meeting) prendre la parole; (make speech) faire un discours; ~ **ill of** dire du mal de; ~**ing for myself** pour ma part; ~ **out** parler à haute voix; parler franchement; ~ **up** parler plus haut; ~ **up for** s/o prendre la défense de qn, parler en faveur de qn; ~ **well for** faire honneur à; **English spoken** (ici) on parle anglais; **nothing to** ~ **of** rien, peu de chose; **without** ~**ing** sans rien dire

**speak-easy** *n US hist* débit *m* de boisson clandestin

**speaker** *n* parleur -euse; (public) orateur *m*; (conversation) interlocuteur

# speaking

-trice; (parliament) président m; (loudspeaker) haut-parleur m

**speaking** adj expressif -ive, parlant, vivant; **they are not on ~ terms** ils ne se parlent pas

**speaking-tube** n tuyau m acoustique

**spear** n lance f, javelot m; vt percer d'un coup de lance; (fish) prendre à la foëne

**spearhead** n fer m de lance; vt mil être le fer de lance de

**spearmint** n menthe verte

**special** adj spécial, particulier -ière; ~ **case** cas m d'espèce; ~ **correspondent** envoyé -e spécial -e; ~ **friend** ami -e intime; ~ **price** prix m de faveur; **take ~ care over sth** apporter des soins particuliers à qch

**specialist** n spécialiste

**speciality** n spécialité f

**specialization** n spécialisation f

**specialize** vt spécialiser; vi se spécialiser

**specially** adv spécialement, surtout, particulièrement

**specialty** n see **speciality**; leg contrat formel sous seing privé

**species** n espèce f, genre m

**specific** adj spécifique; (affirmation) précis, explicite

**specification** n spécification f; description f; devis descriptif

**specify** vt spécifier, préciser, déterminer

**specimen** n spécimen m, exemple m; (sample) échantillon m; coll **he's a queer ~** c'est un drôle de type

**specious** adj spécieux -ieuse, trompeur -euse

**speck** n petite tache, point m; (dust) grain m; fig brin m

**speckled** adj tacheté, moucheté

**specs** npl coll lunettes fpl

**spectacle** n spectacle m; **make a ~ of oneself** se donner en spectacle; ~**s** lunettes fpl

**spectacle-case** n étui m à lunettes

**spectacled** adj à lunettes

**spectacular** adj spectaculaire, impressionnant

**spectator** n spectateur -trice, assistant -e

**spectral** adj spectral

**spectre** n spectre m, fantôme m

**spectrum** n spectre m

**speculate** vi spéculer; méditer

**speculation** n spéculation f; méditation f, conjecture f

**speculative** adj spéculatif -ive, contemplatif -ive

**speculator** n spéculateur -trice

**speech** n (faculty) parole f; (public) discours m; (language) langue f; **make a ~** prononcer (faire) un discours; **parts of ~** parties fpl du discours

**speech-day** n (school) distribution f des

prix

**speechify** vi pérorer, discourir

**speechless** adj (dumb) incapable de parler; (from surprise, etc) interdit, muet -ette

**speech-therapy** n orthophonie f

**speech-training** n cours m de diction

¹**speed** n vitesse f, rapidité f; (haste) hâte f; **at full ~** à toute vitesse; (running) à toutes jambes; **maximum ~** vitesse f limite; mot plafond m; ~ (guest) souhaiter bon voyage à; vi se hâter; faire de la vitesse; ~ **up** accélérer, aller plus vite

²**speed** n ar chance f; succès m; **wish s/o god (good) ~** souhaiter bonne chance à qn; vt obs **God ~ you** que Dieu vous fasse prospérer

**speedboat** n canot m automobile

**speeder** n contrôleur m de vitesse; mot (person) chauffard m

**speedily** adv rapidement, promptement

**speediness** n rapidité f, promptitude f

**speeding** n mot excès m de vitesse

**speed-limit** n limite f de vitesse, vitesse maximale

**speedometer** n mot compteur m, indicateur m de vitesse

**speedway** n autodrome m, piste f d'autodrome; (motorway) autoroute f

**speedy** adj rapide, prompt

**speleologist** n spéléologue

¹**spell** n (words) formule f magique; (magic power) charme m; **cast a ~ on (over) s/o** jeter un sort sur qn

²**spell** n période f; (work) tour m

³**spell** vt (orally) épeler; (writing) orthographier; (signify) signifier; ~ **badly** faire des (beaucoup de) fautes d'orthographe; ~ **out sth** déchiffrer qch; fig expliquer qch; **learn to ~** apprendre l'orthographe

**spellbound** adj ensorcelé, magnétisé

**speller** n be a good (bad) ~ savoir (ne pas savoir) l'orthographe

**spelling** n (written) orthographe f; ~ **mistake** faute f d'orthographe

**spelling-bee** n concours m d'orthographe

**spelling-book** n alphabet m

**spend** vt (money) dépenser; (time) passer; coll ~ **a penny** aller au petit coin, aller faire pipi; ~ **oneself** s'épuiser; ~ **time on sth** consacrer du temps à qch

**spender** n big ~ personne f qui dépense beaucoup

**spendthrift** n dépensier -ière, gaspilleur -euse; adj dépensier -ière, prodigue

**spent** adj (exhausted) épuisé; (storm) calmé; ~ **bullet** balle morte

**sperm** n sperme m

708

**sperm-whale** *n* cachalot *m*

**spew** *vt* + *vi* vomir

**sphere** *n* sphère *f*; *fig* domaine *m*, champ *m*; **limited** ~ cadre restreint

**spherical** *adj* sphérique

**sphincter** *n anat* sphincter *m*

**sphinx** *n* sphinx *m*

**spice** *n* épice *f*, aromate *m*; (tiny bit) soupçon *m*; *vt* épicer

**spicily** *adv* d'une manière piquante

**spiciness** *n* goût piquant; *fig* piquant *m*

**spick-and-span** *adj* propre comme un sou neuf; (person) tiré à quatre épingles

**spicy** *adj* épicé; (fragrant) parfumé; (story) piquant, salé

**spider** *n* araignée *f*; ~ **'s web** toile *f* d'araignée

**spider-crab** *n* araignée *f* de mer

**spidery** *adj* qui ressemble à une araignée; ~ **handwriting** pattes *fpl* de mouches

**spiel** *n coll* boniment *m*

**spigot** *n* fausset *m*

**spike** *n* (sharp point) pointe *f*; (nail) clou *m* à large tête; *bot* épi *m*; *vt* clouer; armer de pointes; (gun) enclouer; *fig* ~ **s/o's guns** déjouer les menées de qn

**spiked** *adj* garni de pointes

**spiky** *adj* à pointe(s) aiguë(s)

¹**spill** *n* culbute *f*, chute *f*; *vt* répandre; (overturn) renverser; *coll* ~ **the beans** (betray secret) vendre la mèche; *vi* se répandre

²**spill** *n* allumette *f* de papier, allume-feu *m invar* en papier roulé

**spin** *n* tournoiement *m*, mouvement *m* de rotation; *aer* vrille *f*; (excursion) promenade *f*, randonnée *f*; *coll* **get into a flat** ~ ne pas savoir où donner de la tête; *vt* (wool) filer; faire tourner; (top) faire aller; (tale) débiter; ~ **a coin** jouer à pile ou face; ~ **out** faire traîner en longueur; *vi* tourner; *aer* descendre en vrille; ~ **along** filer, rouler; ~ **round** pivoter; se retourner vivement; **my head is** ~ **ning** la tête me tourne; **send s/o** ~ **ning** envoyer rouler qn

**spinach** *n* épinards *mpl*

**spinal** *adj* spinal; ~ **column** colonne vertébrale; ~ **cord** cordon *m* médullaire

**spindle** *n* fuseau *m*; *mech* axe *m*, arbre *m*; **axle** ~ fusée *f* d'essieu

**spindle-shanks** *npl* jambes *fpl* de fuseau

**spindly** *adj* très maigre

**spin-drier** *n* essoreuse *f*

**spine** *n anat* épine dorsale; (prickle) épine *f*, piquant *m*

**spineless** *adj fig pej* flasque, mou (*f* molle)

**spinner** *n* (person) fileur -euse; (machine) machine *f* à filer

**spinney, spinny** *n* bosquet *m*, petit bois

**spinning** *n* (thread) filage *m*; (movement) tournoiement *m*, mouvement *m* de rotation

**spinning-wheel** *n* rouet *m*

**spinster** *n* fille non mariée, célibataire *f*; *pej* vieille fille

**spiny** *adj* épineux -euse, couvert d'épines

**spiral** *n* spirale *f*; *aer* montée *f* en spirale; descente *f* en spirale; *adj* spiral

**spirally** *adv* en spirale

**spire** *n* flèche *f*

**spirit** *n* esprit *m*; (soul) âme *f*; (alcohol) alcool *m*, spiritueux *m*; (vivacity) entrain *m*, élan *m*, ardeur *f*; (courage) courage *m*; ~ **s** spiritueux *mpl*; **enter into the** ~ **of sth** entrer de bon cœur dans la partie; **in good** ~ **s** de bonne humeur; **in high** ~ **s** en train; **in low** ~ **s** abattu; **man of** ~ homme *m* de caractère; **recover one's** ~ **s** reprendre courage; **surgical** ~ alcool *m* à 90°; **take sth in the wrong** ~ prendre qch en mauvaise part; *vt* ~ **away** faire disparaître (comme par enchantement)

**spirited** *adj* vif (*f* vive), animé

**spirit-lamp** *n* lampe *f* à alcool; (for heating) réchaud *m* à alcool

**spiritless** *adj* sans vie; abattu; sans courage

**spirit-level** *n* niveau *m* à bulle d'air

**spiritual** *adj* spirituel -elle

**spiritualism** *n* spiritisme *m*; *philos* spiritualisme *m*

**spiritualist** *n* spirite; *philos* spiritualiste

**spirituality** *n* spiritualité *f*

**spiritualize** *vt* spiritualiser

**spiritually** *adv* spirituellement

¹**spit** *n* broche *f*; (modern) rôtissoire *f*; *geog* pointe *f*; *vt* embrocher

²**spit** *n* (spittle) salive *f*, crachat *m*; *coll* **he's the dead** ~ **of his father** c'est son père tout craché; *vt* + *vi* cracher; **it is** ~ **ting (with rain)** il tombe quelques gouttes

**spite** *n* dépit *m*, rancune *f*; (nastiness) méchanceté *f*; **out of** ~ par dépit; par méchanceté; *prep phr* **in** ~ **of** en dépit de, malgré; *vt* contrarier, vexer

**spiteful** *adj* rancunier -ière, vindicatif -ive; méchant

**spitfire** *n* coléreux -euse, rageur -euse

**spittle** *n* salive *f*, crachat *m*

**spittoon** *n* crachoir *m*

**splash** *n* éclaboussement *m*; (mud) éclaboussure *f*; (waves) clapotis *m*; (colour) tache *f*; ~ **headline** grosse manchette; *fig* **make a** ~ faire sensation; *vt* éclabousser; ~ **money about** jeter son argent par les fenêtres; *vi* rejaillir en éclaboussures; (water) clapoter; (child) ~ **about in the water**

barboter dans l'eau; ~ **up** gicler
**splash-down** n amerrissage m
**splay** vt archi ébraser, épanouir; carp couper en biseau; (dislocate) démettre
**spleen** n anat rate f; (bad temper) mauvaise humeur; obs (melancholy) spleen m
**splendid** adj splendide, magnifique; ~! à la bonne heure!
**splendour** n splendeur f, éclat m
**splenetic** adj coléreux -euse; anat splénique
**splice** n épissure f; vt épisser; cin réparer; coll naut ~ **the main-brace** donner une tournée de rhum supplémentaire; coll get ~ **d** se marier
**splint** n éclisse f; **put in** ~ **s** éclisser; vt surg éclisser
**splinter** n (wood, shell) éclat m; (bone) esquille f; (under skin) écharde f; ~ **group** groupe m fractionnaire; vt briser en éclats; vi éclater, voler en éclats
**splinter-proof** adj à l'épreuve des éclats
**splintery** adj plein d'éclats; qui vole en éclats facilement
**split** n fente f, fissure f; (division) division f; (secession) rupture f, scission f; (skin) gerçure f; coll demi-bouteille f; **do the** ~ **s** faire le grand écart; vt fendre; (divide) diviser; (share) partager; (cloth) déchirer; ~ **hairs** couper les cheveux en quatre; ~ **one's sides with laughter** se tordre de rire; ~ **the atom** désintégrer l'atome; vi se fendre; (skin) se gercer; coll moucharder; ~ **in two** se casser en deux; coll ~ **on** s/o dénoncer qn; ~ **up** se fractionner; **my head is** ~ **ting** j'ai un mal de tête terrible
**split-second** adj ultra-rapide; ultra-précis
**splodge, splotch** n tache f
**splurge** n coll épate f; vi coll faire de l'épate; (spend wildly) faire des dépenses extravagantes
**splutter** n bredouillement m; crachement m; vt + vi bredouiller, bafouiller; vi (emit saliva) lancer de la salive en parlant; coll envoyer des postillons
**spoil** vt gâter; (damage) abîmer, endommager; (despoil) dépouiller, piller; ~ s/o's **appetite** couper l'appétit à qn; vi se gâter, s'abîmer; (foodstuffs) s'avarier; coll **be** ~ **ing for a fight** avoir très envie de se battre
**spoils** npl butin m
**spoil-sport** n trouble-fête invar, rabat-joie m invar
**spoke** n rayon m; fig **put a** ~ **in** s/o's **wheel** mettre des bâtons dans les roues à qn
**spokesman** n porte-parole m invar

**spoliation** n spoliation f, dépouillement m
**sponge** n éponge f; fig **throw up the** ~ abandonner, s'avouer vaincu; vt éponger; nettoyer avec une éponge; ~ **down** éponger; ~ **out** enlever à l'éponge; vi coll ~ **on (off)** s/o vivre aux crochets de qn
**sponge-cake** n = biscuit m de Savoie
**sponger** n coll pique-assiette m invar, parasite m
**sponginess** n spongiosité f
**spongy** adj spongieux -ieuse
**sponsor** n garant -e, caution f; (baptism) parrain m, marraine f; theat + rad + TV commanditaire m; vt répondre pour, parrainer; (programme) offrir
**sponsorship** n parrainage m
**spontaneity** n spontanéité f
**spontaneous** adj spontané
**spoof** n coll mystification f, blague f; adj coll faux (f fausse); vt coll mystifier, duper
**spook** n coll fantôme m, revenant m
**spooky** adj coll hanté
**spool** n bobine f
**spoon** n cuiller f, cuillère f; **dessert-**~ cuiller f à dessert; **table-**~ cuiller f à soupe; **tea-**~ petite cuiller; vt ~ **up** manger avec la cuiller; vi sl se faire des mamours
**spoon-feed** vt nourrir à la cuiller; fig mâcher la besogne à
**spoonful** n cuillerée f
**spoor** n piste f, trace f; foulées fpl
**sporadic** adj sporadique
**spore** n spore f
**sport** n sport m; (play) jeu m, divertissement m; (jesting) plaisanterie f, moquerie f; biol variété anormale; **be a** ~! sois chic! invar; coll **be a good** ~ (games) être beau joueur (f belle joueuse); (character) être un chic type (f une chic fille); **be the** ~ **of fortune** être le jouet de la fortune; **for** ~ par plaisanterie; **make** ~ **of** se moquer de; mot ~ **s model** modèle m grand sport; vt coll arborer, exhiber, étaler; vi jouer, se divertir; biol produire une variété anormale
**sportily** adv d'une façon sportive
**sportiness** n caractère sportif
**sporting** adj de sport; (gun) de chasse; (attitude) sportif -ive, sport invar; **a** ~ **chance** une chance raisonnable
**sportive** adj badin, enjoué
**sports-car** n voiture f de sport
**sports-coat, sports-jacket** n veston m sport
**sports-day** n fête sportive
**sports-jacket** n see sports-coat
**sportsman** n amateur m de sport; fig beau joueur

**sportsmanship** n qualités sportives; (behaviour) conduite sportive, esprit sportif

**sportswoman** n (femme) sportive f

**sporty** adj sportif -ive; (decent) chic invar; (colours) voyant

**spot** n (stain) tache f; (place) endroit m, lieu m; (dress) pois m; (rain) goutte f; (on skin) bouton m; **a ~ of** un petit peu de; **a ~ of trouble** un petit ennui; **beauty ~** (on face) grain m de beauté; (place) site m remarquable; coll **be in a ~** être dans une situation dangereuse; **be on the ~** être là, être sur place; **have a soft ~ for** s/o avoir un faible pour qn; coll **knock ~s off** s/o battre qn à plate couture; **pay ~ cash** payer (argent) comptant; **put one's finger on a weak ~** mettre le doigt sur un point faible; vt tacher, tacheter; (notice) apercevoir, repérer; (recognize) reconnaître; **~ the winner** prédire le gagnant

**spot-check** n contrôle-surprise m invar

**spotless** adj sans tache

**spotlight** n projecteur m; vt diriger les projecteurs sur

**spotted** adj tacheté, moucheté

**spotter** n observateur m

**spotty** adj couvert de boutons; (spotted) tacheté

**spouse** n époux m (f épouse)

**spout** n (rain-water) tuyau m de décharge, gargouille f; (kettle, etc) bec m; sl **down the ~** perdu; sl **up the ~** (pawned) chez ma tante; (pregnant) enceinte; vt faire jaillir; coll (speech) dégoiser, déclamer; vi jaillir; coll (speech) pérorer

**sprain** n entorse f, foulure f; vt **~ one's ankle** se donner une entorse; **~ one's wrist** se fouler le poignet

**sprat** n sprat m

**sprawl** vi s'étendre, s'étaler

¹**spray** n poussière f d'eau, embrun m; (perfume, etc) jet pulvérisé; (device) vaporisateur m; coup m de vaporisateur; vt pulvériser, vaporiser; (garden) arroser; (sprinkle) asperger; (plant, etc) passer au vaporisateur

²**spray** n (branch) brin m, brindille f; (jewel) aigrette f

**sprayer** n vaporisateur m, pulvérisateur m

**spray-gun** n pistolet m (à peinture)

**spread** n étendue f; (wings) envergure f; (dissemination) diffusion f, propagation f; coll (feast) régal m, festin m; **cheese ~** fromage m à tartiner; **double-page ~** annonce f sur deux pages; **middle-aged ~** embonpoint m qui vient avec l'âge; vt étendre; (net) tendre; (news, etc) répandre, faire circuler; (sails) déployer; (tablecloth) mettre; **~ out** étaler; **~ over** (stagger) échelonner; vi s'étendre, s'étaler; (news) se répandre; (disease) se propager; **~ to** gagner

**spread-eagle** vt étaler; vi s'étaler, se vautrer

**spreader** n étendeur -euse; (news, ideas) propagateur -trice; (rumours) colporteur -euse

**spree** n **go on a ~** faire la noce, faire la bombe; **go on a spending ~** dépenser des sommes folles (à faire des achats)

**sprig** n brin m, brindille f

**sprightly** adj enjoué, éveillé

**spring** n (season) printemps m; (water) source f; (jump) saut m, bond m; (steel) ressort m; (elasticity) élasticité f; mot **~s** suspension f; vt (trap) faire jouer; (explosive) faire sauter; (oar) faire craquer; US sl faire relâcher, lâcher; naut **~ a leak** commencer à faire eau; **~ a question on** s/o poser une question à qn de façon inattendue; vi (jump) sauter, bondir; (water) jaillir; (grow) pousser; **~ from** provenir de; (be descended from) descendre de; **~ up** (storm) s'élever; (plant) pousser

**springboard** n tremplin m

**springbok** n springbok m

**spring-clean** n nettoyage m à fond au printemps; vt + vi nettoyer à fond au printemps

**spring-cleaning** n grand nettoyage fait au printemps

**springer** n sauteur -euse; (hunting) springer m

**springiness** n élasticité f

**spring-like** adj printanier -ière

**spring-tide** n grande marée

**springtime** n printemps m

**springy** adj élastique

**sprinkle** vt répandre, jeter; (with water) asperger, arroser; (powder) saupoudrer

**sprinkler** n arroseur automatique rotatif, arroseuse f à jet tournant; eccles goupillon m

**sprinkling** n arrosage m, saupoudrage m; (salt, etc) pincée f; (rain) quelques gouttes fpl

**sprint** n sprint m; vi sprinter, faire une course de vitesse

**sprinter** n sprinter m

**sprite** n lutin m, farfadet m

**sprocket** n dent f; **~ wheel** pignon m de chaîne

**sprout** n pousse f, rejeton m; **(Brussels) ~s** choux mpl de Bruxelles; vt pousser; vi pousser, bourgeonner

¹**spruce** n bot sapin m

²**spruce** adj pimpant, tiré à quatre

épingles; vt ~ **oneself up** se pomponner

**spud** n petite bêche; coll pomme f de terre, coll patate f

**spud-bashing** n coll mil corvée f de patates

**spunk** n (tinder) amadou m; coll fig courage m; vulg semence f

**spur** n éperon m; (cock) ergot m; (stimulus) stimulant m, aiguillon m; geog contrefort m, éperon m; **on the ~ of the moment** sous l'impulsion du moment; vt éperonner; fig ~ **on** aiguillonner, stimuler

**spurious** adj faux (f fausse), contrefait

**spurn** vt dédaigner, repousser, rejeter

**spur-road** n bretelle f

**spurt** n jaillissement m, jet m; effort soudain; (race) démarrage m; vi jaillir; ~ **out** gicler

**sputnik** n spoutnik m

**sputter** vt + vi bredouiller; vi (flame) grésiller

**sputum** n med crachat m

**spy** n espion -ionne; vt apercevoir; détecter; ~ **out** explorer; vi espionner; ~ **on** s/o espionner qn

**spy-glass** n longue-vue f (pl longues-vues)

**spy-hole** n (door) judas m

**squabble** n querelle f, prise f de bec; vi se quereller, se chamailler

**squabbler** n chamailleur -euse

**squad** n escouade f; (team) équipe f, groupe m; **firing ~** peloton m d'exécution; **flying ~** brigade f mobile

**squadron** n escadron m; aer escadrille f; naut escadre f

**squadron-leader** n mil commandant m d'escadron; aer chef m d'escadrille

**squalid** adj misérable, sordide, minable

**squall** n (wind) bourrasque f, rafale f; (cry) cri m rauque; fig dispute f, coll grabuge m; vi crier, brailler

**squally** adj à rafales

**squalor** n misère f; aspect m sordide

**squander** vt gaspiller, dilapider

**square** n carré m; (town) place f, square m; (chessboard) case f; (instrument) équerre f; coll personne f vieux jeu; **set-~** équerre f à dessin; **silk ~** foulard m; adj carré; (honest) honnête; coll vieux jeu; ~ **meal** repas copieux; **be ~ with** s/o être quitte envers qn; **get things ~** mettre les choses en ordre; adv à angles droits; vt (stone, wood) équarrir; math carrer; (account) régler; coll (bribe) graisser la patte à, suborner; vi (agree) s'accorder, cadrer; ~ **up** se mettre en posture de combat

**square-bashing** n coll mil exercice m

**squarely** adv carrément; honnêtement

**squareness** n forme carrée; honnêteté f

**squash** n écrasement m; (crowd) cohue f, presse f; (game) squash m; **lemon ~** citronnade f; **orange ~** orangeade f; vt écraser; coll remettre à sa place

**squash-court** n terrain m de squash

**squash-rackets** n squash m

**squashy** adj mou (f molle) et humide

**squat** adj trapu; vi s'accroupir; (game) se tapir; (in premises) occuper une maison (un logement) sans autorisation, squatter

**squatter** n squatter m

**squaw** n femme f peau-rouge

**squawk** n cri m rauque; vi pousser des cris rauques

**squeak** n petit cri aigu; (machine) grincement m; vi pousser des petits cris aigus; (machine) grincer; sl moucharder

**squeaker** n sl mouchard -e

**squeaky** adj qui crie; (machine) qui grince

**squeal** n cri perçant; vi pousser des cris perçants; coll (protest) protester; sl (inform) trahir ses complices

**squealer** n criard -e; sl dénonciateur -trice

**squeamish** adj sujet -ette aux nausées; (sensitive) délicat, difficile

**squeeze** n étreinte f, compression f; (hand) serrement m; (crowd) cohue f; coll econ resserrement m du crédit; vt presser; (hand) serrer; (extort) extorquer; ~ **into** faire entrer dans; ~ **oneself into (through)** se faufiler dans (à travers); ~ **out** extorquer, arracher; (exclude) évincer; vi ~ **into** s'introduire dans; ~ **up** se serrer

**squelch** n giclement m, gargouillement m; vt écraser (en faisant gicler); vi (person) patauger; (thing) gargouiller

**squib** n pétard m; fig satire f

**squid** n calmar m, encornet m

**squiggle** n ligne ondulante; écriture f illisible; fioriture f; (after signature) parafe m

**squiggly** adj (writing) illisible; ondulant

**squint** n strabisme m, louchement m; coll coup m d'œil; vi loucher; ~ **at sth** regarder qch de côté

**squint-eyed** adj strabique

**squire** n (landowner) propriétaire terrien; hist hobereau m; (of knight) écuyer m

**squirm** vi se tordre, se tortiller

**squirrel** n écureuil m

**squirt** n (implement) seringue f; (of liquid) jet m; coll little ~ gringalet m; vt lancer en jet, faire jaillir; vi gicler, jaillir

**squit** n sl nabot m, avorton m

**stab** n coup m de poignard (de couteau); fig ~ **in the back** attaque déloyale; coll

have a ~ at sth tenter qch; *vt* donner un coup de couteau à, poignarder; *vi* (pain) lanciner
**stability** *n* stabilité *f*
**stabilization** *n* stabilisation *f*
**stabilize** *vt* stabiliser
**stabilizer** *n* stabilisateur *m*
¹**stable** *n* écurie *f*; *vt* loger
²**stable** *adj* stable, fixe, solide; (person) constant
**stable-boy** *n* valet *m* d'écurie, palefrenier *m*
**stably** *adv* d'une manière stable
**staccato** *adj* haché, saccadé
**stack** *n* pile *f*, tas *m*; (hay) meule *f*; (chimney) souche *f*, cheminée *f* d'usine; *coll* ~s of beaucoup de; *vt* empiler, entasser; (hay) mettre en meule; ~ the cards tricher aux cartes
**stadium** *n* stade *m*
**staff** *n* (stick) bâton *m*; *mil* état-major *m* (*pl* états-majors); (personnel) personnel *m*; *pl* soutien *m*; *mus* portée *f*; *vt* fournir de (pourvoir en) personnel, recruter du personnel pour
**staff-officer** *n* officier *m* d'état-major
**stag** *n* cerf *m*; ~ party réunion *f* entre hommes
**stag-beetle** *n* cerf-volant *m* (*pl* cerfs-volants)
**stage** *n* (platform) estrade *f*, échafaudage *m*; *theat* scène *f*, plateau *m*; (journey, etc) étape *f*; (step) phase *f*; (period) période *f*, stade *m*; (scene) scène *f*; **at this** ~ à ce point; **fare** ~ section *f*; **go on the** ~ se faire acteur -trice; *vt* (play) monter; (arrange) organiser
**stage-coach** *n* diligence *f*
**stagecraft** *n* technique *f* de la scène
**stage-door** *n* entrée *f* des artistes
**stage-effect** *n* effet *m* scénique
**stage-fright** *n* trac *m*
**stage-hand** *n* machiniste *m*
**stage-manage** *vt theat* faire la régie de; *fig* organiser
**stage-manager** *n* régisseur *m*
**stage-struck** *adj* entiché du théâtre
**stage-whisper** *n* aparté *m*
**stagger** *n* allure chancelante; *vt* consterner, bouleverser; (holidays) étaler, échelonner; (rivets) décaler; *vi* chanceler, tituber
**staggering** *adj* chancelant; *fig* renversant
**stagnant** *adj* stagnant
**stagnate** *vi* être stagnant; (water) croupir
**stagnation** *n* stagnation *f*
**stagy** *adj* théâtral; peu sincère
**staid** *adj* posé, sérieux -ieuse
**stain** *n* tache *f*; (colour) couleur *f*; ~ **remover** détachant *m*; *vt* tacher; *fig* souiller; (dye) teindre; (glass) peindre;

(wood) teinter; *vi* se tacher
**stained-glass** *n* ~ **window** vitrail *m*
**stainless** *adj* (steel) inoxydable; sans tache
**stair** *n* marche *f*, degré *m*
**staircase** *n* escalier *m*; **moving** ~ escalier roulant, escalator *m*
**stair-rod** *n* tringle *f* d'escalier
**stairway** *n* escalier *m*
**stake** *n* pieu *m*, poteau *m*; *hort* tuteur *m*; (gambling) mise *f*, enjeu *m*; (interest) intérêt *m*; **at** ~ en jeu; **be burnt at the** ~ mourir sur le bûcher; **his future is at** ~ il y va de son avenir; *vt* garnir de pieux; *hort* mettre un tuteur à; (gamble) jouer, mettre en jeu; (risk) hasarder; ~ **out** jalonner
**stake-holder** *n* celui qui tient les enjeux
**stalactite** *n* stalactite *f*
**stalagmite** *n* stalagmite *f*
**stale** *adj* (old) vieux (*f* vieille); (bread) rassis; (food) pas frais (*f* fraîche); (air) vicié; (tired) fatigué; *vi* (beer) s'éventer; *fig* perdre son intérêt
**stalemate** *n* impasse *f*; (chess) pat *m*
**staleness** *n* (age) vieillesse *f*; (joke) banalité *f*; (atmosphere) odeur *f* de renfermé; (bread) état rassis
¹**stalk** *n* tige *f*; (cabbage) trognon *m*
²**stalk** *n* (hunting) chasse *f* à l'approche; démarche fière; (striding) marche *f* à grandes enjambées; *vt* traquer, chasser; ~ **s/o** filer qn; *vi* ~ **along** marcher fièrement; marcher à grands pas
**stalker** *n* chasseur *m* à l'approche
¹**stall** *n* (stable) stalle *f*; (cattle) étable *f*; (goods) étalage *m*; (exhibition) stand *m*; *eccles* stalle *f*; (finger) doigtier *m*; *theat* ~s fauteuils *mpl* d'orchestre; **market** ~ boutique *f* en plein vent; **newspaper** ~ kiosque *m* (à journaux); *vt* mettre à l'écurie, établer
²**stall** *vt* + *vi mot* caler; *vi* (delay) chercher à gagner du temps
**stall-holder** *n* marchand -e, étalagiste
**stallion** *n* étalon *m*
**stalwart** *n* costaud *m*; **an old** ~ un vieux de la vieille; *adj* robuste, vigoureux -euse; loyal
**stamen** *n bot* étamine *f*
**stamina** *n* vigueur *f*, résistance *f*
**stammer** *n* bégaiement *m*, balbutiement *m*; *vt* + *vi* bégayer, balbutier
**stammerer** *n* bègue
**stammering** *adj* bègue
**stamp** *n* (with foot) battement *m* de pied, trépignement *m*; (instrument) poinçon *m*; (rubber) tampon *m*; (imprint) timbre *m*; (postage) timbre *m*, timbre-poste *m* (*pl* timbres-poste); (hall-mark) contrôle *m*; (trade-mark) estampille *f*; *fig* empreinte *f*; (character)

trempe *f*; *vt* (documents, etc) timbrer; (letters) affranchir; (passport) viser; (metal, etc) estamper; (silver) poinçonner; (impress) imprimer; ~ **one's foot** frapper du pied; ~ **out** supprimer, étouffer; (fire) étouffer en piétinant; *vi* frapper du pied, piétiner; ~ **on** piétiner

**stamp-album** *n* album *m* de timbres(-poste)

**stamp-collecting** *n* philatélie *f*

**stamp-collector** *n* philatéliste, collectionneur -euse de timbres(-poste)

**stamp-duty** *n* droit *m* de timbre

**stampede** *n* fuite précipitée, débandade *f*; (rush) ruée *f*; *vt* jeter la panique parmi; *vi* fuir en désordre; (rush) se ruer

**stamper** *n* (machine) timbreuse *f*; (person) timbreur -euse

**stance** *n* position *f* des pieds; **take up one's** ~ se mettre en posture

**stanch, staunch** *vt* étancher

**stanchion** *n* étançon *m*; *naut* épontille *f*

**stand** *n* position *f*, place *f*; (resistance) résistance *f*; (stopping) arrêt *m*, halte *f*; (vehicles) lieu *m* de stationnement, station *f*; (sportsground) tribune *f*; (platform) estrade *f*; (stall) étalage *m*; (exhibition) stand *m*; (base) pied *m*, dessous *m*, piédestal *m*; *US* leg barre *f* des témoins; **make a** ~ résister; *theat* **one-night** ~ représentation *f* unique; *sl* aventure passagère; **take one's** ~ se placer; se baser; *vt* (endure) supporter, endurer; (put up with) tolérer; (undergo) subir; (place) mettre, poser; *coll* (pay) payer, offrir; ~ **a chance** avoir une chance; *coll* ~ **an employee off** mettre un employé (*f* une employée) à pied; *coll* ~ **s/o up** faire faux bond à qn; ~ **sth up** mettre qch debout; ~ **the climate** résister au climat; *sl* **I can't** ~ **him** je ne peux pas le sentir; *vi* être debout, se tenir debout; (situation) se trouver, être situé; (building) se dresser; (vehicle) stationner; (remain) rester, demeurer, durer; (stop) s'arrêter; (be valid) être valable; (candidate) se porter; ~ **against** s/o s'opposer à qn; ~ **around** rester à regarder; ~ **aside** se tenir à l'écart, se ranger; *mil* ~ **at ease!** repos!; ~ **back** (withdraw) reculer; ~ **by** (support) défendre, soutenir; (be near) être (au)près de; ~ **down** se retirer; (election) retirer sa candidature; ~ **fast** tenir bon; ~ **for** signifier, vouloir dire; ~ **for nothing** ne compter pour rien; ~ **in for** s/o remplacer qn; ~ **out** ressortir; (project) faire saillie; (resist) résister; (be outstanding) être exceptionnel -elle; ~ **out for sth** s'obstiner à demander qch; ~ **over**

ter en suspens; ~ **to lose nothing** n'avoir rien à perdre; ~ **to reason** aller de soi

**standard** *n* (flag) étendard *m*, pavillon *m*, bannière *f*; (measure) étalon *m*, unité *f*; (model) modèle *m*, type *m*; norme *f*; degré *m*; (level) niveau *m*, taux *m*; *obs* (school) classe *f*; (support) support *m*; *adj* standard *invar*; normal; ~ **measurement** mesure-étalon *f* (*pl* mesures-étalons); ~ **size** taille courante

**standard-bearer** *n* porte-drapeau *m* (*pl* porte-drapeau(x))

**standardization** *n* normalisation *f*, unification *f*, standardisation *f*

**standardize** *vt* normaliser, standardiser

**standard-lamp** *n* lampadaire *m*

**stand-by** *n* ressource *f*, expédient *m*; *adj* de réserve; ~ **flight** vol *m* sans garantie d'embarquement au titulaire d'un billet à tarif réduit

**stand-in** *n* remplaçant -e; *theat* doublure *f*

**standing** *n* station *f* debout; (duration) durée *f*; (social) position *f*, standing *m*; ~ **room** places *fpl* debout; *adj* debout *invar*; (army) permanent; (water) dormant; (crops) sur pied; ~ **joke** plaisanterie courante; ~ **rule** règle *f* fixe; **be left** ~ être laissé sur place

**stand-offish** *adj* distant, réservé

**stand-offishness** *n* réserve *f*, raideur *f*

**standpoint** *n* point *m* de vue

**standstill** *n* arrêt *m*; **come to a** ~ s'arrêter, s'immobiliser

**stanza** *n* stance *f*, strophe *f*

¹**staple** *n* (loop) crampon *m*; (for papers) agrafe *f*; *vt* agrafer; cramponner

²**staple** *n* produit principal; ~ **diet** régime *m* de base; ~ **industry** industrie principale

**stapler** *n* agrafeuse *f*

**star** *n* étoile *f*, astre *m*; *cin* + *theat* vedette *f*, étoile *f*, star *f*; ~ **part** rôle *m* de vedette; **shooting** ~ étoile filante; **the** ~ **s and stripes** la bannière étoilée; *vt* marquer d'une étoile (d'un astérisque); *vi* jouer le rôle principal (l'un des rôles principaux)

**starboard** *n* *naut* tribord *m*; **on the** ~ **bow** par tribord devant; **on the** ~ **side** à tribord

**starch** *n* amidon *m*; (for linen) empois *m*; *cul* fécule *f*; *vt* empeser, amidonner

**starchy** *adj* (food) féculent; *coll* (person) guindé, empesé

**stardom** *n* célébrité *f*; **rise to** ~ devenir une vedette

**stare** *n* regard *m* fixe; *vt* ~ s/o **in the face** dévisager qn; ~ s/o **out** faire baisser les yeux à qn; *coll* **it's staring you in the face** ça vous saute aux yeux; *vi* regarder fixement; ~ **at** s/o regarder qn

fixement, dévisager qn
**starfish** n étoile f de mer
**star-gazer** n fig rêvasseur -euse
**star-gazing** n rêvasserie f
**staring** adj (eyes) fixe, grand ouvert; (look) ébahi, effaré
**stark** adj pur, absolu; adv tout, tout à fait
**stark-naked** adj nu comme un ver
**starless** adj sans étoiles
**starlet** n starlette f
**starlight** n lumière f des étoiles
**starling** n étourneau m
**starred** adj étoilé, parsemé d'étoiles; marqué d'une étoile
**starry** adj étoilé, parsemé d'étoiles
**starry-eyed** adj romanesque, idéaliste
**star-spangled** adj (par)semé d'étoiles; **the ~ banner** la bannière étoilée
**start** n (beginning) commencement m, début m; (departure) départ m; mot démarrage m; (fear) tressaillement m, sursaut m; (handicap) avance f; **flying ~** départ lancé; **for a ~** d'abord, pour commencer; **make a good ~** commencer bien; **make an early ~** commencer de bonne heure; (departure) partir de bonne heure; **wake with a ~** se réveiller en sursaut; vt (begin) commencer; (cake, conversation) entamer; (make depart) faire partir; (engine) faire marcher; mot mettre en marche; (game) lever; (business) lancer, fonder; (rumour) répandre; (cause) provoquer; vi (begin) commencer; (depart) partir, se mettre en route; (engine) démarrer; (fear) tressaillir, sursauter; **~ again from scratch** recommencer à zéro; **~ doing sth** se mettre (commencer) à faire qch; **~ up** se lever en sursaut; **to ~ with** en premier lieu, pour commencer
**starter** n (originator) auteur m; (race) starter m; mot démarreur m; (meal) hors-d'œuvre m invar, premier plat
**starting-handle** n mot manivelle f de mise en marche
**starting-point** n point m de départ
**starting-post** n poteau m de départ
**startle** vt effrayer, alarmer, faire tressaillir
**startling** adj (alarming) effrayant; (surprising) surprenant, sensationnel -elle
**starvation** n faim f, manque m de nourriture; **~ wages** salaire m de famine
**starve** vt faire mourir de faim, priver de nourriture; vi mourir de faim
**starveling** n + adj famélique
**starving** adj affamé
**stash** vt sl cacher
**state** n état m; (nation) État m; condition f, situation f; (rank) rang m, dignité

f; **~ apartments** salons mpl d'apparat; **~ coach** voiture f d'apparat; **~ control** étatisme m; US **State Department** = ministère m des Affaires étrangères; **~ school** école f d'état; **in ~** en grande pompe; **lie in ~** être exposé sur un lit de parade; **live in ~** mener grand train; **that's a fine ~ of affairs!** c'est du joli!; **the married ~** le mariage; hist **the States General** les États généraux; vt déclarer, affirmer; (problem) poser; (complaint) exposer; (fix) arrêter; **~ one's opinion** donner son opinion
**statecraft** n habileté f politique
**stated** adj **at ~ times** à (des) heures fixes; **on ~ days** à jours fixes
**stateless** adj apatride, sans patrie
**stately** adj majestueux -euse, imposant
**statement** n déclaration f; (explanation, account) exposé m, exposition f; (report) rapport m, compte rendu m; (accounts) relevé m de compte
**state-room** n naut cabine f de luxe; (palace) salle f de réception
**statesman** n homme m d'État
**statesmanship** n habileté f politique, science f du gouvernement
**static** adj stationnaire, statique
**station** n (position) position f, place f, poste m; (rank) rang m, condition f; (railway) gare f; (underground) station f; **action ~s** postes mpl de combat; **marry below one's ~** faire une mésalliance; mot **service ~** station-service f (pl stations-service); **the ~s of the Cross** le chemin de (la) Croix; vt placer, mettre; mil poster
**stationary** adj stationnaire, immobile; **~ engine** machine f fixe
**stationer** n papetier -ière; **~'s shop** papeterie f
**stationery** n papeterie f
**station-master** n chef m de gare
**station-wagon** n US mot familiale f, break m
**statistic(al)** adj statistique
**statistician** n statisticien -ienne
**statistics** npl (subject) statistique f; (alleged facts) statistiques fpl
**statuary** n statuaire f; adj statuaire
**statue** n statue f
**statuesque** adj sculptural
**statuette** n statuette f
**stature** n taille f
**status** n rang m, condition f; **~ quo** statu quo m invar; **civil ~** état civil
**statute** n loi f, ordonnance f; **~ s statuts** mpl, règlements mpl
**statute-book** n code m
**statutory** adj établi, réglementaire, statutaire; (offence) prévu par la loi

¹**staunch** *adj* dévoué, ferme; (friend) à toute épreuve; (ship) étanche

²**staunch** *vt see* stanch

**stave** *n* bâton *m*; (barrel) douve *f*; *mus* portée *f*; *vt* ~ **in** défoncer, enfoncer; ~ **off** détourner, écarter; (danger) prévenir

¹**stay** *n* séjour *m*, visite *f*; ~ **of execution** sursis *m*; *vt* (stop) arrêter; *leg* remettre, ajourner; *vi* (remain) rester, demeurer; (visit) habiter, séjourner; (hotel) descendre; ~ **for** attendre; ~ **in** ne pas sortir; ~ **on** rester encore quelque temps; ~ **put** rester sur place; ~ **up** veiller, ne pas se coucher

²**stay** *n* support *m*, soutien *m*; ~ **s** corset *m*; *vt* étayer

³**stay** *n naut* hauban *m*

**stay-at-home** *n* + *adj* casanier -ière

**stayer** *n* (sport) coureur *m* de fond; (horse) stayer *m*; *coll* personne *f* qui ne sait pas partir

**stead** *n* in s/o's ~ à la place de qn; **stand s/o in good** ~ être très utile à qn

**steadfast** *adj* ferme, inébranlable

**steadily** *adv* fermement, régulièrement; (diligently) assidûment

**steadiness** *n* fermeté *f*; assiduité *f*; stabilité *f*

**steady** *adj* (firm) ferme, solide; (constant) constant, soutenu; (person) sûr, rangé, sérieux -ieuse; (regular) régulier -ière; (rain) persistant; *adv* ~! ne bougez pas!; ~ **on**! doucement!; *vt* raffermir, affermir

**steak** *n* tranche *f* de viande, tranche *f* de poisson; (beef) bifteck *m*, entrecôte *f*; **fillet** ~ tournedos *m*; **rump** ~ rom-steck *m*

**steal** *vt* voler, soustraire, dérober; ~ **a glance at s/o** jeter un regard furtif à qn; ~ **a march on s/o** devancer qn; *vi* ~ **away** partir furtivement; ~ **in** entrer à la dérobée; ~ **out** sortir furtivement

**stealth** *n* secret *m*; **by** ~ à la dérobée, furtivement

**stealthy** *adj* furtif -ive

**steam** *n* vapeur *f*; (on window, etc) buée *f*; **at full** ~ à toute vapeur; **get up** ~ chauffer; **keep up** ~ rester sous pression; **let off** ~ lâcher la vapeur; *coll* épancher sa bile; *vt cul* cuire à l'étuvée (à la vapeur); *vi* dégager de la vapeur, fumer; ~ **ahead** avancer rapidement; ~ **up** (window) s'embuer

**steamboat** *n* bateau *m* à vapeur, vapeur *m*

**steam-engine** *n* machine *f* à vapeur

**steamer** *n* navire *m* à vapeur; *cul* marmite *f* à vapeur

**steam-gauge** *n* manomètre *m* de pression

**steam-hammer** *n* marteau-pilon *m* (*pl* marteaux-pilons)

**steaminess** *n* atmosphère embuée; atmosphère *f* humide

**steam-roller** *n* rouleau *m* compresseur

**steamroller** *vt* écraser; ~ **one's way through sth** atteindre son but en forçant tous les obstacles

**steamship** *n* navire *m* à vapeur

**steamy** *adj* plein de vapeur; (atmosphere) humide

**steel** *n* acier *m*; (sharpening) fusil *m*; (sword) lame *f*; ~ **industry** industrie *f* sidérurgique; **heart of** ~ cœur *m* de fer; *vt* aciérer; ~ **oneself against sth** se raidir contre qch; ~ **oneself to do sth** s'armer de courage pour faire qch

**steel-plated** *adj* cuirassé

**steel-rimmed** *adj* (spectacles) à monture d'acier

**steelworks** *n* aciérie *f*

**steely** *adj* d'acier, *fig* dur, inflexible

¹**steep** *adj* raide, escarpé; *coll* **that's a bit** ~ ça, c'est un peu fort

²**steep** *vt* tremper, saturer; ~ **oneself in an atmosphere** se plonger dans une atmosphère; *vi* tremper

**steepen** *vt* augmenter; *vi* devenir plus raide

**steeple** *n* flèche *f*

**steeplechase** *n* course *f* d'obstacles; (racing) steeple-chase *m*

**steeplejack** *n* réparateur *m* de clochers, réparateur *m* de cheminées d'usine

¹**steer** *n* jeune bœuf *m*

²**steer** *vt* conduire, diriger; (ship) gouverner; ~ **a course** mettre le cap sur; *vi* ~ **away from** (clear of) éviter

**steerable** *adj* gouvernable, dirigeable

**steerage** *n* travel ~ voyager dans l'entrepont (en troisième classe)

**steering** *n* direction *f*, conduite *f*; ~ **committee** comité *m* d'organisation; ~ **gear** appareil *m* à gouverner

**steering-column** *n mot* colonne *f* de direction

**steering-wheel** *n mot* volant *m*

**steersman** *n* timonier *m*

**stellar** *adj* stellaire

¹**stem** *n bot* tige *f*; (fruit) queue *f*; (glass) pied *m*; (pipe) tuyau *m*; *naut* avant *m*; *vi* ~ **from** être le résultat de, être issu de

²**stem** *vt* arrêter, contenir; (water) endiguer; (epidemic) enrayer; (brake) freiner; (attack) briser

**stench** *n* puanteur *f*

**stencil** *n* patron *m*; (typing) stencil *m*; (drawing) décoration *f* au poncif; *vt* imprimer au patron, marquer au patron; (typing) tirer au stencil, polycopier stenographer *n* sténographe, *coll* sténo

stenography *n* sténographie *f*

step *n* pas *m*; (stair) marche *f*, degré *m*; (ladder) échelon *m*; (vehicle) marche-pied *m*; (measure) démarche *f*; (door) seuil *m*, pas *m* de la porte; ~ by ~ pas à pas; flight of ~ s escalier *m*; follow in the ~ s of marcher sur les traces de; in ~ au pas; pair of ~ s échelle *f* double; take a ~ faire un pas; take ~ s faire des démarches; that's a good ~ forward c'est déjà un bon pas de fait; *vt* ~ out mesurer au pas; *vi* faire un pas; (walk) marcher; ~ across traverser; ~ aside se ranger, s'écarter; ~ back reculer; ~ down descendre; *fig* démissionner; ~ forward s'avancer; ~ in entrer; ~ off (alight) descendre; *mot* ~ on the gas écraser le champignon; ~ out sortir; (hasten) allonger le pas; ~ over franchir; ~ this way venez par ici; ~ up s'approcher

stepbrother *n* beau-frère *m* (*pl* beaux-frères)

stepchild *n* enfant d'un autre lit

stepdaughter *n* belle-fille *f* (*pl* belles-filles)

stepfather *n* beau-père *m* (*pl* beaux-pères)

step-ladder *n* échelle *f* double

stepmother *n* belle-mère *f* (*pl* belles-mères)

stepping-stone *n* marchepied *m*, tremplin *m*

stepsister *n* demi-sœur *f*

stepson *n* beau-fils *m* (*pl* beaux-fils)

stereo *n* stéréo *f*; *adj* stéréo

stereophonic *adj* stéréophonique

stereophony *n* stéréophonie *f*

stereotype *n* cliché *m*; *fig* stéréotype *m*; *vt* stéréotyper

sterile *adj* stérile

sterility *n* stérilité *f*

sterilization *n* stérilisation *f*

sterilize *vt* stériliser

sterling *n econ* sterling *m*; *adj* vrai, véritable, solide; *econ* sterling

¹stern *n naut* arrière *m*, poupe *f*; *coll* derrière *m*

²stern *adj* sévère, dur

sternly *adv* sévèrement, durement

sternness *n* sévérité *f*, dureté *f*

steroids *npl* stéroïdes *mpl*

stet *vt* (typing) maintenir

stethoscope *n* stéthoscope *m*

stetson *n US* chapeau *m* à très larges bords

stevedore *n* arrimeur *m*, déchargeur *m*

stew *n* ragoût *m*; (game) civet *m*; *coll* be in a ~ être dans tous ses états; *vt* faire cuire en ragoût; (fruit) mettre en compote; *vi* cuire à la casserole; (simmer) mijoter; *coll* (be hot) étouffer

steward *n* économe *m*, intendant *m*; (household) maître *m* d'hôtel; *naut* + *aer* steward *m*; shop ~ délégué syndical

stewardess *n naut* femme *f* de chambre; air ~ hôtesse *f* de l'air

stewardship *n* économat *m*, intendance *f*

stewed *adj* cuit en ragoût; *sl* ivre; ~ beef bœuf *m* en daube; ~ fruit compote *f* de fruits; ~ mutton ragoût *m* de mouton; ~ tea thé trop infusé

¹stick *n* bâton *m*; (walking) canne *f*; (wand) baguette *f*; (handle) manche *m*; (hockey) crosse *f*; (wood) morceau *m* de bois; (beans) rame *f*; (vine) échalas *m*; ~ of bombs chapelet *m* de bombes; bread ~ gressin *m*; *fig* get the wrong end of the ~ avoir mal compris; queer ~ drôle *m* de type; the big ~ le recours à la force

²stick *vt* coller; (attach) attacher; (pierce) percer; (pin) piquer; (fix) fixer; *coll* (put) mettre, *coll* fourrer, *coll* ficher; *coll* (bear) supporter, souffrir; ~ down coller; (write) inscrire; ~ 'em up! haut les mains!; *coll* ~ it tenir le coup; ~ on coller, fixer; ~ one's chest out bomber le torse (la poitrine); ~ out faire dépasser, sortir; *coll* ~ sth out tenir qch jusqu'au bout; ~ up dresser; (notice) afficher; *vi* s'enfoncer, se planter, se piquer; (adhere) tenir, adhérer, rester collé, coller; *coll* ~ around attendre; ~ at s'arrêter devant; (persist) persévérer avec; ~ at doing sth se faire scrupule de faire qch; ~ at nothing ne reculer devant rien; ~ by s/o ne pas abandonner qn, rester fidèle à qn; ~ out ressortir, faire saillie; ~ out for insister sur; *coll* ~ to one's guns ne pas en démordre; ~ to sth persévérer avec qch; ~ to the facts s'en tenir aux faits; ~ up se dresser; *coll* ~ up for s/o prendre la défense de qn

sticker *n* (bills) colleur *m* (d'affiches); (knife) couteau *m* de boucher; *coll* (label) étiquette gommée; *coll* (stayer) crampon *m*; *coll* (worker) travailleur *m*

stickiness *n* viscosité *f*

sticking-plaster *n* sparadrap *m*

stick-insect *n* phasme *m*

stick-in-the-mud *n* + *adj* routinier -ière

stickleback *n* épinoche *f*

stickler *n* rigoriste; be a ~ for être très à cheval sur

sticky *adj* collant, gluant, visqueux -euse; *coll* (person) difficile

stiff *n sl* (corpse) cadavre *m*; *sl* big ~ espèce *f* d'idiot; *adj* raide, rigide, inflexible, dur; (manner) guindé; (difficult) pénible, rude; (numb) engourdi; (muscles) courbaturé; (resistance) opiniâtre; *coll* (price) salé; ~ as a poker raide comme un pieu; **~ neck** torticolis *m*; **become ~** se raidir, s'ankyloser

**stiffen** *vt* raidir; (strengthen) renforcer, raffermir; *cul* lier; *vi* devenir raide, se raidir; (wind) fraîchir

**stiffener** *n* renfort *m*; *coll* verre *m* d'alcool, petit verre

**stiffening** *n* raidissement *m*; (strengthening) renforcement *m*, durcissement *m*

**stiffly** *adv* avec raideur; (manner) d'un air guindé; (resistance) opiniâtrement

**stiff-necked** *adj* entêté, obstiné

**stiffness** *n* raideur *f*, rigidité *f*; (manner) contrainte *f*; (obstinacy) opiniâtreté *f*; (difficulty) difficulté *f*

**stifle** *vt* étouffer; (repress) réprimer; *vi* étouffer, suffoquer

**stigma** *n* infamie *f*; *path* stigmate *m*

**stigmata** *npl eccles* stigmates *mpl*

**stigmatize** *vt* stigmatiser

**stile** *n* échalier *m*

**stiletto** *n* stylet *m*; **~ heel** talon *m* aiguille

**¹still** *n phot* photographie (tirée d'un film); *adj* tranquille, calme; (stationary) immobile; **~ waters run deep** il n'y a pire eau que l'eau qui dort; **keep ~** ne pas bouger; **his heart stood ~** son cœur cessa de battre; *vt* tranquilliser, calmer

**²still** *adv* encore, toujours; *conj* cependant, pourtant, toutefois

**³still** *n* alambic *m*

**still-born** *adj* mort-né (*f* mort-née)

**still-life** *n* nature morte

**stillness** *n* tranquillité *f*, calme *m*, silence *m*

**stilt** *n* échasse *f*; **on ~s** monté sur des échasses

**stilted** *adj* guindé

**stimulant** *n* stimulant *m*, remontant *m*

**stimulate** *vt* stimuler; exciter

**stimulation** *n* stimulation *f*

**stimulative** *adj* stimulateur -trice

**stimulus** *n* stimulant *m*

**sting** *n* (insect) aiguillon *m*, dard *m*; (wound) piqûre *f*; *fig* pointe *f*; (energy) vigueur *f*; *vt* piquer; *sl* **he stung me** il m'a fait payer le prix fort; *vi* cuire

**stinginess** *n* ladrerie *f*, pingrerie *f*

**stingy** *adj* ladre, pingre

**stink** *n* puanteur *f*; *sl* **raise a ~** faire de l'esclandre; *vt* **~ out** enfumer, chasser par la mauvaise odeur; *vi* puer

**stink-bomb** *n* boule puante

**stinker** *n sl* fig sale type *m*

**stinking** *adj* puant; *sl* dégoûtant; *sl* (drunk) ivre

**stint** *n* restriction *f*; (job) tâche *f*, besogne assignée; **without ~** sans limite; *vt* réduire, limiter, restreindre; **~ oneself** se priver du nécessaire

**stipend** *n* traitement *m*

**stipendiary** *adj* qui reçoit des appointements fixes; **~ magistrate** magistrat appointé

**stipulate** *vt* + *vi* stipuler

**stipulation** *n* stipulation *f*

**stir** *n* remuement *m*, mouvement *m*; (agitation) remue-ménage *m*, agitation *f*, émoi *m*; *vt* remuer; (move) bouger; *fig* agiter, exciter; **~ up** fomenter, ameuter; *vi* bouger, remuer; **not ~ out of the house** ne pas sortir de la maison

**stirring** *adj* remuant; (rousing) entraînant, vibrant

**stirrup** *n* étrier *m*

**stirrup-cup** *n* coup *m* de l'étrier

**stirrup-pump** *n* pompe à main portative

**stitch** *n* point *m*; (knitting) maille *f*; *surg* (point *m* de) suture *f*; *med* point *m* de côté; **a ~ in time saves nine** un point à temps en épargne cent; **without a ~ on** tout nu, nu comme un ver; *vt* coudre; *surg* suturer; (book) brocher; **~ up** recoudre

**stoat** *n* hermine *f*

**stock** *n* (goods) marchandises *fpl*, stock *m*; (quantity) quantité *f*; (stores) provision *f*; (race) famille *f*, lignée *f*; (cattle) bétail *m*; (tree) tronc *m*; *hort* portegreffe *m* (*pl* porte-greffe(s)); *bot* giroflée *f*; *cul* bouillon *m*; (gun) fût *m*, bois *m*; *econ* valeurs *fpl*, actions *fpl*; **~s** pilori *m*; *naut* chantier *m*; **~s and shares** valeurs *fpl* de bourse; **in ~** en magasin, en stock; **out of ~** épuisé; **take ~ of** faire l'inventaire de; **take ~ of the situation** faire le point de la situation; *adj* (standard) courant; (goods) de série; **~-car** stock-car *m*; **~ phrase** phrase toute faite; *vt* approvisionner, stocker; (have in stock) tenir en magasin, stocker; (gun) monter; **well ~ed shop** magasin bien approvisionné

**stockade** *n* palissade *f*

**stock-breeder** *n* éleveur -euse

**stockbroker** *n* agent *m* de change, courtier *m* en bourse

**Stock Exchange** *n* Bourse *f*

**stockholder** *n* actionnaire

**stocking** *n* bas *m*

**stockinged** *adj* **in one's ~ feet** sans chaussures

**stock-in-trade** *n* stock *m*; *coll* répertoire *m*

**stockist** *n* stockiste *m*

**stock-market** *n* marché *m* des valeurs

**stockpile** *n* réserve *f*, stocks *mpl* de réserve; *vt* stocker

**stockpot** *n* pot-au-feu *m invar*

**stock-still** *adj* tout à fait immobile

**stock-taking** *n* inventaire *m*; *fig* examen *m* de la situation stocky *adj* trapu

stockyard *n* parc *m* à bestiaux

stodge *n coll* pudding *m*; aliment bourrant

stodginess *n* lourdeur *f*

stodgy *adj* lourd, indigeste; (person) rasoir *invar*

stoic *n* + *adj* stoïcien -ienne, stoïque

stoical *adj* stoïque

stoicism *n* stoïcisme *m*

stoke *vt* charger, chauffer; entretenir; *vi coll* ~ up bouffer

stokehold *n* chaufferie *f*

stoker *n* chauffeur *m*

stole *n* étole *f*

stolid *adj* lourd, flegmatique

stomach *n* estomac *m*; (belly) ventre *m*; (taste) goût *m*, envie *f*, inclination *f*; (courage) courage *m*; on an empty ~ à jeun; on one's ~ à plat ventre; turn s/o's ~ écœurer qn; *vt* supporter, tolérer; (insult) digérer

stomach-pump *n* pompe stomacale

stone *n* pierre *f*; (pebble) caillou *m*; (fruit) noyau *m*; *med* calcul *m*; (mill) meule *f*; (weight) = 6 kilos 38 grammes; a rolling ~ gathers no moss pierre qui roule n'amasse pas mousse; a ~'s throw away à quelques pas; leave no ~ unturned ne rien négliger; precious ~s pierres précieuses; *adj* de pierre; (earthenware) de grès; *vt* lapider; (fruit) dénoyauter

stone-blind *adj* complètement aveugle

stone-cold *adj* froid comme le marbre

stoned *adj sl* ivre; (drugs) chîté

stone-deaf *adj* complètement sourd, *coll* sourd comme un pot

stonemason *n* maçon *m*

stonewall *vi* faire de l'obstruction

stoneware *n* poterie *f* de grès

stonework *n* maçonnerie *f*

stony *adj* pierreux -euse, rocailleux -euse; (hard) dur; (stare) glacé; *coll* (broke) à sec, fauché

stony-broke *adj* fauché, à sec

stony-hearted *adj* insensible, dur

stooge *n coll* dupe *f*; souffre-douleur *m invar*; subalterne *m*; *theat* faire-valoir *m invar*; *vi theat* servir de faire-valoir

stook *n agr* tas *m* de gerbes

stool *n* tabouret *m*; (three-legged) escabeau *m*; *med* ~s selles *fpl*

stool-pigeon *n* appeau *m*; *coll fig* mouchard -e

¹stoop *n* dos voûté; walk with a ~ marcher le dos voûté; *vi* se pencher, se baisser; *fig* s'abaisser; (be round-shouldered) avoir le dos rond

²stoop *n see* stoup

stop *n* arrêt *m*, halte *f*; interruption *f*; (air travel) escale *f*; (punctuation) point *m*;

*mus* jeu *m*; (flute) trou *m*; (door) heurtoir *m*; come to a ~ s'arrêter; *mot* stopper; *coll* pull out all the ~s donner son maximum; put a ~ to mettre fin à; regular ~ arrêt *m* fixe; request ~ arrêt facultatif; *vt* arrêter; (cease) cesser; (prevent) empêcher; (suppress) supprimer; (hole) boucher; (shut) fermer; (road) barrer; (payment) suspendre; (cut off) couper; (tooth) plomber, obturer; ~ a blow parer un coup; ~ thief! au voleur!; get ~ped up se boucher; *vi* s'arrêter; *mot* stopper; *naut* faire escale; (cease) cesser; ~ at nothing ne reculer devant rien; ~ away ne pas venir; ~ for s/o attendre qn; ~ off s'arrêter, faire étape; ~ short s'arrêter tout court; ~ there! restez là!; his knowledge ~s there ses connaissances se bornent là; the matter will not ~ there l'affaire n'en demeurera pas là

stopcock *n* robinet *m*, robinet *m* de fermeture

stopgap *n* bouche-trou *m*

stop-off *n US* arrêt *m*; *aer* escale *f*

stop-light *n* feu *m* rouge; (on vehicle) stop *m*

stop-over *n US* arrêt *m*

stoppage *n* obstruction *f*; *sp* arrêt *m*: (work) suspension *f*; (pay) retenue *f*

stopper *n* bouchon *m*

stopping *n* arrêt *m*; (tooth) plombage *m*; (ceasing) cessation *f*, suspension *f*; (plug) tampon *m*; *adj* ~ train train *m* omnibus

stopping-place *n* arrêt *m*, halte *f*; *aer* escale *f*

stop-press *n* ~ news dernières informations

stop-watch *n* chronomètre *m*

storage *n* emmagasinage *m*, accumulation *f*; (place) entrepôts *mpl*, magasins *mpl*

store *n* provision *f*, approvisionnement *m*; abondance *f*; (place) entrepôt *m*; (furniture) garde-meuble *m* (*pl* garde-meuble(s)); (shop) magasin *m*; ~s provisions *fpl*; keep sth in ~ tenir qch en réserve; have a surprise in ~ for s/o ménager une surprise à qn; set great ~ by faire grand cas de; *vt* emmagasiner; (put in store) mettre en dépôt; (store up) amasser, accumuler

storehouse *n* entrepôt *m*, magasin *m*

storekeeper *n* magasinier *m*

store-room *n* (pantry) office *m*; (warehouse) halle *f* de dépôt

storey *n* étage *m*; first ~ premier étage; *US* deuxième étage *m*

stork *n* cigogne *f*

storm *n* tempête *f*; (thunder) orage *m*; stir up a ~ soulever une tempête; take by

~ prendre d'assaut; *vt* livrer l'assaut à; (capture) prendre d'assaut; *vi* faire rage; (person) tempêter

**storm-bound** *adj* retenu par la tempête

**storm-centre** *n* centre *m* de dépression

**storm-cloud** *n* nuage menaçant

**storminess** *n* caractère orageux

**storm-troops** *npl* troupes *fpl* d'assaut

**stormy** *adj* orageux -euse; (sea) démonté; **it is ~** le vent souffle en tempête

**story** *n* histoire *f*, récit *m*; (short) conte *m*; (plot) intrigue *f*; (lie) mensonge *m*; **it's a long ~** c'est toute une histoire; **tall ~** galéjade *f*; **to cut a long ~ short** en un mot

**storyteller** *n* conteur -euse

**stoup, stoop** *n eccles* bénitier *m*

¹**stout** *n* stout *m*, bière brune forte

²**stout** *adj* fort, vigoureux -euse; (resolute) résolu; (object) solide, résistant; (plump) gros (*f* grosse), corpulent; **get ~** prendre de l'embonpoint

**stout-hearted** *adj* vaillant, courageux -euse

**stoutly** *adv* fortement, vigoureusement

**stoutness** *n* embonpoint *m*, corpulence *f*; courage *m*; vigueur *f*

**stove** *n* poêle *m*, fourneau *m*

**stovepipe** *n* tuyau *m* de poêle

**stow** *vt* ranger, mettre en place; *naut* arrimer

**stowage** *n naut* arrimage *m*

**stowaway** *n* passager clandestin

**straddle** *vt* chevaucher; (horse) enfourcher; **~ one's legs** écarter les jambes

**strafe** *vt* bombarder; *coll* donner une bonne correction à

**straggle** *vi* rester en arrière; **~ along** marcher sans ordre

**straggler** *n* traînard -e

**straggling** *adj* éparpillé, disséminé

**straight** *n* partie droite, bout droit; *adj* droit; (upright) d'aplomb; (in order) en ordre; (honest) intègre, honnête, loyal; (simple) sans complications; **~ left** direct *m* de gauche; **put ~** redresser; (order) arranger, mettre en ordre; *adv* droit; directement; **~ ahead (on)** tout droit; **~ away** immédiatement; **~ off** tout de suite; **~ out** franchement; **I'll be ~ back** je reviens tout de suite; **I'll tell you ~** je vous le dis franchement; **keep a ~ face** ne pas sourciller; **walk ~ in** entrer sans frapper

**straighten** *vt* redresser; (order) arranger, mettre en ordre; *vi* se redresser

**straightforward** *adj* franc (*f* franche), honnête, loyal

**straightness** *n* rectitude *f*; (character) droiture *f*

¹**strain** *n* tension *f*, effort *m*; *med* entorse

*f*, foulure *f*; (tone) ton *m*; mélodie *f*; *mech* rapport *m* de la déformation; *vt* (stretch) tendre; (force) forcer; (filter) filtrer, passer au tamis; **~ oneself** se forcer, faire un grand effort; **~ one's eyes** s'abîmer les yeux; *vi* faire un grand effort; **~ after sth** faire de grands efforts pour atteindre qch

²**strain** *n* race *f*, lignée *f*; qualité inhérente

**strained** *adj* tendu

**strainer** *n* passoire *f*, filtre *m*, tamis *m*

**strait** *n* détroit *m*; **be in dire ~s** (money) être dans la gêne; (trouble) être aux abois; *adj obs* étroit

**strait-jacket** *n* camisole *f* de force

**strait-laced** *adj* collet monté *invar*

¹**strand** *n* (shore) plage *f*, rive *f*, grève *f*; *vt* (ship) échouer; abandonner

²**strand** *n* (rope) toron *m*; (thread) brin *m*; (hair) tresse *f*

**stranded** *adj* (ship) échoué; abandonné; *mot* + *coll* **•g be** ~ être en panne

**strange** *adj* étrange; (peculiar) singulier -ière, curieux -ieuse, bizarre; (unknown) inconnu; (new) nouveau (*f* nouvelle)

**stranger** *n* étranger -ère, inconnu -e; **I'm a ~ here** je ne suis pas d'ici; **you are quite a ~!** on ne vous voit plus!

**strangle** *vt* étrangler

**stranglehold** *n* prise *f* à la gorge; *fig* pouvoir *m* d'empêchement; **have a ~ on** s/o tenir qn par la gorge

**strangler** *n* étrangleur -euse

**strangulate** *vt* étrangler; **~d hernia** hernie étranglée

**strangulation** *n* étranglement *m*

**strap** *n* (leather) courroie *f*; (fabric) bande *f*, sangle *f*; (shoe) barrette *f*; (watch) bracelet *m*

**strap-hanger** *n coll* voyageur -euse debout (*pl* voyageurs -euses debout)

**strapping** *adj* solide, robuste, bien découplé; **~ girl** beau brin de fille

**stratagem** *n* ruse *f*, stratagème *m*

**strategic** *adj* stratégique

**strategist** *n* stratège *m*

**strategy** *n* stratégie *f*

**stratification** *n* stratification *f*

**stratify** *vt* stratifier

**stratosphere** *n* stratosphère *f*

**stratum** *n* couche *f*

**straw** *n* paille *f*, chalumeau *m*; **it's not worth a ~** cela ne vaut rien du tout; **it's the last ~!** c'est le comble!; **man of ~** prête-nom *m*, homme *m* de paille

**strawberry** *n* fraise *f*; (plant) fraisier *m*; **~ ice(-cream)** glace *f* à la fraise; **wild ~** fraise *f* des bois

**stray** *n* bête perdue; (child) enfant perdu -e; (dog) chien perdu; *adj* égaré, errant;

*vi* s'égarer, errer

**streak** *n* raie *f*, bande *f*, strie *f*, trait *m*; (trace) trace *f*; ~ **of lightning** éclair *m*; *vt* rayer, strier; *vi* passer comme un éclair; *coll* courir tout nu (*f* toute nue) (dans un lieu public)

**streaky** *adj* rayé, strié; (bacon) entrelardé

**stream** *n* ruisseau *m*, cours *m* d'eau; (current) courant *m*; (flowing) ruissellement *m*; (lava) coulée *f*; (words, insults) torrent *m*; (school) division *f*; **against the** ~ à contre-courant; **with the** ~ au fil de l'eau; *vt* sélectionner selon l'aptitude; *vi* couler, ruisseler; (flag, hair) flotter; ~ **forth** jaillir; ~ **in** pénétrer à flots; ~ **out** sortir à flots; ~ **with perspiration** être en nage

**streamer** *n* banderole *f*, serpentin *m*

**streaming** *n* sélectionnement *m* selon l'aptitude

**streamline** *vt* (car) caréner; (procedures) moderniser, rationaliser

**streamlined** *adj* caréné; *mot* aérodynamique

**street** *n* rue *f*; ~ **level** rez-de-chaussée *m invar*; **be** ~**s ahead of s/o** avoir devancé qn de beaucoup; **not in the same** ~ **as** pas à comparer avec; **the man in the** ~ l'homme moyen; *coll* **up one's** ~ de sa compétence; **walk the** ~**s** battre le pavé; (prostitute) faire le trottoir

**streetcar** *n US* tramway *m*

**street-door** *n* porte *f* d'entrée

**street-guide** *n* indicateur *m* des rues

**street-lamp** *n* réverbère *m*

**street-lighting** *n* éclairage *m* des rues

**street-urchin** *n* gamin -e des rues

**street-walker** *n* racoleuse *f*

**strength** *n* force *f*, forces *fpl*; (materials) solidité *f*, rigidité *f*; *mil* effectifs *mpl*; (intensity) intensité *f*; ~ **of mind** fermeté *f* d'esprit; ~ **of will** résolution *f*; **at full** ~ au grand complet; **in great** ~ en grand nombre; **on the** ~ **of** sur la foi de; **regain** ~ reprendre des forces; **with all one's** ~ de toutes ses forces

**strengthen** *vt* renforcer, consolider; (body) fortifier; (authority) raffermir

**strenuous** *adj* énergique, actif -ive; (work) ardu, pénible

**streptococcus** *n* (*pl* **streptococci**) streptocoque *m*

**streptomycin** *n* streptomycine *f*

**stress** *n* force *f*, contrainte *f*; (mental) tension *f*; *tech* effort *m*; (emphasis) insistance *f*; *gramm* accent *m* tonique; *med* stress *m*; *mech* **be in** ~ travailler; **lay** ~ **on** insister sur; *vt* souligner, appuyer sur, insister sur; *mech* faire

travailler; *gramm* accentuer

**stretch** *n* (extending) extension *f*, allongement *m*, étirage *m*; (strain) tension *f*; (extent) étendue *f*; ~ **stockings** bas *mpl* extensibles; **at a** ~ tout d'un(e) trait(e); **at full** ~ à toute allure; **by a** ~ **of the imagination** par un effort d'imagination; *coll* **do a** ~ faire de la prison; **for hours at a** ~ pendant des heures d'affilée; **have a** ~ s'étirer; *vt* tendre, tirer; (limbs) allonger, étirer; (widen) élargir; (wings) déployer; (prolong) prolonger; (sense) forcer; (exaggerate) exagérer; ~ **a point** faire une concession; ~ **oneself** s'étirer; ~ **one's legs** se dégourdir les jambes; ~ **out** allonger; *vi* s'étendre, s'élargir, s'allonger; (person) s'étirer

**stretcher** *n* brancard *m*, civière *f*

**stretcher-bearer** *n* brancardier *m*

**stretcher-party** *n* détachement *m* de brancardiers

**strew** *vt* répandre; ~ **with flowers** joncher de fleurs

**strewth** *interj sl* ça alors!

**striate** *vt* strier

**stricken** *adj* accablé, affligé, frappé

**strict** *adj* sévère, rigide; rigoureux -euse; (exact) précis

**strictness** *n* (precision) précision *f*, exactitude *f*; rigueur *f*, sévérité *f*

**stricture** *n* critique *f*; *med* rétrécissement *m*

**stride** *n* enjambée *f*, grand pas; **get into one's** ~ prendre son allure normale; **make great** ~**s** faire de grands progrès; **take sth in one's** ~ faire qch sans le moindre effort; **with giant** ~**s** à pas de géant; *vi* ~ **along** marcher à grandes enjambées; ~ **away** s'éloigner à grands pas; ~ **over** enjamber

**stridency** *n* stridence *f*

**strident** *adj* strident

**strife** *n* lutte *f*; **domestic** ~ querelles *fpl* de ménage

**strike** *n* grève *f*; (attack) raid *m*; **be on** ~ être en grève; **lightning** ~ grève surprise; **sympathy** ~ grève *f* de solidarité; **unofficial** ~ grève non autorisée par le syndicat; *vt* frapper; (match) frotter; (attitude) prendre; (find) trouver; (clock) sonner; ~ **a bargain** conclure un marché; ~ **a chord** plaquer un accord; ~ **against sth** heurter qch; ~ **an average** établir une moyenne; ~ **camp** lever le camp; ~ **down** abattre; ~ **in** enfoncer; ~ **off** abattre; (head) trancher; (name) rayer; ~ **oil** atteindre une nappe pétrolifère; *fig* trouver le filon; ~ **out** rayer, biffer; ~ **terror into s/o** frapper qn de terreur; ~ **the bottom** toucher le fond; ~

the eye attirer le regard; ~ the flag baisser le pavillon; ~ up an acquaintance with lier connaissance avec; ~ up a song entonner une chanson; be struck on s/o être entiché de qn; how does it ~ you? quelle impression cela vous fait-il?; it struck me that l'idée me vint que; you ~ me as being honest vous me paraissez honnête; vi frapper; (clock) sonner; (industry) se mettre en grève, faire grève; ~ across country prendre à travers les champs; ~ home frapper juste; ~ lucky avoir de la chance; ~ out at s/o allonger un coup à qn; ~ out for oneself voler de ses propres ailes; mus ~ up commencer à jouer; ~ while the iron is hot battre le fer pendant qu'il est chaud

**strikebound** adj paralysé par la grève

**strike-breaker** n jaune m, briseur m de grève

**strike-pay** n allocation f de grève

**striker** n gréviste; (device) marteau m; (arms) percuteur m

**striking** n frappement m; (coin) frappe f; (clock) sonnerie f; (rowing) rate of ~ cadence f de nage; adj frappant, remarquable; ~ force force f de frappe; within ~ distance à portée

**string** n ficelle f; (apron, purse) cordon m; (onions) chapelet m; (list) liste f; mus corde f; (beans) fil m; (people) procession f; mus ~s instruments mpl à cordes; ~ bag filet m (à provisions); ~ of beads collier m; eccles chapelet m; have s/o on a ~ tenir qn en lisières; pull ~s faire jouer ses relations; without ~s sans conditions; vt mettre une ficelle à; (parcel) ficeler; (beads) enfiler; (racket) corder; (bow) garnir d'une corde; (beans) effiler; highly strung nerveux -euse; vi coll ~ along with s/o suivre qn

**stringed** adj mus à cordes

**stringency** n rigueur f, sévérité f

**stringent** adj rigoureux -euse

**stringer** n (piano) monteur m de cordes; sl (journalism) pigiste m

**stringy** adj fibreux -euse, filandreux -euse; coll maigre

**strip** n bande f; vt (despoil) dépouiller; (undress) mettre tout nu (f toute nue); (take off) ôter, enlever; (bed) défaire; ~ down démonter; vi (person) se déshabiller; se dévêtir; (come off) se détacher; coll ~ naked se mettre à poil

**strip-cartoon** n bande illustrée

**stripe** n raie f, barre f; mil galon m, rayure f; vt rayer, barrer

**striped** adj à raies, rayé

**stripling** n adolescent m, jeune m

**stripper** n strip-teaseuse f

**strip-poker** n strip-poker m

**strip-tease** n strip-tease m

**strive** vi tâcher, s'efforcer; ~ against lutter contre; ~ for sth essayer d'obtenir qch

**stroboscope** n stroboscope m

**¹stroke** n coup m; (swimming) brassée f; med congestion cérébrale; (rowing) chef m de nage; (drawing) coup m de crayon; (painting) coup m de pinceau; ~ of luck coup m de chance; at one ~ d'un seul coup; breast-~ brasse f; not do a ~ of work ne rien faire de ses dix doigts; on the ~ of three sur le coup de trois heures; with a ~ of the pen d'un trait de plume; vt ~ a boat donner la nage

**²stroke** vt caresser, flatter

**stroll** n petit tour; go for a ~ (aller) faire un petit tour; vi flâner, coll se balader

**strolling** adj errant, vagabond; obs ~ player comédien ambulant

**strong** adj fort, robuste; (object) solide, résistant; (powerful) puissant; (measure) énergique; (drink) fort; (conviction) ferme; (solution) concentré; ~ language langage violent; ~ point fort m; army ten thousand ~ armée forte de dix mille hommes; be ~ enough to être de taille à; have a ~ smell sentir fort; adv be going ~ marcher très bien

**strong-arm** n coll homme fort, brute f; adj coll ~ tactics tactique brutale; vt coll tabasser

**strong-box** n coffre-fort m (pl coffresforts)

**stronghold** n forteresse f; fig citadelle f

**strongly** adv fortement; solidement; vigoureusement, énergiquement; ~ marked accentué; feel ~ about sth attacher une grande importance à qch

**strong-minded** adj résolu, décidé

**strong-room** n cave f des coffres-forts

**strontium** n strontium m

**strop** n cuir m; vt affiler sur le cuir

**structural** adj structural

**structuralism** n structuralisme m

**structure** n structure f; bâtiment m, édifice m

**struggle** n lutte f; vi lutter; se débattre; ~ through surmonter tous les obstacles; se frayer un chemin à travers; ~ up gravir, escalader; ~ with adversity être aux prises avec l'adversité

**strum** vi ~ on the guitar gratter de la guitare; ~ on the piano tapoter un air au piano

**strumpet** n fille f des rues, prostituée f

**¹strut** n démarche fière; vi se pavaner

**²strut** n (support) support m, étai m

**struth** interj sl ça alors!

**strychnine** n strychnine f

**stub** *n* (tree, plant) souche *f*; (pencil) bout *m*; (cigarette) mégot *m*; (cheque) talon *m*; *vt* (roots) extirper; ~ **one's toe** se buter le pied; ~ **out a cigarette** écraser le bout d'une cigarette (pour l'éteindre)

**stubble** *n* chaume *m*; (beard) barbe *f* de plusieurs jours

**stubbly** *adj* couvert de chaume; ~ **beard** barbe *f* de plusieurs jours

**stubborn** *adj* obstiné, entêté, opiniâtre; (will) tenace; **as** ~ **as a mule** têtu comme un mulet

**stubbornness** *n* obstination *f*, opiniâtreté *f*, entêtement *m*

**stubby** *adj* trapu

**stucco** *n* stuc *m*; *vt* enduire de stuc

**stuck** *adj* (pig) égorgé; *coll* **be** ~ ne pas pouvoir avancer, être en panne; *sl* être amoureux -euse

**stuck-up** *adj coll* prétentieux -ieuse, snob *invar*

**¹stud** *n* clou *m* (à grosse tête); **collar** ~ bouton *m* de col; *vt* garnir de clous, clouter

**²stud** *n* (breeding) haras *m*; (racing) écurie *f* de course

**student** *n* étudiant -e

**studentship** *n* bourse *f* d'études

**stud-farm** *n* haras *m*

**studied** *adj* étudié, calculé; recherché

**studio** *n* studio *m*; (photographer, painter) atelier *m*

**studious** *adj* studieux -ieuse

**study** *n* étude *f*; (room) cabinet *m* de travail; (school) salle *f* d'étude; **brown** ~ rêverie *f*; *vt* étudier, faire des études de; (observe) observer; *vi* étudier, faire des études

**stuff** *n* (matter) matière *f*, substance *f*; (textiles) étoffe *f*, tissu *m*; **do one's** ~ faire ce qu'on attend de vous; **know one's** ~ s'y connaître; **that's the** ~ **to give him!** voilà comme il faut agir avec lui!; *vt* bourrer, remplir; (chair) rembourrer; *cul* farcir; (animal) empailler; *vulg* baiser; *sl* ~ **it!** va te faire fiche; *coll* ~ **oneself** bâfrer; *coll* ~ **sth in** fourrer qch dans; ~ **up** boucher; **be a** ~ **ed shirt** être très collet monté

**stuffiness** *n* manque *m* d'air; odeur *f* de renfermé; *fig* manière guindée; pruderie *f*

**stuffing** *n* bourrage *m*; empaillage *m*; (chair) bourre *f*; *cul* farce *f*

**stuffy** *adj* mal aéré; (person) collet monté *invar*; (dreary) ennuyeux -euse

**stultification** *n* abrutissement *m*

**stultify** *vt* rendre stupide, abrutir; (action) rendre inutile; ôter toute signification à

**stumble** *n* trébuchement *m*; *vi* tré-

bucher, faire un faux pas; (horse) broncher; (speech) balbutier; ~ **across** rencontrer, tomber sur; ~ **over sth** buter contre qch; ~ **upon** tomber sur

**stumbling-block** *n* pierre *f* d'achoppement

**stump** *n* tronçon *m*; (limb) moignon *m*; (cabbage) trognon *m*; (tooth) chicot *m*; (pencil) bout *m*; (cigar) mégot *m*; (cricket) piquet *m*; (drawing) estompe *f*; *coll* **stir one's** ~ **s** se remuer, s'activer; *vt* (puzzle) coller; (drawing) estomper; *vi* ~ **along** clopiner; *coll* ~ **up** payer, *coll* casquer

**stumpy** *adj* (person) trapu; (thing) court

**stun** *vt* étourdir, assommer; *fig* abasourdir

**stunner** *n coll* **she's a** ~ elle est sensationnelle

**stunning** *adj* (blow) étourdissant; *coll fig* épatant, renversant, formidable

**¹stunt** *n* tour *m* de force; affaire *f* de publicité; *aer* acrobatie *f*; *vi aer* faire des acrobaties

**²stunt** *vt* arrêter dans sa croissance

**stunted** *adj* rabougri

**stunt-man** *n cin* cascadeur *m*

**stupefaction** *n* stupéfaction *f*

**stupefy** *vt* abrutir, hébéter; *med* stupéfier; **I'm stupefied by that** je n'en reviens pas

**stupendous** *adj* prodigieux -ieuse

**stupid** *adj* stupide, bête, idiot, sot (*f* sotte)

**stupidity** *n* stupidité *f*, sottise *f*, bêtise *f*

**stupidly** *adv* stupidement, sottement

**stupor** *n* stupeur *f*

**sturdy** *adj* vigoureux -euse, robuste

**sturgeon** *n* esturgeon *m*

**stutter** *n* bégaiement *m*; *vt* + *vi* bégayer, bredouiller

**stutterer** *n* bègue

**sty** *n* porcherie *f*; *coll fig* taudis *m*

**sty(e)** *n med* orgelet *m*, *med* compère-loriot *m* (*pl* compères-loriots)

**style** *n* style *m*, manière *f*; ton *m*, chic *m*, élégance *f*; (living) train *m* de maison; (type) type *m*, modèle *m*; (title) titre *m*, nom *m*; **live in fine** ~ mener grand train; **she has** ~ elle a du chic; **win in fine** ~ gagner haut la main; *vt* appeler, dénommer

**stylish** *adj* chic *invar*, élégant

**stylist** *n* styliste

**stylistic** *adj* du style

**stylistics** *npl* stylistique *f*

**stylization** *n* stylisation *f*

**stylize** *vt* styliser

**stylus** *n* style *m*, aiguille *f*

**stymie, stimy** *n* (golf) trou barré; *vt* (golf) barrer le trou; *coll* empêcher

**styptic** *n* styptique *m*; *adj* styptique

suave

**suave** *adj* suave, doux (*f* douce)
**suavity** *n* suavité *f*
**subaltern** *n* mil sous-lieutenant *m*; *adj* subalterne
**subclass** *n* sous-classe *f*
**subcommission** *n* sous-commission *f*
**sub-committee** *n* sous-comité *m*
**subconscious** *n* subconscient *m*; *adj* subconscient
**subconsciousness** *n* subconscience *f*
**subcontinent** *n* sous-continent *m*
**subcontract** *n* contrat *m* en sous-traitance; *vt* sous-traiter
**subcontractor** *n* sous-traitant *m*
**subdivide** *vt* subdiviser; *vi* se subdiviser
**subdivision** *n* subdivision *f*
**subdue** *vt* subjuguer, soumettre; (tame) dompter; (fire) maîtriser; (light) adoucir, atténuer
**subdued** *adj* vaincu; (person) déprimé; ~ **light** demi-jour *m*; **in a ~ voice** à voix basse
**sub-edit** *vt* corriger, mettre au point
**sub-editor** *n* (newspaper) secrétaire de la rédaction
**subgroup** *n* groupement *m* secondaire, sous-groupe *m*
**subheading** *n* sous-titre *m*
**subhuman** *adj* pas tout à fait humain; stupide
**subject** *n* sujet -ette; (topic) sujet *m*, question *f*; *gramm* sujet *m*; (school) matière *f*; **change the ~** changer de sujet; **let us return to the ~** revenons à nos moutons; **on the ~ of** au sujet de; *adj* sujet -ette, exposé; (in subjection) assujetti, soumis; (condition) ~ **to** sous réserve de; *vt* assujettir, subjuguer, soumettre; exposer
**subject-heading** *n* (catalogue) titre *m* selon le sujet
**subjection** *n* sujétion *f*, soumission *f*
**subjective** *adj* subjectif -ive; *gramm* ~ **case** nominatif *m*
**subjectivism** *n* subjectivisme *m*
**subjectivist** *adj* subjectiviste *m*
**subjectivity** *n* subjectivité *f*
**subject-matter** *n* sujet *m*, contenu *m*
**subjugate** *vt* subjuguer, soumettre
**subjugation** *n* subjugation *f*, assujettissement *m*
**subjunctive** *n* subjonctif *m*; *adj* subjonctif -ive
**sub-lease** *n* sous-location *f*; *vt* sous-louer
**sub-let** *vt* sous-louer
**sub-lieutenant** *n* naut enseigne *m*
**sublimate** *vt* sublimer
**sublimation** *n* sublimation *f*
**sublime** *adj* sublime
**subliminal** *adj* subliminal
**sublimity** *n* sublimité *f*
**sub-machine-gun** *n* mitraillette *f*

**submarine** *n* sous-marin *m*; *adj* sous-marin
**submerge** *vt* submerger, immerger, inonder; *vi* plonger
**submission** *n* soumission *f*, résignation *f*
**submissive** *adj* soumis, résigné
**submit** *vt* soumettre, présenter; *vi* se soumettre; (allege) alléguer
**subnormal** *adj* au-dessous de la normale
**subordinate** *adj* subalterne, inférieur; secondaire; *gramm* subordonné; *vt* subordonner
**subordination** *n* subordination *f*, soumission *f*
**suborn** *vt* suborner, séduire
**sub-plot** *n* intrigue *f* secondaire
**subpoena** *n* leg assignation *f* (de témoins); *vt* leg ~ **s/o to appear** assigner qn à comparaître
**subscribe** *vt* souscrire; *vi* ~ **to** souscrire à; (take out subscription) s'abonner à
**subscriber** *n* signataire, souscripteur -trice; (magazine, etc) abonné -e; (payer) contractant -e; ~ **trunk dialling** téléphone *m* automatique
**subscription** *n* souscription *f*; signature *f*; (payment) cotisation *f*; (adherence) adhésion *f*; (magazine, etc) abonnement *m*; **pay a ~** verser une cotisation; **renew a ~** se réabonner; **take out a ~** prendre un abonnement
**subsection** *n* paragraphe *m*
**subsequence** *n* postériorité *f*, conséquence *f*
**subsequent** *adj* qui suit; (later) postérieur, ultérieur
**subservience** *n* servilité *f*, soumission *f*; (use) utilité *f*
**subservient** *adj* servile, obséquieux -ieuse; (useful) utile; (subordinate) subordonné
**subside** *vi* (ground) s'affaisser; (water) baisser; (precipitate) se précipiter; (anger, storm, etc) se calmer, s'apaiser; (stop talking) se taire
**subsidence** *n* (ground) affaissement *m*; (river) décrue *f*; (collapse) effondrement *m*; (anger) apaisement *m*
**subsidiary** *n comm* filiale *f*; *adj* subsidiaire
**subsidize** *vt* subventionner
**subsidy** *n* subvention *f*
**subsist** *vi* subsister; ~ **on sth** vivre de qch
**subsistence** *n* existence *f*, subsistance *f*
**subsoil** *n* sous-sol *m*
**subsonic** *adj* subsonique
**sub-species** *n* sous-espèce *f*
**substance** *n* substance *f*, matière *f*; (main meaning) fond *m*, essentiel *m*; (reality) réalité *f*; (possessions) avoir

724

*m*, biens *mpl*; **man of** ~ homme fortuné

**sub-standard** *adj* inférieur au niveau normal, inférieur

**substantial** *adj* substantiel -ielle, réel -elle; important; (considerable) appréciable; (big and robust) solide; (wealthy) cossu, aisé

**substantiality** *n* solidité *f*; réalité *f*; *leg* bien-fondé *m*

**substantially** *adv* substantiellement, réellement; solidement; (considerably) à un degré considérable

**substantiate** *vt* établir, prouver, justifier

**substantiation** *n* justification *f*

**substantive** *n gramm* substantif *m*; *adj* réel -elle; *gramm* substantif -ive

**sub-station** *n* sous-station *f*

**substitute** *n* remplaçant -e, suppléant -e; (agent) représentant -e; (food, etc) ersatz *m*, succédané *m*; *vt* substituer, remplacer

**substitution** *n* substitution *f*, remplacement *m*

**substratum** *n* couche inférieure

**subterfuge** *n* subterfuge *m*, faux-fuyant *m*

**subterranean** *adj* souterrain

**subtitle** *n* sous-titre *m*; *vt* sous-titrer

**subtle** *adj* subtil; (mind) fin, raffiné; (odour) délicat; (cunning) rusé

**subtlety** *n* subtilité *f*; finesse *f*; ruse *f*

**subtly** *adv* subtilement, avec finesse

**subtract** *vt* soustraire

**subtraction** *n* soustraction *f*

**subtropical** *adj* subtropical

**suburb** *n* faubourg *m*; **outer** ~ **(s)** banlieue *f*

**suburban** *adj* de banlieue, suburbain; (Paris) faubourien -ienne

**suburbanite** *n* banlieusard -e

**suburbia** *n* banlieue *f*

**subvention** *n* subvention *f*

**subversion** *n* subversion *f*, renversement *m*

**subversive** *adj* subversif -ive

**subvert** *vt* subvertir, renverser

**subway** *n* passage souterrain; *US* métro *m*

**succeed** *vt* (follow) succéder à, suivre; *vi* réussir, parvenir

**succeeding** *adj* (following) suivant; (future) à venir, successif -ive

**success** *n* réussite *f*, succès *m*; **her dress is a great** ~ sa robe est très réussie; **make a** ~ **of sth** réussir qch; **wish s/o** ~ souhaiter bonne chance à qn

**successful** *adj* (plan) couronné de succès; (event) heureux -euse; (attempt) réussi; **I am** ~ **in everything** tout me réussit

**succession** *n* succession *f*; (series) suite *f*; (inheritance) héritage *m*; **in rapid** ~

coup sur coup; **in** ~ de suite, successivement

**successive** *adj* successif -ive, consécutif -ive

**successor** *n* successeur *m*

**succinct** *adj* succinct

**succour** *n* secours *m*, aide *f*; *vt* secourir

**succulence** *n* succulence *f*

**succulent** *adj* succulent

**succumb** *vi* succomber

**such** *adj* tel (*f* telle); pareil -eille, semblable; (of that kind) de ce genre; ~ **a foolish man** un homme si stupide; ~ **a man** un tel homme; ~ **as do not like it** ceux qui ne l'aiment pas; ~ **is not the case** il n'en est pas ainsi; **he did no** ~ **thing** il n'a rien fait de la sorte; **her hate was** ~ **that** telle était sa haine que; **in** ~ **a way that** de telle sorte que; **in** ~ **cases** en pareils cas; **no** ~ **thing!** il n'en est rien!; **until** ~ **time as** jusqu'à ce que; **you have** ~ **methods!** vous avez de ces façons de procéder!

**such-and-such** tel et tel (*f* telle et telle)

**suchlike** *adj* semblable, de cette sorte, de ce genre, de cet acabit; **teachers, doctors and** ~ les professeurs, les médecins et autres gens de cette espèce

**suck** *n* action *f* de sucer; **have a** ~ **(at)** sucer; *vt* sucer; (baby) téter; ~ **down** engloutir; ~ **in** absorber, aspirer; *sl* duper, refaire; *fig* ~ **s/o dry** sucer qn jusqu'au dernier sou; ~ **up** sucer, aspirer, absorber; *vi* ~ **at** sucer; (pipe) tirer sur; *sl* ~ **up to s/o** lécher les bottes de qn

**sucker** *n* suceur -euse; *ent* suçoir *m*; *zool* ventouse *f*; *hort* rejeton *m*, surgeon *m*; *coll* blanc-bec *m* (*pl* blancs-becs), poire *f*

**sucking** *adj* qui tète

**sucking-pig** *n* cochon *m* de lait

**suckle** *vt* allaiter

**suckling** *n* allaitement *m*; (baby) nourrisson *m*; (animal) jeune animal *m* qui tète encore

**suction** *n* succion *f*, aspiration *f*

**suction-pump** *n* pompe aspirante

**suction-valve** *n* clapet *m* d'aspiration

**sudden** *adj* soudain, subit; (movement) brusque; **all of a** ~ soudain, tout à coup

**suddenly** *adv* tout à coup, soudain

**suddenness** *n* soudaineté *f*

**suds** *npl* eau *f* de savon; mousse *f* de savon

**sue** *vt leg* poursuivre, intenter un procès à; *vi* ~ **for** demander, solliciter, implorer

**suède** *n* (shoes) daim *m*; (gloves) suède *m*

**suet** *n* graisse *f* de rognon

**suffer** *vt* souffrir; (undergo) subir; (allow) permettre, tolérer; *vi* souffrir; (have losses, damage) subir des pertes (des dégâts); ~ **for one's mistakes** supporter les conséquences de ses erreurs

**sufferance** *n* tolérance *f*, souffrance *f*; **on** ~ par tolérance

**sufferer** *n* (disaster) victime *f*, sinistré -e; (accident) accidenté -e; (illness) malade

**suffering** *n* souffrance *f*

**suffice** *vt* suffire à; *vi* suffire; ~ **it to say that** qu'il suffise de dire que

**sufficiency** *n* suffisance *f*, quantité suffisante

**sufficient** *adj* suffisant, assez; **two are** ~ il suffit de deux

**suffix** *n* suffixe *m*

**suffocate** *vt* + *vi* étouffer, suffoquer

**suffocating** *adj* étouffant, suffocant

**suffocation** *n* suffocation *f*, étouffement *m*

**suffragan** *n eccles* suffragant *m*; *adj* suffragant

**suffrage** *n* suffrage *m*; vote *m*, voix *f*; (right) droit *m* de vote

**suffragette** *n hist* suffragette *f*

**suffuse** *vt* se répandre sur

**sugar** *n* sucre *m*; *fig* flatterie *f*; *sl* (money) fric *m*; **barley** ~ sucre *m* d'orge; **brown** ~ cassonade *f*; **caster** ~ sucre *m* en poudre; **granulated** ~ sucre crystallisé; **lump (loaf)** ~ sucre *m* en morceaux; *vt* sucrer; ~ **the pill** dorer la pilule

**sugar-basin** *n* sucrier *m*

**sugar-beet** *n* betterave *f* à sucre

**sugar-cane** *n* canne *f* à sucre

**sugar-coated** *adj* dragéifié

**sugar-daddy** *n sl* protecteur âgé

**sugariness** *n* goût sucré; *fig* douceur mielleuse

**sugar-plum** *n* bonbon *m* au sucre

**sugary** *adj* sucré; trop sucré; *coll fig* mielleux -euse, flatteur -euse

**suggest** *vt* suggérer, proposer; (idea) inspirer; (advise) conseiller; (hint) insinuer; (evoke) évoquer

**suggestibility** *n* suggestibilité *f*

**suggestible** *adj* que l'on peut suggérer; (person) influençable

**suggestion** *n* suggestion *f*; (tiny bit) pointe *f*, soupçon *m*

**suggestive** *adj* suggestif -ive, évocateur -trice

**suicidal** *adj* de suicide; ~ **attempt** tentative insensée; **it would be** ~ **to** ce serait un véritable suicide de

**suicide** *n* suicide *m*; (person) suicidé -e; **attempted** ~ tentative *f* de suicide; **commit** ~ se suicider

**suit** *n* (clothes) complet *m*, costume *m*; *leg* procès *m*; (request) demande *f*, prière *f*, requête *f*; (marriage) demande *f* en mariage; (cards) couleur *f*; ~ **of armour** armure complète; **bring a** ~ **against s/o** intenter un procès contre

qn; **follow** ~ (cards) jouer de la même couleur; (copy) en faire autant; **lounge** ~ complet-veston *m* (*pl* complets-veston); *vt* convenir à, aller à; (adapt) adapter; *coll* ~ **yourself!** faites comme vous voudrez;. **that** ~ **s me fine** cela m'arrange tout à fait; **they are** ~ **ed to each other** ils sont faits l'un pour l'autre

**suitability** *n* convenance *f*; (relevance) à-propos *m*

**suitable** *adj* convenable; approprié; bon (*f* bonne), propre

**suitcase** *n* valise *f*, mallette *f*

**suite** *n* suite *f*, cortège *m*; *mus* suite *f*; (rooms) appartement *m*; ~ **of furniture** ameublement *m*, ensemble *m*; **drawing-room** ~ salon *m*

**suitor** *n leg* plaideur -euse; (marriage) prétendant *m*

**sulk** *vi* bouder, faire la mine

**sulkily** *adv* d'un air boudeur, en boudant

**sulkiness** *n* bouderie *f*

**sulky** *adj* boudeur -euse, maussade

**sullen** *adj* (person) maussade, morose

**sullenness** *n* air renfrogné

**sully** *vt* souiller, salir, flétrir

**sulphonamide** *n* sulfamide *m*

**sulphur** *n* soufre *m*

**sulphureous** *adj* sulfureux -euse; couleur de soufre *invar*

**sulphuric** *adj* sulfurique

**sulphurous** *adj* sulfureux

**sultan** *n* sultan *m*

**sultana** *n* sultane *f*; (dried grape) raisin *m* de Smyrne

**sultry** *adj* étouffant; (air) lourd, chaud; *coll* sexy

**sum** *n* somme *f*; total *m*, montant *m*; (arithmetic) problème *m*; *vt* ~ **up** résumer; (weigh up) juger, classer; ~ **up a situation** se rendre compte d'une situation; *leg* ~ **up the case** résumer les débats

**summarily** *adv* sommairement

**summarize** *vt* résumer

**summary** *n* sommaire *m*, résumé *m*; *adj* sommaire

**summer** *n* été *m*; ~ **holidays** grandes vacances; ~ **time** heure *f* d'été; ~ **visitor** estivant -e; **Indian** ~ été *m* de la Saint-Martin; **in** ~ en été; *vi* estiver

**summer-house** *n* pavillon *m*

**summer-school** *n* cours *m* d'été

**summer-time** *n* été *m*

**summing-up** *n leg* résumé *m* des débats; évaluation *f*

**summit** *n* sommet *m*, cime *f*; *fig* comble *m*; ~ **conference** conférence *f* au sommet

**summit-level** *n* niveau le plus élevé

**summit-meeting** *n* conférence *f* au sommet

**summon** vt appeler, faire venir; (meeting) convoquer; *leg* sommer de comparaître; (request) sommer; **~ a witness to attend** assigner un témoin; **~ up one's courage** faire appel à tout son courage

**summons** n appel m; *leg* assignation f; (meeting) convocation f; (from police) procès-verbal m (*pl* procès-verbaux); **take out a ~ against s/o** faire assigner qn; vt *leg* assigner, citer à comparaître

**sump** n *mot* fond m de carter; (pit) dépotoir m

**sumptuosity** n somptuosité f

**sumptuous** adj somptueux -euse

**sun** n soleil m; *coll* **get a touch of the ~** prendre un coup de soleil; **take the ~** prendre le soleil; **the ~ is shining** il fait du soleil; vt exposer au soleil; **~ oneself** se chauffer au soleil

**sunbathe** vi prendre des bains de soleil

**sunbathing** n bain m de soleil

**sunbeam** n rayon m de soleil

**sunburn** n (tan) hâle m; (burn) coup m de soleil

**sunburnt** adj hâlé, bronzé

**sundae** n glace f aux fruits, glace f au sirop

**Sunday** n dimanche m; adj du dimanche; **in one's ~ best** dans ses habits du dimanche, *pej* endimanché

**Sunday-school** n école f du dimanche

**sunder** vt séparer, fendre en deux

**sundial** n cadran m solaire

**sundown** n coucher m du soleil

**sundries** npl articles divers; (expenses) frais divers

**sundry** adj divers; **all and ~** tous sans exception

**sunflower** n tournesol m, soleil m

**sun-glasses** npl lunettes fpl de soleil (solaires)

**sun-god** n dieu m du soleil

**sun-hat** n chapeau m à larges bords

**sunk** adj sombré, coulé; *coll* perdu; *sl* foutu

**sunken** adj enfoncé, affaissé; (rock) submergé; (cheeks, road) creux (f creuse)

**sun-lamp** n *med* lampe f à rayons ultra-violets; *cin* sunlight m

**sunless** adj sans soleil

**sunlight** n lumière f du soleil; **in the ~** au soleil, au grand soleil

**sunlit** adj éclairé par le soleil

**sun-lounge** n solarium m

**sunny** adj ensoleillé, exposé au soleil; *fig* riant, radieux -ieuse; **it is ~** il fait du soleil

**sunrise** n lever m du soleil

**sun-roof** n *mot* toit ouvrant

**sunset** n coucher m du soleil, couchant m

**sunshade** n ombrelle f

**sunshine** n lumière f du soleil; *fig* gaieté f; **in the ~** au soleil

**sunspot** n tache f solaire

**sunstroke** n insolation f, coup m de soleil

**sun-tan** n hâle m

**sun-trap** n endroit très ensoleillé

**sun-up** n *US* lever m du soleil

**sup** n petite gorgée; vi souper

**¹super** n *theat* figurant -e

**²super** adj *coll* épatant, formidable

**superabundance** n surabondance f

**superabundant** adj surabondant

**superannuate** vt mettre à la retraite; *coll* mettre au rancart

**superannuated** adj (person) en (à la) retraite; (thing) suranné, démodé

**superannuation** n (action) mise f à la retraite; (pension) pension f de retraite f; **~ fund** caisse f des retraites

**superb** adj superbe, magnifique

**supercharge** vt suralimenter

**supercharger** n *mech* surcompresseur m

**supercilious** adj dédaigneux -euse; (haughty) hautain

**super-duper** adj *coll* formidable

**super-ego** n moi inconscient

**supererogation** n surérogation f

**supererogatory** adj surérogatoire

**superficial** adj superficiel -ielle

**superficiality** n nature superficielle; (shallowness) manque m de profondeur

**superficially** adv superficiellement

**superfluity** n superfluité f

**superfluous** adj superflu

**superhuman** adj surhumain

**superimpose** vt superposer, surimposer

**superintend** vt surveiller, diriger

**superintendent** n surintendant m; chef m; (police) commissaire m

**superior** n supérieur -ieure; adj supérieur -ieure; (person) sourcilleux -euse, arrogant; (condescending) condescendant

**superiority** n supériorité f

**superlative** n superlatif m; adj suprême, magnifique; *gramm* superlatif -ive

**superman** n surhomme m

**supermarket** n supermarché m

**supernational** adj supranational

**supernatural** adj surnaturel -elle

**supernaturalism** n croyance f au surnaturel

**supernaturally** adv surnaturellement

**supernumerary** n surnuméraire; *theat* +*cin* figurant -e; adj en surnombre, surnuméraire

**supersaturate** vt sursaturer

**superscribe** vt apposer une inscription sur

**superscription** *n* (heading) inscription *f*; (address) suscription *f*; (on document) en-tête *m*

**supersede** *vt* remplacer; (render invalid) annuler

**superseded** *adj* périmé; **~ by events** dépassé par les événements

**supersensitive** *adj* hypersensible

**supersonic** *adj* supersonique

**superstition** *n* superstition *f*

**superstitious** *adj* superstitieux -ieuse

**superstructure** *n* superstructure *f*

**supertax** *n* impôt *m* sur le revenu à taux très élevé

**supervene** *vi* survenir

**supervise** *vt* (watch over) surveiller; (control) diriger

**supervision** *n* surveillance *f*; direction *f*

**supervisor** *n* surveillant -e; directeur -trice

¹**supine** *n gramm* supin *m*

²**supine** *adj* couché, sur le dos; (indolent) indolent, inerte

**supper** *n* souper *m*; **have ~** souper; **the Last Supper** la Cène; **the Lord's Supper** la communion

**supplant** *vt* supplanter, évincer

**supple** *adj* souple, flexible; *fig* conciliant, complaisant; *vt* rendre souple

**supplement** *n* supplément *m*; (book) appendice *m*; *vt* compléter, augmenter, ajouter à

**supplementary** *adj* supplémentaire

**suppleness** *n* souplesse *f*; *fig* complaisance *f*

**suppliant** *n* suppliant -e; *adj* suppliant

**supplicant** *n* suppliant -e

**supplicate** *vt + vi* supplier

**supplication** *n* supplication *f*; (petition) supplique *f*

**supplier** *n* fournisseur -euse

¹**supply** *n* provision *f*; (supplying) approvisionnement *m*; *mil* (food) ravitaillement *m*; (person) suppléant -e; **supplies** (accessories) fournitures *fpl*; (stocks) stocks *mpl*; **~ and demand** l'offre *f* et la demande; **~ teacher** remplaçant -e (d'un professeur); **electricity ~** alimentation *f* en électricité; **take in a ~ of** s'approvisionner en; *vt* fournir, munir, approvisionner; (need) répondre à; **~ s/o's needs** pourvoir aux besoins de qn; *vi* **~ for s/o** remplacer qn

²**supply** *adv* avec souplesse, souplement

**support** *n* appui *m*, soutien *m*; (prop) support *m*; *bui* soutènement *m*; **be without means of ~** être sans ressources; **in ~ of** à l'appui de; *vt* soutenir, appuyer, supporter; (keep) maintenir; (life, family) entretenir; (theory) corroborer; (charity) patron-ner; **~ oneself** gagner sa vie

**supportable** *adj* supportable, tolérable; (theory) soutenable

**supporter** *n* (adherent) adhérent -e, partisan -e; *sp* supporter *m*; (device) support *m*

**suppose** *vt + vi* supposer, s'imaginer; (believe) croire; **I ~ so** sans doute, bien probablement; **she is ~d to be ill** elle est censée être malade

**supposed** *adj* supposé, prétendu; (so-called) soi-disant

**supposing** *conj* si, supposé que

**supposition** *n* supposition *f*

**suppository** *n* suppositoire *m*

**suppress** *vt* supprimer, réprimer, étouffer; (hide) dissimuler; (information) taire, ne pas révéler

**suppressible** *adj* supprimable

**suppression** *n* suppression *f*, répression *f*; étouffement *m*; *rad + TV* antiparasitage *m*; (truth) dissimulation *f*

**suppressor** *n* étouffeur *m*; (information) dissimulateur *m*; *rad + TV* dispositif *m* antiparasite

**suppurate** *vi* suppurer

**supranational** *adj* supranational

**supremacy** *n* suprématie *f*

**supreme** *adj* suprême; **reign ~** régner en maître

**surcharge** *n* surtaxe *f*; (stamp) surcharge *f*; *vt* surtaxer; (letter) surcharger

**sure** *adj* sûr, certain; (infallible) infaillible; (success) assuré; *sl* **~ thing!** bien sûr!; **be ~ to do sth** ne pas manquer de faire qch; **for ~** sans faute; **I'm ~ of it** j'en suis convaincu; **it is ~ to be him** c'est sûrement lui; **make ~ of (obtaining) sth** s'assurer qch; **make ~ of sth** s'assurer de qch; **to be ~!** assurément!; *adv* vraiment, certainement; **~ enough!** bien sûr!

**sure-fire** *adj* coll infaillible

**sure-footed** *adj* au pied sûr

**surely** *adv* sûrement; (yes) assurément, bien sûr

**sureness** *n* (safety) sûreté *f*; (certainty) certitude *f*

**surety** *n* garantie *f*, caution *f*; (person) garant -e; **stand ~ for s/o** se porter garant pour qn

**surf** *n* ressac *m*; *vi* faire du surf

**surface** *n* surface *f*; extérieur *m*, dehors *m*; **break ~** revenir en surface; *fig* **on the ~** en apparence; **working ~** surface *f* d'appui; *vt* polir (apprêter) la surface de; (road) revêtir; *vi* revenir en surface

**surfboard** *n* planche *f* de surf

**surfeit** *n* excès *m*, surabondance *f*; satiété *f*; *vt* rassasier, gorger; *vi* se gorger

**surfing** *n* surf *m*

**surf-riding** n surf m

**surge** n houle f, vague f; ~ **of anger** vague f de colère; vi (water) se soulever, déferler; (crowd) déferler, se répandre; ~ **back** refluer

**surgeon** n chirurgien m

**surgery** n chirurgie f; (place) cabinet m de consultation; (hospital) dispensaire m; ~ **hours** heures fpl de consultation

**surgical** adj chirurgical, de chirurgie; ~ **spirit** alcool m (à 90°)

**surliness** n air bourru, caractère hargneux

**surly** adj bourru, hargneux -euse

**surmise** n conjecture f; vt + vi deviner

**surmount** vt surmonter

**surname** n nom m de famille

**surpass** vt surpasser; (exceed) dépasser

**surpassing** adj sans pareil -eille, incomparable

**surplice** n eccles surplis m

**surplus** n excédent m, surplus m; adj de surplus, en surplus

**surprise** n surprise f, étonnement m; **give s/o a** ~ faire une surprise à qn; **take s/o by** ~ prendre qn au dépourvu; **to my** ~ **he appeared** je fus étonné de le voir paraître; adj inattendu; vt étonner, surprendre; **I am** ~**d at you!** vous m'étonnez!

**surprising** adj étonnant, surprenant

**surrealism** n surréalisme m

**surrealist** n surréaliste

**surrealistic** adj surréaliste

**surrender** n mil reddition f; abandon m; leg cession f; (insurance) rachat m; vt mil rendre; leg céder; (renounce) renoncer à; ~ **oneself to** se livrer à; vi se rendre

**surreptitious** adj subreptice, clandestin

**surround** n bordure f; (frame) encadrement m; vt entourer; (encircle) cerner

**surrounding** adj environnant

**surroundings** npl (places) environs mpl, alentours mpl; (people) entourage m, milieu m

**surtax** n surtaxe f; vt surtaxer

**surveillance** n surveillance f

**survey** n aperçu m, vue générale; étude f, enquête f; (land) arpentage m; inspection f, visite f; **make a** ~ **of** sth examiner qch; **make a sample** ~ faire une enquête par sondage; vt regarder, contempler; examiner, inspecter; (note down) faire le relevé de; (land) arpenter

**surveying** n arpentage m

**surveyor** n (land) arpenteur m; inspecteur m, surveillant m

**survival** n survivance f

**survive** vt survivre à; vi survivre

**survivor** n survivant -e; (disaster) rescapé -e

**susceptibility** n (subject to influence) susceptibilité f; sensibilité f; prédisposition f

**susceptible** adj (easily influenced) susceptible; (emotional) sensible; (to disease) prédisposé

**susceptive** adj susceptible

**suspect** n suspect -e; adj suspect; vt soupçonner; s'imaginer; (suppose) se douter de; ~ **danger** flairer le danger

**suspend** vt suspendre

**suspender-belt** n porte-jarretelles m invar

**suspenders** npl jarretelles fpl; US bretelles fpl

**suspense** n suspens m; (anxiety) suspense m; **keep s/o in** ~ tenir qn en suspens

**suspension** n suspension f; ~ **bridge** pont suspendu; ~ **of driving licence** retrait m temporaire du permis de conduire

**suspicion** n soupçon m; leg suspicion f; (mistrust) méfiance f; **above** ~ au-dessus de tout soupçon; **arouse** ~ éveiller les soupçons; **have** ~**s about s/o** soupçonner qn; **lay oneself open to** ~ s'exposer aux soupçons; **with** ~ avec défiance

**suspicious** adj méfiant, soupçonneux -euse; (suspect) suspect, louche

**sustain** vt soutenir; (loss) éprouver, essuyer, subir; (life) entretenir; ~ **an injury** recevoir une blessure

**sustaining** adj ~ **food** nourriture fortifiante

**sustenance** n nourriture f

**suture** n suture f; vt suturer

**swab** n torchon m, serpillière f; naut faubert m; med tampon m; sl lourdaud m; vt essuyer avec un torchon; ~ **down** laver à grande eau

**swaddle** vt emmailloter

**swaddling-clothes** npl langes mpl

**swag** n sl butin m

**swagger** n air crâneur; (boasting) rodomontades fpl; vi se pavaner, crâner

**swagger-stick** n canne f de jonc, stick m

**swain** n poet + joc soupirant m

¹**swallow** n orni hirondelle f; **one** ~ **doesn't make a summer** une hirondelle ne fait pas le printemps

²**swallow** n gorgée f; (gullet) gosier m; vt avaler, gober; ~ **an affront** avaler un affront; ~ **a story** gober une histoire; ~ **one's pride** mettre son orgueil dans sa poche; ~ **one's words** se rétracter; ~ **the wrong way** avaler de travers; ~ **up** dévorer; (engulf) engloutir

**swallow-dive** n saut m de l'ange

**swallow-tail** n ent machaon m, coll grand porte-queue invar

**swamp** n marais m, marécage m; vt inonder; (boat) remplir d'eau; **be ~ed with work** être débordé de travail

**swampy** adj marécageux -euse

**swan** n cygne m; vi coll **~ about (around)** se promener, errer à l'aventure

**swank** n coll prétention f; (person) crâneur -euse; vi coll crâner, se donner des airs

**swan-song** n chant m du cygne

**swap, swop** n coll troc m, échange m; vt coll troquer, échanger

**sward** n gazon m, pelouse f

**swarm** n essaim m; (people) foule f; vi (bees) essaimer; (people) se presser; coll grouiller; **~ up** grimper; **~ with** fourmiller de

**swarthy** adj basané

**swashbuckler** n fanfaron m, rodomont m

**swastika** n croix gammée

**swat** vt coll frapper; (fly) écraser

**swath** n agr andain m

**swathe** n bandage m; agr andain m; vt emmailloter, envelopper

**swatter** n (flies) tapette f (à mouches)

**sway** n balancement m; (rule) domination f, empire m; vt balancer, faire osciller; (rule) gouverner; (influence) influencer; **~ from** détourner; vi se balancer, osciller; (hesitate) balancer, rester indécis

**swear** n coll **have a good ~** lâcher une bordée de jurons; vt jurer; déclarer; **~ in** assermenter; **~ s/o to secrecy** faire jurer le secret à qn; vi jurer; prêter serment; **~ at** maudire, injurier; **~ by sth** jurer sur qch; (extol) vanter; **~ like a trooper** jurer comme un charretier; **~ to sth** affirmer qch sous serment

**swearer** n celui (f celle) qui prête serment; jureur m

**swearing** n attestation f sous serment; (bad language) jurons mpl

**swear-word** n juron m, gros mot

**sweat** n transpiration f, sueur f; coll corvée f; sl mil **an old ~** un vieux troupier; **be in a ~** être trempé de sueur; **by the ~ of one's brow** à la sueur de son front; vt faire suer; fig exploiter; vi suer, transpirer; (work hard) peiner; (wall) suinter; **~ profusely** suer à grosses gouttes

**sweat-band** n (hat) cuir intérieur; sp bandeau m

**sweater** n chandail m

**sweating** n transpiration f; (labour) exploitation f

**sweaty** adj couvert de sueur

**swede** n rutabaga m

**Swede** n Suédois -e

**Sweden** n Suède f

**Swedish** n (language) suédois m; adj suédois

**sweep** n (with broom) coup m de balai; (arm) mouvement m circulaire; (bend) courbe f, boucle f; (chimneys) ramoneur m; (mines) drague f; (extent) étendue f; coll sweepstake m; **at one ~** d'un seul coup; **make a clean ~ of sth** faire table rase de qch; **make a wide ~** décrire une grande courbe; vt balayer; (chimney) ramoner; (mines) draguer; **~ along** entraîner; **~ aside** écarter; **~ away** balayer, emporter; (abolish) abolir; **~ off** emporter; **~ the board** tout rafler; **~ up** balayer, ramasser; vi **~ along (by, past)** passer rapidement; **~ down upon** fondre sur, s'abattre sur; **~ in** (person) entrer d'un air majestueux; **~ on** continuer d'avancer

**sweeper** n (machine) balayeuse f; (person) balayeur m

**sweeping** n balayage m; (chimney) ramonage m; adj rapide; (extensive) complet -ète, entier -ière, important; (exaggerated) un peu exagéré

**sweepings** npl balayures fpl

**sweepstake** n sweepstake m

**sweet** n bonbon m; (at meal) entremets m, dessert m; (person) chéri -e; adj doux (f douce); (sugared) sucré; (person) gentil -ille, charmant; (smell) odorant; (sound) mélodieux -ieuse; **be ~ on s/o** avoir un (le) béguin pour qn; **have a ~ tooth** aimer les douceurs; **it's very ~ of her** c'est très aimable de sa part; coll **keep s/o ~** cultiver la bienveillance de qn; **smell ~** sentir bon

**sweetbread** n cul ris m de veau (d'agneau)

**sweet-corn** n maïs doux

**sweeten** vt sucrer; fig adoucir; sl graisser la patte à; vi s'adoucir

**sweetener** n édulcorant m; sl pot-de-vin m (pl pots-de-vin)

**sweetheart** n amoureux -euse

**sweetie** n coll bonbon m; (person) chérie f

**sweetmeat** n obs bonbon m

**sweetness** n douceur f; (person) gentillesse f

**sweet-pea** n pois m de senteur

**sweet-potato** n patate f

**sweet-scented** adj au parfum doux, odorant

**sweet-shop** n confiserie f

**sweet-william** n bot œillet m de poète

**swell** n gonflement m, bosse f; (sea) houle f; coll élégant m; sl gros personnage; adj coll chic invar; épatant; vt gonfler, enfler; (increase) augmenter; vi s'enfler, se gonfler; (increase) augmenter; (sea) se soulever; med se tuméfier; **~ up** (rise) monter .

**swelling** n enflement m, gonflement m; (river) crue f; (bump) bosse f; grosseur f, tumeur f

**swelter** *vi* étouffer de chaleur; **it's ~ ing!** on étouffe ici!

**swerve** *n* déviation *f*, écart *m*; *vi* faire un écart; *mot* faire une embardée

¹**swift** *n orni* martinet *m*

²**swift** *adj* rapide; prompt

**swift-footed** *adj* au pied léger

**swiftness** *n* rapidité *f*; promptitude *f*

**swig** *n coll* grand trait; *vt coll* boire à grands traits

**swill** *n* lavage *m* à grande eau; (pigswill) pâtée *f* pour les cochons; *vt* laver à grande eau; *sl* boire avidement; **~ out** rincer

**swim** *n* action *f* de nager; *coll* **be in the ~** être dans le mouvement, être à la page; **go for a ~** aller nager; *vt* traverser à la nage; *vi* nager; (be flooded) être inondé; **~ across** traverser à la nage; **~ with the tide** nager dans le sens du courant; *fig* aller dans le sens de la foule; **my head is ~ ming** la tête me tourne

**swimmer** *n* nageur -euse

**swimming** *n* natation *f*, nage *f*

**swimming-bath** *n* piscine *f*

**swimmingly** *adv coll* à merveille, comme sur des roulettes

**swimming-pool** *n* piscine *f*

**swim-suit** *n* costume *m* de bain

**swindle** *n* escroquerie *f*, filouterie *f*; *vt* escroquer, filouter

**swindler** *n* escroc *m*, filou *m*

**swine** *n* cochon *m*, porc *m*; *sl* salaud *m*

**swineherd** *n* porcher -ère

**swing** *n* balancement *m*, oscillation *f*; (child's) balançoire *f*, escarpolette *f*; (opinion) revirement *m*; (music, boxing) swing *m*; **be in full ~** battre son plein; **get into the ~ of things** se mettre au courant; **go with a ~** marcher très bien; (song) être entraînant; **walk with a ~** marcher d'un pas rythmé; *vt* balancer, faire osciller; (turn) faire tourner; (brandish) brandir; (hammock) accrocher; *coll* (fix) arranger; **~ one's arms** balancer les bras en marchant; **~ round** faire pivoter, faire tourner; influencer; *vi* se balancer, osciller, tournoyer; *sl* (hang) être pendu; (door) tourner; changer de direction; **~ along** marcher d'un pas rythmé; **~ back** se rabattre; (pendulum) revenir; *mot* **~ right round** faire un tête-à-queue; **~ round** se retourner; (change mind) faire volte-face; **~ to and fro** osciller, ballotter

**swing-boat** *n* bateau *m* balançoire, balançoire *f*

**swing-bridge** *n* pont tournant

**swing-door** *n* porte *f* va-et-vient

**swingeing** *adj* énorme; (measure) draconien -ienne

**swinging** *adj* oscillant; (arms) ballant; vigoureux -euse; *coll* dans le vent, à la mode; (daring) osé, avancé

**swinish** *adj* de cochon; *sl* grossier -ière, sale

**swipe** *n coll* taloche *f*; *vt coll* donner une taloche à; *sl* (steal) chiper, faucher

**swirl** *n* remous *m*, tourbillon *m*; *vi* tourbillonner

**swish** *n* sifflement *m*; (water, leaves) bruissement *m*; coup *m* de bâton; (dress) froufrou *m*; *adj coll* élégant; *vt* fouetter; (stick) faire siffler; *vi* (water, leaves) bruire; siffler

**Swiss** *n* Suisse -esse; *adj* suisse, helvétique

**switch** *n* (stick) badine *f*; *elect* interrupteur *m*, commutateur *m*; (radio) bouton *m*; (railway) aiguille *f*; (ride) cravache *f*; **two-way ~** interrupteur *m* va-et-vient; *vt* (change) changer; (train) aiguiller; (with stick) donner un coup de badine à; *elect* **~ off** couper, fermer; (light) éteindre; *elect* **~ on** ouvrir; (light) allumer; *mot* **~ on the ignition** mettre le contact; **~ round** changer; *vi* changer; **~ round** se retourner rapidement

**switchback** *n* montagnes *fpl* russes

**switchboard** *n elect* tableau *m* de distribution; (telephone) standard *m*

**Switzerland** *n* Suisse *f*; **French-speaking ~** la Suisse romande; **German-speaking ~** la Suisse allemande (alémanique)

**swivel** *n* émerillon *m*; *vt* faire pivoter, faire tourner; *vi* pivoter, tourner

**swiz(zle)** *n coll* déception *f*, duperie *f*

**swizzle-stick** *n* fouet *m* à champagne

**swollen** *adj* enflé, gonflé; (river) en crue; (face) bouffi

**swollen-headed** *adj* vaniteux -euse

**swoon** *n* évanouissement *m*; *vi obs* s'évanouir

**swoop** *n* descente *f*, attaque *f*; *aer* attaque *f* en piqué; **at one fell ~** d'un (seul) coup; *vi* fondre; **~ down on** s'abattre sur

**swop** *n* + *vt* see **swap**

**sword** *n* épée *f*, sabre *m*; *fig* **cross ~s with s/o** mesurer ses forces avec qn; **put s/o to the ~** passer qn au fil de l'épée

**sword-belt** *n* ceinturon *m*

**sword-dance** *n* danse *f* du sabre

**swordfish** *n* espadon *m*

**swordplay** *n* escrime *f*, maniement *m* de l'épée

**swordsman** *n* escrimeur *m*; **he's a good ~** c'est une fine lame

**swordsmanship** *n* escrime *f*

**sword-swallower** *n* avaleur *m* de sabres

**sworn** *adj* (enemy) juré; (evidence) assermenté

swot

swot *n coll* bûcheur -euse; *vt coll* ~ **up**
piocher; *vi coll* bûcher, piocher
sybarite *n* sybarite
sycamore *n* sycomore *m*
sycophant *n* flagorneur -euse
syllabic *adj* syllabique
syllable *n* syllabe *f*
syllabus *n* programme *m*
syllogism *n* syllogisme *m*
sylph *n* sylphe *m*, sylphide *f*
sylvan *adj* sylvestre
symbol *n* symbole *m*
symbolic(al) *adj* symbolique
symbolism *n* symbolisme *m*
symbolization *n* symbolisation *f*
symbolize *vt* symboliser
symmetric(al) *adj* symétrique
symmetry *n* symétrie *f*
sympathetic *adj* compatissant; *anat*
sympathique; *med* ~ **nerve** grand
sympathique
sympathize *vi* compatir; sympathiser
sympathizer *n* sympathisant -e; (cause)
partisan -e
sympathy *n* compassion *f*; sympathie *f*;
**be in** ~ **with** s/o sympathiser avec qn;
**deepest** ~ condoléances *fpl*
symphonic *adj* symphonique
symphony *n* symphonie *f*
symposium *n* symposium *m*, colloque *m*
symptom *n* symptome *m*, indice *m*
symptomatic *adj* symptomatique
synagogue *n* synagogue *f*
synchromesh *n mot* vitesse synchronisée
synchronism *n* synchronisme *m*
synchronization *n* synchronisation *f*
synchronize *vt* synchroniser; *vi* arriver
simultanément; *elect* être en phase
syncopate *vt* syncoper
syncopation *n* syncope *f*

syndic *n* syndic *m*
syndical *adj* syndical
syndicalism *n* syndicalisme *m*
syndicate *n* syndicat *m*; *vt* syndiquer;
(article) publier simultanément dans
plusieurs journaux
syndrome *n* syndrome *m*
synod *n* concile *m*, synode *m*
synonym *n* synonyme *m*
synonymity, synonymy *n* synonymie *f*
synonymous *adj* synonyme
synonymy *n see* synonymity
synopsis *n* (*pl* synopses) résumé *m*,
abrégé *m*
synoptic *adj* synoptique
synovitis *n med* synovite *f*
syntactic(al) *adj* syntaxique, syntac-
tique
syntax *n* syntaxe *f*
synthesis *n* synthèse *f*
synthesize *vt* synthétiser
synthetic *adj* synthétique, artificiel -ielle
syphilis *n med* syphilis *f*
syphilitic *adj med* syphilitique
Syria *n* Syrie *f*
Syrian *adj* syrien -ienne
syringa *n bot* seringa *m*
syringe *n* seringue *f*; *vt* seringuer, laver à
l'aide d'une seringue
syrup *n* sirop *m*
syrupy *adj* sirupeux -euse
system *n* système *m*, méthode *f*; *anat* organisme *m*; **digestive** ~ appareil digestif; **feudal** ~ régime féodal; **railway** ~
réseau *m* ferroviaire; **road** ~ réseau
routier
systematic *adj* systématique
systematization *n* systématisation *f*
systematize *vt* systématiser
systole *n med* systole *f*

# T

t *n fig* **cross one's** ~ **'s** mettre les points
sur les i; **to a** ~ à la perfection, à merveille
ta *interj coll* merci
tab *n* (clothing) patte *f*; (shoe-lace) ferret
*m*; (label) étiquette *f*; *coll* **keep** ~ **s on**
s/o tenir qn à l'œil; *vt* étiqueter
tabby *n* chat tigré (*f* chatte tigrée)

tabernacle *n* tabernacle *m*
table *n* table *f*; (list) tableau *m*; **clear the**
~ desservir; **lay the** ~ mettre la table,
dresser (mettre) le couvert; **nest of** ~ **s**
table *f* gigogne; **occasional** ~ guéridon
*m*; **turn the** ~ **s on** s/o renverser les
rôles aux dépens de qn; *vt* (bill) déposer; *US* ajourner; cataloguer

732

**tableau** n tableau m

**tablecloth** n nappe f

**table-d'hôte** n table f d'hôte, repas m à prix fixe

**tableland** n geog plateau m

**table-mat** n dessous-de-plat m invar

**tablespoon** n cuiller f (cuillère f) à soupe

**tablespoonful** n cuillerée f à soupe

**tablet** n (writing) tablette f; (plaque) plaque commémorative; med comprimé m

**table-talk** n propos mpl de table, conversation familière

**table-tennis** n tennis m de table, ping-pong m invar

**table-turning** n phénomène m des tables tournantes

**tableware** n vaisselle f

**tabloid** n med comprimé m; (newspaper) journal m de petit format

**taboo, tabu** n tabou m; adj interdit, proscrit; vt déclarer tabou

**tabular** adj tabulaire

**tabulate** vt classifier, disposer en forme de table(s)

**tachometer** n mot compte-tours m; tachymètre m; contrôlographe m

**tacit** adj tacite

**taciturn** adj taciturne

**taciturnity** n taciturnité f

**tack** n petit clou, broquette f; naut amure f; naut (manoeuvre) bordée f; coll **be on the right** ~ être sur la bonne voie; **get down to brass** ~ s en venir au fait; vt clouer; (needlework) bâtir; ~ **sth onto sth** attacher qch à qch; vi naut virer de bord, louvoyer

**tackle** n attirail m, engins mpl; (rugby) placage m; **fishing** ~ attirail m de pêche; (shop) articles mpl de pêche; vt (seize) empoigner, saisir à bras-le-corps; (task) s'attaquer à; (problem) aborder; (rugby) plaquer

**tackling** n (rugby) placage m

**tacky** adj collant, gluant

**tact** n tact m, savoir-faire m

**tactful** adj ~ **person** personne f de tact; **be** ~ avoir du tact

**tactical** adj tactique

**tactician** n tacticien m

**tactics** npl tactique f

**tactile** adj tactile; tangible

**tactless** adj maladroit, indiscret -ète, dépourvu de tact

**tadpole** n têtard m

**taffeta** n taffetas m

**taffy** n US berlingot m, caramel m

**tag** n (shoe-lace) ferret m; (end) bout m qui pend; (string) attache f; (label) étiquette f; (saying) cliché m, citation f; refrain m; (game) chat m; vt (shoe-lace) ferrer; (attach) attacher; vi coll ~ **along behind** s/o suivre qn, traîner derrière qn

**tail** n queue f; (coat) pan m; (coin) pile f; ~ s habit m; **be on** s/o's ~ suivre qn de près, filer qn; coll **keep one's** ~ **up** ne pas se laisser abattre; **turn** ~ s'enfuir; **wear** ~ s porter l'habit; vt suivre de près; enlever la queue (les queues) à; attacher une queue à; vi ~ **away (off)** diminuer; (voice) s'éteindre

**tail-board** n (vehicle) hayon m

**tail-coat** n habit m

**tailed** adj à queue

**tail-end** n extrémité f; queue f; fin f

**tail-light** n mot feu m arrière

**tailor** n tailleur m; vt façonner

**tailor-made** adj fait sur mesure

**tailpiece** n dernier paragraphe

**taint** n corruption f; (stain) souillure f; (hereditary) tare f; (infection) trace f; vt infecter, polluer; (spoil) gâter

**take** n prise f; cin prise f de vue; rad prise f de son; vt prendre; (person) emmener; (catch) attraper; (contain) contenir; (carry) porter; (bear) supporter; (house) louer; (opportunity) saisir; (understand) comprendre; (exam) se présenter à; (paper) s'abonner à; (money) gagner, se faire; (walk) faire; (require) demander; ~ **aback** déconcerter; ~ **a chair** s'asseoir; ~ **an hour to do sth** mettre une heure pour faire qch; ~ **apart** démonter; ~ **aside** prendre à part; ~ **away** emporter, enlever; (person) emmener; (withdraw) retirer; math soustraire; ~ **back** reporter; (person) reconduire; (accept again) reprendre; (words) retirer; ~ **down** descendre; (unhook) décrocher; (write) inscrire; (humiliate) humilier; (demolish) démolir; ~ **hold of** empoigner, saisir; ~ **in** rentrer; (receive) recevoir; (understand, include) comprendre; (lodger) prendre, loger; (cheat) tromper; (garment) reprendre; ~ **into account** tenir compte de; naut ~ **in water** faire eau; ~ **it easy** ne pas se faire de bile; sl se la couler douce; ~ **it from me!** croyez-moi!; ~ **it into one's head to do sth** s'aviser de faire qch; coll fig ~ **it out of** épuiser; coll ~ **it out on** s/o se venger de qn, s'en prendre à qn; ~ **it that** supposer que; ~ **off** ôter, enlever, retirer; (person) emmener; (mimic) imiter; ~ **on** (labour) embaucher; (undertake) entreprendre; (accept) accepter; (lead) mener; ~ **out** sortir; (person) emmener promener; (girl) sortir avec; (tooth) arracher; (insurance) contracter; ~ **over** reprendre, prendre la succession de; (show round) faire visiter; (company) racheter; ~ **pity on** avoir pitié de;

~ **place** avoir lieu; ~ **round** faire visiter; faire faire le tour de; ~ **s/o at his word** prendre qn au mot; ~ **s/o to be fifty** donner cinquante ans à qn; ~ **sth amiss** prendre qch en mauvaise part; ~ **sth from s/o** prendre qch à qn; ~ **that!** attrape ça!; ~ **the chair** présider; ~ **the trouble to do sth** se donner (prendre) la peine de faire qch; ~ **the wrong path** se tromper de chemin; ~ **up** prendre; (pick up) ramasser; (bring up) monter; (person) faire monter; (occupy) occuper, remplir; (remove) enlever; (adopt) adopter; (occupation) commencer, se mettre à; (stitch) relever; (subject) s'occuper de; (sleeve) raccourcir; (career) embrasser; (tell off) reprendre; **be ~n ill** tomber malade; **be ~n up with sth** être occupé à qch; **be ~n with** être attiré (séduit) par; **it ~s courage** il faut du courage; **~n** (occupied) occupé; **taking all in all** à tout prendre; **what do you ~ me for?** pour qui me prenez-vous?; *vi* prendre; (succeed) réussir; ~ **after** ressembler à, tenir de; ~ **off** *aer* décoller; (go away) filer; ~ **on** (worry) s'inquiéter, s'affliger; (get excited) se monter; (succeed) réussir; ~ **over** prendre la succession; ~ **over from s/o** remplacer qn; ~ **to** (affection) s'attacher à; (things) prendre goût à; (get addicted) s'adonner à; (get used to) se faire à; (make for) se diriger vers, se réfugier dans; ~ **upon oneself to do sth** se charger de faire qch; (take liberty) se permettre de faire qch; ~ **up with s/o** se lier d'amitié avec qn; fréquenter qn; (live with) se mettre en ménage avec qn

**take-off** *n aer* décollage *m*; *coll* caricature *f*

**take-over** *n* prise *f* de possession; (business) reprise *f*; ~ **bid** offre publique d'achat

**taker** *n* preneur -euse; (bet) tenant *m*; **any ~s?** y a-t-il quelqu'un que ça intéresse?; y a-t-il preneur?

**taking** *n* prise *f*; *adj* attrayant, séduisant

**takings** *npl* recette *f*

**talc** *n* talc *m*

**talcum** *n* poudre *f* de talc

**tale** *n* conte *m*, récit *m*, histoire *f*; *pej* racontar *m*; **old wives' ~s** histoires *fpl* de bonne femme; **tell ~s** rapporter, *coll* moucharder

**talent** *n* talent *m*; aptitude *f*; don *m*

**talented** *adj* doué, de talent

**tale-teller** *n* rapporteur -euse

**talisman** *n* talisman *m*

**talk** *n* conversation *f*; (chat) causerie *f*; (rumour) bruit *m*; (gossip) bavardage *m*; **have a ~ with s/o** causer avec qn; **have ~s** avoir des entretiens; **he's all ~** ce n'est qu'un bavard; **idle ~** paroles *fpl* en l'air; **there's some ~ of a visit** il est question d'une visite; **there is some ~ that** le bruit court que; *vt* parler; ~ **down** faire taire en parlant plus fort; ~ **English** parler anglais; ~ **s/o into doing sth** persuader qn de faire qch; ~ **s/o round** persuader qn, convaincre qn; *vi* parler; (chat) causer, bavarder; ~ **about** (gossip) jaser de; ~ **away** parler sans arrêt; ~ **big** se vanter; ~ **down to one's listeners** s'abaisser au niveau de son auditoire; ~ **on** continuer à parler; ~ **over** discuter; ~ **through one's hat** dire des bêtises; **now you're ~ing!** voilà qui s'appelle parler! ~**ing of that** à propos de cela

**talkative** *adj* bavard, loquace

**talker** *n* parleur -euse; *coll* **be a great ~** *coll* avoir la langue bien pendue

**talkie** *n coll cin obs* film parlant

**talking** *n* bavardage *m*, conversation *f*; *adj* parlant

**talking-point** *n* sujet *m* de discussion

**talking-to** *n* semonce *f*

**tall** *adj* grand, de haute taille; (building, etc) haut, élevé; *coll* invraisemblable, exagéré

**tallboy** *n* grande commode

**tallness** *n* (person) grande taille; (building, etc) hauteur *f*

**tallow** *n* suif *m*

**tally** *n* pointage *m*; (label) étiquette *f*; (stick) taille *f*; *vt* pointer; (goods) contrôler; *vi* correspondre, s'accorder

**tally-clerk** *n* pointeur -euse

**tally-ho** *n* + *interj* taïaut *m*

**Talmud** *n* Talmud *m*

**talon** *n* (bird) serre *f*; griffe *f*

**tamable** *adj* domptable

**tamarisk** *n bot* tamaris *m*

**tambour** *n mus* grosse caisse; (needlework) tambour *m* à broder

**tambourine** *n* tambourin *m*, tambour *m* de basque

**tame** *adj* (animal) apprivoisé; (person) docile; (poor) faible; (style) monotone; *vt* apprivoiser; (lion, etc) dompter; (passion) mater

**tamely** *adv* faiblement, avec soumission

**tameness** *n* docilité *f*; soumission *f*; caractère soumis; (insipidity) monotonie *f*, fadeur *f*

**tamp** *vt* tasser, damer

**tamper** *vi* ~ **with** toucher à; (document) falsifier; (witness) suborner, corrompre

**tampon** *n* tampon *m*

**tan** *n* tan *m*; (skin) hâle *m*; *adj* tanné; *vt* tanner; (sun) hâler, bronzer; *coll*

étriller; *vi* se hâler, se bronzer
**tandem** *n* tandem *m*
**tang** *n* saveur *f*, goût vif
**tangent** *n* tangente *f*; **fly off at a ~** prendre la tangente; *adj* tangent
**tangential** *adj* tangentiel -ielle
**tangerine** *n* mandarine *f*
**tangibility** *n* tangibilité *f*
**tangible** *adj* tangible
**tangle** *n* confusion *f*, embrouillement *m*, enchevêtrement *m*; (muddle) fouillis *m*; *coll* **be in a ~** ne plus savoir où on est; *coll* **get into a ~** s'embrouiller; *vt* embrouiller, emmêler, enchevêtrer; *vi* s'embrouiller, s'emmêler
**tangly** *adj* embrouillé, emmêlé
**tango** *n* tango *m*
**tank** *n* réservoir *m*; (water) citerne *f*; *mil* tank *m*, char *m* (de combat); *US* **~ truck (car)** camion-citerne *m* (*pl* camions-citernes); **petrol ~** réservoir *m* à essence; **septic ~** fosse *f* septique; *vi* **mot ~ up** faire le plein (d'essence)
**tankard** *n* chope *f*, grand pot
**tanker** *n* (ship) bateau-citerne *m* (*pl* bateaux-citernes); (vehicle) camion-citerne *m* (*pl* camions-citernes)
**¹tanner** *n* tanneur *m*
**²tanner** *n coll ar + obs* pièce *f* de six pence
**tannery** *n* tannerie *f*
**tannin** *n* tan(n)in *m*
**tanning** *n* tannage *m*; *coll* raclée *f*
**Tannoy** *n* système *m* de diffusion par haut-parleur
**tantalization** *n* tentation *f*; provocation *f*
**tantalize** *vt* (tease) taquiner; mettre au supplice, infliger le supplice de Tantale à
**tantalizing** *adj* tentant; provocant
**tantamount** *adj* équivalent; **it is ~ to saying** c'est comme si on disait
**tantrum** *n* accès *m* de colère
**¹tap** *n* (water) robinet *m*; (barrel) fausset *m*, cannelle *f*; **be on ~** être toujours disponible; **on ~** en perce; (wine) au tonneau; **turn off (on) the ~** fermer (ouvrir) le robinet; *vt* (cask) percer, mettre en perce; (tree) gemmer; (wine) tirer; (main) brancher; (phone) écouter
**²tap** *n* tape *f*, petit coup; *vt* taper, tapoter, frapper légèrement; *vi* **~ at** frapper à
**tap-dance** *n* danse *f* à claquettes
**tape** *n* ruban *m*; (recording) bande *f* (magnétique); **adhesive ~** scotch *m*; *coll* **red ~** formalités *fpl* bureaucratiques, fonctionnarisme *m*; *vt* (garment) border; (measure) mesurer au cordeau; (record) enregistrer sur bande; **he's got it all ~d** il a la situation bien en main
**tape-machine** *n* téléimprimeur *m*

**tape-measure** *n* mètre *m* (à ruban)
**taper** *n* bougie filée; *eccles* cierge *m*; *vt* effiler; *vi* aller en diminuant; **~ off** s'effiler
**tape-recorder** *n* magnétophone *m*
**tape-recording** *n* enregistrement *m* sur bande (magnétique)
**tapering** *adj* effilé, en pointe
**tapestry** *n* tapisserie *f*
**tapeworm** *n* ver *m* solitaire, ténia *m*
**tapioca** *n* tapioca *m*
**tappet** *n mech* came *f* de distribution, taquet *m*
**tapping** *n* petits coups; (tree) incision *f*; (cask) mise *f* en perce; *elect* branchement *m*; (message) captation *f*
**tap-room** *n* bar *m*
**tap-root** *n* racine pivotante
**tap-water** *n* eau *f* du robinet, eau *f* de la ville
**tar** *n* goudron *m*; *coll* (sailor) loup *m* de mer; **spoil the ship for a ha'p'orth of ~** faire des économies de bouts de chandelle; *vt* goudronner; *coll* **be ~red with the same brush** avoir les mêmes défauts
**tarantella** *n* tarantelle *f*
**tarantula** *n* tarentule *f*
**tardy** *adj* lent; (lazy) paresseux -euse; (belated) tardif -ive
**¹tare** *n bot* ivraie *f*
**²tare** *n comm* tare *f*; poids *m* à vide
**target** *n* cible *f*; but *m*; objectif *m*; **be the (a) ~ for** être en butte à
**target-practice** *n* tir *m* à la cible
**tariff** *n* tarif *m*; (price-list) liste *f* des prix
**tarmac** *n* goudron *m*, bitume *m*; *aer* (runway) piste *f* d'envol; *aer* aire *f* de stationnement
**tarnish** *n* ternissure *f*; *vt* ternir; *vi* se ternir
**tarpaulin** *n* bâche *f*
**¹tarry** *adj* goudronneux -euse
**²tarry** *vi* s'attarder; (remain) rester, demeurer
**¹tart** *n cul* tarte *f*; (small) tartelette *f*, tourte *f*; *sl* (whore) poule *f*, grue *f*; *vt* **~ oneself up** s'attifer
**²tart** *adj* aigre, acide; (manner) acerbe; (wine) vert
**tartan** *n* tartan *m*
**tartar** *n* tartre *m*
**Tartar** *n* Tartare, Tatar -e; *coll* personne coléreuse
**tartness** *n* aigreur *f*, acidité *f*; (manner) acerbité *f*
**task** *n* tâche *f*, besogne *f*, ouvrage *m*; **take s/o to ~** prendre qn à partie
**task-force** *n* corps *m* expéditionnaire
**taskmaster** *n fig* tyran *m*
**tassel** *n* gland *m*, pompon *m*, houppe *f*; (book) signet *m*

**taste** n goût m, saveur f; (inclination) penchant m, prédilection f; ~ s differ à chacun son goût; **acquire a ~ for** prendre goût à; **have ~** avoir du goût; **in bad ~** de mauvais goût; **just a ~** un tout petit peu, un soupçon; vt goûter, goûter à; (eat a little) manger un petit peu de; (wine) déguster; (perceive a taste) sentir; (happiness, power, etc) connaître; vi ~ **of** avoir un (le) goût de

**taste-bud** n papille gustative

**tasteful** adj de bon goût; (dress) élégant

**tasteless** adj fade, insipide, sans saveur; (in bad taste) de mauvais goût

**taster** n dégustateur -trice

**tasty** adj succulent, savoureux -euse

**tat** vt (needlework) faire en frivolité; vi faire de la frivolité

**ta-ta** interj coll au revoir!

**tatter** n lambeau m; **in ~ s** en lambeaux

**tattered** adj en lambeaux, en loques

**tattiness** n (shabbiness) aspect défraîchi; (untidiness) aspect déguenillé

**tattle** n bavardage m, commérage m; vi cancaner

**tattler** n cancanier -ière

**¹tattoo** n mil retraite f; **beat a ~** tambouriner

**²tattoo** n (marking) tatouage m; vt tatouer

**tatty** adj (shabby) défraîchi; (untidy) déguenillé

**taunt** n reproche m; insulte f, injure f; vt railler, se moquer de; ~ **s/o with sth** reprocher qch à qn

**taut** adj tendu, raide

**tautological** adj tautologique

**tautology** n tautologie f

**tavern** n cabaret m, taverne f

**tawdry** adj clinquant, voyant, d'un mauvais goût criard

**tawny** adj fauve

**tax** n impôt m, taxe f, contribution f; (burden) charge f; **collect ~ es** percevoir des impôts; **direct (indirect) ~ es** contributions directes (indirectes); **value-added ~** taxe f à la valeur ajoutée; vt taxer, imposer; mettre un impôt sur; (accuse) accuser; (strain) mettre à l'épreuve

**taxable** adj imposable

**taxation** n imposition f, taxation f

**tax-collector** n percepteur -trice

**tax-free** adj exempt d'impôts

**taxi** n (also ~ **-cab**) taxi m; vi aer rouler au sol

**taxidermist** n empailleur -euse

**taxidermy** n taxidermie f, naturalisation f d'animaux

**taxi-driver**, **taximan** n chauffeur m de taxi

**taximeter** n taximètre m

**taxi-rank** n station f de taxis

**taxology, taxonomy** n taxonomie f

**tax-payer** n contribuable

**tea** n thé m; (herb) tisane f, infusion f; **afternoon ~** goûter m, five o'clock m; **beef ~** bouillon m; **China ~** thé m de Chine; **come to ~** venir prendre le thé; **Indian ~** thé m de Ceylan; **coll it's not my cup of ~** je n'aime pas ça

**tea-bag** n sachet m de thé

**tea-break** n = pause-café f (pl pauses-café)

**tea-caddy** n boîte f à thé

**teach** vt (subjects, pupils) enseigner, (pupils) instruire, apprendre à; ~ **s/o sth** enseigner (apprendre) qch à qn; **she ~ es** elle est dans l'enseignement

**tea-chest** n caisse f à thé

**teach-in** n débat public dans une université

**teaching** n enseignement m, instruction f; adj ~ **profession** corps enseignant; **the ~ staff** (secondary) les professeurs mpl; (primary) les instituteurs mpl

**tea-cloth** n (wiping) torchon m; (table) napperon m

**tea-cosy** n couvre-théière m

**teacup** n tasse f à thé; **storm in a ~** tempête f dans un verre d'eau

**tea-dance** n thé dansant

**tea-garden** n établissement m où l'on sert le thé en plein air; plantation f de thé

**teak** n teck m

**tea-leaf** n feuille f de thé

**team** n sp équipe f; (horses, etc) attelage m; ~ **spirit** esprit m d'équipe; **home ~** équipe f qui reçoit; vt atteler; vi ~ **up with** se joindre à

**teamwork** n travail m en équipe

**tea-party** n thé m

**teapot** n théière f

**¹tear** n larme f; **be in ~ s** être en larmes; **burst into ~ s** fondre en larmes; **shed ~ s** verser des larmes; **with ~ s in her eyes** les larmes aux yeux

**²tear** n (action) déchirement m; déchirure f; vt déchirer; ~ **away (down, off, from)** arracher; coll ~ **one's hair** s'arracher les cheveux; ~ **open** ouvrir en déchirant; ~ **up** déchirer (en morceaux); (tree) déraciner; (road) défoncer; **be torn between** hésiter entre; vi se déchirer; coll ~ **along** aller à toute vitesse; ~ **at** déchirer, arracher

**tear-drop** n larme f

**tear-duct** n conduit lacrymal

**tearful** adj en pleurs; pej pleurnichant, larmoyant

**tear-gas** n gaz m lacrymogène

**tear-jerker** n coll histoire f (film m, roman m, etc) très sentimental(e)

**tea-room** n salon m de thé

**tea-rose** n rose f thé

**tear-stained** adj barbouillé de larmes

**tease** n taquin -e; vt taquiner; (wool) démêler, carder

**teaser** n taquin -e; coll colle f, problème m difficile

**tea-service, tea-set** n service m à thé

**tea-shop** n salon m de thé

**teaspoon** n cuiller f à thé

**teaspoonful** n cuillerée f à thé; = cuillerée f à café

**tea-strainer** n passe-thé m invar

**teat** n mamelon m, tétin m, téton m; (bottle) tétine f

**tea-table** n table f à thé

**tea-things** npl service m à thé

**tea-towel** n torchon m

**tea-tray** n plateau m

**tea-urn** n = samovar m

**technical** adj technique

**technicality** n détail m technique

**technician** n technicien -ienne

**Technicolor** n Technicolor m

**technique** n technique f

**technocracy** n technocratie f

**technocrat** n technocrate

**technological** adj technologique

**technologist** n technologue

**technology** n technologie f

**techy** adj see **tetchy**

**teddy-bear** n ours m en peluche, coll nounours m

**Te Deum** n Te Deum m

**tedious** adj ennuyeux -euse, fatigant

**tedium, tediousness** n ennui m

**tee** n dé m, tee m; vt surélever

¹**teem** vi abonder, foisonner, fourmiller

²**teem** vt (discharge) déverser

**teenage** adj adolescent

**teenager** n adolescent -e

**teens** npl coll âge m entre douze et vingt ans

**teeny** adj coll tout petit, minuscule

**teeter** vi chanceler, basculer

**teething** n dentition f; adj fig ~ **troubles** difficultés initiales; **be** ~ faire ses dents

**teetotal** adj abstinent; antialcoolique

**teetotalism** n antialcoolisme m, abstention f de boissons alcooliques

**telecast** n émission f de télévision, programme m télévisé

**telecommunications** npl télécommunications fpl

**telegram** n télégramme m, dépêche f

**telegraph** n télégraphe m; vt + vi télégraphier

**telegraphic** adj télégraphique

**telegraphist** n télégraphiste

**telegraph-pole** n poteau m télégraphique

**telegraphy** n télégraphie f; **wireless** ~ télégraphie f sans fils, T.S.F.

**telepathic** adj télépathique

**telepathy** n télépathie f

**telephone** n téléphone m; ~ **call** appel m téléphonique; ~ **number** numéro m de téléphone; **be on the** ~ avoir le téléphone; **he's wanted on the** ~ on le demande au téléphone; vt (person) téléphoner à; (message) téléphoner; vi téléphoner

**telephone-box (booth)** n cabine f téléphonique

**telephone-operator** n téléphoniste, standardiste

**telephonic** adj téléphonique

**telephonist** n téléphoniste, standardiste

**telephony** n téléphonie f

**telephotography** n photographie f au téléobjectif

**telephoto-lens** n téléobjectif m

**teleprint** vt transmettre par téléscripteur

**teleprinter** n téléscripteur m

**telerecord** vt enregistrer à la télévision

**telerecording** n émission de télévision enregistrée

**telescope** n télescope m; vt télescoper

**telescopic** adj télescopique; ~ **lens** téléobjectif m

**teletype** vt transmettre par téléscripteur

**teletypewriter** n téléscripteur m

**televiewer** n téléspectateur -trice

**televise** vt téléviser

**television** n télévision f; ~ **set** poste m de télévision, téléviseur m

**telex** n télex m

**tell** vt dire; (relate) raconter; (inform) apprendre; (announce) proclamer, annoncer; (know) savoir; (distinguish) reconnaître, distinguer; (express) exprimer; (count) compter; ~ **off** (scold) laver la tête à, dire son fait à; (count) énumérer; ~ **s/o sth** dire qch à qn; ~ **s/o to do sth** ordonner (dire, commander) à qn de faire qch; (clock) ~ **the time** marquer l'heure; **all told** tout compris, en tout; **I am told** on me dit; **I told you so!** je vous l'avais bien dit!; **you never can** ~ on ne sait jamais; **you're** ~**ing me!** à qui le dites-vous!; vi produire son effet, porter; ~ **on** affecter, agir sur; coll moucharder

**tellable** adj que l'on peut dire; que l'on ose raconter

**teller** n narrateur -trice, conteur -euse; (bank) caissier -ière; (votes) scrutateur -trice

**telling** n récit m, narration f; (votes) énumération f; **there's no** ~ on ne sait jamais; adj efficace, frappant; ~ **blow** coup m qui porte

**telling-off** n coll semonce f, coll engueulade f

**telltale** n rapporteur -euse, coll cafard

737

-e; *adj* révélateur -trice

**telly** *n* télé *f*

**temerarious** *adj* téméraire

**temerity** *n* témérité *f*

**temp** *n coll* intérimaire

**temper** *n* (humour) humeur *f*; (anger) colère *f*; (disposition) caractère *m*; *metal* trempe *f*; **be in a** ~ être en colère; **have a good** ~ avoir bon caractère; **in a bad (good)** ~ de mauvaise (bonne) humeur; **keep one's** ~ rester calme; **lose one's** ~ se mettre en colère, s'emporter; *vt* (moderate) tempérer, adoucir; (mix) délayer, broyer; *metal* tremper

**temperament** *n* tempérament *m*

**temperamental** *adj* capricieux -ieuse, fantasque

**temperance** *n* (drink) tempérance *f*; modération *f*; ~ **society** ligue *f* antialcoolique

**temperate** *adj* (person) sobre; modéré; (climate) tempéré

**temperature** *n* température *f*

**tempered** *adj* (steel) trempé

**tempest** *n* tempête *f*

**tempestuous** *adj fig* orageux -euse; tempétueux -euse

¹**temple** *n* (church) temple *m*, église *f*

²**temple** *n anat* tempe *f*

**tempo** *n* rythme *m*; *mus* tempo *m*

¹**temporal** *adj anat* temporal

²**temporal** *adj* temporel -elle

**temporality** *n* pouvoir temporel

**temporarily** *adv* provisoirement, temporairement

**temporariness** *n* caractère *m* temporaire

**temporary** *n* intérimaire; *adj* temporaire, provisoire; (transient) passager -ère

**temporize** *vi* temporiser

**tempt** *vt* tenter; **be strongly ~ed to do sth** avoir bien envie de faire qch

**temptation** *n* tentation *f*; **yield to ~** se laisser tenter, succomber à la tentation

**tempter** *n* tentateur *m*

**tempting** *adj* tentant, attrayant, séduisant

**temptress** *n* tentatrice *f*

**ten** *n* dix *m invar*; **about ~** une dizaine; **they came in ~s** ils sont arrivés par dizaines; *adj* dix *invar*

**tenable** *adj* (argument) soutenable; (position) tenable

**tenacious** *adj* tenace

**tenaciously** *adv* avec ténacité

**tenacity** *n* ténacité *f*

**tenancy** *n* location *f*; (lease) bail *m* (*pl* baux)

**tenant** *n* locataire

**tenanted** *adj* occupé, habité (par un locataire)

**tench** *n* tanche *f*

¹**tend** *vt* soigner; (supervise) garder, surveiller; (garden) entretenir

²**tend** *vi* tendre; ~ **to do sth** (be liable to) avoir une tendance à faire qch, être sujet -ette à faire qch; (have tendency to) tendre à faire qch

**tendency** *n* tendance *f*, inclination *f*

**tendentious, tendencious** *adj* tendancieux -ieuse

¹**tender** *n* offre *f*, soumission *f*; **be legal ~** avoir cours; **by ~** par voie d'adjudication; **invite ~s for work** mettre un travail en adjudication; *vt* offrir; *vi comm* faire une soumission

²**tender** *n* (guard) garde *m*, gardien *m*; (locomotive) tender *m*; *naut* bateau *m* annexe; **bar ~** barman *m*

³**tender** *adj* tendre; (to touch) sensible; (subject) délicat; (delicate) fragile; (person) affectueux -euse, tendre; **of ~ years** en bas âge

**tenderfoot** *n* novice

**tender-hearted** *adj* sensible, au cœur tendre

**tenderly** *adv* tendrement, avec tendresse

**tenderness** *n* (feelings) tendresse *f*, affection *f*; (skin, etc) sensibilité *f*; fragilité *f*; (steak, etc) tendreté *f*

**tendon** *n* tendon *m*

**tendril** *n* vrille *f*

**tenement** *n* appartement *m* dans une maison de rapport; ~ **house** maison *f* de rapport

**tenet** *n* doctrine *f*, principe *m*

**tenfold** *adj* décuple; **increase ~** décupler

**tennis** *n* tennis *m*

**tennis-ball** *n* balle *f* de tennis

**tennis-court** *n* court *m* (terrain *m*) de tennis

**tenon** *n carp* tenon *m*

**tenor** *n* teneur *f*, sens général; (content) contenu *m*; *mus* ténor *m*; ~ **of events** cours *m* des événements

¹**tense** *n gramm* temps *m*

²**tense** *adj* tendu, raide

**tenseness** *n* tension *f*, rigidité *f*

**tensile** *adj* extensible, élastique

**tension** *n* tension *f*; rigidité *f*; *elect* voltage *m*

**tent** *n* tente *f*; **pitch a ~** dresser une tente

**tentacle** *n* tentacule *m*

**tentative** *adj* d'essai, expérimental

**tenterhooks** *npl* **on ~** au supplice

**tenth** *n* dixième; (date) dix *m*; *adj* dixième

**tenthly** *adv* en dixième lieu, dixièmement

**tenuous** *adj* ténu, mince

**tenure** *n* possession *f*, occupation *f*; **during his ~ of office** pendant la période où il exerçait ses fonctions

**tepid** *adj* tiède

**tepidity** *n* tiédeur *f*

**tepidly** *adv* tièdement

**tercentenary** *n* tricentenaire *m*; *adj* tricentenaire

**term** *n* terme *m*, limite *f*; (period) temps *m*; (duration) durée *f*; (expression) terme *m*; (school) trimestre *m*; ~s conditions *fpl*; (relations) rapports *mpl*, relations *fpl*; ~s of reference attributions *fpl*; **beginning of** ~ rentrée *f* des classes; **be on good (bad)** ~s **with** être bien (mal) avec; **by the** ~s **of** aux termes de; **come to** ~s **with** s'arranger avec; **contradiction in** ~s contradiction *f* dans les termes; **inclusive** ~s tout compris; **on easy** ~s avec facilités de paiement; **on no** ~s à aucun prix; **on these** ~s à ces conditions; *vt* appeler, nommer

**termagant** *n* mégère *f*

**terminable** *adj* terminable; (contract) résiliable

**terminal** *n* (railway) gare *f* terminus; *aer* aérogare *f*; *elect* borne *f*; *adj* qui termine, terminal, dernier -ière; (school) de trimestre

**terminate** *vt* terminer, mettre fin à; (contract) résilier; *vi* se terminer, finir

**termination** *n* terminaison *f*, conclusion *f*; (stopping) cessation *f*

**terminological** *adj* terminologique

**terminology** *n* terminologie *f*

**terminus** *n* terminus *m*, tête *f* de ligne

**termite** *n* termite *m*

**tern** *n orni* sterne *f*, hirondelle *f* de mer

**terrace** *n* terrasse *f*; (houses) rangée *f* de maisons toutes pareilles; *vt* disposer en terrasses

**terracotta** *n* terre cuite

**terrain** *n* terrain *m*

**terrestrial** *adj* terrestre

**terrible** *adj* terrible, affreux -euse; *coll* excessif -ive

**terribly** *adv* terriblement, affreusement; *coll* très, extrêmement

**terrier** *n* terrier *m*

**terrific** *adj* épouvantable, terrible; *coll* formidable

**terrify** *vt* terrifier, épouvanter; ~ s/o out of his (her) wits rendre qn fou (*f* folle) de terreur

**terrine** *n* terrine *f*

**territorial** *adj* territorial; the ~ army = la réserve (composée de volontaires)

**territory** *n* territoire *m*

**terror** *n* terreur *f*, épouvante *f*; *coll* be a ~ for driving fast conduire à une vitesse terrifiante; *coll* go in ~ of sth avoir une peur bleue de qch; *coll* he's a little ~ c'est un enfant terrible

**terrorism** *n* terrorisme *m*

**terrorist** *n* terroriste

**terrorize** *vt* terroriser

**terror-struck** *adj* saisi de terreur

**terse** *adj* concis, net (*f* nette); (manner) brusque

**tertiary** *adj* tertiaire

**Terylene** *n* Térylène *m*

**test** *n* épreuve *f*; test *m*, examen *m*; ~ case précédent *m*; *leg* cas *m* faisant jurisprudence; *chem* réactif *m*; *fig* acid ~ épreuve concluante; pass a ~ être accepté; put to the ~ mettre à l'épreuve; *vt* éprouver; tester, examiner; mettre à l'épreuve; (try out) essayer; (check) contrôler

**testament** *n* testament *m*

**testator** *n leg* testateur *m*

**testatrix** *n leg* testatrice *f*

**tester** *n* (person) essayeur -euse; (device) appareil *m* de contrôle

**testicle** *n* testicule *m*

**testify** *vt* témoigner; (declare) affirmer; *vi* témoigner; ~ against (in favour of) s/o déposer contre (en faveur de) qn

**testily** *adv* d'un air irrité

**testimonial** *n* (presentation) témoignage *m* d'estime; (reference) certificat *m*, lettre *f* de recommandation

**testimony** *n* témoignage *m*; *leg* déposition *f*, attestation *f*; in ~ of which en foi de quoi

**testiness** *n* irritabilité *f*

**test-pilot** *n* pilote *m* d'essai

**test-tube** *n* éprouvette *f*

**testy** *adj* irritable, irascible

**tetanus** *n* tétanos *m*

**tetchy, techy** *adj* facilement irrité, susceptible

**tête-à-tête** *n* tête-à-tête *m invar*, entretien privé

**tether** *n* attache *f*, longe *f*; be at the end of one's ~ être à bout (à bout de forces, à bout de ressources); *vt* attacher

**Teutonic** *adj* teuton -onne, teutonique

**text** *n* texte *m*; stick to one's ~ s'en tenir au sujet

**text-book** *n* manuel *m*

**textile** *n* textile *m*, tissu *m*; *adj* textile

**textual** *adj* textuel -elle

**texture** *n* texture *f*; (skin) grain *m*

**thalidomide** *n* thalidomide *f*

**than** *conj* que; (with numbers) de; more ~ seven plus de sept; more ~ you plus que vous; more ~ you think plus que vous ne croyez

**thank** *vt* remercier, dire merci à; ~ God! Dieu merci!; ~ s/o for sth remercier qn de qch; he has only himself to ~ for it c'est uniquement de sa faute; no ~ you (non) merci

**thankful** *adj* reconnaissant

**thankfully** *adv* avec reconnaissance

**thankless** *adj* ingrat

**thank-offering** *n* sacrifice *m* d'actions de grâces

**thanks** *npl* remerciements *mpl*; ~! merci!; ~ **to** grâce à; **give her my** ~ remerciez-la de ma part; **give** ~ **to** remercier, rendre grâces à; **many** ~! merci bien!

**thanksgiving** *n* action *f* de grâces

**that** *dem pron* cela, ça; (the one, that one) celui(-là) (*f* celle(-là), *mpl* ceux(-là), *fpl* celles(-là)); ~ **is (to say)** c'est à dire; ~'s ~! et voilà!; ~'s the **house!** voilà la maison!; ~'s why! voilà pourquoi!; **at** ~ (moreover) ce qui plus est; **is** ~ **your father?** est-ce là votre père?; **it has come to** ~ les choses en sont venues là; **what is** ~? qu'est-ce que c'est que cela?; *rel pron* (subject) qui; (object) que; (after prepositions) lequel (*f* laquelle, *mpl* lesquels, *fpl* lesquelles); *adj* ce (cet before vowel or h mute) (*f* cette, *mpl* + *fpl* ces); ~ **house is bigger than this one** cette maison-là est plus grande que celle-ci; **those people who don't care** ceux qui ne s'en soucient pas; *adv* **he's not** ~ **rich** il n'est pas si riche que ça; **she's** ~ **pretty!** elle est si jolie!; *conj* que; (in order that) afin que, pour que; ~ **he should die so young!** dire qu'il est mort si jeune!

**thatch** *n* chaume *m*; *vt* couvrir de chaume; ~ **ed cottage** chaumière *f*

**thaw** *n* dégel *m*; fonte *f* des neiges; *fig* dégel *m*; *vt* + *vi* dégeler, fondre; *vi* (person) perdre sa froideur

**the** *def art* le (*f* la) (both l' before vowel or h mute) (*mpl* + *fpl* les); **of** ~ du (*f* de la) (both de l' before vowel or h mute) (*mpl* + *fpl* des); **to** ~ au (*f* à la) (both à l' before vowel or h mute) (*mpl* + *fpl* aux); ~ **cheek!** quel culot!; **Henry** ~ **Eighth** Henri huit; **it's** *the* **place for winter sports** c'est le meilleur endroit pour les sports d'hiver; *adv* ~ **less he works,** ~ **less he earns** moins il travaille, moins il gagne; ~ **more one has,** ~ **more one wants** plus on a, plus on en veut; ~ **sooner** ~ **better** le plus tôt sera le mieux; **all** ~ **better (more)** d'autant mieux (plus)

**theatre** *n* théâtre *m*; (drama) art *m* dramatique; (lecture) amphithéâtre *m*, *coll* amphi *m*; (operating) salle *f* d'opérations

**theatre-goer** *n* amateur *m* de théâtre

**theatrical** *adj* théâtral; ~ **company** troupe *f* d'acteurs (de comédiens)

**theatricals** *npl* **amateur** ~ spectacle *m* d'amateurs

**thee** *pron ar* + *lit* te; toi

**theft** *n* vol *m*; **petty** ~ larcin *m*

**their** *adj* leur

**theirs** *pron* le leur (*f* la leur), à eux (*f* à elles); **she is a cousin of** ~ c'est une de leurs cousines

**theism** *n* théisme *m*

**theist** *n* théiste

**them** *pron* les; eux (*f* elles); (to them) leur, y; **both of** ~ tous (*f* toutes) les deux; **I'll take half of** ~ j'en prendrai la moitié; **most of** ~ la plupart d'entre eux; **neither of** ~ ni l'un(e) ni l'autre; **of** ~ en

**thematic** *adj* thématique; par sujets

**theme** *n* thème *m*, sujet *m*

**themselves** *pron pl* se; eux-mêmes (*f* elles-mêmes)

**then** *adj* d'alors, de l'époque; *adv* alors, à cette époque, en ce temps-là; (next) puis, ensuite; ~ **and there** immédiatement, sur-le-champ; **before** ~ avant cela; **between now and** ~ d'ici là; **now and** ~ de temps en temps, de temps à autre; **since** ~ depuis ce temps-là; **till** ~ jusqu'alors, jusque-là; **what** ~? et puis après?; *conj* (therefore) donc, par conséquent, alors

**thence** *adv* de là; (therefore) par conséquent

**thenceforth** *adv* désormais

**thenceforward** *adv* à partir de ce temps-là

**theocracy** *n* théocratie *f*

**theodolite** *n* théodolite *m*

**theologian** *n* théologien -ienne

**theological** *adj* théologique

**theology** *n* théologie *f*

**theorem** *n* théorème *m*

**theoretical** *adj* théorique

**theorist** *n* théoricien -ienne

**theorize** *vi* faire de la théorie

**theory** *n* théorie *f*, hypothèse *f*; **in** ~ en principe, en théorie

**theosophy** *n* théosophie *f*

**therapeutic** *adj* thérapeutique

**therapeutics** *npl* thérapeutique *f*

**therapist** *n* praticien -ienne; **occupational** ~ spécialiste de thérapie rééducative

**therapy** *n* thérapie *f*

**there** *impers pron* ~ **is (are)** il y a; ~ **occurred sth terrible** il se passa qch de terrible; ~ **was once upon a time** il était une fois; *adv* là; y; (yonder) là-bas; ~ **and back** aller et retour; ~'s **the problem** c'est là le problème; ~, **take it!** tenez, prenez-le!; ~ **they are!** les voilà!; ~ **they come!** les voilà qui arrivent!; ~ **you are wrong** en cela (quant à cela) vous avez tort; *coll* **be all**

# think

~ être avisé; **go** ~ **and back** aller et revenir; *coll* **he's not all** ~ il n'a pas toute sa tête; **he won't leave** ~ il refuse de partir de là; **in** ~ là-dedans; **out** ~ là-dehors; **over** ~ là-bas; **up** ~ là-haut

**thereabouts** *adv* près de là, par là; (approximately) à peu près, environ

**thereafter** *adv* ensuite, par la suite, après cela

**thereby** *adv* par ce moyen, de cette façon

**therefore** *adv* donc, par conséquent

**therein** *adv* en cela, à cet égard

**thereupon** *adv* là-dessus, sur ce

**therewith** *adv* avec cela

**therm** *n* unité *f* britannique de chaleur

**thermal** *adj* thermal; ~ **baths** thermes *mpl*

**thermodynamics** *npl* thermodynamique *f*

**thermometer** *n* thermomètre *m*

**thermonuclear** *adj* thermonucléaire

**Thermos** *n* Thermos *m* or *f*

**thermostat** *n* thermostat *m*

**thesaurus** *n* thesaurus *m*

**thesis** *n* thèse *f*

**they** *pron* ils (*f* elles); eux (*f* elles); ~ **are good pupils** ce sont de bons élèves; ~ **say on dit; here** ~ **are!** les voici!; **My parents? They don't know!** Mes parents? Eux, ils n'en savent rien!

**thick** *n* partie épaisse; **be in the** ~ **of the fight** être au plus fort du combat; **through** ~ **and thin** à travers toutes les épreuves; *adj* épais (*f* épaisse); (big) gros (*f* grosse); (dense) serré, touffu; (intimate) intime; *coll* stupide; (beard) fourni; (head) lourd; ~ **soup** crème *f*; **be as** ~ **as thieves** s'accorder comme larrons en foire; **be very** ~ **with s/o** être très lié avec qn; **have a** ~ **skin** être peu sensible; *adv* en couche épaisse; (slices) en tranches épaisses; **fall** ~ **and fast** tomber (pleuvoir) dru; **lay it on** ~ exagérer

**thicken** *vt* épaissir; (sauce) lier; *vi* (s') épaissir; (sauce) se lier; (plot) se compliquer

**thickening** *n* épaississement *m*

**thicket** *n* fourré *m*

**thick-headed** *adj* stupide, bête

**thickish** *adj* assez épais (*f* épaisse); *coll* assez stupide

**thickly** *adv* en couche épaisse; (snow, etc) dru

**thickness** *n* épaisseur *f*; (hair) abondance *f*; (liquid) consistance *f*; (layer) couche *f*

**thickset** *adj* épais (*f* épaisse); (person) trapu

**thick-skinned** *adj* à (la) peau épaisse; (person) peu sensible

**thief** *n* voleur -euse; **stop** ~! au voleur!

**thieve** *vt* voler

**thieving** *n* vol *m*; **petty** ~ larcins *mpl*; *adj* voleur -euse

**thievish** *adj* voleur -euse

**thigh** *n* cuisse *f*

**thigh-bone** *n* fémur *m*

**thimble** *n* dé *m* (à coudre)

**thimbleful** *n* *fig* doigt *m*

**thin** *adj* mince, peu épais (*f* épaisse); (person) maigre; (slender) élancé; (tenuous) ténu; (clothing) léger -ère; (sparse) clairsemé, rare; (crowd) peu nombreux -euse; *coll* (argument) peu convaincant, pauvre; ~ **on top** déplumé; **get** ~ maigrir; **have a** ~ **time** passer un temps peu agréable; *vt* amincir, diminuer; (~ **out**) éclaircir; (sauce) allonger; (paint) délayer; *vi* maigrir; (crowd) s'éclaircir

**thine** *pron* le tien (*f* la tienne), à toi

**thing** *n* chose *f*, objet *m*; affaire *f*; ~**s** (clothes) vêtements *mpl*; (belongings) effets *mpl*, affaires *fpl*; (luggage) bagages *mpl*; **as** ~**s are** dans l'état actuel des choses; *coll* **be on to a good** ~ avoir trouvé le filon; **for one** ~ en premier lieu; **how are** ~**s?** comment ça va?; **it's just one of those** ~**s** qu'est-ce que vous voulez, c'est comme ça; **it's not the (done)** ~ ça ne se fait pas; **know a** ~ **or two** être malin (*f* maligne); **look here, old** ~! écoute, mon vieux!; **money's the** ~ c'est l'argent qui compte; **poor little** ~! pauvre petit!; **put on one's** ~**s** s'habiller; **quite another** ~ tout autre chose; **take off one's** ~**s** se déshabiller; *coll* **tell s/o a** ~ **or two** dire son fait à qn; **that's the** ~ **for me!** voilà mon affaire!; **that's the very** ~ c'est tout à fait ce qu'il faut

**thingummy(jig)** *coll* machin *m*, truc *m*, chose *m*

**think** *n* **have a** ~ réfléchir; *coll* **he's got another** ~ **coming** il se fait des illusions; il ferait bien de réfléchir; *vt* penser; (believe) croire; (deem) juger, estimer; ~ **nothing of** compter pour rien; ~ **out** méditer, imaginer; ~ **over** réfléchir à; **he** ~**s a lot of himself** il se prend pour qn; *vi* penser; (believe) croire; (imagine) s'imaginer; (deem) considérer; ~ **about sth** penser à qch; (have opinion of) penser de qch; ~ **better of sth** se raviser de qch, changer d'avis; ~ **little of sth** faire peu de cas de qch; ~ **much of sth** faire grand cas de qch; ~ **nothing of** faire peu de cas de; ~ **of doing sth** penser à faire qch; ~ **too much of sth** attacher trop d'importance à qch; ~ **twice before doing sth** regarder à deux fois avant de faire

741

qch; ~ **up sth** inventer qch; ~ **well (badly) of s/o** avoir bonne (mauvaise) opinion de qn; **as you** ~ comme bon vous semblera; **come to** ~ **of it** à la réflexion; **I** ~ **it's very good** je le trouve très bien; **I** ~ **so** je crois que oui; **I thought as much** c'est bien ce que je pensais, je m'en doutais bien; **just** ~ **!** pensez donc!; **one would** ~ **that** on dirait que

**thinkable** *adj* concevable, imaginable

**thinker** *n* penseur -euse

**thinking** *n* pensée *f*, réflexion *f*; *adj* pensant

**thinly** *adv* clair, légèrement, à peine

**thinness** *n* minceur *f*, peu *m* d'épaisseur; (leanness) maigreur *f*; (liquid) fluidité *f*; (hair) rareté *f*

**thin-skinned** *adj* susceptible

**third** *n* troisième, tiers *m*; *mot* troisième vitesse *f*; (dates, kings) trois *m*; *adj* troisième

**third-degree** *n* passage *m* à tabac

**thirdly** *adv* troisièmement, en troisième lieu

**third-party** *n* leg tiers *m*; *adj* ~ **insurance** assurance *f* au tiers

**third-rate** *adj* très inférieur; de troisième qualité

**thirst** *n* soif *f*; *vi* avoir soif; ~ **after** avoir soif de

**thirsty** *adj* altéré, assoiffé; **be** ~ avoir soif; *coll* **that's** ~ **work** ça donne soif

**thirteen** *n* treize *m invar*; *adj* treize *invar*

**thirteenth** *n* treizième; (date) treize *m*; *adj* treizième

**thirtieth** *n* trentième; (date) trente *m*; *adj* trentième

**thirty** *adj* trente *invar*; **about** ~ une trentaine

**this** *adj* ce (*before vowel or h mute* cet) (*f sing* cette) (*pl* ces); ~ **way** par ici; **I want** ~ **book, not that one** je veux ce livre-ci, pas celui-là; *pron* ceci; ce; (this one) celui-ci (*pl* ceux-ci, *f sing* celle-ci, *fpl* celles-ci); ~ **is where** c'est ici que; **after** ~ ensuite; **what's** ~? qu'est-ce que c'est que ceci?; *adv* ~ **far** jusqu'ici; **he's** ~ **tall** il est grand comme ça

**thistle** *n* chardon *m*

**thither** *adv* là; y

**thong** *n* lanière *f*, courroie *f*

**thorax** *n* thorax *m*

**thorn** *n* épine *f*; *fig* ~ **in the flesh** sujet *m* d'irritation

**thorny** *adj* épineux -euse

**thorough** *adj* (work, person) consciencieux -ieuse; (search) minutieux -ieuse; (profound) profond; (perfect) parfait; (real) vrai; (very bad) achevé, fieffé

**thoroughbred** *n* animal *m* de race, pur-

sang *m invar*; *adj* pur-sang *invar*, de race

**thoroughfare** *n* voie *f* de communication, rue *f*; **no** ~ passage interdit; (temporary) route (rue) barrée

**thoroughgoing** *adj* (out and out) fieffé, accompli; (thorough) consciencieux -ieuse

**thoroughly** *adv* tout à fait; parfaitement; complètement, à fond

**thoroughness** *n* (work) perfection *f*; (search) caractère approfondi

**thou** *pron ar + lit* tu; toi

**though** *adv* (yet) pourtant, tout de même; *conj* quoique, bien que; (even if) quand (même); ~ **he is rich** quoiqu'il soit riche; **as** ~ comme si; **as** ~ **nothing had happened** comme si de rien n'était; **even** ~ **it were to cost me my life** quand cela me coûterait la vie

**thought** *n* pensée *f*; idée *f*; réflexion *f*, considération *f*; (care) souci *m*; (purpose) dessein *m*, intention *f*; **collect one's** ~**s** rassembler ses idées; **on second** ~**s** réflexion faite; **the mere** ~ **of it** rien que d'y penser

**thoughtful** *adj* pensif -ive, rêveur -euse; (considered) réfléchi; (considerate) prévenant; (book) profond

**thoughtless** *adj* (thought) étourdi; (careless) irréfléchi; (inconsiderate) sans égards

**thought-reader** *n* liseur -euse de pensées

**thought-reading** *n* lecture *f* de la pensée

**thousand** *n* mille *m invar*; (dates) mil; *adj* mille; **about a** ~ un millier, quelque mille; **a** ~ **thanks** mille fois merci; ~**s of soldiers** des milliers de soldats

**thousandth** *n + adj* millième

**thrash** *vt* battre; *coll* rosser; ~ **out** débattre

**thrashing** *n* rossée *f*; (grain) battage *m*; (defeat) défaite *f*

**thread** *n* fil *m*; (screw) pas *m*, filet *m*; *vt* enfiler; (screw) fileter; ~ **one's way through (into)** se faufiler à travers (dans)

**threadbare** *adj* râpé, usé jusqu'à la corde; (argument) usé jusqu'à la corde

**threat** *n* menace *f*

**threaten** *vt* menacer; ~ **to do sth** menacer de faire qch

**threatening** *adj* menaçant, de menace

**three** *n* trois *m*; *adj* trois

**three-cornered** *adj* triangulaire; (hat) tricorne

**three-dimensional** *adj* à trois dimensions

**threefold** *adj* triple

**three-legged** *adj* (stool) à trois pieds

**three-piece** *adj* en trois pièces; ~ **suit** costume *m* trois-pièces

**three-quarter** *n sp* trois-quarts *m invar*;

adj (portrait) de trois-quarts; trois-quarts *invar*
**threesome** *n* partie *f* à trois
**three-speed** *adj* à trois vitesses
**thresh** *vt* battre
**thresher** *n* (person) batteur *m* en grange; (machine) batteuse *f*
**threshing** *n* battage *m*
**threshold** *n* seuil *m*, pas *m* de porte; (beginning) début *m*
**thrice** *adv* trois fois
**thrift** *n* économie *f*, frugalité *f*, épargne *f*
**thrifty** *adj* économe; *US* vigoureux -euse
**thrill** *n* tressaillement *m*, frisson *m*; *vt* faire tressaillir, faire frémir, émouvoir; **be ~ed at sth** être ravi de qch; *vi* frissonner, frémir
**thriller** *n* roman *m* (pièce *f*) à sensation; roman policier
**thrilling** *adj* émouvant, passionnant, saisissant
**thrive** *vi* prospérer, réussir; (plant) bien venir; **he ~s on it** il s'en trouve bien
**thriving** *adj* (plant) vigoureux -euse; (person, business) prospère
**throat** *n* gorge *f*, gosier *m*; *fig* **cut one's own ~** travailler à sa propre ruine; **have a sore ~** avoir mal à la gorge; *fig* **jump down s/o's ~** s'attaquer à qn; *fig* **thrust sth down s/o's ~** imposer qch à qn
**throaty** *adj* guttural
**throb** *n* battement *m*, pulsation *f*; (machine) vrombissement *m*; *vi* battre, palpiter; (machine) vrombir
**throes** *npl* douleurs *fpl*; **the ~ of death** les affres *fpl* de la mort, l'agonie *f*
**thrombosis** *n* thrombose *f*
**throne** *n* trône *m*
**throng** *n* foule *f*, cohue *f*; *vt* encombrer; *vi* affluer, se presser
**throttle** *n* *mech* pàpillon *m*; **open (out) the ~** mettre les gaz; *vt* étrangler; *vi* **mot ~ down** mettre le moteur au ralenti
**through** *adj* direct; *US* terminé, fini; (traffic) en transit; *adv* à travers, d'un bout à l'autre; **~ and ~** de part en part; (utterly) complètement; **be ~ with** (finish) avoir fini; (have done with) en avoir fini avec; **get ~ traverser**; **get ~ to s/o** (telephone) avoir la communication avec qn; (be understood) réussir à se faire comprendre de qn; **let s/o ~** laisser passer qn; **she put me ~ to the manager** elle m'a passé le directeur; *prep* à travers, au travers de; par; (because of) à cause de, pour cause de; *US* jusqu'à; **get ~ an examination** être reçu à un examen; **get ~ sth** terminer qch; *coll fig* **go ~ it** en voir de dures; **sleep right ~ the night** dormir toute la nuit; *US* **Sunday ~ Saturday** de dimanche à samedi

**throughout** *adv* (time) tout le temps; (place) partout; *prep* d'un bout à l'autre de
**throughway** *n* *US* autoroute *f*
**throw** *n* jet *m*, lancement *m*; (dice) coup *m* de dés; (wrestling) mise *f* à terre; *vt* jeter, lancer; (hurl) projeter; (wrestling) terrasser; (rider) démonter, désarçonner; **~ about** éparpiller; *coll* **~ a fit** tomber en convulsions; *coll* **~ a party** faire une boum; **~ away** jeter; (waste) gaspiller; (lose) perdre; (chance) laisser passer; **~ back** rejeter; (ball) renvoyer; **~ down** jeter à terre; (person) renverser, terrasser; **~ in** jeter dedans; (add) ajouter; **~ in one's hand** abandonner (la partie); **~ in one's lot with** s/o partager le sort de qn; **~ light on sth** jeter de la lumière sur qch, éclaircir une question; **~ off** rejeter; (clothes) ôter; (illness) se débarrasser de; *fig* **~ oneself at** se jeter à la tête de; **~ oneself into** se lancer dans; **~ open** ouvrir tout grand; **~ out** jeter dehors, chasser; (reject) rejeter; (hint) insinuer; **~ over** jeter pardessus; (upset) renverser; (abandon) abandonner; **~ s/o a kiss** envoyer un baiser à qn; **~ up** jeter en l'air; (abandon) renoncer à; (resign) se démettre de, démissionner de; (build) construire; *coll* (vomit) vomir
**throwaway** *n* *coll* prospectus *m*; *adj* énoncé avec une indifférence calculée
**throwback** *n* retour *m* atavique; (person) cas *m* d'atavisme
**thrower** *n* lanceur -euse
**throw-in** *n* (football) remise *f* en jeu
**throw-out** *n* rebut *m*
¹**thrush** *n* grive *f*
²**thrush** *n* *med* aphtes *mpl*
**thrust** *n* poussée *f*; (fencing) coup *m* d'estoc; *vt* pousser; **~ back** repousser; **~ forward** pousser en avant; **~ in(to)** enfoncer dans; **~ one's hands into one's pockets** fourrer les mains dans ses poches; **~ out** mettre dehors; *vi* **~ at s/o** porter une botte à qn
**thruster** *n* *coll* arriviste
**thrusting** *adj* agressif -ive
**thud** *n* bruit sourd; *vi* tomber avec un bruit sourd
**thug** *n* bandit *m*, apache *m*
**thuggery** *n* banditisme *m*
**thumb** *n* pouce *m*; *coll* **~s up!** chic alors!; *coll* **give s/o the ~s up** indiquer à qn que tout va (ira) bien; **rule of ~** méthode *f* empirique; **twiddle one's ~s** se tourner les pouces; **under s/o's ~** sous la domination de qn; *vt* manier; (books) feuilleter; (dirty) salir
**thumb-index** *n* book bound with **~** livre relié avec encoches

**thumb-nail** *n* ongle *m* du pouce; ~ **sketch** croquis hâtif
**thumbscrew** *n* vis *f* à ailettes
**thumb-tack** *n* US punaise *f*
**thump** *n* coup sourd; (punch) coup *m* de poing; *vt* + *vi* cogner, frapper
**thumping** *adj coll* énorme
**thunder** *n* tonnerre *m*; **clap (peal) of** ~ coup *m* de tonnerre; *coll* **steal s/o's** ~ couper ses effets à qn; *vi* tonner; (person) tonitruer, fulminer
**thunderbolt** *n* foudre *f*, coup *m* de foudre
**thunderclap** *n* coup *m* de tonnerre
**thundercloud** *n* nuage orageux
**thundering** *adj* tonnant; *coll* formidable, à tout casser
**thunderous** *adj* tonnant, de tonnerre; *fig* retentissant
**thunderstorm** *n* orage *m*
**thunderstruck** *adj* sidéré, abasourdi
**thundery** *adj* orageux -euse
**Thursday** *n* jeudi *m*
**thus** *adv* ainsi, comme ça, de cette façon; donc; ~ **far** jusqu'ici; jusque-là
**thwack** *n* coup *m*; *vt* frapper vigoureusement
**¹thwart** *n* banc *m* de nage
**²thwart** *vt* déjouer, contrecarrer
**thy** *adj* ton (*f sing* ta, *mpl* + *fpl* tes)
**thyme** *n* thym *m*
**thyroid** *n* (glande *f*) thyroïde *f*
**thyself** *pron* toi-même; te
**tiara** *n* tiare *f*
**tic** *n* tic *m*
**tichy** *adj coll* tout petit (*f* toute petite)
**¹tick** *n* (clock, etc) tic-tac *m invar*; *coll* instant *m*; (mark) marque *f*; **do sth in two** ~**s** faire qch en moins de rien; *vt* ~ **off** cocher, pointer; *coll* rembarrer; ~ **out** enregistrer; *vi* faire tic-tac; *sl* rouspéter; *mech* ~ **over** tourner au ralenti; *coll* **what makes him** ~? qu'est-ce qui le pousse?
**²tick** *n* (insect) tique *f*
**³tick** *n* (material) coutil *m*, toile *f* à matelas
**⁴tick** *n coll* **on** ~ à crédit
**ticker-tape** *n* bande *f* de téléimprimeur
**ticket** *n* billet *m*; (métro, bus) ticket *m*; (label) étiquette *f*; (traffic offence) papillon *m*; US *pol* liste électorale; **complimentary** ~ billet *m* de faveur; **get a** ~ attraper une contravention; **platform** ~ billet *m* de quai; **return** ~ billet *m* (d')aller et retour; **season** ~ abonnement *m*; **single** ~ billet *m* simple; *coll* **that's the** ~! c'est ça!, à la bonne heure!; *vt* étiqueter
**ticket-collector** *n* contrôleur *m*
**ticket-office** *n* US guichet *m*

**ticking-off** *n coll* semonce *f*
**tickle** *n* chatouillement *m*; *vt* chatouiller; *coll* (amuse) amuser; *vi* chatouiller; (itch) démanger
**tickler** *n* problème difficile, question délicate; *mech* poussoir *m*
**ticklish** *adj* chatouilleux -euse; *fig* susceptible; (task, problem) délicat
**tidal** *adj* qui a à faire avec la marée; (harbour, etc) à marée; ~ **wave** raz *m* de marée; *fig* vague *f*
**tiddler** *n* petit poisson; (stickleback) épinoche *f*; *coll* (child) mioche
**tiddley** *adj coll* ivre, pompette
**tiddley-winks** *npl* jeu *m* de puce
**tide** *n* marée *f*; (course) cours *m*; (time) temps *m*, saison *f*; **go (swim) with the** ~ suivre le courant; **the** ~ **is coming in** la marée monte; **the** ~ **is going out** la marée descend; *vt* ~ **over** aider à surmonter une difficulté, *coll* dépanner
**tidemark** *n* ligne *f* de marée; *fig* (dirt) ligne *f* de crasse
**tidily** *adv* proprement, de façon ordonnée
**tidiness** *n* bon ordre; (person) caractère ordonné
**tidings** *npl ar* nouvelles *fpl*
**tidy** *adj* (place) bien rangé, propre, bien tenu; (person) ordonné; *coll* (fairly good) passable, convenable; *vt* ranger, mettre en ordre; ~ **oneself up** faire un brin de toilette; *vi* ~ **up** mettre de l'ordre partout, tout remettre en place
**tie** *n* (bond) lien *m*, attache *f*; (string) cordon *m*; (garment) cravate *f*; (knot) nœud *m*; (burden) entrave *f*; (game) partie nulle, match nul; US (railway) traverse *f*; *mus* liaison *f*; *vt* lier, attacher; (parcel) ficeler; (knot) faire; *med* ligaturer; ~ **down** immobiliser; assujettir; astreindre; *fig* ~ **s/o's hands** enlever à qn toute liberté d'action; ~ **sth on** attacher qch avec de la (une) ficelle; ~ **up** ficeler, attacher; (person) ligoter; *coll* **be** ~**d up** être très pris (occupé); **be** ~**d up with another firm** avoir des accords avec une autre maison; *coll* **get** ~**d up** s'embrouiller; US **the traffic is** ~**d up** il y a un embouteillage; *vi* ~ **up (in) with** avoir rapport avec
**tie-pin** *n* épingle *f* de cravate
**tier** *n* rangée *f*; (cake) étage *m*
**tie-up** *n coll* rapport *m*; US (traffic) embouteillage *m*
**tiff** *n* petite dispute
**tiger** *n* tigre *m*
**tigerish** *adj* de tigre
**tiger-lily** *n* lis tigré
**tight** *adj* (stretched) tendu, raide; (clothes) collant, étriqué; (not leaking)

744

impermeable; (money) rare; *coll* (drunk) gris, ivre; *adv* (firmly) fermement, étroitement; (stretched) fortement tendu; (sealed) hermétiquement; **draw ~** serrer bien; **hold ~** tenir bien; **hold ~!** tenez-vous bien!; **shut ~** bien fermer; **sit ~** ne pas bouger

**tighten** *vt* serrer, resserrer; (tauten) retendre; **~ one's belt** se serrer la ceinture; **~ up** renforcer; *vi* (screw) se resserrer; (rope) se tendre

**tight-fisted** *adj* ladre, pingre

**tight-lipped** *adj* aux lèvres serrées; à l'air sévère; *fig* discret -ète, cachottier -ière

**tightly** *adv* fortement; étroitement

**tightness** *n* (tension) tension *f*, raideur *f*; (clothing) étroitesse *f*; (leak-proof) étanchéité *f*, imperméabilité *f*; (money) rareté *f*

**tightrope** *n* corde *f* raide

**tights** *npl* collant *m*

**tigress** *n* tigresse *f*

**tike, tyke** *n coll* vilain chien; (dog) clebs *m*; *fig* rustre *m*

**tilde** *n gramm* tilde *m*

**tile** *n* (roof) tuile *f*; (floor, wall) carreau *m*; *coll* chapeau *m* haut de forme; *vt* (roof) couvrir de tuiles; (floor) carreler

¹**till** *vt* labourer, cultiver

¹**till** *n* caisse *f*

³**till** *prep* jusqu'à; **~ now** jusqu'ici; **~ then** jusque-là; **not ~** pas avant; *conj* jusqu'à ce que; **not ~** pas avant que

¹**tiller** *n* laboureur *m*, cultivateur *m*

²**tiller** *n naut* barre *f*

¹**tilt** *n* (slope) inclinaison *f*, pente *f*; *hist* joute *f*; **at full ~** à fond de train; **have a ~ at** s/o jouter contre qn; *vt* incliner, pencher; *vi* s'incliner, pencher; **~ at** s/o critiquer qn; **~ over** se renverser, basculer

²**tilt** *n* (cover) bâche *f*

**timber** *n* bois *m* de construction; **piece of ~** poutre *f*; **standing ~** bois *m* sur pied; *vt* boiser

**timbre** *n* timbre *m*

**time** *n* temps *m*; (occasion) fois *f*; (of day) heure *f*; (period) époque *f*; (moment) moment *m*; (season) saison *f*; (term) terme *m*; *mus* mesure *f*; (pace) pas *m*; **~ after ~** à maintes reprises; **~ will show** (tell) qui vivra verra; *coll* **about ~ too!** ce n'est pas trop tôt!; **after a ~** quelque temps après; **against ~** contre la montre; **another ~** une autre fois; **at all ~s** toujours; **at any ~** à tout moment; **at one ~** autrefois; **at one ~ ... at another ~** tantôt ... tantôt; **at the right ~** au bon moment, à propos; **at the same ~** en même temps; (on the other hand) d'autre part; **beat ~** battre la mesure; **before ~** en

avance; **behind the ~s** arriéré; **by this ~** à l'heure qu'il est; **for a long ~** (now) depuis longtemps; (past) pendant longtemps; **for a ~** pendant quelque temps; **four at a ~** quatre à la fois; (stairs) quatre à quatre; **from ~ to ~** de temps en temps, de temps à autre; **have a bad ~** passer de mauvais moments; **have a good ~** s'amuser bien; *coll* **have no ~ for** s/o trouver qn peu intéressant; **in good ~** bien à l'heure, bien à temps; **in my ~** de mon temps; **in no ~** en un rien de temps, en un clin d'œil; **serve one's ~** faire son temps; **spare ~** loisir *m*; **take ~ to do sth** mettre du temps à faire qch; **this ~ last month** il y a un mois aujourd'hui; **waste ~** perdre du (son) temps; **what's the ~?** quelle heure est-il?; *vt* calculer la durée de, chronométrer; fixer l'heure de; *mot* régler

**time-bomb** *n* bombe *f* à retardement

**time-exposure** *n phot* pose *f*

**time-fuse** *n* fusée *f* à retardement

**time-honoured** *adj* consacré par l'usage, vénérable

**timekeeper** *n* chronométreur *m*; **good ~** (watch) montre *f* qui est toujours à l'heure; (person) personne *f* qui est toujours à l'heure

**time-lag** *n* retard *m*

**timeless** *adj* éternel -elle, sans fin

**timely** *adj* opportun, à propos

**timepiece** *n* montre *f*; (clock) pendule *f*

**timer** *n* chronométreur *m*; (sand) sablier *m*

**timesaving** *adj* qui économise le (du) temps

**timeserver** *n* opportuniste

**timeserving** *n* opportunisme *m*; *adj* opportuniste

**time-signal** *n* signal *m* horaire

**time-switch** *n* minuterie *f*

**timetable** *n* horaire *m*; (trains) indicateur *m*; (personal) emploi *m* du temps

**timeworn** *adj* usé par le temps

**timid** *adj* timide, peureux -euse

**timidity** *n* timidité *f*

**timing** *n* chronométrage *m*; *mech* réglage *m*; **show good ~** bien calculer son temps (son moment)

**timorous** *adj* peureux -euse, craintif -ive

**tin** *n* étain *m*; (can) boîte *f* en fer blanc; *mil* **~ hat** casque *m*; **~ loaf** pain moulé; *vt* étamer; (can) mettre en boîte

**tin-can** *n* boîte *f* en fer blanc

**tincture** *n* (colour) teinte *f*; *med* teinture *f*; *vt* teinter

**tinder** *n* amadou *m*; *ar* mèche *f* de briquet

**tinder-box** *n ar* briquet *m*

**tinfoil** *n* feuille *f* d'étain; *coll* papier *m* d'argent

**ting** *n* tintement *m*; *vi* tinter

**tinge** *n* teinte *f*, nuance *f*; (tiny bit) soupçon *m*; *vt* teinter, nuancer

**tingle** *n* picotement *m*; (ears) tintement *m*; *vi* picoter; (ears) tinter; **my legs are tingling** j'ai des fourmis dans les jambes

**tininess** *n* petitesse *f*

**tinker** *n* rétameur *m*; *vt* (re-tin) rétamer; (try to repair) ~ **with** retaper, rafistoler; *vi* ~ **about** bricoler

**tinkle** *n* tintement *m*; *coll* coup *m* de fil; *vi* tinter

**tinned** *adj* étamé; (canned) en boîte, en conserve

**tinning** *n* mise *f* en boîte

**tinny** *adj* (sound) métallique; (taste) d'étain

**tin-opener** *n* ouvre-boîte(s) *m invar*

**tinpot** *adj coll* misérable, inférieur

**tinsel** *n* paillettes *fpl*; *fig* clinquant *m*; *adj* de clinquant; *vt* garnir de paillettes

**tint** *n* teinte *f*, nuance *f*; *vt* teinter, colorer

**tintack** *n* clou *m* de tapisserie

**tiny** *adj* tout petit (*f* toute petite), minuscule

**tip** *n* (end) bout *m*, extrémité *f*, pointe *f*; (stick) embout *m*; (money) pourboire *m*, gratification *f*; (touch) tape *f*; (advice) conseil *m*; (racing) tuyau *m*; (rubbish) dépotoir *m*; (heap) tas *m*; *vt* (shoe) mettre un bout à; (stick) mettre un embout à; (overturn) renverser, verser; (touch) effleurer, toucher légèrement; (money) donner un pourboire à; ~ **out** déverser; ~ **over** renverser; ~ **up** faire basculer; *vi* ~ **(over)** se renverser, basculer

**tip-off** *n coll* renseignement privé, avertissement privé

**tipple** *n coll* boisson *f* alcoolique; *vi* pinter, picoler

**tipsiness** *n* ivresse *f*

**tipstaff** *n leg* huissier *m*

**tipster** *n* donneur *m* de tuyaux

**tipsy** *adj* gris

**tiptoe** *n* **on** ~ sur la pointe des pieds; *vi* marcher sur la pointe des pieds

**tiptop** *adj coll* extra *invar*

**tirade** *n* tirade *f*

**¹tire** *vt* fatiguer, lasser; (exhaust) épuiser; (bore) ennuyer; *vi* se fatiguer, se lasser; ~ **of sth** se fatiguer de qch

**²tire** *n US see* **tyre**

**tired** *adj* fatigué; **be** ~ (sleepy) avoir sommeil; **get** ~ **of doing sth** se lasser de faire qch; *coll* **he makes me** ~ *sl* il me casse les pieds

**tiredness** *n* fatigue *f*, lassitude *f*

**tireless** *adj* infatigable, inlassable

**tiresome** *adj* fatigant; (boring) ennuyeux -euse; (irritating) exaspérant

**tiring** *adj* fatigant, lassant

**tissue** *n* tissu *m*, étoffe *f*; mouchoir *m* en papier

**tissue-paper** *n* papier *m* de soie

**¹tit** *n* mésange *f*

**²tit** *n sl* mamelle *f*

**Titan** *n* Titan *m*

**titanic** *adj* titanique

**titbit** *n* friandise *f*; (news) canard *m*

**tit-for-tat** *adv* à bon chat bon rat; **give s/o** ~ rendre à qn la pareille

**tithe** *n hist* dîme *f*; dixième *m*

**titillate** *vt* émoustiller, chatouiller

**titillation** *n* chatouillement *m*

**titivate** *vt* pomponner; *vi* se pomponner, se bichonner

**title** *n* titre *m*; (right) droit *m*; (nobility) titre *m* de noblesse; **have a** ~ **to sth** avoir droit à qch; *vt* intituler

**titled** *adj* noble, ayant un titre de noblesse

**title-deed** *n leg* titre *m* de propriété

**title-holder** *n sp* détenteur -trice du titre

**title-page** *n* titre *m*

**title-role** *n theat* rôle *m* qui donne le titre à la pièce

**titmouse** *n* mésange *f*

**titter** *n* (smothered laugh) rire étouffé; (giggle) rire *m* bête; *vi* avoir un rire étouffé; rire bêtement, ricaner

**tittle-tattle** *n* cancans *mpl*, commérages *mpl*

**titular** *adj* titulaire

**tizzy** *n coll* affolement *m*; **all of a** ~ complètement affolé

**T-junction** *n* carrefour *m* en forme de T

**to** *prep* à; (towards) vers; (till, as far as) jusqu'à; en; (in order to) pour, afin de; (against) contre; (feelings, obligations) envers; ~ **be sold** à vendre; ~ **Canada** au Canada; ~ **England** en Angleterre; ~ **the best of my knowledge** autant que je sache; ~ **the day** jour pour jour; ~ **the house (shop) of** chez; ~ **the trains** accès aux quais; **five** ~ **two** cinq contre deux; (time) deux heures moins cinq; **five trees** ~ **each street** cinq arbres par rue; **from town** ~ **town** de ville en ville; **go** ~ **and fro** aller et venir; **I'd like** ~ je voudrais bien; **I want you** ~ **come** je veux que vous veniez; **keep it** ~ **yourself** gardez ça pour vous; **push the door** ~ fermer la porte; **so** ~ **speak** pour ainsi dire; **there's no one** ~ **ask** il n'y a personne à qui on puisse demander; **there's nothing** ~ **it** c'est facile; (not worth it) ça ne vaut pas la peine; **the way** ~ **X** le chemin pour aller à X; **they died** ~ **a**

man ils sont morts jusqu'au dernier;
**trains** ~ **Paris** les trains à destination
de Paris; **walk** ~ **and fro** aller de long
en large; **what's that** ~ **him?** qu'est-ce
que ça peut lui faire?

**toad** n crapaud m

**toad-in-the-hole** n cul saucisses cuites au
four dans une pâte à frire

**toadstool** n champignon vénéneux

**toady** n flagorneur -euse; vt + vi flagorner

**toast** n toast m, pain grillé; (drink) toast
m; (person) personne f à qui on porte
un toast; coll **have s/o on** ~ tenir qn;
vt griller, rôtir; (person) boire à la santé
de, porter un toast à; vi rôtir, griller

**toaster** n grille-pain m invar

**toasting-fork** n fourchette f à toast

**toast-master** n annonceur m des toasts

**toast-rack** n porte-toasts m

**tobacco** n tabac m

**tobacconist** n marchand -e de tabac;
(shop) bureau m de tabac

**tobacco-pouch** n blague f à tabac

**toboggan** n toboggan m, luge f; vi faire
du toboggan

**toccata** n mus toccata f

**tocsin** n tocsin m

**today** adv aujourd'hui; ~ **week** aujourd'hui en huit; **here** ~ **and gone
tomorrow** ce que c'est de nous

**toddle** vi trottiner, marcher à petits pas

**toddler** n coll tout petit (f toute petite)
(enfant); enfant qui commence à marcher

**toddy** n grog chaud

**to-do** n coll remue-ménage m invar;
(scene) scène f; **what a** ~! quelle histoire!, quelle affaire!

**toe** n doigt m de pied, orteil m; (sock)
bout m; (shoe) pointe f; **big** ~ gros
orteil; **from top to** ~ de pied en cap;
**on the tip of one's** ~ **s** sur la pointe des
pieds; fig **tread on s/o's** ~ **s** offenser
qn; vt toucher du bout de l'orteil; ~
**the line** se conformer au mot d'ordre

**toe-cap** n bout rapporté

**toehold** n coll prise f précaire

**toenail** n ongle m de pied

**toff** n coll dandy m; personne huppée

**toffee** n caramel m (au beurre)

**toffee-nosed** adj coll bêcheur -euse

**tog** vt + vi ~ **up** attifer

**toga** n toge f

**together** adv ensemble; (at the same
time) en même temps; ~ **with** avec; en
même temps que; **all** ~ tous (fpl
toutes) ensemble; (united) tous (fpl
toutes) réuni(e)s; (at the same time)
tous (fpl toutes) à la fois; **for weeks** ~
durant des semaines

**togetherness** n unité f, camaraderie f

**toggle** n barrette f; naut cabillot m
(d'amarrage)

**togs** npl coll nippes fpl, frusques fpl

**toil** n peine f, labeur m, travail m
pénible; vi peiner, travailler

**toiler** n travailleur -euse

**toilet** n toilette f; (W.C.) cabinets mpl,
toilettes fpl, waters mpl

**toilet-paper** n papier m hygiénique

**toiletries** npl articles mpl de toilette

**toilet-roll** n rouleau m de papier hygiénique

**toilet-soap** n savon m de toilette

**toilet-table** n coiffeuse f

**toilet-water** n eau f de toilette

**toils** npl filet m, piège m

**toilsome** adj pénible

**token** n signe m, marque f; (coin) jeton
m; (paper) bon m; **in** ~ **of** en signe de;
**love** ~ gage m d'amour; adj nominal,
symbolique; ~ **strike** grève f d'avertissement

**tolerable** adj tolérable, supportable;
(fair) passable

**tolerance** n tolérance f

**tolerant** adj tolérant

**tolerate** vt tolérer, supporter

**toleration** n tolérance f

**¹toll** n péage m, droit m de passage;
(losses) pertes fpl; US ~ **call** communication interurbaine; fig **take** ~ **of**
infliger des pertes à

**²toll** n son m de cloche; vt + vi sonner

**toll-bridge** n pont m à péage

**toll-gate** n barrière f à péage

**toll-road** n route f à péage

**tomahawk** n tomahawk m

**tomato** n tomate f

**tomb** n tombe f; fig mort f

**tombola** n tombola f

**tomboy** n garçon manqué

**tombstone** n pierre tombale

**tom-cat** n matou m

**tome** n tome m

**tomfoolery** n coll bêtises fpl

**tommy-gun** n mitraillette f

**tommy-rot** n coll bêtises fpl

**tomorrow** n lendemain m; adv demain;
~ **week** demain en huit; **the day after**
~ après-demain

**tomtom** n tam-tam m

**ton** n tonne f; naut tonneau m; coll ~ **s**
**of** des tas de, des masses de, beaucoup
de; coll **do the** ~ **(up)** faire du cent-
soixante à l'heure; fig **weigh a** ~ peser
un poids énorme

**tonal** adj tonal

**tonality** n tonalité f

**tone** n ton m; (voice) voix f, accent m;
mus son m; (pitch) timbre m; (muscles)
tonicité f; **in a low** ~ d'un ton bas; **in
that** ~ **of voice** sur ce ton; vt phot

virer; (skin) tonifier; ~ **down** atténuer, adoucir; (sound) baisser; *vi* (colours) s'harmoniser; ~ **down** se radoucir

**tone-control** *n* bouton *m* de tonalité

**tone-deaf** *adj* affligé de surdité musicale

**toneless** *adj* (sound) atone; (colour) sans éclat

**tongs** *npl* pincettes *fpl*, pinces *fpl*, tenailles *fpl*

**tongue** *n* langue *f*; (shoe) languette *f*; (bell) battant *m*; **hold one's ~** se taire; **keep a civil ~ in one's head** rester poli; **put out one's ~** tirer la langue; **with ~ in cheek** de façon ironique

**tongue-tied** *adj* muet -ette, interdit

**tongue-twister** *n* mot *m* (phrase *f*) difficile à prononcer

**tonic** *n* fortifiant *m*, reconstituant *m*; *mus* tonique *f*; *adj* tonique, réconfortant

**tonight** *n* ce soir; *adv* ce soir; cette nuit

**tonnage** *n* tonnage *m*

**tonne** *n* tonne *f*

**tonsil** *n* amygdale *f*

**tonsillitis** *n* angine *f*, amygdalite *f*

**tonsure** *n* tonsure *f*

**too** *adv* trop, par trop; (moreover) d'ailleurs, de plus; (also) aussi, également; ~ **bad!** dommage!; ~ **little** trop peu; ~ **much** trop; *coll* ~ **true!** et comment!; **a hundred francs ~ much** cent francs de trop; *coll* **have had one ~ many** être pompette; *coll* **he's ~ much for me** il est trop fort pour moi

**tool** *n* outil *m*, instrument *m*; (person) créature *f*; *vulg* membre viril, queue *f*; *vt* travailler, usiner; ~ **up** équiper

**tool-bag** *n* sac *m* à outils

**tool-box** *n* boîte *f* à outils

**tool-maker** *n* fabricant *m* d'outils

**tool-shed** *n* cabane *f* à outils

**toot** *n* mot coup *m* de klaxon; *vi* mot klaxonner, avertir

**tooth** *n* (*pl* teeth) dent *f*; ~ **and nail** de toutes ses forces, avec acharnement; *sl* **be fed up to the teeth** en avoir ras le bol; **be long in the ~** n'être plus très jeune; **cast sth in s/o's teeth** reprocher qch à qn; **cut one's teeth** faire ses dents; **fight ~ and nail** se battre avec acharnement; **grind one's teeth** grincer des dents; **grit one's teeth** serrer les dents; **have a sweet ~** aimer les sucreries; **have a ~ out** se faire arracher une dent; **have a ~ stopped** obturer (plomber) une dent; **in the teeth of** malgré, en dépit de; **set of teeth** (natural) denture *f*; (false) dentier *m*

**toothache** *n* mal *m* de dents; **have (a) ~** avoir mal aux dents

**toothbrush** *n* brosse *f* à dents

**toothcomb** *n* peigne fin

**toothless** *adj* sans dents, édenté

**toothpaste** *n* pâte *f* dentifrice

**toothpick** *n* cure-dents *m invar*

**tootle** *vi* klaxonner doucement et de façon continue; *coll* mot ~ **along** rouler doucement

¹**top** *n* sommet *m*, cime *f*; (upper side) dessus *m*, surface *f*; (head, upper end) haut *m*; (lid) couvercle *m*; (tree) tête *f*; (roof) faîte *m*; (bottle) capsule *f*; *naut* hune *f*; **at the ~ of one's voice** à tue-tête; *coll* **blow one's ~** s'emporter, se mettre en colère; **come out on ~** avoir le dessus; **from ~ to bottom** de haut en bas, de fond en comble; **from ~ to toe** de la tête aux pieds; *mot* **hard ~** berline *f*; *mot* **in ~** en prise; **one on ~ of the other** l'un (*f* l'une) sur l'autre; (time) l'un (*f* l'une) après l'autre; **on ~** dessus; **on ~ of it all** pour comble, par-dessus le marché; **on the ~ of one's form** en pleine forme; **sit at the ~ of the table** être assis au bout de la table; *coll* **the ~s** ce qu'il y a de mieux; **work is getting on ~ of him** il est débordé par le travail; *adj* supérieur; principal, premier -ière; du haut, du dessus; ~ **floor** dernier étage; *coll* **be ~ dog** être vainqueur; *vt* (tree) étêter; surmonter, couronner, couvrir; (exceed) dépasser, surpasser; ~ **up** remplir ( jusqu'au bord); *coll* **let me ~ you up!** encore un peu!

²**top** *n* (toy) toupie *f*

**topaz** *n* topaze *f*

**top-boot** *n* botte *f* à revers

**top-coat** *n* pardessus *m*; (paint) couche *f* de finition

**top-dressing** *n* fumure *f* en surface

**toper** *n* *coll* ivrogne *m*, buveur *m*

**top-hat** *n* (chapeau *m*) haut-de-forme *m* (*pl* hauts-de-forme)

**top-heavy** *adj* trop lourd du haut

**topic** *n* sujet *m*, thème *m*

**topical** *adj* courant, d'actualité; *med* topique

**topicality** *n* actualité *f*

**topknot** *n* (hair) chignon *m*; (bird) aigrette *f*

**top-level** *adj* au plus haut niveau, au sommet

**topmast** *n* mât *m* de hune

**topmost** *adj* le plus haut, le plus élevé

**topnotch** *adj* de premier ordre

**topographical** *adj* topographique

**topography** *n* topographie *f*

**topper** *n* *coll* (person) type épatant; (hat) (chapeau *m*) haut-de-forme *m* (*pl* hauts-de-forme)

**topple** *vt* faire tomber; ~ **over** faire

748

tomber, renverser; *vi* ~ **down (over)** tomber, s'écrouler, dégringoler

**topsail** *n naut* hunier *m*

**top-secret** *adj* très secret -ète

**topside** *n cul* tende *f* de tranche

**topsy-turvy** *adj* + *adv* sens dessus dessous

**torch** *n* torche *f*, flambeau *m*; (electric) lampe *f* électrique de poche

**torchlight** *n* **by** ~ à la lueur des flambeaux; ~ **procession** cortège *m* aux flambeaux

**toreador** *n* toréador *m*

**torment** *n* supplice *m*, torture *f*; tourment *m*; **be in** ~ être au supplice; *vt* torturer, tourmenter

**tormentor** *n* bourreau *m*, persécuteur -trice

**tornado** *n* tornade *f*, ouragan *m*

**torpedo** *n* torpille *f*; *vt* torpiller

**torpedo-boat** *n* (small) vedette *f* lance-torpilles, torpilleur *m*

**torpedo-tube** *n* lance-torpilles *m*

**torpid** *adj* engourdi, inerte

**torpidity** *n* engourdissement *m*, inertie *f*, torpeur *f*

**torpidly** *adv* de façon léthargique

**torpor** *n* torpeur *f*

**torque** *n mech* moment *m* de torsion, couple moteur

**torrefy** *vt* torréfier

**torrent** *n* torrent *m*

**torrential** *adj* torrentiel -ielle

**torrid** *adj* torride

**torso** *n* torse *m*

**tort** *n leg* dommage *m*, fait délictueux

**tortoise** *n* tortue *f*

**tortoiseshell** *n* écaille *f* (de tortue)

**tortuosity** *n* tortuosité *f*

**tortuous** *adj* tortueux -euse

**tortuousness** *n see* **tortuosity**

**torture** *n* torture *f*, question *f*, supplice *m*; *vt* torturer, mettre à la torture

**torturer** *n* bourreau *m*, tortionnaire *m*

**tosh** *n coll* bêtises *f pl*

**toss** *n* lancement *m*, jet *m*; (head) mouvement impatient; *sp* tirage *m* au sort; (coin) coup *m* de pile ou face; (fall) chute *f*; **argue the** ~ continuer à argumenter une fois la dispute réglée; *vt* lancer, jeter; (head) secouer; (horse) démonter; *cul* sauter; (salad) fatiguer; ~ **about** ballotter; ~ **a coin** jouer à pile ou face; ~ **aside** jeter de côté; ~ **off** (drink) avaler d'un trait; (work) expédier; *vi* ~ **about** s'agiter, se retourner; ~ **for sth** jouer qch à pile ou face; ~ **on the waves** être ballotté par les vagues; **pitch and** ~ tanguer

**toss-up** *n* (coin) coup *m* de pile ou face; **it's a** ~ c'est une affaire de chance

¹**tot** *n* (person) tout petit (toute petite),

marmot *m*; (drink) petit verre, goutte *f*

²**tot** *vt* ~ **up** additionner; *vi* s'élever

**total** *n* total *m*, montant *m*; *adj* total, entier -ière, complet -ète; *vt* additionner; *vi* totaliser; **it** ~ **s up to a big amount** cela s'élève à une somme considérable

**totalisator** *n see* **totalizator**

**totalitarian** *adj* totalitaire

**totalitarianism** *n* totalitarisme *m*

**totality** *n* totalité *f*

**totalizator, totalisator** *n* totalisateur *m*; *sp* = Pari Mutuel Urbain (P.M.U.)

**totally** *adv* totalement, complètement

**totem** *n* totem *m*

**totter** *vi* chanceler; (building) menacer ruine; ~ **in** entrer d'un pas chancelant

**tottery** *adj* chancelant

**toucan** *n* toucan *m*

**touch** *n* (sense) toucher *m*; (feel) contact *m*; communication *f*, rapport *m*, contact *m*; (painting) touche *f*, coup *m* de pinceau; *mus* toucher *m*; (bit) pointe *f*, soupçon *m*; (tiny blow) léger coup; **finishing** ~ dernière main; **get (keep) in** ~ **with** entrer (rester) en contact avec; *sp* **kick into** ~ envoyer en touche; **out of** ~ **with** pas au courant de; *vt* toucher; (feeling) émouvoir; (affect) affecter, produire de l'effet sur; (reach) atteindre; (meddle, be adjacent to) toucher à; (graze) effleurer; (equal) égaler; ~ **off** faire exploser; *coll* ~ **s/o for a hundred francs** taper qn de cent francs; ~ **up** faire des retouches à, retoucher; *sl* peloter; ~ **wood!** touche du bois!; **there's no one to** ~ **him** personne ne lui arrive à la cheville; **they can't** ~ **me** ils ne peuvent rien contre moi; *vi* se toucher, venir en contact; ~ **down** atterrir; *sp* marquer un essai; ~ **on** effleurer

**touch-and-go** *adj* risqué; **it was** ~! il était moins cinq!

**touchdown** *n* atterrissage *m*; (sea) amerrissage *m*

**touché** *interj* touché!

**touched** *adj* touché, ému; *coll* piqué, timbré

**touchiness** *n* susceptibilité *f*

**touching** *adj* touchant, émouvant; *prep* concernant, touchant

**touch-line** *n* ligne *f* de touche

**touchstone** *n* pierre *f* de touche

**touch-type** *vi* taper au toucher

**touch-typist** *n* dactylo *f* qui tape au toucher

**touchy** *adj* susceptible

**tough** *n* dur *m*; *adj* dur; (hard-wearing) résistant, solide; (work) difficile

**toughen** *vt* durcir; (person) endurcir

**toughly** *adv* avec ténacité, opiniâtrement

**toughness** *n* dureté *f*; résistance *f*, solidité *f*; (work) difficulté *f*

**toupee** *n* toupet *m*

**tour** *n* tour *m*, excursion *f*; *mil*+*theat* tournée *f*; *vt* voyager dans, faire le tour de; *theat* faire une tournée dans; *vi* voyager, faire du tourisme

**tour-de-force** *n* tour *m* de force

**tourer** *n* voiture *f* décapotable

**touring** *n* tourisme *m*; *adj* qui fait du tourisme; (troupe) en tournée

**tourism** *n* tourisme *m*

**tourist** *n* touriste; ~ **office** syndicat *m* d'initiative

**tourmaline** *n min* tourmaline *f*

**tournament** *n* tournoi *m*

**tourniquet** *n* tourniquet *m*

**tour-operator** *n* organisateur *m* de voyages

**tousle** *vt* (hair) ébouriffer

**tout** *n* racoleur *m*; (racing) pronostiqueur *m*; **ticket** ~ revendeur *m* de billets; *vi* (racing) vendre des pronostics; ~ **for** racoler, courir après

**¹tow** *n* (hemp) étoupe *f*

**²tow** *n* remorque *f*; **take a boat in** ~ prendre un bateau à la remorque; *vt* remorquer; (from path) haler; ~ **away** (parked car) mettre en fourrière

**towards, toward** *prep* vers, du côté de; (feelings, etc) envers, à l'égard de; (purpose) pour; ~ **six o'clock** vers six heures

**towel** *n* serviette *f*; (small) essuie-mains *m*; **sanitary** ~ serviette *f* hygiénique; **Turkish** ~ serviette *f* éponge; *vt* essuyer avec une serviette

**towelling** *n* tissu-éponge *m* (*pl* tissus-éponges)

**towel-rail** *n* porte-serviettes *m*

**tower** *n* tour *f*; (church) clocher *m*; ~ **of strength** puissant appui; **water** ~ château *m* d'eau; *vi* s'élever, dominer; ~ **over** dominer

**towering** *adj* très haut; *fig* (rage) terrible, violent

**towline** *n* remorque *f*, corde *f* de halage

**town** *n* ville *f*; **country** ~ ville *f* de province; **county** ~ = ville *f* de préfecture; *coll fig* **go to** ~ bien s'amuser; *coll fig* **go to** ~ **on sth** ne pas regarder à la dépense; (make effort) mettre le paquet; **man about** ~ mondain *m*; *adj* de la ville, urbain, municipal

**town-clerk** *n* secrétaire *m* de mairie

**town-council** *n* conseil municipal

**town-councillor** *n* conseiller -ère municipal -e

**town-crier** *n* tambour *m* de ville

**town-hall** *n* mairie *f*, hôtel *m* de ville

**town-planner** *n* urbaniste

**town-planning** *n* urbanisme *m*

**townsfolk** *npl* habitants *mpl* d'une ville

**township** *n* commune *f*

**townsman** *n* citadin *m*

**townspeople** *npl* habitants *mpl* d'une ville, citadins *mpl*

**towpath** *n* chemin *m* de halage

**tow-rope** *n* corde *f* de halage

**toxaemia** *n* toxémie *f*

**toxic** *adj* toxique

**toxicologist** *n* toxicologue

**toxicology** *n* toxicologie *f*

**toxin** *n* toxine *f*

**toy** *n* jouet *m*, joujou *m*; ~ **soldier** soldat *m* de plomb; ~ **train** petit train; *vi* jouer; ~ **with an idea** caresser une idée; ~ **with one's food** manger du bout des dents

**toyshop** *n* magasin *m* de jouets

**trace** *n* trace *f*, vestige *m*; *vt* tracer; (follow) suivre, suivre la piste de; (recover) recouvrer; (on paper) calquer; ~ **out** esquisser; ~ **sth back to its source** remonter à l'origine de qch

**traceable** *adj* que l'on peut tracer

**tracer** *n* traceur *m*; ~ **bullet** balle traçante

**tracery** *n archi* réseau *m*, entrelacs *m*

**trachea** *n anat* trachée *f*

**tracheotomy** *n* trachéotomie *f*

**tracing** *n* tracé *m*; calque *m*

**tracing-paper** *n* papier-calque *m invar*

**track** *n* (path) chemin *m*, sentier *m*; (animal, footprints) piste *f*, trace *f*; (metal belt wheel) chenille *f*; (rail) voie *f*; (bullet) trajectoire *f*; **be on s/o's** ~ **(s)** être sur la trace de qn; **be on the wrong** ~ faire fausse route; **keep** ~ **of s/o** ne pas perdre qn de vue; *coll* **make** ~ **s** filer; **on the right** ~ sur la bonne voie; *vt* (animal) suivre à la piste; (criminal) traquer; ~ **down** dépister; *vi cin* faire un travel(l)ing

**tracked** *adj* (vehicle) à chenilles

**tracker** *n* traqueur *m*

**tracker-dog** *n* limier *m*, chien policier

**trackless** *adj* sans chemins; (vehicle) sans chenilles

**¹tract** *n* étendue *f*, région *f*; *anat* voie *f*

**²tract** *n* (document) brochure *f*, tract *m*

**tractability** *n* docilité *f*

**tractable** *adj* traitable, docile

**traction** *n* traction *f*

**traction-engine** *n* locomobile *f*

**tractor** *n* tracteur *m*; ~ **-drawn** tracté

**trad** *adj coll* traditionnel -elle

**trade** *n* commerce *m*, affaires *fpl*, négoce *m*; (calling) métier (manuel), emploi *m*; (body) corps *m* de métier; ~ **s** (winds) alizés *mpl*; ~ **secret** secret *m* de fabrication; **be in the** ~ être du métier; **be in** ~ être dans le commerce; **by** ~ de son (leur, etc) état; **each to his**

own ~ chacun son métier; **free ~**
libre-échange *m*; *vt* faire trafic de; ~ **in**
donner en reprise; ~ **sth for sth** troquer qch contre qch; *vi* faire le commerce, faire des affaires, trafiquer

**trade-mark** *n* marque *f* de fabrique;
**registered ~** marque déposée

**trade-name** *n* nom *m* de marque, appellation *f*

**trade-price** *n* prix *m* à la production (fabrique)

**trader** *n* négociant -e, commerçant -e,
marchand -e

**tradesman** *n* marchand *m*, commerçant
*m*; ~ **'s entrance** entrée *f* de service

**trade-union** *n* syndicat (ouvrier)

**trade-unionism** *n* syndicalisme (ouvrier)

**trade-unionist** *n* syndiqué -e, syndi-
caliste, ouvrier -ière syndiqué -e

**trade-wind** *n* vent alizé, alizé *m*

**trading-stamp** *n* timbre-prime *m* (*pl*
timbres-prime)

**tradition** *n* tradition *f*

**traditional** *adj* traditionnel -elle

**traditionalism** *n* traditionalisme *m*

**traditionalist** *n* traditionaliste

**traditionally** *adv* traditionnellement

**traduce** *vt* calomnier, diffamer

**traffic** *n* trafic *m*, commerce *m*, négoce
*m*; (movement) mouvement *m*; (vehicles) circulation (routière); *US* ~ **circle**
rond-point *m* (*pl* ronds-points); ~
**congestion** embouteillage *m*; **one-way**
~ sens *m* unique; **rail ~ transport** *m*
(trafic *m*) ferroviaire; *vi* trafiquer

**trafficator** *n* mot flèche *f* de direction

**traffic-block** *n* embouteillage *m*

**traffic-controller** *n* aer contrôleur -euse
de la navigation aérienne, *coll* aiguilleur *m* du ciel

**traffic-jam** *n* embouteillage *m*, encombrement *m* (de la circulation)

**trafficker** *n* trafiquant -e

**traffic-lights** *npl* feux *mpl* de circulation

**traffic-sign** *n* panneau *m* de signalisation

**traffic-warden** *n* contractuel -elle

**tragedian** *n* auteur *m* tragique; tragédien
-ienne

**tragedy** *n* tragédie *f*; *fig* drame *m*

**tragic** *adj* tragique

**tragi-comedy** *n* tragi-comédie *f*

**tragi-comic** *adj* tragi-comique

**trail** *n* traînée *f*; (track) piste *f*, voie *f*; *US*
sentier *m*; **on the ~ of** sur la piste de;
**pick up the ~** retrouver la piste; *vt*
traquer, suivre à la piste; (drag)
traîner; ~ **sth along** traîner qch après
soi; *vi* traîner; (plants) grimper; ~
**along** se traîner; ~ **off** se perdre

**trailer** *n* (person) traqueur *m*; (vehicle)
remorque *f*; *US* caravane *f*, roulotte *f*;
*cin* extrait de film (projeté à des fins

publicitaires); *US* ~ **park** cara-
van(n)ing *m*; *US* ~ **truck** semi-remor-
que *f*

¹**train** *n* train *m*, convoi *m*; (retinue)
suite *f*; (dress) traîne *f*, queue *f*; (succession) succession *f*, série *f*; (trail)
traînée *f*; ~ **of thought** enchaînement
*m* d'idées; **on the ~** dans le train; **the**
~ **is in** le train est en gare

²**train** *vt* former, instruire; (animal)
dresser; *sp* entraîner; (plant) diriger;
(gun) braquer, pointer; *vi* s'exercer; *sp*
s'entraîner

**train-bearer** *n eccles* caudataire *m*; (wedding) demoiselle *f* d'honneur, page *m*

**trainee** *n* stagiaire, élève

**trainer** *n sp* entraîneur *m*; (animals)
dresseur -euse; *aer* avion-école *m* (*pl*
avions-école)

**train-ferry** *n* ferry-boat *m*

**training** *n sp* entraînement *m*; éducation
*f*, formation *f*, instruction *f*; (animals)
dressage *m*; **physical ~** éducation *f*
physique

**training-college** *n* école normale

**training-ship** *n* navire-école *m* (*pl* navi-
res-école)

**train-sickness** *n* mal *m* de train

**traipse, trapse** *vi coll* se balader, traîner
ça et là; *coll* ~ **in** s'amener

**trait** *n* trait *m* de caractère

**traitor** *n* traître *m*

**traitorous** *adj* traître -esse, perfide

**traitress** *n* traîtresse *f*

**trajectory** *n* trajectoire *f*

**tram** *n* tramway *m*

**tram-car** *n* tram *m*, voiture *f* de tramway

**tramline** *n* voie *f* du tramway; ~**s**
(tennis) couloir *m*

**trammel** *n* entrave *f*; *vt* entraver

**tramp** *n* (noise) bruit *m* de pas; (walk)
marche *f*, excursion *f* à pied; (person)
vagabond -e, clochard -e, chemineau
*m*; *US* prostituée *f*; *naut* cargo *m*; *vt* ~
**the streets** battre le pavé; *vi* marcher
lourdement; (travel) aller à pied

**trample** *vt* ~ **down** piétiner, fouler; ~
**underfoot** fouler aux pieds; *vi* ~ **on**
sth piétiner qch, marcher sur qch

**trampoline** *n* tremplin *m* de gymnastique

**tramway** *n* tramway *m*

**trance** *n* extase *f*; (hypnotic) transe *f*; **fall**
**into a ~** tomber en transe

**tranny** *n coll abbr* transistor *m*

**tranquil** *adj* tranquille, paisible, calme

**tranquillity** *n* tranquillité *f*, calme *m*

**tranquillize** *vt* tranquilliser

**tranquillizer** *n* tranquillisant *m*, calmant
*m*

**transact** *vt* traiter; ~ **business with s/o**
faire des affaires avec qn

transaction

**transaction** *n* transaction *f*, affaire *f*; (action) conduite *f* (d'une affaire), gestion *f*; **commercial** ~ opération commerciale

**transalpine** *adj* transalpin

**transatlantic** *adj* transatlantique

**transcend** *vt* surpasser, aller au delà de; *philos* transcender

**transcendence** *n* transcendance *f*

**transcendent** *adj* transcendant

**transcendental** *adj* transcendantal

**transcendentalism** *n* transcendantalisme *m*

**transcontinental** *adj* transcontinental

**transcribe** *vt* transcrire

**transcript** *n* copie *f*, transcription *f*

**transcription** *n* transcription *f*

**transept** *n* transept *m*

**transfer** *n* transport *m*; (official) déplacement *m*; (shares, rights) transfert *m*; (picture) décalcomanie *f*; (funds) virement *m*; *vt* transférer; (official) déplacer; *leg* céder; (funds) virer; (printing) décalquer

**transferability** *n* transmissibilité *f*

**transferable** *adj* transmissible

**transferee** *n leg* cessionnaire

**transference** *n* transfert *m*

**transfiguration** *n* transfiguration *f*

**transfigure** *vt* transfigurer

**transfix** *vt* transpercer; ~ **with fear** pétrifier de terreur

**transform** *vt* transformer; convertir

**transformation** *n* transformation *f*; conversion *f*

**transformer** *n elect* transformateur *m*

**transfuse** *vt* transfuser

**transfusion** *n* transfusion *f*

**transgress** *vi* transgresser

**transgression** *n* transgression *f*, violation *f*; (sin) péché *m*

**transgressor** *n* transgresseur *m*; (sinner) pécheur (*f* pécheresse)

**transience** *n* caractère *m* transitoire, nature passagère

**transient** *adj* transitoire, éphémère

**transistor** *n* transistor *m*

**transistorize** *vt* transistoriser, équiper de transistors

**transit** *n* (movement) passage *m*; transport *m*; (customs) transit *m*

**transition** *n* transition *f*; ~ **period** période *f* de transition

**transitional** *adj* de transition

**transitive** *adj gramm* transitif -ive

**transitory** *adj* transitoire, passager -ère

**translatable** *adj* traduisible

**translate** *vt* traduire; (bishop) transférer

**translation** *n* traduction *f*; (bishop) translation *f*

**translator** *n* traducteur -trice

**transliterate** *vt* transcrire

**translucence** *n* translucidité *f*

**translucent** *adj* translucide

**transmissible** *adj* transmissible

**transmission** *n* transmission *f*

**transmit** *vt* transmettre

**transmitter** *n* transmetteur *m*; *rad* émetteur *m*

**transmutable** *adj* transmuable

**transmutation** *n* transmutation *f*

**transmute** *vt* transformer

**transom** *n* traverse *f*; (lintel) linteau *m*

**transparence** *n* transparence *f*

**transparency** *n* transparence *f*; *phot* diapositive *f*

**transparent** *adj* transparent; (evident) clair, évident

**transpire** *vt* (liquid) exsuder; (smell) exhaler; *vi* transpirer; (occur) se passer

**transplant** *n surg* greffe *f*; *vt* transplanter; *surg* greffer

**transplantation** *n* transplantation *f*

**transport** *n* transport *m*; ~ **café** restaurant routier, restaurant *m* des routiers; ~ **plane** avion *m* de transport; *vt* transporter; *leg hist* déporter

**transportation** *n US* transport *m*; *leg hist* déportation *f*

**transporter** *n* transporteur *m*; **tank** ~ porte-chars *m invar*

**transporter-bridge** *n* pont transbordeur

**transpose** *vt* transposer

**transposition** *n* transposition *f*

**transubstantiate** *vt* changer en une autre substance

**transubstantiation** *n* transsubstantiation *f*

**transversal** *adj* transversal

**transverse** *adj* transversal, en travers

**transvestism, transvestitism** *n* travestisme *m*

**transvestite** *n* travesti -e

**trap** *n* piège *m*, trappe *f*, traquenard *m*; (rabbits, etc) collet *m*; *fig* piège *m*, ruse *f*; (vehicle) carriole *f*; *sl* gueule *f*; **be caught in the** ~ se laisser prendre au piège; **set a** ~ tendre un piège; **walk into the** ~ donner dans le panneau; *vt* prendre au piège, attraper; (cut off) bloquer, coincer

**trap-door** *n* trappe *f*

**trapeze** *n* trapèze *m*; ~ **artist** trapéziste

**trapper** *n* trappeur *m*

**trappings** *npl* ornements *mpl*; (finery) atours *mpl*

**Trappist** *n* trappiste *m*; *adj* de la Trappe

**trapse** *vi see* **traipse**

**trash** *n* camelote *f*, choses *fpl* sans valeur; *US* détritus *mpl*, ordures *fpl*; *US coll pej* (people) racaille *f*; *US coll pej* **white** ~ blancs (*f* blanches) pauvres

**trash-can** *n US* poubelle *f*

752

**trashy** adj sans valeur

**trauma** n trauma m, traumatisme m

**traumatic** adj traumatique; (distressing) traumatisant

**travail** n peine f; (birth pains) douleurs fpl de l'enfantement; vi peiner; (childbirth) être en travail

**travel** n voyage m, voyages mpl; vt (distance) parcourir, faire; vi voyager; (light) se propager; (news) se répandre; (vehicle) marcher; comm être voyageur de commerce; comm ~ **in wine** être représentant en vins

**travel-agency** n agence f de voyages (tourisme)

**travel-bureau** n bureau m de tourisme

**travelled** adj **much** ~ qui a beaucoup voyagé

**traveller** n voyageur -euse; (commercial) représentant m, voyageur m de commerce; ~'s **cheque** chèque m de voyage; bot ~'s **joy** clématite f des haies

**travelling-bag** n sac m de voyage

**travelogue** n coll documentaire m de voyage

**traversable** adj traversable, franchissable

**traverse** n traversée f; mech traverse f; vt traverser, passer

**travesty** n travestissement m, parodie f

**trawl** n chalut m; vi pêcher au chalut

**trawler** n chalutier m

**tray** n plateau m

**treacherous** adj traître -esse, perfide

**treachery** n perfidie f, trahison f

**treacle** n mélasse f

**tread** n pas m; (sound) bruit m de(s) pas; (stairs) marche f; (tyre) chape f; vt fouler; ~ **underfoot** fouler aux pieds; ~ **water** nager debout; **well-trodden path** chemin battu; vi marcher; ~ **on** poser les pieds sur

**treadle, treddle** n pédale f

**treadmill** n agr trépigneuse f; fig besogne quotidienne, routine ingrate

**treason** n trahison f

**treasonable** adj de trahison, perfide

**treasure** n trésor m; ~ **hunt** chasse f au trésor; vt priser, tenir beaucoup à; (take care of) garder soigneusement

**treasure-house** n trésor m

**treasurer** n trésorier -ière

**treasure-trove** n trésor caché et découvert par hasard

**treasury** n trésorerie f, trésor public; **the Treasury** = le ministère des Finances

**treat** n régal m, plaisir m, fête f; (outing) sortie f; **a** ~ **in store** un plaisir à venir; **stand** ~ **all round** payer la tournée; vt traiter; (drink) payer à boire à; (regale) régaler; med soigner; ~ **oneself to sth**

se payer qch, s'offrir qch; adv phr coll **a** ~ très bien

**treatise** n traité m

**treatment** n traitement m; med traitement médical; ~ **of one's friends** manière f d'agir envers ses amis

**treaty** n traité m; contrat m, accord m

**treble** n triple m; mus soprano m; adj triple; mus de soprano; ~ **clef** clef f de sol; vt + vi tripler

**treddle** n see **treadle**

**tree** n arbre m; (beam) poutre f; fig **be at the top of the** ~ être au haut de l'échelle; coll **be up a** ~ être dans la pétrin; **climb a** ~ grimper sur un arbre; **family** ~ arbre m généalogique; **shoe** ~ tendeur m

**treeless** adj sans arbres

**trek** n voyage (long et pénible); vi ar voyager en chariot; faire un voyage long et pénible

**trellis(-work)** n treillis m, treillage m

**tremble** n frisson m, tremblement m; (voice) tremblotement m; **all of a** ~ tout tremblant; vi trembler, frissonner

**trembler** n trembleur -euse; elect trembleur m

**tremendous** adj énorme, immense; (marvellous) formidable

**tremolo** n mus trémolo m

**tremor** n tremblement m, frémissement m

**tremulous** adj tremblotant, tremblant

**trench** n tranchée f, fossé m; vt creuser un fossé dans; vi ~ **on** empiéter sur

**trenchant** adj tranchant, incisif -ive, mordant

**trench-coat** n trench-coat m

**trend** n tendance f, direction f

**trend-setting** adj à l'avant-garde de la mode

**trendy** adj dans le vent

**trepan** vt trépaner

**trepanning** n surg trépanation f

**trepidation** n trépidation f

**trespass** n leg violation f de propriété; (crime) délit m; (sin) péché m; vi (sin) pécher; ~ **against the law** enfreindre la loi; ~ **on** (domain) empiéter sur; (kindness) abuser de; ~ **on s/o's property** pénétrer sans autorité sur la propriété de qn

**trespasser** n (property) intrus -e; ~ **s will be prosecuted** défense d'entrer sous peine d'amende

**tress** n tresse f, boucle f

**trestle** n tréteau m, chevalet m

**triad** n triade f

**trial** n essai m, épreuve f; (law) procès m, jugement m, cause f; leg **go on** ~ passer en jugement; **on** ~ à l'essai; adj d'essai; ~ **balance** balance f d'inventaire; **~ run** essai *m*

**triangle** *n* triangle *m*

**triangular** *adj* triangulaire

**triangulate** *vt* trianguler

**triangulation** *n* triangulation *f*

**tribal** *adj* de tribu, de la tribu, tribal

**tribalism** *n* tribalisme *m*

**tribe** *n* tribu *f*

**tribesman** *n* membre *m* de la tribu

**tribulation** *n* tribulation *f*

**tribunal** *n* tribunal *m*, cour *f* de justice

**tributary** *n* tributaire *m*; (river) affluent *m*; *adj* tributaire

**tribute** *n* tribut *m*; *fig* hommage *m*

**trice** *n* **in a ~** en un clin d'œil

**trick** *n* tour *m*; (dodge) ruse *f*; (practical joke) farce *f*, blague *f*; (habit) manie *f*, tic *m*, habitude *f*; (cards) levée *f*; **~ of the trade** truc *m*; **conjuring ~** tour *m* de passe-passe; **dirty ~** vilain tour; **know a ~ or two** avoir plus d'un tour dans son sac; **play a ~ on s/o** jouer un tour à qn; **that will do the ~** ça fera l'affaire; *vt* duper, attraper; **~ out** attifer

**trick-cyclist** *n* cycliste-acrobate (*pl* cyclistes-acrobates); *coll* psychiatre

**trickery** *n* tromperie *f*, fourberie *f*

**trickiness** *n* difficulté *f*

**trickle** *n* filet *m*; *vt* laisser dégoutter; *vi* couler (goutte à goutte); **~ in** (liquid) s'infiltrer; (people) entrer par petits groupes

**trickling** *n* écoulement *m*

**trick-rider** *n* voltigeur *m*

**trickster** *n* escroc *m*, fourbe *m*

**tricky** *adj* rusé, astucieux -ieuse; (subtle) fin; compliqué; (difficult) difficile, délicat, épineux -euse

**tricycle** *n* tricycle *m*

**tricyclist** *n* tricycliste

**trident** *n* trident *m*

**tried** *adj* éprouvé

**triennial** *adj* qui a lieu une fois tous les trois ans, trisannuel -elle

**trier** *n coll* **he's a ~** il fait toujours de son mieux

**trifle** *n* bagatelle *f*, rien *m*; *cul* = diplomate *m*; *adv phr* **a ~** un peu; *vi* badiner; **~ away one's time** perdre son temps; **~ with one's health** jouer avec sa santé; **~ with s/o** se jouer de qn

**trifler** *n* personne *f* frivole

**trifling** *adj* insignifiant, peu important

**trigger** *n* détente *f*, gâchette *f*; *vt* **~ off** déclencher

**trigonometry** *n* trigonométrie *f*

**trike** *n coll* tricycle *m*

**trilateral** *adj* trilatéral

**trilby** *n* chapeau *m* en feutre, feutre *m*

**trilingual** *adj* trilingue

**trill** *n mus* trille *f*; *vt mus* triller; *vi mus* faire des trilles

**trilogy** *n* trilogie *f*

**trim** *n* bon ordre; (person) **in good ~** en bonne forme; (things) **in perfect ~** en parfait état; *adj* propre, soigné, en bon ordre, en bon état; *vt* arranger, mettre en ordre; (shape) tailler; (hair) rafraîchir; (dress) orner, garnir, parer; (sails) orienter; (boat) équilibrer, redresser; (lamp) émécher; (cargo) arrimer; **~ up** (hat) garnir à neuf

**trimly** *adv* proprement, en bon ordre

**trimmer** *n* (hats) garnisseur -euse; *naut* arrimeur *m*; *coll* opportuniste

**trimming** *n* arrangement *m*; (hedge) taille *f*; (hats) garnissage *m*; (decoration) ornement *m*, garniture *f*; (cargo) arrimage *m*; (clothes) passementerie *f*; *cul* **~s** garniture *f*

**trimness** *n* élégance *f*, air bien tenu

**trinity** *n* groupe *m* de trois; *eccles* **Trinity** la Trinité

**trinket** *n* colifichet *m*, breloque *f*; (jewel) petit bijou

**trio** *n* trio *m*

**trip** *n* excursion *f*, voyage *m* d'agrément, tour *m*; (stumble) faux pas, faute *f*, croche-pied *m*; *sl* (drugs) trip *m*; **go for a ~** faire une excursion; *vt* faire un croc-en-jambe à; (obstacle) faire trébucher; *fig* **~ s/o up** prendre qn en défaut; *vi* trébucher, faire un faux pas; **~ along** aller d'un pas léger; *fig* **~ up** commettre une faute

**tripartite** *adj* tripartite

**tripe** *n cul* gras-double *m*; *coll fig* bêtises *fpl*; **~ shop** triperie *f*

**triple** *adj* triple

**triplet** *n mus* triolet *m*; *pros* tercet *m*; **~s** triplés *mpl* (*fpl* triplées)

**triplicate** *n* triplicata *m*; **in ~** en triple exemplaire; *adj* triple, triplé; *vt* tripler; rédiger en trois exemplaires

**tripod** *n* trépied *m*

**tripos** *n* = examen *m* de licence (à Cambridge)

**tripper** *n* excursionniste

**tripping** *adj* courant (marchant) d'un pas léger

**triptych** *n* triptyque *m*

**trip-wire** *n* fil *m* de détente, fil tendu

**trisect** *vt* triséquer

**trite** *adj* banal (*pl* banals), rebattu

**triteness** *n* banalité *f*

**triumph** *n* triomphe *m*; succès *m*; *vi* triompher

**triumphal** *adj* triomphal

**triumphant** *adj* triomphant

**triumvirate** *n* triumvirat *m*

**trivet** *n* trépied *m*

**trivia** *npl* riens *mpl*

**trivial** *adj* sans importance, insignifiant

**triviality** *n* insignifiance *f*; (remark) banalité *f*

**trochee** *n pros* trochée *m*

**troglodyte** *n* troglodyte *m*

**Trojan** *n* Troyen -enne; **work like a ~** travailler comme un nègre; *adj* troyen -enne; **~ horse** cheval *m* de Troie; **the ~ War** la guerre de Troie

¹**troll** *n* chanson *f* à reprises; *vt* chantonner; (fishing) pêcher à la cuiller

²**troll** *n* troll *m*

**trolley** *n* chariot *m*; (basket) poussette *f*; (porter) diable *m*; (dishes) table roulante; *elect* trolley *m*; (supermarket) caddie *m*

**trolley-bus** *n* trolleybus *m*

**trollop** *n* souillon *f*, putain *f*

**trombone** *n* trombone *m*

**troop** *n* troupe *f*, bande *f*; **~s** soldats *mpl*, troupes *fpl*; *vt* **~ the colours** présenter le drapeau; *vi* **~ in (out)** entrer (sortir) en bande

**trooper** *n mil* soldat *m* de cavalerie

**troop-ship** *n* transport *m* de troupes

**troop-train** *n* train *m* militaire

**trophy** *n* trophée *m*

**tropic** *n* tropique *m*

**tropical** *adj* tropical

**trot** *n* trot *m*; **at a ~** au trot; **at an easy (a slow) ~** au petit trot; **at full ~** au grand trot; *vt* faire trotter; *coll* **~ sth out** sortir qch; *vi* trotter, aller au trot; **~ away (off)** partir au trot

**trotter** *n* (horse, mare) trotteur -euse; (pig, sheep) pied *m*

**trouble** *n* (grief) chagrin *m*, peine *f*; (difficulty) difficulté *f*, problème *m*; (bother) dérangement *m*, peine *f*, ennui *m*; (worry) inquiétude *f*, souci *m*; *mech* panne *f*, avarie *f*; **ask for ~** se préparer des ennuis; **be in ~** avoir des ennuis; *coll* **get a girl into ~** rendre une fille enceinte; **get into ~** s'attirer des ennuis; **go to a great deal of ~** se donner beaucoup de mal; **have heart (etc) ~** souffrir du cœur (etc); **it's not worth the ~** cela ne vaut pas la peine; **make ~** semer la discorde; **money ~s** soucis *mpl* d'argent; **take the ~ to** se donner la peine de; **that's no ~** cela ne me dérange nullement; **what's the ~?** qu'est-ce qui ne va pas?; *vt* (grieve) affliger, chagriner; (worry) inquiéter, préoccuper; (bother) ennuyer; (disturb) déranger; **~ oneself about sth** se mettre en peine de qch; **~ oneself to do sth** se donner la peine de faire qch; **could I ~ you for the salt?** voudriez-vous s'il vous plaît me passer le sel?; *vi* (worry) s'inquiéter; (inconvenience) se déranger, se donner la peine

**troublemaker** *n* fauteur -trice, provocateur -trice, fomentateur -trice de troubles

**troubleshooter** *n* conciliateur *m*; *mech* dépanneur *m*

**troublesome** *adj* ennuyeux -euse, gênant, incommode

**troublespot** *n* point chaud

**trough** *n* auge *f*; (drinking) abreuvoir *m*; (kneading) pétrin *m*; (wave) creux *m*; *meteor* dépression *f*

**trounce** *vt* rosser, rouer de coups; (defeat) écraser; (scold) réprimander

**troupe** *n* troupe *f*

**trouper** *n* membre *m* d'une troupe, acteur -trice chevronné -e

**trouser-clip** *n* pince *f* à pantalon

**trousered** *adj* à pantalon, portant un pantalon

**trousers** *npl* pantalon *m*, pantalons *mpl*; *coll* **she's the one who wears the ~** c'est elle qui porte le pantalon; **short ~** culottes courtes

**trouser-suit** *n* tailleur-pantalon *m* (*pl* tailleurs-pantalons)

**trousseau** *n* trousseau *m*

**trout** *n* truite *f*

**trowel** *n* truelle *f*

**truancy** *n* absence *f* de l'école sans raison valable

**truant** *n* élève absent -e de l'école sans raison valable; **play ~** faire l'école buissonnière

**truce** *n* trêve *f*

¹**truck** *n* (barter) troc *m*, échange *m*; *US* produits maraîchers; *US* **~ farmer** maraîcher -ère; **have no ~ with** n'avoir rien à faire avec; *vt* troquer, échanger

²**truck** *n* chariot *m*; (railway) wagon *m* à marchandises; *US* camion *m*; *min* benne *f*; *US* **delivery ~** camionnette *f*

**truculence** *n* férocité *f*

**truculent** *adj* féroce, farouche, brutal

**trudge** *n* marche *f* pénible; *vi* marcher péniblement (lourdement)

**true** *n* **out of ~** (post, etc) hors d'aplomb; (axle) faussé; (wheel) décentré; *adj* vrai, véridique; (genuine) véritable, authentique, réel -elle; (faithful) fidèle, loyal; (accurate) juste, exact; *leg* **~ copy** copie *f* conforme; **come ~** se réaliser, se vérifier; **the same holds ~ in respect of** il en est de même pour; *adv* vraiment; (correctly) juste; *vt* ajuster, rectifier

**true-blue** *adj coll* loyal; à toute épreuve

**true-born** *adj* légitime

**true-bred** *adj* de race, (de) pur sang *invar*

**true-hearted** *adj* au cœur fidèle, loyal; sincère

**true-love** *n* bien aimé -e

**truffle** *n* truffe *f*

**truism** *n* truisme *m*, *coll* vérité *f* de la Palisse

**truly** *adv* vraiment; véritablement; justement; **(really and)** ~? vrai de vrai?; **(I am), (Sir), yours** ~ je vous prie de croire, Monsieur, à l'expression de mes sentiments respectueux; *coll* **yours** ~ votre humble serviteur *m*; *sl* bibi *m*

**trump** *n* atout *m*; *coll* bon type; **turn up** ~s (be helpful) être d'un grand secours; faire des merveilles; *vt* (cards) couper; ~ **up** inventer, fabriquer; *vi* jouer atout

**trump-card** *n* atout *m*; *fig* atout (majeur), carte maîtresse

**trumpery** *adj* (goods) sans valeur, de camelote; (argument) spécieux -ieuse

**trumpet** *n* trompette *f*; (person) trompettiste, trompette *m*; **blow one's own** ~ se vanter; *fig* **with a flourish of** ~s à cor et à cri; *vt* publier à son de trompe; ~ **abroad** proclamer; *vi* sonner de la trompette; (elephant) barrir

**trumpet-call** *n* sonnerie *f* de trompette

**trumpeter** *n* *mil* trompette *m*; *mus* trompettiste

**trumpeting** *n* (elephant) barrissement *m*

**truncate** *vt* tronquer

**truncheon** *n* bâton *m*, matraque *f*

**trundle** *vt* faire rouler; (barrow) pousser

**trunk** *n* (tree, body) tronc *m*; (luggage) malle *f*; *US mot* coffre *m*; (elephant) trompe *f*

**trunk-call** *n* (telephone) communication interurbaine

**trunk-line** *n* (railway) grande ligne; (telephone) ligne interurbaine

**trunk-road** *n* route nationale, grande route

**trunks** *npl* slip *m*

**truss** *n* *bui* armature *f*, ferme *f*; (hay) botte *f*; *med* bandage *m* herniaire; *vt* (hay) mettre en bottes; *bui* renforcer; *cul* trousser; (tie) lier

**trust** *n* confiance *f*; (hope) espoir *m*, espérance *f*; (office) charge *f*; (responsibility) responsabilité *f*; (care) garde *f*, dépôt *m*; (industry) trust *m*, cartel *m*; *leg* fidéicommis *m*; *comm* **on** ~ à crédit; *vt* avoir confiance en, se fier à; *comm* faire crédit à; (believe) croire; *iron* ~ **him!** ça, c'est bien lui!; ~ **oneself to do sth** se risquer à faire qch; ~ **one's own eyes (ears)** en croire ses yeux (oreilles); ~ **s/o with sth** confier qch à qn; *vi* ~ **in** mettre sa confiance en; (hope) mettre son espoir en; ~ **to luck** s'en remettre au hasard

**trusted** *adj* de confiance; (method) éprouvé

**trustee** *n* dépositaire, administrateur -trice; *leg* curateur -trice; **board of** ~s conseil *m* d'administration

**trusteeship** *n* administration *f*; *leg* fidéicommis *m*; *pol* tutelle *f*

**trustful** *adj* confiant

**trustiness** *n* fidélité *f*, loyauté *f*

**trustworthiness** *n* (person) loyauté *f*; (information) crédibilité *f*

**trustworthy** *adj* digne de confiance, honnête; (accurate) exact

**trusty** *adj* digne de confiance; fidèle

**truth** *n* vérité *f*; chose vraie; **not a word of** ~ pas un mot de vrai; **tell s/o some home** ~s dire son fait à qn; **there's some** ~ **in it** il y a du vrai là-dedans; **to tell the** ~ à vrai dire

**truthful** *adj* (person) qui dit la vérité; (statement) véridique, vrai; (likeness) fidèle

**try** *n* essai *m*, tentative *f*; **at the first** ~ du premier coup; **be worth a** ~ valoir la peine d'essayer; **have a** ~ **at doing sth** essayer de faire qch; (rugby) **score a** ~ marquer un essai; *vt* essayer, expérimenter; (test) éprouver, mettre à l'épreuve; (tire) fatiguer; (verify) vérifier; *leg* juger; (irritate) vexer; (taste) goûter, déguster; ~ **it on** (bluff) bluffer; ~ **on** essayer; ~ **one's best** faire tout son possible (de son mieux); ~ **one's strength against s/o** se mesurer avec qn; ~ **out** faire l'essai de; *vi* essayer; ~ **for sth** essayer d'obtenir qch

**trying** *adj* difficile, vexant

**try-on** *n* bluff *m*

**tryst** *n* *lit* rendez-vous *m* (d'amour)

**tsar** *n* tsar *m*

**tsetse-fly** *n* mouche *f* tsé-tsé

**T-shirt** *n* T-shirt *m*

**tub** *n* baquet *m*, cuve *f*; (bath) bain *m*, tub *m*; *coll* (boat) rafiot *m*; *vt* mettre dans un baquet; *vi coll* prendre un bain

**tuba** *n* tuba *m*

**tubby** *adj coll* rondelet -ette, pansu

**tube** *n* tube *m*, tuyau *m*; *coll* (underground) = métro *m*; *US télé f*; *surg* drain *m*; *anat* canal *m*; **inner** ~ chambre *f* à air

**tubeless** *adj* sans chambre à air

**tuber** *n* tubercule *f*

**tubercular** *adj* tuberculeux -euse

**tuberculosis** *n* tuberculose *f*

**tuberculous** *adj* tuberculeux -euse

**tube-station** *n* = station *f* de métro

**tube-train** *n* = métro *m*, rame *f* de métro

**tubing** *n* tubage *m*, tuyautage *m*, tubes *mpl*

**tub-thumper** *n* orateur *m* de carrefour

**tub-thumping** *n* discours bruyants et émotifs, discours *mpl* démagogiques;

*adj* porté à faire des discours bruyants et émotifs (démagogiques)

**tubular** *adj* tubulaire

**tuck** *n* pli *m*, rempli *m*; *coll* boustifaille *f*; *vt* (dressmaking) faire des plis à, remplier, plisser; (fold) replier, serrer; ~ **away** cacher; ~ **in** rentrer; (fold) replier; (person) border; ~ **in the bedclothes** border le lit; ~ **up** (skirt) retrousser; *vi coll* ~ **in** s'en mettre jusque-là, bouffer

**tuck-box** *n coll* boîte *f* à provisions

**tuck-shop** *n coll* (school) pâtisserie *f*, boutique *f* de bonbons

**Tuesday** *n* mardi *m*

**tufa** *n geol* tuf *m*

**tuft** *n* touffe *f*; (bird) huppe *f*, aigrette *f*; (wool) flocon *m*

**tufted** *adj* en touffe; (bird) huppé

**tug** *n* traction *f*; (shake) secousse *f*; *naut* ~ **(boat)** remorqueur *m*; *vt* tirer (avec effort); ~ **along** traîner; *naut* remorquer; *vi* tirer (avec effort); ~ **at** tirer sur

**tug-of-war** *n* lutte *f* de traction à la corde

**tuition** *n* enseignement *m*, instruction *f*; **postal** ~ enseignement *m* par correspondance; **private** ~ leçons particulières, cours particuliers

**tulip** *n* tulipe *f*

**tumble** *n* chute *f*, culbute *f*; *vt* bouleverser, déranger; (knock over) faire tomber; (crease) chiffonner; ~ **down** (over) culbuter, renverser; *vi* tomber, culbuter; ~ **down** dégringoler; (building) s'écrouler; ~ **into** se jeter dans; *coll* ~ **on sth** tomber sur qch, trouver qch par hasard; *coll* ~ **to sth** comprendre qch; *sl* piger qch

**tumbledown** *adj coll* délabré, en ruine

**tumbler** *n* (circus) acrobate; verre *m*; *elect* culbuteur *m*

**tumbrel, tumbril** *n* tombereau *m*

**tumefaction** *n* tuméfaction *f*

**tumefy** *vt* tuméfier; *vi* se tuméfier

**tummy** *n coll* ventre *m*; (stomach) estomac *m*

**tumour** *n* tumeur *f*

**tumult** *n* tumulte *m*, agitation *f*

**tumultuous** *adj* tumultueux -euse

**tuna** *n* thon *m*

**tundra** *n* toundra *f*

**tune** *n* air *m*; *fig* **change one's** ~ changer de langage; **in** ~ d'accord; **sing out of (in)** ~ chanter faux (juste); *vt* accorder, mettre d'accord; *mot* mettre au point; ~ **in to a station** capter un poste; *vi* s'accorder

**tuneful** *adj* mélodieux -ieuse

**tuneless** *adj* inharmonieux -ieuse, discordant

**tuner** *n* (piano) accordeur *m*

**tungsten** *n* tungstène *m*

**tunic** *n* tunique *f*

**tuning** *n* accordage *m*; *mot* mise *f* au point

**tuning-fork** *n* diapason *m*

**Tunisia** *n* Tunisie *f*

**Tunisian** *n* Tunisien -ienne; *adj* tunisien -ienne

**tunnel** *n* tunnel *m*, passage souterrain; (mine) galerie *f*; *vt* percer un tunnel dans (à travers); *vi* percer un tunnel

**tunny(-fish)** *n* thon *m*

**turban** *n* turban *m*

**turbid** *adj* trouble

**turbine** *n* turbine *f*

**turbo-jet** *n* turboréacteur *m*

**turbo-prop** *n* turbopropulseur *m*

**turbot** *n* turbot *m*

**turbulence** *n* turbulence *f*

**turbulent** *adj* turbulent; (unruly) insubordonné

**turd** *n* étron *m*; *sl* (person) salaud *m*

**tureen** *n* soupière *f*

**turf** *n* (grass) gazon *m*; (lawn) pelouse *f*; (peat) tourbe *f*; (racing) turf *m*; *vt* gazonner; *coll* ~ **s/o out** flanquer qn dehors

**turf-accountant** *n* bookmaker *m*

**turgid** *adj* enflé; (style) ampoulé

**turgidity** *n* enflure *f*; (style) emphase *f*

**Turk** *n* Turc (*f* Turque)

**Turkey** *n* Turquie *f*

**turkey** *n* dindon *m*; (hen) dinde *f*; *coll* **talk** ~ parler sérieusement; **young** ~ dindonneau *m*

**Turkish** *n* (language) turc *m*; *adj* turc (*f* turque); ~ **bath** bain *m* de vapeur; ~ **delight** loukoum *m*; ~ **towel** serviette *f* éponge

**turmoil** *n* tumulte *m*, agitation *f*

**turn** *n* tour *m*; (wheel) révolution *f*; (road) tournant *m*; (bend) virage *m*; (change) changement *m*; (direction) changement *m* de direction; (walk) promenade *f*; (shock) coup *m*; (act) numéro *m*; (attack) crise *f*; ~ **of mind** tournure *f* d'esprit; **at every** ~ à tout propos, à tout bout de champ; **done to a** ~ cuit à point; **do s/o a bad** ~ jouer un mauvais tour à qn; **do s/o a good** ~ rendre service à qn; **give s/o a** ~ faire peur à qn; **in** ~ à tour de rôle; **play out of** ~ jouer avant son tour; **take a** ~ **for the better (worse)** s'améliorer (empirer); *vt* tourner; (change) transformer, changer; (make revolve) faire tourner; (direct) diriger; (soil) retourner; ~ **aside** détourner, écarter; ~ **away** (deflect) détourner; (dismiss) renvoyer; ~ **back** faire retourner; (send) renvoyer; ~ **down** rabattre; (fold) plier; (volume, gas, light) baisser; (offer, suggestion) repousser;

(candidate) refuser; ~ **in** (fold) replier; (hand over) livrer, rendre; ~ **off** fermer, couper; (light) éteindre; ~ **on** (water) ouvrir; (light) allumer; *sl* stimuler; ~ **one's attention to** porter l'attention sur; ~ **one's stomach** soulever le cœur; ~ **out** (evict) mettre à la porte, expulser; (light) éteindre; (produce) produire; (clean) nettoyer à fond; (empty) vider; ~ **over** (overturn) renverser; (page) tourner; (pages) feuilleter; (hand over) remettre; (think about) réfléchir à; *comm* faire; ~ **round** retourner; ~ **tail** prendre la fuite; ~ **the scale** faire pencher la balance; ~ **up** retourner; (tuck up) retrousser; (collar) relever; (page) trouver; ~ **upside down** mettre sens dessus dessous; *fig* bouleverser; **be** ~ **ed fifty** avoir cinquante ans passés; **it is** ~ **ed five o'clock** il est cinq heures passées; **nicely** ~ **ed out** (person) soigné, élégant; **without** ~ **ing a hair** sans sourciller; *vi* se tourner; (revolve) tourner; (turn round) se retourner; (become) devenir; (wind, tide) changer; (milk) tourner; ~ **about** se retourner, se tourner; ~ **aside** se détourner, s'écarter; ~ **away** se détourner; ~ **back** rebrousser chemin, retourner; (look) regarder en arrière; ~ **down a street** prendre une rue; *coll* ~ **in** aller (se) coucher; ~ **into** se changer en; ~ **off** bifurquer, tourner; ~ **on s/o** se retourner contre qn, attaquer qn; ~ **out** (end) finir, se terminer; (go out) sortir; (become) devenir; (get up) se lever; (happen) arriver; ~ **out well (badly)** bien (mal) tourner; ~ **over** se retourner; (vehicle) verser, capoter; (boat) chavirer; ~ **round** se retourner; ~ **to** (change) se changer en; (refer) se reporter à; (for help) recourir à; *coll* se mettre au travail; ~ **towards** se diriger vers; ~ **up** se relever; *coll* (arrive) arriver (à l'improviste), se présenter; **as it** ~ **ed out** en l'occurrence; **not know which way to** ~ ne savoir où donner de la tête

**turncoat** *n* renégat -e

**turncock** *n* (instrument) clef *f*

**turner** *n* tourneur *m*

**turning** *n* (movement) rotation *f*; (road) tournant *m*; (change) changement *m*; *mot* virage *m*; (action) retournage *m*; (industry) tournage *m*

**turning-point** *n* moment *m* critique, point décisif

**turnip** *n* navet *m*

**turnkey** *n* geôlier -ière

**turn-out** *n* (concourse) assemblée *f*; (clothes) tenue *f*; (outfit) équipage *m*;

(production) rendement *m*, production *f*

**turnover** *n* chiffre *m* d'affaires; (personnel) mouvement *m*; (goods) écoulement *m*; *cul* chausson *m*

**turnpike** *n* US autoroute *f* à péage; *hist* barrière *f* de péage

**turn-round** *n comm* + *naut* rotation *f*

**turnstile** *n* tourniquet *m*

**turntable** *n* (record-player) platine *f*; (railway) plaque tournante

**turn-up** *n* (trousers) revers *m*; *coll* fracas *m*; *coll* surprise *f*

**turpentine** *n* térébenthine *f*

**turpitude** *n* turpitude *f*

**turquoise** *n* turquoise *f*; *adj* turquoise *invar*

**turret** *n* tourelle *f*

**turtle** *n* tortue *f* de mer; **turn** ~ chavirer

**turtle-dove** *n* tourterelle *f*

**Tuscany** *n* Toscane *f*

**tusk** *n* défense *f*

**tussle** *n* lutte *f*, mêlée *f*

**tussock** *n* touffe *f* d'herbe

**tut** *interj* allons donc!

**tutelage** *n* tutelle *f*

**tutelary** *adj* tutélaire

**tutor** *n* (teacher) professeur *m*; (individual) précepteur -trice; (university) directeur -trice d'études; *vt* instruire; donner des cours particuliers à

**tutorial** *n* cours particulier (donné à un étudiant); *adj* d'instruction, d'un précepteur

**tutorship** *n* préceptorat *m*

**tuxedo** *n* US smoking *m*

**twaddle** *n* fadaises *fpl*, futilités *fpl*

**twain** *n lit* **the** ~ les deux; *adj lit* **in** ~ en deux

**twang** *n* bruit sec (d'une corde); **nasal** ~ accent nasillard; *vt* faire résonner; *vi* vibrer, émettre un son vibrant

**tweak** *n* pincement *m*; *vt* pincer

**twee** *adj coll pej* (person) mignard; (object) un peu trop joli

**tweed** *n* tweed *m*

**tweet** *n* pépiement *m*; *vi* pépier

**tweezers** *npl* petite pince, brucelles *fpl*

**twelfth** *n* douzième *m*; (date) douze *m*; *adj* douzième; **Twelfth Night** la fête des Rois; **Twelfth Night cake** galette *f* des Rois

**twelve** *n* douze *m invar*; **about** ~ une douzaine; *adj* douze *invar*

**twentieth** *n* vingtième *m*; (date) vingt *m*; *adj* vingtième

**twenty** *n* vingt *m invar*; *adj* vingt *invar*

**twenty-first** *n* vingt-et-unième; (date) vingt-et-un *m*; *adj* vingt-et-unième

**twerp** *n coll* andouille *f*

**twice** *adv* deux fois, à deux reprises; **not have to be asked** ~ ne pas se faire prier

**twiddle** *vt* tourner; ~ **one's thumbs** se tourner les pouces

**¹twig** *n* brindille *f*

**²twig** *vt* + *vi coll* comprendre; *sl* piger

**twilight** *n* crépuscule *m*; **in the** ~ au crépuscule, entre chien et loup

**twin** *n* + *adj* jumeau -elle; ~ **beds** lits jumeaux; *vt* jumeler

**twine** *n* ficelle *f*; *vt* (twist) tordre; (entwine) entrelacer; (weave) tisser; *vi* se tordre; ~ **round** s'enrouler autour; (road) serpenter

**twin-engined** *adj* à deux moteurs

**twinge** *n* élancement *m*, tiraillement *m*; ~ **of conscience** remords *m*

**twinkle** *n* scintillement *m*; (eyes) pétillement *m*; *vi* scintiller; (eyes) pétiller

**twinkling** *n* scintillement *m*; (eyes) pétillement *m*; **in the** ~ **of an eye** en un clin d'œil

**twin-set** *n* twin-set *m*

**twirl** *n* pirouette *f*, tournoiement *m*; *vt* faire tournoyer, faire tourner; (twist) tortiller; *vi* tournoyer, pirouetter

**twist** *n* torsion *f*; (cotton, etc) cordon *m*, cordonnet *m*; (hair) torsade *f*; (road) coude *m*; (sheet of metal, etc) gondolage *m*; (sense) perversion *f*; (dance) twist *m*; ~ **s and turns** tours *mpl* et détours *mpl*; *vt* tordre, tortiller; (plait) tresser; (sense) altérer; ~ **one's ankle** se fouler la cheville; ~ **s/o round one's little finger** mener qn par le bout du nez; ~ **s/o's arm** tordre le bras à qn; *coll fig* exercer une pression sur qn; *vi* se tordre, se tortiller; (road) faire des détours (lacets); ~ **and turn** (struggle) se débattre; (wind) serpenter

**twister** *n* tordeur -euse; *coll* (person) fourbe; *coll* (problem) question *f* difficile

**twisty** *adj* qui serpente; *coll* malhonnête

**¹twit** *n coll* imbécile, idiot -e

**²twit** *vt* taquiner, railler

**twitch** *n* saccade *f*, secousse *f*; (pain) élancement *m*; (face) tic *m*; (limbs) mouvement convulsif; *vt* (snatch) tirer brusquement; (contort) crisper; *vi* se crisper, se contracter

**twitching** *n see* **twitch** *n*

**twitter** *n* gazouillement *m*; *vi* gazouiller

**twittering** *n see* **twitter** *n*

**two** *n* deux *m invar*; *adj* deux *invar*; ~ **by** ~ deux à deux; **in a day or** ~ dans quelques jours, dans un ou deux jours; **put** ~ **and** ~ **together** tirer ses conclusions

**two-edged** *adj* à deux tranchants, à double tranchant

**two-faced** *adj coll* hypocrite

**twofold** *adj* double; *adv* doublement

**two-handed** *adj* à deux mains

**two-legged** *adj* bipède

**two-piece** *n* deux-pièces *m invar*

**two-ply** *adj* à deux brins

**two-seater** *n aer* avion *m* à deux places; *mot* voiture *f* à deux places

**twosome** *n* (couple) couple *m*; (game) jeu *m* pour deux personnes

**two-step** *n* pas *m* de deux

**two-stroke** *adj mech* à deux temps

**two-timing** *adj US coll* trompeur -euse

**two-way** *adj* (road) à deux sens

**tycoon** *n* grand manitou

**tyke** *n see* **tike**

**tympanum** *n* tympan *m*

**type** *n* type *m*, genre *m*; *typ* caractère *m*; *coll* type *m*, *sl* mec *m*; *vt* + *vi* taper à la machine

**typecast** *adj theat* à qui l'on donne toujours le même genre de rôle

**typescript** *n* manuscrit dactylographié

**type-setter** *n* compositeur -trice, typographe

**typewriter** *n* machine *f* à écrire

**typewriting** *n* dactylographie *f*

**typewritten** *adj* écrit à la machine

**typhoid** *n* (fièvre *f*) typhoïde *f*; *adj* typhoïde

**typhoon** *n* typhon *m*

**typhus** *n* typhus *m*

**typical** *adj* typique

**typify** *vt* représenter; être typique (caractéristique)

**typing** *n* dactylographie *f*

**typing-paper** *n* papier *m* pour machine à écrire

**typist** *n* dactylographe, *coll* dactylo

**typographer** *n* typographe

**typographical** *adj* typographique

**typography** *n* typographie *f*

**typological** *adj* typologique

**typology** *n* typologie *f*

**tyrannical** *adj* tyrannique

**tyrannize** *vt* tyranniser; *vi* agir en tyran, faire le tyran

**tyrannous** *adj* tyrannique

**tyranny** *n* tyrannie *f*

**tyrant** *n* tyran *m*

**tyre**, *US* **tire** *n* (pneumatic) pneu *m*; (solid) bandage *m*

**tyre-gauge** *n* manomètre *m*

**tyro** *n* novice

**Tyrolean** *adj* tyrolien -ienne

759

# U

**u** *n* (snob behaviour, speech) **this is U**
c'est bien, c'est ce qu'il faut; (thought
to be vulgar) **non-U** peu recommandable

**ubiquitous** *adj* omniprésent, qui se
trouve partout, qu'on voit partout

**ubiquity** *n* ubiquité *f*, omniprésence *f*

**udder** *n* mamelle *f*; (cow) pis *m*

**Uganda** *n* Ouganda *m*, Uganda *m*

**ugh** *interj* pouah!

**ugliness** *n* laideur *f*

**ugly** *adj* laid, vilain, disgracieux -ieuse;
(wound) dangereux -euse; **~ as sin**
laid comme un pou; **~ customer** sale
type *m*; **grow ~** enlaidir; **turn ~** se fâcher

**ulcer** *n* ulcère *m*

**ulcerate** *vt* ulcérer; *vi* s'ulcérer

**ulceration** *n* ulcération *f*

**ulcerous** *adj* ulcéreux -euse

**ulna** *n anat* cubitus *m*

**Ulster** *n* Ulster *m*

**ult** *adv abbr see* **ultimo**

**ulterior** *adj* ultérieur; **~ motive** but
secret; **without ~ motive** sans arrière-
pensée

**ultimate** *n* essentiel *m*; point final; **the
~ in refinement** ce qu'il y a de plus
raffiné; *adj* final, définitif -ive; (last) ultime

**ultimatum** *n* ultimatum *m*

**ultimo** *adv* **on the 10th ~** le 10 du mois
dernier

**ultra** *n pol* ultra, extrémiste; *adj* extrême

**ultramarine** *adj* (country, etc) d'outre-
mer; (colour) bleu *m* outremer *invar*

**ultramodern** *adj* ultramoderne

**ultrasonic** *adj* ultrasonique

**ultra-violet** *adj* ultra-violet -ette

**ululate** *vi* (owl) ululer

**ululation** *n* (owl) ululement *m*

**umbilical** *adj* ombilical

**umbilicus** *n anat* ombilic *m*, nombril *m*

**umbrage** *n* ombrage *m*; **take ~ at**
s'offenser de

**umbrella** *n* parapluie *m*

**umbrella-stand** *n* porte-parapluies *m*

**umpire** *n* arbitre *m*, juge *m*; *vt* arbitrer;
*vi* servir d'arbitre

**umpteen** *adj sl* beaucoup de

**unabashed** *adj* aucunement ébranlé, aucunement décontenancé

**unabated** *adj* non diminué

**unable** *adj* incapable; (prevented) empêché

**unabridged** *adj* non abrégé; **~ edition**
édition intégrale

**unaccented** *adj* non accentué

**unacceptable** *adj* inacceptable

**unaccommodating** *adj* peu accommodant

**unaccompanied** *adj* seul, non accompagné; *mus* sans accompagnement

**unaccountable** *adj* inexplicable; (odd)
étrange

**unaccounted** *adj* **~ for** inexpliqué;
(missing) qui manque

**unaccustomed** *adj* (person) peu habitué;
(unusual) inaccoutumé

**unacknowledged** *adj* non reconnu;
(letter) resté sans réponse

**unacquainted** *adj* **be ~ with** ne pas connaître

**unadaptable** *adj* inadaptable

**unaddressed** *adj* sans adresse

**unadorned** *adj* sans ornement

**unadulterated** *adj* pur; sans mélange

**unadvised** *adj* imprudent, mal avisé

**unaffected** *adj* (natural) sans affectation,
naturel -elle, simple; non affecté; **~ by
water** inaltérable à l'eau

**unafraid** *adj* sans peur

**unaided** *adj* sans aide, tout seul (*f* toute
seule); **by one's ~ efforts** par ses
propres efforts

**unalloyed** *adj* pur, parfait

**unalterable** *adj* immuable

**unambiguous** *adj* non équivoque, clair

**unambitious** *adj* sans ambition; (aim,
etc) modeste

**unamenable** *adj* réfractaire

**un-American** *adj* contraire à l'esprit
américain; indigne d'un Américain;
anti-américain

**unanimity** *n* unanimité *f*

**unanimous** *adj* unanime

**unanswerable** *adj* (question) qui
n'admet pas de réponse; (argument)
irréfutable

**unappetizing** *adj* peu appétissant

**unappreciated** *adj* peu estimé, inapprécié

**unappreciative** *adj* insensible, froid

**unapproachable** *adj* inabordable, inaccessible

**unarmed** *adj* non armé; (combat) sans
armes

**unashamed** *adj* sans honte, effronté;
(brazen) éhonté

**unasked** *adj* (guest) sans être invité -e

**unassailable** adj (reputation) inattaquable; (right) indiscutable

**unassisted** adj sans aide, tout seul (f toute seule)

**unassuming** adj modeste, sans prétention(s)

**unattached** adj indépendant; (single) seul, sans attaches

**unattainable** adj impossible à atteindre, inaccessible, hors de portée

**unattended** adj non accompagné; (neglected) négligé; (unmanned) non pourvu de personnel; (not controlled) sans surveillance

**unattractive** adj peu attrayant; (character) peu sympathique, déplaisant

**unauthorized** adj non autorisé; (illegal) illicite

**unavailable** adj introuvable, impossible à obtenir; (person) indisponible, pas libre

**unavailing** adj inutile, vain

**unavoidable** adj inévitable

**unaware** adj ignorant; be ~ of ignorer

**unawares** adv inconsciemment; catch s/o ~ prendre qn au dépourvu

**unbalance** n déséquilibre m; vt déséquilibrer, déranger

**unbar** vt débarrer; fig ouvrir

**unbearable** adj insupportable

**unbeatable** adj imbattable

**unbeaten** adj invaincu, non battu

**unbecoming** adj déplacé, peu convenable; (dress) peu seyant

**unbefriended** adj sans ami(s)

**unbeknown** adj ~ to à l'insu de

**unbelief** n incrédulité f

**unbelievable** adj incroyable

**unbeliever** n incrédule; (religion) incroyant -e

**unbelieving** adj incrédule

**unbend** vt détendre; (straighten) redresser; vi se détendre

**unbending** adj inflexible, intransigeant

**unbiased, unbiassed** adj impartial, objectif -ive, sans prévention

**unbidden** adj non invité; spontané

**unbind** vt délier; (wound) débander

**unblemished** adj sans défaut; fig sans tache

**unblock** vt dégager, déboucher

**unblushing** adj sans vergogne, éhonté

**unbolt** vt déverrouiller

**unborn** adj pas encore né; (future) à venir

**unbosom** vt ~ oneself to s/o ouvrir son cœur à qn

**unbounded** adj sans bornes, illimité

**unbowed** adj fig insoumis

**unbreakable** adj incassable

**unbridled** adj débridé, effréné

**unbroken** adj non cassé, intact; (continuous) continu, ininterrompu; (unsubdued) indompté; (rule) toujours observé; (record) non battu, pas encore battu

**unbuckle** vt dégrafer, déboucler

**unburden** vt alléger, soulager; ~ oneself of sth se soulager de qch

**unbusinesslike** adj peu commerçant; (action) irrégulier -ière; (person) incompétent

**unbutton** vt déboutonner; vi fig se détendre

**uncalculated** adj indéfini; fig inattendu

**uncalled-for** adj (remark, action) déplacé; non justifié, non mérité

**uncanny** adj mystérieux -ieuse, inquiétant

**uncared-for** adj peu soigné, négligé; (abandoned) délaissé

**unceasing** adj incessant, continu; (effort) soutenu, assidu

**unceremonious** adj sans façon; brusque

**uncertain** adj incertain; (undecided) indéterminé, irrésolu; (step) mal assuré; (temper) inégal

**uncertainty** n incertitude f, doute m

**unchain** vt déchaîner

**unchallengeable** adj incontestable

**unchallenged** adj incontesté; (person) que personne ne vient contredire

**unchangeable** adj immuable

**unchanging** adj constant, invariable

**uncharitable** adj peu charitable

**uncharted** adj qui ne figure pas sur la carte; inexploré

**unchecked** adj (unrestrained) sans frein; (unhindered) qui ne rencontre pas d'obstacles; (bill, etc) non vérifié

**unchivalrous** adj peu courtois, peu galant

**unchristian** adj peu chrétien -ienne; coll impossible

**uncircumcised** adj incirconcis

**uncivil** adj impoli

**uncivilized** adj barbare, non civilisé

**uncivilly** adv impoliment

**unclaimed** adj non réclamé

**unclasp** vt dégrafer, défaire; (fist) desserrer

**unclassed** adj non classé

**unclassified** adj non classé

**uncle** n oncle m

**unclean** adj malpropre; impur

**unclench** vt desserrer

**uncloak** vt (plan) découvrir, dévoiler; démasquer

**unclothe** vt déshabiller, dévêtir

**unclouded** adj sans nuages, serein; (liquid) limpide; fig clair

**uncoil** vt dérouler; vi se dérouler

**uncoloured** adj non coloré; (colourless) incolore; fig impartial

**uncomfortable** adj (things) peu confortable, inconfortable; fig désagréable; (person) mal à son aise; (embarrassed) gêné; **feel** ~ être mal à l'aise; **feel** ~ **about sth** être inquiet -iète au sujet de qch; **make things** ~ **for s/o** créer des ennuis pour qn

**uncommitted** *adj* non engagé, indépendant

**uncommon** *adj* rare, singulier -ière, peu commun

**uncommonly** *adv* singulièrement, particulièrement

**uncommunicative** *adj* peu communicatif -ive

**uncomplaining** *adj* qui ne se plaint pas, résigné

**uncomplimentary** *adj* peu flatteur -euse

**uncompromising** *adj* intransigeant, inflexible

**unconcealed** *adj* qui n'est pas caché; (feeling) non dissimulé

**unconcern** *n* indifférence *f*; insouciance *f*

**unconcerned** *adj* indifférent, insouciant

**unconditional** *adj* inconditionnel -elle, sans conditions, absolu

**unconfined** *adj* sans restrictions, illimité

**unconfirmed** *adj* non confirmé

**uncongenial** *adj* (person) peu sympathique, peu agréable; (task) ingrat

**unconnected** *adj* sans rapport; (thoughts) sans suite

**unconquerable** *adj* invincible

**unconquered** *adj* invaincu

**unconscionable** *adj* démesuré, déraisonnable

**unconscious** *n* inconscient *m*; *adj* inconscient; sans connaissance, inanimé; **be** ~ **of sth** ignorer qch

**unconsciously** *adv* inconsciemment

**unconsciousness** *n* inconscience *f*; (faint) évanouissement *m*

**unconsecrated** *adj* non béni

**unconsidered** *adj* (action) irréfléchi; (little valued) peu estimé

**unconstitutional** *adj* anticonstitutionnel -elle

**unconstrained** *adj* non contraint, libre

**uncontested** *adj* non contesté, incontesté.

**uncontrollable** *adj* ingouvernable; (passion) irrésistible; ~ **laughter** fou rire

**uncontrolled** *adj* incontrôlé, libre, indépendant

**unconventional** *adj* original, non-conformiste

**unconventionality** *n* originalité *f*; (manner) liberté *f* d'allures

**unconventionally** *adv* de façon non-conformiste

**unconverted** *adj* non converti

**unconvinced** *adj* sceptique, non convaincu

**unconvincing** *adj* peu convaincant

**uncooked** *adj* pas cuit; (raw) cru

**unco-operative** *adj* peu coopérateur -trice

**unco-ordinated** *adj* non coordonné

**uncork** *vt* déboucher

**uncorrected** *adj* non corrigé

**uncorroborated** *adj* non confirmé

**uncouple** *vt* découpler; (disengage) débrayer

**uncouth** *adj* grossier -ière, rude, fruste

**uncover** *vt* découvrir

**uncritical** *adj* (person) dépourvu de sens critique; (attitude) peu critique

**uncrowned** *adj* non couronné

**uncrushable** *adj* (material) infroissable; impossible à écraser

**unction** *n* onction *f*

**unctuous** *adj* onctueux -euse; *fig pej* mielleux -euse

**uncultivated** *adj* (land) inculte; (person) sans culture

**uncultured** *adj* sans culture; (land) inculte

**uncurl** *vt* défriser, dérouler; *vi* (hair) se défriser; (rope) se dérouler

**uncut** *adj* non coupé; (book) non abrégé; (hedge) non taillé; (diamond) brut; (text) intégral

**undamaged** *adj* intact, non endommagé

**undated** *adj* sans date

**undaunted** *adj* intrépide, non intimidé

**undeceive** *vt* détromper, désabuser

**undecided** *adj* indécis, incertain

**undecipherable** *adj* indéchiffrable

**undeclared** *adj* non déclaré; resté secret -ète, caché

**undefeated** *adj* invaincu

**undefended** *adj* sans défense, non défendu

**undefiled** *adj* pur, sans tache

**undefined** *adj* non défini, vague

**undemonstrative** *adj* peu expansif -ive, réservé

**undeniable** *adj* indéniable, incontestable

**undependable** *adj* sur lequel (*f* laquelle) on ne peut pas compter

**under** *adj* de dessous; (subordinate) subalterne; *prep* sous, au-dessous de; (less than) moins de; (according to) selon; ~ **one's breath** à demi-voix; ~ **repair** en réparation; ~ **sentence of death** condamné à mort; ~ **the circumstances** dans ces circonstances; ~ **the necessity of** dans la nécessité de; ~ **treatment** en traitement; **be** ~ **the doctor** être entre les mains du docteur; **in the phone-book** ~ **Smith** dans l'annuaire parmi les Smith; *adv* dessous, au-dessous, en-dessous; (too little) insuffisamment, trop peu; **keep s/o** ~ tenir qn en soumission; **see** ~ voir ci-dessous

**under-age** *adj* au-dessous de l'âge autorisé, trop jeune

**under-belly** *n* bas-ventre *m*; *fig* région mal protégée

**underbid** *vt* demander moins cher que

**undercarriage** *n aer* train *m* d'atterrissage

**undercharge** *vt* demander trop peu à

**underclothes** *npl*, **underclothing** *n* sous-vêtements *mpl*, linge *m* de corps; (women) lingerie *f*

**undercoat** *n* (paint) couche *f* de fond

**undercover** *adj* secret -ète, clandestin

**undercurrent** *n* courant *m* de fond; *fig* courant sous-jacent

**undercut** *vt* (charge less) faire payer moins cher que; faire des propositions plus avantageuses que

**underdevelop** *vt phot* développer insuffisamment

**underdeveloped** *adj* sous-développé; *phot* insuffisamment développé; (child) retardé dans sa croissance

**underdog** *n* celui (*f* celle) qui est opprimé -e; *collect* les opprimés *mpl*

**underdone** *adj* pas assez cuit; (meat) saignant

**underestimate** *n* sous-estimation *f*; *vt* sous-estimer

**under-exposure** *n phot* sous-exposition *f*

**underfelt** *n* assise *f* de feutre

**underfoot** *adv* sous les pieds; **trample ~** fouler aux pieds

**undergarment** *n* sous-vêtement *m*

**undergo** *vt* subir; (suffering) supporter

**undergraduate** *n* étudiant -e (n'ayant pas encore sa licence)

**underground** *n* = métro *m*; mouvement *m* de résistance clandestine; *adj* souterrain; (secret) clandestin; (mine) ~ **worker** ouvrier *m* du fond; *adv* sous (la) terre; secrètement

**undergrowth** *n* broussailles *fpl*, sous-bois *m*

**underhand** *adj* sournois, dissimulé; *adv* en-dessous, sournoisement

**underlay** *n* (carpet) assise *f* de feutre; *typ* hausse *f*

**underlie** *vt* être au-dessous de; *fig* être à la base de

**underline** *vt* souligner

**underling** *n pej* subalterne *m*

**underlying** *adj* sous-jacent; *fig* profond

**undermanned** *adj* ayant un personnel insuffisant

**undermentioned** *adj* ci-dessous

**undermine** *vt* miner, saper

**undermost** *adj* le plus bas (*f* la plus basse), inférieur

**underneath** *adj* de dessous, inférieur; *adv* au-dessous, dessous; *prep* au-dessous de, sous

**undernourished** *adj* sous-alimenté

**underpaid** *adj* mal rétribué, mal payé

**underpants** *npl* caleçon *m*, slip *m*

**underpass** *n* passage inférieur

**underpay** *vt* payer mal, rétribuer insuffisamment

**underpin** *vt* étayer; (foundations) reprendre en sous-œuvre

**underprivileged** *adj* déshérité

**underrate** *vt* sous-estimer, faire trop peu de cas de

**underscore** *vt* souligner

**under-sea** *adj* sous-marin, sous la mer

**under-secretary** *n* sous-secrétaire *m*

**undersell** *vt* vendre moins cher que

**undershirt** *n US* tricot *m* de corps

**undersigned** *n* + *adj* soussigné -e

**undersized** *adj* d'une taille au-dessous de la moyenne, de petite taille

**underskirt** *n* jupon *m*

**understaffed** *adj* à court de personnel

**understand** *vt* comprendre; (be judge of) se connaître en; **give s/o to ~** donner à entendre à qn; **make oneself understood** se faire comprendre; *vi* comprendre; (agree) convenir

**understandable** *adj* compréhensible

**understanding** *n* entendement *m*, intelligence *f*, jugement *m*, compréhension *f*; (agreement) accord *m*, entente *f*; **come to an ~ with s/o** s'entendre avec qn; **on the ~ that** à condition que; *adj* compréhensif -ive; (sympathetic) bienveillant

**understate** *vt* minimiser l'importance de

**understatement** *n* affirmation *f* qui ne dit pas assez, litote *f*

**understeer** *vi* car that ~s voiture sous-vireuse

**understood** *adj* compris; (agreed) convenu, entendu; *fig* + *gramm* sous-entendu; **that's ~** cela va sans dire

**understudy** *n* doublure *f*; *vt* doubler

**undertake** *vt* entreprendre; (take responsibility for) assumer; ~ **to do sth** se charger de faire qch

**undertaker** *n* entrepreneur *m* de pompes funèbres; *coll* croque-mort *m*

**undertaking** *n* entreprise *f*; (promise) engagement *m*, promesse *f*

**under-the-counter** *adj coll* louche, illégal

**undertone** *n* fond *m*; **in an ~** à voix basse

**undervalue** *vt* sous-évaluer, sous-estimer

**undervest** *n* tricot *m* de corps

**underwater** *adj* sous-marin

**underwear** *n* sous-vêtements *mpl*; (women) lingerie *f*

**underweight** *adj* trop léger -ère; au-dessous du poids voulu, d'un poids insuffisant

763

**underworld** n bas-fonds mpl de la société; coll pègre f; myth enfers mpl

**underwrite** vt garantir, souscrire à

**underwriter** n assureur m; (finance) membre m d'un syndicat de garantie, souscripteur m

**undeserved** adj immérité

**undeserving** adj (person) peu méritant; (cause) peu méritoire

**undesigned** adj involontaire; (unexpected) imprévu

**undesirable** n + adj indésirable

**undetected** adj inaperçu, qui a échappé à l'attention; non détecté

**undetermined** adj indéterminé; (person) indécis

**undeterred** adj aucunement découragé

**undeveloped** adj non développé, non exploité

**undeviating** adj direct, constant

**undigested** adj mal digéré

**undignified** adj manquant de dignité, peu digne

**undiluted** adj non dilué; concentré; pur

**undiminished** adj non diminué, toujours égal

**undimmed** adj non atténué; brillant, clair

**undisciplined** adj indiscipliné

**undisclosed** adj tenu secret -ète, non divulgué

**undiscovered** adj caché, non découvert

**undiscriminating** adj sans discernement

**undisguised** adj non déguisé; (open) franc (f franche), non dissimulé

**undismayed** adj sans peur, non découragé

**undisputed** adj incontesté

**undistinguished** adj médiocre, banal, quelconque

**undisturbed** adj (person) tranquille; (peaceful) paisible; (not moved) qui n'a pas été dérangé (remué); (peace, etc) ininterrompu

**undivided** adj entier -ière, sans partage, indivisé

**undo** vt défaire; (untie) délier, dénouer; (destroy) détruire; (repair) réparer

**undoing** n (act) action f de défaire; (ruin) ruine f, perte f

**undone** adj défait; (not done) pas fait, négligé, inaccompli; (ruined) ruiné, perdu

**undoubted** adj incontestable

**undramatic** adj peu dramatique; fig calme, ordinaire

**undreamed, undreamt** adj ~ of qu'on ne peut s'imaginer; (unsuspected) insoupçonné

**undress** n négligé m, petite tenue; vt déshabiller, dévêtir; vi se déshabiller

**undrinkable** adj (unpalatable) imbu-vable; (unfit to drink) non potable

**undue** adj excessif -ive, exagéré

**undulate** vt + vi onduler, ondoyer

**undulating** adj onduleux -euse

**undulatory** adj ondulatoire; (surface) onduleux -euse

**unduly** adv sans raison; (excessively) à l'excès, outre mesure

**undutiful** adj désobéissant, qui ne remplit pas ses devoirs

**undying** adj immortel -elle; (lasting) impérissable, durable

**unearned** adj non gagné; (reward) immérité; ~ **income** rentes fpl

**unearth** vt déterrer; (discover) dénicher

**unearthly** adj surnaturel -elle, sinistre; coll (hour) indu; coll (terrific) de tous les diables

**uneasiness** n malaise m, gêne f; (worry) inquiétude f

**uneasy** adj mal à l'aise; (worried) inquiet -iète; (situation) gênant; ~ **feeling that** impression déconcertante que

**uneatable** adj immangeable

**uneconomic(al)** adj peu (non) économique; (work) peu (non) rentable

**unedifying** adj peu édifiant

**unedited** adj non édité; (not published) inédit; cin non monté

**uneducated** adj sans instruction; (speech, etc) vulgaire

**unemotional** adj peu émotif -ive

**unemployable** adj inemployable

**unemployed** n the ~ les chômeurs mpl; adj sans travail, sans emploi; (idle) désœuvré; (not used) inemployé

**unemployment** n chômage m, manque m de travail; ~ **benefit** allocation f de chômage

**unending** adj interminable, sans fin

**unendurable** adj insupportable

**un-English** adj contraire à l'esprit anglais (aux coutumes anglaises), peu anglais

**unenlightened** adj ignorant, peu éclairé

**unenterprising** adj peu entreprenant

**unenthusiastic** adj peu enthousiaste

**unenviable** adj peu enviable

**unequal** adj inégal; (irregular) irrégulier -ière; be ~ to doing sth ne pas avoir la force de faire qch; be ~ to the task ne pas être à la hauteur de la tâche

**unequalled** adj sans égal, inégalé

**unequivocal** adj clair, sans équivoque

**unerring** adj sûr, infaillible

**unessential** adj non essentiel -ielle

**unethical** adj immoral, malhonnête

**uneven** adj inégal; (rough) raboteux -euse; (ground) accidenté; (number) impair

**uneventful** adj sans incidents, calme

**unexampled** adj sans exemple; unique

**unexceptionable** *adj* irréprochable
**unexceptional** *adj* ordinaire
**unexciting** *adj* (life) peu passionnant; (boring) monotone, ennuyeux -euse
**unexpected** *adj* inattendu, imprévu
**unexpired** *adj* non expiré; (ticket, etc) encore valable
**unexplained** *adj* inexpliqué
**unexploded** *adj* non éclaté
**unexpressed** *adj* non exprimé, inexprimé
**unexpurgated** *adj* (text) intégral, non expurgé
**unfailing** *adj* (reliable) sûr, infaillible; (source) intarissable
**unfair** *adj* injuste; inéquitable
**unfairness** *n* injustice *f*
**unfaithful** *adj* infidèle
**unfaithfulness** *n* infidélité *f*
**unfaltering** *adj* ferme, assuré
**unfamiliar** *adj* peu familier -ière, inconnu; (little known) mal connu; (strange) étranger -ère
**unfamiliarity** *n* (ignorance) ignorance *f*; nouveauté *f*
**unfashionable** *adj* pas de mode; (out of fashion) démodé
**unfasten** *vt* détacher; (dress) défaire; (door) ouvrir
**unfathomable** *adj* insondable; (character, mystery, etc) impénétrable
**unfavourable** *adj* défavorable; (not propitious) inopportun
**unfeeling** *adj* insensible, impitoyable
**unfeigned** *adj* sincère
**unfettered** *adj* libre, sans liens
**unfinished** *adj* inachevé, incomplet -ète
**unfit** *adj* impropre, inapte; (health) en mauvaise santé; ~ **for traffic** impraticable
**unfitted** *adj* impropre, inapte
**unfitting** *adj* peu convenable, inconvenant, déplacé
**unfix** *vt* détacher, défaire
**unflagging** *adj* inlassable, infatigable; (sustained) soutenu
**unflappable** *adj* imperturbable
**unflattering** *adj* peu flatteur -euse
**unfledged** *adj* (bird) sans plumes; *fig* jeune, sans expérience
**unflinching** *adj* ferme, stoïque
**unfold** *vt* déplier; (unroll) dérouler; (wings) déployer; (reveal) révéler, exposer; *vi* se dérouler; (wings) se déployer; (flower) épanouir
**unforced** *adj* spontané, naturel -elle
**unforeseen** *adj* imprévu, inattendu
**unforgettable** *adj* inoubliable
**unforgivable** *adj* impardonnable
**unforgiving** *adj* implacable
**unforthcoming** *adj* peu aimable, peu avenant
**unfortified** *adj* sans fortifications

**unfortunate** *n* malheureux -euse; *adj* malheureux -euse, infortuné; regrettable
**unfounded** *adj* sans fondement, non fondé
**unfreeze** *vt* dégeler
**unfrequented** *adj* peu fréquenté; (place) isolé
**unfriendliness** *n* hostilité *f*, froideur *f*
**unfriendly** *adj* peu amical, hostile
**unfrock** *vt eccles* défroquer
**unfruitful** *adj* stérile; *fig* infructueux -euse
**unfulfilled** *adj* non accompli; non satisfait; (prophecy) irréalisé
**unfurl** *vt* (flag) déployer; (sail) déferler
**unfurnished** *adj* non meublé; (unprovided) dépourvu
**ungainly** *adj* gauche; (gait) dégingandé
**ungallant** *adj* peu galant
**ungenerous** *adj* peu généreux -euse
**ungentlemanly** *adj* mal élevé, impoli
**un-get-at-able** *adj coll* inaccessible
**ungifted** *adj* peu doué
**ungodliness** *n* impiété *f*
**ungodly** *adj* impie; *coll* terrible, affreux -euse
**ungovernable** *adj* ingouvernable; (rage, etc) effréné; (desire) irrépressible
**ungracious** *adj* peu aimable
**ungrammatical** *adj* incorrect, non grammatical
**ungrateful** *adj* ingrat, peu reconnaissant
**ungrounded** *adj* sans fondement
**ungrudging** *adj* libéral, généreux -euse; (given willingly) donné de bon cœur
**unguarded** *adj* (undefended) sans défense; irréfléchi, indiscret -ète; **in an** ~ **moment** dans un instant d'inattention (d'oubli)
**unguent** *n* onguent *m*
**unhallowed** *adj* non béni; (evil) impie
**unhampered** *adj* libre, non gêné
**unhand** *vt poet* lâcher
**unhandy** *adj* maladroit; (tool) peu maniable
**unhappily** *adv* malheureusement
**unhappiness** *n* malheur *m*, infélicité *f*; (expression) inopportunité *f*
**unhappy** *adj* malheureux -euse, infortuné, triste; (infelicitous) peu heureux -euse, regrettable
**unharmed** *adj* indemne, sain et sauf (*f* saine et sauve)
**unharness** *vt* dételer
**unhealthy** *adj* (person) maladif -ive; (place) insalubre, malsain
**unheard-of** *adj* inouï, extraordinaire
**unheeded** *adj* dédaigné, inaperçu
**unheeding** *adj* insouciant, inattentif -ive
**unhelpful** *adj* (person) peu secourable,

peu coopératif -ive; (no use) peu utile

**unhesitating** *adj* (person) ferme, résolu; (answer, etc) prompt

**unhindered** *adj* sans obstacle, sans empêchement

**unhinge** *vt* (door) enlever de ses gonds; (derange) détraquer

**unhitch** *vt* dételer, détacher

**unholy** *adj* profane; *coll* terrible, affreux -euse

**unhook** *vt* (take down) décrocher; (undo) dégrafer

**unhoped** *adj* ~ **for** inespéré

**unhorse** *vt* désarçonner

**unhurried** *adj* lent

**unhurt** *adj* (person) indemne; (unbroken) intact

**unhygienic** *adj* peu hygiénique

**unicellular** *adj* unicellulaire

**unicorn** *n* licorne *f*

**unidentified** *adj* non identifié; ~ **flying object (UFO)** objet volant non identifié (OVNI)

**unification** *n* unification *f*

**uniform** *n* uniforme *m*; *adj* uniforme, constant

**uniformed** *adj* en uniforme

**uniformity** *n* uniformité *f*

**uniformly** *adv* uniformément

**unify** *vt* unifier

**unilateral** *adj* unilatéral

**unimaginable** *adj* inimaginable, inconcevable

**unimaginative** *adj* dénué d'imagination

**unimpaired** *adj* non affaibli, intact, non diminué

**unimpassioned** *adj* sans passion

**unimpeachable** *adj* irréprochable; (testimony) irrécusable

**unimpeded** *adj* sans empêchement, libre

**unimportant** *adj* sans importance, peu important, insignifiant

**unimposing** *adj* peu imposant

**unimpressed** *adj* peu impressionné, peu convaincu

**unimpressive** *adj* peu frappant, peu impressionnant

**unimproved** *adj* non amélioré

**uninformed** *adj* ignorant, mal renseigné

**uninhabitable** *adj* inhabitable

**uninhabited** *adj* inhabité

**uninhibited** *adj* (person) sans inhibitions; (desire) non refréné

**uninitiated** *npl* profanes; *adj* non initié

**uninjured** *adj* indemne

**uninspired** *adj* sans inspiration; (style) banal (*pl* banals)

**uninsured** *adj* non assuré

**unintelligent** *adj* inintelligent

**unintelligible** *adj* inintelligible

**unintended** *adj* involontaire, inconscient

**unintentional** *adj* involontaire, inconscient

**uninterested** *adj* indifférent, non intéressé

**uninteresting** *adj* sans intérêt, inintéressant, ennuyeux -euse

**uninterrupted** *adj* ininterrompu, continu

**uninvited** *adj* qui n'a pas été invité; ~ **guest** hôte inattendu; **come** ~ venir sans être invité

**uninviting** *adj* peu attrayant; (food) peu appétissant

**union** *n* union *f*; harmonie *f*; mariage *m*; *med* raccord *m*; concorde *f*; (industry) syndicat (ouvrier); **Union Jack** pavillon *m* britannique; *US* **the Union** les États-Unis *mpl*

**unionism** *n* (industry) syndicalisme *m*

**unique** *adj* unique

**unisex** *adj* unisexe

**unison** *n* unisson *m*; **in** ~ à l'unisson

**unit** *n* unité *f*; (furniture) élément *m*; groupe *m*; ~ **trust** société *f* de gestion de portefeuille; **kitchen** ~ bloc *m* cuisine

**Unitarian** *n* + *adj* unitarien -ienne

**unitary** *adj* unitaire

**unite** *vt* unir; (unify) unifier; (in agreement) mettre d'accord; *vi* s'unir, se joindre; (companies) fusionner; *pol* ~ **against** faire bloc contre

**united** *adj* uni, réuni; **the United Kingdom** le Royaume-Uni; **the United Nations** les Nations Unies; **the United States** les États-Unis *mpl*

**unity** *n* unité *f*; concorde *f*, harmonie *f*

**universal** *n* proposition universelle; *adj* universel -elle

**universality** *n* universalité *f*

**universalize** *vt* universaliser

**universally** *adv* universellement

**universe** *n* univers *m*

**university** *n* université *f*; *adj* universitaire

**unjust** *adj* injuste

**unjustifiable** *adj* inexcusable, injustifiable

**unjustified** *adj* injustifié; non motivé

**unkempt** *adj* (hair) mal peigné; (appearance) mal soigné, débraillé

**unkind** *adj* peu aimable, pas gentil -ille; méchant, cruel -elle; **that's** ~ **of you** c'est peu aimable de votre part

**unkindly** *adv* d'une manière peu aimable; méchamment; **take sth** ~ prendre qch en mauvaise part

**unkindness** *n* manque *m* de bienveillance; méchanceté *f*

**unknowable** *adj* inconnaissable

**unknowing** *adj* inconscient

**unknowingly** *adv* sans le savoir, inconsciemment

**unknown** *n* inconnu *m*; *adj* inconnu; ~ **to me (him)** à mon (son) insu

**unlace** *vt* délacer

**unladen** *adj* sans charge, non chargé

**unladylike** *adj* peu distingué

**unlaid** *adj* (table) non mis; non posé; (ghost) non exorcisé; *sl* vierge

**unlatch** *vt* ouvrir

**unlawful** *adj* illégal; (means) illicite

**unlearn** *vt* oublier (ce qu'on a appris), désapprendre

**unlearned** *adj* ignorant; (inexpert) peu versé

**unleash** *vt* lâcher; *fig* déchaîner

**unleavened** *adj* sans levain, azyme

**unless** *conj* à moins que; ~ **he leaves straightaway** à moins qu'il ne parte tout de suite; ~ **I am mistaken** si je ne me trompe; ~ **I hear to the contrary** à moins (sauf) avis contraire

**unlettered** *adj* illettré

**unlicensed** *adj* non autorisé, illicite

**unlike** *adj* différent, dissemblable; *prep* à l'encontre de

**unlikelihood, unlikeliness** *n* improbabilité *f*; invraisemblance *f*

**unlikely** *adj* peu probable, improbable; (implausible) invraisemblable

**unlimited** *adj* illimité, sans bornes

**unload** *vt* décharger; *coll* (get rid of) se défaire de; (shares) vendre; *vi* *mot* décharger (la voiture)

**unlock** *vt* ouvrir; (wheel) débloquer

**unlooked-for** *adj* inattendu, inespéré

**unloose(n)** *vt* délier, détacher, desserrer

**unlovable** *adj* peu attachant

**unlovely** *adj* disgracieux -ieuse, laid, déplaisant

**unloving** *adj* peu affectueux -euse, froid

**unluckily** *adv* malheureusement

**unlucky** *adj* infortuné, malheureux -euse, malencontreux -euse; (star) maléfique; (day) néfaste; **be** ~ **ne pas avoir de chance; be** ~ **to** porter malchance de

**unmade** *adj* pas encore fait (créé); (road) non goudronné

**unmake** *vt* (destroy) détruire; (take to pieces) défaire; ruiner

**unman** *vt* *fig* émasculer, décourager; (castrate) émasculer

**unmanageable** *adj* ingouvernable; (unwieldy) difficile à manier

**unmanly** *adj* peu viril, efféminé; (cowardly) lâche

**unmanned** *adj* découragé, démoralisé; (crewless) sans équipage

**unmannerly** *adj* grossier -ière, malappris, impoli

**unmarked** *adj* ne portant aucune marque; (unstained) sans tache; (schoolwork) non corrigé

**unmarketable** *adj* invendable

**unmarriageable** *adj* immariable, impossible à marier

**unmarried** *adj* célibataire, non marié; ~ **mother** fille-mère *f* (*pl* filles-mères)

**unmask** *vt* démasquer; *vi* se démasquer

**unmatched** *adj* (peerless) sans égal, incomparable

**unmeant** *adj* involontaire

**unmeasured** *adj* non mesuré; (boundless) infini; excessif -ive

**unmentionable** *adj* innommable, horrible

**unmerciful** *adj* sans pitié, impitoyable

**unmerited** *adj* immérité

**unmethodical** *adj* peu méthodique, sans méthode

**unminded** *adj* (neglected) non surveillé; n'ayant pas l'intention

**unmindful** *adj* oublieux -ieuse

**unmistakable** *adj* clair, évident; (likeness) facilement reconnaissable

**unmistakably** *adv* clairement; à ne pas s'y méprendre (tromper)

**unmitigated** *adj* non mitigé; dans toute la force du terme; *coll* parfait, pur; ~ **liar** fieffé menteur (*f* fieffée menteuse)

**unmixed** *adj* sans mélange

**unmolested** *adj* sans être inquiété, tranquille, en paix

**unmounted** *adj* non monté; (picture) non encadré; (jewel) non serti

**unmourned** *adj* non pleuré, non regretté

**unmoved** *adj* impassible, insensible

**unmusical** *adj* (sound) pas mélodieux -ieuse, inharmonieux -ieuse; (person) peu musicien -ienne

**unmuzzle** *vt* démuseler

**unnamable** *adj* innommable

**unnamed** *adj* sans nom; anonyme

**unnatural** *adj* anormal; monstrueux -euse, contre nature; (person) dénaturé

**unnavigable** *adj* (place) non navigable; (ship) que l'on ne peut gouverner (diriger)

**unnecessarily** *adv* inutilement

**unnecessary** *adj* non nécessaire, superflu

**unneighbourly** *adj* peu obligeant, indigne d'un bon voisin

**unnerve** *vt* déconcerter, faire perdre son courage à

**unnoticed** *adj* inaperçu, inobservé

**unnumbered** *adj* (countless) innombrable, sans nombre; non numéroté

**unobjectionable** *adj* irréprochable

**unobservant** *adj* peu observateur -trice

**unobserved** *adj* inaperçu

**unobstructed** *adj* non encombré, libre

**unobtainable** *adj* impossible à obtenir

**unobtrusive** *adj* discret -ète, effacé, modeste

**unoccupied** *adj* inoccupé; (seat) libre; (idle) sans occupation; (house) inhabité

**unoffending** *adj* innocent, inoffensif -ive

**unofficial** *adj* non officiel -ielle; (information) officieux -ieuse; ~ **strike** grève décidée sans l'appui du syndicat, grève *f* sauvage

**unopened** *adj* non ouvert; (letter) non décacheté; (bottle) non débouché

**unopposed** *adj* sans opposition

**unorganized** *adj* sans organisation, mal organisé

**unoriginal** *adj* (work, etc) banal (*pl* banals); (person) dépourvu d'originalité

**unorthodox** *adj* peu orthodoxe; *eccles* hétérodoxe

**unostentatious** *adj* (person) simple; (action) fait sans ostentation

**unpack** *vt* déballer; (luggage) défaire

**unpaid** *adj* non payé; (post) non rétribué; (person) qui ne reçoit pas de salaire; (bill) non acquitté

**unpalatable** *adj* peu agréable au goût; *fig* désagréable

**unparalleled** *adj* incomparable, sans pareil -eille •

**unpardonable** *adj* impardonnable

**unparliamentary** *adj* indigne d'un membre du parlement; (language) grossier -ière

**unpatriotic** *adj* (person) peu patriote; (action) peu patriotique

**unpaved** *adj* non pavé

**unpeg** *vt* dépendre; (prices) permettre l'augmentation de

**unperceived** *adj* inaperçu

**unperformed** *adj* inaccompli, inachevé; *theat* non joué

**unperturbed** *adj* impassible, calme

**unpick** *vt* (sewing) défaire

**unpicked** *adj* (sewing) défait; (flowers, etc) non cueilli; (not chosen) non choisi

**unpin** *vt* enlever les épingles de

**unplaced** *adj* (person) sans emploi; (candidate) non classé; (horse) non placé

**unplanned** *adj* qui n'a pas été organisé à l'avance; accidentel -elle, imprévu

**unplayable** *adj* injouable; *mus* inexécutable

**unpleasant** *adj* désagréable, déplaisant, fâcheux -euse

**unpleasantness** *n* désagrément *m*; (person) caractère déplaisant; (quarrel) brouille *f*

**unpleasing** *adj* peu agréable; (person) qui manque de grâce, déplaisant

**unplug** *vt elect* débrancher

**unpolished** *adj* non poli; (shoes) non ciré; (person) grossier -ière; (glass) dépoli

**unpolluted** *adj* non pollué, pur

**unpopular** *adj* impopulaire

**unpopularity** *n* impopularité *f*

**unpractical** *adj* peu pratique; (task) impraticable

**unprecedented** *adj* sans précédent, inouï

**unpredictable** *adj* imprévisible

**unprejudiced** *adj* sans préjugés, impartial

**unpremeditated** *adj* non prémédité

**unprepared** *adj* non préparé, improvisé; sans préparatifs; (food) inapprêté; **catch s/o** ~ prendre qn au dépourvu

**unprepossessing** *adj* peu engageant, rébarbatif -ive

**unpresentable** *adj* peu présentable

**unpretentious, unpretending** *adj* modeste, sans prétentions

**unpriced** *adj* dont le prix n'est pas marqué

**unprincipled** *adj* sans principes, sans scrupules

**unprintable** *adj* que l'on n'ose pas imprimer; licencieux -ieuse

**unprivileged** *adj* sans privilèges

**unprized** *adj* peu estimé

**unprocurable** *adj* introuvable, impossible à obtenir

**unproductive** *adj* improductif -ive

**unprofessional** *adj* contraire aux usages de la profession (du métier), contraire au code professionnel

**unprofitable** *adj* peu lucratif -ive, peu rentable; (vain) inutile

**unpromising** *adj* peu prometteur -euse

**unprompted** *adj* spontané

**unpronounceable** *adj* imprononçable

**unprotected** *adj* sans protection, sans défense

**unprovable** *adj* impossible à prouver

**unproved** *adj* non prouvé; (not tested) inéprouvé

**unprovided** *adj* dépourvu, dénué; ~ **for** sans ressources

**unprovoked** *adj* non provoqué, gratuit

**unpublished** *adj* inédit

**unpunctual** *adj* inexact; (late) en retard; **always** ~ jamais à l'heure

**unpunctuality** *n* inexactitude *f*, manque *m* de ponctualité

**unpunished** *adj* impuni

**unqualified** *adj* incompétent; n'ayant pas de diplôme(s); (not restricted) sans réserve, sans restriction; *coll* total, absolu

**unquenchable** *adj* (fire) inextinguible; insatiable

**unquenched** *adj* (fire) non éteint; (thirst) non étanché; (desire) inassouvi

unquestionable *adj* indiscutable, indubitable

unquestioned *adj* indisputé, incontesté

unquestioning *adj* inconditionnel -elle, aveugle

unquestioningly *adv* aveuglément

unquiet *adj* agité, inquiet -iète

unquotable *adj* que l'on ne peut citer (répéter)

unquote *vi* fermer les guillemets; **quote** ... ~ début *m* de citation ... fin *f* de citation

unquoted *adj* non cité; (share) non coté

unravel *vt* (thread) effiler, débrouiller; *fig* éclairer; *vi* (thread) s'effiler; *fig* se débrouiller

unreachable *adj* impossible à atteindre

unread *adj* non lu

unreadable *adj* illisible

unreadiness *n* manque *m* de préparation; manque *m* de promptitude

unready *adj* pas prêt; pas préparé; irrésolu

unreal *adj* irréel -elle, sans réalité

unrealistic *adj* peu réaliste

unreality *n* irréalité *f*

unrealizable *adj* irréalisable

unrealized *adj* non réalisé

unreasonable *adj* déraisonnable, peu raisonnable; (exaggerated) exagéré, exorbitant

unrecognizable *adj* méconnaissable

unrecognized *adj* méconnu; (government, etc) non reconnu

unreconciled *adj* irréconcilié

unrecorded *adj* dont on ne trouve aucune mention; (not on tape) non enregistré

unredeemed *adj* non racheté; (promise) non tenu; (pledge) non dégagé

unreel *vt* débobiner, dérouler

unrefined *adj* non raffiné, brut; (person) grossier -ière

unreflecting *adj* (light) non réfléchissant; (thoughtless) étourdi

unreformed *adj* non réformé

unregarded *adj* (not noticed) inaperçu; (of no value) non estimé

unregistered *adj* non enregistré, non inscrit; (letter) non recommandé; (birth) non déclaré; (car) non immatriculé

unrehearsed *adj* impromptu, non préparé; (play) non répété

unrelated *adj* sans rapport; (kinship) sans lien de parenté

unrelenting *adj* implacable, inexorable

unreliability *n* inexactitude *f*; (character) instabilité *f*

unreliable *adj* peu sûr, sur lequel (*f* laquelle) on ne peut pas compter; (information) sujet -ette à caution

unrelieved *adj* sans secours; (pain) constant, non soulagé; (landscape) monotone; (continuous) continu, incessant

unremarkable *adj* peu remarquable, indigne d'attention, médiocre

unremitting *adj* incessant, inlassable

unremittingly *adv* inlassablement, sans cesse, sans relâche

unremunerative *adj* peu rémunérateur -trice, peu lucratif -ive

unrepentant *adj* impénitent

unrepresentative *adj* peu représentatif -ive, peu typique

unrequited *adj* non récompensé; (love) non partagé

unreserved *adj* sans réserve, franc (*f* franche); (seat, etc) non réservé

unresolved *adj* non résolu

unresponsive *adj* insensible, peu sensible, froid

unrest *n* inquiétude *f*, trouble *m*, agitation *f*

unrestrained *adj* libre, sans restriction; immodéré, outrancier -ière

unrestricted *adj* sans restriction, illimité

unrewarded *adj* non récompensé, sans récompense

unrighteous *adj* impie; (unjust) injuste, méchant

unripe *adj* pas mûr, vert; (corn) en herbe

unrivalled *adj* sans rival, incomparable

unroll *vt* dérouler; *vi* se dérouler

unromantic *adj* peu romantique; prosaïque, terre à terre *invar*

unruffled *adj* (person) placide, serein; (sea) calme; (hair) lisse

unruly *adj* indiscipliné, turbulent

unsaddle *vt* (person) désarçonner; (horse) desseller

unsafe *adj* dangereux -euse, peu sûr; hasardeux -euse; en danger

unsaid *adj* **leave sth** ~ passer qch sous silence

unsal(e)able *adj* invendable

unsanctified *adj* non béni

unsanitary *adj* peu hygiénique; (unhealthy) insalubre

unsatisfactory *adj* peu satisfaisant, qui laisse à désirer

unsatisfied *adj* insatisfait; (appetite) inassouvi

unsatisfying *adj* peu satisfaisant; insuffisant

unsavoury *adj* désagréable, mauvais; répugnant; (reputation) équivoque

unsay *vt* rétracter, se dédire de

unscathed *adj* (person) indemne, sain et sauf (*f* saine et sauve)

unscholarly *adj* indigne d'un savant; (person) peu savant

unschooled *adj* peu instruit

unscientific *adj* peu scientifique

## unscramble

**unscramble** vt (signals) décoder; *coll* (plan) annuler

**unscratched** *adj* sans égratignure; *fig* complètement indemne

**unscreened** *adj* (place) exposé; (without screen) sans écran; *cin* qui n'a pas été tourné en film; (not investigated) non examiné

**unscrew** vt dévisser

**unscripted** *adj* sans script, improvisé

**unscrupulous** *adj* sans scrupules, peu scrupuleux -euse

**unscrupulousness** n manque *m* de scrupules

**unseal** vt décacheter

**unsealed** *adj* non cacheté; (not stuck down) ouvert

**unseasonable** *adj* hors de saison; *fig* déplacé, inopportun

**unseat** vt (horseman) désarçonner; faire perdre son siège (sa situation) à

**unseaworthy** *adj* hors d'état de prendre la mer

**unsecured** *adj* (door) mal fermé; (loan) non garanti

**unseeing** *adj* aveugle

**unseemliness** n inconvenance *f*, indécence *f*

**unseemly** *adj* inconvenant, peu convenable, indécent

**unseen** n version *f*; *adj* inaperçu; ~ **translation** *f*

**unselfconscious** *adj* naturel -elle

**unselfish** *adj* sans égoïsme; généreux -euse; (action) désintéressé

**unselfishness** n désintéressement *m*; générosité *f*

**unserviceable** *adj* inutilisable, hors d'état de servir

**unsettle** vt troubler le repos de, perturber; (disturb) déranger

**unsettled** *adj* (person) troublé, inquiet -iète; (weather) variable, incertain; (unpaid) non réglé; (question) indécis

**unsettling** *adj* troublant, inquiétant

**unshackled** *adj* libre, sans entraves

**unshaded** *adj* non ombragé; (lamp) sans abat-jour; (drawing) non hachuré

**unshak(e)able** *adj* inébranlable

**unshaken** *adj* inébranlable

**unshapely** *adj* difforme, mal fait

**unshaven** *adj* non rasé; (bearded) barbu

**unsheathe** vt dégainer

**unsheltered** *adj* non abrité, exposé

**unship** vt décharger

**unshod** *adj* (person) sans chaussures, nu-pieds *invar*; (horse) déferré

**unshrinkable** *adj* irrétrécissable

**unshriven** *adj* die ~ mourir sans confession ni absolution

**unsighted** *adj* inaperçu; (gun) sans hausse

**unsightly** *adj* laid, vilain

**unsigned** *adj* sans signature

**unsinkable** *adj* insubmersible

**unskilful** *adj* inhabile, maladroit

**unskilled** *adj* inexpérimenté, inexpert; ~ **labour** main-d'œuvre (*pl* mains-d'œuvre) non spécialisée; ~ **labourer** (**workman**) manœuvre *m*

**unskimmed** *adj* (milk) non écrémé

**unsleeping** *adj* vigilant

**unsociable** *adj* insociable, farouche

**unsocial** *adj* contre les usages de la société; insociable; ~ **hours** heures anormales

**unsold** *adj* invendu

**unsoldierly** *adj* peu martial

**unsolicited** *adj* non sollicité; spontané

**unsolvable** *adj* insoluble

**unsolved** *adj* non résolu

**unsophisticated** *adj* (manner) naturel -elle; (person) naïf (*f* naïve)

**unsound** *adj* (health) précaire; (mind) dérangé; (opinion) erroné, mal fondé; (weakened) affaibli, peu solide; (business) périclitant

**unsparing** *adj* prodigue; (merciless) impitoyable; be ~ **of sth** ne pas ménager qch

**unspeakable** *adj* inexprimable, indicible; *pej* infect, détestable

**unspecialized** *adj* non spécialisé

**unspecified** *adj* non spécifié

**unspoilt** *adj* (child) non gâté; (unaffected) inaltéré; (object, country-side, etc) qui n'est pas abîmé

**unspoken** *adj* tacite; (understood) sous-entendu

**unsportsmanlike**, **unsporting** *adj* déloyal, indigne d'un sportsman

**unspotted** *adj* sans tache, immaculé; (not seen) inaperçu

**unstable** *adj* instable; (character) inconstant

**unstamped** *adj* (letter) sans timbre, non affranchi

**unstatesmanlike** *adj* indigne d'un homme d'état

**unsteadiness** n instabilité *f*; indécision *f*, irrésolution *f*

**unsteady** *adj* peu solide, peu stable; (character) irrésolu, inconstant; (step) chancelant

**unstick** vt décoller

**unstinted** *adj* abondant, sans limite, sans réserve

**unstinting** *adj* prodigue, libéral

**unstop** vt (bottle) déboucher; (unblock) dégorger

**unstoppable** *adj* qu'on ne peut pas arrêter

**unstoppered** *adj* sans bouchon

**unstrap** *vt* ôter la courroie (les courroies) de

**unstressed** *adj* atone, sans accent

**unstuck** *adj* décollé; **come ~** se décoller; *coll* échouer

**unstudied** *adj* spontané, naturel -elle; **~ in** ignorant de

**unsubdued** *adj* indompté, non maîtrisé

**unsubmissive** *adj* insoumis

**unsubsidized** *adj* non subventionné

**unsubstantial** *adj* insubstantiel -ielle; (not firm) peu solide; (meal) léger -ère

**unsubstantiated** *adj* non prouvé; (rumour) non confirmé

**unsuccessful** *adj* non réussi, raté, infructueux -euse; (person) qui a échoué; (applicant) refusé; *pol* non élu; **be ~** échouer

**unsuccessfully** *adv* sans succès

**unsuitability** *n* impropreté *f*; inaptitude *f*; inopportunité *f*

**unsuitable** *adj* (thing) impropre; (person) inapte; (remark) déplacé, inopportun; (unbecoming) peu convenable

**unsuited** *adj* **~ for** (thing) impropre à; (person) peu fait pour; **they are ~ to each other** ils sont mal assortis

**unsullied** *adj* sans tache, sans souillure

**unsung** *adj fig* méconnu

**unsupported** *adj* (statement) non confirmé; (person, effort) sans soutien, non soutenu; (structure) sans support, non étayé

**unsure** *adj* incertain, peu sûr; **be ~ of oneself** manquer de confiance en soi-même

**unsurpassed** *adj* non surpassé

**unsuspected** *adj* insoupçonné

**unsuspecting** *adj* sans soupçons, sans méfiance

**unsuspicious** *adj* (feeling no suspicion) sans soupçons, peu méfiant; (arousing no suspicion) qui n'évoque aucun soupçon

**unsweetened** *adj* non sucré, sans sucre

**unswerving** *adj* inébranlable, constant

**unsymmetrical** *adj* asymétrique

**unsympathetic** *adj* indifférent, peu compatissant; (unlikeable) antipathique

**unsystematic** *adj* sans méthode, non systématique

**untack** *vt* (seam) défaire

**untainted** *adj* non corrompu; (food) frais (*f* fraîche)

**untamed** *adj* non apprivoisé, farouche; sauvage; (unsubdued) indompté

**untangle** *vt* (string, hair, etc) démêler; *fig* éclaircir, débrouiller

**untapped** *adj fig* inutilisé, inexploité

**untarnished** *adj* non terni; (reputation) sans tache

**untasted** *adj* auquel (*f* à laquelle) on n'a pas goûté

**untaught** *adj* ignorant, sans instruction; **do sth ~** faire qch sans avoir appris, faire qch naturellement

**untaxed** *adj* non imposé; (car) sans vignette; *fig* non surchargé

**unteachable** *adj* (thing) impossible à enseigner; (person) à qui l'on ne peut rien apprendre

**untempered** *adj* (steel) non revenu; non tempéré, non atténué

**untenable** *adj* (theory) insoutenable; (position) intenable

**untenanted** *adj* inoccupé, sans locataire

**untested** *adj* non éprouvé; (result) non vérifié

**untether** *vt* détacher

**unthankful** *adj* ingrat

**unthinkable** *adj* inimaginable, impensable, inconcevable

**unthinking** *adj* irréfléchi, étourdi

**unthought-of** *adj* inattendu

**untidily** *adv* sans ordre, sans soin

**untidiness** *n* désordre *m*; (dress) débraillé *m*

**untidy** *adj* (person) désordonné; (room) en désordre; (hair) mal peigné; (dress) débraillé

**untie** *vt* dénouer, défaire; (person) délier

**until** *prep* jusqu'à; **not do sth ~ after** ne faire qch qu'après; **not ~** pas avant; *conj* jusqu'à ce que; **~ he succeeds** jusqu'à ce qu'il réussisse; **not ~ he succeeds** pas avant qu'il (ne) réussisse

**untimely** *adj* (early) prématuré; (inopportune) inopportun

**untiring** *adj* infatigable; (activity) assidu

**unto** *prep lit see* **to**

**untold** *adj* passé sous silence; (unlimited) incalculable, immense, inouï, inimaginable

**untouchable** *adj* intouchable

**untouched** *adj* non touché; (unharmed) indemne

**untoward** *adj* malencontreux -euse, fâcheux -euse; *ar* (person) indocile

**untraceable** *adj* introuvable

**untrained** *adj* inexercé, inexpérimenté

**untrammelled** *adj* sans entraves, sans contrainte

**untransferable** *adj* non transmissible; *leg* incessible, inaliénable

**untranslatable** *adj* intraduisible

**untravelled** *adj* (person) qui n'a jamais voyagé; (country) inexploré

**untried** *adj* pas encore mis à l'épreuve; *leg* qui n'a pas encore été jugé

**untrodden** *adj* isolé, inexploré; (snow, forest) vierge

**untroubled** *adj* calme, paisible

**untrue** *adj* faux (*f* fausse), erroné; (person) déloyal

**untrustworthy** *adj* indigne de confiance; (memory) peu sûr; (information) douteux -euse

**untruth** *n* mensonge *m*

**untruthful** *adj* menteur -euse; (false) faux (*f* fausse); (statement) mensonger -ère

**untutored** *adj* ignorant, sans instruction, peu instruit

**untwist** *vt* détordre, démêler, défaire

**¹unused** *adj* inutilisé; (word) inusité; (new) neuf (*f* neuve)

**²unused** *adj* (unaccustomed) peu habitué, inaccoutumé

**unusual** *adj* extraordinaire, exceptionnel -elle, insolite, inhabituel -elle; (word) peu usité

**unusually** *adv* exceptionnellement

**unutterable** *adj* indicible

**unvalued** *adj* peu estimé; (not costed) non évalué

**unvaried** *adj* constant, uniforme; monotone

**unvarnished** *adj* non verni; *fig* simple, sans fard

**unvarying** *adj* invariable

**unveil** *vt* dévoiler

**unverifiable** *adj* invérifiable

**unverified** *adj* non vérifié

**unversed** *adj* peu versé, ignorant

**unvoiced** *adj* non exprimé; (consonant) sourd

**unwanted** *adj* non désiré; (surplus) superflu

**unwarily** *adv* imprudemment

**unwariness** *n* imprudence *f*

**unwarlike** *adj* peu guerrier -ière, paisible

**unwarrantable** *adj* inexcusable

**unwarranted** *adj* injustifié; (not guaranteed) sans garantie

**unwary** *adj* imprudent, sans méfiance

**unwashed** *adj* malpropre, non lavé; **the great ~** le peuple, les prolétaires *mpl*

**unwavering** *adj* constant, ferme, inébranlable

**unweaned** *adj* non sevré

**unwearable** *adj* que l'on ne peut pas porter

**unwearied** *adj* non fatigué; infatigable

**unwearying** *adj* inlassable

**unwelcome** *adj* (person) mal venu, importun; (thing) désagréable, fâcheux -euse

**unwell** *adj* souffrant, peu bien

**unwholesome** *adj* malsain; (climate) insalubre

**unwieldy** *adj* (object) peu maniable; (person) gauche, lourd

**unwilling** *adj* peu serviable, pas d'accord; **be ~ to do sth** être peu disposé à faire qch, refuser de faire qch

**unwillingness** *n* mauvaise volonté, répugnance *f*

**unwind** *vt* dérouler; *vi* se dérouler; *sl* se détendre

**unwisdom** *n* imprudence *f*, stupidité *f*

**unwise** *adj* imprudent, malavisé

**unwitting** *adj* inconscient; (unintentional) involontaire

**unwittingly** *adv* sans le savoir, inconsciemment

**unwomanly** *adj* peu féminin

**unwonted** *adj* inaccoutumé, insolite

**unworkable** *adj* impraticable; (land, mine) inexploitable

**unworldly** *adj* détaché de ce monde, qui n'est pas de ce monde

**unworn** *adj* non usé; qui n'a pas été porté

**unworthiness** *n* peu *m* de mérite

**unworthy** *adj* indigne; (worthless) sans valeur, méprisable

**unwounded** *adj* sans blessure, non blessé, indemne

**unwrap** *vt* défaire

**unwritten** *adj* non écrit; **it's an ~ law that** il est accepté que

**unyielding** *adj* qui ne cède pas, ferme; (person) opiniâtre

**unzip** *vt* ouvrir en tirant la fermeture éclair

**up** *n* **~ s and downs** les hauts *mpl* et les bas *mpl*, les vicissitudes *fpl*; *coll* **be on the ~ and ~** être en train de faire son chemin, aller en progressant; *adj* montant, de montée; **the ~** le train qui va en direction de la ville (de la capitale); *vt coll* augmenter; *adv* en haut, vers le haut; (in the air) en l'air; (standing) debout; (out of bed) levé; (time) écoulé, expiré; (prices) en hausse; (tide) haut; (sun, moon) levé; (umbrella) ouvert; (shutters) fermé; à l'université; **~ above** en haut; **~ there** là-haut; **~ to now** jusqu'ici; **all the way ~** jusqu'en haut; *coll* **be ~ against it** être aux prises avec des difficultés; **be ~ all night** ne pas se coucher de la nuit; **be ~ and doing** se mettre à la besogne; **be ~ to sth** (capable) être capable de faire qch; (scheme) mijoter qch, avoir qch en tête; **be well ~ in sth** connaître qch à fond; **business is looking ~** les affaires reprennent; **further ~** (higher) plus haut; (further away) plus loin; **go ~** monter; (increase) augmenter; (to town) aller en ville; **go ~ to s/o** aborder qn, s'approcher de qn; **I don't feel ~ to it** je ne m'en sens pas la force; *coll* **it's all ~ with us** c'en est fait de nous; **it's ~ to him to do it** c'est à lui de le faire; **road ~** route *f* en réparation, travaux *mpl*; *coll* **there's sth ~** il y a qch; **two floors ~** au deuxième étage; *US* au premier étage; **walk ~ and**

**down** aller (marcher) de long en large, faire les cent pas; *coll* **what's ~?** qu'y a-t-il?; *coll* **what's ~ with you?** qu'est-ce qui vous prend?, qu'est-ce que vous avez?; *prep* en haut de

**up-and-coming** *adj* d'avenir, qui avance bien

**upbraid** *vt* reprocher

**upbringing** *n* éducation *f*; formation *f*

**up-country** *adj* de l'intérieur; *fig* naïf (*f* naïve)

**up-date** *vt* moderniser; (report) mettre à jour

**up-end** *vt* mettre debout

**up-grade** *n* montée *f*, pente ascendante; **be on the ~** monter; (improving) reprendre, s'améliorer; *vt* donner un grade supérieur à; (job) revaloriser

**upheaval** *n* bouleversement *m*, agitation *f*; *geol* soulèvement *m*

**uphill** *adj* montant; *fig* dur, pénible, difficile; *adv* en montant

**uphold** *vt* supporter; (theory) soutenir; (confirm) confirmer; (verdict) maintenir; **~ the law** faire observer la loi

**upholster** *vt* tapisser; (chair) rembourrer, capitonner

**upholsterer** *n* tapissier *m*

**upholstery** *n* tapisserie *f* d'ameublement; (chair) rembourrage *m*

**upkeep** *n* entretien *m*; (cost) frais *mpl* d'entretien

**upland** *adj* des montagnes

**uplands** *npl* région montagneuse, hautes terres *fpl*

**uplift** *n* élévation *f*; *iron* élévation morale; *vt* soulever, hausser; *fig* élever, égayer; (morally) édifier

**upon** *prep see* **on**

**upper** *n* (shoe) empeigne *f*; **be down on one's ~s** être dans la dèche; *adj* supérieur, plus élevé, de dessus, haut; *theat* **~ circle** deuxième balcon *m*; **gain the ~ hand** prendre le dessus; **the ~ part** le dessus; **the ~ Volga** la haute Volga

**upper-class** *adj* appartenant aux classes supérieures, typique des classes supérieures

**upper-cut** *n* (boxing) uppercut *m*

**uppermost** *adj* le plus haut (*f* la plus haute); *fig* premier -ière; *adv* au dessus, en dessus; **be ~** prédominer

**uppish** *adj coll* arrogant, présomptueux -euse

**upright** *n* montant *m*; (piano) piano droit; *adj* vertical, droit, perpendiculaire; *fig* honnête

**uprightness** *n* droiture *f*, intégrité *f*; verticalité *f*

**uprising** *n* soulèvement *m*, révolte *f*

**uproar** *n* vacarme *m*, *coll* chahut *m*

**uproarious** *adj* tumultueux -euse, bruyant

**uproot** *vt* déraciner

**uprush** *n see* **upsurge**

**upset** *n* bouleversement *m*, chambardement *m*, remue-ménage *m invar*; (boat) chavirement *m*; (trouble) ennui *m*; (plans) renversement *m*; *adj* bouleversé, ému; (auction) **~ price** mise *f* à prix; *vt* (knock over) renverser; (disturb) bouleverser; (boat) faire chavirer; (arrangements) désorganiser, déranger; (person) troubler, bouleverser; (stomach) déranger; *vi* se renverser

**upsetting** *adj* inquiétant, bouleversant, fâcheux -euse

**upshot** *n* résultat *m*, issue *f*

**upside-down** *adj* renversé; *adv* sens dessus dessous, la tête en bas, à l'envers; *coll fig* en désordre

**upstage** *vt* éclipser; *adj coll* hautain, snob *invar*; *adv theat* derrière les décors, dans les coulisses

**upstairs** *adj* d'en haut; *adv* en haut (de l'escalier); **go ~** monter (l'escalier)

**upstanding** *adj* debout *invar*; *fig* honnête, probe

**upstart** *n* parvenu -e

**upstream** *adv* en amont

**upsurge, uprush** *n* poussée *f*, accès *m*; recrudescence *f*

**uptake** *n* compréhension *f*; *coll* **be quick on the ~** avoir l'esprit éveillé; **be slow on the ~** avoir la compréhension lente

**uptight** *adj sl* tendu

**up-to-date** *adj* moderne, à la page; *coll* dans le vent; (fashion) à la mode, dernier cri *invar*

**up-to-the-minute** *adj* très récent, tout récent (*f* toute récente)

**upturn** *n* amélioration *f*; *vt* retourner, renverser

**upturned** *adj* (nose) retroussé; (edges) relevé

**upward** *adj* ascendant

**upwards** *adv* en montant, vers le haut; (facing) en dessus; **~ of** plus de; **look ~** regarder en l'air; **they cost from fifty francs ~** les prix vont à partir de cinquante francs

**uranium** *n* uranium *m*

**urban** *adj* urbain

**urbane** *adj* poli, courtois

**urbanity** *n* urbanité *f*, courtoisie *f*

**urbanization** *n* urbanisation *f*

**urbanize** *vt* urbaniser

**urchin** *n* gamin -e

**urethra** *n anat* urètre *m*

**urge** *n* impulsion *f*, poussée *f*; *vt* presser, encourager, exhorter, exciter; (advocate) alléguer, faire valoir; (entreat) prier instamment

**urgency** *n* urgence *f*

**urgent** adj urgent, pressant
**urinal** n urinoir m; (pot) urinal m
**urinary** adj urinaire
**urinate** vi uriner
**urination** n acte m d'uriner
**urine** n urine f
**urn** n urne f; (tea, etc) fontaine f
**Uruguay** n Uruguay m
**Uruguayan** n Uruguayen -enne; adj uruguayen -enne
**us** pron nous, nous autres
**usable** adj utilisable
**usage** n (use) traitement m; (custom) coutume f, usage m
**use** n usage m, emploi m; (utility) utilité f; (action) utilisation f; (need) besoin m; (habit) coutume f, habitude f; (right to use) jouissance f; **directions for** ~ mode m d'emploi; **for the** ~ **of** à l'usage de; coll **have no** ~ **for** s/o être embêté par qn, détester qn; **have no** ~ **for sth** n'avoir aucun besoin de qch; **it was no** ~ **me (my) trying** j'avais beau essayer; **make** ~ **of sth** se servir de qch; **not in** ~ pas en service; **out of** ~ hors d'usage, hors de service; **that's no** ~ **at all** ça ne vaut rien du tout, ça ne sert à rien du tout; **what's the** ~ **of doing this?** à quoi bon faire cela?; vt employer, se servir de, utiliser; (treat) en user avec; (consume) consommer; ~ **up** épuiser, finir; **I** ~ **this as a lever** cela me sert de levier; vi **I** ~**d to go** j'allais
**used** adj usagé; (stamp) oblitéré; ~ **to** habitué à; ~ **up** épuisé, fini; **get** ~ **to sth** s'habituer à qch
**useful** adj utile; pratique; profitable
**usefulness** n utilité f
**useless** adj inutile; (vain) vain; (person) bon (f bonne) à rien
**user** n usager -ère, utilisateur -trice
**usher** n huissier m; (doorkeeper) portier m; theat placeur m; vt ~ **s/o in** faire entrer qn; ~ **s/o out** reconduire qn (jusqu'à la porte)
**usherette** n ouvreuse f
**usual** adj habituel -elle, usuel -elle; (customary) d'usage; adv habituellement, d'habitude; **as** ~ comme d'habitude
**usually** adv d'habitude, d'ordinaire, habituellement
**usurer** n usurier -ière
**usurious** adj usuraire
**usurp** vt usurper
**usurpation** n usurpation f
**usurper** n usurpateur -trice
**usury** n usure f
**utensil** n ustensile m
**uterus** n utérus m
**utilitarian** adj utilitaire
**utility** n utilité f; **public** ~ entreprise f de service public; adj utilitaire
**utilizable** adj utilisable
**utilization** n utilisation f
**utilize** vt utiliser
**utmost, uttermost** n dernier degré; **at the** ~ tout au plus; **do one's** ~ **to** faire tout son possible pour; adj dernier -ière, extrême; **of the** ~ **importance** de la dernière importance
**utopia** n utopie f
**utopian** adj utopique
**¹utter** adj complet -ète, absolu, entier -ière; ~ **idiot** parfait imbécile
**²utter** vt (cry) pousser; (word) prononcer, dire; (circulate) mettre en circulation
**utterance** n déclaration f, expression f; articulation f
**utterly** adv complètement, tout à fait
**uttermost** adj see **utmost**
**U-turn** n demi-tour m, retour m en arrière
**uvula** n luette f
**uxorious** adj très attaché à sa femme

# V

**V VD** abbr maladie vénérienne; **V neck** décolleté m en V; **the V sign** le V de la victoire
**vac** n abbr vacances fpl
**vacancy** n (situation) vacance f; (emptiness) vide m; (stupidity) absence f d'idées
**vacant** adj (situation) vacant; (house, etc) inoccupé, vide; (look) distrait, niais, stupide; ~ **possession** libre

possession *f*

**vacate** *vt* quitter, évacuer

**vacation** *n* vacances *fpl*; (university) **long ~** grandes vacances

**vacationist** *n US* vacancier -ière

**vaccinate** *vt* vacciner

**vaccination** *n* vaccination *f*

**vaccine** *n* vaccin *m*

**vacillate** *vi* vaciller, hésiter

**vacillating** *adj* irrésolu, indécis

**vacillation** *n* vacillation *f*, hésitation *f*

**vacuity** *n* vide *m*; *fig* manque *m* d'intelligence

**vacuous** *adj* niais, stupide; (face, eyes) sans expression; (remark) dénué de sens

**vacuum** *n* vide *m*; *phys* vacuum *m*; **~ brake** frein *m* à vide; **~ cleaner** aspirateur *m*; **~ flask** Thermos *m*; **~ packed** emballé sous vide; **~ pump** pompe *f* à vide

**vagabond** *n + adj* vagabond -e

**vagary** *n* caprice *m*, fantaisie *f*

**vagina** *n* vagin *m*

**vaginal** *adj* vaginal; **~ discharge** pertes blanches

**vagrancy** *n* vagabondage *m*

**vagrant** *n + adj* vagabond -e

**vague** *adj* vague; (outline) flou; (person) indécis; **not have the ~st idea** n'avoir pas la moindre idée

**vagueness** *n* vague *m*

**vain** *adj* vain; (useless) inutile; (person) vaniteux -euse; **in ~** en vain, inutilement; **it will be ~ for you to try** vous aurez beau essayer; **take God's name in ~** blasphémer le nom de Dieu

**vainglorious** *adj* orgueilleux -euse, vaniteux -euse

**vainglory** *n* gloriole *f*, prétention *f*

**vainly** *adv* vainement, inutilement

**valance** *n* (bed) tour *m* de lit, frange *f*

**vale** *n poet* val *m*, vallon *m*

**valediction** *n* adieu *m*, adieux *mpl*

**valedictory** *adj* d'adieu

**valency** *n chem* valence *f*

**valentine** *n* amoureux -euse; carte envoyée le jour de la Saint-Valentin

**valet** *n* valet *m* de chambre; *vt* nettoyer, remettre en état

**valetudinarian** *n + adj* valétudinaire

**valiant** *adj* valeureux -euse, vaillant

**valid** *adj* valable, valide; (ticket) **no longer ~** périmé

**validate** *vt* valider

**validity** *n* validité *f*

**valise** *n* sac *m* de voyage, mallette *f*

**valium** *n* valium *m*

**valley** *n* vallée *f*; *bui* noue *f*

**valorous** *adj* valeureux -euse

**valour** *n* vaillance *f*

**valuable** *adj* de valeur, précieux -ieuse

**valuables** *npl* objets *mpl* de valeur

**valuation** *n* évaluation *f*, estimation *f*; valeur estimée; *leg* expertise *f*

**value** *n* valeur *f*, prix *m*; *fig* mérite *m*; **~-added tax (V.A.T.)** taxe *f* à la valeur ajoutée (T.V.A.); **be of little ~** valoir peu de chose; **be of no ~** ne rien valoir; **be of ~** avoir de la valeur; **get good ~ for one's money** en avoir pour son argent; **increase in ~** plus-value *f*; *vt* évaluer, estimer

**valued** *adj* précieux -ieuse, estimé

**valueless** *adj* sans valeur

**valuer** *n* estimateur *m*, expert *m*; **official ~** commissaire-priseur *m* (*pl* commissaires-priseurs)

**valve** *n* soupape *f*; (tyre) valve *f*; *anat* valvule *f*; *rad* lampe *f*; **exhaust (outlet) ~** soupape *f* d'échappement; **inlet ~** soupape *f* d'admission; **safety ~** soupape *f* de sûreté

**valve-cap** *n* capuchon *m*

**valvular** *adj* valvulaire

**vamoose** *vi US coll* décamper, filer

**vamp** *n coll* vamp *f*, femme fatale; *vt* enjôler, envoûter; *coll* vamper

**vampire** *n* vampire *m*

**¹van** *n* (vehicle) fourgon *m*; (light) camionnette *f*; **delivery ~** camionnette *f* de livraison; **furniture (removal) ~** fourgon *m* de déménagement; **guard's ~** fourgon *m* (du chef du train); **luggage ~** fourgon *m* (à bagages)

**²van** *n* avant-garde *f*

**³van** *n abbr* (tennis) avantage *m*

**vandal** *n* vandale *m*

**vandalism** *n* vandalisme *m*

**vandalize** *vt* saccager

**vane** *n* (weather) girouette *f*; (windmill) bras *m*; (ventilator) pale *f*; (turbine) aube *f*

**vanguard** *n* avant-garde *f*

**vanilla** *n* vanille *f*; **~ ice-cream** glace *f* à la vanille

**vanish** *vi* disparaître

**vanishing** *n* disparition *f*; **~ point** point *m* de fuite; **do a ~ trick** disparaître; *adj* **~ cream** crème *f* de jour

**vanity** *n* vanité *f*; futilité *f*

**vanquish** *vt* vaincre

**vanquisher** *n* vainqueur *m*

**vantage** *n* **~ point** position avantageuse

**vapid** *adj* insipide, fade

**vapidity** *n* insipidité *f*, fadeur *f*

**vaporization** *n* vaporisation *f*

**vaporize** *vt* vaporiser; *vi* se vaporiser

**vaporizer** *n* vaporisateur *m*, pulvérisateur *m*, atomiseur *m*

**vaporous** *adj* vaporeux -euse

**vapour** *n* vapeur *f*; (on window) buée *f*, **~ trail** traînée *f* de condensation

**vapourings** *npl* fadaises *fpl*, bavardage *m* inutile

**vapoury** *adj* vaporeux -euse; *fig* imaginaire, fantaisiste

**variability** *n* variabilité *f*

**variable** *n math* variable *f*; *adj* variable, changeant

**variance** *n* désaccord *m*, discorde *f*; (temperature, etc) variation *f*; **at ~ with** en désaccord avec

**variant** *n* variante *f*

**variation** *n* variation *f*, changement *m*

**varicoloured** *adj* de couleurs différentes, bariolé, multicolore

**varicose** *adj* variqueux -euse; **~ veins** varices *fpl*

**varied** *adj* varié, divers

**variegate** *vt* varier, diversifier; (colour) barioler

**variegation** *n* diversité *f* de couleurs, bigarrure *f*

**variety** *n* variété *f*, diversité *f*; **~ entertainment** numéros *mpl* de music-hall; **~ theatre** théâtre *m* de variétés

**variform** *adj* diversiforme

**various** *adj* divers, varié, différent; (several) plusieurs

**varnish** *n* vernis *m*; *vt* vernir; (pottery) vernisser; *fig* cacher, passer sous silence; (gloss over) ✦farder

**vary** *vt* varier, faire varier; *vi* varier, changer; être différent; (disagree) ne pas être d'accord, différer

**vase** *n* vase *m*

**vasectomy** *n* vasectomie *f*

**vaseline** *n* vaseline *f*

**vassal** *n* vassal *m*

**vast** *adj* vaste, immense, énorme

**vastly** *adv* vastement; (very much) infiniment, immensément

**vat** *n* cuve *f*, bac *m*

**Vatican** *n* Vatican *m*; **~ City** Cité *f* du Vatican

**vaudeville** *n* vaudeville *m*

**¹vault** *n archi* voûte *f*; (grave) caveau *m*; (underground place) cave *f*; (bank) chambre forte; **~ of heaven** voûte *f* céleste; *vt* voûter

**²vault** *n* (jump) saut *m*; *vt* sauter; *vi* **~ over** sauter, franchir d'un saut

**vaulted** *adj* voûté, en voûte

**¹vaulting** *n* construction *f* de voûtes

**²vaulting** *n* (jumping) exercice *m* du saut; *adj fig* **~ ambition** ambition démesurée

**vaulting-horse** *n* cheval *m* d'arçons

**vaunt** *vt* vanter, se vanter de

**veal** *n* veau *m*

**vector** *n* vecteur *m*

**veer** *n* changement *m* de direction, virage *m*; (opinion) revirement *m*; *vt naut* faire virer; *vi* (ship) virer; (wind) tourner; *fig* **~ round** changer d'opinion

**vegetable** *n* légume *m*; *bot* végétal *m*; **~ garden** (jardin *m*) potager *m*; **early ~ s** primeurs *fpl*; *adj* végétal; (existence) végétatif- ive

**vegetable-dish** *n* légumier *m*

**vegetarian** *n + adj* végétarien -ienne

**vegetarianism** *n* végétarisme *m*

**vegetative** *adj* végétatif -ive

**vehemence** *n* véhémence *f*

**vehement** *adj* véhément, impétueux -euse

**vehicle** *n* véhicule *m*, voiture *f*; *mil* engin *m*; *med* agent vecteur *m*

**vehicular** *adj* des voitures

**veil** *n* voile *m*; (hat) voilette *f*; *vt* voiler; *fig* cacher, dissimuler

**veiled** *adj* voilé; *fig* caché

**vein** *n* veine *f*; *bot + zool* nervure *f*; *geol* filon *m*; (humour) disposition *f*, humeur *f*; *vt* veiner

**vellum** *n* vélin *m*

**velocity** *n* vélocité *f*, vitesse *f*

**velvet** *n* velours *m*; *coll* **on ~** sur du velours; *adj* de velours

**velveteen** *n* velours *m* de coton, velvet *m*

**velvety** *adj* velouté

**venal** *adj* vénal, corruptible

**vend** *vt* vendre

**vender, vendor** *n* vendeur -euse; *leg* vendeur -eresse

**vendetta** *n* vendetta *f*

**vending** *n* vente *f*; **~ machine** distributeur *m* automatique

**vendor** *n see* **vender**

**veneer** *n* revêtement *m*, placage *m*; *fig* vernis *m*; *vt* plaquer

**veneering** *n* placage *m*

**venerable** *adj* vénérable

**venerate** *vt* vénérer

**veneration** *n* vénération *f*

**venereal** *adj* vénérien -ienne

**Venetian** *n* Vénitien -ienne; *adj* vénitien -ienne; **~ blind** jalousie *f*

**Venezuela** *n* Venezuela *m*

**vengeance** *n* vengeance *f*; **take ~ on** s/o se venger sur (de) qn; **with a ~** furieusement, pour de bon

**vengeful** *adj* vindicatif -ive

**venial** *adj* véniel -ielle, léger- ère

**veniality** *n* caractère véniel

**Venice** *n* Venise *f*

**venison** *n* venaison *f*

**venom** *n* venin *m*

**venomous** *adj* (snake, etc) venimeux -euse; **~ tongue** langue *f* de vipère

**venous** *adj* veineux -euse

**vent** *n* trou *m*, orifice *m*, passage *m*; (coat) fente *f*; *geol* cheminée *f*; **give ~ to** donner libre cours à, manifester, laisser éclater; (sigh, shout) laisser échapper; *vt* (anger) décharger, laisser éclater

**vent-hole** *n* (volcano) évent *m*; (barrel)

trou *m* de fausset

**ventilate** *vt* aérer, ventiler; (blood) oxy-géner; *coll* mettre en discussion, agiter

**ventilation** *n* aération *f*, ventilation *f*; (blood) oxygénation *f*

**ventilator** *n* ventilateur *m*

**ventricle** *n* ventricule *m*

**ventricular** *adj* ventriculaire

**ventriloquism** *n* ventriloquie *f*

**ventriloquist** *n* ventriloque

**venture** *n* risque *m*, aventure risquée; aventure *f*; *comm* spéculation *f*, opération *f*, entreprise risquée; **at a ~** à l'aventure, au hasard; *vt* risquer, hasar-der; *vi* ~ **into** s'aventurer dans; ~ **to do sth** (risk) se risquer (hasarder) à faire qch; (dare) oser (se permettre de) faire qch; ~ **(up)on sth** se risquer à faire qch

**venturesome** *adj* aventureux -euse; (action) risqué, hasardeux -euse

**venue** *n* lieu *m* de réunion, rendez-vous *m*; *leg* lieu *m* du jugement

**Venus** *n* Vénus *f*

**veracious** *adj* véridique

**veracity** *n* véracité *f*

**veranda** *n* véranda *f*

**verb** *n* verbe *m*

**verbal** *adj* verbal; (translation) littéral

**verbalism** *n* verbalisme *m*

**verbalization** *n* expression verbale

**verbalize** *vt* traduire (exprimer) en pa-roles

**verbally** *adv* verbalement; littéralement

**verbatim** *adj* textuel -elle; *adv* textuelle-ment, mot pour mot

**verbena** *n* verveine *f*

**verbiage** *n* verbiage *m*

**verbose** *adj* verbeux -euse, diffus

**verbosity** *n* verbosité *f*

**verdancy** *n* verdure *f*; *fig* naïveté *f*

**verdant** *adj* vert, verdoyant

**verdict** *n* verdict *m*, jugement *m*; (opi-nion) avis *m*

**verdigris** *n* vert-de-gris *m*

**verdure** *n* verdure *f*, herbage *m*; *fig* ver-deur *f*, jeunesse *f*

**verge** *n* bord *m*, bordure *f*; (road) accote-ment *m*; (wood) orée *f*; **on the ~ of di-saster** à deux doigts de la catastrophe; **on the ~ of leaving** sur le point de partir; *vi* incliner, tendre; ~ **on** tou-cher à; (age) friser; (colour) tirer sur

**verger** *n* bedeau *m*

**verifiable** *adj* vérifiable

**verification** *n* vérification *f*, contrôle *m*

**verify** *vt* vérifier

**verily** *adv* *bibl* + *ar* en vérité

**verisimilitude** *n* vraisemblance *f*

**veritable** *adj* véritable

**verity** *n* *lit* vérité *f*

**vermilion** *n* vermillon *m*; *adj* vermillon

*invar*, vermeil -eille

**vermin** *n* vermine *f*

**verminous** *adj* couvert de vermine

**vermouth** *n* vermout(h) *m*

**vernacular** *n* langue *f* du pays, langue *f* vulgaire; *adj* vernaculaire, du pays

**verruca** *n* verrue *f*

**versatile** *adj* aux talents variés; (mind) souple; *bot* + *zool* versatile

**versatility** *n* (person) faculté *f* d'adapta-tion; (mind) souplesse *f* d'esprit

**verse** *n* (line) vers *m*; (stanza) strophe *f*, couplet *m*; *bibl* verset *m*; (poetry) poésie *f*; *pej* poème *m* faible; **blank ~** vers blancs; **free ~** vers *mpl* libres

**versed** *adj* versé

**versification** *n* versification *f*

**versify** *vt* mettre en vers; *vi* faire des vers, versifier

**version** *n* version *f*, traduction *f*; inter-prétation *f*; **according to his ~** selon lui, d'après lui

**verso** *n* (page) verso *m*; (medal, coin) revers *m*

**versus** *prep* contre

**vertebra** *n* ( *pl* **vertebrae**) vertèbre *f*

**vertebrate** *n* vertébré *m*; *adj* vertébré

**vertex** *n* ( *pl* **vertices**) sommet *m*; *anat* vertex *m*

**vertical** *n* verticale *f*; *adj* vertical; ~ **take-off aircraft** avion *m* à décollage vertical

**vertiginous** *adj* vertigineux -euse

**vertigo** *n* vertige *m*

**verve** *n* verve *f*

**very** *adj* vrai, véritable; (selfsame) même; complet -ète; **at the ~ beginning** tout au début; **do one's ~ best** faire tout son possible; **his ~ words** ses propres paroles; **in the ~ middle of** au beau milieu de; **in this ~ place** ici même; **the ~ idea!** ça, par exemple!; **the ~ thing I needed** justement ce qu'il me fallait; **the ~ thought** la seule pensée; **to the ~ day** jour pour jour; *adv* très, fort, bien; tout; ~ **much** beau-coup, bien; **at the ~ latest** au plus tard; **at the ~ least** tout au moins; **at the ~ most** tout au plus; **not ~** pas tellement; **so ~ good** si bon ( *f* bonne); **the ~ best** le meilleur de tous ( *f* la meilleure de toutes); **the ~ first** le tout premier ( *f* la toute première); **the ~ same day** le (ce) jour même

**vesicle** *n* *med* vésicule *f*

**vespers** *npl* vêpres *fpl*

**vessel** *n* (liquid) récipient *m*, vase *m*; (ship) vaisseau *m*, navire *m*; **blood ~** vaisseau sanguin

¹**vest** *n* gilet *m*; (underwear) tricot *m* (de corps); *vt* revêtir

²**vest** *vt* ~ **s/o with authority** investir qn

de l'autorité; *vi leg* ~ **in** échoir à

**vested** *adj* dévolu; (invested) investi; ~ **interests** droits acquis

**vestibule** *n* vestibule *m*, entrée *f*

**vestige** *n* vestige *m*, trace *f*

**vestment** *n* vêtement *m*; *eccles* vêtement sacerdotal

**vestry** *n* sacristie *f*

**¹vet** *n coll* vétérinaire

**²vet** *vt* (person, statement) examiner (minutieusement); (text) corriger

**veteran** *n* vétéran *m*; *adj* vieux (*f* vieille), expérimenté, de vétéran

**veterinarian** *n* vétérinaire

**veterinary** *adj* vétérinaire

**veto** *n* veto *m*; *vt* interdire, mettre son veto à

**vex** *vt* vexer, contrarier, fâcher

**vexation** *n* vexation *f*, ennui *m*, tourment *m*

**vexatious** *adj* contrariant, ennuyeux -euse; *leg* vexatoire

**vexed** *adj* vexé, contrarié; ~ **question** question très débattue

**vexing** *adj* contrariant, vexant, ennuyeux -euse

**via** *prep* via, par

**viability** *n* viabilité *f*

**viable** *adj* viable

**viaduct** *n* viaduc *m*

**vial** *n* fiole *f*

**viands** *npl* aliments *mpl*

**viaticum** *n* viatique *m*

**vibrancy** *n* résonance *f*

**vibrant** *adj* vibrant

**vibraphone** *n* vibraphone *m*

**vibrate** *vt* faire vibrer; *vi* vibrer

**vibration** *n* vibration *f*, oscillation *f*

**vibrato** *n mus* vibrato *m*

**vibrator** *n* vibrateur *m*

**vicar** *n* pasteur *m*, vicaire *m*; (parish priest) = curé *m*; **the Vicar of Christ** le Pape

**vicarage** *n* (protestant) presbytère *m*; (Catholic) = cure *f*

**vicarious** *adj* (authority) délégué; (pleasure) ressenti par un autre; (punishment) souffert par un autre

**vicariously** *adv* à la place d'un autre

**¹vice** *n* vice *m*; (trait) défaut *m*

**²vice** *n* (tool) étau *m*

**³vice** *prep* à la place de; ~ **versa** vice versa, inversement

**vice-chairman** *n* vice-président *m*

**vice-chancellor** *n* vice-chancelier *m*; (university) recteur *m*

**vice-president** *n* vice-président -e

**vice-principal** *n* sous-directeur -trice

**viceroy** *n* vice-roi *m*

**vicinity** *n* voisinage *m*, proximité *f*

**vicious** *adj* dépravé, vicieux -ieuse; (spiteful) méchant; (ill-tempered) hai-

neux -euse; (horse) rétif -ive

**viciousness** *n* méchanceté *f*

**vicissitude** *n* vicissitude *f*, péripétie *f*

**victim** *n* victime *f*; **fall a** ~ **to** être victime de, succomber à

**victimization** *n* représailles *fpl*, oppression *f*

**victimize** *vt* exercer des représailles contre

**victor** *n* vainqueur *m*

**Victorian** *adj* victorien -ienne

**victorious** *adj* victorieux -ieuse

**victory** *n* victoire *f*; **gain a (the)** ~ remporter une (la) victoire

**victual** *vt* ravitailler, approvisionner

**victualler** *n* fournisseur *m* de vivres; **licensed** ~ débitant *m* de boissons

**victuals** *npl* vivres *mpl*, provisions *fpl*

**video** *n* télévision *f*; ~ **recorder** magnétoscope *m*; ~ **recording** enregistrement *m* sur magnétoscope

**vie** *vi* rivaliser, lutter; ~ **in politeness with s/o** faire assaut de politesse avec qn

**Vienna** *n* Vienne *f*

**Vietnam** *n* le Vietnam

**Vietnamese** *n* Vietnamien -ienne; *adj* vietnamien -ienne

**view** *n* vue *f*; coup d'œil *m*; opinion *f*, avis *m*; intention *f*; photo *f*; **get a good** ~ voir bien; **in my** ~ à mon avis; **in** ~ en vue; **in** ~ **of** en considération de, étant donné; **keep in** ~ ne pas perdre de vue; **on** ~ exposé au public; **point of** ~ point *m* de vue; **with a** ~ **to** dans le but de; *vt* regarder; examiner; (house) visiter; envisager

**viewer** *n* spectateur -trice; *TV* téléspectateur -trice

**view-finder** *n phot* viseur *m*

**viewpoint** *n* point *m* de vue; (panorama) belvédère *m*

**vigil** *n* veille *f*; *eccles* vigile *f*; **keep** ~ veiller

**vigilance** *n* vigilance *f*; *US* ~ **committee** comité *m* de surveillance des mœurs

**vigilante** *n* membre *m* d'un comité de vigilance

**vignette** *n* vignette *f*

**vigorous** *adj* vigoureux -euse, robuste

**vigour** *n* vigueur *f*, énergie *f*, vitalité *f*

**Viking** *n* Viking *m*

**vile** *adj* infâme, vil, bas (*f* basse); (worthless) sans valeur; (dreadful) abominable; (temper) exécrable, massacrant

**vileness** *n* bassesse *f*

**vilification** *n* dénigrement *m*, diffamation *f*

**vilify** *vt* dénigrer, diffamer

**villa** *n* villa *f*

**village** n village m; adj de village; de campagne

**villager** n villageois -e

**villain** n scélérat m, bandit m, coquin m

**villainess** n scélérate f, coquine f

**villainous** adj infâme, scélérat; coll exécrable, abominable

**villainy** n infamie f

**vindicate** vt défendre, justifier; prouver

**vindication** n défense f, justification f

**vindicative** adj justificatif -ive

**vindicator** n défenseur m

**vindictive** adj vindicatif -ive, rancunier -ière

**vine** n vigne f; (creeper) plante grimpante

**vine-dresser** n vigneron m

**vinegar** n vinaigre m; ~ sauce vinaigrette f; **wine** ~ vinaigre m de vin

**vinegary** adj vinaigré; coll fig aigre; (person) revêche

**vine-grower** n viticulteur m

**vineyard** n vigne f; (extensive) vignoble m

**vingt-et-un** n (card game) vingt-et-un m

**viniculture** n viniculture f

**vinous** adj vineux -euse

**vintage** n (harvest) vendanges fpl, récolte f du raisin; (crop) vendange f; (year) année f, cru m; adj ~ car voiture f du début du siècle; ~ champagne champagne m d'origine; ~ wine grand vin, grand cru; ~ year grande année

**vintner** n négociant m en vins

**vinyl** n vinyle m

**viol** n mus viole f

**viola** n mus alto m

**violable** adj qui peut être violé

**violate** vt violer; (peace) troubler; (sanctuary) profaner

**violation** n violation f; (sanctuary) profanation f; (order) infraction f; (woman) viol m

**violator** n violateur -trice

**violence** n violence f; **crime of** ~ voie f de fait; **do** ~ **to one's feelings** se faire violence; **resort to** ~ se livrer à des voies de fait, employer la violence; **robbery with** ~ vol m avec coups et blessures

**violent** adj intense, extrême; (colour) voyant, criard; (emotion) vif (f vive); coll (hell of a, rare old) carabiné; **in a** ~ **hurry** extrêmement pressé; **lay** ~ **hands on** s/o attaquer qn brutalement

**violet** n violette f; (colour) violet m; adj violet -ette

**violin** n violon m

**violinist** n violoniste

**violoncellist** n violoncelliste

**violoncello** n violoncelle m

**viper** n vipère f

**viperish** adj (tongue) de vipère

**virago** n mégère f

**virgin** n vierge f; adj de vierge, virginal; ~ **birth** parthénogenèse f

**virginal** adj virginal

**virginia** n ~ **creeper** vigne f vierge

**virginity** n virginité f

**viridescent** adj verdâtre

**virile** adj viril, mâle

**virility** n virilité f

**virology** n virologie f

**virtual** adj vrai, de fait, effectif -ive; (potential) virtuel -elle

**virtually** adv en pratique, effectivement; (almost) presque

**virtue** n vertu f; (property) qualité f, avantage m; (power) pouvoir m, efficacité f; **by** ~ **of** en vertu de, en raison de; **make a** ~ **of necessity** faire de nécessité vertu

**virtuosity** n virtuosité f

**virtuoso** n mus virtuose; amateur m d'art, connaisseur m; adj de virtuose

**virtuous** adj vertueux -euse

**virulence** n virulence f

**virulent** adj virulent

**virus** n virus m; fig poison m

**visa** n visa m; vt viser

**visage** n visage m

**vis-à-vis** n vis-à-vis m; adv vis-à-vis; prep vis-à-vis de, en face de

**viscera** npl viscères mpl

**visceral** adj viscéral

**viscose** n viscose f

**viscosity** n viscosité f

**viscount** n vicomte m

**viscountess** n vicomtesse f

**viscous** adj visqueux -euse, gluant

**visibility** n visibilité f

**visible** adj visible; manifeste

**vision** n vision f; (eyesight) vue f; imagination f; (ghost) fantôme m; **field of** ~ champ m de vue; **man of** ~ homme m qui voit loin; **within the range of** ~ à portée de vue

**visionary** n visionnaire; adj (person) visionnaire; (plan) chimérique

**visit** n visite f; (stay) séjour m; **be on a** ~ être en visite; **pay s/o a** ~ rendre visite à qn; vt rendre visite à, aller voir; (call on) passer chez; (sights, etc) visiter; (inspect) inspecter

**visitant** n visiteur m; (bird) oiseau migrateur m; (ghost) fantôme m

**visitation** n visite f (d'inspection); lit (ghost) apparition f; eccles visite pastorale

**visiting** n visites fpl; **go** ~ faire des visites, aller en visite; adj en visite; ~ **card** carte f de visite; ~ **hours** heures *fpl* de visite; **not be on ~ terms** ne pas se voir

**visitor** *n* visiteur -euse; touriste, voyageur -euse; **~s' book** livre *m* d'or, registre *m*; **have ~s** avoir du monde; **summer ~s** estivants *mpl*; **winter ~s** hivernants *mpl*

**visor, vizor** *n* visière *f*

**vista** *n* (prospect) perspective *f*; (forest) éclaircie *f*, percée *f*

**visual** *adj* visuel -elle; **~ aid** support visuel; **~ distance** distance *f* de visibilité

**visualization** *n* visualisation *f*

**visualize** *vt* se représenter, se faire une image de, visualiser; (foresee) envisager, prévoir; *vi* s'imaginer; (foresee) prévoir, envisager

**visually** *adv* visuellement, de façon visuelle

**vital** *adj* vital, essentiel -ielle; (fatal) irrémédiable, mortel -elle; (lively) énergique; **matter of ~ importance** affaire *f* d'importance capitale

**vitality** *n* vitalité *f*, vigueur *f*

**vitalize** *vt* vitaliser, vivifier

**vitally** *adv* d'une manière vitale, vitalement

**vitals** *npl anat* organes vitaux

**vitamin** *n* vitamine *f*

**vitiate** *vt* vicier

**vitiation** *n* viciation *f*

**viticulture** *n* viticulture *f*

**vitreous** *adj* vitreux -euse

**vitrify** *vt* vitrifier

**vitriol** *n* vitriol *m*

**vitriolic** *adj chem* de vitriol; *fig* mordant; **~ pen** plume trempée dans du vitriol

**vituperate** *vt* injurier; *vi* vitupérer

**vituperation** *n* insultes *fpl*, injures *fpl*

**vituperative** *adj* injurieux -ieuse

**viva** *n coll* examen oral; **~ voce** de vive voix

**vivacious** *adj* vif (*f* vive), animé, enjoué

**vivacity** *n* vivacité *f*, animation *f*

**vivid** *adj* vif (*f* vive), éclatant, frappant

**vividness** *n* vivacité *f*, éclat *m*

**vivify** *vt* vivifier, ranimer

**vivisect** *vt* pratiquer des vivisections sur; *vi* faire de la vivisection

**vivisection** *n* vivisection *f*

**vixen** *n* renarde *f*; *coll fig* mégère *f*

**vixenish** *adj* (woman) méchant; (character) de mégère

**viz** *adv abbr* à savoir, c'est à dire

**vizier** *n* vizir *m*

**vizor** *n see* visor

**vocable** *n* vocable *m*

**vocabulary** *n* vocabulaire *m*

**vocal** *adj* vocal; (communication) verbal; (person) bruyant, qui aime se faire entendre

**vocalist** *n* chanteur -euse; (opera, classical music) cantatrice *f*

**vocalization** *n* vocalisation *f*

**vocalize** *vt* (air) chanter; *ling* vocaliser; *vi mus* faire des vocalises, vocaliser

**vocally** *adv* vocalement; (by speech) oralement

**vocation** *n* vocation *f*; profession *f*

**vocational** *adj* professionnel -elle

**vocative** *n gramm* vocatif *m*; *adj* vocatif -ive

**vociferate** *vt + vi* vociférer

**vociferation** *n* vociférations *fpl*, cris *mpl*

**vociferous** *adj* bruyant, criard

**vodka** *n* vodka *f*

**vogue** *n* vogue *f*, mode *f*; **in ~** en vogue, à la mode

**voice** *n* voix *f*; (tone of) ton *m*; **at the top of one's ~** à tue-tête; **have no ~ in the matter** n'avoir pas voix au chapitre; **in a low ~** à voix basse; **like the sound of one's own ~** aimer à s'entendre parler; **lose one's ~** avoir une extinction de voix; **with one ~** à l'unanimité; *vt* exprimer, énoncer

**voiced** *adj phon* sonore

**voiceless** *adj* sans voix, muet (*f* muette); *phon* sourd

**void** *n* vide *m*; *adj* vide; inoccupé; *leg* nul (*f* nulle); **~ of** dépourvu de; *vt* évacuer

**volatile** *adj* volatil; (person) léger -ère, inconstant

**volatility** *n* volatilité *f*

**volatilize** *vt* volatiliser

**vol-au-vent** *n cul* vol-au-vent *m invar*

**volcanic** *adj* volcanique

**volcano** *n* volcan *m*

**vole** *n* campagnol *m*

**volition** *n* volonté *f*, volition *f*; **do sth of one's own ~** faire qch de son propre gré

**volley** *n* (firing) décharge *f*, salve *f*; (abuse) bordée *f*; *sp* volée *f*; *vt sp* reprendre en volée

**volley-ball** *n* volley(-ball *m*) *m*

**volt** *n* volt *m*

**voltage** *n* voltage *m*

**volte-face** *n* volte-face *f invar*

**voltmeter** *n elect* voltmètre *m*

**volubility** *n* volubilité *f*

**voluble** *adj* (person) volubile, loquace; (speech) facile, aisé

**volume** *n* (book) volume *m*, tome *m*, livre *m*; *sci* volume *m*; (size) grosseur *f*, ampleur *f*; (smoke) nuages *mpl*

**volume-control** *n* bouton *m* de réglage du volume

**voluminous** *adj* volumineux -euse, abondant

**voluntarily** *adv* volontairement, de plein gré

**voluntary** *adj* volontaire; **~ organization** organisation *f* bénévole volunteer *n* volontaire; *vt* offrir volontairement; ~ **an answer** hasarder une réponse; ~ **information** donner spontanément un renseignement; *vi* s'offrir comme volontaire; *mil* s'engager comme volontaire

voluptuary *n* + *adj* voluptueux -euse

voluptuous *adj* voluptueux -euse

vomit *n* vomi *m*; *vt* + *vi* vomir

vomiting *n* vomissement *m*

voodoo *n* vaudou *m*; *adj* vaudou *invar*

voodooism *n* pratique *f* du vaudou

voracious *adj* vorace

voracity *n* voracité *f*

vortex *n* tourbillon *m*

votary *n* fervent -e, adorateur -trice

vote *n* (practice, etc) vote *m*, scrutin *m*; (individual) voix *f*; ~ **of censure** motion *f* de censure; **have the** ~ avoir le droit de vote; **put a question to the** ~ mettre une question aux voix; **take the** ~ procéder au scrutin; *vt* voter, élire; ~ **down (out)** repousser; ~ **in** élire; *vi* voter, aller aux urnes; (suggest) proposer

voter *n* électeur -trice, votant *m*

voting-paper *n* bulletin *m* de vote

votive *adj* votif -ive; ~ **offering** ex-voto *m invar*

vouch *vi* ~ **for** garantir, répondre de

voucher *n* bon *m*, fiche *f*; (receipt) reçu *m*; (confirmatory document) pièce justificative

vouchsafe *vt* accorder; *vi* ~ **to do sth** daigner faire qch

vow *n* vœu *m*, serment *m*; **fulfil a** ~ accomplir un vœu; **take one's** ~s entrer en religion; *vt* + *vi* jurer

vowel *n* voyelle *f*

voyage *n* voyage *m*; (sea) traversée *f*, voyage *m* par mer; *vi* naviguer

voyager *n* voyageur -euse (par mer), passager -ère

voyeur *n* voyeur *m*

voyeurism *n* voyeurisme *m*

vulcanite *n* caoutchouc vulcanisé, ébonite *f*

vulcanize *vt* vulcaniser

vulgar *adj* commun, vulgaire, grossier -ière; (general) très répandu; ~ **fraction** fraction *f* ordinaire

vulgarism *n* mot *m* vulgaire, expression *f* vulgaire

vulgarity *n* vulgarité *f*

vulgarization *n* vulgarisation *f*

vulgarize *vt* vulgariser

vulgarly *adv* vulgairement, grossièrement; (commonly) communément

Vulgate *n* Vulgate *f*

vulnerability *n* vulnérabilité *f*

vulnerable *adj* vulnérable

vulture *n* vautour *m*

vulva *n anat* vulve *f*

vying *n* rivalité *f*

# W

wabble *n* + *vi see* wobble

wacky *adj coll* fou-fou (*f* fofolle)

wad *n* (notes) liasse *f*; (material) bourre *f*; (cotton wool) tampon *m*; *vt* bourrer; ouater; (ears) bourrer de l'ouate dans

wadding *n* rembourrage *m*; (cotton wool) ouate *f*

waddle *n* dandinement *m*; *vi* marcher comme un canard, se dandiner

wade *vt* passer à gué; *vi* marcher dans l'eau (la boue, etc); ~ **across** traverser à gué; ~ **in** entrer dans l'eau; *coll fig* intervenir; ~ **through** traverser; *coll fig* achever péniblement

wader *n orni* échassier *m*; (person) personne *f* qui marche dans l'eau; (boots) ~s bottes *fpl* cuissardes (de pêcheur)

wafer *n cul* gaufrette *f*; *eccles* hostie *f*; (sealing) pain *m* à cacheter

wafer-thin *adj* très mince

¹waffle *n* gaufre *f*

²waffle *n coll* laïus *m*, rabâchage *m*; *vi* raconter des bêtises; écrire (parler) autour du sujet (dans le vague)

waft *n* bouffée *f*; (wind) souffle *m*; *vt* porter (dans l'air)

¹wag *n* farceur -euse, badin -e

²wag *n* agitation *f*, mouvement *m*, frétillement *m*; *vt* agiter; (tail) remuer; (head) branler, secouer; *vi* se remuer,

s'agiter; **set tongues ~ging** faire jaser les gens

¹**wage** n salaire m, paie f; **~s** gages mpl; **minimum living ~** minimum vital; **minimum ~** salaire minimum interprofessionnel de croissance (S.M.I.C.)

²**wage** vt **~ war** faire la guerre

**wage-earner** n salarié -e

**wage-freeze** n blocage m des salaires

**wager** n gageure f, pari m; **lay a ~** faire un pari; vt gager, parier

**waggish** adj blagueur -euse, badin, plaisant

**waggle** vt remuer; secouer

**wagon, waggon** n (railway) wagon m; chariot m, charrette f

**wagtail** n bergeronnette f

**waif** n épave f; **~s and strays** enfants abandonnés

**wail** n gémissement m, plainte f; (baby) vagissement m; vi gémir; (baby) vagir

**wainscot(ing)** n boiserie f, lambris m; vt lambrisser

**waist** n taille f, ceinture f; **~ measurement** tour m de taille; **put one's arm round s/o's ~** prendre qn par la taille

**waistband** n ceinture f

**waistcoat** n gilet m

**waist-deep** adj jusqu'à la taille (la ceinture)

**waistline** n taille f

**wait** n attente f; (between two trains) battement m; **lie in ~** se tenir en embuscade; **lie in ~ for s/o** attendre qn au passage; vt (watch for) guetter; vi attendre; (at table) servir; **~ and see** voir venir; **~ for** attendre; **~ on** servir; **~ on s/o hand and foot** être l'esclave de qn; **~ up** veiller; **~ up for s/o** attendre (le soir) que qn rentre; **keep s/o ~ing** faire attendre qn

**waiter** n garçon m de restaurant (café); **head ~** maître m d'hôtel; **wine ~** sommelier m

**waiting** n attente f; **~ list** liste f d'attente; **lady in ~** dame f d'honneur; **lose nothing by ~** rien perdre pour attendre; **play a ~ game** attendre son heure

**waiting-room** n salle f d'attente

**waitress** n serveuse f; **~!** mademoiselle!

**waive** vt renoncer à, abandonner; (condition) ne pas insister sur

**waiver** n leg abandon m

¹**wake** n (ship) sillage m; **follow in the ~ of s/o** marcher sur les traces de qn; **in the ~ of** à la suite de

²**wake** n veillée f mortuaire; hist fête f de la dédicace d'une église; vt réveiller; ranimer; exciter, provoquer; vi s'éveiller; (state) être éveillé; **~ (up)** se réveiller; **~ up to sth** se rendre enfin compte

de qch; **~ up with a start** se réveiller en sursaut

**wakeful** adj (vigilant) vigilant; éveillé, sans sommeil

**wakefulness** n insomnie f; vigilance f

**waken** vt réveiller; (feeling) éveiller; (suspicion) exciter; vi se réveiller

**wakening** n réveil m

**waking** n réveil m; **on ~** au réveil

**Wales** n le pays de Galles

**walk** n marche f, promenade f; (gait) démarche f; (place) allée f, avenue f, promenade f; **~ of life** position sociale; **at a ~** au pas; **go for a ~** aller se promener, faire une promenade; **take s/o for a ~** emmener qn en promenade; **take the dog for a ~** sortir le chien; vt faire marcher, promener; **~ a kilometre** faire un kilomètre à pied; **~ the streets** courir les rues; (prostitute) faire le trottoir; **I can ~ it in half an hour** j'en ai pour une demi-heure à pied; vi marcher; (stroll) se promener; (go on foot) aller à pied; **~ about** se promener; **~ away** s'en aller, partir; **~ back** retourner à pied; **~ home** rentrer à pied; **~ in** entrer; **~ in one's sleep** être somnambule; **~ off** s'en aller; **~ on** continuer (sa marche); **~ out** sortir; partir; abandonner; **~ round sth** faire le tour de qch (à pied); **~ up** monter à pied; (approach) s'approcher, s'avancer; **~ up and down** se promener de long en large; **go ~ing** aller en promenade

**walkabout** n promenade f parmi la foule, bain m de foule

**walker** n marcheur -euse, promeneur -euse; **be a good ~** être bon marcheur (f bonne marcheuse)

**walkie-talkie** n émetteur-récepteur m (pl émetteurs-récepteurs), talkie-walkie m (pl talkies-walkies), walkie-talkie m (pl walkies-talkies)

**walking** n marche f, promenade f à pied; adj ambulant; **the ~ wounded** les blessés qui peuvent marcher; **at a ~ pace** au pas; **the village is within ~ distance** on peut facilement se rendre au village à pied

**walking-stick** n canne f

**walk-on** adj theat **~ part** rôle m de figurant -e

**walk-out** n coll grève f

**walk-over** n victoire f facile

**wall** n mur m, muraille f; (chest, rock) paroi f; (tyre) flanc m; **~-to-~ carpet** moquette f; **come up against a blank ~** se heurter contre un mur; **dry-stone ~** mur m en pierres sèches; coll **go to the ~** succomber; **tariff ~** barrière douanière; vt **~ in** murer; entourer de murs;

~ **off** séparer par un mur; ~ **up** murer
**wallaby** n wallaby m
**wallet** n portefeuille f
**wall-eye** n (squint) œil m à strabisme divergent; œil m vairon
**wallflower** n giroflée f; coll fig **be a** ~ faire tapisserie
**wall-lamp** n applique f
**Walloon** n Wallon -onne
**wallop** n coll grand coup, sl gnon m, torgnole f; **go down with a** ~ tomber lourdement; vt coll rosser
**walloping** n coll rossée f, volée f de coups; adj coll énorme
**wallow** n trou bourbeux; vi se rouler, se vautrer; ~ **in blood** se plonger dans le sang; coll **be** ~ **ing in money** rouler sur l'or
**wallpaper** n papier peint
**walnut** n noix f
**walrus** n morse m
**waltz** n valse f
**wan** adj blême, pâle
**wand** n baguette f (de fée); verge f
**wander** vt parcourir; vi errer, se promener au hasard; (stray) s'égarer; ~ **about** errer à l'aventure; **his mind is** ~ **ing** il divague, il a le délire; (vague) il est distrait
**wanderer** n vagabond -e, rôdeur -euse
**wandering** n course vagabonde; (straying) égarement m; (mind) délire m; ~ **s** voyages mpl; adj errant, vagabond; (mind) distrait; (tribe) nomade
**wanderlust** n passion f des voyages
**wane** n déclin m; **be on the** ~ (moon) décroître; (person) être sur le déclin; vi décroître, décliner
**wangle** n coll combine f; vt carotter, obtenir par le système D; (falsify) cuisiner; vi resquiller
**wangler** n combinard -e, carotteur -euse
**wangling** n carottage m
**wanly** adv smile ~ sourire d'un air triste
**wanness** n pâleur f
**want** n (lack) manque m, défaut m; (need) besoin m; (poverty) pauvreté f, misère f, indigence f; **attend to s/o's** ~ **s** pourvoir aux besoins de qn; **be in** ~ **of** avoir besoin de; **for** ~ **of** faute de; **in** ~ dans le besoin; vt désirer, vouloir; (need) avoir besoin de; (lack) manquer de; (require) exiger; **he's not** ~ **ed** on ne veut pas de lui; **he** ~ **s a hundred francs for it** il en veut (demande) cent francs; **I have all I** ~ j'ai tout ce qu'il me faut; **that** ~ **s some doing** ce n'est pas facile à faire; **they** ~ **us to go away** ils veulent que nous partions; **you are** ~ **ed** on vous demande; vi ~ **for nothing** ne manquer de rien
**wanted** adj désiré, voulu; demandé;

(sought) recherché; ~, **lady's bicycle** on demande bicyclette de femme
**wanting** adj manquant, qui manque; ~ **in** dépourvu de; **be** ~ faire défaut; **there is sth** ~ le compte n'y est pas
**wanton** n femme légère; adj (woman) impudique; (action) gratuit; (playful) folâtre; (undisciplined) déréglé
**war** n guerre f; ~ **memorial** monument m aux morts; ~ **of words** dispute f de mots; ~ **zone** zone f militaire; **on a** ~ **footing** sur un pied de guerre; **the phoney** ~ la drôle de guerre; vi lutter, faire la guerre
**warble,** n gazouillement m; vi gazouiller; coll (person) chanter
**warbling** n see **warble** n
**war-cry** n cri m de guerre
**ward** n (person) pupille; (hospital) salle f d'hôpital; pol circonscription f; (lock) garde f; **emergency** ~ salle f des urgences; **intensive-care** ~ salle f de réanimation; vt ~ **off** parer, détourner; (illness) prévenir
**war-dance** n danse guerrière
**warden** n (guard) gardien -ienne, surveillant -e; (park) conservateur -trice; (institution) directeur -trice; **air-raid** ~ chef m d'îlot; **traffic** ~ contractuel -elle
**warder** n gardien m (de prison)
**wardress** n gardienne f (de prison)
**wardrobe** n garde-robe f, penderie f, armoire f
**wardrobe-keeper** n theat costumier -ière
**wardroom** n naut carré m des officiers
**ware** npl produits mpl, ustensiles mpl; ~ **s** marchandises fpl
**warehouse** n magasin m, entrepôt m; **bonded** ~ entrepôt m en douane
**warfare** n guerre f
**warhead** n tête f; (rocket) ogive f; **nuclear** ~ tête f nucléaire
**war-horse** n cheval m de bataille; coll fig dur -e à cuire
**warily** adv prudemment, avec prudence
**wariness** n prudence f, circonspection f
**warlike** adj guerrier -ière; (air) martial; (people) belliqueux -euse
**war-lord** n seigneur m de la guerre
**warm** adj chaud; (hearty) chaleureux -euse; (generous) généreux -euse; coll (rich) cossu; **be** ~ (person) avoir chaud; (thing) être chaud; **get** ~ se réchauffer; **it is** ~ (weather) il fait chaud; **keep** ~ se tenir au chaud; vt chauffer; ~ **the cockles of the heart** réjouir le cœur; ~ **up** réchauffer; vi (se) chauffer, se réchauffer; s'animer, s'échauffer; ~ **to s/o** se prendre de sympathie pour qn; ~ **up** (engine) se réchauffer; fig s'animer

**warm-blooded** adj à sang chaud; fig ardent

**warm-hearted** adj généreux -euse, au cœur chaud

**warming-pan** n bassinoire f

**warmly** adv chaudement; (heartily) chaleureusement

**warmonger** n belliciste

**warmongering** n propagande f de guerre

**warmth** n chaleur f; cordialité f; (anger) emportement m; vivacité f

**warn** vt avertir, prévenir; ~ off détourner; ~ s/o against sth mettre qn en garde contre qch; ~ s/o not to do sth conseiller fortement à qn de ne pas faire qch

**warning** n avertissement m; (notice) avis m; (notification) préavis m; (air-raid) alerte f; let this be a ~ to you que cela vous serve de leçon; adj avertisseur -euse

**warp** n (textiles) chaîne f; vt (twist) tordre; (wood) déjeter; fausser; (mind) pervertir; vi se déformer; (wood) se déjeter; (wheel) se voiler

**war-paint** n peinture f de guerre; coll be in one's ~ être sur son trente-et-un, être en grand tralala

**warpath** n coll be on the ~ être parti en campagne, chercher noise à tout le monde

**warrant** n garantie f; autorisation f, justification f; (arrest) mandat m d'arrêt; (money) bon m, mandat m; vt garantir; justifier; I ~ you he'll come je vous assure qu'il viendra; il viendra, je vous en réponds

**warrant-officer** n adjudant m

**warranty** n autorisation f; garantie f

**warren** n garenne f; fig labyrinthe m, dédale m

**warrior** n guerrier m

**Warsaw** n Varsovie f

**warship** n bâtiment m de guerre

**wart** n verrue f

**wartime** n période f (temps m) de guerre

**wary** adj prudent, circonspect; be ~ of se méfier de; keep a ~ eye on surveiller attentivement

**wash** n lavage m; (laundry) lessive f, blanchissage m; (ship) sillage m; (propeller) souffle m; (painting) couche f (d'aquarelle); US ~ cloth gant m de toilette; have a ~ faire sa toilette; vt laver; (clothes) blanchir, laver; (shore) baigner; ~ away enlever par le lavage; ~ down laver à grande eau; coll (drinking) faire descendre; ~ off enlever par le lavage; ~ one's face se débarbouiller; ~ one's hands se laver les mains; ~ out rincer, laver; ~ sth ashore rejeter qch sur le rivage; coll ~ed out vanné; coll ~ed up ruiné, fichu; vi se laver; ~ over

balayer; ~ up faire la vaisselle; (material) ~ well être très lavable, se laver bien; coll that won't ~! ça ne prendra pas!

**washable** adj lavable

**wash-basin** n lavabo m

**wash-board** n planche f à laver

**wash-bowl** n US lavabo m

¹**washer** n (person) laveur -euse; (machine) machine f à laver

²**washer** n mech rondelle f

**washer-up** n (restaurant) plongeur -euse

**washing** n lavage m; (laundry) blanchissage m, lessive f

**wash(ing)-day** n jour m de lessive

**washing-machine** n machine f à laver

**washing-soda** n cristaux mpl de soude

**washing-up** n vaisselle f; (restaurant) plonge f

**wash-leather** n peau f de chamois

**wash-out** n coll fiasco m; (play) four m; (person) raté -e

**wash-stand** n lavabo m

**washy** adj faible, fade, insipide; (colour) délavé

**wasp** n guêpe f; ~s' nest guêpier m

**waspish** adj irascible, irritable

**wastage** n perte f; gaspillage m

**waste** n (loss) perte f; gaspillage m; (refuse) déchets mpl; désert m; terrain m vague, région f inculte; ~ disposal unit broyeur m à ordures; go (run) to ~ se perdre; sheer ~ pure perte; adj (land) désert, inculte; (useless) de rebut; ~ ground terrain m vague; ~ paper vieux papiers m; vt (squander) gaspiller; (time) perdre; (use up) consumer, user; ~ one's words prêcher dans le désert; it's ~d on him c'est trop beau (bon) pour lui; ça ne lui sert à rien; vi ~ away dépérir; maigrir

**wasteful** adj gaspilleur -euse; ~ habit habitude f de gaspillage

**wastefulness** n prodigalité f, habitudes fpl de gaspillage

**waste-paper basket** n corbeille f à papier

**waste-pipe** n (tuyau m de) trop-plein m, tuyau m de dégagement

**waster, wastrel** n vaurien -ienne

**watch** n (guard) garde f; naut quart m; (timepiece) montre f; (staying up) veille f; be on the ~ être sur ses gardes; be on the ~ for guetter, être à l'affût de; keep a good ~ faire bonne garde; vt (look at) regarder, observer; (guard) veiller sur, garder; (game) assister à; ~ closely surveiller de près; ~ one's opportunity guetter l'occasion; ~ your step! prenez garde de tomber!; fig faites attention!; vi veiller; ~ out être sur ses gardes; ~ out for s/o attendre qn; ~ over surveiller

**watchdog** n chien m de garde; fig gardien -ienne

**watcher** n veilleur -euse

**watchful** adj vigilant, attentif -ive, alerte

**watchmaker** n horloger -ère

**watchman** n veilleur m, garde m; **night ~** veilleur m de nuit

**watch-tower** n tour f d'observation; (concentration camp) mirador m

**watchword** n mot m d'ordre

**water** n eau f; **~ on the knee** épanchement m de synovie; **be in low ~** (poor) être dans la dèche; (in a state) être bien bas; **by ~** par mer, par voie d'eau; **cold ~** eau froide; (cool) eau fraîche; **drinking ~** eau potable; **coll get into hot ~** se mettre dans le pétrin; **hard ~** eau dure; **have ~ laid on** faire mettre l'eau courante; **high (low) ~** marée haute (basse); **keep one's head above ~** se maintenir à la surface; fig faire face à ses obligations; **pour cold ~ on an idea** rejeter une idée; **soft ~** eau douce; **take the ~s** faire une cure, prendre les eaux; **turn on the ~** ouvrir l'eau; vt arroser; (animals) abreuver; (wine) couper; (silk) moirer; **~ down** atténuer; vi (eyes) pleurer; **it makes my mouth ~** ça me fait venir l'eau à la bouche

**water-bottle** n carafe f; gourde f; **hot ~** bouillotte f

**water-cannon** n lance f d'incendie

**water-closet** n cabinets mpl, waters mpl

**water-colour** n aquarelle f

**watercress** n cresson m de fontaine

**water-diviner** n sourcier -ière

**watered** adj arrosé; (wet) mouillé; **~ silk** soie moirée

**waterfall** n chute f d'eau, cascade f

**waterfront** n bord m de mer, quai m

**waterglass** n silicate m de potasse

**watering** n arrosage m; (animals) abreuvage m; (drink) dilution f; comm dilution f de capital

**watering-can** n arrosoir m

**watering-place** n (cattle) abreuvoir m; (spa) station f balnéaire, ville f d'eau

**water-level** n niveau m d'eau

**water-lily** n nénuphar m

**waterline** n naut ligne f de flottaison

**waterlogged** adj (ground) détrempé, imbibé d'eau; (ship) plein d'eau

**water-main** n conduite principale (d'eau)

**watermark** n (paper) filigrane m; naut laisse f de haute mer (de basse mer)

**water-melon** n pastèque f, melon m d'eau

**water-mill** n moulin m à eau

**water-pipe** n conduite f d'eau

**water-pistol** n pistolet m à eau

**water-polo** n water-polo m

**water-power** n énergie f hydraulique

**waterproof** n imperméable m; adj imperméable; vt imperméabiliser, rendre imperméable

**water-rat** n rat m d'eau

**water-rate** n impôt perçu par le service des eaux

**watershed** n ligne f de partage des eaux

**waterside** n bord m de l'eau

**water-ski** vi faire du ski nautique

**water-skiing** n ski m nautique

**water-softener** n adoucisseur m d'eau

**water-supply** n approvisionnement m en eau, service m des eaux

**watertight** adj étanche; fig irréfutable, où tout a été prévu

**water-tower** n château m d'eau

**water-wagon** n citerne f mobile; coll **on the ~** ne buvant que de l'eau

**water-wings** npl flotteur m de natation

**waterworks** npl usine f de distribution d'eau; sl **turn on the ~** (cry) chialer

**watery** adj aqueux -euse; (ground) noyé d'eau; (eyes) larmoyant; (clouds) chargé de pluie; (soup) clair

**watt** n watt m

**wattage** n elect puissance f

**¹wattle** n (hurdle) clayonnage m; vt clayonner

**²wattle** n (turkey) fanon m; (fish) barbe f

**wave** n vague f; lit flot m; phys onde f; (hand) signe m; (hair) ondulation f; (movement) ondoiement m; **heat ~** vague f de chaleur; **light ~** onde lumineuse; **long ~s** grandes ondes; **medium ~s** ondes moyennes; **permanent ~** permanente f, indéfrisable f; **short ~s** ondes courtes; **sound ~** onde f sonore; vt agiter; (stick, etc) brandir; (hair) onduler; **~ aside** écarter; **~ one's hand** faire signe de la main; **~ s/o down** faire signe d'arrêter à qn; vi flotter; (hair) onduler; **~ to s/o** faire signe à qn

**wave-length** n longueur f d'onde

**waver** vi hésiter, vaciller; (troops) fléchir

**waverer** n indécis -e

**wavering** n hésitation f; irrésolution f

**wavy** adj onduleux -euse

**¹wax** n cire f; (ear) cérumen m; (ski) fart m; **~ taper** rat m de cave; eccles cierge m; vt cirer; (furniture) encaustiquer; (skis) farter

**²wax** vi croître

**waxen** adj de cire; (complexion) cireux -euse

**waxwork** n modelage m en cire; **~s** figures fpl en cire; musée m de figures en cire

**way** n chemin m, route f, voie f;

(direction) sens *m*, direction *f*, côté *m*; (manner) manière *f*, méthode *f*, façon *f*; (means) moyen *m*; (progress) progrès *m*; (custom) habitude *f*; *naut* erre *f*; **~ down** descente *f*; **~ in** entrée *f*; **~ out** sortie *f*; **~ through** passage *m*; **~ up** montée *f*; **all the ~** tout au long du chemin; (to the end) jusqu'au bout; **a little ~ off** pas trop loin; **a long ~ off** très loin; **be (get) in the ~** gêner; **by a long ~** de beaucoup; **by the ~** en passant, à propos; **down their ~** du côté d'où ils habitent; **feel one's ~** aller à tâtons; *fig* sonder le terrain; **find the ~ to do sth** trouver le moyen de faire qch; **get into the ~ of doing sth** prendre l'habitude de faire qch; **get one's own ~** arriver à ses fins; **give ~** céder; **go one's ~** passer son chemin; **go the shortest ~** prendre par le plus court; **go the wrong ~** faire fausse route; **have one's own ~** faire à sa guise; **if I had my ~** si ce n'était que de moi; **in a ~** en quelque sorte; **in a bad ~** en mauvais état, mal en point; **in many ~s** à bien des égards; **in no ~** nullement; **in the ~ of** en fait de; **in this ~** de cette façon (manière); **keep out of the ~** se tenir à l'écart; **lead the ~** aller devant; **make a ~ through** se frayer un chemin à travers; **make one's ~ by hard work** arriver à force de travail; **make ~ for** faire place à; **not by a long ~** il s'en faut de beaucoup; **on my ~** chemin faisant; **on the ~** en chemin, en allant, en cours de route; **out of the ~** écarté, isolé; *fig* peu ordinaire; **out of the ~!** ôtez-vous de là!, rangez-vous!; **over the ~** en face, vis à vis; **right of ~** droit *m* de passage; **see one's ~** voir clair; *fig* voir comment on peut; **she has a ~ with her** elle est insinuante; *fig* **stand in s/o's ~** gêner qn; **that's the ~!** voilà qui est bien!, à la bonne heure!; **that ~!** par là!; **the other ~** en sens contraire; **the right ~ up** dans le bon sens; **the wrong ~ up** à l'envers, sens dessus dessous; **things are in a bad ~** les choses vont mal; **this ~!** par ici!; **this ~ and that** de-ci, de-là; **which ~?** par où?

**wayfarer** *n* voyageur *m*, passant *m*

**waylay** *vt* guetter au passage, tendre un guet-apens à

**wayside** *n* bord *m* de la route; **fall by the ~** rester en chemin

**wayward** *adj* capricieux -ieuse, obstiné

**W.C.** *n* waters *mpl*, cabinets *mpl*

**we** *pron* nous; (one) on; **here ~ are!** nous voici!

**weak** *adj* faible; (drink) léger -ère; (solution) dilué; (body) chétif -ive

**weaken** *vt* affaiblir; amollir; *vi* s'affaiblir

**weak-kneed** *adj coll fig* sans caractère, mou (*f* molle)

**weakling** *n* être chétif; *coll* femmelette *f*

**weakly** *adj* chétif -ive; *adv* faiblement

**weak-minded** *adj* faible d'esprit

**weakness** *n* faiblesse *f*; **have a ~ for** avoir un faible pour

**weak-spirited** *adj* peu courageux -euse, irrésolu

¹**weal** *n* bien *m*; **the common ~** le bien de tous

²**weal** *n* (mark) marque *f*, trace *f*

**wealth** *n* richesse *f*, fortune *f*

**wealthy** *adj* riche, opulent

**wean** *vt* sevrer

**weapon** *n* arme *f*

**weaponry** *n* armes *fpl*

**wear** *n* usage *m*; (clothes) vêtements *mpl*; **~ and tear** usure *f*; **fair ~ and tear** usure normale; **for evening ~** pour le soir; **the worse for ~** usé; *fig* en piteux état; *vt* porter; (put on) mettre; **~ away** user, ronger; **~ down** user; **~ off** faire disparaître; **~ out** user, épuiser; (patience) lasser; *vi* s'user; (time) traîner; **~ off** disparaître, s'effacer; **~ on** s'écouler, s'avancer; **~ out** s'user; **~ through** se trouer (à force d'être usé); **~ well** faire bon usage; (person) se conserver bien

**wearable** *adj* mettable

**wearily** *adv* d'un air fatigué; péniblement

**weariness** *n* fatigue *f*, lassitude *f*

**wearing** *n* (clothes) port *m*; (wear) usure *f*; *adj* fatigant, lassant

**wearisome** *adj* ennuyeux -euse

**weary** *adj* fatigué, las (*f* lasse)

**weasel** *n* belette *f*

**weather** *n* temps *m*; **~ conditions** conditions *fpl* atmosphériques; **be under the ~** être indisposé; **in this ~** par un temps pareil; **it is fine ~** il fait beau; **make heavy ~ of sth** compliquer les choses; **what's the ~ like?** quel temps fait-il?; *vt* (rocks) désagréger, altérer; (storm) résister à; (survive) survivre à; (wood) faire mûrir; *vi* (rocks) se désagréger; s'altérer

**weather-beaten** *adj* battu par la tempête; (complexion) basané, hâlé

**weather-bound** *adj* retenu par le mauvais temps

**weathercock** *n* girouette *f*

**weather-forecast** *n* prévisions *fpl* du temps, bulletin *m* météorologique, *coll* météo *f*

**weatherman** *n rad* + *TV* personne *f* qui lit le bulletin météorologique; météorologue *m* weatherproof *adj* à l'épreuve du mauvais temps

weather-vane *n* girouette *f*

weave *n* tissage *m*; *vt* tisser; (plot) tramer; (plait) tresser; *vi* ~ **a way through** se faufiler à travers, se frayer un chemin à travers; *coll* **get weaving** s'y mettre

weaver *n* tisserand -e

weaving *n* tissage *m*

weazen(ed) *adj see* wizen(ed)

web *n* tissu *m*; *anat* membrane *f*, palmure *f*; (spider) toile *f*

webbed *adj* palmé

webbing *n* (chairs) sangles *fpl*; (bird) palmure *f*

wed *vt* épouser, se marier avec; (parson) marier; *vi* se marier

wedded *adj* marié; (of marriage) conjugal; (attached) attaché

wedding *n* noce *f*, noces *fpl*, mariage *m*; *adj* nuptial, de mariage; ~ **cake** gâteau *m* de mariage; ~ **day** jour *m* de noces; ~ **night** nuit *f* de noces

wedding-breakfast *n* repas *m* de noces

wedding-dress *n* robe *f* de mariée

wedding-ring *n* alliance *f*

wedge *n* coin *m*; **it's the thin end of the** ~ c'est un premier empiètement; *vt* coincer; caler, enfoncer

wedlock *n* mariage *m*; **born in (out of)** ~ légitime (illégitime)

Wednesday *n* mercredi *m*; **Ash** ~ le mercredi des Cendres

¹wee *adj coll* tout petit (*f* toute petite), minuscule

²wee, wee-wee *n* pipi *m*; *vi* faire pipi

weed *n* mauvaise herbe; *coll* personne chétive et maigre; *vt* désherber; ~ **out** extirper, éliminer

weed-killer *n* désherbant *m*, herbicide *m*

weeds *npl* vêtements *mpl* de deuil

weedy *adj* couvert de mauvaises herbes; *coll* malingre, peu robuste, chétif -ive

week *n* semaine *f*, huit jours *fpl*; **a** ~ **from now** (d')aujourd'hui en huit; **last** ~ la semaine dernière; **today (tomorrow)** ~ aujourd'hui (demain) en huit; **twice a** ~ deux fois par semaine; **yesterday** ~ il y a eu hier huit jours

weekday *n* jour *m* de semaine, jour *m* ouvrable; **on** ~ **s** en semaine

week-end *n* fin *f* de semaine, weekend *m*

weekly *n* revue *f* (journal *m*) hebdomadaire, hebdomadaire *m*; *adj* hebdomadaire; *adv* par semaine, tous les huit jours; **be paid** ~ être payé à la semaine

weeny *adj coll* minuscule

weep *vt* ~ **one's eyes out** pleurer à chaudes larmes; *vi* pleurer; (wall, etc) suinter

weeper *n* pleurer -euse

weeping *n* larmes *fpl*; (wall) suintement *m*; *adj* qui pleure; (wall) suintant; ~ **willow** saule pleureur

weepy *adj coll* larmoyant

weevil *n* charançon

wee-wee *n* + *vi see* ²wee

weigh *vt* peser; (in hand) soupeser; (anchor) lever; ~ **down** (scales) faire pencher; (overload) surcharger; ~ **one's words** peser ses paroles, mesurer ses mots; ~ **out** peser en quantités déterminées; ~ **up** jauger; (consider) considérer, calculer; *vi* peser; (count) compter; ~ **a lot (little)** peser lourd (peu); ~ **in** *sp* se faire peser; (intervene) intervenir; ~ **on the mind** tracasser

weigh-bridge *n* pont-bascule *m* (*pl* ponts-bascules)

weigh-in *n* pesage *m*

weight *n* poids *m*; (weightiness) pesanteur *f*, lourdeur *f*; (power) force *f*; importance *f*; **carry** ~ avoir de l'autorité; **feel the** ~ **of** soupeser; **gain** ~ prendre du poids; **he's worth his** ~ **in gold** il vaut son pesant d'or; **of little** ~ peu important; *fig* **pull one's** ~ y mettre du sien; *sp* **put the** ~ lancer le poids; **set of** ~ **s** série *f* de poids; *vt* charger

weight-lifter *n* haltérophile *m*

weighty *adj* pesant, lourd; important, sérieux -ieuse

weir *n* déversoir *m*; barrage *m*

weird *adj* surnaturel -elle, mystérieux -ieuse; (strange) étrange

weirdie *n coll* excentrique

Welch *n* + *adj see* Welsh

welch *vi see* welsh

welcome *n* bienvenue *f*, accueil *m*; **give s/o a good** ~ faire bon accueil à qn; *adj* bienvenu; (pleasant) agréable; ~ **!** soyez le bienvenu (*f* la bienvenue)!; **you're** ~ à votre service, il n'y a pas de quoi; **you're** ~ **to have a go** libre à vous d'essayer; *vt* souhaiter la bienvenue à, accueillir; (event) se réjouir de

weld *n* soudure *f*; *vt* souder, unir à chaud; *fig* unir; *vi* se souder

welder *n* soudeur *m*

welfare *n* bien-être *m*; ~ **state** État-providence *m*; ~ **work** œuvres sociales; **child** ~ protection *f* de l'enfance

¹well *n* puits *m*; (hollow part) creux *m*; (ship) sentine *f*; **sink a** ~ forer un puits; *vi* ~ **up (out)** jaillir

²well *n* bien *m*; *adj* (good) bon (*f* bonne); (health) en bonne santé, bien, bien portant; (advisable) souhaitable; **all's** ~ **that ends** ~ tout est bien qui finit bien; **be** ~ **again** être rétabli; **look** ~ avoir bonne mine; **that's all very** ~ tout cela est bel et bon, c'est bien joli; *adv* bien;

~! eh bien!; ~ **and good!** à la bonne heure!; ~ **done!** bravo!; ~, **he doesn't know any better** que voulez-vous, il ne sait pas; ~ **I never!** ça alors!, pas possible!; **all being** ~ si tout va bien; **as** ~ aussi; **as** ~ **as** (in addition) ainsi que; **as** ~ **as I can** do mon mieux; **come off** ~ (be lucky) avoir de la chance; (happen) se passer bien; **do** ~ **by s/o** être généreux -euse envers qn; **he can't very** ~ **go away** il ne lui est guère possible de partir; **it's** ~ **past six** il est six heures bien sonnées; **it's** ~ **worth seeing** cela vaut bien la peine d'être vu; **one might as** ~ **do it** autant le faire; **pretty** ~ **finished** presque fini; **you are** ~ **out of it** vous avez bien de la chance d'en être quitte; **you might** ~ **ask** c'est une question qui s'impose

**well-advised** adj (person) bien avisé; (action) sage

**well-appointed** adj bien équipé, bien meublé

**well-balanced** adj bien équilibré

**well-behaved** adj (child) sage; (animal) bien dressé

**well-being** n bien-être m

**well-bred** adj bien élevé; (dog) de race

**well-disposed** adj bien disposé

**well-heeled** adj coll riche

**well-informed** adj bien renseigné; (learned) instruit; **keep (oneself)** ~ se tenir au courant

**Wellingtons** npl bottes fpl en caoutchouc

**well-intended** adj fait à bonne intention

**well-intentioned** adj plein de bonnes intentions

**well-kept** adj bien tenu, soigné

**well-known** adj connu, célèbre

**well-meaning** adj bien intentionné

**well-meant** adj fait avec une bonne intention

**well-nigh** adv lit presque

**well-off** adj aisé, riche, à l'aise; **be** ~ **for sth** être bien pourvu de qch; **you don't know when you are** ~ vous ne savez pas quand vous êtes bien

**well-read** adj (person) cultivé

**well-spoken** adj ayant un accent cultivé

**well-thought-of** adj bien considéré

**well-timed** adj bien calculé

**well-to-do** adj à l'aise, prospère

**well-wisher** n personne f qui vous veut du bien, ami -e

**well-worn** adj très usagé, usé jusqu'à la corde

**Welsh, Welch** n (language) gallois m; adj gallois

**welsh, welch** vi filer sans payer; ~ **on** trahir

**Welshman** n Gallois m

**Welshwoman** n Galloise f

**welt** n (shoe) trépointe f; (glove) bordure f; vt (shoe) mettre des trépointes à; (glove) border; coll rosser

**welter** n confusion f, désordre m

**welter-weight** n poids mi-moyen

**wen** n loupe f

**wend** vt ~ **one's way** diriger ses pas

**werewolf** n loup-garou m (pl loups-garous)

**west** n ouest m, occident m; adj ouest invar, occidental; (wind) d'ouest; **the West Indies** les Antilles fpl; adv à l'ouest; vers l'ouest; **go** ~ se diriger vers l'ouest; coll mourir

**westerly** adj d'ouest

**western** n ciné western m; adj de l'ouest, occidental

**westernize** vt occidentaliser

**westernmost** adj situé le plus à l'occident

**westward** n direction f de l'ouest; adj+adv à l'ouest

**westwards** adv vers l'ouest; à l'ouest

**wet** n (rain) pluie f; humidité f; **go out in the** ~ sortir sous la pluie; adj humide, mouillé; coll ~ **blanket** rabat-joie m invar; (weather) **be** ~ pleuvoir; **be** ~ **through** être trempé jusqu'aux os; **get** ~ se mouiller; vt mouiller, tremper; coll ~ **one's whistle** boire un coup

**wetness** n humidité f

**wet-nurse** n nourrice f

**wetting** n mouillage m

**whack** n bon coup; action f de battre; coll part f; **have a** ~ **at sth** essayer de faire qch; vt rosser, donner des coups à; coll (defeat) battre

**whacked** adj coll éreinté, crevé

**whacking** n coll raclée f; adj coll énorme

**whale** n baleine f; coll as m, expert m; coll a ~ **of a storm** une tempête fantastique; coll **have a** ~ **of a time** s'amuser drôlement bien

**whalebone** n (in garment) fanon m de baleine

**whaler** n baleinier m

**whaling** n pêche f à la baleine

**wharf** n quai m, débarcadère m; vt déposer sur le quai; vi amarrer à quai

**what** adj (interrogative and exclamatory) quel (f quelle); ~ **a house!** quelle maison!; ~ **day of the month is it?** le combien sommes-nous?; ~ **little I have** le peu que je possède; ~ **news?** quoi de nouveau?; ~ **right have you to do this?** de quel droit faites-vous cela?; ~ **silly boys they are!** que ces garçons sont stupides!; ~ **time is it?** quelle heure est-il?; pron rel ce qui, ce que; (interrogative) qu'est-ce qui, qu'est-ce que?, que?; quoi?; comment?; comment!; quel (f quelle); ~ **do you take**

me for? pour qui me prenez-vous?; ~ for? pourquoi?; ~! He's here already! Comment! Il est déjà arrivé?; ~ if he won't? et s'il ne veut pas?; ~ is the number of the house? quel est le numéro de la maison?; ~ is this for? à quoi sert ceci?; ~ 's she like? comment est-elle?; ~ 's that? qu'est-ce que c'est que cela?; ~ 's that to you? qu'est-ce que cela peut vous faire?; ~ 's the good of trying? à quoi bon essayer?; ~ 's the matter? qu'est-ce qu'il y a?; ~ 's the Spanish for 'table'? comment dit-on 'table' en espagnol?; ~ 's to be done? que faire?; ~ 's your name? comment vous appelez-vous?; easy, ~? c'est facile, hein?; eat ~ you like mangez ce que vous voulez; he knows ~ 's ~ c'est un tout malin; I know ~ you're here for je sais pourquoi vous êtes ici; coll so ~? et puis après?

**what-do-you-call-him (her)** n monsieur (madame) machin

**what-do-you-call-it** n machin m

**whatever, whatsoever** adj quelque ... qui, que; aucun; quelconque; ~ shops you see quelques magasins que vous voyiez; **in any way** ~ d'une manière quelconque; **I see no possibility** ~ je ne vois absolument aucune possibilité; **nothing** ~ absolument rien; **on no account** ~ sous aucun prétexte; **will she see any doctor** ~? verra-t-elle un médecin quelconque?; pron quoi que, quel (f quelle) que; tout ce qui, tout ce que; ~ he wants tout ce qu'il voudra; ~ the answer may be quelle que soit la réponse; ~ they say quoi qu'ils disent

**what-for** n give s/o ~ dire à qn de quoi il retourne

**what-have-you** n all his belongings and ~ tous ses effets et tout ce qui s'ensuit

**whatnot** n (furniture) étagère f; coll machin m

**whatsoever** adj+pron see whatever

**wheat** n blé m, froment m

**wheedle** vt cajoler, enjôler

**wheedling** n cajolerie f; adj enjôleur -euse, cajoleur -euse

**wheel** n roue f; (steering) volant m; (ship) barre f; ~s (organization) rouages mpl; ~s within ~s complications fpl; vt tourner, faire tourner, faire pivoter; (cycle) pousser; ~ in apporter; vi tournoyer, tourner; mil faire une conversion

**wheelbarrow** n brouette f

**wheelbase** n empattement m

**wheelchair** n fauteuil roulant

**wheeled** adj à roues, sur roues

**wheeling** n ~ and dealing manigances fpl, combines fpl

**wheelwright** n charron m

**wheeze** n respiration sifflante; sl truc m; vi respirer difficilement; siffler en respirant

**wheezy** adj asthmatique; (horse) poussif -ive

**whelk** n buccin m

**whelp** n petit chien, chiot m; petit m d'un fauve; pej petit morveux

**when** adv quand?; lorsque, quand; où; say ~! dites-moi quand ce sera assez!; conj quand, lorsque; après que; où, que; **the day** ~ le jour où; **the week** ~ he was here la semaine où il était ici

**whence** adv d'où

**whenever** adv+conj chaque fois que, toutes les fois que; ~ will you learn? quand donc apprendras-tu?; **come** ~ you like venez quand vous voudrez

**whensoever** adv à n'importe quel moment où

**where** adv où; là où; ~ does he come from? d'où vient-il?; I go ~ I am welcome je vais là où je suis le bienvenu (f la bienvenue); fig that's ~ he's got to voilà où il en est

**whereabouts** n lieu m où l'on se trouve; adv où; ~ can he be? où donc peut-il être?

**whereas** conj tandis que, alors que; (considering) vu que, attendu que

**whereat** adv sur quoi; à quoi

**whereby** adv par où, par lequel (f laquelle), par quoi

**whereof** adv de quoi, dont

**whereon** adv sur lequel (f laquelle), sur quoi

**wheresoever** adv see wherever

**whereupon** adv sur quoi, sur lequel (f laquelle); après quoi

**wherever, wheresoever** adv partout où; où que

**wherewith** adv avec quoi; avec lequel (f laquelle)

**wherewithal** n nécessaire m; find the ~ fournir les moyens

**whet** vt aiguiser, affiler; (appetite) stimuler; (curiosity, etc) exciter

**whether** conj si; que; ~ he's ill or not qu'il soit malade ou non; ~ ... or soit ...ou que, soit que ... soit que; **I don't know** ~ he's coming je ne sais pas s'il viendra

**whetstone** n pierre f à aiguiser

**whew** interj ouf!

**whey** n petit lait

**whey-faced** adj pâle, blême

**which** adj quel (f quelle); lequel (f laquelle, mpl lesquels, fpl lesquelles); ~ one lequel (f laquelle); he arrived at nine, at ~ time I was having breakfast il est arrivé à neuf heures, heure à laquelle je prenais mon petit déjeuner; *pron* (interrogative) lequel (*f* laquelle); *rel* qui, que, lequel (*f* laquelle); ce qui, ce que; quoi; ~ **are you voting for?** pour lequel (*f* laquelle) votez-vous?; **of** ~ dont; **the books ~ I need** les livres dont j'ai besoin; **the house ~ I can see** la maison que je vois; **the house ~ stands there** la maison qui se trouve là; **the house towards ~ I went** la maison vers laquelle je me dirigeai; **we are going out,** ~ **he hates** nous allons sortir, ce qu'il déteste; **they drink,** ~ **is bad** ils boivent, ce qui est mauvais; **they want to go out,** ~ **I object to** ils veulent sortir, ce à quoi je m'oppose

**whichever, whichsoever** *adj* n'importe quel (*f* quelle), le (*f* la) ... que; quel (*f* quelle) que soit, quel que soit celui (*f* celle) qui (que); *pron* celui (*f* celle) qui, celui (*f* celle) que; n'importe lequel (*f* laquelle)

**whiff** *n* bouffée *f*; (wind) souffle *m*; *coll* petit cigare; *vi* souffler par bouffées; *coll* sentir mauvais, puer

**while** *n* temps *m*; **after a little** ~ au bout de quelque temps, quelque temps après; **a good** ~ assez longtemps, pas mal de temps; **a little** ~ **ago** il y a peu de temps; **be worth** ~ valoir la peine; **in a little** ~ sous peu; **once in a** ~ de temps à autre, une fois de temps en temps; **the** ~ pendant ce temps; *vt* ~ **away the time** faire passer le temps; *conj* pendant que, tandis que; en; (as long as) tant que; (concession) quoique, bien que, tout en; (whereas) tandis que; ~ **admitting he is wrong, he persists** tout en reconnaissant qu'il a tort, il persiste; ~ **eating** en mangeant

**whilst** *conj see* **while** *conj*

**whim** *n* caprice *m*, fantaisie *f*

**whimper** *n* geignement *m*; *coll* pleurnicherie *f*; (pain) plainte *f*; *vi* pleurnicher; (dog) pousser des petits cris plaintifs

**whims(e)y** *n* fantaisie *f*, lubie *f*

**whimsical** *adj* capricieux -ieuse, fantasque; (queer) bizarre

**whimsicality** *n* caractère *m* fantasque; bizarrerie *f*

**whine** *n* plainte *f*, geignement *m*; *vi* se plaindre, geindre; ~ **about sth** se lamenter sur qch

**whinny** *n* hennissement *m*; *vi* hennir

**whip** *n* fouet *m*; coup *m* de fouet; *cul* mousse *f*; *pol* chef *m* de file; *vt* fouetter; (eggs) battre; ~ **off** enlever vivement; ~ **out** sortir vivement; ~ **through** parcourir rapidement; ~ **up**

stimuler; *vi* fouetter; ~ **along** filer à bonne allure; ~ **down** descendre rapidement; ~ **round** se retourner vivement

**whipcord** *n* corde *f* à fouet; (fabric) whipcord *m*

**whiphand** *n* avantage *m*, dessus *m*

**whiplash** *n* mèche *f* (de fouet)

**whipper** *n* fouetteur -euse

**whipper-snapper** *n* (child) petit garnement; freluquet *m*

**whippet** *n* whippet *m*; *mil* char *m* (d'assaut) de type léger

**whipping** *n* fouettement *m*; **get a** ~ être fouetté

**whipping-boy** *n* bouc *m* émissaire

**whip-round** *n* collecte *f*

**whirl** *n* tournoiement *m*, mouvement *m* giratoire; *fig* tourbillon *m*; **my head is in a** ~ la tête me tourne; *vt* faire tournoyer, faire tourbillonner; ~ **s/o along** entraîner (emporter) qn à toute vitesse; *vi* tournoyer, tourbillonner; (on toes) pirouetter; ~ **along** filer à toute allure

**whirligig** *n* (toy) moulin *m* à vent; (merry-go-round) manège *m*; *fig* tourbillon *m*

**whirlpool** *n* tourbillon *m*

**whirlwind** *n* trombe *f*; **come in like a** ~ entrer en trombe

**whir(r)** *n* ronflement *m*, ronronnement *m*, sifflement *m*; *vi* ronfler, ronronner; (turn fast) tourner à toute vitesse

**whisk** *n* (movement) mouvement *m* en coup de fouet; (dusting) époussette *f*, plumeau *m*; *cul* fouet *m*, batteur *m*; *vt* (eggs) battre; (cream) fouetter; ~ **sth away** enlever qch rapidement; ~ **sth up** enlever qch rapidement

**whiskers** *npl* (man) favoris *mpl*; (cat) moustaches *fpl*

**whiskey** *n* whisky irlandais

**whisky** *n* whisky *m*, Scotch *m*

**whisper** *n* chuchotement *m*; *fig* murmure *m*, bruit *m*; **speak in a** ~ parler tout bas; *vt* chuchoter, souffler; *vi* chuchoter, parler tout bas

**whisperer** *n* chuchoteur -euse

**whispering** *n* chuchotement *m*

**whist** *n* whist *m*; ~ **drive** tournoi *m* de whist

**whistle** *n* sifflement *m*, coup *m* de sifflet; (object) sifflet *m*; **blow one's** ~ donner un coup de sifflet; *coll* **wet one's** ~ boire un coup; *vt* siffler, sifflotter; ~ **up** siffler; *fig* faire venir; *vi* siffler; *coll* **you can** ~ **for it** tu peux toujours courir après

**whistler** *n* siffleur *m*

**whistle-stop** *n US* (railway) halte *f*; *US pol* ~ **tour** tournée électorale faite par train spécial

**whit** *n* brin *m*; **every ~** absolument; **not a ~** pas le moins du monde

**Whit** *adj* **~ Monday** le lundi de Pentecôte; **~ Sunday** la Pentecôte

**white** *n* blanc *m*; (race) blanc (*f* blanche); (whiteness) blancheur *f*; **~s** linge *m*; (trousers) pantalon blanc; **~ of the eye** cornée *f*; **dressed in ~** habillé en blanc; *adj* blanc (*f* blanche); (reputation) sans tache; *fig* **~ elephant** rossignol *m*; *US fig* **~ man** homme loyal; **go ~** blanchir; pâlir

**whitebait** *n* blanchaille *f*

**white-collar** *adj* **~ worker** employé -e de bureau

**white-haired** *adj* aux cheveux blancs

**whiten** *vt* + *vi* blanchir

**whitener** *n* blanc *m*

**whiteness** *n* blancheur *f*; (face) pâleur *f*

**whitening** *n* blanchiment *m*; (hair, etc) blanchissement *m*; (powder) blanc *m* d'Espagne

**whitewash** *n* blanc *m* de chaux; *vt* blanchir à la chaux; *fig* blanchir, disculper

**whitewashing** *n* peinture *f* à la chaux; *fig* disculpation *f*

**whither** *adv* où; là où

¹**whiting** *n* (fish) merlan *m*

²**whiting** *n* (bleach) blanc *m* d'Espagne (de Meudon)

**whitish** *adj* blanchâtre

**whitlow** *n* panaris *m*

**Whitsun, Whitsuntide** *n* la Pentecôte; *adj* de Pentecôte

**whittle** *vt* tailler au couteau; **~ away at** diminuer petit à petit; **~ down** diminuer petit à petit, amenuiser

**whiz(z)** *n* sifflement *m*; *vi* siffler; **~ past** passer en sifflant; (speed by) passer à toute allure

**whiz(z)-kid** *n* jeune prodige *m*

**who** *pron* qui?, qui est-ce qui?; quel (*f* quelle)?; *rel* qui; lequel (*f* laquelle, *mpl* lesquels, *fpl* lesquelles); **~ do you think you are?** pour qui vous prenez-vous?; **~ is that man?** quel est cet homme?; **Who's Who** le Who's Who, l'annuaire *m* des notabilités; **I don't know ~'s ~ here** je ne connais personne ici; **my father's cousin, ~ is very rich** le cousin de mon père, lequel est très riche

**whoa** *interj* (to horse) ho!; (to person) holà!

**whodunit** *n* roman policier, roman *m* à suspense

**whoever, whosoever** *pron* (he who) celui qui (*f* celle qui); quiconque; (whoever it may be) qui que, qui que ce soit qui; **~ you may be** qui que vous soyez

**whole** *n* tout *m*, totalité *f*, ensemble *m*; **as a ~** dans l'ensemble; **on the ~** en

somme, à tout prendre; *adj* complet -ète, entier -ière, intégral; (unharmed) sain et sauf (*f* saine et sauve); (undamaged) intact; *coll* **go the ~ hog** aller jusqu'au bout; **the ~ truth** toute la vérité

**whole-hearted** *adj* (sincere) sincère; (single-minded) total

**wholemeal** *n* (bread) complet -ète

**wholesale** *n* vente *f* en gros; *adj* + *adv* en gros, en bloc; *fig* en masse

**wholesaler** *n* grossiste

**wholly** *adv* totalement, entièrement

**whoop** *n* grand cri; (cough) quinte *f* de toux; *vi* pousser de grands cris; tousser de façon prolongée

**whoopee** *n coll* **make ~** faire la noce, faire la bombe; *interj* hourra!

**whooping-cough, hooping-cough** *n* coqueluche *f*

**whoosh** *vi* **~ by** passer à toute allure

**whopper** *n coll* chose *f* énorme

**whopping** *adj coll* énorme, gros (*f* grosse), grand; *adv coll* **a ~ great chap** un type énorme

**whore** *n* putain *f*, prostituée *f*

**whorl** *n* (spiral) spire *f*; (shell) volute *f*; *bot* verticille *m*

**whose** *poss pron* de qui?, à qui?; **~ are they?** à qui sont-ils?; **~ book are you reading?** à qui est le livre que vous lisez?; **~ pupil are you?** de qui êtes-vous l'élève?; *adj rel* dont; de qui, duquel (*f* de laquelle, *mpl* desquels, *fpl* desquelles); **the girl to ~ sister I sent it** la jeune fille à la sœur de qui (de laquelle) je l'ai envoyé

**whosoever** *pron see* **whoever**

**why** *n* pourquoi *m*; **the ~s and wherefores** les pourquoi et les comment; *adv* pourquoi; **~ not?** pourquoi pas?; **that's ~ he came** voilà pourquoi il est venu; **this is ~ he came** voilà pourquoi il est venu; *interj* tiens!; **~, look here!** voyons!; **~, of course!** mais bien sûr!; **~, what do you want?** mais que voulez-vous donc?

**wick** *n* mèche *f*; *coll* **he gets on my ~** il me tape sur les nerfs

**wicked** *adj* méchant, mauvais; (temper) dangereux -euse; (awful) affreux -euse; *coll* (mischievous) malicieux -ieuse; **it's ~!** c'est honteux!

**wickedness** *n* méchanceté *f*

**wicker** *n* rameau *m f*; *adj* en osier

**wickerwork** *n* vannerie *f*; *adj* en osier, d'osier

**wicket** *n* (door) guichet *m*; *sp* (cricket) guichet *m*

**wide** *n* broke to the **~** complètement fauché -e; *adj* large; (extensive) étendu, vaste; (far) loin, éloigné; (great) grand,

vaste; *sl* rusé, futé; **be ~ of the mark** être loin du compte; **how ~ is the garden?** de quelle largeur est le jardin?; **three metres ~ large** de trois mètres; *adv* loin; à côté; **~ open** grand ouvert
**wide-angle** *adj* **~ lens** objectif *m* grand angle *invar*
**wide-apart** *adj* espacé
**wide-awake** *n* chapeau *m* de feutre à larges bords; *adj* alerte
**wide-eyed** *adj* aux yeux grands ouverts, les yeux écarquillés
**widely** *adv* largement; très
**widen** *vt* élargir; (extend) étendre, étendre les limites de; *vi* s'élargir; s'étendre
**wide-ranging** *adj* de grande envergure; divers
**widespread** *adj* répandu, général; (extensive) étendu
**widow** *n* veuve *f*
**widowed** *adj* veuf (*f* veuve)
**widower** *n* veuf *m*
**widowhood** *n* veuvage *m*
**width** *n* largeur *f*; (dress) ampleur *f*
**wield** *vt* manier; **~ power** exercer le pouvoir
**wife** *n* femme *f*, épouse *f*; **take a ~** prendre femme, se marier; **the world and his ~** absolument tout le monde
**wifely** *adj* d'épouse; conjugal
**wig** *n* perruque *f*, postiche *m*
**wigging** *n coll* semonce *f*; **give s/o a good ~** laver la tête à qn
**wiggle** *vt* remuer, tortiller, agiter
**wig-maker** *n* perruquier -ière
**wigwam** *n* wigwam *m*
**wild** *n* état *m* sauvage; **~s** région *f* sauvage; *adj* sauvage; (mad) fou (*f* folle), insensé; (furious) furieux -ieuse; affolé, effaré; (wind) violent; (morals) dissolu, dissipé; (behaviour) déréglé, délirant, extravagant; **go on a ~ goose chase** courir après la lune; **make s/o ~** faire enrager qn; **run ~** courir en liberté
**wildcat** *n* chat *m* sauvage; **~ scheme** projet très risqué; **~ strike** grève *f* sauvage
**wildebeest** *n* gnou *m*
**wilderness** *n* désert *m*
**wild-eyed** *adj* aux yeux effarouchés
**wildfire** *n* **spread like ~** se répandre comme une traînée de poudre
**wildly** *adv* follement, exagérément; complètement
**wildness** *n* état *m* sauvage; férocité *f*; (wind) fureur *f*; (behaviour) dérèglement *m*, extravagance *f*
**wile** *n* ruse *f*; **~s** cajoleries *fpl*
**wilful** *adj* obstiné, entêté; (act) fait exprès, volontaire; *leg* prémédité
**wilfulness** *n* obstination *f*, entêtement *m*

**wilily** *adv* de façon rusée
**wiliness** *n* ruse *f*, astuce *f*
**will** *n* volonté *f*; (choice) gré *m*; testament *m*; **against one's ~** contre son gré; **at ~** à volonté; **bear s/o ill ~** en vouloir à qn; **mention s/o in one's ~** coucher qn sur son testament; **of one's own free ~** de son plein (propre) gré; **the last ~ and testament** les dernières volontés; **where there's a ~ there's a way** vouloir c'est pouvoir; **with a ~** de bon cœur; *vt* vouloir, ordonner; (bequeath) léguer; *vi* + *v aux* vouloir; translated as part of *fut* tense; **~ you come?** – **Yes, I ~** Viendrez-vous? – Oui (je viendrai); **as you ~** comme vous voulez; **do what you ~, it ~ be too late** quoi que vous fassiez, il sera trop tard; **he ~ play the fool at table** il insiste pour faire l'idiot à table; **my brother ~ always help you** mon frère vous aidera toujours; **she ~ have it that she tried** elle insiste qu'elle a essayé; **she would do that!** ça, c'est bien elle!; **she would not budge** elle ne voulait pas bouger; **they would do it if they could** ils le feraient s'ils le pouvaient; **this ~ be him** ce sera lui sans doute; **try to come, ~ you?** essayez de venir, hein?; **won't you come in?** veuillez entrer; **would that he could see you!** je voudrais bien qu'il vous voie (vît); **would to God that he were gone!** plût à Dieu qu'il fût parti!; **would you mind asking him?** voudriez-vous lui demander?; **you won't forget, ~ you?** vous n'oublierez pas, n'est-ce pas?; **you would never cry when you were little** tu ne pleurais jamais quand tu étais petit
**willies** *npl coll* **give s/o the ~** donner les chocottes à qn
**willing** *adj* bien disposé, de bonne volonté; **~ or no(t)** bon gré mal gré; **be ~ to do sth** être prêt à faire qch, vouloir bien faire qch; *coll* **show ~** faire preuve de bonne volonté
**will-o'-the-wisp** *n* feu follet
**willow** *n* saule *m*; **weeping ~** saule pleureur
**willowy** *adj* souple
**will-power** *n* volonté *f*
**willy-nilly** *adv* bon gré mal gré
**wilt** *vi* se flétrir, se faner; (person) dépérir
**wily** *adj* rusé, astucieux -ieuse
**win** *n* victoire *f*; *vt* gagner; (victory) remporter; (gain) acquérir, trouver; **~ back** regagner, reconquérir; **~ over** gagner, s'attirer; **~ round** persuader, convaincre; **~ s/o's love** se faire aimer de qn; *vi* gagner; **~ through** parvenir à son but
**wince** *n* tressaillement *m*; *vi* sourciller;

(pain) faire une grimace de douleur

**winch** *n* manivelle *f*; (hoist) treuil *m*; *vt* ~
**up (down)** monter (descendre) au treuil

**¹wind** *n* vent *m*; (breath) souffle *m*,
haleine *f*, respiration *f*; *med* (belch)
vents *mpl*; (bowels) gaz *mpl*; ~ **instrument** instrument *m* à vent; **get one's
second** ~ reprendre haleine; *coll* **get the**
~ **up** avoir le trac (la frousse); **get** ~ **of**
avoir vent de; **it's all** ~ ce n'est que du
vent; **it's an ill** ~ **that blows no one any
good** à qch malheur est bon; **north** ~
bise *f*; **put the** ~ **up s/o** donner le trac à
qn; *sl* **raise the** ~ se procurer de l'argent; **sail close to the** ~ *naut* serrer le
vent; *fig* friser l'indécence; **sow the** ~
**and reap the whirlwind** semer le vent et
récolter la tempête; **take the** ~ **out of
s/o's sails** couper l'herbe sous les pieds
de qn; *coll* **there's sth in the** ~ il y a quelque anguille sous roche; *vt* (game) avoir
vent de, flairer; (take breath away)
couper le souffle à; ~ **the horn** sonner le
cor

**²wind** *vt* tourner, rouler; (clock) remonter; (thread) dévider; (spool) bobiner;
~ **round** enrouler; ~ **up** (clock)
remonter; *comm* liquider; (meeting)
clore; *vi* tourner; (meander) serpenter;
~ **down (up)** descendre (monter) en
serpentant; *coll* (finish) terminer, finir

**windbreak** *n* brise-vent *m invar*

**wind-cheater** *n* blouson *m*, anorak *m*

**windfall** *n* fruit tombé; *fig* aubaine *f*

**wind-gauge** *n* anémomètre *m*

**winding** *n* détour *m*, cours sinueux,
méandre *m*; (clock) remontage *m*;
(spooling) bobinage *m*; *adj* sinueux
-euse; qui serpente

**winding-sheet** *n* linceul *m*

**wind-instrument** *n* instrument *m* à vent

**windmill** *n* moulin *m* à vent

**window** *n* fenêtre *f*; (vehicle) glace *f*;
(shop) devanture *f*, vitrine *f*; (ticket)
guichet *m*; **French** ~ porte-fenêtre *f* (*pl*
portes-fenêtres); **look out of the** ~
regarder par la fenêtre; *mot* **rear** ~
lunette *f* arrière; **stained-glass** ~ vitrail
*m* (*pl* vitraux)

**window-box** *n* caisse *f* à fleurs, jardinière
*f*

**window-cleaner** *n* laveur *m* de vitres

**window-dresser** *n* étalagiste

**window-dressing** *n* art *m* de l'étalage; *coll
fig* façade *f*, trompe-l'œil *m invar*

**window-frame** *n* chambranle *m*, châssis
*m* de fenêtre

**window-ledge** *n* rebord *m* de fenêtre

**window-pane** *n* carreau *m*, vitre *f*

**window-shopping** *n coll* lèche-vitrines *m*

**window-sill** *n* appui *m* de fenêtre, rebord
*m* de fenêtre

**windpipe** *n* trachée(-artère) *f* (*pl* tra-
chées(-artères)), gosier *m*

**windproof** *adj* qui protège contre le vent

**windscreen** *n mot* pare-brise *m invar*;
*hort* brise-vent *m invar*; ~ **washer** lave-
glace *m*

**windscreen-wiper** *n* essuie-glace *m*

**windshield** *n US mot* pare-brise *m invar*

**wind-sock** *n aer* manche *f* à air

**windsurfer** *n* véliplanchiste; (craft) planche *f* à voile

**windswept** *adj* balayé par le vent

**wind-tunnel** *n* tunnel *m* aérodynamique

**wind-up** *n coll* liquidation *f*

**windward** *n* côté *m* du vent; *adj* + *adv* au
vent

**windy** *adj* venteux -euse; (place) exposé
au vent, balayé par le vent; *coll* (speech)
verbeux -euse; **be** ~ faire du vent; *coll*
(scared) avoir le trac

**wine** *n* vin *m*; ~ **and dine s/o** fêter qn

**wine-butler** *n* sommelier *m*

**wine-cellar** *n* cave *f*

**wineglass** *n* verre *m* à vin

**wine-list** *n* carte *f* des vins

**wine-press** *n* pressoir *m*

**wine-taster** *n* (person) dégustateur -trice;
(cup) taste-vin (tâte-vin) *m invar*

**wine-waiter** *n* sommelier *m*

**wing** *n* aile *f*; *mil* escadre aérienne; *theat*
~**s** coulisses *fpl*; (bird) **be on the** ~
voler; **take s/o under one's** ~ prendre
qn sous sa protection; **take** ~ s'envoler; *vt* (wound) blesser; (arrow)
empenner; ~ **one's way** voler

**winged** *adj* ailé; (wounded) blessé (à
l'aile)

**winger** *n* (football) ailier *m*

**wing-nut** *n* écrou *m* à oreilles

**wing-span, wing-spread** *n* envergure *f*

**wink** *n* clin *m* d'œil, clignement *m* d'œil;
**have forty** ~ **s** faire un petit somme; **not
sleep a** ~ ne pas fermer l'œil; *coll* **tip
s/o the** ~ faire signe de l'œil à qn, avertir qn; *vi* cligner de l'œil; (light) clignoter; *coll fig* ~ **at sth** fermer les yeux
sur qch

**winker** *n mot* clignotant *m*

**winking** *n* clignement *m* de l'œil; *coll* **easy
as** ~ simple comme bonjour; *adj* (light)
clignotant

**winkle** *n* bigorneau *m*; *vt* ~ **out** extraire

**winner** *n* gagnant -e; *coll* **be a** ~ être un
succès assuré

**winning** *adj* gagnant; (ways) séduisant,
attrayant

**winning-post** *n* poteau *m* d'arrivée

**winnow** *vt* (grain) vanner; ~ **the good
from the bad** séparer le bon du mauvais

**winsome** *adj* séduisant

**winter** *n* hiver *m*; ~ **sports** sports *mpl*
d'hiver; **in** ~ en hiver; *vt* hiverner;

(plants) conserver pendant l'hiver; *vi* hiverner, passer l'hiver

**wintry** *adj* d'hiver, hivernal

**wipe** *n* coup *m* de torchon (d'éponge), *coll* taloche *f*; *vt* essuyer; effacer; *sl* frapper; ~ **away** essuyer; ~ **off** essuyer; (debt) acquitter; ~ **out** effacer; *coll* exterminer; *coll* ~ **the floor with** s/o battre qn à plate couture; ~ **up** nettoyer; *vi* ~ **up** essuyer la vaisselle

**wiper** *n* (cloth) torchon *m*; *mot* essuie-glace *m*

**wire** *n* fil *m* de fer, fil *m* métallique; télégramme *m*; ~ **brush** brosse *f* métallique; **he's a live** ~ il est énergique; *fig* **pull the** ~**s** tirer les ficelles; *vt* munir d'un fil métallique; **attacher** avec du fil de fer; (opening) grillager; *elect* faire l'installation électrique de; ~ **up** (batteries) accoupler; *vi* télégraphier

**wire-cutters** *npl* cisailles *fpl*

**wire-haired** *adj* (dog) à poil dur

**wireless** *n* télégraphie *f* sans fil, T.S.F. *f*, radio *f*; **on the** ~ à la T.S.F.

**wire-netting** *n* treillis *m* en fil de fer (métallique)

**wirepuller** *n coll* intrigant -e

**wire-tapping** *n* mise *f* sur écoute d'une ligne téléphonique

**wiriness** *n* vigueur *f*; (hair) raideur *f*

**wiring** *n elect* installation *f* électrique; *rad* montage *m*

**wiry** *adj* sec (*f* sèche) et vigoureux -euse; (hair) raide

**wisdom** *n* sagesse *f*

**wisdom-tooth** *n* dent *f* de sagesse

¹**wise** *n* façon *f*, manière *f*; **in no** ~ aucunement, nullement

²**wise** *adj* sage, prudent, avisé; (well-informed) avisé; (knowledgeable) savant; **be none the** ~**r** n'en être pas plus avancé; **no one will be any the** ~**r** personne n'en saura rien; *coll* **put s/o** ~ **to sth** expliquer qch à qn; **the (three) Wise Men** les Rois mages

**wiseacre** *n* prétendu sage *m*

**wisecrack** *n* bon mot

**wisely** *adv* sagement, prudemment

**wish** *n* désir *m*, vœu *m*, souhait *m*; **best** ~**es** meilleurs vœux; **have no** ~ **to do** sth n'avoir aucune envie de faire qch; *vt* vouloir, désirer, souhaiter; ~ **s/o sth** souhaiter qch à qn; ~ **to do sth** désirer faire qch; *coll* **have sth** ~**ed on one** ne pas pouvoir refuser qch; **I** ~ **I had seen it** j'aurais voulu le voir

**wishbone** *n* fourchette *f*, bréchet *m*

**wishful** *adj* désireux -euse; **indulge in** ~ **thinking** prendre ses désirs pour des réalités

**wishy-washy** *adj coll* faible, fade

**wisp** *n* bouchon *m*, poignée *f*; (thin strand) brin *m*; (smoke) traînée *f*

**wistaria, wisteria** *n* glycine *f*

**wistful** *adj* pensif -ive; (look) d'envie, nostalgique

**wistfully** *adv* d'un air d'envie; d'un air de regret

**wistfulness** *n* envie *f*

¹**wit** *n* esprit *m*, intelligence *f*; (person) bel esprit; **be at one's** ~ '**s end** ne plus savoir à quel saint se vouer; **collect one's** ~**s** se ressaisir; **flash of** ~ trait *m* d'esprit; **keep one's** ~**s about one** avoir toute sa présence d'esprit; **live by one's** ~**s** vivre d'expédients

²**wit** *vt obs* savoir; **to** ~ c'est-à-dire, à savoir

**witch** *n* sorcière *f*; *coll* ensorceleuse *f*

**witchcraft** *n* sorcellerie *f*

**witch-doctor** *n* sorcier guérisseur

**witchery** *n* sorcellerie *f*; fascination *f*

**witch-hunt** *n* chasse *f* aux sorcières

**witching** *adj* charmant, séduisant; magique

**with** *prep* avec; à, de; chez; (despite) malgré; ~ **all due respect** sauf votre respect; ~ **all his kindness** malgré toute sa bonté; ~ **all my heart** de tout mon cœur; ~ **black hair** aux cheveux noirs; ~ **both hands** à deux mains; ~ **child** enceinte; ~ **him you can never be right** à ses yeux, on n'a jamais raison; ~ **his money there's no problem** riche comme il est, il n'y a pas de problème; ~ **regret** à regret; ~ **tears in his eyes** les larmes aux yeux; ~ **the purpose of** dans le but de; ~ **these words** sur ces paroles, là-dessus; *coll* **be** ~ **it** être à la page, être dans le vent; **come** ~ **one's coat on** venir en pardessus; (illness) **go down** ~ attraper, succomber à; **he's** ~ **me there** là, il est d'accord avec moi; **stay** ~ **friends** séjourner chez des amis

**withal** *adv ar* aussi; d'ailleurs; (in spite of it all) en dépit de tout; *prep ar* avec

**withdraw** *vt* retirer, enlever; *vi* se retirer; (move away) s'éloigner; ~ **into oneself** se renfermer en soi-même

**withdrawal** *n* retraite *f*; (money) retrait *m*; (troops) repli *m*; ~ **symptoms** symptômes *mpl* d'abstinence

**withdrawn** *adj* timide, sauvage, renfermé; (absent-minded) distrait

**wither** *vt* flétrir, dessécher; *vi* se flétrir, dessécher; ~ **away** (flowers) se faner; dépérir

**withered** *adj* (dried up) desséché; (limb) atrophié

**withering** *adj* qui flétrit, qui dessèche; (look) foudroyant

**withers** *npl* garrot *m*; *coll* **my** ~ **are unwrung** cela ne me touche pas

**withhold** *vt* retenir, refuser; (not reveal) cacher

**within** *adv* dedans, à l'intérieur; *prep* à l'intérieur de, en dedans de; ~ **an hour** avant une heure; ~ **an inch of death** à deux doigts de la mort; ~ **himself** en son fort intérieur; ~ **reason** dans des limites raisonnables; ~ **ten kilometres** à moins de dix kilomètres; ~ **these walls** entre ces murs; **come** ~ **the provisions of the law** tomber sous le coup de la loi; **live** ~ **one's means** vivre selon ses ressources

**without** *adv* dehors, à l'extérieur; *prep* (outside) en dehors de; sans; ~ **doing it** sans le faire; **be** ~ être sans; (lack) manquer de; **do (go)** ~ se passer de; **that goes** ~ **saying** cela va sans dire

**withstand** *vt* résister à

**witless** *adj* stupide, sans intelligence, imbécile, sot (*f* sotte)

**witness** *n* (person) témoin *m*; (testimony) témoignage *m*; ~ **for the defence (prosecution)** témoin *m* à décharge (charge); **bear** ~ **to** rendre témoignage de; **call s/o as** ~ citer qn comme témoin; **leg in** ~ **thereof** en témoignage de quoi; *vt* être témoin de; (be present at) assister à, attester; ~ **...** voyez ..., regardez ...; *vi* ~ **to sth** témoigner de qch

**witness-box** *n* barre *f* des témoins

**witticism** *n* trait *m* d'esprit, bon mot

**wittily** *adv* spirituellement

**witting** *adj* fait de propos délibéré

**wittingly** *adv* sciemment, en toute connaissance de cause

**witty** *adj* spirituel -elle

**wizard** *n* sorcier *m*, magicien *m*; *adj coll* chic (*f invar*), épatant

**wizardry** *n* sorcellerie *f*, magie *f*

**wizen(ed), weazen(ed)** *adj* desséché, ratatiné

**woad** *n* guède *f*

**wobble, wabble** *n* branlement *m*, tremblement *m*; *mot* shimmy *m*; *vi* branler, ballotter, aller de travers; (stagger) tituber; *fig* hésiter, vaciller, tergiverser

**wobbly** *adj* branlant; vacillant; (furniture) bancal (*pl* bancals)

**wodge** *n coll* gros morceau

**woe** *n* malheur *m*, chagrin *m*; ~ **is me!** pauvre de moi!

**woebegone** *adj* triste, malheureux -euse; (expression) à l'air désolé, abattu

**woeful** *adj* triste, malheureux -euse

**wog** *n pej* Arabe, bicot *m*, moricaud -e; nègre (*f* négresse)

**wold** *n* plaine onduleuse; plateau *m*

**wolf** *n* loup (*f* louve); *coll* homme *m* à femmes; ~ **in sheep's clothing** loup déguisé en brebis; **cry** ~ crier au loup;

**keep the** ~ **from the door** se mettre à l'abri du besoin; *vt* dévorer

**wolf-cub** *n* louveteau *m*

**wolf-dog, wolf-hound** *n* chien *m* de chasse au loup

**wolfish** *adj* de loup; vorace

**wolf-whistle** *n* sifflement admiratif

**woman** *n* (*pl* women) femme *f*; **run after women** courir les filles; **there's a** ~ **in it** cherchez la femme; *adj* femme; ~ **doctor** femme *f* médecin; ~ **friend** amie *f*

**woman-hater** *n* misogyne

**womanhood** *n* état *m* de femme

**womanish** *adj* efféminé

**womanize** *vi coll* être coureur, courir

**womankind, womenkind** *n collect* les femmes *fpl*

**womanly** *adj* de femme, féminin

**womb** *n* matrice *f*, utérus *m*; *fig* sein *m*

**wombat** *n zool* phascolome *m*

**womenfolk** *n* les femmes *fpl*

**womenkind** *n see* **womankind**

**wonder** *n* merveille *f*, prodige *m*; (surprise) étonnement *m*, surprise *f*; **a nine days'** ~ la merveille d'un jour; **it's a** ~ **that he's still alive** c'est un miracle qu'il soit encore vivant; **no** ~ ça n'a rien d'étonnant; **promise** ~s promettre monts et merveilles; *vi* s'étonner, s'émerveiller; (doubt) se demander; (reflect) penser, songer; **I don't** ~ **at it!** cela ne m'étonne nullement

**wonderful** *adj* merveilleux -euse, prodigieux -ieuse, étonnant

**wondering** *adj* émerveillé

**wonderland** *n* pays *m* des merveilles

**wonderment** *n* étonnement *m*

**wonder-struck** *adj* émerveillé

**wondrous** *adj* merveilleux -euse, étonnant, incroyable

**wonky** *adj coll* branlant

**won't** *abbr* will not

**wont** *n* coutume *f*, habitude *f*, usage *m*; *adj* **be** ~ **to do sth** avoir l'habitude de faire qch

**woo** *vt* (woman) courtiser; solliciter

**wood** *n* bois *m*; (bowls) boule *f*; (barrel) tonneau *m*; (beer) **drawn from the** ~ tiré au fût; **they are not yet out of the** ~ ils ne sont pas encore tirés d'affaire; **touch** ~ **!** touchons du bois!

**woodbine** *n bot* chèvrefeuille *m*

**woodcock** *n* bécasse *f*

**woodcraft** *n* connaissance *f* de la forêt

**woodcut** *n* gravure *f* sur bois

**woodcutter** *n* bûcheron -onne

**wooded** *adj* boisé

**wooden** *adj* de bois, en bois; *coll* (stiff) raide; *coll* (stupid) bête, sans intelligence; ~ **shoes** sabots *mpl*

**wood-engraving** *n* gravure *f* sur bois

**wooden-headèd** *adj* stupide

**woodland** *n* bois *m*, pays boisé; *adj* sylvestre, des bois

**woodlouse** *n* (*pl* **woodlice**) cloporte *m*

**woodman** *n* bûcheron *m*

**woodpecker** *n* pic *m*; **green** ~ pivert *m*

**wood-pigeon** *n* (pigeon *m*) ramier *m*

**wood-pulp** *n* pâte *f* de bois

**woodshed** *n* bûcher *m*

**woodwind** *n collect mus* les bois *mpl*

**woodwork** *n* boiserie *f*; (carpentry) menuiserie *f*, ébénisterie *f*

**woodworm** *n* ver *m* du bois

**woody** *adj* boisé; (vegetables) ligneux -euse

**wooer** *n ar* prétendant *m*

**woof** *n* trame *f*

**wooing** *n* cour *f*

**wool** *n* laine *f*; *fig* dyed-in-the- ~ intransigeant; **pull the ~ over s/o's eyes** donner le change à qn; **steel ~** paille *f* de fer

**wool-gathering** *n* rêvasserie *f*

**woollen** *adj* de laine

**woolliness** *n* nature laineuse; *fig* manque *m* de netteté, verbosité *f*

**woolly** *n* vêtement *m* de laine; *adj* laineux -euse, de laine; (fruit) cotonneux -euse; (outline) flou; (style) mou (*f* molle)

**woolly-headed, woolly-minded** *adj* confus, nébuleux -euse

**woozy** *adj sl* un petit peu parti, un peu paf *invar*

**wop** *n sl pej* Italien -ienne, Espagnol -e, *sl* métèque *m*

**word** *n* mot *m*; (spoken) parole *f*; terme *m*; (promise) parole *f*; (information) avis *m*, nouvelle *f*; ~ **for** ~ textuellement; (translation) littéral; ~ **of command** ordre *m*; **a man of his** ~ un homme de parole; **a** ~ **to the wise** à bon entendeur salut; **break one's** ~ manquer à sa parole; **by** ~ **of mouth** de vive voix; **have a** ~ **with s/o** dire un mot à qn; **have** ~ **s with s/o** se disputer avec qn; **in a** ~ en un mot, bref; **in other** ~ s en d'autres termes; **in the** ~ **s of** selon l'expression de; **keep one's** ~ tenir parole; **put in a good** ~ **for s/o** glisser un mot en faveur de qn; **send** ~ envoyer dire; **sharp's the** ~! vite!, dépêchez-vous!; **take my** ~ **for it** croyez-m'en; *eccles* **the Word** le Verbe; **the** ~ **goes round** on se donne le mot; **too stupid for** ~ s stupide au possible; **upon my** ~! ça alors!; **we can't get a** ~ **out of him** nous ne pouvons pas tirer un mot de lui; **without a** ~ sans mot dire; *vt* exprimer, rédiger

**word-blind** *adj* dyslexique

**word-formation** *n* formation *f* des mots

**wordiness** *n* verbosité *f*

**wording** *n* rédaction *f*; mots *mpl*, langage *m*

**wordless** *adj* sans paroles; interdit

**word-perfect** *adj* qui connaît parfaitement son rôle

**word-processing** *n* traitement *m* de texte

**word-processor** *n* machine *f* de traitement de texte

**word-splitting** *n* ergotage *m*, ergoterie *f*

**wordy** *adj* verbeux -euse, diffus

**work** *n* travail *m*; (task) ouvrage *m*, besogne *f*, tâche *f*; (creative) œuvre *f*, ouvrage *m*; *collect* œuvre *m*; (business) affaire *f*; ~ **s** (factory) usine *f*, fabrique *f*, atelier *m*; (wheels) rouages *mpl*; (clockwork) mouvement *m*; (public) travaux *mpl*; ~ **s committee** comité *m* d'entreprise; *coll* **be all in the day's** ~ faire partie de la routine quotidienne; **be at** ~ être au travail; **be out of** ~ être sans travail; **day's** ~ journée *f*; (price) **ex** ~ s **prix** *m* à l'usine; *coll* **give s/o the** ~ s battre qn; (kill) tuer qn; **good** ~ s **bonnes œuvres**; **have lots of** ~ **to do** avoir du pain sur la planche; *coll* **have one's** ~ **cut out** avoir de quoi faire; **road** ~ s **attention travaux!**; **start** ~ se mettre au travail; *coll* **the whole** ~ s tout le bataclan; *vt* (make work) faire travailler; (machine, etc) faire fonctionner, faire marcher; (exploit) exploiter; (materials, etc) travailler; (shape) façonner; (embroider) broder; (cure) opérer; *coll* (fix) arranger; ~ **free** réussir à dégager; ~ **in** faire entrer petit à petit; ~ **into** introduire; ~ **off** se débarrasser de; ~ **oneself to death** se tuer au travail; ~ **one's passage** travailler pour payer son voyage; ~ **out** mener à bien; (idea) développer; (problem) résoudre; (calculation) calculer; (mine) épuiser; ~ **s/o hard** surmener qn; ~ **up** préparer; (person) exciter; *vi* travailler; (machine) fonctionner, marcher; (operate) opérer, agir; *sp* s'entraîner; ~ **in** pénétrer petit à petit; ~ **loose** se desserrer; ~ **off** se détacher; ~ **on** continuer à travailler; ~ **on s/o** agir sur qn; ~ **out** se terminer, aboutir; (cost) ~ **out at** s'élever à, se chiffrer à; ~ **out well** se terminer bien

**workable** *adj* (plan) réalisable, pratique; (mine) exploitable

**workaday** *adj* de tous les jours; (dull) prosaïque

**work-basket** *n* nécessaire *m* à ouvrage

**work-bench** *n* établi *m*

**workday** *n* jour *m* ouvrable

**worked-up** *adj* excité, emballé

**worker** *n* travailleur -euse; (workman)

ouvrier *m*; (working woman) ouvrière *f*; **heavy ~** travailleur *m* de force; **he's a hard ~** c'est un travailleur, il travaille dur

**work-force** *n* main-d'œuvre *f* (*pl* mains-d'œuvre)

**workhouse** *n* hospice *m*

**working** *n* travail *m*; (machine) fonctionnement *m*; *adj* qui travaille, ouvrier -ière; (machine) qui fonctionne; **~ day** jour *m* ouvrable; **~ hours** heures *fpl* de travail; **~ man** travailleur *m*, ouvrier *m*; **~ party** équipe *f*; **not ~** (person) au repos; (machine) en panne; **the ~ class** la classe ouvrière

**working-out** *n* calcul *m*; développement *m*; (outcome) résultat *m*

**work-load** *n* quantité *f* de travail

**workman** *n* (*pl* **workmen**) ouvrier *m*

**workmanlike** *adj* bien fait

**workmanship** *n* exécution *f*, façon *f*

**workpeople** *npl* ouvriers *mpl*, ouvrières *fpl*

**workshop** *n* atelier *m*

**work-shy** *adj coll* flemmard, tire-au-flanc *invar*

**work-to-rule** *n* grève *f* du zèle

**world** *n* monde *m*; milieu *m*; **~ war** guerre mondiale; *coll* **a ~ of** beaucoup de; **give the ~ to do sth** donner n'importe quoi pour faire qch; **go round the ~** faire le tour du monde; **in this ~** ici-bas; **it's a small ~!** que le monde est petit!; **not for (all) the ~** pour rien au monde; *coll fig* **out of this ~** sensationnel -elle, absolument extraordinaire; **such is the way of the ~** ainsi va le monde; **the next ~** l'autre monde; **the whole ~** le monde entier; **the ~ of good** tout le bien du monde; **think the ~ of s/o** avoir une très bonne opinion de qn; **what in the ~ is wrong?** mais qu'est-ce qui ne va donc pas?

**world-famous** *adj* de renommée mondiale

**worldliness** *n* mondanité *f*

**worldly** *adj* du monde, mondain

**worldly-minded** *adj* attaché aux choses de ce monde (aux choses matérielles)

**worldly-wise** *adj* qui a l'expérience du monde (de la vie)

**world-shaking** *adj* stupéfiant

**world-wide** *adj* universel -elle, mondial

**worm** *n* ver *m*; (screw) filet *m*; *coll fig* pauvre type *m*; *vt* **~ one's way into** se faufiler dans, se glisser dans; **~ sth out of s/o** tirer qch de qn

**worm-eaten** *adj* vermoulu, piqué des vers; (fruit) véreux -euse

**worm-powder** *n* poudre *f* vermifuge

**wormwood** *n* absinthe *f*, armoise *f*

absinthe

**wormy** *adj* plein de vers; vermoulu

**worn** *adj* usé; (tired) fatigué, épuisé

**worn-out** *adj* usé; (person) épuisé, exténué

**worried** *adj* inquiet -iète, soucieux -ieuse

**worrier** *n* inquiet -iète, personne *f* qui s'inquiète facilement; *coll* bileux -euse

**worrisome** *adj* ennuyeux -euse, inquiétant

**worry** *n* inquiétude *f*, tracas *m*, tourment *m*; *vt* inquiéter, tourmenter, tracasser; (harry) harceler; *vi* s'inquiéter, se tourmenter, se tracasser; *coll* s'en faire, se faire du mauvais sang

**worrying** *adj* inquiétant

**worse** *n pis m*; **change for the ~** altérer; s'altérer; **so much the ~** tant pis; **they have been through ~ than that** ils en ont vu bien d'autres; *adj* pire; (health) plus malade; **be none the ~ for sth** ne pas s'en porter plus mal; **from bad to ~** de mal en pis; **grow ~** empirer; **to make matters ~** par surcroît de malheur; *adv* pis; plus mal

**worsen** *vt* + *vi* empirer

**worship** *n* culte *m*, adoration *f*; **hours of ~** heures *fpl* des offices; **place of ~** *RC* église *f*; (Protestant) temple *m*; **Your Worship** (mayor) Monsieur le Maire; (judge) Monsieur le Juge; *vt* adorer; rendre un culte à

**worshipful** *adj* honorable

**worshipper** *n* adorateur -trice; (church) **the ~s** les fidèles *mpl*

**worst** *n* pire *m*; *lit* pis *m*; plus mauvais; **at (the) ~** au pis aller; **do your ~!** vous pouvez toujours essayer!; **expect the ~** s'attendre au pire; **get the ~ of it** avoir le dessous; **if the ~ comes to the ~** en mettant les choses au pis; **that's the ~ of plastic furniture** c'est l'inconvénient des meubles en plastique; **the ~ of it is that …** le pis c'est que …; *adj* pire; plus mauvais; **he's the world's ~ driver** comme conducteur, il est zéro; *adv* le pis; le plus mal

**worsted** *n* laine peignée; laine filée

**worth** *n* valeur *f*; prix *m*, mérite *m*; **give me a hundred francs' ~** donnez-m'en pour cent francs; **have one's money's ~** en avoir pour son argent; *adj* **be ~ a lot** avoir une grande valeur; **be ~ sth** valoir qch; **be ~ while (the trouble)** valoir la peine; *coll* **for all one's ~** de toutes ses forces; **he's ~ millions** il est riche à millions; **it's as much as his life is ~** ce serait risquer sa vie; **that's ~ knowing** c'est bon à savoir

**worthily** *adv* dignement

**worthiness** *n* mérite *m*

**worthless** *adj* sans valeur; ~ **person** vaurien -ienne
**worth-while** *adj* qui (en) vaut la peine, *coll* qui vaut le coup
**worthy** *adj* digne, estimable; (praise-worthy) brave
**would** *vi + v aux see* **will**
**would-be** *adj* prétendu, soi- disant *invar*
**wound** *n* blessure *f*, plaie *f*; *vt* blesser
**wow** *n coll* succès éclatant
**wraith** *n* revenant *m*, apparition *f*
**wrangle** *n* dispute *f*, querelle *f*; *vi* se dis-puter, se quereller
**wrangler** *n* querelleur -euse
**wrangling** *n* disputes *fpl*, querelles *fpl*
**wrap** *n* manteau *m*, pèlerine *f*; (blanket) couverture *f*; *vt* envelopper; ~ **oneself up** se couvrir bien; ~ **sth round sth** en-rouler qch dans qch; *vi* ~ **up** s'emmi-toufler
**wrapped** *adj* be ~ **in thought** être absorbé dans ses réflexions; **be ~ up in sth** être entièrement préoccupé de qch, être absorbé par qch
**wrapper** *n* enveloppe *f*; (book) couverture *f*, couvre-livre *m*; (newspaper) bande *f*; *US* (garment) robe *f* de chambre
**wrapping** *n* emballage *m*; enveloppe *f*, couverture *f*
**wrapping-paper** *n* papier *m* d'emballage
**wrath** *n* colère *f*
**wrathful** *adj* furieux -ieuse; *lit* courroucé
**wreak** *vt* ~ **havoc** semer la destruction; ~ **one's wrath on** passer sa colère sur; ~ **vengeance on** se venger de
**wreath** *n* couronne *f*, guirlande *f*; (fune-ral) couronne *f*
**wreathe** *vt* enguirlander, couronner de fleurs
**wreck** *n* (event) naufrage *m*; épave *f*, navire naufragé; (building) ruine *f*; *US* accident *m*; *coll* (person) be a ~ être une loque; *vt* (ship) faire faire naufrage à; (destroy) détruire; (demolish) démo-lir; (train) faire dérailler
**wreckage** *n* épaves *fpl*, débris *mpl*
**wrecker** *n* destructeur -trice; (vandal) casseur -euse
**wren** *n* roitelet *m*
**wrench** *n* (ankle) entorse, *f*, foulure, *f*; (twist) torsion *f*; (snatch) arrachement *m*; (tool) clef *f*; *coll* it will be quite a ~ **to leave** ça me fera de la peine de par-tir; *vt* arracher; (twist) tordre; ~ **open** forcer; ~ **off** arracher; ~ **sth from s/o** arracher qch à qn
**wrest** *vt* arracher; (twist) tordre
**wrestle** *vi* lutter; ~ **with temptation** résis-ter à la tentation
**wrestler** *n* lutteur *m*
**wretch** *n* malheureux -euse, misérable; **poor ~** pauvre diable *m*

**wretched** *adj* malheureux -euse, misé-rable; (pitiful) pitoyable; ~ **weather** temps *m* de chien; **feel ~** être mal en train; **where's that ~ book** où est ce diable de (sacré) livre?
**wriggle** *n* tortillement *m*; *vt* ~ **one's toes** remuer les doigts de pied; ~ **one's way into** se faufiler dans; *vi* se tortiller; (struggle) se débattre; ~ **out of a difficulty** se tirer d'une situation difficile; ~ **through** se faufiler à travers
**wring** *vt* tordre; ~ **one's hands** se tordre les mains; ~ **sth out of s/o** arracher qch à qn; ~ **the neck of an animal** tordre le cou à un animal
**wringer** *n* (washing) essoreuse *f*
**wringing** *adj* ~ **wet** (person) trempé jusqu'aux os; (things) détrempé
**wrinkle** *n* ride *f*; (cloth) faux pli; *coll* (tip) tuyau, *m*; *vt* rider; (cloth) plisser, chiffonner; *vi* se plisser
**wrist** *n* poignet *m*
**wristband** *n* poignet *m*, manchette *f*
**wristlet** *n* bracelet *m*
**wrist-watch** *n* montre-bracelet *f* (*pl* montres-bracelets)
**writ** *n leg* ordonnance *f*, mandat *m*; **Holy Writ** les Saintes Écritures; **serve a ~ on s/o** assigner qn en justice
**write** *vt* écrire; (note down) noter, inscrire; (article) rédiger; ~ **a word in** insérer un mot; ~ **down** (note) inscrire; coucher par écrit; *coll* décrier; ~ **off** (capital) amortir; *comm* défalquer; ~ **out** écrire, transcrire; (prescription) rédiger; ~ **up** rédiger, écrire; (praise) prôner; *vi* écrire; ~ **back to** s/o répon-dre à la lettre de qn; ~ **off for sth** com-mander qch par écrit; **he can read and ~** il sait lire et écrire
**write-off** *n* perte totale, perte sèche
**writer** *n* écrivain *m*, auteur *m*; **be a good ~** (handwriting) avoir une bonne écri-ture
**write-up** *n* article *m*; **a good ~** un article élogieux; *theat* une critique favorable
**writhe** *vi* se tordre, se tortiller
**writing** *n* écriture *f*; ~ **s** écrits *mpl*; ~ **is his life** écrire c'est sa vie; **at the time of ~** au moment où j'écris; **in ~** par écrit
**writing-case** *n* nécessaire *m* de correspon-dence
**writing-desk** *n* bureau *m*, secrétaire *m*
**writing-pad** *n* bloc *m* de papier à lettres
**writing-paper** *n* papier *m* à lettres
**writing-table** *n* bureau *m*
**wrong** *n* mal *m*; (injustice) injustice *f*; *leg* préjudice *m*; **be in the ~** être dans son tort; *adj* mauvais, mal *invar*; (incor-rect) faux (*f* fausse), pas juste; (inaccu-rate) inexact; ~ **side up** sens dessus

dessous; **be on the ~ side of forty** avoir dépassé la quarantaine; **be ~** (person) avoir tort, se tromper; (watch) ne pas être à l'heure; **get on the ~ side of s/o** se faire mal voir de qn; (offend) prendre qn à rebrousse-poil; *coll* **get out of bed on the ~ side** se lever du pied gauche; **it's ~ to do that** c'est mal de faire cela; **say the ~ thing** commettre un impair; **set about things in the ~ way** s'y prendre mal; **sth is ~** il y a qch qui ne va pas; **take the ~ street** se tromper de rue; **what do you find ~ with him?** qu'avez-vous à lui reprocher?; **what's ~?** qu'est-ce qu'il y a qui ne va pas?; **what's ~ with you?** qu'avez-vous?; *adv* mal; (unjustly) à tort, injustement; inexactement, incorrectement;

*coll* **get s/o ~** mal comprendre qn; **go ~** (person) faire fausse route, tourner mal; (machine) se détraquer; (events) aller mal; *vt* faire du tort à; *leg* léser; (be unjust) être injuste envers
**wrongdoer** *n* méchant -e, délinquant -e
**wrongdoing** *n* mal *m*; injustice *f*
**wrongful** *adj* injuste
**wrong-headed** *adj* à l'esprit pervers
**wrongly** *adv* à tort; mal; **rightly or ~** à tort ou à raison
**wrought** *adj* travaillé, façonné; **~ iron** fer forgé
**wrought-up** *adj* agité
**wry** *adj* de travers, tordu; dégoûté; (smile) forcé; **pull a ~ face** faire la grimace
**wryness** *n* dégoût *m*

# X

**xenophobe** *n* xénophobe
**xenophobia** *n* xénophobie *f*
**xerography** *n* xérographie *f*

**Xmas** *n see* **Christmas**
**X-rays** *npl* rayons *mpl* X
**xylophone** *n* xylophone *m*

# Y

**yacht** *n* yacht *m*
**yacht-club** *n* cercle *m* nautique, yacht-club *m*
**yachting** *n* yachting *m*; **go ~** faire du yachting
**yachtsman** *n* yacht(s)man *m* (*pl* yacht(s)men)
**yachtsmanship** *n* qualités *fpl* de yachtsman
**yachtswoman** *n* yacht(s)woman *f* (*pl* yacht(s)women)
**yak** *n* ya(c)k *m*
**yam** *n bot* igname *f*

**yammer** *vi coll* gémir, geindre
**yank** *n* secousse *f*; *vt coll* tirer; **~ off** emmener de force; **~ out** arracher
**Yank(ee)** *n coll* Amerloque, Yankee
**yap** *n* jappement *m*; *vi* japper
¹**yard** *n* (measure) yard *m*; *naut* vergue *f*; **by the ~** au mètre; *fig* à n'en plus finir
²**yard** *n* cour *f*; (works) chantier *m*; (materials) dépôt *m*; *US* jardin *m* de derrière; **the Yard** Scotland Yard *m* = le Quai des Orfèvres
**yardage** *n* métrage *m*
**yardstick** *n* yard *m*; **measure things by**

**one's own ~** mesurer les autres à son aune

**yarn** n fil m; (story) histoire f, longue histoire; **spin a ~** raconter une histoire; vi débiter des histoires

**yaw** n naut embardée f; vi faire des embardées

**yawl** n yole f

**yawn** n bâillement m; vi bâiller; (gape) être béant

**yawning** n bâillement m; adj bâillant; (gaping) béant

**year** n (age, dates) an m, année f; (age) **~s** âge m; **~ by ~** d'année en année; **Happy New Year** bonne (et heureuse) année; **be ten ~s old** avoir dix ans; **by the ~** à l'année; **five a ~** cinq par an (année); **in the ~ X** en l'an X; **last ~** l'année dernière; **leap ~** année bissextile; **see the old ~ out** réveillonner

**year-book** n annuaire m

**yearling** n animal m d'un an; (horse) poulain m d'un an

**year-long** adj durant une année, durant toute une année

**yearly** adj annuel -elle; adv annuellement, chaque année, tous les ans

**yearn** vi **~ for** languir après, soupirer après, avoir envie de; **~ to do sth** avoir très envie de faire qch

**yearning** n envie f, désir ardent

**yeast** n levure f

**yell** n hurlement m; vi hurler, crier à tue-tête

**yellow** n jaune m; adj jaune; **~ fever** fièvre f jaune; **~ pages** = Bottin m; **go (make)** jaunir

**yellow-hammer** n bruant m jaune

**yellowish, yellowy** adj jaunâtre

**yelp** n jappement m, glapissement m; vi japper, glapir

**¹yen** n yen m

**²yen** n coll désir ardent, grande envie

**yeoman** n hist franc tenancier; mil hallebardier m; **do ~ service** fournir un service précieux

**yeomanry** n fermiers propriétaires mpl; mil hist corps de volontaires formé de fermiers propriétaires

**yes** adv oui; (after neg) si; **~, certainly** mais oui; **~, of course** mais bien sûr (que oui); **Didn't you see him?–Yes, I did** Ne l'avez-vous pas vu?–Si

**yes-man** n coll béni-oui-oui m invar

**yesterday** n hier m; adv hier; **~ morning** hier (au) matin; **~ week** hier il y a eu huit jours; **the day before ~** avant-hier

**yet** adv encore; déjà; (notwithstanding) malgré tout; **~ he won't yield** malgré tout il ne veut pas céder; **as ~** jusqu'à présent; **not ~** pas encore; **you're not going ~!** vous ne partez pas déjà!;

conj cependant, pourtant, néanmoins

**yeti** n homme m des neiges, yéti m

**yew** n if m

**yiddish** n (language) yiddish m; adj yiddish invar

**yield** n rendement m, produit m; (crop) récolte f; **give a good ~** rapporter beaucoup; vt (produce) rendre, rapporter, produire; (give) donner, offrir; (give out) exhaler; (surrender) céder, livrer; vi céder, se rendre, se soumettre

**yielding** n rendement m; soumission f; (surrender) reddition f; (soil, etc) affaissement m; adj (person) complaisant, facile; (soft) mou (f molle); (supple) élastique, souple

**yob** n sl pej type m, mec m; butor m

**yodel** n tyrolienne f; vi jodler

**yoga** n yoga m

**yog(h)urt** n yog(h)ourt m, yaourt m

**yogi** n yogi m

**yoke** n joug m; (clothing) empiècement m; (pair) couple m; (oxen) attelage m; vt atteler; accoupler

**yokel** n rustre m

**yolk** n jaune m d'œuf

**yonder** adj ce ...-là (f cette ...-là, pl ces ...-là); adv là-bas

**yore** adv ar **in days of ~** au temps jadis; **of ~** d'autrefois

**you** pron pl, formal sing vous; sing +familiar tu, te, toi; indef on, vous; **~ English** vous autres Anglais; **~ fool!** idiot que tu es!; **away with ~!** allez-vous en!; fig between ~ **and me** entre nous; **if I were ~** à votre place; **people seem strange to ~ when ~ are in a foreign country** les gens vous paraissent bizarres quand on est dans un pays étranger

**young** npl jeunesse f, jeunes mpl; (animals) petits mpl; adj jeune; (animals) petit; (night) peu avancé; (wine) vert; **~ men** jeunes gens mpl; **~er son (daughter)** fils (fille) cadet(te); **grow ~er** rajeunir

**youngish** adj assez jeune

**youngster** n jeune personne f, jeune homme m; garçon m; **he's just a ~** c'est un gamin

**your** adj votre (pl vos); (familiar) ton (f ta, pl tes); indef son (f sa, pl ses); **it's ~ turn** c'est à vous; **please wash ~ hands** veuillez vous laver les mains

**yours** pron le vôtre, (f la vôtre); (familiar) le tien (f la tienne); **a friend of ~** un de vos amis (f une de vos amies); **it's ~** c'est à toi; **is this essay ~?** est-ce que cette dissertation est de vous?

**yourself** pron vous-même; (familiar) toi-même

**youth** n (age) jeunesse f, jeune âge m;

(person) jeune *m*, adolescent *m*, jeune homme *m*; **the fountain of Youth** la fontaine de Jouvence
**youthful** *adj* jeune, juvénile
**youth-hostel** *n* auberge *f* de (la) jeunesse
**youth-hosteller** *n coll* ajiste

**yowl** *n* hurlement *m*; *vi* hurler
**yo-yo** *n* yo-yo *m invar*
**Yugoslav** *n* + *adj see* Jugoslav
**Yugoslavia** *n see* Jugoslavia
**Yule** *n* Noël *m*
**Yule-log** *n* bûche *f* de Noël
**Yuletide** *n obs* époque *f* de Noël

# Z

**zany** *n* bouffon *m*; *adj* idiot, loufoque
**zeal** *n* zèle *m*, ardeur *f*
**zealot** *n* fanatique; *hist* zélote *m*
**zebra** *n* zèbre *m*; ~ **crossing** = passage clouté, passage *m* pour piétons
**Zeitgeist** *n* esprit *m* de l'époque
**Zen** *n* Zen *m*; *adj* zen *invar*
**zenith** *n* zénith *m*; *fig* apogée *f*, sommet *m*
**zephyr** *n* zéphyr *m*
**zeppelin** *n* zeppelin *m*
**zero** *n* zéro *m*
**zest** *n* entrain *m*, enthousiasme *m*; piquant *m*; **eat with** ~ manger avec appétit
**zigzag** *n* zigzag *m*; **in** ~s en zigzag; *vi* zigzaguer
**zinc** *n* zinc *m*
**zinc-ware** *n* zinguerie *f*
**Zionism** *n* sionisme *m*
**zip** *n* (whizz) sifflement *m*; *coll* (energy)

vigueur *f*, énergie *f*; (fastener) fermeture *f* éclair; *vt* ~ **up** fermer la fermeture éclair de; *vi* filer; ~ **by (past)** passer comme un éclair
**zip-fastener** *n* fermeture *f* éclair
**zipper** *n* US fermeture *f* éclair
**zither** *n* cithare *f*
**zodiac** *n* zodiaque *m*
**zombie** *n* zombi *m*
**zonal** *adj* zonal
**zone** *n* zone *f*; *vt* diviser en zones; répartir en zones
**zoning** *n* répartition *f* en zones
**zoo** *n* zoo *m*, jardin *m* zoologique
**zoological** *adj* zoologique
**zoology** *n* zoologie *f*
**zoom** *n* bourdonnement *m*; *aer* montée *f* en chandelle; *vi* (rise fast) monter en flèche; *aer* monter en chandelle; bourdonner, vrombir
**Zulu** *n* Zoulou

# READ MORE IN PENGUIN

In every corner of the world, on every subject under the sun, Penguin represents quality and variety – the very best in publishing today.

For complete information about books available from Penguin – including Puffins, Penguin Classics and Arkana – and how to order them, write to us at the appropriate address below. Please note that for copyright reasons the selection of books varies from country to country.

**In the United Kingdom**: Please write to *Dept. EP, Penguin Books Ltd, Bath Road, Harmondsworth, West Drayton, Middlesex UB7 0DA*

**In the United States**: Please write to *Consumer Services, Penguin Putnam Inc., 405 Murray Hill Parkway, East Rutherford, New Jersey 07073-2136.* VISA and MasterCard holders call 1-800-631-8571 to order Penguin titles

**In Canada**: Please write to *Penguin Books Canada Ltd, 10 Alcorn Avenue, Suite 300, Toronto, Ontario M4V 3B2*

**In Australia**: Please write to *Penguin Books Australia Ltd, 487 Maroondah Highway, Ringwood, Victoria 3134*

**In New Zealand**: Please write to *Penguin Books (NZ) Ltd, Private Bag 102902, North Shore Mail Centre, Auckland 10*

**In India**: Please write to *Penguin Books India Pvt Ltd, 11 Community Centre, Panchsheel Park, New Delhi 110017*

**In the Netherlands**: Please write to *Penguin Books Netherlands bv, Postbus 3507, NL-1001 AH Amsterdam*

**In Germany**: Please write to *Penguin Books Deutschland GmbH, Metzlerstrasse 26, 60594 Frankfurt am Main*

**In Spain**: Please write to *Penguin Books S. A., Bravo Murillo 19, 1°B, 28015 Madrid*

**In Italy**: Please write to *Penguin Italia s.r.l., Via Vittorio Emanuele 45la, 20094 Corsico, Milano*

**In France**: Please write to *Penguin France, 12, Rue Prosper Ferradou, 31700 Blagnac*

**In Japan**: Please write to *Penguin Books Japan Ltd, Iidabashi KM-Bldg, 2-23-9 Koraku, Bunkyo-Ku, Tokyo 112-0004*

**In South Africa**: Please write to *Penguin Books South Africa (Pty) Ltd, P.O. Box 751093, Gardenview, 2047 Johannesburg*

# READ MORE IN PENGUIN

## DICTIONARIES

Abbreviations
Ancient History
Archaeology
Architecture
Art and Artists
Astronomy
Biographical Dictionary of
    Women
Biology
Botany
Building
Business
Challenging Words
Chemistry
Civil Engineering
Classical Mythology
Computers
Contemporary American History
Curious and Interesting Geometry
Curious and Interesting Numbers
Curious and Interesting Words
Design and Designers
Economics
Eighteenth-Century History
Electronics
English and European History
English Idioms
Foreign Terms and Phrases
French
Geography
Geology
German
Historical Slang
Human Geography
Information Technology

International Finance
International Relations
Literary Terms and Literary
    Theory
Mathematics
Modern History 1789–1945
Modern Quotations
Music
Musical Performers
Nineteenth-Century World
    History
Philosophy
Physical Geography
Physics
Politics
Proverbs
Psychology
Quotations
Quotations from Shakespeare
Religions
Rhyming Dictionary
Russian
Saints
Science
Sociology
Spanish
Surnames
Symbols
Synonyms and Antonyms
Telecommunications
Theatre
The Third Reich
Third World Terms
Troublesome Words
Twentieth-Century History
Twentieth-Century Quotations